Florida Rules of Court

Volume II – Federal

2017

Mat #41846028

ISBN 978–0–314–68521–6

PREFACE

Designed for use in the office or courtroom, this pamphlet contains the Florida federal rules.

WHAT'S NEW

Florida Rules of Court, Volume II – Federal, 2017, includes rules and associated material governing practice before the Florida federal courts. It is current with amendments received through February 1, 2017.

CONTACT US

For additional information or research assistance, call the reference attorneys at 1–800–REF–ATTY (1–800–733–2889). Contact our U.S. legal editorial department directly with your questions and suggestions by e-mail at editors.us-legal@tr.com.

Thank you for subscribing to this product. Should you have any questions regarding this product please contact Customer Service at 1–800–328–4880 or by fax at 1–800–340–9378. If you would like to inquire about related publications, or to place an order, please contact us at 1-888-728-7677 or visit us at legalsolutions.thomsonreuters.com.

THE PUBLISHER

March 2017

TABLE OF CONTENTS

FEDERAL RULES OF CIVIL PROCEDURE

Including Amendments Effective December 1, 2016

TITLE I. SCOPE OF RULES; FORM OF ACTION

RULE 1. SCOPE AND PURPOSE

These rules govern the procedure in all civil actions and proceedings in the United States district courts, except as stated in Rule 81. They should be construed, administered, and employed by the court and the parties to secure the just, speedy, and inexpensive determination of every action and proceeding.

(Amended December 29, 1948, effective October 20, 1949; February 28, 1966, effective July 1, 1966; April 22, 1993, effective December 1, 1993; April 30, 2007, effective December 1, 2007; April 29, 2015, effective December 1, 2015.)

RULE 2. ONE FORM OF ACTION

There is one form of action—the civil action.

(Amended April 30, 2007, effective December 1, 2007.)

TITLE II. COMMENCING AN ACTION; SERVICE OF PROCESS, PLEADINGS, MOTIONS, AND ORDERS

RULE 3. COMMENCING AN ACTION

A civil action is commenced by filing a complaint with the court.

(Amended April 30, 2007, effective December 1, 2007.)

RULE 4. SUMMONS

(a) Contents; Amendments.

(1) ***Contents.*** A summons must:

(A) name the court and the parties;

(B) be directed to the defendant;

(C) state the name and address of the plaintiff's attorney or—if unrepresented—of the plaintiff;

(D) state the time within which the defendant must appear and defend;

(E) notify the defendant that a failure to appear and defend will result in a default judgment against the defendant for the relief demanded in the complaint;

(F) be signed by the clerk; and

(G) bear the court's seal.

(2) ***Amendments.*** The court may permit a summons to be amended.

(b) Issuance. On or after filing the complaint, the plaintiff may present a summons to the clerk for signature and seal. If the summons is properly completed, the clerk must sign, seal, and issue it to the plaintiff for service on the defendant. A summons—or a copy of a summons that is addressed to multiple defendants—must be issued for each defendant to be served.

(c) Service.

(1) ***In General.*** A summons must be served with a copy of the complaint. The plaintiff is responsible for having the

summons and complaint served within the time allowed by Rule 4(m) and must furnish the necessary copies to the person who makes service.

(2) ***By Whom.*** Any person who is at least 18 years old and not a party may serve a summons and complaint.

(3) ***By a Marshal or Someone Specially Appointed.*** At the plaintiff's request, the court may order that service be made by a United States marshal or deputy marshal or by a person specially appointed by the court. The court must so order if the plaintiff is authorized to proceed in forma pauperis under 28 U.S.C. § 1915 or as a seaman under 28 U.S.C. § 1916.

(d) Waiving Service.

(1) ***Requesting a Waiver.*** An individual, corporation, or association that is subject to service under Rule 4(e), (f), or (h) has a duty to avoid unnecessary expenses of serving the summons. The plaintiff may notify such a defendant that an action has been commenced and request that the defendant waive service of a summons. The notice and request must:

(A) be in writing and be addressed:

(i) to the individual defendant; or

(ii) for a defendant subject to service under Rule 4(h), to an officer, a managing or general agent, or any other agent authorized by appointment or by law to receive service of process;

(B) name the court where the complaint was filed;

(C) be accompanied by a copy of the complaint, 2 copies of the waiver form appended to this Rule 4, and a prepaid means for returning the form;

(D) inform the defendant, using the form appended to this Rule 4, of the consequences of waiving and not waiving service;

(E) state the date when the request is sent;

(F) give the defendant a reasonable time of at least 30 days after the request was sent—or at least 60 days if sent to the defendant outside any judicial district of the United States—to return the waiver; and

(G) be sent by first-class mail or other reliable means.

(2) ***Failure to Waive.*** If a defendant located within the United States fails, without good cause, to sign and return a waiver requested by a plaintiff located within the United States, the court must impose on the defendant:

(A) the expenses later incurred in making service; and

(B) the reasonable expenses, including attorney's fees, of any motion required to collect those service expenses.

(3) ***Time to Answer After a Waiver.*** A defendant who, before being served with process, timely returns a waiver need not serve an answer to the complaint until 60 days after the request was sent—or until 90 days after it was sent to the defendant outside any judicial district of the United States.

(4) ***Results of Filing a Waiver.*** When the plaintiff files a waiver, proof of service is not required and these rules apply as if a summons and complaint had been served at the time of filing the waiver.

(5) ***Jurisdiction and Venue Not Waived.*** Waiving service of a summons does not waive any objection to personal jurisdiction or to venue.

(e) Serving an Individual Within a Judicial District of the United States. Unless federal law provides otherwise, an individual—other than a minor, an incompetent person, or a person whose waiver has been filed—may be served in a judicial district of the United States by:

(1) following state law for serving a summons in an action brought in courts of general jurisdiction in the state where the district court is located or where service is made; or

(2) doing any of the following:

(A) delivering a copy of the summons and of the complaint to the individual personally;

(B) leaving a copy of each at the individual's dwelling or usual place of abode with someone of suitable age and discretion who resides there; or

(C) delivering a copy of each to an agent authorized by appointment or by law to receive service of process.

(f) Serving an Individual in a Foreign Country. Unless federal law provides otherwise, an individual—other than a minor, an incompetent person, or a person whose waiver has been filed—may be served at a place not within any judicial district of the United States:

(1) by any internationally agreed means of service that is reasonably calculated to give notice, such as those authorized by the Hague Convention on the Service Abroad of Judicial and Extrajudicial Documents;

(2) if there is no internationally agreed means, or if an international agreement allows but does not specify other means, by a method that is reasonably calculated to give notice:

(A) as prescribed by the foreign country's law for service in that country in an action in its courts of general jurisdiction;

(B) as the foreign authority directs in response to a letter rogatory or letter of request; or

(C) unless prohibited by the foreign country's law, by:

(i) delivering a copy of the summons and of the complaint to the individual personally; or

(ii) using any form of mail that the clerk addresses and sends to the individual and that requires a signed receipt; or

(3) by other means not prohibited by international agreement, as the court orders.

(g) Serving a Minor or an Incompetent Person. A minor or an incompetent person in a judicial district of the United States must be served by following state law for serving a summons or like process on such a defendant in an action brought in the courts of general jurisdiction of the state where service is made. A minor or an incompetent person who is not within any judicial district of the United States must be served in the manner prescribed by Rule 4(f)(2)(A), (f)(2)(B), or (f)(3).

(h) Serving a Corporation, Partnership, or Association. Unless federal law provides otherwise or the defendant's waiver has been filed, a domestic or foreign corporation, or a partnership or other unincorporated association that is subject to suit under a common name, must be served:

(1) in a judicial district of the United States:

(A) in the manner prescribed by Rule 4(e)(1) for serving an individual; or

(B) by delivering a copy of the summons and of the complaint to an officer, a managing or general agent, or any other agent authorized by appointment or by law to receive service of process and—if the agent is one authorized by statute and the statute so requires—by also mailing a copy of each to the defendant; or

(2) at a place not within any judicial district of the United States, in any manner prescribed by Rule 4(f) for serving an individual, except personal delivery under (f)(2)(C)(i).

(i) Serving the United States and Its Agencies, Corporations, Officers, or Employees.

(1) ***United States.*** To serve the United States, a party must:

(A)(i) deliver a copy of the summons and of the complaint to the United States attorney for the district where the action is brought—or to an assistant United States attorney or clerical employee whom the United States attorney designates in a writing filed with the court clerk—or

(ii) send a copy of each by registered or certified mail to the civil-process clerk at the United States attorney's office;

(B) send a copy of each by registered or certified mail to the Attorney General of the United States at Washington, D.C.; and

(C) if the action challenges an order of a nonparty agency or officer of the United States, send a copy of each by registered or certified mail to the agency or officer.

(2) ***Agency; Corporation; Officer or Employee Sued in an Official Capacity.*** To serve a United States agency or corporation, or a United States officer or employee sued only in an official capacity, a party must serve the United States and also send a copy of the summons and of the complaint by registered or certified mail to the agency, corporation, officer, or employee.

(3) ***Officer or Employee Sued Individually.*** To serve a United States officer or employee sued in an individual capacity for an act or omission occurring in connection with duties performed on the United States' behalf (whether or not the officer or employee is also sued in an official capacity), a party must serve the United States and also serve the officer or employee under Rule 4(e), (f), or (g).

(4) ***Extending Time.*** The court must allow a party a reasonable time to cure its failure to:

(A) serve a person required to be served under Rule 4(i)(2), if the party has served either the United States attorney or the Attorney General of the United States; or

(B) serve the United States under Rule 4(i)(3), if the party has served the United States officer or employee.

(j) Serving a Foreign, State, or Local Government.

(1) ***Foreign State.*** A foreign state or its political subdivision, agency, or instrumentality must be served in accordance with 28 U.S.C. § 1608.

(2) ***State or Local Government.*** A state, a municipal corporation, or any other state-created governmental organization that is subject to suit must be served by:

(A) delivering a copy of the summons and of the complaint to its chief executive officer; or

(B) serving a copy of each in the manner prescribed by that state's law for serving a summons or like process on such a defendant.

(k) Territorial Limits of Effective Service.

(1) ***In General.*** Serving a summons or filing a waiver of service establishes personal jurisdiction over a defendant:

(A) who is subject to the jurisdiction of a court of general jurisdiction in the state where the district court is located;

(B) who is a party joined under Rule 14 or 19 and is served within a judicial district of the United States and not more than 100 miles from where the summons was issued; or

(C) when authorized by a federal statute.

(2) ***Federal Claim Outside State-Court Jurisdiction.*** For a claim that arises under federal law, serving a summons or filing a waiver of service establishes personal jurisdiction over a defendant if:

(A) the defendant is not subject to jurisdiction in any state's courts of general jurisdiction; and

(B) exercising jurisdiction is consistent with the United States Constitution and laws.

(l) **Proving Service.**

(1) ***Affidavit Required.*** Unless service is waived, proof of service must be made to the court. Except for service by a United States marshal or deputy marshal, proof must be by the server's affidavit.

(2) ***Service Outside the United States.*** Service not within any judicial district of the United States must be proved as follows:

(A) if made under Rule 4(f)(1), as provided in the applicable treaty or convention; or

(B) if made under Rule 4(f)(2) or (f)(3), by a receipt signed by the addressee, or by other evidence satisfying the court that the summons and complaint were delivered to the addressee.

(3) ***Validity of Service; Amending Proof.*** Failure to prove service does not affect the validity of service. The court may permit proof of service to be amended.

(m) Time Limit for Service. If a defendant is not served within 90 days after the complaint is filed, the court—on motion or on its own after notice to the plaintiff—must dismiss the action without prejudice against that defendant or order that service be made within a specified time. But if the plaintiff shows good cause for the failure, the court must extend the time for service for an appropriate period. This subdivision (m) does not apply to service in a foreign country under Rule 4(f), 4(h)(2), or 4(j)(1).*

(n) Asserting Jurisdiction over Property or Assets.

(1) ***Federal Law.*** The court may assert jurisdiction over property if authorized by a federal statute. Notice to claimants of the property must be given as provided in the statute or by serving a summons under this rule.

(2) ***State Law.*** On a showing that personal jurisdiction over a defendant cannot be obtained in the district where the action is brought by reasonable efforts to serve a summons under this rule, the court may assert jurisdiction over the defendant's assets found in the district. Jurisdiction is acquired by seizing the assets under the circumstances and in the manner provided by state law in that district.

Rule 4 Notice of a Lawsuit and Request to Waive Service of Summons.

(Caption)

To (*name the defendant or — if the defendant is a corporation, partnership, or association — name an officer or agent authorized to receive service*):

Why are you getting this?

A lawsuit has been filed against you, or the entity you represent, in this court under the number shown above. A copy of the complaint is attached.

This is not a summons, or an official notice from the court. It is a request that, to avoid expenses, you waive formal service of a summons by signing and returning the enclosed waiver. To avoid these expenses, you must return the signed waiver within (*give at least 30 days or at least 60 days if the defendant is outside any judicial district of the United States*) from the date shown below, which is the date this notice was sent. Two copies of the waiver form are enclosed, along with a stamped, self-addressed envelope or other prepaid means for returning one copy. You may keep the other copy.

What happens next?

If you return the signed waiver, I will file it with the court. The action will then proceed as if you had been served on the date the waiver is filed, but no summons will be served on you and you will have 60 days from the date this notice is sent (see the date below) to answer the complaint (or 90 days if this notice is sent to you outside any judicial district of the United States).

If you do not return the signed waiver within the time indicated, I will arrange to have the summons and complaint served on you. And I will ask the court to require you, or the entity you represent, to pay the expenses of making service.

Please read the enclosed statement about the duty to avoid unnecessary expenses.

I certify that this request is being sent to you on the date below.

Date: __________

____

(Signature of the attorney
or unrepresented party)

____

(Printed name)

____

(Address)

____

(E-mail address)

____

(Telephone number)

Rule 4 Waiver of the Service of Summons.

(Caption)

To (*name the plaintiff's attorney or the unrepresented plaintiff*):

I have received your request to waive service of a summons in this action along with a copy of the complaint, two copies of this waiver form, and a prepaid means of returning one signed copy of the form to you.

I, or the entity I represent, agree to save the expense of serving a summons and complaint in this case.

I understand that I, or the entity I represent, will keep all defenses or objections to the lawsuit, the court's jurisdiction, and the venue of the action, but that I waive any objections to the absence of a summons or of service.

I also understand that I, or the entity I represent, must file and serve an answer or a motion under Rule 12 within 60 days from________, the date when this request was sent (or 90 days if it was sent outside the United States). If I fail to do so, a default judgment will be entered against me or the entity I represent.

Date: __________

____

(Signature of the attorney
or unrepresented party)

____

(Printed name)

____

(Address)

____

(E-mail address)

____

(Telephone number)

(Attach the following)

Duty to Avoid Unnecessary Expenses of Serving a Summons

Rule 4 of the Federal Rules of Civil Procedure requires certain defendants to cooperate in saving unnecessary expenses of serving a summons and complaint. A defendant who is located in the United States and who fails to return a signed waiver of service requested by a plaintiff located in the United States will be required to pay the expenses of service, unless the defendant shows good cause for the failure.

"Good cause" does not include a belief that the lawsuit is groundless, or that it has been brought in an improper venue, or that the court has no jurisdiction over this matter or over the defendant or the defendant's property.

If the waiver is signed and returned, you can still make these and all other defenses and objections, but you cannot object to the absence of a summons or of service.

If you waive service, then you must, within the time specified on the waiver form, serve an answer or a motion under Rule 12 on the plaintiff and file a copy with the court. By signing and returning the waiver form, you are allowed more time to respond than if a summons had been served.

(Amended January 21, 1963, effective July 1, 1963; February 28, 1966, effective July 1, 1966; April 29, 1980, effective August 1, 1980; amended by Pub.L. 97-462, § 2, January 12, 1983, 96 Stat. 2527, effective 45 days after January 12, 1983; amended March 2, 1987, effective August 1, 1987; April 22, 1993, effective December 1, 1993; April 17, 2000, effective December 1, 2000; April 30, 2007, effective December 1, 2007; April 29, 2015, effective December 1, 2015; April 28, 2016, effective December 1, 2016.)

* [**Publisher's Note:** The text "or to service of a notice under Rule 71.1(d)(3)(A)" was added to Rule 4(m) in 2015 and probably should remain part of the rule; however, it was not included in the 2016 Order of the Supreme Court.

The Order of the Supreme Court dated April 29, 2015, amended Rule 4(m) to read:

(m) Time Limit for Service. If a defendant is not served within 90 days after the complaint is filed, the court—on motion or on its own after notice to the plaintiff—must dismiss the action without prejudice against that defendant or order that service be made within a specified time. But if the plaintiff shows good cause for the failure, the court must extend the time for service for an appropriate period. This subdivision (m) does not apply to service in a foreign country under Rule 4(f) or 4(j)(1) or to service of a notice under Rule 71.1(d)(3)(A).

According to the note of the Advisory Committee, the 2015 Order intended, in part, to "make it clear that the reference to Rule 4 in Rule 71.1(d)(3)(A) does not include Rule 4(m)."

The Order of the Supreme Court dated April 28, 2016, amended Rule 4(m) to read:

(m) Time Limit for Service. If a defendant is not served within 90 days after the complaint is filed, the court—on motion or on its own after notice to the plaintiff—must dismiss the action without prejudice against that defendant or order that service be made within a specified time. But if the plaintiff shows good cause for the failure, the court must extend the time for service for an appropriate period. This subdivision (m) does not apply to service in a foreign country under Rule 4(f), 4(h)(2), or 4(j)(1).

According to the note of the Advisory Committee, the 2016 Order intended, in part, to resolve a "possible ambiguity" related to Rule 4(h)(2).

Neither the 2016 Order nor the 2016 note of the Advisory Committee referenced the 2015 Order.]

RULE 4.1. SERVING OTHER PROCESS

(a) In General. Process—other than a summons under Rule 4 or a subpoena under Rule 45—must be served by a United States marshal or deputy marshal or by a person specially appointed for that purpose. It may be served anywhere within the territorial limits of the state where the district court is located and, if authorized by a federal statute, beyond those limits. Proof of service must be made under Rule 4(*l*).

(b) Enforcing Orders: Committing for Civil Contempt. An order committing a person for civil contempt of a decree or injunction issued to enforce federal law may be served and enforced in any district. Any other order in a civil-contempt proceeding may be served only in the state where the issuing court is located or elsewhere in the United States within 100 miles from where the order was issued.

(Adopted April 22, 1993, effective December 1, 1993; amended April 30, 2007, effective December 1, 2007.)

RULE 5. SERVING AND FILING PLEADINGS AND OTHER PAPERS

(a) Service: When Required.

(1) ***In General.*** Unless these rules provide otherwise, each of the following papers must be served on every party:

(A) an order stating that service is required;

(B) a pleading filed after the original complaint, unless the court orders otherwise under Rule 5(c) because there are numerous defendants;

(C) a discovery paper required to be served on a party, unless the court orders otherwise;

(D) a written motion, except one that may be heard ex parte; and

(E) a written notice, appearance, demand, or offer of judgment, or any similar paper.

(2) ***If a Party Fails to Appear.*** No service is required on a party who is in default for failing to appear. But a pleading that asserts a new claim for relief against such a party must be served on that party under Rule 4.

(3) ***Seizing Property.*** If an action is begun by seizing property and no person is or need be named as a defendant, any service required before the filing of an appearance, answer, or claim must be made on the person who had custody or possession of the property when it was seized.

(b) Service: How Made.

(1) ***Serving an Attorney.*** If a party is represented by an attorney, service under this rule must be made on the attorney unless the court orders service on the party.

(2) ***Service in General.*** A paper is served under this rule by:

(A) handing it to the person;

(B) leaving it:

(i) at the person's office with a clerk or other person in charge or, if no one is in charge, in a conspicuous place in the office; or

(ii) if the person has no office or the office is closed, at the person's dwelling or usual place of abode with someone of suitable age and discretion who resides there;

(C) mailing it to the person's last known address—in which event service is complete upon mailing;

(D) leaving it with the court clerk if the person has no known address;

(E) sending it by electronic means if the person consented in writing—in which event service is complete upon transmission, but is not effective if the serving party learns that it did not reach the person to be served; or

(F) delivering it by any other means that the person consented to in writing—in which event service is complete when the person making service delivers it to the agency designated to make delivery.

(3) *Using Court Facilities.* If a local rule so authorizes, a party may use the court's transmission facilities to make service under Rule 5(b)(2)(E).

(c) Serving Numerous Defendants.

(1) *In General.* If an action involves an unusually large number of defendants, the court may, on motion or on its own, order that:

(A) defendants' pleadings and replies to them need not be served on other defendants;

(B) any crossclaim, counterclaim, avoidance, or affirmative defense in those pleadings and replies to them will be treated as denied or avoided by all other parties; and

(C) filing any such pleading and serving it on the plaintiff constitutes notice of the pleading to all parties.

(2) *Notifying Parties.* A copy of every such order must be served on the parties as the court directs.

(d) Filing.

(1) *Required Filings; Certificate of Service.* Any paper after the complaint that is required to be served—together with a certificate of service—must be filed within a reasonable time after service. But disclosures under Rule 26(a)(1) or (2) and the following discovery requests and responses must not be filed until they are used in the proceeding or the court orders filing: depositions, interrogatories, requests for documents or tangible things or to permit entry onto land, and requests for admission.

(2) *How Filing Is Made—In General.* A paper is filed by delivering it:

(A) to the clerk; or

(B) to a judge who agrees to accept it for filing, and who must then note the filing date on the paper and promptly send it to the clerk.

(3) *Electronic Filing, Signing, or Verification.* A court may, by local rule, allow papers to be filed, signed, or verified by electronic means that are consistent with any technical standards established by the Judicial Conference of the United States. A local rule may require electronic filing only if reasonable exceptions are allowed. A paper filed electronically in compliance with a local rule is a written paper for purposes of these rules.

(4) *Acceptance by the Clerk.* The clerk must not refuse to file a paper solely because it is not in the form prescribed by these rules or by a local rule or practice.

(Amended January 21, 1963, effective July 1, 1963; March 30, 1970, effective July 1, 1970; April 29, 1980, effective August 1, 1980; March 2, 1987, effective August 1, 1987; April 30, 1991, effective December 1, 1991; April 22, 1993, effective December 1, 1993; April 23, 1996, effective December 1, 1996; April 17, 2000, effective December 1, 2000; April 23, 2001, effective December 1, 2001; April 12, 2006, effective December 1, 2006; April 30, 2007, effective December 1, 2007.)

RULE 5.1. CONSTITUTIONAL CHALLENGE TO A STATUTE—NOTICE, CERTIFICATION, AND INTERVENTION

(a) Notice by a Party. A party that files a pleading, written motion, or other paper drawing into question the constitutionality of a federal or state statute must promptly:

(1) file a notice of constitutional question stating the question and identifying the paper that raises it, if:

(A) a federal statute is questioned and the parties do not include the United States, one of its agencies, or one of its officers or employees in an official capacity; or

(B) a state statute is questioned and the parties do not include the state, one of its agencies, or one of its officers or employees in an official capacity; and

(2) serve the notice and paper on the Attorney General of the United States if a federal statute is questioned—or on the state attorney general if a state statute is questioned—either by certified or registered mail or by sending it to an electronic address designated by the attorney general for this purpose.

(b) Certification by the Court. The court must, under 28 U.S.C. § 2403, certify to the appropriate attorney general that a statute has been questioned.

(c) Intervention; Final Decision on the Merits. Unless the court sets a later time, the attorney general may intervene within 60 days after the notice is filed or after the court certifies the challenge, whichever is earlier. Before the time to intervene expires, the court may reject the constitutional challenge, but may not enter a final judgment holding the statute unconstitutional.

(d) No Forfeiture. A party's failure to file and serve the notice, or the court's failure to certify, does not forfeit a constitutional claim or defense that is otherwise timely asserted.

(Adopted April 12, 2006, effective December 1, 2006; amended April 30, 2007, effective December 1, 2007.)

RULE 5.2. PRIVACY PROTECTION FOR FILINGS MADE WITH THE COURT

(a) Redacted Filings. Unless the court orders otherwise, in an electronic or paper filing with the court that contains an individual's social-security number, taxpayer-identification number, or birth date, the name of an individual known to be a minor, or a financial-account number, a party or nonparty making the filing may include only:

(1) the last four digits of the social-security number and taxpayer-identification number;

(2) the year of the individual's birth;

(3) the minor's initials; and

(4) the last four digits of the financial-account number.

(b) Exemptions from the Redaction Requirement. The redaction requirement does not apply to the following:

(1) a financial-account number that identifies the property allegedly subject to forfeiture in a forfeiture proceeding;

(2) the record of an administrative or agency proceeding;

(3) the official record of a state-court proceeding;

(4) the record of a court or tribunal, if that record was not subject to the redaction requirement when originally filed;

(5) a filing covered by Rule 5.2(c) or (d); and

(6) a pro se filing in an action brought under 28 U.S.C. §§ 2241, 2254, or 2255.

(c) Limitations on Remote Access to Electronic Files; Social–Security Appeals and Immigration Cases. Unless the court orders otherwise, in an action for benefits under the Social Security Act, and in an action or proceeding relating to an order of removal, to relief from removal, or to immigration benefits or detention, access to an electronic file is authorized as follows:

(1) the parties and their attorneys may have remote electronic access to any part of the case file, including the administrative record;

(2) any other person may have electronic access to the full record at the courthouse, but may have remote electronic access only to:

(A) the docket maintained by the court; and

(B) an opinion, order, judgment, or other disposition of the court, but not any other part of the case file or the administrative record.

(d) Filings Made Under Seal. The court may order that a filing be made under seal without redaction. The court may later unseal the filing or order the person who made the filing to file a redacted version for the public record.

(e) Protective Orders. For good cause, the court may by order in a case:

(1) require redaction of additional information; or

(2) limit or prohibit a nonparty's remote electronic access to a document filed with the court.

(f) Option for Additional Unredacted Filing Under Seal. A person making a redacted filing may also file an unredacted copy under seal. The court must retain the unredacted copy as part of the record.

(g) Option for Filing a Reference List. A filing that contains redacted information may be filed together with a reference list that identifies each item of redacted information and specifies an appropriate identifier that uniquely corresponds to each item listed. The list must be filed under seal and may be amended as of right. Any reference in the case to a listed identifier will be construed to refer to the corresponding item of information.

(h) Waiver of Protection of Identifiers. A person waives the protection of Rule 5.2(a) as to the person's own information by filing it without redaction and not under seal.

(Adopted April 30, 2007, effective December 1, 2007.)

RULE 6. COMPUTING AND EXTENDING TIME; TIME FOR MOTION PAPERS

(a) Computing Time. The following rules apply in computing any time period specified in these rules, in any local rule or court order, or in any statute that does not specify a method of computing time.

(1) ***Period Stated in Days or a Longer Unit.*** When the period is stated in days or a longer unit of time:

(A) exclude the day of the event that triggers the period;

(B) count every day, including intermediate Saturdays, Sundays, and legal holidays; and

(C) include the last day of the period, but if the last day is a Saturday, Sunday, or legal holiday, the period continues to run until the end of the next day that is not a Saturday, Sunday, or legal holiday.

(2) ***Period Stated in Hours.*** When the period is stated in hours:

(A) begin counting immediately on the occurrence of the event that triggers the period;

(B) count every hour, including hours during intermediate Saturdays, Sundays, and legal holidays; and

(C) if the period would end on a Saturday, Sunday, or legal holiday, the period continues to run until the same time on the next day that is not a Saturday, Sunday, or legal holiday.

(3) ***Inaccessibility of the Clerk's Office.*** Unless the court orders otherwise, if the clerk's office is inaccessible:

(A) on the last day for filing under Rule 6(a)(1), then the time for filing is extended to the first accessible day that is not a Saturday, Sunday, or legal holiday; or

(B) during the last hour for filing under Rule 6(a)(2), then the time for filing is extended to the same time on the first accessible day that is not a Saturday, Sunday, or legal holiday.

(4) ***"Last Day" Defined.*** Unless a different time is set by a statute, local rule, or court order, the last day ends:

(A) for electronic filing, at midnight in the court's time zone; and

(B) for filing by other means, when the clerk's office is scheduled to close.

(5) ***"Next Day" Defined.*** The "next day" is determined by continuing to count forward when the period is measured

after an event and backward when measured before an event.

(6) ***"Legal Holiday" Defined.*** "Legal holiday" means:

(A) the day set aside by statute for observing New Year's Day, Martin Luther King Jr.'s Birthday, Washington's Birthday, Memorial Day, Independence Day, Labor Day, Columbus Day, Veterans' Day, Thanksgiving Day, or Christmas Day;

(B) any day declared a holiday by the President or Congress; and

(C) for periods that are measured after an event, any other day declared a holiday by the state where the district court is located.

(b) Extending Time.

(1) ***In General.*** When an act may or must be done within a specified time, the court may, for good cause, extend the time:

(A) with or without motion or notice if the court acts, or if a request is made, before the original time or its extension expires; or

(B) on motion made after the time has expired if the party failed to act because of excusable neglect.

(2) ***Exceptions.*** A court must not extend the time to act under Rules 50(b) and (d), 52(b), 59(b), (d), and (e), and 60(b).

(c) Motions, Notices of Hearing, and Affidavits.

(1) ***In General.*** A written motion and notice of the hearing must be served at least 14 days before the time specified for the hearing, with the following exceptions:

(A) when the motion may be heard ex parte;

(B) when these rules set a different time; or

(C) when a court order—which a party may, for good cause, apply for ex parte—sets a different time.

(2) ***Supporting Affidavit.*** Any affidavit supporting a motion must be served with the motion. Except as Rule 59(c) provides otherwise, any opposing affidavit must be served at least 7 days before the hearing, unless the court permits service at another time.

(d) Additional Time After Certain Kinds of Service. When a party may or must act within a specified time after being served and service is made under Rule 5(b)(2)(C) (mail), (D) (leaving with the clerk), or (F) (other means consented to), 3 days are added after the period would otherwise expire under Rule 6(a).

(Amended December 27, 1946, effective March 19, 1948; January 21, 1963, effective July 1, 1963; February 28, 1966, effective July 1, 1966; December 4, 1967, effective July 1, 1968; March 1, 1971, effective July 1, 1971; April 28, 1983, effective August 1, 1983; April 29, 1985, effective August 1, 1985; March 2, 1987, effective August 1, 1987; April 29, 1999, effective December 1, 1999; April 23, 2001, effective December 1, 2001; April 25, 2005, effective December 1, 2005; April 30, 2007, effective December 1, 2007; March 26, 2009, effective December 1, 2009; April 28, 2016, effective December 1, 2016.)

TITLE III. PLEADINGS AND MOTIONS

RULE 7. PLEADINGS ALLOWED; FORM OF MOTIONS AND OTHER PAPERS

(a) Pleadings. Only these pleadings are allowed:

(1) a complaint;

(2) an answer to a complaint;

(3) an answer to a counterclaim designated as a counterclaim;

(4) an answer to a crossclaim;

(5) a third-party complaint;

(6) an answer to a third-party complaint; and

(7) if the court orders one, a reply to an answer.

(b) Motions and Other Papers.

(1) ***In General.*** A request for a court order must be made by motion. The motion must:

(A) be in writing unless made during a hearing or trial;

(B) state with particularity the grounds for seeking the order; and

(C) state the relief sought.

(2) ***Form.*** The rules governing captions and other matters of form in pleadings apply to motions and other papers.

(Amended December 27, 1946, effective March 19, 1948; January 21, 1963, effective July 1, 1963; April 28, 1983, effective August 1, 1983; April 30, 2007, effective December 1, 2007.)

RULE 7.1. DISCLOSURE STATEMENT

(a) Who Must File; Contents. A nongovernmental corporate party must file two copies of a disclosure statement that:

(1) identifies any parent corporation and any publicly held corporation owning 10% or more of its stock; or

(2) states that there is no such corporation.

(b) Time to File; Supplemental Filing. A party must:

(1) file the disclosure statement with its first appearance, pleading, petition, motion, response, or other request addressed to the court; and

(2) promptly file a supplemental statement if any required information changes.

(Adopted April 29, 2002, effective December 1, 2002; April 30, 2007, effective December 1, 2007.)

RULE 8. GENERAL RULES OF PLEADING

(a) Claim for Relief. A pleading that states a claim for relief must contain:

(1) a short and plain statement of the grounds for the court's jurisdiction, unless the court already has jurisdiction and the claim needs no new jurisdictional support;

(2) a short and plain statement of the claim showing that the pleader is entitled to relief; and

(3) a demand for the relief sought, which may include relief in the alternative or different types of relief.

(b) Defenses; Admissions and Denials.

(1) ***In General.*** In responding to a pleading, a party must:

(A) state in short and plain terms its defenses to each claim asserted against it; and

(B) admit or deny the allegations asserted against it by an opposing party.

(2) ***Denials—Responding to the Substance.*** A denial must fairly respond to the substance of the allegation.

(3) ***General and Specific Denials.*** A party that intends in good faith to deny all the allegations of a pleading—including the jurisdictional grounds—may do so by a general denial. A party that does not intend to deny all the allegations must either specifically deny designated allegations or generally deny all except those specifically admitted.

(4) ***Denying Part of an Allegation.*** A party that intends in good faith to deny only part of an allegation must admit the part that is true and deny the rest.

(5) ***Lacking Knowledge or Information.*** A party that lacks knowledge or information sufficient to form a belief about the truth of an allegation must so state, and the statement has the effect of a denial.

(6) ***Effect of Failing to Deny.*** An allegation—other than one relating to the amount of damages—is admitted if a responsive pleading is required and the allegation is not denied. If a responsive pleading is not required, an allegation is considered denied or avoided.

(c) Affirmative Defenses.

(1) ***In General.*** In responding to a pleading, a party must affirmatively state any avoidance or affirmative defense, including:

- accord and satisfaction;
- arbitration and award;
- assumption of risk;
- contributory negligence;
- duress;
- estoppel;
- failure of consideration;
- fraud;
- illegality;
- injury by fellow servant;
- laches;
- license;
- payment;
- release;
- res judicata;
- statute of frauds;
- statute of limitations; and
- waiver.

(2) ***Mistaken Designation.*** If a party mistakenly designates a defense as a counterclaim, or a counterclaim as a defense, the court must, if justice requires, treat the pleading as though it were correctly designated, and may impose terms for doing so.

(d) Pleading to Be Concise and Direct; Alternative Statements; Inconsistency.

(1) ***In General.*** Each allegation must be simple, concise, and direct. No technical form is required.

(2) ***Alternative Statements of a Claim or Defense.*** A party may set out 2 or more statements of a claim or defense alternatively or hypothetically, either in a single count or defense or in separate ones. If a party makes alternative statements, the pleading is sufficient if any one of them is sufficient.

(3) ***Inconsistent Claims or Defenses.*** A party may state as many separate claims or defenses as it has, regardless of consistency.

(e) Construing Pleadings. Pleadings must be construed so as to do justice.

(Amended February 28, 1966, effective July 1, 1966; March 2, 1987, effective August 1, 1987; April 30, 2007, effective December 1, 2007; April 28, 2010, effective December 1, 2010.)

RULE 9. PLEADING SPECIAL MATTERS

(a) Capacity or Authority to Sue; Legal Existence.

(1) ***In General.*** Except when required to show that the court has jurisdiction, a pleading need not allege:

(A) a party's capacity to sue or be sued;

(B) a party's authority to sue or be sued in a representative capacity; or

(C) the legal existence of an organized association of persons that is made a party.

(2) ***Raising Those Issues.*** To raise any of those issues, a party must do so by a specific denial, which must state any supporting facts that are peculiarly within the party's knowledge.

(b) Fraud or Mistake; Conditions of Mind. In alleging fraud or mistake, a party must state with particularity the circumstances constituting fraud or mistake. Malice, intent, knowledge, and other conditions of a person's mind may be alleged generally.

(c) Conditions Precedent. In pleading conditions precedent, it suffices to allege generally that all conditions precedent have occurred or been performed. But when denying that a condition precedent has occurred or been performed, a party must do so with particularity.

(d) Official Document or Act. In pleading an official document or official act, it suffices to allege that the document was legally issued or the act legally done.

(e) Judgment. In pleading a judgment or decision of a domestic or foreign court, a judicial or quasi-judicial tribunal, or a board or officer, it suffices to plead the judgment or decision without showing jurisdiction to render it.

(f) Time and Place. An allegation of time or place is material when testing the sufficiency of a pleading.

(g) Special Damages. If an item of special damage is claimed, it must be specifically stated.

(h) Admiralty or Maritime Claim.

(1) ***How Designated.*** If a claim for relief is within the admiralty or maritime jurisdiction and also within the court's subject-matter jurisdiction on some other ground, the pleading may designate the claim as an admiralty or maritime claim for purposes of Rules 14(c), 38(e), and 82 and the Supplemental Rules for Admiralty or Maritime Claims and Asset Forfeiture Actions. A claim cognizable only in the admiralty or maritime jurisdiction is an admiralty or maritime claim for those purposes, whether or not so designated.

(2) ***Designation for Appeal.*** A case that includes an admiralty or maritime claim within this subdivision (h) is an admiralty case within 28 U.S.C. § 1292(a)(3).

(Amended February 28, 1966, effective July 1, 1966; December 4, 1967, effective July 1, 1968; March 30, 1970, effective July 1, 1970; March 2, 1987, effective August 1, 1987; April 11, 1997, effective December 1, 1997; April 12, 2006, effective December 1, 2006; April 30, 2007, effective December 1, 2007.)

RULE 10. FORM OF PLEADINGS

(a) Caption; Names of Parties. Every pleading must have a caption with the court's name, a title, a file number, and a Rule 7(a) designation. The title of the complaint must name all the parties; the title of other pleadings, after naming the first party on each side, may refer generally to other parties.

(b) Paragraphs; Separate Statements. A party must state its claims or defenses in numbered paragraphs, each limited as far as practicable to a single set of circumstances. A later pleading may refer by number to a paragraph in an earlier pleading. If doing so would promote clarity, each claim founded on a separate transaction or occurrence—and each defense other than a denial—must be stated in a separate count or defense.

(c) Adoption by Reference; Exhibits. A statement in a pleading may be adopted by reference elsewhere in the same pleading or in any other pleading or motion. A copy of a written instrument that is an exhibit to a pleading is a part of the pleading for all purposes.

(Amended April 30, 2007, effective December 1, 2007.)

RULE 11. SIGNING PLEADINGS, MOTIONS, AND OTHER PAPERS; REPRESENTATIONS TO THE COURT; SANCTIONS

(a) Signature. Every pleading, written motion, and other paper must be signed by at least one attorney of record in the attorney's name—or by a party personally if the party is unrepresented. The paper must state the signer's address, e-mail address, and telephone number. Unless a rule or statute specifically states otherwise, a pleading need not be verified or accompanied by an affidavit. The court must strike an unsigned paper unless the omission is promptly corrected after being called to the attorney's or party's attention.

(b) Representations to the Court. By presenting to the court a pleading, written motion, or other paper—whether by signing, filing, submitting, or later advocating it—an attorney or unrepresented party certifies that to the best of the person's knowledge, information, and belief, formed after an inquiry reasonable under the circumstances:

(1) it is not being presented for any improper purpose, such as to harass, cause unnecessary delay, or needlessly increase the cost of litigation;

(2) the claims, defenses, and other legal contentions are warranted by existing law or by a nonfrivolous argument for extending, modifying, or reversing existing law or for establishing new law;

(3) the factual contentions have evidentiary support or, if specifically so identified, will likely have evidentiary support after a reasonable opportunity for further investigation or discovery; and

(4) the denials of factual contentions are warranted on the evidence or, if specifically so identified, are reasonably based on belief or a lack of information.

(c) Sanctions.

(1) ***In General.*** If, after notice and a reasonable opportunity to respond, the court determines that Rule 11(b) has been violated, the court may impose an appropriate sanction on any attorney, law firm, or party that violated the rule or is responsible for the violation. Absent exceptional circumstances, a law firm must be held jointly responsible for a violation committed by its partner, associate, or employee.

(2) ***Motion for Sanctions.*** A motion for sanctions must be made separately from any other motion and must describe the specific conduct that allegedly violates Rule 11(b). The motion must be served under Rule 5, but it must not be filed or be presented to the court if the challenged paper, claim, defense, contention, or denial is withdrawn or appropriately corrected within 21 days after service or within another time the court sets. If warranted, the court may award to the prevailing party the reasonable expenses, including attorney's fees, incurred for the motion.

(3) ***On the Court's Initiative.*** On its own, the court may order an attorney, law firm, or party to show cause why conduct specifically described in the order has not violated Rule 11(b).

(4) ***Nature of a Sanction.*** A sanction imposed under this rule must be limited to what suffices to deter repetition of the conduct or comparable conduct by others similarly situated. The sanction may include nonmonetary directives; an order to pay a penalty into court; or, if imposed on motion and warranted for effective deterrence, an order directing payment to the movant of part or all of the reasonable attorney's fees and other expenses directly resulting from the violation.

(5) ***Limitations on Monetary Sanctions.*** The court must not impose a monetary sanction:

(A) against a represented party for violating Rule 11(b)(2); or

(B) on its own, unless it issued the show-cause order under Rule 11(c)(3) before voluntary dismissal or settlement of the claims made by or against the party that is, or whose attorneys are, to be sanctioned.

(6) ***Requirements for an Order.*** An order imposing a sanction must describe the sanctioned conduct and explain the basis for the sanction.

(d) Inapplicability to Discovery. This rule does not apply to disclosures and discovery requests, responses, objections, and motions under Rules 26 through 37.

(Amended April 28, 1983, effective August 1, 1983; March 2, 1987, effective August 1, 1987; April 22, 1993, effective December 1, 1993; April 30, 2007, effective December 1, 2007.)

RULE 12. DEFENSES AND OBJECTIONS: WHEN AND HOW PRESENTED; MOTION FOR JUDGMENT ON THE PLEADINGS; CONSOLIDATING MOTIONS; WAIVING DEFENSES; PRETRIAL HEARING

(a) Time to Serve a Responsive Pleading.

(1) ***In General.*** Unless another time is specified by this rule or a federal statute, the time for serving a responsive pleading is as follows:

(A) A defendant must serve an answer:

(i) within 21 days after being served with the summons and complaint; or

(ii) if it has timely waived service under Rule 4(d), within 60 days after the request for a waiver was sent, or within 90 days after it was sent to the defendant outside any judicial district of the United States.

(B) A party must serve an answer to a counterclaim or crossclaim within 21 days after being served with the pleading that states the counterclaim or crossclaim.

(C) A party must serve a reply to an answer within 21 days after being served with an order to reply, unless the order specifies a different time.

(2) ***United States and Its Agencies, Officers, or Employees Sued in an Official Capacity.*** The United States, a United States agency, or a United States officer or employee sued only in an official capacity must serve an answer to a complaint, counterclaim, or crossclaim within 60 days after service on the United States attorney.

(3) ***United States Officers or Employees Sued in an Individual Capacity.*** A United States officer or employee sued in an individual capacity for an act or omission occurring in connection with duties performed on the United States' behalf must serve an answer to a complaint, counterclaim, or crossclaim within 60 days after service on the officer or employee or service on the United States attorney, whichever is later.

(4) ***Effect of a Motion.*** Unless the court sets a different time, serving a motion under this rule alters these periods as follows:

(A) if the court denies the motion or postpones its disposition until trial, the responsive pleading must be served within 14 days after notice of the court's action; or

(B) if the court grants a motion for a more definite statement, the responsive pleading must be served within 14 days after the more definite statement is served.

(b) How to Present Defenses. Every defense to a claim for relief in any pleading must be asserted in the responsive pleading if one is required. But a party may assert the following defenses by motion:

(1) lack of subject-matter jurisdiction;

(2) lack of personal jurisdiction;

(3) improper venue;

(4) insufficient process;

(5) insufficient service of process;

(6) failure to state a claim upon which relief can be granted; and

(7) failure to join a party under Rule 19.

A motion asserting any of these defenses must be made before pleading if a responsive pleading is allowed. If a pleading sets out a claim for relief that does not require a responsive pleading, an opposing party may assert at trial any defense to that claim. No defense or objection is waived by joining it with one or more other defenses or objections in a responsive pleading or in a motion.

(c) Motion for Judgment on the Pleadings. After the pleadings are closed—but early enough not to delay trial—a party may move for judgment on the pleadings.

(d) Result of Presenting Matters Outside the Pleadings. If, on a motion under Rule 12(b)(6) or 12(c), matters outside the pleadings are presented to and not excluded by the court, the motion must be treated as one for summary judgment under Rule 56. All parties must be given a reasonable opportunity to present all the material that is pertinent to the motion.

(e) Motion for a More Definite Statement. A party may move for a more definite statement of a pleading to which a responsive pleading is allowed but which is so vague or ambiguous that the party cannot reasonably prepare a response. The motion must be made before filing a responsive pleading and must point out the defects complained of and the details desired. If the court orders a more definite statement and the order is not obeyed within 14 days after notice of the order or within the time the court sets, the court may strike the pleading or issue any other appropriate order.

(f) Motion to Strike. The court may strike from a pleading an insufficient defense or any redundant, immaterial, impertinent, or scandalous matter. The court may act:

(1) on its own; or

(2) on motion made by a party either before responding to the pleading or, if a response is not allowed, within 21 days after being served with the pleading.

(g) Joining Motions.

(1) ***Right to Join.*** A motion under this rule may be joined with any other motion allowed by this rule.

(2) ***Limitation on Further Motions.*** Except as provided in Rule 12(h)(2) or (3), a party that makes a motion under this rule must not make another motion under this rule raising a defense or objection that was available to the party but omitted from its earlier motion.

(h) Waiving and Preserving Certain Defenses.

(1) ***When Some Are Waived.*** A party waives any defense listed in Rule 12(b)(2)-(5) by:

(A) omitting it from a motion in the circumstances described in Rule 12(g)(2); or

(B) failing to either:

(i) make it by motion under this rule; or

(ii) include it in a responsive pleading or in an amendment allowed by Rule 15(a)(1) as a matter of course.

(2) ***When to Raise Others.*** Failure to state a claim upon which relief can be granted, to join a person required by Rule 19(b), or to state a legal defense to a claim may be raised:

(A) in any pleading allowed or ordered under Rule 7(a);

(B) by a motion under Rule 12(c); or

(C) at trial.

(3) ***Lack of Subject-Matter Jurisdiction.*** If the court determines at any time that it lacks subject-matter jurisdiction, the court must dismiss the action.

(i) Hearing Before Trial. If a party so moves, any defense listed in Rule 12(b)(1)-(7)—whether made in a pleading or by motion—and a motion under Rule 12(c) must be heard and decided before trial unless the court orders a deferral until trial.

(Amended December 27, 1946, effective March 19, 1948; January 21, 1963, effective July 1, 1963; February 28, 1966, effective July 1, 1966; March 2, 1987, effective August 1, 1987; April 22, 1993, effective December 1, 1993; April 17, 2000, effective December 1, 2000; April 30, 2007, effective December 1, 2007; March 26, 2009, effective December 1, 2009.)

RULE 13. COUNTERCLAIM AND CROSSCLAIM

(a) Compulsory Counterclaim.

(1) ***In General.*** A pleading must state as a counterclaim any claim that—at the time of its service—the pleader has against an opposing party if the claim:

(A) arises out of the transaction or occurrence that is the subject matter of the opposing party's claim; and

(B) does not require adding another party over whom the court cannot acquire jurisdiction.

(2) ***Exceptions.*** The pleader need not state the claim if:

(A) when the action was commenced, the claim was the subject of another pending action; or

(B) the opposing party sued on its claim by attachment or other process that did not establish personal jurisdiction over the pleader on that claim, and the pleader does not assert any counterclaim under this rule.

(b) Permissive Counterclaim. A pleading may state as a counterclaim against an opposing party any claim that is not compulsory.

(c) Relief Sought in a Counterclaim. A counterclaim need not diminish or defeat the recovery sought by the opposing party. It may request relief that exceeds in amount or differs in kind from the relief sought by the opposing party.

(d) Counterclaim Against the United States. These rules do not expand the right to assert a counterclaim—or to claim a credit—against the United States or a United States officer or agency.

(e) Counterclaim Maturing or Acquired After Pleading. The court may permit a party to file a supplemental pleading asserting a counterclaim that matured or was acquired by the party after serving an earlier pleading.

(f) [Abrogated]

(g) Crossclaim Against a Coparty. A pleading may state as a crossclaim any claim by one party against a coparty if the claim arises out of the transaction or occurrence that is the subject matter of the original action or of a counterclaim, or if the claim relates to any property that is the subject matter of the original action. The crossclaim may include a claim that the coparty is or may be liable to the cross-claimant for all or part of a claim asserted in the action against the cross-claimant.

(h) Joining Additional Parties. Rules 19 and 20 govern the addition of a person as a party to a counterclaim or crossclaim.

(i) Separate Trials; Separate Judgments. If the court orders separate trials under Rule 42(b), it may enter judgment on a counterclaim or crossclaim under Rule 54(b) when it has jurisdiction to do so, even if the opposing party's claims have been dismissed or otherwise resolved.

(Amended December 27, 1946, effective March 19, 1948; January 21, 1963, effective July 1, 1963; February 28, 1966, effective July 1, 1966; March 2, 1987, effective August 1, 1987; April 30, 2007, effective December 1, 2007; March 26, 2009, effective December 1, 2009.)

RULE 14. THIRD-PARTY PRACTICE

(a) When a Defending Party May Bring in a Third Party.

(1) ***Timing of the Summons and Complaint.*** A defending party may, as third-party plaintiff, serve a summons and complaint on a nonparty who is or may be liable to it for all or part of the claim against it. But the third-party plaintiff must, by motion, obtain the court's leave if it files the third-party complaint more than 14 days after serving its original answer.

(2) ***Third-Party Defendant's Claims and Defenses.*** The person served with the summons and third-party complaint—the "third-party defendant":

(A) must assert any defense against the third-party plaintiff's claim under Rule 12;

(B) must assert any counterclaim against the third-party plaintiff under Rule 13(a), and may assert any counterclaim against the third-party plaintiff under Rule

13(b) or any crossclaim against another third-party defendant under Rule 13(g);

(C) may assert against the plaintiff any defense that the third-party plaintiff has to the plaintiff's claim; and

(D) may also assert against the plaintiff any claim arising out of the transaction or occurrence that is the subject matter of the plaintiff's claim against the third-party plaintiff.

(3) ***Plaintiff's Claims Against a Third-Party Defendant.*** The plaintiff may assert against the third-party defendant any claim arising out of the transaction or occurrence that is the subject matter of the plaintiff's claim against the third-party plaintiff. The third-party defendant must then assert any defense under Rule 12 and any counterclaim under Rule 13(a), and may assert any counterclaim under Rule 13(b) or any crossclaim under Rule 13(g).

(4) ***Motion to Strike, Sever, or Try Separately.*** Any party may move to strike the third-party claim, to sever it, or to try it separately.

(5) ***Third-Party Defendant's Claim Against a Nonparty.*** A third-party defendant may proceed under this rule against a nonparty who is or may be liable to the third-party defendant for all or part of any claim against it.

(6) ***Third-Party Complaint In Rem.*** If it is within the admiralty or maritime jurisdiction, a third-party complaint may be in rem. In that event, a reference in this rule to the "summons" includes the warrant of arrest, and a reference to the defendant or third-party plaintiff includes, when appropriate, a person who asserts a right under Supplemental Rule C(6)(a)(i) in the property arrested.

(b) When a Plaintiff May Bring in a Third Party. When a claim is asserted against a plaintiff, the plaintiff may bring in a third party if this rule would allow a defendant to do so.

(c) Admiralty or Maritime Claim.

(1) ***Scope of Impleader.*** If a plaintiff asserts an admiralty or maritime claim under Rule 9(h), the defendant or a person who asserts a right under Supplemental Rule C(6)(a)(i) may, as a third-party plaintiff, bring in a third-party defendant who may be wholly or partly liable—either to the plaintiff or to the third-party plaintiff—for remedy over, contribution, or otherwise on account of the same transaction, occurrence, or series of transactions or occurrences.

(2) ***Defending Against a Demand for Judgment for the Plaintiff.*** The third-party plaintiff may demand judgment in the plaintiff's favor against the third-party defendant. In that event, the third-party defendant must defend under Rule 12 against the plaintiff's claim as well as the third-party plaintiff's claim; and the action proceeds as if the plaintiff had sued both the third-party defendant and the third-party plaintiff.

(Amended December 27, 1946, effective March 19, 1948; January 21, 1963, effective July 1, 1963; February 28, 1966, effective July 1, 1966; March 2, 1987, effective August 1, 1987; April 17, 2000, effective December 1, 2000; April 12, 2006, effective December 1, 2006; April 30, 2007, effective December 1, 2007; March 26, 2009, effective December 1, 2009.)

RULE 15. AMENDED AND SUPPLEMENTAL PLEADINGS

(a) Amendments Before Trial.

(1) ***Amending as a Matter of Course.*** A party may amend its pleading once as a matter of course within:

(A) 21 days after serving it, or

(B) if the pleading is one to which a responsive pleading is required, 21 days after service of a responsive pleading or 21 days after service of a motion under Rule 12(b), (e), or (f), whichever is earlier.

(2) ***Other Amendments.*** In all other cases, a party may amend its pleading only with the opposing party's written consent or the court's leave. The court should freely give leave when justice so requires.

(3) ***Time to Respond.*** Unless the court orders otherwise, any required response to an amended pleading must be made within the time remaining to respond to the original pleading or within 14 days after service of the amended pleading, whichever is later.

(b) Amendments During and After Trial.

(1) ***Based on an Objection at Trial.*** If, at trial, a party objects that evidence is not within the issues raised in the pleadings, the court may permit the pleadings to be amended. The court should freely permit an amendment when doing so will aid in presenting the merits and the objecting party fails to satisfy the court that the evidence would prejudice that party's action or defense on the merits. The court may grant a continuance to enable the objecting party to meet the evidence.

(2) ***For Issues Tried by Consent.*** When an issue not raised by the pleadings is tried by the parties' express or implied consent, it must be treated in all respects as if raised in the pleadings. A party may move—at any time, even after judgment—to amend the pleadings to conform them to the evidence and to raise an unpleaded issue. But failure to amend does not affect the result of the trial of that issue.

(c) Relation Back of Amendments.

(1) ***When an Amendment Relates Back.*** An amendment to a pleading relates back to the date of the original pleading when:

(A) the law that provides the applicable statute of limitations allows relation back;

(B) the amendment asserts a claim or defense that arose out of the conduct, transaction, or occurrence set out—or attempted to be set out—in the original pleading; or

(C) the amendment changes the party or the naming of the party against whom a claim is asserted, if Rule 15(c)(1)(B) is satisfied and if, within the period provided by Rule 4(m) for serving the summons and complaint, the party to be brought in by amendment:

(i) received such notice of the action that it will not be prejudiced in defending on the merits; and

(ii) knew or should have known that the action would have been brought against it, but for a mistake concerning the proper party's identity.

(2) ***Notice to the United States.*** When the United States or a United States officer or agency is added as a defendant by amendment, the notice requirements of Rule 15(c)(1)(C)(i) and (ii) are satisfied if, during the stated period, process was delivered or mailed to the United States attorney or the United States attorney's designee, to the Attorney General of the United States, or to the officer or agency.

(d) Supplemental Pleadings. On motion and reasonable notice, the court may, on just terms, permit a party to serve a supplemental pleading setting out any transaction, occurrence, or event that happened after the date of the pleading to be supplemented. The court may permit supplementation even though the original pleading is defective in stating a claim or defense. The court may order that the opposing party plead to the supplemental pleading within a specified time.

(Amended January 21, 1963, effective July 1, 1963; February 28, 1966, effective July 1, 1966; March 2, 1987, effective August 1, 1987; April 30, 1991, effective December 1, 1991; amended by Pub.L. 102–198, § 11, December 9, 1991, 105 Stat. 1626; amended April 22, 1993, effective December 1, 1993; April 30, 2007, effective December 1, 2007; March 26, 2009, effective December 1, 2009.)

RULE 16. PRETRIAL CONFERENCES; SCHEDULING; MANAGEMENT

(a) Purposes of a Pretrial Conference. In any action, the court may order the attorneys and any unrepresented parties to appear for one or more pretrial conferences for such purposes as:

(1) expediting disposition of the action;

(2) establishing early and continuing control so that the case will not be protracted because of lack of management;

(3) discouraging wasteful pretrial activities;

(4) improving the quality of the trial through more thorough preparation; and

(5) facilitating settlement.

(b) Scheduling.

(1) ***Scheduling Order.*** Except in categories of actions exempted by local rule, the district judge—or a magistrate judge when authorized by local rule—must issue a scheduling order:

(A) after receiving the parties' report under Rule 26(f); or

(B) after consulting with the parties' attorneys and any unrepresented parties at a scheduling conference.

(2) ***Time to Issue.*** The judge must issue the scheduling order as soon as practicable, but unless the judge finds good cause for delay, the judge must issue it within the earlier of 90 days after any defendant has been served with the complaint or 60 days after any defendant has appeared.

(3) ***Contents of the Order.***

(A) *Required Contents.* The scheduling order must limit the time to join other parties, amend the pleadings, complete discovery, and file motions.

(B) *Permitted Contents.* The scheduling order may:

(i) modify the timing of disclosures under Rules 26(a) and 26(e)(1);

(ii) modify the extent of discovery;

(iii) provide for disclosure, discovery, or preservation of electronically stored information;

(iv) include any agreements the parties reach for asserting claims of privilege or of protection as trial-preparation material after information is produced, including agreements reached under Federal Rule of Evidence 502;

(v) direct that before moving for an order relating to discovery, the movant must request a conference with the court;

(vi) set dates for pretrial conferences and for trial; and

(vii) include other appropriate matters.

(4) ***Modifying a Schedule.*** A schedule may be modified only for good cause and with the judge's consent.

(c) Attendance and Matters for Consideration at a Pretrial Conference.

(1) ***Attendance.*** A represented party must authorize at least one of its attorneys to make stipulations and admissions about all matters that can reasonably be anticipated for discussion at a pretrial conference. If appropriate, the court may require that a party or its representative be present or reasonably available by other means to consider possible settlement.

(2) ***Matters for Consideration.*** At any pretrial conference, the court may consider and take appropriate action on the following matters:

(A) formulating and simplifying the issues, and eliminating frivolous claims or defenses;

(B) amending the pleadings if necessary or desirable;

(C) obtaining admissions and stipulations about facts and documents to avoid unnecessary proof, and ruling in advance on the admissibility of evidence;

(D) avoiding unnecessary proof and cumulative evidence, and limiting the use of testimony under Federal Rule of Evidence 702;

(E) determining the appropriateness and timing of summary adjudication under Rule 56;

(F) controlling and scheduling discovery, including orders affecting disclosures and discovery under Rule 26 and Rules 29 through 37;

(G) identifying witnesses and documents, scheduling the filing and exchange of any pretrial briefs, and setting dates for further conferences and for trial;

(H) referring matters to a magistrate judge or a master;

(I) settling the case and using special procedures to assist in resolving the dispute when authorized by statute or local rule;

(J) determining the form and content of the pretrial order;

(K) disposing of pending motions;

(L) adopting special procedures for managing potentially difficult or protracted actions that may involve complex issues, multiple parties, difficult legal questions, or unusual proof problems;

(M) ordering a separate trial under Rule 42(b) of a claim, counterclaim, crossclaim, third-party claim, or particular issue;

(N) ordering the presentation of evidence early in the trial on a manageable issue that might, on the evidence, be the basis for a judgment as a matter of law under Rule 50(a) or a judgment on partial findings under Rule 52(c);

(O) establishing a reasonable limit on the time allowed to present evidence; and

(P) facilitating in other ways the just, speedy, and inexpensive disposition of the action.

(d) Pretrial Orders. After any conference under this rule, the court should issue an order reciting the action taken. This order controls the course of the action unless the court modifies it.

(e) Final Pretrial Conference and Orders. The court may hold a final pretrial conference to formulate a trial plan, including a plan to facilitate the admission of evidence. The conference must be held as close to the start of trial as is reasonable, and must be attended by at least one attorney who will conduct the trial for each party and by any unrepresented party. The court may modify the order issued after a final pretrial conference only to prevent manifest injustice.

(f) Sanctions.

(1) ***In General.*** On motion or on its own, the court may issue any just orders, including those authorized by Rule 37(b)(2)(A)(ii)-(vii), if a party or its attorney:

(A) fails to appear at a scheduling or other pretrial conference;

(B) is substantially unprepared to participate—or does not participate in good faith—in the conference; or

(C) fails to obey a scheduling or other pretrial order.

(2) ***Imposing Fees and Costs.*** Instead of or in addition to any other sanction, the court must order the party, its attorney, or both to pay the reasonable expenses—including attorney's fees—incurred because of any noncompliance with this rule, unless the noncompliance was substantially justified or other circumstances make an award of expenses unjust.

(Amended April 28, 1983, effective August 1, 1983; March 2, 1987, effective August 1, 1987; April 22, 1993, effective December 1, 1993; April 12, 2006, effective December 1, 2006; April 30, 2007, effective December 1, 2007; April 29, 2015, effective December 1, 2015.)

TITLE IV. PARTIES

RULE 17. PLAINTIFF AND DEFENDANT; CAPACITY; PUBLIC OFFICERS

(a) Real Party in Interest.

(1) ***Designation in General.*** An action must be prosecuted in the name of the real party in interest. The following may sue in their own names without joining the person for whose benefit the action is brought:

(A) an executor;

(B) an administrator;

(C) a guardian;

(D) a bailee;

(E) a trustee of an express trust;

(F) a party with whom or in whose name a contract has been made for another's benefit; and

(G) a party authorized by statute.

(2) ***Action in the Name of the United States for Another's Use or Benefit.*** When a federal statute so provides, an action for another's use or benefit must be brought in the name of the United States.

(3) ***Joinder of the Real Party in Interest.*** The court may not dismiss an action for failure to prosecute in the name of the real party in interest until, after an objection, a reasonable time has been allowed for the real party in interest to ratify, join, or be substituted into the action. After ratification, joinder, or substitution, the action proceeds as if it had been originally commenced by the real party in interest.

(b) Capacity to Sue or Be Sued. Capacity to sue or be sued is determined as follows:

(1) for an individual who is not acting in a representative capacity, by the law of the individual's domicile;

(2) for a corporation, by the law under which it was organized; and

(3) for all other parties, by the law of the state where the court is located, except that:

(A) a partnership or other unincorporated association with no such capacity under that state's law may sue or be sued in its common name to enforce a substantive right existing under the United States Constitution or laws; and

(B) 28 U.S.C. §§ 754 and 959(a) govern the capacity of a receiver appointed by a United States court to sue or be sued in a United States court.

(c) Minor or Incompetent Person.

(1) ***With a Representative.*** The following representatives may sue or defend on behalf of a minor or an incompetent person:

(A) a general guardian;

(B) a committee;

(C) a conservator; or

(D) a like fiduciary.

(2) ***Without a Representative.*** A minor or an incompetent person who does not have a duly appointed representative may sue by a next friend or by a guardian ad litem. The court must appoint a guardian ad litem—or issue another appropriate order—to protect a minor or incompetent person who is unrepresented in an action.

(d) Public Officer's Title and Name. A public officer who sues or is sued in an official capacity may be designated by official title rather than by name, but the court may order that the officer's name be added.

(Amended December 27, 1946, effective March 19, 1948; December 29, 1948, effective October 20, 1949; February 28, 1966, effective July 1, 1966; March 2, 1987, effective August 1, 1987; April 25, 1988, effective August 1, 1988; amended by Pub.L. 100–690, Title VII, § 7049, November 18, 1988, 102 Stat. 4401 (although amendment by Pub.L. 100–690 could not be executed due to prior amendment by Court order which made the same change effective August 1, 1988); April 30, 2007, effective December 1, 2007.)

RULE 18. JOINDER OF CLAIMS

(a) In General. A party asserting a claim, counterclaim, crossclaim, or third-party claim may join, as independent or alternative claims, as many claims as it has against an opposing party.

(b) Joinder of Contingent Claims. A party may join two claims even though one of them is contingent on the disposition of the other; but the court may grant relief only in accordance with the parties' relative substantive rights. In particular, a plaintiff may state a claim for money and a claim to set aside a conveyance that is fraudulent as to that plaintiff, without first obtaining a judgment for the money.

(Amended February 28, 1966, effective July 1, 1966; March 2, 1987, effective August 1, 1987; April 30, 2007, effective December 1, 2007.)

RULE 19. REQUIRED JOINDER OF PARTIES

(a) Persons Required to Be Joined if Feasible.

(1) ***Required Party.*** A person who is subject to service of process and whose joinder will not deprive the court of subject-matter jurisdiction must be joined as a party if:

(A) in that person's absence, the court cannot accord complete relief among existing parties; or

(B) that person claims an interest relating to the subject of the action and is so situated that disposing of the action in the person's absence may:

(i) as a practical matter impair or impede the person's ability to protect the interest; or

(ii) leave an existing party subject to a substantial risk of incurring double, multiple, or otherwise inconsistent obligations because of the interest.

(2) ***Joinder by Court Order.*** If a person has not been joined as required, the court must order that the person be made a party. A person who refuses to join as a plaintiff may be made either a defendant or, in a proper case, an involuntary plaintiff.

(3) ***Venue.*** If a joined party objects to venue and the joinder would make venue improper, the court must dismiss that party.

(b) When Joinder Is Not Feasible. If a person who is required to be joined if feasible cannot be joined, the court must determine whether, in equity and good conscience, the action should proceed among the existing parties or should be dismissed. The factors for the court to consider include:

(1) the extent to which a judgment rendered in the person's absence might prejudice that person or the existing parties;

(2) the extent to which any prejudice could be lessened or avoided by:

(A) protective provisions in the judgment;

(B) shaping the relief; or

(C) other measures;

(3) whether a judgment rendered in the person's absence would be adequate; and

(4) whether the plaintiff would have an adequate remedy if the action were dismissed for nonjoinder.

(c) Pleading the Reasons for Nonjoinder. When asserting a claim for relief, a party must state:

(1) the name, if known, of any person who is required to be joined if feasible but is not joined; and

(2) the reasons for not joining that person.

(d) Exception for Class Actions. This rule is subject to Rule 23.

(Amended February 28, 1966, effective July 1, 1966; March 2, 1987, effective August 1, 1987; April 30, 2007, effective December 1, 2007.)

RULE 20. PERMISSIVE JOINDER OF PARTIES

(a) Persons Who May Join or Be Joined.

(1) ***Plaintiffs.*** Persons may join in one action as plaintiffs if:

(A) they assert any right to relief jointly, severally, or in the alternative with respect to or arising out of the same transaction, occurrence, or series of transactions or occurrences; and

(B) any question of law or fact common to all plaintiffs will arise in the action.

(2) ***Defendants.*** Persons—as well as a vessel, cargo, or other property subject to admiralty process in rem—may be joined in one action as defendants if:

(A) any right to relief is asserted against them jointly, severally, or in the alternative with respect to or arising out of the same transaction, occurrence, or series of transactions or occurrences; and

(B) any question of law or fact common to all defendants will arise in the action.

(3) ***Extent of Relief.*** Neither a plaintiff nor a defendant need be interested in obtaining or defending against all the relief demanded. The court may grant judgment to one or more plaintiffs according to their rights, and against one or more defendants according to their liabilities.

(b) **Protective Measures.** The court may issue orders—including an order for separate trials—to protect a party against embarrassment, delay, expense, or other prejudice that arises from including a person against whom the party asserts no claim and who asserts no claim against the party.

(Amended February 28, 1966, effective July 1, 1966; March 2, 1987, effective August 1, 1987; April 30, 2007, effective December 1, 2007.)

RULE 21. MISJOINDER AND NONJOINDER OF PARTIES

Misjoinder of parties is not a ground for dismissing an action. On motion or on its own, the court may at any time, on just terms, add or drop a party. The court may also sever any claim against a party.

(Amended April 30, 2007, effective December 1, 2007.)

RULE 22. INTERPLEADER

(a) **Grounds.**

(1) ***By a Plaintiff.*** Persons with claims that may expose a plaintiff to double or multiple liability may be joined as defendants and required to interplead. Joinder for interpleader is proper even though:

(A) the claims of the several claimants, or the titles on which their claims depend, lack a common origin or are adverse and independent rather than identical; or

(B) the plaintiff denies liability in whole or in part to any or all of the claimants.

(2) ***By a Defendant.*** A defendant exposed to similar liability may seek interpleader through a crossclaim or counterclaim.

(b) **Relation to Other Rules and Statutes.** This rule supplements—and does not limit—the joinder of parties allowed by Rule 20. The remedy this rule provides is in addition to—and does not supersede or limit—the remedy provided by 28 U.S.C. §§ 1335, 1397, and 2361. An action under those statutes must be conducted under these rules.

(Amended December 29, 1948, effective October 20, 1949; March 2, 1987, effective August 1, 1987; April 30, 2007, effective December 1, 2007.)

RULE 23. CLASS ACTIONS

(a) **Prerequisites.** One or more members of a class may sue or be sued as representative parties on behalf of all members only if:

(1) the class is so numerous that joinder of all members is impracticable;

(2) there are questions of law or fact common to the class;

(3) the claims or defenses of the representative parties are typical of the claims or defenses of the class; and

(4) the representative parties will fairly and adequately protect the interests of the class.

(b) **Types of Class Actions.** A class action may be maintained if Rule 23(a) is satisfied and if:

(1) prosecuting separate actions by or against individual class members would create a risk of:

(A) inconsistent or varying adjudications with respect to individual class members that would establish incompatible standards of conduct for the party opposing the class; or

(B) adjudications with respect to individual class members that, as a practical matter, would be dispositive of the interests of the other members not parties to the individual adjudications or would substantially impair or impede their ability to protect their interests;

(2) the party opposing the class has acted or refused to act on grounds that apply generally to the class, so that final injunctive relief or corresponding declaratory relief is appropriate respecting the class as a whole; or

(3) the court finds that the questions of law or fact common to class members predominate over any questions affecting only individual members, and that a class action is superior to other available methods for fairly and efficiently adjudicating the controversy. The matters pertinent to these findings include:

(A) the class members' interests in individually controlling the prosecution or defense of separate actions;

(B) the extent and nature of any litigation concerning the controversy already begun by or against class members;

(C) the desirability or undesirability of concentrating the litigation of the claims in the particular forum; and

(D) the likely difficulties in managing a class action.

(c) **Certification Order; Notice to Class Members; Judgment; Issues Classes; Subclasses.**

(1) ***Certification Order.***

(A) *Time to Issue.* At an early practicable time after a person sues or is sued as a class representative, the court must determine by order whether to certify the action as a class action.

(B) *Defining the Class; Appointing Class Counsel.* An order that certifies a class action must define the class and the class claims, issues, or defenses, and must appoint class counsel under Rule 23(g).

(C) *Altering or Amending the Order.* An order that grants or denies class certification may be altered or amended before final judgment.

(2) ***Notice.***

(A) *For (b)(1) or (b)(2) Classes.* For any class certified under Rule 23(b)(1) or (b)(2), the court may direct appropriate notice to the class.

(B) *For (b)(3) Classes.* For any class certified under Rule 23(b)(3), the court must direct to class members the best notice that is practicable under the circumstances, including individual notice to all members who can be identified through reasonable effort. The notice must clearly and concisely state in plain, easily understood language:

(i) the nature of the action;

(ii) the definition of the class certified;

(iii) the class claims, issues, or defenses;

(iv) that a class member may enter an appearance through an attorney if the member so desires;

(v) that the court will exclude from the class any member who requests exclusion;

(vi) the time and manner for requesting exclusion; and

(vii) the binding effect of a class judgment on members under Rule 23(c)(3).

(3) ***Judgment.*** Whether or not favorable to the class, the judgment in a class action must:

(A) for any class certified under Rule 23(b)(1) or (b)(2), include and describe those whom the court finds to be class members; and

(B) for any class certified under Rule 23(b)(3), include and specify or describe those to whom the Rule 23(c)(2) notice was directed, who have not requested exclusion, and whom the court finds to be class members.

(4) ***Particular Issues.*** When appropriate, an action may be brought or maintained as a class action with respect to particular issues.

(5) ***Subclasses.*** When appropriate, a class may be divided into subclasses that are each treated as a class under this rule.

(d) Conducting the Action.

(1) ***In General.*** In conducting an action under this rule, the court may issue orders that:

(A) determine the course of proceedings or prescribe measures to prevent undue repetition or complication in presenting evidence or argument;

(B) require—to protect class members and fairly conduct the action—giving appropriate notice to some or all class members of:

(i) any step in the action;

(ii) the proposed extent of the judgment; or

(iii) the members' opportunity to signify whether they consider the representation fair and adequate, to intervene and present claims or defenses, or to otherwise come into the action;

(C) impose conditions on the representative parties or on intervenors;

(D) require that the pleadings be amended to eliminate allegations about representation of absent persons and that the action proceed accordingly; or

(E) deal with similar procedural matters.

(2) ***Combining and Amending Orders.*** An order under Rule 23(d)(1) may be altered or amended from time to time and may be combined with an order under Rule 16.

(e) Settlement, Voluntary Dismissal, or Compromise. The claims, issues, or defenses of a certified class may be settled, voluntarily dismissed, or compromised only with the court's approval. The following procedures apply to a proposed settlement, voluntary dismissal, or compromise:

(1) The court must direct notice in a reasonable manner to all class members who would be bound by the proposal.

(2) If the proposal would bind class members, the court may approve it only after a hearing and on finding that it is fair, reasonable, and adequate.

(3) The parties seeking approval must file a statement identifying any agreement made in connection with the proposal.

(4) If the class action was previously certified under Rule 23(b)(3), the court may refuse to approve a settlement unless it affords a new opportunity to request exclusion to individual class members who had an earlier opportunity to request exclusion but did not do so.

(5) Any class member may object to the proposal if it requires court approval under this subdivision (e); the objection may be withdrawn only with the court's approval.

(f) Appeals. A court of appeals may permit an appeal from an order granting or denying class-action certification under this rule if a petition for permission to appeal is filed with the circuit clerk within 14 days after the order is entered. An appeal does not stay proceedings in the district court unless the district judge or the court of appeals so orders.

(g) Class Counsel.

(1) ***Appointing Class Counsel.*** Unless a statute provides otherwise, a court that certifies a class must appoint class counsel. In appointing class counsel, the court:

(A) must consider:

(i) the work counsel has done in identifying or investigating potential claims in the action;

(ii) counsel's experience in handling class actions, other complex litigation, and the types of claims asserted in the action;

(iii) counsel's knowledge of the applicable law; and

(iv) the resources that counsel will commit to representing the class;

(B) may consider any other matter pertinent to counsel's ability to fairly and adequately represent the interests of the class;

(C) may order potential class counsel to provide information on any subject pertinent to the appointment and to propose terms for attorney's fees and nontaxable costs;

(D) may include in the appointing order provisions about the award of attorney's fees or nontaxable costs under Rule 23(h); and

(E) may make further orders in connection with the appointment.

(2) ***Standard for Appointing Class Counsel.*** When one applicant seeks appointment as class counsel, the court may appoint that applicant only if the applicant is adequate under Rule 23(g)(1) and (4). If more than one adequate applicant seeks appointment, the court must appoint the applicant best able to represent the interests of the class.

(3) ***Interim Counsel.*** The court may designate interim counsel to act on behalf of a putative class before determining whether to certify the action as a class action.

(4) ***Duty of Class Counsel.*** Class counsel must fairly and adequately represent the interests of the class.

(h) Attorney's Fees and Nontaxable Costs. In a certified class action, the court may award reasonable attorney's fees and nontaxable costs that are authorized by law or by the parties' agreement. The following procedures apply:

(1) A claim for an award must be made by motion under Rule 54(d)(2), subject to the provisions of this subdivision (h), at a time the court sets. Notice of the motion must be served on all parties and, for motions by class counsel, directed to class members in a reasonable manner.

(2) A class member, or a party from whom payment is sought, may object to the motion.

(3) The court may hold a hearing and must find the facts and state its legal conclusions under Rule 52(a).

(4) The court may refer issues related to the amount of the award to a special master or a magistrate judge, as provided in Rule 54(d)(2)(D).

(Amended February 28, 1966, effective July 1, 1966; March 2, 1987, effective August 1, 1987; April 24, 1998, effective December 1, 1998; March 27, 2003, effective December 1, 2003; April 30, 2007, effective December 1, 2007; March 26, 2009, effective December 1, 2009.)

RULE 23.1. DERIVATIVE ACTIONS

(a) Prerequisites. This rule applies when one or more shareholders or members of a corporation or an unincorporated association bring a derivative action to enforce a right that the corporation or association may properly assert but has failed to enforce. The derivative action may not be maintained if it appears that the plaintiff does not fairly and adequately represent the interests of shareholders or members who are similarly situated in enforcing the right of the corporation or association.

(b) Pleading Requirements. The complaint must be verified and must:

(1) allege that the plaintiff was a shareholder or member at the time of the transaction complained of, or that the plaintiff's share or membership later devolved on it by operation of law;

(2) allege that the action is not a collusive one to confer jurisdiction that the court would otherwise lack; and

(3) state with particularity:

(A) any effort by the plaintiff to obtain the desired action from the directors or comparable authority and, if necessary, from the shareholders or members; and

(B) the reasons for not obtaining the action or not making the effort.

(c) Settlement, Dismissal, and Compromise. A derivative action may be settled, voluntarily dismissed, or compromised only with the court's approval. Notice of a proposed settlement, voluntary dismissal, or compromise must be given to shareholders or members in the manner that the court orders.

(Adopted February 28, 1966, effective July 1, 1966; amended March 2, 1987, effective August 1, 1987; April 30, 2007, effective December 1, 2007.)

RULE 23.2. ACTIONS RELATING TO UNINCORPORATED ASSOCIATIONS

This rule applies to an action brought by or against the members of an unincorporated association as a class by naming certain members as representative parties. The action may be maintained only if it appears that those parties will fairly and adequately protect the interests of the association and its members. In conducting the action, the court may issue any appropriate orders corresponding with those in Rule 23(d), and the procedure for settlement, voluntary dismissal, or compromise must correspond with the procedure in Rule 23(e).

(Adopted February 28, 1966, effective July 1, 1966; amended April 30, 2007, effective December 1, 2007.)

RULE 24. INTERVENTION

(a) Intervention of Right. On timely motion, the court must permit anyone to intervene who:

(1) is given an unconditional right to intervene by a federal statute; or

(2) claims an interest relating to the property or transaction that is the subject of the action, and is so situated that disposing of the action may as a practical matter impair or impede the movant's ability to protect its interest, unless existing parties adequately represent that interest.

(b) Permissive Intervention.

(1) ***In General.*** On timely motion, the court may permit anyone to intervene who:

(A) is given a conditional right to intervene by a federal statute; or

(B) has a claim or defense that shares with the main action a common question of law or fact.

(2) ***By a Government Officer or Agency.*** On timely motion, the court may permit a federal or state governmental officer or agency to intervene if a party's claim or defense is based on:

(A) a statute or executive order administered by the officer or agency; or

(B) any regulation, order, requirement, or agreement issued or made under the statute or executive order.

(3) ***Delay or Prejudice.*** In exercising its discretion, the court must consider whether the intervention will unduly delay or prejudice the adjudication of the original parties' rights.

(c) Notice and Pleading Required. A motion to intervene must be served on the parties as provided in Rule 5. The motion must state the grounds for intervention and be accompanied by a pleading that sets out the claim or defense for which intervention is sought.

(Amended December 27, 1946, effective March 19, 1948; December 29, 1948, effective October 20, 1949; January 21, 1963, effective July 1, 1963; February 28, 1966, effective July 1, 1966; March 2, 1987, effective August 1, 1987; April 30, 1991, effective December 1, 1991; April 12, 2006, effective December 1, 2006; April 30, 2007, effective December 1, 2007.)

RULE 25. SUBSTITUTION OF PARTIES

(a) Death.

(1) ***Substitution if the Claim Is Not Extinguished.*** If a party dies and the claim is not extinguished, the court may order substitution of the proper party. A motion for substitution may be made by any party or by the decedent's successor or representative. If the motion is not made within 90 days after service of a statement noting the death, the action by or against the decedent must be dismissed.

(2) ***Continuation Among the Remaining Parties.*** After a party's death, if the right sought to be enforced survives only to or against the remaining parties, the action does not abate, but proceeds in favor of or against the remaining parties. The death should be noted on the record.

(3) ***Service.*** A motion to substitute, together with a notice of hearing, must be served on the parties as provided in Rule 5 and on nonparties as provided in Rule 4. A statement noting death must be served in the same manner. Service may be made in any judicial district.

(b) Incompetency. If a party becomes incompetent, the court may, on motion, permit the action to be continued by or against the party's representative. The motion must be served as provided in Rule 25(a)(3).

(c) Transfer of Interest. If an interest is transferred, the action may be continued by or against the original party unless the court, on motion, orders the transferee to be substituted in the action or joined with the original party. The motion must be served as provided in Rule 25(a)(3).

(d) Public Officers; Death or Separation from Office. An action does not abate when a public officer who is a party in an official capacity dies, resigns, or otherwise ceases to hold office while the action is pending. The officer's successor is automatically substituted as a party. Later proceedings should be in the substituted party's name, but any misnomer not affecting the parties' substantial rights must be disregarded. The court may order substitution at any time, but the absence of such an order does not affect the substitution.

(Amended December 29, 1948, effective October 20, 1949; April 17, 1961, effective July 19, 1961; January 21, 1963, effective July 1, 1963; March 2, 1987, effective August 1, 1987; April 30, 2007, effective December 1, 2007.)

TITLE V. DISCLOSURES AND DISCOVERY

RULE 26. DUTY TO DISCLOSE; GENERAL PROVISIONS GOVERNING DISCOVERY

(a) Required Disclosures.

(1) ***Initial Disclosure.***

(A) *In General.* Except as exempted by Rule 26(a)(1)(B) or as otherwise stipulated or ordered by the court, a party must, without awaiting a discovery request, provide to the other parties:

(i) the name and, if known, the address and telephone number of each individual likely to have discoverable information—along with the subjects of that information—that the disclosing party may use to support its claims or defenses, unless the use would be solely for impeachment;

(ii) a copy—or a description by category and location—of all documents, electronically stored information, and tangible things that the disclosing party has in its possession, custody, or control and may use to support its claims or defenses, unless the use would be solely for impeachment;

(iii) a computation of each category of damages claimed by the disclosing party—who must also make available for inspection and copying as under Rule 34 the documents or other evidentiary material, unless privileged or protected from disclosure, on which each computation is based, including materials bearing on the nature and extent of injuries suffered; and

(iv) for inspection and copying as under Rule 34, any insurance agreement under which an insurance business may be liable to satisfy all or part of a possible judgment in the action or to indemnify or reimburse for payments made to satisfy the judgment.

(B) *Proceedings Exempt from Initial Disclosure.* The following proceedings are exempt from initial disclosure:

(i) an action for review on an administrative record;

(ii) a forfeiture action in rem arising from a federal statute;

(iii) a petition for habeas corpus or any other proceeding to challenge a criminal conviction or sentence;

(iv) an action brought without an attorney by a person in the custody of the United States, a state, or a state subdivision;

(v) an action to enforce or quash an administrative summons or subpoena;

(vi) an action by the United States to recover benefit payments;

(vii) an action by the United States to collect on a student loan guaranteed by the United States;

(viii) a proceeding ancillary to a proceeding in another court; and

(ix) an action to enforce an arbitration award.

(C) *Time for Initial Disclosures—In General.* A party must make the initial disclosures at or within 14 days after the parties' Rule 26(f) conference unless a different time is set by stipulation or court order, or unless a party objects during the conference that initial disclosures are not appropriate in this action and states the objection in the proposed discovery plan. In ruling on the objection, the court must determine what disclosures, if any, are to be made and must set the time for disclosure.

(D) *Time for Initial Disclosures—For Parties Served or Joined Later.* A party that is first served or otherwise joined after the Rule 26(f) conference must make the initial disclosures within 30 days after being served or joined, unless a different time is set by stipulation or court order.

(E) *Basis for Initial Disclosure; Unacceptable Excuses.* A party must make its initial disclosures based on the information then reasonably available to it. A party is not excused from making its disclosures because it has not fully investigated the case or because it challenges the sufficiency of another party's disclosures or because another party has not made its disclosures.

(2) ***Disclosure of Expert Testimony.***

(A) *In General.* In addition to the disclosures required by Rule 26(a)(1), a party must disclose to the other parties the identity of any witness it may use at trial to present evidence under Federal Rule of Evidence 702, 703, or 705.

(B) *Witnesses Who Must Provide a Written Report.* Unless otherwise stipulated or ordered by the court, this disclosure must be accompanied by a written report—prepared and signed by the witness—if the witness is one retained or specially employed to provide expert testimony in the case or one whose duties as the party's employee regularly involve giving expert testimony. The report must contain:

(i) a complete statement of all opinions the witness will express and the basis and reasons for them;

(ii) the facts or data considered by the witness in forming them;

(iii) any exhibits that will be used to summarize or support them;

(iv) the witness's qualifications, including a list of all publications authored in the previous 10 years;

(v) a list of all other cases in which, during the previous 4 years, the witness testified as an expert at trial or by deposition; and

(vi) a statement of the compensation to be paid for the study and testimony in the case.

(C) *Witnesses Who Do Not Provide a Written Report.* Unless otherwise stipulated or ordered by the court, if the witness is not required to provide a written report, this disclosure must state:

(i) the subject matter on which the witness is expected to present evidence under Federal Rule of Evidence 702, 703, or 705; and

(ii) a summary of the facts and opinions to which the witness is expected to testify.

(D) *Time to Disclose Expert Testimony.* A party must make these disclosures at the times and in the sequence that the court orders. Absent a stipulation or a court order, the disclosures must be made:

(i) at least 90 days before the date set for trial or for the case to be ready for trial; or

(ii) if the evidence is intended solely to contradict or rebut evidence on the same subject matter identified by another party under Rule 26(a)(2)(B) or (C), within 30 days after the other party's disclosure.

(E) *Supplementing the Disclosure.* The parties must supplement these disclosures when required under Rule 26(e).

(3) ***Pretrial Disclosures.***

(A) *In General.* In addition to the disclosures required by Rule 26(a)(1) and (2), a party must provide to the other parties and promptly file the following information about the evidence that it may present at trial other than solely for impeachment:

(i) the name and, if not previously provided, the address and telephone number of each witness—separately identifying those the party expects to present and those it may call if the need arises;

(ii) the designation of those witnesses whose testimony the party expects to present by deposition and, if not taken stenographically, a transcript of the pertinent parts of the deposition; and

(iii) an identification of each document or other exhibit, including summaries of other evidence—separately identifying those items the party expects to offer and those it may offer if the need arises.

(B) *Time for Pretrial Disclosures; Objections.* Unless the court orders otherwise, these disclosures must be made at least 30 days before trial. Within 14 days after they are made, unless the court sets a different time, a party may serve and promptly file a list of the following objections: any objections to the use under Rule 32(a) of a deposition designated by another party under Rule 26(a)(3)(A)(ii); and any objection, together with the grounds for it, that may be made to the admissibility of materials identified under Rule 26(a)(3)(A)(iii). An objection not so made—except for one under Federal Rule of Evidence 402 or 403—is waived unless excused by the court for good cause.

(4) ***Form of Disclosures.*** Unless the court orders otherwise, all disclosures under Rule 26(a) must be in writing, signed, and served.

(b) Discovery Scope and Limits.

(1) ***Scope in General.*** Unless otherwise limited by court order, the scope of discovery is as follows: Parties may obtain discovery regarding any nonprivileged matter that is relevant to any party's claim or defense and proportional to the needs of the case, considering the importance of the issues at stake in the action, the amount in controversy, the parties' relative access to relevant information, the parties' resources, the importance of the discovery in resolving the issues, and whether the burden or expense of the proposed discovery outweighs its likely benefit. Information within this scope of discovery need not be admissible in evidence to be discoverable.

(2) ***Limitations on Frequency and Extent.***

(A) *When Permitted.* By order, the court may alter the limits in these rules on the number of depositions and interrogatories or on the length of depositions under Rule 30. By order or local rule, the court may also limit the number of requests under Rule 36.

(B) *Specific Limitations on Electronically Stored Information.* A party need not provide discovery of electronically stored information from sources that the party identifies as not reasonably accessible because of undue burden or cost. On motion to compel discovery or for a protective order, the party from whom discovery is sought must show that the information is not reasonably accessible because of undue burden or cost. If that showing is made, the court may nonetheless order discovery from such sources if the requesting party shows good cause, considering the limitations of Rule 26(b)(2)(C). The court may specify conditions for the discovery.

(C) *When Required.* On motion or on its own, the court must limit the frequency or extent of discovery otherwise allowed by these rules or by local rule if it determines that:

(i) the discovery sought is unreasonably cumulative or duplicative, or can be obtained from some other source that is more convenient, less burdensome, or less expensive;

(ii) the party seeking discovery has had ample opportunity to obtain the information by discovery in the action; or

(iii) the proposed discovery is outside the scope permitted by Rule 26(b)(1).

(3) ***Trial Preparation: Materials.***

(A) *Documents and Tangible Things.* Ordinarily, a party may not discover documents and tangible things that are prepared in anticipation of litigation or for trial by or for another party or its representative (including the other party's attorney, consultant, surety, indemnitor, insurer, or agent). But, subject to Rule 26(b)(4), those materials may be discovered if:

(i) they are otherwise discoverable under Rule 26(b)(1); and

(ii) the party shows that it has substantial need for the materials to prepare its case and cannot, without undue hardship, obtain their substantial equivalent by other means.

(B) *Protection Against Disclosure.* If the court orders discovery of those materials, it must protect against disclosure of the mental impressions, conclusions, opinions, or legal theories of a party's attorney or other representative concerning the litigation.

(C) *Previous Statement.* Any party or other person may, on request and without the required showing, obtain the person's own previous statement about the action or its subject matter. If the request is refused, the person may move for a court order, and Rule 37(a)(5) applies to the award of expenses. A previous statement is either:

(i) a written statement that the person has signed or otherwise adopted or approved; or

(ii) a contemporaneous stenographic, mechanical, electrical, or other recording—or a transcription of it—that recites substantially verbatim the person's oral statement.

(4) ***Trial Preparation: Experts.***

(A) *Deposition of an Expert Who May Testify.* A party may depose any person who has been identified as an expert whose opinions may be presented at trial. If Rule 26(a)(2)(B) requires a report from the expert, the deposition may be conducted only after the report is provided.

(B) *Trial–Preparation Protection for Draft Reports or Disclosures.* Rules 26(b)(3)(A) and (B) protect drafts of any report or disclosure required under Rule 26(a)(2), regardless of the form in which the draft is recorded.

(C) *Trial–Preparation Protection for Communications Between a Party's Attorney and Expert Witnesses.* Rules 26(b)(3)(A) and (B) protect communications between the party's attorney and any witness required to provide a report under Rule 26(a)(2)(B), regardless of the form of the communications, except to the extent that the communications:

(i) relate to compensation for the expert's study or testimony;

(ii) identify facts or data that the party's attorney provided and that the expert considered in forming the opinions to be expressed; or

(iii) identify assumptions that the party's attorney provided and that the expert relied on in forming the opinions to be expressed.

(D) *Expert Employed Only for Trial Preparation.* Ordinarily, a party may not, by interrogatories or deposition, discover facts known or opinions held by an expert who has been retained or specially employed by another party in anticipation of litigation or to prepare for trial and who is not expected to be called as a witness at trial. But a party may do so only:

(i) as provided in Rule 35(b); or

(ii) on showing exceptional circumstances under which it is impracticable for the party to obtain facts or opinions on the same subject by other means.

(E) *Payment.* Unless manifest injustice would result, the court must require that the party seeking discovery:

(i) pay the expert a reasonable fee for time spent in responding to discovery under Rule 26(b)(4)(A) or (D); and

(ii) for discovery under (D), also pay the other party a fair portion of the fees and expenses it reasonably incurred in obtaining the expert's facts and opinions.

(5) ***Claiming Privilege or Protecting Trial-Preparation Materials.***

(A) *Information Withheld.* When a party withholds information otherwise discoverable by claiming that the information is privileged or subject to protection as trial-preparation material, the party must:

(i) expressly make the claim; and

(ii) describe the nature of the documents, communications, or tangible things not produced or disclosed—and do so in a manner that, without revealing information itself privileged or protected, will enable other parties to assess the claim.

(B) *Information Produced.* If information produced in discovery is subject to a claim of privilege or of protection as trial-preparation material, the party making the claim may notify any party that received the information of the claim and the basis for it. After being notified, a party must promptly return, sequester, or destroy the specified information and any copies it has; must not use or disclose the information until the claim is resolved; must take reasonable steps to retrieve the information if the party disclosed it before being notified; and may promptly present the information to the court under seal for a determination of the claim. The producing party must preserve the information until the claim is resolved.

(c) Protective Orders.

(1) ***In General.*** A party or any person from whom discovery is sought may move for a protective order in the court where the action is pending — or as an alternative on matters relating to a deposition, in the court for the district where the deposition will be taken. The motion must include a certification that the movant has in good faith conferred or attempted to confer with other affected parties in an effort to resolve the dispute without court action. The court may, for good cause, issue an order to protect a party or person from annoyance, embarrassment, oppression, or undue burden or expense, including one or more of the following:

(A) forbidding the disclosure or discovery;

(B) specifying terms, including time and place or the allocation of expenses, for the disclosure or discovery;

(C) prescribing a discovery method other than the one selected by the party seeking discovery;

(D) forbidding inquiry into certain matters, or limiting the scope of disclosure or discovery to certain matters;

(E) designating the persons who may be present while the discovery is conducted;

(F) requiring that a deposition be sealed and opened only on court order;

(G) requiring that a trade secret or other confidential research, development, or commercial information not be revealed or be revealed only in a specified way; and

(H) requiring that the parties simultaneously file specified documents or information in sealed envelopes, to be opened as the court directs.

(2) ***Ordering Discovery.*** If a motion for a protective order is wholly or partly denied, the court may, on just terms, order that any party or person provide or permit discovery.

(3) ***Awarding Expenses.*** Rule 37(a)(5) applies to the award of expenses.

(d) Timing and Sequence of Discovery.

(1) ***Timing.*** A party may not seek discovery from any source before the parties have conferred as required by Rule 26(f), except in a proceeding exempted from initial disclosure under Rule 26(a)(1)(B), or when authorized by these rules, by stipulation, or by court order.

(2) ***Early Rule 34 Requests.***

(A) **Time to Deliver.** More than 21 days after the summons and complaint are served on a party, a request under Rule 34 may be delivered:

(i) to that party by any other party, and

(ii) by that party to any plaintiff or to any other party that has been served.

(B) ***When Considered Served.*** The request is considered to have been served at the first Rule 26(f) conference.

(3) ***Sequence.*** Unless the parties stipulate or the court orders otherwise for the parties' and witnesses' convenience and in the interests of justice:

(A) methods of discovery may be used in any sequence; and

(B) discovery by one party does not require any other party to delay its discovery.

(e) Supplementing Disclosures and Responses.

(1) ***In General.*** A party who has made a disclosure under Rule 26(a)—or who has responded to an interrogatory, request for production, or request for admission—must supplement or correct its disclosure or response:

(A) in a timely manner if the party learns that in some material respect the disclosure or response is incomplete or incorrect, and if the additional or corrective information has not otherwise been made known to the other parties during the discovery process or in writing; or

(B) as ordered by the court.

(2) ***Expert Witness.*** For an expert whose report must be disclosed under Rule 26(a)(2)(B), the party's duty to supplement extends both to information included in the report and to information given during the expert's deposition. Any additions or changes to this information must be disclosed by the time the party's pretrial disclosures under Rule 26(a)(3) are due.

(f) Conference of the Parties; Planning for Discovery.

(1) ***Conference Timing.*** Except in a proceeding exempted from initial disclosure under Rule 26(a)(1)(B) or when the court orders otherwise, the parties must confer as soon as practicable—and in any event at least 21 days before a scheduling conference is to be held or a scheduling order is due under Rule 16(b).

(2) ***Conference Content; Parties' Responsibilities.*** In conferring, the parties must consider the nature and basis of their claims and defenses and the possibilities for promptly settling or resolving the case; make or arrange for the disclosures required by Rule 26(a)(1); discuss any issues about preserving discoverable information; and develop a proposed discovery plan. The attorneys of record and all unrepresented parties that have appeared in the case are jointly responsible for arranging the conference, for attempting in good faith to agree on the proposed discovery plan, and for submitting to the court within 14 days after the conference a written report outlining the plan. The court may order the parties or attorneys to attend the conference in person.

(3) ***Discovery Plan.*** A discovery plan must state the parties' views and proposals on:

(A) what changes should be made in the timing, form, or requirement for disclosures under Rule 26(a), including a statement of when initial disclosures were made or will be made;

(B) the subjects on which discovery may be needed, when discovery should be completed, and whether discovery should be conducted in phases or be limited to or focused on particular issues;

(C) any issues about disclosure, discovery, or preservation of electronically stored information, including the form or forms in which it should be produced;

(D) any issues about claims of privilege or of protection as trial-preparation materials, including — if the parties agree on a procedure to assert these claims after production — whether to ask the court to include their agreement in an order under Federal Rule of Evidence 502;

(E) what changes should be made in the limitations on discovery imposed under these rules or by local rule, and what other limitations should be imposed; and

(F) any other orders that the court should issue under Rule 26(c) or under Rule 16(b) and (c).

(4) ***Expedited Schedule.*** If necessary to comply with its expedited schedule for Rule 16(b) conferences, a court may by local rule:

(A) require the parties' conference to occur less than 21 days before the scheduling conference is held or a scheduling order is due under Rule 16(b); and

(B) require the written report outlining the discovery plan to be filed less than 14 days after the parties' conference, or excuse the parties from submitting a written report and permit them to report orally on their discovery plan at the Rule 16(b) conference.

(g) Signing Disclosures and Discovery Requests, Responses, and Objections.

(1) ***Signature Required; Effect of Signature.*** Every disclosure under Rule 26(a)(1) or (a)(3) and every discovery request, response, or objection must be signed by at least one attorney of record in the attorney's own name—or by the party personally, if unrepresented—and must state the signer's address, e-mail address, and telephone number. By signing, an attorney or party certifies that to the best of the person's knowledge, information, and belief formed after a reasonable inquiry:

(A) with respect to a disclosure, it is complete and correct as of the time it is made; and

(B) with respect to a discovery request, response, or objection, it is:

(i) consistent with these rules and warranted by existing law or by a nonfrivolous argument for extending, modifying, or reversing existing law, or for establishing new law;

(ii) not interposed for any improper purpose, such as to harass, cause unnecessary delay, or needlessly increase the cost of litigation; and

(iii) neither unreasonable nor unduly burdensome or expensive, considering the needs of the case, prior discovery in the case, the amount in controversy, and the importance of the issues at stake in the action.

(2) ***Failure to Sign.*** Other parties have no duty to act on an unsigned disclosure, request, response, or objection until it is signed, and the court must strike it unless a signature is promptly supplied after the omission is called to the attorney's or party's attention.

(3) ***Sanction for Improper Certification.*** If a certification violates this rule without substantial justification, the court, on motion or on its own, must impose an appropriate sanction on the signer, the party on whose behalf the signer was acting, or both. The sanction may include an order to pay the reasonable expenses, including attorney's fees, caused by the violation.

(Amended December 27, 1946, effective March 19, 1948; January 21, 1963, effective July 1, 1963; February 28, 1966, effective July 1, 1966; March 30, 1970, effective July 1, 1970; April 29, 1980, effective August 1, 1980; April 28, 1983, effective August 1, 1983; March 2, 1987, effective August 1, 1987; April 22, 1993, effective December 1, 1993; April 17, 2000, effective December 1, 2000; April 12, 2006, effective December 1, 2006; April 30, 2007, effective December 1, 2007; April 28, 2010, effective December 1, 2010; April 29, 2015, effective December 1, 2015.)

RULE 27. DEPOSITIONS TO PERPETUATE TESTIMONY

(a) Before an Action Is Filed.

(1) ***Petition.*** A person who wants to perpetuate testimony about any matter cognizable in a United States court may file a verified petition in the district court for the district where any expected adverse party resides. The petition must ask for an order authorizing the petitioner to depose the named persons in order to perpetuate their testimony. The petition must be titled in the petitioner's name and must show:

(A) that the petitioner expects to be a party to an action cognizable in a United States court but cannot presently bring it or cause it to be brought;

(B) the subject matter of the expected action and the petitioner's interest;

(C) the facts that the petitioner wants to establish by the proposed testimony and the reasons to perpetuate it;

(D) the names or a description of the persons whom the petitioner expects to be adverse parties and their addresses, so far as known; and

(E) the name, address, and expected substance of the testimony of each deponent.

(2) ***Notice and Service.*** At least 21 days before the hearing date, the petitioner must serve each expected adverse party with a copy of the petition and a notice stating the time and place of the hearing. The notice may be served either inside or outside the district or state in the manner provided in Rule 4. If that service cannot be made with reasonable diligence on an expected adverse party, the court may order service by publication or otherwise. The court must appoint an attorney to represent persons not served in the manner provided in Rule 4 and to cross-examine the deponent if an unserved person is not otherwise represented. If any expected adverse party is a minor or is incompetent, Rule 17(c) applies.

(3) ***Order and Examination.*** If satisfied that perpetuating the testimony may prevent a failure or delay of justice, the court must issue an order that designates or describes the persons whose depositions may be taken, specifies the subject matter of the examinations, and states whether the depositions will be taken orally or by written interrogatories. The depositions may then be taken under these rules, and the court may issue orders like those authorized by Rules 34 and 35. A reference in these rules to the court where an action is pending means, for purposes of this rule, the court where the petition for the deposition was filed.

(4) ***Using the Deposition.*** A deposition to perpetuate testimony may be used under Rule 32(a) in any later-filed district-court action involving the same subject matter if the deposition either was taken under these rules or, although not so taken, would be admissible in evidence in the courts of the state where it was taken.

(b) Pending Appeal.

(1) ***In General.*** The court where a judgment has been rendered may, if an appeal has been taken or may still be taken, permit a party to depose witnesses to perpetuate their testimony for use in the event of further proceedings in that court.

(2) ***Motion.*** The party who wants to perpetuate testimony may move for leave to take the depositions, on the same notice and service as if the action were pending in the district court. The motion must show:

(A) the name, address, and expected substance of the testimony of each deponent; and

(B) the reasons for perpetuating the testimony.

(3) ***Court Order.*** If the court finds that perpetuating the testimony may prevent a failure or delay of justice, the court may permit the depositions to be taken and may issue orders like those authorized by Rules 34 and 35. The depositions may be taken and used as any other deposition taken in a pending district-court action.

(c) Perpetuation by an Action. This rule does not limit a court's power to entertain an action to perpetuate testimony.

(Amended December 27, 1946, effective March 19, 1948; December 29, 1948, effective October 20, 1949; March 1, 1971, effective July 1, 1971; March 2, 1987, effective August 1, 1987; April 25, 2005, effective December 1, 2005; April 30, 2007, effective December 1, 2007; March 26, 2009, effective December 1, 2009.)

RULE 28. PERSONS BEFORE WHOM DEPOSITIONS MAY BE TAKEN

(a) Within the United States.

(1) ***In General.*** Within the United States or a territory or insular possession subject to United States jurisdiction, a deposition must be taken before:

(A) an officer authorized to administer oaths either by federal law or by the law in the place of examination; or

(B) a person appointed by the court where the action is pending to administer oaths and take testimony.

(2) ***Definition of "Officer".*** The term "officer" in Rules 30, 31, and 32 includes a person appointed by the court under this rule or designated by the parties under Rule 29(a).

(b) In a Foreign Country.

(1) ***In General.*** A deposition may be taken in a foreign country:

(A) under an applicable treaty or convention;

(B) under a letter of request, whether or not captioned a "letter rogatory";

(C) on notice, before a person authorized to administer oaths either by federal law or by the law in the place of examination; or

(D) before a person commissioned by the court to administer any necessary oath and take testimony.

(2) ***Issuing a Letter of Request or a Commission.*** A letter of request, a commission, or both may be issued:

(A) on appropriate terms after an application and notice of it; and

(B) without a showing that taking the deposition in another manner is impracticable or inconvenient.

(3) ***Form of a Request, Notice, or Commission.*** When a letter of request or any other device is used according to a treaty or convention, it must be captioned in the form prescribed by that treaty or convention. A letter of request may be addressed "To the Appropriate Authority in [name of country]." A deposition notice or a commission must designate by name or descriptive title the person before whom the deposition is to be taken.

(4) ***Letter of Request—Admitting Evidence.*** Evidence obtained in response to a letter of request need not be excluded merely because it is not a verbatim transcript, because the testimony was not taken under oath, or because of any similar departure from the requirements for depositions taken within the United States.

(c) Disqualification. A deposition must not be taken before a person who is any party's relative, employee, or attorney; who is related to or employed by any party's attorney; or who is financially interested in the action.

(Amended December 27, 1946, effective March 19, 1948; January 21, 1963, effective July 1, 1963; April 29, 1980, effective August 1, 1980; March 2, 1987, effective August 1, 1987; April 22, 1993, effective December 1, 1993; April 30, 2007, effective December 1, 2007.)

RULE 29. STIPULATIONS ABOUT DISCOVERY PROCEDURE

Unless the court orders otherwise, the parties may stipulate that:

(a) a deposition may be taken before any person, at any time or place, on any notice, and in the manner specified—in which event it may be used in the same way as any other deposition; and

(b) other procedures governing or limiting discovery be modified—but a stipulation extending the time for any form of discovery must have court approval if it would interfere with the time set for completing discovery, for hearing a motion, or for trial.

(Amended March 30, 1970, effective July 1, 1970; April 22, 1993, effective December 1, 1993; April 30, 2007, effective December 1, 2007.)

RULE 30. DEPOSITIONS BY ORAL EXAMINATION

(a) When a Deposition May Be Taken.

(1) ***Without Leave.*** A party may, by oral questions, depose any person, including a party, without leave of court except as provided in Rule 30(a)(2). The deponent's attendance may be compelled by subpoena under Rule 45.

(2) ***With Leave.*** A party must obtain leave of court, and the court must grant leave to the extent consistent with Rule 26(b)(1) and (2):

(A) if the parties have not stipulated to the deposition and:

(i) the deposition would result in more than 10 depositions being taken under this rule or Rule 31 by the plaintiffs, or by the defendants, or by the third-party defendants;

(ii) the deponent has already been deposed in the case; or

(iii) the party seeks to take the deposition before the time specified in Rule 26(d), unless the party certifies in the notice, with supporting facts, that the deponent is expected to leave the United States and be unavailable for examination in this country after that time; or

(B) if the deponent is confined in prison.

(b) Notice of the Deposition; Other Formal Requirements.

(1) ***Notice in General.*** A party who wants to depose a person by oral questions must give reasonable written notice to every other party. The notice must state the time and place of the deposition and, if known, the deponent's name and address. If the name is unknown, the notice must provide a general description sufficient to identify the person or the particular class or group to which the person belongs.

(2) ***Producing Documents.*** If a subpoena duces tecum is to be served on the deponent, the materials designated for production, as set out in the subpoena, must be listed in the notice or in an attachment. The notice to a party deponent may be accompanied by a request under Rule 34 to produce documents and tangible things at the deposition.

(3) ***Method of Recording.***

(A) *Method Stated in the Notice.* The party who notices the deposition must state in the notice the method for recording the testimony. Unless the court orders otherwise, testimony may be recorded by audio, audiovisual, or stenographic means. The noticing party bears the recording costs. Any party may arrange to transcribe a deposition.

(B) *Additional Method.* With prior notice to the deponent and other parties, any party may designate another method for recording the testimony in addition to that specified in the original notice. That party bears the expense of the additional record or transcript unless the court orders otherwise.

(4) ***By Remote Means.*** The parties may stipulate—or the court may on motion order—that a deposition be taken by telephone or other remote means. For the purpose of this rule and Rules 28(a), 37(a)(2), and 37(b)(1), the deposition takes place where the deponent answers the questions.

(5) ***Officer's Duties.***

(A) *Before the Deposition.* Unless the parties stipulate otherwise, a deposition must be conducted before an officer appointed or designated under Rule 28. The officer must begin the deposition with an on-the-record statement that includes:

(i) the officer's name and business address;

(ii) the date, time, and place of the deposition;

(iii) the deponent's name;

(iv) the officer's administration of the oath or affirmation to the deponent; and

(v) the identity of all persons present.

(B) *Conducting the Deposition; Avoiding Distortion.* If the deposition is recorded non-stenographically, the officer must repeat the items in Rule 30(b)(5)(A)(i)-(iii) at the beginning of each unit of the recording medium. The deponent's and attorneys' appearance or demeanor must not be distorted through recording techniques.

(C) *After the Deposition.* At the end of a deposition, the officer must state on the record that the deposition is complete and must set out any stipulations made by the attorneys about custody of the transcript or recording and of the exhibits, or about any other pertinent matters.

(6) ***Notice or Subpoena Directed to an Organization.*** In its notice or subpoena, a party may name as the deponent a public or private corporation, a partnership, an association, a governmental agency, or other entity and must describe with reasonable particularity the matters for examination. The named organization must then designate one or more officers, directors, or managing agents, or designate other persons who consent to testify on its behalf; and it may set out the matters on which each person designated will testify. A subpoena must advise a nonparty organization of its duty to make this designation. The persons designated must testify about information known or reasonably available to the organization. This paragraph (6) does not preclude a deposition by any other procedure allowed by these rules.

(c) Examination and Cross-Examination; Record of the Examination; Objections; Written Questions.

(1) ***Examination and Cross-Examination.*** The examination and cross-examination of a deponent proceed as they would at trial under the Federal Rules of Evidence, except Rules 103 and 615. After putting the deponent under oath or affirmation, the officer must record the testimony by the method designated under Rule 30(b)(3)(A). The testimony must be recorded by the officer personally or by a person acting in the presence and under the direction of the officer.

(2) ***Objections.*** An objection at the time of the examination—whether to evidence, to a party's conduct, to the officer's qualifications, to the manner of taking the deposition, or to any other aspect of the deposition—must be noted on the record, but the examination still proceeds; the testimony is taken subject to any objection. An objection must be stated concisely in a nonargumentative and nonsuggestive manner. A person may instruct a deponent not to answer only when necessary to preserve a privilege, to enforce a limitation ordered by the court, or to present a motion under Rule 30(d)(3).

(3) ***Participating Through Written Questions.*** Instead of participating in the oral examination, a party may serve written questions in a sealed envelope on the party noticing the deposition, who must deliver them to the officer. The officer must ask the deponent those questions and record the answers verbatim.

(d) Duration; Sanction; Motion to Terminate or Limit.

(1) ***Duration.*** Unless otherwise stipulated or ordered by the court, a deposition is limited to one day of 7 hours. The court must allow additional time consistent with Rule 26(b)(1) and (2) if needed to fairly examine the deponent or if the deponent, another person, or any other circumstance impedes or delays the examination.

(2) ***Sanction.*** The court may impose an appropriate sanction—including the reasonable expenses and attorney's fees incurred by any party—on a person who impedes, delays, or frustrates the fair examination of the deponent.

(3) ***Motion to Terminate or Limit.***

(A) *Grounds.* At any time during a deposition, the deponent or a party may move to terminate or limit it on the ground that it is being conducted in bad faith or in a manner that unreasonably annoys, embarrasses, or oppresses the deponent or party. The motion may be filed in the court where the action is pending or the deposition is being taken. If the objecting deponent or party so demands, the deposition must be suspended for the time necessary to obtain an order.

(B) *Order.* The court may order that the deposition be terminated or may limit its scope and manner as provided in Rule 26(c). If terminated, the deposition may be resumed only by order of the court where the action is pending.

(C) *Award of Expenses.* Rule 37(a)(5) applies to the award of expenses.

(e) Review by the Witness; Changes.

(1) ***Review; Statement of Changes.*** On request by the deponent or a party before the deposition is completed, the deponent must be allowed 30 days after being notified by the officer that the transcript or recording is available in which:

(A) to review the transcript or recording; and

(B) if there are changes in form or substance, to sign a statement listing the changes and the reasons for making them.

(2) ***Changes Indicated in the Officer's Certificate.*** The officer must note in the certificate prescribed by Rule 30(f)(1) whether a review was requested and, if so, must attach any changes the deponent makes during the 30–day period.

(f) Certification and Delivery; Exhibits; Copies of the Transcript or Recording; Filing.

(1) ***Certification and Delivery.*** The officer must certify in writing that the witness was duly sworn and that the deposition accurately records the witness's testimony. The certificate must accompany the record of the deposition. Unless the court orders otherwise, the officer must seal the deposition in an envelope or package bearing the title of the action and marked "Deposition of [witness's name]" and must promptly send it to the attorney who arranged for the transcript or recording. The attorney must store it under conditions that will protect it against loss, destruction, tampering, or deterioration.

(2) ***Documents and Tangible Things.***

(A) *Originals and Copies.* Documents and tangible things produced for inspection during a deposition must, on a party's request, be marked for identification and attached to the deposition. Any party may inspect and copy them. But if the person who produced them wants to keep the originals, the person may:

(i) offer copies to be marked, attached to the deposition, and then used as originals—after giving all parties a fair opportunity to verify the copies by comparing them with the originals; or

(ii) give all parties a fair opportunity to inspect and copy the originals after they are marked—in which event the originals may be used as if attached to the deposition.

(B) *Order Regarding the Originals.* Any party may move for an order that the originals be attached to the deposition pending final disposition of the case.

(3) ***Copies of the Transcript or Recording.*** Unless otherwise stipulated or ordered by the court, the officer must retain the stenographic notes of a deposition taken stenographically or a copy of the recording of a deposition taken by another method. When paid reasonable charges, the officer must furnish a copy of the transcript or recording to any party or the deponent.

(4) ***Notice of Filing.*** A party who files the deposition must promptly notify all other parties of the filing.

(g) Failure to Attend a Deposition or Serve a Subpoena; Expenses. A party who, expecting a deposition to be taken, attends in person or by an attorney may recover reasonable expenses for attending, including attorney's fees, if the noticing party failed to:

(1) attend and proceed with the deposition; or

(2) serve a subpoena on a nonparty deponent, who consequently did not attend.

(Amended January 21, 1963, effective July 1, 1963; March 30, 1970, effective July 1, 1970; March 1, 1971, effective July 1, 1971; November 20, 1972, effective July 1, 1975; April 29, 1980, effective August 1, 1980; March 2, 1987, effective August 1, 1987; April 22, 1993, effective December 1, 1993; April 17, 2000, effective December 1, 2000; April 30, 2007, effective December 1, 2007; April 29, 2015, effective December 1, 2015.)

RULE 31. DEPOSITIONS BY WRITTEN QUESTIONS

(a) When a Deposition May Be Taken.

(1) ***Without Leave.*** A party may, by written questions, depose any person, including a party, without leave of court except as provided in Rule 31(a)(2). The deponent's attendance may be compelled by subpoena under Rule 45.

(2) ***With Leave.*** A party must obtain leave of court, and the court must grant leave to the extent consistent with Rule 26(b)(1) and (2):

(A) if the parties have not stipulated to the deposition and:

(i) the deposition would result in more than 10 depositions being taken under this rule or Rule 30 by the plaintiffs, or by the defendants, or by the third-party defendants;

(ii) the deponent has already been deposed in the case; or

(iii) the party seeks to take a deposition before the time specified in Rule 26(d); or

(B) if the deponent is confined in prison.

(3) ***Service; Required Notice.*** A party who wants to depose a person by written questions must serve them on every other party, with a notice stating, if known, the deponent's name and address. If the name is unknown, the notice must provide a general description sufficient to identify the person or the particular class or group to which the person belongs. The notice must also state the name or descriptive title and the address of the officer before whom the deposition will be taken.

(4) ***Questions Directed to an Organization.*** A public or private corporation, a partnership, an association, or a governmental agency may be deposed by written questions in accordance with Rule 30(b)(6).

(5) ***Questions from Other Parties.*** Any questions to the deponent from other parties must be served on all parties as follows: cross-questions, within 14 days after being served with the notice and direct questions; redirect questions, within 7 days after being served with cross-questions; and recross-questions, within 7 days after being served with redirect questions. The court may, for good cause, extend or shorten these times.

(b) Delivery to the Officer; Officer's Duties. The party who noticed the deposition must deliver to the officer a copy of all the questions served and of the notice. The officer must promptly proceed in the manner provided in Rule 30(c), (e), and (f) to:

(1) take the deponent's testimony in response to the questions;

(2) prepare and certify the deposition; and

(3) send it to the party, attaching a copy of the questions and of the notice.

(c) Notice of Completion or Filing.

(1) ***Completion.*** The party who noticed the deposition must notify all other parties when it is completed.

(2) ***Filing.*** A party who files the deposition must promptly notify all other parties of the filing.

(Amended March 30, 1970, effective July 1, 1970; March 2, 1987, effective August 1, 1987; April 22, 1993, effective December 1, 1993; April 30, 2007, effective December 1, 2007; April 29, 2015, effective December 1, 2015.)

RULE 32. USING DEPOSITIONS IN COURT PROCEEDINGS

(a) Using Depositions.

(1) ***In General.*** At a hearing or trial, all or part of a deposition may be used against a party on these conditions:

(A) the party was present or represented at the taking of the deposition or had reasonable notice of it;

(B) it is used to the extent it would be admissible under the Federal Rules of Evidence if the deponent were present and testifying; and

(C) the use is allowed by Rule 32(a)(2) through (8).

(2) ***Impeachment and Other Uses.*** Any party may use a deposition to contradict or impeach the testimony given by the deponent as a witness, or for any other purpose allowed by the Federal Rules of Evidence.

(3) ***Deposition of Party, Agent, or Designee.*** An adverse party may use for any purpose the deposition of a party or anyone who, when deposed, was the party's officer, director, managing agent, or designee under Rule 30(b)(6) or 31(a)(4).

(4) ***Unavailable Witness.*** A party may use for any purpose the deposition of a witness, whether or not a party, if the court finds:

(A) that the witness is dead;

(B) that the witness is more than 100 miles from the place of hearing or trial or is outside the United States, unless it appears that the witness's absence was procured by the party offering the deposition;

(C) that the witness cannot attend or testify because of age, illness, infirmity, or imprisonment;

(D) that the party offering the deposition could not procure the witness's attendance by subpoena; or

(E) on motion and notice, that exceptional circumstances make it desirable—in the interest of justice and with due regard to the importance of live testimony in open court—to permit the deposition to be used.

(5) ***Limitations on Use.***

(A) *Deposition Taken on Short Notice.* A deposition must not be used against a party who, having received less than 14 days' notice of the deposition, promptly moved for a protective order under Rule 26(c)(1)(B) requesting that it not be taken or be taken at a different time or place—and this motion was still pending when the deposition was taken.

(B) *Unavailable Deponent; Party Could Not Obtain an Attorney.* A deposition taken without leave of court under the unavailability provision of Rule 30(a)(2)(A)(iii) must not be used against a party who shows that, when served with the notice, it could not, despite diligent efforts, obtain an attorney to represent it at the deposition.

(6) ***Using Part of a Deposition.*** If a party offers in evidence only part of a deposition, an adverse party may require the offeror to introduce other parts that in fairness should be considered with the part introduced, and any party may itself introduce any other parts.

(7) ***Substituting a Party.*** Substituting a party under Rule 25 does not affect the right to use a deposition previously taken.

(8) ***Deposition Taken in an Earlier Action.*** A deposition lawfully taken and, if required, filed in any federal- or state-court action may be used in a later action involving the same subject matter between the same parties, or their representatives or successors in interest, to the same extent as if taken in the later action. A deposition previously taken may also be used as allowed by the Federal Rules of Evidence.

(b) Objections to Admissibility. Subject to Rules 28(b) and 32(d)(3), an objection may be made at a hearing or trial to the admission of any deposition testimony that would be inadmissible if the witness were present and testifying.

(c) Form of Presentation. Unless the court orders otherwise, a party must provide a transcript of any deposition testimony the party offers, but may provide the court with the testimony in nontranscript form as well. On any party's request, deposition testimony offered in a jury trial for any purpose other than impeachment must be presented in nontranscript form, if available, unless the court for good cause orders otherwise.

(d) Waiver of Objections.

(1) ***To the Notice.*** An objection to an error or irregularity in a deposition notice is waived unless promptly served in writing on the party giving the notice.

(2) ***To the Officer's Qualification.*** An objection based on disqualification of the officer before whom a deposition is to be taken is waived if not made:

(A) before the deposition begins; or

(B) promptly after the basis for disqualification becomes known or, with reasonable diligence, could have been known.

(3) ***To the Taking of the Deposition.***

(A) *Objection to Competence, Relevance, or Materiality.* An objection to a deponent's competence—or to the competence, relevance, or materiality of testimony—is not waived by a failure to make the objection before or during the deposition, unless the ground for it might have been corrected at that time.

(B) *Objection to an Error or Irregularity.* An objection to an error or irregularity at an oral examination is waived if:

(i) it relates to the manner of taking the deposition, the form of a question or answer, the oath or affirmation, a party's conduct, or other matters that might have been corrected at that time; and

(ii) it is not timely made during the deposition.

(C) *Objection to a Written Question.* An objection to the form of a written question under Rule 31 is waived if not served in writing on the party submitting the question within the time for serving responsive questions or, if the question is a recross-question, within 7 days after being served with it.

(4) ***To Completing and Returning the Deposition.*** An objection to how the officer transcribed the testimony—or prepared, signed, certified, sealed, endorsed, sent, or otherwise dealt with the deposition—is waived unless a motion to suppress is made promptly after the error or irregularity becomes known or, with reasonable diligence, could have been known.

(Amended March 30, 1970, effective July 1, 1970; November 20, 1972, effective July 1, 1975; April 29, 1980, effective August 1, 1980; March 2, 1987, effective August 1, 1987; April 22, 1993, effective December 1, 1993; April 30, 2007, effective December 1, 2007; March 26, 2009, effective December 1, 2009.)

RULE 33. INTERROGATORIES TO PARTIES

(a) In General.

(1) ***Number.*** Unless otherwise stipulated or ordered by the court, a party may serve on any other party no more than 25 written interrogatories, including all discrete subparts. Leave to serve additional interrogatories may be granted to the extent consistent with Rule 26(b)(1) and (2).

(2) *Scope.* An interrogatory may relate to any matter that may be inquired into under Rule 26(b). An interrogatory is not objectionable merely because it asks for an opinion or contention that relates to fact or the application of law to fact, but the court may order that the interrogatory need not be answered until designated discovery is complete, or until a pretrial conference or some other time.

(b) Answers and Objections.

(1) ***Responding Party.*** The interrogatories must be answered:

(A) by the party to whom they are directed; or

(B) if that party is a public or private corporation, a partnership, an association, or a governmental agency, by any officer or agent, who must furnish the information available to the party.

(2) ***Time to Respond.*** The responding party must serve its answers and any objections within 30 days after being served with the interrogatories. A shorter or longer time may be stipulated to under Rule 29 or be ordered by the court.

(3) ***Answering Each Interrogatory.*** Each interrogatory must, to the extent it is not objected to, be answered separately and fully in writing under oath.

(4) ***Objections.*** The grounds for objecting to an interrogatory must be stated with specificity. Any ground not stated in a timely objection is waived unless the court, for good cause, excuses the failure.

(5) ***Signature.*** The person who makes the answers must sign them, and the attorney who objects must sign any objections.

(c) Use. An answer to an interrogatory may be used to the extent allowed by the Federal Rules of Evidence.

(d) Option to Produce Business Records. If the answer to an interrogatory may be determined by examining, auditing, compiling, abstracting, or summarizing a party's business records (including electronically stored information), and if the burden of deriving or ascertaining the answer will be substantially the same for either party, the responding party may answer by:

(1) specifying the records that must be reviewed, in sufficient detail to enable the interrogating party to locate and identify them as readily as the responding party could; and

(2) giving the interrogating party a reasonable opportunity to examine and audit the records and to make copies, compilations, abstracts, or summaries.

(Amended December 27, 1946, effective March 19, 1948; March 30, 1970, effective July 1, 1970; April 29, 1980, effective August 1, 1980; April 22, 1993, effective December 1, 1993; April 12, 2006, effective December 1, 2006; April 30, 2007, effective December 1, 2007; April 29, 2015, effective December 1, 2015.)

RULE 34. PRODUCING DOCUMENTS, ELECTRONICALLY STORED INFORMATION, AND TANGIBLE THINGS, OR ENTERING ONTO LAND, FOR INSPECTION AND OTHER PURPOSES

(a) In General. A party may serve on any other party a request within the scope of Rule 26(b):

(1) to produce and permit the requesting party or its representative to inspect, copy, test, or sample the following items in the responding party's possession, custody, or control:

(A) any designated documents or electronically stored information—including writings, drawings, graphs, charts, photographs, sound recordings, images, and other data or data compilations—stored in any medium from which information can be obtained either directly or, if necessary, after translation by the responding party into a reasonably usable form; or

(B) any designated tangible things; or

(2) to permit entry onto designated land or other property possessed or controlled by the responding party, so that the requesting party may inspect, measure, survey, photograph, test, or sample the property or any designated object or operation on it.

(b) Procedure.

(1) ***Contents of the Request.*** The request:

(A) must describe with reasonable particularity each item or category of items to be inspected;

(B) must specify a reasonable time, place, and manner for the inspection and for performing the related acts; and

(C) may specify the form or forms in which electronically stored information is to be produced.

(2) ***Responses and Objections.***

(A) *Time to Respond.* The party to whom the request is directed must respond in writing within 30 days after being served or — if the request was delivered under Rule 26(d)(2) — within 30 days after the parties' first Rule 26(f) conference. A shorter or longer time may be stipulated to under Rule 29 or be ordered by the court.

(B) *Responding to Each Item.* For each item or category, the response must either state that inspection and related activities will be permitted as requested or state with specificity the grounds for objecting to the request, including the reasons. The responding party may state that it will produce copies of documents or of electronically stored information instead of permitting inspection. The production must then be completed no later than the time for inspection specified in the request or another reasonable time specified in the response.

(C) *Objections.* An objection must state whether any responsive materials are being withheld on the basis of that objection. An objection to part of a request must specify the part and permit inspection of the rest.

(D) *Responding to a Request for Production of Electronically Stored Information.* The response may state an objection to a requested form for producing electronically stored information. If the responding party objects to a requested form—or if no form was specified in the request—the party must state the form or forms it intends to use.

(E) *Producing the Documents or Electronically Stored Information.* Unless otherwise stipulated or ordered by the court, these procedures apply to producing documents or electronically stored information:

(i) A party must produce documents as they are kept in the usual course of business or must organize and label them to correspond to the categories in the request;

(ii) If a request does not specify a form for producing electronically stored information, a party must produce it in a form or forms in which it is ordinarily maintained or in a reasonably usable form or forms; and

(iii) A party need not produce the same electronically stored information in more than one form.

(c) Nonparties. As provided in Rule 45, a nonparty may be compelled to produce documents and tangible things or to permit an inspection.

(Amended December 27, 1946, effective March 19, 1948; March 30, 1970, effective July 1, 1970; April 29, 1980, effective August 1, 1980; March 2, 1987, effective August 1, 1987; April 30, 1991, effective December 1, 1991; April 22, 1993, effective December 1, 1993; April 12, 2006, effective December 1, 2006; April 30, 2007, effective December 1, 2007; April 29, 2015, effective December 1, 2015.)

RULE 35. PHYSICAL AND MENTAL EXAMINATIONS

(a) Order for an Examination.

(1) ***In General.*** The court where the action is pending may order a party whose mental or physical condition—including blood group—is in controversy to submit to a physical or mental examination by a suitably licensed or certified examiner. The court has the same authority to order a party to produce for examination a person who is in its custody or under its legal control.

(2) ***Motion and Notice; Contents of the Order.*** The order:

(A) may be made only on motion for good cause and on notice to all parties and the person to be examined; and

(B) must specify the time, place, manner, conditions, and scope of the examination, as well as the person or persons who will perform it.

(b) Examiner's Report.

(1) ***Request by the Party or Person Examined.*** The party who moved for the examination must, on request, deliver to the requester a copy of the examiner's report, together with like reports of all earlier examinations of the same condition. The request may be made by the party against whom the examination order was issued or by the person examined.

(2) ***Contents.*** The examiner's report must be in writing and must set out in detail the examiner's findings, including diagnoses, conclusions, and the results of any tests.

(3) ***Request by the Moving Party.*** After delivering the reports, the party who moved for the examination may request—and is entitled to receive—from the party against whom the examination order was issued like reports of all earlier or later examinations of the same condition. But those reports need not be delivered by the party with custody or control of the person examined if the party shows that it could not obtain them.

(4) ***Waiver of Privilege.*** By requesting and obtaining the examiner's report, or by deposing the examiner, the party examined waives any privilege it may have—in that action or any other action involving the same controversy—concerning testimony about all examinations of the same condition.

(5) ***Failure to Deliver a Report.*** The court on motion may order—on just terms—that a party deliver the report of an examination. If the report is not provided, the court may exclude the examiner's testimony at trial.

(6) ***Scope.*** This subdivision (b) applies also to an examination made by the parties' agreement, unless the agreement states otherwise. This subdivision does not preclude obtaining an examiner's report or deposing an examiner under other rules.

(Amended March 30, 1970, effective July 1, 1970; March 2, 1987, effective August 1, 1987; amended by Pub.L. 100–690, Title VII, § 7047(b), November 18, 1988, 102 Stat. 4401; amended April 30, 1991, effective December 1, 1991; April 30, 2007, effective December 1, 2007.)

RULE 36. REQUESTS FOR ADMISSION

(a) Scope and Procedure.

(1) ***Scope.*** A party may serve on any other party a written request to admit, for purposes of the pending action only, the truth of any matters within the scope of Rule 26(b)(1) relating to:

(A) facts, the application of law to fact, or opinions about either; and

(B) the genuineness of any described documents.

(2) ***Form; Copy of a Document.*** Each matter must be separately stated. A request to admit the genuineness of a document must be accompanied by a copy of the document unless it is, or has been, otherwise furnished or made available for inspection and copying.

(3) ***Time to Respond; Effect of Not Responding.*** A matter is admitted unless, within 30 days after being served, the party to whom the request is directed serves on the requesting party a written answer or objection addressed to the matter and signed by the party or its attorney. A shorter or longer time for responding may be stipulated to under Rule 29 or be ordered by the court.

(4) ***Answer.*** If a matter is not admitted, the answer must specifically deny it or state in detail why the answering party cannot truthfully admit or deny it. A denial must fairly respond to the substance of the matter; and when good faith requires that a party qualify an answer or deny only a part of a matter, the answer must specify the part admitted and qualify or deny the rest. The answering party may assert lack of knowledge or information as a reason for failing to admit or deny only if the party states that it has made reasonable inquiry and that the information it knows or can readily obtain is insufficient to enable it to admit or deny.

(5) ***Objections.*** The grounds for objecting to a request must be stated. A party must not object solely on the ground that the request presents a genuine issue for trial.

(6) ***Motion Regarding the Sufficiency of an Answer or Objection.*** The requesting party may move to determine the sufficiency of an answer or objection. Unless the court finds an objection justified, it must order that an answer be served. On finding that an answer does not comply with this rule, the court may order either that the matter is admitted or that an amended answer be served. The court may defer its final decision until a pretrial conference or a specified time before trial. Rule 37(a)(5) applies to an award of expenses.

(b) Effect of an Admission; Withdrawing or Amending It. A matter admitted under this rule is conclusively established unless the court, on motion, permits the admission to be withdrawn or amended. Subject to Rule 16(e), the court may permit withdrawal or amendment if it would promote the presentation of the merits of the action and if the court is not persuaded that it would prejudice the requesting party in maintaining or defending the action on the merits. An admission under this rule is not an admission for any other purpose and cannot be used against the party in any other proceeding.

(Amended December 27, 1946, effective March 19, 1948; March 30, 1970, effective July 1, 1970; March 2, 1987, effective August 1, 1987; April 22, 1993, effective December 1, 1993; April 30, 2007, effective December 1, 2007.)

RULE 37. FAILURE TO MAKE DISCLOSURES OR TO COOPERATE IN DISCOVERY; SANCTIONS

(a) Motion for an Order Compelling Disclosure or Discovery.

(1) ***In General.*** On notice to other parties and all affected persons, a party may move for an order compelling disclosure or discovery. The motion must include a certification that the movant has in good faith conferred or attempted to confer with the person or party failing to make disclosure or discovery in an effort to obtain it without court action.

(2) ***Appropriate Court.*** A motion for an order to a party must be made in the court where the action is pending. A motion for an order to a nonparty must be made in the court where the discovery is or will be taken.

(3) ***Specific Motions.***

(A) *To Compel Disclosure.* If a party fails to make a disclosure required by Rule 26(a), any other party may move to compel disclosure and for appropriate sanctions.

(B) *To Compel a Discovery Response.* A party seeking discovery may move for an order compelling an answer, designation, production, or inspection. This motion may be made if:

(i) a deponent fails to answer a question asked under Rule 30 or 31;

(ii) a corporation or other entity fails to make a designation under Rule 30(b)(6) or 31(a)(4);

(iii) a party fails to answer an interrogatory submitted under Rule 33; or

(iv) a party fails to produce documents or fails to respond that inspection will be permitted — or fails to permit inspection — as requested under Rule 34.

(C) *Related to a Deposition.* When taking an oral deposition, the party asking a question may complete or adjourn the examination before moving for an order.

(4) ***Evasive or Incomplete Disclosure, Answer, or Response.*** For purposes of this subdivision (a), an evasive or incomplete disclosure, answer, or response must be treated as a failure to disclose, answer, or respond.

(5) ***Payment of Expenses; Protective Orders.***

(A) *If the Motion Is Granted (or Disclosure or Discovery Is Provided After Filing).* If the motion is granted—or if the disclosure or requested discovery is provided after the motion was filed—the court must, after giving an opportunity to be heard, require the party or deponent whose conduct necessitated the motion, the party or attorney advising that conduct, or both to pay the movant's reasonable expenses incurred in making the motion, including attorney's fees. But the court must not order this payment if:

(i) the movant filed the motion before attempting in good faith to obtain the disclosure or discovery without court action;

(ii) the opposing party's nondisclosure, response, or objection was substantially justified; or

(iii) other circumstances make an award of expenses unjust.

(B) *If the Motion Is Denied.* If the motion is denied, the court may issue any protective order authorized under Rule 26(c) and must, after giving an opportunity to be heard, require the movant, the attorney filing the motion, or both to pay the party or deponent who opposed the motion its reasonable expenses incurred in opposing the motion, including attorney's fees. But the court must not order this payment if the motion was substantially justified or other circumstances make an award of expenses unjust.

(C) *If the Motion Is Granted in Part and Denied in Part.* If the motion is granted in part and denied in part, the court may issue any protective order authorized under Rule 26(c) and may, after giving an opportunity to be heard, apportion the reasonable expenses for the motion.

(b) Failure to Comply with a Court Order.

(1) ***Sanctions Sought in the District Where the Deposition Is Taken.*** If the court where the discovery is taken orders a deponent to be sworn or to answer a question and the deponent fails to obey, the failure may be treated as contempt of court. If a deposition-related motion is transferred to the court where the action is pending, and that court orders a deponent to be sworn or to answer a question and the deponent fails to obey, the failure may be treated as contempt of either the court where the discovery is taken or the court where the action is pending.

(2) ***Sanctions Sought in the District Where the Action Is Pending.***

(A) *For Not Obeying a Discovery Order.* If a party or a party's officer, director, or managing agent—or a witness designated under Rule 30(b)(6) or 31(a)(4)—fails to obey an order to provide or permit discovery, including an order under Rule 26(f), 35, or 37(a), the court where the action is pending may issue further just orders. They may include the following:

(i) directing that the matters embraced in the order or other designated facts be taken as established for purposes of the action, as the prevailing party claims;

(ii) prohibiting the disobedient party from supporting or opposing designated claims or defenses, or from introducing designated matters in evidence;

(iii) striking pleadings in whole or in part;

(iv) staying further proceedings until the order is obeyed;

(v) dismissing the action or proceeding in whole or in part;

(vi) rendering a default judgment against the disobedient party; or

(vii) treating as contempt of court the failure to obey any order except an order to submit to a physical or mental examination.

(B) *For Not Producing a Person for Examination.* If a party fails to comply with an order under Rule 35(a) requiring it to produce another person for examination, the court may issue any of the orders listed in Rule 37(b)(2)(A)(i)-(vi), unless the disobedient party shows that it cannot produce the other person.

(C) *Payment of Expenses.* Instead of or in addition to the orders above, the court must order the disobedient party, the attorney advising that party, or both to pay the reasonable expenses, including attorney's fees, caused by the failure, unless the failure was substantially justified or other circumstances make an award of expenses unjust.

(c) Failure to Disclose, to Supplement an Earlier Response, or to Admit.

(1) ***Failure to Disclose or Supplement.*** If a party fails to provide information or identify a witness as required by Rule 26(a) or (e), the party is not allowed to use that information or witness to supply evidence on a motion, at a hearing, or at a trial, unless the failure was substantially justified or is harmless. In addition to or instead of this sanction, the court, on motion and after giving an opportunity to be heard:

(A) may order payment of the reasonable expenses, including attorney's fees, caused by the failure;

(B) may inform the jury of the party's failure; and

(C) may impose other appropriate sanctions, including any of the orders listed in Rule 37(b)(2)(A)(i)-(vi).

(2) ***Failure to Admit.*** If a party fails to admit what is requested under Rule 36 and if the requesting party later proves a document to be genuine or the matter true, the requesting party may move that the party who failed to admit pay the reasonable expenses, including attorney's fees, incurred in making that proof. The court must so order unless:

(A) the request was held objectionable under Rule 36(a);

(B) the admission sought was of no substantial importance;

(C) the party failing to admit had a reasonable ground to believe that it might prevail on the matter; or

(D) there was other good reason for the failure to admit.

(d) Party's Failure to Attend Its Own Deposition, Serve Answers to Interrogatories, or Respond to a Request for Inspection.

(1) ***In General.***

(A) *Motion; Grounds for Sanctions.* The court where the action is pending may, on motion, order sanctions if:

(i) a party or a party's officer, director, or managing agent—or a person designated under Rule 30(b)(6) or 31(a)(4)—fails, after being served with proper notice, to appear for that person's deposition; or

(ii) a party, after being properly served with interrogatories under Rule 33 or a request for inspection under Rule 34, fails to serve its answers, objections, or written response.

(B) *Certification.* A motion for sanctions for failing to answer or respond must include a certification that the movant has in good faith conferred or attempted to confer with the party failing to act in an effort to obtain the answer or response without court action.

(2) ***Unacceptable Excuse for Failing to Act.*** A failure described in Rule 37(d)(1)(A) is not excused on the ground that the discovery sought was objectionable, unless the party failing to act has a pending motion for a protective order under Rule 26(c).

(3) ***Types of Sanctions.*** Sanctions may include any of the orders listed in Rule 37(b)(2)(A)(i)-(vi). Instead of or in addition to these sanctions, the court must require the party failing to act, the attorney advising that party, or both to pay the reasonable expenses, including attorney's fees, caused by the failure, unless the failure was substantially justified or other circumstances make an award of expenses unjust.

(e) Failure to Preserve Electronically Stored Information. If electronically stored information that should have been preserved in the anticipation or conduct of litigation is lost because a party failed to take reasonable steps to preserve it, and it cannot be restored or replaced through additional discovery, the court:

(1) upon finding prejudice to another party from loss of the information, may order measures no greater than necessary to cure the prejudice; or

(2) only upon finding that the party acted with the intent to deprive another party of the information's use in the litigation may:

(A) presume that the lost information was unfavorable to the party;

(B) instruct the jury that it may or must presume the information was unfavorable to the party; or

(C) dismiss the action or enter a default judgment.

(f) Failure to Participate in Framing a Discovery Plan. If a party or its attorney fails to participate in good faith in developing and submitting a proposed discovery plan as required by Rule 26(f), the court may, after giving an opportunity to be heard, require that party or attorney to pay to any other party the reasonable expenses, including attorney's fees, caused by the failure.

(Amended December 29, 1948, effective October 20, 1949; March 30, 1970, effective July 1, 1970; April 29, 1980, effective August 1, 1980; amended by Pub.L. 96–481, Title II, § 205(a), October 21, 1980, 94 Stat. 2330, effective October 1, 1981; amended March 2, 1987, effective August 1, 1987; April 22, 1993, effective December 1, 1993; April 17, 2000, effective December 1, 2000; April 12, 2006, effective December 1, 2006; April 30, 2007, effective December 1, 2007; April 16, 2013, effective December 1, 2013; April 29, 2015, effective December 1, 2015.)

TITLE VI. TRIALS

RULE 38. RIGHT TO A JURY TRIAL; DEMAND

(a) Right Preserved. The right of trial by jury as declared by the Seventh Amendment to the Constitution—or as provided by a federal statute—is preserved to the parties inviolate.

(b) Demand. On any issue triable of right by a jury, a party may demand a jury trial by:

(1) serving the other parties with a written demand—which may be included in a pleading—no later than 14 days after the last pleading directed to the issue is served; and

(2) filing the demand in accordance with Rule 5(d).

(c) Specifying Issues. In its demand, a party may specify the issues that it wishes to have tried by a jury; otherwise, it is considered to have demanded a jury trial on all the issues so triable. If the party has demanded a jury trial on only some issues, any other party may—within 14 days after being served with the demand or within a shorter time ordered by the court—serve a demand for a jury trial on any other or all factual issues triable by jury.

(d) Waiver; Withdrawal. A party waives a jury trial unless its demand is properly served and filed. A proper demand may be withdrawn only if the parties consent.

(e) Admiralty and Maritime Claims. These rules do not create a right to a jury trial on issues in a claim that is an admiralty or maritime claim under Rule 9(h).

(Amended February 28, 1966, effective July 1, 1966; March 2, 1987, effective August 1, 1987; April 22, 1993, effective December 1, 1993; April 30, 2007, effective December 1, 2007; March 26, 2009, effective December 1, 2009.)

RULE 39. TRIAL BY JURY OR BY THE COURT

(a) When a Demand Is Made. When a jury trial has been demanded under Rule 38, the action must be designated on the docket as a jury action. The trial on all issues so demanded must be by jury unless:

(1) the parties or their attorneys file a stipulation to a nonjury trial or so stipulate on the record; or

(2) the court, on motion or on its own, finds that on some or all of those issues there is no federal right to a jury trial.

(b) When No Demand Is Made. Issues on which a jury trial is not properly demanded are to be tried by the court. But the court may, on motion, order a jury trial on any issue for which a jury might have been demanded.

(c) Advisory Jury; Jury Trial by Consent. In an action not triable of right by a jury, the court, on motion or on its own:

(1) may try any issue with an advisory jury; or

(2) may, with the parties' consent, try any issue by a jury whose verdict has the same effect as if a jury trial had been a matter of right, unless the action is against the United States and a federal statute provides for a nonjury trial.

(Amended April 30, 2007, effective December 1, 2007.)

RULE 40. SCHEDULING CASES FOR TRIAL

Each court must provide by rule for scheduling trials. The court must give priority to actions entitled to priority by a federal statute.

(Amended April 30, 2007, effective December 1, 2007.)

RULE 41. DISMISSAL OF ACTIONS

(a) Voluntary Dismissal.

(1) *By the Plaintiff.*

(A) *Without a Court Order.* Subject to Rules 23(e), 23.1(c), 23.2, and 66 and any applicable federal statute, the plaintiff may dismiss an action without a court order by filing:

(i) a notice of dismissal before the opposing party serves either an answer or a motion for summary judgment; or

(ii) a stipulation of dismissal signed by all parties who have appeared.

(B) *Effect.* Unless the notice or stipulation states otherwise, the dismissal is without prejudice. But if the plaintiff previously dismissed any federal- or state-court action based on or including the same claim, a notice of dismissal operates as an adjudication on the merits.

(2) *By Court Order; Effect.* Except as provided in Rule 41(a)(1), an action may be dismissed at the plaintiff's request only by court order, on terms that the court considers proper. If a defendant has pleaded a counterclaim before being served with the plaintiff's motion to dismiss, the action may be dismissed over the defendant's objection only if the counterclaim can remain pending for independent adjudication. Unless the order states otherwise, a dismissal under this paragraph (2) is without prejudice.

(b) Involuntary Dismissal; Effect. If the plaintiff fails to prosecute or to comply with these rules or a court order, a defendant may move to dismiss the action or any claim against it. Unless the dismissal order states otherwise, a dismissal under this subdivision (b) and any dismissal not under this rule—except one for lack of jurisdiction, improper venue, or failure to join a party under Rule 19—operates as an adjudication on the merits.

(c) Dismissing a Counterclaim, Crossclaim, or Third-Party Claim. This rule applies to a dismissal of any counterclaim, crossclaim, or third-party claim. A claimant's voluntary dismissal under Rule 41(a)(1)(A)(i) must be made:

(1) before a responsive pleading is served; or

(2) if there is no responsive pleading, before evidence is introduced at a hearing or trial.

(d) Costs of a Previously Dismissed Action. If a plaintiff who previously dismissed an action in any court files an action based on or including the same claim against the same defendant, the court:

(1) may order the plaintiff to pay all or part of the costs of that previous action; and

(2) may stay the proceedings until the plaintiff has complied.

(Amended December 27, 1946, effective March 19, 1948; January 21, 1963, effective July 1, 1963; February 28, 1966, effective July 1, 1966; December 4, 1967, effective July 1, 1968; March 2, 1987, effective August 1, 1987; April 30, 1991, effective December 1, 1991; April 30, 2007, effective December 1, 2007.)

RULE 42. CONSOLIDATION; SEPARATE TRIALS

(a) Consolidation. If actions before the court involve a common question of law or fact, the court may:

(1) join for hearing or trial any or all matters at issue in the actions;

(2) consolidate the actions; or

(3) issue any other orders to avoid unnecessary cost or delay.

(b) Separate Trials. For convenience, to avoid prejudice, or to expedite and economize, the court may order a separate trial of one or more separate issues, claims, crossclaims, counterclaims, or third-party claims. When ordering a separate trial, the court must preserve any federal right to a jury trial.

(Amended February 28, 1966, effective July 1, 1966; April 30, 2007, effective December 1, 2007.)

RULE 43. TAKING TESTIMONY

(a) In Open Court. At trial, the witnesses' testimony must be taken in open court unless a federal statute, the Federal Rules of Evidence, these rules, or other rules adopted by the Supreme Court provide otherwise. For good cause in compelling circumstances and with appropriate safeguards, the court may permit testimony in open court by contemporaneous transmission from a different location.

(b) Affirmation Instead of an Oath. When these rules require an oath, a solemn affirmation suffices.

(c) Evidence on a Motion. When a motion relies on facts outside the record, the court may hear the matter on affidavits or may hear it wholly or partly on oral testimony or on depositions.

(d) Interpreter. The court may appoint an interpreter of its choosing; fix reasonable compensation to be paid from funds provided by law or by one or more parties; and tax the compensation as costs.

(Amended February 28, 1966, effective July 1, 1966; November 20, 1972, and December 18, 1972, effective July 1, 1975; March 2, 1987, effective August 1, 1987; April 23, 1996, effective December 1, 1996; April 30, 2007, effective December 1, 2007.)

RULE 44. PROVING AN OFFICIAL RECORD

(a) Means of Proving.

(1) ***Domestic Record.*** Each of the following evidences an official record—or an entry in it—that is otherwise admissible and is kept within the United States, any state, district, or commonwealth, or any territory subject to the administrative or judicial jurisdiction of the United States:

(A) an official publication of the record; or

(B) a copy attested by the officer with legal custody of the record—or by the officer's deputy—and accompanied by a certificate that the officer has custody. The certificate must be made under seal:

(i) by a judge of a court of record in the district or political subdivision where the record is kept; or

(ii) by any public officer with a seal of office and with official duties in the district or political subdivision where the record is kept.

(2) ***Foreign Record.***

(A) *In General.* Each of the following evidences a foreign official record—or an entry in it—that is otherwise admissible:

(i) an official publication of the record; or

(ii) the record—or a copy—that is attested by an authorized person and is accompanied either by a final certification of genuineness or by a certification under a treaty or convention to which the United States and the country where the record is located are parties.

(B) *Final Certification of Genuineness.* A final certification must certify the genuineness of the signature and official position of the attester or of any foreign official whose certificate of genuineness relates to the attestation or is in a chain of certificates of genuineness relating to the attestation. A final certification may be made by a secretary of a United States embassy or legation; by a consul general, vice consul, or consular agent of the United States; or by a diplomatic or consular official of the foreign country assigned or accredited to the United States.

(C) *Other Means of Proof.* If all parties have had a reasonable opportunity to investigate a foreign record's authenticity and accuracy, the court may, for good cause, either:

(i) admit an attested copy without final certification; or

(ii) permit the record to be evidenced by an attested summary with or without a final certification.

(b) Lack of a Record. A written statement that a diligent search of designated records revealed no record or entry of a specified tenor is admissible as evidence that the records contain no such record or entry. For domestic records, the statement must be authenticated under Rule 44(a)(1). For foreign records, the statement must comply with (a)(2)(C)(ii).

(c) Other Proof. A party may prove an official record—or an entry or lack of an entry in it—by any other method authorized by law.

(Amended February 28, 1966, effective July 1, 1966; March 2, 1987, effective August 1, 1987; April 30, 1991, effective December 1, 1991; April 30, 2007, effective December 1, 2007.)

RULE 44.1. DETERMINING FOREIGN LAW

A party who intends to raise an issue about a foreign country's law must give notice by a pleading or other writing. In determining foreign law, the court may consider any relevant material or source, including testimony, whether or not submitted by a party or admissible under the Federal Rules of Evidence. The court's determination must be treated as a ruling on a question of law.

(Adopted February 28, 1966, effective July 1, 1966; amended November 20, 1972, effective July 1, 1975; March 2, 1987, effective August 1, 1987; April 30, 2007, effective December 1, 2007.)

RULE 45. SUBPOENA

(a) In General.

(1) ***Form and Contents.***

(A) *Requirements—In General.* Every subpoena must:

(i) state the court from which it issued;

(ii) state the title of the action and its civil-action number;

(iii) command each person to whom it is directed to do the following at a specified time and place: attend and testify; produce designated documents, electronically stored information, or tangible things in that person's possession, custody, or control; or permit the inspection of premises; and

(iv) set out the text of Rule 45(d) and (e).

(B) *Command to Attend a Deposition—Notice of the Recording Method.* A subpoena commanding attendance at a deposition must state the method for recording the testimony.

(C) *Combining or Separating a Command to Produce or to Permit Inspection; Specifying the Form for Electronically Stored Information.* A command to produce documents, electronically stored information, or tangible things or to permit the inspection of premises may be included in a subpoena commanding attendance at a deposition, hearing, or trial, or may be set out in a separate subpoena. A subpoena may specify the form or forms in which electronically stored information is to be produced.

(D) *Command to Produce; Included Obligations.* A command in a subpoena to produce documents, electronically stored information, or tangible things requires the responding person to permit inspection, copying, testing, or sampling of the materials.

(2) ***Issuing Court.*** A subpoena must issue from the court where the action is pending.

(3) ***Issued by Whom.*** The clerk must issue a subpoena, signed but otherwise in blank, to a party who requests it. That party must complete it before service. An attorney also may issue and sign a subpoena if the attorney is authorized to practice in the issuing court.

(4) ***Notice to Other Parties Before Service.*** If the subpoena commands the production of documents, electronically stored information, or tangible things or the inspection of premises before trial, then before it is served on the person to whom it is directed, a notice and a copy of the subpoena must be served on each party.

(b) Service.

(1) ***By Whom and How; Tendering Fees.*** Any person who is at least 18 years old and not a party may serve a subpoena. Serving a subpoena requires delivering a copy to the named person and, if the subpoena requires that person's attendance, tendering the fees for 1 day's attendance and the mileage allowed by law. Fees and mileage need not be tendered when the subpoena issues on behalf of the United States or any of its officers or agencies.

(2) ***Service in the United States.*** A subpoena may be served at any place within the United States.

(3) ***Service in a Foreign Country.*** 28 U.S.C. § 1783 governs issuing and serving a subpoena directed to a United States national or resident who is in a foreign country.

(4) ***Proof of Service.*** Proving service, when necessary, requires filing with the issuing court a statement showing the date and manner of service and the names of the persons served. The statement must be certified by the server.

(c) Place of Compliance.

(1) ***For a Trial, Hearing, or Deposition.*** A subpoena may command a person to attend a trial, hearing, or deposition only as follows:

(A) within 100 miles of where the person resides, is employed, or regularly transacts business in person; or

(B) within the state where the person resides, is employed, or regularly transacts business in person, if the person

(i) is a party or a party's officer; or

(ii) is commanded to attend a trial and would not incur substantial expense.

(2) ***For Other Discovery.*** A subpoena may command:

(A) production of documents, electronically stored information, or tangible things at a place within 100 miles of where the person resides, is employed, or regularly transacts business in person; and

(B) inspection of premises at the premises to be inspected.

(d) Protecting a Person Subject to a Subpoena; Enforcement.

(1) ***Avoiding Undue Burden or Expense; Sanctions.*** A party or attorney responsible for issuing and serving a subpoena must take reasonable steps to avoid imposing undue burden or expense on a person subject to the subpoena. The court for the district where compliance is required must enforce this duty and impose an appropriate sanction—which may include lost earnings and reasonable attorney's fees—on a party or attorney who fails to comply.

(2) ***Command to Produce Materials or Permit Inspection.***

(A) *Appearance Not Required.* A person commanded to produce documents, electronically stored information, or tangible things, or to permit the inspection of premises, need not appear in person at the place of production or inspection unless also commanded to appear for a deposition, hearing, or trial.

(B) *Objections.* A person commanded to produce documents or tangible things or to permit inspection may serve on the party or attorney designated in the subpoena a written objection to inspecting, copying, testing, or sampling any or all of the materials or to inspecting the premises—or to producing electronically stored information in the form or forms requested. The objection must be served before the earlier of the time specified for compliance or 14 days after the subpoena is served. If an objection is made, the following rules apply:

(i) At any time, on notice to the commanded person, the serving party may move the court for the district where compliance is required for an order compelling production or inspection.

(ii) These acts may be required only as directed in the order, and the order must protect a person who is neither a party nor a party's officer from significant expense resulting from compliance.

(3) ***Quashing or Modifying a Subpoena.***

(A) *When Required.* On timely motion, the court for the district where compliance is required must quash or modify a subpoena that:

(i) fails to allow a reasonable time to comply;

(ii) requires a person to comply beyond the geographical limits specified in Rule 45(c);

(iii) requires disclosure of privileged or other protected matter, if no exception or waiver applies; or

(iv) subjects a person to undue burden.

(B) *When Permitted.* To protect a person subject to or affected by a subpoena, the court for the district where compliance is required may, on motion, quash or modify the subpoena if it requires:

(i) disclosing a trade secret or other confidential research, development, or commercial information; or

(ii) disclosing an unretained expert's opinion or information that does not describe specific occurrences in dispute and results from the expert's study that was not requested by a party.

(C) *Specifying Conditions as an Alternative.* In the circumstances described in Rule 45(d)(3)(B), the court may, instead of quashing or modifying a subpoena, order appearance or production under specified conditions if the serving party:

(i) shows a substantial need for the testimony or material that cannot be otherwise met without undue hardship; and

(ii) ensures that the subpoenaed person will be reasonably compensated.

(e) Duties in Responding to a Subpoena.

(1) ***Producing Documents or Electronically Stored Information.*** These procedures apply to producing documents or electronically stored information:

(A) *Documents.* A person responding to a subpoena to produce documents must produce them as they are kept in the ordinary course of business or must organize and label them to correspond to the categories in the demand.

(B) *Form for Producing Electronically Stored Information Not Specified.* If a subpoena does not specify a form for producing electronically stored information, the person responding must produce it in a form or forms in which it is ordinarily maintained or in a reasonably usable form or forms.

(C) *Electronically Stored Information Produced in Only One Form.* The person responding need not produce the same electronically stored information in more than one form.

(D) *Inaccessible Electronically Stored Information.* The person responding need not provide discovery of electronically stored information from sources that the person identifies as not reasonably accessible because of undue burden or cost. On motion to compel discovery or for a protective order, the person responding must show that the information is not reasonably accessible because of undue burden or cost. If that showing is made, the court may nonetheless order discovery from such sources if the requesting party shows good cause, considering the limitations of Rule 26(b)(2)(C). The court may specify conditions for the discovery.

(2) *Claiming Privilege or Protection.*

(A) *Information Withheld.* A person withholding subpoenaed information under a claim that it is privileged or subject to protection as trial-preparation material must:

(i) expressly make the claim; and

(ii) describe the nature of the withheld documents, communications, or tangible things in a manner that, without revealing information itself privileged or protected, will enable the parties to assess the claim.

(B) *Information Produced.* If information produced in response to a subpoena is subject to a claim of privilege or of protection as trial-preparation material, the person making the claim may notify any party that received the information of the claim and the basis for it. After being notified, a party must promptly return, sequester, or destroy the specified information and any copies it has; must not use or disclose the information until the claim is resolved; must take reasonable steps to retrieve the information if the party disclosed it before being notified; and may promptly present the information under seal to the court for the district where compliance is required for a determination of the claim. The person who produced the information must preserve the information until the claim is resolved.

(f) Transferring a Subpoena-Related Motion. When the court where compliance is required did not issue the subpoena, it may transfer a motion under this rule to the issuing court if the person subject to the subpoena consents or if the court finds exceptional circumstances. Then, if the attorney for a person subject to a subpoena is authorized to practice in the court where the motion was made, the attorney may file papers and appear on the motion as an officer of the issuing court. To enforce its order, the issuing court may transfer the order to the court where the motion was made.

(g) Contempt. The court for the district where compliance is required—and also, after a motion is transferred, the issuing court—may hold in contempt a person who, having been served, fails without adequate excuse to obey the subpoena or an order related to it.

(Amended December 27, 1946, effective March 19, 1948; December 29, 1948, effective October 20, 1949; March 30, 1970, effective July 1, 1970; April 29, 1980, effective August 1, 1980; April 29, 1985, effective August 1, 1985; March 2, 1987, effective August 1, 1987; April 30, 1991, effective December 1, 1991; April 25, 2005, effective December 1, 2005; April 12, 2006, effective December 1, 2006; April 30, 2007, effective December 1, 2007; April 16, 2013, effective December 1, 2013.)

RULE 46. OBJECTING TO A RULING OR ORDER

A formal exception to a ruling or order is unnecessary. When the ruling or order is requested or made, a party need only state the action that it wants the court to take or objects to, along with the grounds for the request or objection. Failing to object does not prejudice a party who had no opportunity to do so when the ruling or order was made.

(Amended March 2, 1987, effective August 1, 1987; April 30, 2007, effective December 1, 2007.)

RULE 47. SELECTING JURORS

(a) Examining Jurors. The court may permit the parties or their attorneys to examine prospective jurors or may itself do so. If the court examines the jurors, it must permit the parties or their attorneys to make any further inquiry it considers proper, or must itself ask any of their additional questions it considers proper.

(b) Peremptory Challenges. The court must allow the number of peremptory challenges provided by 28 U.S.C. § 1870.

(c) Excusing a Juror. During trial or deliberation, the court may excuse a juror for good cause.

(Amended February 28, 1966, effective July 1, 1966; April 30, 1991, effective December 1, 1991; April 30, 2007, effective December 1, 2007.)

RULE 48. NUMBER OF JURORS; VERDICT; POLLING

(a) Number of Jurors. A jury must begin with at least 6 and no more than 12 members, and each juror must participate in the verdict unless excused under Rule 47(c).

(b) Verdict. Unless the parties stipulate otherwise, the verdict must be unanimous and must be returned by a jury of at least 6 members.

(c) Polling. After a verdict is returned but before the jury is discharged, the court must on a party's request, or may on its own, poll the jurors individually. If the poll reveals a lack of unanimity or lack of assent by the number of jurors that the parties stipulated to, the court may direct the jury to deliberate further or may order a new trial.

(Amended April 30, 1991, effective December 1, 1991; April 30, 2007, effective December 1, 2007; March 26, 2009, effective December 1, 2009.)

RULE 49. SPECIAL VERDICT; GENERAL VERDICT AND QUESTIONS

(a) Special Verdict.

(1) ***In General.*** The court may require a jury to return only a special verdict in the form of a special written finding on each issue of fact. The court may do so by:

(A) submitting written questions susceptible of a categorical or other brief answer;

(B) submitting written forms of the special findings that might properly be made under the pleadings and evidence; or

(C) using any other method that the court considers appropriate.

(2) ***Instructions.*** The court must give the instructions and explanations necessary to enable the jury to make its findings on each submitted issue.

(3) ***Issues Not Submitted.*** A party waives the right to a jury trial on any issue of fact raised by the pleadings or evidence but not submitted to the jury unless, before the jury retires, the party demands its submission to the jury. If the party does not demand submission, the court may make a finding on the issue. If the court makes no finding, it is considered to have made a finding consistent with its judgment on the special verdict.

(b) General Verdict with Answers to Written Questions.

(1) ***In General.*** The court may submit to the jury forms for a general verdict, together with written questions on one or more issues of fact that the jury must decide. The court must give the instructions and explanations necessary to enable the jury to render a general verdict and answer the questions in writing, and must direct the jury to do both.

(2) ***Verdict and Answers Consistent.*** When the general verdict and the answers are consistent, the court must approve, for entry under Rule 58, an appropriate judgment on the verdict and answers.

(3) ***Answers Inconsistent with the Verdict.*** When the answers are consistent with each other but one or more is inconsistent with the general verdict, the court may:

(A) approve, for entry under Rule 58, an appropriate judgment according to the answers, notwithstanding the general verdict;

(B) direct the jury to further consider its answers and verdict; or

(C) order a new trial.

(4) ***Answers Inconsistent with Each Other and the Verdict.*** When the answers are inconsistent with each other and one or more is also inconsistent with the general verdict, judgment must not be entered; instead, the court must direct the jury to further consider its answers and verdict, or must order a new trial.

(Amended January 21, 1963, effective July 1, 1963; March 2, 1987, effective August 1, 1987; April 30, 2007, effective December 1, 2007.)

RULE 50. JUDGMENT AS A MATTER OF LAW IN A JURY TRIAL; RELATED MOTION FOR A NEW TRIAL; CONDITIONAL RULING

(a) Judgment as a Matter of Law.

(1) ***In General.*** If a party has been fully heard on an issue during a jury trial and the court finds that a reasonable jury would not have a legally sufficient evidentiary basis to find for the party on that issue, the court may:

(A) resolve the issue against the party; and

(B) grant a motion for judgment as a matter of law against the party on a claim or defense that, under the controlling law, can be maintained or defeated only with a favorable finding on that issue.

(2) ***Motion.*** A motion for judgment as a matter of law may be made at any time before the case is submitted to the jury. The motion must specify the judgment sought and the law and facts that entitle the movant to the judgment.

(b) Renewing the Motion After Trial; Alternative Motion for a New Trial. If the court does not grant a motion for judgment as a matter of law made under Rule 50(a), the court is considered to have submitted the action to the jury subject to the court's later deciding the legal questions raised by the motion. No later than 28 days after the entry of judgment—or if the motion addresses a jury issue not decided by a verdict, no later than 28 days after the jury was discharged—the movant may file a renewed motion for judgment as a matter of law and may include an alternative or joint request for a new trial under Rule 59. In ruling on the renewed motion, the court may:

(1) allow judgment on the verdict, if the jury returned a verdict;

(2) order a new trial; or

(3) direct the entry of judgment as a matter of law.

(c) Granting the Renewed Motion; Conditional Ruling on a Motion for a New Trial.

(1) ***In General.*** If the court grants a renewed motion for judgment as a matter of law, it must also conditionally rule on any motion for a new trial by determining whether a new trial should be granted if the judgment is later vacated or reversed. The court must state the grounds for conditionally granting or denying the motion for a new trial.

(2) ***Effect of a Conditional Ruling.*** Conditionally granting the motion for a new trial does not affect the judgment's finality; if the judgment is reversed, the new trial must proceed unless the appellate court orders otherwise. If the motion for a new trial is conditionally denied, the appellee may assert error in that denial; if the judgment is reversed, the case must proceed as the appellate court orders.

(d) Time for a Losing Party's New–Trial Motion. Any motion for a new trial under Rule 59 by a party against whom judgment as a matter of law is rendered must be filed no later than 28 days after the entry of the judgment.

(e) Denying the Motion for Judgment as a Matter of Law; Reversal on Appeal. If the court denies the motion for judgment as a matter of law, the prevailing party may, as appellee, assert grounds entitling it to a new trial should the appellate court conclude that the trial court erred in denying the motion. If the appellate court reverses the judgment, it may order a new trial, direct the trial court to determine whether a new trial should be granted, or direct the entry of judgment.

(Amended January 21, 1963, effective July 1, 1963; March 2, 1987, effective August 1, 1987; April 30, 1991, effective December 1, 1991; April 22, 1993, effective December 1, 1993; April 27, 1995, effective December 1, 1995; April 12, 2006, effective December 1, 2006; April 30, 2007, effective December 1, 2007; March 26, 2009, effective December 1, 2009.)

RULE 51. INSTRUCTIONS TO THE JURY; OBJECTIONS; PRESERVING A CLAIM OF ERROR

(a) Requests.

(1) ***Before or at the Close of the Evidence.*** At the close of the evidence or at any earlier reasonable time that the court orders, a party may file and furnish to every other party written requests for the jury instructions it wants the court to give.

(2) ***After the Close of the Evidence.*** After the close of the evidence, a party may:

(A) file requests for instructions on issues that could not reasonably have been anticipated by an earlier time that the court set for requests; and

(B) with the court's permission, file untimely requests for instructions on any issue.

(b) Instructions. The court:

(1) must inform the parties of its proposed instructions and proposed action on the requests before instructing the jury and before final jury arguments;

(2) must give the parties an opportunity to object on the record and out of the jury's hearing before the instructions and arguments are delivered; and

(3) may instruct the jury at any time before the jury is discharged.

(c) Objections.

(1) ***How to Make.*** A party who objects to an instruction or the failure to give an instruction must do so on the record, stating distinctly the matter objected to and the grounds for the objection.

(2) ***When to Make.*** An objection is timely if:

(A) a party objects at the opportunity provided under Rule 51(b)(2); or

(B) a party was not informed of an instruction or action on a request before that opportunity to object, and the party objects promptly after learning that the instruction or request will be, or has been, given or refused.

(d) Assigning Error; Plain Error.

(1) ***Assigning Error.*** A party may assign as error:

(A) an error in an instruction actually given, if that party properly objected; or

(B) a failure to give an instruction, if that party properly requested it and—unless the court rejected the request in a definitive ruling on the record—also properly objected.

(2) ***Plain Error.*** A court may consider a plain error in the instructions that has not been preserved as required by Rule 51(d)(1) if the error affects substantial rights.

(Amended March 2, 1987, effective August 1, 1987; March 27, 2003, effective December 1, 2003; April 30, 2007, effective December 1, 2007.)

RULE 52. FINDINGS AND CONCLUSIONS BY THE COURT; JUDGMENT ON PARTIAL FINDINGS

(a) Findings and Conclusions.

(1) ***In General.*** In an action tried on the facts without a jury or with an advisory jury, the court must find the facts specially and state its conclusions of law separately. The findings and conclusions may be stated on the record after the close of the evidence or may appear in an opinion or a memorandum of decision filed by the court. Judgment must be entered under Rule 58.

(2) ***For an Interlocutory Injunction.*** In granting or refusing an interlocutory injunction, the court must similarly state the findings and conclusions that support its action.

(3) ***For a Motion.*** The court is not required to state findings or conclusions when ruling on a motion under Rule 12 or 56 or, unless these rules provide otherwise, on any other motion.

(4) ***Effect of a Master's Findings.*** A master's findings, to the extent adopted by the court, must be considered the court's findings.

(5) ***Questioning the Evidentiary Support.*** A party may later question the sufficiency of the evidence supporting the findings, whether or not the party requested findings, objected to them, moved to amend them, or moved for partial findings.

(6) ***Setting Aside the Findings.*** Findings of fact, whether based on oral or other evidence, must not be set aside unless clearly erroneous, and the reviewing court must give due regard to the trial court's opportunity to judge the witnesses' credibility.

(b) Amended or Additional Findings. On a party's motion filed no later than 28 days after the entry of judgment, the court may amend its findings—or make additional findings—and may amend the judgment accordingly. The motion may accompany a motion for a new trial under Rule 59.

(c) Judgment on Partial Findings. If a party has been fully heard on an issue during a nonjury trial and the court finds against the party on that issue, the court may enter judgment against the party on a claim or defense that, under the controlling law, can be maintained or defeated only with a favorable finding on that issue. The court may, however, decline to render any judgment until the close of the evidence. A judgment on partial findings must be supported by findings of fact and conclusions of law as required by Rule 52(a).

(Amended December 27, 1946, effective March 19, 1948; January 21, 1963, effective July 1, 1963; April 28, 1983, effective August 1, 1983; April 29, 1985, effective August 1, 1985; April 30, 1991, effective December 1, 1991; April 22, 1993, effective December 1, 1993; April 27, 1995, effective December 1, 1995; April 30, 2007, effective December 1, 2007; March 26, 2009, effective December 1, 2009.)

RULE 53. MASTERS

(a) Appointment.

(1) ***Scope.*** Unless a statute provides otherwise, a court may appoint a master only to:

(A) perform duties consented to by the parties;

(B) hold trial proceedings and make or recommend findings of fact on issues to be decided without a jury if appointment is warranted by:

(i) some exceptional condition; or

(ii) the need to perform an accounting or resolve a difficult computation of damages; or

(C) address pretrial and posttrial matters that cannot be effectively and timely addressed by an available district judge or magistrate judge of the district.

(2) *Disqualification.* A master must not have a relationship to the parties, attorneys, action, or court that would require disqualification of a judge under 28 U.S.C. § 455, unless the parties, with the court's approval, consent to the appointment after the master discloses any potential grounds for disqualification.

(3) *Possible Expense or Delay.* In appointing a master, the court must consider the fairness of imposing the likely expenses on the parties and must protect against unreasonable expense or delay.

(b) Order Appointing a Master.

(1) *Notice.* Before appointing a master, the court must give the parties notice and an opportunity to be heard. Any party may suggest candidates for appointment.

(2) *Contents.* The appointing order must direct the master to proceed with all reasonable diligence and must state:

(A) the master's duties, including any investigation or enforcement duties, and any limits on the master's authority under Rule 53(c);

(B) the circumstances, if any, in which the master may communicate ex parte with the court or a party;

(C) the nature of the materials to be preserved and filed as the record of the master's activities;

(D) the time limits, method of filing the record, other procedures, and standards for reviewing the master's orders, findings, and recommendations; and

(E) the basis, terms, and procedure for fixing the master's compensation under Rule 53(g).

(3) *Issuing.* The court may issue the order only after:

(A) the master files an affidavit disclosing whether there is any ground for disqualification under 28 U.S.C. § 455; and

(B) if a ground is disclosed, the parties, with the court's approval, waive the disqualification.

(4) *Amending.* The order may be amended at any time after notice to the parties and an opportunity to be heard.

(c) Master's Authority.

(1) *In General.* Unless the appointing order directs otherwise, a master may:

(A) regulate all proceedings;

(B) take all appropriate measures to perform the assigned duties fairly and efficiently; and

(C) if conducting an evidentiary hearing, exercise the appointing court's power to compel, take, and record evidence.

(2) *Sanctions.* The master may by order impose on a party any noncontempt sanction provided by Rule 37 or 45, and may recommend a contempt sanction against a party and sanctions against a nonparty.

(d) Master's Orders. A master who issues an order must file it and promptly serve a copy on each party. The clerk must enter the order on the docket.

(e) Master's Reports. A master must report to the court as required by the appointing order. The master must file the report and promptly serve a copy on each party, unless the court orders otherwise.

(f) Action on the Master's Order, Report, or Recommendations.

(1) *Opportunity for a Hearing; Action in General.* In acting on a master's order, report, or recommendations, the court must give the parties notice and an opportunity to be heard; may receive evidence; and may adopt or affirm, modify, wholly or partly reject or reverse, or resubmit to the master with instructions.

(2) *Time to Object or Move to Adopt or Modify.* A party may file objections to—or a motion to adopt or modify—the master's order, report, or recommendations no later than 21 days after a copy is served, unless the court sets a different time.

(3) *Reviewing Factual Findings.* The court must decide de novo all objections to findings of fact made or recommended by a master, unless the parties, with the court's approval, stipulate that:

(A) the findings will be reviewed for clear error; or

(B) the findings of a master appointed under Rule 53(a)(1)(A) or (C) will be final.

(4) *Reviewing Legal Conclusions.* The court must decide de novo all objections to conclusions of law made or recommended by a master.

(5) *Reviewing Procedural Matters.* Unless the appointing order establishes a different standard of review, the court may set aside a master's ruling on a procedural matter only for an abuse of discretion.

(g) Compensation.

(1) *Fixing Compensation.* Before or after judgment, the court must fix the master's compensation on the basis and terms stated in the appointing order, but the court may set a new basis and terms after giving notice and an opportunity to be heard.

(2) *Payment.* The compensation must be paid either:

(A) by a party or parties; or

(B) from a fund or subject matter of the action within the court's control.

(3) *Allocating Payment.* The court must allocate payment among the parties after considering the nature and amount of the controversy, the parties' means, and the

extent to which any party is more responsible than other parties for the reference to a master. An interim allocation may be amended to reflect a decision on the merits.

(h) Appointing a Magistrate Judge. A magistrate judge is subject to this rule only when the order referring a matter to the magistrate judge states that the reference is made under this rule.

(Amended February 28, 1966, effective July 1, 1966; April 28, 1983, effective August 1, 1983; March 2, 1987, effective August 1, 1987; April 30, 1991, effective December 1, 1991; April 22, 1993, effective December 1, 1993; March 27, 2003, effective December 1, 2003; April 30, 2007, effective December 1, 2007; March 26, 2009, effective December 1, 2009.)

TITLE VII. JUDGMENT

RULE 54. JUDGMENT; COSTS

(a) Definition; Form. "Judgment" as used in these rules includes a decree and any order from which an appeal lies. A judgment should not include recitals of pleadings, a master's report, or a record of prior proceedings.

(b) Judgment on Multiple Claims or Involving Multiple Parties. When an action presents more than one claim for relief—whether as a claim, counterclaim, crossclaim, or third-party claim—or when multiple parties are involved, the court may direct entry of a final judgment as to one or more, but fewer than all, claims or parties only if the court expressly determines that there is no just reason for delay. Otherwise, any order or other decision, however designated, that adjudicates fewer than all the claims or the rights and liabilities of fewer than all the parties does not end the action as to any of the claims or parties and may be revised at any time before the entry of a judgment adjudicating all the claims and all the parties' rights and liabilities.

(c) Demand for Judgment; Relief to Be Granted. A default judgment must not differ in kind from, or exceed in amount, what is demanded in the pleadings. Every other final judgment should grant the relief to which each party is entitled, even if the party has not demanded that relief in its pleadings.

(d) Costs; Attorney's Fees.

(1) *Costs Other Than Attorney's Fees.* Unless a federal statute, these rules, or a court order provides otherwise, costs—other than attorney's fees—should be allowed to the prevailing party. But costs against the United States, its officers, and its agencies may be imposed only to the extent allowed by law. The clerk may tax costs on 14 days' notice. On motion served within the next 7 days, the court may review the clerk's action.

(2) *Attorney's Fees.*

(A) *Claim to Be by Motion.* A claim for attorney's fees and related nontaxable expenses must be made by motion unless the substantive law requires those fees to be proved at trial as an element of damages.

(B) *Timing and Contents of the Motion.* Unless a statute or a court order provides otherwise, the motion must:

(i) be filed no later than 14 days after the entry of judgment;

(ii) specify the judgment and the statute, rule, or other grounds entitling the movant to the award;

(iii) state the amount sought or provide a fair estimate of it; and

(iv) disclose, if the court so orders, the terms of any agreement about fees for the services for which the claim is made.

(C) *Proceedings.* Subject to Rule 23(h), the court must, on a party's request, give an opportunity for adversary submissions on the motion in accordance with Rule 43(c) or 78. The court may decide issues of liability for fees before receiving submissions on the value of services. The court must find the facts and state its conclusions of law as provided in Rule 52(a).

(D) *Special Procedures by Local Rule; Reference to a Master or a Magistrate Judge.* By local rule, the court may establish special procedures to resolve fee-related issues without extensive evidentiary hearings. Also, the court may refer issues concerning the value of services to a special master under Rule 53 without regard to the limitations of Rule 53(a)(1), and may refer a motion for attorney's fees to a magistrate judge under Rule 72(b) as if it were a dispositive pretrial matter.

(E) *Exceptions.* Subparagraphs (A)-(D) do not apply to claims for fees and expenses as sanctions for violating these rules or as sanctions under 28 U.S.C. § 1927.

(Amended December 27, 1946, effective March 19, 1948; April 17, 1961, effective July 19, 1961; March 2, 1987, effective August 1, 1987; April 22, 1993, effective December 1, 1993; April 29, 2002, effective December 1, 2002; March 27, 2003, effective December 1, 2003; April 30, 2007, effective December 1, 2007; March 26, 2009, effective December 1, 2009.)

RULE 55. DEFAULT; DEFAULT JUDGMENT

(a) Entering a Default. When a party against whom a judgment for affirmative relief is sought has failed to plead or otherwise defend, and that failure is shown by affidavit or otherwise, the clerk must enter the party's default.

(b) Entering a Default Judgment.

(1) *By the Clerk.* If the plaintiff's claim is for a sum certain or a sum that can be made certain by computation, the clerk—on the plaintiff's request, with an affidavit showing the amount due—must enter judgment for that amount and costs against a defendant who has been defaulted for not appearing and who is neither a minor nor an incompetent person.

(2) *By the Court.* In all other cases, the party must apply to the court for a default judgment. A default judgment may be entered against a minor or incompetent person only if represented by a general guardian, conservator, or other like fiduciary who has appeared. If the party against whom a default judgment is sought has appeared personally or by a representative, that party or its representative must be served with written notice of the application at least 7 days before the hearing. The court may conduct hearings or make referrals—preserving any federal statutory right to a jury trial—when, to enter or effectuate judgment, it needs to:

(A) conduct an accounting;

(B) determine the amount of damages;

(C) establish the truth of any allegation by evidence; or

(D) investigate any other matter.

(c) Setting Aside a Default or a Default Judgment. The court may set aside an entry of default for good cause, and it may set aside a final default judgment under Rule 60(b).

(d) Judgment Against the United States. A default judgment may be entered against the United States, its officers, or its agencies only if the claimant establishes a claim or right to relief by evidence that satisfies the court.

(Amended March 2, 1987, effective August 1, 1987; April 30, 2007, effective December 1, 2007; March 26, 2009, effective December 1, 2009; April 29, 2015, effective December 1, 2015.)

RULE 56. SUMMARY JUDGMENT

(a) Motion for Summary Judgment or Partial Summary Judgment. A party may move for summary judgment, identifying each claim or defense—or the part of each claim or defense—on which summary judgment is sought. The court shall grant summary judgment if the movant shows that there is no genuine dispute as to any material fact and the movant is entitled to judgment as a matter of law. The court should state on the record the reasons for granting or denying the motion.

(b) Time to File a Motion. Unless a different time is set by local rule or the court orders otherwise, a party may file a motion for summary judgment at any time until 30 days after the close of all discovery.

(c) Procedures.

(1) ***Supporting Factual Positions.*** A party asserting that a fact cannot be or is genuinely disputed must support the assertion by:

(A) citing to particular parts of materials in the record, including depositions, documents, electronically stored information, affidavits or declarations, stipulations (including those made for purposes of the motion only), admissions, interrogatory answers, or other materials; or

(B) showing that the materials cited do not establish the absence or presence of a genuine dispute, or that an adverse party cannot produce admissible evidence to support the fact.

(2) ***Objection That a Fact Is Not Supported by Admissible Evidence.*** A party may object that the material cited to support or dispute a fact cannot be presented in a form that would be admissible in evidence.

(3) ***Materials Not Cited.*** The court need consider only the cited materials, but it may consider other materials in the record.

(4) ***Affidavits or Declarations.*** An affidavit or declaration used to support or oppose a motion must be made on personal knowledge, set out facts that would be admissible in evidence, and show that the affiant or declarant is competent to testify on the matters stated.

(d) When Facts Are Unavailable to the Nonmovant. If a nonmovant shows by affidavit or declaration that, for specified reasons, it cannot present facts essential to justify its opposition, the court may:

(1) defer considering the motion or deny it;

(2) allow time to obtain affidavits or declarations or to take discovery; or

(3) issue any other appropriate order.

(e) Failing to Properly Support or Address a Fact. If a party fails to properly support an assertion of fact or fails to properly address another party's assertion of fact as required by Rule 56(c), the court may:

(1) give an opportunity to properly support or address the fact;

(2) consider the fact undisputed for purposes of the motion;

(3) grant summary judgment if the motion and supporting materials—including the facts considered undisputed—show that the movant is entitled to it; or

(4) issue any other appropriate order.

(f) Judgment Independent of the Motion. After giving notice and a reasonable time to respond, the court may:

(1) grant summary judgment for a nonmovant;

(2) grant the motion on grounds not raised by a party; or

(3) consider summary judgment on its own after identifying for the parties material facts that may not be genuinely in dispute.

(g) Failing to Grant All the Requested Relief. If the court does not grant all the relief requested by the motion, it may enter an order stating any material fact—including an item of damages or other relief—that is not genuinely in dispute and treating the fact as established in the case.

(h) Affidavit or Declaration Submitted in Bad Faith. If satisfied that an affidavit or declaration under this rule is submitted in bad faith or solely for delay, the court—after notice and a reasonable time to respond—may order the submitting party to pay the other party the reasonable expenses, including attorney's fees, it incurred as a result. An offending party or attorney may also be held in contempt or subjected to other appropriate sanctions.

(Amended December 27, 1946, effective March 19, 1948; January 21, 1963, effective July 1, 1963; March 2, 1987, effective August 1, 1987; April 30, 2007, effective December 1, 2007; March 26, 2009, effective December 1, 2009; April 28, 2010, effective December 1, 2010.)

RULE 57. DECLARATORY JUDGMENT

These rules govern the procedure for obtaining a declaratory judgment under 28 U.S.C. § 2201. Rules 38 and 39 govern a demand for a jury trial. The existence of another adequate remedy does not preclude a declaratory judgment that is otherwise appropriate. The court may order a speedy hearing of a declaratory-judgment action.

(Amended December 29, 1948, effective October 20, 1949; April 30, 2007, effective December 1, 2007.)

RULE 58. ENTERING JUDGMENT

(a) Separate Document. Every judgment and amended judgment must be set out in a separate document, but a separate document is not required for an order disposing of a motion:

(1) for judgment under Rule 50(b);

(2) to amend or make additional findings under Rule 52(b);

(3) for attorney's fees under Rule 54;

(4) for a new trial, or to alter or amend the judgment, under Rule 59; or

(5) for relief under Rule 60.

(b) Entering Judgment.

(1) ***Without the Court's Direction.*** Subject to Rule 54(b) and unless the court orders otherwise, the clerk must, without awaiting the court's direction, promptly prepare, sign, and enter the judgment when:

(A) the jury returns a general verdict;

(B) the court awards only costs or a sum certain; or

(C) the court denies all relief.

(2) ***Court's Approval Required.*** Subject to Rule 54(b), the court must promptly approve the form of the judgment, which the clerk must promptly enter, when:

(A) the jury returns a special verdict or a general verdict with answers to written questions; or

(B) the court grants other relief not described in this subdivision (b).

(c) Time of Entry. For purposes of these rules, judgment is entered at the following times:

(1) if a separate document is not required, when the judgment is entered in the civil docket under Rule 79(a); or

(2) if a separate document is required, when the judgment is entered in the civil docket under Rule 79(a) and the earlier of these events occurs:

(A) it is set out in a separate document; or

(B) 150 days have run from the entry in the civil docket.

(d) Request for Entry. A party may request that judgment be set out in a separate document as required by Rule 58(a).

(e) Cost or Fee Awards. Ordinarily, the entry of judgment may not be delayed, nor the time for appeal extended, in order to tax costs or award fees. But if a timely motion for attorney's fees is made under Rule 54(d)(2), the court may act before a notice of appeal has been filed and become effective to order that the motion have the same effect under Federal Rule of Appellate Procedure 4(a)(4) as a timely motion under Rule 59.

(Amended December 27, 1946, effective March 19, 1948; January 21, 1963, effective July 1, 1963; April 22, 1993, effective December 1, 1993; April 29, 2002, effective December 1, 2002; April 30, 2007, effective December 1, 2007.)

RULE 59. NEW TRIAL; ALTERING OR AMENDING A JUDGMENT

(a) In General.

(1) ***Grounds for New Trial.*** The court may, on motion, grant a new trial on all or some of the issues—and to any party—as follows:

(A) after a jury trial, for any reason for which a new trial has heretofore been granted in an action at law in federal court; or

(B) after a nonjury trial, for any reason for which a rehearing has heretofore been granted in a suit in equity in federal court.

(2) ***Further Action After a Nonjury Trial.*** After a nonjury trial, the court may, on motion for a new trial, open the judgment if one has been entered, take additional testimony, amend findings of fact and conclusions of law or make new ones, and direct the entry of a new judgment.

(b) Time to File a Motion for a New Trial. A motion for a new trial must be filed no later than 28 days after the entry of judgment.

(c) Time to Serve Affidavits. When a motion for a new trial is based on affidavits, they must be filed with the motion. The opposing party has 14 days after being served to file opposing affidavits. The court may permit reply affidavits.

(d) New Trial on the Court's Initiative or for Reasons Not in the Motion. No later than 28 days after the entry of judgment, the court, on its own, may order a new trial for any reason that would justify granting one on a party's motion. After giving the parties notice and an opportunity to be heard, the court may grant a timely motion for a new trial for a reason not stated in the motion. In either event, the court must specify the reasons in its order.

(e) Motion to Alter or Amend a Judgment. A motion to alter or amend a judgment must be filed no later than 28 days after the entry of the judgment.

(Amended December 27, 1946, effective March 19, 1948; February 28, 1966, effective July 1, 1966; April 27, 1995, effective December 1, 1995; April 30, 2007, effective December 1, 2007; March 26, 2009, effective December 1, 2009.)

RULE 60. RELIEF FROM A JUDGMENT OR ORDER

(a) Corrections Based on Clerical Mistakes; Oversights and Omissions. The court may correct a clerical mistake or a mistake arising from oversight or omission whenever one is found in a judgment, order, or other part of the record. The court may do so on motion or on its own, with or without notice. But after an appeal has been docketed in the appellate court and while it is pending, such a mistake may be corrected only with the appellate court's leave.

(b) Grounds for Relief from a Final Judgment, Order, or Proceeding. On motion and just terms, the court may relieve a party or its legal representative from a final judgment, order, or proceeding for the following reasons:

(1) mistake, inadvertence, surprise, or excusable neglect;

(2) newly discovered evidence that, with reasonable diligence, could not have been discovered in time to move for a new trial under Rule 59(b);

(3) fraud (whether previously called intrinsic or extrinsic), misrepresentation, or misconduct by an opposing party;

(4) the judgment is void;

(5) the judgment has been satisfied, released or discharged; it is based on an earlier judgment that has been reversed or vacated; or applying it prospectively is no longer equitable; or

(6) any other reason that justifies relief.

(c) Timing and Effect of the Motion.

(1) ***Timing.*** A motion under Rule 60(b) must be made within a reasonable time—and for reasons (1), (2), and (3) no more than a year after the entry of the judgment or order or the date of the proceeding.

(2) ***Effect on Finality.*** The motion does not affect the judgment's finality or suspend its operation.

(d) Other Powers to Grant Relief. This rule does not limit a court's power to:

(1) entertain an independent action to relieve a party from a judgment, order, or proceeding;

(2) grant relief under 28 U.S.C. § 1655 to a defendant who was not personally notified of the action; or

(3) set aside a judgment for fraud on the court.

(e) Bills and Writs Abolished. The following are abolished: bills of review, bills in the nature of bills of review, and writs of coram nobis, coram vobis, and audita querela.

(Amended December 27, 1946, effective March 19, 1948; December 29, 1948, effective October 20, 1949; March 2, 1987, effective August 1, 1987; April 30, 2007, effective December 1, 2007.)

RULE 61. HARMLESS ERROR

Unless justice requires otherwise, no error in admitting or excluding evidence—or any other error by the court or a party—is ground for granting a new trial, for setting aside a verdict, or for vacating, modifying, or otherwise disturbing a judgment or order. At every stage of the proceeding, the court must disregard all errors and defects that do not affect any party's substantial rights.

(Amended April 30, 2007, effective December 1, 2007.)

RULE 62. STAY OF PROCEEDINGS TO ENFORCE A JUDGMENT

(a) Automatic Stay; Exceptions for Injunctions, Receiverships, and Patent Accountings. Except as stated in this rule, no execution may issue on a judgment, nor may proceedings be taken to enforce it, until 14 days have passed after its entry. But unless the court orders otherwise, the following are not stayed after being entered, even if an appeal is taken:

(1) an interlocutory or final judgment in an action for an injunction or a receivership; or

(2) a judgment or order that directs an accounting in an action for patent infringement.

(b) Stay Pending the Disposition of a Motion. On appropriate terms for the opposing party's security, the court may stay the execution of a judgment—or any proceedings to enforce it—pending disposition of any of the following motions:

(1) under Rule 50, for judgment as a matter of law;

(2) under Rule 52(b), to amend the findings or for additional findings;

(3) under Rule 59, for a new trial or to alter or amend a judgment; or

(4) under Rule 60, for relief from a judgment or order.

(c) Injunction Pending an Appeal. While an appeal is pending from an interlocutory order or final judgment that grants, dissolves, or denies an injunction, the court may suspend, modify, restore, or grant an injunction on terms for bond or other terms that secure the opposing party's rights. If the judgment appealed from is rendered by a statutory three-judge district court, the order must be made either:

(1) by that court sitting in open session; or

(2) by the assent of all its judges, as evidenced by their signatures.

(d) Stay with Bond on Appeal. If an appeal is taken, the appellant may obtain a stay by supersedeas bond, except in an action described in Rule 62(a)(1) or (2). The bond may be given upon or after filing the notice of appeal or after obtaining the order allowing the appeal. The stay takes effect when the court approves the bond.

(e) Stay Without Bond on an Appeal by the United States, Its Officers, or Its Agencies. The court must not require a bond, obligation, or other security from the appellant when granting a stay on an appeal by the United States, its officers, or its agencies or on an appeal directed by a department of the federal government.

(f) Stay in Favor of a Judgment Debtor Under State Law. If a judgment is a lien on the judgment debtor's property under the law of the state where the court is located, the judgment debtor is entitled to the same stay of execution the state court would give.

(g) Appellate Court's Power Not Limited. This rule does not limit the power of the appellate court or one of its judges or justices:

(1) to stay proceedings—or suspend, modify, restore, or grant an injunction—while an appeal is pending; or

(2) to issue an order to preserve the status quo or the effectiveness of the judgment to be entered.

(h) Stay with Multiple Claims or Parties. A court may stay the enforcement of a final judgment entered under Rule 54(b) until it enters a later judgment or judgments, and may prescribe terms necessary to secure the benefit of the stayed judgment for the party in whose favor it was entered.

(Amended December 27, 1946, effective March 19, 1948; December 29, 1948, effective October 20, 1949; April 17, 1961, effective July 19, 1961; March 2, 1987, effective August 1, 1987; April 30, 2007, effective December 1, 2007; March 26, 2009, effective December 1, 2009.)

RULE 62.1. INDICATIVE RULING ON A MOTION FOR RELIEF THAT IS BARRED BY A PENDING APPEAL

(a) Relief Pending Appeal. If a timely motion is made for relief that the court lacks authority to grant because of an appeal that has been docketed and is pending, the court may:

(1) defer considering the motion;

(2) deny the motion; or

(3) state either that it would grant the motion if the court of appeals remands for that purpose or that the motion raises a substantial issue.

(b) Notice to the Court of Appeals. The movant must promptly notify the circuit clerk under Federal Rule of Appellate Procedure 12.1 if the district court states that it would grant the motion or that the motion raises a substantial issue.

(c) Remand. The district court may decide the motion if the court of appeals remands for that purpose.

(Added March 26, 2009, effective December 1, 2009.)

RULE 63. JUDGE'S INABILITY TO PROCEED

If a judge conducting a hearing or trial is unable to proceed, any other judge may proceed upon certifying familiarity with the record and determining that the case may be completed without prejudice to the parties. In a hearing or a nonjury trial, the successor judge must, at a party's request, recall any witness whose testimony is material and disputed and who is available to testify again without undue burden. The successor judge may also recall any other witness.

(Amended March 2, 1987, effective August 1, 1987; April 30, 1991, effective December 1, 1991; April 30, 2007, effective December 1, 2007.)

TITLE VIII. PROVISIONAL AND FINAL REMEDIES

RULE 64. SEIZING A PERSON OR PROPERTY

(a) Remedies Under State Law—In General. At the commencement of and throughout an action, every remedy is available that, under the law of the state where the court is located, provides for seizing a person or property to secure satisfaction of the potential judgment. But a federal statute governs to the extent it applies.

(b) Specific Kinds of Remedies. The remedies available under this rule include the following—however designated and regardless of whether state procedure requires an independent action:

- arrest;
- attachment;
- garnishment;
- replevin;
- sequestration; and
- other corresponding or equivalent remedies.

(Amended April 30, 2007, effective December 1, 2007.)

RULE 65. INJUNCTIONS AND RESTRAINING ORDERS

(a) Preliminary Injunction.

(1) ***Notice.*** The court may issue a preliminary injunction only on notice to the adverse party.

(2) ***Consolidating the Hearing with the Trial on the Merits.*** Before or after beginning the hearing on a motion for a preliminary injunction, the court may advance the trial on the merits and consolidate it with the hearing. Even when consolidation is not ordered, evidence that is received on the motion and that would be admissible at trial becomes part of the trial record and need not be repeated at trial. But the court must preserve any party's right to a jury trial.

(b) Temporary Restraining Order.

(1) ***Issuing Without Notice.*** The court may issue a temporary restraining order without written or oral notice to the adverse party or its attorney only if:

(A) specific facts in an affidavit or a verified complaint clearly show that immediate and irreparable injury, loss, or damage will result to the movant before the adverse party can be heard in opposition; and

(B) the movant's attorney certifies in writing any efforts made to give notice and the reasons why it should not be required.

(2) ***Contents; Expiration.*** Every temporary restraining order issued without notice must state the date and hour it was issued; describe the injury and state why it is irreparable; state why the order was issued without notice; and be promptly filed in the clerk's office and entered in the record. The order expires at the time after entry—not to exceed 14 days—that the court sets, unless before that time the court, for good cause, extends it for a like period or the adverse party consents to a longer extension. The reasons for an extension must be entered in the record.

(3) ***Expediting the Preliminary-Injunction Hearing.*** If the order is issued without notice, the motion for a preliminary injunction must be set for hearing at the earliest possible time, taking precedence over all other matters except hearings on older matters of the same character. At the hearing, the party who obtained the order must proceed with the motion; if the party does not, the court must dissolve the order.

(4) ***Motion to Dissolve.*** On 2 days' notice to the party who obtained the order without notice—or on shorter notice set by the court—the adverse party may appear and move to dissolve or modify the order. The court must then hear and decide the motion as promptly as justice requires.

(c) Security. The court may issue a preliminary injunction or a temporary restraining order only if the movant gives security in an amount that the court considers proper to pay the costs and damages sustained by any party found to have been wrongfully enjoined or restrained. The United States, its officers, and its agencies are not required to give security.

(d) Contents and Scope of Every Injunction and Restraining Order.

(1) ***Contents.*** Every order granting an injunction and every restraining order must:

(A) state the reasons why it issued;

(B) state its terms specifically; and

(C) describe in reasonable detail—and not by referring to the complaint or other document—the act or acts restrained or required.

(2) ***Persons Bound.*** The order binds only the following who receive actual notice of it by personal service or otherwise:

(A) the parties;

(B) the parties' officers, agents, servants, employees, and attorneys; and

(C) other persons who are in active concert or participation with anyone described in Rule 65(d)(2)(A) or (B).

(e) Other Laws Not Modified. These rules do not modify the following:

(1) any federal statute relating to temporary restraining orders or preliminary injunctions in actions affecting employer and employee;

(2) 28 U.S.C. § 2361, which relates to preliminary injunctions in actions of interpleader or in the nature of interpleader; or

(3) 28 U.S.C. § 2284, which relates to actions that must be heard and decided by a three-judge district court.

(f) Copyright Impoundment. This rule applies to copyright-impoundment proceedings.

(Amended December 27, 1946, effective March 19, 1948; December 29, 1948, effective October 20, 1949; February 28, 1966, effective July 1, 1966; March 2, 1987, effective August 1, 1987; April 23, 2001, effective December 1, 2001; April 30, 2007, effective December 1, 2007; March 26, 2009, effective December 1, 2009.)

RULE 65.1. PROCEEDINGS AGAINST A SURETY

Whenever these rules (including the Supplemental Rules for Admiralty or Maritime Claims and Asset Forfeiture Actions) require or allow a party to give security, and security is given through a bond or other undertaking with one or more sureties, each surety submits to the court's jurisdiction and irrevocably appoints the court clerk as its agent for receiving service of any papers that affect its liability on the bond or undertaking. The surety's liability may be enforced on motion without an independent action. The motion and any notice that the court orders may be served on the court clerk, who must promptly mail a copy of each to every surety whose address is known.

(Adopted February 28, 1966, effective July 1, 1966; amended March 2, 1987, effective August 1, 1987; April 12, 2006, effective December 1, 2006; April 30, 2007, effective December 1, 2007.)

RULE 66. RECEIVERS

These rules govern an action in which the appointment of a receiver is sought or a receiver sues or is sued. But the practice in administering an estate by a receiver or a similar court-appointed officer must accord with the historical practice in federal courts or with a local rule. An action in which a receiver has been appointed may be dismissed only by court order.

(Amended December 27, 1946, effective March 19, 1948; December 29, 1948, effective October 20, 1949; April 30, 2007, effective December 1, 2007.)

RULE 67. DEPOSIT INTO COURT

(a) Depositing Property. If any part of the relief sought is a money judgment or the disposition of a sum of money or some other deliverable thing, a party—on notice to every other party and by leave of court—may deposit with the court all or part of the money or thing, whether or not that party claims any of it. The depositing party must deliver to the clerk a copy of the order permitting deposit.

(b) Investing and Withdrawing Funds. Money paid into court under this rule must be deposited and withdrawn in accordance with 28 U.S.C. §§ 2041 and 2042 and any like statute. The money must be deposited in an interest-bearing account or invested in a court-approved, interest-bearing instrument.

(Amended December 29, 1948, effective October 20, 1949; April 28, 1983, effective August 1, 1983; April 30, 2007, effective December 1, 2007.)

RULE 68. OFFER OF JUDGMENT

(a) Making an Offer; Judgment on an Accepted Offer. At least 14 days before the date set for trial, a party defending against a claim may serve on an opposing party an offer to allow judgment on specified terms, with the costs then accrued. If, within 14 days after being served, the opposing party serves written notice accepting the offer, either party may then file the offer and notice of acceptance, plus proof of service. The clerk must then enter judgment.

(b) Unaccepted Offer. An unaccepted offer is considered withdrawn, but it does not preclude a later offer. Evidence of an unaccepted offer is not admissible except in a proceeding to determine costs.

(c) Offer After Liability is Determined. When one party's liability to another has been determined but the extent of liability remains to be determined by further proceedings, the party held liable may make an offer of judgment. It must be served within a reasonable time—but at least 14 days—before the date set for a hearing to determine the extent of liability.

(d) Paying Costs After an Unaccepted Offer. If the judgment that the offeree finally obtains is not more favorable than the unaccepted offer, the offeree must pay the costs incurred after the offer was made.

(Amended December 27, 1946, effective March 19, 1948; February 28, 1966, effective July 1, 1966; March 2, 1987, effective August 1, 1987; April 30, 2007, effective December 1, 2007; March 26, 2009, effective December 1, 2009.)

RULE 69. EXECUTION

(a) In General.

(1) ***Money Judgment; Applicable Procedure.*** A money judgment is enforced by a writ of execution, unless the court directs otherwise. The procedure on execution—and in proceedings supplementary to and in aid of judgment or execution—must accord with the procedure of the state where the court is located, but a federal statute governs to the extent it applies.

(2) ***Obtaining Discovery.*** In aid of the judgment or execution, the judgment creditor or a successor in interest whose interest appears of record may obtain discovery from any person—including the judgment debtor—as provided in these rules or by the procedure of the state where the court is located.

(b) Against Certain Public Officers. When a judgment has been entered against a revenue officer in the circumstances stated in 28 U.S.C. § 2006, or against an officer of Congress in the circumstances stated in 2 U.S.C. § 118, the judgment must be satisfied as those statutes provide.

(Amended December 29, 1948, effective October 20, 1949; March 30, 1970, effective July 1, 1970; March 2, 1987 effective August 1, 1987; April 30, 2007, effective December 1, 2007.)

RULE 70. ENFORCING A JUDGMENT FOR A SPECIFIC ACT

(a) Party's Failure to Act; Ordering Another to Act. If a judgment requires a party to convey land, to deliver a deed or other document, or to perform any other specific act and the party fails to comply within the time specified, the court may order the act to be done—at the disobedient party's expense—by another person appointed by the court. When done, the act has the same effect as if done by the party.

(b) Vesting Title. If the real or personal property is within the district, the court—instead of ordering a conveyance—may enter a judgment divesting any party's title and vesting it in others. That judgment has the effect of a legally executed conveyance.

(c) Obtaining a Writ of Attachment or Sequestration. On application by a party entitled to performance of an act, the clerk must issue a writ of attachment or sequestration against the disobedient party's property to compel obedience.

(d) Obtaining a Writ of Execution or Assistance. On application by a party who obtains a judgment or order for possession, the clerk must issue a writ of execution or assistance.

(e) Holding in Contempt. The court may also hold the disobedient party in contempt.

(Amended April 30, 2007, effective December 1, 2007.)

RULE 71. ENFORCING RELIEF FOR OR AGAINST A NONPARTY

When an order grants relief for a nonparty or may be enforced against a nonparty, the procedure for enforcing the order is the same as for a party.

(Amended March 2, 1987, effective August 1, 1987; April 30, 2007, effective December 1, 2007.)

TITLE IX. SPECIAL PROCEEDINGS

RULE 71.1. CONDEMNING REAL OR PERSONAL PROPERTY

(a) Applicability of Other Rules. These rules govern proceedings to condemn real and personal property by eminent domain, except as this rule provides otherwise.

(b) Joinder of Properties. The plaintiff may join separate pieces of property in a single action, no matter whether they are owned by the same persons or sought for the same use.

(c) Complaint.

(1) ***Caption.*** The complaint must contain a caption as provided in Rule 10(a). The plaintiff must, however, name as defendants both the property—designated generally by kind, quantity, and location—and at least one owner of some part of or interest in the property.

(2) ***Contents.*** The complaint must contain a short and plain statement of the following:

(A) the authority for the taking;

(B) the uses for which the property is to be taken;

(C) a description sufficient to identify the property;

(D) the interests to be acquired; and

(E) for each piece of property, a designation of each defendant who has been joined as an owner or owner of an interest in it.

(3) ***Parties.*** When the action commences, the plaintiff need join as defendants only those persons who have or claim an interest in the property and whose names are then known. But before any hearing on compensation, the plaintiff must add as defendants all those persons who have or claim an interest and whose names have become known or can be found by a reasonably diligent search of the records, considering both the property's character and value and the interests to be acquired. All others may be made defendants under the designation "Unknown Owners."

(4) ***Procedure.*** Notice must be served on all defendants as provided in Rule 71.1(d), whether they were named as defendants when the action commenced or were added later. A defendant may answer as provided in Rule 71.1(e). The court, meanwhile, may order any distribution of a deposit that the facts warrant.

(5) *Filing; Additional Copies.* In addition to filing the complaint, the plaintiff must give the clerk at least one copy for the defendants' use and additional copies at the request of the clerk or a defendant.

(d) Process.

(1) *Delivering Notice to the Clerk.* On filing a complaint, the plaintiff must promptly deliver to the clerk joint or several notices directed to the named defendants. When adding defendants, the plaintiff must deliver to the clerk additional notices directed to the new defendants.

(2) *Contents of the Notice.*

(A) *Main Contents.* Each notice must name the court, the title of the action, and the defendant to whom it is directed. It must describe the property sufficiently to identify it, but need not describe any property other than that to be taken from the named defendant. The notice must also state:

(i) that the action is to condemn property;

(ii) the interest to be taken;

(iii) the authority for the taking;

(iv) the uses for which the property is to be taken;

(v) that the defendant may serve an answer on the plaintiff's attorney within 21 days after being served with the notice;

(vi) that the failure to so serve an answer constitutes consent to the taking and to the court's authority to proceed with the action and fix the compensation; and

(vii) that a defendant who does not serve an answer may file a notice of appearance.

(B) *Conclusion.* The notice must conclude with the name, telephone number, and e-mail address of the plaintiff's attorney and an address within the district in which the action is brought where the attorney may be served.

(3) *Serving the Notice.*

(A) *Personal Service.* When a defendant whose address is known resides within the United States or a territory subject to the administrative or judicial jurisdiction of the United States, personal service of the notice (without a copy of the complaint) must be made in accordance with Rule 4.

(B) *Service by Publication.*

(i) A defendant may be served by publication only when the plaintiff's attorney files a certificate stating that the attorney believes the defendant cannot be personally served, because after diligent inquiry within the state where the complaint is filed, the defendant's place of residence is still unknown or, if known, that it is beyond the territorial limits of personal service. Service is then made by publishing the notice—once a week for at least 3 successive weeks—in a newspaper published in the county where the property is located or, if there is no such newspaper, in a newspaper with general circulation where the property is located. Before the last publication, a copy of the notice must also be mailed to every defendant who cannot be personally served but whose place of residence is then known. Unknown owners may be served by publication in the same manner by a notice addressed to "Unknown Owners."

(ii) Service by publication is complete on the date of the last publication. The plaintiff's attorney must prove publication and mailing by a certificate, attach a printed copy of the published notice, and mark on the copy the newspaper's name and the dates of publication.

(4) *Effect of Delivery and Service.* Delivering the notice to the clerk and serving it have the same effect as serving a summons under Rule 4.

(5) *Amending the Notice; Proof of Service and Amending the Proof.* Rule 4(a)(2) governs amending the notice. Rule 4(*l*) governs proof of service and amending it.

(e) Appearance or Answer.

(1) *Notice of Appearance.* A defendant that has no objection or defense to the taking of its property may serve a notice of appearance designating the property in which it claims an interest. The defendant must then be given notice of all later proceedings affecting the defendant.

(2) *Answer.* A defendant that has an objection or defense to the taking must serve an answer within 21 days after being served with the notice. The answer must:

(A) identify the property in which the defendant claims an interest;

(B) state the nature and extent of the interest; and

(C) state all the defendant's objections and defenses to the taking.

(3) *Waiver of Other Objections and Defenses; Evidence on Compensation.* A defendant waives all objections and defenses not stated in its answer. No other pleading or motion asserting an additional objection or defense is allowed. But at the trial on compensation, a defendant—whether or not it has previously appeared or answered—may present evidence on the amount of compensation to be paid and may share in the award.

(f) Amending Pleadings. Without leave of court, the plaintiff may—as often as it wants—amend the complaint at any time before the trial on compensation. But no amendment may be made if it would result in a dismissal inconsistent with Rule 71.1(i)(1) or (2). The plaintiff need not serve a copy of an amendment, but must serve notice of the filing, as provided in Rule 5(b), on every affected party who has appeared and, as provided in Rule 71.1(d), on every affected party who has not appeared. In addition, the plaintiff must give the clerk at least one copy of each amendment for the defendants' use, and additional copies at the request of the clerk or a defendant. A defendant may appear or answer in the time and manner and with the same effect as provided in Rule 71.1(e).

(g) Substituting Parties. If a defendant dies, becomes incompetent, or transfers an interest after being joined, the court may, on motion and notice of hearing, order that the proper party be substituted. Service of the motion and notice on a nonparty must be made as provided in Rule 71.1(d)(3).

(h) Trial of the Issues.

(1) ***Issues Other Than Compensation; Compensation.*** In an action involving eminent domain under federal law, the court tries all issues, including compensation, except when compensation must be determined:

(A) by any tribunal specially constituted by a federal statute to determine compensation; or

(B) if there is no such tribunal, by a jury when a party demands one within the time to answer or within any additional time the court sets, unless the court appoints a commission.

(2) ***Appointing a Commission; Commission's Powers and Report.***

(A) *Reasons for Appointing.* If a party has demanded a jury, the court may instead appoint a three-person commission to determine compensation because of the character, location, or quantity of the property to be condemned or for other just reasons.

(B) *Alternate Commissioners.* The court may appoint up to two additional persons to serve as alternate commissioners to hear the case and replace commissioners who, before a decision is filed, the court finds unable or disqualified to perform their duties. Once the commission renders its final decision, the court must discharge any alternate who has not replaced a commissioner.

(C) *Examining the Prospective Commissioners.* Before making its appointments, the court must advise the parties of the identity and qualifications of each prospective commissioner and alternate, and may permit the parties to examine them. The parties may not suggest appointees, but for good cause may object to a prospective commissioner or alternate.

(D) *Commission's Powers and Report.* A commission has the powers of a master under Rule 53(c). Its action and report are determined by a majority. Rule 53(d), (e), and (f) apply to its action and report.

(i) Dismissal of the Action or a Defendant.

(1) ***Dismissing the Action.***

(A) *By the Plaintiff.* If no compensation hearing on a piece of property has begun, and if the plaintiff has not acquired title or a lesser interest or taken possession, the plaintiff may, without a court order, dismiss the action as to that property by filing a notice of dismissal briefly describing the property.

(B) *By Stipulation.* Before a judgment is entered vesting the plaintiff with title or a lesser interest in or possession of property, the plaintiff and affected defendants may, without a court order, dismiss the action in whole or in part by filing a stipulation of dismissal. And if the parties so stipulate, the court may vacate a judgment already entered.

(C) *By Court Order.* At any time before compensation has been determined and paid, the court may, after a motion and hearing, dismiss the action as to a piece of property. But if the plaintiff has already taken title, a lesser interest, or possession as to any part of it, the court must award compensation for the title, lesser interest, or possession taken.

(2) ***Dismissing a Defendant.*** The court may at any time dismiss a defendant who was unnecessarily or improperly joined.

(3) ***Effect.*** A dismissal is without prejudice unless otherwise stated in the notice, stipulation, or court order.

(j) Deposit and Its Distribution.

(1) ***Deposit.*** The plaintiff must deposit with the court any money required by law as a condition to the exercise of eminent domain and may make a deposit when allowed by statute.

(2) ***Distribution; Adjusting Distribution.*** After a deposit, the court and attorneys must expedite the proceedings so as to distribute the deposit and to determine and pay compensation. If the compensation finally awarded to a defendant exceeds the amount distributed to that defendant, the court must enter judgment against the plaintiff for the deficiency. If the compensation awarded to a defendant is less than the amount distributed to that defendant, the court must enter judgment against that defendant for the overpayment.

(k) Condemnation Under a State's Power of Eminent Domain. This rule governs an action involving eminent domain under state law. But if state law provides for trying an issue by jury—or for trying the issue of compensation by jury or commission or both—that law governs.

(*l*) Costs. Costs are not subject to Rule 54(d).

(Adopted April 30, 1951, effective August 1, 1951; amended January 21, 1963, effective July 1, 1963; April 29, 1985, effective August 1, 1985; March 2, 1987, effective August 1, 1987; April 25, 1988, effective August 1, 1988; amended by Pub.L. 100–690, Title VII, § 7050, November 18, 1988, 102 Stat. 4401 (although amendment by Pub.L. 100–690 could not be executed due to prior amendment by Court order which made the same change effective August 1, 1988); amended April 22, 1993, effective December 1, 1993; March 27, 2003, effective December 1, 2003; April 30, 2007, effective December 1, 2007; March 26, 2009, effective December 1, 2009.)

RULE 72. MAGISTRATE JUDGES: PRETRIAL ORDER

(a) Nondispositive Matters. When a pretrial matter not dispositive of a party's claim or defense is referred to a magistrate judge to hear and decide, the magistrate judge must promptly conduct the required proceedings and, when appropriate, issue a written order stating the decision. A party may serve and file objections to the order within 14 days after being served with a copy. A party may not assign as error a defect in the order not timely objected to. The district judge in the case must consider timely objections and modify or set aside any part of the order that is clearly erroneous or is contrary to law.

(b) Dispositive Motions and Prisoner Petitions.

(1) ***Findings and Recommendations.*** A magistrate judge must promptly conduct the required proceedings when assigned, without the parties' consent, to hear a pretrial matter dispositive of a claim or defense or a prisoner petition challenging the conditions of confinement. A record must be made of all evidentiary proceedings and may, at the magistrate judge's discretion, be made of any other proceedings. The magistrate judge must enter a recommended disposition, including, if appropriate, proposed findings of fact. The clerk must promptly mail a copy to each party.

(2) ***Objections.*** Within 14 days after being served with a copy of the recommended disposition, a party may serve and file specific written objections to the proposed findings and recommendations. A party may respond to another party's objections within 14 days after being served with a copy. Unless the district judge orders otherwise, the objecting party must promptly arrange for transcribing the record, or whatever portions of it the parties agree to or the magistrate judge considers sufficient.

(3) ***Resolving Objections.*** The district judge must determine de novo any part of the magistrate judge's disposition that has been properly objected to. The district judge may accept, reject, or modify the recommended disposition; receive further evidence; or return the matter to the magistrate judge with instructions.

(Former Rule 72 abrogated December 4, 1967, effective July 1, 1968; new Rule 72 adopted April 28, 1983, effective August 1, 1983; amended April 30, 1991, effective December 1, 1991; April 22, 1993, effective December 1, 1993; April 30, 2007, effective December 1, 2007; March 26, 2009, effective December 1, 2009.)

RULE 73. MAGISTRATE JUDGES: TRIAL BY CONSENT; APPEAL

(a) Trial by Consent. When authorized under 28 U.S.C. § 636(c), a magistrate judge may, if all parties consent, conduct a civil action or proceeding, including a jury or nonjury trial. A record must be made in accordance with 28 U.S.C. § 636(c)(5).

(b) Consent Procedure.

(1) ***In General.*** When a magistrate judge has been designated to conduct civil actions or proceedings, the clerk must give the parties written notice of their opportunity to consent under 28 U.S.C. § 636(c). To signify their consent, the parties must jointly or separately file a statement consenting to the referral. A district judge or magistrate judge may be informed of a party's response to the clerk's notice only if all parties have consented to the referral.

(2) ***Reminding the Parties About Consenting.*** A district judge, magistrate judge, or other court official may remind the parties of the magistrate judge's availability, but must also advise them that they are free to withhold consent without adverse substantive consequences.

(3) ***Vacating a Referral.*** On its own for good cause—or when a party shows extraordinary circumstances—the district judge may vacate a referral to a magistrate judge under this rule.

(c) Appealing a Judgment. In accordance with 28 U.S.C. § 636(c)(3), an appeal from a judgment entered at a magistrate judge's direction may be taken to the court of appeals as would any other appeal from a district-court judgment.

(Former Rule 73 abrogated December 4, 1967, effective July 1, 1968; new Rule 73 adopted April 28, 1983, effective August 1, 1983; amended March 2, 1987, effective August 1, 1987; April 22, 1993, effective December 1, 1993; April 11, 1997, effective December 1, 1997; April 30, 2007, effective December 1, 2007.)

RULE 74. METHOD OF APPEAL FROM MAGISTRATE JUDGE TO DISTRICT JUDGE UNDER TITLE 28, U.S.C. § 636(c)(4) AND RULE 73(d) [ABROGATED]

(Former Rule 74 abrogated December 4, 1967, effective July 1, 1968; new Rule 74 adopted April 28, 1983, effective August 1, 1983; amended April 22, 1993, effective December 1, 1993; abrogated April 11, 1997, effective December 1, 1997; April 30, 2007, effective December 1, 2007.)

RULE 75. PROCEEDINGS ON APPEAL FROM MAGISTRATE JUDGE TO DISTRICT JUDGE UNDER RULE 73(d) [ABROGATED]

(Former Rule 75 abrogated December 4, 1967, effective July 1, 1968; new Rule 75 adopted April 28, 1983, effective August 1, 1983; amended March 2, 1987, effective August 1, 1987; April 22, 1993, effective December 1, 1993; abrogated April 11, 1997, effective December 1, 1997; April 30, 2007, effective December 1, 2007.)

RULE 76. JUDGMENT OF THE DISTRICT JUDGE ON THE APPEAL UNDER RULE 73(d) AND COSTS [ABROGATED]

(Former Rule 76 abrogated December 4, 1967, effective July 1, 1968; new Rule 76 adopted April 28, 1983, effective August 1, 1983; amended April 22, 1993, effective December 1, 1993; abrogated April 11, 1997, effective December 1, 1997; April 30, 2007, effective December 1, 2007.)

TITLE X. DISTRICT COURTS AND CLERKS: CONDUCTING BUSINESS; ISSUING ORDERS

RULE 77. CONDUCTING BUSINESS; CLERK'S AUTHORITY; NOTICE OF AN ORDER OR JUDGMENT

(a) When Court Is Open. Every district court is considered always open for filing any paper, issuing and returning process, making a motion, or entering an order.

(b) Place for Trial and Other Proceedings. Every trial on the merits must be conducted in open court and, so far as convenient, in a regular courtroom. Any other act or proceeding may be done or conducted by a judge in chambers, without the attendance of the clerk or other court official, and anywhere inside or outside the district. But no hearing—other than one ex parte—may be conducted outside the district unless all the affected parties consent.

(c) Clerk's Office Hours; Clerk's Orders.

(1) ***Hours.*** The clerk's office—with a clerk or deputy on duty—must be open during business hours every day except Saturdays, Sundays, and legal holidays. But a court may, by local rule or order, require that the office be open for specified hours on Saturday or a particular legal holiday other than one listed in Rule 6(a)(6)(A).

(2) ***Orders.*** Subject to the court's power to suspend, alter, or rescind the clerk's action for good cause, the clerk may:

(A) issue process;

(B) enter a default;

(C) enter a default judgment under Rule 55(b)(1); and

(D) act on any other matter that does not require the court's action.

(d) Serving Notice of an Order or Judgment.

(1) ***Service.*** Immediately after entering an order or judgment, the clerk must serve notice of the entry, as provided in Rule 5(b), on each party who is not in default for failing to appear. The clerk must record the service on the docket. A party also may serve notice of the entry as provided in Rule 5(b).

(2) ***Time to Appeal Not Affected by Lack of Notice.*** Lack of notice of the entry does not affect the time for appeal or relieve—or authorize the court to relieve—a party for failing to appeal within the time allowed, except as allowed by Federal Rule of Appellate Procedure (4)(a).

(Amended December 27, 1946, effective March 19, 1948; January 21, 1963, effective July 1, 1963; December 4, 1967, effective July 1, 1968; March 1, 1971, effective July 1, 1971; March 2, 1987, effective August 1, 1987; April 30, 1991, effective December 1, 1991; April 23, 2001, effective December 1, 2001; April 30, 2007, effective December 1, 2007; April 25, 2014, effective December 1, 2014.)

RULE 78. HEARING MOTIONS; SUBMISSION ON BRIEFS

(a) Providing a Regular Schedule for Oral Hearings. A court may establish regular times and places for oral hearings on motions.

(b) Providing for Submission on Briefs. By rule or order, the court may provide for submitting and determining motions on briefs, without oral hearings.

(Amended March 2, 1987, effective August 1, 1987; April 30, 2007, effective December 1, 2007.)

RULE 79. RECORDS KEPT BY THE CLERK

(a) Civil Docket.

(1) ***In General.*** The clerk must keep a record known as the "civil docket" in the form and manner prescribed by the Director of the Administrative Office of the United States Courts with the approval of the Judicial Conference of the United States. The clerk must enter each civil action in the docket. Actions must be assigned consecutive file numbers, which must be noted in the docket where the first entry of the action is made.

(2) ***Items to be Entered.*** The following items must be marked with the file number and entered chronologically in the docket:

(A) papers filed with the clerk;

(B) process issued, and proofs of service or other returns showing execution; and

(C) appearances, orders, verdicts, and judgments.

(3) ***Contents of Entries; Jury Trial Demanded.*** Each entry must briefly show the nature of the paper filed or writ issued, the substance of each proof of service or other return, and the substance and date of entry of each order and judgment. When a jury trial has been properly demanded or ordered, the clerk must enter the word "jury" in the docket.

(b) Civil Judgments and Orders. The clerk must keep a copy of every final judgment and appealable order; of every order affecting title to or a lien on real or personal property; and of any other order that the court directs to be kept. The clerk must keep these in the form and manner prescribed by the Director of the Administrative Office of the United States Courts with the approval of the Judicial Conference of the United States.

(c) Indexes; Calendars. Under the court's direction, the clerk must:

(1) keep indexes of the docket and of the judgments and orders described in Rule 79(b); and

(2) prepare calendars of all actions ready for trial, distinguishing jury trials from nonjury trials.

(d) Other Records. The clerk must keep any other records required by the Director of the Administrative Office of the United States Courts with the approval of the Judicial Conference of the United States.

(Amended December 27, 1946, effective March 19, 1948; December 29, 1948, effective October 20, 1949; January 21, 1963, effective July 1, 1963; April 30, 2007, effective December 1, 2007.)

RULE 80. STENOGRAPHIC TRANSCRIPT AS EVIDENCE

If stenographically reported testimony at a hearing or trial is admissible in evidence at a later trial, the testimony may be proved by a transcript certified by the person who reported it.

(Amended December 27, 1946, effective March 19, 1948; April 30, 2007, effective December 1, 2007.)

TITLE XI. GENERAL PROVISIONS

RULE 81. APPLICABILITY OF THE RULES IN GENERAL; REMOVED ACTIONS

(a) Applicability to Particular Proceedings.

(1) ***Prize Proceedings.*** These rules do not apply to prize proceedings in admiralty governed by 10 U.S.C. §§ 7651–7681.

(2) ***Bankruptcy.*** These rules apply to bankruptcy proceedings to the extent provided by the Federal Rules of Bankruptcy Procedure.

(3) ***Citizenship.*** These rules apply to proceedings for admission to citizenship to the extent that the practice in those proceedings is not specified in federal statutes and has previously conformed to the practice in civil actions. The provisions of 8 U.S.C. § 1451 for service by publication and for answer apply in proceedings to cancel citizenship certificates.

(4) ***Special Writs.*** These rules apply to proceedings for habeas corpus and for quo warranto to the extent that the practice in those proceedings:

(A) is not specified in a federal statute, the Rules Governing Section 2254 Cases, or the Rules Governing Section 2255 Cases; and

(B) has previously conformed to the practice in civil actions.

(5) ***Proceedings Involving a Subpoena.*** These rules apply to proceedings to compel testimony or the production of documents through a subpoena issued by a United States officer or agency under a federal statute, except as otherwise provided by statute, by local rule, or by court order in the proceedings.

(6) ***Other Proceedings.*** These rules, to the extent applicable, govern proceedings under the following laws, except as these laws provide other procedures:

(A) 7 U.S.C. §§ 292, 499g(c), for reviewing an order of the Secretary of Agriculture;

(B) 9 U.S.C., relating to arbitration;

(C) 15 U.S.C. § 522, for reviewing an order of the Secretary of the Interior;

(D) 15 U.S.C. § 715d(c), for reviewing an order denying a certificate of clearance;

(E) 29 U.S.C. §§ 159, 160, for enforcing an order of the National Labor Relations Board;

(F) 33 U.S.C. §§ 918, 921, for enforcing or reviewing a compensation order under the Longshore and Harbor Workers' Compensation Act; and

(G) 45 U.S.C. § 159, for reviewing an arbitration award in a railway-labor dispute.

(b) Scire Facias and Mandamus. The writs of scire facias and mandamus are abolished. Relief previously available through them may be obtained by appropriate action or motion under these rules.

(c) Removed Actions.

(1) ***Applicability.*** These rules apply to a civil action after it is removed from a state court.

(2) ***Further Pleading.*** After removal, repleading is unnecessary unless the court orders it. A defendant who did not answer before removal must answer or present other defenses or objections under these rules within the longest of these periods:

(A) 21 days after receiving—through service or otherwise—a copy of the initial pleading stating the claim for relief;

(B) 21 days after being served with the summons for an initial pleading on file at the time of service; or

(C) 7 days after the notice of removal is filed.

(3) ***Demand for a Jury Trial.***

(A) *As Affected by State Law.* A party who, before removal, expressly demanded a jury trial in accordance with state law need not renew the demand after removal. If the state law did not require an express demand for a jury trial, a party need not make one after removal unless the court orders the parties to do so within a specified time. The court must so order at a party's request and may so order on its own. A party who fails to make a demand when so ordered waives a jury trial.

(B) *Under Rule 38.* If all necessary pleadings have been served at the time of removal, a party entitled to a jury trial under Rule 38 must be given one if the party serves a demand within 14 days after:

(i) it files a notice of removal; or

(ii) it is served with a notice of removal filed by another party.

(d) Law Applicable.

(1) ***"State Law" Defined.*** When these rules refer to state law, the term "law" includes the state's statutes and the state's judicial decisions.

(2) ***"State" Defined.*** The term "state" includes, where appropriate, the District of Columbia and any United States commonwealth or territory.

(3) ***"Federal Statute" Defined in the District of Columbia.*** In the United States District Court for the District of Columbia, the term "federal statute" includes any Act of Congress that applies locally to the District.

(Amended December 28, 1939, effective April 3, 1941; December 27, 1946, effective March 19, 1948; December 29, 1948, effective October 20, 1949; April 30, 1951, effective August 1, 1951; January 21, 1963, effective July 1, 1963; February 28, 1966, effective July 1, 1966; December 4, 1967, effective July 1, 1968; March 1, 1971, effective July 1, 1971; March 2, 1987, effective August 1, 1987; April 23, 2001, effective December 1, 2001; April 29, 2002, effective December 1, 2002; April 30, 2007, effective December 1, 2007; March 26, 2009, effective December 1, 2009.)

RULE 82. JURISDICTION AND VENUE UNAFFECTED

These rules do not extend or limit the jurisdiction of the district courts or the venue of actions in those courts. An admiralty or maritime claim under Rule 9(h) is governed by 28 U.S.C. § 1390.

(Amended December 29, 1948, effective October 20, 1949; February 28, 1966, effective July 1, 1966; April 23, 2001, effective December 1, 2001; April 30, 2007, effective December 1, 2007; April 28, 2016, effective December 1, 2016.)

RULE 83. RULES BY DISTRICT COURTS; JUDGE'S DIRECTIVES

(a) Local Rules.

(1) ***In General.*** After giving public notice and an opportunity for comment, a district court, acting by a majority of its district judges, may adopt and amend rules governing its practice. A local rule must be consistent with—but not duplicate—federal statutes and rules adopted under 28 U.S.C. §§ 2072 and 2075, and must conform to any uniform numbering system prescribed by the Judicial Conference of the United States. A local rule takes effect on the date specified by the district court and remains in effect unless amended by the court or abrogated by the judicial council of the circuit. Copies of rules and amendments must, on their adoption, be furnished to the judicial council and the Administrative Office of the United States Courts and be made available to the public.

(2) ***Requirement of Form.*** A local rule imposing a requirement of form must not be enforced in a way that causes a party to lose any right because of a nonwillful failure to comply.

(b) Procedure When There Is No Controlling Law. A judge may regulate practice in any manner consistent with federal law, rules adopted under 28 U.S.C. §§ 2072 and 2075, and the district's local rules. No sanction or other disadvantage may be imposed for noncompliance with any requirement not in federal law, federal rules, or the local rules unless the alleged violator has been furnished in the particular case with actual notice of the requirement.

(Amended April 29, 1985, effective August 1, 1985; April 27, 1995, effective December 1, 1995; April 30, 2007, effective December 1, 2007.)

RULE 84. FORMS [ABROGATED]

(Amended December 27, 1946, effective March 19, 1948; April 30, 2007, effective December 1, 2007; abrogated April 29, 2015, effective December 1, 2015.)

RULE 85. TITLE

These rules may be cited as the Federal Rules of Civil Procedure.

(Amended April 30, 2007, effective December 1, 2007.)

RULE 86. EFFECTIVE DATES

(a) In General. These rules and any amendments take effect at the time specified by the Supreme Court, subject to 28 U.S.C. § 2074. They govern:

(1) proceedings in an action commenced after their effective date; and

(2) proceedings after that date in an action then pending unless:

(A) the Supreme Court specifies otherwise; or

(B) the court determines that applying them in a particular action would be infeasible or work an injustice.

(b) December 1, 2007 Amendments. If any provision in Rules 1–5.1, 6–73, or 77–86 conflicts with another law, priority in time for the purpose of 28 U.S.C. § 2072(b) is not affected by the amendments taking effect on December 1, 2007.

(Amended December 27, 1946, effective March 19, 1948; December 29, 1948, effective October 20, 1949; April 17, 1961, effective July 19, 1961; January 21, 1963, and March 18, 1963, effective July 1, 1963; April 30, 2007, effective December 1, 2007.)

APPENDIX OF FORMS [ABROGATED]

SUPPLEMENTAL RULES FOR ADMIRALTY OR MARITIME CLAIMS AND ASSET FORFEITURE ACTIONS

RULE A. SCOPE OF RULES

(1) These Supplemental Rules apply to:

(A) the procedure in admiralty and maritime claims within the meaning of Rule 9(h) with respect to the following remedies:

(i) maritime attachment and garnishment,

(ii) actions in rem,

(iii) possessory, petitory, and partition actions, and

(iv) actions for exoneration from or limitation of liability;

(B) forfeiture actions in rem arising from a federal statute; and

(C) the procedure in statutory condemnation proceedings analogous to maritime actions in rem, whether within the admiralty and maritime jurisdiction or not. Except as otherwise provided, references in these Supplemental Rules to actions in rem include such analogous statutory condemnation proceedings.

(2) The Federal Rules of Civil Procedure also apply to the foregoing proceedings except to the extent that they are inconsistent with these Supplemental Rules.

(Added Feb. 28, 1966, eff. July 1, 1966; amended Apr. 12, 2006, eff. Dec. 1, 2006.)

RULE B. IN PERSONAM ACTIONS: ATTACHMENT AND GARNISHMENT

(1) When Available; Complaint, Affidavit, Judicial Authorization, and Process. In an in personam action:

(a) If a defendant is not found within the district when a verified complaint praying for attachment and the affidavit required by Rule B(1)(b) are filed, a verified complaint may contain a prayer for process to attach the defendant's tangible or intangible personal property—up to the amount sued for—in the hands of garnishees named in the process.

(b) The plaintiff or the plaintiff's attorney must sign and file with the complaint an affidavit stating that, to the affiant's knowledge, or on information and belief, the defendant cannot be found within the district. The court must review the complaint and affidavit and, if the conditions of this Rule B appear to exist, enter an order so stating and authorizing process of attachment and garnishment. The clerk may issue supplemental process enforcing the court's order upon application without further court order.

(c) If the plaintiff or the plaintiff's attorney certifies that exigent circumstances make court review impracticable, the clerk must issue the summons and process of attachment and garnishment. The plaintiff has the burden in any post-attachment hearing under Rule E(4)(f) to show that exigent circumstances existed.

(d)(i) If the property is a vessel or tangible property on board a vessel, the summons, process, and any supplemental process must be delivered to the marshal for service.

(ii) If the property is other tangible or intangible property, the summons, process, and any supplemental process must be delivered to a person or organization authorized to serve it, who may be (A) a marshal; (B) someone under contract with the United States; (C) someone specially appointed by the court for that purpose; or, (D) in an action brought by the United States, any officer or employee of the United States.

(e) The plaintiff may invoke state-law remedies under Rule 64 for seizure of person or property for the purpose of securing satisfaction of the judgment.

(2) Notice to Defendant. No default judgment may be entered except upon proof—which may be by affidavit—that:

(a) the complaint, summons, and process of attachment or garnishment have been served on the defendant in a manner authorized by Rule 4;

(b) the plaintiff or the garnishee has mailed to the defendant the complaint, summons, and process of attachment or garnishment, using any form of mail requiring a return receipt; or

(c) the plaintiff or the garnishee has tried diligently to give notice of the action to the defendant but could not do so.

(3) Answer.

(a) By Garnishee. The garnishee shall serve an answer, together with answers to any interrogatories served with the complaint, within 21 days after service of process upon the garnishee. Interrogatories to the garnishee may be served with the complaint without leave of court. If the garnishee refuses or neglects to answer on oath as to the debts, credits, or effects of the defendant in the garnishee's hands, or any interrogatories concerning such debts, credits, and effects that may be propounded by the plaintiff, the court may award compulsory process against the garnishee. If the garnishee admits any debts, credits, or effects, they shall be held in the garnishee's hands or paid into the registry of the court, and shall be held in either case subject to the further order of the court.

(b) By Defendant. The defendant shall serve an answer within 30 days after process has been executed, whether by attachment of property or service on the garnishee.

(Added Feb. 28, 1966, eff. July 1, 1966; amended Apr. 29, 1985, eff. Aug. 1, 1985; Mar. 2, 1987, eff. Aug. 1, 1987; Apr. 17, 2000, eff. Dec. 1, 2000; Apr. 25, 2005, eff. Dec. 1, 2005; Mar. 26, 2009, eff. Dec. 1, 2009.)

RULE C. IN REM ACTIONS: SPECIAL PROVISIONS

(1) When Available. An action in rem may be brought:

(a) To enforce any maritime lien;

(b) Whenever a statute of the United States provides for a maritime action in rem or a proceeding analogous thereto.

Except as otherwise provided by law a party who may proceed in rem may also, or in the alternative, proceed in personam against any person who may be liable.

Statutory provisions exempting vessels or other property owned or possessed by or operated by or for the United States from arrest or seizure are not affected by this rule. When a statute so provides, an action against the United States or an instrumentality thereof may proceed on in rem principles.

(2) Complaint. In an action in rem the complaint must:

(a) be verified;

(b) describe with reasonable particularity the property that is the subject of the action; and

(c) state that the property is within the district or will be within the district while the action is pending.

(3) Judicial Authorization and Process.

(a) Arrest Warrant.

(i) The court must review the complaint and any supporting papers. If the conditions for an in rem action appear to exist, the court must issue an order directing the clerk to issue a warrant for the arrest of the vessel or other property that is the subject of the action.

(ii) If the plaintiff or the plaintiff's attorney certifies that exigent circumstances make court review impracticable, the clerk must promptly issue a summons and a warrant for the arrest of the vessel or other property that is the subject of the action. The plaintiff has the burden in any post-arrest hearing under Rule E(4)(f) to show that exigent circumstances existed.

(b) Service.

(i) If the property that is the subject of the action is a vessel or tangible property on board a vessel, the warrant and any supplemental process must be delivered to the marshal for service.

(ii) If the property that is the subject of the action is other property, tangible or intangible, the warrant and any supplemental process must be delivered to a person or organization authorized to enforce it, who may be: (A) a marshal; (B) someone under contract with the United States; (C) someone specially appointed by the court for that purpose; or, (D) in an action brought by the United States, any officer or employee of the United States.

(c) Deposit in Court. If the property that is the subject of the action consists in whole or in part of freight, the proceeds of property sold, or other intangible property, the clerk must issue—in addition to the warrant—a summons directing any person controlling the property to show cause why it should not be deposited in court to abide the judgment.

(d) Supplemental Process. The clerk may upon application issue supplemental process to enforce the court's order without further court order.

(4) Notice. No notice other than execution of process is required when the property that is the subject of the action has been released under Rule E(5). If the property is not released within 14 days after execution, the plaintiff must promptly—or within the time that the court allows—give public notice of the action and arrest in a newspaper designated by court order and having general circulation in the district, but publication may be terminated if the property is released before publication is completed. The notice must specify the time under Rule C(6) to file a statement of interest in or right against the seized property and to answer. This rule does not affect the notice requirements in an action to foreclose a preferred ship mortgage under 46 U.S.C. §§ 31301 et seq., as amended.

(5) Ancillary Process. In any action in rem in which process has been served as provided by this rule, if any part of the property that is the subject of the action has not been brought within the control of the court because it has been removed or sold, or because it is intangible property in the hands of a person who has not been served with process, the court may, on motion, order any person having possession or control of such property or its proceeds to show cause why it should not be delivered into the custody of the marshal or other person or organization having a warrant for the arrest of the property, or paid into court to abide the judgment; and, after hearing, the court may enter such judgment as law and justice may require.

(6) Responsive Pleading; Interrogatories.

(a) Statement of Interest; Answer. In an action in rem:

(i) a person who asserts a right of possession or any ownership interest in the property that is the subject of the action must file a verified statement of right or interest:

(A) within 14 days after the execution of process, or

(B) within the time that the court allows;

(ii) the statement of right or interest must describe the interest in the property that supports the person's demand for its restitution or right to defend the action;

(iii) an agent, bailee, or attorney must state the authority to file a statement of right or interest on behalf of another; and

(iv) a person who asserts a right of possession or any ownership interest must serve an answer within 21 days after filing the statement of interest or right.

(b) Interrogatories. Interrogatories may be served with the complaint in an in rem action without leave of court. Answers to the interrogatories must be served with the answer to the complaint.

(Added Feb. 28, 1966, eff. July 1, 1966; amended Apr. 29, 1985, eff. Aug. 1, 1985; Mar. 2, 1987, eff. Aug. 1, 1987; Apr. 30, 1991, eff. Dec. 1, 1991; Apr. 17, 2000, eff. Dec. 1, 2000; Apr. 29, 2002, eff. Dec. 1, 2002; Apr. 25, 2005, eff. Dec. 1, 2005; Apr. 12, 2006, eff. Dec. 1, 2006; Apr. 23, 2008, eff. Dec. 1, 2008; Mar. 26, 2009, eff. Dec. 1, 2009.)

RULE D. POSSESSORY, PETITORY, AND PARTITION ACTIONS

In all actions for possession, partition, and to try title maintainable according to the course of the admiralty practice with respect to a vessel, in all actions so maintainable with respect to the possession of cargo or other maritime property, and in all actions by one or more part owners against the others to obtain security for the return of the vessel from any voyage undertaken without their consent, or by one or more part owners against the others to obtain possession of the vessel for any voyage on giving security for its safe return, the process shall be by a warrant of arrest of the vessel, cargo, or other property, and by notice in the manner provided by Rule B(2) to the adverse party or parties.

(Added Feb. 28, 1966, eff. July 1, 1966.)

RULE E. ACTIONS IN REM AND QUASI IN REM: GENERAL PROVISIONS

(1) Applicability. Except as otherwise provided, this rule applies to actions in personam with process of maritime attachment and garnishment, actions in rem, and petitory, possessory, and partition actions, supplementing Rules B, C, and D.

(2) Complaint; Security.

(a) Complaint. In actions to which this rule is applicable the complaint shall state the circumstances from which the claim arises with such particularity that the defendant or claimant will be able, without moving for a more definite statement, to commence an investigation of the facts and to frame a responsive pleading.

(b) Security for Costs. Subject to the provisions of Rule 54(d) and of relevant statutes, the court may, on the filing of the complaint or on the appearance of any defendant, claimant, or any other party, or at any later time, require the plaintiff, defendant, claimant, or other party to give security, or additional security, in such sum as the court shall direct to pay all costs and expenses that shall be awarded against the party by any interlocutory order or by the final judgment, or on appeal by any appellate court.

(3) Process.

(a) In admiralty and maritime proceedings process in rem or of maritime attachment and garnishment may be served only within the district.

(b) Issuance and Delivery. Issuance and delivery of process in rem, or of maritime attachment and garnishment, shall be held in abeyance if the plaintiff so requests.

(4) Execution of Process; Marshal's Return; Custody of Property; Procedures for Release.

(a) In General. Upon issuance and delivery of the process, or, in the case of summons with process of attachment and garnishment, when it appears that the defendant cannot be found within the district, the marshal or other person or organization having a warrant shall forthwith execute the process in accordance with this subdivision (4), making due and prompt return.

(b) Tangible Property. If tangible property is to be attached or arrested, the marshal or other person or organization having the warrant shall take it into the marshal's possession for safe custody. If the character or situation of the property is such that the taking of actual possession is impracticable, the marshal or other person executing the process shall affix a copy thereof to the property in a conspicuous place and leave a copy of the complaint and process with the person having possession or the person's agent. In furtherance of the marshal's custody of any vessel the marshal is authorized to make a written request to the collector of customs not to grant clearance to such vessel until notified by the marshal or deputy marshal or by the clerk that the vessel has been released in accordance with these rules.

(c) Intangible Property. If intangible property is to be attached or arrested the marshal or other person or organization having the warrant shall execute the process by leaving with the garnishee or other obligor a copy of the complaint and process requiring the garnishee or other obligor to answer as provided in Rules B(3)(a) and C(6); or the marshal may accept for payment into the registry of the court the amount owed to the extent of the amount claimed by the plaintiff with interest and costs, in which event the garnishee or other obligor shall not be required to answer unless alias process shall be served.

(d) Directions With Respect to Property in Custody. The marshal or other person or organization having the warrant may at any time apply to the court for directions with respect to property that has been attached or arrested, and shall give notice of such application to any or all of the parties as the court may direct.

(e) Expenses of Seizing and Keeping Property; Deposit. These rules do not alter the provisions of Title 28, U.S.C., § 1921, as amended, relative to the expenses of seizing and keeping property attached or arrested and to the requirement of deposits to cover such expenses.

(f) Procedure for Release From Arrest or Attachment. Whenever property is arrested or attached, any person claiming an interest in it shall be entitled to a prompt hearing at which the plaintiff shall be required to show why the arrest or attachment should not be vacated or other relief granted consistent with these rules. This subdivision shall have no application to suits for seamen's wages when process is issued upon a certification of sufficient cause filed pursuant to Title 46, U.S.C. §§ 603 and 604 or to actions by the United States for forfeitures for violation of any statute of the United States.

(5) Release of Property.

(a) Special Bond. Whenever process of maritime attachment and garnishment or process in rem is issued the execution of such process shall be stayed, or the property released, on the giving of security, to be approved by the court or clerk, or by stipulation of the parties, conditioned to answer the judgment of the court or of any appellate court. The parties may stipulate the amount and nature of such security. In the event of the inability or refusal of the parties so to stipulate the court shall fix the principal sum of the bond or stipulation at an amount sufficient to cover the amount of the plaintiff's claim fairly stated with accrued interest and costs; but the principal sum shall in no event exceed (i) twice the amount of the plaintiff's claim or (ii) the value of the property on due appraisement, whichever is smaller. The bond or stipulation shall be conditioned for the payment of the principal sum and interest thereon at 6 per cent per annum.

(b) General Bond. The owner of any vessel may file a general bond or stipulation, with sufficient surety, to be approved by the court, conditioned to answer the judgment of such court in all or any actions that may be brought thereafter in such court in which the vessel is attached or arrested. Thereupon the execution of all such process against such vessel shall be stayed so long as the amount secured by such bond or stipulation is at least double the aggregate amount claimed by plaintiffs in all actions begun and pending in which such vessel has been attached or arrested. Judgments and remedies may be had on such bond or stipulation as if a special bond or stipulation had been filed in each of such actions. The district court may make necessary orders to carry this rule into effect, particularly as to the giving of proper notice of any action against or attachment of a vessel for which a general bond has been filed. Such bond or stipulation shall be indorsed by the clerk with a minute of the actions wherein process is so stayed. Further security may be required by the court at any time.

If a special bond or stipulation is given in a particular case, the liability on the general bond or stipulation shall cease as to that case.

(c) Release by Consent or Stipulation; Order of Court or Clerk; Costs. Any vessel, cargo, or other property in the custody of the marshal or other person or organization having the warrant may be released forthwith upon the marshal's acceptance and approval of a stipulation, bond, or other security, signed by the party on whose behalf the property is detained or the party's attorney and expressly authorizing such release, if all costs and charges of the court and its officers shall have first been paid. Otherwise no property in the custody of the marshal, other person or organization having the warrant, or other officer of the court shall be released without an order of the court; but such order may be entered as of course by the clerk, upon the giving of approved security as provided by law and these rules, or upon the dismissal or discontinuance of the action; but the marshal or other person or organization having the warrant shall not deliver any property so released until the costs and charges of the officers of the court shall first have been paid.

(d) Possessory, Petitory, and Partition Actions. The foregoing provisions of this subdivision (5) do not apply to petitory, possessory, and partition actions. In such cases the property arrested shall be released only by order of the court, on such terms and conditions and on the giving of such security as the court may require.

(6) Reduction or Impairment of Security. Whenever security is taken the court may, on motion and hearing, for good cause shown, reduce the amount of security given; and if the surety shall be or become insufficient, new or additional sureties may be required on motion and hearing.

(7) Security on Counterclaim.

(a) When a person who has given security for damages in the original action asserts a counterclaim that arises from the transaction or occurrence that is the subject of the original action, a plaintiff for whose benefit the security has been given must give security for damages demanded in the counterclaim unless the court for cause shown, directs otherwise. Proceedings on the original claim must be stayed until this security is given unless the court directs otherwise.

(b) The plaintiff is required to give security under Rule E(7)(a) when the United States or its corporate instrumentality counterclaims and would have been required to give security to respond in damages if a private party but is relieved by law from giving security.

(8) Restricted Appearance. An appearance to defend against an admiralty and maritime claim with respect to which there has issued process in rem, or process of attachment and garnishment, may be expressly restricted to the defense of such claim, and in that event is not an appearance for the purposes of any other claim with respect to which such process is not available or has not been served.

(9) Disposition of Property; Sales.

(a) Interlocutory Sales; Delivery.

(i) On application of a party, the marshal, or other person having custody of the property, the court may order all or part of the property sold—with the sales proceeds, or as much of them as will satisfy the judgment, paid into court to await further orders of the court—if:

(A) the attached or arrested property is perishable, or liable to deterioration, decay, or injury by being detained in custody pending the action;

(B) the expense of keeping the property is excessive or disproportionate; or

(C) there is an unreasonable delay in securing release of the property.

(ii) In the circumstances described in Rule E(9)(a)(i), the court, on motion by a defendant or a person filing a statement of interest or right under Rule C(6), may order that the property, rather than being sold, be delivered to the movant upon giving security under these rules.

(b) Sales; Proceeds. All sales of property shall be made by the marshal or a deputy marshal, or by other person or organization having the warrant, or by any other person assigned by the court where the marshal or other person or organization having the warrant is a party in interest; and the proceeds of sale shall be forthwith paid into the registry of the court to be disposed of according to law.

(10) Preservation of Property. When the owner or another person remains in possession of property attached or arrested under the provisions of Rule E(4)(b) that permit execution of process without taking actual possession, the court, on a party's motion or on its own, may enter any order necessary to preserve the property and to prevent its removal.

(Added Feb. 28, 1966, eff. July 1, 1966; amended Apr. 29, 1985, eff. Aug. 1, 1985; Mar. 2, 1987, eff. Aug. 1, 1987; Apr. 30, 1991, eff. Dec. 1, 1991; Apr. 17, 2000, eff. Dec. 1, 2000; Apr. 12, 2006, eff. Dec. 1, 2006.)

RULE F. LIMITATION OF LIABILITY

(1) Time for Filing Complaint; Security. Not later than six months after receipt of a claim in writing, any vessel owner may file a complaint in the appropriate district court, as provided in subdivision (9) of this rule, for limitation of liability pursuant to statute. The owner (a) shall deposit with the court, for the benefit of claimants, a sum equal to the amount or value of the owner's interest in the vessel and pending freight, or approved security therefor, and in addition such sums, or approved security therefor, as the court may from time to time fix as necessary to carry out the provisions of the statutes as amended; or (b) at the owner's option shall transfer to a trustee to be appointed by the court, for the benefit of claimants, the owner's interest in the vessel and pending freight, together with such sums, or approved security therefor, as the court may from time to time fix as necessary to carry out the provisions of the statutes as amended. The plaintiff shall also give security for costs and, if the plaintiff elects to give security, for interest at the rate of 6 percent per annum from the date of the security.

(2) Complaint. The complaint shall set forth the facts on the basis of which the right to limit liability is asserted and all facts necessary to enable the court to determine the amount to which the owner's liability shall be limited. The complaint may demand exoneration from as well as limitation of liability. It shall state the voyage if any, on which the demands sought to be limited arose, with the date and place of its termination; the amount of all demands including all unsatisfied liens or claims of lien, in contract or in tort or otherwise, arising on that voyage, so far as known to the plaintiff, and what actions and proceedings, if any, are pending thereon; whether the vessel was damaged, lost, or abandoned, and, if so, when and where; the value of the vessel at the close of the voyage or, in case of wreck, the value of her wreckage, strippings, or proceeds, if any, and where and in whose possession they are; and the amount of any pending freight recovered or recoverable. If the plaintiff elects to transfer the plaintiff's interest in the vessel to a trustee, the complaint must further show any prior paramount liens thereon, and what voyages or trips, if any, she has made since the voyage or trip on which the claims sought to be limited arose, and any existing liens arising upon any such subsequent voyage or trip, with the amounts and causes thereof, and the names and addresses of the lienors, so far as known; and whether the vessel sustained any injury upon or by reason of such subsequent voyage or trip.

(3) Claims Against Owner; Injunction. Upon compliance by the owner with the requirements of subdivision (1) of this rule all claims and proceedings against the owner or the owner's property with respect to the matter in question shall cease. On application of the plaintiff the court shall enjoin the further prosecution of any action or proceeding against the plaintiff or the plaintiff's property with respect to any claim subject to limitation in the action.

(4) Notice to Claimants. Upon the owner's compliance with subdivision (1) of this rule the court shall issue a notice to all persons asserting claims with respect to which the complaint seeks limitation, admonishing them to file their respective claims with the clerk of the court and to serve on the attorneys for the plaintiff a copy thereof on or before a date to be named in the notice. The date so fixed shall not be less than 30 days after issuance of the notice. For cause shown, the court may enlarge the time within which claims may be filed. The notice shall be published in such newspaper or newspapers as the court may direct once a week for four successive weeks prior to the date fixed for the filing of claims. The plaintiff not later than the day of second publication shall also mail a copy of the notice to every person known to have made any claim against the vessel or the plaintiff arising out of the voyage or trip on which the claims sought to be limited arose. In cases involving death a copy of such notice shall be mailed to the decedent at the decedent's last known address, and also to any person who shall be known to have made any claim on account of such death.

(5) Claims and Answer. Claims shall be filed and served on or before the date specified in the notice provided for in subdivision (4) of this rule. Each claim shall specify the facts upon which the claimant relies in support of the claim, the items thereof, and the dates on which the same accrued. If a claimant desires to contest either the right to exoneration from or the right to limitation of liability the claimant shall file and serve an answer to the complaint unless the claim has included an answer.

(6) Information to be Given Claimants. Within 30 days after the date specified in the notice for filing claims, or within such time as the court thereafter may allow, the plaintiff shall mail to the attorney for each claimant (or if the claimant has no attorney to the claimant) a list setting forth (a) the name of each claimant, (b) the name and address of the claimant's attorney (if the claimant is known to have one), (c) the nature of the claim, i.e., whether property loss, property damage, death, personal injury etc., and (d) the amount thereof.

(7) Insufficiency of Fund or Security. Any claimant may by motion demand that the funds deposited in court or the security given by the plaintiff be increased on the ground that they are less than the value of the plaintiff's interest in the vessel and pending freight. Thereupon the court shall cause due appraisement to be made of the value of the plaintiff's interest in the vessel and pending freight; and if the court finds that the deposit or security is either insufficient or excessive it shall order its increase or reduction. In like manner any claimant may demand that the deposit or security be increased on the ground that it is insufficient to carry out the provisions of the statutes relating to claims in respect of loss of life or bodily injury; and, after notice and hearing, the court may similarly order that the deposit or security be increased or reduced.

(8) Objections to Claims: Distribution of Fund. Any interested party may question or controvert any claim without filing an objection thereto. Upon determination of liability the fund deposited or secured, or the proceeds of the vessel and pending freight, shall be divided pro rata, subject to all relevant provisions of law, among the several claimants in proportion to the amounts of their respective claims, duly proved, saving, however, to all parties any priority to which they may be legally entitled.

(9) Venue; Transfer. The complaint shall be filed in any district in which the vessel has been attached or arrested to answer for any claim with respect to which the plaintiff seeks to limit liability; or, if the vessel has not been attached or arrested, then in any district in which the owner has been sued with respect to any such claim. When the vessel has not been attached or arrested to answer the matters aforesaid, and suit has not been commenced against the owner, the proceedings may be had in the district in which the vessel may be, but if the vessel is not within any district and no suit has been commenced in any district, then the complaint may be filed in any district. For the convenience of parties and witnesses, in the interest of justice, the court may transfer the action to any district; if venue is wrongly laid the court shall dismiss or, if it be in the interest of justice, transfer the action to any district in which it could have been brought. If the vessel shall have been sold, the proceeds shall represent the vessel for the purposes of these rules.

(Added Feb. 28, 1966, eff. July 1, 1966; amended Mar. 2, 1987, eff. Aug. 1, 1987.)

RULE G. FORFEITURE ACTIONS IN REM

(1) Scope. This rule governs a forfeiture action in rem arising from a federal statute. To the extent that this rule does not address an issue, Supplemental Rules C and E and the Federal Rules of Civil Procedure also apply.

(2) Complaint. The complaint must:

(a) be verified;

(b) state the grounds for subject-matter jurisdiction, in rem jurisdiction over the defendant property, and venue;

(c) describe the property with reasonable particularity;

(d) if the property is tangible, state its location when any seizure occurred and—if different—its location when the action is filed;

(e) identify the statute under which the forfeiture action is brought; and

(f) state sufficiently detailed facts to support a reasonable belief that the government will be able to meet its burden of proof at trial.

(3) Judicial Authorization and Process.

(a) Real Property. If the defendant is real property, the government must proceed under 18 U.S.C. § 985.

(b) Other Property; Arrest Warrant. If the defendant is not real property:

(i) the clerk must issue a warrant to arrest the property if it is in the government's possession, custody, or control;

(ii) the court—on finding probable cause—must issue a warrant to arrest the property if it is not in the government's possession, custody, or control and is not subject to a judicial restraining order; and

(iii) a warrant is not necessary if the property is subject to a judicial restraining order.

(c) Execution of Process.

(i) The warrant and any supplemental process must be delivered to a person or organization authorized to execute it, who may be: (A) a marshal or any other United States officer or employee; (B) someone under contract with the United States; or (C) someone specially appointed by the court for that purpose.

(ii) The authorized person or organization must execute the warrant and any supplemental process on property in the United States as soon as practicable unless:

(A) the property is in the government's possession, custody, or control; or

(B) the court orders a different time when the complaint is under seal, the action is stayed before the warrant and supplemental process are executed, or the court finds other good cause.

(iii) The warrant and any supplemental process may be executed within the district or, when authorized by statute, outside the district.

(iv) If executing a warrant on property outside the United States is required, the warrant may be transmitted to an appropriate authority for serving process where the property is located.

(4) Notice.

(a) Notice by Publication.

(i) When Publication Is Required. A judgment of forfeiture may be entered only if the government has published notice of the action within a reasonable time after filing the complaint or at a time the court orders. But notice need not be published if:

(A) the defendant property is worth less than $1,000 and direct notice is sent under Rule G(4)(b) to every person the government can reasonably identify as a potential claimant; or

(B) the court finds that the cost of publication exceeds the property's value and that other means of notice would satisfy due process.

(ii) Content of the Notice. Unless the court orders otherwise, the notice must:

(A) describe the property with reasonable particularity;

(B) state the times under Rule G(5) to file a claim and to answer; and

(C) name the government attorney to be served with the claim and answer.

(iii) Frequency of Publication. Published notice must appear:

(A) once a week for three consecutive weeks; or

(B) only once if, before the action was filed, notice of nonjudicial forfeiture of the same property was published on an official internet government forfeiture site for at least 30 consecutive days, or in a newspaper of general circulation for three consecutive weeks in a district where publication is authorized under Rule G(4)(a)(iv).

(iv) Means of Publication. The government should select from the following options a means of publication reasonably calculated to notify potential claimants of the action:

(A) if the property is in the United States, publication in a newspaper generally circulated in the district where the action is filed, where the property was seized, or where property that was not seized is located;

(B) if the property is outside the United States, publication in a newspaper generally circulated in a district where the action is filed, in a newspaper generally circulated in the country where the property is located, or in legal notices published and generally circulated in the country where the property is located; or

(C) instead of (A) or (B), posting a notice on an official internet government forfeiture site for at least 30 consecutive days.

(b) Notice to Known Potential Claimants.

(i) Direct Notice Required. The government must send notice of the action and a copy of the complaint to any person who reasonably appears to be a potential claimant on the facts known to the government before the end of the time for filing a claim under Rule G(5)(a)(ii)(B).

(ii) Content of the Notice. The notice must state:

(A) the date when the notice is sent;

(B) a deadline for filing a claim, at least 35 days after the notice is sent;

(C) that an answer or a motion under Rule 12 must be filed no later than 21 days after filing the claim; and

(D) the name of the government attorney to be served with the claim and answer.

(iii) Sending Notice.

(A) The notice must be sent by means reasonably calculated to reach the potential claimant.

(B) Notice may be sent to the potential claimant or to the attorney representing the potential claimant with respect to the seizure of the property or in a related investigation, administrative forfeiture proceeding, or criminal case.

(C) Notice sent to a potential claimant who is incarcerated must be sent to the place of incarceration.

(D) Notice to a person arrested in connection with an offense giving rise to the forfeiture who is not incarcerated when notice is sent may be sent to the address that person last gave to the agency that arrested or released the person.

(E) Notice to a person from whom the property was seized who is not incarcerated when notice is sent may be sent to the last address that person gave to the agency that seized the property.

(iv) When Notice Is Sent. Notice by the following means is sent on the date when it is placed in the mail, delivered to a commercial carrier, or sent by electronic mail.

(v) Actual Notice. A potential claimant who had actual notice of a forfeiture action may not oppose or seek relief from forfeiture because of the government's failure to send the required notice.

(5) Responsive Pleadings.

(a) Filing a Claim.

(i) A person who asserts an interest in the defendant property may contest the forfeiture by filing a claim in the court where the action is pending. The claim must:

(A) identify the specific property claimed;

(B) identify the claimant and state the claimant's interest in the property;

(C) be signed by the claimant under penalty of perjury; and

(D) be served on the government attorney designated under Rule G(4)(a)(ii)(C) or (b)(ii)(D).

(ii) Unless the court for good cause sets a different time, the claim must be filed:

(A) by the time stated in a direct notice sent under Rule G(4)(b);

(B) if notice was published but direct notice was not sent to the claimant or the claimant's attorney, no later than 30 days after final publication of newspaper notice or legal notice under Rule G(4)(a) or no later than 60 days after the first day of publication on an official internet government forfeiture site; or

(C) if notice was not published and direct notice was not sent to the claimant or the claimant's attorney:

(1) if the property was in the government's possession, custody, or control when the complaint was filed, no later than 60 days after the filing, not counting any time when the complaint was under seal or when the action was stayed before execution of a warrant issued under Rule G(3)(b); or

(2) if the property was not in the government's possession, custody, or control when the complaint was filed, no later than 60 days after the government complied with 18 U.S.C. § 985(c) as to real property, or 60 days after process was executed on the property under Rule G(3).

(iii) A claim filed by a person asserting an interest as a bailee must identify the bailor, and if filed on the bailor's behalf must state the authority to do so.

(b) Answer. A claimant must serve and file an answer to the complaint or a motion under Rule 12 within 21 days after filing the claim. A claimant waives an objection to in rem jurisdiction or to venue if the objection is not made by motion or stated in the answer.

(6) Special Interrogatories.

(a) Time and Scope. The government may serve special interrogatories limited to the claimant's identity and relationship to the defendant property without the court's leave at any time after the claim is filed and before discovery is closed. But if the claimant serves a motion to dismiss the action, the government must serve the interrogatories within 21 days after the motion is served.

(b) Answers or Objections. Answers or objections to these interrogatories must be served within 21 days after the interrogatories are served.

(c) Government's Response Deferred. The government need not respond to a claimant's motion to dismiss the action under Rule G(8)(b) until 21 days after the claimant has answered these interrogatories.

(7) Preserving, Preventing Criminal Use, and Disposing of Property; Sales.

(a) Preserving and Preventing Criminal Use of Property. When the government does not have actual possession of the defendant property the court, on motion or on its own, may enter any order necessary to preserve the property, to prevent its removal or encumbrance, or to prevent its use in a criminal offense.

(b) Interlocutory Sale or Delivery.

(i) Order to Sell. On motion by a party or a person having custody of the property, the court may order all or part of the property sold if:

(A) the property is perishable or at risk of deterioration, decay, or injury by being detained in custody pending the action;

(B) the expense of keeping the property is excessive or is disproportionate to its fair market value;

(C) the property is subject to a mortgage or to taxes on which the owner is in default; or

(D) the court finds other good cause.

(ii) Who Makes the Sale. A sale must be made by a United States agency that has authority to sell the property, by the agency's contractor, or by any person the court designates.

(iii) Sale Procedures. The sale is governed by 28 U.S.C. §§ 2001, 2002, and 2004, unless all parties, with the court's approval, agree to the sale, aspects of the sale, or different procedures.

(iv) Sale Proceeds. Sale proceeds are a substitute res subject to forfeiture in place of the property that was sold. The proceeds must be held in an interest-bearing account maintained by the United States pending the conclusion of the forfeiture action.

(v) Delivery on a Claimant's Motion. The court may order that the property be delivered to the claimant pending the conclusion of the action if the claimant shows circumstances that would permit sale under Rule G(7)(b)(i) and gives security under these rules.

(c) Disposing of Forfeited Property. Upon entry of a forfeiture judgment, the property or proceeds from selling the property must be disposed of as provided by law.

(8) Motions.

(a) Motion To Suppress Use of the Property as Evidence. If the defendant property was seized, a party with standing to contest the lawfulness of the seizure may move to suppress use of the property as evidence. Suppression does not affect forfeiture of the property based on independently derived evidence.

(b) Motion To Dismiss the Action.

(i) A claimant who establishes standing to contest forfeiture may move to dismiss the action under Rule 12(b).

(ii) In an action governed by 18 U.S.C. § 983(a)(3)(D) the complaint may not be dismissed on the ground that the government did not have adequate evidence at the time the complaint was filed to establish the forfeitability of the property. The sufficiency of the complaint is governed by Rule G(2).

(c) Motion To Strike a Claim or Answer.

(i) At any time before trial, the government may move to strike a claim or answer:

(A) for failing to comply with Rule G(5) or (6), or

(B) because the claimant lacks standing.

(ii) The motion:

(A) must be decided before any motion by the claimant to dismiss the action; and

(B) may be presented as a motion for judgment on the pleadings or as a motion to determine after a hearing or by summary judgment whether the claimant can carry the burden of establishing standing by a preponderance of the evidence.

(d) Petition To Release Property.

(i) If a United States agency or an agency's contractor holds property for judicial or nonjudicial forfeiture under a statute governed by 18 U.S.C. § 983(f), a person who has filed a claim to the property may petition for its release under § 983(f).

(ii) If a petition for release is filed before a judicial forfeiture action is filed against the property, the petition may be filed either in the district where the property was seized or in the district where a warrant to seize the property issued. If a judicial forfeiture action against the property is later filed in another district—or if the government shows that the action will be filed in another district—the petition may be transferred to that district under 28 U.S.C. § 1404.

(e) Excessive Fines. A claimant may seek to mitigate a forfeiture under the Excessive Fines Clause of the Eighth Amendment by motion for summary judgment or by motion made after entry of a forfeiture judgment if:

(i) the claimant has pleaded the defense under Rule 8; and

(ii) the parties have had the opportunity to conduct civil discovery on the defense.

(9) Trial. Trial is to the court unless any party demands trial by jury under Rule 38.

(Added Apr. 12, 2006, eff. Dec. 1, 2006; amended Mar. 26, 2009, eff. Dec. 1, 2009.)

INDEX TO
FEDERAL RULES OF CIVIL PROCEDURE

FEDERAL RULES OF EVIDENCE

Including Amendments Received Through December 1, 2016

ARTICLE I. GENERAL PROVISIONS

ARTICLE II. JUDICIAL NOTICE

ARTICLE III. PRESUMPTIONS IN CIVIL CASES

ARTICLE IV. RELEVANCE AND ITS LIMITS

ARTICLE V. PRIVILEGES

ARTICLE VI. WITNESSES

ARTICLE VII. OPINIONS AND EXPERT TESTIMONY

ARTICLE VIII. HEARSAY

ARTICLE IX. AUTHENTICATION AND IDENTIFICATION

ARTICLE X. CONTENTS OF WRITINGS, RECORDINGS, AND PHOTOGRAPHS

ARTICLE XI. MISCELLANEOUS RULES

ARTICLE I. GENERAL PROVISIONS

RULE 101. SCOPE; DEFINITIONS

(a) Scope. These rules apply to proceedings in United States courts. The specific courts and proceedings to which the rules apply, along with exceptions, are set out in Rule 1101.

(b) Definitions. In these rules:

(1) "civil case" means a civil action or proceeding;

(2) "criminal case" includes a criminal proceeding;

(3) "public office" includes a public agency;

(4) "record" includes a memorandum, report, or data compilation;

(5) a "rule prescribed by the Supreme Court" means a rule adopted by the Supreme Court under statutory authority; and

(6) a reference to any kind of written material or any other medium includes electronically stored information.

(Pub.L. 93–595, § 1, Jan. 2, 1975, 88 Stat. 1929; Mar. 2, 1987, eff. Oct. 1, 1987; Apr. 25, 1988, eff. Nov. 1, 1988; Apr. 22, 1993, eff. Dec. 1, 1993; Apr. 26, 2011, eff. Dec. 1, 2011.)

RULE 102. PURPOSE

These rules should be construed so as to administer every proceeding fairly, eliminate unjustifiable expense and delay, and promote the development of evidence law, to the end of ascertaining the truth and securing a just determination.

(Pub.L. 93–595, § 1, Jan. 2, 1975, 88 Stat.1929; Apr. 26, 2011, eff. Dec. 1, 2011.)

RULE 103. RULINGS ON EVIDENCE

(a) Preserving a Claim of Error. A party may claim error in a ruling to admit or exclude evidence only if the error affects a substantial right of the party and:

(1) if the ruling admits evidence, a party, on the record:

(A) timely objects or moves to strike; and

(B) states the specific ground, unless it was apparent from the context; or

(2) if the ruling excludes evidence, a party informs the court of its substance by an offer of proof, unless the substance was apparent from the context.

(b) Not Needing to Renew an Objection or Offer of Proof. Once the court rules definitively on the record—either before or at trial—a party need not renew an objection or offer of proof to preserve a claim of error for appeal.

(c) Court's Statement About the Ruling; Directing an Offer of Proof. The court may make any statement about the character or form of the evidence, the objection made, and the ruling. The court may direct that an offer of proof be made in question-and-answer form.

(d) Preventing the Jury from Hearing Inadmissible Evidence. To the extent practicable, the court must conduct a jury trial so that inadmissible evidence is not suggested to the jury by any means.

(e) Taking Notice of Plain Error. A court may take notice of a plain error affecting a substantial right, even if the claim of error was not properly preserved.

(Pub.L. 93–595, § 1, Jan. 2, 1975, 88 Stat. 1929; Apr. 17, 2000, eff. Dec. 1, 2000; Apr. 26, 2011, eff. Dec. 1, 2011.)

RULE 104. PRELIMINARY QUESTIONS

(a) In General. The court must decide any preliminary question about whether a witness is qualified, a privilege exists, or evidence is admissible. In so deciding, the court is not bound by evidence rules, except those on privilege.

(b) Relevance That Depends on a Fact. When the relevance of evidence depends on whether a fact exists, proof must be introduced sufficient to support a finding that the fact does exist. The court may admit the proposed evidence on the condition that the proof be introduced later.

(c) Conducting a Hearing So That the Jury Cannot Hear It. The court must conduct any hearing on a preliminary question so that the jury cannot hear it if:

(1) the hearing involves the admissibility of a confession;

(2) a defendant in a criminal case is a witness and so requests; or

(3) justice so requires.

(d) Cross-Examining a Defendant in a Criminal Case. By testifying on a preliminary question, a defendant in a criminal case does not become subject to cross-examination on other issues in the case.

(e) Evidence Relevant to Weight and Credibility. This rule does not limit a party's right to introduce before the jury evidence that is relevant to the weight or credibility of other evidence.

(Pub.L. 93–595, § 1, Jan. 2, 1975, 88 Stat.1930; Mar. 2, 1987, eff. Oct. 1, 1987; Apr. 26, 2011, eff. Dec. 1, 2011.)

RULE 105. LIMITING EVIDENCE THAT IS NOT ADMISSIBLE AGAINST OTHER PARTIES OR FOR OTHER PURPOSES

If the court admits evidence that is admissible against a party or for a purpose—but not against another party or for another purpose—the court, on timely request, must restrict the evidence to its proper scope and instruct the jury accordingly.

(Pub.L. 93–595, § 1, Jan. 2, 1975, 88 Stat. 1930; Apr. 26, 2011, eff. Dec. 1, 2011.)

RULE 106. REMAINDER OF OR RELATED WRITINGS OR RECORDED STATEMENTS

If a party introduces all or part of a writing or recorded statement, an adverse party may require the introduction, at that time, of any other part—or any other writing or recorded statement—that in fairness ought to be considered at the same time.

(Pub.L. 93–595, § 1, Jan. 2, 1975, 88 Stat. 1930; Mar. 2, 1987, eff. Oct. 1, 1987; Apr. 26, 2011, eff. Dec. 1, 2011.)

ARTICLE II. JUDICIAL NOTICE

RULE 201. JUDICIAL NOTICE OF ADJUDICATIVE FACTS

(a) Scope. This rule governs judicial notice of an adjudicative fact only, not a legislative fact.

(b) Kinds of Facts That May Be Judicially Noticed. The court may judicially notice a fact that is not subject to reasonable dispute because it:

(1) is generally known within the trial court's territorial jurisdiction; or

(2) can be accurately and readily determined from sources whose accuracy cannot reasonably be questioned.

(c) Taking Notice. The court:

(1) may take judicial notice on its own; or

(2) must take judicial notice if a party requests it and the court is supplied with the necessary information.

(d) Timing. The court may take judicial notice at any stage of the proceeding.

(e) Opportunity to Be Heard. On timely request, a party is entitled to be heard on the propriety of taking judicial notice and the nature of the fact to be noticed. If the court takes judicial notice before notifying a party, the party, on request, is still entitled to be heard.

(f) Instructing the Jury. In a civil case, the court must instruct the jury to accept the noticed fact as conclusive. In a criminal case, the court must instruct the jury that it may or may not accept the noticed fact as conclusive.

(Pub.L. 93–595, § 1, Jan. 2, 1975, 88 Stat. 1930; Apr. 26, 2011, eff. Dec. 1, 2011.)

ARTICLE III. PRESUMPTIONS IN CIVIL CASES

RULE 301. PRESUMPTIONS IN CIVIL CASES GENERALLY

In a civil case, unless a federal statute or these rules provide otherwise, the party against whom a presumption is directed has the burden of producing evidence to rebut the presumption. But this rule does not shift the burden of persuasion, which remains on the party who had it originally.

(Pub.L. 93–595, § 1, Jan. 2, 1975, 88 Stat. 1931; Apr. 26, 2011, eff. Dec. 1, 2011.)

RULE 302. APPLYING STATE LAW TO PRESUMPTIONS IN CIVIL CASES

In a civil case, state law governs the effect of a presumption regarding a claim or defense for which state law supplies the rule of decision.

(Pub.L. 93–595, § 1, Jan. 2, 1975, 88 Stat. 1931; Apr. 26, 2011, eff. Dec. 1, 2011.)

ARTICLE IV. RELEVANCE AND ITS LIMITS

RULE 401. TEST FOR RELEVANT EVIDENCE

Evidence is relevant if:

(a) it has any tendency to make a fact more or less probable than it would be without the evidence; and

(b) the fact is of consequence in determining the action.

(Pub.L. 93–595, § 1, Jan. 2, 1975, 88 Stat. 1931; Apr. 26, 2011, eff. Dec. 1, 2011.)

RULE 402. GENERAL ADMISSIBILITY OF RELEVANT EVIDENCE

Relevant evidence is admissible unless any of the following provides otherwise:

- the United States Constitution;
- a federal statute;
- these rules; or
- other rules prescribed by the Supreme Court.

Irrelevant evidence is not admissible.

(Pub.L. 93–595, § 1, Jan. 2, 1975, 88 Stat. 1931; Apr. 26, 2011, eff. Dec. 1, 2011.)

RULE 403. EXCLUDING RELEVANT EVIDENCE FOR PREJUDICE, CONFUSION, WASTE OF TIME, OR OTHER REASONS

The court may exclude relevant evidence if its probative value is substantially outweighed by a danger of one or more of the following: unfair prejudice, confusing the issues, misleading the jury, undue delay, wasting time, or needlessly presenting cumulative evidence.

(Pub.L. 93–595, § 1, Jan. 2, 1975, 88 Stat. 1932; Apr. 26, 2011, eff. Dec. 1, 2011.)

RULE 404. CHARACTER EVIDENCE; CRIMES OR OTHER ACTS

(a) Character Evidence.

(1) Prohibited Uses. Evidence of a person's character or character trait is not admissible to prove that on a particular occasion the person acted in accordance with the character or trait.

(2) Exceptions for a Defendant or Victim in a Criminal Case. The following exceptions apply in a criminal case:

(A) a defendant may offer evidence of the defendant's pertinent trait, and if the evidence is admitted, the prosecutor may offer evidence to rebut it;

(B) subject to the limitations in Rule 412, a defendant may offer evidence of an alleged victim's pertinent trait, and if the evidence is admitted, the prosecutor may:

(i) offer evidence to rebut it; and

(ii) offer evidence of the defendant's same trait; and

(C) in a homicide case, the prosecutor may offer evidence of the alleged victim's trait of peacefulness to rebut evidence that the victim was the first aggressor.

(3) Exceptions for a Witness. Evidence of a witness's character may be admitted under Rules 607, 608, and 609.

(b) Crimes, Wrongs, or Other Acts.

(1) Prohibited Uses. Evidence of a crime, wrong, or other act is not admissible to prove a person's character in order to show that on a particular occasion the person acted in accordance with the character.

(2) Permitted Uses; Notice in a Criminal Case. This evidence may be admissible for another purpose, such as proving motive, opportunity, intent, preparation, plan, knowledge, identity, absence of mistake, or lack of accident. On request by a defendant in a criminal case, the prosecutor must:

(A) provide reasonable notice of the general nature of any such evidence that the prosecutor intends to offer at trial; and

(B) do so before trial—or during trial if the court, for good cause, excuses lack of pretrial notice.

(Pub.L. 93–595, § 1, Jan. 2, 1975, 88 Stat.1932; Mar. 2, 1987, eff. Oct. 1, 1987; Apr. 30, 1991, eff. Dec. 1, 1991; Apr. 17, 2000, eff. Dec. 1, 2000; Apr. 12, 2006, eff. Dec. 1, 2006; Apr. 26, 2011, eff. Dec. 1, 2011.)

RULE 405. METHODS OF PROVING CHARACTER

(a) By Reputation or Opinion. When evidence of a person's character or character trait is admissible, it may be proved by testimony about the person's reputation or by testimony in the form of an opinion. On cross-examination of the character witness, the court may allow an inquiry into relevant specific instances of the person's conduct.

(b) By Specific Instances of Conduct. When a person's character or character trait is an essential element of a charge, claim, or defense, the character or trait may also be proved by relevant specific instances of the person's conduct.

(Pub.L. 93–595, § 1, Jan. 2, 1975, 88 Stat. 1932; Mar. 2, 1987, eff. Oct. 1, 1987; Apr. 26, 2011, eff. Dec. 1, 2011.)

RULE 406. HABIT; ROUTINE PRACTICE

Evidence of a person's habit or an organization's routine practice may be admitted to prove that on a particular occasion the person or organization acted in accordance with the habit or routine practice. The court may admit this evidence regardless of whether it is corroborated or whether there was an eyewitness.

(Pub.L. 93–595, § 1, Jan. 2, 1975, 88 Stat. 1932; Apr. 26, 2011, eff. Dec. 1, 2011.)

RULE 407. SUBSEQUENT REMEDIAL MEASURES

When measures are taken that would have made an earlier injury or harm less likely to occur, evidence of the subsequent measures is not admissible to prove:

- negligence;
- culpable conduct;
- a defect in a product or its design; or
- a need for a warning or instruction.

But the court may admit this evidence for another purpose, such as impeachment or—if disputed—proving ownership, control, or the feasibility of precautionary measures.

(Pub.L. 93–595, § 1, Jan. 2, 1975, 88 Stat. 1932; Apr. 11, 1997, eff. Dec. 1, 1997; Apr. 26, 2011, eff. Dec. 1, 2011.)

RULE 408. COMPROMISE OFFERS AND NEGOTIATIONS

(a) Prohibited Uses. Evidence of the following is not admissible—on behalf of any party—either to prove or disprove the validity or amount of a disputed claim or to impeach by a prior inconsistent statement or a contradiction:

(1) furnishing, promising, or offering—or accepting, promising to accept, or offering to accept—a valuable consideration in compromising or attempting to compromise the claim; and

(2) conduct or a statement made during compromise negotiations about the claim—except when offered in a criminal case and when the negotiations related to a claim by a public office in the exercise of its regulatory, investigative, or enforcement authority.

(b) Exceptions. The court may admit this evidence for another purpose, such as proving a witness's bias or prejudice, negating a contention of undue delay, or proving an effort to obstruct a criminal investigation or prosecution.

(Pub.L. 93–595, § 1, Jan. 2, 1975, 88 Stat. 1933; Apr. 12, 2006, eff. Dec. 1, 2006; Apr. 26, 2011, eff. Dec. 1, 2011.)

RULE 409. OFFERS TO PAY MEDICAL AND SIMILAR EXPENSES

Evidence of furnishing, promising to pay, or offering to pay medical, hospital, or similar expenses resulting from an injury is not admissible to prove liability for the injury.

(Pub.L. 93–595, § 1, Jan. 2, 1975, 88 Stat.1933; Apr. 26, 2011, eff. Dec. 1, 2011.)

RULE 410. PLEAS, PLEA DISCUSSIONS, AND RELATED STATEMENTS

(a) Prohibited Uses. In a civil or criminal case, evidence of the following is not admissible against the defendant who made the plea or participated in the plea discussions:

(1) a guilty plea that was later withdrawn;

(2) a nolo contendere plea;

(3) a statement made during a proceeding on either of those pleas under Federal Rule of Criminal Procedure 11 or a comparable state procedure; or

(4) a statement made during plea discussions with an attorney for the prosecuting authority if the discussions did not result in a guilty plea or they resulted in a later-withdrawn guilty plea.

(b) Exceptions. The court may admit a statement described in Rule 410(a)(3) or (4):

(1) in any proceeding in which another statement made during the same plea or plea discussions has been introduced, if in fairness the statements ought to be considered together; or

(2) in a criminal proceeding for perjury or false statement, if the defendant made the statement under oath, on the record, and with counsel present.

(Pub.L. 93–595, § 1, Jan. 2, 1975, 88 Stat. 1933; Pub.L. 94–149, § 1(9), Dec. 12, 1975, 89 Stat. 805; Apr. 30, 1979, eff. Dec. 1, 1980; Apr. 26, 2011, eff. Dec. 1, 2011.)

RULE 411. LIABILITY INSURANCE

Evidence that a person was or was not insured against liability is not admissible to prove whether the person acted negligently or otherwise wrongfully. But the court may admit this evidence for another purpose, such as proving a witness's bias or prejudice or proving agency, ownership, or control.

(Pub.L. 93–595, § 1, Jan. 2, 1975, 88 Stat.1933; Mar. 2, 1987, eff. Oct. 1, 1987; Apr. 26, 2011, eff. Dec. 1, 2011.)

RULE 412. SEX-OFFENSE CASES: THE VICTIM'S SEXUAL BEHAVIOR OR PREDISPOSITION

(a) Prohibited Uses. The following evidence is not admissible in a civil or criminal proceeding involving alleged sexual misconduct:

(1) evidence offered to prove that a victim engaged in other sexual behavior; or

(2) evidence offered to prove a victim's sexual predisposition.

(b) Exceptions.

(1) Criminal Cases. The court may admit the following evidence in a criminal case:

(A) evidence of specific instances of a victim's sexual behavior, if offered to prove that someone other than the defendant was the source of semen, injury, or other physical evidence;

(B) evidence of specific instances of a victim's sexual behavior with respect to the person accused of the sexual misconduct, if offered by the defendant to prove consent or if offered by the prosecutor; and

(C) evidence whose exclusion would violate the defendant's constitutional rights.

(2) Civil Cases. In a civil case, the court may admit evidence offered to prove a victim's sexual behavior or sexual predisposition if its probative value substantially outweighs the danger of harm to any victim and of unfair prejudice to any party. The court may admit evidence of a victim's reputation only if the victim has placed it in controversy.

(c) Procedure to Determine Admissibility.

(1) Motion. If a party intends to offer evidence under Rule 412(b), the party must:

(A) file a motion that specifically describes the evidence and states the purpose for which it is to be offered;

(B) do so at least 14 days before trial unless the court, for good cause, sets a different time;

(C) serve the motion on all parties; and

(D) notify the victim or, when appropriate, the victim's guardian or representative.

(2) Hearing. Before admitting evidence under this rule, the court must conduct an in camera hearing and give the victim and parties a right to attend and be heard. Unless the court orders otherwise, the motion, related materials, and the record of the hearing must be and remain sealed.

(d) Definition of "Victim." In this rule, "victim" includes an alleged victim.

(Added Pub.L. 95–540, § 2(a), Oct. 28, 1978, 92 Stat. 2046; amended Pub.L. 100–690, Title VII, § 7046(a), Nov. 18, 1988, 102 Stat. 4400; Apr. 29, 1994, eff. Dec. 1, 1994; Pub.L. 103–322, Title IV, § 40141(b), Sept. 13, 1994, 108 Stat. 1919; Apr. 26, 2011, eff. Dec. 1, 2011.)

RULE 413. SIMILAR CRIMES IN SEXUAL-ASSAULT CASES

(a) Permitted Uses. In a criminal case in which a defendant is accused of a sexual assault, the court may admit evidence that the defendant committed any other sexual assault. The evidence may be considered on any matter to which it is relevant.

(b) Disclosure to the Defendant. If the prosecutor intends to offer this evidence, the prosecutor must disclose it to the defendant, including witnesses' statements or a summary of the expected testimony. The prosecutor must do so at least 15 days before trial or at a later time that the court allows for good cause.

(c) Effect on Other Rules. This rule does not limit the admission or consideration of evidence under any other rule.

(d) Definition of "Sexual Assault." In this rule and Rule 415, "sexual assault" means a crime under federal law or under state law (as "state" is defined in 18 U.S.C. § 513) involving:

(1) any conduct prohibited by 18 U.S.C. chapter 109A;

(2) contact, without consent, between any part of the defendant's body—or an object—and another person's genitals or anus;

(3) contact, without consent, between the defendant's genitals or anus and any part of another person's body;

(4) deriving sexual pleasure or gratification from inflicting death, bodily injury, or physical pain on another person; or

(5) an attempt or conspiracy to engage in conduct described in subparagraphs (1)–(4).

(Added Pub.L. 103–322, Title XXXII, § 320935(a), Sept. 13, 1994, 108 Stat. 2136; Apr. 26, 2011, eff. Dec. 1, 2011.)

RULE 414. SIMILAR CRIMES IN CHILD-MOLESTATION CASES

(a) Permitted Uses. In a criminal case in which a defendant is accused of child molestation, the court may admit evidence that the defendant committed any other child molestation. The evidence may be considered on any matter to which it is relevant.

(b) Disclosure to the Defendant. If the prosecutor intends to offer this evidence, the prosecutor must disclose it to the defendant, including witnesses' statements or a summary of the expected testimony. The prosecutor must do so at least 15 days before trial or at a later time that the court allows for good cause.

(c) Effect on Other Rules. This rule does not limit the admission or consideration of evidence under any other rule.

(d) Definition of "Child" and "Child Molestation." In this rule and Rule 415:

(1) "child" means a person below the age of 14; and

(2) "child molestation" means a crime under federal law or under state law (as "state" is defined in 18 U.S.C. § 513) involving:

(A) any conduct prohibited by 18 U.S.C. chapter 109A and committed with a child;

(B) any conduct prohibited by 18 U.S.C. chapter 110;

(C) contact between any part of the defendant's body—or an object—and a child's genitals or anus;

(D) contact between the defendant's genitals or anus and any part of a child's body;

(E) deriving sexual pleasure or gratification from inflicting death, bodily injury, or physical pain on a child; or

(F) an attempt or conspiracy to engage in conduct described in subparagraphs (A)–(E).

(Added Pub.L. 103–322, Title XXXII, § 320935(a), Sept. 13, 1994, 108 Stat. 2135; Apr. 26, 2011, eff. Dec. 1, 2011.)

RULE 415. SIMILAR ACTS IN CIVIL CASES INVOLVING SEXUAL ASSAULT OR CHILD MOLESTATION

(a) Permitted Uses. In a civil case involving a claim for relief based on a party's alleged sexual assault or child molestation, the court may admit evidence that the party committed any other sexual assault or child molestation. The evidence may be considered as provided in Rules 413 and 414.

(b) Disclosure to the Opponent. If a party intends to offer this evidence, the party must disclose it to the party against whom it will be offered, including witnesses' statements or a summary of the expected testimony. The party must do so at least 15 days before trial or at a later time that the court allows for good cause.

(c) Effect on Other Rules. This rule does not limit the admission or consideration of evidence under any other rule.

(Added Pub.L. 103–322, Title XXXII, § 320935(a), Sept. 13, 1994, 108 Stat. 2137; Apr. 26, 2011, eff. Dec. 1, 2011.)

ARTICLE V. PRIVILEGES

RULE 501. PRIVILEGE IN GENERAL

The common law—as interpreted by United States courts in the light of reason and experience—governs a claim of privilege unless any of the following provides otherwise:

- the United States Constitution;
- a federal statute; or
- rules prescribed by the Supreme Court.

But in a civil case, state law governs privilege regarding a claim or defense for which state law supplies the rule of decision.

(Pub.L. 93–595, § 1, Jan. 2, 1975, 88 Stat. 1933; Apr. 26, 2011, eff. Dec. 1, 2011.)

RULE 502. ATTORNEY–CLIENT PRIVILEGE AND WORK PRODUCT; LIMITATIONS ON WAIVER

The following provisions apply, in the circumstances set out, to disclosure of a communication or information covered by the attorney-client privilege or work-product protection.

(a) Disclosure Made in a Federal Proceeding or to a Federal Office or Agency; Scope of a Waiver. When the disclosure is made in a federal proceeding or to a federal office or agency and waives the attorney-client privilege or work-product protection, the waiver extends to an undisclosed communication or information in a federal or state proceeding only if:

(1) the waiver is intentional;

(2) the disclosed and undisclosed communications or information concern the same subject matter; and

(3) they ought in fairness to be considered together.

(b) Inadvertent Disclosure. When made in a federal proceeding or to a federal office or agency, the disclosure does not operate as a waiver in a federal or state proceeding if:

(1) the disclosure is inadvertent;

(2) the holder of the privilege or protection took reasonable steps to prevent disclosure; and

(3) the holder promptly took reasonable steps to rectify the error, including (if applicable) following Federal Rule of Civil Procedure 26(b)(5)(B).

(c) Disclosure Made in a State Proceeding. When the disclosure is made in a state proceeding and is not the subject of a state-court order concerning waiver, the disclosure does not operate as a waiver in a federal proceeding if the disclosure:

(1) would not be a waiver under this rule if it had been made in a federal proceeding; or

(2) is not a waiver under the law of the state where the disclosure occurred.

(d) Controlling Effect of a Court Order. A federal court may order that the privilege or protection is not waived by disclosure connected with the litigation pending before the court—in which event the disclosure is also not a waiver in any other federal or state proceeding.

(e) Controlling Effect of a Party Agreement. An agreement on the effect of disclosure in a federal proceeding is binding only on the parties to the agreement, unless it is incorporated into a court order.

(f) Controlling Effect of This Rule. Notwithstanding Rules 101 and 1101, this rule applies to state proceedings and to federal court-annexed and federal court-mandated arbitration proceedings, in the circumstances set out in the rule. And notwithstanding Rule 501, this rule applies even if state law provides the rule of decision.

(g) Definitions. In this rule:

(1) "attorney-client privilege" means the protection that applicable law provides for confidential attorney-client communications; and

(2) "work-product protection" means the protection that applicable law provides for tangible material (or its intangible equivalent) prepared in anticipation of litigation or for trial.

(Pub.L. 110–322, § 1(a), Sept. 19, 2008, 122 Stat. 3537; Apr. 26, 2011, eff. Dec. 1, 2011.)

ARTICLE VI. WITNESSES

RULE 601. COMPETENCY TO TESTIFY IN GENERAL

Every person is competent to be a witness unless these rules provide otherwise. But in a civil case, state law governs the witness's competency regarding a claim or defense for which state law supplies the rule of decision.

(Pub.L. 93–595, § 1, Jan. 2, 1975, 88 Stat.1934; Apr. 26, 2011, eff. Dec. 1, 2011.)

RULE 602. NEED FOR PERSONAL KNOWLEDGE

A witness may testify to a matter only if evidence is introduced sufficient to support a finding that the witness has personal knowledge of the matter. Evidence to prove personal knowledge may consist of the witness's own testimony. This rule does not apply to a witness's expert testimony under Rule 703.

(Pub.L. 93–595, § 1, Jan. 2, 1975, 88 Stat. 1934; Mar. 2, 1987, eff. Oct. 1, 1987; Apr. 25, 1988, eff. Nov. 1, 1988; Apr. 26, 2011, eff. Dec. 1, 2011.)

RULE 603. OATH OR AFFIRMATION TO TESTIFY TRUTHFULLY

Before testifying, a witness must give an oath or affirmation to testify truthfully. It must be in a form designed to impress that duty on the witness's conscience.

(Pub.L. 93–595, § 1, Jan. 2, 1975, 88 Stat. 1934; Mar. 2, 1987, eff. Oct. 1, 1987; Apr. 26, 2011, eff. Dec. 1, 2011.)

RULE 604. INTERPRETER

An interpreter must be qualified and must give an oath or affirmation to make a true translation.

(Pub.L. 93–595, § 1, Jan. 2, 1975, 88 Stat. 1934; Mar. 2, 1987, eff. Oct. 1, 1987; Apr. 26, 2011, eff. Dec. 1, 2011.)

RULE 605. JUDGE'S COMPETENCY AS A WITNESS

The presiding judge may not testify as a witness at the trial. A party need not object to preserve the issue.

(Pub.L. 93–595, § 1, Jan. 2, 1975, 88 Stat. 1934; Apr. 26, 2011, eff. Dec. 1, 2011.)

RULE 606. JUROR'S COMPETENCY AS A WITNESS

(a) At the Trial. A juror may not testify as a witness before the other jurors at the trial. If a juror is called to testify, the court must give a party an opportunity to object outside the jury's presence.

(b) During an Inquiry Into the Validity of a Verdict or Indictment.

(1) Prohibited Testimony or Other Evidence. During an inquiry into the validity of a verdict or indictment, a juror may not testify about any statement made or incident that occurred during the jury's deliberations; the effect of anything on that juror's or another juror's vote; or any juror's mental processes concerning the verdict or indictment. The court may not receive a juror's affidavit or evidence of a juror's statement on these matters.

(2) Exceptions. A juror may testify about whether:

(A) extraneous prejudicial information was improperly brought to the jury's attention;

(B) an outside influence was improperly brought to bear on any juror; or

(C) a mistake was made in entering the verdict on the verdict form.

(Pub.L. 93–595, § 1, Jan. 2, 1975, 88 Stat. 1934; Pub.L. 94–149, § 1(10), Dec. 12, 1975, 89 Stat. 805; Mar. 2, 1987, eff. Oct. 1, 1987; Apr. 12, 2006, eff. Dec. 1, 2006; Apr. 26, 2011, eff. Dec. 1, 2011.)

RULE 607. WHO MAY IMPEACH A WITNESS

Any party, including the party that called the witness, may attack the witness's credibility.

(Pub.L. 93–595, § 1, Jan. 2, 1975, 88 Stat.1934; Mar. 2, 1987, eff. Oct. 1, 1987; Apr. 26, 2011, eff. Dec. 1, 2011.)

RULE 608. A WITNESS'S CHARACTER FOR TRUTHFULNESS OR UNTRUTHFULNESS

(a) Reputation or Opinion Evidence. A witness's credibility may be attacked or supported by testimony about the witness's reputation for having a character for truthfulness or untruthfulness, or by testimony in the form of an opinion about that character. But evidence of truthful character is admissible only after the witness's character for truthfulness has been attacked.

(b) Specific Instances of Conduct. Except for a criminal conviction under Rule 609, extrinsic evidence is not admissible to prove specific instances of a witness's conduct in order to attack or support the witness's character for truthfulness. But the court may, on cross-examination, allow them to be inquired into if they are probative of the character for truthfulness or untruthfulness of:

(1) the witness; or

(2) another witness whose character the witness being cross-examined has testified about.

By testifying on another matter, a witness does not waive any privilege against self-incrimination for testimony that relates only to the witness's character for truthfulness.

(Pub.L. 93–595, § 1, Jan. 2, 1975, 88 Stat.1935; Mar. 2, 1987, eff. Oct. 1, 1987; Apr. 25, 1988, eff. Nov. 1, 1988; Mar. 27, 2003, eff. Dec. 1, 2003; Apr. 26, 2011, eff. Dec. 1, 2011.)

RULE 609. IMPEACHMENT BY EVIDENCE OF A CRIMINAL CONVICTION

(a) In General. The following rules apply to attacking a witness's character for truthfulness by evidence of a criminal conviction:

(1) for a crime that, in the convicting jurisdiction, was punishable by death or by imprisonment for more than one year, the evidence:

(A) must be admitted, subject to Rule 403, in a civil case or in a criminal case in which the witness is not a defendant; and

(B) must be admitted in a criminal case in which the witness is a defendant, if the probative value of the evidence outweighs its prejudicial effect to that defendant; and

(2) for any crime regardless of the punishment, the evidence must be admitted if the court can readily determine that establishing the elements of the crime required proving—or the witness's admitting—a dishonest act or false statement.

(b) Limit on Using the Evidence After 10 Years. This subdivision (b) applies if more than 10 years have passed since the witness's conviction or release from confinement for it, whichever is later. Evidence of the conviction is admissible only if:

(1) its probative value, supported by specific facts and circumstances, substantially outweighs its prejudicial effect; and

(2) the proponent gives an adverse party reasonable written notice of the intent to use it so that the party has a fair opportunity to contest its use.

(c) Effect of a Pardon, Annulment, or Certificate of Rehabilitation. Evidence of a conviction is not admissible if:

(1) the conviction has been the subject of a pardon, annulment, certificate of rehabilitation, or other equivalent procedure based on a finding that the person has been rehabilitated, and the person has not been convicted of a later crime punishable by death or by imprisonment for more than one year; or

(2) the conviction has been the subject of a pardon, annulment, or other equivalent procedure based on a finding of innocence.

(d) Juvenile Adjudications. Evidence of a juvenile adjudication is admissible under this rule only if:

(1) it is offered in a criminal case;

(2) the adjudication was of a witness other than the defendant;

(3) an adult's conviction for that offense would be admissible to attack the adult's credibility; and

(4) admitting the evidence is necessary to fairly determine guilt or innocence.

(e) Pendency of an Appeal. A conviction that satisfies this rule is admissible even if an appeal is pending. Evidence of the pendency is also admissible.

(Pub.L. 93–595, § 1, Jan. 2, 1975, 88 Stat.1935; Mar. 2, 1987, eff. Oct. 1, 1987; Jan. 26, 1990, eff. Dec. 1, 1990; Apr. 12, 2006, eff. Dec. 1, 2006; Apr. 26, 2011, eff. Dec. 1, 2011.)

RULE 610. RELIGIOUS BELIEFS OR OPINIONS

Evidence of a witness's religious beliefs or opinions is not admissible to attack or support the witness's credibility.

(Pub.L. 93–595, § 1, Jan. 2, 1975, 88 Stat.1936; Mar. 2, 1987, eff. Oct. 1, 1987; Apr. 26, 2011, eff. Dec. 1, 2011.)

RULE 611. MODE AND ORDER OF EXAMINING WITNESSES AND PRESENTING EVIDENCE

(a) Control by the Court; Purposes. The court should exercise reasonable control over the mode and order of examining witnesses and presenting evidence so as to:

(1) make those procedures effective for determining the truth;

(2) avoid wasting time; and

(3) protect witnesses from harassment or undue embarrassment.

(b) Scope of Cross–Examination. Cross-examination should not go beyond the subject matter of the direct examination and matters affecting the witness's credibility. The court may allow inquiry into additional matters as if on direct examination.

(c) Leading Questions. Leading questions should not be used on direct examination except as necessary to develop the witness's testimony. Ordinarily, the court should allow leading questions:

(1) on cross-examination; and

(2) when a party calls a hostile witness, an adverse party, or a witness identified with an adverse party.

(Pub.L. 93–595, § 1, Jan. 2, 1975, 88 Stat. 1936; Mar. 2, 1987, eff. Oct. 1, 1987; Apr. 26, 2011, eff. Dec. 1, 2011.)

RULE 612. WRITING USED TO REFRESH A WITNESS'S MEMORY

(a) Scope. This rule gives an adverse party certain options when a witness uses a writing to refresh memory:

(1) while testifying; or

(2) before testifying, if the court decides that justice requires the party to have those options.

(b) Adverse Party's Options; Deleting Unrelated Matter. Unless 18 U.S.C. § 3500 provides otherwise in a criminal case, an adverse party is entitled to have the writing produced at the hearing, to inspect it, to cross-examine the witness about it, and to introduce in evidence any portion that relates to the witness's testimony. If the producing party claims that the writing includes unrelated matter, the court must examine the writing in camera, delete any unrelated portion, and order that the rest be delivered to the adverse party. Any portion deleted over objection must be preserved for the record.

(c) Failure to Produce or Deliver the Writing. If a writing is not produced or is not delivered as ordered, the court may issue any appropriate order. But if the prosecution does not comply in a criminal case, the court must strike the witness's testimony or—if justice so requires—declare a mistrial.

(Pub.L. 93–595, § 1, Jan. 2, 1975, 88 Stat. 1936; Mar. 2, 1987, eff. Oct. 1, 1987; Apr. 26, 2011, eff. Dec. 1, 2011.)

RULE 613. WITNESS'S PRIOR STATEMENT

(a) Showing or Disclosing the Statement During Examination. When examining a witness about the witness's prior statement, a party need not show it or disclose its contents to the witness. But the party must, on request, show it or disclose its contents to an adverse party's attorney.

(b) Extrinsic Evidence of a Prior Inconsistent Statement. Extrinsic evidence of a witness's prior inconsistent statement is admissible only if the witness is given an opportunity to explain or deny the statement and an adverse party is given an opportunity to examine the witness about it, or if justice so requires. This subdivision (b) does not apply to an opposing party's statement under Rule 801(d)(2).

(Pub.L. 93–595, § 1, Jan. 2, 1975, 88 Stat.1936; Mar. 2, 1987, eff. Oct. 1, 1987; Apr. 25, 1988, eff. Nov. 1, 1988; Apr. 26, 2011, eff. Dec. 1, 2011.)

RULE 614. COURT'S CALLING OR EXAMINING A WITNESS

(a) Calling. The court may call a witness on its own or at a party's request. Each party is entitled to cross-examine the witness.

(b) Examining. The court may examine a witness regardless of who calls the witness.

(c) Objections. A party may object to the court's calling or examining a witness either at that time or at the next opportunity when the jury is not present.

(Pub.L. 93–595, § 1, Jan. 2, 1975, 88 Stat.1937; Apr. 26, 2011, eff. Dec. 1, 2011.)

RULE 615. EXCLUDING WITNESSES

At a party's request, the court must order witnesses excluded so that they cannot hear other witnesses' testimony. Or the court may do so on its own. But this rule does not authorize excluding:

(a) a party who is a natural person;

(b) an officer or employee of a party that is not a natural person, after being designated as the party's representative by its attorney;

(c) a person whose presence a party shows to be essential to presenting the party's claim or defense; or

(d) a person authorized by statute to be present.

(Pub.L. 93–595, § 1, Jan. 2, 1975, 88 Stat.1937; Mar. 2, 1987, eff. Oct. 1, 1987; Apr. 25, 1988, eff. Nov. 1, 1988; Pub.L. 100–690, Nov. 18, 1988, Title VII, § 7075(a), 102 Stat. 4405; Apr. 24, 1998, eff. Dec. 1, 1998; Apr. 26, 2011, eff. Dec. 1, 2011.)

ARTICLE VII. OPINIONS AND EXPERT TESTIMONY

RULE 701. OPINION TESTIMONY BY LAY WITNESSES

If a witness is not testifying as an expert, testimony in the form of an opinion is limited to one that is:

(a) rationally based on the witness's perception;

(b) helpful to clearly understanding the witness's testimony or to determining a fact in issue; and

(c) not based on scientific, technical, or other specialized knowledge within the scope of Rule 702.

(Pub.L. 93–595, § 1, Jan. 2, 1975, 88 Stat.1937; Mar. 2, 1987, eff. Oct. 1, 1987; Apr. 17, 2000, eff. Dec. 1, 2000; Apr. 26, 2011, eff. Dec. 1, 2011.)

RULE 702. TESTIMONY BY EXPERT WITNESSES

A witness who is qualified as an expert by knowledge, skill, experience, training, or education may testify in the form of an opinion or otherwise if:

(a) the expert's scientific, technical, or other specialized knowledge will help the trier of fact to understand the evidence or to determine a fact in issue;

(b) the testimony is based on sufficient facts or data;

(c) the testimony is the product of reliable principles and methods; and

(d) the expert has reliably applied the principles and methods to the facts of the case.

(Pub.L. 93–595, § 1, Jan. 2, 1975, 88 Stat. 1937; Apr. 17, 2000, eff. Dec. 1, 2000; Apr. 26, 2011, eff. Dec. 1, 2011.)

RULE 703. BASES OF AN EXPERT'S OPINION TESTIMONY

An expert may base an opinion on facts or data in the case that the expert has been made aware of or personally observed. If experts in the particular field would reasonably rely on those kinds of facts or data in forming an opinion on the subject, they need not be admissible for the opinion to be admitted. But if the facts or data would otherwise be inadmissible, the proponent of the opinion may disclose them to the jury only if their probative value in helping the jury evaluate the opinion substantially outweighs their prejudicial effect.

(Pub.L. 93–595, § 1, Jan. 2, 1975, 88 Stat.1937; Mar. 2, 1987, eff. Oct. 1, 1987; Apr. 17, 2000, eff. Dec. 1, 2000; Apr. 26, 2011, eff. Dec. 1, 2011.)

RULE 704. OPINION ON AN ULTIMATE ISSUE

(a) In General—Not Automatically Objectionable. An opinion is not objectionable just because it embraces an ultimate issue.

(b) Exception. In a criminal case, an expert witness must not state an opinion about whether the defendant did or did not have a mental state or condition that constitutes an element of the crime charged or of a defense. Those matters are for the trier of fact alone.

(Pub.L. 93–595, § 1, Jan. 2, 1975, 88 Stat. 1937; Pub.L. 98–473, Title IV, § 406, Oct. 12, 1984, 98 Stat. 2067; Apr. 26, 2011, eff. Dec. 1, 2011.)

RULE 705. DISCLOSING THE FACTS OR DATA UNDERLYING AN EXPERT'S OPINION

Unless the court orders otherwise, an expert may state an opinion—and give the reasons for it—without first testifying to the underlying facts or data. But the expert may be required to disclose those facts or data on cross-examination.

(Pub.L. 93–595, § 1, Jan. 2, 1975, 88 Stat. 1938; Mar. 2, 1987, eff. Oct. 1, 1987; Apr. 22, 1993, eff. Dec. 1, 1993; Apr. 26, 2011, eff. Dec. 1, 2011.)

RULE 706. COURT-APPOINTED EXPERT WITNESSES

(a) Appointment Process. On a party's motion or on its own, the court may order the parties to show cause why expert witnesses should not be appointed and may ask the parties to submit nominations. The court may appoint any expert that the parties agree on and any of its own choosing. But the court may only appoint someone who consents to act.

(b) Expert's Role. The court must inform the expert of the expert's duties. The court may do so in writing and have a copy filed with the clerk or may do so orally at a conference in which the parties have an opportunity to participate. The expert:

(1) must advise the parties of any findings the expert makes;

(2) may be deposed by any party;

(3) may be called to testify by the court or any party; and

(4) may be cross-examined by any party, including the party that called the expert.

(c) Compensation. The expert is entitled to a reasonable compensation, as set by the court. The compensation is payable as follows:

(1) in a criminal case or in a civil case involving just compensation under the Fifth Amendment, from any funds that are provided by law; and

(2) in any other civil case, by the parties in the proportion and at the time that the court directs—and the compensation is then charged like other costs.

(d) Disclosing the Appointment to the Jury. The court may authorize disclosure to the jury that the court appointed the expert.

(e) Parties' Choice of Their Own Experts. This rule does not limit a party in calling its own experts.

(Pub.L. 93–595, § 1, Jan. 2, 1975, 88 Stat.1938; Mar. 2, 1987, eff. Oct. 1, 1987; Apr. 26, 2011, eff. Dec. 1, 2011.)

ARTICLE VIII. HEARSAY

RULE 801. DEFINITIONS THAT APPLY TO THIS ARTICLE; EXCLUSIONS FROM HEARSAY

(a) Statement. "Statement" means a person's oral assertion, written assertion, or nonverbal conduct, if the person intended it as an assertion.

(b) Declarant. "Declarant" means the person who made the statement.

(c) Hearsay. "Hearsay" means a statement that:

(1) the declarant does not make while testifying at the current trial or hearing; and

(2) a party offers in evidence to prove the truth of the matter asserted in the statement.

(d) Statements That Are Not Hearsay. A statement that meets the following conditions is not hearsay:

(1) A Declarant-Witness's Prior Statement. The declarant testifies and is subject to cross-examination about a prior statement, and the statement:

(A) is inconsistent with the declarant's testimony and was given under penalty of perjury at a trial, hearing, or other proceeding or in a deposition;

(B) is consistent with the declarant's testimony and is offered:

(i) to rebut an express or implied charge that the declarant recently fabricated it or acted from a recent improper influence or motive in so testifying; or

(ii) to rehabilitate the declarant's credibility as a witness when attacked on another ground; or

(C) identifies a person as someone the declarant perceived earlier.

(2) An Opposing Party's Statement. The statement is offered against an opposing party and:

(A) was made by the party in an individual or representative capacity;

(B) is one the party manifested that it adopted or believed to be true;

(C) was made by a person whom the party authorized to make a statement on the subject;

(D) was made by the party's agent or employee on a matter within the scope of that relationship and while it existed; or

(E) was made by the party's coconspirator during and in furtherance of the conspiracy.

The statement must be considered but does not by itself establish the declarant's authority under (C); the existence or scope of the relationship under (D); or the existence of the conspiracy or participation in it under (E).

(Pub.L. 93–595, § 1, Jan. 2, 1975, 88 Stat.1938; Pub.L. 94–113, § 1, Oct. 16, 1975, 89 Stat. 576; Mar. 2, 1987, eff. Oct. 1, 1987; Apr. 11, 1997, eff. Dec. 1, 1997; Apr. 26, 2011, eff. Dec. 1, 2011; Apr. 25, 2014, eff. Dec. 1, 2014.)

RULE 802. THE RULE AGAINST HEARSAY

Hearsay is not admissible unless any of the following provides otherwise:

- a federal statute;
- these rules; or
- other rules prescribed by the Supreme Court.

(Pub.L. 93–595, § 1, Jan. 2, 1975, 88 Stat. 1939; Apr. 26, 2011, eff. Dec. 1, 2011.)

RULE 803. EXCEPTIONS TO THE RULE AGAINST HEARSAY—REGARDLESS OF WHETHER THE DECLARANT IS AVAILABLE AS A WITNESS

The following are not excluded by the rule against hearsay, regardless of whether the declarant is available as a witness:

(1) Present Sense Impression. A statement describing or explaining an event or condition, made while or immediately after the declarant perceived it.

(2) Excited Utterance. A statement relating to a startling event or condition, made while the declarant was under the stress of excitement that it caused.

(3) Then-Existing Mental, Emotional, or Physical Condition. A statement of the declarant's then-existing state of mind (such as motive, intent, or plan) or emotional, sensory, or physical condition (such as mental feeling, pain, or bodily health), but not including a statement of memory or belief to prove the fact remembered or believed unless it relates to the validity or terms of the declarant's will.

(4) Statement Made for Medical Diagnosis or Treatment. A statement that:

(A) is made for—and is reasonably pertinent to—medical diagnosis or treatment; and

(B) describes medical history; past or present symptoms or sensations; their inception; or their general cause.

(5) Recorded Recollection. A record that:

(A) is on a matter the witness once knew about but now cannot recall well enough to testify fully and accurately;

(B) was made or adopted by the witness when the matter was fresh in the witness's memory; and

(C) accurately reflects the witness's knowledge.

If admitted, the record may be read into evidence but may be received as an exhibit only if offered by an adverse party.

(6) **Records of a Regularly Conducted Activity.** A record of an act, event, condition, opinion, or diagnosis if:

(A) the record was made at or near the time by—or from information transmitted by—someone with knowledge;

(B) the record was kept in the course of a regularly conducted activity of a business, organization, occupation, or calling, whether or not for profit;

(C) making the record was a regular practice of that activity;

(D) all these conditions are shown by the testimony of the custodian or another qualified witness, or by a certification that complies with Rule 902(11) or (12) or with a statute permitting certification; and

(E) the opponent does not show that the source of information or the method or circumstances of preparation indicate a lack of trustworthiness.

(7) **Absence of a Record of a Regularly Conducted Activity.** Evidence that a matter is not included in a record described in paragraph (6) if:

(A) the evidence is admitted to prove that the matter did not occur or exist;

(B) a record was regularly kept for a matter of that kind; and

(C) the opponent does not show that the possible source of the information or other circumstances indicate a lack of trustworthiness.

(8) **Public Records.** A record or statement of a public office if:

(A) it sets out:

(i) the office's activities;

(ii) a matter observed while under a legal duty to report, but not including, in a criminal case, a matter observed by law-enforcement personnel; or

(iii) in a civil case or against the government in a criminal case, factual findings from a legally authorized investigation; and

(B) the opponent does not show that the source of information or other circumstances indicate a lack of trustworthiness.

(9) **Public Records of Vital Statistics.** A record of a birth, death, or marriage, if reported to a public office in accordance with a legal duty.

(10) **Absence of a Public Record.** Testimony—or a certification under Rule 902—that a diligent search failed to disclose a public record or statement if:

(A) the testimony or certification is admitted to prove that

(i) the record or statement does not exist; or

(ii) a matter did not occur or exist, if a public office regularly kept a record or statement for a matter of that kind; and

(B) in a criminal case, a prosecutor who intends to offer a certification provides written notice of that intent at least 14 days before trial, and the defendant does not object in writing within 7 days of receiving the notice—unless the court sets a different time for the notice or the objection.

(11) **Records of Religious Organizations Concerning Personal or Family History.** A statement of birth, legitimacy, ancestry, marriage, divorce, death, relationship by blood or marriage, or similar facts of personal or family history, contained in a regularly kept record of a religious organization.

(12) **Certificates of Marriage, Baptism, and Similar Ceremonies.** A statement of fact contained in a certificate:

(A) made by a person who is authorized by a religious organization or by law to perform the act certified;

(B) attesting that the person performed a marriage or similar ceremony or administered a sacrament; and

(C) purporting to have been issued at the time of the act or within a reasonable time after it.

(13) **Family Records.** A statement of fact about personal or family history contained in a family record, such as a Bible, genealogy, chart, engraving on a ring, inscription on a portrait, or engraving on an urn or burial marker.

(14) **Records of Documents That Affect an Interest in Property.** The record of a document that purports to establish or affect an interest in property if:

(A) the record is admitted to prove the content of the original recorded document, along with its signing and its delivery by each person who purports to have signed it;

(B) the record is kept in a public office; and

(C) a statute authorizes recording documents of that kind in that office.

(15) **Statements in Documents That Affect an Interest in Property.** A statement contained in a document that purports to establish or affect an interest in property if the matter stated was relevant to the document's purpose—unless later dealings with the property are inconsistent with the truth of the statement or the purport of the document.

(16) **Statements in Ancient Documents.** A statement in a document that is at least 20 years old and whose authenticity is established.

(17) **Market Reports and Similar Commercial Publications.** Market quotations, lists, directories, or other compilations that are generally relied on by the public or by persons in particular occupations.

(18) **Statements in Learned Treatises, Periodicals, or Pamphlets.** A statement contained in a treatise, periodical, or pamphlet if:

(A) the statement is called to the attention of an expert witness on cross-examination or relied on by the expert on direct examination; and

(B) the publication is established as a reliable authority by the expert's admission or testimony, by another expert's testimony, or by judicial notice.

If admitted, the statement may be read into evidence but not received as an exhibit.

(19) **Reputation Concerning Personal or Family History.** A reputation among a person's family by blood, adoption, or marriage—or among a person's associates or in the community—concerning the person's birth, adoption, legitimacy, ancestry, marriage, divorce, death, relationship by blood, adoption, or marriage, or similar facts of personal or family history.

(20) **Reputation Concerning Boundaries or General History.** A reputation in a community—arising before the controversy—concerning boundaries of land in the community or customs that affect the land, or concerning general historical events important to that community, state, or nation.

(21) **Reputation Concerning Character.** A reputation among a person's associates or in the community concerning the person's character.

(22) **Judgment of a Previous Conviction.** Evidence of a final judgment of conviction if:

(A) the judgment was entered after a trial or guilty plea, but not a nolo contendere plea;

(B) the conviction was for a crime punishable by death or by imprisonment for more than a year;

(C) the evidence is admitted to prove any fact essential to the judgment; and

(D) when offered by the prosecutor in a criminal case for a purpose other than impeachment, the judgment was against the defendant.

The pendency of an appeal may be shown but does not affect admissibility.

(23) **Judgments Involving Personal, Family, or General History, or a Boundary.** A judgment that is admitted to prove a matter of personal, family, or general history, or boundaries, if the matter:

(A) was essential to the judgment; and

(B) could be proved by evidence of reputation.

(24) **[Other Exceptions.]** [Transferred to Rule 807.]

(Pub.L. 93–595, § 1, Jan. 2, 1975, 88 Stat. 1939; Pub.L. 94–149, § 1(11), Dec. 12, 1975, 89 Stat. 805; Mar. 2, 1987, eff. Oct. 1, 1987; Apr. 11, 1997, eff. Dec. 1, 1997; Apr. 17, 2000, eff. Dec. 1, 2000; Apr. 26, 2011, eff. Dec. 1, 2011; Apr. 16, 2013, eff. Dec. 1, 2013; Apr. 25, 2014, eff. Dec. 1, 2014.)

RULE 804. EXCEPTIONS TO THE RULE AGAINST HEARSAY—WHEN THE DECLARANT IS UNAVAILABLE AS A WITNESS

(a) **Criteria for Being Unavailable.** A declarant is considered to be unavailable as a witness if the declarant:

(1) is exempted from testifying about the subject matter of the declarant's statement because the court rules that a privilege applies;

(2) refuses to testify about the subject matter despite a court order to do so;

(3) testifies to not remembering the subject matter;

(4) cannot be present or testify at the trial or hearing because of death or a then-existing infirmity, physical illness, or mental illness; or

(5) is absent from the trial or hearing and the statement's proponent has not been able, by process or other reasonable means, to procure:

(A) the declarant's attendance, in the case of a hearsay exception under Rule 804(b)(1) or (6); or

(B) the declarant's attendance or testimony, in the case of a hearsay exception under Rule 804(b)(2), (3), or (4).

But this subdivision (a) does not apply if the statement's proponent procured or wrongfully caused the declarant's unavailability as a witness in order to prevent the declarant from attending or testifying.

(b) **The Exceptions.** The following are not excluded by the rule against hearsay if the declarant is unavailable as a witness:

(1) **Former Testimony.** Testimony that:

(A) was given as a witness at a trial, hearing, or lawful deposition, whether given during the current proceeding or a different one; and

(B) is now offered against a party who had—or, in a civil case, whose predecessor in interest had—an opportunity and similar motive to develop it by direct, cross-, or redirect examination.

(2) **Statement Under the Belief of Imminent Death.** In a prosecution for homicide or in a civil case, a statement that the declarant, while believing the declarant's death to be imminent, made about its cause or circumstances.

(3) **Statement Against Interest.** A statement that:

(A) a reasonable person in the declarant's position would have made only if the person believed it to be true because, when made, it was so contrary to the declarant's proprietary or pecuniary interest or had so great a tendency to invalidate the declarant's claim against someone else or to expose the declarant to civil or criminal liability; and

(B) is supported by corroborating circumstances that clearly indicate its trustworthiness, if it is offered in a criminal case as one that tends to expose the declarant to criminal liability.

(4) **Statement of Personal or Family History.** A statement about:

(A) the declarant's own birth, adoption, legitimacy, ancestry, marriage, divorce, relationship by blood, adoption, or marriage, or similar facts of personal or family history, even though the declarant had no way of acquiring personal knowledge about that fact; or

(B) another person concerning any of these facts, as well as death, if the declarant was related to the person by blood, adoption, or marriage or was so intimately associated with the person's family that the declarant's information is likely to be accurate.

(5) [Other Exceptions.] [Transferred to Rule 807.]

(6) Statement Offered Against a Party That Wrongfully Caused the Declarant's Unavailability. A statement offered against a party that wrongfully caused—or acquiesced in wrongfully causing—the declarant's unavailability as a witness, and did so intending that result.

(Pub.L. 93–595, § 1, Jan. 2, 1975, 88 Stat. 1942; Pub.L. 94–149, § 1(12), (13), Dec. 12, 1975, 89 Stat. 806; Mar. 2, 1987, eff. Oct. 1, 1987; Pub.L. 100–690, Title VII, § 7075(b), Nov. 18, 1988, 102 Stat. 4405; Apr. 11, 1997, eff. Dec. 1, 1997; Apr. 28, 2010, eff. Dec. 1, 2010; Apr. 26, 2011, eff. Dec. 1, 2011.)

RULE 805. HEARSAY WITHIN HEARSAY

Hearsay within hearsay is not excluded by the rule against hearsay if each part of the combined statements conforms with an exception to the rule.

(Pub.L. 93–595, § 1, Jan. 2, 1975, 88 Stat. 1943; Apr. 26, 2011, eff. Dec. 1, 2011.)

RULE 806. ATTACKING AND SUPPORTING THE DECLARANT'S CREDIBILITY

When a hearsay statement—or a statement described in Rule 801(d)(2)(C), (D), or (E)—has been admitted in evidence, the declarant's credibility may be attacked, and then supported, by any evidence that would be admissible for those purposes if the declarant had testified as a witness. The court may admit evidence of the declarant's inconsistent statement or conduct, regardless of when it occurred or whether the declarant had an opportunity to explain or deny it. If the party against whom the statement was admitted calls the declarant as a witness, the party may examine the declarant on the statement as if on cross-examination.

(Pub.L. 93–595, § 1, Jan. 2, 1975, 88 Stat. 1943; Mar. 2, 1987, eff. Oct. 1, 1987; Apr. 11, 1997, eff. Dec. 1, 1997; Apr. 26, 2011, eff. Dec. 1, 2011.)

RULE 807. RESIDUAL EXCEPTION

(a) In General. Under the following circumstances, a hearsay statement is not excluded by the rule against hearsay even if the statement is not specifically covered by a hearsay exception in Rule 803 or 804:

(1) the statement has equivalent circumstantial guarantees of trustworthiness;

(2) it is offered as evidence of a material fact;

(3) it is more probative on the point for which it is offered than any other evidence that the proponent can obtain through reasonable efforts; and

(4) admitting it will best serve the purposes of these rules and the interests of justice.

(b) Notice. The statement is admissible only if, before the trial or hearing, the proponent gives an adverse party reasonable notice of the intent to offer the statement and its particulars, including the declarant's name and address, so that the party has a fair opportunity to meet it.

(Added Apr. 11, 1997, eff. Dec. 1, 1997; Apr. 26, 2011, eff. Dec. 1, 2011.)

ARTICLE IX. AUTHENTICATION AND IDENTIFICATION

RULE 901. AUTHENTICATING OR IDENTIFYING EVIDENCE

(a) In General. To satisfy the requirement of authenticating or identifying an item of evidence, the proponent must produce evidence sufficient to support a finding that the item is what the proponent claims it is.

(b) Examples. The following are examples only—not a complete list—of evidence that satisfies the requirement:

(1) Testimony of a Witness with Knowledge. Testimony that an item is what it is claimed to be.

(2) Nonexpert Opinion About Handwriting. A nonexpert's opinion that handwriting is genuine, based on a familiarity with it that was not acquired for the current litigation.

(3) Comparison by an Expert Witness or the Trier of Fact. A comparison with an authenticated specimen by an expert witness or the trier of fact.

(4) Distinctive Characteristics and the Like. The appearance, contents, substance, internal patterns, or other distinctive characteristics of the item, taken together with all the circumstances.

(5) Opinion About a Voice. An opinion identifying a person's voice—whether heard firsthand or through mechanical or electronic transmission or recording—based on hearing the voice at any time under circumstances that connect it with the alleged speaker.

(6) Evidence About a Telephone Conversation. For a telephone conversation, evidence that a call was made to the number assigned at the time to:

(A) a particular person, if circumstances, including self-identification, show that the person answering was the one called; or

(B) a particular business, if the call was made to a business and the call related to business reasonably transacted over the telephone.

(7) Evidence About Public Records. Evidence that:

(A) a document was recorded or filed in a public office as authorized by law; or

(B) a purported public record or statement is from the office where items of this kind are kept.

(8) Evidence About Ancient Documents or Data Compilations. For a document or data compilation, evidence that it:

(A) is in a condition that creates no suspicion about its authenticity;

(B) was in a place where, if authentic, it would likely be; and

(C) is at least 20 years old when offered.

(9) Evidence About a Process or System. Evidence describing a process or system and showing that it produces an accurate result.

(10) Methods Provided by a Statute or Rule. Any method of authentication or identification allowed by a federal statute or a rule prescribed by the Supreme Court.

(Pub.L. 93–595, § 1, Jan. 2, 1975, 88 Stat.1943; Apr. 26, 2011, eff. Dec. 1, 2011.)

RULE 902. EVIDENCE THAT IS SELF-AUTHENTICATING

The following items of evidence are self-authenticating; they require no extrinsic evidence of authenticity in order to be admitted:

(1) Domestic Public Documents That Are Sealed and Signed. A document that bears:

(A) a seal purporting to be that of the United States; any state, district, commonwealth, territory, or insular possession of the United States; the former Panama Canal Zone; the Trust Territory of the Pacific Islands; a political subdivision of any of these entities; or a department, agency, or officer of any entity named above; and

(B) a signature purporting to be an execution or attestation.

(2) Domestic Public Documents That Are Not Sealed but Are Signed and Certified. A document that bears no seal if:

(A) it bears the signature of an officer or employee of an entity named in Rule 902(1)(A); and

(B) another public officer who has a seal and official duties within that same entity certifies under seal—or its equivalent—that the signer has the official capacity and that the signature is genuine.

(3) Foreign Public Documents. A document that purports to be signed or attested by a person who is authorized by a foreign country's law to do so. The document must be accompanied by a final certification that certifies the genuineness of the signature and official position of the signer or attester—or of any foreign official whose certificate of genuineness relates to the signature or attestation or is in a chain of certificates of genuineness relating to the signature or attestation. The certification may be made by a secretary of a United States embassy or legation; by a consul general, vice consul, or consular agent of the United States; or by a diplomatic or consular official of the foreign country assigned or accredited to the United States. If all parties have been given a reasonable opportunity to investigate the document's authenticity and accuracy, the court may, for good cause, either:

(A) order that it be treated as presumptively authentic without final certification; or

(B) allow it to be evidenced by an attested summary with or without final certification.

(4) Certified Copies of Public Records. A copy of an official record—or a copy of a document that was recorded or filed in a public office as authorized by law—if the copy is certified as correct by:

(A) the custodian or another person authorized to make the certification; or

(B) a certificate that complies with Rule 902(1), (2), or (3), a federal statute, or a rule prescribed by the Supreme Court.

(5) Official Publications. A book, pamphlet, or other publication purporting to be issued by a public authority.

(6) Newspapers and Periodicals. Printed material purporting to be a newspaper or periodical.

(7) Trade Inscriptions and the Like. An inscription, sign, tag, or label purporting to have been affixed in the course of business and indicating origin, ownership, or control.

(8) Acknowledged Documents. A document accompanied by a certificate of acknowledgment that is lawfully executed by a notary public or another officer who is authorized to take acknowledgments.

(9) Commercial Paper and Related Documents. Commercial paper, a signature on it, and related documents, to the extent allowed by general commercial law.

(10) Presumptions Under a Federal Statute. A signature, document, or anything else that a federal statute declares to be presumptively or prima facie genuine or authentic.

(11) Certified Domestic Records of a Regularly Conducted Activity. The original or a copy of a domestic record that meets the requirements of Rule 803(6)(A)–(C), as shown by a certification of the custodian or another qualified person that complies with a federal statute or a rule prescribed by the Supreme Court. Before the trial or hearing, the proponent must give an adverse party reasonable written notice of the intent to offer the record—and must make the record and certification available for inspection—so that the party has a fair opportunity to challenge them.

(12) Certified Foreign Records of a Regularly Conducted Activity. In a civil case, the original or a copy of a foreign record that meets the requirements of Rule 902(11), modified as follows: the certification, rather than complying with a federal statute or Supreme Court rule, must be signed in a manner that, if falsely made, would subject the maker to a criminal penalty in the country where the certification is signed. The proponent must also meet the notice requirements of Rule 902(11).

(Pub.L. 93–595, § 1, Jan. 2, 1975, 88 Stat. 1944; Mar. 2, 1987, eff. Oct. 1, 1987; Apr. 25, 1988, eff. Nov. 1, 1988; Apr. 17, 2000, eff. Dec. 1, 2000; Apr. 26, 2011, eff. Dec. 1, 2011.)

RULE 903. SUBSCRIBING WITNESS'S TESTIMONY

A subscribing witness's testimony is necessary to authenticate a writing only if required by the law of the jurisdiction that governs its validity.

(Pub.L. 93–595, § 1, Jan. 2, 1975, 88 Stat.1945; Apr. 26, 2011, eff. Dec. 1, 2011.)

ARTICLE X. CONTENTS OF WRITINGS, RECORDINGS, AND PHOTOGRAPHS

RULE 1001. DEFINITIONS THAT APPLY TO THIS ARTICLE

In this article:

(a) A "writing" consists of letters, words, numbers, or their equivalent set down in any form.

(b) A "recording" consists of letters, words, numbers, or their equivalent recorded in any manner.

(c) A "photograph" means a photographic image or its equivalent stored in any form.

(d) An "original" of a writing or recording means the writing or recording itself or any counterpart intended to have the same effect by the person who executed or issued it. For electronically stored information, "original" means any printout—or other output readable by sight—if it accurately reflects the information. An "original" of a photograph includes the negative or a print from it.

(e) A "duplicate" means a counterpart produced by a mechanical, photographic, chemical, electronic, or other equivalent process or technique that accurately reproduces the original.

(Pub.L. 93–595, § 1, Jan. 2, 1975, 88 Stat. 1945; Apr. 26, 2011, eff. Dec. 1, 2011.)

RULE 1002. REQUIREMENT OF THE ORIGINAL

An original writing, recording, or photograph is required in order to prove its content unless these rules or a federal statute provides otherwise.

(Pub.L. 93–595, § 1, Jan. 2, 1975, 88 Stat. 1946; Apr. 26, 2011, eff. Dec. 1, 2011.)

RULE 1003. ADMISSIBILITY OF DUPLICATES

A duplicate is admissible to the same extent as the original unless a genuine question is raised about the original's authenticity or the circumstances make it unfair to admit the duplicate.

(Pub.L. 93–595, § 1, Jan. 2, 1975, 88 Stat. 1946; Apr. 26, 2011, eff. Dec. 1, 2011.)

RULE 1004. ADMISSIBILITY OF OTHER EVIDENCE OF CONTENT

An original is not required and other evidence of the content of a writing, recording, or photograph is admissible if:

(a) all the originals are lost or destroyed, and not by the proponent acting in bad faith;

(b) an original cannot be obtained by any available judicial process;

(c) the party against whom the original would be offered had control of the original; was at that time put on notice, by pleadings or otherwise, that the original would be a subject of proof at the trial or hearing; and fails to produce it at the trial or hearing; or

(d) the writing, recording, or photograph is not closely related to a controlling issue.

(Pub.L. 93–595, § 1, Jan. 2, 1975, 88 Stat. 1946; Mar. 2, 1987, eff. Oct. 1, 1987; Apr. 26, 2011, eff. Dec. 1, 2011.)

RULE 1005. COPIES OF PUBLIC RECORDS TO PROVE CONTENT

The proponent may use a copy to prove the content of an official record—or of a document that was recorded or filed in a public office as authorized by law—if these conditions are met: the record or document is otherwise admissible; and the copy is certified as correct in accordance with Rule 902(4) or is testified to be correct by a witness who has compared it with the original. If no such copy can be obtained by reasonable diligence, then the proponent may use other evidence to prove the content.

(Pub.L. 93–595, § 1, Jan. 2, 1975, 88 Stat. 1946; Apr. 26, 2011, eff. Dec. 1, 2011.)

RULE 1006. SUMMARIES TO PROVE CONTENT

The proponent may use a summary, chart, or calculation to prove the content of voluminous writings, recordings, or photographs that cannot be conveniently examined in court. The proponent must make the originals or duplicates available for examination or copying, or both, by other parties at a reasonable time and place. And the court may order the proponent to produce them in court.

(Pub.L. 93–595, § 1, Jan. 2, 1975, 88 Stat. 1946; Apr. 26, 2011, eff. Dec. 1, 2011.)

RULE 1007. TESTIMONY OR STATEMENT OF A PARTY TO PROVE CONTENT

The proponent may prove the content of a writing, recording, or photograph by the testimony, deposition, or written statement of the party against whom the evidence is offered. The proponent need not account for the original.

(Pub.L. 93–595, § 1, Jan. 2, 1975, 88 Stat. 1947; Mar. 2, 1987, eff. Oct. 1, 1987; Apr. 26, 2011, eff. Dec. 1, 2011.)

RULE 1008. FUNCTIONS OF THE COURT AND JURY

Ordinarily, the court determines whether the proponent has fulfilled the factual conditions for admitting other evidence of the content of a writing, recording, or photograph under Rule 1004 or 1005. But in a jury trial, the jury determines—in accordance with Rule 104(b)—any issue about whether:

(a) an asserted writing, recording, or photograph ever existed;

(b) another one produced at the trial or hearing is the original; or

(c) other evidence of content accurately reflects the content.

(Pub.L. 93–595, § 1, Jan. 2, 1975, 88 Stat. 1947; Apr. 26, 2011, eff. Dec. 1, 2011.)

ARTICLE XI. MISCELLANEOUS RULES

RULE 1101. APPLICABILITY OF THE RULES

(a) To Courts and Judges. These rules apply to proceedings before:

- United States district courts;
- United States bankruptcy and magistrate judges;
- United States courts of appeals;
- the United States Court of Federal Claims; and
- the district courts of Guam, the Virgin Islands, and the Northern Mariana Islands.

(b) To Cases and Proceedings. These rules apply in:

- civil cases and proceedings, including bankruptcy, admiralty, and maritime cases;
- criminal cases and proceedings; and
- contempt proceedings, except those in which the court may act summarily.

(c) Rules on Privilege. The rules on privilege apply to all stages of a case or proceeding.

(d) Exceptions. These rules—except for those on privilege—do not apply to the following:

(1) the court's determination, under Rule 104(a), on a preliminary question of fact governing admissibility;

(2) grand-jury proceedings; and

(3) miscellaneous proceedings such as:

- extradition or rendition;
- issuing an arrest warrant, criminal summons, or search warrant;
- a preliminary examination in a criminal case;
- sentencing;
- granting or revoking probation or supervised release; and
- considering whether to release on bail or otherwise.

(e) Other Statutes and Rules. A federal statute or a rule prescribed by the Supreme Court may provide for admitting or excluding evidence independently from these rules.

(Pub.L. 93–595, § 1, Jan. 2, 1975, 88 Stat. 1947; Pub.L. 94–149, § 1(14), Dec. 12, 1975, 89 Stat. 806; Pub.L. 95–598, Title II, § 251, Nov. 6, 1978, 92 Stat. 2673; Pub.L. 97–164, Title I, § 142, Apr. 2, 1982, 96 Stat. 45; Mar. 2, 1987, eff. Oct. 1, 1987; Apr. 25, 1988, eff. Nov. 1, 1988; Pub.L. 100–690, Title VII, § 7075(c), Nov. 18, 1988, 102 Stat. 4405; Apr. 22, 1993, eff. Dec. 1, 1993; Apr. 26, 2011, eff. Dec. 1, 2011.)

RULE 1102. AMENDMENTS

These rules may be amended as provided in 28 U.S.C. § 2072.

(Pub.L. 93–595, § 1, Jan. 2, 1975, 88 Stat.1948; Apr. 30, 1991, eff. Dec. 1, 1991; Apr. 26, 2011, eff. Dec. 1, 2011.)

RULE 1103. TITLE

These rules may be cited as the Federal Rules of Evidence.

(Pub.L. 93–595, § 1, Jan. 2, 1975, 88 Stat.1948; Apr. 26, 2011, eff. Dec. 1, 2011.)

INDEX TO FEDERAL RULES OF EVIDENCE

FEDERAL RULES OF APPELLATE PROCEDURE

Including Amendments Effective December 1, 2016

TITLE I. APPLICABILITY OF RULES

RULE 1. SCOPE OF RULES; DEFINITION; TITLE

(a) Scope of Rules.

(1) These rules govern procedure in the United States courts of appeals.

(2) When these rules provide for filing a motion or other document in the district court, the procedure must comply with the practice of the district court.

(b) Definition. In these rules, "state" includes the District of Columbia and any United States commonwealth or territory.

(c) Title. These rules are to be known as the Federal Rules of Appellate Procedure.

(As amended Apr. 30, 1979, eff. Aug. 1, 1979; Apr. 25, 1989, eff. Dec. 1, 1989; Apr. 29, 1994, eff. Dec. 1, 1994; Apr. 24, 1998, eff. Dec. 1, 1998; Apr. 29, 2002, eff. Dec. 1, 2002; Apr. 28, 2010, eff. Dec. 1, 2010.)

RULE 2. SUSPENSION OF RULES

On its own or a party's motion, a court of appeals may—to expedite its decision or for other good cause—suspend any provision of these rules in a particular case and order proceedings as it directs, except as otherwise provided in Rule 26(b).

(As amended Apr. 24, 1998, eff. Dec. 1, 1998.)

TITLE II. APPEAL FROM A JUDGMENT OR ORDER OF A DISTRICT COURT

RULE 3. APPEAL AS OF RIGHT—HOW TAKEN

(a) Filing the Notice of Appeal.

(1) An appeal permitted by law as of right from a district court to a court of appeals may be taken only by filing a notice of appeal with the district clerk within the time allowed by Rule 4. At the time of filing, the appellant must furnish the clerk with enough copies of the notice to enable the clerk to comply with Rule 3(d).

(2) An appellant's failure to take any step other than the timely filing of a notice of appeal does not affect the validity of the appeal, but is ground only for the court of appeals to act as it considers appropriate, including dismissing the appeal.

(3) An appeal from a judgment by a magistrate judge in a civil case is taken in the same way as an appeal from any other district court judgment.

(4) An appeal by permission under 28 U.S.C. § 1292(b) or an appeal in a bankruptcy case may be taken only in the manner prescribed by Rules 5 and 6, respectively.

(b) Joint or Consolidated Appeals.

(1) When two or more parties are entitled to appeal from a district-court judgment or order, and their interests make joinder practicable, they may file a joint notice of appeal. They may then proceed on appeal as a single appellant.

(2) When the parties have filed separate timely notices of appeal, the appeals may be joined or consolidated by the court of appeals.

(c) Contents of the Notice of Appeal.

(1) The notice of appeal must:

(A) specify the party or parties taking the appeal by naming each one in the caption or body of the notice, but an attorney representing more than one party may describe those parties with such terms as "all plaintiffs," "the defendants," "the plaintiffs A, B, et al.," or "all defendants except X";

(B) designate the judgment, order, or part thereof being appealed; and

(C) name the court to which the appeal is taken.

(2) A pro se notice of appeal is considered filed on behalf of the signer and the signer's spouse and minor children (if they are parties), unless the notice clearly indicates otherwise.

(3) In a class action, whether or not the class has been certified, the notice of appeal is sufficient if it names one person qualified to bring the appeal as representative of the class.

(4) An appeal must not be dismissed for informality of form or title of the notice of appeal, or for failure to name a party whose intent to appeal is otherwise clear from the notice.

(5) Form 1 in the Appendix of Forms is a suggested form of a notice of appeal.

(d) Serving the Notice of Appeal.

(1) The district clerk must serve notice of the filing of a notice of appeal by mailing a copy to each party's counsel of record—excluding the appellant's—or, if a party is proceeding pro se, to the party's last known address. When a defendant in a criminal case appeals, the clerk must also serve a copy of the notice of appeal on the defendant, either by personal service or by mail addressed to the defendant. The clerk must promptly send a copy of the notice of appeal and of the docket entries—and any later docket entries—to the clerk of the court of appeals named in the notice. The district clerk must note, on each copy, the date when the notice of appeal was filed.

(2) If an inmate confined in an institution files a notice of appeal in the manner provided by Rule 4(c), the district clerk must also note the date when the clerk docketed the notice.

(3) The district clerk's failure to serve notice does not affect the validity of the appeal. The clerk must note on the docket the names of the parties to whom the clerk mails

copies, with the date of mailing. Service is sufficient despite the death of a party or the party's counsel.

(e) Payment of Fees. Upon filing a notice of appeal, the appellant must pay the district clerk all required fees. The district clerk receives the appellate docket fee on behalf of the court of appeals.

(As amended Apr. 30, 1979, eff. Aug. 1, 1979; Mar. 10, 1986, eff. July 1, 1986; Apr. 25, 1989, eff. Dec. 1, 1989; Apr. 22, 1993, eff. Dec. 1, 1993; Apr. 29, 1994, eff. Dec. 1, 1994; Apr. 24, 1998, eff. Dec. 1, 1998.)

[RULE 3.1 APPEAL FROM A JUDGMENT OF A MAGISTRATE JUDGE IN A CIVIL CASE (ABROGATED APR. 24, 1998, EFF. DEC. 1, 1998)]

RULE 4. APPEAL AS OF RIGHT—WHEN TAKEN

(a) Appeal in a Civil Case.

(1) Time for Filing a Notice of Appeal.

(A) In a civil case, except as provided in Rules 4(a)(1)(B), 4(a)(4), and 4(c), the notice of appeal required by Rule 3 must be filed with the district clerk within 30 days after entry of the judgment or order appealed from.

(B) The notice of appeal may be filed by any party within 60 days after entry of the judgment or order appealed from if one of the parties is:

(i) the United States;

(ii) a United States agency;

(iii) a United States officer or employee sued in an official capacity; or

(iv) a current or former United States officer or employee sued in an individual capacity for an act or omission occurring in connection with duties performed on the United States' behalf—including all instances in which the United States represents that person when the judgment or order is entered or files the appeal for that person.

(C) An appeal from an order granting or denying an application for a writ of error coram nobis is an appeal in a civil case for purposes of Rule 4(a).

(2) Filing Before Entry of Judgment. A notice of appeal filed after the court announces a decision or order—but before the entry of the judgment or order—is treated as filed on the date of and after the entry.

(3) Multiple Appeals. If one party timely files a notice of appeal, any other party may file a notice of appeal within 14 days after the date when the first notice was filed, or within the time otherwise prescribed by this Rule 4(a), whichever period ends later.

(4) Effect of a Motion on a Notice of Appeal.

(A) If a party files in the district court any of the following motions under the Federal Rules of Civil Procedure—and does so within the time allowed by those rules—the time to file an appeal runs for all parties from the entry of the order disposing of the last such remaining motion:

(i) for judgment under Rule 50(b);

(ii) to amend or make additional factual findings under Rule 52(b), whether or not granting the motion would alter the judgment;

(iii) for attorney's fees under Rule 54 if the district court extends the time to appeal under Rule 58;

(iv) to alter or amend the judgment under Rule 59;

(v) for a new trial under Rule 59; or

(vi) for relief under Rule 60 if the motion is filed no later than 28 days after the judgment is entered.

(B)(i) If a party files a notice of appeal after the court announces or enters a judgment—but before it disposes of any motion listed in Rule 4(a)(4)(A)—the notice becomes effective to appeal a judgment or order, in whole or in part, when the order disposing of the last such remaining motion is entered.

(ii)* A party intending to challenge an order disposing of any motion listed in Rule 4(a)(4)(A), or a judgment's alteration or amendment upon such a motion, must file a notice of appeal, or an amended notice of appeal—in compliance with Rule 3(c)—within the time prescribed by this Rule measured from the entry of the order disposing of the last such remaining motion.

(5) Motion for Extension of Time.

(A) The district court may extend the time to file a notice of appeal if:

(i) a party so moves no later than 30 days after the time prescribed by this Rule 4(a) expires; and

(ii) regardless of whether its motion is filed before or during the 30 days after the time prescribed by this Rule 4(a) expires, that party shows excusable neglect or good cause.

(B) A motion filed before the expiration of the time prescribed in Rule 4(a)(1) or (3) may be ex parte unless the court requires otherwise. If the motion is filed after the expiration of the prescribed time, notice must be given to the other parties in accordance with local rules.

(C) No extension under this Rule 4(a)(5) may exceed 30 days after the prescribed time or 14 days after the date when the order granting the motion is entered, whichever is later.

(6) Reopening the Time to File an Appeal. The district court may reopen the time to file an appeal for a period of 14 days after the date when its order to reopen is entered, but only if all the following conditions are satisfied:

(A) the court finds that the moving party did not receive notice under Federal Rule of Civil Procedure 77(d) of the entry of the judgment or order sought to be appealed within 21 days after entry;

(B) the motion is filed within 180 days after the judgment or order is entered or within 14 days after the moving party receives notice under Federal Rule of Civil Procedure 77(d) of the entry, whichever is earlier; and

(C) the court finds that no party would be prejudiced.

(7) Entry Defined.

(A) A judgment or order is entered for purposes of this Rule 4(a):

(i) if Federal Rule of Civil Procedure 58(a) does not require a separate document, when the judgment or order is entered in the civil docket under Federal Rule of Civil Procedure 79(a); or

(ii) if Federal Rule of Civil Procedure 58(a) requires a separate document, when the judgment or order is entered in the civil docket under Federal Rule of Civil Procedure 79(a) and when the earlier of these events occurs:

- the judgment or order is set forth on a separate document, or
- 150 days have run from entry of the judgment or order in the civil docket under Federal Rule of Civil Procedure 79(a).

(B) A failure to set forth a judgment or order on a separate document when required by Federal Rule of Civil Procedure 58(a) does not affect the validity of an appeal from that judgment or order.

(b) Appeal in a Criminal Case.

(1) Time for Filing a Notice of Appeal.

(A) In a criminal case, a defendant's notice of appeal must be filed in the district court within 14 days after the later of:

(i) the entry of either the judgment or the order being appealed; or

(ii) the filing of the government's notice of appeal.

(B) When the government is entitled to appeal, its notice of appeal must be filed in the district court within 30 days after the later of:

(i) the entry of the judgment or order being appealed; or

(ii) the filing of a notice of appeal by any defendant.

(2) Filing Before Entry of Judgment. A notice of appeal filed after the court announces a decision, sentence, or order—but before the entry of the judgment or order—is treated as filed on the date of and after the entry.

(3) Effect of a Motion on a Notice of Appeal.

(A) If a defendant timely makes any of the following motions under the Federal Rules of Criminal Procedure, the notice of appeal from a judgment of conviction must be filed within 14 days after the entry of the order disposing of the last such remaining motion, or within 14 days after the entry of the judgment of conviction, whichever period ends later. This provision applies to a timely motion:

(i) for judgment of acquittal under Rule 29;

(ii) for a new trial under Rule 33, but if based on newly discovered evidence, only if the motion is made no later than 14 days after the entry of the judgment; or

(iii) for arrest of judgment under Rule 34.

(B) A notice of appeal filed after the court announces a decision, sentence, or order—but before it disposes of any of the motions referred to in Rule 4(b)(3)(A)—becomes effective upon the later of the following:

(i) the entry of the order disposing of the last such remaining motion; or

(ii) the entry of the judgment of conviction.

(C) A valid notice of appeal is effective—without amendment—to appeal from an order disposing of any of the motions referred to in Rule 4(b)(3)(A).

(4) Motion for Extension of Time. Upon a finding of excusable neglect or good cause, the district court may—before or after the time has expired, with or without motion and notice—extend the time to file a notice of appeal for a period not to exceed 30 days from the expiration of the time otherwise prescribed by this Rule 4(b).

(5) Jurisdiction. The filing of a notice of appeal under this Rule 4(b) does not divest a district court of jurisdiction to correct a sentence under Federal Rule of Criminal Procedure 35(a), nor does the filing of a motion under 35(a) affect the validity of a notice of appeal filed before entry of the order disposing of the motion. The filing of a motion under Federal Rule of Criminal Procedure 35(a) does not suspend the time for filing a notice of appeal from a judgment of conviction.

(6) Entry Defined. A judgment or order is entered for purposes of this Rule 4(b) when it is entered on the criminal docket.

(c) Appeal by an Inmate Confined in an Institution.

(1) If an institution has a system designed for legal mail, an inmate confined there must use that system to receive the benefit of this Rule 4(c)(1). If an inmate files a notice of appeal in either a civil or a criminal case, the notice is timely if it is deposited in the institution's internal mail system on or before the last day for filing and:

(A) it is accompanied by:

(i) a declaration in compliance with 28 U.S.C. § 1746—or a notarized statement—setting out the date of deposit and stating that first-class postage is being prepaid; or

(ii) evidence (such as a postmark or date stamp) showing that the notice was so deposited and that postage was prepaid; or

(B) the court of appeals exercises its discretion to permit the later filing of a declaration or notarized statement that satisfies Rule 4(c)(1)(A)(i).

(2) If an inmate files the first notice of appeal in a civil case under this Rule 4(c), the 14-day period provided in Rule 4(a)(3) for another party to file a notice of appeal runs from the date when the district court dockets the first notice.

(3) When a defendant in a criminal case files a notice of appeal under this Rule 4(c), the 30-day period for the government to file its notice of appeal runs from the entry of the judgment or order appealed from or from the district

court's docketing of the defendant's notice of appeal, whichever is later.

(d) Mistaken Filing in the Court of Appeals. If a notice of appeal in either a civil or a criminal case is mistakenly filed in the court of appeals, the clerk of that court must note on the notice the date when it was received and send it to the district clerk. The notice is then considered filed in the district court on the date so noted.

(As amended Apr. 30, 1979, eff. Aug. 1, 1979; Nov. 18, 1988, Pub.L. 100–690, Title VII, § 7111, 102 Stat. 4419; Apr. 30, 1991, eff. Dec. 1, 1991; Apr. 22, 1993, eff. Dec. 1, 1993; Apr. 27, 1995, eff. Dec. 1, 1995; Apr. 24, 1998, eff. Dec. 1, 1998; Apr. 29, 2002, eff. Dec. 1, 2002; Apr. 25, 2005, eff. Dec. 1, 2005; Mar. 26, 2009, eff. Dec. 1, 2009; Apr. 28, 2010, eff. Dec. 1, 2010; Apr. 26, 2011, eff. Dec. 1, 2011; Apr. 28, 2016, eff. Dec. 1, 2016.)

* **[Publisher's Note:** Subdivision (a)(4)(B)(iii) was omitted in the 2009 Order of the Supreme Court amending this Rule. Prior thereto, (a)(4)(B)(iii) read:

"(iii) No additional fee is required to file an amended notice."]

RULE 5. APPEAL BY PERMISSION

(a) Petition for Permission to Appeal.

(1) To request permission to appeal when an appeal is within the court of appeals' discretion, a party must file a petition for permission to appeal. The petition must be filed with the circuit clerk with proof of service on all other parties to the district-court action.

(2) The petition must be filed within the time specified by the statute or rule authorizing the appeal or, if no such time is specified, within the time provided by Rule 4(a) for filing a notice of appeal.

(3) If a party cannot petition for appeal unless the district court first enters an order granting permission to do so or stating that the necessary conditions are met, the district court may amend its order, either on its own or in response to a party's motion, to include the required permission or statement. In that event, the time to petition runs from entry of the amended order.

(b) Contents of the Petition; Answer or Cross-Petition; Oral Argument.

(1) The petition must include the following:

(A) the facts necessary to understand the question presented;

(B) the question itself;

(C) the relief sought;

(D) the reasons why the appeal should be allowed and is authorized by a statute or rule; and

(E) an attached copy of:

(i) the order, decree, or judgment complained of and any related opinion or memorandum, and

(ii) any order stating the district court's permission to appeal or finding that the necessary conditions are met.

(2) A party may file an answer in opposition or a cross-petition within 10 days after the petition is served.

(3) The petition and answer will be submitted without oral argument unless the court of appeals orders otherwise.

(c) Form of Papers; Number of Copies; Length Limits. All papers must conform to Rule 32(c)(2). An original and 3 copies must be filed unless the court requires a different number by local rule or by order in a particular case. Except by the court's permission, and excluding the accompanying documents required by Rule 5(b)(1)(E):

(1) a paper produced using a computer must not exceed 5,200 words; and

(2) a handwritten or typewritten paper must not exceed 20 pages.

(d) Grant of Permission; Fees; Cost Bond; Filing the Record.

(1) Within 14 days after the entry of the order granting permission to appeal, the appellant must:

(A) pay the district clerk all required fees; and

(B) file a cost bond if required under Rule 7.

(2) A notice of appeal need not be filed. The date when the order granting permission to appeal is entered serves as the date of the notice of appeal for calculating time under these rules.

(3) The district clerk must notify the circuit clerk once the petitioner has paid the fees. Upon receiving this notice, the circuit clerk must enter the appeal on the docket. The record must be forwarded and filed in accordance with Rules 11 and 12(c).

(As amended Apr. 30, 1979, eff. Aug. 1, 1979; Apr. 29, 1994, eff. Dec. 1, 1994; Apr. 24, 1998, eff. Dec. 1, 1998; Apr. 29, 2002, eff. Dec. 1, 2002; Mar. 26, 2009, eff. Dec. 1, 2009; Apr. 28, 2016, eff. Dec. 1, 2016.)

[RULE 5.1 APPEAL BY LEAVE UNDER 28 U.S.C. § 636(C)(5) (ABROGATED APR. 24, 1998, EFF. DEC. 1, 1998)]

RULE 6. APPEAL IN A BANKRUPTCY CASE

(a) Appeal From a Judgment, Order, or Decree of a District Court Exercising Original Jurisdiction in a Bankruptcy Case. An appeal to a court of appeals from a final judgment, order, or decree of a district court exercising jurisdiction under 28 U.S.C. § 1334 is taken as any other civil appeal under these rules.

(b) Appeal From a Judgment, Order, or Decree of a District Court or Bankruptcy Appellate Panel Exercising Appellate Jurisdiction in a Bankruptcy Case.

(1) **Applicability of Other Rules.** These rules apply to an appeal to a court of appeals under 28 U.S.C. § 158(d)(1) from a final judgment, order, or decree of a district court or bankruptcy appellate panel exercising appellate jurisdiction under 28 U.S.C. § 158(a) or (b), but with these qualifications:

(A) Rules 4(a)(4), 4(b), 9, 10, 11, 12(c), 13–20, 22–23, and 24(b) do not apply;

(B) the reference in Rule 3(c) to "Form 1 in the Appendix of Forms" must be read as a reference to Form 5;

(C) when the appeal is from a bankruptcy appellate panel, "district court," as used in any applicable rule, means "appellate panel"; and

(D) in Rule 12.1, "district court" includes a bankruptcy court or bankruptcy appellate panel.

(2) **Additional Rules.** In addition to the rules made applicable by Rule 6(b)(1), the following rules apply:

(A) **Motion for Rehearing.**

(i) If a timely motion for rehearing under Bankruptcy Rule 8022 is filed, the time to appeal for all parties runs from the entry of the order disposing of the motion. A notice of appeal filed after the district court or bankruptcy appellate panel announces or enters a judgment, order, or decree—but before disposition of the motion for rehearing—becomes effective when the order disposing of the motion for rehearing is entered.

(ii) If a party intends to challenge the order disposing of the motion—or the alteration or amendment of a judgment, order, or decree upon the motion—then the party, in compliance with Rules 3(c) and 6(b)(1)(B), must file a notice of appeal or amended notice of appeal. The notice or amended notice must be filed within the time prescribed by Rule 4—excluding Rules 4(a)(4) and 4(b)—measured from the entry of the order disposing of the motion.

(iii) No additional fee is required to file an amended notice.

(B) **The Record on Appeal.**

(i) Within 14 days after filing the notice of appeal, the appellant must file with the clerk possessing the record assembled in accordance with Bankruptcy Rule 8009—and serve on the appellee—a statement of the issues to be presented on appeal and a designation of the record to be certified and made available to the circuit clerk.

(ii) An appellee who believes that other parts of the record are necessary must, within 14 days after being served with the appellant's designation, file with the clerk and serve on the appellant a designation of additional parts to be included.

(iii) The record on appeal consists of:

- the redesignated record as provided above;
- the proceedings in the district court or bankruptcy appellate panel; and
- a certified copy of the docket entries prepared by the clerk under Rule 3(d).

(C) **Making the Record Available.**

(i) When the record is complete, the district clerk or bankruptcy-appellate-panel clerk must number the documents constituting the record and promptly make it available to the circuit clerk. If the clerk makes the record available in paper form, the clerk will not send documents of unusual bulk or weight, physical exhibits other than documents, or other parts of the record designated for omission by local rule of the court of appeals, unless directed to do so by a party or the circuit clerk. If unusually bulky or heavy exhibits are to be made available in paper form, a party must arrange with the clerks in advance for their transportation and receipt.

(ii) All parties must do whatever else is necessary to enable the clerk to assemble the record and make it available. When the record is made available in paper form, the court of appeals may provide by rule or order that a certified copy of the docket entries be made available in place of the redesignated record. But any party may request at any time during the pendency of the appeal that the redesignated record be made available.

(D) **Filing the Record.** When the district clerk or bankruptcy-appellate-panel clerk has made the record available, the circuit clerk must note that fact on the docket. The date noted on the docket serves as the filing date of the record. The circuit clerk must immediately notify all parties of the filing date.

(c) **Direct Review by Permission Under 28 U.S.C. § 158(d)(2).**

(1) **Applicability of Other Rules.** These rules apply to a direct appeal by permission under 28 U.S.C. § 158(d)(2), but with these qualifications:

(A) Rules 3–4, 5(a)(3), 6(a), 6(b), 8(a), 8(c), 9–12, 13–20, 22–23, and 24(b) do not apply;

(B) as used in any applicable rule, "district court" or "district clerk" includes—to the extent appropriate—a bankruptcy court or bankruptcy appellate panel or its clerk; and

(C) the reference to "Rules 11 and 12(c)" in Rule 5(d)(3) must be read as a reference to Rules 6(c)(2)(B) and (C).

(2) **Additional Rules.** In addition, the following rules apply:

(A) **The Record on Appeal.** Bankruptcy Rule 8009 governs the record on appeal.

(B) **Making the Record Available.** Bankruptcy Rule 8010 governs completing the record and making it available.

(C) **Stays Pending Appeal.** Bankruptcy Rule 8007 applies to stays pending appeal.

(D) **Duties of the Circuit Clerk.** When the bankruptcy clerk has made the record available, the circuit clerk must note that fact on the docket. The date noted on the docket serves as the filing date of the record. The circuit clerk must immediately notify all parties of the filing date.

(E) **Filing a Representation Statement.** Unless the court of appeals designates another time, within 14 days after entry of the order granting permission to appeal, the attorney who sought permission must file a statement with the circuit clerk naming the parties that the attorney represents on appeal.

(Added Apr. 25, 1989, eff. Dec. 1, 1989; amended Apr. 30, 1991, eff. Dec. 1, 1991; Apr. 22, 1993, eff. Dec. 1, 1993; Apr. 24, 1998, eff. Dec. 1, 1998; Mar. 26, 2009, eff. Dec. 1, 2009; Apr. 25, 2014, eff. Dec. 1, 2014.)

RULE 7. BOND FOR COSTS ON APPEAL IN A CIVIL CASE

In a civil case, the district court may require an appellant to file a bond or provide other security in any form and amount necessary to ensure payment of costs on appeal. Rule 8(b) applies to a surety on a bond given under this rule.

(As amended Apr. 30, 1979, eff. Aug. 1, 1979; Apr. 24, 1998, eff. Dec. 1, 1998.)

RULE 8. STAY OR INJUNCTION PENDING APPEAL

(a) Motion for Stay.

(1) Initial Motion in the District Court. A party must ordinarily move first in the district court for the following relief:

(A) a stay of the judgment or order of a district court pending appeal;

(B) approval of a supersedeas bond; or

(C) an order suspending, modifying, restoring, or granting an injunction while an appeal is pending.

(2) Motion in the Court of Appeals; Conditions on Relief. A motion for the relief mentioned in Rule 8(a)(1) may be made to the court of appeals or to one of its judges.

(A) The motion must:

(i) show that moving first in the district court would be impracticable; or

(ii) state that, a motion having been made, the district court denied the motion or failed to afford the relief requested and state any reasons given by the district court for its action.

(B) The motion must also include:

(i) the reasons for granting the relief requested and the facts relied on;

(ii) originals or copies of affidavits or other sworn statements supporting facts subject to dispute; and

(iii) relevant parts of the record.

(C) The moving party must give reasonable notice of the motion to all parties.

(D) A motion under this Rule 8(a)(2) must be filed with the circuit clerk and normally will be considered by a panel of the court. But in an exceptional case in which time requirements make that procedure impracticable, the motion may be made to and considered by a single judge.

(E) The court may condition relief on a party's filing a bond or other appropriate security in the district court.

(b) Proceeding Against a Surety. If a party gives security in the form of a bond or stipulation or other undertaking with one or more sureties, each surety submits to the jurisdiction of the district court and irrevocably appoints the district clerk as the surety's agent on whom any papers affecting the surety's liability on the bond or undertaking may be served. On motion, a surety's liability may be enforced in the district court without the necessity of an independent action. The motion and any notice that the district court prescribes may be served on the district clerk, who must promptly mail a copy to each surety whose address is known.

(c) Stay in a Criminal Case. Rule 38 of the Federal Rules of Criminal Procedure governs a stay in a criminal case.

(As amended Mar. 10, 1986, eff. July 1, 1986; Apr. 27, 1995, eff. Dec. 1, 1995; Apr. 24, 1998, eff. Dec. 1, 1998.)

RULE 9. RELEASE IN A CRIMINAL CASE

(a) Release Before Judgment of Conviction.

(1) The district court must state in writing, or orally on the record, the reasons for an order regarding the release or detention of a defendant in a criminal case. A party appealing from the order must file with the court of appeals a copy of the district court's order and the court's statement of reasons as soon as practicable after filing the notice of appeal. An appellant who questions the factual basis for the district court's order must file a transcript of the release proceedings or an explanation of why a transcript was not obtained.

(2) After reasonable notice to the appellee, the court of appeals must promptly determine the appeal on the basis of the papers, affidavits, and parts of the record that the parties present or the court requires. Unless the court so orders, briefs need not be filed.

(3) The court of appeals or one of its judges may order the defendant's release pending the disposition of the appeal.

(b) Release After Judgment of Conviction. A party entitled to do so may obtain review of a district-court order regarding release after a judgment of conviction by filing a notice of appeal from that order in the district court, or by filing a motion in the court of appeals if the party has already filed a notice of appeal from the judgment of conviction. Both the order and the review are subject to Rule 9(a). The papers filed by the party seeking review must include a copy of the judgment of conviction.

(c) Criteria for Release. The court must make its decision regarding release in accordance with the applicable provisions of 18 U.S.C. §§ 3142, 3143, and 3145(c).

(As amended Apr. 24, 1972, eff. Oct. 1, 1972; Oct. 12, 1984, Pub.L. 98–473, Title II, § 210, 98 Stat. 1987; Apr. 29, 1994, eff. Dec. 1, 1994; Apr. 24, 1998, eff. Dec. 1, 1998.)

RULE 10. THE RECORD ON APPEAL

(a) Composition of the Record on Appeal. The following items constitute the record on appeal:

(1) the original papers and exhibits filed in the district court;

(2) the transcript of proceedings, if any; and

(3) a certified copy of the docket entries prepared by the district clerk.

(b) The Transcript of Proceedings.

(1) Appellant's Duty to Order. Within 14 days after filing the notice of appeal or entry of an order disposing of the last timely remaining motion of a type specified in Rule 4(a)(4)(A), whichever is later, the appellant must do either of the following:

(A) order from the reporter a transcript of such parts of the proceedings not already on file as the appellant considers necessary, subject to a local rule of the court of appeals and with the following qualifications:

(i) the order must be in writing;

(ii) if the cost of the transcript is to be paid by the United States under the Criminal Justice Act, the order must so state; and

(iii) the appellant must, within the same period, file a copy of the order with the district clerk; or

(B) file a certificate stating that no transcript will be ordered.

(2) Unsupported Finding or Conclusion. If the appellant intends to urge on appeal that a finding or conclusion is unsupported by the evidence or is contrary to the evidence, the appellant must include in the record a transcript of all evidence relevant to that finding or conclusion.

(3) Partial Transcript. Unless the entire transcript is ordered:

(A) the appellant must—within the 14 days provided in Rule 10(b)(1)—file a statement of the issues that the appellant intends to present on the appeal and must serve on the appellee a copy of both the order or certificate and the statement;

(B) if the appellee considers it necessary to have a transcript of other parts of the proceedings, the appellee must, within 14 days after the service of the order or certificate and the statement of the issues, file and serve on the appellant a designation of additional parts to be ordered; and

(C) unless within 14 days after service of that designation the appellant has ordered all such parts, and has so notified the appellee, the appellee may within the following 14 days either order the parts or move in the district court for an order requiring the appellant to do so.

(4) Payment. At the time of ordering, a party must make satisfactory arrangements with the reporter for paying the cost of the transcript.

(c) Statement of the Evidence When the Proceedings Were Not Recorded or When a Transcript Is Unavailable. If the transcript of a hearing or trial is unavailable, the appellant may prepare a statement of the evidence or proceedings from the best available means, including the appellant's recollection. The statement must be served on the appellee, who may serve objections or proposed amendments within 14 days after being served. The statement and any objections or proposed amendments must then be submitted to the district court for settlement and approval. As settled and approved, the statement must be included by the district clerk in the record on appeal.

(d) Agreed Statement as the Record on Appeal. In place of the record on appeal as defined in Rule 10(a), the parties may prepare, sign, and submit to the district court a statement of the case showing how the issues presented by the appeal arose and were decided in the district court. The statement must set forth only those facts averred and proved or sought to be proved that are essential to the court's resolution of the issues. If the statement is truthful, it—together with any additions that the district court may consider necessary to a full presentation of the issues on appeal—must be approved by the district court and must then be certified to the court of appeals as the record on appeal. The district clerk must then send it to the circuit clerk within the time provided by Rule 11. A copy of the agreed statement may be filed in place of the appendix required by Rule 30.

(e) Correction or Modification of the Record.

(1) If any difference arises about whether the record truly discloses what occurred in the district court, the difference must be submitted to and settled by that court and the record conformed accordingly.

(2) If anything material to either party is omitted from or misstated in the record by error or accident, the omission or misstatement may be corrected and a supplemental record may be certified and forwarded:

(A) on stipulation of the parties;

(B) by the district court before or after the record has been forwarded; or

(C) by the court of appeals.

(3) All other questions as to the form and content of the record must be presented to the court of appeals.

(As amended Apr. 30, 1979, eff. Aug. 1, 1979; Mar. 10, 1986, eff. July 1, 1986; Apr. 30, 1991, eff. Dec. 1, 1991; Apr. 22, 1993, eff. Dec. 1, 1993; Apr. 27, 1995, eff. Dec. 1, 1995; Apr. 24, 1998, eff. Dec. 1, 1998; Mar. 26, 2009, eff. Dec. 1, 2009.)

RULE 11. FORWARDING THE RECORD

(a) Appellant's Duty. An appellant filing a notice of appeal must comply with Rule 10(b) and must do whatever else is necessary to enable the clerk to assemble and forward the record. If there are multiple appeals from a judgment or order, the clerk must forward a single record.

(b) Duties of Reporter and District Clerk.

(1) Reporter's Duty to Prepare and File a Transcript. The reporter must prepare and file a transcript as follows:

(A) Upon receiving an order for a transcript, the reporter must enter at the foot of the order the date of its receipt and the expected completion date and send a copy, so endorsed, to the circuit clerk.

(B) If the transcript cannot be completed within 30 days of the reporter's receipt of the order, the reporter may request the circuit clerk to grant additional time to complete it. The clerk must note on the docket the action taken and notify the parties.

(C) When a transcript is complete, the reporter must file it with the district clerk and notify the circuit clerk of the filing.

(D) If the reporter fails to file the transcript on time, the circuit clerk must notify the district judge and do whatever else the court of appeals directs.

(2) District Clerk's Duty to Forward. When the record is complete, the district clerk must number the documents constituting the record and send them promptly to the circuit clerk together with a list of the documents correspondingly numbered and reasonably identified. Unless directed to do so by a party or the circuit clerk, the district clerk will not send to the court of appeals documents of unusual bulk or weight, physical exhibits other than documents, or other parts of the record designated for omission by local rule of the court of appeals. If the exhibits are unusually bulky or heavy, a party must arrange with the clerks in advance for their transportation and receipt.

(c) Retaining the Record Temporarily in the District Court for Use in Preparing the Appeal. The parties may stipulate, or the district court on motion may order, that the district clerk retain the record temporarily for the parties to use in preparing the papers on appeal. In that event the district clerk must certify to the circuit clerk that the record on appeal is complete. Upon receipt of the appellee's brief, or earlier if the court orders or the parties agree, the appellant must request the district clerk to forward the record.

(d) [Abrogated.]

(e) Retaining the Record by Court Order.

(1) The court of appeals may, by order or local rule, provide that a certified copy of the docket entries be forwarded instead of the entire record. But a party may at any time during the appeal request that designated parts of the record be forwarded.

(2) The district court may order the record or some part of it retained if the court needs it while the appeal is pending, subject, however, to call by the court of appeals.

(3) If part or all of the record is ordered retained, the district clerk must send to the court of appeals a copy of the order and the docket entries together with the parts of the original record allowed by the district court and copies of any parts of the record designated by the parties.

(f) Retaining Parts of the Record in the District Court by Stipulation of the Parties. The parties may agree by written stipulation filed in the district court that designated parts of the record be retained in the district court subject to call by the court of appeals or request by a party. The parts of the record so designated remain a part of the record on appeal.

(g) Record for a Preliminary Motion in the Court of Appeals. If, before the record is forwarded, a party makes any of the following motions in the court of appeals:

- for dismissal;
- for release;
- for a stay pending appeal;
- for additional security on the bond on appeal or on a supersedeas bond; or
- for any other intermediate order—

the district clerk must send the court of appeals any parts of the record designated by any party.

(As amended Apr. 30, 1979, eff. Aug. 1, 1979; Mar. 10, 1986, eff. July 1, 1986; Apr. 24, 1998, eff. Dec. 1, 1998.)

RULE 12. DOCKETING THE APPEAL; FILING A REPRESENTATION STATEMENT; FILING THE RECORD

(a) Docketing the Appeal. Upon receiving the copy of the notice of appeal and the docket entries from the district clerk under Rule 3(d), the circuit clerk must docket the appeal under the title of the district-court action and must identify the appellant, adding the appellant's name if necessary.

(b) Filing a Representation Statement. Unless the court of appeals designates another time, the attorney who filed the notice of appeal must, within 14 days after filing the notice, file a statement with the circuit clerk naming the parties that the attorney represents on appeal.

(c) Filing the Record, Partial Record, or Certificate. Upon receiving the record, partial record, or district clerk's certificate as provided in Rule 11, the circuit clerk must file it and immediately notify all parties of the filing date.

(As amended Apr. 30, 1979, eff. Aug. 1, 1979; Mar. 10, 1986, eff. July 1, 1986; Apr. 22, 1993, eff. Dec. 1, 1993; Apr. 24, 1998, eff. Dec. 1, 1998; Mar. 26, 2009, eff. Dec. 1, 2009.)

RULE 12.1 REMAND AFTER AN INDICATIVE RULING BY THE DISTRICT COURT ON A MOTION FOR RELIEF THAT IS BARRED BY A PENDING APPEAL

(a) Notice to the Court of Appeals. If a timely motion is made in the district court for relief that it lacks authority to grant because of an appeal that has been docketed and is pending, the movant must promptly notify the circuit clerk if the district court states either that it would grant the motion or that the motion raises a substantial issue.

(b) Remand After an Indicative Ruling. If the district court states that it would grant the motion or that the motion raises a substantial issue, the court of appeals may remand for further proceedings but retains jurisdiction unless it expressly dismisses the appeal. If the court of appeals remands but retains jurisdiction, the parties must promptly notify the circuit clerk when the district court has decided the motion on remand.

(Added Mar. 26, 2009, eff. Dec. 1, 2009.)

TITLE III. APPEALS FROM THE UNITED STATES TAX COURT

RULE 13. APPEALS FROM THE TAX COURT

(a) Appeal as of Right.

(1) How Obtained; Time for Filing a Notice of Appeal.

(A) An appeal as of right from the United States Tax Court is commenced by filing a notice of appeal with the Tax Court clerk within 90 days after the entry of the Tax Court's decision. At the time of filing, the appellant must furnish the clerk with enough copies of the notice to enable the clerk to comply with Rule 3(d). If one party files a timely notice of appeal, any other party may file a notice of appeal within 120 days after the Tax Court's decision is entered.

(B) If, under Tax Court rules, a party makes a timely motion to vacate or revise the Tax Court's decision, the time to file a notice of appeal runs from the entry of the order disposing of the motion or from the entry of a new decision, whichever is later.

(2) Notice of Appeal; How Filed. The notice of appeal may be filed either at the Tax Court clerk's office in the District of Columbia or by mail addressed to the clerk. If sent by mail the notice is considered filed on the postmark date, subject to § 7502 of the Internal Revenue Code, as amended, and the applicable regulations.

(3) Contents of the Notice of Appeal; Service; Effect of Filing and Service. Rule 3 prescribes the contents of a notice of appeal, the manner of service, and the effect of its filing and service. Form 2 in the Appendix of Forms is a suggested form of a notice of appeal.

(4) The Record on Appeal; Forwarding; Filing.

(A) Except as otherwise provided under Tax Court rules for the transcript of proceedings, the appeal is governed by the parts of Rules 10, 11, and 12 regarding the record on appeal from a district court, the time and manner of forwarding and filing, and the docketing in the court of appeals.

(B) If an appeal is taken to more than one court of appeals, the original record must be sent to the court named in the first notice of appeal filed. In an appeal to any other court of appeals, the appellant must apply to that other court to make provision for the record.

(b) Appeal by Permission. An appeal by permission is governed by Rule 5.

(As amended Apr. 30, 1979, eff. Aug. 1, 1979; Apr. 29, 1994, eff. Dec. 1, 1994; Apr. 24, 1998, eff. Dec. 1, 1998; Apr. 16, 2013, eff. Dec. 1, 2013.)

RULE 14. APPLICABILITY OF OTHER RULES TO APPEALS FROM THE TAX COURT

All provisions of these rules, except Rules 4, 6–9, 15–20, and 22–23, apply to appeals from the Tax Court. References in any applicable rule (other than Rule 24(a)) to the district court and district clerk are to be read as referring to the Tax Court and its clerk.

(As amended Apr. 24, 1998, eff. Dec. 1, 1998; Apr. 16, 2013, eff. Dec. 1, 2013.)

TITLE IV. REVIEW OR ENFORCEMENT OF AN ORDER OF AN ADMINISTRATIVE AGENCY, BOARD, COMMISSION, OR OFFICER

RULE 15. REVIEW OR ENFORCEMENT OF AN AGENCY ORDER—HOW OBTAINED; INTERVENTION

(a) Petition for Review; Joint Petition.

(1) Review of an agency order is commenced by filing, within the time prescribed by law, a petition for review with the clerk of a court of appeals authorized to review the agency order. If their interests make joinder practicable, two or more persons may join in a petition to the same court to review the same order.

(2) The petition must:

(A) name each party seeking review either in the caption or the body of the petition—using such terms as "et al.," "petitioners," or "respondents" does not effectively name the parties;

(B) name the agency as a respondent (even though not named in the petition, the United States is a respondent if required by statute); and

(C) specify the order or part thereof to be reviewed.

(3) Form 3 in the Appendix of Forms is a suggested form of a petition for review.

(4) In this rule "agency" includes an agency, board, commission, or officer; "petition for review" includes a petition to enjoin, suspend, modify, or otherwise review, or a notice of appeal, whichever form is indicated by the applicable statute.

(b) Application or Cross-Application to Enforce an Order; Answer; Default.

(1) An application to enforce an agency order must be filed with the clerk of a court of appeals authorized to enforce the order. If a petition is filed to review an agency order that the court may enforce, a party opposing the petition may file a cross-application for enforcement.

(2) Within 21 days after the application for enforcement is filed, the respondent must serve on the applicant an answer to the application and file it with the clerk. If the respondent fails to answer in time, the court will enter judgment for the relief requested.

(3) The application must contain a concise statement of the proceedings in which the order was entered, the facts upon which venue is based, and the relief requested.

(c) Service of the Petition or Application. The circuit clerk must serve a copy of the petition for review, or an application or cross-application to enforce an agency order, on each respondent as prescribed by Rule 3(d), unless a different manner of service is prescribed by statute. At the time of filing, the petitioner must:

(1) serve, or have served, a copy on each party admitted to participate in the agency proceedings, except for the respondents;

(2) file with the clerk a list of those so served; and

(3) give the clerk enough copies of the petition or application to serve each respondent.

(d) Intervention. Unless a statute provides another method, a person who wants to intervene in a proceeding under this rule must file a motion for leave to intervene with the circuit clerk and serve a copy on all parties. The motion—or other notice of intervention authorized by statute—must be filed within 30 days after the petition for review is filed and must contain a concise statement of the interest of the moving party and the grounds for intervention.

(e) Payment of Fees. When filing any separate or joint petition for review in a court of appeals, the petitioner must pay the circuit clerk all required fees.

(As amended Apr. 22, 1993, eff. Dec. 1, 1993; Apr. 24, 1998, eff. Dec. 1, 1998; Mar. 26, 2009, eff. Dec. 1, 2009.)

RULE 15.1 BRIEFS AND ORAL ARGUMENT IN A NATIONAL LABOR RELATIONS BOARD PROCEEDING

In either an enforcement or a review proceeding, a party adverse to the National Labor Relations Board proceeds first on briefing and at oral argument, unless the court orders otherwise.

(Added Mar. 10, 1986, eff. July 1, 1986; amended Apr. 24, 1998, eff. Dec. 1, 1998.)

RULE 16. THE RECORD ON REVIEW OR ENFORCEMENT

(a) Composition of the Record. The record on review or enforcement of an agency order consists of:

(1) the order involved;

(2) any findings or report on which it is based; and

(3) the pleadings, evidence, and other parts of the proceedings before the agency.

(b) Omissions From or Misstatements in the Record. The parties may at any time, by stipulation, supply any omission from the record or correct a misstatement, or the court may so direct. If necessary, the court may direct that a supplemental record be prepared and filed.

(As amended Apr. 24, 1998, eff. Dec. 1, 1998.)

RULE 17. FILING THE RECORD

(a) Agency to File; Time for Filing; Notice of Filing. The agency must file the record with the circuit clerk within 40 days after being served with a petition for review, unless the statute authorizing review provides otherwise, or within 40 days after it files an application for enforcement unless the respondent fails to answer or the court orders otherwise. The court may shorten or extend the time to file the record. The clerk must notify all parties of the date when the record is filed.

(b) Filing—What Constitutes.

(1) The agency must file:

(A) the original or a certified copy of the entire record or parts designated by the parties; or

(B) a certified list adequately describing all documents, transcripts of testimony, exhibits, and other material constituting the record, or describing those parts designated by the parties.

(2) The parties may stipulate in writing that no record or certified list be filed. The date when the stipulation is filed with the circuit clerk is treated as the date when the record is filed.

(3) The agency must retain any portion of the record not filed with the clerk. All parts of the record retained by the agency are a part of the record on review for all purposes and, if the court or a party so requests, must be sent to the court regardless of any prior stipulation.

(As amended Apr. 24, 1998, eff. Dec. 1, 1998.)

RULE 18. STAY PENDING REVIEW

(a) Motion for a Stay.

(1) **Initial Motion Before the Agency.** A petitioner must ordinarily move first before the agency for a stay pending review of its decision or order.

(2) **Motion in the Court of Appeals.** A motion for a stay may be made to the court of appeals or one of its judges.

(A) The motion must:

(i) show that moving first before the agency would be impracticable; or

(ii) state that, a motion having been made, the agency denied the motion or failed to afford the relief requested and state any reasons given by the agency for its action.

(B) The motion must also include:

(i) the reasons for granting the relief requested and the facts relied on;

(ii) originals or copies of affidavits or other sworn statements supporting facts subject to dispute; and

(iii) relevant parts of the record.

(C) The moving party must give reasonable notice of the motion to all parties.

(D) The motion must be filed with the circuit clerk and normally will be considered by a panel of the court. But in an exceptional case in which time requirements make that procedure impracticable, the motion may be made to and considered by a single judge.

(b) **Bond.** The court may condition relief on the filing of a bond or other appropriate security.

(As amended Apr. 24, 1998, eff. Dec. 1, 1998.)

RULE 19. SETTLEMENT OF A JUDGMENT ENFORCING AN AGENCY ORDER IN PART

When the court files an opinion directing entry of judgment enforcing the agency's order in part, the agency must within 14 days file with the clerk and serve on each other party a proposed judgment conforming to the opinion. A party who disagrees with the agency's proposed judgment must within 10 days file with the clerk and serve the agency with a proposed judgment that the party believes conforms to the opinion. The court will settle the judgment and direct entry without further hearing or argument.

(As amended Mar. 10, 1986, eff. July 1, 1986; Apr. 24, 1998, eff. Dec. 1, 1998; Mar. 26, 2009, eff. Dec. 1, 2009.)

RULE 20. APPLICABILITY OF RULES TO THE REVIEW OR ENFORCEMENT OF AN AGENCY ORDER

All provisions of these rules, except Rules 3–14 and 22–23, apply to the review or enforcement of an agency order. In these rules, "appellant" includes a petitioner or applicant, and "appellee" includes a respondent.

(As amended Apr. 24, 1998, eff. Dec. 1, 1998.)

TITLE V. EXTRAORDINARY WRITS

RULE 21. WRITS OF MANDAMUS AND PROHIBITION, AND OTHER EXTRAORDINARY WRITS

(a) **Mandamus or Prohibition to a Court: Petition, Filing, Service, and Docketing.**

(1) A party petitioning for a writ of mandamus or prohibition directed to a court must file a petition with the circuit clerk with proof of service on all parties to the proceeding in the trial court. The party must also provide a copy to the trial-court judge. All parties to the proceeding in the trial court other than the petitioner are respondents for all purposes.

(2)(A) The petition must be titled "In re [name of petitioner]."

(B) The petition must state:

(i) the relief sought;

(ii) the issues presented;

(iii) the facts necessary to understand the issue presented by the petition; and

(iv) the reasons why the writ should issue.

(C) The petition must include a copy of any order or opinion or parts of the record that may be essential to understand the matters set forth in the petition.

(3) Upon receiving the prescribed docket fee, the clerk must docket the petition and submit it to the court.

(b) **Denial; Order Directing Answer; Briefs; Precedence.**

(1) The court may deny the petition without an answer. Otherwise, it must order the respondent, if any, to answer within a fixed time.

(2) The clerk must serve the order to respond on all persons directed to respond.

(3) Two or more respondents may answer jointly.

(4) The court of appeals may invite or order the trial-court judge to address the petition or may invite an amicus curiae to do so. The trial-court judge may request permission to address the petition but may not do so unless invited or ordered to do so by the court of appeals.

(5) If briefing or oral argument is required, the clerk must advise the parties, and when appropriate, the trial-court judge or amicus curiae.

(6) The proceeding must be given preference over ordinary civil cases.

(7) The circuit clerk must send a copy of the final disposition to the trial-court judge.

(c) **Other Extraordinary Writs.** An application for an extraordinary writ other than one provided for in Rule 21(a) must be made by filing a petition with the circuit clerk with proof of service on the respondents. Proceedings on the application must conform, so far as is practicable, to the procedures prescribed in Rule 21(a) and (b).

(d) **Form of Papers; Number of Copies; Length Limits.** All papers must conform to Rule 32(c)(2). An original and 3 copies must be filed unless the court requires the filing of a different number by local rule or by order in a particular case. Except by the court's permission, and excluding the accompanying documents required by Rule 21(a)(2)(C):

(1) a paper produced using a computer must not exceed 7,800 words; and

(2) a handwritten or typewritten paper must not exceed 30 pages.

(As amended Apr. 29, 1994, eff. Dec. 1, 1994; Apr. 23, 1996, eff. Dec. 1, 1996; Apr. 24, 1998, eff. Dec. 1, 1998; Apr. 29, 2002, eff. Dec. 1, 2002; Apr. 28, 2016, eff. Dec. 1, 2016.)

TITLE VI. HABEAS CORPUS; PROCEEDINGS IN FORMA PAUPERIS

RULE 22. HABEAS CORPUS AND SECTION 2255 PROCEEDINGS

(a) Application for the Original Writ. An application for a writ of habeas corpus must be made to the appropriate district court. If made to a circuit judge, the application must be transferred to the appropriate district court. If a district court denies an application made or transferred to it, renewal of the application before a circuit judge is not permitted. The applicant may, under 28 U.S.C. § 2253, appeal to the court of appeals from the district court's order denying the application.

(b) Certificate of Appealability.

(1) In a habeas corpus proceeding in which the detention complained of arises from process issued by a state court, or in a 28 U.S.C. § 2255 proceeding, the applicant cannot take an appeal unless a circuit justice or a circuit or district judge issues a certificate of appealability under 28 U.S.C. § 2253(c). If an applicant files a notice of appeal, the district clerk must send to the court of appeals the certificate (if any) and the statement described in Rule 11(a) of the Rules Governing Proceedings Under 28 U.S.C. § 2254 or § 2255 (if any), along with the notice of appeal and the file of the district-court proceedings. If the district judge has denied the certificate, the applicant may request a circuit judge to issue it.

(2) A request addressed to the court of appeals may be considered by a circuit judge or judges, as the court prescribes. If no express request for a certificate is filed, the notice of appeal constitutes a request addressed to the judges of the court of appeals.

(3) A certificate of appealability is not required when a state or its representative or the United States or its representative appeals.

(As amended Pub.L. 104–132, Title I, § 103, Apr. 24, 1996, 110 Stat. 1218; Apr. 24, 1998, eff. Dec. 1, 1998; Mar. 26, 2009, eff. Dec. 1, 2009.)

RULE 23. CUSTODY OR RELEASE OF A PRISONER IN A HABEAS CORPUS PROCEEDING

(a) Transfer of Custody Pending Review. Pending review of a decision in a habeas corpus proceeding commenced before a court, justice, or judge of the United States for the release of a prisoner, the person having custody of the prisoner must not transfer custody to another unless a transfer is directed in accordance with this rule. When, upon application, a custodian shows the need for a transfer, the court, justice, or judge rendering the decision under review may authorize the transfer and substitute the successor custodian as a party.

(b) Detention or Release Pending Review of Decision Not to Release. While a decision not to release a prisoner is under review, the court or judge rendering the decision, or the court of appeals, or the Supreme Court, or a judge or justice of either court, may order that the prisoner be:

(1) detained in the custody from which release is sought;

(2) detained in other appropriate custody; or

(3) released on personal recognizance, with or without surety.

(c) Release Pending Review of Decision Ordering Release. While a decision ordering the release of a prisoner is under review, the prisoner must—unless the court or judge rendering the decision, or the court of appeals, or the Supreme Court, or a judge or justice of either court orders otherwise—be released on personal recognizance, with or without surety.

(d) Modification of the Initial Order on Custody. An initial order governing the prisoner's custody or release, including any recognizance or surety, continues in effect pending review unless for special reasons shown to the court of appeals or the Supreme Court, or to a judge or justice of either court, the order is modified or an independent order regarding custody, release, or surety is issued.

(As amended Mar. 10, 1986, eff. July 1, 1986; Apr. 24, 1998, eff. Dec. 1, 1998.)

RULE 24. PROCEEDING IN FORMA PAUPERIS

(a) Leave to Proceed In Forma Pauperis.

(1) Motion in the District Court. Except as stated in Rule 24(a)(3), a party to a district-court action who desires to appeal in forma pauperis must file a motion in the district court. The party must attach an affidavit that:

(A) shows in the detail prescribed by Form 4 of the Appendix of Forms the party's inability to pay or to give security for fees and costs;

(B) claims an entitlement to redress; and

(C) states the issues that the party intends to present on appeal.

(2) Action on the Motion. If the district court grants the motion, the party may proceed on appeal without prepaying or giving security for fees and costs, unless a statute provides otherwise. If the district court denies the motion, it must state its reasons in writing.

(3) Prior Approval. A party who was permitted to proceed in forma pauperis in the district-court action, or who was determined to be financially unable to obtain an adequate defense in a criminal case, may proceed on appeal in forma pauperis without further authorization, unless:

(A) the district court—before or after the notice of appeal is filed—certifies that the appeal is not taken in good faith or finds that the party is not otherwise entitled to proceed in forma pauperis and states in writing its reasons for the certification or finding; or

(B) a statute provides otherwise.

(4) Notice of District Court's Denial. The district clerk must immediately notify the parties and the court of appeals when the district court does any of the following:

(A) denies a motion to proceed on appeal in forma pauperis;

(B) certifies that the appeal is not taken in good faith; or

(C) finds that the party is not otherwise entitled to proceed in forma pauperis.

(5) Motion in the Court of Appeals. A party may file a motion to proceed on appeal in forma pauperis in the court of appeals within 30 days after service of the notice prescribed in Rule 24(a)(4). The motion must include a copy of the affidavit filed in the district court and the district court's statement of reasons for its action. If no affidavit was filed in the district court, the party must include the affidavit prescribed by Rule 24(a)(1).

(b) Leave to Proceed In Forma Pauperis on Appeal from the United States Tax Court or on Appeal or Review of an Administrative–Agency Proceeding. A party may file in the court of appeals a motion for leave to proceed on appeal in forma pauperis with an affidavit prescribed by Rule 24(a)(1):

(1) in an appeal from the United States Tax Court; and

(2) when an appeal or review of a proceeding before an administrative agency, board, commission, or officer proceeds directly in the court of appeals.

(c) Leave to Use Original Record. A party allowed to proceed on appeal in forma pauperis may request that the appeal be heard on the original record without reproducing any part.

(As amended Apr. 30, 1979, eff. Aug. 1, 1979; Mar. 10, 1986, eff. July 1, 1986; Apr. 24, 1998, eff. Dec. 1, 1998; Apr. 29, 2002, eff. Dec. 1, 2002; Apr. 16, 2013, eff. Dec. 1, 2013.)

TITLE VII. GENERAL PROVISIONS

RULE 25. FILING AND SERVICE

(a) Filing.

(1) Filing with the Clerk. A paper required or permitted to be filed in a court of appeals must be filed with the clerk.

(2) Filing: Method and Timeliness.

(A) In general. Filing may be accomplished by mail addressed to the clerk, but filing is not timely unless the clerk receives the papers within the time fixed for filing.

(B) A brief or appendix. A brief or appendix is timely filed, however, if on or before the last day for filing, it is:

(i) mailed to the clerk by First–Class Mail, or other class of mail that is at least as expeditious, postage prepaid; or

(ii) dispatched to a third-party commercial carrier for delivery to the clerk within 3 days.

(C) Inmate Filing. If an institution has a system designed for legal mail, an inmate confined there must use that system to receive the benefit of this Rule 25(a)(2)(C). A paper filed by an inmate is timely if it is deposited in the institution's internal mail system on or before the last day for filing and:

(i) it is accompanied by:

• a declaration in compliance with 28 U.S.C. § 1746—or a notarized statement—setting out the date of deposit and stating that first-class postage is being prepaid; or

• evidence (such as a postmark or date stamp) showing that the paper was so deposited and that postage was prepaid; or

(ii) the court of appeals exercises its discretion to permit the later filing of a declaration or notarized statement that satisfies Rule 25(a)(2)(C)(i).

(D) Electronic filing. A court of appeals may by local rule permit or require papers to be filed, signed, or verified by electronic means that are consistent with technical standards, if any, that the Judicial Conference of the United States establishes. A local rule may require filing by electronic means only if reasonable exceptions are allowed. A paper filed by electronic means in compliance with a local rule constitutes a written paper for the purpose of applying these rules.

(3) Filing a Motion with a Judge. If a motion requests relief that may be granted by a single judge, the judge may permit the motion to be filed with the judge; the judge must note the filing date on the motion and give it to the clerk.

(4) Clerk's Refusal of Documents. The clerk must not refuse to accept for filing any paper presented for that purpose solely because it is not presented in proper form as required by these rules or by any local rule or practice.

(5) Privacy Protection. An appeal in a case whose privacy protection was governed by Federal Rule of Bankruptcy Procedure 9037, Federal Rule of Civil Procedure 5.2, or Federal Rule of Criminal Procedure 49.1 is governed by the same rule on appeal. In all other proceedings, privacy protection is governed by Federal Rule of Civil Procedure 5.2, except that Federal Rule of Criminal Procedure 49.1 governs when an extraordinary writ is sought in a criminal case.

(b) Service of All Papers Required. Unless a rule requires service by the clerk, a party must, at or before the time of filing a paper, serve a copy on the other parties to the appeal or review. Service on a party represented by counsel must be made on the party's counsel.

(c) Manner of Service.

(1) Service may be any of the following:

(A) personal, including delivery to a responsible person at the office of counsel;

(B) by mail;

(C) by third-party commercial carrier for delivery within 3 days; or

(D) by electronic means, if the party being served consents in writing.

(2) If authorized by local rule, a party may use the court's transmission equipment to make electronic service under Rule 25(c)(1)(D).

(3) When reasonable considering such factors as the immediacy of the relief sought, distance, and cost, service on a party must be by a manner at least as expeditious as the manner used to file the paper with the court.

(4) Service by mail or by commercial carrier is complete on mailing or delivery to the carrier. Service by electronic means is complete on transmission, unless the party making service is notified that the paper was not received by the party served.

(d) Proof of Service.

(1) A paper presented for filing must contain either of the following:

(A) an acknowledgment of service by the person served; or

(B) proof of service consisting of a statement by the person who made service certifying:

(i) the date and manner of service;

(ii) the names of the persons served; and

(iii) their mail or electronic addresses, facsimile numbers, or the addresses of the places of delivery, as appropriate for the manner of service.

(2) When a brief or appendix is filed by mailing or dispatch in accordance with Rule 25(a)(2)(B), the proof of service must also state the date and manner by which the document was mailed or dispatched to the clerk.

(3) Proof of service may appear on or be affixed to the papers filed.

(e) Number of Copies. When these rules require the filing or furnishing of a number of copies, a court may require a different number by local rule or by order in a particular case.

(As amended Mar. 10, 1986, eff. July 1, 1986; Apr. 30, 1991, eff. Dec. 1, 1991; Apr. 22, 1993, eff. Dec. 1, 1993; Apr. 29, 1994, eff. Dec. 1, 1994; Apr. 23, 1996, eff. Dec. 1, 1996; Apr. 24, 1998, eff. Dec. 1, 1998; Apr. 29, 2002, eff. Dec. 1, 2002; Apr. 12, 2006, eff. Dec. 1, 2006; Apr. 30, 2007, eff. Dec. 1, 2007; Mar. 26, 2009, eff. Dec. 1, 2009; Apr. 28, 2016, eff. Dec. 1, 2016.)

RULE 26. COMPUTING AND EXTENDING TIME

(a) Computing Time. The following rules apply in computing any time period specified in these rules, in any local rule or court order, or in any statute that does not specify a method of computing time.

(1) **Period Stated in Days or a Longer Unit.** When the period is stated in days or a longer unit of time:

(A) exclude the day of the event that triggers the period;

(B) count every day, including intermediate Saturdays, Sundays, and legal holidays; and

(C) include the last day of the period, but if the last day is a Saturday, Sunday, or legal holiday, the period continues to run until the end of the next day that is not a Saturday, Sunday, or legal holiday.

(2) **Period Stated in Hours.** When the period is stated in hours:

(A) begin counting immediately on the occurrence of the event that triggers the period;

(B) count every hour, including hours during intermediate Saturdays, Sundays, and legal holidays; and

(C) if the period would end on a Saturday, Sunday, or legal holiday, the period continues to run until the same time on the next day that is not a Saturday, Sunday, or legal holiday.

(3) **Inaccessibility of the Clerk's Office.** Unless the court orders otherwise, if the clerk's office is inaccessible:

(A) on the last day for filing under Rule 26(a)(1), then the time for filing is extended to the first accessible day that is not a Saturday, Sunday, or legal holiday; or

(B) during the last hour for filing under Rule 26(a)(2), then the time for filing is extended to the same time on the first accessible day that is not a Saturday, Sunday, or legal holiday.

(4) **"Last Day" Defined.** Unless a different time is set by a statute, local rule, or court order, the last day ends:

(A) for electronic filing in the district court, at midnight in the court's time zone;

(B) for electronic filing in the court of appeals, at midnight in the time zone of the circuit clerk's principal office;

(C) for filing under Rules 4(c)(1), 25(a)(2)(B), and 25(a)(2)(C)—and filing by mail under Rule 13(a)(2)—at the latest time for the method chosen for delivery to the post office, third-party commercial carrier, or prison mailing system; and

(D) for filing by other means, when the clerk's office is scheduled to close.

(5) **"Next Day" Defined.** The "next day" is determined by continuing to count forward when the period is measured after an event and backward when measured before an event.

(6) **"Legal Holiday" Defined.** "Legal holiday" means:

(A) the day set aside by statute for observing New Year's Day, Martin Luther King Jr.'s Birthday, Washington's Birthday, Memorial Day, Independence Day, Labor Day, Columbus Day, Veterans' Day, Thanksgiving Day, or Christmas Day;

(B) any day declared a holiday by the President or Congress; and

(C) for periods that are measured after an event, any other day declared a holiday by the state where either of the following is located: the district court that rendered the challenged judgment or order, or the circuit clerk's principal office.

(b) Extending Time. For good cause, the court may extend the time prescribed by these rules or by its order to perform any act, or may permit an act to be done after that time expires. But the court may not extend the time to file:

(1) a notice of appeal (except as authorized in Rule 4) or a petition for permission to appeal; or

(2) a notice of appeal from or a petition to enjoin, set aside, suspend, modify, enforce, or otherwise review an order of an administrative agency, board, commission, or officer of the United States, unless specifically authorized by law.

(c) Additional Time after Certain Kinds of Service. When a party may or must act within a specified time after being served, 3 days are added after the period would otherwise expire under Rule 26(a), unless the paper is delivered on the date of service stated in the proof of service. For purposes of this Rule 26(c), a paper that is served electronically is treated as delivered on the date of service stated in the proof of service.

(As amended Mar. 1, 1971, eff. July 1, 1971; Mar. 10, 1986, eff. July 1, 1986; Apr. 25, 1989, eff. Dec. 1, 1989; Apr. 30, 1991, eff. Dec. 1, 1991; Apr. 23, 1996, eff. Dec. 1, 1996; Apr. 24, 1998, eff. Dec. 1, 1998; Apr. 29, 2002, eff. Dec. 1, 2002; Apr. 25, 2005, eff. Dec. 1, 2005; Mar. 26, 2009, eff. Dec. 1, 2009; Apr. 28, 2016, eff. Dec. 1, 2016.)

RULE 26.1 CORPORATE DISCLOSURE STATEMENT

(a) Who Must File. Any nongovernmental corporate party to a proceeding in a court of appeals must file a statement that identifies any parent corporation and any publicly held corporation that owns 10% or more of its stock or states that there is no such corporation.

(b) Time for Filing; Supplemental Filing. A party must file the Rule 26.1(a) statement with the principal brief or upon filing a motion, response, petition, or answer in the court of appeals, whichever occurs first, unless a local rule requires earlier filing. Even if the statement has already been filed, the party's principal brief must include the statement before the table of contents. A party must supplement its statement whenever the information that must be disclosed under Rule 26.1(a) changes.

(c) Number of Copies. If the Rule 26.1(a) statement is filed before the principal brief, or if a supplemental statement is filed, the party must file an original and 3 copies unless the court requires a different number by local rule or by order in a particular case.

(Added Apr. 25, 1989, eff. Dec. 1, 1989; amended Apr. 30, 1991, eff. Dec. 1, 1991; Apr. 29, 1994, eff. Dec. 1, 1994; Apr. 24, 1998, eff. Dec. 1, 1998; Apr. 29, 2002, eff. Dec. 1, 2002.)

RULE 27. MOTIONS

(a) In General.

(1) Application for Relief. An application for an order or other relief is made by motion unless these rules prescribe another form. A motion must be in writing unless the court permits otherwise.

(2) Contents of a Motion.

(A) Grounds and relief sought. A motion must state with particularity the grounds for the motion, the relief sought, and the legal argument necessary to support it.

(B) Accompanying documents.

(i) Any affidavit or other paper necessary to support a motion must be served and filed with the motion.

(ii) An affidavit must contain only factual information, not legal argument.

(iii) A motion seeking substantive relief must include a copy of the trial court's opinion or agency's decision as a separate exhibit.

(C) Documents barred or not required.

(i) A separate brief supporting or responding to a motion must not be filed.

(ii) A notice of motion is not required.

(iii) A proposed order is not required.

(3) Response.

(A) Time to file. Any party may file a response to a motion; Rule 27(a)(2) governs its contents. The response must be filed within 10 days after service of the motion unless the court shortens or extends the time. A motion authorized by Rules 8, 9, 18, or 41 may be granted before the 10-day period runs only if the court gives reasonable notice to the parties that it intends to act sooner.

(B) Request for affirmative relief. A response may include a motion for affirmative relief. The time to respond to the new motion, and to reply to that response, are governed by Rule 27(a)(3)(A) and (a)(4). The title of the response must alert the court to the request for relief.

(4) Reply to Response. Any reply to a response must be filed within 7 days after service of the response. A reply must not present matters that do not relate to the response.

(b) Disposition of a Motion for a Procedural Order. The court may act on a motion for a procedural order—including a motion under Rule 26(b)—at any time without awaiting a response, and may, by rule or by order in a particular case, authorize its clerk to act on specified types of procedural motions. A party adversely affected by the court's, or the clerk's, action may file a motion to reconsider, vacate, or modify that action. Timely opposition filed after the motion is granted in whole or in part does not constitute a request to reconsider, vacate, or modify the disposition; a motion requesting that relief must be filed.

(c) Power of a Single Judge to Entertain a Motion. A circuit judge may act alone on any motion, but may not dismiss or otherwise determine an appeal or other proceeding. A court of appeals may provide by rule or by order in a particular case that only the court may act on any motion or class of motions. The court may review the action of a single judge.

(d) Form of Papers; Length Limits; Number of Copies.

(1) Format.

(A) Reproduction. A motion, response, or reply may be reproduced by any process that yields a clear black image on light paper. The paper must be opaque and unglazed. Only one side of the paper may be used.

(B) Cover. A cover is not required, but there must be a caption that includes the case number, the name of the court, the title of the case, and a brief descriptive title indicating the purpose of the motion and identifying the party or parties for whom it is filed. If a cover is used, it must be white.

(C) Binding. The document must be bound in any manner that is secure, does not obscure the text, and permits the document to lie reasonably flat when open.

(D) Paper size, line spacing, and margins. The document must be on 8½ by 11 inch paper. The text must be double-spaced, but quotations more than two lines long may be indented and single-spaced. Headings and footnotes may be single-spaced. Margins must be at least one inch on all four sides. Page numbers may be placed in the margins, but no text may appear there.

(E) Typeface and type styles. The document must comply with the typeface requirements of Rule 32(a)(5) and the type-style requirements of Rule 32(a)(6).

(2) Length Limits. Except by the court's permission, and excluding the accompanying documents authorized by Rule 27(a)(2)(B):

(A) a motion or response to a motion produced using a computer must not exceed 5,200 words;

(B) a handwritten or typewritten motion or response to a motion must not exceed 20 pages;

(C) a reply produced using a computer must not exceed 2,600 words; and

(D) a handwritten or typewritten reply to a response must not exceed 10 pages.

(3) Number of Copies. An original and 3 copies must be filed unless the court requires a different number by local rule or by order in a particular case.

(e) Oral Argument. A motion will be decided without oral argument unless the court orders otherwise.

(As amended Apr. 30, 1979, eff. Aug. 1, 1979; Apr. 25, 1989, eff. Dec. 1, 1989; Apr. 29, 1994, eff. Dec. 1, 1994; Apr. 24, 1998, eff. Dec. 1, 1998; Apr. 29, 2002, eff. Dec. 1, 2002; Apr. 25, 2005, eff. Dec. 1, 2005; Mar. 26, 2009, eff. Dec. 1, 2009; Apr. 28, 2016, eff. Dec. 1, 2016.)

RULE 28. BRIEFS

(a) Appellant's Brief. The appellant's brief must contain, under appropriate headings and in the order indicated:

(1) a corporate disclosure statement if required by Rule 26.1;

(2) a table of contents, with page references;

(3) a table of authorities—cases (alphabetically arranged), statutes, and other authorities—with references to the pages of the brief where they are cited;

(4) a jurisdictional statement, including:

(A) the basis for the district court's or agency's subject-matter jurisdiction, with citations to applicable statutory provisions and stating relevant facts establishing jurisdiction;

(B) the basis for the court of appeals' jurisdiction, with citations to applicable statutory provisions and stating relevant facts establishing jurisdiction;

(C) the filing dates establishing the timeliness of the appeal or petition for review; and

(D) an assertion that the appeal is from a final order or judgment that disposes of all parties' claims, or information establishing the court of appeals' jurisdiction on some other basis;

(5) a statement of the issues presented for review;

(6) a concise statement of the case setting out the facts relevant to the issues submitted for review, describing the relevant procedural history, and identifying the rulings presented for review, with appropriate references to the record (see Rule 28(e));

(7) a summary of the argument, which must contain a succinct, clear, and accurate statement of the arguments made in the body of the brief, and which must not merely repeat the argument headings;

(8) the argument, which must contain:

(A) appellant's contentions and the reasons for them, with citations to the authorities and parts of the record on which the appellant relies; and

(B) for each issue, a concise statement of the applicable standard of review (which may appear in the discussion of the issue or under a separate heading placed before the discussion of the issues);

(9) a short conclusion stating the precise relief sought; and

(10) the certificate of compliance, if required by Rule 32(g)(1).

(b) Appellee's Brief. The appellee's brief must conform to the requirements of Rule 28(a)(1)–(8) and (10), except that none of the following need appear unless the appellee is dissatisfied with the appellant's statement:

(1) the jurisdictional statement;

(2) the statement of the issues;

(3) the statement of the case; and

(4) the statement of the standard of review.

(c) Reply Brief. The appellant may file a brief in reply to the appellee's brief. Unless the court permits, no further briefs may be filed. A reply brief must contain a table of contents, with page references, and a table of authorities—cases (alphabetically arranged), statutes, and other authorities—with references to the pages of the reply brief where they are cited.

(d) References to Parties. In briefs and at oral argument, counsel should minimize use of the terms "appellant" and "appellee." To make briefs clear, counsel should use the parties' actual names or the designations used in the lower court or agency proceeding, or such descriptive terms as "the employee," "the injured person," "the taxpayer," "the ship," "the stevedore."

(e) References to the Record. References to the parts of the record contained in the appendix filed with the appellant's brief must be to the pages of the appendix. If the appendix is prepared after the briefs are filed, a party referring to the record must follow one of the methods detailed in Rule 30(c). If the original record is used under Rule 30(f) and is not consecutively paginated, or if the brief refers to an unreproduced part of the record, any reference must be to the page of the original document. For example:

- Answer p. 7;
- Motion for Judgment p. 2;
- Transcript p. 231.

Only clear abbreviations may be used. A party referring to evidence whose admissibility is in controversy must cite the pages of the appendix or of the transcript at which the evidence was identified, offered, and received or rejected.

(f) Reproduction of Statutes, Rules, Regulations, etc. If the court's determination of the issues presented requires the study of statutes, rules, regulations, etc., the relevant parts must be set out in the brief or in an addendum at the end, or may be supplied to the court in pamphlet form.

(g) [Reserved]

(h) [Deleted]

(i) Briefs in a Case Involving Multiple Appellants or Appellees. In a case involving more than one appellant or appellee, including consolidated cases, any number of appellants or appellees may join in a brief, and any party may adopt by reference a part of another's brief. Parties may also join in reply briefs.

(j) Citation of Supplemental Authorities. If pertinent and significant authorities come to a party's attention after the party's brief has been filed—or after oral argument but before decision—a party may promptly advise the circuit clerk by letter, with a copy to all other parties, setting forth the citations. The letter must state the reasons for the supplemental citations, referring either to the page of the brief or to a point argued orally. The body of the letter must not exceed 350 words. Any response must be made promptly and must be similarly limited.

(As amended Apr. 30, 1979, eff. Aug. 1, 1979; Mar. 10, 1986, eff. July 1, 1986; Apr. 25, 1989, eff. Dec. 1, 1989; Apr. 30, 1991, eff. Dec. 1, 1991; Apr. 22, 1993, eff. Dec. 1, 1993; Apr. 29, 1994, eff. Dec. 1, 1994; Apr. 24, 1998, eff. Dec. 1, 1998; Apr. 29, 2002, eff. Dec. 1, 2002; Apr. 25, 2005, eff. Dec. 1, 2005; Apr. 16, 2013, eff. Dec. 1, 2013; Apr. 28, 2016, eff. Dec. 1, 2016.)

RULE 28.1 CROSS–APPEALS

(a) Applicability. This rule applies to a case in which a cross-appeal is filed. Rules 28(a)-(c), 31(a)(1), 32(a)(2), and 32(a)(7)(A)-(B) do not apply to such a case, except as otherwise provided in this rule.

(b) Designation of Appellant. The party who files a notice of appeal first is the appellant for the purposes of this rule and Rules 30 and 34. If notices are filed on the same day, the plaintiff in the proceeding below is the appellant. These designations may be modified by the parties' agreement or by court order.

(c) Briefs. In a case involving a cross-appeal:

(1) Appellant's Principal Brief. The appellant must file a principal brief in the appeal. That brief must comply with Rule 28(a).

(2) Appellee's Principal and Response Brief. The appellee must file a principal brief in the cross-appeal and must, in the same brief, respond to the principal brief in the appeal. That appellee's brief must comply with Rule 28(a), except that the brief need not include a statement of the case unless the appellee is dissatisfied with the appellant's statement.

(3) Appellant's Response and Reply Brief. The appellant must file a brief that responds to the principal brief in the cross-appeal and may, in the same brief, reply to the response in the appeal. That brief must comply with Rule 28(a)(2)–(8) and (10), except that none of the following need appear unless the appellant is dissatisfied with the appellee's statement in the cross-appeal:

(A) the jurisdictional statement;

(B) the statement of the issues;

(C) the statement of the case; and

(D) the statement of the standard of review.

(4) Appellee's Reply Brief. The appellee may file a brief in reply to the response in the cross-appeal. That brief must comply with Rule 28(a)(2)–(3) and (10) and must be limited to the issues presented by the cross-appeal.

(5) No Further Briefs. Unless the court permits, no further briefs may be filed in a case involving a cross-appeal.

(d) Cover. Except for filings by unrepresented parties, the cover of the appellant's principal brief must be blue; the appellee's principal and response brief, red; the appellant's response and reply brief, yellow; the appellee's reply brief, gray; an intervenor's or amicus curiae's brief, green; and any supplemental brief, tan. The front cover of a brief must contain the information required by Rule 32(a)(2).

(e) Length.

(1) Page Limitation. Unless it complies with Rule 28.1(e)(2), the appellant's principal brief must not exceed 30 pages; the appellee's principal and response brief, 35 pages; the appellant's response and reply brief, 30 pages; and the appellee's reply brief, 15 pages.

(2) Type-Volume Limitation.

(A) The appellant's principal brief or the appellant's response and reply brief is acceptable if it:

(i) contains no more than 13,000 words; or

(ii) uses a monospaced face and contains no more than 1,300 lines of text.

(B) The appellee's principal and response brief is acceptable if it:

(i) contains no more than 15,300 words; or

(ii) uses a monospaced face and contains no more than 1,500 lines of text.

(C) The appellee's reply brief is acceptable if it contains no more than half of the type volume specified in Rule 28.1(e)(2)(A).

(f) Time to Serve and File a Brief. Briefs must be served and filed as follows:

(1) the appellant's principal brief, within 40 days after the record is filed;

(2) the appellee's principal and response brief, within 30 days after the appellant's principal brief is served;

(3) the appellant's response and reply brief, within 30 days after the appellee's principal and response brief is served; and

(4) the appellee's reply brief, within 14 days after the appellant's response and reply brief is served, but at least 7 days before argument unless the court, for good cause, allows a later filing.

(As added April 25, 2005, eff. Dec. 1, 2005; amended Mar. 26, 2009, eff. Dec. 1, 2009; Apr. 16, 2013, eff. Dec. 1, 2013; Apr. 28, 2016, eff. Dec. 1, 2016.)

RULE 29. BRIEF OF AN AMICUS CURIAE

(a) During Initial Consideration of a Case on the Merits.

(1) Applicability. This Rule 29(a) governs amicus filings during a court's initial consideration of a case on the merits.

(2) When Permitted. The United States or its officer or agency or a state may file an amicus-curiae brief without the consent of the parties or leave of court. Any other amicus curiae may file a brief only by leave of court or if the brief states that all parties have consented to its filing.

(3) Motion for Leave to File. The motion must be accompanied by the proposed brief and state:

(A) the movant's interest; and

(B) the reason why an amicus brief is desirable and why the matters asserted are relevant to the disposition of the case.

(4) Contents and Form. An amicus brief must comply with Rule 32. In addition to the requirements of Rule 32, the cover must identify the party or parties supported and indicate whether the brief supports affirmance or reversal. An amicus brief need not comply with Rule 28, but must include the following:

(A) if the amicus curiae is a corporation, a disclosure statement like that required of parties by Rule 26.1;

(B) a table of contents, with page references;

(C) a table of authorities—cases (alphabetically arranged), statutes, and other authorities— with references to the pages of the brief where they are cited;

(D) a concise statement of the identity of the amicus curiae, its interest in the case, and the source of its authority to file;

(E) unless the amicus curiae is one listed in the first sentence of Rule 29(a)(2), a statement that indicates whether:

(i) a party's counsel authored the brief in whole or in part;

(ii) a party or a party's counsel contributed money that was intended to fund preparing or submitting the brief; and

(iii) a person—other than the amicus curiae, its members, or its counsel—contributed money that was intended to fund preparing or submitting the brief and, if so, identifies each such person;

(F) an argument, which may be preceded by a summary and which need not include a statement of the applicable standard of review; and

(G) a certificate of compliance under Rule 32(g)(1), if length is computed using a word or line limit.

(5) Length. Except by the court's permission, an amicus brief may be no more than one-half the maximum length authorized by these rules for a party's principal brief. If the court grants a party permission to file a longer brief, that extension does not affect the length of an amicus brief.

(6) Time for Filing. An amicus curiae must file its brief, accompanied by a motion for filing when necessary, no later than 7 days after the principal brief of the party being supported is filed. An amicus curiae that does not support either party must file its brief no later than 7 days after the appellant's or petitioner's principal brief is filed. A court may grant leave for later filing, specifying the time within which an opposing party may answer.

(7) Reply Brief. Except by the court's permission, an amicus curiae may not file a reply brief.

(8) Oral Argument. An amicus curiae may participate in oral argument only with the court's permission.

(b) During Consideration of Whether to Grant Rehearing.

(1) Applicability. This Rule 29(b) governs amicus filings during a court's consideration of whether to grant panel rehearing or rehearing en banc, unless a local rule or order in a case provides otherwise.

(2) When Permitted. The United States or its officer or agency or a state may file an amicus-curiae brief without the consent of the parties or leave of court. Any other amicus curiae may file a brief only by leave of court.

(3) Motion for Leave to File. Rule 29(a)(3) applies to a motion for leave.

(4) Contents, Form, and Length. Rule 29(a)(4) applies to the amicus brief. The brief must not exceed 2,600 words.

(5) Time for Filing. An amicus curiae supporting the petition for rehearing or supporting neither party must file its brief, accompanied by a motion for filing when necessary, no later than 7 days after the petition is filed. An amicus curiae opposing the petition must file its brief, accompanied by a motion for filing when necessary, no later than the date set by the court for the response.

(As amended Apr. 24, 1998, eff. Dec. 1, 1998; Apr. 28, 2010, eff. Dec. 1, 2010; Apr. 28, 2016, eff. Dec. 1, 2016.)

RULE 30. APPENDIX TO THE BRIEFS

(a) Appellant's Responsibility.

(1) Contents of the Appendix. The appellant must prepare and file an appendix to the briefs containing:

(A) the relevant docket entries in the proceeding below;

(B) the relevant portions of the pleadings, charge, findings, or opinion;

(C) the judgment, order, or decision in question; and

(D) other parts of the record to which the parties wish to direct the court's attention.

(2) Excluded Material. Memoranda of law in the district court should not be included in the appendix unless they have independent relevance. Parts of the record may be relied on by the court or the parties even though not included in the appendix.

(3) Time to File; Number of Copies. Unless filing is deferred under Rule 30(c), the appellant must file 10 copies of the appendix with the brief and must serve one copy on counsel for each party separately represented. An unrepresented party proceeding in forma pauperis must file 4 legible copies with the clerk, and one copy must be served on counsel for each separately represented party. The court may by local rule or by order in a particular case require the filing or service of a different number.

(b) All Parties' Responsibilities.

(1) Determining the Contents of the Appendix. The parties are encouraged to agree on the contents of the appendix. In the absence of an agreement, the appellant must, within 14 days after the record is filed, serve on the appellee a designation of the parts of the record the appellant intends to include in the appendix and a statement of the issues the appellant intends to present for review. The appellee may, within 14 days after receiving the designation, serve on the appellant a designation of additional parts to which it wishes to direct the court's attention. The appellant must include the designated parts in the appendix. The parties must not engage in unnecessary designation of parts of the record, because the entire record is available to the court. This paragraph applies also to a cross-appellant and a cross-appellee.

(2) Costs of Appendix. Unless the parties agree otherwise, the appellant must pay the cost of the appendix. If the appellant considers parts of the record designated by the appellee to be unnecessary, the appellant may advise the appellee, who must then advance the cost of including those parts. The cost of the appendix is a taxable cost. But if any party causes unnecessary parts of the record to be included in the appendix, the court may impose the cost of those parts on that party. Each circuit must, by local rule, provide for sanctions against attorneys who unreasonably and vexatiously increase litigation costs by including unnecessary material in the appendix.

(c) Deferred Appendix.

(1) Deferral Until After Briefs Are Filed. The court may provide by rule for classes of cases or by order in a particular case that preparation of the appendix may be deferred until after the briefs have been filed and that the appendix may be filed 21 days after the appellee's brief is served. Even though the filing of the appendix may be deferred, Rule 30(b) applies; except that a party must designate the parts of the record it wants included in the appendix when it serves its brief, and need not include a statement of the issues presented.

(2) References to the Record.

(A) If the deferred appendix is used, the parties may cite in their briefs the pertinent pages of the record. When the appendix is prepared, the record pages cited in the briefs must be indicated by inserting record page numbers, in brackets, at places in the appendix where those pages of the record appear.

(B) A party who wants to refer directly to pages of the appendix may serve and file copies of the brief within the time required by Rule 31(a), containing appropriate references to pertinent pages of the record. In that event, within 14 days after the appendix is filed, the party must serve and file copies of the brief, containing references to the pages of the appendix in place of or in addition to the references to the pertinent pages of the record. Except for the correction of typographical errors, no other changes may be made to the brief.

(d) Format of the Appendix. The appendix must begin with a table of contents identifying the page at which each part begins. The relevant docket entries must follow the table of contents. Other parts of the record must follow chronologically. When pages from the transcript of proceedings are placed in the appendix, the transcript page numbers must be shown in brackets immediately before the included pages. Omissions in the text of papers or of the transcript must be indicated by asterisks. Immaterial formal matters (captions, subscriptions, acknowledgments, etc.) should be omitted.

(e) Reproduction of Exhibits. Exhibits designated for inclusion in the appendix may be reproduced in a separate volume, or volumes, suitably indexed. Four copies must be filed with the appendix, and one copy must be served on counsel for each separately represented party. If a transcript of a proceeding before an administrative agency, board, commission, or officer was used in a district-court action and has been designated for inclusion in the appendix, the transcript must be placed in the appendix as an exhibit.

(f) Appeal on the Original Record Without an Appendix. The court may, either by rule for all cases or classes of cases or by order in a particular case, dispense with the appendix and permit an appeal to proceed on the original record with any copies of the record, or relevant parts, that the court may order the parties to file.

(As amended Mar. 30, 1970, eff. July 1, 1970; Mar. 10, 1986, eff. July 1, 1986; Apr. 30, 1991, eff. Dec. 1, 1991; Apr. 29, 1994, eff. Dec. 1, 1994; Apr. 24, 1998, eff. Dec. 1, 1998; Mar. 26, 2009, eff. Dec. 1, 2009.)

RULE 31. SERVING AND FILING BRIEFS

(a) Time to Serve and File a Brief.

(1) The appellant must serve and file a brief within 40 days after the record is filed. The appellee must serve and file a brief within 30 days after the appellant's brief is served. The appellant may serve and file a reply brief within 14 days after service of the appellee's brief but a reply brief must be filed at least 7 days before argument, unless the court, for good cause, allows a later filing.

(2) A court of appeals that routinely considers cases on the merits promptly after the briefs are filed may shorten the time to serve and file briefs, either by local rule or by order in a particular case.

(b) Number of Copies. Twenty-five copies of each brief must be filed with the clerk and 2 copies must be served on each unrepresented party and on counsel for each separately represented party. An unrepresented party proceeding in forma pauperis must file 4 legible copies with the clerk, and one copy must be served on each unrepresented party and on counsel for each separately represented party. The court may by local rule or by order in a particular case require the filing or service of a different number.

(c) Consequence of Failure to File. If an appellant fails to file a brief within the time provided by this rule, or within an extended time, an appellee may move to dismiss the appeal. An appellee who fails to file a brief will not be heard at oral argument unless the court grants permission.

(As amended Mar. 30, 1970, eff. July 1, 1970; Mar. 10, 1986, eff. July 1, 1986; Apr. 29, 1994, eff. Dec. 1, 1994; Apr. 24, 1998, eff. Dec. 1, 1998; Apr. 29, 2002, eff. Dec. 1, 2002; Mar. 26, 2009, eff. Dec. 1, 2009.)

RULE 32. FORM OF BRIEFS, APPENDICES, AND OTHER PAPERS

(a) Form of a Brief.

(1) Reproduction.

(A) A brief may be reproduced by any process that yields a clear black image on light paper. The paper must be opaque and unglazed. Only one side of the paper may be used.

(B) Text must be reproduced with a clarity that equals or exceeds the output of a laser printer.

(C) Photographs, illustrations, and tables may be reproduced by any method that results in a good copy of the original; a glossy finish is acceptable if the original is glossy.

(2) Cover. Except for filings by unrepresented parties, the cover of the appellant's brief must be blue; the appellee's, red; an intervenor's or amicus curiae's, green; any reply brief, gray; and any supplemental brief, tan. The front cover of a brief must contain:

(A) the number of the case centered at the top;

(B) the name of the court;

(C) the title of the case (see Rule 12(a));

(D) the nature of the proceeding (e.g., Appeal, Petition for Review) and the name of the court, agency, or board below;

(E) the title of the brief, identifying the party or parties for whom the brief is filed; and

(F) the name, office address, and telephone number of counsel representing the party for whom the brief is filed.

(3) Binding. The brief must be bound in any manner that is secure, does not obscure the text, and permits the brief to lie reasonably flat when open.

(4) Paper Size, Line Spacing, and Margins. The brief must be on 8½ by 11 inch paper. The text must be double-spaced, but quotations more than two lines long may be indented and single-spaced. Headings and footnotes may be single-spaced. Margins must be at least one inch on all four sides. Page numbers may be placed in the margins, but no text may appear there.

(5) Typeface. Either a proportionally spaced or a monospaced face may be used.

(A) A proportionally spaced face must include serifs, but sans-serif type may be used in headings and captions. A proportionally spaced face must be 14-point or larger.

(B) A monospaced face may not contain more than 10½ characters per inch.

(6) Type Styles. A brief must be set in a plain, roman style, although italics or boldface may be used for emphasis. Case names must be italicized or underlined.

(7) Length.

(A) Page Limitation. A principal brief may not exceed 30 pages, or a reply brief 15 pages, unless it complies with Rule 32(a)(7)(B).

(B) Type-Volume Limitation.

(i) A principal brief is acceptable if it:

- contains no more than 13,000 words; or
- uses a monospaced face and contains no more than 1,300 lines of text.

(ii) A reply brief is acceptable if it contains no more than half of the type volume specified in Rule 32(a)(7)(B)(i).

(b) Form of an Appendix. An appendix must comply with Rule 32(a)(1), (2), (3), and (4), with the following exceptions:

(1) The cover of a separately bound appendix must be white.

(2) An appendix may include a legible photocopy of any document found in the record or of a printed judicial or agency decision.

(3) When necessary to facilitate inclusion of odd-sized documents such as technical drawings, an appendix may be a size other than 8½ by 11 inches, and need not lie reasonably flat when opened.

(c) Form of Other Papers.

(1) Motion. The form of a motion is governed by Rule 27(d).

(2) Other Papers. Any other paper, including a petition for panel rehearing and a petition for hearing or rehearing en banc, and any response to such a petition, must be reproduced in the manner prescribed by Rule 32(a), with the following exceptions:

(A) A cover is not necessary if the caption and signature page of the paper together contain the information required by Rule 32(a)(2). If a cover is used, it must be white.

(B) Rule 32(a)(7) does not apply.

(d) Signature. Every brief, motion, or other paper filed with the court must be signed by the party filing the paper or, if the party is represented, by one of the party's attorneys.

(e) Local Variation. Every court of appeals must accept documents that comply with the form requirements of this rule and the length limits set by these rules. By local rule or order in a particular case, a court of appeals may accept documents that do not meet all the form requirements of this rule or the length limits set by these rules.

(f) Items Excluded from Length. In computing any length limit, headings, footnotes, and quotations count toward the limit but the following items do not:

- the cover page;
- a corporate disclosure statement;
- a table of contents;
- a table of citations;
- a statement regarding oral argument;
- an addendum containing statutes, rules, or regulations;
- certificates of counsel;
- the signature block;
- the proof of service; and
- any item specifically excluded by these rules or by local rule.

(g) Certificate of Compliance.

(1) Briefs and Papers That Require a Certificate. A brief submitted under Rules 28.1(e)(2), 29(b)(4), or 32(a)(7)(B)—and a paper submitted under Rules 5(c)(1), 21(d)(1), 27(d)(2)(A), 27(d)(2)(C), 35(b)(2)(A), or 40(b)(1)—must include a certificate by the attorney, or an unrepresented party, that the document complies with the type-volume limitation. The person preparing the certificate may rely on the word or line count of the word-processing system used to prepare the document. The certificate must state the number of words—or the number of lines of monospaced type—in the document.

(2) Acceptable Form. Form 6 in the Appendix of Forms meets the requirements for a certificate of compliance.

(As amended Apr. 24, 1998, eff. Dec. 1, 1998; Apr. 29, 2002, eff. Dec. 1, 2002; Apr. 25, 2005, eff. Dec. 1, 2005; Apr. 28, 2016, eff. Dec. 1, 2016.)

RULE 32.1 CITING JUDICIAL DISPOSITIONS

(a) Citation Permitted. A court may not prohibit or restrict the citation of federal judicial opinions, orders, judgments, or other written dispositions that have been:

(i) designated as "unpublished," "not for publication," "non-precedential," "not precedent," or the like; and

(ii) issued on or after January 1, 2007.

(b) Copies Required. If a party cites a federal judicial opinion, order, judgment, or other written disposition that is not available in a publicly accessible electronic database, the party must file and serve a copy of that opinion, order, judgment, or disposition with the brief or other paper in which it is cited.

(Added Apr. 12, 2006, eff. Dec. 1, 2006.)

RULE 33. APPEAL CONFERENCES

The court may direct the attorneys—and, when appropriate, the parties—to participate in one or more conferences to address any matter that may aid in disposing of the proceedings, including simplifying the issues and discussing settlement. A judge or other person designated by the court may preside over the conference, which may be conducted in person or by telephone. Before a settlement conference, the attorneys must consult with their clients and obtain as much authority as feasible to settle the case. The court may, as a result of the conference, enter an order controlling the course of the proceedings or implementing any settlement agreement.

(As amended Apr. 29, 1994, eff. Dec. 1, 1994; Apr. 24, 1998, eff. Dec. 1, 1998.)

RULE 34. ORAL ARGUMENT

(a) In General.

(1) Party's Statement. Any party may file, or a court may require by local rule, a statement explaining why oral argument should, or need not, be permitted.

(2) Standards. Oral argument must be allowed in every case unless a panel of three judges who have examined the briefs and record unanimously agrees that oral argument is unnecessary for any of the following reasons:

(A) the appeal is frivolous;

(B) the dispositive issue or issues have been authoritatively decided; or

(C) the facts and legal arguments are adequately presented in the briefs and record, and the decisional process would not be significantly aided by oral argument.

(b) Notice of Argument; Postponement. The clerk must advise all parties whether oral argument will be scheduled, and, if so, the date, time, and place for it, and the time allowed for each side. A motion to postpone the argument or to allow longer argument must be filed reasonably in advance of the hearing date.

(c) Order and Contents of Argument. The appellant opens and concludes the argument. Counsel must not read at length from briefs, records, or authorities.

(d) Cross-Appeals and Separate Appeals. If there is a cross-appeal, Rule 28.1(b) determines which party is the appellant and which is the appellee for purposes of oral argument. Unless the court directs otherwise, a cross-appeal or separate appeal must be argued when the initial appeal is argued. Separate parties should avoid duplicative argument.

(e) Nonappearance of a Party. If the appellee fails to appear for argument, the court must hear appellant's argument. If the appellant fails to appear for argument, the court may hear the appellee's argument. If neither party appears, the case will be decided on the briefs, unless the court orders otherwise.

(f) Submission on Briefs. The parties may agree to submit a case for decision on the briefs, but the court may direct that the case be argued.

(g) Use of Physical Exhibits at Argument; Removal. Counsel intending to use physical exhibits other than documents at the argument must arrange to place them in the courtroom on the day of the argument before the court convenes. After the argument, counsel must remove the exhibits from the courtroom, unless the court directs otherwise. The clerk may destroy or dispose of the exhibits if counsel does not reclaim them within a reasonable time after the clerk gives notice to remove them.

(As amended Apr. 30, 1979, eff. Aug. 1, 1979; Mar. 10, 1986, eff. July 1, 1986; Apr. 30, 1991, eff. Dec. 1, 1991; Apr. 22, 1993, eff. Dec. 1, 1993; Apr. 24, 1998, eff. Dec. 1, 1998; Apr. 25, 2005, eff. Dec. 1, 2005.)

RULE 35. EN BANC DETERMINATION

(a) When Hearing or Rehearing En Banc May Be Ordered. A majority of the circuit judges who are in regular active service and who are not disqualified may order that an appeal or other proceeding be heard or reheard by the court of appeals en banc. An en banc hearing or rehearing is not favored and ordinarily will not be ordered unless:

(1) en banc consideration is necessary to secure or maintain uniformity of the court's decisions; or

(2) the proceeding involves a question of exceptional importance.

(b) Petition for Hearing or Rehearing En Banc. A party may petition for a hearing or rehearing en banc.

(1) The petition must begin with a statement that either:

(A) the panel decision conflicts with a decision of the United States Supreme Court or of the court to which the petition is addressed (with citation to the conflicting case or cases) and consideration by the full court is therefore necessary to secure and maintain uniformity of the court's decisions; or

(B) the proceeding involves one or more questions of exceptional importance, each of which must be concisely stated; for example, a petition may assert that a proceeding presents a question of exceptional importance if it involves an issue on which the panel decision conflicts with the authoritative decisions of other United States Courts of Appeals that have addressed the issue.

(2) Except by the court's permission:

(A) a petition for an en banc hearing or rehearing produced using a computer must not exceed 3,900 words; and

(B) a handwritten or typewritten petition for an en banc hearing or rehearing must not exceed 15 pages.

(3) For purposes of the limits in Rule 35(b)(2), if a party files both a petition for panel rehearing and a petition for rehearing en banc, they are considered a single document even if they are filed separately, unless separate filing is required by local rule.

(c) Time for Petition for Hearing or Rehearing En Banc. A petition that an appeal be heard initially en banc must be filed by the date when the appellee's brief is due. A petition for a rehearing en banc must be filed within the time prescribed by Rule 40 for filing a petition for rehearing.

(d) Number of Copies. The number of copies to be filed must be prescribed by local rule and may be altered by order in a particular case.

(e) Response. No response may be filed to a petition for an en banc consideration unless the court orders a response.

(f) Call for a Vote. A vote need not be taken to determine whether the case will be heard or reheard en banc unless a judge calls for a vote.

(As amended Apr. 30, 1979, eff. Aug. 1, 1979; Apr. 29, 1994, eff. Dec. 1, 1994; Apr. 24, 1998, eff. Dec. 1, 1998; Apr. 25, 2005, eff. Dec. 1, 2005; Apr. 28, 2016, eff. Dec. 1, 2016.)

RULE 36. ENTRY OF JUDGMENT; NOTICE

(a) Entry. A judgment is entered when it is noted on the docket. The clerk must prepare, sign, and enter the judgment:

(1) after receiving the court's opinion—but if settlement of the judgment's form is required, after final settlement; or

(2) if a judgment is rendered without an opinion, as the court instructs.

(b) Notice. On the date when judgment is entered, the clerk must serve on all parties a copy of the opinion—or the judgment, if no opinion was written—and a notice of the date when the judgment was entered.

(As amended Apr. 24, 1998, eff. Dec. 1, 1998; Apr. 29, 2002, eff. Dec. 1, 2002.)

RULE 37. INTEREST ON JUDGMENT

(a) When the Court Affirms. Unless the law provides otherwise, if a money judgment in a civil case is affirmed, whatever interest is allowed by law is payable from the date when the district court's judgment was entered.

(b) When the Court Reverses. If the court modifies or reverses a judgment with a direction that a money judgment be entered in the district court, the mandate must contain instructions about the allowance of interest.

(As amended Apr. 24, 1998, eff. Dec. 1, 1998.)

RULE 38. FRIVOLOUS APPEAL—DAMAGES AND COSTS

If a court of appeals determines that an appeal is frivolous, it may, after a separately filed motion or notice from the court and reasonable opportunity to respond, award just damages and single or double costs to the appellee.

(As amended Apr. 29, 1994, eff. Dec. 1, 1994; Apr. 24, 1998, eff. Dec. 1, 1998.)

RULE 39. COSTS

(a) Against Whom Assessed. The following rules apply unless the law provides or the court orders otherwise:

(1) if an appeal is dismissed, costs are taxed against the appellant, unless the parties agree otherwise;

(2) if a judgment is affirmed, costs are taxed against the appellant;

(3) if a judgment is reversed, costs are taxed against the appellee;

(4) if a judgment is affirmed in part, reversed in part, modified, or vacated, costs are taxed only as the court orders.

(b) Costs For and Against the United States. Costs for or against the United States, its agency, or officer will be assessed under Rule 39(a) only if authorized by law.

(c) Costs of Copies. Each court of appeals must, by local rule, fix the maximum rate for taxing the cost of producing necessary copies of a brief or appendix, or copies of records authorized by Rule 30(f). The rate must not exceed that generally charged for such work in the area where the clerk's office is located and should encourage economical methods of copying.

(d) Bill of Costs: Objections; Insertion in Mandate.

(1) A party who wants costs taxed must—within 14 days after entry of judgment—file with the circuit clerk, with proof of service, an itemized and verified bill of costs.

(2) Objections must be filed within 14 days after service of the bill of costs, unless the court extends the time.

(3) The clerk must prepare and certify an itemized statement of costs for insertion in the mandate, but issuance of the mandate must not be delayed for taxing costs. If the mandate issues before costs are finally determined, the district clerk must—upon the circuit clerk's request—add the statement of costs, or any amendment of it, to the mandate.

(e) Costs on Appeal Taxable in the District Court. The following costs on appeal are taxable in the district court for the benefit of the party entitled to costs under this rule:

(1) the preparation and transmission of the record;

(2) the reporter's transcript, if needed to determine the appeal;

(3) premiums paid for a supersedeas bond or other bond to preserve rights pending appeal; and

(4) the fee for filing the notice of appeal.

(As amended Apr. 30, 1979, eff. Aug. 1, 1979; Mar. 10, 1986, eff. July 1, 1986; Apr. 24, 1998, eff. Dec. 1, 1998; Mar. 26, 2009, eff. Dec. 1, 2009.)

RULE 40. PETITION FOR PANEL REHEARING

(a) Time to File; Contents; Answer; Action by the Court if Granted.

(1) **Time.** Unless the time is shortened or extended by order or local rule, a petition for panel rehearing may be filed within 14 days after entry of judgment. But in a civil case, unless an order shortens or extends the time, the petition may be filed by any party within 45 days after entry of judgment if one of the parties is:

(A) the United States;

(B) a United States agency;

(C) a United States officer or employee sued in an official capacity; or

(D) a current or former United States officer or employee sued in an individual capacity for an act or omission occurring in connection with duties performed on the United States' behalf—including all instances in which the United States represents that person when the court of appeals' judgment is entered or files the petition for that person.

(2) **Contents.** The petition must state with particularity each point of law or fact that the petitioner believes the court has overlooked or misapprehended and must argue in support of the petition. Oral argument is not permitted.

(3) **Answer.** Unless the court requests, no answer to a petition for panel rehearing is permitted. But ordinarily rehearing will not be granted in the absence of such a request.

(4) **Action by the Court.** If a petition for panel rehearing is granted, the court may do any of the following:

(A) make a final disposition of the case without reargument;

(B) restore the case to the calendar for reargument or resubmission; or

(C) issue any other appropriate order.

(b) Form of Petition; Length. The petition must comply in form with Rule 32. Copies must be served and filed as Rule 31 prescribes. Except by the court's permission:

(1) a petition for panel rehearing produced using a computer must not exceed 3,900 words; and

(2) a handwritten or typewritten petition for panel rehearing must not exceed 15 pages.

(As amended Apr. 30, 1979, eff. Aug. 1, 1979; Apr. 29, 1994, eff. Dec. 1, 1994; Apr. 24, 1998, eff. Dec. 1, 1998; Apr. 26, 2011, eff. Dec. 1, 2011; Apr. 28, 2016, eff. Dec. 1, 2016.)

RULE 41. MANDATE: CONTENTS; ISSUANCE AND EFFECTIVE DATE; STAY

(a) Contents. Unless the court directs that a formal mandate issue, the mandate consists of a certified copy of the judgment, a copy of the court's opinion, if any, and any direction about costs.

(b) When Issued. The court's mandate must issue 7 days after the time to file a petition for rehearing expires, or 7 days after entry of an order denying a timely petition for panel rehearing, petition for rehearing en banc, or motion for stay of mandate, whichever is later. The court may shorten or extend the time.

(c) Effective Date. The mandate is effective when issued.

(d) Staying the Mandate.

(1) On Petition for Rehearing or Motion. The timely filing of a petition for panel rehearing, petition for rehearing en banc, or motion for stay of mandate, stays the mandate until disposition of the petition or motion, unless the court orders otherwise.

(2) Pending Petition for Certiorari.

(A) A party may move to stay the mandate pending the filing of a petition for a writ of certiorari in the Supreme Court. The motion must be served on all parties and must show that the certiorari petition would present a substantial question and that there is good cause for a stay.

(B) The stay must not exceed 90 days, unless the period is extended for good cause or unless the party who obtained the stay files a petition for the writ and so notifies the circuit clerk in writing within the period of the stay. In that case, the stay continues until the Supreme Court's final disposition.

(C) The court may require a bond or other security as a condition to granting or continuing a stay of the mandate.

(D) The court of appeals must issue the mandate immediately when a copy of a Supreme Court order denying the petition for writ of certiorari is filed.

(As amended Apr. 29, 1994, eff. Dec. 1, 1994; Apr. 24, 1998, eff. Dec. 1, 1998; Apr. 29, 2002, eff. Dec. 1, 2002; Mar. 26, 2009, eff. Dec. 1, 2009.)

RULE 42. VOLUNTARY DISMISSAL

(a) Dismissal in the District Court. Before an appeal has been docketed by the circuit clerk, the district court may dismiss the appeal on the filing of a stipulation signed by all parties or on the appellant's motion with notice to all parties.

(b) Dismissal in the Court of Appeals. The circuit clerk may dismiss a docketed appeal if the parties file a signed dismissal agreement specifying how costs are to be paid and pay any fees that are due. But no mandate or other process may issue without a court order. An appeal may be dismissed on the appellant's motion on terms agreed to by the parties or fixed by the court.

(As amended Apr. 24, 1998, eff. Dec. 1, 1998.)

RULE 43. SUBSTITUTION OF PARTIES

(a) Death of a Party.

(1) After Notice of Appeal Is Filed. If a party dies after a notice of appeal has been filed or while a proceeding is pending in the court of appeals, the decedent's personal representative may be substituted as a party on motion filed with the circuit clerk by the representative or by any party. A party's motion must be served on the representative in accordance with Rule 25. If the decedent has no representative, any party may suggest the death on the record, and the court of appeals may then direct appropriate proceedings.

(2) Before Notice of Appeal Is Filed—Potential Appellant. If a party entitled to appeal dies before filing a notice of appeal, the decedent's personal representative—or, if there is no personal representative, the decedent's attorney of record—may file a notice of appeal within the time prescribed by these rules. After the notice of appeal is filed, substitution must be in accordance with Rule 43(a)(1).

(3) Before Notice of Appeal Is Filed—Potential Appellee. If a party against whom an appeal may be taken dies after entry of a judgment or order in the district court, but before a notice of appeal is filed, an appellant may proceed as if the death had not occurred. After the notice of appeal is filed, substitution must be in accordance with Rule 43(a)(1).

(b) Substitution for a Reason Other Than Death. If a party needs to be substituted for any reason other than death, the procedure prescribed in Rule 43(a) applies.

(c) Public Officer: Identification; Substitution.

(1) Identification of Party. A public officer who is a party to an appeal or other proceeding in an official capacity may be described as a party by the public officer's official title rather than by name. But the court may require the public officer's name to be added.

(2) Automatic Substitution of Officeholder. When a public officer who is a party to an appeal or other proceeding in an official capacity dies, resigns, or otherwise ceases to hold office, the action does not abate. The public officer's successor is automatically substituted as a party. Proceedings following the substitution are to be in the name of the substituted party, but any misnomer that does not affect the substantial rights of the parties may be disregarded. An order of substitution may be entered at any time, but failure to enter an order does not affect the substitution.

(As amended Mar. 10, 1986, eff. July 1, 1986; Apr. 24, 1998, eff. Dec. 1, 1998.)

RULE 44. CASE INVOLVING A CONSTITUTIONAL QUESTION WHEN THE UNITED STATES OR THE RELEVANT STATE IS NOT A PARTY

(a) Constitutional Challenge to Federal Statute. If a party questions the constitutionality of an Act of Congress in a proceeding in which the United States or its agency, officer, or employee is not a party in an official capacity, the questioning party must give written notice to the circuit clerk immediately upon the filing of the record or as soon as the question is raised in the court of appeals. The clerk must then certify that fact to the Attorney General.

(b) Constitutional Challenge to State Statute. If a party questions the constitutionality of a statute of a State in a proceeding in which that State or its agency, officer, or employee is not a party in an official capacity, the questioning party must give written notice to the circuit clerk immediately upon the filing of the record or as soon as the question is raised in the court of appeals. The clerk must then certify that fact to the attorney general of the State.

(As amended Apr. 24, 1998, eff. Dec. 1, 1998; Apr. 29, 2002, eff. Dec. 1, 2002.)

RULE 45. CLERK'S DUTIES

(a) General Provisions.

(1) Qualifications. The circuit clerk must take the oath and post any bond required by law. Neither the clerk nor any deputy clerk may practice as an attorney or counselor in any court while in office.

(2) When Court Is Open. The court of appeals is always open for filing any paper, issuing and returning process, making a motion, and entering an order. The clerk's office with the clerk or a deputy in attendance must be open during business hours on all days except Saturdays, Sundays, and legal holidays. A court may provide by local rule or by order that the clerk's office be open for specified hours on Saturdays or on legal holidays other than New Year's Day, Martin Luther King, Jr.'s Birthday, Washington's Birthday, Memorial Day, Independence Day, Labor Day, Columbus Day, Veterans' Day, Thanksgiving Day, and Christmas Day.

(b) Records.

(1) The Docket. The circuit clerk must maintain a docket and an index of all docketed cases in the manner prescribed by the Director of the Administrative Office of the United States Courts. The clerk must record all papers filed with the clerk and all process, orders, and judgments.

(2) Calendar. Under the court's direction, the clerk must prepare a calendar of cases awaiting argument. In placing cases on the calendar for argument, the clerk must give preference to appeals in criminal cases and to other proceedings and appeals entitled to preference by law.

(3) Other Records. The clerk must keep other books and records required by the Director of the Administrative Office of the United States Courts, with the approval of the Judicial Conference of the United States, or by the court.

(c) Notice of an Order or Judgment. Upon the entry of an order or judgment, the circuit clerk must immediately serve a notice of entry on each party, with a copy of any opinion, and must note the date of service on the docket. Service on a party represented by counsel must be made on counsel.

(d) Custody of Records and Papers. The circuit clerk has custody of the court's records and papers. Unless the court orders or instructs otherwise, the clerk must not permit an original record or paper to be taken from the clerk's office. Upon disposition of the case, original papers constituting the record on appeal or review must be returned to the court or agency from which they were received. The clerk must preserve a copy of any brief, appendix, or other paper that has been filed.

(As amended Mar. 1, 1971, eff. July 1, 1971; Mar. 10, 1986, eff. July 1, 1986; Apr. 24, 1998, eff. Dec. 1, 1998; Apr. 29, 2002, eff. Dec. 1, 2002; Apr. 25, 2005, eff. Dec. 1, 2005.)

RULE 46. ATTORNEYS

(a) Admission to the Bar.

(1) Eligibility. An attorney is eligible for admission to the bar of a court of appeals if that attorney is of good moral and professional character and is admitted to practice before the Supreme Court of the United States, the highest court of a state, another United States court of appeals, or a United States district court (including the district courts for Guam, the Northern Mariana Islands, and the Virgin Islands).

(2) Application. An applicant must file an application for admission, on a form approved by the court that contains the applicant's personal statement showing eligibility for membership. The applicant must subscribe to the following oath or affirmation:

"I, _______________, do solemnly swear [or affirm] that I will conduct myself as an attorney and counselor of this court, uprightly and according to law; and that I will support the Constitution of the United States."

(3) Admission Procedures. On written or oral motion of a member of the court's bar, the court will act on the application. An applicant may be admitted by oral motion in open court. But, unless the court orders otherwise, an applicant need not appear before the court to be admitted. Upon admission, an applicant must pay the clerk the fee prescribed by local rule or court order.

(b) Suspension or Disbarment.

(1) Standard. A member of the court's bar is subject to suspension or disbarment by the court if the member:

(A) has been suspended or disbarred from practice in any other court; or

(B) is guilty of conduct unbecoming a member of the court's bar.

(2) Procedure. The member must be given an opportunity to show good cause, within the time prescribed by the court, why the member should not be suspended or disbarred.

(3) Order. The court must enter an appropriate order after the member responds and a hearing is held, if requested, or after the time prescribed for a response expires, if no response is made.

(c) Discipline. A court of appeals may discipline an attorney who practices before it for conduct unbecoming a member of the bar or for failure to comply with any court rule. First, however, the court must afford the attorney reasonable notice, an opportunity to show cause to the contrary, and, if requested, a hearing.

(As amended Mar. 10, 1986, eff. July 1, 1986; Apr. 24, 1998, eff. Dec. 1, 1998.)

RULE 47. LOCAL RULES BY COURTS OF APPEALS

(a) Local Rules.

(1) Each court of appeals acting by a majority of its judges in regular active service may, after giving appropriate public notice and opportunity for comment, make and amend rules governing its practice. A generally applicable direction to parties or lawyers regarding practice before a court must be in a local rule rather than an internal operating procedure or standing order. A local rule must be consistent with—but not duplicative of—Acts of Congress and rules adopted under 28 U.S.C. § 2072 and must conform to any uniform numbering system prescribed by the Judicial Conference of the United States. Each circuit clerk must send the Administrative Office of the United States Courts a copy of each local rule and internal operating procedure when it is promulgated or amended.

(2) A local rule imposing a requirement of form must not be enforced in a manner that causes a party to lose rights because of a nonwillful failure to comply with the requirement.

(b) Procedure When There Is No Controlling Law. A court of appeals may regulate practice in a particular case in any manner consistent with federal law, these rules, and local rules of the circuit. No sanction or other disadvantage may be imposed for noncompliance with any requirement not in federal law, federal rules, or the local circuit rules unless the alleged violator has been furnished in the particular case with actual notice of the requirement.

(As amended Apr. 27, 1995, eff. Dec. 1, 1995; Apr. 24, 1998, eff. Dec. 1, 1998.)

RULE 48. MASTERS

(a) Appointment; Powers. A court of appeals may appoint a special master to hold hearings, if necessary, and to recommend factual findings and disposition in matters ancillary to proceedings in the court. Unless the order referring a matter to a master specifies or limits the master's powers, those powers include, but are not limited to, the following:

(1) regulating all aspects of a hearing;

(2) taking all appropriate action for the efficient performance of the master's duties under the order;

(3) requiring the production of evidence on all matters embraced in the reference; and

(4) administering oaths and examining witnesses and parties.

(b) Compensation. If the master is not a judge or court employee, the court must determine the master's compensation and whether the cost is to be charged to any party.

(As amended Apr. 29, 1994, eff. Dec. 1, 1994; Apr. 24, 1998, eff. Dec. 1, 1998.)

APPENDIX OF FORMS

FORM 1. NOTICE OF APPEAL TO A COURT OF APPEALS FROM A JUDGMENT OR ORDER OF A DISTRICT COURT

United States District Court for the ______
District of ______
File Number ______

A.B., Plaintiff)
)
v.) *Notice of Appeal*
)
C.D., Defendant)

Notice is hereby given that [(here name all parties taking the appeal)], (plaintiffs) (defendants) in the above named case,*] hereby appeal to the United States Court of Appeals for the ______ Circuit (from the final judgment) (from an order (describing it)) entered in this action on the ______ day of ______, 20___.

(s) ______
Attorney for [______]
[Address: ______]

*[**Note to inmate filers:** If you are an inmate confined in an institution and you seek the timing benefit of Fed. R. App. P. 4(c)(1), complete Form 7 (Declaration of Inmate Filing) and file that declaration along with this Notice of Appeal.]*

* See Rule 3(c) for permissible ways of identifying appellants.

(As amended Apr. 22, 1993, eff. Dec. 1, 1993; Mar. 27, 2003, eff. Dec. 1, 2003; Apr. 28, 2016, eff. Dec. 1, 2016.)

FORM 2. NOTICE OF APPEAL TO A COURT OF APPEALS FROM A DECISION OF THE UNITED STATES TAX COURT

UNITED STATES TAX COURT

Washington, D.C.

A.B., Petitioner	)	
	)	
v.	)	Docket No. ________________
	)	
Commissioner of Internal Revenue, Respondent	)	

Notice of Appeal

Notice is hereby given that [here name all parties taking the appeal[1]], hereby appeals to the United States Court of Appeals for the ______ Circuit from (that part of) the decision of this court entered in the above captioned proceeding on the ______ day of ______, 20___ (relating to ______).

(s) ________________________
Counsel for [________________]
[Address:________________]

(As amended Apr. 22, 1993, eff. Dec. 1, 1993; Mar. 27, 2003, eff. Dec. 1, 2003.)

1 See Rule 3(c) for permissible ways of identifying appellants.

FORM 3. PETITION FOR REVIEW OF ORDER OF AN AGENCY, BOARD, COMMISSION OR OFFICER

United States Court of Appeals for the _____ Circuit

A.B., Petitioner)
)
v.) Petition for Review
XYZ Commission, Respondent)

[(here name all parties bringing the petition[1])] hereby petitions the court for review of the Order of the XYZ Commission (describe the order) entered on _____, 20__.

[(s)] ______________________
Attorney for Petitioners
Address:______________________

(As amended Apr. 22, 1993, eff. Dec. 1, 1993; Mar. 27, 2003, eff. Dec. 1, 2003.)

[1] See Rule 15.

FORM 4. AFFIDAVIT ACCOMPANYING MOTION FOR PERMISSION TO APPEAL IN FORMA PAUPERIS

UNITED STATES DISTRICT COURT
for the
<________> DISTRICT OF <________>

<Name(s) of plaintiff(s)>,	)	
	)	
Plaintiff(s)	)	
	)	
v.	)	
	)	Case No. <Number>
<Name(s) of defendant(s)>,	)	
Defendant(s)	)	
	)	

Affidavit in Support of Motion

I swear or affirm under penalty of perjury that, because of my poverty, I cannot prepay the docket fees of my appeal or post a bond for them. I believe I am entitled to redress. I swear or affirm under penalty of perjury under United States laws that my answers on this form are true and correct. (28 U.S.C. § 1746; 18 U.S.C. § 1621.)

Signed: ____________________

Instructions

Complete all questions in this application and then sign it. Do not leave any blanks: if the answer to a question is "0," "none," or "not applicable (N/A)," write in that response. If you need more space to answer a question or to explain your answer, attach a separate sheet of paper identified with your name, your case's docket number, and the question number.

Date: ____________________

My issues on appeal are:

1. *For both you and your spouse estimate the average amount of money received from each of the following sources during the past 12 months. Adjust any amount that was received weekly, biweekly, quarterly, semiannually, or annually to show the monthly rate. Use gross amounts, that is, amounts before any deductions for taxes or otherwise.*

Income source	**Average monthly amount during the past 12 months**		**Amount expected next month**	
	You	**Spouse**	**You**	**Spouse**
Employment	$____	$____	$____	$____
Self-employment	$____	$____	$____	$____
Income from real property (such as rental income)	$____	$____	$____	$____
Interest and dividends	$____	$____	$____	$____
Gifts	$____	$____	$____	$____
Alimony	$____	$____	$____	$____
Child support	$____	$____	$____	$____
Retirement (such as social security, pensions, annuities, insurance)	$____	$____	$____	$____
Disability (such as social security, insurance payments)	$____	$____	$____	$____
Unemployment payments	$____	$____	$____	$____
Public-assistance (such as welfare)	$____	$____	$____	$____

Other (specify):	$	$	$	$
Total monthly income:	$	$	$	$

2. *List your employment history for the past two years, most recent employer first. (Gross monthly pay is before taxes or other deductions.)*

Employer	Address	Dates of employment	Gross monthly pay

3. *List your spouse's employment history for the past two years, most recent employer first. (Gross monthly pay is before taxes or other deductions.)*

Employer	Address	Dates of employment	Gross monthly pay

4. *How much cash do you and your spouse have?* $________
Below, state any money you or your spouse have in bank accounts or in any other financial institution.

Financial institution	Type of account	Amount you have	Amount your spouse has
		$	$
		$	$
		$	$

If you are a prisoner seeking to appeal a judgment in a civil action or proceeding, you must attach a statement certified by the appropriate institutional officer showing all receipts, expenditures, and balances during the last six months in your institutional accounts. If you have multiple accounts, perhaps because you have been in multiple institutions, attach one certified statement of each account.

5. *List the assets, and their values, which you own or your spouse owns. Do not list clothing and ordinary household furnishings.*

Home	(Value)	**Other real estate**	(Value)	**Motor vehicle #1**	(Value)
				Make & year:	
				Model:	
				Registration #:	

Motor vehicle #2	(Value)	**Other assets**	(Value)	**Other assets**	(Value)
Make & year:					
Model:					
Registration #:					

6. *State every person, business, or organization owing you or your spouse money, and the amount owed.*

Person owing you or your spouse money	Amount owed to you	Amount owed to your spouse

7. *State the persons who rely on you or your spouse for support.*

Name [or, if under 18, initials only]	**Relationship**	**Age**

8. *Estimate the average monthly expenses of you and your family. Show separately the amounts paid by your spouse. Adjust any payments that are made weekly, biweekly, quarterly, semiannually, or annually to show the monthly rate.*

	You	**Your Spouse**
Rent or home-mortgage payment (include lot rented for mobile home)	$____	$____
Are real-estate taxes included? ☐ Yes ☐ No		
Is property insurance included? ☐ Yes ☐ No		
Utilities (electricity, heating fuel, water, sewer, and Telephone)	$____	$____
Home maintenance (repairs and upkeep)	$____	$____
Food	$____	$____
Clothing	$____	$____
Laundry and dry-cleaning	$____	$____
Medical and dental expenses	$____	$____
Transportation (not including motor vehicle payments)	$____	$____
Recreation, entertainment, newspapers, magazines, etc.	$____	$____
Insurance (not deducted from wages or included in mortgage payments)	$____	$____
Homeowner's or renter's:	$____	$____
Life:	$____	$____
Health:	$____	$____
Motor Vehicle:	$____	$____
Other: ________	$____	$____
Taxes (not deducted from wages or included in mortgage payments) (specify): __	$____	$____
Installment payments	$____	$____
Motor Vehicle:	$____	$____
Credit card (name): ________	$____	$____
Department store (name): ______	$____	$____
Other: ________	$____	$____
Alimony, maintenance, and support paid to others	$____	$____
Regular expenses for operation of business, profession, or farm (attach detailed statement)	$____	$____
Other (specify): ________	$____	$____
Total monthly expenses:	$____	$____

9. *Do you expect any major changes to your monthly income or expenses or in your assets or liabilities during the next 12 months?*

☐ Yes ☐ No   If yes, describe on an attached sheet.

10. *Have you spent—or will you be spending—any money for expenses or attorney fees in connection with this lawsuit?* ☐ Yes ☐ No

If yes, how much? $______

11. *Provide any other information that will help explain why you cannot pay the docket fees for your appeal.*

12. *State the city and state of your legal residence.*

Your daytime phone number: (___) ______
Your age: ______ *Your years of schooling:* ______
Last four digits of your social-security number: ____________

(As amended Apr. 24, 1998, eff. Dec. 1, 1998; Apr. 28, 2010, eff. Dec. 1, 2010; Apr. 16, 2013, eff. Dec. 1, 2013.)

FORM 5. NOTICE OF APPEAL TO A COURT OF APPEALS FROM A JUDGMENT OR ORDER OF A DISTRICT COURT OR A BANKRUPTCY APPELLATE PANEL

United States District Court for the ....
District of ....

In re)
)
....,)
Debtor)
) File No. ....
....,)
Plaintiff)
)
v.)
)
....,)
Defendant)

Notice of Appeal to
United States Court of Appeals
for the .... Circuit

.........................., the plaintiff [or defendant or other party] appeals to the United States Court of Appeals for the .... Circuit from the final judgment [or order or decree] of the district court for the district of .... [or bankruptcy appellate panel of the .... circuit], entered in this case on ...., 20.... [here describe the judgment, order, or decree] ....

The parties to the judgment [or order or decree] appealed from and the names and addresses of their respective attorneys are as follows:

Dated ....
Signed ....
Attorney for Appellant

Address: ....
....

*[**Note to inmate filers:** If you are an inmate confined in an institution and you seek the timing benefit of Fed. R. App. P. 4(c)(1), complete Form 7 (Declaration of Inmate Filing) and file that declaration along with this Notice of Appeal.]*

(Added Apr. 25, 1989, eff. Dec. 1, 1989; amended Mar. 27, 2003, eff. Dec. 1, 2003; Apr. 28, 2016, eff. Dec. 1, 2016.)

FORM 6. CERTIFICATE OF COMPLIANCE WITH TYPE–VOLUME LIMIT

Certificate of Compliance With Type-Volume Limit, Typeface Requirements, and Type-Style Requirements

1. This document complies with [the type-volume limit of Fed. R. App. P. [*insert Rule citation; e.g., 32(a)(7)(B)*]] [the word limit of Fed. R. App. P. [*insert Rule citation; e.g., 5(c)(1)*]] because, excluding the parts of the document exempted by Fed. R. App. P. 32(f) [and [*insert applicable Rule citation, if any*]]:

☐ this document contains [*state the number of*] words, **or**

☐ this brief uses a monospaced typeface and contains [*state the number of*] lines of text.

2. This document complies with the typeface requirements of Fed. R. App. P. 32(a)(5) and the type-style requirements of Fed. R. App. P. 32(a)(6) because:

☐ this document has been prepared in a proportionally spaced typeface using [*state name and version of word-processing program*] in [*state font size and name of type style*], **or**

☐ this document has been prepared in a monospaced typeface using [*state name and version of word-processing program*] with [*state number of characters per inch and name of type*].

(s)____________________

Attorney for ____________________

Dated: ____________

(Added Apr. 29, 2002, eff. Dec. 1, 2002; amended Apr. 28, 2016, eff. Dec. 1, 2016.)

FORM 7. DECLARATION OF INMATE FILING

_______________ *[insert name of court; for example, United States District Court for the District of Minnesota]*

A.B., Plaintiff)
)
v.) *Case No.* _______________
)
C.D., Defendant)

I am an inmate confined in an institution. Today, _______________ *[insert date]*, I am depositing the _______________ *[insert title of document; for example, "notice of appeal"]* in this case in the institution's internal mail system. First-class postage is being prepaid either by me or by the institution on my behalf.

I declare under penalty of perjury that the foregoing is true and correct (see 28 U.S.C. § 1746; 18 U.S.C. § 1621).

Sign your name here _______________

Signed on _______________ *[insert date]*

*[**Note to inmate filers:** If your institution has a system designed for legal mail, you must use that system in order to receive the timing benefit of Fed. R. App. P. 4(c)(1) or Fed. R. App. P. 25(a)(2)(C).]*

(Added Apr. 28, 2016, eff. Dec. 1, 2016.)

APPENDIX

This chart summarizes the length limits stated in the Federal Rules of Appellate Procedure. Please refer to the rules for precise requirements, and bear in mind the following:

- In computing these limits, you can exclude the items listed in Rule 32(f).
- If you use a word limit or a line limit (other than the word limit in Rule 28(j)), you must file the certificate required by Rule 32(g).
- For the limits in Rules 5, 21, 27, 35, and 40:
  - You must use the word limit if you produce your document on a computer; and
  - You must use the page limit if you handwrite your document or type it on a typewriter.
- For the limits in Rules 28.1, 29(a)(5), and 32:
  - You may use the word limit or page limit, regardless of how you produce the document; or
  - You may use the line limit if you type or print your document with a monospaced typeface. A typeface is monospaced when each character occupies the same amount of horizontal space.

	Rule	Document type	Word limit	Page limit	Line limit
Permission to appeal	5(c)	• Petition for permission to appeal • Answer in opposition • Cross-petition	5,200	20	Not applicable
Extraordinary writs	21(d)	• Petition for writ of mandamus or prohibition or other extraordinary writ • Answer	7,800	30	Not applicable
Motions	27(d)(2)	• Motion • Response to a motion	5,200	20	Not applicable
	27(d)(2)	• Reply to a response to a motion	2,600	10	Not applicable
Parties' briefs (where no cross-appeal)	32(a)(7)	• Principal brief	13,000	30	1,300
	32(a)(7)	• Reply brief	6,500	15	650
Parties' briefs (where cross-appeal)	28.1(e)	• Appellant's principal brief • Appellant's response and reply brief	13,000	30	1,300
	28.1(e)	• Appellee's principal and response brief	15,300	35	1,500
	28.1(e)	• Appellee's reply brief	6,500	15	650
Party's supplemental letter	28(j)	• Letter citing supplemental authorities	350	Not applicable	Not applicable
Amicus briefs	29(a)(5)	• Amicus brief during initial consideration of case on merits	One-half the length set by the Appellate Rules for a party's principal brief	One-half the length set by the Appellate Rules for a party's principal brief	One-half the length set by the Appellate Rules for a party's principal brief
	29(b)(4)	• Amicus brief during consideration of whether to grant rehearing	2,600	Not applicable	Not applicable

	Rule	Document type	Word limit	Page limit	Line limit
Rehearing and en banc filings	35(b)(2) & 40(b)	• Petition for hearing en banc • Petition for panel rehearing; petition for rehearing en banc	3,900	15	Not applicable

(Added Apr. 28, 2016, eff. Dec. 1, 2016.)

INDEX TO FEDERAL RULES OF APPELLATE PROCEDURE

UNITED STATES COURT OF APPEALS
FOR THE
ELEVENTH CIRCUIT

Including Amendments Received Through February 1, 2017

APPENDIX OF FORMS

ADDENDA

INTRODUCTION

Both the court of appeals, by action of a majority of the circuit judges in regular service (see generally 28 U.S.C. chapters 3, 13, 15, 21, 47, 57, and Federal Rules of Appellate Procedure 47), and the judicial council of the circuit (membership of which has been fixed pursuant to statute to include nine active circuit judges, one active judge from each of the nine district courts, and the circuit chief judge) have certain responsibilities for the effective and expeditious administration of justice within the circuit. Contained herein are rules relevant to the court of appeals adopted by the court and by action of the judicial council.

The United States Court of Appeals for the Eleventh Circuit has adopted these rules pursuant to Federal Rules of Appellate Procedure (FRAP) 47. They supplement the provisions of law and FRAP. To properly proceed in this court, counsel should read and follow FRAP, these rules, and the court's Internal Operating Procedures (IOP) which describe the internal workings of the clerk's office and the court. Although there are necessary exceptions, an effort has been made by the court not to duplicate in the Circuit Rules or the IOPs either FRAP or each other. Circuit rules not inconsistent with FRAP govern. The word "appeal" as used in these rules and IOPs includes, where appropriate, any proceeding in this court, including petitions for review and applications for enforcement of agency orders, and writs of mandamus and prohibition, and other extraordinary writs.

Available addenda as adopted by the court are:

ONE: Rules for Conduct of and Representation and Participation at the Eleventh Circuit Judicial Conference

TWO: Procedures in Proceedings for Review of Orders of the Federal Energy Regulatory Commission

FIVE: Non-Criminal Justice Act Counsel Appointments

SEVEN: Regulations of the United States Court of Appeals for the Eleventh Circuit for the Selection and Appointment or the Reappointment of Federal Public Defenders

EIGHT: Rules Governing Attorney Discipline in the U.S. Court of Appeals for the Eleventh Circuit

NINE: Regulations of the U.S. Court of Appeals for the Eleventh Circuit for the Selection and Appointment or the Reappointment of Bankruptcy Administrators

The judicial council of the Eleventh Circuit pursuant to its statutory authority has appointed a circuit executive (11th Cir. R. 47-2), adopted rules for the conduct of complaint proceedings under 28 U.S.C. §§ 351-364 (Addendum Three), adopted a plan and guidelines under the Criminal Justice Act (11th Cir. R. 24-1 and Addendum Four), and adopted rules and regulations for selection and appointment of bankruptcy judges (Addendum Six).

Available addenda as adopted by the judicial council are:

THREE: Rules for Judicial-Conduct and Judicial-Disability Proceedings with Eleventh Circuit Judicial Conduct and Disability Rules

FOUR: Eleventh Circuit Plan under the Criminal Justice Act and Guidelines for Counsel Supplementing the Eleventh Circuit Plan under the Criminal Justice Act

SIX: Rules and Regulations of the Judicial Council and the United States Court of Appeals for the Eleventh Circuit for the Selection of Nominees, the Appointment of Bankruptcy Judges, and the Reappointment of Bankruptcy Judges

The rules, internal operating procedures, and addenda are available on the Internet at www.ca11.uscourts.gov.

[Amended effective April 1, 1991; April 1, 1994; January 2, 1996; December 1, 1998; January 1, 2000; January 1, 2003; December 1, 2009; August 1, 2013; December 1, 2013.]

TITLE I. APPLICABILITY OF RULES

FRAP 1. SCOPE OF RULES; DEFINITION; TITLE

[For text of rule, see the Federal Rules of Appellate Procedure]

FRAP 2. SUSPENSION OF RULES

[For text of rule, see the Federal Rules of Appellate Procedure]

RULE 2-1. COURT ACTION

In lieu of the procedures described in the Eleventh Circuit Rules and Internal Operating Procedures, the court may take such other or different action as it deems appropriate.

[Effective January 1, 2000.]

TITLE II. APPEAL FROM A JUDGMENT OR ORDER OF A DISTRICT COURT

FRAP 3. APPEAL AS OF RIGHT—HOW TAKEN

[For text of rule, see the Federal Rules of Appellate Procedure]

RULE 3-1. FAILURE TO OBJECT TO A MAGISTRATE JUDGE'S FINDINGS OR RECOMMENDATIONS

A party failing to object to a magistrate judge's findings or recommendations contained in a report and recommendation in accordance with the provisions of 28 U.S.C. § 636(b)(1) waives the right to challenge on appeal the district court's order based on unobjected-to factual and legal conclusions if the party was informed of the time period for objecting and the consequences on appeal for failing to object. In the absence of a proper objection, however, the court may review on appeal for plain error if necessary in the interests of justice.

[Effective December 1, 2014.]

IOP—CIR. RULE 3

*1. **Payment of Fees.** When the notice of appeal is filed in the district court, counsel must pay to the district court clerk, pursuant to FRAP 3(e), the court of appeals docketing fee prescribed by the Judicial Conference of the United States in the Court of Appeals Miscellaneous Fee Schedule issued pursuant to 28 U.S.C. § 1913, plus the district court filing fee required by 28 U.S.C. § 1917. Upon receipt of a copy of a notice of appeal, the clerk of the court of appeals will transmit to counsel a notice advising of other requirements of the rules. See FRAP 13, 15, and 21 for information on payment of fees for Tax Court appeals, petitions for review of agency orders or writs of mandamus or other writs.*

*2. **Opportunity to Seek Extension of Time to File Objections.** The parties may seek an extension of time to file written objections to a magistrate judge's report and recommendation, provided they do so before the deadline for filing written objections passes.*

*3. **Notice to Accompany Magistrate Judge's Findings or Recommendations.** A magistrate judge's findings or recommendations under 28 U.S.C. § 636(b)(1) must be accompanied by clear notice to the parties of the time period for objecting or seeking an extension of time to file written objections and notice that failure to object in accordance with the provisions of § 636(b)(1) waives the right to challenge on appeal the district court's order based on unobjected-to factual and legal conclusions.*

Cross-Reference: FRAP 12, 13, 15, 21

[Amended effective April 1, 1991; December 1, 1998; December 1, 2003; April 9, 2006; August 1, 2014; December 1, 2014.]

FRAP 3.1. APPEAL FROM A JUDGMENT OF A MAGISTRATE JUDGE IN A CIVIL CASE [ABROGATED]

[For text of rule, see the Federal Rules of Appellate Procedure]

FRAP 4. APPEAL AS OF RIGHT—WHEN TAKEN

[For text of rule, see the Federal Rules of Appellate Procedure]

IOP—CIR. RULE 4

***Timely Filing Required.** Except for notices of appeal filed by inmates of correctional institutions as provided in FRAP 4(c), notices of appeal must be timely filed in the office of the clerk of the district court.*

Cross-Reference: Fed.R.Civ.P. 54, 58, 79(a); 28 U.S.C. § 1292

[Amended effective January 2, 1996; December 1, 2009.]

FRAP 5. APPEAL BY PERMISSION

[For text of rule, see the Federal Rules of Appellate Procedure]

RULE 5-1. CERTIFICATE REQUIRED

The petition and answer shall contain a Certificate of Interested Persons and Corporate Disclosure Statement as described in FRAP 26.1 and the accompanying circuit rules.

[Former 11th Cir. R. 5-1 deleted effective December 1, 1998. Former 11th Cir. R. 5-2 adopted effective April 1, 1991. Redesignated 11th Cir. R. 5-1 effective December 1, 1998.]

IOP—CIR. RULE 5

*1. **Appeals by Permission.** When the petition is granted, counsel must pay to the district court clerk the court of appeals docketing fee prescribed by the Judicial Conference of the United States in the Court of Appeals Miscellaneous Fee Schedule issued pursuant to 28 U.S.C. § 1913, plus the district court filing fee required by 28 U.S.C. § 1917.*

*2. **Pro Hac Vice Admission.** When an application to appear pro hac vice is granted while a petition for permission to appeal is pending, the attorney's pro hac vice admission continues in effect for the appeal if the petition is granted. See 11th Cir. R. 46-4.*

Cross-Reference: FRAP 3, 26.1

[Amended effective December 1, 2003; April 9, 2006; December 1, 2008; August 1, 2014.]

FRAP 5.1. APPEAL BY PERMISSION UNDER 28 U.S.C. § 636(c)(5) [ABROGATED]

[For text of rule, see the Federal Rules of Appellate Procedure]

FRAP 6. APPEAL IN A BANKRUPTCY CASE FROM A FINAL JUDGMENT, ORDER, OR DECREE OF A DISTRICT COURT OR BANKRUPTCY APPELLATE PANEL

[For text of rule, see the Federal Rules of Appellate Procedure]

IOP—CIR. RULE 6

Direct Appeal. *The Judicial Council of the Eleventh Circuit has not established a bankruptcy appellate panel. A direct appeal from a bankruptcy court to the court of appeals is available only as authorized by statute. See 28 U.S.C. § 158(d).*

Cross–Reference: FRAP 3, 4

[Amended effective April 1, 1991; April 1, 2006.]

FRAP 7. BOND FOR COSTS ON APPEAL IN A CIVIL CASE

[For text of rule, see the Federal Rules of Appellate Procedure]

FRAP 8. STAY OR INJUNCTION PENDING APPEAL

[For text of rule, see the Federal Rules of Appellate Procedure]

RULE 8–1. MOTIONS

Motions for stay or injunction pending appeal must include a copy of the judgment or order from which relief is sought and of any opinion or findings of the district court, and shall otherwise comply with the rules.

RULE 8–2. MOTION FOR RECONSIDERATION

A motion to reconsider, vacate, or modify an order granting or denying relief under FRAP 8 must be filed within 21 days of the entry of such order. No additional time shall be allowed for mailing.

[Effective January 1, 2002.]

IOP—CIR. RULE 8

Proof of Service Required. *Motions for stay or injunction pending appeal must include proof of service on all parties appearing below.*

Cross–Reference: FRAP 27

FRAP 9. RELEASE IN A CRIMINAL CASE

[For text of rule, see the Federal Rules of Appellate Procedure]

RULE 9–1. MOTIONS

Parties seeking review of a district court's order on release in a criminal case under FRAP 9(a) must file a motion with this court, within seven days of filing the notice of appeal, setting out the reasons why the party believes the order should be reversed. The opposing party must file a response within ten days, unless otherwise ordered by the court. Any replies shall be filed no later than seven days after the filing of the response, unless otherwise ordered by the court. All motions for release or for modification of the conditions of release, whether filed under FRAP 9(a) or 9(b), must include a copy of the judgment or order from which relief is sought and of any opinion or findings of the district court.

[Amended effective April 1, 2016.]

IOP—CIR. RULE 9

Proof of Service Required. *Motions for release or for modification of the conditions of release must include proof of service on all parties appearing below.*

Cross–Reference: FRAP 23, 27

FRAP 10. THE RECORD ON APPEAL

[For text of rule, see the Federal Rules of Appellate Procedure]

RULE 10–1. ORDERING THE TRANSCRIPT—DUTIES OF APPELLANT AND APPELLEE

Appellant's written order for a transcript or certification that no transcript will be ordered, as required by FRAP 10(b), shall be on a form prescribed by the court of appeals. Counsel and pro se parties shall file the form with the district court clerk and the clerk of the court of appeals, and send copies to the appropriate court reporter(s) and all parties, in conformance with instructions included on the form. The form must be filed and sent as indicated above within 14 days after filing the notice of appeal or after entry of an order disposing of the last timely motion of a type specified in FRAP 4(a)(4).

If a transcript is to be ordered by counsel appointed under the Criminal Justice Act, and counsel has not yet submitted to the district judge for approval a CJA Form 24, "Authorization and Voucher for Payment of Transcript," counsel shall attach to the transcript order form filed with the district court an original completed and signed CJA 24 form requesting authorization for government payment of the transcript. The district court clerk will submit the CJA 24 to the appropriate district judge for a ruling.

If an appellee designates additional parts of the proceedings to be ordered, orders additional parts of the proceedings, or moves in the district court for an order requiring appellant to do so, as provided by FRAP 10(b), a copy of such designation, transcript order, or motion shall be simultaneously sent to the clerk of this court in addition to being filed and served on other parties as provided by FRAP 10(b).

[Amended effective April 1, 1991; January 2, 1996; April 1, 1999; December 1, 2009; August 1, 2013.]

IOP—CIR. RULE 10

Ordering the Transcript. *The transcript order form prescribed by the court of appeals may be obtained from the court's website at www.ca11.uscourts.gov. Financial arrangements for payment of the costs of the transcript which are satisfactory to the reporter must be made before the transcript order is complete and signed by appellant.*

[Amended effective April 1, 1999; December 1, 2013.]

FRAP 11. FORWARDING THE RECORD

[For text of rule, see the Federal Rules of Appellate Procedure]

RULE 11-1. DUTIES OF COURT REPORTERS; EXTENSIONS OF TIME

In each case in which a transcript is ordered, the court reporter shall furnish the following information on a form prescribed by the clerk of this court:

(a) acknowledge that the reporter has received the order for the transcript and the date of the order;

(b) state whether adequate financial arrangements have been made under CJA or otherwise;

(c) state the number of trial or hearing days involved in the transcript and an estimate of the number of pages;

(d) give the estimated date on which the transcript is to be completed.

The court reporter shall notify the ordering party and the clerk of this court at the time that ordered transcripts are filed in the district court. A court reporter who requests an extension of time for filing the transcript beyond the 30 day period fixed by FRAP 11(b) shall file a written application with the clerk of the court of appeals on a form provided by the clerk of this court and shall specify in detail the amount of work that has been accomplished on the transcript, list all outstanding transcripts due to this and other courts and the due date for filing each and set forth the reasons which make an extension of time for filing the transcript appropriate. The court reporter shall certify that the court reporter has sent a copy of the application to both the Chief District Judge of that district, to the district judge who tried the case, and to all counsel of record. In some cases this court may require written approval of the request by the appropriate district judge. The clerk of the court of appeals shall also send a copy of the clerk's action on the application to both the appropriate Chief District Judge and the district judge. If the court reporter files the transcript beyond the 30 day period fixed by FRAP 11(b) without having obtained an extension of time to do so, the clerk of the court of appeals shall so notify the appropriate Chief District Judge as well as the district judge.

[Amended effective April 1, 1991; April 1, 1994; January 2, 1996; April 1, 1999; January 1, 2002.]

RULE 11-2. CERTIFICATION AND TRANSMISSION OF RECORD—DUTIES OF DISTRICT COURT CLERK

The clerk of the district court is responsible for determining when the record on appeal is complete for purposes of the appeal. Upon completion of the record the clerk of the district court shall temporarily retain the record for use by the parties in preparing appellate papers. Whether the record is in electronic or paper form, the clerk of the district court shall certify to the parties on appeal and to the clerk of this court that the record (including the transcript or parts thereof designated for inclusion, and all necessary exhibits) is complete for purposes of appeal. Unless the required certification can be transmitted to the clerk of this court within 14 days from the filing by appellant of a certificate that no transcript is necessary or 14 days after the filing of the transcript of trial proceedings if one has been ordered, whichever is later, the clerk of the district court shall advise the clerk of this court of the reasons for delay and request additional time for filing the required certification. Upon notification from this court that the brief of the appellee has been filed, the clerk of the district court shall forthwith transmit those portions of the original record that are in paper.

[Amended effective April 1, 1991; April 1, 1999; January 1, 2002; April 1, 2004; December 1, 2013.]

RULE 11-3. PREPARATION AND TRANSMISSION OF EXHIBITS—DUTIES OF DISTRICT COURT CLERK

The clerk of the district court is responsible for transmitting with the record to the clerk of this court a list of exhibits correspondingly numbered and identified with reasonable definiteness. The district court clerk must include in the electronic record on appeal electronic versions of all documentary exhibits admitted into evidence at trial or any evidentiary hearing. The district court clerk must ensure that no such documentary exhibits are returned to the parties before electronic versions of those exhibits have been entered into the electronic record on appeal. In appeals from the Tax Court, which files only a paper record, the Tax Court clerk is required to transmit to this court in paper all documentary exhibits admitted into evidence at trial or any evidentiary hearing.

If any documentary exhibits have been sealed or marked confidential by the district court or the district court clerk, the district court clerk must transmit any such sealed or confidential documentary exhibits to this court either in their original form or in electronic form provided the electronic access is appropriately restricted, unless otherwise directed by the clerk of this court. If audio or video files were entered into evidence at trial or any evidentiary hearing, such files and any transcripts must be retained by the district court clerk during the period in which a notice of appeal may be timely filed and transmitted to this court as part of the record on appeal.

As to non-documentary physical exhibits, the parties are required to include photographs or other reproductions of such exhibits in the electronic record on appeal. The parties may submit such photographs or other reproductions in paper or electronic form. The district court clerk must make advance arrangements with the clerk of this court prior to sending any exhibit containing wiring or electronic components (such as a beeper, cellular phone, etc.). Exhibits of unusual size or weight which are contained in a box larger than 14 3/4″ × 12″ × 9 1/2″ shall not be transmitted by the district court clerk until and unless directed to do so by the clerk of this court. A party must make advance arrangements with the clerks for the transportation and receipt of exhibits of unusual size or weight. If transmittal has been authorized, a party may be requested to personally transfer oversized exhibits to the clerk of this court.

[Amended effective January 2, 1996; December 1, 1998; April 1, 1999; December 1, 2016.]

RULE 11–4. FORM OF PAPER RECORD

When the record on appeal is in paper, the record shall be bound securely with durable front and back covers in a manner that will facilitate reading. The clerk of the district court or bankruptcy court as applicable shall index the record by means of document numbers in consecutive order. In civil appeals, including bankruptcy and prisoner (civil and habeas) appeals, to facilitate use of the record by the court and by counsel, the district court or bankruptcy court as applicable shall affix indexing tabs bearing those document numbers to identify orders and significant filings. Indexing tabs are not required to be affixed to records in criminal appeals.

[Amended effective April 1, 1991; April 1, 1999; December 1, 2013.]

IOP—CIR. RULE 11

1. ***Duties of Court Reporters; Extensions of Time.*** *The appellant is not required to seek extensions of time for filing the transcript if the reporter cannot prepare it within 30 days from receipt of the appellant's purchase order. The matter of filing the transcript is between the reporter, the clerk of the Eleventh Circuit, the clerk of the district court, and the district judge. Counsel will be informed when an extension of time is allowed on request made by the court reporter.*

2. ***Preparation of Paper Record; Duties of District Court Clerk.*** *When the record on appeal is in paper, at the time that the record is complete for purposes of appeal and before transmitting certification that the record is complete, the district court will assemble the record into one or more volumes, and identify by a separate document number each filing contained therein. Each volume of the record should generally contain less than 250 pages. The district court docket sheet, so numbered, will be provided to the parties upon request to facilitate citation to the original record by reference to the file copies maintained by the parties. Prior to transmitting the record to the clerk of the court of appeals, the district court docket sheet shall be marked to identify by number the volume into which documents have been placed, and the cover of each volume of the record shall indicate the volume number and the document numbers of the first and last document contained therein (e.g., Vol. 2, Documents 26—49). The district court docket sheet, so marked, will be included in the record transmitted to the clerk of the court of appeals. Transcripts will be sequentially arranged in separate numbered volumes, with volume numbers noted on the docket sheet index. In civil appeals, including bankruptcy and prisoner (civil and habeas) appeals, standard commercially–available indexing tabs or their equivalent which extend beyond the edge of the page shall be affixed to the first page of orders and of significant filings in the record to identify and assist in locating the papers. Tabs should be visible and staggered in sequence from top to bottom along the right-hand side. Tab numbers should correspond to the document numbers assigned by the district court.*

3. ***Oversized Exhibits.*** *Ordinarily, oversized exhibits must be transmitted at the expense of the party requesting same, following approval from the clerks of this court and the district court. Requests to transmit oversized exhibits are discouraged. In lieu of arranging for transmittal by the district court of oversized physical exhibits, parties are encouraged to substitute photographs, diagrams, or models of lesser size and weight, or to stipulate to the nature and content of such exhibits. The clerk of this court may dispose of oversized exhibits without further notice unless a party makes arrangements with the clerk for their return within 30 days of issuance of the mandate.*

Cross–Reference: FRAP 16

[Amended effective April 1, 1991; April 1, 1994; January 2, 1996; December 1, 1998; April 1, 1999; January 1, 2003; December 1, 2013; December 1, 2016.]

FRAP 12. DOCKETING THE APPEAL; FILING A REPRESENTATION STATEMENT; FILING THE RECORD

[For text of rule, see the Federal Rules of Appellate Procedure]

RULE 12–1. FILING THE RECORD

In an appeal from a district court in which a transcript is ordered, the record is deemed completed and filed on the date the court reporter files the transcript with the district court. In an appeal from a district court in which there was no hearing below (including an appeal from summary judgment), or all necessary transcripts are already on file, or a transcript is not ordered, the record is deemed completed and filed on the date the appeal is docketed in the court of appeals pursuant to FRAP 12(a). The provisions of this rule also apply to the review of a Tax Court decision. [See 11th Cir. R. 31–1 for the time for serving and filing briefs.]

[Effective April 1, 1999.]

IOP—CIR. RULE 12

1. ***Docketing an Appeal.*** *Appeals are immediately docketed upon receipt of the notice of appeal and district court docket entries. A general docket number is assigned and all* *counsel and pro se parties are so advised. Failure to pay the docket fee does not prevent the appeal from being docketed but is grounds for dismissal of the appeal by the clerk under the authority of 11th Cir. R. 42–1.*

*2. **Appearance of Counsel Form.** An Appearance of Counsel Form is the required form for the Representation Statement required to be filed by FRAP 12(b). See 11th Cir. R. 46–5.*

Cross–Reference: FRAP 3, 13, 46

[Amended effective April 1, 1994; January 1, 2002; August 1, 2005; April 1, 2010.]

FRAP 12.1. REMAND AFTER AN INDICATIVE RULING BY THE DISTRICT COURT ON A MOTION FOR RELIEF THAT IS BARRED BY A PENDING APPEAL

[For text of rule, see the Federal Rules of Appellate Procedure]

RULE 12.1–1 INDICATIVE RULING BY THE DISTRICT COURT

(a) A party who files a motion in the district court that the district court lacks authority to grant because an appeal is pending must, within 14 days after filing the motion, serve and file a motion in this court to stay the appeal until the district court rules on the motion before it. If this court stays the appeal, the party who filed the motion in the district court must, unless this court orders otherwise, file written status reports at 30–day intervals from the date of this court's order informing this court of the status of the district court proceedings.

(b) If the motion filed in the district court is one that does not request substantive relief from the order or judgment under appeal, such as a motion to correct a clerical error pursuant to Fed.R.Civ.P. 60(a), any party to the appeal may file a motion for a limited remand to give the district court authority to rule on the motion, without waiting for the district court to signify its intentions on the motion. A response and reply may be filed in compliance with FRAP 27 and the corresponding local rules of this court.

(c) If the motion filed in the district court requests substantive relief from the order or judgment under appeal, such as a motion to modify a preliminary injunction or a motion for relief from judgment pursuant to Fed.R.Civ.P. 60(b), the district court may consider whether to grant or deny the motion without obtaining a remand from this court.

(1) If the district court determines that the motion should be denied, the district court may deny the motion without a remand by this court.

(2) If the district court determines that the motion should be granted, the district court should enter an order stating that it intends to grant the motion if this court returns jurisdiction to it.

(i) Any appellant or cross-appellant may file an objection to remand with this court within 14 days after entry of the district court's order.

(ii) If no objection to remand is filed with this court within 14 days after entry of the district court's order, this court may remand the case in full to the district court for entry of an order granting relief and will direct the clerk to close the appeal. Any such order shall constitute an express dismissal of the appeal for purposes of FRAP 12.1.

(iii) If an objection to remand is filed with this court within 14 days after entry of the district court's order, that objection will be treated as a motion for the court to retain jurisdiction. A response and reply may be filed in compliance with FRAP 27 and the corresponding local rules of this court. Upon consideration of the objections and any responses and replies, the court will determine whether to retain jurisdiction over the appeal.

(iv) If the district court enters an order on remand that fails to grant the relief the district court had stated it would grant, any appellant or cross-appellant may, within 30 days after entry of the district court's order, file a motion in this court to reopen and reinstate the closed appeal.

(d) With respect to any motion described in section (c) of this rule, if the district court determines that the motion raises a substantial issue that warrants further consideration, the district court should enter an order so stating. The district court may without a remand conduct such further proceedings as are necessary to determine whether the motion should be granted or denied.

(1) While such proceedings are pending in the district court, the appeal will remain stayed unless this court orders otherwise.

(2) If the district court thereafter determines that the motion should be denied, the district court may deny the motion without a remand by this court.

(3) If the district court thereafter determines that the motion should be granted, the provisions of section (c)(2) of this rule apply.

(e) Upon the district court's entry of any order addressing any motion described in FRAP 12.1, the parties must promptly notify this court of such order.

[Adopted effective December 1, 2009.]

TITLE III. APPEALS FROM THE UNITED STATES TAX COURT

FRAP 13. APPEALS FROM THE TAX COURT

[For text of rule, see the Federal Rules of Appellate Procedure]

IOP—CIR. RULE 13

***Payment of Fees.** When the notice of appeal is filed in the Tax Court, counsel must pay to the Tax Court the court of appeals docketing fee prescribed by the Judicial Conference of* *the United States in the Court of Appeals Miscellaneous Fee Schedule issued pursuant to 28 U.S.C. § 1913. Upon receipt of a copy of a notice of appeal, the clerk of the court of appeals will transmit to counsel a notice advising of other requirements of the rules.*

Cross-Reference: FRAP 3, 10, 11, 12

[Amended effective April 1, 1991; December 1, 1998; December 1, 2003; April 9, 2006; August 1, 2014.]

FRAP 14. APPLICABILITY OF OTHER RULES TO APPEALS FROM THE TAX COURT

[For text of rule, see the Federal Rules of Appellate Procedure]

RULE 14-1. APPLICABILITY OF OTHER CIRCUIT RULES TO APPEALS FROM THE TAX COURT

All provisions of the Eleventh Circuit Rules, except any Eleventh Circuit Rules accompanying FRAP 4, 6–9, 15–20, and 22–23, apply to appeals from the Tax Court. Except as otherwise indicated, as used in any applicable Eleventh Circuit Rule the term "district court" includes the Tax Court, the term "district judge" includes a judge of the Tax Court, and the term "district court clerk" includes the Tax Court clerk.

[Adopted effective April 1, 2016.]

TITLE IV. REVIEW OR ENFORCEMENT OF AN ORDER OF AN ADMINISTRATIVE AGENCY, BOARD, COMMISSION, OR OFFICER

FRAP 15. REVIEW OR ENFORCEMENT OF AN AGENCY ORDER—HOW OBTAINED; INTERVENTION

[For text of rule, see the Federal Rules of Appellate Procedure]

RULE 15-1. PROCEDURES IN PROCEEDINGS FOR REVIEW OF ORDERS OF THE FEDERAL ENERGY REGULATORY COMMISSION

This court has adopted special rules for these proceedings. See Addendum Two.

[Amended effective December 1, 1998.]

RULE 15-2. PETITIONS FOR REVIEW AND APPLICATIONS FOR ENFORCEMENT

A copy of the order(s) sought to be reviewed or enforced shall be attached to each petition or application which is filed. In an immigration appeal, the petitioner or applicant shall also attach a copy of the Immigration Judge's order and the Notice to Appear.

[Adopted effective April 1, 1991. Amended effective December 1, 2003.]

RULE 15-3. ANSWER TO APPLICATION FOR ENFORCEMENT

An answer to an application for enforcement may be served on the petitioner and filed with the clerk within 21 days after the application is filed.

[Adopted effective April 1, 1991. Amended effective January 1, 2002.]

RULE 15-4. MOTION FOR LEAVE TO INTERVENE

A motion for leave to intervene or other notice of intervention authorized by applicable statute may be filed within 30 days of the date on which the petition for review is filed.

[Effective January 1, 2002. Amended effective December 1, 2003.]

IOP—CIR. RULE 15

*1. **Payment of Fees.** The court of appeals docketing fee prescribed by the Judicial Conference of the United States in the Court of Appeals Miscellaneous Fee Schedule, issued pursuant to 28 U.S.C. § 1913, is due upon filing of the petition. Checks should be made payable to Clerk, U.S. Court of Appeals, Eleventh Circuit. Applications to file a petition in forma pauperis are governed by FRAP 24(b).*

*2. **Notice of Origin.** Counsel are requested to advise the clerk, at the time of filing, of the petitioner's place of residence, principal place of business, domicile, or other information concerning place of origin.*

*3. **Federal Energy Regulatory Commission Proceedings.** Because these matters usually involve multiple parties before the court, it has adopted special procedures of (a) simplifying and defining issues, (b) agreeing on an appendix and record, (c) assigning joint briefing responsibilities and scheduling briefs, and (d) such other matters as may aid in the disposition of the proceeding. See 11th Cir. R. 15-1 and Addendum Two.*

*4. **National Labor Relations Board Original Contempt Proceedings.***

a. Assignment to Panel. *When the Board files a petition for adjudication of a respondent for civil contempt of a previously issued order or mandate of this court, the clerk normally refers it back to the original panel which previously heard or decided the matter on its merits. That panel, through the initiating judge, is then responsible for issuance of all preliminary orders including among others the order to show cause fixing the time for filing a response to the pleadings or answer.*

If the former panel determines that good reason exists for not assuming direction of the matter (e.g., death or retirement of a panel member or serious legal issue warranting all active judge determination in the event of a visiting judge on the panel), the clerk is notified and under the direction of the chief judge selects by lot a panel of active judges.

b. Where Evidentiary Hearing Required. *If the matter indicates that disputed issues of fact are involved requiring an evidentiary hearing, the initiating judge of the panel at that stage usually enters for the panel the Board's proposed order of reference of the matter for hearing before a special master. The order specifies the nature of the conditions, the hearing, the master's powers and duties, the filing of the master's report, including findings of fact, conclusions, and recommendations of the special master.*

c. Proceedings After Master's Report. *Once the special master's report is filed, the parties are advised thereof and of the order of reference fixing the time for filing of any objections, responses to objections, and supporting briefs in support or opposition thereto. When ripe for submission the matter is usually then handled by the court under its usual procedures.*

[Amended effective April 1, 1991; April 1, 1994; December 1, 1998; December 1, 2003; April 9, 2006; April 1, 2010; August 1, 2013; August 1, 2014.]

FRAP 15.1. BRIEFS AND ORAL ARGUMENT IN A NATIONAL LABOR RELATIONS BOARD PROCEEDING

[For text of rule, see the Federal Rules of Appellate Procedure]

RULE 15.1–1. FAILURE TO PROSECUTE

In an enforcement proceeding, if a party adverse to the National Labor Relations Board fails to file or correct the brief or appendix within the time permitted by the rules, the court may take such action as it deems appropriate including, but not limited to, entry of judgment enforcing the Board's order.

[Adopted effective April 1, 2006. Amended effective December 1, 2013.]

FRAP 16. THE RECORD ON REVIEW OR ENFORCEMENT

[For text of rule, see the Federal Rules of Appellate Procedure]

RULE 16–1. FORM OF PAPER RECORD

When the record on appeal is in paper, the record shall be bound securely with durable front and back covers in a manner that will facilitate reading. The agency shall index the record by means of document numbers in consecutive order.

Cross–Reference: FRAP 10

[Amended effective April 1, 2016.]

FRAP 17. FILING THE RECORD

[For text of rule, see the Federal Rules of Appellate Procedure]

RULE 17–1. CERTIFIED EXTRACTS OF THE RECORD

If a certified list of documents comprising the record is filed in lieu of the formal record, petitioner shall obtain from the agency, board, or commission a certified copy of the portions of the record relied upon by the parties in their briefs, to be numbered and indexed and filed within 21 days from the date of filing of respondent's brief, with a front and back durable (at least 90#) cover. The front cover shall contain the information specified in 11th Cir. R. 28–1(a) and be captioned "Certified Extracts of the Record."

[Amended effective December 1, 1998; April 1, 1999.]

FRAP 18. STAY PENDING REVIEW

[For text of rule, see the Federal Rules of Appellate Procedure]

RULE 18–1. MOTIONS

Motions for stay or injunction pending review must include a copy of the decision or order from which relief is sought and of any opinion or findings of the agency.

RULE 18–2. MOTION FOR RECONSIDERATION

A motion to reconsider, vacate, or modify an order granting or denying relief under FRAP 18 must be filed within 21 days of the entry of such order. No additional time shall be allowed for mailing.

[Effective January 1, 2002.]

IOP—CIR. RULE 18

Proof of Service Required. *Motions for stay or injunction pending review must include proof of service on all parties appearing below.*

Cross–Reference: FRAP 27

FRAP 19. SETTLEMENT OF A JUDGMENT ENFORCING AN AGENCY ORDER IN PART

[For text of rule, see the Federal Rules of Appellate Procedure]

FRAP 20. APPLICABILITY OF RULES TO THE REVIEW OR ENFORCEMENT OF AN AGENCY ORDER

[For text of rule, see the Federal Rules of Appellate Procedure]

RULE 20–1. APPLICABILITY OF OTHER CIRCUIT RULES TO THE REVIEW OR ENFORCEMENT OF AN AGENCY ORDER

All provisions of the Eleventh Circuit Rules, except any Eleventh Circuit Rules accompanying FRAP 3–14 and 22–23, apply to the review or enforcement of any agency order. Except as otherwise indicated, as used in any applicable Eleventh Circuit Rule the term "appellant" includes a petitioner, applicant, or movant, the term "appellee" includes a respondent, and the term "appeal" includes a petition for review or enforcement.

[Adopted effective April 1, 2016.]

TITLE V. EXTRAORDINARY WRITS

FRAP 21. WRITS OF MANDAMUS AND PROHIBITION, AND OTHER EXTRAORDINARY WRITS

[For text of rule, see the Federal Rules of Appellate Procedure]

RULE 21-1. WRITS OF MANDAMUS AND PROHIBITION AND OTHER EXTRAORDINARY WRITS

(a) As part of the required showing of the reasons why the writ should issue, the petition should include a showing that mandamus is appropriate because there is no other adequate remedy available.

(b) The petition shall include a Certificate of Interested Persons and Corporate Disclosure Statement as described in FRAP 26.1 and the accompanying circuit rules.

(c) The petition shall include a proof of service showing that the petition was served on all parties to the proceeding in the district court, and that a copy was provided to the district court judge. Service is the responsibility of the petitioner, not the clerk.

[Amended effective April 1, 1991; December 1, 1998.]

IOP—CIR. RULE 21

Payment of Fees. *The court of appeals docketing fee prescribed by the Judicial Conference of the United States in the Court of Appeals Miscellaneous Fee Schedule, issued pursuant to 28 U.S.C. § 1913, is due upon filing of the petition. Checks should be made payable to Clerk, U.S. Court of Appeals, Eleventh Circuit.*

Cross-Reference: FRAP 26.1

[Amended effective April 1, 1994; December 1, 1998; April 1, 1999; December 1, 2003; August 1, 2014.]

TITLE VI. HABEAS CORPUS; PROCEEDINGS IN FORMA PAUPERIS

FRAP 22. HABEAS CORPUS AND SECTION 2255 PROCEEDINGS

[For text of rule, see the Federal Rules of Appellate Procedure]

RULE 22-1. CERTIFICATE OF APPEALABILITY

In all cases brought pursuant to 28 U.S.C. §§ 2241, 2254, or 2255, a timely notice of appeal must be filed.

(a) A party must file a timely notice of appeal even if the district court issues a certificate of appealability. The district court or the court of appeals will construe a party's filing of an application for a certificate of appealability, or other document indicating an intent to appeal, as the filing of a notice of appeal. If the notice of appeal or its equivalent is filed in the court of appeals, the clerk of that court will note the date it was received and send it to the district court, pursuant to FRAP 4(d).

(b) If the district court denies a certificate of appealability, a party may seek a certificate of appealability from the court of appeals. In the event that a party does not file an application for such a certificate, the court of appeals will construe a party's filing of a timely notice of appeal as an application to the court of appeals for a certificate of appealability.

(c) An application to the court of appeals for a certificate of appealability may be considered by a single circuit judge. The denial of a certificate of appealability, whether by a single circuit judge or by a panel, may be the subject of a motion for reconsideration but may not be the subject of a petition for panel rehearing or a petition for rehearing en banc.

[Amended effective December 1, 1998; April 1, 1999; April 1, 2003; April 1, 2010.]

RULE 22-2. LENGTH OF APPLICATION FOR A CERTIFICATE OF APPEALABILITY

An application to the court of appeals for a certificate of appealability and a brief in support thereof (whether or not they are combined in a single document) collectively may not exceed the maximum length authorized for a party's principal brief [see FRAP 32(a)(7)]. A response and brief opposing an application is subject to the same limitations.

[Effective April 1, 2004.]

RULE 22-3. APPLICATION FOR LEAVE TO FILE A SECOND OR SUCCESSIVE HABEAS CORPUS PETITION OR MOTION TO VACATE, SET ASIDE OR CORRECT SENTENCE

(a) Form. An applicant seeking leave to file a second or successive habeas corpus petition or motion to vacate, set aside or correct sentence must use the appropriate form provided by the clerk of this court, except in a case in which the sentence imposed is death. In a death sentence case, the use of the form is optional.

(b) Finality of Determination. Consistent with 28 U.S.C. § 2244(b)(3)(E), the grant or denial of an authorization by a court of appeals to file a second or successive habeas corpus petition or a motion pursuant to 28 U.S.C. § 2255 is not appealable and shall not be the subject of a motion for reconsideration, a petition for panel rehearing, or a petition for rehearing en banc.

[Amended effective December 1, 1998; April 1, 2003. Renumbered effective April 1, 2004. Amended effective April 1, 2007; December 1, 2016.]

RULE 22-4. PETITIONS IN CAPITAL CASES PURSUANT TO 28 U.S.C. §§ 2254 AND 2255

(a) Stay Cases.

(1) The following rules shall apply to cases brought pursuant to 28 U.S.C. §§ 2254 and 2255 in which a court has imposed a sentence of death, execution has been ordered, a United States District Court has denied a motion to stay execution pending appeal, and the petitioner has appealed to this court and has applied for a stay of execution. Except as changed by these rules the provisions of 11th Cir. R. 27-1 shall apply.

(2) Upon the filing of the notice of appeal in a case where the district court has denied a stay, the clerk of the district court shall immediately notify the clerk of this court by telephone of such filing.

(3) A motion for stay of execution and application for a certificate of appealability (if not granted by the district court) shall be filed with the clerk of this court together with documents required by 11th Cir. R. 27-1.

(4) Upon receipt of the notice of appeal and motion for stay (and application for a certificate of appealability, if not granted by the district court), the clerk shall docket the appeal and assign it to a panel constituted by the court from a roster of the active judges of the court maintained for the purposes of these rules. The clerk shall notify the judges of the panel of their assignment by telephone or other expeditious means. The panel to which the appeal is assigned shall handle all matters pertaining to the motion to stay, application for a certificate of appealability, the merits, second or successive petitions, remands from the Supreme Court of the United States, and all incidental and collateral matters, including any separate proceedings questioning the conviction or sentence.

(5) The panel shall consider an application for a certificate of appealability, shall determine whether oral argument will be heard on the motion to stay, and shall determine all other matters pertaining to the appeal.

(6) If the district court has refused to grant a certificate of appealability, and this court also denies a certificate of appealability, no further action need be taken by the court.

(7) If a certificate of appealability is granted by the district court or by this court, the panel may grant a temporary stay pending consideration of the merits of the appeal if necessary to prevent mooting the appeal.

(b) Non-Stay Cases.

(1) Applications, petitions, and appeals in capital cases that are not governed by section (a) of this rule shall proceed under the Federal Rules of Appellate Procedure, the Eleventh Circuit Rules, and the usual policies of this court. The ordinary briefing schedule for appeals will be followed to the extent feasible.

(c) Application for an Order Authorizing Second or Successive Habeas Corpus Petition. An application in the court of appeals for an order authorizing the district court to consider a second or successive habeas corpus petition shall be assigned to the panel constituted under section (a)(4) of this Rule to consider habeas corpus appeals, petitions or other related matters with respect to the same petitioner.

[Amended effective May 1, 1996; December 1, 1998; April 1, 2003. Renumbered effective April 1, 2004. Amended effective December 1, 2004; August 1, 2011; August 1, 2013; April 1, 2014.]

IOP—CIR. RULE 22

1. Certificate of Appealability. *Consistent with FRAP 2, the court may suspend the provisions of 11th Cir. R. 22-1(c) and order proceedings in accordance with the court's direction.*

2. Oral Argument in Capital Cases. *The presiding judge of the panel will notify the clerk at the appropriate time whether or not there will be oral argument in the case, and if so, the date for oral argument and the amount of oral argument time allotted to each side. A capital case appeal will include oral argument on the merits unless the panel decides unanimously that oral argument is not needed.*

Cross-Reference: FRAP 27; 28 U.S.C. §§ 2244, 2254, 2255; Rules 9 and 11 of the Rules Governing Section 2254 and Section 2255 Cases in the United States District Courts

[Effective December 1, 1998. Amended effective April 1, 2003; August 1, 2011.]

FRAP 23. CUSTODY OR RELEASE OF A PRISONER IN A HABEAS CORPUS PROCEEDING

[For text of rule, see the Federal Rules of Appellate Procedure]

FRAP 24. PROCEEDING IN FORMA PAUPERIS

[For text of rule, see the Federal Rules of Appellate Procedure]

RULE 24-1. APPEALS IN FORMA PAUPERIS AND UNDER THE CRIMINAL JUSTICE ACT

(a) To meet the requirements of the Criminal Justice Act of 1964, as amended, 18 U.S.C. § 3006A, the judicial council of this circuit has adopted a plan that supplements the various plans that have been adopted by the United States district courts of this circuit by providing for representation on appeal of parties financially unable to obtain adequate representation. The circuit's CJA plan, and the guidelines for counsel, appear as Addendum Four to these rules.

(b) If counsel was appointed for a party in the district court under the Criminal Justice Act, the party may appeal without prepaying costs and without establishing the right to proceed in forma pauperis. 18 U.S.C. § 3006A(d)(6). This policy also applies to all in forma pauperis appeals from judgments of conviction.

[Amended effective April 1, 1991.]

RULE 24–2. MOTION FOR LEAVE TO PROCEED ON APPEAL IN FORMA PAUPERIS

A motion for leave to proceed on appeal in forma pauperis may be filed in the court of appeals within 30 days after service of notice of the action of the district court denying leave to proceed on appeal in forma pauperis.

[Adopted effective April 1, 1991. Amended effective January 1, 2003.]

IOP—CIR. RULE 24

Prison Litigation Reform Act. *In all civil appeals by prisoners, the Prison Litigation Reform Act of 1995 (hereinafter "the Act"), 28 U.S.C. § 1915 (as amended), requires payment of the court of appeals docketing fee prescribed by the Judicial Conference of the United States in the Court of Appeals Miscellaneous Fee Schedule, issued pursuant to 28 U.S.C. § 1913, plus the district court filing fee required by 28 U.S.C. § 1917, payable to the clerk of the United States District Court where the prisoner/appellant filed the notice of appeal. Likewise, prior to the filing of a petition for a writ of mandamus (or other writ) the Act requires payment of the court of appeals docketing fee prescribed by the Judicial Conference of the United States in the Court of Appeals Miscellaneous Fee Schedule issued pursuant to 28 U.S.C. § 1913, payable to Clerk, U.S. Court of Appeals, Eleventh Circuit. If a prisoner is unable to pay the required fee in full at the time of filing a notice of appeal or petition for a writ, the appropriate district court (if a notice of appeal is filed) or this court (if a petition for a writ is filed) may allow the prison or other institution of confinement to pay the fee in installments from the prisoner's account.*

[Effective December 1, 1998. Amended effective December 1, 2003; April 9, 2006; August 1, 2014.]

TITLE VII. GENERAL PROVISIONS

FRAP 25. FILING AND SERVICE

[For text of rule, see the Federal Rules of Appellate Procedure]

RULE 25–1. FILINGS FROM PARTY REPRESENTED BY COUNSEL

When a party is represented by counsel, the clerk may not accept filings from the party.

RULE 25–2. FILING OF PAPERS TRANSMITTED BY ALTERNATE MEANS

The clerk may specially authorize the filing of papers transmitted by alternate means in emergencies and for other compelling circumstances. In such cases, signed originals must thereafter also be furnished by conventional means. Provided that the clerk had given prior authorization for transmission by alternate means and the papers conform to the requirements of FRAP and circuit rules, the signed originals will be filed nunc pro tunc to the receipt date of the papers transmitted by alternate means. The court may act upon the papers transmitted by alternate means prior to receipt of the signed originals.

[Adopted effective April 1, 1994. Amended effective December 1, 2013.]

RULE 25–3. ELECTRONIC CASE FILES (ECF) SYSTEM

(a) Electronic Filing and Service. It is mandatory that all counsel of record use the court's Electronic Case Files (ECF) system. Documents must be filed and served electronically by counsel in accordance with the procedures adopted by the court and set forth in the Eleventh Circuit Guide to Electronic Filing. The Eleventh Circuit Guide to Electronic Filing, and information and training materials related to electronic filing, are available on the court's website at www.ca11.uscourts.gov.

The notice generated and e-mailed by the ECF system constitutes service of all electronically filed documents on attorneys registered to use the ECF system. Independent service, either by paper or otherwise, need not be made on those attorneys. Pro se litigants and attorneys who are exempt from electronic filing must be served by the filing party through the conventional means of service set forth in FRAP 25. A document filed electronically through the ECF system still must contain a certificate of service conforming to the requirements of FRAP 25.

(b) Exemption. Upon motion and a showing of good cause, the court may exempt an attorney from the electronic filing requirements and authorize filing and service by means other than the use of the ECF system. The motion, which need not be filed or served electronically, must be filed at least 14 days before the brief, petition, or other document is due. Also see 11th Cir. R. 31–5.

[Effective December 1, 1998. Amended effective January 1, 2003; August 1, 2013; December 1, 2014.]

RULE 25–4. INFORMATION AND SIGNATURE REQUIRED

All papers filed, including motions and briefs, must contain the name, office address, and telephone number of an attorney or a party proceeding pro se, and be signed by an attorney or by a party proceeding pro se. Inmate filings must be signed by the inmate and should contain name, prisoner number, institution, and street address.

[Effective December 1, 1998. Amended effective January 1, 2002.]

RULE 25-5. MAINTAINING PRIVACY OF PERSONAL DATA

In order to promote electronic access to case files while also protecting personal privacy and other legitimate interests, parties shall refrain from including, or shall partially redact where inclusion is necessary, the following personal data identifiers from all pleadings filed with the court, including exhibits thereto, whether filed electronically or in paper, unless otherwise ordered by the court.

a. Social Security Numbers and Taxpayer Identification Numbers. If an individual's social security number or taxpayer identification number must be included in a pleading, only the last four digits of that number should be used.

b. Names of Minor Children. If the involvement of a minor child must be mentioned, only the initials of that child should be used. For purposes of this rule, a minor child is any person under the age of eighteen years, unless otherwise provided by statute or court order.

c. Dates of Birth. If an individual's date of birth must be included in a pleading, only the year should be used.

d. Financial Account Numbers. If financial account numbers are relevant, only the last four digits of these numbers should be used.

e. Home Addresses. If a home address must be included, only the city and state should be used.

Subject to the exemptions from the redaction requirement contained in the Federal Rules of Civil, Criminal, and Bankruptcy Procedure, as made applicable to the courts of appeals through FRAP 25(a)(5), a party filing a document containing the personal data identifiers listed above shall file a redacted document for the public file and either:

(1) a reference list under seal. The reference list shall contain the complete personal data identifier and the redacted identifier used in its place in the redacted filing. All references in the filing to the redacted identifiers included in the reference list will be construed to refer to the corresponding complete personal data identifiers. The reference list must be filed under seal, may be amended as of right, and shall be retained by the court as part of the record. A motion to file the reference list under seal is not required. Or

(2) an unredacted document under seal, along with a motion to file the unredacted document under seal specifying the type of personal data identifier included in the document and why the party believes that including it in the document is necessary or relevant. If permitted to be filed, both the redacted and unredacted documents shall be retained by the court as part of the record.

The responsibility for redacting these personal data identifiers rests solely with counsel and the parties. The clerk will not review each pleading for compliance with this rule. A person waives the protection of this rule as to the person's own information by filing it without redaction and not under seal.

Consistent with FRAP 25(a)(5), electronic public access is not provided to pleadings filed with the court in social security appeals and immigration appeals. Therefore, parties in social security appeals and immigration appeals are exempt from the requirements of this rule.

In addition to the foregoing, a party should exercise caution when filing a document that contains any of the following information. A party filing a redacted document that contains any of the following information must comply with the rules for filing an unredacted document as described in numbered paragraph (2) above.

- Personal identifying number, such as driver's license number;
- medical records, treatment and diagnosis;
- employment history;
- individual financial information;
- proprietary or trade secret information;
- information regarding an individual's cooperation with the government;
- national security information;
- sensitive security information as described in 49 U.S.C. § 114(s).

[Effective December 1, 2003. Amended effective December 1, 2004; April 1, 2005. Renumbered from 31-6, effective December 1, 2006. Amended effective December 1, 2007.]

RULE 25-6. COURT ACTION WITH RESPECT TO IMPERMISSIBLE LANGUAGE OR INFORMATION IN FILINGS

(a) When any paper filed with the court, including motions and briefs, contains:

(1) *ad hominem* or defamatory language; or

(2) information the public disclosure of which would constitute a clearly unwarranted invasion of personal privacy; or

(3) information the public disclosure of which would violate legally protected interests,

the court on motion of a party or on its own motion, may without prior notice take appropriate action.

(b) The appropriate action the court may take in the circumstances described above includes ordering that: the document be sealed; specified language or information be stricken from the document; the document be struck from the record; the clerk be directed to remove the document from electronic public access; the party who filed the document either explain why including the specified language or disclosing the specified information in the document is relevant, necessary, and appropriate or file a redacted or replacement document.

(c) When the court takes such action under this rule without prior notice, the party may within 14 days from the date the court order is issued file a motion to restore language or information stricken or removed from the document or file the document without redaction, setting forth with particularity any reasons why the action taken by the court was unwarranted. The timely filing of such motion will postpone the due date for filing any redacted or replacement document until the court rules on the motion.

[Effective April 1, 2007. Amended effective December 1, 2015.]

IOP—CIR. RULE 25

*1. **Timely Filing of Papers.** Except as otherwise provided by FRAP 25(a) for inmate filings and for briefs and appendices, all other papers, including petitions for rehearing, shall not be timely unless they are actually received in the clerk's office within the time fixed for filing.*

*2. **Acknowledgment of Filings.** The clerk will acknowledge paper filings if a stamped self-addressed envelope is provided.*

*3. **Filing With the Clerk.** The clerk's office in Atlanta is the proper place for the filing of all court documents that are exempt from electronic filing. It is open for business from 8:30 a.m. until 5:00 p.m., Eastern time, Monday through Friday (except legal holidays). Staff is available during these hours to receive filings and to respond to over-the-counter and telephone inquiries. Outside of normal business hours, an emergency telephone message system is available through which a deputy clerk may be reached by dialing the main clerk's office telephone number and following recorded instructions.*

*4. **Papers Sent Directly to Judges' Chambers.** When an attorney or party sends papers related to a pending appeal directly to a judge's chambers without having received prior approval from the court to do so, the judge shall forward the papers to the clerk for appropriate processing. The clerk will advise the attorney or party that the papers have been received by the clerk, and that the clerk's office in Atlanta is the proper place for the filing of appellate papers.*

*5. **Miami Satellite Office.** The clerk maintains a satellite office in Miami, Florida, to assist parties and counsel to access the record on appeal in appeals being briefed, and to provide other related assistance. It is open for business from 8:30 a.m. until 5:00 p.m., Eastern time, Monday through Friday (except legal holidays).*

All filings and case-related inquiries should be directed to the clerk's principal office in Atlanta, except that counsel who receive a calendar assigning an appeal to a specific day of oral argument in Miami should direct filings and case-related inquiries up to the date of oral argument to the Miami satellite office. Inquiries concerning bar membership, renewal of bar membership, and application for admission to the bar are to be directed to the clerk's principal office in Atlanta.

Cross–Reference: FRAP 26, 45, "E–Government Act of 2002," Pub. L. No. 107–347

Cross–Reference for 11th Cir. R. 25–6(a)(2): See 5 U.S.C. § 552b(c)(6) [personal privacy exception to the Freedom of Information Act]

[Amended effective April 1, 1991; April 1, 1994; December 1, 1998; January 1, 2002; December 1, 2004; December 1, 2009; December 1, 2013; December 1, 2015.]

FRAP 26. COMPUTING AND EXTENDING TIME

[For text of rule, see the Federal Rules of Appellate Procedure]

RULE 26–1. MOTION FOR EXTENSION OF TIME

A motion for extension of time made pursuant to FRAP 26(b) shall contain a statement that movant's counsel has consulted opposing counsel and that either opposing counsel has no objection to the relief sought, or will or will not promptly file an objection. In criminal appeals, counsel must state whether the party they represent is incarcerated.

[Amended effective April 1, 1991; December 1, 1998.]

IOP—CIR. RULE 26

*1. **Extensions of Time.** The court expects the timely filing of all papers within the period of time allowed by the rules, without granting extensions of time. Requests for extensions of time to file the brief or appendix are governed by 11th Cir. R. 31–2. Failure to timely file required documents may cause the appeal to be dismissed for want of prosecution, under the provisions of 11th Cir. R. 42–1, 42–2, or 42–3, or may result in possible disciplinary action against counsel as described in Addendum Eight, or both.*

*2. **Inaccessibility of Clerk's Office.** The court, by order of the chief judge, may determine that inclement weather or other extraordinary conditions have made the clerk's office inaccessible. If such a determination is made, any filings due to be made on such a day will automatically be processed as timely if received on the day that the clerk's office reopens for business. Counsel need not make any special application or request for such treatment. Further, parties and their counsel should note that ordinarily local conditions at the place from which filings are sent do not trigger the additional time for filing provisions of FRAP 26(a) except upon application to the clerk and order of court.*

Cross–Reference: FRAP 25, 27, 31, 42, 45

[Amended effective April 1, 1991; April 1, 1994; January 2, 1996; December 1, 1998; January 1, 2000; April 9, 2006; December 1, 2013.]

FRAP 26.1. CORPORATE DISCLOSURE STATEMENT

[For text of rule, see the Federal Rules of Appellate Procedure]

RULE 26.1–1. CERTIFICATE OF INTERESTED PERSONS AND CORPORATE DISCLOSURE STATEMENT (CIP): FILING REQUIREMENTS

(a) Paper or E–Filed CIPs.

(1) Every party and amicus curiae ("filers") must include a certificate of interested persons and corporate disclosure statement ("CIP") within every motion, petition, brief, answer, response, and reply filed.

(2) In addition, appellants and petitioners must file a CIP within 14 days after the date the case or appeal is docketed in this court.

(3) Also, all appellees, intervenors, respondents, and all other parties to the case or appeal must file a CIP within 28 days after the date the case or appeal is docketed in this court, regardless of whether appellants and petitioners have filed a CIP. If appellants and petitioners have already filed a CIP, appellees, intervenors, respondents, and all other parties may file a notice either indicating that the CIP is correct and complete, or adding any interested persons or entities omitted from the CIP.

(b) Web-based CIP. On the same day any filer represented by counsel first files its paper or e-filed CIP, that filer must also complete the court's web-based CIP at www.ca11.uscourts.gov. At the website, counsel for filers will log into the web-based CIP where they will enter stock ("ticker") symbol information for publicly traded corporations to be used by the court in electronically checking for recusals. If there is no publicly traded corporation involved, and thus no stock ticker symbol to enter, the filer still must complete the web-based CIP by entering "nothing to declare."

Failure to complete the web-based CIP will delay processing of the motion, case, or appeal, and may result in other sanctions under 11th Cir. R. 26.1-5(c).

The e-filing of a CIP by an attorney registered to use the ECF system does not relieve that attorney of the requirement to complete and keep updated the web-based CIP. Pro se filers (except attorneys appearing in particular cases as pro se parties) are not required or authorized to complete the web-based CIP.

[Adopted effective April 1, 1991. Amended effective April 1, 1994; January 2, 1996; December 1, 1998; January 1, 2003; April 1, 2003; December 1, 2015; December 1, 2016.]

RULE 26.1-2 CIP: CONTENTS

(a) General. A CIP must contain a complete list of all trial judges, attorneys, persons, associations of persons, firms, partnerships, or corporations that have an interest in the outcome of the particular case or appeal, including subsidiaries, conglomerates, affiliates, parent corporations, any publicly held corporation that owns 10% or more of the party's stock, and other identifiable legal entities related to a party.

In criminal and criminal-related appeals, the CIP must also disclose the identity of any victims. In bankruptcy appeals, the CIP must also identify the debtor, the members of the creditor's committee, any entity which is an active participant in the proceedings, and other entities whose stock or equity value may be substantially affected by the outcome of the proceedings.

(b) CIPs in Briefs. The CIP contained in the first brief filed must include a complete list of all persons and entities known to that filer to have an interest in the outcome of the particular case or appeal. The CIP contained in the second and all subsequent briefs filed may include only persons and entities omitted from the CIP contained in the first brief filed and in any other brief that has been filed. Filers who believe that the CIP contained in the first brief filed and in any other brief that has been filed is complete must certify to that effect.

(c) CIPs in Motions or Petitions. The CIP contained in each motion or petition filed must include a complete list of all persons and entities known to that filer to have an interest in the outcome of the particular case or appeal. The CIP contained in a response or answer to a motion or petition, or a reply to a response, may include only persons and entities that were omitted from the CIP contained in the motion or petition. Filers who believe that the CIP contained in the motion or petition is complete must certify to that effect.

(d) CIPs in Petitions for En Banc Consideration. In a petition for en banc consideration, the petitioner's CIP must also compile and include a complete list of all persons and entities listed on all CIPs previously filed in the case or appeal prior to the date of filing of the petition for en banc consideration. Eleventh Circuit Rule 26.1-2(b) applies to all en banc briefs.

[Adopted effective April 1, 1991. Amended effective January 2, 1996; January 1, 2003; March 6, 2007, effective for all appeals docketed, or in which the record is deemed filed per 11th Cir.R. 12-1, on or after April 1, 2007; August 1, 2007; December 1, 2009; December 1, 2010; December 1, 2015.]

RULE 26.1-3. CIP: FORM

(a) The CIP must list persons (last name first) and entities in alphabetical order, have only one column, and be double-spaced.

(b) A corporate entity must be identified by its full corporate name as registered with a secretary of state's office and, if its stock is publicly listed, its stock ("ticker") symbol must be provided after the corporate name. If no publicly traded company or corporation has an interest in the outcome of the case or appeal, a statement certifying to that effect must be included at the end of the CIP and must be entered into the web-based CIP.

(c) At the top of each page, the court of appeals docket number and short style must be noted (name of first-listed plaintiff or petitioner v. name of first-listed defendant or respondent). Each page of the CIP must be separately sequentially numbered to indicate the total number of pages comprising the CIP (e.g., C-1 of 3, C-2 of 3, C-3 of 3). These pages do not count against any length limitations imposed on the papers filed.

(d) When being included in a document, the CIP must immediately follow the cover page within a brief, and must precede the text in a petition, answer, motion, response, or reply.

[Adopted effective April 1, 1991. Amended effective April 1, 1994; December 1, 1998; March 6, 2007, effective for all appeals docketed, or in which the record is deemed filed per 11 Cir.R. 12-1, on or after April 1, 2007; December 1, 2015; December 1, 2016.]

RULE 26.1-4 CIP: AMENDMENTS

Every filer is required to notify the court immediately of any additions, deletions, corrections, or other changes that should be made to its CIP. A filer must do so by filing an amended CIP with the court and by including an amended CIP with all subsequent filings. A filer:

- must prominently indicate on the amended CIP the fact that the CIP has been amended;
- must clearly identify the person or entity that has been added, deleted, corrected, or otherwise changed; and
- if represented by counsel, must update the web-based CIP to reflect the amendments on the same day the amended CIP is filed.

If an amended CIP that deletes a person or entity is filed, every other party must, within 10 days after the filing of the amended CIP, file a notice indicating whether or not it agrees that the deletion is proper.

[Effective December 1, 2015.]

RULE 26.1-5 FAILURE TO SUBMIT A CIP OR COMPLETE THE WEB-BASED CIP

(a) The court will not act upon any papers requiring a CIP, including emergency filings, until the CIP is filed and the web-based CIP is completed, except to prevent manifest injustice.

(b) The clerk is not authorized to submit to the court any brief, petition, answer, motion, response, or reply that does not contain the CIP, or any of those papers in a case or appeal where the web-based CIP has not been completed, but may receive and retain the papers pending supplementation of the papers with the required CIP and pending completion of the web-based CIP.

(c) The failure to comply with 11th Cir. Rules 26.1-1 through 26.1-4 may result in dismissal of the case or appeal under 11th Cir. R. 42-1(b), return of deficient documents without action, or other sanctions on counsel, the party, or both.

Cross-Reference: FRAP 5, 5.1, 21, 27, 28, 29, 35

[Effective December 1, 2015.]

FRAP 27. MOTIONS

[For text of rule, see the Federal Rules of Appellate Procedure]

RULE 27-1. MOTIONS

(a) Number of Copies and Form of Motion.

(1) When a motion is filed in paper, an original and three copies of the motion and supporting papers must be filed if the motion requires panel action. An original and one copy of the motion and supporting papers must be filed if the motion may be acted upon by a single judge or by the clerk [see 11th Cir. R. 27-1(c) and (d)].

(2) A motion filed in paper must contain proof of service on all parties, and should ordinarily be served on other parties by means which are as equally expeditious as those used to file the motion with the court.

(3) A motion shall be accompanied by, and the opposing party shall be served with, supporting documentation required by FRAP 27, including relevant materials from previous judicial or administrative proceedings in the case or appeal. A party moving for a stay must include a copy of the judgment or order from which relief is sought and any opinion and findings of the district court.

(4) In addition to matters required by FRAP 27, a motion shall contain a brief recitation of prior actions of this or any other court or judge to which the motion, or a substantially similar or related application for relief, has been made.

(5) A motion for extension of time made pursuant to FRAP 26(b) shall, and other motions where appropriate may, contain a statement that movant's counsel has consulted opposing counsel and that either opposing counsel has no objection to the relief sought, or will or will not promptly file an objection.

(6) In criminal appeals, counsel must state whether the party they represent is incarcerated.

(7) Both retained and appointed counsel who seek leave to withdraw from or to dismiss a criminal appeal must recite in the motion that the party they represent has been informed of the motion and either approves or disapproves of the relief sought and show service of the motion on the party they represent.

(8) Appointed counsel who seek leave to withdraw from representation in a criminal appeal must follow procedures set forth by the Supreme Court in *Anders v. California*, 386 U.S. 738, 87 S.Ct. 1396, 18 L.Ed.2d 493 (1967). It is counsel's responsibility to ensure that the record contains transcripts of *relevant* proceedings in the case, including pre-trial proceedings, trial proceedings (including opening and closing arguments and jury instructions), and sentencing proceedings. Counsel's brief in support of a motion to withdraw under *Anders* must contain a certificate of service indicating service on the party represented as well as on the other parties to the appeal.

(9) All motions filed with the court shall include a Certificate of Interested Persons and Corporate Disclosure Statement as described in FRAP 26.1 and the accompanying circuit rules.

(10) A motion must comply with the typeface and type style requirements of FRAP 32(a)(5) and 32(a)(6).

(b) Emergency Motions.

(1) Except in capital cases in which execution has been scheduled, a motion will be treated as an emergency motion only when **both** of the following conditions are present:

1. The motion will be moot unless a ruling is obtained within seven days; and

2. If the order sought to be reviewed is a district court order or action, the motion is being filed within seven days of the filing of the district court order or action sought to be reviewed.

Motions that do not meet these two conditions but in which a ruling is required by a date certain may be treated as "time sensitive" motions.

(2) A party requesting emergency action shall label the motion as "Emergency Motion" and state the nature of the emergency and the date by which action is necessary. The

motion or accompanying memorandum shall state the reasons for granting the requested relief and must specifically discuss:

(i) the likelihood the moving party will prevail on the merits;

(ii) the prospect of irreparable injury to the moving party if relief is withheld;

(iii) the possibility of harm to other parties if relief is granted; and

(iv) the public interest.

Counsel filing the motion shall make every possible effort to serve the motion personally; if this is not possible, counsel shall notify opposing counsel promptly by telephone.

(3) If the emergency motion raises any issue theretofore raised in a district court, counsel for the moving party shall furnish copies of all pleadings, briefs, memoranda or other papers filed in the district court supporting or opposing the position taken by the moving party in the motion and copies of any order or memorandum decision of the district court relating thereto. If compliance is impossible or impractical due to time restraints or otherwise, the reason for non-compliance shall be stated.

(4) An emergency motion, whether addressed to the court or an individual judge, ordinarily should be filed with the clerk and not with an individual judge. To expedite consideration by the court in a genuine emergency, counsel may telephone the clerk and describe a motion that has not yet been filed in writing. This is not a substitute for the filing required by FRAP 27(a).

(5) Except in capital cases in which execution has been scheduled, counsel will be permitted to file an emergency motion outside of normal business hours only when **both** of the following conditions are present:

1. The motion will be moot unless a ruling is obtained prior to noon [Eastern Time] of the next business day; and

2. If the order or action sought to be reviewed is a district court order or action, the motion is being filed within two business days of the filing of the district court order or action sought to be reviewed.

(c) Motions for Procedural Orders Acted Upon by the Clerk. The clerk is authorized, subject to review by the court, to act for the court on the following unopposed procedural motions:

(1) to extend the time for filing briefs or other papers in appeals not yet assigned or under submission;

(2) to withdraw appearances except for court-appointed counsel;

(3) to make corrections at the request of counsel in briefs or pleadings filed in this court;

(4) to extend the time for filing petitions for rehearing for not longer than 28 days, but only when the court's opinion is unpublished;

(5) to abate or stay further proceedings in appeals, provided that the requesting party files a written status report with the clerk at 30-day intervals, indicating whether the abatement or stay should continue;

(6) to supplement or correct records;

(7) to consolidate appeals from the same district court;

(8) to incorporate records or briefs from former appeals;

(9) to grant leave to file further reply or supplemental briefs before argument in addition to the single reply brief permitted by FRAP 28(c);

(10) to reinstate appeals dismissed by the clerk;

(11) to enter orders continuing on appeal district court appointments of counsel for purposes of compensation;

(12) to file briefs in excess of the page and type-volume limitations set forth in FRAP 32(a)(7), but only upon a showing of extraordinary circumstances;

(13) to extend the time for filing Bills of Costs;

(14) to permit the release of the record from the clerk's custody but only upon a showing of extraordinary circumstances;

(15) to grant leave to adopt by reference any part of the brief of another;

(16) to intervene in a proceeding seeking review or enforcement of an agency order;

(17) to intervene pursuant to 28 U.S.C. § 2403;

(18) for substitution of parties.

The clerk is authorized, subject to review by the court, to act for the court on the following opposed procedural motions:

(19) to grant moderate extensions of time for filing briefs or other papers in appeals not yet assigned or under submission unless substantial reasons for opposition are advanced;

(20) to expedite briefing in a direct appeal of a criminal conviction and/or sentence when it appears that an incarcerated defendant's projected release is expected to occur prior to the conclusion of appellate proceedings.

The clerk is also authorized to carry a motion with the case where there is no need for court action prior to the time the matter is considered on the merits by a panel.

(d) Motions Acted Upon by a Single Judge. Under FRAP 27(c), a single judge may, subject to review by the court, act upon any request for relief that may be sought by motion, except to dismiss or otherwise determine an appeal or other proceeding. Without limiting this authority, a single judge is authorized to act, subject to review by the court, on the following motions:

(1) where opposed, motions that are subject to action by the clerk under part (c) of this rule;

(2) for certificates of appealability under FRAP 22(b) and 28 U.S.C. § 2254;

(3) to appeal in forma pauperis pursuant to FRAP 24 and 28 U.S.C. § 1915(a);

(4) to appoint counsel for indigent persons appealing from judgments of conviction or from denial of writs of habeas corpus or petitions filed under 28 U.S.C. § 2255, or to permit court appointed counsel to withdraw;

(5) to extend the length of briefs except in capital cases, and to extend the length of petitions for rehearing or rehearing en banc;

(6) to extend the times prescribed by the rules of this court for good cause shown (note that FRAP 26(b) forbids the court to enlarge the time for taking various actions, including the time for filing a notice of appeal); in criminal appeals, counsel requesting an extension of time to file a brief must state whether the party they represent is incarcerated;

(7) to exercise the power granted in FRAP 8 and 9 with respect to stays or injunctions or releases in criminal cases pending appeal but subject to the restrictions set out therein, and under FRAP 18 with respect to stays pending review of decisions or orders of agencies but subject to the restrictions on the power of a single judge contained therein;

(8) to stay the issuance of mandates or recall mandates pending certiorari;

(9) to expedite appeals;

(10) to file briefs as amicus curiae prior to issuance of a panel opinion.

(e) Two–Judge Motions Panels. Specified motions as determined by the court may be acted upon by a panel of two judges.

(f) Motions Shall Not Be Argued. Unless ordered by the court no motion shall be orally argued.

(g) Effect of a Ruling on a Motion. A ruling on a motion or other interlocutory matter, whether entered by a single judge or a panel, is not binding upon the panel to which the appeal is assigned on the merits, and the merits panel may alter, amend, or vacate it.

[Amended effective April 1, 1991; April 1, 1994; January 2, 1996; December 1, 1998; January 1, 2002; January 1, 2003; December 1, 2003; December 1, 2004; August 1, 2013; December 1, 2013.]

RULE 27–2. MOTION FOR RECONSIDERATION

A motion to reconsider, vacate, or modify an order must be filed within 21 days of the entry of such order. No additional time shall be allowed for mailing.

[Effective January 1, 2002. Amended effective January 1, 2003; April 1, 2009.]

RULE 27–3. SUCCESSIVE MOTIONS FOR RECONSIDERATION NOT PERMITTED

A party may file only one motion for reconsideration with respect to the same order. Likewise, a party may not request reconsideration of an order disposing of a motion for reconsideration previously filed by that party.

[Effective January 1, 2002.]

RULE 27–4. SANCTIONS FOR FILING A FRIVOLOUS MOTION

When a party or an attorney practicing before this court files a frivolous motion, the court may, on motion of a party, or on its own motion after notice and a reasonable opportunity to respond, impose an appropriate sanction on the party, the attorney, or both. For purposes of this rule, a motion is frivolous if:

(a) it is without legal merit and cannot be supported by a reasonable argument for an extension, modification, or reversal of existing law, or the establishment of new law; or

(b) it contains assertions of material facts that are false or unsupported by the record; or

(c) it is presented for an improper purpose, such as to harass or to cause unnecessary delay or needless increase in the cost of litigation.

Sanctions may be monetary or nonmonetary in nature. Monetary sanctions may include an order to pay a penalty into the court, or an order directing payment to another party of some or all of the attorney's fees and expenses incurred by that party as a result of the frivolous motion, or both.

When a motion to impose sanctions is filed under this rule, the court may, if warranted, award to the party prevailing on the motion reasonable attorney's fees and expenses incurred in presenting or opposing the motion.

[Effective January 1, 2003.]

IOP—CIR. RULE 27

*1. **Routing Procedures to Judges.** Pre–submission motions requiring consideration by judges are assigned to motions panels. Composition of these panels is changed at the beginning of each court year in October, and upon a change in the court's membership. The clerk submits the motion papers to the judges assigned in rotation from a routing log, the effect of which is to route motions randomly to judges based on filing date. In matters requiring panel action, the papers are sent to the first judge (initiating judge), who will transmit them to the second judge with a recommendation. The second judge in turn sends them on to the third judge who returns the file and an appropriate order to the clerk.*

*2. **Emergency Motion Procedure.** Emergency motions are assigned in rotation from a separate emergency routing log. The papers are forwarded to all panel members simultaneously. If the matter requires that counsel contact panel members individually, the clerk after first securing panel approval will advise counsel (or parties) of the identity of the panel members to whom the appeal is assigned.*

*3. **Motions to Expedite Appeals.** Except as otherwise provided in these rules, and unless the court directs otherwise, an appeal may be expedited only by the court upon motion and for good cause shown. Unless the court otherwise specifies, the clerk will fix an appropriate briefing schedule which will permit the appeal to be heard at an early date.*

*4. **Motions after Assignment of Appeal to Calendar.** After an appeal is assigned to a non-argument or oral argument calendar, motions in that appeal are circulated to that panel rather than to an administrative motions panel.*

*5. **Signature Required.** 11th Cir. R. 25–4 requires motions to be signed by an attorney or by a party proceeding pro se.*

6. ***Acknowledgment of Motions.*** *The clerk will acknowledge filing of a motion if a stamped selfaddressed envelope is provided.*

7. ***Withdrawing Motions.*** *If a party no longer requires a ruling by the court on a pending motion, the filing party should file a motion to withdraw the motion.*

Cross-Reference: FRAP 8, 9, 18, 26, 26.1, 32, 43; U.S. Sup. Ct. Rule 43

[Amended effective April 1, 1994; January 2, 1996; December 1, 1998; January 1, 2002; April 1, 2016; December 1, 2016.]

FRAP 28. BRIEFS

[For text of rule, see the Federal Rules of Appellate Procedure]

RULE 28-1. BRIEFS—CONTENTS

Each principal brief shall consist, in the order listed, of the following:

(a) Cover Page. Elements to be shown on the cover page include the court of appeals docket number centered at the top; the name of this court; the title of the case [see FRAP 12(a)]; the nature of the proceeding [e.g., Appeal, Petition for Review]; the name of the court, agency, or board below; the title of the brief, identifying the party or parties for whom the brief is filed; and the name, office address, and telephone number of the attorney. See FRAP 32(a)(2).

(b) Certificate of Interested Persons and Corporate Disclosure Statement. A Certificate of Interested Persons and Corporate Disclosure Statement ("CIP") is required of every party and amicus curiae. The CIP shall comply with FRAP 26.1 and the accompanying circuit rules, and shall be included within each brief immediately following the cover page.

(c) Statement Regarding Oral Argument. Appellant's brief shall include a short statement of whether or not oral argument is desired, and if so, the reasons why oral argument should be heard. Appellee's brief shall include a similar statement. The court will accord these statements due, though not controlling, weight in determining whether oral argument will be heard. See FRAP 34(a) and (f) and 11th Cir. R. 34-3(c).

(d) Table of Contents. The table of contents shall include page references to each section required by this rule to be included within the brief. The table shall also include specific page references to each heading or subheading of each issue argued.

(e) Table of Citations. The Table of Citations shall show the locations in the brief of citations, and shall contain asterisks in the margin identifying the citations upon which the party primarily relies.

(f) Statement Regarding Adoption of Briefs of Other Parties. A party who adopts by reference any part of the brief of another party pursuant to FRAP 28(i) shall include a statement describing in detail which briefs and which portions of those briefs are adopted.

(g) Statement of Subject-Matter and Appellate Jurisdiction. The jurisdictional statement must contain all information required by FRAP 28(a)(4)(A) through (D).

(h) Statement of the Issues.

(i) Statement of the Case. In the statement of the case, as in all other sections of the brief, every assertion regarding matter in the record shall be supported by a reference to the volume number (if available), document number, and page number of the original record where the matter relied upon is to be found. The statement of the case shall briefly recite the nature of the case and shall then include:

(i) the course of proceedings and dispositions in the court below. IN CRIMINAL APPEALS, COUNSEL MUST STATE WHETHER THE PARTY THEY REPRESENT IS INCARCERATED;

(ii) a statement of the facts. A proper statement of facts reflects a high standard of professionalism. It must state the facts accurately, those favorable and those unfavorable to the party. Inferences drawn from facts must be identified as such;

(iii) a statement of the standard or scope of review for each contention. For example, where the appeal is from an exercise of district court discretion, there shall be a statement that the standard of review is whether the district court abused its discretion. The appropriate standard or scope of review for other contentions should be similarly indicated, e.g., that the district court erred in formulating or applying a rule of law; or that there is insufficient evidence to support a verdict; or that fact findings of the trial judge are clearly erroneous under Fed.R.Civ.P. 52(a); or that there is a lack of substantial evidence in the record as a whole to support the factual findings of an administrative agency; or that the agency's action, findings and conclusions should be held unlawful and set aside for the reasons set forth in 5 U.S.C. § 706(2).

(j) Summary of the Argument. The opening briefs of the parties shall also contain a summary of argument, suitably paragraphed, which should be a clear, accurate and succinct condensation of the argument actually made in the body of the brief. It should not be a mere repetition of the headings under which the argument is arranged. It should seldom exceed two and never five pages.

(k) Argument and Citations of Authority. Citations of authority in the brief shall comply with the rules of citation in the latest edition of either the "Bluebook" (A Uniform System of Citation) or the "ALWD Guide" (Association of Legal Writing Directors' Guide to Legal Citation). Citations shall reference the specific page number(s) which relate to the proposition for which the case is cited. For state reported cases the national reporter series should be cross referenced (e.g., Southern Reporter, Southeast Reporter).

(*l*) Conclusion.

(m) Certificate of Compliance. The certificate described in FRAP 32(g), if required by that rule.

(n) Certificate of Service.

[Former 11th Cir. R. 28–2 amended effective April 1, 1991. Amended effective April 1, 1994; January 2, 1996; December 1, 1998. Redesignated 11th Cir. R. 28–1 and amended effective April 1, 1999. Amended effective January 1, 2002; April 1, 2004; August 1, 2011; December 1, 2015; August 1, 2016; December 1, 2016.]

RULE 28–2. APPELLEE'S BRIEF

An appellee's brief need not contain items (g), (h), and (i) of 11th Cir. R. 28–1 if the appellee is satisfied with the appellant's statement.

[Adopted effective December 1, 2005.]

RULE 28–3. REPLY BRIEF

A reply brief need contain only items (a), (b), (d), (e), (k), (m) and (n) of 11th Cir. R. 28–1.

[Former 11th Cir. R. 28–3 amended effective April 1, 1991; April 1, 1994; January 2, 1996; December 1, 1998. Redesignated 11th Cir. R. 28–2 and amended effective April 1, 1999. Redesignated 11th Cir.R. 28–3 effective December 1, 2005. Amended effective August 1, 2016.]

RULE 28–4. BRIEFS FROM PARTY REPRESENTED BY COUNSEL

When a party is represented by counsel, the clerk may not accept a brief from the party.

[Former 11th Cir. R. 28–4 redesignated 11th Cir. R. 28–3 effective April 1, 1999. Redesignated 11th Cir.R. 28–4 effective December 1, 2005.]

RULE 28–5. REFERENCES TO THE RECORD

References to the record in a brief shall be to volume number (if available), document number, and page number. A reference may (but need not) contain the full or abbreviated name of a document.

[Effective April 1, 1999. Redesignated 11th Cir.R. 28–5 effective December 1, 2005.]

IOP—CIR. RULE 28

1. ***Signature Required.*** *11th Cir. R. 25–4 requires briefs to be signed by an attorney or by a party proceeding pro se.*

2. ***"One Attorney, One Brief".*** *Unless otherwise directed by the court, an attorney representing more than one party in an appeal may only file one principal brief (and one reply brief, if authorized), which will include argument as to all of the parties represented by that attorney in that appeal, and one (combined) appendix. A single party responding to more than one brief, or represented by more than one attorney, is similarly bound.*

3. ***Adoption of Briefs of Other Parties.*** *The adoption by reference of any part of the brief of another party pursuant to FRAP 28(i) does not fulfill the obligation of a party to file a separate brief which conforms to 11th Cir. R. 28–1, except upon written motion granted by the court.*

4. ***Waiver of Reply Brief.*** *A party may waive the right to file a reply brief. Immediate notice of such waiver to the clerk will expedite submission of the appeal to the court.*

5. ***Supplemental Briefs.*** *Supplemental briefs may not be filed without leave of court. The court may, particularly after an appeal is orally argued or submitted on the non-argument calendar, call for supplemental briefs on specific issues.*

6. ***Citation of Supplemental Authorities.*** *After a party's brief has been filed, counsel may direct a letter to the clerk with citations to supplemental authorities. See FRAP 28(j). The body of the letter must not exceed 350 words, including footnotes. If a new case is not reported, copies should be appended. When such a letter is filed in paper, four copies must be filed, with service on opposing counsel.*

7. ***Briefs in Consolidated Cases and Appeals.*** *Unless the parties otherwise agree or the court otherwise orders, the party who filed the first notice of appeal shall be deemed the appellant for purposes of FRAP 28, 30, and 31 and the accompanying circuit rules.*

8. ***Corporate Reorganization—Chapter 11.*** *The first appeal is handled in the usual manner. Counsel shall state in their briefs whether the proceeding is likely to be complex and protracted so that the panel can determine whether it should enter an order directing that it will be the permanent panel for subsequent appeals in the same matter. If there are likely to be successive appeals, a single panel may thus become fully familiar with the case making the handling of future appeals more expeditious and economical for litigants, counsel and court.*

9. ***Requesting Copies of the Record.*** *Pursuant to FRAP 45(d), where there is an original paper record on appeal, that record may not be circulated to counsel or parties. Counsel or parties may obtain copies of specified portions of the record upon payment of the per page copy fee prescribed by the Judicial Conference of the United States in the Court of Appeals Miscellaneous Fee Schedule issued pursuant to 28 U.S.C. § 1913. The copy fee is not automatically waived simply because a party has been allowed to proceed on appeal in forma pauperis, but may be waived by court order upon an appropriate motion supported by an affidavit of indigency which substantially complies with Form 4 in the Appendix to the FRAP Rules.*

Requests for copies must be in writing and should identify the items to be copied by reference to the district court docket sheet or the agency's list of documents comprising the record. Upon receipt of such a written request, this office will advise the requesting party of the total number of pages to be copied and the cost. Upon payment of the required copying fee, the requested copies will be sent.

Cross–Reference: FRAP 26.1, 32.1, 36

[Amended effective April 1, 1991; April 1, 1994; December 1, 1998; April 1, 1999; January 1, 2002; December 1, 2005; August 1, 2013; December 1, 2013.]

FRAP 28.1. CROSS–APPEALS

[For text of rule, see the Federal Rules of Appellate Procedure]

RULE 28.1-1 BRIEFS IN CROSS-APPEALS

In addition to the requirements of FRAP 28.1, briefs in cross-appeals are also governed by 11th Cir. R. 28-1 through 28-5 and the Internal Operating Procedures corresponding to those rules.

[Adopted effective December 1, 2005.]

RULE 28.1-2 BRIEFING SCHEDULE IN CROSS-APPEALS

Except as otherwise provided by 11th Cir. R. 31-1, the initial brief of appellant/cross-appellee shall be served and filed within 40 days after the date on which the record is deemed filed as provided by 11th Cir. R. 12-1. The brief of appellee/cross-appellant shall be served and filed within 30 days after service of the last appellant's brief. The second brief of appellant/cross-appellee shall be served and filed within 30 days after service of the last appellee/cross-appellant's brief. Appellee/cross-appellant's reply brief shall be served and filed within 14 days after service of the last appellant/cross-appellee's second brief.

[Adopted effective December 1, 2005.]

IOP—CIR. RULE 28.1

1. Designation of Appellant in Cross-Appeals. *If parties agree to modify the designation of appellant pursuant to FRAP 28.1(b), counsel are expected to advise the clerk in writing, upon commencement of the briefing schedule, which party will file the first brief.*

2. Color of Covers of Briefs in Cross-Appeals. *In cross-appeals the color of the covers of briefs shall be as follows:*

brief of appellant—blue

brief of appellee-cross-appellant—red

brief of cross-appellee and reply brief for appellant—yellow

reply brief of cross-appellant—gray

amicus—green

appellate intervenor—green

If supplemental briefs are allowed to be filed by order of the court, the color of their covers shall be tan.

[Adopted effective December 1, 2005.]

FRAP 29. BRIEF OF AN AMICUS CURIAE

[For text of rule, see the Federal Rules of Appellate Procedure]

RULE 29-1. MOTIONS FOR LEAVE

Motions for leave to file a brief of amicus curiae must comply with FRAP 27 and 11th Cir. R. 27-1, including the requirement of a Certificate of Interested Persons and Corporate Disclosure Statement as described in FRAP 26.1 and the accompanying circuit rules.

[Amended effective April 1, 1991.]

RULE 29-2. AMICUS BRIEF

In addition to the requirements of FRAP 29(a)(4), an amicus brief must contain items (a), (b), (d), (e), (h), (j), (k), (*l*), (m) and (n) of 11th Cir. R. 28-1.

[Adopted effective April 1, 1994. Amended effective January 2, 1996; December 1, 1998; April 1, 1999; January 1, 2003; December 1, 2016.]

RULE 29-3. MOTION FOR LEAVE TO FILE AMICUS BRIEF IN SUPPORT OF PETITION FOR REHEARING EN BANC.

A request for leave to file an amicus brief in support of a petition for rehearing en banc must be made by motion accompanied by the proposed brief in conformance with 11th Cir. R. 35-5, except that subsections (f) and (k) may be omitted. The proposed amicus brief must not exceed the length limits set out in FRAP 29(b)(4), exclusive of items required by 11th Cir. R. 35-5(a), (b), (c), (d), and (j). The cover must be green. An amicus curiae must file its proposed brief, accompanied by a motion for filing when necessary, no later than 10 days after the petition for rehearing en banc being supported is filed.

[Former 11th Cir. R. 35-6 effective April 1, 2007. Amended effective December 1, 2009; December 1, 2010. Redesignated as 11th Cir. R. 29-3 and amended effective December 1, 2016.]

RULE 29-4. MOTION FOR LEAVE TO FILE AMICUS BRIEF IN SUPPORT OF PETITION FOR PANEL REHEARING.

A request for leave to file an amicus brief in support of a petition for panel rehearing must be made by motion accompanied by the proposed brief in conformance with FRAP 29(a)(3) and (a)(4) and the corresponding circuit rules. The proposed amicus brief must not exceed the length limits set out in FRAP 29(b)(4), exclusive of items that do not count towards page limitations as described in 11th Cir. R. 32-4. The cover must be green. An amicus curiae must file its proposed brief, accompanied by a motion for filing when necessary, no later than 10 days after the petition for panel rehearing being supported is filed.

[Former 11th Cir. R. 40-6 effective April 1, 2007. Amended effective December 1, 2009; December 1, 2010. Redesignated as 11th Cir. R. 29-4 and amended effective December 1, 2016.]

IOP—CIR. RULE 29

1. Citation of Supplemental Authorities. *After an amicus brief has been filed, counsel for amicus may direct a letter to the clerk with citations to supplemental authorities. See FRAP 28(j). The body of the letter must not exceed 350 words, including footnotes. If a new case is not reported, copies should be appended. When such a letter is filed in paper, four copies must be filed, with service on counsel for the parties and other amicus curiae in the appeal.*

2. Length of Amicus Brief in a Cross-Appeal. *The maximum length of an amicus brief in a cross-appeal, regardless of the party supported, is one-half the maximum length* *authorized by FRAP 28.1(e) for an appellant/cross-appellee's principal brief.*

Cross-Reference: FRAP 26.1

[Adopted effective December 1, 2004. Amended effective April 1, 2006; August 1, 2013.]

FRAP 30. APPENDIX TO THE BRIEFS

[For text of rule, see the Federal Rules of Appellate Procedure]

RULE 30-1. APPENDIX—APPEALS FROM DISTRICT COURT AND TAX COURT

(a) Contents. In appeals from district courts and the tax court, the appellant must file an appendix containing those items required by FRAP 30(a)(1), which are:

- the relevant docket entries in the proceeding below;
- the relevant portions of the pleadings, charge, findings, or opinion;
- the judgment, order, or decision in question; and
- other parts of the record to which the parties wish to direct the court's attention.

Other than FRAP 30(a)(1), the requirements in FRAP 30 do not apply in this circuit.

Consistent with the requirements of FRAP 30(a)(1) that the appendix contain relevant docket entries and relevant portions of the record, this court has determined that the following items are either relevant docket entries or relevant portions of the record in the types of appeals specified below and thus must be included in the appendix:

(1) the district court or tax court docket sheet, including, in bankruptcy appeals, the bankruptcy court docket sheet;

(2) in an appeal in a criminal case, the indictment, information, or petition as amended;

(3) in an appeal in a civil case, the complaint, answer, response, counterclaim, cross-claim, and any amendments to such items;

(4) those parts of any pretrial order relevant to the issues on appeal;

(5) the judgment or interlocutory order appealed from;

(6) any other order or orders sought to be reviewed, including, in bankruptcy appeals, the order(s) of the bankruptcy court appealed to the district court;

(7) in an appeal from the grant or denial of a petition for a writ of habeas corpus under 28 U.S.C. § 2254, all opinions by any state court previously rendered in the criminal prosecution and related collateral proceedings and appeals, and any state court orders addressing any claims and defenses brought by the petitioner in the federal action. This requirement applies whether or not the state court opinions and orders are contained in the district court record;

(8) any supporting opinion, findings of fact and conclusions of law filed or delivered orally by the court;

(9) if the correctness of a jury instruction is in issue, the instruction in question and any other relevant part of the jury charge;

(10) a magistrate's report and recommendation, when appealing a court order adopting same in whole or in part;

(11) findings and conclusions of an administrative law judge, when appealing a court order reviewing an administrative agency determination involving same;

(12) the relevant parts of any document, such as an insurance policy, contract, agreement, or ERISA plan, whose interpretation is relevant to the issues on appeal;

(13) in an appeal in a criminal case in which any issue is raised concerning the guilty plea, the transcript of the guilty plea colloquy and any written plea agreement;

(14) in an appeal in a criminal case in which any issue is raised concerning the sentence, the transcript of the sentencing proceeding, and the presentence investigation report and addenda (under seal in a separate envelope); and

(15) any other pleadings, affidavits, transcripts, filings, documents, or exhibits that any one of the parties believes will be helpful to this court in deciding the appeal.

Except as otherwise permitted by subsection (a)(7) of this rule, under no circumstances should a document be included in the appendix that was not submitted to the trial court.

(b) Appellee's Responsibility. If the appellant's appendix is deficient or if the appellee's brief, to support its position on an issue, relies on parts of the record not included in appellant's appendix, the appellee must file its own supplemental appendix within seven days of filing its brief. The appellee's supplemental appendix must not duplicate any documents in the appellant's appendix.

In an appeal by an incarcerated pro se party, counsel for appellee must submit an appendix that includes the specific pages of any record materials referred to in the argument section of appellee's brief and those referred to in the argument section of the appellant's brief that are relevant to the resolution of an issue on appeal.

(c) Time for Filing. A party must file an appendix or supplemental appendix within seven days of filing the party's brief.

(d) Number of Copies. A pro se party proceeding in forma pauperis may file only one paper copy of the appendix or supplemental appendix, except that an incarcerated pro se party is not required to file an appendix.

Every other party must file two paper copies of the appendix or supplemental appendix within seven days of filing the party's brief, and if the appeal is classed for oral argument, such party must file an additional three identical paper copies of the appendix previously filed within seven days after the date on the notice from the clerk that the appeal has been classed for oral argument. One copy shall be served on counsel for each party separately represented, and on each pro se party. Where multiple parties are on one side of an appeal, they are strongly urged to file a joint appendix.

For counsel using the ECF system, the electronically filed appendix is the official record copy of the appendix. Use of the ECF system does not modify the requirement that counsel must provide to the court the required number of paper copies of the appendix. Counsel will be considered to have complied with this requirement if, on the day the electronic appendix is filed, counsel sends two paper copies to the clerk using one of the methods outlined in FRAP 25(a)(2)(B). If the appeal is classed for oral argument, counsel must file an additional three identical paper copies of the appendix in accordance with the preceding paragraph. Also see 11th Cir. R. 25-3(a).

(e) Form. The paper appendix shall be reproduced on white paper by any duplicating or copying process capable of producing a clear black image, with a cover containing the information specified in 11th Cir. R. 28-1(a) and captioned "Appendix." The appendix shall be assembled with a front and back durable (at least 90#) white covering and shall be bound across the top with a secure fastener. Indexing tabs shall be affixed to the first page of each document in the appendix to identify and assist in locating the document. An index identifying each document contained in the appendix and its tab number shall be included immediately following the cover page. The appendix shall include a certificate of service consistent with FRAP 25(d).

[Amended effective April 1, 1991; April 1, 1994; January 2, 1996; June 22, 1998; December 1, 1998; April 1, 1999; August 1, 2011; December 1, 2013; August 1, 2014; December 1, 2014; December 1, 2015.]

RULE 30-2. APPENDIX—AGENCY REVIEW PROCEEDINGS

Except in review proceedings covered by 11th Cir. R. 15-1, in proceedings for review of orders of an agency, board, commission or officer, the petitioner must file an appendix containing those items required by FRAP 30(a)(1), which are:

- the relevant docket entries in the proceeding below;
- the relevant portions of the pleadings, charge, findings, or opinion;
- the judgment, order, or decision in question; and
- other parts of the record to which the parties wish to direct the court's attention.

Other than FRAP 30(a)(1), the requirements in FRAP 30 do not apply in this circuit.

The requirements concerning the time for filing, number of copies, and form, set out in 11th Cir. R. 30-1(c), (d), and (e), also apply in agency proceedings. In a National Labor Relations Board enforcement proceeding, the party adverse to the Board shall be considered a petitioner for purposes of this rule.

[Amended effective April 1, 1991; April 1, 1994; January 2, 1996; December 1, 1998; April 1, 2006; December 1, 2013.]

RULE 30-3. ELECTRONIC APPENDIX SUBMISSION

This rule only applies to attorneys who have been granted an exemption from the use of the ECF system under 11th Cir. R. 25-3(b). On the day the attorney's paper appendix is served, the attorney must provide the court with an electronic appendix in accordance with directions provided by the clerk. The time for serving and filing an appendix is determined by service and filing of the paper appendix. If corrections are required to be made to the paper appendix, a corrected copy of the electronic appendix must be provided. The certificate of service shall indicate the date of service of the appendix in paper format.

[Effective August 1, 2014.]

IOP—CIR. RULE 30

1. ***Indexing Tabs on an Appendix.*** *For paper appendices, standard commercially-available indexing tabs or their equivalent which extend beyond the edge of the page should be staggered in sequence from top to bottom along the right-hand side. Tab numbers should correspond to the original document numbers assigned by the district court and noted on the district court docket sheet. The district court docket sheet should also be tabbed and identified. For electronic appendices, separator pages showing the appropriate tab numbers should be used in place of indexing tabs.*

2. ***Appendices in Cross-Appeals.*** *In cross-appeals the appellee-cross-appellant may (but is not required to) file an appendix within seven days of filing their first brief.*

[Effective April 1, 1991. Amended effective December 1, 1998; August 1, 2011; December 1, 2013; August 1, 2014.]

FRAP 31. SERVING AND FILING BRIEFS

[For text of rule, see the Federal Rules of Appellate Procedure]

RULE 31-1. BRIEFS—TIME FOR SERVING AND FILING

(a) Briefing Schedule. Except as otherwise provided herein, the appellant shall serve and file a brief within 40 days after the date on which the record is deemed filed as provided by 11th Cir. R. 12-1. The appellee shall serve and file a brief within 30 days after service of the brief of the last appellant. The appellant may serve and file a reply brief within 14 days after service of the brief of the last appellee.

(b) Pending Motions. If any of the following motions or matters are pending in either the district court or the court of appeals at the time the appeal is docketed in the court of appeals or thereafter, the appellant (or appellant/cross-appellee) shall serve and file a brief within 40 days after the date on which the district court or the court of appeals rules on the motion or resolves the matter, and the appeal is allowed to proceed, or within 40 days after the date on which the record is deemed filed as provided by 11th Cir. R. 12-1, whichever is later:

- Motion to proceed In Forma Pauperis
- Motion for a Certificate of Appealability or to expand a Certificate of Appealability
- Motion of a type specified in FRAP 4(a)(4)(A) or FRAP 4(b)(3)(A)
- Determination of excusable neglect or good cause as specified in FRAP 4(a)(5)(A) or FRAP 4(b)(4)

- Assessment of fees pursuant to the Prisoner Litigation Reform Act
- Appointment and/or withdrawal of counsel
- Request for transcript at government expense
- Designation by appellee of additional parts of the proceedings to be ordered from the court reporter, order by appellee of such parts, or motion by appellee for an order requiring appellant to order such parts, as provided by FRAP 10(b)(3)(B) and (C)
- Motion to consolidate appeals, provided that such motion is filed on or before the date the appellant's brief is due in any of the appeals which are the subject of such motion

Except as otherwise provided below, if any of the foregoing motions or matters are pending in either the district court or the court of appeals after the appellant (or appellant/cross-appellee) has served and filed a brief, the appellee (or appellee/cross-appellant) shall serve and file a brief within 30 days after the date on which the district court or the court of appeals rules on the motion or resolves the matter, and the appeal is allowed to proceed, or within 30 days after the date on which the supplemental record is deemed filed as provided by 11th Cir. R. 12–1, whichever is later.

When a motion to consolidate appeals is filed or is pending after an appellant has served and filed a brief in any of the appeals which are the subject of such motion, the due date for filing appellee's brief shall be postponed until the court rules on such motion. If the motion is granted, the appellee (or appellee/cross-appellant) shall serve and file a brief in the consolidated appeals within 30 days after the date on which the court rules on the motion, or within 30 days after service of the last appellant's brief, whichever is later. If the motion is denied, the appellee (or appellee/cross-appellant) shall serve and file a brief in each separate appeal within 30 days after the date on which the court rules on the motion, or within 30 days after service of the last appellant's brief in that separate appeal, whichever is later.

(c) Effect of Other Pending Motions on Time for Serving and Filing Brief. Except as otherwise provided in this rule, a pending motion does not postpone the time for serving and filing any brief. For example, the appellee's brief remains due within 30 days after service of the appellant's brief even though a motion to file appellant's brief out-of-time or to file a brief which does not comply with the court's rules is pending. However, the filing of a motion to dismiss a criminal appeal based on an appeal waiver in a plea agreement shall postpone the due date for filing appellee's brief until the court rules on such motion. In addition, a motion to file a replacement brief under 11th Cir. R. 31–6(b) shall postpone the due date for filing an opposing party's response brief or reply brief until the court rules on such motion. When the court rules on the motion, a new due date will be set for filing the next brief.

(d) Jurisdictional Question. If, upon review of the district court docket entries, order and/or judgment appealed from, and the notice of appeal, it appears that this court may lack jurisdiction over the appeal, the court may request counsel and pro se parties to advise the court in writing of their position with respect to the jurisdictional question(s) raised. The issuance of a jurisdictional question does not stay the time for filing appellant's brief otherwise provided by this rule. The due date for filing appellee's brief shall be postponed until the court determines that the appeal shall proceed or directs counsel and pro se parties to address the jurisdictional question(s) in their briefs on the merits. When the court rules on a jurisdictional question, a new due date will be set for filing appellee's brief if the appeal is allowed to proceed.

[Adopted effective April 1, 1991. Amended effective January 2, 1996; June 3, 1997; December 1, 1998; April 1, 1999; January 1, 2000; January 1, 2002; January 1, 2003; April 1, 2003; December 1, 2003; December 1, 2004; December 1, 2005; December 1, 2009.]

RULE 31-2. BRIEFS AND APPENDICES—MOTION TO EXTEND TIME

(a) First Request for an Extension of Time. A party's first request for an extension of time to file its brief or appendix or to correct a deficiency in the brief or appendix must set forth good cause. A first request for an extension of 14 days or less may be made by telephone or in writing, is not subject to 11th Cir. R. 26–1, and may be granted by the clerk. A first request for an extension of more than 14 days must be made by written motion setting forth with particularity the facts demonstrating good cause, and will only be acted upon by the court. When a briefing schedule has been established by court order, a first request for an extension must be made by written motion and will only be acted upon by the court. Any motion for extension of time by the court shall be subject to 11th Cir. R. 26–1.

(b) First Request Filed 14 or More Days in Advance. When a party's first request for an extension of time to file its brief or appendix is filed 14 or more days in advance of the due date for filing the brief or appendix and the requested extension of time is denied in full on a date that is seven or fewer days before the due date or is after the due date has passed, the time for filing the party's brief or appendix will be extended an additional seven days beyond the initial due date or the date the court order is issued, whichever is later, unless the court orders otherwise.

(c) Seven Days in Advance Requirement. If a party's first request for an extension of time to file its brief or appendix seeks an extension of more than 14 days, the motion must be filed at least seven days in advance of the due date for filing the brief or appendix. Such a motion received by the clerk less than seven days in advance of the due date for filing the brief or appendix will generally be denied by the court, unless the motion demonstrates that the good cause on which the motion is based did not exist earlier or was not and with due diligence could not have been known earlier or communicated to the court earlier.

(d) Second Request for an Extension of Time. A party's second request for an extension of time to file its brief or appendix or to correct a deficiency in its brief or appendix is extremely disfavored and is granted rarely. A party's second request for an extension will be granted only upon a showing of extraordinary circumstances that were not foreseeable at the time the first request was made. A second request must be made by written motion and will only be acted upon by the court.

(e) Extension of Time Must Be Requested Prior to Due Date. A request for an extension of time to file the brief or appendix pursuant to this rule must be made or filed prior to the expiration of the due date for filing the brief or appendix. The clerk is without authority to file an appellant's motion for an extension of time to file the brief or appendix received by the clerk after the expiration of the due date for filing the brief or appendix. A request for an extension of time to correct a deficiency in the brief or appendix pursuant this rule must be made or filed within 14 days of the clerk's notice as provided in 11th Cir. R. 42-3. The clerk is without authority to file an appellant's motion for an extension of time to correct a deficiency in the brief or appendix received by the clerk after the expiration of the 14-day period provided by that rule. [See 11th Cir. R. 42-2 and 42-3 concerning dismissal for failure to prosecute in a civil appeal.]

[Effective January 1, 2000. Amended effective January 1, 2002; August 1, 2005; December 1, 2006; December 1, 2013; December 1, 2015.]

RULE 31-3. BRIEFS—NUMBER OF COPIES

One originally signed brief and six copies (total of seven) shall be filed in all appeals, except that pro se parties proceeding in forma pauperis may file one originally signed brief and three copies (total of four). One copy must be served on counsel for each party separately represented.

For counsel using the ECF system, the electronically filed brief is the official record copy of the brief. Use of the ECF system does not modify the requirement that counsel must provide to the court seven paper copies of a brief. Counsel will be considered to have complied with this requirement if, on the day the electronic brief is filed, counsel sends seven paper copies to the clerk using one of the methods outlined in FRAP 25(a)(2)(B). Also see 11th Cir. R. 25-3(a).

[Former 11th Cir.R. 31-1 redesignated as 11th Cir.R. 31-2 effective April 1, 1991. Amended effective December 1, 1998. Renumbered effective January 1, 2000. Amended effective April 1, 2014; December 1, 2014.]

RULE 31-4. EXPEDITED BRIEFING IN CRIMINAL APPEALS

The clerk is authorized to expedite briefing when it appears that an incarcerated defendant's projected release is expected to occur prior to the conclusion of appellate proceedings.

[Effective December 1, 1998. Renumbered effective January 1, 2000.]

RULE 31-5. ELECTRONIC BRIEF SUBMISSION

This rule only applies to attorneys who have been granted an exemption from the use of the ECF system under 11th Cir. R. 25-3(b). On the day the attorney's paper brief is served, the attorney must provide the court with an electronic brief in accordance with directions provided by the clerk. The time for serving and filing a brief is determined by service and filing of the paper brief. If corrections are required to be made to the paper brief, a corrected copy of the electronic brief must be provided. The certificate of service shall indicate the date of service of the brief in paper format.

[Effective December 1, 1998. Renumbered effective January 1, 2000. Amended effective January 1, 2003; August 1, 2007; August 1, 2013; April 1, 2014; December 1, 2014.]

RULE 31-6. REPLACEMENT BRIEFS

(a) Replacement Briefs From Counsel Appointed to Represent a Pro Se Party. When an attorney is appointed to represent a pro se party in an appeal in which the party has filed a pro se brief, the attorney must file a new brief that will replace the brief filed by the pro se party, unless otherwise directed by the court.

(b) Replacement Briefs in Other Circumstances. Except as otherwise provided in subsection (a) of this rule, when a pro se party or the party's prior counsel has already filed a brief, a newly retained or appointed attorney may file a replacement brief only upon motion and with leave of court. If permission to file a replacement brief is granted, the brief filed by the pro se party or prior counsel will not be considered by the court; therefore, no portion of the prior brief may be adopted by reference. However, the new attorney may replicate any portion of the prior brief into the replacement brief as an integral part thereof. A motion to file a replacement brief generally will be denied if an opposing party has already filed an appellee's principal brief or an appellant's reply brief, or if the appeal has already been submitted to a non-argument panel or assigned to an oral argument panel.

[Effective April 1, 2009. Amended effective August 1, 2013.]

IOP—CIR. RULE 31

Briefing Schedule. *The clerk's office will send counsel and pro se parties a letter confirming the due date for filing appellant's brief consistent with the provisions of 11th Cir. R. 12-1 and 11th Cir. R. 31-1, but delay in or failure to receive such a letter does not affect the obligation of counsel and pro se parties to file the brief within the time permitted by 11th Cir. R. 31-1. The clerk's office will also advise counsel and pro se parties of the rules and procedures governing the form of briefs.*

Cross-Reference: FRAP 25, 26, 27; "E-Government Act of 2002," Pub. L. No. 107-347

[Amended effective April 1, 1994; April 1, 1999.]

FRAP 32. FORM OF BRIEFS, APPENDICES, AND OTHER PAPERS

[For text of rule, see the Federal Rules of Appellate Procedure]

RULE 32-1. BINDING OF PAPERS

Except as otherwise provided by 11th Cir. R. 30-1(e) for appendices, all papers shall be stapled or bound on the left. All copies presented to the court must be legible.

[Amended effective January 2, 1996; December 1, 1998; December 1, 2013.]

RULE 32-2. BRIEFS—COVER

The cover of the brief must clearly indicate the name of the party on whose behalf the brief is filed. Each copy must comply with FRAP, have a cover of durable quality (at least 90#) on both front and back sides, and be securely bound along the left-hand margin so as to insure that the bound copy will not loosen or fall apart or the cover be detached by shipping and use. Exposed metal prong paper fasteners are prohibited on briefs.

[Former 11th Cir. R. 32-2 deleted effective December 1, 1998. Former 11th Cir. R. 32-3 amended effective April 1, 1991; April 1, 1994; January 2, 1996. Redesignated 11th Cir. R. 32-2 and amended effective December 1, 1998. Amended effective January 1, 2000.]

RULE 32-3. BRIEFS—FORM

Only the cover page, the certificate of service, direct quotes, headings and footnotes may be single-spaced. All other typed matter must be double-spaced, including the Table of Contents and the Table of Citations. The court may reject or require recomposition of a brief for failure to comply.

The clerk may exercise very limited discretion to permit the filing of briefs in which the violation of FRAP and circuit rules governing the format of briefs is exceedingly minor if in the judgment of the clerk recomposition of the brief would be unwarranted.

Except as otherwise provided in the preceding paragraph, unless each copy of the brief, in the judgment of the clerk, conforms to this rule and to provisions of FRAP 32(a), the clerk may conditionally file the brief, subject to the requirement that the party file in the office of the clerk a complete set of replacement briefs which comply with FRAP and circuit rules within 14 days of issuance of notice by the clerk that the briefs have been conditionally filed. The clerk's notice shall specify the matters requiring correction. No substantive changes may be made to the brief. The time for filing of the opposing party's brief runs from the date of service of the conditionally filed brief and is unaffected by the later substitution of corrected copies pursuant to this rule.

[Former 11th Cir. R. 32-4 adopted effective January 2, 1996. Redesignated 11th Cir. R. 32-3 and amended effective December 1, 1998. Amended effective January 1, 2000; August 1, 2007.]

RULE 32-4. BRIEFS—PAGE NUMBERING AND LENGTH

The pages of each brief shall be consecutively numbered except that materials referred to in 11th Cir. R. 28-1(a), (b), (c), (d), (e), (f), (g), (m) and (n) and any addendum containing statutes, rules, or regulations need not be numbered and do not count towards page limitations or type-volume limitations. Motions for leave to file briefs which do not comply with the limitations set forth in FRAP 28.1(e) or FRAP 32(a)(7), as applicable, must be filed at least seven days in advance of the due date of the brief. The court looks with disfavor upon such motions and will only grant such a motion for extraordinary and compelling reasons.

[Former 11th Cir. R. 28-2 amended effective April 1, 1991; April 1, 1994; January 2, 1996; December 1, 1998. Redesignated 11th Cir. R. 32-4 and amended effective April 1, 1999. Amended effective January 1, 2000; December 1, 2005.]

IOP—CIR. RULE 32

*1. **Color of Covers of Briefs.** The covers of briefs operate for a busy court like traffic signals. It is important to efficient paper flow for those signals to be correct. The color of the covers of briefs shall be as follows:*

brief of appellant—blue

brief of appellee—red

reply brief of appellant—gray

amicus—green

appellate intervenor—green

If supplemental briefs are allowed to be filed by order of the court, the color of their covers shall be tan.

For cross-appeals, see I.O.P. 2, Color of Covers of Briefs in Cross-Appeals, following FRAP 28.1.

*2. **Form of Printing—Legibility.** While the court encourages inexpensive forms of reproduction to minimize costs, counsel should personally check each copy of the brief for legibility, completeness, and a proper binding since copies distributed to the court are selected at random. It is also essential that the size type conform to the requirements of FRAP 32(a).*

*3. **Briefs—Miscellaneous Information.***

a. Certificate of Service. *The certificate of service required by FRAP 25(d) must be shown at the conclusion of the brief.*

b. Acknowledgment of Briefs. *The clerk will acknowledge filing of a brief if a stamped self-addressed envelope is provided.*

c. Sample Briefs and Appendices. *Upon request, the clerk's office will loan to counsel sample briefs and appendices that comply with the prescribed form.*

[Amended effective April 1, 1991; April 1, 1994; January 2, 1996; December 1, 1998; January 1, 2003; December 1, 2005; December 1, 2013.]

FRAP 32.1. CITING JUDICIAL DISPOSITIONS

[For text of rule, see the Federal Rules of Appellate Procedure]

FRAP 33. APPEAL CONFERENCES

[For text of rule, see the Federal Rules of Appellate Procedure]

RULE 33–1. KINNARD MEDIATION CENTER

(a) Filing Civil Appeal Statement. A Civil Appeal Statement is required in all civil appeals, except as provided in section (a)(3) below.

(1) *Civil Appeals From United States District Courts.* When notice of the filing of a notice of appeal is served pursuant to FRAP 3(d), the clerk of the district court shall notify the appellant(s) (and cross-appellant(s)) that a Civil Appeal Statement form is available as provided in section (a)(4) below. The appellant(s) (and cross-appellant(s)) shall file with the clerk of the court of appeals, with service on all other parties, an original and one copy of a completed Civil Appeal Statement within 14 days after the date the appeal is docketed in this court. The completed Civil Appeal Statement shall set forth information necessary for an understanding of the nature of the appeal and shall be accompanied by the portion of the district court record described in 11th Cir. R. 33–1(b)(1). Any appellee may file an original and one copy of a response with the court of appeals within 10 days of the receipt of the completed Civil Appeal Statement and shall serve a copy of the response on all other parties.

(2) *Review of Administrative Agency Orders and Appeals From the United States Tax Court.* When the clerk of the court of appeals notifies the parties that an appeal or petition has been docketed, the clerk shall also notify the appellant(s)/petitioner(s) (and cross-appellant(s)/cross-petitioner(s)) that a Civil Appeal Statement form is available as provided in section (a)(4) below. The appellant(s)/petitioner(s) (and cross-appellant(s)/cross-petitioner(s)) shall file with the clerk of the court of appeals, with service on all other parties, an original and one copy of a completed Civil Appeal Statement within 14 days from the date the notice was transmitted by the clerk of the court of appeals. The completed Civil Appeal Statement shall set forth information necessary for an understanding of the nature of the appeal or petition and shall be accompanied by the portion of the record described in 11th Cir. R. 33–1(b). Any appellee/respondent may file an original and one copy of a response with the court of appeals within 10 days of the receipt of the completed Civil Appeal Statement and shall serve a copy of the response on all other parties.

(3) A Civil Appeal Statement is not required to be filed in (1) appeals or petitions in which any party is proceeding without the assistance of counsel or in which any party is incarcerated; (2) appeals from habeas corpus actions filed under 28 U.S.C. §§ 2241, 2254, and 2255; and (3) immigration appeals.

(4) *Availability of Civil Appeal Statement Forms.* The Civil Appeal Statement form is available on the Internet at www.ca11.uscourts.gov. Copies may also be obtained from the clerk of the court of appeals and from the clerk of each district court within the Eleventh Circuit.

(b) Portions of Record to Accompany Completed Civil Appeal Statement.

(1) *Civil Appeals From United States District Courts and the United States Tax Court.* The appellant shall file with each completed Civil Appeal Statement the following portions of the district court or tax court record:

(i) the judgment or order appealed from;

(ii) any other order or orders sought to be reviewed, including, in bankruptcy appeals, the order(s) of the bankruptcy court appealed to the district court;

(iii) any supporting opinion, findings of fact, and conclusions of law filed by the court;

(iv) the magistrate judge's report and recommendation, when appealing a court order adopting same in whole or in part; and

(v) findings and conclusions of an administrative law judge, when appealing a court order reviewing an administrative agency determination involving same.

(2) *Review of Administrative Agency Orders.* The petitioner shall file with each completed Civil Appeal Statement the following portions of the agency record:

(i) the agency docket sheet, or index of documents comprising the record, if one exists;

(ii) any order or orders sought to be reviewed; and

(iii) any supporting opinion, findings of fact, and conclusions of law filed by the agency, board, commission, or officer.

(c) Mediation.

(1) An active or senior judge of the court of appeals, a panel of judges (either before or after oral argument), or the Kinnard Mediation Center, by appointment of the court, may direct counsel and parties in an appeal to participate in mediation conducted by the court's circuit mediators. Mediations are official court proceedings and the Kinnard Mediation Center circuit mediators act on behalf of the court. Counsel for any party may request mediation in an appeal in which a Civil Appeal Statement is required to be filed if he or she thinks it would be helpful. Such requests will not be disclosed by the Kinnard Mediation Center to opposing counsel without permission of the requesting party. The purposes of the mediation are to explore the possibility of settlement of the dispute, to prevent unnecessary motions or delay by attempting to resolve any procedural problems in the appeal, and to identify and clarify issues presented in the appeal. Mediation sessions are held in person or by telephone. Counsel must, except as waived by the mediator in advance of the mediation date, have the party available during the mediation. Should waiver of party availability be granted by the mediator, counsel must have the authority to respond to settlement proposals consistent with the party's interests. The mediator may require the physical presence of the party at an in-person mediation or the telephone participation of the party in a telephone mediation. For a governmental or other entity for which settlement decisions must be made collectively, the availability, presence, or participation requirement may be satisfied by a representative authorized to negotiate on behalf of that entity and to make recommendations to it concerning settlement.

(2) A judge who participates in the mediation or becomes involved in the settlement discussions pursuant to this rule will not sit on a judicial panel that deals with that appeal.

(3) Communications made during the mediation and any subsequent communications related thereto shall be confiden-

tial. Such communications shall not be disclosed by any party or participant in the mediation in motions, briefs, or argument to the Eleventh Circuit Court of Appeals or to any court or adjudicative body that might address the appeal's merits, except as necessary for enforcement of Rule 33-1 under paragraph (f)(2), nor shall such communications be disclosed to anyone not involved in the mediation or otherwise not entitled to be kept informed about the mediation by reason of a position or relationship with a party unless the written consent of each mediation participant is obtained. Counsel's motions, briefs, or argument to the court shall not contain any reference to the Kinnard Mediation Center.

(d) Confidential Mediation Statement. The court requires, except as waived by the circuit mediator, that counsel in appeals selected for mediation send a confidential mediation statement assessing the appeal to the Kinnard Mediation Center before the mediation. The Kinnard Mediation Center will not share the confidential mediation statement with the other side, and it will not become part of the court file.

(e) Filing Deadlines. The filing of a Civil Appeal Statement or the scheduling of mediation does not extend the time for ordering any necessary transcript (pursuant to 11th Cir. R. 10-1) or for filing briefs (pursuant to 11th Cir. R. 31-1). Such time may be extended by a circuit mediator to comply with these rules if there is a substantial probability the appeal will settle and the extension will prevent the unnecessary expenditure of time and resources by counsel, the parties, and the court.

(f) Noncompliance Sanctions.

(1) If the appellant or petitioner has not taken the action specified in paragraph (a) of this rule within the time specified, the appeal or petition may be dismissed by the clerk of the court of appeals after appropriate notice pursuant to 11th Cir. R. 42-1.

(2) Upon failure of a party or attorney to comply with the provisions of this rule or the provisions of the court's notice of mediation, the court may assess reasonable expenses caused by the failure, including attorney's fees; assess all or a portion of the appellate costs; dismiss the appeal; or take such other appropriate action as the circumstances may warrant.

(g) Use of Private Mediators.

(1) Upon agreement of all parties, a private mediator may be employed by the parties, at their expense, to mediate an appeal that has been selected for mediation by the Kinnard Mediation Center.

(2) Such private mediator (i) shall have been certified or registered as a mediator by either the State of Alabama, Florida, or Georgia for the preceding five years; (ii) shall have been admitted to practice law in either the State of Alabama, Florida, or Georgia for the preceding fifteen years and be currently in good standing; and (iii) shall be currently admitted to the bar of this court.

(3) All persons while employed as private mediators shall follow the private mediator procedures as set forth by the Kinnard Mediation Center.

(4) The provisions of this subsection (g) shall be in effect until discontinued by the Chief Circuit Mediator or by the court.

[Adopted effective October, 1992. Amended effective December 1, 1998; April 1, 1999; January 1, 2000; January 1, 2002; April 1, 2003; December 1, 2003; October 1, 2004; December 1, 2004; August 1, 2005; April 1, 2007; August 1, 2007; December 1, 2009.]

FRAP 34. ORAL ARGUMENT

[For text of rule, see the Federal Rules of Appellate Procedure]

RULE 34-1. SESSIONS

(a) At least one session of the court shall ordinarily be held each court year in each state of the circuit. Sessions may be scheduled at any location having adequate facilities. The court may assign the hearing of any appeal to another time or place of sitting.

(b) Regular and special sessions of the court may be held at the following places: Atlanta, Jacksonville, Miami, Montgomery, Tallahassee and Tampa.

[Amended effective April 1, 1991.]

RULE 34-2. QUORUM

Unless otherwise directed, a panel of the court shall consist of three judges. When an appeal is assigned to an oral argument panel, at least two judges shall be judges of this court unless such judges cannot sit because recused or disqualified or unless the chief judge certifies that there is an emergency including, but not limited to, the unavailability of a judge of the court because of illness. Any two judges of a panel constitute a quorum. If a judge of a panel that has taken an appeal or matter under submission is not able to participate in a decision, the two remaining judges, whether or not they are both judges of this court, may decide the appeal or may request the chief judge or a delegate of the chief judge to designate another judge to sit in place of the judge unable to participate. No further argument will be had or briefs received unless ordered.

Prior to oral argument, if a judge of an oral argument panel to which an appeal has been assigned determines that he or she cannot sit for reasons other than recusal or disqualification, the two remaining judges, whether or not they are both judges of this court, may hear oral argument. If the third judge is thereafter able to participate as a panel member, the third judge may listen to the oral argument recording and participate in the decision. If the third judge is thereafter not able to participate as a panel member, the two remaining judges may proceed as provided in the paragraph above.

Prior to oral argument, if a judge of an oral argument panel to which an appeal has been assigned determines that he or she cannot sit because recused or disqualified, the two remaining judges, whether or not they are both judges of this court, may: (1) proceed by quorum to hear oral argument and decide the appeal; (2) return the appeal to the clerk for placement on another calendar; or (3) request the chief judge or a delegate of the chief judge to designate another judge to sit in place of the recused or disqualified judge. For purposes of this rule, an appeal is considered assigned to an oral argument panel when the clerk notifies counsel of the specific day of the week on which oral argument in the appeal is scheduled to be heard. Prior to that time, a recusal or disqualification will ordinarily result in the appeal being transferred to another calendar.

Following the issuance of an opinion by a panel of three judges, if a judge of the panel recuses or is disqualified, the two remaining judges, whether or not they are both judges of this court, may proceed by quorum to take such further actions as are deemed appropriate.

[Amended effective April 1, 1994; January 1, 2002; April 1, 2004; August 1, 2008; December 1, 2009.]

RULE 34-3. NON-ARGUMENT CALENDAR

(a) The court maintains a two-calendar system for consideration and decision of appeals in the interest of efficient and appropriate use of judicial resources, control of the docket by the court, minimizing unnecessary expenditure of government funds, and lessening delay in decisions.

(b) When a panel of judges of the court unanimously determines, after an examination of the briefs and records, that an appeal of a party falls within one of the three categories of FRAP 34(a)(2):

(1) the appeal is frivolous; or

(2) the dispositive issue or set of issues has been authoritatively determined; or

(3) the facts and legal arguments are adequately presented in the briefs and record and the decisional process will not be significantly aided by oral argument; that appeal will be placed on the non-argument calendar for submission and decision without oral argument. If at any time before decision a judge on the non-argument panel concludes that oral argument is desired, that appeal will be transferred to the oral argument calendar. Except as provided in subparagraphs (d) and (f) of this rule, decision without oral argument must be unanimous, and no dissenting or special concurring opinion may be filed.

(c) Any party may request in his or her brief that oral argument be heard, as provided in 11th Cir. R. 28-1(c).

(d) Pursuant to FRAP 34(f), if parties state that they do not desire oral argument or otherwise agree that an appeal shall be submitted on briefs, that appeal may be placed on the non-argument calendar even though it does not fall within one of the requirements of FRAP 34(a). The decision in that appeal need not be unanimous and a dissent or special concurrence may be filed.

(e) Panels of three judges are drawn to serve as non-argument panels to determine whether appeals should be placed on the non-argument calendar and to receive submission of and decide non-argument appeals. In appeals involving multiple parties, a non-argument panel judge may determine that the appeals of fewer than all parties shall be scheduled for oral argument, and that the appeals of the remaining parties shall be submitted to the assigned oral argument panel for decision on the briefs. Or, a non-argument panel may decide the appeals of fewer than all parties without oral argument and may schedule the appeals of the remaining parties for oral argument.

(f) When an appeal is assigned to an oral argument panel, the oral argument panel, whether or not composed of only active judges, may by unanimous vote determine that the appeal will be decided by the panel without oral argument, or transfer the appeal to the non-argument calendar. In appeals involving multiple parties, an oral argument panel may by unanimous vote determine that the appeals of fewer than all parties will be decided by the panel without oral argument, and that the appeals of the remaining parties will be scheduled for oral argument.

[Amended effective April 1, 1991; April 1, 1994; December 1, 1998; April 1, 1999; January 1, 2002; April 1, 2004; August 1, 2013.]

RULE 34-4. ORAL ARGUMENT CALENDAR

(a) **General.** All appeals not assigned to the non-argument calendar shall be assigned to the oral argument calendar. Appeals to be orally argued will be calendared by the clerk based upon the court's calendaring priorities. Counsel for each party scheduled to present oral argument to the court must appear for oral argument unless excused by the court for good cause shown. The oral argument calendar will show the time the court has allotted for each argument.

(b) **Waiver or Submission Without Argument.** After an appeal has been scheduled for oral argument, argument may only be waived by the court upon motion filed in advance of the date set for hearing. If counsel for parties agree to submit the appeal on briefs, that appeal will be governed by FRAP 34(f).

(c) **Failure to Appear for Oral Argument.** If counsel for appellant fails to appear in an appeal from criminal conviction, the court will not hear argument from the United States; in all other appeals, the court may hear argument from counsel present.

(d) **Number of Counsel to Be Heard.** Only two counsel will be heard for each party whose appeal is scheduled to be argued, and the time allowed may be apportioned between counsel at their discretion.

(e) **Expediting Appeals.** The court may, on its own motion or for good cause shown on motion of a party, advance an appeal for hearing and prescribe an abbreviated briefing schedule.

(f) **Continuance of Hearing.** After an appeal has been set for hearing it may not be continued by stipulation of the parties or their counsel but only by an order of the court on good cause shown. Usually the engagement of counsel in other courts will not be considered good cause.

(g) **Recording Oral Arguments.** With advance approval of the court, counsel may arrange and pay for a qualified court reporter to be present to record and transcribe the oral argument for counsel's personal use. When counsel has received such approval, counsel must provide the court with a copy of the transcript without delay and at no expense to the court. Except as otherwise provided in this rule, recording of court proceedings by anyone other than the court is prohibited. Also see I.O.P. 16, CD Recordings of Oral Arguments, following this rule.

(h) Citation of Supplemental Authorities During Oral Argument. If counsel intend to cite supplemental authorities during oral argument that were not provided to the court and opposing counsel prior to the day of oral argument, counsel must bring to oral argument a sufficient number of paper copies of the opinion(s) or other authorities being cited to permit distribution to panel members and opposing counsel.

[Amended effective April 1, 1994; December 1, 1998; January 1, 2003; August 1, 2012.]

IOP—CIR. RULE 34

1. Non-Argument Calendar. *When the last brief is filed an appeal is sent to the office of staff attorney for classification. If the staff attorney is of the opinion that the appeal of a party does not warrant oral argument, a brief memorandum is prepared and the appeal is returned to the clerk for routing to one of the court's active judges, selected in rotation. In appeals involving multiple parties, the staff attorney may recommend that appeals of fewer than all parties be decided without oral argument but that the appeals of the remaining parties be scheduled for oral argument. If the judge to whom an appeal is directed for such consideration agrees that the appeal of a party does not warrant oral argument, that judge forwards the briefs, together with a proposed opinion, to the two other judges on the non-argument panel. If a party requests oral argument, all panel judges must concur not only that the appeal of that party does not warrant oral argument, but also in the panel opinion as a proper disposition without any special concurrence or dissent. If a party does not request oral argument, all panel judges must concur that the appeal of that party does not warrant oral argument.*

In other appeals, when oral argument is requested by a party and the staff attorney is of the opinion that oral argument should be heard, the staff attorney may recommend that an appeal be assigned to the oral argument calendar, subject to later review by the assigned oral argument panel.

If a determination is made that oral argument should be heard, the appeal is placed on the next appropriate calendar, consistent with the court's calendaring priorities. At that time a determination is made of the oral argument time to be allotted to each side.

The assignment of an appeal to the non-argument calendar does not mean that it is considered to be an appeal of less importance than an orally argued appeal.

2. Oral Argument.

a. Court Year Schedule. *A proposed court schedule for an entire year is prepared by the circuit executive in collaboration with the clerk's office, and then approved by the scheduling committee of the court which consists of active judges. The court schedule does not consider what specific appeals are to be heard, but only sets the weeks of court in relation to the probable volume of appeals and judgeship availability for the year.*

b. Separation of Assignment of Judges and Calendaring of Appeals. *To insure complete objectivity in the assignment of judges and the calendaring of appeals, the two functions of judge assignment to panels and calendaring of appeals are intentionally separated. The circuit executive and the scheduling committee take into account a fixed number of weeks for each active judge and the available sittings from the court's senior judges, visiting circuit judges, and district judges. After this determination, names of the active judges for the sessions of the court are drawn by lot from a matrix for the entire court year.*

This schedule is available only to judges and the circuit executive for their advance planning, not to the clerk. The clerk is not furnished with names of the panel members for any session until after the court calendars of appeals have been prepared and approved as described below.

3. Preparation and Issuing of Calendars.

a. General. *The clerk's office prepares oral argument calendars approximately one month in advance of oral argument.*

b. Calendaring by Case Type. *The clerk attempts to balance the calendars by dividing the appeals scheduled for oral argument among the panels by case type so that each panel for a particular week has an equitable number of different types of litigation for consideration.*

c. Non–Preference Appeals. *Appeals are calendared for hearing in accordance with the court's "first-in first-out" rule. Absent special priority, those appeals which are oldest in point of time of availability of briefs are calendared first for hearing, insofar as practicable with other requirements of the docket.*

d. Number of Appeals Assigned. *Ordinarily the court hears argument Tuesday through Friday. A regular oral argument session consists of up to 22 appeals with up to 6 appeals scheduled per day.*

e. Advance Notice. *Counsel are provided the maximum advance notice of scheduling for oral argument practicable. Ordinarily counsel will receive notice of oral argument at least three weeks in advance. Counsel are expected to make all reasonable efforts to adjust conflicts in their schedule which will permit them to attend oral argument as scheduled. Motions for continuance are disfavored in recognition of the difficulty in scheduling panels and the commitment of the court to dispose of appeals as promptly as possible and of the fact that there is no backlog of appeals awaiting oral argument.*

4. Location of Court Sessions—Convenience of Counsel. *Appeals to be assigned to oral argument sessions are, if possible, selected from the area where the session is to be held.*

5. Forwarding Briefs to Judges. *Immediately after issuance of the calendar and receipt by the clerk of names of the panel members, the clerk forwards to panel members copies of the briefs for the appeals set on the calendar.*

6. Pre–Argument Preparation. *The judges read the briefs prior to oral argument.*

7. Identity of Panel. *The clerk's office may disclose the names of the panel members for a particular session two weeks in advance of the session, or earlier as determined by* *the court. At the time the clerk issues a calendar assigning an appeal to a specific day of oral argument, the clerk will advise counsel of when the clerk's office may be contacted to learn the identity of the panel members.*

8. ***Checking In with Clerk's Office.*** *On the day of hearing counsel should check in with the clerk's office at least 30 minutes in advance of the convening of court to advise the courtroom deputy of the name of the attorney or attorneys who will present argument for each party and how the argument time will be divided between opening and rebuttal. Timely check-in is necessary so that the clerk can inform the panel of the names of attorneys presenting argument and their time division.*

9. ***Submission Without Argument.*** *When an appeal is placed on the oral argument calendar, a judge of the court has determined that oral argument would be helpful in that particular appeal. Therefore, requests by the parties to waive oral argument are not looked upon with favor, and counsel may be excused only by the court for good cause shown. Attorneys appointed by the court under the Criminal Justice Act must personally appear for oral argument unless excused by the court for good cause shown.*

10. ***Time for Oral Argument.*** *The time for oral argument will be indicated on the calendar. The time specified is per side. In the event that more than one attorney will present oral argument per side, arrangements among counsel regarding the division of time and the order of presentation should be made before counsel check in with the clerk's office.*

11. ***Additional Time for Oral Argument.*** *Additional time for oral argument is sparingly permitted. Requests for additional time for oral argument should be set forth in a motion to the clerk filed well in advance of the oral argument.*

12. ***Calling the Calendar.*** *Usually the court hears the appeals in the order in which they appear on the calendar, and will not call the calendar unless there are some special problems requiring attention. All counsel, however, must be present at the beginning of the court session for the day.*

13. ***Presenting Argument.*** *Counsel should prepare oral arguments with the knowledge that the judges have already studied the briefs. Reading from briefs, decisions or the record is not permitted except in unusual circumstances. Counsel should be prepared to answer questions by the court. The essay Twenty Pages and Twenty Minutes Revisited by Judge John C. Godbold is available from the clerk on request.*

14. ***Timer and Lighting Signal Procedure.*** *The courtroom deputy will monitor time and use lighting signals. In Atlanta, Miami, and Montgomery, and sometimes in other locations where court is held, an easily readable timer visible both to counsel and the court is also used.*

a. Appellant's Argument. *A green light signals the beginning of the opening argument of appellant. Two minutes prior to expiration of the time allowed for opening argument, the green light goes off and a yellow light comes on. When the time reserved for opening has expired, the yellow light goes off and a red light comes on.*

b. Appellee's Argument. *The same procedure as outlined above for appellant is used.*

c. Appellant's Rebuttal. *A green light signals commencement of time; a red light comes on when the time expires. No yellow caution light is displayed for this argument.*

15. ***Appeals Conference and Designation of Writing Judge.*** *At the conclusion of each day's arguments the panel usually has a conference on the appeals heard that day. A tentative decision is usually reached, a tentative determination is made as to the kind of opinion necessary and the presiding judge, when in the majority, makes opinion writing assignments. Judges do not specialize. Writing assignments are made so as to equalize the workload of the entire session.*

16. ***CD Recordings of Oral Arguments.*** *Oral argument is recorded for the use of the court. Although the court is not in the court reporting or audio recording business, copies of the court's audio recordings of oral arguments are available for purchase on CD upon payment of the fee prescribed by the Judicial Conference of the United States in the Court of Appeals Miscellaneous Fee Schedule issued pursuant to 28 U.S.C. § 1913, payable to Clerk, U.S. Court of Appeals, Eleventh Circuit. CD recordings of oral arguments are available for oral arguments held after August 1, 2012. The court makes no representations about the quality of the CD recordings or about how quickly they will become available. Oral argument recordings are retained for a limited time by the court for its use and then the recordings are destroyed.*

Cross-Reference: FRAP 45; 28 U.S.C. §§ 46, 48

[Amended effective April 1, 1991; April 1, 1994; January 2, 1996; December 1, 1998; April 1, 1999; January 1, 2002; August 1, 2012; August 1, 2013; April 1, 2014; August 1, 2016.]

FRAP 35. EN BANC DETERMINATION

[For text of rule, see the Federal Rules of Appellate Procedure]

RULE 35-1. NUMBER OF COPIES AND LENGTH

Fifteen copies of a petition for en banc consideration pursuant to FRAP 35 shall be filed whether for initial hearing or rehearing. A petition for en banc consideration shall not exceed the length limitations set out in FRAP 35(b)(2), exclusive of items required by 11th Cir. R. 35-5(a), (b), (c), (d), (j), and (k). If a petition for en banc consideration is made with a petition for rehearing (whether or not they are combined in a single document) the combined documents shall not exceed the length limitations set out in FRAP 35(b)(2), exclusive of items required by 11th Cir. R. 35-5(a), (b), (c), (d), (j), and (k).

Use of the ECF system does not modify the requirement that counsel must provide to the court 15 paper copies of a petition for en banc consideration, whether for initial hearing or rehearing. Counsel will be considered to have complied with this requirement if, on the day the electronic petition is filed, counsel sends 15 paper copies to the clerk using one of the methods outlined in FRAP 25(a)(2)(B).

[Amended effective April 1, 1991; April 1, 1994; December 1, 1998; April 1, 2014; December 1, 2014; December 1, 2016.]

RULE 35-2. TIME—EXTENSIONS

A petition for en banc rehearing must be filed within 21 days of entry of judgment, except that a petition for en banc rehearing in a civil appeal in which the United States or an agency or officer thereof is a party must be filed within 45 days of entry of judgment. Judgment is entered on the opinion filing date. No additional time is allowed for mailing. Counsel should not request extensions of time except for the most compelling reasons. For purposes of this rule, a "civil appeal" is one that falls within the scope of 11th Cir. R. 42-2(a).

[Amended effective April 1, 1991; January 2, 1996; December 1, 1998; December 1, 2004; April 1, 2007.]

RULE 35-3. EXTRAORDINARY NATURE OF PETITIONS FOR EN BANC CONSIDERATION

A petition for en banc consideration, whether upon initial hearing or rehearing, is an extraordinary procedure intended to bring to the attention of the entire court a precedent-setting error of exceptional importance in an appeal or other proceeding, and, with specific reference to a petition for en banc consideration upon rehearing, is intended to bring to the attention of the entire court a panel opinion that is allegedly in direct conflict with precedent of the Supreme Court or of this circuit. Alleged errors in a panel's determination of state law, or in the facts of the case (including sufficiency of the evidence), or error asserted in the panel's misapplication of correct precedent to the facts of the case, are matters for rehearing before the panel but not for en banc consideration.

Counsel are reminded that the duty of counsel is fully discharged without filing a petition for rehearing en banc if the rigid standards of FRAP 35(a) are not met, and that the filing of a petition for rehearing or rehearing en banc is not a prerequisite to filing a petition for writ of certiorari.

[Amended effective April 1, 1991; December 1, 1998.]

RULE 35-4. MATTERS NOT CONSIDERED EN BANC

A petition for rehearing en banc tendered with respect to any of the following orders will not be considered by the court en banc, but will be referred as a motion for reconsideration to the judge or panel that entered the order sought to be reheard:

(a) Administrative or interim orders, including but not limited to orders ruling on requests for the following relief: stay or injunction pending appeal; appointment of counsel; leave to appeal in forma pauperis; and, permission to appeal when an appeal is within the court's discretion.

(b) Any order dismissing an appeal that is not published including, but not limited to, dismissal for failure to prosecute or because an appeal is frivolous.

[Amended effective April 1, 1991; December 1, 1998; December 1, 2008.]

RULE 35-5. FORM OF PETITION

A petition for en banc consideration shall be bound in a white cover which is clearly labeled with the title "Petition for Rehearing (or Hearing) En Banc." A petition for en banc consideration shall contain the following items in this sequence:

(a) a cover page as described in 11th Cir. R. 28-1(a);

(b) a Certificate of Interested Persons and Corporate Disclosure Statement as described in FRAP 26.1 and the accompanying circuit rules;

(c) where the party petitioning for en banc consideration is represented by counsel, one or both of the following statements of counsel as applicable:

I express a belief, based on a reasoned and studied professional judgment, that the panel decision is contrary to the following decision(s) of the Supreme Court of the United States or the precedents of this circuit and that consideration by the full court is necessary to secure and maintain uniformity of decisions in this court: [cite specifically the case or cases]

I express a belief, based on a reasoned and studied professional judgment, that this appeal involves one or more questions of exceptional importance: [set forth each question in one sentence]

/s/____________________

ATTORNEY OF RECORD FOR

____

(d) table of contents and citations;

(e) statement of the issue(s) asserted to merit en banc consideration;

(f) statement of the course of proceedings and disposition of the case;

(g) statement of any facts necessary to argument of the issues;

(h) argument and authorities. These shall concern only the issues and shall address specifically not only their merit but why they are contended to be worthy of en banc consideration;

(i) conclusion;

(j) certificate of service;

(k) a copy of the opinion sought to be reheard.

[Amended effective April 1, 1991; December 1, 1998; April 1, 1999; January 1, 2002. Redesignated as 11th Cir. R. 35-5 effective December 1, 2004. Amended effective December 1, 2015.]

RULE 35-6. RESPONSE TO PETITION

A response to a petition for en banc consideration may not be filed unless requested by the court.

[Former 11th Cir. R. 35-8 deleted effective April 1, 1994. Former 11th Cir. R. 35-7 amended effective April 1, 1991. Redesignated as new 11th Cir. R. 35-8 effective April 1, 1994. Redesignated as new 11th Cir. R. 35-7 and amended effective December 1, 1998. Redesignated as 11th Cir. R. 35-6 effective December 1, 2004. Redesignated as 11th Cir. R. 35-7 effective April 1, 2007. Redesignated as 11th Cir. R. 35-6 effective December 1, 2016.]

RULE 35-7. EN BANC BRIEFS

An en banc briefing schedule shall be set by the clerk for all appeals in which rehearing en banc is granted by the court.

Twenty copies of en banc briefs are required, and must be filed in the clerk's office, and served on counsel, according to the schedule established. En banc briefs should be prepared in the same manner and form as opening briefs and conform to the requirements of FRAP 28 and 32. The covers of all en banc briefs shall be of the color required by FRAP 32 and shall contain the title "En Banc Brief." Unless otherwise directed by the court, the page and type-volume limitations described in FRAP 32(a)(7) apply to en banc briefs. Counsel are also required to furnish 20 additional copies of each brief previously filed by them.

[Former 11th Cir. R. 35-9 amended effective April 1, 1991; April 1, 1994. Redesignated 11th Cir. R. 35-8 and amended effective December 1, 1998. Amended effective April 1, 1999; January 1, 2002. Redesignated as 11th Cir. R. 35-7 effective December 1, 2004. Redesignated as 11th Cir. R. 35-8 effective April 1, 2007. Redesignated as 11th Cir. R. 35-7 effective December 1, 2016.]

RULE 35-8. EN BANC AMICUS BRIEFS

The United States or its officer or agency or a state may file an en banc amicus brief without the consent of the parties or leave of court. Any other amicus curiae must request leave of court by filing a motion accompanied by the proposed brief in conformance with FRAP 29(a)(3) through (a)(5) and the corresponding circuit rules. An amicus curiae must file its en banc brief, accompanied by a motion for filing when necessary, no later than the due date of the principal en banc brief of the party being supported. An amicus curiae that does not support either party must file its en banc brief, accompanied by a motion for filing when necessary, no later than the due date of the appellant's or petitioner's principal en banc brief. An amicus curiae must also comply with 11th Cir. R. 35-7.

[Adopted effective April 1, 2006. Redesignated as 11th Cir. R. 35-9 effective April 1, 2007. Amended effective December 1, 2010. Redesignated as 11th Cir. R. 35-8 effective December 1, 2016.]

RULE 35-9. SENIOR CIRCUIT JUDGES' PARTICIPATION

Senior circuit judges of the Eleventh Circuit assigned to duty pursuant to statute and court rules may sit en banc reviewing decisions of panels of which they were members and may continue to participate in the decision of a case that was heard or reheard by the court en banc at a time when such judge was in regular active service.

[Former 11th Cir. R. 35-10 amended effective April 1, 1991. Redesignated as 11th Cir. R. 35-9 and amended effective December 1, 1998. Redesignated as 11th Cir. R. 35-8 effective December 1, 2004. Redesignated as 11th Cir. R. 35-9 effective April 1, 2006. Redesignated as 11th Cir. R. 35-10 effective April 1, 2007. Redesignated as 11th Cir. R. 35-9 effective December 1, 2016.]

RULE 35-10. EFFECT OF GRANTING REHEARING EN BANC

Unless otherwise expressly provided, the effect of granting a rehearing en banc is to vacate the panel opinion and to stay the mandate.

[Former 11th Cir. R. 35-11 amended effective April 1, 1991. Redesignated as 11th Cir. R. 35-10 effective December 1, 1998. Redesignated as 11th Cir. R. 35-9 effective December 1, 2004. Redesignated as 11th Cir. R. 35-10 effective April 1, 2006. Redesignated as 11th Cir. R. 35-11 effective April 1, 2007. Redesignated as 11th Cir. R. 35-10 effective December 1, 2016.]

RULE 35-11. [RESCINDED]

IOP—CIR. RULE 35

*1. **Time.** Except as otherwise provided by FRAP 25(a) for inmate filings, a petition for rehearing en banc whether or not combined with a petition for rehearing is timely only if received by the clerk within the time specified in 11th Cir. R. 35-2.*

*2. **Panel Has Control.** A petition for rehearing en banc will also be treated as a petition for rehearing before the original panel. Although a copy of the petition for rehearing en banc is distributed to each panel judge and every active judge of the court, the filing of a petition for rehearing en banc does not take the appeal out of plenary control of the panel deciding the appeal. The panel may, on its own, grant rehearing by the panel and may do so without action by the full court. A petition for rehearing will not be treated as a petition for rehearing en banc.*

*3. **Requesting a Poll.** Within 30 days of the date that the clerk transmits the petition for rehearing en banc, any active Eleventh Circuit judge may advise the "notify judge" that in the event the panel declines to grant rehearing, the judge requests that a poll be taken regarding en banc consideration. The "notify judge" is the writing judge if that judge is a member of this court. If the writing judge is a visiting judge, the notify judge will be the senior active judge of this court on the panel or, if none, the senior non-active judge of this court on the panel. At the same time the judge may notify the clerk to withhold the mandate.*

If the panel, after such notice, concludes not to grant rehearing, the notify judge will inform the chief judge of that fact and that a request was made that a poll be taken regarding en banc consideration. The chief judge then polls the court by written ballot on whether rehearing en banc is to be granted.

*4. **No Poll Request.** If after expiration of the specified time for requesting a poll, the notify judge has not received a poll request from any active member of the court, the panel, without further notice, may take such action as it deems appropriate on the petition for rehearing en banc. In its order disposing of the appeal or other matter and the petition, the panel must note that no poll was requested by any judge of the court in regular active service.*

*5. **Requesting a Poll on Court's Own Motion.** Any active Eleventh Circuit judge may request that the court be polled on whether rehearing en banc should be granted whether or not a petition for rehearing en banc has been filed by a party. This is ordinarily done by a letter from the requesting judge to the chief judge with copies to the other active and senior judges of the court and any other panel member. At the same time the judge may notify the clerk to withhold the mandate. If a petition for rehearing or a petition for rehearing en banc has not been filed by the date that mandate would otherwise issue, the Clerk will make an entry on the docket to advise the parties that a judge has notified the clerk to withhold the mandate. The identity of the judge will not be disclosed.*

*6. **Polling the Court.** Upon request to poll, the chief judge conducts a poll. Each active judge receives a form ballot that is used to cast a vote. A copy of each judge's ballot* *is sent to all other active judges. The ballot form indicates whether the judge voting desires oral argument if en banc is granted.*

7. ***Effect of Recusal or Disqualification on Number of Votes Required.*** *A recused or disqualified judge is not counted in the base when calculating whether a majority of circuit judges in regular active service have voted to rehear an appeal en banc. If, for example, there are 12 circuit judges in regular active service on this court, and five of them are recused or disqualified in an appeal, rehearing en banc may be granted by affirmative vote of four judges (a majority of the seven non-recused and non-disqualified judges).*

8. ***Negative Poll.*** *If the vote on the poll is unfavorable to en banc consideration, the chief judge enters the appropriate order.*

9. ***En Banc Rehearing Procedures Following Affirmative Poll.***

a. Appeal Managers. When an appeal is voted to be reheard en banc, the chief judge shall designate as appeal managers a group of active judges of this court. The chief judge will ordinarily designate the judge who authored the panel opinion, the judge who requested that the court be polled regarding whether the appeal should be reheard en banc, and a judge who dissented from or specially concurred in the panel opinion, if they are active circuit judges of this court. The chief judge may, however, designate other active circuit judges as appeal managers.

b. Initial Notice to Counsel. The clerk meanwhile notifies counsel that rehearing en banc has been granted but that they should not prepare en banc briefs until they are advised of the issue(s) to be briefed and length limitations on briefs.

c. Notice of Issue(s) to be Briefed. The appeal managers prepare and circulate to the other members of the en banc court a proposed notice to the parties advising which issue(s) should be briefed to the en banc court, length limitations on briefs, and whether the appeal will be orally argued or submitted on briefs. The notice may also set the time limits for oral argument. In appeals with multiple appellants or appellees, the notice may direct parties to file a single joint appellants' or appellees' en banc brief. In such cases the side directed to file a single joint brief may be allotted some extension of the length limitations that would otherwise apply to the brief. Members of the en banc court thereafter advise the appeal managers of any suggested changes in the proposed notice. Provided that no member of the en banc court objects, counsel may be advised that the en banc court will decide only specified issues, and after deciding them, remand other issues to the panel. Once the form of the notice has been approved by the court, the clerk issues the notice to counsel.

d. Oral Argument. Appeals to be reheard en banc will ordinarily be orally argued unless fewer than three of the judges of the en banc court determine that argument should be heard.

Cross–Reference: FRAP 40, 41

[Amended effective April 1, 1991; April 1, 1994; January 2, 1996; December 1, 1998; January 1, 2002; January 1, 2003; December 1, 2004; December 1, 2005; December 1, 2006; August 1, 2010; August 1, 2013; December 1, 2015; August 1, 2016; December 1, 2016.]

FRAP 36. ENTRY OF JUDGMENT; NOTICE

[For text of rule, see the Federal Rules of Appellate Procedure]

RULE 36–1. AFFIRMANCE WITHOUT OPINION [RESCINDED]

RULE 36–2. UNPUBLISHED OPINIONS

An opinion shall be unpublished unless a majority of the panel decides to publish it. Unpublished opinions are not considered binding precedent, but they may be cited as persuasive authority. If the text of an unpublished opinion is not available on the internet, a copy of the unpublished opinion must be attached to or incorporated within the brief, petition, motion or response in which such citation is made. But see I.O.P. 7, Citation to Unpublished Opinions by the Court, following this rule.

[Adopted effective April 1, 1991. Amended effective January 2, 1996; December 1, 2004; April 1, 2006.]

RULE 36–3. PUBLISHING UNPUBLISHED OPINIONS

At any time before the mandate has issued, the panel, on its own motion or upon the motion of a party, may by unanimous vote order a previously unpublished opinion to be published. The timely filing of a motion to publish shall stay issuance of the mandate until disposition thereof unless otherwise ordered by the court. The time for issuance of the mandate and for filing a petition for rehearing or petition for rehearing en banc shall begin running anew from the date of any order directing publication.

[Adopted effective January 2, 1996. Amended effective December 1, 1998.]

IOP—CIR. RULE 36

1. ***Motion to Amend, Correct, or Settle the Judgment.*** *These motions are referred to the panel members.*

2. ***Effect of Mandate on Precedential Value of Opinion.*** *Under the law of this circuit, published opinions are binding precedent. The issuance or non-issuance of the mandate does not affect this result. See Martin v. Singletary, 965 F.2d 944, 945 n.1 (11th Cir. 1992). For information concerning the precedential value of opinions of the former Fifth Circuit, see Bonner v. City of Prichard, Alabama, 661 F.2d 1206 (11th Cir. 1981) (en banc) and Stein v. Reynolds Securities, Inc., 667 F.2d 33 (11th Cir. 1982).*

3. ***Processing of Opinions.*** *After the draft opinion has been prepared, the opinion writing judge circulates the proposed opinion to each of the other two judges on the panel. Review of another judge's proposed opinion is given high priority by the other members of the panel. When the writing judge has received concurrences from the other judges or in the case of dissent, or special concurrences, sufficient concurrence(s) to constitute a majority, the writing judge then sends the opinion to the clerk , along with the concurrences, dissent, or special concurrence, as the case may be.*

*4. **Circulation of Opinions to Non-Panel Members.** Copies of proposed opinions are not normally circulated to non-panel members. In special cases, however, a panel or member thereof may circulate a proposed opinion to other members of the court.*

*5. **Publication of Opinions.** The policy of the court is: The unlimited proliferation of published opinions is undesirable because it tends to impair the development of the cohesive body of law. To meet this serious problem it is declared to be the basic policy of this court to exercise imaginative and innovative resourcefulness in fashioning new methods to increase judicial efficiency and reduce the volume of published opinions. Judges of this court will exercise appropriate discipline to reduce the length of opinions by the use of those techniques which result in brevity without sacrifice of quality.*

*6. **Unpublished Opinions.** A majority of the panel determine whether an opinion should be published. Opinions that the panel believes to have no precedential value are not published. Although unpublished opinions may be cited as persuasive authority, they are not considered binding precedent. The court will not give the unpublished opinion of another circuit more weight than the decision is to be given in that circuit under its own rules. Parties may request publication of an unpublished opinion by filing a motion to that effect in compliance with FRAP 27 and the corresponding circuit rules.*

*7. **Citation to Unpublished Opinions by the Court.** The court generally does not cite to its "unpublished" opinions because they are not binding precedent. The court may cite to them where they are specifically relevant to determine whether the predicates for res judicata, collateral estoppel, or double jeopardy exist in the case, to ascertain the law of the case, or to establish the procedural history or facts of the case.*

*8. **Release of Opinions.** Prior to issuance of an opinion, information concerning the date a decision by the court may be expected is not available to counsel.*

Opinions are generally released from the clerk's office in Atlanta. Upon release of an opinion, a copy is mailed to counsel and made available to the press and public at the clerk's office and at the circuit libraries. On request, the clerk will also notify counsel by telephone. Opinions are available on the Internet at www.ca11.uscourts.gov.

Opinions are subject to typographical and printing errors. Cooperation of the bar in calling apparent errors to the attention of the clerk's office is solicited.

*9. **Citation to Internet Materials in an Opinion.** When an opinion of the court includes a citation to materials available on a website, the writing judge will send a copy of the cited internet materials to the clerk for placement on the docket.*

Cross-Reference: FRAP 28, 32.1, 41

[Amended effective April 1, 1991; April 1, 1994; January 2, 1996; December 1, 1998; April 1, 1999; January 1, 2002; December 1, 2003; December 1, 2004; August 1, 2005; December 1, 2005; December 1, 2006; April 1, 2009; April 1, 2016.]

FRAP 37. INTEREST ON JUDGMENT

[For text of rule, see the Federal Rules of Appellate Procedure]

FRAP 38. FRIVOLOUS APPEAL—DAMAGES AND COSTS

[For text of rule, see the Federal Rules of Appellate Procedure]

RULE 38-1. TIME FOR FILING MOTIONS

Motions for damages and costs pursuant to FRAP 38 must be filed no later than the filing of appellee's brief.

[Effective December 1, 1998.]

IOP—CIR. RULE 38

***Motions for Damages and Costs.** Such motions shall not be contained in appellee's brief but shall be filed separately consistent with the requirements of FRAP 27 and the corresponding circuit rules. When the motion is filed in paper, an original and three copies must be filed.*

Cross-Reference: FRAP 42; 28 U.S.C. § 1927

[Effective December 1, 1998. Amended effective August 1, 2013.]

FRAP 39. COSTS

[For text of rule, see the Federal Rules of Appellate Procedure]

RULE 39-1. COSTS

In taxing costs for printing or reproduction and binding pursuant to FRAP 39(c) the clerk shall tax such costs at rates not higher than those determined by the clerk from time to time by reference to the rates generally charged for the most economical methods of printing or reproduction and binding in the principal cities of the circuit, or at actual cost, whichever is less.

Unless advance approval for additional copies is secured from the clerk, costs will be taxed only for the number of copies of the brief and appendix required by the rules to be filed and served, plus two copies for each party signing the brief.

All costs shall be paid and mailed directly to the party to whom costs have been awarded. Costs should not be mailed to the clerk of the court.

[Amended effective December 1, 1998; December 1, 2013.]

RULE 39-2. ATTORNEY'S FEES

(a) Time for Filing. Except as otherwise provided herein or by statute or court order, an application for attorney's fees must be filed with the clerk within 14 days after the time to file a petition for rehearing or rehearing en banc expires, or within 14 days after entry of an order disposing of a timely petition for rehearing or denying a timely petition for rehearing en banc, whichever is later. For purposes of this rule, the term "attorney's fees" includes fees and expenses authorized by statute, but excludes damages and costs sought pursuant to FRAP 38, costs taxed pursuant to FRAP 39, and sanctions sought pursuant to 11th Cir. R. 27–4.

(b) Required Documentation. An application for attorney's fees must be supported by a memorandum showing that the party seeking attorney's fees is legally entitled to them. The application must also include a summary of work performed, on a form available from the clerk, supported by contemporaneous time records recording all work for which a fee is claimed. An affidavit attesting to the truthfulness of the information contained in the application and demonstrating the basis for the hourly rate requested must also accompany the application. Exceptions may be made only to avoid an unconscionable result. If contemporaneous time records are not available, the court may approve only the minimum amount of fees necessary, in the court's judgment, to adequately compensate the attorney.

(c) Objection to Application. Any party from whom attorney's fees are sought may file an objection to the application. An objection must be filed with the clerk within 14 days after service of the application. The party seeking attorney's fees may file a reply to the objection within 10 days after service of the objection.

(d) Motion to Transfer. Any party who is or may be eligible for attorney's fees on appeal may, within the time for filing an application provided by this rule, file a motion to transfer consideration of attorney's fees on appeal to the district court or administrative agency from which the appeal was taken.

(e) Remand for Further Proceedings. When a reversal on appeal, in whole or in part, results in a remand to the district court for trial or other further proceedings (e.g., reversal of order granting summary judgment, or denying a new trial), a party who may be eligible for attorney's fees on appeal after prevailing on the merits upon remand may, in lieu of filing an application for attorney's fees in this court, request attorney's fees for the appeal in a timely application filed with the district court upon disposition of the matter on remand.

[Effective January 1, 2003. Amended effective December 1, 2009.]

RULE 39–3. FEE AWARDS TO PREVAILING PARTIES UNDER THE EQUAL ACCESS TO JUSTICE ACT

(a) An application to this court for an award of fees and expenses pursuant to 28 U.S.C. § 2412(d)(1)(B) must be filed within the time specified in the statute. The application must identify the applicant, show the nature and extent of services rendered, that the applicant has prevailed, and shall identify the position of the United States Government or an agency thereof which the applicant alleges was not substantially justified.

(b) An application to the court pursuant to 5 U.S.C. § 504(c)(2) shall be upon the factual record made before the agency, which shall be filed with this court under the procedures established in FRAP 11 and associated circuit rules. Unless the court establishes a schedule for filing formal briefs upon motion of a party, such proceedings shall be upon the application papers, together with such supporting papers, including memorandum briefs, as the appellant shall submit within 14 days of filing of the record of agency proceedings and upon any response filed by the United States in opposition thereto within the succeeding 14 days.

[Effective January 1, 2003.]

IOP—CIR. RULE 39

*1. **Time—Extensions.** Except as otherwise provided by FRAP 25(a) for inmate filings, a bill of costs is timely only if received by the clerk within 14 days of entry of judgment. Judgment is entered on the opinion filing date. The filing of a petition for rehearing or petition for rehearing en banc does not extend the time for filing a bill of costs. A motion to extend the time to file a bill of costs may be considered by the clerk.*

*2. **Costs for or Against the United States.** When costs are sought for or against the United States, the statutory or other authority relied upon for such an award must be set forth as an attachment to the Bill of Costs.*

*3. **Reproduction of Statutes, Rules, and Regulations.** Costs will be taxed for the reproduction of statutes, rules, and regulations in conformity with FRAP 28(f). Costs will not be taxed for the reproduction of papers not required or allowed to be filed pursuant to FRAP 28 and 30 and the corresponding circuit rules, even though the brief or appendix within which said papers are included was accepted for filing by the clerk.*

[Amended effective April 1, 1991; April 1, 1994; January 2, 1996; December 1, 1998; December 1, 2013; April 1, 2016.]

FRAP 40. PETITION FOR PANEL REHEARING

[For text of rule, see the Federal Rules of Appellate Procedure]

RULE 40–1. CONTENTS

A copy of the opinion sought to be reheard shall be included as an addendum to each petition for rehearing, following the certificate of service. This addendum does not count towards length limitations.

[Amended effective January 1, 2002; December 1, 2016.]

RULE 40–2. NUMBER OF COPIES

Four copies of a petition for rehearing pursuant to FRAP 40 shall be filed. Use of the ECF system does not modify the requirement that counsel must provide to the court four paper copies of a petition for rehearing. Counsel will be considered to have complied with this requirement if, on the day the electronic petition is filed, counsel sends four paper copies to the clerk using one of the methods outlined in FRAP 25(a)(2)(B).

[Formerly 11th Cir. R. 40–1, renumbered effective January 1, 2002. Amended effective April 1, 2014.]

RULE 40-3. TIME—EXTENSIONS

A petition for rehearing must be filed within 21 days of entry of judgment, except that a petition for rehearing in a civil appeal in which the United States or an officer or agency thereof is a party must be filed within 45 days of entry of judgment. Judgment is entered on the opinion filing date. No additional time shall be allowed for mailing. Counsel should not request extensions of time except for the most compelling reasons. For purposes of this rule, a "civil appeal" is one that falls within the scope of 11th Cir. R. 42-2(a).

[Amended effective April 1, 1991; January 2, 1996. Formerly 11th Cir. R. 40-2, renumbered effective January 1, 2002. Amended effective December 1, 2004; April 1, 2007.]

RULE 40-4. [RESCINDED]

RULE 40-5. SUPPLEMENTAL AUTHORITIES

If pertinent and significant authorities come to a party's attention while a party's petition for rehearing or petition for rehearing en banc is pending, a party may promptly advise the clerk by letter, with a copy to all other parties. The body of the letter must not exceed 350 words, including footnotes. If a new case is not reported, copies should be appended. When such a letter is filed in paper, four copies must be filed.

[Effective January 1, 2002. Amended effective January 1, 2003; August 1, 2013.]

RULE 40-6. [RESCINDED]

IOP—CIR. RULE 40

*1. **Necessity for Filing.** As indicated in 11th Cir. R. 35-3, it is not necessary to file a petition for rehearing or petition for rehearing en banc in the court of appeals as a prerequisite to the filing of a petition for writ of certiorari in the Supreme Court of the United States. Counsel are also reminded that the duty of counsel is fully discharged without filing a petition for rehearing en banc if the rigid standards of FRAP 35(a) are not met.*

*2. **Petition for Panel Rehearing.** A petition for rehearing is intended to bring to the attention of the panel claimed errors of fact or law in the opinion. It is not to be used for reargument of the issues previously presented or to attack the court's non-argument calendar procedures. Petitions for rehearing are reviewed by panel members only.*

*3. **Time.** Except as otherwise provided by FRAP 25(a) for inmate filings, a petition for rehearing is timely only if received by the clerk within the time specified in 11th Cir. R. 40-3.*

*4. **Form of Petition for Panel Rehearing.** The form of a petition for panel rehearing is governed by FRAP 32(c)(2).*

Cross-Reference: FRAP 35

[Amended effective April 1, 1991; April 1, 1994; January 2, 1996; December 1, 1998; January 1, 2002; April 1, 2007.]

FRAP 41. MANDATE: CONTENTS; ISSUANCE AND EFFECTIVE DATE; STAY

[For text of rule, see the Federal Rules of Appellate Procedure]

RULE 41-1. STAY OR RECALL OF MANDATE

(a) A motion filed under FRAP 41 for a stay of the issuance of a mandate in a direct criminal appeal shall not be granted simply upon request. Ordinarily the motion will be denied unless it shows that it is not frivolous, not filed merely for delay, and shows that a substantial question is to be presented to the Supreme Court or otherwise sets forth good cause for a stay.

(b) A mandate once issued shall not be recalled except to prevent injustice.

(c) When a motion to recall a mandate is tendered for filing more than one year after issuance of the mandate, the clerk shall not accept the motion for filing unless the motion states with specificity why it was not filed sooner. The court will not grant the motion unless the movant has established good cause for the delay in filing the motion.

(d) Unless otherwise expressly provided, granting a petition for rehearing en banc vacates the panel opinion and stays the mandate.

[Amended effective April 1, 1991; April 1, 1994; December 1, 1998; January 1, 2003.]

RULE 41-2. EXPEDITING ISSUANCE OF MANDATE

In any appeal in which a published opinion has issued, the time for issuance of mandate may be shortened only after all circuit judges in regular active service who are not recused or disqualified have been provided with reasonable notice and an opportunity to notify the clerk to withhold issuance of the mandate.

[Adopted effective April 1, 2003.]

RULE 41-3. PUBLISHED ORDER DISMISSING APPEAL OR DISPOSING OF A PETITION FOR A WRIT OF MANDAMUS OR PROHIBITION OR OTHER EXTRAORDINARY WRIT

When any of the following orders is published, the time for issuance of the mandate is governed by FRAP 41(b):

(a) An order dismissing an appeal.

(b) An order disposing of a petition for a writ of mandamus or prohibition or other extraordinary writ.

[Adopted effective December 1, 2003. Amended effective April 1, 2009; August 1, 2010.]

RULE 41-4. NON-PUBLISHED ORDER DISMISSING APPEAL OR DISPOSING OF A PETITION FOR A WRIT OF MANDAMUS OR PROHIBITION OR OTHER EXTRAORDINARY WRIT

When any of the following orders is not published, the clerk shall issue a copy to the district court clerk or agency as the mandate:

(a) An order dismissing an appeal, including an order dismissing an appeal for want of prosecution.

(b) An order disposing of a petition for a writ of mandamus or prohibition or other extraordinary writ.

[Adopted effective December 1, 2003. Amended effective August 1, 2010.]

IOP—CIR. RULE 41

1. Stay or Recall of Mandate. *A motion for stay or recall of mandate is disposed of by a single judge. See 11th Cir. R. 27-1(d).*

2. Return of Record. *The original record and any exhibits are returned to the clerk of the district court or agency with the mandate.*

3. Certified Records for Supreme Court of the United States. *Pursuant to Rule 12.7 of the Rules of the Supreme Court of the United States, the clerks of the courts of appeals are deemed to be the custodial agents of the record pending consideration of a petition for a writ of certiorari. Therefore, the clerk's office does not prepare a certified record unless specifically requested to do so by the Clerk of the Supreme Court. If certiorari is granted, the Clerk of the Supreme Court will request the clerk of the court of appeals to certify and transmit the record. See Rule 16.2 of the Rules of the Supreme Court of the United States.*

Cross-Reference: FRAP 35, 36, 40

[Amended effective April 1, 1991; April 1, 1994; January 2, 1996; December 1, 1998; January 1, 2002.]

FRAP 42. VOLUNTARY DISMISSAL

[For text of rule, see the Federal Rules of Appellate Procedure]

RULE 42-1. DISMISSAL OF APPEALS

(a) Motions to Dismiss by Appellants or Petitioners and Joint Motions to Dismiss. If an appellant or petitioner files an unopposed motion to dismiss an appeal, petition, or agency proceeding, or if both parties file a joint motion to dismiss an appeal, petition, or agency proceeding, and the matter has not yet been assigned to a panel on the merits, the clerk may clerically dismiss the appeal, petition, or agency proceeding and in such circumstances will issue a copy of the order as and for the mandate. By issuing such a dismissal, the clerk expresses no opinion on the effect of that dismissal. If the appeal, petition, or agency proceeding has been assigned to a panel on the merits, any motion to dismiss will be submitted to that panel.

A joint motion to dismiss must be signed by counsel for each party encompassed by the motion, or by the party itself if proceeding pro se. All motions to dismiss must contain a Certificate of Interested Persons and Corporate Disclosure Statement in compliance with FRAP 26.1 and the accompanying circuit rules. If an appellant's or petitioner's motion to dismiss is opposed, it will be submitted to the court. For motions to dismiss criminal appeals, see also 11th Cir. R. 27-1(a)(7) and 27-1(a)(8).

(b) Dismissal for Failure to Prosecute. Except as otherwise provided for briefs and appendices in civil appeals in 11th Cir. R. 42-2 and 42-3, when appellant fails to file a brief or other required papers within the time permitted, or otherwise fails to comply with the applicable rules, the clerk shall issue a notice to counsel, or to pro se appellant, that upon expiration of 14 days from the date thereof the appeal will be dismissed for want of prosecution if the default has not been remedied by filing the brief or other required papers and a motion to file documents out of time. Within that 14-day notice period a party in default must seek leave of the court, by appropriate motion, to file documents out of time or otherwise remedy the default. Failure to timely file such motion will result in dismissal for want of prosecution.

The clerk shall not dismiss an appeal during the pendency of a timely filed motion for an extension of time to file appellant's brief or appendix, but if the court denies such leave after the expiration of the due date for filing the brief or appendix, the clerk shall dismiss the appeal forthwith. The clerk shall not dismiss an appeal during the pendency of a timely filed motion to file documents out of time or otherwise remedy the default which is accompanied by the brief or other required papers, but if the court denies such leave the clerk shall dismiss the appeal forthwith.

If an appellant is represented by appointed counsel, the clerk may refer the matter to the Chief Judge for consideration of possible disciplinary action against counsel in lieu of dismissal.

[Amended effective January 2, 1996; January 1, 2000; January 1, 2002; January 1, 2003; December 1, 2003; December 1, 2004; December 1, 2013; August 1, 2016.]

RULE 42-2. DISMISSAL IN A CIVIL APPEAL FOR APPELLANT'S FAILURE TO FILE BRIEF OR APPENDIX BY DUE DATE

(a) Applicability of Rule. The provisions of this rule apply to all civil appeals, including Tax Court appeals, bankruptcy appeals, appeals in cases brought pursuant to 28 U.S.C. §§ 2254 and 2255, review of agency orders, and petitions for extraordinary writs when briefing has been ordered, but not including appeals of orders revoking supervised release or of orders entered pursuant to Rule 35 of the Federal Rules of Criminal Procedure or 18 U.S.C. § 3582.

(b) Notice of Due Date for Filing Brief and Appendix. Eleventh Circuit Rules 30-1(c) and 31-1 establish the due dates for filing the brief and appendix. To facilitate compliance, the clerk will send counsel and pro se parties a notice confirming the due date for filing appellant's brief and appendix consistent with 11th Cir. R. 30-1(c) and 31-1. However, delay in or failure to receive such notice does not affect the obligation of counsel and pro se parties to file the brief and appendix within the time permitted by the rules.

(c) Dismissal Without Further Notice. When an appellant has failed to file the brief or appendix by the due date as established by 11th Cir. R. 30-1(c) and 31-1 and set forth in the clerk's notice, or, if the due date has been extended by the court, within the time so extended, an appeal shall be treated as dismissed for failure to prosecute on the first business day following the due date. The clerk thereafter will enter an order dismissing the appeal and mail a copy of that order to counsel and pro se parties. If an appellant is represented by appointed counsel, the clerk may refer the matter to the Chief Judge for consideration of possible disciplinary action against counsel in lieu of dismissal.

(d) Effect of Pending Motion to Extend Time. The clerk shall not dismiss an appeal during the pendency of a timely filed motion for an extension of time to file appellant's brief or appendix, but if the court denies such leave after the expiration of the due date for filing the brief or appendix, the clerk shall dismiss the appeal.

(e) Motion to Set Aside Dismissal and Remedy Default. An appeal dismissed pursuant to this rule may be reinstated only upon the timely filing of a motion to set aside the dismissal and remedy the default showing extraordinary circumstances, accompanied by the required brief and appendix. Such a motion showing extraordinary circumstances, accompanied by the required brief and appendix, must be filed within 14 days of the date the clerk enters the order dismissing the appeal. The timely filing of such a motion, accompanied by the required brief and appendix, and a showing of extraordinary circumstances, is the exclusive method of seeking to set aside a dismissal entered pursuant to this rule. An untimely filed motion to set aside dismissal and remedy default must be denied unless the motion demonstrates extraordinary circumstances justifying the delay in filing the motion, and no further filings shall be accepted by the clerk in that dismissed appeal.

(f) Failure of Appellee to File Brief by Due Date. When an appellee fails to file a brief by the due date as established by 11th Cir. R. 31–1, or, if the due date has been extended by the court, within the time so extended, the appeal will be submitted to the court for decision without further delay, and the appellee will not be heard at oral argument (if oral argument is scheduled to be heard) unless otherwise ordered by the court.

[Amended effective January 1, 2002; April 1, 2007; December 1, 2013.]

RULE 42–3. DISMISSAL IN A CIVIL APPEAL FOR APPELLANT'S FAILURE TO CORRECT A DEFICIENCY IN BRIEFS OR APPENDICES WITHIN 14 DAYS OF NOTICE

(a) Applicability of Rule. The provisions of this rule apply to all civil appeals, including Tax Court appeals, bankruptcy appeals, appeals in cases brought pursuant to 28 U.S.C. §§ 2254 and 2255, review of agency orders, and petitions for extraordinary writs when briefing has been ordered, but not including appeals of orders revoking supervised release or of orders entered pursuant to Rule 35 of the Federal Rules of Criminal Procedure or 18 U.S.C. § 3582.

(b) Notice to Correct a Deficiency in Briefs or Appendices. If briefs or appendices do not comply with the rules governing the form of briefs and appendices, the clerk will send counsel and pro se parties a notice specifying the matters requiring correction. A complete corrected set of replacement briefs or appendices must be filed in the office of the clerk within 14 days of the date of the clerk's notice.

(c) Dismissal Without Further Notice. When an appellant has failed to correct the brief or appendix within 14 days of the clerk's notice, or, if the due date has been extended by the court, within the time so extended, an appeal shall be treated as dismissed for failure to prosecute on the first business day following the due date. The clerk thereafter will enter an order dismissing the appeal and mail a copy of that order to counsel and pro se parties. If an appellant is represented by appointed counsel, the clerk may refer the matter to the Chief Judge for consideration of possible disciplinary action against counsel in lieu of dismissal.

(d) Effect of Pending Motion to Extend Time. The clerk shall not dismiss an appeal during the pendency of a timely filed motion for an extension of time to correct a deficiency in appellant's brief or appendix, but if the court denies such leave after the expiration of the due date for correcting a deficiency in the brief or appendix, the clerk shall dismiss the appeal.

(e) Motion to Set Aside Dismissal and Remedy Default. An appeal dismissed pursuant to this rule may be reinstated only upon the filing of a motion to set aside the dismissal and remedy the default showing extraordinary circumstances, accompanied by the required corrected brief or appendix. Such a motion showing extraordinary circumstances, accompanied by the required corrected brief or appendix, must be filed within 14 days of the date the clerk enters the order dismissing the appeal. The timely filing of such a motion, accompanied by the required corrected brief or appendix, and a showing of extraordinary circumstances, is the exclusive method of seeking to set aside a dismissal entered pursuant to this rule. An untimely filed motion to set aside dismissal and remedy default must be denied unless the motion demonstrates extraordinary circumstances justifying the delay in filing the motion, and no further filings shall be accepted by the clerk in that dismissed appeal.

(f) Failure of Appellee to File Corrected Brief Within 14 Days of Notice. When an appellee fails to file a corrected brief within 14 days of the clerk's notice, or, if that date has been extended by the court, within the time so extended, the appeal will be submitted to the court for decision without further delay, and the appellee will not be heard at oral argument (if oral argument is scheduled to be heard) unless otherwise ordered by the court.

[Amended effective January 1, 2002; April 1, 2007; December 1, 2013.]

RULE 42–4. FRIVOLOUS APPEALS

If it shall appear to the court at any time that an appeal is frivolous and entirely without merit, the appeal may be dismissed.

[Effective January 1, 2000.]

IOP—CIR. RULE 42

Dismissal Rules Apply to Principal Briefs. *The rules that provide for dismissal of an appeal for appellant's failure to file a brief by the due date, or to correct deficiencies in a brief within 14 days of notice, apply to appellant's or cross-*

appellant's principal (first) brief only, unless the court orders otherwise.

Cross-Reference: FRAP 3, 38; 28 U.S.C. § 1927

[Adopted effective January 1, 2000. Amended effective December 1, 2004; December 1, 2008; August 1, 2016.]

FRAP 43. SUBSTITUTION OF PARTIES

[For text of rule, see the Federal Rules of Appellate Procedure]

FRAP 44. CASE INVOLVING A CONSTITUTIONAL QUESTION WHEN THE UNITED STATES OR THE RELEVANT STATE IS NOT A PARTY

[For text of rule, see the Federal Rules of Appellate Procedure]

FRAP 45. CLERK'S DUTIES

[For text of rule, see the Federal Rules of Appellate Procedure]

RULE 45-1. CLERK

(a) Location. The clerk's principal office shall be in the city of Atlanta, Georgia.

(b) Office to Be Open. The office of the clerk, with the clerk or a deputy in attendance, shall be open for business from 8:30 a.m. to 5:00 p.m., Eastern time, on all days except Saturdays, Sundays, New Year's Day, Birthday of Martin Luther King, Jr., Washington's Birthday, Memorial Day, Independence Day, Labor Day, Columbus Day, Veterans Day, Thanksgiving Day, and Christmas Day.

[Amended effective April 1, 1991; December 1, 2013.]

IOP—CIR. RULE 45

1. Telephone Inquiries. *The clerk's office welcomes telephone inquiries from counsel concerning rules and procedures. Counsel may contact the appropriate deputy clerk by calling the clerk's office. The clerk is also available to confer with counsel on special problems.*

2. Emergency Telephone Inquiries After Hours. *In emergency situations arising outside normal office hours, or on weekends, the deputy clerk on duty may be reached by dialing the clerk's office and following recorded instructions.*

3. Miami Satellite Office. *The clerk maintains a satellite office in Miami, Florida. See I.O.P. 5, Miami Satellite Office, following FRAP 25.*

Cross-Reference: FRAP 25, 26, 34; 28 U.S.C. §§ 452, 711, 956

[Amended effective April 1, 1994; April 1, 2014.]

FRAP 46. ATTORNEYS

[For text of rule, see the Federal Rules of Appellate Procedure]

RULE 46-1. BAR ADMISSION AND FEES

Only attorneys admitted to the bar of this court may practice before the court, except as otherwise provided in these rules. Admission is governed by FRAP 46 and this Eleventh Circuit Rule, and attorneys must also meet the requirements of 11th Cir. R. 46-7. To request admission to the bar, an attorney must complete an application form, available on the Internet at www.ca11.uscourts.gov, and submit the form to the clerk's principal office in Atlanta. The application form must be accompanied by:

- a certificate of good standing issued within the previous six months from a court described in FRAP 46(a)(1); and
- the non-refundable fee set by the court and posted on the court's website, payable to Clerk, U.S. Court of Appeals, Eleventh Circuit.

Each member of the bar has a continuing obligation to keep this court informed of any changes to addresses, phone numbers, fax numbers, and e-mail addresses.

[Amended effective April 1, 1991; April 1, 1994; December 1, 1998; January 1, 2002; April 1, 2005; August 1, 2005; April 1, 2006; December 1, 2007; August 1, 2012; December 1, 2015.]

RULE 46-2. RENEWAL OF BAR MEMBERSHIP; INACTIVE STATUS

Each attorney admitted to the bar of this court shall pay a bar membership renewal fee of $10.00 every five years from the date of admission. A new certificate of admission will *not* issue upon payment of this fee. During the first week of the month in which an attorney's renewal fee is due, the clerk shall send by mail, e-mail, or other means a notice to the attorney using the contact information on the roll of attorneys admitted to practice before this court (attorney roll), and advise the attorney that payment of the renewal fee is due by the last day of that month. If the notice is returned undelivered due to incorrect or invalid contact information, no further notice will be sent. If the renewal fee is not paid by the last day of the month in which the notice is sent, the attorney's membership in the bar of this court will be placed in inactive status for a period of 12 months, beginning on the first day of the next month. An attorney whose bar membership is in inactive status may not practice before the court. To renew a bar membership, including one in inactive status, an attorney must complete a bar membership renewal form, available at www.ca11.uscourts.gov. The renewal form must be accompanied by a non-refundable bar membership renewal fee of $10.00. All attorneys must use the court's Electronic Case Files (ECF) system to submit their renewal forms and payments.

After 12 months in inactive status, if an attorney has not paid the bar membership renewal fee, the clerk shall strike the attorney's name from the attorney roll. An attorney whose name is stricken from the attorney roll due to nonpayment of the renewal fee who thereafter wishes to practice before the court must apply for admission to the bar pursuant to 11th

Cir. R. 46–1, unless the attorney is eligible to be admitted for a particular proceeding pursuant to 11th Cir. R. 46–3.

[Effective December 1, 2007. Amended effective December 1, 2015; December 1, 2016.]

RULE 46–3. ADMISSION FOR PARTICULAR PROCEEDING

The following attorneys shall be admitted for the particular proceeding in which they are appearing without the necessity of formal application or payment of the admission fee: an attorney appearing on behalf of the United States, a federal public defender, an attorney appointed by a federal court under the Criminal Justice Act or appointed to represent a party in forma pauperis.

[Effective December 1, 2007. Amended effective April 1, 2016.]

RULE 46–4. PRO HAC VICE ADMISSION

An attorney who does not reside in the circuit but is otherwise eligible for admission to the bar pursuant to FRAP 46 and these rules, and also meets the requirements of 11th Cir. R. 46–7, may apply to appear pro hac vice in a particular proceeding. The following items must be provided:

- a completed Application to Appear Pro Hac Vice form, available on the Internet at www.ca11.uscourts.gov, with proof of service;
- a certificate of good standing issued within the previous six months from a court described in FRAP 46(a)(1); and
- a non-refundable pro hac vice application fee of $50.00, payable to U.S. Court of Appeals, Non-Appropriated Fund, 11th Circuit.

An attorney may apply to appear before this court pro hac vice only two times.

To practice before the court, an attorney who resides in the circuit or who has two times previously applied to appear before this court pro hac vice, must apply for admission to the bar pursuant to 11th Cir. R. 46–1, unless the attorney is eligible to be admitted for a particular proceeding pursuant to 11th Cir. R. 46–3.

The clerk is authorized to grant an application to appear pro hac vice in an appeal not yet assigned or under submission, in such circumstances as determined by the court, when an attorney meets the requirements of the rules.

[Effective December 1, 2007. Amended effective December 1, 2013; December 1, 2015.]

RULE 46–5. ENTRY OF APPEARANCE

Every attorney, except one appointed by the court for a specific case, must file an Appearance of Counsel Form in order to participate in a case before the court. The form must be filed within 14 days after the date on the notice from the clerk that the Appearance of Counsel Form must be filed. With a court-appointed attorney, the order of appointment will be treated as the appearance form.

Except for those who are court-appointed, an attorney who has not previously filed an Appearance of Counsel Form in a case will not be permitted to participate in oral argument of the case until the appearance form is filed.

[Effective December 1, 2007. Amended effective April 1, 2009.]

RULE 46–6. CLERK'S AUTHORITY TO ACCEPT FILINGS

(a) Filings From an Attorney Who Is Not a Member of the Eleventh Circuit Bar.

(1) Subject to the provisions of this rule, the clerk may conditionally file the following papers received from an attorney who is not a member of the circuit bar and who is not admitted for the particular proceeding pursuant to 11th Cir. R. 46–3:

- a petition or application that initiates a proceeding in this court;
- an emergency motion as described in 11th Cir. R. 27–1(b);
- a motion or petition that is treated by the clerk as "time sensitive" as that term is used in 11th Cir. R. 27–1(b).

(2) Upon filing the petition, application, or motion, the clerk will mail a notice to the attorney, stating that in order to participate in the appeal the attorney must be properly admitted either to the bar of this court or for the particular proceeding pursuant to 11th Cir. R. 46–4, and that the attorney must submit an appropriate application for admission within fourteen (14) days from the date of such notice.

(3) Within the 14–day notice period, the clerk may conditionally file motions and other papers received from the attorney, subject to receipt of an appropriate application for admission within that period. At the expiration of the 14–day notice period, if an appropriate application for admission has not been received, the clerk will return any such motions and other papers to the attorney and enter that action on the docket, and the motions and other papers will be treated as though they were never filed.

(4) When an appropriate application for admission is received within the 14–day notice period, the clerk may continue to conditionally file motions and other papers received from the attorney, subject to the court's approval of the attorney's application for admission. If the attorney's application is denied, the clerk will return any such motions and other papers to the attorney and enter that action on the docket, and the motions and other papers will be treated as though they were never filed. Before taking that action, the clerk may stay further proceedings in the appeal for 30 days, if necessary, to allow the attorney's client to seek new counsel.

(b) Filings From an Attorney Who Has Not Filed an Appearance of Counsel Form Within 14 Days After Notice Is Mailed by the Clerk. When an attorney fails to file a required Appearance of Counsel Form within 14 days after notice of that requirement is mailed by the clerk, the clerk may not accept any further filings (except for a brief) from the attorney until the attorney files an Appearance of Counsel Form. When an attorney who has not filed an Appearance of Counsel Form tenders a brief for filing, the clerk will treat the failure to file an Appearance of Counsel Form as a deficiency in the form of the brief. An Appearance of Counsel Form need not be accompanied by a motion to file out of time.

[Effective December 1, 2007.]

RULE 46-7. ACTIVE MEMBERSHIP IN GOOD STANDING WITH STATE BAR REQUIRED TO PRACTICE; CHANGES IN STATUS OF BAR MEMBERSHIP MUST BE REPORTED

In addition to the requirements of FRAP 46 and the corresponding circuit rules, and Addendum Eight, an attorney may not practice before this court if the attorney is not an active member in good standing with a state bar or the bar of the highest court of a state, or the District of Columbia (hereinafter, "state bar"). When an attorney's active membership in good standing with a state bar lapses for any reason, including but not limited to retirement, placement in inactive status, failure to pay bar membership fees, or failure to complete continuing education requirements, the attorney must notify the clerk of this court within 14 days. That notification must also list every other state bar and federal bar of which the attorney is a member, including state bar numbers and the attorney's status with that bar (e.g., active, inactive, retired, etc.). Members of the Eleventh Circuit bar have a continuing obligation to provide such notification, and attorneys appearing pro hac vice in a particular case or appeal must provide such notification while that case or appeal is pending. Upon receipt of that notification, the court may take any action it deems appropriate, including placing the attorney's bar membership in inactive status until the attorney provides documentation of active membership in good standing with a state bar.

[Effective December 1, 2007. Amended effective December 1, 2015.]

RULE 46-8. CERTIFICATE OF ADMISSION

Upon admission to the bar of this court, the clerk will send the attorney a certificate of admission. A duplicate certificate of admission is available for purchase upon payment of the fee prescribed by the Judicial Conference of the United States in the Court of Appeals Miscellaneous Fee Schedule issued pursuant to 28 U.S.C. § 1913, payable to Clerk, U.S. Court of Appeals, Eleventh Circuit.

[Effective December 1, 2007. Amended effective August 1, 2012.]

RULE 46-9. ATTORNEY DISCIPLINE

This court has adopted rules governing attorney conduct and discipline. See Addendum Eight.

[Effective December 1, 2007.]

RULE 46-10. APPOINTMENT OR WITHDRAWAL OF COUNSEL

(a) Appellate Obligations of Retained Counsel. Retained counsel for a criminal defendant has an obligation to continue to represent that defendant until successor counsel either enters an appearance or is appointed under the Criminal Justice Act, and may not abandon or cease representation of a defendant except upon order of the court.

(b) Habeas Corpus or 28 U.S.C. § 2255 Pauper Appeals. When any pro se appeal for either habeas corpus or 2255 relief is classified for oral argument, counsel will normally be appointed under the Criminal Justice Act before the appeal is calendared. The non-argument panel that classifies the appeal for oral argument will advise the clerk who will then obtain counsel under the regular procedure.

(c) Relieving Court Appointed Counsel on Appeal. Counsel appointed by the trial court shall not be relieved on appeal except in the event of incompatibility between attorney and client or other serious circumstances.

(d) Criminal Justice Act Appointments. The Judicial Council of this circuit has adopted the Eleventh Circuit Plan under the Criminal Justice Act and Guidelines for Counsel Supplementing the Eleventh Circuit Plan under the Criminal Justice Act. See Addendum Four.

(e) Non-Criminal Justice Act Appointments. This court has adopted rules governing Non-Criminal Justice Act Appointments. See Addendum Five.

[Effective December 1, 2007. Amended effective August 1, 2013.]

RULE 46-11. APPEARANCE AND ARGUMENT BY ELIGIBLE LAW STUDENTS

(a) Scope of Legal Assistance.

(1) *Notice of Appearance.* An eligible law student, as described below, acting under a supervising attorney of record, may enter an appearance in this court on behalf of any indigent person, the United States, or a governmental agency in any civil or criminal case, provided that the party on whose behalf the student appears and the supervising attorney of record has consented thereto in writing. The written consent of the party (or the party's representative) and the supervising attorney of record must be filed with this court.

(2) *Briefs.* An eligible law student may assist in the preparation of briefs and other documents to be filed in this court, but such briefs or documents must be reviewed, approved entirely, and signed by the supervising attorney of record. Names of students participating in the preparation of briefs may, however, be added to the briefs.

(3) *Oral Argument.* Except, on behalf of the accused, in a direct appeal from a criminal prosecution, an eligible law student may also participate in oral argument, but only in the presence of the supervising attorney of record.

(b) Law Student Eligibility Requirements. In order to appear before this court, the law student must:

(1) Be enrolled in a law school approved by the American Bar Association;

(2) Have completed legal studies for which the student has received at least 48 semester hours or 72 quarter hours of academic credit or the equivalent if the school is on some other basis;

(3) Be certified by the dean of the law student's law school as qualified to provide the legal representation permitted by this rule. This certification, which shall be filed with the clerk, may be withdrawn by the dean at any time by mailing a notice

to the clerk or by termination by this court without notice or hearing and without any showing of cause;

(4) Neither ask for nor receive any compensation or remuneration of any kind for the student's services from the person on whose behalf the student renders services, but this shall not prevent an attorney, legal aid bureau, law school, public defender agency, a State, or the United States from paying compensation to the eligible law student, nor shall it prevent these entities from making proper charges for its services;

(5) Certify in writing that the student has read and is familiar with the Code of Professional Responsibility of the American Bar Association, the Federal Rules of Appellate Procedure, and the rules of this court; and

(6) File all of the certifications and consents necessary under this rule with the clerk of this court prior to the submission of any briefs or documents containing the law student's name and the law student's appearance at oral argument.

(c) Supervising Attorney of Record Requirements.

(1) The supervising attorney of record must be a member in good standing of the bar of this court.

(2) With respect to the law student's appearance, the supervising attorney of record shall certify in writing to this court that he or she:

(A) consents to the participation of the law student and agrees to supervise the law student;

(B) assumes full, personal professional responsibility for the case and for the quality of the law student's work;

(C) will assist the student to the extent necessary; and

(D) will appear with the student in all written and oral proceedings before this court and be prepared to supplement any written or oral statement made by the student to this court or opposing counsel.

[Effective December 1, 2010.]

IOP—CIR. RULE 46

1. Admissions. *There is no formal swearing-in ceremony.*

2. Payment Returned or Denied for Insufficient Funds. *When a payment of a fee is returned unpaid or denied by a financial institution due to insufficient funds, counsel must thereafter pay the fee by money order or cashier's check made payable to the same entity or account as the returned check or denied payment. In addition, counsel must also remit by separate money order or cashier's check the returned-or-denied-payment fee prescribed by the Judicial Conference of the United States in the Court of Appeals Miscellaneous Fee Schedule issued pursuant to 28 U.S.C. § 1913, payable to Clerk, U.S. Court of Appeals, Eleventh Circuit.*

3. Components of Attorney Admission Fee. *The attorney admission fee is composed of two separate fees. A national admission fee has been prescribed by the Judicial Conference of the United States in the Court of Appeals Miscellaneous Fee Schedule issued pursuant to 28 U.S.C. § 1913. This fee is remitted to the federal judiciary. A local admission fee has been prescribed by this court pursuant to FRAP 46(a)(3), and is posted on the court's website. This fee is deposited in the court's non-appropriated fund account to be used for the benefit of the bench and bar in the administration of justice.*

[Effective January 1, 2002. Amended effective August 1, 2005; August 1, 2012; August 1, 2014.]

FRAP 47. LOCAL RULES BY COURTS OF APPEALS

[For text of rule, see the Federal Rules of Appellate Procedure]

RULE 47-1. NAME, SEAL, AND PROCESS

(a) Name. The name of this court is "United States Court of Appeals for the Eleventh Circuit."

(b) Seal. Centered upon a blue disc a representation of the American eagle in its proper colors with wings displayed and inverted standing upon a closed book with gold page ends and maroon cover; also standing upon the book and in front of the eagle's right wing a gold balance embellished with three white stars, one above each of the pans and one atop the centerpost and below the book on a gold semi-circular scroll in blue letters the inscription EQUAL JUSTICE UNDER LAW; all enclosed by a gold-edged white border inscribed in blue with the words UNITED STATES COURT OF APPEALS above two gold rosettes of blue and gold and the words ELEVENTH CIRCUIT also in blue.

(c) Writs and Process. Writs and process of this court shall be under the seal of the court and signed by the clerk.

RULE 47-2. CIRCUIT EXECUTIVE

The judicial council has appointed a circuit executive pursuant to 28 U.S.C. § 332 as secretary of the judicial council and of the judicial conference.

The circuit executive is designated as the court's manager for all matters pertaining to administrative planning, organizing and budgeting. The clerk, the director of the staff attorney's office, and the circuit librarian shall coordinate fully with the circuit executive on those administrative matters pertaining to their areas of responsibility that appropriately warrant judicial attention or administrative action.

The circuit executive shall maintain an office in Atlanta, Georgia.

RULE 47-3. CIRCUIT LIBRARIAN

Under the direction of a circuit librarian the court will maintain a library in Atlanta, Georgia, and approve regulations for its use. All persons admitted to practice before the court shall be authorized to use the library. Libraries may be maintained at other places in the circuit designated by the judicial council.

[Amended effective December 1, 1998.]

RULE 47-4. STAFF ATTORNEYS

Under the supervision of a senior staff attorney, a central staff of attorneys shall be maintained at Atlanta, Georgia, to assist the court in legal research, analysis of appellate records and study of particular legal problems, and such other duties as the court directs.

[Former 11th Cir. R. 47-4(b) redesignated new 11th Cir. R. 47-4 effective December 1, 1998.]

RULE 47-5. JUDICIAL CONFERENCE

The rules of this court for having and conducting the conference and for representation and active participation at the conference by judges and members of the bar appear as Addendum One.

[Former 11th Cir. R. 47-4 amended effective April 1, 1994. Redesignated 11th Cir. R. 47-5 effective December 1, 1998.]

RULE 47-6. RESTRICTIONS ON PRACTICE BY CURRENT AND FORMER EMPLOYEES

Consistent with the Consolidated Code of Conduct for Judicial Employees adopted by the Judicial Conference of the United States, no employee of the court shall engage in the practice of law. A former employee of the court may not participate by way of representation, consultation, or assistance, in any matter which was pending in the court during the employee's term of employment.

[Former 11th Cir. R. 47-6 adopted effective April 1, 1991. Redesignated 11th Cir. R. 47-7 and amended effective December 1, 1998. Redesignated 11th Cir. R. 47-6 effective January 1, 2003.]

IOP—CIR. RULE 47

*1. **Physical Facilities.** The headquarters of the United States Court of Appeals for the Eleventh Circuit is located at 56 Forsyth Street, N.W., Atlanta, Georgia 30303, in the Elbert P. Tuttle U.S. Court of Appeals Building. The courthouse contains three courtrooms, chambers for judges, the Kinnard Mediation Center, and the library. The John C. Godbold Federal Building, which contains the circuit executive's office, the clerk's office, and the office of the staff attorneys, is located at 96 Poplar Street, N.W., Atlanta, Georgia 30303, and is directly behind the Elbert P. Tuttle U.S. Court of Appeals Building.*

*2. **Judges.** The Eleventh Circuit has 12 authorized active judges. Each active judge's office, maintained in the place of residence, is authorized three law clerks and two secretaries or four law clerks and one secretary. The chief judge is authorized one additional law clerk or secretary. Several senior judges maintain offices and staffs commensurate with the judicial work they choose to do, and sit on oral argument panels several times during the year. Senior judges do not normally participate in the administrative work of the court, although they are authorized by law to do so.*

*3. **Circuit Executive.** The circuit executive is the chief administrative officer of the court. The circuit executive's office contains staff assistants and secretaries. See 28 U.S.C. § 332.*

*4. **Office of Staff Attorneys.** The office is comprised of a senior staff attorney, staff attorneys, and supporting clerical personnel. This office assists the court in legal research, analysis of appellate records, and studies of particular legal problems. It also assists in handling pro se prisoner matters. In many cases the office prepares memoranda to assist the judges.*

*5. **Library.** The library is staffed by the circuit librarian and assistant librarians. Library hours are from 8:30 a.m. to 4:30 p.m., Monday through Friday.*

All persons admitted to practice before the court are authorized to use the library. Under regulations approved by the court, others may use the library by special permission only. Books and materials may not be removed from the library without permission of the librarian.

*6. **Judicial Conference.** Pursuant to 28 U.S.C. § 333 there is held biennially, and may be held annually, at such time and place as designated by the chief judge of the court, a conference of all circuit, district and bankruptcy judges of the circuit for the purpose of considering the business of the courts and advising means of improving the administration of justice within the circuit. See Addendum One to the circuit rules.*

*7. **Judicial Council.** The judicial council established by 28 U.S.C. § 332 is composed of nineteen members: one active judge from each of the nine district courts, nine active circuit judges, and the circuit chief judge. The judicial council meets on call of the chief judge approximately three times a year to consider and to make orders for the effective and expeditious administration of the courts within the circuit. The council is responsible for considering complaints against judges.*

*8. **Fifth Circuit Court of Appeals Reorganization Act of 1980 (P.L. 96-452, October 4, 1980).** Section 9 of the Fifth Circuit Court of Appeals Reorganization Act of 1980 determines appellate case processing after October 1, 1981, in terms of the "submitted for decision" date of each appeal.*

The date an appeal assigned to the oral argument calendar is submitted for decision, is the date on which the initial argument of the appeal is heard. The date an appeal decided on the summary or non-argument calendar is submitted for decision, is the date on which the last panel judge concurs in summary or nonargument calendar disposition.

*9. **Recusal or Disqualification of Judges.***

a. Grounds. *A judge may recuse himself or herself under any circumstances considered sufficient to require such action. A judge is disqualified under circumstances set forth in 28 U.S.C. § 455 or in accordance with Canon 3C, Code of Conduct for United States Judges as approved by the Judicial Conference of the United States, April 1973, as amended.*

b. Administrative Motions Procedure.

(1) Single Judge Matter. If a judge who is the initiating judge recuses himself or herself from considering or is disqualified to consider an administrative motion, the file is returned to the clerk who then sends it to the next initiating judge listed on the administrative routing log.

(2) Panel Matter. If a judge who is the initiating judge recuses himself or herself from considering or is disqualified to consider an administrative motion, the file is forwarded by the recused judge directly to the next judge (who then becomes the initiating judge) for decision by quorum of the panel. If these remaining judges cannot agree as to disposition of the matter or if the appeal is deemed more appropriate for a full panel, the quorum may submit the matter to the backup judge. If at any point there are insufficient, unrecused judges on a panel to constitute a quorum, the file is returned to the clerk for appointment of a new panel from the administrative routing log.

c. Non–Argument Calendar Appeals. *The same procedure is followed as in paragraph (b)(2) above, except that a backup judge is ordinarily called in since the court's practice is that appeals are not ordinarily disposed of on the merits by only two judges.*

d. Oral Argument Calendar Appeals. *Prior to issuance of the court calendar, each judge on the panel is furnished with a copy for each appeal of the Certificate of Interested Persons and Corporate Disclosure Statement described in FRAP 26.1 and the accompanying circuit rules, for each judge's advance study to determine if the judge should recuse himself or herself or is disqualified in any of the appeals.*

10. Complaints Against Judges. *This court's rule for the conduct of complaint proceedings under 28 U.S.C. §§ 351–364 is outlined in Addendum Three.*

11. Pro Se Applications. *The clerk's office processes and answers prisoner and other pro se correspondence with the assistance of the staff attorneys' office. When a pro se petition is in the proper form for docketing and processing, it is routed to the staff attorneys' office. This office prepares legal memoranda for the court on such interlocutory matters as applications for leave to appeal in forma pauperis, certificates of appealability, and appointment of counsel, and on other pro se matters.*

12. Statistics. *The clerk periodically prepares statistical reports for the court and for the Administrative Office of the United States Courts. These reports are used to manage the internal affairs of the court and to provide information for purposes of determining personnel and equipment needs, the number of oral argument sessions to be scheduled, the workload of the judges and staff, and other management concerns. The reports are distributed to the judges and the circuit executive, and are discussed at judicial council meetings.*

Cross–Reference: 28 U.S.C. §§ 41–48, 57, 291–296, 332, 333, 372, 455, 713, 1691

[Amended effective April 1, 1991; April 1, 1994; December 1, 1998; April 1, 1999; April 1, 1999; January 1, 2003; December 1, 2006; August 1, 2008; December 1, 2008; December 1, 2009; August 1, 2013; April 1, 2014; December 1, 2015.]

FRAP 48. MASTERS

[For text of rule, see the Federal Rules of Appellate Procedure]

APPENDIX OF FORMS

FORM 1. NOTICE OF APPEAL TO A COURT OF APPEALS FROM A JUDGMENT OR ORDER OF A DISTRICT COURT

[For text of form, see the Federal Rules of Appellate Procedure]

FORM 2. NOTICE OF APPEAL TO A COURT OF APPEALS FROM A DECISION OF THE UNITED STATES TAX COURT

[For text of form, see the Federal Rules of Appellate Procedure]

FORM 3. PETITION FOR REVIEW OF ORDER OF AN AGENCY, BOARD, COMMISSION OR OFFICER

[For text of form, see the Federal Rules of Appellate Procedure]

FORM 4. AFFIDAVIT ACCOMPANYING MOTION FOR PERMISSION TO APPEAL IN FORMA PAUPERIS

[For text of form, see the Federal Rules of Appellate Procedure]

FORM 5. NOTICE OF APPEAL TO A COURT OF APPEALS FROM A JUDGMENT OR ORDER OF A DISTRICT COURT OR A BANKRUPTCY APPELLATE PANEL

[For text of form, see the Federal Rules of Appellate Procedure]

FORM 6. CERTIFICATE OF COMPLIANCE WITH RULE 32(A)

[For text of form, see the Federal Rules of Appellate Procedure]

ADDENDA

ADDENDUM ONE. RULES FOR CONDUCT OF AND REPRESENTATION AND PARTICIPATION AT THE ELEVENTH CIRCUIT JUDICIAL CONFERENCE

(a) Planning and Conducting the Conference. The judicial council shall have the responsibility for planning and conducting judicial conferences. The long-range plans for conducting judicial conferences shall be made on recommendation of a judicial conference committee of the judicial council appointed by the chief judge with judicial council approval. Each annual conference shall be planned and conducted by a judicial conference planning chair, appointed by the committee with judicial council approval. The chair, with approval of the chief judge, shall appoint such committees as may be necessary for efficient and effective operation of the conference.

(b) Members of the Conference. The judicial conference of this circuit shall consist of the following:

(1) ex officio

a. the active circuit and district judges, bankruptcy judges, and full-time magistrates of the circuit;

b. the circuit justice;

c. the senior and retired circuit, district and bankruptcy judges and magistrates of the circuit;

d. the circuit executive of the circuit;

e. the clerk of the circuit court or a designated deputy;

f. the staff attorney of the court;

g. the circuit librarian;

h. presidents and presidents-elect of the state bars of the states within the circuit;

i. three official representatives chosen by each state bar of the states comprising the circuit;

j. the chief justices of the state supreme courts of each state within the circuit, or their designees;

k. the members of the lawyers advisory committee of the circuit;

l. the executive director of each state bar of the states within the circuit;

m. each United States attorney of the circuit;

n. the federal public defender of any district within the circuit, and a representative of a community defender organization in any district, designated by the president of such organization;

o. the dean of each accredited law school within the circuit;

p. any retired justice of the Supreme Court of the United States residing or practicing within the circuit;

q. any current or former attorney general of the United States residing or practicing within the circuit;

r. any lawyer who has been nominated to a circuit, district or bankruptcy court judgeship within the circuit, whether or not yet confirmed or inducted;

s. the president, or personal designee, of the American Bar Association;

t. former presidents of the American Bar Association residing or practicing in the circuit;

u. the current members of the board of governors of the American Bar Association from the circuit;

v. the current members of the American Bar Association judiciary committee who reside in the circuit;

w. the president, or personal designee, of the Federal Bar Association and the regional representatives;

x. the president, or personal designee, of the National Bar Association and the regional representatives;

y. the executive director and the attorney board members of the historical society;

z. state attorneys general or their designees;

aa. chief judge of the United States Tax Court or designee;

bb. directors of capital case resource centers.

(2) One or more lawyers, as indicated below, who actively practice in the federal courts of the circuit as selected by the judges of the courts hereinafter designated. As the Congress may change the number of active judges from time to time, the number of designees shall be adjusted correspondingly:

	Number of Designees
Eleventh Circuit Court of Appeals	12
Northern District of Alabama	
–District	7
–Bankruptcy	5
Middle District of Alabama	
–District	3
–Bankruptcy	2
Southern District of Alabama	
–District	3
–Bankruptcy	2
Northern District of Florida	

–District	3
–Bankruptcy	1
Middle District of Florida	
–District	9
–Bankruptcy	4
Southern District of Florida	
–District	15
–Bankruptcy	3
Northern District of Georgia	
–District	11
–Bankruptcy	6
Middle District of Georgia	
–District	2
–Bankruptcy	2
Southern District of Georgia	
–District	3
–Bankruptcy	2

The standards used in selecting representative lawyers as members of the conference must bear a direct relationship to the following minimum requirements:

a. the lawyer-members must constitute a fair cross-section of the practitioners of the court, giving due consideration to qualified individuals regardless of race, color, sex, religion, or national origin;

b. each lawyer-member must be interested in the purposes and work of the conference and be willing and able to actively contribute to this end; and

c. each lawyer-member must be willing to assist in implementing conference programs with the local bar.

A court may invite the same lawyer representative to the judicial conference for not more than three years during any five year period, but only if such representative is fully performing the three requirements referred to above and if approved by the circuit chief judge.

(c) Open Judicial Conference. From time to time the Court of Appeals may conduct a judicial conference at which any attorney admitted to practice in one of the several district courts within the Eleventh Circuit or the Eleventh Circuit Court of Appeals may be invited to attend.

(d) Registration Fee. A non-reimbursable registration fee in an amount fixed by the judicial council shall be collected from each member attending the conference. The sums so collected shall be used to defray conference expenses. Any excess shall be placed in a separately maintained Eleventh Circuit Judicial Conference Fund that shall be used for the purpose of paying the expense of other conference or future conference-related activities.

(e) Secretary of the Conference. The circuit executive, who shall be secretary of the conference, shall be responsible for collection and disbursement of conference funds, for all records and accounts of the conference, and for the staff support required for conducting the conference, and shall perform such other duties as may be necessary to ensure efficient operation of the conference.

[Amended effective February 26, 1986; April 1, 1991.]

ADDENDUM TWO. PROCEDURES IN PROCEEDINGS FOR REVIEW OF ORDERS OF THE FEDERAL ENERGY REGULATORY COMMISSION

(a) Petition for Review. The petition for review shall specify as a part of its caption the number, date, and identification of the order to be reviewed and append the service list required by FRAP 15(c). The petition shall contain a Certificate of Interested Persons and Corporate Disclosure Statement as described in FRAP 26.1 and the accompanying circuit rules.

(b) Docketing. Petitions for review and other documents concerning commission orders in the same number series (i.e., 699, 699A, 699B) shall be assigned to the same docket in this court.

(c) Intervention.

(1) *Party.* A party to a commission proceeding may intervene in a review of the same proceeding in this court by filing a notice of intervention in the docket assigned to the petition for review of any order entered in such proceeding. The notice shall state whether the intervenor is a petitioner who objects to the order or a respondent who supports the order. A notice of intervention shall confer petitioner or respondent status on the intervening party as to all proceedings in the docket.

(2) *Nonparty.* One not a party to a commission proceeding who desires to intervene in a review of that proceeding in this court shall file with the clerk and serve upon all parties to the proceeding a motion for leave to intervene. The motion shall contain a concise statement of the interest of the moving party, the grounds upon which intervention is sought, and a statement why the interest asserted is not adequately protected by existing parties. Any opposition to the motion shall be filed within 10 days of service.

(d) Docketing Statement. Within 30 days of the initial petition for review but not later than 10 days after the expiration of the period permitted for filing a petition for review, all parties filing petitions for review shall file a joint docketing statement that shall:

(1) list each issue to be raised in the review;

(2) list any other review proceeding pending as to the same order in any other court, and

(3) append copies of the order to be reviewed.

A petitioner who files for review after a docketing statement has been filed shall specify in the petition for review any exceptions taken or additions to the issues listed in the docketing statement. A party who intervenes after a docketing statement has been filed shall specify in the notice of intervention any exceptions taken to the issues listed in the docketing statement.

(e) Venue. Upon the filing with the judicial panel on multidistrict litigation of notice that petitions for review have been filed in more than one court, further proceedings in this court shall be governed by 28 U.S.C. § 2112.

(f) Prehearing Conference. Ten days after the filing of a docketing statement or 10 days after entry of an order by the court deciding a venue issue, whichever is later, the clerk may notice a prehearing conference to:

(1) simplify and define issues;

(2) agree on an appendix and record;

(3) assign joint briefing responsibilities and schedule briefs, and;

(4) handle such other matters as may aid in disposing of the proceeding. Except for good cause shown a party who petitions for review or intervenes in a docket after prehearing conference has been held will be bound by the result of the prehearing conference.

(g) Severance. A petitioner or respondent may move to sever parties or issues on a showing of prejudice.

(For other provisions governing review of administrative agencies, boards, and commissions, see FRAP 15.)

[Amended effective April 1, 1991.]

ADDENDUM THREE. RULES FOR JUDICIAL–CONDUCT AND JUDICIAL–DISABILITY PROCEEDINGS

PREFACE

These Rules were promulgated by the Judicial Conference of the United States, after public comment, pursuant to 28 U.S.C. §§ 331 and 358, to establish standards and procedures for addressing complaints filed by complainants or identified by chief judges under the Judicial Conduct and Disability Act, 28 U.S.C. §§ 351–364.

[Adopted March 11, 2008, effective April 10, 2008.]

ARTICLE I. GENERAL PROVISIONS

RULE 1. SCOPE

These Rules govern proceedings under the Judicial Conduct and Disability Act (the Act), 28 U.S.C. §§ 351–364, to determine whether a covered judge has engaged in conduct prejudicial to the effective and expeditious administration of the business of the courts or is unable to discharge the duties of office because of mental or physical disability.

[Adopted March 11, 2008, effective April 10, 2008. Amended effective September 17, 2015.]

Commentary on Rule 1

In September 2006, the Judicial Conduct and Disability Act Study Committee ("Breyer Committee"), appointed in 2004 by Chief Justice Rehnquist, presented a report ("Breyer Committee Report"), 239 F.R.D. 116 (Sept. 2006), to Chief Justice Roberts that evaluated implementation of the Judicial Conduct and Disability Act of 1980, 28 U.S.C. §§ 351–364. The Breyer Committee had been formed in response to criticism from the public and Congress regarding the effectiveness of the Act's implementation. The Executive Committee of the Judicial Conference directed its Committee on Judicial Conduct and Disability to consider the Breyer Committee's recommendations and to report on their implementation to the Conference.

The Breyer Committee found that it could not evaluate implementation of the Act without establishing interpretive standards, Breyer Committee Report, 239 F.R.D. at 132, and that a major problem faced by chief judges in implementing the Act was the lack of authoritative interpretive standards. *Id.* at 212–15. The Breyer Committee then established standards to guide its evaluation, some of which were new formulations and some of which were taken from the "Illustrative Rules Governing Complaints of Judicial Misconduct and Disability," discussed below. The principal standards used by the Breyer Committee are in Appendix E of its Report. *Id.* at 238.

Based on the Breyer Committee's findings, the Committee on Judicial Conduct and Disability concluded that there was a need for the Judicial Conference to exercise its power under Section 358 of the Act to fashion standards guiding the various officers and bodies that must exercise responsibility under the Act. To that end, the Committee on Judicial Conduct and Disability proposed rules that were based largely on Appendix E of the Breyer Committee Report and the Illustrative Rules.

The Illustrative Rules were originally prepared in 1986 by the Special Committee of the Conference of Chief Judges of the United States Courts of Appeals, and were subsequently revised and amended, most recently in 2000, by the predecessor to the Committee on Judicial Conduct and Disability. The Illustrative Rules were adopted, with minor variations, by circuit judicial councils, to govern complaints under the Judicial Conduct and Disability Act.

After being submitted for public comment pursuant to 28 U.S.C. § 358(c), the Judicial Conference promulgated the present Rules on March 11, 2008. They were amended on September 17, 2015.

RULE 2. EFFECT AND CONSTRUCTION

(a) Generally. These Rules are mandatory; they supersede any conflicting judicial-council rules. Judicial councils may promulgate additional rules to implement the Act as long as those rules do not conflict with these Rules.

(b) Exception. A Rule will not apply if, when performing duties authorized by the Act, a chief judge, a special committee, a judicial council, the Committee on Judicial Conduct and Disability, or the Judicial Conference expressly finds that exceptional circumstances render application of that Rule in a particular proceeding manifestly unjust or contrary to the purposes of the Act or these Rules.

[Adopted March 11, 2008, effective April 10, 2008. Amended effective September 17, 2015.]

Commentary on Rule 2

Unlike the Illustrative Rules, these Rules provide mandatory and nationally uniform provisions governing the substantive and procedural aspects of misconduct and disability proceedings under the Act. The mandatory nature of these Rules is authorized by 28 U.S.C. §§ 358(a) and (c). Judicial councils retain the power to promulgate rules consistent with these Rules. For example, a local rule may authorize the electronic distribution of materials pursuant to Rule 8(b).

Rule 2(b) recognizes that unforeseen and exceptional circumstances may call for a different approach in particular cases.

RULE 3. DEFINITIONS

(a) Chief Judge. "Chief judge" means the chief judge of a United States court of appeals, of the United States Court of International Trade, or of the United States Court of Federal Claims.

(b) Circuit Clerk. "Circuit clerk" means a clerk of a United States court of appeals, the clerk of the United States Court of International Trade, the clerk of the United States Court of Federal Claims, or the circuit executive of the United States Court of Appeals for the Federal Circuit.

(c) Complaint. A complaint is:

(1) a document that, in accordance with Rule 6, is filed by any person in his or her individual capacity or on behalf of a professional organization; or

(2) information from any source, other than a document described in (c)(1), that gives a chief judge probable cause to believe that a covered judge, as defined in Rule 4, has engaged in misconduct or may have a disability, whether or not the information is framed as or is intended to be an allegation of misconduct or disability.

(d) Court of Appeals, District Court, and District Judge. "Court of appeals," "district court," and "district judge," where appropriate, include the United States Court of Federal Claims, the United States Court of International Trade, and the judges thereof.

(e) Disability. "Disability" is a temporary or permanent impairment, physical or mental, rendering a judge unable to discharge the duties of the particular judicial office. Examples of disability include substance abuse, the inability to stay awake during court proceedings, or impairment of cognitive abilities that renders the judge unable to function effectively.

(f) Judicial Council and Circuit. "Judicial council" and "circuit," where appropriate, include any courts designated in 28 U.S.C. § 363.

(g) Magistrate Judge. "Magistrate judge," where appropriate, includes a special master appointed by the Court of Federal Claims under 42 U.S.C. § 300aa–12(c).

(h) Misconduct. Cognizable misconduct:

(1) is conduct prejudicial to the effective and expeditious administration of the business of the courts. Misconduct includes, but is not limited to:

(A) using the judge's office to obtain special treatment for friends or relatives;

(B) accepting bribes, gifts, or other personal favors related to the judicial office;

(C) having improper discussions with parties or counsel for one side in a case;

(D) treating litigants, attorneys, or others in a demonstrably egregious and hostile manner;

(E) engaging in partisan political activity or making inappropriately partisan statements;

(F) soliciting funds for organizations;

(G) retaliating against complainants, witnesses, or others for their participation in this complaint process;

(H) refusing, without good cause shown, to cooperate in the investigation of a complaint under these Rules; or

(I) violating other specific, mandatory standards of judicial conduct, such as those pertaining to restrictions on outside income and requirements for financial disclosure.

(2) is conduct occurring outside the performance of official duties if the conduct might have a prejudicial effect on the administration of the business of the courts, including a substantial and widespread lowering of public confidence in the courts among reasonable people.

(3) does not include:

(A) an allegation that is directly related to the merits of a decision or procedural ruling. An allegation that calls into question the correctness of a judge's ruling, including a failure to recuse, without more, is merits-related. If the decision or ruling is alleged to be the result of an improper motive, *e.g.*, a bribe, ex parte contact, racial or ethnic bias, or improper conduct in rendering a decision or ruling, such as personally derogatory remarks irrelevant to the issues, the complaint is not cognizable to the extent that it attacks the merits.

(B) an allegation about delay in rendering a decision or ruling, unless the allegation concerns an improper motive in delaying a particular decision or habitual delay in a significant number of unrelated cases.

(i) Subject Judge. "Subject judge" means any judge described in Rule 4 who is the subject of a complaint.

[Adopted March 11, 2008, effective April 10, 2008. Amended effective September 17, 2015.]

Commentary on Rule 3

Rule 3 is derived and adapted from the Breyer Committee Report and the Illustrative Rules.

Unless otherwise specified or the context otherwise indicates, the term "complaint" is used in these Rules to refer both to complaints identified by a chief judge under Rule 5 and to complaints filed by a complainant under Rule 6.

Under the Act, a "complaint" may be filed by "any person" or "identified" by a chief judge. *See* 28 U.S.C. §§ 351(a), (b). Under Rule 3(c)(1), complaints may be submitted by a person, in his or her individual capacity, or by a professional organization. Generally, the word "complaint" brings to mind the commencement of an adversary proceeding in which the contending parties are left to present the evidence and legal arguments, and judges play the role of an essentially passive arbiter. The Act, however, establishes an administrative, inquisitorial process. For example, even absent a complaint under Rule 6, chief judges are expected in some circumstances to trigger the process—"identify a complaint," *see* 28 U.S.C. § 351(b) and Rule 5—and conduct an investigation without becoming a party. *See* 28 U.S.C. § 352(a); Breyer Committee Report, 239 F.R.D. at 214; Illustrative Rule 2(j). Even when a complaint is filed by someone other than the chief judge, the complainant lacks many rights that a litigant would have, and the chief judge, instead of being limited to the "four corners of the complaint," must, under Rule 11, proceed as though misconduct or disability has been alleged where the complainant reveals information of misconduct or disability but does not claim it as such. *See* Breyer Committee Report, 239 F.R.D. at 183–84.

An allegation of misconduct or disability filed under Rule 6 is a "complaint," and the Rule so provides in subsection (c)(1). However, both the nature of the process and the use of the term "identify" suggest that the word "complaint" covers more than a document formally triggering the process. The process relies on chief judges considering known information and triggering the process when appropriate. "Identifying" a "complaint," therefore, is best understood as the chief judge's concluding that information known to the judge constitutes probable cause to believe that misconduct occurred or a disability exists, whether or not the information is framed as, or intended to be, an accusation. This definition is codified in subsection (c)(2).

Rule 3(e) relates to disability and provides only the most general definition, recognizing that a fact-specific approach is the only one available. A mental disability could involve cognitive impairment or any psychiatric or psychological condition that renders the judge unable to discharge the duties of office. Such duties may include those that are administrative. If, for example, the judge is a chief judge, the judicial council, fulfilling its obligation under 28 U.S.C. § 332(d)(1) to make "necessary and appropriate orders for the effective and expeditious administration of justice," may find, under 28 U.S.C. § 45(d) or § 136(e), that the judge is "temporarily unable to perform" his or her chief-judge duties. In that event, an appropriate remedy could involve, under Rule 20(b)(1)(D)(vii), temporary reassignment of chief-judge duties to the next judge statutorily eligible to perform them.

The phrase "prejudicial to the effective and expeditious administration of the business of the courts" is not subject to precise definition, and subsection (h)(1) therefore provides some specific examples. Although the Code of Conduct for United States Judges may be informative, its main precepts are highly general; the Code is in many potential applications aspirational rather than a set of disciplinary rules. Ultimately, the responsibility for determining what constitutes misconduct under the statute is the province of the judicial council of the circuit, subject to such review and limitations as are ordained by the statute and by these Rules.

Even where specific, mandatory rules exist—for example, governing the receipt of gifts by judges, outside earned income, and financial disclosure obligations—the distinction between the misconduct statute and these specific, mandatory rules must be borne in mind. For example, an inadvertent, minor violation of any one of these rules, promptly remedied when called to the attention of the judge, might still be a violation but might not rise to the level of misconduct under the statute. By contrast, a pattern of such violations of the Code might well rise to the level of misconduct.

Under Rule 3(h)(1)(G), a judge's efforts to retaliate against any person for his or her involvement in the complaint process may constitute cognizable misconduct. The Rule makes this explicit in the interest of public confidence in the complaint process.

Rule 3(h)(1)(H) provides that a judge's refusal, without good cause shown, to cooperate in the investigation of a complaint under these Rules may constitute cognizable misconduct. While the exercise of rights under the Fifth Amendment to the Constitution would constitute good cause under Rule 3(h)(1)(H), given the fact-specific nature of the inquiry, it is not possible to otherwise anticipate all circumstances that might also constitute good cause. The Commentary on Rule 13 provides additional discussion regarding Rule 3(h)(1)(H). The Rules contemplate that judicial councils will not consider commencing proceedings under Rule 3(h)(1)(H) except as necessary after other means to acquire the information have been tried or have proven futile.

Rule 3(h)(2) reflects that an allegation can meet the statutory standard even though the judge's alleged conduct did not occur in the course of the performance of official duties. And some conduct in the categories listed under subsection (h)(1), or in categories not listed, might, depending on the circumstances, amount to "misconduct" under subsection (h)(2), or under both subsection (h)(1) and subsection (h)(2). Also, the Code of Conduct for United States Judges expressly covers a wide range of extra-official activities, and some of these activities may constitute misconduct. For example, allegations that a judge solicited funds for a charity or participated in a partisan political event are cognizable under the Act.

On the other hand, judges are entitled to some leeway in extra-official activities. For example, misconduct may not include a judge being repeatedly and publicly discourteous to a spouse (not including physical abuse) even though this might cause some reasonable people to have diminished confidence in the courts. Rule 3(h)(2) states that conduct of this sort is covered, for example, when it might lead to a "substantial and widespread" lowering of such confidence.

Rule 3(h)(3)(A) tracks the Act, 28 U.S.C. § 352(b)(1)(A)(ii), in excluding from the definition of misconduct allegations "[d]irectly related to the merits of a decision or procedural ruling." This exclusion preserves the independence of judges in the exercise of judicial power by ensuring that the complaint procedure is not used to collaterally attack the substance of a judge's ruling. Any allegation that calls into question the correctness of an official action of a judge—without more—is merits-related. The phrase "decision or procedural ruling" is not limited to rulings issued in deciding Article III cases or controversies. Thus, a complaint challenging the correctness of a chief judge's determination to dismiss a prior misconduct complaint would be properly dismissed as merits-related—in other words, as challenging the substance of the judge's administrative determination to dismiss the complaint—even though it does not concern the judge's rulings in Article III litigation. Similarly, an allegation that a judge had incorrectly declined to approve a Criminal Justice Act voucher is merits-related under this standard.

Conversely, an allegation—however unsupported—that a judge conspired with a prosecutor to make a particular ruling is not merits-related, even though it "relates" to a ruling in a colloquial sense. Such an allegation attacks the propriety of conspiring with the prosecutor and goes beyond a challenge to the correctness—"the merits"—of the ruling itself. An allegation that a judge ruled against the complainant because the complainant is a member of a particular racial or ethnic group, or because the judge dislikes the complainant personally, is also not merits-related. Such an allegation attacks the propriety of arriving at rulings with an illicit or improper motive. Similarly, an allegation that a judge used an inappropriate term to refer to a class of people is not merits-related even if the judge used it on the bench or in an opinion; the correctness of the judge's rulings is not at stake. An allegation that a judge treated litigants, attorneys, or others in a demonstrably egregious and hostile manner while on the bench is also not merits-related.

The existence of an appellate remedy is usually irrelevant to whether an allegation is merits-related. The merits-related ground for dismissal exists to protect judges' independence in making rulings, not to protect or promote the appellate process. A complaint alleging an incorrect ruling is merits-related even though the complainant has no recourse from that ruling. By the same token, an allegation that is otherwise cognizable under the Act should not be dismissed merely because an appellate remedy appears to exist (for example, vacating a ruling that resulted from an improper *ex parte* communication). However, there may be occasions when appellate and misconduct proceedings overlap, and consideration and disposition of a complaint under these Rules may be properly deferred by the chief judge until the appellate proceedings are concluded in order to avoid inconsistent decisions, among other things.

Because of the special need to protect judges' independence in deciding what to say in an opinion or ruling, a somewhat different standard applies to determine the merits-relatedness of a non-frivolous allegation that a judge's language in a ruling reflected an improper motive. If the judge's language was relevant to the case at hand—for example, a statement that a claim is legally or factually "frivolous"—then the judge's choice of language is presumptively merits-related and excluded, absent evidence apart from the ruling itself suggesting an improper motive. If, on the other hand, the challenged language does not seem relevant on its face, then an additional inquiry under Rule 11 is necessary.

With regard to Rule 3(h)(3)(B), a complaint of delay in a single case is excluded as merits-related. Such an allegation may be said to challenge the correctness of an official action of the judge—in other words, assigning a low priority to deciding the particular case. But, by the same token, an allegation of a habitual pattern of delay in a significant number of unrelated cases, or an allegation of deliberate delay in a single case arising out of an illicit motive, is not merits-related.

The remaining subsections of Rule 3 provide technical definitions clarifying the application of the Rules to the various kinds of courts covered.

RULE 4. COVERED JUDGES

A complaint under these Rules may concern the actions or capacity only of judges of United States courts of appeals, judges of United States district courts, judges of United States bankruptcy courts, United States magistrate judges, and judges of the courts specified in 28 U.S.C. § 363.

[Adopted March 11, 2008, effective April 10, 2008.]

Commentary on Rule 4

This Rule tracks the Act. Rule 8(c) and (d) contain provisions as to the handling of complaints against persons not covered by the Act, such as other court personnel, or against both covered judges and noncovered persons.

ARTICLE II. INITIATION OF A COMPLAINT

RULE 5. IDENTIFICATION OF COMPLAINT

(a) Identification. When a chief judge has information constituting reasonable grounds for inquiry into whether a covered judge has engaged in misconduct or has a disability, the chief judge may conduct an inquiry, as he or she deems appropriate, into the accuracy of the information even if no related complaint has been filed. A chief judge who finds probable cause to believe that misconduct has occurred or that a disability exists may seek an informal resolution that he or she finds satisfactory. If no informal resolution is achieved or is feasible, the chief judge may identify a complaint and, by written order stating the reasons, begin the review provided in Rule 11. If the evidence of misconduct is clear and convincing and no informal resolution is achieved or is feasible, the chief judge must identify a complaint. A chief judge must not decline to identify a complaint merely because the person making the allegation has not filed a complaint under Rule 6. This Rule is subject to Rule 7.

(b) Submission Not Fully Complying With Rule 6. A legible submission in substantial but not full compliance with Rule 6 must be considered as possible grounds for the identification of a complaint under Rule 5(a).

[Adopted March 11, 2008, effective April 10, 2008. Amended effective September 17, 2015.]

Commentary on Rule 5

This Rule is adapted from the Breyer Committee Report, 239 F.R.D. at 245–46.

The Act authorizes a chief judge, by written order stating reasons, to identify a complaint and thereby dispense with the filing of a written complaint. *See* 28 U.S.C. § 351(b). Under Rule 5, when a chief judge becomes aware of information constituting reasonable grounds to inquire into possible misconduct or disability on the part of a covered judge, and no formal complaint has been filed, the chief judge has the power in his or her discretion to begin an appropriate inquiry. A chief judge's decision whether to informally seek a resolution and/or to identify a complaint is guided by the results of that inquiry. If the chief judge concludes that there is probable cause to believe that misconduct has occurred or a disability exists, the chief judge may seek an informal resolution, if feasible, and if failing in that, may identify a complaint. Discretion is accorded largely for the reasons police officers and prosecutors have discretion in making arrests or bringing charges. The matter may be trivial and isolated, based on marginal evidence, or otherwise highly unlikely to lead to a misconduct or disability finding. On the other hand, if the inquiry leads the chief judge to conclude that there is clear and convincing evidence of misconduct or a disability, and no satisfactory informal resolution has been achieved or is feasible, the chief judge is required to identify a complaint.

An informal resolution is one agreed to by the subject judge and found satisfactory by the chief judge. Because an informal resolution under Rule 5 reached before a complaint is filed under Rule 6 will generally cause a subsequent Rule 6 complaint alleging the identical matter to be concluded, *see* Rule 11(d), the chief judge must be sure that the resolution is fully appropriate before endorsing it. In doing so, the chief judge must balance the seriousness of the matter against the particular judge's alacrity in addressing the issue. The availability of this procedure should encourage attempts at swift remedial action before a formal complaint is filed.

When a chief judge identifies a complaint, a written order stating the reasons for the identification must be provided; this begins the process articulated in Rule 11. Rule 11 provides that once a chief judge has identified a complaint, the chief judge, subject to the disqualification provisions of Rule 25, will perform, with respect to that complaint, all functions assigned to the chief judge for the determination of complaints filed by a complainant.

In high-visibility situations, it may be desirable for a chief judge to identify a complaint without first seeking an informal resolution (and then, if the circumstances warrant, dismiss or conclude the identified complaint without appointment of a special committee) in order to assure the public that the allegations have not been ignored.

A chief judge's decision not to identify a complaint under Rule 5 is not appealable and is subject to Rule 3(h)(3)(A), which excludes merits-related complaints from the definition of misconduct.

A chief judge may not decline to identify a complaint solely on the basis that the unfiled allegations could be raised by one or more persons in a filed complaint, but none of these persons has opted to do so.

Subsection (a) concludes by stating that this Rule is "subject to Rule 7." This is intended to establish that only (i) the chief judge of the home circuit of a potential subject judge, or (ii) the chief judge of a circuit in which misconduct is alleged to have occurred in the course of official business while the potential subject judge was sitting by designation, shall have the power or a duty under this Rule to identify a complaint.

Subsection (b) provides that submissions that do not comply with the requirements of Rule 6(d) must be considered under Rule 5(a). For instance, if a complaint has been filed but the form submitted is unsigned, or the truth of the statements therein are not verified in writing under penalty of perjury, then a chief judge must nevertheless consider the allegations as known information and as a possible basis for the identification of a complaint under the process described in Rule 5(a).

RULE 6. FILING OF COMPLAINT

(a) Form. A complainant may use the form reproduced in the appendix to these Rules or a form designated by the rules of the judicial council in the circuit in which the complaint is filed. A complaint form is also available on each court of appeals' website or may be obtained from the circuit clerk or any district court or bankruptcy court within the circuit. A form is not necessary to file a complaint, but the complaint must be written and must include the information described in (b).

(b) Brief Statement of Facts. A complaint must contain a concise statement that details the specific facts on which the claim of misconduct or disability is based. The statement of facts should include a description of:

(1) what happened;

(2) when and where the relevant events happened;

(3) any information that would help an investigator check the facts; and

(4) for an allegation of disability, any additional facts that form the basis of that allegation.

(c) Legibility. A complaint should be typewritten if possible. If not typewritten, it must be legible. An illegible complaint will be returned to the complainant with a request to resubmit it in legible form. If a resubmitted complaint is still illegible, it will not be accepted for filing.

(d) Complainant's Address and Signature; Verification. The complainant must provide a contact address and sign the complaint. The truth of the statements made in the complaint must be verified in writing under penalty of perjury. If any of these requirements are not met, the submission will be accepted, but it will be reviewed under only Rule 5(b).

(e) Number of Copies; Envelope Marking. The complainant shall provide the number of copies of the complaint required by local rule. Each copy should be in an envelope marked "Complaint of Misconduct" or "Complaint of Disability." The envelope must not show the name of any subject judge.

[Adopted March 11, 2008, effective April 10, 2008. Amended effective September 17, 2015.]

Commentary on Rule 6

The Rule is adapted from the Illustrative Rules and is self-explanatory.

RULE 6.1. FORM [11TH CIR. JCDR 6.1]

Complaints may be filed on the form contained in the Appendix to these Rules, and available from these other sources:

- on the court's web site at www.ca11.uscourts.gov;
- by telephoning the court's Clerk's Office at 404–335–6577;
- by visiting or writing to the court's Clerk's Office at the address shown in 11th Cir. JCDR 6.6; or
- from the clerk of any district court or bankruptcy court within the Eleventh Circuit.

[Adopted effective April 1, 2009.]

RULE 6.2. STATEMENT OF FACTS: LENGTH; FORMAT [11TH CIR. JCDR 6.2]

The required statement of facts should be attached to the complaint form, and should not exceed five (5) pages. To assure legibility, the statement of facts should conform to the following technical requirements:

- 8½ × 11 inch paper;
- Only one side of the paper should be used;
- The text should be double-spaced, but quotations more than two lines long may be indented and single-spaced; headings and footnotes may be single-spaced;
- Margins should be at least one inch on all four sides; page numbers may appear in the margins but no text should appear there;
- If typed, either a proportionally spaced or monospaced typeface may be used; a proportionally spaced typeface should be 14–point or larger; a monospaced typeface should not contain more than 10½ characters per inch.

[Adopted effective April 1, 2009.]

RULE 6.3. SUBMISSION OF DOCUMENTS [11TH CIR. JCDR 6.3]

Documents referred to in the statement of facts may be filed with the complaint. The statement should cite the page(s) of such document(s) that the complainant deems pertinent to the allegations of the complaint.

[Adopted effective April 1, 2009.]

RULE 6.4. NUMBER OF COPIES [11TH CIR. JCDR 6.4]

Four copies each of the complaint, statement of facts, and any document(s) filed therewith must be filed with the Clerk.

[Adopted effective April 1, 2009.]

RULE 6.5. ANONYMOUS COMPLAINTS [11TH CIR. JCDR 6.5]

An anonymous complaint will not be accepted for filing by the Clerk. Nevertheless, the Clerk will forward such a complaint to the Chief Judge.

[Adopted effective April 1, 2009.]

RULE 6.6. PLACE OF FILING [11TH CIR. JCDR 6.6]

A complaint must be delivered or mailed in an envelope to:

Clerk
United States Court of Appeals
56 Forsyth Street, N.W.
Atlanta, Georgia 30303

The envelope should be marked "Complaint of Misconduct" or "Complaint of Disability." The name of the subject judge must not appear on the envelope.

[Adopted effective April 1, 2009.]

RULE 6.7. SUPPLEMENTATION [11TH CIR. JCDR 6.7]

Once filed, a complaint may not be supplemented or modified by additional statements or documents unless authorized by order of the Chief Judge.

[Adopted effective April 1, 2009.]

RULE 6.8. NO FILING FEE [11TH CIR. JCDR 6.8]

There is no filing fee for a complaint of misconduct or disability.

[Adopted effective April 1, 2009.]

RULE 7. WHERE TO INITIATE COMPLAINT

(a) Where to File. Except as provided in (b),

(1) a complaint against a judge of a United States court of appeals, a United States district court, a United States bankruptcy court, or a United States magistrate judge must be filed with the circuit clerk in the jurisdiction in which the subject judge holds office.

(2) a complaint against a judge of the United States Court of International Trade or the United States Court of Federal Claims must be filed with the respective clerk of that court.

(3) a complaint against a judge of the United States Court of Appeals for the Federal Circuit must be filed with the circuit executive of that court.

(b) Misconduct in Another Circuit; Transfer. If a complaint alleges misconduct in the course of official business while the subject judge was sitting on a court by designation under 28 U.S.C. §§ 291–293 and 294(d), the complaint may be filed or identified with the circuit clerk of that circuit or of the subject judge's home circuit. The proceeding will continue in the circuit of the first-filed or first-identified complaint. The judicial council of the circuit where the complaint was first filed or first identified may transfer the complaint to the subject judge's home circuit or to the circuit where the alleged misconduct occurred, as the case may be.

[Adopted March 11, 2008, effective April 10, 2008. Amended effective September 17, 2015.]

Commentary on Rule 7

Title 28 U.S.C. § 351 states that complaints are to be filed with "the clerk of the court of appeals for the circuit." However, in many circuits, this role is filled by circuit executives. Accordingly, the term "circuit clerk," as defined in Rule 3(b) and used throughout these Rules, applies to circuit executives.

Section 351 uses the term "the circuit" in a way that suggests that either the home circuit of the subject judge or the circuit in which misconduct is alleged to have occurred is the proper venue for complaints. With an exception for judges sitting by designation, the Rule requires the filing or identification of a misconduct or disability complaint in the circuit in which the judge holds office, largely based on the administrative perspective of the Act. Given the Act's emphasis on the future conduct of the business of the courts, the circuit in which the judge holds office is the appropriate forum because that circuit is likely best able to influence a judge's future behavior in constructive ways.

However, when judges sit by designation, the non-home circuit has a strong interest in redressing misconduct in the course of official business, and where allegations also involve a member of the bar—*ex parte* contact between an attorney and a judge, for example—it may often be desirable to have the judicial and bar misconduct proceedings take place in the same venue. Rule 7(b), therefore, allows transfer to, or filing or identification of a complaint in, the non-home circuit. The proceeding may be transferred by the judicial council of the filing or identified circuit to the other circuit.

RULE 8. ACTION BY CIRCUIT CLERK

(a) Receipt of Complaint. Upon receiving a complaint against a judge filed under Rule 6 or identified under Rule 5, the circuit clerk must open a file, assign a docket number according to a uniform numbering scheme promulgated by the Committee on Judicial Conduct and Disability, and acknowledge the complaint's receipt.

(b) Distribution of Copies. The circuit clerk must promptly send copies of a complaint filed under Rule 6 to the chief judge or the judge authorized to act as chief judge under Rule 25(f), and copies of complaints filed under Rule 6 or identified under Rule 5 to each subject judge. The circuit clerk must retain the original complaint. Any further distribution should be as provided by local rule.

(c) Complaint Against Noncovered Person. If the circuit clerk receives a complaint about a person not holding an office described in Rule 4, the clerk must not accept the complaint under these Rules.

(d) Complaint Against Judge and Another Noncovered Person. If the circuit clerk receives a complaint about a judge described in Rule 4 and a person not holding an office described in Rule 4, the clerk must accept the complaint under these Rules only with regard to the judge and must so inform the complainant.

[Adopted March 11, 2008, effective April 10, 2008. Amended effective September 17, 2015.]

Commentary on Rule 8

This Rule is adapted from the Illustrative Rules and is largely self-explanatory.

The uniform docketing scheme described in subsection (a) should take into account potential problems associated with a complaint that names multiple judges. One solution may be to provide separate docket numbers for each subject judge. Separate docket numbers would help avoid difficulties in tracking cases, particularly if a complaint is dismissed with respect to some, but not all of the named judges.

Complaints against noncovered persons are not to be accepted for processing under these Rules but may, of course, be accepted under other circuit rules or procedures for grievances.

RULE 8.1. RECEIPT OF COMPLAINT NOT IN PROPER FORM [11TH CIR. JCDR 8.1]

Upon receipt of a complaint not filed in the form required by the Rules for Judicial–Conduct and Judicial–Disability Proceedings adopted by the Judicial Conference of the United States, the Clerk shall return the complaint to the complainant and explain why it was returned.

[Adopted effective April 1, 2009.]

RULE 9. TIME FOR FILING OR IDENTIFYING COMPLAINT

A complaint may be filed or identified at any time. If the passage of time has made an accurate and fair investigation of a complaint impracticable, the complaint must be dismissed under Rule 11(c)(1)(E).

[Adopted March 11, 2008, effective April 10, 2008. Amended effective September 17, 2015.]

Commentary on Rule 9

This Rule is adapted from the Act, 28 U.S.C. §§ 351, 352(b)(1)(A)(iii), and the Illustrative Rules.

RULE 10. ABUSE OF COMPLAINT PROCEDURE

(a) Abusive Complaints. A complainant who has filed repetitive, harassing, or frivolous complaints, or has otherwise abused the complaint procedure, may be restricted from filing further complaints. After giving the complainant an opportunity to show cause in writing why his or her right to file further complaints should not be limited, the judicial council may prohibit, restrict, or impose conditions on the complainant's use of the complaint procedure. Upon written request of the complainant, the judicial council may revise or withdraw any prohibition, restriction, or condition previously imposed.

(b) Orchestrated Complaints. When many essentially identical complaints from different complainants are received and appear to be part of an orchestrated campaign, the chief judge may recommend that the judicial council issue a written order instructing the circuit clerk to accept only a certain number of such complaints for filing and to refuse to accept additional complaints. The circuit clerk must send a copy of any such order to anyone whose complaint was not accepted.

[Adopted March 11, 2008, effective April 10, 2008. Amended effective September 17, 2015.]

Commentary on Rule 10

This Rule is adapted from the Illustrative Rules.

Rule 10(a) provides a mechanism for a judicial council to restrict the filing of further complaints by a single complainant who has abused the complaint procedure. In some instances, however, the complaint procedure may be abused in a manner for which the remedy provided in Rule 10(a) may not be appropriate. For example, some circuits have been inundated with submissions of dozens or hundreds of essentially identical complaints against the same judge or judges, all submitted by different complainants. In many of these instances, persons with grievances against a particular judge or judges used the Internet or other technology to orchestrate mass complaint-filing campaigns against them. If each complaint submitted as part of such a campaign were accepted for filing and processed according to these Rules, there would be a serious drain on court resources without any benefit to the adjudication of the underlying merits.

A judicial council may, therefore, respond to such mass filings under Rule 10(b) by declining to accept repetitive complaints for filing, regardless of the fact that the complaints are nominally submitted by different complainants. When the first complaint or complaints have been dismissed on the merits, and when further, essentially identical submissions follow, the judicial council may issue a second order noting that these are identical or repetitive complaints, directing the circuit clerk not to accept these complaints or any further such complaints for filing, and directing the clerk to send each putative complainant copies of both orders.

ARTICLE III. REVIEW OF A COMPLAINT BY THE CHIEF JUDGE

RULE 11. CHIEF JUDGE'S REVIEW

(a) Purpose of Chief Judge's Review. When a complaint is identified by the chief judge or is filed, the chief judge must review it unless the chief judge is disqualified under Rule 25. If a complaint contains information constituting evidence of misconduct or disability, but the complainant does not claim it as such, the chief judge must treat the complaint as if it did allege misconduct or disability and give notice to the subject judge. After reviewing a complaint, the chief judge must determine whether it should be:

(1) dismissed;

(2) concluded on the ground that voluntary corrective action has been taken;

(3) concluded because intervening events have made action on the complaint no longer necessary; or

(4) referred to a special committee.

(b) Chief Judge's Inquiry. In determining what action to take under Rule 11(a), the chief judge may conduct a limited inquiry. The chief judge, or a designee, may communicate orally or in writing with the complainant, the subject judge, and any others who may have knowledge of the matter, and may obtain and review transcripts and other relevant documents. In conducting the inquiry, the chief judge must not determine any reasonably disputed issue. Any such determination must be left to a special committee appointed under Rule 11(f) and to the judicial council that considers the special committee's report.

(c) Dismissal.

(1) *Permissible Grounds.* A complaint must be dismissed in whole or in part to the extent that the chief judge concludes that the complaint:

(A) alleges conduct that, even if true, is not prejudicial to the effective and expeditious administration of the business of the courts and does not indicate a mental or physical disability resulting in the inability to discharge the duties of judicial office;

(B) is directly related to the merits of a decision or procedural ruling;

(C) is frivolous;

(D) is based on allegations lacking sufficient evidence to raise an inference that misconduct has occurred or that a disability exists;

(E) is based on allegations that are incapable of being established through investigation;

(F) has been filed in the wrong circuit under Rule 7; or

(G) is otherwise not appropriate for consideration under the Act.

(2) *Impermissible Grounds.* A complaint must not be dismissed solely because it repeats allegations of a previously dismissed complaint if it also contains material information not previously considered and does not constitute harassment of the subject judge.

(d) Corrective Action. The chief judge may conclude a complaint proceeding in whole or in part if:

(1) an informal resolution under Rule 5 satisfactory to the chief judge was reached before the complaint was filed under Rule 6; or

(2) the chief judge determines that the subject judge has taken appropriate voluntary corrective action that acknowledges and remedies the problems raised by the complaint.

(e) Intervening Events. The chief judge may conclude a complaint proceeding in whole or in part upon determining that intervening events render some or all of the allegations moot or make remedial action impossible.

(f) Appointment of Special Committee. If some or all of a complaint is not dismissed or concluded, the chief judge must promptly appoint a special committee to investigate the complaint or any relevant portion of it and to make recommendations to the judicial council. Before appointing a special committee, the chief judge must invite the subject judge to respond to the complaint either orally or in writing if the judge was not given an opportunity during the limited inquiry. In the chief judge's discretion, separate complaints may be joined and assigned to a single special committee. Similarly, a single complaint about more than one judge may be severed and more than one special committee appointed.

(g) Notice of Chief Judge's Action; Petition for Review.

(1) *When Chief Judge Appoints Special Committee.* If the chief judge appoints a special committee, the chief judge must notify the complainant and the subject judge that the matter has been referred to a committee, notify the complainant of a complainant's rights under Rule 16, and identify the members of the committee. A copy of the order appointing the special committee must be sent to the Committee on Judicial Conduct and Disability.

(2) *When Chief Judge Disposes of Complaint Without Appointing Special Committee.* If the chief judge disposes of a complaint under Rule 11(c), (d), or (e), the chief judge must prepare a supporting memorandum that sets forth the reasons for the disposition. If the complaint was initiated by identification under Rule 5, the memorandum must so indicate. Except as authorized by 28 U.S.C. § 360, the memorandum must not include the name of the complainant or of the subject judge. The order and memoranda incorporated by reference in the order must be promptly sent to the complainant, the subject judge, and the Committee on Judicial Conduct and Disability.

(3) *Right to Petition for Review.* If the chief judge disposes of a complaint under Rule 11(c), (d), or (e), the complainant and the subject judge must be notified of the right to petition the judicial council for review of the disposition, as provided in Rule 18. If the chief judge so disposes of a complaint that was identified under Rule 5 or filed by its subject judge, the chief judge must transmit the order and memoranda incorporated by reference in the order to the judicial council for review in accordance with Rule 19. In the event of such a transmission, the subject judge may make a written submission to the judicial council but will have no further right of review except as allowed under Rule 21(b)(1)(B). When a disposition is to be reviewed by the judicial council, the chief judge must promptly transmit all materials obtained in connection with the inquiry under Rule 11(b) to the circuit clerk for transmittal to the council.

(h) Public Availability of Chief Judge's Decision. The chief judge's decision must be made public to the extent, at the time, and in the manner provided in Rule 24.

[Adopted March 11, 2008, effective April 10, 2008. Amended effective September 17, 2015.]

Commentary on Rule 11

This Rule describes complaint-review actions available either to a chief judge or, where that judge is the subject judge or is otherwise disqualified under Rule 25, to the judge designated under Rule 25(f) to perform the chief judge's duties under these Rules. Subsection (a) of this Rule provides that where a complaint has been filed under Rule 6, the ordinary doctrines of waiver do not apply. The chief judge must identify as a complaint any misconduct or disability issues raised by the factual allegations of the complaint even if the complainant makes no such claim with regard to those issues. For example, an allegation limited to misconduct in fact-finding that mentions periods during a trial when the judge was asleep must be treated as a complaint regarding disability. Some formal order giving notice of the expanded scope of the proceeding must be given to the subject judge.

Subsection (b) describes the nature of the chief judge's inquiry. It is based largely on the Breyer Committee Report, 239 F.R.D. at 243–45. The Act states that dismissal is appropriate "when a limited inquiry . . . demonstrates that the allegations in the complaint lack any factual foundation or are conclusively refuted by objective evidence." 28 U.S.C. § 352(b)(1)(B). At the same time, however, Section 352(a) states that "[t]he chief judge shall not undertake to make findings of fact about any matter that is reasonably in dispute." These two statutory standards should be read together, so that a matter is not "reasonably" in dispute if a limited inquiry shows that the allegations do not constitute misconduct or disability, that they lack any reliable factual foundation, or that they are conclusively refuted by objective evidence.

In conducting a limited inquiry under subsection (b), the chief judge must avoid determinations of reasonably disputed issues, including reasonably disputed issues as to whether the facts alleged constitute misconduct or disability, which are ordinarily left to the judicial council and its special committee. An allegation of fact is ordinarily not "refuted" simply because the subject judge denies it. The limited inquiry must reveal something more in the way of refutation before it is appropriate to dismiss a complaint that is otherwise cognizable. If it is the complainant's word against the subject judge's—in other words, there is simply no other significant evidence of what happened or of the complainant's unreliability—then there must be a special-committee investigation. Such a credibility issue is a matter "reasonably in dispute" within the meaning of the Act.

However, dismissal following a limited inquiry may occur when a complaint refers to transcripts or to witnesses and the chief judge determines that the transcripts and witnesses all support the subject judge. Breyer Committee Report, 239 F.R.D. at 243. For example, consider a complaint alleging that the subject judge said X, and the complaint mentions, or it is independently clear, that five people may have heard what the judge said. *Id.* The chief judge is told by the subject judge and one witness that the judge did not say X, and the chief judge dismisses the complaint without questioning the other four possible witnesses. *Id.* In this example, the matter remains reasonably in dispute. If all five witnesses say the subject judge did not say X, dismissal is appropriate, but if potential witnesses who are reasonably accessible have not been questioned, then the matter remains reasonably in dispute. *Id.*

Similarly, under subsection (c)(1)(A), if it is clear that the conduct or disability alleged, even if true, is not cognizable under these Rules, the complaint should be dismissed. If that issue is reasonably in dispute, however, dismissal under subsection (c)(1)(A) is inappropriate.

Essentially, the standard articulated in subsection (b) is that used to decide motions for summary judgment pursuant to Fed. R. Civ. P. 56. Genuine issues of material fact are not resolved at the summary judgment stage. A material fact is one that "might affect the outcome of the suit under the governing law," and a dispute is "genuine" if "the evidence is such that a reasonable jury could return a verdict for the nonmoving party." *Anderson v. Liberty Lobby*, 477 U.S. 242, 248 (1986). Similarly, the chief judge may not resolve a genuine issue concerning a material fact or the existence of misconduct or a disability when conducting a limited inquiry pursuant to subsection (b).

Subsection (c) describes the grounds on which a complaint may be dismissed. These are adapted from the Act, 28 U.S.C. § 352(b), and the Breyer Committee Report, 239 F.R.D. at 239–45. Subsection (c)(1)(A) permits dismissal of an allegation that, even if true, does not constitute misconduct or disability under the statutory standard. The proper standards are set out in Rule 3 and discussed in the Commentary on that Rule. Subsection (c)(1)(B) permits dismissal of complaints related to the merits of a decision by a subject judge; this standard is also governed by Rule 3 and its accompanying Commentary.

Subsections (c)(1)(C)–(E) implement the statute by allowing dismissal of complaints that are "frivolous, lacking sufficient evidence to raise an inference that misconduct has occurred, or containing allegations which are incapable of being established through investigation." 28 U.S.C. § 352(b)(1)(A)(iii).

Dismissal of a complaint as "frivolous" under Rule 11(c)(1)(C) will generally occur without any inquiry beyond the face of the complaint. For instance, when the allegations are facially incredible or so lacking in indicia of reliability that no further inquiry is warranted, dismissal under this subsection is appropriate.

A complaint warranting dismissal under Rule 11(c)(1)(D) is illustrated by the following example. Consider a complainant who alleges an impropriety and asserts that he knows of it because it was observed and reported to him by a person who is identified. The subject judge denies that the event occurred. When contacted, the source also denies it. In such a case, the chief judge's proper course of action may turn on whether the source had any role in the allegedly improper conduct. If the complaint was based on a lawyer's statement that he or she had an improper *ex parte* contact with a judge, the lawyer's denial of the impropriety might not be taken as wholly persuasive, and it would be appropriate to conclude that a real factual issue is raised. On the other hand, if the complaint quoted a disinterested third party and that disinterested party denied that the statement had been made, there would be no value in opening a formal investigation. In such a case, it would be appropriate to dismiss the complaint under Rule 11(c)(1)(D).

Rule 11(c)(1)(E) is intended, among other things, to cover situations when no evidence is offered or identified, or when the only identified source is unavailable. Breyer Committee Report, 239 F.R.D. at 243. For example, a complaint alleges that an unnamed attorney told the complainant that the subject judge did X. *Id.* The subject judge denies it. The chief judge requests that the complainant (who does not purport to have observed the subject judge do X) identify the unnamed witness, or that the unnamed witness come forward so that the chief judge can learn the unnamed witness's account. *Id.* The complainant responds that he has spoken with the unnamed witness, that the unnamed witness is an attorney who practices in federal court, and that the unnamed witness is unwilling to be identified or to come forward. *Id.* at 243–44. The allegation is then properly dismissed as containing allegations that are incapable of being established through investigation. *Id.*

If, however, the situation involves a reasonable dispute over credibility, the matter should proceed. For example, the complainant alleges an impropriety and alleges that he or she observed it and that there were no other witnesses; the subject judge denies that the event occurred. Unless the complainant's allegations are facially incredible or so lacking indicia of reliability as to warrant dismissal under Rule 11(c)(1)(C), a special committee must be appointed because there is a material factual question that is reasonably in dispute.

Dismissal is also appropriate when a complaint is filed so long after an alleged event that memory loss, death, or changes to unknown residences prevent a proper investigation.

Subsection (c)(2) indicates that the investigative nature of the process prevents the application of claim preclusion principles where new and material evidence becomes available. However, it also recognizes that at some point a renewed investigation may constitute harassment of the subject judge and should not be undertaken, depending of course on the seriousness of the issues and the weight of the new evidence.

Rule 11(d) implements the Act's provision for dismissal if voluntary appropriate corrective action has been taken. It is largely adapted from the Breyer Committee Report, 239 F.R.D. at 244–45. The Act authorizes the chief judge to conclude the complaint proceedings if "appropriate corrective action has been taken." 28 U.S.C. § 352(b)(2). Under the Rule, action taken after a complaint is filed is "appropriate" when it acknowledges and remedies the problem raised by the complaint. Breyer Committee Report, 239 F.R.D. at 244. Because the Act deals with the conduct of judges, the emphasis is on correction of the judicial conduct that was the subject of the complaint. *Id.* Terminating a complaint based on corrective action is premised on the implicit understanding that voluntary self-correction or redress of misconduct or a disability is preferable to sanctions. *Id.* The chief judge may facilitate this process by giving the subject judge an objective view of the appearance of the judicial conduct in question and by suggesting appropriate corrective measures. *Id.* Moreover, when corrective action is taken under Rule 5 satisfactory to the chief judge before a complaint is filed, that informal resolution will be sufficient to conclude a subsequent complaint based on identical conduct.

"Corrective action" must be voluntary action taken by the subject judge. Breyer Committee Report, 239 F.R.D. at 244. A remedial action directed by the chief judge or by an appellate court without the participation of the subject judge in formulating the directive or without the subject judge's subsequent agreement to such action does not constitute the requisite voluntary corrective action. *Id.* Neither the chief judge nor an appellate court has authority under the Act to impose a formal remedy or sanction; only the judicial council can impose a formal remedy or sanction under 28 U.S.C. § 354(a)(2). *Id.* Compliance with a previous judicial-council order may serve as corrective action allowing conclusion of a later complaint about the same behavior. *Id.*

Where a subject judge's conduct has resulted in identifiable, particularized harm to the complainant or another individual, appropriate corrective action should include steps taken by that judge to acknowledge and redress the harm, if possible, such as by an apology, recusal from a case, or a pledge to refrain from similar conduct in the future. *Id.* While the Act is generally forward-looking, any corrective action should, to the extent possible, serve to correct a specific harm to an individual, if such harm can reasonably be remedied. *Id.* In some cases, corrective action may not be "appropriate" to justify conclusion of a complaint unless the complainant or other individual harmed is meaningfully apprised of the nature of the corrective action in the chief judge's order, in a direct communication from the subject judge, or otherwise. *Id.*

Voluntary corrective action should be proportionate to any plausible allegations of misconduct in a complaint. The form of corrective action should also be proportionate to any sanctions that the judicial council might impose under Rule 20(b), such as a private or public reprimand or a change in case assignments. Breyer Committee Report, 239 F.R.D at 244–5. In other words, minor corrective action will not suffice to dispose of a serious matter. *Id.*

Rule 11(e) implements Section 352(b)(2) of the Act, which permits the chief judge to "conclude the proceeding" if "action on the complaint is no longer necessary because of intervening events," such as a resignation from judicial office. Ordinarily, however, stepping down from an administrative post such as chief judge, judicial-council member, or court-committee chair does not constitute an event rendering unnecessary any further action on a complaint alleging judicial misconduct. Breyer Committee Report, 239 F.R.D. at 245. As long as the subject of a complaint performs judicial duties, a complaint alleging judicial misconduct must be addressed. *Id.*

If a complaint is not disposed of pursuant to Rule 11(c), (d), or (e), a special committee must be appointed. Rule 11(f) states that a subject judge must be invited to respond to the complaint before a special committee is appointed, if no earlier response was invited.

Subject judges, of course, receive copies of complaints at the same time that they are referred to the chief judge, and they are free to volunteer responses to them. Under Rule 11(b), the chief judge may request a response if it is thought necessary. However, many complaints are clear candidates for dismissal even if their allegations are accepted as true, and there is no need for the subject judge to devote time to a defense.

The Act requires that the order dismissing a complaint or concluding a proceeding contain a statement of reasons and that a copy of the order be sent to the complainant. 28 U.S.C. § 352(b). Rule 24, dealing with availability of information to the public, contemplates that the order will be made public, usually without disclosing the names of the complainant or the subject judge. If desired for administrative purposes, more identifying information can be included in a non-public version of the order.

When a complaint is disposed of by the chief judge, the statutory purposes are best served by providing the complainant with a full, particularized, but concise explanation, giving reasons for the conclusions reached. *See also* Commentary on Rule 24 (dealing with public availability).

Rule 11(g) provides that the complainant and the subject judge must be notified, in the case of a disposition by the chief judge, of the right to petition the judicial council for review. Because an identified complaint has no "complainant" to petition for review, the chief judge's dispositive order on such a complaint will be transmitted to the judicial council for review. The same will apply where a complaint was filed by its subject judge. A copy of the chief judge's order, and memoranda incorporated by reference in the order, disposing of a complaint must be sent by the circuit clerk to the Committee on Judicial Conduct and Disability.

ARTICLE IV. INVESTIGATION AND REPORT BY SPECIAL COMMITTEE

RULE 12. SPECIAL COMMITTEE'S COMPOSITION

(a) Membership. Except as provided in (e), a special committee appointed under Rule 11(f) must consist of the chief judge and equal numbers of circuit and district judges. These judges may include senior judges. If the complaint is about a district judge, bankruptcy judge, or magistrate judge, then, when possible, the district-judge members of the special committee must be from districts other than the district of the subject judge. For the courts named in 28 U.S.C. § 363, the special committee must be selected from the judges serving on the subject judge's court.

(b) Presiding Officer. When appointing the special committee, the chief judge may serve as the presiding officer or else must designate a committee member as the presiding officer.

(c) Bankruptcy Judge or Magistrate Judge as Adviser. If the subject judge is a bankruptcy judge or magistrate judge, he or she may, within 14 days after being notified of the special committee's appointment, ask the chief judge to designate as a committee adviser another bankruptcy judge or magistrate judge, as the case may be. The chief judge must grant such a request but may otherwise use discretion in naming the adviser. Unless the adviser is a Court of Federal Claims special master appointed under 42 U.S.C. § 300aa–12(c), the adviser must be from a district other than the district of the subject bankruptcy judge or subject magistrate judge. The adviser cannot vote but has the other privileges of a special-committee member.

(d) Provision of Documents. The chief judge must certify to each other member of the special committee and to any adviser copies of the complaint and statement of facts, in whole or relevant part, and any other relevant documents on file.

(e) Continuing Qualification of Special-Committee Member. A member of a special committee may continue to serve on the committee even though the member relinquishes the position of chief judge, active circuit judge, or active district judge, as the case may be, but only if the member continues to hold office under Article III, Section 1, of the Constitution of the United States, or under 28 U.S.C. § 171.

(f) Inability of Special-Committee Member to Complete Service. If a member of a special committee can no longer serve because of death, disability, disqualification, resignation, retirement from office, or other reason, the chief judge must decide whether to appoint a replacement member, either a circuit or district judge as needed under (a). No special committee appointed under these Rules may function with only a single member, and the votes of a two-member committee must be unanimous.

(g) Voting. All actions by a special committee must be by vote of a majority of all members of the committee.

[Adopted March 11, 2008, effective April 10, 2008. Amended effective September 17, 2015.]

Commentary on Rule 12

This Rule is adapted from the Act and the Illustrative Rules.

Rule 12 leaves the size of a special committee flexible, to be determined on a case-by-case basis. The question of the size of a special committee is one that should be weighed with care in view of the potential for consuming the members' time; a large committee should be appointed only if there is a special reason to do so. Rule 12(a) acknowledges the common practice of including senior judges in the membership of a special committee.

Although the Act requires that the chief judge be a member of each special committee, 28 U.S.C. § 353(a)(1), it does not require that the chief judge preside. Accordingly, Rule 12(b) provides that if the chief judge does not preside, he or she must designate another member of the special committee as the presiding officer.

Rule 12(c) provides that the chief judge must appoint a bankruptcy judge or magistrate judge as an adviser to a special committee at the request of a bankruptcy or magistrate subject judge. Subsection (c) also provides that the adviser will have all the privileges of a member of the special committee except a vote. The adviser, therefore, may participate in all deliberations of the special committee, question witnesses at hearings, and write a separate statement to accompany the committee's report to the judicial council.

Rule 12(e) provides that a member of a special committee who remains an Article III judge may continue to serve on the committee even though the member's status otherwise changes. Thus, a special committee that originally consisted of the chief judge and an equal number of circuit and district judges, as required by the law, may continue to function even though changes of status alter that composition. This provision reflects the belief that stability of membership will contribute to the quality of the work of such committees.

Stability of membership is also the principal concern animating Rule 12(f), which deals with the case in which a special committee loses a member before its work is complete. The Rule permits the chief judge to determine whether a replacement member should be appointed. Generally, appointment of a replacement member is desirable in these situations unless the special committee has conducted evidentiary hearings before the vacancy occurs. However, cases may arise in which a special committee is in the late stages of its work, and in which it would be difficult for a new member to play a meaningful role. The Rule also preserves the collegial character of the special-committee process by prohibiting a single surviving member from serving as a committee and by providing that a committee of two surviving members will, in essence, operate under a unanimity rule.

Rule 12(g) provides that actions of a special committee must be by vote of a majority of all the members. All the members of a special committee should participate in committee decisions. In that circumstance, it seems reasonable to require that special-committee decisions be made by a majority of the membership, rather than a majority of some smaller quorum.

RULE 13. CONDUCT OF SPECIAL–COMMITTEE INVESTIGATION

(a) Extent and Methods of Special–Committee Investigation. A special committee should determine the appropriate extent and methods of its investigation in light of the allegations of the complaint and its preliminary inquiry. The investigation may include use of appropriate experts or other professionals. If, in the course of the investigation, the special committee has cause to believe that the subject judge may have engaged in misconduct or has a disability that is beyond the scope of the complaint, the committee must refer the new matter to the chief judge for a determination of whether action under Rule 5 or Rule 11 is necessary before the committee's investigation is expanded to include the new matter.

(b) Criminal Conduct. If the special committee's investigation concerns conduct that may be a crime, the committee must consult with the appropriate prosecutorial authorities to the extent permitted by the Act to avoid compromising any criminal investigation. The special committee has final authority over the timing and extent of its investigation and the formulation of its recommendations.

(c) Staff. The special committee may arrange for staff assistance to conduct the investigation. It may use existing staff of the Judiciary or may hire special staff through the Director of the Administrative Office of the United States Courts.

(d) Delegation of Subpoena Power; Contempt. The chief judge may delegate the authority to exercise the subpoena powers of the special committee. The judicial council or special committee may institute a contempt proceeding under 28 U.S.C. § 332(d) against anyone who fails to comply with a subpoena.

[Adopted March 11, 2008, effective April 10, 2008. Amended effective September 17, 2015.]

Commentary on Rule 13

This Rule is adapted from the Illustrative Rules.

Rule 13, as well as Rules 14, 15, and 16, are concerned with the way in which the special committee carries out its mission. They reflect the view that the special committee has two roles that are separated in ordinary litigation. First, the special committee has an investigative role of the kind that is characteristically left to executive branch agencies or discovery by civil litigants. 28 U.S.C. § 353(c). Second, it has a formalized fact-finding and recommendation-of-disposition role that is characteristically left to juries, judges, or arbitrators. *Id.* Rule 13 generally governs the investigative stage. Even though the same body has responsibility for both roles under the Act, it is important to distinguish between them in order to ensure that appropriate rights are afforded at appropriate times to the subject judge.

Rule 13(a) includes a provision making clear that a special committee may choose to consult appropriate experts or other professionals if it determines that such a consultation is warranted. If, for example, the special committee has cause to believe that the subject judge may be unable to discharge all of the duties of office by reason of mental or physical disability, the committee could ask the subject judge to respond to inquiries and, if necessary, request the judge to undergo a medical or psychological examination. In advance of any such examination, the special committee may enter into an agreement with the subject judge as to the scope and use that may be made of the examination results. In addition or in the alternative, the special committee may ask to review existing records, including medical records.

The extent of the subject judge's cooperation in the investigation may be taken into account in the consideration of the underlying complaint. If, for example, the subject judge impedes reasonable efforts to confirm or disconfirm the presence of a disability, the special committee may still consider whether the conduct alleged in the complaint and confirmed in the investigation constitutes disability. The same would be true of a complaint alleging misconduct.

The special committee may also consider whether such a judge might be in violation of his or her duty to cooperate in an investigation under these Rules, a duty rooted not only in the Act's definition of misconduct but also in the Code of Conduct for United States Judges, which emphasizes the need to maintain public confidence in the

Judiciary, *see* Canon 2(A) and Canon 1 cmt., and requires judges to "facilitate the performance of the administrative responsibilities of other judges and court personnel," Canon 3(B)(1). If the special committee finds a breach of the duty to cooperate and believes that the breach may amount to misconduct under Rule 3(h)(1)(H), it should determine, under the final sentence of Rule 13(a), whether that possibility should be referred to the chief judge for consideration of action under Rule 5 or Rule 11. *See also* Commentary on Rule 3.

One of the difficult questions that can arise is the relationship between proceedings under the Act and criminal investigations. Rule 13(b) assigns responsibility for coordination to the special committee in cases in which criminal conduct is suspected, but gives the committee the authority to determine the appropriate pace of its activity in light of any criminal investigation.

Title 28 U.S.C. § 356(a) provides that a special committee will have full subpoena powers as provided in 28 U.S.C. § 332(d). Section 332(d)(1) provides that subpoenas will be issued on behalf of a judicial council by the circuit clerk "at the direction of the chief judge of the circuit or his designee." Rule 13(d) contemplates that, where the chief judge designates someone else as presiding officer of the special committee, the presiding officer also be delegated the authority to direct the circuit clerk to issue subpoenas related to committee proceedings. That is not intended to imply, however, that the decision to use the subpoena power is exercisable by the presiding officer alone. *See* Rule 12(g).

RULE 14. CONDUCT OF SPECIAL-COMMITTEE HEARINGS

(a) Purpose of Hearings. The special committee may hold hearings to take testimony and receive other evidence, to hear argument, or both. If the special committee is investigating allegations against more than one judge, it may hold joint or separate hearings.

(b) Special-Committee Evidence. Subject to Rule 15, the special committee must obtain material, nonredundant evidence in the form it considers appropriate. In the special committee's discretion, evidence may be obtained by committee members, staff, or both. Witnesses offering testimonial evidence may include the complainant and the subject judge.

(c) Counsel for Witnesses. The subject judge has the right to counsel. The special committee has discretion to decide whether other witnesses may have counsel present when they testify.

(d) Witness Fees. Witness fees must be paid as provided in 28 U.S.C. § 1821.

(e) Oath. All testimony taken at a hearing must be given under oath or affirmation.

(f) Rules of Evidence. The Federal Rules of Evidence do not apply to special-committee hearings.

(g) Record and Transcript. A record and transcript must be made of all hearings.

[Adopted March 11, 2008, effective April 10, 2008. Amended effective September 17, 2015.]

Commentary on Rule 14

This Rule is adapted from the Act, 28 U.S.C. § 353, and the Illustrative Rules.

Rule 14 is concerned with the conduct of fact-finding hearings. Special-committee hearings will normally be held only after the investigative work has been completed and the committee has concluded that there is sufficient evidence to warrant a formal fact-finding proceeding. Special-committee proceedings are primarily inquisitorial rather than adversarial. Accordingly, the Federal Rules of Evidence do not apply to such hearings. Inevitably, a hearing will have something of an adversary character. Nevertheless, that tendency should be moderated to the extent possible. Even though a proceeding will commonly have investigative and hearing stages, special-committee members should not regard themselves as prosecutors one day and judges the next. Their duty—and that of their staff—is at all times to be impartial seekers of the truth.

Rule 14(b) contemplates that material evidence will be obtained by the special committee and presented in the form of affidavits, live testimony, etc. Staff or others who are organizing the hearings should regard it as their role to present evidence representing the entire picture. With respect to testimonial evidence, the subject judge should normally be called as a special-committee witness. Cases may arise in which the subject judge will not testify voluntarily. In such cases, subpoena powers are available, subject to the normal testimonial privileges. Although Rule 15(c) recognizes the subject judge's statutory right to call witnesses on his or her own behalf, exercise of this right should not usually be necessary.

RULE 15. SUBJECT JUDGE'S RIGHTS

(a) Notice.

(1) *Generally.* The subject judge must receive written notice of:

(A) the appointment of a special committee under Rule 11(f);

(B) the expansion of the scope of an investigation under Rule 13(a);

(C) any hearing under Rule 14, including its purposes, the names of any witnesses the special committee intends to call, and the text of any statements that have been taken from those witnesses.

(2) *Suggestion of Additional Witnesses.* The subject judge may suggest additional witnesses to the special committee.

(b) Special-Committee Report. The subject judge must be sent a copy of the special committee's report when it is filed with the judicial council.

(c) Presentation of Evidence. At any hearing held under Rule 14, the subject judge has the right to present evidence, to compel the attendance of witnesses, and to compel the production of documents. At the request of the subject judge, the chief judge or the judge's designee must direct the circuit clerk to issue a subpoena to a witness under 28 U.S.C. § 332(d)(1). The subject judge must be given the opportunity to cross-examine special-committee witnesses, in person or by counsel.

(d) Presentation of Argument. The subject judge may submit written argument to the special committee and must be given a reasonable opportunity to present oral argument at an appropriate stage of the investigation.

(e) Attendance at Hearings. The subject judge has the right to attend any hearing held under Rule 14 and to receive copies of the transcript, of any documents introduced, and of any written arguments submitted by the complainant to the special committee.

(f) Representation by Counsel. The subject judge may choose to be represented by counsel in the exercise of any right enumerated in this Rule. As provided in Rule 20(e), the United States may bear the costs of the representation.

[Adopted March 11, 2008, effective April 10, 2008. Amended effective September 17, 2015.]

Commentary on Rule 15

This Rule is adapted from the Act and the Illustrative Rules.

The Act states that these Rules must contain provisions requiring that "the judge whose conduct is the subject of a complaint ... be afforded an opportunity to appear (in person or by counsel) at proceedings conducted by the investigating panel, to present oral and documentary evidence, to compel the attendance of witnesses or the production of documents, to cross-examine witnesses, and to present argument orally or in writing." 28 U.S.C. § 358(b)(2). To implement this provision, Rule 15(e) gives the subject judge the right to attend any hearing held for the purpose of receiving evidence of record or hearing argument under Rule 14.

The Act does not require that the subject judge be permitted to attend all proceedings of the special committee. Accordingly, the Rules do not give a right to attend other proceedings—for example, meetings at which the special committee is engaged in investigative activity, such as interviewing persons to learn whether they ought to be called as witnesses or examining for relevance purposes documents delivered pursuant to a subpoena duces tecum, or meetings in which the committee is deliberating on the evidence or its recommendations.

RULE 16. COMPLAINANT'S RIGHTS IN INVESTIGATION

(a) Notice. The complainant must receive written notice of the investigation as provided in Rule 11(g)(1). When the special committee's report to the judicial council is filed, the complainant must be notified of the filing. The judicial council may, in its discretion, provide a copy of the report of a special committee to the complainant.

(b) Opportunity to Provide Evidence. If the complainant knows of relevant evidence not already before the special committee, the complainant may briefly explain in writing the basis of that knowledge and the nature of that evidence. If the special committee determines that the complainant has information not already known to the committee that would assist in the committee's investigation, a representative of the committee must interview the complainant.

(c) Presentation of Argument. The complainant may submit written argument to the special committee. In its discretion, the special committee may permit the complainant to offer oral argument.

(d) Representation by Counsel. A complainant may submit written argument through counsel and, if permitted to offer oral argument, may do so through counsel.

(e) Cooperation. In exercising its discretion under this Rule, the special committee may take into account the degree of the complainant's cooperation in preserving the confidentiality of the proceedings, including the identity of the subject judge.

[Adopted March 11, 2008, effective April 10, 2008. Amended effective September 17, 2015.]

Commentary on Rule 16

This Rule is adapted from the Act and the Illustrative Rules.

In accordance with the view of the process as fundamentally administrative and inquisitorial, these Rules do not give the complainant the rights of a party to litigation and leave the complainant's role largely to the discretion of the special committee. However, Rule 16(b) gives the complainant the prerogative to make a brief written submission showing that he or she is aware of relevant evidence not already known to the special committee. (Such a submission may precede any written or oral argument the complainant provides under Rule 16(c), or it may accompany that argument.) If the special committee determines, independently or from the complainant's submission, that the complainant has information that would assist the committee in its investigation, the complainant must be interviewed by a representative of the committee. Such an interview may be in person or by telephone, and the representative of the special committee may be either a member or staff.

Rule 16 does not contemplate that the complainant will ordinarily be permitted to attend proceedings of the special committee except when testifying or presenting oral argument. A special committee may exercise its discretion to permit the complainant to be present at its proceedings, or to permit the complainant, individually or through counsel, to participate in the examination or cross-examination of witnesses.

The Act authorizes an exception to the normal confidentiality provisions where the judicial council in its discretion provides a copy of the report of the special committee to the complainant and to the subject judge. 28 U.S.C. § 360(a)(1). However, the Rules do not entitle the complainant to a copy of the special committee's report.

In exercising their discretion regarding the role of the complainant, the special committee and the judicial council should protect the confidentiality of the complaint process. As a consequence, subsection (e) provides that the special committee may consider the degree to which a complainant has cooperated in preserving the confidentiality of the proceedings in determining what role beyond the minimum required by these Rules should be given to that complainant.

RULE 17. SPECIAL-COMMITTEE REPORT

The special committee must file with the judicial council a comprehensive report of its investigation, including findings and recommendations for council action. The report must be accompanied by a statement of the vote by which it was adopted, any separate or dissenting statements of special-committee members, and the record of any hearings held under Rule 14. In addition to being sent to the subject judge under Rule 15(b), a copy of the report and any accompanying statements and documents must be sent to the Committee on Judicial Conduct and Disability.

[Adopted March 11, 2008, effective April 10, 2008. Amended effective September 17, 2015.]

Commentary on Rule 17

This Rule is adapted from the Illustrative Rules and is self-explanatory. The provision for sending a copy of the special-committee report and accompanying statements and documents to the Committee on Judicial Conduct and Disability is new.

ARTICLE V. JUDICIAL–COUNCIL REVIEW

RULE 18. PETITION FOR REVIEW OF CHIEF JUDGE DISPOSITION UNDER RULE 11(C), (D), OR (E)

(a) Petition for Review. After the chief judge issues an order under Rule 11(c), (d), or (e), the complainant or the subject judge may petition the judicial council of the circuit to review the order. By rules promulgated under 28 U.S.C. § 358, the judicial council may refer a petition for review filed under this Rule to a panel of no fewer than five members of the council, at least two of whom must be district judges.

(b) When to File; Form; Where to File. A petition for review must be filed in the office of the circuit clerk within 42 days after the date of the chief judge's order. The petition for review should be in letter form, addressed to the circuit clerk, and in an envelope marked "Misconduct Petition" or "Disability Petition." The name of the subject judge must not be shown on the envelope. The petition for review should be typewritten or otherwise legible. It should begin with "I hereby petition the judicial council for review of . . ." and state the reasons why the petition should be granted. It must be signed.

(c) Receipt and Distribution of Petition. A circuit clerk who receives a petition for review filed in accordance with this Rule must:

(1) acknowledge its receipt and send a copy to the complainant or subject judge, as the case may be;

(2) promptly distribute to each member of the judicial council, or its relevant panel, except for any member disqualified under Rule 25, or make available in the manner provided by local rule, the following materials:

(A) copies of the complaint;

(B) all materials obtained by the chief judge in connection with the inquiry;

(C) the chief judge's order disposing of the complaint;

(D) any memorandum in support of the chief judge's order;

(E) the petition for review; and

(F) an appropriate ballot; and

(3) send the petition for review to the Committee on Judicial Conduct and Disability. Unless the Committee on Judicial Conduct and Disability requests them, the circuit clerk will not send copies of the materials obtained by the chief judge.

(d) Untimely Petition. The circuit clerk must refuse to accept a petition that is received after the time allowed in (b).

(e) Timely Petition Not in Proper Form. When the circuit clerk receives a petition for review filed within the time allowed but in a form that is improper to a degree that would substantially impair its consideration by the judicial council—such as a document that is ambiguous about whether it is intended to be a petition for review—the circuit clerk must acknowledge its receipt, call the filer's attention to the deficiencies, and give the filer the opportunity to correct the deficiencies within the original time allowed for filing the petition or within 21 days after the date on which a notice of the deficiencies was sent to the complainant, whichever is later. If the deficiencies are corrected within the time allowed, the circuit clerk will proceed according to paragraphs (a) and (c) of this Rule. If the deficiencies are not corrected, the circuit clerk must reject the petition.

[Adopted March 11, 2008, effective April 10, 2008. Amended effective September 17, 2015.]

Commentary on Rule 18

Rule 18 is adapted largely from the Illustrative Rules.

Subsection (a) permits the subject judge, as well as the complainant, to petition for review of the chief judge's order dismissing a complaint under Rule 11(c), or concluding that appropriate corrective action or intervening events have remedied or mooted the problems raised by the complaint pursuant to Rule 11(d) or (e). Although the subject judge may ostensibly be vindicated by the dismissal or conclusion of a complaint, the chief judge's order may include language disagreeable to the subject judge. For example, an order may dismiss a complaint, but state that the subject judge did in fact engage in misconduct. Accordingly, a subject judge may wish to object to the content of the order and is given the opportunity to petition the judicial council of the circuit for review.

Subsection (b) contains a time limit of 42 days to file a petition for review. It is important to establish a time limit on petitions for review of chief judges' dispositions in order to provide finality to the process. If the complaint requires an investigation, the investigation should proceed; if it does not, the subject judge should know that the matter is closed.

The standards for timely filing under the Federal Rules of Appellate Procedure should be applied to petitions for review. *See* Fed. R. App. P. 25(a)(2)(A), (C).

Rule 18(e) provides for an automatic extension of the time limit imposed under subsection (b) if a person files a petition that is rejected for failure to comply with formal requirements.

RULE 18.1. PETITION FOR REVIEW: LENGTH; FORMAT [11TH CIR. JCDR 18.1]

The petition should not exceed five (5) pages, and should not include attachments. To assure legibility, the petition should conform to the following technical requirements:

- 8½ × 11 inch paper;
- Only one side of the paper should be used;
- The text should be double-spaced, but quotations more than two lines long may be indented and single-spaced; headings and footnotes may be single-spaced;
- Margins should be at least one inch on all four sides; page numbers may appear in the margins but no text should appear there;
- If typed, either a proportionally spaced or monospaced typeface may be used; a proportionally spaced typeface should be 14-point or larger; a monospaced typeface should not contain more than 10½ characters per inch.

[Adopted effective April 1, 2009.]

RULE 18.2. PLACE OF FILING [11TH CIR. JCDR 18.2]

A petition for review must be delivered or mailed in an envelope to:

Clerk
United States Court of Appeals
56 Forsyth Street, N.W.
Atlanta, Georgia 30303

The envelope should be marked "Misconduct Petition" or "Disability Petition." The name of the subject judge must not appear on the envelope.

[Adopted effective April 1, 2009.]

RULE 19. JUDICIAL–COUNCIL DISPOSITION OF PETITION FOR REVIEW

(a) Rights of Subject Judge. At any time after a complainant files a petition for review, the subject judge may file a written response with the circuit clerk. The circuit clerk must promptly distribute copies of the response to each member of the judicial council or of the relevant panel, unless that member is disqualified under Rule 25. Copies must also be distributed to the chief judge, to the complainant, and to the Committee on Judicial Conduct and Disability. The subject judge must not otherwise communicate with individual judicial-council members about the matter. The subject judge must be given copies of any communications to the judicial council from the complainant.

(b) Judicial–Council Action. After considering a petition for review and the materials before it, the judicial council may:

(1) affirm the chief judge's disposition by denying the petition;

(2) return the matter to the chief judge with directions to conduct a further inquiry under Rule 11(b) or to identify a complaint under Rule 5;

(3) return the matter to the chief judge with directions to appoint a special committee under Rule 11(f); or

(4) in exceptional circumstances, take other appropriate action.

(c) Notice of Judicial–Council Decision. Copies of the judicial council's order, together with memoranda incorporated by reference in the order and separate concurring or dissenting statements, must be given to the complainant, the subject judge, and the Committee on Judicial Conduct and Disability.

(d) Memorandum of Judicial–Council Decision. If the judicial council's order affirms the chief judge's disposition, a supporting memorandum must be prepared only if the council concludes that there is a need to supplement the chief judge's explanation. A memorandum supporting a judicial-council order must not include the name of the complainant or the subject judge.

(e) Review of Judicial–Council Decision. If the judicial council's decision is adverse to the petitioner, and if no member of the council dissented, the complainant must be notified that he or she has no right to seek review of the decision. If there was a dissent, the petitioner must be informed that he or she can file a petition for review under Rule 21(b).

(f) Public Availability of Judicial–Council Decision. Materials related to the judicial council's decision must be made public to the extent, at the time, and in the manner set forth in Rule 24.

[Adopted March 11, 2008, effective April 10, 2008. Amended effective September 17, 2015.]

Commentary on Rule 19

This Rule is adapted largely from the Act and is self-explanatory.

The judicial council should ordinarily review the decision of the chief judge on the merits, treating the petition for review for all practical purposes as an appeal. The judicial council may respond to a petition for review by affirming the chief judge's order, remanding the matter, or, in exceptional cases, taking other appropriate action. A petition for review of a judicial council's decision may be filed under Rule 21(b) in any matter in which one or more members of the council dissented from the order.

RULE 20. JUDICIAL–COUNCIL ACTION FOLLOWING APPOINTMENT OF SPECIAL COMMITTEE

(a) Subject Judge's Rights. Within 21 days after the filing of the report of a special committee, the subject judge may send a written response to the members of the judicial council. The subject judge must also be given an opportunity to present argument, personally or through counsel, written or oral, as determined by the judicial council. The subject judge must not otherwise communicate with judicial-council members about the matter.

(b) Judicial–Council Action.

(1) *Discretionary Actions.* Subject to the subject judge's rights set forth in subsection (a), the judicial council may:

(A) dismiss the complaint because:

(i) even if the claim is true, the claimed conduct is not conduct prejudicial to the effective and expeditious administration of the business of the courts and does not indicate a mental or physical disability resulting in inability to discharge the duties of office;

(ii) the complaint is directly related to the merits of a decision or procedural ruling;

(iii) the facts on which the complaint is based have not been established; or

(iv) the complaint is otherwise not appropriate for consideration under 28 U.S.C. §§ 351–364.

(B) conclude the proceeding because appropriate corrective action has been taken or intervening events have made the proceeding unnecessary.

(C) refer the complaint to the Judicial Conference with the judicial council's recommendations for action.

(D) take remedial action to ensure the effective and expeditious administration of the business of the courts, including:

(i) censuring or reprimanding the subject judge, either by private communication or by public announcement;

(ii) ordering that no new cases be assigned to the subject judge for a limited, fixed period;

(iii) in the case of a magistrate judge, ordering the chief judge of the district court to take action specified by the council, including the initiation of removal proceedings under 28 U.S.C. § 631(i) or 42 U.S.C. § 300aa–12(c)(2);

(iv) in the case of a bankruptcy judge, removing the judge from office under 28 U.S.C. § 152(e);

(v) in the case of a circuit or district judge, requesting the judge to retire voluntarily with the provision (if necessary) that ordinary length-of-service requirements be waived;

(vi) in the case of a circuit or district judge who is eligible to retire but does not do so, certifying the disability of the judge under 28 U.S.C. § 372(b) so that an additional judge may be appointed; and

(vii) in the case of a circuit chief judge or district chief judge, finding that the judge is temporarily unable to perform chief-judge duties, with the result that those duties devolve to the next eligible judge in accordance with 28 U.S.C. § 45(d) or § 136(e).

(E) take any combination of actions described in (b)(1)(A)–(D) of this Rule that is within its power.

(2) *Mandatory Actions.* A judicial council must refer a complaint to the Judicial Conference if the council determines that a circuit judge or district judge may have engaged in conduct that:

(A) might constitute ground for impeachment; or

(B) in the interest of justice, is not amenable to resolution by the judicial council.

(c) Inadequate Basis for Decision. If the judicial council finds that a special committee's report, recommendations, and record provide an inadequate basis for decision, it may return the matter to the committee for further investigation and a new report, or it may conduct further investigation. If the judicial council decides to conduct further investigation, the subject judge must be given adequate prior notice in writing of that decision and of the general scope and purpose of the additional investigation. The judicial council's conduct of the additional investigation must generally accord with the procedures and powers set forth in Rules 13 through 16 for the conduct of an investigation by a special committee.

(d) Judicial–Council Vote. Judicial-council action must be taken by a majority of those members of the council who are not disqualified. A decision to remove a bankruptcy judge from office requires a majority vote of all the members of the judicial council.

(e) Recommendation for Fee Reimbursement. If the complaint has been finally dismissed or concluded under (b)(1)(A) or (B) of this Rule, and if the subject judge so requests, the judicial council may recommend that the Director of the Administrative Office use funds appropriated to the Judiciary to reimburse the judge for reasonable expenses incurred during the investigation, when those expenses would not have been incurred but for the requirements of the Act and these Rules. Reasonable expenses include attorneys' fees and expenses related to a successful defense or prosecution of a proceeding under Rule 21(a) or (b).

(f) Judicial–Council Order. Judicial-council action must be by written order. Unless the judicial council finds that extraordinary reasons would make it contrary to the interests of justice, the order must be accompanied by a memorandum setting forth the factual determinations on which it is based and the reasons for the council action. Such a memorandum may incorporate all or part of any underlying special-committee report. If the complaint was initiated by identification under Rule 5, the memorandum must so indicate. The order and memoranda incorporated by reference in the order must be provided to the complainant, the subject judge, and the Committee on Judicial Conduct and Disability. The complainant and the subject judge must be notified of any right to review of the judicial council's decision as provided in Rule 21(b). If the complaint was identified under Rule 5 or filed by its subject judge, the judicial council must transmit the order and memoranda incorporated by reference in the order to the Committee on Judicial Conduct and Disability for review in accordance with Rule 21. In the event of such a transmission, the subject judge may make a written submission to the Committee on Judicial Conduct and Disability but will have no further right of review.

[Adopted March 11, 2008, effective April 10, 2008. Amended effective September 17, 2015.]

Commentary on Rule 20

This Rule is largely adapted from the Illustrative Rules.

Rule 20(a) provides that within 21 days after the filing of the report of a special committee, the subject judge may address a written response to all of the members of the judicial council. The subject judge must also be given an opportunity to present argument to the judicial council, personally or through counsel, or both, at the direction of the council. Whether that argument is written or oral would be for the judicial council to determine. The subject judge may not otherwise communicate with judicial-council members about the matter.

Rule 20(b)(1)(D) recites the remedial actions enumerated in 28 U.S.C. § 354(a)(2) while making clear that this list is not exhaustive. A judicial council may consider lesser remedies. Some remedies may be unique to senior judges, whose caseloads can be modified by agreement or through statutory designation and certification processes.

Under 28 U.S.C. §§ 45(d) and 136(e), which provide for succession where "a chief judge is temporarily unable to perform his duties as such," the determination whether such an inability exists is not expressly reserved to the chief judge. Nor, indeed, is it assigned to any particular judge or court-governance body. Clearly, however, a chief judge's inability to function as chief could implicate "the effective and expeditious administration of justice," which the judicial council of the circuit must, under 28 U.S.C. § 332(d)(1), "make all necessary and appropriate orders" to secure. For this reason, such reassignment is among a judicial council's remedial options, as subsection (b)(1)(D)(vii) makes clear. Consistent with 28 U.S.C. §§ 45(d) and 136(e), however, any reassignment of chief-judge duties must not outlast the subject judge's inability to perform them. Nor can such reassignment result in any extension of the subject judge's term as chief judge.

Rule 20(c) provides that if the judicial council decides to conduct an additional investigation, the subject judge must be given adequate prior notice in writing of that decision and of the general scope and purpose of the additional investigation. The conduct of the investigation will be generally in accordance with the procedures set forth in Rules 13 through 16 for the conduct of an investigation by a special committee. However, if hearings are held, the judicial council may limit testimony or the presentation of evidence to avoid unnecessary repetition of testimony and evidence before the special committee.

Rule 20(d) provides that judicial-council action must be taken by a majority of those members of the council who are not disqualified, except that a decision to remove a bankruptcy judge from office requires a majority of all the members of the council as required by 28 U.S.C. § 152(e). However, it is inappropriate to apply a similar rule to the less severe actions that a judicial council may take under the Act. If some members of the judicial council are disqualified in the matter, their disqualification should not be given the effect of a vote against council action.

With regard to Rule 20(e), the judicial council, on the request of the subject judge, may recommend to the Director of the Administrative Office that the subject judge be reimbursed for reasonable expenses incurred, including attorneys' fees. The judicial council has the authority to recommend such reimbursement where, after investigation by a special committee, the complaint has been finally dismissed or concluded under subsection (b)(1)(A) or (B) of this Rule. It is contemplated that such reimbursement may be provided for the successful prosecution or defense of a proceeding under Rule 21(a) or (b), in other words, one that results in a Rule 20(b)(1)(A) or (B) dismissal or conclusion.

Rule 20(f) requires that judicial-council action be by order and, normally, that it be supported with a memorandum of factual determinations and reasons. Notice of the action must be given to the complainant and the subject judge, and must include notice of any right to petition for review of the judicial council's decision under Rule 21(b). Because an identified complaint has no "complainant" to petition for review, a judicial council's dispositive order on an identified complaint on which a special committee has been appointed must be transmitted to the Committee on Judicial Conduct and Disability for review. The same will apply where a complaint was filed by its subject judge.

ARTICLE VI. REVIEW BY JUDICIAL CONFERENCE COMMITTEE ON CONDUCT AND DISABILITY

RULE 21. COMMITTEE ON JUDICIAL CONDUCT AND DISABILITY

(a) Committee Review. The Committee on Judicial Conduct and Disability, consisting of seven members, considers and disposes of all petitions for review under (b) of this Rule, in conformity with the Committee's jurisdictional statement. Its review of judicial-council orders is for errors of law, clear errors of fact, or abuse of discretion. Its disposition of petitions for review is ordinarily final. The Judicial Conference may, in its sole discretion, review any such Committee decision, but a complainant or subject judge does not have a right to this review.

(b) Reviewable Matters.

(1) *Upon Petition.* A complainant or subject judge may petition the Committee for review of a judicial-council order entered in accordance with:

(A) Rule 20(b)(1)(A), (B), (D), or (E); or

(B) Rule 19(b)(1) or (4) if one or more members of the judicial council dissented from the order.

(2) *Upon Committee's Initiative.* At its initiative and in its sole discretion, the Committee may review any judicial-council order entered under Rule 19(b)(1) or (4), but only to determine whether a special committee should be appointed. Before undertaking the review, the Committee must invite that judicial council to explain why it believes the appointment of a special committee is unnecessary, unless the reasons are clearly stated in the council's order denying the petition for review. If the Committee believes that it would benefit from a submission by the subject judge, it may issue an appropriate request. If the Committee determines that a special committee should be appointed, the Committee must issue a written decision giving its reasons.

(c) Committee Vote. Any member of the Committee from the same circuit as the subject judge is disqualified from considering or voting on a petition for review related to that subject judge. Committee decisions under (b) of this Rule must be by majority vote of the qualified Committee members. Those members hearing the petition for review should serve in that capacity until final disposition of the petition, whether or not their term of Committee membership has ended. If only six members are qualified to consider a petition for review, the Chief Justice shall select an additional judge to join the qualified members to consider the petition. If four or fewer members are qualified to consider a petition for review, the Chief Justice shall select a panel of five judges, including the qualified Committee members, to consider it.

(d) Additional Investigation. Except in extraordinary circumstances, the Committee will not conduct an additional investigation. The Committee may return the matter to the judicial council with directions to undertake an additional investigation. If the Committee conducts an additional investigation, it will exercise the powers of the Judicial Conference under 28 U.S.C. § 331.

(e) Oral Argument; Personal Appearance. There is ordinarily no oral argument or personal appearance before the Committee. In its discretion, the Committee may permit written submissions.

(f) Committee Decision. A Committee decision under this Rule must be transmitted promptly to the Judicial Conference. Other distribution will be by the Administrative Office at the direction of the Committee chair.

(g) Finality. All orders of the Judicial Conference or of the Committee (when the Conference does not exercise its power of review) are final.

[Adopted March 11, 2008, effective April 10, 2008. Amended effective September 17, 2015.]

Commentary on Rule 21

This Rule is largely self-explanatory.

Rule 21(a) is intended to clarify that the delegation of power to the Committee on Judicial Conduct and Disability to dispose of petitions for review does not preclude review of such dispositions by the Judicial Conference. However, there is no right to such review in any party.

Rules 21(b)(1)(B) and (b)(2) are intended to fill a jurisdictional gap as to review of a dismissal or a conclusion of a complaint under Rule 19(b)(1) or (4). Where one or more members of a judicial council reviewing a petition have dissented, the complainant or the subject judge has the right to petition for review by the Committee. Under Rule 21(b)(2), the Committee may review such a dismissal or conclusion in its sole discretion, whether or not a dissent occurred, and only as to the appointment of a special committee. Any review under Rule 21(b)(2) will be conducted as soon as practicable after the dismissal or conclusion at issue. No party has a right to such review, and such review will be rare.

Rule 21(c) provides for review only by Committee members from circuits other than that of the subject judge. The Rule provides that every petition for review must be considered and voted on by at least five, and if possible by seven, qualified Committee members to avoid the possibility of tie votes. If six, or four or fewer, members are qualified, the Chief Justice shall appoint other judges to join the qualified members to consider the petition for review. To the extent possible, the judges whom the Chief Justice selects to join the qualified members should be drawn from among former members of the Committee.

Under this Rule, all Committee decisions are final in that they are unreviewable unless the Judicial Conference, in its discretion, decides to review a decision. Committee decisions, however, do not necessarily constitute final action on a complaint for purposes of Rule 24.

RULE 22. PROCEDURES FOR REVIEW

(a) Filing Petition for Review. A petition for review of a judicial-council decision on a complaint referred to a special committee may be filed by sending a brief written statement to the Committee on Judicial Conduct and Disability at JCD_PetitionforReview@ao.uscourts.gov or to:

Judicial Conference Committee on Judicial Conduct and Disability
Attn: Office of General Counsel
Administrative Office of the United States Courts
One Columbus Circle, NE
Washington, D.C. 20544

The Administrative Office will send a copy of the petition for review to the complainant or subject judge, as the case may be.

(b) Form and Contents of Petition. No particular form is required. The petition for review must contain a short statement of the basic facts underlying the complaint, the history of its consideration before the appropriate judicial council, a copy of the council's decision, and the grounds on which the petitioner seeks review. The petition for review must specify the date and docket number of the judicial council order for which review is sought. The petitioner may attach any documents or correspondence arising in the course of the proceeding before the judicial council or its special committee. A petition for review should not normally exceed 20 pages plus necessary attachments. A petition for review must be signed by the petitioner or his or her attorney.

(c) Time. A petition for review must be submitted within 42 days after the date of the order for which review is sought.

(d) Action on Receipt of Petition. When a petition for review of a judicial-council decision on a complaint referred to a special committee is submitted in accordance with this Rule, the Administrative Office shall acknowledge its receipt, notify the chair of the Committee on Judicial Conduct and Disability, and distribute the petition to the members of the Committee for their deliberation.

[Adopted March 11, 2008, effective April 10, 2008. Amended effective September 17, 2015.]

Commentary on Rule 22

Rule 22 is self-explanatory.

ARTICLE VII. MISCELLANEOUS RULES

RULE 23. CONFIDENTIALITY

(a) General Rule. The consideration of a complaint by a chief judge, a special committee, a judicial council, or the Committee on Judicial Conduct and Disability is confidential. Information about this consideration must not be disclosed by any judge or employee of the Judiciary or by any person who records or transcribes testimony except as allowed by these Rules. A chief judge may disclose the existence of a proceeding under these Rules when necessary or appropriate to maintain public confidence in the Judiciary's ability to redress misconduct or disability.

(b) Files. All files related to a complaint must be separately maintained with appropriate security precautions to ensure confidentiality.

(c) Disclosure in Decisions. Except as otherwise provided in Rule 24, written decisions of a chief judge, a judicial council, or the Committee on Judicial Conduct and Disability, and dissenting opinions or separate statements of members of a council or the Committee may contain information and exhibits that the authors consider appropriate for inclusion, and the information and exhibits may be made public.

(d) Availability to Judicial Conference. On request of the Judicial Conference or its Committee on Judicial Conduct and Disability, the circuit clerk must furnish any requested records related to a complaint. For auditing purposes, the circuit clerk must provide access to the Committee on Judicial Conduct and Disability to records of proceedings under the Act at the site where the records are kept.

(e) Availability to District Court. If the judicial council directs the initiation of proceedings for removal of a magistrate judge under Rule 20(b)(1)(D)(iii), the circuit clerk must provide to the chief judge of the district court copies of the report of the special committee and any other documents and records that were before the council at the time of its decision. On request of the chief judge of the district court, the judicial council may authorize release to that chief judge of any other records relating to the investigation.

(f) Impeachment Proceedings. If the Judicial Conference determines that consideration of impeachment may be warranted, it must transmit the record of all relevant proceedings to the Speaker of the House of Representatives.

(g) Subject Judge's Consent. If both the subject judge and the chief judge consent in writing, any materials from the files may be disclosed to any person. In any such disclosure, the chief judge may require that the identity of the complainant, or of witnesses in an investigation conducted under these Rules, not be revealed.

(h) Disclosure in Special Circumstances. The Judicial Conference, its Committee on Judicial Conduct and Disability, or a judicial council may authorize disclosure of information about the consideration of a complaint, including the papers, documents, and transcripts relating to the investigation, to the extent that disclosure is justified by special circumstances and is not prohibited by the Act. Disclosure may be made to judicial researchers engaged in the study or evaluation of experience under the Act and related modes of judicial discipline, but only where the study or evaluation has been specifically approved by the Judicial Conference or by the Committee on Judicial Conduct and Disability. Appropriate steps must be taken to protect the identities of the subject judge, the complainant, and witnesses from public disclosure. Other appropriate safeguards to protect against the dissemination of confidential information may be imposed.

(i) Disclosure of Identity by Subject Judge. Nothing in this Rule precludes the subject judge from acknowledging that he or she is the judge referred to in documents made public under Rule 24.

(j) Assistance and Consultation. Nothing in this Rule prohibits a chief judge, a special committee, a judicial council, or the Judicial Conference or its Committee on Judicial Conduct and Disability, in the performance of any function authorized under the Act or these Rules, from seeking the help of qualified staff or experts or from consulting other judges who may be helpful regarding the performance of that function.

[Adopted March 11, 2008, effective April 10, 2008. Amended effective September 17, 2015.]

Commentary on Rule 23

Rule 23 was adapted from the Illustrative Rules.

The Act applies a rule of confidentiality to "papers, documents, and records of proceedings related to investigations conducted under this chapter" and states that they may not be disclosed "by any person in any proceeding," with enumerated exceptions. 28 U.S.C. § 360(a). Three questions arise: Who is bound by the confidentiality rule, what proceedings are subject to the rule, and who is within the circle of people who may have access to information without breaching the rule?

With regard to the first question, Rule 23(a) provides that judges, employees of the Judiciary, and those persons involved in recording proceedings and preparing transcripts are obliged to respect the confidentiality requirement. This of course includes subject judges who do not consent to identification under Rule 23(i).

With regard to the second question, Rule 23(a) applies the rule of confidentiality broadly to consideration of a complaint at any stage.

With regard to the third question, there is no barrier of confidentiality among a chief judge, a judicial council, the Judicial Conference, and the Committee on Judicial Conduct and Disability. Each may have access to any of the confidential records for use in their consideration of a referred matter, a petition for review, or monitoring the administration of the Act. A district court may have similar access if the judicial council orders the district court to initiate proceedings to remove a magistrate judge from office, and Rule 23(e) so provides.

In extraordinary circumstances, a chief judge may disclose the existence of a proceeding under these Rules. The disclosure of such information in high-visibility or controversial cases is to reassure the public that the Judiciary is capable of redressing judicial misconduct or disability. Moreover, the confidentiality requirement does not prevent the chief judge from "communicat[ing] orally or in writing with . . . [persons] who may have knowledge of the matter" as part of a limited inquiry conducted by the chief judge under Rule 11(b).

Rule 23 recognizes that there must be some exceptions to the Act's confidentiality requirement. For example, the Act requires that certain orders and the reasons for them must be made public. 28 U.S.C. § 360(b). Rule 23(c) makes it explicit that written decisions, as well as dissenting opinions and separate statements, may contain references to information that would otherwise be confidential and that such information may be made public. However, subsection (c) is subject to Rule 24(a), which provides the general rule regarding the public availability of decisions. For example, the name of a subject judge cannot be made public in a decision if disclosure of the name is prohibited by that Rule.

The Act makes clear that there is a barrier of confidentiality between the judicial branch and the legislative branch. It provides that material may be disclosed to Congress only if it is believed necessary to an impeachment investigation or trial of a judge. 28 U.S.C. § 360(a)(2). Accordingly, Section 355(b) of the Act requires the Judicial Conference to transmit the record of a proceeding to the House of Representatives if the Conference believes that impeachment of a subject judge may be appropriate. Rule 23(f) implements this requirement.

The Act provides that confidential materials may be disclosed if authorized in writing by the subject judge and by the chief judge. 28 U.S.C. § 360(a)(3). Rule 23(g) implements this requirement. Once the subject judge has consented to the disclosure of confidential materials related to a complaint, the chief judge ordinarily will refuse consent only to the extent necessary to protect the confidentiality interests of the complainant or of witnesses who have testified in investigatory proceedings or who have provided information in response to a limited inquiry undertaken pursuant to Rule 11. It will generally be necessary, therefore, for the chief judge to require that the identities of the complainant or of such witnesses, as well as any identifying information, be shielded in any materials disclosed, except insofar as the chief judge has secured the consent of the complainant or of a particular witness to disclosure, or there is a demonstrated need for disclosure of the information that, in the judgment of the chief judge, outweighs the confidentiality interest of the complainant or of a particular witness (as may be the case where the complainant is delusional or where the complainant or a particular witness has already demonstrated a lack of concern about maintaining the confidentiality of the proceedings).

Rule 23(h) permits disclosure of additional information in circumstances not enumerated. For example, disclosure may be appropriate to permit a prosecution for perjury based on testimony given before a special committee. Another example might involve evidence of criminal conduct by a judge discovered by a special committee.

Subsection (h) also permits the authorization of disclosure of information about the consideration of a complaint, including the papers, documents, and transcripts relating to the investigation, to judicial researchers engaged in the study or evaluation of experience under the Act and related modes of judicial discipline. The Rule envisions disclosure of information from the official record of a complaint proceeding to a limited category of persons for appropriately authorized research purposes only, and with appropriate safeguards to protect individual identities in any published research results. In authorizing disclosure, a judicial council may refuse to release particular materials when such release would be contrary to the interests of justice, or when those materials constitute purely internal communications. The Rule does not envision disclosure of purely internal communications between judges and their colleagues and staff.

Under Rule 23(j), any of the specified judges or entities performing a function authorized under these Rules may seek expert or staff assistance or may consult with other judges who may be helpful regarding performance of that function; the confidentiality requirement does not preclude this. A chief judge, for example, may properly seek the advice and assistance of another judge who the chief judge deems to be in the best position to communicate with the subject judge in an attempt to bring about corrective action. As another example, a new chief judge may wish to confer with a predecessor to learn how similar complaints have been handled. In consulting with other judges, of course, a chief judge should disclose information regarding the complaint only to the extent the chief judge deems necessary under the circumstances.

RULE 24. PUBLIC AVAILABILITY OF DECISIONS

(a) General Rule; Specific Cases. When final action has been taken on a complaint and it is no longer subject to review, all orders entered by the chief judge and judicial council, including memoranda incorporated by reference in those orders and any dissenting opinions or separate statements by members of the judicial council, but excluding any orders under Rule 5 or 11(f), must be made public, with the following exceptions:

(1) if the complaint is finally dismissed under Rule 11(c) without the appointment of a special committee, or if it is concluded under Rule 11(d) because of voluntary corrective action, the publicly available materials must not disclose the name of the subject judge without his or her consent.

(2) if the complaint is concluded because of intervening events, or dismissed at any time after a special committee is appointed, the judicial council must determine whether the name of the subject judge should be disclosed.

(3) if the complaint is finally disposed of by a privately communicated censure or reprimand, the publicly available materials must not disclose either the name of the subject judge or the text of the reprimand.

(4) if the complaint is finally disposed of under Rule 20(b)(1)(D) by any action other than private censure or reprimand, the text of the dispositive order must be included in the materials made public, and the name of the subject judge must be disclosed.

(5) the name of the complainant must not be disclosed in materials made public under this Rule unless the chief judge orders disclosure.

(b) Manner of Making Public. The orders described in (a) must be made public by placing them in a publicly accessible file in the office of the circuit clerk and by placing the orders on the court's public website. If the orders appear to have precedential value, the chief judge may cause them to be published. In addition, the Committee on Judicial Conduct and Disability will make available on the Judiciary's website, www.uscourts.gov, selected illustrative orders described in paragraph (a), appropriately redacted, to provide additional information to the public on how complaints are addressed under the Act.

(c) Orders of Committee on Judicial Conduct and Disability. Orders of the Committee on Judicial Conduct and Disability constituting final action in a complaint proceeding arising from a particular circuit will be made available to the public in the office of the circuit clerk of the relevant court of appeals. The Committee on Judicial Conduct and Disability will also make such orders available on the Judiciary's website, www.uscourts.gov. When authorized by the Committee on Judicial Conduct and Disability, other orders related to complaint proceedings will similarly be made available.

(d) Complaint Referred to Judicial Conference. If a complaint is referred to the Judicial Conference under Rule 20(b)(1)(C) or 20(b)(2), materials relating to the complaint will be made public only if ordered by the Judicial Conference.

[Adopted March 11, 2008, effective April 10, 2008. Amended effective September 17, 2015.]

Commentary on Rule 24

Rule 24 is adapted from the Illustrative Rules and the recommendations of the Breyer Committee.

The Act requires the circuits to make available only written orders of a judicial council or the Judicial Conference imposing some form of sanction. 28 U.S.C. § 360(b). The Judicial Conference, however, has long recognized the desirability of public availability of a broader range of orders and other materials. In 1994, the Judicial Conference "urge[d] all circuits and courts covered by the Act to submit to the West Publishing Company, for publication in Federal Reporter 3d, and to Lexis all orders issued pursuant to [the Act] that are deemed by the issuing circuit or court to have significant precedential value to other circuits and courts covered by the Act." Report of the Proceedings of the Judicial Conference of the United States, Mar. 1994, at 28. Following this recommendation, the 2000 revision of the Illustrative Rules contained a public availability provision very similar to Rule 24. In 2002, the Judicial Conference again voted to encourage the circuits "to submit non-routine public orders disposing of complaints of judicial misconduct or disability for publication by on-line and print services." Report of the Proceedings of the Judicial Conference of the United States, Sept. 2002, at 58. The Breyer Committee Report further emphasized that "[p]osting such orders on the judicial branch's public website would not only benefit judges directly, it would also encourage scholarly commentary and analysis of the orders." Breyer Committee Report, 239 F.R.D. at 216. With these considerations in mind, Rule 24 provides for public availability of a wide range of materials.

Rule 24 provides for public availability of orders of a chief judge, a judicial council, and the Committee on Judicial Conduct and Disability, as well as the texts of memoranda incorporated by reference in those orders, together with any dissenting opinions or separate statements by members of the judicial council. No memoranda other than those incorporated by reference in those orders shall be disclosed. However, these orders and memoranda are to be made public only when final action on the complaint has been taken and any right of review has been exhausted. The provision that decisions will be made public only after final action has been taken is designed in part to avoid public disclosure of the existence of pending proceedings. Whether the name of the subject judge is disclosed will then depend on the nature of the final action. If the final action is an order predicated on a finding of misconduct or disability (other than a privately communicated censure or reprimand) the name of the subject judge must be made public. If the final action is dismissal of the complaint, the name of the subject judge must not be disclosed. Rule 24(a)(1) provides that where a proceeding is concluded under Rule 11(d) by the chief judge on the basis of voluntary corrective action, the name of the subject judge must not be disclosed. Shielding the name of the subject judge in this circumstance should encourage informal disposition.

If a complaint is dismissed as moot, or because intervening events have made action on the complaint unnecessary, after appointment of a special committee, Rule 24(a)(2) allows the judicial council to determine whether the subject judge will be identified. In such a case, no final decision has been rendered on the merits, but it may be in the public interest—particularly if a judicial officer resigns in the course of an investigation—to make the identity of the subject judge known.

Once a special committee has been appointed, and a proceeding is concluded by the full judicial council on the basis of a remedial order of the council, Rule 24(a)(4) provides for disclosure of the name of the subject judge.

Rule 24(a)(5) provides that the identity of the complainant will be disclosed only if the chief judge so orders. Identifying the complainant when the subject judge is not identified would increase the likelihood that the identity of the subject judge would become publicly known, thus circumventing the policy of nondisclosure. It may not always be practicable to shield the complainant's identity while making public disclosure of the judicial council's order and supporting memoranda; in some circumstances, moreover, the complainant may consent to public identification.

Rule 24(b) makes clear that circuits must post on their external websites all orders required to be made public under Rule 24(a).

Matters involving orders issued following a special-committee investigation often involve highly sensitive situations, and it is important that judicial councils have every opportunity to reach a correct and just outcome. This would include the ability to reach informal resolution before a subject judge's identity must be released. But there must also come a point of procedural finality. The date of finality—and thus the time at which other safeguards and rules such as the publication requirement are triggered—is the date on which the judicial council issues a Final Order. *See In re Complaint of Judicial Misconduct*, 751 F.3d 611, 617 (2014) (requiring publication of a judicial-council order "[e]ven though the period for review had not yet elapsed" and concluding that "the order was a final decision because the Council had adjudicated the matter on the merits after having received a report from a special investigating committee"). As determined in the cited case, modifications of this kind to a final order are subject to review by the Committee on Judicial Conduct and Disability.

RULE 25. DISQUALIFICATION

(a) General Rule. Any judge is disqualified from participating in any proceeding under these Rules if the judge, in his or her discretion, concludes that circumstances warrant disqualification. If a complaint is filed by a judge, that judge is disqualified from participating in any consideration of the complaint except to the extent that these Rules provide for a complainant's participation. A chief judge who has identified a complaint under Rule 5 is not automatically disqualified from considering the complaint.

(b) Subject Judge. A subject judge is disqualified from considering a complaint except to the extent that these Rules provide for participation by a subject judge.

(c) Chief Judge Disqualified From Considering Petition for Review of Chief Judge's Order. If a petition for review of the chief judge's order entered under Rule 11(c), (d), or (e) is filed with the judicial council in accordance with Rule 18, the chief judge is disqualified from participating in the council's consideration of the petition.

(d) Member of Special Committee Not Disqualified. A member of the judicial council who serves on a special committee, including the chief judge, is not disqualified from participating in council consideration of the committee's report.

(e) Subject Judge's Disqualification After Appointment of Special Committee. Upon appointment of a special committee, the subject judge is disqualified from participating in the identification or consideration of any complaint, related or unrelated to the pending matter, under the Act or these Rules. The disqualification continues until all proceedings on the complaint against the subject judge are finally terminated with no further right of review.

(f) Substitute for Disqualified Chief Judge. If the chief judge is disqualified from performing duties that the Act and these Rules assign to a chief judge, those duties must be assigned to the most-senior active circuit judge not disqualified. If all circuit judges in regular active service are disqualified, the judicial council may determine whether to request a transfer under Rule 26, or, in the interest of sound judicial administration, to permit the chief judge to dispose of the complaint on the merits. Members of the judicial council who are named in the complaint may participate in this determination if necessary to obtain a quorum of the council.

(g) Judicial–Council Action When Multiple Judges Disqualified. Notwithstanding any other provision in these Rules to the contrary,

(1) a member of the judicial council who is a subject judge may participate in its disposition if:

(A) participation by one or more subject judges is necessary to obtain a quorum of the judicial council;

(B) the judicial council finds that the lack of a quorum is due to the naming of one or more judges in the complaint for the purpose of disqualifying that judge or those judges, or to the naming of one or more judges based on their participation in a decision excluded from the definition of misconduct under Rule 3(h)(3); and

(C) the judicial council votes that it is necessary, appropriate, and in the interest of sound judicial administration that one or more subject judges be eligible to act.

(2) otherwise disqualified members may participate in votes taken under (g)(1)(B) and (g)(1)(C).

(h) Disqualification of Members of Committee on Judicial Conduct and Disability. No member of the Committee on Judicial Conduct and Disability is disqualified from participating in any proceeding under the Act or these Rules because of consultations with a chief judge, a member of a special committee, or a member of a judicial council about the interpretation or application of the Act or these Rules, unless the member believes that the consultation would prevent fair-minded participation.

[Adopted March 11, 2008, effective April 10, 2008. Amended effective September 17, 2015.]

Commentary on Rule 25

While a subject judge is barred by Rule 25(b) from participating in the disposition of the complaint in which he or she is named, Rule 25(e) recognizes that participation in proceedings arising under the Act or these Rules by a judge who is the subject of a special committee investigation may lead to an appearance of self-interest in creating substantive and procedural precedents governing such proceedings. Rule 25(e) bars such participation.

Under the Act, a complaint against the chief judge is to be handled by "that circuit judge in regular active service next senior in date of commission." 28 U.S.C. § 351(c). The Rules do not purport to prescribe who is to preside over meetings of the judicial council. Consequently, where the presiding member of the judicial council is disqualified from participating under these Rules, the order of precedence prescribed by Rule 25(f) for performing "the duties and responsibilities of the chief circuit judge under these Rules" does not apply to determine the acting presiding member of the council. That is a matter left to the internal rules or operating practices of each judicial council. In most cases the most senior active circuit judge who is a member of the judicial council and who is not disqualified will preside.

Sometimes a single complaint is filed against a large group of judges. If the normal disqualification rules are observed in such a case, no court of appeals judge can serve as acting chief judge of the circuit, and the judicial council will be without appellate members. Where the complaint is against all circuit and district judges, under normal rules no member of the judicial council can perform the duties assigned to the council under the statute.

A similar problem is created by successive complaints arising out of the same underlying grievance. For example, a complainant files a complaint against a district judge based on alleged misconduct, and the complaint is dismissed by the chief judge under the statute. The complainant may then file a complaint against the chief judge for dismissing the first complaint, and when that complaint is dismissed by the next senior judge, still a third complaint may be filed. The threat is that the complainant will bump down the seniority ladder until, once again, there is no member of the court of appeals who can serve as acting chief judge for the purpose of the next complaint. Similarly, complaints involving the merits of litigation may involve a series of decisions in which many judges participated or in which a rehearing en banc was denied by the court of appeals, and the complaint may name a majority of the judicial council as subject judges.

In recognition that these multiple-judge complaints are virtually always meritless, the judicial council is given discretion to determine: (1) whether it is necessary, appropriate, and in the interest of sound judicial administration to permit the chief judge to dispose of a complaint where it would otherwise be impossible for any active circuit judge in the circuit to act, and (2) whether it is necessary, appropriate, and in the interest of sound judicial administration, after appropriate findings as to need and justification are made, to permit subject judges of the judicial council to participate in the disposition of a petition for review where it would otherwise be impossible to obtain a quorum.

Applying a rule of necessity in these situations is consistent with the appearance of justice. *See, e.g., In re Complaint of Doe*, 2 F.3d 308 (8th Cir. Jud. Council 1993) (invoking the rule of necessity); *In re Complaint of Judicial Misconduct*, No. 91–80464 (9th Cir. Jud. Council 1992) (same). There is no unfairness in permitting the chief judge to dispose of a patently insubstantial complaint that names all active circuit judges in the circuit.

Similarly, there is no unfairness in permitting subject judges, in these circumstances, to participate in the review of the chief judge's dismissal of an insubstantial complaint. The remaining option is to assign the matter to another body. Among other alternatives, the judicial council may request a transfer of the petition under Rule 26. Given the administrative inconvenience and delay involved in these alternatives, it is desirable to request a transfer only if the judicial council determines that the petition for review is substantial enough to warrant such action.

In the unlikely event that a quorum of the judicial council cannot be obtained to consider the report of a special committee, it would normally be necessary to request a transfer under Rule 26.

Rule 25(h) recognizes that the jurisdictional statement of the Committee on Judicial Conduct and Disability contemplates consultation between members of the Committee and judicial participants in proceedings under the Act and these Rules. Such consultation should not automatically preclude participation by a member in that proceeding.

RULE 26. TRANSFER TO ANOTHER JUDICIAL COUNCIL

In exceptional circumstances, the chief judge or the judicial council may ask the Chief Justice to transfer a proceeding based on a complaint identified under Rule 5 or filed under Rule 6 to the judicial council of another circuit. The request for a transfer may be made at any stage of the proceeding before a reference to the Judicial Conference under Rule 20(b)(1)(C) or 20(b)(2) or a petition for review is filed under Rule 22. Upon receiving such a request, the Chief Justice may refuse the request or select the transferee judicial council, which may then exercise the powers of a judicial council under these Rules.

[Adopted March 11, 2008, effective April 10, 2008. Amended effective September 17, 2015.]

Commentary on Rule 26

Rule 26 is new; it implements the Breyer Committee's recommended use of transfers. Breyer Committee Report, 239 F.R.D. at 214–15.

Rule 26 authorizes the transfer of a complaint proceeding to another judicial council selected by the Chief Justice. Such transfers may be appropriate, for example, in the case of a serious complaint where there are multiple disqualifications among the original judicial council, where the issues are highly visible and a local disposition may weaken public confidence in the process, where internal tensions arising in the council as a result of the complaint render disposition by a less involved council appropriate, or where a complaint calls into question policies or governance of the home court of appeals. The power to effect a transfer is lodged in the Chief Justice to avoid disputes in a judicial council over where to transfer a sensitive matter and to ensure that the transferee council accepts the matter.

Upon receipt of a transferred proceeding, the transferee judicial council shall determine the proper stage at which to begin consideration of the complaint—for example, reference to the transferee chief judge, appointment of a special committee, etc.

RULE 27. WITHDRAWAL OF COMPLAINT OR PETITION FOR REVIEW

(a) Complaint Pending Before Chief Judge. With the chief judge's consent, the complainant may withdraw a complaint that is before the chief judge for a decision under Rule 11. The withdrawal of a complaint will not prevent the chief judge from identifying or having to identify a complaint under Rule 5 based on the withdrawn complaint.

(b) Complaint Pending Before Special Committee or Judicial Council. After a complaint has been referred to the special committee for investigation and before the committee files its report, the complainant may withdraw the complaint only with the consent of both the subject judge and either the special committee or the judicial council.

(c) Petition for Review. A petition for review addressed to the judicial council under Rule 18, or the Committee on Judicial Conduct and Disability under Rule 22, may be withdrawn if no action on the petition has been taken.

[Adopted March 11, 2008, effective April 10, 2008. Amended effective September 17, 2015.]

Commentary on Rule 27

Rule 27 is adapted from the Illustrative Rules and treats the complaint proceeding, once begun, as a matter of public business rather than as the property of the complainant. Accordingly, the chief judge or the judicial council remains responsible for addressing any complaint under the Act, even a complaint that has been formally withdrawn by the complainant.

Under subsection (a), a complaint pending before the chief judge may be withdrawn if the chief judge consents. Where the complaint clearly lacked merit, the chief judge may accordingly be saved the burden of preparing a formal order and supporting memorandum. However, the chief judge may, or be obligated under Rule 5, to identify a complaint based on allegations in a withdrawn complaint.

If the chief judge appoints a special committee, Rule 27(b) provides that the complaint may be withdrawn only with the consent of both the body before which it is pending (the special committee or the judicial council) and the subject judge. Once a complaint has reached the stage of appointment of a special committee, a resolution of the issues may be necessary to preserve public confidence. Moreover, the subject judge is given the right to insist that the matter be resolved on the merits, thereby eliminating any ambiguity that might remain if the proceeding were terminated by withdrawal of the complaint.

With regard to all petitions for review, Rule 27(c) grants the petitioner unrestricted authority to withdraw the petition. It is thought that the public's interest in the proceeding is adequately protected, because there will necessarily have been a decision by the chief judge and often by the judicial council as well in such a case.

RULE 28. AVAILABILITY OF RULES AND FORMS

These Rules and copies of the complaint form as provided in Rule 6(a) must be available without charge in the office of the circuit clerk of each court of appeals, district court, bankruptcy court, or other federal court whose judges are subject to the Act. Each court must also make these Rules, the complaint form, and complaint-filing instructions available on the court's website, or provide an Internet link to these items on the appropriate court of appeals website or on www.uscourts.gov.

[Adopted March 11, 2008, effective April 10, 2008. Amended effective September 17, 2015.]

RULE 29. EFFECTIVE DATE

These Rules will become effective 30 days after promulgation by the Judicial Conference of the United States.

[Adopted March 11, 2008, effective April 10, 2008.]

APPENDIX

COMPLAINT FORM

Judicial Council of the ______________ Circuit

COMPLAINT OF JUDICIAL MISCONDUCT OR DISABILITY

To begin the complaint process, complete this form and prepare the brief statement of facts described in item 4 (below). The Rules for Judicial-Conduct and Judicial-Disability Proceedings, adopted by the Judicial Conference of the United States, contain information on what to include in a complaint (Rule 6), where to file a complaint (Rule 7), and other important matters. The Rules are available in federal court clerks' offices, on individual federal courts' websites, and on www.uscourts.gov.

Your complaint (this form and the statement of facts) should be typewritten and must be legible. For the number of copies to file, consult the local rules or clerk's office of the court in which your complaint is required to be filed. Enclose each copy of the complaint in an envelope marked "COMPLAINT OF MISCONDUCT" or "COMPLAINT OF DISABILITY" and submit it to the appropriate clerk of court. **Do not put the name of any judge on the envelope.**

1. Name of Complainant: ______________________

   Contact Address: ______________________

   ____

   Daytime telephone: (__) ____________

2. Name(s) of Judge(s): ______________________

   Court: ______________________

3. Does this complaint concern the behavior of the judge(s) in a particular lawsuit or lawsuits?

   [ ] Yes [ ] No

   If "yes," give the following information about each lawsuit:

   Court: ______________________

   Case Number: ______________________

   Docket number of any appeal to the ____ Circuit: ____________

   Are (were) you a party or lawyer in the lawsuit?

   [ ] Party [ ] Lawyer [ ] Neither

If you are (were) a party and have (had) a lawyer, give the lawyer's name, address, and telephone number:

____

____

____

4. **Brief Statement of Facts.** Attach a brief statement of the specific facts on which the claim of judicial misconduct or disability is based. Include what happened, when and where it happened, and any information that would help an investigator check the facts. If the complaint alleges judicial disability, also include any additional facts that form the basis of that allegation.

5. **Declaration and signature:**

I declare under penalty of perjury that the statements made in this complaint are true and correct to the best of my knowledge.

(Signature)______________________ (Date)__________

[Adopted March 11, 2008, effective April 10, 2008. Revised September 17, 2015.]

ADDENDUM FOUR. ELEVENTH CIRCUIT PLAN UNDER THE CRIMINAL JUSTICE ACT

The U.S. Court of Appeals for the Eleventh Circuit, with the approval of the judicial council, adopts this plan for furnishing representation for persons financially unable to obtain adequate representation in the cases and situations described in 18 U.S.C. § 3006A(a), as amended. This plan supplements the CJA plans of the several districts of the circuit concerning provisions for representation on appeal and the guidelines set forth in Volume 7 of the Guide to Judiciary Policies and Procedures. These guidelines are available on the internet via a link on the court of appeals web site at www.ca11.uscourts.gov, and for inspection in the office of the clerk of each court within the circuit, in the Circuit Library, and in the satellite libraries maintained throughout the circuit.

(a) Philosophy of the Act. Hourly rates of compensation fixed by the amended Act are designated and intended to be maximum rates and should be so treated. The rates were not intended to change the basic and underlying philosophy of the Act that the bar of the nation owes a responsibility to represent persons financially unable to retain counsel. The compensation provided under the Act is not intended to equate with private counsel fees.

(b) Relation to District Court Plans. The provisions of the plans of the various district courts within the Eleventh Circuit shall also be applicable on appeals from such courts except insofar as they may be inconsistent with some provision of this plan, in which case this plan shall prevail.

(c) Determination of Need. In determining need for appointment of counsel under the Act, the court shall not be governed by a requirement of indigency on the part of the party but rather within the spirit and purpose of the Act by financial inability to employ counsel and by congressional intent in formulating this program.

(d) Appointment of Counsel.

(1) Pursuant to subsection (b) of the Act, counsel furnishing representation under this plan shall be selected from the panels of attorneys designated or approved by the district courts of the Eleventh Circuit, which are hereby approved by this court, or from a bar association, legal aid agency, or federal public defender organization or community defender organization approved by a district court plan and authorized to furnish representation under the Act. In addition, when the interests of justice require, any judge of this court may appoint competent counsel not otherwise included in the preceding categories. In accordance, however, with subsection (a)(3) of the Act and with the directives of the Judicial Conference of the United States, at least 25% of all such appointments shall be assigned to members of the private bar. The clerk of this court shall ensure that the proration guideline is satisfied. All qualified attorneys shall be encouraged to participate in the furnishing of representation under the Act without regard to race, color, religion, sex, age, national origin, or disabling condition.

(2) If a party was represented in the district court by counsel appointed under the Act, such counsel shall be mindful of the obligation and responsibility to continue representation on appeal until either successor counsel is appointed under the Act or counsel is relieved by order of this court. See § (e)(1) below. Retained counsel for a criminal defendant has an obligation to continue to represent that defendant until successor counsel either enters an appearance or is appointed under the Act, and may not abandon or cease representation of a defendant except upon order of this court. Unless approved in advance by this court, the district court is not authorized to appoint counsel on appeal to represent a defendant who was represented in the district court by retained counsel without first conducting an *in camera* review of the financial circumstances of the defendant and of the fee arrangements between the defendant and retained trial counsel. Appointment of counsel on appeal may be requested in this court by filing an appropriate motion supported by an affidavit which substantially complies with Form 4 in the Appendix to the FRAP Rules. Also see § (e)(1) of this plan.

(3) In all classes of cases to which the Act applies (except classes enumerated in subsection (a)(2)(B) of the Act or arising under 18 U.S.C. § 4245) where an appellant was not represented by counsel in the court below, the clerk shall notify the appellant of the right to be represented on appeal by counsel and that an attorney will be appointed as a representative if appellant is financially unable to obtain representation.

(4) Any person subject to revocation of parole, in custody as a material witness, or seeking relief under 28 U.S.C. § 2241, § 2254 or § 2255, or 18 U.S.C. § 4245 may apply to this court to be furnished representation. The court may approve such representation on a determination that the interests of justice so require and that the person is financially unable to obtain representation.

(5) In all cases under the Act in which the party has been found by the district court to be financially unable to obtain representation, the court of appeals may accept this finding and appoint an attorney without further proof. Counsel appointed under the Act are under a continuing duty to disclose to this court any change in defendant's circumstances which may render them ineligible for continued representation under the Act.

(6) In all cases appealed by counsel appointed by the district court under the Act, if such counsel has not previously been relieved by this court, the clerk shall continue trial counsel's appointment for purposes of further representation on appeal.

(7) The court or any judge thereof who resides in the state in which is located the district court from which the appeal is taken may enter an appropriate order appointing any new counsel required by order of the court to be provided on appeal for a party financially unable to obtain counsel.

(8) In cases where appointment of counsel under the Act is to be made for the first time on appeal, before submitting the order of appointment to the appropriate judge of this court, the clerk shall request the party to execute an affidavit

specifying the party's financial inability to employ counsel. Upon the party's return of the duly executed affidavit, the clerk will serve a copy upon opposing counsel, with advice that within 14 days (unless this time is extended by the court or the clerk for the court), counsel may furnish proof that the affidavit is false. Further action may thereafter be taken or directed by the appropriate judge upon receiving the clerk's submission of the available papers and evidence.

(9) If at any stage of the proceedings on appeal the court finds a party is financially unable to pay counsel already retained by the party, the court may appoint counsel as provided in subsection (b) of the Act and authorize payment as provided in subsection (d) of the Act, pursuant to subsection (c) of the Act.

(10) In appeals under the Act involving more than one party, if the court finds the need, because of conflicting interests of parties or because circumstances otherwise warrant, separate counsel may be appointed for any one or more of the parties as required for their adequate representation.

(11) The court may at its discretion and in the interest of justice substitute one appointed counsel for another at any stage of the proceedings on appeal.

(12) The court may at its discretion and where circumstances warrant make appointments of counsel retroactive so as to include representation furnished prior to appointment, and it may authorize compensation therefor pursuant to subsections (c) and (d) of the Act.

(e) Withdrawal or Release of Appointed Counsel.

(1) As stated in § (d)(2) of this plan, counsel appointed under the Act to represent a party in district court shall continue such representation until either successor counsel is appointed under the Act or counsel is relieved by order of the court of appeals.

(2) If trial counsel appointed under the Act by the district court wishes to be relieved from the duty of representing the party on appeal, counsel shall file with the clerk of the court of appeals an original and one copy of a motion asking for such relief and stating the grounds therefor, but shall nevertheless continue to represent the party on appeal until relieved by the court of appeals. The district court may also relieve counsel appointed under the Act provided it substitutes counsel as provided under subsection (c) of the Act. Also see § (d)(2) of this plan.

(3) If a party for whom counsel was appointed by the district court under the Act wishes appointed counsel relieved and replacement counsel appointed, the party shall file with the clerk of the court of appeals a motion requesting such relief, and the clerk shall submit this motion to the court for ruling.

(f) Duties of Appointed Counsel.

(1) In all cases appealed under the Act or in forma pauperis where trial counsel has been appointed by the district court under the Act, the appointed counsel shall file with the district court the appropriate CJA Form 24 for the court reporter's furnishing the transcript of testimony at the expense of the United States.

(2) Appointed counsel shall furnish the party represented, upon written request, with a copy of motion papers and briefs filed for the party on the appeal, and shall send the party a copy of the court's decision when issued; the clerk will send appointed counsel an extra copy of the decision for this purpose.

(3) If oral argument is scheduled, appointed counsel shall appear unless otherwise directed by the court.

(4) Appointed counsel shall advise the party represented in each case covered by the Act that, if the party wishes to appeal to the court of appeals or file a petition for a writ of certiorari with the Supreme Court, the right exists under the Act to do so without prepayment of fees and costs or giving security therefor and without filing the affidavit of financial inability to pay such costs required by 28 U.S.C. § 1915(a).

(5) If the decision of this court is adverse to the client, counsel shall inform the client of the right to file a petition for rehearing or petition for rehearing en banc in this court, or to petition the Supreme Court of the United States for a writ of certiorari. Counsel shall file a petition for rehearing, a petition for rehearing en banc, or a petition for a writ of certiorari if requested to do so by the client in writing, but only if in counsel's considered judgment sufficient grounds exist. Sufficient grounds for requesting rehearing en banc do not exist unless the suggestion would satisfy the standards of FRAP 35(a). See 11th Cir. R. 35-3. Sufficient grounds for filing a petition for a writ of certiorari do not exist unless in counsel's considered judgment there are grounds that are not frivolous and are consistent with the standards for filing a petition under the Rules of the Supreme Court and applicable case law. If counsel concludes that there are *not* sufficient grounds to seek further review of a type requested by the client, counsel shall so inform the client and shall advise the client that such review will not be sought by counsel. In such circumstances, counsel is not required to move to withdraw. If the client petitions the Supreme Court of the United States for a writ of certiorari, and the Supreme Court grants certiorari and remands the matter to this court for further consideration, counsel shall resume representation of the client in proceedings before this court.

(6) No appointed representative under this plan shall accept any payment from or on behalf of the person represented in this court without prior authorization by a United States circuit judge. All such authorized payments shall be received subject to the directions contained in any such order and pursuant to the provisions of subsection (f) of the Act.

(g) Payment of Claims for Compensation and Expenses.

(1) In all appeals covered by the Act, the court of appeals may authorize compensation for services and reimbursement of necessary expenses reasonably incurred in representing a party on appeal within the limitations of the Act, by any private attorney, bar association, legal aid agency, federal public defender organization or community defender organization appointed by the court. In fixing compensation the court will be mindful that the hourly rates of compensation allowed by the Act are intended as maximum rates. Hourly rates for representation on appeal shall in no event exceed the amounts fixed in the statutes. In fixing compensation the court may

take into account factors other than the hours expended multiplied by the hourly rate allowed under the Act. Factors considered in authorizing fees include cases involving comparable issues, comparable records, comparable days at trial, work by other lawyers on the same case, and other matters where comparisons may be fairly drawn. Adequate compensation is the benchmark in making such awards.

(2) Except as provided in subsection (3) of this section, for representation of a party under the Act, compensation shall not exceed for each attorney in each court the amount fixed by statute.

(3) Payments for representation on appeal in excess of the total limitations contained in the Act may be made for extended or complex representation, provided payment is approved by the chief judge of the circuit or the chief judge's designee.

(4) Travel expenses and other expenses reasonably incurred and necessary for adequate representation on appeal may be claimed by an appointed attorney or other legal representative under this plan. The clerk of court shall furnish each attorney or other representative at the time of appointment with information as to expenses currently allowable under the Act in accordance with rules, regulations and guidelines promulgated by the Judicial Conference of the United States. Per diem may not be claimed in lieu of actual travel and subsistence expenses. Meal and lodging expenses incurred incident to representation on appeal, necessary long distance telephone calls or telegrams, and the cost of photocopying (but not printing), are reimbursable expenses within the guidelines established by the court. Expenses of general office overhead, personal items, filing fees and expenses for printing of briefs are not reimbursable (parties represented in cases covered by the Act are not required to pay filing fees or to print their briefs on appeal). Expenses of travel by private automobile may be claimed on a straight mileage basis at the authorized rate. See § (b) of the guidelines, below. Parking fees and toll expenses are allowable. Transportation other than by private automobile may be claimed on an actual cost basis, but first class fare is not permitted unless absolutely necessary and documentation is provided that tourist or economy fares were not available.

(5) Unless otherwise ordered by the court for good cause shown, travel expenses other than those incurred in connection with attending oral argument will not be reimbursed without a prior ex parte application to and approval by the court.

(6) All claims for compensation and reimbursement of expenses for representation on appeal shall be itemized in detail and filed with the clerk of court on officially approved forms that the clerk's office will provide. A CJA voucher claiming compensation for time spent on appeal should be filed no later than **60 days** after either issuance of mandate *or* filing with the U.S. Supreme Court of a petition for a writ of certiorari (whichever is later). Failure to file a CJA voucher within the time permitted by these rules **may result in a reduction in the fees awarded** pursuant to the Act.

(7) After approval of allowable compensation and reimbursable expenses payment will be made by the Administrative Office of the United States Courts.

(8) Time and expenses required for preparation of a petition for writ of certiorari, a response to a petition for a writ of certiorari, or a reply to a response to a petition for a writ of certiorari, should be claimed on the voucher as an expense incident to representation before the court of appeals rather than claimed in the Supreme Court. See § (f)(4), above.

(9) When it is considered necessary and appropriate in a specific case, the court on motion of counsel may approve interim payments under the Act. Such interim payments are designed to strike a balance between the interest in relieving court-appointed counsel of financial hardship in extended and complex cases, and the practical application of the statutorily imposed responsibility of the chief judge of the circuit to provide a meaningful review of claims for excess compensation. See § (g)(3), above. Absent exceptional circumstances such interim compensation as may be approved will not ordinarily exceed the amounts specified in 18 U.S.C. § 3006A(d)(2). At the conclusion of representation, counsel should submit a final voucher claiming time and expenses not previously approved, including any amounts claimed on interim vouchers which were not compensated.

[Adopted effective January 24, 1985. Amended effective May 9, 1985; April 1, 1991; January 2, 1996; December 1, 1998; January 1, 2000; January 1, 2002; December, 2006.]

GUIDELINES FOR COUNSEL SUPPLEMENTING THE ELEVENTH CIRCUIT PLAN UNDER THE CRIMINAL JUSTICE ACT

(a) Compensation for Legal Services.

(1) *Maximum Compensation.* Allowable compensation rates for counsel are set out in 18 U.S.C. § 3006A(d). The Judicial Council may from time to time authorize special rates of compensation for certain classes of cases, or for counsel practicing in certain locations. Special rates have been established for capital cases. Information regarding special rates is available from the clerk.

(2) *Writ of Certiorari.* Counsel claiming time and expenses for preparation of a petition for a writ of certiorari, a response to a petition for a writ of certiorari, or a reply to a response to a petition for a writ of certiorari, must include a copy of the petition, response, or reply with the voucher.

(3) *Compensation for Substitute Attorneys.* If an attorney is substituted for one previously appointed in the same case the total compensation that may be paid to both attorneys shall not exceed the statutory maximum for one defendant, unless the case involves extended or complex representation. In such a case vouchers for counsels' services shall not be approved until the conclusion of the appeal.

(4) *Itemized Listing of Hours Expended.* Counsel shall submit with the CJA voucher an itemized memorandum detailing how the hours claimed were expended.

(5) *Travel Time.* Reasonable and necessary travel time consistent with guidelines established by the Judicial Conference of the United States is compensable at the out of court hourly rate.

(b) Compensation for Reimbursable Expenses.

(1) *Travel and Transportation Expenses.* Travel and transportation must be accomplished by the most economical means available. Only actual expenses may be claimed.

(i) Air Transportation. The clerk's office will arrange for counsel to obtain air transportation at the government rate charged to the court's account. At the time the appeal is scheduled for oral argument, the clerk's office provides counsel with an Air Travel Authorization that may be used to obtain government rate airline tickets from the government's contract travel agency. If counsel decides not to make air travel arrangements in this manner, reimbursement for air travel may not exceed the government rate that could have been obtained by following the procedures provided by the clerk's office.

(ii) Automobile Transportation. The total mileage cost shall not exceed the fare authorized for travel by tourist or economy air transport except in an emergency or for other compelling reasons. Travel by privately owned automobile shall not exceed the current government authorized rate for official travel per mile on a straight mileage basis, plus parking fees, ferry, bridge, road, and tunnel fares.

(iii) Local Transportation. Local travel will be accomplished by the most economical means available and only actual expenses may be claimed. Transportation to and from an airport should be by airport shuttle, if available.

(iv) Meals and Lodging. Reasonable compensation for hotel or motel accommodations and meals will be allowed on an actual expense basis subject to the limitations governing compensation for federal employees traveling to the same destination. Counsel will be notified by the clerk prior to the scheduled oral argument session of the current limitations. A copy of the hotel or motel bill shall be attached to the voucher.

(2) *Photocopying.* Actual costs not to exceed 25 cents per page will be paid if the copying bill is submitted. For in-house copying, actual costs not to exceed 15 cents per page will be paid.

(3) *Express Mail and Other Special Arrangements.* For delivery of items that could have been mailed via U.S. Postal Service first class mail, additional expenses will be reimbursed only if a satisfactory explanation is given why first class mail service was not utilized. In non-emergency cases routine documents such as briefs and motions should be prepared early enough to permit use of first class mail. (See also FRAP 25(a).)

(4) *Computer Assisted Legal Research.*

(i) By Court Appointed Counsel. The cost of use, by appointed counsel, of computer assisted legal research services, may be allowed as a reimbursable out-of-pocket expense, provided that the amount claimed is reasonable. Whenever appointed counsel incurs charges for computer assisted legal research, counsel should attach to the compensation voucher a copy of the bill and receipt for the use of the legal research services or an explanation of the precise basis of the charge (e.g., indicating the extent to which it was derived by proration of monthly charges, or by charges identifiable to the specific research). If the amount claimed is in excess of $500 or if it includes costs for downloading or printing, counsel should include a brief statement of justification.

(ii) By Commercial Computer Assisted Legal Research Services. The court may in advance authorize counsel to obtain computer assisted legal research services, where the research is performed by employees of a commercial legal research firm or organization rather than by appointed counsel, provided that the total amount charged for computer assisted legal research services is reasonable. Requests by counsel for authorization to obtain such computer assisted legal research services should include the following:

a—a brief explanation of the need for the research services; and

b—an estimate of the charges.

(5) *Miscellaneous Expenses.* The lowest possible cost for expenses such as postage, telephone calls, brief supplies, and parking, shall be incurred.

(6) *Briefs.* Reimbursement will be provided only for the number of copies of briefs and record excerpts required by the rules to be filed and served, plus two copies for each party signing the brief. The number of copies and number of pages must be itemized on the voucher.

[Adopted effective January 24, 1985. Amended effective May 9, 1985; April 1, 1991; January 1, 2002; December, 2006; December 1, 2009.]

ADDENDUM FIVE. NON-CRIMINAL JUSTICE ACT COUNSEL APPOINTMENTS

The court adopts these provisions for furnishing representation for persons financially unable to obtain adequate representation in cases and situations which do not fall within the scope of 18 U.S.C. § 3006A, as amended—but in which the court believes that the interests of justice will be served by the presence of counsel.

(a) Determination of Need. In determining need for appointment of counsel, the court shall generally be governed by the guidelines outlined in 18 U.S.C. § 3006A.

(b) Appointment of Counsel.

(1) Counsel shall be selected from the same panels of attorneys designated or approved by the district courts of the Eleventh Circuit as described in Addendum Four, which are hereby approved by this court, or from a bar association, legal aid agency, or other approved organization. In addition, any judge of this court may appoint competent counsel not otherwise included in the preceding categories.

(2) Any person seeking relief under 29 U.S.C. § 621, 42 U.S.C. § 1981, 42 U.S.C. § 1982, 42 U.S.C. § 1983, 42 U.S.C. § 1985, 42 U.S.C. § 1986, 42 U.S.C. § 2000a, 42 U.S.C. § 2000d, and 42 U.S.C. § 2000e or in such other cases as the court shall determine to be appropriate may be eligible for representation. The court may approve such representation on a determination that the interests of justice so require and that the person is financially unable to obtain representation.

(3) The court may at its discretion and in the interest of justice substitute one appointed counsel for another at any stage of the proceedings on appeal.

(4) The court may at its discretion and where circumstances warrant make appointments of counsel retroactive so as to include representation furnished prior to appointment.

(c) Withdrawal or Release of Appointed Counsel. Counsel appointed under this rule to represent a party shall continue such representation until relieved by order of the court of appeals.

(d) Duties of Appointed Counsel.

(1) Appointed counsel shall furnish the party represented, upon written request, with a copy of motion papers and briefs filed for the party on the appeal, and shall send the party a copy of the court's decision when issued; the clerk will send appointed counsel an extra copy of the decision for this purpose.

(2) Appointed counsel shall appear for oral argument only when directed by the court.

(3) In the event of affirmance or other decision adverse to the party represented appointed counsel shall promptly advise the party in writing of the right to seek further review by the filing of a petition for writ of certiorari with the Supreme Court.

(4) Appointed counsel shall advise the party represented in each case that, if the party wishes to file a petition for a writ of certiorari with the Supreme Court, the party may have the right to do so without prepayment of fees and costs or giving security therefor.

(5) No appointed representative under this rule shall accept a payment from or on behalf of the person represented in this court without prior authorization by a United States circuit judge.

(e) Payment of Claims for Expenses.

(1) In all appeals covered by this rule, the court of appeals may authorize reimbursement of necessary expenses reasonably incurred in representing a party on appeal, consistent with the limitations contained in the Criminal Justice Act, by any private attorney, bar association, legal aid agency, or other approved organization appointed by the court for the purpose of representing a party on appeal pursuant to this addendum. Compensation for attorney services as a fee for either in-court or out-of-court time is not authorized.

(2) Travel expenses and other expenses reasonably incurred and necessary for adequate representation on appeal may be claimed by an appointed attorney or other legal representative. The clerk of court shall furnish each attorney or other representative at the time of appointment with information as to expenses currently allowable and in accordance with rules, regulations and guidelines promulgated by the Judicial Conference of the United States. Per diem may not be claimed in lieu of actual travel and subsistence expenses. Meal and lodging expenses incurred incident to representation on appeal, necessary long distance telephone calls or telegrams, and the cost of photocopying (but not printing), are reimbursable expenses within the guidelines established by the court. Expenses of general office overhead, personal items, filing fees and expenses of printing of briefs are not reimbursable. Expenses of travel by private automobile may be claimed on a straight mileage basis at the authorized rate. See § (6) of the guidelines, below. Parking fees and toll expenses are allowable. Transportation other than by private automobile may be claimed on an actual cost basis, but first class fare is not permitted unless absolutely necessary and documentation is provided that tourist or economy fares were not available.

(3) Unless otherwise ordered by the court for good cause shown, travel expenses other than those incurred in connection with attending oral argument will not be reimbursed without a prior ex parte application to and approval by the court.

(4) All claims for reimbursement of expenses for representation on appeal shall be itemized in detail and filed with the clerk of court on officially approved forms that the clerk's office will provide. Claims should be filed as promptly as possible and in no event later than 60 days after issuance of the mandate.

(5) After approval of allowable reimbursable expenses by the court, the claim form will be forwarded to the circuit executive for payment.

(6) *Reimbursable Expenses.*

(a) Travel and Transportation Expenses. Travel and transportation must be accomplished by the most economical means available. Only actual expenses may be claimed.

(i) Air Transportation. Tourist or economy accommodations must be used except where unavailable. A copy of the ticket must be attached to the claim form. If travel by first class air transportation is claimed a detailed explanation of the reasons therefor must be provided with the ticket copy.

(ii) Automobile Transportation. The total mileage cost shall not exceed the fare authorized for travel by tourist or economy air transport except in an emergency or for other compelling reasons. Travel by privately owned automobile shall not exceed the current government authorized rate for official travel per mile on a straight mileage basis, plus parking fees, ferry, bridge, road, and tunnel fares.

(iii) Local Transportation. Local travel will be accomplished by the most economical means available and only actual expenses may be claimed. Transportation to and from an airport should be by airport shuttle, if available.

(iv) Meals and Lodging. Reasonable compensation for hotel or motel accommodations and meals will be allowed on an actual expense basis subject to the limitations governing compensation for federal employees traveling to the same destination. Counsel will be notified by the clerk prior to the scheduled oral argument session of the current limitations. A copy of the hotel or motel bill shall be attached to the claim form.

(b) Photocopying. Actual costs not to exceed 25 cents per page will be paid if copy bill is submitted. For in-house copying, actual costs not to exceed 15 cents per page will be paid.

(c) Express Mail and Other Special Arrangements. For delivery of items that could have been mailed via U.S. Postal Service first class mail, additional expenses will be reimbursed only if a satisfactory explanation is given why first class mail service was not utilized. In non-emergency cases routine documents such as briefs and motions should be prepared early enough to permit use of first class mail.

(d) Computer Assisted Legal Research.

(i) By Court Appointed Counsel. The cost of use, by appointed counsel, of computer assisted legal research services, may be allowed as a reimbursable out-of-pocket expense, provided that the amount claimed is reasonable. Whenever appointed counsel incurs charges for computer assisted legal research, counsel should attach to the claim form a copy of the bill and receipt for the use of the legal research services or an explanation of the precise basis of the charge (e.g., indicating the extent to which it was derived by proration of monthly charges, or by charges identifiable to the specific research). If the amount claimed is in excess of $500 or if it includes costs for downloading or printing, counsel should include a brief statement of justification.

(ii) By Commercial Computer Assisted Legal Research Services. The court may in advance authorize counsel to obtain computer assisted legal research services, where the research is performed by employees of a commercial legal research firm or organization rather than by appointed counsel, provided that the total amount charged for computer assisted legal research services is reasonable. Requests by counsel for authority to obtain such computer assisted legal research services should include the following:

a—a brief explanation of the need for the research services; and

b—an estimate of the charges.

(e) Miscellaneous Expenses. The lowest possible cost for expenses such as postage, telephone calls, brief supplies, and parking, shall be incurred.

(f) Briefs. Reimbursement will be provided only for the number of copies of briefs and record excerpts required by the rules to be filed and served, plus two copies for each party signing the brief. The number of copies and number of pages must be itemized on the claim form.

(g) Funding. By resolution the court may allocate from time to time certain monies from its nonappropriated fund account to support this program of non-CJA counsel appointments.

[Adopted effective January 24, 1985. Amended effective May 9, 1985; April 1, 1991; October, 1992; August 1, 2007.]

ADDENDUM SIX. RULES AND REGULATIONS OF THE JUDICIAL COUNCIL AND THE UNITED STATES COURT OF APPEALS FOR THE ELEVENTH CIRCUIT FOR THE SELECTION OF NOMINEES, THE APPOINTMENT OF BANKRUPTCY JUDGES, AND THE REAPPOINTMENT OF BANKRUPTCY JUDGES

PURPOSE

United States bankruptcy judges exercise important judicial powers and responsibilities as officers of the United States district courts. It is therefore imperative that only highly qualified individuals be selected as bankruptcy judges. These regulations are adopted in accordance with the Regulations of the Judicial Conference of the United States for the Selection, Appointment and Reappointment of United States Bankruptcy Judges and governing statutes. These regulations set forth procedural guidelines that create no vested rights for any prospective or incumbent bankruptcy judge.

Bankruptcy judges will be appointed without regard to race, color, sex, religion, or national origin.

PART A. SELECTION AND APPOINTMENT OF BANKRUPTCY JUDGES

1. Establishment of Committee. Upon notification of a bankruptcy judge vacancy, the procedures of Chapter 3 of the Rules and Regulations of the Judicial Conference of the United States for the Selection, Appointment and Reappointment of United States Bankruptcy Judges shall be initiated and conducted by a committee consisting of the resident members of the Council in the state in which the vacancy exists.

2. Public Notice of Position Vacancy. The circuit executive will be responsible for advertising each vacancy in accordance with the regulations established by the Judicial Conference of the United States for the selection of United States Bankruptcy Judge nominees. After the deadline for applications, the circuit executive will forward all applications received to the committee.

3. Committee Duties.

a. *General.* The committee shall determine for the Judicial Council that:

1. public notice of such vacancy has been given and an effort has been made, in the case of each such vacancy to identify qualified candidates, without regard to race, color, sex, religion, or national origin;

2. such persons are members in good standing of at least one State bar, or the District of Columbia bar, and members in good standing of every bar of which they are members;

3. such persons possess, and have a reputation for, integrity and good character;

4. such persons are of sound physical and mental health;

5. such persons possess and have demonstrated commitment to equal justice under law;

6. such persons possess and have demonstrated outstanding legal ability and competence, as evidenced by substantial legal experience, ability to deal with complex legal problems, aptitude for legal scholarship and writing, and familiarity with courts and court processes; and

7. such person's demeanor, character, and personality indicate they would exhibit judicial temperament if appointed to the position of United States bankruptcy judge.

b. *Procedures.*

1. The committee shall interview such a number of qualified applicants as it deems appropriate. As a general rule, the committee will have interviewed those applicants whom it recommends as "best qualified."

2. The committee shall: (a) give the names of all applicants with brief resumes to the Council, (b) report with supporting information all nominees who are considered "best qualified," (c) designate the nominee(s) it recommends be submitted by the Council to the Court, and (d) recommend the nominee(s) whom it thinks should be interviewed by the Court.

3. The committee report will provide deadlines for objection by Council members and recommend deadlines for objection to the Council report by Court members. Such deadlines shall reasonably meet the time required for a study of the report. Procedures for modification of the reports of either the committee or the Council may be conducted by telephone in order to meet the time set for Court interviews.

c. The application of a sitting bankruptcy judge should not be considered for any position within that judge's district other than the one the judge occupies.

4. Duties of the Judicial Council. Except for other duties as provided in the Act or in the Judicial Conference regulations, the committee report shall be the Council report unless a Council member objects and the report is modified on motion passed by a majority vote of the Council.

5. Duties of the Court of Appeals.

a. Following receipt of the names of the nominees, the Court shall interview the nominee(s) recommended in the Council report, unless a Court member objects and the recommendation is modified by motion of any Court member passed by majority vote. In no event will any appointment be made without the appointee having been personally interviewed by the Court.

b. One person shall be selected by the Court of Appeals for appointment and that person's name shall be submitted to the Director of the Administrative Office, who shall request investigations by the Federal Bureau of Investigation and the Internal Revenue Service. It is contemplated that the investigation by the FBI shall be a full-field investigation.

c. Information received from the FBI and IRS shall be reviewed by the Chief Judge of the circuit. If the Chief Judge of the circuit determines that information in the FBI and IRS reports warrants review, the Chief Judge shall send the reports to the Court of Appeals judges who served on the Judicial Council's screening committee or the full Court. If the Chief Judge of the circuit determines that the FBI and IRS reports contain no negative information, the Chief Judge may issue an order of appointment on behalf of the Court. If the IRS report is not received in a timely manner, the Chief Judge may waive the report, provided that the Chief Judge is satisfied and so reports to the other members of the Court that tax returns have been filed by the selectee as required.

d. The appointment of the bankruptcy judge shall be entered of record in the Court of Appeals and the pertinent district court or courts, and notice of such appointment shall be given at once by the clerk of the Court of Appeals to the Director of the Administrative Office. The clerk will, at that time, provide the Director a copy of the public notice.

6. Confidentiality of Public Comments.

a. If a member of the public makes a comment concerning the qualifications of a bankruptcy judge candidate, the person making the comment may request that their identity be kept confidential. The applicant will, however, be provided with a general description of the source and nature of any comments.

b. The selection committee or the Court of Appeals may determine, at its sole discretion, that the identity of a person making a comment should be disclosed to the candidate in order to afford the applicant a fair opportunity to respond to the comment. In that event, the person making the comment will be given an opportunity to withdraw the comment before the commenter's identity is disclosed to the candidate. If the comment is withdrawn, it will not be considered by the selection committee or the Court of Appeals, and the identity of the person making the comment will remain confidential. If the person making the comment waives confidentiality, the commenter's name will be revealed to the candidate, along with the substance of the comment.

PART B. REAPPOINTMENT OF BANKRUPTCY JUDGES

1. Incumbent's Written Notice. The Court requires incumbents seeking reappointment to submit a written notification of willingness to accept reappointment twelve months before the bankruptcy judge's term expires. Receipt of the notification by the Court will commence the reappointment process. The circuit executive, on behalf of the Chief Judge, will forward the Questionnaire for Reappointment as United States Bankruptcy Judge to the incumbent for completion and return to the circuit executive. The incumbent judge, however, must also submit Official Form Per–74 not earlier than nine months and not later than six months before expiration of the judge's term as required by the Guide to Judiciary Policy in order to protect retirement benefits pursuant to 28 U.S.C. § 377(b). The Court may reappoint an incumbent bankruptcy judge to a new 14–year term of office without considering other potentially qualified candidates.

2. Establishment of Committee. Upon notification of an incumbent bankruptcy judge's willingness to accept reappointment to a new 14–year term of office, the procedures of Chapter 5 of the Regulations of the Judicial Conference of the United States for the Selection, Appointment and Reappointment of United States Bankruptcy Judges shall be initiated and conducted by a committee consisting of the resident members of the Council in the state in which the incumbent sits.

3. Public Notice Soliciting Comments. Within 60 days of receipt of the timely Official Form Per–74, the circuit executive shall cause to be published a public notice in accordance with the regulations established by the Judicial Conference of the United States for the reappointment of United States Bankruptcy Judges. The comment period shall not exceed 45 days. The circuit executive will submit the comments from the public to the reappointment committee within 10 days after the deadline for submission of comments.

4. Committee Duties. The committee will seek comments from members of the bar and the public regarding their assessment of the incumbent judge's: 1) judicial conduct; 2) effectiveness as a bankruptcy judge; 3) effectiveness as a supervisor of judicial employees; and 4) suitability for reappointment to another 14–year term as bankruptcy judge. The committee may interview the incumbent bankruptcy judge as it deems appropriate. The committee will report to the Council on the measures taken to obtain public comment, a summary of the comments received, and the committee's recommendation regarding the reappointment. The committee report will provide deadlines for objection by Council members and recommend deadlines for objection to the Council report by Court members.

5. Duties of the Judicial Council. Except for other duties as provided in the Act or in the Judicial Conference Regulations, the committee report shall be the Council report unless a Council member objects and the report is modified on motion passed by majority vote of the Council.

6. Duties of the Court of Appeals. Not later than 60 days after the Court of Appeals receives from the circuit executive the comments of the members of the bar and public, and after due consideration of those comments, the active judges of the Court of Appeals shall vote whether to reappoint the incumbent. Following receipt of the Council report, the Court also may interview the incumbent bankruptcy judge. The reappointment decision will be determined by a vote of the active judges of the Court of Appeals as set forth in Section 5.03 of the Judicial Conference of the United States Regulations. Upon reappointment, the Court will issue an order of appointment which shall be entered of record in the Court of Appeals and the pertinent district court or courts, and notice of such appointment shall be given at once by the Clerk of the Court of Appeals to the Director of the Administrative Office.

7. Confidentiality of Public Comments.

a. If a member of the public makes a comment concerning the qualifications of the incumbent, the person making the comment may request that their identity be kept confidential.

The incumbent will, however, be provided with a general description of the source and nature of any comments.

b. The selection committee or the Court of Appeals may determine, at its sole discretion, that the identity of a person making a comment should be disclosed to the incumbent in order to afford the incumbent a fair opportunity to respond to the comment. In that event, the person making the comment will be given an opportunity to withdraw the comment before the commenter's identity is disclosed to the incumbent. If the comment is withdrawn, it will not be considered by the selection committee or the Court of Appeals, and the identity of the person making the comment will remain confidential. If the person making the comment waives confidentiality, the commenter's name will be revealed to the incumbent, along with the substance of the comment.

[Adopted effective January 24, 1985. Amended effective October 19, 1987; October, 1992; December 1, 2009; May 7, 2010; November 20, 2012.]

ADDENDUM SEVEN. REGULATIONS OF THE UNITED STATES COURT OF APPEALS FOR THE ELEVENTH CIRCUIT FOR THE SELECTION AND APPOINTMENT OR THE REAPPOINTMENT OF FEDERAL PUBLIC DEFENDERS

1. Purpose. Federal public defenders exercise important powers and responsibilities as officers of the United States Courts. It is imperative that highly qualified individuals be selected and retained as public defenders. For the expeditious and orderly achievement of this end, as well as to ensure that federal public defenders provide competent, independent counsel and vigorous representation to indigent persons, the United States Court of Appeals for the Eleventh Circuit has adopted the regulations set forth herein. These regulations shall be administered through a Federal Public Defender Committee appointed by the Chief Judge of the Eleventh Circuit Court of Appeals pursuant to Section 3 of these regulations.

2. Authority. The Criminal Justice Act, 18 U.S.C. § 3006A(g), provides that "A Federal Public Defender Organization ... shall be supervised by a Federal Public Defender appointed by the court of appeals of the circuit ... after considering recommendations from the district court or courts to be served."

3. Federal Public Defender Committee.

a. *Appointment of Federal Public Defender Committee.* The Chief Judge of the U.S. Court of Appeals shall appoint a Federal Public Defender Committee [hereinafter "Committee"]. The Committee shall consist of a U.S. Circuit Judge, a U.S. District Judge from each district which has established a Federal Public Defender Organization pursuant to 18 U.S.C. § 3006A(g)(2)(A), and one or more lawyers from each such district who specialize in the practice of criminal law and are themselves qualified for appointment as a Federal Public Defender under Section 5 of these regulations.

b. *Terms of Committee Members.* The U.S. Circuit Judge and each district judge appointed to the Committee shall serve for a term of two years. One–third of the lawyers first appointed shall serve a term of one year, one-third for two years, and the remainder and all thereafter appointed for a term of three years. Each member shall serve until his or her successor has been appointed. The Chief Judge of the U.S. Court of Appeals may vacate an appointment at any time.

c. *Functions of Committee.*

(1) The Committee shall determine which applicants meet the qualifications for appointment as a federal public defender as set forth in Section 5 of these regulations.

(2) The Committee shall examine applications and evaluate all qualified candidates without regard to race, color, age, gender, religion, disability, or national origin.

(3) If a federal public defender has applied for an additional four-year term, the Committee shall also consider public comments received and the results of the survey conducted pursuant to Section 6 of these regulations in its evaluation of the Federal Public Defender's application.

(4) The Committee shall interview at least four of the applicants determined to be qualified. If the Committee determines that less than four qualified persons have applied for the position, it may either reopen the application process or report to the Chief Judge of the U.S. Court of Appeals why fewer than four qualified persons could reasonably be expected to apply for the position.

d. *Committee Chair, Votes, and Quorum.*

(1) The Chief Judge of the U.S. Court of Appeals shall designate one of the members of the Committee to serve as Chair.

(2) Decisions of the Committee shall be made by a majority of those participating.

(3) A majority of the Committee shall constitute a quorum.

4. Term of Appointment of Federal Public Defenders. The Criminal Justice Act provides that the U.S. Court of Appeals shall appoint a person to serve as Federal Public Defender for a four-year term. The expiration date of a four-year term is the day prior to the fourth anniversary of the date the oath of office was administered. The Administrative Office of the United States Courts determines the precise expiration date of a four-year term of office.

5. Qualifications for Appointment as Federal Public Defender. To be qualified for appointment as Federal Public Defender, applicants must:

a. be members in good standing of at least one state bar, or the District of Columbia, or Virgin Islands bar, and members in good standing of every other bar of which they are members;

b. have been engaged in the active practice of criminal law for a period of at least five years, preferably with significant federal criminal trial and appellate experience;

c. possess the ability to administer a federal public defender's office effectively;

d. possess, and have a reputation for:

(1) integrity and good character;

(2) sound physical and mental health;

(3) commitment to equal justice under law and vigorous representation of his or her clients;

(4) outstanding legal ability and competence (evidenced by substantial legal experience, ability to deal with complex legal problems, aptitude for legal scholarship and writing, and familiarity with courts and court processes);

e. have a commitment to the vigorous representation of those unable to afford counsel; and

f. not be related by blood or marriage to a judge of the Eleventh Circuit Court of Appeals or to a judge of the district court to be served, within the degrees specified in Title 28, United States Code, Section 458 at the time of the initial appointment.

The Federal Public Defender Committee will resolve any questions regarding the qualifications of applicants.

6. Federal Public Defender Committee's Evaluation of the Performance of the Incumbent Federal Public Defender.

a. Prior to the conclusion of the third year of each four-year term, the Federal Public Defender Committee shall conduct an evaluation of the administration of the Federal Public Defender's office. The purpose of this evaluation is to identify strengths and weaknesses in the administration of the office and to provide the Federal Public Defender with an opportunity to initiate corrective measures if any administrative deficiencies are discovered. The performance of the Federal Public Defender will be evaluated in terms of the quality of representation, the level of commitment to vigorous representation and service to clients, and administrative efficiency of the office. This evaluation will be based on information received through a solicitation for public comment and a written survey designed and administered by the Committee.

(1) A solicitation for public comment regarding the performance of the Federal Public Defender and his or her office will be placed by the Committee in the major metropolitan or legal newspapers within the district served by the Federal Public Defender.

(2) The Committee shall also conduct a written survey of the administration of the office of the Federal Public Defender. That survey shall be distributed to district judges, magistrate judges, the Defender Services Division of the Administrative Office of the United States Courts, and to any other persons whose employment places them in a position to observe the performance of the Federal Public Defender, the quality of representation, the level of commitment to vigorous representation and service to clients, and administrative efficiency of the Federal Public Defender's office.

(3) The Committee may make such additional inquiry as it considers appropriate concerning the quality of services provided by the Federal Public Defender office in the district. With the prior approval of the Chief Judge of the U.S. Court of Appeals, the Committee may appoint consultants to assist it in its evaluation of the administration of a federal public defender's office.

(4) At the conclusion of the survey period the Committee shall prepare a statistical summary of the results of its survey and a narrative summary of the responses to the solicitation for public comment.

(5) The Federal Public Defender shall be afforded an opportunity to review and respond to the statistical summary and narrative summary prepared by the Committee.

(6) The Committee should meet with the Federal Public Defender to discuss the evaluation of his or her office, if such conference is warranted by the responses to the request for public comment or the survey.

7. Incumbent Federal Public Defenders.

a. *Eligibility of Federal Public Defenders for Reappointment.* The Criminal Justice Act permits appointment of an incumbent Federal Public Defender to an additional four-year term. There is not, however, a legitimate expectation of a right to reappointment or a presumption that the Federal Public Defender is the best qualified applicant for a subsequent four-year term.

b. *Application by Federal Public Defender for Additional Four-Year Term.* Approximately one year prior to expiration of the four-year term of office, the Administrative Office of the United States Courts advises the Chief Judge of the U.S. Court of Appeals of the expiration date of each four-year term. Upon receipt of this notice, the Chief Judge of the U.S. Court of Appeals shall write to the incumbent Federal Public Defender to inquire whether he or she intends to again apply for appointment at the expiration of his or her term of office. The Federal Public Defender shall notify the Chief Judge of the U.S. Court of Appeals whether he or she wishes to apply for an additional four-year term within 35 days of the receipt of the inquiry from the Chief Judge of the U.S. Court of Appeals.

c. *Evaluation Statement to Accompany Application.* If the Federal Public Defender applies for appointment for an additional four-year term, such application shall be accompanied by a written statement prepared by the Federal Public Defender setting forth an evaluation of his or her administration of the office of Federal Public Defender. This statement shall assess the strengths and weaknesses of his or her administration of the office of Federal Public Defender and the steps that should be taken to eliminate any deficiencies and strengthen the administration of the office.

8. Public Recruitment of Qualified Candidates.

a. *Public Notice.* At the end of each four-year term, or when a vacancy occurs due to the resignation, removal, or incapacity of the occupant of the office of Federal Public Defender, a public notice shall issue announcing that applications are being accepted for a four-year term for the position of Federal Public Defender for the particular district. The public notice shall advise all applicants that the U.S. Court of Appeals for the Eleventh Circuit is searching for the best qualified person currently available for this position and that the U.S. Court of Appeals for the Eleventh Circuit encourages applications from all qualified persons including women, members of minority groups, and individuals with disabilities. If the Federal Public Defender has applied for an additional four-year term, the notice shall also state that the Federal Public Defender has applied for reappointment and that his or her application will be reviewed under the same standards applied to all other applicants.

b. *Publication of Public Notice.* The Committee shall seek qualified applicants who reflect the makeup in the relevant national labor market and will use adequate means to publicize the existence of a vacancy to all segments of the relevant national labor market.

(1) The Committee shall publish a notice that applications are being accepted for a four-year term as Federal Public Defender in a national publication for the legal profession.

(2) Whenever possible, the Committee shall also advertise in publications from each of the following categories: (1) state bar journal, newsletter, or similar publication; (2) general local newspaper or similar publication; (3) local bar journal, newsletter, or legal periodical.

c. *Posting and Distribution of Notice.* The public notice shall also be posted in the offices of the Clerk of the U.S. Court of Appeals and in each district court clerk's office within the Eleventh Circuit. A copy of the notice shall also be provided to each district judge and magistrate judge of the circuit, requesting that the judges recruit attorneys whom they feel may be qualified for the position, especially females, members of minority groups, and individuals with disabilities. The Defender Services Division of the Administrative Office of the United States Courts shall also be provided with a copy of the notice for nationwide distribution.

d. *Availability of Applications.* The Committee shall devise and provide federal public defender application forms to the Clerk of the U.S. Court of Appeals and to each district court clerk's office within the Eleventh Circuit when a vacancy occurs.

e. *Timely Submission of Application.* To be considered, applications must be received by the Committee by the posted deadline.

f. *Review of Completed Applications.* After the closing date for receipt of applications, the Committee shall review all timely applications.

9. Report to U.S. Court of Appeals. Upon completion of the duties set forth in Sections 6 and 8 of these regulations, the Federal Public Defender Committee shall submit a report to the Chief Judge of the U.S. Court of Appeals and to the active judges of the Court. The report shall constitute the recommendations of the Committee concerning the appointment of the federal public defender in that district, and shall include the following:

a. a description of actions taken pursuant to Section 8 of these regulations regarding giving notice of the position;

b. the names of all persons who submitted applications and the names of those deemed by the Committee to be qualified for appointment pursuant to Section 5 of these regulations;

c. the results of the Committee's investigation into the background of the qualified candidates;

d. the names of the qualified candidates who were interviewed by the Committee; and

e. a preferential ranking of not less than three nor more than five best qualified persons from among those the Committee considered qualified for appointment under Section 5 of these regulations. The Committee shall set forth the basis for its ranking of each of the persons it found to be the best qualified applicants.

10. District Court Recommendations.

a. *Solicitation of Recommendations.* Following receipt of all applications, the Chair of the Federal Public Defender Committee shall send a list of the names of all applicants determined by the Committee to be qualified, its preferential ranking of the not less than three nor more than five applicants considered to be best qualified and if the Federal Public Defender has applied for an additional four-year term a copy of the summary of the results of the survey concerning his or her last four-year term and of the summary of the responses to the solicitation for public comment to the Chief Judge of the district in which the Federal Public Defender is to be appointed, soliciting the recommendations of that district. The district court shall submit to the Chair of the Committee and to the Chief Judge of the U.S. Court of Appeals its written recommendation, if any, within 35 days after receipt of the Committee's letter. Extensions of time to respond may be granted by the Chair of the Committee upon application by a chief judge of the district court.

b. *Suggested Procedures for the District Court.*

(1) The Chief Judge of the district court may circulate to the members of his or her court the names of all applicants and the summary of the results of the survey if the Federal Public Defender has applied for an additional four-year term.

(2) The district court may wish to consider the summaries of the results of the survey and responses to the solicitation for public comment, if conducted, in arriving at its recommendation. The district court may, in its discretion, conduct its own inquiry concerning any qualified applicant. Within 35 days of receipt of the Committee's report, the district court may either:

(a) submit its written recommendation(s) to the Chair of the Committee; or

(b) notify the Chief Judge of the U.S. Court of Appeals and the Committee that the district court declines to make a recommendation.

(3) If the district court decides to submit a recommendation, its report should include:

(a) a preferential ranking of the applicants whom the district court found to be the best qualified for appointment if different from the ranking recommended by the Committee. The district court may set forth the reasons for its ranking. The district court should consider only those applicants determined by the Committee to have been qualified; and

(b) a summary of the district court's inquiry, if any, concerning the qualified applicants.

11. Vote by U.S. Court of Appeals and Background Investigation on Nominee.

a. If the Federal Public Defender Committee's recommendation is in accord with that submitted by the district court and if time constraints or exceptional circumstances warrant it, a vote of the judges of the U.S. Court of Appeals may be conducted by mail or by telephone. Otherwise the Committee's recommendations on the nomination to a vacancy, together with the recommendations of the district court, shall be presented at a regularly scheduled U.S. Court of Appeals Administrative Meeting.

b. After voting to nominate a candidate to fill a vacancy,

(1) the name of the nominee shall be submitted by the Chief Judge of the U.S. Court of Appeals to the Director of

the Administrative Office of the United States Courts for background investigations by the Federal Bureau of Investigation and the Internal Revenue Service;

(2) The Administrative Office of United States Courts will send the FBI and IRS reports to the Chief Judge of the U.S. Court of Appeals, who shall refer the reports to the Committee;

(3) The candidate will complete the required financial disclosure forms and will send them to the Chief Judge of the U.S. Court of Appeals and to the Administrative Office of United States Courts;

(4) After reviewing the FBI and IRS reports, the Committee shall submit its recommendation to the U.S. Court of Appeals on whether the nomination should be confirmed;

c. Upon receipt of the Committee's recommendation on confirmation, the U.S. Court of Appeals shall vote on whether to confirm the nomination. The confirmation vote of the U.S. Court of Appeals may be conducted either by mail or at a regularly scheduled court administrative meeting.

12. Confidentiality. If a member of the public makes a comment concerning the qualifications of the incumbent Federal Public Defender or the administration of his or her office, or about an applicant for that position, in a survey or otherwise, the person making the comment may request that their identity be kept confidential. The incumbent or applicant will, however, be provided with a general description of the source and nature of any comments.

The Federal Public Defender Committee or the Court of Appeals may determine, at its sole discretion, that the identity of a person making a comment should be disclosed to the incumbent or applicant in order to afford that person a fair opportunity to respond to the comment. In that event, the person making the comment will be given an opportunity to withdraw the comment before the commenter's identity is disclosed to the incumbent or applicant. If the comment is withdrawn, it will not be considered by the Committee or the Court of Appeals, and the identity of the person making the comment will remain confidential. If the person making the comment waives confidentiality, the commenter's name will be revealed to the incumbent or the applicant, along with the substance of the comment.

All information made available to the members of the Federal Public Defender Committee in the performance of their duties, including the Committee's report and the names recommended therein, shall be kept in strict confidence by the persons authorized by these procedures to receive this information, unless other provisions of these procedures or the U.S. Court of Appeals specifically authorize a disclosure.

If the Committee, with the consent of the Chief Judge of the U.S. Court of Appeals, decides to appoint consultants pursuant to Section 6(a)(3) of these regulations to assist it in considering the appointment of a federal public defender, it may provide any confidential information to the consultants as it considers necessary or appropriate.

13. Interim Appointment. A federal public defender whose four-year term of office has expired may continue to perform the duties of his or her office until a successor is chosen or until one year passes, whichever is earlier, upon approval of such an extension by a majority of the judges of the U.S. Court of Appeals.

[Adopted effective October 22, 1985. Amended effective October, 1992; January 1, 2002; October 26, 2012.]

ADDENDUM EIGHT. RULES GOVERNING ATTORNEY DISCIPLINE IN THE U.S. COURT OF APPEALS FOR THE ELEVENTH CIRCUIT

PREFATORY STATEMENT

Nothing contained in these rules shall be construed to deny the U.S. Court of Appeals for the Eleventh Circuit (the Court) its inherent power to maintain control over proceedings conducted before it or to deny the Court those powers derived from statute, rules of procedure, or rules of court. References herein to a panel are to a three-judge panel of the Court who shall act by majority vote.

When alleged attorney misconduct is brought to the attention of the Court, whether by a judge of the Court, a lawyer admitted to practice before the Court, an officer or employee of the Court, or otherwise, the Court may dispose of the matter through the use of its inherent, statutory, or other powers; refer the matter to an appropriate state bar agency for investigation and disposition; refer the matter to the Court's Committee on Lawyer Qualifications and Conduct as hereinafter defined; or take any other action the Court deems appropriate. These procedures are not mutually exclusive.

[Adopted effective October, 1992.]

RULE 1. STANDARDS FOR PROFESSIONAL CONDUCT

A. An act or omission of an attorney admitted to practice before the Court, committed individually or in concert with any other person or persons, that violates the Code of Professional Responsibility or Rules of Professional Conduct adopted by this Court, shall constitute misconduct and shall be grounds for discipline, whether or not the act or omission occurred in the course of an attorney-client relationship. Except as otherwise provided by a specific rule of the Court, attorneys practicing before the Court shall be governed by the Federal Rules of Appellate Procedure, the Court's local rules, the American Bar Association Model Rules of Professional Conduct, and the rules of professional conduct adopted by the highest court of the state(s) in which the attorney is admitted to practice to the extent that those state rules are not inconsistent with the American Bar Association Model Rules of Professional Conduct, in which case the model rules shall govern.

B. Discipline for misconduct defined in these rules may consist of disbarment, suspension, reprimand, monetary sanctions (including payment of the costs of disciplinary proceedings), removal from district court Criminal Justice Act panels, removal from the Court's roster of attorneys eligible for practice before the Court and for appointment under the Criminal Justice Act, or any other sanction the Court may deem appropriate.

[Adopted effective October, 1992. Amended effective January 2, 1996.]

RULE 2. COMMITTEE ON LAWYER QUALIFICATIONS AND CONDUCT

A. The Court may appoint a standing committee consisting of nine members of the bar of the Court, three from each state of the circuit, to be known as the "Committee on Lawyer Qualifications and Conduct" (the Committee). Three of those first appointed shall serve a term of one year; three shall serve a term of two years; and the remainder and all thereafter appointed shall serve a term of three years. Each member shall serve until the member's successor is appointed. The Court may vacate any such appointment at any time. The Court shall designate one of the members to serve as chairman. A majority of the Committee shall constitute a quorum.

B. The purpose and function of the Committee is to conduct, on referral by the Court through the Chief Judge or the Chief Judge's designee (hereinafter the Chief Judge unless otherwise provided in these rules), investigations of alleged misconduct by any member of the bar of the Court, or any attorney appearing and participating in any proceeding before the Court; to conduct and preside over disciplinary hearings when appropriate and as hereinafter provided; to conduct, on referral by the Court through the Chief Judge, inquiries and investigations of allegations of inadequate performance by an attorney practicing before the Court as hereinafter provided; and to submit written findings and recommendations to the Court for appropriate action. The members of the Committee, while serving in their official capacities, shall be considered representatives of the Court and as acting under the powers and immunities of the Court, and shall enjoy all such immunities while acting in good faith and in their official capacities.

C. The Court through the Chief Judge may refer to the Committee any accusation or evidence of misconduct that may constitute a violation of the disciplinary rules by any member of the bar with respect to any professional matter before the Court for such investigation, hearing, and report as the Court deems advisable. In addition to or instead of referring a disciplinary matter to the Committee, the Court through the Chief Judge may refer a complaint to the chief judge of the appropriate district court of the Eleventh Circuit for referral to that court's committee on lawyer qualifications and conduct. The Committee may refer disciplinary matters to an appropriate state bar for preliminary investigation, or may request the Court to appoint special counsel to assist in or exclusively to conduct disciplinary proceedings, as provided in Rule 11., infra. The Court through the Chief Judge also may refer to the Committee any matter concerning an attorney's failure to maintain an adequate level of competency in the attorney's practice before the Court, as provided in Rule 8., infra. Under no circumstances may the Committee investigate or initiate proceedings concerning these matters without prior referral by the Court through the Chief Judge.

D. The Committee shall be vested with such powers as are necessary to conduct the proper and expeditious disposition of any matter referred by the Court, including, but not limited to, the power to compel the attendance of witnesses; to take or cause to be taken the deposition of witnesses; to order the production of books, records, or other documentary evidence; and any power prescribed elsewhere in these rules. The chairman, or in the chairman's absence each member of the Committee, shall have the power to administer oaths and affirmations to witnesses. The Committee may constitute itself into investigative panels, each investigative panel ordinarily consisting of the three members residing in the same state, for the purpose of investigating allegations of misconduct and inquiring into inadequate performance, and submitting written findings and recommendations to the Committee and to the Court. Hearings shall ordinarily be held before the Committee and not an investigative panel.

E. Except as provided in Rule 13(C), unless and until otherwise ordered by the Chief Judge, all reports, records of proceedings, and other materials presented by the Court, the Committee, or any person to the Clerk of the Court (the Clerk) for filing shall be filed and maintained as sealed and confidential documents and shall be labeled accordingly by the Court, the Committee, or the person presenting such matters for filing.

[Adopted effective October, 1992. Amended effective January 2, 1996; January 1, 2002.]

RULE 3. DISCIPLINARY PROCEEDINGS

A(1). When misconduct or an allegation of misconduct that, if substantiated, may warrant discipline against an attorney admitted to practice before the Court comes to the attention of a judge of the Court, whether by complaint or otherwise, the judge may refer the matter to the Court through the Chief Judge for possible referral to the Committee for investigation and, if probable cause is found that the attorney has engaged in such misconduct, for initiation of formal disciplinary proceedings. In addition to or instead of referring the disciplinary matter to the Committee, the Court through the Chief Judge may refer the matter to the chief judge of the appropriate district court of the Eleventh Circuit for disposition.

A(2). The Court through the Chief Judge may, prior to referring the matter to the Committee, direct the Clerk to issue an order requiring the attorney to show cause within 14 days from the date of the order why the attorney should not be disciplined. Such order may further provide that if the attorney fails to file a verified response within the time allowed, the attorney shall be indefinitely suspended from practice before the Court.

The attorney's response to such order shall be verified by a signed declaration similar to the following: "I swear (or affirm) that all statements made herein, including those made in attachments which are incorporated herein by reference, are true and correct to the best of my knowledge, information, and belief." When an attorney is suspended upon failure timely to file a verified response the matter need not be referred to the Committee. If an attorney timely files a verified response, the Clerk shall refer the matter to the Chief Judge, who shall determine whether to refer the matter to the Committee or take other appropriate action.

B(1). If the Committee concludes, after investigation, that no probable cause exists to believe that the attorney has engaged in misconduct, and, therefore, that a formal disciplinary proceeding should not be initiated, the Committee in a report filed with the Clerk shall recommend a disposition of the matter—for example, that the Court dismiss the complaint, that further action on the complaint be deferred, or that other action be taken. The Committee's report and all material received or generated by the Committee in the course of its investigation shall be confidential unless and until otherwise ordered by the Court through the Chief Judge.

B(2). With respect to matters referred to the Committee under Rule 3(A)(2), if the Committee concludes, after investigation, that the attorney has demonstrated sufficient justification why discipline should not be imposed, the Committee in a report filed with the Clerk shall request the Court to close the matter with no discipline imposed, stating its reasons therefor.

C(1). If the Committee concludes, after investigation, that probable cause exists to believe that the attorney has engaged in misconduct, the Committee shall file with the Clerk a report of its investigation, stating with specificity the facts supporting its conclusion, and shall apply to the Court for the issuance of an order requiring the attorney to show cause within 14 days after service of that order why the attorney should not be disciplined. The order to show cause, issued by the Chief Judge, shall set forth the particular misconduct for which the attorney is sought to be disciplined. A copy of the Committee's report and the order to show cause shall be served on the attorney as provided in Rule 12., infra. The attorney may file with the Clerk, within 14 days of service of the order to show cause, a written response thereto. After considering the attorney's response, if any, the Committee may request the Court to rescind the order to show cause. If the Committee does not request the Court to rescind the order to show cause, or if a panel of the Court convened by the Chief Judge denies the Committee's request that it rescind the order to show cause, the Committee shall hold a hearing on the matter, giving the attorney at least 14 days notice as provided in Rule 12., infra. All proceedings before the Committee shall be recorded and the record thereof made available to the attorney. Such proceedings, the record thereof, and all materials received or generated by the Committee shall be confidential unless and until otherwise ordered by the Court through the Chief Judge.

C(2). With respect to matters referred to the Committee under Rule 3(A)(2), if the Committee concludes, after investigation, that the attorney has failed to demonstrate sufficient justification why discipline should not be imposed, or if a panel of the Court convened by the Chief Judge denies the Committee's request that it rescind the order to show cause, the Committee shall hold a hearing on the matter, giving the attorney at least 14 days notice as provided in Rule 12., infra.

C(3). An attorney may waive a hearing before the Committee by agreeing to the imposition of specific discipline to be recommended by the Committee in a report filed with the Clerk pursuant to Rule 3(E). When an attorney waives a hearing pursuant to this rule, an order to show cause pursuant to Rule 3(F), infra, need not issue.

D. Attorney misconduct shall be established by clear and convincing evidence. Except as otherwise ordered by the Court or provided in these rules, the Committee, in receiving evidence, shall be guided by the spirit of the Federal Rules of Evidence. The attorney, personally or through counsel, shall have the right to confront and cross-examine all witnesses appearing before the Committee and to present witnesses or other evidence. The Committee may require the attorney to testify or otherwise to make under oath specific and complete disclosure of all matters material to the alleged misconduct, subject to any privilege or right against such disclosure the attorney may assert pursuant to federal or state law.

E. Upon completion of a disciplinary proceeding, the Committee shall file with the Clerk the record of that proceeding and the Committee's report to the Court. The report shall include the Committee's findings of fact regarding the alleged misconduct and its recommendation as to whether the attorney should be found guilty of misconduct and disciplined. A copy of the report and recommendations shall be served on the attorney as provided in Rule 12., infra.

F. Upon receipt of the Committee's finding that misconduct warranting discipline occurred, a panel of the Court convened by the Chief Judge shall issue an order requiring the attorney to show cause why the Committee's recommendation should not be accepted and implemented. After considering the attorney's response, the panel may adopt, modify, or reject the Committee's finding or take other appropriate action as provided in Rule 1.B., supra.

[Adopted effective October, 1992. Amended effective January 2, 1996; January 1, 2002.]

RULE 4. ATTORNEYS CONVICTED OF CRIMES

A. When an attorney admitted to practice before the Court has been convicted in a court of the United States or the District of Columbia or of a state, territory, commonwealth, or possession of the United States (another court) of a serious crime as defined in this rule, the Clerk, upon receipt of a copy of the judgment of such conviction, shall issue and serve on the attorney as provided in Rule 12., infra, an order to show cause why the attorney should not be disbarred. The order shall state that unless the attorney files a response to the order with the Clerk within 14 days after service the attorney shall be disbarred. The order shall further state that if a response is filed the attorney shall be suspended from the bar of the Court until a panel of the Court convened by the Chief Judge otherwise orders. The panel, after considering the attorney's response, (1) may rescind the order to show cause and lift the suspension, (2) may suspend or disbar the attorney, or (3) may refer the matter to the Committee with instructions to initiate a disciplinary proceeding; provided, however, that the panel shall not disbar the attorney or refer the matter to the Committee until any direct appeal from the attorney's conviction has been concluded and the conviction becomes final.

B. The term "serious" crime shall include any felony, or any attempt, conspiracy, or solicitation of another to commit a felony, and any lesser crime an essential element of which, as determined by the statutory or common-law definition of such crime in the jurisdiction in which it occurred, involves false swearing, misrepresentation, fraud, deceit, dishonesty, bribery, extortion, misappropriation, or theft.

C. An attorney suspended or disbarred pursuant to the provisions of this rule shall be reinstated immediately upon the filing with the Clerk of proof that the attorney's conviction has been set aside; such reinstatement, however, shall not terminate any disciplinary proceeding that has been initiated pursuant to this rule.

[Adopted effective October, 1992.]

RULE 5. DISCIPLINE IMPOSED BY OTHER COURTS

A. When an attorney admitted to practice before the Court has been suspended or disbarred by another court, the attorney shall file a copy of the judgment or order imposing such discipline with the Clerk. Upon receipt of a copy of such judgment or order, whether from the attorney or another source, the Clerk shall issue and serve on the attorney as provided in Rule 12., infra, an order to show cause why the Court should not discipline the attorney in the same manner. The order shall state that unless the attorney files a response to the order with the Clerk within 14 days after service the attorney shall be disciplined accordingly. The order further shall state that if a response is filed the attorney shall be suspended from the bar of the Court until a panel of the Court convened by the Chief Judge otherwise orders. The panel, after considering the attorney's response, (1) may rescind the order to show cause and lift the suspension, (2) may suspend or disbar the attorney, or (3) may refer the matter to the Committee; provided, however, that the panel shall not suspend or disbar the attorney or refer the matter to the Committee until any stay of discipline granted by a court having jurisdiction has been lifted.

B. A determination by another court that an attorney has engaged in misconduct shall establish such conduct conclusively for purposes of a disciplinary proceeding pursuant to these rules, unless the attorney demonstrates and the Court is satisfied that:

1. the procedure used to make such determination was so lacking in notice or opportunity to be heard as to constitute a deprivation of the attorney's due process rights; or

2. the proof was so insufficient that the Court, consistent with its duty, could not accept as final the conclusion of the other court that the attorney engaged in such misconduct.

C. Discipline imposed by another court, whether suspension or disbarment, shall likewise be imposed by this Court unless the attorney demonstrates and the Court is satisfied that:

1. the imposition of the same discipline by the Court would result in grave injustice; or

2. the misconduct warrants substantially different discipline by the Court.

D. The Court at any time may direct the Committee to conduct disciplinary proceedings or to make recommendations to the Court for appropriate action in light of the imposition of professional discipline by another court.

[Adopted effective October, 1992.]

RULE 6. DISBARMENT ON CONSENT OR RESIGNATION IN OTHER COURTS

A. When an attorney admitted to practice before the Court has been disbarred on consent or has resigned from the bar of another court pending an investigation of allegations of misconduct, the attorney promptly shall inform the Clerk in writing of such disbarment on consent or such resignation.

B. Upon receipt of written notice, whether from the attorney or another source, that an attorney admitted to practice before the Court has been disbarred on consent or has resigned from the bar of another court pending an investigation of allegations of misconduct, the Clerk shall issue and serve on the attorney as provided in Rule 12., infra, an order to show cause why the Court should not disbar the attorney. The order shall state that unless the attorney files a response to the order with the Clerk within 14 days after service the attorney shall be disbarred. The order shall further state that if a response is filed the attorney shall be suspended from the bar of the Court until a panel of the Court convened by the Chief Judge otherwise orders. The panel, after considering the attorney's response, (1) may rescind the order to show cause and lift the suspension, (2) may suspend or disbar the attorney, or (3) may refer the matter to the Committee.

[Adopted effective October, 1992.]

RULE 7. DISBARMENT ON CONSENT WHILE UNDER DISCIPLINARY INVESTIGATION OR PROSECUTION

A. An attorney admitted to practice before the Court who is the subject of an investigation or of a pending proceeding involving allegations of misconduct may consent to disbarment by filing with the Clerk an affidavit stating that the attorney freely and voluntarily consents to disbarment by the Court.

B. Upon the Clerk's receipt of such affidavit, a panel of the Court convened by the Chief Judge shall enter an order disbarring the attorney.

C. The order disbarring the attorney on consent shall be a matter of public record. The affidavit required pursuant to the provisions of this rule, however, shall be confidential unless and until otherwise ordered by the Court through the Chief Judge.

[Adopted effective October, 1992.]

RULE 8. ATTORNEY COMPETENCY AND INCAPACITY

A. When it appears that an attorney, for whatever reason, is failing to perform at an adequate level of competency necessary to protect the interests of the attorney's client (a competency matter), a panel of the Court convened by the Chief Judge may take any remedial action that it deems appropriate, including but not limited to referral of the attorney to appropriate institutions and professional personnel for assistance in raising the attorney's level of competency. The panel, through the Chief Judge, may also refer the matter to the Committee for investigation and recommendation.

B. A competency matter is not a disciplinary matter and thus shall not implicate the formal procedures described elsewhere in these rules. Upon referral of a competency matter, the Committee may conduct a preliminary inquiry and may request an informal meeting with the attorney to discuss the circumstances relating to the referral.

C. If, after conducting a preliminary inquiry, including meeting with the attorney if it elects to do so, the Committee determines that further action is not warranted, the Committee shall so notify the attorney and the referring panel and the matter shall be considered terminated unless the referring panel otherwise directs.

D. If the Committee determines, with or without a preliminary inquiry, that the matter warrants formal action, the Committee may recommend to the attorney in writing that steps be taken to improve the quality of the attorney's professional performance and may recommend that specific actions be taken to effect such improvement. Upon receipt of the Committee's recommendation, the Clerk shall forthwith serve it upon the attorney as provided in Rule 12., infra. The attorney may file a written response to the Committee's recommendation with the Clerk within 14 days of such service, seeking review or revocation of the Committee's recommendation or suggesting alternatives thereto. If the attorney does not file such a response, the Committee's recommendation shall become the decision of the Committee. If the attorney does file such a response, the Committee may modify, revoke, or adhere to its recommendation, and that determination shall become the decision of the Committee. Upon receipt of the Committee's decision, the Clerk shall forthwith serve it upon the attorney as provided in Rule 12., infra. If the attorney agrees to comply with the Committee's decision, the Committee shall report to the referring panel that the attorney has agreed to its resolution of the matter. The Committee may monitor the attorney's compliance with its decision and may request the assistance of the Court to ensure such compliance.

E. If the attorney objects to the Committee's decision, the attorney may file a written response with the Clerk within 14 days of service of the decision. The referring panel shall consider the Committee's decision and the objection of the attorney and may adopt, modify, or reject the Committee's decision or take other appropriate action.

F. If the Committee finds that there is a substantial likelihood that the attorney's continued practice of law before the Court may result in serious harm to the attorney's clients, it may recommend that, pending compliance with its decision, the Court consider limiting or otherwise imposing appropriate restrictions on the attorney's continued practice before the Court. The referring panel may take any action that it deems appropriate with respect to the Committee's recommendation.

G. All information, reports, records, and recommendations gathered, possessed, or generated by or on behalf of the Committee in relation to the referral of a competency matter shall be confidential unless and until otherwise ordered by the Court through the Chief Judge.

H. Nothing contained in this rule or any action taken pursuant to this rule shall be construed to interfere with or substitute for any procedure relating to the discipline of any attorney as elsewhere provided in these rules. Disciplinary proceedings shall occur separately from competency proceedings held pursuant to this rule.

[Adopted effective October, 1992.]

RULE 9. REINSTATEMENT AFTER DISBARMENT OR SUSPENSION

A. An attorney suspended for 90 days or less shall be reinstated by the Clerk at the end of the suspension period upon filing with the Clerk an affidavit of compliance with the provisions of the suspension order. An attorney suspended for more than 90 days or disbarred may not resume the practice of law before the Court until reinstated by order of the Court. An attorney who has been disbarred may not apply for reinstatement until the expiration of at least five years from the effective date of disbarment.

B. A petition for reinstatement filed by a suspended or disbarred attorney pursuant to this rule shall be filed with the Clerk and referred to the Chief Judge of the Court. If an attorney's suspension or disbarment in this Court was reciprocally imposed pursuant to Rule 5, supra, and the attorney has been reinstated to practice in the other court, the Chief Judge may grant the petition if deemed appropriate. In other circumstances, the Chief Judge may submit a petition to a panel of the Court or may refer a petition to the Committee. When a petition is referred to it, the Committee shall schedule a hearing, giving at least 14 days notice as provided in Rule 12., infra.

C. At the hearing the petitioner shall have the burden of establishing by clear and convincing evidence that the petitioner has the moral qualifications, competency, and learning in the law required for admission to practice before the Court and that the petitioner's resumption of the practice of law will not be detrimental to the integrity and standing of the bar, to the administration of justice, or to the public interest. The petitioner, personally or through counsel, shall have the right to present witnesses or other evidence. The Committee may require the petitioner to testify or otherwise to make under oath specific and complete disclosure of all matters material to the petition for reinstatement, subject to any privilege or right against such disclosure the petitioner may assert under federal or state law.

D. Upon completion of the hearing, the Committee shall file with the Clerk the Committee's report to the Court. The report shall include the Committee's findings of fact regarding the petitioner's fitness to resume the practice of law and its recommendation regarding whether or not the petitioner should be reinstated. A copy of the report and recommendation shall be served on the petitioner as provided in Rule 12., infra. The Committee's report and all material received or generated by the Committee in the course of its proceedings shall be confidential unless and until otherwise ordered by the Court through the Chief Judge.

E. If, after considering the Committee's report and recommendation, a panel of the Court convened by the Chief Judge finds that the petitioner is unfit to resume the practice of law, the panel shall dismiss the petition. If, after considering the Committee's report and recommendation, the panel finds that the petitioner is fit to resume the practice of law, the panel shall reinstate the petitioner. The panel's order may condition reinstatement upon the petitioner paying all or part of the costs of the proceedings and making partial or complete restitution to all parties harmed by the petitioner's conduct that led to the suspension or disbarment. Further, if the petitioner has been suspended for five or more years, or disbarred, the panel may condition reinstatement upon the petitioner furnishing proof of competency and learning in the law. Such proof may include certification by the bar examiners of a state or other jurisdiction that the petitioner successfully completed an examination for admission to practice subsequent to the date of suspension or disbarment. Reinstatement may be subject to any conditions that the panel in its discretion deems appropriate.

F. No petition for reinstatement filed pursuant to this rule shall be filed within one year following an adverse judgment on a petition for reinstatement filed by the same person.

G. Petitions for reinstatement filed pursuant to this rule shall be accompanied by a deposit in an amount sufficient to cover anticipated costs of the reinstatement proceeding. The Court through the Chief Judge, in consultation with the Committee, shall set and may periodically adjust the amount of such deposits.

[Adopted effective October, 1992. Amended effective January 1, 2002.]

RULE 10. ATTORNEYS SPECIALLY ADMITTED

Whenever an attorney applies for admission to the bar of the Court or is admitted for purposes of a particular proceeding pursuant to 11th Cir. R. 46–3 (including admission pro hac vice), the attorney thereby confers disciplinary jurisdiction upon the Court for any alleged misconduct arising in the course of or in the preparation for such a proceeding that may constitute a violation of the Code of Professional Responsibility and Rules of Professional Conduct adopted by the Court as provided in Rule 1., supra.

[Adopted effective October, 1992.]

RULE 11. SPECIAL COUNSEL

A. Whenever pursuant to these rules the Court directs or the Committee requests appointment of special counsel to investigate or assist in the investigation of misconduct, to prosecute or assist in the prosecution of disciplinary proceedings, or to assist in the disposition of a reinstatement petition filed by a disciplined attorney, a panel of the Court convened by the Chief Judge may appoint as special counsel any active member of the bar of the Court, the disciplinary agency of the highest court of any state in which the attorney is admitted to practice, or any other disciplinary agency having jurisdiction.

B. The Court, acting in its administrative capacity, may allocate from time to time certain monies from its nonappropriated fund account to support the operations of the Committee, including payment of any expenses incurred by the Committee and of any fees authorized to be paid to Special Counsel pursuant to these rules.

[Adopted effective October, 1992.]

RULE 12. SERVICE OF PAPERS AND OTHER NOTICES

Service of an order to show cause instituting a formal disciplinary proceeding shall be made by personal service or by registered or certified mail addressed to the attorney at the address shown on the roll of attorneys admitted to practice before the Court. Service of any other paper or notice required by these rules shall be deemed to have been made if such paper or notice is mailed by first-class mail to the attorney at the address shown on the roll of attorneys admitted to practice before the Court, or to the attorney's counsel at the address indicated in the most recent pleading or document filed by such counsel in the course of any proceeding pursuant to these rules.

[Adopted effective October, 1992.]

RULE 13. ADDITIONAL DUTIES OF THE CLERK

A. When informed that an attorney admitted to practice before the Court has been convicted of a serious crime as defined in Rule 4., supra, the Clerk promptly shall obtain and file with the Court a copy of the judgment of such conviction.

B. When informed that an attorney admitted to practice before the Court has been disciplined by another court, the Clerk promptly shall obtain and file with the Court a copy of the judgment or order imposing such discipline.

C. Whenever it appears that an attorney who has been disbarred, suspended, or publicly reprimanded by the Court is admitted to practice law in another jurisdiction or before another court, the Clerk shall, within 14 days of such public discipline transmit to the disciplinary authority in such other court or jurisdiction, as well as to the disciplined attorney as provided in Rule 12, supra, a copy of this Court's order imposing public discipline. A copy of an order imposing discipline other than disbarment, suspension, or public reprimand shall not be transmitted to the disciplinary authority in such other court or jurisdiction unless so ordered by the Court.

D. The Clerk promptly shall notify the National Discipline Data Bank of the American Bar Association of any order imposing public discipline on an attorney admitted to practice before the Court.

[Adopted effective October, 1992. Amended effective January 2, 1996; January 1, 2002.]

ADDENDUM NINE. REGULATIONS OF THE UNITED STATES COURT OF APPEALS FOR THE ELEVENTH CIRCUIT FOR THE SELECTION AND APPOINTMENT OR THE REAPPOINTMENT OF BANKRUPTCY ADMINISTRATORS

PURPOSE

United States bankruptcy administrators oversee trustees and estate administration in bankruptcy cases for the three judicial districts in Alabama. Their duties are essentially the same as those of the U.S. trustees in the Department of Justice, who serve in all other judicial districts in the Eleventh Circuit. It is imperative that only highly qualified individuals be selected as bankruptcy administrators. These regulations supplement the Regulations of the Judicial Conference of the United States for the Selection, Appointment and Reappointment of Bankruptcy Administrators, the Guide to Judiciary Policy, and governing statutes. These regulations set forth procedural guidelines that create no vested rights for any prospective or incumbent bankruptcy administrator.

Bankruptcy administrators will be appointed without regard to race, color, sex, religion, or national origin.

CONFIDENTIALITY OF PUBLIC COMMENTS

If a member of the public makes a comment concerning the qualifications of the incumbent bankruptcy administrator or an applicant for that position, in response to a survey solicitation, public notice, or otherwise, the person making the comment may request that their identity be kept confidential. The incumbent or applicant will, however, be provided with a general description of the source and nature of any comments.

The Court of Appeals may determine, at its sole discretion, that the identity of a person making a comment should be disclosed to the incumbent or applicant in order to afford that person a fair opportunity to respond to the comment. In that event, the person making the comment will be given an opportunity to withdraw the comment before the commenter's identity is disclosed to the incumbent or applicant. If the comment is withdrawn, it will not be considered by the Court of Appeals, and the identity of the person making the comment will remain confidential. If the person making the comment waives confidentiality, the commenter's name will be revealed to the incumbent or applicant, along with the substance of the comment.

[Effective October 26, 2012.]

ELECTRONIC CASE FILING

ELEVENTH CIRCUIT GUIDE TO ELECTRONIC FILING

Introduction

The United States Court of Appeals for the Eleventh Circuit requires attorneys to file documents electronically, subject to exceptions set forth in the Eleventh Circuit Rules and this Guide, using the Electronic Case Files ("ECF") system.

Participation in the ECF System

Participation in the ECF system by attorneys is mandatory. See 11th Cir. R. 25–3 and General Order 38. Reasonable exceptions will be allowed, upon motion and a showing of good cause.

1. Definitions

1.1. Attorney Filer means an attorney who has registered as described in Section 2 of this Guide and is therefore authorized to file documents electronically and to receive service through the ECF system.

1.2. Document means any order, opinion, judgment, petition, application, notice, transcript, motion, brief, or other document filed in a case.

1.3. ECF (Electronic Case Files) means the system maintained by the Court for receiving and storing documents in electronic format.

1.4. NDA (Notice of Docket Activity) is a notice generated automatically by the ECF system at the time a document is filed and a docket entry results. This notice sets forth the time of filing, the text of the docket entry, and the names of the attorneys required to receive notice of the filing. If a PDF document is attached to the docket entry, the NDA will also identify the person filing the document and the type of document, and will contain a hyperlink to the filed document. Any document filed by the Court will similarly list those to whom electronic notice of the filing is being sent.

1.5. PACER (Public Access to Court Electronic Records) is an electronic system that allows Internet users to view, print, and download electronically maintained docket information and federal court documents.

1.6. PDF (Portable Document Format) means a non-modifiable electronic file containing the ".pdf" file extension. Text–Searchable PDF means a PDF file generated from an original word-processing file rather than scanned.

2. Registration/Passwords

2.1. Unless an attorney is granted an exemption, an attorney must register to file and serve documents electronically using the ECF system.

2.2. To register as a user of the ECF system, an attorney must be a member of the Eleventh Circuit bar in good standing, admitted for a particular proceeding under 11th Cir. R. 46–3, admitted pro hac vice in a particular case, or appearing in a particular case as a pro se party. An attorney must also have submitted to the PACER Service Center a completed ECF Attorney Registration form. PACER Service Center contact information is shown in Section 13.

2.3. In addition to ECF registration, the attorney or the attorney's firm must have a PACER account and an e-mail address. The PACER Service Center assigns two sets of log-ins and passwords—one for PACER access and one for ECF access. The log-in and password for ECF access will be used to file documents electronically with the Court.

2.4. Upon receipt of the attorney's registration information from the PACER Service Center, the clerk will determine eligibility and activate the Attorney Filer's account. Authorized use of an attorney's log-in and password by another is deemed to be the act of the attorney. If a log-in and/or password should become compromised, the attorney is responsible for notifying the PACER Service Center (see contact information in Section 13).

2.5. An Attorney Filer whose e-mail address, mailing address, telephone number, or fax number changes from that disclosed on the attorney's original ECF Attorney Registration form must promptly notify the PACER Service Center. Service by the clerk on an obsolete e-mail address will still constitute valid service on an Attorney Filer if the attorney has failed to notify the PACER Service Center of a new e-mail address.

3. Signatures

3.1. Attorneys—An Attorney Filer's use of the assigned log-in and password to submit a document electronically serves as that attorney's signature on that document for all purposes. The identity of the Attorney Filer submitting the electronically filed document must be reflected at the end of the document by means of an "s/[attorney's name]" block showing the attorney's name, followed by the attorney's business address, telephone number, and e-mail address. Graphic and other electronic signatures are discouraged.

3.2. Multiple Attorney Signatures—The Attorney Filer of any electronically filed document requiring multiple signatures (e.g., stipulations) must list thereon all the names of other attorney signatories by means of an "s/[attorney's name]" block for each. By submitting such a document, the Attorney Filer certifies that each of the other attorneys has expressly agreed to the form and substance of the document, and that the Attorney Filer has their authority to submit the document electronically.

3.3. Clerk of Court and Deputy Clerks—The electronic filing of any document by the clerk of court or a deputy clerk by use of that individual's log-in and password shall be deemed the filing of a signed original document for all purposes.

4. Electronic Filing/Exceptions

4.1. Except as otherwise required by circuit rule, this Guide, or by order of the Court, all documents submitted by attorneys in cases filed with the Eleventh Circuit must be filed electronically, using the Electronic Case Files ("ECF") system. The circuit rules and this Guide govern electronic filings.

4.2. All electronically filed documents must be in PDF form and must conform to all technical and format requirements established by the Court and, if any, the Judicial Conference of the United States. Whenever possible, documents must be in Text–Searchable PDF and not created by scanning.

4.3. The maximum size of a document that may be filed electronically is 25 MB (megabytes). If a document exceeds 25 MB, it must be filed in separate volumes, each not to exceed 25 MB.

4.4. The electronic filing of a Certificate of Interested Persons (CIP) in the ECF system does not relieve an Attorney Filer of the requirement to also complete and keep updated the web-based CIP on the Court's website. To complete the web-based CIP, counsel must obtain from the clerk an Eleventh Circuit EDF number that is independent of PACER and ECF passwords.

4.5. The following documents are exempted from the electronic filing requirement and are to be filed in paper format:

(1) Any document filed by a party who is not represented by counsel;

(2) A petition for permission to appeal under FRAP 5;

(3) A petition for review of an agency order under FRAP 15;

(4) A petition for a writ of mandamus, writ of prohibition, or other extraordinary writ under FRAP 21;

(5) Any other document initiating an original action in the court of appeals;

(6) An application for leave to file a second or successive habeas corpus petition or motion to vacate, set aside or correct sentence;

(7) A document filed under seal or requested to be filed under seal; and

(8) A voucher and associated documents pertaining to a claim for compensation and reimbursement of expenses when representation is provided under the Criminal Justice Act or Addendum Five.

4.6. No unrepresented party (except an attorney appearing in a particular case as a pro se party) may file electronically; unrepresented parties must submit documents in paper format. The clerk will scan such documents into the ECF system, and the electronic version scanned in by the clerk will constitute the official record of the Court as reflected on its docket. The clerk may divide an oversized pro se document into separate volumes for purposes of scanning.

5. Entry on the Docket/Official Court Record

5.1. The electronic transmission of a document, together with transmission of the NDA from the Court, in accordance with the policies and procedures adopted by the Court, constitutes the filing of the document under the Federal Rules of Appellate Procedure and constitutes the entry of that document onto the official docket of the Court maintained by the clerk pursuant to FRAP 45(b)(1).

5.2. The electronic version of filed documents, whether filed electronically in the first instance or received by the clerk in paper format and subsequently scanned into electronic format, constitutes the official record in the case.

5.3. Later modification of a filed document or docket entry by the Attorney Filer is not permitted except as authorized by the Court. The clerk may edit the docket entry to correct or supplement the text. A notation will be made indicating the entry was edited. A document submitted electronically is deemed to have been filed on the date and at the time indicated in the system-generated NDA.

5.4. When the clerk scans a document into the ECF system, the clerk will discard the paper document once it has been scanned and made a part of the official record, unless the electronic file thereby produced is incomplete or of questionable quality.

5.5. Except as otherwise provided by circuit rule or Court order, all orders, decrees, judgments, and proceedings of the Court relating to cases filed and maintained in the ECF system will be filed in accordance with the circuit rules and this Guide and will constitute entry on the docket kept by the clerk and service on parties under FRAP 36, 45(b)(1), and 45(c). Any order or other court-issued document filed electronically without the original signature of a judge or authorized Court personnel has the same force and effect as if the judge or clerk had signed a paper copy of the order.

6. Filing Deadlines/Technical Failure

6.1. Filing documents electronically does not in any way alter any filing deadlines. When a specific time of day deadline is set by Court order or stipulation, the electronic filing must be completed by that time. Otherwise, electronic filing must be completed by 11:59 p.m. Eastern Time to be considered timely filed that day. An electronically filed document is deemed filed upon completion of the transmission and issuance of an NDA.

6.2. The uploading of an incorrect document, or the filing of a document in the wrong case, does not constitute compliance with filing deadlines. In the event that an Attorney Filer uploads an incorrect document, or files a document in the wrong case, the clerk will send the Attorney Filer notice of the error. If the Attorney Filer corrects the error within 5 days of the clerk's notice, a motion to file the document out of time is not required. Otherwise, the Attorney Filer must also electronically file in the case a motion to file the document out of time.

6.3. When a correction to an electronically filed document (e.g., motion, brief, or appendix) is necessary, counsel must upload the entire new document, and not just the corrected pages.

6.4. An Attorney Filer whose filing is untimely as the result of a technical failure may seek appropriate relief from the Court. To resolve a technical failure that may be attributable to the PACER Service Center or the Court, counsel should communicate with the appropriate contact person as shown in Section 13:

a. Technical issues such as log-in and password questions, and creating and uploading PDF documents, should be directed to the PACER Service Center help desk.

b. Procedural questions concerning how to docket a specific event should be directed to the Eleventh Circuit ECF help desk. This includes any instance in which an Attorney Filer has transmitted a document to the ECF system and did not thereafter receive an NDA.

7. Service of Documents

7.1. Registration to use the ECF system constitutes consent to receive electronic service of all documents as provided by the Federal Rules of Appellate Procedure and the circuit rules, as well as to receive electronic notice of correspondence, orders, and opinions issued by the Court.

7.2. A certificate of service is required for all documents, and an Attorney Filer must comply with FRAP 25 when filing electronically. The ECF system will automatically generate and send by e-mail an NDA to all Attorney Filers participating in the case. This notice constitutes service on those Attorney Filers. Independent service, either by paper or otherwise, need not be made on any Attorney Filer. The NDA generated by the ECF system does not replace the certificate of service required by FRAP 25. In other words, a document filed electronically by an Attorney Filer must still contain a certificate of service conforming to the requirements of FRAP 25.

7.3. Pro se litigants and attorneys who are exempt from electronic filing must be served by the filing party through the conventional means of service set forth in FRAP 25.

7.4. Except as may otherwise be provided by circuit rule or Court order, all orders, opinions, judgments, and other Court-issued documents in cases maintained in the ECF system will be filed and served on Attorney Filers electronically.

8. Access to Documents

8.1. Access to all documents maintained electronically, except those under seal, is available to any person through the PACER system. PACER accounts are established through the PACER Service Center. See contact information in Section 13.

9. Documents Under Seal

9.1. A motion to file documents under seal may be filed electronically unless prohibited by law, circuit rule, or Court order. Do not attach to the motion the sealed documents or documents requested to be sealed. Documents requested to be sealed must be submitted in paper format in a sealed envelope, and must be received by the clerk within 10 days of filing the motion. The face of the envelope containing such documents must contain a conspicuous notation that it contains "DOCUMENTS UNDER SEAL", or substantially similar language.

9.2. Documents filed under seal in the court from which an appeal is taken will continue to be filed under seal on appeal to this Court.

10. Briefs/Petitions for Rehearing/Petitions for En Banc Consideration

10.1. The electronically filed brief is the official record copy of the brief.

10.2. Use of the ECF system does not modify the requirements of the circuit rules that counsel must provide to the Court the required number of paper copies of a brief, a petition for rehearing, a petition for initial en banc consideration, or a petition for rehearing en banc, specified in the circuit rules. Counsel will be considered to have complied with this requirement if, on the day the electronic brief or petition is filed, counsel sends the required number of paper copies to the clerk using one of the following methods outlined in FRAP 25(a)(2)(B):

a. mail to the clerk by First-Class Mail, or other class of mail that is at least as expeditious, postage prepaid; or

b. dispatch to a third-party commercial carrier for delivery to the clerk within three days.

11. Appendices

11.1. The electronically filed appendix is the official record copy of the appendix. Use of the ECF system does not modify the requirements of 11th Cir. Rules 30–1 and 30–2 that counsel must provide to the Court the required number of paper copies of an appendix specified in those rules. Counsel will be considered to have complied with this requirement if, on the day the electronic appendix is filed, counsel sends two paper copies to the clerk using one of the methods outlined in FRAP 25(a)(2)(B). If the appeal is classed for oral argument, counsel must file an additional three identical paper copies of the appendix in accordance with 11th Cir. R. 30–1(d).

12. Privacy Protection and Redactions

12.1. In accordance with FRAP 25(a)(5) and 11th Cir. R. 25–5, an Attorney Filer must redact all documents, including briefs, consistent with the privacy policy of the Judicial Conference of the United States. Required redactions include social security numbers and taxpayer identification numbers (use last four digits only), names of minor children (use initials only), birth dates (use year of birth only), financial account numbers (use last four digits only), and home addresses (use city and state only). It is the responsibility of the filer to redact pleadings appropriately.

12.2. Pursuant to the privacy policy of the Judicial Conference of the United States and applicable statutory provisions, remote electronic access to immigration and social security dockets is limited. In this regard, the clerk will restrict electronic public access in these cases to judges, Court staff, and the parties and attorneys in the appeal or agency proceeding. The Court will not restrict access to orders and opinions in these cases. Parties seeking to restrict access to orders and opinions must file a motion explaining why that relief is required in a given case.

13. Contacts

<u>PACER Service Center</u>

Technical issues such as log-in and password questions, and creating PDF documents, should be directed to the PACER Service Center help desk:

PACER Service Center
P.O. Box 780549
San Antonio, TX 78278
Tel. 800–676–6856 or 210–301–6440
www.pacer.gov

<u>Eleventh Circuit ECF help desk</u>

Procedural questions concerning how to docket a specific event should be directed to the Eleventh Circuit ECF help desk at 404–335–6125. This includes any instance in which an Attorney Filer has transmitted a document to the ECF system and did not thereafter receive an NDA. The ECF help desk is available while the Clerk's Office is open per 11th Cir. R. 45–1(b).

[Dated: April 9, 2013. Amended effective August 26, 2013; March, 2014.]

GENERAL ORDER 38. IN RE: ELECTRONIC CASE FILES

Before: DUBINA, Chief Judge, TJOFLAT, CARNES, BARKETT, HULL, MARCUS, WILSON, PRYOR, MARTIN, and JORDAN, Circuit Judges.

In October 2011, the Court approved General Order 37 authorizing counsel voluntarily to file documents electronically in cases using the Court's Electronic Case Files ("ECF") system. Counsel's voluntary participation in the ECF system has worked well, and the Court now determines that electronic filing should be mandatory for all counsel.

Effective 1 April 2013, counsel are required to file documents electronically in appeals pending on that date and in appeals docketed in this Court on or after that date, following the procedures set out in the "Eleventh Circuit Guide to Electronic Filing" ("the Guide"). Reasonable exceptions to the requirement will be allowed, upon motion and a showing of good cause.

The Guide will be posted on the Court's website, www.call.uscourts.gov, and may be amended, as necessary, without prior notice.

[Dated: February 26, 2013.]

GENERAL ORDER 39. IN RE: ELECTRONIC RECORDS ON APPEAL

Before: DUBINA, Chief Judge, TJOFLAT, CARNES, BARKETT, HULL, MARCUS, WILSON, PRYOR, MARTIN, and JORDAN, Circuit Judges.

On 26 February 2007, this Court issued General Order 33 continuing in effect an Electronic Records on Appeal Pilot Program in the Southern District of Alabama through 30 November 2007, unless earlier modified or extended by the Court. On 23 October 2007, the Court made several changes to the components of the pilot program as reflected in General Order 35. As of 1 April 2013, all district courts in this circuit are participating in the Electronic Records on Appeal Program for civil and criminal cases being appealed from the district court.

As a result of further evaluation of the Electronic Records on Appeal Program and after receiving input from the bar in this circuit, the Court now vacates General Order 35 and adopts the attached "Appendix on Appeal" requirements for appeals where the district court is now filing only an electronic record on appeal. The requirements of the Electronic Records on Appeal Program Components have been significantly changed and reduced in content to only those items now set forth in the attached "Appendix on Appeal" requirements.

APPENDIX ON APPEAL WHERE ONLY ELECTRONIC RECORD FILED BY DISTRICT COURT

Appendix Requirements.

(a) *Contents.* In appeals from district courts, the appellant must file a paper appendix containing those items required by FRAP 30(a)(1), which are:

- the relevant docket entries in the proceeding below;
- the relevant portions of the pleadings, charge, findings, or opinion;
- the judgment, order, or decision in question; and
- other parts of the record to which the parties wish to direct the court's attention.

Other than FRAP 30(a)(1), the requirements in FRAP 30 do not apply in this circuit.

Consistent with the requirements of FRAP 30(a)(1) that the appendix contain relevant docket entries and relevant portions of the record, this Court has determined that the following items are either relevant docket entries or relevant portions of the record in the types of appeals specified below and thus must be included in the appendix.

Items 1–12 below are already required by 11th Cir. R. 30–1. Items 13–14 were added as part of the original Electronic Records on Appeal Program requirements, but those original requirements have now been significantly changed and reduced in content:

(1) the district court docket sheet, including, in bankruptcy appeals, the bankruptcy court docket sheet;

(2) in an appeal in a criminal case, the indictment, information, or petition as amended;

(3) in an appeal in a civil case, the complaint, answer, response, counterclaim, cross-claim, and any amendments to such items;

(4) those parts of any pretrial order relevant to the issues on appeal;

(5) the judgment or interlocutory order appealed from;

(6) any other order or orders sought to be reviewed, including, in bankruptcy appeals, the order(s) of the bankruptcy court appealed to the district court;

(7) in an appeal from the grant or denial of a petition for a writ of habeas corpus under 28 U.S.C. § 2254, all opinions by any state court previously rendered in the criminal prosecution and related collateral proceedings and appeals, and any state court orders addressing any claims and defenses brought by the petitioner in the federal action. This requirement applies whether or not the state court opinions and orders are contained in the district court record;

(8) any supporting opinion, findings of fact and conclusions of law filed or delivered orally by the court;

(9) if the correctness of a jury instruction is in issue, the instruction in question and any other relevant part of the jury charge;

(10) a magistrate's report and recommendation, when appealing a court order adopting same in whole or in part;

(11) findings and conclusions of an administrative law judge, when appealing a court order reviewing an administrative agency determination involving same;

(12) the relevant parts of any document, such as an insurance policy, contract, agreement, or ERISA plan, whose interpretation is relevant to the issues on appeal;

(13) in an appeal in a criminal case in which any issue is raised concerning the guilty plea, the transcript of the guilty plea colloquy and any written plea agreement;

(14) in an appeal in a criminal case in which any issue is raised concerning the sentence, the transcript of the sentencing proceeding, and the presentence investigation report and addenda (under seal in a separate envelope); and

(15) any other pleadings, affidavits, transcripts, filings, documents, or exhibits that any one of the parties believes will be helpful to this Court in deciding the appeal.

Except as otherwise permitted by subsection (a)(7) above, under no circumstances should a document be included in the appendix that was not submitted to the trial court.

(b) *Appellee's Responsibility.* If the appellant's appendix is deficient or if the appellee's brief, to support its position on an issue, relies on parts of the record not included in appellant's appendix, the appellee must file its own supplemental appendix within seven days of filing its brief. The appellee's supplemental appendix must not duplicate any documents in the appellant's appendix.

In an appeal by an incarcerated pro se party, counsel for appellee must submit an appendix that includes the specific pages of any record materials referred to in the argument section of appellee's brief and those referred to in the argument section of the appellant's brief that are relevant to the resolution of an issue on appeal.

(c) *Time for Filing.* A party must file an appendix or supplemental appendix within seven calendar days of filing the party's brief.

(d) *Number of Copies.* A pro se party proceeding in forma pauperis may file only one copy of the appendix or supplemental appendix, except that an incarcerated pro se party is not required to file an appendix.

Every other party must file two copies of the appendix or supplemental appendix within seven calendar days of filing the party's brief, and if the appeal is classed for oral argument, an additional three identical copies of the appendix previously filed by the party within seven calendar days after the date on the notice from the Clerk that the appeal has been classed for oral argument. One copy shall be served on counsel for each party separately represented, and on each pro se party. Where multiple parties are on one side of an appeal, they are strongly urged to file a joint appendix.

(e) *Form.* The appendix shall be reproduced on white paper by any duplicating or copying process capable of producing a clear black image, with a cover containing the information specified in 11th Cir. R. 28–1(a) and captioned "Appendix." The appendix shall be assembled with a front and back durable (at least 90#) white covering and shall be bound across the top with a secure fastener. Indexing tabs shall be affixed to the first page of each document in the appendix to identify and assist in locating the document. An index identifying each document contained in the appendix and its tab number shall be included immediately following the cover page. The appendix shall include a certificate of service consistent with FRAP 25(d).

District Court Items.

(a) The district court is not required to certify and transmit an entire paper record on appeal as required by FRAP 11 and the corresponding circuit rules, unless requested to do so by the Clerk of this Court in a particular case; but the district court is still required to certify when the record is complete for purposes of appeal.

(b) The district court is required to transmit in paper any document in the record that is not available to this Court electronically, including depositions, sealed records, PSIs, and any paper exhibits that have not been scanned into CM/ECF by the district court. Such documents must be transmitted at the time the district court certifies that the record is complete for purposes of appeal, unless the Clerk of this Court requests earlier transmittal in a particular case.

(c) When the Supreme Court requests a paper record in a case, it is the responsibility of the district court to provide one.

(d) This Court will rely on the electronic record on appeal to access any necessary documents not contained in the parties' appendices, or when access to the record is required prior to briefing.

(e) The Clerk's Office will not print documents from the electronic record, but the staff attorneys and chambers staff may do so.

(f) The electronic record, including any hearing or trial proceedings, will be available in a text-searchable format.

(g) There will be an ongoing evaluation of the program by judges, chambers staff and staff attorneys to determine whether the objectives have been met.

[Dated: June 26, 2013.]

SELECTED GENERAL ORDERS

GENERAL ORDER 36. [CHANGE OF COUNSEL]*

Before: DUBINA, Chief Judge, TJOFLAT, EDMONDSON, CARNES, BARKETT, HULL, MARCUS, WILSON, PRYOR, and MARTIN, Circuit Judges.

After an appeal has been assigned to an oral argument panel, any change in or addition to counsel in the appeal requires leave of court. For purposes of this General Order, an appeal is considered assigned to an oral argument panel when the clerk notifies counsel of the specific day of the week on which oral argument in the appeal is scheduled to be heard.

[Dated: June 16, 2011.]

* **[Publisher's Note:** Title editorially supplied.]

INDEX TO UNITED STATES COURT OF APPEALS FOR THE ELEVENTH CIRCUIT

UNITED STATES DISTRICT COURT FOR THE NORTHERN DISTRICT OF FLORIDA

Including Amendments Received Through February 1, 2017

GENERAL RULES

RULE 1.1 SCOPE OF THE RULES; CITATION

These rules apply to all proceedings in the United States District Court for the Northern District of Florida. But they apply to proceedings in the Bankruptcy Court only when not inconsistent with the Bankruptcy Court's own local rules. These rules may be cited as "N.D. Fla. Loc. R." Administrative orders that govern matters not addressed in these rules are available on the District's website.

[Adopted November 24, 2015.]

RULE 2.1 DEFINITIONS

In these rules:

(A) "this District" or "the District" means the Northern District of Florida;

(B) "the Clerk" means the Clerk of Court, Northern District of Florida;

(C) the "Court" means an assigned judge in a case;

(D) an "assigned judge" includes each judge assigned to a case (and in most cases, this includes both a district judge and a magistrate judge);

(E) a reference to any kind of written material or any other medium includes electronically stored information; and

(F) references to an "attorney" include a party proceeding pro se unless the context clearly indicates the contrary.

[Adopted November 24, 2015.]

RULE 3.1 DIVISIONS

(A) **Boundaries.** The District has four divisions:

(1) the Pensacola Division includes Escambia, Santa Rosa, Okaloosa, and Walton Counties;

(2) the Panama City Division includes Jackson, Holmes, Washington, Bay, Calhoun, and Gulf Counties;

(3) the Tallahassee Division includes Leon, Gadsden, Liberty, Franklin, Wakulla, Jefferson, Taylor, and Madison Counties; and

(4) the Gainesville Division includes Alachua, Lafayette, Dixie, Gilchrist, and Levy Counties.

(B) **Place of Filing Original and Removed Cases.** An original case must be filed in a division in which venue would be proper if the division was a stand-alone district. A removed case must be filed in the division that includes the county where the case was pending in state court.

(C) **Transfer; Place of Keeping a File.** A case will remain pending in the division where it was filed unless the Court enters an order transferring it. When there is a physical file, the Clerk may keep it in a division that includes an assigned judge's principal office, even if the case is pending in another division. A physical file may not be withdrawn from the Clerk's office by anyone other than a judge or judge's employee.

(D) **Place of Trial or Hearing.** A trial or hearing will occur in the division where a case is pending, unless the Court directs otherwise.

[Adopted November 24, 2015.]

RULE 4.1 SERVING PROCESS ON BEHALF OF A PARTY PROCEEDING *IN FORMA PAUPERIS*

(A) **Court Authorization Required.** A party who is not represented by an attorney and who has moved or intends to move for leave to proceed *in forma pauperis* must not serve process—and must not request a waiver of service under Federal Rule of Civil Procedure 4(d)(1)—until the Court enters an order authorizing it. The Court may direct the manner of serving process or requesting a waiver.

(B) **Serving a Correctional Officer or Employee.** The Court may direct the manner of personal service on a correctional officer or other employee of a correctional facility and may require the use of a process server designated for a specific correctional facility.

[Adopted November 24, 2015.]

RULE 5.1 FORM OF DOCUMENTS

(A) **Scope of the Rule.** This rule sets out the required form of each document filed in a case other than an exhibit or other material not created for filing in the case.

(B) **Case Style and Heading.** The first page of a document must begin with the case style. The case style must include the name of the court, the case number (including the initials of any assigned judges), and the name of at least one party on each side of the case (as framed by the first pleading or amended by an order or by substitution of a party under Federal Rule of Civil Procedure 25(d)). The document must include a heading after the case style but before any other content. The heading must clearly identify the document.

(C) **Format.** A document must be double spaced with at least 14-point font and at least one-inch margins on the top, bottom, left, and right of each page. Pages must be numbered. Handwritten documents must be legible with adequate spacing between lines. Hard copies should be securely fastened in the upper left-hand corner.

(D) Signature Block for an Attorney. A document filed by an attorney must include a signature block with the attorney's handwritten or electronic signature, typed name, bar number, street and email addresses, and telephone number. The signature block must identify by name or category the parties on whose behalf the document is filed.

(E) Signature Block for a Pro Se Party. A document filed by a pro se party must include a signature block with the party's handwritten signature, typed or printed name, street address, email address if the party has one, and telephone number if the party has one. But the signature may be electronic if an administrative rule or court order allows the party to file the document electronically.

(F) Certificate of Service. A document must include a certificate of service—with an electronic or handwritten signature—setting out the date and method of service. But a certificate of service is not required if:

(1) each party on whom the document will be served either (a) is represented by an attorney who will be served through the electronic filing system, or (b) has not yet appeared and will be served through formal service of process; or

(2) the document is properly being filed *ex parte*.

[Adopted November 24, 2015.]

RULE 5.2 CIVIL COVER SHEET

An attorney who files or removes a civil case must simultaneously file a civil cover sheet on a form available without charge from the Clerk or on the District's website. But the Court may allow the civil cover sheet to be filed later. A pro se party need not file a civil cover sheet.

[Adopted November 24, 2015.]

RULE 5.3 PAYING A FILING FEE OR PROCEEDING *IN FORMA PAUPERIS*

A party who files or removes a civil case must simultaneously either pay any fee required under 28 U.S.C. § 1914 or move for leave to proceed *in forma pauperis* under 28 U.S.C. § 1915. The Clerk must open the case and refer any motion for leave to proceed *in forma pauperis* to an assigned judge. A party who moves for leave to proceed *in forma pauperis* must simultaneously file a financial affidavit on a form available without charge from the Clerk or on the District's website. The motion must also be on a form available without charge from the Clerk or the District's website unless filed by an attorney. Unless otherwise ordered, a person in custody will not be excused from paying the $5 fee for filing a habeas petition if the person has a prison account with a balance of $25 or more.

[Adopted November 24, 2015.]

RULE 5.4 ELECTRONIC FILING

(A) When Required. Unless the Court orders otherwise, every document submitted for filing must be submitted through the electronic filing system, not in hard copy or by facsimile or other means, except that the following documents may—and if so required by an administrative order or an order in a case must—be filed in hard copy:

(1) An exhibit introduced at a trial or hearing;

(2) A document filed under seal;

(3) A document filed by a party pro se.

(B) As Effective as a Hard Copy. An order, sworn document, or other document that is electronically filed in the proper case file has exactly the same effect as would a substantively identical hard copy.

(C) Responsibility for Electronically Filed Signatures. An attorney who electronically files a document with the attorney's handwritten or electronic signature—or who authorizes another person to electronically file such a document—is responsible for the document just as if it had been filed in hard copy with the attorney's handwritten signature. And a party is responsible for a document electronically filed on the party's behalf with the party's or an attorney's handwritten or electronic signature, just as if the document had been filed in hard copy with the party's or attorney's handwritten signature.

(D) Sworn Documents. By electronically filing a copy of a document with an original seal or certification or a sworn original signature, an attorney certifies that the attorney has custody of the original. The attorney must make the original available for inspection and copying by any other party or the Court and must file the original if the Court so orders. If the original is not filed, the attorney must retain the original for at least two years after the litigation—including all appeals—has ended.

(E) Effective Date of an Electronic Filing. A document is electronically filed when the filing is accepted by the District's electronic filing system. A filing is made on a date if it is made prior to midnight on that date in local time at the place of holding court in the division where the case is pending.

(F) Service on Other Parties. A document that is electronically filed and that is electronically served on a party through the electronic filing system need not be served on that party by any other means, unless the Court so orders. An attorney's participation in the electronic filing system constitutes consent to accept service through the electronic filing system.

(G) Responsibility for a Filing and for the Accuracy of the Docket. The attorney who authorizes the electronic filing of a document is responsible for it under this rule regardless of whether the attorney actually makes the electronic filing or authorizes another person to do so. And the attorney must ensure that the document is accurately docketed.

[Adopted November 24, 2015.]

RULE 5.5 SEALING CASE FILES AND DOCUMENTS; REDACTING DOCUMENTS

(A) General Rule. Each case file and each document filed in it is public unless one of these provides otherwise: a statute, court rule, administrative order, or order in the case. The Court may, by an order in the case, modify any sealing or redaction requirement set out in an administrative order or this rule.

(B) Documents That May Be Sealed Without an Order. When a statute, court rule, or administrative order requires the sealing of a category of documents, a party may submit a document in that category for filing under seal, without moving for leave to file the document under seal. The Clerk must maintain the document under seal unless the Court orders otherwise.

(C) Documents That May Be Sealed Only With an Order. A party who wishes to file any other document under seal must, if feasible, move in advance for leave to file the document under seal. The party may submit the document for filing under seal only if the Court authorizes it. If a party submits a document for filing under seal before the Court authorizes it—either because obtaining advance authorization was not feasible or in violation of this rule—the Clerk must promptly refer the sealing issue to the Court and must maintain the document under seal until otherwise ordered.

(D) Filing Redacted Versions of Sealed Documents. When feasible, a party who files a document under seal must file a redacted version that will become part of the public file. Filing a redacted version is feasible unless (1) a person could infer from the redacted version the substance or import of the information that called for sealing the original or (2) the redacted version would include so little information that publicly filing it would serve no purpose.

(E) Redacting Documents That Are Improperly Filed with Personal Identifiers. If a party violates Federal Rule of Civil Procedure 5.2 or Federal Rule of Criminal Procedure 49.1 by failing to redact a personal identifier, the party must promptly file a properly redacted substitute. When the substitute is filed, the Clerk must seal the unredacted original.

[Adopted November 24, 2015.]

RULE 5.6 NOTICE OF A PRIOR OR SIMILAR CASE

A party who files or removes a case must file a notice—and if the party fails to do so any other party with knowledge of the circumstances must file a notice—if:

(A) a case in this District that includes an identical claim—or a similar claim—between some or all of the same or related parties was previously terminated by any means; or

(B) the new case involves issues of fact or law in common with the issues in another case pending in the District.

[Adopted November 24, 2015.]

RULE 5.7 PRO SE CIVIL-RIGHTS CASES AND COLLATERAL ATTACKS ON CRIMINAL CONVICTIONS

(A) Required Forms. A party not represented by an attorney must file any of these only on a form available without charge from the Clerk or on the District's website: a petition for a writ of habeas corpus, a motion for relief under 28 U.S.C. § 2255, or a complaint in a civil-rights case. A case is a civil-rights case if it asserts a claim under the United States Constitution or a statute creating individual rights, including, for example, 42 U.S.C. § 1983 or the Civil Rights Act of 1964. The Court need not—and ordinarily will not—consider a petition, motion, or complaint that is not filed on the proper form.

(B) Requirement to Set Out Claims and Facts as Part of the Form; Memorandum Optional. A petition, motion, or complaint described in subdivision (A) must set out specific claims and supporting facts and may not make reference to a memorandum. A party may, but need not, also file a memorandum with the petition, motion, or complaint. A petition, motion, or complaint, together with any memorandum, must not exceed 25 pages, unless the Court authorizes it.

(C) Applicability of Federal Rules in Collateral Attacks. The Rules Governing Section 2254 Cases in the United States District Courts, as adopted by the Supreme Court, apply to all habeas corpus petitions in this District whether or not filed under section 2254. The Rules Governing Section 2255 Proceedings for the United States District Courts, as adopted by the Supreme Court, apply to all section 2255 motions.

[Adopted November 24, 2015.]

RULE 5.8 SPECIAL PROCEDURAL AND FILING REQUIREMENTS APPLICABLE TO HABEAS CORPUS INVOLVING THE DEATH PENALTY

(A) In habeas corpus cases involving the death penalty, it is the responsibility of the party who first makes reference in a pleading or instrument to a deposition or an exhibit to:

(1) Obtain either the original or a certified copy of that deposition and include that deposition or exhibit as an exhibit to their pleading or instrument; or

(2) To file a certificate indicating why the deposition or exhibit is not included as an exhibit to the pleading or instrument.

(B) It is the responsibility of the party offering for filing any portion of a prior state or federal court record or transcript to:

(1) Obtain from the Clerk's office a habeas corpus checklist and review the various phases of court proceedings identified on the checklist.

(2) Review each prior state or federal court record to be submitted and identify, within each record, the first page of every portion of the submitted record identified on the checklist, using the colored tabs and numbering scheme as indicated below:

(a) Petitioner shall use red index tabs and shall sequentially number the index tabs commencing with the number "P–1," "P–2," etc.

(b) Respondent shall employ blue index tabs and shall sequentially number the index tabs commencing with the number "R–1," "R–2," etc.

(c) Amicus curiae or other parties permitted to intervene or otherwise participate shall employ green index tabs and shall sequentially number the index tabs commencing with the number "X–1," "X–2," etc.

(3) Cross-reference the index tab number to the checklist.

(4) File a completed checklist concurrently with the filing of the first pleading or instrument which makes reference to any portion of a prior state or federal court record or transcript.

(5) Serve a copy of the checklist on all parties and file a certificate of service along with the checklist, indicating service upon all parties.

(C) In order to facilitate the timely and efficient processing of habeas corpus capital cases, checklists and index tabs may be obtained in advance of filing from the Clerk's office.

[Adopted November 24, 2015.]

RULE 5.9 TRIAL AND HEARING EXHIBITS

(A) Tendering and Maintaining Exhibits. An exhibit tendered or received in evidence during a trial or hearing must be delivered to the Clerk, and the Clerk must maintain custody of the exhibit, with these exceptions:

(1) the Court may order otherwise;

(2) a sensitive exhibit—such as a weapon, drug, cash, pornography, or thing of high value—may be retained by the law enforcement agency or party who offered it, and in that event the agency or party must maintain the integrity of the exhibit;

(3) the Clerk may release an exhibit temporarily to an assigned judge, the judge's staff, or the court reporter.

(B) Retrieving Exhibits After the Litigation. Within 90 days after a case is closed and all appeals have been exhausted, the party who offered an exhibit must retrieve it from the Clerk. The Clerk may destroy an exhibit not timely retrieved.

[Adopted November 24, 2015.]

RULE 6.1 EXTENSIONS OF TIME AND CONTINUANCES

Only the Court may continue a trial, hearing, or other proceeding. A stipulation to extend a deadline is effective only with Court approval. But the parties may stipulate, without Court approval, to extend a deadline for responding to a specific discovery request or for making a Federal Rule of Civil Procedure 26 disclosure if the extension does not interfere with the time set for any of these: completing discovery, submitting or responding to a motion, or trial.

[Adopted November 24, 2015.]

RULE 7.1 MOTIONS

(A) How Made. An oral motion may be made during a properly noticed trial or hearing. Any other motion must be in writing in the form required by Local Rule 5.1 and this Local Rule 7.1. A request for action of any kind relating to a case can never be made by a letter to a judge.

(B) Attorney Conference Required. Before filing a motion raising an issue, an attorney for the moving party must attempt in good faith to resolve the issue through a meaningful conference with an attorney for the adverse party. The adverse party's attorney must participate in the conference in good faith. The conference may be conducted in person, by telephone, in writing, or electronically, but an oral conference is encouraged. An email or other writing sent at or near the time of filing the motion is not a meaningful conference. When a conference is conducted in writing or electronically, an attorney ordinarily should be afforded at least 24 hours—as calculated under Federal Rule of Civil Procedure 6—to respond to a communication. This Rule 7.1(B) applies to an unrepresented (pro se) party only if the party is not in custody.

(C) Certificate Required. A motion or supporting memorandum must include a certificate—under a separate heading—confirming that the moving party complied with the attorney-conference requirement of Local Rule 7.1(B) and setting out the results.

(D) Exceptions: Attorney Conference and Certificate Not Required. An attorney conference and certificate are not required for a motion that would determine the outcome of a case or a claim, for a motion for leave to proceed *in forma pauperis*, or for a motion that properly may be submitted *ex parte*.

(E) Supporting and Opposing Memoranda Required; Deadline. A party who files a written motion must file a supporting memorandum in the same document with, or at the same time as, the motion. A party who opposes the motion must file a memorandum in opposition. Unless otherwise ordered, the deadline for a memorandum opposing a motion (other than a summary-judgment motion) is 14 days after service of the motion, without a 3-day extension based on electronic service of the motion. The deadline and other requirements that apply to a summary judgment motion are set out in Local Rule 56.1.

(F) Word Limit. A memorandum must not exceed 8,000 words and must include a certificate stating the number of words in the memorandum. The person preparing the certificate may rely on the word count of the word-processing system used to prepare the memorandum. Headings, footnotes, and quotations count toward the word limit. The case style, signature block, and any certificate of service do not count toward the word limit. If a motion itself exceeds 500 words, the words in the motion count toward the limitation on words in the supporting memorandum. In extraordinary circumstances, the Court may grant leave to file a longer memorandum, but doing so is disfavored. A party who moves for leave to file a longer memorandum may attach the proposed memorandum to the motion if all opposing parties consent to the motion; otherwise the party must obtain leave to file the longer memorandum before tendering the longer memorandum.

(G) Exceptions: Memoranda Not Required. Supporting and opposing memoranda are not required for:

(1) an unopposed motion;

(2) a motion for leave to proceed *in forma pauperis*;

(3) a motion for leave for an attorney to appear pro hac vice or withdraw or for substitution of counsel;

(4) a motion to withdraw or substitute exhibits;

(5) a motion to exceed a word or page limit or for leave to file a reply memorandum.

(H) Failing to File a Required Memorandum. The Court may deny a moving party's motion if the party does not file a memorandum as required by this rule. The Court may grant a motion by default if an opposing party does not file a memorandum as required by this rule.

(I) Reply Memoranda. A party ordinarily may not file a reply memorandum in support of a motion. But a party may file a reply memorandum in support of a summary-judgment motion under Local Rule 56.1(D). And in extraordinary circumstances, the Court may grant leave to file a reply memorandum in support of another motion. A reply memorandum must not exceed 3200 words (counted and certified as under Local Rule 7.1(F)) unless the Court sets a higher limit. When leave to file a reply memorandum is required, a party must obtain leave before tendering the reply memorandum.

(J) Notices of Supplemental Authority. If a pertinent and significant authority comes to a party's attention after the party's memorandum has been filed—or after a hearing but before decision—the party may file a notice of supplemental authority. The notice must not exceed 350 words. A copy of the cited authority may be attached. Any response must be made promptly and must be similarly limited.

(K) Oral Argument. The Court may—and most often does—rule on a motion without oral argument, even if a party requests oral argument. But the Court may set an oral argument on its own or at the request of a party. A request may be made as part of the motion or supporting or opposing memorandum, should be set out under a separate heading, and should include an estimate of the required time.

(L) Emergencies. A motion that requires a ruling more promptly than would occur in the ordinary course of business may be labeled an emergency. The motion or supporting memorandum should explain the emergency. The moving party should orally advise the Clerk's office that the emergency motion has been filed. The Court may require an expedited response or otherwise amend the schedule as appropriate.

(M) Sending Letters—or Copies of Letters—to the Judge. A party or victim may address a letter to the judge about a forthcoming sentencing, but the letter must be provided to the probation office—not directly to the judge. A party must not address or send any other letter to the judge. A copy of a letter to and from others—including a letter between attorneys—may be filed with the Clerk as an exhibit when relevant to an issue that is being submitted. But filing letters between attorneys is discouraged. For purposes of this rule, a "letter" includes correspondence of any kind, including email.

[Adopted November 24, 2015.]

RULE 7.2 REMOVING A CASE FROM STATE COURT

(A) Filing State–Court Papers. At the time of a case's removal from state court, if feasible, and in any event within 14 days after removal, the removing party must file a copy of each paper filed or served in the state court.

(B) Pending Motions. For a motion that was pending in state court at the time of removal, the attorneys must confer and the parties must file supporting and opposing memoranda, unless (1) these steps were already taken in state court or (2) Local Rule 7.1 would not have required these steps for a motion originally filed in this District. The deadline for a supporting memorandum is 14 days after removal. The deadline for an opposing memorandum is 14 days after the later of the removal or the filing of the supporting memorandum.

[Adopted November 24, 2015.]

RULE 11.1 ATTORNEYS

(A) Qualification for Admission to the District's Bar. An attorney is qualified for admission to the District's bar only if the attorney is a member in good standing of The Florida Bar. But an attorney who was previously admitted to the District's bar may remain a member so long as (1) the attorney does not violate Florida law on the unauthorized practice of law and (2) there are no other grounds for the attorney's removal from the District's bar.

(B) Applying for Admission. An application for admission to the District's bar must be under oath and must be submitted to the Clerk in the form the Clerk directs. The applicant must submit proof of membership in The Florida Bar in the form the Clerk directs. The applicant must pay the fee set by administrative order, except that an applicant who is an employee of the United States or a state or local government need not pay the fee.

(C) Appearing Pro Hac Vice. An attorney who is a member in good standing of the bar of a jurisdiction where the attorney resides or regularly practices law may file a motion in a case for leave to appear pro hac vice. The attorney must pay the fee set by administrative order and must file proof of bar membership in the form the Clerk directs. Admission pro hac vice does not change the attorney's obligation to comply with Florida law on the unauthorized practice of law.

(D) Other Appearances Prohibited; Exceptions for Emergencies and for Attorneys Representing the United States. An attorney must not file a document or appear at a trial or hearing unless the attorney is a member of the District's bar or has been granted leave to appear in the case pro hac vice. But in an emergency, an attorney may file a document or appear while seeking admission to the District's bar or leave to appear pro hac vice. And an attorney may appear for the United States—or for a federal agency or federal employee on matters within the scope of employment—without being a member of the District's bar or being admitted pro hac vice.

(E) Education. By administrative order, the District may require an attorney to successfully complete a tutorial on the local rules—or to meet a similar requirement—before being admitted to the District's bar, appearing pro hac vice, or appearing for the United States. By administrative order, the District may require an attorney to successfully complete a tutorial on the electronic filing system—or to meet a similar requirement—before filing materials electronically.

(F) Participation by a Represented Party Prohibited. A party who is represented by an attorney must appear only through the attorney; the party may not file documents or participate in a trial or hearing on the party's own behalf. A party who appears pro se may not be represented jointly or intermittently by an attorney. But an attorney may enter an appearance and thus end a party's pro se status, so long as the appearance will not delay a trial or other proceeding, and the Court may allow an attorney to withdraw even if doing so will leave the party without an attorney.

(G) Professional Conduct, Disbarment, and Other Discipline.

(1) *Professional Conduct.* An attorney must comply with the Rules of Professional Conduct that are part of the Rules Regulating The Florida Bar, as amended from time to time, or with any set of rules adopted by The Florida Bar in their place, unless federal law provides otherwise.

(2) *Notifying the District of Any Disbarment or Suspension.* An attorney who is disbarred or suspended from any jurisdiction's bar must immediately notify the district by letter to the Clerk or Chief Judge, enclosing a copy of the disbarment or suspension.

(3) *Effect of Disbarment or Suspension by The Florida Bar.* An attorney who is disbarred or suspended by The Florida Bar stands automatically disbarred or suspended from the district's bar, without further action, effective at the same time as disbarment or suspension from The Florida Bar. Reinstatement to The Florida Bar after a suspension automatically reinstates the attorney to the district's bar. An attorney who is readmitted to The Florida Bar after disbarment may become a member of the district's bar only by reapplying.

(4) *Disbarment or Suspension on Other Grounds.* An attorney will be removed or suspended from the District's bar on any other ground only after notice and an opportunity to be heard. At the District's option, the opportunity to be heard may be limited to submitting argument or evidence in writing. The attorney may be prohibited from acting on a case in this District after notice is given and while the attorney's removal or suspension is under consideration. Grounds for disbarment or suspension include:

(a) disbarment or suspension from any jurisdiction's bar;

(b) conviction of, entry of a plea of guilty or nolo contendere to, or commission of a felony or misdemeanor;

(c) a finding of, or conduct constituting, contempt of this or any other court;

(d) a violation of the professional-conduct standards that apply under this rule's paragraph (G)(1); or

(e) other conduct inconsistent with the high level of professionalism expected in this District.

(5) *Withdrawing from the District's Bar.* An attorney may withdraw from the District's bar by giving notice to the Clerk.

(6) *Reinstatement.* The District may reinstate a removed or suspended attorney, or an attorney who has withdrawn, with or without conditions. A reinstated attorney must pay the admission fee unless the attorney is automatically reinstated under Local Rule 11.1(G)(3).

(7) *Contempt.* A person may be held in contempt of court if the person (a) acts as an attorney in this District in violation of this rule or (b) pretends to be entitled to act as an attorney in this District but is not.

(8) *Other Restrictions or Discipline.* For good cause, the District may limit an attorney's activities in the District or impose other discipline, and the Court may limit an attorney's activities or impose discipline in a case, after giving any appropriate notice and opportunity to be heard.

(H) Withdrawing in a Case.

(1) *When Court Approval Required.* An attorney who has appeared in a case may not withdraw unless:

(a) the Court grants leave to withdraw; or

(b) the client consents and the withdrawal will leave the client with another attorney of record who intends to continue in the case.

(2) *Prior Notice.* An attorney must not move for leave to withdraw without first giving 14 days' notice to the client, unless giving notice is impossible. The motion must set out the client's position on the motion.

(3) *Nonpayment of Fees.* An attorney ordinarily will not be allowed to withdraw based on a client's failure to pay attorney's fees or expenses if the withdrawal will delay a trial or hearing. And in a criminal case, a motion to withdraw based on a defendant's failure to pay attorney's fees or expenses ordinarily will be denied if made more than 7 days after the defendant's first arraignment.

(I) Responsibility of Retained Counsel in Criminal Cases.

(1) Unless the Court, within 7 days after arraignment, is notified in writing of counsel's withdrawal because of the defendant's failure to make satisfactory financial arrangements, the Court will expect retained criminal defense counsel to represent the defendant until the conclusion of the case. Failure of a defendant to pay sums owed for attorney's fees or failure of counsel to collect a sum sufficient to compensate for all the services usually required of defense counsel will not constitute good cause for withdrawal after the 7-day period has expired.

(2) If a defendant moves the Court to proceed on appeal *in forma pauperis* and/or for appointment of Criminal Justice Act appellate counsel, counsel retained for trial will, in addition to the information required under Form 4 of the Rules of Appellate Procedure, be required to fully disclose in camera (a) the attorney's fee agreement and the total amount of such fees and costs paid to date, in cash or otherwise; (b) by whom fees and costs were paid; (c) any fees and costs remaining

unpaid and the complete terms of agreements concerning payment thereof; (d) the costs actually incurred to date; and (e) a detailed description of services actually rendered to date, including a record of the itemized time (to the nearest 1/10 of an hour) for each service, both in-court and out-of-court, and the total time. All such information submitted will be viewed in camera by the Court for the purpose of deciding the defendant's motion and will be a part of the record (sealed if requested) in the case.

[Adopted November 24, 2015.]

RULE 15.1 AMENDING A PLEADING

(A) Complete Copy Required. A pleading may be amended only by filing a complete copy of the amended pleading. Allegations in a prior pleading that are not set out in the amended pleading are deemed abandoned, with this exception: if, in a definitive ruling, the Court has dismissed a claim or struck a defense without leave to amend, the claim or defense must not be included in a later amended pleading.

(B) Separately Docketing a Motion for Leave and the Amended Pleading. When a pleading may be amended only by leave of court, the amending party must file a motion for leave to amend and must simultaneously file the proposed amended pleading itself. The proposed amended pleading will become effective only if the Court grants leave to amend.

[Adopted November 24, 2015.]

RULE 16.1 RULE 26(f) ATTORNEY CONFERENCE; PRIOR DISCOVERY

In a civil case in which the attorneys must confer under Federal Rule of Civil Procedure 26(f), the conference must occur as soon as practicable. The Court may—and ordinarily will—enter an order modifying the deadline for the conference. If an order has not been entered, the deadline is determined by the Federal Rules and is ordinarily the earlier of 69 days after any defendant has appeared or 99 days after the first service of process on any defendant. A party may seek discovery before the conference only when authorized by the Federal Rules, by stipulation, or by an order in the case.

[Adopted November 24, 2015.]

RULE 16.2 NOTICE OF A SETTLEMENT OR INTENT TO PLEAD GUILTY OR MOTION TO CONTINUE; ASSESSING COSTS

(A) Duty to Give Notice. Each attorney of record must ensure that the Court is notified immediately when:

(1) A civil case is settled;

(2) A defendant elects to enter a guilty plea;

(3) The parties resolve by agreement a motion or other dispute that is under submission; or

(4) A party expects to move for continuance of a trial or hearing.

(B) Manner of Giving Notice. Actual notice must be given in a manner that ensures that the judge and court personnel do not unnecessarily work on a settled case or issue and that jurors are not unnecessarily required to appear. When a trial or hearing is imminent or a matter is under submission, filing an electronic notice may not be sufficient; telephone notice may be required. A party must give notice to all other parties at least as promptly as to the Court.

(C) Expenses. If a party fails to give notice at least two days—calculated under Federal Rule of Civil Procedure 6—before a jury panel is scheduled to report for jury selection, juror attendance and mileage fees will be assessed against the party or the party's attorney or both, unless the Court orders otherwise for good cause. Other expenses incurred as a result of any failure to give timely notice under this rule—including witness fees, travel expenses, and expenses incurred by the United States Marshal or for court security—may also be assessed. Expenses assessed against an attorney appointed under the Criminal Justice Act may be offset against the attorney's fee.

[Adopted November 24, 2015.]

RULE 16.3 MEDIATION

The Court may order the parties to mediate a civil case. The parties may agree to mediate a civil case even when the Court has not ordered them to do so. Mediation must be conducted in accordance with the Rules for Certified and Court-Appointed Mediators adopted by the Florida Supreme Court, except as otherwise ordered, but this sentence does not apply to a settlement conference—even if called "mediation"—conducted by a district or magistrate judge. Everything said during a mediation or settlement conference—other than the terms of any settlement agreement itself—is confidential and inadmissible as a settlement negotiation.

[Adopted November 24, 2015.]

RULE 23.1 CLASS ACTIONS

A pleading that asserts a claim on behalf of or against a class must set out the proposed definition of the class and must allege facts showing that the claim or defense may be so maintained. The pleader must file a motion to certify the class, together with a memorandum and evidence showing the class certification is appropriate, within 90 days after filing the pleading. The Court may change the deadline by an order in the case. The filing of an amended pleading does not extend the deadline.

[Adopted November 24, 2015.]

RULE 24.1 CONSTITUTIONAL CHALLENGES TO STATUTES, RULES, AND ORDINANCES

A party who files a pleading, written motion, or other paper drawing into question the constitutionality of a federal or state statute or rule must promptly file and serve a notice under Federal Rule of Civil Procedure 5.1(a). A party who files a pleading, written motion, or other paper calling into question the constitutionality of a political subdivision's ordinance or rule must file a notice and serve it on the state attorney general, the state attorney with jurisdiction in the political subdivision's geographic area, and the attorney for the political subdivision.

[Adopted November 24, 2015.]

RULE 26.1 DISCOVERY IN CIVIL CASES

(A) Discovery Materials Not To Be Filed; Exceptions. A party may conduct discovery but must not file a discovery request or response or a deposition transcript unless:

(1) the Court orders the filing;

(2) the material is needed for determination of a pending motion or issue; or

(3) the material is admitted into evidence at a trial or hearing.

(B) Place of Depositions. Unless the Court orders otherwise for cause,

(1) a party who asserts a claim for affirmative relief—other than costs and attorney's fees—can be required to appear once in this District for a deposition; and

(2) any other party can be required to appear for a deposition only where a nonparty witness could be required to appear.

(C) Objections to Written Discovery Requests. An objection to an interrogatory, production request, or admission request must be set out specifically for the individual interrogatory, production request, or admission request; an objection cannot be set out generally for an entire set of discovery requests. Boilerplate objections are strongly disfavored.

(D) Motions To Compel. A discovery motion must frame the dispute clearly and, if feasible, must, for each discovery request at issue:

(1) quote the discovery request verbatim;

(2) quote each objection specifically directed to the discovery request; and

(3) set out the reasons why the discovery should be compelled.

[Adopted November 24, 2015.]

RULE 26.2 DISCOVERY IN CRIMINAL CASES

(A) Policy. It is the District's policy to rely on the standard discovery procedure as set forth in this rule as the sole means for the exchange of discovery in criminal cases except in extraordinary circumstances. This rule is intended to promote the efficient exchange of discovery without altering the rights and obligations of the parties, but at the same time eliminating the practice of routinely filing voluminous and duplicative discovery motions. Best practices consistent with this rule may be addressed by administrative order.

(B) Discovery Upon Defendant's Request. At the earliest opportunity and no later than 7 days after arraignment, the defendant's attorney shall contact the government's attorney and make a good faith attempt to have all properly discoverable material and information promptly disclosed or provided for inspection or copying. In addition, upon request of the defendant, the government shall specifically provide the following within 7 days after the request:

(1) *Defendant's Statements Under Fed. R. Crim. P. 16(a)(1)(A)(B), and (C).* Any written or recorded statements made by the defendant; the substance of any oral statement made by the defendant before or after the defendant's arrest in response to interrogation by a then known-to-be government agent which the government intends to offer in evidence at trial; and any recorded grand jury testimony of the defendant relating to the offenses charged.

(2) *Defendant's Prior Record Under Fed. R. Crim. P. 16(a)(1)(D).* The defendant's complete arrest and conviction record, as known to the government.

(3) *Documents and Tangible Objects Under Fed. R. Crim. P. 16(a)(1)(E).* Books, papers, documents, photographs, tangible objects, buildings or places, or copies or portions thereof, which the government intends to use as evidence-in-chief at trial, which are material to the preparation of the defendant's defense, or which were obtained from or belong to the defendant.

(4) *Reports of Examinations and Tests Under Fed. R. Crim. P. 16(a)(1)(F).* Results or reports of physical or mental examinations and of scientific tests or experiments, or copies thereof, which are material to the preparation of the defendant's defense or are intended for use by the government as evidence-in-chief at trial.

(5) *Expert Witnesses Under Fed. R. Crim. P. 16(a)(1)(G).* A written summary of testimony the government intends to use under Rules 702, 703, or 705 of the Federal Rules of Evidence.

(C) Defendant's Discovery Obligations. If the defendant requests disclosure under subdivisions (a)(1)(C), (D), or (E) of Fed. R. Crim. P. 16, or if the defendant has given notice under Fed. R. Crim. P. 12.2 of an intent to present expert testimony on the defendant's mental condition, the government shall make its requests as allowed by Fed. R. Crim. P. 16 within 3 days after compliance with the defendant's request or after receipt of defendant's notice of intent to present expert testimony on the defendant's mental condition pursuant to Fed. R. Crim. P. 12.2, and the defendant shall provide, by the deadline set out below, the following:

(1) *Documents and Tangible Objects Under Fed. R. Crim. P. 16(b)(1)(A).* Within 7 days after government's request, books, papers, documents, photographs, tangible objects, or copies or portions thereof, which the defendant intends to introduce as evidence-in-chief at trial.

(2) *Reports of Examinations and Tests Under Fed. R. Crim. P. 16(b)(1)(B).* At least 30 days before the trial, results or reports of physical or mental examinations, and of scientific tests or experiments, or copies thereof, which the defendant intends to introduce as evidence-in-chief at trial, or which were prepared by a witness whom the defendant intends to call at trial and which relate to that witness's testimony.

(3) *Expert Witnesses Under Fed. R. Crim. P. 16(b)(1)(C).* Within 14 days after the government's request, a written

summary of testimony the defendant intends to use under Rules 702, 703, or 705 of the Federal Rules of Evidence.

(D) Other Disclosure Obligations of the Government. The government's attorney shall provide the following within 7 days after the defendant's arraignment, or promptly after acquiring knowledge thereof:

(1) *Brady Material.* All information and material known to the government which may be favorable to the defendant on the issues of guilt or punishment, without regard to materiality, that is within the scope of *Brady v. Maryland,* 373 U.S. 83 (1963) and *United States v. Agurs,* 427 U.S. 97 (1976).

(2) *Giglio Material.* The existence and substance of any payments, promises of immunity, leniency, preferential treatment, or other inducements made to prospective witnesses, within the scope of *United States v. Giglio,* 405 U.S. 150 (1972) and *Napus v. Illinois,* 360 U.S. 264 (1959).

(3) *Testifying Informant's Convictions.* A record of prior convictions of any alleged informant who will testify for the government at trial.

(4) *Defendant's Identification.* If a lineup, showup, photo spread or similar procedure was used in attempting to identify the defendant, the exact procedure and participants shall be described and the results, together with any pictures and photographs, shall be disclosed.

(5) *Inspection of Vehicles, Vessels, or Aircraft.* If any vehicle, vessel, or aircraft was allegedly utilized in the commission of any offenses charged, the government shall permit the defendant's counsel and any experts selected by the defense to inspect it, if it is in the custody of any governmental authority.

(6) *Defendant's Latent Prints.* If latent fingerprints, or prints of any type, have been identified by a government expert as those of the defendant, copies thereof shall be provided.

(E) Obligations of the Government.

(1) The government shall advise all government agents and officers involved in the case to preserve all rough notes and electronically stored information.

(2) The government shall advise the defendant of its intention to introduce evidence at trial, pursuant to Rule 404(b), Federal Rules of Evidence.

(3) If the defendant was an "aggrieved person" as defined in 18 U.S.C. § 2510(11), the government shall so advise the defendant and set forth the detailed circumstances thereof.

(4) The government shall anticipate the need for, and arrange for the transcription of, the grand jury testimony of all witnesses who will testify in the government's case-in-chief, if subject to Fed. R. Crim. P. 26.2 and to 18 U.S.C. § 3500. *Jencks* Act materials and witnesses' statements shall be provided as required by Fed. R. Crim. P. 26.2 and § 3500. However, the government, and where applicable, the defendant, is requested to make such materials and statements available to the other party sufficiently in advance so as to avoid any delays or interruptions at trial.

(F) Obligations of the Defendant.

(1) *Insanity.* If a defendant intends to rely upon the defense of insanity at the time of the alleged crime, or intends to introduce expert testimony relating to a mental disease, defect, or other mental condition bearing upon the issue of guilt, or, in a capital case, punishment, the defendant shall give written notice thereof to the government within 14 days after arraignment.

(2) *Alibi.* If the attorney for the government makes demand for notice of defendant's intent to offer a defense of an alibi, the defendant shall respond within 14 days after the demand.

(3) *Entrapment.* If the defendant intends to rely upon the defense of entrapment, such intention shall be disclosed by written notice to the government's attorney at least 14 days before the trial. *See United States v. Webster,* 649 F.2d 346 (5th Cir. 1981).

(G) Joint Obligations of Attorneys.

(1) *Conference and Joint Report.* The attorneys for the government and the defendant shall confer at least 7 days prior to the scheduled date for jury selection and shall discuss all discovery requested and provided. They shall also make every possible effort in good faith to stipulate to facts, to points of law, and to the authenticity of exhibits (particularly regarding those exhibits for which records custodian witnesses may be avoided). A joint written statement, signed by the attorney for each defendant and the government, shall be prepared and filed prior to commencement of trial. It shall generally describe all discovery material exchanged and shall set forth all stipulations. No stipulation made shall be used against a defendant unless the stipulation is in writing and signed by both the defendant and the defendant's attorney.

(2) *Newly Discovered Evidence.* It shall be the duty of counsel for both sides to immediately reveal to opposing counsel all newly discovered information, evidence, or other material within the scope of this rule, and there is a continuing duty upon each attorney to disclose by the speediest means available.

(3) *Discovery Motions Prohibited.* No attorney shall file a discovery motion without first conferring with opposing counsel, and no motion will be considered by the Court unless it is accompanied by a certification of such conference and a statement of the moving party's good faith efforts to resolve the subject matter of the motion by agreement with opposing counsel. No discovery motions should be filed for information or material within the scope of this rule.

(4) *Filing of Requests.* Discovery requests made pursuant to Fed. R. Crim. P. 16 and this local rule require no action on the part of the Court and should not be filed with the Clerk, unless needed for consideration of a motion or to preserve an issue for appeal.

(5) *Protected Material.* When the government believes that public disclosure of *Giglio* material or testifying-informant convictions poses a danger to a witness, it may provide this information in an envelope separate from other discovery material and marked "*Giglio* material/informant convictions—DISTRIBUTION OUTSIDE THE DEFENSE TEAM IS PROHIBITED." Information designated in this manner shall not be distributed by the attorney for the defendant, except to

those working on the attorney's behalf. While it is information that is necessarily shared with the defendant, copies of this information shall not be provided to the defendant.

[Adopted November 24, 2015.]

RULE 41.1 DISMISSAL FOR FAILURE TO COMPLY WITH A RULE OR COURT ORDER

If a party fails to comply with an applicable rule or a court order, the Court may strike a pleading, dismiss a claim, enter a default on a claim, take other appropriate action, or issue an order to show cause why any of these actions should not be taken.

[Adopted November 24, 2015.]

RULE 54.1 MOTIONS FOR ATTORNEY'S FEES

(A) Bifurcated Procedure. A party who seeks an award of attorney's fees must first move for a determination of the party's *entitlement* to a fee award and may move for a determination of the *amount* of an award only after the Court determines the party's entitlement to an award. Local Rule 7.1, including the requirement for the attorneys to confer in a good-faith effort to resolve the dispute, applies in full.

(B) Deadline for an Entitlement Motion. The deadline for moving for a determination of entitlement is 14 days after the entry of the judgment or, if there is no judgment, 14 days after the case is closed. An appeal does not extend the deadline unless the Court so orders.

(C) Maintaining Time Records. No award of attorney's fees will be made based in whole or part on time devoted to a case unless the attorney or other timekeeper made a contemporaneous, detailed record of the time to the nearest tenth hour. A detailed record must provide enough information to allow the Court to evaluate reasonableness; an entry like "research" or "conference" without a description of the subject will not do.

(D) Filing and Disclosing Time Records. Unless an assigned judge orders otherwise, the time records must not be filed with the Clerk until necessary for the determination of a fee motion. But a party must promptly disclose to another party—on a request made at any time—the total number of hours that have been devoted to the case by the party's attorneys and other timekeepers through the end of the month preceding the request.

(E) Required Filings in Support of a Motion to Determine the Fee Amount. If the Court determines that a party is entitled to a fee award, the party must file within 30 days:

(1) A declaration setting out the time devoted to the case by date and task, specifically identifying the timekeeper and the timekeeper's claimed hourly rate. The declaration must include sufficient detail to allow a determination of reasonableness. And the declaration must include sufficient detail to allow the maximum feasible separation of time devoted to matters that are and are not compensable and matters on which the party did and did not prevail.

(2) A declaration of an independent attorney addressing the reasonableness of the claimed time and rates.

(F) Required Filings in Opposition to a Motion to Determine the Fee Amount. A party who opposes a motion to determine the fee amount must file within 30 days after the motion is served a memorandum specifically identifying any objection to the claimed amount. If the party objects to a timekeeper's claimed hourly rate, the memorandum must set out the rate that the party asserts is reasonable. If the party asserts that hours should be reduced or not compensated, the memorandum must identify the hours or otherwise specifically describe the proposed reduction. The memorandum must set out the fee award the party asserts would be reasonable—and by doing so the party will not be deemed to waive the party's objection that fees should not be awarded at all.

(G) Additional Conference and Notice. After a party files a memorandum in opposition to the motion to determine the fee amount, the attorneys must confer again in a good-faith effort to resolve the dispute—on amount if not also on entitlement. The parties must file a notice of whether they have reached any agreement. The deadline for the notice is 14 days after the memorandum in opposition was filed.

[Adopted November 24, 2015.]

RULE 54.2 TAXATION OF COSTS

(A) Bill of Costs Required; Objections; Deadlines. A party who seeks taxation of costs—other than attorney's fees—must file a verified bill of costs on a form available from the Clerk or on the District's website. The deadline for filing the bill of costs is 14 days after the entry of the judgment or, if there is no judgment, 14 days after the case is closed. The party may simultaneously file a memorandum in support of the bill of costs. Any other party may file a memorandum in opposition within 14 days after the bill of costs is filed. An appeal does not extend these deadline unless the Court so orders.

(B) Taxation by the Clerk or the Court. Unless the Court orders otherwise, the Clerk will review and take appropriate action on the bill of costs, after the deadline for filing objections.

(C) Review by the Court. On motion filed within 7 days after the Clerk's action, the Court may review the action.

(D) Administrative Order. An administrative order may provide guidance to the Clerk and parties on the taxation of categories of costs, but the administrative order will have no legal effect in any dispute over whether a cost legally can or should be taxed in a case.

[Adopted November 24, 2015.]

RULE 56.1 SUMMARY JUDGMENT MOTIONS

(A) Federal Rule 56. A summary-judgment motion is governed by Federal Rule of Civil Procedure 56 and, unless the Court orders otherwise, this rule.

(B) Motion and Supporting Memorandum. A party who moves for summary judgment must file at the same time a memorandum of up to 8,000 words and any supporting evidence not already in the record. The memorandum must include a statement of facts generally in the form that would be appropriate in an appellate brief. A statement of facts must not be set out in a separate document.

(C) Opposing Memorandum. An opposing party must file within 21 days—without a 3-day extension based on electronic service of the motion—a memorandum of up to 8,000 words and any opposing evidence not already in the record. The memorandum must respond to the moving party's statement of facts as would be appropriate in an appellate brief. The opposing party must not file a separate document setting out the facts or responding to the moving party's statement of facts.

(D) Reply Memorandum. The moving party may file a reply memorandum of up to 3,200 words. The moving party should do so only if the opposing memorandum raised new matters not addressed in the original supporting memorandum. The deadline for a reply memorandum is 7 days after the opposing memorandum is filed—without a 3-day extension based on electronic service of the opposing memorandum.

(E) Word Limits. Words are counted under this rule, and a certificate of compliance is required, in the same manner as under Local Rule 7.1(F).

(F) Pinpoint Record Citations Required. Each memorandum must include pinpoint citations to the record evidence supporting each factual assertion. The Court may, but need not, consider record evidence that has not been properly cited.

(G) Ruling Without a Hearing; Time for a Ruling. A motion may be resolved against a party without a hearing—and without further notice—at any time after the party has had an opportunity to file a memorandum and evidence under this rule.

[Adopted November 24, 2015.]

RULE 72.1 AUTHORITY OF UNITED STATES MAGISTRATE JUDGES

(A) Duties Under 28 U.S.C. § 636; Effect of a Ruling by a Magistrate Judge.

(1) A magistrate judge is a judicial officer of the district court. All United States magistrate judges serving within the territorial jurisdiction of the Northern District of Florida have the authority conferred by 28 U.S.C. § 636 and may exercise all other powers and duties conferred or imposed by law and the federal procedure rules.

(2) A magistrate judge's ruling or order in a matter heard and determined by a magistrate judge is the court's ruling and will remain in effect unless and until reversed, vacated, modified, or stayed. The filing of a motion for reconsideration does not stay the magistrate judge's ruling or order.

(B) Designation for Trial of Misdemeanor Cases Upon Consent Under 18 U.S.C. § 3401. All United States magistrate judges serving within the territorial jurisdiction of the Northern District of Florida are hereby designated to try persons accused of, and sentence persons convicted of, misdemeanors and petty offenses committed within this District, in accordance with 18 U.S.C. § 3401 and Fed. R. Crim. P. 58.

(C) Designation for Trial of Civil Cases Upon Consent Pursuant to 28 U.S.C. § 636(c). With the consent of the parties, full-time magistrate judges are hereby designated to conduct civil trials, including the entry of final judgment.

[Adopted November 24, 2015.]

RULE 72.2 REFERRAL OF MATTERS TO MAGISTRATE JUDGES BY THIS RULE

(A) Misdemeanor Cases. All misdemeanor cases, including those transferred to this District pursuant to Fed. R. Crim. P. 20, shall be assigned by the Clerk, upon the filing of an information, complaint, or violation notice, or the return of an indictment, to a magistrate judge, who shall proceed in accordance with the provisions of 18 U.S.C. § 3401 and of Fed. R. Crim. P. 58.

(B) Applications for Post–Trial Relief by Persons Convicted of Criminal Offenses and Other Cases Filed Under 28 U.S.C. §§ 2241, 2254, and 2255. Except in cases in which the death penalty has been imposed, all cases seeking post-trial or postconviction relief by persons convicted of state or federal offenses and all other cases arising under 28 U.S.C. §§ 2241, 2254, or 2255, shall be assigned to a district judge and, unless otherwise ordered, shall be referred by the Clerk to a full-time magistrate judge for all proceedings, including preliminary orders, conduct of necessary evidentiary hearings, and filing of a report and recommendation containing proposed findings of fact and conclusions of law and recommending disposition of the application or petition.

(C) Civil Rights Cases Filed by Prisoners. All prisoner petitions and complaints challenging conditions of confinement pursuant to 42 U.S.C. § 1983 and 28 U.S.C. § 1331 *(Bivens* actions), or pursuant to similar statutes, shall be assigned to a district judge and, unless otherwise ordered, shall be referred by the Clerk to a full-time magistrate judge for all proceedings, including preliminary orders, conduct of necessary evidentiary hearings, and filing of a report and recommendation containing proposed findings of fact and conclusions of law and recommending disposition of the complaint.

(D) Social Security Cases and Other Administrative Proceedings. All actions brought under section 205(g) of the Social Security Act, 42 U.S.C. § 405(g) and related statutes, and all other actions to review administrative determinations on a developed administrative record shall be assigned to a district judge and, unless otherwise ordered, shall be referred by the Clerk to a magistrate judge for all proceedings, including preliminary orders, conduct of necessary hearings, and filing of a report and recommendation containing proposed findings of fact and conclusions of law and recommending disposition of the petition or complaint.

(E) Civil Cases Filed by Non–Prisoner Pro Se Litigants. All civil cases filed where one or more of the parties is a non-prisoner pro se litigant shall be assigned to a district judge and, unless otherwise ordered, shall be referred by the Clerk to a full time magistrate judge for all proceedings, including preliminary orders, conduct of necessary hearings, and filing of a report and recommendation containing proposed findings of fact and conclusions of law and recommending disposition of the case.

(F) Additional Duties. Absent an order by a district judge in a specific case to the contrary, the following additional matters shall routinely be referred by the Clerk to magistrate judges serving within the territorial jurisdiction of the Northern District of Florida when a magistrate judge is available, and magistrate judges to whom such matters have been referred shall have authority to:

(1) Issue criminal complaints and issue appropriate arrest warrants or summons;

(2) Issue search warrants pursuant to Fed. R. Crim. P. 41, and issue administrative search or inspection warrants;

(3) Review for probable cause and issue process upon any other application by the United States (for example, for seizure of real property in rem) for which there is evolving legal precedent indicating a need for a judicial finding of probable cause before proceeding;

(4) Issue warrants and orders as authorized by 18 U.S.C. § 2703 (disclosure of customer communications or records), 18 U.S.C. § 3123 (a pen register or a trap and trace device), or orders and writs pursuant to 28 U.S.C. § 1651(a) (all writs necessary or appropriate in aid of jurisdiction);

(5) Conduct initial appearances in felony cases, consider and determine motions for detention, impose conditions of release pursuant to 18 U.S.C. § 3142, conduct arraignments upon indictments for purposes of taking a not guilty plea, and issue scheduling orders setting trial;

(6) Appoint counsel for indigent persons pursuant to 18 U.S.C. § 3006A;

(7) Consider and determine motions for detention and impose conditions of release for material witnesses pursuant to 18 U.S.C. § 3144;

(8) Conduct preliminary hearings upon criminal complaints and determine probable cause;

(9) Conduct and determine removal hearings and issue warrants of removal;

(10) Conduct first appearances and preliminary hearings, by whatever name called, in proceedings for the revocation of parole, supervised release, mandatory release, or probation;

(11) Receive the return of indictments by the grand jury and issue process thereon;

(12) Hear and order discharge of indigent prisoners or persons imprisoned for debt under process or execution issued by a federal court pursuant to 18 U.S.C. § 3569 (repealed 1987) and 28 U.S.C. § 2007;

(13) Appoint interpreters in cases pending before a magistrate judge initiated by the United States pursuant to 28 U.S.C. §§ 1827 and 1828;

(14) Issue warrants and conduct extradition proceedings pursuant to 18 U.S.C. § 3184;

(15) Perform the functions specified in 18 U.S.C. §§ 4107, 4108, and 4109, regarding proceedings for verification of consent by offenders to transfer to or from the United States and the appointment of counsel therein;

(16) Institute proceedings against persons violating certain civil rights statutes under 42 U.S.C. §§ 1987 and 1989;

(17) Issue subpoenas, writs of habeas corpus ad testificandum or habeas corpus ad prosequendum, or other orders necessary to obtain the presence of parties, witnesses or evidence needed for court proceedings in any civil and criminal cases;

(18) Issue attachment or other orders to enforce obedience to an Internal Revenue Service summons to produce records or give testimony pursuant to 26 U.S.C. § 7604(a) and (b);

(19) Settle and certify the nonpayment of seaman's wages and conduct proceedings for the disposition of deceased seaman's effects under 46 U.S.C. § 10101 *et seq.*;

(20) Enforce awards of foreign consul and arbitrate differences between captains and crews of vessels of the consul's nations under 22 U.S.C. § 358a;

(21) Review prisoner correspondence;

(22) Enter court orders to withdraw funds from the registry of the court in matters handled by the magistrate judge;

(23) Preside at naturalization ceremonies and issue orders granting motions for naturalization;

(24) Preside at attorney admission ceremonies and issue orders granting applications for admission to the District's bar;

(25) Adopt schedules for forfeiture of collateral under Fed. R. Crim. P. 58(d)(1);

(26) Issue warrants of arrest in rem, attachment, garnishment, or other process in admiralty; and

(27) Determine actions to be taken regarding non-complying documents submitted for filing under N.D. Fla. Loc. R. 5.1, or the Federal Rules of Civil or Criminal Procedure.

[Adopted November 24, 2015.]

RULE 72.3 SPECIFIC REFERRALS OF MATTERS TO MAGISTRATE JUDGES

Any district judge may assign any matter, civil or criminal, to a magistrate judge of this District to the full extent permitted by 28 U.S.C. § 636. Specifically included is the taking of guilty pleas in felony cases with the consent of the defendant and recommending the acceptance or rejection of such pleas to the district judge, and ordering a presentence investigation report. The assignment and designation of duties to magistrate judges by district judges may be made by written standing order entered jointly by the resident district judges of the District or of any division of the District or through oral directive or written order by any individual district judge in any case, cases, or category of cases assigned to that judge.

[Adopted November 24, 2015.]

RULE 72.4 FULL-TIME AND PART-TIME MAGISTRATE JUDGES

Any reference in these local rules to magistrate judges includes both full-time and part-time magistrate judges unless otherwise expressly stated in these rules or in the applicable general law or rules of procedure.

[Adopted November 24, 2015.]

RULE 73.1 PROCEDURES FOR CONSENT TO TRIAL BEFORE A MAGISTRATE JUDGE

(A) Notice. In all civil cases, as may be provided by Administrative Order, the Clerk shall notify the parties that, pursuant to 28 U.S.C. § 636(c), they may consent to have a full-time magistrate judge conduct any or all proceedings in the case and order the entry of a final judgment. The notice shall state that the parties are free to withhold their consent without adverse substantive consequences.

(B) Execution of Consent. Any party who consents to trial of any or all of the civil case by a magistrate judge must execute a consent form and return it to the office of the Clerk within 45 days of the date of service of the notice. The form shall not be returned if the party does not consent. No magistrate judge, district judge, or other court official may attempt to coerce any party to consent to the reference of any matter to a full-time magistrate judge. This rule, however, shall not preclude any district judge or magistrate judge from informing the parties that they may have the option of having a case referred to a full-time magistrate judge for all proceedings, including trial.

(C) Reference. Cases in which the parties have timely filed a fully executed consent form shall be referred to the full-time magistrate judge assigned to the case, and notice thereof shall be made a part of the file, with copies furnished to the parties.

[Adopted November 24, 2015.]

RULE 77.1 PHOTOGRAPHING, RECORDING, AND BROADCASTING PROCEEDINGS

(A) Proceedings must not be photographed, recorded, broadcast, or transmitted by any means, except as authorized by this rule.

(B) Investitures, naturalizations, and ceremonial proceedings may be photographed or recorded, unless the Court prohibits it.

(C) Proceedings may be transmitted to or recorded by the United States Marshals Service for security purposes.

(D) The court reporter may make an audio recording for use in preparing an official transcript. And other court personnel may make an audio recording when the recording will be the official record of a proceeding.

(E) The Court may authorize any other photograph, recording, broadcast, or transmission if consistent with any applicable policies of the Judicial Conference of the United States and Eleventh Circuit Judicial Council.

[Adopted November 24, 2015.]

RULE 77.2 ELECTRONIC DEVICES

(A) This rule applies to devices that are capable of remote communication (including cellular telephones, laptops, and electronic tablets). This rule also applies to devices that are capable of photographing, recording, broadcasting, or transmitting proceedings. Such devices must not be brought into a United States Courthouse in this District, except as authorized by this rule.

(B) Court employees and employees of an agency with an office in a courthouse may bring devices into the courthouse but may not bring devices into a courtroom unless otherwise authorized by this rule.

(C) Officers providing security may bring devices into a courtroom.

(D) The attorneys of record in a case and members of their staffs may bring devices into the courthouse and into a courtroom. While in the courtroom, attorneys and staff members may use devices only in connection with the proceeding and otherwise must keep devices off or in silent mode. Cellular telephones and other hand-held devices must be kept out of sight while court is in session. Devices may be used outside a courtroom or in other parts of the building so long as court proceedings are not disturbed. The Court may change these provisions by an order in a case.

(E) Members of the media may request the same authority to bring in and use devices as attorneys and their staffs have under this rule's paragraph (D). A request may be made orally or in writing to the Clerk. The Clerk may grant the request under guidelines established by an administrative order or as authorized by the Court in a case. Unless the Clerk grants such a request or the Court gives greater authority under this rule's paragraph (G), members of the media have the same rights, and are subject to the same obligations, as members of the public.

(F) Devices may be brought into a courthouse for photographing, recording, broadcasting, or transmitting proceedings as authorized by Local Rule 77.1.

(G) The Court may authorize devices to be brought into the courthouse or courtroom on other specific occasions and may authorize or restrict their use.

(H) The United States Marshals Service may agree to store a device that cannot properly be brought into the courthouse under this rule. And as part of its control over the courthouse grounds, the Marshals Service may ban or restrict devices on the grounds.

[Adopted November 24, 2015.]

RULE 77.3 VIDEO AND AUDIO PROCEEDINGS

The Court may conduct a trial or hearing—and may receive testimony and other evidence—by video or audio transmission from a remote location, unless contrary to law.

[Adopted November 24, 2015.]

RULE 77.4 RELEASE OF INFORMATION IN CRIMINAL AND CIVIL CASES

(A) Release of Information by Officials in General. No judicial branch employee (including a judge's staff, clerks, probation officers, and court reporters), no officer, employee or representative of the United States Marshals Service or court security officer, nor any state, local, or federal law enforcement officer or employee associated with or assisting in the preparation or trial of a criminal case, may disseminate by any means of public communication, without authorization by the Court, information relating to an imminent or pending criminal or civil case that is not part of the public records of the court.

(B) Release of Information by Attorneys in Criminal Cases.

(1) It is the duty of attorneys, including the United States Attorney, who represent parties in criminal cases, and their respective staffs, not to release or authorize the release of information or opinion which a reasonable person would expect to be disseminated by means of public communication, in connection with pending or imminent criminal litigation with which the attorney is associated, if there is a substantial likelihood that such dissemination will cause material prejudice to a fair trial or otherwise cause material prejudice to the due administration of justice.

(2) With respect to a grand jury or other pending investigation of any criminal matter, an attorney participating in or associated with the investigation shall refrain from making any extrajudicial statement which a reasonable person would expect to be disseminated by means of public communication, that goes beyond the public record or that is not necessary to inform the public that the investigation is underway, to describe the general scope of the investigation, to obtain assistance in the apprehension of a suspect, to warn the public of any dangers, or otherwise to aid in the investigation.

(3) From the time of arrest, issuance of an arrest warrant, or the filing of a complaint, information, or indictment in any criminal matter until the commencement of trial or disposition without trial, no attorney nor others associated with the prosecution or defense shall release or authorize the release of any extrajudicial statement which a reasonable person would expect to be disseminated by means of public communication, relating to that matter and concerning:

(a) The prior criminal record (including arrests, indictment, or other charges of crime) or the character or reputation of the accused, except that the attorney may make a factual statement of the accused's name, age, residence, occupation, and family status. If the accused has not been apprehended, an attorney associated with the prosecution may release any information necessary to aid in apprehension of the accused or to warn the public of any dangers the accused may present;

(b) The existence or contents of any confession, admission, or statement given by the accused, or the refusal or failure of the accused to make any statement;

(c) The performance of any examinations or tests or the accused's refusal or failure to submit to an examination or test;

(d) The identity, testimony, or credibility of prospective witnesses, except that the attorney may announce the identity of the victim if the announcement is not otherwise prohibited by law;

(e) The possibility of a plea of guilty to the offense charged or a lesser offense;

(f) Any opinion as to the accused's guilt or innocence or as to the merits of the case or the evidence in the case.

(4) These prohibitions shall not be construed to preclude the attorney, in the proper discharge of official or professional obligations, from announcing the fact and circumstances of arrest (including time and place of arrest, resistance, pursuit, and use of weapons), the identity of the investigating and arresting officer or agency, and the length of the investigation; from making an announcement, at the time of seizure of any physical evidence other than a confession, admission, or statement, which is limited to a description of the evidence seized; from disclosing the nature, substance, or text of the charge, including a brief description of the offense charged; from quoting or referring without comment to public records of the court in the case; from announcing the scheduling or result of any stage in the judicial process; from requesting assistance in obtaining evidence; or from announcing without further comment that the accused denies the charges.

(5) During the trial of any criminal matter, including the period of selection of the jury, no attorney associated with the prosecution or defense shall give or authorize any extrajudicial statement or interview, relating to the trial or the parties or issues in the trial which a reasonable person would expect to be disseminated by means of public communication, except that an attorney may quote from or refer without comment to public records of the court in the case.

(6) After the completion of a trial or disposition without trial of any criminal matter, and prior to the imposition of sentence, an attorney associated with the prosecution or defense shall refrain from making or authorizing any extrajudicial statement which a reasonable person would expect to be disseminated by means of public communication if there is a substantial likelihood that such dissemination will materially prejudice the imposition of sentence.

(7) Nothing in this rule is intended to preclude the formulation or application of more restrictive rules relating to the release of information about juvenile or other offenders, to preclude the holding of hearings or the lawful issuance of reports by legislative, administrative, or investigative, or to preclude any attorney who represented a party from replying to charges, made public, of attorney misconduct.

(C) Release of Information by Attorneys in Civil Cases. An attorney associated with a civil action shall not during its investigation or litigation make or participate in making an extrajudicial statement, other than a quotation from or reference to public records, which a reasonable person would expect to be disseminated by means of public communication if there is a substantial likelihood that such dissemination will cause material prejudice to a fair trial and which relates to:

(1) Evidence regarding the occurrence or transaction involved;

(2) The character, credibility, or criminal record of a party, witness, or prospective witness;

(3) The performance of results or any examinations or tests or the refusal or failure of a party to submit to such;

(4) An opinion as to the merits of the claims or defenses of a party, except as required by law or administrative rule; or

(5) Any other matter reasonably likely to interfere with a fair trial of the action.

(D) Special Orders in Widely Publicized and Sensational Cases. In a widely publicized or sensational case, the Court on motion of either party or on its own motion, may issue a special order governing such matters as: (1) extrajudicial statements by parties and witnesses likely to interfere with the rights of the accused to a fair trial by an impartial jury, (2) the seating and conduct in the courtroom of spectators and news media representatives, (3) management and sequestration of jurors and witnesses, and (4) any other matters which the Court may deem appropriate for inclusion in such an order.

(E) Sealed Indictments in Criminal Cases. Sealed indictments will be automatically unsealed by the Clerk at the first appearance of any defendant named in that indictment unless otherwise ordered by a judicial officer.

(F) Disposition of Sealed Documents in Civil Cases at the Conclusion of the Case. Thirty days after the conclusion of a civil case (expiration of the time to appeal, if no appeal is filed, or voluntary dismissal of the appeal, or receipt of the mandate after an appeal and expiration of the time in which to seek certiorari review in the Supreme Court, if an appeal is taken) all sealed documents maintained in paper form will be returned to the party who submitted them, and the party shall retain the documents for 3 years thereafter.

[Adopted November 24, 2015.]

RULE 77.5 MARSHAL TO ATTEND COURT

Unless excused by the presiding judge, the United States Marshal of this District, or deputy, or, as an alternative in civil cases only, a court security officer, shall be in attendance during all sessions of any kind conducted in open court.

[Adopted November 24, 2015.]

RULE 87.1 APPEALS IN BANKRUPTCY CASES

The Federal Rules of Bankruptcy Procedure govern the schedule for an appeal to the district court in a bankruptcy case except as otherwise ordered by the Court.

[Adopted November 24, 2015.]

RULE 88.1 PRESENTENCE INVESTIGATION REPORTS, PRESENTENCING PROCEDURES, PROVISIONS OF PRETRIAL SERVICES

(A) Ordinarily, sentencing will occur approximately 70 days following the defendant's plea of guilty or *nolo contendere,* or upon being found guilty, subject to the time limitations and other provisions of Fed. R. Crim. P. 32, and following the preparation of a presentence report by the probation officer.

(B) The presentence report shall be disclosed only as permitted under Fed. R. Crim. P. 32; however, the probation officer's recommendation, if any, on the sentence, shall be disclosed only to the sentencing judge.

(C) The presentence report shall be deemed to have been disclosed (1) when a copy of the report is physically or electronically delivered; or (2) one day after the report's availability for inspection is orally communicated; or (3) three days after a copy of the report or notice of its availability is mailed. A party must make objections or give notice that it has no objections as required by Fed. R. Crim. P. 32(f).

(D) No confidential records of the court maintained at the probation office, including presentence reports and probation supervision reports, shall be sought by any applicant except by written request to the Court establishing with particularity the need for specific information believed to be contained in such records. When a demand for disclosure of such information or such records is made by way of subpoena or other judicial process served upon a probation officer of this court, the probation officer may file a petition seeking instruction from the Court with respect to the manner in which that officer should respond to such subpoena or such process.

(E) Any party filing an appeal or cross appeal in any criminal case in which it is expected that an issue will be asserted pursuant to 18 U.S.C. § 3742 concerning the sentence imposed by the Court shall immediately notify the probation officer who shall then file with the Clerk for inclusion in the record *in camera* a copy of the presentence investigation report. The probation officer shall also furnish, at the same time, a copy of the presentence report to the United States and to the defendant.

(F) Pretrial services within the purview of 18 U.S.C. § 3152 *et seq.* shall be supervised and provided by the chief probation/pretrial services officer of this court pursuant to 18 U.S.C. § 3152(a). Any federal officer taking or receiving custody of a defendant in the Northern District of Florida shall immediately notify the probation office of such detention, the name of the defendant, the charge(s) against the defendant, and the place in which the defendant is being detained. A pretrial services officer shall then interview the defendant as soon as practicable at this place of confinement or, if the defendant has been released, at such other places as the pretrial services officer shall specify.

(G) A party may file a sentencing memorandum. The deadline for doing so is three days before the sentencing hearing.

[Adopted November 24, 2015.]

RULE 88.2 APPEAL OF A MAGISTRATE JUDGE'S RULINGS IN CONSENT MISDEMEANOR CASES

(A) Appeals from any decision, order, judgment, or sentence entered by a magistrate judge in a misdemeanor criminal case, including petty offenses, as to which the defendant has consented to proceed before a magistrate judge shall be governed by Fed. R. Crim. P. 58.

(B) Upon receipt of the notice of appeal, the Clerk shall docket the appeal and assign the case to a district judge.

(C) Unless excused by order of the district judge, every appellant shall be responsible for preparation of a typewritten transcript of the proceedings before the magistrate judge from which an appeal has been taken. If such transcript has been prepared from an audio tape recording, the transcript shall be submitted to the magistrate judge for certification of its accuracy. After certification by the magistrate judge, the transcript shall be forwarded to the Clerk for filing, and the Clerk shall promptly notify the parties of the filing. A copy of the record of such proceedings shall be made available, at the expense of the court, to a person who establishes by affidavit the inability to pay or give security therefor.

(D) Within 15 days of the date on which the transcript is filed in the Clerk's office, or if there is to be no transcript, within 15 days of the filing of the notice of appeal, the appellant shall serve and file a brief which shall enumerate each reversible error claimed to have occurred in the proceedings before the magistrate judge. Within 15 days of service of appellant's brief, the appellee shall serve and file a brief. The appellant may serve and file a reply brief within 7 days of service of appellee's brief.

(E) The district judge to whom the appeal is assigned may hear oral argument or may decide the appeal on the briefs. Requests for oral argument shall be made at the time briefs are filed and shall be granted at the discretion of the district judge.

[Adopted November 24, 2015.]

RULE 88.3 PATENT RULES

The Northern District of Georgia Local Patent Rules, as amended from time to time, apply in a patent case unless the Court orders otherwise.

[Adopted November 24, 2015.]

ADDENDUM

CUSTOMARY AND TRADITIONAL CONDUCT AND DECORUM IN THE UNITED STATES DISTRICT COURT

(A) The purpose of this addendum is to state for the guidance of those heretofore unfamiliar with the traditions of this United States District Court certain basic principles concerning courtroom conduct and decorum. These standards are minimal and not all-inclusive. They are intended to emphasize and supplement, not supplant or limit, the ethical obligations of counsel under the Code of Professional Responsibility or the time honored customs of experienced trial counsel.

(B) When appearing in this United States district court, all counsel and all persons at counsel table should conduct themselves in the following customary and traditional manner:

(1) Stand as court is opened, recessed, or adjourned.

(2) Stand when the jury enters or retires from the courtroom.

(3) Stand when addressing, or being addressed by, the court.

(4) Address all remarks to the court, not to opposing counsel.

(5) Avoid disparaging remarks or acrimony toward opposing counsel and remain wholly detached from any ill feeling between litigants and witnesses.

(6) Refer to all persons, including witnesses, other counsel and the parties, by their surnames and not by their first or given names.

(7) Counsel should request permission before approaching the bench; and any document counsel wish to have the court examine should be handed to the clerk.

(8) Unless opposing counsel has previously shown exhibits, any exhibit offered in evidence should, at the time of such offer, be handed to opposing counsel.

(9) In making objections, counsel should state only the legal grounds for the objection and should withhold all further comment or argument unless elaboration is requested by the court.

(10) In examining a witness, counsel shall not repeat or echo the answer given by the witness.

(11) Offers of, or requests for, a stipulation should be made privately, not within the hearing of the jury.

(12) In opening statements and in arguments to the jury, counsel shall not express personal knowledge or opinion concerning any matter in issue, shall not read or purport to read from deposition or trial manuscripts, and shall not suggest to the jury, directly or indirectly, that it may or should request transcripts or the reading of any testimony by the reporter.

(13) Counsel shall admonish and discourage all persons at counsel table from making gestures, facial expressions, audible comments, or the like, as manifestations of approval or disapproval during the testimony of witnesses, or at any other time.

(14) Smoking, eating, food and drink are prohibited in the courtroom at any time.

[Adopted effective April 1, 1995. Amended effective November 24, 2015.]

ADMIRALTY AND MARITIME RULES

RULE A. GENERAL PROVISIONS

(1) Scope of the Local Admiralty and Maritime Rules. The local admiralty and maritime rules apply to the procedures in admiralty and maritime claims within the meaning of Fed.R.Civ.P. 9(h), which in turn are governed by the Supplemental Rules for Certain Admiralty and Maritime Claims of the Federal Rules of Civil Procedure.

(2) Citation Format.

(a) The Supplemental Rules for Certain Admiralty and Maritime Claims of the Federal Rules of Civil Procedure shall be cited as "Supplemental Rule (___)".

(b) The Local Rules of the Northern District of Florida shall be cited as "Local Rule (___)".

(c) The Local Admiralty and Maritime Rules shall be cited as "Local Admiralty Rule (___)".

(3) Application of Local Admiralty and Maritime Rules. The Local Admiralty Rules shall apply to all actions governed by Local Admiralty Rule A(1), and to the extent possible should be construed to be consistent with the other local rules of this Court. To the extent that a Local Admiralty Rule conflicts with another local rule of this Court, the Local Admiralty Rule shall control.

(4) Designation of "In Admiralty" Proceedings. Every complaint filed as a Fed. R. Civ. P. 9(h) action shall boldly set forth the words "IN ADMIRALTY" following the designation of the Court. This requirement is in addition to any statements which may be contained in the body of the complaint.

(5) Verification of Pleadings, Claims and Answers to Interrogatories. Every complaint and claim filed pursuant to Supplemental Rules (B), (C) and/or (D) shall be verified on oath or solemn affirmation by a party, or an officer of a corporate party.

If a party or corporate officer is not within the district, verification of a complaint, claim and/or answers to interrogatories may be made by an agent, an attorney-in-fact, or the attorney of record. Such person shall state briefly the source of his or her knowledge, or information and belief, and shall declare that the document affirmed is true to the best of his or her knowledge, and/or information and belief. Additionally, such person shall state that he or she is authorized to make this representation on behalf of the party or corporate officer, and shall indicate why verification is not made by a party or a corporate officer. Such verification will be deemed to have been made by the party to whom the document might apply as if verified personally.

Any interested party may move the Court, with or without a request for stay, for the personal oath or affirmation of a party or all parties, or that of a corporate officer. If required by the Court, such verification may be obtained by commission, or as otherwise provided by Court order.

(6) Issuance of Process. Except as limited by the provisions of Supplemental Rule (B)(1) and Local Admiralty Rule B(3) or Supplemental Rule (C)(3) and Local Admiralty Rule C(2); or in suits prosecuted in forma pauperis and sought to be filed without prepayment of fees or costs, or without security; all process shall be issued by the Court without further notice of Court.

(7) Publication of Notices. Unless otherwise required by the Court, or applicable Local Admiralty or Supplemental Rule, whenever a notice is required to be published by any statute of the United States, or by any Supplemental Rule or Local Admiralty Rule, such notice shall be published at least once, without further order of Court, in an approved newspaper in the county or counties where the vessel or property was located at the time of arrest, attachment, or seizure, and if different, in the county within the Northern District of Florida where the lawsuit is pending. Publication of Notice of Sale shall be as provided in Local Admiralty Rule E(16). Upon a showing of good cause, the Court may require additional publications if necessary to provide reasonable notice. The newspaper of largest circulation in a county in the Northern District is rebuttably presumed to be a newspaper of general circulation in that same county.

For purposes of this subsection, an approved newspaper shall be a newspaper of general circulation, designated from time to time by the Court. A listing of these approved newspapers will be made available in the Clerk's Office during normal business hours.

(8) Form and Return of Process in In Personam Actions. Unless otherwise ordered by the Court, Fed.R.Civ.P. 9(h) process shall be by civil summons, and shall be returnable twenty (20) days after service of process; except that process issued in accordance with Supplemental Rule (B) shall conform to the requirements of that rule.

(9) Judicial Officer Defined. As used in these Local Admiralty Rules, the term "judicial officer" or "Court" shall mean either a United States District Judge or a United States Magistrate Judge.

(10) Appendix of Forms. The forms presented in the Appendix provide an illustration of the format and content of papers filed in admiralty and maritime actions within the Northern District of Florida. While the forms are sufficient, they are neither mandatory nor exhaustive.

[Adopted November 24, 2015.]

RULE B. ATTACHMENT AND GARNISHMENT: SPECIAL PROVISIONS

(1) Definition of "Not Found Within the District". In an action in personam filed pursuant to Supplemental Rule (B), a defendant shall be considered "not found within the district" if the defendant cannot be served within the Northern District of Florida with the summons and complaint as provided by Fed.R.Civ.P. 4(d)(1), (2), (3), or (6).

(2) Verification of Complaint Required. In addition to the specific requirements of Local Admiralty Rule A(5), whenever verification is made by the plaintiff's attorney or agent, and that person does not have personal knowledge, or knowledge acquired in the ordinary course of business of the facts alleged in the complaint, the attorney or agent shall also state the circumstances which make it necessary for that person to make the verification, and shall indicate the source of the attorney's or agent's information.

(3) Pre-seizure Requirements. In accordance with Supplemental Rule (B)(1), the process of attachment and garnishment shall issue only after one of the following conditions has been met:

(a) *Judicial Review Prior to Issuance.* Except as provided in Local Admiralty Rule B(3)(b), a judicial officer shall first review the verified complaint, and any other relevant case papers, prior to the Clerk issuing the requested process of attachment and garnishment. No notice of this pre-arrest judicial review is required to be given to any person or prospective party.

If the Court finds that probable cause exists to issue the process of attachment and garnishment, plaintiff shall prepare an order for the Court's signature directing the Clerk to issue the process. This order shall substantially conform in format and content to the form identified as NDF 1 in the Appendix of these Local Admiralty Rules.

Upon receipt of the signed order, the Clerk shall file the order and, in accordance with Local Admiralty Rule B(3)(c), issue the summons and process of attachment and garnishment. Thereafter the Clerk may issue supplemental process without further order of Court.

(b) *Certification of Exigent Circumstances.* If the plaintiff files a written certification that exigent circumstances make review by the Court impracticable, the Clerk shall, in accordance with Local Admiralty Rule B(3)(c), issue a summons and the process of attachment and garnishment.

Thereafter at any post-attachment proceedings under Supplemental Rule (E)(4)(f) and Local Admiralty Rule B(5), plaintiff shall have the burden of showing that probable cause existed for the issuance of process, and that exigent circumstances existed which precluded judicial review in accordance with Local Admiralty Rule B(3)(a).

(c) *Preparation and Issuance of the Process of Attachment and Garnishment.* Plaintiff shall prepare the summons and the process of attachment and garnishment, and deliver the documents to the Clerk for filing and issuance.

The process of attachment and garnishment shall substantially conform in format and content to the form identified as NDF 2 in the Appendix to these Local Admiralty Rules, and shall in all cases give adequate notice of the post seizure provisions of Local Admiralty Rule B(5).

(d) *Marshal's Return of Service.* The Marshal shall file a return of service indicating the date and manner in which service was perfected and, if service was perfected upon a garnishee, the Marshal shall indicate in the return the name, address, and telephone number of the garnishee.

(4) Notification of Seizure to Defendant. In an in personam action under Supplemental Rule (B), it is expected that plaintiff and/or garnishee will initially attempt to perfect service of the notice in accordance with Supplemental Rule (B)(2)(a) or (b).

However, when service of the notice cannot be perfected in accordance with Supplemental Rule (B)(2)(a) or (b), plaintiff and/or garnishee should then attempt to perfect service in accordance with Supplemental Rule (B)(2)(c). In this regard, service of process shall be sufficiently served by leaving a copy of the process of attachment and garnishment with the defendant or garnishee at his or her usual place of business.

(5) Post-attachment Review Proceedings.

(a) *Filing a Required Answer.* In accordance with Supplemental Rule (E)(4)(f), any person who claims an interest in property seized pursuant to Supplemental Rule (B) must file an answer and claim against the property. The answer and claim shall describe the nature of the claimant's interest in the property, and shall articulate reasons why the seizure should be vacated. The claimant shall serve a copy of the answer and claim upon plaintiff's counsel, the Marshal, and any other party to the litigation. The claimant shall also file a Certificate of Service indicating the date and manner in which service was perfected.

(b) *Hearing on the Answer and Claim.* The claimant may be heard before a judicial officer not less than three (3) days after the answer and claim has been filed and service has been perfected upon the plaintiff.

If the Court orders that the seizure be vacated, the judicial officer shall also award attorney's fees, costs, and other expenses incurred by any party as a result of the seizure.

If the seizure was predicated upon a showing of "exigent circumstances" under Local Admiralty Rule B(3)(b), and the Court finds that such exigent circumstances did not exist, the judicial officer shall award attorney's fees, costs, and other expenses incurred by any party as a result of the seizure. Upon an award of attorney's fees under this rule, the parties will be directed to comply with Local Rule 54.1(E)

(6) Procedural Requirement for the Entry of Default. In accordance with Rule 55, Fed.R.Civ.P., a party seeking the entry of default in a Supplemental Rule (B) action shall file a motion and supporting legal memorandum and shall offer other proof sufficient to demonstrate that due notice of the action and seizure have been given in accordance with Local Admiralty Rule B(4).

Upon review of the motion, memorandum, and other proof, the Clerk shall, where appropriate, enter default in accordance with Rule 55(a), Fed.R.Civ.P. Thereafter, the Clerk shall serve notice of the entry of default upon all parties represented in the action.

(7) Procedural Requirements for the Entry of Default Judgment. Not later than thirty (30) days following notice of the entry of default, the party seeking the entry of default judgment shall file a motion and supporting legal memorandum, along with other appropriate exhibits to the motion sufficient to support the entry of default judgment. The moving party shall serve these papers upon every other party to the action and file a Certificate of Service indicating the date and manner in which service was perfected.

A party opposing the entry of default judgment shall have five (5) days from the receipt of the motion to file written opposition with the Court. Thereafter, unless otherwise ordered by the Court, the motion for the entry of default judgment will be heard without oral argument.

If the Court grants the motion and enters the default judgment, such judgment shall establish a right on the part of the party or parties in which favor it is entered. The judgment shall be considered prior to any claims of the owner of the defendant property against which it is entered, and to the remnants and surpluses thereof; providing, however, that such a judgment shall not establish any entitlement to the defendant property having priority over non-possessory lien claimants. Obtaining a judgment by default shall not preclude the party in whose favor it is entered from contending and proving that all, or any portion, of the claim or claims encompassed within the judgment are prior to any such non-possessory lien claims.

[Adopted November 24, 2015.]

RULE C. ACTION IN REM

(1) Verification Requirements. Every complaint and claim filed in an in rem proceeding pursuant to Supplemental Rule (C) shall be verified in accordance with Local Admiralty Rules A(5) and B(2).

(2) Pre-seizure Requirements. In accordance with Supplemental Rule (C)(3), the process of arrest in rem shall issue only after one of the following conditions has been met:

(a) *Judicial Review Prior to Issuance.* Except as provided in Local Admiralty Rule C(2)(b), a judicial officer shall first review the verified complaint, and any other relevant case papers, prior to the Clerk issuing the warrant of arrest and/or summons in rem. No notice of this pre-seizure judicial review is required to be given to any person or prospective party.

If the Court finds that probable cause exists for an action in rem, plaintiff shall prepare an order for the Court's signature directing the Clerk to issue a warrant of arrest and/or summons. This order shall substantially conform in format and content to the form identified as NDF 2 in the Appendix to these Local Admiralty Rules.

Upon receipt of the signed order, the Clerk shall file the order and, in accordance with Local Admiralty Rule C(2)(c), issue the warrant of arrest and/or summons. Thereafter the Clerk may issue supplemental process without further order of the Court.

(b) *Certification of Exigent Circumstances.* If the plaintiff files a written certification that exigent circumstances make review by the Court impracticable, the Clerk shall, in accordance with Local Admiralty Rule B(3)(b), issue a warrant of arrest and/or summons.

Thereafter at any post-arrest proceedings under Supplemental Rule (E)(4)(f) and Local Admiralty Rule C(7), plaintiff shall have the burden of showing that probable cause existed for the issuance of process, and that exigent circumstances existed which precluded judicial review in accordance with Local Admiralty Rule C(2)(a).

(c) *Preparation and Issuance of the Warrant of Arrest and/or Summons.* Plaintiff shall prepare the warrant of arrest and/or summons, and deliver them to the Clerk for filing and issuance.

The warrant of arrest shall substantially conform in format and content to the form identified as NDF 4 in the Appendix to these Local Admiralty Rules, and shall in all cases give adequate notice of the post-arrest provisions of Local Admiralty Rule C(7).

(3) Special Requirements for Actions Involving Freight, Proceeds and/or Intangible Property.

(a) *Instructions to Be Contained in the Summons.* Unless otherwise ordered by the Court, the summons shall order the person having control of the freight, proceeds and/or intangible property to either:

(1) File a claim within ten (10) days after service of the summons in accordance with Local Admiralty Rule C(6)(a); or

(2) Deliver or pay over to the Marshal, the freight, proceeds, and/or intangible property, or a part thereof, sufficient to satisfy plaintiff's claim.

The summons shall also inform the person having control of the freight, proceeds, and/or intangible property that service of the summons has the effect of arresting the property, thereby preventing the release, disposal, or other distribution of the property without prior order of the Court.

(b) *Requirements for Claims to Prevent the Delivery of Property to the Marshal.* Any claim filed in accordance with Supplemental Rule (E)(4) and Local Admiralty Rule C(6)(a) shall describe the nature of claimant's interest in the property, and shall articulate reasons why the seizure should be vacated. The claim shall be served upon the plaintiff, the Marshal, and all other parties to the litigation. Additionally, the claimant shall file a Certificate of Service indicating the date and manner in which service was perfected.

(c) *Delivery or Payment of the Freight, Proceeds, and/or Intangible Property to the U.S. Marshal.* Unless a claim is filed in accordance with Supplemental Rule (E)(4)(f), and Local Admiralty Rule C(6)(a), any person served with a summons issued pursuant to Local Admiralty Rule C(2)(a) or (b), shall within ten (10) days after execution of service, deliver or pay over to the Marshal all, or part of, the freight, proceeds, and/or intangible property sufficient to satisfy plaintiff's claim.

Unless otherwise ordered by the Court, the person tendering control of the freight, proceeds, and/or intangible property shall be excused from any further duty with respect to the property in question.

(4) Publishing Notice of the Arrest as Required by Supplemental Rule (C)(4).

(a) *Time for Publication.* If the property is not released within ten (10) days after the execution of process, the notice required by Supplemental Rule (C)(4) shall be published by the plaintiff in accordance with Local Admiralty Rule A(7). Such notice, unless otherwise ordered by the Court, shall be published within seventeen (17) days after execution of process. The notice shall substantially conform to the form identified as NDF 7 in the Appendix to these Local Admiralty Rules.

(b) *Proof of Publication.* Plaintiff shall file proof of publication with the Clerk not later than ten (10) days following the last day of publication. It shall be sufficient proof for the plaintiff to file the sworn statement by, or on behalf of, the publisher or editor, indicating the dates of publication, along with a copy or reproduction of the actual publication.

(5) Undertaking in Lieu of Arrest. If, before or after the commencement of an action, a party accepts any written undertaking to respond on behalf of the vessel and/or other property in return for foregoing the arrest, the undertaking shall only respond to orders or judgments in favor of the party accepting the undertaking, and any parties expressly named therein, to the extent of the benefit thereby conferred.

(6) Time for Filing Claim or Answer. Unless otherwise ordered by the court, any claimant of property subject to an action in rem shall:

(a) File the claim within ten (10) days after process has been executed; and

(b) Serve an answer within twenty (20) days after the filing of the claim.

(7) Post-arrest Proceedings. Coincident with the filing of a claim pursuant to Supplemental Rule (E)(4)(f), and Local Admiralty Rule C(6)(a), the claimant may also file a motion and proposed order directing plaintiff to show cause why the arrest should not be vacated. If the Court grants the order, the Court shall set a date and time for a show cause hearing. Thereafter, if the Court orders the arrest to be vacated, the Court shall award attorney's fees, costs, and other expenses incurred by any party as a result of the arrest.

Additionally, if the seizure was predicated upon a showing of "exigent circumstances" under Local Admiralty Rule C(6)(b), and the Court finds that such exigent circumstances did not exist, the Court shall award attorney's fees, costs and other expenses incurred by any party as a result of the seizure. Upon an award of attorney's fees under this rule, the parties will be directed to comply with Local Rule 54.1(E).

(8) Procedural Requirements Prior to the Entry of Default. In accordance with Rule 55, Fed.R.Civ.P., a party seeking the entry of default judgment in rem shall first file a motion and supporting legal memorandum. The party seeking the entry of default shall also file such other proof sufficient to demonstrate that due notice of the action and arrest have been given by:

(a) Service upon the master or other person having custody of the property;

(b) Delivery, or by certified mail, return receipt requested (or international effective equivalent), to every other person, including any known owner, who has not appeared or intervened in the action, and who is known to have, or claims to have, a possessory interest in the property. The party seeking entry of default judgment under Local Rule C(8) may be excused for failing to give notice to such "other person" upon a satisfactory showing that diligent effort was made to give notice without success; and

(c) Publication as required by Supplemental Rule (C)(4) and Local Admiralty Rule C(4). Upon review of the motion, memorandum, and other proof, the Clerk may, where appropriate, enter default in accordance with Rule 55, Fed.R.Civ.P. Thereafter, the Clerk shall serve notice of the entry of default upon all parties represented in the action.

(9) Procedural Requirements for the Entry of Default Judgment. Not later than thirty (30) days following notice of the entry of default, the moving party shall file a motion, and supporting legal documents, for the entry of default judgment pursuant to Rule 55(b), Fed.R.Civ.P. The moving party may also file as exhibits for the motion such other documentation as may be required to support the entry of default judgment. Thereafter the court will consider the motion as indicated below:

(a) *When No Person Has Filed a Claim or Answer.* Unless otherwise ordered by the court, the motion for default judgment will be considered by the court without oral argument.

(b) *When Any Person Has Filed an Appearance, But Does Not Join in the Motion for Entry of Default Judgment.* If any person has filed an appearance in accordance with Local Admiralty Rule C(6), but does not join in the motion for entry of default judgment, the party seeking the entry of default judgment shall serve notice of the motion upon the party not joining in the motion, and thereafter the opposing party shall have five (5) days from receipt of the notice to file written opposition with the court.

If the court grants the motion and enters the default judgment, such judgment shall establish a right on the part of the party or parties in whose favor it is entered. The judgment shall be considered prior to any claims of the owner of the defendant property against which it is entered, and to the remnants and surpluses thereof; providing, however, that such a judgment shall not establish any entitlement to the defendant property having priority over non-possessory lien claimants. Obtaining a judgment by default shall not preclude the party in whose favor it is entered from contending and proving that all, or any portion, of the claim or claims encompassed within the judgment are prior to any such non-possessory lien claims.

[Adopted November 24, 2015.]

RULE D. POSSESSORY, PETITORY AND PARTITION ACTIONS

(1) Establishing Dates for the Return of Process. In possessory actions filed pursuant to Supplemental Rule (D), the Court may order that process be returnable at a time shorter than that prescribed by Rule 12(a), Fed.R.Civ.P.

If the Court shortens the time, the Court shall specify the date upon which the answer must be filed, and may also set a hearing date to expedite the disposition of the possessory action. When possible, possessory actions shall be given preference on a judicial officer's calendar.

[Adopted November 24, 2015.]

RULE E. ACTIONS IN REM AND QUASI IN REM: GENERAL PROVISIONS

(1) Statement of Itemized Damages and Expenses Required. Every complaint in a Supplemental Rule (B) and (C) action shall state the amount of the debt, damages, or salvage for which the action is brought. In addition, the statement shall also specify the amount of any unliquidated claims, including attorneys' fees.

(2) Requirements and Procedures for Effecting Intervention. Whenever a vessel or other property is arrested or attached in accordance with any Supplemental Rule, and the vessel or property is in the custody of the U.S. Marshal or duly authorized substitute custodian, any other person having a claim against the vessel or property shall be required to present their claim as indicated below:

(a) *Intervention of Right When No Sale of the Vessel or Property Is Pending.* Except as limited by Local Admiralty Rule E(2)(b), any person having a claim against a vessel or property previously arrested or attached by the Marshal may, as a matter of right, file an intervening complaint at any time before an order is entered by the Court scheduling the vessel or property for sale.

Coincident with the filing of an intervening complaint, the offering party shall prepare and file a supplemental warrant of arrest and/or a supplemental process of attachment and garnishment.

Upon receipt of the intervening complaint and supplemental process, the Clerk shall conform a copy of the intervening complaint and shall issue the supplemental process. Thereafter, the offering party shall deliver the conformed copy of the intervening complaint and supplemental process to the Marshal for execution. Upon receipt of the intervening complaint and supplemental process, the Marshal shall re-arrest or re-attach the vessel or property in the name of the intervening plaintiff.

Counsel for the intervening party shall serve a copy of the intervening complaint, and copies of all process and exhibits upon all other counsel of record, and shall thereafter file a certificate of service with the Clerk indicating the manner and date of service.

(b) *Permissive Intervention When the Vessel or Property Has Been Scheduled for Sale by the Court.* Except as indicated below, and subject to any other rule or order of this Court, no person shall have an automatic right to intervene in an action where the Court has ordered the sale of the vessel or property, and the date of the sale is set within fifteen (15) days from the date the party moves for permission to intervene in accordance with this subsection. In such cases, the person seeking permission to intervene must:

(1) File a motion to intervene and indicate in the caption of the motion a request for expedited hearing when appropriate;

(2) Include a copy of the anticipated intervening complaint as an exhibit to the motion to intervene;

(3) Prepare and offer for filing a supplemental warrant of arrest and/or a supplemental process of attachment and garnishment;

(4) Serve copies of the motion to intervene, with exhibits and proposed supplemental process upon every other party to the litigation; and

(5) File a certificate of service indicating the date and manner of service.

Thereafter, the Court may permit intervention under such conditions and terms as are equitable to the interests of all parties; and if intervention is permitted, shall also direct the Clerk to issue the supplemental process.

Upon receipt of the order permitting intervention, the Clerk shall file the originally signed intervening complaint, conform a copy of the intervening complaint and issue the supplemental process.

Thereafter, the offering party shall deliver the conformed copy of the intervening complaint and supplemental process to the Marshal for execution. Upon receipt of the intervening complaint and supplemental process, the Marshal shall re-arrest or re-attach the vessel or property in the name of the intervening plaintiff.

Counsel for the intervening party shall also serve a copy of the intervening complaint, exhibits, and supplemental process upon every other party of record and shall thereafter file a Certificate of Service with the Clerk indicating the manner and date of service.

(3) Special Requirements for Salvage Actions. In cases of salvage, the complaint shall also state to the extent known, the value of the hull, cargo, freight, and other property salvaged, the amount claimed, the names of the principal salvors, and that the suit is instituted in their behalf and in behalf of all other persons associated with them.

In addition to these special pleading requirements, plaintiff shall attach as an exhibit to the complaint a list of all known salvors, and all persons believed entitled to share in the salvage. Plaintiff shall also attach a copy of any agreement of consortship available and known to exist among them collegially or individually.

(4) Form and Amount of Stipulation or Bonds. Stipulations or bonds in admiralty and maritime actions need not be under seal and may be executed by the agent or attorney of the stipulator or obligor. Stipulations for costs with corporate surety need not be signed or executed by the party, but may be signed by the party's agent or attorney.

(a) Seaman's Wage Claims: Actions initiated by seamen pursuant to 28 U.S.C. 1916 may be filed without prepaying fees or costs or furnishing security therefor.

(b) Security for Costs: In an action under the Supplemental Rules, other than an action solely in personam, the plaintiff, and any intervenor, shall file with its initial pleading a stipulation for costs in the principal sum of $500.00 as security for all costs awarded against the plaintiff or intervenor by this court or any appellate court which shall be deposited into the registry of the court. No motion made by a plaintiff or intervenor will be considered by the Court until the security for costs is deposited. A party may move for an order increasing the amount of security for costs or for return of the balance upon conclusion of the action. In an action for limitation of liability, the amount of security for costs under Supplemental Rule F(1) may be combined with the security for value and interest unless otherwise ordered.

(c) Actions In Forma Pauperis: An action under these rules may be maintained in forma pauperis by express allowance of the court upon motion by the party. Where a party is allowed to proceed in forma pauperis, no stipulation for costs shall be required.

(5) Deposit of Marshal's Fees and Expenses Required Prior to Effecting Arrest, Attachment and/or Garnishment.

(a) *Deposit Required Before Seizure.* Any party seeking the arrest or attachment of property in accordance with Supplemental Rule (E) shall deposit a sum with the Marshal sufficient to cover the Marshal's estimated fees and expenses of arresting and keeping the property for at least ten (10) days. The Marshal is not required to execute process until the deposit is made.

(b) *Proration of Marshal's Fees and Expenses Upon Intervention.* When one or more parties intervene pursuant to Local Admiralty Rule E(2)(a) or (b), the burden of advancing sums to the Marshal sufficient to cover the Marshal's fees and expenses shall be allocated equitably between the original plaintiff, and the intervening party or parties as indicated below:

(1) Stipulation for the Allocation and Payment of the Marshal's Fees and Expenses. Immediately upon the filing of the intervening complaint, counsel for the intervening plaintiff shall arrange for a conference between all other parties to the action, at which time a good faith effort shall be made to allocate fees and expenses among the parties. Any resulting stipulation between the parties shall be codified and filed with the Court and a copy served upon the Marshal.

(2) Allocation of Costs and Expenses in the Event That Counsel Cannot Stipulate. The Court expects that counsel will resolve the allocation of costs and expenses in accordance with the preceding paragraph. In the event that such an arrangement cannot be made, the parties shall share in the fees and expenses of the Marshal in proportion to their claims as stated in the original and intervening complaints.

In order to determine the proportionate shares of each party, counsel for the last intervening plaintiff shall determine the total amounts claimed by each party. The individual claims shall be determined from the original and amended complaint, and all other intervening complaints subsequently accepted and processed by the Marshal in accordance with Local Admiralty Rule E(2)(a) or (b).

Thereafter, counsel for the last intervening plaintiff shall deliver to the Marshal a list which summarizes each party's claim, and the proportion which each party's claim bears to the aggregate claims asserted in the litigation, determined to the nearest one-tenth of one percentage point.

Upon receipt of this listing, the Marshal shall determine the total expenses incurred to date and shall estimate the expenses to be incurred during the next ten (10) days. For the purpose of making this calculation, the total fees and expenses shall be calculated from the date when continuous and uninterrupted arrest or attachment of the property began, and not prorated from the date a particular party's intervening complaint was filed.

The Marshal shall then apply the percentages determined in the listing, and shall compute the amount of the intervening party's initial deposit requirements. The Marshal shall also utilize this listing to compute any additional deposit requirements which may be necessary pursuant to Local Admiralty Rule E(5)(c).

The Marshal need not re-arrest or re-attach the vessel and/or property until the deposit is received from the intervening plaintiff.

(c) *Additional Deposit Requirements.* Until the property arrested or attached and garnished has been released or otherwise disposed of in accordance with Supplemental Rule (E), the Marshal may require from any original and intervening party who has caused the arrest or attachment and garnishment of a vessel or property, to post such additional deposits as the Marshal determines necessary to cover any additional estimated fees or expenses.

(d) *Judicial Relief From Deposit Requirements.* Any party aggrieved by the deposit requirements of Local Admiralty Rule E(5)(b) may apply to the Court for relief. Such application shall be predicated upon a showing that owing to the relative priorities of the claims asserted against the vessel or other property, the deposit requirements operate to impose a burden disproportionate to the aggrieved party's recovery potential.

The judicial officer may adjust the deposit requirements, but in no event shall the proportion required of an aggrieved party be reduced to a percentage less than that imposed upon the claimant whose claim is the smallest among that of claims which the aggrieved party stipulates as having priority over its claim; or, in the absence of such stipulation, the greatest percentage imposed upon any claimant participating in the deposit requirements.

(e) *Consequence of Failing to Comply With Additional Deposit Requirements.* Any party who fails to make the additional deposit as requested by the Marshal may not participate further in the proceeding, except for the purpose of seeking relief from this rule. Additionally, the Marshal shall notify the Court in writing whenever any party fails to make additional deposits as required by Local Admiralty Rule E(5)(c).

In the event that a party questions its obligations to advance monies required by this rule, the Marshal may apply to the Court for instructions concerning that party's obligation under the rule.

(6) Property in Possession of a United States Officer. Whenever the property to be arrested or attached is in custody of a U.S. officer, the Marshal shall serve the appropriate process upon the officer or employee; or, if the officer or employee is not found within the district, then to the custodian of the property within the district. The Marshal shall direct the officer, employee or custodian not to relinquish custody of the property until ordered to do so by the Court.

(7) Process Held in Abeyance.

(a) *When Permitted.* In accordance with Supplemental Rule (E)(3)(b), a plaintiff may ask the Clerk not to issue process, but rather to hold the process in abeyance. The

Clerk shall docket this request, and thereafter shall not be responsible for ensuring that process is issued at a later date.

(b) *When Intervention Is Subsequently Required.* It is the intention of these rules that a vessel or other property should be arrested or attached pursuant to process issued and effected in only one civil action. Therefore, if while process is held in abeyance on one action, the vessel or property is arrested or attached in another action, it shall be the responsibility of the plaintiff who originally requested process be held in abeyance in the first action to voluntarily dismiss without prejudice the first action, insofar as that action seeks to proceed against the property arrested or attached in the second action, and promptly intervene in the second action pursuant to Local Admiralty Rule E(2)(a) or (b).

In order to prevent undue hardship or manifest injustice, motions to consolidate in rem actions against the same vessel or property will be granted only in exceptional circumstances.

(8) Release of Property in Accordance With Supplemental Rule (E)(5).

(a) *Release by Consent or Stipulation.* Subject to the limitations imposed by Supplemental Rule (E)(5)(c), the Marshal may release any vessel, cargo or property in the Marshal's possession to the party on whose behalf the property is detained. However, as a precondition to release, the Marshal shall require a stipulation, bond, or other security, expressly authorizing the release. The authorizing instrument shall be signed by the party, or the party's attorney, on whose behalf the property is detained.

The stipulation, bond, or other security shall be posted in an amount equal to, or greater than, the amount required for the following types of action:

(1) Actions Entirely for a Sum Certain. The amount alleged to be due in the complaint, with interest at six percent (6%) per annum from the date claimed to be due to a date twenty-four (24) months after the date the claim was filed, or by filing an approved stipulation, or bond for the amount alleged plus interest as computed in this subsection.

The stipulation or bond shall be conditioned to abide by all orders of the Court, and to pay the amount of any final judgment entered by this Court or any appellate Court, with interest.

(2) Actions Other Than Possessory, Petitory or Partition. Unless otherwise ordered by the Court, the amount of the appraised or agreed value of the property seized, with interest. If an appraised value cannot be agreed upon by the parties, the Court shall order an appraisal in accordance with Local Admiralty Rule F(3).

The stipulation or bond shall be conditioned to abide by all orders of the Court, and to pay the amount of any final judgment entered by this Court or any appellate Court, with interest.

The person consenting or stipulating to the release shall also file a claim in accordance with Local Admiralty Rule E(2)(a) or (b).

(3) Possessory, Petitory or Partition Actions. The Marshal may release property in these actions only upon order of Court, and upon the subsequent deposit of security and compliance with such terms and/or conditions as the Court deems appropriate.

(b) *Release Pursuant to Court Order.* In accordance with Supplemental Rule (E)(5)(c), a party may petition to release the vessel pursuant to Court order. A party making such application shall file a Request for Release which shall substantially conform in format and content to the form identified as NDF 8 in the Appendix to these Local Admiralty Rules. Additionally, the party shall prepare, and offer for filing, a proposed order directing the release. This order shall substantially conform in format and content to the form identified as NDF 9 in the Appendix to these Local Admiralty Rules.

However, as a precondition to the release, the Marshal shall require a stipulation, bond, or other security, as specified in Local Admiralty Rule E(8)(a)(1), (2) or (3), as appropriate.

(c) *Upon the Dismissal or Discontinuance of an Action.* Upon dismissal of an action by an order of the Court or upon filing a notice of voluntary dismissal, a party may obtain release of any vessel, cargo, or property by coordinating with the Marshal to ensure that all costs and charges of the Court and its officers have first been paid.

(d) *Release Subsequent to the Posting of a General Bond.*

(1) Requirements of a General Bond. General bonds filed pursuant to Supplemental Rule (E)(5)(b) shall identify the vessel by name, nationality, dimensions, official number or registration number, hailing port and port of documentation.

(2) Responsibility for Maintaining a Current Listing of General Bonds. The Clerk shall maintain a current listing of all general bonds. This listing should be maintained in alphabetical order by name of the vessel. The listing will be available for inspection during normal business hours.

(3) Execution of Process. The arrest of a vessel covered by a general bond shall be stayed in accordance with Supplemental Rule (E)(5)(b), however, the Marshal shall serve a copy of the complaint upon the master or other person in whose charge or custody the vessel is found. If neither the master nor another person in charge of custody is found aboard the vessel, the Marshal shall make the return accordingly.

Thereafter, it shall be plaintiff's responsibility to advise the owner or designated agent, at the address furnished in the general bond, of (1) the case number, (2) nature of the action and the amount claimed; (3) the plaintiff and name and address of plaintiff's attorney; and (4) the return date for filing a claim.

(9) Application to Modify Security for Value and Interest. At any time, any party having an interest in the subject matter of the action may move the Court, on due notice and for cause, for greater, better or lesser security, and any such order may be enforced by attachment or as otherwise provided by law.

(10) Custody and Safekeeping.

(a) *Initial Responsibility.* The Marshal shall initially take custody of any vessel, cargo and/or other property arrested, or attached in accordance with these rules. Thereafter, and until such time as substitute custodians may be authorized in accordance with Local Admiralty Rule E(10)(c), the Marshal shall be responsible for providing adequate and necessary security for the safekeeping of the vessel or property. In the discretion of the Marshal, adequate and necessary security may include the placing of keepers on or near the vessel and/or the appointment of a facility or person to serve as a custodian of the vessel or property.

(b) *Limitations on the Handling, Repairing and Subsequent Movement of Vessels or Property.* Subsequent to the arrest or attachment of a vessel or property, and except as provided in Local Admiralty Rule E(10)(a), no person may handle cargo, conduct repairs, or move a vessel without prior order of Court. Notwithstanding the foregoing, the custodian or substitute custodian is obligated to comply with any orders issued by the Captain of the Port, United States Coast Guard, including an order to move the vessel; and to comply with any applicable federal, state, or local laws or regulations pertaining to vessel and port safety. Any movement of a vessel pursuant to such requirements must not remove the vessel from the Northern District of Florida and shall be reported to the Court within twenty-four (24) hours of the vessel's movement.

(c) *Procedures for Changing Custody Arrangements.* Any party may petition the Court to dispense with keepers, remove or place the vessel, cargo and/or other property at a specified facility, designate a substitute custodian for the vessel or cargo, or for other similar relief. The motion shall substantially conform in format and content to the form identified as NDF 5 in the Appendix of these Local Admiralty Rules.

(1) Notification of the Marshal Required. When an application for change in custody arrangements is filed, either before or after the Marshal has taken custody of the vessel or property, the filing party shall serve notice of the application on the Marshal in sufficient time to permit the Marshal to review the indemnification and insurance arrangements of the filing party and substitute custodian. The application shall also be served upon all other parties to the litigation.

(2) Indemnification Requirements. Any motion for the appointment of a substitute custodian or facility shall include as an exhibit to the motion, a consent and indemnification agreement signed by both the filing party, or the filing party's attorney, and the proposed substitute custodian.

The consent and indemnification agreement shall expressly release the Marshal from any and all liability and responsibility for the care and custody of the property while in the hands of the substitute custodian; and shall expressly hold the Marshal harmless from any and all claims whatsoever arising from the substitute custodianship. The agreement shall substantially conform in format and content to the form identified as NDF 6 in the Appendix to these Local Admiralty Rules.

(3) **Court Approval Required.** The motion to change custody arrangements, and indemnification and consent agreement shall be referred to a judicial officer who shall determine whether the facility or substitute custodian is capable of safely keeping the vessel, cargo and/or property.

(d) *Insurance Requirements.*

(1) Responsibility for Initially Obtaining Insurance. Concurrent with the arrest or attachment of a vessel or property, the Marshal shall obtain insurance to protect the Marshal, the Marshal's deputies, keepers, and custodians from liability arising from the arrest or attachment.

The insurance shall also protect the Marshal and the Marshal's deputies or agents from any liability arising from performing services undertaken to protect the vessel, cargo and/or property while that property is in the custody of the Court.

(2) Payment of Insurance Premiums. It shall be the responsibility of the party applying for the arrest or attachment of a vessel, cargo and/or property to promptly reimburse the Marshal for premiums paid to effect the necessary insurance.

The party applying for change in custody arrangements shall be responsible for paying the Marshal for any additional premium associated with the change.

(3) Taxation of Insurance Premiums. The premiums charged for the liability insurance will be taxed as an expense of custody while the vessel, cargo and/or property is in *custodia legis.*

(11) Preservation, Humanitarian and Repatriation Expenses.

(a) *Limitations on Reimbursement for Services and/or Supplies Provided to a Vessel or Property in Custody.* Except in cases of emergency or undue hardship, no person will be entitled to claim as an expense of administration the costs of services or supplies furnished to a vessel, cargo and/or property unless such services or supplies have been furnished to the Marshal upon the Marshal's order, or pursuant to an order of this Court.

Any order issued pursuant to this subsection shall require the person furnishing the services or supplies to file a weekly invoice. This invoice shall be set forth in the format prescribed in Local Admiralty Rule E(11)(e).

(b) *Preservation Expenses for the Vessel and Cargo.* The Marshal, or substitute custodian, is authorized to incur expenses reasonably deemed necessary in maintaining the vessel, cargo and/or property in custody for the purpose of preventing the vessel, cargo and/or property from suffering loss or undue deterioration.

(c) *Expenses for Care and Maintenance of a Crew.* Except in an emergency, or upon the authorization of a judicial officer, neither the Marshal nor substitute custodian shall incur expenses for feeding or otherwise maintaining the crew.

Applications for providing food, water and necessary medical services for the maintenance of the crew may be submitted, and decided ex parte by a judicial officer, providing such an application is made by some person other than the owner, manager or general agent of the vessel.

Such applications must be filed within thirty (30) days from the date of the vessel's initial seizure. Otherwise, except in the case of an emergency, such applications shall be filed and served upon all parties, who in turn shall have ten (10) days from receipt of the application to file a written response. Expenses for feeding or otherwise maintaining the crew, when incurred in accordance with this subsection, shall be taxed as an expense of administration and not as an expense of custody.

(d) *Repatriation Expenses.* Absent an order of Court expressly ordering the repatriation of the crew and/or passengers, and directing that the expenses be taxed as a cost of administration, no person shall be entitled to claim these expenses as expenses of administration.

(e) *Claim by a Supplier for Payment of Charges.* Any person who claims payment for furnishing services or supplies in compliance with Local Admiralty Rule E(11), shall submit an invoice to the Marshal's office for review and approval.

The claim shall be presented in the form of a verified claim, and shall be submitted within a reasonable time after furnishing the services or supplies, but in no event shall a claim be accepted after the vessel, or property has been released. The claimant shall file a copy of the verified claim with the Marshal, and also serve the substitute custodian and all other parties to the litigation.

The Marshal shall review the claim, make adjustments or recommendations to the claim as are appropriate, and shall thereafter forward the claim to the Court for approval. The Court may postpone the hearing on an individual claim until a hearing can be set to consolidate other claims against the property.

(12) Property in Incidental Custody and Otherwise Not Subject to the Arrest or Attachment.

(a) *Authority to Preserve Cargo in Incidental Custody.* The Marshal, or an authorized substitute custodian, shall be responsible for securing, maintaining and preserving all property incidentally taken into custody as a result of the arrest or attachment of a vessel or property. Incidental property may include, but shall not be limited to, laden cargo not itself the subject of the arrest or attachment.

The Marshal or other custodian shall maintain a separate account of all costs and expenses associated with the care and maintenance of property incidentally taken into custody.

Any person claiming entitlement to possession of property incidentally taken into custody shall be required, as a precondition of receiving possession, to reimburse the Marshal for such separately accounted expenses. Funds received by the Marshal will be credited against both the expense of custody and administration.

(b) *Separation, Storage and Preservation of Property in Incidental Custody.* Any party, or the Marshal, may petition the Court to permit the separation and storage of property in incidental custody from the property actually arrested or attached.

When separation of the property is ordered to protect the incidentally seized property from undue deterioration; provide for safer storage; meet an emergency; reduce the expenses of custody; or to facilitate a sale of the vessel or other property pursuant to Local Admiralty Rule E(16); the costs of such separation shall be treated as an expense of preservation and taxed as a cost of custody.

(c) *Disposal of Unclaimed Property.* Property incidentally in custody and not subsequently claimed by any person entitled to possession, shall be disposed of in accordance with the laws governing the disposition of property abandoned to the United States of America.

Except when prohibited by prevailing federal statute, the resulting net proceeds associated with the disposition of abandoned property shall be applied to offset the expense of administration, with the remainder escheating to the United States of America as provided by law.

(13) Dismissal.

(1) *By Consent.* No action may be dismissed pursuant to Fed.R.Civ.P. 41(a) unless all costs and expenses of the Court and its officials have first been paid.

Additionally, if there is more than one plaintiff or intervening plaintiff, no dismissal may be taken by a plaintiff unless that party's proportionate share of costs and expenses has been paid in accordance with Local Admiralty Rule E(6).

(2) *Involuntary Dismissal.* If the Court enters a dismissal pursuant to Fed.R.Civ.P. 41(b), the Court shall also designate the costs and expenses to be paid by the party or parties so dismissed.

(14) Judgments.

(1) *Expenses of Sureties as Costs.* If costs are awarded to any party, then all reasonable premiums or expenses paid by the prevailing party on bonds, stipulations and/or other security shall be taxed as costs in the case.

(2) *Costs of Arrest or Attachment.* If costs are awarded to any party, then all reasonable expenses paid by the prevailing party incidental to, or arising from the arrest or attachment of any vessel, property and/or cargo shall be taxed as costs in the case.

(15) Stay of Final Order.

(a) *Automatic Stay for Ten (10) Days.* In accordance with Fed.R.Civ.P. 62(a), no execution shall issue upon a judgment, nor shall seized property be released pursuant to a judgment or dismissal, until ten (10) days after the entry of the judgment or order of dismissal.

(b) *Stays Beyond the Ten (10) Day Period.* If within the ten (10) day period established by Fed.R.Civ.P. 62(a), a party files any of the motions contemplated in Fed.R.Civ.P. 62(b), or a notice of appeal, then unless otherwise ordered by the Court, a further stay shall exist for a period not to exceed thirty (30) days from the entry of the judgment or order. The purpose of this additional stay is to permit the Court to consider an application for the establishment of a supersedeas bond, and to order the date upon which the bond shall be filed with the Court.

(16) Notice of Sale.

(a) *Publication of Notice.* In an action in rem or quasi in rem, and except in suits on behalf of the United States of America where other notice is prescribed by statute, the Marshal shall publish notice in any of the newspapers approved pursuant to Local Admiralty Rule A(7).

(b) *Duration of Publication.* Unless otherwise ordered by the Court, applicable Supplemental Rule, or Local Admiralty Rule, publication of the notice of sale shall be made at least twice; the first publication shall be at least one (1) calendar week prior to the date of the sale, and the second at least three (3) calendar days prior to the date of the sale.

(17) Sale of a Vessel or Property.

(a) *Payment of the Purchase Price.* Unless otherwise provided in the order of sale, the person whose bid is accepted shall pay the Marshal the purchase price in the manner provided below;

(1) If the Bid Is Not More Than $500.00. The successful bidder shall immediately pay the full purchase price.

(2) If the Bid Is More Than $500.00. The bidder shall immediately deposit with the Marshal $500.00, or 10% of the bid, whichever sum is greater. Thereafter the bidder shall pay the remaining purchase price within three (3) working days.

If an objection to the sale is filed within the time permitted by Local Admiralty Rule E(17)(g), the successful bidder is excused from paying the remaining purchase price until three (3) working days after the Court confirms the sale.

(b) *Method of Payment.* Unless otherwise ordered by the Court, payments to the Marshal shall be made in cash, certified check or cashier's check.

(c) *Custodial Costs Pending Payment.* When a successful bidder fails to pay the balance of the bid within the time allowed by Local Admiralty Rule E (17)(a)(2), or within the time permitted by order of the Court, the Marshal shall charge the successful bidder for the cost of keeping the property from the date payment of the balance was due, to the date the bidder takes delivery of the property.

The Marshal may refuse to release the property until these additional charges have been paid.

(d) *Default for Failure to Pay the Balance.* The person who fails to pay the balance of the bid within the time allowed shall be deemed to be in default. Thereafter a judicial officer may order that the sale be awarded to the second highest bidder, or may order a new sale as appropriate.

Any sum deposited by the bidder in default shall be forfeited, and the amount shall be applied by the Marshal to any additional costs incurred because of the forfeiture and default, including costs incident to resale. The balance of the deposit, if any, shall be retained in the registry and subject to further order of the Court.

(e) *Marshal's Report of Sale.* At the conclusion of the sale, the Marshal shall file a written report of the sale to include the date of the sale, the price obtained, and the name and address of the buyer.

(f) *Confirmation of Sale.* Unless an objection is timely filed in accordance with this rule, or the purchaser is in default for failing to pay the balance of the purchase price, plaintiff shall proceed to have the sale confirmed on the day following the last day for filing objections.

In order to confirm the sale, plaintiff's counsel shall file a "Request for Confirmation of Sale" following the last day for filing an objection. The "Request for Confirmation of Sale" shall substantially conform in format and content to the form identified as NDF 10 in the Appendix to these Local Admiralty Rules. Plaintiff's counsel shall also prepare and offer for filing a "Confirmation of the Sale". The "Confirmation of Sale" shall substantially conform in format and content to the form identified as NDF 11 in the Appendix to these Local Admiralty Rules. Thereafter, the Clerk shall file and docket the confirmation and shall promptly transmit a certified copy of the "Confirmation of Sale" to the Marshal's office.

Unless otherwise ordered by the Court, if the plaintiff fails to timely file the "Request for Confirmation of Sale" and proposed "Confirmation of Sale", the Marshal shall assess any continuing costs or expenses for custody of the vessel or property against the plaintiff.

(g) *Objections to Confirmation.*

(1) Time for Filing Objections. Unless otherwise permitted by the Court, an objection must be filed within three (3) working days following the sale. The party or person filing an objection shall serve a copy of the objection upon the Marshal and all other parties to the action, and shall also file a Certificate of Service indicating the date and manner of service. Opposition to the objection must be filed within five (5) days after receipt of the objection of the sale.

The Court shall consider the objection, and any opposition to the objection, and shall confirm the sale, order a new sale, or grant other relief as appropriate.

(2) Deposit of Preservation or Maintenance Costs. In addition to filing written objections, any person objecting to the sale shall also deposit with the Marshal the cost of keeping the property for at least seven (7) days. Proof of the deposit with the Marshal's office shall be delivered to the Clerk's office by the moving party. The Court will not consider the objection without proof of this deposit.

If the objection is sustained, the objector will be reimbursed for the expense of keeping the property from the proceeds of any subsequent sale, and any remaining deposit will be returned to the objector upon Court order.

If the objection is denied, the sum deposited by the objector will be applied to pay the fees and expenses incurred by the Marshal in keeping the property from the date the objection was filed until the sale is confirmed. Any remaining deposit will be returned to the objector upon order of Court.

(h) *Confirmation of Title.* Failure of a party to give the required notice of an action and arrest of a vessel, property and/or cargo, or failure to give required notice of a sale, may afford grounds for objecting to the sale, but such failure does not affect the title of a good faith purchaser of the property.

(18) Post-sale Claim. Claims against the proceeds of a sale authorized by these rules, except for seamen's wages, will not be admitted on behalf of lienors who file their claims after the sale.

Unless otherwise ordered by the Court, any claims filed after the date of the sale shall be limited to the remnants and surplus arising from the sale.

[Adopted November 24, 2015.]

RULE F. ACTIONS TO LIMIT LIABILITY

(1) Publication of the Notice. Immediately upon the commencement of an action to limit liability pursuant to Supplemental Rule (F), plaintiff shall, without further order of Court, effect publication of the notice in accordance with the provisions set forth in Supplemental Rule (F)(4) and Local Admiralty Rule A(7).

(2) Proof of Publication. Plaintiff shall file proof of publication not later than the return date. It shall be sufficient proof for plaintiff to file the sworn statement by, or on behalf of, the publisher or editor, indicating the dates of publication, along with a copy or reproduction of the actual publication.

(3) Appraisals Pursuant to Supplemental Rule (F)(7). Upon the filing of a claimant's motion pursuant to Supplemental Rule (F)(7), demanding an increase in the funds deposited in Court or the security given by plaintiff, the Court shall order an appraisement of the value of the plaintiff's interest in the vessel and pending cargo. Upon receipt of the order directing the appraisal, the parties shall have three (3) working days to file a written stipulation to an appraiser. In the event that the parties do not file a stipulation, the Court shall appoint the appraiser.

The appraiser shall promptly conduct an appraisal and thereafter file the appraisal with the Clerk and serve a copy of the appraisal upon the moving party and the plaintiff. The appraiser shall also file a Certificate of Service indicating the date and manner in which service was perfected.

(4) Objections to the Appraisal. Any party may move to set aside the appraisal within ten (10) days following the filing of the appraisal with the Clerk.

(5) Fees of the Appraiser. The Court shall establish the fee to be paid the appraiser. Unless otherwise ordered by the Court, the fee shall be taxed against the party seeking relief under Supplemental Rule (F)(7).

[Adopted November 24, 2015.]

APPENDIX OF FORMS. ADMIRALTY AND MARITIME RULES

FORM 1. ORDER DIRECTING THE ISSUANCE OF THE PROCESS OF ATTACHMENT AND GARNISHMENT

UNITED STATES DISTRICT COURT
NORTHERN DISTRICT OF FLORIDA
Case No. ____-Civ or Cr-(USDJ's last name/USMJ's last name)
"IN ADMIRALTY"

Plaintiff,
v.
Defendant.
____

Pursuant to Supplemental Rule (B)(1) and Local Admiralty Rule B(3)(a), the Clerk is directed to issue the summons and process of attachment and garnishment in the above-styled action.
DONE AND ORDERED at ____________, Florida, this ______ day of _____________, ________.

____
United States District Judge

UNITED STATES DISTRICT COURT
NORTHERN DISTRICT OF FLORIDA
Case No. ____-Civ or Cr-(USDJ's last name/USMJ's last name)
"IN ADMIRALTY"

Plaintiff,
v.
Defendant.
____

PROCESS OF ATTACHMENT AND GARNISHMENT

The complaint in the above-styled case was filed in the __________ Division of this Court on __________, ______.

In accordance with Supplemental Rule (B) of Certain Admiralty and Maritime Claims of the Federal Rules of Civil Procedure and Local Admiralty Rule B, you are directed to attach and garnish the property indicated below:
DESCRIPTION
(Describe the property to be attached and garnished in sufficient detail, including location of the property, to permit the U.S. Marshal to effect the seizure.)

You shall also give notice of the attachment and garnishment to every person required by

[Amended November 24, 2015.]

FORM 2. PROCESS OF ATTACHMENT AND GARNISHMENT

appropriate Supplemental Rule, Local Admiralty Rule, and the practices of your office.

DATED at ___________, Florida, this ______ day of ___________, _____.
CLERK
By:__________________
Deputy Clerk
(Name of Plaintiff's Attorney)
(Florida Bar Number, if admitted in Fla.)
(Firm Name, if applicable)
(Mailing Address)
(City, State & Zip Code)
(Telephone Number)
(Facsimile Number)
(E-Mail Address)

SPECIAL NOTICE
Any person claiming an interest in property seized pursuant to this process of attachment and garnishment must file a claim in accordance with the post-seizure review provisions of Local Admiralty Rule B(5).

[Amended November 24, 2015.]

FORM 3. ORDER DIRECTING THE ISSUANCE OF THE WARRANT OF ARREST

UNITED STATES DISTRICT COURT
NORTHERN DISTRICT OF FLORIDA
Case No. ____-Civ or Cr-(USDJ's last name/USMJ's last name)
"IN ADMIRALTY"

Plaintiff,
v.
Defendant.

____

ORDER DIRECTING THE ISSUANCE OF THE WARRANT OF ARREST AND/OR SUMMONS

Pursuant to Supplemental Rule (C)(1) and Local Admiralty Rule C(2)(a), the Clerk is directed to issue a warrant of arrest and/or summons in the above-styled action.

DONE AND ORDERED at ________, Florida, this ____ day of ________, ______.

____
United States District Judge

[Amended November 24, 2015.]

FORM 4. WARRANT FOR ARREST IN REM

UNITED STATES DISTRICT COURT
NORTHERN DISTRICT OF FLORIDA
Case No. ____-Civ or Cr-(USDJ's last name/USMJ's last name)
"IN ADMIRALTY'

Plaintiff,
v.
Defendant.
____

WARRANT FOR ARREST IN REM
TO THE UNITED STATES MARSHAL
FOR THE UNITED STATES DISTRICT COURT
FOR THE NORTHERN DISTRICT OF FLORIDA

The complaint in the above-styled in rem proceeding was filed in the __________ Division of this Court on ________.

In accordance with Supplemental Rule (C) for Certain Admiralty and Maritime Claims of the Federal Rules of Civil Procedure and Local Admiralty Rule C, you are directed to arrest the Defendant vessel, her boats, tackle, apparel and furniture, engines and appurtenances, and to detain the same in your custody pending further order of the Court.

You shall also give notice of the arrest to all persons required by appropriate Supplemental Rule, Local Admiralty Rule, and the practices of your office.

ORDERED at ____________, Florida, this ______ day of ________, ____.
CLERK
By: ____________________
Deputy Clerk
(Name of Plaintiff's Attorney)
(Florida Bar Number, if admitted in Fla.)
(Firm Name, if applicable)
(Mailing Address)
(City, State & Zip Code)
(Telephone Number)
(Facsimile Number)
(E-Mail Address)
cc: Counsel of Record

SPECIAL NOTICE
In accordance with Local Admiralty Rule C(6), any person claiming an interest in the vessel and/or property shall be required to file a claim within ten (10) days after process has been executed, and shall also be required to file an answer within twenty (20) days after the filing of his claim.

Any persons claiming an interest in the vessel and/or property may also pursue the post-arrest remedies set forth in Local Admiralty Rule C(7).

[Amended November 24, 2015.]

FORM 5. MOTION FOR APPOINTMENT OF SUBSTITUTE CUSTODIAN

UNITED STATES DISTRICT COURT
NORTHERN DISTRICT OF FLORIDA
Case No. ____-Civ or Cr-(USDJ's last name/USMJ's last name)
"IN ADMIRALTY"

Plaintiff,
v.
Defendant.
____

MOTION FOR APPOINTMENT OF SUBSTITUTE CUSTODIAN

Pursuant to Local Admiralty Rule E(10)(c), Plaintiff __________________, by and through the undersigned attorney, represents the following:

(1) On _____________, _____, Plaintiff initiated the above-styled action against the vessel_______________________________, her boats, tackle, apparel, furniture and furnishings, equipment, engines and appurtenances.

(2) On _____________, _____, the Clerk of the District Court issued a Warrant of Arrest against the vessel ________________________, directing the U.S. Marshal to take custody of the vessel, and to retain custody of the vessel pending further order of this Court.

(3)(a) Subsequent to the issuance of the Warrant of Arrest, the marshal will take steps to immediately seize the vessel. Thereafter, continual custody by the marshal will require the services of at least one custodian at a cost of at least $__________ per day. (This paragraph would be applicable only when the motion for appointment is filed concurrent with the complaint and application for the warrant of arrest.)
-or-
(3)(b) Pursuant to the previously issued Warrant of Arrest, the Marshal has already arrested the vessel. Continued custody by the Marshal requires the services of ___________ custodians at a cost of at least $___________ per day. (This paragraph would be applicable in all cases where the Marshal has previously arrested the vessel.)

(4) The vessel is currently berthed at ____________, and subject to the approval of the Court, the substitute custodian is prepared to provide security, wharfage, and routine services for the safekeeping of the vessel at a cost substantially less than that presently required by the Marshal. The substitute custodian has also agreed to continue to provide these services pending further order of this Court.

(5) The substitute custodian has adequate facilities for the care, maintenance and security of the vessel. In discharging its obligation to care for, maintain and secure the vessel, the Substitute Custodian shall comply with all orders of the Captain of the Port, United States Coast Guard, including but not limited to, an order to move the vessel; and any applicable federal, state, and local laws, regulations and requirements pertaining to vessel and port safety. The Substitute Custodian shall advise the Court, the parties to the action, and the United States Marshal, of any movement of

the vessel pursuant to an order of the Captain of the Port, within twenty-four (24) hours of such vessel movement.

(6) Concurrent with the Court's approval of the Motion for Appointment of the Substitute Custodian, Plaintiff and the Substitute Custodian will file a Consent and Indemnification Agreement in accordance with Local Admiralty Rule E(10)(c)(2).

THEREFORE, in accordance with the representations set forth in this instrument, and subject to the filing of the indemnification agreement noted in paragraph (6) above, Plaintiff requests this Court to enter an order appointing ____________ as the Substitute Custodian for the vessel ______________________.

DATED at ____________, Florida, this _______ day of ____________, _____.

____
SIGNATURE OF COUNSEL OF RECORD
Typed Name of Counsel
Fla. Bar ID No. (if admitted in Fla.)
Firm or Business Name
Mailing Address
City, State, Zip Code
Telephone Number
Facsimile Number
E-Mail Address
cc: Counsel of Record
Substitute Custodian

SPECIAL NOTE
Plaintiff's attorney shall also prepare for the Court=s signature and subsequent filing, a proposed order for the Appointment of Substitute Custodian.

[Amended November 24, 2015.]

FORM 6. CONSENT AND INDEMNIFICATION AGREEMENT FOR THE APPOINTMENT OF A SUBSTITUTE CUSTODIAN

UNITED STATES DISTRICT COURT
NORTHERN DISTRICT OF FLORIDA
Case No. ____-Civ or Cr-(USDJ's last name/USMJ's last name)
"IN ADMIRALTY"

Plaintiff,
v.
Defendant.
____

CONSENT AND INDEMNIFICATION AGREEMENT FOR THE APPOINTMENT OF A SUBSTITUTE CUSTODIAN

Plaintiff ____________________, (by the undersigned attorney) and ____________________, the proposed Substitute Custodian, hereby expressly release the U.S. Marshal for this district, and the U.S. Marshal's Service, from any and all liability and responsibility for the care and custody of ____________________ (describe the property) while in the hands of ____________________ (substitute custodian).

Plaintiff and ____________________ (substitute custodian) also expressly agree to hold the U.S. Marshal for this district, and the U.S. Marshal's Service, harmless from any and all claims whatsoever arising during the period of the substitute custodianship.

As counsel of record in this action, the undersigned attorney represents that he has been expressly authorized by the Plaintiff to sign this Consent and Indemnification Agreement for, and on behalf of the Plaintiff.

SIGNED this ______ day of _____________, ________, at _____________, Florida.

______________________	______________________
PLAINTIFF'S ATTORNEY	SUBSTITUTE CUSTODIAN
Typed Name	Typed Name
Fla. Bar ID No. (if admitted in Fla.)	Fla. Bar ID No. (if admitted in Fla.)
Firm or Business	Name Firm or Business Name
Mailing Address	Mailing Address
City, State, Zip Code	City, State, Zip Code
Telephone Number	Telephone Number
Facsimile Number	Facsimile Number
E-Mail Address	E-Mail Address

cc: Counsel of Record

[Amended November 24, 2015.]

FORM 7. NOTICE OF ACTION IN REM AND ARREST OF VESSEL

UNITED STATES DISTRICT COURT
NORTHERN DISTRICT OF FLORIDA
Case No. ____-Civ or Cr-(USDJ's last name/USMJ's last name)
"IN ADMIRALTY"

Plaintiff,
v.
Defendant.
____

NOTICE OF ACTION IN REM AND ARREST OF VESSEL

In accordance with Supplemental Rule (C)(4) for Certain Admiralty and Maritime Action of the Federal Rules of Civil Procedure, and Local Admiralty Rule C(4), notice is hereby given of the arrest of ______________, on __________, ______, in accordance with a Warrant of Arrest issued on __________, ________.

Pursuant to Supplemental Rule (C)(6), and Local Admiralty Rule C(6), any person having a claim against the vessel and/or property shall file a claim with the Court not later than ten (10) days after process has been effected, or as otherwise provided in Supplemental Rule (C)(6), and shall serve an answer within twenty (20) days from the date of filing their claim.

DATED at __________, Florida, this _____ day of __________, _____.

____
SIGNED NAME OF PLAINTIFF'S ATTORNEY
Typed Name of Counsel
Fla. Bar ID No. (if admitted in Fla.)
Firm or Business Name
Mailing Address
City, State, Zip Code
Telephone Number
Facsimile Number
E-Mail Address

cc: Counsel of Record

[Amended November 24, 2015.]

FORM 8. MOTION FOR RELEASE OF A VESSEL OR PROPERTY IN ACCORDANCE WITH SUPPLEMENTAL RULE (E)(5)

UNITED STATES DISTRICT COURT
NORTHERN DISTRICT OF FLORIDA
Case No. ____-Civ or Cr-(USDJ's last name/USMJ's last name)
"IN ADMIRALTY"

Plaintiff,
v.
Defendant.
____

MOTION FOR RELEASE OF A VESSEL OR PROPERTY IN ACCORDANCE WITH SUPPLEMENTAL RULE (E)(5)

In accordance with Supplemental Rule (E)(5) and Local Admiralty Rule E(8)(b), plaintiff, on whose behalf property has been seized, requests the Court to enter an Order directing the United States Marshal for the Northern District of Florida to release the property. This request is made for the following reasons:

(Describe the reasons in sufficient detail to permit the Court to enter an appropriate order.)

DATED at ____________, Florida, this ________ day of ________, ____.

____
SIGNED NAME OF PLAINTIFF'S ATTORNEY
Typed Name of Counsel
Fla. Bar ID No. (if admitted in Fla.)
Firm or Business Name
Mailing Address
City, State, Zip Code
Telephone Number
Facsimile Number
E-Mail Address
cc: Counsel of Record

[Amended November 24, 2015.]

FORM 9. ORDER DIRECTING THE RELEASE OF A VESSEL OR PROPERTY IN ACCORDANCE WITH SUPPLEMENTAL RULE (E)(5)

UNITED STATES DISTRICT COURT
NORTHERN DISTRICT OF FLORIDA
Case No. ____-Civ or Cr-(USDJ's last name/USMJ's last name)
"IN ADMIRALTY"

Plaintiff,
v.
Defendant.
____________________/

ORDER DIRECTING THE RELEASE OF A VESSEL OR PROPERTY IN ACCORDANCE WITH SUPPLEMENTAL RULE (E)(5)

In accordance with Supplemental Rule (E)(5) and Local Admiralty Rule E(8)(a), and pursuant to the Request for Release filed on ____________, ______, the United States Marshal is directed to release the vessel and/or property currently being held in his custody in the above-styled action.

ORDERED at ____________, Florida, this ____ day of ____________, ______.

____
United States District Judge

cc: Counsel of Record

[Amended November 24, 2015.]

FORM 10. REQUEST FOR CONFIRMATION OF SALE

UNITED STATES DISTRICT COURT
Northern DISTRICT OF FLORIDA
Case No. ___-Civ or Cr-(USDJ's last name/USMJ's last name)
"IN ADMIRALTY"

Plaintiff,
v.
Defendant.
____

REQUEST FOR CONFIRMATION OF SALE

Plaintiff, by and through its undersigned attorney certifies the following:
(1) *Date of Sale:* In accordance with the Court's previous Order of Sale, plaintiff represents that the sale of ________________ (describe the property) was conducted by the Marshal on __________, _____.

(2) *Last Day for Filing Objections:* Pursuant to Local Admiralty Rule E(17)(g)(1), the last day for filing objections to the sale was __________, _____.

(3) *Survey of Court Records:* Plaintiff has surveyed the docket and records of this case, and has confirmed that as of __________, _____, there were no objections to the sale on file with the Clerk of Court.

THEREFORE, in light of the facts presented above, plaintiff requests the Clerk to enter a Confirmation of Sale and to transmit the confirmation to the Marshal for processing.

DATED at __________, Florida, this _____ day of __________, _____.

____
SIGNED NAME OF PLAINTIFF'S ATTORNEY
Typed Name of Counsel
Fla. Bar ID No. (if admitted in Fla.)
Firm or Business Name
Mailing Address
City, State, Zip Code
Telephone Number
Facsimile Number
E-Mail Address

cc: Counsel of Record

[Amended November 24, 2015.]

FORM 11. CONFIRMATION OF SALE

UNITED STATES DISTRICT COURT
NORTHERN DISTRICT OF FLORIDA
Case No. ___-Civ or Cr-(USDJ's last name/USMJ's last name)
"IN ADMIRALTY"

Plaintiff,
v.
Defendant.

CONFIRMATION OF SALE

The records in this action indicate that no objection has been filed to the sale of property conducted by the U.S. Marshal on ________, ____.

THEREFORE, in accordance with Local Admiralty Rule E(17)(f), the sale shall stand confirmed as of ________, ____.

DONE at __________, Florida, this ____ day of ________, ____.

CLERK

By:
Deputy Clerk

cc: U.S. Marshal
Counsel of Record

[Amended November 24, 2015.]

FORM 12. SUMMONS AND PROCESS OF MARITIME ATTACHMENT AND GARNISHMENT

UNITED STATES DISTRICT COURT
NORTHERN DISTRICT OF FLORIDA
Case No. ____-Civ or Cr-(USDJ's last name/USMJ's last name)
SUMMONS AND PROCESS OF MARITIME ATTACHMENT AND GARNISHMENT
THE PRESIDENT OF THE UNITED
STATES OF AMERICA

TO: THE UNITED STATES MARSHAL FOR THE NORTHERN DISTRICT OF FLORIDA.

GREETING:
WHEREAS, on the ________ day of ____________, ______, ____________________ filed a complaint against ____ for reasons in said complaint mentioned for the sum of and praying for process of marine attachment and garnishment against the said defendant and ____________________,

WHEREAS, this process is issued pursuant to such prayer and requires that a garnishee shall serve his answer within twenty (20) days after service of process upon him and requires that a defendant shall serve his answer within thirty (30) days after process has been executed, whether by attachment of property or service on the garnishee,

NOW, THEREFORE, you are hereby commanded that if the said defendant cannot be found within the District you attach goods, chattels, credits and effects located and to be found at ______and described as follows:____________________________, or in the hands of ________________________, the garnishee, up to the amount sued for, to-wit:

and how you shall have executed this process, make known to this Court with your certificate of execution thereof written.

WITNESS THE HONORABLE

____
Judge of said Court at __________, Florida,
in said District, this ________ day of
__________, ______.

______________________________,

CLERK

BY: ____________________
Deputy Clerk

NOTE: This process is issued pursuant to Rule B(1) of the Supplemental Rules for Certain Admiralty and Maritime Claims of the Federal Rules of Civil Procedure.

[Amended November 24, 2015.]

FORM 13. MARITIME SUMMONS TO SHOW CAUSE RESPECTING INTANGIBLE PROPERTY

UNITED STATES DISTRICT COURT
NORTHERN DISTRICT OF FLORIDA
Case No. ____-Civ or Cr-(USDJ's last name/USMJ's last name)
MARITIME SUMMONS TO SHOW CAUSE
RESPECTING INTANGIBLE PROPERTY

Plaintiff,
vs.
Defendant(s).

TO ALL PERSONS having control of the freight of the vessel ________ or control of the proceeds of the sale of said vessel or control of the proceeds of the sale of any property appurtenant thereto or control of any other intangible property appurtenant thereto.

You are hereby summoned to interpose in writing a claim, by attorney or in proper person, at the Clerk's Office in said District within ten (10) days after the service, and therewith or thereafter within twenty (20) days following such claim or thirty (30) days after the service, whichever is less, a responsive pleading to the complaint herewith served upon you and to show cause why said property under your control should not be paid into court to abide the judgment; and you are required so also to serve copy thereof upon ___________, plaintiff's attorney(s) whose address is __________________; or if you do not claim said property then to so serve and show cause why said property under your control should not be paid into court to abide the judgment.

The service of this summons upon you brings said property within the control of the Court.

Service of this summons is ineffective unless made in time to give notice of the required appearance or such shorter period as the Court may fix by making and signing the form of order provided below:

WITNESS THE HONORABLE

____

Judge of said Court at _________, Florida,
in said District, this ________ day of

_____________, ______.

____________________________,

CLERK

BY: __________________________
Deputy Clerk

Date:

Good cause for shortening the periods required by the foregoing summons having been shown by affidavit of ___________, verified the ______ day of ___________, ______, the period of notice of the appearance in all respects required by the foregoing summons is hereby fixed as ______ days.

Dated at ______, Florida, the _______ day of ___________, ______.

____
UNITED STATES DISTRICT JUDGE

NOTE: This summons is issued pursuant to Rule C(3) of the Supplemental Rules for Certain Admiralty Maritime Claims of the Federal Rules of Civil Procedure.

[Amended November 24, 2015.]

FORM 14. AFFIDAVIT–FOREIGN ATTACHMENT

UNITED STATES DISTRICT COURT
NORTHERN DISTRICT OF FLORIDA

Case No. ____-Civ or Cr-(USDJ's last name/USMJ's last name)

Plaintiff,
v.
Defendant(s).

AFFIDAVIT
(Foreign Attachment)

This affidavit is executed by the undersigned in order to secure the issuance and execution of a Writ of Foreign Attachment in the above-styled in personam cause in admiralty.

As attorney for the above-styled plaintiff, the undersigned does hereby certify to the Court, the Clerk and the Marshal that the undersigned has made a diligent search and inquiry to ascertain the name and address of a person or party upon whom can be served process in personam which will bind the above-styled defendant.

That based upon such diligent search and inquiry the undersigned has been unable to ascertain the name and address of any person or party within the Northern District of Florida upon whom service of process would bind said defendant.

The Clerk of this Court is hereby requested to issue a Writ of Foreign Attachment and deliver the same to the Marshal.

The Marshal is hereby directed to promptly serve said Writ of Foreign Attachment upon ____________ (name of vessel) which vessel is presently located at ____________.

____
Attorney for Plaintiff
Sworn and subscribed to this ______ day of ____________, ______.

Clerk, U.S. District Court
Northern District of Florida

By:
Deputy Clerk

[Amended November 24, 2015.]

ELECTRONIC CASE FILING

ADMINISTRATIVE ORDER ELECTRONIC CASE FILING

Courts are authorized to establish practices and procedures for the filing, signing, and verification of documents by electronic means. See, e.g., Rules 5 and 83, Fed. R. Civ. P., and Rules 49 and 57, Fed. R. Crim. P. This Court elects to do so through its Local Rules and through this administrative order. It is, therefore, ORDERED:

(1) The docketing and case management system for the Northern District of Florida shall be the judiciary's Case Management and Electronic Case Files (CM/ECF) program and the official record of the court shall be the electronic file maintained by the court and such paper files as are permitted by the Clerk's *Attorney User's Manual (User's Manual).*

(2) The Clerk of this Court is authorized to implement and publish *Electronic Case Filing Policies and Procedures (User's Manual) for Civil Cases,* and *Electronic Case Filing Policies and Procedures (User's Manual) for Criminal Cases.* All documents in civil and criminal cases shall be filed as outlined in the current version of the User's Manuals. The provisions in this Administrative Order and the *User's Manuals* are intended to be consistent with the Federal Rules of Civil and Criminal Procedure and this Court's Local Rules. Any conflicts should be brought to the Court's attention immediately.

(3) Commencement of Action.

(A) Civil Cases are commenced with the filing of a complaint. Attorneys may commence a civil case electronically. The procedures for commencing a civil case are contained in the *User's Manual.*

(B) Criminal Cases are commenced with filing of an indictment or information by the government. The procedures for commencing a criminal case are contained in the *User's Manual.*

(4) The electronic filing of a pleading, motion, or other paper by an attorney who is a registered participant in the Electronic Case Filing System shall constitute the signature of the attorney under Federal Rules of Civil and Criminal Procedure.

(5) No attorney shall knowingly permit or cause to permit his/her password to be utilized by any unauthorized person.

(6) The electronic filing of a pleading, motion, or other paper in accordance with the *User's Manuals* shall constitute entry of that document on the docket kept by the Clerk under Federal Rules of Civil Procedure 79.

(7) The Office of Clerk shall enter orders, decrees, judgments, and proceedings of the court in accordance with the *User's Manuals*, which shall constitute entry of the order, decree, judgments, or proceeding on the docket kept by the Clerk under Federal Rule of Civil Procedure 58, and Federal Rules of Criminal Procedure 55.

(8) Registration in the Electronic Filing System and receipt of a password from the court shall constitute consent to receive service and notices electronically.

(9) Service.

(A) Transmission of a notice of electronic filing constitutes service of the filed document upon each party in the case who is registered as a filing user.

(B) Service by electronic means is complete on transmission. Service by electronic means is not effective if the party making service receives an error message or otherwise learns that the attempted service did not reach the person to be served.

(C) Service to a non-filing user shall be carried out through traditional means such as first class mail or hand delivery, or other means.

(10) Attorneys shall not cause any notice, pleading, or other document to be filed on the court's electronic filing system which is not authorized or required by statute or rule.

(11) Public Access to Files.

(A) All documents filed in a case, whether in paper or electronic form, other than sealed documents, may be viewed by any person in the Clerk's Office. Paper documents may be examined only in the division of the Clerk's Office where the paper file, to the extent there is one, is maintained. A person may also obtain access to the CM/ECF system by obtaining a *Public Access to*

Court Electronic Records (PACER) log-in user name and password. A person who has PACER access may view and retrieve docket sheets in civil and criminal cases and documents in civil cases (except Social Security cases). Only counsel for the government and for a defendant may retrieve electronic documents in criminal cases.

(12) A document filed in the court's electronic filing system must be received prior to midnight local time in the division where the case is pending in order to be considered timely filed on that day.

(13) Attorneys and parties shall retain any documents filed electronically where an original signature is required for two years after the document is filed.

(14) *Pro se* litigants who are not attorneys must file all documents with the court in paper form.

This Administrative Order shall be effective on and after **November 12, 2003.**

[Dated: November 28, 2003.]

NOTICE OF ELECTRONIC AVAILABILITY OF CIVIL AND CRIMINAL CASE FILE INFORMATION

The United States District Court for the Northern District of Florida accepts electronically filed pleadings and makes the content of these pleadings available on the court's Internet website via the Case Management/Electronic Case Files ("CM/ECF") system and/or PACER.[1] Any subscriber to CM/ECF and/or PACER will be able to read, download, store, and print the full content of electronically filed documents. The clerk's office will not make electronically available documents that have been sealed or otherwise restricted by court order.

You should not include sensitive information in any document filed with the court unless such inclusion is necessary and relevant to the case. You must remember that any personal information not otherwise protected will be made available over the Internet via CM/ECF and/or WebPACER. If sensitive information must be included, the following personal data identifiers must be partially redacted from the document, whether it is filed traditionally or electronically: Social Security numbers, financial account numbers, dates of birth, the names of minor children, and home addresses of parties. Disclosure of financial account and real property information in public electronic records, as is necessary to properly identify property in foreclosure and forfeiture proceedings, is an allowable exception.

In compliance with the E–Government Act of 2002, a party wishing to file a document containing the personal data identifiers specified above may

(a) file an unredacted document under seal, or

(b) file a reference list under seal.

The court may, however, still require the party to file a redacted copy for the public file.

In addition, exercise caution when filing documents that contain the following:

1. Personal identifying number, such as driver's license number;
2. Medical records, treatment and diagnosis;
3. Employment history;
4. Individual financial information; and
5. Proprietary or trade secret information.

Counsel are strongly urged to share this notice with all clients so that an informed decision about the inclusion of certain materials may be made. If a redacted document is filed, it is the **sole responsibility of counsel and the parties** to be sure that all pleadings comply with this notice requiring redaction of personal data identifiers. Likewise, counsel and the parties will be solely responsible for any unredacted documents filed. **The Clerk's Office will *not* review documents for compliance with this notice, seal on its own motion documents containing personal identifiers, or redact documents, whether filed electronically or on paper.**

1 Remote electronic access to pleadings filed in civil social security cases is limited to counsel of record and court staff. Non–parties have direct access to the pleadings on file at the Clerk's Office.

[Effective November 1, 2004. Amended effective November 14, 2006.]

MISCELLANEOUS ORDERS AND NOTICES

PRO HAC VICE ATTORNEY ADMISSION FEE

This Court has approved a new Local Rule 11.1 regarding admission of attorneys to the bar of this Court, and has changed the requirements for pro hac vice admissions to coincide with admission requirements for regularly admitted attorneys, including allowing attorneys admitted pro hac vice to remain as member of the bar of this Court after their original case has concluded. Therefore, the Clerk is hereby directed to collect a pro hac vice admission fee in the amount of One Hundred Seventy Dollars ($170), payable to the Clerk of this Court.

The $170 pro hac vice fee shall be submitted in accordance with Local Rule 11.1(C)(2), and shall be collected for, and remitted by the Clerk to, the Federal Bench and Bar Fund of the District. This order will be effective June 1, 2004.

All of the judges of this District concur in the entry of this order.

[Effective May 19, 2004.]

MISC. NO. 4:95mc40111. ELECTRONIC DISCLOSURE OF PRESENTENCE REPORTS

The Probation Office for the Northern District of Florida, having developed a secure procedure for disclosing presentence investigation reports to defense counsel representing defendants in criminal cases in this district, has asked for authorization to electronically transmit the presentence investigation reports. The transmission will be accomplished to ensure complete confidentiality of the report in accordance with Local Rule 88.1.

Upon consideration, It is ORDERED that the Probation Office for the Northern District of Florida may electronically transmit presentence investigation reports to defense counsel via the procedure approved by the judges of this district. This procedure shall become effective on July 1, 2004.

This order is entered with the concurrence of all the United States District Judges for the Northern District of Florida.

[Effective June 21, 2004.]

ALLOWABLE ITEMS FOR TAXATION OF COSTS

Under Local Rule 54.2, costs are taxable in the first instance by the clerk of the court, subject to review by the court on motion filed within five days after entry of the clerk's decision. Recognizing that taxation of costs is subject to various interpretations, but recognizing that some guidance is necessary to assist the clerk in performing the duty to initially determine what costs are to be taxed, the following guidelines are implemented to assist the clerk in performing such duty, while preserving to the litigants the right to seek, or oppose, taxation of any item, and are not meant to remove or restrict the discretion of any judge in determining the taxability of such item on review of the clerk's decision. The clerk will tax costs based on the standards set forth in this administrative order and subject to the clerk's determination of the reasonableness of the amounts claimed. Requests for departure from these standards shall be noted in the original request for (or objection to) taxation of costs by the clerk and then included in a motion for review by the court after entry of the clerk's decision. Inclusion or exclusion of a category of costs from these standards expresses no view of the court on whether such costs ultimately should or should not be taxed on review by the court in a particular case; the intent of this order is to create a clear rule that will be followed by the clerk, with any appropriate adjustments made by the court based on applicable law separate and apart from this order. Costs incurred in a state court prior to removal are taxable to the same extent as if incurred in this court after removal.

The clerk will tax the following costs:

1. Filing fees paid to the clerk of court.

2. Fees for service of process in an amount not exceeding the amount that would be charged by the United States Marshal for performing the same service.

3. Fees of a court reporter for attendance at, and for the original and a party's first copy of a transcript of, any trial, hearing, or deposition in the case at bar.

4. Fees actually paid to witnesses who were subpoenaed and testified at a trial, hearing, or deposition, for attendance and travel, in an amount not exceeding the statutory rate, and fees for service of subpoenas on such witnesses. Expert witness fees in excess of those payable to nonexpert witnesses are not taxable.

5. The fee paid or cost incurred internally for copies made for the court and adverse parties of exhibits, pleadings, or other papers filed with the court, not including copies of papers that were or properly should have been filed and served electronically. The cost of enlargements, special graphics, computer presentations and animations, and physical exhibits or models will not be taxed by the clerk.

6. The fee of an interpreter incurred in connection with the testimony of a non-English speaking witness at a trial, hearing, or deposition.

7. The fee of a competent translator of a non-English document that is filed or admitted into evidence.

8. Fees taxable under 28 U.S.C. § 1923.

This order is entered with the concurrence of the judges of the Court.

[Effective September 21, 2004.]

MEDIA GUIDELINES

(1) Court Orders/Web Page/Electronic Access to Court Records. The Court speaks through its orders. Copies of court orders, pleadings, and other court file documents are available in the Clerk's Offices in the Northern District of Florida. The cost is 50 cents per page. The Court's web site, www. flnd.uscourts.gov, contains information pertaining to orders, schedules, notices, and filings. Current docket sheets and documents in most pending civil and criminal cases are also available electronically over the Internet through the Court's CM/ECF system. In order to access the system, you will need a national PACER (Public Access to Court Electronic Records) account. To obtain a PACER account, contact the PACER Service Center at:

PACER Service Center, P.O. Box 780549
San Antonio, TX 78278
(800) 676–6856 or (210) 301–6440
www.pacer.psc.uscourts.gov

(2) Cameras and Recording Equipment. Cameras and video or sound recording equipment are permitted in a courthouse of the United States District Court for the Northern District of Florida only if a judicial officer of the Court, or a court-authorized official, has approved in advance the use of the equipment within the courthouse. Such approval for limited use is normally given upon request for Naturalization Ceremonies, Investitures, and other ceremonial events.

(3) Cell Phones and Electronic Equipment. Cellular phones, pagers, two-way radios, laptop computers, and other electronic equipment must be checked in at the courthouse entrance security desk, and any use thereof is only permitted within the entrance lobby and within plain view of the entrance area security officers, unless prior authorization has been received from the presiding judicial officer. Court approval for courtroom use of laptop computers by attorneys will normally be granted upon request.

(4) Interviews. Media interviews may be conducted in the area outside the front entrances to the courthouses of the U.S. District Court for the Northern District of Florida, as long as there is no interference with normal ingress and egress and no harassment of persons involved in, or observing, court proceedings. No media interviews shall be conducted within the courthouses without the prior approval of the presiding judicial officer. In the event of inclement weather, interviews may upon request be permitted in the lobbies of the courthouses, subject to any conditions set by the Court. In high profile or highly publicized cases, and with prior authorization by the presiding judicial officer, the counsel of record may arrange for press conferences or media interviews to be conducted, subject to any conditions set by the Court.

(5) Communications With Jurors. Media representatives shall not communicate with jurors or their families during any jury selection or trial and are prohibited from communicating at any time with grand jurors about any matter which occurred or may occur before the grand jury, including after the grand jury has completed its service. Media representatives are prohibited from entering the jury assembly areas, grand jury rooms, and the jury deliberation room at any time during jury selection and trial (including recesses).

(6) Security in Courthouses. All persons, including media representatives, entering the federal courthouses in the Northern District of Florida are required to pass through an electronic metal detector and present any bags, parcels, brief cases, equipment, etc. for inspection. Presentation of photo identification is also required.

(7) Compliance. The Court and the United States Marshals Service will enforce these guidelines. Failure to comply with any of these guidelines may result in sanctions.

(8) Approval by Court. These guidelines were approved by the Court on March 26th, 2004 and are effective immediately.

[Effective March 26, 2004.]

MISC. NO. 4:95mc40111. IN RE: POLICY AND PROCEDURES REGARDING REFUND OF FEES PAID ELECTRONICALLY (PAY.GOV)

The Judicial Conference of the United States has a long-standing policy prohibiting the refund of fees. This policy was relatively easy to administer in a paper environment; however, issues have been raised since the implementation of Case Management/ Electronic Case Filing (CM/ECF), which encompasses the ability to collect filing fees electronically using a credit card via Pay.gov. Difficulties with the application of the refund policy have greatly increased as filing parties can inadvertently make erroneous or duplicate payments on line.

The Judicial Conference has endorsed a process which addresses only limited refund authority by the court when user errors in electronic payments are made. This policy is intended to serve as guidance to the Clerk of Court in determining when to exercise his discretion in addressing refund of fees paid electronically via Pay.gov.

- ♦ This policy addresses only limited refund authority by the court when errors in electronic payments are made.
- ♦ If the court discovers an erroneous filing for which a fee has not yet been collected, the court may correct the erroneous filing administratively and not collect the fee.
- ♦ Requests for refunds after the fee has already been collected must be made by written application to the Clerk of Court.
- ♦ If a refund request is granted, the refund will be processed through the electronic credit card system, Pay.gov; no refunds will be issued through the use of Treasury checks.
- ♦ If the Clerk determines that a refund is not warranted and the party disagrees, a motion may be filed with the court within ten (10) days of such determination requesting that the Chief Judge review the same.

[Effective October 9, 2007.]

IN RE: STANDING ORDER OF REFERENCE REGARDING TITLE 11

Pursuant to 28 U.S.C. Section 157(a) all cases under Title 11 (Bankruptcy) and all proceedings arising under Title 11 (Bankruptcy) or arising in or related to a case under Title 11 (Bankruptcy) are referred to the bankruptcy judge(s) of this district.

If a bankruptcy judge or district judge determines that entry of a final order or judgment by a bankruptcy judge in a particular proceeding referred under this order and determined to be a core matter would not be consistent with Article III of the United States Constitution, the bankruptcy judge shall, unless otherwise ordered by the district court, hear the proceeding and submit proposed findings of fact and conclusions of law to the district court. The district court may treat any order of the bankruptcy court as proposed findings of fact and conclusions of law in the event the district court concludes that the bankruptcy judge could not have entered a final order or judgment consistent with Article III of the United States Constitution.

[Effective June 5, 2012.]

CRIMINAL JUSTICE ACT PLAN

I. AUTHORITY. Pursuant to the Criminal Justice Act of 1964 (18 U.S.C. § 3006A) [hereinafter referred to as CJA], and the *Guidelines for the Administration of the Criminal Justice Act,* Volume VII, *Guide to Judiciary Policies and Procedures* (CJA Guidelines), the Judges of the United States District Court for the Northern District of Florida adopt the following amended plan for furnishing representation in federal court to any person financially unable to obtain adequate representation.

II. STATEMENT OF POLICY.

A. Objectives.

1. The principal objective of this Plan is to attain the goal of equality before the law for all persons. This plan, therefore, shall be administered so that those accused of crime, or otherwise eligible for service pursuant to the CJA, will not be deprived, because they are financially unable to pay for adequate representation, of any element of representation necessary to an effective defense.

2. The further objective of this Plan is to particularize the requirements of the CJA and the CJA Guidelines in a way that meets the needs of this District.

B. Compliance.

1. The Court, its Clerk, the Federal Public Defender's Office, and private attorneys appointed under the CJA shall comply with the CJA Guidelines approved by the Judicial Conference of the United States and/or its Committee on Defender Services and with this Plan.

2. Each private attorney shall be provided by the Clerk of Court with a then-current copy of this Plan upon the attorney's first appointment under the CJA or designation as a member of the Panel of Private Attorneys under the Criminal Justice Act (CJA Panel). The Clerk shall maintain a current copy of the CJA Guidelines for the use of members of the CJA Panel and shall make known to such attorneys its availability.

III. PROVISION OF REPRESENTATION.

A. Representation *shall* be provided in this District for any financially eligible person who:

1. is charged with a felony;

2. is charged with a misdemeanor, unless the charge is a petty offense for which incarceration will not be imposed;

3. is a juvenile alleged to have committed an act of juvenile delinquency as defined in 18 U.S.C. § 5031;

4. is charged with a violation of probation or supervised release in a felony case or a misdemeanor case in which a term of imprisonment may be imposed (unless the presiding judicial officer announces in advance that a term of imprisonment will not be imposed);

5. is under arrest, when such representation is required by law;

6. is entitled to appointment of counsel in parole proceedings;

7. is subject to a mental condition hearing under 18 U.S.C. § 4241–4247;

8. is in custody as a material witness;

9. is seeking to set aside or vacate a death sentence under Sections 2254 or 2255 of Title 28, United States Code;

10. is entitled to appointment of counsel in verification of consent proceedings pursuant to a transfer of an offender to or from the United States for the execution of a penal sentence under 18 U.S.C. § 4109;

11. is entitled to appointment of counsel under the Sixth Amendment to the Constitution; or

12. faces loss of liberty in a case, and federal law requires the appointment of counsel.

B. Whenever the judicial officer determines that the interests of justice so require, representation *may* be provided in this District for a financially eligible person who

1. is charged with a petty offense (Class B or C misdemeanor, or an infraction) for which a sentence to confinement is authorized;

2. is seeking relief, other than to set aside or vacate a death sentence under 28 U.S.C. § 2241, 2254, or 2255;

3. is charged with civil or criminal contempt and faces a loss of liberty;

4. has been called as a witness before a grand jury, a court, the Congress, or a federal agency or commission which has the power to compel testimony, and there is reason to believe, either prior to or during testimony, that the witness could be subject to a criminal prosecution, a civil or criminal contempt proceeding, or faces a loss of liberty;

5. is proposed by the United States Attorney for processing under a pretrial diversion program; or

6. is held for international extradition under Chapter 209 of Title 18, United States Code.

IV. ESTABLISHMENT OF THE FEDERAL PUBLIC DEFENDER ORGANIZATION. The Court continues to find that the use of a Federal Public Defender Organization in this District, as defined in 18 U.S.C. § 3006A(g)(2)(A), is appropriate and should continue. The Federal Public Defender shall submit to the Director of the Administrative Office of the United States Courts, at the time and in the form prescribed, reports of the office's activities and the financial position and proposed budget of the office. Copies of the reports shall be furnished to this Court and to the Judicial Council for the Eleventh Circuit. Neither the Federal Public Defender, nor any staff attorney appointed as an Assistant Federal Public Defender, may engage in the private practice of law.

V. CRIMINAL JUSTICE ACT PANEL.

A. *Formation of a Standing Committee to Oversee the Criminal Justice Act Panel.*

1. The Judges of the United States District Court for the Northern District of Florida hereby create a standing committee to oversee the CJA Panel. This committee shall consist of the Federal Public Defender or his or her designee and four attorneys who are engaged in the private practice of law and appointed by the Chief Judge of the District. Preferably, each of the private attorneys should come from a different division within the district. Each member of the standing committee shall be a voting member, and possess sufficient experience and interest in the federal criminal justice system to administer the CJA Panel.

2. The Federal Public Defender or his or her representative shall be a permanent member of the committee. The Clerk of Court or his or her designee shall be an ex officio, non-voting member of the committee.

3. Appointments will be made for two-year terms. The standing committee will be permitted to use the staff of the Clerk for clerical and record-keeping matters.

4. The standing committee shall meet formally at least twice a year. In addition to reviewing panel membership, the committee shall identify and define any operating difficulties encountered in the administration of the Panel and make recommendations to the Court for appropriate changes.

5. The standing committee shall also coordinate with the Federal Public Defender's Office, and the panel representative, training efforts for the CJA Panel. Such training shall include correspondence with panel attorneys on substantive and procedural changes in the law, local rules, and other matters affecting the panel attorneys. The training shall also include an annual seminar. The Federal Public Defender shall be responsible for presenting the training seminar to the panel attorneys.

B. *Membership of the CJA Panel.*

1. Pursuant to the terms of this Plan, CJA panel attorneys shall be members of the bar of this District. In addition to bar membership, the panel attorneys should have prior federal and/or state criminal trial experience, significant involvement in serious or complex criminal cases, knowledge of the Sentencing Guidelines and the Bail Reform Act, and knowledge of other relevant areas of criminal practice.

2. The Panel shall consist of attorneys recommended by the standing committee and approved by a judge of the District.

3. Those attorneys approved by a District Judge are appointed for a three-year term. As the expiration of the three-year term approaches, the standing committee shall provide the Chief Judge with the names of those lawyers that, in the view of the committee, should continue for another three-year term. The Chief Judge shall consider the recommendations of the committee,

and issue a letter or order reappointing those attorneys the Chief Judge wishes to continue serving on the panel. The responsibility for initiating this process rests with the standing committee, and there is no need for a panel member to reapply for appointment.

4. To maintain their continued eligibility to serve on the Panel each attorney shall attend annually the training seminar presented by the Federal Public Defender's Office, or inform the Office of the Public Defender of their participation in a seminar or training session that addresses the practice of federal criminal law.

5. An attorney may, during his or her three-year term, be removed from the Panel by a majority vote of the district judges.

VI. ASSIGNMENT OF CASES TO THE CJA PANEL.

A. The Federal Public Defender's Office shall be responsible for overseeing the assignment of cases to panel attorneys. That responsibility shall include the obligation to contact the panel member regarding the assignment, to secure the panel member's agreement to represent the defendant, and to notify the Clerk of the assignment. It also includes the obligation of assisting the Court in its assignment of the appropriate number of cases to panel members. Assignments shall be made on a rotational basis except where, due to the nature and complexity of the case, an attorney's experience, and geographical considerations, require otherwise.

B. The Federal Public Defender's Office shall maintain a master list of CJA appointments, which will include the date of each appointment, the case name, the date of each refusal ("pass") by a panel attorney, and the reason for each pass.

C. If the Federal Public Defender's Office determines that a panel member has repeatedly passed assignments, the Federal Public Defender's Office may refer the name of the attorney to the standing committee. The standing committee shall then consider the information provided by the Federal Public Defender's Office and make such further inquiry as it deems appropriate.

D. The Federal Public Defender's Office shall also maintain a public record of assignments to the Federal Public Defender's Office and to the CJA Panel, as well as current statistical data reflecting the proration of appointments.

VII. DUTIES OF LAW ENFORCEMENT AND RELATED AGENCIES.

A. *Presentation of Accused for Appointment of Counsel.* The United States Attorney or designee or the United States Marshal or designee shall contact the Clerk of the Court and arrange to have the arrested person promptly presented before a judicial officer for determination of financial eligibility and appointment of counsel.

B. *Pretrial Service Interview.* Prior to any probation officer or pretrial services officer interviewing a person subject to proceedings under 18 U.S.C. § 3142 et seq., the officer shall ask any person who is in custody, or who otherwise may be entitled to counsel under the Criminal Justice Act, whether he or she is financially able to secure representation. In those cases where the person says that he or she is unable to do so, the officer shall notify the Federal Public Defender's Office. The Federal Public Defender or his or her representative may offer advice to the person prior to the pretrial interview or may also attend the interview itself for the purpose of providing assistance. If a representative from the Federal Public Defender's Office chooses to be present for the interview, he or she must report promptly to the interview so as to afford the pretrial services officer adequate time to complete the interview and verify information prior to the court appearance. Should there be no one available from the Federal Public Defender's Office who can promptly appear, or should the Federal Public Defender's Office choose not to appear, the pretrial officer may begin and complete the interview.

C. *Notice of Indictment or Criminal Information.* The Clerk of the Court shall, no later than first appearance, provide the accused with a copy of the applicable indictment, information, or petition to modify or revoke probation.

VIII. DETERMINATION OF NEED FOR COUNSEL.

A. *Counsel for Persons Appearing Without an Attorney.* In every case in which a person is eligible for appointment of counsel pursuant to 18 U.S.C. § 3006A(a) and the person appears without counsel, the judicial officer shall advise that person that he or she has a right to be represented by counsel throughout the case and that counsel will be appointed to represent the person if so desired, if he or she is financially unable to obtain counsel.

Whenever the person states that he or she is financially unable to obtain counsel and desires the appointment of counsel, the judicial officer shall inquire into and make a finding as to whether the person is financially able to obtain counsel.

B. *Counsel for Persons Appearing With an Attorney.* Where an arrested person has been represented by counsel before his or her presentation before a judicial officer under circumstances where such representation is authorized by 18 U.S.C. § 3006A(a), counsel may subsequently apply to the judicial officer for approval of compensation. If an application is made to a Magistrate Judge, the Magistrate Judge shall submit a recommendation to a Judge of this Court for final approval. If the Judge finds that the person has been and is then financially unable to obtain an adequate defense, and that representation was required by law, compensation will be made retroactive pursuant to 18 U.S.C. § 3006A(b).

IX. APPOINTMENT OF COUNSEL.

A. *The Judicial Officer.*

1. In every case in which appointment of counsel pursuant to 18 U.S.C. § 3006A(a) is appropriate, the judicial officer shall appoint counsel promptly if it is found that the person is financially unable to obtain an attorney, unless the person waives his or her right to be represented by counsel.

2. The judicial officer shall appoint the Federal Public Defender's Office or counsel from the CJA Panel, except in circumstances where, in the interest of justice, it becomes necessary to appoint some other qualified counsel. The person shall not have the right to select his or her appointed counsel from the Federal Public Defender's Office, from the CJA Panel, or otherwise.

3. Pursuant to 18 U.S.C. § 3005, a person charged with a capital offense is entitled to the appointment of two attorneys, at least one of whom shall be learned in the law applicable to capital cases. In appointing counsel in federal capital prosecutions, the Court shall consider the recommendation of the Federal Public Defender. If following the appointment of counsel in a case in which a defendant was charged with an offense that may be punishable by death, it is determined that the death penalty will not be sought, the Court may reconsider the question of the number of counsel needed.

4. If, at any time after the appointment of counsel, the judicial officer finds that the person is financially able to obtain counsel or make partial payment for the representation, the judicial officer may terminate the appointment of counsel or recommend that any funds available to the person be ordered paid as provided in 18 U.S.C. § 3006A(f).

5. If at any stage of the trial proceedings, the judicial officer finds that the person is financially unable to continue to pay retained counsel, the judicial officer may make an original appointment of counsel in accordance with the general procedure set forth in this Plan.

6. If a person having a right to counsel (i.e., where the appointment is not a matter of discretion) is not represented by counsel before the judicial officer and seeks to waive his or her right to have appointed counsel, the judicial officer shall make appropriate inquiry regarding such a waiver. If the person admits or the judicial officer finds that the person is financially able to obtain counsel but declines to do so, the judicial officer shall certify that fact in the record of the proceedings.

B. *The Clerk.* If a person having a right to counsel desires to have counsel appointed, then

(a) if no affidavit of financial ability to employ counsel has been filed with the Clerk, a form of affidavit shall promptly be sent to the person, to be filled out by the person and returned to the Clerk; or

(b) if the notice to the Clerk includes an affidavit of financial inability to employ counsel, the Clerk shall promptly communicate with a judicial officer for consideration of the appointment of counsel.

C. *Obligation of Counsel.*

1. The services to be rendered a person represented by appointed counsel shall be commensurate with those rendered if counsel were privately employed by the person.

2. Attorneys appointed pursuant to the CJA shall conform to the highest standards of professional conduct, including but not limited to the provisions of The Florida Bar's Rules of Professional Conduct and Guidelines for Professional Conduct.

3. Counsel appointed by a judicial officer shall, unless excused by order of court, continue to act for the person throughout the proceedings in this Court. Appointed counsel is expected to appear personally at all proceedings, with substitutions or the filing of additional appearances permitted only with leave of the Court. The judicial officer before whom a case is pending may, in the interest of justice, substitute one appointed counsel for another at any stage of the proceedings.

4. If at any time after appointment, counsel obtains information that a client is financially able to make payment, in whole or in part, for legal or other services in connection with his or her representation, and the source of the attorney's information is not protected as a privileged communication, counsel shall advise the Court.

5. In all criminal cases, appointed counsel shall advise the defendant of the right to appeal and of the right to counsel on appeal. If requested to do so by the defendant in a criminal case, counsel shall file a timely Notice of Appeal, and shall continue to represent the defendant, unless, or until, relieved by the district court or the court of appeals.

X. INVESTIGATIVE, EXPERT, AND OTHER SERVICES. Counsel (whether or not appointed under the Act) for a person who is financially unable to obtain investigative, expert, or other services necessary for an adequate defense in his or her case may request such services in an ex parte application before a judicial officer, as provided in 18 U.S.C. § 3006A(e)(1). Upon finding that the services are necessary, and that the person is financially unable to obtain them, the judicial officer shall authorize counsel to obtain the services.

Appointed counsel may obtain, subject to later judicial review, investigative, expert, or other services without prior authorization, pursuant to the dollar limitation set out in 18 U.S.C. § 3006A(e)(2).

Counsel shall comply with all provisions regarding financial limitations and requests for services, as set forth in 18 U.S.C. § 3006A(e), and any guidelines or regulations approved by the Judicial Conference of the United States.

XI. COMPENSATION. Payment of fees and expenses to counsel appointed under this Plan (other than to the Federal Public Defender's Office), and payment for investigative, expert, and other services incurred, shall be made in accordance with any statutory limitations and such rules, regulations, and guidelines, as have been or may be prescribed from time to time by the Judicial Conference of the United States, and in accordance with the fiscal policies of the Administrative Office of the United States Courts. No appointed counsel may request or accept any payment or promise of payment for assisting in the representation of a person, unless such payment is approved by order of court. Payment in excess of any maximum amount provided by statute or otherwise may be made for extended or complex representation, whenever the court in which the representation was rendered certifies that the amount of the excess payment is necessary to provide fair compensation, and the payment is approved by the Chief Judge of the Eleventh Circuit or the Chief Judge's designee.

Claims for compensation of private attorneys providing representation under the CJA shall be submitted on the appropriate CJA form to the office of the Clerk of Court. That office shall review the claim form for mathematical and technical accuracy and for conformity with the CJA Guidelines and, if the claim is correct in form, shall forward the claim form for the consideration of the appropriate judge or magistrate judge. After review of any submissions by appointed counsel and the completion of any other steps deemed appropriate by the Court, the judicial officer shall take action on the voucher, consistent with this Plan, the CJA, and the interests of justice.

XII. FORMS. Where standard forms have been approved by the Judicial Conference of the United States or an appropriate committee thereof, and have been distributed by the Administrative Office, such forms shall be used by the Court, the Clerk, the judicial officers, the Federal Public Defender's Office, and counsel.

XIII. EFFECTIVE DATE. This Plan, as amended this 27th day of June, 2000, shall take effect when approved by the Judicial Council of the Eleventh Circuit. This Plan supersedes all prior Criminal Justice Act plans of this Court.

PLAN FOR THE RANDOM SELECTION OF GRAND AND PETIT JURORS

Pursuant to the Jury Selection and Service Act of 1968, Title 28, U.S. Code, Section 1861, et seq., as amended ("the Act"), the following Plan for the Random Selection of Grand and Petit Jurors ("Plan") is hereby adopted by the United States District Court for the Northern District of Florida.

I. Effective Date and Duration. This Plan supersedes any and all plans and amendments heretofore adopted and shall become effective upon approval by the Eleventh Circuit Reviewing Panel, as provided in Title 28, U.S. Code, Section 1863(a). It shall remain in force and effect until modified by the Court with the approval of the Reviewing Panel.

II. Policy.

A. The purpose of this Plan is to implement the policies of the United States as set forth in Title 28, U.S. Code, Section 1861:

1. That all litigants in federal courts entitled to trial by jury shall have the right to grand and petit juries selected at random from a fair cross section of the community in the district or division wherein the court convenes;

2. That all citizens shall have the opportunity to be considered for service on grand and petit juries in the district courts of the United States; and

3. That all citizens shall have an obligation to serve as jurors when summonsed for that purpose.

B. It is further the purpose of this Plan to implement the prohibition against discrimination contained in Title 28, U.S. Code, Section 1862. That section provides that no citizen shall be excluded from service as a grand or petit juror in the district courts of the United States on account of race, color, religion, sex, national origin, or economic status.

III. Definitions. For purposes of this Plan:

A. "Clerk" or "Clerk of Court" shall mean the Clerk of the United States District Court for the Northern District of Florida, any authorized deputy clerk, and any other person authorized by the court to assist the Clerk in the performance of duties pursuant to this Plan;

B. "Chief Judge" shall mean the Chief Judge of the United States District Court for the Northern District of Florida;

C. "Voter registration lists" shall mean the official records maintained by state or county election officials of persons registered to vote in either the most recent state or the most recent federal general election;

D. "Master jury wheel" or "master wheel" is a term designating all names selected directly from official voter registration lists in a manner prescribed in this Plan;

E. "Qualified jury wheel" or "qualified wheel" is a term designating the names of all persons determined to be qualified to serve as grand or petit jurors according to the manner prescribed in this Plan;

F. "Qualification form" or "qualification questionnaire" shall mean a form prescribed by the Administrative Office of the United States Courts and approved by the Judicial Conference of the United States, which shall elicit certain information about a prospective juror;

G. "Jury summons" shall mean a summons issued by the Clerk, containing a preprinted or stamped seal of the court, the name of the Clerk, and instructions to appear for jury service;

H. "Petit juror" shall mean a juror summonsed to serve at a civil or criminal trial proceeding; and

I. "Grand juror" shall mean a juror summonsed to serve on a grand jury in one of the divisions of this court.

IV. Applicability. The Northern District of Florida is hereby divided for jury selection purposes into four divisions, which are identical with the statutory composition of the district. Those divisions are:

A. Pensacola Division which consists of the counties of Escambia, Okaloosa, Santa Rosa, and Walton;

B. Tallahassee Division which consists of the counties of Franklin, Gadsden, Jefferson, Leon, Liberty, Madison, Taylor, and Wakulla;

C. Gainesville Division which consists of the counties of Alachua, Dixie, Gilchrist, Lafayette, and Levy; and

D. Panama City Division which consists of the counties of Bay, Calhoun, Gulf, Holmes, Jackson, and Washington.

The provisions of this Plan apply to all the divisions of the district unless otherwise indicated.

V. Management and Supervision of the Jury Selection Process. The Clerk, under the supervision and control of the Chief Judge or any judge or judges that the Chief Judges may designate, shall manage the jury selection process. Such management shall be consistent with this Plan and Title 28, U.S.C. Section 1861, et seq. The Clerk may use computers and other automation technologies in implementing this Plan and shall maintain operational guidelines to govern such use. The Clerk also may hire or contract with persons or entities to perform the duties set forth in this Plan, as long as the Clerk supervises the work of such persons or entities and receives written certification from them that work has been completed pursuant to the instructions of the Clerk.

VI. Formula for the Method and Manner of Random Selection of Jurors.

A. At the option of the Clerk, and after consultation with the Court, the selection of names from complete source list databases in electronic media for the master jury wheels may be accomplished by a purely randomized process through a properly programmed electronic data processing system. Similarly, at the option of the Clerk, and after consultation with the Court, a properly programmed electronic data processing system for a purely randomized selection may be used to select names from the master wheels for the purpose of determining qualification for jury service and from the qualified wheels for summonsing persons to serve as grand or petit jurors. Such random selections of names from the source lists for inclusion in the master wheels by data computer personnel must ensure that each county within each division is substantially proportionally represented in the master wheels in accordance with Title 28, U.S. Code, Section 1863(b)(3). The selections of names from the source lists, the master wheels, and the qualified wheels must ensure that the mathematical odds of any single name being selected are substantially equal.

B. Alternatively, the random selection of names from the source lists, master wheels, and qualified wheels may be accomplished through a properly programmed electronic data processing system using a "starting number" and "quotient" formula. This formula will ensure that any group of names selected will represent all segments of source records from which names are drawn and that the mathematical odds of any single name being selected are substantially equal.

1. The "quotient" is the number of names in the source list or wheel, divided by the number of names wanted in any one drawing; i.e., the increment of names passed for each name selected. For example, if there are 200,000 names on the voter registration list, and 4,000 of those names are necessary to establish the master wheel, the "quotient" for this drawing would be 50 (200,000 divided by 4,000 equals 50). Or, if there are 2,000 names in the qualified wheel and the court wishes to summons 100 jurors, the "quotient" for this drawing would be 20 (2,000 divided by 100 equals 20).

2. The "starting number" is a number drawn by lot from a box containing consecutively numbered cards covering the same range of numbers as the "quotient." For example, in the qualified wheel drawing mentioned above, the Clerk would place consecutively numbered cards from 1 to 20 in a box and draw one number. If the randomly picked number was 5, the 5th name in the wheel would be selected and every 20th name thereafter would be selected; i.e., 5th name, 25th name, 45th name, etc.

3. Randomly drawing a "starting number" by lot establishes the location on the list or wheel from which the first name is selected; removes the possibility of human discretion or choice in selection of any individual name, making individual name selection unpredictable and unpredeterminable; and ensures that, at the outset of the drawing, mathematical odds of being picked are substantially equal for all names in the source from which drawn.

VII. Master Wheels.

A. *Source Lists.* The Court finds that the voter registration lists contain names which represent a fair cross-section of the community in the Northern District of Florida and that the policy, purpose and intent of the Act will be fully accomplished and implemented by the use of voter registration lists as the source for names of prospective grand and petit jurors. Accordingly, the names of all grand

and petit jurors shall be selected at random from the voter registration lists maintained in machine readable forms by the by the various county supervisors of election or the Division of Elections of the Department of State of the State of Florida.

Such random selections of grand and petit jurors from voter registration lists may be made by either of the following methods, so long as they comply in all respects with this Plan:

1. The Clerk may obtain copies of the complete voter registration lists from the various county supervisors of election or the Division of Elections of the Department of State of the State of Florida. The Clerk shall make the random selection of names pursuant to this Plan from such list or lists; or,

2. The Clerk may authorize the various county supervisors of election or the Division of Elections of the Department of State of the State of Florida, acting in accordance with specific instructions from the Clerk, to select at random the required number of names from the voter registration lists of the counties that comprise the Northern District of Florida.

B. *Establishment of Master Wheels.* The names which are chosen through either of the two methods listed above will be used to fill the appropriate master wheels. The Clerk is required to maintain a separate master wheel for each division in the district, as described in Section IV of this Plan. The names and addresses of all persons randomly selected from the voter registration lists from each division shall be placed in the respective master wheel for each division.

C. *Number of Names to Be Drawn.* The master wheels shall be emptied and refilled between January 1 and September 1 of each odd-numbered year (2001, 2003, etc.) unless the Chief Judge directs otherwise. The total number of names drawn for each division shall be sufficient, as determined by the Clerk, to accommodate all grand and petit jurors required in the district for a period of two years after each refill, but at a minimum the total number of names shall be at least one half of 1 percent of the total number of names on the voter registration lists for each division. The Chief Judge may order additional names to be placed in any master wheel at any time.

VIII. Qualified Wheels.

A. *Establishment of Qualified Wheels.*

1. The Clerk shall maintain a separate qualified wheel for each division in the district.

2. From time to time as the need arises, the Clerk shall publicly draw at random from the master wheel of each division in the manner set forth in Section VI of this Plan the names of persons to whom questionnaires will be sent for the purpose of examining their qualifications for jury service.

3. The Clerk shall place in the qualified wheel for each division the names of all persons drawn from the master wheel of that division who, upon return of their questionnaires, are found not to be disqualified, exempt, or excused pursuant to this Plan. The Clerk shall ensure that at all times a sufficient number of names is contained in each of the divisional qualified wheels so that the grand and petit jury pools may be drawn at any time required by the Court.

4. Unless the Chief Judge directs otherwise, the qualified wheel of each division shall be emptied and refilled during each odd-numbered year as soon as the process of qualifying jurors from the new master wheels has produced a sufficient number of qualified jurors who represent a fair cross section of the community to meet the needs of the court.

B. *Qualification Questionnaires.*

1. After determining the number of names to be drawn from the master wheel of each division, as determined by the Clerk to meet the needs of the court, a qualification questionnaire shall be mailed by the Clerk to each person whose name has been drawn from the master wheels. The qualification questionnaire shall be executed and returned within ten days of receipt by the juror. If the person to whom the qualification questionnaire is sent is unable to complete it, another person shall complete it and indicate on the qualification questionnaire why such action was necessary.

2. Whenever an omission, ambiguity, or error in the execution of the qualification questionnaire is apparent, the Clerk shall return the form to the prospective juror, with instructions to make any necessary corrections and to return the corrected form to the Clerk within ten days.

3. Pursuant to Title 28 U.S. Code, Section 1864(a), a person who fails to return a completed qualification questionnaire as instructed may be summonsed by the Clerk to fill out a qualification questionnaire.

C. *Determination of Qualification for Jury Service.*

1. The Clerk, under the supervision of the court, shall determine solely on the basis of information provided on the qualification questionnaire whether a person is qualified for jury service, or unqualified for, or exempt, or to be excused from jury service. The Clerk shall record such determination on the qualification questionnaire or on the person's record in the court's electronic database. The Clerk shall also note the failure of a prospective juror to return the qualification questionnaire or to appear in response to a summons because of failure to return the qualification questionnaire as instructed.

2. Pursuant to Title 28, U.S. Code, Section 1865(b), any person shall be determined to be qualified to serve as a grand or petit juror in this district unless he or she:

a. Is not a citizen of the United States;

b. Is not 18 years old or older;

c. Has not resided for a period of one year within this district;

d. Is unable to read, write and understand the English language with a degree of proficiency sufficient to complete satisfactorily the qualification questionnaire;

e. Is unable to speak the English language;

f. Is incapable, by reason of mental or physical infirmity, to render satisfactory jury service;

g. Has a charge pending against him or her for the commission of a crime punishable by imprisonment for more than one year; or

h. Has been convicted in a state or federal court of record of a crime punishable by imprisonment for more than one year and has not had his or her civil rights restored.

D. *Exemptions From Jury Service.* Pursuant to Title 28, U.S. Code, Section 1863(b)(6), the Court finds that exempting the following groups of persons or occupational classes from jury service is in the public interest and would not be inconsistent with the Act:

1. Members in active service of the Armed Forces of the United States;

2. Members of the fire or police departments of any state, district, territory or possession, or any subdivision thereof, but not members of any voluntary organizations;

3. Public officers in the executive, legislative, or judicial branches of the government of the United States, or any state, district, territory; or possession, or any subdivision thereof who are actively engaged in the performance of official duties. Public officer shall mean a person who is either elected to public office or who is an officer directly appointed by a person elected to public office.

E. *Excuses From Jury Service.*

1. Permanent Excuses for Life of the Master Wheels. Pursuant to Title 28, U.S. Code, Section 1863(b)(5)(A) and (B), the Court hereby finds that members of the following occupational classes or groups of persons would endure undue hardship or extreme inconvenience if required to perform jury service and, therefore, shall be excused from such service upon individual request:

a. A person over 70 years of age;

b. A person who has served as a grand or petit juror in federal court within the last two years;

c. A person having active care and custody of a child or children under 10 years of age, whose health and/or safety would be jeopardized by any absence for jury service;

d. A person having active care and custody of, or who is essential to the care of, aged or infirm persons;

e. A person whose services are so essential to the operation of a commercial or agricultural enterprise that it would close or cease to function if such person were required to perform jury service; or

f. A person who serves as a volunteer firefighter, rescue squad member or ambulance crew member in an official capacity, without compensation, in a public agency. Public agency means the United States, or any state, district, territory or possession, or any subdivision thereof.

2. Temporary Excuses.

a. Any person summonsed for jury service may be excused temporarily by the Clerk upon a showing of undue hardship or extreme inconvenience. Such excuse may be for specific dates within the term for which the juror was summonsed or for such period of time as the Clerk or the Court deems necessary.

b. If a juror is excused temporarily, the name of the juror shall be returned to the qualified wheel for selection or deferred to a specific date.

c. A juror shall be notified, orally or in writing or both, whether or not his or her request to be excused has been granted.

F. *Exclusions From Jury Service.* Pursuant to Title 28, U.S. Code, Section 1866(c), any juror who has been summonsed for jury service may be excluded by the Court upon a finding by the Court:

1. That such person may be unable to render impartial jury service or that his or her service as a juror would possibly disrupt the proceedings;

2. That such person is peremptorily challenged as provided by law;

3. That such person should be excluded pursuant to the procedure specified by law upon a challenge by any party for good cause shown; or

4. That such person would be likely to threaten the secrecy of the proceedings, or otherwise adversely affect the integrity of jury deliberations; provided that no person shall be excluded under this subparagraph unless the Judge, in open court, determines exclusion is warranted and will not be inconsistent with Title 28, U.S. Code, Sections 1861 and 1862. The names of persons excluded under this subparagraph, together with detailed explanations for the exclusions, shall be forwarded immediately to the Judicial Council of the Eleventh Circuit for disposition under the provisions of Title 28, U.S. Code, section 1866(c).

5. Such person excluded from a particular jury under the provisions of subparagraphs 1 through 3 of this subsection F shall be eligible to sit on another jury if the basis for the initial exclusion would not be relevant to the ability of such person to serve on another jury.

IX. Drawing of Names for Issuance of Summons.

A. *Summons.* Once the qualified wheel of a division is filled, the names of persons contained in that qualified wheel may be summonsed at random for service on either a grand jury or a petit jury.

B. *Grand Juries.* Three separate and distinct geographic areas of this district are hereby established for the summonsing of grand jurors:

1. Unless otherwise specifically ordered by the Chief Judge, a grand jury for the Pensacola and Panama City Divisions shall sit at Pensacola. An equal number of names shall be publicly drawn at random from the qualified wheels of each of these two divisions only.

2. Unless otherwise specifically ordered by the Chief Judge, a grand jury for the Tallahassee Division shall sit in Tallahassee, and names shall be publicly drawn at random from the qualified wheel of this division only.

3. Unless otherwise specifically ordered by the Chief Judge, a grand jury for the Gainesville Division shall sit in Gainesville, and names shall be publicly drawn at random from the qualified wheel of this division only.

C. *Petit Juries.*

1. The Clerk shall publicly draw at random names for a petit jury panel from the qualified wheel of the division in which trial is scheduled to be held.

2. The number of names drawn shall be consistent with the number of jurors required to serve the needs of the Court.

3. Except when necessary to complete service in a particular case, no person shall be required to serve or attend court for prospective service as a petit juror for a total of more than thirty days.

X. Maintenance and Inspection of Records.

A. *Disclosure of Names.* Unless otherwise ordered by the Court, the names drawn from any qualified wheel to serve as grand or petit jurors shall not be disclosed or made available to the public. The names of grand jurors may be provided to the United States Attorney by the Clerk. The Court may order the names of jurors to be kept confidential in any case when the interests of justice so require. The names of prospective jurors shall not be disclosed except as provided in Title 28, U.S. Code, Sections 1867 and 1868.

B. *Records.*

1. The names in the master wheels, the qualified wheels, and on grand and petit jury panels may be maintained in printed form or on electronic data storage devices.

2. The Clerk shall retain and, when requested, provide public access to this Plan, including a verbal description of the methods used to refill the master and qualified wheels and to summons jurors.

3. The contents of records or papers used by the Clerk in connection with the jury selection process shall not be disclosed, except pursuant to this Plan or as may be necessary in the preparation or presentation of a motion under Title 28, U.S. Code, Sections 1867(a), (b) or (c).

4. After the master wheels are emptied and refilled pursuant to this Plan, and after all persons selected to serve as jurors before the master wheels were emptied have completed such service, all records and papers compiled and maintained by the Clerk before the master wheels were emptied shall be preserved in the custody of the Clerk for four years and shall be available for public inspection for the purpose of determining the validity of the selection of any jury. Thereafter, the Clerk may dispose of all such records following applicable records disposition policies.

XI. Incorporation of Amendments. Incorporated herein by reference is Title 28, U.S. Code, Sections 1861, et seq., together with all amendments which may hereafter be made, and all laws hereafter enacted relating to grand and petit juries and trial by jury in the United States.

[Effective July 26, 2004.]

INDEX TO UNITED STATES DISTRICT COURT FOR THE NORTHERN DISTRICT OF FLORIDA

UNITED STATES BANKRUPTCY COURT FOR THE NORTHERN DISTRICT OF FLORIDA

Including Amendments Received Through February 1, 2017

I. RULES

II. ADDENDA

III. LOCAL FORMS

A. ADMINISTRATIVE FORMS

B. INSTRUCTIONAL DOCUMENTS

C. LOCAL FORMS (ALL CASES)

2. Corporate Ownership Statement.
3. Verified Ex Parte Motion for Mortgage Modification Mediation ("MMM").
3PS. Verified Ex Parte Motion for Mortgage Modification Mediation ("MMM").
4. Certificate of Service.
5. Exhibit Tag/Cover Sheet.
6. Exhibit List.
7. Statement of Need for Emergency Hearing.
12. Notice of Address to Be Used in Specific Case Pursuant to 11 U.S.C.§ 342(e).
16. Statement of No Employment Income.
17. Notice of Change of Address of Debtor.
18. Motion for Determination and Waiver of Debtor's Duty to Comply With the Credit Counseling Requirement Under 11 U.S.C. Section 109(h)(4).
19. Request for Notice Pursuant to Bankruptcy Rule 2002(g).
20. Notice of Appearance.
32. Motion for Protective Order to Restrict Access and Allow for Redaction of Information.
35. Pro Se Debtor(s)' Statement Regarding Conversion to Chapter 7 Pursuant to Fed. R. Bankr. P. 1019 and N.D. Fla. LBR 1019.
36. Verification of Creditor Mailing Matrix.

D. CHAPTER 7 FORMS

7–7. Report and Notice of Trustee's Intention to Abandon Property of the Estate.
7–8. Report and Notice of Intention to Sell Property of the Estate.
7–15. Certificate and Affidavit for Adding Creditors in a Closed Case.

E. CHAPTER 11 FORMS

11–5. Chapter 11—Vote on Plan.
11–6. Cover Sheet for Application for Attorney Compensation and Reimbursement of Expenses.
11–26. Individual Debtor(s) Motion for Entry of Discharge, Certificate of Compliance and Notice of Time to Object.
11–37. Statement/Certification Regarding Requirements for Discharge in an Individual Chapter 11 Case.

F. CHAPTER 12 FORMS

12–9. Chapter 12 Case—Summary of Operations—Family Farmer.
12–10. Chapter 12 Case—Monthly Cash Receipts and Disbursements.
12–37. Statement/Certification Regarding Requirements for Discharge in a Chapter 12 Case.

G. CHAPTER 13 FORMS

13–1. Optional Plan Language.
13–13. Pre-Confirmation Statement Regarding Individual Debtor's Domestic Support Obligations and Filing of Tax Returns, as Applicable, Pursuant to Code and Rule Requirements.
13–21. Chapter 13 Plan.
13–22. Annual Statement.
13–23. Motion to Modify Chapter 13 Plan.
13–27. Supplemental Disclosure to Schedules I and/or J Regarding Listed Expenses.
13–28. Agreed Motion to Abate Plan Payments to Address Accrued Delinquency.
13–29. Debtor(s)' Election to Abate Plan Payments Pursuant to Confirmed Plan Terms.
13–30. Debtor(s)' Election to Use a Portion of Tax Refund Pursuant to Confirmed Plan Terms.
13–31. Debtor(s)' Notice of Chapter 13 Plan Payment Change Pursuant to Creditor's Notice of Payment Change on Debtor(s)' Principal Mortgage.
13–33. Motion to Deem Mortgage Current.
13–34. Secured Creditor's Notice of Payment Change.
13–37. Statement/Certification Regarding Requirements for Discharge in a Chapter 13 Case.
13–38. Motion for Referral to Mortgage Modification Mediation.
13–38–PS. Motion for Referral to Mortgage Modification Mediation.
13–39. Notice of Scheduled Mortgage Mediation.

MORTGAGE MODIFICATION MEDIATION PROGRAM

Memorandum re: Uniform Mortgage Modification Mediation Procedures in the Bankruptcy Court for the Northern District of Florida [Modified by Order 2015–1, effective October 1, 2015].

20. In Re: Guidelines and Procedures for Mortgage Modification Mediators.

Administrative Order 2015–1. In re: Administrative Order Prescribing Procedures for Mortgage Modification.

STANDING ORDERS

10. In re: Courtroom Computer Usage.
11. Relating to Electronic Case Filing.
17. In re: Investment of Registry Funds.
19. In Re: Chapter 13 Attorneys Fees, Adequate Protection Payments, Annual Statements, Form Plan, and Tax Returns.

SELECTED ADMINISTRATIVE ORDERS

05–001. Establishing Initial Procedures in Chapter 11 Cases.
10–001. In re: Final Reports—Cases Converted From Chapter 13 to Chapter 7.
12–002. In re: Adoption of Interim Rule 1007–I.

Proposed Orders Guidelines.

13–001. Order Adopting Negative Notice List Pursuant to L.R. 2002–2A(7).
13–004. In re: Order Vacating Standing Orders Number 9, 13, and 15.

Administrative Order No. 15–002. In Re: Motions to Extend or Impose the Automatic Stay Under 11 U.S.C. 362(c)(3) and 362(c)(4).

I. RULES

RULE 1001-1. INTRODUCTION AND GENERAL STATEMENT OF ADOPTION AND APPLICATION OF LOCAL RULES

A. The title of these rules is "Local Rules, United States Bankruptcy Court, Northern District of Florida." They may be cited as "N.D. Fla. LBR ___."

B. These rules shall take effect on December 1, 2011, and shall apply in said United States Bankruptcy Court to all cases, and to all matters and proceedings arising in or related to cases under Title 11, United States Code (the Bankruptcy Code) then pending and thereafter filed, except to the extent that in the opinion of the Court their application in a pending case, matter or proceeding would not be feasible or would work an injustice.

C. For cause, on motion of a party in interest or sua sponte, the Court may direct that one or more provisions of these rules not apply in a case, matter, or proceeding.

D. The Local Rules of the United States District Court, Northern District of Florida shall apply in all bankruptcy cases, including contested matters and adversary proceedings, to the extent applicable and to the extent not inconsistent with the bankruptcy rules and the local bankruptcy rules for the Northern District of Florida.

E. Definitions. The terms "Court," "Clerk," and "Judge," when those appear in applicable District Court Local Rules, shall mean the Bankruptcy Court, Bankruptcy Clerk, and Bankruptcy Judge, respectively, unless inconsistent with the language or meaning of the particular District Court Local Rule.

[Effective June 1, 1997. Amended effective October 6, 2003; April 1, 2005; September 1, 2006; December 1, 2009; December 1, 2011.]

RULE 1005-1. PETITION—CAPTION

A petition filed on behalf of an individual or an individual and such individual's spouse shall not include the name of any corporation, partnership, limited partnership, or joint venture.

[Effective June 1, 1997.]

RULE 1006-1. FILING FEE

The filing fee must be paid by an attorney's office or trust account, check, cash, money order, or preapproved credit card. Documents filed electronically require payment on-line by credit card at the time of filing. If paid by check, there should be a separate check for each petition or item filed. Direct payments from debtors may only be by cash, cashier's check or money order—no personal checks, credit cards or debit cards from debtors will be accepted.

[Effective December 1, 2009.]

RULE 1007-1. LISTS, SCHEDULES, STATEMENTS, AND OTHER DOCUMENTS

The following shall be filed at the same time as, but separately from, the petition and submitted on the most current version of the prescribed form:

A. Chapter 7, 12, or 13.

(1) List of Creditors (Names and Addresses) unless the petition is accompanied by a schedule of liabilities or a Chapter 13 statement.

(2) Master Mailing Matrix (see Local Rule 1007-2).

(3) Filing Fee.

(4) Unless the U.S. Trustee has determined that the credit counseling requirement of § 109(h) does not apply in the district, a Statement of Compliance as prescribed by the appropriate form (see local forms page on Court internet site) by individual debtors, which must include one of the following:

(a) an attached Certificate and Debt Repayment Plan, if any, required by § 521(b);

(b) a Statement that the debtor has received the credit counseling briefing required by § 109(h)(1) but does not have the certificate required by § 521(b);

(c) a Certification under § 109(h)(3); or

(d) a Request for a determination by the Court under § 109(h)(4).

(5) If the debtor is unable to comply with the requirement under 11 U.S.C. § 521(a)(1)(B)(iv) because he/she has no income, a Certificate or Statement noting the lack of income. (Form available on Court's internet site.)

(6) If the debtor is a corporation other than a governmental unit, a Corporate Ownership Statement must be filed with the petition. This Statement should disclose all corporations that directly or indirectly own 10% or more of the class of the corporation's equity interests. The Statement must be provided even if there are no entities to report. (Form available on Court's internet site.)

Note:

- **Statement of Social Security Number.** Failure of a pro se debtor to submit the Statement of Social Security Number (official form B-21) may lead to dismissal of the case. In cases filed electronically, the Statement is not required to be filed with the Court and shall be maintained by the registered user/attorney in accordance with Section II.M.1. of the Administrative Procedures (a link to the Admin. Procedures will be added to the PDF version of the rules).
- **Format for Paper Filings.** Per USDC Local Rule 5.1B(3)—Except for forms provided by this court, all documents tendered for filing, or filed electronically, shall be double-spaced, if typewritten, no smaller than 12 point font, and on plain white letter-sized (8 1/2″ × 11″) paper with approximately one and one-fourth (1 1/4) inch margins. The first page of every pleading or document filed in paper form shall, however, allow approximately a two (2) inch margin at the bottom of the page where the clerk shall date stamp such pleading or document filed.

B. Chapter 9 or 11.

(1) List of Creditors (Names and Addresses) unless the petition is accompanied by a schedule of liabilities.

(2) Exhibit "A" to Official Form No. 1, if debtor is a corporation.

(3) List of twenty largest unsecured creditors excluding insiders.

(4) Master mailing matrix (see Local Rule 1007-2).

(5) Filing Fee.

(6) Unless the U.S. Trustee has determined that the credit counseling requirement of § 109(h) does not apply in the district, a Statement of Compliance as prescribed by the appropriate form (see local forms page on Court internet site) by individual debtors, which must include one of the following:

(a) an attached Certificate and Debt Repayment Plan, if any, required by § 521(b);

(b) a Statement that the debtor has received the credit counseling briefing required by § 109(h)(1) but does not have the Certificate required by § 521(b);

(c) a Certification under § 109(h)(3); or

(d) a Request for a determination by the Court under § 109(h)(4).

(7) If the Chapter 11 individual debtor is unable to comply with the requirements of 11 U.S.C. § 521(a)(1)(B)(iv) because he/she has no income, a Certificate or Statement noting the lack of income. (Form available on Court's internet site.)

(8) If the debtor is a corporation other than a governmental unit, a Corporate Ownership Statement must be filed with the petition. This Statement should disclose all corporations that directly or indirectly own 10% or more of the class of the corporation's equity interests. The Statement must be provided even if there are no entities to report. (Form available on Court's internet site.)

[Effective June 1, 1997. Amended effective October 6, 2003; April 1, 2005. Amended, on an interim basis, effective October 17, 2005. Amended effective September 1, 2006; December 1, 2009; December 1, 2011.]

RULE 1007-2. MAILING LIST OR MATRIX

The debtor shall file separately, but at the same time as the petition, a list containing the name and address of each creditor which shall serve as a mailing matrix. The mailing matrix shall be signature verified and submitted in the format specified by the Clerk's Office (see "MAILING MATRIX FILING INSTRUCTIONS" on local forms page on Court internet site).

[Effective June 1, 1997. Amended effective October 6, 2003; April 1, 2005; September 1, 2006; December 1, 2009; December 1, 2011.]

RULE 1007-3. STATEMENT OF INTENTION

The debtor's statement of intention (any and amendment thereto), filed pursuant to 11 U.S.C. § 521(a)(2), shall include the terms under which the stated intentions will be accomplished by the debtor.

[Effective September 1, 2006.]

RULE 1009-1. AMENDMENTS OF VOLUNTARY PETITIONS, LISTS, SCHEDULES AND STATEMENTS

A. Amendments to Voluntary Petitions, Lists, Schedules and Statements may be made by filing the original with the Clerk. Amendments must contain a caption which includes the case number, case name and the title of the document. The amendment must be executed and acknowledged by the debtor and attorney of record in the same manner that the item being amended was originally executed. Amended schedules should be filed in their entirety for clarity and to simplify the record. Any changes, additions or deletions must be clearly indicated.

B. The debtor shall notice the amendment to any entity affected thereby, the trustee, and to the U.S. Trustee's office. A certificate of service shall be filed with the Clerk.

C. Amendments adding additional creditors to the schedules require the appropriate filing fee and shall be accompanied by an additional mailing matrix which contains the names and addresses of only the creditors being added.

D. Adding Creditors in a Closed No Asset Case: If the case is a closed Chapter 7 case with no distribution to creditors, a "Certificate and Affidavit for Adding Creditors to Schedules in a Closed No Asset Case" must be completed and filed (see local forms page on Court internet site).

E. An amended Statement of Social Security Number (Form 21) should be completed to correct a previously filed social security or individual taxpayer identification number and kept on file for four years after the case or proceeding is closed with a copy of the amended form mailed to the Clerk's Office.

Note: As with the original Form, the amended Form should NOT be filed on the system or sent via e-mail. In addition, under the Federal Rules of Bankruptcy Procedure, a notice of the correct number needs to be sent to all creditors, the United States Trustee, and the case trustee. A truncated or redacted copy of the notice showing only the last four digits should be filed with the Court. **Only** with an error in the last four digits of the SSN that appear on the petition should the debtor file an amended petition with notice to all parties.

[Effective June 1, 1997. Amended effective April 1, 2005; September 1, 2006; December 1, 2009.]

RULE 1014-1. CHANGE OF VENUE

In accordance with Local Rule 3.1(C) of the U.S. District Court for the Northern District of Florida, attorneys desiring to transfer a new Chapter 7 or 13 petition to another division within the District must select the division at case opening where they want the case administered and contemporaneously file a Motion to Transfer.

Note: Detailed instructions can be provided by the clerk's office upon request. Nothing in the local rule is intended to apply to new Chapter 11 petitions.

[Effective December 1, 2011.]

RULE 1015-1. JOINT ADMINISTRATION

A. Time for Filing Objection to Joint Administration. All cases involving two or more related debtors will be jointly administered in accordance with Bankruptcy Rule 1015. However a creditor or party in interest may file an objection to joint administration no later than 30 days after the first date set for the meeting of creditors under 11 U.S.C. § 341(a).

B. Extension of Time. On motion of any party in interest, after hearing on notice, the Court may for cause extend the time to file an objection to joint administration. The motion shall be filed before the time has expired.

C. Until the Order Consolidating is entered, all items are to be filed as applicable in each involved case.

[Effective October 6, 2003. Amended effective December 1, 2011.]

RULE 1017-1. DISMISSAL—CASE OR PROCEEDINGS

Failure to comply with these Rules may be grounds for dismissal of a case or conversion to a case under Chapter 7 of Title 11.

[Effective June 1, 1997. Amended effective October 6, 2003; December 1, 2009.]

RULE 1019-1. CONVERSION

A. In cases converted to Chapter 7,

(1) the debtor-in-possession or the trustee shall file an original of all lists, schedules, statements, and other documents required by Bankruptcy Rule 1007, on the most current version of the official forms with the debtor's signatures, which accurately reflects the condition of the debtor's estate at the time of conversion.

(2) The lists, schedules, statements, and other documents shall be filed within the time provided in Bankruptcy Rule 1007 and 1019(1)(A). The final report and schedule of post-petition debts shall be filed within the time provided in Bankruptcy Rule 1019(1)(A).

(3) If the debtor has acquired no debt or property since the filing of the case and prior to conversion, the debtor shall obviate the need for filing new and/or amended schedules and statements by filing a statement that he or she has acquired no debts or property since the case was filed.

Note: If there are changes or amendments to be made, this process is not applicable and the debtor shall comply with all other requirements of Bankruptcy Rule 1019.

B. The applicable current monthly income form (Form B 22A, 22B, or 22C) shall be filed in all cases within fourteen (14) days of conversion.

[Effective June 1, 1997. Amended effective October 6, 2003; April 1, 2005. Amended, on an interim basis, effective October 17, 2005. Amended effective September 1, 2006; December 1, 2009; December 1, 2011.]

RULE 1070-1. JURISDICTION

Motions other than those filed in adversary proceedings shall be deemed to be core proceedings unless a response asserting that the matter should be treated as a non-core proceeding is filed within the time provided in Local Rule 9013-1.

[Effective June 1, 1997. Amended effective December 1, 2011.]

RULE 2002-1. NOTICE TO CREDITORS AND OTHER INTERESTED PARTIES

A party in interest who desires to receive copies of pleadings and notices to which it is entitled under Bankruptcy Rule 2002 shall:

A. File a request with the Clerk;

B. Serve a copy of the request on the debtor, debtor's attorney, the attorney for the debtor-in-possession, the trustee, the attorney for the trustee and the U.S. Trustee; and

C. Attach to the request filed with the Clerk a certificate of service which states to whom a copy of the request has been given.

[Effective June 1, 1997. Amended effective October 6, 2003; September 1, 2006.]

RULE 2002-2. NEGATIVE NOTICE PROCEDURE

A. The following motions, objections, and other pleadings not already specifically provided for by a similar negative notice procedure in these rules may be considered by the Court without an actual hearing under the negative notice procedure described in this rule if no party in interest requests a hearing:

(1) Motion to approve agreements relating to relief from the automatic stay, prohibiting or conditioning the use, sale, or lease of property, providing adequate protection, use of cash collateral, and obtaining credit pursuant to Bankruptcy Rule 4001(d).

(2) Motion to avoid liens on exempt property pursuant to Bankruptcy Rule 4003(d).

(3) Motion to use, sell, or lease property not in the ordinary course of business pursuant to Bankruptcy Rule 6004(a) but not motions to sell property free and clear of liens or other interests pursuant to Bankruptcy Rule 6004(c).

(4) Notices of abandonment pursuant to Bankruptcy Rule 6007(a) and motion to compel abandonment pursuant to Bankruptcy Rule 6007(b).

(5) Motion to approve compromises or settlements pursuant to Bankruptcy Rule 9019(a).

(6) Motion to extend time under Local Rule 3002-1.

(7) Other motions, objections, and matters if permitted by the presiding judge.*

B. Motions, objections, and other matters filed pursuant to this negative notice procedure shall:

(1) Be served in the manner and on the parties as required by the provisions of the Federal Rules of Bankruptcy Procedure, Local Rule, or any order of Court applicable to motions, objections, or matters of the type made and shall be filed with the proof of such service in accordance with the provisions of Local Rule 7004-1.

(2) To the extent permitted under the Federal Rules of Bankruptcy Procedures, Local Rules, or any order of the Court, a Filing User may make use of these Negative Notice Procedures by serving motions, objections, and other matters

by electronic means to any other Filing User or other party who consents to receive service by electronic means.

(3) Contain a negative notice legend prominently displayed on the face of the first page of the paper. The negative notice legend shall be in a form substantially as follows:

NOTICE OF OPPORTUNITY TO OBJECT AND FOR HEARING

Pursuant to Local Rule 2002-2, the Court will consider this motion, objection, or other matter without further notice or hearing unless a party in interest files an objection within twenty-one (21) days from the date of service of this paper. If you object to the relief requested in this paper, you must file your objection with the Clerk of the Court at 110 E. Park Avenue, Tallahassee, FL 32301, and serve a copy on the movant's attorney, (name and address, and any other appropriate persons).

If you file and serve an objection within the time permitted, the Court may schedule a hearing and you will be notified. If you do not file an objection within the time permitted, the Court will consider that you do not oppose the granting of the relief requested in the paper, and will proceed to consider the paper without further notice or hearing, and may grant the relief requested.

C. For the purpose of completing the above negative notice legend, the number of days during which parties may object that is placed in the negative notice legend shall be twenty-one (21) days.

(1) In the event a party in interest files an objection within the time permitted in the negative notice legend, the Court may schedule a hearing on the motion, objection, or other matter upon notice to the movant's attorney, the objecting party or parties, and others as may be appropriate.

(2) In the event no party in interest files an objection within the time permitted in the negative notice legend as computed under Bankruptcy Rule 9006(a) and (f), the Court will consider the matter in chambers without further notice or hearing upon the submission by the movant of a proposed form of order granting relief. The movant shall submit the proposed order not later than fourteen (14) days after the expiration of the objection period. In the event the movant fails to submit a proposed form of order within this time, the Court may enter an order denying the matter without prejudice for lack of prosecution. In addition to any other requirements, the proposed form of order shall recite that:

(a) The motion, objection, or other matter was served upon all interested parties with the Local Rule 2002-2 negative notice legend informing the parties of their opportunity to object within the proper days of the date of service;

(b) No party filed an objection within the time permitted; and

(c) The Court therefore considers the matter to be unopposed.

D. Nothing in this rule is intended to preclude the Court from conducting a hearing on the motion, objection, or other matter even if no objection is filed within the time permitted in the negative notice legend.

[Effective December 1, 2009. Amended effective December 1, 2011.]

* [Publisher's Note: *See* Administrative Order No. 13-001, *post.*]

RULE 2002-3. PREFERRED ADDRESS NOTIFICATION

A. An entity and a notice provider may agree that when the notice provider is directed by the Court to give notice to that entity, the notice provider shall give the notice to the entity in the manner agreed to and at the address or addresses the entity supplies to the notice provider. That address is conclusively presumed to be a proper address for the notice. The notice provider's failure to use the supplied address does not invalidate any notice that is otherwise effective under applicable law.

B. The filing of a notice of preferred address pursuant to 11 U.S.C. § 342(f) by the creditor directly with the agency or agencies that provide noticing services for the Bankruptcy Court will constitute the filing of such notice with the Court.

C. Registration with the National Creditor Registration Service must be accomplished through the Bankruptcy Noticing Center, the agency that provides noticing services for the Bankruptcy Court for the Northern District of Florida. Forms and registration information are available at https://www.ncrsuscourts.com.

D. A local form for use by creditors for filing the notice of preferred address under 11 U.S.C. § 342(e) is available on the Court's website.

[Effective December 1, 2011.]

RULE 2003-1. MEETING OF CREDITORS AND EQUITY SECURITY HOLDERS

Section 341 Meetings will not be continued except for good cause shown. All requests for continuances must be made through the U.S. Trustee's Office in Chapter 11 cases and through the trustee in Chapter 7, 12, or 13 cases.

[Effective June 1, 1997.]

RULE 2015-1. DEBTOR IN POSSESSION DUTIES

A. A debtor-in-possession or a trustee who operates a business shall file signed monthly financial reports in the form and containing the information as set forth by the Office of the U.S. Trustee (see local forms page on Court internet site).

B. A debtor-in-possession in a Chapter 11 case who is an individual not engaged in business shall file signed monthly financial reports in the form and containing the information as set forth by the Office of the U.S. Trustee (see local forms page on Court internet site).

C. The monthly reports shall be filed no later than the 20th day of each month commencing with the month following the filing of the petition and shall reflect all transactions during the immediately preceding month.

D. The attorney for the debtor-in-possession shall not be required to sign the monthly financial reports or file any notice of their filing.

E. The debtor-in-possession or trustee in a Chapter 11 case shall file the original monthly financial report with the Clerk and serve a copy of the reports and financial statements upon the U.S. Trustee, the members of the creditors' committee, if one has been appointed, the attorney for the creditors' committee, if one has been employed, and such other person or persons as the Court may from time to time direct. The debtor-in-possession in Chapter 12 and Chapter 13 business cases shall serve a copy of the reports and financial statements upon the trustee, the U.S. Trustee and upon such other person or persons as the Court may from time to time direct.

F. In Chapter 12 cases the debtor shall file signed Monthly Cash Receipts and Disbursements Statements as set forth by the Office of the U.S. Trustee (see local forms page on Court internet site). The debtor shall file the original with the Clerk and provide a copy to the Chapter 12 Trustee and the U.S. Trustee beginning with the filing of the bankruptcy petition and ending when the payments under the Plan are complete. The reports shall be filed by the debtor no later than the 15th day following the end of the month and shall include all of the debtor's receipts or income, in cash or by check, received during the month. The receipts should be itemized by kind, quantity, and dollar amount. All expenses paid in cash or by check should be itemized.

G. Failure to comply with this rule may be grounds for conversion to Chapter 7, if permitted by law, or for dismissal of the case.

[Effective June 1, 1997. Amended effective October 6, 2003; December 1, 2009.]

RULE 2016-1. COMPENSATION OF PROFESSIONALS

A. Applications for Compensation in Chapter 7 Cases.

(1)(a) Final applications for fees and expenses of all professionals incurred during the administration of the Chapter 7 cases and allowable under 11 U.S.C. § 503(b) must be filed not later than twenty-one (21) days after service of notification by the trustee that the case is ready to close.

(b) In cases that have been converted to Chapter 7, all final applications of professionals for fees, costs, and expenses incurred in the superseded case must be filed within ninety (90) days after the date of the order converting the case.

(2) All applications for fees and expenses, whether interim or final, shall contain the amounts requested and a detailed itemization of the work performed including:

(a) the name of the individual performing the work;

(b) the amount of time expended for each item of work;

(c) the hourly rate requested; and

(d) a discussion of the criterion that are relevant in determining the compensation to be awarded.

(3)(a) Applications for fees and expenses totaling $1,000 or less will be determined after notice and an opportunity for a hearing. Notice shall go to all creditors, the U.S. Trustee, and all other parties in interest. A hearing will not be held unless a timely objection is filed with the Court.

(b) Applications for fees and expenses under 11 U.S.C. § 326 will be determined after notice and an opportunity for a hearing. Notice shall go to all creditors, the U.S. Trustee, and all other parties in interest. A hearing will not be held unless a timely objection is filed with the Court.

B. Applications for Compensation in Chapter 11 Cases.

(1) Applications of attorneys, accountants, auctioneers, appraisers, and other professionals for compensation from the estate of the debtor allowable under 11 U.S.C. § 503(b), should be filed no later than twenty-one (21) days after the entry of an order scheduling the confirmation hearing, except for applications for fees and expenses totaling $1,000 or less, which may be heard and determined pursuant to Local Rule 2016-1. A copy of the application shall be served upon the trustee, the attorney for the trustee, the debtor-in-possession, the attorney for the creditors' committee, and the U.S. Trustee. Nothing herein shall preclude an application not filed pursuant to this rule; provided, however, that debtor shall not be required to pay for such services at the time of confirmation.

(2) All applications for compensation of professionals, including interim applications, shall contain a detailed itemization of the work performed. Applications by attorneys and accountants shall include the individual performing the item of work, a description of the work performed for each item, the amount of time expended for each item, the hourly rate requested, and a discussion of the criteria that are relevant in determining the compensation to be awarded.

(3) All disclosures required to be transmitted to the United States Trustee under Bankruptcy Rule 1026(b) shall be served on the case trustee within the time required for service on the United States Trustee.

[Effective June 1, 1997. Amended effective October 6, 2003. Amended, on an interim basis, effective October 17, 2005. Amended effective September 1, 2006; December 1, 2009.]

RULE 2071-1. COMMITTEES

A. Upon appointment of a committee of creditors pursuant to 11 U.S.C. § 1102, those creditors willing to serve shall have an organizational meeting and elect a chairman who shall preside at meetings of the creditors' committee.

B. The meetings of the creditors' committee may be held by telephone.

C. The U.S. Trustee shall notice the Clerk of the Bankruptcy Court of the names, addresses, and telephone numbers of the members of the committee. If no committee is appointed, the U.S. Trustee's Office shall notice the Clerk of the Bankruptcy Court that no committee has been appointed. A copy of the appropriate notice shall be served upon the attorney for the debtor and the members of the committee.

[Effective June 1, 1997. Amended effective April 1, 2005.]

RULE 2081-1. CHAPTER 11—GENERAL

Note: Please see Administrative Order 05-001—*Administrative Order Establishing Initial Procedures in Chapter 11 Cases* on the Court's website* in conjunction with this Local Rule.

A. Authority to Operate Business/Manage Financial Affairs.

(1) The operation of a business by a debtor-in-possession in cases filed under Chapter 11 shall be subject to the terms and conditions of an order continuing the debtor-in-possession to be entered upon the filing of the petition or entry of the Order for Relief. The debtor-in-possession shall also deposit taxes and file tax returns in compliance with the terms of the Order to File Federal and State Employment Tax Returns and To Deposit State and Federal Taxes (see local forms page on Court internet site).

(2) Individual Chapter 11 debtors not engaged in business shall be subject to the terms and conditions of the order authorizing individual debtors to manage financial affairs to be entered upon the filing of the petition or entry of the order for relief.

(3) All Chapter 11 voluntary debtors must comply with the Administrative Order Establishing Initial Procedures in Chapter 11 Cases (see Administrative Order No. 05-001 on the Court internet site).

B. Post-Confirmation Matters.

(1) Within twenty-one (21) days after the hearing confirming the plan, the attorney for the proponent of the plan shall prepare the Order of Confirmation and submit it to the Court. Copies of the proposed order shall be served upon the U.S. Trustee, any party in interest who filed an objection to the confirmation and to any other person designated by the Court. The Order Confirming the Plan will be distributed by the Court to all parties in interest. The proponent of the plan shall then be responsible for the distribution of copies of the confirmed plan to all creditors, the U.S. Trustee, and other parties as may be designated by the Court.

(2)(a) In addition to the report required by Bankruptcy Rule 2015(a) and (b), in those instances where the plan requires longer than one hundred twenty (120) days for consummation, the plan proponent shall file a Confirmed Plan Status Report beginning the third month after the effective date of the plan and every three (3) months thereafter. This report shall disclose any distributions made, including the amount of each distribution to creditors as identified in the plan, as well as a description of all other matters which must be consummated in order to close the estate.

(b) If the plan provides for payments to any class of creditors over a period of time which is longer than one hundred eighty (180) days from the date of confirmation, the plan proponent shall execute an instrument evidencing the indebtedness and deliver such instrument to each creditor or other party interest. Such instrument shall provide for payment of the amount due under the plan upon the terms set forth in the plan. Delivery of instruments shall be deemed commencement of distribution under the plan for purposes of closing the estate pursuant to 11 U.S.C. § 1101(c). Such instruments shall be delivered to creditors in each class within thirty (30) days after all objections to claims in that class have been resolved or, if there are no objections to claims in any class, then within sixty (60) days after the entry of an Order of Confirmation.

(c) Upon substantial consummation of the plan for cases other than those for an individual, the plan proponent shall file an application for final decree which shall certify compliance with 11 U.S.C. § 1101.

(d) After the last plan payment has been made in an individual case, the debtor shall file:

(1) a certification that the final payment has been made (see local forms page on Court internet site);

(2) an application for final decree which shall certify compliance with 11 U.S.C. § 1101.

[Effective June 1, 1997. Amended effective October 6, 2003; September 1, 2006; December 1, 2009; December 1, 2011.]

* [**Publisher's Note:** Administrative Order 05-001 is reproduced herein, *post*.]

RULE 2082-1. CHAPTER 12—GENERAL

A. Duties of the Chapter 12 Debtor.

(1) At least seven (7) days before the first meeting of creditors, the debtor must file and provide the Chapter 12 Trustee with the Summary of Operations for Chapter 12 Case (see local forms page on Court internet site) and the Income Tax Returns for the two (2) years immediately preceding the filing of the bankruptcy petition.

(2) At least seven (7) days before the confirmation hearing, the debtor must file and provide a copy to the Chapter 12 Trustee of the Farm/Fisherman Plan for a three (3) year period indicating projected disposable income, and a liquidation analysis reflecting the distributions to unsecured creditors if the case proceeds as a Chapter 7.

(3) The debtor shall file and provide a copy to the Chapter 12 Trustee the Monthly Cash Receipts and Disbursements Statement (see local forms page on Court internet site) beginning with the filing of the bankruptcy petition and ending when the payments under the plan are complete. The Statements shall be filed by the debtor no later than the fifteenth (15th) day following the end of the month and shall include all of the debtor's receipts and/or income, in cash or by check, received during the month. The receipts should be itemized by kind, quantity, and dollar amount. All expenses paid in cash or by check should be itemized.

(4) Within sixty (60) days after the end of a calendar year (or fiscal year), the debtor must complete and file with the Clerk and the Chapter 12 Trustee, Internal Revenue Service Form Schedule 1040 F together with all supporting schedules of Schedule F, and Form 4835, for any part of the calendar or taxable period ending after the date on which the Chapter 12 petition was filed. The Schedule F and Form 4835 must report all income and all expenses to the end of the calendar (or fiscal) year.

(5) All payments to the Chapter 12 Trustee shall be in the form of a cashier's check or money order.

B. Pre-Confirmation Matters in Chapter 12.

(1) In all cases filed under Chapter 12, the debtor shall file a statement which contains "adequate information" about: (a) the debtor's ability to make all of the payments under the plan and to comply with the plan, (b) the financial condition of the debtor, including assets and liabilities of the debtor as well as the income and expenses of the debtor for the preceding calendar year, (c) the value of any property of the estate, whether being retained by the debtor or surrendered, which is subject to a lien or security interest as well as a description of the basis for such value, (d) an analysis of the amount which would be received by unsecured creditors if the estate of the debtor were to be liquidated under Chapter 7 of Title 11, and (e) a projection of the net disposable income of the debtor for the term of the plan.

(2) For purposes of this section, "adequate information" shall mean information of a kind, and in sufficient detail, as far as reasonably practicable in light of the nature and history of the debtor and the condition of the debtor's books and records, that will enable creditors and the trustee to make an informed judgment about confirmation of the plan.

(3) In a Chapter 12 case, the pre-confirmation statement shall be filed upon the filing of a plan. Copies of the pre-confirmation statement shall be served upon all creditors, the trustee, the U.S. Trustee, and other persons who have requested notice pursuant to Bankruptcy Rule 2002.

(4) All Chapter 12 individual debtors shall file with the Court and serve on the Chapter 12 Trustee a certification that the debtor has paid all amounts to be paid under a domestic support obligation that first became payable after the date of the filing of the Chapter 12 petition if the debtor is required by a judicial or administrative order, or by statute, to pay such domestic support obligation. If the debtor is not required to pay any amounts under a domestic support obligation, then the debtor shall file a certification stating that the debtor is not required to pay said amounts. (Form available on Court internet site.)

C. Local Rule 2081-1(B) shall apply in Chapter 12 cases.

[Effective June 1, 1997. Amended effective October 6, 2003; April 1, 2005; December 1, 2009; December 1, 2011.]

RULE 2083-1. CHAPTER 13—GENERAL

Note:

- Please see Standing Order #13—*Chapter 13 Cases Governed by the Bankruptcy Abuse Prevention and Consumer Protection Act (Adequate Protection)* on the Court's website in conjunction with this Local Rule

- Please see Standing Order #15—*Adopting Form Chapter 13 Plan and Related Provisions (Annual Statement)* on the Court's website in conjunction with this Local Rule.*

A. Pre-Confirmation Matters in Chapter 13. In all cases filed under Chapter 13 where the debtor is required to file monthly operating reports, the debtor shall file a statement which contains "adequate information" about:

(1) the debtor's ability to make all of the payments under the plan and to comply with the plan,

(2) the financial condition of the debtor, including assets and liabilities of the debtor as well as the income and expenses of the debtor for the preceding calendar year,

(3) the value of any property of the estate, whether being retained by the debtor or surrendered, which is subject to a lien or security interest as well as a description of the basis for such value,

(4) an analysis of the amount which would be received by unsecured creditors if the estate of the debtor were to be liquidated under Chapter 7 of Title 11, and

(5) a projection of the net disposable income of the debtor for the term of the plan.

B. For purposes of this section, "adequate information" shall mean information of a kind, and in sufficient detail, as far as reasonably practicable in light of the nature and history of the debtor and the condition of the debtor's books and records, that will enable creditors and the trustee to make an informed judgment about confirmation of the plan.

C. In business Chapter 13 cases, the pre-confirmation statement shall be filed twenty-one (21) days prior to the confirmation hearing. Copies of the pre-confirmation statement shall be served upon all creditors, the trustee, the U.S. Trustee, and other persons who have requested notice pursuant to Bankruptcy Rule 2002.

[Effective June 1, 1997. Amended effective December 1, 2009; December 1, 2011.]

* [**Publisher's Note:** So in original. *But see* Administrative Order 13-004, *post.*]

RULE 2090-1. ATTORNEYS—ADMISSION TO PRACTICE

A. General Admission. Except as provided herein, Local Rule 11.1 of the United States District Court for the Northern District of Florida governs the admission and appearance of attorneys before the Bankruptcy Court. All attorneys admitted to practice or approved to appear Pro Hac Vice in the United States District Court for the Northern District of Florida are by virtue thereof admitted to practice in the Bankruptcy Court.

Note: With the advent of electronic case filing, the United States District Court no longer draws any substantive distinction between membership in the bar of this district and pro hac vice admission. An attorney admitted pro hac vice will be treated as a member of the bar of this district and will remain a member, even after termination of the case, until such time as the attorney affirmatively withdraws from the bar of this district or no longer meets the admission qualifications.

B. Admission Not Required.

(1) An attorney representing the United States, or any agency thereof, having the authority of the Government to appear as its counsel, may appear and be heard in any case or proceeding in which the Government or such agency thereof is a party-in-interest.

(2) An attorney who is not admitted to the United States District Court, Northern District of Florida, but is an active member in good standing of the bar of a Court of general jurisdiction in any state or territory of the United States, may appear on behalf of a creditor in the following instances:

(a) Preparation and filing of a notice of appearance and request for service of notices pursuant to Bankruptcy Rule 2002; and

(b) The preparation and filing of a proof of claim.

C. Conduct. All attorneys appearing in the Bankruptcy Court and all persons at counsel table are expected to observe the same customary and traditional Rules of Conduct and Decorum applicable in the United States District Court, as set forth in Addendum A for convenient reference.

D. Attorneys—Appearance and Withdrawal; Representation by an Attorney—When Required.

(1) No attorney, having made an appearance for a creditor in a contested matter or adversary proceeding or having filed a petition on behalf of a debtor, shall thereafter abandon the case or proceeding in which the appearance was made or withdraw as counsel for any party therein, except by leave of Court obtained after giving fourteen (14) days notice to the party or client affected thereby and to opposing counsel.

(2)(a) The disclosure statement required by Bankruptcy Rule 2016(b) shall include a statement as to whether the attorney has been retained to represent the debtor in discharge and dischargeability proceedings including those initiated via motion under Bankruptcy Rule 4004.

(b) If the disclosure statement recites that the attorney has not been retained to represent the debtor in proceedings as described in D.(2)(a), the attorney shall not be required to represent the debtor in such proceedings.

(c) If the disclosure statement fails to recite whether the attorney has been retained to represent the debtor in proceedings as described in D.(2)(a), the attorney shall be deemed to represent the debtor in such proceedings and shall not be allowed to withdraw from such proceedings except as provided in paragraph (1).

(3) Unless allowed to withdraw from a case, matter, or proceeding by order of the Court, counsel filing a petition on behalf of a debtor shall attend all hearings and meetings scheduled in the case or proceeding at which the debtor is required to attend under any provision of the Bankruptcy Code, the Bankruptcy Rules, or order of the Court; provided, however, counsel need not attend a hearing in regard to a matter in which the debtor is not a party and whose attendance has only been required as a witness.

(4) Any party for whom a general appearance of counsel has been made shall not thereafter take any step or be heard in the case in proper person absent prior leave of Court, nor shall any natural person, having previously elected to proceed in proper person, be permitted to obtain special or intermittent appearances of counsel except upon such conditions as the Court may specify.

(5) An entity other than a natural person may not file any petition or pleading, except a proof of claim or a ballot, or otherwise appear except through an attorney; provided, however, that any creditor or party in interest may participate in a Section 341 Meeting of Creditors without an attorney.

[Effective June 1, 1997. Amended effective April 1, 2005; December 1, 2009; December 1, 2011.]

RULE 3001–2. TRANSFER/ASSIGNMENT OF CLAIM

A. Scope of Rule. This Local Rule applies to the transfer or assignment of any claim or interest filed pursuant to Bankruptcy Rule 3001, 3002, 3003 or Local Rule 3002–1. Nothing in this Local Rule shall be construed as an extension of any time limit for filing a Proof of Claim or Interest.

B. Required Form and Content. Transfers or assignments of claim pursuant to Bankruptcy Rule 3001(e)(2) shall be filed using Procedural Bankruptcy Form B 210A or a form that substantially conforms to it. The transfer of claim form shall be accompanied by evidence of the transfer and shall include:

(1) The name and address of the transferee (entity that purchased or otherwise acquired the claim);

(2) The name and address of the transferor (entity that sold or otherwise relinquished the claim;

(3) The amount of claim;

(4) The date claim filed;

(5) An actual or electronic signature(s) of the transferee; and,

(6) A reference to the claim number for the claim to be transferred.

Note: When the transfer or assignment of claim is filed in CM/ECF on the main case docket, the filing event should also reference the claim number of the claim to be transferred so that information will appear on the claim register.

C. Service and Notice Requirement.

(1) Any entity filing a Transfer of Claim or Assignment of Claim pursuant to Bankruptcy Rule 3001(e)(2) shall immediately serve upon the transferor, the trustee and the debtor or debtor's attorney a copy of the Transfer of Claim or Assignment of Claim and supporting evidence of the transfer.

(2) At the same time of service as required in section C.(1), the entity shall also immediately serve upon the transferor, the trustee and the debtor or debtor's attorney a Notice of Transfer of Claim. The Notice of Transfer of Claim shall include:

(a) The claim number of the transferor;

(b) The name and address of the transferor;

(c) The name and address of the transferee;

(d) The date of the filing of the Transfer of Claim (typically form B 210A); and

(e) A statement prominently displayed on the face of the first page of the notice which states that any objections to the transfer must be filed within twenty-one (21) days of the mailing of the notice. The notice shall substantially conform with the following:

United States Bankruptcy Court
Northern District of Florida

In re ____________ Case No. ____________

NOTICE OF TRANSFER OF CLAIM OTHER THAN FOR SECURITY

Claim No. ___ (if known) was filed or deemed filed under 11 U.S.C. § 1111(a) in this case by the alleged transferor. As evidence of the transfer of that claim, the transferee filed a Transfer of Claim Other than for Security in the clerk's office of this court on ________ (date).

Name of Alleged Transferor
Name of Transferee
Address of Alleged Transferor:
Address of Transferee:

DEADLINE TO OBJECT TO TRANSFER

The alleged transferor of the claim is hereby notified that objections must be filed with the court within twenty-one (21) days of the mailing of this notice. If no objection is timely received by the court, the transferee will be substituted as the original claimant without further Order of the court.

Date: ____________ ____________
Signature of Transferee

D. Objection and Hearing.

(1) Any party objecting to the Transfer of Claim or Assignment of Claim shall file an objection no more than twenty-one (21) days from the filing of the Notice of Transfer of Claim. Any timely objection will be set for hearing.

(2) Failure to timely object will result in the transferee being substituted for the transferor as the holder of the claim without further notice or hearing.

E. Alternative to Notice Requirement.

(1) As an alternative to the notice requirement in section C.(2) above, the Transfer of Claim or Assignment of Claim may include a Waiver of Notice wherein the transferor waives the right to receive notice of and object to the filing of the Transfer of Claim or Assignment of Claim.

(2) Any signed statement by the transferor waiving notice of the transfer shall be deemed a declination of the opportunity to object to the transfer or assignment of claim and shall be deemed as a request by the transferor to substitute the transferee as the holder of the claim identified in the Notice of Transfer.

[Effective December 1, 2011.]

RULE 3002–1. FILING PROOF OF CLAIM OR INTEREST

A. Upon confirmation of the Chapter 13 Plan that provides for surrender of secured collateral back to a creditor:

(1) The secured creditor shall have sixty (60) days from confirmation of the Chapter 13 Plan to file an unsecured proof of claim regarding any deficiency balance that may occur upon the sale of the subject collateral if the collateral consists of personal property that was not liquidated within the claims bar date period;

(2) The secured creditor shall have ninety (90) days from confirmation of the Chapter 13 Plan to file an unsecured proof of claim regarding any deficiency balance that may occur upon the sale of the subject collateral if the collateral consists of real property that was not liquidated within the claims bar date period;

(3) The time periods provided above may be extended by Court Order upon the creditor filing an appropriate Motion using negative notice stating the circumstances necessitating a need for a longer period of time and an estimated deficiency;

(4) If no unsecured proof of claim is filed within the given time period and no Motion to Extend the Time is filed, the creditor will then be barred from filing an unsecured proof of claim. If a proof of claim is subsequently filed in violation of this Rule, then that claim is automatically disallowed and the Chapter 13 Trustee shall make no disbursement on such claim unless a Motion and Order allowing the filing of the claim has been entered.

(5) If the plan filed by the debtor(s) provides for the surrender of collateral, that plan shall constitute the debtor(s) consent to the immediate termination of the automatic stay.

B. If a Chapter 13 Plan does not provide for the surrender of property:

(1) The secured creditor shall have sixty (60) days from the date of an Order terminating the automatic stay to file an unsecured proof of claim regarding any deficiency balance that may occur upon the sale of the subject collateral if the collateral consists of personal property that was not liquidated within the claims bar date period;

(2) The secured creditor shall have ninety (90) days from the date of an Order terminating the automatic stay to file an unsecured proof of claim regarding any deficiency balance that may occur upon the sale of the subject collateral if the collateral consists of real property that was not liquidated within the claims bar date period;

(3) The time periods provided above may be extended by Court Order upon the creditor filing an appropriate Motion using negative notice stating the circumstances necessitating a need for a longer period of time and an estimated deficiency;

(4) If no unsecured proof of claim is filed within the given time period and no Motion to Extend the Time is filed, the creditor will then be barred from filing an unsecured proof of claim. If a proof of claim is subsequently filed in violation of this Rule, then that claim is automatically disallowed and the Chapter 13 Trustee shall make no disbursement on such claim unless a Motion and Order allowing the filing of the claim has been entered.

[Effective December 1, 2009. Amended effective December 1, 2011.]

RULE 3002.1–1 NOTICE RELATING TO CLAIMS SECURED BY SECURITY INTEREST IN THE DEBTOR'S PRINCIPAL RESIDENCE

A. In addition to the relief provided in Bankruptcy Rule 3002.1(i)(1) and (2), the holder of the claim may not seek to collect any fees, expenses and/or changes included in the omitted information required by Bankruptcy Rule 3002.1(b), (c) or (g).

B. All notices required pursuant to Bankruptcy Rule 3002.1 shall be provided to debtor, debtor's counsel and trustee in accordance with Bankruptcy Rule 2002 and shall include a certificate of service. If filing the required notices as a supplement to the holder's proof of claim does not result in notice to the debtor, debtor's counsel and trustee via the Electronic Case Filing (CM/ECF) system, the holder of the claim shall serve the unnoticed party by alternative means and so indicate on the certificate of service filed with the notice.

[Effective December 1, 2009. Amended effective December 1, 2011.]

RULE 3007-1. CLAIMS OBJECTIONS

A. Objections to timely-filed claims shall be subject to Bankruptcy Rule 9014 and Local Rule 9013-1, except that the initial pleading need not contain or be accompanied by citations of authority.

B. Objections to claim shall contain the legend set forth in Local Rule 2002-2.B(3) and shall be filed individually for each claim objected to and may name only one creditor.

Note: Objections which include multiple claims, except with respect to duplicate claims, cannot be accurately processed and tracked in the Court's electronic filing system.

C. All responsive pleadings to an objection to claim shall contain or be accompanied by citations of authority.

D. If no response to an objection to a claim is filed pursuant to Local Rule 9013-1 and the objection contained the legend set forth in Local Rule 2002-2.B(3), the Court may grant relief to the objecting party without the necessity of an evidentiary hearing if relief is otherwise proper.

E. All proposed orders on objections to claims shall recite in the ordering paragraph that the objection is either sustained or denied, that the claim is either allowed or disallowed, and if allowed, the amount and class of each such allowed claim.

F. In all cases filed under Chapter 13, unless extended by the Court, objections to timely-filed claims shall be filed no later than the hearing on Confirmation of the plan.

G. In all cases filed under Chapter 11, unless extended by the Court, objections to claims shall be filed not less than forty-five (45) days prior to the entry of an Order of Confirmation.

Note: As guidance to practitioners utilizing this Local Rule, this procedure should be used only for routine objections to claims and in no instance shall this rule be used in filing objections to claims of federal governmental units.

[Effective June 1, 1997. Amended effective October 6, 2003; April 1, 2005; December 1, 2009; December 1, 2011.]

RULE 3012-1. VALUATION OF COLLATERAL

A. In cases filed under Chapter 11:

(1) All secured creditors shall be served a copy of any plan and disclosure statement or any amendment thereto filed in the case. The value of property set forth in the disclosure statement filed pursuant to 11 U.S.C. § 1125 shall be deemed at confirmation to be the value of the property for purposes of the plan and confirmation of the plan, including the treatment of creditors under the plan, unless seven (7) days prior to the hearing on confirmation a party in interest has filed a motion pursuant to Bankruptcy Rule 3012, in which event such values shall be as determined by the Court.

(2) The disclosure statement shall include the plan proponent's basis or justification for all values shown.

B. In cases filed under Chapter 12 or 13: Upon the filing of the plan or within seven (7) days thereafter, the debtor shall file a notice to secured creditors whose claims are being impaired under the plan of the value of the collateral which secures their claim. The notice shall contain the legend set forth in Local Rule 2002-2.B(3) and the following information:

(1) The value of the collateral and the basis or justification for the value shown;

(2) In a case under Chapter 13, whether the collateral is or is not of a kind described in § 1325(a)(9);

(3) The proposed use or disposition of the collateral, i.e., retain or surrender; and

(4) If the debtor proposes to surrender the collateral in satisfaction of all or a portion of the claim based on the valuation, the notice shall so state.

The attorney for the debtor shall file a certificate of service to evidence service of the notice pursuant to this rule. Notice shall be given as provided by Bankruptcy Rule 9014 and Rule 7004. The value of property subject to liens or security interests as noticed shall be deemed to be the value of the property for purposes of confirmation and treatment of such creditor pursuant to a plan unless no later than thirty (30) days after such notice any party in interest files a motion to value collateral or motion to determine secured status pursuant to Bankruptcy Rule 3012. The notice sent to a secured creditor pursuant to this rule shall notify such creditor that failure to file a timely motion to value collateral or motion to determine secured status will result in such collateral being valued at the amount listed for purposes of confirmation of the plan and treatment of such creditor's claim pursuant to the plan.

C. A motion to value property or motion to determine secured status of property of the estate shall state the value of the property as alleged by the moving party and all facts or circumstances supporting such value and shall be accompanied by an appraisal or other evidence of value. A motion to value or motion to determine secured status of property shall include a certification as required by Local Rule 7007-1. The appraisal or other evidence shall be filed and a copy served upon all adverse parties who are required to be served with a copy of the motion. Any adverse party who contests the motion and desires to appear and be heard on the issue of value shall file a response to such motion within thirty (30) days prior to the hearing on the motion and shall file and serve not later than seven (7) days prior to the hearing an appraisal or other evidence of value.

D. In any proceeding in which the value of real property is an issue and where a party intends to present appraisal testimony, the appraisal report and a statement of the qualifications of the appraisal witness shall be filed with the Court and served on all opposing parties as soon as the report first becomes available but in no case less than seven (7) days before the trial or hearing wherein the testimony is to be presented.

E. All objections to the admissibility of the appraisal report or the qualifications of the appraiser as an expert shall be filed and served upon the appraisal's proponent no less than two (2) days prior to the trial or hearing wherein the testimony is to be presented. Absent any objections, the report shall be admitted into evidence without further testimony.

F. Admission into evidence of an appraisal report shall constitute the complete direct examination of an appraiser witness. Cross examination of the witness will begin immediately upon admission of the report followed by redirect and recross.

Note: Local Rule 3012–1B does not apply to cases when the sole impairment of the claim is the debtor's proposed change in the interest rate.

[Effective June 1, 1997. Amended effective October 6, 2003; April 1, 2005. Amended, on an interim basis, effective October 17, 2005. Amended effective September 1, 2006; December 1, 2009.]

RULE 3012–2. VALUATION OF COLLATERAL—LIEN STRIPPING IN CHAPTER 13'S

In chapter 13 cases, motions to value claims cases secured by junior liens on the debtor's principal residence and to strip off those liens may be filed as an exception to Local Rule 3012–1.B and on negative notice pursuant to Local Rule 2002–2.

A. The following guidelines and procedures are to be used with regard to the Motion:

(1) Motions to value claims secured by junior liens on the debtor's principal residence at $0.00 and to "strip off" such liens shall not be filed before the earlier of the time when:

(a) the affected creditor has filed a proof of claim or

(b) the expiration of the time to file claims (claims bar date). A premature motion to value will be denied without prejudice.

(2) The motion shall:

(a) clearly state

(i) all known parties who may have an interest in the mortgage,

(ii) the loan number (formatted as xxxx1234) and recording information of all mortgage lien(s) affected by the Motion,

(iii) the legal description and street address of the subject property, and

(iv) the basis of the valuation—private appraisal, county valuation, or other,

(v) the balance of the first mortgage;

(b) be verified, or supported by an affidavit or declaration (pursuant to 28 U.S.C. § 1746) of the debtor;

(c) include on the first page the required negative notice legend giving interested parties thirty (30) days to file an objection;

(d) certify service on:

(i) the appropriate persons required by Bankruptcy Rule 7004(b) (note in particular the requirement to serve insured depository institutions by certified mail),

(ii) on the person who filed the mortgagee's proof of claim,

(iii) the attorney, if any, for such creditor, and

(iv) the Chapter 13 trustee; and

(e) be docketed in the Electronic Case Filing System (CM/ECF) using the Motion to "Determine Secured Status and Strip Junior Lien on Debtor's Principal Residence" docket event.

(3) The negative notice legend should be substantially compliant with the one found under Local Rule 2002–2.B.(3) except that the objection period is to be set to thirty (30) days.

B. The movant shall submit a proposed order to the Clerk's Office no later than fourteen (14) days after the expiration of the thirty (30) day objection period.

C. The debtor's Chapter 13 plan shall provide for the stripping off of the lien, conditioned on the debtor's obtaining a discharge or upon further Order of the Court.

[Effective December 1, 2011.]

RULE 3015–1. CERTIFICATION REQUIRED BY CHAPTER 13 DEBTOR FOR CONFIRMATION

A. All Chapter 13 debtors shall file with the Court and serve on the Chapter 13 Trustee a certification that the debtor has paid all amounts to be paid under a domestic support obligation that first became payable after the date of the filing of the Chapter 13 petition if the debtor is required by a judicial or administrative order, or by statute, to pay such domestic support obligation. If the debtor is not required to pay any amounts under a domestic support obligation, then the debtor shall file a certification stating that the debtor is not required to pay said amounts.

B. All Chapter 13 debtors shall file with the Court and serve on the Chapter 13 Trustee a certification that all applicable Federal, State and local tax returns as required by section 1308 and 1325(a)(9) have been filed.

[Adopted, on an interim basis, effective October 17, 2005. Amended effective December 1, 2009.]

RULE 3017–1. DISCLOSURE STATEMENT—APPROVAL

A. Upon the filing of the disclosure statement in cases under Chapter 11, the proponent of the plan shall serve copies of the disclosure statement and plan upon the debtor (if not the proponent), the debtor's attorney (if the debtor is not the proponent), the trustee (if any), the attorney for the creditors committee (if any), each member of the creditors committee, the Internal Revenue, Special Procedures Staff, the Securities and Exchange Commission, Chapter 11 Bankruptcy Filings, Washington, D.C. 20549, the U.S. Trustee, all parties required under Local Rule 3012-1A(1) and all parties in interest who have filed with the Clerk a request that notice be sent to them pursuant to Bankruptcy Rule 2002. A certificate of such service shall be filed with the Clerk.

B. The attorney for the debtor shall send copies of the disclosure statement and plan to any other party in interest who requests a copy and may charge such party in interest a reasonable charge for copying and mailing not to exceed the amount charged by the Clerk's Office.

C. Objections to the proposed disclosure statement shall be filed and served on the debtor, the debtor's attorney, the attorney for the proponent of the plan (if other than the debtor), the U.S. Trustee, and all parties entitled to be served copies of the disclosure statement and plan as listed above at least seven (7) days prior to the hearing on the disclosure statement. Any objections not timely filed shall be deemed waived.

[Effective June 1, 1997. Amended effective April 1, 2005; December 1, 2009.]

RULE 3017.1-1 DISCLOSURE STATEMENT—SMALL BUSINESS

A. Conditional Approval. In a small business case, the Court may, on application of the plan proponent, conditionally approve a disclosure statement filed in accordance with Bankruptcy Rule 3016. On or before conditional approval of the disclosure statement, the Court shall

(1) fix a time within which the holders of claims and interests may accept or reject the plan;

(2) fix a time for filing objections to the disclosure statement;

(3) fix a date for the hearing on final approval of the disclosure statement to be held if a timely objection is filed; and

(4) fix a date for the hearing on confirmation.

B. If the plan proponent files a plan with the Court that is intended to provide adequate information, as defined by 11 U.S.C. § 1125(a)(1), instead of filing a separate disclosure statement, the plan proponent shall simultaneously file a separate Request to Consider Plan with Adequate Information along with the plan filed.

C. Application of Bankruptcy Rule 3017. If the disclosure statement is conditionally approved, Bankruptcy Rule 3017(a), (b), (c), and (e) do not apply. Conditional approval of the disclosure statement is considered approval of the disclosure statement for the purpose of applying Bankruptcy Rule 3017(d).

D. Objections and Hearing on Final Approval. Notice of the time fixed for filing objections and the hearing to consider final approval of the disclosure statement shall be given in accordance with Bankruptcy Rule 2002 and may be combined with notice of the hearing on confirmation of the plan. Objections to the disclosure statement shall be filed, transmitted to the U.S. Trustee, and served on the debtor, the trustee, any committee appointed under the Bankruptcy Code and any other entity designated by the Court at any time before final approval of the disclosure statement or by an earlier date as the Court may fix. If a timely objection to the disclosure statement is filed, the Court shall hold a hearing to consider final approval before or combined with the hearing on confirmation of the plan.

Note: If the debtor is a small business, § 1125(f) permits the Court to conditionally approve a disclosure statement subject to final approval after notice and a hearing. If a disclosure statement is conditionally approved, and no timely objection to the disclosure statement is filed, it is not necessary for the Court to hold a hearing on final approval.

[Effective September 1, 2006. Amended effective December 1, 2009.]

RULE 3020-1. CHAPTER 11—CONFIRMATION

A. Objections to confirmation shall be governed by Bankruptcy Rule 9014 and shall be filed and served not less than seven (7) days before the hearing on confirmation or within such time as may otherwise be ordered by the Court. A copy of any objection shall be served upon each of the persons set forth in Bankruptcy Rule 3020(b), the U.S. Trustee, and the proponent of the plan (if other than the debtor).

B. All acceptances and rejections shall be sent to the proponent of the plan at least seven (7) days prior to the confirmation hearing, and, if the plan proponent is not the debtor, a copy of all ballots shall be served upon the debtor. Prior to the hearing on confirmation in Chapter 11 cases, the attorney for the plan proponent shall tabulate the acceptances and rejections of the plan on a Chapter 11 Ballot Tabulation form (see local forms page on Court internet site). The ballot tabulation shall then be filed with the Court prior to the confirmation hearing. The attorney for the plan proponent shall certify that the tabulation is accurate and that all ballots received have been accounted for in the tabulation. The original ballots shall be retained for the time period required under Section II.M.1.a of the Administrative Procedures for ECF and will be made available in a format as directed by the Court for the confirmation hearing or other required proceeding if so requested.

C. In tabulating the acceptances and rejections, the following rules shall govern:

(1) Ballots which are not signed or which do not identify the creditor will not count as either an acceptance or rejection;

(2) Ballots which do not show a choice of either acceptance or rejection will not be counted either as an acceptance or a rejection;

(3) Ballots which are filed after the last date set for filing of ballots will not be counted as either an acceptance or rejection except upon leave of the Court; and

(4) Where duplicate ballots are filed and one elects acceptance and one elects rejection, then, absent leave of the Court, neither ballot will be counted unless the latter one is designated as amending the prior one.

D. A summary of the tabulations shall be filed with the Court which shall list for each class: the total number of claims voting, total dollar amount of claims accepting, percentages of claims voting which accept the plan, and percentage of dollar amount of claims voting which accept the plan. Such summary shall also indicate for each class whether they are impaired or unimpaired and whether or not the requisite vote has been attained for each class.

E. All Chapter 11 individual debtors shall file with the Court and serve on the U.S. Trustee a certification that the debtor has paid all amounts that are required to be paid under a domestic support obligation that first became payable after the date of the filing of the Chapter 11 petition if the debtor is required by a judicial or administrative order, or by statute, to pay such domestic support obligation. If the debtor is not required to pay any amounts under a domestic support obligation, then the debtor shall file a certification stating that the debtor is not required to pay said amounts. (Form available on Court internet site.)

[Effective June 1, 1997. Amended effective October 6, 2003; April 1, 2005; September 1, 2006; December 1, 2009; December 1, 2011.]

RULE 4001-1. AUTOMATIC STAY—RELIEF FROM

A. Unless otherwise stated in the notice of hearing, a preliminary, non-evidentiary hearing under 11 U.S.C. § 362(e) will be restricted to the pleadings, affidavits and documents of record, and argument of counsel.

B. The movant shall file with the Motion, or within seven (7) days after service of the notice of hearing, the following as appropriate in the circumstances:

(1) An affidavit of indebtedness;

(2) Copies of documents, including filing and recording information necessary to establish a perfected secured interest;

(3) An appraisal or other evidence of value together with the qualifications of the appraiser;

(4) An affidavit showing such facts as may be necessary to demonstrate the movant's right to relief from stay;

(5) A statement showing the debtor's payment history.

C. If the motion is opposed, the debtor or the trustee shall file a response within fifteen (15) days after entry of the Court's order and notice of preliminary hearing; said response shall be accompanied by such appraisals, affidavits and documents as may be necessary to demonstrate the movant is not entitled to relief from the stay. If no response is filed within the time provided by this rule, the Court may grant the motion without a hearing.

D. In final hearings under 11 U.S.C. § 362(e), respective counsel shall present competent evidence admissible under the Federal Rules of Evidence either in support of, or in opposition to, the motion.

E. Not less than fourteen (14) days prior to the final hearing, each party shall furnish a list of the names and addresses of all witnesses (designating expert witnesses as such) and copies of all exhibits that such party intends to introduce at trial.

F. A party who intends to introduce the testimony of an expert witness shall make such witness available for deposition upon reasonable notice.

G. The moving party may, without leave of Court, take a deposition of the trustee, debtor, and debtor-in-possession fourteen (14) days after the date of service of the motion. Leave of Court must be obtained only if the moving party seeks to take the deposition of the trustee, debtor, or the debtor-in-possession prior to the expiration of fourteen (14) days after the date of service of the motion. Leave of Court is not required if a trustee, debtor, or debtor-in-possession has served a notice of taking deposition or otherwise sought discovery after service of the motion.

H. Any party in interest shall be entitled to inspect the property which is the subject of a motion under this rule upon reasonable notice. The notice shall provide for inspection not less than seven (7) days from the date of service of such notice unless the time is shortened or extended by the Court.

I. For the purpose of this rule, the time for responding under Bankruptcy Rule 7033, 7034 and 7036, is reduced to twenty-one (21) days unless otherwise directed by the Court.

[Effective June 1, 1997. Amended effective April 1, 2005. Amended, on an interim basis, effective October 17, 2005. Amended effective September 1, 2006; December 1, 2009.]

RULE 4001-2. AUTOMATIC STAY—CONFIRMATION OF NO STAY

If the party in interest contends the debtor is a repeat filer under § 362(c)(3) or § 362(c)(4), the party shall provide the following as appropriate in the circumstances for each prior case:

A. If prior filing was in this Court, the complete case caption, date of filing and date of dismissal;

B. If prior filing was in any other Court, then, in addition to the requirements of subsection A, the movant shall also file relevant copies of all Court records reflecting the information provided in subsection A.

[Effective September 1, 2006. Amended effective December 1, 2009.]

RULE 4001-3. IMPOSING OR EXTENDING AUTOMATIC STAY

A motion to impose or extend the automatic stay under 11 U.S.C. § 362(c)(3) shall be filed within five (5) days of the filing of the petition. The debtor shall serve all interested parties simultaneously with the filing of the motion. Interested parties shall include, but not be limited to, the U.S. Trustee, the case trustee, any co-owner of all affected property, and all lien holders of all affected property.

[Effective September 1, 2006. Amended effective December 1, 2009.]

RULE 4001-4. AUTOMATIC STAY—CO-DEBTOR RELIEF FROM

A. The movant shall file with the Motion the following as appropriate in the circumstances:

(1) An affidavit of indebtedness;

(2) Copies of documents, including filing and recording information necessary to establish:

(a) as between the debtor and the individual protected under 11 U.S.C. § 1301(a), such individual received the consideration for the claim held by the movant;

(b) the plan filed by the debtor proposes not to pay such claim; or

(c) the movant's interest would be irreparably harmed by continuation of such stay.

(3) An affidavit showing such facts as may be necessary to demonstrate the movant's right to relief from stay.

B. For the purpose of this rule, the time for responding under Bankruptcy Rule 7033, 7034 and 7036, is reduced to twenty-one (21) days unless otherwise directed by the Court.

[Effective December 1, 2009.]

RULE 4002-1. TAX RETURNS

A. Except as otherwise provided, debtors shall provide copies of documents to the trustee. The trustee is authorized to dispose of such copies at such time and in such manner as the trustee deems appropriate. Nothing in this rule shall prohibit or limit the trustee from requesting original documents. It is the intent of this rule to relieve trustees of the burden of storage of documents such as tax returns and to further relieve the trustee from any need to return documents to the debtor.

B. Copies of tax information provided by the debtor are confidential and dissemination of the tax information should be done only as appropriate under the circumstances of the particular case. At the discretion of the Court, sanctions may be imposed for improper use, disclosure, or dissemination of the tax information.

C. For parties to obtain access to tax information filed with the Bankruptcy Court, a motion is to be filed with the Court which shall include:

(1) A description of the movant's status in the case, to allow the Court to ascertain whether the movant may properly be given access to the required tax information;

(2) A description of the specific tax information sought;

(3) A statement indicating that the information cannot be obtained by the movant from any other sources;

(4) A statement showing a demonstrated need for tax information; and

(5) The name and address for mailing of confidential information.

Note: The order granting a motion for access to tax information will include language that the tax information obtained is confidential and will condition dissemination of the tax information as appropriate under the circumstances of the particular case. At the discretion of the Court, the order will state that sanctions may be imposed for improper use, disclosure, or dissemination of the tax information.

[Adopted, on an interim basis, effective October 17, 2005.]

RULE 4003-1. LIEN AVOIDANCE

A. A motion to avoid a lien under 11 U.S.C. § 522(f) and Bankruptcy Rule 4003(d) may name only one creditor as respondent. A separate motion is required for each creditor whose lien or transfer is sought to be avoided.

B. The debtor shall serve a copy of the motion on the respondent in accordance with Bankruptcy Rule 7004.

C. The respondent shall have twenty-one (21) days within which to file and serve on the debtor a response to the motion.

D. If a timely response is filed, the matter will be noticed for an evidentiary hearing. If the respondent fails to file a timely response and the legend set forth in Local Rule 2002-2.B(3) was included in the motion, the motion may be granted without further notice or hearing.

[Effective June 1, 1997. Amended effective April 1, 2005; September 1, 2006; December 1, 2009.]

RULE 4004-1. GRANT OR DENIAL OF DISCHARGE

A. When the debtor's Certification of Completion of Instructional Course Concerning Personal Financial Management is filed stating that no personal financial management course is required due to incapacitation or disability as defined in 11 U.S.C. § 109(h) or being on active duty in a military combat zone, an affidavit shall be filed at the same time providing all necessary information denoting personal knowledge to substantiate this certification.

B. All Chapter 13 debtors shall file with the Court and serve on the Chapter 13 Trustee a certification that the debtor has paid all amounts that are required to be paid under a domestic support obligation as required by a judicial or administrative order, or by statute, that were due on or before the date of the certification, including amounts due before the petition was filed, but only to the extent provided for by the Chapter 13 Plan. If the debtor is not required to pay any amounts under a domestic support obligation, then the debtor shall file a certification stating that the debtor is not required to pay said amounts.

The debtor shall also certify compliance with 11 U.S.C. § 1328(h) using the following language:

(1) The debtor has not claimed an exemption under § 522(b)(3) in an amount which exceeds the specified § 522(q) dollar amount in value in property of the kind described in § 522(q)(1) [generally the Debtor's homestead];

or

(2) The debtor has claimed an exemption under § 522(b)(3) in an amount which exceeds the specified § 522(q) dollar amount in value in property of the kind described in § 522(q)(1) but there is no pending proceeding in which the debtor may be found guilty of a felony of a kind described in § 522(q)(1)(A) or found liable for a debt of the kind described in § 522(q)(1)(B).

C. In an individual Chapter 11 the debtor shall certify compliance with 11 U.S.C. § 1141(d)(5)(C):

(1) The debtor has not claimed an exemption under § 522(b)(3) in an amount which exceeds the specified § 522(q) dollar amount in value in property of the kind described in § 522(q)(1) [generally the Debtor's homestead];

or

(2) The debtor has claimed an exemption under § 522(b)(3) in an amount which exceeds the specified § 522(q) dollar amount in value in property of the kind described in § 522(q)(1) but there is no pending proceeding in which the debtor may be found guilty of a felony of a kind described in § 522(q)(1)(A) or found liable for a debt of the kind described in § 522(q)(1)(B).

D. All Chapter 12 debtors shall file with the Court and serve on the Chapter 12 Trustee a certification that the debtor has paid all amounts that are required to be paid under a domestic support obligation as required by a judicial or administrative order, or by statute, that were due on or before the date of the certification, including amounts due before the petition was filed, but only to the extent provided for by the Chapter 12 Plan. If the debtor is not required to pay any amounts under a domestic support obligation, then the debtor shall file a certification stating that the debtor is not required to pay said amounts.

The debtor shall also certify compliance with 11 U.S.C. § 1228(f) (Chapter 12):

(1) The debtor has not claimed an exemption under § 522(b)(3) in an amount which exceeds the specified § 522(q) dollar amount in value in property of the kind described in § 522(q)(1) [generally the Debtor's homestead];

or

(2) The debtor has claimed an exemption under § 522(b)(3) in an amount which exceeds the specified § 522(q) dollar amount in value in property of the kind described in § 522(q)(1) but there is no pending proceeding in which the Debtor may be found guilty of a felony of a kind described in § 522(q)(1)(A) or found liable for a debt of the kind described in § 522(q)(1)(B).

Note: The dollar amounts listed in this Rule shall be adjusted as set out in 11 U.S.C. § 104.

[Adopted, on an interim basis, effective October 17, 2005. Amended effective September 1, 2006; December 1, 2011.]

RULE 5005-1. ELECTRONIC FILING

Note: Please see Standing Order #11—*Relating to Electronic Case Filing AND Administrative Procedures for Filing, Signing, Verifying Pleadings and Papers by Electronic Means* on the Court's website in conjunction with this Local Rule.

The Clerk of the Bankruptcy Court may accept for filing documents submitted, signed, verified or served by electronic means that are consistent with technical standards, if any, that the Judicial Conference of the United States establishes and that comply with the administrative procedures established by the Bankruptcy Court.

[Effective October 6, 2003. Amended effective December 1, 2011.]

RULE 5007-1. TRANSCRIPTS

A. Hard copy access to all transcripts provided to the Court by a court reporter or transcriber will initially be restricted to Court users and case participants for a period of 90 days from the date of filing to allow interested parties the opportunity to review the transcript and file a request for redaction, requesting that personal data identifiers be redacted prior to the transcript being made available to the public. Such personal identifiers are:

(1) Social security numbers

(2) Financial account numbers

(3) Names of minor children

(4) Dates of birth

(5) Home addresses of individuals

B. The clerk's office will be prohibited from providing electronic access as well as paper and/or electronic copies of such transcripts until 90 days from the date the transcripts were filed.

(1) Individuals wishing to purchase a copy of the transcript within the 90–day period must contact the transcriber directly.

(2) An attorney who purchases the transcript during the 90–day period will be given remote electronic access to the on-line transcript available at that time.

(3) Members of the general public, including pro se parties who purchase the transcript, will not be given remote electronic access to the transcript during the 90–day period.

After the 90–day period expires, transcripts will be available for public access through the PACER system.

C. Within seven (7) calendar days of the filing of the official transcript on the docket, each party shall inform the Court, by filing a notice of intent to request redaction with the clerk and serving a copy on the transcriber, of the party's intent to redact personal data identifiers from the electronic transcript of the court proceeding. The party then has twenty-one (21) calendar days from the date of the filing of the official transcript to file a request for redaction with a listing indicating where the personal identifiers to be redacted appear in the transcript and serve a copy on the transcriber. The transcriber will then have 31 calendar days from the date of the filing of the official transcript to file a redacted version of the transcript. Parties are reminded not to include in their public filing the information they want redacted. The transcriber must redact the identifiers as directed by the party as follows:

(1) Social security numbers will be limited to the last four digits

(2) Financial account numbers

(3) Names of minor children

(4) Dates of birth and

(5) Home addresses of individuals

D. If no request for redaction is filed within the allotted time, the Court will conclude that the parties to the action have no objection to the inclusion of personal data identifiers in the transcript and the transcript will be made electronically available on the 91st calendar day unless the Court for good cause, related to the application of the Judicial Conference policy on privacy and public access to electronic case files, finds that a transcript should not be made available.

E. If a timely request for redaction is filed with the clerk's office by any party to the proceeding following the filing of the official transcript, the official un-redacted transcript will not be made available. However, the redacted transcript will be made electronically available to the general public on the 91st day following the filing of the official transcript.

F. During the 90 day period, or longer if the Court so orders, any attorney who wishes to redact information not covered in Bankruptcy Rule 9037(a), must file a motion for protective order pursuant to part (d) of the Rule. A transcript will not be electronically available until the Court has ruled on the intervening motions for extension of time or for protective orders related to the transcript.

G. The cost of any redactions and the responsibility for monitoring the docket to know when the electronic transcript of their hearing has been filed shall be the sole responsibility of the parties to the hearing who have requested the redaction.

H. It is the responsibility of the parties to avoid introducing personal identifier information into the record, and attorneys are instructed to avoid eliciting information from or formulating questions to witnesses during court hearings that include personal identifier data and are further directed to be sensitive to the importance of protecting such personal data during the conduct of hearings that are being transcribed.

[Amended effective December 1, 2011.]

RULE 5011-1. WITHDRAWAL AND ABSTENTION FROM HEARING A PROCEEDING

A. Cases.

(1) A case referred to the Bankruptcy Court may be withdrawn by the District Court for cause shown on a timely motion filed by any party in interest. The motion to withdraw the reference of a case, in whole or in part, shall be filed with the Clerk of the Bankruptcy Court no later than thirty (30) days after the 11 U.S.C. § 341(a) Meeting of Creditors is concluded. Parties in interest without notice or actual knowledge of the pendency of the case may move to withdraw the reference not later than twenty-one (21) days after having acquired actual knowledge of the pendency of the case.

(2) Upon filing of a Motion to Withdraw Reference, the Clerk of the Bankruptcy Court shall forthwith transmit the motion to the Clerk of the District Court together with the pertinent record and any subsequent responses.

(3) The motion shall be served on counsel of record for the debtor or, if the debtor has no attorney, on the debtor and U.S. Trustee. The debtor shall have fourteen (14) days after service of the motion to file a response. The District Court may dispose of the motion with or without a hearing.

(4) Upon final disposition of a case transmitted to the District Court pursuant to an Order Withdrawing Reference of the case, the Clerk of the District Court shall transmit to the Bankruptcy Court a copy of the entire case file originally transmitted to the District Court together with the order, judgment, or decree entered by the District Court.

(5) In the event the Motion to Withdraw Reference is denied, the Clerk of the District Court shall forthwith retransmit the motion to the Clerk of the Bankruptcy Court together with the matters originally transmitted.

B. Proceedings.

(1) A proceeding arising in, under or related to a case referred to the Bankruptcy Court pursuant to the Order of General Reference may be withdrawn by the District Court for cause shown on a timely motion filed by a party in interest. The Motion to Withdraw Proceeding must be filed with the Clerk of the Bankruptcy Court not later than the date set for filing an answer under Bankruptcy Rule 7012 or within twenty-one (21) days after the Bankruptcy Court has made a determination that a proceeding is a non-core matter.

(2) A Motion to Withdraw Proceeding must specifically identify the proceeding sought to be withdrawn, setting forth the exact style, title, and adversary number where applicable.

(3) Immediately upon docketing the Motion to Withdraw Proceeding, the Clerk of the Bankruptcy Court shall forthwith forward the motion to the District Court together with all papers pertaining to the proceeding sought to be withdrawn.

(4) A Motion to Withdraw Proceeding shall be served on counsel of record for the debtor or, if the debtor has no attorney, on the debtor. The debtor shall have fourteen (14) days after service of the motion to file a response. The District Court may dispose of the motion with or without a hearing.

(5) Upon final disposition of a proceeding transmitted to the District Court pursuant to an Order Withdrawing Reference, the Clerk of the District Court shall transmit to the Bankruptcy Court a copy of the entire record originally transmitted to the District Court together with any order, judgment, or decree entered by the District Court.

(6) In the event that the reference of a proceeding is withdrawn by the District Court and the bankruptcy case is subsequently dismissed by order of the Bankruptcy Court, the Clerk of the Bankruptcy Court shall immediately certify to the District Court that an order of dismissal has been entered.

C. Abstention.

(1) Unless otherwise ordered by the Bankruptcy Court, a Motion for Abstention under 11 U.S.C. § 305 of the Code shall not toll, suspend, or otherwise change the time period for filing responsive pleadings or motions in pending matters.

(2) An Order of Abstention shall have the effect of closing the file of the case.

(3) All requests for the Court to abstain in a case under Title 11 shall be filed no later than thirty (30) days after the 11 U.S.C. § 341(a) Meeting of Creditors is concluded.

[Effective June 1, 1997. Amended effective December 1, 2009; December 1, 2011.]

RULE 6004-1. SALE OF ESTATE PROPERTY

A. In sales of property of the estate, other than

(1) in the ordinary course of business or

(2) of personal identifiable information under § 363(b)(1)(B), the trustee shall prepare and file a Report and Notice of Intention to Sell Property of the Estate (see local forms page on Court internet site). Where the value of the estate's interest in the property is less than $1,000.00, notice need be given only to the debtor, debtor's attorney, any committee or its authorized agent, the U.S. Trustee's Office, and to any creditor and equity security holders who file a request that all notices be sent to them.

B. Sales or leases of personally identifiable information under § 363(b)(1)(B) shall be governed by Bankruptcy Rule 6004(g).

C. Sales of property of the estate free and clear of liens pursuant to 11 U.S.C. § 363(f) and Bankruptcy Rule 6004(c) shall be accomplished in the following manner:

(1) File a motion pursuant to Rule 6004(c) for authority to sell property free and clear of liens or other interest, and serve the motion on the parties thereto who have liens or other interest in the property to be sold; and

(2) File a notice of sale containing the legend found in Local Rule 2002-2.B(3) (see local forms page on Court internet site) as provided in Rule 6004(a), and serve the notice on all creditors and parties in interest.

D. All objections to the sale, whether by a party with an interest in the property or otherwise, shall be set for hearing at the same time. If no objections to the sale are filed, the motion shall be granted without a hearing and the sale may proceed without further notice or hearing.

[Effective June 1, 1997. Amended effective October 6, 2003; April 1, 2005. Amended, on an interim basis, effective October 17, 2005. Amended effective December 1, 2009.]

RULE 6007-1. ABANDONMENT

A. Any party in interest, other than a trustee, who seeks to have property abandoned from the estate may do so by complying with the following:

(1) Prepare a Report and Notice of Trustee's Intention to Abandon Property of Estate (see local forms page on Court internet site). Present the original prepared Report and Notice to the trustee and enclose the following documentation or information:

(a) Evidence of indebtedness owed including promissory notes, statements of account or the like;

(b) Affidavit of amount due with calculations set forth in detail;

(c) Evidence of perfection of the lien or encumbrance including mortgages, security agreements, UCC filings and copies of titles showing liens; and

(d) Evidence as to value.

(2) The party in interest seeking abandonment of the property shall serve the Report and Notice of Trustee's Intention to Abandon Property of Estate on all creditors and parties in interest, except:

(a) If the property to be abandoned is encumbered by liens greater than the value of the property, notice shall be given only to the debtor, debtor's attorney, any known lien holders, the creditors' committee, if any, and the U.S. Trustee's Office.

(b) If the property to be abandoned is not encumbered by any liens but has a value totaling less than $500.00, notice shall be given to the debtor, debtor's attorney, the creditors' committee, if any, and the U.S. Trustee's Office.

(3) The party in interest who has requested the abandonment shall file the Report and Notice and a Certificate of Service with the Clerk.

B. A trustee who seeks to abandon property from the estate may do so by complying with the following:

(1) Prepare a Report and Notice of Trustee's Intention to Abandon Property of Estate;

(2) The trustee shall serve the Report and Notice of Trustee's Intention to Abandon Property of Estate on all creditors and parties in interest, except:

(a) If the property to be abandoned is encumbered by liens greater than the value of the property, notice shall be given only to the debtor, debtor's attorney, any known lien holders, the creditors' committee, if any, and the U.S. Trustee's Office.

(b) If the property to be abandoned is not encumbered by any liens but has a value totaling less than $500.00, notice shall be given to the debtor, debtor's attorney, the creditors' committee, if any, and the U.S. Trustee's Office.

(3) The trustee shall file the Report and Notice and a Certificate of Service with the Clerk.

C. Unless an objection is filed within twenty-one (21) days of the filing of the notice which contained the legend set forth in Local Rule 2002-2.B.(3) or within such other time fixed by the Court, the abandonment will be deemed final and no order will be issued.

[Effective June 1, 1997. Amended effective October 6, 2003; April 1, 2005; December 1, 2009; December 1, 2011.]

RULE 7001-1. ADVERSARY PROCEEDINGS

An adversary proceeding governed by Part VII of the Bankruptcy Rules shall be commenced by the filing of a complaint. The filing shall include the Adversary Proceeding Cover Sheet (Form B 104) and the appropriate filing fee. The caption of the complaint shall conform substantially with Official Form No. B 16D. Upon the filing of the adversary complaint and cover sheet, the Clerk's office shall issue the summons. The plaintiff's attorney shall receive the summons electronically and shall be responsible for printing and serving the summons along with a copy of the complaint upon the defendant(s) in accordance with Bankruptcy Rule 7004(b)(9). If the plaintiff is not represented by an attorney, the summons will be mailed to plaintiff for service upon the defendant(s).

[Effective June 1, 1997. Amended effective October 6, 2003; September 1, 2006.]

RULE 7004-1. SERVICE OF PROCESS

Service is the responsibility of the plaintiff's attorney and must be affected in accordance with Bankruptcy Rule 7004. Upon completion of service, a certificate of service showing compliance with Bankruptcy Rule 7004 must be executed and filed and a copy of the certificate provided to the defendant. The back of the original Summons may be used for this purpose.

[Effective June 1, 1997.]

RULE 7007-1. MOTION PRACTICE

A. In adversary proceedings, counsel for the moving party shall confer with counsel for the opposing party and shall file with the Court at the time of filing a motion, or within three (3) days thereafter, a statement certifying that he has conferred with counsel for the opposing party in a good faith effort to resolve by agreement the issues raised and the result thereof. If certain of the issues have been resolved by agreement, the certificate shall specify the issue so resolved and those remaining for resolution. Counsel shall clearly identify those motions which are consented to in their entirety. The statement shall specify the amount of time requested for hearing on the motion.

B. Each motion shall contain no more than one claim or request for relief unless the prayer is seeking alternative relief provided for in a single section of the Bankruptcy Code or Rules.

[Effective June 1, 1997. Amended effective December 1, 2011.]

RULE 7008-1. CORE/NON-CORE PROCEEDINGS

If an issue is raised under Bankruptcy Rule 7008(a) as to whether a proceeding is core or non-core, the party instituting the proceeding shall, within twenty-one (21) days after the service of the pleading creating the issue, file a motion seeking a determination as to whether the proceeding is core or non-core.

[Effective June 1, 1997. Amended effective December 1, 2009.]

RULE 7016-1. PRE-TRIAL/MEDIATION PROCEDURES

Local Rule 16.3 of the United States District Court for the Northern District of Florida, concerning Mediation, shall be applicable in all adversary proceedings and contested matters as directed by the Bankruptcy Court (see Addendum B).

[Effective June 1, 1997. Amended effective December 1, 2009; December 1, 2011.]

RULE 7026-1. DISCOVERY—GENERAL

A. Before filing a motion to compel pursuant to Bankruptcy Rule 7037, or a motion for protective order pursuant to Bankruptcy Rule 7026, counsel for the moving party shall confer with counsel for the opposing party in a good faith effort to resolve by agreement the issues raised, and shall file with the Court at the time of filing the motion a statement certifying that counsel has so conferred with opposing counsel and that counsel have been unable to resolve this dispute.

B. Motions to compel discovery pursuant to Bankruptcy Rule 7037 shall:

(1) quote in full each interrogatory, question on deposition, request for admission, or request for production to which the motion is addressed;

(2) the objection and grounds therefore as stated by the opposing party; and

(3) the reasons such objection should be overruled and the motion granted.

C. For the guidance of counsel in preparing or opposing contemplated motions for a protective order pursuant to Bankruptcy Rule 7026, related to the place of taking a party litigant's deposition, or the deposition of the managing agent of a party, it is the general policy of the Court that a nonresident plaintiff may reasonably be deposed at least once in this District during the discovery stages of the case; and that a nonresident defendant who intends to be present in person at trial may reasonably be deposed at least once in this District either during the discovery stages of the case or within a week prior to trial as the circumstances seem to suggest. A nonresident, within the meaning of this rule, is a person residing outside the Northern District of the State of Florida.

[Effective June 1, 1997.]

RULE 7041-1. DISMISSAL—FAILURE TO PROSECUTE

Whenever, in any civil action, it appears that no activity by filing of pleadings, orders of the Court or otherwise has occurred for a period of more than ninety (90) days, the Court may, on motion of any party in interest or on its own motion, enter an order to show cause why the action should not be dismissed, and if no satisfactory cause is shown, the action may be dismissed by the Court for want of prosecution.

[Effective June 1, 1997.]

RULE 7042-1. CONSOLIDATION OF ADVERSARY PROCEEDINGS

A. Rule 42 Fed.R.Civ.P. applies in adversary proceedings.

B. Until the Order Consolidating is entered, all items are to be filed as applicable in each involved adversary proceeding.

[Effective December 1, 2011.]

RULE 7054-1. COST—TAXATION/PAYMENT

When appropriate, motions to tax costs and attorney fees in actions or proceedings shall be filed not later than thirty (30) days after termination of such actions or proceedings.

[Effective June 1, 1997.]

RULE 7055-1. DEFAULT

A. A party seeking entry of a default by the Clerk shall file a motion which shall state:

(1) Upon whom, how, and when service was made, with reference to the applicable Bankruptcy Rule;

(2) The date on which a responsive pleading was due;

(3) That no extension of time was sought or obtained by the adverse party; and

(4) That the movant seeks an entry of default.

B. The party seeking a judgment by default shall file the following:

(1) An affidavit in support of the allegations set forth in the complaint;

(2) An affidavit of non-military service (where applicable);

(3) A motion for entry of default final judgment;

(4) A proposed order granting the motion for entry of default final judgment setting forth the relief to be provided in the final judgment; and

(5) A separate judgment in accordance with Fed.R.Civ.P. 58(a).

[Effective June 1, 1997. Amended effective December 1, 2009.]

RULE 7067-1. REGISTRY FUND

A. Whenever a party seeks a Court order for money to be deposited by the Clerk in an interest-bearing account or investment, the party shall file with the Clerk's Office its motion along with a proposed order.

B. The Clerk is directed to deduct from the income earned on the deposit a fee not exceeding that authorized by the Judicial Conference of the United States and set by the Director of the Administrative Office of the U.S. Courts in accordance with the schedule which shall be published periodically by the Director in the Federal Register. This assessment shall apply to all registry fund investments regardless of the nature of the case underlying the investment at the conclusion of the case.

[Effective June 1, 1997. Amended effective October 6, 2003; April 1, 2005; December 1, 2009.]

RULE 9004-1. DISMISSAL—CAPTION—DOCUMENTS

A. If a pleading contains a prayer for injunctive relief pursuant to Bankruptcy Rule 7065, the title of the pleading shall include the words: *"AND PRAYER FOR INJUNCTIVE RELIEF."*

B. The caption of a motion shall identify the filing party and designate the matter at issue. If the motion contains a memorandum, the caption shall so state. For example, *"TRUSTEE'S MOTION TO COMPROMISE AND SETTLE CONTROVERSY AND MEMORANDUM."*

C. Unless otherwise directed by the Court, any party permitted to amend a pleading, motion, or other document filed with the Court shall file the amended pleading in its entirety, and relate it back in the system to the originally filed pleading. It shall be styled: "Amended & Restated (Name of Pleading)."

[Effective June 1, 1997. Amended, on an interim basis, effective October 17, 2005. Amended effective December 1, 2009.]

RULE 9006-1. TIME PERIODS

A. All time periods established in these rules may be extended or shortened by the Court upon a showing of cause.

B. In computing any period of time prescribed or allowed by an order of this Court, the date such period shall commence is the date the order is docketed by the Clerk pursuant to Rule 5003 of the Bankruptcy Rules.

[Effective June 1, 1997.]

RULE 9013-1. BRIEFS AND MEMORANDA OF LAW

A. A moving party shall serve and file with every motion or application in a contested matter or adversary proceeding a memorandum of law or other citation of authority in support of the motion.

B. (1) Each party objecting to the relief being sought shall file and serve, within fifteen (15) days after service of the motion or application, a response and memorandum with citation of the authorities. Failure to file a response and such memorandum may be sufficient cause for the granting of the motion by default.

(2) *Certificate of No Objection.* After the objection deadline has passed with no objection having been filed or served, counsel for the movant may file a Certificate of No Objection stating that no objection has been filed or served on the movant. By filing such certification, counsel for the movant is representing to the Court that the movant is unaware of any objection to the motion or application and that counsel has reviewed the Court's docket and no objection appears thereon. Upon receipt of the Certificate of No Objection, the Court may enter the Order accompanying the motion or application without further pleading or hearing and, once the Order is entered, the hearing scheduled on the motion or application shall be canceled without further notice.

C. Absent prior permission of the Court, no party shall file any brief or legal memorandum in excess of twenty (20) pages (exclusive of exhibits).

[Effective June 1, 1997. Amended effective September 1, 2006; December 1, 2009.]

RULE 9014-1. WITNESSES AND EVIDENTIARY HEARINGS

If a party has determined an evidentiary hearing is required at the time of filing a motion, counsel shall immediately notify the appropriate chambers by telephone in conjunction with the requirements stated on the ECF system when filing the motion. This includes information as to the estimated amount of time required for scheduling purposes. Failure to notify the Court may result in unnecessary delays and continuances due to improper noticing.

[Effective October 6, 2003. Amended effective April 1, 2005. Amended, on an interim basis, effective October 17, 2005. Amended effective December 1, 2009.]

RULE 9015-1. JURY TRIAL

A. Applicability of Certain Federal Rules of Civil Procedure. Rules 38, 39, 47–49 and 51 Fed.R.Civ.P. and Rule 81(c) Fed.R.Civ.P. insofar as it applies to jury trials, apply in all cases and proceedings, except that a demand made under Rule 38(b) Fed.R.Civ.P. shall be filed in accordance with Bankruptcy Rule 5005.

B. A demand for a jury trial shall include a statement indicating the demanding party's consent or non-consent to have the jury trial conducted by a bankruptcy judge. The adverse party shall file a statement of consent or non-consent within twenty-one (21) days after the case or matter is at issue or within fourteen (14) days after the final determination of a right to a jury trial by the Bankruptcy Court, whichever date is later.

C. Pursuant to the "Order Designating Bankruptcy Judges to Conduct Jury Trials" entered by the United States District Court for the Northern District of Florida on January 3, 1995, the Federal Rules of Civil Procedure, Federal Rules of Evidence, and the Northern District of Florida Local Rules shall apply to the conduct of all proceedings involving a jury trial in the Bankruptcy Court. A copy of the Order of the District Court can be found on the Court internet site.

Note: This rule provides procedures relating to jury trials. This rule is not intended to expand or create any right to trial by jury where such right does not otherwise exist.

[Effective June 1, 1997. Amended effective December 1, 2009.]

RULE 9020-1. CONTEMPT PROCEEDINGS

A. A party moving for an order of contempt shall file:

(1) A verified motion for contempt stating with specificity the grounds, act or violation alleged to have been committed by the opposing party.

(2) An affidavit in support of the facts stated in the motion.

(3) Any other documents or evidence attached as exhibits which support the motion for contempt.

(4) A certificate of service reflecting compliance with Bankruptcy Rule 7004.

B. In addition, parties shall submit a proposed Order to Show Cause directing the opposing party to appear at an evidentiary hearing (to be noticed by the Court) and show cause as to why the Court should not grant the motion and find the opposing party in contempt for the alleged conduct that is the grounds for the motion.

[Effective December 1, 2011.]

RULE 9037-1. PRIVACY PROTECTION FOR FILINGS MADE WITH THE COURT

Procedures to protect personal identifiers and information are governed in accordance with Bankruptcy Rule 9037 and this Court's *Administrative Procedures for Electronic Filing, Signing and Verifying Pleadings and Papers by Electronic Means*. If a document containing information in violation of those provisions is filed, a Motion for Protective Order to Restrict Remote Electronic Access and Provide for Redaction of Information should be filed along with a proposed Order. Upon entry of the Order, access to the original document will be restricted on the system. The filer must then file an amended document in which the private information has been properly redacted.

[Effective December 1, 2009.]

RULE 9070-1. EXHIBITS

A. No later than three (3) business days prior to trial or an evidentiary hearing, counsel for the parties shall mark, list, file, and exchange all exhibits which they plan to introduce into evidence. If for some reason the exhibit or a facsimile of the exhibit cannot be filed, clarifying information for the non-filing is to be provided with the items that are filed.

B. Each exhibit shall be tagged separately with a tag containing the following information:

RECEIVED AS PLAINTIFF / / DEFENDANT / / JOINT / /
EXHIBIT NO. ________
CASE NO. ________
ADVERSARY NO. ________
FOR ID. ________ IN EVIDENCE ________
DATE REC'D ________

C. Exhibits shall be identified numerically commencing with number 1.

D. All exhibits must be listed in order on a separate sheet of paper using the exhibit form (see local forms page on Court internet site) and filed with the Court no later than three (3) business days prior to the commencement of the hearing.

E. The original, hard copy and/or printable version of the documentary exhibits and listing of exhibits shall be furnished to the Clerk at the commencement of the hearing or trial. Additional copies shall be made available for use by the presiding Judge, law clerk, and witnesses. In lieu of separate copies for the witnesses, counsel are encouraged to utilize the Court's electronic exhibit display equipment. In addition, copies of documentary exhibits and the listing of exhibits shall be exchanged between counsel prior to the hearing.

F. All exhibits produced at hearing or trial which are not pre-marked shall be tendered to and marked by the Court Clerk as they are presented in evidence. Sufficient copies pursuant to Section E shall be provided by counsel.

G. Upon the expiration of thirty (30) days after an order or judgment concluding a contested matter an adversary proceeding is entered, including the entry of an order disposing of any post-judgment motions, provided that no appeal is pending, or if an appeal is taken, upon filing of the mandate, the Clerk shall give notice to all parties to reclaim their exhibits. The parties shall have thirty (30) days from the date of said notice to either reclaim their exhibits or to make arrangements with the Clerk to do so. Exhibits which are not reclaimed shall be discarded or destroyed.

[Effective June 1, 1997. Amended effective October 6, 2003; April 1, 2005; September 1, 2006; December 1, 2009.]

RULE 9071-1. STIPULATIONS

No stipulation or agreement between any parties or their attorneys, the existence of which is not conceded, in relation to any aspect of any pending case, will be considered by the Court unless the same is made before the Court or is reduced to writing and subscribed by the party or attorney against whom it is asserted.

[Effective June 1, 1997.]

RULE 9072-1. ORDERS—PROPOSED

A. All proposed orders shall carry a full, descriptive title detailing the nature of the matter ruled upon. The name of the preparer shall appear in the lower left hand corner of the signature page. All parties on whom service of the order is to be made shall be listed under the signature block.

B. No order or judgment will be entered where the date or signature of the Court is the only text on a page.

C. Proposed orders and judgments shall be submitted electronically via the Orders link on the ECF system or similar link as part of the ECF Central program. Hard copies may be submitted only by non-ECF participants. Specifications regarding formatting, consent language and naming conventions are described in the Administrative Procedures for ECF and must be strictly adhered to in all cases. (See Addendum C.)

D. The proposed order shall be furnished electronically to the parties in interest with respect to the proposed order (i.e., those parties in interest affected by the order).

E. All orders should be submitted within three (3) business days after the date of the hearing or expiration of the response deadline, unless directed otherwise by the Court or under a separate order-related provision contained within these rules.

[Effective June 1, 1997. Amended effective April 1, 2005; December 1, 2009.]

RULE 9073-1. HEARINGS

A. If a movant seeks a hearing on a motion, or if the motion does not request a hearing, and an entity filing a response desires a hearing, the title of the motion or response shall include the following language: "... And Request For Hearing."

B. (1) When filing a motion, response to a motion, or pleading which seeks an emergency hearing, the docket text should be modified to include the words "Emergency Motion." Pursuant to instructions included on the electronic filing screen, the Judge's chambers should be contacted by telephone if an emergency hearing is required.

(2) Emergency hearings shall ordinarily be held only where direct, immediate, and substantial harm will occur to:

(a) the interest of an entity in property;

(b) the estate; or

(c) the debtor's ability to reorganize if the parties are not able to obtain an immediate resolution of the dispute.

(3) A motion seeking an emergency hearing shall be accompanied by a "Statement of Need For Emergency Hearing" stating:

(a) why the relief requested requires an emergency hearing;

(b) that the need for an emergency hearing is not caused by lack of due diligence by the party, or its counsel, seeking the relief; and

(c) that efforts have been made to resolve the issue without an emergency hearing.

C. All hearings may be adjourned or continued from time to time by announcement made in open Court without further written notice.

[Effective June 1, 1997. Amended effective October 6, 2003; April 1, 2005; September 1, 2006.]

II. ADDENDA

ADDENDUM A. CUSTOMARY AND TRADITIONAL CONDUCT AND DECORUM IN THE UNITED STATES DISTRICT COURT [N.D. FLA. LOC. R. ADDENDUM]

A. The purpose of this addendum is to state for the guidance of those heretofore unfamiliar with the traditions of this United States District Court certain basic principles concerning courtroom conduct and decorum. These standards are minimal and not all-inclusive. They are intended to emphasize and supplement, not supplant or limit, the ethical obligations of counsel under the Code of Professional Responsibility or the time honored customs of experienced trial counsel.

B. When appearing in the United States District Court, all counsel and all persons at counsel table should conduct themselves in the following customary and traditional manner:

(1) Stand as court is opened, recessed or adjourned.

(2) Stand when the jury enters or retires from the courtroom.

(3) Stand when addressing, or being addressed by, the Court.

(4) Address all remarks to the Court, not to opposing counsel.

(5) Avoid disparaging personal remarks or acrimony toward opposing counsel and remain wholly detached from any ill feeling between the litigants or witnesses.

(6) Refer to all persons, including witnesses, other counsel and the parties, by their surnames and not by their first or given names.

(7) Counsel should request permission before approaching the bench; and any document counsel wishes to have the Court examine should be handed to the clerk.

(8) Unless opposing counsel has previously been shown exhibits, any exhibit offered in evidence should, at the time of such offer, be handed to opposing counsel.

(9) In making objections, counsel should state only the legal grounds for the objection and should withhold all further comment or argument unless elaboration is requested by the Court.

(10) In examining a witness, counsel shall not repeat or echo the answer given by the witness.

(11) Offers of, or requests for, a stipulation should be made privately, not within the hearing of the jury.

(12) In opening statements and in arguments to the jury, counsel shall not express personal knowledge or opinion concerning any matter in issue, shall not read or purport to read from deposition or trial manuscripts, and shall not suggest to the jury directly or indirectly that it may or should request transcripts or the reading of any testimony by the reporter.

(13) Counsel shall admonish and discourage all persons at counsel table from making gestures, facial expressions, audible comments, or the like, as manifestations of approval or disapproval during the testimony of witnesses, or at any other time.

(14) Smoking, eating, food and drink are prohibited in the courtroom at any time.

[Effective June 1, 1997.]

ADDENDUM B. MEDIATION [N.D. FLA. LOC. R. 16.3]

(A) Definition. Mediation is an opportunity for the parties to negotiate their own settlement. Mediation is a supervised settlement conference presided over by a neutral mediator to promote conciliation, compromise and the ultimate settlement of a civil action. The mediator may be a mediator certified in accordance with these rules or any person mutually agreed upon by all parties. The mediator's role in the settlement is to suggest alternatives, analyze issues, question perceptions, conduct private caucuses, stimulate negotiations between opposing sides, and keep order. The mediation process does not allow for testimony of witnesses. The mediator does not review or rule upon questions of fact or law, or render any final decision in the case. Absent a settlement or consent of the parties, the mediator will only report to the presiding judge whether the case settled, was adjourned or continued for further mediation, or was terminated because settlement was not possible and the mediator declared an impasse.

(B) Purpose. Mediation is intended as an alternative method to resolve civil cases, thereby saving time and cost without sacrificing the quality of justice to be rendered or the right of the litigants to a full trial in the event of an impasse following mediation.

(C) Qualifications of Mediators. Any person who is certified and remains in good standing as a circuit court mediator under the rules adopted by the Supreme Court of Florida is qualified to serve as a mediator in this district. By mutual agreement and with Court approval, any other person may be a mediator in a specific case.

(D) Standards of Professional Conduct for Mediators. All mediators, whether certified or not, who mediate in cases pending in this district shall be governed by standards of professional conduct and ethical rules adopted by the Supreme Court of Florida for circuit court mediators.

(E) Disqualification of a Mediator. After reasonable notice and hearing, and for good cause, the presiding judge shall have discretion and authority to disqualify any mediator from serving as mediator in a particular case. Good cause may include violation of the standards of professional conduct for mediators. Additionally, any person selected as a mediator may be disqualified for bias or prejudice as provided in 28 U.S.C. § 144, and shall be disqualified in any case in which such action would be required by a justice, district judge, or magistrate judge governed by 28 U.S.C. § 455.

(F) Compensation of Mediators. Absent agreement by all parties to the contrary, mediators shall be compensated and reimbursed for expenses at the rate set by the Court. Further, absent agreement of the parties to the contrary or order of the Court for good cause shown, the cost of the mediator's services shall be paid equally by the parties to the mediation conference.

(G) Limitations on Acceptance of Compensation or Other Reimbursement. Except as provided by these rules, no mediator shall charge or accept in connection with the mediation of any particular case, any compensation, fee, or any other thing of value from any other source without prior written approval of the Court.

(H) Mediators as Counsel in Other Cases. Any member of the bar who is certified or selected as a mediator pursuant to these rules shall not, for that reason alone, be disqualified from appearing and acting as counsel in any other case pending in this district.

(I) Referral to Mediation. Any pending civil case may be referred to mediation by the presiding judicial officer at such time as the judicial officer may determine to be in the interests of justice. The parties may request the Court to submit any pending civil case to mediation at any time.

[Effective June 1, 1997.]

ADDENDUM C. STANDING ORDER #11 RELATING TO ELECTRONIC CASE FILING

Federal Rule of Civil Procedure 5(e) and Federal Rules of Bankruptcy Procedure 5005(a)(2), 9011, 9029, and Local Bankruptcy Rule 5005–1 authorize this court to establish practices and procedures for the filing, signing, and verification of pleadings and papers by electronic means. This Order sets out those practices and procedures.

IT IS ORDERED that:

1. The Administrative Procedures for Filing, Signing, and Verifying Pleadings and Papers by Electronic Means have been presented to this court and are hereby approved.

2. The provisions of this Order shall apply to all cases previously filed, proceedings presently pending and those subsequently filed in the United States Bankruptcy Court for the Northern District of Florida.

3. Any Order signed electronically and hence without the original signature of a judge shall have the same force and effect as if the judge had affixed his signature to a paper copy of the Order and entered it in a conventional manner. This provision also applies to Administrative Orders that are granted and routinely entered by the Clerk's Office.

4. Documents may be filed on-line at any time. Such filings will constitute entry of that pleading or other paper on the docket kept by the Clerk of Court in accordance with FRBP 5003. Documents to be filed at either location of the Clerk's Office shall be filed within the regular business hours of the Clerk's Office. The time zone of the division in which a case is filed will be the official time zone for filing and noticing purposes.

5. The electronic filing of documents shall be suspended if, under extraordinary circumstances, the system is out of service. The Clerk's Office will maintain a log of these occurrences for reference purposes. During such periods, filing conventionally via hard copy will be permitted. For emergency filing situations when the system is out of service during non-business hours, filers can make arrangements with the Clerk or the Clerk's designee for the acceptance of filings.

6. If the Clerk's Office deems it necessary to electronically scan a paper document into the Electronic Case Filing System, the electronically scanned document shall constitute the official record of the court, and the paper document may be discarded without further notice.

7. Amendments to this Order and the Administrative Procedures for Filing, Signing, and Verifying Pleadings and Papers by Electronic Means may be entered from time to time in keeping with the needs of the court.

8. Nothing contained in this Order is intended, or shall be construed to alter or modify any party's duties under the provisions of the Bankruptcy Code or the Federal Rules of Bankruptcy Procedure.

[Dated: November 4, 2003, effective November 12, 2003.]

UNITED STATES BANKRUPTCY COURT
NORTHERN DISTRICT OF FLORIDA

Tenth Amended

ADMINISTRATIVE PROCEDURES FOR FILING, SIGNING AND VERIFYING PLEADINGS AND PAPERS BY ELECTRONIC MEANS

I. REGISTRATION FOR THE ELECTRONIC FILING SYSTEM

A. Designation of Cases.

1. The court shall designate which cases shall be assigned to the Electronic Case Filing System ("System" or "ECF"). The conversion to the System took place on November 12, 2003, and cases on the System can be accessed through www.flnb.uscourts.gov.

B. Passwords.

1. All attorneys, filing agents, and limited use filers are required to use a court-provided login and password to participate in the electronic retrieval and filing of pleadings and other papers in accordance with the System. Registration for a login and password is governed by Paragraph I.C.

2. No attorney or filing agent shall knowingly permit or cause to permit his/her password to be utilized by anyone other than an authorized employee of his/her law firm.

3. No person shall knowingly utilize or cause another person to utilize the password of a registered attorney unless that person is an authorized employee of that attorney's law firm.

4. Your password can be reset using a link available through www.flnb.uscourts.gov if it has been forgotten or compromised. Contact the Clerk's Office if you receive a message that your account has been locked. For security purposes, passwords will not be provided over the telephone. If a password must be reissued, information will be sent electronically to the primary email address for the account.

C. User Registration and Responsibilities.

1. Each attorney or limited filer desiring to file pleadings or other papers electronically ("e-file") must:

a. Complete System training. This requirement can be met by having attended a court-provided CM/ECF training seminar, completing the Court's online training module, or by already being a registered CM/ECF user in another U.S. Bankruptcy or U.S. District Court.

b. Register online for an account through the Court's website (www.flnb.uscourts.gov) agreeing to abide by the Court's requirements. Further instructions are provided through the CM/ECF Registration Program software. You will be required to provide the Court with a current email address for use with the System and to comply with Paragraph II.D.

c. Agree to keep your contact information current by using the "Maintain My ECF Account" link found in CM/ECF.

2. Once registered, you are required to:

a. Maintain all applicable user account information on the System including your current address, telephone numbers, and email address(es). If there is evidence that a user account is not being maintained as required, it may be deactivated by the Court.

b. Notify the Court of any changes in user status or changes in firm affiliation so that updates to applicable case- and user-related information can be made.

3. Limited filing is available for the following list of filers:

a. Attorneys appearing pro hac vice;

b. Individuals authorized to prepare and file a Proof of Claim(s) and related attachments/supplements;

c. Individuals authorized to appear on behalf of a child support creditor;

d. Individuals authorized to file *Motions to Withdraw Unclaimed Funds*;

e. Individuals authorized to submit *Reaffirmation Agreements*; and

f. Court reporters or employees of transcription services required to file transcripts.

4. Withdrawing from Participation

a. Filers may withdraw from participation in the System by providing the Court with written notice of such withdrawal. Upon receipt, and if no order is required to be entered by the Court, the Clerk's Office will immediately cancel the account and will delete the user's name from any applicable electronic service list. **IMPORTANT NOTE: An order is required for an attorney to withdraw if the attorney has filed a case or has made an appearance for a party. See Local Rule 2090–1D.**

II. Filing and Service of Documents

A. Filing.

1. All petitions, motions, pleadings, memoranda of law, or other documents, except for creditor matrices and orders, are to be converted into portable document format (.PDF) and filed directly on the System (otherwise known as e–filing). Exceptions may be directed or approved by the Court on a case by case basis. Creditor matrices are to be filed in a similar manner, but in text (.TXT) format. Information regarding the formatting of orders can be found in Paragraph II.F and on the Court's website at www.flnb.uscourts.gov.

2. Judicial waiver will be required for counsel to file documents in hard copy format. If hard copies are submitted without a waiver, the Clerk's Office will proceed with steps to possibly strike the document.

3. For corporate entities that file more than 20 Proof of Claims in a calendar year, a judicial waiver *will be required* to file documents in hard copy format. If hard copies are submitted without a waiver, the Clerk's Office will proceed with steps to possibly strike the document.

4. Pleadings or other papers presented for filing by unregistered attorneys and/or parties via compact disk (CD) must contain a scanned or electronic copy of all original signatures. All CDs will be scanned for viruses. Infected disks will not be returned to the filer and will be destroyed.

5. Parties not represented by counsel (known as pro se parties) may file documents in hard copy format *except for those entities that fall under Paragraph II.A.3.* These documents will be scanned into .PDF format by the Clerk's Office and docketed into the System. Paper documents will be discarded once processed without further notice, except for those under Paragraph II.H.

6. Emergency or expedited motions must be accompanied by a "Statement of Need for Emergency Hearing".

a. See the Court's website at www.flnb.uscourts.gov for additional information concerning emergency matters.

b. Parties and attorneys are *not* permitted to contact the presiding judge or members of chambers staff concerning emergency or other matters as that action would constitute ex parte communication.

7. Additional requirements may be reviewed on the Court's website located at www.flnb.uscourts.gov. Please make specific note of the information found at http://www.flnb.uscourts.gov/filing–requirements/ instructions–and–procedures–chambers.

B. Service.

1. Participation in the System by a receipt of a court-issued login and password shall constitute a request for service and notice by electronic means pursuant to FRBP 9036. Registered participants of the System, by possessing a password from the Court, agree to receive notice and service by electronic means both from the Court and from other System participants, wherever located. Service by other means requires non-participation in the System, and judicial waiver is required under Paragraph II.A.2.

2. Whenever a pleading or other paper is e-filed through the System in accordance with these procedures, the filer will cause the System to automatically generate and serve to electronic case participants a "Notice of Electronic Filing" (NEF) at the time of docketing. Such service will be considered the equivalent of service by first class mail, postage prepaid, *if and only if* the recipient of the NEF is a registered participant in the System. If not, then the filer must have obtain the service

recipient's written agreement to accept electronic service in lieu of service by first class mail. The filer will also be responsible for carrying out the electronic service outside of the System.

3. For all remaining parties and non-registered participants, the filing attorney shall serve the pleading or other paper upon all entitled in accordance with applicable Rules and Court policies. (See www.flnb.uscourts.gov.)

4. **A Certificate of Service is required to be included with or filed subsequent to all pleadings and other documents filed through the System and must state the names of all parties served and the method of service, including a party's mailing address or email address if served electronically via NEF.** The following language is recommended for Certificate of Service purposes. Additional procedural instructions and a stand-alone Certificate of Service fillable PDF may be found on the Court's website:

The following parties were served either by electronic or standard first class mail:

(Then show the name of each party to whom service was rendered together with their respective mailing address, email address, or fax number, as applicable.)

IMPORTANT NOTE:

The Bankruptcy Noticing Center (BNC), established by the Administrative Office of the U.S. Courts (AOUSC), provides *the court* with a centralized service for preparing, producing, and sending documents by mail or electronic notification. Use of BNC services for the dissemination of pleadings or other papers by the public is not authorized, however, there are other noticing services available to you for a fee. The Clerk's Office does not recommend or endorse mail/noticing services and suggests that you contact your colleagues who may be utilizing this type of service for a recommendation.

C. Signatures.

1. Signatures for the e-filing of a petition, pleading, motion, claim, or other paper by an attorney or unrepresented party who is a registered participant of the System for FRBP 9011 and other applicable Rules are valid only when the filing is accompanied via their authorized System login, **and** the .PDF document filed contains either a scanned image of any original signature(s) or the text "/s/ user name" where an original signature should occur.

2. Petitions, lists, schedules, statements, amendments, pleadings, affidavits and other documents that must contain original signatures or that require verification under FRBP 1008 or an unsworn declaration as provided in 28 U.S.C. § 1746 may be e-filed by attorneys registered in the System. Applicable retention requirements can be found in Paragraph II.L.

D. Email Address in Pleadings.

1. All registered System participants must include a working email address on all filed pleadings and other papers so that parties may communicate as needed on applicable case-related issues.

E. Fees Payable to the Clerk.

1. All fees are due at the time of filing on the System. Users must settle their online accounts for any outstanding fees by midnight Eastern Time on the day of filing. If fees are not received in a timely manner, steps will be taken to either strike the pleading or dismiss the case, whichever is applicable.

F. Orders.

1. All orders are to be submitted electronically via *ECF Central* or the "Proposed Order Submission" link on the System menu.

2. Order submissions must conform to the specifications maintained on the Court's website at http://www.flnb.uscourts.gov/sites/default/ files/filing_requirements/4–inst.pdf.

G. Attachments to Pleadings and Proof(s) of Claim.

1. If a filed document includes exhibits or attachments, then such exhibits or attachments are to be attached to the document submitted for filing. Filers submitting attachments electronically are required to complete the "Category" **and** "Description" fields for each uploaded file. The information in these fields aids the Court *significantly* in its review of the case file.

2. If the filed document is set for hearing, hard copies of the exhibits or attachments shall be introduced at the hearing for possible admission to the official record. See Local Rule 9071–1(E) for details.

3. Similarly, exhibits, attachments and/or supporting documentation for a Proof of Claim(s) are to be attached to the Proof of Claim when submitted for filing. The creditor must provide a copy of the original documentation to any party objecting to its claim. In the event of a hearing on an objection to the claim, the Proof of Claim along with all original exhibits, attachments and supporting documentation shall be introduced at the hearing for possible admission to the official record.

4. Exhibits and attachments that are not in proper format should be photographed so that they can be scanned or converted by the filer into portable document format (.PDF) for subsequent e-filing.

H. Documents Filed Under Seal.

1. Motions to file documents under seal may be e-filed; however, the actual document(s) to be filed under seal must be presented on paper for the Court's consideration. If the motion is granted, then the Clerk will scan, e-file and seal the document(s) in the System, setting appropriate restrictions so that the document may not be viewed by anyone other than the judge assigned to the case. The original paper document(s) will be attached to a paper copy of the order, logged, and stored in a sealed document safe. If the motion is denied, the paper documents will be disposed of in accordance with the order or Court policy.

I. Title of Docket Entries.

1. An attorney who e-files a pleading or other document shall be responsible for designating a docket entry title for the document by using one of the docket event categories prescribed by the Court and reflected in the System.

J. Correcting Errors in Electronic Filings.

1. Electronic filings appear on the court docket immediately upon submission through the System. Notices of Electronic Filing (NEFs) are produced concurrently with document submission. If a document contains an error or is filed in error, corrective action may be required from the filer before the pleading will be considered by the Court.

a. Submission error. If an action is required from the filer, the error notification will come in the form of a *"Submission Error Notification"* (SEN) entered on the docket by Clerk's Office staff. This docket entry automatically generates an email notice to the registered user who filed the pleading.

IMPORTANT: This is the only notice you will receive advising you that corrective action is necessary.

The email will identify the nature of the error and will inform the filer if an action on their part is necessary in order for the filing to be considered by the Court as well as any applicable time frame in which the action needs to be taken.

b. Corrective entries. Some errors can be corrected by Clerk's Office staff making it unnecessary for the filer to take corrective action. In those instances, the Court will generally make the necessary corrections. To maintain the integrity of the court docket, any changes made by court staff will be noted on the docket with the text *"Corrective Entry."* The entry will identify the nature of any changes made by the Clerk's Office. It is not necessary for the filing party to take any additional action to correct the entry.

K. Interrogatories.

1. E–file a "Notice of Service of Interrogatories" only. Do not e-file the entire set of interrogatories. Upon request of the Court or party, the filer may be required to produce the interrogatories at issue in open court or at another location.

L. Retention Requirements.

1. *E–filed Documents by registered users:*

a. All petitions, lists, schedules, statements, pleadings, affidavits and other documents requiring verification under FRBP 1008 and an unsworn declaration as provided in 28 U.S.C. § 1746 must be retained with the original signatures by the attorney or other registered user who e-files such a document or other paper for four years after the closing of the case.

b. With respect to e-filed petitions, the filing attorney shall retain an originally executed copy of Official Form 21 until four years after the closing of the case.

2. *Pro Se Filings:*

a. The Court will retain pro se filings that must contain original signatures, that require verification under FRBP 1008, or unsworn declarations as provided in 28 U.S.C. § 1746 until four years after the closing of the case.

b. The Court will retain the original Official Form 21 until four years after the closing of the case.

III. Public Access at the Courthouse

A. Public Access at the Courthouse.

1. Access to the electronic docket and documents filed in the System is available to the public at no charge through terminals located within District and Bankruptcy Court Clerk's Office Intake lobbies.

2. Assistance with bankruptcy cases is available at the two staffed Northern District of Florida Bankruptcy Court divisional offices located in Tallahassee and Pensacola. While Bankruptcy hearings are held in the Gainesville and Panama City divisions, Bankruptcy staff in those locations is unavailable.

B. Internet Access.

1. Although any person can retrieve and view documents in the System and access information from it without charge at the Clerk's Offices, electronic access to the System for viewing purposes is otherwise limited to subscribers of the Public Access to Court Electronic Records (PACER) System. PACER information may be found at https://www.pacer.gov/.

C. Conventional and Certified Copies of Documents.

1. Conventional and certified copies of electronically filed documents may be purchased at the Clerk's Office. The fee for copying and certification will be in accordance with 28 U.S.C. § 1930.

D. Privacy Provisions.

1. In accordance with the E–Government Act of 2002, and its own policy regarding privacy and public access, the Judiciary Conference of the United States (JCUS), at its September 2003 session, promulgated Official Bankruptcy Form 21 (Official Form 21), Statement of Social Security Number(s). This form has been created to satisfy the requirement set forth in FRBP 1007(f) that a debtor must submit a verified statement of his or her Social Security number (SSN) along with the debtor's petition.

a. With respect to e-filed petitions, the debtor's signature declaring under penalty of perjury that information in the petition is true and correct shall apply to the debtor's SSN as e-filed with the petition.

b. With respect to petitions filed by electronic means on a computer disk, the debtor's attorney shall submit a copy of Official Form 21 as a separate paper document with the Clerk at the same time as the petition is filed.

c. Attorneys shall not file or submit any additional statements or verifications of the debtor's SSN.

d. With respect to petitions filed on paper by unrepresented (pro se) debtors, the debtor shall submit an original Official Form 21 as a separate paper document with the Clerk at the same time the petition is filed.

e. Originally executed copies of Official Form 21 will not be accessible to parties, the bar, or the public.

2. In order to protect personal privacy and other legitimate interests under FRBP 9037, parties shall refrain from including, or shall partial redact, the following personally identifiable information (PII) from all documents and pleadings filed with the Court, including attachments thereto, unless required by statute, FRBP, official bankruptcy forms, or otherwise ordered by the Court:

a. Social Security Number (SSN). If an individual's SSN must be included in a pleading, only the last four digits of that number should be used except when submitting Official Form 21 on which the entire SSN should appear.

b. Names of minor children. If the involvement of a minor child must be mentioned, only the initials of that child should be used. On Schedule I of Official Form 6, list the relationship and age of the debtor's dependents, i.e., "son, age 6".

c. Dates of birth. If an individual's date of birth must be included in a pleading, only the year should be used.

3. The responsibility for redacting personal identifiers described above rests solely with legal counsel and parties filing documents with the Court. The Clerk's Office will not alter, review, or inspect any document for compliance with privacy rules and has no responsibility to do so.

4. If a document containing information in violation of FRBP 9037 happens to be filed, a "Motion for Protective Order to Restrict Remote Electronic Access and Provide for Redaction of Information" will need to be filed along with the proposed order and applicable fees. (See www.flnb.uscourts.gov for fee information.) Upon entry of the order, access to the original document will be restricted. The filer may then file an amended document in which the private information has been properly redacted.

IV. Definitions and Abbreviations Used in this Document

A. Definitions.

1. *ECF Central*

a. Software designed to allow attorneys to submit proposed orders.

2. *E-file or E-filing.*

a. The act of filing pleadings or other papers electronically through the System.

3. *Pro Se*

a. A Latin phrase meaning "for oneself" or "on one's own behalf". Applied here, it refers to parties proceeding without an attorney.

4. *System.*

a. The electronic case filing system software known as Case Management/Electronic Case Files, CM/ECF, ECF or the System.

B. Abbreviations.

1. *BNC.*

a. Bankruptcy Noticing Center

2. *NEF.*

a. Notice of Electronic Filing

3. *PACER.*

a. A system called "Public Access to Court Electronic Records" that allows registered users to access System (CM/ECF) databases across the country and review public documents and docket reports for a fee.

4. *PII.*

a. Personally Identifiable Information—Information such as Social Security numbers, dates of birth, and financial account information that uniquely identifies you or aspects of your financial life.

5. *SEN.*

a. Submission Error Notification—the only the notice you will receive advising you that corrective action is necessary concerning an issue with your e-filing.

6. *SSN.*

a. Social Security Number

[Dated: March 27, 2015.]

III. LOCAL FORMS

*[**Publisher's Note:** The Court may have reformatted and/or updated forms found herein; however, the form date may not reflect this update. Please see publisher's credit at end of each form for currentness.]*

A. ADMINISTRATIVE FORMS

FORM A1. CREDIT CARD ONE TIME AUTHORIZATION FORM

FLNB Local Form A-1 (Rev. 03/16)

INSTRUCTIONS FOR COMPLETING FORM: This form must be typed. The signature field must be signed by the person whose signature appears on the back of the credit card. If you are mailing or faxing this form, you must photocopy your credit card (BOTH SIDES) and include the copy with this form.

United States Bankruptcy Court - Northern District of Florida
CREDIT CARD ONE TIME AUTHORIZATION FORM

I hereby authorize the U.S. Bankruptcy Court for the Northern District of Florida to charge the credit card listed below for payment of fees, costs, and expenses as designated on this form. I certify that I am authorized to use this credit card. The U.S. Bankruptcy Court will maintain this form in the court's safe.

Card Holder Name: ______________________________

Signature: ______________________________ Date: ______________

Address: ______________________________

______________________________ Telephone: ______________

CARD TYPE:

○ MasterCard ○ VISA ○ Discover ○ American Express* ○ Diners Club

* American Express ID Number: ________ *(This four digit number is printed on your card above the embossed account number.)*

Account Number: ______________________________ Expiration Date: ________

CHARGE INFORMATION: *Please list the appropriate amounts for each applicable charge. The current fee schedule is available on the court's website at* **http://www.flnb.uscourts.gov/court-resources/filing-fees**.

Filing Fee (for new cases)	$ ________
Motion Fee	$ ________
Conversion Fee	$ ________
Search Fee	$ ________
Copies & Certifications made by Court	$ ________
Appeal Fee	$ ________
File Retrieval from Archives	$ ________
Complaint Fee	$ ________
Other: ________________	$ ________
TOTAL CHARGES	$ ________

This Credit Card One Time Authorization Form (A1) along with the Copy Work Request Form (A8) may be mailed to the Tallahassee office located at 100 E. Park Ave., Ste. 100, Tallahassee, FL 32301 or faxed to (850) 521-5004.

Please contact the Clerk's Office at (850) 521-5001 or (866) 639-4615 if you have any questions or concerns.

[Revised March 2016.]

FORM A6. APPLICATION FOR FILING AGENT ACCOUNT(S)

FLNB Local Form A-6 (10/15)

UNITED STATES BANKRUPTCY COURT
NORTHERN DISTRICT OF FLORIDA

APPLICATION FOR FILING AGENT ACCOUNT(S)

I, ______________________________, an active ◯ attorney or ◯ trustee CM/ECF user in good standing with the Northern District of Florida, request that the following person(s) be provided a login and password to the CM/ECF system in the Northern District of Florida as a Filing Agent on my behalf.

1. By requesting Filing Agent access for a person in my employ, I understand and agree to accept full responsibility for any and all cases, documents and/or pleadings filed by this/these person(s).

2. I affirm that I have provided the necessary CM/ECF training to or have requested that the Court provide CM/ECF training to this/these person(s) to ensure the correct filing of cases, documents and/or pleadings.

3. I affirm that this/these person(s) have read and are familiar with the Local Rules for the U.S. Bankruptcy Court for the Northern District of Florida.

4. Furthermore, I agree to immediately notify the Court of the need to deactivate the account(s) in the event the Filing Agent leaves my employ or should no longer file cases, documents and/or pleadings on my behalf.

Date: ____________________

CM/ECF Login: ____________________

Please do not include your password

/s/ ____________________

Attorney or Trustee Signature

Firm:

Address: ____________________

____

Phone: ____________________

Email this completed application to:
Samantha_Kiser@flnb.uscourts.gov

NOTE: The login(s) and password(s) will be sent to the primary email address in CM/ECF for the attorney submitting this application.

[Amended effective April, 2014; January 2015; October 2015.]

FORM A7. APPLICATION FOR LOGIN AND PASSWORD FOR CHILD SUPPORT CREDITOR OR REPRESENTATIVE

FLNB Local Form A-7 (2/2012)

UNITED STATES BANKRUPTCY COURT
NORTHERN DISTRICT OF FLORIDA

APPLICATION FOR LOGIN AND PASSWORD
FOR CHILD SUPPORT CREDITOR OR REPRESENTATIVE

Applicant Name: ______________________________

Address: ______________________________

City: ______________ State: ________ Zip: ________

Bar ID, if applicable: ______________ State of: ________

Case(s) in the Northern District of Florida in which you will be filing (debtor name(s) and case number(s):

____

Are you requesting reactivation of a login and password previously issued to you by the U.S. Bankruptcy Court for the Northern District of Florida? ◯ Yes ◯ No

If yes, provide the login to be reactivated: ______________

1. I affirm that I am authorized to prepare and file documents and pleadings on behalf of the child support creditor, ______________________________.

2. I understand that my use of the login and password to file a document or pleading in the record of the bankruptcy case(s) or proceeding(s) noted above constitutes my signature and my signing of those documents and/or pleadings for all purposes authorized and required by law, including, without limitation, the United States Code, Federal Rules of Civil Procedure, Federal Rules of Bankruptcy Procedure, Federal Rules of Criminal Procedure and any applicable non-bankruptcy law.

3. I understand that I must retain all documents bearing my original signature and which are filed using my login and password, and all documents and pleadings bearing the original signature of any signer on whose behalf I file the documents and pleadings using my login and password, for a period of four years after the closing of the case or proceeding in which the documents or pleadings were filed.

4. I understand that it is my responsibility to protect and secure the confidentiality of my password. If I believe my password has been compromised, I understand that I am to notify the Court in writing immediately.

5. I understand that it is my responsibility to notify the Court immediate or any change in my address, telephone number, fax number, or email address.

6. I understand that the issuance of a password to me constitutes waiver of conventional service pursuant to the Federal Rules of Bankruptcy Procedure 9036 and the Court's Electronic Case Filing general order. I agree to accept a Notice of Electronic Filing by hand, facsimile, first class mail, or authorized email in lieu of conventional service. In doing so, I also agree to maintain a current and active email address by which to receive such notification.

7. I understand that in cases wherein service of documents filed electronically is required to be made on the United States and its agencies, corporations or officers, full compliance with Rules 2002(j) and 7004(b)(4), (5) and (6) of the Federal Rules of Bankruptcy Procedure, and Rule 4(I) and (j) of the Federal Rules of Civil Procedure is also required.

8. I understand that all documents and/or pleadings filed in the Electronic Case Filing system which contain an individual's social security number, taxpayer identification number, birthdate, the name of an individual other than the debtor(s) known to be and identified as a minor, or a financial account number must be redacted in accordance with Fed. R. Bankr. P. 9037.

9. I affirm that I have read and understand, and agree to adhere to the Court's guidelines for the Electronic Case Filing system (the Administrative Procedures Regarding Electronic Case Filing) and the Local Rules for the U.S. Bankruptcy Court for the Northern District of Florida.

Date: ______________________ ______________________________
Applicant Signature

Return completed application to Samantha Kiser:
Fax: (850) 521-5004
Email: Samantha_Kiser@flnb.uscourts
U.S. Mail: U.S. Bankruptcy Court, 110 E. Park Ave., Ste. 100, Tallahassee, FL 32301

Your login and password will be emailed to you at the email address provided above. If you wish to request online training, please contact Samantha Kiser (Samantha_Kiser@flnb.uscourts.gov or 866-639-4615) for access to the training database.

Electronic Case Filing access is provided pursuant to § 304(g) of the Bankruptcy Reform Act of 1994 (Pub.L. No. 103-394) and will be terminated by the Court at the conclusion of the case(s) or proceeding(s) noted above.

AO Form 281 (08/06)
FLNB Local Form A-7 (Attachment)

UNITED STATES BANKRUPTCY COURT
NORTHERN DISTRICT OF FLORIDA

In re: Case No.:

Chapter:

Debtor(s)

APPEARANCE OF CHILD SUPPORT CREDITOR*
OR REPRESENTATIVE

I certify under penalty of perjury that I am a child support creditor* of the above-named debtor, or the authorized representative of such child support creditor, with respect to the child support obligation which is set out below.

Name: ____________________

Organization:

Address: ____________________

Telephone Number: ____________________

Date: __________ ____________________

Child Support Creditor* or Authorized Representative

Summary of Child Support Obligation

Amount in arrears:

$ ____________________

Amount currently due per week or per month on a continuing basis:

$ ____________________
(per week)(per month)

If Child Support has been assigned:

Amount of Support which is owed under assignments:

$ ____________________

Amount owed primary child support creditor (balance not assigned):

$ ____________________

Attach an itemized statement of account. Do not disclose the name of a minor child. See 11 U.S.C. § 112. If a social security number or taxpayer identification number is included, set out only the last four digits of the number. Judicial Conference Privacy Policy (09/01).

*** Child support creditor includes both creditor to whom the debtor has a primary obligation to pay child support as well as any entity to whom such support has been assigned, if pursuant to Section 402(a)(26) of the Social Security Act or if such debt has been assigned to the Federal Government or to any State or political subdivision of a State.**

[Amended effective April, 2014; October 2015]

FORM A8. REQUEST FOR COPIES

FLNB Local Form A-8 (01/17)

UNITED STATES BANKRUPCTY COURT
NORTHERN DISTRICT OF FLORIDA

REQUEST FOR COPIES

All requests for copies must be made in writing; telephonic requests will not be accepted. This form must be filled out in its entirety and submitted to the Clerk's Office with the appropriate payment (see fees below). Copy work will be completed within two (2) days of receipt of the request.

A "One Time Credit Card Authorization" form is located on our website at www.flnb.uscourts.gov. You may fax this form and the one time authorization to charge your credit card to 850-521-5004 or mail this form and payment to the address provided below. Checks must be made payable to "Clerk, U.S. Bankruptcy Court." **Be advised that we cannot accept checks or credit card authorization forms from debtors in pending bankruptcy cases.**

PAYMENT MUST BE MADE IN ADVANCE.

Note that copies are also available from the public terminals located in the lobby of each U.S. Bankruptcy or U.S. District Courthouse in the Northern District of Florida at a charge of $.10 per page. There is no search fee required for obtaining copies from the public terminals.

DEBTOR(S) NAME(S): ______________________ CASE NO(S).: ____________

Indicate the document name and document or claim number of the item(s) requested and which, if any, are to be certified. If you do not know the document number, please clearly identify the document, e.g. "Order Confirming Plan":

SEARCH FEE (per name or item searched):	$31.00 x ______	Case(s)	= $ ______
COPIES (per page)	$ .50 x ______	Page(s)	= $ ______
CERTIFICATION (per document):	$11.00 x ______	Certification(s)	= $ ______
EXEMPLIFICATION CERTIFICATE (for registering Judgments):	$22.00 x ______	Exemplification(s)	= $ ______
ARCHIVE RETRIEVAL (retrieval only, does not include copies):	$64.00 x ______	File(s) Requested	= $ ______
		Total Fees Due:	$ ______

YOUR NAME: ______________________ DATE: ____________

PHONE and/or EMAIL: ______________________

MAIL COPIES TO (Name & Address): ______________________

For additional assistance, please contact our help desk at CMECF_HelpDesk@flnb.uscourts.gov or by phone at (850) 521-5001 or (888) 765-1752.

Request for Copies
U.S. Bankruptcy Court, NDFL
110 E. Park Avenue, Suite 100
Tallahassee, FL 32301

[Amended effective December, 2012; February, 2013; April, 2014; January, 2017.]

FORM A9. APPLICATION FOR ADMISSION TO REGISTRY OF MEDIATORS QUALIFIED UNDER FLORIDA NORTHERN MORTGAGE MODIFICATION MEDIATION PROGRAM

FLNB Local Form A-9 (03/2015)

APPLICATION FOR ADMISSION
TO REGISTERY OF MEDIATORS QUALIFIED UNDER
FLORIDA NORTHERN MORTGAGE MODIFICATION MEDIATION PROGRAM

1. Name: ______________________________

2. Address: ______________________________

   City: ______________ State: ________ Zip: ________

3. Phone: ______________ 4. Email: ______________

5. Date certified as a Florida Supreme Court Certified Circuit Court Mediator: ______________
   ☐ Proof of certification attached

6. Date completed training course of at least eight (8) additional hours focused on modifying residential mortgages in bankruptcy proceedings: ______________ ☐ Proof of completion attached.

7. I agree to accept two (2) mortgage modification mediation assignments per calendar year when one or more of the parties cannot pay the mediation fee.

I certify that I meet the qualifications for membership to the Florida Northern mortgage modification registry as outlined in Standing Order No. 20 and that the foregoing statements are true and correct.

______________ ______________
Date Signature

YOU MUST attach appropriate proof of certification and training completion in conjunction with items 5 and 6.

Mail to:
FLNB Mediation Coordinator
United States Bankruptcy Court
110 East Park Ave., #100
Tallahassee, FL 32301

[Amended effective March, 2014, April 9, 2014, March 16, 2015.]

NATF 90. ARCHIVES REQUEST

National Archives Trust Fund Board NATF Form 90 (last modified: 11-2012)

NATIONAL ARCHIVES AND RECORDS ADMINISTRATION (NARA)
Order BANKRUPTCY CASES *Instructions*

Save time by ordering online: https://eservices.archives.gov/orderonline/

Copy Packages Available

Pre-Selected Documents (Individual only): Includes the following documents, to the extent that they are contained in the case file: **Discharge of Debtor** (or Order of Dismissal or Final Decree), **Voluntary Petition**, **Summary of Debts and Property**, **Schedules D, E** and **F** (Note in some jurisdictions Schedules may be listed as A1, A2 and A3). No substitutions will be made for these documents.

Entire Case File: Includes all documents in a Business and Individual case file.

Docket Sheet: A list of documents filed in a Bankruptcy case; an outline of the case.

Certification: A seal certifying copies to be a valid reproduction of the file. This is available for an additional charge of $15.00 for all packages delivered by mail or express shipping. Certification for faxed and scanned copies is not available.

General Information

- Use a separate NATF Form 90 for each file you request. Steps 1-6 must be completed on the order form to perform a search for the file. Steps 1-6 begin on page 2. Please discard this instruction sheet; only return pages 2 and 3. Allow 1-3 work days from receipt of payment for processing your order.
- When paying by check or money order for your request, a separate payment is required for each individual request. If paying by credit card, you may fax your request form to the fax number provided in Step 1.
- Orders can be sent by overnight delivery at an additional charge.
- In addition to photocopies, orders can be faxed and/or scanned. Faxed and scanned orders cannot be certified.
- Request may be returned if the necessary information is not supplied or if the credit card is declined. Case information must be obtained from the Court where the case was filed.
- Please note that contents of recent cases may be in both electronic and paper form. If NARA cannot provide you with documents you requested, we will refer you to the Court that adjudicated the case.
- The *Entire Case File* option in Step 2 includes up to the first 150 pages. Copies of additional pages are subject to an additional labor charge of $22.00 per 15 minutes of work done. You will be notified of any additional labor charges before they are incurred.
- Please do not send credit card information via email.

Additional information may be found here: http://www.archives.gov/research/court-records/

PRIVACY ACT STATEMENT

Collection of this information is authorized by 44 U.S.C. 2108. Disclosure of the information is voluntary; however, we will be unable to respond to your request if you do not furnish your name and address and the minimum required information about the records. The information is used by NARA employees to search for the record; to respond to you; to maintain control over information requests received and answered; and to facilitate preparation of internal statistical reports. If you provide credit card information, that information is used to bill you for copies.

National Archives Trust Fund Board NATF Form 90 (last modified 11-2012)

NATIONAL ARCHIVES AND RECORDS ADMINISTRATION (NARA)
BANKRUPTCY CASES *ORDER FORM*

STEP 1. SELECT THE AREA WHERE THE CASE FILE IS HELD *(select only one)*

SELECT	AREA SERVED	ADDRESS TO SEND COMPLETED FORM
☐	Connecticut Maine Massachusetts New Hampshire Rhode Island Vermont	NARA, Northeast Region — Boston, Research Room 380 Trapelo Road Waltham, MA 02452-6399 Telephone: 781-663-0378 Fax: 781-663-0155 Email: waltham.courts@nara.gov
☐	Delaware Maryland Pennsylvania Virginia West Virginia.	NARA, Mid-Atlantic Region 14700 Townsend Road Philadelphia PA 19154-1025 Telephone: 215-305-2000 Fax: 215-305-2038 Email: philadelphia.reference@nara.gov
☐	Alabama Florida Georgia Kentucky Mississippi North and South Carolina Tennessee	NARA, Southeast Region – U.S. Court Reference Program 4712 Southpark Boulevard Ellenwood, GA 30294 Telephone: 404-736-2900 Fax: 404-736-2927 Email: atlanta.reference@nara.gov
☐	Illinois Indiana Michigan Minnesota Ohio Wisconsin	NARA, Great Lakes Region — FRC, AIS Operation 7358 S. Pulaski Road Chicago, IL 60629 Telephone: 773-948-9030 Fax: 773-948-9051 Email: chicago.reference@nara.gov
☐	Ohio Indiana Michigan IRS and Defense Finance Facilities Nationwide	NARA, Great Lakes Region – Dayton FRC 3150 Springboro Road Dayton, OH 45439 Phone: -937-425-0606 Fax: 937-425-0640 Email dayton.reference@nara.gov
☐	New York New Jersey Puerto Rico Virgin Islands	NARA, Central Plains Region 200 Space Center Drive Lee's Summit, MO 64064 Telephone: 816-268-8100 Fax: 816-268-8159 Email: leessummit.reference@nara.gov
☐	Iowa Kansas Missouri Nebraska	NARA, Central Plains Region 17501 W. 98th Street, Ste. 47-48 Lenexa, KS 66219 Telephone: 913-563-7600 Fax: 913-563-7691 Email: kansascity.reference@nara.gov
☐	Texas Arkansas Oklahoma Louisiana	NARA, Southwest Region 1400 John Burgess Drive Fort Worth, Texas 76140 Telephone: 817-551-2035 Fax: 817-551-2037 Email: tercs.ftworth@nara.gov
☐	Colorado Wyoming Montana Utah North and South Dakota New Mexico	NARA, Rocky Mountain Region Research Room Denver Federal Center Bldg 48 Lakewood, CO 80225 Telephone: 303-407-5740 Fax: 303-407-5709 Email: denver.reference@nara.gov
☐	Arizona Southern California Clark County, Nevada	NARA, Pacific Region — Riverside, Trust Fund Unit 23123 Cajalco Road Perris, CA 92570-7298 Telephone: 951-956-2023 Fax: 951-956-2029 Email: riverside.trustfund@nara.gov
☐	Hawaii Nevada (except Clark County) Northern California	NARA - Pacific Region, San Francisco Federal Records Center (Attn: TF Copy Service) 1000 Commodore Drive San Bruno, CA 94066-2350 Telephone: 650-238-3500 Fax: 650-238-3507 Email: sanbruno.reference@nara.gov
☐	Alaska Idaho Oregon Washington	NARA, Pacific Alaska Region 6125 Sand Point Way N. E. Seattle, WA 98115-7999 Telephone: 206-336-5134 Fax: 206-336-5113 Email: seattle.reference@nara.gov
☐	District of Columbia	NARA, Washington National Records Center 4205 Suitland Road Suitland, MD 20746-8001 Telephone: 301-778-1520 Fax: 301-778-1534 Email: Suitland.Courts@nara.gov

National Archives Trust Fund Board NATF Form 90 (last modified: 11-2012)

NATIONAL ARCHIVES AND RECORDS ADMINISTRATION (NARA)
BANKRUPTCY CASES ORDER FORM

Save time by ordering online: https://eservices.archives.gov/orderonline/

STEP 2. SELECT COPY PACKAGE *(select only one)*

Copy Package – Not Certified	*Copy Package – Certified*
☐ Pre-Selected Documents — **$35.00** ☐ Entire Case File — **$90.00** (150 page maximum) ☐ Docket Sheet — **$35.00**	(Certification for faxed, emailed and scanned copies is **not** available) ☐ Pre-Selected Documents Certified — **$50.00** ☐ Entire Case File Certified — **$105.00** ☐ Docket Sheet — **$50.00**

STEP 3. CASE INFORMATION *(obtain from the court in which the case was filed)*

COURT LOCATION (city & state)	DEBTOR NAME(S)	CASE NUMBER
TRANSFER NUMBER	BOX NUMBER	

STEP 4. DELIVERY OPTIONS

Delivery Method: *(select one)*

☐ Fax ☐ Mail ☐ Email

Delivery Type: *(select one)*

☐ Paper Copies ☐ Scanned on CD/DVD ☐ Email *(if no selection is made, paper copies will be delivered via mail)*

Expedited Delivery: *(optional, select one)*

☐ Overnight express (additional $30.00)

☐ Charge Fed Ex Account - # ____________________

☐ Charge UPS Account - # ____________________

STEP 5. YOUR DELIVERY INFORMATION

MAIL COPIES TO:	*FAX COPIES TO:*	*EMAIL COPIES TO:*
NAME	FAX NUMBER	EMAIL ADDRESS
STREET ADDRESS - APT. # / SUITE #		
CITY	ATTENTION	DAYTIME TELEPHONE NUMBER (required)
STATE AND ZIP		
DAYTIME TELEPHONE NUMBER (required)	DAYTIME TELEPHONE NUMBER (required)	ALTERNATE TELEPHONE NUMBER (preferred)
ALTERNATE TELEPHONE NUMBER (preferred)	ALTERNATE TELEPHONE NUMBER (preferred)	

STEP 6. YOUR PAYMENT INFORMATION

Credit Card *(please do not send credit card information via email)*		***Check or Money Order***
CARD TYPE ☐ VISA ☐ MasterCard ☐ American Express ☐ Discover		Make your check or money order payable to: ***National Archives Trust Fund (NATF)*** Mail your request **with payment** to the address shown in **Step 1** on the previous page.
ACCOUNT NUMBER	EXPIRATION DATE	
NAME ON CARD		
SIGNATURE or THREE DIGIT SECURITY CODE (on back of charge card). Order cannot be processed if one of these two items is not provided.		

NARA USE ONLY

SEARCHER	DATE	PAYMENT:
REMARKS	☐ Review – Date: Time:	☐ Paid Check # ________

[Amended effective November 21, 2012.]

B. INSTRUCTIONAL DOCUMENTS

1–INST. INSTRUCTIONS FOR CREDITOR MATRIX CD OR DISK

U.S. Bankruptcy Court for the Northern District of Florida
FLNB LF 1-Inst Rev. 12/1/15

INSTRUCTIONS FOR CREATING A MAILING MATRIX

A *mailing matrix*, or sometimes called a "creditor matrix" or "matrix," is a list containing each creditor's name and mailing address. The matrix is required pursuant to N.D. Fla. LBR 1007-2. Although the Court uses sophisticated equipment and software to ensure accuracy in creditor matrix readings, certain problems can still occur. Following these guidelines will reduce the likelihood of errors and avoid delay in mailing notices:

- Names and addresses must be typed in a standard typeface or print style (no italics or cursive style print). *The matrix cannot be handwritten per Local Rule 1007-2.*
- Names should be in upper and lower case. Do not use all capital letters.
- Matrix must be typed in a single column down the page.
- Names and addresses must be **left justified. Do not center.**
- Addresses must not exceed five (5) lines and each line must contain no more than 40 characters, including spaces.
- Do not place spaces at the beginning of a line. Do not use special characters such as ½ or accent marks. The pound/number (#) and ampersand (&) signs are acceptable.
- Do not include account numbers on the matrix.
- "Attention" lines should be placed on the second line of the creditor's address.
- City, state, and ZIP code must be on the last line, must contain only one space between components, and must not contain tabbed spacing (see example below).
- Nine-digit ZIP codes must have a hyphen separating the two groups of digits.
- States must be indicated using two-letter abbreviations.
- Separate creditors by one blank line (i.e., double space between creditors).
- Use a minimum of 1/2 inch margins.
- DO NOT include the name(s) of the debtor, joint debtor, or attorney for the debtor(s) on the matrix. They will be added automatically by CM/ECF. Do not include page numbers, headers, or footers.
- Save the file in text format (.txt) using the debtor's last name (e.g., Smith.txt). Petition preparation software programs often save the matrix using a ".scn" extension which is also acceptable. Matrices will not be accepted in Portable Document Format (.pdf).

IF YOU ARE PROVIDING THE MATRIX ON A CD: If your CD is unreadable by the Court, it will be returned to you and a deficiency notice will be issued. If your CD is found to contain malicious software such as a virus, it will be destroyed and you will be contacted by our office.

Things to avoid when submitting a matrix on paper:

- Extra marks on the document such as letterhead, dates, coffee or soda stains, and handwritten marks
- Non-standard paper such as onion skin, half- or legal-sized, or colored paper
- Poor quality type caused by carbon or photocopies, using an exhausted typewriter or a typewriter with a fabric ribbon, or documents from a printer with low toner
- Unreadable type face or print styles such as proportionally spaced fonts, dot-matrix print, or non-standard fonts (e.g., Old English or Script). **Courier font works best.**

U.S. Bankruptcy Court for the Northern District of Florida
FLNB LF 1-Inst Rev. 12/1/15

Example Creditor Matrix (using Courier font):

INCORRECT FORM:	CORRECT FORM:
Attn: Insolvency ME-128 Internal Revenue Service 301 W. Wisconsin Ave. Milwaukee, WI **532022221**	Internal Revenue Service **Attn: Insolvency ME-128** 310 W. Wisconsin Ave. Milwaukee, WI **53202-2221**
General Welding Supply Attn: Accounting P.O. Box 3657 **Baltimore MD 20984**	General Welding Supply Attn: Accounting P.O. Box 3657 **Baltimore, MD 20984**
Peterboro Food & Beverage **1300 Exchange Bldg.** **Suite 700** 401 S. Adams St. P.O. Box 55672 Buffalo, NY 20009	Peterboro Food & Beverage **1300 Exchange Bldg., Ste. 700** 401 S. Adams St. P.O. Box 55672 Buffalo, NY 20009
Flex Northwest Seattle, **Washington** **98372**	Flex Northwest Seattle, **WA 98372**
First National Bank **Acct # 123-456-7890** P.O. Box 3391 Beaumont, TX 77704	First National Bank P.O. Box 3391 Beaumont, TX 77704

[Effective December 1, 2015.]

3–INST. CM/ECF GROUP PERMISSIONS

If you have any questions, concerns and/or other comments regarding group permissions please feel free to contact Ne'Shoni Foulks via email at NeShoni_Foulks@flnb.uscourts.gov.

Introduction

Hello and welcome to the Northern District of Florida—Bankruptcy Court. The Northern District became an online court in November 2003 per Standing Order #11. CM/ECF is comprised of several distinct "User Groups", all of which hold unique permissions and restrictions. The most common of these groups are as follows: Attorney, Attorney and Creditor, Creditor, U.S. Trustee and Trustee. In the past, there has been some confusion as to the permissions and restrictions which come with each of the filing groups; therefore, we have put together some information which will address any questions or concerns.

Attorney

In general, "Attorney" permissions are granted to Attorneys who solely represent Debtors in Bankruptcy proceedings. Attorney access can only be granted to an Attorney in good standing who is admitted to practice in the Northern District of Florida—District Court. Pro Hac Vice applicants must refer to Local Rule 11.1C(2) U.S.D.C. Attorneys must complete the "ECF Application—Attorney" form located on the internet to begin their admission process in our court. Once an Attorney receives his/her Login and Password they have full access to file both Bankruptcy and Adversary proceedings in our court. Using their ECF Login and Password, attorneys have access to the Bankruptcy, Adversary, Utilities and Search Menu. A separate Login and Password must be obtained from PACER in order for Attorneys to access and view filed documents by way of the Query and/or Reports Menu. Pursuant to F.R.B.P. 9036, Attorneys will receive all court notifications electronically in lieu of conventional service; therefore, they are required to maintain a current and active e-mail address at all times. Attorneys are expected to update their contact information and/or make any changes necessary should their current information change.

Attorney and Creditor

In general, "Attorney & Creditor" permissions are granted to Attorneys who represent Debtors and/or Creditors in Bankruptcy proceedings. Attorney and Creditor access can only be granted to an Attorney in good standing who is admitted to practice in the Northern District of Florida—District Court. Pro Hac Vice applicants must refer to Local Rule 11.1C(2) U.S.D.C. Attorney's must complete the "ECF Application—Combination" form located on the internet to begin their admission process in our court. Once an Attorney receives his/her Login and Password they have full access to file both Bankruptcy and Adversary proceedings in our court. Using their ECF Login and Password, attorneys have access to the Bankruptcy, Adversary, Utilities and Search Menu. A separate Login and Password must be obtained from PACER in order for Attorneys to access and view filed documents by way of the Query and/or Reports Menu. Pursuant to F.R.B.P. 9036, Attorneys will receive all court notifications electronically in lieu of conventional service; therefore, they are required to maintain a current and active email address at all times. Attorneys are expected to update their contact information and/or make any changes necessary should their current information change.

Creditor/Limited User

In general, "Creditor" permissions are granted to Creditors and/or Attorneys who are not admitted to practice in the Northern District of Florida—District Court. Creditors must complete the "ECF Application—Limited Use" form located on the internet to begin their admission process in our court. Once a Creditor receives his/her Login and Password they have access to file a handful of pre-selected Bankruptcy proceedings, including but not limited to: Proofs of Claim, Requests for Notice, Reaffirmation Agreements, etc. Using their ECF Login and Password, Creditors have access to the Bankruptcy, Utilities and Search Menu. A separate Login and Password must be obtained from PACER in order for Creditors to access and view filed documents by way of the Query and/or Reports Menu. Unlike Attorneys, Creditors in this category do not receive electronic notifications from the court. If a "Notice of Appearance and Request for Notice" is filed, Creditors will receive court notifications pursuant to F.R.B.P. 2002 (all creditor notices) by way of USPS conventional service. Creditors do not have access to maintain their ECF account; therefore, it is their responsibility to notify the court immediately of any change of address, telephone or fax number and/or e-mail address.

Child Support Creditor

In general, "Child Support Creditor" permissions are granted to Creditors and/or Attorneys per Section 304(g) of the Bankruptcy Reform Act of 1994 (Public Law No. 103–394). Child Support Creditors may apply for admission to our electronic case filing system without necessity of being admitted to practice in the U.S. District Court for the Northern District of Florida; however, compliance with all other provisions of the Administrative Procedures and Standing Order No. 11 is required. Child Support Creditors must complete Local Form A7 "Child Support Creditor" located on the internet to begin their admission process. Once a Child Support Creditor receives his/her Login and Password they have full access to file both Bankruptcy and Adversary proceedings in our court. Using their ECF Login and Password, Child Support Creditors have access to the Bankruptcy, Adversary, Utilities and Search Menu. A separate Login and Password must be obtained from PACER in order for Child Support Creditors to access and view filed documents by way of the Query and/or Reports Menu. Pursuant to F.R.B.P. 9036, Child Support Creditors will receive all court notifications electronically in lieu of conventional service; therefore, they are required to maintain a current and active e-mail address at all times. Attorneys are expected to update their contact information and/or make any changes necessary should their current information change. Applicants in this category should also be aware that their accounts will only remain active while the case they are involved in is open in our court and that accounts will be deactivated up case closing.

Filing Agent

In general, "Filing Agent" permissions are granted to Attorneys' paralegals, assistants and/or office staff who file on behalf of the Attorney. Attorneys who wish to have their personnel set up with Filing Agent accounts must complete Local Form A6 "Filing Agent for Attorney" located on the internet to begin their admission process. Once a Filing Agent receives his/her Login and Password they have full access to file both Bankruptcy and Adversary proceedings on behalf of their Attorney in our court. Using their ECF Login and Password, Filing Agents have access to the Bankruptcy, Adversary, Utilities and Search Menu. A separate Login and Password must be obtained from PACER in order for Filing Agents to access and view filed documents by way of the Query and/or Reports Menu. Pursuant to F.R.B.P. 9036, Filing Agents will receive all court notifications electronically in lieu of conventional service; therefore, they are required to maintain a current and active e-mail address at all times. Attorneys are expected to update their contact information and/or make any changes necessary should their current information change.

U.S. Trustee

In general, "U.S. Trustee" permissions are granted to U.S. Trustees who oversee Bankruptcy proceedings. U.S. Trustee access can only be granted to an Attorney in good standing who is admitted to practice in the Northern District of Florida—District Court. Pro Hac Vice applicants must refer to Local Rule 11.1C(2) U.S.D.C. U.S. Trustees must complete the "ECF Application—Attorney" form located on the internet to begin their admission process in our court. Once a U.S. Trustee receives his/her Login and Password they have full access to file both Bankruptcy and Adversary proceedings in our court. Using their ECF Login and Password, U.S. Trustees have access to an extended list of Bankruptcy Events, as well as the Adversary, Utilities and Search Menu. A separate Login and Password must be obtained from PACER in order for U.S. Trustees to access and view filed documents by way of the Query and/or Reports Menu. Pursuant to F.R.B.P. 9036, U.S. Trustees will receive all court notifications electronically in lieu of conventional service; therefore, they are required to maintain a current and active e-mail address at all times. U.S. Trustees are expected to update their contact information and/or make any changes necessary should their current information change.

Trustee

In general, "Trustee" permissions are granted to Chapter Trustees who oversee Bankruptcy and Adversary proceedings. Trustee's access can only be granted to an Attorney in good standing who is admitted to practice in the Northern District of Florida—District Court. Pro Hac Vice applicants must refer to Local Rule 11.1C(2) U.S.D.C. Trustees must complete the "ECF Application—Attorney" form located on the internet to begin their admission process in our court. Once a Trustee receives his/her Login and Password they have full access to file both Bankruptcy and Adversary proceedings in our court. Using their ECF Login and Password, Trustees have access to an extended list of Bankruptcy Events, as well as the Adversary, Utilities and Search Menu. A separate Login and Password must be obtained from PACER in order for Trustees to access and view filed documents by way of the Query and/or Reports Menu. Pursuant to F.R.B.P. 9036,

Trustees will receive all court notifications electronically in lieu of conventional service; therefore, they are required to maintain a current and active e-mail address at all times. Trustees are expected to update their contact information and/or make any changes necessary should their current information change.

***Court Reporter**

We are currently in the process of establishing CM/ECF access for Court Reporters. Once completed, the rights and permissions will be much the same as the Limited User group (*please see above). Before a login/password can be issued, Court Reporters must be fingerprinted and have an established relationship with the court or one the firms that currently provide reporting services for our court. If you meet the requirements and are interested in obtaining a login/password as a Court Reporter, please complete the "ECF Application—Limited User" and submit to the Court. All applications received will be held in pending status until the Court Reporter group has been officially implemented in CM/ECF.

4–INST. PROPOSED ORDER GUIDELINES

United States Bankruptcy Court
Northern District of Florida

Proposed Order Guidelines

(Rev. 08/17/16)

CASE STYLE: The case style must include the chapter, complete and correct debtor or plaintiff and defendant name(s), and case number including the assigned judge's initials once known.

TITLE: The title of the proposed order should contain the disposition of the motion, contain the name of the movant and the docket number of the motion, and should completely match the title of the related motion (ONLY ONE MOTION PER ORDER):

- Order Granting ABC Bank's Motion for Relief from Stay (Doc. 51)
- Order Approving Trustee's Application for Compensation (Doc. 123)
- Orders "on" a motion/application/objection will not be accepted; they must include a disposition

DISPOSITION: The correct disposition terminology should be used:

- Motions are granted or denied
- Objections are sustained or overruled
- Applications are approved or disapproved
- Non-dispositional language such as "Order on Motion" will not be accepted

BODY: The opening paragraph of the proposed order should contain the document number of the motion or document to which the order is related:

- *"This case came before the Court on Creditor ABC Bank's Motion to Dismiss Case (Doc. 57)..."*

PREPARED BY: The name of the attorney who prepared the proposed order is to be indicated at the end of the document.

AMENDED ORDERS: Amended orders must contain a footnote explaining why the original order is being amended.

REFERENCED DOCUMENTS: Proposed orders which contain references to Proofs of Claim or items on the docket such as responses, amendments, etc., should contain the name(s) and docket or claim number(s) of those items as shown in the examples above.

OBJECTIONS TO CLAIMS: Orders sustaining objections to claims should clearly indicate the amount of the claim to be disallowed. Do not simply state "claim is disallowed in its entirety."

SERVICE LANGUAGE: Proposed orders will be required to include one of these service statements:

- **For an Attorney**: "Attorney [Name of submitting attorney] is directed to serve a copy of this order on interested parties and file a certificate of service within 3 business days of entry of the order"
- **For a Trustee**: "Trustee [Name of submitting trustee] is directed to serve a copy of this order on interested parties and file a certificate of service within 3 business days of entry of the order"

The statement should be located after the signature block with two hard returns preceding it. Proposed orders that do not include this statement will be rejected and the submitting party will be required to submit a new order with the appropriate language included. Failure to serve an order within the time allotted may result in the order being vacated.

SUBMISSION RULES: Proposed orders should be submitted in Word (preferably), WordPerfect, or other compatible word processing format. PDF FILES WILL NOT BE ACCEPTED. Use the electronic submission link through CM/ECF **only** to submit proposed orders.

COMPETING ORDERS: If there is a dispute between counsel about all or a portion of a proposed order that cannot be resolved by the time the proposed order is to be submitted, then the submitting attorney must check a box located on the CM/ECF proposed order document upload screen labeled "Competing order may be submitted." In addition, a letter must be included (as the first page of the proposed order) that states:

- The order is not agreed to by opposing counsel;
- Whether a competing order is expected; and
- The issue that is in dispute.

The letter and the proposed order must be copied to opposing counsel.

PLAIN LANGUAGE: Utilize plain language as follows:

- **CORRECT:** "It is Ordered."
- **INCORRECT:** Accordingly; Hereby; Therefore; Adjudged and Decreed; Whereas
- **INCORRECT:** "The Court is of the opinion…"
- **CORRECT:** "No party filed an objection within the prescribed time period, the court considers the matter unopposed."
- **INCORRECT:** "No response having been filed, the court is of the opinion that the Motion is due to be granted."

FORMAT:

- Documents must be double spaced and contain only basic formatting.
- Use the same font type and size throughout the document (preferably 14 pt. font).
- Ensure that the correct judge's initials appear after the case number within the header.
- Ensure that the Chapter identification, e.g., Chapter 7, appears above or below the case number within the header.
- When using properly spelled Latin terms (e.g. *in rem*), you must either underline the term or use Italic font.
- The name of the attorney who prepared the order is to be indicated at the end of the document.
- To save space, position the judge's signature line approximately one (1) inch below the date line.
- Use the following date and judge signature block format on all proposed orders:

[Indent] DONE AND ORDERED on <blank line - court to add date>

[Tab Right] ____________________
[Tab Right] KAREN K. SPECIE
[Tab Right] U.S. Bankruptcy Judge

EXAMPLE:

DONE AND ORDERED on November 19, 2012 .

____

KAREN K. SPECIE
U.S. Bankruptcy Judge

[Effective September 14, 2012. Amended effective March 31, 2014; October 23, 2014; February 26, 2015; August 17, 2016.]

5–Inst. CERTIFICATE OF SERVICE—EXPLANATION & SAMPLE

5-Inst (2/15)

UNITED STATES BANKRUPTCY COURT
NORTHERN DISTRICT OF FLORIDA

CERTIFICATE OF SERVICE - EXPLANATION & SAMPLE

What is a Certificate of Service/Proof of Service?
A Certificate of Service is a signed piece of paper that verifies that you have attempted to deliver a document regarding your case to the parties and/or creditors involved in your bankruptcy case.

Why is a Certificate of Service needed?
The Certificate of Service confirms that a copy of the document you are filing with the court has been provided to everyone connected with the case or the proceeding. If the papers are not served in the correct way at the correct time, the court cannot proceed with your case or proceeding.

When is a Certificate of Service used?
A Certificate of Service must be attached to every document you file in the bankruptcy case or filed after you have served a document at the direction of the court.

How are documents served?
The person serving the documents may use the following methods:

- First class, U.S. Mail
- Overnight mail
- Personal delivery
- Email or fax, if the parties agree to service by that method

To whom should I serve the documents?
The general requirements for serving documents in your bankruptcy case are set forth in the Fed. R. Bankr. P. 7004. Neither the Court nor the Clerk's Office staff can tell you who you are required to serve however, as a general rule, any person or entity affected by the document should be served with a copy.

When should service be executed?
Service of motions or other documents filed with the court must be performed at the time of filing the document and the Certificate of Service, if not attached to the document, must be filed immediately thereafter.

Service of notices, orders, or other documents as directed by the court should be performed as soon as possible and a Certificate of Service filed with the court within three days.

Is there a form I should use to create a Certificate of Service?
Yes. Local Form 4 may be used to create a Certificate of Service of a document for which the court has directed that you are to serve (e.g., hearing notices, orders, or other documents). The Certificate of Service of a motion or application, objection, or other pleading should be attached to the back of the document being filed. Sample formas for both types of Certificate of Service follow these instructions.

Sample LF 4 - To be used to file Certificate of Service of documents you are directed by the Court to serve.

UNITED STATES BANKRUPTCY COURT
NORTHERN DISTRICT OF FLORIDA
__________ DIVISION

In Re: Case Number:
Chapter:

Debtor Name(s)

Debtor(s)

CERTIFICATE OF SERVICE

I, (name of person certifying service), hereby certify that a true and correct copy of the (document name) was served on the following in the manner stated below:

1. **Served by the Court via Notice of Electronic Filing (NEF):** I have confirmed that the foregoing document was served by the Court via NEF on (date) to the following person(s) at the email address(es) noted herein:

   John Doe (JohnDoe@gmail.com)
   Joe Schmo (JoeSchmo@lawfirm.net)

   ☐ No persons/entities served by Notice of Electronic Filing

2. **Served by U.S. Mail:** The foregoing document was served by first class, postage prepaid, U.S. Mail on (date) to the persons and/or entities at the addresses noted herein as obtained from a current mailing matrix obtained from the court's CM/ECF system:

   Mary Smith
   PO Box 123
   Atlanta, GA 30303

   Brad Turner
   576 N. Main St.
   Tallahassee, FL 32301

   ☐ See attached mailing matrix
   ☐ No persons/entities served by U.S. Mail

3. **Served by Personal Delivery, Overnight Mail, Facsimile Transmission or Email** (state method for each person or entity served): Service was executed on ___(date)_________ to the following persons and/or entities via the means noted below:

   Mike Brown by fax at 800-867-5309

   Jim Johnston by email at JimmyJ@hotmail.com

   Sue Swanson by overnight delivery (FedEx) c/o Credit One, 4467 Peachtree St., Atlanta, GA 30303

   □ No persons/entities served by personal delivery, overnight mail, facsimile transmission or email (excluding NEF transmission)

I declare under penalty of perjury that the foregoing is true and correct.

_________________________________ Date: _______________

Signature of Person Certifying Service

Sample Certificate of Service to be used as an attachment to filing motions, applications, responses, or other pleadings in a bankruptcy case or adversary proceeding. NOTE: This format may not be used to file a Certificate of Service that is not part of another document.

Certificate of Service

The following parties were served either by electronic or standard first class mail:

John Doe (JohnDoe@gmail.com)
Joe Schmo (JoeSchmo@lawfirm.net)

Mary Smith
PO Box 123
Atlanta, GA 30303

Brad Turner
576 N. Main St.
Tallahassee, FL 32301

______________________________ Date: ________________

Signature of Person Certifying Service

[Dated: February 2015.]

C. LOCAL FORMS (ALL CASES)

LOCAL FORM 1. DEBTOR'S STATEMENT OF ASSISTANCE RECEIVED IN CONNECTION WITH THE FILING OF THIS CASE

FLNB Local Form 1 (05/07)

United States Bankruptcy Court
Northern District of Florida

IN RE:

Case No.: ______________
Chapter: ______________

Debtor(s)

DEBTOR'S STATEMENT OF ASSISTANCE RECEIVED IN CONNECTION WITH THE FILING OF THIS CASE

☐ I DID NOT RECEIVE ANY ASSISTANCE IN PREPARING THIS CASE FOR FILING.

☐ I DID RECEIVE ASSISTANCE IN PREPARING THIS CASE FOR FILING.

1. The person or firm that assisted is:
   Name: ______________________________
   Address: ______________________________
   City: ______________ ST: ______ Zip: ______
   Telephone:
2. I paid the sum of $ ______________
3. I still owe the sum of $ ______________
4. I agreed to turn over or give a security interest in the following property:

I (we) ______________________________, the Debtor(s), do hereby declare under penalty of perjury,that the statements made are true and correct.

Executed this ______ day of ______________, 20 ____.
(Day) (Month) (Year)

____
Signature of Debtor

____
Signature of Joint Debtor

[Adopted effective October, 2005. Amended effective May, 2007; April, 2014.]

LOCAL FORM 2. CORPORATE OWNERSHIP STATEMENT

FLNB Local Form 2

UNITED STATES BANKRUPTCY COURT
NORTHERN DISTRICT OF FLORIDA
GAINESVILLE DIVISION

In re: Case No.:

Chapter:

Debtor(s)

CORPORATE OWNERSHIP STATEMENT

Pursuant to Bankruptcy Rule 1007(a) or Bankruptcy Rule 7007.1, ______________________________

____, a

- ☐ Corporate Debtor
- ☐ Party to an adversary proceeding
- ☐ Party to a contested matter
- ☐ Member of committee of creditors

makes the following disclosure(s):

All corporations, other than a governmental unit, that directly or indirectly own ten percent (10%) or more of any class of the corporation's equity interests, are listed below:

OR

☐ There are no entities that directly or indirectly own ten percent (10%) or more of any class of the corporation's equity interest.

______________________ By: ______________________

Date

[Amended effective April, 2014.]

LOCAL FORM 3. VERIFIED EX PARTE MOTION FOR MORTGAGE MODIFICATION MEDIATION ("MMM")

FLNB Local Form 3 (09/14)

UNITED STATES BANKRUPTCY COURT
NORTHERN DISTRICT OF FLORIDA
______________________ **DIVISION**

In re:

Case No.:
Chapter:

Debtor(s)

VERIFIED EX PARTE MOTION FOR MORTGAGE MODIFICATION MEDIATION ("MMM")

The Debtor(s) request entry of an order referring the Debtor and Lender,

____

("Lender") to Mortgage Modification Mediation ("MMM"), and alleges:

1. Debtor is an individual who filed for bankruptcy relief under, or converted to chapter ____ on ______________________.
2. Debtor requests MMM for real property ("Property") located at the following street address:

   ____

   a. The account number(s) for this Property is ______________(last four digits of all account numbers for the same Lender).

   b. The Property is (check one box):

   ◯ The Debtor's primary residence

   ◯ Not the Debtor's primary residence

   c. The Lender's full name and current address are:

   ____

   ____

* *All references to "Debtor" shall include and refer to both debtors in a case filed jointly by two individuals.*

d. Borrowers obligated on the promissory note and mortgage on the Property are:

○ Debtor only

○ Debtor and non-filing co-obligor/co-borrower/third party (within ten (10) days of the date of this Order, debtor must provide Lender the names, addresses, telephone numbers, and email addresses, if any, of any non-Debtors who are co-obligors, co-borrowers, or third parties to the obligation(s) to be modified.)

3. **Debtor and debtor's counsel, if applicable, intends to comply with the procedures and guidelines contained within the Court's *Uniform District-wide Mortgage Modification Mediation Procedures* available at *www.flnb.uscourts.gov/mortgage-modification-mediation*.**

4. Debtor consents to Lender communicating directly with Debtor's attorney for any and all aspects of the MMM program. The parties may communicate outside the Portal orally, but all written communication shall occur through the Portal.

5. Prior to filing this motion, Debtor or Debtor's attorney has collected all of the required supporting documentation along with the appropriate modification forms via the MMM Portal. Within seven (7) days after the selection of a Mediator or the Lender's registration on the MMM Portal, the Debtor or Debtor's attorney shall upload and submit through the MMM portal all forms needed for MMM with the Lender, and shall pay the non-refundable MMM Portal submission fee; and will upload this Order to the MMM Portal as part of the submission of Debtor's documentation.

6. The Debtor certifies that the Debtor's portion of the required mediator's fee is in hand, or has been remitted to Debtor's attorney. Debtor understands and acknowledges that after the mediator is designated, the mediator's fee is not refundable for any reason at any time.

7. The Debtor's filing fee for this case and any prior case filed in this district has been paid in full or has been waived by court order.

Wherefore, Debtor requests the entry of an order granting this Ex Parte Motion, and requests such other and further relief as this Court deems just and proper.

____
Date

/s/ Attorney Name
Bar No.:
Firm Name
Address
City, ST Zip
Phone and Fax
Email

DEBTOR'S VERIFICATION

Pursuant to 28 U.S.C. § 1746, I declare under penalty of perjury the foregoing is true and correct on_________________, 20___.

____
Debtor

____
Joint Debtor

CERTIFICATE OF SERVICE

I HEREBY CERTIFY that a true and correct copy of the **Verified Ex Parte Motion for Mortgage Modification Mediation (MMM)** was served by U.S., first class Mail, upon the parties listed below on________________ ,20___ .

/s/ Attorney Name
Bar No.:
Firm Name
Address
City, ST Zip
Phone and Fax
Email

Copies to:

Lender (identify name of Lender and where notice sent)
Lender's Counsel (if known)

[Dated: September 2014.]

LOCAL FORM 3PS. VERIFIED EX PARTE MOTION FOR MORTGAGE MODIFICATION MEDIATION ("MMM")

FLNB Local Form 3PS (09/14)

UNITED STATES BANKRUPTCY COURT
NORTHERN DISTRICT OF FLORIDA
_______________ DIVISION

In re: **Case No.:**

Chapter:

Debtor(s)

VERIFIED EX PARTE MOTION FOR MORTGAGE MODIFICATION MEDIATION ("MMM")

The Debtor(s) request entry of an order referring the Debtor and Lender,

____

("Lender") to Mortgage Modification Mediation ("MMM"), and alleges:

1. Debtor is an individual who filed for bankruptcy relief under, or converted to chapter ____ on _______________.

2. Debtor requests MMM for real property ("Property") located at the following street address:

____

a. The account number(s) for this Property is _______________ (last four digits of all account numbers for the same Lender).

b. The Property is (check one box):

◯ The Debtor's primary residence

◯ Not the Debtor's primary residence

c. The Lender's full name and current address are:

____

____

* *All references to "Debtor" shall include and refer to both debtors in a case filed jointly by two individuals.*

d. Borrowers obligated on the promissory note and mortgage on the Property are:

◯ Debtor only

◯ Debtor and non-filing co-obligor/co-borrower/third party (within ten (10) days of the date of this Order, debtor must provide Lender the names, addresses, telephone numbers, and email addresses, if any, of any non-Debtors who are co-obligors, co-borrowers, or third parties to the obligation(s) to be modified.)

3. **Debtor and debtor's counsel, if applicable, intends to comply with the procedures and guidelines contained within the Court's *Uniform District-wide Mortgage Modification Mediation Procedures* available at *www.flnb.uscourts.gov/mortgage-modification-mediation*.**

4. Debtor consents to Lender communicating directly with Debtor's attorney for any and all aspects of the MMM program. The parties may communicate outside the Portal orally, but all written communication shall occur through the Portal.

5. Prior to filing this motion, Debtor or Debtor's attorney has collected all of the required supporting documentation along with the appropriate modification forms via the MMM Portal. Within seven (7) days after the selection of a Mediator or the Lender's registration on the MMM Portal, the Debtor or Debtor's attorney shall upload and submit through the MMM portal all forms needed for MMM with the Lender, and shall pay the non-refundable MMM Portal submission fee; and will upload this Order to the MMM Portal as part of the submission of Debtor's documentation.

6. The Debtor certifies that the Debtor's portion of the required mediator's fee is in hand, or has been remitted to Debtor's attorney. Debtor understands and acknowledges that after the mediato is designated, the mediator's fee is not refundable for any reason at any time.

7. The Debtor's filing fee for this case and any prior case filed in this district has been paid in full or has been waived by court order.

Wherefore, Debtor requests the entry of an order granting this Ex Parte Motion, and requests such other and further relief as this Court deems just and proper.

____
Date

____
Debtor's Signature
Address
City, ST Zip
Telephone
Email

____
Joint Debtor's Signature
Address
City, ST Zip
Telephone
Email

DEBTOR'S VERIFICATION

Pursuant to 28 U.S.C. § 1746, I declare under penalty of perjury the foregoing is true and correct on ________________, 20___.

____
Debtor's Signature

____
Joint Debtor's Signature

CERTIFICATE OF SERVICE

I HEREBY CERTIFY that a true and correct copy of the **Verified Ex Parte Motion for Mortgage Modification Mediation (MMM)** was served by U.S., first class Mail, upon the parties listed below on ______________ 20___.

____
Debtor's Signature

____
Joint Debtor's Signature

Copies to:

Lender (identify name of Lender and where notice sent)
Lender's Counsel (if known)

[Dated: September 2014.]

LOCAL FORM 4. CERTIFICATE OF SERVICE

FLNB Local Form 4 (02/15)

UNITED STATES BANKRUPTCY COURT
NORTHERN DISTRICT OF FLORIDA
_________________ DIVISION

In Re: Case Number:
Chapter:

Debtor(s)

CERTIFICATE OF SERVICE

I, ______________________________________, hereby certify that a true and correct copy of the ____ was served on the following in the manner stated below:

1. **Served by the Court via Notice of Electronic Filing (NEF):** I have confirmed that the foregoing document was served by the Court via NEF on _______________ to the following person(s) at the email address(es) noted herein:

☐ No persons/entities served by Notice of Electronic Filing

2. **Served by U.S. Mail:** The foregoing document was served by first class, postage prepaid, U.S. Mail on _______________ to the persons and/or entities at the addresses noted herein as obtained from a current mailing matrix obtained from the court's CM/ECF system:

☐ See attached mailing matrix or additional sheets
☐ No persons/entities served by U.S. Mail

3. **Served by Personal Delivery, Overnight Mail, Facsimile Transmission or Email** (state method for each person or entity served): Service was executed on _______________ to the following persons and/or entities via the means noted below:

☐ No persons/entities served by personal delivery, overnight mail, facsimile transmission or email (excluding NEF transmission)

I declare under penalty of perjury that the foregoing is true and correct.

_________________________________ Date: ____________________

Signature of Person Certifying Service

[Dated: February 2015]

LOCAL FORM 5. EXHIBIT TAG/COVER SHEET

FLNB Local Form 5

Exhibit Tag/ Cover Sheet

Party submitting: ________________ Ex. #___

Admitted: Yes or No (circle one)

Debtor:________________________________

Case No.:______________________________

***Adv. No.:*______________________________**

Nature of Hearing/
Docket No:______________________________

____

Dated ____________ , 20___.

By:____________________, Deputy Clerk

[Effective July, 2014.]

LOCAL FORM 6. EXHIBIT LIST

FLNB Local Form 6

United States Bankruptcy Court

Northern District of Florida

EXHIBIT LIST

v.

Case Number:

PRESIDING JUDGE	PLAINTIFF'S ATTORNEY	DEFENDANT'S ATTORNEY
HEARING/TRAIL DATE(S)	COURT REPORTER	COURTROOM DEPUTY

PLF. NO.	DEF. NO.	DATE OFFERED	MARKED	ADMITTED	DESCRIPTION OF EXHIBITS*

*Include a notation as to the location of any exhibit not held with the case file or not available because of size.

Page 1 of ________ Pages

FLNB Local Form 6

EXHIBIT LIST - CONTINUATION

vs.					CASE NO.
PLF. NO.	DEF. NO.	DATE OFFERED	MARKED	ADMITTED	DESCRIPTION OF EXHIBITS

Page ___ of ____ Pages

[Effective June 1, 1997. Amended effective April 11, 2003. Renumbered effective January 1, 2006. Amended effective July, 2014.]

LOCAL FORM 7. STATEMENT OF NEED FOR EMERGENCY HEARING

FLNB Local Form 7 (Rev. 12/15)

UNITED STATES BANKRUPTCY COURT
NORTHERN DISTRICT OF FLORIDA
DIVISION
www.flnb.uscourts.gov

In re: **Case No.:**

Chapter:

Debtor(s)

STATEMENT OF NEED FOR EMERGENCY HEARING

I, THE UNDERSIGNED, REQUEST AN EMERGENCY HEARING ON

(title of pleading)

I REQUEST THE MATTER BE HEARD ON OR BEFORE

(insert date)

1. I UNDERSTAND AND AGREE that emergency hearings shall ordinarily be held only where direct, immediate, and substantial harm will occur to (a) the interest of an entity in property; (b) the estate; or (c) the debtor's ability to reorganize if the parties are not able to obtain an immediate resolution of the dispute (N.D. Fla. LBR 9073-1 B.). I HEREBY CERTIFY:

2. There is a true necessity for an emergency hearing because direct, immediate, and substantial harm will occur to: *Check the appropriate box(es) and insert explanation of facts:*

☐ the interest of an entity in property;

☐ the estate; or

☐ the debtor's ability to reorganize if parties are not able to obtain an immediate resolution of the dispute.

3. The relief requested is:

4. This matter must be heard on an emergency basis specifically because:

5. Pursuant to the Local Rules of this Court and the District Court for the Northern District of Florida (N.D. Fla. Loc. R. 7.1(B)), I have conferred with opposing counsel before requesting an emergency hearing.

6. As a member of the Bar of the Court, that I have carefully examined the matter under consideration and to the best of my knowledge, information, and belief formed after reasonable inquiry, all allegations are well grounded in fact and all contentions are warranted by existing law or a good faith argument for the extension, modification, or reversal of existing law can be made. The matter under consideration is not interposed for any improper purpose, such as to harass, or to cause delay.

7. The necessity of this emergency hearing has not been caused by a lack of due diligence on my part, but has been brought about by circumstances beyond my control or that of my client.

8. This motion is filed with full understanding of F.R.B.P. 9011 and the consequences of noncompliance with the same.

DATED this _____ day of _____________________ , _______.

/s/ ________________________________

(signature block)

[Effective July 21, 2015. Amended effective December 1, 2015.]

LOCAL FORM 12. NOTICE OF ADDRESS TO BE USED IN SPECIFIC CASE PURSUANT TO 11 U.S.C.§ 342(e)

FLNB Local Form 12 (10/05)

United States Bankruptcy Court
Northern District of Florida
Gainesville Division

IN RE:

Case Number:

Chapter:

Debtor(s)

NOTICE OF ADDRESS TO BE USED IN SPECIFIC CASE PURSUANT TO 11 U.S.C. § 342(e)

Requestor's Name:

Current Address of Record:

Phone Number:

Address to be added as preferred address for this case:

Creditor Name:

Address Line 1:

Address Line 2:

Address Line 3:

City, State:

Zip:

Email:

I have served a copy of this Notice of Address to be Used in Specific Case Pursuant to11 U.S.C. § 342(e) on the debtor in the above-referenced case.

Under penalty of perjury, I, the undersigned affirm that I am authorized to request this address change.

Name: ______________________________

Signature: ______________________________

Date: ______________________________

[Effective October, 2005. Amended April, 2014.]

LOCAL FORM 16. STATEMENT OF NO EMPLOYMENT INCOME

FLNB Local Form 16 (Rev. 07/11)

UNITED STATES BANKRUPTCY COURT
NORTHERN DISTRICT OF FLORIDA
DIVISION

In Re: Case No:
Chapter:

Debtor(s)

STATEMENT OF NO EMPLOYMENT INCOME

Check box if statement applies to debtor ☐ Debtor, ________________________, is not required to submit payment advices or other evidence of payment under 11 U.S.C. 521(a)(1)(B)(iv) and certifies as follows:

☐ Debtor was not employed and had no income from an employer within 60 days prior to the filing of the petition.

☐ Debtor was self-employed and had no income from an employer within 60 days prior to the filing of the petition.

Check box if statement applies to joint-debtor ☐ Joint-debtor, ________________________, is not required to submit payment advices or other evidence of payment under 11 U.S.C. 521(a)(1)(B)(iv) and certifies as follows:

☐ Debtor was not employed and had no income from an employer within 60 days prior to the filing of the petition.

☐ Debtor was self-employed and had no income from an employer within 60 days prior to the filing of the petition.

I declare under penalty of perjury that the foregoing is true and correct.

Date: Signature of Debtor: /s/ ________________________

Date: Signature of Joint-Debtor: /s/ ________________________

By: /s/ ________________________
ATTORNEY SIGNATURE IF REPRESENTED BY COUNSEL

[Amended effective May, 2007; April, 2014.]

LOCAL FORM 17. NOTICE OF CHANGE OF ADDRESS OF DEBTOR

FLNB Local Form 17 (Rev. 05/07)

UNITED STATES BANKRUPTCY COURT
NORTHERN DISTRICT OF FLORIDA
Gainesville **DIVISION**

In re: **Case No.:**
Chapter:

Debtor(s)

Notice of Change of Address of Debtor(s)

Debtor's former mailing address:

Name:

Address:

Please be advised that effective ______________________, the debtor(s)' new mailing address is:

Name:

Address:

New address applies to (check one): ◯ Debtor Only ◯ Joint Debtor Only ◯ Both Debtors

____
Debtor Signature (if *pro se*)

____
Debtor Name Printed

/s/ ______________________________
Attorney Signature

____
Bar ID No.

[Amended effective May, 2007; April, 2014.]

LOCAL FORM 18. MOTION FOR DETERMINATION AND WAIVER OF DEBTOR'S DUTY TO COMPLY WITH THE CREDIT COUNSELING REQUIREMENT UNDER 11 U.S.C. SECTION 109(h)(4)

FLNB Local Form 18 (Rev. 07/11)

UNITED STATES BANKRUPTCY COURT
NORTHERN DISTRICT OF FLORIDA
GAINESVILLE DIVISION

In Re: Case No.:

Chapter:

Debtor(s)

MOTION FOR DETERMINATION AND WAIVER OF DEBTOR'S DUTY TO COMPLY WITH THE CREDIT COUNSELING REQUIREMENT UNDER 11 U.S.C. SECTION 109(h)(4)

In accordance with Section 109(h)(4) of the Bankruptcy Code, I hereby request that the Court determine that I may be relieved of the credit counseling requirement imposed by Section 109(h)(4) of the Bankruptcy Code due to an ***incapacity, disability*** or because I am engaged in ***active military duty in a military combat zone***. For the purposes of making this request under Section 109(h)(4), I understand that "incapacity" means that the debtor is impaired by reason of mental illness or mental deficiency so that he or she is incapable of realizing and making rational decisions with respect to his or her financial responsibilities; and "disability" means that the debtor is so physically impaired as to be unable, after reasonable effort, to participate in an in-person, telephone, or internet briefing as required by statute.

My request is based on one of the following (Please check one of the boxes below):

☐ I have an incapacity.

☐ I have a disability.

☐ I am engaged in active military duty in a military combat zone.

[In the space provided on the next page, please furnish a detailed explanation setting forth the basis for your request. Attach any documentation that will assist the Court in making a determination. Please do not include any unnecessary private information such as the names of your minor children or your full Social Security Number (include only the last four numbers of your Social Security Number). If both the debtor and joint debtor are making a request under Section 109(h)(4), each debtor should file a separate request with the Court. Please note that this waiver only applies to the debtor making the request. A joint debtor to whom this waiver does not apply must still satisfy the credit counseling requirement.]

Explanation:

Signature of Attorney

Date

Name of Attorney

Signature of Debtor or Joint Debtor, as applicable

Date

Name of Debtor or Joint Debtor, as applicable

[Amended effective July, 2011; April, 2014.]

LOCAL FORM 19. REQUEST FOR NOTICE PURSUANT TO BANKRUPTCY RULE 2002(g)

FLNB Local Form 19 (Rev. 05/07)

UNITED STATES BANKRUPTCY COURT
NORTHERN DISTRICT OF FLORIDA
Gainesville **DIVISION**

In re: **Case No.:**

Chapter:

Debtor(s)

REQUEST FOR NOTICE PURSUANT TO BANKRUPTCY RULE 2002(g)

1. This request is filed pursuant to Bankruptcy Rule 2002(g) for the purpose of ensuring that the creditor listed below receives all notices required to be mailed under Bankruptcy Rule 2002 at the address listed below.

2. The address to which all such notices should be sent:

Name:

Address:

Date: ______________________ /s/______________________
Creditor/Representative Signature

____
Creditor/Representative Printed

[Amended effective May, 2007; April, 2014.]

LOCAL FORM 20. NOTICE OF APPEARANCE

FLNB Local Form 20 (Rev. 05/07)

UNITED STATES BANKRUPTCY COURT
NORTHERN DISTRICT OF FLORIDA
GAINESVILLE **DIVISION**

In re:

Case No.:
Chapter:

Debtor(s)

NOTICE OF APPEARANCE

______________________________, a creditor in the above styled proceeding, hereby requests that all matters which must be noticed to creditors, any creditors committees, and any other parties-in-interest pursuant to FRBP 2002, whether sent by the Court, the Debtors, or any other party in the case, be sent to the undersigned; and pursuant to FRBP 2002(g), requests that the following be added to the Court's Master Mailing List:

Name: ______________________________

Address: ______________________________

____

City: ______________ ST: _____ Zip: ______

Dated this ______ day of ______________, ______.

____
Attorney Signature

____
Attorney Name Printed

____
Bar ID No.

[Amended effective May, 2007; April, 2014.]

LOCAL FORM 32. MOTION FOR PROTECTIVE ORDER TO RESTRICT ACCESS AND ALLOW FOR REDACTION OF INFORMATION

FLNB Local Form 32 (Rev. 07/10)

UNITED STATES BANKRUPTCY COURT
NORTHERN DISTRICT OF FLORIDA
DIVISION

In re: Case No.:
Chapter:

Debtor(s)

MOTION FOR PROTECTIVE ORDER TO RESTRICT ACCESS
AND ALLOW FOR REDACTION OF INFORMATION

COMES NOW ______________________________ and moves this Court for the entry of an order restricting access and allowing for redaction of information pursuant to Fed. R. Bankr. P. 9037, and as grounds therefore states as follows:

1. A ______________________________ was filed in the record of this court on ______________, and is listed as number _____ on the ◯ docket or ◯ claims register.
2. The above named document contained a name, social security number, and/or account number which is prohibited under Fed. R. Bankr. P. 9037.
3. Upon entry of the order granting this motion, the movant will file an amended document or claim with the personal information redacted.

WHEREFORE, the movant respectfully requests this Court enter an order directing the Clerk to restrict electronic access to the document/claim named in item number 1 above, and allow the movant to refile the document or claim with the information redacted.

RESPECTFULLY SUBMITTED this ______ day of ______________, 20 ___.

Attorney Signature

FLNB Local Form 32

CERTIFICATE OF SERVICE

I HEREBY certify that a true and accurate copy of the foregoing has been furnished by electronic filing or first class mail to:

on this ______ day of ____________________ 20 ____ .

____

[Effective December, 2009. Amended effective July, 2010, April, 2014.]

LOCAL FORM 35. PRO SE DEBTOR(S)' STATEMENT REGARDING CONVERSION TO CHAPTER 7 PURSUANT TO FED. R. BANKR. P. 1019 AND N.D. FLA. LBR 1019

FLNB Local Form 7-35 (02/11)

UNITED STATES BANKRUPTCY COURT
NORTHERN DISTRICT OF FLORIDA
GAINESVILLE **DIVISION**

In re: **Case No.:**
Chapter:

Debtor(s)

PRO SE DEBTOR(S)' STATEMENT REGARDING CONVERSION TO CHAPTER 7 PURSUANT TO FED. R. BANKR. P. 1019 AND N.D. FLA. LBR 1019

COMES NOW THE DEBTOR(S), having converted to a case under Chapter 7 of Title 11, to declare there has been no acquisition of property nor debts or leases incurred since the filing of the initial petition under Chapter ____ .

Respectfully submitted this ________ day of ____________________________ , 20____.

____
Debtor

____
Joint Debtor

[Amended effective April, 2014.]

LOCAL FORM 36. VERIFICATION OF CREDITOR MAILING MATRIX

FLNB Local Form 36 (05/11)

UNITED STATES BANKRUPTCY COURT
NORTHERN DISTRICT OF FLORIDA
GAINESVILLE **DIVISION**

In re: **Case No.:**

Chapter:

Debtor(s)

VERIFICATION OF CREDITOR MAILING MATRIX

I/We, the above named debtor(s), do hereby verify under penalty of perjury that the mailing matrix (list of creditors) attached or previously filed in this case is true and correct to the best of my/our knowledge.

Debtor's Signature Date:

Printed Name of Debtor

Joint Debtor's Signature Date:

Printed Name of Joint Debtor

[Amended effective April, 2014.]

D. CHAPTER 7 FORMS

LOCAL FORM 7–7. REPORT AND NOTICE OF TRUSTEE'S INTENTION TO ABANDON PROPERTY OF THE ESTATE

FLNB Local Form 7-7 (Rev. 03/10)

UNITED STATES BANKRUPTCY COURT
NORTHERN DISTRICT OF FLORIDA
DIVISION

In re: **Case No.:**

Chapter:

Debtor(s)

REPORT AND NOTICE OF TRUSTEE'S
INTENTION TO ABANDON PROPERTY OF THE ESTATE

TO: Debtor(s), Creditors, and Parties in Interest

NOTICE OF OPPORTUNITY TO
OBJECT AND FOR HEARING

Pursuant to Local Rule 2002-2, the court will consider this motion, objection or other matter without further notice or hearing unless a party in interest files an objection within twenty-one (21) days from the date of service of this paper. If you object to the relief requested in this paper, you must file your objection with the clerk of the Court at 110 E. Park Avenue, Tallahassee, FL 32301, and serve a copy on the trustee, ______________________ at ______________________.

If you file and serve an objection within the time permitted, the Court may schedule a hearing and you will be notified. If you do not file an objection within the time permitted, the Court will consider that you do not oppose the granting of the relief requested in the paper, and will proceed to consider the paper without further notice of hearing, and may grant the relief requested.

NOTICE IS HEREBY GIVEN that the trustee/debtor-in-possession intends to abandon the following property(ies) of the estate:

Item No. Value	Property Description	Lienholder(s) Name & Address	Amount of Secured Claim	Fair Market

Said property is being abandoned for the following reasons:

1) The secured creditors hold a valid, perfected security interest on the property and the balance due exceeds the fair market value of the property; or

2) The property(ies) are worthless and unsaleable.

3) The cost of preservation and cost of sale of the property(ies) is greater than the price which could be realized from liquidation of same.

Dated: ______________________ ______________________________

Trustee

Name:

Address:

Phone No.

[Renumbered effective January 1, 2006. Amended effective December, 2009; March, 2010; April, 2014.]

LOCAL FORM 7-8. REPORT AND NOTICE OF INTENTION TO SELL PROPERTY OF THE ESTATE

FLNB Local Form 7-8 (Rev. 02/10)

UNITED STATES BANKRUPTCY COURT
NORTHERN DISTRICT OF FLORIDA
DIVISION

In re: **Case No.:**
Chapter:

Debtor(s)

REPORT AND NOTICE OF TRUSTEE'S INTENTION TO SELL PROPERTY OF THE ESTATE

TO: Debtor(s), Creditors, and Parties in Interest

NOTICE OF OPPORTUNITY TO OBJECT AND FOR HEARING

Pursuant to Local Rule 2002-2, the court will consider this motion, objection or other matter without further notice or hearing unless a party in interest files an objection within twenty-one (21) days from the date of service of this paper. If you object to the relief requested in this paper, you must file your objection with the clerk of the Court at 110 E. Park Avenue, Tallahassee, FL 32301, and serve a copy on the trustee, ______________________ at ______________________.

If you file and serve an objection within the time permitted, the Court may schedule a hearing and you will be notified. If you do not file an objection within the time permitted, the Court will consider that you do not oppose the granting of the relief requested in the paper, and will proceed to consider the paper without further notice of hearing, and may grant the relief requested.

NOTICE IS HEREBY GIVEN that the trustee/debtor-in-possession intends to sell the following property(ies) of the estate of the debtor(s), under the terms and conditions set forth below.

1. Description of property:

2. Manner of Sale: ○ Private* ○ Public Auction

3. Terms of Sale (include purchaser, if know, price, terms, whether or not sale is free and clear of liens, names and addresses or lienors, and all other pertinent information):

*(Applicable to private sales only) The trustee will entertain any higher bids for the purchase of the assets of the debtor(s) which the trustee proposes to sell. Such bids must be in writing and accompanied by a deposit of _______ % of the proposed higher purchase price. Any higher bid must be received by the trustee at the address listed below no later than the close of business on _________________________.

NOTICE IS HEREBY GIVEN that all objections to the same must state the basis for the objection. If no objection is filed, the sale described above will take place.

Dated: ___________________________ ___________________________

Trustee

Name:

Address:

Phone No.

[Renumbered effective January 1, 2006. Amended effective December, 2009; February, 2010; April, 2014.]

LOCAL FORM 7-15. CERTIFICATE AND AFFIDAVIT FOR ADDING CREDITORS IN A CLOSED CASE

FLNB Local Form 7-15 (04/11)

UNITED STATES BANKRUPTCY COURT
NORTHERN DISTRICT OF FLORIDA
DIVISION

In re:

Case No.:
Chapter 7

Debtor(s)

CERTIFICATE AND AFFIDAVIT FOR ADDING CREDITORS IN A CLOSED CASE

1. The undersigned *pro se* debtor(s) or the undersigned member of the bar of this Court who represents the debtor(s), hereby certifies that:
   a. The above-captioned case was filed under or converted to a Chapter 7 of the Bankruptcy Code ("Chapter 7") and remained a case under Chapter 7 until closing;
   b. After filing or conversion to Chapter 7, a notice of no dividend, contained in the Notice of First Meeting of Creditors, was sent to the creditors listed on the schedules informing the creditors they need not file claims in the above-captioned case;
   c. The Chapter 7 Trustee has filed a Report of No Distribution and, subsequent to the filing of that report, no assets of the estate have been recovered or administered; a discharge was entered and the case was subsequently closed;
   d. The purpose of filing this Certificate is to amend the schedules to add only the pre-petition creditor(s) listed on the attached sheet.
   e. Due notice of items b and c above has been sent to such creditor(s) and no response has been received from the creditor(s) within the thirty (30) day response period.

2. The debtor(s) signing below, under penalty of perjury, further certifies that:
   a. Such debtor(s) did not intentionally omit the creditor(s) listed on the attached sheet from the schedules filed in the above-referenced case; and
   b. Such debtor(s) did not intend to hinder, delay or default said creditor(s).

Signature of Attorney

Signature of Debtor

Printed Name of Attorney

Signature of Joint Debtor

Date

[Amended effective April, 2011; April, 2014.]

E. CHAPTER 11 FORMS

LOCAL FORM 11–5. CHAPTER 11—VOTE ON PLAN

FLNB LF 11 5 (01/14)

CHAPTER 11 BALLOT TABULATION

DEBTOR: ______________________________

CASE NUMBER: ______________________

LAST DATE FOR BALLOTS: ______________

DATE OF HEARING TO TABULATE VOTE: __________

Name of Creditor and Class Number	Amount of Claim	Claim No.	Accept	Reject

CHAPTER 11 BALLOT TABULATION

DEBTOR: ______________________________

CASE NUMBER: ______________________

SUMMARY

CLASS

TOTAL NUMBER OF CLAIMS VOTING: ______________

TOTAL NUMBER OF CLAIMS ACCEPTING: ______________

TOTAL DOLLAR AMOUNT OF CLAIMS VOTING: ______________

TOTAL DOLLAR AMOUNT OF CLAIMS ACCEPTING: ______________

*

CLASS

TOTAL NUMBER OF CLAIMS VOTING: ______________

TOTAL NUMBER OF CLAIMS ACCEPTING: ______________

TOTAL DOLLAR AMOUNT OF CLAIMS VOTING: ______________

TOTAL DOLLAR AMOUNT OF CLAIMS ACCEPTING: ______________

*

CLASS

TOTAL NUMBER OF CLAIMS VOTING: ______________

TOTAL NUMBER OF CLAIMS ACCEPTING: ______________

TOTAL DOLLAR AMOUNT OF CLAIMS VOTING: ______________

TOTAL DOLLAR AMOUNT OF CLAIMS ACCEPTING: ______________

*

CLASS

TOTAL NUMBER OF CLAIMS VOTING: ______________

TOTAL NUMBER OF CLAIMS ACCEPTING: ______________

TOTAL DOLLAR AMOUNT OF CLAIMS VOTING: ______________

TOTAL DOLLAR AMOUNT OF CLAIMS ACCEPTING: ______________

*

***Indicate if more or less than 2/3 of amount voting**

[Renumbered effective January 1, 2006. Amended effective January 2014.]

LOCAL FORM 11-6. COVER SHEET FOR APPLICATION FOR ATTORNEY COMPENSATION AND REIMBURSEMENT OF EXPENSES

FLNB Local Form 11-6 (04/14)

UNITED STATES BANKRUPTCY COURT
NORTHERN DISTRICT OF FLORIDA
DIVISION

In Re: ____________________ Case No.
____________________ Chapter: 11
____
____

Debtor(s)

Cover Sheet for
Application by ____________________ for Compensation for Services Rendered and Reimbursement of Expenses as Counsel to the ____________ for the Period from ____________ through ____________

Name of Applicant: ____________________

Services Provided to: ____________________

Date of Retention: ____________________

Period for this Application: ____________________

Amount of Compensation Sought: ____________________

Amount of Expense Reimbursement: ____________________

Amount of Original Retainer: ____________ Current Balance: ____________

Blended Hourly Rate this Application: ____________ Cumulative: ____________

This is an ◯ interim ◯ final Application

Disclose the following for each prior application:

		Requested				Approved		Paid		Holdback
Filed	Period	Fees	Hrs.	Rate	Exps.	Fees	Exps.	Fees	Exps.	
Total:										

[Effective April, 2014.]

LOCAL FORM 11–26. INDIVIDUAL DEBTOR(S) MOTION FOR ENTRY OF DISCHARGE, CERTIFICATE OF COMPLIANCE AND NOTICE OF TIME TO OBJECT

FLNB Local Form 11-26 (Rev. 09/10)

UNITED STATES BANKRUPTCY COURT
NORTHERN DISTRICT OF FLORIDA
DIVISION

In re: **Case No.:**
Chapter 11

Debtor(s)
Last 4 Digits of Debtor's SSN: XXX-XX-
Last 4 Digits of Joint Debtor's SSN: XXX-XX-

Individual Debtor(s) Motion for Entry of Discharge,
Certificate of Compliance and Notice of Time to Object

Notice of Time to Object

Any interested party who fails to file and serve a written objection to this motion within twenty-one (21) days after the date of service of this motion shall be deemed to have consented to the entry of an order of discharge. If no objection is filed, a discharge pursuant to 11 U.S.C. § 1141(d)(5)(A) may be entered without further notice or hearing.

I/We, the undersigned debtor(s), move the court for entry of a discharge in this case pursuant to 11 U.S.C. § 1141(d)(5)(A) by certifying under penalty of perjury that:

1. All plan payments have been completed.

2. Compliance with 11 U.S.C. § 1141(d)(5)(C):

☐ I/We did not have, either at the time of filing this bankruptcy case or at the present time, equity in excess of the dollar amount specified in § 522(q), in the type of property described in 11 U.S.C. § 522(p)(1).

OR

☐ A. There has been no conviction in any proceeding and there is not currently pending a proceeding in which the debtor(s) may be found guilty of a felony or liable for a debt of a kind described in 11 U.S.C. §522(q)(1)(A) [circumstances showing that the filing of this case was an abuse of the Bankruptcy Code], and

FLNB Local Form 11-26 (Rev. 09/10)

☐ B. Neither I (individual case) nor either of us (joint case) is liable for a debt of the kind described in 11 U.S.C. § 522(q)(1)(B) [securities law violations; civil remedies under 18 U.S.C. § 1964; or criminal, intentional, or reckless misconduct that caused death or serious physical injury to an individual in the past five (5) years].

I declare under penalty of perjury that the information contained in this Certificate is true and correct.

/s/____________________________
Debtor Signature

/s/____________________________
Joint Debtor Signature

CERTIFICATE OF SERVICE

The undersigned hereby certifies that on the_____day of__________, 20____, a true and correct copy of the Motion for Entry of Discharge, Certificate of Compliance and Notice of Time to Object was served upon all creditors and parties in interested listed on the attached service list by either first-class, U.S. Mail or via the CM/ECF system of the United States Bankruptcy Court. If the debtor is appearing pro se, the Clerk's Office will serve the Motion and Certificate on all creditors and parties in interest.

/s/____________________________
Attorney Signature OR Debtor, if Pro se

[Amended effective December, 2009; September, 2010; April, 2014.]

LOCAL FORM 11–37. STATEMENT/CERTIFICATION REGARDING REQUIREMENTS FOR DISCHARGE IN AN INDIVIDUAL CHAPTER 11 CASE

FLNB Local Form 11-37 (08/11)

UNITED STATES BANKRUPTCY COURT
NORTHERN DISTRICT OF FLORIDA
GAINESVILLE DIVISION

In re: **Case No.:**
Chapter 11

Debtor(s)

STATEMENT/CERTIFICATION REGARDING REQUIREMENTS FOR DISCHARGE IN AN INDIVIDUAL CHAPTER 11 CASE

Pursuant to 11 U.S.C. § 1141(d) and/or Local Rule 4004-1, concerning compliance with the requirements for discharge in an individual chapter 11 case, the debtor(s) hereby state and certify that as to

1. Plan payments:

   ☐ I/We have completed all plan payments;

   OR

   ☐ I/We have been granted a hardship discharge pursuant to the provisions of 11 U.S.C. § 1141(d)(5)(B).

2. Compliance with 11 U.S.C. § 1141(d)(5)(C) [regarding exemptions]:

   ☐ I/We **did not** have either at the time of filing this bankruptcy case or at the present time, equity in excess of the dollar amount specified in 11 U.S.C. § 522(q), in the type of property described in 11 U.S.C. § 522(p)(1);

   OR

   ☐ I/We **did have** at the time of the filing of this bankruptcy case or **do have at the present time**, equity in excess of the dollar amount specified in 11 U.S.C. § 522(q), in the type of property described in 11 U.S.C. § 522(p)(1), but

   a. there has been no conviction in any proceeding and there is not currently a pending proceeding in which the debtor(s) may be found guilty of a felony or liable for a debt of a kind described in 11 U.S.C. § 522(q)(1)(A) [circumstances showing that the filing of this case was an abuse of the provisions of this title], **AND**

   b. the debtor(s) is/are not liable for a debt of the kind described in 11 U.S.C. § 522(q)(1)(B) [securities law violations, civil remedies under 18 U.S.C. § 1964; or criminal, intentional, or reckless misconduct that caused death or serious injury to an individual in the past five (5) years].

FLNB Local Form 11-37 (08/11)

3. Post-petition Instructional Course in Personal Financial Management:

☐ I/We have completed a post-petition instructional course in personal financial management and have filed with the court an Official Form 23, Debtor's Certification of Completion of Postpetition Instructional Course Concerning Personal Financial Management and/or the certificate issued by the course provider, for each debtor, if applicable, pursuant to Fed. R. Bankr. P. 4004(c)(4).

I/We declare under penalty of perjury that the statements and certifications contained herein are true and correct.

________________________ ________________
Signature of Debtor Date

________________________ ________________
Signature of Joint Debtor, if applicable Date

[Effective August 1, 2011. Amended effective April, 2014.]

F. CHAPTER 12 FORMS

LOCAL FORM 12-9. CHAPTER 12 CASE—SUMMARY OF OPERATIONS—FAMILY FARMER

FLNB Local Form 9
Rev. 12/2009

CHAPTER 12 CASE
SUMMARY OF OPERATIONS - FAMILY FARMER

(This report must be filed with the Chapter 12 Trustee seven (7) days before the First Meeting of Creditors)

NAME OF DEBTOR: ______________________

CASE NO. ____________

I. NUMBER OF ACRES:

Owned: ________

Leased (list by parcel)	Amount or % of Rent Received by Debtor
____________________	____________________
____________________	____________________
____________________	____________________

II. LIVESTOCK AND POULTRY

Number of (list by kind)

III. RESULTS OF LAST CROP SEASON:

A. Crop Grown:

NUMBER ACRES CROP PLANTED	YIELD PER ACRE	YIELD AMOUNT SOLD	TOTAL SALES PRICE	QUANTITY SOLD OR SEALED	AMOUNT LIEN ON STORE CROP
(List by crop)					

B. Livestock and Poultry Sold Last Year:

Livestock	Number	Total Price
(List by kind)	$__________	

C. Total Income Last Year from Products Sold:
(i.e. milk, eggs, wool, hides, etc.)

(List by kind) $

Have you made an assignment of proceeds? ________________ (Yes/No)

If yes, to whom: ______________________________

____

____

IV. CURRENT OR PROPOSED FARMING SEASON:

______A. Crops:

CROP	NO. OF ACRES	ESTIMATED* YIELD	ESTIMATED** PRICE PER UNIT	TOTAL PROCEEDS
(list by kind)				

Total Proceeds - all crops $ ________________

* Assuming normal moisture and growing conditions
**State your estimate of market price per unit or government support (loan) price if you are eligible for government support program

B. Estimated Income From livestock and Poultry Operation:

Livestock and Poultry	Number to be Sold	Estimated Total Price
(list by kind)		

Total Livestock and Poultry Sales Price $________________

C. Total Estimated Crop, Livestock and Poultry Income $________________

V. CURRENT OR PROPOSED CROP SEASON - ESTIMATED EXPENSES

A. Operating Expenses:

EXPENSES	AMOUNT
Fuel	$ ________
Seed	________
Feed	________
Herbicides, Pesticides Or other Chemicals	________
Equipment Rental	________
Electric & Phone Bills	________
Repairs	________
Crop Insurance	________
Other Insurance	________
Real Estate Taxes	________
Cash Rent on Leased Land	________
Combining and/or Drying Expense	________
Processing costs	________
Hired Labor	________
Other	________
Total Estimated Operating Expenses	$ ________

If you have an operating loan for the current or proposed crop season, state amount $ ________
and name and address of lender ____

and security given or pledged ____

B. Payments on Secured Debt.

Cash rents (if not included in Part A above): $ ________

Crop Share Rents - State # of bushels/pounds and dollar value: $ ________

Real Estate Mortgage and Contract for Deed (purchase agreement) payments:

To whom: Amount

____

____

____

____

______________________ Total Amount $__________

Annual Payment due on Equipment Purchase Contracts:

To whom: Amount

____

____

____

____

______________________ Total Amount $__________

Payments on Loans Secured by Equipment, Crops or Livestock:

To whom: Amount

____

____

____

____

______________________ Total Amount $__________

Total Payments on Secured Debt $__________

C. Total Operating Expenses and Payments on Secured Debt $__________

VI. NET ESTIMATED OPERATING PROFIT OR LOSS
(Total Receipts from Item IV(C) less Total Expenses & Payments from Item V(C)) $__________

A. Estimated Household and Family Cash Living Expenses (subtract from net profit or add to net loss) $__________

B. Estimated state, local and Federal Income Taxes on Net Profit $__________

C. Total of A and B $__________

D. Disposable Income from Farming (Subtract C from amount entered on line at VII) $__________

E. Income from other than Farming $__________

F. Total Disposable Income $__________

[Renumbered effective January 1, 2006. Amended effective December, 2009.]

LOCAL FORM 12–10. CHAPTER 12 CASE—MONTHLY CASH RECEIPTS AND DISBURSEMENTS

1/06

Local Form #10

Month of ____________, 20__

CHAPTER 12 CASE

NAME OF DEBTOR: ____

MONTHLY CASH RECEIPTS AND DISBURSEMENTS

(Report on a cash basis, unless you keep financial records on an accrual basis)

I. Cash Received During Month (Itemize):

Item & Quantity Sold	Amount
____________________	$________
____________________	________
____________________	________
____________________	________
New loan received this month (if any)	
Wages earned from outside work	
Other receipts:	________

TOTAL CASH RECEIPTS $____________

II. Expenses Paid:

Total amount paid for household or living expense $____________

Item	Amount
____________________	$________
____________________	________
____________________	________
____________________	________

Plan payments made to Chapter 12 Trustee $________

TOTAL EXPENSES PAID DURING MONTH $____________

Losses due to crop failure or damage $________

Losses due to death or disease of livestock or poultry $________

PROFIT (OR LOSS) FOR MONTH $____________

III. Cash Reconciliation:

Cash and Bank Accounts Balance at beginning of Month: $________

Income (or Loss) During Month $________

_____ Cash and Bank Account Balance at End of Month $____________

IV. Expenses Charged But Not Paid During Month (Itemize)

Item	Amount
________________________	$________
________________________	________
________________________	________

I CERTIFY UNDER PENALTY OF PERJURY THAT I HAVE READ THE FOREGOING STATEMENT, AND IT IS TRUE AND CORRECT TO THE BEST OF MY KNOWLEDGE, INFORMATION, AND BELIEF.

____

Date **Debtor/Officer of Debtor**

[Renumbered effective January 1, 2006.]

LOCAL FORM 12–37. STATEMENT/CERTIFICATION REGARDING REQUIREMENTS FOR DISCHARGE IN A CHAPTER 12 CASE

FLNB Local Form 37-12 (08/11)

UNITED STATES BANKRUPTCY COURT
NORTHERN DISTRICT OF FLORIDA
DIVISION

In re: **Case No.:**
Chapter 12

Debtor(s)

STATEMENT/CERTIFICATION REGARDING REQUIREMENTS FOR DISCHARGE IN A CHAPTER 12 CASE

Pursuant to 11 U.S.C. § 1228 and/or Local Rule 4004-1, concerning compliance with the requirements for discharge in a chapter 12 case, the debtor(s) hereby state and certify that as to

1. Plan payments:

☐ I/We have completed all plan payments;

OR

☐ I/We have been granted a hardship discharge pursuant to the provisions of 11 U.S.C. § 1228(b).

2. Compliance with 11 U.S.C. § 1228(f) [regarding exemptions]:

☐ I/We **did not** have either at the time of filing this bankruptcy case or at the present time, equity in excess of the dollar amount specified in 11 U.S.C. § 522(p)(1);

OR

☐ I/We **did have** at the time of the filing of this bankruptcy case or **do have at the present time**, equity in excess of the dollar amount specified in 11 U.S.C. § 522(q), in the type of property described in 11 U.S.C. § 522(p)(1), but

a. there has been no conviction in any proceeding and there is not currently a pending in which the debtor(s) may be found guilty of a felony or liable for a debt of a kind described in 11 U.S.C. § 522(q)(1)(A) [circumstances showing that the filing of this case was an abuse of the provisions of this title], **AND**

b. the debtor(s) is/are not liable for a debt of the kind described in 11 U.S.C. § 522(q)(1)(B) [securities law violations, civil remedies under 18 U.S.C. § 1964; or criminal, intentional, or reckless misconduct that caused death or serious injury to an individual in the past five (5) years].

3. Domestic Support Obligations:

☐ The **debtor** is not required to pay any amounts under a domestic support obligation; OR

☐ The **joint debtor**, if applicable, is not required to pay any amounts under a domestic support obligation; OR

☐ All amounts to be paid by the **debtor** under a domestic support obligation that first became payable after the date of the filing of the petition, if the debtor is required by a judicial or administrative order or by statute to pay such domestic support obligation, have been paid. *Provide the following information:*

☐ All amounts to be paid by the **joint debtor**, if applicable, under a domestic support obligation that first became payable after the date of the filing of the petition, if the debtor is required by a judicial or admin- istrative order or by statute to pay such domestic support obligation, have been paid. *Provide the following information:*

Debtor's Current Address:

Joint Debtor's Current Address:

Debtor's Employer & Employer's Address:

Joint Debtor's Employer & Employer's Address:

I/We declare under penalty of perjury that the statements and certifications contained herein are true and correct.

Signature of Debtor Date

Signature of Joint Debtor, if applicable Date

[Effective August 1, 2011. Amended effective April, 2014.]

G. CHAPTER 13 FORMS

LOCAL FORM 13–1. OPTIONAL PLAN LANGUAGE

FLNB Local Form 13-1 (12/09)

U.S. Bankruptcy Court
Northern Dsitrcit of Florida
OPTIONAL PLAN LANGUAGE

The excerpts below, or substantively similar language, have been approved by the Chapter 13 Trustee and can be added to the Chapter 13 Form Plan in the Northern District of Florida in the "Other Provisions" section:

Abatement of Plan Payment Procedures Where the Plan Payment is Ultimately Returned to the Estate by the Debtor

During the life of the plan, and with notice only to the Chapter 13 Trustee, the debtor may file the Debtor's Election to Abate Plan Payment in a maximum of three (3) plan payments in a 36 month term case, and for a maximum of seven (7) plan payments in a 60 month case. The election can only be used for payment of necessary expenses, or loss of job, and must provide in the Debtor's Election the method to replace the estate funds, unless the Debtor's Election states that the plan is and will remain a 100% repayment plan notwithstanding the current and prior abatements. The Debtor's Election may not be used to abate more than two (2) consecutive payments at any one time. This election does not prohibit the debtor from filing and noticing to all creditors a Motion to Abate for a plan payment abatement which does not meet the criteria of this plan provision. However, the Debtor's Election may not be used in any case in which the Trustee is paying the regular monthly mortgage payment through the Plan unless the abatement is only for a portion of the plan payment which will still allow payment of the mortgage payment and the trustee's fee. The Trustee is authorized to adjust the Debtor(s)' pay schedules as set forth in the Election by the Debtor upon the filing of the Election by the Debtor.

Use of Tax Refunds

During the life of the plan, and with notice only to the Chapter 13 Trustee, the debtor may file the Debtor's Election to Use Tax Refund for a maximum of thirty percent (30%) of each tax refund per year in a 36 month term case, plus an additional forty percent (40%) of each additional tax refund per year in a 60 month case. The election can only be used for payment of necessary expenses, or job loss, and must provide in the Debtor's Election to Use Tax Refund the method to replace the estate funds, unless the Debtor's Election states that the plan is and will remain a 100% repayment plan notwithstanding the current and prior abatements. This election does not prohibit the debtor from filing and noticing to all creditors a Motion to Use Tax Refunds for refunds which do not meet the criteria of this plan provision. This Plan provision does not relieve the Debtor of the duty to file and serve tax returns on the Trustee. The Trustee is authorized to adjust the Debtor(s)' pay schedules as set forth in the Election by the Debtor.

[Amended effective December, 2009. Amended effective April, 2014.]

LOCAL FORM 13–13. PRE–CONFIRMATION STATEMENT REGARDING INDIVIDUAL DEBTOR'S DOMESTIC SUPPORT OBLIGATIONS AND FILING OF TAX RETURNS, AS APPLICABLE, PURSUANT TO CODE AND RULE REQUIREMENTS

FLNB Local Form 13-13 (Rev. 08/11)

UNITED STATES BANKRUPTCY COURT
NORTHERN DISTRICT OF FLORIDA
DIVISION

In re: Case No.:

Chapter:

Debtor(s)

PRE-CONFIRMATION STATEMENT REGARDING INDIVIDUAL DEBTOR'S DOMESTIC SUPPORT OBLIGATIONS AND FILING OF TAX RETURNS, AS APPLICABLE, PURSUANT TO CODE AND RULE REQUIREMENTS

NOTICE IS HEREBY given that

A. pursuant to Local Rule ____________, the debtor(s) make(s) the following certification(s) as to domestic support obligations:

☐ The **debtor** is not required to pay any amounts under a domestic support obligation; OR

☐ All amounts to be paid by the **debtor** under a domestic support obligation that first became payable after the date of the filing of the petition, if the debtor is required by a judicial or administrative order or by statute to pay such domestic support obligation, have been paid. *Provide the following information:*

Debtor's Current Address

Debtor's Employer & Employer's Address:

☐ The **joint debtor**, if applicable, is not required to pay any amounts under a domestic support obligation; OR

☐ All amounts to be paid by the **joint debtor** under a domestic support obligation that first became payable after the date of the filing of the petition, if the debtor is required by a judicial or administrative order or by statute to pay such domestic support obligation, have been paid. *Provide the following information:*

Joint Debtor's Current Address:

Joint Debtor's Employer & Employer's Address:

B. pursuant to 11 U.S.C. § 1325(a)(9), if applicable, the chapter 13 debtor(s) certifies that:

☐ The **debtor** has filed all Federal, State and local tax returns as required by § 1308.

☐ The **joint debtor**, if applicable, has filed all Federal, State and local tax returns as required by § 1308.

I/We declare under penalty of perjury that the foregoing is true and correct.

______________________ ______________________
Debtor's Signature Date

______________________ ______________________
Joint Debtor's Signature Date

[Amended effective August 1, 2011. Amended effective April, 2014.]

LOCAL FORM 13–21. CHAPTER 13 PLAN*

FLNB Local Form 13-21

United States Bankruptcy Court
Northern District of Florida

In re ______________________________ **Case No.** __________
Debtor(s) **Chapter 13**

CHAPTER 13 PLAN

1. **Payments to the Trustee:** The future earnings or other future income of the Debtor is submitted to the supervision and control of the trustee. The Debtor (or the Debtor's employer) shall pay to the trustee the sum of $________ per month for________ months, then $________ per month for________ months. The Debtor shall pay to the Trustee the tax refunds for ______ years.

Total of base plan payments: $__________________

2. **Plan Length:** The term of the plan is for________months.

3. Allowed claims against the Debtor shall be paid in accordance with the provisions of the Bankruptcy Code and this Plan.

a. Secured creditors shall retain their mortgage, lien or security interest in collateral until the earlier of (a) the payment of the underlying debt determined under non-bankruptcy law, or (b) discharge under 11 U.S.C. § 1328.

b. Creditors who have co-signers, co-makers, or guarantors ("Co-Obligors") from whom they are enjoined from collection under 11 U.S.C. §1301, and which are separately classified and shall file their claims, including all of the contractual interest which is due or will become due during the consummation of the Plan, and payment of the amount specified in the proof of claim to the creditor shall constitute full payment of the debt as to the Debtor.

c. All priority creditors under 11 U.S.C. § 507 shall be paid in full in deferred cash payments.

4. From the payments received under the plan, the trustee shall make disbursements as follows:

a. Administrative Expenses/ Priority Claims

(1) Trustee's Fee: As determined by the Attorney General of the United States.

(2) Filing Fee (unpaid portion): ______________

(3) Priority Claims under 11 U.S.C. §507 – Domestic Support Obligations

(a) Debtor is required to pay all post-petition domestic support obligations directly to the holder of the claim.

(b) The name(s) of the holder of any domestic support obligation are as follows (11 U.S.C. §§ 101(14A) and 1302(b)(6)):

____

(c) Anticipated Domestic Support Obligation Arrearage Claims. Unless otherwise specified in this Plan, priority claims under 11 U.S.C. § 507(a)(1) will be paid in full pursuant to 11 U.S.C. § 1322(a)(2).

Creditor (Name)	Estimated Arrearage Claim

(d) Pursuant to 11 U.S.C. §§ 507(a)(1)(B) and 1322(a)(4), the following domestic support obligation claims are assigned to, owed to, or recoverable by a governmental unit.

Claimant and proposed treatment: ______________________________

(4) Attorney's Fee (unpaid portion): ____________________

Pursuant to Standing Order of this Court, the Debtor's attorney may seek additional fees for the applicable amount as stated in the Order upon the filing of the required annual statement each year. If the Plan is modified due to an increase in income shown on the annual statement, the Debtor's attorney may seek additional fees for the applicable amount as stated in the Order. In either of these events, no further notice will be given to creditors.

(5) Other Priority Claims.

Name	Amount of Claim	Interest Rate (If specified)

b. Secured Claims

(1) Secured Debts Which Will Not Extend Beyond the Length of the Plan

(a) Secured Claims Subject to Valuation Under 11 U.S.C. §506. Each of the following secured claims shall be paid through the plan as set forth below, until the secured value or the amount of the claim, whichever is less, has been paid in full. Any remaining portion of the allowed claim shall be treated as a general unsecured claim.

Name	Proposed Total Amount of Allowed Secured Claim	Interest Rate (If specified)

(b) Secured Claims Not Subject to Valuation Under 11 U.S.C. §506. Each of the following claims shall be paid through the plan as set forth below until the amount of the claim as set forth below has been paid in full.

Name	Amount of Secured Claim	Interest Rate (If specified)

(2) Secured Debts Which Will Extend Beyond the Length of the Plan

Name	Amount of Claim	Monthly Payment	Interest Rate (If specified)

c. Unsecured Claims

General Nonpriority Unsecured: Unsecured debts shall be paid approximately ________ cents on the dollar and paid pro rata.

5. The Debtor proposes to cure defaults to the following creditors by means of monthly payments by the trustee:

Creditor	Amount of Default to be Cured	Interest Rate (If specified)

6. The Debtor shall make regular payments directly to the following creditors:

Name	Amount of Claim	Monthly Payment	Interest Rate (If specified)

7. The following executory contracts of the debtor are rejected:

Other Party	Description of Contract or Lease

8. Property to Be Surrendered to Secured Creditor for which the creditor shall be entitled to file a deficiency claim:

Name	Amount of Claim	Description of Property

9. Title to the Debtor's property shall revest in Debtor on confirmation of a plan unless otherwise provided in paragraph 11.

10. As used herein, the term "Debtor" shall include both debtors in a joint case.

11. Non-Standard Provisions (all non-standard provisions must be inserted in this paragraph).

12. Other Provisions:

Unsecured claims shall be paid interest to the extent available, if any, not to exceed 6%.

The provisions of paragraph 3 are not intended to modify the rights of the holders of any mortgages on any real property owned by Debtor. The terms of all notes and mortgages on Debtor's real property shall remain in full force and effect.

PAYMENT OF THE FOREGOING ARREARAGES UNDER THIS PLAN SHALL CONCLUSIVELY CONSTITUTE PAYMENT OF ALL PRE-PETITION ARREARAGES.

Pursuant to 11 U.S.C. §521(f)(4)(B) and Standing Order of this Court, the required annual statement as described shall be filed.

Date ________________________ Signature____
Debtor(s)

[Effective December 1, 2008. Amended effective December, 2009; April, 2014.]

* **[Publisher's Note:** For Optional Plan Language, *see* Form 13–1, *ante*.]

LOCAL FORM 13-22. ANNUAL STATEMENT

FLNB Local Form 13-22 (Rev. 08/2011)

UNITED STATES BANKRUPTCY COURT
NORTHERN DISTRICT OF FLORIDA
DIVISION

In re:

Case No.:
Chapter: 13

Debtor(s)

ANNUAL STATEMENT
(Pursuant to 11 U.S.C. § 521(f) and Standing Order of this Court)

COMES NOW the Debtor(s), by and through the undersigned attorney(s), if applicable, and files this Annual Statement in accordance with 11 U.S.C. § 521(f) and Standing Order of this Court, and hereby states as follows:

1. The income and expenditures of the Debtor(s) during the tax year most recently concluded before this Annual Statement is filed are detailed on the attached Schedule I and J worksheets. The method of calculation of the Debtor(s)' monthly income and expenditures is detailed on the attached Schedules I and J worksheets. The attached Schedule I and J worksheets are not intended to amend previously filed schedules.
2. The Debtor(s)' monthly income is disclosed as follows:
   a. The amount and source of income of the Debtor(s):

   b. The identity of any person who shares responsibility for the support of any dependent(s) of the Debtor(s):

   c. The identity of any person who contributed, and the amount contributed, to the household in which the Debtor(s) resides:

3. The debtor(s) ☐ will or ☐ will not be filing a Motion to Modify Chapter 13 Plan due to changes in income and expenses as shown on the attached Schedules I and J worksheets.

4. The Debtor(s) has complied with related provisions for the submission of tax returns to the Chapter 13 Trustee. The Debtor(s)' attorney, if Debtor(s) is represented, is now eligible for disbursement of $250.00, and the Trustee is authorized to disburse said funds, if available.

RESPECTFULLY SUBMITTED this _____ day of ________________, 20___.

____
Debtor OR Debtor(s)' Attorney Signature

CERTIFICATE OF SERVICE

I HEREBY certify that a true and accurate copy of the foregoing has been furnished by electronic filing or first class mail to:

on the _____ day of ______________________, ________.

____

[Effective May, 2007. Amended effective December, 2009; August, 2011.]

LOCAL FORM 13–23. MOTION TO MODIFY CHAPTER 13 PLAN

FLNB Local Form 13-23 (12/09)

UNITED STATES BANKRUPTCY COURT
NORTHERN DISTRICT OF FLORIDA
DIVISION

In re:

Case No.:
Chapter 13

Debtor(s)

MOTION TO MODIFY CHAPTER 13 PLAN
Due to Changes in Income and/or Expenses as Shown on Annual Statement filed Pursuant to 11 U.S.C. § 521(f) and Standing Order of this Court

COMES NOW the Debtor(s), ______________________________, by and through the undersigned attorney, and moves this Court to enter an Order Modifying the Confirmed Plan, and as grounds therefore would show:

1. The Motion to Modify is due to a change in the Debtor(s)' income and/or expense and the availability of additional income.
2. All of the terms and conditions in the confirmed Plan are incorporated and shall remain in full force and effect, except as set forth herein.
3. The Debtor(s)' Plan payments will increase by $ _________ per month. This will result in the Debtor(s)' monthly Plan payment being $ __________ commencing with the __________ payment and continuing for _____ months for a total plan base of $ __________.

4. Upon entry of the order approving modification of the confirmed plan, the Debtor(s)' attorney shall be entitled to attorney's fees of $500.00 for the filing and approval of this modification which increases the Plan base.

RESPECTFULLY SUBMITTED this ______ day of __________________ , ______.

____
Attorney for the Debtor(s)

I HEREBY certify that a true and accurate copy of the foregoing has been furnished by electronic filing or first class mail to the following on the same date as reflected on the Court's docket as the electronic filing date for this document.

____
Attorney for the Debtor(s)

[Effective May, 2007. Amended effective December, 2009.]

LOCAL FORM 13–27. SUPPLEMENTAL DISCLOSURE TO SCHEDULES I AND/OR J REGARDING LISTED EXPENSES

FLNB Local Form 13-27 (11/09)

Case Number:__________________
Debtor Name(s): ____

SUPPLEMENTAL DISCLOSURE TO SCHEDULES I AND/OR J REGARDING LISTED EXPENSES

Check the applicable boxes and provide details as needed:

☐ **Child Care:** Disclose the category of the child's/children's age(s), if not indicated on the petition, and the type of child care received (e.g., infant to preschool, after school care, summer care and after school care).

☐ **Life Insurance:**

☐ Term

☐ Whole Life

☐ **Home Maintenance** - Describe debtor(s)' home and/or home maintenance needs (e.g., debtor has 25 year old roof with shingle problems; house is 50 years old with original appliances, etc.)

☐ **Medical & Dental:** Disclose extenuating circumstances such as "Debtor has medical problems including diabetes and their maximum out of pocket expense per their policy is $xxx.xx." or "Policy does not include payment of prescriptions."

☐ **Transportation:**

- Age(s) of debtor's vehicle(s):

- Warranty details:

- Other:

☐ **401(k) Loan:**

☐ The debtor(s) has had a 401(k) loan since __________________ and the loan does not payout during the life of the plan.

☐ The 401(k) loan will pay out ______________________ and the funds are dedicated to the plan.

☐ **Alimony:**

☐ Per Case Number ___________________________, the debtor is required to pay alimony and/or child support.

☐ These payments will continue during the life of the plan.

☐ These payments will end ___________________________ and the plan and the increase is included in the plan payments.

☐ **Adult Dependents:**

☐ The debtor(s) has claimed an adult dependent who is age _______ and who is living at home.

☐ The adult is a dependent of the debtor due to:

☐ Medical issues

☐ Attendance at a post-secondary school

- Anticipated graduation: ______________________

- Adult dependent is ________ employed.

☐ Other reason:

☐ This dependant will remain a dependant for the life of the plan; or

☐ Debtor will dedicate the additional income during the life of the plan.

☐ **Business & Operating Reports:**

☐ The debtor is operating a business with gross receipts of $__________________

☐ **Income Discrepancy & Overtime or One-time Income:** Indicate how the debtor(s) intends to alleviate the need to object to facially apparent income discrepancies (e.g., The debtor agrees to dedicate and pay any additional income above 8%.)

☐ **Non-Filing Co-Debtor:**

- ☐ The income and expenses have been divided on a pro-rate share of each spouse's income.
- ☐ Each spouse's income has been divided by the total income to determine a pro-rata share.
- ☐ The total income will be reduced by the total joint expenses (Form B22C, if applicable).
- ☐ The remaining sum will be divided by each spouse's pro-rate share to determine the amount due to the chapter 13 plan.
- ☐ Other:

[Effective November, 2009. Amended effective April, 2014.]

LOCAL FORM 13-28. AGREED MOTION TO ABATE PLAN PAYMENTS TO ADDRESS ACCRUED DELINQUENCY

FLNB Local Form 13-28

UNITED STATES BANKRUPTCY COURT
NORTHERN DISTRICT OF FLORIDA
DIVISION

In re: **Case No.:**
Chapter 13

Debtor(s)

AGREED MOTION TO ABATE PLAN PAYMENTS TO ADDRESS ACCRUED DELINQUENCY

COMES NOW the Debtor(s), by and through the undersigned attorney, and hereby files this Agreed Motion to Abate Plan Payments to Address Accrued Delinquency, and hereby states in support thereof:

1. The Debtor(s) was unable to make the plan payment(s) due to circumstances beyond their control arising from either the payment of unexpected, necessary expenses or due to an interruption of plan income.
2. The Debtor(s) request an abatement for the following plan payments:

   ______________________ Amount: $________________

   Amount: $

3. The Debtor(s) shall cure the abated payments in the amount of $______________ by the following method:

4. The Debtor(s) agrees to be bound by the terms and conditions stated within this Agreed Motion to Abate Plan Payments once an order is entered adopting this Agreed Motion.

5. The Debtor(s) agrees to Strict Compliance in accordance with the terms of this motion.

WHEREFORE, the Debtor(s) pray that the Court enter an Order Granting the Agreed Motion to Abate Plan Payments pursuant to the terms and conditions set forth herein, or for such other relief as deemed mete and proper.

RESPECTFULLY SUBMITTED this________ day of _________________________, ________.

Debtor's Attorney or Debtor, if pro se

CERTIFICATE OF SERVICE

I HEREBY certify that a true and accurate copy of the foregoing has been furnished by electronic filing or first class mail to:

on the same date as the electronic filing date for this document as reflected on the Court's docket.

[Effective November, 2009. Amended effective May, 2014.]

LOCAL FORM 13–29. DEBTOR(S)' ELECTION TO ABATE PLAN PAYMENTS PURSUANT TO CONFIRMED PLAN TERMS

FLNB Local Form 13-29

UNITED STATES BANKRUPTCY COURT
NORTHERN DISTRICT OF FLORIDA
DIVISION

In re: Case No.:

Chapter: 13

Debtor(s)

DEBTOR(S)' ELECTION TO ABATE PLAN PAYMENTS
PURSUANT TO CONFIRMED PLAN TERMS

COMES NOW the Debtor(s) by and through the undersigned attorney, and hereby files the Election to Abate Plan Payments Pursuant to Confirmed Plan Terms, and states as follows:

1. The confirmed plan allows the Debtor(s) to abate a maximum of three (3) plan payments in a 36 month term case and a maximum of seven (7) plan payments in a 60 month case.
2. The plan term for this case is _____ months.
3. This is the Debtor(s)' _____ election in this case.
4. The Debtor(s) is electing to abate the plan payment for __________ in the amount of $ _______ .
5. The Debtor(s) is not attempting to elect to abate more than two (2) consecutive plan payments at one time.
6. This election is being made due to the need for payment of necessary expenses, and or due to the loss of income.
7. The Debtor(s)' plan is a 100% plan and will remain the same notwithstanding any abated plan payments, or in the alternative, the Debtor(s) cures the abated plan payments by the

following method:

The Debtor(s) shall pay the above delinquent sum by ______________________.

8. The Trustee is not paying the regular mortgage payment, or in the alternative, the Debtor(s) is not seeking to abate the amount of the regular monthly mortgage payment being paid by the Trustee.

RESPECTFULLY SUBMITTED this ____day of ________________, 20 __.

____
Debtor's Attorney or Debtor, if pro se

CERTIFICATE OF SERVICE

I HEREBY Certify that a true and accurate copy of the foregoing has been furnished by electronic filing or first class mail to:

on the same date as reflected on the Court's docket as the electronic filing date for this document.

[Effective November, 2009. Amended effective April, 2014.]

LOCAL FORM 13–30. DEBTOR(S)' ELECTION TO USE A PORTION OF TAX REFUND PURSUANT TO CONFIRMED PLAN TERMS

FLNB Local Form 13-30

UNITED STATES BANKRUPTCY COURT
NORTHERN DISTRICT OF FLORIDA
DIVISION

In re:

Case No.:
Chapter 13

Debtor(s) ____________________

DEBTOR(S)' ELECTION TO USE A PORTION OF TAX REFUND PURSUANT TO CONFIRMED PLAN TERMS

COMES NOW the Debtor by and through the undersigned attorney, and hereby files the Election to Use a Portion of Tax Refund Pursuant to Confirmed Plan Terms, and states as follows:

1. The confirmed plan allows the Debtor to use thirty percent (30%) of a tax refund each year for the first three (3) years in a 36 month term case, plus an additional forty percent (40%) of each year's tax refund for each year thereafter in a 60-month term case.
2. The plan term in this case is __________ months.
3. This is the Debtor's ___________ election in this case for the year _________.
4. The Debtor is electing to use $____________________ of the total tax refund for tax year ________. The remainder shall be transmitted forthwith to the Chapter 13 Trustee.
5. The Debtor agrees that the plan base shall be adjusted by the total amount of the United States Income Tax Refund ($_________________) and shall be paid to the Trustee as set forth below:

a. Portion used ($___________) to be submitted *(explain terms of repayment)*:

b. Remainder ($___________) to be submitted within ten (10) days from the date of receipt of the refund.

6. This election is being made due to the need for payment of necessary expenses and/or due to the loss of income.

RESPECTFULLY SUBMITTED this _________ day of ____________________, ______.

____
Debtor(s) or Debtor(s)' Attorney

CERTIFICATE OF SERVICE

I HEREBY certify that a true and accurate copy of the foregoing has been furnished by electronic filing or first class mail to:

on the same date as the document was filed electronically as reflected on the Court's docket.

____
Debtor(s) or Debtor(s)' Attorney

[Effective April, 2011. Amended effective April, 2014.]

LOCAL FORM 13–31. DEBTOR(S)' NOTICE OF CHAPTER 13 PLAN PAYMENT CHANGE PURSUANT TO CREDITOR'S NOTICE OF PAYMENT CHANGE ON DEBTOR(S)' PRINCIPAL MORTGAGE

FLNB Local Form 13-31 (12/09)

UNITED STATES BANKRUPTCY COURT
NORTHERN DISTRICT OF FLORIDA
DIVISION

In re: **Case No.:**

Chapter: 13

Debtor(s)

DEBTOR'S NOTICE OF CHAPTER 13 PLAN PAYMENT CHANGE PURSUANT TO CREDITOR'S NOTICE OF PAYMENT CHANGE ON DEBTOR'S PRINCIPLE MORTGAGE

COMES NOW the Debtor by and through the undersigned attorney and hereby files the Debtor's Notice of Chapter 13 Plan Payment Change Pursuant to Creditor's Notice of Payment Change on Debtor's Principle Residence, and states as follows:

1. The Debtor is filing this Notice of Chapter 13 Plan Payment Change Pursuant to the Creditor's Notice of Payment Change on the Debtor's Principle Residence to increase the Chapter 13 plan payments to the Trustee.

2. The confirmed plan provides for the Debtor to pay the sum of $ ________________ for _____ months. The plan payment amount will be increased as follows: Commencing on _____________, the new Chapter 13 plan payment shall be $ ________ for the remaining _____ months of the plan. The new minimum plan base will be $ _____________. This notice does not alleviate the Debtor's obligation to pay any other sums due under the confirmed Chapter 13 plan (i.e., tax refunds, etc.).

RESPECTFULLY SUBMITTED this ____ day of __________________, 20 ___.

____
Debtor's Attorney

Certificate of Service

I HEREBY certify that a true and accurate copy of the foregoing has been furnished by electronic filing or first class mail on the same date as the document was electronically filed as reflected on the Court's docket to the following:

____
Debtor's Attorney

[Effective December, 2009. Amended effective April, 2014.]

LOCAL FORM 13–33. MOTION TO DEEM MORTGAGE CURRENT

FLNB Local Form 13-33

UNITED STATES BANKRUPTCY COURT
NORTHERN DISTRICT OF FLORIDA
DIVISION

In re:

Case No.:
Chapter: 13

Debtor(s)

MOTION TO DEEM MORTGAGE CURRENT

NOTICE OF OPPORTUNITY TO OBJECT AND FOR HEARING

Pursuant to Local Rule 2002-2, the Court will consider this motion without further notice or hearing unless a party in interest files an objection within 21 days from the date of service of this paper. If you object to the relief requested in this paper, you must file your objection with the Clerk of Court at 110 E. Park Avenue, Suite 100, Tallahassee, FL 32301, and serve a copy on the movant's attorney and any other appropriate persons.

If you file and serve and objection within the time permitted, the Court may schedule a hearing and you will be notified. If you do not file an objection within the time permitted, the Court will consider that you do not oppose the granting of the relief requested in the paper and will proceed to consider the paper without further notice or hearing and may grant the relief requested.

Comes now the Debtor(s) through the undersigned attorney and certifies according to the Trustee's records, the Debtor has paid and the Trustee has disbursed all arrears and regular on-going payments to ______________________________ (the "Mortgagee") pursuant to the terms of the most current confirmed plan. The current confirmed plan provided for arrears in the total amount of $__________ , and regular on-going payments to be paid directly to the Mortgagee by the Debtor. Since the Trustee's records reflect these arrearage payments are completed, and the Debtor certifies by the filing of the Motion that all post-petition payments, fees, expenses, and charges have been made, the mortgage debt to Mortgagee should be current as of ______________ (month following the last cure payment) except for specified fees and charges.

Note any exceptions here:

All parties wishing to be heard shall appear at the scheduled hearing. If there is a dispute as to the status of the mortgage, the Court may take evidence at the hearing or treat the hearing as a preliminary hearing and set a further evidentiary hearing on a different date.

RESPECTFULLY SUBMITTED this ___ day of ________________, 20 __.

____
Debtor's Attorney

Certificate of Service

I HEREBY certify that a true and accurate copy of the foregoing has been furnished by electronic filing or first class mail on the same date as the document was electronically filed as reflected on the Court's docket to the following:

____
Debtor's Attorney

[Effective December, 2009. Amended effective April, 2014.]

LOCAL FORM 13–34. SECURED CREDITOR'S NOTICE OF PAYMENT CHANGE

FLNB Local Form 13-34 (12/09)

UNITED STATES BANKRUPTCY COURT
NORTHERN DISTRICT OF FLORIDA
DIVISION

In re: **Case No.:**
Chapter: 13

Debtor(s)

SECURED CREDITOR'S NOTICE OF PAYMENT CHANGE

Comes now ______________________________, a secured creditor, and hereby gives notice under Local Rule 3002.1-1 that pursuant to Section ______________ of the *[identify the appropriate association document, e.g., mortgage]* ________________________________, the regular monthly payment amount will change effective ________________. The new regular monthly mortgage payment is $ __________ effective ________________. The new regular monthly mortgage payment is comprised of principal and interest in the amount of $ __________, and escrow payment for *[specify composition of escrow payment, i.e., taxes and/or insurance]* ____ of $ __________.

Documentation to support the increased regular mortgage payment is attached hereto as Exhibit A. The secured creditor requests that the necessary action be taken to ensure that the correct payments are provided for by the debtor. Any questions regarding this change should be directed to:

____

Date:

____
Attorney for Secured Creditor
Address:

Phone:
Fax:
Email:

CERTIFICATE OF SERVICE

I HEREBY certify that a true and accurate copy of the Notice of Payment Change has been furnished to the Debtor(s) via U.S. Mail on ________________, the Chapter 13 Trustee, and the attorney for the Debtor(s), if applicable, via ________________________ on ________________________.

____

Attorney for Secured Creditor

Address:

Phone:

Fax:

Email:

[Effective December, 2009. Amended effective May, 2014.]

LOCAL FORM 13–37. STATEMENT/CERTIFICATION REGARDING REQUIREMENTS FOR DISCHARGE IN A CHAPTER 13 CASE

FLNB Local Form 13-37 (08/11)

UNITED STATES BANKRUPTCY COURT
NORTHERN DISTRICT OF FLORIDA
DIVISION

In re: **Case No.:**
Chapter 13

Debtor(s)

STATEMENT/CERTIFICATION REGARDING REQUIREMENTS FOR DISCHARGE IN A CHAPTER 13 CASE

Pursuant to 11 U.S.C. § 1328 and/or Local Rule 4004-1, concerning compliance with the requirements for discharge in a chapter 13 case, the debtor and/or joint debtor, if applicable, hereby state and certify that as to

1. Plan payments:

☐ I/We have completed all plan payments; OR

☐ I/We have been granted a hardship discharge pursuant to the provisions of 11 U.S.C. § 1328(b).

2. Compliance with 11 U.S.C. § 1328(h) [regarding exemptions]:

☐ I/We **did not** have either at the time of filing this bankruptcy case or at the present time, equity in excess of the dollar amount specified in 11 U.S.C. § 522(q), in the type of property described in 11 U.S.C. § 522(p)(1);

OR

☐ I/We **did have** at the time of the filing of this bankruptcy case or **do have at the present time**, equity in excess of the dollar amount specified in 11 U.S.C. § 522(q), in the type of property described in 11 U.S.C. § 522(p)(1), but

a. there has been no conviction in any proceeding and there is not currently a pending proceeding in which the debtor(s) may be found guilty of a felony or liable for a debt of a kind described in 11 U.S.C. § 522(q)(1)(A) [circumstances showing that the filing of this case was an abuse of the provisions of this title], **AND**

b. the debtor(s) is/are not liable for a debt of the kind described in 11 U.S.C. § 522(q)(1)(B) [securities law violations, civil remedies under 18 U.S.C. § 1964; or criminal, intentional, or reckless misconduct that caused death or serious injury to an individual in the past five (5) years].

3. Post-petition instructional course in personal financial management:

☐ I/We have completed a post-petition instructional course in personal financial management and have filed with the court an Official Form 23, Debtor's Certification of Completion of Postpetition Instructional Course Concerning Personal Financial Management and/or the certificate issued by the course provider, for each debtor, if applicable, within the timelines specified in 11 U.S.C. § 1328(g).

4. Domestic Support Obligations (11 U.S.C. 1328(a)):

☐ The **debtor** is not required to pay any amounts under a domestic support obligation; OR

☐ All amounts to be paid by the **debtor** under a domestic support obligation that first became payable after the date of the filing of the petition, if the debtor is required by a judicial or adminis- trative order or by statute to pay such domestic support obligation, have been paid. *Provide the following information:*

Debtor's Current Address:

Debtor's Employer & Employer's Address:

☐ The **joint debtor**, if applicable, is not required to pay any amounts under a domestic support obligation; OR

☐ All amounts to be paid by the **joint debtor** under a domestic support obligation that first became payable after the date of the filing of the petition, if the debtor is required by a judicial or adminis- trative order or by statute to pay such domestic support obligation, have been paid. *Provide the following information:*

Joint Debtor's Current Address:

Joint Debtor's Employer & Employer's Address:

5. Previous Discharge:

☐ The **debtor** has not received a prior discharge of the kind noted in 11 U.S.C. § 1328(f).

☐ The **joint debtor**, if applicable, has not received a prior discharge of the kind noted in 11 U.S.C. § 1328(f).

I/We declare under penalty of perjury that the statements and certifications contained herein are true and correct.

______________________________ ______________________
Signature of Debtor Date

______________________________ ______________________
Signature of Joint Debtor, if applicable Date

[Effective August 1, 2011. Amended effective May, 2014.]

LOCAL FORM 13-38. MOTION FOR REFERRAL TO MORTGAGE MODIFICATION MEDIATION

FLNB Local Form 13-38 (06/13)

UNITED STATES BANKRUPTCY COURT
NORTHERN DISTRICT OF FLORIDA
______________ **DIVISION**

In re: **Case No.:**

Chapter 13

Debtor(s)

MOTION FOR REFERRAL TO MORTGAGE MODIFICATION MEDIATION

The debtor(s) request entry of an order referring the debtor(s) and [List creditors with mortgages encumbering the debtor(s)' primary residence] ______________ to mortgage modification mediation, and in support state:

1. The debtor(s) filed this Chapter 13 case in an attempt to retain their primary residence.

2. The debtor(s) would like to modify the terms of the mortgage(s) encumbering their primary residence. The debtor(s)' income will allow them to contribute as much as 31 percent of their current gross income to payment of their modified mortgage debt.

3. Mediation pursuant to Addendum B of the Local Rules of the United States Bankruptcy Court for the Northern District of Florida will assist the parties in negotiation of a modification of the relevant mortgage(s).

4. Debtor(s) will pay $385.00 mediation cost to the Chapter 13 Trustee prior to attending attending any scheduled mediation.

Wherefore, debtor(s) request the entry of an order referring this case to mediation for and for such other and further relief as this Court deems just and proper.

____
Date

/s/ Attorney Name
Bar No.:
Firm Name
Address
City, ST Zip
Phone and Fax
Email

[Effective June, 2013. Amended effective May, 2014.]

LOCAL FORM 13–38–PS. MOTION FOR REFERRAL TO MORTGAGE MODIFICATION MEDIATION

FLNB Local Form 13-38-PS (Pro Se) (06/13)

UNITED STATES BANKRUPTCY COURT
NORTHERN DISTRICT OF FLORIDA
DIVISION

In re:

Case No.:
Chapter 13

Debtor(s)

MOTION FOR REFERRAL TO MORTGAGE MODIFICATION MEDIATION

The debtor(s) request entry of an order referring the debtor(s) and
[List creditors with mortgages encumbering the debtor(s)' primary residence]
____
to mortgage modification mediation, and in support state:

1. The debtor(s) filed this Chapter 13 case in an attempt to retain their primary residence.

2. The debtor(s) would like to modify the terms of the mortgage(s) encumbering their primary residence. The debtor(s)' income will allow them to contribute as much as 31 percent of their current gross income to payment of their modified mortgage debt.

3. Mediation pursuant to Addendum B of the Local Rules of the United States Bankruptcy Court for the Northern District of Florida will assist the parties in negotiation of a modification of the relevant mortgage(s).

4. Debtor(s) will pay $385.00 mediation cost to the Chapter 13 Trustee prior to attending attending any scheduled mediation.

Wherefore, debtor(s) request the entry of an order referring this case to mediation for and for such other and further relief as this Court deems just and proper.

____
Date

____
Signature of Debtor

____
Signature of Joint Debtor

Address
City, ST Zip
Phone
Email

[Effective June, 2013. Amended effective May, 2014.]

LOCAL FORM 13-39. NOTICE OF SCHEDULED MORTGAGE MEDIATION

FLNB Local Form 13-39 (06/13)

UNITED STATES BANKRUPTCY COURT
NORTHERN DISTRICT OF FLORIDA
DIVISION

In re:

Case No.:
Chapter 13

Debtor(s)

NOTICE OF SCHEDULED MORTGAGE MEDIATION

TO: **All parties named on the attached service list.**

NOTICE IS HEREBY GIVEN that mediation has been set in the above-styled case as follows:

Date of Mediation: ________________

Time of Mediation: ________________

Mediator Assigned: ________________

Mediator Telephone: ________________

Location of Mediation: ________________

All parties are authorized to appear by video or telephone conference pursuant to the Order Granting Motion for Referral to Mortgage Modification Mediation.

________________ /s/ Attorney Name
Date

Bar Number:
Firm Name
Address
City, ST Zip
Phone and Fax
Email

[Effective June, 2013. Amended effective May, 2014.]

MORTGAGE MODIFICATION MEDIATION PROGRAM

MEMORANDUM RE: UNIFORM MORTGAGE MODIFICATION MEDIATION PROCEDURES IN THE BANKRUPTCY COURT FOR THE NORTHERN DISTRICT OF FLORIDA [MODIFIED BY ORDER 2015–1, EFFECTIVE OCTOBER 1, 2015]

AMENDED STANDING ORDER NO. 20. IN RE: GUIDELINES AND PROCEDURES FOR MORTGAGE MODIFICATION MEDIATORS

Standing Order No. 20 signed on May 31, 2013, was entered in order to implement mortgage modification mediation for Chapter 13 Debtor(s) and allow for the local rules to be amended. The order is now being amended to reflect that the Mortgage Modification Mediation (MMM) Program is available in all cases and for any type of real property. In addition, the list of mediator qualifications below has been amended. All changes are effective September 22, 2014.

A. Appointment of Mortgage Modification Mediators.

(1) *Qualifications of Mediator.* To qualify for service as a mortgage modification mediator, individuals must:

(a) Be a Florida Supreme Court Certified Circuit Civil Court Mediator;

(b) Have completed at least eight (8) hours of additional training focused on modifying residential mortgages in bankruptcy proceedings; and

(c) Agree to accept two mediation assignments, involving at least one party not being able to pay the mediation fee, per calendar year.

(2) *Mediator Application Procedures.* The application for admission to the registry of qualified mortgage mediators is posted on the Court's website. Completed applications shall be submitted by mail to the Clerk of Court, together with the following supporting documents:

(a) Proof of current Florida Supreme Court Circuit Civil Mediator certification; and

(b) Proof of completion of at least eight (8) hours of additional training focused on modifying residential mortgages in bankruptcy proceedings.

B. Mediation Registry.

(1) The Clerk of Court shall establish and maintain a registry of qualified persons to serve as mediators for mortgage modification in approved cases pending in the Court. This registry will be posted on the Court's website.

(2) *Removal.* The Clerk shall remove an approved mediator from the registry at the mediator's request or at the direction of the Court in the exercise of its discretion. If removed at the mediator's own request, the mediator thereafter may request to be reappointed to the registry without the necessity of submitting a new application. Upon receipt of such request, the Clerk shall reassign such qualified mediator to the registry.

(3) *Disqualification.* Any person selected as a mediator may be disqualified for bias or prejudice as provided in 28 U.S.C. § 144 and shall be disqualified in any action in which the mediator would be required to do so if the mediator were a judicial officer governed by 28 U.S.C. § 455.

[Dated: October 6, 2014.]

ADMINISTRATIVE ORDER 2015–1. IN RE: ADMINISTRATIVE ORDER PRESCRIBING PROCEDURES FOR MORTGAGE MODIFICATION

Effective September 22, 2014, the Bankruptcy Court for the Northern District of Florida adopted its mortgage modification mediation ("MMM") procedures.[1] Finding it appropriate and necessary to modify the MMM procedures, it is

ORDERED:

1. Effective October 1, 2015, all parties participating in the MMM process in the Northern District of Florida shall comply with the amended and modified MMM procedures set forth below.

2. MMM is available in all cases and for any type of real property.

3. A motion seeking MMM shall include, **on the first page**, a complete address of the property as to which the mortgage may be modified and the last four digits of the mortgage loan number(s). If this information is not included, the motion will be denied without prejudice or abated until an amended motion containing the required information is filed.

4. No negative notice is required for a motion seeking MMM. Lenders may seek reconsideration for cause within 14 days of entry of an order granting an MMM Motion.

5. A motion seeking MMM shall be filed within 90 days of the filing or conversion of the case. The Court will prepare and enter an order directing MMM on timely filed motions. If the MMM motion is not filed timely, the Court may set a hearing and will grant the request only if good cause is demonstrated for the delay.

6. The parties shall conclude the MMM process within 150 days of the filing or conversion of the case unless that time is enlarged by written consent on the Portal (described below), by stipulation of the parties, or by Court order.

7. Parties shall have 14 days after the entry of the order directing MMM to jointly select a Mediator qualified pursuant to Amended Standing Order No. 20. If the parties cannot agree on a Mediator, the Debtor shall select a Mediator and the lender may file an objection within seven (7) days. If a timely objection to a Mediator is filed, the Chapter 12 or 13 Trustee or the Clerk of Court in a Chapter 7 or 11 case will select the Mediator from the Approved Mediator Registry on a random, rotating basis.

8. Debtor and Lender shall each pay $250 directly to the Mediator within 7 days of designating the Mediator. Parties shall also equally pay the Mediator for any additional hourly fees incurred from MMM conferences that extend beyond two one-hour sessions. The Mediator shall file a report within seven (7) days of each mediation conference indicating the current status of the mediation. If a Mediator fails to comply with this reporting requirement, upon motion, notice, and hearing, the Court may order a Mediator to disgorge mediation fees and the Mediator's removal from the Approved Mediator Registry.

9. Parties shall use the secure portal (the "Portal;" https://www.dclmwp.com/Home) for submission of documents to initiate the MMM and follow guidelines included in the Court's Order directing MMM entered in each individual case.

10. The parties may communicate outside the Portal orally, but all written communication shall occur through the Portal.

11. Parties may submit a proposed order simultaneously with a motion seeking approval of a *temporary* MMM agreement without need for notice or a hearing.

12. Using the Court's Negative Notice procedures, Debtor shall file a motion to approve a *permanent* MMM agreement. The motion must contain the agreed terms of the modification, the new mortgage payments, and the lender's mailing address.

13. Orders approving permanent MMM agreements (i) shall be in a format that can be recorded in the official records of the county where the property is located, and (ii) should be recorded by the Debtor within 90 days of the entry of the order, unless the parties agree otherwise.

14. In all cases, Debtors seeking MMM shall provide adequate protection to the lenders. For *homestead* properties, Debtors shall pay the lesser of (1) 31% of their gross disposable income (after deducting homeowner association fees), or (2) the normal monthly contractual mortgage payment. For *non-homestead* income producing property, Debtors shall pay 75% of the gross rental income generated by the property. In Chapter 12 and 13 cases, Debtors shall make the adequate protection payments to the Chapter 12 or 13 Trustee, who shall hold the funds pending either further order of the Court, a Notice of Adequate Protection filed by the Debtor, or a joint stipulation of the parties as to distribution. In all other Chapters, Debtors shall make the adequate protection payments directly to the lender with no requirement for Court approval or modification of the automatic stay.

15. Unless the parties agree in writing to the contrary, MMM payments made during the MMM process will be applied in accordance with the applicable loan documents and non-bankruptcy law.

16. Debtors who seek to participate in MMM must have paid all current and prior bankruptcy filing fee(s) in full prior to filing a Motion seeking MMM.

17. The referral of a matter to MMM does not relieve the parties from complying with other Orders, applicable provisions of the Bankruptcy Code, the Federal Rules of Bankruptcy Procedure,

or Local Rules. Entry of an Order authorizing MMM shall not stay the Debtor's bankruptcy case. If the Debtor's case is otherwise in a posture for administrative closing, the case shall remain open during the pendency of MMM, unless otherwise ordered by the Court. The Clerk may enter a discharge in the ordinary course of a case unless entry of the discharge is delayed pursuant to a motion made by the Debtor or the lender and an order of the Court.

18. MMM is deemed concluded upon the earliest of: (a) the filing of a final report by the Mediator, (b) an order approving a permanent mortgage modification, or (c) other order of the Court indicating the MMM concluded. Upon conclusion of the MMM in a Chapter 12 or 13, any payments not yet disbursed to the lender by the Chapter 12 or 13 Trustee shall be disbursed:

a. if MMM resulted in a permanent mortgage modification agreement, which may include the lender's decision to decline receipt of additional funds, then as specifically agreed to by the Debtor and lender.

b. if MMM did not result in a permanent mortgage modification agreement, then:

i. to the lender to be applied in accordance with the trial modification agreement, if any; otherwise in accordance with the applicable loan documents and non-bankruptcy law, or

ii. if the lender affirmatively rejects the undisbursed funds, as provided by the Chapter 12 or 13 Plan or Confirmation Order.

19. Notwithstanding the foregoing, if a Chapter 12 or 13 case is dismissed or converted to a Chapter 7 or 11 case, the Chapter 12 or 13 Trustee shall disburse any funds remaining in the Trustee's possession to the Debtor; if the Debtor is represented by an attorney, the Trustee shall mail the funds to the Debtor in care of the Debtor's attorney.

20. In Chapter 11, 12 and 13 cases, the Court may confirm a plan of reorganization subject to pending MMM.

21. The MMM procedures do not affect amounts of allowed attorney fees for Debtor and creditor attorneys participating in the MMM program. In the event the parties reach a final resolution, or if no agreement has been reached, attorneys for Debtors shall be permitted to charge an attorney's fee not to exceed $2,500 and costs not to exceed $100 for MMM, or such other amounts as may be set forth in any Administrative Order on attorneys' fees in effect upon conclusion of MMM, subject to the compensation requirements for the chapter under which the case is filed. The MMM attorney's fee shall include: (a) filing of the MMM Motion and submission of the Order authorizing MMM; (b) preparation of all forms and providing all information required for mediation; (c) filing of other required pleadings and preparation of proposed orders and settlement papers, as applicable; (d) communicating with the lender or its attorney and the Mediator, via the Portal and otherwise as appropriate; (e) attendance at all MMM conferences and Court hearings; (f) review of all modified loan documents; and (g) preparation of trial and final MMM motions and Orders.

22. If the lender and the Debtor fail to reach a settlement, then no later than 14 calendar days after the Mediator's Final Report is filed, in a Chapter 12 or 13 case the Debtor will amend or modify the plan to (a) conform to the lender's Proof of Claim (if the lender has filed a Proof of Claim), without limiting the Debtor's right to object to the claim or proceed with a motion to value; (b) provide that the real property will be "treated outside the plan"; or (c) provide that the real property will be surrendered. If the property is surrendered or "treated outside the plan," the lender will be entitled to *in rem* stay relief to pursue available state court remedies against the property. Notwithstanding the foregoing, lender may file a motion to confirm that the automatic stay is not in effect as to the real property using the Court's Negative Notice procedures.

[Dated: September 22, 2015.]

1 Prior to this Administrative Order, the MMM procedures for the Northern District of Florida have been governed by the September 10, 2014 Memorandum entitled "Uniform Mortgage Modification Procedures in the Bankruptcy Court for the Northern District of Florida": http://www.flnb.uscourts.gov/sites/default/files/courtresources/mmmprocedures.pdf.

STANDING ORDERS

STANDING ORDER NO. 10. IN RE: COURTROOM COMPUTER USAGE

In the interest of increased efficiency and in light of the technology available to practitioners appearing before the Court, it is:

ORDERED:

1. Any party, counsel, or counsel's staff is permitted to bring all portable personal computing devices, such as laptop computers, iPads, notebooks, etc., in the courtroom gallery.

2. Prior to entering the courtroom, any such party, counsel, or staff must turn on the portable personal computing device and otherwise comply with any security requests of the Court Security Officers.

3. If any party, counsel, or counsel's staff abuses the privilege or in any other way disrupts the courtroom through the use of such portable personal computing devices, the Court will direct the party or their counsel to remove the equipment from the courtroom.

4. The devices may not be used to record video or audio of any portion of any hearing or take still photos inside the courtroom gallery.

[Effective April 28, 2006. Amended effective January 21, 2014.]

STANDING ORDER NO. 11. RELATING TO ELECTRONIC CASE FILING

Federal Rule of Civil Procedure 5(e) and Federal Rules of Bankruptcy Procedure 5005(a)(2), 9011, 9029, and Local Bankruptcy Rule 5005–1 authorize this court to establish practices and procedures for the filing, signing, and verification of pleadings and papers by electronic means. This Order sets out those practices and procedures.

IT IS ORDERED that:

1. The *Administrative Procedures for Filing, Signing, and Verifying Pleadings and Papers by Electronic Means** have been presented to this court and are hereby approved.
2. The provisions of this Order shall apply to all cases previously filed, proceedings presently pending and those subsequently filed in the United States Bankruptcy Court for the Northern District of Florida.
3. Any Order signed electronically and hence without the original signature of a judge shall have the same force and effect as if the judge had affixed his signature to a paper copy of the Order and entered it in a conventional manner. This provision also applies to Administrative Orders that are granted and routinely entered by the Clerk's Office.
4. Documents may be filed on-line at any time. Such filings will constitute entry of that pleading or other paper on the docket kept by the Clerk of Court in accordance with FRBP 5003. Documents to be filed at either location of the Clerk's Office shall be filed within the regular business hours of the Clerk's Office. The time zone of the division in which a case is filed will be the official time zone for filing and noticing purposes.
5. The electronic filing of documents shall be suspended if, under extraordinary circumstances, the system is out of service. The Clerk's Office will maintain a log of these occurrences for reference purposes. During such periods, filing conventionally via hard copy will be permitted. For emergency filing situations when the system is out of service during non-business hours, filers can make arrangements with the Clerk or the Clerk's designee for the acceptance of filings.
6. If the Clerk's Office deems it necessary to electronically scan a paper document into the Electronic Case Filing System, the electronically scanned document shall constitute the official record of the court, and the paper document may be discarded without further notice.
7. Amendments to this Order and the *Administrative Procedures for Filing, Signing, and Verifying Pleadings and Papers by Electronic Means* may be entered from time to time in keeping with the needs of the court.

8. Nothing contained in this Order is intended, or shall be construed to alter or modify any party's duties under the provisions of the Bankruptcy Code or the Federal Rules of Bankruptcy Procedure.

[Dated: November 4, 2003, effective November 12, 2003.]

* [**Publisher's Note:** For the Court's ECF administrative procedures, *see* Addendum C, *ante.*]

FIRST AMENDED STANDING ORDER NO. 17. IN RE: INVESTMENT OF REGISTRY FUNDS

AMENDED ORDER REGARDING DEPOSIT AND INVESTMENT OF REGISTRY FUNDS

The Court, having determined that it is necessary to amend local procedures to reflect the transition of accountability and administration of the Court Registry Investment System ("CRIS") from the United States District Court for the Southern District of Texas to the Administrative Office of the United States Courts, as well as ensure the continued uniformity in the deposit and investment of funds in the Court's Registry,

IT IS ORDERED that the following shall govern the receipt, deposit and investment of registry funds:

I. Receipt of Funds.

A. No money shall be sent to the Court or its officers for deposit in the Court's registry without a court order signed by the presiding judge in the case or proceeding.

B. Unless provided for elsewhere in this Order, all monies ordered to be paid to the Court or received by its officers in any case pending or adjudicated shall be deposited with the Treasurer of the United States in the name and to the credit of this Court pursuant to 28 U.S.C. § 2041 through depositories designated by the Treasury to accept such deposit on its behalf.

C. The party making the deposit or transferring funds to the Court's registry shall serve the order permitting the deposit or transfer on the Clerk of Court.

II. Investment of Registry Funds.

A. Where, by order of the Court, funds on deposit with the Court are to be placed in some form of interest-bearing account, CRIS, administered by the Administrative Office of the United States Courts, shall be the only investment mechanism authorized.

B. Money from each case deposited in CRIS shall be "pooled" together with those on deposit with Treasury to the credit of other courts in CRIS and used to purchase Government Account Series securities through the Bureau of Public Debt, which will be held at Treasury, in an account in the name and to the credit of the Director of Administrative Office of the United States Courts, hereby designated as custodian for CRIS.

C. An account for each case will be established in CRIS titled in the name of the case giving rise to the investment in the fund. Income generated from fund investments will be distributed to each case based on the ratio each account's principal and earnings has to the aggregate principal and income total in the fund. Reports showing the interest earned and the principal amounts contributed in each case will be prepared and distributed to each court participating in CRIS and made available to litigants and/or their counsel.

III. Deductions of Fees.

A. The custodian is authorized and directed by this Order to deduct the registry fee for maintaining accounts in CRIS and the investment services fee for the management of investments. The proper registry fee is to be determined on the basis of the rates published by the Director of the Administrative Office of United States Courts as approved by the Judicial Conference. The investment services fee is assessed from interest earning according to the Court's Miscellaneous Fee Schedule.

B. If registry fees were assessed against the case under the old 45-day requirement prior to deposit in CRIS, no additional registry fee will be assessed.

IV. Transition From Former Investment Procedure. This Order shall become effective May 19, 2011, and supercedes and abrogates all prior orders of this Court regarding the deposit and investment of registry funds.

[Effective May 9, 2011.]

STANDING ORDER NO. 19. IN RE: CHAPTER 13 ATTORNEYS FEES, ADEQUATE PROTECTION PAYMENTS, ANNUAL STATEMENTS, FORM PLAN, AND TAX RETURNS

AMENDED

This Order pertains to all Chapter 13 cases in the Northern District of Florida filed on and after June 1, 2013. In order to fairly compensate attorneys providing competent representation of debtors in cases filed under Chapter 13, to provide fair treatment to creditors receiving payments under Chapter 13 plans, and to limit the administrative burdens placed on the Court, the Chapter 13 Trustee and attorneys, the following guidelines and procedures are hereby adopted:

1. Attorneys Fees.

a. Attorney's fees, excluding costs, in the amount listed on the court's website as of the date of filing the Chapter 13 Petition shall be considered "normal and customary" in "routine" cases under chapter 13 and may be paid by pre-petition retainer, through the plan, or through a combination of the two, without further application to the Court.

b. A "routine" case will normally be one in which the attorney has prepared and filed the petition, lists, schedules, plan and all other required documents; attends the 11 U.S.C. § 341 meeting of creditors; attends the hearing on confirmation; prepares and serves notices of valuation pursuant to Local Bankruptcy Rule 3012–1 B; prepares and serves motions to avoid liens pursuant to 11 U.S.C. § 522(f); negotiates adequate protection agreements, if necessary, for one automobile and for the homestead; and files uncontested objections to claims.

c. An attorney seeking fees in excess of the amount listed on the Court's website shall file an application in accordance with 11 U.S.C. § 330 and Local Bankruptcy Rule 2016–1 B(2). The application shall be supported by contemporaneous time records and shall specifically identify services required to comply with the provisions of BAPCPA and any other factors to justify a departure from the presumptively reasonable fee. Applications for additional fees of less than $1,000.00 in excess of the presumptively reasonable fee may be considered by the Court without a hearing pursuant to this Court's Local Rules on 21 days negative notice to the trustee and parties in interest. Additional fees may be awarded upon order of the Court; attorneys' fees will not be awarded based on excessive time caused by inefficient use of the attorney's time.

d. The United States Trustee or Chapter 13 Trustee may object to payment of the normal and customary fee in any case in which it appears that such fee is excessive based on the amount of income available to fund a plan, the nature and amount of debt dealt within the plan or for other cause shown. The Court may, sua sponte or at the request of the Chapter 13 Trustee, reduce the fees to be paid to the attorney under a plan if confirmation is delayed due to lack of diligence by the attorney in preparation for confirmation.

e. Attorney's fees may be paid by the Chapter 13 Trustee ahead of payments to other creditors except for payments of regular mortgage payments on the Debtor's homestead if provided for under the plan and payments of adequate protection to creditors holding automobile liens, or as otherwise ordered by the Court.

2. Adequate Protection Payments. Pursuant to 11 U.S.C. § 1326(a)(1):

a. Adequate protection payments required to be made by the Debtor pursuant to 11 U.S.C. § 1326(a)(1)(C) shall be paid by the Chapter 13 Trustee from plan payments paid by the Debtor to the Trustee;

b. Within 15 days of the filing of the order for relief, the Debtor shall file a Notice of Adequate Protection ("Notice") with this Court. The notice should include how each pre-confirmation adequate protection payment was calculated, the amount of the adequate protection payment, the creditor's name, the creditor's payment address, and account number, if known (the Debtor may redact any account number as permitted by applicable law);

c. Each Notice of Adequate Protection shall be sent via U.S. Mail, postage prepaid, to the creditor at the address listed in the Notice;

d. For the purposes of this Order, unless the parties agree otherwise, adequate protection for motor vehicles shall equal:

(1) at a minimum, the retail value of said motor vehicle pursuant to 11 U.S.C. § 506 without interest, divided by 60; or

(2) in the alternative, the Notice may designate the monthly plan payment as adequate protection if it is at least equal to the designated monthly payment in subsection (1);

e. Notwithstanding any other provision in the Order, an affected creditor may file a motion pursuant to 11 U.S.C. § 1326(a)(3) for an order changing said adequate protection payments;

f. Notwithstanding any other provision in this Order, the parties may stipulate to a different payment amount for the adequate protection payments to be made pursuant to 11 U.S.C. § 1326. For purposes of these stipulations, a stipulation entered into prior to the filing of the petition shall be effective if filed with the Court within 15 days of the order for relief;

g. Upon the filing of the Notice of Adequate Protection described above, the Chapter 13 Trustee shall be authorized to commence making adequate protection payments to the creditor(s) named in each Adequate Protection Notice as provided in each such Notice; and

h. The Chapter 13 Standing Trustee shall be allowed to collect a percentage fee from all payments received by such individual under plans in the cases under chapter 13 of title 11 for which such individual serves as standing trustee. The rate shall be determined by the Attorney General through the Office of the United States Trustee. Provided, however, if the Trustee does not take the percentage fee on the receipt, then the Trustee shall be allowed to collect compensation and expenses at the rate determined by the Attorney General through the Office of the United States Trustee.

3. **Annual Statements.** The Chapter 13 Trustee's standing request for annual statements pursuant to 11 U.S.C. § 521(f) is granted. Except as otherwise provided in this Order:

a. The Chapter 13 Debtor shall file with the Court an annual statement of the income and expenditures of the Debtor during the tax year most recently concluded before such statement is filed. Debtors shall also file a statement of their monthly income that details how income, expenditures, and monthly income are calculated using an annual statement worksheet that substantially complies with the form found on the Court's website.

b. The annual statement shall be filed on the date that is either 90 days after the end of the most recent tax year or one (1) year after the date of the commencement of the case, whichever is later, if the plan is not confirmed before such later date; and annually after the plan is confirmed and until the case is closed, no later than the date that is 45 days before the anniversary of the confirmation of the plan.

c. The annual statement shall disclose:

(1) the amount and sources of the income of Debtor(s);

(2) the identity of any person responsible with the Debtor(s) for the support of any dependent of the Debtor(s); and

(3) the amount of contributions made for the household in which the Debtor resides; and

(4) the identity of the persons who made such contributions made for the household in which the Debtor resides.

d. Upon the Debtor's compliance with paragraphs a, b and c of this Section, the Chapter 13 Trustee shall be authorized to disburse to the Debtor's attorney, if funds are available, the amount then shown on the Court's website as compensation for the "normal and customary" fee for this service in "routine" cases.

e. Upon entry of an Order modifying the Plan to increase the Plan base as a result of increased income shown by the annual statement, where the Plan contains a provision for additional attorney's fees in the amount shown on the court's website on the date of modification, the Trustee shall be authorized to disburse said sum to the Debtor(s)' attorney.

4. **Form Plan.** The Chapter 13 Debtor shall file a Chapter 13 Plan conforming to the Court approved form Plan posted on the Court's website on the date of the original filing of the Chapter 13 petition.

E.[1] **Tax Returns.** Pursuant to 11 U.S.C. § 1308:

a. *Pre–Petition Tax Returns.* The Debtor shall provide to the Chapter 13 Trustee their Federal income tax returns for all tax periods during the two (2) year period ending on the date of the filing of the Petition.

b. *Post–Petition Tax Returns.* The Debtor shall also provide to the Chapter 13 Trustee:

(1) at the same time filed with the taxing authority, a copy of each Federal income tax return required under applicable law (or at the election of the Debtor, a transcript of such tax return) with respect to each tax year of the Debtor ending while the case is pending under such chapter;

(2) at the same time filed with the taxing authority, each Federal income tax return required under applicable law (or at the election of the Debtor, a transcript of such tax return) that had not been filed with such authority as of the date of the commencement of the case and that was subsequently filed for any tax year of the Debtor(s) during the three (3) year period prior to the date of the commencement of the case;

(3) a copy of each amendment to any Federal income tax return or transcript provided to the Trustee under paragraph (1) or (2) of this Section.

[Dated: May 31, 2013. Amended effective September 30, 2014.]

[1] So in original.

SELECTED ADMINISTRATIVE ORDERS

ADMINISTRATIVE ORDER 05–001. ESTABLISHING INITIAL PROCEDURES IN CHAPTER 11 CASES

Chapter 11 cases typically are filed by active businesses with numerous employees and complex creditor relationships. To protect the interests of competing constituencies, the Court must give special attention to Chapter 11 cases shortly after the petition is filed.

At these early hearings, the Court must balance the various competing interests while striving to assure prompt attention to the debtor's reorganization effort. This order is entered to facilitate early hearings in all Chapter 11 cases filed in all divisions of the United States Bankruptcy Court of the Northern District of Florida.

A. Operations—Chapter 11 Case Management Summary. The trustee or debtor-in-possession in a Chapter 11 case may operate the business of the debtor pursuant to 11 U.S.C. § 1108 and subject to any order of the Court specifying terms and conditions of the operation of the debtor's business. The Court and other parties must have prompt information about the debtor's operations. Accordingly, the debtor-in-possession is directed to file with the Court within the earlier of three business days following the petition date or the date of the first scheduled hearing, a Chapter 11 Case Management Summary providing the following information:

1. Description of the debtor's business;
2. Locations of debtor's operations and whether leased or owned;
3. Reasons for filing Chapter 11;
4. List of officers and directors, if applicable, and their salaries and benefits at the time of filing and during the 1 year prior to filing;
5. Debtor's annual gross revenues;
6. Amounts owed to various classes of creditors:
   a. Obligations owed to priority creditors such as governmental creditors for taxes,
   b. Identity, collateral, and amounts owed to secured creditors, and
   c. Amount of unsecured claims.
7. General description and approximate value of the debtor's current and fixed assets;
8. Number of employees and amounts of wages owed as of petition date;
9. Status of debtor's payroll and sales tax obligations, if applicable; and
10. Anticipated emergency relief to be requested within 14 days from the petition date.

B. Employee Salaries. Upon the filing of a Chapter 11 petition, all employees (including managers, agents, or officers who are not affiliates, within the meaning of 11 U.S.C. § 101(2)(A)), may be paid a salary and receive benefits accruing post-petition in the ordinary course of business. The Court may review, and grant appropriate relief, if such salaries or benefits are later determined to be unreasonable.

An officer, manager, or employee who also qualifies as an affiliate (collectively, "Affiliate Officer"), must file a motion and obtain Court approval of his or her salary and benefits, in advance of payment. Court authority for payment of any salary or benefits shall not constitute an assumption of any existing employment agreement. A motion for authority for the payment of any prepetition wages or for Affiliate Officer's salary may be filed pursuant to the expedited procedures set forth in section (C) below. Authorization for payment may be retroactive to the petition date if the motion so requests.

C. Expedited Motions. The following motions shall be scheduled for hearing within three business days, if reasonably possible and if the motions are served electronically or by facsimile transmission on requisite parties.

1. *Motion Seeking Authority to Use Cash Collateral.* A motion seeking authority to use cash collateral pursuant to 11 U.S.C. § 363 shall comply with Bankruptcy Rule 4001(b) or (d) and include the following information:

   a. Typical Terms. The motion to use cash collateral should include the following provisions:

(1) Identification of each secured creditor having a security interest in the cash collateral, the basis upon which each secured creditor is entitled to assert a security interest in the cash collateral, and the amount owed to each secured creditor;

(2) The type of adequate protection the debtor is offering each secured creditor (e.g., replacement lien, insurance);

(3) The amounts and types of cash collateral on the petition date;

(4) The amount of cash collateral which the debtor seeks authority to use from the date of the preliminary hearing on the motion through and until the final hearing on the motion, if the debtor seeks the use of cash collateral sooner than 15 days after service of the motion;

(5) A budget setting forth the projected cash flow of the debtor for the period of time for which the use of cash collateral is sought;

(6) Reasonable reporting requirements; and

(7) Provisions defining an event of default and consequences of default (e.g., the right to require the debtor to cease the use of cash collateral immediately upon default and obtain an expedited hearing to obtain appropriate relief).

b. Extraordinary Terms. The following provisions are considered extraordinary, must be detailed with specificity, and will generally not be approved absent compelling circumstances:

(1) Any cross-collateralization provision that would secure the repayment of pre-petition debt with post-petition assets;

(2) A waiver of any claims to include avoidance actions against any secured creditor;

(3) A waiver of any rights the estate may have under 11 U.S.C. § 506(c);

(4) Any factual stipulations or findings that bind the estate or parties in interest with respect to the validity, priority, and extent of secured creditor's liens;

(5) Immediate relief from stay under the order approving use of cash collateral or automatic relief from stay upon default;

(6) Granting of liens on avoidance action recoveries;

(7) Validation of any secured creditor's security interest in its collateral or within a limited period of time after the appointment of a committee pursuant to 11 U.S.C. § 1102; or

(8) Any subordination of administrative priority claims arising under 11 U.S.C. § 726(c);

2. *Motion for Approval of Post Petition Financing.* A motion seeking approval of post petition financing pursuant to 11 U.S.C. § 364 shall comply with Bankruptcy Rule 4001(c) and (d) and must include:

a. The identity of the proposed lender and its relationship to any of the parties;

b. The terms of the debt to be incurred ("DIP Loan") including:

(1) The collateral in which the lender is seeking to obtain a security interest and whether the lender is seeking to prime existing liens;

(2) The amount of the loan proposed to be extended by the lender;

(3) The applicable interest rate and all other charges to be made in connection with the DIP Loan; and

(4) The payment terms and duration of the DIP Loan of the proposed credit;

c. The amount of credit which the debtor seeks authority to obtain from the date of the preliminary hearing on the motion through and until the final hearing on the motion, if the debtor seeks authority to obtain credit sooner than 15 days after service of the motion. (The debtor shall attach a budget setting forth the projected cash flow of the debtor for the period of time for which the credit is sought);

d. The efforts made to obtain financing from other lenders;

e. The debtor's ability to repay the DIP Loan; and

f. The inclusion of any of the terms listed in C.1.b. above.

3. *Motion for Authority for the Payment of Prepetition Wages.* A motion seeking authority to pay employees of the debtor prepetition wages outstanding as of the petition date shall include a schedule setting forth:

a. The name of each employee to whom such wages are sought to be paid;

b. The amount due such employee(s) as of the petition date;

c. The amounts to be withheld from such wages, including all applicable payroll taxes and related benefits;

d. The period of time for which prepetition wages are due;

e. Whether the employee is presently employed by the debtor; and

f. Whether any of the employees are insiders as defined in 11 U.S.C. § 101(31).

The motion shall also include a representation by the debtor that all applicable payroll taxes and related benefits due to the debtor's employees will be paid concurrently with payment of the wages.

4. *Motion to Pay Critical Vendors.* A motion seeking authority to pay prepetition claims deemed critical by the debtor is deemed extraordinary, will generally not be approved absent compelling circumstances supported by evidentiary findings, and any relief requested will be evaluated considering the distribution scheme in the Bankruptcy Code. Any such motion shall include:

a. The schedule of the names of each claimant;

b. The amount due each claimant;

c. A description of the goods or services provided to the debtor by each claimant;

d. Facts and law supporting payment of the prepetition debt under the doctrine of necessity; and

e. Whether the claimant has made any concession or other agreement in consideration for the proposed payment, including the extension of postpetition trade credit.

5. *Motion for Authority to Maintain Prepetition Bank Accounts.* A motion seeking authority to maintain prepetition bank accounts shall include:

a. A schedule listing each prepetition bank account which the debtor seeks to maintain post petition;

b. The reason for seeking such authority;

c. The amount on deposit in each such account as of the petition date;

d. Whether the depository is an authorized depository pursuant to 11 U.S.C. § 345(b); and

e. A representation that the debtor has consulted with the Office of the United States Trustee regarding the continued maintenance of prepetition bank accounts and the United States Trustee has not consented to the proposed maintenance or use of such accounts.

If the debtor is unable to provide the foregoing information, the motion shall set forth the reason why such information is not available, and provide an estimate as to when the debtor will supplement its motion with such information.

6. *Motion for Authority to Pay Affiliate Officer Salaries.* A motion to pay, on an interim basis, the salary of any officer, manager, or employee, who also qualifies as an affiliate under 11 U.S.C. § 101(2)(A) shall include:

a. The name of the Affiliate Officer, the officer's position and job responsibilities;

b. The nature of the Affiliate Officer's relationship to the debtor;

c. The salary received by the Affiliate Officer during the 12 months prior to the filing of the debtor's Chapter 11 petition, including a description of any prepetition employment agreement;

d. A description of any services performed for any third party or compensation received or which will be received by the Affiliate Officer from any source other than the debtor-in-possession after the date of the petition;

e. The salary proposed to be paid to the Affiliate Officer, including all benefits; and

f. The amounts to be withheld from such salary of the Affiliate Officer, including all applicable payroll taxes and related benefits.

An interim order to authorize the payment of salaries to Affiliate Officers is subject to review or reconsideration at any time upon the motion of a party in interest or by the Court sua sponte.

D. Use of Property. Subject to the provisions of 11 U.S.C. §§ 363 and 365, the debtor-in-possession may use, sell, or lease property of the estate. The debtor-in-possession is authorized to pay all necessary and current expenses of operating its business, including tax and lease payments, to the extent that such payments are necessary to preserve the assets or operate the business and provided that the payments are for only the postpetition period.

E. Bank Accounts. The debtor-in-possession, consistent with 11 U.S.C. § 345, is authorized to open and maintain bank accounts for the deposit, investment, and disbursement of monies of the estate; provided, however, that the debtor-in-possession shall segregate all monies withheld from employees or collected for taxes in a separate bank account/s and shall pay these funds to the proper authority when due.

[Effective May 9, 2005.]

ADMINISTRATIVE ORDER 10-001. IN RE: FINAL REPORTS—CASES CONVERTED FROM CHAPTER 13 TO CHAPTER 7

FED. R. BANKR. P. 1019(5)(B)(ii) provides in part that "[u]nless the court directs otherwise, if a chapter 13 case is converted to chapter 7,"

(ii) the trustee, not later than 30 days after conversion of the case, shall file and transmit to the United States trustee a final report and account...

IN ORDER TO facilitate the procedural provisions of Rule 1019(5)(B)(ii) and to reduce the administrative burden placed on the Northern District's Chapter 13 Trustee for filing final reports in cases converted from a Chapter 13 to a Chapter 7 proceeding, it is

ORDERED that the Chapter 13 Trustee shall file and transmit to the United States Trustee, a Final Report and Account no later than forty-five (45) days from entry of the date of the Order Converting Case.

[Effective July 6, 2010.]

ADMINISTRATIVE ORDER 12-002. IN RE: ADOPTION OF INTERIM RULE 1007-I

Whereas, the Judicial Conference of the United States approved Interim Rule 1007-I for adoption to implement the *National Guard and Reservists Debt Relief Act of 2008* which became effective December 19, 2008; and

The general effective date of the Act did not provide sufficient time to promulgate rules after appropriate public notice and an opportunity for comment, this court agreed to adopt Interim Rule 1007-I under Administrative Order 09-001. Since that time, additional conforming amendments have been made to the interim rule.

NOW THEREFORE, IT IS ORDERED that Interim Rule 1007-I is adopted* and shall remain in effect until further order of this Court.

[Effective December 1, 2012.]

* **[Publisher's Note:** Interim Rule 1007-I, as published by the Judicial Conference of the United States, and as amended December 1, 2012, is reproduced below.]

Interim Rule 1007-I.[1] Lists, Schedules, Statements, and Other Documents; Time Limits; Expiration of Temporary Means Testing Exclusion[2]

* * * * *

(b) Schedules, Statements, and Other Documents Required.

* * * * *

(4) *Unless either*: (A) § 707(b)(2)(D)(I) applies, or (B) § 707(b)(2)(D)(ii) applies and the exclusion from means testing granted therein extends beyond the period specified by Rule 1017(e), an individual debtor in a chapter 7 case shall file a statement of current monthly income prepared as prescribed by the appropriate Official Form, and, if the current monthly income exceeds the median

family income for the applicable state and household size, the information, including calculations, required by § 707(b), prepared as prescribed by the appropriate Official Form.

* * * * *

(c) Time Limits. In a voluntary case, the schedules, statements, and other documents required by subdivision (b)(1), (4), (5), and (6) shall be filed with the petition or within 14 days thereafter, except as otherwise provided in subdivisions (d), (e), (f), (h), and (n) of this rule. In an involuntary case, the schedules, statements, and other documents required by subdivision (b)(1) shall be filed by the debtor within 14 days of the entry of the order for relief. In a voluntary case, the documents required by paragraphs (A), (C), and (D) of subdivision (b)(3) shall be filed with the petition. Unless the court orders otherwise, a debtor who has filed a statement under subdivision (b)(3)(B), shall file the documents required by subdivision (b)(3)(A) within 14 days of the order for relief. In a chapter 7 case, the debtor shall file the statement required by subdivision (b)(7) within 60 days after the first date set for the meeting of creditors under § 341 of the Code, and in a chapter 11 or 13 case no later than the date when the last payment was made by the debtor as required by the plan or the filing of a motion for a discharge under § 1141(d)(5)(B) or § 1328(b) of the Code. The court may, at any time and in its discretion, enlarge the time to file the statement required by subdivision (b)(7). The debtor shall file the statement required by subdivision (b)(8) no earlier than the date of the last payment made under the plan or the date of the filing of a motion for a discharge under §§ 1141(d)(5)(B), 1228(b), or 1328(b) of the Code. Lists, schedules, statements, and other documents filed prior to the conversion of a case to another chapter shall be deemed filed in the converted case unless the court directs otherwise. Except as provided in § 1116(3), any extension of time to file schedules, statements, and other documents required under this rule may be granted only on motion for cause shown and on notice to the United States trustee, any committee elected under § 705 or appointed under § 1102 of the Code, trustee, examiner, or other party as the court may direct. Notice of an extension shall be given to the United States trustee and to any committee, trustee, or other party as the court may direct.

* * * * *

(n) Time Limits for, and Notice to, Debtors Temporarily Excluded From Means Testing.

(1) An individual debtor who is temporarily excluded from means testing pursuant to § 707(b)(2)(D)(ii) of the Code shall file any statement and calculations required by subdivision (b)(4) no later than14 days after the expiration of the temporary exclusion if the expiration occurs within the time specified by Rule 1017(e) for filing a motion pursuant to § 707(b)(2).

(2) If the temporary exclusion from means testing under § 707(b)(2)(D)(ii) terminates due to the circumstances specified in subdivision (n)(1), and if the debtor has not previously filed a statement and calculations required by subdivision (b)(4), the clerk shall promptly notify the debtor that the required statement and calculations must be filed within the time specified in subdivision (n)(1).

1 Interim Rule 1007–I has been adopted by the bankruptcy courts to implement the National Guard and Reservists Debt Relief Act of 2008, Public Law No: 110–438, as amended by Public Law No. 112–64. The amended Act, which provides a temporary exclusion from the application of the means test for certain members of the National Guard and reserve components of the Armed Forces, applies to bankruptcy cases commenced in the seven-year period beginning December 19, 2008.

2 Incorporates (1) time amendments to Rule 1007 which took effect on December 1, 2009, (2) an amendment, effective December 1, 2010, which extended the time to file the statement of completion of a course in personal financial management in a chapter 7 case filed by an individual debtor, and (3) a conforming amendment, effective December 1, 2012, which removed an inconsistency created by the 2010 amendment.

PROPOSED ORDERS GUIDELINES

Please note the following new proposed order guidelines effective immediately:

TITLE: The title of the proposed order should contain the disposition of the motion, contain the name of the movant and the docket number of the motion, and should completely match the title of the related motion:

- Order Granting ABC Bank's Motion for Relief from Stay (Doc. 51)
- Order Approving Trustee's Application for Compensation (Doc. 123)
- Orders "on" a motion/application/objection will not be accepted; they must include a disposition

DISPOSITION: The correct disposition terminology should be used:

- Motions are granted or denied

- Objections are sustained or overruled
- Applications are approved or disapproved
- Non-dispositional language such as "Order on Motion" will not be accepted

BODY: The opening paragraph of the proposed order should contain the document number of the motion or document to which the order is related

- *"This case came before the Court on Creditor ABC Bank's Motion to Dismiss Case (Doc. 57)"*

PREPARED BY: The name of the attorney who prepared the proposed order is to be indicated at the end of the document.

AMENDED ORDERS: Amended orders must contain a footnote explaining why the original order is being amended.

REFERENCED DOCUMENTS: Proposed orders which contain references to Proofs of Claim or items on the docket such as responses, amendments, etc., should contain the name(s) and docket or claim number(s) of those items as shown in the examples above.

OBJECTIONS TO CLAIMS: Orders sustaining objections to claim should include the claimant's address upon which notice was served and should clearly indicate the amount of the claim to be disallowed. Do not simply state "claim is disallowed in its entirety."

ELECTRONIC FORMAT: As always, proposed orders should be submitted in Word (preferably), WordPerfect, or other compatible word processing format.

[Effective October 16, 2012.]

ADMINISTRATIVE ORDER NO. 13–001. ORDER ADOPTING NEGATIVE NOTICE LIST PURSUANT TO L.R. 2002–2A(7)

The Court permits and encourages service of certain motions, objections and other matters by negative notice, pursuant to L.R. 2002–2. Local Rule 2002–2(A)(7) provides that "[o]ther motions, objections, and matters" may be filed on negative notice if permitted by the presiding judge. The Court has adopted a list of motions and papers that may be filed using negative notice pursuant to Local Rule 2002–2.

The Negative Notice List is posted on the Court's website and may be amended or updated from time to time.

AS REQUIRED BY L.R. 2002–2B(3), ALL PAPERS SERVED BY NEGATIVE NOTICE MUST CONTAIN THE NEGATIVE NOTICE LEGEND ON THE TOP OF THE FIRST PAGE AND MUST PROVIDE FOR A TWENTY–ONE (21) DAY OBJECTION PERIOD UNLESS OTHERWISE STATED ON THE NEGATIVE NOTICE LIST. Motions and papers that are not on the Negative Notice List may be set for hearing or, if appropriate, granted or denied without a hearing. Parties and counsel are reminded of the Court's discretion to set any matter for hearing, even if no objection is filed. Negative notice is not appropriate for emergency matters.

[Dated: February 27, 2013.]

UNITED STATES
BANKRUPTCY COURT
NORTHERN DISTRICT OF FLORIDA

PERMISSIVE USE OF NEGATIVE NOTICE
Revision effective April 10, 2014

The Court permits and encourages service of the following papers using negative notice as permitted by Local Rule 2002–2. You are reminded, however, of the Court's discretion to set any matter for hearing, even if no objection is filed. Negative notice is not appropriate for emergency matters. The negative notice legend shall provide for a **21–day** objection period unless stated otherwise below, and shall be prominently displayed on the face of the first page of the document.

Chapter 7

Application for Payment of Administrative Expenses (Interim)

Motion by Chapter 7 Trustee to Authorize Interim Distribution to Creditors and to Pay Administrative Expenses

Motion for Order Confirming that the Automatic Stay is Terminated (11 U.S.C. 362(c) and (j))
Motion for Relief from Stay

Motion to Approve Agreements Relating to Relief from Stay, Prohibiting or Conditioning the Use, Sale of Lease of Property, Providing Adequate Protection, Use of Cash Collateral and Obtaining Credit pursuant to Fed. R. Bankr. P. 4001(d)

Notice of Intent to Abandon Property filed by Trustee

Motion to Compel Abandonment

Motion to Approve Compromise or Settlement

Motion to Avoid Lien on Exempt Property

Motion to Assume Lease/Executory Contract

Motion to Confirm Priority of Modified Mortgage

Motion to Determine Secured Status/Value Property (30 day notice required)

Motion to Determine Secured Status/Strip Lien on Real Property (30 day notice required)

Motion to Dismiss for Failure to Attend 341 Meeting (filed by Trustee)

Motion Objecting to Discharge pursuant to Rule 4004(a) re Sect. 727(a)(8), (a)(9)

Motion to Redeem

Motion/Notice to Sell or Lease Property (does not apply to sales free and clear of interests)

Motion for Turnover of Property by Trustee

Objection to Claim (excludes objections to claims of federal government units)

Objection to Exemptions

Chapter 11

Motion to Approve Agreements Relating to Relief from Stay, Prohibiting or Conditioning the Use, Sale of Lease of Property, Providing Adequate Protection, Use of Cash Collateral and Obtaining Credit pursuant to Fed. R. Bankr. P. 4001(d)

Motion to Avoid Lien on Exempt Property

Motion to Approve Compromise or Settlement

Motion to Administratively Close Individual Chapter 11 Case

Motion to Determine Secured Status/Value Property (30-day notice required)

Motion to Determine Secured Status/Strip Lien on Real Property (30-day notice required)

Objection to Claim (excludes objections to claims of federal government units)

Chapter 12 and 13

Motion for Relief from Co-Debtor Stay

Motion for Relief from Stay as to the Debtor*

Motion for Order Confirming that the Automatic Stay is Terminated (§ 362(c) and (j))
Motion Objecting to Discharge pursuant to Rule 4004(a) re Sect. 1328(f)

Motion to Approve Agreements Relating to Relief from Stay, Prohibiting or Conditioning the Use, Sale of Lease of Property, Providing Adequate Protection, Use of Cash Collateral and Obtaining Credit pursuant to Fed. R. Bankr. P. 4001(d)

Motion to Approve Compromise or Settlement

Motion to Approve Proposed Mortgage Modification (post mediation)

Motion to Assume Lease/Executory Contract

Motion to Avoid Lien on Exempt Property

Motion to Confirm Priority of Modified Mortgage

Motion to Deem Mortgage Current

Motion to Determine Secured Status/Value Property (30 day notice required)

Motion to Determine Secured Status/Strip Lien on Real Property (30 day notice required)

Motion to Dismiss for Failure to Attend 341 Meeting (filed by Trustee)

Motion to Dismiss for Failure to Make Plan Payments (filed by Trustee)

Motion to Extend Time Under Local Rule 3002-1

Motion to Modify Mortgage (not via the Mortgage Modification Mediation program)

Motion to Modify Plan Post Confirmation

Motion to Refinance Homestead

Motion to Offset Funds filed by Trustee

Motion for Turnover of Property by Trustee (30 day notice required)

Motion/Notice to Sell or Lease Property (does not apply to sales free and clear of interests)

Objection to Claim (excludes objections to claims of federal government units)

[Effective March 1, 2013. Amended effective April 10, 2014.]

* If a Chapter 13 Plan surrenders collateral, the plan constitutes the debtor(s) consent to relief from stay pursuant to Local Rule 3002–1A.(5).

ADMINISTRATIVE ORDER NO. 13–004. IN RE: ORDER VACATING STANDING ORDERS NUMBER 9, 13, AND 15

On June 1, 2013 the Court entered Standing Order No. 19, entitled "Chapter 13 Attorneys Fees, Adequate Protection Payments, Annual Statements, Form Plan and Tax Returns." Because Standing Order No. 19 combines the provisions included in prior Standing Orders No. 9, 13 and 15, it is:

ORDERED: Standing Order No. 9 dated October 27, 2009, Standing Order No. 13 dated October 14, 2005, and Standing Order No. 15 dated October 26, 2009, are VACATED.

[Dated: May 31, 2013.]

ADMINISTRATIVE ORDER NO. 15–002. IN RE: MOTIONS TO EXTEND OR IMPOSE THE AUTOMATIC STAY UNDER 11 U.S.C. 362(C)(3) AND 362(C)(4)

ADMINISTRATIVE ORDER ADOPTING INTERIM PROCEDURES FOR MOTIONS TO EXTEND OR IMPOSE THE AUTOMATIC STAY UNDER 11 U.S.C. § 362(C)(3) AND § 362(C)(4)

Because of the difficulties inherent in scheduling evidentiary hearings on all motions to impose or extend the automatic stay in the four Divisions within this District, the Court deems it necessary and appropriate to implement new procedures for such motions. This Administrative Order supplements Local Rule 4001–3.

The following procedures are adopted effective as to all Motions to Extend or Impose the Automatic Stay Under 11 U.S.C. § 362(c)(3) and § 362(c)(4) ("Motion") filed on and after October 1, 2015:

1. Deadline to File. Except for good cause shown in the Motion,a Motion filed pursuant to 11 U.S.C. § 362(c)(3) or § 362(c)(4) shall be filed within five (5) days of the date of the filing of the petition.

2. Contents of Motion; Affidavit Required if Presumption Arises Under 11 U.S.C. § 362(c)(3)(C) OR § 362(c)(4)(D).

a. *Contents of Motion.* A Motion to Extend or Impose the Automatic Stay filed pursuant to this Order shall include the following information:

i. the number of previous cases under the Bankruptcy Code involving the debtor and pending within the one-year period preceding the filing of the current case;

ii. the jurisdiction and case number of each such case;

iii. the date and reason(s) for dismissal of each such previous case;

iv. an express statement whether any presumption of lack of good faith arises pursuant to § 362(c)(3)(C) or § 362(c)(4)(D); and

v. the facts upon which the movant relies to (i) rebut any presumption of bad faith and (ii) demonstrate that the filing of the latter case is in good faith as to any creditors to be stayed.

b. *Affidavit or Declaration Required if Presumption Arises Under § 362(c)(3)(C) or § 362(c)(4)(D).* The movant shall attach a notarized Affidavit signed under penalty of perjury containing the facts upon which the movant relies to rebut any presumption under § 362(c)(3)(C) or § 362(c)(4)(D). In lieu of an Affidavit, the movant may file an Unsworn Declaration Under Penalty of Perjury pursuant to 28 U.S.C. § 1746.

3. Notice of Hearing. Upon the filing of a Motion subject to this Order, the Court will set a hearing to occur no later than 30 days from the date the petition was filed.

4. Service of the Motion and Notice of Hearing.

a. The movant shall promptly serve the Motion (and any Affidavit or Declaration) in the manner required by the Bankruptcy Code, the Federal Rules of Bankruptcy Procedure, and this Court's Local Rules upon each party against whom the movant seeks to extend or impose the stay, and creditors and parties in interest as may be required by the applicable rules. The movant shall file a certificate of service with the Motion, or no later than three (3) days after filing the Motion. The movant shall not delay service of the Motion pending resolution of a motion for expedited hearing or a motion to shorten time to respond to the Motion.

b. The movant shall serve the notice of hearing in the same manner as required for service of the Motion.

5. Objection to Motion. Unless otherwise ordered, any objection to a Motion subject to this Order shall be filed within 14 days after service of the Motion.

6. Order Entered Without Hearing. The Court may grant the Motion in accordance with Fed. R. Civ. P. 43(c) and Fed. R. Bankr. P. 9017 without hearing only if:

a. the movant files and serves with the Motion the Affidavit or Declaration signed by the movant containing the facts upon which the movant relies to rebut any presumption under § 362(c)(3)(C) or § 362(c)(4)(D);

b. no objection to the Motion is filed within 14 days subsequent to the service of the Motion (or such shorter time as is ordered); and

c. the Court determines that the Motion complies with this Order and that the information contained in the Affidavit or Declaration is sufficient to rebut any presumption under § 362(c)(3)(C) or § 362(c)(4)(D).

7. No Trustee Approval. If the Trustee has not objected to the Motion, the Trustee need not have approved the order granting the Motion prior to it being uploaded.

8. Hearing if no Order Entered. The Movant is responsible for submitting an order granting the Motion prior to the hearing if all other requirements of this Administrative Order are met. **The hearing will be held as scheduled unless an Order granting the Motion has been entered.** Movant's failure to appear at the hearing may result in the Motion being denied. If an objecting party fails to appear at any hearing, its objection will be deemed withdrawn.

[Effective September 24, 2015.]

UNITED STATES DISTRICT COURT FOR THE MIDDLE DISTRICT OF FLORIDA

Including Amendments Received Through February 1, 2017

CHAPTER ONE. ADMINISTRATION OF COURT BUSINESS

RULE 1.01 SCOPE AND CONSTRUCTION OF RULES

(a) These rules, made pursuant to the authority of 28 U.S.C. Section 2071, Rule 83, Fed.R.Civ.P., and Rule 57, Fed.R.Cr.P., shall apply to all proceedings in this Court, whether civil or criminal, unless specifically provided to the contrary or necessarily restricted by inference from the context. The Court may prescribe by administrative order procedures for electronic filing and related matters in civil and criminal cases. The administrative order shall govern, notwithstanding these rules, which otherwise will govern to the extent not inconsistent with the administrative order.

(b) These rules are intended to supplement and complement the Federal Rules of Civil Procedure, the Federal Rules of Criminal Procedure, and other controlling statutes and rules of Court. They shall be applied, construed and enforced to avoid inconsistency with other governing statutes and rules of court, and shall be employed to provide fairness and simplicity in procedure, to avoid technical and unjustified delay, and to secure just, expeditious and inexpensive determination of all proceedings.

(c) The Court may suspend application and enforcement of these rules, in whole or in part, in the interests of justice in individual cases by written order. When a judge of this Court in a specific case issues any order which is not consistent with these rules, such order shall constitute a suspension of the rules with respect to the case only, and only to the extent that such order is inconsistent with the rules.

(d) In all circumstances in which these rules, the Federal Rules of Civil Procedure, the Federal Rules of Criminal Procedure, other rules as prescribed by the Supreme Court of the United States, or any statute of the United States, or the Federal Common Law, do not apply, the practices, pleadings, forms and modes of proceedings then existing in like causes in the Courts of the State of Florida shall be followed.

[Amended effective May 15, 2004.]

RULE 1.02 DIVISIONS OF THE COURT

(a) The Middle District of Florida consists of those counties and places of holding court as designated in 28 U.S.C. Section 89.

(b) The District shall be divided into five Divisions to be known as the Jacksonville, Ocala, Orlando, Tampa and Ft. Myers Divisions, as follows:

(1) The Jacksonville Division shall consist of the following counties: Baker, Bradford, Clay, Columbia, Duval, Flagler, Hamilton, Nassau, Putnam, St. Johns, Suwannee and Union. The place of holding court shall be Jacksonville.

(2) The Ocala Division shall consist of the following counties: Citrus, Lake, Marion and Sumter. The place of holding court shall be Ocala.

(3) The Orlando Division shall consist of the following counties: Brevard, Orange, Osceola, Seminole and Volusia. The place of holding court shall be Orlando.

(4) The Tampa Division shall consist of the following counties: Hardee, Hernando, Hillsborough, Manatee, Pasco, Pinellas, Polk and Sarasota. The place of holding court shall be Tampa.

(5) The Fort Myers Division shall consist of the following counties: Charlotte, Collier, DeSoto, Glades, Hendry and Lee. The place of holding court shall be Fort Myers.

(c) All civil proceedings of any kind shall be instituted in that Division encompassing the county or counties having the greatest nexus with the cause, giving due regard to the place where the claim arose and the residence or principal place of business of the parties.

(d) All criminal proceedings of any kind shall be docketed and tried in that Division encompassing the county or counties in which the alleged offense or offenses were committed; provided, however, an indictment returned in any Division shall be valid regardless of the county or counties within the District in which the alleged offense or offenses were committed.

(e) The Court may, within its discretion, or upon good cause shown by any interested party, order that any case, civil or criminal, be transferred from one Division to any other Division for trial, or from one place of holding court to another place of holding court in the same Division.

[Amended effective February 19, 1989; July 1, 1993; July 1, 2002.]

RULE 1.03 DOCKETING AND ASSIGNMENT OF CASES

(a) Upon the filing of the initial paper or pleading in any case the Clerk shall docket the proceeding as a civil, criminal or miscellaneous action. Each case or proceeding shall be given a six-part docket number, which includes: (1) the one-digit number indicating the division of the Court; (2) the two-digit number indicating the year in which the proceeding is initiated; (3) the code indicating the docket to which the case is assigned; (4) the sequence number of the case or proceeding; (5) a designation consisting of a letter or series of letters disclosing the division in which the proceeding is pending; and (6) the code indicating the judge to whom the case is assigned (the code shall conform to the code assigned by the Administrative Office of the United States Courts) followed by the initials of the magistrate judge to whom the case is assigned.

(b) Each case, upon the filing of the initial paper or pleading, shall be assigned by the Clerk to an individual judge of the Court who shall thereafter be the presiding judge with respect to that cause. Individual assignment of cases within each Division shall be made at random or by lot in such proportions as the judges of the Court from time to time direct. Neither the Clerk nor any member of his staff shall have any power or discretion in determining the judge to whom any case is assigned. The method of assignment shall be designed to prevent anyone from choosing the judge to whom a case is to be assigned, and all persons shall conscientiously refrain from attempting to circumvent this rule.

(c) No application for any order of court shall be made until the case or controversy in which the matter arises has been docketed and assigned by the Clerk as prescribed by subsection (b) of this rule, and then only to the judge to whom the case has been assigned; provided, however:

(1) When no case has previously been initiated, docketed and assigned, emergency applications arising during days or hours that the Clerk's Office is closed may be submitted to any available judge resident in the appropriate Division, or, if no judge is available in the Division, to any other judge in the District, but the case shall then be docketed and assigned by the Clerk on the next business day and shall thereafter be conducted by the judge to whom it is assigned in accordance with subsection (b) of this rule.

(2) When the judge to whom a case has been assigned is temporarily unavailable due to illness, absence or prolonged engagement in other judicial business, emergency applications arising in the case may be made to the other resident judge in the Division or, if more than one, to the judge who is junior in commission in that Division. If no other judge is available in the Division such applications may be made to any other available judge in the District.

(d) The judge to whom any case is assigned may, at any time, reassign the case to any other consenting judge for any limited purpose or for all further purposes.

(e) The Clerk shall accept for filing all prisoner cases filed with or without the required filing fee or application to proceed in forma pauperis. However, a prisoner case will be subject to dismissal by the Court, sua sponte, if the filing fee is not paid or if the application is not filed within 30 days of the commencement of the action.

[Amended effective July 1, 1998; July 1, 2002.]

RULE 1.04 SIMILAR OR SUCCESSIVE CASES; DUTY OF COUNSEL

(a) Whenever a case, once docketed and assigned, is terminated by any means and is thereafter refiled without substantial change in issues or parties, it shall be assigned, or reassigned if need be, to the judge to whom the original case was assigned. Whenever a second or subsequent case seeking post-conviction or other relief by petition for writ of habeas corpus is filed by the same petitioner involving the same conviction, it shall be assigned, or reassigned if need be, to the same judge to whom the original case was assigned. All motions under 28 U.S.C. Section 2255 shall be assigned to the judge to whom the original criminal case was assigned.

(b) Transfer of Related Cases Before Two or More Judges. If cases assigned to different judges are related because of either a common question of fact or any other prospective duplication in the prosecution or resolution of the cases, a party may move to transfer any related case to the judge assigned to the first-filed among the related cases. The moving party shall file a notice of filing the motion to transfer, including a copy of the motion to transfer, in each related case. The proposed transferor judge shall dispose of the motion to transfer but shall grant the motion only with the consent of the transferee judge. If the transferee judge determines that the same magistrate judge should preside in some or all respects in some or all of the related cases, the Clerk shall assign the magistrate judge assigned to the first-filed among the affected cases to preside in that respect in those cases.

(c) Consolidation of Related Cases Before One Judge. If cases assigned to a judge are related because of either a common question of law or fact or any other prospective duplication in the prosecution or resolution of the cases, a party may move to consolidate the cases for any or all purposes in accord with Rule 42, Fed.R.Civ.P., or Rule 13, Fed.R.Cr.P. The moving party shall file a notice of filing the motion to consolidate, including a copy of the motion to consolidate, in each related case. If the presiding judge determines that the same magistrate judge should preside in some or all respects in some or all of the consolidated cases, the Clerk shall assign the magistrate judge assigned to the first-filed among the affected cases to preside in that respect in those cases.

(d) All counsel of record in any case have a continuing duty promptly to inform the Court and counsel of the existence of any other case within the purview of this rule, as well as the existence of any similar or related case or proceeding pending before any other court or administrative agency. Counsel shall notify the Court by filing and serving a "Notice of Pendency of Related Actions" that identifies and describes any related case.

[Amended effective July 1, 2002; May 11, 2006.]

RULE 1.05 FORM OF PLEADINGS; GENERAL REQUIREMENTS

(a) Although a quotation of three (3) lines or more may be single-spaced and indented and a footnote shall be single-spaced in no smaller than ten-point type, all pleadings and other papers tendered by counsel for filing shall be typewritten, double-spaced, in at least twelve-point type, and, if filed on paper, shall be on opaque, unglazed, white paper eight and one-half inches wide by eleven inches long (8½ × 11), with one and one-fourth inch top, bottom and left margins and a one to one and one-fourth inch right margin. Only one side of the paper may be used.

(b) All pleadings, motions, briefs, applications, and orders tendered by counsel for filing shall contain on the first page a caption as prescribed by Rule 10(a), Fed.R.Civ.P., and in addition thereto shall state in the title the name and designation of the party (as Plaintiff or Defendant or the like) in whose behalf the paper is submitted.

(c) The first pleading filed on behalf of any party or parties represented by counsel shall be signed by at least one attorney in his individual name with the designation "Trial Counsel", or the equivalent. Thereafter, until seasonable notice to the contrary is filed with the Court and served upon opposing counsel, such attorney shall be the person responsible for the case with full authority, individually, to conduct all proceedings including trial.

(d) All pleadings, motions, briefs, applications and other papers tendered by counsel for filing shall be signed personally by counsel as required by Rule 11, Fed.R.Civ.P. Immediately under every signature line, additional information shall be given as indicated in the example below:

(Signature of Counsel)
Typed Name of Counsel
Florida Bar Identification Number (if admitted to practice in Florida)
Firm or Business Name
Mailing Address
City, State, Zip Code
Telephone Number
Facsimile Phone Number (if available)
E-mail address

(e) The Clerk is authorized and directed to require a complete and executed AO Form JS44, Civil Cover Sheet, which shall accompany each civil case as a condition to the filing thereof. State and federal prisoners, and other persons filing civil cases pro se are exempt from the requirements of this subsection.

[Amended effective April 1, 1988; February 1, 1994; February 1, 1995; July 1, 1998; July 1, 2002; May 11, 2006.]

RULE 1.06 FORM OF PLEADINGS; SPECIAL REQUIREMENTS

(a) If demand for jury trial is contained within a pleading pursuant to Rule 38(b), Fed.R.Civ.P., the title of the pleading shall include the words "And Demand for Jury Trial" or the equivalent.

(b) If a pleading contains a prayer for injunctive relief pursuant to Rule 65, Fed.R.Civ.P., the title of the pleading shall include the words "Injunctive Relief Sought" or the equivalent. (See also Rules 4.05 and 4.06.)

(c) To enable the Court to comply with the provisions of 28 U.S.C. Section 2284, in any case which a party believes may require a three-judge district court, the words, "Three–Judge District Court Requested" or the equivalent shall be included within the title of the first pleading filed by that party. If a three-judge district court is convened all subsequent pleading, motions, briefs, applications and orders shall be tendered for filing in quadruplicate (the original and three copies).

(d) To enable the Court to comply with 28 U.S.C. Section 2403, in any case to which the United States or any agency, officer or employee thereof is not a party, any party who shall draw into question the constitutionality of any Act of Congress affecting the public interest shall forthwith so notify the Clerk in writing, stating the title of the case, its docket number, the Act of Congress in question and the grounds upon which it is assailed.

RULE 1.07 PREPARATION, SERVICE AND RETURN OF PROCESS; SERVICE OF PLEADINGS SUBSEQUENT TO ORIGINAL COMPLAINT

(a) Counsel shall prepare all process and present it to the Clerk for certification.

(b) When service of process has been effected but no appearance or response is made within the time and manner provided by Rule 12, Fed.R.Civ.P., the party effecting service shall promptly apply to the Clerk for entry of default pursuant to Rule 55(a), Fed.R.Civ.P., and shall then proceed without delay to apply for a judgment pursuant to Rule 55(b), Fed. R.Civ.P., failing which the case shall be subject to dismissal sixty (60) days after such service without notice and without prejudice; provided, however, such time may be extended by order of the Court on reasonable application with good cause shown.

(c) Service of a pleading or paper subsequent to the original complaint may be made by transmitting it by facsimile to the attorney's or party's office with a cover sheet containing the sender's name, firm, address, telephone number, and facsimile number, and the number of pages transmitted. When service is made by facsimile, a copy shall also be served by any other method permitted by Rule 5, Fed. R. Civ. P. Service by delivery after 5:00 p.m. shall be deemed to have been made on the next business day.

[Amended effective December 14, 1984; February 1, 1994; May 1, 2006.]

RULE 1.08 INTEGRITY OF FILES AND RECORDS

(a) No person, other than the Clerk or his authorized deputies, shall insert or delete, or deface, or make any entry or correction by interlineation or otherwise, in, from or upon any file or other record of the Court unless expressly permitted or ordered to do so by the Court.

(b) Court files or other papers or records in the possession of the Clerk may be removed from the Clerk's Office only upon written permission or order of the Court which shall specify the time within which the same shall be returned.

RULE 1.09 FILING UNDER SEAL

(a) Unless filing under seal is authorized by statute, rule, or order, a party seeking to file under seal any paper or other matter in any civil case shall file and serve a motion, the title of which includes the words "Motion to Seal" and which includes (i) an identification and description of each item proposed for sealing; (ii) the reason that filing each item is necessary; (iii) the reason that sealing each item is necessary; (iv) the reason that a means other than sealing is unavailable or unsatisfactory to preserve the interest advanced by the movant in support of the seal; (v) a statement of the proposed duration of the seal; and (vi) a memorandum of legal authority supporting the seal. The movant shall not file or otherwise tender to the Clerk any item proposed for sealing unless the Court has granted the motion required by this section. No settlement agreement shall be sealed absent extraordinary circumstances, such as the preservation of national security, protection of trade secrets or other valuable proprietary information, protection of especially vulnerable persons including minors or persons with disabilities, or protection of non-parties without either the opportunity or ability to protect themselves. Every order sealing any item pursuant this section shall state the particular reason the seal is required.

(b) If filing under seal is authorized by statute, rule, or order (including an order requiring or permitting a seal and obtained pursuant to (a) of this rule), a party seeking to file under seal any paper or other matter in any civil case shall file and serve a motion, the title of which includes the words "Motion to Seal Pursuant to [Statute, Rule, or Order]" and which includes (i) a citation to the statute, rule, or order authorizing the seal; (ii) an identification and description of each item submitted for sealing; (iii) a statement of the proposed duration of the seal; and (iv) a statement establishing that the items submitted for sealing are within the identified statute, rule, or order the movant cites as authorizing the seal. The movant shall submit to the Clerk along with a motion under this section each item proposed for sealing. Every order sealing any item pursuant to this section shall state the particular reason the seal is required and shall identify the statute, rule, or order authorizing the seal.

(c) Unless otherwise ordered by the Court for good cause shown, no order sealing any item pursuant to this section shall extend beyond one year, although a seal is renewable by a motion that complies with (b) of this rule, identifies the expiration of the seal, and is filed before the expiration of the seal.

(d) The Clerk shall return to the movant any matter for which sealing is denied.

[Effective May 11, 2006.]

CHAPTER TWO. ATTORNEYS

RULE 2.01 GENERAL ADMISSION TO PRACTICE

(a) No person shall be permitted to appear or be heard as counsel for another in any proceeding in this Court unless first admitted to practice in the Court pursuant to this rule (or heretofore admitted under prior rules of the Court).

(b) Only those persons who are members in good standing of The Florida Bar shall be eligible for general admission to the bar of the Court. If a person ceases to be a member in good standing of The Florida Bar, that person will be suspended from the bar of the Court until that person is reinstated to The Florida Bar. However, if the suspension from The Florida Bar is 90 days or less, the person will be automatically reinstated. If the suspension is 91 days or more, that person must apply with the Clerk of Court for reinstatement. Each applicant for general admission shall file with the Clerk a written petition setting forth his residence and office address, his general and legal education, and the Courts to which he has previously been admitted to practice. The petition shall be accompanied by the certificates of two members in good standing of the bar of the Court attesting that the applicant is of good moral character and is otherwise competent and eligible for general admission to practice in the Court (provided, however, members in good standing of the bars of the Northern or Southern Districts of Florida shall be admitted on petition without necessity of such certificates). In addition, each applicant shall furnish a certificate certifying that the applicant has read and is familiar with each of the following: The Federal Rules of Evidence, the Federal Rules of Civil Procedure, the Federal Rules of Criminal Procedure, and the Local Rules of the Middle District of Florida.

(c) Petitions for general admission to practice shall be called from time to time in open Court on notice to the applicants; except that, under special circumstances, any United States District Judge or United States Magistrate Judge of the Court may entertain a petition at any time. Upon taking the prescribed oath and payment of the prescribed enrollment fee, the applicant shall then be enrolled as a member of the bar of the Court and the Clerk shall issue a suitable certificate to that effect.

(d) To maintain good standing in the bar of this Court, each attorney admitted under this rule, beginning in the year following the year of the attorney's admission, must pay a periodic fee set by administrative order and, unless exempted by the Chief Judge for good cause, must register with the Clerk of Court and maintain an e-mail address for electronic service by the Clerk during the attorney's membership in the bar of this Court. An attorney who fails to pay timely the periodic fee or fails without exemption to maintain a registered e-mail address is subject to removal from membership in the bar of this Court.

[Amended effective July 1, 1998; July 1, 2002; May 15, 2004; May 11, 2006.]

RULE 2.02 SPECIAL ADMISSION TO PRACTICE

(a) Any attorney who is not a resident of Florida but who is a member in good standing of the bar of any District Court of the United States; outside Florida; may appear specially as counsel of record; without formal or general admission; provided, however, such privilege is not abused by appearances in separate cases to such a degree as to constitute the maintenance of a regular practice of law in Florida; and provided further that whenever appearing as counsel by filing any pleading or paper in any case pending in this Court, a non-resident attorney shall file within fourteen (14) days a written designation and consent-to-act on the part of some member of the bar of this Court, resident in Florida, upon whom all notices and papers may be served and who will be responsible for the progress of the case, including the trial in default of the non-resident attorney. In addition to filing the written designation, the non-resident attorney shall comply with both the fee and e-mail registration requirements of Rule 2.01(d), and the written designation shall certify the non-resident attorney's compliance.

(b) An attorney employed full-time by either the United States, an agency of the United States, or a public entity established under the laws of the United States may appear within the course and scope of the attorney's employment as counsel without general or other formal admission.

(c) Any attorney who appears specially in this Court pursuant to subsections (a) or (b) of this rule shall be deemed to be familiar with, and shall be governed by, these rules in general, including Rule 2.04 hereof in particular; and shall also be deemed to be familiar with and governed by the Code of Professional Responsibility and other ethical limitations or requirements then governing the professional behavior of members of The Florida Bar.

(d) In an extraordinary circumstance (such as the hearing of an emergency matter) a lawyer who is not a member of the Middle District bar may move *instanter* for temporary admission provided the lawyer appears eligible for membership in the Middle District bar and simultaneously initiates proceedings for general or special admission to the Middle District bar. Temporary admission expires in thirty days or upon determination of the application for general or special admission, whichever is earlier.

[Amended effective May 15, 2004; May 11, 2006; December 1, 2009.]

RULE 2.03 APPEARANCE AND WITHDRAWAL

(a) Every pleading or paper of any kind filed by an attorney in this Court shall conform and be subject to the requirements of Rule 11, Fed.R.Civ.P., and unless otherwise expressly stated therein, shall constitute a general appearance on behalf of the persons or parties for whom the pleading or paper is filed.

(b) No attorney, having made a general appearance under subsection (a) of this rule, shall thereafter abandon the case or proceeding in which the appearance was made, or withdraw as counsel for any party therein, except by written leave of Court obtained after giving ten (10) days' notice to the party or client affected thereby, and to opposing counsel.

(c) In all criminal cases non-payment of attorney's fees shall not be sufficient justification for seeking leave to withdraw if the withdrawal of counsel is likely to cause a continuance of a scheduled trial date; nor shall leave be given to withdraw in any other case, absent compelling ethical considerations, if such withdrawal would likely cause continuance or delay. If a party discharges an attorney it shall be the responsibility of that party to proceed pro se or obtain the appearance of substitute counsel in sufficient time to meet established trial dates or other regularly scheduled proceedings as the Court may direct.

(d) Any party for whom a general appearance of counsel has been made shall not thereafter take any step or be heard in the case in proper person, absent prior leave of Court; nor shall any party, having previously elected to proceed in proper person, be permitted to obtain special or intermittent appearances of counsel except upon such conditions as the Court may specify.

(e) A corporation may appear and be heard only through counsel admitted to practice in the Court pursuant to Rule 2.01 or Rule 2.02.

[Amended effective May 11, 2006.]

RULE 2.04 DISCIPLINE

(a) Any member of the bar of this Court, admitted generally under Rule 2.01 or specially under Rule 2.02, may, after hearing and for good cause shown, be disbarred, suspended, reprimanded or subjected to such other discipline as the Court may deem proper.

(b) Whenever it appears to the Court that any member of its bar, admitted generally under Rule 2.01 or then appearing specially under Rule 2.02, has been disbarred or suspended from practice by the Supreme Court of Florida, or by any other court of competent jurisdiction, as the case might be, or has been disbarred on consent or resigned from the bar of any other court while an investigation into allegations of misconduct is pending, or has been convicted of a felony in any court, such disbarment, suspension, resignation, or conviction shall, twenty-one (21) days thereafter, operate as an automatic suspension of such attorney's right to practice in this Court; provided, however, the attorney may file, within such twenty-one (21) day period, a petition, with a copy served upon the United States Attorney, seeking relief from the operation of this rule, and if a timely petition is filed, suspension shall be stayed until the petition is determined. If such petition is filed by an attorney who has been admitted to practice generally under Rule 2.01 of these rules, it shall be heard and determined by the Chief Judge of the Court sitting with any two or more of other judges of the District as the Chief Judge shall designate. If such petition is filed by an attorney who has been admitted to practice specially under Rule 2.02 of these rules, it shall be heard and determined by the judge assigned to the case in which such special appearance has been made.

(c) Any attorney admitted to practice before this Court, upon being subjected to public discipline by any other Court of the United States or the District of Columbia, or by a court of any state, territory, commonwealth, or possession of the United States, including any attorney who is disbarred on consent or resigns from any bar while an investigation into allegations of misconduct is pending, shall promptly inform the Clerk of this Court of such action.

(d) The professional conduct of all members of the bar of this Court, admitted generally under Rule 2.01 or specially under Rule 2.02, shall be governed by the Model Rules of Professional Conduct of the American Bar Association as modified and adopted by the Supreme Court of Florida to govern the professional behavior of the members of The Florida Bar.

(e) The Court may appoint a Grievance Committee in each Division of the Court to conduct investigations of alleged misconduct on the part of any member of its bar, whether admitted generally under Rule 2.01 or specially under Rule 2.02. Each Grievance Committee shall consist of not less than five members of the bar of this Court regularly practicing in that Division, three of whom shall constitute a quorum. Appointments shall be for three (3) years. The Court shall designate the Chairman of the Committee in each Division, but each Committee shall otherwise organize itself as it sees fit. All proceedings before the Committees may be conducted informally, but shall remain confidential unless otherwise ordered by the Court. Each Committee shall function as follows:

(1) Any matter or question touching upon the professional behavior of a member of the bar may be referred at any time to the Chairman of the appropriate Committee by any judge of the Court. The Chairman of the Committee will promptly designate himself, or some other member, to investigate the matter and make a preliminary report to the Committee as a whole for the Committee's determination as to whether (i) the inquiry should be terminated because the question raised is unsupported or insubstantial; or (ii) the question raised justifies further inquiry but should be referred to the appropriate grievance committee of The Florida Bar; or (iii) the question raised justifies further inquiry and should be pursued by the Committee due to distinctly Federal features or other appropriate reason. The Chairman of the Committee shall then report the Committee's preliminary recommendation to the referring judge and shall follow his direction.

(2) If a Committee is directed by the referring judge to pursue its inquiry, it shall proceed with dispatch to make such further investigation as it deems necessary to make a final report to the Court as to whether there is, or is not, probable cause to believe that the subject member of the bar has been guilty of unprofessional or unethical conduct justifying disciplinary action by the Court. If the Committee makes a report of probable cause, such report shall then be transmitted to the United States Attorney (or, if the United States Attorney be disqualified by interest, to another member of the bar appointed by the Chief Judge for that purpose) who shall file and serve a petition for an order to show cause upon the accused attorney. Such petition, and all further proceedings thereon, shall be heard and determined by the Chief Judge of the District sitting together with any two or more judges of the District as the Chief Judge shall designate.

(f) It shall be the duty of every member of the bar of the Court, admitted generally under Rule 2.01 or specially under Rule 2.02, to respond to and cooperate fully with any Grievance Committee of the Court during the course of any investigation being conducted pursuant to subsection (d) of this rule; provided, however, no attorney shall be entitled as of right to notice of the pendency of any such investigation unless and until he is named in a petition to show cause filed pursuant to subsection (e)(2) of this rule.

(g) Nothing in this rule shall be construed as providing an exclusive procedure for the discipline of members of the bar in appropriate cases, nor as a limitation upon the power of the Court to punish for contempt in appropriate cases.

(h) Attorneys and litigants should conduct themselves with civility and in a spirit of cooperation in order to reduce unnecessary cost and delay.

[Amended effective May 2, 1988; February 1, 1994; July 1, 2002; May 11, 2006; December 1, 2009.]

RULE 2.05 APPEARANCE BY LAW STUDENTS

(a) The purpose of this rule is to authorize, under certain circumstances, the appearance of eligible law students in this Court as a means of providing assistance to lawyers who represent clients unable to pay for such services, and to encourage participating law schools to provide clinical instruction in the conduct of litigation in federal court.

(b) An eligible law student, as hereafter defined, may appear and be heard in this Court on behalf of any person found by the Court to be indigent and who consents in writing to such appearance. The written consent of the client and his or her attorney of record (the supervising attorney) shall be filed in the case; and, absent excusal by the Court, all such appearances shall be made in the presence of the supervising attorney. An eligible law student shall neither ask for nor receive any compensation or remuneration of any kind for services rendered pursuant to this rule, whether in court or out-of-court.

(c) In addition to appearance in Court, an eligible law student, having the written consent of the client and the supervising attorney as provided in subsection (b) of this rule, may engage in other activities outside the presence, but under the general supervision and direction of the supervising attorney including preparation of pleadings, legal research and brief writing, and preparation of discovery requests and responses. Any paper filed with the Court or served upon the opposing party should reflect the name of the eligible law student, if any, who participated in its preparation, and any such paper must be signed by the supervising attorney as counsel of record. An eligible law student may also engage in the conduct of any informal discovery or investigation authorized by the supervising attorney; may participate in reviewing and inspecting discovery materials; and may participate in oral depositions (provided that the supervising attorney shall be present at all depositions).

(d) An eligible law student is one who (1) is enrolled in a participating law school accredited by the American Bar Association; (2) has completed legal studies amounting to at least four semesters or six quarters for which the student has received not less than 48 semester hours or 72 quarter hours of academic credit; (3) has read and is familiar with the Federal Rules of Civil and Criminal Procedures, the Federal Rules of Evidence, the Code of Professional Responsibility and the Rules of this Court; and (4) is certified by the Dean of the participating law school as being of good character, competent legal ability, adequately trained to perform as a legal intern, and is otherwise qualified under the terms of this rule.

(e) The certification of a student or students by the participating law school Dean shall be filed with the Clerk and, unless sooner withdrawn, shall remain in effect for so long as the student continues to be enrolled as an active student in the participating law school. Any certification of a student may be withdrawn by the Dean at any time on notice to the Clerk without statement of cause. Similarly, any certification of a student may be terminated by the Court at any time on notice to the Dean without statement of cause.

[Effective August 15, 1986.]

CHAPTER THREE. MOTIONS, DISCOVERY AND PRETRIAL PROCEEDINGS

RULE 3.01 MOTIONS; BRIEFS AND HEARINGS

(a) In a motion or other application for an order, the movant shall include a concise statement of the precise relief requested, a statement of the basis for the request, and a memorandum of legal authority in support of the request, all of which the movant shall include in a single document not more than twenty-five (25) pages.

(b) Each party opposing a motion or application shall file within fourteen (14) days after service of the motion or application a response that includes a memorandum of legal authority in opposition to the request, all of which the respondent shall include in a document not more than twenty (20) pages.

(c) No party shall file any reply or further memorandum directed to the motion or response allowed in (a) and (b) unless the Court grants leave.

(d) A motion requesting leave to file either a motion in excess of twenty-five (25) pages, a response in excess of twenty (20) pages, or a reply or further memorandum shall not exceed three (3) pages, shall specify the length of the proposed filing, and shall not include, as an attachment or otherwise, the proposed motion, response, reply, or other paper.

(e) Motions of an emergency nature may be considered and determined by the Court at any time, in its discretion (see also, Rule 4.05). The unwarranted designation of a motion as an emergency motion may result in the imposition of sanctions.

(f) All applications to the Court (i) requesting relief in any form, or (ii) citing authorities or presenting argument with respect to any matter awaiting decision, shall be made in writing (except as provided in Rule 7(b) of the Federal Rules of Civil Procedure) in accordance with this rule and in appropriate form pursuant to Rule 1.05; and, unless invited or directed by the presiding judge, shall not be addressed or presented to the Court in the form of a letter or the like. All pleadings and papers to be filed shall be filed with the Clerk of the Court and not with the judge thereof, except as provided by Rule 1.03(c) of these Rules.

(g) Before filing any motion in a civil case, except a motion for injunctive relief, for judgment on the pleadings, for summary judgment, to dismiss or to permit maintenance of a class action, to dismiss for failure to state a claim upon which relief can be granted, or to involuntarily dismiss an action, the moving party shall confer with counsel for the opposing party in a good faith effort to resolve the issues raised by the motion, and shall file with the motion a statement (1) certifying that the moving counsel has conferred with opposing counsel and (2) stating whether counsel agree on the resolution of the motion. A certification to the effect that opposing counsel was unavailable for a conference before filing a motion is insufficient to satisfy the parties' obligation to confer. The moving party retains the duty to contact opposing counsel expeditiously after filing and to supplement the motion promptly with a statement certifying whether or to what extent the parties have resolved the issue(s) presented in the motion. If the interested parties agree to all or part of the relief sought in any motion, the caption of the motion shall include the word "unopposed," "agreed," or "stipulated" or otherwise succinctly inform the reader that, as to all or part of the requested relief, no opposition exists.

(h) All dispositive motions must be so designated in the caption of the motion. All dispositive motions which are not decided within one hundred and eighty (180) days of the responsive filing (or the expiration of the time allowed for its filing under the local rules) shall be brought to the attention of the district judge by the movant by filing a "Notice To the Court" within ten days after the time for deciding the motion has expired. Movant shall file an additional "Notice To The Court" after the expiration of each and every additional thirty day period during which the motion remains undecided. Movant shall provide the Chief Judge of the Middle District with a copy of each and every "Notice To The Court" which movant is required to file under this rule.

(i) The use of telephonic hearings and conferences is encouraged, whenever possible, particularly when counsel are located in different cities.

(j) Motions and other applications will ordinarily be determined by the Court on the basis of the motion papers and briefs or legal memoranda; provided, however, the Court may allow oral argument upon the written request of any interested party or upon the Court's own motion. Requests for oral argument shall accompany the motion, or the opposing brief or legal memorandum, and shall estimate the time required for argument. All hearings on motions shall be noticed by the Clerk, as directed by the judge assigned to the case, either on regular motion days if practicable (pursuant to Rule 78, Fed. R.Civ.P.), or at such other times as the Court shall direct.

[Amended effective December 1, 1992; February 1, 1994; July 1, 1998; July 1, 2002; May 11, 2006; December 1, 2009.]

RULE 3.02 NOTICE OF DEPOSITIONS

Unless otherwise stipulated by all interested parties pursuant to Rule 29, Fed.R.Civ.P., and excepting the circumstances governed by Rule 30(a), Fed.R.Civ.P., a party desiring to take the deposition of any person upon oral examination shall give at least fourteen (14) days notice in writing to every other party to the action and to the deponent (if the deponent is not a party).

[Amended effective February 1, 1994; May 1, 2006; December 1, 2009.]

RULE 3.03 WRITTEN INTERROGATORIES; FILING OF DISCOVERY MATERIAL; EXCHANGE OF DISCOVERY REQUEST BY COMPUTER DISK

(a) Written interrogatories shall be so prepared and arranged that a blank space shall be provided after each separately numbered interrogatory. The space shall be reasonably calculated to enable the answering party to insert the answer within the space.

(b) The original of the written interrogatories and a copy shall be served on the party to whom the interrogatories are directed, and copies on all other parties. No copy of the written interrogatories shall be filed with the Court by the party propounding them. The answering party shall use the original of the written interrogatories for his answers and objections, if any; and the original shall be returned to the party propounding the interrogatories with copies served upon all other parties. The interrogatories as answered or objected to shall not be filed with the Court as a matter of course, but may later be filed by any party in whole or in part if necessary to presentation and consideration of a motion to compel, a motion for summary judgment, a motion for injunctive relief, or other similar proceedings.

(c) Notices of the taking of oral depositions shall not be filed with the Court as a matter of course (except as necessary to presentation and consideration of motions to compel); and transcripts of oral depositions shall not be filed unless and until requested by a party or ordered by the Court.

(d) Requests for the production of documents and other things, matters disclosed pursuant to Fed.R.Civ.P. 26, and requests for admission, and answers and responses thereto, shall not be filed with the Court as a matter of course but may later be filed in whole or in part if necessary to presentation and consideration of a motion to compel, a motion for summary judgment, a motion for injunctive relief, or other similar proceedings.

(e) Litigants' counsel should utilize computer technology to the maximum extent possible in all phases of litigation i.e., to serve interrogatories on opposing counsel with a copy of the questions on computer disk in addition to the required printed copy.

[Amended effective February 1, 1994; February 1, 1994; July 1, 2002; May 11, 2006.]

RULE 3.04 MOTIONS TO COMPEL AND FOR PROTECTIVE ORDER

(a) A motion to compel discovery pursuant to Rule 36 or Rule 37, Fed.R.Civ.P., shall include quotation in full of each interrogatory, question on deposition, request for admission, or request for production to which the motion is addressed; each of which shall be followed immediately by quotation in full of the objection and grounds therefor as stated by the opposing party; or the answer or response which is asserted to be insufficient, immediately followed by a statement of the reason the motion should be granted. The opposing party shall then respond as required by Rule 3.01(b) of these rules.

(b) For the guidance of counsel in preparing or opposing contemplated motions for a protective order pursuant to Rule 26(c), Fed.R.Civ.P., related to the place of taking a party-litigant's deposition, or the deposition of the managing agent of a party, it is the general policy of the Court that a non-resident plaintiff may reasonably be deposed at least once in this District during the discovery stages of the case; and that a non-resident defendant who intends to be present in person at trial may reasonably be deposed at least once in this District either during the discovery stages of the case or within a week prior to trial as the circumstances seem to suggest. Otherwise, depositions of parties should usually be taken as in the case of other witnesses pursuant to Rule 45(d), Fed.R.Civ.P. A non-resident, within the meaning of this rule, is a person residing outside the State of Florida.

[Amended effective October 22, 1984; December 3, 1990; December 1, 1992; July 1, 2002; May 11, 2006.]

RULE 3.05 CASE MANAGEMENT

(a) As soon as practicable after the filing of any civil action, the Clerk shall designate the case for future management on one of three tracks. The Clerk will notify the Plaintiff of such designation and the Plaintiff must then serve that notice upon all other parties. However, in cases governed by Rule 4.02, the Clerk will notify the party effecting removal, as specified in Rule 4.02(b), who then must serve that notice upon all other parties. The presiding judge may thereafter direct at any time that a case be redesignated from one track to a different track.

(b) Cases shall be designated by the Clerk to their appropriate tracks as follows:

(1) The following categories of proceedings are Track One Cases:

(A) an action for review on an administrative record;

(B) a petition for habeas corpus or other proceeding to challenge a criminal conviction or sentence;

(C) an action brought without counsel by a person in custody of the United States, a state, or a state subdivision;

(D) an action to enforce or quash an administrative summons or subpoena;

(E) an action by the United States to recover benefit payments;

(F) an action by the United States to collect on a student loan guaranteed by the United States;

(G) a proceeding ancillary to proceedings in other courts; and

(H) an action to enforce an arbitration award.

(2) Track Two cases shall include all cases not designated as Track One Cases, and not within the definition of Track Three Cases as hereafter stated. Track Two Cases will normally consist of non-complex actions which will require a trial, either jury or non-jury, absent earlier settlement or disposition by summary judgment or some other means.

(3) Track Three Cases shall include those cases involving class action or antitrust claims, securities litigation, mass disaster or other complex tort cases, or those actions presenting factual or legal issues arising from the presence of multiple parties or multiple claims portending extensive discovery procedures or numerous legal issues such that the management techniques recommended in the current edition of the Manual For Complex Litigation should be considered and applied as appropriate to the circumstances of the case. Track Three Cases shall also include any action so imminently affecting the public interest (e.g., legislative redistricting, school desegregation, voting rights) as to warrant heightened judicial attention or expedited treatment.

(c) The following procedures shall apply depending upon the Track to which a case has been designated:

(1) Track One Cases—

(A) Government foreclosure or recovery cases, motions to withdraw references to the Bankruptcy Court, and proceedings under 28 U.S.C. § 2255 will normally be managed by the presiding District Judge pursuant to notices or orders entered by the Judge, or by the Clerk under the Court's direction, in each such case.

(B) Other Track One cases will normally be referred at the time of filing to the Magistrate Judges for management by them in accordance with other provisions of these local rules or standing orders entered in each Division of the Court governing the duties and responsibilities of the Magistrate Judges. Such cases will then be managed by them pursuant to notices or orders entered by the Magistrate Judge, or by the Clerk under the Court's direction, in each such case.

(2) Track Two Cases—

(A) All Rule 12, F.R.Civ.P., motions will be promptly considered by the Court and will normally be decided within sixty (60) days after receipt of the last paper directed to the motion.

(B) Counsel and any unrepresented party shall meet within 60 days after service of the complaint upon any defendant, or the first appearance of any defendant, regardless of the pendency of any undecided motions, for the purpose of preparing and filing a Case Management Report in the form prescribed below. Unless the Court orders otherwise, parties represented by counsel are permitted, but are not required, to attend the case management meeting. The Case Management Report must be filed within 14 days after the meeting. Unless otherwise ordered by the Court, a party may not seek discovery from any source before the meeting.

(C) The Case Management Report shall include:

(i) The date(s) and time(s) of the meetings of the parties and the identity of the persons present.

(ii) A date by which the parties have agreed to pre-discovery disclosures of core information, either voluntarily or as may be required by the Federal Rules of Civil Procedure or other provisions of these rules, and a detailed description of the information scheduled for disclosure.

(iii) A discovery plan which shall include a detailed description of the discovery each party intends to pursue (requests for admission, requests for production or inspection, written interrogatories, oral depositions), the time during which each form of discovery will be pursued, the proposed date for completion of discovery, and such other matters relating to discovery as the parties may agree upon (e.g., handling of confidential information, limits on the number or length of depositions, assertion of privileges).

(iv) A final date for the filing of all motions for leave to file third party claims or to join other parties and specification of a final date for the filing of any motions for summary judgment.

(v) A statement concerning the intent of the parties regarding alternative dispute resolution (settlement negotiations, court annexed arbitration under Chapter Eight or court annexed mediation under Chapter Nine of these rules), and specification of a date by which the parties will either report to the court concerning prospective settlement or apply for an order invoking arbitration or mediation.

(vi) A date by which the parties will be ready for a final pretrial conference and subsequent trial.

(vii) The signature of all counsel and all unrepresented parties either in a single document or duplicate originals.

(viii) A statement assessing the need for a preliminary pretrial conference before entry of a Case Management and Scheduling Order.

(D) Upon receipt of the Case Management Report the court will either (i) schedule a preliminary pretrial conference to further discuss the content of the report and the subjects enumerated in Rule 16, F.R.Civ.P., before the entry of a Case Management and Scheduling Order, or (ii) enter a Case Management and Scheduling Order. The Case Management and Scheduling Order will establish a discovery plan and a schedule of dates including the dates of a final pretrial conference and trial (or specify dates after which a pretrial conference or trial may be scheduled on twenty-one (21) days' notice).

(E) It is the goal of the court that a trial will be conducted in all Track Two Cases within two years after the filing of the complaint, and that most such cases will be tried within one year after the filing of the complaint. A motion to amend any pleading or a motion for continuance of any pretrial conference, hearing, or trial is distinctly disfavored after entry of the Case Management and Scheduling Order.

(3) Track Three Cases—

(A) The provisions of subsections (c)(2)(A), (B) and (C)(i)–(vii) of this rule shall apply to all Track Three Cases.

(B) Upon receipt of the Case Management Report, if not sooner in some cases, the Court will schedule and conduct a preliminary pretrial conference to discuss with the parties the content of the report and the subjects enumerated in Rule 16, F.R.Civ.P., before the entry of a Case Management and Scheduling Order.

(C) The Case Management and Scheduling Order will establish a discovery plan and will also schedule such additional preliminary pretrial conferences as may seem necessary as well as a final pretrial conference and trial (or specify dates after which a pretrial conference or trial may be scheduled on twenty-one (21) days' notice).

(D) It is the goal of the court that a trial will be conducted in all Track Three Cases within three years after the filing of the complaint, and that most such cases will be tried within two (2) years after the filing of the complaint or on an acutely accelerated schedule if the public interest requires. A motion to amend any pleading or to continue any pretrial conference, hearing or trial is severely disfavored because, in light of the need for special judicial attention, counsel should prosecute or defend a Track Three Case only if able to accommodate the scheduling demands.

(d) The disclosures required by Fed.R.Civ.P. 26 (including the initial disclosures specified in Rule 26(a)(1)) shall be made in Track Two and Track Three Cases in the time and manner required by that rule unless otherwise ordered by the Court or stipulated by the parties. If the parties stipulate not to exchange initial disclosures, the Court may order the parties to exchange similar information pursuant to Fed.R.Civ.P. 16. Track One Cases are exempt from the initial disclosures provisions of Rule 26(a)(1).

[Amended effective February 1, 1994; July 1, 1998; July 1, 2002; December 1, 2009.]

RULE 3.06 FINAL PRETRIAL PROCEDURES

(a) Final pretrial conferences may be scheduled by the Court pursuant to Rule 16(d), Fed.R.Civ.P., in any civil case on not less than twenty-one (21) days notice.

(b) In any case in which a final pretrial conference is scheduled by the Court (or in any case in which the Court directs the preparation and filing of a pretrial statement in accordance with this rule, but without scheduling a pretrial conference), it shall be the responsibility of counsel for all parties to meet together no later than fourteen (14) days before the date of the final pretrial conference (or at such other time as the Court may direct) in a good faith effort to:

(1) discuss the possibility of settlement;

(2) stipulate to as many facts or issues as possible;

(3) examine all exhibits and Rule 5.04 exhibit substitutes or documents and other items of tangible evidence to be offered by any party at trial;

(4) exchange the names and addresses of all witnesses; and

(5) prepare a pretrial statement in accordance with subsection (c) of this rule.

(c) The pretrial statement shall be filed with the Court no later than seven (7) days before the date of the final pretrial conference (or at such other time as the Court may direct), and shall contain:

(1) the basis of federal jurisdiction;

(2) a concise statement of the nature of the action;

(3) a brief, general statement of each party's case;

(4) a list of all exhibits and Rule 5.04 exhibit substitutes to be offered at trial with notation of all objections thereto;

(5) a list of all witnesses who may be called at trial;

(6) a list of all expert witnesses including, as to each such witness, a statement of the subject matter and a summary of the substance of his or her testimony;

(7) in cases in which any party claims money damages, a statement of the elements of each such claim and the amount being sought with respect to each such element;

(8) a list of all depositions to be offered in evidence at trial (as distinguished from possible use for impeachment), including a designation of the pages and lines to be offered from each deposition;

(9) a concise statement of those facts which are admitted and will require no proof at trial, together with any reservations directed to such admissions;

(10) a concise statement of applicable principles of law on which there is agreement;

(11) a concise statement of those issues of fact which remain to be litigated (without incorporation by reference to prior pleadings and memoranda);

(12) a concise statement of those issues of law which remain for determination by the Court (without incorporation by reference to prior pleadings or memoranda);

(13) a concise statement of any disagreement as to the application of the Federal Rules of Evidence or the Federal Rules of Civil Procedure;

(14) a list of all motions or other matters which require action by the Court; and

(15) the signatures of counsel for all parties.

(d) If a final pretrial conference is scheduled by the Court, lead trial counsel for each party shall attend.

(e) All pleadings filed by any party prior to filing of the pretrial statement shall be deemed to be merged therein, or in any subsequent pretrial order entered by the Court. The pretrial statement and the pretrial order, if any, will control the course of the trial and may not be amended except by order of the Court in the furtherance of justice. If new evidence or witnesses are discovered after filing of the pretrial statement, the party desiring to use the same shall immediately notify opposing counsel and the Court, and such use shall be permitted only by order of the Court in the furtherance of justice.

[Amended effective April 1, 1991; July 1, 2002; December 1, 2009.]

RULE 3.07 MARKING AND LISTING EXHIBITS

(a) In advance of trial and, when reasonable, in advance of evidentiary hearing, counsel for each party in any case shall obtain from the Clerk (or from an outside source in the format utilized by the Clerk or in a format approved by the presiding judge), tabs or labels. These tabs or labels shall be used for the marking and identification of each exhibit proposed to be offered in evidence or otherwise tendered to any witness during trial and evidentiary hearing and for the marking and identification of photographs and reductions proposed to be offered with exhibits in accordance with Rule 5.04. Counsel shall identify a photograph or reduction offered with an exhibit with the number identifying the exhibit.

(b) Upon marking exhibits, counsel shall also prepare a list of such exhibits, in sequence, with a descriptive notation sufficient to identify each separate numbered exhibit. Counsel shall furnish copies of the list to opposing counsel and three copies to the Court at the commencement of trial and, when reasonable, at the commencement of evidentiary hearing. (See also Rules 5.03 and 5.04.)

[Amended effective April 1, 1991.]

RULE 3.08 NOTICE OF SETTLEMENTS; DISMISSAL

(a) It shall be the duty of all counsel to immediately notify the Court upon the settlement of any case.

(b) When notified that a case has been settled and for purposes of administratively closing the file, the Court may order that a case be dismissed subject to the right of any party to move the Court within sixty (60) days thereafter (or within such other period of time as the Court may specify) for the purpose of entering a stipulated form of final order or judgment; or, on good cause shown, to reopen the case for further proceedings.

RULE 3.09 CONTINUANCES

(a) No trial, hearing or other proceeding shall be continued upon stipulation of counsel alone, but a continuance may be allowed by order of the Court for good cause shown.

(b) Failure to complete discovery procedures within the time established pursuant to Rule 3.05 of these rules shall not constitute cause for continuance unless such failure or inability is brought to the attention of the Court at least sixty (60) days in advance of any scheduled trial date and is not the result of lack of diligence in pursuing such discovery.

(c) Except for good cause shown, no continuance shall be granted on the ground that a party or witness has not been served with process or a subpoena, as the case might be, unless the moving party, at least seven (7) days before the return date, has delivered the papers to be served to the Marshal (or other appropriate person) for that purpose.

(d) Motions to continue trial must be signed by the attorney of record who shall certify that the moving party has been informed of the motion and has consented to it.

[Amended effective February 1, 1994; December 1, 2009.]

RULE 3.10 FAILURE TO PROSECUTE: DISMISSAL

(a)* Whenever it appears that any case is not being diligently prosecuted the Court may, on motion of any party or on its own motion, enter an order to show cause why the case should not be dismissed, and if no satisfactory cause is shown, the case may be dismissed by the Court for want of prosecution.

* So in original. No subparagraph (b) was promulgated.

CHAPTER FOUR. SPECIAL RULES

RULE 4.01 AMENDMENTS OF PLEADINGS

(a)* Unless otherwise directed by the Court, any party permitted to amend a pleading shall file the amended pleading in its entirety with the amendments incorporated therein.

* So in original. No subparagraph (b) was promulgated.

RULE 4.02 REMOVAL OF CASES FROM STATE COURT

(a) All cases removed to this Court from the courts of the State of Florida shall be docketed and assigned, in accordance with Rule 1.03 of these rules, in the Division encompassing the county of the State in which the case was pending.

(b) The party effecting removal shall file with the notice of removal a true and legible copy of all process, pleadings, orders, and other papers or exhibits of every kind, including depositions, then on file in the state court.

(c) When a case is removed to this Court with pending motions on which briefs or legal memoranda have not been submitted, the moving party shall file and serve a supporting brief within fourteen (14) days after the removal in accordance with Rule 3.01(a) of these rules, and the party or parties opposing the motion shall then comply with Rule 3.01(b) of these rules.

[Amended effective March 15, 1989; December 1, 2009.]

RULE 4.03 TIME OF MOTION TO JOIN THIRD PARTIES

(a) Any motion by a defendant for leave to join a third-party defendant pursuant to Rule 14(a), Fed.R.Civ.P., shall be made within six (6) months from the date of service of the moving defendant's answer to the complaint, or at least sixty (60) days prior to a scheduled trial date, whichever first occurs.

(b) A motion by a plaintiff for leave to join a third-party defendant pursuant to Rule 14(b), Fed.R.Civ.P., shall be made within six (6) months from the date of service of the moving plaintiff's reply to the counterclaim, or at least sixty (60) days prior to a scheduled trial date, whichever first occurs.

(c) The provision of this rule may be suspended upon a showing of good cause therefor.

RULE 4.04 CLASS ACTIONS

(a) In any case sought to be maintained as a class action pursuant to Rule 23, Fed.R.Civ.P., the complaint shall contain, under a separate heading styled "CLASS ACTION ALLEGATIONS", detailed allegations of fact showing the existence of the several prerequisites to a class action as enumerated in Rule 23(a) and (b), Fed.R.Civ.P.

(b) Within ninety (90) days following the filing of the initial complaint in such an action, unless the time is extended by the Court for cause shown, the named plaintiff or plaintiffs shall move for a determination under Rule 23(c)(1) as to whether the case is to be maintained as a class action. The motion shall be supported by a memorandum as required by Rule 3.01(a) of these rules; and, in addition to a showing of the prerequisites as required by subsection (a) of this rule, the motion shall contain a detailed description or definition of the class (and sub-classes, if any), and the number of persons in the class. If a determination is sought that the action shall be maintained under Rule 23(b)(3), the motion shall also suggest a means of providing, and defraying the cost of, the notice required by Rule 23(c)(2), Fed.R.Civ.P. If discovery relating to class action issues is needed, the parties may move the Court for leave to take such discovery prior to the case management meeting.

(c) In ruling upon a motion made under subsection (b) of this rule, the Court may allow the class action, may disallow and strike the class action allegations, or may order postponement of the determination pending additional discovery or such other preliminary procedures as may appear appropriate in the circumstances.

(d) The foregoing provisions of this rule shall apply, with appropriate adaptations, to any complaint alleged to be brought against a class, and to counterclaims or cross-claims brought for a class.

[Amended effective February 1, 1995; July 1, 2002.]

RULE 4.05 TEMPORARY RESTRAINING ORDERS

(a) Pursuant to Rule 65(b), Fed.R.Civ.P., temporary restraining orders may be issued without notice to be effective for a period of fourteen (14) days unless extended or sooner dissolved. Such orders will be entered only in emergency cases to maintain the status quo until the requisite notice may be given and an opportunity is afforded to opposing parties to respond to the application for a preliminary injunction. (See Rule 4.06 of these rules.)

(b) Due to previously scheduled business it will not ordinarily be possible for the Court to interrupt its daily calendar in order to conduct a hearing or entertain oral presentation and argument incident to an application for a temporary restraining order. The Court's decision, of necessity, will usually be made solely on the basis of the complaint and other supporting papers submitted pursuant to this rule. Accordingly, all applications for temporary restraining orders must be presented as follows:

(1) The request for the issuance of the temporary restraining order should be made by a separate motion entitled "Motion for Temporary Restraining Order."

(2) The motion must be supported by allegations of specific facts shown in the verified complaint or accompanying affidavits, not only that the moving party is threatened with irreparable injury, but that such injury is so imminent that notice and a hearing on the application for preliminary injunction is impractical if not impossible (Rule 65(b), Fed.R.Civ.P.).

(3) The motion should also: (i) describe precisely the conduct sought to be enjoined; (ii) set forth facts on which the Court can make a reasoned determination as to the amount of security which must be posted pursuant to Rule 65(c), Fed. R.Civ.P.; (iii) be accompanied by a proposed form of temporary restraining order prepared in strict accordance with the several requirements contained in Rule 65(b) and (d), Fed. R.Civ.P.; and (iv) should contain or be accompanied by a supporting legal memorandum or brief.

(4) The brief or legal memorandum submitted in support of the motion must address the following issues: (i) the likelihood that the moving party will ultimately prevail on the merits of the claim; (ii) the irreparable nature of the threatened injury and the reason that notice cannot be given; (iii) the potential harm that might be caused to the opposing parties or others if the order is issued; and (iv) the public interest, if any.

(5) If a temporary restraining order is issued by the Court it will be the responsibility of the successful movant to obtain immediate service of process upon the defendants, or parties enjoined, pursuant to Rule 4, Fed.R.Civ.P. In addition to the summons, complaint and temporary restraining order, the papers served must also include all motions, briefs, affidavits and exhibits submitted to the Court, as well as such additional affidavits or other papers upon which the moving party will rely in seeking to convert the temporary restraining order into a preliminary injunction. The papers so served must also include a notice of the hearing time fixed by the Court for consideration of the application for preliminary injunction. The hearing will usually be scheduled within fourteen (14) days or prior to expiration of the temporary restraining order under Rule 65(b), Fed.R.Civ.P.

(6) If a temporary restraining order is denied; and if the reason for the denial would not, as a matter of law, also preclude the issuance of a preliminary injunction; and if the

moving party desires to pursue the request for a preliminary injunction; then the requirements of the preceding paragraph (5), and the remaining provisions of this rule, shall apply to the same extent as if a temporary restraining order had been issued.

[Amended effective December 1, 2009.]

RULE 4.06 PRELIMINARY INJUNCTIONS

(a) A preliminary injunction may not be issued absent notice (Rule 65(a)(1), Fed.R.Civ.P.), which must be given at least fourteen (14) days in advance of the hearing (Rule 6(c), Fed.R.Civ.P.).

(b) All hearings scheduled on applications for a preliminary injunction will be limited in the usual course to argument of counsel unless the Court grants express leave to the contrary in advance of the hearing pursuant to Rule 43(e), Fed.R.Civ.P. In order to develop a record and the positions of the parties in advance of the hearing, the following procedure shall apply:

(1) The party applying for the preliminary injunction shall fully comply with the procedural requirements of Rule 4.05(b)(1) through (b)(5) of these rules pertaining to temporary restraining orders.

(2) Service of all papers and affidavits upon which the moving party intends to rely must be served with the motion (Rule 6(c), Fed.R.Civ.P.).

(3) The party or parties opposing the application must file with the Clerk's Office, and deliver to the moving party, all counter or opposing affidavits, and a responsive brief, not later than at least seven (7) days before the hearing (Rule 6(c), Fed.R.Civ.P.).

(4) Lengthy briefs, affidavits and other papers are counter-productive and should be avoided. If the parties desire additional time to prepare, and so stipulate in writing, the scheduled hearing may be postponed and the temporary restraining order (if one has been issued) will be extended as provided in Rule 65(b), Fed.R.Civ.P. In the event the hearing is postponed, any additional papers must be filed in advance of the rescheduled hearing according to the time periods specified in paragraphs (2) and (3) above (as required by Rule 6(d), Fed.R.Civ.P.).

[Amended effective December 1, 2009.]

RULE 4.07 IN FORMA PAUPERIS PROCEEDINGS

(a) Cases commenced in forma pauperis with appropriate affidavit of indigency pursuant to 28 U.S.C. Section 1915, or other applicable statutes (including such proceedings initiated by prisoners under 28 U.S.C. Sections 2254 or 2255), shall be docketed and assigned by the Clerk in accordance with Rules 1.03 or 1.04 as in any other case; provided, however, the case shall then be transmitted, prior to issuance of any process, to the judge to whom the case has been assigned. The Court may dismiss the case if satisfied that the action is frivolous or malicious, as provided by 28 U.S.C. Section 1915(e); or may enter such other orders as shall seem appropriate to the pendency of the cause, including an order that the party seeking leave to proceed in forma pauperis shall pay a stated portion of the Clerk's and/or Marshal's fees within a prescribed time, failing which the action may be dismissed without prejudice. (See also Rule 4.14.)

(b) All persons applying to proceed in forma pauperis shall be deemed to have consented to the entry of an order by the Court directing payment of all non-prepaid fees and costs out of any recovery, including a reasonable attorney's fee if counsel has been appointed by the Court to represent such person.

[Amended effective July 1, 2002.]

RULE 4.08 SERVICE OF SUBPOENAS ON STATE AND FEDERAL OFFICERS

(a)* Absent prior permission of the Court, no party shall cause to be issued and served any subpoena requiring the attendance, for deposition or for trial, of any state or federal judicial officer, or other person then holding an elective state or federal office.

* So in original. No subparagraph (b) was promulgated.

RULE 4.09 MARSHAL'S DEEDS

(a)* Unless otherwise ordered by the Court, Marshal's deeds for property sold in execution or upon foreclosure or other order or decree of the Court shall not be acknowledged or delivered until ten (10) days after the date of sale and thereafter pending a ruling by the Court upon objections or other applications, if any, filed within such fourteen (14) day period.

* So in original. No subparagraph (b) was promulgated.

[Amended effective December 1, 2009.]

RULE 4.10 RELEASE OF INFORMATION

(a) All government personnel, including Marshals, Deputy Marshals, Court Clerks, Deputy Clerks, Probation Officers, and Court Reporters, among others, together with state or federal law enforcement personnel associated or assisting in the preparation or trial of a criminal case, are prohibited from disclosing for dissemination by any means of public communication, without authorization by the Court, information relating to an imminent or pending criminal case that is not part of the public records of the Court.

(b) It is the duty of the lawyer not to release or authorize the release of information or opinion for dissemination by any means of public communication in connection with pending or imminent criminal litigation with which he is associated, if there is a reasonable likelihood that such dissemination will interfere with a fair trial or otherwise prejudice the due administration of justice. Where there is any such reasonable likelihood, the following will apply:

(1) With respect to a grand jury or other pending investigation of any criminal matter, a lawyer participating in the investigation shall refrain from making any extrajudicial statement, for dissemination by any means of public communication, that goes beyond the public record or that is not necessary to inform the public that the investigation is underway, to describe the general scope of the investigation, to obtain

assistance in the apprehension of a suspect, to warn the public of any dangers, or otherwise to aid in the investigation.

(2) From the time of arrest, issuance of an arrest warrant, or the filing of a complaint, information, or indictment in any criminal matter until the commencement of trial or disposition without trial, a lawyer associated with the prosecution or defense shall not release or authorize release of any extrajudicial statement, for dissemination by any means of public communication, relating to that matter and concerning: (i) the prior criminal record (including arrests, indictments, or other charges of crime), or the character or reputation of the accused, except that the lawyer may make a factual statement of the accused's name, age, residence, occupation, and family status, and if the accused has not been apprehended, a lawyer associated with the prosecution may release any information necessary to aid in his apprehension or to warn the public of any dangers he may present; (ii) the existence or contents of any confession, admission, or statement given by the accused, or the refusal or failure of the accused to make any statement; (iii) the performance of any examinations or tests or the accused's refusal or failure to submit to an examination or test; (iv) the identity, testimony or credibility of prospective witnesses, except that the lawyer may announce the identity of the victim if the announcement is not otherwise prohibited by law; (v) the possibility of a plea of guilty to the offense charged or a lesser offense; or (vi) any opinion as to the accused's guilt or innocence or as to the merits of the case or the evidence in the case.

(c) The foregoing provisions of subsection (b) of this rule shall not be construed to preclude the lawyer, in the proper discharge of his official or professional obligations, from announcing the fact and circumstances of arrest (including time and place of arrest, resistance, pursuit, and use of weapons), the identity of the investigating and arresting officer or agency, and the length of time of seizure of any physical evidence other than a confession, admission, or statement, which is limited to a description of the evidence seized; from disclosing the nature, substance, or text of the charge, including a brief description of the offense charged; from quoting or referring without comment to public records of the court in the case; from announcing the scheduling or result of any stage in the judicial process; from requesting assistance in obtaining evidence; or from announcing without further comment that the accused denies the charges made against him.

(d) During the trial of any criminal matter, including the period of selection of the jury, no lawyer associated with the prosecution or defense shall give or authorize any extrajudicial statement or interview, relating to the trial or the parties or issues in the trial, for dissemination by any means of public communication, except that the lawyer may quote from or refer without comment to public records of the court in the case.

(e) Unless otherwise provided by law, all preliminary criminal proceedings including preliminary examinations and hearings on pretrial motions, shall be held in open court and shall be available for attendance and observation by the public; provided that, upon motion made or agreed to by the defense, the Court, in the exercise of its discretion, may order that a pretrial proceeding be closed to the public in whole or in part, on the grounds:

(1) that there is a reasonable likelihood that the dissemination of information disclosed at such proceeding would impair the defendant's right to a fair trial; and

(2) that reasonable alternatives to closure will not adequately protect defendant's right to a fair trial.

If the Court so orders, it shall state for the record its specific findings concerning the need for closure.

(f) Nothing in this rule is intended to preclude the formulation or application of more restrictive rules relating to the release of information about juvenile or other offenders, to preclude the holding of hearings or the lawful issuance of reports by legislative, administrative, or investigative bodies, or to preclude any lawyer from replying to charges of misconduct that are publicly made against him.

(g) In a widely publicized or sensational case, the Court on motion of either party or on its own motion, may issue a special order governing such matters as extrajudicial statements by parties and witnesses likely to interfere with the rights of any party to a fair trial by an impartial jury, the seating and conduct in the courtroom of spectators and news media representatives, the management and sequestration of jurors and witnesses, and any other matters which the Court may deem appropriate for inclusion in such an order.

RULE 4.11 PHOTOGRAPHS; BROADCASTING OR TELEVISING; USE OF COMPUTERS AND COMMUNICATION DEVICES

(a)(1) As approved by the Judicial Conference of the United States at its March, 1979 meeting, the taking of photographs and the recording or taping of ceremonies for the investing of judicial officers and of naturalization proceedings and the possession of necessary equipment therefor is authorized in courtrooms of this Court and the environs thereof. At least three (3) hours prior notice of the use of recording or television equipment shall be given to the presiding judge who may control the placement of such equipment in the courtroom.

(a)(2) Otherwise, the taking of photographs, the operation of recording or transmission devices, and the broadcasting or televising of proceedings in any courtroom or hearing room of this Court, or the environs thereof, either while the Court is in session or at recesses between sessions when Court officials, attorneys, jurors, witnesses or other persons connected with judicial proceedings of any kind are present, are prohibited.

(b) In order to facilitate the enforcement of subsection (a)(2) of this rule, no photographic, broadcasting, television, sound or recording equipment of any kind (except that of Court personnel and as authorized by subsection (a)(1) hereof) will be permitted in that part of any building where federal judicial proceedings of any kind are usually conducted in this District, as is designated by the resident judges of the Division in which such building is located. Such designation shall be made by order, filed in the office of the Clerk in such division. Except that of Court personnel, cellular telephones and computer equipment are likewise prohibited in that part of any building where federal judicial proceedings of any kind are usually conducted in this District, as designated by the resident judges in the manner set forth in the preceding sentence, unless otherwise permitted by the judicial officer before whom the particular case or proceeding is pending. This rule does not prohibit the possession of telephonic pagers in such locations, provided that such pagers are either switched off or placed in a silent activation mode while in such locations.

(c) Employees of other federal agencies resident within the security perimeters of buildings in this District housing federal courts or proceedings, with valid agency identification, are permitted to transport any of the equipment identified above through security checkpoints for the purpose of using same, in their official capacities, within areas of such buildings not covered by subsection (b) of this rule. Said equipment shall be subject to inspection by the United States Marshals Service.

[Amended effective October 1, 1997.]

RULE 4.12 PRE–SENTENCE INVESTIGATION REPORTS; PRE–SENTENCING PROCEDURES

(a) Ordinarily, sentencing will occur within seventy-five (75) calendar days following the defendant's plea of guilt or nolo contendere, or upon being found guilty. The Court may either shorten or lengthen for good cause the time limits prescribed in this rule. On request, the defendant's counsel is entitled to notice and a reasonable opportunity to attend any interview of the defendant by the probation officer in the course of a presentence investigation.

(b) Not less than thirty-five (35) days prior to the date set for sentencing, the probation officer shall disclose the presentence investigation report to the defendant and to counsel for the defendant and the Government, unless the defendant waives this minimum period. Within fourteen (14) days thereafter, counsel (or the defendant if acting pro se) shall communicate in writing to the probation officer and to each other any objections they may have as to any material information, sentencing classifications, sentencing guideline ranges, and policy statements contained in or omitted from the report.

(c) After receiving counsel's objections, the probation officer shall conduct any further investigation and make any revisions to the presentence report that may be necessary. The officer may require counsel for both parties as well as the defendant and/or the case agent to meet with the officer to discuss unresolved factual and legal issues. All counsel shall make themselves available to the officer for this purpose on short notice regardless of place of residence.

(d) No later than seven (7) days prior to the date of the sentencing hearing, the probation officer shall submit the presentence report to the sentencing judge. The report shall be accompanied by an addendum setting forth any objections counsel may have made that have not been resolved, together with the officer's comments thereon. The probation officer shall certify that the contents of the report including any revisions thereof, have been disclosed to the defendant and to counsel for the defendant and the Government, that the content of the addendum has been communicated to the defendant and to counsel, and that the addendum fairly states any remaining objections.

(e) Except for any objection made under subdivision (b) that has not been resolved, the Court, at the sentencing, may accept the presentence report as its findings of fact. The Court, however, for good cause shown, may allow a new objection to be raised at any time before the imposition of sentence. In resolving disputed issues of fact, the Court may consider any reliable information presented by the probation officer, the defendant or the Government.

(f) The Court directs the probation officer not to disclose the probation officer's recommendation, if any, on the sentence, pursuant to its authority in Rule 32(e)(3).

(g) The presentence report shall be deemed to have been disclosed:

1. When a copy of the report is physically delivered.

2. One day after the report's availability for inspection is orally communicated.

3. Three (3) days after a copy of the report or notice of its availability is mailed.

(h) No confidential records of the Court maintained at the probation office, including presentence reports and probation supervision reports, shall be sought by any applicant except by written petition to the Court establishing with particularity the need for specific information believed to be contained in such records. When a demand for disclosure of such information for such records is made by way of subpoena or other judicial process served upon a probation officer of this Court, the probation officer may file a petition seeking instruction from the Court with respect to the manner in which he should respond to such subpoena or such process.

(i) Any party filing an appeal or cross appeal in any criminal case in which it is expected that an issue will be asserted pursuant to 18 U.S.C. Section 3742 concerning the sentence imposed by the Court shall immediately notify the probation officer who shall then file with the Clerk for inclusion in the record in camera a copy of the presentence investigation report. The probation officer shall also furnish, at the same time, a copy of the presentence report to the Government and to the defendant.

[Amended effective January 1, 1988; January 1, 1989; March 1, 1991; February 1, 1995; May 11, 2006.]

RULE 4.13 COURT PLANS

(a) Pursuant to the requirements of the Criminal Justice Act of 1964, as amended, 18 U.S.C. Section 3006A, the Court has adopted, with the approval of the Judicial Council of the Eleventh Circuit, a plan for the assignment of counsel to represent indigent defendants in criminal proceedings pursuant to Rule 44, Fed.R.Cr.P. A copy of the plan, as amended, shall be available for inspection in the Clerk's offices during regular business hours.

(b) Pursuant to the requirements of the Jury Selection and Service Act of 1968, as amended, 28 U.S.C. Section 1863, the Court has adopted, with the approval of the Judicial Council of the Eleventh Circuit, a plan for the random selection of grand

and petit jurors. A copy of the plan, as amended, shall be available for inspection in the Clerk's offices during regular business hours.

(c) Pursuant to the requirements of the Speedy Trial Act of 1974, 18 U.S.C. Section 3165, and Rule 50(b), Fed.R.Cr.P., the Court has adopted, with the approval of the Judicial Council of the Eleventh Circuit, a plan to minimize undue delay and further prompt disposition of criminal cases. A copy of the plan, as amended, shall be available for inspection in the Clerk's offices during regular business hours.

RULE 4.14 PROCEEDINGS UNDER 28 U.S.C. SECTIONS 2254 AND 2255

(a) All proceedings instituted in this Court pursuant to 28 U.S.C. Sections 2254 and 2255, respectively, shall be governed by the Rules pertaining to such proceedings as prescribed by the Supreme Court of the United States, including the model forms appended thereto.

(b) In proceedings instituted in forma pauperis under 28 U.S.C. Section 2254 and 42 U.S.C. Section 1983 by persons in custody, the Court may order, as a condition to allowing the case to proceed, that the Clerk's and Marshal's fees be paid by the petitioner if it appears that he has $25.00 or more to his credit (in Section 2254 cases), or $120.00 or more to his credit (in Section 1983 cases), in any account maintained for him by custodial authorities.

RULE 4.15 WRITTEN STIPULATIONS REQUIRED

(a)* No stipulation or agreement between any parties or their attorneys, the existence of which is not conceded, in relation to any aspect of any pending case, will be considered by the Court unless the same is made before the Court and noted in the record or is reduced to writing and subscribed by the party or attorney against whom it is asserted.

* So in original. No subparagraph (b) was promulgated.

RULE 4.16 MANAGEMENT OF FUNDS HELD ON DEPOSIT WITH THIS COURT

(a) Any party wishing to deposit funds pursuant to Rule 67, Fed.R.Civ.P., may do so upon notice to every other party and upon leave of Court. The party making the deposit should prepare an order for entry by the Court. Absent good cause shown, the order should direct the Clerk of Court to deposit the funds into a special interest bearing account. Pursuant to Rule 67, Fed.R.Civ.P., the party making the deposit shall also serve a copy of the order upon either the Clerk of Court, the Chief Deputy Clerk, the Chief Financial Deputy Clerk, or the appropriate resident clerk's office Division Manager. Absent personal service upon one of those individuals, the Clerk of Court and members of his staff shall be relieved and discharged of any personal liability which might result from non-compliance with the deposit instructions contained in the order or in this Rule.

(b) Except for funds held by the Clerk as non-appropriated funds, as provided in the Guidelines and Plan for the Administration of Non–Appropriated Funds adopted by the Middle District of Florida, funds deposited with the Court that are not governed by subsection (a) of this Rule shall be deposited by the Clerk into the treasury of the United States; provided, however, that the Court may, by administrative order, permit deposit of registry funds into interest bearing accounts when the amount to be deposited exceeds a minimum sum stated in the administrative order. Final disposition of such deposits, as well as any earned interest, shall be determined by subsequent order of the Court.

[Amended effective January 1, 1988; May 15, 2004.]

RULE 4.17 SPECIAL FILING AND PROCEDURAL REQUIREMENTS APPLICABLE TO HABEAS CORPUS CAPITAL CASES

(a) Applicability. The provisions of this Rule shall only apply to those habeas corpus capital cases brought pursuant to 28 U.S.C. Section 2254 in which a Florida state court has imposed a sentence of death, a death warrant has been signed and the petitioner's execution has been scheduled.

In view of the limited time normally available to the Court to fully consider the merits of a habeas corpus petition under such conditions, special filing and procedural requirements addressed in this Rule shall apply, except to the extent that in the opinion of the assigned judge their application in a particular proceeding would not be feasible or would work an injustice.

(b) Responsibility for Lodging a Complete Copy of the State Court Record. In any habeas corpus capital case falling within the scope of this Rule, the Attorney General's Office for the State of Florida shall promptly lodge with the appropriate divisional clerk's office an "Advance Appendix" containing a complete copy of the state court record. The appendix shall include, but not be limited to the record of: pretrial proceedings; guilt/innocence phase of trial proceedings; sentencing proceedings; and direct state court appeal and collateral proceedings including the appeal of post-trial motions. Any portion of the state court record that is not immediately available due to ongoing state court proceedings, shall be lodged immediately thereafter in the form of a "Supplemental Appendix."

(c) Responsibility for Indexing and Tabbing the Appendices. Coincident with the lodging of any appendices, the Attorney General's Office shall also be responsible for:

(1) Preparing and lodging a Master Index to each appendix;

(2) Tabbing the first page of every appendix document and cross referencing the index tab number to the appropriate item on the Index; and

(3) Serving a copy of each Index on counsel for the petitioner and lodging a Certificate of Service to indicate compliance with this requirement.

(d) Manner of Service. In order to facilitate the timely and efficient processing of habeas corpus capital cases, all pleadings and other papers tendered for filing shall be served on opposing counsel by the most expeditious means available, including use of overnight mail delivery service.

(e) Order to Answer. Counsel for the respondent is hereby directed to file an answer to the petition immediately following receipt of the served petition and shall not await further Court order.

(f) Disposition of Appendices. The petition and/or answer may refer to any portion of the appendices lodged with the Clerk by citing to the appropriate tab number and page. All appendices lodged with the Clerk pursuant to Rule 4.17(b) shall be filed in the district court record upon the receipt and filing of a petition for writ of habeas corpus.

In the event the petitioner receives a stay of execution at the state court level, the Clerk shall return the lodged appendices to the Attorney General's Office.

[Added effective February 1, 1986.]

RULE 4.18 APPLICATIONS FOR COSTS OR ATTORNEY'S FEES

(a)* In accordance with Fed.R.Civ.P. 54, all claims for costs or attorney's fees preserved by appropriate pleading or pretrial stipulation shall be asserted by separate motion or petition filed not later than fourteen (14) days following the entry of judgment. The pendency of an appeal from the judgment shall not postpone the filing of a timely application pursuant to this rule.**

[Added effective March 15, 1989. Amended effective February 1, 1994.]

* So in original. No subparagraph (b) was promulgated.

** **[Publisher's Note:** With respect to attorney fee applications in Social Security matters, see the Court's order dated November 13, 2012, In re: Procedures for Applying for Attorney's Fees Under 42 U.S.C. §§ 406(b) and 1382(d)(2), *post.*]

RULE 4.19 PROVISION OF PRETRIAL SERVICES

(a) Pretrial services within the purview of 18 U.S.C. Section 3152 et seq. shall be supervised and provided by the Chief Pretrial Services Officer of this Court pursuant to 18 U.S.C. Section 3152(a). Any federal officer taking or receiving custody of a defendant in the Middle District of Florida shall immediately notify the pretrial services office of such detention, the name of the defendant, the charge(s) against him, and the place in which the defendant is being detained. A pretrial services officer shall then interview the defendant as soon as practicable at his place of confinement or, if the defendant has been released, at such other places as the pretrial services office shall specify.

(b) No confidential records of the Court maintained at the pretrial services office shall be sought by any applicant except by written petition to the Court establishing with particularity the need for specific information believed to be contained in such records. When a demand for disclosure of such information or such records is made by way of subpoena or other judicial process served upon a pretrial services officer of this Court, the pretrial services officer may file a petition seeking instruction from the Court with respect to the manner in which he should respond to such subpoena or such process.

[Added effective March 1, 1991. Amended effective May 11, 2006.]

CHAPTER FIVE. TRIAL AND COURTROOM PROCEDURES

RULE 5.01 JURIES—SELECTION; INSTRUCTIONS; PROHIBITION OF POST–TRIAL INTERVIEWS

(a) In all civil cases tried by jury, in accordance with Fed.R.Civ.P. 48, the jury shall consist of 6 to 12 persons as the Court may specify.

(b) The method of voir dire examination and exercise of challenges in selection of the jury shall be as specified by the presiding judge. A list of the venire will be furnished to counsel only at the time the case is called for trial, and prior to commencement of voir dire examination (unless otherwise required by governing rule or statute), and must be returned to the Clerk when the jury is empaneled. No person shall copy from or reproduce, in whole or in part, any list of veniremen.

(c) All requests for instructions to the jury shall be submitted in writing within the time specified by the presiding judge. Such requests, and supplemental requests, if any, shall be marked with the name and number of the case; shall designate the party submitting the request; shall be numbered in sequence; and shall contain citation of supporting authorities, if any.

(d) No attorney or party shall undertake, directly or indirectly, to interview any juror after trial in any civil or criminal case except as permitted by this Rule. If a party believes that grounds for legal challenge to a verdict exist, he may move for an order permitting an interview of a juror or jurors to determine whether the verdict is subject to the challenge. The motion shall be served within fourteen (14) days after rendition of the verdict unless good cause is shown for the failure to make the motion within that time. The motion shall state the name and address of each juror to be interviewed and the grounds for the challenge that the moving party believes may exist. The presiding judge may conduct such hearings, if any, as necessary, and shall enter an order denying the motion or permitting the interview. If the interview is permitted, the Court may prescribe the place, manner, conditions, and scope of the interview.

[Amended effective May 2, 1988; February 1, 1993; December 1, 2009.]

RULE 5.02 MARSHAL TO ATTEND COURT

(a)* Unless excused by the presiding judge, the United States Marshal of this District, or his Deputy, shall be in attendance during all sessions of any kind conducted in open court.

* So in original. No subparagraph (b) was promulgated.

RULE 5.03 COURTROOM DECORUM

(a) The purpose of this rule is to state, for the guidance of those heretofore unfamiliar with the traditions of this Court, certain basic principles concerning courtroom behavior and decorum. The requirements stated in this rule are minimal, not all-inclusive; and are intended to emphasize and supplement, not supplant or limit, the ethical obligations of counsel under the Code of Professional Responsibility or the time honored customs of experienced trial counsel. Individual judges of the Court may, in any case, or generally, announce and enforce additional prohibitions or requirements; or may excuse compliance with any one or more of the provisions of this rule.

(b) When appearing in this Court, unless excused by the presiding Judge, all counsel (including, where the context applies, all persons at counsel table) shall abide by the following:

(1) Stand as Court is opened, recessed or adjourned.

(2) Stand when the jury enters or retires from the courtroom.

(3) Stand when addressing, or being addressed by, the Court.

(4) Stand at the lectern while examining any witness; except that counsel may approach the Clerk's desk or the witness for purposes of handling or tendering exhibits.

(5) Stand at the lectern while making opening statements or closing arguments.

(6) Address all remarks to the Court, not to opposing counsel.

(7) Avoid disparaging personal remarks or acrimony toward opposing counsel and remain wholly detached from any ill feeling between the litigants or witnesses.

(8) Refer to all persons, including witnesses, other counsel and the parties by their surnames and not by their first or given names.

(9) Only one attorney for each party shall examine, or cross examine each witness. The attorney stating objections, if any, during direct examination, shall be the attorney recognized for cross examination.

(10) Counsel should request permission before approaching the bench; and any documents counsel wish to have the Court examine should be handed to the Clerk.

(11) Any paper or exhibit not previously marked for identification (see Rule 3.07) should first be handed to the Clerk to be marked before it is tendered to a witness for his examination; and any exhibit offered in evidence should, at the time of such offer, be handed to opposing counsel.

(12) In making objections counsel should state only the legal grounds for the objection and should withhold all further comment or argument unless elaboration is requested by the Court.

(13) In examining a witness, counsel shall not repeat or echo the answer given by the witness.

(14) Offers of, or requests for, a stipulation should be made privately, not within the hearing of the jury.

(15) In opening statements and in arguments to the jury, counsel shall not express personal knowledge or opinion concerning any matter in issue; shall not read or purport to read from deposition or trial transcripts, and shall not suggest to the jury, directly or indirectly, that it may or should request transcripts or the reading of any testimony by the reporter.

(16) Counsel shall admonish all persons at counsel table that gestures, facial expressions, audible comments, or the like, as manifestations of approval or disapproval during the testimony of witnesses, or at any other time, are absolutely prohibited.

RULE 5.04 DISPOSITION OF EXHIBITS AND DISCOVERY MATERIALS

(a) Sensitive Exhibits and Exhibits Other Than Documents. Sensitive exhibits shall include, but are not necessarily limited to, drugs, weapons, currency, exhibits of a pornographic nature, and articles of high monetary value. When offering sensitive exhibits and exhibits other than documents into evidence, offering counsel shall also offer photographs of the exhibits. Counsel will be deemed by the Court to stipulate to substitution of the photographs for the exhibits in the record on appeal, unless otherwise ordered by the Court.

(b) Documentary Exhibits Larger Than 8½″ × 11″. When offering into evidence a documentary exhibit larger or smaller than 8½″ × 11″, counsel shall also offer an 8½″ × 11″ reduction or enlargement of the exhibit. Counsel will be deemed by the Court to stipulate to the substitution of the 8½″ × 11″ reduction or enlargement for the exhibits in the record on appeal, unless otherwise ordered by the Court.

(c) Clerk's Disposition Schedule. The Clerk shall dispose of exhibits in accordance with the following schedule:

(1) *Sensitive Exhibits.* Sensitive exhibits offered or received into evidence or otherwise filed with the Clerk during any proceeding in this Court shall be maintained in the custody of the Clerk during the hours in which the Court is in session. At the conclusion of each daily proceeding, and when Court recesses if the presiding judge so directs, the Clerk shall return all sensitive exhibits to offering counsel or their delegates who shall then be responsible for maintaining custody and the integrity of such exhibits until the next session of Court at which time they shall be returned to the Clerk. After a verdict is rendered in a jury case or final order is entered in a non-jury case, with the approval of the presiding judge, the Clerk shall immediately return custody of sensitive exhibits to the offering or filing counsel. It shall be the responsibility of counsel to safely maintain all exhibits thus returned during the time permitted for an appeal and thereafter during the pendency of an appeal should one be taken.

(2) *Documents Larger Than 8½″ × 11″ and Exhibits Other Than Documents.* A document larger or smaller than 8½″ × 11″ or an exhibit other than a document offered or received into evidence or otherwise filed with the Clerk during any proceeding in this Court shall be delivered to and kept by the Clerk until a verdict is rendered in a jury case or until the entry of a final order by the Court in a non-jury case. Thereafter, unless otherwise ordered by the Court, the Clerk shall immediately return custody of the exhibit to the offering or filing counsel. It shall be the responsibility of counsel to safely maintain all exhibits thus returned to counsel during the time permitted for filing an appeal and during the pendency of

any appeal should one be taken. The Clerk shall handle and dispose of any photograph or reduction offered with an exhibit in the manner described in subsection (3) below unless otherwise ordered by the Court.

(3) *Other Exhibits and Discovery Materials.* Other exhibits and discovery materials offered or received in evidence or otherwise filed with the Clerk during any proceeding in this Court and any photographs or reductions offered pursuant to subsections (a) and (b) shall be delivered to the Clerk who shall keep them in custody unless otherwise ordered by the Court, except that the Clerk may, without special order, permit an official court reporter to retain custody pending preparation of the transcript and transmit such items to a court of appeals. All such exhibits, discovery materials, photographs and reductions remaining in the custody of the Clerk shall be taken away by counsel within three (3) months after the case is finally decided, unless an appeal is taken in the United States Court of Appeals for the Eleventh Circuit. It shall be the responsibility of counsel to safely maintain exhibits thus taken away during the time permitted for an appeal with any other court and thereafter during the pendency of an appeal with such court should one be taken. In all cases in which an appeal is taken with the United States Court of Appeals for the Eleventh Circuit, all exhibits, photographs and reductions shall be taken away within thirty (30) days after the filing and recording of the mandate of that court.

(d) Destruction of Exhibits. The Clerk may notify counsel in writing of the requirement that exhibits, discovery materials, photographs, and reductions be removed, and if they are not removed within thirty (30) days, the Clerk may destroy them or make such other disposition as the Court may direct.

[Former Rule 5.04 deleted January 18, 1991, effective April 1, 1991. New Rule 5.04 added January 18, 1991, effective April 1, 1991. Amended effective July 1, 2002.]

CHAPTER SIX. UNITED STATES MAGISTRATE JUDGES

RULE 6.01 DUTIES OF UNITED STATES MAGISTRATE JUDGES

(a) In addition to the powers and duties set forth in 28 U.S.C. Section 636(a), the United States Magistrate Judges are hereby authorized, pursuant to 28 U.S.C. Section 636(b), to perform any and all additional duties, as may be assigned to them from time to time by any judge of this Court, which are not inconsistent with the Constitution and laws of the United States.

(b) The assignment of duties to United States Magistrate Judges by the judges of the Court may be made by standing order entered jointly by the resident judges in any Division of the Court; or by any individual judge, in any case or cases assigned to him, through written order or oral directive made or given with respect to such case or cases.

(c) The duties authorized to be performed by United States Magistrate Judges, when assigned to them pursuant to subsection (b) of this rule, shall include, but are not limited to:

(1) Issuance of search warrants upon a determination that probable cause exists, pursuant to Rule 41, Fed.R.Cr.P., and issuance of administrative search warrants upon proper application meeting the requirements of applicable law.

(2) Processing of complaints and issuing appropriate summonses or arrest warrants for the named defendants. (Rule 4, Fed.R.Cr.P.)

(3) Conduct of initial appearance proceedings for defendants, informing them of their rights, admitting them to bail and imposing conditions of release. (Rule 5, Fed.R.Cr.P. and 18 U.S.C. Section 3146.)

(4) Appointment of counsel for indigent persons and administration of the Court's Criminal Justice Act Plan, including maintenance of a register of eligible attorneys and the approval of attorneys' compensation and expense vouchers. (18 U.S.C. Section 3006A; Rule 44, Fed.R.Cr.P.; and Rule 4.13(a) of these rules.)

(5) Conduct of full preliminary examinations. (Rule 5.1, Fed.R.Cr.P. and 18 U.S.C. Section 3060.)

(6) Conduct of removal hearings for defendants charged in other districts, including the issuance of warrants of removal. (Rule 40, Fed.R.Cr.P.)

(7) Issuance of writs of habeas corpus ad testificandum and habeas corpus ad prosequendum. (28 U.S.C. Section 2241(c)(5).)

(8) Setting of bail for material witnesses and holding others to security of the peace and for good behavior. (18 U.S.C. Section 3149 and 18 U.S.C. Section 3043.)

(9) Issuance of warrants and conduct of extradition proceedings pursuant to 18 U.S.C. Section 3184.

(10) The discharge of indigent prisoners or persons imprisoned for debt under process or execution issued by a federal court. (18 U.S.C. Section 3569 and 28 U.S.C. Section 2007.)

(11) Issuance of an attachment or other orders to enforce obedience to an Internal Revenue Service summons to produce records or give testimony. (26 U.S.C. Section 7604(a) and (b).)

(12) Conduct of post-indictment arraignments, acceptance of not guilty pleas, acceptance of guilty pleas in felony cases with the consent of the Defendant, and the ordering of a presentence investigation report concerning any defendant who signifies the desire to plead guilty. (Rules 10, 11(a) and 32(c), Fed.R.Cr.P.)

(13) Acceptance of the return of an indictment by the grand jury, issuance of process thereon and, on motion of the United States, ordering dismissal of an indictment or any separate count thereof. (Rules 6(f) and 48(a), Fed.R.Cr.P.)

(14) Supervision and determination of all pretrial proceedings and motions made in criminal cases through the Court's Omnibus Hearing procedure or otherwise including, without limitation, motions and orders made pursuant to Rules 12, 12.2(c), 15, 16, 17, 17.1 and 28, Fed.R.Cr.P., 18 U.S.C. Section 4244, orders determining excludable time under 18 U.S.C.

Section 3161, and orders dismissing a complaint without prejudice for failure to return a timely indictment under 18 U.S.C. Section 3162; except that a magistrate judge shall not grant a motion to dismiss or quash an indictment or information made by the defendant, or a motion to suppress evidence, but may make recommendations to the Court concerning them.

(15) Conduct of hearings and issuance of orders upon motions arising out of grand jury proceedings including orders entered pursuant to 18 U.S.C. Section 6003, and orders involving enforcement or modification of subpoenas, directing or regulating lineups, photographs, handwriting exemplars, fingerprinting, palm printing, voice identification, medical examinations, and the taking of blood, urine, fingernail, hair and bodily secretion samples (with appropriate medical safeguards).

(16) Conduct of preliminary and final hearings in all probation revocation proceedings, and the preparation of a report and recommendation to the Court as to whether the petition should be granted or denied. (Rule 32.1, Fed.R.Cr.P. and 18 U.S.C. Section 3653.)

(17) Processing and review of habeas corpus petitions filed pursuant to 28 U.S.C. Section 2241, et seq., those filed by state prisoners pursuant to 28 U.S.C. Section 2254, or by federal prisoners pursuant to 28 U.S.C. Section 2255, and civil suits filed by state prisoners under 42 U.S.C. Section 1983, with authority to require responses, issue orders to show cause and such other orders as are necessary to develop a complete record, including the conduct of evidentiary hearings, and the preparation of a report and recommendation to the Court as to appropriate disposition of the petition or claim.

(18) Supervision and determination of all pretrial proceedings and motions made in civil cases including, without limitation, rulings upon all procedural and discovery motions, and conducting pretrial conferences; except that a magistrate judge (absent a stipulation entered into by all affected parties) shall not appoint a receiver, issue an injunctive order pursuant to Rule 65, Fed.R.Civ.P., enter an order dismissing or permitting maintenance of a class action pursuant to Rule 23, Fed. R.Civ.P., enter any order granting judgment on the pleadings or summary judgment in whole or in part pursuant to Rules 12(c) or 56, Fed.R.Civ.P., enter an order of involuntary dismissal pursuant to Rule 41(b) or (c), Fed.R.Civ.P., or enter any other final order or judgment that would be appealable if entered by a judge of the Court, but may make recommendations to the Court concerning them.

(19) Conduct of all proceedings in civil suits, before or after judgment, incident to the issuance of writs of replevin, garnishment, attachment or execution pursuant to governing state or federal law, and the conduct of all proceedings and the entry of all necessary orders in aid of execution pursuant to Rule 69, Fed.R.Civ.P.

(20) Conduct or preside over the voir dire examination and empanelment of trial juries in civil and criminal cases.

(21) Processing and review of all suits instituted under any law of the United States providing for judicial review of final decisions of administrative officers or agencies on the basis of the record of administrative proceedings, and the preparation of a report and recommendation to the Court concerning the disposition of the case.

(22) Serving as a master for the taking of testimony and evidence and the preparation of a report and recommendation for the assessment of damages in admiralty cases, non-jury proceedings under Rule 55(b)(2), Fed.R.Civ.P., or in any other case in which a special reference is made pursuant to Rule 53, Fed.R.Civ.P.

(23) In admiralty cases, entering orders (i) appointing substitute custodians of vessels or property seized in rem; (ii) fixing the amount of security, pursuant to Rule E(5), Supplemental Rules for Certain Admiralty and Maritime Claims, which must be posted by the claimant of a vessel or property seized in rem; (iii) in limitation of liability proceedings, for monition and restraining order including approval of the ad interim stipulation filed with the complaint, establishment of the means of notice to potential claimants and a deadline for the filing of claims; and (iv) to restrain further proceedings against the plaintiff in limitation except by means of the filing of a claim in the limitation proceeding.

(24) Appointing persons to serve process pursuant to Rule 4(c), Fed.R.Civ.P., except that, as to in rem process, such appointments shall be made only when the Marshal has no deputy immediately available to execute the same and the individual appointed has been approved by the Marshal for such purpose.

(25) Processing and review of petitions in civil commitment proceedings under the Narcotic Addict Rehabilitation Act, and the preparation of a report and recommendation concerning the disposition of the petition.

(26) Conduct of proceedings and imposition of civil fines and penalties under the Federal Boat Safety Act. (46 U.S.C. Section 1484(d).)

[Amended effective October 16, 1984; January 1, 1992.]

RULE 6.02 REVIEW OF MAGISTRATE JUDGES' REPORTS AND RECOMMENDATIONS

(a)* In any case in which the magistrate judge is not authorized to enter an operative order pursuant to Rule 6.01, 28 U.S.C. Section 636 or any standing or special order of the Court entered thereunder, but is authorized or directed to file a report or recommendation to the District Judge to whom the case has been assigned, a copy of such report and recommendation shall be furnished, upon filing, to the District Judge and to all parties. Within fourteen (14) days after such service, any party may file and serve written objections thereto; and any party desiring to oppose such objections shall have fourteen (14) days thereafter within which to file and serve a written response. The District Judge may accept, reject, or modify in whole or in part, the report and recommendation of the magistrate judge or may receive further evidence or recommit the matter to the magistrate judge with instructions.

[Amended effective February 1, 1995; December 1, 2009.]

* So in original. No subparagraph (b) was promulgated.

RULE 6.03 MISDEMEANOR AND PETTY OFFENSES

(a) Pursuant to 18 U.S.C. Section 3401, any full time United States Magistrate Judge of this District, sitting with or without a jury, shall have jurisdiction to try persons accused of, and sentence persons convicted of, petty offenses. With consent of the parties, any full time United States Magistrate Judge of this District, sitting with or without a jury, shall have jurisdiction to try persons accused of, and sentence persons convicted of a Class A misdemeanor committed within the District whether originating under an applicable Federal statute or regulation or a state statute or regulation made applicable by 18 U.S.C. Section 13. Cases of misdemeanors may, upon transfer into this District under Rule 20, Fed.R.Cr.P., be referred to a full time United States Magistrate Judge of this District for plea and sentence, upon defendant's consent. In a petty offense case involving a juvenile, any full time United States Magistrate Judge of this District may exercise all powers granted to the District Court under Chapter 403 of Title 18 of the United States Code. In cases of any misdemeanor, other than a petty offense involving a juvenile, in which consent to trial before a Magistrate Judge has been filed, a Magistrate Judge may exercise all powers granted to the District Court under Chapter 403 of Title 18 of the United States Code.

(b) Any person charged with a petty offense as defined in 18 U.S.C. Section 19 may, in lieu of appearance post collateral in the amount indicated for the offense, waive appearance before a magistrate judge, and consent to forfeiture of the collateral. The offenses for which collateral may be posted and forfeited in lieu of appearance by the person charged, together with the amounts of collateral to be posted, shall be specified in standing orders of the Court, in each Division of the Court, copies of which shall be maintained in the offices of the Clerk and the magistrate judges, respectively. For all petty offenses not specified in such standing orders, the person charged must appear before a magistrate judge; and further, nothing contained in this rule shall prohibit a law enforcement officer from arresting a person for the commission of any offense, including those for which collateral may be posted and forfeited, and requiring the person charged to appear before a magistrate judge or, upon arrest, taking him immediately before a magistrate judge.

(c) In the trial of all cases pursuant to this rule, Rule 58, Federal Rules of Criminal Procedure, governs practice and procedure.

[Amended effective July 1, 1984; July 1, 2002.]

RULE 6.04 [RESERVED EFFECTIVE MAY 11, 2006]

RULE 6.05 TRIAL OF CIVIL CASES

(a) Pursuant to 28 U.S.C. Section 636(c)(1), and subject to the provisions of this rule, all full time United States Magistrate Judges in the District are hereby specially designated to conduct any or all proceedings in any jury or nonjury civil matter and order the entry of judgment in the case.

(b) Upon the filing of any civil case the Clerk shall deliver to the Plaintiff(s) written notice of the right of the parties to consent to disposition of the case by a United States Magistrate Judge pursuant to 28 U.S.C. Section 636(c) and the provisions of this rule. The Clerk shall also issue or supply at that time, for each Defendant in the case, copies of such notice which shall be attached to the summons and thereafter served upon the Defendant(s) in the manner provided by Rule 4, Fed.R.Civ.P.; provided, however, that a failure to serve a copy of such notice upon any Defendant shall not affect the validity of the service of process or the jurisdiction of the Court to proceed. If, after the initial filing of a civil case, new or additional parties enter or join in the action pursuant to the operation of any statute, rule or order of the Court, the Clerk shall immediately mail or otherwise deliver a copy of such notice to each such party.

(c) The written notice contemplated by subsection (b) of this rule shall be in such form as the judges of the Court from time to time direct. In addition, the Clerk shall maintain on hand, in a form or forms to be approved by the judges of the Court, written consent agreements for the use of the parties in communicating to the Clerk their unanimous and voluntary consent, upon entry of an order of reference by the presiding district judge, to have all further proceedings in the case, including trial with or without a jury, and the entry of judgment, conducted by a United States Magistrate Judge. One form of such consent agreements shall provide for appeal to the United States Court of Appeals (28 U.S.C. Section 636(c)(3)), and another shall provide for appeal to the presiding district judge (28 U.S.C. Section 636(c)(4)).

(d) If the parties in any civil case unanimously consent to disposition of the case by a United States Magistrate Judge pursuant to 28 U.S.C. Section 636(c) and this rule, such consent must be communicated to the Clerk on an appropriate form (provided by the Clerk in accordance with subsection (c) of this rule). The Clerk shall not accept or file any consent except in the form and manner, and within the time, prescribed by this rule.

(e) In the event the parties file a unanimous consent pursuant to subsection (d) of this rule, the Clerk shall immediately notify the presiding district judge who will promptly (1) enter an order of reference to a United States magistrate judge, or (2) enter an order declining to do so; provided, however, the judges of the Court shall not decline to make an order or orders of reference for the purpose of limiting the types of cases to be tried by the United States magistrate judges pursuant to this rule. In making or in declining to make an order of reference the presiding judge may consider, among other things, the current allocation of pending judicial business between the judges of the Court and the magistrate judges; the judicial economy, if any, to be gained by the reference as measured in part by the extent of prior judicial labor expended and familiarity accumulated in the case by the judge or the magistrate judge, as the case might be; the extent to which the magistrate judge(s) may have time available to devote to the case giving due regard to the necessity of diligent performance of other judicial duties regularly assigned to the magistrate judges; and any other features peculiar to the individual case which suggest, in the interest of justice or judicial economy, that a reference should or should not be made.

(f) In any case in which an order of reference has been made, the presiding judge may, for cause shown on his own motion, or under extraordinary circumstances shown by any party, vacate the order of reference and restore the case to the calendar of the presiding judge.

(g) In all cases in which an order of reference has been made on the basis of a consent agreement providing for appeal to the presiding judge of the District Court pursuant to 28 U.S.C. Section 636(c)(4), any such appeal shall be governed by the applicable Federal Rules of Appellate Procedure relating to appeals in civil cases from the District Court to the Court of Appeals, except that Rules 30, 31(b), and 32, Fed.R.App.P., shall not apply.

(h) Nothing in this rule shall be construed to limit or affect the right of any judge or judges of the Court to assign judicial duties or responsibilities to a United States magistrate judge or magistrate judges pursuant to Rule 6.01, or any standing order entered under that rule, with or without the consent of the parties.

[Amended effective February 1, 1994.]

CHAPTER SEVEN. ADMIRALTY AND MARITIME RULES

RULE 7.01 GENERAL PROVISIONS

(a) Scope of the Local Admiralty and Maritime Rules. The local admiralty and maritime rules apply to the procedures in admiralty and maritime claims within the meaning of Fed.R.Civ.P. 9(h), which in turn are governed by the Supplemental Rules for Certain Admiralty and Maritime Claims of the Federal Rules of Civil Procedure.

(b) Citation Format.

(1) The Supplemental Rules for Certain Admiralty and Maritime Claims of the Federal Rules of Civil Procedure shall be cited as "Supplemental Rule (___)".

(2) The Local Rules of the Middle District of Florida shall be cited as "Local Rule (___)".

(3) The Local Admiralty and Maritime Rules shall be cited as "Local Admiralty Rule (___)".

(c) Application of Local Admiralty and Maritime Rules. The Local Admiralty Rules shall apply to all actions governed by Local Admiralty Rule 7.01(a), and to the extent possible should be construed to be consistent with the other local rules of this Court. To the extent that a Local Admiralty Rule conflicts with another local rule of this Court, the Local Admiralty Rule shall control.

(d) Designation of "In Admiralty" Proceedings. Every complaint filed as a Fed.R.Civ.P. 9(h) action shall boldly set forth the words "IN ADMIRALTY" following the designation of the Court. This requirement is in addition to any statements which may be contained in the body of the complaint.

(e) Verification of Pleadings, Claims and Answers to Interrogatories. Every complaint and claim filed pursuant to Supplemental Rules (B), (C) and/or (D) shall be verified on oath or solemn affirmation by a party, or an officer of a corporate party.

If a party or corporate officer is not within the district, verification of a complaint, claim and/or answers to interrogatories may be made by an agent, an attorney-in-fact, or the attorney of record. Such person shall state briefly the source of his knowledge, or information and belief, and shall declare that the document affirmed is true to the best of his knowledge, and/or information and belief. Additionally, such person shall state that he is authorized to make this representation on behalf of the party or corporate officer, and shall indicate why verification is not made by a party or a corporate officer. Such verification will be deemed to have been made by the party to whom the document might apply as if verified personally.

Any interested party may move the Court, with or without a request for stay, for the personal oath or affirmation of a party or all parties, or that of a corporate officer. If required by the Court, such verification may be obtained by commission, or as otherwise provided by Court order.

(f) Issuance of Process. Except as limited by the provisions of Supplemental Rule (B)(1) and Local Admiralty Rule 7.02(c); or Supplemental Rule (C)(3) and Local Admiralty Rule 7.03(b); or in suits prosecuted in forma pauperis and sought to be filed without prepayment of fees or costs, or without security; all process shall be issued by the Court without further notice of Court.

(g) Publication of Notices. Unless otherwise required by the Court, or applicable Local Admiralty or Supplemental Rule, whenever a notice is required to be published by any statute of the United States, or by any Supplemental Rule or Local Admiralty Rule, such notice shall be published at least once, without further order of Court, in an approved newspaper in the county or counties where the vessel or property was located at the time of arrest, attachment, or seizure, and if different, in the county within the Middle District of Florida where the lawsuit is pending.

For the purposes of this subsection, an approved newspaper shall be a newspaper of general circulation. The newspaper of largest circulation in a county in the Middle District is rebuttably presumed to be a newspaper of general circulation in that same county. For cause shown by a party or on its own motion, the court may require publication in one or more additional publications if necessary to provide notice reasonably calculated to inform interested parties.

(h) Form and Return of Process in In Personam Actions. Unless otherwise ordered by the Court, Fed.R.Civ.P. 9(h) process shall be by civil summons, and shall be returnable twenty-one (21) days after service of process; except that process issued in accordance with Supplemental Rule (B) shall conform to the requirements of that rule.

(i) Judicial Officer Defined. As used in these Local Admiralty Rules, the term "judicial officer" or "Court" shall mean either a United States district judge or a United States magistrate judge.

(j) Appendix of Forms. The forms presented in the Appendix provide an illustration of the format and content of papers filed in admiralty and maritime actions within the Middle District of Florida. While the forms are sufficient, they are neither mandatory nor exhaustive.

(k) Advisory Committee Notes. Chapter Seven of these Rules was prepared and submitted to the Court, at its request, by a Subcommittee of the Admiralty Law Committee of The Florida Bar. The work product of the Subcommittee, as transmitted to the Court, contained explanatory comments following each rule entitled "Notes of Advisory Committee on Local Rules." Such notes have not been adopted by the Court as a part of the Local Admiralty Rules, however, copies of the advisory notes are available in the Office of the Clerk.

[Chapter 7 revised effective February 1, 1986. Amended effective July 1, 1998; December 1, 2009.]

RULE 7.02 ATTACHMENT AND GARNISHMENT: SPECIAL PROVISIONS

(a) Definition of "Not Found Within the District". In an action in personam filed pursuant to Supplemental Rule (B), a defendant shall be considered "not found within the district" if he cannot be served within the Middle District of Florida with the summons and complaint as provided by Fed.R.Civ.P. 4(e)(1) or (2), (g), (h)(1), or (j)(1) or (2).

(b) Verification of Complaint Required. In addition to the specific requirements of Local Admiralty Rule 7.01(e), whenever verification is made by the plaintiff's attorney or agent, and that person does not have personal knowledge, or knowledge acquired in the ordinary course of business of the facts alleged in the complaint, the attorney or agent shall also state the circumstances which make it necessary for that person to make the verification, and shall indicate the source of the attorney's or agent's information.

(c) Pre–Seizure Requirements. In accordance with Supplemental Rule (B)(1), the process of attachment and garnishment shall issue only after one of the following conditions has been met:

(1) *Judicial Review Prior to Issuance.* Except as provided in Local Admiralty Rule 7.02(c)(2), a judicial officer shall first review the verified complaint, and any other relevant case papers, prior to the Clerk issuing the requested process of attachment and garnishment. No notice of this pre-arrest judicial review is required to be given to any person or prospective party.

If the Court finds that probable cause exists to issue the process of attachment and garnishment, plaintiff shall prepare an order for the Court's signature directing the Clerk to issue the process. This order shall substantially conform in format and content to the form identified as MDF 700 in the Appendix of these Local Admiralty Rules.

Upon receipt of the signed order, the Clerk shall file the order and, in accordance with Local Admiralty Rule 7.02(c)(3), issue the summons and process of attachment and garnishment. Thereafter the Clerk may issue supplemental process without further order of Court.

(2) *Certification of Exigent Circumstances.* If the plaintiff files a written certification that exigent circumstances make review by the Court impracticable, the Clerk shall, in accordance with Local Admiralty Rule 7.02(c)(3), issue a summons and the process of attachment and garnishment.

Thereafter at any post-attachment proceedings under Supplemental Rule (E)(4)(f) and Local Admiralty Rule 7.02(e), plaintiff shall have the burden of showing that probable cause existed for the issuance of process, and that exigent circumstances existed which precluded judicial review in accordance with Local Admiralty Rule 7.02(c)(1).

(3) *Preparation and Issuance of the Process of Attachment and Garnishment.* Plaintiff shall prepare the summons and the process of attachment and garnishment, and deliver the documents to the Clerk for filing and issuance.

The process of attachment and garnishment shall substantially conform in format and content to the form identified as MDF 701 in the Appendix to these Local Admiralty Rules, and shall in all cases give adequate notice of the post-seizure provisions of Local Admiralty Rule 7.02(e).

(4) *Marshal's Return of Service.* The Marshal shall file a return of service indicating the date and manner in which service was perfected and, if service was perfected upon a garnishee, the Marshal shall indicate in his return the name, address, and telephone number of the garnishee.

(d) Notification of Seizure to Defendant. In an in personam action under Supplemental Rule (B), it is expected that plaintiff and/or garnishee will initially attempt to perfect service of the notice in accordance with Supplemental Rule (B)(2)(a) or (b).

However, when service of the notice cannot be perfected in accordance with Supplemental Rule (B)(2)(a) or (b), plaintiff and/or garnishee should then attempt to perfect service in accordance with Supplemental Rule (B)(2)(c). In this regard, service of process shall be sufficiently served by leaving a copy of the process of attachment and garnishment with the defendant or garnishee at his usual place of business.

(e) Post–Attachment Review Proceedings.

(1) *Filing a Required Answer.* In accordance with Supplemental Rule (E)(4)(f), any person who claims an interest in property seized pursuant to Supplemental Rule (B) must file an answer and claim against the property. The answer and claim shall describe the nature of the claimant's interest in the property, and shall articulate reasons why the seizure should be vacated. The claimant shall serve a copy of the answer and claim upon plaintiff's counsel, the Marshal, and any other party to the litigation. The claimant shall also file a Certificate of Service indicating the date and manner in which service was perfected.

(2) *Hearing on the Answer and Claim.* The claimant may be heard before a judicial officer not less than three (3) days after the answer and claim has been filed and service has been perfected upon the plaintiff.

If the Court orders that the seizure be vacated, the judicial officer shall also award attorney's fees, costs and other expenses incurred by any party as a result of the seizure.

If the seizure was predicated upon a showing of "exigent circumstances" under Local Admiralty Rule 7.02(c)(2), and the Court finds that such exigent circumstances did not exist, the judicial officer shall award attorney's fees, costs, and other expenses incurred by any party as a result of the seizure.

(f) Procedural Requirements for the Entry of Default. In accordance with Rule 55, Fed.R.Civ.P. and Local Rule 1.07(b), a party seeking the entry of default in a Supplemental Rule (B) action shall file a motion and supporting legal memorandum in accordance with Local Rule 3.01, and shall offer other proof sufficient to demonstrate that due notice of the action and seizure have been given in accordance with Local Admiralty Rule 7.02(d).

Upon review of the motion, memorandum, and other proof, the Clerk shall, where appropriate, enter default in accordance with Rule 55(a), Fed.R.Civ.P. Thereafter, the Clerk shall serve notice of the entry of default upon all parties represented in the action.

(g) Procedural Requirements for the Entry of Default Judgment. Not sooner than seven (7) nor later than thirty (30) days following notice of the entry of default, the party seeking the entry of default judgment shall file a motion and supporting legal memorandum in accordance with Local Rule 3.01, along with other appropriate exhibits to the motion sufficient to support the entry of default judgment. The moving party shall serve these papers upon every other party to the action and file a Certificate of Service indicating the date and manner in which service was perfected.

A party opposing the entry of default judgment shall have seven (7) days from the receipt of the motion to file written opposition with the Court. Thereafter, unless otherwise ordered by the Court, the motion for the entry of default judgment will be heard without oral argument.

If the Court grants the motion and enters the default judgment, such judgment shall establish a right on the part of the party or parties in which favor it is entered. The judgment shall be considered prior to any claims of the owner of the defendant property against which it is entered, and to the remnants and surpluses thereof; providing, however, that such a judgment shall not establish any entitlement to the defendant property having priority over non-possessory lien claimants. Obtaining a judgment by default shall not preclude the party in whose favor it is entered from contending and proving that all, or any portion, of the claim or claims encompassed within the judgment are prior to any such non-possessory lien claims.

[Chapter 7 revised effective February 1, 1986. Amended effective February 1, 1995; December 1, 2009.]

RULE 7.03 ACTION IN REM

(a) Verification Requirements. Every complaint and claim filed in an in rem proceeding pursuant to Supplemental Rule (C) shall be verified in accordance with Local Admiralty Rules 7.01(e) and 7.02(b).

(b) Pre–Seizure Requirements. In accordance with Supplemental Rule (C)(3), the process of arrest in rem shall issue only after one of the following conditions has been met:

(1) *Judicial Review Prior to Issuance.* Except as provided in Local Admiralty Rule 7.03(b)(2), a judicial officer shall first review the verified complaint, and any other relevant case papers, prior to the Clerk issuing the warrant of arrest and/or summons in rem. No notice of this pre-seizure judicial review is required to be given to any person or prospective party.

If the Court finds that probable cause exists for an action in rem, plaintiff shall prepare an order for the Court's signature directing the Clerk to issue a warrant of arrest and/or summons. This order shall substantially conform in format and content to the form identified as MDF 702 in the Appendix to these Local Admiralty Rules.

Upon receipt of the signed order, the Clerk shall file the order and, in accordance with Local Admiralty Rule 7.03(b)(3) issue the warrant of arrest and/or summons. Thereafter the Clerk may issue supplemental process without further order of the Court.

(2) *Certification of Exigent Circumstances.* If the plaintiff files a written certification that exigent circumstances make review by the Court impracticable, the Clerk shall, in accordance with Local Admiralty Rule 7.03(b)(3), issue a warrant of arrest and/or summons.

Thereafter at any post-arrest proceedings under Supplemental Rule (E)(4)(f) and Local Admiralty Rule 7.03(g), plaintiff shall have the burden of showing that probable cause existed for the issuance of process, and that exigent circumstances existed which precluded judicial review in accordance with Local Admiralty Rule 7.03(b)(1).

(3) *Preparation and Issuance of the Warrant of Arrest and/or Summons.* Plaintiff shall prepare the warrant of arrest and/or summons, and deliver them to the Clerk for filing and issuance.

The warrant of arrest shall substantially conform in format and content to the form identified as MDF 703 in the Appendix to these Local Admiralty Rules, and shall in all cases give adequate notice of the post-arrest provisions of Local Admiralty Rule 7.03(g).

(c) Special Requirements for Actions Involving Freight, Proceeds and/or Intangible Property.

(1) *Instructions to Be Contained in the Summons.* Unless otherwise ordered by the Court, the summons shall order the person having control of the freight, proceeds and/or intangible property to either:

(A) File a claim within fourteen (14) days after service of the summons in accordance with Local Admiralty Rule 7.03(f)(1); or

(B) Deliver or pay over to the Marshal, the freight, proceeds, and/or intangible property, or a part thereof, sufficient to satisfy plaintiff's claim.

The summons shall also inform the person having control of the freight, proceeds, and/or intangible property that service of the summons has the effect of arresting the property, thereby preventing the release, disposal or other distribution of the property without prior order of the Court.

(2) *Requirements for Claims to Prevent the Delivery of Property to the Marshal.* Any claim filed in accordance with

Supplemental Rule (E)(4) and Local Admiralty Rule 7.03(f)(1) shall describe the nature of claimant's interest in the property, and shall articulate reasons why the seizure should be vacated.

The claim shall be served upon the plaintiff, Marshal, and all other parties to the litigation. Additionally, the claimant shall file a Certificate of Service indicating the date and manner in which service was perfected.

(3) *Delivery or Payment of the Freight, Proceeds, and/or Intangible Property to the U.S. Marshal.* Unless a claim is filed in accordance with Supplemental Rule (E)(4)(f), and Local Admiralty Rule 7.03(f)(1), any person served with a summons issued pursuant to Local Admiralty Rule 7.03(b)(1) or (2), shall within fourteen (14) days after execution of service, deliver or pay over to the Marshal all, or part of, the freight, proceeds, and/or intangible property sufficient to satisfy plaintiff's claim.

Unless otherwise ordered by the Court, the person tendering control of the freight, proceeds, and/or intangible property shall be excused from any further duty with respect to the property in question.

(d) Publishing Notice of the Arrest as Required by Supplemental Rule (C)(4).

(1) *Time for Publication.* If the property is not released within fourteen (14) days after the execution of process, the notice required by Supplemental Rule (C)(4) shall be published by the plaintiff in accordance with Local Admiralty Rule 7.01(g). Such notice shall be published within twenty-one (21) days after execution of process. The notice shall substantially conform to the form identified as MDF 706 in the Appendix to these Local Admiralty Rules.

(2) *Proof of Publication.* Plaintiff shall file with the Clerk, proof of publication not later than fourteen (14) days following the last day of publication. It shall be sufficient proof for the plaintiff to file the sworn statement by, or on behalf of, the publisher or editor, indicating the dates of publication, along with a copy or reproduction of the actual publication.

(e) Undertaking in Lieu of Arrest. If, before or after the commencement of an action, a party accepts any written undertaking to respond on behalf of the vessel and/or other property in return for foregoing the arrest, the undertaking shall be substituted for the vessel or other property sued in rem.

The undertaking shall be referred to under the name of the vessel or other property in any pleading, order, or judgment; providing, however, that the undertaking shall only respond to orders or judgments in favor of the party accepting the undertaking, and any parties expressly named therein, to the extent of the benefit thereby conferred.

(f) Time for Filing Claim or Answer. Unless otherwise ordered by the court, any claimant of property subject to an action in rem shall:

(1) File his claim within fourteen (14) days after process has been executed; and

(2) Serve his answer within twenty-one (21) days after the filing of the claim.

(g) Post–Arrest Proceedings. Coincident with the filing of a claim pursuant to Supplemental Rule (E)(4)(f), and Local Admiralty Rule 7.03(f)(1), the claimant may also file a motion and proposed order directing plaintiff to show cause why the arrest should not be vacated. If the court grants the order, the court shall set a date and time for a show cause hearing. Thereafter, if the court orders the arrest to be vacated, the court shall award attorney's fees, costs, and other expenses incurred by any party as a result of the arrest.

Additionally, if the seizure was predicated upon a showing of "exigent circumstances" under Local Admiralty Rule 7.03(b)(2), and the court finds that such exigent circumstances did not exist, the court shall award attorneys' fees, costs and other expenses incurred by any party as a result of the seizure.

(h) Procedural Requirements Prior to the Entry of Default. In accordance with Rule 55, Fed.R.Civ.P. and Local Rule 1.07(b), a party seeking the entry of default in rem shall first file a motion and supporting legal memorandum in accordance with Local Rule 3.01.

The party seeking the entry of default shall also file such other proof sufficient to demonstrate that due notice of the action and arrest have been given by:

(1) Service upon the master or other person having custody of the property; and

(2) Delivery, or by certified mail, return receipt requested (or international effective equivalent), to every other person, including any known owner, who has not appeared or intervened in the action, and who is known to have, or claims to have, a possessory interest in the property.

The party seeking entry of default judgment under Local Admiralty Rule 7.03(i) may be excused for failing to give notice to such "other person" upon a satisfactory showing that diligent effort was made to give notice without success; and

(3) Publication as required by Supplemental Rule (C)(4) and Local Admiralty Rule 7.03(d).

Upon review of the motion, memorandum, and other proof, the Clerk, may, where appropriate, enter default in accordance with Rule 55, Fed.R.Civ.P. Thereafter, the Clerk shall serve notice of the entry of default upon all parties represented in the action.

(i) Procedural Requirements for the Entry of Default Judgment. Not sooner than seven (7) nor later than thirty (30) days following notice of the entry of default, the moving party shall file a motion, and supporting legal documents, for the entry of default judgment pursuant to Rule 55(b), Fed. R.Civ.P. The moving party may also file as exhibits for the motion such other documentation as may be required to support the entry of default judgment. Thereafter the court will consider the motion as indicated below:

(1) *When No Person Has Filed a Claim or Answer.* Unless otherwise ordered by the court, the motion for default judgment will be considered by the court without oral argument.

(2) *When Any Person Has Filed an Appearance, But Does Not Join in the Motion for Entry of Default Judgment.* If any person has filed an appearance in accordance with Local Admiralty Rule 7.03(f), but does not join in the motion for

entry of default judgment, the party seeking the entry of default judgment shall serve notice of the motion upon the party not joining in the motion, and thereafter the opposing party shall have seven (7) days from receipt of the notice to file written opposition with the court.

If the court grants the motion and enters the default judgment, such judgment shall establish a right on the part of the party or parties in whose favor it is entered. The judgment shall be considered prior to any claims of the owner of the defendant property against which it is entered, and to the remnants and surpluses thereof; providing, however, that such a judgment shall not establish any entitlement to the defendant property against which it is entered, and to the remnants and surpluses thereof; providing, however, that such a judgment shall not establish any entitlement to the defendant property having priority over non-possessory lien claimants. Obtaining a judgment by default shall not preclude the party in whose favor it is entered from contending and proving that all, or any portion, of the claim or claims encompassed within the judgment are prior to any such non-possessory lien claims.

[Chapter 7 revised effective February 1, 1986. Amended effective July 1, 2002; December 1, 2009.]

RULE 7.04 POSSESSORY, PETITORY AND PARTITION ACTIONS

(a) Establishing Dates for the Return of Process. In possessory actions filed pursuant to Supplemental Rule (D), the Court may order that process be returnable at a time shorter than that prescribed by Rule 12(a), Fed.R.Civ.P.

If the Court shortens the time, the Court shall specify the date upon which the answer must be filed, and may also set a hearing date to expedite the disposition of the possessory action. When possible, possessory actions shall be given preference on a judicial officer's calendar.

(b) Service of Notice. Notice of all possessory, petitory and/or partition actions pursuant to Supplemental Rule (D) shall be made in accordance with Local Admiralty Rule 7.01(g).

[Chapter 7 revised effective February 1, 1986.]

RULE 7.05 ACTIONS IN REM AND QUASI IN REM: GENERAL PROVISIONS

(a) Statement of Itemized Damages and Expenses Required. Every complaint in a Supplemental Rule (B) or (C) action shall state the amount of the debt, damages, or salvage for which the action is brought. In addition, the statement shall also specify the amount of any unliquidated claims, including attorneys' fees.

(b) Requirements and Procedures for Effecting Intervention. Whenever a vessel or other property is arrested or attached in accordance with any Supplemental Rule, and the vessel or property is in the custody of the U.S. Marshal, or duly authorized substitute custodian, any other person having a claim against the vessel or property shall be required to present their claim as indicated below:

(1) *Intervention of Right When No Sale of the Vessel or Property Is Pending.* Except as limited by Local Admiralty Rule 7.05(b)(2), any person having a claim against a vessel or property previously arrested or attached by the Marshal may, as a matter of right, file an intervening complaint at any time before an order is entered by the Court scheduling the vessel or property for sale.

Coincident with the filing of an intervening complaint, the offering party shall prepare and file a supplemental warrant of arrest and/or a supplemental process of attachment and garnishment.

Upon receipt of the intervening complaint and supplemental process, the Clerk shall conform a copy of the intervening complaint and shall issue the supplemental process. Thereafter, the offering party shall deliver the conformed copy of the intervening complaint and supplemental process to the Marshal for execution. Upon receipt of the intervening complaint and supplemental process, the Marshal shall re-arrest or re-attach the vessel or property in the name of the intervening plaintiff.

Counsel for the intervening party shall serve a copy of the intervening complaint, and copies of all process and exhibits upon all other counsel of record, and shall thereafter file a certificate of service with the Clerk indicating the manner and date of service.

(2) *Permissive Intervention When the Vessel or Property Has Been Scheduled for Sale by the Court.* Except as indicated below, and subject to any other rule or order of this Court, no person shall have an automatic right to intervene in an action when the Court has ordered the sale of the vessel or property, and the date of the sale is set within fourteen (14) days from the date the party moves for permission to intervene in accordance with this subsection. In such cases, the person seeking permission to intervene must:

(A) File a motion to intervene and indicate in the caption of the motion a request for expedited hearing when appropriate.

(B) Include a copy of the anticipated intervening complaint as an exhibit to the motion to intervene.

(C) Prepare and offer for filing a supplemental warrant of arrest and/or a supplemental process of attachment and garnishment.

(D) Serve copies of the motion to intervene, with exhibits and proposed supplemental process upon every other party to the litigation.

(E) File a certificate of service indicating the date and manner of service.

Thereafter, the Court may permit intervention under such conditions and terms as are equitable to the interests of all parties; and if intervention is permitted, shall also direct the Clerk to issue the supplemental process.

Upon receipt of the order permitting intervention, the Clerk shall file the originally signed intervening complaint, conform a copy of the intervening complaint and issue the supplemental process.

Thereafter, the offering party shall deliver the conformed copy of the intervening complaint and supplemental process to the Marshal for execution. Upon receipt of the intervening complaint and supplemental process, the Marshal shall re-arrest or re-attach the vessel or property in the name of the intervening plaintiff.

Counsel for the intervening party shall also serve a copy of the intervening complaint, exhibits, and supplemental process upon every other party of record, and shall thereafter file a Certificate of Service with the Clerk indicating the manner and date of service.

(c) Special Requirements for Salvage Actions. In cases of salvage, the complaint shall also state to the extent known, the value of the hull, cargo, freight, and other property salved, the amount claimed, the names of the principal salvors, and that the suit is instituted in their behalf and in behalf of all other persons associated with them.

In addition to these special pleading requirements, plaintiff shall attach as an exhibit to the complaint a list of all known salvors, and all persons believed entitled to share in the salvage. Plaintiff shall also attach a copy of any agreement of consortship available and known to exist among them collegially or individually.

(d) Form of Stipulations or Bonds. Except in cases instituted by the United States through information, or complaint of information upon seizures for any breach of the revenues, navigation, or other laws of the United States, stipulations or bonds in admiralty and maritime actions need not be under seal and may be executed by the agent or attorney of the stipulator or obligor.

Stipulations for costs with corporate surety need not be signed or executed by the party, but may be signed by the party's agent or attorney.

(e) Stipulation for Costs.

(1) *Seaman's Wage Claims.* Actions initiated by seamen pursuant to 28 U.S.C. Section 1916 may be filed without the posting of a stipulation for costs.

(2) *Security for Costs.* In an action under the Supplemental Rules, a party may move upon notice to all parties for an order to compel an adverse party to post security for costs with the clerk pursuant to Supplemental Rule E(2)(b). Unless otherwise ordered, the amount of security shall be $250. The party so ordered shall post the security within seven (7) days after the order is entered. A party who fails to post security when due may not participate further in the proceedings. A party may move for an order increasing the amount of security for costs.

(3) *Security for Costs and Limitation of Liability Proceedings.* The amount of security for costs under Supplemental Rule F(1) shall be $250, and it may be combined with the security for value and interest, unless otherwise ordered.

(f) Deposit of Marshal's Fees and Expenses Required Prior to Effecting Arrest, Attachment and/or Garnishment.

(1) *Deposit Required Before Seizure.* Any party seeking the arrest or attachment of property in accordance with Supplemental Rule (E) shall deposit a sum with the Marshal sufficient to cover the Marshal's estimated fees and expenses of arresting and keeping the property for at least fourteen (14) days. The Marshal is not required to execute process until the deposit is made.

(2) *Proration of Marshal's Fees and Expenses Upon Intervention.* When one or more parties intervene pursuant to Local Admiralty Rule 7.05(b)(1) or (2), the burden of advancing sums to the Marshal sufficient to cover the Marshal's fees and expenses shall be allocated equitably between the original plaintiff, and the intervening party or parties as indicated below:

(A) Stipulation for the Allocation and Payment of the Marshal's Fees and Expenses. Immediately upon the filing of the intervening complaint, counsel for the intervening plaintiff shall arrange for a conference between all other parties to the action, at which time a good faith effort shall be made to allocate fees and expenses among the parties. Any resulting stipulation between the parties shall be codified and filed with the Court and a copy served upon the Marshal.

(B) Upon receipt of this listing, the Marshal shall determine the total expenses incurred to date, and shall estimate the expenses to be incurred during the next fourteen (14) days. For the purpose of making this calculation, the total fees and expenses shall be calculated from the date when continuous and uninterrupted arrest or attachment of the property began, and not prorated from the date a particular party's intervening complaint was filed.

In order to determine the proportionate shares of each party, counsel for the last intervening plaintiff shall determine the total amounts claimed by each party. The individual claims shall be determined from the original and amended complaint, and all other intervening complaints subsequently accepted and processed by the Marshal in accordance with Local Admiralty Rule 7.05(b)(1) or (2).

Thereafter, counsel for the last intervening plaintiff shall deliver to the Marshal a list which summarizes each party's claim, and the proportion which each party's claim bears to the aggregate claims asserted in the litigation, determined to the nearest one-tenth of one percentage point.

Upon receipt of this listing, the Marshal shall determine the total expenses incurred to date, and shall estimate the expenses to be incurred during the next ten (10) days. For the purpose of making this calculation, the total fees and expenses shall be calculated from the date when continuous and uninterrupted arrest or attachment of the property began, and not prorated from the date a particular party's intervening complaint was filed.

The Marshal shall then apply the percentages determined in the listing, and shall compute the amount of the intervening party's initial deposit requirements. The Marshal shall also utilize this listing to compute any additional deposit requirements which may be necessary pursuant to Local Admiralty Rule 7.05(f)(3).

The Marshal need not re-arrest or re-attach the vessel and/or property until the deposit is received from the intervening plaintiff.

(3) *Additional Deposit Requirements.* Until the property arrested or attached and garnished has been released or otherwise disposed of in accordance with Supplemental Rule (E), the Marshal may require from any original and intervening party who has caused the arrest or attachment and garnishment of a vessel or property, to post such additional deposits as the Marshal determines necessary to cover any additional estimated fees or expenses.

(4) *Judicial Relief From Deposit Requirements.* Any party aggrieved by the deposit requirements of Local Admiralty Rule 7.05(f)(2) may apply to the Court for relief. Such an application shall be predicated upon a showing that owing to the relative priorities of the claims asserted against the vessel or other property, the deposit requirements operate to impose a burden disproportionate to the aggrieved party's recovery potential.

The judicial officer may adjust the deposit requirements, but in no event shall the proportion required of an aggrieved party be reduced to a percentage less than that imposed upon the claimant whose claim is the smallest among that of claims which the aggrieved party stipulates as having priority over its claim; or, in the absence of such stipulation, the greatest percentage imposed upon any claimant participating in the deposit requirements.

(5) *Consequence of Failing to Comply With Additional Deposit Requirements.* Any party who fails to make the additional deposit as requested by the Marshal may not participate further in the proceeding, except for the purpose of seeking relief from this rule. Additionally, the Marshal shall notify the Court in writing whenever any party fails to make additional deposits as required by Local Admiralty Rule 7.05(f)(3).

In the event that a party questions its obligations to advance monies required by this rule, the Marshal may apply to the Court for instructions concerning that party's obligation under the rule.

(g) Property in Possession of a United States Officer. Whenever the property to be arrested or attached is in the custody of a U.S. officer, the Marshal shall serve the appropriate process upon the officer or employee; or, if the officer or employee is not found within the district, then to the custodian of the property within the district.

The Marshal shall direct the officer, employee or custodian not to relinquish custody of the property until ordered to do so by the Court.

(h) Process Held in Abeyance.

(1) *When Permitted.* In accordance with Supplemental Rule (E)(3)(b), a plaintiff may ask the Clerk not to issue process, but rather to hold the process in abeyance. The Clerk shall docket this request, and thereafter shall not be responsible for ensuring that process is issued at a later date.

(2) *When Intervention Is Subsequently Required.* It is the intention of these rules that a vessel or other property should be arrested or attached pursuant to process issued and effected in only one civil action. Therefore, if while process is held in abeyance in one action, the vessel or property is arrested or attached in another action, it shall be the responsibility of the plaintiff who originally requested process be held in abeyance in the first action to voluntarily dismiss without prejudice the first action, insofar as that action seeks to proceed against the property arrested or attached in the second action, and promptly intervene in the second action pursuant to Local Admiralty Rule 7.05(b)(1) or (2).

In order to prevent undue hardship or manifest injustice, motions to consolidate in rem actions against the same vessel or property will be granted only in exceptional circumstances.

(i) Release of Property in Accordance With Supplemental Rule (E)(5).

(1) *Release by Consent or Stipulation.* Subject to the limitations imposed by Supplemental Rule (E)(5)(c), the Marshal may release any vessel, cargo or property in his possession to the party on whose behalf the property is detained. However, as a precondition to release, the Marshal shall require a stipulation, bond, or other security, expressly authorizing the release. The authorizing instrument shall be signed by the party, or his attorney, on whose behalf the property is detained.

The stipulation, bond, or other security shall be posted in an amount equal to, or greater than, the amount required for the following types of action:

(A) Actions Entirely for a Sum Certain. The amount alleged to be due in the complaint, with interest at six percent (6%) per annum from the date claimed to be due to a date forty-eight (48) months after the date the claim was filed, or by filing an approved stipulation, or bond for the amount alleged plus interest as computed in this subsection.

The stipulation or bond shall be conditioned to abide by all orders of the Court, and to pay the amount of any final judgment entered by this Court or any appellate Court, with interest.

(B) Actions Other Than Possessory, Petitory or Partition. Unless otherwise ordered by the Court, the amount of the appraised or agreed value of the property seized, with interest. If an appraised value cannot be agreed upon by the parties, the Court shall order an appraisal in accordance with Local Admiralty Rule 7.06(c).

The stipulation or bond shall be conditioned to abide by all orders of the Court, and to pay the amount of any final judgment entered by this Court or any appellate Court, with interest.

The person consenting or stipulating to the release shall also file a claim in accordance with Local Admiralty Rule 7.05(b)(1) or (2).

(C) Possessory, Petitory or Partition Actions. The Marshal may release property in these actions only upon order of Court, and upon the subsequent deposit of security and compliance with such terms and/or conditions as the Court deems appropriate.

(2) *Release Pursuant to Court Order.* In accordance with Supplemental Rule (E)(5)(c), a party may petition to release the vessel pursuant to Court order. A party making such application shall file a Request for Release which shall substantially conform in format and content to the form identified as MDF 707 in the Appendix to these Local Admiralty Rules.

Additionally, the party shall prepare, and offer for filing, a proposed order directing the release. This order shall substantially conform in format and content to the form identified as MDF 708 in the Appendix to these Local Admiralty Rules.

However, as a precondition to the release, the Marshal shall require a stipulation, bond, or other security, as specified in Local Admiralty Rule 7.05(i)(1)(A), (B) or (C), as appropriate.

(3) *Upon the Dismissal or Discontinuance of an Action.* By coordinating with the Marshal to ensure that all costs and charges of the Court and its officers have first been paid.

(4) *Release Subsequent to the Posting of a General Bond.*

(A) Requirements of a General Bond. General bonds filed pursuant to Supplemental Rule (E)(5)(b) shall identify the vessel by name, nationality, dimensions, official number or registration number, hailing port and port of documentation.

(B) Responsibility for Maintaining a Current Listing of General Bonds. The Clerk shall maintain a current listing of all general bonds. This listing should be maintained in alphabetical order by name of the vessel. The listing will be available for inspection during normal business hours.

(C) Execution of Process. The arrest of a vessel covered by a general bond shall be stayed in accordance with Supplemental Rule (E)(5)(b), however, the Marshal shall serve a copy of the complaint upon the master or other person in whose charge or custody the vessel is found. If neither the master nor another person in charge of custody is found aboard the vessel, the Marshal shall make his return accordingly.

Thereafter, it shall be plaintiff's responsibility to advise the owner or designated agent, at the address furnished in the general bond, of (1) the case number; (2) nature of the action and the amount claimed; (3) the plaintiff and name and address of plaintiff's attorney; and (4) the return date for filing a claim.

(j) Application to Modify Security for Value and Interest. At any time, any party having an interest in the subject matter of the action may move the Court, on due notice and for cause, for greater, better or lesser security, and any such order may be enforced by attachment or as otherwise provided by law.

(k) Custody and Safekeeping.

(1) *Initial Responsibility.* The Marshal shall initially take custody of any vessel, cargo and/or other property arrested, or attached in accordance with these rules. Thereafter, and until such time as substitute custodians may be authorized in accordance with Local Admiralty Rule 7.05(k)(3), the Marshal shall be responsible for providing adequate and necessary security for the safekeeping of the vessel or property.

In the discretion of the Marshal, adequate and necessary security may include the placing of keepers on or near the vessel and/or the appointment of a facility or person to serve as a custodian of the vessel or property.

(2) *Limitations on the Handling, Repairing and Subsequent Movement of Vessels or Property.* Subsequent to the arrest or attachment of a vessel or property, and except as provided in Local Admiralty Rule 7.05(k)(1), no person may handle cargo, conduct repairs, or move a vessel without prior order of Court.

(3) *Procedures for Changing Custody Arrangements.* Any party may petition the Court to dispense with keepers, remove or place the vessel, cargo and/or other property at a specified facility, designate a substitute custodian for the vessel or cargo, or for other similar relief. The motion shall substantially conform in format and content to the form identified as MDF 704 in the Appendix of these Local Admiralty Rules.

(A) Notification of the Marshal Required. When an application for change in custody arrangements is filed, either before or after the Marshal has taken custody of the vessel or property, the filing party shall serve notice of the application on the Marshal in sufficient time to permit the Marshal to review the indemnification and insurance arrangements of the filing party and substitute custodians. The application shall also be served upon all other parties to the litigation.

(B) Indemnification Requirements. Any motion for the appointment of a substitute custodian or facility shall include as an exhibit to the motion, a consent and indemnification agreement signed by both the filing party, or his attorney, and the proposed substitute custodian.

The consent and indemnification agreement shall expressly release the Marshal from any and all liability and responsibility for the care and custody of the property while in the hands of the substitute custodian; and shall expressly hold the Marshal harmless from any and all claims whatsoever arising from the substitute custodianship. The agreement shall substantially conform in format and content to the form identified as MDF 705 in the Appendix to these Local Admiralty Rules.

(C) Court Approval Required. The motion to change custody arrangements, and indemnification and consent agreement shall be referred to a judicial officer who shall determine whether the facility or substitute custodian is capable of safely keeping the vessel, cargo and/or property.

(4) *Insurance Requirements.*

(A) Responsibility for Initially Obtaining Insurance. Concurrent with the arrest or attachment of a vessel or property, the Marshal shall obtain insurance to protect the Marshal, his deputies, keepers, and custodians from liability arising from the arrest or attachment.

The insurance shall also protect the Marshal and his deputies or agents from any liability arising from performing services undertaken to protect the vessel, cargo and/or property while that property is in the custody of the Court.

(B) Payment of Insurance Premiums. It shall be the responsibility of the party applying for the arrest or attachment of a vessel, cargo and/or property to promptly reimburse the Marshal for premiums paid to effect the necessary insurance.

The party applying for change in custody arrangements shall be responsible for paying the Marshal for any additional premium associated with the change.

(C) Taxation of Insurance Premiums. The premiums charged for the liability insurance will be taxed as an expense of custody while the vessel, cargo and/or property is in custodia legis.

(5) *Contribution by Intervening Parties to Expenses of Substitute Custodian.* When a substitute custodian has been authorized under Local Admiralty Rule 7.05(k)(3), the Court in its discretion may require contribution by intervening parties (a) to all expenses of the substitute custodian and (b) to insurance premiums required under Local Admiralty Rule 7.05(k)(4) upon equitable terms. In addition to all relevant facts, the Court may consider the provisions of Local Admiralty Rule 7.05(f)(2)(B).

(*l*) Preservation, Humanitarian and Repatriation Expenses.

(1) *Limitations on Reimbursement for Services and/or Supplies Provided to a Vessel or Property in Custody.* Except in cases of emergency or undue hardship, no person will be entitled to claim as an expense of administration the costs of services or supplies furnished to a vessel, cargo and/or property unless such services or supplies have been furnished to the Marshal upon his order, or pursuant to an order of this Court.

Any order issued pursuant to this subsection shall require the person furnishing the services or supplies to file a weekly invoice. This invoice shall be set forth in the format prescribed in Local Admiralty Rule 7.05(*l*)(5).

(2) *Preservation Expenses for the Vessel and Cargo.* The Marshal, or substitute custodian, is authorized to incur expenses reasonably deemed necessary in maintaining the vessel, cargo and/or property in custody for the purpose of preventing the vessel, cargo and/or property from suffering loss or undue deterioration.

(3) *Expenses for Care and Maintenance of a Crew.* Except in an emergency, or upon the authorization of a judicial officer, neither the Marshal nor substitute custodian shall incur expenses for feeding or otherwise maintaining the crew.

Applications for providing food, water and necessary medical services for the maintenance of the crew may be submitted, and decided ex parte by a judicial officer, providing such an application is made by some person other than the owner, manager or general agent of the vessel.

Such applications must be filed within thirty (30) days from the date of the vessel's initial seizure. Otherwise, except in the case of an emergency, such applications shall be filed and served upon all parties, who in turn shall have fourteen (14) days from receipt of the application to file a written response.

Expenses for feeding or otherwise maintaining the crew, when incurred in accordance with this subsection, shall be taxed as an expense of administration and not as an expense of custody.

(4) *Repatriation Expenses.* Absent an order of Court expressly ordering the repatriation of the crew and/or passengers, and directing that the expenses be taxed as a cost of administration, no person shall be entitled to claim these expenses as expenses of administration.

(5) *Claim by a Supplier for Payment of Charges.* Any person who claims payment for furnishing services or supplies in compliance with Local Admiralty Rule 7.05(*l*), shall submit an invoice to the Marshal's office for review and approval.

The claim shall be presented in the form of a verified claim, and shall be submitted within a reasonable time after furnishing the services or supplies, but in no event shall a claim be accepted after the vessel, or property has been released. The claimant shall file a copy of the verified claim with the Marshal, and also serve the substitute custodian and all other parties to the litigation.

The Marshal shall review the claim, make adjustments or recommendations to the claim as are appropriate, and shall thereafter forward the claim to the Court for approval. The Court may postpone the hearing on an individual claim until a hearing can be set to consolidate other claims against the property.

(m) Property in Incidental Custody and Otherwise Not Subject to the Arrest or Attachment.

(1) *Authority to Preserve Cargo in Incidental Custody.* The Marshal, or an authorized substitute custodian, shall be responsible for securing, maintaining and preserving all property incidentally taken into custody as a result of the arrest or attachment of a vessel or property. Incidental property may include, but shall not be limited to, laden cargo not itself the subject of the arrest or attachment.

The Marshal or other custodian shall maintain a separate account of all costs and expenses associated with the care and maintenance of property incidentally taken into custody.

Any person claiming entitlement to possession of property incidentally taken into custody shall be required, as a precondition of receiving possession, to reimburse the Marshal for such separately accounted expenses. Monies received by the Marshal will be credited against both the expense of custody and administration.

(2) *Separation, Storage and Preservation of Property in Incidental Custody.* Any party, or the Marshal, may petition the Court to permit the separation and storage of property in incidental custody from the property actually arrested or attached.

When separation of the property is ordered to protect the incidentally seized property from undue deterioration; provide for safer storage; meet an emergency; reduce the expenses of custody; or to facilitate a sale of the vessel or other property pursuant to Local Admiralty Rule 7.05(q); the costs of such separation shall be treated as an expense of preservation and taxed as a cost of custody.

(3) *Disposal of Unclaimed Property.* Property incidentally in custody and not subsequently claimed by any person entitled to possession, shall be disposed of in accordance with the laws governing the disposition of property abandoned to the United States of America.

Except when prohibited by prevailing federal statute, the resulting net proceeds associated with the disposition of abandoned property shall be applied to offset the expense of administration, with the remainder escheating to the United States of America as provided by law.

(n) Dismissal.

(1) *By Consent.* No action may be dismissed pursuant to Fed.R.Civ.P. 41(a) unless all costs and expenses of the Court and its officials have first been paid.

Additionally, if there is more than one plaintiff or intervening plaintiff, no dismissal may be taken by a plaintiff unless that party's proportionate share of costs and expenses has been paid in accordance with Local Admiralty Rule 7.05(f).

(2) *Involuntary Dismissal.* If the Court enters a dismissal pursuant to Fed.R.Civ.P. 41(b), the Court shall also designate the costs and expenses to be paid by the party or parties so dismissed.

(*o*) Judgments.

(1) *Expenses of Sureties as Costs.* If costs are awarded to any party, then all reasonable premiums or expenses paid by the prevailing party on bonds, stipulations and/or other security shall be taxed as costs in the case.

(2) *Costs of Arrest or Attachment.* If costs are awarded to any party, then all reasonable expenses paid by the prevailing party incidental to, or arising from the arrest or attachment of any vessel, property and/or cargo shall be taxed as costs in the case.

(p) Stay of Final Order.

(1) *Automatic Stay for Fourteen (14) Days.* In accordance with Fed.R.Civ.P. 62(a), no execution shall issue upon a judgment, nor shall seized property be released pursuant to a judgment or dismissal, until fourteen (14) days after the entry of the judgment or order of dismissal.

(2) *Stays Beyond the Fourteen (14) Day Period.* If within the fourteen (14) day period established by Fed.R.Civ.P. 62(a), a party files any of the motions contemplated in Fed.R.Civ.P. 62(b), or a notice of appeal, then unless otherwise ordered by the Court, a further stay shall exist for a period not to exceed thirty (30) days from the entry of the judgment or order. The purpose of this additional stay is to permit the Court to consider an application for the establishment of a supersedeas bond, and to order the date upon which the bond shall be filed with the Court.

(q) Notice of Sale.

(1) *Publication of Notice.* In an action in rem or quasi in rem, and except in suits on behalf of the United States of America where other notice is prescribed by statute, the Marshal shall publish notice in any of the newspapers approved pursuant to Local Admiralty Rule 7.01(g).

(2) *Duration of Publication.* Unless otherwise ordered by the Court, applicable Supplemental Rule, or Local Admiralty Rule, publication of the notice of sale shall be made at least twice; the first publication shall be at least one (1) calendar week prior to the date of the sale, and the second at least three (3) calendar days prior to the date of the sale.

(r) Sale of a Vessel or Property.

(1) *Payment of the Purchase Price.* Unless otherwise provided in the order of sale, the person whose bid is accepted shall pay the Marshal the purchase price in the manner provided below:

(A) If the Bid is Not More Than $500.00. The successful bidder shall immediately pay the full purchase price.

(B) If the Bid is More Than $500.00. The bidder shall immediately deposit with the Marshal $500.00, or 10% of the bid, whichever sum is greater. Thereafter the bidder shall pay the remaining purchase price within three (3) working days.

If an objection to the sale is filed within the time permitted by Local Admiralty Rule 7.05(r)(7), the successful bidder is excused from paying the remaining purchase price until three (3) working days after the Court confirms the sale.

(2) *Method of Payment.* Unless otherwise ordered by the Court, payments to the Marshal shall be made in cash, certified check or cashier's check.

(3) *Custodial Costs Pending Payment.* When a successful bidder fails to pay the balance of the bid within the time allowed by Local Admiralty Rule 7.05(r)(1)(B), or within the time permitted by order of the Court, the Marshal shall charge the successful bidder for the cost of keeping the property from the date payment of the balance was due, to the date the bidder takes delivery of the property.

The Marshal may refuse to release the property until these additional charges have been paid.

(4) *Default for Failure to Pay the Balance.* The person who fails to pay the balance of the bid within the time allowed shall be deemed to be in default. Thereafter a judicial officer may order that the sale be awarded to the second highest bidder, or may order a new sale as appropriate.

Any sum deposited by the bidder in default shall be forfeited, and the amount shall be applied by the Marshal to any additional costs incurred because of the forfeiture and default, including costs incident to resale. The balance of the deposit, if any, shall be retained in the registry and subject to further order of the Court.

(5) *Marshal's Report of Sale.* At the conclusion of the sale, the Marshal shall file a written report of the sale to include the date of the sale, the price obtained, and the name and address of the buyer.

(6) *Confirmation of Sale.* Unless an objection is timely filed in accordance with this rule, or the purchaser is in default for failing to pay the balance of the purchase price, plaintiff shall proceed to have the sale confirmed on the day following the last day for filing objections.

In order to confirm the sale, plaintiff's counsel shall file a "Request for Confirmation of Sale" on the day following the last day for filing an objection. The "Request for Confirmation of Sale" shall substantially conform in format and content to the form identified as MDF 709 in the Appendix to these Local Admiralty Rules. Plaintiff's counsel shall also prepare and offer for filing a "Confirmation of Sale". The "Confirmation of Sale" shall substantially conform in format and content to the form identified as MDF 710 in the Appendix to these Local Admiralty Rules. Thereafter the Clerk shall file and docket the confirmation and shall promptly transmit a certified copy of the "Confirmation of Sale" to the Marshal's office.

Unless otherwise ordered by the Court, if the plaintiff fails to timely file the "Request for Confirmation of Sale" and proposed "Confirmation of Sale", the Marshal shall assess any continuing costs or expenses for custody of the vessel or property against the plaintiff.

(7) *Objections to Confirmation.*

(A) Time for Filing Objections. Unless otherwise permitted by the Court, an objection must be filed within three (3) working days following the sale. The party or person filing an objection shall serve a copy of the objection upon the Marshal and all other parties to the action, and shall also file a Certificate of Service indicating the date and manner of service. Opposition to the objection must be filed within five (5) days after receipt of the objection of the sale.

The Court shall consider the objection, and any opposition to the objection, and shall confirm the sale, order a new sale, or grant other relief as appropriate.

(B) Deposit of Preservation or Maintenance Costs. In addition to filing written objections, any person objecting to the sale shall also deposit with the Marshal the cost of keeping the property for at least seven (7) days. Proof of the deposit with the Marshal's office shall be delivered to the Clerk's office by the moving party. The Court will not consider the objection without proof of this deposit.

If the objection is sustained, the objector will be reimbursed for the expense of keeping the property from the proceeds of any subsequent sale, and any remaining deposit will be returned to the objector upon Court order.

If the objection is denied, the sum deposited by the objector will be applied to pay the fees and expenses incurred by the Marshal in keeping the property from the date the objection was filed until the sale is confirmed. Any remaining deposit will be returned to the objector upon order of Court.

(8) *Confirmation of Title.* Failure of a party to give the required notice of an action and arrest of a vessel, property and/or cargo, or failure to give required notice of a sale, may afford grounds for objecting to the sale, but such failure does not affect the title of a good faith purchaser of the property.

(s) Post–Sale Claim. Claims against the proceeds of a sale authorized by these rules, except for seamen's wages, will not be admitted on behalf of lienors who file their claims after the sale.

Unless otherwise ordered by the Court, any claims filed after the date of the sale shall be limited to the remnants and surplus arising from the sale.

[Chapter 7 revised effective February 1, 1986. Amended effective January 1, 1992; July 1, 1998; December 1, 2009.]

RULE 7.06 ACTIONS TO LIMIT LIABILITY

(a) Publication of the Notice. Immediately upon the commencement of an action to limit liability pursuant to Supplemental Rule (F), plaintiff shall, without further order of Court, effect publication of the notice in accordance with the provisions set forth in Supplemental Rule (F)(4) and Local Admiralty Rule 7.01(g).

(b) Proof of Publication. Plaintiff shall file proof of publication not later than the return date. It shall be sufficient proof for plaintiff to file the sworn statement by, or on behalf of, the publisher or editor, indicating the dates of publication, along with a copy or reproduction of the actual publication.

(c) Appraisals Pursuant to Supplemental Rule (F)(7). Upon the filing of a claimant's motion pursuant to Supplemental Rule (F)(7), demanding an increase in the funds deposited in Court or the security given by plaintiff, the Court shall order an appraisement of the value of the plaintiff's interest in the vessel and pending cargo.

Upon receipt of the order directing the appraisal, the parties shall have seven (7) days to file a written stipulation to an appraiser. In the event that the parties do not file a stipulation, the Court shall appoint the appraiser.

The appraiser shall promptly conduct an appraisal and thereafter file the appraisal with the Clerk and serve a copy of the appraisal upon the moving party and the plaintiff. The appraiser shall also file a Certificate of Service indicating the date and manner in which service was perfected.

(d) Objections to the Appraisal. Any party may move to set aside the appraisal within fourteen (14) days following the filing of the appraisal with the Clerk.

(e) Fees of the Appraiser. The Court shall establish the fee to be paid the appraiser. Unless otherwise ordered by the Court, the fee shall be taxed against the party seeking relief under Supplemental Rule (F)(7).

[Chapter 7 revised effective February 1, 1986. Amended effective December 1, 2009.]

Advisory Notes

7.06(a): This section incorporates the publication provisions of Local Admiralty Rule 7.01(g), and applies them to limitation of liability actions. The rule provides for the publication of the notice required by Supplemental Rule (F)(4) without further order of the Court. The Committee believes that this self-executing aspect of the rule will save judicial time and at the time will not impair the rights of any party or claimant.

7.06(b): The Committee determined that filing proof of publication with the clerk was essential in order to establish an adequate record of the publication.

APPENDIX OF FORMS. ADMIRALTY AND MARITIME RULES

NOTE: ALL ORDERS MUST BE PREPARED IN ACCORDANCE WITH LOCAL RULE 1.05(a).

MDF 700. ORDER DIRECTING THE ISSUANCE OF THE PROCESS OF ATTACHMENT AND GARNISHMENT

UNITED STATES DISTRICT COURT
MIDDLE DISTRICT OF FLORIDA
___________ Division

"IN ADMIRALTY"

Plaintiff,

v. CASE NO. ________________

Defendant.

____

ORDER DIRECTING THE ISSUANCE OF THE PROCESS OF ATTACHMENT AND GARNISHMENT

Pursuant to Supplemental Rule (B)(1) and Local Admiralty Rule 7.02(c)(1), the Clerk is directed to issue the summons and process of attachment and garnishment in the above-styled action.

ORDERED at ________, Florida, this ____ day of ________, 20____.

____
United States Magistrate Judge

MDF 701. PROCESS OF ATTACHMENT AND GARNISHMENT

UNITED STATES DISTRICT COURT
MIDDLE DISTRICT OF FLORIDA
__________ Division

"IN ADMIRALTY"

Plaintiff,

v. CASE NO. ____________________

Defendant.
____

PROCESS OF ATTACHMENT AND GARNISHMENT

The complaint in the above-styled case was filed in the ________ Division of this Court on ______________________, 20___.

In accordance with Supplemental Rule (B) of Certain Admiralty and Maritime Claims of the Federal Rules of Civil Procedure and Local Admiralty Rule 7.02, you are directed to attach and garnish the property indicated below:

DESCRIPTION

(Describe the property to be attached and garnished in sufficient detail, including location of the property, to permit the U.S. Marshal to effect the seizure.)

You shall also give notice of the attachment and garnishment to every person required by appropriate Supplemental Rule, Local Admiralty Rule, and the practices of your office.

DATED at ______________, Florida, this ____ day of _______________, 20____.

[Name of Clerk], CLERK

By: ____________________________________
Deputy Clerk

(Name of Plaintiff's Attorney)
(Florida Bar Number, if admitted in Fla.)
(Firm Name, if applicable)
(Mailing Address)
(City, State & Zip Code)
(Telephone Number)
(Facsimile Phone Number, if available)

SPECIAL NOTICE

Any person claiming an interest in property seized pursuant to this process of attachment and garnishment must file a claim in accordance with the post-seizure review provisions of Local Admiralty Rule 7.02(e).

[Amended effective July 1, 2002.]

MDF 702. ORDER DIRECTING THE ISSUANCE OF THE WARRANT OF ARREST AND/OR SUMMONS

UNITED STATES DISTRICT COURT
MIDDLE DISTRICT OF FLORIDA
___________ Division

"IN ADMIRALTY"

____

Plaintiff,

v. CASE NO. __________________________

Defendant.

____

ORDER DIRECTING THE ISSUANCE OF
THE WARRANT OF ARREST AND/OR SUMMONS

Pursuant to Supplemental Rule (C)(1) and Local Admiralty Rule 7.03(b)(1), the Clerk is directed to issue a warrant of arrest and/or summons in the above-styled action.

ORDERED at _______________, Florida, this _______ day of ___________, 20 ___.

____
United States Magistrate Judge

MDF 703. WARRANT FOR ARREST IN REM

UNITED STATES DISTRICT COURT
MIDDLE DISTRICT OF FLORIDA
__________ Division

"IN ADMIRALTY"

Plaintiff,

v. CASE NO. ______________________

Defendant.
____

WARRANT FOR ARREST IN REM

TO THE UNITED STATES MARSHAL FOR THE UNITED STATES DISTRICT COURT FOR THE MIDDLE DISTRICT OF FLORIDA:

The complaint in the above-styled in rem proceeding was filed in the ________ Division of this Court on ____________________, 20__.

In accordance with Supplemental Rule (C) for Certain Admiralty and Maritime Claims of the Federal Rules of Civil Procedure and Local Admiralty Rule 7.03, you are directed to arrest the defendant vessel, her boats, tackle, apparel and furniture, engines and appurtenances, and to detain the same in your custody pending further order of the Court.

You shall also give notice of the arrest to all persons required by appropriate Supplemental Rule, Local Admiralty Rule, and the practices of your office.

ORDERED at __________, Florida, this _____ day of __________, 20____.

[Name of Clerk], CLERK

By: ____________________________

(Name of Plaintiff's Attorney)
(Florida Bar Number, if admitted in Fla.)
(Firm Name, if applicable)
(Mailing Address)
(City, State & Zip Code)
(Telephone Number)
(Facsimile Phone Number, if available)

cc: Counsel of Record

SPECIAL NOTICE

In accordance with Local Admiralty Rule 7.03(f), any person claiming an interest in the vessel and/or property shall be required to file a claim within fourteen (14) days after process has been executed, and shall also be required to file an answer within twenty-one (21) days after the filing of his claim. Any persons claiming an interest in the vessel and/or property may also pursue the post-arrest remedies set forth in Local Admiralty Rule 7.03(g).

[Amended effective July 1, 2002; December 1, 2009.]

MDF 704. MOTION FOR APPOINTMENT OF SUBSTITUTE CUSTODIAN

UNITED STATES DISTRICT COURT
MIDDLE DISTRICT OF FLORIDA
____________ Division

"IN ADMIRALTY"

Plaintiff,

v. CASE NO. __________________________

Defendant.
____

MOTION FOR APPOINTMENT OF SUBSTITUTE CUSTODIAN

Pursuant to Local Admiralty Rule 7.05(k)(3), Plaintiff _______________, by and through the undersigned attorney, represents the following:

(1) On __________________, 20____, Plaintiff initiated the above-styled action against the vessel __________________________, her boats, tackle, apparel, furniture and furnishings, equipment, engines and appurtenances.

(2) On __________________, 20____, the Clerk of the District Court issued a Warrant of Arrest against the vessel, directing the U.S. Marshal to take custody of the vessel __________________, and to retain custody of the vessel pending further order of this Court.

(3)(a) Subsequent to the issuance of the Warrant of Arrest, the Marshal will take steps to immediately seize the vessel. Thereafter, continual custody by the Marshal will require the services of at least one custodian at a cost of at least $___________ per day. (This paragraph would be applicable only when the motion for appointment is filed concurrent with the complaint and application for the warrant of arrest.)

- or -

(3)(b) Pursuant to the previously issued Warrant of Arrest, the Marshal has already arrested the vessel. Continued custody by the Marshal requires the services of ________ custodians at a cost of at least $__________ per day. (This paragraph would be applicable in all cases where the Marshal has previously arrested the vessel.)

(4) The vessel is currently berthed at __________________, and subject to the approval of the Court, the substitute custodian is prepared to provide security, wharfage, and routine services for the safekeeping of the vessel at a cost substantially less than that presently required by the Marshal. The substitute custodian has also agreed to continue to provide these services pending further order of this Court.

(continued on page 2)

(5) The substitute custodian has adequate facilities for the care, maintenance and security of the vessel.

(6) Concurrent with the Court's approval of the Motion for Appointment of the Substitute Custodian, Plaintiff and the Substitute Custodian will file a Consent and Indemnification Agreement in accordance with Local Admiralty Rule 7.05(k)(3)(B).

THEREFORE, in accordance with the representations set forth in this instrument, and subject to the filing of the indemnification agreement noted in paragraph (6) above, Plaintiff requests this Court to enter an order appointing ________________________________ as the Substitute Custodian for the vessel ________________________.

DATED at _______________, Florida, this _______ day of ___________, 20 _____.

____
SIGNATURE OF COUNSEL OF RECORD
Typed Name of Counsel
Fla. Bar ID No. (if admitted in Fla.)
Firm or Business Name
Mailing Address
City, State, Zip Code
Telephone Number
Facsimile Phone Number (if available)

cc: Counsel of Record
Substitute Custodian

SPECIAL NOTE

Plaintiff's attorney shall also prepare for the Court's signature and subsequent filing, a proposed order for the Appointment of Substitute Custodian.

MDF 705. CONSENT AND INDEMNIFICATION AGREEMENT FOR THE APPOINTMENT OF A SUBSTITUTE CUSTODIAN

UNITED STATES DISTRICT COURT
MIDDLE DISTRICT OF FLORIDA
_________ Division

"IN ADMIRALTY"

Plaintiff,

v. CASE NO. _________

Defendant.
____

CONSENT AND INDEMNIFICATION AGREEMENT
FOR THE APPOINTMENT OF A SUBSTITUTE CUSTODIAN

Plaintiff, ______________, (by the undersigned attorney) and ______________, the proposed Substitute Custodian, hereby expressly release the U.S. Marshal for this district, and the U.S. Marshal's Service, from any and all liability and responsibility for the care and custody of ______________ (describe the property) while in the hands of ______________ (substitute custodian).

Plaintiff and ______________ (substitute custodian) also expressly agree to hold the U.S. Marshal for this district, and the U.S. Marshal's Service, harmless from any and all claims whatsoever arising during the period of the substitute custodianship.

As counsel of record in this action, the undersigned attorney represents that he has been expressly authorized by the Plaintiff to sign this Consent and Indemnification Agreement for, and on behalf of the Plaintiff.

SIGNED this _____ day of ______________, 20____, at ______________, Florida.

______________________________	______________________________
PLAINTIFF'S ATTORNEY	SUBSTITUTE CUSTODIAN
Typed Name	Typed Name
Fla. Bar ID No. (if admitted in Fla.)	Fla. Bar ID No. (if admitted in Fla.)
Firm or Business Name	Firm or Business Name
Mailing Address	Mailing Address
City, State, Zip Code	City, State, Zip Code
Telephone Number	Telephone Number
Facsimile Phone Number (if available)	Facsimile Phone Number (if available)

cc: Counsel of Record

MDF 706. NOTICE OF ACTION IN REM AND ARREST OF VESSEL

UNITED STATES DISTRICT COURT
MIDDLE DISTRICT OF FLORIDA
________ Division

"IN ADMIRALTY"

Plaintiff,

v. CASE NO. ________________________

Defendant.
____

NOTICE OF ACTION IN REM AND ARREST OF VESSEL

In accordance with Supplemental Rule (C)(4) for Certain Admiralty and Maritime Action of the Federal Rules of Civil Procedure, and Local Admiralty Rule 7.03(d), notice is hereby given of the arrest of _______________, in accordance with a Warrant of Arrest issued on ____________, 20__.

Pursuant to Supplemental Rule (C)(6), and Local Admiralty Rule 703(f), any person having a claim against the vessel and/or property shall file a claim with the Court not later than fourteen (14) days after process has been effected, and shall file an answer within twenty-one (21) days from the date of filing their claim.

DATED at ________________, Florida, this _____ day of _________, 20______.

____
SIGNED NAME OF PLAINTIFF'S ATTORNEY
Typed Name of Counsel
Fla. Bar ID No. (if admitted in Fla.)
Firm or Business Name
Mailing Address
City, State, Zip Code
Telephone Number
Facsimile Phone Number (if available)

cc: Counsel of Record

[Amended effective December 1, 2009.]

MDF 707. MOTION FOR RELEASE OF A VESSEL OR PROPERTY IN ACCORDANCE WITH SUPPLEMENTAL RULE (E)(5)

UNITED STATES DISTRICT COURT
MIDDLE DISTRICT OF FLORIDA
__________ Division

"IN ADMIRALTY"

____

Plaintiff,

v. CASE NO. ________________________

Defendant.
____

MOTION FOR RELEASE OF A VESSEL OR PROPERTY
IN ACCORDANCE WITH SUPPLEMENTAL RULE (E)(5)

In accordance with Supplemental Rule (E)(5) and Local Admiralty Rule 7.05(i)(2), plaintiff, on whose behalf property has been seized, requests the Court to enter an Order directing the United States Marshal for the Middle District of Florida to release the property. This request is made for the following reasons:

(Describe the reasons in sufficient detail to permit the Court to enter an appropriate order.)

DATED at __________, Florida, this _____ day of ____________, 20____.

____
SIGNED NAME OF PLAINTIFF'S ATTORNEY
Typed Name of Counsel
Fla. Bar ID No. (if admitted in Fla.)
Firm or Business Name
Mailing Address
City, State, Zip Code
Telephone Number
Facsimile Phone Number (if available)

cc: Counsel of Record

MDF 708. ORDER DIRECTING THE RELEASE OF A VESSEL OR PROPERTY IN ACCORDANCE WITH SUPPLEMENTAL RULE (E)(5)

UNITED STATES DISTRICT COURT
MIDDLE DISTRICT OF FLORIDA
____________ Division

"IN ADMIRALTY"

Plaintiff,

v. CASE NO. ________________________

Defendant.
____

ORDER DIRECTING THE RELEASE OF A VESSEL OR
PROPERTY IN ACCORDANCE WITH SUPPLEMENTAL RULE (E)(5)

In accordance with Supplemental Rule (E)(5) and Local Admiralty Rule 7.05(i)(1), and pursuant to the Request for Release filed on ____________, 20 ____, the United States Marshal is directed to release the vessel and/or property currently being held in his custody in the above-styled action.

ORDERED at ______________, Florida, this ______ day of ________, 20_____.

____
United States Magistrate Judge

cc: Counsel of Record

MDF 709. REQUEST FOR CONFIRMATION OF SALE

UNITED STATES DISTRICT COURT
MIDDLE DISTRICT OF FLORIDA
___________ Division

"IN ADMIRALTY"

Plaintiff,

v. CASE NO. ________________________

Defendant.

____

REQUEST FOR CONFIRMATION OF SALE

Plaintiff, by and through its undersigned attorney, certifies the following:

(1) **Date of Sale**: In accordance with the Court's previous Order of Sale, plaintiff represents that the sale of __________ (describe the property) was conducted by the Marshal on __________, 20____.

(2) **Last Day for Filing Objections:** Pursuant to Local Admiralty Rule 7.05(r)(7)(A), the last day for filing objections to the sale was __________, 20____.

(3) **Survey of Court Records:** Plaintiff has surveyed the docket and records of this case, and has confirmed that as of ________________, 20____, there were no objections to the sale on file with the Clerk of Court.

THEREFORE, in light of the facts presented above, plaintiff requests the Clerk to enter a Confirmation of Sale and to transmit the confirmation to the Marshal for processing.

DATED at ____________, Florida, this ______ day of _______________, 20 _____.

____
SIGNED NAME OF PLAINTIFF'S ATTORNEY
Typed Name of Counsel
Fla. Bar ID No. (if admitted in Fla.)
Firm or Business Name
Mailing Address
City, State, Zip Code
Telephone Number
Facsimile Phone Number (if available)

cc: Counsel of Record

MDF 710. CONFIRMATION OF SALE

UNITED STATES DISTRICT COURT
MIDDLE DISTRICT OF FLORIDA
__________ Division

"IN ADMIRALTY"

Plaintiff,

v. CASE NO. ____________________

Defendant.

CONFIRMATION OF SALE

The records in this action indicate that no objection has been filed to the sale of property conducted by the U.S. Marshal on ____________________, 20____.

THEREFORE, in accordance with Local Admiralty Rule 7.05(r)(6), the sale to (identify the purchaser) shall stand confirmed as of ____________________, 20____.

DONE at ____________, Florida, this _____ day of ______________, 20______.

[Name of Clerk], CLERK

By: ______________________________
Deputy Clerk

cc: U.S. Marshal
Counsel of Record

[Amended effective July 1, 2002.]

CHAPTER EIGHT. COURT ANNEXED ARBITRATION

RULE 8.01 ARBITRATION

(a) It is the purpose of the Court, through adoption and implementation of this rule, to provide an alternative mechanism for the resolution of civil disputes in accord with 28 U.S.C. Sections 651–658.

(b) The Chief Judge shall certify those persons who are eligible and qualified to serve as arbitrators under this rule. An individual may be certified to serve as an arbitrator under this rule if admitted to The Florida Bar for at least five (5) years, admitted to practice before this Court, and determined by the Chief Judge competent to perform the duties of an arbitrator.

An advisory committee or committees comprised of members of the bar in each Division of the Court, respectively, may be constituted to assist the Chief Judge in screening applicants and aiding in the formulation and application of standards for selecting arbitrators.

(c) Each individual certified as an arbitrator shall take the oath or affirmation prescribed by 28 U.S.C. Section 453 before serving as an arbitrator. Depending upon the availability of funds from the Administrative Office of the United States Courts, or other appropriate agency, arbitrators may be compensated for their services in such amounts and in such manner as the Chief Judge shall specify from time to time. No arbitrator shall charge or accept for services any fee or reimbursement from any other source. Any member of the bar who is certified and designated as an arbitrator pursuant to these rules shall not for that reason be disqualified from appearing and acting as counsel in any other case pending before the Court.

[Amended effective May 11, 2006.]

RULE 8.02 CASES FOR ARBITRATION

(a) Any civil action may be referred to arbitration in accordance with this rule if the parties consent in writing to arbitration, except that referral to arbitration may not occur if:

(1) the action is based on an alleged violation of a right secured by the Constitution of the United States;

(2) jurisdiction is based in whole or in part on 28 U.S.C. Section 1343; or

(3) the relief sought consists of money damages in an amount greater than $150,000.

(b) No party or attorney can be prejudiced for refusing to participate in arbitration by consent.

[Amended effective January 1, 1989; June 15, 1989; February 1, 1994; May 11, 2006.]

RULE 8.03 REFERRAL TO ARBITRATION

Within twenty-one (21) days after referral to arbitration, the Court shall select three (3) certified arbitrators to conduct the arbitration proceedings. Not more than one member or associate of a firm or association of attorneys shall be appointed to the same panel of arbitrators. Any person selected as an arbitrator may be disqualified for bias or prejudice as provided in 28 U.S.C. Section 144, and shall disqualify himself in any action in which he would be required to do so if he were a justice, judge, or magistrate judge governed by 28 U.S.C. Section 455.

[Amended effective May 11, 2006; December 1, 2009.]

RULE 8.04 ARBITRATION HEARING

(a) Immediately upon selection and designation of the arbitrators pursuant to Rule 8.03, the Clerk shall communicate with the parties and the arbitrators in an effort to ascertain a mutually convenient date for a hearing, and shall then schedule and give notice of the date and time of the arbitration hearing which may be held in space provided in the United States Courthouse. The hearing shall be scheduled within ninety (90) days from the date of the selection and designation of the arbitrators on at least twenty-one (21) days notice to the parties. Any continuance of the hearing beyond that ninety (90) day period may be allowed only by order of the Court for good cause shown.

(b) At least fourteen (14) days prior to the arbitration hearing each party shall furnish to every other party a list of witnesses, if any, and copies (or photographs) of all exhibits to be offered at the hearing. The arbitrators may refuse to consider any witness or exhibit which has not been so disclosed.

(c) Individual parties or authorized representatives of corporate parties shall attend the arbitration hearing unless excused in advance by the arbitrators for good cause shown. The hearing shall be conducted informally; the Federal Rules of Evidence shall be a guide, but shall not be binding. It is contemplated by the Court that the presentation of testimony shall be kept to a minimum, and that cases shall be presented to the arbitrators primarily through the statements and arguments of counsel.

(d) Any party may have a recording and transcript made of the arbitration hearing at the party's expense.

[Amended effective May 11, 2006; December 1, 2009.]

RULE 8.05 ARBITRATION AWARD AND JUDGMENT

(a) The award of the arbitrators shall be filed with the Clerk within fourteen (14) days following the hearing, and the Clerk shall give immediate notice to the parties. The award shall state the result reached by the arbitrators without necessity of factual findings or legal conclusions. A majority determination shall control the award.

(b) At the end of thirty (30) days after the filing of the arbitrator's award the Clerk shall enter judgment on the award if no timely demand for trial de novo has been made. If the parties have previously stipulated in writing that the award shall be final and binding, the Clerk shall enter judgment on the award when filed.

(c) Pursuant to 28 U.S.C. Section 657(b), the contents of any arbitration award shall be sealed and shall remain unknown to any judge assigned to the case—

(1) Except as necessary for the Court to determine whether to assess costs or attorney fees under 28 U.S.C. Section 655 or

(2) Until the District Court has entered final judgment in the action or the action has been otherwise terminated, at which time the award shall be unsealed.

[Amended effective June 15, 1989; May 11, 2006; December 1, 2009.]

RULE 8.06 TRIAL DE NOVO

(a) Within thirty (30) days after the filing of the arbitration award with the Clerk, any party may demand a trial de novo in the District Court. Written notification of such a demand shall be filed with the Clerk and a copy shall be served by the moving party upon all other parties.

(b) Upon a demand for a trial de novo the action shall be placed on the calendar of the Court and treated for all purposes as if it had not been referred to arbitration, and any right of trial by jury shall be preserved inviolate.

(c) At the trial de novo the Court shall not admit evidence that there has been an arbitration proceeding, the nature or amount of the award, or any other matter concerning the conduct of the arbitration proceeding, except that testimony given at an arbitration hearing may be used for any purpose otherwise permitted by the Federal Rules of Evidence, or the Federal Rules of Civil Procedure.

(d) No penalty for demanding a trial de novo shall be assessed by the Court.

[Amended effective September 12, 1986; June 15, 1989; May 11, 2006.]

CHAPTER NINE. COURT ANNEXED MEDIATION

RULE 9.01 GENERAL PROVISIONS

(a) Definitions. Mediation is a supervised settlement conference presided over by a qualified, certified and neutral mediator to promote conciliation, compromise and the ultimate settlement of a civil action.

The mediator is an attorney, certified by the chief judge in accordance with these rules, who possesses the unique skills required to facilitate the mediation process including the ability to suggest alternatives, analyze issues, question perceptions, use logic, conduct private caucuses, stimulate negotiations between opposing sides and keep order.

The mediation process does not allow for testimony of witnesses. The mediator does not review or rule upon questions of fact or law, or render any final decision in the case. Absent a settlement, the mediator will report only to the presiding judge as to whether the case settled, was adjourned for further mediation (by agreement of the parties), or that the mediator declared an impasse.

(b) Purpose. It is the purpose of the Court, through adoption and implementation of this rule, to provide an alternative mechanism for the resolution of civil disputes (a Court annexed, mandatory mediation procedure) leading to disposition before trial of many civil cases with resultant savings in time and costs to the litigants and to the Court, but without sacrificing the quality of justice to be rendered or the right of the litigants to a full trial in the event of an impasse following mediation.

[Added effective November 15, 1989.]

RULE 9.02 CERTIFICATION; QUALIFICATION AND COMPENSATION OF MEDIATORS

(a) Certification of Mediators. The chief judge shall certify those persons who are eligible and qualified to serve as mediators under this rule, in such numbers as the chief judge shall deem appropriate. Thereafter, the chief judge shall have complete discretion and authority to withdraw the certification of any mediator at any time.

(b) Lists of Certified Mediators. Lists of certified mediators shall be maintained in each division of the Court, and shall be made available to counsel and the public upon request.

(c) Qualifications of Mediators. An individual may be certified to serve as a mediator if:

(1) He or she is a former state court judge who presided in a court of general jurisdiction and was also a member of the bar in the state in which he presided; or

(2) He or she is a retired federal judicial officer; or

(3) He or she has been a member of a state bar or the bar of the District of Columbia for at least ten (10) years and is currently admitted to the Bar of this Court.

In addition, an applicant for certification must have completed a minimum of 40 hours in the Florida Circuit Court Mediation Training Course certified by the Florida Supreme Court and be found competent by the chief judge to perform mediation duties.

At the direction of the chief judge, an advisory committee may be constituted to assist in formulating policy and additional standards relating to the qualification of mediators and to assist in reviewing applications of prospective mediators.

(d) Oath Required. Every mediator shall take the oath or affirmation prescribed by 28 U.S.C. Section 453 upon qualifying as a mediator.

(e) Disqualification of a Mediator. Any person selected as a mediator may be disqualified for bias or prejudice as provided in 28 U.S.C. Section 144, and shall be disqualified in any case in which such action would be required by a justice, judge, or magistrate judge governed by 28 U.S.C. Section 455.

(f) Compensation of Mediators. Absent agreement of the parties and the mediator, mediators shall be compensated at a reasonable hourly rate provided by order of the Court after consideration of the amount in controversy, the nature of the dispute, the resources of the parties, the prevailing market rate for mediators in the applicable market, the skill and experience of the mediator, and other pertinent factors. Unless altered by order of the Court, the cost of the mediator's services shall be borne equally by the parties to the mediation conference.

(g) Limitations on Acceptance of Compensation or Other Reimbursement. Except as provided by these rules, no mediator shall charge or accept in connection with the mediation of any particular case, any fee or thing of value from any other source whatever, absent written approval of the Court given in advance of the receipt of any such payment or thing of value.

(h) Mediators as Counsel in Other Cases. Any member of the bar who is certified and designated as a mediator pursuant to these rules shall not for that reason be disqualified from appearing and acting as counsel in any other case pending before the Court.

[Added effective November 15, 1989. Amended effective December 1, 1992; February 1, 1994; July 1, 2002.]

RULE 9.03 TYPES OF CASES SUBJECT TO MEDIATION; WITHDRAWAL

(a) Court Referral. Upon order by the presiding judge, any civil action or claim may be referred by the Court to a mediation conference, providing the action or claim has not already been arbitrated in accordance with Chapter Eight of the Rules of the Middle District of Florida, except:

(1) Appeals from rulings of administrative agencies.

(2) Habeas corpus and/or extraordinary writs.

(3) Forfeitures of seized property.

(4) Bankruptcy appeals.

(b) Stipulation of Counsel. Any action or claim may be referred to a mediation conference upon the stipulation of counsel of record. Such application shall also certify agreement to pay the mediator's fee in accordance with these rules.

(c) Withdrawal From Mediation. Any civil action or claim referred to mediation pursuant to this rule may be exempt or withdrawn from mediation by the presiding judge at any time, before or after reference, upon a determination for any reason that the case is not suitable for mediation.

[Added effective November 15, 1989.]

RULE 9.04 PROCEDURES TO REFER A CASE OR CLAIM TO MEDIATION

(a)* Order of Referral. In every case in which the Court determines that referral to mediation is appropriate pursuant to Rule 9.03(a) or (b), the Court shall enter an order of referral which shall:

(1) Designate the mediator if one has previously been selected by the parties or, if not, allow fourteen (14) days for the parties to make such selection and notify the Court.

(2) Define the window of time in which the mediation conference may be conducted, preferably not sooner than 45 days and not later than fourteen (14) days before the scheduled trial date.

(3) Designate an attorney as lead counsel, who shall be responsible for coordinating two alternate mediation conference dates agreeable to the mediator and all counsel of record.

[Added effective November 15, 1989. Amended effective December 1, 1992; December 1, 2009.]

* So in original. No subparagraph (b) was promulgated.

RULE 9.05 SCHEDULING THE MEDIATION CONFERENCE

(a) Report of Lead Counsel. Not later than twenty-one (21) days after the entry of the order of referral pursuant to Rule 9.04(a), lead counsel shall file a report indicating the agreeable alternate mediation conference dates.

(b) Scheduling Mediation Conference Date. Upon receipt of the report of lead counsel, or upon failure of lead counsel to either file the report or secure mutually agreeable mediation conference dates, the Court shall fix the date for the mediation conference by order. Unless otherwise provided by order, the mediation conference shall be conducted in the United States Courthouse.

(c) Party Attendance Required. Unless otherwise excused by the presiding judge in writing, all parties, corporate representatives, and any other required claims professionals (insurance adjusters, etc.), shall be present at the Mediation Conference with full authority to negotiate a settlement. Failure to comply with the attendance or settlement authority requirements may subject a party to sanctions by the Court.

(d) Continuance of Mediation Conference Date. Subject to the availability of mediation conference space in the Courthouse, the mediator may, with the consent of all parties and counsel, reschedule the mediation conference to a date certain not later than fourteen (14) days prior to the scheduled trial date. Any continuance beyond that time must be approved by the presiding judge.

(e) Mediation Absent Party Attendance. Subject to approval of the mediator, the mediation conference may proceed in the absence of a party who, after due notice, fails to be present. Upon the recommendation of the mediator, sanctions may be imposed by the Court on any party who, absent good cause shown, failed to attend the mediation conference.

[Added effective November 15, 1989. Amended effective December 1, 2009.]

RULE 9.06 MEDIATION REPORT; NOTICE OF SETTLEMENT; JUDGMENT

(a) Mediation Report. Within seven (7) days following the conclusion of the mediation conference, the mediator shall file a Mediation Report indicating whether all required parties were present and had authority to settle the case. The report shall also indicate whether the case settled, was continued with the consent of the parties, or whether the mediator was forced to declare an impasse.

(b) Notice of Settlement. In the event that the parties reach an agreement to settle the case or claim, lead counsel shall promptly notify the Court of the settlement in accordance with Local Rule 3.08, and the Clerk shall enter judgment accordingly.

[Added effective November 15, 1989. Amended effective December 1, 2009.]

RULE 9.07 TRIAL DE NOVO

(a) Trial De Novo Upon Impasse. If the mediation conference ends in an impasse, the case will be tried as originally scheduled.

(b) Restrictions on the Use of Information Derived During the Mediation Conference. All proceedings of the mediation conference, including statements made by any party, attorney, or other participant, are privileged in all respects. The proceedings may not be reported, recorded, placed into evidence, made known to the trial court or jury, or construed for any purpose as an admission against interest. A party is not bound by anything said or done at the conference, unless a settlement is reached.

[Added effective November 15, 1989.]

ELECTRONIC CASE FILING

ADMINISTRATIVE PROCEDURES FOR ELECTRONIC FILING

I. INTRODUCTION

Since July 12, 2004, the United States District Court for the Middle District of Florida (the "Court") has mandated electronic filing through the Case Management/Electronic Case Files ("CM/ECF") system. Unless otherwise permitted by these Administrative Procedures, a Court order, or the Local Rules of the Middle District of Florida ("Local Rules"), all documents submitted for filing in civil, criminal, and miscellaneous cases must be filed electronically through CM/ECF. Eligible attorneys and pro se litigants authorized by Court order to file electronically are referred to in these Administrative Procedures as "E–filers."

These mandatory procedures provide attorneys and litigants directions on using CM/ECF. In addition, the Court's *Electronic Case Files CM/ECF User Manual* provides step-by-step instructions on the electronic filing process. Attorneys and litigants may also call the appropriate divisional Clerk's Office with any questions.

The Court may modify these Administrative Procedures at any time without prior notice. The Clerk or any judge of this Court may depart from these procedures without prior notice.

II. REGISTRATION FOR CM/ECF

A. Eligibility to File Electronically.

1. An attorney admitted to practice in this Court, including an attorney admitted pro hac vice under the Local Rules, is eligible to file electronically and must register on CM/ECF as an E–filer.

2. A pro se litigant (i.e., an individual proceeding without legal representation) is not permitted to file electronically, absent authorization by the Court. A pro se litigant must file all pleadings and documents in paper format with the appropriate divisional Clerk's Office. The Clerk will scan a pro se litigant's documents and file them in CM/ECF.

B. Registration.

1. To register for CM/ECF, an eligible attorney or authorized pro se litigant must complete and submit the "ECF Registration Form" found on the Court's website at *http://www.flmd.uscourts.gov/CMECF/register.cfm.* The Court does not require CM/ECF training. But, it encourages E–filers to review the training tutorials found on the Court's website at *http://www.flmd.uscourts.gov/CMECF/tutorials_video.htm.*

2. By registering for CM/ECF, an E–filer consents to electronic service of all documents in accordance with the Federal Rules of Procedure, and waives the right to personal service or service by mail. Registration, however, does not constitute consent to electronic service of a document that is not filed with the Court (e.g., Rule 26 disclosure or a discovery request). An E–filer may consent to electronic service of such documents separately, in writing, in accordance with the Federal Rules of Procedure.

C. Login Name and Password.

1. Once registered, an E–filer will be issued a login name and password. The Clerk will email the login name and password to the primary email address provided on the ECF Registration Form.

2. Once an E–filer receives a login name and password, the E–filer is responsible for all documents filed using the login name and password, and is subject to sanctions under the Federal Rules of Procedure for any misuse.

3. A pro se E–filer must not knowingly permit or cause to permit any other person to use the pro se E–filer's login name and password. However, an attorney E–filer may permit an authorized employee of the attorney's office to use the attorney's login name and password on the attorney's behalf.

4. An attorney does not need to re-register for a new CM/ECF login name and password if the attorney changes law firms. The login name and password remain valid. But, the Court strongly encourages an attorney to change the attorney's password upon changing firms.

5. An E–filer may terminate a CM/ECF password by sending a written notice of termination to the appropriate divisional Clerk's Office. Upon receipt of the notice of termination, the Clerk will immediately terminate the E–filer's CM/ECF password. However, for attorney E–filers, filing a notice of termination is separate and distinct from withdrawing as an attorney of record in a case, which is permitted only by Court order.

6. The Court may disable an E–filer's login name and password if:

a) the E–filer is an attorney who fails to maintain active status as a member of the bar of the United States District Court for the Middle District of Florida or is suspended for disciplinary reasons;

b) the email sent to the E–filer's primary email address is returned as undeliverable, and the E–filer has not provided a correct email address;

c) the Court determines the login name and password have been used in violation of these administrative procedures; or

d) the E–filer is a pro se litigant whose authorization to file electronically has terminated.

D. Contact Information.

1. All attorneys and pro se litigants must maintain current information in CM/ECF including name, email address, mailing address, telephone number, fax number, and where applicable, firm name or affiliation. An E–filer must immediately update CM/ECF with any change to the E–filer's contact information. In addition, an E–Filer should inform the Court and parties of such a change by using the "Notice of Change of Address" event in CM/ECF for each active case. Pro se litigants who are not authorized to file electronically must submit a "Notice of Change of Address" in paper format.

2. When an attorney changes firms, both the attorney and firm should be aware of the implications for CM/ECF's noticing system.

a) For cases that will remain with the departing attorney, the attorney must immediately change the attorney's email address in CM/ECF, and submit either the "Change of Address" form, available on the Court's website at *http://www.flmd.uscourts.gov/CMECF/default.htm*, or a written change of address to the appropriate divisional Clerk's Office.

b) For cases that will remain with the firm of the departing attorney, another attorney from that firm must file a notice of appearance (unless the attorney has already appeared). The departing attorney or other attorney who has appeared must file a motion for approval of the departing attorney's withdrawal so the case docket properly reflects the attorney of record.

3. An attorney may add a secondary email address to the attorney's account so other individuals (e.g., legal staff) may receive notices.

4. To add an attorney of record after the initial pleadings are filed, a notice of appearance must be electronically filed in accordance with the Local Rules.

III. FILING AND SERVICE

A. Electronic Filing.

1. All documents must be filed electronically in CM/ECF, unless otherwise provided by these Administrative Procedures, the Local Rules, or a Court order. Documents filed electronically have the same legal status and effect as documents filed in paper format. Emailing or faxing a document to the Clerk's Office or to the assigned judge does not constitute an official filing of the document.

a) An E–filer must verify the accuracy and readability of a document before filing it in CM/ECF.

b) If an E–filer is unable to file a document or item electronically because the document or item cannot be scanned, the E–filer must file that document or item with the Clerk's Office and submit a Notice of Filing Electronically.

2. A document filed electronically must comply with the requirements of the Federal Rules of Procedure and the Local Rules. Documents filed electronically are also subject to any page limitation set by Court order or Rule.

3. A document is not filed until CM/ECF generates a Notice of Electronic Filing ("NEF"). A document filed electronically is deemed filed as of the time and date printed on the NEF.

4. When filing a document considered to be an emergency or otherwise urgent or time-sensitive, the E–filer must immediately contact the appropriate divisional Clerk's Office.

B. Notice of Electronic Filing.

1. When a document is filed electronically, CM/ECF automatically emails an NEF to all E–filers who are of record in the case. The NEF constitutes proof of filing. The NEF includes the docket entry, unique electronic document stamp, list of the recipients receiving the email notification of the filing, and hyperlink to the filed document(s). Some orders and docket entries do not have separate documents and consist only of the NEF.

2. A document filed electronically can be viewed the first time for free from the hyperlink. The hyperlink expires after the earlier of two events: the first use or fifteen (15) days after the NEF is emailed. To view a hyperlink after it has expired, an E–filer must use the Public Access to Court Electronic Records ("PACER") program and will be charged to view the document.

3. The Clerk will mail paper copies of orders, judgments, and notices to pro se litigants who are not E–filers.

4. An attorney who has properly withdrawn from a case under the Local Rules or whose client(s) has been terminated from a case but continues to receive NEFs may file a notice requesting the Court to remove the attorney from the service list in that case.

C. Filing in Paper Format.

1. A document presented to the Court in paper format for filing will be scanned as a PDF and docketed electronically in CM/ECF thereby generating an NEF. The scanned PDF image is the official court record.

2. A document presented to the Court for filing is deemed filed at the time received by the Clerk.

3. The following documents must be presented in paper format to the appropriate divisional Clerk's Office for conventional filing:

a) Initiating documents in civil and miscellaneous cases. Initiating documents (e.g., complaints, petitions, and notices of removal) and the civil cover sheets must be filed in paper format or PDF format on CD–ROM, DVD, or other medium as the Court directs. An attorney or pro se litigant may mail or deliver initiating documents to the Clerk. Upon receipt, the Clerk will scan and file the initiating document(s) electronically in CM/ECF.

(1) Notices of removal. When filing a notice of removal, the filing party must include all documents required to be filed pursuant to *28 U.S.C. §§ 1446–47* as separate PDF documents on a CD–ROM, DVD, or other medium.

(2) Once the Clerk opens the case, an E–filer must file any additional portions of the state court record electronically.

b) Documents filed ex parte. When a document is filed ex parte, the opposing party will not receive notice of the filing. Also, when the Court rules on an ex parte document, only the filing party will receive notice of the Court's decision.

c) Documents filed under seal. A document filed under seal must be filed in paper format and in accordance with the Local Rules. The document must be clearly designated as "UNDER SEAL" or "IN CAMERA." An E–filer, however, may file a "Motion to Seal" either electronically or in paper format. If a motion to seal is filed electronically, the E–filer must file each document being proposed for sealing in paper format. If the Court grants a motion to seal, it will enter an order authorizing the filing of the document in paper format under seal.

d) Documents filed ex parte and under seal. If the Court grants an application to file a document ex parte and under seal, the ex parte sealed document must be filed in paper format. An application and all related ex parte documents must be clearly designated as "EX PARTE AND UNDER SEAL." The opposing party will neither receive notice of the filing nor be able to view the document filed under seal at the appropriate divisional Clerk's Office or in CM/ECF.

e) Charging documents, warrants, or summonses in criminal cases. A charging document in a criminal case (e.g., indictment, superseding indictment, information, and complaint) must be presented in paper format. Where applicable, an attorney must present a warrant and summons to the Clerk for filing along with the charging document. The Clerk will thereafter issue the warrant or summons to the United States Marshal for service.

f) Pro se litigant's documents. All documents filed by a pro se litigant (including prisoners) must be submitted in paper format to the appropriate divisional Clerk's Office, unless the pro se litigant has been granted authorization by the Court to file electronically.

D. Filing Fees. Any fee payable to the Clerk must be paid by a certified bank check, cashier's check, money order, or cash. Personal checks are not accepted, but law firms may remit payments using business checks. Checks and money orders must be made payable to "Clerk, United States District Court." If paying with cash, the exact amount must be tendered. The Court accepts neither credit or debit cards nor electronic billing or debit accounts.

E. Service.

1. *Summons.* Upon filing a civil complaint, the filing attorney or pro se litigant must submit a paper summons for each defendant to be served to the Clerk for issuance. The filing party is responsible for assuring that service of process is accomplished in accordance with the Federal Rules of Procedure. Service of process is not accomplished via CM/ECF. A returned summons, however, may be imaged and filed electronically or in paper format.

2. *Service through CM/ECF.* Service through CM/ECF is considered service by mail under the Federal Rules of Procedure.

3. *Service on a Party Who is Not CM/ECF Registered.* An E–filer must serve paper copies of a document filed electronically on a party not registered for CM/ECF in accordance with the Federal Rules of Procedure.

4. *Serving by Other Means.* If a filing party submits documents in paper format to the Clerk, the party must serve the documents in accordance with the Federal Rules of Procedure.

5. *Certificate of Service.* All documents filed electronically and in paper format must include a certificate of service. The NEF does not constitute a certificate of service. The certificate of service must state the manner in which service was accomplished on each party. A certificate of service may be filed as an attachment to the parent document. *See* Form A for sample certificates of service.

F. Retention of Paper Records. Paper records will be maintained and disposed of in accordance with the policies of the Administrative Office of the United States Courts and this Court's Administrative Order.

IV. PREPARING DOCUMENTS FOR ELECTRONIC FILING

A. General Filing Standards.

1. When electronically filing in CM/ECF, an E–filer must submit all documents as a PDF.

2. When scanning a document not created on a word processing system, an E–filer should configure the scanner for black and white at 300 dots per inch ("dpi"), rather than color or gray scale scanning, unless those settings are needed to display the image of data in the PDF properly. An exhibit may be scanned in color (e.g., a color photograph). An E–filer is responsible for ensuring the accuracy and readability of a scanned document.

3. Documents submitted on CD–ROM, DVD, or other medium as the Court directs, must contain only documents relating to a single case and be labeled with the E–filer's name, case number, case name, a brief description of the documents on the medium, and the telephone number of the E–filer. Each PDF file name on a disk must be titled with a sufficient description so it may be readily identified. Each PDF document submitted must be within the ten (10) megabytes size limit.

4. No proposed order or judgment may be submitted unless authorized by the assigned judge.

B. Hyperlinks.

1. The use of hyperlinks in documents filed electronically is permitted. When filing a document containing hyperlinks, the E–filer is encouraged to:

a) hyperlink to other portions of the same document;

b) hyperlink to other documents electronically filed with the Court (or to any other federal court's e-filing system); and

c) hyperlink to cited legal authority located on recognized electronic research services like Westlaw, LexisNexis, FindLaw, and official government websites. Hyperlinks to cited authority do not replace standard citation format.

2. Hyperlinks are convenient mechanisms for accessing material cited in a document filed in CM/ECF. However, neither a hyperlink nor any website to which it refers will be considered part of the record.

3. The Court accepts no responsibility for, and does not endorse, any product, organization, or content at any hyperlinked website, or at any website to which that website may be linked.

C. Technical Requirements.

1. No single document may exceed ten (10) megabytes in size. A document exceeding ten (10) megabytes must be divided and filed as separate attachments or docket entries.

2. Electronically filed documents must be converted to PDF format using Adobe Acrobat or similar PDF conversion software and not scanned to PDF. The table below identifies recommended PDF creation methods.

Document Format	Recommended PDF Creation Method
Documents in Word, WordPerfect, or other word-processing software	PDF conversion (rather than scanned)
Transcripts in text format on disk or in email	PDF conversion
Maps and photos in electronic format	PDF conversion (when appropriate)
Websites	PDF conversion
Printed copies of documents, contracts, statements, transcripts, etc., if an electronic copy is not readily available	Scanning to PDF
Map, photos, and other materials, if an electronic copy is not readily available	Scanning to PDF

3. When possible, an E–filer should scan documents with Optical Character Recognition ("OCR"). OCR converts scanned images into text and provides the ability to "text-search" and "copy and paste" in a document. OCR is available in most scanning and PDF creation software packages. OCR is most effective on primarily text-based documents, and is generally not beneficial for maps, photographs, charts, graphs, financial statements, and other non-text documents. An E–filer using OCR is responsible for verifying reasonable accuracy and readability of the document.

D. Redactions.

1. *Responsibility for Redactions.* It is the responsibility of every attorney and pro se litigant to redact personal identifiers before filing pleadings, motions, memoranda, exhibits, and other documents with the Court. The attorney or pro se litigant is responsible for verifying that appropriate and effective methods of redaction have been used. Attorneys and pro se litigants must review the Judicial Conference Privacy Policy and applicable Court rules at *http://www.privacy.uscourts.gov/*. Upon logging into CM/ECF, the system will prompt E–filers to acknowledge compliance with the redaction rules under the Federal Rules of Procedure.

2. *Redaction Rules.* Unless the Court orders otherwise, documents filed electronically that include a social security number, individual's tax identification number, name of an individual known to be a minor, financial account, individual's birth date, or home address (in criminal case) may include only the following:

a) social security number—the last four numbers;

b) tax identification number—the last four numbers;

c) name of minor children—the initials;

d) financial account number—the last four numbers;

e) date of birth—the year; and

f) home address (in criminal cases)—the city and state.

3. *Exemptions from the Redaction Rules.* The above redaction rules do not apply to:

a) a financial account number or a real property address that identifies the property alleged to be subject to forfeiture in a forfeiture proceeding;

b) a record of an administrative or agency proceeding;

c) an official record of a state court proceeding;

d) the record of a court or tribunal, if that record was not subject to redaction when originally filed;

e) a filing exempted under the Federal Rules of Procedure;

f) a pro se litigant filing an action brought under *28 U.S.C. §§ 2241, 2254, or 2255*;

g) an arrest or search warrant; and

h) a charging document and an affidavit filed in support of any charging document.

4. *Correcting a Failure to Redact.* If the Clerk notifies an attorney or pro se litigant that a document contains a personal identifier, the filer must promptly file a redacted document. Note, however, the Clerk is not responsible for reviewing any document filed to determine whether it includes personal information.

5. *Waiver of Protection of Identifiers.* A party waives the protection against disclosure of personal identifiers as to the party's own information to the extent that the party files personal information not under seal and without redaction.

6. *Sealed Filings.* The Court may order a filing to be made under seal without redaction. The Court may later unseal a filing or order a filing of a redacted version for the public record.

7. *Protective Orders.* If necessary to protect private or sensitive information that is otherwise unprotected, the Court may require redaction of additional information, or limit or prohibit remote electronic access.

E. Attaching Exhibits to Documents.

1. An E–filer must file an exhibit attached to a pleading, motion, memorandum, declaration, affidavit, or other document electronically as a PDF. The resulting file must be less than ten (10) megabytes.

2. An E–filer must verify the readability of scanned exhibits before filing them with the Court. Text PDF files are preferred, but image PDF documents are accepted.

3. An E–filer filing a document with numerous exhibits totaling more than ten (10) pages is encouraged to use the following procedures:

a) create an index to the exhibits, including the exhibit number and title of the exhibit. File the index as an attachment to the parent document. *See* Form B for sample exhibit index.

b) title and number each exhibit, then attach each exhibit separately to the parent document. Each exhibit must have a descriptive title.

c) divide any single exhibit larger than ten (10) megabytes into clearly labeled parts smaller than ten (10) megabytes. File each part or section as separate attachments to the memorandum.

d) use PDF bookmarks.

F. Electronic Signatures.

1. *Signatures of Filing Parties.* Every pleading, motion, memorandum of law, or other document must be signed by the pro se litigant authorized by the Court to file electronically or at least one attorney of record. A signature must appear in documents filed electronically in one of the following manners:

a) "/s/ (E–filer's first and last name)";

b) an electronic image of the E–filer's signature that is pasted into the signature block on the document; or

c) a conventional signature (when the document is scanned).

The submission of a document (i) signed with "/s/ (E–filer's first and last name)," an electronic image of the E–filer's signature, or a conventional signature, and (ii) filed under that E–filer's login name and password constitutes an original signature under the Federal Rules of Procedure.

2. *Signatures of Non-Filing Attorneys.* The filing attorney is permitted to file a document that requires the signature of another attorney (e.g., stipulation), if the filing attorney obtains approval from the non-filing attorney that he/she authorizes the filing attorney to sign the document electronically. The filing attorney may indicate such approval by one of the following:

a) Oral Approval for Electronic Signature.

/s/ (non–filing attorney's first and last name)

(Signed by Filing Attorney with permission of Non-filing Attorney)

Electronic Signature or /s/ (filing attorney's first and last name)

The filing attorney must maintain a record of when and how permission was obtained to sign the non-filing attorney's name until all appeals have been exhausted or the time for seeking appellate review has expired.

b) Approval by signature. The filing attorney may obtain and keep a paper copy of the document the non-filing attorney signed. Possession of a signed copy must be indicated as follows:

/s/ (non–filing attorney's first and last name)

(*I certify that I maintain a signed copy of the document bearing the signature of (non–filing attorney's first and last name) in my office.)

Electronic Signature or /s/ (filing attorney's first and last name)

The filing attorney must maintain the signed copy of the document until all appeals have been exhausted or the time for seeking appellate review has expired.

c) Scanned signature. The filing attorney may obtain an original signature, scan the signature page, and file it as an attachment to the document. The filing attorney must maintain the signed original until all appeals have been exhausted or the time for seeking appellate review has expired.

3. *Signatures of Non–Attorneys.* The filing attorney is permitted to file a document that requires the signature of a non-attorney or an individual who is not counsel of record (e.g., verified pleadings, contracts, and affidavits) in electronic format in any of the following ways, provided the filing attorney maintains the signed original until all appeals have been exhausted or the time for seeking appellate review has expired:

a) An electronic version of a document bearing "/s/ (first and last name)" filed with a statement that the original has been signed.

/s/ Party Smith*

(*I certify that I have the signed original of this document that is available for inspection during normal business hours by the Court or a party to this action.)

Electronic Signature or /s/ (filing attorney's first and last name)

b) A document bearing "/s/ (first and last name)" may be filed with a scanned copy of the signature page as an attachment.

c) If a document containing original signatures is not digitally available, it may be scanned and filed electronically.

4. *Signatures in Criminal Cases.* A document in a criminal case that requires the signature of a non-attorney (e.g., grand jury foreperson, defendant, third-party custodian, sureties on a bond, United States Marshal, or officer from the Court's Probation or Pretrial Services Office) must be presented in paper format to the Clerk, scanned by the Clerk, docketed in CM/ECF, and retained in paper format.

5. *Signatures of Judges and Court Officials.* The submission of a document that is signed (i) with "/s/ (judge's or court official's first and last name)" or an electronic image of a judge's or court official's traditional signature, and (ii) filed using the judge's or court official's login name and password constitutes an original signature for all purposes.

V. PROBLEMS IN ELECTRONIC FILING

A. Correcting Errors.

1. Once a document is filed in CM/ECF, only the Clerk may change or correct the document or docket entry.

a) If an E–filer discovers an error after completing the electronic filing process, the E–filer should immediately contact the appropriate divisional Clerk's Office with the case number and document number of the erroneous filing.

b) If the Clerk discovers an error with a document filed, the Clerk may (i) alert the E–filer of the error and, if necessary, the manner in which to proceed (e.g., refile a document with a new document number or file a motion to strike); and (ii) note the error and any instructions provided to the E–filer in the docket entry.

c) An E–filer notified by the Clerk to correct an error is responsible for doing so immediately.

2. If, after filing, an E–filer determines a document or exhibit should have been filed under seal, that E–filer must comply with the Local Rules and obtain a Court order to seal the document or exhibit. Absent a Court order, the document will not be sealed.

B. Technical Failures.

1. If an E–filer experiences a technical failure with, for example telephone lines, Internet Service, or other hardware and software problems, the E–filer is responsible for filing the document in paper format.

2. If a technical failure with CM/ECF results in an untimely filing, the E–filer may move the Court for appropriate relief. CM/ECF is available twenty-four hours per day, seven days per week except during scheduled maintenance or power outages. Scheduled maintenance and power outages will be posted on the Court's website. The Clerk will maintain a log of all periods of technical failure.

VI. PUBLIC ACCESS TO COURT ELECTRONIC RECORDS

Remote public electronic access to case dockets and documents filed in CM/ECF is available through PACER. PACER is available to anyone who registers for an account including attorneys, law firms, pro se litigants, government agencies, data collectors, the media, and the general public. To receive an PACER account, a person must register at ***www.pacer.gov***.

A paper copy and a certified copy of an electronically filed document may be purchased at the Clerk's Office.

FORM A—Sample Certificate of Service Language

Sample A—Attorney E–filer

I hereby certify that on (date), I electronically filed the foregoing with the Clerk of the Court by using the CM/ECF system. I further certify that I mailed the foregoing document and the notice of electronic filing by first-class mail to the following non–CM/ECF participants: ________.

/s/ (Attorney's first and last name)
Attorney's first and last name
Attorney's Bar Number
Attorney for Plaintiff/Defendant
Law Firm Name
Law Firm Address
Phone Number
Fax Number
Attorney's Email Address

Sample B—Attorney E–filer

I hereby certify that on (date), I presented the foregoing to the Clerk of the Court for filing and uploading to the CM/ECF system. I further certify that I mailed the foregoing document and the notice of electronic filing by first-class mail to the following non–CM/ECF participants: ________.

/s/ (Attorney's first and last name)
Attorney's first and last name
Attorney's Bar Number
Attorney for Plaintiff/Defendant
Law Firm Name
Law Firm Address
Phone Number
Fax Number
Attorney's Email Address

Sample C—Authorized Pro Se E–filer

I hereby certify that on (date), I electronically filed the foregoing with the Clerk of the Court by using the CM/ECF system. I further certify that I mailed the foregoing document and the notice of electronic filing by first-class mail to the following non–CM/ECF participants: ______.

/s/ (Pro se e-filer's first and last name)
Pro se e-filer's first and last name
Plaintiff/Defendant
Address
Phone Number
Fax Number
Email Address

Sample D—Authorized Pro Se E–filer

I hereby certify that on (date), I presented the foregoing to the Clerk of the Court for filing and uploading to the CM/ECF system. I further certify that I mailed the foregoing document and the notice of electronic filing by first-class mail to the following non–CM/ECF participants: ______.

/s/ (Pro se e-filer's first and last name)
Pro se e-filer's first and last name
Plaintiff/Defendant
Address
Phone Number
Fax Number
Email Address

FORM B—SAMPLE EXHIBIT INDEX

Exhibit Index

Number	Title
1	Affidavit of John Smith
2	Excerpts from Jane Doe's Deposition
3–A	Contract Between XYZ Company and ABC Company (Part 1, Pages 1–15)
3–B	Contract Between XYZ Company and ABC Company (Part 2, Pages 16–24)
4	XYZ Company General Ledgers

[Effective March 15, 2007. Amended effective June 5, 2015.]

CRIMINAL JUSTICE ACT PLAN

CHAPTER ONE

SECTION 1.01 AUTHORITY

The Criminal Justice Act Plan, hereinafter referred to as the Plan, is adopted pursuant to the authority of the Criminal Justice Act of 1984, as subsequently amended by Acts of Congress and codified in Chapter 201 of Title 18, United States Code, and Volume VII of the Guide to Judiciary Policies and Procedures.

SECTION 1.02 EFFECTIVE DATE OF IMPLEMENTATION

In accordance with 18 U.S.C. § 3006A(a), this Plan has been adopted by the United States District Court for the Middle District of Florida and will be implemented on the day the plan is approved by the Judicial Council of the Eleventh Circuit.

SECTION 1.03 COURT DEFINED

Except as limited by specific statutory requirements, reference throughout this Plan to the "Court" shall mean that either a district judge or United States magistrate is authorized to perform the particular function.

SECTION 1.04 PROVISION FOR THE REPRESENTATION OF DEFENDANTS

(a) Authorized Representation: In accordance with 18 U.S.C. § 3006A(a), this Plan is adopted to ensure the adequate representation of any person financially unable to obtain adequate representation, and:

(1) Who is charged with a felony and/or a misdemeanor (other than a petty offense as defined in Title 18 of the United States Code unless a loss of liberty is possible), or with juvenile delinquency by the commission of an act which, if committed by an adult, would be such a felony or misdemeanor or with a violation of probation; or

(2) Who is under arrest, when such representation is required by law; or

(3) Who is subject to revocation of parole, in custody as a material witness, or seeking collateral relief, as provided by 18 U.S.C. § 3006A(a)(1)(g); or

(4) Whose mental condition is the subject of a hearing pursuant to Chapter 313 of Title 18, United States Code; or

(5) For whom the Fifth or Sixth Amendment to the Constitution requires the appointment of counsel or for whom, in a case in which the person faces loss of liberty, any Federal law requires the appointment of counsel.

(b) Scope of Representation: Representation provided under this Plan shall include counsel and investigative, expert, and/or other services necessary for an adequate defense.

(c) Source of Representation:

(1) *Federal Defender Organization:* A Federal Public Defender Organization has been established to provide representation in accordance with 18 U.S.C. § 3006A(g)(2)(A). This Plan contemplates that approximately 75% of the annual appointments, as calculated on a fiscal year basis, shall be assigned to the Federal Defender Organization.

(2) *Criminal Justice Act (CJA) Panel Attorneys:* This Plan contemplates that approximately 25% of the annual appointments, calculated on a fiscal year basis, shall be assigned to CJA panel members. Membership of the divisional CJA panels shall be established by:

(A) Regular Panel Membership: In accordance with 18 U.S.C. § 3006A(b), each Division of this Court shall prepare and maintain a panel listing of attorneys who are willing to accept appointments in accordance with this Plan, and who are competent to give adequate representation to indigent defendants. Attorneys appointed to regular membership on the divisional CJA panels shall serve at the pleasure of the Court.

(1) Criteria For Panel Membership: The minimum criteria for membership on any divisional CJA Panel are that each attorney:

(a) Be a member in good standing of the Bar of the United States District Court for the Middle District of Florida and the Florida Bar;

(b) Have at least two years experience as an attorney licensed to practice in any state or the District of Columbia;

(c) Have sufficient competence to furnish high quality representation to criminal defendants in the District Court;

(d) Be familiar with:

(1) the Federal Rules of Criminal Procedure;

(2) the Federal Rules of Evidence;

(3) the Bail Reform Act of 1984;

(4) the Federal Sentencing Guidelines; and,

(5) legislation, rules, or guidelines which supersede, amend, or supplement (1) through (4) above;

(e) Have attended and completed at least one live or video-taped course or seminar on the topic of the Federal Sentencing Guidelines, and its application, within the twelve months prior to application. If such training course or seminar is not sponsored by the Jacksonville, Orlando, Tampa, or Ft. Myers Chapters of the Federal Bar Association, the program for the seminar or training must be approved by the Federal Public Defender of the Middle District of Florida;

(f) Have attended and completed at least one Public Defender-approved continuing legal education seminar on federal court criminal practice within the twelve months prior to application, or have reviewed an approved video presentation concerning criminal practice in the Middle District of Florida which shall be on file in each Federal Public Defender Office in the District; and

(g) Have participated as counsel of record, either as prosecutor or defense attorney, in at least one criminal jury trial in any federal court. Alternatively, this requirement may be satisfied by the applicant's having participated in a federal criminal jury trial by sitting "second chair" to a member of a divisional Mentor Panel; and

(h) Effective July 1, 1997, all members of the CJA panel must attend and complete at least one continuing legal education program annually. The program must emphasize Federal Sentencing Guidelines and other aspects of federal criminal trial practice and be approved by the Federal Public Defender of the Middle District of Florida.

(2) The Federal Public Defender shall be responsible for certifying to the Court compliance by the applicant with the continuing education requirements of subsections (e), (f), and (h) hereof. In order to facilitate satisfaction of this oversight responsibility, the applicant shall be required to furnish written evidence of the applicant's attendance or participation in any such training course or seminar to the Federal Public Defender in such form or manner specified by the Federal Public Defender.

(3) The Federal Public Defender shall be responsible for providing educational materials including the video presentation concerning criminal practice for the Middle District of Florida for use by CJA panel applicants and members, and other members of the Bar. Such training is important for enhancing the quality of representation of indigents and for making the CJA panel accessible to able attorneys who have limited federal criminal experience. Similarly, the Federal Public Defender shall serve as a central repository for materials which may be helpful to the members of the CJA panel, such as legal memoranda on recurring issues and jury instructions.

(4) In considering an applicant for membership on the CJA panel, the Court may, in its discretion, waive any of the requirements of section (1)(b), (e), (f), (g), and (h).

(B) The Mentor Panel: The District Court shall establish a Mentor Panel in each Division consisting of attorneys with substantial experience in criminal matters in the District Court and who are willing to serve as "Mentors". Membership on the Mentor Panel shall not preclude an attorney from also serving on the CJA Panel. Appointments to the Mentor Panels shall be made by the Chief Judge of the District, upon recommendations by the United States magistrates. The number of attorneys serving on the divisional Mentor Panels shall be determined by the Chief Judge, depending on the needs and workload of each division. Mentors shall serve for a term of three years. However, Mentors may be reappointed to succeeding terms at the discretion of the Chief Judge. The Federal Public Defender and his attorney assistants shall, by virtue of such positions, be members of the Mentor Panel in their respective divisions; provided, however, that any such attorney may "opt out" as a Mentor. Mentors, who shall serve without compensation, shall be willing to:

(1) Permit applicants for the CJA Panel who do not meet the minimal trial experience requirement to sit "second chair" during the trial of a federal criminal case (subject to the consent of the Mentor's client and approval of the presiding judge) and furnish to the applicant at the conclusion of the trial a letter certifying that the applicant has done so;

(2) Assist the Federal Public Defender and pertinent Federal Bar Association chapters in planning and/or participation in criminal justice training programs for CJA Panel attorneys and those who desire to become CJA Panel attorneys;

(3) Advise and consult with CJA Panel members on matters of federal criminal procedure and practice, as well as on issues regarding ethical considerations; and,

(4) Provide the Court with such assistance and advice as the Court may from time to time request regarding methods and means for enhancing the quality of criminal defense representation in the District.

(C) Panel Member Terms and Reappointment:

(1) Members of the CJA Panel serve at the pleasure of the Court.

(2) After three years of service on a CJA Panel, the Panel member may reapply and be reappointed for succeeding three-year terms if, in the discretion of the Board of Judges, that the member continues to meet the qualifications delineated in section (A)(1) above.

(D) Pro Hac Vice Appointments: When the Court determines that the appointment of an attorney, who is not a member of the CJA panel, is in the interest of justice, judicial economy or continuity of representation, or there is some other compelling circumstance warranting the appointment, the attorney may be admitted to the CJA panel pro hac vice and appointed to represent the defendant. Such appointments shall be made only in exceptional and compelling circumstances. Attorneys appointed under the special provisions of this paragraph shall not thereby attain regular membership status on the CJA panel.

(E) Removal: The Board of Judges, in its discretion, may remove a CJA panel attorney for conduct incompatible with the goals of the Criminal Justice Act, the requirements set out in section 1.04(c)(2) of this Plan, or the standards imposed by Local Rule 2.01. A complaint regarding a CJA panel attorney should be forwarded to the Chief Judge, who may refer the matter to the appropriate committee (or subcommittee) for consideration. That committee (or subcommittee) may then make such inquiry as it deems warranted and issue a report and recommendation of action for the Board of Judges to consider. When a complaint is forwarded by the Chief Judge to a committee (or subcommittee) for consideration, a copy of the complaint shall be provided to the CJA panel attorney. The CJA panel attorney who is the subject of the complaint may submit a response to the Chair of committee (or subcommittee) within fourteen days from the certified mailing date of the complaint.

CHAPTER TWO

APPOINTMENT AND PAYMENT OF COUNSEL

SECTION 2.01 MAINTENANCE OF THE DIVISIONAL CJA PANELS

In accordance with Local Rule 6.01(c)(4) of the Middle District of Florida, responsibility for maintenance of the divisional CJA panels is delegated to the United States magistrates.

In this regard, the United States magistrates may make additions to, or deletions from, the approved CJA panel of attorneys. Such action should ensure that the CJA panel is large enough to provide a sufficient number of experienced attorneys to handle the CJA caseload, yet small enough so that panel members receive an adequate number of appointments to maintain their proficiency in criminal defense work.

SECTION 2.02 APPOINTMENT OF COUNSEL IN A CRIMINAL CASE

(a) Advice of Right to Counsel: The Court shall advise a defendant of the right to be represented by counsel and that counsel will be appointed if requested, and if the defendant is financially unable to obtain counsel in every criminal case in which a defendant appears without counsel and is entitled to representation as provided in Chapter One of this Plan.

(b) Fact Finding and Financial Inquiry: Unless representation by counsel is waived in writing by the defendant, the Court shall conduct a fact finding inquiry into the defendant's financial status. If, after appropriate inquiry, the Court determines that the defendant is financially unable to obtain counsel, counsel shall be appointed in accordance with this Plan.

(c) Retroactive Appointment: Appointment of counsel may be made retroactive to include any representation furnished pursuant to the Plan prior to appointment.

(d) Continuity and Duration of Appointment: A person for whom counsel is appointed shall be represented by such appointed counsel at every stage of the proceedings from initial appearance through appeal, including ancillary matters appropriate to the proceedings, until relieved and discharged by the Court or by the Court of Appeals.

(e) Substitution of Appointed Counsel by the Court: The Court may, in the interests of justice, substitute one appointed counsel for another at any stage of the proceedings.

(f) Prohibition for Accepting Payment by Appointed Counsel: Unless permitted in advance by court order, counsel appointed under the provisions of this Plan may not require, request, or accept any payment or promise of payment for representing a party.

(g) Responsibility of Appointed Counsel Upon Conviction: Prior to the entry of a plea of guilty or upon conviction following trial, appointed counsel shall advise the defendant of the right of appeal, if any, and of the right to counsel on appeal. If requested by defendant, appointed counsel shall file a timely notice of appeal and shall continue representation of the defendant throughout the appellate process.

SECTION 2.03 PARTIAL PAYMENT AND/OR REIMBURSEMENT FOR THE COST OF APPOINTED COUNSEL

If at any time the Court finds that a person is financially able to obtain counsel or to make full or partial payment for representation, or that funds are available for payment from or on behalf of a person furnished representation, the Court may terminate the appointment of counsel and may direct or authorize payment as provided in 18 U.S.C. § 3006A(f).

If appointed counsel obtains information that a client is financially able to make payment, in whole or in part, for legal or other services in connection with the representation, and the source of the attorney's information is not protected as a privileged communication, counsel shall promptly advise the Court.

SECTION 2.04 APPOINTMENT OF PREVIOUSLY RETAINED COUNSEL

Pursuant to Local Rule 2.03(c) of the Middle District of Florida, after appearing in a criminal proceeding, retained counsel will not ordinarily be permitted to withdraw by reason of non-payment of attorney's fees. When retained counsel is permitted to withdraw after trial or, under exceptional circumstances, at some other stage of the proceeding, and the Court finds that the defendant is then qualified for the appointment of counsel pursuant to this Plan, counsel may so be appointed. If there are other persons in the same case or proceeding then being represented by appointed counsel, the same counsel may be appointed for the unrepresented defendant in the absence of a conflict of interest. Otherwise, the appointment shall be made as in the usual course of administering this Plan; previously retained counsel shall not be appointed as a matter of course.

CHAPTER THREE

REQUEST FOR SERVICES OTHER THAN COUNSEL

SECTION 3.01 OBTAINING SERVICES OTHER THAN COUNSEL UPON REQUEST

(a) Eligibility: Counsel (whether appointed under the provisions of this Plan or privately retained) or persons who are otherwise eligible for representation under this Plan, but who have elected to proceed pro se, may request services in an ex parte application in accordance with 18 U.S.C. § 3006A(e)(1).

(b) Ex Parte Application Procedure: Except as permitted by section 3.02 below, ex parte applications for expert, investigative, or other services necessary for an adequate defense shall be submitted to the Court prior to the performance of such services. The Court will consider the ex parte application and, upon finding that such services are necessary for an adequate defense and that the person is financially unable to obtain the services, may authorize the services.

SECTION 3.02 OBTAINING SERVICES OTHER THAN COUNSEL WITHOUT OBTAINING COURT APPROVAL

(a) Eligibility: In accordance with 18 U.S.C. § 3006A(e)(2), only counsel appointed under the provisions of this Plan may obtain, subject to later review, investigative, expert, or other services without prior authorization.

(b) Procedure for Ratification of Expenses: Counsel may request ratification for compensation of services provided in accordance with this section by submitting an ex parte application to a district judge, or United States magistrate if the services rendered were in conjunction with a matter over which the United States magistrate has jurisdiction.

The Court will consider the ex parte application and, upon finding that such services are necessary for an adequate defense and that the person is financially unable to obtain the services, may authorize payment for the services subject to the limitations imposed by 18 U.S.C. § 3006A(e).

SECTION 3.03 WAIVER OF LIMITS TO THE FEDERAL PUBLIC DEFENDER ORGANIZATION

The Federal Public Defender's organization may obtain investigative, expert, or other services without regard to the requirements and limitations of this Chapter, provided that total expenditures of the organization for investigative, expert, and other services do not exceed its budget authorization for these specific categories. In the event that such expenditures exceed budget authorization, applications must be made on an ex parte application basis in accordance with this Chapter, and shall be subject to the limitations imposed therein.

CHAPTER FOUR

COMPENSATION TO CJA PANEL ATTORNEYS

SECTION 4.01 MANDATORY USE OF CJA FORMS

Applications for compensation shall be submitted on the appropriate CJA Forms. Forms may be obtained during normal business hours from the Office of the Clerk of Court.

SECTION 4.02 SCHEDULE OF MAXIMUM FEES AND EXPENSES FOR COUNSEL

The fees payable to counsel appointed pursuant to this Plan, and the payment of expenses incurred in providing representation pursuant to such appointment, shall be made in such amounts and in the manner prescribed from time to time by the Criminal Justice Act, as amended, and in accordance with the rules, regulations, and guidelines prescribed from time to time by the Judicial Conference of the United States.

[Dated: October 21, 2010. Approved by the Judicial Council of the Eleventh Circuit January 12, 2011.]

JURY PLAN

PLAN FOR THE QUALIFICATION AND RANDOM SELECTION OF GRAND AND PETIT JURORS

CHAPTER ONE. GENERAL POLICY MATTERS

1.01. Adoption and Implementation. Pursuant to the Jury Selection and Service Act of 1968 (Public Law 90–274), 28 U.S.C. Section 1861 et seq., the following Plan for the Qualification and Random Selection of Grand and Petit Jurors, hereinafter referred to as the Plan, is adopted, as amended, by this Court. The Plan shall be placed into operation upon approval by a reviewing panel of the United States Court of Appeals for the Eleventh Circuit.

This Plan is intended to conform to all relevant statutes and guidelines adopted by the Judicial Conference of the United States.

1.02. Declaration of Policy. This Plan is intended to incorporate and implement the policies set forth in 28 U.S.C. Section 1861, namely:

(a) That all litigants appearing before the United States District Court for the Middle District of Florida, who may be entitled to a trial by jury, shall have the right to grand and petit juries selected at random from a fair cross-section of the community in the division wherein the Court convenes.

(b) That all citizens shall have the opportunity to be considered for service on grand and petit juries and shall have an obligation to serve when summoned for that purpose.

1.03. Use of Automated Data Processing Equipment in the Juror Qualification and Selection Process. The Court finds that automated data processing systems, to include the use of optical scanning technology, can be utilized effectively in the selection, copying, and processing of names from the individual county source lists identified in Section 4.04 of this Plan, and in all other aspects of the juror qualification and selection process.

Therefore, the Clerk may elect to utilize automated data processing systems, or a combination of a manual and automated data processing systems, to assist in the juror qualification and selection process.

1.04. Use of Non–Court Personnel in the Juror Qualification and Selection Process.

(a) *Non–Court Personnel Defined.* The Court finds that it may be necessary, or otherwise advantageous, for the Clerk to secure the services of non-court personnel to assist in the juror qualification and selection process. Such non-court personnel may include, but are not limited to:

(1) The Florida Department of State, Division of Elections, county officials, and their employees, responsible for custody and maintenance of the source lists identified in Section 4.04 of this Plan.

(2) Operators of automated data processing and optical scanning facilities and their employees and/or agents.

(3) Other administrative or clerical persons whose services may be necessary to select, process, and/or mail the various documents and records involved in the juror qualification and selection process.

(b) *Direction of Non–Court Personnel.* If the Clerk determines that it is necessary to secure the services of such non-court personnel, the Clerk shall, at a minimum:

(1) Issue written instructions to the individual(s) describing the operations or activities to be conducted.

(2) Require non-court personnel to execute an affidavit, under penalty of perjury, certifying compliance with the written instructions.

(3) Receive the written instructions and affidavit into the jury records of the Court.

CHAPTER TWO. ESTABLISHMENT OF JURY DIVISIONS

2.01. Establishment of Jury Divisions.

(a) *Authority.* In accordance with 28 U.S.C. Section 1869(e)(2), and Local Rule 1.02, the following jury divisions are established within the Middle District of Florida:

(1) Tampa Jury Division

(2) Ft. Myers Jury Division

(3) Orlando Jury Division

(4) Jacksonville Jury Division

(5) Ocala Jury Division

(b) *Composition of Jury Divisions.* In accordance with Local Rule 1.02(b), the counties which comprise the Middle District of Florida shall be grouped into the foregoing jury divisions as provided in such Local Rule.

CHAPTER THREE. SUPERVISION AND MANAGEMENT

3.01. Responsibility for Supervision of the Juror Qualification and Selection Process. In accordance with 28 U.S.C. Section 1863(b)(1), the Chief Judge of the Court shall be responsible for the overall supervision of the District's juror qualification and selection process.

Notwithstanding the responsibility vested in the Chief Judge, it is the intention of this Plan that supervision of the divisional juror qualification and selection process shall be separately accomplished within each of the jury divisions by a District Judge appointed by the Chief Judge.

3.02. Management of the Juror Qualification and Selection Process. In accordance with 28 U.S.C. Section 1863(b)(1), the Clerk shall act under the supervision and control of the Chief Judge to manage the District's juror qualification and selection process, and under the supervision and control of the individual Supervising Judges to manage the day-to-day divisional juror qualification and selection process.

In accordance with 28 U.S.C. Section 1869(a), the Clerk may delegate responsibility for the day-to-day management of the district or divisional juror qualification and selection process to any authorized deputy clerk.

CHAPTER FOUR. ESTABLISHMENT OF MASTER JURY WHEELS

4.01. Master Jury Wheel Defined. In accordance with 28 U.S.C. Section 1869(g), a "master jury wheel" shall mean any device or automated data processing system into which shall be placed the names of all the individuals randomly selected from the various source lists in accordance with Chapter Five of this Plan.

4.02. Establishment of Divisional Master Jury Wheels. In accordance with 28 U.S.C. Section 1863(b)(4), the Clerk shall establish and maintain a master jury wheel for each jury division established pursuant to Section 2.01 of this Plan.

4.03. Emptying and Refilling the Master Jury Wheels. Unless otherwise ordered by the Court, the Clerk is directed to empty and then refill the divisional master jury wheels between January 1, 1989, and October 31, 1989, and every odd numbered year thereafter between January 1 and October 31.

4.04. Source Lists to Be Utilized in Filling the Master Jury Wheels.

(a) *Primary Source Lists.* In accordance with 28 U.S.C. Section 1863(b)(2), voter registration lists shall be utilized as the primary source lists for filling the divisional master jury wheels.

(b) *Alternate Source Lists.* In accordance with 28 U.S.C. Section 1863(b)(2), if the Clerk determines that a particular county does not maintain a voter registration list, then the Clerk shall utilize the list of actual voters as an alternate source list for selecting names of prospective jurors to be placed in the master jury wheels.

CHAPTER FIVE. FILLING THE MASTER JURY WHEELS

5.01. Filling the Master Jury Wheels. In accordance with 28 U.S.C. Section 1863(b)(4), the Clerk shall initially fill the divisional master jury wheels with the minimum number of names indicated below. The Court finds that these totals are sufficient to meet the administrative requirements associated with the juror qualification and selection process and that additional names would be cumbersome and unnecessary.

(a)	Tampa Master Jury Wheel	80,000 names
(b)	Ft. Myers Master Jury Wheel	25,000 names
(c)	Orlando Master Jury Wheel	50,000 names
(d)	Jacksonville Master Jury Wheel	45,000 names
(e)	Ocala Master Jury Wheel	25,000 names

5.02. Placement of Additional Names in the Master Jury Wheels. From time to time it may be necessary to supplement the names within a particular divisional master jury wheel. In such a case, either the Chief Judge, or a Supervising Judge, may order the Clerk to obtain additional names from the primary or alternate source lists identified in Section 4.04 of the Plan to be placed into the divisional master jury wheel.

5.03. Procedures to Ensure Proportional Representation and Random Selection of Names From the Source Lists.

(a) *Calculation of an Interval Number.* The Clerk may employ the following minimum steps to ensure that substantial proportional representation exists between the counties comprising a particular jury division:

(1) Identify for each of the individual counties comprising a particular jury division, the state, local, and/or federal official having custody, possession, or control of the source lists identified in Section 4.04 of this Plan.

(2) Communicate with the appropriate official identified in the preceding subsection to determine:

(A) Whether the particular county maintains current voter registration lists, and if such lists are maintained, the total number of names contained on the voter registration lists as of the most recent general election.

In the event that the particular county periodically updates its voter registration lists, then the Clerk shall determine the total number of names on the voter registration lists as of a date to be specified by the Clerk following the most recent general election; or

(B) In the event that a particular county does not maintain current voter registration lists, the total number of actual voters who voted in the most recent general election.

In the event that the county periodically updates and corrects its list of actual voters, then the Clerk shall determine the total number of names on the list of actual voters as of a date to be specified by the Clerk following the most recent general election.

(3) After determining the total number of names for each county, segregate the counties into the jury divisions defined in Section 2.01 of this Plan.

(4) Calculate the total number of names for all of the counties with a particular jury division.

(5) Divide the total number of names contained on all of the source lists in a particular jury division by the total number of names required to be initially placed in that jury division's master jury wheel pursuant to Section 5.01 of this Plan. The resultant value produced by this calculation shall be referred to as the **interval number**. The interval number represents the interval between selected names on the various source lists, e.g.:

Assume that there are 660,000 names on the combined source lists for the counties comprising a particular jury division, and the total number of names required to be placed into that division's master jury wheel is 6,000, then the Clerk would divide 660,000 by 6,000. This calculation would produce an **interval number** of 110.

(6) Selection of a Random Starting Number: After calculating the interval number for each jury division, the Clerk would then publicly draw at random a **starting number** from a range of numbers which shall include the number one through the interval number for each particular jury division. The starting number represents the first name to be selected from each county's source list.

(7) Use of the Starting Number and Interval Number to Randomly Select Names From the Source Lists: After calculating the interval and starting numbers, the Clerk shall arrange to select the first name from each county's source list which corresponds to the starting number, and thereafter, shall select every subsequent name throughout the remainder of the source list which corresponds to the interval number, e.g.:

Assuming that the starting number for a particular jury division was 10, and the interval number for that jury division was 110, the Clerk would arrange that the tenth name from each county's source list be selected, and thereafter every 110th name throughout the remainder of the source lists for each county be selected, e.g., 10, 120, 230, 340, etc.

(b) *Alternative Method of Random Selection.* At the Clerk's option, and after consultation with the Court, the selection of names from complete source list databases in electronic media for the master jury wheel may be accomplished by a purely randomized process through a properly programmed electronic data processing system. Similarly, at the option of the Clerk and after consultation with the Court, a properly programmed electronic data processing system for pure randomized selection may be used to select names from the master wheel for the purpose of determining qualification for jury service, and from the qualified wheel for summoning persons to serve as grand or petit jurors. Such random selections of names from the source list for inclusion in the master wheel by data computer personnel must insure that each county within the jury division is substantially proportionally represented in the master jury wheel in accordance with 28 United States Code, Section 1863(b)(3). The selections of names from the source list, the master wheel, and the qualified wheel must also insure that the mathematical odds of any single name being picked are substantially equal.

5.04. Placing Names Into the Master Jury Wheels. Each name selected pursuant to Section 5.03 shall be placed into the appropriate divisional master jury wheel.

CHAPTER SIX. DRAWING NAMES FROM THE MASTER JURY WHEELS

6.01. Drawing of Names From the Master Jury Wheels. In accordance with 28 U.S.C. Section 1864(a), the Clerk shall post a general notice for public review in the clerk's office and on the court's website explaining the process by which names are periodically and randomly drawn.

6.02. Mailing of Juror Qualification Questionnaires. In accordance with 28 U.S.C. Section 1864(a), the Clerk shall mail a juror qualification questionnaire to every person whose name is drawn from a master jury wheel.

6.03. Actions to Be Taken When a Questionnaire Has Been Returned as "Undeliverable". When a questionnaire is returned as undeliverable, the Clerk shall verify the address on the questionnaire with the address for the particular juror contained in the records of the master jury wheel.

If the address on the questionnaire is not the same as that contained in the master jury wheel, the Clerk shall re-issue a new questionnaire with the corrected address; otherwise, the Clerk shall recommend, and the Court may find, that the person is not qualified for jury service pursuant to Section 7.01 of this Plan.

6.04. Actions to Be Taken When a Questionnaire Has Not Been Returned. In accordance with 28 U.S.C. Section 1864(a), any person who fails to return a completed questionnaire may be summoned by the Clerk to appear before the Clerk in order to fill out a questionnaire. However, it is not the intention of the Court to require the Clerk to summon every person who has failed to return their questionnaire.

In order to determine whether any particular person shall be summoned, the Clerk should first determine whether there have been sufficient numbers of returned questionnaires to permit the Court to qualify sufficient jurors for placement into the appropriate qualified jury wheel established pursuant to Section 8.01 of this Plan.

If the Clerk determines that sufficient numbers of questionnaires have been returned, the Clerk shall recommend, and the Court may order, that the name of the person who failed to return the questionnaire be returned to the appropriate master jury wheel.

CHAPTER SEVEN. DETERMINING QUALIFICATION FOR JURY SERVICE

7.01. Determining Qualification Status of Prospective Jurors. In accordance with 28 U.S.C. Section 1865(a), the Chief Judge or Supervising Judge, on his or her initiative or upon recommendation of the Clerk, or the Clerk under supervision of the court, shall determine, solely on the basis of information provided on the questionnaire and other competent evidence, whether a person is qualified, unqualified, exempt from, or should be excused from jury service.

To assist the Court in evaluating the qualification status of prospective jurors, the Clerk shall initially review all returned questionnaires and shall evaluate each questionnaire in accordance with the qualification criteria established in this Plan.

After such review, the Clerk shall recommend a qualification determination for each prospective juror to either the Chief Judge or the Supervising Judge, who in turn shall be responsible for a final ruling upon the qualification of each prospective juror.

7.02. Actions to Be Taken When the Questionnaire Has Erroneous, Ambiguous or Omitted Answers. In accordance with 28 U.S.C. § 1865(a), if the Clerk determines that a questionnaire has been returned with erroneous, ambiguous or omitted answers, and that such answers are essential to determining the qualification status of a prospective juror, the Clerk shall return the questionnaire to the prospective juror with instructions to explain, complete or correct the appropriate answer, and to return the questionnaire by mail within ten (10) days.

7.03. Qualifications for Jury Service. In accordance with 28 U.S.C. § 1865(b), the Clerk shall recommend, and the Chief Judge or the Supervising Judge shall find, that every person is qualified for jury service unless that person:

(a) Is not a citizen of the United States eighteen (18) years old who has resided for a period of one year within the Middle District of Florida; or

(b) Is unable to read, write, and understand the English language with a degree of proficiency sufficient to fill out satisfactorily the questionnaire; or

(c) Is unable to speak the English language; or

(d) Is incapable, by reason of mental or physical infirmity, to render satisfactory jury service; or

(e) Has a charge pending against him or her for the commission of, or has been convicted in a State or Federal court of record, of a crime punishable by imprisonment for more than one year, and that his or her civil rights have not been restored.

7.04. Exemption From Jury Service. In accordance with 28 U.S.C. Section 1863(b)(6), the Court finds that individuals who comprise the following groups of persons or occupational classes shall, in the public interest, be exempt from performing jury service, and that their exemption is not inconsistent with the policies set forth in 28 U.S.C. Sections 1861 and 1862.

(a) Members in active service in the Armed Forces of the United States;

(b) Members of the fire or police departments of any state, district, territory, possession, or subdivision thereof; or

(c) Public officers in the executive, legislative, or judicial branches of the Government of the United States, or any state, district, territory, or possession or subdivision thereof, who are actively engaged in the performance of their official duties.

7.05. Persons Who May Be Excused From Jury Service.

(a) *Permanent Excuse Upon Individual Request.* In accordance with 28 U.S.C. Section 1863(b)(5), the Court finds that service by the following persons or members of the following occupational classes would entail undue hardship or extreme inconvenience to such individuals, and that granting individual requests for permanent excuse from such persons would not be inconsistent with the policies set forth in 28 U.S.C. Sections 1861 and 1862.

(1) Persons over 70 years of age; or

(2) Persons having responsibility for providing in-home care and custody of a child or children under the age of ten (10); or

(3) Persons who are essential to the care of aged or infirm persons; or

(4) Persons who have served as a grand or petit juror in a federal court within the past two years; or

(5) Voluntary safety personnel serving a public agency as a non-compensated fire fighter or member of an ambulance or rescue squad; or

(6) Persons with arrest powers who are not otherwise exempt pursuant to Section 7.04 of this Plan.

(b) *Deferral Upon Individual Request.* In accordance with 28 U.S.C. Section 1866(c)(1), the Court, or the clerk under supervision of the Court, may defer any qualified juror from jury service.

Requests for deferral by individual jurors should ordinarily be presented in writing, and should present a showing of undue hardship or extreme inconvenience.

The name of any juror deferred shall be returned to the qualified jury wheel, unless otherwise ordered by the Court.

CHAPTER EIGHT. ESTABLISHMENT OF QUALIFIED JURY WHEELS

8.01. Qualified Jury Wheel Defined. In accordance with 28 U.S.C. Section 1869(g), a "qualified jury wheel" shall mean any device or automated data processing system, into which shall be placed the names of all persons determined to be qualified for jury service pursuant to Chapter Seven of this Plan.

8.02. Establishment of Divisional Qualified Jury Wheels. In accordance with 28 U.S.C. Section 1866(a), the Clerk shall establish and maintain a qualified jury wheel for each jury division established pursuant to Section 2.01 of this Plan.

8.03. Emptying and Refilling the Qualified Jury Wheels. Unless otherwise ordered by the Court, the Clerk shall empty and refill the qualified jury wheels between January 1, 1989, and October 31, 1989, and every odd year thereafter between January 1 and October 31.

When delays occur between the emptying and refilling of the master and qualified jury wheels, the Court may order that names of qualified jurors presently in the qualified jury wheels be retained and summoned for jury service until the Clerk can complete the operations necessary to refill the qualified jury wheels.

8.04. Placing Names in the Qualified Jury Wheels. In accordance with 28 U.S.C. Section 1866(a), the names of all persons determined to be qualified for jury service shall be placed into the appropriate qualified jury wheel.

If a person relocates within the district, that person's name may be transferred to the divisional jury wheel in which they now reside since the statutory residency requirement has not been compromised.

CHAPTER NINE. SELECTING AND SUMMONING JURORS FOR JURY SERVICE

9.01. Drawing of Names From the Qualified Jury Wheels. In accordance with 28 U.S.C. Section 1866(a), the Clerk shall post a general notice for public review in the clerk's office and on the court's website explaining the process by which names required from time to time for assignment to grand and petit jury panels are periodically and randomly drawn.

9.02. Summoning Jurors. The Clerk may issue a summons to each juror in any manner permitted by 28 U.S.C. Section 1866(b).

CHAPTER TEN. SELECTION AND IMPANELMENT OF REGULAR AND SPECIAL JURIES

10.01. Selection and Impanelment of Grand Juries.

(a) *Regular Grand Juries.*

(1) Fort Myers Jury Division: In accordance with Fed.R.Cr.P. 6(a), the Court shall order that one or more regular grand juries be drawn at random, and summoned to serve the Fort Myers Jury Division.

(2) Jacksonville Jury Division: In accordance with Fed.R.Cr.P. 6(a), the Court shall order that one or more regular grand juries be drawn at random, and summoned to serve the Jacksonville Division.

(3) Ocala Jury Division: In accordance with Fed.R.Cr.P. 6(a), the Court shall order that one or more regular grand juries be drawn at random, and summoned to serve the Ocala Jury Division.

(4) Orlando Jury Division: In accordance with Fed.R.Cr.P. 6(a), the Court shall order that one or more regular grand juries be drawn at random, and summoned to serve the Orlando Jury Division.

(5) Tampa Jury Division: In accordance with Fed.R.Cr.P. 6(a), the Court shall order that one or more regular grand juries be drawn at random, and summoned to serve the Tampa Jury Division.

(b) *Special Grand Juries.*

(1) Authority to Convene: In accordance with 18 U.S.C. Section 3331, the Court may order that a special grand jury be empaneled to sit in a particular jury division, however, any such special grand jury shall be empowered to serve throughout the entire district.

(2) Selection Procedures: Unless otherwise ordered by the Court, when selecting names of jurors to be summoned for a special grand jury venire, the Clerk shall first determine the division in which the special grand jury will be empaneled, and thereafter, shall draw at random a sufficient number of prospective jurors from that division to serve on impanelment day.

(c) *In Camera Proceedings Relating to Grand Jury Impanelment.* In accordance with 28 U.S.C. Section 1863(b)(7), and unless otherwise directed by the Court, the actual impanelment of either a regular or special grand jury shall not be held in open Court or within public view.

CHAPTER ELEVEN. DISCLOSURE OF JURY SELECTION RECORDS

11.01. Disclosure of Juror Names.

(a) *Names of Jurors Assigned to Petit Jury Panels.* In accordance with 28 U.S.C. Section 1863(b)(7) and the Rules of this Court, and subject to 18 U.S.C. Section 3432 dealing with capital cases, the names of persons assigned to petit jury panels may be disclosed by the Clerk to counsel at the time of assignment. The Clerk may provide the names to the parties and to the public only after receiving permission from the presiding judge. The Court shall allow the names to be disclosed to the parties and to the public unless the Court specifies on the record or in a written order the reason that the interest of justice requires that the names remain confidential.

(b) *Names of Jurors Assigned to Grand Jury Panels.* In accordance with 28 U.S.C. Section 1863(b)(7), the names of jurors selected for either a grand jury venire, or for actual service on a particular grand jury, shall not be disclosed to any person except upon written order of the District Court, and only then upon a showing that exceptional circumstances have created a demonstrated need for disclosure.

11.02. Disclosure of Information and Records Relating to the Juror Qualification and Selection Process.

(a) *Prior to the Emptying and Refilling of the Master Jury Wheel(s).* In accordance with 28 U.S.C. Section 1867(f), the contents of records and papers used by the Clerk in connection with the juror qualification and selection process shall not be disclosed, except upon written order of the District Court.

(b) *Subsequent to the Emptying and Refilling of the Master Jury Wheels.* In accordance with 28 U.S.C. Section 1868, the Clerk shall keep all records and papers relating to the juror qualification and selection process for four years following the emptying and refilling of the master jury wheels, or for such longer period of time as the Court may require.

Upon written request from any person attempting to determine the validity of the selection of any jury, the Court may order the Clerk to make such records available during normal business hours.

[Dated: October 22, 2009; approved by the Judicial Counsel of the Eleventh Circuit January 15, 2010.]

SELECTED ORDERS AND NOTICES

GENERAL ORDER 6:13–MC–94–011–22. IN RE: POSSESSION AND USE OF PERSONAL ELECTRONIC DEVICES IN FEDERAL COURTHOUSES IN THE MIDDLE DISTRICT OF FLORIDA

This Order sets forth the Court's policy concerning the possession and use of personal electronic devices in the federal courthouses in the Middle District of Florida. Personal electronic devices are things like cellular telephones, "smart phones," laptop computers, and tablet computers.

1. **General Policy.** No one may bring a personal electronic device beyond a courthouse's security checkpoint.

2. **Exceptions.** The following exceptions to the general policy apply. Any personal electronic device carried beyond a courthouse's security checkpoint based on an exception remains subject to inspection, to Fed. R. Crim. P. 53 (prohibiting courtroom photography and broadcasting in criminal cases), and to Local Rule 4.11(a)(2) (prohibiting courtroom photography and broadcasting in all cases). Further, any person who brings in a personal electronic device under an exception, (a) must keep the personal electronic device on silent mode, (b) may not share it with anyone, (c) may not use it in a manner that disrupts any judicial proceeding, (d) may not use it to search for information about a potential or seated juror, and (e) may not bring it into the courtroom for the United States Court of Appeals for the Eleventh Circuit in the Bryan Simpson United States Courthouse in Jacksonville.

2.1. *Court–Ordered Permission.* Anyone may bring a personal electronic device beyond a courthouse's security checkpoint by presenting an order from a judge of the Court giving him or her permission to do so. The order must specify the person, place, purpose, and time frame.

2.2. *Employees.* Any agency employee who works in a courthouse office, a U.S. Trustee, any attorney of the United State's Attorney's Office or the Federal Defender's Office, or any law enforcement officer on official business may bring a personal electronic device beyond the courthouse's security checkpoint by presenting valid agency identification.

2.3. *Jurors.* At the presiding judge's discretion, any seated petit or grand juror may bring a personal electronic device beyond the courthouse's security checkpoint during his or her service. The juror (a) must store the device in a designated receptacle at all times except during breaks, (b) may use the device only in designated areas or in the jury assembly room; and (c) may use the device only for non-case matters. The judge must provide the United States Marshals Service and the lead Court Security Officer with a memorandum setting forth the list of jurors, the case name, the case number, the beginning date of service, and the expected end date of service.

2.4. *Attorneys.* Any attorney permitted to practice law in the Middle District of Florida may bring any personal electronic device beyond the courthouse's security checkpoint by presenting a valid Florida Bar identification card or pro hac vice order. In addition to the restrictions set forth in paragraph 2, attorneys may not use personal electronic devices directly outside of any courtroom when court is in session.

2.5. *Judicial Discretion.* Any presiding judge may modify these procedures or suspend any person's privileges granted by this Order at any time for any reason.

[Filed: October 1, 2013.]

IN RE: PROCEDURES FOR APPLYING FOR ATTORNEY'S FEES UNDER 42 U.S.C. §§ 406(b) AND 1383(d)(2)

Section 406(b) and section 1383(d)(2) with regard to Title XVI claims of Title 42 govern motions for attorney's fees in Social Security disability cases. Section 406(b) provides in relevant part that "the court may determine and allow as part of its judgment a reasonable fee for [an attorney's] representation, not in excess of 25 percent of the total of the past-due benefits to which the claimant is entitled by reason of such judgment." 42 U.S.C. § 406(b)(1)(A). However, at the time the judgment is entered, the specific amount of past-due benefits, if any, is unknown.

Federal Rule of Civil Procedure 54(d)(2)(B) applies to the filing of a request for attorney's fees, pursuant to Sections 406(b) and 1383(d)(2), and it requires a motion for attorney's fees to be filed within fourteen (14) days after judgment unless provided otherwise by statute or order of the court. Fed.R.Civ.P. 54(d)(2)(B). Because the amount of past-due benefits and attorney's fees is unknown at the time of judgment, the Court adopts the following procedures and filing schedule with regard to section 406(b) (and section 1383(d)(2)) motions for attorney's fees:

(I) If the plaintiff's attorney seeks attorney's fees under 42 U.S.C. §§ 406(b) or 1383(d)(2), he or she must file a motion for approval of such fees no later than thirty (30) days after the date of the Social Security letter sent to the plaintiff's counsel of record at the conclusion of the Agency's past-due benefit calculation slating the amount withheld for attorney's fees.

(II) Any response to the motion shall be filed within the time provided in the Local Rules. The motion shall state the amount (if any) of attorney's fees awarded or sought by Plaintiff pursuant to 42 U.S.C. § 406(a) and any amount previously awarded by the court, pursuant to the Equal Access to Justice Act.

(III) Plaintiff shall file any reply within ten (10) days of service of defendant's response.

(IV) Counsel are reminded of the requirement to comply with Local Rule 3.01(g) prior to filing any motion which often expedites disposition of the fee request.

[Effective November 13, 2012.]

IN RE: POLICY GOVERNING LIMITED PERSONAL USE OF SUPPLIED BROADBAND WIRELESS CONNECTION FOR REGISTERED COURTROOM USERS

CONDITIONS APPLICABLE TO USING INTERNET

In order to provide access to supplied broadband wireless internet within the courtrooms of the United States Courthouses in this District, registered attorneys and other users who have obtained permission to access the connection are subject to the terms and conditions set forth herein. While the Court recognizes the bar's expressed desire to be able to utilize the internet in court for case specific and other related purposes, the Court has an obligation to ensure that, to the extent the connection implicates government property and resources, they are used appropriately and for purposes not adverse to the public interest. The Clerk of Court is responsible for authorizing attorneys to use the internet connection by verifying that all attorneys and other users who use this service have obtained Court permission. At all times, use of internet access shall be controlled by and subject to directions of the presiding judge.

All users are governed by the following terms of use:

1. The use of the provided broadband internet connection shall be available, upon prior court approval, to a) bar members, including those attorneys admitted specially; b) paralegals or other assistants or employees of bar members, upon the agreement of the bar member to be responsible for their use of the internet connection; and, c) any other approved user. Any and all users agree to be bound by the limitations set forth in this Order.

2. Internet access in the courtrooms should be used for business reasons only, ideally business related to the court case. This includes e-mail, electronic case filing (CM/ECF) and PACER access. It is the responsibility of the registered user to ensure that he or she is not giving the false impression that they are acting in an official capacity on behalf of the Federal courts when they are using the supplied broadband connection.

3. Authorized bar members and other users under this Policy are expected to conduct themselves professionally and to refrain from using the internet connection for activities that are strongly discouraged or prohibited. Such improper activities include:

- Any personal use that could cause congestion, delay, or disruption of service to any government system or equipment. For example, greeting cards, video, sound or other large file attachments can degrade the performance of the entire network. "Push" technology on the Internet and other continuous data streams would also degrade the performance of the entire network and be an inappropriate use (including music or video files or logging onto radio or other broadcast services).
- Using the internet connection to access social media sites, such as Facebook, Twitter, and LinkedIn, unless it is related to a legitimate business use.

- Using peer-to-peer file sharing (Napster, Grokster, Morpheous, and certain interactive internet games), or chat rooms.
- Using the internet connection as a staging ground or platform to gain unauthorized access to other systems.
- The creation, copying, transmission, or retransmission of chain letters or other unauthorized mass mailings regardless of the subject matter.
- Using the internet connection for activities that are illegal, inappropriate, or offensive to fellow bar members or the public. Such activities include, but are not limited to: hate speech or material that ridicules others on the basis of race, creed, religion, color, sex, disability, national origin, or sexual orientation.
- The creation, download, viewing, storage, copying, or transmission of sexually explicit or sexually oriented materials.
- The creation, download, viewing, storage, copying, transmission of materials related to illegal gambling, illegal weapons, terrorist activities, and any other illegal activities otherwise prohibited, etc.
- Use for commercial purposes not related to the case (e.g., sales or administration of business transactions, sale of goods or services).
- Engaging in any outside fund-raising activity, endorsing any product or service, participating in any lobbying activity, or engaging in any prohibited partisan political activity.
- Use for posting information to external newsgroups, bulletin boards or other public forums. This includes any use that could create the perception that the communication is "endorsed" by the Federal Courts.
- The unauthorized acquisition, use, reproduction, transmission, or distribution of any controlled information including computer software and data, that includes privacy information, copyrighted, trade marked or material with other intellectual property rights (beyond fair use), proprietary data, or export controlled software or data.

Unauthorized or improper use of the internet connection may result in the imposition of sanctions, which may include the loss of use or limitations on use of the connection, criminal penalties, and/or being held financially liable for the cost of improper use. Bar members are expected to supervise any employees authorized on their motion to use the internet connection.

4. Users are expected to use their private laptop or notebook computer (or other approved access device) in the courtroom; the Court will not provide such equipment. Moreover, due to liability issues, the Court's IT staff will not be able to assist in specific problems with the user's equipment. The Court provides no guarantee of the availability of or quality of the internet connection provided and use of the internet connection constitutes an acknowledgment by the user that the Court is not liable for any damages to personal equipment or any other damage that may result directly or indirectly from the use of the provided broadband connection.

5. Internet browsing and e-mail transmissions are subject to inspection by a variety of persons and mechanisms, authorized and otherwise. Registered users using the broadband internet connection have neither a right nor an expectation of absolute privacy while accessing the Internet and using email in the courtroom. Electronic communications and Internet activity may be monitored at any time for any purpose, including compliance with acceptable use policies. If such monitoring reveals possible evidence of criminal activity court personnel may provide the evidence of such monitoring to law enforcement personnel. All persons accessing the system expressly consent to this monitoring.

6. Bar members and other approved users have no inherent right to use the internet connection. Under all circumstances limited personal use is a privilege not a right. This privilege to use the internet connection for non-government purposes may be revoked or limited at any time by the District Court, Middle District of Florida.

[Effective July 28, 2011.]

PUBLIC NOTICE. POLICY ON SENSITIVE INFORMATION IN CASE FILES ACCESSIBLE THROUGH PACER

Effective November 1, 2004, the United States District Court for the Middle District of Florida enhanced its Public Access to Court Electronic Records (PACER)[1] service by providing electronic remote access to documents filed in criminal cases before this court. Any subscriber to PACER or WebPACER will be able to read, download, store, and print the full content of these electronic documents. Please note that documents sealed or otherwise restricted by court order, will not be available through PACER or WebPACER.

Litigants should not include sensitive information in any document filed with the court unless such inclusion is necessary and relevant to the case. Litigants must remember that any personal information not otherwise protected will be made available over the Internet via PACER or WebPACER. If sensitive information must be included, the following personal data and identifiers must be partially redacted from the pleading:

- Social Security Numbers. If an individual's social security number must be included in a document, only the last four digits of that number should be used.
- Names of Minor Children. If the involvement of a minor child must be mentioned, only the initials of the child should be used.
- Dates of Birth. If an individual's date of birth must be included in a document, only the year should be used.
- Financial Account Numbers. If financial account numbers are relevant, only the last four digits of these numbers should be used.

In compliance with the E–Government Act of 2002, a party wishing to file a document containing the personal data identifiers specified above may file an unredacted document under seal, which will be retained by the court as part of the record. In that circumstance, the court requires the party to file a redacted copy for the public file.

In addition, exercise caution when filing documents that contain the following:

- Personal identifying number, such as driver's license number;
- Medical records, treatment and diagnosis;
- Employment history;
- Individual financial information; and
- Proprietary or trade secret information.

Counsel is strongly urged to share this notice with all clients, so that an informed decision about the inclusion of certain materials may be made. If a redacted document is filed, it is the sole responsibility of counsel and the parties to be sure that all pleadings comply with the rules of this court requiring redaction of personal data identifiers. The Clerk of Court will not review each pleading for redaction.

This policy does not create a private right of action against the Court, the Clerk of Court, counsel, or any other individual or entity on behalf of any individual or entity that may have identifying information erroneously included in a filed document that is made available on PACER or WebPACER.

[Effective November 1, 2004.]

1 PACER is an electronic public access service that allows users to obtain case information from the federal courts. PACER allows a registered user to access case information through the Internet or a dial-up connection. For more information, please visit pacer.flmd.uscourts.gov.

NOTICE REGARDING MEDIATION PROGRAM AND MEDIATOR'S APPLICATION FORM

UNITED STATES DISTRICT COURT
MIDDLE DISTRICT OF FLORIDA **MEDIATOR'S APPLICATION FORM**

In accordance with Rule 9.02 of the Rules of the Middle District of Florida, I am applying for certification as a mediator with the United States District Court for the Middle District of Florida. I qualify by the following:

☐ Former State Judge and Bar Member of that state

☐ Retired Federal Judicial Officer

☐ Bar Member of any state or DC for 10 years
AND current member of USDC–FLM Bar

The following information is supplied in support of this application:

Last Name: ____________ Fla. Bar ID No.: ____________

First/MI: ____________

Firm's Name: ____________

Mailing Address: ____________

____

City: ________ Zip Code + Ext. ____________

- ____________

Office Phone No: ____________

Office FAX No: ____________

List names and dates of membership with any state bars or the bar of the District Columbia:

____

Are you a member in good standing of the bar associations listed above? ☐ Yes ☐ No

Date admitted to the Bar of this Court: ____________
(mm/dd/yy)

Date the State Supreme Court's Mediator Certification Program completed: ____________

Number of mediation conferences held to date: ____________

Check all of areas of legal practice or experience which best describes your legal background.

☐ Administrative Law	☐ Insurance	☐ Products Liability
☐ Admiralty	☐ Intellectual Property	☐ Professional Liability
☐ Business Litigation	☐ Labor	☐ Real Property
☐ Civil Rights	☐ Personal Injury	☐ Social Security
☐ Contracts	☐ Personal Property	☐ Tax
☐ Environmental Law		

Please indicate the Divisions in the Middle District in which you would be willing to serve as a mediator:

☐ Ft. Myers ☐ Jacksonville ☐ Ocala ☐ Orlando ☐ Tampa

____________ ____________
E-mail Signature

FOR COURT USE ONLY

Date certified by the chief judge as a mediator: ____________

UNITED STATES DISTRICT COURT
MIDDLE DISTRICT OF FLORIDA
OFFICE OF THE CLERK
United States Courthouse
401 W Central Blvd
Orlando, Florida 32801–0210

Anne C. Conway
Chief Judge

Sheryl Loesch
Clerk

(407) 835-4200

NOTICE REGARDING THE MEDIATION PROGRAM IN THE MIDDLE DISTRICT OF FLORIDA

The Middle District of Florida has adopted a Mediation Program. This Program consists of a supervised settlement conference presided over by a qualified, certified and neutral mediator to promote conciliation, compromise and the ultimate settlement of a civil action. Pursuant to Local Rule 9.02, the chief judge of the District shall certify those persons who are eligible and qualified to serve as mediators under this rule, in such numbers as the chief judge shall deem appropriate. An individual may be certified to serve as a mediator if:

(1) He or she is a former state court judge who presided in a court of general jurisdiction and was also a member of the bar in the state in which he presided; or

(2) He or she is a retired federal judicial officer; or

(3) He or she has been a member of a state bar or the bar of the District of Columbia for at least ten (10) years and is currently admitted to the Bar of this Court.

In addition, an applicant for certification must have completed a minimum of 40 hours in the Florida Circuit Court Mediation Training Course certified by the Florida Supreme Court and be found competent by the chief judge to perform mediation duties.

If you are interested in becoming a mediator for the Middle District of Florida, and meet the above requirements, please complete the application form on the reverse side, and return to:

United States District Court
Middle District of Florida
United States Courthouse
401 W Central Blvd—Ste 2100
Orlando, Florida 32801–021

Attention: Joan Calcutt

Application deadlines established by the Court are the first business days in January and July. Applications will be considered by the Court on the first deadline after submission. Applicants will be notified in writing regarding the disposition of applications, and each successful applicant will receive a copy of the Court order certifying the applicant as a mediator. Names of certified mediators are included on a roster which is available to the public at the intake section of each division.

[Amended effective February 1, 1994; April 24, 2003; October 2, 2008.]

INDEX TO UNITED STATES DISTRICT COURT FOR THE MIDDLE DISTRICT OF FLORIDA

UNITED STATES BANKRUPTCY COURT FOR THE MIDDLE DISTRICT OF FLORIDA

Including Amendments Received Through February 1, 2017

PART VIII. APPEALS TO DISTRICT COURT OR BANKRUPTCY APPELLATE PANEL

PART IX. GENERAL PROVISIONS

SELECTED APPENDICES

RULE 2081–1—APPENDIX

RULE 9070–1—APPENDIX

SELECTED NOTICES AND ADMINISTRATIVE ORDERS

RULE 1001–1. SCOPE OF RULES; SHORT TITLE

(a) Promulgation and Application. These rules are promulgated in accordance with Fed. R. Bankr. P. 9029. These rules apply to all cases under title 11 and in all civil proceedings arising under title 11, or arising in or related to cases under title 11 in the United States Bankruptcy Court for the Middle District of Florida ("Court").

(b) Implementation. These rules are intended to supplement and complement the Bankruptcy Code and Federal Rules of Bankruptcy Procedure. These rules shall be construed, administered, and employed by the Court and the parties to secure the just, speedy, and inexpensive determination of every case, contested matter, and adversary proceeding.

(c) Failure to Comply. The Court, on its own motion or on the motion of any party in interest, may impose sanctions for failure to comply with these rules, including, without limitation, dismissal of the case or the proceeding, conversion of the case, denial of the motion filed by the party, striking of pleadings or other submissions, the staying of any further proceedings until verification of compliance with these rules has been filed with the Court or as may otherwise be appropriate under the circumstances. However, notwithstanding the foregoing, for good cause, the Court may suspend the requirements set forth in these rules and may order proceedings in accordance with its direction.

(d) Local Rules of the District Court. The local rules of the United States District Court for the Middle District of Florida governing civil and criminal proceedings shall not apply to cases or proceedings in this Court except as provided for in these rules or otherwise ordered by this Court.

(e) Citation. These rules shall be cited as "Local Rules."

[Effective June 15, 1997. Amended effective December 1, 2004; July 1, 2015; July 1, 2016.]

Notes of Advisory Committee

2016 Amendment

This amendment includes a revision to section (b) that is consistent with the 2015 amendment to Fed. R. Civ. P. 1 and new section (c), which incorporates the provisions regarding sanctions for failure to comply with the Local Rules set forth in abrogated Local Rule 9011–3 Sanctions. This amended rule is effective July 1, 2016.

2015 Amendment

The amendments to this rule are stylistic and effective July 1, 2015.

2004 Amendment

This rule is amended to reflect conformity in the citation of Fed. R. Bankr. P. and Local Rules.

1997 Amendment

This amendment conforms the existing Local Rules to the uniform numbering system prescribed by the Judicial Conference of the United States and to the model system suggested and approved by the Advisory Committee on Bankruptcy Rules of the Judicial Conference's Committee on Rules of Practice and Procedure. In renumbering the Local Rules to conform to the uniform numbering system, no change in substance is intended. This amendment was effective on April 15, 1997. Paragraphs (a) through (d) of this rule were formerly Local Rule 1.01(a) through (d). Paragraph (e) of this rule was formerly Local Rule 1.01(f). The Advisory Committee Notes to the superseded rules may be helpful in interpreting and applying the current rules.

1995 Amendment[1]

The amendments to subparagraphs (a) and (b) of Local Rule 1.01 are stylistic. No substantive change is intended.

A new subparagraph (e) is added to specify that the definitions of words and phrases contained in 11 U.S.C. §§ 101, 902, and 1101, and Fed. R. Bankr. P. 9001, and the rules of construction contained in 11 U.S.C. § 102 also apply in the Local Rules.

Subparagraph (f) has been amended to expand the method of citation of the Local Rules to include the designation "(Bankr. M.D. Fla.)." References to the "Local Rules" as used herein shall mean the Local Rules (Bankr. M.D. Fla.).

These amendments were effective on February 15, 1995. The Court's Order Amending Local Rules of the United States Bankruptcy Court for the Middle District of Florida, No. 95–001–MIS–TPA, entered on February 2, 1995, adopting these amendments provides that "[t]hese amendments govern all cases and proceedings commenced on or after February 15, 1995, and, insofar as practicable, all cases and proceedings then pending."

[1] Pursuant to the Order Reconstituting Local Rules Lawyers' Advisory Committee, No. 94–004–MIS–TPA, dated February 23, 1994, the Court reconstituted the membership of the Local Rules Lawyers' Advisory Committee (which shall be referred to herein as the "Advisory Committee") and requested the Advisory Committee to make such recommendations as appropriate generally concerning the Local Rules and specifically concerning the impact of the December 1, 1993, amendments to the Federal Rules of Civil Procedure. The Advisory Committee has drafted these notes with their proposed amendments to assist the Court, the bar, and the public in understanding the proposed amendments and in interpreting and following the rules if adopted by the Court.

RULE 1001–2. CASE MANAGEMENT AND ELECTRONIC CASE FILING SYSTEM—CM/ECF

(a) Case Management/Electronic Case Filing System. The Court has established an online case management and electronic case filing system ("CM/ECF"), on which the Court maintains paperless court files and dockets and which allows a party with a log-in and password issued by the Clerk ("Electronic Filing User") to electronically file papers in court files.

(b) Electronic Filing Users. Attorneys filing papers with the Court must be Electronic Filing Users. Those persons entitled to become Electronic Filing Users include attorneys admitted to practice in the United States District Court for the Middle District of Florida, United States Trustees and their assistants, private trustees, governmental units, commercial claim filers, or others as may be provided by administrative order. To become an Electronic Filing User, attorneys and other parties must complete CM/ECF training and register with the Clerk. The Clerk shall establish registration, training, and certification procedures, which shall include administering a CM/ECF training program. The Clerk shall keep a registry of authorized Electronic Filing Users. Electronic Filing Users shall adhere to all requirements as promulgated by the Clerk and posted on the Court's website, www.flmb.uscourts.gov. The Clerk shall maintain and promulgate the requirements and guidelines as necessary.

(c) Restriction on Use of User Login and Password. No Electronic Filing User or other person may knowingly permit or cause to permit an Electronic Filing User's password to be used by anyone other than an authorized agent of the Electronic Filing User. An attorney is not permitted to use another attorney's password to file a paper with the Court using CM/ECF. An Electronic Filing User agrees to protect the security of the Electronic Filing User's login and password and shall immediately notify the Clerk if the security of their password has been compromised. An Electronic Filing User may be subject to sanctions for failure to comply with this provision.

(d) Format. Papers filed electronically shall be submitted in Portable Document Format (PDF). Papers in electronic format shall be converted to PDF from the word processing original, not scanned, to permit text searches and to facilitate transmission and retrieval. If only a paper copy of a paper to be filed with the Court (*e.g.,* an original or copy of an exhibit) is available, it may be converted to PDF format by scanning.

(e) Signatures.

(1) *CM/ECF User Login and Password Serve as Attorney's Signature.* The name of the Electronic Filing User under whose login and password the document is submitted shall be preceded by "/s/" typed in the space where the signature would otherwise appear. The user login and password re-

quired to submit documents via CM/ECF serve as the Electronic Filing User's signature on all electronic documents filed with the Court. They also serve as a signature for purposes of Fed. R. Bankr. P. 9011, the Federal Rules of Bankruptcy Procedure, the Local Rules, and for any other purpose for which a signature is required in connection with proceedings before the Court.

(2) *Client Signatures.* Attorneys may file papers signed by their clients by including a scanned paper bearing the client's signature or, subject to the retention requirements of paragraph (f) of this rule, by typing the client's name preceded by "/s/" where the signature would otherwise appear.

(3) *Papers Requiring More Than One Signature.* Electronically filed papers requiring signatures of more than one party shall be filed:

(i) by submitting a scanned paper containing all necessary signatures;

(ii) by including an attestation by the filing attorney that concurrence in the filing of the paper has been obtained from each of the other signatories. The filing attorney's attestation may be included after the signature block of the additional signatory or may take the form of a declaration attached to the paper. An acceptable form of attestation is:

"Filer's Attestation: Pursuant to Local Rule 1001–2(e)(3) regarding signatures, [name of filing attorney] attests that concurrence in the filing of this paper has been obtained."; or

(iii) in any other manner approved by the Court.

(f) Retention of Original Papers. Electronic Filing Users shall retain paper copies bearing original signatures of the following papers for two years after the closing of the case:

(1) petitions, lists, schedules, statements of financial affairs, including the Statement of Social Security Number(s) (Official Form 121); and

(2) affidavits, and other papers that require verification under Fed. R. Bankr. P.1008, and unsworn declarations as provided for in 28 U.S.C. § 1746.

On request, the Electronic Filing User shall provide original documents for review to the Court, the Office of the United States Trustee, or any party in interest as ordered by the Court.

(g) Proofs of Service. Proofs of Service executed by a non-lawyer in compliance with Local Rule 9013–1 shall be filed by the attorney for the party on whose behalf service is made by filing a scanned copy of the original signature page via CM/ECF.

(h) Waiver of Service by Mail. Registration as an Electronic Filing User constitutes (1) waiver of the right to receive notice by first-class mail and the right to service by first-class mail or personal service and (2) consent to receive notice electronically and consent to electronic service, except with regard to service of a summons and complaint under Fed. R. Bankr. P. 7004. Waiver of service and notice by first-class mail applies to notice of the entry of an order or judgment under Fed. R. Bankr. P. 9022.

(i) Electronic Filing of Proofs of Claim and Related Documents. Claimants who are not Electronic Filing Users may file proofs of claim in paper or through the eProof of Claim hyperlink on the Court's website, www.flmb.uscourts.gov. All claimants who have filed or expect to file ten or more claims and/or claim-related papers, such as transfers of claims and withdrawals of claims, within any one-year period, shall file these claims and documents electronically through CM/ECF or the eProof of Claim hyperlink.

(j) Electronic Ballot Filing in Chapter 11 Cases. Parties may file paper ballots with the Court under Local Rule 3018–1, but are encouraged to electronically file ballots through the Chapter 11 eBallots hyperlink on the Court's website, www.flmb.uscourts.gov.

(k) Filing Papers Under Seal. Local Rule 5005–4 governs the filing of papers under seal.

(*l*) Unavailability of CM/ECF or Hyperlinks. Electronic Filing Users may file paper documents whenever CM/ECF is inaccessible or an Electronic Filing User's computer system is not functioning. Filers of proofs of claim who cannot access the Court's eProof of Claim hyperlink and filers of ballots who cannot access the Court's eBallot hyperlink may file paper proofs of claim and ballots. After–hours emergency filing procedures are set forth in Local Rule 5001–2.

(m) Access to CM/ECF by Non–Electronic Filing Users.

(1) *PACER Access.* Any person or organization, including parties appearing before the Court *pro se*, may access CM/ECF at the Court's website by obtaining a log-in and password from PACER (Public Access to Court Electronic Records), available at www.pacer.gov. Those who have PACER access but who are not Electronic Filing Users may retrieve docket sheets and court papers but may not file documents electronically.

(2) *Request by Pro Se Debtors to Receive Electronic Notification.* Individual *pro se* debtors who have an Internet email address may request to receive electronic notification of filings made in their bankruptcy cases by submitting the form available on the Court's website at www.flmb.uscourts.gov/cmecf.

[Effective December 1, 2004. Amended effective July 1, 2013; July 1, 2014; July 1, 2015; December 1, 2015; July 1, 2016.]

Notes of Advisory Committee

2016 Amendment

This amendment incorporates the provisions regarding the signature of papers filed via CM/ECF set forth in abrogated Local Rule 9011–4 Signatures. The amendment also cross-references Local Rule 5005–4 Sealed Papers. Other revisions are stylistic. This amended rule is effective July 1, 2016.

2015 Amendment

New section (c) of the rule requires Electronic Filing Users to convert papers maintained in electronic format from the word processing original to Portable Document Format (PDF). This does not apply to papers originally in paper form, such as client records or exhibits. In addition, section (d) reduces the time during which Electronic Filing Users must retain paper copies bearing original signature from four years to two years. This amendment is effective July 1, 2015.

2014 Amendment

This amendment revises section (e) to provide that claimants who have filed or expect to file ten or more claims (reduced from 25) with a one-year period shall file their claims and claims-related papers electronically. This amendment is effective July 1, 2014.

2013 Amendment

This amendment reflects current CM/ECF practices and electronic filing procedures, including the requirement that attorneys filing papers with the Court be Electronic Filing Users. This amendment supersedes and replaces archived Administrative Orders FLMB 2003–4, FTM 2005–2, JAX–2004–2, ORL–2004–2, and TPA 2005–05 (establishing deadlines for attorneys to participate in CM/ECF) and archived Administrative Orders FTM–2008–1, JAX–2006–5, ORL–2008–1, and TPA–2008–10 (establishing deadlines for claimants to electronically file proofs of claim and related papers).

2004 Amendment

This amendment is adapted from the "Model Local Bankruptcy Court Rules for Electronic Case Filing" approved on September 11, 2001 by the Judicial Conference of the United States Courts. This amendment sets out overall electronic filing guidance and requirements, yet allows the Clerk flexibility in managing the details of this system. It is contemplated that the Clerk will actively coordinate such activities with members of the Bankruptcy Bar in the District.

This amendment also establishes a presumption that once attorneys or others become an "Electronic Filing User," they will file all documents in cases assigned to CM/ECF by electronic means only. Consistent with Fed. R. Bankr. P. 5005, this rule strongly encourages attorney participation while not making electronic filing mandatory. (Fed. R. Bankr. P. 5005 in part states that a court "may permit" papers to be filed electronically, and provides that the Clerk "shall not refuse to accept for filing any paper presented . . . solely because it is not presented in proper form.")

RULE 1001–3. PRIVACY POLICY REGARDING PUBLIC ACCESS TO ELECTRONIC CASE FILES

(a) Application of Rule. In compliance with the policy of the Judicial Conference of the United States, and the E-Government Act of 2002, parties shall not include, or shall partially redact where inclusion is necessary, the following personal data identifiers from documents and pleadings filed with the Court, including exhibits thereto, whether filed electronically or in paper, unless otherwise ordered by the Court or required by statute, the Federal Rules of Bankruptcy Procedure, or the Official Forms. This rule applies to:

(1) *Social Security Numbers.* If an individual's Social Security number must be included in a pleading, only the last four digits of that number shall be used.

(2) *Names of Minor Children.* If the involvement of a minor child must be mentioned, only the initials of that child shall be used.

(3) *Dates of Birth.* If an individual's date of birth must be included in a pleading, only the year shall be used.

(4) *Financial Account Numbers.* If financial account numbers are relevant, only the last four digits of these numbers shall be used.

(b) Responsibility. The responsibility for redacting these personal identifiers rests solely with counsel and the parties. The Clerk will not review papers for compliance with this rule.

(c) Unredacted Papers May Be Filed Under Seal. In compliance with the E–Government Act of 2002, a party wishing to file a paper containing the personal data identifiers listed above may file an unredacted paper under seal. This paper shall be retained by the Court as part of the record. The party shall also file a redacted copy via CM/ECF.

[Effective December 1, 2004. Amended effective July 1, 2015.]

Notes of Advisory Committee

2015 Amendment

The amendments to this rule are stylistic and effective July 1, 2015.

2004 Amendment

This amendment serves as guidance for implementing the Judicial Conference Privacy Policy and the E–Government Act of 2002.

PART I. COMMENCEMENT OF CASE; PROCEEDINGS RELATING TO PETITION AND ORDER FOR RELIEF

RULE 1002–1. FILING OF THE PETITION [ABROGATED EFFECTIVE JULY 1, 2015]

Notes of Advisory Committee

2015

This rule is abrogated effective July 1, 2015, as it is duplicative of other rules.

RULE 1007–1. LISTS, SCHEDULES, STATEMENTS, AND OTHER REQUIRED DOCUMENTS

(a) Requirements at Commencement of Case. The following shall be submitted at the commencement of a case for relief:

(1) *Chapter 7, 9, 13, or 12.* The petition and a list of creditors or a master mailing matrix, in accordance with Local Rule 1007–2.

(2) *Chapter 11.* The petition, a list of creditors or a master mailing matrix, a list of equity security holders, and a list of creditors holding the twenty largest unsecured claims, in accordance with Local Rule 1007–2.

(3) *All Chapters.* Individual debtors are required to file a Statement of Social Security Number (Official Form 121) signed under penalty of perjury by the individual debtor. In cases filed by Electronic Filing Users, the Electronic Filing User shall maintain the original Statement of Social Security Number for a period of four years after closing the case. Failure to submit the Statement of Social Security Number may lead to dismissal of the case.

(b) Payment Advices Not Filed With the Court Unless Ordered. Copies of payment advices or other evidence of payment ("Payment Advices") shall not be filed with the Court unless otherwise ordered. Pursuant to 11 U.S.C. § 521(a)(1)(B)(iv) and Fed. R. Bankr. P. 1007(b)(1)(E), unless the Court orders otherwise, the debtor is required to file with the Court copies of all Payment Advices or other evidence of payment received within 60 days before the date of the filing of the petition by the debtor from any employer of the debtor. The purpose of this requirement is accomplished by requiring that Payment Advices be provided to the United States Trustee, the trustee, or any creditor requesting copies. Additionally, privacy concerns are accommodated by not requiring the filing of the Payment Advices.

(c) Requirement to Provide Payment Advices to the Trustee. The debtor shall provide Payment Advices to the trustee and, if requested, to the United States Trustee, and to any creditor who timely requests copies of the Payment Advices, at least seven days before the time of the meeting of creditors conducted pursuant to 11 U.S.C. § 341. To be considered timely, a creditor's request must be received at least 14 days before the first date set for the meeting of creditors.

[Effective June 15, 1997. Amended effective December 1, 2004; March 15, 2012; July 1, 2013; December 1, 2015.]

Notes of Advisory Committee

2013 Amendment

This amendment specifies that a list of creditors or a master mailing matrix must be filed with bankruptcy petitions. Local Rule 1007-2 provides that debtors who are not represented by an attorney must submit a master mailing matrix with their petition. This amendment is effective July 1, 2013.

2012 Amendment

This amendment incorporates archived Administrative Orders FLMB-2010-1 and JAX-2006-1 "Orders on Filing Payment Advices Pursuant to 11 U.S.C. § 521(a)(1)(B)(iv)." The amendment exercises the Court's discretion provided by Section 521(a)(1)(B)(iv) and Fed. R. Bankr. P. 1007(b)(1)(E) to waive the requirement of filing Payment Advices with the Court. In doing so, the Court recognizes that the underlying purpose of these provisions is accomplished by requiring that Payment Advices be provided to the United States Trustee, the trustee, or any creditor requesting copies. Additionally, privacy concerns are addressed by avoiding filing Payment Advices in the public record. The addition of headings and subheadings is a stylistic rather than substantive change.

This amendment is effective March 15, 2012.

2004 Amendment

This amendment deletes the requirement to submit additional paper copies of petitions, schedules, or creditor lists. Those copies, which were distributed to case trustees, Internal Revenue Service, Securities and Exchange, or to the United States Trustee, will now be accessible on the Court's Electronic Filing System. It also deletes the requirement for an individual debtor not represented by an attorney to file a statement of assistance received in connection with the filing of the case. Fed. R. Bankr. P. 2016(c) requires every bankruptcy petition preparer to file a declaration under penalty of perjury disclosing any fee received from or on behalf of the debtor in compliance with Section 110(h)(1). Further, in compliance with the Judicial Conference's policy on privacy, the rule requires the debtor's Social Security number be "submitted" to the court, rather than "filed." An Electronic Filing User is responsible for submitting the Statement of Social Security Number containing an image of the debtor's original signature as a separate non-viewable entry in CM/ECF and for submitting the debtor's full Social Security number during the case filing or case upload process.

1997 Amendment

This amendment conforms the existing Local Rules to the uniform numbering system prescribed by the Judicial Conference of the United States and to the model system suggested and approved by the Advisory Committee on Bankruptcy Rules of the Judicial Conference's Committee on Rules of Practice and Procedure. In renumbering the Local Rules to conform to the uniform numbering system, no change in substance is intended. This amendment was effective on April 15, 1997.

Paragraph (a) of this rule was formerly Local Rule 2.04(g). Paragraph (b) of this rule was formerly Local Rule 2.04(c). The Advisory Committee Notes to the superseded rules may be helpful in interpreting and applying the current rules.

1995 Amendment

New subparagraph (c) to Local Rule 2.04 adds a requirement that individuals in bankruptcy cases who are not represented by an attorney are required to file with the petition an executed statement of assistance received in connection with the filing of the case in a form available from the Clerk's Office.

These amendments were effective on February 15, 1995.

RULE 1007-2. MAILING—LIST OR MATRIX

(a) Master Mailing Matrix.

(1) *Debtors Not Represented by Counsel.* Debtors who are not represented by an attorney must submit a master mailing matrix with their petition. The master mailing matrix shall be provided in a computer-readable format as designated by the Clerk and published on the Court's website, www.flmb.uscourts.gov. In the event a pro se debtor is unable to provide the matrix in computer-readable format, the debtor shall follow such directions as the Clerk may reasonably give to facilitate conversion of the matrix into computer-readable format.

(2) *Contents of the Matrix.* The matrix shall not include the names and addresses of the debtor, any joint debtor, the attorney for the debtor or debtors, or the United States Trustee. The matrix shall include the names and complete mailing addresses of all creditors and any general partners of the debtor.

(b) Chapter 11 Local Rule 1007-2 Parties in Interest List. In Chapter 11 cases, the Clerk shall maintain the list of creditors holding the 20 largest unsecured claims filed by the debtor pursuant to Fed. R. Bankr. P. 1007(d) and shall designate this list as the "Local Rule 1007-2 Parties in Interest List" in CM/ECF. Upon appointment of a committee of unsecured creditors, the Clerk shall add the names and addresses of the committee members, counsel for the committee, if any, and authorized agents of the committee, if any, to the Local Rule 1007-2 Parties in Interest List and shall remove the names and addresses of the creditors holding the 20 largest unsecured claims. The Clerk shall also add to this list the names and addresses of parties who have filed requests for notice pursuant to Rule 2002-1(d) of these rules.

(c) Equity Security Holders Mailing Matrix. In Chapter 11 cases in which there are equity security holders (except publicly traded equity securities), the Clerk shall maintain the list of equity security holders filed by the debtor pursuant to Fed. R. Bankr. P. 1007(a)(3) in CM/ECF and shall designate this list as the "Equity Security Holders Matrix."

[Effective June 15, 1997. Amended effective December 1, 2004; July 1, 2013.]

Notes of Advisory Committee

2013 Amendment

This amendment clarifies that only debtors not represented by an attorney are required to file a master mailing matrix with their petitions. Attorneys are required to file petitions electronically via CM/ECF. The computer software and CM/ECF system generate the required matrixes.

This amendment is effective July 1, 2013.

2004 Amendment

This amendment removes the requirement for Electronic Filing Users to file matrices in paper or on computer diskettes because Electronic Filing Users are able to file matrices directly into CM/ECF.

1997 Amendment

This amendment conforms the existing Local Rules to the uniform numbering system prescribed by the Judicial Conference of the United States and to the model system suggested and approved by the Advisory Committee on Bankruptcy Rules of the Judicial Conference's Committee on Rules of Practice and Procedure. In renumbering the Local Rules to conform to the uniform numbering system, no change in substance is intended. This amendment was effective on April 15, 1997.

Paragraphs (a) and (b) of this rule were formerly paragraphs (e) and (f) of Local Rule 2.04. The Advisory Committee Notes to the superseded rules may be helpful in interpreting and applying the current rules.

1995 Amendment

Local Rule 2.04(e)(1) has been amended to require that in any case in which the number of creditors exceeds fifty (50), the master mailing matrix shall be provided in a computer-readable format designated and published from time to time by the Clerk. In all other cases, the master mailing matrix may be provided in either the computer-readable format or on an Avery Label 5351, 33 block, or similar product as may be from time to time designated and published by the Clerk.

Local Rule 2.04(e)(3) has been amended to provide, consistent with current practice, that upon appointment of a committee, the Clerk shall add to the mailing matrix the names and addresses of the committee members, counsel for the committee, and any authorized agents of the committee, and shall delete therefrom the names and addresses of the creditors holding the twenty (20) largest unsecured claims.

These amendments were effective on February 15, 1995.

RULE 1009-1. AMENDMENTS TO LISTS & SCHEDULES

(a) Applicability of Rule. This rule applies to amendments to schedules, petitions, lists, matrices, statements of social security number, and statements of financial affairs.

(b) Content of Amendments. Amendments shall contain a caption including the case number and the title and shall be marked "Amended." Amendments to Schedule A or Schedule B shall set forth all of the debtor's real and personal property and shall state both the assets added and the assets deleted in the amendment. Amendments to Schedule C shall set forth all exemptions claimed by the debtor. Amendments to Schedules D, E, F, G and H shall set forth additional, new information, i.e., additional creditors, or deleted information.

(c) Execution and Verification. Amendments shall be executed and verified under penalty of perjury by the debtor and attorney of record in the same manner that the item being amended was originally executed.

(d) Amendments Adding Ten or More Creditors. Amendments that add ten or more creditors shall comply with the provisions of Local Rule 1007-2(a) applicable to the submission of the master mailing matrix with the original petition.

(e) Service of Amendments. The debtor shall serve notice of amendments to any persons or entities affected thereby, and file a proof of service with the Clerk in accordance with the provisions of Local Rule 9013-1. Amendments to Schedules D, E, and F shall be served upon the newly added creditor(s), together with a copy of the Notice of Commencement of Bankruptcy Case, Meeting of Creditors, & Deadlines, the Notice of Deadline to File Proof of Claim, if any, and in Chapter 13 cases, a copy of the most recently filed Chapter 13 plan.

(f) Amendments to Statement of Social Security Number. In compliance with the policy of the United States Judicial Conference to protect personal data identifiers, any amendment to the debtor's Statement of Social Security Number will be filed on the docket as a restricted entry. The debtor/debtor's attorney shall (i) serve a copy of the amended statement on all parties who were served with the Notice of Bankruptcy Case, Meeting of Creditors, & Deadlines, and (ii) file a proof of service with the Clerk. Electronic Filing Users shall maintain the original signed and verified amended statement setting out the debtor's full social security number for a period of four years after the case is closed.

(g) Filing Fees. Amendments to the debtor's schedules of creditors, lists of creditors, matrix, or mailing list require the prescribed filing fee unless the nature of the amendment is to change the address of a creditor or an attorney listed for a creditor.

[Effective June 15, 1997. Amended effective December 1, 2004; July 1, 2013; July 1, 2015.]

Notes of Advisory Committee

2015 Amendment

Amended section (e) requires service of the Notice of Deadline to File Proof of Claim, if any, upon newly added creditors in Schedules D, E, and F. This amendment is effective July 1, 2015.

2013 Amendment

This amendment requires that amendments to bankruptcy schedules indicate the information that has been added and/or deleted.

This amendment is effective July 1, 2013.

2004 Amendment

This amendment to the Local Rule above, as with similar amendments removes the requirement to submit additional paper copies of documents because those parties requiring copies will have access to these documents under CM/ECF. It also adds instructions for filing an amendment to the debtor's Statement of Social Security Number. Further, it clarifies when a filing fee is due with an amendment.

1997 Amendment

This amendment conforms the existing Local Rules to the uniform numbering system prescribed by the Judicial Conference of the United States and to the model system suggested and approved by the Advisory Committee on Bankruptcy Rules of the Judicial Conference's Committee on Rules of Practice and Procedure. In renumbering the Local Rules to conform to the uniform numbering system, no change in substance is intended. This amendment was effective on April 15, 1997.

This rule was formerly Local Rule 2.06. The Advisory Committee Notes to the superseded rules may be helpful in interpreting and applying the current rules.

1995 Amendment

This rule is amended to substitute the term "proof of service" for "certificate of service" as required by amended Rule 2.19(a). The other amendment to Local Rule 2.06(d) is stylistic. No substantive change is intended.

These amendments were effective on February 15, 1995.

RULE 1015–1. JOINT ADMINISTRATION OF CASES

(a) Joint Petition by Married Couple. If a married couple files a joint petition, or if an involuntary petition is filed against a married couple, the trustee shall administer the estates jointly without order of the Court. If the trustee, a debtor, or any other party in interest desires that the trustee administer the estates separately, that party may move for an order of separate administration.

(b) Joint Administration Generally. Except in the case of a joint petition by a married couple, a party seeking joint administration shall file a motion for joint administration. A motion for joint administration filed in a Chapter 11 case may be considered with or without a hearing at the Court's discretion.

(c) Manner of Joint Administration. Jointly administered cases shall be administered as follows:

(1) *Designation of Lead Case.* The earliest filed case assigned to a judge shall be designated in the joint administration order as the "lead case," except as otherwise ordered by the Court.

(2) *Captions.* All papers shall be captioned with the name and case number of the lead case name followed by the words ("Jointly Administered with") beneath the case number, and shall include the case names and numbers of each case that is subject to joint administration, unless otherwise ordered. However, a proof of claim shall indicate only the case name and number of the case in which the claim is filed. The caption shall not use the word "Consolidated" to refer to joint administration.

UNITED STATES BANKRUPTCY COURT
MIDDLE DISTRICT OF FLORIDA
DIVISION

In re:

	Chapter 11
ABC Company, Inc.,	Case No. 8:12–bk–00001–XXX
	Jointly Administered with
ABC Holding Co.	Case No. 8:12–bk–00002–XXX
ABC Operating Co.	Case No. 8:12–bk–00003–XXX

Debtors.
_______________________/

(3) *Docket.* With such exceptions as may be determined by the Court, a single case docket shall be maintained after the entry of the order for joint administration under the case number of the case designated in the joint administration order as the lead case.

(4) *Claims.* A separate claims register shall be maintained for each case. A separate claim must be filed in each jointly administered case in which a creditor asserts a claim.

(5) *Monthly Operating Reports.* In Chapter 11 cases, unless otherwise ordered, a separate Monthly Operating Report shall be filed for each of the jointly administered cases. The Monthly Reports shall be filed in the lead case.

(d) Severance of Jointly Administered Cases. If at any time, the trustee, a debtor, or any other party in interest desires that jointly administered cases be administered separately, that party may move for an order to sever the joint administration.

[Effective June 15, 1997. Amended effective March 15, 2012; July 1, 2013.]

Notes of Advisory Committee

2013 Amendment

This amendment clarifies the requirement that Monthly Operating Reports be filed in the lead case and adds subsection (d) to permit the severance of jointly administered cases.

This amendment is effective July 1, 2013.

2012 Amendment

This amendment establishes procedures for the joint administration of estates of persons other than married petitioners. The term "husband and wife" has been changed to "married couple." The addition of headings and subheadings is a stylistic rather than substantive change.

This amendment is effective March 15, 2012.

1997 Amendment

This amendment conforms the existing Local Rules to the uniform numbering system prescribed by the Judicial Conference of the United States and to the model system suggested and approved by the Advisory Committee on Bankruptcy Rules of the Judicial Conference's Committee on Rules of Practice and Procedure. In renumbering the Local Rules to conform to the uniform numbering system, no change in substance is intended. This amendment was effective on April 15, 1997.

This rule was formerly Local Rule 2.05. The Advisory Committee Notes to the superseded rules may be helpful in interpreting and applying the current rules.

1995 Amendment

New subparagraph (c) to Local Rule 2.04 adds a requirement that individuals in bankruptcy cases who are not represented by an attorney are required to file with the petition an executed statement of assistance received in connection with the filing of the case in a form available from the Clerk's Office. These amendments were effective on February 15, 1995.

These amendments were effective on February 15, 1995.

RULE 1019-1. CONVERSION—PROCEDURE FOLLOWING CHAPTER 11 CONFIRMATION [ABROGATED EFFECTIVE JULY 1, 2015]

Notes of Advisory Committee

2015

This rule is abrogated effective July 1, 2015, as it is duplicative of Fed. R. Bankr. P. 2002(a)(4).

RULE 1020-1. CHAPTER 11 SMALL BUSINESS CASES—GENERAL [ABROGATED EFFECTIVE OCTOBER 15, 1998]

Notes of Advisory Committee

1998 Amendment

On December 1, 1997, amendments to the Federal Rules of Bankruptcy Procedure added new Rule 1020, entitled "Election to be Considered a Small Business in a Chapter 11 Reorganization Case." This new rule was made necessary by the amendments to the Bankruptcy Code included in the Bankruptcy Reform Act of 1994, Pub. L. No. 103-394. The Court had adopted Local Rule 1020-1 in 1995 as an interim matter pending amendment of the Federal Rules of Bankruptcy Procedure. The local rule is now abrogated as duplicative of national rules effective October 15, 1998.

RULE 1071-1. DIVISIONS—BANKRUPTCY COURT

(a) Middle District of Florida. The Middle District of Florida consists of those counties and places of holding court as designated in 28 U.S.C. § 89.

(b) Divisions. The Middle District shall be divided into four Divisions to be known as the Jacksonville, Orlando, Tampa, and Fort Myers Divisions, as follows:

(1) *Jacksonville Division.* The Jacksonville Division consists of the following counties: Baker, Bradford, Citrus, Clay, Columbia, Duval, Flagler, Hamilton, Marion, Nassau, Putnam, St. Johns, Sumter, Suwannee, and Union. The place of holding court shall be Jacksonville.

(2) *Orlando Division.* The Orlando Division consists of the following counties: Brevard, Lake, Orange, Osceola, Seminole, and Volusia. The place of holding court shall be Orlando.

(3) *Tampa Division.* The Tampa Division consists of the following counties: Hardee, Hernando, Hillsborough, Manatee, Pasco, Pinellas, Polk, and Sarasota. The place of holding court shall be Tampa.

(4) *Fort Myers Division.* The Fort Myers Division consists of the following counties: Charlotte, DeSoto, Glades, Collier, Hendry, and Lee. The place of holding court shall be Fort Myers or as determined by the presiding judge.

(c) Assignment of Division. The Clerk's Office shall assign each case to the appropriate Division as determined by the debtor's county of residence or principal place of business as set forth on the bankruptcy petition. The Court, upon motion of any party in interest or the Court's own motion, may order that the case be transferred to a different Division if the Court determines that the transfer is in the interest of justice or for the convenience of the parties.

[Effective June 15, 1997. Amended effective August 1, 2014.]

Notes of Advisory Committee

2014 Amendment

This amendment changes the assignment of Volusia County from the Jacksonville Division to the Orlando Division so as to be consistent with the designation of divisions of the United States District Court for the Middle District of Florida. Section (c) clarifies the Court's procedure of assigning cases to the appropriate division based upon the information set forth on the bankruptcy petition. This amendment is effective August 1, 2014.

1997 Amendment

This amendment conforms the existing Local Rules to the uniform numbering system prescribed by the Judicial Conference of the United States and to the model system suggested and approved by the Advisory Committee on Bankruptcy Rules of the Judicial Conference's Committee on Rules of Practice and Procedure. In renumbering the Local Rules to conform to the uniform numbering system, no change in substance is intended. This amendment was effective on April 15, 1997.

This rule was formerly Local Rule 1.03. The Advisory Committee Notes to the superseded rules may be helpful in interpreting and applying the current rules.

1995 Amendment

This amendment abolishes the Ocala Division as a separate, free-standing division of the Court and reassigns to the Jacksonville Divisions the counties that presently comprise the Ocala Division. Because of the lack of facilities available to the Court in Ocala, bankruptcy court has not been conducted in Ocala for some considerable period of time. For this reason, cases from counties comprising the Ocala Division have been treated by the Court as filed in and assigned to the Jacksonville Division. In March, 1994, the Judicial Conference of the United States deleted Ocala from the List of approved places for holding bankruptcy court. This amendment, therefore, merely conforms the Local Rules to existing practice.

These amendments were effective on February 15, 1995.

RULE 1073-1. ASSIGNMENT OF CASES

(a) Initial Assignment of Cases — General. In a Division with two or more resident judges, the Clerk shall assign cases to an individual judge using a blind draw system to ensure the random assignment of cases or as directed by the Chief Judge. Neither the Clerk nor any member of the Clerk's staff shall have any power or discretion in determining the judge to whom any case is assigned. This method of assignment is designed to prevent anyone from choosing the judge to whom a case is to be assigned and all persons shall conscientiously refrain from attempting to circumvent this rule.

(b) Initial Assignment of Cases Special Provisions. Notwithstanding any provision of subsection (a) to the contrary,

(1) Cases filed only under a certain chapter or chapters of the Bankruptcy Code may be assigned to a particular judge as the Court may from time to time direct.

(2) Cases may be assigned to judges under the blind draw system in such proportions as the Court may from time to time direct.

(3) Successive cases filed by or against the same debtor and multiple cases filed by or against related entities or affiliates shall be assigned to the judge assigned the first filed case if the successive cases are filed in the same Division as the first case. If a successive case is filed in a Division other than the Division in which the previous case was filed, any interested party may move to transfer venue to the original Division for assignment to the judge assigned to the first case.

(c) Reassignment of Matters due to Judge's Temporary Unavailability. When the judge to whom a case or proceeding has been assigned is temporarily unavailable due to illness, absence, or prolonged engagement in other judicial business, emergency applications and motions arising in the case or proceeding may be assigned to any other resident judge in the Division, generally to the judge who is junior in date of appointment in that Division. If no other judge is available in the Division, such applications or motions may be assigned to any other available judge in the District.

(d) Reassignment of Cases and Proceedings Due to Disqualification or Recusal. If a judge is unable, because of the entry of an order of disqualification or recusal, to preside in a case or proceeding pending in—

(1) a Division with more than two resident judges, the Clerk shall reassign the case or proceeding to another judge resident in that Division selected by utilization of a blind draw system.

(2) a Division with two resident judges, the Clerk shall reassign the case or proceeding to the other judge resident in that Division.

(3) a Division with one resident judge, the Clerk shall reassign the case or proceeding to a judge in another Division as designated by the Chief Judge.

(e) Successive Reassignment of Cases and Proceedings Due to Disqualification or Recusal. If a successor judge who is reassigned a case or proceeding cannot preside because of the entry of an order of disqualification or recusal, the Clerk shall reassign the case or proceeding —

(1) to another judge resident in that Division, if there is one who is able to preside (by utilization of a blind draw system if there is more than one remaining judge able to preside); or

(2) to another judge selected by the Chief Judge if there is no other judge resident in that Division who is able to preside.

(f) Reassignment of Cases and Proceedings for Other Reasons.

(1) Nothing in this rule shall limit the authority of the Chief Judge under 28 U.S.C. § 154(b) to assign or reassign cases and proceedings as may be necessary to ensure that the business of the Court is handled effectively and expeditiously or of any judge to reassign cases and proceedings for other appropriate reasons, such as to equalize caseloads among judges, distribute cases to new judges, etc.

(2) The judge to whom any case or proceeding is assigned may, at any time, reassign the case or proceeding to any other consenting judge for any limited purpose or for all further purposes.

[Effective June 15, 1997. Amended effective December 1, 2004; July 1, 2015.]

Notes of Advisory Committee

2015 Amendment

This amendment clarifies that a successive case filed by or against a debtor will be assigned to the judge assigned to the previously filed case unless the successive case is filed in a different Division. In that event, the case will not be reassigned to the Division of the previous case, but parties in interest may move for a transfer of venue to the original venue and assigned judge. The amendment also clarifies that the Chief Judge shall designate the judge to whom the Clerk shall assign Fort Myers cases. This amendment is effective July 1, 2015.

2004 Amendment

This amendment clarifies that the Chief Judge will assign a judge resident in the Tampa Division to Ft. Myers cases and deletes the requirement for a general standing order in the assignment of cases.

1997 Amendment

This amendment conforms the existing Local Rules to the uniform numbering system prescribed by the Judicial Conference of the United States and to the model system suggested and approved by the Advisory Committee on Bankruptcy Rules of the Judicial Conference's Committee on Rules of Practice and Procedure. In renumbering the Local Rules to conform to the uniform numbering system, no change in substance is intended. This amendment was effective on April 15, 1997.

This rule was formerly Local Rule 1.04. The Advisory Committee Notes to the superseded rules may be helpful in interpreting and applying the current rules.

1995 Amendment

This amendment simply makes technical and grammatical changes necessary because of the abolition of the Ocala Division as contained in the amendment to Local Rule 1.03.

These amendments were effective on February 15, 1995.

1993 Amendment

This rule was substantially modified effective February 1, 1993, in anticipation of the arrival of new judges as a result of the expansion of the membership of the court that was authorized by the Congress.

RULE 1074–1. CORPORATIONS AND OTHER NON-INDIVIDUAL PERSONS

Corporations, partnerships, trusts, and other persons who are not individuals may appear and be heard only through counsel permitted to practice in the Court under Local Rule 2090–1. Subject to this general rule, agents of non-individual persons may attend meetings of creditors under section 341(a) of the Bankruptcy Code and may, with the Court's permission, appear in connection with objections to claims and other limited matters.

[Effective June 15, 1997. Amended effective July 1, 2015.]

Notes of Advisory Committee

2015 Amendment

This amendment incorporates the Court's current practice permitting agents, such as employees or principals, of non-individual persons (*e.g.*, corporations, limited liability companies, etc.) to attend meetings of creditors and, with the Court's permission, other hearings on objections to claims and other limited matters. This amendment is effective July 1, 2015.

1997 Amendment

This amendment conforms the existing Local Rules to the uniform numbering system prescribed by the Judicial Conference of the United States and to the model system suggested and approved by the Advisory Committee on Bankruptcy Rules of the Judicial Conference's Committee on Rules of Practice and Procedure. In renumbering the Local Rules to conform to the uniform numbering system, no change in substance is intended. This amendment was effective on April 15, 1997.

This rule was formerly Local Rule 1.08(d). The Advisory Committee Notes to the superseded rules may be helpful in interpreting and applying the current rules.

PART II. OFFICERS AND ADMINISTRATION; NOTICES; MEETINGS; EXAMINATIONS; ELECTIONS; ATTORNEYS AND ACCOUNTANTS

RULE 2002-1. NOTICE TO CREDITORS AND OTHER INTERESTED PARTIES

(a) Mailing of Notice. The Clerk may require the debtor, the trustee, or other party in interest filing a petition, a complaint, an objection, or other pleading for which a notice may be required to prepare and mail such notice as the Court may designate and to file with the Clerk proof of service in accordance with the provisions of Local Rule 9013-1.

(b) Notices in Chapter 11 Cases in Which Committees Have Been Appointed. Pursuant to Fed. R. Bankr. P. 2002(i) and unless otherwise ordered by the Court, the notices required by Fed. R. Bankr. P. 2002(a)(2), (3), and (6) may be delivered only to the parties on the Local Rule 1007-2 Parties in Interest List.

(c) Notices in Chapter 7 Cases. In Chapter 7 cases, pursuant to Fed. R. Bankr. P. 2002(h) and unless otherwise ordered by the Court, after 90 days following the first date set for the meeting of creditors under 11 U.S.C. § 341, all notices required by Fed. R. Bankr. P. 2002(a) need only be served upon the debtor, the trustee, all indenture trustees, creditors that hold claims for which proofs of claim have been filed, creditors, if any, that are still permitted to file claims by reason of an extension granted pursuant to Fed. R. Bankr. P. 3002(c)(1) or (c)(2), and parties who have filed a request for notice pursuant to section (d) of this rule.

(d) Requests for Notice. A party who files a request for notice pursuant to Fed. R. Bankr. P. 2002(g) shall be placed on the master mailing matrix and, in Chapter 11 cases, on the Local Rule 1007-2 Parties in Interest List. Requests for notice shall be served on the debtor and the trustee.

(e) Form of Notice. Notices shall be in such form as may be directed by the Clerk or as may be ordered by the Court.

(f) Return Address Required. Envelopes containing notices or orders served by the Bankruptcy Noticing Center, the debtor's attorney, or the debtor if the debtor is acting *pro se*, shall bear the return address of the debtor's attorney or the *pro se* debtor.

(g) Returned Notices. If the debtor's attorney or *pro se* debtor receives a piece of mail from the United States Post Office that was addressed to a party to the case but has been returned as undeliverable, the debtor's attorney or the *pro se* debtor shall immediately determine the correct address of the party, mail a copy of the returned piece of mail to the party, and promptly thereafter file proof of such service with the Clerk. The debtor's attorney or the *pro se* debtor shall also immediately file with the Clerk a notice of the corrected address for the creditor.

(h) Service of Orders and Notices. If the Court directs an attorney or a party to serve an order or a notice, the attorney or party shall serve the order or notice within three days of its having been entered by the Court, and the attorney or party shall thereafter promptly file a proof of such service in accordance with the provisions of Local Rule 9013-1.

(i) Notices as Directed by the Court. If a party is authorized by the Federal Rules of Bankruptcy Procedure, Local Rule, or order of the Court to give notice of a hearing or the time in which an objection or request for hearing is required, such notice shall be on the face of the first page of such notice, pleading, or other paper.

(j) Administrative Expense. The cost or expense incurred in serving notices and orders may be an administrative expense to be paid or reimbursed pursuant to 11 U.S.C. § 503(a).

[Effective June 15, 1997. Amended effective December 1, 2004; March 15, 2012; July 1, 2013; December 1, 2015.]

Notes of Advisory Committee

2013 Amendment

This amendment adds new section (c) which applies to Chapter 7 cases and limits service of notices required by Fed. R. Bankr. P. 2002(a), after 90 days following the first date set for the meeting of creditors, to the debtor, the trustee, all indenture trustees, creditors that hold claims for which proofs of claim have been filed, and creditors, if any, that are still permitted to file claims by reason of an extension granted pursuant to Fed. R. Bankr. P. 3001(c)(1) or (c)(2). This is consistent with Fed. R. Bankr. P. 2002(h).

This amendment is effective July 1, 2013.

2012 Amendment

This amendment incorporates archived Administrative Order FLMB-2003-1 "General Order Regarding the Return Address of Notices and Orders Mailed by the Bankruptcy Noticing Center." The addition of headings and subheadings is intended to be a stylistic rather than substantive change.

This amendment is effective March 15, 2012.

2004 Amendment

This amendment corrects the Bankruptcy Rules citation to that of the currently used citation. This amendment, 2002-1(a), recognizes that the Clerk may more expeditiously give notice to creditors or parties in interest through the Bankruptcy Noticing Center (BNC). For practical purposes, only when the Clerk cannot reasonably process notices through BNC, would the Clerk request the moving party to send notice to creditors or other parties in interest.

This amendment, 2002-1(d), adds a provision permitting Electronic Filing Users the ability to complete service of pleadings by electronic means.

1997 Amendment

This amendment conforms the existing Local Rules to the uniform numbering system prescribed by the Judicial Conference of the United States and to the model system suggested and approved by the Advisory Committee on Bankruptcy Rules of the Judicial Conference's Committee on Rules of Practice and Procedure. In renumbering the Local Rules to conform to the uniform numbering system, no change in substance is intended. This amendment was effective on April 15, 1997.

Paragraph (a) of this rule was formerly Local Rule 3.03. Paragraphs (b) through (g) of this rule were formerly paragraphs (b) through (f) and (h) of Local Rule 2.19. The Advisory Committee Notes to the superseded rules may be helpful in interpreting and applying the current rules.

1995 Amendment

This rule is amended to substitute the term "proof of service" for "certificate of service" as required by amended Rule 2.19(a). The provisions as to the content of the proof and the time for filing the proof are deleted because those subjects are now contained in amended rule 2.19(a).

These amendments were effective on February 15, 1995.

RULE 2002-4. NEGATIVE NOTICE PROCEDURE

(a) Matters Authorized to Be Considered on Negative Notice. The Court has established a list (the "Negative Notice List") of motions, objections, and other papers that may be considered by the Court without an actual hearing under the negative notice procedure described in this rule if no party in interest files a response to the relief requested. The Negative Notice List is posted on the Court's website, www.flmb.uscourts.gov, and may be supplemented or otherwise amended by the Court from time to time. Other motions, objections, and other matters may be considered by the Court using the negative notice procedure if permitted by the presiding judge.

(b) Manner of Service. Motions, objections, and other papers filed pursuant to this negative notice procedure shall:

(1) Be served in the manner and on the parties as required by the applicable provisions of the Federal Rules of Bankruptcy Procedure, Local Rules, or Court order, and shall be filed with proof of such service in accordance with the provisions of Local Rule 9013-1; and

(2) Contain a negative notice legend prominently displayed on the face of the first page of the paper. The negative notice legend shall be in the following form:

NOTICE OF OPPORTUNITY TO OBJECT AND REQUEST FOR HEARING

Pursuant to Local Rule 2002-4, the Court will consider this motion, objection, or other matter without further notice or hearing unless a party in interest files a response within [number] days from the date set forth on the proof of service attached to this paper plus an additional three days for service. If you object to the relief requested in this paper, you must file your response with the Clerk of the Court at [address] and serve a copy on the movant's attorney, [name and address], and any other appropriate persons within the time allowed.

If you file and serve a response within the time permitted, the Court may schedule and notify you of a hearing, or the Court may consider the response and may grant or deny the relief requested without a hearing. If you do not file a response within the time permitted, the Court will consider that you do not oppose the relief requested in the paper, will proceed to consider the paper without further notice or hearing, and may grant the relief requested.

(c) Time for Filing Responses. For the purpose of completing the negative notice legend, the number of days during which parties may respond that is placed in the negative notice legend shall be 21 days, except as set forth on the Negative Notice List.

(d) Hearings. In the event a party in interest files a response within the time permitted in the negative notice legend, the Court may, but need not, schedule a hearing on the motion, objection, or other matter upon notice to the movant's attorney, the objecting party or parties, and others as may be appropriate.

(e) Consideration Without a Hearing. If no response is filed within the time permitted in the negative notice legend as computed under Fed. R. Bankr. P. 9006(a) and (f), the Court will consider the matter in chambers without further notice or hearing upon the submission by the movant of a proposed form of order granting the relief. The movant shall submit the proposed order after the expiration of the response period and within three business days of such expiration. If the movant fails to submit a proposed form of order within this time, the Court may enter an order denying, disapproving, or overruling the matter without prejudice for lack of prosecution. In addition to any other requirements, the proposed order shall recite that:

(1) The motion, objection, or other matter was served upon all interested parties with the Local Rule 2002-4 negative notice legend informing the parties of their opportunity to respond within 21 (or other) days of the date of service;

(2) No party filed a response within the time permitted; and

(3) The Court therefore considers the matter to be unopposed.

(f) Court May Schedule a Hearing Even if No Response is Filed. Nothing in this rule is intended to preclude the Court from conducting a hearing on the motion, objection, or other matter even if no response is filed within the time permitted in the negative notice legend.

[Effective June 15, 1997. Amended effective December 1, 2004; December 1, 2009; October 6, 2011; July 1, 2013; July 1, 2014; December 1, 2015.]

Notes of Advisory Committee

2014 Amendment

The amendment revises the negative notice legend to add an additional three days for service to the response period. Revised section (e) provides that the movant shall submit a proposed order days after the expiration of the response period and within three business days of such expiration. This amendment is effective July 1, 2014.

2013 Amendment

This amendment refers parties to the Negative Notice List posted on the Court's website for a complete list of the motions, objections, and other matters that have been approved by the Court for consideration using negative notice procedures and for the applicable number of days in the objection period. This amendment is effective July 1, 2013.

2004 Amendment

This amendment corrects the Bankruptcy Rules citation to that of the currently used citation. Further, this amendment under section (b)(2) above allows Electronic Filing Users, i.e. those registered with the Court to file pleadings electronically, to take further advantage of using Negative Notice procedures within the electronic filing environment. Together with other Local Rule changes, these amendments are designed to assist attorneys in fulfilling the new electronic filing requirements. Former section (b)(2) is renumbered to (b)(3).

1997 Amendment

This amendment conforms the existing Local Rules to the uniform numbering system prescribed by the Judicial Conference of the United States and to the model system suggested and approved by the Advisory Committee on Bankruptcy Rules of the Judicial Conference's Committee on Rules of Practice and Procedure. In renumbering the Local Rules to conform to the uniform numbering system, no change in substance is intended. This amendment was effective on April 15, 1997.

This rule was formerly Local Rule 2.19A. The Advisory Committee Notes to the superseded rules may be helpful in interpreting and applying the current rules.

1995 Amendment

The rule codifies the negative notice procedure that has been in use, in varying degrees, in the Court for some time. As authorized by 11 U.S.C. § 102(1), orders required to be entered "after notice and a hearing," or a similar phrase in the Bankruptcy Code or Federal Rules of Bankruptcy Procedure, may be entered without an actual hearing if appropriate notice is given and no party-in-interest requests a hearing. This rule is intended to give effect to this authorization in those kinds of matters that experience teaches frequently trigger no opposition. The Advisory Committee considers that this rule will substantially enhance the efficiency and economy of the practice in the Court.

Subparagraph (a)(6) contemplates that the list of motions authorized to be made under the negative notice procedure, as set forth in subparagraph (a)(1) through (a)(5), may be expanded if authorized by the presiding judge for matters heard by that judge.

Although the Advisory Committee foresees that the rule will normally be used in connection with motions, it is intended by the drafters that the rule would also apply if a judge authorizes its use in matters in which an objection rather than a motion initiates the matter. For example, if authorized by a judge for matters before that judge, it could apply to objections to proofs of claim under Fed. R. Bankr. P. 3007. In that case, the party filing an objection to claim would be the "movant" and the objection to claim would be the "motion" for purposes of interpreting and applying the rule.

The rule further contemplates that, when no objection to the motion is filed within the prescribed period, the Court will review the motion for procedural and substantive regularity upon the movant's submission of a proposed form of order granting the motion. The Court may schedule a hearing on the motion if the Court, for any reason, determines that the circumstances make a hearing necessary or desirable.

These amendments were effective on February 15, 1995.

RULE 2004-1. EXAMINATION OF DEBTOR AND OTHERS

(a) This Rule Does Not Apply in Adversary Proceedings and Contested Matters. This rule applies only to examinations conducted pursuant to Fed. R. Bankr. P. 2004. The rules governing discovery in adversary proceedings and contested matters are set forth in Part VII of the Federal Rules of Bankruptcy Procedure and Local Rules 7026-1, 7030-1, 7033-1 and 7037-1.

(b) Manner of Setting Examination. A Court order is not necessary to authorize an examination pursuant to Fed. R. Bankr. P. 2004 or to require production of documents at the examination. Examinations shall be scheduled upon notice filed with the Court and served on the trustee, the debtor, the debtor's attorney, and the party to be examined.

(c) Reasonable Notice. The attendance of the examinee and the production of documents may not be required less than 21 days after service of the notice, except by agreement of the parties or order of the Court. To the extent that a request for production of documents under this rule may be construed as a request under Fed. R. Bankr. P. 7034, the time to respond is shortened to 21 days. The notice of examination may provide for the production of documents in advance of the examination, but in no event shall the production of documents be required less than 21 days from service of the notice of examination, unless otherwise agreed to by the parties or ordered by the Court.

(d) Who May Attend. Any party in interest who wishes to attend an examination scheduled under this rule may do so by filing and serving a cross-notice of examination at least 14 days in advance of the scheduled examination.

(e) Motion for Protective Order. An interested party may file, prior to the date of the proposed examination or production of documents, a motion for protective order stating the reasons for prohibiting, limiting, or rescheduling the examination or production of documents. A motion for protective order shall be filed as an emergency motion under Local Rule 9004-2(e). The examination and/or production of documents shall be stayed until the Court rules on the motion.

(f) Subpoena. No subpoena is necessary to compel the attendance of, or the production of documents by, the debtor at an examination of the debtor. A subpoena is necessary to compel the attendance of, or production of documents by, a witness other than the debtor. The provisions of Fed. R. Civ. P. 45 apply to subpoenas issued under this rule.

(g) Videotaped Examinations. Examinations may be videotaped if the notice of examination or subpoena states that the examination will be videotaped and whether it will also be recorded stenographically.

[Effective July 1, 2014. Amended effective December 1, 2015; July 1, 2016.]

Notes of Advisory Committee

2016 Amendment

This amendment clarifies that parties shall schedule examinations under Fed. R. Bankr. P. 2004 notice rather than by motion. This amended rule is effective July 1, 2016.

2014

This new rule is effective July 1, 2014.

RULE 2007.1–1 TRUSTEES & EXAMINERS (CH. 11) [ABROGATED EFFECTIVE OCTOBER 15, 1998]

Notes of Advisory Committee

1998 Amendment

On December 1, 1997, amendments to the Federal Rules of Bankruptcy Procedure amended Rule 2007.1. These amendments were made necessary by amendments to the Bankruptcy Code included in the Bankruptcy Reform Act of 1994, Pub. L. 103–394. The Court had adopted Local Rule 2007.1–1 in 1995 as an interim matter pending amendment to the Federal Rules of Bankruptcy Procedure. The local rule is now abrogated as duplicative of the national rule.

RULE 2015–1. TRUSTEE EXPENDITURES

(a) Chapter 7 Trustee's Limited Authority to Expend Funds. Chapter 7 trustees may incur and pay expenses directly related to the administration of the estate not to exceed $500 in the aggregate without order of the Court. The Trustee's Final Report shall itemize all expenses incurred and paid during the administration of the estate and shall be subject to review by the Court.

(b) Bank Servicing Fees. A trustee may pay bank servicing fees to the extent authorized by the Uniform Depository Agreement that exists between the bank used by the trustee as a depository for estate funds and the United States Trustee. These fees may be assessed against the trustee's bankruptcy accounts.

(c) Court Filing Fees. A trustee may pay any unpaid filing fees to the Court without order of the Court.

[Amended effective July 1, 2015.]

Notes of Advisory Committee

2015 Amendment

The amendment in section (c) authorizes Chapter 7 trustees to pay any unpaid filing fees from available funds in cases where the debtor is either not required to pay a filing fee or has failed to do so. This amendment is effective July 1, 2015.

2012 Adoption

This rule incorporates archived Administrative Order FLMB 2011–1 "Administrative Order Providing Limited Authority to Expend Funds," which permitted Chapter 7 trustees to incur and pay routine expenses. It increases the amount permitted from $300 to $500 without order of the Court. It requires the Trustee's Final Report to itemize all expenses incurred rather than the preliminary report, and permits the payment of bank servicing fees. This rule is effective March 15, 2012.

RULE 2015–3. CHAPTER 7 TRUSTEES—NOTICE OF DISPOSITION OF RECORDS

Except with respect to the disposal of patient records pursuant to 11 U.S.C. § 351, the trustee in Chapter 7 cases, in addition to complying with the applicable requirements of the United States Trustee's Handbook for Chapter 7 Trustees, shall give 30 days' written notice to the debtor, the debtor's attorney, the Internal Revenue Service, and the United States Trustee prior to destroying any of the debtor's books and records in the trustee's possession.

[Effective June 15, 1997. Amended effective March 15, 2012.]

Notes of Advisory Committee

2012 Amendment

This amendment incorporates the addition of 11 U.S.C. § 351 by the Bankruptcy Abuse Prevention and Consumer Protection Act of 2005, Pub. L. 109–8. The amendment also clarifies the trustee's duty to meet the requirements of the United States Trustee's Handbook for Chapter 7 Trustees with respect to the destruction of books and records.

This amendment is effective March 15, 2012.

1997 Amendment

This amendment conforms the existing Local Rules to the uniform numbering system prescribed by the Judicial Conference of the United States and to the model system suggested and approved by the Advisory Committee on Bankruptcy Rules of the Judicial Conference's Committee on Rules of Practice and Procedure. In renumbering the Local Rules to conform to the uniform numbering system, no change in substance is intended. This amendment was effective on April 15, 1997.

This rule was formerly Local Rule 2.19(g). The Advisory Committee Notes to the superseded rules may be helpful in interpreting and applying the current rules.

RULE 2016–1. COMPENSATION OF PROFESSIONALS

(a) General. Requests for compensation for professional services and reimbursement of expenses are governed by Fed. R. Bankr. P. 2016 and this rule.

(b) Retainers. Professionals may apply prepetition and approved postpetition retainers in the ordinary course towards compensation for professional services and reimbursement of expenses without a separate order; however, professionals must fully disclose and account for all retainers in their Rule 2016 Disclosure Statement and in all subsequent applications for compensation. This rule does not relieve professionals from the obligation to file interim and/or final fee applications. The Court may order disgorgement of applied fees and costs at any time. This rule does not preclude any challenge to the entitlement or the reasonableness of any retainer.

(c) Applications for Compensation for Professional Services and Reimbursement of Expenses.

(1) *Chapter 7 Cases.*

(i) Except as provided for in Local Rule 2015–1, professionals employed by a Chapter 7 trustee shall file final applications for fees and expenses incurred during a Chapter 7 case upon completion of services or upon notification by the trustee that the case is ready to close.

(ii) In cases that have been converted to Chapter 7, all final applications of professionals for fees and expenses incurred in the case prior to conversion shall be filed within 90 days after the date of the order converting the case.

(iii) All applications, whether interim or final, shall contain the amounts requested and a detailed itemization of the work performed including: (1) the name of the individual performing the work; (2) the amount of time expended for each item of work; (3) the hourly rate requested; (4) the date of employment; (5) a discussion of the criteria that are relevant in determining the compensation to be awarded; (6) a detail of reimbursable costs; and (7) a verification stating that the fees and costs for which reimbursement is sought are reasonable for the work performed, and that the application is true and accurate.

(2) *Chapter 11 Cases.*

(i) General Information Requirements. Applications for interim or final compensation of less than $5,000 shall conform to the requirements of section (c)(1)(iii) of this rule. Applications for compensation that exceed $5,000 in the aggregate shall also contain the information set forth below unless ordered otherwise.

1. The first page of the application shall be the Chapter 11 Fee Application Summary available on the Court's website. However, if the application is served using the negative notice procedures of Local Rule 2002–4, the negative notice legend and the title of the application shall be located on the first page of the application and the Summary shall be the second page of the application.

2. Time shall be itemized by project category. Examples of project categories include General Case Administration, Asset Sales, Claims Administration and Objections, Fee Applications and Objections, Cash Collateral, Relief from Stay Proceedings, Avoidance Actions, Plan and Disclosure Statement, and Valuation.

3. The narrative portion of the application shall provide information by project category as to the types of services performed, the necessity for performing the services, the results obtained, the benefit to the estate, and other information that is not apparent from the activity descriptions or that the applicant wishes to bring to the attention of the Court. In addition, the narrative portion of the application may describe special employment terms, billing policies, expense policies, voluntary reductions, reasons for the use of multiple professionals for a particular activity, or reasons for substantial time billed relating to a specific activity.

4. All applications shall include complete and detailed activity descriptions billed in tenths of an hour (six minutes). Each activity description shall include the type of activity (*e.g.*, phone call, research) and the subject matter (*e.g.*, cash collateral motion, § 341 meeting, etc.). Activity descriptions shall not be lumped—each activity shall have a separate description and a time allotment.

(ii) Applications to Permit Monthly Payment of Interim Fee Applications. In larger Chapter 11 cases, upon motion and after notice and hearing, the Court may consider the approval of procedures for monthly payment of interim fee applications for professionals.

(iii) Final Applications. To be considered at the confirmation hearing, a professional fee application shall be filed 30 days prior to the confirmation hearing unless ordered otherwise. The Court will not consider any application for compensation unless all creditors receive at least 21 days' notice of the hearing. The notice of hearing shall at a minimum identify the applicant and the amounts requested. A final application may include an estimate of the amount of additional fees and costs to be incurred through confirmation. The final application may be supplemented at, or prior to, the confirmation hearing, so long as the amount sought is within the estimate. Final applications may be supplemented up to 14 days after entry of the confirmation order for work performed beyond the amount estimated and allowed at confirmation. Supplements to final applications shall be subject to Court approval after notice and hearing.

(iv) Post Confirmation Professional Fees. Unless otherwise ordered by the Court, professional fees and costs incurred after confirmation in connection with actions against third parties are subject to Court approval.

(3) *Chapter 13 Cases.* Compensation for professional services or reimbursement of expenses by attorneys for Chapter 13 debtors shall be governed by the prevailing practice in the Division in which the case is pending.

(d) *Creditors' Attorney's Fees.* Applications for attorney's fees made on behalf of a creditor, other than requests under 11 U.S.C. § 503(b)(2), (3), and (4), are not governed by this rule. Nevertheless, any party in interest may seek a judicial determination of such fees.

(e) *Expense Reimbursement Guidelines.* The Court may establish expense reimbursement guidelines to address expenses such as photocopying, facsimile transmissions, computerized research, and meals and travel. Such guidelines will be posted on the Court's web site.

(f) *Waiver Procedure.* An application to employ a professional within the scope of this rule may include a request that the Court waive, for cause, one or more of the information requirements of this rule. Such waivers may be appropriate for ordinary course professionals and professionals seeking de minimus payments and may be granted at the Court's discretion.

[Effective June 15, 1997. Amended effective March 15, 2012; July 1, 2014; July 1, 2015.]

Notes of Advisory Committee

2015 Amendment

This amendment provides that when fee applications are served using the negative notice procedures of Local Rule 2002-4, the negative notice legend and the title of the application shall be located on the first page of the application and the Chapter 11 Fee Application Summary [previously titled the Chapter 11 Fee Application Cover Page] shall be the second page of the application. This amendment is effective July 1, 2015.

2014 Amendment

This amendment adds subsection (c)(2)(iv), requiring Court approval for post confirmation professional fees and costs, unless otherwise ordered by the Court. This amendment is effective July 1, 2014.

2012 Amendment

This amendment establishes the procedures to be used by professionals in seeking compensation in Chapter 7, 11, and 13 cases. Local Rule 2015-1 authorizes Chapter 7 trustees to incur and pay expenses, including payments to professionals, not to exceed $500 in the aggregate without order of the Court.

This amendment is effective March 15, 2012.

1997 Amendment

This amendment conforms the existing Local Rules to the uniform numbering system prescribed by the Judicial Conference of the United States and to the model system suggested and approved by the Advisory Committee on Bankruptcy Rules of the Judicial Conference's Committee on Rules of Practice and Procedure. In renumbering the Local Rules to conform to the uniform numbering system, no change in substance is intended. This amendment was effective on April 15, 1997.

This rule was formerly Local Rule 3.04. The Advisory Committee Notes to the superseded rules may be helpful in interpreting and applying the current rules.

1995 Amendment

This amendment to Local Rule 3.04 requires that applications of professionals for compensation also be served on the debtor, debtor's attorney, and any trustee appointed under 11 U.S.C. §§ 1104, 1202, or 1302.

These amendments were effective on February 15, 1995.

RULE 2081-1. CHAPTER 11—GENERAL

(a) Operations. The trustee or debtor-in-possession in a Chapter 11 case may operate the business of the debtor pursuant to 11 U.S.C. § 1108 and any order of the Court specifying terms and conditions of the operation of the debtor's business.

(b) Case Management Summary. Within the earlier of three business days following the petition date, or the date that the debtor-in-possession first files a motion requesting affirmative relief, the debtor-in-possession shall file a Chapter 11 Case Management Summary providing the following information:

(1) description of the debtor's business;

(2) locations of the debtor's operations and whether leased or owned;

(3) reasons for filing Chapter 11;

(4) list of officers, directors and insiders (including relatives of insiders), if applicable, and their salaries and benefits at the time of filing and during the one year prior to filing;

(5) the debtor's annual gross revenues;

(6) amounts owed to various creditors, including current year to date and prior fiscal year:

(i) priority creditors such as governmental creditors for taxes,

(ii) secured creditors and their respective collateral, and

(iii) unsecured creditors;

(7) general description and approximate value of the debtor's current and fixed assets;

(8) number of employees and gross amounts of wages owed as of petition date;

(9) status of the debtor's payroll and sales tax obligation, if applicable;

(10) anticipated emergency relief to be requested within the first 14 days after the petition date; and

(11) the debtor's strategic objectives, i.e., refinancing, cram down, surrender/sale of assets or business.

(c) Initial Status Conference. The Court may schedule an initial status conference at which debtor's counsel should be prepared to address the following: status of the case and reason for the bankruptcy case, deadlines for filing a plan and disclosure statement, special noticing issues, the need for scheduling regular status conferences, and the scheduling of pending motions.

(d) Monthly Operating Reports in Small Business Cases. Each month, Small Business Debtors as defined in 11 U.S.C. § 101(51D) shall file a Schedule of Receipts and Disbursements (also required of Chapter 11 Business Debtors), following as Appendix A. The Schedule may be filed without the referenced attachments. This requirement is in addition to the Small Business Monthly Operating Report prescribed or promulgated by the Judicial Conference.

(e) Employee Salaries. Upon the filing of a Chapter 11 petition, all employees (including managers, agents, or officers who are not affiliates, within the meaning of 11 U.S.C. § 101(2)(A)), may be paid a salary and receive benefits accruing post-petition in the ordinary course of business. The Court may review, and grant appropriate relief, if such salaries are later determined to be unreasonable.

An officer, manager, or employee who also qualifies as an affiliate (collectively, "Affiliate Officer") must file a motion to have his or her salary and benefits approved by the Court in advance of payment. Court authority for payment of any salary or benefits shall not constitute the assumption of any existing employment agreement. A motion for authority for the payment of any prepetition wages or Affiliate Officer's salary may be filed pursuant to the expedited procedures set forth in section (f)(6) of this rule. Authorization for payment may be retroactive to the petition date if the motion so requests.

(f) Expedited Motions. The following motions shall be scheduled for hearing within three business days, if reasonably possible and if the motions are served electronically or by facsimile transmission. Expedited motions must be served by facsimile or hand delivery on the Office of United States Trustee, with telephonic notice of the hearing date and time, unless service by another means is agreed to by the Office of the United States Trustee.

(1) *Motion Seeking Authority to Use Cash Collateral.* A motion seeking authority to use cash collateral pursuant to 11 U.S.C. § 363 shall comply with Fed. R. Bankr. P. 4001(b) or (d) and include the following information:

(i) Typical Terms. The motion to use cash collateral should include the following provisions:

1. identification of each secured creditor having a security interest in the cash collateral, the basis upon which the secured creditor is entitled to assert a security interest in the cash collateral, and the amount owed to the secured creditor;

2. the type of adequate protection the debtor is offering each secured creditor (e.g., replacement lien, insurance);

3. the amounts and types of cash collateral on the petition date;

4. the amount of cash collateral that the debtor seeks authority to use from the date of the preliminary hearing on the motion through and until the final hearing on the motion, if the debtor seeks the use of cash collateral sooner than 14 days after service of the motion;

5. a budget setting forth the projected cash flow of the debtor for the period of time for which the use of cash collateral is sought;

6. reasonable reporting requirements; and

7. proposed consequences of default.

(ii) Extraordinary Terms. The following provisions will generally not be approved absent compelling circumstances:

1. any cross-collateralization provision that would secure the repayment of prepetition debt with post-petition assets;

2. a waiver of any claims to include avoidance actions against any secured creditor;

3. a waiver of any rights the estate may have under 11 U.S.C. § 506(c);

4. any factual stipulations or findings that bind the estate or parties in interest with respect to the validity, priority, and extent of secured creditor's liens;

5. immediate relief from stay under the order approving use of cash collateral or automatic relief from stay upon default;

6. granting of liens on avoidance action recoveries;

7. validation of any secured creditor's security interest in its collateral or within a limited period of time after the appointment of a committee pursuant to 11 U.S.C. § 1102; or

8. any subordination of administrative priority claims arising under 11 U.S.C. § 726(c).

(2) *Motion for Approval of Post Petition Financing.* A motion seeking approval of post petition financing pursuant to 11 U.S.C. § 364 shall comply with Fed. R. Bankr. P. 4001(c) and (d) and must include:

(i) the identity of the proposed lender and its relationship to any of the parties;

(ii) a copy of the DIP loan agreement, together with a summary of the terms of the debt to be incurred ("DIP Loan") including:

1. the collateral in which the lender is seeking to obtain a security interest and whether the lender is seeking to prime existing liens;

2. the amount of the loan proposed to be extended by the lender;

3. the applicable interest rate and all other charges to be made in connection with the DIP Loan; and

4. the payment terms and duration of the DIP Loan.

(iii) the amount of credit that the debtor seeks authority to obtain from the date of the preliminary hearing on the motion through and until the final hearing on the motion, if the debtor seeks authority to obtain credit sooner than 14 days after service of the motion. (The debtor shall attach a budget setting forth the projected cash flow of the debtor for the period of time for which the credit is sought.);

(iv) the efforts made to obtain financing from other lenders;

(v) the debtor's ability to repay the DIP Loan; and

(vi) the inclusion of any of the terms listed in subsection (f)(1)(ii) above.

(3) *Motion for Authority to Pay Prepetition Wages.* A motion seeking authority to pay employees of the debtor prepetition wages outstanding as of the petition date shall include a schedule setting forth:

(i) the name of each employee to whom such wages are sought to be paid;

(ii) the amount due such employee(s) as of the petition date;

(iii) the amounts to be withheld from such wages, including all applicable payroll taxes and related benefits;

(iv) the period of time for which prepetition wages are due;

(v) whether the employee is presently employed by the debtor;

(vi) the irreparable harm that will result if the relief is not granted; and

(vii) whether any of the employees are insiders as defined in 11 U.S.C. § 101(31).

The motion shall also include a representation by the debtor that all applicable payroll taxes and related benefits due to the debtor's employees will be paid concurrently with payment of the wages.

(4) *Motion for Authority to Maintain Prepetition Bank Accounts.* A motion seeking authority to maintain prepetition bank accounts shall include:

(i) a schedule listing each prepetition bank account that the debtor seeks to maintain post petition;

(ii) the reason for seeking such authority;

(iii) the amount on deposit in each such account as of the petition date;

(iv) whether the depository is an authorized depository pursuant to 11 U.S.C. § 345(b); and

(v) a representation that the debtor has consulted with the Office of the United States Trustee regarding the continued maintenance of prepetition bank accounts and the United States Trustee has not consented to the proposed maintenance of use of such accounts.

If the debtor is unable to provide the foregoing information, the motion shall set forth the reason why such information is not available and provide an estimate as to when the debtor will supplement its motion with such information.

(5) *Motion for Authority to Pay Critical Vendors.* A motion seeking authority to pay prepetition claims deemed critical by the debtor will generally not be approved absent compelling circumstances supported by evidentiary findings. Any such motion shall include:

(i) a schedule of the names of each claimant;

(ii) the amount due each claimant;

(iii) a description of the goods or services provided to the debtor by each claimant;

(iv) facts and law supporting payment of the prepetition debt under the doctrine of necessity;

(v) the irreparable harm that will result if the relief is not granted; and

(vi) whether the claimant has made any concession or other agreement in consideration for the proposed payment, including the extension of postpetition trade credit.

(6) *Motion for Authority to Pay Affiliate Officer Salaries.* A motion to pay, on an interim basis, the salary of any officer, manager, or employee, who also qualifies as an affiliate under 11 U.S.C. § 101(2)(A) shall include:

(i) the name of the Affiliate Officer, the officer's position and job responsibilities;

(ii) the nature of the Affiliate Officer's relationship to the debtor;

(iii) the salary received by the Affiliate Officer during the 12 months prior to the filing of the debtor's Chapter 11 petition, including a description of any pre-petition employment agreement;

(iv) a description of any services performed for any third party or compensation received or that will be received by the Affiliate Officer from any source other than the debtor-in-possession after the date of the petition;

(v) the salary proposed to be paid to the Affiliate Officer, including all benefits; and

(vi) the amounts to be withheld from such salary of the Affiliate Officer, including all applicable payroll taxes and related benefits.

An interim order to authorize the payment of salaries to Affiliate Officers is subject to review or reconsideration at any time upon the motion of a party in interest or by the Court sua sponte.

(7) *Motion to Determine Adequate Assurance for Payment of Utility Services or, in the Alternative, Establishing the Procedure for Determining Adequate Assurance.*

(i) Content of the Motion. A motion to determine adequate assurance of payment of the debtor's utility services shall include:

1. a schedule of the names and addresses of the utilities;

2. whether the debtor is current in the payment of its utility;

3. an estimate of average monthly utility expense;

4. the amount owed to each utility; and

5. the method by which the debtor will provide adequate assurance of timely payment.

(ii) Proposed Order Conditionally Approving Motion. The motion shall be accompanied by a proposed order that provides for conditional approval of the motion subject to a 30-day objection period, which shall be set forth in the order by including above the preamble and below the title of the order the following bulletin in print either highlighted or bold so as to make it more prominent than the remainder of the text:

Any interested party who fails to file and serve a written objection to the motion (as conditionally approved by this Order) within 30 days after entry of the Order, shall be deemed to have consented to the provisions of this Order.

(iii) Objections. Timely objections will be scheduled for hearing. If no timely objection is filed the order shall be deemed final, and no further notice, hearing, or order shall be required.

(g) Use of Property. Subject to the provisions of 11 U.S.C. §§ 363 and 365, the debtor-in-possession may use, sell, or lease property of the estate. The debtor-in-possession is authorized to pay all necessary and current expenses of operating its business, including tax and lease payments, to the extent that such payments are necessary to preserve the assets or operate the business and provided that the payments are for only the postpetition period.

(h) Bank Accounts. The debtor-in-possession, consistent with 11 U.S.C. § 345, is authorized to open and maintain bank accounts for the deposit, investment, and disbursement of monies of the estate; provided, however, that the debtor-in-possession shall segregate all monies withheld from employees or collected for taxes in a separate bank account(s) and shall pay these funds to the proper authority when due.

[Effective June 15, 1997. Amended effective March 15, 2012; July 1, 2013.]

Notes of Advisory Committee

2013 Amendment

This amendment requires that a Case Management Summary be filed in advance of the filing of any motion in the case and sets forth the matters that the Court may wish to address if an Initial Status Conference is scheduled.

This amendment is effective July 1, 2013.

2012 Amendment

This amendment establishes a rule that is consistent with Administrative Order FLMB-2009-1 "Administrative Order Establishing Initial Procedures in Chapter 11 Cases Filed in the United States Bankruptcy Court of the Middle District of Florida." Additionally, the rule requires that Small Business Debtors file a Schedule of Receipts and Disbursements in addition to Small Business Monthly Operating Reports.

Federal Rules of Bankruptcy Procedure 6003 and 4001 should be considered with regard to "first-day" motions. Consideration should also be given to the Court's general procedures for emergency hearings.

The addition of headings and subheadings is a stylistic rather than a substantive change.

This amendment is effective March 15, 2012.

1997 Amendment

This amendment conforms the existing Local Rule to the uniform numbering system prescribed by the Judicial Conference of the United States and to the model system suggested and approved by the Advisory Committee on Bankruptcy Rules of the Judicial Conference's Committee on Rules of Practice and Procedure. In renumbering the Local Rules to conform to the uniform numbering system, no change in substance is intended. This amendment was effective on April 15, 1997.

This rule was formerly Local Rule 3.02. The Advisory Committee Notes to the superseded rules may be helpful in interpreting and applying the current rules.

1995 Amendment

The amendment dispenses with the requirement for the filing of a motion for authority to operate the business of the debtor. Consistent with current practice, it is contemplated that the court will enter an order sua sponte setting forth the requirements for operating the business of the debtor. It was the view of the Advisory Committee that dispensing with the requirement of filing a motion would reduce needless paperwork for counsel and the Clerk's office.

These amendments were effective on February 15, 1995.

RULE 2090-1. ATTORNEYS—ADMISSION TO PRACTICE

(a) Admission to the District Court Required. Except as set forth in this rule, an attorney who wishes to appear or be heard as counsel for another in any case or proceeding in the Court must first be admitted to practice in the United States District Court for the Middle District of Florida pursuant to Rule 2.01 of the Local Rules for the United States District Court for the Middle District of Florida.

(b) Limited Appearances by Attorneys not Admitted to the Middle District. An attorney residing outside the Middle District of Florida who is not admitted to practice in the United States District Court for the Middle District of Florida may appear without general or special admission to practice in the following limited instances:

(1) the preparation and filing of a notice of appearance and request for service of notices pursuant to Fed. R. Bankr. P. 2002;

(2) the preparation and filing of a proof of claim;

(3) the attendance and inquiry at the meeting of creditors held under 11 U.S.C. § 341; and

(4) the attendance and representation of a creditor at a hearing that has been noticed to all creditors other than the representation of a party in a contested matter or adversary proceeding.

(c) Special Admission to Practice.

(1) *Attorneys not Admitted to Practice in the Middle District.* An attorney who is a member in good standing of the bar of a District Court of the United States other than the Middle District of Florida (a "Non-Resident Attorney") may appear *pro hac vice* upon motion to the Court provided that such privilege is not abused by frequent or regular appearances in separate cases to such a degree as to constitute the maintenance of a regular practice of law in the Middle District of Florida. Motions to appear *pro hac vice* shall be accompanied by a written designation of an attorney admitted to practice in the Middle District and that attorney's consent to act as local counsel. A form motion to appear *pro hac vice*, a form written designation, and a form order granting the motion are available on the Court's website, www.flmb.uscourts.gov.

(2) *Government Attorneys* Any attorney representing the United States, or any agency thereof, having the authority of the Government to appear as its counsel, may appear specially and be heard in any case or proceeding in which the Government or such agency thereof is a party in interest, without formal or general admission.

(3) *Separate Requirements for Electronic Filing Users.* A Non-Resident Attorney who is admitted to practice *pro hac vice* and wishes to file papers with the Court must be an Electronic Filing User as set forth in Local Rule 1001-2. Otherwise, local counsel may file papers on behalf of Non-Resident Attorneys who do not wish to become Electronic Filing Users.

(4) *Admission Fees.* The Non-Resident Attorney shall pay to the District Court any admission fee required by the District Court of the Middle District of Florida.

(d) Conduct of Attorneys. All attorneys who appear in this Court shall be deemed to be familiar with and shall be governed by these Local Rules, the Rules of Professional Conduct, and other requirements governing the professional behavior of members of The Florida Bar. Such attorneys shall be subject to the disciplinary powers of the Court, including the processes and procedures set forth in Local Rule 2090-2. Attorneys should conduct themselves with civility and in a spirit of cooperation in order to reduce unnecessary cost and delay.

(e) Attorneys Who Become Ineligible to Practice Law.

(1) *Voluntary Resignation.* An attorney admitted to appear or be heard as counsel for another who resigns from the practice of law in the State of Florida, or from the bar of any state, the District of Columbia or territory upon whose admission the attorney's eligibility to practice law in this Court relies, shall immediately notify the Court of such resignation. Upon such notification, the Court shall suspend the attorney's right to practice before the Court in accordance with Local Rule 2090–2(b).

(2) *Involuntary Ineligibility to Practice Law.* An attorney admitted to appear or be heard as counsel for another who becomes ineligible to practice law because of disbarment or suspension by the bar of any state, the District of Columbia, or territory, or any federal district court or other court of competent jurisdiction, shall immediately notify the Court of such disbarment or suspension. Upon such notification, the Court shall suspend the attorney's right to practice before this Court in accordance with Local Rule 2090–2(b).

[Effective June 15, 1997. Amended effective December 1, 2004; December 1, 2009; July 1, 2014; July 1, 2015; July 1, 2016.]

Notes of Advisory Committee

2016 Amendment

This amendment clarifies the procedure to be followed by attorneys who wish to appear before the Court but who are not admitted to practice in the Middle District of Florida. The amendment also instructs counsel that the District Court requires a filing fee to be paid for special admission to practice. This amended rule is effective July 1, 2016.

2015 Amendment

New section (d) was previously section (a) of Local Rule 2090–2 Attorneys—Discipline. This amendment is effective July 1, 2015.

2014 Amendment

This amendment adds new section (d), requiring any attorney admitted to practice before the Court who becomes ineligible to practice law to so advise the Court. This amendment is effective July 1, 2014.

2004 Amendment

This amendment corrects the Bankruptcy Rules citation to that of the currently used citation.

1997 Amendment

This amendment conforms the existing Local Rules to the uniform numbering system prescribed by the Judicial Conference of the United States and to the model system suggested and approved by the Advisory Committee on Bankruptcy Rules of the Judicial Conference's Committee on Rules of Practice and Procedure. In renumbering the Local Rules to conform to the uniform numbering system, no change in substance is intended. This amendment was effective on April 15, 1997.

This rule was formerly Local Rule 1.07(a)–(c)(1)–(2). The Advisory Committee Notes to the superseded rules may be helpful in interpreting and applying the current rules.

The reference in paragraph (a) of this rule is to District Court Local Rule 2.01. At the time of this amendment, the District Court had not taken action to renumber its local rules. In the event the District Court renumbers its local rules, this rule should be interpreted to refer to the renumbered successor to current District Court Local Rule 2.01.

1995 Amendment

The amendment to Local Rule 1.07(b) is stylistic. No substantive change is intended.

The amendment to Local Rule 1.07 (c)(1) specifies that the attorney executing the written designation and consent-to-act on behalf of the non-resident attorney be resident in the Middle District of Florida.

The amendment to Local Rule 1.07(c)(3) is intended to clarify that an attorney appearing specially is subject to the same disciplinary process as a member of the bar of the District Court.

These amendments were effective on February 15, 1995.

RULE 2090–2. ATTORNEYS—DISCIPLINE

(a) General. Any attorney who appears before the Court, either generally under Local Rule 2090–1(a) or (b) or specially under Local Rule 2090–1(c), may, after hearing and for good cause shown, be reprimanded, suspended (temporarily or permanently) from practice before the Court, or subjected to such other discipline as a judge of the Court may deem proper. Nothing in this rule shall be construed as providing exclusive procedures for the discipline of an attorney in appropriate cases or as a limitation upon the power of the Court to punish for contempt in appropriate cases.

(b) Suspension or Disbarment in Another Court. Whenever the Court is notified that an attorney who appears before the Court (i) has been disbarred or suspended from practice by the Supreme Court of Florida, or by any other court of competent jurisdiction, (ii) has been disbarred on consent or resigned from the bar of any other court while an investigation into allegations of misconduct is pending, or (iii) has been convicted of a felony in any court, the Court shall enter an order that suspends the attorney from practice before the Court and terminates the attorney's CM/ECF filing privileges effective 14 days from the date of the order. However, within the 14–day period, the attorney may file a motion, with a copy served upon the United States Attorney, seeking relief from the operation of the suspension order. If a timely motion is filed, the suspension shall be stayed until the Court determines the motion.

(1) *Attorneys Admitted Generally.* If the attorney is admitted to practice generally under Local Rule 2090–1(a) or (b), the motion for relief from the suspension order shall be heard and determined by the Chief Judge or such other judge of the Court as the Chief Judge shall designate.

(2) *Attorneys Admitted Specially.* If the attorney is admitted to practice specially under Local Rule 2090–1(c), the motion for relief from the suspension order shall be heard and determined by the judge assigned to the case in which such special appearance has been made.

(c) Duty to Inform the Court of Disciplinary Proceedings. Any attorney who appears in this Court, upon being subjected to public discipline by any other Court of the United States or the District of Columbia, or by a court of any state, territory, commonwealth, or possession of the United States, including any attorney who is disbarred on consent or resigns from any bar while an investigation into allegations of misconduct is pending, shall promptly inform the Clerk of this Court of such action.

(d) Chief Judge May Convene a Grievance Committee. Without limiting a judge's ability to discipline an attorney as provided in subsection (a) of this rule, and in addition to or as an alternative to such ability, upon request of a judge of this Court, the Chief Judge of this Court shall convene and appoint a Grievance Committee in the requesting judge's Division of the Court to conduct an investigation of alleged misconduct on the part of an attorney who appears in this Court, whether appearing generally under Local Rule 2090-1(a) or (b) or specially under Local Rule 2090-1(c). Each Grievance Committee so appointed shall consist of not less than five attorneys regularly practicing in that Division, three of whom shall constitute a quorum. Appointments shall be for the period of time necessary to conclude the investigation for which the Grievance Committee was appointed. The Court shall designate the Chairman of the Committee, but each Committee shall otherwise organize itself as it sees fit. All proceedings before the Committee may be conducted informally, but shall remain confidential unless otherwise ordered by the Court. Each Committee shall function as follows:

(1) *Investigation by Grievance Committee.* When a requesting judge refers for investigation by a Committee any matter or question touching upon the professional behavior of an attorney, the Chairman of the Committee will promptly designate a member to investigate the matter and make a report to the Committee as a whole for the Committee's determination as to whether (i) the inquiry should be terminated because the question raised is unsupported or insubstantial; or (ii) the question raised justifies further inquiry but should be referred to the appropriate grievance committee of The Florida Bar; or (iii) the question raised should be pursued because there is probable cause to believe that the subject attorney has been guilty of unprofessional conduct justifying disciplinary action by the Court. The Chairman of the Committee shall then report the Committee's recommendation to the requesting judge and shall follow his or her direction.

(2) *Referral to United States Attorney.* If the requesting judge directs prosecution under this rule, such report shall then be transmitted to the United States Attorney (or, if the United States Attorney be disqualified by interest, to another member of the bar appointed by the Chief Judge of this Court for that purpose) who shall file and serve a motion for an order to show cause upon the accused attorney. Such motion, and all further proceedings thereon, shall be heard and determined by the Chief Judge of this Court sitting together with any two or more judges of this Court as the Chief Judge of this Court shall designate.

(e) Duty to Respond. It shall be the duty of every attorney who appears in this Court, either generally under Local Rule 2090-1(a) or (b) or specially under Local Rule 2090-1(c), to respond to the Court in any proceeding under subsection (a) of this rule or any Grievance Committee of the Court or the United States Attorney during the course of any investigation or prosecution being conducted pursuant to subsection (d) of this rule; provided, however, no attorney shall be entitled as of right to notice of the pendency of any such investigation unless and until the attorney is named in an order to show cause filed pursuant to subsection (d)(2) of this rule.

(f) Report to the District Court. Any discipline imposed under subsection (a) or (d) of this rule will be reported to the District Court for the Middle District of Florida.

[Effective June 15, 1997. Amended effective April 19, 2009; July 1, 2015; July 1, 2016.]

Notes of Advisory Committee

2016 Amendment

This amendment clarifies the procedures to be used when an attorney admitted to practice before the Court, either generally or specially, is disbarred or suspended from practice by the Supreme Court of Florida or another court. This amended rule is effective July 1, 2016.

2015 Amendment

Former section (a) is now incorporated into Local Rule 2090-1(d) effective July 1, 2015.

2009 Amendment

This amendment adds a local disciplinary rule. Although bankruptcy courts possess the inherent power to discipline attorneys and impose sanctions, this rule is meant to address the policy and recommendation of the American Bar Association (ABA) that "the Federal Rules of Bankruptcy Procedure ... be amended ... to clarify the authority of bankruptcy courts to discipline attorneys ... and require ... bankruptcy courts to adopt and enforce local disciplinary rules with respect to attorneys practicing before them ..." American Bar Association, Report and Recommendation 117 at 2 (adopted August 2006). As of the date of this amendment, the Federal Rules of Bankruptcy Procedure have not been so amended. Nonetheless, for reasons recited in the ABA report as well as the Court's desire to provide formal, systemic disciplinary procedures as an option to the use of sua sponte discipline by one of the Court's bankruptcy judges, this Court has elected to act on the recommendation that a local disciplinary rule be adopted. Although attorneys who practice in the Bankruptcy Court must be admitted to practice in the United States District of Court for the Middle District of Florida, subject to that court's Rule 2.04(e)(1), only a portion of such attorneys actually appear in the District Court. Therefore, this Court deems it advisable to adopt its own grievance process pursuant to which this Court will address misconduct issues arising in cases in this Court. This amendment was effective on April 19, 2009.

1997 Amendment

This amendment conforms the existing Local Rules to the uniform numbering system prescribed by the Judicial Conference of the United States and to the model system suggested and approved by the Advisory Committee on Bankruptcy Rules of the Judicial Conference's Committee on Rules of Practice and Procedure. In renumbering the Local Rules to conform to the uniform numbering system, no change in substance is intended. This amendment was effective on April 15, 1997.

This rule was formerly Local Rule 1.07(c)(3). The Advisory Committee Notes to the superseded rules may be helpful in interpreting and applying the current rules.

The reference in this rule is to District Court Local Rule 2.04. At the time of this amendment, the District Court had not taken action to renumber its local rules. In the event the District Court renumbers its local rules, this rule should be interpreted to refer to the renumbered successor to current District Court Local Rule 2.04.

Formerly cited as FL R USBCTSD Rule 9011-1.

RULE 2091-1. ATTORNEYS—DUTIES OF DEBTOR'S COUNSEL

Unless the Court has permitted the withdrawal of the attorney under Local Rule 2091-2, an attorney who files a petition on behalf of a debtor shall attend all hearings in the case that the debtor is required to attend under any provision of the Bankruptcy Code, the Federal Rules of Bankruptcy Procedure, these rules, or order of the Court. However, counsel need not attend a hearing regarding a matter to which the debtor is not a party and whose attendance has only been required as a witness.

[Former Rule 9011-1, effective June 15, 1997. Amended and renumbered effective July 1, 2016.]

Notes of Advisory Committee

2016 Amendment

This amendment renumbers the rule from 9011-1 to 2091-1 and revises the title of the rule to indicate that the rule applies to debtor's counsel. Other revisions are stylistic. This amended rule is effective July 1, 2016.

1997 Amendment

This amendment conforms the existing Local Rules to the uniform numbering system prescribed by the Judicial Conference of the United States and to the model system suggested and approved by the Advisory Committee on Bankruptcy Rules of the Judicial Conference's Committee on Rules of Practice and Procedure. In renumbering the Local Rules to conform to the uniform numbering system, no change in substance is intended. This amendment was effective on April 15, 1997.

This rule was formerly Local Rule 1.08(b). The Advisory Committee Notes to the superseded rules may be helpful in interpreting and applying the current rules.

Formerly cited as FL R USBCTSD Rule 2091-1.

RULE 2091-2. ATTORNEYS—WITHDRAWALS AND SUBSTITUTIONS

(a) Withdrawal Generally. Except as otherwise provided in this rule or by order of the Court, an attorney may not withdraw in any case or proceeding except by leave of Court. A motion for leave to withdraw shall be filed and served using the negative notice procedures of Local Rule 2002-4. The negative notice legend shall provide for a 14-day response period and shall be served on the client, parties in interest affected thereby, and opposing counsel.

(b) Withdrawal for Party in Interest Other Than the Debtor. An attorney for a party in interest other than the debtor who is not a party to any pending contested matter or adversary proceeding may withdraw his or her appearance without court order by filing a notice of withdrawal as attorney, stating the name and mailing address of the client, and serving copies of the notice on the client, the debtor, the trustee, the United States Trustee, and their attorneys.

(c) Withdrawal of Co-Counsel. An attorney seeking to withdraw from representing a client in a case or proceeding at a time when such client is represented by other counsel of record in such matter may withdraw his or her appearance by filing a notice of withdrawal that is approved and signed by the client and other counsel of record for the client, and serving copies of the notice on parties in interest entitled to notice.

(d) Substitution of Counsel. Counsel seeking to withdraw from representation of a client may file a joint motion with counsel seeking to be substituted in as counsel for such client, in the relevant case or proceedings, requesting authority of the Court for substitution of counsel. Such motion shall certify that the client has consented to the substitution or be signed by the client, and such motion shall be served on the client and parties in interest entitled to notice. The Court may grant a joint motion for substitution of counsel without a hearing. Substitution of counsel is subject to the requirements of the Bankruptcy Code, the Bankruptcy Rules, and this Court's Local Rules with regard to retention of professionals, disclosure, payment of professionals, and related matters.

[Former Rule 2091-1, effective June 15, 1997. Amended effective December 1, 2009; July 1, 2013. Amended and renumbered effective July 1, 2016.]

Notes of Advisory Committee

2016 Amendment

This amendment renumbers the rule from 2091-1 to 2091-2 and clarifies that motions for leave to withdraw shall be filed using the negative notice procedures of Local Rule 2004-2. This amended rule is effective July 1, 2016.

2013 Amendment

This amendment establishes procedures for the withdrawal of an attorney for a party in interest other than the debtor who is not a party to any pending contested matter or proceeding, the withdrawal of an attorney when the party is represented by another attorney, and the substitution of one attorney for another.

This amendment is effective July 1, 2013.

1997 Amendment

This amendment conforms the existing Local Rules to the uniform numbering system prescribed by the Judicial Conference of the United States and to the model system suggested and approved by the Advisory Committee on Bankruptcy Rules of the Judicial Conference's Committee on Rules of Practice and Procedure. In renumbering the Local Rules to conform to the uniform numbering system, no change in substance is intended. This amendment was effective on April 15, 1997.

This rule was formerly Local Rule 1.08(a). The Advisory Committee Notes to the superseded rules may be helpful in interpreting and applying the current rules.

1995 Amendment

The amendments to Local Rule 1.08 are stylistic. No substantive change is intended.

These amendments were effective on February 15, 1995.

RULE 2092-1. APPEARANCES BY LAW STUDENTS

(a) Purpose. In the interest of providing assistance to lawyers who represent clients unable to pay for legal services, and encouraging participating law schools to provide clinical instruction in the conduct of litigation in bankruptcy court, this rule establishes the rules and procedures by which eligible law students may appear in this Court ("Qualified Law Student").

(b) Qualified Law Students. Except as otherwise provided herein, the requirements of M.D. Fla. R. 2.05 shall govern the limited admission of Qualified Law Students to practice before the Court for the purpose of representing indigent persons. This limited admission to practice before the Court may be revoked at any time upon the Court's own motion.

(c) Participation Under Supervision. A Qualified Law Student may participate in all court proceedings, including depositions, provided that a supervising lawyer or another lawyer from the same office as the supervising lawyer ("Supervising Lawyer") is present. The Supervising Lawyer shall be present while a qualified law student is participating in court proceedings.

(d) Requirements of Supervising Lawyer. The Supervising Lawyer shall be admitted to practice before this Court as an Electronic Filing User. The Supervising Lawyer shall direct, supervise, and review all of the work of the Qualified Law Student and shall assume personal professional responsibility for any work undertaken by the Qualified Law Student while under the Supervising Lawyer's supervision. All pleadings, motions, briefs, and other papers prepared by the Qualified Law Student shall be reviewed by the Supervising Lawyer, and shall be filed with the Court electronically using that lawyer's CM/ECF User ID.

(e) Termination of Supervising Lawyer. A lawyer currently acting as a Supervising Lawyer may be terminated as a Supervising Lawyer at the discretion of the Court. When a Qualified Law Student's Supervising Lawyer is so terminated, the student shall cease performing any services under this rule until written notice of a substitute Supervising Lawyer, signed by the Qualified Law Student and by the Supervising Lawyer, is filed with the Court.

(f) Signature on Court Filings. When a Qualified Law Student signs any correspondence or legal document, the Qualified Law Student's signature shall be followed by the title "Law Student," and if the document is prepared for presentation to a court or for filing with the clerk thereof, the document shall also be signed by the Supervising Lawyer.

(g) Judicial Determination of Indigency Not Required for Referral to a Qualified Law Student. A judicial determination of indigency is not required, and no motion for a judicial determination of indigency need be filed, with respect to any person who has been referred to a Qualified Law Student by a not-for-profit legal aid organization or legal aid clinic operated by a participating law school.

(h) Law Student and Supervising Attorney Not "Debt Relief Agencies." The performance of pro bono legal services to debtors or other persons who are unable to pay for such legal services, in accordance with this rule, shall not cause the Qualified Law Student, the sponsoring legal aid organization or law school, or the Supervising Lawyer to be deemed a "debt relief agency" as defined in 11 U.S.C. § 101(12A).

[Effective July 1, 2013. Amended effective July 1, 2015.]

Notes of Advisory Committee

2015 Amendment

This amendment eliminates the requirement that qualified law students comply with applicable requirements promulgated by the Supreme Court of Florida and the Florida Bar. This amendment also clarifies that, in addition to the requirement that the supervising lawyer or a lawyer with the same law firm as the supervising lawyer review all papers prepared by the qualified law student, the papers shall be filed using that lawyer's CM/ECF User ID. This amendment is effective July 1, 2015.

2013 Adoption

This rule establishes procedures by which supervised law students may appear before the Court. This rule is effective July 1, 2013.

PART III. CLAIMS AND DISTRIBUTION TO CREDITORS AND EQUITY INTEREST HOLDERS; PLANS

RULE 3002-1. TIME FOR FILING PROOFS OF CLAIM IN REINSTATED CASES

If a case is dismissed before the deadline for filing proofs of claim has expired and the case is later reinstated, the deadline in Fed. R. Bankr. P. 3002(c) for filing a proof of claim is modified as follows:

(a) Dismissal Before § 341 Meeting. In a case that is dismissed before the § 341 meeting is held, the new deadline for filing a proof of claim or interest shall be the later of 60 calendar days after the rescheduled § 341 meeting or the original deadline for filing a proof of claim.

(b) Dismissal After § 341 Meeting. In a case that is dismissed after the § 341 meeting is held, the new deadline for filing a proof of claim or interest shall be the later of 60 calendar days from the date of entry of the order that vacates the order of dismissal and reinstates the case or the original deadline for filing a proof of claim.

[Effective March 15, 2012. Amended effective July 1, 2016.]

Notes of Advisory Committee

2016 Amendment

This amendment extends the deadlines for filing proofs of claim in reinstated cases from 28 to 60 days and is now applicable to cases filed under all chapters. This amended rule is effective July 1, 2016.

2012 Adoption

This rule provides for new deadlines for filing proofs of claims in bankruptcy cases that are dismissed and thereafter reinstated before the expiration of the claims bar date. This rule is effective March 15, 2012.

RULE 3007–1. CLAIMS—OBJECTIONS

(a) Contents. Objections to claims shall state the legal and factual basis for the objection and the amount of the debt conceded, if any.

(b) Service. Objections to claims shall be served on the claimant by mail or via CM/ECF as follows:

(1) to the attorney for the claimant, if the attorney has filed a notice of appearance and request for notice pursuant to Fed. R. Bankr. P. 2002(g); and

(2) to the agent or representative of the claimant who executed the proof of claim. If the name and address of the agent or representative are not legibly set forth in the proof of claim, the claimant shall be served at all addresses given for the claimant in the proof of claim.

(3) When the claimant is a domestic or foreign corporation, a partnership, or other unincorporated association, or a governmental entity or an insured depository, the objection shall also be served in the manner required by Fed. R. Bankr. P. 7004.

(c) Orders on Objections to Claims. Proposed orders on objections to claims shall recite that (1) the objection is either sustained or overruled and (2) that the claim is either allowed or disallowed.

[Effective June 15, 1997. Amended effective December 1, 2000; December 1, 2004; July 1, 2015.]

Notes of Advisory Committee

2015 Amendment

This amendment is stylistic and effective July 1, 2015.

2004 Amendment

This amendment corrects the Bankruptcy Rules citation to that of the currently used citation. Further, this amendment, 3007(e) adds a provision permitting the Electronic Filing Users the ability to complete service of pleadings by electronic means.

2000 Amendment

As set forth in new paragraph (b)(1) of this rule, objections to claim are to be served on the attorney for the claimant if the claimant's attorney has filed a F.R.B.P. 2000(g) notice of appearance and request for notice. Service on the claimant's attorney of record is in addition to service on the claimant as previously required by former paragraphs (b)(1) and (b)(2) of the rule. Under this amendment, these former paragraphs are renumbered as subparagraphs (b)(2)(i) and (b)(2)(ii).

The additional service requirement contained in this amendment is designed to remedy problems arising when an objecting party properly serves the objection on the claimant but does not also serve the claimant's counsel of record. Claimants who employ counsel in a bankruptcy case reasonably expect that their attorneys will receive notice of actions affecting their claims. *See, e.g.*, Fed. R. Civ. P. 5(b). Yet attorneys who have properly entered their appearances are not regularly served when parties object to their clients' claims. This failure to notice counsel has led to the unnecessary continuation of hearings and the setting aside of orders sustaining objections when counsel for the claimant, who has received no notice, fails to respond or appear.

This amendment also harmonizes service of objections to claims with service upon a debtor under Fed. R. Bankr. P. 7004(b)(9), which requires service on both the debtor and the debtor's counsel.

This amendment was effective on December 1, 2000.

1997 Amendment

This amendment conforms the existing Local Rules to the uniform numbering system prescribed by the Judicial Conference of the United States and to the model system suggested and approved by the Advisory Committee on Bankruptcy Rules of the Judicial Conference's Committee on Rules of Practice and Procedure. In renumbering the Local Rules to conform to the uniform numbering system, no change in substance is intended. This amendment was effective on April 15, 1997.

This rule was formerly Local Rule 2.10. The Advisory Committee Notes to the superseded rules may be helpful in interpreting and applying the current rules.

1995 Amendment

Fed. R. Bankr. P. 3007 requires that objections to the allowance of claims be served on "the claimant, the debtor or the debtor in possession and the trustee." Local Rule 2.10 deals with how the claimant who has filed a proof of claim is to be served with such an objection.

The amendment to subparagraph (b)(1) clarifies that objections to proofs of claim must be served on the agent or representative of the claimant who executed the proof of claim if that person's name and address are legibly stated in the proof of claim.

The amendment to subparagraph (b)(2) clarifies that, if this information is not legibly contained in the proof of claim, then the claimant must be served at all addresses given for the claimant in the proof of claim. This amendment also makes clear that, when the claimant is a corporation, partnership, or other unincorporated association, such an objection must be mailed to the attention of an officer, a managing or general agent, or other authorized agent of the claimant.

The amendment to subparagraph (c) is necessitated by Section 114 of the Bankruptcy Reform Act of 1994. This legislation amended Fed. R. Bankr. P. 7004 by providing additional certified mail service requirements for insured depository institutions. In addition, the amendment continues the existing requirement that governmental entities also must be served in the special manners set forth in Fed. R. Bankr. P. 7004.

These amendments were effective on February 15, 1995.

RULE 3012–1. MOTIONS TO DETERMINE SECURED STATUS—SERVICE

Motions to determine the secured status of a claim under 11 U.S.C. § 506 and Fed. R. Bankr. P. 3012 shall be served on the holder of the secured claim in both the manner required by Local Rule 3007–1(b) and the manner required by Fed. R. Bankr. P. 7004.

[Effective December 1, 2000. Amended effective December 1, 2004; July 1, 2015.]

Notes of Advisory Committee

2015 Amendment

This amendment is stylistic and effective July 1, 2015.

2004 Amendment

This amendment corrects the Bankruptcy Rules citation to that of the currently used citation.

2000 Amendment

This new local rule is designed to ensure that a motion to determine the secured status of a claim is served on the person who filed the proof of claim and the claimant's attorney, just as an objection to a claim is served on the person who filed the proof of claim and the claimant's attorney. *See* Local Rule 3007-1(b) and (c).

In the past, parties have served such motions on corporate claimants in an appropriate manner under Fed. R. Bankr. P. 7004, but the person within the organization with knowledge of the claim has not received the motion until well after the court has already acted on the motion. In these circumstances, the Court has had to revisit the matter, and the work of the parties and the Court has been duplicated. By ensuring that a party also serves the motion on the individual who filed the proof of claim, it is thought that problems of this sort experienced in the past can be eliminated.

This rule is effective on December 1, 2000.

RULE 3017-2. DISCLOSURE STATEMENT—SMALL BUSINESS CASES [ABROGATED EFFECTIVE OCTOBER 15, 1998]

Notes of Advisory Committee

1998 Amendment

On December 1, 1997, amendments to the Federal Rules of Bankruptcy Procedure amended Rule 2007.1. These amendments were made necessary by amendments to the Bankruptcy Code included in the Bankruptcy Reform Act of 1994, Pub. L. 103-394. The Court had adopted Local Rule 2007.1-1 in 1995 as an interim matter pending amendment to the Federal Rules of Bankruptcy Procedure. The local rule is now abrogated as duplicative of the national rule. This amendment was effective on October 15, 1998.

RULE 3018-1. BALLOTS—VOTING ON PLANS

(a) Form of Ballot. The form of ballot distributed to creditors shall include both the Court's physical address and information regarding the Chapter 11 eBallot hyperlink on the Court's website, and shall state that ballots must be received by the Clerk no later than the deadline established by order of the Court.

(b) Filing of Ballots. Ballots may be filed in paper with the Court, or may be electronically filed with the Clerk's Office via the Chapter 11 eBallot hyperlink on the Court's website, www.flmb.uscourts.gov. A report of all ballots filed may be viewed on CM/ECF.

(c) Late-Filed Ballots. Any ballot received after the last day to file ballots shall be considered as a late-filed ballot, and its acceptance shall be left to the discretion of the judge.

(d) Ballot Tabulation. The attorney for the proponent of the Chapter 11 plan shall prepare a tabulation of the acceptances and rejections of the plan. The ballot tabulation shall be filed not later than two days prior to the confirmation hearing. The tabulation shall be in the form available on the Court's website, www.flmb.uscourts.gov, and shall list the following for each class: total number of claims voting; total number of claims accepting; total dollar amount of claims voting; total dollar amount of claims accepting; percentages of claims voting that accept the plan; and percentage of dollar amount of claims voting that accept the plan. The ballot tabulation shall also indicate, for each class, whether the class is impaired or unimpaired, and whether the requisite vote has been attained.

(e) Rules Governing Ballot Tabulation. In tabulating the ballots, the following rules shall govern:

(1) Although CM/ECF creates a ballot report, it may include late-filed or otherwise invalid ballots. The responsibility for independently reviewing and tabulating acceptances and rejections for the plan remains with the attorney for the plan proponent.

(2) Ballots that are not signed, or where a company name is not shown on the signature line (when applicable), will not be counted either as an acceptance or as a rejection.

(3) If the amount of the creditor's claim shown on the ballot differs from the debtor's schedules and a proof of claim has been filed, unless an objection to the amount set forth on the proof of claim has been filed, the amount shown on the proof of claim will be used to determine the amount voting. If no proof of claim has been filed, the amount of the claim on the schedules will be used.

(4) If an objection to a proof of claim has been filed, absent court order to the contrary, the ballot filed by the claimant shall not be counted as either an acceptance or a rejection, but information regarding the ballot shall be included on the ballot tabulation.

(5) Ballots that do not show a choice of either acceptance or rejection will not be counted either as an acceptance or as a rejection.

(6) Ballots filed after the last date set for filing for ballots will not be counted either as an acceptance or as a rejection, unless leave of Court is granted.

(7) If duplicate ballots are filed, with one electing acceptance and the other electing rejection, neither ballot will be counted unless the later ballot is designated as amending the prior one.

[Effective June 15, 1997. Amended effective December 1, 2004; December 1, 2009; July 1, 2013; July 1, 2015.]

Notes of Advisory Committee

2015 Amendment

The amendment to section (d) prescribes a form of ballot tabulation available on the Court's website and specifies that the ballot tabulation shall be filed with the Court two days prior to the confirmation hearing. This amendment is effective July 1, 2015.

2013 Amendment

This amendment recognizes the Court's current practice, which permits ballots to be electronically filed via CM/ECF or via the Chapter 11 eBallot hyperlink located on the Court's website. The amendment also clarifies the rules governing ballot tabulations. This amendment is effective July 1, 2013.

RULE 3020-1. CHAPTER 11—CONFIRMATION

(a) Amendments to the Plan. Amendments to the plan shall be filed with the Court either as a single integrated amended plan or incorporated in the order of confirmation.

(b) Objections to Confirmation. Unless otherwise ordered by the Court, any objections to confirmation in a

Chapter 11 case shall be filed and served seven days before the date of the hearing on confirmation. The objection shall be served upon the debtor, the debtor's attorney, the trustee or examiner (if any), the proponent of the plan (if not the debtor), counsel for any official committee, and the United States Trustee.

(c) Confirmation Order. The plan proponent shall be responsible for preparing the order of confirmation and submitting it to the Court for entry. The order shall be submitted to the Court within 14 days after the hearing on confirmation.

(1) *Contents.* The confirmation order shall include the following if applicable: a schedule summarizing the timing and amount of payments to be made to each class of creditors under the plan; notice of any scheduled post-confirmation status conference; and the form of Post-Confirmation Avoidance & Claim Litigation Report to be filed in connection with post-confirmation status conferences conducted in the case. The form is available on the Court's website, www.flmb.uscourts.gov.

(2) *Service.* The plan proponent shall serve a conformed copy of the confirmation order together with a copy of the confirmed plan to all creditors, the United States Trustee, those persons on the Local Rule 1007-2 Parties in Interest List, and other parties as may be designated by the Court and file a proof of such service in accordance with the provisions of Local Rule 9013-1 within 14 days of the entry of the order of confirmation on the docket.

(d) Deadline for Filing Adversary Proceedings and Objections to Claims. Unless otherwise ordered by the Court, any adversary proceeding or contested matter contemplated by the Chapter 11 plan of reorganization and any objection to claim shall be filed no later than 60 days after the entry of the order of confirmation.

[Effective June 15, 1997. Amended effective December 1, 2009; July 1, 2014; December 1, 2015; July 1, 2016.]

Notes of Advisory Committee

2016 Amendment

This amendment requires orders confirming plans in Chapter 11 cases to include a summary of the timing and amount of payments to be made to each class of creditors under the plan. The amendment also changes the deadline from 30 days to 60 days for filing any adversary proceeding or contested matter contemplated by the Chapter 11 plan and any objection to claim. Other revisions are stylistic. This amended rule is effective July 1, 2016.

2014 Amendment

This amendment adds new section (a), requiring that plan modifications and amendments be filed in a single integrated plan or be incorporated in the order of confirmation. The purpose of this amendment is to clarify the terms of the plan as confirmed. The amendment also adds new section (d), requiring that the order of confirmation include notice of the first scheduled post confirmation status conference and the filing of post confirmation avoidance and claim litigation reports. This amendment is effective July 1, 2014.

1997 Amendment

This amendment conforms the existing Local Rules to the uniform numbering system prescribed by the Judicial Conference of the United States and to the model system suggested and approved by the Advisory Committee on Bankruptcy Rules of the Judicial Conference's Committee on Rules of Practice and Procedure. In renumbering the Local Rules to conform to the uniform numbering system, no change in substance is intended. This amendment was effective on April 15, 1997.

Paragraph (a) of this rule was formerly Local Rule 3.05(a). Paragraph (b) of this rule was formerly Local Rule 3.06(b). Paragraph (c) of this rule was formerly Local Rule 3.06(a). The Advisory Committee Notes to the superseded rules may be helpful in interpreting and applying the current rules.

1995 Amendment

Local Rule 3.06(a) has been amended to include the requirement that the debtor file any adversary proceedings or contested matters contemplated by the plan of reorganization no later than thirty (30) days after the entry of an order of confirmation.

Local Rule 3.06(c) has been amended to include contested matters and adversary proceedings within the matters which must be concluded before entry of a final decree.

Local Rule 3.06(d) has been added to make clear the requirement that a debtor who desires to convert a Chapter 11 case after confirmation of a plan of reorganization may do so only on motion and hearing with notice to all creditors and parties in interest. This is consistent with Bankruptcy Code § 1112(a)(1) which precludes the debtor from converting a case from Chapter 11 to Chapter 7 as a matter of right if the debtor is not a debtor in possession, Fed. R. Bankr. P. 9013 which requires that a request for an order be made by motion, and Fed. R. Bankr. P. 2002(a)(5) which requires that parties in interest receive twenty days' notice of a hearing on conversion of a case to another chapter. It is not intended that this Local Rule create any substantive rights not otherwise available under existing law.

These amendments were effective February 15, 1995.

RULE 3021-1. DISPOSITION OF UNCLAIMED OR UNDISTRIBUTABLE FUNDS IN A CHAPTER 11 LIQUIDATING PLAN

(a) Disposition of Unclaimed Funds or Undistributable Funds under a Chapter 11 Liquidating Plan. A Chapter 11 liquidating plan shall provide for the disposition of unclaimed funds and undistributable funds. The plan may provide that any unclaimed funds or undistributable funds be redistributed to other creditors or administrative claimants, or be donated to a not-for-profit, non-religious organization identified in the plan or disclosure statement accompanying the plan.

(b) Unclaimed Funds. Unclaimed funds are distributions to creditors left unclaimed 120 days after the final distribution under the plan.

(c) Undistributable Funds. Undistributable funds are any funds other than unclaimed funds, including, but not limited to, funds that cannot be disbursed because: (1) a creditor has affirmatively rejected a distribution; (2) the administrative costs of distribution make distribution uneconomical; or (3) all creditors, including administrative claimants, have been paid in full and there is no one that has a right to the funds.

(d) Failure of Liquidating Plan to Provide for Disposition of Unclaimed Funds or Undistributable Funds. If a Chapter 11 liquidating plan does not provide for the disposition of unclaimed funds or undistributable funds, and if there are any such funds at the time of final distribution under the plan, the disbursing agent shall file a motion, upon notice and hearing, proposing disposition of such funds, including as described in section (a) of this rule.

[Effective July 1, 2013. Amended effective December 1, 2015.]

Notes of Advisory Committee

2013

This rule permits liquidating Chapter 11 plans to provide that unclaimed and undistributable funds be redistributed to other creditors or donated to a non-profit organization. This rule is effective July 1, 2013.

RULE 3022–1. FINAL REPORT/DECREE (CHAPTER 11)

(a) Non–Individual Debtors. Unless extended by the Court, on or before the later of 30 days after the order of confirmation in a case under Chapter 11, or 30 days after the disposition of all adversary proceedings, contested matters, and objections to claims, the debtor's attorney shall file a certificate of substantial consummation together with a motion for final decree.

(b) Individual Debtors. After the entry of an order of confirmation and the disposition of all adversary proceedings, contested matters, and objections to claims, individual debtors may file a motion to administratively close the Chapter 11 case. The debtor may move to reopen the case for the purpose of obtaining a discharge and entry of a final decree after the completion of all payments under the plan, or for the purpose of seeking a hardship discharge. In addition, the debtor, any creditor, or any other party in interest may file a motion to reopen an administratively closed case at any time without the necessity of paying a filing fee.

[Effective June 15, 1997. Amended effective July 1, 2013.]

Notes of Advisory Committee

2013 Amendment

This amendment permits individual debtors, who, pursuant to 11 U.S.C. § 1141(d)(5), are not eligible to receive a discharge until the debtor has completed all payments under the plan or has obtained a hardship discharge, to obtain an order that administratively closes the case.

This amendment is effective July 1, 2013.

1997 Amendment

This amendment conforms the existing Local Rules to the uniform numbering system prescribed by the Judicial Conference of the United States and to the model system suggested and approved by the Advisory Committee on Bankruptcy Rules of the Judicial Conference's Committee on Rules of Practice and Procedure. In renumbering the Local Rules to conform to the uniform numbering system, no change in substance is intended. This amendment was effective on April 15, 1997.

This rule was formerly Local Rule 3.06(c). The Advisory Committee Notes to the superseded rules may be helpful in interpreting and applying the current rules.

RULE 3071–1. APPLICATIONS FOR ADMINISTRATIVE EXPENSES

Requests for administrative expenses pursuant to 11 U.S.C. § 503(b)(1) shall be made by application as follows:

(a) Chapter 7 Cases. In Chapter 7 cases, applications for administrative expenses shall be filed before the later of:

(1) the claims bar date;

(2) for administrative expenses arising from the use of premises by a trustee, within 30 days after the surrender of the premises from the trustee; or

(3) thirty days after the occurrence of the last event giving rise to the claim.

(b) Chapter 11, 12, and 13 Cases. In Chapter 11, 12, and 13 cases, applications for administrative expenses shall be filed before the later of:

(1) twenty–one days prior to the hearing on confirmation or, to the extent that the claim arose after the initial deadline, twenty-one days before any continued hearing on confirmation; or

(2) thirty days after the occurrence of the last event giving rise to the claim.

(c) All Other Chapters. In cases under all other chapters of the Bankruptcy Code, applications for administrative expenses shall be filed as specified by the Court.

[Effective June 15, 1997. Amended effective December 1, 2009; July 1, 2015.]

Notes of Advisory Committee

2015 Amendment

The amendment to section (b) specifies that applications for administrative expenses in Chapter 11, 12, and 13 cases must be filed before the later of 21 days in advance of the confirmation hearing, or with respect expenses arising after the original deadline, 21 days in advance of a continued confirmation hearing, and 30 days after the last event giving rise to the claim. This amendment is effective July 1, 2015.

1997 Amendment

This amendment conforms the existing Local Rules to the uniform numbering system prescribed by the Judicial Conference of the United States and to the model system suggested and approved by the Advisory Committee on Bankruptcy Rules of the Judicial Conference's Committee on Rules of Practice and Procedure. In renumbering the Local Rules to conform to the uniform numbering system, no change in substance is intended. This amendment was effective on April 15, 1997.

This rule was formerly Local Rule 2.20. The Advisory Committee Notes to the superseded rules may be helpful in interpreting and applying the current rules.

PART IV. THE DEBTOR: DUTIES AND BENEFITS

RULE 4001-1. AUTOMATIC STAY

(a) Motions to Extend or Impose the Automatic Stay. A motion to extend the automatic stay under 11 U.S.C. § 362(c)(3) shall be filed and served upon interested parties within seven days of the filing of the petition. A motion to impose the automatic stay under 11 U.S.C. § 362(c)(4) shall be filed and served upon interested parties as soon as practicable after the filing of the petition.

(b) Motions to Confirm That No Automatic Stay Is in Effect. Motions filed under 11 U.S.C. § 362(j) for an order confirming that the automatic stay is terminated under 11 U.S.C. § 362(c)(3) or did not become effective under § 362(c)(4) shall include the complete case caption, date of filing, and date of dismissal of the debtor's prior bankruptcy filing(s), and if the prior bankruptcy filing(s) were in another district, relevant copies of court records reflecting this information.

(c) Motions for Relief From Stay.

(1) *Chapters 7 and 11.* Motions for relief from the automatic stay in Chapter 7 and 11 cases shall include the following:

(i) Copies of loan documents, including filing and recording information necessary to establish a perfected security interest;

(ii) If the basis for the motion is lack of equity under 11 U.S.C. § 362(d)(2)(A), evidence of value; and

(iii) A statement of indebtedness, including information regarding any default under the loan.

(2) *Chapters 12 and 13.*

(i) Generally. The Court discourages secured creditors whose claims are being paid through the debtor's Chapter 12 or Chapter 13 plan payments from seeking relief from the automatic stay based upon the debtor's default in plan payments. In most instances, the Court will rely upon the trustee to monitor payments under the plan and to file a motion to dismiss, if appropriate.

(ii) Plan Provides for Surrender of Property, Direct Payment to Secured Creditor, or Does Not Provide for Claim. If the debtor's Chapter 12 or Chapter 13 plan provides for the surrender of collateral to the movant, for the debt to be paid by the debtor directly to the movant rather than through the Chapter 13 trustee's office, or does not provide for the movant's claim under the plan, the movant shall include a statement to that effect. If the statement is in the form of an affidavit or declaration by the movant's attorney, the Court's negative notice procedures do not apply and an order granting the motion will be entered without a hearing. If the stay has terminated as a result of the treatment of the movant's claim under the plan and a prior order of the Court, the movant may use this procedure to file a motion for an order confirming that the automatic stay is not in effect.

(iii) Motions for Relief from Codebtor Stay. Motions for relief from the codebtor stay imposed by 11 U.S.C. §§ 1201(a) or 1301(a) shall establish that the debtor's Chapter 13 plan does not provide for payment in full of the movant's claim or that the movant's interest will be irreparably harmed by the continuation of the codebtor stay. A motion for relief from the automatic stay shall not be combined with a motion for relief from the codebtor stay.

(3) *Standing.* Unless the issue of standing is actually litigated and determined by the Court, the Court's order granting or denying a motion for relief from stay will not make a determination that the movant has standing to seek the relief requested in the motion or any related action pending in another court.

(4) *Effect of Conversion on Pending Motion.* If a case is converted from one chapter to another while a motion for relief from stay is pending, the Court's order of conversion will provide for the abatement of the motion until the movant files an amended motion and serves the amended motion upon all appropriate parties, including the trustee appointed in the converted case. No filing fee will be assessed for the amended motion.

(5) *Effect of Dismissal on Pending Motion.* If a case is dismissed while a motion for relief from stay is pending, the Court's dismissal order will confirm that the stay is terminated by operation of law upon the effective date of the dismissal order and will deny all pending motions for relief from stay. However, the Court will retain jurisdiction to consider motions for relief from stay that request an order binding upon the debtor in subsequently filed cases and to consider any pending order to show cause for dismissal with prejudice. If the motion is served using the negative notice provisions of Local Rule 2004-2, and the negative notice period expires prior to the date on which the dismissal order becomes final, the Court will process an order granting the motion in the usual course.

(6) *Inspection of Property.* Upon reasonable notice, the moving party shall be entitled to inspect the property that is the subject of a motion for relief from the automatic stay. The notice shall provide for inspection not less than seven days from the date of service of such notice unless the time is shortened by the Court.

(7) *Discovery Response Time.* For the purpose of this rule, the time for responding to discovery requests under Fed. R. Bankr. P. 7030, 7034, and 7036 is reduced to 21 days, unless otherwise directed by the Court.

(8) *Expert Witness Testimony.* A party who intends to introduce the testimony of an expert witness at trial shall make such witness available for deposition upon reasonable notice.

[Effective July 1, 2014.]

Notes of Advisory Committee

2014 Amendment

This rule is effective July 1, 2014.

RULE 4003-2. LIEN AVOIDANCE

(a) Title and Contents of Motion. The title of the motion shall identify the creditor whose lien is sought to be avoided. The motion shall be verified or be accompanied with an affidavit and shall describe with specificity the nature of the lien, recording information, if applicable, and the property affected with legal description, as appropriate.

(b) Motion Directed to a Single Creditor. A separate motion is required for each creditor whose lien is sought to be avoided.

(c) Service. A motion to avoid a lien under 11 U.S.C. § 522(f) shall be served in accordance with Fed. R. Bankr. P. 7004 and 9014.

[Effective June 15, 1997. Amended effective December 1, 2004; July 1, 2015.]

Notes of Advisory Committee

2015 Amendment

This amendment is stylistic and conforms the rule to current practice and is effective July 1, 2015.

2004 Amendment

This amendment corrects the Bankruptcy Rules citation to that of the currently used citation.

1997 Amendment

This amendment conforms the existing Local Rules to the uniform numbering system prescribed by the Judicial Conference of the United States and to the model system suggested and approved by the Advisory Committee on Bankruptcy Rules of the Judicial Conference's Committee on Rules of Practice and Procedure. In renumbering the Local Rules to conform to the uniform numbering system, no change in substance is intended. This amendment was effective on April 15, 1997.

This rule was formerly Local Rule 2.12. The Advisory Committee Notes to the superseded rules may be helpful in interpreting and applying the current rules.

1995 Amendment

The amendment is stylistic. No substantive change is intended. These amendments were effective on February 15, 1995.

RULE 4008-1. REAFFIRMATION AGREEMENTS

(a) Form of Reaffirmation Agreement. The Court requires the use of the official forms available on the Court's website, www.flmb.uscourts.gov, and will consider the failure to use the official forms on a case-by-case basis.

(b) Execution. The Court does not require creditors to sign proposed reaffirmation agreements prior to sending them to debtors. If a debtor receives a reaffirmation from a creditor that the creditor has not signed, the debtor shall return the reaffirmation agreement to the creditor for final signature and filing with the Court.

(c) Debtors Not Represented by Counsel. Reaffirmation agreements by debtors not represented by counsel may be scheduled for hearing.

(d) Debtors Represented by Counsel. Reaffirmation agreements by debtors represented by counsel will be scheduled for hearing only if (1) the attorney has not signed the reaffirmation agreement or (2) the attorney indicates on the cover sheet to the reaffirmation agreement that a presumption of undue hardship arises, unless the Court has reviewed the reaffirmation agreement and has determined that no hearing is necessary to address the stated undue hardship.

(e) Extension of Time to Enter into Reaffirmation Agreement. The Court routinely grants motions under Fed. R. Bankr. P. 4008(a) for extensions of time to file reaffirmation agreements of up to 60 days, provided that the motion is filed prior to entry of the discharge. The Court may set a hearing on a request for an extension that exceeds 60 days to allow the movant to establish good cause for the length of the request.

(f) Parties Must Agree to Reaffirm Debts Prior to Entry of Discharge. Absent extraordinary circumstances, the Court will not set aside discharges to consider untimely agreements to reaffirm a debt and will not set hearings on reaffirmation agreements made after entry of the discharge. However, the Court will consider reaffirmation agreements made before the entry of the discharge even if the written agreement is filed after entry of the discharge.

(g) Reaffirmation Agreements Filed After Case Is Closed. Motions to reopen closed Chapter 7 cases to file reaffirmation agreements timely reached but not filed prior to the entry of the discharge and closing of the case need not be served upon creditors and will be considered without a hearing. An order granting the motion may be submitted when the motion to reopen is filed. Absent a showing of good cause, the Court will not waive the case reopening fee.

(h) No Presumption of Enforceability. The Court's approval of a reaffirmation agreement shall not constitute a presumption that the terms of the reaffirmation agreement are enforceable against the debtor.

[Effective July 1, 2015.]

Notes of Advisory Committee

2015

This rule incorporates procedures adopted by the Court as set forth in a memorandum to counsel from Chief Judge Jennemann dated August 27, 2014 (available under Emailed Blast Notifications on the Court's website). This rule is effective July 1, 2015.

PART V. COURTS AND CLERKS

RULE 5001-1. UNAVAILABILITY OF ELECTRONIC FILING SYSTEM ("CM/ECF") [ABROGATED EFFECTIVE MARCH 15, 2012]

Notes of Advisory Committee

2012 Amendment

This rule was abrogated effective March 15, 2012. Its content has been incorporated in Local Rule 5001-2 "Clerk's Office Locations, Hours, and Procedures After-Hours Filing in Case of Emergency." These amendments conform the Local Rules to the uniform numbering system prescribed by the Judicial Conference of the United States and to the model system suggested and approved by the Advisory Committee on Bankruptcy Rules of Practice and Procedure.

RULE 5001-2. CLERK'S OFFICE LOCATIONS, HOURS, AND PROCEDURES FOR AFTER-HOURS FILING IN CASE OF EMERGENCY

(a) Locations. The Clerk's offices, located in Tampa, Jacksonville, and Orlando, are open to the public during times posted on the Court's website at http://www.flmb.uscourts.gov/locations/. Access to the Court's online Case Management/Electronic Court Filing ("CM/ECF") system is generally available 24 hours a day, 7 days a week.

(b) After-Hours Filings in Cases of Emergency and by Non-Electronic Filing Users. If CM/ECF is inaccessible, an Electronic Filing User's system is inoperable, or an emergency requires the paper filing of a document to meet a filing deadline, the Court will permit the after-hours filing of paper documents by facsimile. Non-Electronic Filing Users are also permitted to file paper documents by facsimile after hours to meet filing deadlines.

(1) *Faxing First Page and Signature Page.* The first page and the signature page of petitions and other papers must be received by facsimile after 4:00 p.m. Eastern Standard Time and before 12:00 a.m. (midnight) Eastern Standard Time. Only the first page and the signature page of the document should be transmitted to the Court by facsimile.

(2) *Where to Fax Documents.* The pages must be transmitted to the Division assigned to handle the case. The facsimile machine telephone numbers can be found through the Court's website located at www.flmb.uscourts.gov/procedures/documents/afterhoursfiling.pdf.

(3) *Untimely Filed Documents Discarded.* Any document received by facsimile between the hours of 12:00 a.m. (midnight) and 4:00 p.m. will be discarded by the Clerk's Office.

(4) *Requirement to Timely File Original Document.* The original document together with any required fee must be received and time stamped by the Office of the Clerk of the Court in the Division in which the case is assigned, or must be filed electronically using CM/ECF, no later than 12:00 p.m. (noon) Eastern Standard Time on the Court's next business day.

(5) *Date and Time Filed.* Documents filed in accordance with the above procedures will be deemed filed on the date and at the time printed on the document by the facsimile machine in the Office of the Clerk of Court in the Division in which the document is filed. Upon the timely receipt of the original document and any required filing fee, the Court will stamp the original document (or in the case of an electronically filed document, make an appropriate docket entry) with the following notation:

This document is deemed filed on _______ pursuant to Local Rule 5001-2 governing after-hours filing.

(6) *Untimely Documents of No Force or Effect.* If the original document is not timely received, the Clerk will note that fact and the facsimile will have no force or effect.

(7) *Case Number Assignment.* The Clerk's Office will not assign a case number to a bankruptcy petition or an adversary number to an adversary complaint until the original document is filed with the Court. The Clerk shall not acknowledge the filing of the document to any creditor or other party until the original is filed.

[Effective March 15, 2012.]

Notes of Advisory Committee

2012 Adoption

This rule incorporates abrogated Local Rule 5001-1 "Unavailability of Electronic Filing System ('CM/ECF')" and archived Administrative Order FLMB-2003-2 "Order Prescribing Administrative Procedures for After-Hours Filing in the Bankruptcy Court, Middle District of Florida."

This rule is effective March 15, 2012.

RULE 5003-1. ELECTRONIC DOCUMENTS—ENTRY OF [ABROGATED EFFECTIVE JULY 1, 2015]

Notes of Advisory Committee

2015

This rule is abrogated effective July 1, 2015, as it is superseded by Local Rule 1001-2.

RULE 5003-2. COURT ORDERS—ENTRY OF [ABROGATED EFFECTIVE JULY 1, 2015]

Notes of Advisory Committee

2015

This rule is abrogated effective July 1, 2015, as it is superseded by current CM/ECF procedures.

RULE 5003-3. COURT PAPERS—REMOVAL OF

(a) Paper Files May Be Reviewed in the Clerk's Office. Any person may review in the Clerk's office Court files maintained in paper form or other papers or records in the possession of the Clerk.

(b) Clerk's Permission Required to Remove Files. Paper files may be removed from the Clerk's office only in emergency situations or as needed in connection with a related criminal or civil court proceeding upon written permission by the Clerk that shall specify the time within which files shall be returned.

(c) Court Permission Required to Make Entry or Corrections to Paper Files. No person shall insert or delete, tamper or deface, make any entry or correction by interlineation or otherwise, in, from or upon any file or other record of the Court unless expressly permitted or ordered to do so by the Court. No person other than the Clerk or authorized deputies or an official copy service shall unfasten any paper in any Court file.

[Effective June 15, 1997. Amended effective December 1, 2004; July 1, 2015.]

Notes of Advisory Committee

2015 Amendment

This amendment is stylistic and effective July 1, 2015.

2004 Amendment

This rule was formerly Local Rule 5003-2.

1997 Amendment

This amendment conforms the existing Local Rules to the uniform numbering system prescribed by the Judicial Conference of the United States and to the model system suggested and approved by the Advisory Committee on Bankruptcy Rules of the Judicial Conference's Committee on Rules of Practice and Procedure. In renumbering the Local Rules to conform to the uniform numbering system, no change in substance is intended. This amendment was effective on April 15, 1997.

This rule was formerly Local Rule 1.10. The Advisory Committee Notes to the superseded rules may be helpful in interpreting and applying the current rules.

1995 Amendment

The amendment to Local Rule 1.10(b) makes this rule consistent with actual practice. These amendments were effective on February 15, 1995.

RULE 5005-1. FILING PAPERS—REQUIREMENTS

(a) Attorneys Required to File via CM/ECF. Attorneys shall file papers with the Court via CM/ECF as set forth in Local Rule 1001-2.

(b) Pro Se Debtors Shall File in Paper Form. Debtors not represented by attorneys shall file petitions commencing cases under the Code and all other papers in paper form.

(c) Petitions Received by Mail. Petitions received by the Clerk's Office via the United States Mail shall be stamped "Filed via Mail" and shall be deemed filed as of 10:00 a.m. Eastern Standard or Eastern Daylight Savings Time on the day received.

(d) Requirements for Paper Filings. Papers tendered for filing shall be typewritten, or if produced by computer-generated software, be printed by letter quality printers. Papers shall be singled-sided, void of tabs, and shall be on white paper approximately 8 1/2 inches wide by 11 inches long, with one-inch margins. The Clerk shall convert any filed paper document to an electronic format by an electronic scanning process. The Clerk shall retain all scanned paper documents for 60 days for quality control purposes and shall destroy or discard such documents after the expiration of such time period.

[Effective December 1, 2004. Amended effective July 1, 2015.]

Notes of Advisory Committee

2015 Amendment

This amendment is stylistic and conforms the rule to the uniform numbering system prescribed by the Judicial Conference of the United States and to the model system suggested and approved by the Advisory Committee on Bankruptcy Rules of the Judicial Conference's Committee on Rules of Practice and Procedure. This amendment incorporates portions of text previously included in Local Rules 5005-2 and 5005-3. This amendment is effective July 1, 2015.

2004 Amendment

This addition is authorized by Rules 5005 and 7005 of the Federal Rules of Bankruptcy Procedure, and is occasioned by the implementation in the Middle District of Florida of the case management/electronic case filing system of the United States Courts.

RULE 5005-2. FILING OF PETITION AND OTHER PAPERS [ABROGATED EFFECTIVE JULY 1, 2015]

Notes of Advisory Committee

2015

This rule is abrogated effective July 1, 2015. Relevant provisions are incorporated in amended Local Rule 5001-1, also effective July 1, 2015.

RULE 5005-3. FILING PAPERS—SIZE OF PAPERS [ABROGATED EFFECTIVE JULY 1, 2015]

Notes of Advisory Committee

2015

This rule is abrogated effective July 1, 2015. Relevant provisions that have not been superseded by current CM/ECF practices are incorporated in amended Local Rule 5005-1, also effective on July 1, 2015.

RULE 5005-4. SEALED PAPERS

(a) Motion to File Paper under Seal and Order on the Motion. A party who seeks to file a paper under seal ("moving party") shall file a motion via CM/ECF using the "Motion to File Paper under Seal" docket event and shall submit a proposed order using the order submission procedures posted on the Court's website, www.flmb.uscourts.gov. The paper to be filed under seal shall not be attached to or submitted with the motion to file paper under seal. During the docketing process, the moving party shall select whether the docket entry and image of the motion to file paper under seal will have unrestricted viewing access (*i.e.*, accessible to anyone with a CM/ECF or PACER login) or whether viewing access will be restricted to the filer, the judge assigned to the case, such staff members (*e.g.*, law clerk, judicial assistant) as the judge may designate, internal Clerk's Office staff, the U.S. Trustee, the trustee assigned to the case, and any auditor serving under 28 U.S.C. § 586(f). If access is restricted to the motion to file paper under seal, access shall also be limited to the resulting order on the motion. Upon entry of an order granting motion to file paper under seal, the Court will notify the moving party, who may then file the sealed paper.

(b) Filing of Sealed Paper. An order granting the motion to file paper under seal must be entered before the sealed paper is filed. Unless directed otherwise by the Court, a paper permitted to be filed under seal shall be filed via CM/ECF using the "Sealed Paper" docket event. The Clerk's Office will notify the staff of the judge assigned to the case when the sealed paper has been filed. Unless otherwise ordered by the Court, the docket entry and the image of the sealed paper will be viewable only by the moving party, the assigned judge and such staff members (*e.g.*, law clerk, judicial assistant) as the judge may designate, the U.S. Trustee, the trustee assigned to the case, and any auditor serving under 28 U.S.C. § 586(f).

(c) Sealed Orders. If the sealed paper is a motion or application that seeks the entry of a sealed Court order, the proposed order may be submitted using the order submission procedures posted on the Court's website, www.flmb.uscourts.gov. The Court will notify the moving party of the entry of the sealed order. Unless otherwise ordered by the Court, the docket entry and image of the order will be viewable only by the moving party, the assigned judge and such staff members (*e.g.*, law clerk, judicial assistant) as the judge may designate, the U.S. Trustee, and the trustee assigned to the case, and any auditor serving under 28 U.S.C. § 586(f).

(d) Access to Sealed Papers and Orders Shall be Determined on a Case–by–Case Basis. Notwithstanding the foregoing, the Court will consider, on a case-by-case basis, the papers filed under seal; the Court shall determine who may have access to the sealed paper and related orders and if and when restrictions on access should be terminated.

[Effective December 1, 2004. Amended effective July 1, 2016.]

Notes of Advisory Committee

2016 Amendment

This amendment conforms the rule to current practice as set forth in the Procedure for Filing Papers under Seal adopted by the Court on June 11, 2015. Access to sealed papers is consistent with 11 U.S.C. § 107(c)(3). This amended rule is effective July 1, 2016.

2004 Amendment

This new rule sets out that sealed documents must remain in paper form and not made part of CM/ECF. It also instructs the Clerk on maintenance of sealed documents.

RULE 5011–1. WITHDRAWAL OF REFERENCE

(a) Contents of Motions for Withdrawal of Reference and Responses. Every written motion for withdrawal of the reference of a case or proceeding under 28 U.S.C. § 157(b)(5) or (d) and response thereto shall be accompanied by a legal memorandum with citation of supporting authorities. Absent prior permission of the District Court, no party shall file any legal memorandum over 20 pages in length.

(b) Deadline for Filing Motion for Withdrawal of Reference of Bankruptcy Case. A motion for withdrawal, in whole or in part, of the reference of a bankruptcy case shall be filed with the Clerk not later than 21 days after the date of the notice of the meeting of creditors mandated by 11 U.S.C. § 341 and Fed. R. Bankr. P. 2003(a). Parties in interest without notice or without actual knowledge of the pendency of the case may move for withdrawal of the reference not later than 21 days after having acquired actual knowledge of the pendency of the case.

(c) Deadline for Filing Motion for Withdrawal of Reference of Adversary Proceeding or Contested Matter. A motion for withdrawal of the reference of an adversary proceeding or contested matter arising in, under, or related to a case that is a subject of the Order of General Reference must be filed with the Clerk not later than 30 days after the filing of the initial pleading or other paper commencing the proceeding or contested matter. The United States or an officer or agency thereof shall move for withdrawal of the reference no later than 35 days after the filing of the initial pleading or other paper commencing the proceeding or contested matter.

(d) Service of Motion for Withdrawal of Reference. A motion for withdrawal of an adversary proceeding or contested matter shall be served on counsel of record for all parties to the proceeding or contested matter or, if a party has no counsel, on the party, and on counsel of record for the debtor, the debtor, and the United States Trustee.

(e) Deadline for Filing Response to Motion to Withdraw the Reference. The opposing parties shall have 14 days after the entry of the motion on the docket to file a responsive pleading and legal memorandum.

(f) Transmission to the District Court. After expiration of the time allowed for a response, the Clerk shall transmit the motion and legal memorandum, response and legal memorandum, if any, and such other pleadings as the parties request to the Clerk of the District Court.

(g) Bankruptcy Case Retains Jurisdiction Pending the District Court's Ruling on the Motion. Until and unless the Court or the District Court orders otherwise, the Court shall continue to hear the case or proceeding while the motion for withdrawal is under consideration in the District Court.

[Effective June 15, 1997. Amended effective December 1, 2004; December 1, 2009; July 1, 2015.]

Notes of Advisory Committee

2015 Amendment

The revisions to this rule are primarily stylistic. This amendment is effective July 1, 2015.

2004 Amendment

This amendment corrects the Bankruptcy Rules citation to that of the currently used citation.

1997 Amendment

This amendment conforms the existing Local Rules to the uniform numbering system prescribed by the Judicial Conference of the United States and to the model system suggested and approved by the

Advisory Committee on Bankruptcy Rules of the Judicial Conference's Committee on Rules of Practice and Procedure. In renumbering the Local Rules to conform to the uniform numbering system, no change in substance is intended. This amendment was effective on April 15, 1997.

This rule was formerly Local Rule 1.05. The Advisory Committee Notes to the superseded rules may be helpful in interpreting and applying the current rules.

1995 Amendment

The amendment to Local Rule 1.05 to delete the term "brief" when used in conjunction with "legal memorandum" as redundant is stylistic as is the addition of term "contested matter" where the term "proceeding" is used. No substantive change is intended.

Local Rule 1.05 (b)(2) has been amended to specify that a motion for withdrawal of a proceeding or contested matter must be filed with the Clerk not later than thirty (30) days, or thirty-five (35) days in the case of the federal government, after the filing of the initial pleading or other paper commencing the proceeding or contested matter. In adversary proceedings, this corresponds to the time an answer or motion is due pursuant to Fed. R. Bankr. P. 7012(a). The amendment makes clear that motions to withdraw the reference of contested matters must be filed within the same period despite the inapplicability of Fed. R. Bankr. P. 7012 to contested matter.

Local Rule 1.05 (b)(3) has been amended to specify that a motion for withdrawal of a proceeding or contested matter shall be served on all parties to the proceeding or contested matter or, if a party has no counsel, on the party, in addition to counsel of record for the debtor, the debtor, and the United States Trustee. These amendments were effective on February 15, 1995.

1993 Amendment

This amendment added a requirement for the filing of briefs or legal memoranda in certain circumstances to harmonize the practice in the Bankruptcy Court with the practice in the District Court and to facilitate the hearing and determination in the District Court of motions for withdrawal of the reference, objections to proposed findings of fact and conclusions of law in non-core proceedings, and other motions, applications, objections, and the like that are filed in the Bankruptcy Court but heard and determined in the District Court. The amendment was effective August 15, 1993.

RULE 5011-2. ABSTENTION

(a) General Deadlines. A motion to abstain from a case, adversary proceeding, or contested matter under 11 U.S.C. § 305 or 28 U.S.C. § 1334(c) shall be filed with the Clerk not later than the time set for filing a motion to withdraw the reference pursuant to Local Rule 5011-1.

(b) Deadline in Removed Adversary Proceeding. A motion to abstain from hearing a removed adversary shall be timely if filed not later 21 days following the filing of the notice of removal of the proceeding pursuant to 28 U.S.C. § 1452.

[Effective June 15, 1997. Amended effective December 1, 2009; July 1, 2015.]

Notes of Advisory Committee

2015 Amendment

This amendment is stylistic and effective July 1, 2015.

1997 Amendment

This amendment conforms the existing Local Rules to the uniform numbering system prescribed by the Judicial Conference of the United States and to the model system suggested and approved by the Advisory Committee on Bankruptcy Rules of the Judicial Conference's Committee on Rules of Practice and Procedure. In renumbering the Local Rules to conform to the uniform numbering system, no change in substance is intended. This amendment was effective on April 15, 1997.

This rule was formerly Local Rule 1.06. The Advisory Committee Notes to the superseded rules may be helpful in interpreting and applying the current rules.

1995 Amendment

The amendment to Local Rule 1.06 is stylistic. No substantive change is intended.

These amendments were effective on February 15, 1995.

RULE 5071-1. CONTINUANCES

(a) Court Order Required for Continuance of Hearing. Trials or hearings shall not be continued upon stipulation of counsel alone, but a continuance may be allowed by order of the Court for good cause shown.

(b) Motions for Continuance. Motions for continuance shall set forth the date and time of the hearing requested to be continued and the reason for the request, the amount of time requested to elapse before the matter is to be rescheduled and the reasons therefor, a statement that the movant has conferred with counsel for opposing parties concerning the requested continuance, and the position of other parties concerning the request.

(c) Proposed Orders. At the time that the motion for continuance is filed, counsel shall submit a proposed order containing blank spaces for the Clerk to enter the date of the continued hearing.

(d) Hearings on Motions for Relief from Stay. A motion for the continuance of the hearing on a motion for relief from the automatic stay will only be granted if the party seeking relief from the automatic stay waives the time limitations set forth in 11 U.S.C. § 362(e).

(e) Hearings Continued Without Written Notice. Hearings may be continued from time to time by announcement made in open Court without further written notice. Electronic Filing Users will receive electronic notification of the entry of any docket entry continuing the hearing.

(f) Creditors' Meetings. All requests for continuances of creditors' meetings scheduled pursuant to 11 U.S.C. § 341 shall be directed to the trustee assigned to the case.

[Effective June 15, 1997. Amended effective December 1, 2004; July 1, 2015.]

Notes of Advisory Committee

2015 Amendment

This amendment is stylistic and effective July 1, 2015.

2004 Amendment

This amendment 5071-1(c) deletes the requirement to submit copies and self-addressed stamped envelopes since the Court can serve order via BNC.

1997 Amendment

This amendment conforms the existing Local Rules to the uniform numbering system prescribed by the Judicial Conference of the United States and to the model system suggested and approved by the Advisory Committee on Bankruptcy Rules of the Judicial Conference's Committee on Rules of Practice and Procedure. In renumbering the Local Rules to conform to the uniform numbering system, no change in substance is intended. This amendment was effective on April 15, 1997.

This rule was formerly Local Rule 2.08(a) through (h). The Advisory Committee Notes to the superseded rules may be helpful in interpreting and applying the current rules.

RULE 5072-1. COURTROOM DECORUM

(a) Purpose of Rule. The purpose of this rule is to state, for the guidance of those unfamiliar with the traditions of this Court, certain basic principles concerning courtroom behavior and decorum. The requirements stated in this rule are minimal, not all-inclusive, and are intended to emphasize and supplement, not supplant or limit, the ethical obligations of counsel under the Rules of Professional Conduct or the time-honored customs of experienced trial counsel. Individual judges of the Court may, in any case, or generally, announce and enforce additional prohibitions or requirements, or may excuse compliance with any one or more of the provisions of this rule.

(b) Courtroom Conduct and Decorum. When appearing in this Court, unless excused by the presiding judge, all counsel (including, where the context applies, all persons at counsel table) shall abide by the following:

(1) Stand as court is opened, recessed, or adjourned.

(2) Stand when addressing or being addressed by the Court.

(3) Stand at the lectern while examining any witness, except that counsel may approach the Clerk's desk or the witness for purposes of handling or tendering exhibits.

(4) Stand at the lectern while making opening statements or closing arguments.

(5) Address all remarks to the Court, not to opposing counsel.

(6) Avoid disparaging personal remarks or acrimony toward opposing counsel and remain wholly detached from any ill feeling between the litigants or witnesses.

(7) Refer to all persons, including witnesses, other counsel, and the parties by their surnames and not by their first or given names.

(8) Only one attorney for each party shall examine or cross-examine each witness. The attorney stating objections, if any, during direct examination shall be the attorney recognized for cross-examination.

(9) Counsel should request permission before approaching the bench, and any documents counsel wish to have the Court examine should be handed to the Clerk.

(10) Any paper or exhibit not previously marked for identification (see Local Rule 9070-1) should be handed first to the Clerk to be marked before it is tendered to a witness for examination; and any exhibit offered in evidence should, at the time of such offer, be handed to opposing counsel.

(11) In making objections, counsel should state only the legal grounds for the objection and should withhold all further comment or argument unless elaboration is requested by the Court.

(12) In examining a witness, counsel shall not repeat or echo the answer given by the witness.

(13) Counsel and parties attending hearings by telephone shall comply with the Court's Policies and Procedures on Telephonic Appearances available on the Court's website, www.flmb.uscourts.gov.

(14) In a case tried before a jury, offers of, or requests for, a stipulation should be made privately, not within the hearing of the jury.

(15) Counsel shall instruct all persons at counsel table that gestures, facial expressions, audible comments, or the like, as manifestations of approval or disapproval during the testimony of witnesses, or at any other time, are absolutely prohibited.

(16) Attorneys and litigants should conduct themselves with civility and in a spirit of cooperation in order to reduce unnecessary cost and delay.

(17) The proceedings of the Court are serious and dignified. All persons appearing in Court should therefore dress in appropriate business attire consistent with their financial abilities.

[Effective June 15, 1997. Amended effective July 1, 2015.]

Notes of Advisory Committee

2015 Amendment

This amendment is primarily stylistic. New section (b)(13) directs counsel and parties to the Court's Policies and Procedures on Telephonic Appearances. This amendment is effective July 1, 2015.

1997 Amendment

This amendment conforms the existing Local Rules to the uniform numbering system prescribed by the Judicial Conference of the United States and to the model system suggested and approved by the Advisory Committee on Bankruptcy Rules of the Judicial Conference's Committee on Rules of Practice and Procedure. In renumbering the Local Rules to conform to the uniform numbering system, no change in substance is intended. This amendment was effective on April 15, 1997.

This rule was formerly Local Rule 2.22. The Advisory Committee Notes to the superseded rules may be helpful in interpreting and applying the current rules.

RULE 5073-1. PHOTOGRAPHS; BROADCASTING OR TELEVISING; USE OF COMPUTERS AND COMMUNICATION DEVICES

Rule 4.11 of the Local Rules of the United States District Court for the Middle District of Florida and General Order 6:13-MC-94-ORL-22 posted on the Court's website, www.flmb.uscourts.gov, apply to all cases and proceedings in the Court.

[Effective June 15, 1997. Amended effective October 15, 1998; July 1, 2016.]

Notes of Advisory Committee

2016 Amendment

This amendment brings the rule current with Court practices. This amended rule is effective July 1, 2016.

1998 Amendment

The local rules of the District Court generally do not apply in the Bankruptcy Court. *See* Local Rule 1001-1(d). In most instances within the district, the Bankruptcy Court's facilities are now located in the same federal courthouse in which the District Court's facilities are located. It is therefore desirable to have the same rules apply in both the District Court and the Bankruptcy Court that govern the photographing, broadcasting, and televising of court proceedings, the use of computers and communication devices in court facilities, and the introduction of such equipment and devices into the building in which court proceedings are conducted. Accordingly, this amendment simply deletes the Bankruptcy Court's rule on these subjects and applies in the Bankruptcy Court the provisions of the District Court's corresponding local rule. This amendment was effective on October 15, 1998.

1997 Amendment

This amendment conforms the existing Local Rules to the uniform numbering system prescribed by the Judicial Conference of the United States and to the model system suggested and approved by the Advisory Committee on Bankruptcy Rules of the Judicial Conference's Committee on Rules of Practice and Procedure. In renumbering the Local Rules to conform to the uniform numbering system, no change in substance is intended. This amendment was effective on April 15, 1997.

This rule was formerly Local Rule 1.09. The Advisory Committee Notes to the superseded rules may be helpful in interpreting and applying the current rules.

1995 Amendment

The amendment which adds new subparagraph 1.09(c) makes clear that the prohibition of recording and photographic equipment is not intended to prohibit the use of dictation equipment in conjunction with the review of the Clerk's Office files or the use of computer equipment, subject to Court control, generally. These amendments were effective on February 15, 1995.

PART VI. COLLECTION AND LIQUIDATION OF THE ESTATE

RULE 6004-1. SALE OF ESTATE PROPERTY

(a) Sales of Estate Property. Other than a sale free and clear of liens under 11 U.S.C. § 363(f), the trustee in a Chapter 7 case may sell property of the estate under 11 U.S.C. § 363(b) without order of the Court provided that the trustee complies with sections (b) and (c) of this rule.

(b) Report and Notice of Intention to Sell. The trustee may file a report and notice of intention to sell property of the estate ("report and notice") without further notice of hearing. The report and notice shall state that if no objection or request for hearing is filed and served within 21 days of the date of service, the specified property will be sold without further hearing or notice.

(c) Service. The report and notice shall be served on all creditors in compliance with Fed. R. Bankr. P. 2002 and Local Rule 2002-1.

(d) Objections. If an objection or request for hearing is filed and served within 21 days from the date of the report and notice, the objection will be set for hearing by the Court. [Effective June 15, 1997. Amended effective December 1, 2004; December 1, 2009; July 1, 2015.]

Notes of Advisory Committee

2015 Amendment

This amendment is stylistic and effective July 1, 2015.

2004 Amendment

This amendment corrects the Bankruptcy Rules citation to that of the currently used citation. Further, this amendment, 6004-1(b), adds a provision permitting Electronic Filing Users the ability to complete service of pleadings by electronic means.

1997 Amendment

This amendment conforms the existing Local Rules to the uniform numbering system prescribed by the Judicial Conference of the United States and to the model system suggested and approved by the Advisory Committee on Bankruptcy Rules of the Judicial Conference's Committee on Rules of Practice and Procedure. In renumbering the Local Rules to conform to the uniform numbering system, no change in substance is intended. This amendment was effective on April 15, 1997.

This rule was formerly Local Rule 2.21. The Advisory Committee Notes to the superseded rules may be helpful in interpreting and applying the current rules.

PART VII. ADVERSARY PROCEEDINGS

RULE 7001-1. ADVERSARY PROCEEDINGS—PROCEDURES

(a) General. This rule applies to all adversary proceedings and, if ordered by the Court, to contested matters. To the extent that the time periods set forth in this rule conflict with those set forth in the Federal Rules of Civil Procedure, the Federal Rules of Bankruptcy Procedure, or other Local Rules, this rule controls.

(b) Service. Plaintiff shall serve the summons issued by the Clerk, the complaint, and a copy of this rule within seven days after the summons is issued as required by Fed. R. Bankr. P. 7004(e). If the initial summons and accompanying papers are not timely served, plaintiff shall promptly request the issuance of an alias summons and serve the alias summons together with the complaint and a copy of this rule. Plaintiff must serve all defendants no later than 28 days after the complaint is filed. If an additional party is thereafter named as a plaintiff or a defendant, plaintiff shall serve a copy of this rule on each additional party within seven days of the date that the additional party is named.

(c) Proof of Service. Plaintiff shall promptly file a proof of service indicating the service of each summons, the complaint, and this rule on each defendant.

(d) Failure to Effect Service. If plaintiff does not complete timely and effective service of the summons and complaint, the Court may dismiss the adversary proceeding for lack of prosecution without further notice or hearing. If plaintiff requires additional time to effect service, plaintiff shall file a motion for extension of time.

(e) Defaults. If a defendant has not filed a timely response, plaintiff shall seek entry of a Clerk's default of that defendant and move for judgment by default no later than 60 days after the complaint is filed. If plaintiff requires additional time to apply for the entry of default or to move for judgment by default, plaintiff shall file a motion for extension of time.

(f) Initial Disclosures. Pursuant to Fed. R. Civ. P. 26(f), at or prior to the Meeting of Parties described below, and without any formal discovery requests, each party shall:

(1) identify in writing the name and, if known, the address and telephone number of each individual with discoverable information relevant to the disputed facts;

(2) provide copies of or a written description by category and location of all documents that are relevant to the disputed facts;

(3) provide a written computation of any damages claimed; and

(4) provide a copy of any insurance agreement that may be available to satisfy all or part of a possible judgment in the action or to indemnify or reimburse for payments made to satisfy the judgment.

(g) Meeting of Parties. At least 14 days prior to the initial status or pretrial conference, the attorneys for the parties or the parties, if not represented by an attorney, shall meet (the "Meeting of Parties") to discuss:

(1) the parties' claims and defenses;

(2) the possibility of settlement;

(3) the initial disclosures required in subsection (f) above; and

(4) a discovery plan as required by Fed. R. Civ. P. 26(f). Unless otherwise ordered by the Court, the parties may orally announce their discovery plan at the pretrial or status conference and need not file a written report.

(h) Pretrial or Status Conference. The Court will conduct a status or pretrial conference at any time after a responsive pleading is filed but, in any event, approximately 90 days after the complaint is filed. The parties may not introduce testimony or documentary evidence at the status conference. The Court, however, may consider relevant undisputed facts, affidavits offered without objection from the opposing parties, judicial notice items, and admissions made during the status conference by parties either directly or through counsel.

(i) Discovery.

(1) *General.* Parties should be familiar with the Local Rules regarding discovery, including Local Rules 7026-1, 7030-1, and 7037-1.

(2) *Commencement of Discovery.* Absent leave of Court, discovery may not commence until the conclusion of the Meeting of Parties.

(3) *Discovery Deadline.* Parties shall complete discovery no later than seven days before the trial date except that the parties may complete previously scheduled depositions up to the trial date.

(4) *Discovery Disputes.* If a discovery dispute occurs, the parties shall first, as required by Fed. R. Civ. P. 37(a)(1), as incorporated by Fed. R. Bankr. P. 7037, confer in good faith to attempt to resolve the issues. If the parties are unable to resolve the dispute, any party may request a telephone conference with the Court so that the Court may render an informal, preliminary ruling on the discovery dispute, without prejudice to the right of any party to file a formal motion.

(j) Motions.

(1) *Motions shall be Served Using the Court's Negative Notice Procedures.* All motions, except for the following types of motions, shall be filed and served using the negative notice procedures of Local Rule 2002-4:

(i) stipulated, joint, or consent motions;

(ii) motions for enlargement of time;

(iii) motions for continuance;

(iv) motions seeking emergency or expedited relief;

(v) motions for entry of default and for default judgment; and

(vi) motions for withdrawal of the reference governed by Local Rule 5011-1.

The negative notice legend shall provide for a 14-day response period, except for motions for summary judgment for which the response time shall be 21 days, unless otherwise ordered by the Court. The moving party may file a reply, if desired, no later than seven days after the response is filed.

(2) *Format.* All motions, responses, and replies shall comply with the Court's Style Guide posted on the Court's website, www.flmb.uscourts.gov. Papers shall be double spaced and, where appropriate, include a legal memorandum containing argument and citations of authorities. Absent leave of Court, motions and supporting memoranda shall not exceed ten pages in length.

(3) *Emergency Motions.* The Court will consider emergency motions at any time in its discretion. Emergency motions shall comply with Local Rule 9004-2(e) and shall be filed using the Emergency Filings/Matters/Motions link on the Court's website, www.flmb.uscourts.gov.

(4) *Motions to Determine Whether Case is Core.* A party who objects to the entry of final orders or judgments by the Bankruptcy Court on any issue in the adversary proceeding shall, not later than the date set for filing a response to the complaint, file a motion requesting that the Court determine whether the proceeding is a core proceeding or otherwise subject to the entry of final orders or judgments by this Court. A party who fails to file a motion on or before the date set for filing a response to the complaint shall be deemed to have consented to the Bankruptcy Court's entering final orders and

judgments in the proceeding, subject only to appeal under 28 U.S.C. § 158.

(5) *Motions for Summary Judgment.* Motions for summary judgment shall be filed no later than 60 days prior to trial. The Court may or may not set a hearing on the motion for summary judgment. Absent order of the Court, the trial will proceed as scheduled even if a motion for summary judgment is pending.

(k) Pretrial Disclosures of Witnesses and the Use of Depositions. Fed. R. Civ. P. 26(a)(3) (except with respect to time limits) shall govern pretrial disclosures regarding witnesses and use of depositions. Parties shall file and exchange names, telephone numbers, and addresses for witnesses, and any designations of depositions at least 28 days before trial. Objections to the use of depositions shall be filed within 14 days of the disclosure. Parties shall confer on any factual or evidentiary stipulations prior to trial.

(*l*) Exhibits.

(1) *Exhibits to be Filed and Exchanged via CM/ECF.* Parties shall prepare exhibits in compliance with Local Rule 9070-1 and Administrative Order FLMB-2015-6 addressing Electronically Stored Exhibits and shall exchange exhibits no later than seven days before the date set for trial. Unless written objection to the admissibility of any exhibit is filed no later than the close of business on the second day before trial, any objection to admissibility (other than under Fed. R. Evid. 402 and 403) shall be deemed waived.

(2) *Self-Authentication of Records of Regularly Conducted Activity.* A party who intends to rely upon the self-authentication procedures of Fed. R. Evid. 902(11) or (12) to introduce into evidence records of regularly conducted activities under Fed. R. Evid. 803(6) shall, within least 28 days before trial, file with the Court and serve on other parties the written declaration required by Fed. R. Evid. 902(11) or (12) and a copy of all records sought to be admitted.

(m) Expert Witness Testimony. Unless the Court orders otherwise, a party who wishes to offer expert testimony at trial shall comply with the requirements of Fed. R. Civ. P. 26(a)(2).

(n) Stipulations. All stipulations of the parties shall be made in writing, signed, and promptly filed with the Court.

(*o*) Supplementation of Disclosures. Parties are under a duty to supplement or correct their Initial Disclosures and their Pretrial Disclosures in accordance with Fed. R. Civ. P. 26(e).

(p) Sanctions. Failure to comply with all requirements of this rule may result in the imposition of sanctions that could include the striking of a party's pleading or the denial of the right to introduce evidence or witness testimony.

(q) Settlements. Pursuant to Local Rule 9019-1, parties shall immediately notify the Court of any settlement and promptly file and serve a motion to approve the compromise in the debtor's main case, not in the adversary proceeding. If the complaint asserts claims under 11 U.S.C. § 523 only, a motion to approve the compromise is not necessary. However, if desired, the parties may seek approval of the settlement by filing a motion in the adversary proceeding.

[Effective July 1, 2016.]

Notes of Advisory Committee

2016

This new rule incorporates the provisions of archived Administrative Order FLMB-2014-10 "Administrative Order Prescribing Procedures for Adversary Proceedings." In addition, section (f)(4) regarding pretrial disclosures is now consistent with Fed. R. Civ. P. 26(f). The rule also clarifies the requirement that motions in adversary proceedings be filed and served using the negative notice procedures of Local Rule 2002-4. This rule is effective July 1, 2016.

RULE 7005-1. PROOF OF SERVICE [ABROGATED EFFECTIVE JULY 1, 2015]

Notes of Advisory Committee

2015

This rule is abrogated effective July 1, 2015. Relevant provisions are incorporated in new Local Rule 9013-1, also effective on July 1, 2015.

RULE 7005-2. FILING OF DISCOVERY MATERIAL [ABROGATED EFFECTIVE DECEMBER 1, 2000]

Notes of Advisory Committee

2000 Amendment

The Court's local rules may not conflict with or duplicate the Federal Rules of Bankruptcy Procedure. *See* Fed.R.Bankr.P. 9029(a)(1). This amendment deletes the provisions of this rule that prohibited the filing of discovery materials until they are used in a proceeding or matter. The deletion is required because the December 1, 2000, amendments to Fed.R.Civ.P. 5(d) provide that disclosures under Rule 26(a)(1) and (2) and discovery requests and responses under Rules 30, 31, 33, 34, and 36 must not be filed until they are used in the action. Disclosures under Rule 26(a)(3), however, are to be filed with the Court.

Pursuant to Fed.R.Bankr.P. 7005, Fed.R.Civ.P. 5 applies in adversary proceedings. Pursuant to Local Rule 9014-1, Fed.R.Civ.P. 5(a)-(d) applies in contested matters. Thus, disclosures and discovery materials in adversary proceedings and contested matters are to be filed—or not filed—as provided in Fed.R.Civ.P. 5(d).

This amendment is effective on December 1, 2000.

RULE 7005-3. SERVICE BY ELECTRONIC MEANS UNDER RULE 5(b)(2)(E) [AMENDED EFFECTIVE JULY 1, 2015]

Notes of Advisory Committee

2015

This rule is abrogated effective July 1, 2015, as it has been superseded by Local Rule 1001-2.

RULE 7026-1. DISCOVERY—GENERAL

(a) General. Local Rule 7001-1 addresses numerous discovery issues in adversary proceedings and, if ordered by the Court, in complex contested matters.

(b) Contested Matters. Unless otherwise ordered by the Court, the disclosure requirements of Fed. R. Civ. P. 26(a) and the conference and reporting requirements of Fed. R. Civ. P. 26(f) do not apply in contested matters. Unless the Court orders otherwise, the parties may commence discovery immediately after service of the paper initiating the contested matter is accomplished under Fed. R. Bankr. P. 7004.

[Effective June 15, 1997. Amended effective December 1, 2000; December 1, 2004; December 1, 2009; July 1, 2016.]

Notes of Advisory Committee

2016 Amendment

This amendment refers parties, in section (a), to Local Rule 7001-1 Adversary Proceedings—Procedures for issues relating to discovery. The amendment also clarifies that, absent order of the Court otherwise, the conference and reporting requirements of Fed. R. Civ. P. 26 do not apply to contested matters. Former section (c) regarding the depositions of nonresident parties has migrated to Rule 7030-1 Depositions upon Oral Examination. This amended rule is effective July 1, 2016.

2004 Amendment

This amendment corrects the Bankruptcy Rules citation to that of the currently used citation.

2000 Amendment

This amendment is made necessary by the December 1, 2000, amendments to the Federal Rules of Civil Procedure.

Under Fed. R. Bankr. P. 7026, Fed. R. Civ. P. 26 applies in adversary proceedings. Under Fed. R. Bankr. P. 9014, Fed. R. Bankr. P. 7026 also applies in contested matters. Fed. R. Bankr. P. 9029(a)(1) further provides that the Court's local rules may not be inconsistent with the Federal Rules of Bankruptcy Procedure.

The December 1, 2000, amendments to Fed. R. Civ. P. 26 eliminate the provisions of that rule that permit courts to "opt out" of certain of its provisions that became effective on December 1, 1993. The Court is required, therefore, to rescind the provisions of its local rules by which it "opted out" of the mandatory disclosure and conference requirements contained in Fed. R. Civ. P. 26(a)(1)–(3) and (f). These "opt out" provisions are presently contained in paragraphs (a) and (b) of this local rule. Because of these required rescissions, the Court is also required to rescind the initiation of discovery provisions contained in paragraph (c) of this local rule.

As a consequence of this amendment, the provisions of Fed. R. Civ. P. 26 are fully applicable in adversary proceedings in the Court, although the terms of the rule set forth circumstances in which the parties may stipulate or the Court may order variations in individual cases. The Court may not do so, however, by local rule or standing order. Thus, the disclosures required by Fed. R. Civ. P. 26(a)(1) through (3) are generally applicable in adversary proceedings; the parties must meet as required by Fed. R. Civ. P. 26(f); and, pursuant to Fed. R. Civ. P. 26(d), the parties may not seek discovery before the parties have conferred as required by Fed. R. Civ. P. 26(f).

Pursuant to Fed. R. Bankr. P. 7005 and Fed. R. Civ. P. 5(d), the parties may not file with the Court the disclosures required by Fed. R. Civ. P. 26(a)(1) and (2) until they are used in the proceeding. The parties must file, however, the disclosures required by Fed. R. Civ. P. 26(a)(3).

Pursuant to Fed. R. Bankr. P. 9014, Fed. R. Bankr. P. 7026 applies in contested matters "unless the court otherwise directs." Thus, the Court retains the ability to direct by local rule that only portions of Fed. R. Bankr. P. 7026 apply in contested matters. The Court has therefore contemporaneously promulgated new Local Rule 9014-2 that applies Fed. R. Bankr. P. 7026 to contested matters only to the extent permitted before this amendment to this local rule. Under Local Rule 9014-2, therefore, the mandatory disclosure provisions of Fed. R. Civ. P. 26(a)(1)–(3) do not apply in contested matters, the parties are not required to confer as set forth in Fed. R. Civ. P. 26(f), and the parties may immediately seek discovery. Of course, the Court may direct the application of these Rule 26 provisions by specific order, and the parties may agree that they apply.

"If necessary to comply with [the Court's] expedited schedule for Rule 16(b) conferences," Fed. R. Civ. P. 26(f) does permit the Court to make local rules as to certain matters related to the Rule 26(f) conference and the discovery plan. Unlike the timing and pace of litigation in civil actions in the district court, litigation in adversary proceedings in the bankruptcy court is handled on an expedited basis. In the new provisions of this local rule appearing as new paragraphs (a) and (b), therefore, the Court exercises this discretion in the manner the Committee believes is appropriate. The Court, of course, can vary these times by individual order.

The last paragraph of this local rule is relettered to reflect the rescission of old paragraphs (a) through (c) and the substitution of new paragraphs (a) and (b).

This amendment was effective on December 1, 2000.

1997 Amendment

This amendment conforms the existing Local Rules to the uniform numbering system prescribed by the Judicial Conference of the United States and to the model system suggested and approved by the Advisory Committee on Bankruptcy Rules of the Judicial Conference's Committee on Rules of Practice and Procedure. In renumbering the Local Rules to conform to the uniform numbering system, no change in substance is intended. This amendment was effective on April 15, 1997.

Paragraphs (a) through (c) of this rule were formerly paragraphs (a) through (c) of Local Rule 2.15. Paragraph (d) of this rule was formerly Local Rule 2.16(b). The Advisory Committee Notes to the superseded rules may be helpful in interpreting and applying the current rules.

1995 Amendment

Introduction

This rule is amended to reflect the Advisory Committee's judgment as to the desirability of applying the December 1, 1993, amendments to the Federal Rules of Civil Procedure to contested matters and adversary proceedings and to make other desirable technical changes.

The December 1, 1993, amendments to the Federal Rules of Civil Procedure greatly affect practice in contested matters and in adversary proceedings. Fed. R. Bankr. P. 7016, 7026, 7030, 7031, and 7033 extend the application of Fed. R. Civ. P. 16, 26, 30, 31 and 33 to adversary proceedings. In addition, unless the Court otherwise directs, Fed. R. Bankr. P. 9014 extends the application of Fed. R. Civ. P. 26, 30, 31, and 33 to contested matters pursuant to Fed. R. Bankr. P. 7026, 7030, 7031 and 7033. Although the Advisory Committee deems certain of the December 1, 1993, amendments to be desirable and beneficial to practice in contested matters and adversary proceedings in this Court, it believes that other of the amendments may not be practically or beneficially implemented. The Advisory Committee therefore intends here that the Court "opt out" of certain of these amendments to the Federal Rules of Civil Procedures as they are made applicable to contested matters and adversary proceedings.

Disclosure and Meeting of Counsel

Fed. R. Civ. P. 26(a)(1–4) now mandates the disclosure of certain relevant information. Paragraph (a) of Local Rule 2.15 therefore provides that these new disclosure requirements apply to contested matters and adversary proceedings only if the parties agree or if the Court orders that some or all of the disclosure requirements apply. Fed. R. Civ. P. 26(f) now requires a meeting of the parties and the filing of a proposed discovery plan within certain prescribed time limits. Paragraph (b) of Local Rule 2.15 therefore provides that these meetings and reporting requirements apply in contested matters and in adversary proceedings only upon the agreement of the parties or upon order of the Court.

Initiation of Discovery

Fed. R. Civ. P. 26(d), 30(a)(2)(C), 31(a)(2)(C), 33(a), 34(b), and 36(a) now generally preclude the initiation of any method of discovery until after the parties meet as required by Fed. R. Civ. P. 26(f), unless the parties agree or the Court otherwise orders. Because the Court has eliminated, in paragraph (b), the meeting of the parties requirement of Fed. R. Civ. P. 26(f) unless the Court specifically orders its application, paragraph (c) provides that the parties may initiate discovery immediately after service of the motion or other paper initiating contested matters and the summons and complaint in adversary proceedings. If the Court orders the application of the meeting of the parties requirement of Fed. R. Civ. P. 26(f), however, the early initiation of discovery authorized in paragraph (c) would not apply and the parties would be precluded from initiating discovery until after the Fed. R. Civ. P. 26(f) meeting unless they agreed or the Court orders to the contrary. Paragraph (c) also continues the meaning and the intent of former Rule 2.14 as to depositions upon oral examination.

These amendments were effective on February 15, 1995.

RULE 7030–1. DEPOSITIONS UPON ORAL EXAMINATION

(a) Notice. Unless the Court orders otherwise, depositions upon oral examination of any person may be noticed on no less than 14–days' notice in writing to every other party to the contested matter or adversary proceeding and to the deponent.

(b) Location. For the guidance of counsel in preparing or opposing contemplated motions for protective order under Fed. R. Bankr. P. 7026 that relates to the place of taking a party litigant's deposition or the deposition of the managing agent of a party, the Court's general policy is

(i) a non-resident plaintiff or moving party may reasonably be deposed at least once in this District during the discovery stages of the case; and

(ii) a non-resident defendant or respondent who intends to be present in person at trial may reasonably be deposed at least once in this District either during the discovery stages of the case or within a week prior to trial as the parties agree or the Court deems appropriate.

A non-resident, within the meaning of this rule, is a person residing outside the Middle District of Florida.

[Effective June 15, 1997. Amended effective December 1, 2009; July 1, 2016.]

Notes of Advisory Committee

2016 Amendment

Section (b) incorporates former section (c) of Local Rule 7026–1 Discovery—General regarding the location of depositions of non-resident parties. The definition of "non-resident" has been changed from "a person residing outside the State of Florida" to "a person residing outside the Middle District of Florida." Other amendments to the rule are stylistic. This amended rule is effective July 1, 2016.

1997 Amendment

This amendment conforms the existing Local Rules to the uniform numbering system prescribed by the Judicial Conference of the United States and to the model system suggested and approved by the Advisory Committee on Bankruptcy Rules of the Judicial Conference's Committee on Rules of Practice and Procedure. In renumbering the Local Rules to conform to the uniform numbering system, no change in substance is intended. This amendment was effective on April 15, 1997.

This rule was formerly Local Rule 2.15(d). The Advisory Committee Notes to the superseded rules may be helpful in interpreting and applying the current rules.

1995 Amendment

Paragraph (d) continues the policy of former Rule 2.14 that depositions be noticed on no less than ten days written notice.

Fed. R. Civ. P. 30(a)(2)(A) and Fed. R. Civ. P. 31(a)(2)(A) now limit to a total of ten the number of depositions upon oral examination and written questions unless the Court authorizes or the parties stipulate to a greater number. The Advisory Committee believes this to be the appropriate presumptive number of depositions in contested matters and adversary proceedings, and the Advisory Committee therefore has not proposed an amendment setting a different presumptive number.

These amendments were effective on February 15, 1995.

RULE 7033–1. INTERROGATORIES TO PARTIES

Parties serving written interrogatories shall provide the responding party's attorney, or the party if unrepresented by an attorney, with a copy of the interrogatories in Word or WordPerfect format to enable the responding party to insert the answers to each interrogatory at the conclusion of that interrogatory.

[Effective June 15, 1997. Amended effective July 1, 2015.]

Notes of Advisory Committee

2015 Amendment

This amendment reflects the changes in word processing technology. This amendment is effective July 1, 2015.

1997 Amendment

This amendment conforms the existing Local Rules to the uniform numbering system prescribed by the Judicial Conference of the United States and to the model system suggested and approved by the Advisory Committee on Bankruptcy Rules of the Judicial Conference's Committee on Rules of Practice and Procedure. In renumbering the Local Rules to conform to the uniform numbering system, no change in substance is intended. This amendment was effective on April 15, 1997.

This rule is derived from Local Rule 2.15(e) and (f). The Advisory Committee Notes to the superseded rules may be helpful in interpreting and applying the current rules.

1995 Amendment

Fed. R. Civ. P. 33(a) now limits each party to 25 written interrogatories including all discreet subparts unless, by order of the Court or written stipulation, a greater number is authorized. The Advisory Committee agrees that this is the appropriate presumptive number of interrogatories in contested matters and in adversary proceedings. As a consequence, the Advisory Committee has deleted the provisions of former paragraph (a) that allowed 50 written interrogatories.

These amendments were effective on February 15, 1995.

Paragraphs (e) and (f) are former paragraphs (b) and (c) without substantial change. They continue the manner in which interrogatories are to be prepared, served, and answered.

RULE 7037-1. FAILURE TO MAKE DISCOVERY: MOTIONS TO COMPEL DISCOVERY

Motions to compel discovery pursuant to Fed. R. Bankr. P. 7037 shall quote in full (1) each interrogatory, question on deposition, request for admission or request for production to which the motion is addressed; (2) the objection and grounds therefor as stated by the opposing party; and (3) the reasons such objections should be overruled and the motion granted.

[Effective June 15, 1997. Amended effective December 1, 2004.]

Notes of Advisory Committee

2004 Amendment

This amendment corrects the Bankruptcy Rules citation to that of the currently used citation.

1997 Amendment

This amendment conforms the existing Local Rules to the uniform numbering system prescribed by the Judicial Conference of the United States and to the model system suggested and approved by the Advisory Committee on Bankruptcy Rules of the Judicial Conference's Committee on Rules of Practice and Procedure. In renumbering the Local Rules to conform to the uniform numbering system, no change in substance is intended. This amendment was effective on April 15, 1997.

This rule was formerly Local Rule 2.16(a). The Advisory Committee Notes to the superseded rules may be helpful in interpreting and applying the current rules.

1995 Amendment

Former subparagraph (a) required that motions to compel discovery or for protective order contain a certificate of counsel's failed good faith efforts to resolve the dispute amicably. Substantially identical requirements now appear in Fed. R. Civ. P. 26(c) and 37(a)(2)(A) and are applicable to adversary proceedings and contested matter through Fed. R. Bankr. P. 7026, 7037, and 9014. The provisions of former subparagraph (a) are therefore deleted as redundant.

These amendments were effective February 15, 1995.

RULE 7054-1. COSTS—TAXATION/PAYMENT; ATTORNEY'S FEES [ABROGATED]

Notes of Advisory Committee

2004 Amendment

This amendment corrects the Bankruptcy Rules citation to that of the currently used citation.

1997 Amendment

This amendment conforms the existing Local Rules to the uniform numbering system prescribed by the Judicial Conference of the United States and to the model system suggested and approved by the Advisory Committee on Bankruptcy Rules of the Judicial Conference's Committee on Rules of Practice and Procedure. In renumbering the Local Rules to conform to the uniform numbering system, no change in substance is intended. This amendment was effective on April 15, 1997.

This rule was formerly Local Rule 2.24. The Advisory Committee Notes to the superseded rules may be helpful in interpreting and applying the current rules.

1995 Amendment

This rule is new. It is derived from District Court Local Rule 4.18 with appropriate modification for bankruptcy practice. These amendments were effective February 15, 1995.

RULE 7055-2. JUDGMENTS BY DEFAULT

When a defendant fails to respond after being timely served with a summons and complaint, cross-complaint, or third party complaint, the plaintiff shall seek entry of a clerk's default and a default judgment as follows:

(a) Motion for Entry of Clerk's Default. Motions for entry of clerk's default shall (1) state that timely service was duly effectuated in compliance with the Federal Rules of Bankruptcy Procedure and that the defendant failed to file a responsive pleading or motion before the expiration of the time specified or any extension of time obtained and (2) where applicable, include a sworn statement of non-military service based upon personal knowledge or a certification from the Servicemembers Civil Relief Act Centralized Verification Service that the defendant is not on active military duty.

(b) Motion for Judgment by Default. Motions for judgment by default shall include a sworn statement supporting the allegations of the complaint, cross-complaint, or third party complaint, and be accompanied by (1) a proposed order granting motion for judgment by default and (2) a proposed judgment.

[Effective June 15, 1997. Amended effective July 1, 2015.]

Notes of Advisory Committee

2015 Amendment

The amendments are stylistic and state the requirements for statements of non-military status. This amendment is effective July 1, 2015.

2004 Amendment

This amendment corrects the Bankruptcy Rules citation to that of the currently used citation. Further, this amendment adds definitions for new words and phrases created in these local rules specifically because of the newly implemented electronic filing system, CM/ECF.

1997 Amendment

This amendment conforms the existing Local Rules to the uniform numbering system prescribed by the Judicial Conference of the United States and to the model system suggested and approved by the Advisory Committee on Bankruptcy Rules of the Judicial Conference's

Committee on Rules of Practice and Procedure. In renumbering the Local Rules to conform to the uniform numbering system, no change in substance is intended. This amendment was effective on April 15, 1997.

This rule was formerly Local Rule 1.01(e). The Advisory Committee Notes to the superseded rules may be helpful in interpreting and applying the current rules.

RULE 7067-1. REGISTRY FUND [ABROGATED]

Notes of Advisory Committee

2004 Amendment

This amendment sets out how parties can place funds in the registry of the court and what steps are needed to withdraw funds from the registry of the court.

PART VIII. APPEALS TO DISTRICT COURT OR BANKRUPTCY APPELLATE PANEL

RULE 8001-1. NOTICE OF APPEAL [ABROGATED]

[Effective June 15, 1997. Amended effective July 1, 2013. Abrogated effective July 1, 2015.]

Notes of Advisory Committee

2015

Effective July 1, 2015, this rule is renumbered as Local Rule 8003-1 to correspond to the amendments and renumbering of the rules in Part VIII of the Federal Rules of Bankruptcy Procedure.

2013 Amendment

This amendment provides information regarding the availability of the appeal cover sheet on the Court's website.

This amendment is effective July 1, 2013.

1997 Amendment

This amendment conforms the existing Local Rules to the uniform numbering system prescribed by the Judicial Conference of the United States and to the model system suggested and approved by the Advisory Committee on Bankruptcy Rules of the Judicial Conference's Committee on Rules of Practice and Procedure. In renumbering the Local Rules to conform to the uniform numbering system, no change in substance is intended. This amendment was effective on April 15, 1997.

This rule was formerly Local Rule 4.02. The Advisory Committee Notes to the superseded rules may be helpful in interpreting and applying the current rules.

RULE 8003-1. NOTICE OF APPEAL

Notices of appeal filed under Fed. R. Bankr. P. 8003 and 8004 shall be accompanied by an appeal cover sheet. The appeal cover sheet form is available on the Court's website, www.flmb.uscourts.gov.

[Effective July 1, 2015.]

Notes of Advisory Committee

2015

This rule was formerly Local Rule 8001-1. It is amended and renumbered to correspond to the amendments and renumbering of the rules in Part VIII of the Federal Rules of Bankruptcy Procedure. This amendment is effective July 1, 2015.

RULE 8006-1. DESIGNATION OF RECORD—APPEAL [ABROGATED]

[Effective June 15, 1997. Amended effective December 1, 2004. Abrogated effective July 1, 2013.]

Notes of Advisory Committee

2013 Amendment

This rule was superseded by Rule 8007-1 effective July 1, 2013.

RULE 8007-1. COMPLETION OF RECORD—APPEAL [ABROGATED]

[Effective July 1, 2013. Abrogated effective July 1, 2015.]

Notes of Advisory Committee

2015

Effective July 1, 2015, this rule is renumbered as Local Rule 8009-1 to correspond to the amendments and renumbering of the rules in Part VIII of the Federal Rules of Bankruptcy Procedure.

2013 Adoption

This new rule supersedes abrogated Local Rule 8006-1 to (a) conform the Local Rules to the uniform numbering system prescribed by the Judicial Conference of the United States and to the model system suggested and approved by the Advisory Committee on Bankruptcy Rules of the Judicial Conference's Committee on Rules of Practice and Procedure, and (b) to recognize the implementation of a CM/ECF system by the United States District Court for the Middle District of Florida.

This rule is effective July 1, 2013.

RULE 8009-1. COMPLETION OF RECORD—APPEAL

Requests for Transcripts. A transcript purchase order form, available on the Court's website, www.flmb.uscourts.gov, shall accompany a request for transcript filed under Fed. R. Bankr. P. 8009(b).

[Effective July 1, 2015.]

Notes of Advisory Committee

2015

This rule was formerly Local Rule 8007-1. It is renumbered to correspond to the amendments and renumbering of the rules in Part VIII of the Federal Rules of Bankruptcy Procedure. This amendment is effective July 1, 2015.

PART IX. GENERAL PROVISIONS

RULE 9001–1. DEFINITIONS

The definitions of words and phrases contained in 11 U.S.C. §§ 101, 902, and 1101, and Fed. R. Bankr. P. 9001, and the rules of construction contained in 11 U.S.C. § 102 shall also apply in these rules. The following words and phrases used in these rules have the meaning indicated:

(a) "CM/ECF" means the court's online case management and electronic filing system.

(b) "Electronic Filing User" means an attorney or other entity given a Court-issued login and password, who is thereby given authority to file papers through CM/ECF. As set forth in Local Rule 1001–2(e), Electronic Filing Users are deemed to have consented to electronic service via CM/ECF.

(c) "Electronic Transmission" or "Email" means delivery through electronic communication of papers to be filed with the Court or to be served on creditors or other parties in interest.

(d) "File" or "Filed" means the legal receipt of documents by the Court; by paper, acknowledged by date stamp affixed to the paper by the Clerk or Judge; or by electronic transmission, acknowledged by the date verified by CM/ECF.

(e) "Electronic Means" or "Electronic Methods" means a non-paper system of delivering documents to and from the Court and to and from attorneys and other parties, the original form of which may also be electronic. Such systems include the use of facsimile machines, Internet email systems, and CM/ECF.

(f) "Notice of Electronic Filing" means an electronic document produced by CM/ECF that certifies each filing with the Court.

[Effective June 15, 1997. Amended effective December 1, 2004; July 1, 2015.]

Notes of Advisory Committee

2015 Amendment

This amendment is primarily stylistic. In addition, section (a) defines "CM/ECF." This amendment is effective July 1, 2015.

2004 Amendment

This amendment corrects the Bankruptcy Rules citation to that of the currently used citation. Further, this amendment adds definitions for new words and phrases created in these local rules specifically because of the newly implemented electronic filing system, CM/ECF.

1997 Amendment

This amendment conforms the existing Local Rules to the uniform numbering system prescribed by the Judicial Conference of the United States and to the model system suggested and approved by the Advisory Committee on Bankruptcy Rules of the Judicial Conference's Committee on Rules of Practice and Procedure. In renumbering the Local Rules to conform to the uniform numbering system, no change in substance is intended. This amendment was effective on April 15, 1997.

This rule was formerly Local Rule 1.01(e). The Advisory Committee Notes to the superseded rules may be helpful in interpreting and applying the current rules.

RULE 9004–2. CAPTION—PAPERS, GENERAL

(a) Caption. The first page of all petitions, pleadings, motions, and other papers filed with the Court shall contain a caption as in the Official Forms and in addition shall state in the title the name and designation of the party (*e.g.*, Debtor, Creditor [name], Plaintiff, Defendant, or the like) on whose behalf the paper is submitted, and a title descriptive of the paper's contents.

(b) Motions. A motion filed with the Court shall request only one form of relief unless the request seeks alternative forms of relief under the same provision of the Bankruptcy Code or Federal Rules of Bankruptcy Procedure (*e.g.*, motion to dismiss or convert; motion for relief from stay, or in the alternative adequate protection; motion to enforce automatic stay and for sanctions).

(c) Demand for Jury Trial. If demand for jury trial is contained within a pleading, the title of the pleading shall include the words "Demand for Jury Trial" or the equivalent.

(d) Injunctive Relief. If a pleading contains a prayer for injunctive relief pursuant to Fed. R. Bankr. P. 7065, the title of the pleading shall include the words "Injunctive Relief Sought" or the equivalent.

(e) Emergency Hearings. If a motion or pleading requests an emergency hearing, the title of the motion or pleading shall include the words "Emergency Hearing Requested" or the equivalent. Emergency hearings shall only be held where direct, immediate, and substantial harm will occur to the interest of an entity in property, to the bankruptcy estate, or to the debtor's ability to reorganize if the parties are not able to obtain an immediate resolution of any dispute. An emergency motion will not be acted upon or set for an emergency hearing without completion and filing of a Certification of Necessity of Request for Emergency Hearing in the form available on the Court's website, www.flmb.uscourts.gov/forms, setting forth sufficient facts justifying the need for an emergency hearing. In addition, the filer shall also alert the Clerk's office that an emergency paper has been filed by completing and submitting the "Emergency Matters—Electronic Case Filing" form on the Court's website at www.flmb.uscourts.gov/procedures.

[Effective June 15, 1997. Amended effective December 1, 2004; July 1, 2015.]

Notes of Advisory Committee

2015 Amendment

This amendment is primarily stylistic. Section (b) clarifies that motions filed with the Court shall request only one form of relief unless the request seeks alternative forms of relief under the same provision of the Bankruptcy Code or Federal Rules of Bankruptcy Procedure. This amendment is effective July 1, 2015.

2004 Amendment

This amendment corrects the Bankruptcy Rules citation to that of the currently used citation.

1997 Amendment

This amendment conforms the existing Local Rules to the uniform numbering system prescribed by the Judicial Conference of the United States and to the model system suggested and approved by the Advisory Committee on Bankruptcy Rules of the Judicial Conference's Committee on Rules of Practice and Procedure. In renumbering the Local Rules to conform to the uniform numbering system, no change in substance is intended. This amendment was effective on April 15, 1997.

Paragraph (a) of this rule formerly was Local Rule 2.02(b). Paragraphs (b) through (f) of this rule formerly were paragraphs (a) through (e) of Local Rule 2.03. The Advisory Committee Notes to the superseded rules may be helpful in interpreting and applying the current rules.

1995 Amendment

Local Rule 2.03(c) has been amended to make clear that the Certificate of Necessity of Request for Emergency Hearing which must be filed in connection with an emergency motion must set forth sufficient facts to justify the need for an emergency hearing.

These amendments were effective on February 15, 1995.

RULE 9004-3. PAPERS—AMENDMENTS

(a) Amended Papers Shall Be Fully Integrated. Except for amendments to schedules, petitions, lists, matrices, and statements of financial affairs subject to the provisions of Local Rule 1009-1, unless otherwise directed by the Court, any party permitted to amend a pleading, motion, or other paper filed with the Court shall file the amended paper as a fully integrated paper with the amendments incorporated therein.

(b) Reference to Docket Number of Original Paper. The first page of the amended paper shall also include a reference to the CM/ECF docket number of the original paper.

(c) Minor Amendments. If the reason for the amendment is to correct a minor error in the original paper (*e.g.*, typographical errors or errors in citations or legal descriptions), the first page of the amended paper shall include a footnote that states the reason for the amendment.

[Effective June 15, 1997. Amended effective July 1, 2015.]

Notes of Advisory Committee

2015 Amendment

This amendment is stylistic and is effective July 1, 2015.

1997 Amendment

This amendment conforms the existing Local Rules to the uniform numbering system prescribed by the Judicial Conference of the United States and to the model system suggested and approved by the Advisory Committee on Bankruptcy Rules of the Judicial Conference's Committee on Rules of Practice and Procedure. In renumbering the Local Rules to conform to the uniform numbering system, no change in substance is intended. This amendment was effective on April 15, 1997.

This rule was formerly Local Rule 2.07. The Advisory Committee Notes to the superseded rules may be helpful in interpreting and applying the current rules.

RULE 9011-2. REPRESENTED PARTIES; PRO SE PARTIES

(a) Represented Parties. Any party for whom a general appearance of counsel has been made shall not thereafter take any step or be heard in the case in proper person, that is on his or her own behalf, absent prior leave of Court.

(b) Pro Se Parties. A party who has elected to proceed in proper person, that is to represent himself or herself without an attorney, shall not be permitted to obtain special or intermittent appearances of counsel except upon such conditions as the Court may specify.

[Effective June 15, 1997. Amended effective July 1, 2015.]

Notes of Advisory Committee

2015 Amendment

This amendment is stylistic and is effective July 1, 2015.

1997 Amendment

This amendment conforms the existing Local Rules to the uniform numbering system prescribed by the Judicial Conference of the United States and to the model system suggested and approved by the Advisory Committee on Bankruptcy Rules of the Judicial Conference's Committee on Rules of Practice and Procedure. In renumbering the Local Rules to conform to the uniform numbering system, no change in substance is intended. This amendment was effective on April 15, 1997.

This rule was formerly Local Rule 1.08(c). The Advisory Committee Notes to the superseded rules may be helpful in interpreting and applying the current rules.

RULE 9011-3. SANCTIONS [ABROGATED]

Notes of Advisory Committee

1997 Amendment

This amendment conforms the existing Local Rules to the uniform numbering system prescribed by the Judicial Conference of the United States and to the model system suggested and approved by the Advisory Committee on Bankruptcy Rules of the Judicial Conference's Committee on Rules of Practice and Procedure. In renumbering the Local Rules to conform to the uniform numbering system, no change in substance is intended. This amendment was effective on April 15, 1997.

This rule was formerly Local Rule 1.02. The Advisory Committee Notes to the superseded rules may be helpful in interpreting and applying the current rules.

RULE 9011-4. SIGNATURES [ABROGATED]

Notes of Advisory Committee

2015 Amendment

The amendment to section (a) requires attorneys to include their telephone number in their signature block and eliminates the requirement that they include their fax number. This amendment is effective July 1, 2015.

2014 Amendment

This amendment adds section (d)(2), which authorizes an attorney to file a paper containing the electronic signature of another party by attesting that the party has concurred in the filing of the paper. This amendment is effective July 1, 2014.

2013 Amendment

This amendment clarifies the requirements and formatting of signatures on pleadings and papers filed with the Court using CM/ECF. The amendment also eliminates the provision of former Rule 9011–4(e), which required attorneys to file a Declaration Under Penalty of Perjury for Electronic Filing for any verified paper that was not filed with an original signature, and establishes the procedure for filing Proofs of Service executed by a non-lawyer in compliance with Local Rule 7005–1. This amendment is effective July 1, 2013.

2004 Amendment

This amendment corrects the Bankruptcy Rules citation to that of the currently used citation. Further, this amendment added as section (a) requests attorneys to list their Internet email addresses if available to assist the Clerk in noting such information to be used for notification purposes.

The amendments under sections (b) through (d) are new and are adapted from the "Model Local Bankruptcy Court Rules for Electronic Case Filing" approved on September 11, 2001 by the Judicial Conference of the United States Courts. Signature issues are a subject of considerable interest and concern. The CM/ECF system is designed to require a login and password to file a document. This Rule provides that use of the login and password constitutes a signature, and assures that such a signature has the same force and effect as a written signature for purposes of the Federal Rules of Bankruptcy Procedure, including Fed. R. Bankr. P. 9011, and any other purpose for which a signature is required on a document in connection with proceedings before the court.

At the present time, other forms of digital or other electronic signature have received only limited acceptance. It is possible that over time and with further technological development, a system of digital signature may replace the current password system.

Some users of electronic filing systems have questioned whether an s-slash requirement is worth retaining. The better view is that an s-slash is necessary; otherwise there is no indication that documents printed out from the website were ever signed. The s-slash provides some indication when the filed document is viewed or printed that the original was in fact signed.

An attorney or other Electronic Filing User is not required to personally file his or her own documents. The task of electronic filing can be delegated to an authorized agent, who may use the login and password to make the filing. However, use of the login and password to make the filing constitutes a signature by the Electronic Filing User under the Rule, even though the Electronic Filing User does not do the physical act of filing.

1997 Amendment

This amendment conforms the existing Local Rules to the uniform numbering system prescribed by the Judicial Conference of the United States and to the model system suggested and approved by the Advisory Committee on Bankruptcy Rules of the Judicial Conference's Committee on Rules of Practice and Procedure. In renumbering the Local Rules to conform to the uniform numbering system, no change in substance is intended. This amendment was effective on April 15, 1997.

This rule was formerly Local Rule 2.02(d). The Advisory Committee Notes to the superseded rules may be helpful in interpreting and applying the current rules.

1995 Amendment

The amendment to Local Rule 2.02(d) adds the requirement that an attorney's facsimile phone number (if available) be listed on any pleading or other submission to the court. These amendments were effective on February 15, 1995.

RULE 9013–1. PROOF OF SERVICE IN BANKRUPTCY CASES, ADVERSARY PROCEEDINGS, AND CONTESTED MATTERS

(a) **Applicability.** This rule applies to proofs of service required by the Federal Rules of Bankruptcy Procedure, Local Rule, or order of the Court other than proof of initial service of a summons and complaint pursuant to Fed. R. Bankr. P. 9014 or of a contested matter under Fed. R. Bankr. P. 7004.

(b) **Service in Adversary Proceedings and Contested Matters.** In adversary proceedings and contested matters in which all parties are represented by counsel or have consented to service via CM/ECF, service of papers and Court orders will be effectuated upon the parties by CM/ECF; counsel are not required to file a separate proof of service reflecting such service.

(c) **Proof of Service by an Attorney.** If proof of service is made by an attorney appearing in the case or proceeding pursuant to the provisions of Local Rule 2090–1, the attorney may make a certificate of service stating the date and manner of service and the name and address of the person served, certified by the signature of the attorney who made the service.

(d) **Proof of Service by a Non–Attorney.** If proof of service is made by a person other than an attorney appearing in the case or proceeding pursuant to the provisions of Local Rule 2090–1, the non-attorney shall make a statement under penalty of perjury stating the date and manner of service and the name and address of the person served, signed, and sworn to by the non-attorney who made the service and including the non-attorney's name, address, and relation to the party on whose behalf the service is made.

(e) **Service on Mailing Matrix.** Where a reference is made to service on a group such as "to all creditors on the matrix," the proof of service shall attach a copy of the mailing matrix obtained from CM/ECF at the time of service.

(f) **Reference to Paper Served.** The proof of service shall refer to the pleading or other paper being served.

(g) **Proof of Service Shall Be Promptly Filed.** Proof of service, whether affixed to the paper served or separately filed, shall be filed promptly after the making of the service.

(h) **Prima Facie Evidence of Service.** Proof of service made in accordance with the provisions of this rule shall be taken as prima facie proof of service.

[Effective July 1, 2015.]

Notes of Advisory Committee

2015

This new rule substantially replaces former Local Rules 7005–1 and 9014–1 which are abrogated. This amendment is effective July 1, 2015.

RULE 9014–1. SERVICE AND PROOF OF SERVICE — CONTESTED MATTERS [ABROGATED]

[Effective June 15, 1997. Amended effective December 1, 2000; December 1, 2004. Abrogated effective July 1, 2015.]

Notes of Advisory Committee

2015

This rule is abrogated effective July 1, 2015. It is replaced by new Local Rule 9013-1, also effective July 1, 2015.

RULE 9014-2. GENERAL PROVISIONS REGARDING DISCOVERY—CONTESTED MATTERS [ABROGATED]

Notes of Advisory Committee

2004 Amendment

This amendment corrects the Bankruptcy Rules citation to that of the currently used citation.

2000 Amendment

Pursuant to Fed.R.Bankr.P. 9014, Fed.R.Bankr.P. 7026 applies in contested matters "unless the court otherwise directs." This new local rule reflects the judgment of the Committee that the mandatory disclosure requirements of Fed.R.Civ.P. 26(a)(1) through (3) are burdensome, unwieldy, and of no benefit in routine contested matters. In an exercise of the Court's discretion under Fed.R.Bankr.P. 9014, therefore, the Court directs in paragraph (a) that these provisions are not mandatory in contested matters. The Court retains the ability to order these disclosures in individual contested matters, and the parties retain the ability to agree to apply the disclosure provisions in individual contested matters.

The provisions of paragraphs (b) and (c) logically flow from the elimination of the mandatory disclosure requirements as provided in paragraph (a). Without the mandatory disclosure requirements, the conference and reporting requirements of Fed.R.Civ.P. 26(f) are unnecessary. Similarly, there is no need for a discovery moratorium before that conference.

The new local rule contained here is made necessary by the December 1, 2000, amendments to the Fed.R.Civ.P. 26 and Local Rule 7026-1. *See* the Notes of Advisory Committee as to the December 1, 2000, amendments to Local Rule 7026-1. Although mandatory disclosures, Rule 26(f) conferences and reports, and discovery moratoriums now apply in adversary proceedings, they do not apply in contested matters as a consequence of this new local rule.

Pursuant to Local Rule 9014-1, those portions of Fed.R.Bankr.P. 7005 applying Fed.R.Civ.P. 5(a)-(d) apply in contested matters. As part of the December 1, 2000, amendments to the Federal Rules of Civil Procedure, Fed.R.Civ.P. 5 was amended as to the filing of disclosure and discovery materials. Under Rule 5(d), as amended, disclosures under Rule 26(a)(1) and (2) and discovery requests and responses under Rules 30, 31, 33, 34, and 36 must not be filed until they are used in the action. Disclosures under Rule 26(a)(3), however, are to be filed with the Court. Because Fed.R.Civ.P. 5(d) applies in contested matters by virtue of Local Rule 9014-1 and applies in adversary proceedings by virtue of Fed.R.Bankr.P. 7005, disclosure and discovery papers in contested matters are filed—or not filed—in the same circumstances as disclosure and discovery papers in adversary proceedings. Local Rule 7005-2 formerly addressed this issue, but the Court abrogated that rule effective on December 1, 2000. *See* Notes of Advisory Committee as to the December 1, 2000, amendments to Local Rule 7005-2.

This amendment was effective on December 1, 2000.

RULE 9015-1. JURY TRIAL

(a) Voir Dire. The method of voir dire examination and exercise of challenges in selection of the jury shall be as specified by the Court. A list of the venire will be furnished to counsel only at the time the case is called for trial, and prior to commencement of voir dire examination (unless otherwise required by governing rule or statute), and must be returned to the Clerk when the jury is empaneled. No person shall copy from or reproduce, in whole or in part, a list of the venire.

(b) Instructions to the Jury. All requests for instructions to the jury shall be submitted in writing within the time specified by the Court. Such requests, and supplemental requests, if any, shall be marked with the name and number of the case, shall designate the party submitting the request, shall be numbered in sequence, and shall contain citation of supporting authorities, if any.

(c) Juror Interviews. No attorney or party shall undertake, directly or indirectly, to interview any juror after trial in any civil case except as permitted by this rule. If a party believes that grounds for legal challenge to a verdict exist, the party may move for an order permitting an interview of a juror or jurors to determine whether the verdict is subject to the challenge. The motion shall be served within 14 days after rendition of the verdict unless good cause is shown for the failure to make the motion within that time. The motion shall state the name and address of each juror to be interviewed and the grounds for the challenge that the moving party believes may exist. The presiding judge may conduct such hearings, if any, as necessary, and shall enter an order denying the motion or permitting the interview. If the interview is permitted, the Court may prescribe the place, manner, conditions, and scope of the interview.

[Effective June 15, 1997. Amended effective October 15, 1998; December 1, 2009; July 1, 2015.]

Notes of Advisory Committee

2015 Amendment

This amendment is stylistic and is effective July 1, 2015.

1998 Amendment

On December 1, 1997, amendments to the Federal Rules of Bankruptcy Procedure added new Rule 9015, entitled "Jury Trials." This new rule was made necessary by the addition of 28 U.S.C. § 157(e) contained in the Bankruptcy Reform Act of 1994, Pub. L. 103-394. The Court had adopted paragraphs (a) through (e) of Local Rule 9015-1 because their subject matter was not covered in the Federal Rules of Bankruptcy Procedure. These paragraphs of the local rule are now abrogated as duplicative of the national rule.

The remaining parts of the local rule, paragraphs (f) through (h), are derived from the comparable District Court Local Rule 5.01. These paragraphs are redesignated paragraphs (a) through (c), respectively.

The District Court has specifically designated all of the bankruptcy judges of the Court to conduct jury trials pursuant to 28 U.S.C. § 157(e). *See* District Court Order No. 94-127-MISC-J-16, entered on December 1, 1994. Although Fed. R. Bankr. P. 9015(b) contemplates that the Court by local rule might establish a time by which the parties must consent to a jury trial conducted by a bankruptcy judge, this amendment does not attempt to establish such a time. Instead, the Committee is of the view that the parties and the Court should have the flexibility to allow consent to be given at any time.

This amendment was effective on October 15, 1998.

1997 Amendment

This amendment conforms the existing Local Rules to the uniform numbering system prescribed by the Judicial Conference of the United States and to the model system suggested and approved by the Advisory Committee on Bankruptcy Rules of the Judicial Conference's Committee on Rules of Practice and Procedure. In renumbering the Local Rules to conform to the uniform numbering system, no change in substance is intended. This amendment was effective on April 15, 1997.

This rule was formerly Local Rule 2.18. The Advisory Committee Notes to the superseded rules may be helpful in interpreting and applying the current rules.

RULE 9016-1. SUBPOENAS BEFORE TRIAL

Absent order of Court to the contrary, subpoenas before trial shall be filed with the Court and, as required by Fed. R. Civ. P. 45(a)(4) incorporated by Fed. R. Bankr. P. 9016, served on each party to the adversary proceeding or contested matter prior to being served on the person to whom the subpoena is directed.

[Effective July 1, 2015.]

Notes of the Advisory Committee

2015

This new rule requires subpoenas before trial to be filed with the Court in addition to being served on each party to the adversary proceeding or contested matter. This amendment is effective July 1, 2015.

RULE 9019-1. SETTLEMENTS

(a) Court to be Advised of Settlement of Pending Matters. When the parties to a pending adversary proceeding or contested matter reach a settlement that will resolve all issues in the pending matter, counsel for the plaintiff or movant shall immediately notify the Clerk's office or chambers personnel that the matter has been settled. The Court in its discretion may cancel any scheduled hearing in the adversary or contested matter or may require counsel to appear at the time set for the hearing to announce the terms of the settlement on the record. The parties shall promptly file papers to conclude the matter.

(b) Dismissal of Adversary Proceedings upon Settlement. When notified that an adversary proceeding has been settled, the Court may order that the proceeding be dismissed subject to the right of any party to file a motion within 14 days thereafter (or within such other period of time as the Court may specify) for the purpose of entering a stipulated form of final order or judgment; or, on good cause shown, to reopen the adversary proceeding for further action.

[Effective June 15, 1997. Amended effective December 1, 2009; July 1, 2015.]

Notes of Advisory Committee

2015 Amendment

This amendment is stylistic and is effective July 1, 2015.

1997 Amendment

This amendment conforms the existing Local Rules to the uniform numbering system prescribed by the Judicial Conference of the United States and to the model system suggested and approved by the Advisory Committee on Bankruptcy Rules of the Judicial Conference's Committee on Rules of Practice and Procedure. In renumbering the Local Rules to conform to the uniform numbering system, no change in substance is intended. This amendment was effective on April 15, 1997.

This rule was formerly Local Rule 2.08(i) and (j). The Advisory Committee Notes to the superseded rules may be helpful in interpreting and applying the current rules.

1995 Amendment

Local Rule 2.08(g) has been moved and renumbered 2.08(i). No substantive change is intended.

Local Rule 2.08(j) is new. It provides that, upon notification that an adversary proceeding has been settled, the proceeding may be administratively closed. For purposes of entering a stipulated form of final order or judgment or in the event that the parties are unable to satisfactorily conclude documentation of the settlement, the Court may reopen the proceeding. The amendment is substantially similar to District Court Local Rule 3.08(b).

These amendments were effective on February 15, 1995.

RULE 9019-2. ALTERNATIVE DISPUTE RESOLUTION (ADR); MEDIATION

(a) Definition. Mediation is an opportunity for the parties to negotiate their own settlement consistent with the mediation policy of self-determination. Mediation is a confidential process that includes a supervised settlement conference presided over by an impartial, neutral mediator to promote conciliation, compromise and the ultimate settlement of a civil action. The mediator's role in the settlement is to suggest alternatives, analyze issues, question perceptions, conduct private caucuses, stimulate negotiations between opposing sides, and keep order. The mediation process does not allow for testimony of witnesses. The mediator should not opine or rule upon questions of fact or law, or render any final decision in the case. At the conclusion of the mediation, the mediator shall report to the Court (1) the identity of the parties in attendance at the mediation, and (2) that parties either reached an agreement in whole or in part or that the mediation was terminated without the parties' coming to an agreement.

(b) Purpose. Mediation is intended as an alternative method to resolve civil cases, saving time and cost without sacrificing the quality of justice to be rendered or the right of the litigants to a full trial in the event that mediation does not resolve the dispute.

(c) Qualifications; Conflicts.

(1) *Qualifications of Mediators.* The parties may select any person to serve as mediator. Parties are encouraged to choose a mediator who has sufficient knowledge and experience in mediations and in bankruptcy law. Notwithstanding the foregoing, the Court, by administrative order, may establish qualifications and maintain a list of those persons eligible to serve as mediator in a residential mortgage modification mediation.

(2) *Conflicts of Interest.* The mediator must disclose all actual or potential conflicts of interest involving the parties participating in the mediation process. The parties may waive a mediator's actual or potential conflict of interest, provided that the mediator concludes in good faith that the mediator's impartiality will not be compromised. The unique nature of bankruptcy cases favors the parties' ability to waive conflicts and supersedes the concept of non-waivable conflicts.

(d) Standards of Professional Conduct for Mediators. All mediators who mediate in cases pending in this District, whether or not certified under the rules adopted by the Supreme Court of Florida, shall be governed by standards of professional conduct and ethical rules adopted by the Supreme Court of Florida for circuit court mediators.

(e) Disqualification of a Mediator. After reasonable notice and hearing, and for good cause, the presiding judge shall have discretion and authority to disqualify any mediator from serving as mediator in a particular case. Good cause may include violation of the standards of professional conduct for mediators.

(f) Compensation of Mediators. Unless otherwise indicated in an order appointing a mediator, an order directing parties to mediate, or other similar court order, the mediator shall be compensated for fees and expenses as established and agreed to by the parties to the mediation. Absent agreement of the parties or order of the Court to the contrary, the cost of the mediator's services shall be paid equally by the parties to the mediation.

In cases in which one or more parties to the mediation is a Chapter 11 trustee or debtor-in-possession, payment of the mediator's charges attributable to that party shall be authorized without the necessity of filing an application with the Court.

(g) Confidentiality.

(1) *Definitions.* As used in this section (g), "Mediation Communication" means an oral or written statement, or nonverbal conduct intended to make an assertion, by or to a participant in a mediation made during the course of the mediation, or prior to a mediation if made in furtherance of a mediation; "Mediation Participant" means a mediation party or a person who attends a mediation in person or by telephone, videoconference, or other electronic means; "Mediation Party" means a person participating in a mediation directly or through a designated representative, and who is a named party, a real party in interest, or who would be a named party or real party in interest if an action relating to the subject matter of the mediation were brought in a court of law; and "Subsequent Proceeding" means an adjudicative process that follows a mediation, including related discovery.

(2) *Confidential Mediation Communications.* Except as provided in this section (g), all Mediation Communications are confidential, and the mediator and the Mediation Participants shall not disclose outside of the mediation any Mediation Communication, and no person may introduce in any Subsequent Proceeding evidence pertaining to any aspect of the mediation effort. However, information that is otherwise admissible or subject to discovery does not become inadmissible or protected from discovery because of its disclosure or use in mediation.

(3) *Evidence Rules and Laws.* Without limiting subsection (2), Rule 408 of the Federal Rules of Evidence and any applicable federal or state statute, rule, common law, or judicial precedent relating to the privileged nature of settlement discussions or mediations apply.

(4) *Settlement Agreements.* Notwithstanding subsections (2) and (3), no confidentiality attaches to a signed, written agreement reached during or as a result of a mediation, unless the mediation parties agree otherwise, or to any communication for which the confidentiality or privilege against disclosure has been waived by all Mediation Parties.

(5) *Preservation of Privileges.* The disclosure by a Mediation Participant or Mediation Party of privileged information to the mediator or to another Mediation Participant or Mediation Party does not waive or otherwise adversely affect the privileged nature of the information.

(6) *Disclosures by Mediator.* The mediator shall not be compelled to disclose to the Court or to any person outside the mediation conference any Mediation Communications, nor shall the mediator be required to testify in regard to the mediation in connection with any Subsequent Proceeding or be a party to any Subsequent Proceeding.

(7) *Disclosure of Communications.* A Mediation Participant who makes a representation about a Mediation Communication waives that privilege, but only to the extent necessary for another Mediation Participant to respond to the disclosure.

(h) Mediators as Counsel in Other Cases. Any member of the bar who selected as a mediator pursuant to this rule shall not, for that reason alone, be disqualified from appearing and acting as counsel in another unrelated case pending in this District.

(i) Referral to Mediation. Any pending case, proceeding, or contested matter may be referred to mediation by the Court at such time as the Court may determine to be in the interests of justice. The parties may request the Court to submit any pending case, proceeding, or contested matter to mediation at any time.

(j) Mortgage Modification Mediations and Other Specialty Mediations. When deemed necessary, the Court shall establish procedures, policies and necessary orders to deal with the mediation of emerging bankruptcy trends, such as residential mortgage modifications.

(k) Participation of Parties at Mediation. All parties to the mediation are required to attend the mediation in person, unless authorized by the Court or the mediator to attend by telephone. Parties are encouraged to participate in the mediation in a good faith attempt to resolve the issues between them. Parties who are not individuals shall participate in mediations through the presence of a representative with full authority to settle the matter that is the subject of the mediation.

[Effective June 15, 1997. Amended effective December 1, 2009; July 1, 2013.]

Notes of Advisory Committee

2013 Amendment

The amendments to this rule significantly modify the rule as originally promulgated in 1989 and amended in 1995 and 1997. The amendments reflect the development of the mediation process in the Middle District of Florida.

Section (c)(2): The parties' ability to waive a mediator's actual or potential conflict of interest in bankruptcy cases differs from the Rules for Certified and Court Appointed Mediators adopted by the Florida Supreme Court, Rules 10.100 et seq., and the opinions of the Mediator Ethics Advisory Committee.

Section (g): The confidentiality provisions of section (g) are adapted in significant part from Florida's Mediation Confidentiality and Privilege Act, Sections 44.401–44.405, Florida Statutes. Although the civil remedies provisions contained in Section 44.406 are not incorporated in this rule, parties are reminded that violations of this rule may be sanctionable under Local Rule 9011–3. By way of example, permissible disclosures in a subsequent proceeding would include statements made at a mediation to the extent necessary to support or oppose a reformation or declaratory relief action concerning an ambiguity in a settlement agreement. Additionally, a confidential settlement agreement is subject to disclosure if required by a subpoena or order of a court of competent jurisdiction.

This amendment is effective July 1, 2013.

RULE 9027–1. REMOVAL/REMAND

(a) State Court Record to be Filed with Notice of Removal. The party filing a notice of removal of a claim or cause of action under 28 U.S.C. § 1452 and Fed. R. Bankr. P. 9027 shall file a complete copy of the state court record, including copies of all papers on file in the state court, with the notice of removal.

(b) Operative Pleadings and Other Relevant Papers to be Separately Docketed. In addition to filing a complete copy of the state court record, within seven days of filing the notice of removal, the party who filed the notice of removal shall also file, as separate docket entries, the operative pleadings, substantive rulings, and any pending motions and responses included in the state court record.

[Effective June 15, 1997. Amended effective December 1, 2004; July 1, 2015.]

Notes of Advisory Committee

2015 Amendment

This amendment requires the removing party, in addition to filing the state court record with the notice of removal, to also file the operative pleadings, etc. as separate docket entries. This amendment is effective July 1, 2015.

2004 Amendment

This amendment corrects the Bankruptcy Rules citation to that of the currently used citation.

1997 Amendment

This amendment conforms the existing Local Rules to the uniform numbering system prescribed by the Judicial Conference of the United States and to the model system suggested and approved by the Advisory Committee on Bankruptcy Rules of the Judicial Conference's Committee on Rules of Practice and Procedure. In renumbering the Local Rules to conform to the uniform numbering system, no change in substance is intended. This amendment was effective on April 15, 1997.

RULE 9033–1. REVIEW OF PROPOSED FINDINGS OF FACT AND CONCLUSIONS OF LAW IN NON–CORE PROCEEDINGS [ABROGATED]

[Effective June 15, 1997. Amended effective December 1, 2004. Abrogated effective July 1, 2015.]

Notes of Advisory Committee

2015

This rule is abrogated effective July 1, 2015. Fed. R. Bankr. P. 9033 addresses objections to proposed findings of fact and conclusions of law.

RULE 9036–1. NOTICE BY ELECTRONIC TRANSMISSION; SERVICE BY FACSIMILE [ABROGATED]

[Effective June 15, 1997. Amended effective December 1, 2004. Abrogated effective July 1, 2015.]

Notes of Advisory Committee

2015

This rule is abrogated effective July 1, 2015, as it has been superseded by Local Rule 1001–2.

RULE 9070–1. EXHIBITS

[Publisher's Note: For Appendices associated with this rule, please refer to the section entitled "Appendices", *post.*]

(a) Marking Exhibits. Prior to the trial of an adversary proceeding or a contested matter, counsel for the parties shall mark and list any exhibits proposed to be introduced into evidence in compliance with this rule.

(b) Numbering Exhibits. Exhibits shall be identified numerically commencing with number 1.

(c) Exhibit List. All exhibits shall be listed, in order, on a separate sheet of paper that shall include the case number, adversary number, the debtor's name, designation as to plaintiff and defendant, and columns with the following headings: Exhibit Number (Exh. #), Document Description, Date Identified, Date Admitted, and With or Without Objection (Appendix A). No markings should be made on the "Identified" and "Admitted" lines; this is for the Court's use.

(d) Exhibit Cover Sheet. Each exhibit shall be preceded by an 8 1/2 x 11-inch Exhibit Cover Sheet (Appendix B).

(e) Submitting Exhibits. At the commencement of a hearing or trial, each party shall submit to the courtroom deputy the original and one copy of all exhibits and the Exhibit List. Original exhibits shall not be stapled or permanently bound. Additional copies, appropriately stapled or in binders, shall be available for use by witnesses and provided to opposing counsel. Parties should confirm the preferred procedure for preparing exhibit binders with the assigned judge's chambers. Any exhibits produced at hearing or trial that are not pre-marked shall be tendered to and marked by the courtroom deputy as they are presented in evidence.

(f) Large Items or Exhibits Other Than Paper Documents. Items to be introduced into evidence other than paper documents should be photographed, accompanied by an Exhibit Cover Sheet, and listed on the Exhibit List. Paper documents larger than 8 1/2 x 14 inches should be listed on the Exhibit List and accompanied by a reduced 8 1/2 x 11-inch copy and an Exhibit Cover Sheet. Counsel shall attach Exhibit Cover Sheets to both exhibits and substitutes, identifying corresponding exhibits and substitutes with the same number. Unless the Court orders otherwise, at the conclusion of the trial or hearing at which the exhibits are offered, if the Clerk has custody of substitutes, the Clerk will return the corresponding original exhibits to counsel. If an appeal is taken, substitutes will be included in the record on appeal.

(g) Disposal of Exhibits. The Clerk, with or without notice, may dispose of any unclaimed exhibits in any matter or proceeding unless notified by the appropriate party within 30 days after an order or judgment concluding a contested matter or an adversary proceeding is entered, including the entry of an order determining any post-judgment motions, provided that no appeal is pending, or if an appeal is taken, upon filing of the mandate. Parties shall bear all costs associated with reclaiming exhibits.

[Effective June 15, 1997. Amended effective March 15, 2012.]

Notes of Advisory Committee

2012 Amendment

This amendment adopts new procedures to accommodate the use of electronic scanning of exhibits, which can be impaired by the use of permanently bound or stapled originals. Paragraph (g) was amended to permit the Clerk to dispose of exhibits left unclaimed for 30 days. This amendment incorporates archived Administrative Orders 99-0001-MIS-ORL and 99-00001-MIS-JAX "General Order for Disposal of Unclaimed Exhibits." A sample Exhibit List (Appendix A) and Exhibit Cover Sheet (Appendix B) are provided. The addition of headings and subheadings is intended to be a stylistic rather than substantive change.

This amendment is effective March 15, 2012.

1997 Amendment

This amendment conforms the existing Local Rules to the uniform numbering system prescribed by the Judicial Conference of the United States and to the model system suggested and approved by the Advisory Committee on Bankruptcy Rules of the Judicial Conference's Committee on Rules of Practice and Procedure. In renumbering the Local Rules to conform to the uniform numbering system, no change in substance is intended. This amendment was effective on April 15, 1997.

This rule was formerly Local Rule 2.13. The Advisory Committee Notes to the superseded rules may be helpful in interpreting and applying the current rules.

1995 Amendment

The amendment to Local Rule 2.13(e) requires that additional copies of exhibits shall be made available for use by witnesses. The deletion of the word "period" after "trial" is stylistic; no substantive change is intended.

The provisions in Local Rule 2.13(h), which dealt with notification to counsel of the obligation to pick up exhibits and the consequence of the failure to do so, have been deleted as this is now dealt with exclusively by Local Rule 2.13(i).

For purposes of Local Rule 2.13(i), the term "post-judgment motion" shall mean a timely motion; (1) to amend or make additional findings of fact under Fed. R. Bankr. P. 7052, whether or not granting the motion would alter the judgment; (2) to alter or amend the judgment under Fed. R. Bankr. P. 9023; (3) for a new trial under Fed. R. Bankr. P. 9023; or (4) for relief under Fed. R. Bankr. P. 9024 if the motion is filed no later than ten (10) days after the entry of judgment.

These amendments were effective on February 15, 1995.

RULE 9070-2. ATTACHMENTS—ELECTRONIC SUBMISSION OF [ABROGATED]

[Effective December 1, 2004. Abrogated effective July 1, 2015.]

Notes of Advisory Committee

2015 Amendment

This rule is abrogated effective July 1, 2015, as it is superseded by Local Rule 1001-2.

RULE 9071-1. STIPULATIONS

All factual and procedural stipulations must either be in writing and filed with the Court or stated on the record in open court.

[Effective June 15, 1997. Amended effective July 1, 2015.]

Notes of Advisory Committee

2015 Amendment

The amendments are stylistic. This amendment is effective July 1, 2015.

1997 Amendment

This amendment conforms the existing Local Rules to the uniform numbering system prescribed by the Judicial Conference of the United States and to the model system suggested and approved by the Advisory Committee on Bankruptcy Rules of the Judicial Conference's Committee on Rules of Practice and Procedure. In renumbering the Local Rules to conform to the uniform numbering system, no change in substance is intended. This amendment was effective on April 15, 1997.

This rule was formerly Local Rule 2.17. The Advisory Committee Notes to the superseded rules may be helpful in interpreting and applying the current rules.

RULE 9072-1. ORDERS—PROPOSED

(a) Format. Proposed orders should follow the format set forth in the Court's Style Guide available on the Court's website, www.flmb.uscourts.gov, and shall include the following:

(1) case name and full case number;

(2) descriptive title, including name and docket number of the matter ruled upon and substance of the Court's ruling, *e.g.*, granted or denied;

(3) if the matter was heard by the Court, the date of the hearing;

(4) if the matter was served using the negative notice provisions of Local Rule 2002–4, the language set forth in Local Rule 2002–4(e); and

(5) the following sentence at the end of the order:

Attorney [or Trustee] [insert name of attorney/trustee] is directed to serve a copy of this order on interested parties who are non–CM/ECF users and to file a proof of service within three days of entry of the order.

(b) Submission of Orders.

(1) *"Accompanying Orders" That May Be Submitted Upon the Filing of Motion or Application.* The Court has designated a list, available on the Court's website, www.flmb.uscourts.gov, of the types of motions and applications that do not ordinarily require notice and a hearing. At the time that a listed motion or application is filed, counsel, following the Court's guidelines for the submission of proposed orders, may submit a proposed order. Notwithstanding the foregoing, the Court may schedule a hearing on the motion or application.

(2) *Negative Notice.* Orders on papers served using the Negative Notice Procedures of Local Rule 2002–4 shall be submitted electronically to the Court after the expiration of the response period and within three business days of such expiration.

(3) *After Hearing.* Orders resulting from a hearing shall be submitted within three business days of the hearing.

(c) Agreed Orders. Agreed or consent orders may be submitted if:

(1) The parties have previously filed an agreed or joint motion that is signed by all necessary parties;

(2) The movant represents in the motion that the movant has obtained consent of the other parties to the entry of a proposed order attached to the motion;

(3) A separate consent with the signature of all necessary parties is filed;

(4) An agreed order signed by all necessary parties is submitted (no prior motion required); or

(5) The movant submits an order that recites in the preamble that the submitting party represents that the other parties have agreed to the form and content of the order, *e.g.*, "By submission of this order for entry, the submitting counsel represents that the opposing party consents to its entry."

(d) Amended Orders. If a party requires the substantive amendment of a previously entered order, the party may file a motion for entry of an amended order together with an amended order, or submit an agreed amended order. Amended orders shall include a footnote on the order's first page that states the reason for the amendment. If the amendment does not affect the substance of the ruling (*e.g.*, merely to correct a legal description), a party may submit an amended order with a footnote on the order's first page that sets forth the reason for the amendment.

[Effective June 15, 1997. Amended effective December 1, 2004; July 1, 2014; July 1, 2015.]

Notes of Advisory Committee

2015 Amendment

This amendment includes section (b)(1) and refers to the "Accompanying Orders" list posted on the Court's website. The amendment is effective July 1, 2015.

2014 Amendment

This amendment clarifies the information to be included in proposed orders submitted to the Court, provides that orders on papers served using the negative notice procedures of Local Rule 2002–4 shall be submitted after the expiration of the response period and within three business days of the response period, changes the time for submission of orders after hearings to three "business" days, and establishes procedures for the submission of agreed and amended orders. This amendment is effective July 1, 2014.

2004 Amendment

This amendment allows Electronic Filing Users to submit proposed orders to the Court by electronic means. The Clerk will be responsible for setting up an electronic acceptance system in order to transmit proposed orders from parties to judges' chambers.

1997 Amendment

This amendment conforms the existing Local Rules to the uniform numbering system prescribed by the Judicial Conference of the United States and to the model system suggested and approved by the Advisory Committee on Bankruptcy Rules of the Judicial Conference's Committee on Rules of Practice and Procedure. In renumbering the Local Rules to conform to the uniform numbering system, no change in substance is intended. This amendment was effective on April 15, 1997.

This rule was formerly Local Rule 2.11. The Advisory Committee Notes to the superseded rules may be helpful in interpreting and applying the current rules.

1995 Amendment

The amendments are stylistic. No substantive change is intended. These amendments were effective on February 15, 1995.

SELECTED APPENDICES

RULE 2081–1—APPENDIX

APPENDIX A. SCHEDULE OF RECEIPTS & DISBURSEMENTS

SCHEDULE OF RECEIPTS AND DISBURSEMENTS
FOR THE PERIOD BEGINNING ________ AND ENDING ________

Name of Debtor: ________________ Case Number
Date of Petition: ________________

	CURRENT MONTH	CUMULATIVE PETITION TO DATE
1. FUNDS AT BEGINNING OF PERIOD	________(a)	________(b)
2. RECEIPTS:		
A. Cash Sales	________	________
Minus: Cash Refunds	(-)________	________
Net Cash Sales	________	________
B. Accounts Receivable	________	________
C. Other Receipts *(See MOR-3)* (If you receive rental income, you must attach a rent roll.)	________	________
3. TOTAL RECEIPTS *(Lines 2A+2B+2C)*	________	________
4. TOTAL FUNDS AVAILABLE FOR OPERATIONS *(Line 1 Line 3)*	________	________
5. DISBURSEMENTS		
A. Advertising	________	________
B. Bank Charges	________	________
C. Contract Labor	________	________
D. Fixed Asset Payments (not incl. in "N")	________	________
E. Insurance	________	________
F. Inventory Payments	________	________
G. Leases	________	________
H. Manufacturing Supplies	________	________
I. Office Supplies	________	________
J. Payroll – Net	________	________
K. Professional Fees (Accounting & Legal)	________	________
L. Rent	________	________
M. Repairs & Maintenance	________	________
N. Secured Creditor Payments	________	________
O. Taxes Paid – Payroll	________	________
P. Taxes Paid - Sales & Use	________	________
Q. Taxes Paid - Other	________	________
R. Telephone	________	________
S. Travel & Entertainment	________	________
Y. U.S. Trustee Quarterly Fees	________	________
U. Utilities	________	________
V. Vehicle Expenses	________	________
W. Other Operating Expenses *(See MOR-3)*	________	________
6. TOTAL DISBURSEMENTS *(Sum of 5A thru W)*	________	________
7. ENDING BALANCE *(Line 4 Minus Line 6)*	________(c)	________(c)

I declare under penalty of perjury that this statement and the accompanying documents and reports are true and correct to the best of my knowledge and belief.

This ____ day of ________, 20__.

____
(Signature)

(a)This number is carried forward from last month's report. For the first report only, this number will be the balance as of the petition date.

(b)This figure will not change from month to month. It is always the amount of funds on hand as of the date of the petition.

(c)These two amounts will always be the same if form is completed correctly.

MOR-2

APPENDIX A

MONTHLY SCHEDULE OF RECEIPTS AND DISBURSEMENTS (cont'd)

Detail of Other Receipts and Other Disbursements

OTHER RECEIPTS:

Describe Each Item of Other Receipt and List Amount of Receipt. Write totals on Page MOR-2, Line 2C.

Description	Current Month	Cumulative Petition to Date
TOTAL OTHER RECEIPTS		

"Other Receipts" includes Loans from Insiders and other sources (i.e. Officer/Owner, related parties, directors, related corporations, etc.). Please describe below:

Loan Amount	Source of Funds	Purpose	Repayment Schedule

OTHER DISBURSEMENTS:

Describe Each Item of Other Disbursement and List Amount of Disbursement. Write totals on Page MOR-2, Line 5W.

Description	Current Month	Cumulative Petition to Date
TOTAL OTHER DISBURSEMENTS		

MOR-3

[Effective March 15, 2012. Amended effective July 1, 2013; June 30, 2015.]

RULE 9070–1—APPENDIX

APPENDIX A. [PLAINTIFF/DEFENDANT'S] EXHIBIT LIST

UNITED STATES BANKRUPTCY COURT
MIDDLE DISTRICT OF FLORIDA
DIVISION

In Re: Case No._______
Chapter

____
[Name of Debtor(s)],

Debtor*.

____

[Name of Plaintiff], Adv. No. __________

Plaintiff,

v.

[Name of Defendant],

Defendant.

____

[Plaintiff/Defendant's] Exhibit List
(Hearing on Acme Bank's
Complaint to Determine Dischargeability (Doc. No. 1))
Hearing Date:

Exh. #	Document Description	Date Identified	Date Admitted	With or Without Objection
1	Promissory Note			

*All references to "Debtor" shall include and refer to both debtors in a case filed jointly by two individuals.

APPENDIX A

APPENDIX B. EXHIBIT COVER SHEET

Exhibit Cover Sheet

Party submitting: ________________ **Ex. #**___

Admitted: Yes or No (circle one)

Debtor:______________________________

Case No.:______________________________

Adv. No.:______________________________

Nature of Hearing/
Docket No:______________________________

____

United States Bankruptcy Court
Middle District of Florida

Dated ____________ **, 20**___**.**

By:____________________**, Deputy Clerk**

APPENDIX B

[Effective March 15, 2012.]

SELECTED NOTICES AND ADMINISTRATIVE ORDERS

GENERAL ORDER ESTABLISHING PROTOCOL FOR PROCESSING UNTIMELY BANKRUPTCY APPEALS [DISTRICT COURT ORDER]

The judges of the court have considered problems associated with the untimely filing of bankruptcy appeals. Acting upon the report and recommendation of the bankruptcy judges, upon thorough consideration, and to ensure the just, speedy, and inexpensive processing of bankruptcy appeals, the court establishes the following protocol:

1. Whenever an appellant files in the bankruptcy court a notice of appeal that is untimely on its face pursuant to the time provisions of F.R.B.P. 8002(a) or (b), the presiding bankruptcy judge may enter an order dismissing the appeal for untimeliness. Unless the district court grants relief from that order pursuant to the provisions of paragraph 2 below, the entry of the order of dismissal shall have the effect of dismissing the appeal; and the clerk of the bankruptcy court shall not transmit the notice of appeal, the order of dismissal, or the record to the clerk of the district court.

2. A party in interest aggrieved by the entry by the bankruptcy judge of an order dismissing the appeal for untimeliness may file in the bankruptcy court a motion for review by the district judge. Such a motion for review shall be filed with the clerk of the bankruptcy court within 10 days of the date of the entry of the order of dismissal for untimeliness. Upon the filing of such a motion for review, the clerk of the bankruptcy court shall transmit to the clerk of the district court a record sufficient to permit the district judge to review the bankruptcy judge's order of dismissal for untimeliness.

[Effective September 25, 1996.]

GENERAL ORDER ESTABLISHING PROTOCOL FOR PROCESSING BANKRUPTCY APPEALS WITHOUT PAYMENT OF FILING FEES [DISTRICT COURT ORDER]

The judges of the court have considered problems associated with the filing of bankruptcy appeals without the required filing fees. Acting upon the report and recommendation of the bankruptcy judges, upon thorough consideration, and to ensure the just, speedy, and inexpensive processing of bankruptcy appeals, the court establishes the following protocol:

A. Motions to Proceed on Appeal In Forma Pauperis:

1. Motions made in the bankruptcy court to proceed on appeal in forma pauperis pursuant to the provisions of 28 U.S.C. § 1915 shall be heard and determined by the presiding bankruptcy judge.

2. A party in interest aggrieved by the entry by the bankruptcy judge of an order determining a motion to proceed on appeal in forma pauperis may file in the bankruptcy court a motion for review by the district judge. Such a motion for review shall be filed with the clerk of the bankruptcy court within 10 days of the date of the entry of the order sought to be reviewed. Upon the filing of such a motion for review, the clerk of the bankruptcy court shall transmit to the clerk of the district court a record sufficient to permit the district judge to review the bankruptcy judge's order.

B. Failure to Pay Required Fees:

1. In the event an appellant who has not obtained leave to proceed on appeal in forma pauperis files a notice of appeal without paying the filing fees required by 28 U.S.C. § 1930(c), F.R.B.P. 8001(a), and the Bankruptcy Court Miscellaneous Fee Schedule, the presiding bankruptcy judge may enter a conditional order of dismissal of the appeal. The conditional order of dismissal shall direct the appellant to pay the required filing fees within 10 days of the date of the entry of the conditional order of dismissal, failing which the appeal shall stand and be taken as dismissed without further order of the court.

2. If the appellant pays the filing fees as required by the order, the processing of the appeal will proceed in the usual course under the Federal Rules of Bankruptcy Procedure.

3. If the appellant fails to pay the filing fees as required by the order, the appeal shall be deemed dismissed without further order of the bankruptcy court or the district court; and the clerk of the bankruptcy court shall not transmit the notice of appeal, the conditional order of dismissal, or the record to the clerk of the district court.

4. A party in interest aggrieved by the entry by the bankruptcy judge of a conditional order of dismissal may file in the bankruptcy court a motion for review by the district judge. Such a motion for review shall be filed with the clerk of the bankruptcy court within 10 days of the date of the entry of the order of conditional dismissal. Upon the filing of such a motion for review, the clerk of the bankruptcy court shall transmit to the clerk of the district court a record sufficient to permit the district judge to review the bankruptcy judge's conditional order of dismissal.

[Effective September 25, 1996.]

ADMINISTRATIVE ORDER FLMB–2009–7. IN RE: POLICY ON ELECTRONIC AVAILABILITY OF TRANSCRIPTS OF COURT PROCEEDINGS

Effective December 1, 2009, time periods in the Federal Rules of Bankruptcy Procedure and in the Local Rules and Administrative Orders of the Bankruptcy Court of the Middle District of Florida are amended to provide that time periods of under 30 days are measured in actual days rather than business days, and generally in periods of 7, 14, and 21 days. To accommodate these changes, the Court's Administrative Order Setting Forth Policy of Electronic Availability of Transcripts of Court Proceedings, Administrative Order 2008–1, is replaced entirely by this Order.

The Judicial Conference of the United States has a national policy addressing electronic availability of transcripts of court proceedings filed with the court. The Judicial Conference Policy on Electronic Availability of Transcripts applies to any transcript of a court proceeding that is subsequently filed with the court and made available to the public via electronic access. The Judicial Conference of the United States has revised the policy to restrict the copying of a transcript for 90 days after delivery to the clerk's office. Accordingly, in accordance with the policy and effective for any transcript filed on or after June 15, 2007 (regardless of when the proceeding took place), it is **ORDERED** as follows:

1. Transcripts of court proceedings may only be filed by the court reporter. Transcripts shall, at the time of the initial filing, be docketed in the court record for that case utilizing a "private" event code which restricts access to the filed transcript to court staff only.

2. Upon the docketing of the transcript as set forth in paragraph 1, the clerk shall prepare and serve on all parties listed as appearances on the transcript a form "Notice Regarding Filing of Transcript and Deadline for Filing Notice of Intent to Request Redaction of Transcript" (Exhibit 1) which shall establish a deadline of 7 calendar days from docketing of the transcript, for the filing of a local form "Notice of Intent to Request Redaction of Transcript" (Exhibit 2). A party is responsible for reviewing and indicating redactions in the testimony of the witnesses that party called and for the party's own statements.

3. Parties timely filing the local form "Notice of Intent to Request Redaction of Transcript" shall, within 21 calendar days of the date the transcript was docketed, unless otherwise ordered by the court, file a "Statement of Personal Data Identifier Redaction Request" ("Statement") which shall indicate, by page and line number, the location of the personal data identifiers for which redaction is being requested. For purposes of this procedure, personal data identifiers shall include: social security numbers, financial account numbers, names of minor children, and dates of birth. Since the "Statement" once filed, will appear as a public document on the docket, the "Statement" should be worded so as not to contain unredacted personal identifiers. A copy of the "Statement" shall be served on the court reporter. Only these personal identifiers may be automatically redacted as provided by paragraph 8 below. Parties seeking to redact other information shall file a motion as required under paragraph 5 below.

4. Parties to the case who are (or represent) persons whose personal data identifier may appear in the transcript and who wish to review the unredacted transcript may either purchase a copy of the transcript from the court reporter or view a copy of the transcript at no charge in any of the clerk's three divisional offices.

5. Any party who filed a "Notice of Intent to Request Redaction of Transcript" during the 7 calendar day period set forth in paragraph 2 above may also file, within the 21 calendar day period set forth in paragraph 3 above, a "Motion for Additional Redactions" to request redaction of information other than personal data identifiers. If appropriate, the motion should be filed in accordance with Local Rule 5005–4 "Sealed Documents." A copy of the motion shall be served on the court reporter.

6. If a "Notice of Intent to Request Redaction of Transcript" is not filed within the initial 7 calendar day deadline set forth in paragraph 2 above and 90 days from the date of filing of the transcript has passed, the unredacted transcript will appear on the docket as a public document available electronically to the public in accordance with existing policies and subject to applicable access fees, unless the court, for good cause related to the Judicial Conference policy, finds that the transcript should not be made remotely available electronically for up to a period of 60 calendar days from the date the unredacted transcript was originally filed by the court reporter.

7. If a "Statement" or "Motion for Additional Redactions" is not filed within the 21 calendar day deadline set forth in paragraphs 3 and 5 above and 90 days from the date of filing of the transcript has passed, the unredacted transcript will appear on the docket as a public document available electronically to the public in accordance with existing policies and subject to applicable access fees, unless the court, for good cause related to the application of the Judicial Conference policy, finds that the transcript should not be made remotely available electronically for up to a period of 60 calendar days from the date the unredacted transcript was originally filed by the court reporter.

8. If a "Notice of Intent to Request Redaction of Transcript" has been filed and subsequently a "Statement" is filed within the 21 calendar day deadline set forth in paragraph 3, the court reporter shall partially redact the personal data identifiers identified in the "Statement" as follows:

- for Social Security numbers, use only the last four digits;
- for financial account numbers, use only the last four digits;
- for names of minor children, use only their initials; and
- for dates of birth, use only the year.

Once a "Statement" is filed, the court reporter has 31 calendar days from the date of the filing of the transcript to file a redacted transcript with an amended certification indicating that the transcript was amended by the redaction of certain personal identifiers at the request of the parties.

9. If a "Motion for Additional Redactions" was filed within the 21 calendar day deadline set forth in paragraph 5 above, or if the court has extended the deadline, the transcript shall remain restricted until the court has ruled upon any such motion and 90 days from the date of filing of the transcript has passed.

10. If a transcript is redacted in accordance with this order, the initially filed unredacted transcript shall be maintained by the clerk as a restricted document, not accessible by parties to the case or the general public. This unredacted transcript shall, if requested, be made available to an appellate court.

11. The policy set forth in this order:

A. Does not affect in any way the obligation of the court reporter to file promptly with the clerk of court the court reporter's original records of a proceeding or the inclusion of a filed transcript with the records of the court pursuant to 28 U.S.C. Section 753.

B. Except for a period of 90 days after delivery of the official transcript, does not affect the obligation of the clerk to make the official transcript included in the court file available for copying by the public without further compensation to the court reporter pursuant to Judicial Conference policy.

C. Is not intended to create a private right of action.

D. Is intended to apply the Judicial Conference policy on privacy and public access to electronic case files to transcripts that are electronically available to the public. It is not intended to change any rules or policies with respect to sealing or redaction of court records for any other purpose.

E. Does not prevent the production of a transcript on an expedited basis for a party, or any other person or entity, that may order such a transcript, subject to whatever court rules or orders are currently imposed to protect sealed materials. Any non-party that orders a transcript on an expedited basis should be alerted to the Judicial Conference policy on privacy and public access to electronic case files by the entity providing the transcript to the party.

[Effective December 1, 2009.]

EXHIBIT 1

UNITED STATES BANKRUPTCY COURT
MIDDLE DISTRICT OF FLORIDA
DIVISION

Case Number:

IN RE:

JOHN S. DOE

Debtor(s)

NOTICE REGARDING FILING OF TRANSCRIPT AND DEADLINE FOR FILING NOTICE OF INTENT TO REQUEST REDACTION OF TRANSCRIPT

Notice is hereby given that an official transcript of a proceeding held on November 15, 2009, has been filed on December 1, 2009, by the court reporter in the above captioned matter.

Under Administrative Order 2009-7, within seven (7) calendar days of the date of service of this notice, the parties shall file with the court a local form "Notice of Intent to Request Redaction of Transcript." Parties timely filing the local form "Notice of Intent to Request Redaction of Transcript" shall, within 21 calendar days of the date the transcript was docketed, unless otherwise ordered by the court, file a "Statement of Personal Data Identifier Redaction Request" which shall indicate, by page and line number, the location of the personal data identifiers for which redaction is being requested. Since the "Statement" once filed, will appear as a public document on the docket, the "Statement" should be worded so as not to contain unredacted personal identifiers.

Parties seeking to review the unredacted transcript filed with the court may either purchase a copy of the transcript from the court reporter or view a copy of the transcript at no charge in any of the clerk's three divisional offices.

If a "Notice of Intent to Request Redaction of Transcript" has not been filed by the deadline indicated above, absent further order of the court, the transcript will be made available on the docket as a publicly accessible document, subject to applicable access charges.

DATED _______________, at _______________, Florida.

LEE ANN BENNETT, Clerk of Court
Sam M. Gibbons United States Courthouse
801 North Florida Avenue, Suite 727
Tampa, Florida 33602

Copies to:

EXHIBIT 2

UNITED STATES BANKRUPTCY COURT
MIDDLE DISTRICT OF FLORIDA
_______________ DIVISION

Case Number:

IN RE:

JOHN S. DOE

_______________ Debtor(s)

NOTICE REGARDING FILING OF TRANSCRIPT AND DEADLINE FOR FILING NOTICE OF INTENT TO REQUEST REDACTION OF TRANSCRIPT

Notice is hereby given that a Statement of Personal Data Identifier Redaction Request and/or a Motion for Additional Redactions with respect to the official transcript of the proceeding held on _______________, in the above referenced case or proceeding will be filed with the court within 21 calendar days from the date the unredacted transcript was filed by the court reporter with the clerk of court.

____
Name

____
Address

____
City, State, Zip Code

____
Appearing on behalf of

DATED _______________, at _______________, Florida.

LEE ANN BENNETT, Clerk of Court
Sam M. Gibbons United States Courthouse
801 North Florida Avenue, Suite 727
Tampa, Florida 33602

Copies to:

ADMINISTRATIVE ORDER FLMB-2013-1. IN RE ORDER REGARDING INTERIM BANKRUPTCY RULE 1007-I

ORDER ADOPTING INTERIM RULE 1007-I AND ADOPTING CONFORMING AMENDMENTS

On October 20, 2008, Congress enacted the *National Guard and Reservists Debt Relief Act of 2008*, which provides a temporary exclusion for certain members of the National Guard and Reservists from the means test in Chapter 7 bankruptcy case. The Act, which now applies through December 18, 2015, is provided for in 11 U.S.C. § 707(2)(D)(ii) of the Bankruptcy Code. To clarify the Act's effect, the Executive Committee of the Judicial Conference of the United States adopted Interim Rule 1007-I to set forth the time required to comply with the means test after the temporary exclusion expires.

On December 12, 2012, Congress amended Bankruptcy Rule 1007 to clarify an inconsistency in the time limit to file a list of creditors in an involuntary bankruptcy. Bankruptcy Rule 1007(c) affects Interim Rule 7001-I and those parties affected by the *National Guard and Reservists Debt Relief Act* because it fixes the time required to file schedules, statements, and other documents with the Court, which become effective after the temporary exclusion of the Act expires. To provide further guidance to those parties affected by *National Guard and Reservists Debt Relief Act*, it is:

ORDERED:

Interim Bankruptcy Rule 1007-I is adopted, effective December 12, 2012, and shall remain in effect until further order of this Court. A copy of the current Interim Rule 1007-1 is attached as Exhibit A.

[Effective January 15, 2013.]

Exhibit "A"

Interim Rule 1007-I.[1] Lists, Schedules, Statements, and Other Documents; Time Limits; Expiration of Temporary Means Testing Exclusion[2]

* * * * *

(b) Schedules, Statements, and Other Documents Required.

* * * * *

(4) *Unless either*: (A) § 707(b)(2)(D)(i) applies, or (B) § 707(b)(2)(D)(ii) applies and the exclusion from means testing granted therein extends beyond the period specified by Rule 1017(e), an individual debtor in a chapter 7 case shall file a statement of current monthly income prepared as prescribed by the appropriate Official Form, and, if the current monthly income exceeds the median family income for the applicable state and household size, the information, including calculations, required by § 707(b), prepared as prescribed by the appropriate Official Form.

* * * * *

(c) Time Limits. In a voluntary case, the schedules, statements, and other documents required by subdivision (b)(1), (4), (5), and (6) shall be filed with the petition or within 14 days thereafter, except as otherwise provided in subdivisions (d), (e), (f), (h), and (n) of this rule. In an involuntary case, the list in subdivision (a)(2), and the schedules, statements, and other documents required by subdivision (b)(1) shall be filed by the debtor within 14 days of the entry of the order for relief. In a voluntary case, the documents required by paragraphs (A), (C), and (D) of subdivision (b)(3) shall be filed with the petition. Unless the court orders otherwise, a debtor who has filed a statement under subdivision (b)(3)(B), shall file the documents required by subdivision (b)(3)(A) within 14 days of the order for relief. In a chapter 7 case, the debtor shall file the statement required by subdivision (b)(7) within 45 days after the first date set for the meeting of creditors under § 341 of the Code, and in a chapter 11 or 13 case no later than the date when the last payment was made by the debtor as required by the plan or the filing of a motion for a discharge under § 1141(d)(5)(B) or § 1328(b) of the Code. The court may, at any time and in its discretion, enlarge the time to file the statement required by subdivision (b)(7). The debtor shall file the statement required by subdivision (b)(8) no earlier than the date of the last payment made under the plan or the date of the filing of a motion for a discharge under §§ 1141(d)(5)(B), 1228(b), or 1328(b) of the Code. Lists, schedules, statements, and other documents filed prior to the conversion of a case to another chapter shall be deemed filed in the converted case unless the court directs otherwise. Except as provided in § 1116(3), any extension of time to file schedules, statements, and other documents required under this rule may be granted only on motion for cause shown and on notice to the United States trustee, any committee elected under § 705 or appointed under § 1102 of the Code, trustee, examiner, or other party as the court may direct. Notice of an extension shall be given to the United States trustee and to any committee, trustee, or other party as the court may direct.

* * * * *

(n) Time Limits for, and Notice to, Debtors Temporarily Excluded from Means Testing.

(1) An individual debtor who is temporarily excluded from means testing pursuant to § 707(b)(2)(D)(ii) of the Code shall file any statement and calculations required by subdivision (b)(4) no later than 14 days after the expiration of the temporary exclusion if the expiration occurs within the time specified by Rule 1017(e) for filing a motion pursuant to § 707(b)(2).

(2) If the temporary exclusion from means testing under § 707(b)(2)(D)(ii) terminates due to the circumstances specified in subdivision (n)(1), and if the debtor has not previously filed a statement and calculations required by subdivision (b)(4), the clerk shall promptly notify the debtor that the required statement and calculations must be filed within the time specified in subdivision (n)(1).

1 Interim Rule 1007–I was adopted by the bankruptcy courts to implement the National Guard and Reservists Debt Relief Act of 2008, Public Law No: 110–438. The Act, which provides a temporary exclusion from the application of the means test for certain members of the National Guard and reserve components of the Armed Forces, applies to bankruptcy cases commenced in the three-year period beginning December 19, 2008.

2 Incorporates time amendments to Rule 1007 which took effect on December 1, 2009.

Committee Note

This rule is amended to take account of the enactment of the National Guard and Reservists Debt Relief Act of 2008, which amended § 707(b)(2)(D) of the Code to provide a temporary exclusion from the application of the means test for certain members of the National Guard and reserve components of the Armed Forces. This exclusion applies to qualifying debtors while they remain on active duty or are performing a homeland defense activity, and for a period of 540 days thereafter. For some debtors initially covered by the exclusion, the protection from means testing will expire while their chapter 7 cases are pending, and at a point when a timely motion to dismiss under § 707(b)(2) can still be filed. Under the amended rule, these debtors are required to file the statement and calculations required by subdivision (b)(4) no later than 14 days after the expiration of their exclusion.

Subdivisions (b)(4) and (c) are amended to relieve debtors qualifying for an exclusion under § 707(b)(2)(D)(ii) from the obligation to file a statement of current monthly income and required calculations within the time period specified in subdivision (c).

Subdivision (n)(1) is added to specify the time for filing of the information required by subdivision (b)(4) by a debtor who initially qualifies for the means test exclusion under § 707(b)(2)(D)(ii), but whose exclusion expires during the time that a motion to dismiss under § 707(b)(2) may still be made under Rule 1017(e). If, upon the expiration of the temporary exclusion, a debtor has not already filed the required statement and calculations, subdivision (n)(2) directs the clerk to provide prompt notice to the debtor of the time for filing as set forth in subdivision (n)(1).

IN RE: STANDING ORDER OF REFERENCE, CASES ARISING UNDER TITLE 11, UNITED STATES CODE [DISTRICT COURT ORDER][1]

Pursuant to 28 U.S.C. Section 157(a) any or all cases under title 11 and any or all proceedings arising under title 11 or arising in or related to a case under title 11 are referred to the bankruptcy judges for this district.

If a bankruptcy judge or district judge determines that entry of a final order or judgment by a bankruptcy judge would not be consistent with Article III of the United States Constitution in a particular proceeding referred under this order and determined to be a core matter, the bankruptcy judge shall, unless otherwise ordered by the district court, hear the proceeding and submit proposed findings of fact and conclusions of law to the district court made in compliance with Fed. R. Civ. P. 52(a)(1) in the form of findings and conclusions stated on the record or in an opinion or memorandum of decision.

The district court may treat any order of the bankruptcy court as proposed findings of fact and conclusions of law in the event the district court concludes that the bankruptcy judge could not have entered a final order or judgment consistent with Article III of the United States Constitution.

[Effective February 2, 2012.]

[1] This Order amends and supersedes the Standing Order of Reference entered by the Hon. W. Terrell Hodges on July 11, 1984, 84–MISC–152.

PERMISSIVE USE OF NEGATIVE NOTICE

The Court permits and encourages service of the following papers using negative notice as permitted by Local Rule 2002–4. The negative notice legend shall provide for a 21–day objection period unless stated otherwise below.

Chapter 7

Motion to Approve Agreements Relating to Relief from Stay, Prohibiting or Conditioning the Use, Sale or Lease of Property, Providing Adequate Protection, Use of Cash Collateral and Obtaining Credit pursuant to Fed. R. Bankr. P. 4001(d) **(14–day notice)**

Motion for Order Confirming that the Automatic Stay is Terminated (362(c) and (j))

Motion for Relief from Stay

Application/Motion to Pay

Application for Payment of Administrative Expenses (Interim)

Motion/Notice of Intent to Abandon Property filed by Trustee (**14–day notice,** pursuant to Fed. R. Bankr. P. 6007)

Motion to Approve Compromise or Settlement

Motion to Assume or Reject Lease/Executory Contract

Motion by Chapter 7 Trustee to Authorize Interim Distribution to Creditors or to Pay Administrative Expenses

Motion to Avoid Lien on Exempt Property

Motion to Compel Abandonment

Motion to Confirm Priority of Modified Mortgage

Motion to Determine Property is of Consequential Value to Estate filed by Trustee (362(h)(2))

Motion to Determine Secured Status/Strip Lien on Real Property **(30–day notice required)**

Motion to Determine Secured Status/Value Property **(30–day notice required)**

Motion to Dismiss for Failure to Attend 341 Meeting filed by Trustee

Motion Objecting to Discharge pursuant to Rule 4004(a)

Motion to Reclassify Claims

Motion to Redeem

Motion/Notice to Sell or Lease Property (does not apply to sales free and clear of interests)

Motion for Turnover **(30–day notice required)**

Objection to Claim **(30–day notice required)**

Objection to Exemptions (However, in Tampa, Orlando, and Ft. Myers the Court will enter an order sustaining an objection that relates **solely** to the value of personal property claimed exempt without a hearing.)

Chapter 11

Application for Final Compensation (must be accompanied by the Chapter 11 Fee Application Cover Page available on the Court's website, www.flmb.uscourts.gov/forms).

Application for Interim Compensation (must be accompanied by the Chapter 11 Fee Application Cover Page available on the Court's website, www.flmb.uscourts.gov/forms).

Application/Motion to Pay

Motion to Administratively Close Individual Chapter 11 Case

Motion to Approve Agreements Relating to Relief from Stay, Prohibiting or Conditioning the Use, Sale or Lease of Property, Providing Adequate

Protection, Use of Cash Collateral and Obtaining Credit pursuant to Fed. R. Bankr. P. 4001(d) **(14–day notice)**

Motion to Approve Compromise or Settlement

Motion to Avoid Lien on Exempt Property

Motion to Determine Secured Status/Strip Lien on Real Property **(30–day notice required)**

Motion to Determine Secured Status /Value Property **(30–day notice required)**

Motion for Turnover **(30–day notice required)**

Objection to Claim **(30–day notice required)**

Chapter 12 and Chapter 13

Motion to Approve Agreements Relating to Relief from Stay, Prohibiting or Conditioning the Use, Sale or Lease of Property, Providing Adequate Protection, Use of Cash Collateral and Obtaining Credit pursuant to Fed. R. Bankr. P. 4001(d) **(14–day notice)**

Motion for Order Confirming that the Automatic Stay is Terminated (362(c) and (j))

Motion for Relief from Co–Debtor Stay **(14–day notice)**

Motion for Relief from Stay as to the Debtor

Application for Compensation filed by Chapter 7 Trustee's Attorney

Application for Quantum Meruit Compensation filed by Chapter 7 Trustee

Application/Motion to Pay

Motion to Approve Compromise or Settlement

Motion to Assume or Reject Lease/Executory Contract

Motion to Avoid Lien on Exempt Property

Motion to Confirm Priority of Modified Mortgage

Motion to Declare Debtor Current and Reinstated on Secured Claim

Motion to Determine Secured Status/Strip Lien on Real Property **(30–day notice required)**

Motion to Determine Secured Status /Value Property **(30–day notice required)**

Motion to Dismiss by Trustee

Motion to Modify Confirmed Plan (Except in Tampa and Ft. Myers)

Motion to Modify Mortgage

Motion Objecting to Discharge pursuant to Rule 4004(a)

Motion to Offset Funds Filed by Trustee

Motion to Sell or Lease Property (does not apply to sales free and clear of interests)

Motion for Turnover **(30–day notice required)**

Objection to Claim **(30–day notice required)**

[Amended effective July 23, 2012; August 28, 2012; March 25, 2013; August 1, 2013; September 5, 2013; October 15, 2013; July 1, 2014.]

ADMINISTRATIVE ORDER FLMB–2013–4. IN RE ADMINISTRATIVE ORDER REGARDING DEPOSIT AND INVESTMENT OF REGISTRY FUNDS [SUPERSEDED BY ADMINISTRATIVE ORDER FLMB–2016–2]

ADMINISTRATIVE ORDER FLMB–2014–10. IN RE ADMINISTRATIVE ORDER PRESCRIBING PROCEDURES FOR ADVERSARY PROCEEDINGS

This Administrative Order establishes uniform procedures for adversary proceedings filed in this district after February 1, 2015. Accordingly, it is

ORDERED:

1. **Service of Summons, Complaint, and Administrative Order.** Plaintiff shall serve the summons issued by the Clerk, a copy of this Administrative Order Prescribing Procedures for Adversary Proceedings, and the complaint initiating an adversary proceeding within seven days after the summons is issued as required by Fed. R. Bankr. P. 7004(e). If the initial summons and accompanying papers are not timely served, the Plaintiff promptly shall request and serve a new summons together with the Complaint and a copy of this Administrative Order. Parties must effect service on all defendants no later than 28 days after the complaint was filed, notwithstanding Fed. R. Civ. P. 4(m). If additional parties are added later, the plaintiff shall serve a copy of this order on each additional party within seven days of the date the additional party is added.

2. **Proof of Service.** Plaintiff shall promptly file a proof of service indicating service of each summons, the complaint, and this Administrative Order on each defendant.

3. **Failure to Effect Service.** If plaintiff does not complete timely and effective service of the summons and complaint, the Court may, without further notice or hearing, dismiss the adversary proceeding for lack of prosecution.

4. **Defaults.** Plaintiff shall seek entry of a Clerk's default and move for a judgment by default no later than 60 days after the complaint is filed if a defendant has not filed a timely response.

5. **Extensions of Time.** Plaintiff must file any motion for an extension of time to effect service or to apply for the entry of default no later than 60 days after the complaint is filed and must demonstrate good cause for the requested extension.

6. **Motions.** The negative notice procedures set forth in Local Rule 2002–4 shall apply to all motions other than motions for withdrawal of the reference that are governed by Local Rule 5011–1. The response time shall be 14 days, except for summary judgment motions for which the response time shall be 21 days. Parties may file a reply, if desired, no later than seven days after a response is filed.

a. *Format.* All motions, responses, and replies shall comply with the Court's Style Guide, be double spaced, and where appropriate, include a legal memorandum containing argument and citations of authorities. Absent leave of Court, motions and supporting memoranda shall not exceed ten pages in length.

b. *Emergency Motions.* The Court will consider emergency motions at any time in its discretion. Emergency motions shall comply with Local Rule 9004–2(d) and shall be filed using the Emergency Filings/Matters/Motions link on the Court's website, www.flmb.uscourts.gov/procedures.

c. *Summary Judgment.* Parties shall file motions for summary judgment no later than 60 days prior to trial. The Court may or may not set a hearing on the motion for summary judgment. The trial will proceed as scheduled even if a motion for summary judgment is pending, absent order of the Court.

7. **Motions to Determine Whether Case is Core.** Not later than the date set for filing a response to the complaint, any party objecting to the entry of final orders or judgments by the Bankruptcy Court on any issue in the adversary proceeding shall file a motion requesting that the Court determine whether the proceeding is a core proceeding or otherwise subject to the entry of final orders or judgments by this Court. Failure of any party to file a motion on or before the deadline set forth in this paragraph shall be deemed consent by such party to the Bankruptcy Court entering all appropriate final orders and judgments in the proceeding subject to review under 28 U.S.C. § 158.

8. Meeting of Parties. At least 14 days prior to the initial status or pretrial conference, attorneys for represented parties or unrepresented parties shall meet (the "Meeting of Parties") to discuss:

a. The claims and defenses;

b. The possibility of settlement;

c. The initial disclosures required in Paragraph 10 below; and

d. A discovery plan as required by Fed. R. Civ. P. 26(f).

9. Commencement of Discovery. Discovery may not commence until the conclusion of the Meeting of Parties, absent leave of Court.

10. Initial Disclosures. Pursuant to Fed. R. Civ. P. 26(f), at or prior to the Meeting of Parties, and without any formal discovery requests, each party shall:

a. Identify in writing each person with discoverable information relevant to the disputed facts;

b. Provide copies of or a written description by category and location of all documents that are relevant to the disputed facts;

c. Formulate a joint discovery plan, if possible; and

d. Provide a written computation of any damages claimed.

11. Pretrial or Status Conference. The Court will conduct a status or pretrial conference at any time after a responsive pleading is filed but, in any event, no later than approximately 90 days after the Complaint is filed. Parties may not introduce testimony or documentary evidence at the status conference. The Court, however, will consider relevant undisputed facts, affidavits offered without objection from the opposing parties, judicial notice items, and admissions made during the status conference by parties either directly or through counsel.

12. Pretrial Disclosures and Exhibits.

a. *Witness List and Use of Depositions.* Fed. R. Civ. P. 26(a)(3) shall govern pretrial disclosures regarding witnesses and use of depositions. Parties shall file and exchange names, telephone numbers, and addresses for witnesses, any designations of depositions at least 28 days before trial. Objections to the use of depositions shall be filed within 14 days of the disclosure. Parties shall confer on any factual or evidentiary stipulations prior to trial.

b. *Exhibits.* Parties shall prepare exhibits in compliance with Local Rule 9070–1 and Administrative Order 2014–6 addressing Electronically Stored Exhibits and shall exchange exhibits no later than seven days before the date set for trial. Unless written objection to the admissibility of any exhibit is filed no later than the close of business on the second day before trial, any objection to admissibility (other than under Fed. R. Evid. 402 and 403) shall be deemed waived.

c. *Self–Authentication of Records of Regularly Conducted Activity.* If a party intends to rely upon the self-authentication procedures of Fed. R. Evid. 902(11) or (12) with respect to the introduction into evidence of records of regularly conducted activities pursuant to Fed. R. Evid. 803(6), the party shall file with the Court and serve on other parties the written declaration required by Fed. R. Evid. 902(11) or (12) and a copy of all records sought to be admitted at least 28 days before trial.

13. Expert Witness Testimony. As a condition of using expert testimony at trial, parties must comply with Fed. R. Civ. P. 26(a)(2) no later than 28 days before trial.

14. Stipulations. All stipulations of the parties shall be made in writing, signed, and promptly filed with the Court.

15. Supplementation of Disclosures. Parties are under a duty to supplement or correct their Initial Disclosures and their Pretrial Disclosures in accordance with Fed. R. Civ. P. 26(e).

16. Discovery Deadline. Parties shall complete discovery no later than seven days before the trial date except that the parties may complete previously scheduled depositions up to the trial date.

17. Discovery Disputes. If a discovery dispute occurs, the parties shall first, as required by Fed. R. Bankr. P. 7037(a)(1), confer in good faith to attempt to resolve the issues. If unsuccessful, any party may request a telephone conference with the Court so that the Court may render an informal, preliminary ruling on the discovery dispute, without prejudice to the right of any party to file a formal motion.

18. Sanctions. Failure to comply with all requirements of this Administrative Order may result in the imposition of sanctions that could include the striking of a party's pleading or the denial of the right to introduce evidence or witness testimony.

19. Settlements. Pursuant to Local Rule 9019–1, parties immediately shall notify the Court of any settlement and promptly file a motion to approve the compromise in the Debtor's main case, not in the adversary proceeding, with one exception. If the adversary proceeding only asserts claims under 11 U.S.C. Section 523, a motion to approve the compromise is not necessary but, if the parties desire, they may seek approval of the settlement by filing a motion in the adversary proceeding.

[Amended effective February 1, 2015.]

ADMINISTRATIVE ORDER FLMB–2015–1. IN RE ADMINISTRATIVE ORDER PRESCRIBING PROCEDURES FOR MORTGAGE MODIFICATION MEDIATION

The Bankruptcy Court for the Middle District of Florida has unified its mortgage modification mediation ("MMM") procedures throughout the district. Effective August 15, 2014, all parties participating in mortgage modification mediation process in the Middle District of Florida shall comply with these procedures. Accordingly, it is

ORDERED:

1. MMM is available in all cases and for any type of real property.

2. A motion seeking MMM shall include, **on the first page of the motion,** a complete property address of the relevant property and the last four digits of the mortgage loan number. If not included, the motion will be abated until an amended motion containing the required information is filed.

3. No negative notice is required for a motion seeking MMM but lenders may seek reconsideration for cause within 14 days of entry of an order directing MMM.

4. A motion seeking MMM shall be filed within 90 days of the filing or conversion of the case. The Court will prepare and enter an order directing MMM on timely filed motions. If not timely filed, the Court will set a hearing and will grant the request only if good cause is demonstrated for the delay.

5. The parties will conclude the MMM process within 150 days of the filing or conversion of the case, unless that time is enlarged by written consent on the portal, by stipulation of the parties, or by Court order.

6. Parties shall have 14 days after the entry of the order directing MMM to jointly select a mediator qualified pursuant to Administrative Order FLMB–2013–3 or to object to the mediator selection process. If the parties cannot agree on a mediator, the Debtor will select a mediator, and the lender may file an objection within 7 days. If a timely objection to a mediator is filed, the Chapter 12 or 13 Trustee or the Clerk in a Chapter 7 or 11 case will select the mediator.

7. Both Debtor and Lender each shall pay $250 directly to the mediator within seven days of the designation of the mediator. Parties also shall equally pay the Mediator for any additional hourly fees incurred from MMM conferences that extend beyond two, one-hour sessions.

8. Parties must use the secure portal (the "Portal") (e.g. https://www.dclmwp.com/Home) for submission of documents to initiate the MMM and follow guidelines included in the Court's order directing MMM entered in each individual case.

9. The parties may communicate outside the Portal orally, but all written communication shall occur through the Portal.

10. Parties may submit a proposed order simultaneously with a motion seeking approval *of a temporary* MMM agreement without need of negative notice or hearing.

11. Parties may use negative notice when filing a motion seeking approval of a *permanent* MMM agreement.

12. An order approving a permanent MMM agreement (i) shall be in a format that can be recorded in the public records of the county where the relevant property is located, and (ii) should be recorded by the Debtor within 90 days of the entry of the order, unless the parties agree otherwise.

13. Debtors seeking MMM must provide adequate protection to the lenders. For homestead properties, the Debtor must pay the lesser of (1) 31% of their gross disposable income (after deducting homeowner association fees), or (2) the normal monthly contractual mortgage payment. For non-homestead income producing property, the Debtor shall pay 75% of the gross rental income generated by the property. In Chapter 12 and 13 cases, the Debtor shall make the adequate protection payments to the Chapter 12 or 13 Trustee who shall hold the funds pending either further order of the Court or a joint stipulation of the parties. In all other chapters, the Debtor shall make the trial payments directly to the lender as agreed between the parties and without requiring Court approval or any modification of the automatic stay.

14. Unless the parties have agreed to the contrary, MMM payments made during the MMM process will be applied in accordance with the applicable loan documents and non-bankruptcy law.

15. When the MMM is concluded, if all payments provided by a Chapter 12 or Chapter 13 bankruptcy plan have not been distributed to the lender then the balance held by the trustee shall be distributed:

A. If MMM is successful, as specifically agreed to by the parties in the agreement reached by the parties (which may include the lender's decision to decline receipt of additional funds);

B. If MMM is *not* successful, then the balance:

(i) shall be distributed to the lender to be applied by the lender in accordance with the applicable loan documents and non-bankruptcy law, or

(ii) the lender may affirmatively reject the balance of the payments and the trustee shall distribute payments as provided by the Chapter 13 Plan or Confirmation Order.

16. In Chapter 12 and 13 cases, the Court may confirm a plan of reorganization subject to pending MMM.

17. The MMM procedures do not affect amounts of allowed attorney fees for debtor and creditor attorneys participating in the MMM program. Divisional practices and limitations on such fees still control.

[Effective March 9, 2015.]

ADMINISTRATIVE ORDER FLMB-2015-3. IN RE ADMINISTRATIVE ORDER PRESCRIBING PROCEDURES FOR FILING PAPERS UNDER SEAL

ADMINISTRATIVE ORDER PRESCRIBING PROCEDURES FOR FILING PAPERS UNDER SEAL

Effective June 15, 2015, parties seeking to file papers under seal in the Middle District of Florida shall comply with the following procedures. Accordingly, it is

ORDERED:

1. Motion to File Paper Under Seal. If a party seeks to file a paper under seal, the party shall electronically file via CM/ECF a motion for authority to file the paper under seal ("Motion to Seal") using the "Motion to Seal" docket event and shall submit a proposed order using the order submission procedures posted on the Court's website. The moving party shall not file the paper requested to be placed under seal until the order granting the Motion to Seal is entered.

2. Papers Filed Under Seal Pursuant to Court Order Shall be Filed Electronically. If the Motion to Seal is granted, unless otherwise specifically directed otherwise by the Court, the paper permitted to be filed under seal shall be filed in a portable document format (PDF) via CM/ECF using the "Sealed Document" docket event.

3. Viewing Restrictions. The Clerk shall restrict CM/ECF access to the Motion to Seal, the order granting or denying the Motion to Seal, and any papers filed under seal to the judge assigned to the case or adversary proceeding until the Court lifts the viewing restriction.

[Dated: May 19, 2015.]

ADMINISTRATIVE ORDER FLMB–2015–5. AMENDED ADMINISTRATIVE ORDER PRESCRIBING PROCEDURES FOR RESIDENTIAL MORTGAGE FORECLOSURE MEDIATORS CERTIFICATION *

The Bankruptcy Court for the Middle District of Florida is a national leader in using mediation to assist parties modify residential mortgages. The Court perceives the need to expand the panel of qualified mediators. Accordingly, it is

ORDERED:

1. Beginning February 1, 2013, the Clerk of Court shall maintain a list of mediators in each Division of this Court who are certified to mediate modifications of residential mortgages involved in foreclosure actions ("Mortgage Mediator").

2. To be certified by the Court as a Mortgage Mediator, the Mortgage Mediator must:

A. Be a Florida Supreme Court Certified Circuit Court Mediator;

B. Have completed at least 8 hours of training approved by the Chief Bankruptcy Judge or her designee that focuses on modifying residential mortgages in bankruptcy proceedings; and

C. Agree to accept two mediation assignments per year without compensation; and

D. Submit an application to the Clerk of Court together with appropriate proof of compliance with Section 2(A, B & C).

[Dated: July 6, 2015.]

*__Publisher's Note:__ *See* Memorandum, dated April 13, 2014, re: Uniform State–Wide Procedures on mediating mortgage modifications, set forth in this publication following the local forms of the United States Bankruptcy Court for the Northern District of Florida, *ante*.

ADMINISTRATIVE ORDER FLMB–2015–6. IN RE AMENDED ADMINISTRATIVE ORDER ON THE USE OF ELECTRONICALLY STORED EXHIBITS IN EVIDENTIARY HEARINGS AND TRIALS

AMENDED ADMINISTRATIVE ORDER SUPPLEMENTING LOCAL RULE 9070–1 TO PROVIDE FOR THE SUBMISSION OF EXHIBITS IN ELECTRONICALLY STORED FORMAT

Many of the evidentiary hearings and trials conducted in this Court involve the use of voluminous and burdensome paper exhibits. The parties, the Court, and court staff spend considerable time handling paper exhibits during the hearing or trial and in post-trial proceedings. To alleviate this burden, this Administrative Order provides procedures for the use of electronically stored exhibits in evidentiary hearings and trials. This Administrative Order incorporates the existing requirements of Local Rule 9070–1 with respect to paper exhibits and supplements those requirements for the use of electronically stored exhibits.

Accordingly, it is **ORDERED:**

Effective **August 3, 2015**, parties in evidentiary hearings and trials shall follow these procedures in the use of exhibits:

(a) General Provisions.

(1) *Submission of Exhibits in Electronic or Paper Format.* If all parties in an adversary proceeding or contested matter are represented by counsel, unless the Court orders otherwise, exhibits shall be exchanged and submitted to the Court in electronic format. Electronically stored exhibits shall not be used in adversary proceedings or contested matters in which any of the parties are pro se.

(2) *Redaction of Personal Data Identifiers.* In compliance with Local Rule 1001–3, the following personal data identifiers shall be redacted from all exhibits submitted to the Court whether in paper or electronic format: Social Security numbers, names of minor children, dates of birth, and financial account numbers other than the last four digits of the account number.

(3) *Numbering Exhibits and Exhibit Cover Sheet.* Exhibits, whether submitted in paper or electronic format, shall be numbered commencing with Arabic numeral 1. Each exhibit shall be preceded by an 8 1/2 × 11–inch Exhibit Cover Sheet (Appendix B to Local Rule 9070–1).

(4) *Exhibit List.* Each party shall prepare a separate Exhibit List in the form attached as Appendix A to Local Rule 9070–1. The Exhibit List shall list each exhibit in numerical order and include the following: case caption, identity of the party submitting the exhibits (*e.g.*, plaintiff, defendant, debtor, creditor, etc.), and columns with the following headings: "Exhibit Number," "Document Description," "Date Identified," "Date Admitted," and "With or Without Objection." No markings should be made in the "Date Identified" and "Date Admitted" columns, which shall be used by the courtroom deputy to record the exhibits that are identified and offered into evidence and those that are received into evidence. Each party shall provide two copies of the Exhibit List to the courtroom deputy before the start of the evidentiary hearing or trial. After the conclusion of the evidentiary hearing or trial, the courtroom deputy will file a completed Exhibit List on the case or adversary proceeding docket.

(b) Procedure for Use of Electronically Stored Exhibits.

(1) *Format of Exhibits.* Each exhibit, together with the Exhibit Cover sheet, shall be electronically stored in an individual Portable Document Format (PDF) file. Each PDF file shall have a unique identification name and number (*e.g.*, "Debtor's Exhibit 1"). To facilitate the filing of exhibits via CM/ECF, the individual PDF files should be contained in a single folder.

(2) *CM/ECF Electronic Exhibit Upload.* Parties shall file their Exhibit List and all electronic exhibits using the CM/ECF Electronically Stored Exhibit Upload by the time set forth in the Administrative Order Prescribing Procedures for Adversary Proceedings, FLMB–2014–10, for the exchange of exhibits. The filing of the Exhibit List and exhibits via CM/ECF Electronically Stored Exhibit Upload shall effectuate a party's delivery of exhibits to opposing part[ies]. Instructions on CM/ECF Electronically Stored Exhibit Upload are located on the Court's website at http://www.flmb.uscourts.gov/procedures/electronicexhibitupload.pdf.

(3) *Use of Electronically Stored Exhibits in Court.* The Electronically Stored Exhibits filed via CM/ECF Electronic Exhibit Upload are the official exhibits for purposes of the evidentiary hearing or trial. However, a party using exhibits during the examination of a witness shall, at the commencement of the examination, provide paper copies of the exhibits to be used during the examination to the Court, the witness, and other parties. Paper exhibits that are not removed from the courtroom following their use will be disposed of by the courtroom deputy.

(4) *Additional Exhibits.* In the event that additional exhibits that were not uploaded via CM/ECF Electronic Exhibit Upload are offered or introduced into evidence during the course of the evidentiary hearing or trial, a complete set of such additional exhibits shall be filed via CM/ECF Electronic Exhibit Upload with the title "[Party's Name]'s Additional Exhibits" within seven days following the conclusion of the evidentiary hearing or trial.

(c) Procedure for Use of Exhibits Submitted In Paper Format.

(1) *Submitting Exhibits to the Court.* At the commencement of an evidentiary hearing or trial, each party shall deliver to the courtroom deputy two copies of the Exhibit List and the exhibits to be introduced into evidence in paper format. Original exhibits shall not be stapled or permanently bound. Additional copies of the exhibits, which may be stapled or placed in binders or folders, shall be provided for use by witnesses, to opposing counsel, and the judge. Parties should confirm the preferred procedure for preparing exhibit binders with the assigned judge's chambers. Any exhibits introduced at an evidentiary hearing or trial that have not been pre-marked shall be tendered to and marked by the courtroom deputy as they are presented in evidence.

(2) *Large Items or Exhibits Other than Paper Documents.* Objects other than paper documents to be introduced into evidence shall be photographed, accompanied by an Exhibit Cover Sheet, and listed on the Exhibit List. Paper documents larger than 8 1/2 × 11 inches shall be listed on the Exhibit List and accompanied by a reduced 8 1/2 × 11–inch copy. Counsel shall attach Exhibit Cover Sheets to both the original physical exhibit and the photograph or reduced copy of the exhibit ("substitutes"), using the same exhibit number for both the original exhibits and the corresponding substitute. Unless the Court orders otherwise, at the conclusion of the trial or hearing at which the exhibits are offered, if the Clerk has custody of substitutes, the Clerk will return the corresponding original exhibits to counsel. If an appeal is taken, only the substitutes will be included in the record on appeal.

(3) *Disposal of Paper Exhibits.* The Clerk, with or without notice, may dispose of any unclaimed paper exhibits unless the Clerk is notified by a party that it intends to reclaim that party's exhibits within 30 days after the later of the entry of an order or judgment concluding the matter or proceeding, the entry of an order determining any post-judgment motions if no appeal is pending, or

if a notice of appeal has been filed, the filing of the mandate. Parties shall bear any costs associated with reclaiming exhibits.

[Effective July 23, 2015.]

ADMINISTRATIVE ORDER FLMB-2016-1. IN RE AMENDED ADMINISTRATIVE ORDER PRESCRIBING PROCEDURES FOR CHAPTER 13 CASES [SUPERSEDED BY ADMINISTRATIVE ORDER FLMB-2016-2]

ADMINISTRATIVE ORDER FLMB-2016-2. IN RE AMENDED ADMINISTRATIVE ORDER PRESCRIBING PROCEDURES FOR CHAPTER 13 CASES [SUPERSEDED BY ADMINISTRATIVE ORDER FLMB-2016-3]

ADMINISTRATIVE ORDER FLMB-2016-3. IN RE: ADMINISTRATIVE ORDER PRESCRIBING PROCEDURES FOR CHAPTER 13 CASES

THIRD AMENDED ADMINISTRATIVE ORDER PRESCRIBING PROCEDURES FOR CHAPTER 13 CASES

This Third Amended Administrative Order establishes uniform procedures for all Chapter 13 cases filed in this District on or after September 6, 2016. Accordingly, it is

ORDERED:

Debtor's failure to timely make payments to the Chapter 13 Trustee (the "Trustee") or to comply with any of the other requirements of this Order may result in dismissal or conversion of the case.

1. **Additional Information Required to Be Filed with the Court.** No later than 14 days from the petition date, Debtor shall file with the Court the lists, statements, and schedules required by Rule 1007.

2. **Service of this Administrative Order to Debtor.** Debtor's attorney or, if Debtor has no attorney, the Trustee shall provide a copy of this Administrative Order to Debtor within seven days of the petition date.

3. **Chapter 13 Plan.** No later than 14 days from the petition date or the date the case converts to Chapter 13, Debtor shall file a Chapter 13 plan (the "Plan") using the form Model Chapter 13 Plan available on the Trustee's and the Court's website. Any modifications to the Model Chapter 13 Plan shall be included in the "Additional Provisions" section of the Plan. Plans that are filed with the petition will be served on creditors by the Clerk; if the Plan is not filed with the petition, Debtor shall serve a copy of the Plan upon all parties in interest and promptly file a proof of service.

4. **Plan Payments.** Payments under the Plan shall be made through the Trustee's office and shall include *all* payments to secured creditors that will come due after filing the petition (and will serve as adequate protection to such creditors) as follows:

a. For claims secured by real or personal property that are valued in the Plan, the monthly Plan payment shall include adequate protection payments based upon the proposed value of the collateral with interest.

b. For claims secured by mortgages for which the Plan proposes mortgage modification mediation ("MMM"), unless otherwise ordered by the Court, the monthly Plan payment shall include:

i. For *homestead* properties, until the MMM is concluded, the lesser of:

A. 31% of gross monthly income of Debtor and non-filing spouse, if any (after deducting homeowner association fees), or

B. The normal monthly contractual mortgage payment.

ii. For *non-homestead,* income-producing property, until the MMM is concluded, 75% of the gross rental income generated from the property.

c. If Debtor is successful in obtaining a mortgage modification at any time during the case, payments on the modified mortgage shall be paid through the Plan.

d. If the MMM does not result in a modified mortgage, then within 14 days of the filing of the mediator's final report, Debtor shall file an amended or modified Plan that proposes treatment of the mortgage claim and the appropriate payment, if any.

e. For claims secured by mortgages for which the Plan proposes to cure prepetition arrearages, the Plan payment shall include the regular postpetition contractual payment and the total arrearages paid in monthly installments over the term of the Plan.

f. The Plan payment need not include postpetition payments on claims secured by property to be surrendered in the Plan or by junior liens on Debtor's principal residence that Debtor intends to value and to strip.

g. The Plan may provide for Debtor to make postpetition payments directly to secured creditors or lessors only on claims that are not in default, for which no arrearages are being cured through the Plan, and that the Plan does not modify. Debtor shall make direct payments via automatic debit/draft from a bank account and provide documentation to the Trustee upon request. The establishment of an automatic/debit draft at Debtor's request is not a violation of the automatic stay. IF THE PLAN PROVIDES FOR DEBTOR TO MAKE DIRECT PAYMENTS TO A SECURED CREDITOR OR LESSOR, THE AUTOMATIC STAY IS TERMINATED, *IN REM*, AS TO THAT CREDITOR.

5. Payments to Trustee. Debtor, not later than 30 days after the petition date, shall make Plan payments to the Trustee as directed in the **Notice of Chapter 13 Bankruptcy Case, Meeting of Creditors, and Deadlines**, and on the same day of each succeeding month. **If the Trustee does not receive payment when due, the Trustee may seek dismissal of the case.** All payments must be made to the Trustee by approved electronic transfer, cashier's check, money order, or employee wage deduction. Each payment shall include Debtor's name, legibly printed, and the case number. The Trustee is authorized to pay from these funds any fees and charges assessed against the estate by law as authorized by § 1326(b) and to collect from all receipts the Trustee's fee authorized by 28 U.S.C. § 586 ("Trustee's commission"). The Trustee's commission shall be earned upon receipt of each payment from the Debtor and may be distributed to the Trustee upon receipt of the payment. The Trustee shall hold the remaining funds pending entry of the order confirming the Plan, except as set forth in this Order.

6. Adequate Protection for Secured Creditors. Pending confirmation of a Plan and as a condition of Debtor's continued possession or use of real or personal property subject to a security interest, the following, when taken collectively, shall constitute adequate protection to each such secured creditor:

a. Under § 1326(a)(1), Debtor shall include all adequate protection payments required by § 1326(a)(1)(C) as Plan payments and make those payments directly to the Trustee, who then will pay secured creditors as ordered by the Court.

b. Debtor shall timely file the Plan and all required information.

c. Debtor shall make all payments due to the Trustee on time.

d. All payments proposed in the initial or any amended Plan to the holders of secured claims are allowed as costs and expenses of preserving the estate within the meaning of § 503(b)(1)(A).

e. The Trustee shall make monthly disbursements of adequate protection payments to secured creditors prior to confirmation of the Plan, as soon as practicable, if:

i. The Plan provides for such payment to the secured creditor;

ii. The secured creditor has filed a proof of claim OR Debtor or the Trustee has filed a proof of claim under § 501(c);

iii. No objection to the proof of claim is pending; and

iv. As provided for in the Court's Administrative Order Prescribing Procedures for Mortgage Modification Mediation, if the Plan provides for MMM of the secured claim.

f. All disbursements to secured creditors are deemed adequate protection payments. Acceptance of such payments is not a waiver of creditors' rights to contest confirmation or Debtor's valuation of collateral, to request relief from the automatic stay on grounds other than a default in payments, or to request additional adequate protection.

g. If a secured creditor desires to receive payments at an address other than the address in the secured creditor's proof of claim, the secured creditor must file a Notice of Payment Address Change with the Clerk and provide written notice to the Trustee.

h. Creditors holding a security interest in the Debtor's principal residence provided for in the Plan under § 1322(b)(5) shall comply with Rule 3002.1 with respect to payment changes and requests for postpetition fees and costs. The Trustee may adjust the Plan payments accordingly and notify Debtor of any such payment change. However, if a secured creditor is subject to an MMM order, the implementation of any notice under Rule 3002.1 is abated until the conclusion of the mediation.

i. Within 14 days of a written request by a secured creditor, Debtor must provide proof of insurance to the secured creditor as required by the loan documents.

j. Within 72 hours of any telephonic request by a secured creditor, Debtor must allow inspection of the collateral if required by the loan documents.

7. Refund of Plan Payments to Debtor if Case Is Converted or Dismissed. Notwithstanding the provisions of paragraph 6, if Debtor files a notice of conversion of this case to a Chapter 7 or the Court orders the conversion of this case to a Chapter 11 or its dismissal, any undistributed funds in the Trustee's possession on the date of conversion or dismissal shall be payable to Debtor and, if Debtor is represented by counsel, mailed to Debtor in care of Debtor's attorney.

8. Executory Contracts and Unexpired Leases. The Plan must provide for the assumption or rejection of executory contracts and lease obligations.

9. Termination of the Automatic Stay. If the Plan provides for (a) the surrender of collateral to the secured creditor or lessor, (b) for payments to be made by Debtor directly to the secured creditor or lessor, (c) that Debtor does not intend to make payments to the creditor, or (d) fails to provide for the claim of the secured creditor or lessor, such secured creditor or lessor is granted *in rem* relief from the automatic stay to pursue its remedies against the property that is security for the claim or the subject of the lease and both *in rem* and *in personam* relief against any codebtor. If Debtor later amends or modifies the Plan to provide for the secured creditor or lessor, Debtor must move to re-impose the stay.

10. Modification of the Automatic Stay. The automatic stay is modified to permit creditors whose claims are secured by mortgages on Debtor's real property to communicate directly with Debtor in good faith regarding the possible modification or refinance of the mortgage obligation.

11. Meeting of Creditors and Documents to Be Submitted to Trustee. Debtor shall appear at the meeting of creditors scheduled under § 341(a) and Rule 2003(a). No later than seven days before the initial meeting of creditors, Debtor shall provide the Trustee with copies of tax returns for the two years preceding the petition date (or an affidavit that Debtor is not required to file tax returns) and copies of all pay stubs, advices, or documentation of income sources for the six-month period ending on the last day of the month preceding the month of the petition date. The Trustee may request other documentation including information about the non-debtor spouse's income, other documents required by the Bankruptcy Code or other local court order, or information needed to administer a Chapter 13 case.

12. Confirmation Hearing. The Clerk is directed to schedule a confirmation hearing between 20 and 45 days after the date first set for the meeting of creditors. Debtor shall be current in payments to the Trustee and ensure that the case is ready for confirmation, if possible, at the initial confirmation hearing. Following the meeting of creditors, the Trustee may file and serve a Recommendation Concerning Confirmation of the Plan. Debtor shall correct any deficiencies or problems in the Recommendation Concerning Confirmation of the Plan at least seven days prior to the initial confirmation hearing. At the initial or any subsequent confirmation hearing, the Court will consider confirmation of the Plan and, on a preliminary, non-evidentiary basis, all pending motions and objections, including any motion to dismiss, objection to confirmation, or objection to claim. If an evidentiary hearing is needed or if cause exists to defer confirmation, the Court will note the date for the continued confirmation hearing on the docket. The Trustee may raise objections to confirmation of the Plan at any confirmation hearing.

13. Pre-Confirmation Deadline for Filing Amended Plans and Certain Motions. The following shall be filed no later than 28 days after the claims bar date:

a. An amended Plan, if necessary to obtain confirmation;

b. Motions to determine secured status of claim; and

c. Motions to avoid liens, if necessary to obtain confirmation.

14. Deadline for Filing Objections to Claims. Debtor shall file objections to any claims that Debtor seeks to have disallowed, in whole or in part, no later than 28 days after the claims bar date or 14 days after the filing of an amended proof of claim.

15. Deadline to Seek Mortgage Modification Mediation. Any party seeking MMM shall file a motion making this request within 90 days of the petition or conversion date.

16. Service Requirements. Debtor shall serve a copy of any amended Plan upon the Trustee and all other parties in interest and promptly file proof of service. Debtor shall serve a copy of any motion or objection on the Trustee and the affected creditor in the manner required by Rule 7004.

17. Duties of Debtor's Attorney and Payment of Attorney's Fees. Debtor's attorney must assist Debtor in all matters related to this case unless the Court has granted the attorney's motion to withdraw from the case. Debtor's counsel shall not withhold legal advice or service from Debtor because of lack of payment and may not demand payment from Debtor or any person on behalf of Debtor as a condition of providing legal advice or service. If the case is converted or dismissed, the Court shall retain jurisdiction to review the total amount of attorney's fees requested by or paid to Debtor's attorney.

As required by Rule 2016(b), Debtor's attorney must disclose:

a. Any prepetition retainer paid to the attorney by Debtor or any other person for Debtor's benefit;

b. Filing fees collected from Debtor and remitted to the Court; and

c. Postpetition payments made to the attorney by Debtor or other person for Debtor's benefit. Such payments shall be held in the attorney's trust account pending Court approval.

If Debtor's attorney fails to timely and completely file these disclosures or to comply with all requirements in this Order, the Court may order a reduction in the amount of attorney's fees requested or the disgorgement of fees.

18. Tax Returns and Refunds. No later than the day before the initial meeting of creditors, Debtor shall file any delinquent tax returns for any tax period concluding within the four years before the petition date. Debtor shall immediately provide a copy of the returns or a statement that Debtor is not required to file tax returns to the Trustee. During the pendency of the Chapter 13 case, Debtor shall timely file all tax returns and make all tax payments and deposits when due. For each tax return that becomes due after the case is filed, Debtor shall provide to the Trustee, within 14 days of the filing of the return, a complete copy of the tax return, including business returns if Debtor owns a business, together with all related W–2s and Form 1099s. Unless otherwise consented to by the Trustee or ordered by the Court, Debtor shall turn over to the Trustee all tax refunds in addition to regular Plan payments. Debtor shall not instruct the Internal Revenue Service or other taxing agency to apply a refund to the following year's tax liability. **Debtor shall spend no tax refunds without first having obtained the Trustee's consent or court approval.**

19. Filing Claims on Behalf of Creditors. Under Rule 3004, within 30 days after the expiration of the claims bar date, Debtor may file a proof of claim on behalf of a creditor if the creditor has not timely filed a claim and Debtor proposes to make payments to the creditor under the Plan.

20. Extension of Time to File Objections to Debtor's Claims o f Exemption. To assure proper administration if the Chapter 13 case converts to another chapter, under § 105, the Court extends the time for the Trustee or any party in interest to file objections to property claimed as exempt by Debtor to not later than (a) 30 days after the conclusion of the meeting of creditors after conversion of the case to a case under another chapter, or (b) 30 days after Debtor amends the list of property claimed as exempt, whichever is later, unless within such period, further time is granted by the Court. However, this extension does not limit the right of any party in interest to object to entry of a discharge under § 1328(h) on the ground that § 522(q)(1) is applicable. To the extent necessary, the extension of time to object to Debtor's claim of exemptions includes and extends beyond the confirmation hearing in every Chapter 13 case; Trustee or any party in interest may contest Debtor's claimed exemptions in objecting to confirmation of the Plan.

21. Cooperation With Trustee. Debtor and Debtor's attorney shall cooperate with the Trustee to the greatest extent possible during the pendency of a Chapter 13 case, both before and after the Plan is confirmed. Upon the Trustee's oral or written request, Debtor shall provide to the Trustee any requested information, including books, documents, records, and papers, relating to property of the estate. Within 28 days of the Trustee's request, Debtor shall, at Debtor's expense, obtain and deliver to the Trustee a current appraisal of real or personal property performed by a qualified appraiser in an acceptable format. Debtor may file, if needed, a motion to employ professionals under § 327.

22. Debtor's Duty to Supplement. Debtor shall promptly disclose to the Trustee and file amendments with the Court reporting all changes of Debtor's financial circumstances, including, but not limited to, inheritances, personal injury settlements, new or additional employment, loss of employment, or reduction or increase to income.

23. Notice of Domestic Support Obligations. At the initial meeting of creditors, Debtor shall inform the Trustee of any domestic support obligation, as defined in § 101(14A), and provide the following information: the name of the holder of claim, the address of the holder of the claim, the state court case number (if applicable), and the telephone number of the holder of claim. Debtor promptly shall provide the same information to the Trustee for any domestic support obligation that arises after the meeting of creditors.

24. Notice to Creditors and Other Interested Parties. All parties must comply with the noticing and service requirements of Local Rule 2002-1. Failure to timely serve orders and notices may cause the denial of the party's motion without prejudice.

25. Default. If Debtor fails to make payments to the Trustee when due or to timely comply with any of the requirements of this Order, the case may be dismissed or converted to a case under Chapter 7 of the Bankruptcy Code upon motion by the Trustee or a party in interest.

*All references to "Debtor" shall include and refer to both debtors in a case filed jointly by two individuals.

**All references to "Plan" shall include any amended plan, which shall supersede all previously filed plans.

***All statutory references are to the Bankruptcy Code, Title 11 of the United States Code, unless otherwise noted. References to rules are to the Federal Rules of Bankruptcy Procedure.

[DATED: September 1, 2016.]

ADMINISTRATIVE ORDER FLMB-2016-4. IN RE AMENDED ADMINISTRATIVE ORDER REGARDING DEPOSIT AND INVESTMENT OF REGISTRY FUNDS

The Court, having determined that it is necessary to adopt local procedures to ensure uniformity in the deposit, investment and tax administration of funds in the Court's Registry,

IT IS ORDERED that the following shall govern the receipt, deposit, and investment of registry funds:

I. Receipt of Funds.

A. No money shall be sent to the Court or its officers for deposit in the Court's registry without a court order signed by the presiding judge in the case or proceeding.

B. The party making the deposit or transferring funds to the Court's registry shall serve the order permitting the deposit or transfer on the Clerk of Court.

C. Unless provided for elsewhere in this Order, all monies ordered to be paid to the Court or received by its officers in any case pending or adjudicated shall be deposited with the Treasurer of the United States in the name and to the credit of this Court pursuant to 28 U.S.C. § 2041 through depositories designated by the Treasury to accept such deposit on its behalf.

II. Investment of Registry Funds.

A. Where, by order of the Court, funds on deposit with the Court are to be placed in some form of interest-bearing account or invested in a court-approved, interest-bearing instrument in accordance with Rule 67 of the Federal Rules of Civil Procedure, the Court Registry Investment System ("CRIS"), administered by the Administrative Office of the United States Courts under 28 U.S.C. § 2045, shall be the only investment mechanism authorized.

B. Interpleader funds deposited under 28 U.S.C. § 1335 meet the IRS definition of a "Disputed Ownership Fund" (DOF), a taxable entity that requires tax administration. Unless otherwise ordered by the Court, interpleader funds shall be deposited in the DOF established within the CRIS and administered by the Administrative Office of the United States Courts, which shall be responsible for meeting all DOF tax administration requirements.

C. The Director of Administrative Office of the United States Courts is designated as custodian for all CRIS funds. The Director or the Director's designee shall perform the duties of custodian. Funds held in the CRIS remain subject to the control and jurisdiction of the Court.

D. Money from each case deposited in the CRIS shall be "pooled" together with those on deposit with Treasury to the credit of other courts in the CRIS and used to purchase Government Account Series securities through the Bureau of Public Debt, which will be held at Treasury, in an account in the name and to the credit of the Director of Administrative Office of the United States Courts. The pooled funds will be invested in accordance with the principals of the CRIS Investment Policy as approved by the Registry Monitoring Group.

E. An account will be established in the CRIS Liquidity Fund titled in the name of the case giving rise to the deposit invested in the fund. Income generated from fund investments will be distributed to each case based on the ratio each account's principal and earnings has to the aggregate principal and income total in the fund after the CRIS fee has been applied. Reports showing the interest earned and the principal amounts contributed in each case will be prepared and distributed to each court participating in the CRIS and made available to litigants and/or their counsel.

F. For each interpleader case, an account shall be established in the CRIS Disputed Ownership Fund, titled in the name of the case giving rise to the deposit invested in the fund. Income generated from fund investments will be distributed to each case after the DOF fee has been applied and tax withholdings have been deducted from the fund. Reports showing the interest earned and the principal amounts contributed in each case will be available through the FedInvest/CMS application for each court participating in the CRIS and made available to litigants and/or their counsel. On appointment of an administrator authorized to incur expenses on behalf of the DOF in a case, the case DOF funds should be transferred to another investment account as directed by court order.

III. Fees and Taxes.

A. The custodian is authorized and directed by this Order to deduct the CRIS fee of an annualized 10 basis points on assets on deposit for all CRIS funds, excluding the case funds held in the DOF, for the management of investments in the CRIS. According to the Court's Miscellaneous Fee Schedule, the CRIS fee is assessed from interest earnings to the pool before a pro rata distribution of earnings is made to court cases.

B. The custodian is authorized and directed by this Order to deduct the DOF fee of an annualized 20 basis points on assets on deposit in the DOF for management of investments and tax administration. According to the Court's Miscellaneous Fee Schedule, the DOF fee is assessed from interest earnings to the pool before a pro rata distribution of earnings is made to court cases. The custodian is further authorized and directed by this Order to withhold and pay federal taxes due on behalf of the DOF.

IV. Transition From Former Investment Procedure.

A. The Clerk of Court is further directed to develop a systematic method of redemption of all existing investments and their transfer to the CRIS.

B. Deposits to the CRIS DOF will not be transferred from any existing CRIS Funds. Only new deposits pursuant to 29 U.S.C. § 1335 from the effective date of this Order will be placed in the CRIS DOF.

C. Parties not wishing to transfer certain existing registry deposits into the CRIS may seek leave to transfer them to the litigants or their designees on proper motion and approval of the judge assigned to the specific case.

D. This Order supersedes and abrogates all prior orders of this Court regarding the deposit and investment of registry funds.

E. The effective date of this Order is the date the CRIS DOF begins accepting deposits.

[Dated: October 6, 2016.]

UNITED STATES DISTRICT COURT FOR THE SOUTHERN DISTRICT OF FLORIDA

Including Amendments Received Through February 1, 2017

GENERAL RULES

SELECTED LOCAL FORMS

ADMIRALTY AND MARITIME RULES

APPENDIX OF FORMS. ADMIRALTY AND MARITIME RULES

MAGISTRATE JUDGE RULES

MAGISTRATE FORMS

SPECIAL RULES GOVERNING THE ADMISSION AND PRACTICE OF ATTORNEYS

RULES GOVERNING ATTORNEY DISCIPLINE

INTERNAL OPERATING PROCEDURES

ELECTRONIC CASE FILING

PLAN FOR THE RANDOM SELECTION OF GRAND AND PETIT JURORS

SELECTED ADMINISTRATIVE ORDERS

GENERAL RULES

INTRODUCTORY STATEMENT

Members of the bar and the Court are proud of the long tradition of courteous practice in the Southern District of Florida. Indeed, it is a fundamental tenet of this Court that attorneys in this District be governed at all times by a spirit of cooperation, professionalism, and civility. For example, and without limiting the foregoing, it remains the Court's expectation that counsel will seek to accommodate their fellow practitioners, including in matters of scheduling, whenever reasonably possible and that counsel will work to eliminate disputes by reasonable agreement to the fullest extent permitted by the bounds of zealous representation and ethical practice.

[Effective December 1, 2014.]

RULE 1.1 SCOPE OF THE LOCAL RULES

These Local Rules shall apply in all proceedings in civil and criminal actions except where otherwise indicated.

When used in these Local Rules, the word "counsel" shall be construed to apply to a party if that party is proceeding pro se.

[Effective December 1, 1994. Amended effective April 15, 1996; April 15, 1997; April 15, 1998; April 15, 1999; April 15, 2000; April 15, 2001; April 15, 2002; April 15, 2003; April 15, 2004; April 15, 2005; April 15, 2006; April 15, 2007; April 15, 2008; April 15, 2009; April 15, 2010; December 1, 2011; December 1, 2014; December 1, 2015.]

Authority

(1993) Model Rule 1.1 (All references to "Model Rules" refer to the Local Rules Project of the Committee on Rules of Practice and Procedure of the Judicial Conference of the United States.)

RULE 3.1 DOCKETING AND TRIAL

Actions and proceedings shall be tried in their county of origin, except that Highlands, Indian River, Martin, Okeechobee and St. Lucie County actions and proceedings shall be tried at Fort Pierce, Florida.

Notwithstanding the foregoing, any civil or criminal proceeding or trial may, upon Order of Court and in the interest of justice, the status of the docket, or to assure compliance with requirements imposed under the Speedy Trial Act, be conducted at any jury division within the District.

[Effective December 1, 1994. Amended effective April 15, 2007; April 15, 2010; December 1, 2011; December 1, 2015.]

Authority

(1993) Former Local Rules 1 and 2. Collier, Hendry and Glades Counties were transferred to the Middle District of Florida by P.L. 100–702.

RULE 3.3 CIVIL COVER SHEET

Every Complaint or other document initiating a civil action shall be accompanied by a completed civil cover sheet. *See* form available on the Court's website (www.flsd.uscourts.gov). This requirement is solely for administrative purposes, and matters appearing only on the civil cover sheet have no legal effect in the action. If counsel becomes aware of an error in the civil cover sheet counsel shall file and serve a written notice that identifies the error.

[Effective December 1, 1994. Amended effective April 15, 2007; December 3, 2012; December 1, 2015.]

Authority

(1993) Former Local Rule 4. Model Rule 3.1; paragraph allowing for filing certain cover sheets to be added nunc pro tunc and pro se exemption omitted.

RULE 3.8 NOTICE OF TRANSFER OF REFILED AND SIMILAR ACTIONS AND PROCEDURES

It shall be the continuing duty of the attorneys of record in every action or proceeding to bring promptly to the attention of the Court and opposing counsel the existence of other actions or proceedings as described in Section 2.15.00 of the Court's Internal Operating Procedures, as well as the existence of any similar actions or proceedings then pending before another court or administrative agency. Such notice shall be given by filing with the Court and serving a "Notice of Pending, Refiled, Related or Similar Actions," containing a list and description thereof sufficient for identification.

[Effective December 1, 1994. Amended effective April 15, 2006; April 15, 2007; December 1, 2015.]

Authority

(1993) Former Local Rule 6.

RULE 5.1 FILING AND COPIES

(a) Form of Conventionally Filed Documents. All civil and criminal pleadings, motions, and other papers exempted from the requirement that they be filed via CM/ECF and that are instead tendered for conventional (non–CM/ECF) filing shall:

(1) Be bound only by easily-removable paper or spring-type binder clips, and not stapled or mechanically bound or fastened in any way. Voluminous pleadings, motions, or documents may be bound with a rubber band. Attachments may not be tabbed; reference characters should be printed or typed on a blank sheet of paper separating each attached document.

(2) When filing a civil complaint for which issuance of initial process is requested, one (1) copy of the complaint must be submitted for each summons.

(3) Be on standard size 8–1/2″ × 11″ white, opaque paper.

(4) Be plainly typed or written on one (1) side with 1" margins on top, bottom, and each side. All typewritten documents, except for quoted material of fifty words or more and footnotes, both of which may be single-spaced, shall have not less than one and one-half (1 1/2) spaces between lines. Fonts for typewritten documents, including footnotes and quotations, must be no smaller than twelve (12) point. All typewritten documents must be paginated properly and consecutively at the bottom center of each page. Only one (1) side of the paper may be used.

(5) Include a caption with:

(A) The name of the Court centered across the page;

(B) The docket number, category (civil or criminal), and the last names of the assigned District Judge and Magistrate Judge, centered across the page;

(C) The style of the action, which fills no more than the left side of the page, leaving sufficient space on the right side for the Clerk of the Court to affix a filing stamp; and

(D) The title of the document, including the name and designation of the party (as plaintiff or defendant or the like) on whose behalf the document is submitted, centered across the page.

Exception:

The requirements of (a)(3)–(a)(5) do not apply to: (i) exhibits submitted for filing; (ii) papers filed in removed actions prior to removal from the state courts; and (iii) forms provided by the Court.

(6) Include (A) a signature block with the name, street address, telephone number, facsimile telephone number, e-mail address, and Florida Bar identification number of all counsel for the party and (B) a certificate of service that contains the name, street address, telephone number, facsimile telephone number, and e-mail address of all counsel for all parties, including the attorney filing the pleading, motion, or other paper. *See* form available on the Court's website (www.flsd.uscourts.gov).

(7) Not be transmitted to the Clerk of the Court or any Judge by facsimile telecopier.

(8) Be submitted with sufficient copies to be filed and docketed in each matter if styled in consolidated cases.

(b) Form of CM/ECF Filed Documents. Except those documents exempted under Section 5 of the CM/ECF Administrative Procedures, all documents required to be served shall be filed in compliance with the CM/ECF Administrative Procedures; however, pro se parties are exempted from this requirement pursuant to Section 2C of the CM/ECF Administrative Procedures. The requirements of paragraphs (a)(2)–(a)(5) above shall apply to documents filed via CM/ECF. *See* Section 3A of the CM/ECF Administrative Procedures.

(c) Restriction on Courtesy Copies. Counsel shall not deliver extra courtesy copies to a Judge's Chambers except when requested by a Judge's office.

(d) Notices of Filing; Form and Content. The title of a notice of filing shall include (1) the name and designation of the party (as plaintiff or defendant or the like) on whose behalf the filing is submitted, and (2) a description of the document being filed. A notice of filing shall identify by title the pleading, motion or other paper to which the document filed pertains and the purpose of the filing, such as in support of or in opposition to a pending motion or the like.

(e) Consent to Service. Registration as an electronic filing user pursuant to Southern District of Florida CM/ECF Administrative Procedures § 3B constitutes consent to receive service electronically pursuant to Fed. R. Civ. P. 5(b)(2)(E) and Fed. R. Crim. P. 49 and waiver of any right to receive service by any other means. Service of papers required to be served pursuant to Fed. R. Civ. P. 5(a) and Fed. R. Crim. P. 39 but not filed, such as discovery requests, may be made via email to the address designated by an attorney for receipt of notices of electronic filings.

[Effective December 1, 1994. Amended effective April 15, 1996; April 15, 1998; April 15, 1999; April 15, 2000; April 15, 2001; Paragraph E added effective April 15, 2003; April 15, 2007; April 15, 2009; April 15, 2010; April 15, 2011; December 1, 2011; December 1, 2015; December 1, 2016.]

Authority

(1993) Former Local Rule 7; Model Rule 5.1; Administrative Order 90–64 (A.6, B).

RULE 5.2 PROOF OF SERVICE AND SERVICE BY PUBLICATION

(a) Certification of Service. Each pleading or paper required by Federal Rule of Civil Procedure 5 to be served on the other parties shall include a certificate of service that complies with Form B to the CM/ECF Administrative Procedures and, if service includes a method other than CM/ECF, that states the persons or firms served, their relationship to the action or proceeding, the date, method and address of service. Signature by the party or its attorney on the original constitutes a representation that service has been made.

(b) Multiple Copies Unnecessary. Any document permitted to be filed via CM/ECF, including the corporate disclosure statement required by Federal Rule of Civil Procedure 7.1, shall be deemed to have been delivered in multiple if multiple copies are required to be filed.

(c) Publication. Publication required by law or rule of court shall be made in a newspaper of general circulation. *The Daily Business Review* and such other newspapers as the Court from time to time may indicate are designated as official newspapers for the publication of notices pertaining to proceedings in this Court; provided, however, that publication shall not be restricted to the aforesaid periodicals unless an order for publication specifically so provides.

[Effective December 1, 1994. Amended effective December 1, 2001; April 15, 2007; April 15, 2010; April 15, 2011; December 1, 2015.]

Authority

(1993) Former Local Rule 7; Model Rule 5.2 (does not require certificate of service); Clerk of the Court's administrative rule on issuance of initial process.

(1994) D. Rule 1.07(c), Local Rules, Middle District of Florida.

RULE 5.3 FILES AND EXHIBITS

(a) Removal of Original Papers. No original papers in the custody of the Clerk of the Court shall be removed by anyone without order of the Court until final adjudication of the action or proceeding and disposition of the appeal, if one is filed, or expiration of the appeal period without appeal being filed, and then only with permission and on terms of the Clerk of the Court. However, official court reporters, special masters, or commissioners may remove original papers as may be necessary.

(b) Exhibits. Except as provided by Section 5H of the CM/ECF Administrative Procedures, all exhibits received or offered in evidence at any hearing shall be delivered to the Clerk of the Court, who shall keep them in the Clerk of the Court's custody, except that any narcotics, cash, counterfeit notes, weapons, precious stones received, including but not limited to other exhibits which, because of size or nature, require special handling, shall remain in possession of the party introducing same during pendency of the proceeding and any appeal. Nothing contained in this Local Rule shall prevent the Court from entering an order with respect to the handling, custody or storage of any exhibit. The Clerk of the Court shall permit United States Magistrate Judges and official court reporters to have custody of exhibits as may be necessary.

(c) Removal of Exhibits. All models, diagrams, books, or other exhibits received in evidence or marked for identification in any action or proceeding shall be removed by the filing party within three (3) months after final adjudication of the action or proceeding and disposition of any appeal. Otherwise, such exhibits may be destroyed or otherwise disposed of as the Clerk of the Court may deem proper.

[Subsection (d) has been moved to Court's I.O.P]

[Effective December 1, 1994. Amended effective April 15, 2007; April 15, 2010; December 1, 2015.]

Authority

(1993) Former Local Rule 8, as amended by Administrative Order 91–54.

RULE 5.4 FILINGS UNDER SEAL; DISPOSAL OF SEALED MATERIALS

(a) General Policy. Unless otherwise provided by law, Court rule, or Court order, proceedings in the United States District Court are public and Court filings are matters of public record. Where not so provided, a party seeking to file matters under seal and/or ex parte shall follow the procedures prescribed by this Local Rule and Sections 5A, 5K, 9A–D, and 10B, as applicable, of the CM/ECF Administrative Procedures. In criminal matters, the procedures prescribed by this Local Rule and by the CM/ECF Administrative Procedures concerning the filing of ex parte documents shall only apply to cases in which a person already has been charged by criminal complaint, criminal information, or indictment.

(b) Procedure for Filing Under Seal in Civil Cases. A party seeking to make a filing under seal in a civil case shall:

(1) In a case that is not otherwise sealed in its entirety as permitted or required by federal law, file electronically via CM/ECF a motion to seal that sets forth the factual and legal basis for departing from the policy that Court filings be public and that describes the proposed sealed filing with as much particularity as possible without revealing the confidential information. The motion shall specify the proposed duration of the requested sealing. The motion to seal (but not the proposed sealed filing) and the docket text shall be publicly available on the docket. The proposed sealed filing must be filed electronically as a sealed document in CM/ECF using events specifically earmarked for sealed civil filings as described in detail in Section 9 of the CM/ECF Administrative Procedures. The filer must complete any required service of the sealed document(s) conventionally, indicating the corresponding document number of the sealed document(s).

A party appearing pro se must file a motion to seal and proposed sealed documents conventionally. Proposed sealed documents shall be submitted in a plain envelope clearly marked "sealed document" with the case number and style of the case noted on the outside. The filer must complete any required service of the sealed document(s) conventionally.

(2) Requests to seal a case in its entirety require a motion to seal that is filed conventionally in a plain envelope clearly marked "sealed document" with the style of the case noted on the outside. The motion must set forth the factual and legal basis for departing from the policy that Court filings be public, describe the proposed sealed filing with as much particularity as possible without revealing the confidential information, and specify the proposed duration of the requested sealing. If the motion is granted, subsequent filings shall be filed conventionally as sealed documents in a plain envelope clearly marked "sealed document" with the case number and style of the case noted on the outside. The filer must complete any required service of the sealed document(s) conventionally.

(c) Procedure for Filing Under Seal in Criminal Cases. A party seeking to make a filing under seal in a criminal case shall:

(1) Conventionally file a motion to seal that sets forth the factual and legal basis for departing from the policy that Court filings be public and that describes the proposed sealed filing with as much particularity as possible without revealing the confidential information. The motion shall specify the proposed duration of the requested sealing. Unless the Court expressly orders otherwise, the motion to seal will itself be sealed from public view and the docket text appearing on the public docket shall reflect only that a sealed filing has been made.

(2) Conventionally file the proposed sealed filing in a plain envelope clearly marked "sealed document" with the case number and style of the case noted on the outside.

(d) Procedure for Filing Ex Parte. A party submitting an ex parte filing shall:

(1) Include the words "ex parte" in the title of the motion and explain the reasons for ex parte treatment. Upon submission, unless the Court directs otherwise the ex-parte filing will be restricted from public view and the docket text appearing on the public docket will reflect only that a restricted filing has been made. Counsel need not serve motions filed ex parte and related documents unless and until the Court so orders.

(2) In criminal matters, conventionally file the ex parte filing in a plain envelope clearly marked "ex parte" with the case number and style of the case noted on the outside.

(3) In civil matters, electronically file the ex parte filing via CM/ECF as a restricted document using the events specifically earmarked for ex parte filings as described in Section 9 of the CM/ECF Administrative Procedures.

(4) A party appearing pro se must file documents conventionally.

(e) Court Ruling.

(1) *Sealed Filings.* An order granting a motion to seal shall state the period of time that the sealed filing shall be sealed. If the Court denies the motion to seal, the proposed sealed filing shall not be public and shall be deleted from the docket by the Clerk's Office.

(2) *Ex Parte Filings.* Access to ex parte motions and related filings will remain restricted unless the Court orders otherwise.

[Effective April 15, 2000. Amended effective April 15, 2001; April 15, 2005; April 15, 2007; April 15, 2010; December 2, 2013; December 1, 2014; December 1, 2015.]

RULE 7.1 MOTIONS, GENERAL

(a) Filing.

(1) Every motion when filed shall incorporate a memorandum of law citing supporting authorities, except that the following motions need not incorporate a memorandum:

(A) petition for writ of habeas corpus ad testificandum or ad prosequendum;

(B) motion for out-of-state process;

(C) motion for order of publication for process;

(D) application for default;

(E) motion for judgment upon default;

(F) motion to withdraw or substitute counsel;

(G) motion for continuance, provided the good cause supporting it is set forth in the motion and affidavit required by Local Rule 7.6;

(H) motion for confirmation of sale;

(I) motion to withdraw or substitute exhibits;

(J) motion for extensions of time providing the good cause supporting it is set forth in the motion;

(K) motion for refund of bond, provided the good cause supporting it is set forth in the motion; and

(L) application for leave to proceed in forma pauperis.

(2) Those motions listed in (a)(1) above shall be accompanied by a proposed order that is filed and submitted via e-mail to the Court as prescribed by Section 3I(6) of the CM/ECF Administrative Procedures.

(3) *Pre-filing Conferences Required of Counsel.* Prior to filing any motion in a civil case, except a motion for injunctive relief, for judgment on the pleadings, for summary judgment, to dismiss or to permit maintenance of a class action, to dismiss for failure to state a claim upon which relief can be granted, or to involuntarily dismiss an action, for garnishment or other relief under Federal Rule of Civil Procedure 64, or otherwise properly filed ex parte under the Federal Rules of Civil Procedure and these Local Rules, or a petition to enforce or vacate an arbitration award, counsel for the movant shall confer (orally or in writing), or make reasonable effort to confer (orally or in writing), with all parties or non-parties who may be affected by the relief sought in the motion in a good faith effort to resolve by agreement the issues to be raised in the motion. Counsel conferring with movant's counsel shall cooperate and act in good faith in attempting to resolve the dispute. At the end of the motion, and above the signature block, counsel for the moving party shall certify either: (A) that counsel for the movant has conferred with all parties or non-parties who may be affected by the relief sought in the motion in a good faith effort to resolve the issues raised in the motion and has been unable to do so; or (B) that counsel for the movant has made reasonable efforts to confer with all parties or non-parties who may be affected by the relief sought in the motion, which efforts shall be identified with specificity in the statement (including the date, time, and manner of each effort), but has been unable to do so. If certain of the issues have been resolved by agreement, the certification shall specify the issues so resolved and the issues remaining unresolved. Failure to comply with the requirements of this Local Rule may be cause for the Court to grant or deny the motion and impose on counsel an appropriate sanction, which may include an order to pay the amount of the reasonable expenses incurred because of the violation, including a reasonable attorney's fee. *See* forms available on the Court's website (www.flsd.uscourts.gov).

(b) Hearings.

(1) No hearing will be held on motions unless set by the Court.

(2) A party who desires oral argument or a hearing of any motion shall request it within the motion or opposing memorandum in a separate section titled "request for hearing." The request shall set forth in detail the reasons why a hearing is desired and would be helpful to the Court and shall estimate the time required for argument. The Court in its discretion may grant or deny a hearing as requested, upon consideration of both the request and any response thereto by an opposing party.

(3) Discovery motions may be referred to and heard by a United States Magistrate Judge.

(4) With respect to:

(A) any motion or other matter which has been pending and fully briefed with no hearing set thereon for a period of ninety (90) days, and

(B) any motion or other matter as to which the Court has conducted a hearing but has not entered an order or otherwise determined the motion or matter within ninety (90) days of the hearing, the movant or applicant, whether party or non-party, shall serve on all parties and any affected non-parties within fourteen (14) days thereafter a "Notification of Ninety Days Expiring" which shall contain the following information:

(i) the title and docket entry number of the subject motion or other application, along with the dates of service and filing;

(ii) the title and docket number of any and all responses or opposing memoranda, along with the dates of service and filing, or if no such papers have been filed, the date on which such papers were due;

(iii) the title and docket entry number of any reply memoranda, or any other papers filed in connection with the motion or other matter, as well as the dates of service and filing; and

(iv) the date of any hearing held on the motion or other matter.

(c) Memorandum of Law. For all motions, except motions served with the summons and complaint, each party opposing a motion shall serve an opposing memorandum of law no later than fourteen (14) days after service of the motion. Failure to do so may be deemed sufficient cause for granting the motion by default. The movant may, within seven (7) days after service of an opposing memorandum of law, serve a reply memorandum in support of the motion, which reply memorandum shall be strictly limited to rebuttal of matters raised in the memorandum in opposition without reargument of matters covered in the movant's initial memorandum of law. No further or additional memoranda of law shall be filed without prior leave of Court. All materials in support of any motion, response, or reply, including affidavits and declarations, shall be served with the filing. For a motion served with the summons and complaint, the opposing memorandum of law shall be due on the day the response to the complaint is due.

(1) *Time.* Time shall be computed under this Local Rule as follows:

(A) If the motion or memorandum was filed via CM/ECF or served by hand-delivery, count fourteen (14) days (seven (7) days for a reply) beginning the day after the motion, response, or memorandum was filed via CM/ECF or certified as having been served by hand-delivery. The last day is the due date. If the last day falls on a Saturday, Sunday, or legal holiday, the period continues to run until the next business day, which is the due date for the opposing memorandum or reply.

(B) If the motion or memorandum was served only by mail, count fourteen (14) days (seven (7) days for a reply) beginning the day after the motion, response, or memorandum was certified as having been mailed. Count three (3) more days. The third day is the due date for the opposing memorandum or reply. If the third day falls on a Saturday, Sunday, or legal holiday, the due date is the next business day.

(2) *Length.* Absent prior permission of the Court, neither a motion and its incorporated memorandum of law nor the opposing memorandum of law shall exceed twenty (20) pages; a reply memorandum shall not exceed ten (10) pages. Title pages preceding the first page of text, "request for hearing" sections, signature pages, certificates of good faith conferences, and certificates of service shall not be counted as pages for purposes of this rule. Filing multiple motions for partial summary judgment is prohibited, absent prior permission of the Court. This prohibition does not preclude a party from filing both a motion for summary judgment asserting an immunity from suit and a later motion for summary judgment addressing any issues that may remain in the case. This prohibition also is not triggered when, as permitted by Fed. R. Civ. P. 12(d), the Court elects to treat a motion filed pursuant to Fed. R. Civ. P. 12(b) or 12(c) as a summary judgment motion.

(d) Emergency Motions. The Court may, upon written motion and good cause shown, waive the time requirements of this Local Rule and grant an immediate hearing on any matter requiring such expedited procedure. The motion shall set forth in detail the necessity for such expedited procedure and be accompanied by the Certification of Emergency form available on the Court's website (www.flsd.uscourts.gov).

As prescribed by Section 10 of the CM/ECF Administrative Procedures, a party seeking to file an emergency motion must file the documents electronically via CM/ECF using the events specifically earmarked for emergency matters. The filer must certify that the matter is a true emergency. Motions are not considered emergencies if the urgency arises due to the attorney's or party's own dilatory conduct. A Certification of Emergency form must be signed and filed as an attachment to the emergency motion in CM/ECF.

Emergency motions in criminal cases that are also ex parte or sealed must be conventionally filed. A party appearing pro se must file emergency matters conventionally.

(e) Applications Previously Refused. Whenever any motion or application has been made to any Judge or Magistrate Judge and has been refused in whole or in part, or has been granted conditionally, and a subsequent motion or application is made to a different District Judge or Magistrate Judge for the same relief in whole or in part, upon the same or any alleged different state of facts, it shall be the continuing duty of each party and attorney seeking such relief to present to the District Judge or Magistrate Judge to whom the subsequent application is made an affidavit setting forth the material facts and circumstances surrounding each prior application, including: (1) when and to what District Judge or Magistrate Judge the application was made; (2) what ruling was made thereon; and (3) what new or different facts and circumstances are claimed to exist which did not exist, or were not shown, upon the prior application. For failure to comply with the requirements of this Local Rule, any ruling made on the subsequent application may be set aside sua sponte or on ex parte motion.

[Effective December 1, 1994. Amended effective April 15, 1996; April 15, 1997; April 15, 2000; April 1, 2004; April 15, 2005; April 15, 2006; April 15, 2007; April 15, 2009; April 15, 2010; April 15, 2011; December 1, 2011; December 1, 2014; December 1, 2015; December 1, 2016.]

RULE 7.2 MOTIONS PENDING ON REMOVAL OR TRANSFER TO THIS COURT

When a court transfers or a party removes an action to this Court, a true and legible copy of: (a) any pending motion and all documents previously filed in support thereof; and (b) any opposition to any such motion and all documents previously filed in opposition to any such motion, shall be filed by the moving party within seven (7) days of the entry of the order of transfer or the filing of the notice of removal , unless those materials already have been made part of the case file in this Court. If there is a motion pending upon transfer or removal for which the moving party has not submitted a memorandum in support, the moving party shall file such memorandum within fourteen (14) days after the filing of the notice of removal or the entry of the order of transfer. If the moving party filed a memorandum in support of the motion prior to removal but any party opposing the motion has not yet filed a memorandum in opposition, any party opposing the motion shall file such memorandum within fourteen (14) days after the filing of the notice of removal or the entry of the order of transfer. All parties shall then comply with the briefing deadlines provided in Local Rule 7.1(c).

[Effective December 1, 1994. Amended effective April 15, 2003; April 15, 2007; April 15, 2010; December 1, 2015.]

Authority

(1993) Former Local Rule 10D.

RULE 7.3 ATTORNEYS FEES AND COSTS

(a) Motions for Attorneys Fees and/or Non-Taxable Expenses and Costs. This rule provides a mechanism to assist parties in resolving attorneys fee and costs disputes by agreement. A motion for an award of attorneys fees and/or non-taxable expenses and costs arising from the entry of a final judgment or order shall not be filed until a good faith effort to resolve the motion, as described in paragraph (b) below, has been completed. The motion shall:

(1) be filed within sixty (60) days of the entry of the final judgment or order giving rise to the claim, regardless of the prospect or pendency of supplemental review or appellate proceedings;

(2) identify the judgment or other order which gives rise to the motion, as well as the statute, rule, or other grounds entitling the moving party to the award;

(3) state the amount sought;

(4) disclose the terms of any applicable fee agreement;

(5) provide:

(A) the identity, experience, and qualifications for each timekeeper for whom fees are sought;

(B) the number of hours reasonably expended by each such timekeeper;

(C) a description of the tasks done during those hours; and

(D) the hourly rate(s)claimed for each timekeeper;

(6) describe and document with invoices all incurred and claimed fees and expenses not taxable under 28 U.S.C. § 1920;

(7) be verified; and

(8) certify that a good faith effort to resolve issues by agreement occurred pursuant to Local Rule 7.3(b), describing what was and was not resolved by agreement and addressing separately the issues of entitlement to fees and amount.

Within fourteen (14) days after filing and service of the motion, the respondent shall describe with reasonable particularity each time entry or nontaxable expense to which it objects, both as to issues of entitlement and as to amount, and shall provide supporting legal authority. If a party objects to an hourly rate, its counsel must submit an affidavit giving its firm's hourly rates for the matter and include any contingency, partial contingency, or other arrangements that could change the effective hourly rate. Pursuant to Federal Rule of Civil Procedure 54(d)(2)(C), either party may move the Court to determine entitlement prior to submission on the issue of amount. This Local Rule's requirements of disclosure are not intended to require the disclosure of privileged, immune, or protected material.

A party shall seek costs that are taxable under 28 U.S.C. § 1920 by filing a bill of costs and supporting memorandum in accordance with paragraph 7.3(c) below. The costs and expenses sought in a motion under this paragraph shall not include any cost sought in a bill of costs.

(b) Good Faith Effort to Resolve Issues by Agreement. Except as to any aspect of a fee claim upon which the parties agree, a draft motion compliant with Local Rule 7.3(a)(1)–(8) must be served but not filed at least thirty (30) days prior to the deadline for filing any motion for attorneys fees and/or costs that is governed by this Local Rule. Within twenty-one (21) days of service of the draft motion, the parties shall confer and attempt in good faith to agree on entitlement to and the amount of fees and expenses not taxable under 28 U.S.C. § 1920. The respondent shall describe in writing and with reasonable particularity each time entry or nontaxable expense to which it objects, both as to issues of entitlement and as to amount, and shall provide supporting legal authority. If a federal statute provides a deadline of fewer than sixty (60) days for a motion governed by Local Rule 7.3(a), the parties need not comply with this paragraph's requirements.

(c) Bill of Costs. A bill of costs pursuant to 28 U.S.C. § 1920 shall be filed and served within thirty (30) days of entry of final judgment or other appealable order that gives rise to a right to tax costs under the circumstances listed in 28 U.S.C. § 1920. Prior to filing the bill of costs, the moving party shall confer with affected parties under the procedure outlined in S.D.Fla.L.R. 7.1(a)(3) in a good faith effort to resolve the items of costs being sought.

An application for a bill of costs must be submitted on form (or in form substantially similar to) AO 133 of the Administrative Office of the United States Courts and shall be limited to the costs permitted by 28 U.S.C. § 1920. Expenses and costs that the party believes are recoverable although not identified in § 1920 shall be moved for as provided in paragraph 7.3(a) above. The bill of costs shall attach copies of any documentation showing the amount of costs and shall be supported by a memorandum not exceeding ten (10) pages. The prospects or pendency of supplemental review or appellate proceedings shall not toll or otherwise extend the time for filing a bill of costs with the Court.

[Effective December 1, 1994. Amended effective April 15, 1999; April 15, 2001; April 15, 2005; April 15, 2006; April 15, 2007; April 15, 2010; April 15, 2011; December 1, 2011; December 3, 2012; December 1, 2015.]

Authority

(1993) Former Local Rule 10F, renumbered per Model Rules.

RULE 7.6 CONTINUANCES OF TRIALS AND HEARINGS

A continuance of any trial, pretrial conference, or other hearing will be granted only on exceptional circumstances. No such continuance will be granted on stipulation of counsel alone. However, upon written notice served and filed at the earliest practical date prior to the trial, pretrial conference, or other hearing, and supported by affidavit setting forth a full showing of good cause, a continuance may be granted by the Court.

[Effective December 1, 1994.]

Authority

(1993) Former Local Rule 11. Renumbered in accordance with Model Rules.

RULE 7.7 CORRESPONDENCE TO THE COURT

Unless invited or directed by the presiding Judge, attorneys and any party represented by an attorney shall not: (a) address or present to the Court in the form of a letter or the like any application requesting relief in any form, citing authorities, or presenting arguments; or (b) furnish the Court with copies of correspondence between or among counsel, or any party represented by an attorney, except when necessary as an exhibit when seeking relief from the Court. Local Rule 5.1(c) above governs the provision of "courtesy copies" to a Judge.

[Effective December 1, 1994. Amended effective April 15, 2003; April 15, 2007; December 1, 2015.]

Authority

(1993) Former Local Rule 10M.

RULE 11.1 ATTORNEYS

(a) Roll of Attorneys. The Bar of this Court shall consist of those persons heretofore admitted and those who may hereafter be admitted in accordance with the Special Rules Governing the Admission and Practice of Attorneys in this District.

(b) Contempt of Court. Any person who before his or her admission to the Bar of this Court or during his or her disbarment or suspension exercises in this District in any action or proceeding pending in this Court any of the privileges of a member of the Bar, or who pretends to be entitled to do so, may be found guilty of contempt of Court.

(c) Professional Conduct. The standards of professional conduct of members of the Bar of this Court shall include the current Rules Regulating The Florida Bar. For a violation of any of these canons in connection with any matter pending before this Court, an attorney may be subjected to appropriate disciplinary action.

(d) Appearance by Attorney.

(1) The filing of any pleading shall, unless otherwise specified, constitute an appearance by the person who signs such pleading.

(2) An attorney representing a witness in any civil action or criminal proceeding, including a grand jury proceeding, or representing a defendant in a grand jury proceeding, shall file a notice of appearance, with consent of the client endorsed thereon, with the Clerk of the Court on a form to be prescribed and furnished by the Court, except that the notice need not be filed when such appearance has previously been evidenced by the filing of pleadings in the action or proceeding. The notice shall be filed by the attorney promptly upon undertaking the representation and prior to the attorney's appearance on behalf of the attorney's client at any hearing or grand jury session. When the appearance is in connection with a grand jury session, the notice of appearance shall be filed with the Clerk of the Court in such manner as to maintain the secrecy requirements of grand jury proceedings.

(3) No attorney shall withdraw the attorney's appearance in any action or proceeding except by leave of Court after notice served on the attorney's client and opposing counsel. A motion to withdraw shall include a current mailing address for the attorney's client or the client's counsel.

(4) Whenever a party has appeared by attorney, the party cannot thereafter appear or act on the party's own behalf in the action or proceeding, or take any step therein, unless an order of substitution shall first have been made by the Court, after notice to the attorney of such party, and to the opposite party; provided, that the Court may in its discretion hear a party in open court, notwithstanding the fact that the party has appeared or is represented by an attorney.

(5) When an attorney dies, or is removed or suspended, or ceases to act as such, a party to an action or proceeding for whom the attorney was acting as counsel must, before any further proceedings are had in the action on the party's behalf, appoint another attorney or appear in person, unless such party is already represented by another attorney.

(6) No agreement between parties or their attorneys, the existence of which is not conceded, in relation to the proceedings or evidence in an action, will be considered by the Court unless the same is made before the Court and noted in the record or is reduced to writing and subscribed by the party or attorney against whom it is asserted.

(7) Only one (1) attorney on each side shall examine or cross-examine a witness, and not more than two (2) attorneys on each side shall argue the merits of the action or proceeding unless the Court shall otherwise permit.

(e) Relations With Jury. Before and during the trial, a lawyer shall avoid communicating with a juror in a case with which a lawyer is connected about any subject, whether pertaining to the case or not. After the jury has been discharged, a lawyer shall not communicate with a member of the jury about a case with which the lawyer and the juror have been connected without leave of Court granted for good cause shown. In such case, the Court may allow counsel to interview jurors to determine whether their verdict is subject to legal challenge, and may limit the time, place, and circumstances under which the interviews may be conducted. The Court also may authorize certain other post-trial lawyer/jury communications in specific cases as the Court may determine to be appropriate under the circumstances. During any Court-conducted or -authorized inquiry, a lawyer shall not ask questions of or make comments to a juror that are calculated to harass or embarrass the juror or to influence the juror's actions in future jury service. Nothing in this rule shall prohibit a lawyer from communicating with a juror after the jury has been discharged where the communication is not related to the case and either the juror initiates the communication or the lawyer encounters the juror in a social or business setting unrelated to the case.

(f) Relation to Other Rules. This Local Rule governing attorneys is supplemented by the Special Rules Governing the Admission and Practice of Attorneys and the Rules Governing Attorney Discipline of this District.

(g) Responsibility to Maintain Current Contact Information. Each member of the Bar of the Southern District, any attorney appearance *pro hac* vice, and any party appearing *pro se* shall maintain current contact information with the Clerk of Court. Each attorney shall update contact information including e-mail address within seven (7) days of a change. Counsel appearing *pro hac vice* and a party appearing *pro se* shall conventionally file a Notice of Current Address with updated contact information within seven (7) days of a change. The failure to comply shall not constitute grounds for relief from deadlines imposed by Rule or by the Court. All Court Orders and Notices will be deemed to be appropriately served if directed either electronically or by conventional mail consistent with information on file with the Clerk of Court.

[Effective December 1, 1994. Amended effective April 15, 2002; April 15, 2007; April 15, 2010; April 15, 2011; December 1, 2011; December 1, 2015; December 1, 2016.]

Authority

(1993) Former Local Rule 16. Renumbered per Model Rules.

RULE 15.1 FORM OF A MOTION TO AMEND AND ITS SUPPORTING DOCUMENTATION

A party who moves to amend a pleading shall attach the original of the amendment to the motion in the manner prescribed by Section 3I(1) of the CM/ECF Administrative Procedures. Any amendment to a pleading, whether filed as a matter of course or upon a successful motion to amend, must, except by leave of Court, reproduce the entire pleading as amended, and may not incorporate any prior pleading by reference. When a motion to amend is granted, the amended pleading shall be separately filed and served forthwith.

[Effective December 1, 1994. Amended effective April 15, 2007; December 1, 2015.]

Authority

(1993) Model Local Rule 15.1.

RULE 16.1 PRETRIAL PROCEDURE IN CIVIL ACTIONS

(a) Differentiated Case Management in Civil Actions.

(1) *Definition.* "Differentiated Case Management" is a system for managing cases based on the complexity of each case and the requirement for judicial involvement. Civil cases having similar characteristics are identified, grouped and assigned to designated tracks. Each track employs a case management plan tailored to the general requirements of similarly situated cases.

(2) *Case Management Tracks.* There shall be three (3) case management tracks, as follows:

(A) Expedited—a relatively non-complex case requiring only one (1) to three (3) days of trial may be assigned to an expedited track in which discovery shall be completed within the period of ninety (90) to 179 days from the date of the Scheduling Order.

(B) Standard Track—a case requiring three (3) to ten (10) days of trial may be assigned to a standard track in which discovery shall be completed within 180 to 269 days from the date of the Scheduling Order.

(C) Complex Track—an unusually complex case requiring over ten (10) days of trial may be assigned to the complex track in which discovery shall be completed within 270 to 365 days from the date of the Scheduling Order.

(3) *Evaluation and Assignment of Cases.* The following factors shall be considered in evaluating and assigning cases to a particular track: the complexity of the case, number of parties, number of expert witnesses, volume of evidence, problems locating or preserving evidence, time estimated by the parties for discovery and time reasonably required for trial, among other factors. The majority of civil cases will be assigned to a standard track.

(4) The parties shall recommend to the Court in their proposed Scheduling Order filed pursuant to Local Rule 16.1(b), to which particular track the case should be assigned.

(b) Scheduling Conference and Order.

(1) *Party Conference.* Except in categories of proceedings exempted from initial disclosures under Federal Rule of Civil Procedure 26(a)(1)(B), or when otherwise ordered, counsel for the parties (or the party, if proceeding pro se), as soon as practicable and in any event at least twenty-one (21) days before a scheduling conference is held or a scheduling order is due under Federal Rule of Civil Procedure 16(b), *must* meet in person, by telephone, or by other comparable means, for the purposes prescribed by Federal Rule of Civil Procedure 26(f).

(2) *Conference Report.* The attorneys of record and all unrepresented parties that have appeared in the case are jointly responsible for submitting to the Court, within fourteen (14) days of the conference, a written report outlining the discovery plan and discussing:

(A) the likelihood of settlement;

(B) the likelihood of appearance in the action of additional parties;

(C) proposed limits on the time:

(i) to join other parties and to amend the pleadings;

(ii) to file and hear motions; and

(iii) to complete discovery.

(D) proposals for the formulation and simplification of issues, including the elimination of frivolous claims or defenses, and the number and timing of motions for summary judgment or partial summary judgment;

(E) the necessity or desirability of amendments to the pleadings;

(F) the possibility of obtaining admissions of fact and of documents, electronically stored information or things which will avoid unnecessary proof, stipulations regarding authenticity of documents, electronically stored information or things, and the need for advance rulings from the Court on admissibility of evidence;

(G) suggestions for the avoidance of unnecessary proof and of cumulative evidence;

(H) suggestions on the advisability of referring matters to a Magistrate Judge or master;

(I) a preliminary estimate of the time required for trial;

(J) requested date or dates for conferences before trial, a final pretrial conference, and trial; and

(K) any other information that might be helpful to the Court in setting the case for status or pretrial conference.

(3) *Joint Proposed Scheduling Order.* The Report shall be accompanied by a Joint Proposed Scheduling Order which shall contain the following information:

(A) Assignment of the case to a particular track pursuant to Local Rule 16.1(a) above;

(B) The detailed discovery schedule agreed to by the parties;

(C) Any agreements or issues to be decided by the Court regarding the preservation, disclosure, and discovery of documents, electronically stored information, or things;

(D) Any agreements the parties reach for asserting claims of privilege or protection of trial preparation material after production;

(E) A limitation of the time to join additional parties and to amend the pleadings;

(F) A space for insertion of a date certain for filing all pretrial motions;

(G) A space for insertion of a date certain for resolution of all pretrial motions by the Court;

(H) Any proposed use of the Manual on Complex Litigation and any other need for rule variations, such as on deposition length or number of depositions;

(I) A space for insertion of a date certain for the date of pretrial conference (if one is to be held); and

(J) A space for insertion of the date certain for trial.

In all civil cases (except those expressly exempted below) the Court shall enter a Scheduling Order as soon as practicable but in any event within ninety (90) days after the appearance of a defendant and within 120 days after the complaint has been served on a defendant. It is within the discretion of each Judge to decide whether to hold a scheduling conference with the parties prior to entering the Scheduling Order.

(4) *Notice of Requirement.* Counsel for plaintiff, or plaintiff if proceeding pro se, shall be responsible for giving notice of the requirements of this subsection to each defendant or counsel for each defendant as soon as possible after such defendant's first appearance.

(5) *Exempt Actions.* The categories of proceedings exempted from initial disclosures under Federal Rule of Civil Procedure 26(a)(1)(B) are exempt from the requirements of this subsection. The Court shall have the discretion to enter a Scheduling Order or hold a Scheduling Conference in any case even if such case is within an exempt category.

(6) *Compliance With Pretrial Orders.* Regardless of whether the action is exempt pursuant to Federal Rule of Civil Procedure 26(a)(1)(B), the parties are required to comply with any pretrial orders by the Court and the requirements of this Local Rule including, but not limited to, orders setting pretrial conferences and establishing deadlines by which the parties' counsel must meet, prepare and submit pretrial stipulations, complete discovery, exchange reports of expert witnesses, and submit memoranda of law and proposed jury instructions.

(c) Pretrial Conference Mandatory. A pretrial conference pursuant to Federal Rule of Civil Procedure 16(a), shall be held in every civil action unless the Court specifically orders otherwise. Each party shall be represented at the pretrial conference and at meetings held pursuant to paragraph (d) hereof by the attorney who will conduct the trial, except for good cause shown a party may be represented by another attorney who has complete information about the action and is authorized to bind the party.

(d) Pretrial Disclosures and Meeting of Counsel. Unless otherwise directed by the Court, at least thirty (30) days before trial each party must provide to the other party and promptly file with the Court the information prescribed by Federal Rule of Civil Procedure 26(a)(3). No later than fourteen (14) days prior to the date of the pretrial conference, or if no pretrial conference is held, fourteen (14) days prior to the call of the calendar, counsel shall meet at a mutually convenient time and place and:

(1) Discuss settlement.

(2) Prepare a pretrial stipulation in accordance with paragraph (e) of this Local Rule.

(3) Simplify the issues and stipulate to as many facts and issues as possible.

(4) Examine all trial exhibits, except that impeachment exhibits need not be revealed.

(5) Exchange any additional information as may expedite the trial.

(e) Pretrial Stipulation Must Be Filed. It shall be the duty of counsel to see that the pretrial stipulation is drawn, executed by counsel for all parties, and filed with the Court no later than seven (7) days prior to the pretrial conference, or if no pretrial conference is held, seven (7) days prior to the call of the calendar. The pretrial stipulation shall contain the following statements in separate numbered paragraphs as indicated:

(1) A short concise statement of the case by each party in the action.

(2) The basis of federal jurisdiction.

(3) The pleadings raising the issues.

(4) A list of all undisposed of motions or other matters requiring action by the Court.

(5) A concise statement of uncontested facts which will require no proof at trial, with reservations, if any.

(6) A statement in reasonable detail of issues of fact which remain to be litigated at trial. By way of example, reasonable details of issues of fact would include: (A) As to negligence or contributory negligence, the specific acts or omissions relied upon; (B) As to damages, the precise nature and extent of damages claimed; (C) As to unseaworthiness or unsafe condition of a vessel or its equipment, the material facts and circumstances relied upon; (D) As to breach of contract, the specific acts or omissions relied upon.

(7) A concise statement of issues of law on which there is agreement.

(8) A concise statement of issues of law which remain for determination by the Court.

(9) Each party's numbered list of trial exhibits, other than impeachment exhibits, with objections, if any, to each exhibit, including the basis of all objections to each document, electronically stored information and thing. The list of exhibits shall be on separate schedules attached to the stipulation, should identify those which the party expects to offer and those which the party may offer if the need arises, and should identify concisely the basis for objection. In noting the basis for objections, the following codes should be used:

A–Authenticity

I–Contains inadmissible matter (mentions insurance, prior conviction, etc.)

R–Relevancy

H–Hearsay

UP–Unduly prejudicial—probative value outweighed by undue prejudice

P–Privileged

Counsel may agree on any other abbreviations for objections, and shall identify such codes in the exhibit listing them.

(10) Each party's numbered list of trial witnesses, with their addresses, separately identifying those whom the party expects to present and those whom the party may call if the need arises. Witnesses whose testimony is expected to be presented by means of a deposition shall be so designated. Impeachment witnesses need not be listed. Expert witnesses shall be so designated.

(11) Estimated trial time.

(12) Where attorney's fees may be awarded to the prevailing party, an estimate of each party as to the maximum amount properly allowable.

(f) Unilateral Filing of Pretrial Stipulation Where Counsel Do Not Agree. If for any reason the pretrial stipulation is not executed by all counsel, each counsel shall file and serve separate proposed pretrial stipulations not later than seven (7) days prior to the pretrial conference, or if no pretrial conference is held, seven (7) days prior to the call of the calendar, with a statement of reasons no agreement was reached thereon.

(g) Record of Pretrial Conference Is Part of Trial Record. Upon the conclusion of the final pretrial conference, the Court will enter further orders as may be appropriate. Thereafter the pretrial stipulation as so modified will control the course of the trial, and may be thereafter amended by the Court only to prevent manifest injustice. The record made upon the pretrial conference shall be deemed a part of the trial record; provided, however, any statement made concerning possible compromise settlement of any claim shall not be a part of the trial record, unless consented to by all parties appearing.

(h) Discovery Proceedings. All discovery proceedings must be completed no later than fourteen (14) days prior to the date of the pretrial conference, or if no pretrial conference is held, fourteen (14) days prior to the call of the calendar, unless further time is allowed by order of the Court for good cause shown.

(i) Newly Discovered Evidence or Witnesses. If new evidence or witnesses are discovered after the pretrial conference, the party desiring their use shall immediately furnish complete details thereof and the reason for late discovery to the Court and to opposing counsel. Use may be allowed by the Court in furtherance of the ends of justice.

(j) Memoranda of Law. Counsel shall serve and file memoranda treating any unusual questions of law, including motions in limine, no later than seven (7) days prior to the pretrial conference, or if no pretrial conference is held, seven (7) days prior to the call of the calendar.

(k) Proposed Jury Instructions or Proposed Findings of Facts and Conclusions of Law. At the close of the evidence or at an earlier reasonable time that the Court directs, counsel may submit proposed jury instructions or, where appropriate, proposed findings of fact and conclusions of law to the Court, with copies to all other counsel. At the close of the evidence, a party may file additional instructions covering matters occurring at the trial that could not reasonably be anticipated; and with the Court's permission, file untimely requests for instructions on any issue.

(*l*) Penalty for Failure to Comply. Failure to comply with the requirements of this Local Rule will subject the party or counsel to appropriate penalties, including but not limited to dismissal of the cause, or the striking of defenses and entry of judgment.

[Effective December 1, 1994. Amended effective April 15, 1996; April 15, 1997; April 15, 1998; April 15, 2001; April 15, 2004; April 15, 2007; April 15, 2010; April 15, 2011; December 1, 2011; December 3, 2012; December 1, 2015.]

Authority

(1993) Former Local Rule 17.

RULE 16.2 COURT ANNEXED MEDIATION

(a) General Provisions.

(1) *Definitions.* Mediation is a supervised settlement conference presided over by a qualified, certified, and neutral mediator, or anyone else whom the parties agree upon to serve as a mediator, to promote conciliation, compromise and the ultimate settlement of a civil action.

A certified mediator is an attorney, certified by the Chief Judge in accordance with these Local Rules, who possesses the unique skills required to facilitate the mediation process including the ability to suggest alternatives, analyze issues, question perceptions, use logic, conduct private caucuses, stimulate negotiations between opposing sides, and keep order.

The mediation process does not allow for testimony of witnesses. The mediator does not review or rule upon questions of fact or law, or render any final decision in the case. Absent a settlement, the mediator will report to the presiding Judge only as to whether the case settled (in full or in part) or was adjourned for further mediation, whether the mediator declared an impasse, and pursuant to Local Rule 16.2(e), whether any party failed to attend the mediation.

(2) *Purpose.* It is the purpose of the Court, through adoption and implementation of this Local Rule, to provide an alternative mechanism for the resolution of civil disputes leading to disposition before trial of many civil cases with resultant savings in time and costs to litigants and to the Court, but without sacrificing the quality of justice to be rendered or the right of the litigants to a full trial in the event of an impasse following mediation. Mediation also enables litigants to take control of their dispute and encourages amicable resolution of disputes.

(b) Certification; Qualification of Certified Mediators; Compensation of Mediators.

(1) *Certification of Mediators.* The Chief Judge shall certify those persons who are eligible and qualified to serve as mediators under this Local Rule, in such numbers as the Chief Judge shall deem appropriate. Thereafter, the Chief Judge

shall have complete discretion and authority to withdraw the certification of any mediator at any time.

(2) *Lists of Certified Mediators.* Lists of certified mediators shall be maintained in the offices of the Clerk of the Court and shall be made available to counsel and the public upon request.

(3) *Qualifications of Certified Mediators.* An individual may be certified to serve as a mediator in this District provided that the individual shall:

(A) be an attorney who has been admitted for at least ten (10) consecutive years to one or more State Bars or the Bar of the District of Columbia; and

(B) currently be a member in good standing of The Florida Bar and the Bar of this Court; and

(C) have substantial experience either as a lawyer or mediator in matters brought in any United States District Court or Bankruptcy Court; and

(D) have been certified and remain in good standing as a circuit court mediator under the rules adopted by the Supreme Court of Florida; and

(E) have substantial experience as a mediator.

The advisory committee may recommend for certification an attorney to serve as a mediator in this District if it determines that, for exceptional circumstances, the applicant should be certified who is not otherwise eligible for certification under this section.

Any individual who seeks certification as a mediator shall agree to accept at least two (2) mediation assignments per year in cases where at least one (1) party lacks the ability to compensate the mediator, in which case the mediator's fees shall be reduced accordingly or the mediator shall serve pro bono (if no litigant is able to contribute compensation).

The Chief Judge shall constitute an advisory committee from lawyers who represent those categories of civil litigants who may utilize the mediation program and lay persons to assist in formulating policy and additional standards relating to the qualification of mediators and the operation of the mediation program and to review applications of prospective mediators and to recommend certification to the Chief Judge as appropriate.

(4) *Standards of Professional Conduct for Mediators.* All individuals who mediate cases pending in this District shall be governed by the Standards of Professional Conduct in the Florida Rules for Certified and Court–Appointed Mediators adopted by the Florida Supreme Court (the "Florida Rules") and shall be subject to discipline and the procedures therefor set forth in the Florida Rules. Every mediator who mediates a case in this District consents to the jurisdiction of the Florida Dispute Resolution Center and the committees and panels authorized thereby for determining the merits of any complaint made against any mediator in this District.

(5) *Oath Required.* Every certified mediator shall take the oath or affirmation prescribed by 28 U.S.C. § 453 upon qualifying as a mediator.

(6) *Disqualification of a Mediator.* Any person selected as a mediator may be disqualified for bias or prejudice as provided in 28 U.S.C. § 144, and shall be disqualified in any case in which such action would be required of a justice, judge, or Magistrate Judge governed by 28 U.S.C. § 455.

(7) *Compensation of Mediators.* Mediators shall be compensated (a) at the rate provided by standing order of the Court, as amended from time to time by the Chief Judge, if the mediator is appointed by the Court without input or at the request of the parties; or (b) at such rate as may be agreed to in writing by the parties and the mediator, if the mediator is selected by the parties. Absent agreement of the parties to the contrary, the cost of the mediator's services shall be borne equally by the parties to the mediation conference. A mediator shall not negotiate or mediate the waiver or shifting of responsibility for payment of mediation fees from one party to the other. All mediation fees payable under this rule shall be due within forty-five (45) days of invoice and shall be enforceable by the Court upon motion.

(c) Types of Cases Subject to Mediation. Unless expressly ordered by the Court, the following types of cases shall not be subject to mediation pursuant to this rule:

(1) Habeas corpus cases;

(2) Motion to vacate sentence under 28 U.S.C. § 2255;

(3) Social Security cases;

(4) Civil forfeiture matters;

(5) IRS summons enforcement actions;

(6) Land condemnation cases;

(7) Default proceedings;

(8) Student loan cases;

(9) Naturalization proceedings filed as civil actions;

(10) Statutory interpleader actions;

(11) Truth–in–Lending Act cases not brought as class actions;

(12) Letters rogatory; and

(13) Registration of foreign judgments.

(d) Procedures to Refer a Case or Claim to Mediation.

(1) *Order of Referral.* In every civil case excepting those listed in Local Rule 16.2(c), the Court shall enter an order of referral similar in form to the proposed order available on the Court's website (www.flsd.uscourts.gov), which shall:

(A) Direct mediation be conducted not later than sixty (60) days before the scheduled trial date which shall be established no later than the date of the issuance of the order of referral.

(B) Direct the parties, within fourteen (14) days of the date of the order of referral, to agree upon a mediator. The parties are encouraged to utilize the list of certified mediators established in connection with Local Rule 16.2(b) but may by mutual agreement select any individual as mediator. The parties shall file a "Notice of Selection of Mediator" within that period of time. If the parties are unable to agree upon a mediator, plaintiff's counsel, or plaintiff if self-represented, shall file a "Request For Clerk To Appoint

Mediator," and the Clerk will designate a mediator from the list of certified mediators on a blind, random basis.

(C) Direct that, at least fourteen (14) days prior to the mediation date, each party give the mediator a confidential written summary of the case identifying issues to be resolved.

(2) *Coordination of Mediation Conference.* Plaintiff's counsel (or another attorney agreed upon by all counsel of record) shall be responsible for coordinating the mediation conference date and location agreeable to the mediator and all counsel of record.

(3) *Stipulation of Counsel.* Any action or claim may be referred to mediation upon stipulation of the parties.

(4) *Withdrawal From Mediation.* Any civil action or claim referred to mediation pursuant to this rule may be exempt or withdrawn from mediation by the presiding Judge at any time, before or after reference, upon application of a party and/or determination for any reason that the case is not suitable for mediation.

(e) Party Attendance Required. Unless excused in writing by the presiding Judge all parties and required claims professionals (*e.g.*, insurance adjusters) shall be physically present at the mediation conference (*i.e.*, in person if the party is a natural person or by personal attendance of a corporate representative if the party is an entity) with full authority to negotiate a settlement. If a party to a mediation is a public entity required to conduct its business pursuant to Florida Statutes Chapter 286, and is a defendant or counterclaim defendant in the litigation, that party shall be deemed to appear at a mediation conference by the physical presence of a representative with full authority to negotiate on behalf of the entity and to recommend settlement to the appropriate decision-making body of the entity. The representative shall not be solely the public entity's counsel (or firm) of record, however, the representative may be the public entity's in-house counsel where another counsel of record for the public entity is also present. In cases where the in-house counsel is counsel of record, that counsel and another representative may act as duly authorized representatives of the public entity. In cases where the parties include a public entity and/or individuals who were or are employed by a public entity or elected officials of a public entity, such individual parties do not need to attend the mediation conference if all claims asserted against the individuals are covered by insurance or by an indemnification from the public entity for purposes of mediation. Notwithstanding the foregoing, counsel representing the individual defendants shall provide the individual defendants with notice of the mediation conference and the individual defendants shall have the right to attend the mediation conference. The mediator shall report non-attendance to the Court. Failure to comply with the attendance or settlement authority requirements may subject a party to sanctions by the Court.

(f) Mediation Report; Notice of Settlement; Judgment.

(1) *Mediation Report.* Within seven (7) days following the mediation conference, the mediator, if an authorized user of the Court's electronic filing system (CM/ECF), shall electronically file a Mediation Report. If the mediator is not an authorized CM/ECF user, the mediator shall file the Mediation Report in the conventional manner. The report shall indicate whether all required parties were present and whether the case settled (in full or in part), whether the mediation was adjourned, or whether the case did not settle.

(2) *Notice of Settlement.* In the event that the parties reach an agreement to settle the case or claim, counsel shall promptly notify the Court of the settlement by filing a notice of settlement signed by counsel of record within fourteen (14) days of the mediation conference. Thereafter the parties shall forthwith submit an appropriate pleading concluding the case.

(g) Trial Upon Failure to Settle.

(1) *Trial Upon Failure to Settle.* If the mediation conference fails to result in a settlement, the case will be tried as originally scheduled.

(2) *Restrictions on the Use of Information Derived During the Mediation Conference.* All proceedings of the mediation shall be confidential and are privileged in all respects as provided under federal law and Florida Statutes § 44.405. The proceedings may not be reported, recorded, placed into evidence, made known to the Court or jury, or construed for any purpose as an admission against interest. A party is not bound by anything said or done at the conference, unless a written settlement is reached, in which case only the terms of the settlement are binding.

[Effective December 1, 1994. Amended effective April 15, 1996; April 15, 1997; April 15, 1999; April 15, 2004; April 15, 2005; April 15, 2007; April 15, 2009; April 15, 2010; December 1, 2011; December 3, 2012; December 1, 2014; December 1, 2015.]

RULE 16.3 CALENDAR CONFLICTS

Calendar conflicts will be resolved and notice shall be given in accordance with the Resolution of the Florida State–Federal Council Regarding Calendar Conflicts Between State and Federal Courts (available on the Court's website: www.flsd.uscourts.gov) or as otherwise agreed to between the Judges in a given case.

[Effective April 15, 2000. Amended effective April 15, 2006; April 15, 2007; December 1, 2011; December 1, 2015.]

Authority

(2000) Resolution of the Florida State–Federal Council Regarding Calendar Conflicts Between State and Federal Courts. *See also* Fla.R.Jud.Admin. 2.052.

(2006) *Krasnow v. Navarro*, 9 F.2d 451 (11th Cir. 1990).

RULE 23.1 CLASS ACTIONS

In any case sought to be maintained as a class action:

(a) The pleading shall bear next to its caption the legend "Class Action."

(b) The pleading shall contain under a separate heading, styled "Class Action Allegations:"

(1) A reference to the portion or portions of Federal Rule of Civil Procedure 23 under which it is claimed that the suit is properly maintainable as a class action.

(2) Appropriate allegations thought to justify such claim, including, but not necessarily limited to:

(A) the size (or approximate size) and definition of the alleged class

(B) the basis upon which the plaintiff (or plaintiffs) claims

(i) to be an adequate representative of the class, or

(ii) if the class is composed of defendants, that those named as parties are adequate representatives of the class

(C) the alleged questions of law and fact claimed to be common to the class, and

(D) in actions claimed to be maintainable as class actions under Federal Rule of Civil Procedure 23(b)(3), allegations thought to support the findings required by that subdivision.

(c) In ruling on any motion by a putative class action plaintiff for a determination under Federal Rule of Civil Procedure 23(c)(1) as to whether an action is to be maintained as a class action, the Court may allow the action to be so maintained, may disallow and strike the class action allegations, or may order postponement of the determination pending discovery or such other preliminary procedures as appear to be appropriate and necessary in the circumstances. Whenever possible, where it is held that the determination should be postponed, a date will be fixed by the Court for renewal of the motion.

[Effective December 1, 1994. Amended effective April 15, 1996; April 15, 2001; April 15, 2004; April 15, 2007; April 15, 2010; December 1, 2011; December 1, 2015.]

Authority

(1993) Former Local Rule 19. Renumbered per Model Rules. In accordance with Model Rule 23.1.

RULE 24.1 CONSTITUTIONAL CHALLENGE TO ACT OF CONGRESS OR STATE STATUTE

(a) Act of Congress. Upon the filing of any action in which the constitutionality of an Act of Congress affecting the public interest is challenged, and to which action the United States or an agency, officer, or employee thereof is not a party in its or their official capacity, counsel representing the party who challenges the Act shall forthwith notify the Court of the existence of the constitutional question. The notice shall contain the full title and number of the action and shall designate the statute assailed and the grounds upon which it is assailed, so that the Court may comply with its statutory duty to certify the fact to the Attorney General of the United States as required by 28 U.S.C. § 2403. The party challenging constitutionality shall also so indicate on the pleading or paper which first does so by stating, immediately following the title of the pleading or paper, "Claim of Unconstitutionality."

(b) State Statute. Upon the filing of any action in which the constitutionality of a state statute, charter, ordinance, or franchise is challenged, counsel shall comply with the notice provisions of Florida Statutes § 86.091.

(c) No Waiver. Failure to comply with this Local Rule will not be grounds for waiving the constitutional issue or for waiving any other right the party may have. Any notice provided under this rule, or lack of notice, will not serve as a substitute for, or as a waiver of, any pleading requirements set forth in the Federal Rules of Civil Procedure or statutes.

[Effective December 1, 1994. Amended effective April 15, 2007; April 15, 2010; December 1, 2015.]

Authority

(1993) Former Local Rule 9; Model Rule 24.1.

RULE 26.1 DISCOVERY AND DISCOVERY MATERIAL (CIVIL)

(a) Generally. Parties may stipulate in writing to modify any practice or procedure governing discovery hereunder unless doing so would violate a Court-ordered deadline, obligation, or restriction.

(b) Service and Filing of Discovery Material. Initial and expert disclosures and the following discovery requests, responses, objections, notices, or any associated proof of service shall not be filed until they are used in the proceeding or the court orders their filing: (1) deposition transcripts; (2) interrogatories; (3) requests for documents, electronically stored information or things, or to permit entry upon land; (4) requests for admission ; and (5) notices of taking depositions or notices of serving subpoenas.

(c) Discovery Material to Be Filed at Outset of Trial or at Filing of Pre-trial or Post-trial Motions. If any written discovery is to be used at trial or is necessary to a pre-trial or post-trial motion, the portions to be used shall be filed with the Clerk of the Court at the outset of the trial or at the filing of the motion insofar as their use can be reasonably anticipated by the parties having custody thereof.

(d) Completion of Discovery. Party and non-party depositions must be scheduled to occur, and written discovery requests and subpoenas seeking the production of documents must be served, in sufficient time that the response is due on or before the discovery cutoff date. Failure by the party seeking discovery to comply with this paragraph obviates the need to respond or object to the discovery, appear at the deposition, or move for a protective order.

(e) Interrogatories and Production Requests.

(1) Each interrogatory objection and/or response must immediately follow the quoted interrogatory, and no part of an interrogatory shall be left unanswered merely because an objection is interposed to another part of the interrogatory.

(2)(A) Where an objection is made to any interrogatory or subpart thereof or to any production request under Federal Rule of Civil Procedure 34, the objection shall state with specificity all grounds. Any ground not stated in an objection within the time provided by the Federal Rules of Civil Procedure, or any extensions thereof, shall be waived.

(B) Where a claim of privilege is asserted in objecting to any interrogatory or production demand, or sub-part thereof, and an answer is not provided on the basis of such assertion:

(i) The attorney asserting the privilege shall in the objection to the interrogatory or document demand, or subpart thereof, identify the nature of the privilege (including work product) which is being claimed and if the privilege is being asserted in connection with a claim or defense governed by state law, indicate the state's privilege rule being invoked; and

(ii) The following information shall be provided in the objection, unless divulgence of such information would cause disclosure of the allegedly privileged information:

(a) For documents or electronically stored information, to the extent the information is readily obtainable from the witness being deposed or otherwise: (1) the type of document (e.g., letter or memorandum) and, if electronically stored information, the software application used to create it (e.g., MS Word, MS Excel); (2) general subject matter of the document or electronically stored information; (3) the date of the document or electronically stored information; and (4) such other information as is sufficient to identify the document or electronically stored information for a subpoena duces tecum, including, where appropriate, the author, addressee, and any other recipient of the document or electronically stored information, and, where not apparent, the relationship of the author, addressee, and any other recipient to each other;

(b) For oral communications: (1) the name of the person making the communication and the names of persons present while the communication was made and, where not apparent, the relationship of the persons present to the person making the communication; (2) the date and the place of communication; and (3) the general subject matter of the communication.

(C) This rule requires preparation of a privilege log with respect to all documents, electronically stored information, things and oral communications withheld on the basis of a claim of privilege or work product protection except the following: written and oral communications between a party and its counsel after commencement of the action and work product material created after commencement of the action.

(3) Whenever a party answers any interrogatory by reference to records or materials from which the answer may be derived or ascertained, as permitted in Federal Rule of Civil Procedure 33(d), the answering party shall make available:

(A) any electronically stored information or summaries thereof that it either has or can adduce by a relatively simple procedure, unless those materials are privileged or otherwise immune from discovery.

(B) any relevant compilations, abstracts or summaries in its custody or readily obtainable by it, unless those materials are privileged or otherwise immune from discovery.

(C) the records and materials for inspection and copying within fourteen (14) days after service of the answers to interrogatories or at a date agreed upon by the parties.

(4) A party need not provide discovery of electronically stored information from sources that the party identifies as not reasonably accessible because of undue burden or cost. On motion to compel discovery or for a protective order, the party from whom discovery is sought must show that the information is not reasonably accessible because of undue burden or cost. If that showing is made, the Court may nonetheless order discovery from such sources if the requesting party shows good cause, considering the limitations of Federal Rule of Civil Procedure 26(b)(2)(C). The Court may specify conditions for the discovery. Absent exceptional circumstances, the Court may not impose sanctions under these Local Rules on a party for failing to provide electronically stored information lost as a result of the routine, good faith operation of an electronic information system.

(5) The documents, electronically stored information, or things should be referenced to specific paragraphs of a request for production where practicable, unless the producing party exercises its option under Federal Rule of Civil Procedure 34(b) to produce documents as they are kept in the usual course of business. The party producing documents in response to a request for production has an obligation to explain the general scheme of record-keeping to the inspecting party. The objective is to acquaint the inspecting party generally with how and where the documents, electronically stored information, or things are maintained.

(6) Each page of any document produced in a non-electronic format must be individually identified by a sequential number that will allow the document to be identified but that does not impair review of the document.

(f) Invocation of Privilege during Depositions.

(1) Where a claim of privilege is asserted during a deposition and information is not provided on the basis of such assertion, upon request the attorney or deponent asserting the privilege shall state the specific nature of the privilege being claimed unless divulgence of such information would cause disclosure of privileged information.

(2) After a claim of privilege has been asserted, unless divulgence of requested information would cause disclosure of privileged information, the attorney or party seeking disclosure shall have reasonable latitude during the deposition to question the witness to establish other relevant information concerning the assertion of the privilege, including questions about the topics set forth in Local Rule 26.1(e)(2)(B)(ii), above.

(g) Discovery Motions.

(1) *Time for Filing.* All disputes related to discovery shall be presented to the Court by motion (or, if the Court has established a different practice for presenting discovery disputes, by other Court-approved method) within (30) days from the: (a) original due date (or later date if extended by the Court or the parties) of the response or objection to the discovery request that is the subject of the dispute; (b) date of the deposition in which the dispute arose: or (c) date on which a party first learned of or should have learned of a purported deficiency concerning the production of discovery materials. Failure to present the dispute to the Court within that timeframe, absent a showing of good cause for the delay, may constitute a waiver of the relief sought at the Court's discretion. The thirty- (30) day period set forth in this rule may be extended once for up to seven (7) additional days by an unfiled, written stipulation between the parties, provided that the stipulation does not conflict with a Court order.

(2) *Motions to Compel.* Except for motions grounded upon complete failure to respond to the discovery sought to be compelled or upon assertion of general or blanket objections to discovery, motions to compel discovery in accordance with

Federal Rules of Civil Procedure 33, 34, 36 and 37, or to compel compliance with subpoenas for production or inspection pursuant to Federal Rule of Civil Procedure 45(c)(2)(B), shall, for each separate interrogatory, question, request for production, request for admission, subpoena request, or deposition question, state: (A) verbatim the specific item to be compelled; (B) the specific objections; (C) the grounds assigned for the objection (if not apparent from the objection); and (D) the reasons assigned as supporting the motion as it relates to that specific item. The party shall write this information in immediate succession to enable the Court to rule separately on each individual item in the motion.

(3) *Motions for Protective Order.* Except for motions for an order to protect a party or other person from whom discovery is sought from having to respond to an entire set of written discovery, from having to appear at a deposition, or from having to comply with an entire subpoena for production or inspection, motions for protective order under Federal Rule of Civil Procedure 26(c) shall, for each separate interrogatory question, request for production, request for admission, subpoena request, or deposition question, state: (A) verbatim the specific item of discovery; (B) the type of protection the party requests; and (C) the reasons supporting the protection. The party shall write this information in immediate succession to enable the Court to rule separately on each individual item in the motion.

(h) Reasonable Notice of Taking Depositions. Unless otherwise stipulated by all interested parties, pursuant to Federal Rule of Civil Procedure 29, and excepting the circumstances governed by Federal Rule of Civil Procedure 30(a), a party desiring to take the deposition within the State of Florida of any person upon oral examination shall give at least seven (7) days' notice in writing to every other party to the action and to the deponent (if the deposition is not of a party), and a party desiring to take the deposition in another State of any person upon oral examination shall give at least fourteen (14) days' notice in writing to every other party to the action and the deponent (if the deposition is not of a party).

Failure to comply with this rule obviates the need for protective order.

Notwithstanding the foregoing, in accordance with Federal Rule of Civil Procedure 32(a)(5)(A), no deposition shall be used against a party who, having received less than eleven (11) calendar days' notice of a deposition as computed under Federal Rule of Civil Procedure 6(a), has promptly upon receiving such notice filed a motion for protective order under Federal Rule of Civil Procedure 26(c)(1)(B) requesting that the deposition not be held or be held at a different time or place and such motion is pending at the time the deposition is held.

[Effective December 1, 1994. Amended effective April 15, 1996; April 15, 1998; April 15, 2001; paragraph G.3 amended effective April 15, 2003; April 15, 2004; April 15, 2005; April 15, 2007; April 15, 2009; April 15, 2010; April 15, 2011; December 1, 2011; December 1, 2014; December 1, 2015; December 1, 2016.]

Authority

(1993) Former Local Rule 10I. New portions of Section E [1994, now Subsections G.2–8] are based on S.D.N.Y. local rule.

RULE 47.1 TAXATION OF COSTS FOR UNDUE INCONVENIENCE TO JURIES

Whenever a civil case that has been set for jury trial is settled or otherwise disposed of, counsel shall so inform the office of the Judge assigned to the case at least one (1) full business day prior to the day the jury is scheduled to be selected or the trial is scheduled to commence, in order that the jurors may be notified not to attend. If such notice is not given to the Clerk of the Court's Office, then except for good cause shown, juror costs, including attendance fees, mileage, and subsistence, may be assessed equally against the parties and their counsel, or otherwise assessed as directed by the Court.

[Effective December 1, 1994. Amended effective April 15, 2007; April 15, 2010; December 1, 2011; December 1, 2015.]

Authority

(1993) Former Local Rule 15.

RULE 56.1 MOTIONS FOR SUMMARY JUDGMENT

(a) Statement of Material Facts. A motion for summary judgment and the opposition thereto shall be accompanied by a statement of material facts as to which it is contended that there does not exist a genuine issue to be tried or there does exist a genuine issue to be tried, respectively. The statement shall:

(1) Not exceed ten (10) pages in length;

(2) Be supported by specific references to pleadings, depositions, answers to interrogatories, admissions, and affidavits on file with the Court; and

(3) Consist of separately numbered paragraphs.

Statements of material facts submitted in opposition to a motion for summary judgment shall correspond with the order and with the paragraph numbering scheme used by the movant, but need not repeat the text of the movant's paragraphs. Additional facts which the party opposing summary judgment contends are material shall be numbered and placed at the end of the opposing party's statement of material facts; the movant shall use that numbering scheme if those additional facts are addressed in the reply.

(b) Effect of Failure to Controvert Statement of Undisputed Facts. All material facts set forth in the movant's statement filed and supported as required above will be deemed admitted unless controverted by the opposing party's statement, provided that the Court finds that the movant's statement is supported by evidence in the record.

[Effective December 1, 1994. Amended effective April 15, 2007; April 15, 2010; April 15, 2011; December 1, 2015.]

Authority

(1993) Former Local Rule 10J.

RULE 62.1 APPEAL BONDS; AUTOMATIC STAY

(a) Appeal Bond. A supersedeas bond staying execution of a money judgment shall be in the amount of 110% of the judgment, to provide security for interest, costs, and any award of damages for delay. Upon its own motion or upon application of a party the Court may direct otherwise.

(b) Extension of Automatic Stay When Notice of Appeal Filed. If within the fourteen (14) day period established by Federal Rule of Civil Procedure 62(a), a party files any of the motions contemplated in Federal Rule of Civil Procedure 62(b), or a notice of appeal, then unless otherwise ordered by the Court, a further stay shall exist for a period not to exceed thirty (30) days from the entry of the judgment or order. The purpose of this additional stay is to permit the filing of a supersedeas bond, which shall be filed by the end of the thirty (30) day period provided herein.

[Effective April 15, 2000. Amended effective April 15, 2007; April 15, 2010; December 1, 2015.]

RULE 67.1 COURT REGISTRY AND WRITS OF GARNISHMENT

(a) Upon the issuance of any Order of Disbursement on the Court registry, the concerned party shall provide a copy of such Order to the Clerk of the Court's Financial Administrator or other designated deputy.

(b) In any case where an Order of Court directs the Clerk of the Court to handle a specific investment in a different manner than specified by Internal Operating Procedures, the interested party shall serve a copy of the Order upon the Clerk of the Court personally or a deputy clerk specifically designated in accordance with the wording of Federal Rule of Civil Procedure 67, to–wit:

"The party making the deposit shall serve the Order permitting deposit on the Clerk of this Court."

(c) A party applying for the issuance of a writ of garnishment shall pay the amount prescribed by applicable Florida law to the garnishee. The payment is for the attorneys' fees of the garnishee. Monies previously required to be deposited in the non-interest bearing registry of the Court shall be disbursed as follows:

(1) The Clerk of the Court shall pay such deposit to the garnishee (or garnishee's counsel, if so requested) for the payment or partial payment of attorney's fees which the garnishee expends or agrees to expend in obtaining representation in response to the writ. Such payment shall be made upon the garnishee's demand, in writing, at any time after the service of the writ, unless otherwise directed by the Court.

(2) In cases of a pre-judgment writ of garnishment, if the garnishee fails to make written demand within sixty (60) days of the conclusion of the case, including all appeals, the Clerk of the Court shall return such deposit to the depositing party (or their counsel) without further order or request, unless otherwise directed by the Court.

(3) In cases of a post-judgment writ of attachment, if the garnishee fails to make written demand within sixty (60) days after post-judgment proceedings on the writ have concluded, including all appeals concerning the writ, the Clerk of the Court shall return such deposit to the depositing party (or their counsel) without further order or request, unless otherwise directed by the Court.

(4) If garnishment cost deposit monies remain on deposit with the Clerk of the Court more than five (5) years after the conclusion of a case or post-judgment proceedings, including all appeals, and if the Clerk of the Court has made reasonable attempts to provide notice to the depositing party or to distribute those monies without success, those unclaimed monies shall be moved into the appropriate U.S. Treasury Unclaimed Funds account pursuant to Title 28, United States Code, Section 2042, without further order of Court. Any monies deposited with the U.S. Treasury under these provisions as unclaimed are available for immediate disbursement to any party by the Clerk of the Court upon application and further Court order.

[Effective December 1, 1994. Amended effective April 15, 2002; April 15, 2007; April 15, 2010; December 1, 2011; December 1, 2014; December 1, 2015.]

Authority

(1993) Former Local Rule 24. Renumbered per Model Rules project.

(2002) Federal Rule of Civil Procedure 69, Florida Statute Section 77.28, and Administrative Orders 90–104, 98–51 and 2001–69.

RULE 77.1 PHOTOGRAPHING, BROADCASTING, TELEVISING

Other than required by authorized personnel in the discharge of official duties, all forms of equipment or means of photographing, tape-recording, broadcasting or televising within the environs of any place of holding court in the District, including courtrooms, chambers, adjacent rooms, hallways, doorways, stairways, elevators or offices of supporting personnel, whether the Court is in session or at recess, is prohibited; except that (a) photographing in connection with naturalization hearings or other special proceedings, as approved by a Judge of this Court, will be permitted; and (b) Judges participating in the Judicial Conference of the United States pilot program may permit recording, broadcasting, and publishing of proceedings in accordance with program guidelines.

[Effective December 1, 1994. Amended effective April 15, 2007; December 1, 2011; December 1, 2015.]

Authority

(1993) Former Local Rule 20.

(2011) Amended to provide for participation in pilot program for the study of camera use in district courtrooms pursuant to those guidelines issued by the Judicial Conference Committee on Court Administration and Case Management (www.uscourts.gov).

RULE 77.2 RELEASE OF INFORMATION IN CRIMINAL AND CIVIL PROCEEDINGS

(a) It is the duty of the lawyer or law firm not to release or authorize the release of information or opinion which a reasonable person would expect to be disseminated by means of public communication, in connection with pending or imminent criminal litigation with which the lawyer or the firm is associated, if there is a reasonable likelihood that such dissemination will interfere with a fair trial or otherwise prejudice the due administration of justice.

(b) With respect to a grand jury or other pending investigation of any criminal matter, a lawyer participating in or associated with the investigation shall refrain from making any extrajudicial statement which a reasonable person would expect to be disseminated by means of public communication, that goes beyond the public record or that is not necessary to inform the public that the investigation is underway, to describe the general scope of the investigation, to obtain assistance in the apprehension of a suspect, to warn the public of any dangers, or otherwise to aid in the investigation.

(c) From the time of arrest, issuance of an arrest warrant, or the filing of a complaint, information, or indictment in any criminal matter until the commencement of trial or disposition without trial, a lawyer or law firm associated with the prosecution or defense shall not release or authorize the release of any extrajudicial statement which a reasonable person would expect to be disseminated by means of public communication, relating to that matter and concerning:

(1) The prior criminal record (including arrests, indictments, or other charges of crime), or the character or reputation of the accused, except that the lawyer or law firm may make a factual statement of the accused's name, age, residence, occupation, and family status, and if the accused has not been apprehended, a lawyer associated with the prosecution may release any information necessary to aid apprehension or to warn the public of any dangers the accused may present.

(2) The existence or contents of any confession, admission, or statement given by the accused, or the refusal or failure of the accused to make any statement.

(3) The performance of any examinations or tests or the accused's refusal or failure to submit to an examination or test.

(4) The identity, testimony, or credibility of prospective witnesses, except that the lawyer or law firm may announce the identity of the victim if the announcement is not otherwise prohibited by law.

(5) The possibility of a plea of guilty to the offense charged or a lesser offense.

(6) Any opinion as to the accused's guilt or innocence or as to the merits of the case or the evidence in the case.

The foregoing shall not be construed to preclude the lawyer or law firm during this period, in the proper discharge of the lawyer's or its official or professional obligations, from announcing the fact and circumstances of arrest (including time and place of arrest, resistance, pursuit, and use of weapons), the identity of the investigating and arresting officer or agency, and the length of the investigation; from making an announcement, at the time of seizure of any physical evidence other than a confession, admission, or statement, which is limited to a description of the evidence seized; from disclosing the nature, substance, or text of the charge, including a brief description of the offense charged; from quoting or referring without comment to public records of the Court in the case; from announcing the scheduling or result of any stage in the judicial process; from requesting assistance in obtaining evidence; or from announcing without further comment that the accused denies the charges made against the accused.

(d) During the trial of any criminal matter, including the period of selection of the jury, no lawyer or law firm associated with the prosecution or defense shall give or authorize any extrajudicial statement or interview, relating to the trial or the parties or issues in the trial which a reasonable person would expect to be disseminated by means of public communication, except that the lawyer or law firm may quote from or refer without comment to public records of the Court in the case.

(e) After the completion of a trial or disposition without trial of any criminal matter, and prior to the imposition of sentence, a lawyer or law firm associated with the prosecution or defense shall refrain from making or authorizing any extrajudicial statement which a reasonable person would expect to be disseminated by means of public communication if there is a reasonable likelihood that such dissemination will affect the imposition of sentence.

(f) Nothing in this Local Rule is intended to preclude the formulation or application of more restrictive rules relating to the release of information about juvenile or other offenders, to preclude the holding of hearings or the lawful issuance of reports by legislative, administrative, or investigative bodies, or to preclude any lawyers from replying to charges of misconduct that are publicly made against the lawyer or law firm.

(g) A lawyer or law firm associated with a civil action shall not during its investigation or litigation make or participate in making an extrajudicial statement, other than a quotation from or reference to public records, which a reasonable person would expect to be disseminated by means of public communication if there is a reasonable likelihood that such dissemination will interfere with a fair trial and which relates to:

(1) Evidence regarding the occurrence or transaction involved.

(2) The character, credibility, or criminal record of a party, witness, or prospective witness.

(3) The performance or results of any examinations or tests or the refusal or failure of a party to submit to such.

(4) The lawyer's opinion as to the merits of the claims or defenses of a party, except as required by law or administrative rule.

(5) Any other matter reasonably likely to interfere with a fair trial of the action.

[Effective December 1, 1994. Amended effective April 15, 2007; April 15, 2010; December 1, 2011; December 1, 2015.]

Authority

(1993) Former Local Rule 21. Rule 4-3.6 of the Rules Regulating The Florida Bar.

RULE 87.1 AUTHORITY OF BANKRUPTCY JUDGES TO MAKE LOCAL RULES

The Bankruptcy Judges of the United States Bankruptcy Court in this District may, by action of a majority of the Bankruptcy Judges, make local rules of practice and procedure to govern all cases, proceedings and other matters in the Bankruptcy Court.

[Effective December 1, 1994. Amended effective April 15, 2007; December 1, 2015.]

RULE 87.2 REFERENCE OF BANKRUPTCY MATTERS

(a) General Order of Reference. Pursuant to 28 U.S.C. § 157(a) and the Order of Reference entered March 27, 2012 (*see* Order of Reference available on the Court's website, www.flsd.uscourts.gov), all cases under Title 11, United States Code, and all proceedings under Title 11, United States Code or arising in or related to cases under Title 11, United States Code, are referred to the Bankruptcy Judges for this District and shall be commenced in the Bankruptcy Court pursuant to the Local Bankruptcy Rules. The Order of Reference also applies to notices of removal pursuant to 28 U.S.C. § 1452(a), which shall be filed with the Clerk of the Bankruptcy Court for the Division of the District where such civil action is pending. The removed claim or cause of action shall be assigned as an adversary proceeding in the Bankruptcy Court.

(b) Authority of Bankruptcy Judges. If a Bankruptcy Judge or District Judge determines that entry of a final order or judgment by a Bankruptcy Judge would not be consistent with Article III of the United States Constitution in a particular case or proceeding referred under the Order of Reference and determined to be a core matter, the Bankruptcy Judge shall, unless otherwise ordered by the District Court, hear the case or proceeding and submit proposed findings of fact and conclusions of law stated on the record or in an opinion or memorandum of decision.

(c) Authority of District Court to Treat Final Orders as Proposed Findings and Conclusions. The District Court may treat any order of the Bankruptcy Court as proposed findings of fact and conclusions of law if the District Court concludes that the Bankruptcy Judge could not have entered a final order or judgment consistent with Article III of the United States Constitution.

[Former Local Rule 87.2 amended and renumbered as Local Rule 87.4, and new Local Rule 87.2 adopted effective April 15, 1996. Amended effective April 15, 2007; April 15, 2010; December 1, 2015.]

RULE 87.3 MOTIONS FOR WITHDRAWAL OF REFERENCE OF CASE OR PROCEEDING FROM THE BANKRUPTCY COURT

A motion to withdraw the reference pursuant to 28 U.S.C. § 157(d) shall be filed with the Clerk of the Bankruptcy Court in accordance with the requirements of Local Bankruptcy Rule 5011–1. Subsequently filed motions for withdrawal of reference in the same case or proceeding shall be regarded as similar actions and proceedings under Local Rule 3.8 and the attorneys of record shall notify the District Court of all such pending actions and proceedings in compliance with Local Rule 3.8. and, if applicable, provide the notice required by Local Rule 7.1(f).

[Effective April 15, 1996. Amended effective April 15, 1999; April 15, 2007; April 15, 2010; December 1, 2015.]

RULE 87.4 BANKRUPTCY APPEALS

Bankruptcy appeals to the District Court are governed by the Federal Rules of Bankruptcy Procedure, particularly Rules 8001 through 8028, and the Local Rules of the Bankruptcy Court. As is authorized by Federal Rule of Bankruptcy Procedure 8026, those rules are supplemented as follows:

(a) Assignment. Appeals from orders or judgments entered by the Bankruptcy Court shall generally be assigned in accordance with the Court's Internal Operating Procedures. Appeals from orders in a bankruptcy case or proceeding in which appeals have been taken from prior orders in the same case or proceeding shall be regarded as similar actions and proceedings under Local Rule 3.8 and it will be the continuing obligation of the Clerk of the District Court and the attorneys of record to comply with Local Rule 3.8.

(b) Docketing of Notice of Appeal in District Court. **All notices of appeal filed in the Bankruptcy Court under Federal Rule of Bankruptcy Procedure 8003 and 8004 shall be transmitted promptly to the Clerk of the District Court for docketing and the opening of a new civil case.**

(c) Limited Authority of Bankruptcy Court to Enter Orders Prior to Transmittal of Record to District Court. After the notice of appeal is transmitted to the District Court and a civil case is opened but before the record is transmitted to the District Court, the Bankruptcy Court is authorized and directed to dismiss an appeal for appellant's: (1) failure to pay the prescribed filing fees; (2) failure to comply with the time limitations specified in Federal Rule of Bankruptcy Procedure 8002; or (3) failure to file a designation of the items for the record or copies thereof or a statement of the issues as required by Federal Rule of Bankruptcy Procedure 8009 and Local Bankruptcy Rule 8009–1. The Bankruptcy Court is further authorized and directed to hear, under Federal Rule of Bankruptcy Procedure 9006(b), motions to extend the foregoing deadlines and to consolidate appeals that present similar issues from a common record. The Bankruptcy Court is also authorized to consider motions for stay pending appeal filed under Federal Rule of Bankruptcy Procedure 8007(a). Bankruptcy Court orders entered under this subsection shall be docketed in the Bankruptcy Court docket and transmitted to the District Court for docketing in the District Court case. Bankruptcy Court orders entered under this subsection may be reviewed by the District Court on motion filed in the District Court within fourteen (14) days after entry of the order on the District Court docket. A motion seeking review shall be filed pursuant to section (d) of this Local Rule.

(d) Motions for Stay and Other Intermediate Requests for Relief. Motions for stay pending appeal filed in the District Court pursuant to Federal Rule of Bankruptcy Procedure 8007(b), motions to review Bankruptcy Court orders entered under Federal Rule of Bankruptcy Procedure 9006(b), and other motions requesting intermediate relief as set forth in Federal Rule of Bankruptcy Procedure 8010(c) shall be filed in the District Court case opened upon transmittal to the District Court of the notice of appeal. The movant shall provide copies of any relevant portions of the Bankruptcy Court record necessary for the District Court to rule on the motion. It shall be the duty of the Clerk of the District Court immediately to transmit a copy of the order ruling on said motion to the Clerk of the Bankruptcy Court. Local Rules 5.1 and 7.1 shall apply to motions for stay and other motions seeking intermediate appellate relief from the District Court.

(e) Motions for Leave to Appeal. A motion for leave to appeal and notice of appeal shall be filed in the Bankruptcy Court pursuant to Local Bankruptcy Rule 8004–1. Upon transmittal of the notice, motion, and related documents to the District Court, a civil case shall be opened as provided in subsection (b) of this Local Rule.

Upon disposition of the motion, the Clerk of the District Court immediately shall transmit a copy of the District Court order to the Clerk of the Bankruptcy Court. If the motion for leave to appeal is granted, the appeal will proceed under the original case number and the Clerk of the Bankruptcy Court will prepare and transmit the record on appeal.

(f) Briefs.

(1) *Briefing Schedule.* The briefing schedule specified by Federal Rule of Bankruptcy Procedure 8018 may be altered only by order of the District Court. If the Clerk of the District Court does not receive appellant's brief within the time specified by Federal Rule of Bankruptcy Procedure 8018, and there is no motion for extension of time pending, the Clerk of the District Court shall furnish to the judge to whom the appeal is assigned a proposed order for dismissal of the appeal.

(2) *Form and Length of Briefs.* The form and length of briefs specified by Federal Rule of Bankruptcy Procedure 8015 may be altered only by the order of the District Court. Failure to comply with Federal Rule of Bankruptcy Procedure 8015 may result in the striking of a brief. District Court Local Rules 5.1 and 7.1 do not apply to briefs governed by Federal Rule of Bankruptcy Procedure 8015.

(g) Oral Argument. Any party requesting oral argument shall make the request within the body of the principal or reply brief, not by separate motion. The setting of oral argument is within the discretion of the District Court.

(h) Judgment. Upon receipt of the District Court's opinion, the Clerk of the District Court shall enter judgment in accordance with Federal Rule of Bankruptcy Procedure 8024(a) and, in accordance with Federal Rule of Bankruptcy Procedure 8024(b), immediately shall transmit to each party and to the Clerk of the Bankruptcy Court a notice of entry together with a copy of the District Court's opinion.

(i) Appeal. If an appeal remains pending three (3) months after its entry on the District Court docket, the appealing party shall file and serve on all parties a "Notice of 90 Days Expiring" in the manner prescribed by Local Rule 7.1(b)(4).

(j) Notice. The Clerk of the Bankruptcy Court is directed to enclose a copy of this Local Rule with the notice of appeal provided to each party in accordance with Federal Rule of Bankruptcy Procedure 8003(c)(1). Failure to receive such a copy will not excuse compliance with all provisions of this Local Rule.

(k) Court Discretion. This Local Rule is not intended to exhaust or restrict the District Court's discretion as to any aspect of any appeal.

(*l*) Sealed Documents. Pursuant to Federal Rule of Bankruptcy Procedure 8009(f), if a document sealed by the Bankruptcy Court is to be included in the record on appeal, a motion must be filed in the District Court to accept the sealed document. If the motion is granted, the Bankruptcy Clerk promptly will transmit the sealed document to the District Court Clerk.

[Former Local Rule 87.2 redesignated as Local Rule 87.4 and amended effective April 15, 1996. Amended effective April 15, 1999; April 15, 2007; April 15, 2009; April 15, 2010; December 1, 2011; December 1, 2015.]

Authority

Former Local Rule 27; (1996) renumbered from Local Rule 87.2 (1993).

RULE 87.5 DESIGNATION OF BANKRUPTCY JUDGES TO CONDUCT JURY TRIALS

The Bankruptcy Judges of this District are specially designated to conduct jury trials, with the express consent of all parties, in all proceedings under 28 U.S.C. § 157 in which the right to a jury trial applies. Pleading and responding to a jury trial demand in bankruptcy cases is governed by Local Bankruptcy Rule 9015–1. Local Rule 47.1 shall apply to jury trials conducted by Bankruptcy Judges under this rule.

[Effective April 15, 1999. Amended effective April 15, 2007; April 15, 2010; December 1, 2015.]

Comment

(1999) Incorporates the provisions of Administrative Order 96–03 "In re: Designation of Bankruptcy Judges to Conduct Jury Trials," available on the Court's website (www.flsd.uscourts.gov).

RULE 88.1 APPOINTMENT OF COUNSEL FOR INDIGENT DEFENDANTS IN CRIMINAL PROCEEDINGS

The appointment of counsel and counsel's obligations in the representation of indigent defendants in criminal proceedings pursuant to Federal Rule of Criminal Procedure 44 shall be in accordance with the "Plan of the United States District Court for the Southern District of Florida Pursuant to the Criminal Justice Act of 1964, as Amended." The current plan is available on the Court's website (www.flsd.uscourts.gov).

[Effective December 1, 1994. Amended effective April 15, 2007; December 3, 2012; December 1, 2015.]

Authority

(1993) Former Local Rule 17, updated.

RULE 88.2 POST CONVICTION, HABEAS CORPUS, AND CIVIL RIGHTS PROCEEDINGS

(a) The following petitions, motions, and complaints must substantially follow the forms, if any, prescribed by the Court and obtained from the Clerk of the Court upon request:

(1) Petitions for writ of habeas corpus pursuant to 28 U.S.C. § 2241 (common law habeas corpus),

(2) Petitions for writ of habeas corpus pursuant to 28 U.S.C. § 2254 (state prisoner attacking conviction),

(3) Motions to Vacate pursuant to 28 U.S.C. § 2255 (federal prisoner attacking conviction),

(4) Civil rights complaints pursuant to 42 U.S.C. § 1983 (Constitutional deprivation under color of state law),

(5) Civil rights complaints pursuant to *Bivens v. Six Unknown Federal Narcotics Agents*, 403 U.S. 388 (1971) (Constitutional deprivation under color of federal law).

Each must be signed under penalty of perjury by petitioner/movant or by a person authorized to sign it for petitioner/movant and, together with filing fee, if any, shall be filed in the Clerk's Office.

(b) When a petition, motion to vacate, or complaint is submitted in forma pauperis, the petitioner/movant/plaintiff shall submit the form "Application to Proceed Without Prepayment of Fees and Affidavit," which may be obtained from the Clerk of the Court, or an affidavit which substantially follows the form, and shall, under oath, set forth information which establishes that he or she is unable to pay the fees and costs of the proceedings referenced above.

[Effective December 1, 1994. Amended effective April 15, 2007; April 15, 2010; April 15, 2011; December 1, 2011; December 1, 2015.]

Authority

(1993) Former Local Rule 18.

RULE 88.3 PETTY AND CERTAIN MISDEMEANOR OFFENSES

(a) Covered Offenses. This Rule shall apply to petty offenses, as defined in 18 U.S.C. § 19, and to certain misdemeanors as shall be identified from time to time by the Court in collateral schedules. Collectively, these petty offenses and identified misdemeanors shall be referred to for purposes of this Rule as "covered offenses."

(b) Collateral and Mandatory Appearance.

(1) Covered offenses that are committed on or within the perimeter of Federally-owned or controlled buildings or within the boundaries of National Parks, Preserves, Historic Sites, or Government Reservations, including but not limited to military installations, and violations under various Treaties and Wildlife Acts, for which collateral may be posted and forfeited in lieu of appearance by the person charged, together with the amount of collateral to be posted and offenses for which a mandatory appearance is required shall be in accordance with schedules which may from time to time be approved by the Court and filed with the Clerk of the Court.

(2) Collateral may not be posted for any covered offense if the alleged violator has previously been convicted of any such offense.

(c) Forfeiture of Collateral.

(1) Any person issued a violation notice for a covered offense for which collateral can be posted may, upon request of the issuing officer, post the required amount by placing cash, personal check or money order in the official violation notice envelope and, after sealing same, delivering it to authorized personnel at a designated office where a receipt will be given. All such envelopes received will be forwarded via mail each day, except for those containing cash which shall be personally delivered to the Clerk of the Court.

(2) The posting of collateral shall signify that the offender does not wish to appear nor request a hearing before the Judge. Collateral so posted shall be forfeited to the United States and the proceedings shall be terminated.

(d) Failure to Post Collateral.

(1) If a person charged with a covered offense for which collateral is required fails to post and forfeit collateral, any punishment, including fine, imprisonment or probation may be imposed within the limits established by law upon conviction by plea or after trial.

(2) No person shall be detained for failure to post collateral for a covered offense for which collateral may be posted unless the person is placed under arrest.

(e) Arrest. Nothing contained in these Local Rules shall prohibit a law enforcement officer from arresting an alleged violator for the commission of any offense, including those for which collateral may be posted or mandatory appearance required, and forthwith notifying a Magistrate Judge for the purpose of appearance or setting bail.

(Schedule of fines and mandatory appearance is on file with Clerk's Office and agencies charged with enforcement thereof.)

[Effective December 1, 1994. Amended effective April 15, 2006; April 15, 2007; April 15, 2009; April 15, 2010; December 1, 2011; December 1, 2015.]

Authority

(1993) Former Local Rule 22.

Comments

(2011) Amended to merge Local Rule 88.4 into Local Rule 88.3.

RULE 88.5 SPEEDY TRIAL REPORTS

Counsel for the Government and counsel for each defendant shall, within twenty-one (21) days after arraignment and every twenty-one (21) days thereafter until trial or plea of guilty or nolo contendere, file with the Court a status report as to each defendant which shall include a concise statement of:

(a) All excludable time as recorded on the docket on which there is agreement, including the applicable statutes. Such agreement shall be conclusive as between the parties, unless it has no basis in fact or law.

(b) All excludable time as recorded on the docket on which there is conflict, including the applicable statutes or law.

(c) Computation of the gross time, excludable time, net time remaining, and the final date upon which the defendant can be tried in compliance with the Speedy Trial Plan of this Court.

(d) Any agreement by the parties as to excludable time which exceeds the amount recorded on the docket shall have no effect unless approved by the Court.

[Effective December 1, 1994. Amended effective April 15, 1998; April 15, 1999; April 15, 2007; April 15, 2010; December 1, 2011; December 1, 2015.]

Authority

(1993) Former Local Rule 25. Title 18, United States Code, Section 3161.

Comments

(2011) Amended to eliminate authority of Court to accept a waiver of Speedy Trial rights. *See Zedner v. United States*, 547 U.S. 489 (2006).

RULE 88.7 RETAINED CRIMINAL DEFENSE ATTORNEYS

(a) Retained criminal defense attorneys are expected to make financial arrangements satisfactory to themselves and sufficient to provide for representation of each defendant until the conclusion of the defendant's case at the trial level. Failure of a defendant to pay sums owed for attorney's fees, or failure of counsel to collect a sum sufficient to compensate him for all the services usually required of defense counsel, will not constitute good cause for withdrawal after arraignment. Every defendant, of course, has a right to appeal from any conviction.

(b) All notices of permanent appearance in the District Court, and motions for substitution of counsel, shall state whether the appearance of counsel is for trial only or for trial and appeal.

(c) At arraignment, the Magistrate Judge will inquire of each defendant and counsel whether counsel has been retained for trial only or for trial and appeal. Where counsel indicates that he or she has been retained only for trial, the defendant will be notified that it is the defendant's responsibility to arrange for counsel for any necessary appeals.

(d) In cases where the defendant moves the Court to proceed in forma pauperis on appeal, or for appointment of Criminal Justice Act appellate counsel, the Court will consider, in passing upon such applications, factors such as (i) the defendant's qualified Sixth Amendment right to counsel of choice, recognizing the distinction between choosing a trial lawyer and choosing an appellate lawyer; (ii) the contract between the defendant and trial counsel; (iii) the defendant's present financial condition and ability to have retained only trial counsel; (iv) retained counsel's appellate experience; (v) the financial burden that prosecuting the appeal would impose upon trial counsel, in view of the fee received and the professional services rendered; and (vi) all other relevant factors, including any constitutional guarantees of the defendant.

(e) In assessing whether the legal fees previously paid to defense counsel should reasonably encompass appellate representation, the Court is to apply the provisions of Rule 4–1.5 of the Rules Regulating The Florida Bar. The Court is to consider the following factors as guides in determining the reasonableness of the fee: (i) the time and labor required, the novelty, complexity, and difficulty of the questions involved, and the skill requisite to perform the legal service proffered; (ii) the likelihood that the acceptance of the particular employment precluded other employment by the lawyer; (iii) the fee, or rate of fee, customarily charged in the locality for legal services of a comparable or similar nature; (iv) the significance of, or amount involved in, the subject matter of the representation, the responsibility involved in the representation, and the results obtained; (v) the time limitations imposed by the client or by the circumstances and, as between attorney and client, any additional or special time demands or requests of the attorney by the client; (vi) the nature and length of the professional relationship of the client; and (vii) the experience, reputation, diligence and ability of the lawyer or lawyers performing the service and the skill, expertise or efficiency of efforts reflected in the actual providing of such services.

In determining a reasonable fee, the time devoted to the representation and the customary rate of fee are not the sole or controlling factors; nor should the determination be governed by fees or rates of fee provided under the Criminal Justice Act. All factors set out in this Local Rule and in the Rules Regulating The Florida Bar should be considered, and may be applied, in justification of a fee higher or lower than that which would result from application of only the time and rate factors.

(f) Those parts of proceedings undertaken pursuant to paragraphs (d) and (e) of this Local Rule that involve confidential or privileged information or communications shall be held in camera, ex-parte, and under seal.

[Effective December 1, 1994. Amended effective April 15, 2007; April 15, 2010; April 15, 2011; December 2, 2013; December 1, 2015.]

Authority

(1993) New rule added at the request of the Eleventh Circuit.

RULE 88.8 PRESENTENCE INVESTIGATIONS

(a) Within seven (7) days following entry of a guilty plea or a verdict of guilty, counsel for the defendant and the probation officer will have made arrangements for the initial interview of the defendant for the PSI.

(b) Counsel for the parties shall confer no later than seven (7) days prior to the scheduled sentencing hearing proceeding with respect to the anticipated length of the sentencing and the number of witnesses to be called. If either party reasonably anticipates that the sentencing proceeding will exceed one hour, the party shall file a notice with the Clerk of the Court and shall hand deliver a courtesy copy to the United States Probation Office no later than five (5) days prior to the sentencing proceeding. The notice shall advise the Court of the number of witnesses to be called and the estimated time required for the sentencing proceeding. Additionally, counsel for the parties shall file within the same time period any notice for enhancement of sentence or requests for departure.

(c) The recommendation as to sentencing made to the Court by the United States Probation Office shall remain confidential.

(d) Counsel for the parties may retain the PSI in their custody, and counsel for the defendant shall provide a copy to the defendant. However, the PSI is a confidential document and neither the parties nor their counsel are authorized to duplicate or disseminate it to third parties without prior permission of the Court.

[Effective December 1, 1994. Amended effective April 15, 2007; April 15, 2010; December 1, 2011; December 1, 2015.]

Authority

Administrative Order 95-02.

RULE 88.9 MOTIONS IN CRIMINAL CASES

(a) Motions in criminal cases are subject to the requirements of, and shall comply with, Local Rule 7.1. with the following exceptions:

Section 7.1(a)(3), which is superseded by this Local Rule.

Section 7.1(b), which pertains to hearings. Hearings on criminal motions may be set by the Court upon appropriate request or as required by the Federal Rules of Criminal Procedure and/or Constitutional Law.

In addition, at the time of filing motions in criminal cases, counsel for the moving party shall file with the Clerk of the Court a statement certifying either: (1) that counsel have conferred in a good faith effort to resolve the issues raised in the motion and have been unable to do so; or (2) that counsel for the moving party has made reasonable effort (which shall be identified with specificity in the statement) to confer with the opposing party but has been unable to do so. This requirement to confer shall not apply to ex parte filings.

(b) Motions in criminal cases which require evidentiary support shall be accompanied by a concise statement of the material facts upon which the motion is based.

(c) Motions in criminal cases shall be filed within twenty-eight (28) days from the arraignment of the defendant to whom the motion applies, except that motions arising from a post-arraignment event shall be filed within a reasonable time after the event.

[Effective December 1, 1994. Amended effective April 15, 1996; April 15, 1997; April 15, 1998; April 15, 2003; April 15, 2007; April 15, 2010; December 1, 2014; December 1, 2015.]

Authority

(1994) Formerly Local Rule 10G; inadvertently omitted in 1993 revision.

(1996) B. From Local Rule 7.5 and former Local Rule 10.H.

RULE 88.10 CRIMINAL DISCOVERY

(a) A defendant's request to the Court for entry of the Standing Discovery Order shall constitute a discovery request by the defendant under Fed. R. Crim. P. 16(a)(1)(A), (B), (C), (D), (E), and (F), and, following entry of the Standing Discovery Order, the government shall comply with the obligations imposed upon it by Fed. R. Crim. P. 16(a)(1)(A)–(F), and shall permit the defendant to inspect and copy the written or recorded statements made by the defendant, or copies thereof, or supply copies thereof, which are within the possession, custody or control of the government, the existence of which is known or by the exercise of due diligence may become known to the government, all subject to the provisions of Fed. R. Crim. P. 16(a)(2).

(b) Following a defendant's request to the Court for entry of the Standing Discovery Order and the Court's entry of the Standing Discovery Order, the defendant, subject to the provisions of Fed. R. Crim. P. 16(b)(2), shall:

(1) after the government complies with Fed. R. Crim. P. 16(a)(1)(E), comply with the obligations that arise under Fed. R. Crim. P. 16(b)(1)(A): and

(2) after the government complies with Fed. R. Crim. P. 16(a)(1)(F). comply with the obligations that arise under Fed. R. Crim. P. 16(b)(1)(B).

(c) The government shall reveal to the defendant and permit inspection and copying of all information and material known to the government which may be favorable to the defendant on the issues of guilt or punishment within the scope of *Brady v. Maryland*, 373 U.S. 83 (1963), and *United States v. Agurs*, 427 U.S. 97 (1976).

(d) The government shall disclose to the defendant the existence and substance of any payments, promises of immunity, leniency, preferential treatment, or other inducements made to prospective government witnesses, within the scope of *Giglio v. United States*, 405 U.S. 150 (1972), and *Napue v. Illinois*, 360 U.S. 264 (1959).

(e) The government shall supply the defendant with a record of prior convictions of any alleged informant who will testify for the government at trial.

(f) The government shall state whether defendant was identified in any lineup, showup, photo array or similar identification proceeding, and produce any pictures utilized or resulting therefrom.

(g) The government shall advise its agents and officers involved in this case to preserve all rough notes.

(h) The government shall advise the defendant(s) of its intention to introduce extrinsic act evidence pursuant to Federal Rule of Evidence 404(b). The government shall provide notice regardless of how it intends to use the extrinsic act evidence at trial, i.e. during its case-in-chief, for impeachment, or for possible rebuttal. Furthermore, the government shall apprise the defense of the general nature of the evidence of the extrinsic acts.

(i) The government shall state whether the defendant was an aggrieved person, as defined in 18 U.S.C. § 2510(11), of any relevant electronic surveillance that was authorized pursuant to 18 U.S.C. § 2516 and 18 U.S.C. § 2518 and that has been unsealed in accordance with 18 U.S.C. § 2518, and if so, shall set forth in detail the circumstances thereof.

(j) The government shall have transcribed the grand jury testimony of all witnesses who will testify for the government at the trial of this cause, preparatory to a timely motion for discovery.

(k) The government shall, upon request, deliver to any chemist selected by the defense, who is presently registered with the Attorney General in compliance with 21 U.S.C. §§ 822 and 823, and 21 C.F.R. § 101.22(8), a sufficient representative sample of any alleged contraband which is the subject of this indictment, to allow independent chemical analysis of such sample.

(*l*) The government shall permit the defendant, his counsel and any experts selected by the defense to inspect any automobile, vessel, or aircraft allegedly utilized in the commission of any offenses charged. Government counsel shall, if necessary, assist defense counsel in arranging such inspection at a reasonable time and place, by advising the government authority having custody of the thing to be inspected that such inspection has been ordered by the court.

(m) The government shall provide the defense, for independent expert examination, copies of all latent fingerprints or palm prints which have been identified by a government expert as those of the defendant.

(n) The parties shall make every possible effort in good faith to stipulate to all facts or points of law the truth and existence of which is not contested and the early resolution of which will expedite the trial.

(*o*) Schedule of Discovery.

(1) Discovery which is to be made in connection with a pre-trial hearing other than a bail or pre-trial detention hearing shall be made not later than forty-eight (48) hours prior to the hearing. Discovery which is to be made in connection with a bail or pre-trial detention hearing shall be made not later than the commencement of the hearing.

(2) Discovery which is to be made in connection with trial shall be made not later than fourteen (14) days after the arraignment, or such other time as ordered by the court.

(3) Discovery which is to be made in connection with post-trial hearings (including, by way of example only, sentencing hearings) shall be made not later than seven (7) days prior to the hearing. This discovery rule shall not affect the provisions of Local Rule 88.8 regarding presentence investigation reports.

(4) It shall be the continuing duty of counsel for both sides to immediately reveal to opposing counsel all newly discovered information or other material within the scope of this Local Rule.

[Effective December 1, 1994. Amended effective April 15, 1996; April 15, 1998; April 15, 2000; April 15, 2003; April 15, 2005; April 15, 2007; April 15, 2010; December 2, 2013; December 1, 2015; December 1, 2016.]

Authority

(1994) Former Standing Order on Criminal Discovery of the Southern District, as amended after public hearing in 1994.

Comments

(2000) With regard to discovery practices related to search warrants in criminal cases *see* September 7, 1999, letter from the then United States Attorney for the Southern District of Florida which has been posted at the U.S. Attorney's website at http://www.usdoj.gov/usao/fls/DiscoveryPractices.html.

RULE 88.11 AFTER HOURS CRIMINAL DUTY PROCEDURES

When a defendant is arrested after hours (in the evening, on the weekend, on a holiday, or in the daytime during the business week at a time that does not permit an appearance at the prescribed session of Magistrate Court), the Duty Assistant United States Attorney shall contact the Duty Magistrate Judge for the purpose of having a bond set.

Once the Duty Magistrate Judge sets a bond, the Duty Assistant United States Attorney shall transmit the bond information to the Duty Marshal and/or to the arresting agents who shall transmit the bond information to the booking officials at the receiving institution. A "permanent" bond shall be set for the defendant at the next available prescribed Duty Magistrate Judge Court session when the defendant appears for initial appearance.

For arrests that occur during the business week, prior to the end of the business day but subsequent to a time when an initial appearance at the prescribed session of Magistrate Judge Court can be made, the Duty Assistant United States Attorney shall contact the Duty Magistrate Judge in chambers for the purpose of having a temporary bond set. As with after hours arrests, the Duty Assistant United States Attorney shall transmit the bond information to the Duty Marshal and/or the arresting agents. If the Duty Magistrate Judge is on the bench when a Duty Assistant United States Attorney calls for the purpose of having a temporary bond set, the Duty Magistrate Judge will return the Duty Assistant United States Attorneys call as soon as the Duty Magistrate Judge gets off the bench.

For after hours arrests, the Duty Assistant United States Attorney shall leave a message on the Duty Magistrate Judge's beeper or cell phone. If by beeper, the call will be returned by the Duty Magistrate Judge. Once the Duty Magistrate Judge sets a bond, the Duty Assistant United States Attorney shall transmit the bond information to the Duty Marshal and/or the arresting agents for transmittal to the receiving institution. Routine arrests occurring after 10:00 p.m. need not be communicated to the Duty Magistrate Judge that night, but shall be reported by the Duty Assistant United States Attorney to the Duty Magistrate Judge the following morning. In emergency situations, the Duty Magistrate Judge may be contacted directly at any hour.

Since a probable causes determination must be made within forty-eight (48) hours of all arrests, except as Federal Rule of Criminal Procedure 4.1 may otherwise provide, a criminal complaint must be presented directly to a Magistrate Judge-for review and approval in all cases where the initial appearance will not take place within forty-eight (48) hours of an arrest.

All after-hours Duty arrests (including but not limited to arrests on warrants where bonds have already been endorsed/set) shall be reported to the Duty Magistrate Judge by the Duty Assistant United States Attorney.

[Effective April 15, 2006. Amended effective April 15, 2007; December 1, 2011; December 1, 2015.]

SELECTED LOCAL FORMS

FORM 5.1. TITLE OF DOCUMENT/SERVICE LIST

SAMPLE FORM FOLLOWING RULE 5.1

(1" from top of page, and centered, begin title of Court)

UNITED STATES DISTRICT COURT
SOUTHERN DISTRICT OF FLORIDA

Case No. ____–Civ or Cr–(USDJ's last name/USMJ's last name)

A.B.,

Plaintiff

vs.

C.D.,

Defendant.

TITLE OF DOCUMENT

Dated: Month, day, year

Respectfully submitted,

____

Attorney Name (Bar Number)
Attorney E-mail Address
Firm Name
Street Address
City, State, Zip Code
Telephone: (xxx)xxx–xxxx
Facsimile: (xxx)xxx–xxxx
Attorneys for Plaintiff/Defendant [Party Name(s)]

Certificate of Service

I hereby certify that a true and correct copy of the foregoing was served by [specify method of service] on [date] on all counsel or parties of record on the Service List below.

____
Attorney Name

SERVICE LIST

Attorney Name
Attorney E–mail Address
Firm Name
Street Address
City, State, Zip Code
Telephone: (xxx)xxx–xxxx
Facsimile: (xxx)xxx–xxxx
Attorneys for Plaintiff/Defendant
[Party's Name(s)]

Attorney Name
Attorney E–mail Address
Firm Name
Street Address
City, State, Zip Code
Telephone: (xxx)xxx–xxxx
Facsimile: (xxx)xxx–xxxx
Attorneys for Plaintiff/Defendant
[Party's Name(s)]

FORM 7.1 CERTIFICATE OF GOOD FAITH CONFERENCE; CONFERRED BUT UNABLE TO RESOLVE ISSUES PRESENTED IN THE MOTION

SAMPLE FORM FOLLOWING RULE 7.1

CERTIFICATE OF GOOD FAITH CONFERENCE; CONFERRED BUT UNABLE TO RESOLVE ISSUES PRESENTED IN THE MOTION

Pursuant to Local Rule 7.1(a)(3)(A), I hereby certify that counsel for the movant has conferred with all parties or non-parties who may be affected by the relief sought in this motion in a good faith effort to resolve the issues but has been unable to resolve the issues.

____
Attorney Name

ALTERNATIVELY,

CERTIFICATE OF GOOD FAITH CONFERENCE; UNABLE TO CONFER

Pursuant to Local Rule 7.1(a)(3)(B), I hereby certify that counsel for the movant has made reasonable efforts to confer with all parties and non-parties who may be affected by the relief sought in the motion but has been unable to do so. The reasonable efforts made were specifically as follows:

____

____.

____
Attorney Name

[FORM 16.2]* SAMPLE FORM. ORDER OF REFERRAL

SAMPLE FORM

UNITED STATES DISTRICT COURT
SOUTHERN DISTRICT OF FLORIDA

Case No. ___ –CIV–[JUDGE/MAGISTRATE]

Plaintiff

vs

Defendant
_________________________/

ORDER OF REFERRAL

Trial having been set in this matter for __________, 20 ___, pursuant to Federal Rule of Civil Procedure 16 and Local Rule 16.2, it is hereby

ORDERED AND ADJUDGED as follows:

1. All parties are required to participate in mediation. The mediation shall be completed no later than sixty (60) days before the scheduled trial date.

2. Plaintiff's counsel, or another attorney agreed upon by all counsel of record and any unrepresented parties, shall be responsible for scheduling the mediation conference. The parties are encouraged to avail themselves of the services of any mediator on the List of Certified Mediators, maintained in the office of the Clerk of the Court, but may select any other mediator. The parties shall agree upon a mediator within fourteen (14) days from the date hereof. If there is no agreement, lead counsel shall promptly notify the Clerk of the Court in writing and the Clerk of the Court shall designate a mediator from the List of Certified Mediators, which designation shall be made on a blind rotation basis.

3. A place, date and time for mediation convenient to the mediator, counsel of record, and unrepresented parties shall be established. The lead attorney shall complete the form order attached and submit it to the Court.

4. Unless excused in writing by the presiding Judge all parties and required claims professionals (e.g., insurance adjusters) shall be physically present at the mediation conference (i.e., in person if the party is a natural person or by personal attendance of a corporate representative if the party is an entity) with full authority to negotiate a settlement. If a party to a mediation is a public entity required to conduct its business pursuant to Florida Statutes Chapter 286, and is a defendant or counterclaim defendant in the litigation, that party shall be deemed to appear at a mediation conference by the physical presence of a representative with full authority to negotiate on behalf of the entity and to recommend settlement to the appropriate decision-making body of the entity. The representative shall not be solely the public entity's counsel (or firm) of record, however, the representative may be the public entity's in-house counsel where another counsel of record for the public entity is also present. In cases where the in-house counsel is counsel of

record, that counsel and another representative may act as duly authorized representatives of the public entity. In cases where the parties include a public entity and/or individuals who were or are employed by a public entity or elected officials of a public entity, such individual parties do not need to attend the mediation conference if all claims asserted against the individuals are covered by insurance or by an indemnification from the public entity for purposes of mediation. Notwithstanding the foregoing, counsel representing the individual defendants shall provide the individual defendants with notice of the mediation conference and the individual defendants shall have the right to attend the mediation conference. The mediator shall report non-attendance to the Court.

5. All proceedings of the mediation shall be confidential and privileged.

6. At least fourteen (14) days prior to the mediation date, each party shall present to the mediator a confidential brief written summary of the case identifying issues to be resolved.

7. The Court may impose sanctions against parties and/or counsel who do not comply with the attendance or settlement authority requirements herein who otherwise violate the terms of this Order. The mediator shall report non-attendance and may recommend imposition of sanctions by the Court for non-attendance.

8. The mediator shall be compensated in accordance with the standing order of the Court entered pursuant to Local Rule 16.2(b)(6), or on such basis as may be agreed to in writing by the parties and the mediator selected by the parties. The cost of mediation shall be shared equally by the parties unless otherwise ordered by the Court. All payments shall be remitted to the mediator within forty-five (45) days of the date of the bill. Notice to the mediator of cancellation or settlement prior to the scheduled mediation conference must be given at least three (3) full business days in advance. Failure to do so will result in imposition of a fee for two (2) hours.

9. If a full or partial settlement is reached in this case, counsel shall promptly notify the Court of the settlement in accordance with Local Rule 16. 2(f), by the filing of a notice of settlement signed by counsel of record within fourteen (14) days of the mediation conference. Thereafter the parties shall forthwith submit an appropriate pleading concluding the case.

10. Within seven (7) days following the mediation conference, the mediator shall file a Mediation Report indicating whether all required parties were present. The report shall also indicate whether the case settled (in full or in part), was adjourned, or whether the case did not settle.

11. If mediation is not conducted, the case may be stricken from the trial calendar, and other sanctions may be imposed.

DONE AND ORDERED this ___ day of ________, 20__.

____
U.S. District Judge

Copies furnished:
All counsel of record

* Form number editorially supplied.

FORM 88.7 NOTICE OF PERMANENT APPEARANCE

SAMPLE FORM FOLLOWING RULE 88.7

UNITED STATES DISTRICT COURT
SOUTHERN DISTRICT OF FLORIDA
CASE NO:

UNITED STATES OF AMERICA

v.

____

NOTICE OF PERMANENT APPEARANCE

(Name of counsel) ______________ files this appearance as counsel for the above-named defendant. Counsel agrees to represent the defendant for:

________ TRIAL AND ALL PROCEEDINGS IN THE DISTRICT COURT

or

________ TRIAL, ALL PROCEEDINGS IN THE DISTRICT COURT, AND ON APPEAL

Counsel acknowledges responsibility to advise the defendant of the right to appeal, and to file a timely notice of appeal if requested to do so by the defendant.

Counsel hereby states that this appearance is in conformity with the requirements of Local General Rule 11.1 and the Special Rules Governing the Admission and Practice of Attorneys.

FEE DISPUTES BETWEEN COUNSEL AND CLIENT SHALL NOT BE A BASIS FOR WITHDRAWAL FROM THIS REPRESENTATION.

Attorney: ______________
Florida Bar Number: ______________
Street Address: ______________
City/State/Zip Code: ______________
Email: ______________
Telephone: ______________

I hereby acknowledge that I have read this form and consent to the representation of the above counsel as noted above.

____
Defendant

Effective April 15, 2011.

ADMIRALTY AND MARITIME RULES

RULE A. GENERAL PROVISIONS

(1) Scope of the Local Admiralty and Maritime Rules. The Local Admiralty and Maritime Rules apply to the procedures in admiralty and maritime claims within the meaning of Federal Rule of Civil Procedure 9(h), which in turn are governed by the Supplemental Rules for Certain Admiralty and Maritime Claims of the Federal Rules of Civil Procedure.

(2) Citation Format.

(a) *The Supplemental Rules* for Certain Admiralty and Maritime Claims of the Federal Rules of Civil Procedure shall be cited as "Supplemental Rule (___)".

(b) The Local Admiralty and Maritime Rules shall be cited as "Local Admiralty Rule (________)".

(3) Application of Local Admiralty and Maritime Rules. The Local Admiralty Rules shall apply to all actions governed by Local Admiralty Rule A(1), and to the extent possible should be construed to be consistent with the other Local Rules of this Court. To the extent that a Local Admiralty Rule conflicts with another Local Rule of this Court, the Local Admiralty Rule shall control.

(4) Designation of "In Admiralty" Proceedings. Every complaint filed as a Federal Rule of Civil Procedure 9(h) action shall boldly set forth the words "IN ADMIRALTY" following the designation of the Court. This requirement is in addition to any statements which may be contained in the body of the complaint.

(5) Verification of Pleadings, Claims and Answers to Interrogatories. Every complaint and claim filed pursuant to Supplemental Rules B, C and/or D shall be verified on oath or solemn affirmation by a party, or an officer of a corporate party.

If a party or corporate officer is not within the District, verification of a complaint, claim and/or answers to interrogatories may be made by an agent, an attorney-in-fact, or the attorney of record. Such person shall state briefly the source of his or her knowledge, or information and belief, and shall declare that the document affirmed is true to the best of his or her knowledge, and/or information and belief. Additionally, such person shall state that he or she is authorized to make this representation on behalf of the party or corporate officer, and shall indicate why verification is not made by a party or a corporate officer. Such verification will be deemed to have been made by the party to whom the document might apply as if verified personally.

Any interested party may move the Court, with or without a request for stay, for the personal oath or affirmation of a party or all parties, or that of a corporate officer. If required by the Court, such verification may be obtained by commission, or as otherwise provided by Court order.

(6) Issuance of Process. Except as limited by the provisions of Supplemental Rule B(1) and Local Admiralty Rule B(3) or Supplemental Rule C(3) and Local Admiralty Rule C(2); or in suits prosecuted in forma pauperis and sought to be filed without prepayment of fees or costs, or without security; all process shall be issued by the Court without further notice of Court.

(7) Publication of Notices. Unless otherwise required by the Court, or applicable Local Admiralty or Supplemental Rule, whenever a notice is required to be published by any statute of the United States, or by any Supplemental Rule or Local Admiralty Rule, such notice shall be published at least once, without further order of Court, in an approved newspaper in the county or counties where the vessel or property was located at the time of arrest, attachment, or seizure, and if different, in the county within the Southern District of Florida where the lawsuit is pending.

For purposes of this subsection, an approved newspaper shall be a newspaper of general circulation, designated from time to time by the Court. A listing of these approved newspapers will be made available in the Clerk's Office during normal business hours.

(8) Form and Return of Process in In Personam Actions. Unless otherwise ordered by the Court, Federal Rule of Civil Procedure 9(h) process shall be by civil summons, and shall be returnable twenty-one (21) days after service of process; except that process issued in accordance with Supplemental Rule B shall conform to the requirements of that rule.

(9) Judicial Officer Defined. As used in these Local Admiralty Rules, the term "judicial officer" or "Court" shall mean either a United States District Judge or a United States Magistrate Judge.

(10) Forms. The forms presented on the Court's website (www.flsd.uscourts.gov) provide an illustration of the format and content of papers filed in admiralty and maritime actions within the Southern District of Florida. While the forms are sufficient, they are neither mandatory nor exhaustive.

[Effective December 1, 1994. Amended effective April 15, 2007; April 15, 2010; April 15, 2011; December 1, 2015.]

Advisory Notes

(1994) These Local Admiralty Rules were amended in 1994 to make them gender neutral.

(1993) (a) **General Comments.** These Local Admiralty Rules were prepared and submitted to the Court through the Rules Committee of the Southern District of Florida, at the request of a Subcommittee of the Admiralty Law Committee of The Florida Bar.

The Local Admiralty and Maritime Rules are promulgated pursuant to this Court's rule making authority under Federal Rule of Civil Procedure 83, and have been drafted to complement the Supplemental Rules for Certain Admiralty and Maritime Claims of the Federal Rules of Civil Procedure.

The Committee has arranged these Local Admiralty Rules to correspond generally with the ordering of the Supplemental Rules, e.g., Local Admiralty Rule A corresponds generally with Supplemental Rule A, and each sequentially lettered Local Admiralty Rule addresses the subject matter of the corresponding next-in-order Supplemental Rule.

Reference to the former Local Admiralty Rules refers to the former Local Rules of the Southern District of Florida.

(b) Comments on Specific Sections. These Local Admiralty Rules are substantially similar to the Local Rules for the Middle District and therefore provide for consistency and uniformity in admiralty and maritime claims in the state.

A(1) and A(3) continue in substance former Local Admiralty Rule 1(a).

A(4) continues the "IN ADMIRALTY" designation requirements of former Local Admiralty Rule 7(a). Under the revised rule, the "IN ADMIRALTY" designation is required to be posted to all complaints even if the complaint is filed as a Federal Rule of Civil Procedure 9(h) action and jurisdiction would exist on another basis, e.g., federal question or diversity jurisdiction.

A(5) continues the requirements of former Local Admiralty Rule 8.

A(6) continues the requirements of former Local Admiralty Rule 2(a).

A(7) enlarges upon former Local Admiralty Rule 3(a) which addressed notice by publication only in cases filed pursuant to Supplemental Rule C(4). The revised rule extends the publication provisions to all Federal Rule of Civil Procedure 9(h) actions for which notice by publication is required.

In addition, the existing provisions have been altered to require that the publication shall be made both in the county where the vessel, or other property, was located at the time of arrest, attachment or seizure; and if different, in the county within the Division of this Court in which the suit is pending.

A(8) continues the requirements of former Local Admiralty Rule 2(c).

A(9) adopts the definition of "Court" provided in the Advisory Notes to the August 1, 1985, amendments to the Supplemental Rules.

As defined in these Local Admiralty Rules, the terms "Court" or "judicial officer" shall extend to United States Magistrates Judges assigned to the Southern District of Florida. The committee notes that the delegation of the duties contemplated by this definition are consistent with the jurisdictional grant to the United States Magistrate Judges as set forth in Title 28, United States Code, Section 636(a).

Where the terms "Court" and "judicial officer" are not used, these Local Admiralty Rules contemplate that without further order of Court, the responsibility of taking the specific action shall be vested with a District Judge.

A(10) provides for that forms pertinent to the Local Admiralty Rules are found at the Court's website (www.flsd.uscourts.gov). The former Local Admiralty Rules incorporated the text of some forms within the specific Local Admiralty Rules and included some forms in an appendix. The forms (now found on the Court's website) provide an alternate method of presenting the format and content of necessary admiralty forms.

As noted in the revised Local Admiralty Rules, these forms are provided as examples, and are not intended to be mandatory. In addition to the specific forms referred to in the Local Admiralty Rules, the Court's website also includes other commonly used admiralty forms for the use and convenience of counsel.

(1998) These Local Admiralty Rules are amended in 1998 to correct scrivener's errors and to require the custodian or substitute custodian to comply with orders of the Captain of the Port, United States Coast Guard.

(2010) Amended to conform tabulation to the style used in the federal rules of procedure.

RULE B. ATTACHMENT AND GARNISHMENT: SPECIAL PROVISIONS

(1) Definition of "Not Found Within the District." In an action in personam filed pursuant to Supplemental Rule B, a defendant shall be considered "not found within the District" if the defendant cannot be served within the Southern District of Florida with the summons and complaint as provided by Federal Rule of Civil Procedure 4(e)(1) or (2), (g), or h(1).

(2) Verification of Complaint Required. In addition to the specific requirements of Local Admiralty Rule A(5), whenever verification is made by the plaintiff's attorney or agent, and that person does not have personal knowledge, or knowledge acquired in the ordinary course of business of the facts alleged in the complaint, the attorney or agent shall also state the circumstances which make it necessary for that person to make the verification, and shall indicate the source of the attorney's or agent's information.

(3) Pre-seizure Requirements. In accordance with Supplemental Rule B(1), the process of attachment and garnishment shall issue only after one of the following conditions has been met:

(a) *Judicial Review Prior to Issuance.* Except as provided in Local Admiralty Rule B(3)(b), a judicial officer shall first review the verified complaint, and any other relevant case papers, prior to the Clerk of the Court issuing the requested process of attachment and garnishment. No notice of this pre-arrest judicial review is required to be given to any person or prospective party.

If the Court finds that probable cause exists to issue the process of attachment and garnishment, plaintiff shall prepare an order for the Court's signature directing the Clerk of the Court to issue the process. This order shall substantially conform in format and content to the form identified as SDF 1 on Court's website (www.flsd.uscourts.gov).

Upon receipt of the signed order, the Clerk of the Court shall file the order and, in accordance with Local Admiralty Rule B(3)(c), issue the summons and process of attachment and garnishment. Thereafter the Clerk of the Court may issue supplemental process without further order of Court.

(b) *Certification of Exigent Circumstances.* If the plaintiff files a written certification that exigent circumstances make review by the Court impracticable, the Clerk of the Court shall, in accordance with Local Admiralty Rule B(3)(c), issue a summons and the process of attachment and garnishment.

Thereafter at any post-attachment proceedings under Supplemental Rule E(4)(f) and Local Admiralty Rule B(5), plaintiff shall have the burden of showing that probable cause existed for the issuance of process, and that exigent circumstances existed which precluded judicial review in accordance with Local Admiralty Rule B(3)(a).

(c) *Preparation and Issuance of the Process of Attachment and Garnishment.* Plaintiff shall prepare the summons and the process of attachment and garnishment, and deliver the documents to the Clerk of the Court for filing and issuance.

The process of attachment and garnishment shall substantially conform in format and content to the form identified as

SDF 2 on the Court's website (www.flsd.uscourts.gov), and shall in all cases give adequate notice of the postseizure provisions of Local Admiralty Rule B(5).

(d) *Marshal's Return of Service.* The Marshal shall file a return of service indicating the date and manner in which service was perfected and, if service was perfected upon a garnishee, the Marshal shall indicate in the return the name, address, and telephone number of the garnishee.

(4) Notification of Seizure to Defendant. In an in personam action under Supplemental Rule B, it is expected that plaintiff and/or garnishee will initially attempt to perfect service of the notice in accordance with Supplemental Rule B(2)(a) or (b).

However, when service of the notice cannot be perfected in accordance with Supplemental Rule B(2)(a) or (b), plaintiff and/or garnishee should then attempt to perfect service in accordance with Supplemental Rule B(2)(c). In this regard, service of process shall be sufficiently served by leaving a copy of the process of attachment and garnishment with the defendant or garnishee at his or her usual place of business.

(5) Post-attachment Review Proceedings.

(a) *Filing a Required Answer.* In accordance with Supplemental Rule E(4)(f), any person who claims an interest in property seized pursuant to Supplemental Rule B must file an answer and claim against the property. The answer and claim shall describe the nature of the claimant's interest in the property, and shall articulate reasons why the seizure should be vacated. The claimant shall serve a copy of the answer and claim upon plaintiff's counsel, the Marshal, and any other party to the litigation. The claimant shall also file a Certificate of Service indicating the date and manner in which service was perfected.

(b) *Hearing on the Answer and Claim.* The claimant may be heard before a judicial officer not less than seven (7) days after the answer and claim has been filed and service has been perfected upon the plaintiff.

If the Court orders that the seizure be vacated, the judicial officer shall also award attorney's fees, costs and other expenses incurred by any party as a result of the seizure.

If the seizure was predicated upon a showing of "exigent circumstances" under Local Admiralty Rule B(3)(b), and the Court finds that such exigent circumstances did not exist, the judicial officer shall award attorney's fees, costs, and other expenses incurred by any party as a result of the seizure.

(6) Procedural Requirement for the Entry of Default. In accordance with Federal Rule of Civil Procedure 55, a party seeking the entry of default in a Supplemental Rule B action shall file a motion and supporting legal memorandum and shall offer other proof sufficient to demonstrate that due notice of the action and seizure have been given in accordance with Local Admiralty Rule B(4).

Upon review of the motion, memorandum, and other proof, the Clerk of the Court shall, where appropriate, enter default in accordance with Federal Rule of Civil Procedure 55(a). Thereafter, the Clerk of the Court shall serve notice of the entry of default upon all parties represented in the action.

(7) Procedural Requirements for the Entry of Default Judgment. Not later than thirty (30) days following notice of the entry of default, the party seeking the entry of default judgment shall file a motion and supporting legal memorandum, along with other appropriate exhibits to the motion sufficient to support the entry of default judgment. The moving party shall serve these papers upon every other party to the action and file a Certificate of Service indicating the date and manner in which service was perfected.

A party opposing the entry of default judgment shall have seven (7) days from the receipt of the motion to file written opposition with the Court. Thereafter, unless otherwise ordered by the Court, the motion for the entry of default judgment will be heard without oral argument.

If the Court grants the motion and enters the default judgment, such judgment shall establish a right on the part of the party or parties in which favor it is entered. The judgment shall be considered prior to any claims of the owner of the defendant property against which it is entered, and to the remnants and surpluses thereof; providing, however, that such a judgment shall not establish any entitlement to the defendant property having priority over non-possessory lien claimants. Obtaining a judgment by default shall not preclude the party in whose favor it is entered from contending and proving that all, or any portion, of the claim or claims encompassed within the judgment are prior to any such non-possessory lien claims.

[Effective December 1, 1994. Amended effective April 15, 1998; April 15, 2000; April 15, 2007; April 15, 2010; April 15, 2011; December 1, 2014; December 1, 2015.]

Advisory Notes

(1993) **(a) General Comments.** Local Admiralty Rule B is intended to enhance and codify the local procedural requirements uniquely applicable to actions of maritime attachment and garnishment under Supplemental Rule B. Other local procedural requirements involving actions in rem and quasi in rem proceedings can be found in Local Admiralty Rule E.

When read in conjunction with Supplemental Rule B and E, Local Admiralty Rules B and E are intended to provide a uniform and comprehensive method for constitutionally implementing the longstanding and peculiar maritime rights of attachment and garnishment. The Committee believes that Local Admiralty Rules B and E correct the deficiencies perceived by some courts to exist in the implementation of this unique maritime provision. *Schiffahartsgesellschaft Leonhardt & Co. v. A. Bottacchi S.A. de Navegacion,* 552 F.Supp. 771 (S.D.Ga.1982); *Cooper Shipping Company v. Century 21,* 1983 A.M.C. 244 (M.D.Fla.1982); *Crysen Shipping Co. v. Bona Shipping Co., Ltd.,* 553 F.Supp. 139 (N.D.Fla.1982); and *Grand Bahama Petroleum Co. v. Canadian Transportation Agencies, Ltd.,* 450 F.Supp. 447 (W.D.Wa. 1978), discussing Supplemental Rule (B) proceedings in light of *Fuentes v. Shevin,* 407 U.S. 67, [92 S.Ct. 1983, 32 L.Ed.2d 556] (1972) and *Sniadach v. Family Finance Corp.,* 395 U.S. 337, [89 S.Ct. 1820, 23 L.Ed.2d 349] (1969).

Although the Committee is aware of the Eleventh Circuit's decision in *Schiffahartsgesellschaft Leonhardt & Co. v. A. Bottacchi S.A. de Navegacion,* 732 F.2d 1543 (1984), the Committee believes that from both a commercial and legal viewpoint, the better practice is to incorporate the pre-seizure scrutiny and post-attachment review provisions provided by this Local Admiralty Rule. These provisions protect the rights of any person claiming an interest in the seized property by permitting such persons to file a claim against the property, and thereafter permitting a judicial determination of the propriety of the seizure.

(b) Comments on Specific Sections. Local Admiralty Rule B(1) codifies the governing law of this Circuit as set forth in *LaBanca v. Ostermunchner*, 664 F.2d 65 (5th Cir., Unit B, 1981).

Local Admiralty Rule B(2) codifies the verification requirements of Supplemental Rule B(1) and former Local Admiralty Rule 8.

B(3) incorporates the "pre-seizure" and "exigent circumstances" provisions of the August 1, 1985, revision to Local Supplemental Rule B(1). In the routine case, the rule contemplates that issuance of the process of attachment and garnishment be preconditioned upon the exercise of judicial review. This ensures that plaintiff can make an appropriate maritime claim, and present proof that the defendant cannot be found within the District. The rule also contemplates that upon a finding of probable cause, a simple order directing the Clerk of the Court to issue the process shall be entered by the Court.

This rule also incorporates the "exigent circumstances" provision of Supplemental Rule B(1). Read in conjunction with Local Admiralty Rule B(5)(b), this rule requires that the plaintiff carry the burden of proof at any post-attachment proceedings to establish not only the prima facie conditions of a maritime attachment and garnishment action under Supplemental Rule B, but also that "exigent circumstances" precluded judicial review under Local Admiralty Rule B(3)(a). The Committee believes that this additional requirement will place upon plaintiff's counsel a burden of extra caution before invoking the "exigent circumstance" provision of the rule.

Local Admiralty Rule B(5) establishes the post-attachment review provisions potentially applicable to maritime attachment and garnishment proceedings. These proceedings may be invoked by any person claiming an interest in the seized property.

(2000) Local Admiralty Rule B(7) is amended to give the party seeking entry of a default judgment up to thirty days, rather than five days, to file a motion and supporting legal memorandum.

(2010) Amended to conform tabulation to the style used in the federal rules of procedure.

(2014) Local Admiralty Rule (B)(1) amended to update references to the Federal Rules of Civil Procedure.

RULE C. ACTION IN REM

(1) Verification Requirements. Every complaint and claim filed in an in rem proceeding pursuant to Supplemental Rule C shall be verified in accordance with Local Admiralty Rules A(5) and B(2).

(2) Pre-seizure Requirements. In accordance with Supplemental Rule C(3), the process of arrest in rem shall issue only after one of the following conditions has been met:

(a) *Judicial Review Prior to Issuance.* Except as provided in Local Admiralty Rule 3(b)(2), a judicial officer shall first review the verified complaint, and any other relevant case papers, prior to the Clerk of the Court issuing the warrant of arrest and/or summons in rem. No notice of this pre-seizure judicial review is required to be given to any person or prospective party.

If the Court finds that probable cause exists for an action in rem, plaintiff shall prepare an order for the Court's signature directing the Clerk of the Court to issue a warrant of arrest and/or summons. This order shall substantially conform in format and content to the form identified as SDF 2 on the Court's website (www.flsd.uscourts.gov).

Upon receipt of the signed order, the Clerk of the Court shall file the order and, in accordance with Local Admiralty Rule 3(b)(3), issue the warrant of arrest and/or summons. Thereafter the Clerk of the Court may issue supplemental process without further order of the Court.

(b) *Certification of Exigent Circumstances.* If the plaintiff files a written certification that exigent circumstances make review by the Court impracticable, the Clerk of the Court shall, in accordance with Local Admiralty Rule B(3)(b), issue a warrant of arrest and/or summons.

Thereafter at any post-arrest proceedings under Supplemental Rule E(4)(f) and Local Admiralty Rule C(7), plaintiff shall have the burden of showing that probable cause existed for the issuance of process, and that exigent circumstances existed which precluded judicial review in accordance with Local Admiralty Rule C(2)(a).

(c) *Preparation and Issuance of the Warrant of Arrest and/or Summons.* Plaintiff shall prepare the warrant of arrest and/or summons and file them electronically with the Clerk of the Court for issuance. If a filing is an emergency matter, the documents must be electronically filed using the events specifically earmarked for emergency motions as described in Section 10 of the CM/ECF Administrative Procedures. A party appearing pro se must file such matters conventionally.

The warrant of arrest shall substantially conform in format and content to the form identified as SDF 4 on the Court's website (www.flsd.uscourts.gov), and shall in all cases give adequate notice of the post-arrest provisions of Local Admiralty Rule C(7).

(3) Special Requirements for Actions Involving Freight, Proceeds and/or Intangible Property.

(a) *Instructions to Be Contained in the Summons.* Unless otherwise ordered by the Court, the summons shall order the person having control of the freight, proceeds and/or intangible property to either:

(i) File a claim within fourteen (14) days, beginning on the next calendar day, including Saturday, Sunday, or a legal holiday, count fourteen days after service of the summons in accordance with Local Admiralty Rule D(6)(a); or

(ii) Deliver or pay over to the Marshal, the freight, proceeds, and/or intangible property, or a part thereof, sufficient to satisfy plaintiff's claim.

The summons shall also inform the person having control of the freight, proceeds, and/or intangible property that service of the summons has the effect of arresting the property, thereby preventing the release, disposal or other distribution of the property without prior order of the Court.

(b) *Requirements for Claims to Prevent the Delivery of Property to the Marshal.* Any claim filed in accordance with Supplemental Rule E(4) and Local Admiralty Rule C(5)(a) shall describe the nature of claimant's interest in the property, and shall articulate reasons why the seizure should be vacated.

The claim shall be served upon the plaintiff, the Marshal, and all other parties to the litigation. Additionally, the claimant shall file a Certificate of Service indicating the date and manner in which service was perfected.

(c) *Delivery or Payment of the Freight, Proceeds, and/or Intangible Property to the United States Marshal.* Unless a claim is filed in accordance with Supplemental Rule E(4)(f), and Local Admiralty Rule C(6)(a), any person served with a summons issued pursuant to Local Admiralty Rule C(2)(a) or C(2)(b), shall within fourteen (14) days, beginning on the next calendar day, including Saturday, Sunday, or a legal holiday, after execution of service, deliver or pay over to the Marshal all, or part of, the freight, proceeds, and/or intangible property sufficient to satisfy plaintiff's claim.

Unless otherwise ordered by the Court, the person tendering control of the freight, proceeds, and/or intangible property shall be excused from any further duty with respect to the property in question.

(4) Publishing Notice of the Arrest as Required by Supplemental Rule C(4).

(a) *Time for Publication.* If the property is not released within fourteen (14) days after the execution of process, the notice required by Supplemental Rule C(4) shall be published by the plaintiff in accordance with Local Admiralty Rule A(7). Such notice shall be published within twenty-one (21) days after execution of process. The notice shall substantially conform to the form identified as SDF 7 on the Court's website (www.flsd.uscourts.gov).

(b) *Proof of Publication.* Plaintiff shall file with the Clerk of the Court proof of publication not later than fourteen (14) days following the last day of publication. It shall be sufficient proof for the plaintiff to file the sworn statement by, or on behalf of, the publisher or editor, indicating the dates of publication, along with a copy or reproduction of the actual publication.

(5) Undertaking in Lieu of Arrest. If, before or after the commencement of an action, a party accepts any written undertaking to respond on behalf of the vessel and/or other property in return for foregoing the arrest, the undertaking shall only respond to orders or judgments in favor of the party accepting the undertaking, and any parties expressly named therein, to the extent of the benefit thereby conferred.

(6) Time for Filing Claim or Answer. Unless otherwise ordered by the Court, any claimant of property subject to an action in rem shall:

(a) File the claim within fourteen (14) days, beginning on the next calendar day, including Saturday, Sunday, or a legal holiday, after process has been executed; and

(b) Serve an answer within twenty-one (21) days after the filing of the claim.

(7) Post-Arrest Proceedings. Coincident with the filing of a claim pursuant to Supplemental Rule E(4)(f), and Local Admiralty Rule C(6)(a), the claimant may also file a motion and proposed order directing plaintiff to show cause why the arrest should not be vacated. If the Court grants the order, the Court shall set a date and time for a show cause hearing. Thereafter, if the Court orders the arrest to be vacated, the Court shall award attorney's fees, costs, and other expenses incurred by any party as a result of the arrest.

Additionally, if the seizure was predicated upon a showing of "exigent circumstances" under Local Admiralty Rule C(2)(b), and the Court finds that such exigent circumstances did not exist, the Court shall award attorneys' fees, costs and other expenses incurred by any party as a result of the seizure.

(8) Procedural Requirements Prior to the Entry of Default. In accordance with Federal Rule of Civil Procedure 55, a party seeking the entry of default judgment in rem shall first file a motion and supporting legal memorandum.

The party seeking the entry of default shall also file such other proof sufficient to demonstrate that due notice of the action and arrest have been given by:

(a) Service upon the master or other person having custody of the property; and

(b) Delivery, or by certified mail, return receipt requested (or international effective equivalent), to every other person, including any known owner, who has not appeared or intervened in the action, and who is known to have, or claims to have, a possessory interest in the property.

The party seeking entry of default judgment under Local Rule 3(h) may be excused for failing to give notice to such "other person" upon a satisfactory showing that diligent effort was made to give notice without success; and

(c) Publication as required by Supplemental Rule C(4) and Local Admiralty Rule C(4).

Upon review of the motion, memorandum, and other proof, the Clerk of the Court may, where appropriate, enter default in accordance with Federal Rule of Civil Procedure 55. Thereafter, the Clerk of the Court shall serve notice of the entry of default upon all parties represented in the action.

(9) Procedural Requirements for the Entry of Default Judgment. Not later than thirty (30) days following notice of the entry of default, the moving party shall file a motion, and supporting legal documents, for the entry of default judgment pursuant to Federal Rule of Civil Procedure 55(b). The moving party may also file as exhibits for the motion such other documentation as may be required to support the entry of default judgment. Thereafter the Court will consider the motion as indicated below:

(a) *When No Person Has Filed a Claim or Answer.* Unless otherwise ordered by the Court, the motion for default judgment will be considered by the Court without oral argument.

(b) *When Any Person Has Filed an Appearance, But Does Not Join in the Motion for Entry of Default Judgment.* If any person has filed an appearance in accordance with Local Admiralty Rule C(6), but does not join in the motion for entry of default judgment, the party seeking the entry of default judgment shall serve notice of the motion upon the party not joining in the motion, and thereafter the opposing party shall have seven (7) days from receipt of the notice to file written opposition with the Court.

If the Court grants the motion and enters the default judgment, such judgment shall establish a right on the part of the party or parties in whose favor it is entered. The judgment shall be considered prior to any claims of the owner of the defendant property against which it is entered, and to the remnants and surpluses thereof; providing, however, that such a judgment shall not establish any entitlement to the defendant property having priority over non-possessory lien claimants. Obtaining a judgment by default shall not preclude the party in whose favor it is entered from contending and proving that all, or any portion, of the claim or claims encompassed within the judgment are prior to any such non-possessory lien claims.

[Effective December 1, 1994. Amended effective April 15, 1998; April 15, 2000; April 15, 2001; April 15, 2007; April 15, 2010; April 15, 2011; December 3, 2012; December 1, 2015.]

Advisory Notes

(1993) C(2). Well-reasoned authority has upheld Supplemental Rule C, specifically holding that a pre-seizure judicial hearing is not required where a vessel, freight, or intangible property is proceeded against to enforce a maritime lien. *Amstar Corporation v. SS Alexandros T,* 664 F.2d 904 (4th Cir.1981); Merchants *Nat'l Bank v. Dredge Gen. G.L. Gillespie,* 663 F.2d 1338 (5th Cir. Unit A, 1981); *Schiffahartsgesellschaft Leonhardt & Co. v. A. Bottacchi S.A. de Navegacion,* 732 F.2d 1543 (11th Cir.1984).

The desirability of providing by local admiralty rule an available avenue for reasonably prompt and effective post-arrest judicial relief is indicated. *See, Merchants Nat'l Bank v. Dredge Gen. G.L. Gillespie,* supra, at 1334, 1350. This provision is incorporated in Local Admiralty Rule C(7).

This procedure made available through this rule has proven effective. *Maryland Ship Building & Dry–Dock Co. v. Pacific Ruler Corp.,* 201 F.Supp. 858 (SDNY 1962). In fact, the procedure established by this local rule goes beyond that encountered in *Merchants Nat'l Bank v. Dredge Gen. G.L. Gillespie,* supra, or *Maryland Ship Building & Dry–Dock Co. v. Pacific Ruler Corp.,* supra.

Under this rule, the claimant or intervenor may petition the Court to order the plaintiff to establish probable cause for the arrest of the property. Therefore at an early stage of the litigation, plaintiff can be required to establish a prima facie case that he is asserting a claim which is entitled to the dignity and status of a maritime lien against the arrested property. This rule contemplates the entry of an order with conclusory findings following the post-arrest proceedings. More detailed findings may be requested by any party.

The rule is not intended to provide a method for contesting the amount of security to be posted for the release of the vessel. Once a prima facie case for the maritime lien has been established, or the question of lien status remains uncontested, the matter of security is left to the provisions of Local Admiralty Rule E.

C(3). Supplemental Rule C(3) also addresses the less commonly encountered action in rem to enforce a maritime lien against freights, proceeds or other intangible property. The revision to this rule designates the United States Marshal to take custody of all tangible and intangible properties arrested in accordance with this rule, and to bring these properties under the control of the Court. This is the practice in many other districts, and when implemented will provide the greatest uniformity in the treatment of tangible and intangible property.

C(4). The substance of former Local Admiralty Rule 3(c) is continued.

C(5). Although this section is new to the local rules, it reflects the current local practice with respect to undertakings and stipulations in lieu of arrest. Such undertakings and stipulations have been held effective to permit a Court to exercise its in rem admiralty jurisdiction so long as either at the time the undertaking or stipulation is given, or at any subsequent time prior to the filing of the action, the vessel or other property is, or will be, present within the District.

C(6). The substance of former Local Admiralty Rule 2(b) is continued.

C(7). See the comments for Local Admiralty Rule C(2).

C(8) **and** (9). These sections are designed to mesh Supplemental Rule (C) with Federal Rule of Civil Procedure 55. For purpose of default and default judgments, the rule recognizes two distinct groups of in rem claimants.

The first category of claimants include those who by ownership or otherwise, would, but for the arrest of the property, be entitled to its possession. Pursuant to Supplemental Rule C(6), these claimants must file a claim setting forth their interest in the property, demand their right to receive possession, and to appear and defend the action. In the case of such claimants, the operation of standard default procedures foreclose their rights to contest positions of the party in whose favor the default is rendered, and the entry of default judgment is both fair and appropriate.

The second category of claimants embodies a potentially numerous and varying class of claimants. The claims of these other claimants do not give rise to a right of possession of the vessel from the marshal or other appropriate custodian, but rather invoke the power of the Court in admiralty to foreclose against the property by the ultimate rendering of a judgment in rem against property entitlements. Such judgments would be predicated upon non-possessory liens.

The time in which the second category of claimants may intervene is governed by the provisions of Local Admiralty Rule E. Such lien claimants are not obligated, and indeed are probably not entitled to file a claim of possession to the vessel, or to answer and defend in the name of the vessel. As to them, in accordance with Federal Rule of Civil Procedure 8, the essential averments of all the complaints are taken as automatically denied.

No default judgments entered pursuant to this rule will operate to adjudicate priorities among competing non-possessory lien claimants.

In attempting to reconcile the traditional notions of default and default judgments with the concept of in rem proceedings, the final language has been formulated to maintain the efficacy of the default procedure without resulting in premature adjudication effecting priorities and distributions.

The default procedure establishes in favor of the holder of such a default judgment, a lien position against the proceeds of the property, resulting from any sale or disposition, or, if currency is involved, the ultimate adjudication, inferior to all other competing priorities, except the otherwise escheating right of the property owner to the remnants and surpluses after all full-claims satisfactions. At the same time, the right of a person obtaining a default judgment to contend and compete with other claimants for priority distribution remains unaffected.

(2000) Local Admiralty Rule C(9) is amended to give the party seeking entry of a default judgment up to thirty days, rather than five days, to file a motion and supporting legal memorandum.

(2001) Corrections to rule number references.

(2010) Amended to conform tabulation to the style used in the Federal Rules of Civil Procedure.

(2012) Amended to correct tabulation and internal citation errors in C(6) and C(7) and to relocate appendix of forms to the Court's website.

RULE D. POSSESSORY, PETITORY AND PARTITION ACTIONS

(1) Establishing Dates for the Return of Process. In possessory actions filed pursuant to Supplemental Rule D, the Court may order that process be returnable at a time shorter than that prescribed by Federal Rule of Civil Procedure 12(a).

If the Court shortens the time, the Court shall specify the date upon which the answer must be filed, and may also set a hearing date to expedite the disposition of the possessory action. When possible, possessory actions shall be given preference on a judicial officer's calendar.

[Effective December 1, 1994. Amended effective April 15, 2007; April 15, 2010; April 15, 2011.]

Advisory Notes

(1993) This rule continues in substance the provisions of former Local Admiralty Rule 15.

The rule recognizes the equity in allowing for a prompt resolution in possessory actions. Since a possessory action is brought to reinstate an owner of a vessel alleging wrongful deprivation of property, rather than to allow original possession, the rule permits the Court to expedite these actions, thereby providing a quick remedy for the one wrongfully deprived of his rightful property. *See Silver v. Sloop Silver Cloud,* 259 F.Supp. 187 (S.D.N.Y. 1966).

Since a petitory and possessory action can be joined to obtain original possession, *The Friendship,* Fed.Cas. No. 5,123 (CCD Maine, 1855), this rule contemplates that an expedited hearing will only occur in purely possessory actions.

(2010) Amended to conform tabulation to the style used in the federal rules of procedure.

RULE E. ACTIONS IN REM AND QUASI IN REM: GENERAL PROVISIONS

(1) Statement of Itemized Damages and Expenses Required. Every complaint in a Supplemental Rule B and C action shall state the amount of the debt, damages, or salvage for which the action is brought. In addition, the statement shall also specify the amount of any unliquidated claims, including attorneys' fees.

(2) Requirements and Procedures for Effecting Intervention. Whenever a vessel or other property is arrested or attached in accordance with any Supplemental Rule, and the vessel or property is in the custody of the United States Marshal, or duly authorized substitute custodian, any other person having a claim against the vessel or property shall be required to present their claim as indicated below:

(a) *Intervention of Right When No Sale of the Vessel or Property Is Pending.* Except as limited by Local Admiralty Rule E(2)(b), any person having a claim against a vessel or property previously arrested or attached by the Marshal may, as a matter of right, file an intervening complaint at any time before an order is entered by the Court scheduling the vessel or property for sale.

Coincident with the filing of an intervening complaint, the offering party shall prepare and file a supplemental warrant of arrest and/or a supplemental process of attachment and garnishment.

Upon receipt of the intervening complaint and supplemental process, the Clerk of the Court shall conform a copy of the intervening complaint and shall issue the supplemental process. Thereafter, the offering party shall deliver the conformed copy of the intervening complaint and supplemental process to the Marshal for execution. Upon receipt of the intervening complaint and supplemental process, the Marshal shall re-arrest or re-attach the vessel or property in the name of the intervening plaintiff.

Counsel for the intervening party shall serve a copy of the intervening complaint, and copies of all process and exhibits upon all other counsel of record, and shall thereafter file a certificate of service with the Clerk of the Court indicating the manner and date of service.

(b) *Permissive Intervention When the Vessel or Property Has Been Scheduled for Sale by the Court.* Except as indicated below, and subject to any other rule or order of this Court, no person shall have an automatic right to intervene in an action where the Court has ordered the sale of the vessel or property, and the date of the sale is set within twenty-one (21) days from the date the party moves for permission to intervene in accordance with this subsection. In such cases, the person seeking permission to intervene must:

(i) File a motion to intervene and indicate in the caption of the motion a request for expedited hearing when appropriate.

(ii) Include a copy of the anticipated intervening complaint as an exhibit to the motion to intervene.

(iii) Prepare and offer for filing a supplemental warrant of arrest and/or a supplemental process of attachment and garnishment.

(iv) Serve copies of the motion to intervene, with exhibits and proposed supplemental process upon every other party to the litigation.

(v) File a certificate of service indicating the date and manner of service.

Thereafter, the Court may permit intervention under such conditions and terms as are equitable to the interests of all parties; and if intervention is permitted, shall also direct the Clerk of the Court to issue the supplemental process.

Upon receipt of the order permitting intervention, the Clerk of the Court shall file the originally signed intervening complaint, conform a copy of the intervening complaint and issue the supplemental process.

Thereafter, the offering party shall deliver the conformed copy of the intervening complaint and supplemental process to the Marshal for execution. Upon receipt of the intervening complaint and supplemental process, the Marshal shall re-arrest or re-attach the vessel or property in the name of the intervening plaintiff.

Counsel for the intervening party shall also serve a copy of the intervening complaint, exhibits, and supplemental process upon every other party of record and shall thereafter file a Certificate of Service with the Clerk of the Court indicating the manner and date of service.

(3) Special Requirements for Salvage Actions. In cases of salvage, the complaint shall also state to the extent known, the value of the hull, cargo, freight, and other property salvaged, the amount claimed, the names of the principal salvors, and that the suit is instituted in their behalf and in behalf of all other persons associated with them.

In addition to these special pleading requirements, plaintiff shall attach as an exhibit to the complaint a list of all known salvors, and all persons believed entitled to share in the salvage. Plaintiff shall also attach a copy of any agreement of consortship available and known to exist among them collegially or individually.

(4) Form of Stipulation or Bonds. Except in cases instituted by the United States through information, or complaint of information upon seizures for any breach of the revenues, navigation, or other laws of the United States, stipulations or bonds in admiralty and maritime actions need not be under seal and may be executed by the agent or attorney of the stipulator or obligor.

(5) Deposit of Marshal's Fees and Expenses Required Prior to Effecting Arrest, Attachment and/or Garnishment.

(a) *Deposit Required Before Seizure.* Any party seeking the arrest or attachment of property in accordance with Supplemental Rule E shall deposit a sum with the Marshal sufficient to cover the Marshal's estimated fees and expenses of arresting and keeping the property for at least fourteen (14) days. The Marshal is not required to execute process until the deposit is made.

(b) *Proration of Marshal's Fees and Expenses upon Intervention.* When one or more parties intervene pursuant to Local Admiralty Rule E(2)(a) or (b), the burden of advancing sums to the Marshal sufficient to cover the Marshal's fees and expenses shall be allocated equitably between the original plaintiff, and the intervening party or parties as indicated below:

(i) Stipulation for the Allocation and Payment of the Marshal's Fees and Expenses. Immediately upon the filing of the intervening complaint, counsel for the intervening plaintiff shall arrange for a conference between all other parties to the action, at which time a good faith effort shall be made to allocate fees and expenses among the parties. Any resulting stipulation between the parties shall be codified and filed with the Court and a copy served upon the Marshal.

(ii) Allocation of Costs and Expenses in the Event That Counsel Cannot Stipulate. The Court expects that counsel will resolve the allocation of costs and expenses in accordance with the preceding paragraph. In the event that such an arrangement cannot be made, the parties shall share in the fees and expenses of the Marshal in proportion to their claims as stated in the original and intervening complaints.

In order to determine the proportionate shares of each party, counsel for the last intervening plaintiff shall determine the total amounts claimed by each party. The individual claims shall be determined from the original and amended complaint, and all other intervening complaints subsequently accepted and processed by the Marshal in accordance with Local Admiralty Rule E(2)(a) or (b).

Thereafter, counsel for the last intervening plaintiff shall deliver to the Marshal a list which summarizes each party's claim, and the proportion which each party's claim bears to the aggregate claims asserted in the litigation, determined to the nearest one-tenth of one percentage point.

Upon receipt of this listing, the Marshal shall determine the total expenses incurred to date and shall estimate the expenses to be incurred during the next fourteen (14) days. For the purpose of making this calculation, the total fees and expenses shall be calculated from the date when continuous and uninterrupted arrest or attachment of the property began, and not prorated from the date a particular party's intervening complaint was filed.

The Marshal shall then apply the percentages determined in the listing, and shall compute the amount of the intervening party's initial deposit requirements. The Marshal shall also utilize this listing to compute any additional deposit requirements which may be necessary pursuant to Local Admiralty Rule E(5)(c).

The Marshal need not re-arrest or re-attach the vessel and/or property until the deposit is received from the intervening plaintiff.

(c) *Additional Deposit Requirements.* Until the property arrested or attached and garnished has been released or otherwise disposed of in accordance with Supplemental Rule E, the Marshal may require from any original and intervening party who has caused the arrest or attachment and garnishment of a vessel or property, to post such additional deposits as the Marshal determines necessary to cover any additional estimated fees or expenses.

(d) *Judicial Relief from Deposit Requirements.* Any party aggrieved by the deposit requirements of Local Admiralty Rule E(5)(b) may apply to the Court for relief. Such application shall be predicated upon a showing that owing to the relative priorities of the claims asserted against the vessel or other property, the deposit requirements operate to impose a burden disproportionate to the aggrieved party's recovery potential.

The judicial officer may adjust the deposit requirements, but in no event shall the proportion required of an aggrieved party be reduced to a percentage less than that imposed upon the claimant whose claim is the smallest among that of claims which the aggrieved party stipulates as having priority over its claim; or, in the absence of such stipulation, the greatest percentage imposed upon any claimant participating in the deposit requirements.

(e) *Consequence of Failing to Comply With Additional Deposit Requirements.* Any party who fails to make the additional deposit as requested by the Marshal may not participate further in the proceeding, except for the purpose of seeking relief from this rule.

Additionally, the Marshal shall notify the Court in writing whenever any party fails to make additional deposits as required by Local Admiralty Rule E(5)(c).

In the event that a party questions its obligations to advance monies required by this rule, the Marshal may apply to the Court for instructions concerning that party's obligation under the rule.

(6) Property in Possession of a United States Officer. Whenever the property to be arrested or attached is in custody of a United States officer, the Marshal shall serve the appropriate process upon the officer or employee; or, if the officer or employee is not found within the District, then to the custodian of the property within the District.

The Marshal shall direct the officer, employee or custodian not to relinquish custody of the property until ordered to do so by the Court.

(7) Process Held in Abeyance.

(a) *When Permitted.* In accordance with Supplemental Rule E(3)(b), a plaintiff may ask the Clerk of the Court not to issue process, but rather to hold the process in abeyance. The Clerk of the Court shall docket this request, and thereafter shall not be responsible for ensuring that process is issued at a later date.

(b) *When Intervention Is Subsequently Required.* It is the intention of these rules that a vessel or other property should be arrested or attached pursuant to process issued and effected in only one civil action. Therefore, if while process is held in abeyance on one action, the vessel or property is arrested or attached in another action, it shall be the responsibility of the plaintiff who originally requested process be held in abeyance in the first action to voluntarily dismiss without prejudice the first action, insofar as that action seeks to proceed against the property arrested or attached in the second action, and promptly intervene in the second action pursuant to Local Admiralty Rule E(2)(a) or (b).

In order to prevent undue hardship or manifest injustice, motions to consolidate in rem actions against the same vessel or property will be granted only in exceptional circumstances.

(8) Release of Property in Accordance With Supplemental Rule E(5).

(a) *Release by Consent or Stipulation.* Subject to the limitations imposed by Supplemental Rule E(5)(c), the Marshal may release any vessel, cargo or property in the Marshal's possession to the party on whose behalf the property is detained. However, as a precondition to release, the Marshal shall require a stipulation, bond, or other security, expressly authorizing the release. The authorizing instrument shall be signed by the party, or the party's attorney, on whose behalf the property is detained.

The stipulation, bond, or other security shall be posted in an amount equal to, or greater than, the amount required for the following types of action:

(i) Actions Entirely for a Sum Certain. The amount alleged to be due in the complaint, with interest at six percent per annum from the date claimed to be due to a date twenty-four months after the date the claim was filed, or by filing an approved stipulation, or bond for the amount alleged plus interest as computed in this subsection.

The stipulation or bond shall be conditioned to abide by all orders of the Court, and to pay the amount of any final judgment entered by this Court or any appellate Court, with interest.

(ii) Actions other than Possessory, Petitory or Partition. Unless otherwise ordered by the Court, the amount of the appraised or agreed value of the property seized, with interest. If an appraised value cannot be agreed upon by the parties, the Court shall order an appraisal in accordance with Local Admiralty Rule F(3).

The stipulation or bond shall be conditioned to abide by all orders of the Court, and to pay the amount of any final judgment entered by this Court or any appellate Court, with interest.

The person consenting or stipulating to the release shall also file a claim in accordance with Local Admiralty Rule E(2)(a) or (b).

(iii) Possessory, Petitory or Partition Actions. The Marshal may release property in these actions only upon order of Court, and upon the subsequent deposit of security and compliance with such terms and/or conditions as the Court deems appropriate.

(b) *Release Pursuant to Court Order.* In accordance with Supplemental Rule E(5)(c), a party may petition to release the vessel pursuant to Court order. A party making such application shall file a Request for Release which shall substantially conform in format and content to the form identified as SDF 8 on the Court's website (www.flsd.uscourts.gov). Additionally, the party shall prepare, and offer for filing, a proposed order directing the release. This order shall substantially conform in format and content to the form identified as SDF 9 on the Court's website (www.flsd.uscourts.gov).

However, as a precondition to the release, the Marshal shall require a stipulation, bond, or other security, as specified in Local Admiralty Rule E(8)(a)(i), (ii), or (iii), as appropriate.

(c) *Upon the Dismissal or Discontinuance of an Action.* By coordinating with the Marshal to ensure that all costs and charges of the Court and its officers have first been paid.

(d) *Release Subsequent to the Posting of a General Bond.*

(i) Requirements of a General Bond. General bonds filed pursuant to Supplemental Rule E(5)(b) shall identify the vessel by name, nationality, dimensions, official number or registration number, hailing port and port of documentation.

(ii) Responsibility for Maintaining a Current Listing of General Bonds. The Clerk of the Court shall maintain a current listing of all general bonds. This listing should be maintained in alphabetical order by name of the vessel. The listing will be available for inspection during normal business hours.

(iii) Execution of Process. The arrest of a vessel covered by a general bond shall be stayed in accordance with Supplemental Rule E(5)(b), however, the Marshal shall serve a copy of the complaint upon the master or other person in whose charge or custody the vessel is found. If neither the master nor another person in charge of custody is found aboard the vessel, the Marshal shall make the return accordingly.

Thereafter, it shall be plaintiff's responsibility to advise the owner or designated agent, at the address furnished in the general bond, of (1) the case number; (2) nature of the action and the amount claimed; (3) the plaintiff and name and address of plaintiff's attorney; and (4) the return date for filing a claim.

(9) Application to Modify Security for Value and Interest. At any time, any party having an interest in the subject matter of the action may move the Court, on due notice and for cause, for greater, better or lesser security, and any such order may be enforced by attachment or as otherwise provided by law.

(10) Custody and Safekeeping.

(a) *Initial Responsibility.* The Marshal shall initially take custody of any vessel, cargo and/or other property arrested, or attached in accordance with these rules. Thereafter, and until such time as substitute custodians may be authorized in accordance with Local Admiralty Rule E(10)(c), the Marshal shall be responsible for providing adequate and necessary security for the safekeeping of the vessel or property.

In the discretion of the Marshal, adequate and necessary security may include the placing of keepers on or near the vessel and/or the appointment of a facility or person to serve as a custodian of the vessel or property.

(b) *Limitations on the Handling, Repairing and Subsequent Movement of Vessels or Property.* Subsequent to the arrest or attachment of a vessel or property, and except as provided in Local Admiralty Rule E(10)(a), no person may handle cargo, conduct repairs, or move a vessel without prior order of Court. Notwithstanding the foregoing, the custodian or substitute custodian is obligated to comply with any orders issued by the Captain of the Port, United States Coast Guard, including an order to move the vessel; and to comply with any applicable federal, state, or local laws or regulations pertaining to vessel and port safety. Any movement of a vessel pursuant to such requirements must not remove the vessel from the District and shall be reported to the Court within twenty-four hours of the vessel's movement.

(c) *Procedures for Changing Custody Arrangements.* Any party may petition the Court to dispense with keepers, remove or place the vessel, cargo and/or other property at a specified facility, designate a substitute custodian for the vessel or cargo, or for other similar relief. The motion shall substantially conform in format and content to the form identified as SDF 5 on the Court's website (www.flsd.uscourts.gov).

(i) Notification of the Marshal Required. When an application for change in custody arrangements is filed, either before or after the Marshal has taken custody of the vessel or property, the filing party shall serve notice of the application on the Marshal in sufficient time to permit the Marshal to review the indemnification and insurance arrangements of the filing party and substitute custodian. The application shall also be served upon all other parties to the litigation.

(ii) Indemnification Requirements. Any motion for the appointment of a substitute custodian or facility shall include as an exhibit to the motion, a consent and indemnification agreement signed by both the filing party, or the filing party's attorney, and the proposed substitute custodian.

The consent and indemnification agreement shall expressly release the Marshal from any and all liability and responsibility for the care and custody of the property while in the hands of the substitute custodian; and shall expressly hold the Marshal harmless from any and all claims whatsoever arising from the substitute custodianship. The agreement shall substantially conform in format and content to the form identified as SDF 6 on the Court's website (www.flsd.uscourts.gov).

(iii) Court Approval Required. The motion to change custody arrangements, and indemnification and consent agreement shall be referred to a judicial officer who shall determine whether the facility or substitute custodian is capable of safely keeping the vessel, cargo and/or property.

(d) *Insurance Requirements.*

(i) Responsibility for Initially Obtaining Insurance. Concurrent with the arrest or attachment of a vessel or property, the Marshal shall obtain insurance to protect the Marshal, the Marshal's deputies, keepers, and custodians from liability arising from the arrest or attachment.

The insurance shall also protect the Marshal and the Marshal's deputies or agents from any liability arising from performing services undertaken to protect the vessel, cargo and/or property while that property is in the custody of the Court.

(ii) Payment of Insurance Premiums. It shall be the responsibility of the party applying for the arrest or attachment of a vessel, cargo and/or property to promptly reimburse the Marshal for premiums paid to effect the necessary insurance.

The party applying for change in custody arrangements shall be responsible for paying the Marshal for any additional premium associated with the change.

(iii) Taxation of Insurance Premiums. The premiums charged for the liability insurance will be taxed as an expense of custody while the vessel, cargo and/or property is in custodia legis.

(11) Preservation, Humanitarian and Repatriation Expenses.

(a) *Limitations on Reimbursement for Services and/or Supplies Provided to a Vessel or Property in Custody.* Except in cases of emergency or undue hardship, no person will be entitled to claim as an expense of administration the costs of services or supplies furnished to a vessel, cargo and/or property unless such services or supplies have been furnished to the Marshal upon the Marshal's order, or pursuant to an order of this Court.

Any order issued pursuant to this subsection shall require the person furnishing the services or supplies to file a weekly invoice. This invoice shall be set forth in the format prescribed in Local Admiralty Rule E(11)(e).

(b) *Preservation Expenses for the Vessel and Cargo.* The Marshal, or substitute custodian, is authorized to incur expenses reasonably deemed necessary in maintaining the vessel, cargo and/or property in custody for the purpose of preventing the vessel, cargo and/or property from suffering loss or undue deterioration.

(c) *Expenses for Care and Maintenance of a Crew.* Except in an emergency, or upon the authorization of a judicial officer, neither the Marshal nor substitute custodian shall incur expenses for feeding or otherwise maintaining the crew.

Applications for providing food, water and necessary medical services for the maintenance of the crew may be submitted, and decided ex parte by a judicial officer, providing such an application is made by some person other than the owner, manager or general agent of the vessel.

Such applications must be filed within thirty (30) days from the date of the vessel's initial seizure. Otherwise, except in the case of an emergency, such applications shall be filed and served upon all parties, who in turn shall have fourteen (14) days from receipt of the application to file a written response, beginning on the next calendar day, including Saturday, Sunday, or a legal holiday.

Expenses for feeding or otherwise maintaining the crew, when incurred in accordance with this subsection, shall be taxed as an expense of administration and not as an expense of custody.

(d) *Repatriation Expenses.* Absent an order of Court expressly ordering the repatriation of the crew and/or passengers, and directing that the expenses be taxed as a cost of administration, no person shall be entitled to claim these expenses as expenses of administration.

(e) *Claim by a Supplier for Payment of Charges.* Any person who claims payment for furnishing services or supplies in compliance with Local Admiralty Rule E(11), shall submit an invoice to the Marshal's Office for review and approval.

The claim shall be presented in the form of a verified claim, and shall be submitted within a reasonable time after furnishing the services or supplies, but in no event shall a claim be accepted after the vessel, or property has been released. The claimant shall file a copy of the verified claim with the Marshal, and also serve the substitute custodian and all other parties to the litigation.

The Marshal shall review the claim, make adjustments or recommendations to the claim as are appropriate, and shall thereafter forward the claim to the Court for approval. The Court may postpone the hearing on an individual claim until a hearing can be set to consolidate other claims against the property.

(12) Property in Incidental Custody and Otherwise Not Subject to the Arrest or Attachment.

(a) *Authority to Preserve Cargo in Incidental Custody.* The Marshal, or an authorized substitute custodian, shall be responsible for securing, maintaining and preserving all property incidentally taken into custody as a result of the arrest or attachment of a vessel or property. Incidental property may include, but shall not be limited to, laden cargo not itself the subject of the arrest or attachment.

The Marshal or other custodian shall maintain a separate account of all costs and expenses associated with the care and maintenance of property incidentally taken into custody.

Any person claiming entitlement to possession of property incidentally taken into custody shall be required, as a precondition of receiving possession, to reimburse the Marshal for such separately accounted expenses. Monies received by the Marshal will be credited against both the expense of custody and administration.

(b) *Separation, Storage and Preservation of Property in Incidental Custody.* Any party, or the Marshal, may petition the Court to permit the separation and storage of property in incidental custody from the property actually arrested or attached.

When separation of the property is ordered to protect the incidentally seized property from undue deterioration; provide for safer storage; meet an emergency; reduce the expenses of custody; or to facilitate a sale of the vessel or other property pursuant to Local Admiralty Rule E(16); the costs of such separation shall be treated as an expense of preservation and taxed as a cost of custody.

(c) *Disposal of Unclaimed Property.* Property incidentally in custody and not subsequently claimed by any person entitled to possession, shall be disposed of in accordance with the laws governing the disposition of property abandoned to the United States of America.

Except when prohibited by prevailing federal statute, the resulting net proceeds associated with the disposition of abandoned property shall be applied to offset the expense of administration, with the remainder escheating to the United States of America as provided by law.

(13) Dismissal.

(a) *By Consent.* No action may be dismissed pursuant to Federal Rule of Civil Procedure 41(a) unless all costs and expenses of the Court and its officials have first been paid.

Additionally, if there is more than one plaintiff or intervening plaintiff, no dismissal may be taken by a plaintiff unless that party's proportionate share of costs and expenses has been paid in accordance with Local Admiralty Rule E(6).

(b) *Involuntary Dismissal.* If the Court enters a dismissal pursuant to Federal Rule of Civil Procedure 41(b), the Court shall also designate the costs and expenses to be paid by the party or parties so dismissed.

(14) Judgments.

(a) *Expenses of Sureties as Costs.* If costs are awarded to any party, then all reasonable premiums or expenses paid by the prevailing party on bonds, stipulations and/or other security shall be taxed as costs in the case.

(b) *Costs of Arrest or Attachment.* If costs are awarded to any party, then all reasonable expenses paid by the prevailing party incidental to, or arising from the arrest or attachment of any vessel, property and/or cargo shall be taxed as costs in the case.

(15) Stay of Final Order.

(a) *Automatic Stay for Fourteen Days.* In accordance with Federal Rule of Civil Procedure 62(a), no execution shall issue upon a judgment, nor shall seized property be released pursuant to a judgment or dismissal, until fourteen (14) days after the entry of the judgment or order of dismissal.

(b) *Stays Beyond the Fourteen Day Period.* If within the fourteen (14) day period established by Federal Rule of Civil Procedure 62(a), a party files any of the motions contemplated in Federal Rule of Civil Procedure 62(b), or a notice of appeal, then unless otherwise ordered by the Court, a further stay shall exist for a period not to exceed thirty (30) days from the entry of the judgment or order. The purpose of this additional stay is to permit the Court to consider an application for the establishment of a supersedeas bond and to order the date upon which the bond shall be filed with the Court.

(16) Notice of Sale.

(a) *Publication of Notice.* In an action in rem or quasi in rem, and except in suits on behalf of the United States of America where other notice is prescribed by statute, the Marshal shall publish notice in any of the newspapers approved pursuant to Local Admiralty Rule A(7).

(b) *Duration of Publication.* Unless otherwise ordered by the Court, applicable Supplemental Rule, or Local Admiralty Rule, publication of the notice of sale shall be made at least twice; the first publication shall be at least fourteen (14) days prior to the date of the sale, and the second at least seven (7) days prior to the date of the sale.

(17) Sale of a Vessel or Property.

(a) *Payment of the Purchase Price.* Unless otherwise provided in the order of sale, the person whose bid is accepted shall pay the Marshal the purchase price in the manner provided below;

(i) If the Bid Is Not More Than $500.00. The successful bidder shall immediately pay the full purchase price.

(ii) If the Bid Is More Than $500.00. The bidder shall immediately deposit with the Marshal $500.00, or ten percent of the bid, whichever sum is greater. Thereafter the bidder shall pay the remaining purchase price within seven (7) days.

If an objection to the sale is filed within the time permitted by Local Admiralty Rule E(17)(g), the successful bidder is excused from paying the remaining purchase price until seven (7) days after the Court confirms the sale.

(b) *Method of Payment.* Unless otherwise ordered by the Court, payments to the Marshal shall be made in cash, certified check or cashier's check.

(c) *Custodial Costs Pending Payment.* When a successful bidder fails to pay the balance of the bid within the time allowed by Local Admiralty Rule E(17)(a)(ii), or within the time permitted by order of the Court, the Marshal shall charge the successful bidder for the cost of keeping the property from the date payment of the balance was due, to the date the bidder takes delivery of the property.

The Marshal may refuse to release the property until these additional charges have been paid.

(d) *Default for Failure to Pay the Balance.* The person who fails to pay the balance of the bid within the time allowed shall be deemed to be in default. Thereafter a judicial officer may order that the sale be awarded to the second highest bidder, or may order a new sale as appropriate.

Any sum deposited by the bidder in default shall be forfeited, and the amount shall be applied by the Marshal to any additional costs incurred because of the forfeiture and default, including costs incident to resale. The balance of the deposit, if any, shall be retained in the registry and subject to further order of the Court.

(e) *Marshal's Report of Sale.* At the conclusion of the sale, the Marshal shall file a written report of the sale to include the date of the sale, the price obtained, and the name and address of the buyer.

(f) *Confirmation of Sale.* Unless an objection is timely filed in accordance with this rule, or the purchaser is in default for failing to pay the balance of the purchase price, plaintiff shall proceed to have the sale confirmed on the day following the last day for filing objections.

In order to confirm the sale, plaintiff's counsel shall file a "Request for Confirmation of Sale" on the day following the last day for filing an objection. *See* forms available on the Court's website (www.flsd.uscourts.gov). Plaintiff's counsel shall also prepare and offer for filing a "Confirmation of the Sale." *See* forms available on the Court's website (www.flsd.uscourts.gov). Thereafter the Clerk of the Court shall file and docket the confirmation and shall promptly transmit a certified copy of the "Confirmation of Sale" to the Marshal's Office.

Unless otherwise ordered by the Court, if the plaintiff fails to timely file the "Request for Confirmation of Sale" and proposed "Confirmation of Sale," the Marshal shall assess any continuing costs or expenses for custody of the vessel or property against the plaintiff.

(g) *Objections to Confirmation.*

(i) Time for Filing Objections. Unless otherwise permitted by the Court, an objection must be filed within seven (7) days following the sale. The party or person filing an objection shall serve a copy of the objection upon the Marshal and all other parties to the action, and shall also file a Certificate of Service indicating the date and manner of service. Opposition to the objection must be filed within seven (7) days after receipt of the objection of the sale.

The Court shall consider the objection, and any opposition to the objection, and shall confirm the sale, order a new sale, or grant other relief as appropriate.

(ii) Deposit of Preservation or Maintenance Costs. In addition to filing written objections, any person objecting to the sale shall also deposit with the Marshal the cost of keeping the property for at least fourteen (14) days. Proof of the deposit with the Marshal's Office shall be delivered to the Clerk of the Court's Office by the moving party. The Court will not consider the objection without proof of this deposit.

If the objection is sustained, the objector will be reimbursed for the expense of keeping the property from the proceeds of any subsequent sale, and any remaining deposit will be returned to the objector upon Court order.

If the objection is denied, the sum deposited by the objector will be applied to pay the fees and expenses incurred by the Marshal in keeping the property from the date the objection was filed until the sale is confirmed. Any remaining deposit will be returned to the objector upon order of Court.

(h) *Confirmation of Title.* Failure of a party to give the required notice of an action and arrest of a vessel, property and/or cargo, or failure to give required notice of a sale, may afford grounds for objecting to the sale, but such failure does not affect the title of a good faith purchaser of the property.

(18) Post–Sale Claim. Claims against the proceeds of a sale authorized by these rules, except for seamen's wages, will not be admitted on behalf of lienors who file their claims after the sale.

Unless otherwise ordered by the Court, any claims filed after the date of the sale shall be limited to the remnants and surplus arising from the sale.

[Effective December 1, 1994. Amended effective April 15, 1998; April 15, 2007; April 15, 2010; April 15, 2011; December 1, 2014; December 1, 2015.]

Advisory Notes

(1993) **Local Admiralty Rule E(1).** This section continues the provisions of former Local Rule 7(c).

Local Admiralty Rule E(2). This section is new. The rules do not require an intervening plaintiff to undertake the formal steps required to issue the original process of arrest or attachment pursuant to Local Admiralty Rule B(3) or C(2); rather the Committee believes that intervening parties need only apply for supplemental process, which in accordance with the August 1, 1985, amendments to Supplemental Rule B and C, may be issued by the Clerk of the Court without further order of the Court. The Committee recommends the re-arrest or re-attachment provisions of this rule in order to accommodate the administrative and records keeping requirements of the Marshal's Office.

The revision also reflects the elimination of the initial security deposit formerly required by Local Admiralty Rule 5(e). The Marshal shall, however, assess custodial costs against the intervening plaintiff in accordance with Local Admiralty Rule E(5)(b).

Local Admiralty Rule E(3). This section continues the provisions of former Local Rule 7(e).

Local Admiralty Rule E(4). This section continues the provisions of former Local Rule 6.

Local Admiralty Rule E(5). The Marshal, as an officer of the Court whose fiscal affairs are regulated by statute and order, is precluded by law from expending funds of the United States to maintain custody of vessels or other property pursuant to claims being asserted by the several states, any foreign sovereigns, or any private parties. This prohibition extends to incurring obligations which, if not satisfied, otherwise might be asserted as a claim against the United States. Consequently, before undertaking to arrest or attach property, the Marshal must receive funds in advance of incurring such obligations sufficient to satisfy them.

Past experience indicates that not infrequently vessels or other properties arrested for nonpayment of incurred obligations will be ultimately sold for satisfaction, to the extent possible, of pending claims. In such cases, substitute security is never given, and the property must be retained in custody for a sufficient period of time to permit the Court to determine the status of the situation and to order appropriate procedures. In such instances, custodial costs tend to be substantial and, by the very nature of the circumstances, the claimants and potential claimants can be both large in number and will vary markedly in the amounts of their respective individual claims. Apportioning the obligation to make advances against custodial costs over this range of claims and claimants has resulted in frequent calls for judicial intervention.

It was the Committee's view that a system initially self-executing and ministerial would minimize situations calling for judicial intervention while affording the Marshal the protection of assured and certain procedures. At the same time, the Committee was strongly of the opinion that the rules should do substantial equity as between claims showing wide variation in amounts and potential priorities and, at the same time, should be so structured as to require all potential claimants to come forward and share in the cost of custody, discouraging the sometime practice of claimants' waiting to intervene until the last moment in order to allow other parties to bear the burdens of making such advances.

A concern was expressed about the position of parties having large, but clearly inferior claims, who, in equity should not be required to share on a prorated value-of-the-claim-asserted basis with claimants who have obvious priority. A typical example of such a situation would involve a mortgagee of a foreign-flag vessel appearing as a claimant in an action along with lien claimants alleging to have supplied necessaries to a vessel in ports of the United States, the mortgagee's position being subordinated by virtue of Title 46, United States Code, Section 951. After considering all possible alternatives, it was obvious that this limited range of situations could not be addressed through a mechanism for automatic administration and, consequently, the provision providing for judicial relief in the event of hardship or inequity was included.

Local Admiralty Rule E(6). Section (6) is new. It reflects the approach embodied in the local rules of those districts which have addressed the question of properties subject to arrest but already in the possession of an officer of the United States.

Local Admiralty Rule E(7). The provisions of Section (7) are new. Paragraph (a), following rules promulgated in other districts, states what is understood by the Advisory Committee to have been the practice in this District. Paragraph (b) is designed to mesh the concept of process held in abeyance with the requirements of Local Admiralty Rule E(2) regarding intervening claims, and is designed to foreclose the possibility of a vessel or other property being arrested or attached in the District as a result of more than one civil action. Since under Local Rule 5(b), the automatic, permissive intervention is not triggered until the vessel or other property has been arrested, attached or seized, a suit in rem in which process is held in abeyance will not form the basis for such an intervention. On the other hand, once the property is arrested, attached or seized, the issuance of process in the earlier suit would be destructive of the "only one civil action" concept, and, consequently paragraph (b) requires a party whose process was held in abeyance to refile as an intervenor pursuant to Local Admiralty Rule E(2), making provision for the proper disposition of the earlier action.

Local Admiralty Rule E(8). Section (8) continues the provisions of former Local Rule 11.

Local Admiralty Rule E(9). Section (9) is new. The provisions of Section (j) are expressly authorized by Supplemental Rule E(6) and offer some potential relief from the automatic operations and other provisions of Supplemental Rule E regarding security for value and interest. The decision in *Industria Nacional del Papel, C.A. M V Albert F.*, 730 F.2d 622 (11th Cir. 1984), indicates that such an application must be made prior to the entry of judgment.

Local Admiralty Rule E(10). Section (10) is new. It is designed to reflect the actual practice in the District, and follows the rules promulgated in several other districts. In formulating this Local Admiralty Rule, the Committee studied Section 6.3 of the "Marshal's Manual," the internal operating guide for the United States Marshal's Service. Section 10(b) was amended in 1998 to permit substitute custodians to move arrested vessels, pursuant to an order of the United States Coast Guard Captain of the Port ("COTP"), without first obtaining permission from the Court. The change was prompted by instances where substitute custodians declined to obey a COTP order to move an arrested vessel, citing Local Admiralty Rule E(10)(b) and its requirement that Court permission be first obtained. Any movement of a vessel pursuant to a COTP order must not take the vessel out of the District. A corresponding change was made in Form 5, paragraph (5).

Local Admiralty Rule E(11). Section (11) is new. It addresses areas which in recent litigation in the District have called excessively for interim judicial administration. While the subject matter is covered in the rules promulgated in other districts, Section (11) differs from the approach of other districts in providing for a more positive control of expenses being incurred in connection with vessels or other property in the custody of the Court, and is designed to avoid accumulated costs being advanced for the first time well after having been incurred.

Local Admiralty Rule E(12). Section (12) is new. It addresses a situation which has arisen in the District in the past and which can be foreseen as possibly arising in the future. While the subject is not addressed in other local rules studied by any oft-cited leading cases, it was the opinion of the Advisory Committee that the area should be addressed by Local Admiralty Rule and that the provisions of Section (12) are both consistent with the general maritime laws of the United States and designed to permit efficient administration without the necessity for undue judicial intervention. As with the claims of intervenors and the allocation of deposits against custodial costs, the provisions of Section (12), in keeping with the design of these Local Admiralty Rules, are intended to be essentially self-executing, with the emphasis on the ministerial role of Court officers and services.

Local Admiralty Rule E(13). Section (13) continues the provisions of former Local Rule 17(a). It follows Federal Rule of Civil Procedure 41, and addresses the necessarily greater concern for costs and expenses inherent in the in rem admiralty procedure.

Local Admiralty Rule E(14). Section (14) continues the provisions of former Local Rule 13.

Local Admiralty Rule E(15). Section (15) incorporates the provisions of former Local Rule 14.

Local Admiralty Rule E(16) and (17). The provisions of former Local Rule 4 have been expanded to provide a standardized procedure governing sales of property, which procedure the Court, at its option, may utilize, in whole or in part, thus shortening and simplifying orders related to sales and accompanying procedures.

Local Admiralty Rule E(18). Consistent with the provision of Local Admiralty Rule E(2), this section gives express notice of the distinct positions of claims pre-sale and post-sale.

(2010) Local Admiralty Rule E(16)(b). The dates of publication were changed to conform with the 2009 changes to the deadline calculations of the Federal Rules.

(2014) Local Admiralty Rule (E)(17) was amended to clarify that forms referenced in the rule are found on the Court's website rather than in the Appendix.

RULE F. ACTIONS TO LIMIT LIABILITY

(1) Monition, Injunction and Publication of the Notice. Upon the plaintiff's filing of an Ad Interim Stipulation of Value or otherwise posting a deposit or transfer in compliance with Supplemental Rules F(1) and F(2), the Court shall immediately issue a Monition and Injunction pursuant to Supplemental Rule F(3). The Monition and Injunction shall: enjoin the further prosecution of any action or proceeding against the plaintiff or the plaintiff's property with respect to any claim subject to limitation in the action; order that all persons asserting claims with respect to which the complaint seeks limitation to file their respective claims pursuant to Supplemental Rule F(4); order that public notice be effectuated by the plaintiff pursuant to Supplemental Rule F(4); and approve the Ad Interim Stipulation of Value or other form of deposit, transfer or security if it meets the requirements of Supplemental Rules F(1) and F(2). Upon the issuance of the Monition and Injunction by the Court, the plaintiff shall effect publication of the notice in accordance with the provisions set forth in Supplemental Rule F(4) and Local Admiralty Rule A(7). This Local Rule does not affect a claimant's right to assert the insufficiency of the fund or security under Supplemental Rule F(7).

(2) Proof of Publication. Plaintiff shall file proof of publication of the notice to claimants with the Court within seven (7) days after the date fixed by the Court pursuant to Supplemental Rule F(4). It shall be sufficient proof for plaintiff to file the sworn statement or a declaration pursuant to 28 U.S.C. § 1746 by, or on behalf of, the publisher or editor, indicating the dates of publication, along with a copy or reproduction of the actual publication.

(3) Security and Appraisals Pursuant to Supplemental Rule F(7). Upon the filing of a claimant's motion pursuant to Supplemental Rule F(7) demanding an increase in the funds deposited in Court or the security given by plaintiff, the Court shall order an appraisement of the value of the plaintiff's interest in the vessel and pending freight.

Upon receipt of the order directing the appraisal, the parties shall have seven (7) days to file a written stipulation to an appraiser. In the event that the parties do not file a stipulation, the Court shall appoint the appraiser.

The appraiser shall promptly conduct an appraisal and thereafter file the appraisal with the Clerk of the Court and serve a copy of the appraisal upon the moving party and the plaintiff. The appraiser shall also file a Certificate of Service indicating the date and manner in which service was perfected.

At such time that the parties agree to the quantum of the plaintiff's Ad Interim Stipulation of Value, deposit or security, or alternatively, the Court finds that the plaintiff's Ad Interim Stipulation of Value is insufficient or excessive, the Court shall order that a deposit or security be effectuated for the amount agreed by the parties or the amount found by the Court to be sufficient, after the date for objections to the appraisal under Supplemental Rule F(4) has passed and the Court has ruled on the objections. The Joint Stipulation of the Parties as to the Value of the Vessel shall substantially conform to the form identified as SDF 18 on the Court's website (www.flsd.uscourts.gov).

(4) Objections to the Appraisal. Any party may move to set aside the appraisal within fourteen (14) days following the filing of the appraisal with the Clerk of the Court.

(5) Fees of the Appraiser. The Court shall establish the fee to be paid the appraiser. Unless otherwise ordered by the Court, the fee shall be taxed against the party seeking relief under Supplemental Rule F(7).

(6) Order of Proof at Trial. In an action where plaintiff seeks to limit liability, the claimants shall offer their proof at trial first, whether the right to limit arises as a claim or as a defense.

[Effective December 1, 1994. Amended effective April 15, 2007; April 15, 2010; April 15, 2011; December 1, 2015.]

Advisory Notes

(1993) **Local Admiralty Rule F(1).** This section incorporates the publication provisions of Local Admiralty Rule A(7), and applies them to limitation of liability actions. The rule provides for the publication of the notice required by Supplemental Rule F(4) without further order of the Court. The Advisory Committee believes that this self-executing aspect of the rule will save judicial time and at the same time will not impair the rights of any party or claimant.

Local Admiralty Rule F(2). The Advisory Committee determined that filing proof of publication with the Clerk of the Court was essential in order to establish an adequate record of the publication.

Local Admiralty Rule F(3). This section continues in substance the provisions of former Local Admiralty Rule 10.

(2010) **Local Admiralty Rule F(1).** The Advisory Committee determined that the publication of the notice without court order did not meet the self-executing aspect of the rule as contemplated in 1993.

Amended to conform tabulation to the style used in the federal rules of procedure.

Local Admiralty Rule F(2). The advisory Committee believes that the previous language "not later than the return date" was vague. The language was changed to remove any confusion on the definition of "return date" and the time by which the plaintiff is required to file the proof of publication. The addition of the language "or a declaration pursuant to 28 U.S.C. § 1746" was added to deal with any exigent circumstances.

Local Admiralty Rule F(3). The Advisory Committee determined that while the previous Local Rule references a claimant's demand for an increase, it fails to consider instances where the claimants accept the plaintiff's Ad Interim Stipulation of Value, obviating the need to post further security.

Local Admiralty Rule F(6). The Maritime Law Association of the United States ("MLA") has approved Model Local Admiralty Rules dated May 2, 2008. The Advisory Committee has adopted MLA Model Local Admiralty Rule F(2) because the Committee believes that although petitioners in limitation of liability proceedings are the plaintiffs, in practice they are defending claims of claimants and therefore the claimants should offer proof at trial first.

APPENDIX OF FORMS. ADMIRALTY AND MARITIME RULES

FORM 1. ORDER DIRECTING THE ISSUANCE OF THE PROCESS OF ATTACHMENT AND GARNISHMENT

UNITED STATES DISTRICT COURT
SOUTHERN DISTRICT OF FLORIDA

Case No. ___ –Civ or Cr –(USDJ's last name/USMJ's last name)

"IN ADMIRALTY"

Plaintiff,

v.

Defendant.

ORDER DIRECTING THE ISSUANCE OF THE PROCESS OF ATTACHMENT AND GARNISHMENT

Pursuant to Supplemental Rule B(1) and Local Admiralty Rule B(3)(a), the Clerk of the Court is directed to issue the summons and process of attachment and garnishment in the above-styled action.

DONE AND ORDERED at ______, Florida, this ______ day of ______, ______.

____
United States District Judge

[Effective December 1, 1994. Amended effective April 15, 2001; April 15, 2007; April 15, 2010; April 15, 2011.]

FORM 2. PROCESS OF ATTACHMENT AND GARNISHMENT

UNITED STATES DISTRICT COURT
SOUTHERN DISTRICT OF FLORIDA

Case No. ___ –Civ or Cr–(USDJ's last name/USMJ's last name)

"IN ADMIRALTY"

Plaintiff,

v.

Defendant.

____

PROCESS OF ATTACHMENT AND GARNISHMENT

The complaint in the above-styled case was filed in the ___ Division of this Court on __________, __________.

In accordance with Supplemental Rule B of Certain Admiralty and Maritime Claims of the Federal Rules of Civil Procedure and Local Admiralty Rule B, you are directed to attach and garnish the property indicated below:

DESCRIPTION

(Describe the property to be attached and garnished in sufficient detail, including location of the property, to permit the United States Marshal to effect the seizure.)

You shall also give notice of the attachment and garnishment to every person required by appropriate Supplemental Rule, Local Admiralty Rule, and the practices of your office.

DATED at _______, Florida, this _______ day of ________, ____.

CLERK

By: ______________________
Deputy Clerk

Attorney Name (Bar Number)
Attorney E-mail Address
Firm Name
Street Address
City, State, Zip Code
Telephone: (xxx)xxx-xxxx
Facsimile: (xxx)xxx-xxxx
Attorneys for Plaintiff [Party Name(s)]

SPECIAL NOTICE

Any person claiming an interest in property seized pursuant to this process of attachment and garnishment must file a claim in accordance with the post-seizure review provisions of Local Admiralty Rule B(5).

[Effective December 1, 1994. Amended effective April 15, 2001; April 15, 2007; April 15, 2010; April 15, 2011.]

FORM 3. ORDER DIRECTING THE ISSUANCE OF THE WARRANT OF ARREST

UNITED STATES DISTRICT COURT
SOUTHERN DISTRICT OF FLORIDA

Case No. ___ –Civ or Cr–(USDJ's last name/USMJ's last name)

"IN ADMIRALTY"

Plaintiff,

v.

Defendant.

____

ORDER DIRECTING THE ISSUANCE OF THE WARRANT OF ARREST AND/OR SUMMONS

Pursuant to Supplemental Rule C(1) and Local Admiralty Rule C(2)(a), the Clerk of the Court is directed to issue a warrant of arrest and/or summons in the above-styled action.

DONE AND ORDERED at __________, Florida, this ___ day of __________, ____.

United States District Judge

[Effective December 1, 1994. Amended effective April 15, 2001; April 15, 2007; April 15, 2010; April 15, 2011.]

FORM 4. WARRANT FOR ARREST IN REM

UNITED STATES DISTRICT COURT
SOUTHERN DISTRICT OF FLORIDA

Case No.___–Civ or Cr–(USDJ's last name/USMJ's last name)

"IN ADMIRALTY"

Plaintiff,

v.

Defendant.

____

WARRANT FOR ARREST IN REM

TO THE UNITED STATES MARSHAL FOR THE UNITED STATES DISTRICT COURT FOR THE SOUTHERN DISTRICT OF FLORIDA

The complaint in the above-styled in rem proceeding was filed in the ___ Division of this Court on __________, _________.

In accordance with Supplemental Rule C for Certain Admiralty and Maritime Claims of the Federal Rules of Civil Procedure and Local Admiralty Rule C, you are directed to arrest the Defendant vessel, her boats, tackle, apparel and furniture, engines and appurtenances, and to detain the same in your custody pending further order of the Court.

You shall also give notice of the arrest to all persons required by appropriate Supplemental Rule, Local Admiralty Rule, and the practices of your office.

ORDERED at _______, Florida, this _______ day of ________, ___.

CLERK

By: ______________________
Deputy Clerk

Attorney Name (Bar Number)
Attorney E–mail Address
Firm Name
Street Address
City, State, Zip Code
Telephone: (xxx)xxx-xxxx
Facsimile: (xxx)xxx-xxxx
Attorneys for Plaintiff [Party Name(s)]

cc: Counsel of Record

SPECIAL NOTICE

In accordance with Local Admiralty Rule C(6), any person claiming an interest in the vessel and/or property shall be required to file a claim within fourteen (14) days after process has been executed, and shall also be required to file an answer within twenty-one (21) days after the filing of this claim.

Any persons claiming an interest in the vessel and/or property may also pursue the post-arrest remedies set forth in Local Admiralty Rule C(7).

[Effective December 1, 1994. Amended effective April 15, 2001; April 15, 2007; April 15, 2010; April 15, 2011.]

FORM 5. MOTION FOR APPOINTMENT OF SUBSTITUTE CUSTODIAN

UNITED STATES DISTRICT COURT
SOUTHERN DISTRICT OF FLORIDA

Case No. ___–Civ or Cr–(USDJ's last name/USMJ's last name)

"IN ADMIRALTY"

Plaintiff,

v.

Defendant.

____

MOTION FOR APPOINTMENT OF SUBSTITUTE CUSTODIAN

Pursuant to Local Admiralty Rule E(10)(c), Plaintiff _________, by and through the undersigned attorney, represents the following:

(1) On _________, _________, Plaintiff initiated the above-styled action against the vessel _________, her boats, tackle, apparel, furniture and furnishings, equipment, engines and appurtenances.

(2) On _________, _________, the Clerk of the Court issued a Warrant of Arrest against the vessel _________, directing the United States Marshal to take custody of the vessel, and to retain custody of the vessel pending further order of this Court.

(3)(a) Subsequent to the issuance of the Warrant of Arrest, the Marshal will take steps to immediately seize the vessel. Thereafter, continual custody by the Marshal will require the services of at least one custodian at a cost of at least $ ___ per day. (This paragraph would be applicable only when the motion for appointment is filed concurrent with the complaint and application for the warrant of arrest.)

-or-

(3)(b) Pursuant to the previously issued Warrant of Arrest, the Marshal has already arrested the vessel. Continued custody by the Marshal requires the services of _________ custodians at a cost of at least $ ___ per day. (This paragraph would be applicable in all cases where the Marshal has previously arrested the vessel.)

(4) The vessel is currently berthed at _________, and subject to the approval of the Court, the substitute custodian is prepared to provide security, wharfage, and routine services for the safekeeping of the vessel at a cost substantially less than that presently required by the Marshal. The substitute custodian has also agreed to continue to provide these services pending further order of this Court.

(5) The substitute custodian has adequate facilities for the care, maintenance and security of the vessel. In discharging its obligation to care for, maintain and secure the vessel, the substitute custodian shall comply with all orders of the Captain of the Port, United States Coast Guard, including but not limited to, an order to move the vessel; and any applicable federal, state, and local laws, regulations and requirements pertaining to vessel and port safety. The substitute custodian shall advise the Court, the parties to the action, and the United States Marshal, of any movement of the vessel pursuant to an order of the Captain of the Port, United States Coast Guard within twenty-four hours of such vessel movement.

(6) Concurrent with the Court's approval of the Motion for Appointment of the Substitute Custodian, Plaintiff and the substitute custodian will file a Consent and Indemnification Agreement in accordance with Local Admiralty Rule E(10)(C)(ii).

THEREFORE, in accordance with the representations set forth in this instrument, and subject to the filing of the indemnification agreement noted in paragraph (6) above, Plaintiff requests this Court to enter an order appointing __________ as the Substitute Custodian for the vessel __________.

DATED at __________, Florida, this ___ day of __________, ___.

SIGNATURE OF COUNSEL OF RECORD
Attorney Name (Bar Number)
Attorney E-mail Address
Firm Name
Street Address
City, State, Zip Code
Telephone: (xxx)xxx–xxxx
Facsimile: (xxx)xxx–xxxx
Attorneys for Plaintiff [Party Name(s)]

cc: Counsel of Record
Substitute Custodian

SPECIAL NOTE

Plaintiff's attorney shall also prepare for the Court's signature and subsequent filing, a proposed order for the Appointment of Substitute Custodian.

[Effective December 1, 1994. Amended effective April 15, 1998; April 15, 2001; April 15, 2007; April 15, 2010; April 15, 2011.]

FORM 6. CONSENT AND INDEMNIFICATION AGREEMENT FOR THE APPOINTMENT OF A SUBSTITUTE CUSTODIAN

UNITED STATES DISTRICT COURT
SOUTHERN DISTRICT OF FLORIDA

Case No. ___–Civ or Cr–(USDJ's last name/USMJ's last name)

"IN ADMIRALTY"

Plaintiff,

v.

Defendant.
____

CONSENT AND INDEMNIFICATION AGREEMENT FOR THE APPOINTMENT OF A SUBSTITUTE CUSTODIAN

Plaintiff _________________, (by the undersigned attorney) and _________________, the proposed Substitute Custodian, hereby expressly release the United States Marshal for this District, and the United States Marshal's Service, from any and all liability and responsibility for the care and custody of _________________ (describe the property) while in the hands of _____________ (substitute custodian).

Plaintiff and _____________ (substitute custodian) also expressly agree to hold the United States Marshal for this District, and the United States Marshal's Service, harmless from any and all claims whatsoever arising during the period of the substitute custodianship.

As counsel of record in this action, the undersigned attorney represents that he has been expressly authorized by the Plaintiff to sign this Consent and Indemnification Agreement for, and on behalf of the Plaintiff.

SIGNED this ___ day of ___________, ______, at __________, Florida.

PLAINTIFF'S ATTORNEY
CUSTODIAN
Attorney Name (Bar Number)
Attorney E-mail Address
Firm Name
Street Address
City, State, Zip Code
Telephone: (xxx)xxx-xxxx
Facsimilee: (xxx)xxx-xxxx
Attorneys for Plaintiff [Party Name(s)]

SUBSTITUTE
Typed Name
Fla. Bar ID No.
(if admitted in Fla.)
Firm or Business Name
Mailing Address
City, State, Zip Code
Telephone Number
Facsimile Number
E–Mail Address

cc: Counsel of Record

[Effective December 1, 1994. Amended effective April 15, 2001; April 15, 2007; April 15, 2010; April 15, 2011.]

FORM 7. NOTICE OF ACTION IN REM AND ARREST OF VESSEL

UNITED STATES DISTRICT COURT
SOUTHERN DISTRICT OF FLORIDA

Case No. ___ –Civ or Cr–(USDJ's last name/USMJ's last name)

"IN ADMIRALTY"

Plaintiff,

v.

Defendant.

____

NOTICE OF ACTION IN REM AND ARREST OF VESSEL

In accordance with Supplemental Rule C(4) for Certain Admiralty and Maritime Action of the Federal Rules of Civil Procedure, and Local Admiralty Rule C(4), notice is hereby given of the arrest of ________, in accordance with a Warrant of Arrest issued on _______, ________.

Pursuant to Supplemental Rule C(6), and Local Admiralty Rule C(6), any person having a claim against the vessel and/or property shall file a claim with the Court not later than fourteen (14) days after process has been effected, and shall file an answer within twenty-one (21) days from the date of filing their claim.

DATED at _______, Florida, this _______ day of ________, _______.

____
SIGNED NAME OF PLAINTIFF'S ATTORNEY
Attorney Name (Bar Number)
Attorney E-mail Address
Firm Name
Street Address
City, State, Zip Code
Telephone: (xxx)xxx-xxxx
Facsimile: (xxx)xxx-xxxx
Attorneys for Plaintiff [Party Name(s)]

cc: Counsel of Record

[Effective December 1, 1994. Amended effective April 15, 2001; April 15, 2007; April 15, 2010; April 15, 2011.]

FORM 8. MOTION FOR RELEASE OF A VESSEL OR PROPERTY IN ACCORDANCE WITH SUPPLEMENTAL RULE E(5)

UNITED STATES DISTRICT COURT
SOUTHERN DISTRICT OF FLORIDA

Case No. ___ –Civ or Cr–(USDJ's last name/USMJ's last name)

"IN ADMIRALTY"

Plaintiff,

v.

Defendant.

____

MOTION FOR RELEASE OF A VESSEL OR PROPERTY IN ACCORDANCE WITH SUPPLEMENTAL RULE E(5)

In accordance with Supplemental Rule E(5) and Local Admiralty Rule E(8)(b), plaintiff, on whose behalf property has been seized, requests the Court to enter an Order directing the United States Marshal for the Southern District of Florida to release the property. This request is made for the following reasons:

(Describe the reasons in sufficient detail to permit the Court to enter an appropriate order.)

DATED at _________, Florida, this ___ day of _________, _______.

____
SIGNED NAME OF PLAINTIFF'S ATTORNEY
Attorney Name (Bar Number)
Attorney E-mail Address
Firm Name
Street Address
City, State, Zip Code
Telephone: (xxx)xxx-xxxx
Facsimile: (xxx)xxx-xxxx
Attorneys for Plaintiff [Party Name(s)]

cc: Counsel of Record

[Effective December 1, 1994. Amended effective April 15, 2001; April 15, 2007; April 15, 2010; April 15, 2011.]

FORM 9. ORDER DIRECTING THE RELEASE OF A VESSEL OR PROPERTY IN ACCORDANCE WITH SUPPLEMENTAL RULE E(5)

UNITED STATES DISTRICT COURT
SOUTHERN DISTRICT OF FLORIDA

Case No. ___–Civ or Cr–(USDJ's last name/USMJ's last name)

"IN ADMIRALTY"

Plaintiff,

v.

Defendant.

____

ORDER DIRECTING THE RELEASE OF A VESSEL OR PROPERTY IN ACCORDANCE WITH SUPPLEMENTAL RULE E(5)

In accordance with Supplemental Rule E(5) and Local Admiralty Rule E(8)(a), and pursuant to the Request for Release filed on ______________, ____, the United States Marshal is directed to release the vessel and/or property currently being held in his custody in the above-styled action.

ORDERED at __________, Florida, this ___ day of _________, ____.

____
U.S. District Judge

cc: Counsel of Record

[Effective December 1, 1994. Amended effective April 15, 2001; April 15, 2010; April 15, 2011.]

FORM 10. REQUEST FOR CONFIRMATION OF SALE

ADMIRALTY AND MARITIME RULES
SAMPLE FORM

UNITED STATES DISTRICT COURT
SOUTHERN DISTRICT OF FLORIDA
Case No. ___–Civ or Cr–(USDJ's last name/USMJ's last name)
"IN ADMIRALTY"

Plaintiff,

v.

Defendant.

REQUEST FOR CONFIRMATION OF SALE

Plaintiff, by and through its undersigned attorney certifies the following:

(1) *Date of Sale:* In accordance with the Court's previous Order of Sale, plaintiff represents that the sale of __________ (describe the property) was conducted by the United States Marshal on __________, __________.

(2) *Last Day for Filing Objections:* Pursuant to Local Admiralty Rule E(17)(g)(i), the last day for filing objections to the sale was __________, __________.

(3) *Survey of Court Records:* Plaintiff has surveyed the docket and records of this case, and has confirmed that as of __________, __________, there were no objections to the sale on file with the Clerk of the Court.

THEREFORE, in light of the facts presented above and pursuant to Local Admiralty Rule E(17)(f), plaintiff requests the Clerk of the Court to enter a Confirmation of Sale and to transmit the confirmation to the Marshal for processing.

DATED at _______, Florida, this _______ day of _______, _______.

____
SIGNED NAME OF PLAINTIFF'S ATTORNEY
Attorney Name (Bar Number)
Attorney E-mail Address
Firm Name
Street Address
City, State, Zip Code
Telephone: (xxx)xxx–xxxx
Facsimile: (xxx)xxx–xxxx
Attorneys for Plaintiff [Party Name(s)]

cc: Counsel of Record

[Effective December 1, 1994. Amended effective April 15, 2001; April 15, 2007; April 15, 2010; April 15, 2011; December 1, 2014.]

FORM 11. CONFIRMATION OF SALE

ADMIRALTY AND MARITIME RULES

SAMPLE FORM

UNITED STATES DISTRICT COURT
SOUTHERN DISTRICT OF FLORIDA
Case No. ___–Civ or Cr–(USDJ's last name/USMJ's last name)
"IN ADMIRALTY"

Plaintiff,

v.

Defendant.
_________________________________/

CLERK'S CONFIRMATION OF SALE

The records in this action indicate that no objection has been filed to the sale of property conducted by the United States Marshal on __________, __________.

THEREFORE, upon the request of plaintiff's counsel and in accordance with Local Admiralty Rule E(17)(f), the sale shall stand confirmed as of the date of this filing.

DONE at ______, Florida, this ______ day of ______, ____.

CLERK

By: ______________
Deputy Clerk

cc: United States Marshal
Counsel of Record

[Effective December 1, 1994. Amended effective April 15, 2001; April 15, 2007; April 15, 2010; April 15, 2011; December 1, 2014.]

FORM 12. SUMMONS AND PROCESS OF MARITIME ATTACHMENT AND GARNISHMENT

UNITED STATES DISTRICT COURT
SOUTHERN DISTRICT OF FLORIDA

Case No. ___ –Civ or Cr–(USDJ's last name/USMJ's last name)

Plaintiff,

v.

Defendant.

____

SUMMONS AND PROCESS OF MARITIME ATTACHMENT AND GARNISHMENT THE PRESIDENT OF THE UNITED STATES OF AMERICA

TO: THE UNITED STATES MARSHAL FOR THE SOUTHERN DISTRICT OF FLORIDA.

GREETING:

WHEREAS, on the ___ day of __________, ___ filed a complaint against _________ _________ for reasons in said complaint mentioned for the sum of _________ _________ and praying for process of marine attachment and garnishment against the said defendant and __________,

WHEREAS, this process is issued pursuant to such prayer and requires that a garnishee shall serve his answer within twenty-one (21) days after service of process upon him and requires that a defendant shall serve his answer within thirty (30) days after process has been executed, whether by attachment of property or service on the garnishee,

NOW, THEREFORE, you are hereby commanded that if the said defendant cannot be found within the District you attach goods, chattels, credits and effects located and to be found at _________ and described as follows: _________, or in the hands of _________, the garnishee, up to the amount sued for, to-wit: _________ and how you shall have executed this process, make known to this Court with your certificate of execution thereof written.

WITNESS THE HONORABLE

____
Judge of said Court at _______, Florida,
in said District, this _______ day of _______, _______.

__________________, CLERK
BY: ______________________
Deputy Clerk

NOTE: This process is issued pursuant to Rule B(1) of the Supplemental Rules for Certain Admiralty and Maritime Claims of the Federal Rules of Civil Procedure.

[Effective December 1, 1994. Amended effective April 15, 2001; April 15, 2007; April 15, 2010.]

FORM 13. MARITIME SUMMONS TO SHOW CAUSE RESPECTING INTANGIBLE PROPERTY

UNITED STATES DISTRICT COURT
SOUTHERN DISTRICT OF FLORIDA

Case No. ___ –Civ or Cr–(USDJ's last name/USMJ's last name)

Plaintiff,

v.

Defendant.

____

MARITIME SUMMONS TO SHOW CAUSE RESPECTING INTANGIBLE PROPERTY

TO ALL PERSONS having control of the freight of the vessel _________ or control of the proceeds of the sale of said vessel or control of the proceeds of the sale of any property appurtenant thereto or control of any other intangible property appurtenant thereto.

You are hereby summoned to interpose in writing a claim, by attorney or in proper person, at the Clerk's of the Court's Office in said District within fourteen (14) days after the service, and therewith or thereafter within twenty-one (21) days following such claim or thirty (30) days after the service, whichever is less, a responsive pleading to the complaint herewith served upon you and to show cause why said property under your control should not be paid into Court to abide the judgment; and you are required so also to serve copy thereof upon _________, plaintiff's attorney(s) whose address is _________; or if you do not claim said property then to so serve and show cause why said property under your control should not be paid into Court to abide the judgment.

The service of this summons upon you brings said property within the control of the Court.

Service of this summons is ineffective unless made in time to give notice of the required appearance or such shorter period as the Court may fix by making and signing the form of order provided below:

WITNESS THE HONORABLE

____
Judge of said Court at _______, Florida,
in said District, this _______ day of _______, _______.

_____________________, CLERK
BY: __________
Deputy Clerk

Date:

Good cause for shortening the periods required by the foregoing summons having been shown by affidavit of __________, verified the ________ day of __________, __________, the period of notice of the appearance in all respects required by the foregoing summons is hereby fixed as ___ days.

Dated at ______, Florida, the ______ day of ________, ______.

____
UNITED STATES DISTRICT JUDGE

NOTE: This summons is issued pursuant to Rule C(3) of the Supplemental Rules for Certain Admiralty Maritime Claims of the Federal Rules of Civil Procedure.

[Effective December 1, 1994. Amended effective April 15, 2001; April 15, 2007; April 15, 2010.]

FORM 14. AFFIDAVIT—FOREIGN ATTACHMENT

UNITED STATES DISTRICT COURT
SOUTHERN DISTRICT OF FLORIDA

Case No. ___ –Civ or Cr–(USDJ's last name/USMJ's last name)

Plaintiff,

v.

Defendant.

____

AFFIDAVIT
(Foreign Attachment)

This affidavit is executed by the undersigned in order to secure the issuance and execution of a Writ of Foreign Attachment in the above-styled in personam cause in admiralty.

As attorney for the above-styled plaintiff, the undersigned does hereby certify to the Court, the Clerk of the Court and the United States Marshal that the undersigned has made a diligent search and inquiry to ascertain the name and address of a person or party upon whom can be served process in personam which will bind the above-styled defendant.

That based upon such diligent search and inquiry the undersigned has been unable to ascertain the name and address of any person or party within the District upon whom service of process would bind said defendant.

The Clerk of the Court is hereby requested to issue a Writ of Foreign Attachment and deliver the same to the United States Marshal.

The United States Marshal is hereby directed to promptly serve said Writ of Foreign Attachment upon ______ (name of vessel) which vessel is presently located at ______.

____
Attorney Name (Bar Number)
Attorney E-mail Address
Firm Name
Street Address
City, State, Zip Code
Telephone: (xxx)xxx–xxxx
Facsimile: (xxx)xxx–xxxx
Attorneys for Plaintiff [Party Name(s)]

Sworn and subscribed to this ___ day of ______, ____.

Clerk, U.S. District Court
Southern District of Florida
By: ______________
Deputy Clerk

[Effective December 1, 1994. Amended effective April 15, 2001; April 15, 2007; April 15, 2010.]

FORM 15. AD INTERIM STIPULATION OF VALUE AND STIPULATION FOR COSTS

UNITED STATES DISTRICT COURT
SOUTHERN DISTRICT OF FLORIDA

Case No. ___ –Civ or Cr–(USDJ's last name/USMJ's last name)

IN ADMIRALTY

IN THE MATTER OF:

Petitioner. /

AD INTERIM STIPULATION OF VALUE AND STIPULATION FOR COSTS

WHEREAS [name of Owner] (the "Petitioner"), as Owner of the [name of vessel] (the "Vessel"), has instituted a proceeding in this Court for limitation of or exoneration from liability with respect to all losses, damages, injuries or destruction allegedly resulting from the casualty described in the Petition, in which the Petitioner requests, among other things, that a Monition may issue to all persons or corporations asserting claims for loss, injuries or damages arising out of said accident and voyage, admonishing them to appear and make due proof of their respective claims and also to appear and answer the allegations of Petitioner herein, and that an Injunction be issued restraining commencement and prosecution of any and all actions, claims or proceedings against Petitioner, the Vessel, or any other property of the Petitioner as a result of the incident described in the Petition, except pursuant to the Monition granted herein;

WHEREAS Petitioner wishes to provide an Ad Interim Stipulation for the value of its interest in the Vessel as security for all those who may file claims herein, pending the ascertainment by reference of the amount or value of Petitioner's interest in the Vessel.

NOW THEREFORE, the Petitioner, stipulates that it will deposit no more than the sum of [amount of stipulation], in the form of a surety bond with the Court's registry with interest at the rate of 6% per annum from the date hereof and costs, and Petitioner will pay said sum and/or deposit said bond into the Court within fifteen (15) days after the demand thereof by any Claimant.

Further, Petitioner will pay and/or deposit a surety bond in the Court's registry, within fifteen (15) days after the entry of an Order confirming the report of a commissioner to be appointed to appraise the amount of value of the Petitioner's interest in the Vessel, the amount or value of such interest is thus ascertained and ordering the posting of said bond, if demanded by any Claimant, or alternatively will file in this proceeding a Joint Stipulation for Value in the usual form, and that after giving of the Joint Stipulation for Value in the usual form, this Ad Interim Stipulation shall stand as security for all claims in the said limitation of liability proceeding *in lieu* of said bond, until such time as any Claimant demands the posting of a bond or the Court so orders.

THUS DONE AND EXECUTED this _____ day of [month], [year].

Respectfully submitted,

____
Attorney-in-fact
[Owner]
Owner of [vessel]

[Effective April 15, 2011.]

FORM 16. ORDER APPROVING AD INTERIM STIPULATION OF VALUE, DIRECTING ISSUANCE OF MONITION AND INJUNCTION

UNITED STATES COURT FOR THE
SOUTHERN DISTRICT OF FLORIDA

Case No. ___ -Civ or Cr-(USDJ's last name/USMJ's last name)

IN ADMIRALTY

IN THE MATTER OF:

Petitioner. /

ORDER APPROVING AD INTERIM STIPULATION OF VALUE, DIRECTING ISSUANCE OF MONITION AND INJUNCTION

A Complaint having been filed herein on the _____ day of [month], [year], by [Petitioner], as Owner of the [vessel] (the "Vessel"), for exoneration from and/or limitation of liability as provided for in the Act of Congress embodied in 46 U.S.C. §§ 30501 *et seq.* and pursuant to Rule F of the Supplemental Rules for Certain Admiralty and Maritime Claims of the Federal Rules of Civil Procedure, together with the statutes supplemental thereto and amendatory thereof, and also contesting its liability independently of the limitation of liability claims under said Acts, Treaty or Code for any loss, damages, deaths, personal injuries, damage or destruction of property or other occurrences arising from the incident which occurred on or about [date of incident], on the navigable waterways of [county] as further described in the Petition for Limitation, and said Complaint also stating the alleged facts and circumstances on which such exoneration from or limitation of liability is claimed;

And Petitioner having deposited with the Court as security for the benefit of Claims, an Ad Interim Stipulation of Value not less than or equal to the amount or value of its interest in the Vessel, as required by the rules of this Court and by the law;

IT IS ORDERED AND ADJUDGED that the Ad Interim Stipulation for the value of Petitioner's interest in the Vessel, for no more than the amount of [amount], including costs of court and interest at the rate of six percent (6%) per annum from date hereof, and filed herein by Petitioner, be accepted as Ad Interim Stipulation for the purpose of this action and that it be approved as to form and quantum.

IT IS FURTHER ORDERED AND ADJUDGED that Petitioner and any Claimant who may properly become a party hereto may contest the amount of value of Petitioner's interest in the Vessel as fixed in said Ad Interim Stipulation, subject to such increases or decreases in the amount of such Stipulation, together with adequate security, as the Court may from time to time order according to the rules and practices of this Court may adjudge.

IT IS FURTHER ORDERED AND ADJUDGED that if the amount of the Ad Interim Stipulation is not contested by any Claimant herein, said Stipulation shall stand as a Stipulation for Value and an appraisal by a Commissioner will not be required.

NOW, THEREFORE, it is ordered that a Monition issue out of and under the seal of this Court against all persons or corporations claiming damage for any and all loss, destruction, damage, injuries, and/or death allegedly as a result of the occurrences and happenings recited in the Complaint, to file their respective claims with the Clerk of this Court and to serve on or mail to the attorneys for Petitioner copies thereof on or before [date], and that all persons or corporations so presenting claims and desiring to contest the allegations of the Complaint shall file an answer to the Complaint in this Court and shall serve on or mail to the attorneys for the Petitioner copies thereof, or be defaulted.

IT IS FURTHER ORDERED that a public notice of said Monition be given by publication as required by Rule F of the Supplemental Rules for Certain Admiralty and Maritime Claims of the Federal Rules of Civil Procedure and the Local Rules of the United States District Court for the Southern District of Florida, once each week for four successive weeks in the "Daily Business Review – [county] Edition" prior to the date fixed for the filing of claims in accordance with Supplemental Rule F and that not later than the date of the second weekly publication, a copy of said notice to be mailed by Petitioner to every person or corporation known by the Petitioner to have a claim against Petitioner arising out of the accident set forth in the Complaint.

IT IS FURTHER ORDERED that the commencement or further prosecution of any action, suit or proceeding in any court whatsoever, and the institution and prosecution of any suits, actions or legal proceedings, of any nature or description whatsoever, in any court whatsoever, except in these proceedings, in respect to any claim arising out of, or connected with the casualty set forth in the Complaint herein, be and the same are hereby STAYED AND RESTRAINED until the final determination of this proceeding.

IT IS FINALLY ORDERED that the service of this Order as a restraining order in this District may be made in the usual manner as any other district of the United States by delivery by the Marshal of the United States for such District of a certified copy of this Order on the person or persons to be restrained or to their respective attorneys, or alternatively, by mailing a conformed copy of it to the person or persons to be restrained or to their respective attorney.

DONE AND ORDERED in Chambers at ______________, Florida this ____ day of [month], [year].

____
UNITED STATES DISTRICT JUDGE

[Effective April 15, 2011.]

FORM 17. AFFIDAVIT OF VALUE

UNITED STATES DISTRICT COURT
SOUTHERN DISTRICT OF FLORIDA

Case No. ___ –Civ or Cr–(USDJ's last name/USMJ's last name)

IN ADMIRALTY

IN THE MATTER OF:

Petitioner. /

AFFIDAVIT OF VALUE

STATE OF FLORIDA

COUNTY OF ___________

Before me, the undersigned authority, a notary public, personally came and appeared [name of expert] who, being duly sworn, did depose and state as follows:

1. I am [name of expert], and I am over eighteen (18) years of age.

2. I am a marine surveyor employed with [name of employer] located in [name of county] County, Florida.

3. I have been actively working as a marine surveyor in [name of county] County for more than [number of years] years and in such capacity I am familiar with and have determined the value of vessels such as the [name of vessel].

4. I examined the [name of vessel] on [date], immediately after the alleged accident as stated in the Complaint. I have reviewed certain documentation information concerning the vessel and determined that the fair market value of the vessel on [date of inspection], immediately after the accident was no more than [value].

____
[name of expert]

STATE OF FLORIDA

COUNTY OF ___________

BEFORE ME, the undersigned authority, personally appeared ______________ who ( ) is personally known to me, or ( ) who produced a copy of ______________________________ as proof of identification.

SWORN TO AND SUBSCRIBED before me this _______ day of _______________, 20____.

____
Notary Public – State of Florida

My Commission Expires:

[Effective April 15, 2011.]

FORM 18. JOINT STIPULATION OF THE PARTIES AS TO THE VALUE OF THE [VESSEL]

UNITED STATES DISTRICT COURT
SOUTHERN DISTRICT OF FLORIDA

Case No. ___ –Civ or Cr–(USDJ's last name/USMJ's last name)

IN ADMIRALTY

IN THE MATTER OF:

Petitioner. /

JOINT STIPULATION OF THE PARTIES AS TO THE VALUE OF THE [VESSEL]

COME NOW the parties, [name of Petitioner] (the "Petitioner"), as Owner of the [description of vessel], the [vessel name] (the "Vessel"), by and through h[is][er] undersigned counsel, Claimants [names of Claimants], by and through their undersigned counsel, and jointly stipulate and agree as follows:

1. On or about [date of incident], Petitioner, as owner of the Vessel, timely filed a Petition for Exoneration From or Limitation of Liability in the U.S. District Court for the Southern District of Florida.

2. Pursuant to the proceeding for exoneration from or limitation of liability filed by Petitioner, Petitioner sought to be exonerated from or to limit his liability for any and all claims, losses, damages, injuries, costs, fees, or other expenses arising from an incident which occurred on or about [date of accident] on the navigable waters of the United States, pursuant to the provisions of the Shipowners Limitation of Liability Act, Title 46, U.S. Code §30501 *et sequentia.*

3. Pursuant to the provisions of Rule F of the Supplemental Rules for Certain Admiralty and Maritime Claims, Petitioner filed an Ad Interim Stipulation for Value setting forth the value of the Vessel following the incident which forms the subject matter of this litigation, and at the conclusion of the voyage during which said incident occurred, as being [dollar amount].

4. Having duly considered the provisions of the Ad Interim Stipulation for Value and the documentation filed in support thereof, the parties jointly stipulate and agree that the value or the Vessel at the conclusion of the voyage of [date] occurred did not exceed the sum of [dollar amount] and, was, in fact, [amount] U.S. dollars.

5. It is further stipulated and agreed by the parties, by and through their undersigned counsel, that the entry by the parties to this Joint Stipulation is without prejudice to, and with full reservation of, all rights, claims, and defenses of the parties including, without limit, any and all defenses of Petitioner and Claimants.

6. Inasmuch as there have been no other claims filed in this Court pursuant to the Monition and Injunction entered by the Court and that there are no other creditors, claimants or alleged lienors whether in contract or in tort who have filed claims against the Petitioner, it is stipulated and agreed by the parties, by and through their undersigned counsel, that no other claims have been timely filed in this proceeding and that all other non-filing claimants should be defaulted by the Court.

WHEREFORE, the parties, [owner], as owner of the [vessel], by and through h[is][er] undersigned counsel, [Claimants], by and through their undersigned counsel, stipulate and agree to the facts set forth herein and to the matters jointly set forth herein as well as the entry by the Court of appropriate Orders as stipulated thereto by the parties.

Respectfully submitted,

______________________	______________________
Claimant's Attorney	Petitioner's Attorney

[Effective April 15, 2011.]

MAGISTRATE JUDGE RULES

RULE 1. AUTHORITY OF UNITED STATES MAGISTRATE JUDGES

(a) Duties Under 28 U.S.C. § 636(a). Each United States Magistrate Judge of this Court is authorized to perform the duties prescribed by 28 U.S.C. § 636(a), and may—

(1) Exercise all the powers and duties conferred or imposed upon United States Commissioners by law and the Federal Rules of Criminal Procedure;

(2) Administer oaths and affirmations, impose conditions of release under 18 U.S.C. § 3146, and take acknowledgments, affidavits, and depositions; and

(3) Conduct extradition proceedings, in accordance with 18 U.S.C. § 3184.

(b) Disposition of Misdemeanor Cases—18 U.S.C. § 3401; Federal Rule of Criminal Procedure 58. A Magistrate Judge may—

(1) Arraign and try persons accused of, and sentence persons convicted of, misdemeanors committed within this District in accordance with 18 U.S.C. § 3401 and Federal Rule of Criminal Procedure 58;

(2) Direct the Probation Office of the Court to conduct a presentence investigation in any misdemeanor case; and

(3) Conduct a jury trial in any misdemeanor case where the defendant so requests and is entitled to trial by jury under the Constitution and laws of the United States.

(c) Determination of Non-Dispositive Pretrial Matters—28 U.S.C. § 636(b)(1)(A). A Magistrate Judge may hear and determine any procedural or discovery motion or other pretrial matter in a civil or criminal case, other than the motions which are specified in subsection 1(d), infra, of these rules.

(d) Recommendations Regarding Case-Dispositive Motions—28 U.S.C. § 636(b)(1)(B).

(1) A Magistrate Judge may submit to a District Judge of the Court a report containing proposed findings of fact and recommendations for disposition by the District Judge of the following pretrial motions in civil and criminal cases:

(A) Motions for injunctive relief, including temporary restraining orders and preliminary and permanent injunctions;

(B) Motions for judgment on the pleadings;

(C) Motions for summary judgment;

(D) Motions to dismiss or permit the maintenance of a class action;

(E) Motions to dismiss for failure to state a claim upon which relief may be granted;

(F) Motions to involuntarily dismiss an action;

(G) Motions for review of default judgments;

(H) Motions to dismiss or quash an indictment or information made by a defendant; and

(I) Motions to suppress evidence in a criminal case.

(2) A Magistrate Judge may determine any preliminary matters and conduct any necessary evidentiary hearing or other proceeding arising in the exercise of the authority conferred by this subsection.

(e) Prisoner Cases Under 28 U.S.C. §§ 2254 and 2255. A Magistrate Judge may perform any or all of the duties imposed upon a District Judge by the rules governing proceedings in 28 U.S.C. §§ 2254 and 2255. In so doing, a Magistrate Judge may issue any preliminary orders and conduct any necessary evidentiary hearing or other appropriate proceeding and shall submit to a District Judge a report containing proposed findings of fact and recommendations for disposition of the petition by the District Judge. Any order disposing of the petition may only be made by a District Judge.

(f) Prisoner Cases Under 42 U.S.C. § 1983. A Magistrate Judge may issue any preliminary orders and conduct any necessary evidentiary hearing or other appropriate proceeding and shall submit to a District Judge a report containing proposed findings of fact and recommendation for the disposition of petitions filed by prisoners challenging the conditions of their confinement.

(g) Special Master References. A Magistrate Judge may be designated by a District Judge to serve as a special master in appropriate civil cases in accordance with 28 U.S.C. § 636(b)(2) and Federal Rules of Civil Procedure 53. Upon the consent of the parties, a Magistrate Judge may be designated by a District Judge to serve as a special master in any civil case, notwithstanding the limitations of Federal Rule of Civil Procedure 53(b).

(h) Conduct of Trials and Disposition of Civil Cases Upon Consent of the Parties—28 U.S.C. § 636(c). Upon the consent of the parties, a full-time Magistrate Judge may conduct any or all proceedings in any civil case which is filed in this Court, including the conduct of a jury or nonjury trial, and may order the entry of a final judgment, in accordance with 28 U.S.C. § 636(c). In the course of conducting such proceedings upon consent of the parties, a Magistrate Judge may hear and determine any and all pre-trial and post-trial motions which are filed by the parties, including case-dispositive motions.

(i) Other Duties. A Magistrate Judge is also authorized to—

(1) Exercise general supervision of civil and criminal calendars, conduct calendar and status calls, and determine motions to expedite or postpone the trial of cases for the District Judges;

(2) Conduct pretrial conferences, settlement conferences, omnibus hearings, and related pretrial proceedings in civil and criminal cases;

(3) Conduct arraignments in criminal cases not triable by the Magistrate Judge and take not guilty pleas in such cases;

(4) Receive grand jury returns in accordance with Federal Rule of Criminal Procedure 6(f);

(5) Accept waivers of indictment, pursuant to Federal Rule of Criminal Procedure 7(b);

(6) Conduct voir dire and select petit juries for the Court;

(7) Accept petit jury verdicts in civil cases in the absence of a District Judge;

(8) Conduct necessary proceedings leading to the potential revocation of probation;

(9) Issue subpoenas, writs of habeas corpus ad testificandum or habeas corpus ad prosequendum, or other orders necessary to obtain the presence of parties, witnesses or evidence needed for Court proceedings;

(10) Order the exoneration or forfeiture of bonds;

(11) Conduct proceedings for the collection of civil penalties of not more than $200 assessed under the Federal Boat Safety Act of 1971, in accordance with 46 U.S.C. § 1484(d);

(12) Conduct examinations of judgment debtors in accordance with Federal Rule of Civil Procedure 69;

(13) Conduct proceedings for initial commitment of narcotics addicts under Title III of the Narcotic Addict Rehabilitation Act;

(14) Perform the functions specified in 18 U.S.C. §§ 4107, 4108 and 4109, regarding proceedings for verification of consent by offenders to transfer to or from the United States and the appointment of counsel therein;

(15) Preside at naturalization hearings and ceremonies; and

(16) Perform any additional duty as is not inconsistent with the Constitution and laws of the United States.

[Effective December 1, 1994. Amended effective April 15, 1998; April 15, 2007; April 15, 2010; December 1, 2015.]

RULE 2. ASSIGNMENT OF MATTERS TO MAGISTRATE JUDGES

All civil and criminal cases in this District shall be filed with the Clerk of the Court and assigned to a District Judge in accordance with Local Rules 1 through 7. Responsibility for the case remains with the District Judge throughout its duration, except that the District Judge may refer to a Magistrate Judge any matter within the scope of these Magistrate Judge Rules.

No specific order of reference shall be required except as otherwise provided in these Magistrate Judge Rules.

Nothing in these Magistrate Judge Rules shall preclude a District Judge from reserving any proceeding for conduct by a District Judge rather than a Magistrate Judge.

[Effective December 1, 1994. Amended effective April 15, 2007.]

RULE 3. PROCEDURES BEFORE THE MAGISTRATE JUDGE

(a) In General. In performing duties for the Court, a Magistrate Judge shall conform to all applicable provisions of federal statutes and rules, to the general procedural rules of this Court, and to the requirements specified in any order of reference from a District Judge.

(b) Special Provisions for the Disposition of Civil Cases by a Magistrate Judge on Consent of the Parties—Title 28, United States Code, Section 636(c).

(1) *Notice.* The Clerk of the Court shall notify the parties in all civil cases that they may consent to have the Magistrate Judge who is assigned to the case at the time of the consent conduct any or all proceedings in the case and order the entry of a final judgment. Such notices shall be handed or mailed to the plaintiff or his representative at the time an action is filed and to other parties as attachments to copies of the complaint and summons, when served. Additional notices may be furnished to the parties at later stages of the proceedings, and may be included with pretrial notices and instructions.

(2) *Execution of Consent.* The Clerk of the Court shall not accept a consent form unless it has been signed by all the parties in a case. The plaintiff shall be responsible for securing the execution of a consent form by the parties and for filing such form with the Clerk of the Court. No consent form will be made available, nor will its contents be made known, to any District Judge or Magistrate Judge, unless all parties have consented to the reference to a Magistrate Judge. No Magistrate Judge, District Judge, or other Court official may attempt to persuade or induce any party to consent to the reference of any matter to a Magistrate Judge. This rule, however, shall not preclude a District Judge or Magistrate Judge from informing the parties that they may have the option of referring a case to a Magistrate Judge.

(3) *References.* After the consent form has been executed and filed, the Clerk of the Court shall transmit it to the District Judge to whom the case has been assigned for consideration of approval and possible referral of the case to the Magistrate Judge assigned to the case, by specific order of reference. Once the case has been assigned to that Magistrate Judge, the Magistrate Judge shall have the authority to conduct any and all proceedings to which the parties have consented and to direct the Clerk of the Court to enter a final judgment in the same manner as if a District Judge had presided.

[Effective December 1, 1994. Amended effective April 15, 2007; December 1, 2011; December 1, 2015.]

RULE 4. REVIEW AND APPEAL

(a) Appeal of Non-dispositive Matters—Government Appeal of Release Order.

(1) *Appeal of Non-Dispositive Matters—28 U.S.C. § 636(b)(1)(A).* Any party may appeal from a Magistrate Judge's order determining a motion or matter under subsection 1(c) of these rules, supra, within fourteen (14) days after being served with the Magistrate Judge's order, unless a different time is prescribed by the Magistrate Judge or District Judge. Such party shall file with the Clerk of the Court, and serve on all parties, written objections which shall specifically set forth the order, or part thereof, appealed from a concise statement of the alleged error in the Magistrate Judge's ruling, and statutory, rule, or case authority, in support of the moving party's position. Any party may respond to another party's objections within fourteen (14) days after being served with a copy thereof. The objecting party may

file a reply within seven (7) days after service of the response. Absent prior permission from the Court, no party shall file any objections or responses to another party's objections exceeding twenty pages in length. The District Judge shall consider the appeal and shall set aside any portion of the Magistrate Judge's order found to be clearly erroneous or contrary to law. The District Judge may also reconsider sua sponte any matter determined by a Magistrate Judge under this rule.

(2) *Government Appeal of Release Order.* At the conclusion of a hearing pursuant to 18 U.S.C. § 3142 in which a Magistrate Judge has entered an order granting pretrial release, the government may make an ore tenus motion that the Magistrate Judge exercise discretion to stay the release order for a reasonable time, to allow the government to pursue review or appeal of the release order, in accordance with 18 U.S.C. § 3145.

If a stay is ordered pursuant to this rule, the Clerk of the Court is directed to obtain the tape recording or cassette immediately after the hearing and deliver the cassettes or tapes promptly to the appropriate court reporter so that an expedited transcript can be delivered to the District Judge within forty-eight (48) hours of the hearing at which the release order is entered. The United States Attorney's Office is to pay the court reporter's charges.

(b) Review of Case–Dispositive Motions and Prisoner Litigation—28 U.S.C. § 636(b)(1)(B). Any party may object to a Magistrate Judge's proposed findings, recommendations or report under subsections 1(d), (e), and (f) of these rules, supra, within fourteen (14) days after being served with a copy thereof, or within such other time as may be allowed by the Magistrate Judge or District Judge. Such party shall file with the Clerk of the Court, and serve on all parties, written objections which shall specifically identify the portions of the proposed findings, recommendations or report to which objection is made, the specific basis for such objections, and supporting legal authority. Any party may respond to another party's objections within fourteen (14) days after being served with a copy thereof, or within such other time as may be allowed by the Magistrate Judge or District Judge. Absent prior permission from the Court, no party shall file any objections or responses to another party's objections exceeding twenty (20) pages in length. A District Judge shall make a de novo determination of those portions of the report or specified proposed findings or recommendations to which objection is made and may accept, reject, or modify, in whole or in part, the findings or recommendations made by the Magistrate Judge. The District Judge, however, need conduct a new hearing only in his discretion or where required by law, and may consider the record developed before the Magistrate Judge, making his own determination on the basis of that record. The District Judge may also receive further evidence, recall witnesses, or recommit the matter to the Magistrate Judge with instructions.

(c) Special Master Reports—28 U.S.C. § 636(b)(2). Any party may seek review of, or action on, a special master report filed by a Magistrate Judge in accordance with the provisions of Federal Rules of Civil Procedure 53(e).

(d) Appeal From Judgments in Misdemeanor Cases—18 U.S.C. § 3402 [Deleted]. Replaced by Federal Rule of Criminal Procedure 58.

(e) Appeal From Judgments in Civil Cases Disposed of on Consent of the Parties—28 U.S.C. § 636(c).

(1) *Appeal to the Court of Appeals.* Upon the entry of judgment in any civil case disposed of by a Magistrate Judge on consent of the parties under authority of 28 U.S.C. § 636(c) and subsection 1(h) of these rules, supra, an aggrieved party shall appeal directly to the United States Court of Appeals for this Circuit in the same manner as an appeal from any other judgment of this Court.

(2) *Appeal to a District Judge [Deleted].* See Pub.L. No. 104–317 § 207, 110 Stat. 3847 (Oct. 19, 1996) (repealing 28 U.S.C. § 636(c)(4) and (5).

[Effective December 1, 1994. Amended effective April 15, 1996; April 15, 1997; April 15, 1998; April 15, 1999; April 15, 2007; April 15, 2010; December 1, 2011; December 1, 2015.]

MAGISTRATE FORMS

NOTICE OF RIGHT TO CONSENT TO DISPOSITION OF A CIVIL CASE BY A UNITED STATES MAGISTRATE JUDGE

UNITED STATES DISTRICT COURT
SOUTHERN DISTRICT OF FLORIDA

In accordance with the provisions of 28 U.S.C. § 636(c), you are hereby notified that the full-time Magistrate Judges of this District, in addition to their other duties, may, upon the consent of all the parties in a civil case, conduct any or all proceedings in a civil case, including a jury or non-jury trial, and order the entry of a final judgment. Copies of appropriate consent forms for this purpose are available from the Clerk of the Court.

You should be aware that your decision to consent, or not to consent, to the referral of your case to the Magistrate Judge assigned to the case for disposition is entirely voluntary and should be communicated solely to the Clerk of the Court. Only if all the parties to the case consent to the reference to the Magistrate Judge will either the District Judge or Magistrate Judge be informed of your decision.

Your opportunity to have your case disposed of by the Magistrate Judge is subject to the discretion of the Court. Accordingly, the District Judge to whom your case is assigned must approve the reference of the case to a Magistrate Judge for disposition, by Order of Reference.

[Effective December 1, 1994. Amended effective April 15, 2007; December 1, 2011.]

Comment

(2011) Amended to clarify that consent applied only to the Magistrate Judge then assigned to the case.

CONSENT TO PROCEED BEFORE A UNITED STATES MAGISTRATE JUDGE

UNITED STATES DISTRICT COURT
SOUTHERN DISTRICT OF FLORIDA

CASE NO. ________

________________________)
Plaintiff,)
)
vs.)
________________________)
Defendant.)
________________________)

CONSENT TO PROCEED BEFORE A UNITED STATES MAGISTRATE JUDGE

In accordance with the provisions of 28 U.S.C. § 636(c), the parties to the above-captioned civil matter hereby waive their right to proceed before a District Judge of this Court and consent to have the Magistrate Judge currently assigned to the case [INSERT MAGISTRATE JUDGE'S NAME] conduct any and all further proceedings in the case (including the trial) and order the entry of judgment. The parties do not consent to the reassignment to any other or successor Magistrate Judge.

____
Attorney Name (Bar Number)
Attorney E–mail Address
Firm Name
Street Address
City, State, Zip Code
Telephone: (xxx)xxx–xxxx
Facsimile: (xxx)xxx–xxxx
Attorneys for Plaintiff
[Party Name(s)]

____
Attorney Name (Bar Number)
Attorney E–mail Address
Firm Name
Street Address
City, State, Zip Code
Telephone: (xxx)xxx–xxxx
Facsimile: (xxx)xxx–xxxx
Attorneys for Defendant
[Party Name(s)]

NOTE: Return this form to the Clerk of the Court only if it has been executed by all parties to the case.

ORDER OF REFERENCE

IT IS HEREBY ORDERED that the above-captioned matter be referred to Magistrate Judge ________ for the conduct of all further proceedings and the entry of judgment in accordance with Title 28 United States Code Section 636(c) and the foregoing consent of the parties.

____
Date

____
United States Magistrate Judge

[Effective December 1, 1994. Amended effective April 15, 2006; April 15, 2007; December 1, 2011.]

Comments

(2006) The form for Consent to Proceed Before a United States Magistrate Judge is amended to reflect the amendments to Title 28, United States Code, Section 636(c), which eliminated appeals by consent of the parties to District Judges.

(2011) Amended to clarify that consent applied only to the Magistrate Judge then assigned to the case.

SPECIAL RULES GOVERNING THE ADMISSION AND PRACTICE OF ATTORNEYS

RULE 1. QUALIFICATIONS FOR ADMISSION

An attorney is qualified for admission to the bar of this District if the attorney is currently a member in good standing of The Florida Bar.

[Effective December 1, 1994. Amended effective January 1, 1996; April 15, 2002; April 15, 2006; April 15, 2007; December 3, 2012; December 1, 2015.]

RULE 2. PROCEDURE FOR APPLYING FOR ADMISSION AND PROOF OF QUALIFICATIONS

Each applicant for admission shall submit a verified petition setting forth the information specified on the form available on the Court's website (www.flsd.uscourts.gov) together with an application fee in the amount set by the Court. Upon receipt of the application fee, the Clerk of the Court shall require each qualified practitioner to sign the oath of admission and shall place such applicant on the roll of attorneys of the bar of this Court.

[Effective December 1, 1994. Amended effective January 1, 1996; April 15, 2007; December 3, 2012; December 1, 2015.]

RULE 3. RETENTION OF MEMBERSHIP IN THE BAR OF THIS COURT

To remain an attorney in good standing of the bar of this Court, each member must remain an active attorney in good standing of The Florida Bar, specifically including compliance with all requirements of the Rules Regulating The Florida Bar, as promulgated by the Supreme Court of Florida, and submit timely payment of the attorney renewal fee every other year commencing March 15, 2012, or as otherwise ordered by the Court. Attorneys who are not in good standing of the bar of this Court may not practice before the Court.

[Effective December 1, 1994. Amended effective January 1, 1996; April 15, 2007; December 1, 2011; December 1, 2015.]

RULE 4. APPEARANCES

(a) Who May Appear Generally. Except when an appearance pro hac vice is permitted by the Court, only members of the bar of this Court may appear as attorneys in the Courts of this District. Attorneys residing and practicing within this District are expected to be members of the bar of this Court.

(b) Appearance Pro Hac Vice.

(1) Any attorney who is a member in good standing of the bar of any United States Court, or of the highest Court of any State or Territory or Insular Possession of the United States, but is not admitted to practice in the Southern District of Florida may, upon written application filed by counsel admitted to practice in this District, be permitted to appear and participate in a particular case. A certification that the applicant has studied the Local Rules shall accompany the application together with such appearance fee as may be required by administrative order. If permission to appear pro hac vice is granted, such appearance shall not constitute formal admission or authorize the attorney to file documents via CM/ECF.

(2) Lawyers who are not members of the bar of this Court shall not be permitted to engage in general practice in this District. For purposes of this rule, more than three appearances within a 365–day period in separate representations before the Courts of this District shall be presumed to be a "general practice." Upon written motion and for good cause shown the Court may waive or modify this prohibition.

(3) The application shall designate a member of the bar of this Court and who is authorized to file through the Court's electronic filing system, with whom the Court and opposing counsel may readily communicate regarding the conduct of the case, upon whom filings shall be served, and who shall be required to electronically file and serve all documents and things that may be filed and served electronically, and who shall be responsible for filing and serving documents in compliance with the CM/ECF Administrative Procedures. *See* Section 2B of the CM/ECF Administrative Procedures. The application must be accompanied by a written statement consenting to the designation, and the address and telephone number of the named designee. Upon written motion and for good cause shown the Court may waive or modify the requirements of such designation.

(c) Appearance Ad Hoc. A member of the bar of this Court acting on behalf of its Volunteer Lawyers' Project may, upon written motion and by leave of court, be permitted to appear for an individual proceeding pro se in a civil matter for the sole purpose of assisting in the discovery process. If the appearance is permitted, when its purpose has been completed the attorney shall give notice to the Court, the pro se civil litigant, and opposing counsel that the ad hoc appearance is terminated.

(d) Government Attorneys. Any full-time United States Attorney, Assistant United States Attorney, Federal Public Defender and Assistant Federal Public Defender and attorney employed full time by and representing the United States government, or any agency thereof, and any Attorney General and Assistant Attorney General of the State of Florida may appear and participate in particular actions or proceedings on behalf of the attorney's employer in the attorney's official capacity without petition for admission. Any attorney so appearing is subject to all rules of this Court.

[Effective December 1, 1994. Amended effective January 1, 1996; April 15, 2007; April 15, 2010; December 1, 2014; December 1, 2015.]

RULE 5. PEER REVIEW

(a) Purpose. It is recognized that the Court and the bar have a joint obligation to improve the level of professional performance in the courtroom. To this end, the purposes to be accomplished through the Ad Hoc Committee on Attorney Admissions, Peer Review and Attorney Grievance (the "Committee") are to determine whether individual attorneys are failing to perform to an adequate level of competence necessary to protect the interests of their clients, to establish and administer a remedial program designed to raise the competence of an attorney who is not performing adequately, to refer such attorneys to appropriate institutions and professional personnel for assistance in raising his or her level of competency, to determine through evaluation, testing or other appropriate means whether an attorney who has been referred for assistance has attained an adequate level of competency, and to report to the Court any attorney who refuses to cooperate by participating in a remedial program to raise his or her level of competence, or fails to achieve an adequate level of competence within a reasonable time.

(b) Duties and Responsibilities of the Committee.

(1) *Referral.* Any District Judge, Magistrate Judge, or Bankruptcy Judge shall refer in writing to the Committee the name of any attorney he or she has observed practicing law in a manner which raises a significant question as to the adequacy of such attorney's ability to represent clients in a competent manner. The referral shall be accompanied by a statement of the reasons why such question is raised.

(2) *Initial Screening.* Promptly after receipt of such a reference the Chairman of the Committee shall advise the attorney that it has been made. Thereafter an Initial Screening Committee shall be selected consisting of three members of the Committee. The Initial Screening Committee may request that the attorney meet with it informally to explain the circumstances which gave rise to the reference and may conduct such preliminary inquiries as it deems advisable. If after such preliminary inquiry the Initial Screening Committee determines that further attention is not needed it shall mark the matter "closed" with notation explaining its determination. Upon closing a matter the Chairman shall notify the referring judge and the attorney.

(3) *Remedial Action.* If the Initial Screening Committee deems that the matter warrants further action, it shall so advise the Chairman who shall then cause a Review Committee to be selected consisting of three members (other than those who served on the Initial Screening Committee). The Review Committee may pursue such inquiries as it deems appropriate and may recommend to the attorney that the attorney take steps to improve the quality of the attorney's professional performance and if so the nature of the recommended action designed to effect such improvement. The attorney shall be advised of any such recommendation in writing and be given the opportunity to respond thereto, to seek revision or revocation of the recommendation or to suggest alternatives thereto. The Review Committee after receiving such response may modify, amend, revoke or adhere to its original recommendation and shall notify the attorney of its final recommendation. Any attorney who takes exception to the proposed Review Committee's final recommendation shall have the right to have it considered by the full Committee. Any recommendation finally promulgated shall be entered in the records of the Committee. The Committee may develop an appropriate remedial program, including, but not limited to, mandatory participation in continuing legal education programs and participation in group and individual study programs. The Committee may monitor the attorney's progress in following the remedial program developed for him or her. If the attorney's lack of competency relates to drug or alcohol abuse, the Committee may require the attorney to seek treatment for that condition and require the attorney to submit periodic reports from the individuals responsible for such treatment.

(c) Referral to the Court. If the Committee finds that there is a substantial likelihood that the attorney's continued practice of law may result in serious harm to the attorney's clients pending completion of a remedial program, it may recommend that the Court consider limiting or otherwise imposing appropriate restrictions on the attorney's continued practice in the District Court.

(d) Obligation to Cooperate With Committee. It shall be the obligation of all members of the bar of this District to cooperate with the Committee so that it may effectively assist members of the bar to improve the quality of their professional performance. Any member of the bar of this Court, who is the subject of a reference under Administrative and Practice Rule 5 or who is asked by the Committee to furnish it with relevant information concerning such a reference shall regard it to be an obligation as an officer of this Court to cooperate fully with the Committee which constitutes an official arm of the Court.

(e) Failure to Respond to Committee. If an attorney shall refuse to meet with the Committee, furnish it with an explanation of the circumstances which gave rise to the referral, or otherwise cooperate with the Committee, the Court shall be so advised and the attorney's failure to cooperate shall be recorded in the records of the Committee. The Committee shall refer to the Court for appropriate action any attorney who refuses to cooperate in participating in a remedial program, or who fails to achieve an adequate level of competence within a reasonable time.

(f) Confidentiality. All matters referred to the Committee, all information in the possession of the Committee and all recommendations or other actions taken by the Committee are matters relating to the administration of the Court and shall be confidential, and shall be disclosed only by order of the Court. Correspondence, records and all written material coming to the Committee shall be retained in an office designated by the Court and are documents of the Court and shall be kept confidential unless the Court directs otherwise. No statement made by the attorney to the Committee shall be admissible in any action for malpractice against the attorney, nor shall any part of the Committee's investigative files be admissible in such proceedings. No statement made by the attorney to the Committee shall be admissible in any action under 28 U.S.C. § 2255 collateral attack for incompetency of counsel in a criminal case, nor shall any part of the Committee's investigative files be admissible in proceedings under 28 U.S.C. § 2255. Likewise, any information given by a client of the attorney to the Committee shall be privileged to the same extent as if the statements were made by the client to the attorney.

(g) Separation From Disciplinary Proceedings. Nothing contained herein and no action hereunder shall be construed to interfere with or substitute for any procedure relating to the discipline of any attorney. Any disciplinary actions relating to the inadequacy of an attorney's performance shall occur apart from the proceedings of the Committee in accordance with law and as directed by the Court.

(h) Committee Immunity. Any Committee determination that a referred attorney is adequately competent does not render the Committee potentially liable as a guarantor of the validity of that determination. The Committee is not liable for the misconduct or nonconduct of any referred attorney. Committee members are immune from prosecution for actions taken within the scope of the duties and responsibilities of the Committee as prescribed by the Court. Unauthorized disclosure of confidential information is outside the scope of the Committee's responsibilities.

(i) Report to the Court. Upon completion of the Committee's activities in respect to each attorney referred by the Court, the Committee shall make a report to the Court. The Committee shall make such interim reports or periodic reports relative to its activities as may be requested by the Court.

[Effective December 1, 1994. Amended effective April 15, 2000; April 15, 2002; April 15, 2007; April 15, 2010; December 1, 2015.]

RULE 6. STUDENT PRACTICE

(a) Purpose. The following Rule for Student Practice is designed to encourage law schools to provide clinical instructions in litigation of varying kinds, and thereby enhance the competence of lawyers in practice before the United States courts.

(b) Student Requirements. An eligible student must:

(1) be duly enrolled in a law school;

(2) have completed at least four semesters of legal studies or the equivalent;

(3) have knowledge of the Federal Rules of Civil and Criminal Procedure and of Evidence, and the Code of Professional Responsibility;

(4) be enrolled for credit in a law school clinical program which has been certified by the Court;

(5) be certified by the dean of the law school, or the dean's designee, as being of good character and sufficient legal ability, and as being adequately trained, in accordance with paragraphs (1)–(4) above, to fulfill his or her other responsibilities as a legal intern to both his or her client and the Court;

(6) be certified by the Court to practice pursuant to this Rule;

(7) neither ask for nor receive any compensation or remuneration of any kind for his or her services from the person on whose behalf he or she renders services, but this shall not prevent a lawyer, legal aid bureau, law school, public defender agency, or the state from paying compensation to the eligible law student (nor shall it prevent any agency from making such charges for its services as it may otherwise properly require).

(c) Program Requirements. The program:

(1) must be a law school clinical practice program for credit, in which a law student obtains academic and practice advocacy training, under supervision of qualified attorneys including federal or state government attorneys or private practitioners;

(2) must be certified by the Court;

(3) must be conducted in such a manner as not to conflict with normal Court schedules;

(4) must be under the direction of a member or members of the regular or adjunct faculty of the law school;

(5) must arrange for the designation and maintenance of an office in this District to which may be sent all notices which the Court may from time to time have occasion or need to send in connection with this Rule or any legal representation provided pursuant to this Rule.

(d) Supervisor Requirements. A supervising attorney must:

(1) be a lawyer whose service as a supervising attorney for this program is approved by the dean of the law school in which the law student is enrolled and who is a member of The Florida Bar in good standing;

(2) be a member of the bar of this Court;

(3) be certified by the Court as a student supervisor;

(4) be present with the student when required by the Court;

(5) co-sign all pleadings or other documents filed with this Court;

(6) assume full personal professional responsibility for a student's guidance in any work undertaken and for the quality of a student's work, and be available for consultation with represented clients;

(7) assist the student in his preparation to the extent the supervising attorney considers it necessary.

(e) Certification of Student, Program and Supervising Attorneys.

(1) *Students.*

(A) Certification by the law school dean or his designee, if said certification is approved by the Court, shall be filed with the Clerk of the Court, and unless it is sooner withdrawn, shall remain in effect until the expiration of eighteen months;

(B) Certification to appear in a particular case may be withdrawn by the Court at any time, in the discretion of the Court, and without any showing of cause. Notice of termination may be filed with the Clerk of the Court.

(2) *Program.*

(A) Certification of a program by the Court shall be filed with the Clerk of the Court and shall remain in effect indefinitely unless withdrawn by the Court;

(B) Certification of a program may be withdrawn by the Court at the end of any academic year without cause, or at any time, provided notice stating the cause for such withdrawal is furnished to the law school dean.

(3) *Supervising Attorney.*

(A) Certification of a supervising attorney by the law school dean, if said certification is approved by the Court, shall be filed with the Clerk of the Court, and shall remain in effect indefinitely unless withdrawn by the dean or by the Court;

(B) Certification of a supervising attorney may be withdrawn by the Court at the end of any academic year without cause, or at any time upon notice and a showing of cause;

(C) Certification of a supervising attorney may be withdrawn by the dean at any time by mailing of notice to that effect to the Clerk of the Court;

(D) Any Judge of this Court retains the authority to withdraw or limit a supervising attorney's participation in any individual case before the Judge.

(f) Activities.

(1) An eligible law student may appear in this Court on behalf of any indigent person if the person on whose behalf he or she is appearing has indicated in writing his or her consent to that appearance and the supervising attorney has also indicated in writing approval of that appearance.

(2) An eligible law student may also appear in any criminal matter on behalf of the government with the written approval of the prosecuting attorney or his or her authorized representative and of the supervising attorney.

(3) An eligible law student may also appear in this Court in any civil matter on behalf of the government, with the written approval of the attorney representing that entity.

(4) In each case, the written consent and approval referred to above shall be filed in the record of the case and shall be brought to the attention of the Judge.

(5) The Board of Governors of The Florida Bar shall fix the standards by which indigency is determined under this Rule upon the recommendation of the largest voluntary bar association located in the state judicial circuit in which this program is implemented.

(6) In addition, an eligible law student may engage in other activities, under the general supervision of a member of the bar of this Court, but outside the personal presence of that lawyer, including:

(A) preparation of pleadings and other documents to be filed in any matter in which the student is eligible to appear, but such pleadings or documents must be signed by the supervising attorney;

(B) preparation of briefs, abstracts and other documents to be filed in appellate courts, but such documents must be signed by the supervising attorney;

(C) except when the assignment of counsel in the matter is required by any constitutional provision, statute or rule of this Court, assistance to indigent inmates of correctional institutions or other persons who request such assistance in preparing applications for and supporting documents for post-conviction relief. If there is an attorney of record in the matter, all such assistance must be supervised by the attorney of record, and all documents submitted to the Court on behalf of such a client must be signed by the attorney of record;

(D) each document or pleading must contain the name of the eligible law student who has participated in drafting it. If he or she participated in drafting only a portion of it, that fact may be mentioned.

(g) Court Administration. The Chief Judge, or one or more members of the Court appointed by the Chief Judge, shall act on behalf of the Court in connection with any function of this Court under this Rule. The Ad Hoc Committee on Attorney Admissions, Peer Review and Attorney Grievance shall assist the Court to administer this Rule including the review of applications and continuing eligibility for certification of programs, supervising attorneys, and students.

[Effective December 1, 1994. Amended effective April 15, 1996; April 15, 2002; April 15, 2007; April 15, 2010; December 1, 2015.]

RULE 7. AD HOC COMMITTEE ON ATTORNEY ADMISSIONS, PEER REVIEW AND ATTORNEY GRIEVANCE

(a) Establishment and Function. There shall be an Ad Hoc Committee on Attorney Admissions, Peer Review and Attorney Grievance (the "Committee"). Subject to the direction of the Court, the Committee shall have the authority and perform the functions assigned by these Rules and shall otherwise assist the Court in the implementation and evaluation of these Rules.

(b) Memberships. The Committee shall consist of a group of law school professors and attorneys practicing within this District. The Chief Judge, or one or more members of the Court appointed by the Chief Judge, shall appoint the members of the Committee. The Chief Judge shall select the Committee Chair. Selections shall be made by Administrative Order entered by the Chief Judge. All persons appointed to the Committee shall serve at the pleasure of the Court.

[Effective December 1, 1994. Amended effective April 15, 1996; April 15, 2002; April 15, 2007; April 15, 2010; December 1, 2015.]

RULE 8. EFFECTIVE DATES

These Rules shall become effective and shall apply to all members of and applicants for admission to the bar as of January 1, 1996.

[Effective December 1, 1994. Amended effective April 15, 1996; December 1, 2015.]

RULES GOVERNING ATTORNEY DISCIPLINE

PREFATORY STATEMENT

Nothing contained in these Rules shall be construed to deny the Court its inherent power to maintain control over the proceedings conducted before it nor to deny the Court those powers derived from statute, rule or procedure, or other rules of court. When alleged attorney misconduct is brought to the attention of the Court, whether by a Judge of the Court, any lawyer admitted to practice before the Court, any officer or employee of the Court, or otherwise, the Court may, in its discretion, dispose of the matter through the use of its inherent, statutory, or other powers; refer the matter to an appropriate state bar agency for investigation and disposition; refer the matter to the Ad Hoc Committee on Attorney Admissions, Peer Review and Attorney Grievance as hereinafter defined; or take any other action the Court deems appropriate. These procedures are not mutually exclusive.

[Effective December 1, 1994. Amended effective April 15, 2002; April 15, 2007; December 1, 2015.]

Source

(1993) Ad Hoc Committee on Attorney Discipline.

RULE 1. STANDARDS FOR PROFESSIONAL CONDUCT

(a) Acts and omissions by an attorney admitted to practice before this Court, individually or in concert with any other person or persons, which violate the Rules of Professional Conduct, Chapter 4 of the Rules Regulating The Florida Bar shall constitute misconduct and shall be grounds for discipline, whether or not the act or omission occurred in the course of an attorney/client relationship. Attorneys practicing before this Court shall be governed by this Court's Local Rules, by the Rules of Professional Conduct, as amended from time to time, and, to the extent not inconsistent with the preceding, the American Bar Association Model Rules of Professional Conduct, except as otherwise provided by specific Rule of this Court. [Attorneys practicing before the Court of Appeals shall be governed by that Court's Local Rules and the American Bar Association Model Rules of Professional Conduct, except as otherwise provided by Rule of the Court.]

(b) Discipline for misconduct defined in these Rules may consist of (1) disbarment, (2) suspension, (3) reprimand, (4) monetary sanctions, (5) removal from this Court's roster of attorneys eligible for practice before this Court, or (6) any other sanction the Court may deem appropriate.

[Effective December 1, 1994. Amended effective April 15, 1996; April 15, 2007; April 15, 2010; December 1, 2015.]

RULE 2. AD HOC COMMITTEE ON ATTORNEY ADMISSIONS, PEER REVIEW AND ATTORNEY GRIEVANCE

(a) Establishment and Membership. There shall be an Ad Hoc Committee on Attorney Admissions, Peer Review and Attorney Grievance (the "Committee"), as established under Rule 7 of the Special Rules Governing the Admission and Practice of Attorneys.

(b) Purpose and Function. The purpose and function of the Committee is to conduct, upon referral by the Court, a District Judge, Magistrate Judge or Bankruptcy Judge of the Court, investigations of alleged misconduct of any member of the Bar of this Court, or any attorney appearing and participating in any proceeding before the Court; to conduct, upon referral by the Court, a District Judge, Magistrate Judge or Bankruptcy Judge of the Court, inquiries and investigations into allegations of inadequate performance by an attorney practicing before the Court, as hereinafter provided; to conduct and preside over disciplinary hearings when appropriate and as hereinafter provided; and to submit written findings and recommendations to the Court or referring District Judge, Magistrate Judge or Bankruptcy Judge for appropriate action by the Court, except as otherwise described herein. The members of the Committee, while serving in their official capacities, shall be considered to be representatives of and acting under the powers and immunities of the Court, and shall enjoy all such immunities while acting in good faith and in their official capacities.

(c) Jurisdiction and Powers.

(1) The Court may, in its discretion, refer to the Committee any accusation or evidence of misconduct by way of violation of the disciplinary rules on the part of any member of the bar with respect to any professional matter before this Court for such investigation, hearing, and report as the Court deems advisable. [The Court of Appeals may, in addition to or instead of referring a disciplinary matter to its own Grievance Committee, refer a complaint to the Chief Judge of a District Court for referral to the District Court's Committee.] The Committee may, in its discretion, refer such matters to an appropriate state bar for preliminary investigation, or may request the Court to appoint special counsel to assist in or exclusively conduct such proceedings, as hereinafter provided in these Rules. (See Rule 11, infra.) The Court may also, in its discretion, refer to the Committee any matter concerning an attorney's failure to maintain an adequate level of competency in his or her practice before this Court, as hereinafter provided. (See Rule 8, infra.) The Committee may under no circumstances initiate and investigate such matters without prior referral by the Court.

(2) The Committee shall be vested with such powers as are necessary to conduct the proper and expeditious disposition of any matter referred by the Court, including the power to compel the attendance of witnesses, to take or cause to be taken the deposition of any witnesses, and to order the production of books, records, or other documentary evidence, and those powers described elsewhere in these Rules. The Chairman, or in his or her absence each member of the Committee, has the power to administer oaths and affirmations to witnesses.

[Effective December 1, 1994. Amended effective April 15, 2000; April 15, 2002; April 15, 2007; April 15, 2010; December 1, 2015.]

RULE 3. DISCIPLINARY PROCEEDINGS

(a) When misconduct or allegations of misconduct which, if substantiated, would warrant discipline on the part of an attorney admitted to practice before this Court shall come to the attention of a District Judge, Magistrate Judge or Bankruptcy Judge of this Court, whether by complaint or otherwise, the District Judge, Magistrate Judge or Bankruptcy Judge may, in his or her discretion, refer the matter to the Committee for investigation and, if warranted, the prosecution of formal disciplinary proceedings or the formulation of such other recommendation as may be appropriate. [The Court of Appeals may, in addition to or instead of referring a disciplinary matter to its own Grievance Committee, refer a complaint to the Chief Judge of a District Court for consideration.]

(b) Should the Committee conclude, after investigation and review, that a formal disciplinary proceeding should not be initiated against an attorney because sufficient evidence is not present or for any other valid reason, the Committee shall file with the Court a recommendation for disposition of the matter, whether by dismissal, admonition, deferral, or any other action. In cases of dismissal, the attorney who is the subject of the investigation need not be notified that a complaint has been submitted or of its ultimate disposition. All investigative reports, records, and recommendations generated by or on behalf of the Committee under such circumstances shall remain strictly confidential.

(c) If the Committee concludes from preliminary investigation, or otherwise, that probable cause exists, the Committee shall file with the Court a written report of its investigation, stating with specificity the facts supporting its conclusion, and shall apply to the Court for the issuance of an order requiring the attorney to show cause within thirty (30) days after service of that order why the attorney should not be disciplined. The order to show cause shall set forth the particular act or acts of conduct for which he or she is sought to be disciplined. A copy of the Committee's written report should be provided to the attorney along with the show cause order. The accused attorney may file with the Committee within fourteen (14) days' of service of the order a written response to the order to show cause. After receipt of the attorney's response, if any, the Committee may request that the Court rescind its previously issued order to show cause. If the show cause order is not rescinded, and upon at least fourteen (14) days' notice, the cause shall be set for hearing before the Committee. A record of all proceedings before the Committee shall be made, and shall be made available to the attorney. That record, and all other materials generated by or on behalf of the Committee or in relation to any disciplinary proceedings before the Committee, shall in all other respects remain strictly confidential unless and until otherwise ordered by the Court. In the event the attorney does not appear, the Committee may recommend summary action and shall report its recommendation forthwith to the Court. In the event that the attorney does appear, he or she shall be entitled to be represented by counsel, to present witnesses and other evidence on his or her behalf, and to confront and cross examine witnesses against him. Except as otherwise ordered by the Court or provided in these Rules, the disciplinary proceedings before the Committee shall be guided by the spirit of the Federal Rules of Evidence. Unless he or she asserts a privilege or right properly available to him or her under applicable federal or state law, the accused attorney may be called as a witness by the Committee to make specific and complete disclosure of all matters material to the charge of misconduct.

(d) Upon completion of a disciplinary proceeding, the Committee shall make a full written report to the Court. The Committee shall include its findings of fact as to the charges of misconduct, recommendations as to whether or not the accused attorney should be found guilty of misconduct justifying disciplinary actions by the Court, and recommendations as to the disciplinary measures to be applied by the Court. The report shall be accompanied by a transcript of the proceedings before the Committee, all pleadings, and all evidentiary exhibits. A copy of the report and recommendation shall also be furnished the attorney. The Committee's written report, transcripts of the proceedings, and all related materials shall remain confidential unless and until otherwise ordered by the Court.

(e) Upon receipt of the Committee's finding that misconduct occurred, the Court shall issue an order requiring the attorney to show cause why the Committee's recommendation should not be adopted by the Court. The Court may, after considering the attorney's response, by majority vote of the active District Judges thereof, adopt, modify, or reject the Committee's findings that misconduct occurred, and may either impose those sanctions recommended by the Committee or fashion whatever penalties provided by the rules which it deems appropriate.

[Effective December 1, 1994. Amended effective April 15, 2000; April 15, 2002; April 15, 2007; April 15, 2010; December 1, 2015.]

RULE 4. ATTORNEYS CONVICTED OF CRIMES

(a) Upon the filing with this Court of a certified copy of a judgment of conviction demonstrating that any attorney admitted to practice before the Court has been convicted in any court of the United States, or the District of Columbia, or of any state, territory, commonwealth, or possession of the United States of any serious crime as herein defined, the Court shall enter an order immediately suspending that attorney, whether the conviction resulted from a plea of guilty, nolo contendere, verdict after trial, or otherwise, and regardless of the pendency of any appeal. The suspension so ordered shall remain in effect until final disposition of the disciplinary proceedings to be commenced upon such conviction. A copy of such order shall be immediately served upon the attorney. Upon good cause shown, the Court may set aside such order when it appears in the interest of justice to do so.

(b) The term "serious" crime shall include any felony and any lesser crime a necessary element of which, as determined by the statutory or common law definition of such crime in the jurisdiction in which it was entered, involves false swearing, misrepresentation, fraud, deceit, bribery, extortion, misappropriation, theft, or the use of dishonesty, or an attempt, conspiracy, or solicitation of another to commit a "serious crime."

(c) A certified copy of a judgment of conviction of an attorney for any crime shall be conclusive evidence of the commission of that crime in any disciplinary proceeding instituted against that attorney based on the conviction.

(d) Upon the filing of a certified copy of a judgment of conviction of an attorney for a serious crime, the Court may, in addition to suspending that attorney in accordance with the provisions of this Rule, also refer the matter to the Committee for institution of disciplinary proceedings in which the sole issue to be determined shall be the extent of the final discipline to be imposed as a result of the conduct resulting in the conviction, provided that a disciplinary proceeding so instituted will not be brought to final hearing until all appeals from the conviction are concluded.

(e) An attorney suspended under the provisions of this Rule will be reinstated immediately upon the filing of a certificate demonstrating that the underlying conviction of a serious crime has been reversed, but the reinstatement will not terminate any disciplinary proceedings then pending against the attorney, the disposition of which shall be determined by the Committee on the basis of all available evidence pertaining to both guilt and the extent of the discipline to be imposed.

[Effective December 1, 1994. Amended effective April 15, 2002; April 15, 2007; April 15, 2010; December 1, 2015.]

RULE 5. DISCIPLINE IMPOSED BY OTHER COURTS

(a) An attorney admitted to practice before this Court shall, upon being subjected to suspension or disbarment by a court of any state, territory, commonwealth, or possession of the United States, or upon being subject to any form of public discipline, including but not limited to suspension or disbarment, by any other court of the United States or the District of Columbia, promptly inform the Clerk of the Court of such action.

(b) Upon the filing of a certified copy of a judgment or order demonstrating that an attorney admitted to practice before this Court has been disciplined by another court as described above, this Court may refer the matter to the Committee for a recommendation for appropriate action, or may issue a notice directed to the attorney containing:

(1) A copy of the judgment or order from the other court, and

(2) An order to show cause directing that the attorney inform this Court, within thirty (30) days after service of that order upon the attorney, of any claim by the attorney predicated upon the grounds set forth in subsection E, supra, that the imposition of identical discipline by the Court would be unwarranted and the reasons therefor.

(c) In the event that the discipline imposed in the other jurisdiction has been stayed there, any reciprocal disciplinary proceedings instituted or discipline imposed in this Court shall be deferred until such stay expires.

(d) After consideration of the response called for by the order issued pursuant to subsection B, supra, or after expiration of the time specified in that order, the Court may impose the identical discipline or may impose any other sanction the Court may deem appropriate.

(e) A final adjudication in another court that an attorney has been guilty of misconduct shall establish conclusively the misconduct for purpose of a disciplinary proceeding in this Court, unless the attorney demonstrates and the Court is satisfied that upon the face of the record upon which the discipline in another jurisdiction is predicated it clearly appears that:

(1) the procedure in that other jurisdiction was so lacking in notice or opportunity to be heard as to constitute a deprivation of due process; or

(2) there was such an infirmity of proof establishing misconduct as to give rise to the clear conviction that this Court could not, consistent with its duty, accept as final the conclusion on that subject; or

(3) the imposition of the same discipline by this Court would result in grave injustice; or

(4) the misconduct established is deemed by this Court to warrant substantially different discipline.

(f) This Court may at any stage ask the Committee to conduct disciplinary proceedings or to make recommendations to the Court for appropriate action in light of the imposition of professional discipline by another court.

[Effective December 1, 1994. Amended effective April 15, 2002; April 15, 2007; April 15, 2010; December 1, 2015.]

RULE 6. DISCIPLINE ON CONSENT OR RESIGNATION IN OTHER COURTS

(a) Any attorney admitted to practice before this Court shall, upon being suspended or disbarred on consent or resigning from any other bar while an investigation into allegations of misconduct is pending, promptly inform the Clerk of the Court of such suspension or disbarment on consent or resignation.

(b) An attorney admitted to practice before this Court who shall be suspended or disbarred on consent or resign from the bar of any other court of the United States or the District of Columbia, or from the bar of any state, territory, commonwealth, or possession of the United States while an investigation into allegations of misconduct is pending shall, upon the filing with this Court of a certified copy of the judgment or order accepting such suspension or disbarment on consent or resignation, cease to be permitted to practice before this Court and be stricken from the roll of attorneys admitted to practice before this Court.

[Effective December 1, 1994. Amended effective April 15, 2007; April 15, 2010; April 15, 2011; December 1, 2015.]

RULE 7. DISCIPLINE ON CONSENT WHILE UNDER DISCIPLINARY INVESTIGATION OR PROSECUTION

(a) Any attorney admitted to practice before this Court who is the subject of an investigation into, or a pending proceeding involving, allegations of misconduct may consent to suspension or disbarment, but only by delivering to this Court an affidavit stating that the attorney desires to consent to suspension or disbarment and that:

(1) the attorney's consent is freely and voluntarily rendered; the attorney is not being subjected to coercion or duress; the attorney is fully aware of the implications of so consenting;

(2) the attorney is aware that there is a presently pending investigation or proceeding involving allegations that there exist grounds for the attorney's discipline the nature of which the attorney shall specifically set forth;

(3) the attorney acknowledges that the material facts so alleged are true; and

(4) the attorney so consents because the attorney knows that if charges were predicated upon the matters under investigation, or if the proceeding were prosecuted, the attorney could not successfully defend himself.

(b) Upon receipt of the required affidavit, this Court shall enter an order suspending or disbarring the attorney.

(c) The order suspending or disbarring the attorney on consent shall be a matter of public record. However, the affidavit required pursuant to the provisions of this Rule shall not be publicly disclosed or made available for use in any other proceeding except upon order of this Court.

[Effective December 1, 1994. Amended effective April 15, 2007; April 15, 2010; April 15, 2011; December 1, 2015.]

RULE 8. INCOMPETENCE AND INCAPACITY

(a) When it appears that an attorney for whatever reason is failing to perform to an adequate level of competence necessary to protect his or her client's interests, the Court may take any remedial action which it deems appropriate, including but not limited to referral of the affected attorney to appropriate institutions and professional personnel for assistance in raising the affected attorney's level of competency. The Court may also, in its discretion, refer the matter to the Committee for further investigation and recommendation.

(b) A referral to the Committee of any matter concerning an attorney's failure to maintain an adequate level of competency in his or her practice before this Court is not a disciplinary matter and does not implicate the formal procedures previously described in these Rules. Upon a referral of this sort, the Committee may request that the attorney meet with it informally and explain the circumstances which gave rise to the referral and may conduct such preliminary inquiries as it deems advisable. If after meeting with the attorney and conducting its preliminary inquiries the Committee determines that further attention is not needed, the Committee shall so notify the referring Judge and consider all inquiries terminated.

(c) If after meeting with the attorney and conducting its preliminary inquiries the Committee deems the matter warrants further action, it may recommend to the attorney that the attorney take steps to improve the quality of his or her professional performance and shall specify the nature of the recommended action designed to effect such improvement. The attorney shall be advised of any such recommendation in writing and be given the opportunity to respond thereto, to seek review or revocation of the recommendation, or to suggest alternatives thereto. The Committee may, after receiving such response, modify, amend, revoke, or adhere to its original recommendation. If the attorney agrees to comply with the Committee's final recommendation, the Committee shall report to the referring Judge that the matter has been resolved by the consent of the affected attorney. The Committee may monitor the affected attorney's compliance with its recommendation and may request the assistance of the Court in ensuring that the attorney is complying with the final recommendation.

(d) If the Committee finds that there is a substantial likelihood that the affected attorney's continued practice of law may result in serious harm to the attorney's clients pending completion of the remedial program, it may recommend that the Court consider limiting or otherwise imposing appropriate restrictions on the attorney's continuing practice before the Court. The Court may take any action which it deems appropriate to effectuate the Committee's recommendation.

(e) Any attorney who takes exception with the Committee's final recommendation shall have the right to have the Court, consisting of the active Judges thereof, consider the recommendation and the response of the affected attorney. The Court may, after considering the attorney's response, by majority vote of the active Judges thereof, adopt, modify, or reject the Committee's recommendations as to the necessary remedial actions and may take whatever actions it deems appropriate to ensure the attorney's compliance.

(f) All information, reports, records, and recommendations gathered, possessed, or generated by or on behalf of the Committee in relation to the referral of a matter concerning an attorney's failure to maintain an adequate level of competency in his or her practice before this Court shall be confidential unless and until otherwise ordered by the Court.

(g) Nothing contained herein and no action taken hereunder shall be construed to interfere with or substitute for any procedure relating to the discipline of any attorney as elsewhere provided in these Rules. Any disciplinary actions relating to the inadequacy of an attorney's performance shall occur apart from the proceedings of the Committee in accordance with law and as directed by the Court.

[Effective December 1, 1994. Amended effective April 15, 2002; April 15, 2007; April 15, 2010; December 1, 2015.]

RULE 9. REINSTATEMENT

(a) After Disbarment or Suspension. An attorney suspended for three months or less shall be automatically reinstated at the end of the period of suspension upon the filing with this Court of an affidavit of compliance with the provisions of the order. An attorney suspended for more than three months or disbarred may not resume the practice of law before this Court until reinstated by order of the Court. An attorney seeking reinstatement after reciprocal disbarment or suspension must meet the same criteria as an attorney seeking original admission under Rule 1 of the Special Rules Governing the Admission and Practice of Attorneys, in that he or she must first seek and obtain reinstatement by The Florida Bar.

(b) Time of Application Following Disbarment. An attorney who has been disbarred after hearing or consent may not apply for reinstatement until the expiration of at least five years from the effective date of disbarment.

(c) Hearing on Application. Petitions for reinstatement by a disbarred or suspended attorney under this Rule shall be filed with the Chief Judge of this Court. The Chief Judge may submit the petition to the Court or may, in his or her discretion, refer the petition to the Committee which shall within thirty (30) days of the referral schedule a hearing at which the petitioner shall have the burden of establishing by clear and convincing evidence that he or she has the moral qualifications, competency, and learning in the law required for admission to practice before this Court and that his or her resumption of the practice of law will not be detrimental to the integrity and standing of the bar or the administration of justice, or subversive of the public interest. Upon completion of the hearing the Committee shall make a full report to the Court. The Committee shall include its findings of fact as to the petitioner's fitness to resume the practice of law and its recommendations as to whether or not the petitioner should be reinstated.

(d) Conditions of Reinstatement. If after consideration of the Committee's report and recommendation the Court finds that the petitioner is unfit to resume the practice of law, the petition shall be dismissed. If after consideration of the Committee's report and recommendation the Court finds that the petitioner is fit to resume the practice of law, the Court shall reinstate him or her, provided that the judgment may make reinstatement conditional upon the payment of all or part of the costs of the proceedings, and on the making of partial or complete restitution to all parties harmed by the petitioner whose conduct led to the suspension or disbarment. Provided further, that if the petitioner has been suspended or disbarred for five years or more, reinstatement may be conditioned, in the discretion of the Court, upon the furnishing of proof of competency and learning in the law, which proof may include certification by the bar examiners of a state or other jurisdiction of the attorney's successful completion of an examination for admission to practice subsequent to the date of suspension or disbarment. Provided further that any reinstatement may be subject to any conditions which the Court in its discretion deems appropriate.

(e) Successive Petitions. No petition for reinstatement under this Rule shall be filed within one year following an adverse judgment upon a petition for reinstatement filed by or on behalf of the same person.

(f) Deposit for Costs of Proceeding. Petitions for reinstatement under this Rule shall be accompanied by a deposit in an amount to be set from time to time by the Court in consultation with the Committee to cover anticipated costs of the reinstatement proceeding.

[Effective December 1, 1994. Amended effective April 15, 2002; April 15, 2006; April 15, 2007; April 15, 2010; December 1, 2015.]

RULE 10. ATTORNEYS SPECIALLY ADMITTED

Whenever an attorney applies to be admitted or is admitted to this Court for purposes of a particular proceeding (pro hac vice), the attorney shall be deemed thereby to have conferred disciplinary jurisdiction upon this Court for any alleged misconduct arising in the course of or in the preparation for such a proceeding which is a violation of this Court's Local Rules and/or the Rules of Professional Conduct adopted by this Court as provided in these Rules.

[Effective December 1, 1994. Amended effective April 15, 2010.]

RULE 11. APPOINTMENT OF COUNSEL

Whenever, at the direction of the Court or upon request of the Committee, counsel is to be appointed pursuant to these rules to investigate or assist in the investigation of misconduct, to prosecute or assist in the prosecution of disciplinary proceedings, or to assist in the disposition of a reinstatement petition filed by a disciplined attorney, this Court, by a majority vote of the active Judges thereof, may appoint as counsel any active member of the bar of this Court, or may, in its discretion, appoint the disciplinary agency of the highest court of the state wherein the Court sits, or other disciplinary agency having jurisdiction.

[Effective December 1, 1994. Amended effective April 15, 2002; April 15, 2010.]

RULE 12. SERVICE OF PAPER AND OTHER NOTICES

Service of an order to show cause instituting a formal disciplinary proceeding shall be made by personal service or by registered or certified mail addressed to the affected attorney at the address shown on the roll of attorneys admitted to practice before this Court or by email upon consent of the affected attorney to waive formal service. Service of any other papers or notices required by these Rules subsequent to the original order to show cause shall be deemed to have been made if such paper or notice is mailed to the attorney at the address shown on the roll of attorneys admitted to practice before the Court, or to counsel or the respondent's attorney at the address indicated in the most recent pleading or document filed by them in the course of any proceeding, or any other method permitted by Federal Rule of Civil Procedure 5(b).

[Effective December 1, 1994. Amended effective April 15, 2007; April 15, 2010; April 15, 2011; December 1, 2015.]

RULE 13. DUTIES OF THE CLERK

(a) Upon being informed that an attorney admitted to practice before this Court has been convicted of any crime, the Clerk of the Court shall determine whether the court in which such conviction occurred has forwarded a certificate of such conviction to this Court. If a certificate has not been so forwarded, the Clerk of the Court shall promptly obtain a certificate and file it with this Court.

(b) Upon being informed that an attorney admitted to practice before this Court has been subjected to discipline by another court, the Clerk of the Court shall determine whether a certified or exemplified copy of the disciplinary judgment or order has been filed with this Court, and, if not, the Clerk of the Court shall promptly obtain a certified or exemplified copy of the disciplinary judgment or order and file it with this Court.

(c) Whenever it appears that any person who has been convicted of any crime or disbarred or suspended or censured or disbarred on consent by this Court is admitted to practice law in any other jurisdiction or before any other court, this Court shall, within fourteen (14) days of that conviction, disbarment, suspension, censure, or disbarment on consent, transmit to the disciplinary authority in such other jurisdiction, or for such other court, a certificate of the conviction or a certified or exemplified copy of the judgment or order of disbarment, suspension, censure, or disbarment on consent, as well as the last known office and residence addresses of the disciplined attorney.

(d) The Clerk of the Court shall, likewise, promptly notify the National Discipline Bank operated by the American Bar Association of any order imposing public discipline on any attorney admitted to practice before this Court.

[Effective December 1, 1994. Amended effective April 15, 2007; April 15, 2010; December 1, 2015.]

INTERNAL OPERATING PROCEDURES

INTRODUCTION

These are the procedures for the Court's internal operations, compiling in summary form various administrative orders, minutes of Executive Committee and Judges' meetings, and previously unwritten customs and practices of the Court. They set out the procedures generally to be used by chambers and the Office of the Clerk of the Court in performing certain administrative tasks.

While the procedures are public and available on request, litigants acquire no rights under them. A current copy of these procedures is also available at the Court's web site http://www.flsd.uscourts.gov/. The judges of the Court have agreed to observe all Local Rules and these internal operating procedures in the conduct of Court business.

[Adopted effective July 1991. Amended effective June 12, 2014.]

IOP 1.00.00. ADMINISTRATIVE ORDERS

The Clerk of Court, who is responsible for the care, custody, and safekeeping of court records, shall, upon receipt of originals of administrative orders signed by the Chief Judge, file stamp and log them in. Original administrative orders shall be maintained in binders in the Clerk's Office. Copies shall be maintained by the Circuit Librarian and made available to the public.

When an administrative order is sent to the Chief Judge for signature, it must include a date and a sequential number obtained from the Clerk of Court.

The Clerk of Court will make distribution of the orders, unless the Chief Judge elects to do so. The Clerk's Office will publicize administrative orders by providing them to the Daily Business Review, as appropriate, and posting them on the Court's website and in public areas of the Clerk's Office.

IOP 1.01.00 Internal Operating Procedures. The Clerk of Court is responsible for maintaining the original Internal Operating Procedures ("IOPs"), notifying the Court of all subsequent changes in the IOPS, and making sure all new judges receive copies of the IOPs.

[Adopted effective July 1991. Amended effective June 12, 2014.]

IOP 2.00.00. RANDOM ASSIGNMENT OF NEW CASES

IOP 2.01.00 Wheel Consolidation. In an effort to ensure equitable distribution of cases, the criminal and civil wheels were consolidated effective January 1, 2002, as follows: (1) The civil A & B wheels are combined into a single wheel from which all new civil cases, but for capital habeas petitions, will now be assigned; (2) The criminal categories I–II, III, IV, and V wheels are likewise consolidated into a single criminal wheel from which all new criminal cases will now be assigned.

IOP 2.01.01 *Assignment of Actions and Proceedings.*

(a) All civil and criminal cases, including those within a weighted category, shall be assigned on a blind random basis so that the District workload is fairly and equally distributed among the active Judges irrespective of jury division; provided that, whenever necessary in the interest of justice and expediency, the Court may modify the assignments made to active or senior Judges.

(b) The Clerk of the Court shall not have any power or discretion in determining the Judge to whom any action or proceeding is assigned, the Clerk of the Court's duties being ministerial only. The method of assignment shall assure that the identity of the assigned Judge shall not be disclosed to the Clerk of the Court nor to any other person, until after filing.

(c) The assignment schedule shall be designed to prevent any litigant from choosing the Judge to whom an action or proceeding is to be assigned, and all attorneys shall conscientiously refrain from attempting to vary this Local Rule.

(d) The District is divided into five (5) Divisions: the Fort Pierce Division (Highlands, Indian River, Martin, Okeechobee and St. Lucie Counties); the West Palm Beach Division (Palm Beach County); the Fort Lauderdale Division (Broward County); the Miami Division (Miami–Dade County); and the Key West Division (Monroe County). Cases are assigned by the Automated Case Assignment System to provide for blind, random assignment of cases and to equitably distribute the District's case load. Each Judge in the District has chambers in one (1) of three (3) Divisions (Miami, Fort Lauderdale or West Palm Beach). A Judge with chambers in one (1) Division may be assigned a case with venue in another Division.

IOP 2.01.02 *Responsibility for Actions and Proceedings.* Every application for an order, including those made in connection with appellate proceedings, shall be made to the Judge to whom the action or proceeding is assigned. The assigned Judge shall have full charge thereof and no changes in assignment shall be made except by order of the Judges affected; provided, that upon the failure or inability of any Judge to act by reason of death or disability, a change in assignment may be made by the Chief Judge.

IOP 2.02.00 "One Division" Rule. In the interest of reducing the expense and inconvenience to litigants and counsel associated with holding and attending court in distant locations, the Court will, to the extent possible, limit the assignment of cases outside of the division of their origination. Although the distribution of judges and filings across the District rules out a system in which each judge's caseload is equal and is composed entirely of cases originating in the division in which the judge sits, it is possible to limit case assignments to the originating division or an immediately contiguous division. Stated more simply, under this rule, when a newly-filed case must be assigned to a judge outside of the division of its origination, it will be assigned to a judge who sits in a neighboring division. Under this rule, hereafter referred to as the "one division rule," no Miami cases will be assigned to a judge who sits in the Palm Beach division, and vice versa. When, for example, there is a need to assign a

Palm Beach case to a Judge outside that division, only Fort Lauderdale Judges will be chosen for assignment.

IOP 2.02.01 *Implementation of One Division Rule.* The "One Division Rule" will commence with the first wheel replenishments occurring after January 1, 2002. Thereafter, every attempt will be made to assign the maximum numbers of cases arising in a particular venue to the judges who preside in that venue.

IOP 2.02.02 *Exceptions to the One Division Rule.* The rule does not consider the Key West and Fort Pierce wheels, in which participation is voluntary, nor does it prohibit senior judges from taking assignments in any division they might prefer. Moreover, as an accommodation to the Court, active Judges may from time to time be authorized to accept new assignments in a manner contrary to the rule. For example, Judge Middlebrooks is currently, as an accommodation to the Court, taking a fixed percentage of criminal cases originating in Miami, although he now presides in West Palm Beach. Finally, there may well be unanticipated emergencies which might require some limited two-division spillover assignment to maintain equality of caseload. The existence of an emergency sufficient to require varying from the rule, however, will be determined only by the Clerk in consultation with the Court.

IOP 2.03.00 Calculation of Senior Judge Participation. Senior judge participation in the case assignment system shall be calculated as a percentage of an active judge's average.

IOP 2.04.00 Assignment of Cases to Newly Appointed Judges. Newly appointed judges shall be placed on the case assignment wheel no later than fifteen (15) days after they are first sworn to perform their judicial duties.

IOP 2.05.00 Transfer of Cases to Newly Appointed Judges.

IOP 2.05.01 *Civil.* The average number of pending civil cases per active judge shall be determined by dividing all civil cases pending before active judges as of a given date by the number of active judges. **Example:** 1000 pending civil cases divided by 15 judges, equals 67 cases per judge.

The same process is then applied after adding the number of new judges to the number of active judges. Example: Two new judges are appointed. 1000 pending civil cases divided by 17 judges, equals 59 cases per judge.

Each active judge will transfer the difference in the average number of pending cases after accounting for the new judges. Example: Using the above formula, four new cases are transferred to each new judge, for a total of eight transferred cases.

The Clerk of Court will randomly select the cases to be transferred in consideration of the new judge's divisional location. Every attempt will be made to give the new judge the same proportion of "home" division cases as the other active judges in that division, as appropriate.

IOP 2.05.02 *Criminal.* Each judge shall transfer to the new judge a number of criminal cases to be determined by the Court. The Clerk of Court will randomly select the cases to be transferred in consideration of the new judge's divisional location. The list of cases selected for transfer for each judge shall be disseminated to all judges. See IOP 2.05.04 for procedures for transferring cases from the list provided by the Clerk of Court. If a case selected by the Clerk of Court is not appropriate for transfer, the transferring judge shall select the next case in sequence on the list that is eligible for transfer and transfer that case to the new judge. The Clerk's list shall be strictly followed in the order provided. Judges may not randomly select cases to be transferred to the new judge.

IOP 2.05.03 *Cases Excluded from Reassignment.* All Fort Pierce and Key West cases, sealed cases and cases received via transfer or recusal are excluded from the reassignment process. Criminal cases which the United States Attorney's Office has declared or which the judge anticipates will require 21 or more days to try, criminal cases involving bond jumping and criminal cases in trial or awaiting sentencing (intervals P4, P5) are excluded from the reassignment process.

Habeas corpus death cases (nature of suit 535), consolidated cases including multi-district litigation cases, 2255s, cases involving CIPA clearance, and civil cases pending 18 months or longer are also excluded from the reassignment process.

In addition, the transferring judge may exclude from transfer any case that has involved a substantial amount of judicial effort or in which any motion is pending that is ripe for disposition by that judge.

IOP 2.05.04 *Procedures for Reassignment.* The Clerk of Court shall furnish each transferring judge with a list of civil and criminal cases to be transferred as of a date certain (the "transfer date"). The transfer lists prepared for each judge shall be disseminated to all judges.

After receiving the list of cases to be transferred, the transferring judge shall, within 30 days, rule upon all pending ripe motions that have not been referred to the paired magistrate judge and which are fully briefed. Judges should then and transfer those cases selected by the Clerk to the newly-appointed judge. If any case on the list is excluded from transfer, pursuant to IOP 2.05.03, or is for other reasons not an appropriate case for transfer, the transferring judge shall select the next case in sequence on his or her list that is eligible for transfer and transfer it to the new judge. Thereafter, the transferring judge shall make no adjustments. Judges do not need to transfer all cases at the same time, as long as the total number of cases transferred does not exceed the total permitted.

Judges shall not issue "boiler-plate" orders denying pending motions without prejudice to review same before the new judge.

All transferring judges must complete a status sheet in the form prepared by the Clerk for every case transferred. All magistrate judges must rule on all pending motions that became ripe on or before the date of the transferring judge's order of reassignment. Magistrate judges should also prepare a certification/order of transfer after cases with applicable ripe pending motions have been disposed.

IOP 2.05.05 *Recusals After Transfer.* New judges receiving transferred cases should make reasonable efforts within the first 120 days following transfer to determine if grounds exist requiring recusals. If, within the first 120 days following transfer, a new judge determines that he or she must recuse, the new judge shall enter an order of recusal, and send the case back to the transferring judge. The transferring judge shall select and transfer a substitute case. If, after the expiration of 120 days following transfer, a new judge determines that he or she must recuse, the new judge shall enter an order of recusal, and the case shall be reassigned by the Clerk following normal procedures.

IOP 2.06.00 *Transfer of Higher-Numbered Cases.* Each division in the Southern District of Florida has its own series of numbers which are sequentially assigned to cases. Therefore, for the purpose of higher-numbered transfers, the "lower-numbered" case refers to the earlier-filed case.

The judge assigned the higher-numbered case shall prepare a proposed Order of Transfer and a Notice to the parties that the higher-numbered case is transferred to the docket of the judge having the lower-numbered case, effective upon that judge's consent to the transfer.

The transferring judge shall forward a copy of the transfer order to the transferee judge for review. The transferee judge must respond to the proposed transfer within thirty days from the date the transferring judge forwards the file. A case will be automatically assigned to the receiving judge if that judge has not responded to the transfer request within thirty days. The transferring judge shall use a form providing for signature by the accepting judge.

Subject to the above time limitation, the transfer of the higher-numbered case must be with the consent and approval of the receiving judge.

No higher-numbered transfer shall be initiated by a judge ordering the Clerk of Court to reassign the case to another judge.

IOP 2.07.00 Miscellaneous Transfers and Reassignments. Judges may confer and directly transfer all or any part of a case on the judge's docket to any consenting judge. Notice shall be provided to all parties.

IOP 2.07.01 *Reassignment of Cases Due to Recusal, Temporary Assignment or Emergency*

(a) The procedure for reassignment of cases due to recusal, temporary assignment or emergency shall be similar to the blind filing assignment for newly-filed cases and shall be administered in a manner approved by the Court so as to assure fair and equitable distribution of all such matters throughout the District.

(b) Any emergency matter arising in a case pending before a Judge who is physically absent from the District or who is unavailable due to illness, or is on vacation may, upon written certification as to each matter from the Judge's office setting forth such grounds therefor, be referred to the Clerk of the Court for reassignment under a blind random assignment procedure. Such assignment, when effected, shall be of temporary duration, limited only to the immediate relief sought, and the case for all other purposes or proceedings shall remain on the docket of the Judge to whom it was originally assigned.

(c) Uncontested matters wherein the parties cannot be prejudiced through delay occasioned by the normal course of business shall not be deemed emergency matters for referral.

(d) The Clerk of the Court shall not have any discretion in determining the Judge to whom any such matter is assigned, nor shall the Clerk of the Court disclose the name of the Judge to attorneys or other persons until after the assignment has been made.

IOP 2.08.00 Assignment of Cases and Referrals to Magistrate Judges.

IOP 2.08.01 *Magistrate Judge Pairing Plan.* The judges shall be paired to individual magistrate judges by the Chief Judge in consideration of the following:

(a) the equal distribution of workload among the magistrate judges and,

(b) the preferences of the district judges, including senior judges, taking into consideration their seniority and their past referral practices.

The pairing shall be for a period of three years in order to promote continuity in the processing of cases, while allowing each magistrate judge to have exposure to several district judges during his or her term.

As of April 1, 2002, and subsequently at the end of each three year period in all cases assigned to district judges with whom the magistrate judge is not paired, each magistrate judge shall retain until disposition all previously referred fully briefed motions. In addition, each magistrate judge shall dispose of all other referred motions that become ripe for disposition in such cases until all fully briefed motions have been ruled upon by the magistrate judge. Upon the magistrate judge's disposition of all fully briefed motions in any case assigned to a district judge with whom the magistrate judge is not paired, the magistrate judge shall certify to the district judge to whom the case is assigned that all such motions have been ruled upon and the district judge will then issue an order directing the clerk of court to transfer the case to the "paired magistrate judge." The magistrate judges shall use their best efforts to dispose of all motions in cases assigned to district judges with whom they are not paired within 60 days of the commencement of the three year rotation.

1. In the event of a higher-numbered case transfer or a recusal by a district judge within 30 days of a case assignment, the Clerk's Office shall concurrently reassign the case to a district judge and the magistrate judge with whom the newly-assigned district judge is paired. In the case of all other district judge recusals, the procedures set forth above with respect to the disposition of fully briefed motions prior to transfer shall apply.

2. In any case filed after April 1, 2002, from which a magistrate judge recuses himself or herself, the Clerk's Office shall randomly assign another magistrate judge to the case. For any case filed before April 1, 2002, which is subject to transfer pursuant to the Court's Magistrate Judge Pairing Plan, but with respect to which the transferee magistrate judge recuses himself or herself, the case shall be returned to the transferor magistrate judge.

3. District judges shall retain full discretion concerning the type and volume of matters referred. However, referrals shall be only to the "paired" magistrate judge, unless a district judge after conferring with and obtaining

the agreement of the district judges with whom another magistrate judge is paired determines that a case or motions should be assigned to or remain with such other magistrate judge (e.g., because of a prior related case, because a magistrate judge has devoted substantial time to an unusually complex case, or for some other meritorious reason), and so notify the Clerk's Office in writing.

4. Any consent trial, consent motion for summary judgment, and other "consent motion" shall remain with the magistrate judge who was assigned to the case when the consent was given.

IOP 2.09.00 Motions for Travel Referrals to a Magistrate Judge. Any motion for travel by a defendant released on bond will be ruled on by the district judge to whom the defendant's case is assigned unless that district judge specifically refers the matter to the magistrate judge with whom the district judge is paired for criminal matters. Magistrate judges must have an order of referral prior to acting on such a motion.

IOP 2.10.00 Assignment by Reason of Disability, Disqualification, or Death of a Judge. Reassignments necessitated by the death, retirement, resignation, or incapacity of any judge, or by any other circumstances, shall be determined at the discretion of the Chief Judge.

IOP 2.11.00 Assignment to Visiting Judges. Cases may be assigned to visiting judges at the discretion of the Chief Judge.

IOP 2.12.00 Death Penalty/Habeas Corpus Cases. Each active judge shall have one case assignment ballot in the death penalty/habeas corpus wheel and may not be assigned another death penalty/habeas corpus case until every other judge has received one and the wheel has been refilled. In the event the judge whose ballot is drawn is out of the district, his ballot will be reinserted into the wheel and another ballot will be drawn.

Once the Governor signs a death warrant, but before the case is filed, a judge will be drawn from the capital wheel. If the case does not come to federal court, that judge's ballot will be reinserted in the wheel.

In all death cases, an initial status conference shall be scheduled within five business days after assignment to a judge. If an evidentiary hearing is required, or if additional oral argument is scheduled, that hearing shall be conducted no later than thirty days after the initial hearing. In addition, the assigned judge will, in appropriate circumstances, enter the following:

(a) An order directing the respondent to file a response and furnish transcripts of the trial and other hearings within five days from the date the petition is filed;

(b) An order directing the parties to complete the habeas corpus check list recommended by the Eleventh Circuit Court of Appeals within twenty-four hours of the filing of the petition.

(c) The judge shall render a final written opinion within five months of the conclusion of the last hearing held. All habeas corpus death cases shall be decided in the Southern District of Florida within a maximum period of six months and five days from the date of the filing of the petition. If a judge is unable to complete a final written opinion within five months of the final hearing, that judge will notify the Chief Judge in writing. The notification shall describe the reasons for the delay and the expected completion date.

The Chief Judge may assist the assigned judge by reassigning any other criminal cases assigned to that judge until the completion of the death case. If a petition for rehearing is filed, it shall be ruled on within sixty days from the date of filing. The Clerk shall notify the assigned judge and the Chief Judge in the event the deadline is not met.

IOP 2.13.00 Court Policy for Scheduling Trials and Calendar Conflicts Arising in the Southern District of Florida. In resolving any calendar conflicts among the judges of this district and between judges of this district and state judges, the following procedures and priorities are established:

(a) Criminal cases shall prevail over civil cases.

(b) Jury trials shall prevail over non-jury trials.

(c) Court of Appeals arguments and hearings shall prevail over trials.

(d) The case in which the trial date has been first scheduled in writing shall take precedence over any later written or oral order scheduling trial.

(e) A trial in progress prevails over those that have not yet begun.

(f) Circumstances such as cost, number of witnesses and attorneys involved, travel, length of trial, age of case, and other relevant matters may warrant deviation from this policy. Such matters should be resolved through communication between the judges involved.

(g) Unless precluded by constitutional or statutory considerations, scheduling conflicts of Criminal Justice Act (CJA) attorneys should be given priority during any given calendar. Judges should be sensitive to the competing commitments of a Criminal Justice Act attorney's caseload absent compelling circumstances which militate against accommodating that attorney's scheduling request.

(h) The Court should entertain motions for continuances, timely notices of scheduling conflicts, and/or notices of emergency proceedings in another court, either federal or state, on a timely basis and grant such relief when requested.

IOP 2.14.00 Emergency Matters. Any emergency matter arising in a case pending before a judge who is physically absent from the Southern District of Florida, or who is on vacation, may, upon written certification of unavailability from the judge's chambers, be referred to the Clerk for reassignment under a blind random assignment procedure. Such reassignment shall be limited only to the immediate relief sought, and the case for all other purposes and proceedings shall remain on the docket of the judge to whom it was originally assigned.

IOP 2.15.00 Transfer of Refiled and Similar Actions and Procedures.

(a) *Refiled.* Whenever an action or proceeding previously dismissed without prejudice is refiled without a substantial change in issues or parties, judges should confer and discuss whether the case should be transferred to the judge who previously dismissed the action or proceeding and, upon agreement, it shall be transferred to the judge who previously dismissed the action or proceeding.

(b) *Post-Conviction Relief, Criminal.* Whenever a second or subsequent action seeking post-conviction or other relief petition for writ of habeas corpus is filed by the same applicant involving the same offense, the action shall be transferred to the Judge who took the action from which review is sought, or any successor Judge. All motions under 28 U.S.C. § 2255 shall be assigned to the Judge who took the action from which review is sought, or any successor Judge.

(c) *Similar.* Whenever an action or proceeding is filed in the Court which involves subject matter which is a material part of the subject matter of another action or proceeding then pending before this Court, or for other reasons the disposition thereof would appear to entail the unnecessary duplication of judicial labor if heard by a different Judge, the Judges involved shall determine whether the newly filed action or proceeding shall be transferred to the Judge to whom the earlier filed action or proceeding is assigned.

IOP 2.16.00 Recusals. Recusal orders may refer to Title 28 U.S.C. § 455 as grounds for recusal. Whether to recite additional reasons for recusal shall be left to the sound discretion of the recusing judge.

In the event of recusal in any matter, the assigned Judge shall enter the fact of recusal on the record and refer the matter to the Clerk of the Court for permanent reassignment to another Judge in accordance with the blind random assignment system.

IOP 2.16.01 *Recusals in Cases Pending Two Years or More.* When a judge receives a case on reassignment from a recusing judge and the case has been in the recusing judge's inventory two years or more, the receiving judge may transfer a like case to the recusing judge.

IOP 2.17.00 Assignment of Cases to Chief Judge. The Chief Judge may elect to take a reduced caseload in consideration of the increased administrative duties for which the Chief Judge is responsible.

IOP 2.18.00 Expedited Review of Petitions Under The Hague Convention. Under the Hague Convention on the Civil Aspects of International Child Abduction, Oct. 25, 1980, T.I.A.S. No. 11670 (Convention), as implemented by Congress in the International Child Abduction Remedies Act (ICARA), *see* 42 U.S.C. § 11601(b)(4), petitions requesting the return of children who have been wrongfully taken or retained must be decided in an expeditious manner. Consistent with directives of the United States Supreme Court and the Eleventh Circuit Court of Appeals, *see Chafin v. Chafin*, ___ U.S. ___, 133 S. Ct. 1017, 1028 (2013), *on remand*, Chafin v. Chafin, 742 F.3d 934 (11th Cir. 2013), the Southern District adopts as a policy the goal of a six-week timeframe from the initial filing of the petition to a decision regarding return of the child. Upon the filing of a petition under the Convention and ICARA, the Clerk shall promptly bring this policy of expedited review to the attention of the Court and the parties via electronic notice filed in the CM/ECF system.

[Adopted effective July 1991. Amended effective June 12, 2014; September 16, 2014.]

IOP 3.00.00. ADMINISTRATIVE DUTIES AND RESPONSIBILITIES OF THE CHIEF JUDGE

IOP 3.01.00 Judicial Administration. The Chief Judge shall have the following powers and duties:

- To convene and preside at the meetings of the judges, regular and special.
- To set and preside over all en banc and ceremonial sessions of the Court.
- To be an ex officio, voting member of each Standing or Ad Hoc Court Committee.
- To be the spokesperson for the Court to the public, the Bar, other government agencies and the judicial establishment.
- To appoint the Chief Bankruptcy Judge and the Chief Magistrate Judge and to determine the term for each.
- To promulgate duty rosters for all duty positions established by the Court.
- In the event of natural disaster or other serious emergency, to close all operations of the Court at any or all of the facilities in which the Court operates.
- To exercise such other powers and duties as may be assigned to the Chief Judge from time to time by the Court or by statute.
- Whenever an active judge retires from the Court, or a courtroom and chambers becomes available in any division of the Court, the Chief Judge shall poll the active judges to determine which, if any of them, seek assignment to the vacant position. When more than one active judge seeks assignment to a vacant or newly available position, the Chief Judge shall assign the position to the most senior active judge seeking it.
- The Chief Judge provides direction and supervision for the District's component offices including:

  United States Bankruptcy Court

  United States Magistrate Judges

  Clerk's Office

  United States Probation Office

  United States Pretrial Services Office
- The Chief Judge is responsible for implementing and enforcing all administrative policies of the United States District Court for the Southern District of Florida, the Eleventh Circuit Judicial Council, and the Judicial Conference of the United States, and all statutes and regulations pertaining to administrative matters of the Court.
- The Chief Judge may appoint "any officer of the Court" (i.e., Clerk of Court and Chief Probation Officer) when a majority of the Court cannot agree on the appointment.
- The Chief Judge, or his designee, shall consider and approve annual and sick leave requests and authorize travel for the Clerk of Court, Chief Probation Officer, Chief Pretrial Services Officer and other employees as may be required by law or Judicial Conference policy.

- The Chief Judge is responsible for the review and approval of all construction projects for the Court and all architectural plans and drawings for such construction.
- In emergency situations, the Chief Judge, after consulting with the Early Dismissal Committee, will implement the Emergency Notification Procedures. Emergency situations are those deemed by the Chief Judge to be of sufficient magnitude to cause serious and hazardous conditions to the health and safety of Federal employees. **The decision for early dismissal or closure will be at the sole discretion of the Chief Judge.** A decision by the Chief Judge for early dismissal or closure related to weather conditions affecting Miami, Fort Lauderdale, or West Palm Beach will apply to all Court locations in the District. Once the decision is made for early dismissal or closure, all Clerk's Office staff must be released.
- The Chief Judge monitors, reviews, and recommends amendments to the Local Rules of Court as well as the following District operating plans:

  Jury Utilization

  Jury Selection and Service Act

  Court Reporter Management Plan

  Speedy Trial Act

  Attorney Admissions

  Automation

  Equal Employment Opportunity

  Emergency Notification Procedures
- The budgeting process contemplates that spending plan requests submitted by judges will be solicited, compiled, and submitted to the Committee on Budget and Fiscal Management for consideration in a timely fashion.
- The Chief Judge chairs the District's Standing Committee on Court Security and Hurricane Preparedness. The United States Marshal, the Federal Bureau of Investigation, the Drug Enforcement Administration, and all other federal agencies are required to immediately notify the Chief Judge concerning any threat to the person, property, welfare, or security of any judge or court employee.
- The Chief Judge is responsible for approving requests of probation and pretrial services officers, submitted through the chiefs of those departments, for approval to carry firearms.
- The Chief Judge, in concert with the Eleventh Judicial Council, is responsible for providing Congress with specific data supporting any request to establish a location for holding court.
- The Chief Judge, or his designee, reviews the Employment Dispute Resolution Coordinator's findings as to complaints of discrimination and presides over any necessary proceedings. The Chief Judge, or his designee, sits as the appeals officer for EDR actions and terminations.
- The Chief Judge must concur in any request to the Circuit Judicial Council for additional temporary assistance based on a declaration of a judicial emergency by a district judge, bankruptcy judge, or magistrate judge.
- The Chief Judge reviews complaints of judicial misconduct or disability pursuant to Addendum Three, Local Rules of the Eleventh Circuit Court of Appeals.
- The Chief Judge certifies to the Chief Judge of the Eleventh Circuit and the Inter–Circuit Assignment Committee of the Judicial Conference of the United States, the need for visiting judges in the Southern District of Florida, and prepares and supervises the fair and equitable distribution of cases to visiting judges. The Clerk of Court shall arrange for staff, chambers, and trial-ready cases pursuant to the directions of the Chief Judge. The Chief Judge, or a designee, may conduct calendar calls for visiting judges.
- The Chief Judge is responsible for making all committee appointments. Traditionally, the Chief Judge has sought the advice and counsel of other judges respecting membership on the Court Committees.

IOP 3.02.00 Bankruptcy. The Chief Judge designates a Chief Bankruptcy Judge whenever a majority of the district judges are unable to agree in the designation.

IOP 3.02.01 *Implementation of Set Term for Chief Bankruptcy Judge.* The Chief Judge shall set the term for the Chief Bankruptcy Judge.

IOP 3.03.00 Case Assignments and Case Management. The Chief Judge, or his designee, (together with the Circuit's Judicial Council and the Administrative Office) receives and reviews the Circuit Executive's separate quarterly reports on district, magistrate, and bankruptcy cases and motions held under advisement for more than sixty days.

The Chief Judge ensures the case assignment system promotes the effective disposition of protracted, difficult, or unusual cases.

The Chief Judge should be informed about and should inform the other district judges when matters concerning the district are before the Eleventh Circuit Judicial Council.

The Chief Judge oversees implementation of the Court's rules for case assignment, and ensures an equal division of the business of the Court among the judges insofar as the Court's rules and orders do not otherwise prescribe.

IOP 3.04.00 Jury Administration. The Chief Judge, or his designee, is responsible for reviewing from time to time and supervising the implementation of the Court's Jury Plan.

The Chief Judge signs all orders for the summonsing of jury pools for grand and petit juries in Miami, Fort Lauderdale, West Palm Beach, Key West, and Fort Pierce.

IOP 3.04.01 *Jury Policy.* The Court has agreed that the below guidelines will be followed in connection with the utilization of jury panels:

(a) Any judge who is willing to volunteer to commence jury selection in the afternoon (noon or later) should advise the Jury Administrator.

(b) Judges should only request the number of jurors that can reasonably be inquired of on a particular day (e.g., with a "high-profile" case, or one that will involve extensive jury voir dire do not request all the jurors that may eventually be necessary). For example, even though a large or special panel of 200 or more may be necessary for a particular case, usually no more than 50 jurors can usually be questioned on a single day.

(c) Judges should not unnecessarily direct the excusal of jurors (e.g., if some jurors are excused or challenged during voir dire, they should not be instructed to go home, go to lunch, or come back on a day certain as the jury staff may want to utilize those jurors in another way).

(d) No jury panel should be summoned on Fridays. Additionally, if judges compress their jury selections on Monday through Wednesday, the Jury Administrator can more effectively "pool" jury panels for use by more than one judge.

(e) During the winter months, the Court should be mindful of releasing jurors after dark.

IOP 3.05.00 United States Magistrate Judges. The Chief Judge may appoint or reappoint United States magistrate judges if there is no concurrence among the judges.

The Chief Judge must certify that no full-time magistrate judge is available when parties request a part-time magistrate judge to preside over a civil proceeding in accordance with 28 U.S.C. § 636(c)(1).

The Chief Judge must agree to a temporary emergency assignment of a magistrate judge from one district to another.

The Chief Judge shall take such actions as the Court considers appropriate in the case of a magistrate judge whose conduct becomes the object of an official circuit council committee investigation.

The Chief Judge is responsible for certifying to the Administrative Office the names of persons selected to be United States magistrate judges and requesting FBI or other background security checks on the individuals selected by the Court.

[Adopted effective July 1991. Amended effective June 12, 2014.]

IOP 4.00.00. DUTIES AND RESPONSIBILITIES OF MAGISTRATE JUDGES

IOP 4.01.00 Duties of the Chief Magistrate Judge. Serves as liaison between the district judges and magistrate judges.

Schedules and presides over meetings of the magistrate judges.

Serves on committees as the Chief Judge may determine.

Coordinates magistrate judge leave requests, duty responsibilities, and emergency assignments as necessary.

IOP 4.02.00 Magistrate Judges

Conditions of Employment:

The United States magistrate judges are appointed by the Court in accordance with the provisions of 28 U.S.C. § 631. Full-time magistrate judges serve a term of eight years and part-time magistrate judges serve for four years. The procedures for the appointment or removal of a magistrate judge are governed by statute. The district judges may select one full-time magistrate judge to serve as the Chief Magistrate Judge performing administrative functions.

Duties:

The United States magistrate judges of the Southern District of Florida are authorized to perform the full range of functions permitted by the jurisdictional statute, 28 U.S.C. § 636, as implemented by the Magistrate Section of the Local Rules of Court.

In Miami, when a civil or criminal case is filed, the Clerk of Court assigns a magistrate judge for the purpose of handling matters referred by the assigned district judge pursuant to the Miami Magistrate Judge Pairing Assignment Plan.

When a civil case is filed in Fort Lauderdale, West Palm Beach, or Fort Pierce, the Clerk of Court assigns a magistrate judge for the purpose of handling matters referred by the assigned district judge pursuant to the Central (Fort Lauderdale) and Northern (West Palm Beach, Fort Pierce) Divisions Pairing Plan.

In civil and criminal matters not yet filed with the Clerk of Court, such as applications for seizure warrants, pen register and trap and trace, administrative inspection warrants, electronic transponders, and search warrants, the magistrate judges shall perform all functions within their jurisdiction.

A Duty Magistrate Judge shall be available at all times to perform such functions. The Duty Magistrate Judge shall be reasonably available at the Courthouse during regular business hours and by telephone at all other times. The Duty Magistrate Judge should handle *emergency* arrest warrants in connection with pretrial supervision matters rather than referring such matters to the judge to whom the case is assigned.

[Adopted effective July 1991. Amended effective June 12, 2014.]

IOP 5.00.00. COMMITTEE ASSIGNMENTS

The size of each Court Committee shall be determined and the Chair of each Committee shall be appointed by the Chief Judge. To create greater participation and collegiality within the Court, magistrate judges may serve as voting members of both Standing and Ad Hoc Committees.

The Chief Judge shall be an ex-officio voting member of all of the Standing Committees.

IOP 5.01.00 Standing Committees. There shall be certain Standing Committees as an integral part of the Court's operation. Standing Committees shall remain in existence and operate continuously provided, however, that the Chief Judge, at any time, may terminate the existence of a Standing Committee, create one or more new Standing Committees, or combine the functions of Standing Committees already in existence.

IOP 5.02.00 Ad Hoc Committees. There shall be such Ad Hoc Committees as the Chief Judge and/or the Court shall from time to time create. At the time of the creation of an Ad Hoc Committee, its purpose and function shall be defined. It shall remain in existence until the Chief Judge determines that its purpose and function have been completed or for the term set for its existence.

[Adopted effective July 1991. Amended effective June 12, 2014.]

IOP 6.00.00. COURT REPORTERS

The official court reporters of the Southern District of Florida will comply with the requirements of the Court Reporter Plan established by the Court December 1, 1982, and revised March 14, 2002, and by the Guide to Judiciary Policies and Procedures, Volume I, Chapter IV, part A, effective January 1, 1983.

Court reporters who are "in trial" should be left in trial rather than assigned to other judges.

Court reporters who are not certified for "real time" reporting cannot be paid the real time rate.

[Adopted effective July 1991. Amended effective June 12, 2014.]

IOP 7.00.00. COURTROOM SCHEDULING

The Clerk of Court will maintain a master list of courtroom assignments wherein each district judge shall be assigned his or her own courtroom.

Should a judge be involved in a trial in which his or her courtroom space is inadequate, the judge shall immediately contact the Clerk of Court and request a larger courtroom.

When a Southern District judge finds he or she must try a case in another division of the district, the judge will contact the Clerk of Court to obtain an available courtroom. If the case is expected to be protracted, the request must be in writing and signed by the judge. In the event the particular space requested has already been reserved by another judge, the Clerk of Court shall notify the requesting judge, both orally and in writing, that the space is not available.

It shall be the responsibility of any judge who has reserved space to immediately notify the Clerk of Court of the cancellation of such reservation in the event that the space is not needed.

A judge may be assigned to only one courtroom at a given time. There will be no double reservation of courtrooms unless a judge is simultaneously presiding over separate trials.

Any judge requiring additional temporary space for use by trial counsel, or for storage of sensitive trial materials, irrespective of the courtroom assigned for his or her use, shall request temporary assignment of additional space through the Chief Judge.

[Adopted effective July 1991. Amended effective June 12, 2014.]

IOP 8.00.00. DUTY JUDGE

On a monthly rotating basis, the Court shall designate from, the active resident judges, a Duty Judge for the Miami, Fort Lauderdale, and West Palm Beach Divisions.

The Duty Judge should be present in the district and available for handling Duty Judge matters at all times during the month assigned. If it is necessary for the Duty Judge to be out of the district for a short period of time during the assignment month, it is the Duty Judge's responsibility to make arrangements with another judge to handle all Duty Judge matters, and to notify the Chief Judge and Clerk of Court of his or her absence.

IOP 8.01.00 The Duty Judge's functions are as follows:

- Handle all grand jury matters. This includes convening grand juries and ruling on matters affecting those grand juries during each month's duty. Grand jury matters, and all matters reasonably related to the original grand jury matter, will be handled by the district judge before whom the original matter was filed. The Clerk's Office will call the offices of the Duty Judge to attempt to arrange a time convenient to the Judge for the empanelment of the grand jury (if one is scheduled for that month), but if the jurors have already been summoned, the date will be firm and the Judge will adjust his or her schedule accordingly. Once the date for the empanelment is set by the Duty Judge in consultation with the clerk, the date will be firm and not subject to change. Rule 6(f) of the Federal Rules of Criminal Procedure makes provisions for a grand jury return to be taken by a United States Magistrate Judge. However, whether the District Judge or the Magistrate Judge will take a return will be determined by the Duty Judge. Until Rule 6(f) is further construed, a District Judge should handle immunization of witnesses and all matters that pertain to contempt.
- Preside over all court naturalization ceremonies and emergency naturalization matters in the Duty Judge's Division.
- Preside over matters arising from Magistrate Judges' proceedings which are not assigned to a District Judge, including but not limited to, applications for review of bonds and competency examinations.
- Transfer of Probation from foreign districts.
- Swearing in of attorneys to practice.
- Preside over wiretap applications in matters not assigned to any District Judge, with the exception that trap-and-trace and pen register orders will continue to be handled by the Magistrate Judges. All extensions, including all matters reasonably related to the original investigation, will be handled by the District Judge who granted the original application.
- Approval of issuance of warrants of arrest in admiralty cases in any division where the assigned judge is out of the district or is otherwise unavailable.
- The Duty Judge may preside over emergency petitions for writ of habeas corpus involving a petitioner's claim to immediate release, where the assigned judge is in the district, but otherwise unavailable to rule on the petition. After ruling on the emergency relief sought, and for all other purposes and proceedings, the case shall remain on the docket of the judge to whom it was originally assigned.
- The Duty Judge, his or her designee, or the Clerk's designee, as appropriate, determines the validity of juror qualifications, exemptions, or excuses.
- If the Duty Judge rescues him or herself from a Duty Judge matter, the matter will be referred to the next upcoming Judge assigned to duty matters. If that Judge is unavailable, the duty assignment roster will be followed in order until another company Judge is found who can handle the matter.

[Adopted effective July 1991. Amended effective June 12, 2014; June 29, 2015.]

IOP 10.00.00. DUTIES AND RESPONSIBILITIES OF COURT EMPLOYEES

Pursuant to the Internet Policy adopted by the Court, judges are asked to look after use of the Internet resource by their staff, and to be aware of the need to adhere to the District's policy.

IOP 10.01.00 Release of Information in Criminal and Civil Proceedings by Courthouse Personnel. All courthouse personnel, including the marshal, deputy marshals, the Clerk of the Court, deputy court clerks, probation officers, court reporters, law clerks, and secretaries, among others, are prohibited from disclosing to any person, without authorization by the Court, information relating to a pending criminal proceeding that is not part of the public records of the Court.

[Adopted effective July 1991. Amended effective June 12, 2014.]

IOP 11.00.00. COURT REGISTRY

IOP 11.01.00 Authorized Depository Banks.

(a) Whenever attorneys, litigants or any other persons or entities are directed to deposit funds within the interest-bearing Court registry, such funds shall be placed by the Clerk of the Court with the Court-designated depository bank.

(b) The Court-designated depository bank shall comply with all applicable statutes, orders, rules and requirements of the Court.

(c) All funds placed by the Clerk of the Court in the Court-designated depository bank shall earn interest at a competitive market rate negotiated by the Clerk of the Court for similar deposits. However, the Chief Judge may determine from time to time a minimum amount below which funds need not be deposited in an interest-bearing account. Deposits for attorney's fees, costs and expenses required before the issuance of any writs of garnishment are exempt from this requirement and will be placed in a non-interest bearing U.S. Treasury account. At the time of disbursement of funds from the registry, the litigant shall advise the Court as to the proper recipient of any earned interest and prior to the release of funds shall provide the Clerk of the Court's Financial Administrator or other designated deputy clerk with the proper tax number or tax status of the recipient for subsequent reporting to the Internal Revenue Service.

(d) The Clerk of the Court shall assess a user's fee as promulgated by the Judicial Conference of the United States on deposits in the interest-bearing Court registry. Such fees shall be deducted at disbursement and be deposited into a special fund established to reimburse the Judiciary for maintaining registry accounts.

(e) Nothing in this rule shall prevent the Court from granting the motion of interested parties for special arrangements for investment of funds. If such investments are in the name of or assigned to the Clerk of the Court, the account will be subject to the collateral provisions of Treasury Circular 176 (31 C.F.R. § 202) and the requirements of Local Rule 67.1(b) as well as other applicable statutes, orders, rules and requirements of the Court.

[Adopted effective July 1991. Amended effective June 12, 2014.]

ELECTRONIC CASE FILING

CM/ECF ADMINISTRATIVE PROCEDURES

Southern District of Florida

Section 1—INTRODUCTION

1A. Terms.

CM/ECF: the federal judiciary's electronic case filing system known as Case Management/Electronic Case Filing (see our website).

Conventional manner: the method used to file documents that cannot or should not be filed electronically via CM/ECF and must be filed by other means (e.g., in person or by U.S. mail). Conventionally filed documents are hard copies containing an original, handwritten (wet) signature of the filing attorney or pro se party.

Document: shall include pleadings, motions, exhibits, declarations, affidavits, memoranda, papers, orders, notices, and any other Court filing.

Electronic filing: uploading a document directly from a CM/ECF User's computer into CM/ECF, thereby filing the document in the Court's electronic case file. (Sending a document to the Court via e-mail or on diskette does not constitute "electronic filing.")

E-mail address of record: the internet e-mail address of each authorized CM/ECF User or party otherwise authorized to electronically receive Notices of Electronic Filing (e.g., attorneys admitted pro hac vice).

Judge: a United States District Judge or Magistrate Judge for the Southern District of Florida.

Notice of Electronic Filing: a notice generated automatically by CM/ECF upon completion of an electronic filing. The Notice of Electronic Filing, when transmitted to an e-mail address of record in a case, constitutes proof of service.

PACER ("Public Access to Court Electronic Records"): an electronic public access service that allows users to obtain case and docket information. Additional information is available at http://pacer.psc.uscourts.gov.

PDF ("Portable Document Format"): a PDF document allows anyone to open a converted document across a broad range of hardware and software, with layout, format, links, and images intact. PDF is the only document format acceptable for electronic filing in CM/ECF. For information on PDF, CM/ECF Users may wish to visit the websites of PDF vendors.

Procedures: the instant Administrative Procedures for Electronically Filing Documents.

User(s): anyone (including attorneys, the Court, and the Clerk of the Court) who is authorized to use the CM/ECF system in the Southern District of Florida.

1B. The Electronic Record and the Authorization for Electronic Filing.

In 1996, the Southern District of Florida began to convert its paper Court files into an electronic format, while continuing to maintain the paper file as the official record. Though the file was converted to an electronic format once received by the Clerk's Office, the filing itself was still accomplished in the conventional manner, creating parallel paper and electronic records. By 2002, technology had advanced to the point that Administrative Order 2002–36 authorized attorneys in this District to use an optional electronic filing system developed by local staff; however, both electronic and paper records continued to be maintained for all cases.

In 2004, Administrative Order 2004–39 sought to alleviate the fiscal and administrative burdens of maintaining the largely duplicative paper and electronic records created up to that time by establishing that the electronic record would become the official Court record as of October 28, 2004. The Order designated as part of the official record all documents transmitted to the Court in electronic format, as well as documents filed in paper form, then scanned and converted to an electronic image by the Clerk's Office. With the exception of various categories of documents specified, it was ordered that the Clerk's Office cease maintaining as part of the paper case file any document filed after October 27, 2004.

The evolutionary process has continued, and, in conjunction with Federal Rule of Civil Procedure 5(d)(3) and Federal Rule of Criminal Procedure 57, the electronic filing system known as CM/ECF has been designated for use nationwide by the United States Courts.

Section 2—FILER CATEGORIES AND ELIGIBILITY TO FILE ELECTRONICALLY

2A. Attorneys Admitted to Practice in the Southern District of Florida. Electronic filing is mandatory for all attorneys admitted to practice in the Southern District of Florida.

2B. Attorneys Appearing Pro Hac Vice. An attorney who has been permitted to appear pro hac vice will **not** be permitted to register as a User in this District, but may access the electronic record through the PACER System (see Section 7B). All documents, including the motion to appear pro hac vice, must be filed electronically through their local counsel (who must be associated with the case pursuant to Local Rule 4(b) of the Rules Governing the Admission and Practice of Attorneys).

Although attorneys admitted pro hac vice will not be permitted to **file** electronically, they will be able to electronically **receive** Notices of Electronic Filing. Such requests should be included in motions to appear pro hac vice and in the accompanying proposed order. E-mail addresses must be provided in both the motion and proposed order in order to receive electronic notices.

2C. Pro Se Litigants. Pro se litigants will **not** be permitted to register as Users at this time. Pro se litigants must file their documents in the conventional manner. Pro se litigants may access the electronic record at the public counter in the Clerk's Office in all divisions or through PACER. Pro se litigants will be served and noticed by U.S. mail or in person (or, if agreed, by facsimile or e-mail).

Section 3—USER INFORMATION AND RESPONSIBILITIES

3A. General Requirements. All documents shall be filed electronically in CM/ECF except as otherwise provided by these Procedures. E-mailing a document to the Clerk's Office or to a Judge shall **not** constitute "filing" the document. A document shall not be considered "filed" for purposes of the Federal Rules of Civil Procedure until the filing party receives a Notice of Electronic Filing (see Section 3J).

Documents filed electronically must meet the requirements of Federal Rule of Civil Procedure 10 (Form of Pleadings) and Local Rule 5.1 (Filing and Copies), as if they had been submitted on paper. Each Judge will instruct litigants if it is necessary to provide paper copies for the Judge. Documents filed electronically are also subject to any page limitation set forth by Court order or by Local Rule 7.1(c)(2).

3B. Registration. Attorneys admitted to practice in the Southern District of Florida (see the Southern District of Florida's Special Rules Governing the Admission and Practice of Attorneys within the Local Rules) must register to use CM/ECF. Eligible attorneys must register electronically on the Court's website at http://www.flsd.uscourts.gov/?page_ID=21. User logins and passwords will be issued upon registration and completion of training. Registration is free of charge.

A PACER login is required **in addition to** the CM/ECF password and login. To register for PACER, a User must complete the form available on the PACER website at http://pacer.psc.uscourts.gov.

3C. Login and Password. Each User will be issued one login and password. When a User files a document electronically using his/her login and password, that document shall be considered signed by the attorney to whom the login and password were issued for purposes of the Local Rules and Federal Rules of Civil Procedure and Federal Rules of Criminal Procedure, including Rule 11 of the Federal Rules of Civil Procedure. After registering, Users may change their passwords. Users shall be responsible for all documents filed with their passwords, whether by Users or any other person.

No User shall permit his/her password to be used by anyone other than an authorized employee of the User's office. If, at any time, a User believes that his/her password has been compromised, the User must immediately change the password and contact the Help Desk. In such case, the User should also generate a CM/ECF report to identify unauthorized documents that may have been filed under the User's password and to notify the Court of the existence of such documents.

3D. Changes of Address and Contact Information. Users shall maintain current contact information (Local Rule 11.1(g) and Administrative Order 2005–38). Upon the change of a User's e-mail address, mailing address, telephone or fax number, the User shall complete the following whenever such a change occurs:

- Electronically file a Notice of Change of Address in all the User's pending cases;
- Update the User's email address in CM/ECF Maintain User Account; and
- Update the User's mailing address, telephone and fax numbers in CM/ECF Maintain User Account. If the system does not allow the User to update the mailing address, the Attorney Admissions Clerk will update the information upon the filing of a Notice of Change of Address in all the User's pending cases.
- Electronically file a Notice of Removal in all cases in which the attorney is no longer the attorney of record.

Also, parties appearing pro se and counsel appearing pro hac vice must file, in each pending case, a notice of change of mailing address or contact information whenever such a change occurs (Administrative Order 2005–38). If court notices sent via the U.S. mail are returned as undeliverable TWICE in a case, notices will no longer be sent to that party until a current mailing address is provided.

3E. Government Attorneys. Upon request and pursuant to Local Rule 4(d), CM/ECF log-ins/passwords are issued to attorneys employed by government agencies. Upon transfer to different government agencies, Users must notify the Attorney Admissions Clerk and update their U.S. mail and email addresses in order for their logins/passwords to remain valid. Users who leave government agencies and do not transfer to other government agencies must notify the Attorney Admissions Clerk so that their log-ins/passwords may be deactivated. See the Court's website (http://www.flsd.uscourts.gov/?page_ID=582) for additional information regarding Government Attorneys and notifying the Attorney Admissions Clerk.

Users associated with government agencies who leave government practice must already be or become members of the Bar of the Southern District of Florida in order to register for CM/ECF logins/passwords. Click here for information on becoming a member of the Southern District of Florida Bar.

Government agencies must also notify the Attorney Admissions Clerk when Users leave their agencies. A notice of substitution of counsel must be filed in order for a government agency to receive future CM/ECF notices regarding case activity associated with a User who is no longer with their agency.

3F. Changes of Name. Requests for name changes must be made in writing and forwarded to the Attorney Admissions Clerk. In order for the Clerk's Office to process a name change request, the request must be accompanied by a copy of a name change order from the Supreme Court of Florida. In the absence of such an order, a name change request will not be processed and a User must continue to file under the name listed on the roll of attorneys of the Bar of the Southern District of Florida. Further, if the name change order is not submitted, Attorney Admissions may be unable to verify that a User is listed on the roll of attorneys.

3G. Technical Specifications.

(1) *Hardware/Software Generally Required for Electronic Filing.*

- A computer running a Windows or Macintosh operating system;
- Word processing software, such as WordPerfect or Microsoft Word, that can convert documents to PDF without the need for scanning;
- PDF reader software, such as Adobe, which may be obtained free of charge from the Adobe website or the Court's website. Users may find it useful to purchase PDF writer software which has additional features for creating, editing, and saving PDF documents. Various companies market PDF writer software and the cost and features vary. Note: PDF documents must be printable and must not contain water marks or advertising which may be generated as a result of the use of free or trial run PDF conversion software;
- Access to a JavaScript enabled browser; Internet Explorer and Firefox browsers have been tested with CM/ECF (for specific versions that are support, see our CM/ECF FAQ);

- High speed internet access is strongly recommended over dial-up internet service. High-speed service will reduce the amount of time necessary to make entries into CM/ECF and download lengthy documents;
- A scanner is necessary to convert paper documents to text-searchable PDF format. Users should make certain their scanners are configured for 300 dpi and 300 pixels per inch. The color setting should be configured for black and white rather than color scanning; however, if the document being filed contains color images (e.g. JPEG, GIF, PNG), the color setting may be configured for color scanning. The page size must be set at 8 ½ × 11 inches. The scanner must be set to convert scanned documents to text-searchable PDF format.

(2) *Electronic Mailbox.* It is the responsibility of the User to maintain an electronic mailbox of sufficient capacity to receive all documents transmitted electronically to counsel.

(3) *Size Limitation for Any Electronically–Filed Document.* CM/ECF will inform Users if they are attempting to file a document larger than 50 megabytes (50 MB). Any document over this size will be rejected by the system due to its inability to upload/download properly; thus, the document must be saved and transmitted in segments or attachments not exceeding 50 megabytes. Please contact the Help Desk if further instruction is needed.

(4) *Hyperlinks.* Pursuant to the policy set forth in Rule 13 of the Model Local Rules for Electronic Case Filing, endorsed by the Judicial Conference in October 2005, a hyperlink contained in a filing is no more than a convenient mechanism for accessing material cited in a document. A hyperlink reference is extraneous to any filed document and is not part of the Court's record. In order to preserve the integrity of the Court record, Users wishing to insert hyperlinks in Court filings shall continue to use the conventional citation method for the cited authority, in addition to the hyperlink.

(5) *Text Searchable Requirement.* Effective January 1, 2012, court filings made via the CM/ECF system must be in a text searchable format. Filings are text searchable if they are converted to PDF format directly from a word processing program (Microsoft Word, WordPerfect, etc) using Adobe Acrobat or similar software. If documents in paper format are scanned into PDF format, the scanning software must have Optical Character Recognition (OCR) functionality and the option must be turned on (OCR functionality is sometimes referred to as text layering).

3H. Filing Information.

(1) *Date Electronic Document is Filed.* A document will be deemed "filed" on a particular date if uploaded to CM/ECF prior to midnight on that date as evidenced by receipt of the Notice of Electronic Filing, unless otherwise ordered by a Judge.

(2) *Abolishment of the Nightbox Policy.* With the implementation of CM/ECF the Court's nightbox policy, as provided for in Administrative Order 2003–10, will be abolished. Electronic documents will be considered "filed" as stated above in 3G(1). Documents filed in the conventional manner will be considered "filed" on the date they are physically received by the Court.

(3) *Court CM/ECF System Hours and Help Desk Information.* CM/ECF is designed to provide system access 24 hours a day; however, parties are encouraged to file documents in advance of filing deadlines and during normal business hours. Users may access the CM/ECF Help Desk either by telephone, 1–888–318–2260, or in person. The Help Desk will respond to questions regarding the electronic filing system and registration process. Please refer to the Help Desk website for further information.

(4) *Technical Failure of the Court's CM/ECF System.* If CM/ECF is unable to accept electronic filings for a continuous period of approximately one hour during regular business hours, a notice of the system outage/technical failure will be posted on the CM/ECF website and/or on the Court's website (www.flsd.uscourts.gov). Should circumstances prevent posting of an outage notification on either of the Court's website, the notification will be placed on the CM/ECF Help Desk telephone line.

The outage notice will inform Users of the expected duration of the outage and will provide alternative filing instructions if the outage is of such a nature to cause alternative filing to be necessary. Generally, alternative filing instructions will advise Users to file in the conventional manner on the same day. Should Users be instructed to file in the conventional manner, the conventional filing **must** be accompanied by Form A (attached hereto). In the event that conventional filing is required, such filings may be delivered to any courthouse in the District, with the exception of emergency matters. Emergency motions and hearings must be filed conventionally **in the division where the Judge is chambered** (see Section 5F).

In the unlikely event that a technical failure occurs after regular business hours on the day a User's filing is due or a filing is otherwise made untimely as a result of a CM/ECF technical failure, Users may have to seek relief from the Court. Users are cautioned that in some circumstances, the Court lacks the authority to grant an extension of time to file (see e.g., Rule 6(b) of the Federal Rules of Civil Procedure); thus, Users are strongly encouraged to file documents in advance of filing deadlines and during regular business hours.

(5) *Failure of User's System.* Problems with a **User's** hardware, software, or Internet Service Provider will not constitute a technical failure under these Procedures. If a User experiences a technical problem that prevents electronic filing from the User's regular workplace, the User should try to file electronically from other computers in the vicinity that have internet access.

(6) *Availability of CM/ECF Workstations and Scanners at Courthouses.* **[DELETED]**

(7) *Filings May Not Be Submitted on CD, DVD, Cassette, or VHS Tape.* Filings submitted on CD, DVD, cassette or VHS tape (or other multi-media format) will not be accepted for filing, unless they were previously submitted as evidence or unless filed pursuant to Court order.

(8) *Documents Written in Foreign Languages Must Be Accompanied With Translation.* Documents not written in English (i.e., foreign language, braille) must be accompanied by a translation, unless a waiver has been granted by the Court.

(9) *Additional User Information.* Additional information for using CM/ECF can be found on the Court's website at http://www.flsd.uscourts.gov/?page_ID=21.

3I. Filings That Require Special Attention.

(1) *Motions Requesting Leave of the Court to File a Document.* If a document to be filed requires a motion requesting leave of the Court (e.g., an amended complaint, a document to be filed out of time, or a document exceeding the page limitation), the proposed document shall be submitted as a PDF attachment to the motion. If the motion to file the proposed document is granted, the filing party must electronically refile the document.

(2) *Documents that Include Personal Identifiers.* See Section 6 for special requirements for filing documents that contain personal data identifiers.

(3) *Materials Inappropriate for Display or Distribution to the Public, Including Minors.* See Section 6E for restrictions regarding documents containing inappropriate materials, including images (not textual descriptions) depicting sexual acts or excretory acts that could be described as pornography or indecent or vulgar even if not legally obscene.

(4) *Discovery Material.* Only discovery materials authorized by Local Rule 26.1(b) will be accepted by this Court and must be filed electronically.

(5) *Mediation.* A request for the Clerk of Court to appoint a mediator pursuant to Local Rule 16.2(d)(1)(b) shall be submitted electronically as a "Request for Clerk to Appoint Mediator". This request category may be found on the CM/ECF website, under "Civil," "Other Filings," "Mediation Documents." Such a request shall *not* be filed as a motion.

Within seven (7) days following a mediation conference, the mediator, if a User, shall electronically file a Mediation Report. If the mediator is not a User, the mediator shall file the Mediation Report in the conventional manner. The report shall indicate whether all required parties were present and whether the case settled (in full or in part), whether the mediation was adjourned, or whether the mediator declared an impasse.

(6) *Proposed Documents.* In addition to being filed in accordance with these procedures, proposed findings of fact and conclusions of law, jury instructions, and proposed orders, **unless otherwise directed by a Judge**, shall be filed initially as an attachment to a motion, notice, or other filing in PDF format as required for electronic filings; however, the **final version** of the proposed document must be e-mailed to the appropriate Judge at the e-mail address listed below. Users must submit the final version of the proposed document by e-mail in Word format (not in PDF format). The **e-mail subject line** and the **name of the attachment** should include the case number, followed by a short description of the attachment (e.g., 05–cv–20534 Order). All counsel must be copied on the e-mail to the Judge. The final document, if approved by the Court, will be filed with the Clerk of Court.

The following e-mail addresses are to be used **only** to submit documents as described above unless otherwise specifically permitted by the Judge.

District Judges	**Magistrate Judges**
moore@flsd.uscourts.gov	lynch@flsd.uscourts.gov
zloch@flsd.uscourts.gov	turnoff@flsd.uscourts.gov
moreno@flsd.uscourts.gov	snow@flsd.uscourts.gov
ungaro@flsd.uscourts.gov	seltzer@flsd.uscourts.gov
lenard@flsd.uscourts.gov	simonton@flsd.uscourts.gov
middlebrooks@flsd.uscourts.gov	o'sullivan@flsd.uscourts.gov
dimitrouleas@flsd.uscourts.gov	white@flsd.uscourts.gov
marra@flsd.uscourts.gov	hopkins@flsd.uscourts.gov
martinez@flsd.uscourts.gov	torres@flsd.uscourts.gov
altonaga@flsd.uscourts.gov	mcaliley@flsd.uscourts.gov
cooke@flsd.uscourts.gov	goodman@flsd.uscourts.gov
williams@flsd.uscourts.gov	brannon@flsd.uscourts.gov
scola@flsd.uscourts.gov	otazo-reyes@flsd.uscourts.gov
gayles@flsd.uscourts.gov	matthewman@flsd.uscourts.gov
bloom@flsd.uscourts.gov	hunt@flsd.uscourts.gov
rosenberg@flsd.uscourts.gov	valle@flsd.uscourts.gov
king@flsd.uscourts.gov	garber@flsd.uscourts.gov
gonzalez@flsd.uscourts.gov	
graham@flsd.uscourts.gov	
hurley@flsd.uscourts.gov	
seitz@flsd.uscourts.gov	
huck@flsd.uscourts.gov	
cohn@flsd.uscourts.gov	

(7) *Consent to Jurisdiction.* Parties who consent to having a Magistrate Judge conduct civil proceedings may file a Consent to Jurisdiction electronically ***only*** if the consent is signed by *both* parties on the same form. If a party has only one signature—the consent *must* be filed in the conventional manner.

3J. Signatures and Affidavits or Declarations.

(1) *Attorney's Signature Block.* A document filed electronically, requiring an attorney's signature, shall be signed according to the format below. An "s/" signature has the same force and effect as an original signature.

s/Pat T. Lawyer
Pat T. Lawyer (Florida Bar Number: 12345)
Attorney E-mail address: pat_lawyer@law.com
XYZ Law Firm
123 Main Street
Miami, Florida 33128
Telephone: (305) 123–4567
Facsimile: (786) 123–4567
Attorneys for Plaintiff/Defendant [Party Name(s)]

(2) *Documents Requiring Original Signatures.* Documents that require original signatures or that require either verification or a sworn declaration under any rule or statute shall be filed electronically with the originally-executed documents maintained by the filer. The document filed electronically shall indicate a signature (e.g., "s/Jane Doe"). Alternatively, the original signed document may be scanned and electronically filed. The User shall retain the paper document containing the original signature(s) for a period of one year after final resolution of the action, including final disposition of all appeals.

(3) *Stipulations or Other Documents Requiring Two or More Signatures.* In the case of a stipulation or other document to be signed by two or more persons, the filer should: submit a scanned document containing all necessary signatures; or, indicate the consent of the other parties on the document; or, file the document identifying the parties whose signatures are required and submit a notice of endorsement by the other parties no later than three business days after the filing. A model form (Form C) is attached hereto. The filing party or attorney shall retain the paper copy

of the document containing the original signatures for a period of one year after final resolution of the action, including final disposition of all appeals.

(4) *Documents Requiring a Judge's Signature.* Documents requiring a Judge's signature may be signed with "s/" Judge's Name, a digitized signature, or an original signature. An "s/" or digitized signature has the same force and effect as an original signature.

3K. Service of Documents and Notices of Electronic Filing.

(1) *Determining Whether Another Party is a User or Otherwise Authorized to Receive Notices of Electronic Filing.* When a document is filed electronically, CM/ECF will generate a Notice of Electronic Filing to: the filing party; any party who is a User; parties otherwise authorized to receive Notices of Electronic Filing (e.g., pro hac vice attorneys); and, the assigned Judge. To determine whether another party is a User or otherwise authorized to receive Notices of Electronic Filing, the filer should: select "Utilities" from the CM/ECF menu; click on "Mailings"; click on "Mailing Information for a Case"; and, enter the case number. The notification information will appear stating whether the filer must mail a copy to the party or if CM/ECF will issue a Notice of Electronic Filing.

(2) *Notices of Electronic Filing and "One Free Look".* If the recipient is a User or otherwise authorized to electronically receive Notices of Electronic Filing (e.g., a pro hac vice attorney), CM/ECF will produce a Notice of Electronic Filing for that party. The Notice of Electronic Filing will contain a hyperlink to the document in PACER. **Under the conditions set forth in the paragraph below**, recipients of Notices of Electronic Filing will be allowed one "free look" at the document and may view, print, or download it. After the one "free look," normal PACER usage fees apply. The hyperlink to access the document will expire after the earlier of these two events: the first use or 15 days. (**CAUTION**: **double** clicking the hyperlink instead of single clicking it will use up the one "free look.")

Only Users who are listed as **active attorneys** on a particular case, will receive Notices of Electronic Filing (at both their primary and secondary e-mail addresses) that contain hyperlinks allowing them one free look at documents filed in that case. Users who have tagged cases on which they are **not** listed as **active attorneys** but for which they, nevertheless, wish to receive Notices of Electronic Filing, will also receive Notices of Electronic Filing (at both their primary and secondary e-mail addresses) that contain hyperlinks allowing them to view documents filed in the cases tagged. **CAUTION:** Users who are **not** listed as **active attorneys** on cases for which they have chosen to receive Notices of Electronic Filing will **automatically incur PACER charges by clicking on the hyperlink.** Regular PACER usage fees will apply.

(3) *Service and Notice of Electronic Filing for Parties Who Are Not Authorized to Electronically Receive Notices of Electronic Filing.* A party who is not a User or is not otherwise authorized to electronically receive Notices of Electronic Filing is entitled to a paper copy of any electronically-filed document. It is the responsibility of the filing party to provide the party with the electronically-filed document according to the Federal Rules of Civil Procedure. When mailing paper copies of documents that have been electronically filed, the filing party must include the Notice of Electronic Filing to provide the recipient with proof of the filing.

Service of a Notice of Electronic Filing on a party who is not a User or otherwise authorized to electronically receive Notices of Electronic Filing may be accomplished by e-mail, subject to the additional service requirements of Federal Rules of Civil Procedure 6(d) and Federal Rules of Criminal Procedure 49(d).

Parties served by non-electronic means may be entitled to additional time to respond. See Federal Rules of Civil Procedure 6(d), Federal Rules of Criminal Procedure 45(c), and Local Rule 7.1(c)(1)(A). Parties are advised that deadlines to respond automatically calculated in CM/ECF do NOT account for and may not be accurate when service is by mail. Parties may NOT rely on response times calculated in CM/ECF, which are only a general guide, and must calculate response deadlines themselves.

(4) *Certificates of Service.* A certificate of service on all parties entitled to service or notice is still required when a party files a document electronically. The certificate must state the manner in which service or notice was accomplished on each party. A model form (Form B) is attached hereto.

Attorneys should be aware that response and reply deadlines which appear in docket text or deadline queries are for Court use only.

(5) *Notices of Electronic Filing Are Not Sent to Terminated Attorneys.* A User who is terminated as an attorney on a case in the Southern District of Florida will not receive notices regarding future case activity; however, Users will continue to receive NEFs after cases are closed as long as they have not been terminated as attorneys on the closed cases. This affects notices to Users who receive notices electronically and to attorneys who receive notices through the U.S. mail.

Users who want to continue receiving electronic notices in a case after they have been terminated must take the following steps:

- Access the Court's CM/ECF website at http://ecf.flsd.uscourts.gov;
- Under "Utilities", select "Maintain Your Account";
- Select "Email Information";
- Click on the primary e-mail address hyperlink, in the left pane;
- In the right pane, type in the case number in the "Add additional cases for noticing" field;
- Press the [Find This Case] button;
- Once the case number has been located, press the [Add Case(s)] button;
- Select the [Return to Person Information Screen] button;
- Press [Submit].

Users who no longer want to continue receiving electronic notices in cases where the parties they represent have been terminated, must take the following steps:

- Contact the CM/ECF Help Desk at 1–888–318–2260;
- Provide the name of the party represented and the date they were terminated from the case;
- Request termination of electronic noticing in that case.

Attorneys may also track the status of cases through PACER.

3L. Docket Entries.

(1) *Making a Docket Entry.* The party filing a document electronically shall be responsible for designating a docket entry title for the document by using one of the docket event categories prescribed by the Court. A user may view the selection of a docket event category categories by: accessing the Court's website at www.flsd.uscourts.gov; clicking on the "CM/ECF tab"; selecting "User Information"; and then selecting "Civil Event List" or "Criminal Event List." website link; and then clicking on "CM/ECF Civil and Criminal Menus for Attorneys."

(2) *Describing an Attachment to a Docket Entry.* A party filing an attachment to a document shall select one of the prescribed attachment categories from the drop-down menu (e.g., affidavit, transcript), provide an alphabetical or numerical designation (e.g., Exhibit A, Exhibit 1), and descriptively name each attachment (e.g., Exhibit 1—Affidavit of Boo Radley) in a manner that enables the Court to easily locate and distinguish attachments. The following is illustrative:

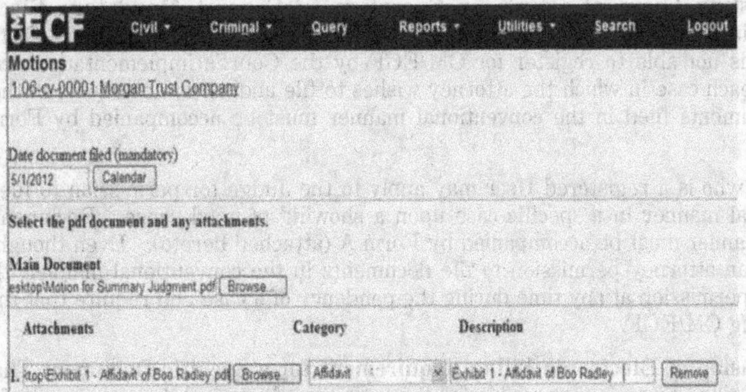

(3) *Correcting a Docket Entry.* CM/ECF will not permit the filing party to make changes to a document or docket entry once the transaction has been accepted. A document filed incorrectly may

be the result of posting the wrong PDF file to a docket entry, selecting the wrong document type from the menu, or entering the wrong case number and not catching the error before the transaction is completed.

If a User makes an error during the filing process, the User should contact the CM/ECF Help Desk, 1–888–318–2260, as soon as possible with the case number and document number for which the correction is being requested. If appropriate, the Clerk's Office will make an entry indicating the document was filed in error. The filing party will be advised if the document needs to be re-filed.

If an error is discovered by the Clerk's Office during the quality control process, the Clerk's Office will docket a "Notice of Instructions to Filer" informing the filer of the error and the manner in which to proceed. The Clerk's Office will not strike or delete attorney entries, unless directed to do so by the Court.

3M. Retention of Original Documents by Users. Original documents that require scanning in order to be filed electronically must be retained by the filing party or attorney for a period of one year after final resolution of the action, including final disposition of all appeals.

3N. Electronic Submission of Exhibits. Most exhibits must be submitted in CM/ECF electronically within three (3) days of the close of trial or proceeding, unless otherwise ordered by the presiding Judge.

Summary of General Directions Re Filing Exhibits in CM/ECF

	Documentary Exhibits	Sealed Exhibits	Non–Documentary Exhibits, e.g. Contraband, Guns, Oversized	Audio/Video Recordings
Civil	Electronic	Electronic*	Electronically file photograph	Conventionally file copy on CD, DVD
Criminal	Electronic	Conventional	Electronically file photograph	Conventionally file copy on CD, DVD

* *Only use sealed events; conventionally file if entire case is sealed*

Source: Administrative Order 2016–70 posted on the Court's website under General Information/Administrative Orders. For additional information, refer to the "Quick Reference Guide to Electronically Filing Trial Exhibits" which can be found on the Court's website under CM/ECF Policies and Procedures.

Section 4—EXCEPTIONS TO MANDATORY ELECTRONIC FILING REQUIREMENT

4A. Requesting Leave of Court for Exception to General Mandatory Electronic Filing Requirement in a Specific Case. An attorney who is a member of the Southern District of Florida Bar, and who is not able to register for CM/ECF by the Court's implementation date, must show good cause in each case in which the attorney wishes to file and serve documents in the conventional manner. Documents filed in the conventional manner must be accompanied by Form A (attached hereto).

An attorney who is a registered User may apply to the Judge for permission to file documents in the conventional manner in a specific case upon a showing of good cause. Documents filed in the conventional manner must be accompanied by Form A (attached hereto). Even though a Judge may initially grant an attorney permission to file documents in the conventional manner, the Judge may withdraw that permission at any time during the pendency of a case and require that the attorney file documents using CM/ECF.

4B. Suspension of Electronic Filing Requirement for a Specific Document That Cannot Be Scanned. The filing party is responsible for the legibility of scanned documents. If, for any reason, a document cannot be easily read after scanning, the filing party should not electronically file the document. Instead, the filing party must conventionally file the document with the Clerk's Office along with Form A (attached hereto). (For a listing of categories of documents that **can never** be filed electronically, see Section 5 below.)

Section 5—DOCUMENTS THAT CANNOT BE FILED ELECTRONICALLY

5A. Cases Filed Under Seal and Sealed Documents in Criminal Cases. Effective December 1, 2015, attorneys authorized to file electronically in the CM/ECF system must file sealed documents electronically via CM/ECF in civil cases that are otherwise open to the public (See Section 9). If the entire civil case is sealed, the initial complaint or other initiating document as well as subsequent sealed filings must continue to be filed conventionally. Attorneys are prohibited from filing sealed documents in criminal actions electronically. Sealed documents in criminal actions shall be filed in the conventional paper format accompanied by a motion to seal as described in Local Rule 5.4. In criminal actions, motions to seal documents previously filed and on the docket must also be filed conventionally. Motions to unseal documents in criminal actions or criminal cases must be filed conventionally and must not be filed electronically.

Documents filed under seal will *not* be available for inspection by case participants or the public. Litigants must serve a notice of filing upon all other parties by conventional means and must file such notice with the sealed document. For complete procedures for filing under seal, see Local Rule 5.4.

5B. Documents Related to Habeas Cases. [Deleted]

5C. Civil Complaints Filed by Pro Se Litigants. *Pro se* litigants must file all documents, including new civil complaints and other civil case initiating documents, in the conventional manner. Complaints filed by attorneys are subject to Administrative Order 2009–36, which requires the electronic filing of new civil complaints or other civil case initiating documents via the CM/ECF system (See Section 8).

A complaint or other initiating documents filed in the conventional manner may be sent through the U.S. mail or personally delivered to the Clerk's Office. It must be accompanied by a civil cover sheet (JS44) and either the required filing fee or Application to Proceed in District Court Without Paying Fees or Costs. (Filing fees are payable by cash, check, money order, or credit card.) The Clerk's Office will scan paper complaints and cover sheets and upload them to CM/ECF. For additional filing requirements, see the Civil Case Filing Requirements.

A complaint filed conventionally will be considered filed on the same day it is received if such filing is in compliance with the Local Rules and these Procedures. A complaint filed conventionally and received before 2:00 p.m. will normally be available for viewing on CM/ECF (PACER) the same day while those received between 2:00 p.m. and close of business will normally be available for viewing in CM/ECF (PACER) no later than 12:00 noon on the next business day.

5D. Criminal Matters.

(1) *Criminal Complaints.* Criminal complaints must be presented in paper form by the U.S. Attorney's Office to the Duty Magistrate Judge. The Clerk's Office will scan the complaint, open the case and upload the PDF to CM/ECF.

(2) *Indictments.* Indictments will be presented by the U.S. Attorney's Office in paper form during the Grand Jury return. The Clerk's Office will then scan the documents, open the criminal case, and upload the PDF to CM/ECF.

(3) *Criminal Information.* Criminal information that initiates a case must be filed in the conventional manner by the U.S. Attorney's Office.

(4) *Plea Agreements.* Fully executed plea agreements must be filed in the conventional manner.

(5) *Filing and Uploading of Criminal Matters—Time and Date.* New criminal matters are deemed filed the day the Clerk's Office receives the initiating document. The U.S. Attorney's Office will be notified electronically when a new case has been opened and a number and Judge assigned. New criminal complaints/cases received before 2:00 p.m. will normally be available for viewing on CM/ECF the same day while those received between 2:00 p.m. and close of business, will normally be available for viewing on CM/ECF no later than 12:00 noon the next business day.

5E. Emergency Motions/Requests for Emergency Hearing. [DELETED—See Section 10]

5F. Summonses Filed by Pro Se Litigants. Summonses are available on the Court's website in the "Forms" section. Pro se litigants must file all documents, including summonses, in the conventional manner. Summonses filed by attorneys are subject to Administrative Order 2009–36 which requires the electronic filing of new civil complaints or other civil case initiating documents via the CM/ECF system (See Section 8). A pro se party requesting the summons must complete the top portion of the summons form and forward the summons to the Clerk's Office in the conventional manner. If sending the summons by U.S. mail, the pro se party must also submit a stamped, self-addressed envelope. The Clerk's Office will issue the summons, make an entry on the Court docket indicating that a summons was issued, and return the issued summons to the requesting party for service in person or by U.S. mail.

5G. Surety Bonds. The Clerk of Court must maintain the original surety bond with the original power of attorney for bonds attached in the Court file until such time as a Judge orders that it be returned to the filing party.

5H. Proposed Trial Exhibits. [DELETED]

5I. Materials Inappropriate for Display or Distribution to the Public, Including Minors. See Section 6E for restrictions regarding documents containing inappropriate materials, including images (not textual descriptions) depicting sexual acts or excretory acts that could be described as pornography or indecent or vulgar even if not legally obscene.

5J. Motion to Appear Pro Hac Vice. [DELETED]

5K. Ex Parte Filings in Criminal Actions. Ex parte filings in criminal actions must be filed conventionally in conformity with Local Rule 5.4. (Note: ex parte filings in civil actions must be filed electronically pursuant to Section 9). At the time of filing, ex parte filings will appear on the docket as "restricted" with electronic access limited to the Court, but will thereafter be treated in the manner set forth in Local Rule 5.4.

Section 6—REDACTION OF PERSONAL INFORMATION, PRIVACY POLICY, AND INAPPROPRIATE MATERIALS

6A. Filing Documents Containing Personal Data Identifiers. Filers must exclude or redact personal information from documents filed with the Court as required by Federal Rule of Criminal Procedure 49.1 and Federal Rule of Civil Procedure 5.2. Unless specifically exempted by the rules or by court order, the personal data identifiers noted below must be redacted to show **only** the following: **Social Security number**: last four digits only; **taxpayer ID number**: last four digits only; **financial account numbers**: last four digits only; **date of birth**: year only; **minor's name:** initials only; **home address:** city and state only (for criminal cases only). Consult the applicable rules for complete instructions on redaction.

6B. Internet Availability of Unprotected Personal Information. It must be remembered that any personal information not otherwise protected will be made available over the internet via PACER. Thus, filers should *exercise caution* when filing documents that contain the following:

- Personal identifying numbers, such as a driver's license number;
- Medical records, including treatment and diagnosis records;
- Employment history;
- Individual financial information;
- Proprietary or trade secret information;
- Information regarding the individual's cooperation with the government;
- Information regarding the victim of any criminal activity;
- National security information;
- Sensitive security information as described in 49 USC § 114(s); and
- Other data as permitted by order of the Court.

Counsel is strongly urged to share this information with all clients so that an informed decision about the inclusion, redaction, and/or exclusion of certain materials may be made. It is the **sole responsibility of counsel and the parties** to ensure the redaction of personal identifiers. The Clerk's Office **will not** review any document for redaction purposes. **SPECIAL NOTICE:** It is the filing party's responsibility to provide the U.S. Attorney's Office with the social security number of the plaintiff upon the filing of a new social security case.

6C. Certain Documents in Criminal Cases Not Accessible to the Public. Pursuant to the Judicial Conference Policy on Privacy and Public Access to Electronic Case Files, [Click here] certain documents in criminal cases shall not be included in the public case file and should not be made available to the public at the courthouse or via remote electronic access.

6D. Redaction of Electronic Transcripts of Court Proceedings. Filers are responsible for redacting personal data identifiers from transcripts of court proceedings filed with the Court as required by the Judicial Conference Policy on Privacy and Public Access to Electronic Case Files [Click here] and Administrative Order 2008–31 of the Southern District of Florida [Click here].

6E. Filing of Materials, Including Images, Inappropriate for Display or Distribution to the Public, Including Minors. Pursuant to Administrative Order 2007–50, Users shall not electronically file materials which would otherwise be inappropriate for display or distribution to the public, including minors, through PACER or the CM/ECF System. These inappropriate materials include images (not textual descriptions) depicting sexual acts or excretory acts that could be described as pornography or indecent or vulgar even if not legally obscene. A document containing such visual materials may only be filed electronically in a redacted version describing in words the images, but removing all images. Alternatively, such documents may be filed in the conventional manner, along with a motion to seal. Counsel and parties are cautioned that failure to protect such images from public dissemination, which includes minors, may subject them to the disciplinary authority of the Court.

Section 7—PUBLIC ACCESS TO THE ELECTRONIC RECORD

7A. Access at the Courthouse. The electronic docket and documents in CM/ECF can be viewed by the public at no charge at the Clerk's Office during regular business hours. A copy fee for an electronic reproduction is required in accordance with 28 U.S.C. § 1930.

7B. Access to Pacer Via the Internet. Remote electronic access to CM/ECF for viewing and printing purposes is available only to PACER system subscribers. A fee will be charged to access any document on the PACER system. Trial and hearing transcripts are not available on PACER at this time and may only be obtained from court reporters. Please refer to the PACER website at www.pacer.psc.uscourts.gov for further information.

7C. Certified Documents. Documents available in PACER are only copies of the Court record. Certified copies are only available through the Clerk's Office.

Section 8—ELECTRONIC FILING OF NEW CIVIL COMPLAINTS

8A. Electronic Filing Civil Complaints or Case Initiating Documents. Pursuant to Administrative Order 2009–36, as of April 5, 2010, attorneys authorized to electronically file in the CM/ECF system must electronically file new civil complaints or other civil case initiating documents via the CM/ECF system. Pro se litigants must continue to file all documents, including new civil complaints and other civil case initiating documents, in the conventional manner.

Any new civil complaint or other civil case initiating document that is to be automatically *sealed* by statute or operation of law, or that is accompanied by a motion or other request to seal the civil case in its entirety, *must be filed conventionally* and must not be filed electronically.

8B. Electronically Filed Civil Complaints—Filing Date. New civil complaints and other civil case initiating documents filed electronically will be deemed filed on a particular date if electronically received prior to midnight on that date and if the filings are in compliance with the Local Rules and these Procedures. New civil cases received electronically on or before 2:00 p.m. during business days will normally be available for viewing on CM/ECF (PACER) the same day. New civil cases electronically filed after 2:00 p.m. on business days, or on weekends or holidays will normally be available for viewing on CM/ECF (PACER) no later than 12:00 noon on the next business day. Until the case opening process is completed, new civil case filings will not be accessible to the public in CM/ECF (PACER). Attorneys electronically filing new civil complaints or other civil case initiating documents are responsible for complying with the instructions posted on the Court's website at http://www.flsd.uscourts.gov/?page_ID=21. Failure to attach the appropriate documents, submit the appropriate filing fees, and comply with such instructions will delay the case opening process until the appropriate remedial action is taken.

8C. Filing Fees Processed Using Pay.gov. The filing fees for new civil complaints, other civil case initiating documents, motions to appear pro hac vice, and other documents that require a filing fee and are filed electronically by Users will be processed using "Pay.gov", a secure government-wide collection portal. Through "Pay.gov," filers may pay the applicable filing fees with a credit card, debit card, or electronic debit from a checking or savings account. Please refer to the Court's website at http://www.flsd.uscourts.gov/?page_ID=21 for additional information regarding "Pay.gov" and Filing Instructions for the Southern District of Florida.

Section 9—ELECTRONIC FILING OF SEALED AND EX PARTE DOCUMENTS IN CIVIL MATTERS

9A. Electronic Filing of Motions to Seal and Proposed Orders. Effective December 1, 2015, attorneys authorized to file electronically in the CM/ECF system must file sealed documents electronically in cases otherwise open to the public and civil ex parte matters.

Attorneys must upload motions to seal and the proposed order via CM/ECF using the "Motion to Seal" (public) event. Notices of Electronic Filing will be sent to CM/ECF users. Attorneys must continue to provide service to pro se parties and other non-ECF users.

If the motion to seal is denied, the Clerk's Office will process the matter as directed by the Court (*e.g.*, replace the image of the proposed sealed filing with an image indicating the document has been replaced pursuant to Court order denying the motion to seal).

Attorneys requesting to file a motion to seal such that the motion itself will be "under seal" must file the request as a motion to seal and the proposed motion to seal (which will itself be sealed) must be filed as a proposed sealed document as instructed below.

In instances where the entire civil case is sealed, the initial complaint or other initiating document as well as subsequent sealed filings must continue to be filed conventionally (See Section 5).

9B. Proposed Sealed Filings and Subsequent Sealed Documents. Attorneys must file electronically proposed sealed filings separate from the motion to seal (which is public record), using "Sealed Motion or Sealed Document" events in CM/ECF. Attorneys also must electronically file any subsequent sealed filings required by Court order and motions to unseal using the "Sealed Motion or Sealed Document" events in CM/ECF. When uploading sealed documents, attorneys must indicate the authority under which the documents are being filed under seal (*e.g.*, Local Rule 5.4(b), sealed per previously entered protective order, or other Court order), and the date and docket entry number of any applicable order.

Attorneys will not have access to their sealed filings via PACER. Attorneys must complete any required service of a sealed document conventionally, indicating the corresponding docket entry number of the sealed document. Service of sealed filings is not completed via CM/ECF. The public docket will reflect that a restricted/sealed document has been filed.

If a sealed document is erroneously filed as a public document, attorneys must immediately call the CM/ECF Help Desk (1–888–318–2260).

9C. Ex Parte Filings. Attorneys must file electronically ex parte motions and proposed orders in civil cases using the "Ex parte Document or Ex parte Motion" events in CM/ECF. Ex parte filings will be restricted from public view unless otherwise directed by the Court. The public docket will reflect that a restricted document has been filed.

9D. Summary of Electronic Filing Requirement for Attorneys. The following is a summary of the electronic filing requirements for sealed, ex parte, and emergency matters. When filing sealed or ex parte matters electronically, attorneys must be certain to use the correct CM/ECF events. Otherwise the filing may be subject to public view rather than restricted. Please contact the CM/ECF Help Desk (1–888–318–2260) if there is any question about which CM/ECF event to use.

	Sealed Filings	**Ex Parte Filings**	**Emergency Matters**
Civil	Electronic*	Electronic	Electronic
Criminal	Conventional	Conventional	Electronic (unless also sealed or ex parte)

* *If the entire case is sealed, civil sealed filings must be conventionally filed.*

Section 10—EMERGENCY MOTIONS/REQUESTS FOR EMERGENCY HEARINGS

10A. Electronic Filing of Emergency Matters.

(1) *Emergency Motion/Certification of Emergency.* Effective December 1, 2015, attorneys authorized to file electronically in the CM/ECF system must file emergency matters electronically.

Emergency matters in criminal cases that are also ex parte or sealed must be conventionally filed. A party appearing pro se must continue to file emergency matters conventionally.

Attorneys must file emergency motions electronically in CM/ECF using the event "Emergency Motion/Certification of Emergency" (which will be accessible to the public on the docket). Notices of Electronic Filing will be sent to CM/ECF users. Attorneys must continue to provide service to pro se parties and other non-CM/ECF users. Filers must certify that the matter is a true emergency. Motions are not considered emergencies if the urgency arises due to the attorney's or party's own dilatory conduct. A Certification of Emergency form must be signed and filed as an attachment to the emergency motion in CM/ECF.

If the filer believes that the matter is an emergency that cannot wait until the assigned District Judge returns, a signed and docketed Certification of Emergency authorizes the Clerk's Office to assign temporarily the emergency matter to another Judge if the assigned Judge is not available.

(2) *Attorneys Must Contact The Clerk's Office.* If an emergency matter is being docketed during business hours, the attorney **must** immediately contact the CM/ECF Help Desk via telephone (1–888–318–2260) to alert the Clerk's Office that an Emergency Motion/Certification of Emergency has been docketed in CM/ECF.

The Clerk's Office will contact the chambers of the District Judge assigned to the case and verify that the Judge is aware of the emergency matter. If a signed Certification of Emergency is not on the docket, the Clerk's Office will bring the matter to the Judge's attention.

If an emergency matter must be filed after hours, the filer must contact the Clerk's Office for instruction. (Refer to the Court's website for additional information.)

(3) *Assigned Judge Unavailable.* If the District Judge assigned to the case is unavailable, the Clerk's Office will verify that a signed Certification of Emergency has been docketed. If a signed Certification of Emergency is on the docket, the Clerk's Office will assign the matter to another Judge from the emergency assignment wheel and contact that chambers to ensure that the Judge is aware of the emergency matter. The Clerk's Office will docket the "Certification of Emergency/Clerk's Notice of Assignment Due to Judge Unavailability" in CM/ECF.

If a signed Certification of Emergency is not on the docket, the Clerk's Office will contact the filer and docket a Clerk's Notice of Non–Compliance. The emergency matter will not be processed until the filer has signed and docketed a Certification of Emergency.

10B. Conventional Filing of Emergency Matters in Criminal Actions that are also Ex Parte or Sealed and by Pro Se Parties.

(1) *Emergency Motion/Certification of Emergency.* Emergency motions in criminal cases that are also ex parte or sealed must be conventionally filed. A party appearing pro se must file emergency motions conventionally. When the emergency motion is filed, a signed Certification of Emergency must also be filed. (The form can be found on the Court's website at http://www.flsd.uscourts.gov). If the filer believes that the matter is an emergency that cannot wait until the assigned District Judge returns, a signed Certification of Emergency authorizes the Clerk's Office to temporarily assign the emergency matter to another Judge if the assigned Judge is not available. The Clerk's Office will docket the Emergency Motion/Certification of Emergency.

The Clerk's Office will contact the chambers of the District Judge assigned to the case to determine how the emergency matter should be handled. If the Certification of Emergency was not filed, the Clerk's Office will notify chambers. If an emergency matter must be filed after hours, refer to the Court's website for contact information. Additional instructions will be provided to filers via telephone.

(2) *Assigned Judge Unavailable.* If the District Judge assigned to the case is unavailable, the Clerk's Office will verify that a signed Certification of Emergency has been filed. If a signed Certification of Emergency has been filed, the Clerk's Office will assign another Judge from the emergency assignment wheel and contact that chambers to ensure that the Judge is aware of the emergency matter. The Clerk's Office will docket the "Certification of Emergency/Clerk's Notice of Assignment Due to Judge Unavailability" in CM/ECF.

If a signed Certification of Emergency is not on the docket, the Clerk's Office will contact the filer. The emergency matter will not be processed until the filer has filed a signed Certification of Emergency.

10C. Summary of Electronic Filing Requirement for Attorneys. The following is a summary of the electronic filing requirements for sealed, ex parte, and emergency matters. When filing sealed or ex parte matters electronically, attorneys must be certain to use the correct CM/ECF events. Otherwise the filing may be subject to public view rather than restricted. Please contact the CM/ECF Help Desk (1–888–318–2260) if there is any question about which CM/ECF event to use.

	Sealed Filings	Ex Parte Filings	Emergency Matters
Civil	Electronic*	Electronic	Electronic
Criminal	Conventional	Conventional	Electronic (unless also sealed or ex parte)

****If the entire case is sealed, civil sealed filings must be conventionally filed.***

FORM A

UNITED STATES DISTRICT COURT
SOUTHERN DISTRICT OF FLORIDA

Case No. ___ Civ or CR–(USDJ's last name/USMJ's last name)

A. B.
Plaintiff(s),

vs

C.D.
Defendant(s). /

NOTICE OF CONVENTIONAL FILING

Please take notice that the foregoing [name of document] is being filed conventionally for the following reason:

☐ A Court Order (copy attached).

☐ It cannot be converted to an electronic format.

☐ A technical failure of the Court's CM/ECF website on date .

Respectfully submitted,
s/[Name of Password Registrant]
(Florida Bar Number)
Attorney E-mail address: xxx@xxx.xxx
Firm Name
Street Address
City, State, Zip Code
Telephone: (xxx) xxx-xxxx
Facsimile: (xxx) xxx-xxxx
Attorneys for Plaintiff/Defendant [Party Name(s)]

FORM B

(1" from top of page, and centered, begin title of Court)
UNITED STATES DISTRICT COURT
SOUTHERN DISTRICT OF FLORIDA
Case No. ________ –Civ or Cr–(USDJ's last name/USMJ's last name)

A.B.,
Plaintiffvs.
C.D.,
Defendant.
____________________________________/

TITLE OF DOCUMENT

Dated: Month, day, year Respectfully submitted,

____
Attorney Name (Bar Number)
Attorney E-mail Address
Firm Name
Street Address
City, State, Zip Code
Telephone: (xxx)xxx–xxxx
Facsimile: (xxx)xxx–xxxx
Attorneys for Plaintiff/Defendant [Party Name(s)]

Certificate of Service

I hereby certify that a true and correct copy of the foregoing was served by [specify method of service] on [date] on all counsel or parties of record on the Service List below.

____
Attorney Name

SERVICE LIST

Attorney Name
Attorney E-mail Address
Firm Name
Street Address
City, State, Zip Code
Telephone: (xxx)xxx–xxxx
Facsimile: (xxx)xxx–xxxx
Attorneys for Plaintiff/Defendant
[Party's Name(s)]

Attorney Name
Attorney E-mail Address
Firm Name
Street Address
City, State, Zip Code
Telephone: (xxx)xxx–xxxx
Facsimile: (xxx)xxx–xxxx
Attorneys for Plaintiff/Defendant
[Party's Name(s)]

FORM C

UNITED STATES DISTRICT COURT
SOUTHERN DISTRICT OF FLORIDA

Case No. ___ Civ or CR–(District/Magistrate Judges' Last Name)

A,B.

Plaintiff,

v.

C.D.,

Defendant.

____________________/

NOTICE OF ENDORSEMENT

Pursuant to the CM/ECF Administrative Procedures, I, , hereby certify that my original signature was placed on the following document which was electronically filed on ______.

___ Joint Proposed Scheduling Order

___ Stipulation of Dismissal

___ Joint Motion

Other: ____

On behalf of __________.

Respectfully submitted,

s/[Name of Password Registrant] (Florida Bar Number)
Attorney E-mail address: xxx@xxx.xxx
Firm Name
Street Address
City, State, Zip Code
Telephone: (xxx) xxx-xxxx
Facsimile: (xxx) xxx-xxxx
Attorneys for Plaintiff/Defendant [Party Name(s)]

Summary of Changes to the Administrative Procedures

Change Date: December 1, 2016

Section 3G(3) Size Limitation for Any Electronically–Filed Document

Modified to reflect the size limitation for electronically-filed documents has been increased from 10 megabytes (MB) to 50 megabytes (MB).

Section 3I(6) Proposed Documents

The list of email addresses used to submit proposed documents was modified to remove the email address for Senior U.S. District Judge Kenneth L. Ryskamp who retired from the U.S. Court.

Section 3K(2) Service of Documents and Notice of Electronic Filing

Modified to remove language that Notice of Electronic Filing is equivalent to service by U.S. mail pursuant to revisions to FRCP 6(d) which no longer provides three (3) additional days for service by electronic means.

Section 3K(3) Service and Notice of Electronic Filing for Parties Who Are Not Authorized to Electronically Receive Notices of Electronic Filing

Modified to indicate that parties served by non-electronic means may be entitled to additional time to respond. This reflects amendments to the federal and local rules. Also modified to clarify that parties are not to rely on response deadlines calculated in CM/ECF which are only a general guide.

Section 3N: Electronic Submission of Exhibits

New section added to reflect new policy that most exhibits must be electronically filed within three (3) days of the conclusion of any trial or proceeding, unless otherwise ordered by the presiding Judge, pursuant to Administrative Order 2016–70.

Section 5H: Proposed Trial Exhibits

Section deleted as trial exhibits must now be electronically filed with the Court. See Section 3N.

Change Date: December 1, 2015

Section 2B Attorneys Appearing Pro Hac Vice

Modified to reflect that motions to appear pro hac vice must be filed electronically by local counsel and the filing fee must be paid electronically via pay.gov.

Section 3(I)(5) Mediation

Modified to reflect mediation reports must be filed within 7 days following a mediation conference, consistent with Local Rule 16.2(f)(1).

Section 3(J)(4) Documents Requiring a Judge's Signature

Modified to reflect that digitized signatures also have the same force and effect as an original signature.

Section 5A Cases Filed Under Seal and Sealed Documents in Criminal Cases

Modified to reflect that attorneys must file electronically sealed documents in civil cases that are otherwise open to the public, as outlined in Section 9. However, if the entire civil case is sealed, documents must continue to be filed conventionally. In addition, sealed documents in criminal actions must be filed conventionally.

Section 5E Emergency Motions/Requests for Emergency Hearings

Deleted from Section 5 "Documents That Cannot Be Filed Electronically". Attorneys must file emergency matters electronically. However, emergency matters in criminal cases that are also ex parte or sealed must be filed conventionally. See Section 10 for additional information.

Section 5J Motion to Appear Pro Hac Vice

Deleted from Section 5 "Documents That Cannnot Be Filed Electronically". Motions to appear pro hac vice must be filed electronically through local counsel. See Section 2B.

Section 5K Ex Parte Filings in Criminal Actions

Modified to reflect that ex parte filings in criminal actions must continue to be filed conventionally. However, ex parte filings in civil cases must be filed electronically as outlined in Section 9.

Section 8C Filing Fees Processed via Pay.gov

Modified to reflect that filing fees for documents filed electronically, including motions to appear pro hac vice, must be paid via "pay.gov."

Section 9 Electronic Filing of Civil Sealed Documents and Civil Ex Parte Documents

New section added to reflect the new policy that requires attorneys to file electronically sealed documents in civil cases that are otherwise open to the public, as well as ex parte documents in civil cases. Additional instruction provided regarding the filing of sealed matters.

Section 10 Emergency Motions/Requests for Emergency Hearings

New section added to reflect new policy requiring attorneys to file emergency matters electronically. However, emergency matters in criminal cases that are also sealed or ex parte must continue to be filed conventionally. Additional instruction provided regarding the filing of emergency matters.

Change Date: December 1, 2014

Section 5K Ex parte Filings

Modified to indicate that at the time of filing, *ex parte* filings will appear on the docket as "restricted" with electronic access limited to the Court, but will thereafter be treated in the manner set forth in Local Rule 5.4.

Section 3I(6) Proposed Documents

The list of email addresses used to submit proposed documents was modified to add email addresses for the recently appointed U.S. District Judge Darrin P. Gayles, U.S. District Judge Beth Bloom, and U.S. District Judge Robin L. Rosenberg. In addition, email addresses were removed for Judge Robin S. Rosenbaum due to her elevation to the Eleventh Circuit Court of Appeals, for U.S. Senior District Judge William M. Hoeveler due to his retirement, and for U.S. Senior District Judge Alan S. Gold due to the closure of his chambers.

Change Date: December 3, 2013

Section 1A Terms

The term "conventional manner" in Section IA was modified to clarify that documents filed in the conventional matter must contain an original, handwritten (wet) signature.

Section 3H Filing Information

Section 3H(5) "Failure of User's System" was modified by removing the reference to CM/ECF workstations/scanners being available to Users at Courthouse locations.

Section 3H(6) "Availability of CM/ECF Workstations and Scanners at Courthouses" was deleted. CM/ECF workstations and scanners are no longer available to Users at Courthouse locations. (Note: Public Terminals to query are still available at Courthouse locations.)

Section 3I(6) Proposed Documents

Section 3I(6) was modified to reflect a policy change adopted by the Court that final versions of proposed documents must be submitted in Word format only, and may no longer be submitted in Word Perfect format.

In addition, the list of email addresses used to submit proposed documents was modified to remove the email addresses for U.S. Magistrate Judge Ted E. Bandstra and U.S. Magistrate Judge Robert L. Dube who retired from the District Court. The list was also modified to add email addresses for the recently appointed U.S. Magistrate Judge Patrick M. Hunt and U.S. Magistrate Judge Alicia O. Valle.

Section 5A Documents and Cases Filed Under Seal

Modified to remove the requirement that sealed documents and motions to seal be accompanied by a sealed document tracking form and copies for Judges pursuant to modifications to Local Rule 5.4.

Section 5C Civil Complaints Filed by Pro Se Litigants

Section 5C was modified to replace "Motions to Proceed Informa Pauperis" with "Application to Proceed in District Court Without Paying Fees or Costs", to reflect current language in Local Rules.

Section 5H Proposed Trial Exhibits

Clarified language to reflect "proposed" exhibits offered at trial.

Change Date: December 1, 2012

Section 3H(7) Filings May Not be Submitted on CD, DVD, Cassette, or VHS Tape

Added to reflect the new policy adopted by the Court in February 2012.

Section 3H(8) Documents Written in Foreign Languages Must be Accompanied with Translation

Added to reflect the new policy adopted by the Court in February 2012.

Section 3H (9) Additional User Information

Section number changed from number 7 to 9 to adjust for the above new policies.

Section 3I(6) Proposed Documents

The list of email addresses used to submit proposed documents was modified to remove the email addresses for (1) U.S. District Judge Alberto Jordan who was elevated to the Eleventh Circuit Court of Appeals; (2) U.S. Magistrate Judge Stephen T. Brown who retired from the District Court; (3) U.S. Magistrate Judge Linnea R. Johnson who retired from the District Court; and (4) U.S.

Magistrate Judge Ann E. Vituanc who retired from the District Court. In addition, the email address for U.S. District Judge Robin S. Rosenbaum was moved to the District Judge list to reflect her recent appointment as a District Judge (her email address remains the same).

The list was also modified to add email addresses for the recently appointed U.S. Magistrate Judge Dave Lee Brannon, U.S. Magistrate Judge Alicia M. Otazo–Reyes, and U.S. Magistrate Judge William Matthewman.

Section 3L Docket Entries

Subsection (1) modified to clarify location of docket event categories on the Court's website. Subsection (2) added to provide instructions on describing an attachment to a docket entry. Subsection (3) numbering changed from 2 to 3 in relation to the above changes.

Section 5E Emergency Motions\Requests for Emergency Hearing

Modified to indicate that filers should refer to the Court's website for contact information if emergency matters must be filed after-hours.

Change Date: December 13, 2011

Section 3G(3) Size Limitation for Any Electronically–Filed Document

Modified to reflect the size limitation for documents filed in CM/ECF will increase from 5 MB to 10 MB, effective January 1, 2012.

Change Date: December 1, 2011

Section 3G(1) Hardware/Software Generally Required for Electronic Filing

Modified to refer Users to Court's website for specific versions of Internet Explorer and Firefox which are supported by CM/ECF. Also modified to indicate page size "must" be set at 8 ½ × 11 inches and scanners must be set to convert scanned documents to text-searchable PDF format.

Section 3G(5) Text Searchable Requirement

Section added to reflect that effective January 1, 2012, filings made via the CM/ECF system must be in text-searchable format.

Section 3I(6) Proposed Documents

Modified to clarify proposed orders must be submitted as an attachment to a motion, notice, or other filing "in PDF format"; however the final version of the proposed document must be emailed to the designated email address for the Judge in WordPerfect or Word format and "must not in be PDF format". Also modified to add email addresses for U.S. District Judge Kathleen M. Williams and Judge Robert N. Scola, Jr.

Change Date: April 15, 2011

Section 1B Electronic Record and Authorization for Electronic Filing

Modified to correct reference to Federal Rules of Civil Procedure. Reference to Rule 5(e) deleted and replaced with reference to Rule 5(d)(3).

Section 2B Attorneys Appearing Pro Hac Vice

Modified to reflect 2010 amendments to the Local Rules correcting the usage of "limited appearance" which is now properly referred to as "appearance pro hac vice". Reference to Local Rules modified to reflect change in tabulation style used in the Local Rules.

Section 3A General Requirements

Reference to Local Rules modified to reflect change in tabulation style used in the Local Rules.

Section 3D Changes of Address and Contact Information

Modified to include reference to addition of 11.1(g) to the Local Rules.

Sections 3I(4) Discovery Material and (5) Mediation

Reference to Local Rules modified to reflect change in tabulation style used in the Local Rules.

Section 3I(6) Proposed Documents

Modified to reflect requirement that all counsel must be copied on the e-mail to the Judge. Modified to reflect that final versions of proposed documents for the recently appointed U.S. Magistrate Judge Jonathan Goodman should be sent to the following email address: goodman@flsd.uscourts.gov. Also modified to reflect changes related to senior and retired Judges.

Section 3K(4) Certificates of Service

Reference to Federal Rule of Civil Procedure 6(e) and service by mail deleted from Section.

Section 3K(5) Notices of Electronic Filing Are Not Sent to Terminated Attorneys

Modified to clarify procedures for users who no longer want to continue receiving electronic notices in cases where the parties represented have been terminated.

Section 5A Documents and Cases Filed Under Seal

Modified to clarify that motions to seal documents previously filed and on the docket, as well as motions unseal documents/cases must also be filed conventionally and must not be filed electronically. Reference to Local Rules modified to reflect change in tabulation style used in the Local Rules.

Section 5B Documents Related to Habeas Cases

Entire section deleted. Eliminated the requirement that transcripts and exhibits filed in state habeas cases must be filed conventionally. Such documents may now be filed electronically via CM/ECF or conventionally.

Section 5C Civil Complaints Filed by Pro Se Litigants

Modified to reflect that pursuant to Administrative Order 2009–36, the pilot project for the electronic filing of new civil cases was terminated and effective April 5, 2010, attorneys are required to electronically file all new civil complaints or other civil case initiating documents, except as provided in the Administrative Order.

Section 5J Motion to Appear Pro Hac Vice

Modified to reflect 2010 amendments to the Local Rules correcting the usage of "limited appearance" which is now properly referred to as "appearance pro hac vice".

Section 5K Ex parte Filings

Modified to correct duplicate numbering (previously 5J).

Section 8A Electronic Filing of New Civil Complaints

Modified to reflect that pursuant to Administrative Order 2009–36, the pilot project for the electronic filing of new civil cases was terminated and effective April 5, 2010, attorneys are required to electronically file all new civil complaints or other civil case initiating documents, except as provided in the Administrative Order.

Section 8C Filing Fees Processed Using Pay.gov

Modified to reflect that attorneys may pay the applicable fees via "Pay.gov" with a credit card, debit card, or electronic debit from a checking of savings account.

Form B Certificate of Service

Modified to conform with Certificate of Service form following Local Rule 5.1. Changes include eliminating the requirement that filers "attach" a Service List on a separate page.

Change Date: 11/13/2009

Section 5C Civil Complaints

Modified to reflect that complaints filed by attorneys are subject to Administrative Order 2009–36, which establishes a pilot project for the electronic filing of civil complaints or other civil case initiating documents via the CM/ECF system. Pro se litigants are required to file all documents, including new civil complaints a other civil case initiating documents, in the conventional manner.

Section 5F Summonses

Modified to reflect that pro se litigants must file all documents, including summonses, in the conventional manner. Summons filed by attorneys are subject to Administrative Order 2009–36, which establishes a pilot project for electronic filing of new civil complaints or other civil case initiating documents via the CM/ECF system.

Section 5J Ex Parte Filings

Added to clarify that ex parte filings must be filed in the conventional manner and must not be filed electronically.

Section 8 Electronic Filing of New Civil Complaints

Entire section added to comply with Administrative Order 2009-36, which establishes a pilot project for the electronic filing of new civil complaint or other civil case initiating documents via the CM/ECF system.

Change Date: 10/5/2009

Section 3D Change of Address and Contact Information

Modified to show that parties appearing pro se and counsel appearing pro hac vice must also maintain current contact information. Also modified to indicate that any change in contact information must be updated whenever such a change occurs.

Section 3G(1) Hardware/Software Generally Required for Electronic Filing

Modified to update scanner configurations. Also modified to indicate that PDF documents must be printable.

Section 3K(2) Notices of Electronic Filing Are Not Sent to Terminated Attorneys

Modified to reflect revised instructions for Users to continue receiving NEFs after they have been terminated in a case, in accordance with Release 4.0.2.

Section 3K(2) Notices of Electronic Filing and "One Free Look"

Modified to include PACER's policy that hyperlinks to view documents referenced in NEFs expire after the earlier of two events: first use or 15 days.

Section 5J Motion to Make Limited Appearance (Pro Hac Vice)

Added to reflect that a motion to make a limited appearance must be filed in the conventional manner according to Section 2B. Such motions cannot be filed electronically.

Change Date: 5/12/2009

Section 6 Redaction of Personal Information, Privacy Policy, and Inappropriate Materials

Entire section revised to comply with changes to Judicial Conference Policy and to the Federal Rule of Criminal Procedure 49.1 and Federal Rule of Civil Procedure 5.2.

Change Date: 5/27/2008

Section 3K(2) NEF and One Free Look

Modified to show that, upon the implementation of CM/ECF Version 3.1, only Users who are listed as active attorneys on a given case will receive "one free look" at case documents.

Section 5B Documents Related to Habeas Cases and Social Security Cases

Modified pursuant to Rule 5.2 of the Federal Rules of Civil Procedure to remove the requirement that social security transcripts and exhibits be filed conventionally and to remove language restricting PACER access to social security cases to counsel of record and court staff due to privacy issues.

Section 5I Proposed Trial Exhibits

Modified to show that the Court will continue its pre-CM/ECF practice of conventionally filing trial exhibits admitted into the public record.

Section 5K Consent to Jurisdiction

5K was renamed 3I(7) and was changed to clarify that parties may electronically file a Consent to Jurisdiction only if both parties sign the same form.

Change Date: 10/15/2007

Section 3D Changes of Address and Contact Information

Modified to clarify that Users can generally update contact information directly in CM/ECF.

Section 3E Government Attorneys Who Leave Their Agencies

Added to indicate that CM/ECF logins and passwords issued to attorneys employed by government agencies are valid only for filings on behalf of the specified agency.

Section 3I(5) Mediation

Modified to bring to the attention of Users that requests for the Clerk to appoint a mediator must be filed using the event "Request for Clerk to Appoint Mediator." Such requests should not be filed as motions.

Section 3K(5) NEFs Not Sent to Terminated Attorneys

Added to indicate that NEFs will no longer be sent to attorneys terminated in a case.

Section 5K Consent to Jurisdiction

Added to clarify that parties who consented to have a magistrate judge conduct a civil proceeding must file a consent in the conventional manner, after both parties have signed the consent.

Section 6B Exemptions from the Redaction Requirement

Exemptions from the Privacy Policy redaction requirement were added to comply with the Federal Criminal and Civil Rules, effective December 1, 2007.

Section 6C Filing of Inappropriate Materials

As directed by Administrative Order 2007–50, the section was added to address the filing of inappropriate materials. (The subject is also referenced in Sections 3I(3) and 5J.)

[Amended effective August 18, 2006; October 12, 2006; October 10, 2007; October 15, 2007; May 27, 2008; May 12, 2009; October 5, 2009; November 13, 2009; February 1, 2011; April 15, 2011; December 1, 2011; April 26, 2012; July 12, 2012; December 1, 2012; February 21, 2013; December 2, 2013; June 30, 2014; August 11, 2014; December 1, 2014; December 1, 2015; December 1, 2016.]

PLAN FOR THE RANDOM SELECTION OF GRAND AND PETIT JURORS

Pursuant to the Jury Selection and Service Act (Public Law 90–274), a Jury Plan was adopted by this Court and approved by the Fifth Circuit Judicial Council on September 10, 1968. The Plan was amended and approved by the Fifth Circuit Judicial Council through April 27, 1981. The Plan was subsequently amended and approved by the Eleventh Circuit Judicial Council on January 31, 1997, June 14, 2002, and again on January 31, 2007.

Subject to approval by the Reviewing Panel of the Eleventh Circuit Judicial Council, the present Plan is hereby further amended in its entirety by substituting in lieu thereof the following Jury Plan for the Southern District of Florida:

I. APPLICABILITY OF PLAN

This Plan is applicable to the Southern District of Florida, which consists of nine counties, as follows:

County	County Seat
Broward	Fort Lauderdale
Miami–Dade	Miami
Highlands	Sebring
Indian River	Vero Beach
Martin	Stuart
Monroe	Key West
Okeechobee	Okeechobee City
Palm Beach	West Palm Beach
St. Lucie	Fort Pierce

Title 28 U.S.C. Section 89(c) provides that "Court for the Southern District of Florida shall be held at Fort Lauderdale, Fort Pierce, Key West, Miami, and West Palm Beach." Special sessions may be held at such places in the District as the nature of the business may require (28 U.S.C. Section 141). Pursuant to this statutory requirement and in compliance with Section 1869(e) of the Jury Selection and Service Act, as amended, the Southern District of Florida is hereby divided into five (5) divisions as follows:

Miami Division, consisting of Miami–Dade County;

Fort Lauderdale Division, consisting of Broward County;

West Palm Beach Division, consisting of Palm Beach County;

Fort Pierce Division, consisting of the Counties of St. Lucie, Martin, Indian River, Okeechobee, and Highlands;

Key West Division, consisting of Monroe County.

In conformance with the Local Rules of this Court, civil and criminal proceedings or trials may upon order of the Court, for the purpose of ensuring compliance with the requirements of the Speedy Trial Act and for such other compelling, justifiable reasons as the Court may determine, be accordingly transferred and conducted within any of the foregoing divisions.

II. POLICY

This Plan is adopted pursuant to and in recognition of the Congressional policy declared in 28 U.S.C., as follows:

"Section 1861 Declaration of Policy"

"It is the policy of the United States that all litigants in Federal courts entitled to trial by jury shall have the right to grand and petit juries selected at random from a fair cross section of the community in the district or division wherein the court convenes. It is further the policy of the

United States that all citizens shall have the opportunity to be considered for service on grand and petit juries in the district courts of the United States, and shall have an obligation to serve as jurors when summoned for that purpose."

"Section 1862 Discrimination Prohibited"

"No citizen shall be excluded from service as a grand or petit juror in the district courts of the United States on account of race, color, religion, sex, national origin, or economic status."

III. MANAGEMENT AND SUPERVISION OF THE JURY SELECTION PROCESS

The Clerk of the Court shall manage the jury selection process under the supervision and control of the Chief Judge of this District. The use of the word "Clerk" in this Plan contemplates the Clerk of the Court and any and all of his deputies, including duly authorized non-court officials. The phrase "Chief Judge" wherever used in this Plan shall mean the Chief Judge of this District or, in his absence, disability or inability to act, the active District Court Judge who is present in the District and has been in service the greatest length of time. Wherever the Jury Selection and Service Act, as amended, requires or authorizes the Plan to designate a District Court Judge to act instead of the Chief Judge, the above definition shall apply and such active District Court Judge above mentioned is hereby designated to act.

The United States District Judge of this Court who shall be designated by Order of the Chief Judge to preside over a particular jury division of this Court, shall supervise and control the management, selection, impaneling process of both grand and petit jurors of this District.

IV. COMPOSITION, SUPPLEMENTATION AND DURATION OF MASTER JURY WHEELS

Voter registration lists represent a fair cross section of the community in each jury division of the Southern District of Florida. Accordingly, names of grand and petit jurors shall be selected at random for each jury division from the voter registration lists of all of the counties in that jury division. Every two years, the Clerk shall obtain, following the general election, a list of registered voters for each county in each jury division.

The Clerk shall maintain, or cause to be maintained, a master jury wheel for each of the divisions within the District. The Clerk shall utilize electronic data processing technology to perform the selection procedures set forth in this Plan.

The Clerk shall make, or cause to be made, the random selection of names for the master jury wheels as follows. The following number of names shall be selected for the master jury wheel as a minimum for each division:

Miami Division	250,000
Fort Lauderdale Division	150,000
West Palm Beach Division	100,000
Fort Pierce Division	18,000
Key West Division	35,000

The minimum number of names for each division shall be at least one-half of one percent of the total number of registered voters for the division. The Court may order additional names to be placed in the master jury wheels from time to time as necessary.

The Clerk shall ascertain the total number of registered voters for each division and divide that number by the number of names to be selected for the master jury wheel from that division. For example, if there are 900,000 registered voters in the Miami Division and if it is necessary to place 250,000 names in the master wheel for the Miami Division for the period in question, that number, 250,000, will be divided into 900,000, thus producing a "quotient" of 4 rounded off to the nearest integer. The Clerk shall then prepare and deposit into a closed container separate slips numbered 1 to 4 inclusive from which the Clerk shall draw by lot one of said numbers for a "starting number." Thus, if the starting number drawn is 2, the Clerk will designate the 2nd name appearing upon the voter registration list of each county for that division, and then the 6th, 10th, 14th, and each and every 4th name which appears thereafter to be placed into the master jury wheel for that division.

At the Clerk's option, and after consultation with the Court, the selection of names for the master jury wheel from complete source list databases in electronic media may be accomplished by either a systematic or a purely randomized process through a properly programmed electronic data processing system. Such random selections of names from the source lists for inclusion in the master wheel by data computer personnel must ensure that each county within the jury division is substantially proportionally represented in the master jury wheel in accordance with 28 U.S.C. Section 1863(b)(3). These selections must also ensure that mathematical odds of any single name being picked are substantially equal.

Each master jury wheel for each jury division of this Court shall be emptied and refilled every two years, specifically during the odd numbered years following a November general election. These master jury wheels will be filled with names obtained from the voter registration lists of each county within the respective jury division.

As required by the Judicial Conference of the United States, a report will be compiled within six months after each periodic refilling of the master jury wheel for each jury division, or upon implementation of any amendment such as to affect the composition of the master jury wheel on forms approved by the Judicial Conference giving general data relating to the respective master jury wheel, the time and manner of juror name selection, the source and number of names placed in the wheel and related information including an analysis of the race, sex and ethnicity of prospective jurors based on returns from a minimum of 300 juror summons and questionnaire forms of those persons drawn at random from each master jury wheel.

This Plan is based on the conclusion and judgment that the policy, purpose and intent of the Jury Selection and Service Act, as amended, will be fully accomplished and implemented by the use of voter registration lists as the source of a random selection of prospective grand and petit jurors who represent a fair cross section of each of the five Jury Divisions of this District. This determination is supported by all the information this Court has been able to obtain after diligent effort on its part, and after full consultation with the Judicial Council of the Eleventh Circuit.

V. USE OF AUTOMATED DATA PROCESSING METHODS FOR JURY ADMINISTRATION

This Court finds that automated data processing methods are more efficient, effective, and economical in performing many of the procedures outlined heretofore in this Plan. In addition, as authorized by 28 U.S.C. Section 1869(a) as amended, the Clerk may employ a private computing firm to assist these automated functions. Therefore, an automated data processing system shall be used to select names for the master wheel from voter registration lists of all counties in the District. The operator of the data processing system shall certify that the names for the master jury wheel are randomly selected from voter registration lists in accordance with this Plan and such additional written instructions as provided by the Clerk.

Similarly, an automated data processing system shall be used to select names from the master wheel for summoning persons to serve as grand or petit jurors, and for the creation of those documents or records required to administer the selection, summoning, qualification, and payment of jurors. Finally, the Clerk is authorized to utilize change of address software to update the addresses of prospective jurors, when deemed necessary.

VI. PROCEDURE FOR THE RANDOM SELECTION OF NAMES FOR SUMMONS

The name selection system shall be planned and programmed according to the same starting number and quotient formula utilized above in the construction of the master wheels, or, at the option of the Clerk and after consultation with the Court, a properly programmed electronic data processing system for pure randomized selection may be used to select names from the master wheels for the purpose of summoning persons to serve as grand or petit jurors. The selection of names from the master wheels must ensure that the mathematical odds of any single name being picked are substantially equal.

VII. DRAWING OF NAMES FROM THE MASTER JURY WHEEL; COMPLETION OF JUROR SUMMONS AND QUESTIONNAIRE FORM

Pursuant to 28 U.S.C. Section 1878, at the option of this District Court, jurors are summoned and qualified in a single procedure, in lieu of the two separate procedures otherwise provided for by the Jury Selection and Service Act.

This Plan hereby incorporates the provisions of 28 U.S.C. Section 1864, which reads as follows:

(a) From time to time as directed by the district court, the clerk or a district judge shall draw at random from the master jury wheel the names of as many persons as may be required for jury service. The clerk or jury commission shall post a general notice for public review in the clerk's office and on the court's website explaining the process by which names are periodically and randomly drawn. The clerk ... may, upon order of the court, prepare an alphabetical list of the names drawn ... the clerk ... shall mail to every person whose name is drawn from the master jury wheel a juror qualification form accompanied by instructions to fill out and return the form, duly signed and sworn, to the clerk ... within ten days. If the person is unable to fill out the form, another shall do it for him, and shall indicate that he has done so and the reason therefor. In any case in which it appears that there is omission, ambiguity, or error in a form, the clerk ... shall return the form with instructions to the person to make such additions or corrections as may be necessary and to return the form to the clerk ... within ten days. Any person who fails to return a completed juror qualification form as instructed may be summoned by the clerk ... forthwith to appear before the clerk ... fill out another juror qualification form in the presence of ... the clerk or the court, at which time, in such cases as it appears warranted, the person may be questioned, but only with regard to his responses to questions contained on the form. Any information thus acquired by the clerk ... may be noted on the juror qualification form and transmitted to the chief judge or such district court judge as the plan may provide.

(b) Any person summoned pursuant to subsection (a) of this section who fails to appear as directed shall be ordered by the district court forthwith to appear and show cause for his failure to comply with the summons. Any person who fails to appear pursuant to such order, or who fails to show good cause for noncompliance with the summons may be fined not more than $1000, imprisoned not more than three days, ordered to perform community service, or any combination thereof. Any person who willfully misrepresents a material fact on a juror qualification form for the purpose of avoiding or securing service as a juror may be fined not more than $1000, imprisoned not more than three days, ordered to perform community service, or any combination thereof.

VIII. DETERMINATION OF QUALIFICATIONS, DISQUALIFICATIONS, EXEMPTIONS, EXCUSES AND DEFERRALS

This Plan hereby incorporates the provisions of 28 U.S.C. Section 1865, as amended. The Clerk, under the supervision of the Court:

(a) ... shall determine solely on the basis of information provided on the juror qualification form and other competent evidence whether a person is unqualified for, or exempt, or to be excused from jury service. The clerk shall enter such determination in the space provided on the juror qualification form and in any alphabetical list of names drawn from the master jury wheel. If a person did not appear in response to a summons, such facts shall be noted on said list.

(b) ... shall deem any person qualified to serve on grand and petit juries in the district court unless he—

(1) is not a citizen of the United States, eighteen years old who has resided for a period of one year within the judicial district;

(2) is unable to read, write and understand the English language with a degree of proficiency sufficient to fill out satisfactorily the juror qualification form;

(3) is unable to speak the English language;

(4) is incapable, by reason of mental or physical infirmity, to render satisfactory jury service; or

(5) has a charge pending against him for the commission of, or has been convicted in a State or Federal court of record of, a crime punishable for more than one year and his civil rights have not been restored.

This Court finds and hereby states that the exemption of the following occupational classes or groups of persons is in the public interest, consistent with the Act, and shall be automatically granted, pursuant to 28 U.S.C. Section 1863(b)(6):

(1) Members in active service of the Armed Forces of the United States;

(2) Members of the fire or police departments of any State, district, territory, possession or subdivision thereof;

(3) Public officers in the executive, legislative, or judicial branches of the Government of the United States, or any State, District, Territory, Possession or subdivision thereof who are actively engaged in the performance of official duties (public officer shall mean a person who is either elected to public office or who is an officer who is directly appointed by a person elected to public office).

This Court finds and hereby states that jury service by members of the following occupational classes or groups of persons would entail undue hardship and extreme inconvenience to the members thereof, and serious obstruction and delay in the fair and impartial administration of justice, and that their excusal will not be inconsistent with the Act and may be claimed, if desired and shall be granted upon individual request, pursuant to 28 U.S.C. Section 1863(b)(5):

(1) Persons over 70 years of age at the time they request excuse;

(2) Volunteer safety personnel who serve without compensation as firefighters, members of a rescue squad or ambulance crew of the United States or any unit of a state or local government;

(3) Persons who have served as grand or petit jurors in a federal court during the past two years immediately preceding their call to serve.

Additionally, the Clerk may, under supervision of the Court, excuse persons summoned for jury service upon a showing of undue hardship, extreme inconvenience, or other ground of excusal as set forth in 28 U.S.C. Section 1866(c)(1) and Section 1869(j), for such period of time as the Court may deem necessary and proper. This Court finds and hereby states that jury service by members of the following groups of persons would entail undue hardship and extreme inconvenience to the members thereof:

(1) Persons who have active care and custody of a child or children under the age of 10 whose health and/or safety would be jeopardized by absence of juror, or a person who is essential to the care of aged, elderly or infirmed persons.

(2) Persons whose services are so essential to the operation of a business, commercial or agricultural enterprise that it may close or cease to function if they were required to perform jury duty.

(3) Persons having no access to a private vehicle and residing in a remote location, where public transportation is unavailable or is not feasible.

This Court finds and hereby states that the Clerk may excuse jurors under the categories defined in this Plan only. Categories not so defined shall be referred to the Court for disposition.

This Court finds and hereby states that the Clerk may, under the supervision of the Court, grant temporary excuses (deferrals) to persons summoned for jury service upon a showing of undue hardship, extreme inconvenience, or other grounds for such period of time as the Court may deem necessary and proper. At the conclusion of the deferral period, these jurors may be re-summoned.

IX. EFFECTIVE DATE

The effective date of this Plan shall be established by a separate Order of this Court after this Plan has been approved by the Judicial Council of the Eleventh Circuit. The current Jury Plan of this Court shall remain effective and operative until the effective date of this revision. Nothing in this Plan shall affect the composition or preclude the service of any juror duly summoned or impaneled on or before the date upon which this Jury Plan shall become effective.

X. PUBLIC ACCESS AND DISCLOSURE

The office of the Clerk of the Court shall retain and, when requested, provide public access to the following:

- the Court's "Plan for the Random Selection of Grand and Petit Jurors."
- a verbal or graphically charted description of the procedure employed in the automated selection system.

- a copy of the Court's authorization and instruction order to the person or computer service organization which carries out automated name selection tasks for the Court.
- the venire list for a particular panel. However, the Court may at any time order that a venire list or lists be kept confidential in any case where the interest of justice so requires. 28 U.S.C. Sect. 1863(b)(7).
- a copy of the report on the Operation of the Jury Selection Plan, JS–12., in addition, the Clerk may disclose for grand juries: impanelment dates, dates of service, and expiration dates.

All other juror information is to be kept confidential, and may not be released to the parties or the public without a Court order.

[Amended March 17, 2010; approved by the Judicial Council of the Eleventh Circuit May 5, 2010.]

SELECTED ADMINISTRATIVE ORDERS

ADMINISTRATIVE ORDER 2004–39. ELECTRONIC CASE RECORDS

This Court currently maintains an official paper record in all cases. Since 1996, the Court has also maintained a parallel electronic record which largely duplicates the aforementioned official paper record. With the advances in technologies over the last decade, the advent of electronic filing, and this District's long experience in creating and maintaining a parallel electronic record, the process of maintaining the paper record has become redundant and the allocation of resources to continue the process inordinately expensive. It is thus herein

ORDERED that, effective October 28, 2004, the official record of the Court shall be the electronic file and, where practicable, documents shall be maintained on the Court's servers. This shall include documents filed with the Court in electronic form as well as documents filed in paper form and converted to an electronic image by the Clerk's Office. It is further

ORDERED that the Clerk's Office cease maintaining as part of the paper case file any case documents filed after October 27, 2004, except as otherwise provided below:

1. Transcripts prepared and filed with the Clerk by Southern District of Florida court reporters shall not be scanned, and shall be maintained as a paper supplement to the electronic record;

2. Sealed filings shall not become part of the publicly-accessible electronic record;

3. Exhibits or attachments that are voluminous and contain materials that may be difficult to convert to an electronic image (e.g., two-sided copy or irregularly sized paper) may, at the discretion of the Clerk, be maintained as a paper supplement to the electronic record;

4. Handwritten documents filed by pro se litigants, the legibility of which would be compromised by conversion may, at the discretion of the Clerk, be maintained in a paper supplement to the electronic record;

5. Administrative records that are voluminous and contain materials that may be difficult to convert to an electronic record may, at the discretion of the Clerk, be maintained as a paper supplement to the electronic record;

6. State Court records submitted in connection with habeas corpus cases pursuant to 28 U.S.C. § 2254 that are voluminous and contain materials that may be difficult to convert to an electronic record may, at the discretion of the Clerk, be maintained as a paper supplement to the electronic record;

7. Non-documentary or otherwise inconvertible exhibits which are introduced at any proceeding before this Court and thereafter become admitted as part of the public record shall be maintained in their original form by the Clerk until case closing, or, if an appeal is taken, until the conclusion of the appeal, at which time they will be returned to the filer.

It is further ORDERED that all paper documents received and converted to an electronic image be maintained on site in original form, indexed by date of entry on this Court's docket, by the Clerk of Court for at least 90 days, after which such documents shall be sent to the Federal Records Center for archiving.

[Effective October 14, 2004.]

ADMINISTRATIVE ORDER 2005–38. IN RE: ATTORNEY CONTACT INFORMATION

This Court increasingly relies on its automated systems to disseminate Orders and Notices to counsel of record and/or parties to actions pending before the Court. The information upon which these systems rely resides primarily in the Court's attorney database, which is maintained by the Clerk of the Court. This and other databases contain mailing and e-mail addresses and telephone and facsimile numbers for all members of the Southern District of Florida bar and all counsel of record in all cases pending before this Court. The efficacy of the Court's automated notification systems relies on the accuracy and currency of the attorney contact information residing in these databases. Thus, the Court depends on counsel not only to furnish accurate mailing and e-mail addresses and facsimile and telephone numbers in connection with initial bar membership, but also to update this information within a reasonable time of any change in this contact information, whether permanent or temporary. For these purposes, a reasonable time is no more than five business days after the change in contact information occurs.

It is therefore **ORDERED** that the contact information provided by attorneys in connection with Southern District of Florida bar membership shall constitute the address information of record in all cases where an appearance is filed until such time as an attorney's bar membership contact information is updated or corrected. Accordingly, all Orders and Notices disseminated by the Court will be deemed to be appropriately served if directed to counsel consistent with the information of record.

It is further **ORDERED** that Southern District of Florida bar members provide the Clerk of Court with updated or corrected contact information in writing within five business days of any change, and that counsel simultaneously provide the Clerk of Court with an accurate listing of all pending cases in which counsel has filed an appearance.

It is further **ORDERED** that all counsel appearing pro hac vice and parties appearing pro se provide the Court with accurate contact information at the time of first appearance, and case-specific notice in writing within five days of any change in contact information.

Finally, it is **ORDERED** that the failure of counsel or any party appearing pro se to provide such information to the Clerk of Court as herein prescribed shall not constitute grounds for relief from deadlines imposed by Rule or by the Court. It is counsels' responsibility to regularly review the docket in all matters pending before the Court for which an appearance has been filed.

[Effective September 13, 2005.]

ADMINISTRATIVE ORDER 2006–16. IN RE: CELLULAR PHONE AND ELECTRONIC EQUIPMENT USAGE IN THE COURTHOUSE

At a regularly scheduled Judges' Meeting, the current United States Marshals Service policy regarding cellular phones and electronic devices in the federal courthouse facilities within the Southern District of Florida was reviewed. Upon consideration, it is further

ORDERED that the following procedures will be strictly adhered to regarding the introduction of electronic equipment into the federal courthouse facilities within the Southern District of Florida:

I. Electronic Devices. All electronic devices including but not limited to Cellular Phones, Pagers, Personal Data Assistants (PDA), Laptop Computers, Tape Recorders, etc., are prohibited from being brought into any federal courthouse facility within the Southern District of Florida with the following exceptions:

A. A written request signed by a judge or other designated authority, forwarded to the United States Marshal for verification, allowing a specific person access to the courthouse with a specific electronic device for a specific purpose and period of time; or,

B. Any federal courthouse employee (United States Probation, Clerk's Office, Chambers Staff, and United States Marshals Service) with valid permanent government employee identification; or,

C. Any attorney of the United States Attorney's Office or the Federal Public Defender's Office with a valid identification card issued from that office; or,

D. Any Special Agent for the United States Government or other law enforcement officer authorized to enforce the law within the Southern District of Florida, having official business within the courthouse facility and possessing a valid agency/department issued identification badge; or,

E. Any attorney permitted to practice law within the Southern District of Florida with a valid Florida Bar identification card or pro *hac* vice order having business within the facility. This applies to attorneys only and precludes staff, investigators, clients, etc.; and,

F.* Prospective jurors and seated jurors and witnesses with subpoenas shall be permitted to bring into the Federal Courthouses their cellular phones (with or without their integrated cameras) and electronic book readers of any kind, including but not limited to Kindles, Nooks, iPads, and any type of electronic tablet reading device. A judge **must** provide the United States Marshals Service with a list of seated jurors who will be allowed to bring cellular phones to the courthouse during a trial. The list must indicate the judge, case number, courthouse, dates of empanelment, and each juror's name and regular cellular phone number or camera cellular phone number and should be provided to the Marshals Service in the form accompanying this Administrative Order as Attachment A.

It will be the responsibility of the judge to have the cellular phones collected from the jurors in the morning before trial begins, to distribute them to the jurors during breaks (if necessary), and to collect them upon the conclusion of those breaks. Jurors will not be permitted to leave the floor with their cellular phones on lunch or other breaks. The United States Marshals Service will not be responsible for collecting or storing the cellular phones of seated jurors.

II. Cameras and Cellular Phones With Integrated Camera Device. Pursuant to Southern District of Florida Local Rule 77.1, cameras of any type are not allowed in any of the federal courthouse facilities without a written order signed by a judge and verified by the United States Marshals Service. Notwithstanding that local rule, those persons permitted to bring a cellular phone into a federal courthouse facility, pursuant to the exceptions listed, may bring that cellular phone, even if it contains an integrated camera device, into any federal courthouse facility. **No cellular phones of any kind may be used in a courtroom or jury deliberations room and no photographs of any kind may be taken in any federal courthouse facility.**

The United States Marshals Service is to continue to inspect all cellular phones and other electronic equipment as they are brought into the federal courthouse facilities as directed to protect the Bench, Bar, and public from harm. It is further

ORDERED that persons not meeting at least one of the exceptions listed will not be permitted to bring an electronic device of any kind, including a cellular phone, into the federal courthouse facilities within the Southern District of Florida (i.e., the general public, etc.). It is further

ORDERED that the penalty for violating this Administrative Order includes a sentence of 30 days in jail and/or a fine of $5,000.00; and/or punishment for contempt of court. See Local Rule 77.1; 41 C.F.R. §§ 102-74.385; 102-74.420; 102-74.450; 18 U.S.C. § 401.

This Order shall be effective immediately and supersedes Administrative Order 2003-92.

[Effective July 31, 2006. Amended effective March 2008; December 23, 2011.]

* **[Publisher's Note:** *See also* Administrative Order 2008-07 and Administrative Order 2009-12, *post.*]

ADMINISTRATIVE ORDER 2006-26. IN RE: REQUIREMENT THAT SOUTHERN DISTRICT OF FLORIDA BAR MEMBERS FILE DOCUMENTS ELECTRONICALLY

The Clerk's Office for the United States District Court for the Southern District of Florida implemented its Case Management/Electronic Case Filing (CM/ECF) system on October 12, 2006. Under Administrative Procedures adopted in connection with this system, Section 2A specifies that it is mandatory for members of the District's Bar to file documents electronically. Section 3B further requires that Bar members register to receive a system login.

CM/ECF system registration was opened to Bar members on the Court's Internet site on February 17, 2006. Southern District of Florida Bar members were specifically advised of registration and training requirements through a Clerk's Notice sent to their last-known office address on or about April 10, 2006. The attorney registration and training requirement has also be published in the Daily Business Review and reference to it has been posted on the District's Internet site.

The first general training session for Bar members was offered on March 7, 2006 in Miami, and training has been offered continuously in Miami and Fort Lauderdale throughout the spring and summer. The training sessions collectively offered the capacity to conduct training for over 5,400 members of the District's Bar.

Inasmuch as members of the Districts Bar are expected to file documents electronically to the CM/ECF system in accordance with the District's Administrative procedures; the impending implementation of the system, Bar training requirements, and availability of training were posted and made well-known to members of the Bar; and the system is now available for use for purposes of electronically filing documents with the Clerk of Court,

It is **ORDERED** that except as to those categories of documents which must be filed conventionally pursuant to Section 5 of the Court's Administrative Procedures which include documents filed under seal; transcripts and exhibits filed in social security cases and in habeas cases; and plea agreements, members of the Southern district of Florida Bar shall file all other court documents electronically; and

It is further **ORDERED** that any member of the Southern District of Florida Bar who seeks to file a document in the conventionally manner because the attorney has not obtained a CM/ECF system login must appear in-person at the nearest Court Division Clerk's Office during published business hours with proper identification and Florida Bar credentials to conventionally file the document; and

It is further **ORDERED** that effective November 6, 2006 and until further notice, except for documents which must be filed conventionally pursuant to Section 5 of the Administrative Procedures, The Clerk of Court shall issue and Order to Show Cause before me to any member of the District's Bar who submits a document for filing in he conventional manner.

[Effective October 25, 2006.]

ADMINISTRATIVE ORDER 2008-07. IN RE: CELLULAR PHONE AND ELECTRONIC EQUIPMENT USAGE IN THE COURTHOUSE*

On July 31, 2006, former Chief Judge William J. Zloch issued Administrative Order 2006-16, which superseded Administrative Order 2003-92. The 2006-16 Order shall be amended as follows:

Paragraph I.F. shall be deleted and replaced with the following language.

F. Prospective jurors and seated jurors and witnesses with subpoenas shall be permitted to bring into the Federal Courthouses their cellular phones—with or without their integrated cameras.

The clear intent of this order is to expand the list of individuals permitted to bring cellular telephones into the courthouse. In the past, only judges were permitted to bring cellular telephones into the courthouse. Subsequently, members of the Bar, Assistant United States Attorneys, Federal Public Defenders, courthouse employees, and Special Agents of the Federal Government were added to the list of those permitted to bring their cellular telephones into the courthouse. Jurors as "judges of the facts," to whom we entrust to decide the most important decisions in the courthouse should likewise be included in the list of permitted cellular telephone carriers. Witnesses, with proper identification and a copy of a subpoena that requires their presence in the courthouse, should also be on that list.

Permitting jurors and witnesses to bring in their cellular telephones is consistent with the efficient administration of judicial proceedings. Judges may need to contact jurors quickly during long recesses. Attorneys may need to contact witnesses on short notice. Because the United States Marshal will continue to inspect all cellular telephones as they are brought into the federal courthouse, the Bench, the Bar, and public will continue to be protected from harm. This proper balance between security and convenience has been reached for those who are involuntarily summoned (jurors and witnesses) into the courthouse.

In today's modern world, security concerns are paramount. Yet these security concerns are satisfied by airlines, the White House, and the majority of courthouses in the United States where cellular telephones are permitted. Expanding the list to include these individuals will not diminish the security provided to the occupants of the courthouse, while at the same time enhance the availability of jurors and witnesses to participate in our court proceedings.

All other provisions of the prior Order 2006-16 shall remain in effect, including the prohibition of the use of cellular phones in a courtroom or jury deliberations room, or the use of any recording device or camera in the courthouse. Violators shall continue to be subject to the contempt order issued by former Chief Judge William J. Zloch in Administrative Order 2006-16.

Any District Judge can, of course, modify this order as it relates to the possession of cellular telephones within the courtroom over which that judge is presiding. Any modification, however, should consider the fact that a uniform rule assists the Deputy United States Marshals and the Court Security Officers in enforcing the rules and protecting us.

[Effective March, 2008.]

* **[Publisher's Note:** *See also* Administrative Order 2009-12, *post.*]

ADMINISTRATIVE ORDER 2008–08. IN RE: ORDER ESTABLISHING NEW COMPENSATION RATE FOR MEDIATORS CERTIFIED UNDER LOCAL RULE 16.2

It has been more than ten years since the Court last set the rate at which mediators, certified under S.D. Fla. L.R. 16.2, would be compensated if appointed by the Clerk of the Court, in accordance with S.D. Fla. L.R. 16. 2.B.(7) and D.1.(b), on a blind rotating basis from the Southern District's list of certified mediators. With the recommendation of the Court's Ad Hoc Advisory Committee on Court Annexed Mediation, and in consideration of the rate of inflation over the last ten years and current prevailing hourly rates for mediators in the Southern District of Florida, it is

ADJUDGED that Administrative Order 97–09 is superseded. It is also

ADJUDGED that, in cases where the parties have not agreed on the selection of a mediator which results in the Clerk of the Court designating a mediator on a blind rotating basis under S.D. Fla. L.R. 16.2.D.1.(b) after the date of this Order, such designated mediators shall be compensated at the rate of Two Hundred Fifty Dollars ($250) per hour, which includes the mediator's time preparing for and conducting the mediation.

[Effective March 13, 2008.]

ADMINISTRATIVE ORDER 2008–31. IN RE: POLICY ON ELECTRONIC AVAILABILITY OF TRANSCRIPTS OF COURT PROCEEDINGS

The Judicial Conference of the United States has revised its national policy addressing electronic availability of transcripts of court proceedings filed with the court. The Judicial Conference Policy on Electronic Availability of Transcripts applies to any transcript of a court proceeding that is subsequently filed with the court and made available to the public via electronic access. In furtherance of the implementation of this policy locally, effective for any transcript filed on or after the date of this order (regardless of when the proceeding took place) it is

ORDERED that transcripts of proceedings before the United States District Court for the Southern District of Florida taken or transcribed by Official Court Reporters and Contract Court Reporters are now required to be filed with the Court in electronic format. The Court will follow the Judicial Conference Policy on Electronic Availability of Transcripts of court proceedings before making official transcripts electronically available to the public. The policy will apply to all transcripts of proceedings or parts of proceedings ordered on or after this date, regardless of when the proceeding took place, unless otherwise ordered by the Court. For specifics as to the policy, please see the attached New Transcript Policy;

It is **FURTHER ORDERED** that the policy set forth in this order:

A. Does not affect in any way the obligation of the court reporter to file promptly with the Clerk of Court the court reporter's original records of a proceeding or the inclusion of a filed transcript with the records of the court pursuant to 28 U.S.C. § 753.

B. Does not affect the obligation of the Clerk to make the official transcript available for copying by the public without further compensation to the court reporter 90 days after the transcript is filed pursuant to Judicial Conference policy.

C. Is not intended to create a private right of action.

D. Is intended to apply the Judicial Conference policy on privacy and public access to electronic case files to transcripts that are electronically available to the public. It is not intended to change any rules or policies with respect to sealing or redaction of court records for any other purpose.

E. Does not prevent the production of a transcript on an expedited basis for a party, or any other person or entity, that may order such a transcript, subject to whatever court rules or orders are currently imposed to protect sealed materials. Any non-party that orders a transcript on an expedited basis should be alerted to the Judicial Conference policy on privacy and public access to electronic case files by the entity providing the transcript to the party.

[Effective September 29, 2008.]

UNITED STATES DISTRICT COURT
SOUTHERN DISTRICT OF FLORIDA

New Transcript Policy
Effective September 30, 2008

At its September 2007 session, the U.S. Judicial Conference approved a new policy regarding the availability of transcripts of court proceedings. A new release of CM/ECF, Version 3.2., includes software that facilitates the implementation of this policy. The policy states:

(1) A transcript provided to a court by a court reporter or transcriber will be available at the office of the clerk of court for inspection only, for a period of 90 days after it is delivered to the clerk.

(2) During the 90–day period, a copy of the transcript may be obtained from the court reporter or transcriber at the rate established by the Judicial Conference, the transcript will be available within the court for internal use, and an attorney who obtains the transcript from the court reporter or transcriber may obtain remote electronic access to the transcript through the court's CM/ECF system for purposes of creating hyperlinks to the transcript in court filings and for other purposes.

(3) After the 90–day period has ended, the filed transcript will be available for inspection and copying in the clerk's office and for download from the court's CM/ECF system through the judiciary's PACER system.

Transcripts must be compliant with the new Federal Privacy Rules, Civ. 5.2 and Crim. 49.1. The Judicial Conference approved procedures for applying the redaction requirements to transcripts of court proceedings and CM/ECF Version 3.2 has been designed to include those procedures.

Pursuant to 28 U.S.C. § 753(b), the court reporter or transcriber must deliver promptly a certified copy of any transcript made to the clerk of court for the records of the court. The Notice of Electronic Filing (NEF) informs parties and attorneys of record of the 90–day restriction and how to obtain the transcript during the restriction period. The starting point for all deadlines begins the date the transcript is submitted. The redaction period for transcripts and the 90–day restriction policy apply to transcripts of federal court proceedings only.

During the 90–day period (which may be extended by the court), access to the transcript in CM/ECF is restricted to the following users:

- court staff
- public terminal users
- attorneys of record or parties who have purchased the transcript from the court reporter or transcriber; and
- other persons as directed by the court.

Except for public terminal viewers, persons authorized to view or download the transcript can also create hyperlinks to the transcript.

Court reporters will either email a PDF version of the transcript to the clerk's office for uploading/docketing or the court reporter will upload /docket transcript into CM/ECF. When an official transcript of a court proceeding has been filed, parties will be notified via CM/ECF notice of electronic filing (NEF) which will include various standard deadlines:

- 21 calendar days after the filing of the transcript, party to file the Redaction Request, if necessary;
- 31 calendar days after the filing of the transcript, court reporter to file the redacted transcript, if requested;
- 90 calendar days after the filing of the transcript, normal release of remote restrictions, unless redaction issues are pending.

Redaction responsibilities apply to the attorneys even when the requestor of the transcript is a judge or a member of the public/media.

Any party needing to review the transcript for redaction purposes may purchase a copy from the court reporter/transcriber or view the transcript at the courthouse using a public terminal. If a party purchases the transcript from the court reporter, and he or she is an attorney on the case, he or she will be given remote access to the transcript via CM/ECF and PACER. PACER fees apply at all times when accessing transcripts remotely. The clerk's office will grant remote access upon notification from the court reporter that payment was received.

There is no obligation on the part of the Clerk's office to perform any redaction. Instead, it rests on the attorneys to tell the court reporter where to redact, and on the court reporter to perform the redaction.

Unless otherwise ordered by the court, the attorney is responsible for privacy compliance of the following portions of the transcript:

- opening and closing statements made on the party's behalf;
- statements of the party;
- the testimony of any witness called by the party;
- sentencing proceedings;[1]
- any other portion of the transcript ordered by the court.

Only the following personal identifiers listed by the Judicial Conference in its policy on the Electronic Availability of Transcripts may be redacted through this part of the process:

1. Minors' names: use the minor's initials;
2. Financial account numbers: use only the last four numbers of the account;
3. Social Security numbers: use only the last four numbers;
4. Dates of birth: use only the year; and
5. Home addresses: use only the city and state (applicable in criminal cases only).

If redaction is requested within 21 calendar days of the transcripts' delivery to the clerk, or longer if so ordered by the Court, the parties must file with the court a Transcript Redaction Request (sample attached). A copy of the Transcript Redaction Request must be either faxed, e-mailed, or mailed to the court reporter. The request should indicate where the personal identifiers to be redacted appear on the transcript.

For example, if a party wanted to redact the Social Security number 123–45–6789 on page 10, line 12 of a transcript the Redaction Request would include the information: Page 10, line 12, SSN to read xxx–xx–6789. Access to the Transcript Redaction Request document will be restricted in PACER and CM/ECF to the court and the attorneys of record in the case.

Redacted Transcript Within 31 Calendar Days

Within 31 calendar days from the filing of the transcript with the Clerk (or longer if ordered by the court), if redaction is requested, the court reporter will file the redacted transcript.

Motion to Redact (other than five listed personal identifiers within 21 days)

If a party wishes to redact additional information (that is not listed by the Judicial Conference) he or she may make a motion to the court. The transcript will not be electronically available until the court has ruled on any such motion, even though the 90–day restriction period may have ended.

The original un-redacted electronic transcript should be retained by the clerk of court as a restricted document. The court will monitor this deadline to ensure that the redacted transcript is available for the parties and attorneys should there be an appeal.

[1] Both the government and the defendant are responsible for privacy compliance of sentencing proceedings.

SAMPLE REDACTION REQUEST FORMAT

Note: the Event is Located on CM/ECF by Clicking:
Civil or Criminal>OTHER DOCUMENTS or APPEALS DOCUMENTS>Redaction Request—Transcript

UNITED STATES DISTRICT COURT
SOUTHERN DISTRICT OF FLORIDA

Case No. ___ –Civ or Cr–(USDJ's last name/USMJ's last name)

Plaintiff(s)

v.

Defendant(s)
________________________________/

TRANSCRIPT REDACTION REQUEST

Pursuant to Fed.R.Civ.P.5.2/Fed.R.Crim.P.49.1, Plaintiff/Defendant requests that the following personal identifiers be redacted from the transcript filed on (Date):

Doc#	Page	Line	Identifier	Redaction Requested
53	15	10	Social Security Number	xxxx–xx–1234
53	25	2	Taxpayer ID Number	xx–xxxx5678
70	32	14	Date of Birth	xx/xx/1954
72	24	23	Minor Child's Name	Pxxx Txxxx
80	56	11	Financial Account Number	xxx–xxx–xxxx2689
93	89	8	Home Address	City, State

Respectfully submitted,

/s/ [Name of Password Registrant](Florida Bar Number)
Attorney e-mail address
Firm Name
Street Address
City, State, Zip Code
Telephone: (xxx) xxx-xxxx
Facsimile: (xxx) xxx-xxxx
Attorneys for Plaintiff/Defendant [Party Name(s)]

Certificate of Service

I hereby certify that on (date), I electronically filed the foregoing document with the Clerk of the Court using CM/ECF and I hereby certify that I have served by some other authorized manner the document to the following Court Reporter: Name of Court Reporter or Court Reporter Coordinator. I also certify that the foregoing document is being served this day on all counsel of record or pro se parties identified on the attached Service List in the manner specified, either via transmission of Notices of Electronic Filing generated by CM/ECF or in some other authorized manner for those counsel or parties who are not authorized to receive electronically Notices of Electronic Filing.

ADMINISTRATIVE ORDER 2009–02. IN RE: REMOTE ELECTRONIC ACCESS TO PLEA AGREEMENTS

On January 15, 2009, the Court conducted an en banc hearing on proposed amendments to this Court's Local Rules. The Report of the Ad Hoc Committee on Rules and Procedures prepared for that hearing contained a Subcommittee Report on the topic of Public Electronic Access to Unsealed Plea Agreements. The topic of remote access to plea agreements has been the subject of extensive national debate. Instead of adopting a national policy, the Judicial Conference of the United States Courts, through its Committee on Court Administration and Case Management, asked "each court to consider adopting a local policy that protects information about cooperation in law enforcement activities but that also recognizes the need to preserve legitimate public access to court files."

This Court currently has a policy in place granting limited remote access to plea agreements to the parties of a case, with only the paper copies of plea agreements available for public viewing at the courthouse. This policy was implemented as an interim measure after the Court initiated its new CM/ECF electronic case management and docketing system. Consistent with the Judicial Conference's admonitions, this Court's Ad Hoc Committee on Rules and Procedures was asked to make recommendations for updating or changing that interim policy if necessary. The Subcommittee that considered the issue in this District was comprised of equal representation of both the prosecution and the defense bars. After consideration of all relevant issues, both the Subcommittee and the Ad Hoc Committee as a whole were unable to make a consensus recommendation to this Court as to changes to make in the existing interim policy.

The Court heard oral argument at the *en banc* hearing from representatives of both the U.S. Attorney's Office and the defense bar. After the hearing, a substantial majority of the District Judges voted to rescind the interim policy and to provide complete remote electronic access to plea agreements. The sense of the Court is that the public's interest in access must prevail in this instance and that restricting access to all plea agreements is overly broad. Other means are available to the prosecution and defense to insure that the public record does not contain information about cooperation arrangements in those instances where the interests of safety or other considerations require different treatment. This applies to plea agreements that are NOT sealed. Each district judge may, in accordance with the law, order specific plea agreements sealed and those sealed plea agreements will not be accessible electronically. Accordingly, it is

ORDERED AND ADJUDGED that as of February 20, 2009, the Southern District of Florida's current policy of providing limited electronic access to plea agreements is rescinded. All plea agreements filed on or after February 20, 2009 will be public documents, with full remote access available to all members of the public and the bar, unless the Court has entered an Order in advance directing the sealing or otherwise restricting a plea agreement;

IT IS FURTHER ORDERED that as to plea agreements filed prior to February 20, 2009, the Court's prior policy shall remain in full force and effect, and those plea agreements will not be available to the public for remote electronic viewing but will remain available for viewing in paper format at the courthouse where filed.

[Effective January 22, 2009.]

ADMINISTRATIVE ORDER 2009-12. IN RE: PROHIBITION ON ELECTRONIC TRANSMISSIONS AND CELLULAR PHONE USE INSIDE COURTROOMS*

In view of the Judicial Conference of the United States's policy and the prohibitions contained in Federal Rule of Criminal Procedure 53 and Southern District of Florida Local Rule 77.1 against live broadcasting from inside courtrooms, this Order amends Administrative Orders 2006-16 and 2008-07 to prohibit text messaging, emailing, twittering, typing, and any cellular phone use from inside courtrooms. These actions by persons inside the courtroom violate the sanctity of the courtroom and disrupt ongoing judicial proceedings.

The Court, however, must balance the interests of preserving the conduct of judicial proceedings against the public's right to know what happens inside courtrooms. Accordingly, it is

ADJUDGED that emailing, text messaging, twittering, typing, and using cellular phones shall continue to be prohibited inside the District's courtrooms. It is also

ADJUDGED that to balance the interest in preserving the sanctity and conduct of judicial proceedings against the public's right to know what occurs inside the District's courtrooms, this Order amends Administrative Orders 2006-16 and 2008-07 to allow news reporters to bring cellular phones, Blackberries, iPhones, Palm Pilots, and other similar electronic personal digital assistants (PDAs) into the courthouse consistent with what is permitted of attorneys, as long as the news reporters agree in writing not to email, text message, twitter, type, or use their cellular phones or other electronic device inside the District's courtrooms. A violation of the agreement will result in contempt of court. The Clerk of Court shall keep the list of reporters who have signed such agreement and make that list available to Court security personnel assigned to each courthouse. The Clerk of Court shall also make space available in each courthouse for those listed reporters to use their cellular phones and other electronic devices outside of the courtrooms. Of course, District and Magistrate Judges retain the discretion to maintain order in their courtrooms, which includes the right to lock their courtrooms should the entry and exit of news reporters become disruptive in a particular proceeding.

[Effective March 23, 2009.]

* **[Publisher's Note: See also Administrative Orders 2006-16 and 2008-07, *ante*.]**

ADMINISTRATIVE ORDER 2009-36. IN RE: ELECTRONIC FILING OF NEW CIVIL CASES

As recommended by the Clerk's Office Committee and adopted by the Judges of the Southern District of Florida at their regularly scheduled meeting, the Court shall adopt the use of the CM/ECF system to electronically receive new civil complaints or other civil case initiating documents from attorneys who are admitted to practice in the Southern District of Florida. As the first step of this implementation, the Court has authorized a three-month pilot project as set forth below. At the completion of the pilot project, attorneys who are admitted to practice in the Southern District of Florida will be required to electronically submit all new civil complaints or other civil case initiating documents in accordance with this Administrative Order, except as provided below.

Effective **January 4, 2010**, it is hereby **ORDERED AND ADJUDGED** that during the pilot project for three months following January 4, 2010, attorneys authorized to electronically file in the CM/ECF system in the Southern District of Florida will have the option to electronically submit new civil complaints or other civil case initiating documents via the CM/ECF system. New civil complaints and other initiating documents will be deemed filed on a particular date if electronically received prior to midnight on that date and if the filings are in compliance with the Local Rules and the CM/ECF Administrative Procedures. [Instructions for electronically submitting new civil case filings are contained on the Court's website.]

It is **FURTHER ORDERED** that required filing fees for new civil complaints or other civil case initiating documents submitted electronically in the CM/ECF system will be processed using "Pay.gov", a secure government-wide collection portal. [Information regarding Pay.gov is contained on the Court's website.]

It is **FURTHER ORDERED** that any new civil complaint or other civil case initiating document that is to be automatically sealed by statute or operation of law, or that is accompanied by a motion or other request to seal the civil case in its entirety, *shall only be filed conventionally* and shall *not* be filed electronically by counsel. Such matters shall continue to be filed conventionally until such time as this Administrative Order is amended or otherwise changed by further Order.

It is **FURTHER ORDERED** that all subsequent civil filings shall be filed as required in the CM/ECF Administrative Procedures and the Local Rules. Pro se litigants must continue to file all documents in the conventional manner, including new civil complaints.

It is **FURTHER ORDERED** that at the completion of the pilot project and effective **April 5, 2010**, attorneys authorized to electronically file in the CM/ECF system will be required to electronically submit new civil complaints or other civil initiating documents (unless sealed or requested to be sealed, as set forth above) in accordance with this Administrative Order.

[Effective October 8, 2009.]

ADMINISTRATIVE ORDER 2012–001. IN RE: VIDEO RECORDING OF COURT PROCEEDINGS UNDER THE CAMERAS PILOT PROJECT

This District has been selected to participate in a national pilot project to permit recording of proceedings in civil matters, This Administrative Order supplements the Judicial Conference Committee on Court Administration and Case Management Guidelines for the Cameras Pilot Project in the District Courts ("the Guidelines"; available at http://www.flsd.uscourts.gov/?page_ID=5838. All recordings of court proceedings must comply with both this Administrative Order and the Guidelines; where they are believed to conflict, the Guidelines will prevail.

1. Participating Judges. Video recording will occur only in proceedings presided over by District Judges who have chosen to participate in the Pilot Project. All further references to "Judge" or "presiding Judge" in this Order include only participating District Judges. A list of participating Judges can be found on the Court's website at: http://www.flsd.uscourts.gov/?page_ID=5838.

2. Proceedings Eligible for Recording. A Judge who is presiding over a civil case proceeding that is held in open court, other than those excluded under the Guidelines, will determine whether to request that the proceeding be recorded. In general, trials and evidentiary hearings will be recorded unless a party does not give consent.

3. Notification of Parties. Unless otherwise ordered by the Judge, at least 10 days prior to each civil case proceeding that the Judge has identified as eligible for recording, the Judge will send each party, or the party's attorney if represented by counsel, a notice ("NOTIFICATION OF REQUEST FOR VIDEO RECORDING") that he or she is requesting that the proceeding be recorded under the pilot project. Alternatively, the Judge may provide such notice by such other means as appropriate, such as through a scheduling order, or at a conference with counsel or with parties proceeding without counsel.

4. Consent of Parties. After each notification, each party will submit a form ("PARTY RESPONSE TO REQUEST FOR VIDEO RECORDING") on which to indicate whether that party consents to the recording of all, part, or none of the proceeding. Parties may indicate as well that they wish to have no recording of specified witnesses on another form ("REQUEST TO EXEMPT WITNESS(ES) FROM VIDEO RECORDING.") Counsel for each party, or the party itself if proceeding pro se, will return the form on behalf of all persons who will appear for that party at the proceeding to be recorded. For data collection purposes, parties who do not consent to recording will be asked to describe their reasons. Unless otherwise ordered by the Judge, the form should be returned via e-mail to the presiding Judge's e-mail address set up for this purpose at least 5 days prior to the proceeding. These forms should NOT be filed via the CM/ECF system, but rather should be sent via e-mail to the appropriate address which can be found on the Court's website at: http://www.flsd.uscourts.gov/?page_ID=5838. The subject line of the e-mail should reflect the case number and the nature of the form being transmitted (e.g., 11–12345 Consent, 11–12345 No Consent or 11–12345 Recording Request). Unless otherwise directed, the forms should be e-mailed to the appropriate e-mail address for each presiding Judges' cases, and this e-mail address should be used for no other purpose unless otherwise directed by that Judge:

5. Hearing on Consent. If some or all parties do not consent to recording a proceeding that the Judge has identified as eligible for recording, the Judge may, in his or her discretion, hold a hearing to discuss the parties' concerns and determine if there are conditions under which the party(ies) would agree to recording some or all of the proceeding. The hearing will be held on the record.

6. Requests for Recording From Parties or Outside Entities. Parties, members of the media, or other outside entities may submit a request that a proceeding be recorded. A request should be submitted to the presiding Judge at least 10 days before the date of the proceeding using the e-mail address which can be found on the Court's website at: http://www.flsd.uscourts.gov/?page_ID=5838. For proceedings that arise with little notice, the request should be made as soon as practicable. The request should be made using the "REQUEST FOR VIDEO RECORDING OF COURT PROCEEDING" form (available at http://www.flsd.uscourts.gov/?page_ID=5838). The presiding Judge will determine whether to deny the request or to seek consent from the parties under the procedures outlined above. The person or entity making the request will be advised of the outcome of the request at least 3 days prior to the proceeding, unless otherwise ordered by the presiding Judge.

7. Data Collection. The completed "PARTY RESPONSE TO REQUEST FOR VIDEO RECORDING" forms, "REQUEST TO EXEMPT WITNESS(ES) FROM VIDEO RECORDING" forms, and "REQUEST FOR VIDEO RECORDING OF COURT PROCEEDING" forms will be made available to researchers at the Federal Judicial Center who are conducting an evaluation of the Cameras Pilot Project on behalf of the Judicial Conference Committee on Court Administration and Case Management.

[Effective January 19, 2012.]

ADMINISTRATIVE ORDER 2012–4. IN RE: ELIMINATION OF ATTORNEY ADMISSIONS EXAMINATIONS

Rule 1 of the Southern District of Florida's Special Rules Governing The Admission and Practice of Attorneys establishes as a prerequisite that attorneys take and pass an examination prior to admission to this Court's bar. This District is only one of approximately four federal district courts nationwide that requires an admission examination. At a regularly scheduled meeting of the Judges of this District held on February 23, 2012, the Judges have determined that requiring a local examination to a large degree duplicates matters found on the Florida Bar exam and no longer accomplishes the purposes it was intended to serve. A substantial majority of Judges of this Court have voted to eliminate Rule 1's examination requirement. Accordingly,

IT IS HEREBY ORDERED that the examination requirement stated in Rule 1 of the Southern District of Florida's Special Rules Governing The Admission and Practice of Attorneys is hereby suspended, effective immediately. Attorneys who satisfy all other requirements for admission to this Court's bar, and who have paid all required admission fees, shall be admitted to the bar of this Court without the necessity of passing an examination; and

IT IS FURTHER ORDERED that the Clerk of Court is directed to provide notice of this Administrative Order through the CM/ECF noticing system and other appropriate means such as publication, and to post revised procedures for admission to the Court's bar on the Southern District's website www.flsd.uscourts.gov as soon as reasonably practicable.

[Effective February 20, 2012.]

ADMINISTRATIVE ORDER 2012-25. ORDER OF REFERENCE

Pursuant to 28 U.S.C. Section 157(a), any and all cases under title 11 and any and all proceedings arising under title 11 or arising in or related to a case under title 11 are referred to the bankruptcy judges of this district. If a bankruptcy judge or district judge determines that entry of a final order or judgment by a bankruptcy judge would not be consistent with Article III of the United States Constitution in a particular proceeding referred under this order and determined to be a core matter, the bankruptcy judge shall, unless otherwise ordered by the district court, hear the proceeding and submit proposed findings of fact and conclusions of law to the district court made in compliance with Fed. R. Civ. P. 52(a)(1) in the form of findings of fact and conclusions stated on the record or in an opinion or memorandum of decision.

The district court may treat any order of the bankruptcy court as proposed findings of fact and conclusions of law in the event that the district court concludes that the bankruptcy judge could not have entered a final order or judgment consistent with Article III of the United States Constitution.

This Order of Reference amends and supersedes the Order of Reference entered by this Court on July 11, 1984, 84-12-Civ-Misc.

[Effective March 27, 2012.]

ADMINISTRATIVE ORDER 2013-4. IN RE: POLICY GOVERNING INITIAL APPEARANCES OF DEFENDANTS

Former Chief Judge William Zloch set forth the policy governing the initial appearances of defendants in this District in a 2003 Memorandum in response to problems that had arisen under the rules that required defendants to be taken to the "nearest available" magistrate judge. The revised rule provides that defendants be taken "without unnecessary delay" before a magistrate judge. The prior rule had resulted in agents and prosecutors having to appear in different divisions for initial appearances and bond hearings.

The 2003 Memorandum directed that:

1. Where a defendant is arrested on a complaint or indictment, that defendant should be presented before the duty magistrate judge in the division where the magistrate judge whose name appears on the charging document is sitting.

2. When a defendant is arrested before a complaint or indictment is filed, the defendant should be presented in the division where the prosecutor overseeing the case is based.

3. The bond hearing should be held before the duty magistrate judge in the division where the initial appearance was held, unless a later-filed indictment results in the transfer of the prosecution from one division to another. In that event, any deferred bond hearing should occur in the division where the indictment is assigned.

Because the assigned prosecutor may not always be based in the division in which the case will be prosecuted, this order revises the policy as follows:

1. Where a defendant is arrested on a warrant issued pursuant to an indictment, that defendant should be presented for an initial appearance before the duty magistrate judge in the division where the assigned district judge sits.

2. Where a defendant is arrested on a warrant issued pursuant to a criminal complaint, that defendant should be presented for an initial appearance before the duty magistrate judge in the division where the magistrate judge who signed the complaint sits.

3. Where a defendant is not arrested on a warrant, but solely on probable cause, the defendant should be presented for an initial appearance before the duty magistrate judge in the division where the criminal complaint will be sought and the case prosecuted.

4. Where a bond hearing has not been held at the initial appearance, a defendant should receive such hearing in the same division as the initial appearance, unless an indictment returned thereafter

is assigned to a district judge in a different division. In that instance, any hearing should be held in the division in which the assigned district judge sits.

5. In exceptional cases, where compliance with the above practices may raise serious safety concerns relating to the transport or housing of defendants or create significant hardships for law enforcement or U.S. Marshals personnel, the assigned Assistant United States Attorney may seek an exception from the Court, providing for the initial appearance to be held in a different division. In those few instances, the assigned Assistant United States Attorney must first obtain supervisory approval. That supervisor must then personally contact the duty magistrate judge, who would normally be conducting the initial proceedings, to formally request that an exception be granted. The transferring magistrate judge may then, with the consent of the receiving magistrate judge, transfer the proceeding.

[Effective January 15, 2013.]

ADMINISTRATIVE ORDER 2014-69. IN RE: REVIEW OF SEALED DOCUMENTS/CASES AND ACCESS VIA CM/ECF TO DOCUMENTS SUBSEQUENTLY UNSEALED

At a locally scheduled Judges' Meeting, the Court reconsidered the process for reviewing civil and criminal documents filed under seal with the Court in light of proposed amendments to Local Rule 5.4 regarding the filing, disposal, and unsealing of documents, which subsequently went into effect December 2, 2013. The review of documents filed under seal was previously addressed in Administrative Orders 2012-87 and 2013-36. This Administrative Order is entered to facilitate the process of reviewing civil and criminal documents filed under seal with this Court **prior to December 2, 2013.** This policy is intended to balance the interests of parties to file documents under seal with public policy interests for access to court filings. This policy is effective July 8, 2014. It is hereby

ORDERED that the Clerk's Office is directed to facilitate the review of sealed documents in cases that have been closed for at least one year and in which the appeal period has expired, or one year after the issuance of the mandate following an appeal. The Clerk's Office will send to the filing party a Notice of Intent to Unseal Document via U.S. mail. The notice will include the filing date of the sealed document(s), caption of the sealed document(s), and docket entry number(s). Attorneys and pro se parties are reminded that they are responsible for maintaining a current mailing address, pursuant to Administrative Order 2005-38 and this Court's CM/ECF Administrative Procedures. It is further

ORDERED that sealed documents identified in the Clerk's Notice will be unsealed and accessible to the public via the CM/ECF system unless objections are filed within 14 days of the Clerk's Notice. Objections must be filed with this Court in the conventional manner and must include justification regarding why the specified document(s) should not be unsealed and be accessible to the public via the CM/ECF system. The presiding Judge will review any objections and determine the disposition of the sealed documents. It is further

ORDERED that the filing party is responsible for notifying the Court if the documents to be unsealed contain personal identifiers and for filing a redacted copy of documents to be unsealed within the 14 days noted in the Clerk's Notice. It is further

ORDERED that if no objections are filed, or following the resolution of any objections, the Clerk's Office is instructed to unseal the electronic records in CM/ECF, making such records accessible to the public via PACER. The Clerk's Office is further instructed to destroy any existing paper copies of such records according to protocol established by the Clerk's Office. It is further

ORDERED that this Administrative Order supersedes the Local Rules, Internal Operating Procedures, Administrative Orders 2013-36 and 2012-87, and any other previous Administrative Orders.

[Dated: July 8, 2014.]

ADMINISTRATIVE ORDER 2016-70. IN RE: ELECTRONIC SUBMISSION OF EXHIBITS

Effective December 1, 2016, the United States Court of Appeals for the Eleventh Circuit is adopting changes to its Local Rules and Internal Operating Procedures that impact the manner in which trial or hearing exhibits are transmitted to the Court of Appeals for purposes of the Record on Appeal in both criminal and civil cases. In order to comply with the Eleventh Circuit's new requirements, set forth in 11th Cir. R. 11-3, effective December 1, 2016, it is

ORDERED AND ADJUDGED that unless otherwise ordered by the presiding Judge, within three (3) days of the conclusion of a trial or other proceeding, parties must file in the CM/ECF system electronic versions of documentary exhibits admitted into evidence, including photographs of non-documentary physical exhibits; it is

FURTHER ORDERED that this requirement for electronic filing excludes sealed exhibits in criminal cases, sealed exhibits in criminal cases will be conventionally filed; it is

FURTHER ORDERED that this requirement for electronic filing excludes contraband and audio/video recordings, and the filing party will file with the Clerk a CD, DVD or other electronic medium containing a copy of any exhibit that is an audio or video recording; it is

FURTHER ORDERED that at the time of filing the electronic exhibits, an attorney for each party shall also complete and file the attached Certification of Compliance Re Admitted Evidence; after electronically filing exhibits, the parties shall make arrangements with the Clerk to retrieve all original exhibits; it is

FURTHER ORDERED that electronically filed exhibits are subject to CM/ECF Administrative Procedures, Section 6, Redaction of Personal Information, Privacy Policy, and Inappropriate Materials; it is

FURTHER ORDERED that the failure to file the electronic exhibits and a Certification of Compliance within three (3) days of the conclusion of trial or proceeding as provided in this order may result in the imposition of sanctions; it is

FURTHER ORDERED that any original exhibits that have been returned to or retained by the filing party after electronic filing shall be kept for safe keeping until the conclusion of any appeals; upon order of the Court, the filing party must return the original exhibits to the Clerk of Court; it is

FURTHER ORDERED that this Administrative Order is intended to implement interim procedures to enable the Court to comply with the Eleventh Circuit's new rules adopted effective December 1, 2016. As such, these interim procedures shall remain in effect until such time as this Court's Local Rules Committee has had an opportunity to solicit input from the bar and propose permanent procedures for adoption by the full Court.

UNITED STATES DISTRICT COURT
FOR THE SOUTHERN DISTRICT OF FLORIDA

CASE NO. XX-CV/CR-XXXXX-JUDGE

__________________,
Plaintiff

v.

__________________,
Defendant.

CERTIFICATE OF COMPLIANCE RE ADMITTED EVIDENCE

I, ______________________________________, as counsel for the plaintiff/defendant, ______________________________________, hereby certify the following:

Check the applicable sections:

☐ ALL EXHIBITS E-FILED: All documentary exhibits and photographs of non-documentary physical exhibits admitted into evidence have been electronically filed in CM/ECF.

☐ EXHIBITS NOT E-FILED: Some documentary exhibits and/or other physical exhibits admitted into evidence cannot be electronically filed in CM/ECF. This includes sealed criminal exhibits and contraband. The following identifies those exhibit numbers that have been retained by the Clerk, and separately identifies those exhibit numbers retained by this filing party. (Itemize or attach a list).

Retained by the Clerk: ______________________________

Retained by filing party: ______________________________

☐ AUDIO/VIDEO EXHIBITS: The following audio and/or video exhibits were entered into evidence during these proceedings. The filing party has conventionally filed with the Clerk of Court a CD or DVD containing the audio or video recording. (Itemize or attach a list.) ____________

Any original exhibits that have been returned to or retained by the filing party after electronic filing shall be kept for safe keeping until the conclusion of any appeals. Upon order of court, the filing party agrees to return the original exhibits to the Clerk of Court.

This Certificate shall be filed within three (3) days of the conclusion of trial or relevant proceedings. Failure to timely comply with the requirements of Administrative Order 2016–70 governing the Electronic Filing of Exhibits may result in the imposition of sanctions.

Signature: ______________________________ Date: ____________

[Dated: November 22, 2016.]

INDEX TO UNITED STATES DISTRICT COURT FOR THE SOUTHERN DISTRICT OF FLORIDA

UNITED STATES BANKRUPTCY COURT FOR THE SOUTHERN DISTRICT OF FLORIDA

Including Amendments Received Through February 1, 2017

LOCAL FORMS, CLERK'S INSTRUCTIONS AND COURT GUIDELINES

tificate of Amount Deposited and Payment of Fees.
LF–35. Final Report and Motion for Entry of Final Decree.
LF–36. Notice of Late Filing of Paper Pursuant to Local Rule 5005–1(F)(2).
LF–37. Order Reopening Case to Amend Schedules to add Omitted Creditor(s).
LF–38. Order Reopening Case to Administer Additional Assets and Directing United States Trustee to Appoint a Trustee.
LF–41. Bill of Costs.
LF–44. Motion to Appear Pro Hac Vice.
LF–45. Order Admitting Attorney Pro Hac Vice.
LF–46. Certificate of Service and [If Service of Notice of Hearing] Certificate of Compliance With Local Rule 9073–1(D).
LF–47. Certificate of Contested Matter.
LF–49. Exhibit Register.
LF–50. Verification of Qualification to Act as Mediator.
LF–51. Order of Referral to Mediation.
LF–52. Notice of Selection of Mediator.
LF–53. Notice of Clerk's Designation of Mediator.
LF–54. Report of Mediator.
LF–57. Writ of Execution to the United States Marshall.
LF–58A. Order Jointly Administering Chapter 7 Cases.
LF–58B. Order Jointly Administering Chapter 11 Cases.
LF–59. Request for Copies of Archived Case Files From U.S. Bankruptcy Court, Southern District of Florida.
LF–60. Request to Expedite Appeal.
LF–61. Notice of Intent to Request Redaction of Transcript.
LF–62. Confirmation Affidavit of [Name of Affiant].
LF–63A. Pretrial Order.
LF–63B. Direct Testimony of John Smith.
LF–63C. Joint Pretrial Stipulation.
LF–64A. Order Conditionally Approving Disclosure Statement, Setting Hearing on Final Approval of Disclosure Statement and Confirmation of Chapter 11 Plan, Setting Various Deadlines and Describing Plan Proponent's Obligations.
LF–64B. Order Setting Hearing on Approval of Disclosure Statement and Confirmation of Chapter 11 Plan, Setting Various Deadlines and Describing Plan Proponent's Obligations.
LF–65. Chapter 7 Trustee's Motion to Dismiss Case for Failure by Debtor to Appear at the First Meeting of Creditors.
LF–66. Order Reinstating Chapter 13 Case.
LF–67. Debtor Certificate of Compliance and Request for Confirmation of Chapter 13 Plan.
LF–69. Application for Compensation for Professional Services or Reimbursement of Expenses by Attorney for Chapter 13 Debtor.
LF–70. Objection to Claim on Shortened Notice.
LF–71. Individual Debtor Certificate for Confirmation Regarding Payment of Domestic Support Obligations and [for Chapter 11 Cases] Filing of Required Tax Returns.
LF–72. Cover Sheet to Accompany Items Submitted for Sealing or In Camera Review.
LF–73. Notice to Defendant of Right Against Garnishment of Wages, Money and Other Property.
LF–74. Third–Party Summons.
LF–75. Agreed Order to Employer to Deduct and Remit and for Related Matters.
LF–76. Notice of Compliance by Attorney for Debtor With Local Rule 2083–1(B) Claims Review Requirement.
LF–77. Motion to Value and Determine Secured Status of Lien on Real Property.
LF–78. Debtor's Notice of Filing Payroll and Sales Tax Reports.
LF–81. Order Determining Debtor has Cured Default and Paid all Required Postpetition Amounts to [Insert Name Of Creditor Here].
LF–84. Subpoena for Rule 2004 Examination.
LF–85. Application for Search of Bankruptcy Records.
LF–88. Archives Request Form.
LF–89. Summary of [First] Interim [or Final] Fee Application of [ ] [Counsel] [Accountant].
LF–90. Rights and Responsibilities Agreement Between Chapter 13 Debtor(s) and Chapter 13 Debtor(s)' Attorney for Cases Filed in the United States Bankruptcy Court, Southern District of Florida.
LF–91. Order Establishing Procedures to Permit Monthly Payment of Interim Fee Applications of Chapter 11 Professionals.
LF–92. Order Granting Motion to Value and Determine Secured Status of Lien on Real Property.
LF–93. Chapter 11 Case Management Summary.
LF–94. Acknowledgment of Responsibility and Request for Login ID and Password for Live Access to CM/ECF With Trustee/US Trustee Filing Privileges.
LF–95. Acknowledgment of Responsibility and Request for Login ID and Password for Live Access to CM/ECF With Full Attorney Filing Privileges.
LF–96. Acknowledgment of Responsibility and Request for Login ID and Password for Live Access to CM/ECF With Limited Filing Privileges.
LF–97A. Debtor's Certificate of Compliance, Motion for Issuance of Discharge and Notice of Deadline to Object.
LF–97B. Debtor's Certificate of Compliance, Motion for Issuance of Discharge Before Completion of Plan Payments, and Notice of Deadline to Object.
LF–98. Ex Parte Motion to Excuse Compliance Under Local Rule 5005–4(B).
LF–99. Order Granting Ex Parte Motion to Excuse Compliance Under Local Rule 5005–4.
LF–100. Trustee's Summary of Requested Fees and Expenses.
LF–101. Notice Regarding Opposing Motions for Summary Judgment.
LF–102. Motion to Value and Determine Secured Status of Lien on Personal Property.
LF–103. Order Granting Motion to Value and Determine Secured Status of Lien on Personal Property.
LF–104. Order Awarding Final Trustee's Fees and Expenses.
LF–105. Order Awarding Final Trustee and Professional Fees and Expenses.
LF–106. Order Jointly Administering Chapter 15 Cases.
LF–107. Order Converting Case Under Chapter 13 to Case Under Chapter 11.
CI–1. Clerk's Filing Instructions.
CI–2. Clerk's Summary of Fees (See also 28 USC § 1930).
CI–3. Clerk's Instructions for Preparing, Submitting and Obtaining Service Matrices.

SELECTED ADMINISTRATIVE ORDERS

RULE 1001–1. SCOPE OF RULES; SANCTIONS; WAIVER; DEFINITIONS; ACRONYMS

(A) Scope. These local rules are promulgated in accordance with Bankruptcy Rule 9029. They shall apply to all cases and proceedings arising in, under, or related to cases pending under Title 11 of the United States Code in the United States Bankruptcy Court for the Southern District of Florida.

[Comment: These local rules are sequentially numbered to correspond to certain of the Bankruptcy Rules, if applicable, except that a dash and a fifth digit has been added in accordance with the directive of the Committee on Rules of Practice and Procedure of the Judicial Conference of the United States. If no related national rule number exists, the local rule has been assigned a number for the related topic in accordance with the Judicial Conference of the United States Uniform Numbering System for Local Bankruptcy Rules.]

(B) District Court Rules. The Local Rules of the United States District Court for the Southern District of Florida shall not apply to cases or proceedings in the Bankruptcy Court, except to the extent that Local Rules 87.1 through 87.5 of the District Court govern bankruptcy matters.

[Comment: See Local Rule 87.1 of the United States District Court (giving bankruptcy court authority to enact local rules).]

(C) Incorporation by Reference. Reference in these rules to administrative orders, local forms, court guidelines or clerk's instructions shall mean the referenced administrative order, form, guideline or instruction as revised or amended.

(D) Sanctions. The court, on its own motion or on the motion of any interested party, may impose sanctions for failure to comply with these rules, including; striking of papers filed with the court, dismissal of proceedings, dismissal or conversion of cases, or as may otherwise be appropriate under the circumstances.

(E) Waiver in Appropriate Circumstances. Upon motion of a party in interest or sua sponte, the court may suspend the requirements of any of these rules in appropriate circumstances.

(F) Definitions. Acronyms.

(1) The terms "court", "judge", "clerk", "local rule", "local form" and "administrative order" shall refer to the United States Bankruptcy Court for the Southern District of Florida and the judges, clerk, local rules, and local forms, and local administrative orders respectively, of this Bankruptcy Court, unless otherwise specifically noted. The term "clerk" means the clerk of court or members of the clerk of court's staff. Reference to district court shall refer to the United States District Court, Southern District of Florida.

(2) "Bankruptcy Rules" shall mean the Federal Rules of Bankruptcy Procedure. Where an Interim Bankruptcy Rule is cited in these rules and that rule is subsequently adopted as a Bankruptcy Rule, the use of "Interim Bankruptcy Rule" shall mean the Bankruptcy Rule as subsequently adopted.

(3) "Individual" shall mean natural person, and "non-individual" shall mean corporation, partnership, trust, or other legal entity which is not a natural person.

(4) "Parties of record", when used by the clerk to designate service, shall mean all parties listed on the "creditor mailing matrix" as described in the "Clerk's Instructions for Preparing, Submitting and Obtaining Service Matrices", except that registered users listed on "Mailing Information for a Case" matrix will receive service from the clerk via their designated

email address, not the U.S. mail address listed on the "creditor mailing matrix".

(5) "Registered user" is an interested party who has been approved to electronically file papers in this court.

(6) "CM/ECF" is an acronym for the "Case Management/Electronic Case Files" system used in this court.

(7) "Electronic filing" is a filing submitted via the Internet by a registered user of CM/ECF in this court.

(8) "Conventional filing" is a filing submitted in paper.

(9) "NEF" is an acronym for "Notice of Electronic Filing" which is an electronic notice generated automatically by the CM/ECF system upon the electronic filing of a document in a case or docketing of a "virtual" public docket event. It contains the names and email addresses of parties who were served electronically. The NEF may also be viewed on the court docket by PACER subscribers.

(10) "BNC" is an acronym for "Bankruptcy Noticing Center", a centralized noticing service authorized by the Administrative Office of the United States Courts and contracted to an entity who provides service of notices on behalf of the United States bankruptcy courts.

(11) "NCRS" is an acronym for "National Creditor Registration Service", a non-fee registration service provided by the BNC that allows bankruptcy court notices to be transmitted electronically to parties in a case. NCRS also maintains preferred mailing address lists for creditors pursuant to 11 U.S.C. § 342(f).

(12) "PDF" is an acronym for "portable document format", a special file format created by Adobe Systems Inc.

(13) "Business day" shall mean any day not a Saturday, Sunday, or a legal holiday. Otherwise, the definitions of words in 11 U.S.C. § 101 and § 1101 and Bankruptcy Rule 9001, and the rules of construction in 11 U.S.C. § 102, govern their use in these rules.

(14) "EBN" is an acronym for Electronic Bankruptcy Noticing which permits any party filing conventionally to receive clerk-served notices electronically via the BNC instead of by U.S. Mail. Parties register for EBN directly with the BNC, not with the court.

(15) "DeBN" is an acronym for Debtor Electronic Bankruptcy Noticing which permits debtors to receive clerk-served notices electronically via the BNC instead of by U.S. Mail. Debtors register for DeBN directly with the clerk of court by filing the Local Form "Debtor's Request to Receive Notices Electronically Under DeBN Program".

[Effective December 1, 1998. Amended effective December 1, 2002; June 2, 2008; December 1, 2009; August 1, 2011. Amended on an interim basis effective June 1, 2016.]

RULE 1002-1. COMMENCEMENT OF CASE

(A) Petition Requirements. At the time of filing, each voluntary petition shall:

(1) comply with requirements as set forth in the "Clerk's Filing Instructions";

(2) be accompanied by a corporate ownership statement as required by Bankruptcy Rule 1007(a)(1) if the debtor is a corporation, limited partnership, limited liability company, limited liability partnership, joint venture, general partnership or any other entity that meets the definition of "corporation" under 11 U.S.C. § 101(9);

(3) if the case is being filed after dismissal of the debtor's previous case by any bankruptcy court, be accompanied by a copy of the dismissal order and any other orders which set forth the conditions under which the subsequent case may be filed; and

(4) be accompanied by an Official Bankruptcy Form "Statement About Your Social Security Numbers" verified in accordance with Local Rule 9011-4(D).

[Comment: See also Bankruptcy Rules 1002, 1007 (schedules), and 9009 (official forms), and Local Rules 1006-1 (installment payments and chapter 7 fee waivers), 1074-1 (corporations), 5080-1 and 5081-1 (filing fees), 5005-1(A)(2) (compliance with Federal Judiciary Privacy Policy), 5005-1(B) (place of filing), 5005-1(C) (deficient petitions) 5005-3, 5005-4, 9004-1, 9004-2 (format), 9009-1 (local forms) and 9011-4 (signatures), 2090-1 (representation by attorney), and 9010-1(B)(1) (corporations, partnerships, trusts, and other business entities must be represented by an attorney).]

(B) Clerk Authorized to Refuse for Filing Certain Voluntary Petitions Filed Conventionally. Dismissal of Electronically Filed Voluntary Petitions.

(1) The clerk shall refuse for filing any conventionally submitted voluntary petition:

(a) from a debtor who had a prior case dismissed by an order which prohibited the debtor from filing for a period of time that has not yet expired, or where a court order sets forth conditions for refiling and those conditions have not been met;

(b) from a debtor which is accompanied by an application to pay filing fee in installments if filing fees remain due from any previous cases filed by that debtor unless the application is accompanied by payment of all previously due fees;

(c) that does not contain the debtor(s)' required original signature(s) and address(es); or

(d) from a pro se individual debtor that is not accompanied by documentary proof of the debtor's identity required by the court as set forth in the "Clerk's Filing Instructions".

(2) *Dismissal of Electronically Filed Petitions.* Any electronically filed voluntary petition filed with any of the deficiencies listed in subdivision (1) above shall be subject to dismissal without notice or hearing.

[Comment: See also Local Rules 1006-1(A) (refusal of petitions) and 5005-1(C) (deficient petitions and papers.)]

[Effective December 1, 1998. Amended effective December 1, 2002; July 1, 2004; June 2, 2008; December 1, 2009; August 1, 2011; December 1, 2015.]

RULE 1003-1. INVOLUNTARY PETITIONS

(A) Petition Requirements. Each involuntary petition must comply with requirements set forth in the "Clerk's Filing Instructions".

(B) Joint Debtors. An involuntary petition shall not be filed against joint debtors.

(C) Clerk Authorized to Refuse Unsigned Petitions. The clerk shall refuse for filing an involuntary petition that is not signed by all of the petitioning creditors.

[Comment: See also Bankruptcy Rules 1005, 1007 and 9009, and Local Rules 5080-1 and 5081-1 (filing fees), 5005-1(A)(2) (compliance with federal judiciary privacy policy), 5005-1(C) (deficient petitions), 5005-3 (format), 5005-4 (electronic filing), 9004-1, 9004-2, and 9011-4 (format requirements), 2090-1(B) (special or limited appearance by attorney), and 9010-1(B)(1) (corporations, partnerships, trusts, and other business entities must be represented by an attorney).]

[Effective December 1, 1998. Amended effective December 1, 2002; July 1, 2004; June 2, 2008; December 1, 2015.]

RULE 1006-1. INSTALLMENT PAYMENTS AND CHAPTER 7 FEE WAIVERS

A voluntary petition in an individual or joint case presented for filing and not accompanied by the required full filing fee will not be accepted by the clerk unless, at the time the petition is filed, application to pay the fee in installments is sought under subdivision (A) of this rule or, if the case is being filed under chapter 7, a waiver of the fee is sought under subdivision (B) of this rule.

(A) Installment Payments.

(1) *Application Requirements.* A voluntary petition submitted in an individual or joint case seeking to pay the filing fee in installments must be accompanied by the Local Form "Application for Individuals to Pay the Filing Fee in Installments".

(2) *Approval of Application by Clerk.* The clerk shall review the application and shall be authorized to sign the order in the name of the clerk on behalf of the court where the following conditions are met:

(a) The application conforms to the local form required under subdivision (A)(1) of this rule;

(b) The first installment payment accompanies the application;

(c) The petition accompanying the application contains the required information regarding disclosure of prior bankruptcy cases;

(d) Copies of any orders required by Local Rule 1002-1(A)(3) accompany the petition;

(e) The petition has not been filed within a "with prejudice" period or subject to any other court imposed refiling restriction still in effect; and

(f) The debtor does not have any previous or pending cases where filing fees are owed.

(3) *Refusal of Petition. Referral of Application to Court.*

(a) Refusal of Petition. The clerk shall refuse for filing any conventionally submitted petition accompanied by an application to pay the filing fee in installments where the requirements of subdivision (A)(2) (e) or (f) of this rule have not been met. If the application has been electronically filed and these requirements were not met, the clerk will refer the matter to the judge assigned to the case.

(b) Denial of Application by Clerk. Referral of Application to Court. If the requirements of subdivision (A)(2) are not complied with at the time of filing of the application, unless a motion setting forth justification as to why the debtor is unable to comply with one or more of these requirements accompanied the filing of the application, the clerk shall not approve the application pursuant to subdivision (A)(2) of this rule. Instead, the clerk is authorized to enter an order denying application on behalf of the court. If the application was accompanied by a motion to waive requirements of subdivision (A)(2), the application shall be referred to the court for review.

(4) *Dismissal of Case Upon Failure to Pay Installment Payment. Balance of Filing Fee Due on Dismissal.* The court shall dismiss without any further notice any case where an installment payment is not timely made in the required manner. The balance of the filing fee shall become due immediately upon the dismissal of a case or upon the failure to timely pay any installments.

[Comment: See also Local Rule 1002-1(B)—Clerk Authorized to Refuse for Filing Certain Voluntary Petitions, Local Rule 1017-2(D)—Failure to Timely Remit Installment Payment and Local Rule 2002-1(C)(1)—clerk's notice to contain notice of intent to dismiss for failure to pay installment payment.]

(B) Chapter 7 Fee Waiver Applications. Applications to waive the filing fee in chapter 7 cases shall be submitted on the Official Bankruptcy Form "Application to Have the Chapter 7 Filing Fee Waived" in accordance with the following requirements:

(1) Applications which do not substantially conform to the Official Bankruptcy Form or that are otherwise defective shall be noted as deficient and the debtor shall have 14 days to file an amended application.

(2) Unless otherwise ordered by the court, the application will be considered on an ex parte basis.

(3) If the fee waiver application is denied and the court directs the debtor to pay the fee in installments, the initial payment shall be due 14 days after entry of the order denying the fee waiver request. Failure to timely remit the payment will result in the case being dismissed without further notice or hearing.

(4) Debtors who had previously been granted permission to pay the filing fee in installments, including a debtor whose chapter 13 case is converted to chapter 7, and who later seeks waiver of the filing fee, must file the waiver application prior to the next installment payment date to avoid dismissal of the case for nonpayment.

(5) If a debtor is granted a chapter 7 fee waiver and the case is converted to chapter 12 or 13, the debtor shall pay, as applicable, the full chapter 12 or 13 filing fee or file an application to pay the fee in installments within 14 days after entry of the conversion order.

(6) The court may vacate an order waiving the filing fee if developments in the case or administration of the case demonstrate that the waiver was or becomes unwarranted. In the event this occurs, the debtor shall pay the full filing fee or, if the order permits, file an application to pay the fee in installments within 14 days after entry of the order.

(7) Entry of an order waiving the chapter 7 filing fee shall be deemed an order waiving other fees scheduled by the Judicial Conference under 28 U.S.C. §§ 1930(b) and (c) unless otherwise ordered by the court.

(8) The court may direct the clerk not to accept petitions under the chapter 7 fee waiver provisions if the court determines that the debtor is filing petitions in a manner that would constitute abuse of the bankruptcy system.

[Effective December 1, 1998. Amended effective December 1, 2002; October 21, 2003; July 1, 2004; June 2, 2008; December 1, 2009; August 1, 2011; December 1, 2015.]

RULE 1007-1. LISTS, SCHEDULES, STATEMENTS AND OTHER REQUIRED DOCUMENTS; EXTENSION OF TIME TO FILE

(A) General. Lists, schedules, statements or other required documents shall conform to any additional requirements set forth in the "Clerk's Filing Instructions".

(B) Extension of Time to File. Motions, pursuant to Bankruptcy Rule 1007(c) or 9006(b), to extend the time to file lists, schedules, statements or other documents, must set forth the date of the scheduled meeting of creditors. If no date has yet been set, the motion should so state. Motions which seek to extend the time within seven days before the § 341 meeting will be granted only after a hearing and only upon a showing of exceptional circumstances. This rule does not apply to motions to extend the time to file a certificate of credit counseling, which extensions are governed by 11 U.S.C. § 109(h), Bankruptcy Rule 1007(b)(3) and Local Rule 1007-1(E).

[Comment: See also Local Rule 5005-1(A)(2) (compliance with federal judiciary privacy policy) and Local Rule 9013-1(C)(2) (no hearing necessary).]

(C) Local Form Must Accompany Filing of Schedules. If Schedules D, and E/F were not filed with the petition, Local Form "Debtor's Notice of Compliance with Requirements for Amending Creditor Information" is required when Schedules D, and E/F are filed or the case may be dismissed.

(D) Consumer Credit Counseling.

(1) Requirement of Debtor to Complete Part 5 of the Voluntary Bankruptcy Petition Regarding Consumer Credit Counseling Requirement. Individual debtors must comply with credit counseling requirements under 11 U.S.C. §§ 109(h) and 521(b), and Bankruptcy Rule 1007(b)(3), and indicate the debtor's status by completing Part 5 of the Official Bankruptcy Form "Voluntary Petition for Individuals Filing for Bankruptcy".

(2) *Failure to Comply with Consumer Credit Counseling Requirements.*

(a) Failure to File Credit Counseling Certificate. If the debtor fails to complete Part 5 of the individual petition or checks the first box indicating credit counseling was received and the debtor does not file a conforming credit counseling certificate with the petition, the petition will be considered nonconforming and the clerk is directed to serve a notice of deadline to correct deficiency. In such case, if the debtor fails to file a conforming credit counseling certificate by the deadline set in the notice, the case may be dismissed without further notice or hearing. If the second box of Part 5 of the voluntary petition is checked indicating that credit counseling was received but the debtor does not have a certificate, and a conforming credit counseling certificate is not filed within 14 days from the date the petition is filed, the case may be dismissed without further notice or hearing.

(b) Failure to Designate Exigent Circumstances or File Motion. If the third box of Part 5 of the voluntary petition is checked indicating that the debtor was not able to obtain credit counseling due to exigent circumstances and does not attach to the voluntary petition a separate sheet explaining what efforts the debtor made to obtain the briefing, why the debtor was unable to obtain it before filing for bankruptcy, and what exigent circumstances required the debtor to file this case, the case may be dismissed without further notice or hearing.

(c) Failure to File a Motion for Waiver of Credit Counseling Requirement. If the fourth box of Part 5 of the voluntary petition is checked and indicates the reason the debtor is eligible for waiver of the credit counseling requirement and the voluntary petition is not accompanied by the required motion for waiver of credit requirement the case may be dismissed without further notice or hearing.

(E) Payment Advices Required Under 11 U.S.C. § 521(a)(1)(B)(iv). Payment advices should be accompanied by the Local Form "Declaration Regarding Payment Advices". If the debtor was unemployed, self-employed or otherwise did not receive or is unable to produce payment advices or evidence of payment from any employer of the debtor reflecting such payment within 60 days before the date of the filing of the petition, the debtor should also submit the Local Form "Declaration Regarding Payment Advices" and indicate on the form the debtor's status regarding payment advices to avoid automatic dismissal of the case. Before filing, privacy information in payment advices and other documents filed in compliance with this provision, should be redacted in accordance with Local Rule 5005-1(A)(2).

(F) Requests for Copies of Debtor's Tax Information. Requests for copies of the debtor's tax information under 11 U.S.C. § 521 or for individual debtors under 11 U.S.C. § 1116(1)(A), shall be made in accordance with the Administrative Office of the United States Courts "Director's Interim Guidance Regarding Tax Information Under 11 U.S.C. § 521" dated September 20, 2005, and any subsequent directives issued. This document is posted on the court website. In any case where the court directs the clerk to provide a party with a copy of a tax return which was ordered to be filed with the clerk, the clerk shall, unless otherwise ordered, provide such copy via U.S. mail. Any party receiving such copy shall comply with the guidelines addressing privacy of tax information.

[Comment: See also Local Rule 1017-2 (C) "Dismissal Under 11 U.S.C. § 521(e)(2)(B) for Failure to Provide Tax Return" and Local Rule 5005-1(A)(2) (compliance with federal judiciary privacy policy).]

[Effective December 1, 1998. Amended effective December 1, 2002; July 1, 2004; June 2, 2008; December 1, 2009; December 1, 2015.]

RULE 1007–2. MAILING—LIST OR MATRIX

(A) Service Matrix to Accompany Petition. Petitions shall be accompanied by a creditor service matrix prepared in the format required by the "Clerk's Instructions for Preparing, Submitting and Obtaining Service Matrices".

(B) Amendments to Initial Creditor Service Matrix. Amendments to the initial creditor service matrix must comply with Bankruptcy Rule 1009 and Local Rule 1009–1.

[Effective December 1, 1998. Amended effective December 1, 2002; June 2, 2008; August 1, 2011; December 1, 2015.]

RULE 1007–3. STATEMENT OF INTENTION

If a creditor is required to provide a reaffirmation agreement or other information necessary for the debtor to timely perform his or her statement of intention under § 521(a)(2), and the creditor refuses to provide the agreement or information, then the debtor may, but is not required to, file a motion to compel the creditor to supply the required agreement or information.

[Effective June 2, 2008.]

RULE 1009–1. AMENDMENTS TO PETITIONS, LISTS, SCHEDULES, AND STATEMENTS

(A) General.

(1) *Amendments to Correct Clerk's Scrivener's Error.* The clerk shall, without court order, correct any scrivener's error by the clerk occurring during entry of debtor information into the court's records and serve notice of the correction on all parties of record.

(2) *Debtor(s)' Signatures Required.* Amendments to summaries, schedules, statement of income and expenses, lists, statement of financial affairs, or statement of intent shall be signed by each debtor pursuant to Bankruptcy Rule 1008. Each debtor must also, if required, sign the local forms required by subdivision (D)(1) of this rule.

(B) Amendment to Petition to Correct Debtor's Name. A debtor or debtors seeking to amend a petition to change a debtor's name (including designation of other or different names under the category "all other names" required to be listed on the petition), or to delete the name of a debtor, shall file a motion with the court requesting approval of such amendment. The movant shall serve any order adding, deleting or changing any debtor's name in a petition upon all parties of record and file a certificate of service thereof. A debtor may not file a motion to amend a petition to add a joint debtor; the additional debtor shall file a separate petition, and may file a motion for joint administration and/or a motion for substantive consolidation with a pending case.

(C) Amendments to Social Security Number or Other Individual Taxpayer Identification Number.

(1) *Amendments Prior to Entry of Discharge.* A request for change in a debtor's social security number or other individual taxpayer identification number presented for filing prior to entry of a "Discharge of Debtor", and prior to the administrative closing of the case, shall be processed by the clerk if such request is accompanied by an Official Bankruptcy Form "Statement About Your Social Security Numbers" reflecting the amended status on the form and a certificate of service in accordance with Local Rule 2002–1(F), reflecting service on all parties of record.

(2) *Amendments Subsequent to Entry of Discharge.* A request for a change in a debtor's social security number or other individual taxpayer identification number presented for filing subsequent to entry of a "Discharge of Debtor" or the administrative closing of the case, shall only be considered by the court upon the filing of a motion, accompanied by an Official Bankruptcy Form "Statement About Your Social Security Numbers", reflecting the amended status on the form, and a certificate of service in accordance with Local Rule 2002–1(F), reflecting service on all parties of record. The motion shall indicate whether an amended discharge is requested. If the case has been administratively closed, the request must also be accompanied by a motion to reopen case to correct social security number or other individual taxpayer identification number and must be accompanied by the applicable re-opening fee. Amendments to a debtor's social security number or other individual taxpayer identification number shall not be made to the official court record, and amended discharges shall not be issued, absent entry of an order of the court directing such changes.

(3) *Requests Must Comply with Privacy Policy.* In accordance with the federal judiciary privacy policy, any papers (other than the Official Bankruptcy Form "Statement About Your Social Security Numbers" filed with the clerk to reflect the amended social security number (or other individual taxpayer identification number) in conjunction with a request to amend social security number or other individual taxpayer identification number, shall be redacted with respect to the social security number or other individual taxpayer identification number of any debtor.

(D) Amendments to Schedules, Statements and Lists.

(1) *Amendments to Creditors' Information Must Be Accompanied by Required Forms.* Either Official Bankruptcy Form "Declaration About an Individual Debtor's Schedules" or Official Bankruptcy Form "Declaration Under Penalty of Perjury for Non–Individual Debtors," as applicable shall accompany any paper required by Bankruptcy Rule 1007 or 1009. As set forth in the "Clerk's Instructions for Preparing, Submitting and Obtaining Service Matrices", the Local Form "Debtor's Notice of Compliance with Requirements for Amending Creditor Information" is required when schedules D, or E/F are filed or amended subsequent to the filing of the petition. The requirement to file Local Form "Debtor's Notice of Compliance with Requirements for Amending Creditor Information" does not apply when corrections to creditor mailing addresses submitted by the debtor or debtor's attorney using either a "Bypass Notice" or "Notifications of Returned Mail" form provided by the BNC for use in changing or correcting creditors' mailing address information deemed to be "undeliverable" by the BNC. Failure to file Local Form "Debtor's Notice of Compliance with Requirements for Amending Creditor Information" or either Official Bankruptcy Form "Declaration About an Individual Debtor's Schedules" or Official Bankruptcy Form "Declaration Under Penalty of Perjury for Non–

Individual Debtors," as applicable when required may result in the required schedules (along with all other documents filed with them) being stricken.

(2) *Service on Affected Parties Required.* If schedules or lists are amended to add or modify a creditor's name or address, a copy of the notice of the meeting of creditors (or any such amended notice) containing the complete social security number of the debtor shall be served on all affected parties, even if the meeting has already been held. A certificate of service must be filed in compliance with Local Rule 2002-1(F).

(3) *Amendment of Claimed Exemptions.* The debtor shall serve notice of all amendments to the schedule of property claimed as exempt, as provided in Local Rule 4003-1.

(4) *Deadline for Amendments in Unconfirmed Chapter 13 Cases.* Amended schedules and statements in a chapter 13 case that are necessary for confirmation must be filed no later than 14 days prior to the scheduled confirmation hearing. Copies of amended schedules and statements must be served as provided by subdivision (D)(2) of this rule.

[Comment: See also Local Rules 5005-1(F)(1) and (F)(3) (two-day submission requirement on responses to motions and emergency filing procedures do not apply).]

[Effective December 1, 1998. Amended effective December 1, 2002; July 1, 2004; June 2, 2008; December 1, 2009; August 1, 2011; December 1, 2015.]

RULE 1010-1. SUMMONS IN INVOLUNTARY CASES

The clerk will generate and docket the summons in an involuntary case and electronically transmit it to the petitioner(s). The electronic summons is a valid summons, signed, sealed and issued by the clerk and it must be served in accordance with Bankruptcy Rule 1010, along with the involuntary petition.

[Effective December 1, 1998. Amended effective December 1, 2002; June 2, 2008; August 1, 2011. Amended on an interim basis December 1, 2016.]

RULE 1013-1. HEARING AND DISPOSITION IN INVOLUNTARY CASES

(A) Contested Petition. If the debtor files a timely answer contesting the petition, the court will then set the contested petition for trial or, at its discretion, for pretrial conference and trial.

(B) Motion to Convert Involuntary Chapter 7 Case. A motion to convert by the debtor in an involuntary chapter 7 proceeding shall be deemed a consent to entry of an order for relief under the chapter to which the case is being converted.

(C) Debtor's Failure to File Lists, Schedules, Statements, and Matrix. If the debtor has failed to comply with (1) the requirements of Bankruptcy Rule 1007 and Local Rules 1007-1 and 1007-2, and (2) the order for relief, the court shall issue an order to show cause against the debtor or other person designated by the court. The court shall not set any required deadlines and the § 341 notice shall not be issued until a complete service matrix is filed in the format required by the "Clerk's Instructions for Preparing, Submitting and Obtaining Service Matrices".

[Comment: See also 11 U.S.C. §§ 706(a), 1112(a), 1208(a), and 1307(a), Bankruptcy Rule 1019 and Local Rules 1019-1 (converted cases), 1017-2(B) (dismissal of involuntary case for failure to appear at meeting of creditors), and 1074-1 (corporations).]

[Effective December 1, 1998. Amended effective December 1, 2002; July 1, 2004; June 2, 2008.]

RULE 1014-1. TRANSFER OF CASES

(A) Related Cases and Adversary Proceedings. Unless provided for in the order, the transfer of a case shall not include the transfer of any related case unless substantively consolidated, but shall include the transfer of any adversary proceeding in the transferred case, and the transfer of an adversary proceeding shall not include the transfer of any related case or proceeding.

(B) Notice of Transfer. The attorney for the debtor, or clerk of court if the debtor is pro se, shall provide notice to all parties of record of the transfer.

[Comment: See Local Rules 2002-1(F) and 5005-1(G)(2) (Certificate of service required).]

(C) Cases Transferred to This Court. Cases or proceedings transferred to this court shall be assigned to a division and judge pursuant to Local Rule 1073-1.

[Effective December 1, 1998. Amended effective December 1, 2002; June 2, 2008.]

RULE 1015-1. JOINT ADMINISTRATION OR TRANSFER; SUBSTANTIVE CONSOLIDATION

(A) Joint Administration or Transfer.

(1) *Motion.*

(a) Where Filed. A party seeking joint administration of related cases shall file a motion seeking such relief in all affected cases. If all affected cases have not been assigned to the same judge, the party shall file a separate motion in each case assigned to a judge not presiding over the first-filed case, requesting transfer of each such case to the judge presiding over the first-filed case. In matters where joint administration is not at issue, a party seeking transfer of related cases to a single judge may file a motion seeking such relief in the case or cases to be transferred.

(b) Content. Motions for joint administration shall include a statement as to whether joint administration will give rise to any conflict of interest among the estates of the cases to be jointly administered. Motions for intra-district transfer will specify with particularity why a case or cases for which transfer is sought is or are related to a case or cases before the judge to whom transfer is requested, and why the transfer should be to that particular judge rather than the judge presiding over the case for which intra-district transfer is sought.

(2) *Consideration of Motion by Court.*

(a) Chapter 11 Cases. A motion for joint administration may be considered by the court ex parte if filed in accordance with Local Rule 5005-1(G)(1)(a) and Local Rule 9013-1(C)(14), except that a motion requesting joint administration of a chapter 11 case of an individual with one or more related chapter 11 cases shall be considered by the court pursuant to Local Rule 9013-1(D)(4)(i), and in accordance with Local Rule 9073-1.

(b) Cases Other Than Chapter 11. A motion for joint administration filed in other than a chapter 11 case shall be considered by the court after hearing on notice pursuant to Local Rule 9013-1(D)(4)(i), and in accordance with Local Rule 9073-1.

(3) *Local Form Order Required.* A proposed order jointly administering a case shall conform to the applicable local form order jointly administering cases.

(4) *Filing Papers in Cases With Pending Motions for Joint Administration of Non Individual Chapter 11 Cases.* Pending determination of a motion for joint administration of cases where all debtors subject to the motion are non individual chapter 11 debtors, parties in interest shall file documents (other than claims) in the case requested in such motion to be designated the lead case as though the motion has been granted.

(5) *Manner of Joint Administration.* Jointly administered cases shall be administered as follows:

(a) Designation of Lead Case. For cases filed at the same time, the first case assigned to a judge shall be designated in the joint administration order as the "lead case". For cases jointly administered subsequent to the original filing date, the order for joint administration shall designate the "lead case".

(b) Caption. Court papers filed after joint administration shall be captioned as provided in Local Rule 9004-2.

(c) Docket. A single case docket shall be maintained after the entry of the order for joint administration, under the case number of the case designated in the joint administration order as the "lead case". If docketing prior to entry of the order for joint administration commenced under (A)(4) and the motion is subsequently denied, any intervening document filed and docketed in the presumed lead case shall not be redocketed in the intended "member" case. Instead, the clerk shall annotate the member case docket to reflect that papers filed during the pendency of the motion and docketed in the presumed lead case are deemed filed in the intended case as of the date originally filed and shall remain under case number (presumed lead case) and shall not be redocketed.

(d) Claims. A separate claims register shall be maintained for each case. Claims shall be filed only in the name and case number of the debtor against which the claim is asserted. A separate claim must be filed in each jointly administered case in which a claim is asserted against the particular debtor.

(e) Ballots. Ballots shall be styled only in the case name and number of the member case for which the plan being voted on was filed.

(B) Substantive Consolidation. Court papers filed after substantive consolidation shall be styled as provided in Local Rule 9004-2. Any proof of claim filed and docketed prior to the consolidation shall remain docketed on the register for the case number for which it was submitted.

[Comment: See Local Rules 1073-1(B) (divisional assignment of cases), 9004-1 (style of papers) and 9004-2 (caption of papers).]

[Effective December 1, 1998. Amended effective December 1, 2002; June 2, 2008; August 1, 2011; December 1, 2015.]

RULE 1017-1. CONVERSION—REQUEST FOR/NOTICE OF

(A) Orders for Conversions Not Requiring a Hearing. The filing of a motion to convert, either ex parte or on negative notice, must be accompanied by the applicable local form order of conversion in accordance with the court's "Guidelines for Preparing, Submitting and Serving Orders". Where conversion is effected upon the filing of a notice of conversion under § 1208(a) or § 1307(a), the court shall prepare the order upon conversion.

(B) Orders for Conversions Requiring a Hearing. Any party directed to submit a conversion order for conversions requiring a hearing shall submit a proposed order which conforms to the applicable local form order of conversion, modified as necessary to reflect the hearing date and any additional directives of the court, and submitted in accordance with the court's "Guidelines for Preparing, Submitting and Serving Orders".

(C) Required Fees.

(1) *Trustee Fee.* An additional fee intended for payment to chapter 7 trustees under the "Bankruptcy Court Miscellaneous Fee Schedule" is due when the motion or notice of conversion to convert to chapter 7 is filed.

(2) *Conversion Fee.* If applicable, a fee shall be charged at the time a motion to convert is filed in the amount of the difference between the current filing fee for the chapter under which the case was originally commenced and the current filing fee for the chapter to which the case is requested to be converted if the converted to case chapter fee is greater.

[Comment: See "Clerk's Summary of Fees".]

[Effective December 1, 1998. Amended effective December 1, 2002; June 2, 2008.]

RULE 1017-2. DISMISSAL OF A CASE

(A) Failure to File Required Papers.

(1) *After Service of Notice of Deficiency.* The court may dismiss a voluntary case under any chapter without further notice or hearing for failure by the debtor to file required schedules, statements or lists or other documents, and may dismiss a chapter 13 case for failure to file a chapter 13 plan, upon determination that:

(a) notice of the deficiency and a warning that the case will be subject to dismissal without further notice has been provided to the debtor and the debtor's attorney prior to the expiration of the deadline for filing; and

(b) the debtor has failed to file the required papers by the deadline and no timely filed request for an extension of time is pending before the court.

(2) *"Automatic Dismissal" Under 11 U.S.C. § 521(i).* The "automatic dismissal" provision under 11 U.S.C. § 521(i), shall be implemented in this court in an individual chapter 7 or 13 case in accordance with the following requirements:

(a) The assigned trustee shall review each such case to determine whether the debtor has complied with all filing requirements set forth in 11 U.S.C. § 521(a)(1), to the satisfaction of the trustee.

(b) If the debtor has met these requirements:

(i) Except as provided in subdivision (c) below, the trustee shall file an electronic statement with the court as follows: "The information required by 11 U.S.C. § 521(a)(1) as provided by the debtor(s) in this case is complete to the satisfaction of the trustee. No creditor or other party in interest has filed a request for an order of dismissal pursuant to 11 U.S.C. § 521(i)(2) and the trustee does not believe that this case is subject to automatic dismissal pursuant to 11 U.S.C. § 521(i)". The chapter 7 trustee shall file this statement no later than the deadline established by the court for filing complaints objecting to the discharge and the chapter 13 trustee shall file this statement prior to entry of an order confirming the plan.

(ii) Upon the filing of this statement by the trustee, the court shall enter an "Order Determining Debtor's Compliance With Filing Requirements of § 521(a)(1)", to be served on all creditors and parties in interest, stating that the case is not subject to automatic dismissal under 11 U.S.C. § 521(i)(1) or (2). If any creditor or party in interest has any reason to contest the court's finding that the debtor has filed all information required by 11 U.S.C. § 521(a)(1), that party shall file an objection to the order not later than 21 days from the date of entry of the order, and serve such objection on the trustee, the U.S. Trustee, the debtor and the debtor's attorney, if any. The objection should specifically identify the information and document(s) required by 11 U.S.C. § 521(a)(1), that the debtor has failed to file.

(iii) Each creditor or other party in interest served with the order who does not file an objection within the 21 day deadline set forth above, has waived the right to file a motion to dismiss this bankruptcy case for the debtor's failure to comply with 11 U.S.C. § 521(a)(1).

(c) If the trustee has determined that the debtor has not met the filing requirements of 11 U.S.C. § 521(a)(1), and the court has not otherwise waived or extended the deadline for filing, the trustee shall file a motion to dismiss the case no later than the deadlines established for filing the trustee statement in subdivision (b)(i) above.

(d) Notwithstanding this rule, the court shall continue to dismiss cases under this court's local rules and procedures earlier than the 46th day if there are any filing deficiencies.

(e) The trustee assigned to a converted case shall comply with these certification requirements by the deadlines established under the chapter to which the case was converted, unless the certification was filed in the prior case.

(B) Failure to Appear at Meeting of Creditors.

(1) *In Chapter 7, 11, and 12 Cases.* The court may dismiss a voluntary case under chapter 7, 11 or 12, without further notice or hearing, for failure of the debtor (or in the case of a non-individual debtor, the debtor's president, managing partner or other knowledgeable officer) to appear at the meeting of creditors, in a chapter 7 case, upon the filing by the trustee of the Local Form "Chapter 7 Trustee's Motion to Dismiss Case for Failure by Debtor to Appear at the § 341 Meeting"; or in a chapter 11 or 12 case, upon the filing of a motion by the U.S. Trustee and upon determination that:

(a) the clerk has served notice of the intended action, by warning in the § 341 or post-conversion meeting notice served under Local Rule 2002–1(C)(1);

(b) there is no motion pending, pursuant to Local Rule 2003–1, to reconsider the trustee's or U.S. Trustee's denial of a request for continuance of the meeting; and

(c) the case was not commenced as an involuntary case. In an involuntary case, a motion to dismiss for failure of the debtor (or in the case of a non-individual debtor, the debtor's president, managing partner or other knowledgeable officer) to appear at the § 341 meeting shall be scheduled for hearing in accordance with Local Rule 9073–1.

(2) *In Chapter 13 Cases.* The court may dismiss a case under chapter 13, without further notice or hearing, for failure by the debtor to appear at the § 341 or post-conversion meeting, if the clerk served notice of the intended dismissal on the debtor in the notice of commencement of case served by the clerk under Local Rule 2002–1(C)(1).

(C) Dismissal Under 11 U.S.C. § 521(e)(2)(B) for Failure to Provide Tax Return. The court will dismiss cases under section 521(e)(2)(B), only upon motion and after a hearing on notice to the debtor. Any motion to dismiss filed by a creditor must recite that the creditor timely requested a copy of the return under Bankruptcy Rule 4002(b)(4).

(D) Failure to Timely Remit Installment Payment or Other Filing Fees Due From Debtor. The court may dismiss a case without further notice or hearing where the debtor has failed to remit a required installment fee payment or other filing fee due from debtor, including filing fees due upon conversion of a case, upon denial of a chapter 7 fee waiver application or upon revocation of an order permitting waiver of the chapter 7 filing fee.

(E) Fees Outstanding at Time of Dismissal. The balance of any statutory or court-ordered fees, including filing fees, conversion fees, and U.S. Trustee's fees, due and owing at the time of dismissal, must be immediately paid in full.

(F) Disposition of Funds by Chapter 12 or 13 Trustee Upon Dismissal of Case. Upon the dismissal of a case under Chapter 12 or Chapter 13 of the Bankruptcy Code, the trustee shall dispose of funds remaining, after payment to the trustee of approved fees and costs and upon payment of any other court authorized administrative expenses, in the following manner:

(1) If there is a confirmed plan in the case, the trustee shall pay any funds received prior to the entry of the order dismissing the case to creditors pursuant to the terms of the plan. All funds received after the entry of the order shall be paid or returned to the debtor.

(2) If there is neither a confirmed plan nor an order directing otherwise, the trustee shall pay all funds,

(a) in a chapter 12 case to the debtor; and

(b) in a chapter 13 case to the debtor except:

(i) the chapter 13 trustee shall disburse all pre-confirmation adequate protection payments and lease payments to the secured creditors described in § 1326(a)(1)(C), and lessors described in § 1326(a)(1)(B), in accordance with the last filed plan. If there are insufficient funds, payment shall be pro rata; and

(ii) where the court has entered an order pre-confirmation that all pre-confirmation interim payments made to the chapter 13 trustee are vested and non-refundable if the plan is not confirmed and the case is dismissed, the pre-confirmation payments held by the trustee at the time of a dismissal shall be disbursed pro rata in accordance with the last filed plan to the lessors and secured creditors protected by § 1326(a)(1)(B) and (C), and to the other creditors and parties protected by the vesting order.

(3) Notwithstanding subdivisions (1) and (2), any remaining balance owed by the debtor to the court for filing fees and clerk's fees shall be paid by the trustee to the court prior to making any refund to the debtor.

[Comment: See also 11 U.S.C. § 347(a) (unclaimed funds), and Local Rule 2002–1(C)(6) (clerk to serve notice of dismissal).]

(G) Deadline in Reinstated Cases for Filing Motions to Dismiss or for Serving Notices of Hearings Pursuant to Bankruptcy Rule 1017(e). If a case is dismissed prior to the expiration of the deadline for filing a motion to dismiss a case for abuse pursuant to Bankruptcy Rule 1017(e)(1), or for service of notice of a hearing on the court's own motion to dismiss a case for abuse pursuant to Bankruptcy Rule 1017(e)(2), and subsequently reinstated, the deadline shall be modified as follows:

(1) In a case dismissed before the meeting of creditors is held, the new deadline shall be 60 days after the rescheduled meeting of creditors.

(2) In a case dismissed after the meeting of creditors is held, the new deadline shall be 60 days from entry of the order reinstating the case.

[Effective December 1, 1998. Amended effective December 1, 2002; July 1, 2004; June 2, 2008; December 1, 2009; August 1, 2011.]

RULE 1019–1. CONVERSION AND RECONVERSION—PROCEDURE FOLLOWING

(A) Extension of Time to File Post–Conversion Schedules. Any motion pursuant to Bankruptcy Rules 1019 and 9006(b), to extend the time to file lists, schedules, statements or payment advices must set forth, if known, the date of the scheduled post-conversion meeting of creditors. If no date has been set, the motion should so state. Motions that seek to extend the time within seven days before the post-conversion meeting of creditors will be granted only after notice and hearing completed before the beginning of such seven day period.

(B) Schedule of Postpetition Debts and Service Matrix and Notice Requirements. The schedule of postpetition debts required by Bankruptcy Rule 1019(5) or subdivision (C) of this rule, shall be accompanied by a supplemental service matrix and notice to the affected parties shall be given as required by the "Clerk's Instructions for Preparing, Submitting and Obtaining Service Matrices" and Bankruptcy Rule 1009. If no unpaid debts have been incurred since the commencement of the case, a certification to this effect shall be filed.

(C) Cases Converted to Chapters 11, 12, or 13. Upon conversion to chapter 11, 12, or 13, and except as otherwise ordered, and subject to subdivisions (D) and (E) of this rule, all property shall be turned over to the debtor in a chapter 13 case or to the trustee or debtor in possession in a chapter 11 or 12 case. Upon conversion to chapter 11, 12, or 13, new time periods shall commence under Bankruptcy Rules 3002, 4004 and 4007. The final report and schedule of unpaid debts required by Bankruptcy Rule 1019(5), shall be filed by the trustee in a case converted from chapter 7, and by the trustee or debtor in possession in a case converted from chapter 11 or 12. In a case converted from chapter 13, the trustee shall file the final report and the debtor shall file the schedule of unpaid debts. The deadline for fee applications arising from the superseded case is provided in Local Rule 2016–1(C)(2) and (4)(c).

(D) Disposition of Funds by Chapter 12 Trustee Upon Conversion of Case. Upon the conversion of a case under chapter 12 of the Bankruptcy Code, the trustee shall dispose of funds remaining after payment to the trustee of approved fees in costs, and upon payment of any other court authorized administrative expenses, in the same manner as provided for disposition of funds upon entry of the order dismissing case under Local Rule 1017–2(F).

(E) Disposition of Funds by Chapter 13 Trustee Upon Conversion of Case to Chapter 7. Upon the conversion of a case under chapter 13 of the Bankruptcy Code to chapter 7, the trustee shall dispose of funds remaining after payment to the trustee of approved fees and costs, subject to provisions of subdivisions (F) and (G) of this rule, as follows:

(1) if the conversion occurs pre-confirmation, distribute the balance of the funds to the debtor after first paying

(a) any funds held by the chapter 13 trustee in trust in accordance with any vesting order entered in the case; and

(b) any unpaid claim allowed under 11 U.S.C. § 503(b).

(2) if the conversion occurs post-confirmation, distribute the balance of the funds to the debtor after first paying

(a) any administrative creditor that the debtor has directed the chapter 13 trustee pay in accordance with an assignment valid under applicable non-bankruptcy law or other written direction signed by the debtor which assignment or written direction must be filed after the notice of conversion has been filed but no later than seven days after the notice of conversion has been filed; and

(b) to secured creditors any funds that are being held in trust for such secured creditor in accordance with a court approved vesting order,

(3) During the 90 days following the notice of conversion, the trustee shall not distribute any funds that are needed to cover checks issued by the trustee before the notice of conversion was filed. Any checks returned during the 90 day period may not be reissued by the trustee except in accordance with 11 U.S.C. § 1326(a)(3), and if there are any checks still unnegotiated 90 days after the notice of conversion was filed the trustee must put a stop payment on those checks.

(F) Temporary Retention of Funds by Chapter 13 Trustee upon Conversion by Notice of Conversion. Upon the debtor's filing of a notice of conversion pursuant to 11 U.S.C. § 1307(a), and for the purposes of determining what funds are to be turned over to the trustee in the converted case, the chapter 13 trustee shall continue to hold the funds not yet distributed, and not needed to cover outstanding checks, for a period not to exceed 30 days, unless extended by court order, or pending resolution of any motion filed in accordance with subdivision (G) of this rule.

(G) Objection Motions Relating to the Notice to Convert. Any party in interest, including a chapter 7 trustee in the converted case, but not the chapter 13 trustee, shall have 14 days from the filing of the notice of conversion to file either of the following motions (the "objection motions") in the chapter 7 case:

(1) a motion to determine whether the conversion was in bad faith such that all funds held by the chapter 13 trustee that would otherwise be returned to the debtor should be turned over to the chapter 7 trustee, or

(2) a motion to determine whether any or all of the funds held by the chapter 13 trustee were derived from a source other than the debtor's post-petition wages.

If no objection motion is filed, then the chapter 13 trustee shall distribute the funds in accordance with subdivision (E) of this rule. If an objection motion is filed the funds will be distributed as ordered by the court.

(H) Extension of Chapter 13 Trustee Final Report Deadline. If an objection motion is filed, the deadline for the chapter 13 trustee to file a final report in accordance with Bankruptcy Rule 1019(5)(B)(ii) shall be extended until 30 days after the hold period expires or such later date as the court orders.

(I) Filing Claims in Cases Converted From Chapter 13 to Chapter 7. Chapter 13 cases converted to chapter 7 shall be designated as no asset cases. Upon the filing of a "Notice of Assets" by the chapter 7 trustee in a case converted from chapter 13, a claims bar deadline shall be established pursuant to Bankruptcy Rule 3002(c)(5).

(J) Deadline for Filing Postpetition Claims.

(1) *In Converted Cases.* Pursuant to Bankruptcy Rule 1019(6), the deadline for filing by a non-government unit of a request for payment of an administrative expense or a claim filed pursuant to § 348(d) of the Bankruptcy Code, shall be 90 days from the date of the post-conversion meeting. This deadline shall be subject to modification, as applicable, by the provisions of subdivisions (E) or (F)(2) of this rule, and Local Rules 3002-1, and 3003-1.

(2) *In Reconverted Cases.* In asset cases where a schedule of unpaid debts has been filed pursuant to Bankruptcy Rule 1019(5), and where a new claims bar deadline will not be set for all creditors since the original claims bar date had expired prior to conversion, the party filing the schedule of postpetition debts required by Bankruptcy Rule 1019(5) or subdivision (B) of this rule, shall file a timely motion requesting that the court set a deadline for postpetition creditors to file claims in accordance with Bankruptcy Rule 1019(6) and this subdivision. Service of the order setting deadline shall be provided by the party filing the motion.

(K) Extension of Deadline to Object to Exemptions in Converted Cases. The deadline for objection to exemptions in converted cases shall be extended pursuant to Local Rule 4003-1(B).

(L) Filing of Chapter Applicable Official Bankruptcy Forms 122A-1, 122A-1 Supp, 122A-2, 122-B, 122C-1, and 122C-2 Upon Conversion of Case. Individual debtors converting to another chapter shall file any Official Bankruptcy Forms numbered 122A-1, 122A-1 Supp, 122A-2, 122B, 122C-1, and 122C-2 that are applicable to the chapter the case is being converted to within 14 days of entry of the conversion order.

[Comment: The court has noted the split of authority regarding applicability of the means test upon conversion of a case. Reference in this local rule to the filing of Official Bankruptcy Form upon conversion does not constitute any conclusion by this court on this substantive issue.]

[Comment: See Bankruptcy Rules 1017(f) (proceeding to convert case) and 4003(b) (clerk's deadline for objecting to exemptions), Local Rule 2002-1 (C)(1) (notifications of deadlines required in notices), Local Rule 3002-1 (A) (claims deadline in cases converted from chapter 13 to chapter 7) and Local Rule 9013-1(D)(3)(h) (conversion of chapter 7 case by debtor on negative notice).]

[Effective December 1, 1998. Amended effective December 1, 2002; June 2, 2008; December 1, 2009. Amended, on an interim basis, effective December 1, 2010. Amended effective August 1, 2011; December 1, 2015. Amended on an interim basis effective March 11, 2016.]

RULE 1071-1. DIVISIONS—BANKRUPTCY COURT

The court maintains permanent offices located in Miami, Ft. Lauderdale and West Palm Beach. At the time of filing or transfer, cases are assigned to one of three divisions: the Miami Division, consisting of Miami-Dade and Monroe Counties; the Fort Lauderdale Division, consisting of Broward County; and the West Palm Beach Division, consisting of

Palm Beach, Highlands, Indian River, Martin, Okeechobee, and St. Lucie Counties.

[Effective December 1, 1998. Amended effective December 1, 2002; June 2, 2008.]

RULE 1073-1. DIVISIONAL AND JUDICIAL ASSIGNMENT OF CASES

(A) Divisional Assignment. All cases shall be reviewed by the clerk upon filing to verify correct divisional assignment and, where appropriate and absent other order of the court, the clerk shall issue a notice of divisional transfer to enable the case to be re-assigned:

(1) if the debtor is an individual, to the division where the first address listed by the debtor on the petition is located; or

(2) if the debtor is a non-individual, to the division where the principle place of business address listed by the debtor on the petition is located.

If a party in interest believes that the case should be assigned to a different division within this district, such party shall file a motion requesting transfer to the desired division and state the reasons therefor.

[Comment: See Local Rules 1015-1(A) (addressing judicial assignment of cases and joint administration or transfer and 1071-1 (divisions of court).]

(B) Judicial Assignment.

(1) All cases shall be assigned on a blind rotation basis, within each chapter category, to a judge assigned to hear cases in the division to which the case has been assigned pursuant to subdivision (A).

(2) A matter from which a judge has been recused or disqualified shall be reassigned by the clerk:

(a) first to another judge resident in the same division, or

(b) to another division if the judge being recused or disqualified is the only resident judge in that division.

(3) Assignment to a specific judge without regard to divisional classification shall be considered by the court on motion by a party in the following cases upon the filing of a motion:

(a) all husband and wife cases, whether filed jointly or severally: and

(b) cases that may be jointly administered pursuant to Bankruptcy Rule 1015.

(4) Notice of reassignment of a case to another judge shall be provided to all parties of record by the clerk of court.

[Effective December 1, 1998. Amended effective December 1, 2002; June 2, 2008; August 1, 2011; December 1, 2015. Amended on an interim basis January 25, 2017.]

RULE 1074-1. CORPORATIONS

A voluntary petition or consent to an involuntary petition filed by a corporation shall be accompanied by a copy of the duly attested corporate resolution (or other appropriate authorization) authorizing the action.

[Comment: See also Local Rule 9010-1(B)(1) (corporations must be represented by an attorney).]

[Effective December 1, 1998. Amended effective December 1, 2002; June 2, 2008; December 1, 2015.]

RULE 1075-1. CLERK'S NOTICE TO CONSUMER DEBTORS REQUIRED UNDER 11 U.S.C. § 342(b)

The clerk shall be deemed to be in compliance with 11 U.S.C. § 342(b), by posting in each public intake area of the clerk's office and by making available to all requesting parties, copies of the Administrative Office of the United States Courts Director's Procedural Form "Notice Required by 11 U.S.C. § 342(b) for Individuals Filing for Bankruptcy".

[Effective December 1, 1998. Amended effective December 1, 2002; June 2, 2008; December 1, 2009; December 1, 2015.]

RULE 2002-1. NOTICES

(A) By Whom Served. Unless otherwise provided by these rules or order of the court:

(1) The proponent of any action in any case or proceeding shall serve notice of the proposed action on all parties to whom notice of the proposed action is mandated by the Bankruptcy Rules or by these rules and on all directly affected parties. The proponent shall serve notice of any hearing scheduled on the proposed action on the same parties in the manner provided by Local Rule 9073-1 or, if applicable, subdivision (H) of this rule. The debtor shall ensure that the mailing matrix required by Local Rule 1007-2, includes those parties required to be served pursuant to Bankruptcy Rule 2002(j).

(2) If the proponent of any action is the U.S. Trustee, or a trustee in a case designated in the § 341 or post-conversion meeting notice as a no-asset case, and the rules require service upon all parties of record, the proponent shall prepare the notice and the clerk shall provide the required service.

[Comment: See also Local Rules 2002-1(F) (certificate of service required), 9073-1 (notices of hearing), 9013-1(C) (motions for which no hearing is necessary), and 9076-1 (electronic service).]

(B) Notices Required to be Served by Clerk or Other Person. Unless otherwise directed by the court, wherever the Bankruptcy Rules or local rules require that the clerk or some other person as the court may direct shall provide notice pursuant to that rule, the clerk is authorized to designate a trustee, debtor in possession, or other party to provide any notice required to interested parties where the interests of justice and efficiency are served. The clerk is further authorized to review the form of all such notices to ensure that the notice complies with the requirements of the court and appropriate rules.

(C) Form, Content, and Manner of Service of Particular Notices.

(1) *Clerk's Notices of Bankruptcy Case, § 341 Meeting or Post-Conversion Meeting, Chapter 13 Confirmation Hearing, Deadlines, and Intended Actions.* The clerk shall prepare and serve the Official Bankruptcy Form 9 Notice of Bankruptcy Case (as modified locally by this court), (and if applicable,

the local initial notice of chapter 13 case and filing requirements of debtor) in each new and converted case.

[Comment: The clerk's notice of bankruptcy case which is mailed to all parties of record pursuant to Local Rule 2002-1(C)(1) shall, on the service copy, contain the complete social security number or individual taxpayer identification number of a debtor, however, the original retained in the court records shall be a redacted copy, containing only the last four digits of the number. Any party required to serve a copy of this notice on additional parties pursuant to Local Rule 1009-1(D)(2) shall serve a copy containing the complete social security number or other individual taxpayer identification number.]

(2) *Notice of Sale.* The trustee or debtor in possession shall prepare and serve a notice of use, sale or lease of any property as provided by Local Rule 6004-1.

(3) *Notice of Continued or Rescheduled § 341 Meeting, Post-Conversion Meeting or Chapter 13 Confirmation Hearing.* The party requesting the rescheduling shall provide notice of any rescheduled § 341 meeting, post-conversion meeting, or chapter 13 confirmation hearing, but no written notice shall be necessary for a § 341 meeting, post-conversion meeting, or chapter 13 confirmation hearing continued after it begins if the continued date is announced at the meeting or hearing.

[Comment: See also Local Rule 2002-1(C)(8) (notice of continued chapter 11 confirmation hearings).]

(4) *Notices Related to Discharge.* In a chapter 7, 12 or 13 case, the clerk, or the clerk's designee under subdivision (B), shall provide notice of entry of an order of discharge or an order denying, waiving or revoking discharge by serving the order on all creditors and other parties. In a chapter 11 case, notice of entry of the discharge, if applicable, shall be provided for non-individual cases in the order confirming plan and for individual cases, in the final decree. In an individual chapter 7, 12, or 13 case closed without entry of discharge for failure to meet the requirements of Bankruptcy Rule 1007(b)(7) or Local Rule 4004-3(A)(3) or (4), the clerk shall serve notice that the case was closed without entry of a discharge.

[Comment: The discharge, order denying discharge or notice closing case without discharge which is mailed to all parties of record pursuant to Local Rule 2002-1(C)(4) shall, on the service copy, contain the redacted social security or other individual taxpayer identification number of a debtor which will consist of the last four digits of the number.]

(5) *Chapter 13 Plan; Amended Plan.* The clerk, or the trustee if the clerk so designates, shall serve the Local Form "Chapter 13 Plan" filed pursuant to Local Rule 3015-1(B). The attorney for the debtor or clerk, if the debtor is pro se, shall serve any subsequently filed amended plan or modified plan and any notice of hearing thereon on all affected parties.

[Comment: See Bankruptcy Rule 3015 and Local Rules 3015-1(B) and 3015-2 (form, notice and deadline requirements for chapter 13 plans and amended plans).]

(6) *Notice of Entry of Order Dismissing Case or Order Reinstating Chapter 13 Case.* The clerk, or the clerk's designee under subdivision (B), shall serve the order of dismissal or order reinstating the case entered in any case on all parties of record.

(7) *Notice of Claims Deadline in Chapter 7 Cases Reopened to Administer Additional Assets or Former No Asset Chapter 7 Cases.* The clerk, or the clerk's designee under subdivision (B), shall serve any order or notice setting a deadline pursuant to Local Rule 3002-1 for filing claims in a chapter 7 case reopened to administer additional assets or a chapter 7 no asset case where the chapter 7 trustee has filed a "Notice of Assets".

(8) *Notice of Chapter 11 Disclosure Statement and Confirmation Hearings and Continued Hearings.* The proponent of the chapter 11 plan and disclosure statement shall provide the notice of the order required pursuant to Bankruptcy Rules 2002(b)(1), 2002(b)(2), 2002(d)(5), 2002(d)(6), 2002(d)(7) and 3017, by serving the court orders described in Local Rules 3016-2 or 3017-2. The party seeking the continuance of any chapter 11 disclosure statement hearing or confirmation hearing shall provide notice of the continued hearing, but no notice shall be necessary for a disclosure statement hearing or confirmation hearing continued after it begins if the continued date is announced at the noticed hearing.

[Comment: See also Local Rules 3017-1 and 3017-2 (service of disclosure statement, plan, and ballot).]

(9) *Notice of Fee Applications in Chapter 11 Case.* The proponent of a chapter 11 plan shall serve a list of fee applicants in the form prescribed by Bankruptcy Rule 2002(c)(2), in accordance with Bankruptcy Rule 2002(a)(6) or, if applicable, Local Rule 2002-1(H), at least 14 days before the date of the confirmation hearing or within such other time set by the court.

[Comment: See also Bankruptcy Rules 2002(a)(6) (service on trustee and all creditors required) and 2002(k) (service on U.S. Trustee required) and Local Rule 2016-1(C)(1) (deadline for filing fee applications).]

(10) *Notice of Trustee's Final Report and Applications for Compensation and Setting Deadline for Objections.* In chapter 7 cases in which the amount of net proceeds realized exceeds the amount set forth in Bankruptcy Rule 2002(f)(8), or the amount of any application for compensation exceeds the amount set forth in Bankruptcy Rule 2002(a)(6), the chapter 7 trustee shall provide notice of the trustee's final report of estate, the court's intention to approve the fee applications, and the 21 day deadline for objecting to the final report or the fee applications by serving the "Notice of Trustee's Final Report and Applications for Compensation (NFR)," accompanied by the Local Form "Trustee's Summary of Requested Fees and Expenses".

[Comment: See also Bankruptcy Rules 2002(a)(6) and (f)(8) (notice of fee applications and notice of final report) and Local Rules 2016-1(C)(2) (deadline for fee applications) and 3009-1 (trustee's final report and proposed dividend).]

(11) *Service of Order Confirming Plan.* In a chapter 11 or 12 case, the proponent of the plan shall serve the order confirming plan. In a chapter 13 case, the clerk, or some other person as the court may direct, shall serve the order confirming plan. Orders confirming plans shall be served on all parties of record.

[Comment: See Bankruptcy Rule 3020(c) (notice of entry of confirmation order) and Local Rule 5005-1(G)(2) (service of orders generally).]

(12) *Service of Chapter 13 Local Form "Debtor's Certificate of Compliance, Motion for Issuance of Discharge and Notice*

of Deadline to Object". The attorney for the debtor (or clerk of court, if the debtor is pro se) shall serve a copy of the Local Form "Debtor's Certificate of Compliance, Motion for Issuance of Discharge and Notice of Deadline to Object" or, if applicable, the Local Form "Debtor's Certificate of Compliance, Motion for Issuance of Discharge Before Completion of Plan Payments, and Notice of Deadline to Object," on all parties of record as required under Local Rule 4004–3(A)(3).

(13) *Service in Chapter 11 or 12 Cases of Local Form "Notice of Deadline to Object to Debtor's Statement Re: 11 U.S.C. § 522(q)(1) Applicability, Payment of Domestic Support Obligations, and [For Chapter 11 Cases Only] Applicability of Financial Management Course and Statement Regarding Eligibility to Receive a Discharge".* In cases involving an individual debtor, the attorney for the debtor (or clerk of court, if the debtor is pro se) shall serve a copy of the Local Form "Notice of Deadline to Object to Debtor's Statement Re: 11 U.S.C. § 522(q)(1) Applicability, Payment of Domestic Support Obligations, and [For Chapter 11 Cases Only] Applicability of Financial Management Course and Statement Regarding Eligibility to Receive a Discharge" on all parties of record as required under Local Rule 4004–3(A)(4).

(14) *Clerk's Notice Under 11 U.S.C. § 362(l)(4)(B) Advising Debtor and Lessor That Automatic Stay is Not in Effect Under 11 U.S.C. § 362(b)(22).* The clerk shall provide the notice required under 11 U.S.C. § 362(*l*)(4)(B), that the stay is not in effect, immediately upon determination that the debtor has not filed either Official Bankruptcy Form "Initial Statement About an Eviction Judgment Against You" containing the certification required under 11 U.S.C. § 362(*l*)(1), or Official Bankruptcy Form "Statement About Payment of an Eviction Judgment Against You" containing the certification required under 11 U.S.C. § 362(*l*)(2). The notice shall also advise parties that if any funds were deposited under § 362(*l*), the court shall order the clerk to disburse the funds only upon the filing of a motion served on all affected parties.

(D) Service Matrices Maintained Under CM/ECF. The types of service lists available in CM/ECF are described in the "Clerk's Instructions for Preparing, Submitting and Obtaining Service Matrices". Verification that a particular party appears accurately on any service matrix, appearance list or claims register is the responsibility of the party providing notice and the party listed. Omissions of parties on any service list maintained under CM/ECF due to failure by the debtor or other responsible party to provide the clerk with supplemental matrices, or where applicable, notices of change of address, shall be the responsibility of that party to correct. Determination as to the appropriate parties to serve shall be the responsibility of the party providing service.

(E) Multi-paged Notices. Multiple page one-sided papers may be condensed to two-sided papers for noticing purposes, but the first page of a paper may not be printed on the reverse side of a separate paper, except by the clerk.

(F) "Certificate of Service" Substantially Conforming to Local Form Required. A party who provides notice of any requested relief, proposed action or other service pursuant to the Bankruptcy Rules, these rules, or by order of the court, shall file with the court, within two business days after service, a certificate of service substantially conforming to the Local Form "Certificate of Service", that shall list the names and addresses and date and manner of service of all parties required to be served. The "Notice of Electronic Filing" (NEF) is not a substitute for the filing of a separate certificate of service but may be incorporated by reference in the certificate of service for the purpose of identifying those parties who were served electronically, even if, by such incorporation, the result is inclusion in the certificate of service of some case participants who received electronic service but were not required to be served. The certificate of service must reflect that non-registered users or registered users who have yet to appear electronically in a specific case were served by conventional paper or other manner of service required under the federal rules and this court's local rules. Papers previously filed with the court that are the subject of the certificate of service shall be referenced as provided under Local Rule 9004–1(D) and not attached to the certificate of service filed with the court. A certificate of service conforming with this local rule may be incorporated into a motion, application or other paper filed with the court.

[Comment: See also Bankruptcy Rule 2002 and Local Rules 5005–1(G) (service of orders), and 9013–1(B) (service of motions).]

(G) Changes of Address. Parties seeking to change their own U.S. Mail address in cases and proceedings in this court must file a signed Notice of Change of Address in each case or proceeding in which the change is to be effected. Parties registered directly with the BNC to receive notices under the EBN program must also notify the BNC directly of any changes in service information. Debtors registered directly with the clerk under the DeBN program must also notify the court directly of a change in the email service address by filing with the clerk an updated Local Form "Debtor's Request to Receive Notices Electronically Under DeBN Program".

[Comment: See Local Rule 9036–1(C). Debtor Electronic Bankruptcy Noticing (DeBN).]

(H) Designation of "Master Service List" in Chapter 11 Cases.

(1) In a chapter 11 case having more than 75 parties of record, a party responsible for service may, at the server's option and in lieu of service on all parties of record, or must, if the court or these rules direct, serve the following parties:

(a) The U.S. Trustee;

(b) The debtor;

(c) The debtor's attorney;

(d) Any indenture trustees;

(e) The members of and attorneys to any official committee established pursuant to 11 U.S.C. § 1102, and, before such appointment, the creditors shown on the list required by Bankruptcy Rule 1007(d);

(f) Creditors holding claims known to be secured by property in which the estate has an interest;

(g) The United States and its agencies as required by Bankruptcy Rule 2002(j);

(h) Those parties and attorneys who have formally requested notice by filing with the court and serving upon debtor's attorney a notice of appearance or request for service of notices and papers in the case;

(i) Any examiner or trustee (and their attorneys) appointed in the case; and

(j) Any parties and entities (including local governmental units) previously known to the debtor to have a particularized interest in the subject of the notice(s) required to be served.

A certificate of service must be filed pursuant to subdivision (F) of this Rule.

(2) The names and addresses for the parties listed in subdivision (H)(1), shall constitute the "Master Service List" in each case. This list shall be maintained by the debtor's attorney, or if applicable, by the chapter 11 trustee's attorney, who shall update the list no less than once each month, by adding or modifying the names and addresses of those parties listed in subdivision (H)(1) during the previous month. An updated "Master Service List" shall be filed with the clerk and a copy served upon all parties listed. In addition, if a party added to, or modified on, the "Master Service List" is a creditor, the debtor's attorney or, if applicable, the chapter 11 trustee, shall file amended schedules in accordance with Bankruptcy Rule 1009 and Local Rule 1009-1. If the added or modified party is not a creditor, the debtor's attorney, or if applicable, the chapter 11 trustee, shall advise the party in writing that the party must file directly with the court, as applicable, a claim, notice of appearance or notice of change of address, in order to be added to, or correctly reflected in, the service databases maintained by the clerk and to receive any notices other than those pursuant to this Rule. Notice in the case will at all times be deemed proper and adequate if papers, and the notices related to such papers, are timely served upon any party whose interests are directly affected by a specific paper, and upon those parties on the "Master Service List". Notwithstanding the provisions of this rule, the service databases maintained by the clerk, as set forth in Local Rule 2002-1(E), shall not be updated by the clerk upon the filing of a "Master Service List". Additions to, or modifications of, the clerk's service databases shall only occur upon the filing with the clerk of, as applicable, amended schedules, claims, notices of appearance or changes of address pursuant to, and in accordance with, the provisions of the Bankruptcy Rules and the local rules, including Local Rules 1007-2, 1009-1, 1019-1, 2002-1, 3002-1 and 3003-1.

(3) Except as otherwise provided by these rules or the court, subdivision (H)(1) shall not apply to notices required to be served on the debtor, the trustee, equity security holders, and all creditors and indenture trustees pursuant to Bankruptcy Rule 2002, including, without limitation, the notice of

(a) commencement and the meeting of creditors under 11 U.S.C. §§ 341 or 1104(b);

(b) a proposed use, sale or lease of all or substantially all of the property of the estate;

(c) the time fixed for filing objections and the hearing to consider approval of a disclosure statement pursuant to Bankruptcy Rule 3017 and Local Rules 3017-1 or 3017-2;

(d) the time fixed for filing objections and the hearing to consider confirmation of a plan pursuant to Bankruptcy Rule 3020 and Local Rules 3017-1 or 3017-2 and 3020-1;

(e) the hearing on the dismissal or conversion of the case to another chapter; and

(f) entry of an order confirming a plan.

(4) Upon timely motion of any party of record, the court may consider, for cause shown, application of this rule to a chapter 11 case with fewer than 75 parties.

[Comment: registered users are deemed served if they have filed an electronic appearance in the case and separate mail notice is not required under this rule. See Local Rule 9076-1.]

(I) Authority to Limit Service for Certain Chapter 7 Notices. A party in a chapter 7 case directed to serve notice under Bankruptcy Rules 2002(a)(2), (a)(3), or (a)(4), is authorized to limit service under Bankruptcy Rule 2002(h). If the limited service option is utilized, the certificate of service shall include a statement to that effect.

(J) Requests for Service by Creditors Under 11 U.S.C. § 342(f). A creditor filing a notice pursuant to 11 U.S.C. § 342(f), shall file such notice directly with the National Creditor Registration Service (NCRS) established by the Administrative Office of the United States Courts for this purpose. The clerk shall forward any such requests filed in this court to the NCRS for processing. A link to the NCRS website and the toll free number shall be maintained on the court website.

[Effective December 1, 1998. Amended effective December 1, 2002; July 1, 2004; June 2, 2008; May 1, 2009; December 1, 2009; August 1, 2011; December 1, 2011; December 1, 2015. Amended on an interim basis effective June 1, 2016.]

RULE 2003-1. MEETING OF CREDITORS

Requests to reschedule the § 341 or post-conversion meeting of creditors must be directed to the trustee, with a copy to the U.S. Trustee, or, in chapter 11 cases, to the U.S. Trustee. Only if the request is denied may the debtor file with the court a motion to reschedule. If the request is granted, notice of the rescheduled § 341 meeting shall be provided pursuant to Local Rule 2002-1(C)(3).

[Effective December 1, 1998. Amended effective December 1, 2002; June 2, 2008.]

RULE 2004-1. EXAMINATIONS OF DEBTOR AND OTHERS

(A) Manner of Setting Examination. No order will be necessary to authorize an examination pursuant to Bankruptcy Rule 2004, or to require production of documents at the examination. Examinations may be scheduled by filing the Local Form "Notice of Rule 2004 Examination" and serving the notice on the trustee, the debtor, the debtor's attorney and the party to be examined, and, if applicable, the subpoena required by subdivision (D) of this Rule.

(B) Reasonable Notice. The attendance of the examinee and the production of documents may not be required less than 14 days after actual delivery of the notice, except by agreement of the parties or order of the court. However, an examination may be scheduled on shorter notice if the notice provides that the party to be examined need not file any objection to the short notice but must notify the examining party promptly of the inadequate notice and must offer a reasonable opportunity to be examined on another date. To the extent that a request for production of documents under this rule may be construed as a request under Bankruptcy Rule 7034, the time to respond is shortened to 14 days.

(C) Motion for Protective Order. An interested party may file, prior to the date of the proposed examination, a motion for protective order stating the reasons for prohibiting, limiting or rescheduling the examination, and the examination shall be stayed until the court rules on the motion.

(D) Subpoena. No subpoena shall be necessary to compel attendance of, or production of documents from, the debtor at an examination of the debtor, but a Local Form "Subpoena for Rule 2004 Examination" shall be necessary to compel the attendance of, or production of documents by, a witness other than the debtor.

(E) Videotaped Examinations. Examinations may be videotaped. The notice or subpoena must indicate that the examination is to be videotaped and whether it will also be recorded stenographically.

[Comment: See also Bankruptcy Rules 7026–7037 and 9014 and Local Rule 7026–1 (discovery in adversary proceedings and contested matters.)]

[Effective December 1, 1998. Amended effective December 1, 2002; June 2, 2008; December 1, 2009; December 1, 2015.]

RULE 2007–1. COMMITTEE ACCESS TO INFORMATION

(A) During the 21 day period immediately following the date of formation of a committee under 11 U.S.C. § 1102(a), the committee shall not be required to provide access to information under § 1102(b)(3)(A), to the extent such information has been reasonably designated by the party providing such information as non-public, proprietary, privileged, work product or otherwise confidential. At any time during or after this 21 day "safe harbor" the committee may move the court for entry of an order clarifying the type and extent of access to information the committee shall be required to provide under § 1102(b)(3)(A). Provided the committee has filed a motion requesting such relief prior to the expiration of the 21 days safe harbor, the committee shall not be required to provide access to information under § 1102(b)(3)(A), to the extent such information has been reasonably designated by the party providing such information as non-public proprietary, privileged, work product or otherwise confidential until such times as the court enters an order on such motion.

(B) Upon motion by the committee, and upon notice and a hearing, the court may determine the appropriate media for solicitation and receipt of comments from creditors including, without limitation, a designated e-mail address, phone number, or website to which creditors and parties-in-interest may direct comments to the committee.

(C) Nothing in this local rule is intended to limit, expand or otherwise affect the right of any creditor of the kind described in § 1102(b)(3)(A), to seek relief under § 1102(b)(3)(C), at any time.

[Effective June 2, 2008. Amended effective December 1, 2009; December 1, 2015.]

RULE 2014–1. EMPLOYMENT OF PROFESSIONALS

(A) Attorneys. Applications seeking approval to employ an attorney for a debtor in possession or trustee will be considered only upon submission of the Local Form "Debtor in Possession's Application for Employment of Attorney" or "Trustee's Application for Employment of Attorney" accompanied by the Local Forms "Affidavit of Proposed Attorney for Debtor in Possession/Trustee" and "Order Approving Employment of [Debtor in Possession's/Trustee's] Attorney". Applications shall also include a copy of any executed Engagement Letter or Retention Agreement. If an Engagement Letter or Retention Agreement is supplemented or modified in writing, applicant *shall* timely file a copy of the supplement or modification.

(B) Auctioneers. Applications seeking approval to employ an auctioneer will be considered only upon submission of the Local Form "Application for Approval of Employment of Auctioneer" in accordance with Local Rule 6005–1.

[Comment: See also Bankruptcy Rule 2014(a) (all professionals' applications shall be accompanied by a verified statement of disinterestedness) and Bankruptcy Rule 6003(a) (interim and final relief following commencement of case—applications for employment) and Local Rules 2016–1 (compensation of professionals), 6005–1 (auctioneers), and 2090–1 and 9010–1 (attorneys).]

[Effective December 1, 1998. Amended effective December 1, 2002; June 2, 2008; December 1, 2015.]

RULE 2015–1. REPORTS

The trustee or debtor in possession shall file financial reports of the estate according to the format and time schedule provided by the U.S. Trustee, and shall serve a copy on the U.S. Trustee. The reports shall contain a statement of all receipts and disbursements, and payments (including wage withholding, unemployment and social security taxes) to employees, and such other information as is required by the U.S. Trustee.

[Comment: See also 11 U.S.C. § 704(a)(8), § 1107(a), and § 1203, Bankruptcy Rule 2015 and Local Rule 2081–1 (chapter 11 debtor's payroll and sales tax report).]

[Effective December 1, 1998. Amended effective December 1, 2002; June 2, 2008; December 1, 2015.]

RULE 2016–1. COMPENSATION FOR SERVICES RENDERED AND REIMBURSEMENT OF EXPENSES

(A) General. Requests for compensation for professional services or reimbursement of expenses from the estate are governed by Bankruptcy Rule 2016 and this rule, except that applications for compensation by auctioneers are governed by Local Rule 6005–1. Subject to later review by the court and the U.S. Trustee, chapter 7 trustees are authorized to pay, without prior approval of the court, those expenses as provided in, and pursuant to, the court's "Guidelines for Reimbursement to Chapter 7 Trustees for Costs Without Prior Court Order". Disclosure of compensation by the attorney for debtor shall conform to the Official Bankruptcy Form "Disclosure of Compensation of Attorney for Debtor".

(B) Requirements for Compensation.

(1) *Applications for Compensation for Professional Services or Reimbursement of Expenses other than by Attorneys for Chapter 13 Debtors.* Applications for compensation of attorneys (other than by attorneys for chapter 13 debtors), accountants, and other professionals submitted pursuant to Bankruptcy Rule 2016 shall conform substantially to the court's "Guidelines for Fee Applications for Professionals in the Southern District of Florida in Bankruptcy Cases" and the local forms described in the guidelines; provided, however, that applications for cumulative compensation that do not exceed $2,500 need not include a breakdown by categories of work performed. Applications for compensation by creditors' attorneys, other than under 11 U.S.C. § 503(b)(2), (3) and (4), are not governed by this subdivision but may be incorporated into the creditor's claim, request for payment of administrative expense, or motion to determine value of secured claim.

(2) *Compensation for Professional Services or Reimbursement of Expenses by Attorney for Chapter 13 Debtor.* Sanctions.

(a) General. Compensation for professional services or reimbursement of expenses by attorneys for chapter 13 debtors shall comply with the court's "Guidelines for Compensation for Professional Services or Reimbursement of Expenses by Attorneys for Chapter 13 Debtors Pursuant to Local Rule 2016-1(B)(2)(a)" ("Chapter 13 Fee Guidelines") and the local forms described in the "Chapter 13 Fee Guidelines". Chapter 13 debtors and their attorneys must execute the Local Form "Rights and Responsibilities Agreement Between Chapter 13 Debtor(s) and Chapter 13 Debtor(s)' Attorney for Cases Filed in the United States Bankruptcy Court, Southern District of Florida" prior to filing a chapter 13 case in this court. The form shall be retained by the parties and not filed with the court. A copy of the agreement must be made available to the chapter 13 trustee at the meeting of creditors.

(b) Sanctions. The failure of an attorney to timely file the plan or schedules, to attend the meeting of creditors, to promptly and timely file amendments, or to appear at confirmation hearings or at any other scheduled meetings or hearings shall result in the reduction of the attorney's fee, for each such occurrence, in such amount as the court finds to be appropriate.

(3) *Interim Compensation in Chapter 11 Cases.*

(a) General. Applications for interim compensation shall comply with the "Guidelines for Fee Applications for Professionals in the Southern District of Florida in Bankruptcy Cases" for final applications unless otherwise ordered by the court.

(b) Motions to Permit Monthly Payment of Interim Fee Applications. In larger chapter 11 cases, upon motion of a chapter 11 debtor, the court, upon notice and hearing, may consider approval of procedures for monthly payment of interim fee applications of chapter 11 professionals. The motion and proposed Local Form "Order Establishing Procedures to Permit Monthly Payment of Interim Fee Applications of Chapter 11 Professionals" shall be served on the U.S. Trustee, the attorney for each official committee (or if no committee is appointed, the 20 largest unsecured creditors), attorneys for all postpetition lenders (or attorneys for their agents) and all parties who have filed a notice of appearance.

(C) Deadlines for Filing Applications in All Chapter Cases. Unless otherwise ordered by the court, the final application for compensation of any professional must be filed:

(1) in chapter 11 cases, not later than 21 days prior to the date of the confirmation hearing, and in cases involving small business debtors not later than 14 days prior to the date of the confirmation hearing, though the applicant may supplement the application with additional supporting documentation under the guidelines at, or prior to, the confirmation hearing, if the application included an estimate of the additional fees and costs necessary through confirmation;

(2) in chapter 7 cases converted or reconverted from chapter 11, 12, or 13 cases, for those services rendered and costs incurred during the superseded case, not later than 90 days after the post-conversion meeting of creditors, in accordance with Bankruptcy Rule 3002(c);

(3) in chapter 12 cases, not later than two business days prior to the confirmation hearing; and

(4) in chapter 13 cases where applications are required:

(a) Prior to confirmation, a local form fee application shall be filed and served on the debtor no later than 14 days prior to the confirmation hearing and notice provided to all interested parties that the fee application will be heard at the confirmation hearing.

(b) Subsequent to confirmation, a local form fee application for fees in conjunction with filing modifications to the plan after confirmation shall be filed and served on the debtor no later than 14 days prior to the hearing on the modified plan, and notice provided to all interested parties that the fee application will be heard with the motion to modify the confirmed plan. Any additional requests for compensation which exceed the amounts permitted under the "Chapter 13 Fee Guidelines" referenced in subdivision (B)(2)(a) of this rule, shall require application and approval in accordance with the "Chapter 13 Fee Guidelines" and shall comply with the notice and hearing requirements of Local Rule 9073-1.

(c) Upon dismissal or conversion of a case prior to confirmation of a plan, a local form fee application shall be filed and served on the debtor by an attorney seeking compensation in excess of the amounts set forth in paragraph (A)(1) of the "Chapter 13 Fee Guidelines". The application must be filed and served no later than 14 days after entry of the order of dismissal or conversion, and the applicant shall comply with the notice and hearing requirements of Local Rule 9073-1.

(D) Bankruptcy Petition Preparers Disclosure of Compensation. Bankruptcy petition preparers must submit fee disclosure information pursuant to 11 U.S.C. § 110(h), in a format conforming to Administrative Office of the United States Courts Director's Procedural Form "Disclosure of Compensation of Bankruptcy Petition Preparer". The Official

Bankruptcy Form "Bankruptcy Petition Preparer's Notice, Declaration, and Signature" must be filed with each document prepared for filing by the bankruptcy petition preparer as required by 11 U.S.C. § 110. If more than one petition preparer works on a case, both petition preparers must file the required fee disclosure information. A petition preparer is only entitled to be compensated if that petition preparer actually does work as a petition preparer. No referral fees are permitted.

[Comment: See also Bankruptcy Rule 2002(c)(2) (notice of fee applications) and Local Rules 1019-1(F) (deadline for filing postpetition claims), 2002-1(C)(9) (service of fee application), 7054-1(F) (motion for fees and costs in adversary proceeding), 8014-1(F) (motion for fees and costs in appeals), 9013-1(C)(3) (ex parte motions to approve employment) and 9013-1(D)(4)(c) (hearing required).]

[Effective December 1, 1998. Amended effective December 1, 2002; July 1, 2004; June 2, 2008; December 1, 2009; December 1, 2015.]

RULE 2081-1. CHAPTER 11—GENERAL

(A) Required Payroll and Sales Tax Reports.

(1) *Content of Reports.* Chapter 11 debtors (other than individuals not engaged in business) shall file a Local Form "Debtor's Notice of Filing Payroll and Sales Tax Reports" certifying the amount of payroll and sales tax payments made and those that remain unpaid for the six months preceding the bankruptcy filing (the "Filing Date"). The debtor shall attach to the certified report proof of all payments made for payroll and sales taxes for the six months preceding the Filing Date. The reports shall certify the following:

(a) the total amount of payroll taxes that accrued during the six months preceding the filing date, the date(s), amount(s) and place of payment of the payroll taxes for the six months preceding the filing date, and the total amount of payroll taxes still due and owing, if any, as of the filing date, whether owed for the period six months prior to the filing date or from any earlier period; and

(b) the total amount of all gross sales subject to sales tax for the six months preceding the filing date, the date(s) and amount(s) of payment of sales tax for the six months preceding the bankruptcy filing, and the total amount of sales tax still due and owing, if any, as of the filing date, whether owed for the period six months prior to the filing date or from any earlier period.

(2) *Deadline for Filing.* The report and attachments required by this rule shall be filed within 14 days from the date of filing of the chapter 11 petition, entry of an order for relief under chapter 11 in an involuntary case, entry of an order reinstating the case or entry of an order converting the case to chapter 11.

(3) *Required Service.* A copy of the certified report shall be served upon the U.S. Trustee, the Internal Revenue Service, the Florida Department of Revenue and any other taxing authority named in the report, and the report shall include a certificate verifying service on these parties.

[Comment: See also Local Rule 2015-1 (reports).]

(B) Required Chapter 11 Case Management Summary.

(1) *Local Form.* The debtor-in-possession (or chapter 11 trustee, if applicable) is directed to file with the court a completed Local Form "Chapter 11 Case Management Summary" providing the information as set forth in the form.

(2) *Deadline for Filing.* The summary shall be filed within the earlier of three business days after relief is entered under chapter 11, or one business day prior to the date of the first scheduled hearing.

(3) *Service.* The summary shall be served on all parties of record.

[Effective December 1, 1998. Amended effective December 1, 2002; June 2, 2008; December 1, 2009.]

RULE 2082-1. CHAPTER 12—FINAL DECREE AND DISCHARGE

(A) Trustees Final Report Required. Upon completion of administration of a case, the trustee shall file a final report and account.

(B) Local Form "Statement in Individual Cases". In an individual chapter 12 case, not later than 30 days after the filing of a final report by the trustee, the debtor shall file the required Local Form "Notice of Deadline to Object to Debtor's Statement Re: 11 U.S.C. § 522(q)(1) Applicability, Payment of Domestic Support Obligations, and [For Chapter 11 Cases Only] Applicability of Financial Management Course and Statement Regarding Eligibility to Receive a Discharge". This statement shall be served on negative notice on all parties of record. Any interested party who fails to file and serve a written objection within 30 days of the filing of the debtor's statement shall be deemed to have consented to entry of the final decree and discharge of debtor. A certificate of service shall be filed as provided by Local Rule 2002-1(F).

[Effective June 2, 2008. Amended effective December 1, 2009.]

RULE 2083-1. CHAPTER 13—GENERAL

(A) Duty of Tax Collector in Dismissed or Converted Cases or Where Stay Relief Has Been Granted to Certificate Holder. In some cases, tax certificate holders may receive payments from the chapter 13 trustee, even if the plan is not confirmed. Any order dismissing or converting such cases or granting stay relief to the certificate holder prior to confirmation may direct that upon receipt by the tax collector of such order, the tax collector shall request or access the chapter 13 trustee's ledger reflecting the amounts paid to certificate holders. Likewise, in any such case, the order may provide that the tax collector shall adjust the county tax records in the same manner required for payments under a confirmed plan.

(B) Required Review of Claims by Attorney for Debtor.

(1) *Scope of Review Required.* Not later than 21 days after expiration of the claims bar date, the attorney shall examine, from records maintained by the clerk, the claims register and all claims filed in the case to determine whether additional action is necessary, including the filing and service in accordance with all applicable rules of:

(a) an amended plan if the plan has not been confirmed;

(b) a motion to modify the confirmed plan; or

(c) objections to nonconforming claims.

(2) *Attorney for Debtor's Notice of Compliance with Claims Review Requirement.* A Local Form "Notice of Compliance by Attorney for Debtor With Local Rule 2083–1(B) Claims Review Requirement" certifying that the review required by subdivision (B)(1) of this rule has been completed shall be filed with the court and served on the trustee and the debtor.

(3) *Failure to Comply.* If the provisions of this rule are not complied with, the trustee may serve upon the attorney for the debtor (with a copy also served on the debtor), a "Trustee's Notice to Attorney for Debtor of Deficiency" which shall provide a 20 day deadline from the date of the notice for the attorney for the debtor to comply. If the deficiency is not cured, the trustee shall file a "Trustee's Report of Non–Compliance with Claims Review Requirement" and the court may dismiss the case without further notice or hearing.

(4) *Pro Se Debtors.* The provisions of this rule do not apply to debtors not represented by an attorney.

[Effective December 1, 1998. Amended effective December 1, 2002; July 1, 2004; June 2, 2008; December 1, 2009; August 1, 2011.]

RULE 2090–1. ATTORNEYS

(A) Qualifications to Practice. Except as provided in subdivision (C) of this rule, to be qualified to practice in this court an attorney must:

(1) be a member of the Bar of the United States District Court for the Southern District of Florida under the Special Rules Governing the Admission and Practice of Attorneys in the District Court;

(2) read and remain familiar with these rules, administrative orders, the Federal Rules of Bankruptcy Procedure, the Federal Rules of Civil Procedure, the Federal Rules of Evidence, The Florida Bar's Rules of Professional Conduct, and the Bankruptcy Code; and

(3) earn at least 12 credit hours by

(a) attending or participating in Florida Bar CLE courses related to the subject area of "Bankruptcy Law" during each attorney's Florida Bar three-year CLE reporting requirement; and/or

(b) performing eligible pro bono legal services for clients unable to afford counsel pursuant to criteria set forth under subdivision (B) below.

This provision will not preclude an attorney from appearing who is within a three-year CLE reporting period but has not yet earned the required 12 credit hours for that period.

Attorneys appearing pursuant to this subdivision who are not registered users of CM/ECF must include on all papers the certification contained in Local Rule 9011–4(B).

(B) CLE Credit for Pro Bono Legal Services. Attorneys may earn up to three CLE credit hours during any one three year cycle towards this court's legal education credit-hour requirement specified in subdivision (A)(3) of this Rule by performing eligible pro bono legal services for clients unable to afford counsel in cases pending or eligible to be filed before this court pursuant to assignment by this court, or by participation in pro bono cases taken in this District through eligible pro bono programs.

(1) *Definitions.*

(a) Eligible pro bono legal services are legal services for which there is **no compensation** to the attorney performing the legal services or for which the attorney has served as a registered mentor to a newer bankruptcy attorney or non-bankruptcy practitioner to take a bankruptcy case on a pro bono basis. Legal services provided by assigned counsel who receive compensation for those services from any source, legal services provided by counsel only when compelled by court order, or legal services provided by legal services organization attorneys within the scope of their employment, are not eligible pro bono legal services.

(b) Eligible pro bono programs are those in which a program, activity or case is sponsored by, and to which attorneys are assigned bankruptcy cases in our District on a pro bono basis by legal services organizations whose primary purpose is the furnishing of legal services to indigent persons of our community, and in which all recipients of the legal services provided by the program have been screened for financial eligibility to receive pro bono services. Such pro bono programs include, but are not limited to, those sponsored by the Put Something Back Program or the Bankruptcy Bar Foundation's Pro Bono Program in our District.

(2) *Pro Bono CLE Credit.* Credit for eligible pro bono legal services may be earned as follows:

(a) Taking Pro Bono Cases. Pro bono CLE Credit may be earned for the provision of eligible pro bono legal services to clients unable to afford counsel by taking pro bono bankruptcy cases from providers of eligible pro bono programs. A maximum of three pro bono CLE credit hours may be earned during any one reporting three year cycle, and only one credit per case absent extraordinary circumstances.

(b) Serving as a Registered Mentor. Pro bono CLE Credit may be earned by providing mentorship services to newer bankruptcy attorneys and non-bankruptcy attorneys who are providing eligible pro bono services through eligible pro bono programs. A maximum of three pro bono CLE credits hours may be earned during any one reporting three-year cycle by the registered attorney mentoring such newer bankruptcy attorney or non-bankruptcy attorney in three pro bono bankruptcy cases during the span of each such reporting three-year cycle by showing proof of its registration for the provider of eligible pro bono programs.

(c) Court Assignment. Pro bono CLE Credit may be earned for the provision of eligible pro bono legal services to clients unable to afford counsel pursuant to assignment by a court. A maximum of three pro bono CLE credits hours may be earned during any one reporting three-year cycle for taking such cases. Attorneys, however, will not be given any credits for performing pro bono legal services pursuant to a sanction or by any order of this court providing otherwise.

(C) Appearances Permitted as Exceptions to Qualification Requirements. An attorney who has not fulfilled the qualifications to practice set forth in subdivision (A) above, may only appear as set forth in this subdivision. Any attorney who appears pursuant to this rule shall be deemed to be familiar with, and shall be governed by, these rules, and the Rules of Professional Conduct and other ethical limitations or requirements governing the professional behavior of members of The Florida Bar.

(1) *Appearances in Limited Instances.* An attorney may appear in the following limited instances without resort to the requirements contained in subdivision (A) or (C)(2) of this rule: (a) the preparation and filing of a notice of appearance (pursuant to Bankruptcy Rule 9010); (b) a request for service of notices (pursuant to Bankruptcy Rule 2002); (c) the preparation and filing of a proof of claim in chapter 7, 11, 12 or 13 cases, or ballots in chapter 11 cases; (d) the filing of notices under Local Rule 3070–1(B); (e) attendance and inquiry at the meeting of creditors held under 11 U.S.C. § 341; and (f) attendance and representation of a creditor at a hearing which has been noticed to all creditors generally, except for representation of a party in a contested matter governed by Bankruptcy Rule 9014, or an adversary proceeding governed by Part VII of the Bankruptcy Rules.

(2) *Pro Hac Vice Appearances.* Any attorney who is a member in good standing of the bar of any state, territory or insular possession of the United States, and who is qualified to practice in this court but is not a member of the bar of the United States District Court for the Southern District of Florida (a "visiting attorney"), may seek to appear pro hac vice in any case or proceeding before this court. Any applicable fee authorized under the Local Rules or General Orders of the United States District Court for the Southern District of Florida for pro hac vice appearances in the bankruptcy court must be paid at the filing of a motion to appear pro hac vice. Such visiting attorney shall associate with an attorney who is qualified to practice with this court, is a member in good standing of the bar of the United States District Court for the Southern District of Florida and qualified to practice before this court, and who maintains an office in this district for the practice of law (a "local attorney"). Such local attorney shall file the Local Form "Motion to Appear Pro Hac Vice" and proposed Local Form "Order Admitting Attorney Pro Hac Vice" in the relevant main bankruptcy case, unless the visiting attorney intends to appear only in a specific adversary proceeding in which case the motion shall be filed only in such adversary proceeding and the local form motion and proposed order may be edited accordingly. In the motion, the local attorney shall certify that he or she is a member in good standing of the bar of the United States District Court for the Southern District of Florida and qualified to practice before this court, that he or she is willing to act as local counsel, and that he or she will participate in the preparation and presentation of, and accept service of all papers in, the case in which the motion is filed and any adversary proceedings in which the visiting attorney appears on behalf of the same client or clients (unless the motion is limited to a particular adversary proceeding). If the motion is filed in the main case, the local attorney must acknowledge that if he or she declines to serve as local counsel in any adversary proceeding involving the same client or clients, separate local counsel must file an additional Motion to Appear Pro Hac Vice, and that absent such separate motion and an order of this court approving the same he or she will continue to act as local counsel for the client(s) in all such proceedings.

In a separate affidavit filed with or as part of the motion, the proposed visiting attorney shall certify that he or she is qualified to practice before this court, and that he or she is a member in good standing of the bar of at least one state, territory, or insular possession of the United States, and a member in good standing of the bar of at least one United States District Court, and indicate such jurisdictions. The proposed visiting attorney must certify that he or she has never been disbarred, that he or she is not currently suspended from the practice of law in the State of Florida or any other state, territory, or insular possession of the United States, and that he or she is not currently suspended from the practice of law before any United States Court of Appeals, United States District Court, or United States Bankruptcy Court. The proposed visiting attorney shall designate local counsel consistent with this local rule. The proposed visiting attorney shall acknowledge that local counsel is required to participate in the preparation and the presentation of, and accept service in, the case and any adversary proceedings in which the visiting attorney appears on behalf of the same client or clients, unless and until other local counsel is designated under this local rule (except where the motion is limited to a particular adversary proceeding). The proposed visiting attorney shall certify that he or she is familiar with and shall be governed by the local rules of this court, the rules of professional conduct and all other requirements governing the professional behavior of members of the Florida Bar.

District Court Local Rule 4(b)(2) applies to pro hac vice appearances before this court as the bankruptcy court is a court of the Southern District of Florida.

The court may waive the requirement of association with a local attorney upon good cause shown after the filing of a motion requesting such relief. The Local Form "Motion to Appear Pro Hac Vice" and proposed Local Form "Order Admitting Attorney Pro Hac Vice" may be modified as necessary for this purpose.

[Comment: See also Local Rule 9011–4(B)(2), required certification.]

(3) *Appearances by Government Attorneys.* Any attorney who is an employee of the United States government, an agency thereof, or a state, municipality or agency or political subdivision thereof, may appear and participate in particular actions or proceedings before the court on behalf of such entity in the attorney's official capacity. Any attorney so appearing is subject to all of the rules of this court.

(D) Attendance at Hearings Required for Debtor's Counsel. An attorney who makes an appearance on behalf of a debtor must attend all hearings scheduled in the debtor's case that the debtor is required to attend under any provision of the Bankruptcy Code, the Bankruptcy Rules, the Local Rules, or order of the court, unless the court has granted a motion to withdraw pursuant to Local Rule 2091–1.

(1) *Attendance at Initial Debtor Interview (IDI) and Meeting of Creditors (341 Meeting).* The attorney attending the IDI or meeting of creditors must be familiar with the facts and schedules and have met and conferred with the client prior to appearing.

(2) *Attendance at Hearing Required for Debtor's Counsel.* An attorney who makes an appearance on behalf of a debtor, or a member of his or her firm who is familiar with the client and the file, must attend all hearings scheduled in the debtor's case that the debtor is required to attend under any provision of the Bankruptcy Code, the Bankruptcy Rules, the Local Rules, or order of the court, unless the court has granted a motion to withdraw pursuant to Local Rule 2091-1. The attorney may not use appearance counsel for any hearing unless (a) the client consents in advance to the use of the appearance attorney, (b) the client does not incur any additional expense associated with the use of an appearance attorney, (c) the appearance attorney complies with all applicable rules regarding disclosure of any fee sharing arrangements, and (d) appearance counsel is familiar with the debtor's schedules and statement of financial affairs and is otherwise familiar with the facts of the case.

(E) Duties of Debtor's Counsel. Unless the attorney has withdrawn as attorney for the debtor pursuant to Local Rule 2091-1, an attorney who files a petition on behalf of a debtor must advise the debtor of, and assist the debtor in complying with, all duties of a debtor under 11 U.S.C. § 521.

[Effective December 1, 1998. Amended effective December 1, 2002; June 2, 2008; August 1, 2011. Amended on an interim basis effective February 14, 2014; June 16, 2015. Amended effective December 1, 2015. Amended on an interim basis effective December 1, 2016.]

RULE 2090-2. ATTORNEY DISCIPLINE

(A) Contempt of Court. Nothing in this rule shall be construed as providing an exclusive procedure for the discipline of attorneys appearing before the court in appropriate cases, nor as a limitation upon the power of the court to punish for contempt in appropriate cases.

(B) Disciplinary Action.

(1) Upon order to show cause entered by at least one judge, any attorney appearing before the court may, after 30 days' notice and hearing and for good cause shown, be suspended from practice before the court, reprimanded or otherwise disciplined, by a judge whose order to show cause initiated the disciplinary proceedings.

(2) Whenever it appears to the court that any attorney appearing before the court has been (a) disbarred or suspended from practice by the Supreme Court of Florida, (b) disbarred or suspended, for moral turpitude or ethical violations, by the highest court in any state or by any federal court, or (c) convicted of a felony in any court, such disbarment, suspension or conviction shall, 21 days afterwards, operate as an automatic suspension of the attorney's right to practice in this court. The attorney may file, within such 21 day period, a petition seeking relief from the operation of this subdivision, and if a timely petition is filed, suspension shall be stayed until the petition is heard and determined by a majority vote of the judges of this court.

(C) Peer Review and Grievance Committee. Any of the judges of this court may chose to refer an attorney to the committee established pursuant to the district court's "Special Rules Governing the Admission and Practice of Attorneys" for proceedings by this committee and by the district court under those rules, which are adopted into these rules by reference for the purpose of such referrals.

(D) Professional Conduct. The professional conduct of attorneys appearing before this court shall be governed by the Model Rules of Professional Conduct of the American Bar Association as modified and adopted by the Supreme Court of Florida to govern the professional behavior of the members of The Florida Bar.

(E) Courtroom Decorum. The courtroom conduct of all attorneys, including, where the context applies, all persons at the counsel table, shall be governed by the guidelines set forth in the court's "Guidelines for Courtroom Decorum".

(F) Waiver in Exceptional Cases. In an exceptional case, when the interest of justice is best served, the judge before whom the matter is pending may waive the requirements of these rules.

[Comment: See also Bankruptcy Rules 2014 (employment of professionals), 2016 (compensation of professionals) and 9011 (effect of attorney's signature), and Local Rules 2014-1, 2016-1, and 9011-4(A)(1) (attorney's signature block).]

[Effective December 1, 1998. Amended effective December 1, 2002; January 26, 2004; June 2, 2008; December 1, 2009.]

RULE 2091-1. ATTORNEYS—CHANGES IN ATTORNEY OF RECORD FOR PARTIES IN CASES OR PROCEEDINGS

Withdrawal from representation of a client shall require leave of court, after notice served on all affected parties, except in the following instances:

(A) Withdrawal by Attorney for Creditor in an Uncontested Matter. An attorney representing a creditor who is not a party to any pending contested matter or adversary proceeding may file a notice of withdrawal of his or her appearance in each affected case or proceeding. Copies of the notice must be served on all interested parties.

(B) Joint Notice of Substitution of Counsel in a Contested Matter. An attorney for a creditor or chapter 7 or 13 debtor seeking to withdraw from representing a client in a case or proceeding at a time when such client is represented by new counsel of record may file a joint notice with counsel seeking to be substituted as counsel of record for the client, in each affected case or proceeding. Such notice shall contain a statement that the client has consented to the substitution or be signed by the client, and be served on all interested parties.

(C) Substitution of Attorney in Same Firm. An attorney with the same firm as an attorney initially employed by a client pursuant to Local Rule 2014-1, may substitute as counsel for that client by filing a notice in each affected case or proceeding containing a statement that the client has consented to the substitution, and serving the notice on all interested parties, unless the attorney initially employed was the signatory to the "Affidavit of Proposed Attorney for Debtor in

Possession/Trustee" or new counsel, if applicable, is not disinterested or represents a materially adverse interest.

The provisions of this rule shall be subject to the requirements of the Bankruptcy Code, the Bankruptcy Rules and this court's Local Rules with regard to retention of professionals, disclosure, payment of professionals and related matters and is not intended as an exception to any other requirement.

[Comment: See also Local Rules 2002–1(G) (attorney change of address) and 2002–1(H) ("Master Service List" in chapter 11 cases) and 2014 –1 (A) Employment of Professionals and 2090–1 "Attorneys".]

[Effective December 1, 1998. Amended effective December 1, 2002; June 2, 2008; August 1, 2011; December 1, 2015.]

RULE 3001–1. PROOF OF CLAIM

(A) Form. A proof of claim shall conform to the requirements of Bankruptcy Rule 3001(a) and Local Rule 9004–1, and the Official Bankruptcy Form "Proof of Claim", and must be signed by the claimant or the claimant's agent. A proof of claim may be conventionally or electronically filed. Electronically filed claims are deemed signed upon electronic submission as provided under Local Rule 5005–4(D).

(B) Administrative Claims. Unless otherwise ordered by the court, requests for payment of administrative expenses shall comply with the requirements of Local Rule 1019–1(F), 2016–1(C)(2), 9013–1, 9013–3 and 9073–1, which requirements include the filing of a motion or application for payment, except as provided under 11 U.S.C. § 503(b)(1)(D). A claim filed on the Official Bankruptcy Form "Proof of Claim" alleging a § 503 administrative claim does not comply with these requirements, is not effective, and shall not be set for hearing, even though such form may be docketed on the claims register.

(C) Transferred Claim.

(1) *Submission Requirements.* Any assignment or other evidence of a transfer of claim filed after a proof of claim has been filed, shall include the claim number of the claim to be transferred. In chapter 11 cases, any assignment or other evidence of a transfer of claim filed where no proof of claim has been filed, shall include reference to the scheduled claim, including classification and amount.

(2) *Order Not Required.* Absent any timely filed objection to the notice of transfer served by the clerk, the claim shall be, without any further order of the court, noted as transferred on the records of the court.

(3) *Notice Not Required.* Where evidence of full or partial transfer of a claim is filed which contains the signatures of both the transferor and transferee, and such evidence of transfer is filed pursuant to Bankruptcy Rule 3001(e)(2) and (4), and in accordance with the local rules, the clerk shall not provide notice of the filing of evidence of the transfer and no objection deadline shall be established. The transferor shall be deemed to have waived any objections to the transfer and the claim shall be noted as transferred in the records of the court.

[Effective December 1, 1998. Amended effective December 1, 2002; July 1, 2004; June 2, 2008; December 1, 2009; August 1, 2011; December 1, 2015.]

RULE 3002–1. FILING PROOF OF CLAIM OR INTEREST IN CHAPTER 7, 12, OR 13 CASES

(A) Chapter 7 No–Asset Cases. Claims Deadline in Cases Converted from Chapter 13 to Chapter 7. Upon the filing of a "Notice of Assets", a deadline for filing claims shall be established as provided by Bankruptcy Rule 3002(c)(5), and noticed pursuant to Local Rule 2002–1(C)(7). Claims deadlines in chapter 13 cases converted to chapter 7 cases shall be established as provided by Bankruptcy Rule 3002(c)(5) and Local Rule 1019–1(E).

(B) Modification of Claims Deadline. The deadline in Bankruptcy Rule 3002(c) for filing a proof of claim in a chapter 7, 12 or 13 case is modified in the following circumstances for nongovernmental unit claimants:

[Comment: See 11 U.S.C. § 502(b)(9) (claims deadline for governmental units).]

(1) *Meeting of Creditors Untimely Noticed.* If service of the § 341 or post-conversion meeting notice is not timely provided pursuant to Bankruptcy Rule 2002(a), and as a result of this failure to provide notice, the § 341 meeting must be rescheduled before another notice can be served, the deadline for filing a proof of claim or interest shall be 90 days after the rescheduled date of the § 341 meeting.

(2) *Case Dismissed and Reinstated.* If a case is dismissed prior to the expiration of the claims deadline and subsequently reinstated:

(a) In a case dismissed before the § 341 meeting is held, the new deadline for filing a proof of claim or interest shall be 90 days after the rescheduled § 341 meeting; and

(b) In a case dismissed after the § 341 meeting is held, the new deadline for filing a proof of claim or interest shall be 90 days from entry of the order reinstating the case. Local Form "Order Reinstating Chapter 13 Case" is required for any reinstated chapter 13 case and Local Form "Order Reinstating Chapter 7 Case" is required for any reinstated chapter 7 case.

(C) Deadline for Claims Arising from Rejection of Contracts or Leases. Unless otherwise ordered by the court, any proof of claim arising pursuant to 11 U.S.C. § 502(g), from the rejection of an executory contract or unexpired lease, must be filed on or before the latest of: i) the time for filing a proof of claim pursuant to Bankruptcy Rule 3002(c) or Local Rule 3002–1(A), whichever is applicable; ii) 30 days after the entry of the order compelling or approving the rejection of the contract or lease; or iii) 30 days after the effective date of the rejection of the contract or lease. The order of rejection shall contain the notice mandated by Local Rule 6006–1.

[Comment: See Bankruptcy Rule 3002(c)(4) (deadline for claims arising from rejection).]

(D) Deadline for Filing Claims in Chapter 7 Cases Reopened to Administer Assets. Upon the filing by a trustee of a "Notice of Assets" in a reopened chapter 7 case:

(1) If no claims deadline was established in the original case or if a claims deadline was established and rendered moot by the filing of a "Report of No Distribution" by the trustee in the original case, the court shall set a deadline of 90 days from issuance of the clerk's Notice of Deadline to File Claims. For governmental units, the deadline shall be this deadline or 180 days after relief was ordered in the original chapter 7 case, whichever is later. Any claims filed during the pendency of the original case shall be deemed filed in the reopened case.

(2) If a claims deadline established in the original case expired prior to the filing of a "Report of No Distribution" by the trustee, or if a distribution was made to creditors by the trustee subsequent to the expiration of a claims deadline in the original case, no additional claims deadline shall be established. Creditors considered for distributions shall be those creditors who filed claims in the original case.

(E) Service of a Proof of Claim in Chapter 13 Cases. In a chapter 13 case where the debtor is pro se, the party filing a proof of claim shall serve, via U.S. mail, a copy of the claim, including all attachments required, upon the debtor. Service on the chapter 13 trustee or the attorney for the debtor is not required since these parties will automatically receive access to the claim and attachments electronically in CM/ECF.

[Comment: See Local Rules 1019–1(F) (deadline for filing postpetition claim in reconverted case) and 2083–1(B) (additional review of claims and service of copies by attorney for chapter 13 debtor required).]

[Effective December 1, 1998. Amended effective December 1, 2002; June 2, 2008; December 1, 2009; August 1, 2011; December 1, 2015.]

RULE 3003–1. FILING PROOF OF CLAIM OR INTEREST IN CHAPTER 11 CASES

(A) Deadline. Unless otherwise ordered by the court and except as provided by 11 U.S.C. § 502(b)(9), the deadline for filing a proof of claim or interest required by Bankruptcy Rule 3003(c)(2) shall be 90 days after the first date scheduled for the meeting of creditors. Notice of this deadline shall be provided, pursuant to Bankruptcy Rules 2002(a)(7) and 2002(f)(3) and Local Rule 2002–1(C)(1), in the § 341 or post-conversion meeting notice.

[Comment: See 11 U.S.C. § 502(b)(9) (claims deadline for governmental units).]

(B) Modification of Claims Deadline. The deadline set pursuant to subdivision (A) of this rule or by order of the court for filing a proof of claim or interest in chapter 11 cases is modified in the following instances for non-governmental unit claimants:

(1) *Meeting of Creditors Untimely Noticed.* If service of the § 341 or post-conversion meeting notice is not timely provided pursuant to Bankruptcy Rule 2002(a) and Local Rule 2002–1(C)(1), and as a result of this failure to provide notice the § 341 meeting must be rescheduled before another notice can be served, the deadline for filing a proof of claim or interest shall be 90 days after the rescheduled date of the § 341 meeting.

(2) *Case Dismissed and Reinstated.* If a chapter 11 case is dismissed prior to the expiration of the claims deadline and subsequently reinstated:

(a) In a case dismissed before the § 341 meeting is held, the new deadline for filing a proof of claim or interest shall be 90 days after the rescheduled § 341 meeting.

(b) In a case dismissed after the § 341 meeting is held, the new deadline for filing a proof of claim or interest shall be 90 days from entry of the order reinstating the case.

Any other proposed order reinstating a case submitted for consideration by the court in chapter 11 cases must contain the new deadlines prescribed by this rule for reinstated cases. The clerk shall provide notice of the new deadline.

(C) Deadline for Claims Arising from Rejection of Contracts or Leases. Unless otherwise ordered by the court, a proof of claim arising pursuant to 11 U.S.C. § 502(g), from the rejection of an executory contract or unexpired lease, must be filed on or before the latest of: i) the time for filing a proof of claim pursuant to Bankruptcy Rule 3002(c); ii) 30 days after the entry of the order compelling or approving the rejection of the contract or lease; or iii) 30 days after the effective date of the rejection of the contract or lease. The order of rejection shall contain the notice mandated by Local Rule 6006–1.

[Comment: See Local Rule 6006–1 (deadline notice to be included in orders rejecting executory contracts).]

[Effective December 1, 1998. Amended effective December 1, 2002; June 2, 2008; December 1, 2009; August 1, 2011; December 1, 2015.]

RULE 3007–1. OBJECTIONS TO CLAIMS

(A) Service. A party filing an objection to claim shall serve a copy of the objection on (1) the claimant at the claimant's address of record or, if the claim has been transferred, at the transferee's address of record, and on (2) any attorney of record in the bankruptcy case for the claim holder. If the claim holder is the United States, service shall also be made as prescribed by Bankruptcy Rule 7004(b)(4).

[Comment: See Local Rule 3001–1(C) (transferred claim).]

(B) Deadline for Filing Objections.

(1) *Chapter 11 Cases.* Except as otherwise ordered by the court, in a chapter 11 case, objections to claims must be filed not later than the deadline set in the orders required to be served in standard or small business cases under Local Rules 3017–1 and 3017–2.

(2) *Chapter 13 Cases—Objections.* Objections to claims in chapter 13 cases which are filed and served on the claimant and the debtor at least 14 days prior to the confirmation hearing shall be designated as "timely pre-confirmation objections". "Timely pre-confirmation objections" shall be heard at the confirmation hearing and the provisions of subdivisions (C) and (D) of this rule, including the 30 day notice requirement, shall not apply. Objections filed pursuant to this rule must comply with Bankruptcy Rule 3007, and must substantially conform to the Local Form "Objection to Claim on Shortened Notice". Notwithstanding the requirements of Bankruptcy

Rule 3007, up to five objections to claim may be included in one pleading, excluding any objections to a claim for which a motion to value collateral has been filed. Objections to claims filed less than 14 days before the confirmation hearing or filed after a plan is confirmed, shall require at least 30 days notice and be filed in accordance with the provisions of subdivisions (A), (C), (D) and (E) of this rule.

(C) Content of Objections. Objections to claims, other than those filed pursuant to subdivision (B)(2) of this rule, must comply with Bankruptcy Rule 3007, and must conform substantially to the Local Form "Objection to Claim". A certificate of service shall be filed in accordance with Local Rule 2002–1(F). Notwithstanding the requirements of Bankruptcy Rule 3007, up to five objections to claim may be included in one pleading.

(D) Relief Without Hearing; Hearings.

(1) If no written response contesting the objection is filed within 30 days after the date of service, the failure to respond shall be deemed a consent by the affected claimant and the court may grant the relief requested by the objecting party without hearing.

(2) It shall be the responsibility of the objecting party, after the claimant's time to respond has expired, to submit, as appropriate, either or both:

(a) the Local Form "Certificate of Contested Matter", regarding claimants who contested the objection;

(b) the Local Form "Order Sustaining Objection to Claims" regarding claimants who did not contest the objection.

(E) Orders. Proposed orders on objections to claims shall recite in the body:

(1) the claim holder's name and claim number;

(2) whether the objection to the claim is sustained or overruled;

(3) whether the claim is allowed or disallowed; and

(4) the allowed amount and priority, if any, of the allowed claim.

[Comment: See also Local Rule 3015–3(A)(4) Chapter 13 valuation of collateral securing claims—Treatment of Unsecured Portion of Collateralized Obligation.]

[Effective December 1, 1998. Amended effective December 1, 2002; June 2, 2008; December 1, 2009; December 1, 2015.]

RULE 3009-1. PREPARATION, FILING, AND SERVICE OF FINAL REPORT BY TRUSTEE

Deadline for Objection to Report of Estate.

(A) Preparation, Filing, and Service of Final Report By Trustee. A "Notice of Trustee's Final Report and Applications for Compensation (NFR)" shall be prepared, filed and served, as may be required under Bankruptcy Rules 2002(a)(6) and 2002(f)(8), by the assigned chapter 7 trustee not later than 14 days after the "Trustee's Final Report (TFR)" is filed with the court. A certificate of service of the "Notice of Trustee's Final Report and Applications for Compensation (NFR)" shall also be filed by the trustee as required under Local Rule 2002–1(F).

(B) Required Local Form "Trustee's Summary of Requested Fees and Expenses." Local Form "Trustee's Summary of Requested Fees and Expenses" shall be filed by the trustee within 14 days after the "Trustee's Final Report (TFR)" is filed with the court. If the trustee is required to prepare, file and serve the "Notice of Trustee's Final Report and Applications for Compensation (NFR)," the Local Form "Trustee's Summary of Requested Fees and Expenses" must also be served along with the "Notice of Trustee's Final Report and Applications for Compensation (NFR)".

(C) Deadline for Objection to Report of Estate. Any objections to the final report or applications for compensation listed in the "Notice of Trustee's Final Report and Applications for Compensation (NFR)" shall be filed not later than 21 days after the service of the notice.

[Comment: No notice of the trustee's final report will be provided to creditors if the net proceeds realized do not exceed the amount set forth in Bankruptcy Rule 2002(f)(8) and if no application for compensation or reimbursement of expenses totals in excess of the amount set forth in Bankruptcy Rule 2002(a)(6). See also Bankruptcy Rules 2016(a) (copy of fee applications to be served on U.S. Trustee) and 9034(k) (U.S. Trustee's authority to require notice) and Local Rules 1019–1(F) (deadline for filing postpetition claims), 2002–1(C)(10) (when notice of final accounts and notice of final fee applications required) and 2016–1(C) (deadline for fee applications).]

[Effective December 1, 1998. Amended effective December 1, 2002; June 2, 2008; May 1, 2009; December 1, 2009; December 1, 2015.]

RULE 3010-1. DEPOSIT OF SMALL DIVIDENDS

The trustee shall pay over to the court any funds left undistributed pursuant to Bankruptcy Rule 3010, accompanied by the Local Form "Notice of Deposit of Funds with the U.S. Bankruptcy Clerk".

[Effective December 1, 1998. Amended effective December 1, 2002; June 2, 2008.]

RULE 3011-1. UNCLAIMED FUNDS

(A) Deposit by Chapter 7, 12, or 13 Trustee. The chapter 7, 12, or 13 trustee shall deposit with the court any funds left undistributed pursuant to Bankruptcy Rule 3011, accompanied by the Local Form "Notice of Deposit of Funds with the U.S. Bankruptcy Clerk".

[Comment: See also 11 U.S.C. § 347(a) (deposit of unclaimed funds after final distribution).]

(B) Disposition of Unclaimed Funds Under A Chapter 11 Liquidating Plan.

(1) The disbursing agent under a chapter 11 plan which provides for the complete liquidation of the property of the debtor shall, when making final distribution under the plan:

(a) Notify such entity, if any, that purchased all of the debtor's assets under the chapter 11 plan, of its potential right to the unclaimed funds to the extent the disbursing agent can identify such an entity.

(b) Unless the plan otherwise provides, pay over to the court any funds left unclaimed 120 days after the final distribution under the plan, accompanied by the Local Form "Notice of Deposit of Funds with the U.S. Bankruptcy Clerk".

(c) File a final account under 11 U.S.C. § 1106(a)(7), prior to the expiration of time provided in 11 U.S.C. § 1143, and all other reports required by Local Rule 3022-1.

(2) A chapter 11 liquidating plan may provide that any unclaimed funds may be redistributed to other creditors or administrative claimants or donated to a not-for-profit, non-religious organization identified in the plan or disclosure statement accompanying the plan.

(C) Disposition of Undistributable Funds Under a Chapter 11 Liquidating Plan.

(1) Undistributable funds are any funds other than unclaimed funds, including, but not limited to, funds that cannot be disbursed because: (a) a creditor has affirmatively rejected a distribution, (b) the administrative costs of distribution effectively interfere with distribution, or (c) all creditors, including administrative claimants, have been paid in full and there is no one that has a right to the funds.

(2) A chapter 11 liquidating plan may provide that any undistributable funds, if applicable or practicable, may be redistributed to other creditors or administrative claimants or donated to a not-for-profit, non-religious organization identified in the plan or disclosure statement accompanying the plan.

(3) If a chapter 11 liquidating plan does not provide for the disposition of undistributable funds then, if there are any such funds at the time of final distribution under the plan, the disbursing agent shall file a motion, upon notice and hearing, proposing disposition of such funds, including as described in subdivision (C)(2) of this local rule.

[Comment: Compare 11 U.S.C. § 347(b) (return of unclaimed funds to debtor in reorganization cases).]

(D) Withdrawal of Unclaimed Funds. The court shall consider a request for withdrawal of unclaimed funds submitted in accordance with the "Clerk's Instructions for Deposits Into and Withdrawal From Unclaimed Funds".

[Effective December 1, 1998. Amended effective December 1, 2002; July 1, 2004; June 2, 2008; December 1, 2009.]

RULE 3012-1. VALUATION OF COLLATERAL

Motions to value collateral pursuant to Bankruptcy Rule 3012 shall be served on the affected creditors in accordance with Bankruptcy Rule 7004. In a chapter 13 case, valuation of secured property shall also be in accordance with Local Rule 3015-3(A). A separate motion to value collateral that is an interest in real property, a motor vehicle, a motor home, a boat, a ship or a manufactured home, is required for each such asset for which relief is sought; any motion seeking valuation of more than one asset may be denied without hearing. Motions to value personal property other than a motor vehicle, a motor home, a boat, a ship or a manufactured home may seek to value more than one item of personal property, but each item of personal property must be identified, even if the property is valued as a group.

[Comment: Motions to value collateral may only seek to value one piece of collateral. However, parties may include more than one piece of collateral for most items of personal property so long as each item of property is identified (e.g., "chairs" would not be acceptable, but "five straight back chairs and one armchair" would be).]

[Effective December 1, 1998. Amended effective December 1, 2002; June 2, 2008.]

RULE 3015-1. CHAPTER 12 AND CHAPTER 13 PLANS

(A) Chapter 12 Case.

(1) *Service of Order Setting Confirmation Hearing.* The "Order (I) Setting Hearing on Confirmation of Plan; (II) Setting Deadline for Filing Objections to Confirmation; (III) Setting Hearing on Fee Applications; and (IV) Directing Debtor to Serve Notice" shall be served, along with a copy of the plan, by the plan proponent in accordance with the provisions of the order.

(2) *Objections to Confirmation.* Objections to confirmation of the plan must be filed at least three business days prior to the confirmation hearing.

[Comment: See Local Rule 2002-1(C)(11) (service of order confirming plan).]

(B) Chapter 13 Case.

(1) *Filing of Plan.* A chapter 13 plan must conform to the Local Form "Chapter 13 Plan".

(2) *Service of Plan on Trustee.* Copies of the Local Form "Chapter 13 Plan" shall be served as provided by Local Rule 2002-1(C)(5).

[Comment: See also Local Rules 3012-1 and 3015-3(A) (valuation of collateral), 3070-1 (plan payments must commence to the chapter 13 trustee not later than 30 days after filing the petition).]

[Effective December 1, 1998. Amended effective December 1, 2002; June 2, 2008; December 1, 2009; December 1, 2015.]

RULE 3015-2. AMENDMENTS TO CHAPTER 13 PLANS

(A) Deadline for Filing Amended Plans. An amended plan must be filed and served as required by these rules at least 14 days prior to the confirmation hearing in order to be considered.

[Comment: See also Local Rules 5005-1(F)(1) and (F)(2) (Two-day submission requirement on response to motions and emergency filing procedures do not apply) and Local Rule 9013-1(D)(4) (Chapter 13 plan may not be amended on negative notice).]

(B) Notice. Copies of the amended plan shall be served as provided by Local Rule 2002-1(C)(5).

[Effective December 1, 1998. Amended effective December 1, 2002; June 2, 2008; December 1, 2009.]

RULE 3015-3. CHAPTER 13 VALUATION OF COLLATERAL. CHAPTER 13 CONFIRMATION

(A) Valuation of Collateral Securing Claims.

(1) *Valuation of Collateral.* A chapter 13 debtor seeking to value collateral securing a claim in a chapter 13 plan pursuant to 11 U.S.C. § 506(a) and Bankruptcy Rule 3012, must file a motion requesting such relief. If the collateral consists of real property, the debtor shall file the Local Form "Motion to Value and Determine Secured Status of Lien on Real Property." If the collateral consists of personal property, the debtor shall file the Local Form "Motion to Value and Determine Secured Status of Lien on Personal Property." The movant shall schedule the motion for hearing in accordance with this court's self-calendaring guidelines, allowing for at least 21 days service of the motion and notice of hearing. The debtor must serve the motion, notice of hearing and the chapter 13 plan on the affected creditor in accordance with Bankruptcy Rule 7004.

(2) *Objections to Debtor's Declared Valuation.* Any objections to the valuation of collateral contained in a chapter 13 plan and in a motion to value collateral must be filed with the court and served on the chapter 13 trustee, the debtor and counsel for the debtor, if any, at least two business days before the date of the hearing on the motion to value collateral. If no timely objection to the proposed valuation is filed, the valuation specified in the plan will be binding upon the affected secured creditor, and the debtor shall submit a proposed order. If the collateral consists of real property, the debtor shall submit a proposed order consistent with the Local Form "Order Granting Motion to Value and Determine Secured Status of Lien on Real Property Held By ___." If the collateral consists of personal property, the debtor shall submit a proposed order consistent with the Local Form "Order Granting Motion to Value and Determine Secured Status of Lien on Personal Property Held By ___."

(3) *Hearing on Objections to Valuation.* Objections to the debtor's proposed valuation pursuant to 11 U.S.C. § 506(a) shall be heard at the evidentiary hearing set on the motion to value collateral. The debtor shall submit a proposed order. If the collateral consists of real property, the debtor shall submit a proposed order consistent with the Local Form "Order Granting Motion to Value and Determine Secured Status of Lien on Real Property Held By ___." If the collateral consists of personal property, the debtor shall submit a proposed order consistent with the Local Form "Order Granting Motion to Value and Determine Secured Status of Lien on Personal Property Held By ___."

(4) *Treatment of Unsecured Portion of Collateralized Obligation.*

(a) If the creditor filed a proof of claim prior to the filing of the motion to value collateral, if the debtor has an objection to the claim, the debtor must file an objection to the claim at the same time, or prior to, the filing of the motion to value collateral. If the debtor does not file an objection to the claim, that portion of the debt that is found to be unsecured shall be allowed as an unsecured claim in the debtor's chapter 13 case and be paid in accordance with the debtor's chapter 13 plan. The order on the motion to value shall specify the amount of the creditor's secured claim and the amount of the creditor's unsecured claim.

(b) If the creditor did not file a proof of claim prior to the filing of the motion to value collateral, the creditor will have until the later of the claims bar date or 21 days from the date the motion to value collateral is served, to file a proof of claim for the unsecured amount of the claim, or the creditor will be deemed to have waived the right to payment of the unsecured claim. The creditor will participate in distributions on account of the unsecured claim only from the date the claim is filed, and the chapter 13 trustee will not be required to seek return of any portion of prior distributions to other unsecured creditors. The debtor or the trustee has the right to object to the proof of claim.

(B) Confirmation Process.

(1) *Objections to Confirmation.* Except for objections to confirmation based on valuation of collateral in the plan filed under section (A) of this Rule, objections to confirmation of the plan must be in writing and filed no later than 14 days prior to the date first scheduled for hearing on confirmation. Any timely filed objection shall constitute an objection to any amended plan. Should an amended plan be filed changing the treatment of any claim, the affected creditor may raise its objection orally at the hearing to consider confirmation of that amended plan.

(2) *Deadline for Debtor to File Local Form Certificate.* Prior to confirmation, Debtors must file the Local Form "Debtor Certificate of Compliance and Request for Confirmation of Chapter 13 Plan".

(3) *Order Confirming Plan.* An order confirming plan shall contain the provisions addressing payment to tax certificate holders and requirements for tax collectors required under Local Rule 2083-1(A) and shall be served pursuant to Local Rule 2002-1(C)(11).

[Comment: See also Local Rules 6006-1(B) (confirmation order shall contain language regarding status of executory contracts or unexpired leases of chapter 13 debtors).]

[Effective December 1, 1998. Amended effective December 1, 2002; July 1, 2004; June 2, 2008; December 1, 2009; January 8, 2010. Amended, on an interim basis, effective April 26, 2010. Amended effective August 1, 2011; December 1, 2015.]

RULE 3016-1. FILING OF PLAN AND DISCLOSURE STATEMENT IN SMALL BUSINESS CHAPTER 11 CASES

In small business chapter 11 cases, a chapter 11 plan and disclosure statement filed by any plan proponent must conform to the Official Bankruptcy Forms "Plan of Reorganization in Small Business Case under Chapter 11" and "Disclosure Statement in Small Business Case under Chapter 11."

[Effective June 2, 2008. Amended effective December 1, 2009.]

RULE 3016-2. FILING OF PLAN AND DISCLOSURE STATEMENT IN STANDARD CHAPTER 11 CASES

(A) Order Setting Disclosure Hearing. In all standard (non-small business) chapter 11 cases, the court shall enter an "Order (I) Setting Hearing to Consider Approval of Disclosure Statement; (II) Setting Deadline for Filing Objections to Disclosure Statement; and (III) Directing Plan Proponent to

Serve Notice" which must be served by the proponent of the chapter 11 plan.

(B) Order Setting Confirmation Hearing. Upon approval of the disclosure statement, the court shall enter the "Order (I) Approving Disclosure Statement; (II) Setting Hearing on Confirmation of Plan; (III) Setting Hearing on Fee Applications; (IV) Setting Various Deadlines; and (V) Describing Plan Proponent's Obligations" which must be served by the plan proponent.

[Comment: See also "Guidelines for Preparing, Submitting, and Serving Orders" (blanks for deadlines in form order shall be left blank).]

[Effective December 1, 1998. Amended effective December 1, 2002; June 2, 2008.]

RULE 3017-1. DISCLOSURE STATEMENT AND CONFIRMATION HEARING—STANDARD CHAPTER 11 CASES

The provisions in this subdivision apply to any chapter 11 plan and disclosure statement filed by any plan proponent other than a small business debtor.

[Comment: See also Bankruptcy Rules 3017(a) and (f) (service of plan and disclosure statement on other parties required).]

(A) Deadline for Objecting to Disclosure Statement. Objections to a disclosure statement must be filed, and a copy delivered to the plan proponent, at least seven days before the hearing on approval of the disclosure statement. The objecting party shall confer with the plan proponent at least three business days before the hearing in an effort to resolve any objections to the disclosure statement. The objection shall include a request for dismissal or conversion of the case if the objecting party will be seeking that relief at the disclosure hearing.

(B) Service of Plan, Disclosure Statement, Ballot, and Notice; Deadline for Service.

(1) At least 30 days before the date set for the hearing on approval of the disclosure statement, the plan proponent shall serve the "Order (I) Setting Hearing to Consider Approval of Disclosure Statement; (II) Setting Deadline for Filing Objections to Disclosure Statement; and (III) Directing Plan Proponent to Serve Notice" on the parties required by Bankruptcy Rules 2002(b), 2002(d), and 2002(j), and on the U.S. Trustee, and shall serve the plan and disclosure statement as required by Bankruptcy Rule 3017(a) and (f).

(2) After court approval of the disclosure statement and at least 40 days before the date set for the confirmation hearing, or as otherwise directed by the court, the plan proponent shall serve the "Order (I) Approving Disclosure Statement; (II) Setting Hearing on Confirmation of Plan; (III) Setting Hearing on Fee Applications; (IV) Setting Various Deadlines; and (V) Describing Plan Proponent's Obligations" together with the plan and disclosure statement, on the parties required by Bankruptcy Rule 3017(d) and shall serve a ballot in the form required by Local Rule 3018-1 on all creditors and equity security holders entitled to vote on the plan. The proponent of the plan must serve the customized ballot and instructions via U.S. Mail on any party who has received the order and copies of the plan and disclosure statement electronically.

[Effective December 1, 1998. Amended effective December 1, 2002; June 2, 2008; December 1, 2009.]

RULE 3017-2. DISCLOSURE STATEMENT APPROVAL AND CONFIRMATION—SMALL BUSINESS CASES

The provisions in this subdivision apply to any chapter 11 plan and disclosure statement filed by a small business debtor.

(A) Procedures for Conditional Approval of Disclosure Statement. Upon filing a plan and disclosure statement, a combined plan and disclosure statement or a plan that contains the disclosures required by 11 U.S.C. § 1125(a) (each being referred to as a "Proposed Disclosure Document"), the plan proponent shall serve a copy of the Proposed Disclosure Document on the U.S. Trustee and each party in interest that is entitled to receive a copy thereof, together with a notice that objections based on inadequate disclosure under Bankruptcy Code § 1125(a), must be filed within 14 days after service of the Proposed Disclosure Document. If no objection is filed within 14 days after service of the Proposed Disclosure Document, and the court does not otherwise determine to set a hearing on approval, the court may issue its "Order (I) Conditionally Approving Proposed Disclosure Document; (II) Setting Hearing on Final Approval of Proposed Disclosure Document and Confirmation of Plan; (III) Setting Hearing on Fee Applications; (IV) Setting Various Deadlines and (V) Describing Plan Proponent's Obligations" which the plan proponent shall serve as provided under subdivision (B) below. If an objection to the adequacy of the Proposed Disclosure Document is timely filed, the court may, in its sole discretion, enter the order described in this subparagraph, or set a final hearing to determine the adequacy of the Proposed Disclosure Document prior to transmission of the plan pursuant to Bankruptcy Rule 3017(d).

(B) Combined Hearing on Approval of the Disclosure Statement and Confirmation of the Plan. If a plan proponent files with this court a separate chapter 11 plan and disclosure statement, or a combined chapter 11 plan and disclosure statement, the form of which has been approved for use in small business cases by this court, then the plan proponent may request that the court combine the hearing on approval of the disclosure statement with the hearing on confirmation of the chapter 11 plan. Upon approval of the request and entry of an "Order (I) Setting Hearing on Approval of the Disclosure Statement and Confirmation of Plan; (II) Setting Hearing on Fee Applications; (III) Setting Various Deadlines; and (IV) Describing Plan Proponent's Obligations", the plan proponent shall serve the foregoing order on the parties required by Bankruptcy Rule 3017(d), along with a ballot in the form required by Local Rule 3018-1, on all creditors and equity security holders entitled to vote on the plan, as well as the U.S. Trustee. The order shall schedule a hearing on confirmation no later than 30 days from its issuance. Objections to the disclosure statement based on inadequate disclosure under Bankruptcy Code § 1125(a), or to confirmation of the chapter 11 plan under §§ 1122, 1123, 1124, 1126, 1127 or 1129 of the Bankruptcy Code, shall be filed with the court within three business days prior to the confirmation hearing. Even if no timely objections are filed, the court shall proceed with the confirmation hearing at the scheduled date and time. The proponent of the plan must serve the customized ballot and instructions via U.S. mail on all parties who have received the order and copies of the plan and disclosure statement electronically.

[Comment: The small business debtor who elects to use the court approved forms for small business plans and disclosure statements, or a combined court approved form, may follow the procedure described in Local Rule 3017-2(B) and bypass the process described in Local Rule 3017-2(A). All other plans that include disclosure information, whether or not titled as a combined plan and disclosure statement, or plans and disclosure statements filed separately, will be subject to the approval procedure set forth in Local Rule 3017-2(A). See also Bankruptcy Rules 2002(b) and (d) and 3017(a) and (d) and Local Rule 2002-1(C)(8) (service of plan, disclosure statement, ballot, and local form order required) and Bankruptcy Rules 2002(k) and 9034 (service on U.S. Trustee required). See also Local Rule 2002-1(C)(9) (service of notice of fee applications).]

[Effective December 1, 1998. Amended effective December 1, 2002; June 2, 2008; December 1, 2009.]

RULE 3017-3. DISCLOSURE STATEMENT APPROVAL AND CONFIRMATION HEARING—PREPACKAGED CHAPTER 11 CASES

A debtor seeking authority to confirm a "Prepackaged Chapter 11 Case" as contemplated by 11 U.S.C. § 1126(b) shall comply with the court's "Guidelines for Prepackaged Chapter 11 Cases".

[Effective June 2, 2008.]

RULE 3018-1. BALLOTS. VOTING ON CHAPTER 11 PLAN—DEADLINE

(A) General. Ballots shall conform to the Local Form "Ballot and Deadline For Filing Ballot Accepting Or Rejecting Plan" and shall be customized prior to service via U.S. Mail on each creditor by the plan proponent to reflect the class of that creditor. Ballots shall be filed electronically by registered users or conventionally and entered on the electronic docket by the clerk. Ballots will appear on the docket on the date filed. The CM/ECF system will generate a ballot summary report of all ballots filed in the case with a hyperlink to each PDF ballot image.

(B) Deadline for Filing. Except as otherwise ordered by the court, ballots accepting or rejecting a chapter 11 plan shall be filed with the court at least 14 days before the confirmation hearing; provided, however, that in small business cases ballots shall be filed at least seven days before the confirmation hearing.

[Comment: See also Local Rules 3017-1(B) (service of ballot), 3020-1(A) (deadline for objecting to confirmation).]

[Effective December 1, 1998. Amended effective December 1, 2002; June 2, 2008; December 1, 2009.]

RULE 3020-1. CONFIRMATION OF CHAPTER 11 PLANS

(A) Deadline for Objections to Confirmation. Objections to confirmation of a plan shall be filed at least 14 days before the confirmation hearing; provided, however, that in a small business case, objections shall be filed at least three business days before the confirmation hearing.

(B) Proponent's Report, Confirmation Affidavit, and for Individual Debtors, Certificate re Domestic Support Obligations and Filing of Tax Returns. The proponent of a chapter 11 plan shall file the Local Form "Certificate of Proponent of Plan on Acceptance of Plan, Report on Amount to be Deposited, Certificate of Amount Deposited and Payment of Fees" and the Local Form "Confirmation Affidavit" at least three business days before the confirmation hearing. If the debtor is an individual, the debtor shall also file the Local Form "Individual Debtor Certificate for Confirmation Regarding Payment of Domestic Support Obligations and [for Chapter 11 Cases] Filing of Required Tax Returns" at least three business days before the confirmation hearing.

(C) Payment of Clerk's and U.S. Trustee's Fees. A plan shall not be confirmed unless the plan proponent's report required by this rule certifies that all outstanding fees payable to the clerk and the U.S. Trustee under 28 U.S.C. § 1930 have been paid.

(D) Order to Be Served. The order confirming plan shall be served pursuant to Bankruptcy Rule 3017(f) and Local Rule 2002-1(C)(11).

[Effective December 1, 1998. Amended effective December 1, 2002; June 2, 2008; December 1, 2009.]

RULE 3022-1. FINAL DECREE IN CHAPTER 11 CASES

(A) Deadline for Filing Final Report and Motion for Entry of Final Decree. Unless otherwise provided in the confirmation order, the proponent of the plan shall file the Local Form "Final Report and Motion for Entry of Final Decree", in a non-individual chapter 11 case, not later than 60 days after the order confirming the plan becomes final, and in an individual chapter 11 case, upon completion of all payments under the confirmed plan, or if applicable, upon the filing of a motion by an individual debtor seeking entry of a discharge prior to completion of payments under the plan under 11 U.S.C. § 1141(d)(5).

(B) Required Local Form Statement in Individual Cases. In an individual chapter 11 case, not later than 60 days after completion of all payments under the confirmed plan, or if applicable, upon the filing of a motion seeking entry of a discharge prior to completion of payments under the plan under 11 U.S.C. § 1141(d)(5), the debtor shall also file the Local Form "Notice of Deadline to Object to Debtor's Statement Re: 11 U.S.C. § 522(q)(1) Applicability, Payment of Domestic Support Obligations, and [For Chapter 11 Cases Only] Applicability of Financial Management Course and Statement Regarding Eligibility to Receive a Discharge". This statement shall be served on negative notice on all parties of record. Any interested party who fails to file and serve a written objection to the statement within 30 days shall be deemed to have consented to entry of the final decree and discharge of debtor. A certificate of service shall be filed as provided by Local Rule 2002-1(F).

[Effective December 1, 1998. Amended effective December 1, 2002; June 2, 2008; April 27, 2009; December 1, 2009.]

RULE 3070-1. CHAPTER 13 PAYMENTS

(A) Commencement of Payments.

(1) *Deadline to Commence.* Payments to the chapter 13 trustee pursuant to the proposed plan, as may be amended, shall commence not later than 30 days after filing the petition. If the case was converted to a chapter 13 case, payments shall commence not later than 30 days after entry of the conversion order. Payments shall be made directly to the trustee in the manner prescribed by the trustee.

(2) *Scope of Payments.*

(a) Payments of personal property leases governed by 11 U.S.C. § 1326(a)(1)(B), shall only be made directly by the debtor to the lessor if the debtor's plan so provides or if no plan provision addresses payment of the debtor's lease obligation. If the plan provides for payment of the lease obligation by the trustee, the debtor shall make the pre-confirmation lease payments to the chapter 13 trustee in accordance with the filed chapter 13 plan.

(b) Pre-confirmation adequate protection payments governed by 11 U.S.C. § 1326(a)(1)(C), shall only be made directly by the debtor to the secured creditor if the debtor's plan so provides or if no plan provision addresses payment of the secured claim. If the plan provides for payment of the secured claim by the trustee, the debtor shall make the pre-confirmation payments to the chapter 13 trustee in accordance with the filed chapter 13 plan.

(3) *Pre-confirmation Payments to be Held by Trustee.* Unless otherwise ordered by the court, to facilitate the administration of chapter 13 cases, all pre-confirmation payments shall be held by the chapter 13 trustee pending confirmation, conversion or dismissal of the case and where applicable, Local Rules 1017-2(F) and 1019-1(D) shall apply.

B) Post Confirmation Payment Changes or Charges.

(1) *Applicability of Bankruptcy Rule 3002.1 to Additional Types of Claims Related to Real Property.* The provisions of Bankruptcy Rule 3002.1 shall also apply to claims that are:

(a) secured by a security interest on real property of the debtor other than the debtor's principal residence (including without limitation claims of condominium associations and homeowner's associations); and

(b) for which the plan provides that either the trustee or the debtor will make contractual installment payments and which payments are subject to change.

[Comment: Bankruptcy Rule 3002.1 by its terms requires the filing of payment change and certain other notices relating only to security interests in the debtor's primary residence, and only where the plan provides that either the trustee or the debtor will make contractual installment payments. The local rule extends that filing requirement from claims secured by primary residences to claims secured by any real properties. However, the trustee does not care to receive, and the secured creditor must not file, notices of payment change where the plan payments to that creditor are not through the trustee or are not going to change under the loan documents.]

(2) If the plan's treatment of a claim secured by a security interest in real property is not covered by subsection (B)(1) of this rule, filing of notices of payment change is prohibited.

(3) With respect to claims in connection with which creditors are directed not to file notices of payment change under subsection (B)(2) of this rule, the holder of the claim may send notices of payment change and escrow notices directly to the debtor without violating the automatic stay.

(4) Upon motion by the debtor, the court will consider awarding sanctions against a creditor that files a notice of payment change not required under Bankruptcy Rule 3002.1 and that is expressly deemed unnecessary under this rule.

(5) *Modifications to Official Bankruptcy Form "Notice of Mortgage Payment Change" Required.* When a notice of payment change is filed addressing a claim covered under subdivision (B)(1) of this Rule, the Official Bankruptcy Form "Notice of Mortgage Payment Change" shall be modified accordingly to reflect the actual type of claim for which the notice is being filed.

[Comment: In this district, payments on mortgages and other voluntary liens on real property are often cured and maintained under Section 1322(b)(5) by payments through the trustee under the plan. Bankruptcy Rule 3002.1 by its terms requires the filing of payment change and certain other notices only to security interests in the debtor's primary residence, and only where the plan payments are for cure and maintenance under Section 1322(b)(5). The local rule now extends that filing requirement from claims secured by primary residences to claims secured by any real properties, and from cure-and-maintenance treatment under Section 1322(b)(5) to all treatment of such claims where the payments through the trustee are subject to change. However, the trustee does not care to receive, and the secured creditor must not file, notices of payment change where the plan payments to that creditor are not through the trustee or are not going to change under the loan documents.]

(C) Dismissal of Case for Failure to Timely Remit Payments.

(1) *Dismissal at the Meeting of Creditors.* If, at the meeting of creditors, the debtor is not current in plan payments under the plan as originally filed, the chapter 13 trustee is authorized by the court to docket in the case a virtual paperless entry titled "Trustee's Request for Entry of Order Dismissing Case" and the case may be dismissed without further notice or hearing. Dismissal shall be with prejudice to the debtor filing any bankruptcy case for a period of 180 days from entry of the order of dismissal, or the expiration of any prejudice period set in any previous order still in effect, whichever is later.

(2) *Dismissal Subsequent to Confirmation.*

(a) Notice of Delinquency. The trustee may, upon the debtor's failure to timely make any payment, serve a notice of delinquency upon the debtor and the debtor's attorney, along with a copy of this rule.

(b) Deadline to Cure Delinquency. The debtor shall have 45 days from the date of the notice of delinquency to make all payments due under the plan, including any payments that become due within the 45-day period. If applicable, the debtor may, within 14 days of the notice of delinquency, file a motion to modify the confirmed plan.

(c) Failure to Cure. If the debtor is not current in plan payments on the 45th day after the date of the notice of delinquency, the trustee shall file and serve a report of noncompliance and the case shall be dismissed without further notice or hearing, with prejudice to the debtors filing any bankruptcy proceeding for a period of 180 days from entry of the order of dismissal, or the expiration of any prejudice period set in any previous order still in effect, whichever is later.

(D) Wage Deduction Orders—Deadline for Submission of Local Form. A debtor who is not self-employed must submit a proposed Local Form "Agreed Order to Employer to Deduct and Remit and for Related Matters" to the court prior to the meeting of creditors. The proposed order must be signed by the debtor and debtor's attorney. If the proposed order is submitted to the court in electronic format, the order must contain the actual imaged signature of the debtor. The attorney for the debtor, or clerk of court, if the debtor is pro se, shall serve the order on the employer. If a wage deduction order has not been entered the court will conduct an evidentiary hearing to determine feasibility at the confirmation hearing. The court will not confirm a case without a wage deduction order in place, absent extenuating circumstances.

(E) Determination of Final Cure Payment.

(1) *Applicability of Bankruptcy Rule 3002.1.* The provisions of Bankruptcy Rule 3002.1 shall also apply to any chapter 13 case where the debtor's plan provided for the curing of defaults on a claim secured by a security interest on real property other than the debtor's principal residence.

(2) *Local Form Order Required.* A proposed order confirming a claim secured by a security interest in real property is current, submitted by a party to the court under Bankruptcy Rule 3002.1 or this local rule, shall substantially conform to this court's Local Form "Order Determining Debtor has Cured Default and Paid All Required Postpetition Amounts".

[Effective December 1, 1998. Amended effective December 1, 2002; June 2, 2008; December 1, 2009; December 1, 2011; December 3, 2012; December 1, 2015. Amended on an interim basis December 1, 2016.]

RULE 4001-1. RELIEF FROM AUTOMATIC STAY

(A) Notice Requirements. In cases other than chapter 11 cases, notice of any motion seeking relief from the automatic stay, pursuant to 11 U.S.C. § 362(d), shall be sufficient if served on the debtor, the debtor's attorney, the trustee, and any person known to the moving party to claim a legal or equitable interest in any property which may be the subject of the motion. In a chapter 11 case, when applicable, service must be in accordance with Local Rule 2002-1(H), otherwise, the notice must be served on the debtor, the debtor's attorney, the trustee, if any, the U.S. Trustee, the members of the creditors' committee or the committee's attorney and any other person known to the moving party to claim a legal or equitable interest in any property which may be the subject of the motion; however, if no creditors' committee has been formed then the notice shall be served on the creditors holding the 7 largest unsecured claims according to the debtor's list of 20 largest creditors filed in the case.

(B) Contents of Motion. Motions for relief from the automatic stay must comply with this court's "Guidelines for Motions for Relief From the Automatic Stay".

(C) Requests for Relief on Negative Notice. Subject to the limitation in chapter 7 cases set forth below, creditors in chapter 7, 11, or 12 cases, in which the debtor is represented by an attorney, may seek relief from stay on negative notice if the motion meets the requirements of the Guidelines referred to in subdivision (B) above, is served in accordance with subdivision (A) above, and includes above the preamble and below the title of the motion the following bulletin in **bold print** so as to make it more prominent than the remainder of the text:

Any interested party who fails to file and serve a written response to this motion within 14 days after the date of service stated in this motion shall, pursuant to Local Rule 4001-1(C), be deemed to have consented to the entry of an order granting the relief requested in the motion.

In a chapter 7 case, negative notice under this rule is not available for a motion for relief from stay filed prior to the commencement of the meeting of creditors in the case.

When this bulletin is included in the motion, no hearing will be scheduled unless a response is filed. Notwithstanding Bankruptcy Rule 9006(f), the failure of parties, properly served, to file a response within 14 days after service of the motion shall be deemed a consent to the granting of the requested relief. After the time to respond has expired, the moving party shall either (a) promptly submit a proposed order pursuant to Local Rule 5005-1(G), including the following language in the order's preamble:

> "and the movant by submitting this form of order having represented that the motion was served on all parties required by Local Rule 4001-1, that the 14-day response time provided by that rule has expired, that no one has filed, or served on the movant, a response to the motion, and that [either] the form of order was attached as an exhibit to the motion [or] the relief to be granted in this order is the identical relief requested in the motion,"

or (b) promptly file the Local Form "Certificate of Contested Matter". If a certificate of contested matter is filed, the court will schedule a hearing in accordance with the procedures contained in Local Rule 9073-1(A). The "Notice of Hearing" shall be served by movant in accordance with the procedures contained in Local Rule 9073-1(B). The option provided in this paragraph is not intended to limit the court's ability to grant or deny relief sooner than 14 days after service of the motion, or the court's discretion to grant relief without a hearing either by consent of the parties or on verified motions which allege pursuant to 11 U.S.C. § 362(f), that immediate irreparable harm will result from the failure to grant emergency relief without a hearing. A party filing a motion for relief from stay pursuant to this subdivision is deemed to have consented to voluntarily extending, to a date 60 days after the filing of a Local Form "Certificate of Contested Matter" by the party filing the motion for relief from stay, the provision of

11 U.S.C. § 362(e), which provides for termination of the automatic stay within 60 days absent an order of the court continuing the stay.

(D) Contested Motions; Response. A response which objects to the granting of the requested relief shall identify the motion, the movant's attorney, and the motion's service date, and shall set forth a short and plain statement of the facts countervailing the motion, including:

(1) a statement of indebtedness, if the amount of debt is in dispute;

(2) a specific statement of any objection to the authenticity, accuracy or completeness of the moving party's exhibits; and

(3) a statement of how the responding party proposes to adequately protect the moving party's security interest, if it is the debtor who objected and adequate protection may be necessary; however, the objection of a chapter 7 trustee prior to the § 341 meeting need state only that the § 341 meeting has not yet been held and that the trustee lacks the necessary information to adequately respond further.

The response must be served on the movant's attorney and on the same parties on whom the motion was served. Notice, pursuant to Local Rule 9073-1(B), shall be served on the same parties on whom the motion was served.

(E) Hearing. An evidentiary hearing scheduled on a motion for relief from the automatic stay will be a final evidentiary hearing unless the court otherwise notifies the parties in advance. If the court designates the initial hearing as a non-evidentiary hearing, the hearing shall be restricted to the pleadings, affidavits and papers of record and to the arguments of attorneys.

(F) Cooperation of Parties in Preparation for Hearing. At least two business days prior to an evidentiary hearing, the parties or their attorneys must meet in an effort to identify those specific issues of fact or law genuinely in dispute, to exchange copies of appraisals and other exhibits and the names and addresses of witnesses the parties intend to offer at the hearing, and to discuss the possibilities of settlement. At the commencement of the hearing, the parties shall present an exhibit register in accordance with Local Rule 9070-1, and shall announce any stipulations of fact or law.

(G) Discovery. A party may take deposition testimony of any party or witness and may request the production of documents or things and inspection of land, upon actual delivery of at least 14 days' notice, and the minimum time requirements of Bankruptcy Rules 7030 and 7034 shall not apply. The parties shall make their appraisers or other experts and fact witnesses, if any, available for deposition, without the need for subpoena, at least two business days before an evidentiary hearing, and the parties are expected to cooperate in exchanging information and documents without the need for formal discovery procedures. In extraordinary circumstances the court, upon motion of a party but without notice or hearing, may authorize the use of interrogatories or other discovery procedures, and may shorten the notice requirements of any applicable rule.

(H) Continuances. Continuances are governed by Local Rule 5071-1. A party seeking relief from the automatic stay who moves for, or consents to, continuance of the hearing waives the right to enforce the 30 or 60 day rules contained in 11 U.S.C. § 362(e), and the 30 or 60 day hearing requirements shall be deemed extended until the court's ruling at the rescheduled hearing.

[Comment: See also 28 U.S.C. § 1930 (clerk's fee required for motions for stay relief), Bankruptcy Rule 9014 (contested matters governed by general rules of discovery) and Local Rules 5071-1 (continuances), 7026-1 (discovery), and the court's "Guidelines for Preparing, Submitting, and Serving Orders".]

(I) Negotiations Related to Potential Modification of Loan; Automatic Stay Not Applicable. The automatic stay is not applicable, and it shall not be necessary to seek relief from the automatic stay, for a lender with a claim secured by property of the estate to negotiate with a pro se debtor or with debtor's counsel regarding potential modification of the loan.

[Effective December 1, 1998. Amended effective December 1, 2002; June 2, 2008; December 1, 2009; August 1, 2011; December 1, 2015.]

RULE 4001-2. CASH COLLATERAL

A motion seeking authority to use cash collateral pursuant to 11 U.S.C. § 363, shall comply with Bankruptcy Rule 4001(b) or (d), Local Rules 9013-1(F) and (G), and the court's "Guidelines for Motions Seeking Authority to Use Cash Collateral and Motions Seeking Approval of Postpetition Financing".

[Effective December 1, 1998. Amended effective December 1, 2002; July 1, 2004; June 2, 2008.]

RULE 4001-3. OBTAINING CREDIT

A motion seeking approval of postpetition financing pursuant to 11 U.S.C. § 364, shall comply with Bankruptcy Rule 4001(c) and (d), Local Rules 9013-1(F) and (H), and the court's "Guidelines for Motions Seeking Authority to Use Cash Collateral and Motions Seeking Approval of Postpetition Financing".

[Effective December 1, 1998. Amended effective December 1, 2002; July 1, 2004; June 2, 2008.]

RULE 4002-1. DEBTOR'S DUTY TO PROVIDE TAX RETURNS TO TRUSTEE AND CREDITORS

Copies of the debtor's tax returns under 11 U.S.C. § 1116(1)(A), Bankruptcy Rule 4002(b)(3) and (4), shall be provided in accordance with Local Rule 5005-1(A)(2).

[Effective June 2, 2008.]

RULE 4003-1. EXEMPTIONS

(A) Amendment of Claimed Exemptions; Modification of Deadline to Object to Claimed Exemptions. When amending the schedule of property claimed as exempt to add assets not previously listed, the debtor shall serve a copy of the schedule on the trustee, and shall serve notice on all creditors and attorneys of record, or if applicable, those parties required to be served pursuant to Local Rule 2002-1(H), of the filing of the amendment and the extended deadline described in Bankruptcy Rule 4003(b) and subdivision (B) of this rule, and file a certificate of service in accordance with Local Rule 2002-1(F).

(B) Deadline to Object in Converted Cases. Except as provided in Bankruptcy Rule 1019(2)(B), upon conversion of an individual case, a new deadline to object to property claimed as exempt shall be 30 days after the conclusion of the post-conversion meeting of creditors or within 30 days after any amendment to the list or supplemental schedule is filed, whichever is later.

[Comment: See also Bankruptcy Rule 1009 and Local Rules 1009-1 (amendments to schedules) and 2002-1(F) (Certificate of service required).]

2011 Amendment: Subdivision (B) is amended to incorporate provisions adopted by this court's Administrative Order 10-5 which were necessitated by December 1, 2010 amendments to Bankruptcy Rule 1019.

[Effective December 1, 1998. Amended effective December 1, 2002; June 2, 2008; December 1, 2009. Amended, on an interim basis, effective December 1, 2010. Amended effective August 1, 2011.]

RULE 4003-2. AVOIDANCE OF LIENS ON EXEMPT PROPERTY

A debtor's motion to avoid a lien on exempt property under 11 U.S.C. § 522(f) and Bankruptcy Rule 4003(d), shall provide a full legal description of the property, and shall include as an exhibit a copy of the security agreement, judgment or other judicial paper giving rise to the lien and showing recordation information. The motion shall be served on the affected parties in accordance with Bankruptcy Rule 7004, and pursuant to either Local Rule 9013-1(D)(3)(f) or Local Rule 9073-1, and a certificate of service shall be filed in accordance with Local Rule 2002-1(F).

[Comment: See also Local Rule 5010-1 (reopening case to avoid a judicial lien).]

[Effective December 1, 1998. Amended effective December 1, 2002; June 2, 2008.]

RULE 4004-1. RESERVED

[Note: 4004-1 is a reserved rule number.]

RULE 4004-2. MODIFICATION OF DEADLINE FOR OBJECTIONS

The deadlines set pursuant to Bankruptcy Rule 4004(a) for filing a complaint or motion objecting to discharge under § 727, and for filing a motion objecting to discharge under § 1328(f), are modified in the following circumstances:

(A) Meeting of Creditors Untimely Noticed. If service of the § 341 or post-conversion meeting notice is not timely provided pursuant to Bankruptcy Rule 2002(a) and Local Rule 2002-1(C)(1), and as a result of this failure to provide notice the § 341 meeting must be rescheduled before another notice can be served, the deadline for objecting to discharge under §§ 727(a) or 1328(f) shall be 60 days after the rescheduled date of the § 341 meeting.

(B) Case Dismissed and Reinstated. If a case is dismissed prior to the expiration of the deadline for objecting to discharge and subsequently reinstated:

(1) in a case dismissed before the § 341 meeting is held, the new deadline for objecting to discharge under §§ 727 or 1328(f) shall be 60 days after the rescheduled § 341 meeting; or

(2) in a case dismissed after the § 341 meeting is held, the new deadline for objecting to discharge under §§ 727 or 1328(f) shall be 60 days from entry of the order reinstating the case.

(C) Notice of New Deadline. The clerk shall provide notice of new deadlines established under this rule.

[Effective December 1, 1998. Amended effective December 1, 2002; June 2, 2008; December 1, 2009. Amended, on an interim basis, effective December 1, 2010. Amended effective August 1, 2011; December 1, 2015.]

RULE 4004-3. DISCHARGE IN GENERAL

(A) The individual debtor shall be discharged upon determination that the debtor is eligible to receive a discharge under the Bankruptcy Code and Bankruptcy Rules (including without limitation the provisions of 11 U.S.C. §§ 707, 727, 1141, 1228, and 1328, and Bankruptcy Rule 4004(c), as applicable), and subject to any established court procedures that provide for delay of entry of the discharge, including but not limited to the following requirements:

(1) in a chapter 12 case, the trustee has filed a final report certifying that all payments have been made pursuant to the confirmed plan;

(2) in a chapter 13 case, unless the debtor is seeking a hardship discharge under 11 U.S.C. § 1328(b), the trustee has filed a "Notice of Completion of Plan Payments";

(3) in a chapter 13 case, the debtor has filed, as appropriate, either the Local Form "Debtor's Certificate of Compliance, Motion for Issuance of Discharge and Notice of Deadline to Object" or the Local Form "Debtor's Certificate of Compliance, Motion for Issuance of Discharge Before Completion of Plan Payments, and Notice of Deadline to Object," as required under Local Rule 2002-1 (C)(12) has served a copy on all parties of record providing a 21 day objection deadline and, if any objections were filed, they have been resolved to permit issuance of a discharge; and

(4) in an individual chapter 11 or 12 case the debtor has submitted the required Local Form "Notice of Deadline to Object to Debtor's Statement Re: 11 U.S.C. § 522(q)(1) Applicability, Payment of Domestic Support Obligations, and [For Chapter 11 Cases Only] Applicability of Financial Management Course and Statement Regarding Eligibility to Receive a Discharge" and a copy was served on all parties of record as required under Local Rule 2002-1(C)(13), and for chapter 11 cases Local Rule 3022-1(B), and for chapter 12 cases Local Rule 2082-1.

(B) Notice of Discharge. The clerk shall serve the order of discharge in all chapter 7, 12 and 13 cases subject to the provisions of Local Rule 2002-1(C)(4). In a chapter 11 non-individual case, the order confirming a plan shall contain notice of the grant or denial of the discharge. In a chapter 11 individual case, the final decree shall contain notice of the grant or denial of the discharge.

[Effective December 1, 1998. Amended effective December 1, 2002; June 2, 2008; December 1, 2009; August 1, 2011; December 1, 2011; March 31, 2015.]

RULE 4006-1. NOTICE OF NO DISCHARGE OR WAIVER OR REVOCATION OF DISCHARGE

Orders denying, revoking or waiving discharge shall be served as provided in Rule 2002-1(C)(4). The clerk may close an individual chapter 7, 12, or 13 case where no discharge was issued due to debtor's failure to comply with the requirements under Bankruptcy Rule 1007(b)(7) or Local Rule 4004-3(A)(3) or (4), and serve notice as provided in Local Rule 2002-1(C)(4).

[Comment: See also Local Rule 5010-1(H).]

[Effective December 1, 1998. Amended effective December 1, 2002; June 2, 2008; December 1, 2009.]

RULE 4007-1. MODIFICATION OF DEADLINE FOR OBJECTING TO DISCHARGEABILITY OF A DEBT

The deadline set pursuant to Bankruptcy Rule 4007(c), for filing a complaint objecting to dischargeability of a debt is modified in the following circumstances:

(A) Meeting of Creditors Untimely Noticed. If service of the § 341 or post-conversion meeting notice is not timely provided pursuant to Bankruptcy Rule 2002(a), and as a result of this failure to provide notice the § 341 meeting must be rescheduled before another notice can be served, the deadline for filing objections to dischargeability of a debt shall be 60 days after the rescheduled date of the § 341 meeting.

(B) Case Dismissed and Reinstated. If a case is dismissed prior to the expiration of the deadline for objecting to dischargeability and subsequently reinstated:

(1) in a case dismissed before the § 341 meeting is held, the new deadline for filing objections to dischargeability shall be 60 days after the rescheduled § 341 meeting, and the clerk shall serve a new § 341 notice which notifies all creditors of the deadline; or

(2) in a case dismissed after the § 341 meeting is held, the new deadline for filing objections to dischargeability shall be 60 days from entry of the order reinstating the case.

(C) Notice of New Deadline. The clerk shall provide notice of any new deadlines established under this rule.

[Effective December 1, 1998. Amended effective December 1, 2002; June 2, 2008; December 1, 2009; August 1, 2011; December 1, 2015.]

RULE 4008-1. REAFFIRMATION

(A) Official Bankruptcy and Director Forms Required; No Notice, Hearing or Order Required to Confirm Enforceability. Reaffirmation agreements shall be filed utilizing the Official Bankruptcy Form "Cover Sheet for Reaffirmation Agreement" and, if applicable, any other Administrative Office of the U.S. Courts Director's Procedural Forms for reaffirmation agreements. No notice, hearing or order shall be necessary to confirm the enforceability of a reaffirmation agreement filed with the court that is signed by all parties to the agreement, that conforms to the requirements of 11 U.S.C. §§ 524(c)(1), (2), and (4), and that is accompanied by a declaration or affidavit of the attorney who represented the debtor during the negotiation of the agreement pursuant to 11 U.S.C. § 524(c)(3). Notwithstanding the foregoing, the court may set a hearing on a reaffirmation agreement as permitted by 11 U.S.C. § 524 and applicable law.

(B) Debtor Must Appear at Reaffirmation Hearing. If the court sets a hearing to consider a reaffirmation agreement, the debtor must appear at the hearing. The hearing will be evidentiary.

(C) Reaffirmation Agreement Made Subsequent to Entry of Discharge. A reaffirmation agreement made by a debtor subsequent to entry of the discharge shall be declared invalid by the court.

(D) Duties of Debtor's Counsel. Unless the attorney has withdrawn as attorney for the debtor pursuant to Local Rule 2091-1, an attorney who files a petition on behalf of a debtor must represent the debtor during the negotiation and filing of any reaffirmation agreements, and appear at any hearings on reaffirmation agreements.

[Comment: See also Local Rule 2090-1(C) and (D).]

[Effective December 1, 1998. Amended effective December 1, 2002; June 2, 2008; December 1, 2009; August 1, 2011; December 1, 2015.]

RULE 5001-1. COURT ADMINISTRATION—ACTING CHIEF JUDGE; ALTERNATE JUDGE

(A) Acting Chief Judge. If the chief judge is absent from the district or is unable to perform required duties, such duties shall be performed by the judge in active service, present in the district and willing to act, who is most senior on the date of the judge's commission, other than a recalled judge. Such judge is designated as the acting chief judge on such occasions.

(B) Alternate Judge. If a judge is unable to perform required duties, such duties may, with the consent of both judges, be performed by the judge designated by the chief judge as the "alternate judge" for that judge.

[Effective December 1, 1998. Amended effective December 1, 2002; June 2, 2008.]

RULE 5001-2. CLERK'S OFFICE LOCATIONS. ACCESS TO CLERK'S OFFICE FOR EMERGENCY OR TIME SENSITIVE FILINGS

(A) Clerk's Office Locations. The main office of the clerk is located in Miami. Divisional offices are located in Ft. Lauderdale and West Palm Beach.

(B) Access to Clerk's Office for Emergency or Time Sensitive Filings. Any party seeking to conventionally file an emergency or otherwise time sensitive paper during a time period when the clerk's office is not open to the public, shall, in advance, contact the clerk or chief deputy clerk to request after hours, holiday or weekend filing accommodations.

[Effective December 1, 1998. Amended effective December 1, 2002; July 1, 2004; August 18, 2006; September 20, 2006; June 2, 2008.]

RULE 5003-1. RECORDS KEPT BY THE CLERK. CERTIFIED COPIES OF COURT RECORDS [ABROGATED EFFECTIVE DECEMBER 1, 2015]

RULE 5003-2. COURT PAPERS—REMOVAL OF [ABROGATED]

RULE 5005-1. FILING AND TRANSMITTAL OF PAPERS

(A) General Requirements.

(1) *Format.* All documents must comply with the format requirements of the Bankruptcy Code, the Bankruptcy Rules and these rules. Documents filed or submitted in cases or proceedings shall be either filed electronically in PDF by a registered user, or filed in conventional paper format by non-registered users and then converted to PDF by the clerk. Any exceptions to the requirement that a document be electronically filed by a registered user shall be set forth in the Clerk's Filing Instructions or in the court's "Guidelines for Preparing, Submitting and Serving Orders".

(2) *Compliance with Federal Judiciary Privacy Policy.* All papers submitted for filing must comply with the federal judiciary privacy policy and the Bankruptcy Rules which address the extent to which personal information will be required to be submitted or included in the public records of the court.

(a) Papers Filed with the Court. Filers of papers shall be responsible for redacting Social Security or other individual taxpayer identification numbers and other personal identifiers such as dates of birth, financial account numbers, and names of minor children from documents filed with the court. Unless otherwise ordered by the court, any documents which include personal identifiers should be redacted to exclude the personal information or, if such redaction is not practical, the party may seek to submit them as sealed records pursuant to Local Rule 5003-1(D); however, the court may still require submission of a redacted copy for inclusion in the public records. Redaction guidelines for personal information not addressed by the Bankruptcy Rules or forms include:

(i) Social Security or other individual taxpayer identification numbers. If an individual's social security or other individual taxpayer identification number must be included in a pleading, only the last four digits of that number should be used.

(ii) Names of minor children. If the involvement of a minor child must be mentioned, only the initials of that child should be used. When completing Official Bankruptcy Forms requiring information on minors, follow the form instructions regarding how to indicate this information.

(iii) Dates of birth. If an individual's date of birth must be included in a pleading, only the year should be used. When completing Official Bankruptcy Forms requiring information on minors, follow the form instructions regarding how to indicate this information.

(iv) Financial account numbers. If financial account numbers are relevant, only the last four digits of these numbers should be used.

(b) Electronic Availability of Electronic Transcripts and Redaction of Transcripts Filed with the Court. Transcripts of court proceedings shall only be filed with the court by the official court reporter. Filed transcripts shall be made available, and shall, where required to comply with privacy requirements, be redacted in accordance with this court's guidelines setting forth the policies on electronic availability of transcripts of court proceedings and redaction of transcripts filed with the court.

(c) Privacy and Redaction of Tax Returns Provided by Individual Debtor Directly to Parties Under 11 U.S.C. §§ 521(e)(2)(A) or (f) or 11 U.S.C. § 1116(1)(A). Requests for copies of the debtor's tax information under 11 U.S.C. § 521, or for tax returns submitted by individual debtors under 11 U.S.C. § 1116(1)(A), and docketed as a non-public "restricted" document, shall be in accordance with the Administrative Office of the United States Courts "Director's Interim Guidance Regarding Tax Information Under 11 U.S.C. § 521" dated September 20, 2005, as amended or supplemented by any subsequent directives issued. This document will be posted on the court website.

[Comment: See also 11 U.S.C. § 110 (bankruptcy petition preparers must continue to submit their complete social security or other individual taxpayer identification numbers, where required, on papers submitted to the court), Bankruptcy Rules 1005 (only last four digits of social security or other individual taxpayer identification numbers included in caption of petition), 1007(f) (verified statement of social security or other individual taxpayer identification numbers must be submitted) and 9037 (Privacy Protection for Filings Made With the Court).]

(3) *Ex Parte Motions to Redact Personal Information.* A party seeking to redact personal information as set forth in subdivision (A)(2) of this Rule may file an ex parte motion, accompanied by the required filing fee, requesting an order directing the clerk to restrict the unredacted document from public view. If the motion is being filed in a closed case, a motion to reopen case is not required if the sole purpose of the reopening is to file a motion to redact personal information. Simultaneously with the filing of the ex parte motion, the movant shall file the amended redacted document and submit a proposed order granting the motion. The clerk may restrict public access to the document containing personal identifiers pending entry of an order granting the ex parte motion. Unless the motion is being filed under seal, the motion should not repeat the actual personal information for which redaction is sought. A copy of the motion and entered order shall be served by the movant on the debtor, any individual whose personal identifiers have been exposed, the case trustee (if any), and the U.S. trustee. The original filed document shall remain restricted to preserve the full record.

[Comment: See Local Rule 5005-4(E) (Official Case Record) and Local Rule 5005-1(G)(1)(a) (submittal of proposed orders). See also

Bankruptcy Rule 9037 (Privacy Protection for Filings Made with the Court).]

(4) *Sealed Records.* Records or other court papers shall be sealed only upon order of the court directing the clerk as to the length of time during which the records shall remain sealed.

(a) Local Form Cover Sheet Required. The Local Form "Cover Sheet to Accompany Items Submitted for Sealing or In Camera Review" shall accompany:

(i) a sealed motion, filed either in advance of filing a sealed document or accompanied by the sealed document (if both the motion and the document are filed together);

(ii) an unsealed motion and a sealed document; or

(iii) a sealed document being filed pursuant to a previously entered order allowing the document to be filed as sealed. If a sealed document is being filed pursuant to a previously entered court order, a notice of filing sealed item and a copy of the order directing sealing (unless order is sealed) must accompany the cover sheet and sealed documents.

(b) Motion Required. The Local Form "Cover Sheet to Accompany Items Submitted for Sealing or In Camera Review", is to be filed in addition to, not in place of, a motion to seal or grant in camera inspection. If the movant requests that the documents remain under seal after closing, the motion should include this request.

(c) Disposition of Sealed Documents Upon Case Closing. Upon administrative closing, the court may issue an order setting a deadline for parties to request that sealed documents remain under seal or to request return of the sealed document(s) to the filing party. If no timely requests are filed, the document(s) will be unsealed.

(5) *Form Used for Submission of Social Security or Other Individual Taxpayer Identification Numbers.* The Official Bankruptcy Form "Statement About Your Social Security Numbers" as required by the Bankruptcy Rules or this court, shall be retained by the clerk as a non-public record.

(B) Place of Filing. Unless otherwise directed by the court, all papers to be filed or received conventionally by the court shall be delivered to the clerk's office, and not to a judge's chambers.

[Comment: See also Local Rule 5005-1(F)(2) (emergency submittal).]

(C) Deficient Petitions and Papers.

(1) *Petitions.* Petitions presented for filing which do not conform to the official form, are filed without an attorney (non-individual debtors only), do not indicate the last four digits of the social security number or other individual taxpayer identification number and/or an identification number on the petition, are not accompanied by the Official Bankruptcy Form "Statement About Your Social Security Numbers"(individual debtors only), are not accompanied by a creditor matrix, list of 20 largest unsecured creditors (chapter 11 cases), are not accompanied by a corporate ownership statement as required by Bankruptcy Rule 1007(a)(1) and Local Rule 1002-1(A)(2), or other document required at the time of filing shall be accepted for filing as deficient. The clerk shall, as provided by subdivision (C)(3) of this rule, serve a notice of deficiency giving the debtor a deadline to correct the deficiency to avoid dismissal of the case without further notice.

(2) *Other Papers.* Any other paper which is otherwise presented in improper form may, depending upon the nature of the deficiency, be either docketed as deficient and, without notice or hearing, be subject to entry of an order striking the paper, or, if filed in a closed case, returned without filing.

(3) *Clerk's Deficiency Notices.*

(a) Authority of Clerk to Prepare and Serve Deficiency Notices. The clerk is authorized to prepare notices which establish deadlines for correction of filing deficiencies for service on parties filing papers not prepared or submitted in compliance with the administrative requirements contained in the Bankruptcy Code, Bankruptcy Rules, Local Rules, Court Administrative Orders or other procedures of this court.

(b) Content of Deficiency Notices. A deficiency notice shall indicate the nature of the deficiencies, establish a deadline for correction of the deficiencies and set forth the consequences, including possible dismissal of the case without further notice, of failure to correct the stated deficiencies within the time indicated. Registered users may also receive notification via an electronic docket entry "Notice to Filer of Apparent Filing Deficiency" that a deficient or incorrect docket entry has been entered. An electronic deficiency notice may establish a deadline for corrective action to be taken or indicate that the error has been corrected by the clerk and no further action is required.

(c) Deadline to Correct Deficiency. The deadline established pursuant to this rule for any deficiencies with respect to schedules and statements required to be filed pursuant to Bankruptcy Rule 1007(b)(1), shall be the 14 day deadline from the date of filing the petition established by Bankruptcy Rule 1007(c), or as extended by the court. All other deadlines for correction of deficiencies pursuant to this rule shall be a date no less than seven days from the date of filing of the deficient paper. The actual deadline established by the clerk shall depend upon the nature of the deficiency to be corrected.

(d) Clerk Corrected Deficiency(ies). At the discretion of the clerk, certain electronically docketed entries will be corrected by the clerk (e.g., incorrect party filer, incorrect document linkage, etc.). The clerk will enter on docket an electronic entry "Notice to Filer of Apparent Filing Deficiency" which will indicate the item was corrected and that no further action is required by the registered user.

[Comment: See Local Rules 1002-1(B) (clerk authorized to refuse for filing certain voluntary petitions, 1006-1(A)(3) (refusal of installment application and petition by clerk), 5080-1 (fees required).]

(D) Papers Filed in Closed Cases. The clerk may return, without docketing, to the filing party any paper which is tendered for filing after the administrative closing of a case or proceeding, except a motion to reopen or other paper specifically authorized by the order disposing of the case or proceeding. If the paper is filed electronically, the clerk will enter an electronic docket entry "Notice to Filer of Apparent Filing

Deficiency" advising that no further action will be taken by the court.

(E) File Stamping of Copies. The clerk shall provide a filed-stamped copy of any conventionally filed paper to the filing party if an additional copy of the paper and an adequately sized, self-addressed stamped envelope is also supplied at the time of filing.

(F) Submission of Papers in Matters Already Set for Hearing.

(1) *Deadline for Filing. Form of Response.* Memoranda, affidavits and other papers intended for consideration at any hearing already set before the court, shall be filed and served so as to be received by the movant and the court not later than 4:30 p.m. on the second business day prior to the hearing, or the papers submitted may not be considered at the hearing. All responsive papers shall set forth any applicable defenses or objections in law or fact on which the respondent relies. All responsive papers shall be served in accordance with these local rules. This subdivision shall not apply to affidavits filed pursuant to Bankruptcy Rule 7056.

(2) *Emergency Submittal.* Memoranda, affidavits or other papers not filed prior to the deadline established in subdivision (1), but which the filing party deems necessary for the court's consideration at the scheduled hearing, may be considered at the hearing only if accompanied by the Local Form "Notice of Late Filing of Paper Pursuant to Local Rule 5005-1(F)(2)", noting the emergency nature of the filing or stating the exceptional circumstances for the untimely filing.

This provision does not apply to amended chapter 13 plans, schedules or statements filed prior to a scheduled confirmation hearing under the deadlines established by Local Rules 1009-1(D)(4) and 3015-2(A).

[Comment: See subdivision (B) (all papers to be delivered to clerk, not to judge).]

(3) *Rule Not Applicable to Exhibits.* This rule shall not be construed to modify Local Rule 9070-1, regarding the presentation of papers introduced as evidence in a trial or evidentiary hearing.

(G) Submittal and Service of Orders. Unless otherwise directed by the court, the "Guidelines for Preparing, Submitting, and Serving Orders" apply to matters before this court.

(1) *Submittal of Proposed Orders.* Unless otherwise directed by the court or by these rules:

(a) Requests for relief which may be considered immediately by the court without opportunity for objection or hearing must be accompanied by a proposed order submitted in accordance with the "Guidelines for Preparing, Submitting, and Serving Orders".

[Comment: See Local Rule 9013-1(C) (motions which may be considered without opportunity for hearing).]

(b) The proponent and any opponent of any requested relief set for hearing on an emergency basis shall bring to the hearing a proposed order granting or denying the relief requested. Otherwise, the proposed order shall be uploaded in electronic format using the E-orders program in CM/ECF.

(c) The prevailing party in a hearing or trial shall submit a proposed order, in the manner directed by the court, conforming to the decision of the court, not later than 4:30 p.m. on the seventh day following the hearing or trial. At the time of submittal, unless otherwise directed by the court the proponent must provide a copy of the proposed order and any covering memo to all adverse parties unless the order conforms strictly to a local form. If a party fails to timely submit a proposed order, the court may dismiss the underlying matter for failure to prosecute or take other action. If the court requests or permits submittal of competing proposed orders each party submitting a proposed order shall provide a copy of the proposed order and any covering memo to all adverse parties no later than two business days following the last date set for submission to the court.

[Comment: See also "Guidelines for Preparing, Submitting, and Serving Orders" and Local Rule 2002-1(A) (notice of proposed relief must be served on all directly affected parties) and Local Rule 9072-1 (form of orders).]

(2) *Service of Entered Orders.* Where the clerk is required to serve orders under these rules, service will be accomplished via the BNC or, via the NEF (for registered users who have appeared in the case). Where the clerk is not required to serve orders under these rules, the clerk will provide, via the BNC or via the NEF (for registered users who have appeared in the case), a copy of the order for use by the designated serving party. It is the responsibility of the designated serving party to timely serve the order on all required parties within three business days from entry and file a certificate of service in accordance with Local Rule 2002-1(F). A proposed order must not indicate in the service section that the clerk will serve the order unless the clerk is required to provide service under these rules or directed by the court for a specific case or order.

[Comment: See also "Guidelines for Preparing, Submitting, and Serving Orders" and Local Rules 2002-1(C) (service of particular orders), 2002-1(H) "Master Service List" in chapter 11 cases, and 9076-1 (electronic service).]

[Effective December 1, 1998. Amended effective December 1, 2002; July 1, 2004; June 2, 2008; December 1, 2009; August 1, 2011; November 19, 2014; December 1, 2015.]

RULE 5005-3. FILING PAPERS—SIZE OF PAPERS

All conventionally filed papers, including attachments and exhibits, shall be 8 1/2 × 11 inches (letter-sized); attachments and exhibits may be photo-reduced if necessary. This subdivision is not intended to preclude the introduction of oversize exhibits at a trial or evidentiary hearing.

[Comment: See also Local Rule 9070-1(B) (oversize exhibits at trial).]

[Effective December 1, 1998. Amended effective December 1, 2002; June 2, 2008.]

RULE 5005-4. ELECTRONIC FILING

(A) Authority. As permitted under Bankruptcy Rules 5005(a)(2), 7005, 9011, 9022, 9029 and 9036, this court, through these rules, court administrative orders, court guidelines, clerk's instructions, local forms, and other clerk or court issued directives has established practices and procedures that permit filing, signing, verifying and serving documents electronically in this court.

(B) Access to Electronic Filing. Access to electronic filing in this district is required, encouraged or prohibited as follows:

(1) All trustees assigned to cases in this district and attorneys appearing in cases in this district under Local Rules 2090–1(A) and 2090–1(B)(3), except for government attorneys appearing for those limited purposes under Local Rule 2090–1(B)(1), and those attorneys excepted under either provision (B)(5) or (B)(6) below, must complete court approved CM/ECF training to become registered users and file documents using CM/ECF.

(2) If the court grants a pro hac vice appearance in a case under Local Rule 2090–1(B)(2), the attorney may apply to become a registered user in this district with full filing privileges and enter an electronic appearance in that case. The court grants pro hac vice appearance on a case by case basis. Attorneys granted pro hac vice appearance who subsequently become registered users with full filing privileges may only enter an electronic appearance in a case in which an order granting pro hac vice has been entered.

(3) The court encourages attorneys appearing under Local Rule 2090–1(B)(1), and creditors without attorneys, to become registered users with limited creditor filing privileges ("limited filer"), permitting them to electronically file notices of appearance, changes of address, requests for service of notices, proofs of claim and other documents related to proofs of claim (not including responses to objections to claims), notices provided pursuant to Local Rule 3070–1(B), reaffirmation agreements, chapter 11 ballots, and other papers as authorized by the court. In addition, without the necessity of becoming a registered user, any claimant or the claimant's agent may utilize the feature available on the court website for electronic submission of a proof of claim form, and the effect of such electronic submission shall be as provided under section (D) of this Rule.

(4) Currently, pro se debtors and bankruptcy petition preparers are ineligible to use CM/ECF to file documents electronically.

(5) Notwithstanding provision (B)(1) of this rule, any attorney who files ten or fewer documents in the court during a twelve month period shall be exempt from the requirement to become a registered user without further order of the court. The term "documents" shall not include petitions or adversary proceedings. An attorney who files a bankruptcy petition under chapter 7, 11, 12, 13 or 15, or an adversary proceeding, shall not be exempt from becoming a registered user.

(6) Notwithstanding provision (B)(1) of this rule, attorneys appearing pro bono on behalf of debtors may seek waiver of the requirement to become a registered user if the attorney does not intend to file non pro bono bankruptcy petitions or other documents that might otherwise require the attorney to become a registered user. Such waiver may be sought by filing the petition accompanied by the Local Form "Ex Parte Motion to Excuse Compliance with Local Rule 5005–4" and the Local Form "Order Granting Ex Parte Motion to Excuse Compliance with Local Rule 5005–4". Waiver of the electronic filing requirement will be on a case by case basis and shall only apply to the case in which the order granting waiver was entered. If applicable, the attorney shall also file the Local Form "Motion to Appear Pro Hac Vice" required under Local Rule 2090–1(B)(2). An attorney who is granted a waiver of the electronic filing requirement must otherwise comply with all Local Rules, including with respect to service of all papers and filing certificates of service.

(C) Retention of Original Signed Documents by Registered Users. Documents that are electronically filed and require original signatures other than that of the registered user must be maintained in paper form at least five years from the date of discharge of the debtor, dismissal of the case or final resolution of all appeals pending in the case, whichever is later. This retention neither affects nor replaces any other retention period required by other laws or rules of procedure. The court may require the production of original documents for review by the court, a trustee, the U.S. Trustee, or any interested party.

(D) Effect of Electronically Filed Document. Any document signed and filed electronically, or filed conventionally and converted to an electronic document by the clerk, including a proof of claim filed electronically on this court's website, shall constitute the filer's approved signature and have the same force and effect as if the individual signed a paper copy of the document. Documents required to be verified or contain an unsworn declaration that are filed electronically shall be treated, for all purposes (both civil and criminal, including penalties for perjury), the same as though signed or subscribed.

(E) Official Case Record. Regardless of whether an interested party files the document electronically or files it conventionally and the clerk converts it to an electronic document, the resulting electronic document and docket entry are deemed to be the court's official record under Bankruptcy Rule 5003. Deletions, substitutions, or public access restrictions of electronic docket entries or PDF images are permitted only with leave of court. The clerk will review documents filed electronically and, when appropriate, will issue a notice of electronic filing deficiency under Local Rule 5005–1(C).

(F) Virtual Docket Entries. A virtual document consists entirely of the text contained in the docket entry and includes no text of any other document. The docket entry for a virtual document is fully effective despite the absence of a separate PDF document attached to the docket entry. Only trustees, the office of the U.S. Trustee, and court staff may enter a virtual docket entry.

(G) Electronic Filing Date and Technical Difficulties.

(1) *Electronic Filing Date.* Unless the court orders otherwise, a document filed in CM/ECF is deemed filed on the date in which the electronic transmission of the document is completed by midnight Eastern Standard time (or Eastern Daylight Saving, whichever is in place at the time the filing is effected). An electronic filing is confirmed as complete when the NEF is generated. The date and time reflected on the NEF as the "entered on" date is the date the court received

the electronic filing. A document filed conventionally, then converted to electronic format by the clerk, is deemed filed on the date stamped by the clerk on the paper document, not the date it is converted to electronic format. The NEF for conventionally filed paper documents will reflect both the date the party filed the paper document and the date the clerk entered the document on the electronic docket.

(2) *Technical Difficulties.* Parties are strongly encouraged to file documents electronically during normal business hours, in case a technical problem is encountered. If a party is unable to file electronically as a result of a technical difficulty with the court's system, the party must contact the clerk's office CM/ECF Help Desk at the telephone number posted on the court's website during normal business hours. If required to meet a filing deadline, a registered user is permitted to conventionally file a paper document only when the CM/ECF system is inaccessible or the registered user's computer system is inoperable. A registered user whose filing is made untimely as the result of a technical failure may seek, or the court on its own motion may grant, appropriate relief. No filing deadline shall be deemed to be extended due to technical problems except by court order. The clerk shall, whenever possible, post notice of any scheduled maintenance or technical problems which renders the system incapable of receiving electronic filings. Registered users are expected to monitor these postings and take any required action necessary to ensure the timely filing of documents.

[Effective December 1, 1998. Amended effective December 1, 2002; June 2, 2008; December 1, 2009; August 1, 2011; December 1, 2015.]

RULE 5007-1. INTERPRETERS; SERVICES FOR PERSONS WITH COMMUNICATIONS DISABILITIES

Except for proceedings initiated by the United States or for those persons with communications disabilities, the court shall not provide interpreters or other accommodation. There is no requirement that an interpreter provided by any party be federally certified. Persons with communications disabilities needing interpretation services may contact the clerk of court for information on obtaining such services.

[Comment: The U.S. Trustee's office will provide interpreter services for the meeting of creditors.]

[Effective December 1, 1998. Amended effective December 1, 2002; June 2, 2008.]

RULE 5010-1. REOPENING CASES

(A) Fees. A motion to reopen a case must be accompanied by the filing fee in effect at that time, unless: (1) the case is being reopened to correct an administrative error or for actions affecting the discharge of the debtor, (2) the motion is being filed by a trustee and contains a request for deferral of payment of fee until assets are recovered from the estate, (3) the motion is seeking to shorten the "with prejudice" period provision of a prior order of dismissal, or (4) the motion is seeking to reopen a chapter 11 case involving an individual debtor whose case was previously closed after confirmation of a plan but prior to entry of discharge.

[Comment: See "Clerk's Summary of Fees".]

(B) Reopening to Amend Schedules to Add an Omitted Creditor. In a no-asset individual chapter 7 case, a motion to reopen a case to amend schedules to add an omitted creditor (1) must be accompanied by the filing fee required by subdivision (A) of this rule, (2) must be accompanied by a proposed order conforming to the Local Form "Order Reopening Case to Amend Schedules to Add Omitted Creditor," and (3) must state why the debtor did not schedule the affected creditor or creditors prior to entry of the debtor's discharge. The motion must be served in accordance with Bankruptcy Rule 7004, using the procedures set forth in either Local Rule 9013-1(D)(3)(i) or Local Rule 9073-1. Any affected creditor may object on any appropriate ground including, without limitation, that the subject debt is of a kind specified in paragraph (2), (4), or (6) of section 523(a) of the Bankruptcy Code and the creditor did not have notice or actual knowledge of the case sufficient to timely request a determination of dischargeability. No trustee shall be appointed. If the debtor fails timely to comply with the order, the case shall be reclosed without further notice.

[Comment: See also 11 U.S.C. § 523(a) (dischargeability of debt) and Local Rule 9013-1(D)(3)(ij) (matters for which negative notice can be used).]

(C) Reopening to Administer Additional Assets. In a chapter 7 case, a motion to reopen a case to administer additional assets may be filed without a reopening fee only if the trustee files a request for deferral of the fee pending recovery of assets. The filing fee shall be paid from any assets recovered.

(D) Motions to Reopen Chapter 13 Cases. A motion to reopen a chapter 13 case for the purposes of reinstating the case must comply with the provisions of Local Rule 9013-1(E).

(E) Reopening to Correct Social Security or other Individual Taxpayer Identification Number of Debtor. A motion to reopen a case to correct the social security or other individual taxpayer identification number of the debtor must be accompanied by the required reopening fee and must be filed in accordance with the provisions of Local Rule 1009-1(C).

(F) Reopening Case to Avoid a Judicial Lien. A multipart motion to reopen case and to avoid judicial lien must be accompanied by the fee required by subdivision (A) of this rule. The motion to reopen case and to avoid judicial lien must comply with Local Rule 4003-2, and must be served in accordance with Bankruptcy Rule 7004, using the procedures set forth in either Local Rule 9013-1(D)(3)(f) or Local Rule 9073-1. Upon entry of an order on the motion to reopen case and to avoid judicial lien, the case shall be reclosed without further order of the court.

[Comment: See also 11 U.S.C. § 350(b) (reopening case).]

(G) Reopening Case to File Official Bankruptcy Form "Certification About a Financial Management Course". If proof of completion of the required financial management course is not filed by the time the case is administratively ready for closing, the case shall be closed without entry of the discharge. If the debtor subsequently completes the requirement, the debtor may file the certificate accompanied by a motion to reopen case to request entry of discharge and payment of any required reopening fee as permitted under Local Rule 9013-1(C)(21).

(H) Reopening Case to File Required Local Forms for Issuance of Discharge. In chapter 7, 12 or 13 cases closed without entry of a discharge under Local Rule 4006-1, for failure to comply with certification and statement requirements under Bankruptcy Rule 1007(b)(7) or Local Rule 4004-3(A)(3), or (4), the debtor may seek to reopen a case for the purposes of obtaining a discharge upon the payment of any required reopening fee and the filing and service of the local forms required under Bankruptcy Rule 1007(b)(7) and Local Rule 4004-3(A)(3), or (4).

[Effective December 1, 1998. Amended effective December 1, 2002; June 2, 2008; December 1, 2009; August 1, 2011; December 1, 2015.]

RULE 5011-1. MOTIONS TO WITHDRAW REFERENCE

(A) Place for Filing. Fee Required. A request for withdrawal in whole or in part of the reference of a case or proceeding, other than a sua sponte request by the judge, shall be filed by motion with the clerk of this court, accompanied by the required filing fee.

(B) Designation of Record; Response to Motion.

(1) *Designation of Record.* Motions for withdrawal of reference shall include a designation of those portions of the record of the case or proceeding that the moving party believes will reasonably be necessary or pertinent to the district court's consideration of the motion.

(2) *Response to Motion; Reply.* Within 14 days after service of the motion and designation, any other party may file and serve a response to the motion and a supplemental designation of record. The moving party may file and serve a reply to the response within 14 days after service of the response.

(3) *Transcripts.* If the record designated by any party includes a transcript of any untranscribed bankruptcy court hearing, that party shall immediately after filing the designation, electronically submit to the court reporter and file with the clerk of this court, the Local Form "Transcript Request Form" and make satisfactory arrangements for payment of its cost.

(C) Transmittal to District Court.

(1) *Transmittal of Record.* When the record is complete for purposes of transmittal, and after the time for filing a response or reply has expired, the clerk of this court shall promptly transmit to the clerk of the district court the motion to withdraw, all timely filed responses and memoranda, and the portions of the record designated.

(2) *Filing of Papers After Transmittal of Record.* After the opening of a docket in the district court, papers pertaining to the matter under review by the district court shall be filed with the clerk of the district court, but all papers relating to other matters in the bankruptcy case or adversary proceeding or contested matter shall continue to be filed with the clerk of this court.

(3) *Transmittal of File.* Unless otherwise directed by the district court judge:

(a) if the district court withdraws the reference of the entire case (including all adversary proceedings) or an entire adversary proceeding, this court's clerk shall immediately transmit the entire case or proceeding file to the clerk of the district court; and

(b) if the district court withdraws a portion of the case or proceeding, this court's clerk shall immediately transmit to the clerk of the district court such portions of the case or proceeding file as the parties designate.

[Comment: The General Order of the United States District Court for the Southern District of Florida referring all cases and proceedings arising under or related to Title 11, U.S.C. has been codified into District Court Local Rule 87.2.]

[Effective December 1, 1998. Amended effective December 1, 2002; June 2, 2008; December 1, 2009; December 1, 2015.]

RULE 5011-2. ABSTENTION

(A) Deadline for Motion; Tolling of Time to Answer. A motion to abstain from a case, under either 11 U.S.C. § 305 or 28 U.S.C. § 1334, shall be filed not later than 30 days following the first date set for the meeting of creditors. A motion to abstain from an adversary proceeding shall be filed not later than the date set for filing a response under Bankruptcy Rule 7012 and these local rules. If the adversary proceeding is an action removed to this court pursuant to 28 U.S.C. § 1452, a motion to abstain must be filed within 21 days after the notice of removal is filed with this court. If a motion for abstention is filed in an adversary proceeding, the time for filing an answer or other responsive pleading shall be extended until 14 days after entry of an order denying such motion.

2011 Amendment: Subdivision (A) of this rule is amended to correct scrivener's errors and to make provision clearer.

(B) Abstention Treated as Dismissal. An order of abstention from the case shall operate as a dismissal of the case or proceeding.

[Effective December 1, 1998. Amended effective December 1, 2002; June 2, 2008; December 1, 2009; August 1, 2011.]

RULE 5071-1. CONTINUANCES

Requests for continuances of scheduled hearings shall be in the form of a motion, and must:

(A) state with particularity the grounds for the motion;

(B) indicate whether a continuance previously has been granted and whether the opposing party consents;

(C) certify that the client consents to the continuance; and

(D) be filed at the earliest practical opportunity prior to the hearing.

The moving party shall submit a proposed order which provides blank spaces for the date and time of the rescheduled hearing in the event that the court grants the motion for continuance without hearing. Motions for continuance will be granted only under exceptional circumstances, and may be considered by the court without a hearing. The stipulation of all parties is not sufficient grounds, standing alone, for a continuance.

[Comment: Compare Local Rule 7090–1 (continuance of trial and pre-trial conferences). See also Local Rule 9013–1(C)(8) (no hearing necessary on motion for continuance).]

[Effective December 1, 1998. Amended effective December 1, 2002; June 2, 2008.]

RULE 5072–2. COURT SECURITY

(A) Prohibited Materials. No weapons (guns, knives or any other item which may be used as a weapon) or electronic devices as set forth in subdivision (C), shall be permitted in the courtroom, chambers and/or other environs of this court. No items may be left unattended in the court environs. Neither the United States Marshals Service nor the court shall be required to provide storage areas for visitors possessing prohibited items. Visitors to court environs housed in federal buildings shall be required to comply with, and are subject to prosecution for violation of, any existing law, order or other regulation in effect in the respective federal building.

(B) Smoking. Electronic Cigarettes. Smoking, including use of electronic cigarettes is prohibited in all environs of the court. Electronic cigarettes may not be brought into courthouses of the Southern District, except by those permitted to bring electronic devices into courthouses under subdivision (C)(2) of this Rule. This exception is subject to any additional prohibitions or permissions on this matter enacted by the U.S. District Court, Southern District of Florida in buildings shared by both the district and bankruptcy courts.

(C) Electronic Devices.

(1) *General Prohibition.* Electronic devices including but not limited to cameras of any type (including cellular phones which have an integrated camera device), cellular phones, pagers, personal data assistants (PDA), iPads or tablets, laptop computers, tape recorders, etc., are prohibited from being brought into any federal courthouse facility within the Southern District of Florida, including the West Palm Beach Bankruptcy Court facility.

(2) *Exceptions.* Notwithstanding subdivision (A) above:

(a) The restrictions against cellular phones (including phones with integrated camera devices), pagers, personal data assistants (PDA), iPads or tablets, laptop computers, tape recorders, etc., do not apply to individuals having official business within the court environs and possessing valid identification identifying them as belonging to the following categories: federal courthouse employees with valid permanent government employee identification; any attorney of the U.S. Trustee's Office with a valid identification card issued from that office; any attorney permitted to practice law within the Southern District of Florida with a valid Florida Bar identification card or pro hac vice order that has business within the facility, any special agent of the United States government or other law enforcement officer authorized to enforce the law within the Southern District of Florida, U.S. Trustees' Office staff and non-attorney bankruptcy trustees who have been authorized by the U.S. District Court, Southern District of Florida, to enter a federal courthouse facility with electronic devices, and court authorized court reporters. Absent permission of the presiding judge, recording and communications devices must remain off while court is in session.

(b) A judge or other designated authority may, by signed request forwarded to the U.S. Marshal for verification, allow a specific person access to the courthouse with a specific electronic device for a specific purpose and period of time.

(c) In the event a jury panel is seated in a case or proceeding before this court, the exception set forth in paragraph I(F) of Administrative Order 2006–16 of the United States District Court, Southern District of Florida with respect to cellular phones and jurors (or any subsequently entered administrative order or local rule) shall apply.

[Comment: See also Administrative Order 2011–108, United States District Court, Southern District of Florida, regarding book readers.]

(D) Penalty for Violations. The penalty provisions set forth in Administrative Order 2006–16 of the United States District Court, Southern District of Florida (and any subsequently issued administrative order or local rule), shall apply in this court for violations of this rule.

[Comment: See also Administrative Order 2009–12, United States District Court, Southern District of Florida, relating to news reporters.]

[Effective June 2, 2008. Amended effective December 1, 2015. Amended on an interim basis effective March 11, 2016.]

RULE 5073–1. PHOTOGRAPHY, RECORDING, AND BROADCASTING—USE OF DEVICES PROHIBITED

Notwithstanding the provisions of Local Rule 5072–2(C)(2)(a), which permit certain parties to enter areas of the court environs with electronic devices capable of recording, photographing, broadcasting, or televising, except as required by authorized personnel in the discharge of official duties or as permitted under Local Rule 5072–2(C)(2)(b), use of these devices within the vicinity of any location designated for the holding of court in the district, is prohibited.

[Comment: Substantially conforms to Local Rule 77.1 of the district court, see also Local Rule 5072–2.]

[Effective December 1, 1998. Amended effective December 1, 2002; June 2, 2008; December 1, 2009.]

RULE 5080–1. FEES

The clerk shall not be required to accept any papers for filing, render any service, or deposit or disburse any funds from the registry of the court, unless any fee or service charge prescribed by statute or by the Judicial Conference of the United States is paid in advance or contemporaneously, except that child support creditors or their representatives may file papers without the required fees if the Administrative Office of the U.S. Courts Director's Form "Appearance of Child Support Creditor or Representative" has been filed with the court.

[Comment: See Local Rules 1006–1 (installment payments and chapter 7 fee waivers) and 7067–1 (registry funds) and "Clerk's Summary of Fees".]

[Effective December 1, 1998. Amended effective December 1, 2002; June 2, 2008.]

RULE 5081–1. FEES—FORM OF PAYMENT

(A) Payment from Conventional Filers (And Other Filers Exempted or Suspended from Credit Card Payment). Fees or other charges to be paid to the clerk, and any deposits to be deposited with the clerk, must be tendered in one of the following forms:

(1) U.S. legal currency (cash may not be remitted by mail);

(2) check, cashier's check or money order in U.S. funds made payable to "Clerk, United States Court". Only checks drawn on attorney's trust or operating account (unless the maker is a debtor in a bankruptcy case), on an account of the trustee appointed to the case for which the payment is remitted, or on any United States, state or local government account, will be accepted for payment of filing fees. The clerk **will accept** a personal or business check for payment of copy, certification or research fees, and fees for compact discs of court proceedings upon presentation of an official government issued photo identification card of the person who is presenting the check. The clerk reserves the right to rescind or amend this policy of acceptance of personal checks without further notice. Payments must be remitted in the exact amount due for the fee owed. No change will be provided for cash, money order, check or other payment remittances.

(B) Payments from Registered Users of CM/ECF.

(1) *Payment by Credit Card Required.* Registered users (other than case trustees, government agencies and other entities which are specifically exempted by the court or registered users with suspended accounts) must use the CM/ECF credit card module to pay fees and make other required deposits for documents filed in CM/ECF.

(2) *Payment Deadline. Sanctions.* The registered user must pay any and all fees for CM/ECF transactions on the date filed. Failing to do so will cause the registered user's electronic filing privileges to be suspended and may result in a bankruptcy petition being dismissed, a document being stricken or sanctions being imposed.

(C) NSF Checks. If any check is returned for insufficient funds or other valid reason by the depository upon which drawn, a returned check fee will be assessed and the clerk may thereafter require cash, cashier's check, or money order from the payor.

(D) Payment Errors.

(1) *Overpayment of Fees.* Overpayments of fees of $25.00 or less will not be refunded by the court. Refunds of overpayments in excess of $25.00 must be requested in writing within 30 days.

(2) *Credit Card Payment Errors.* Filing fees paid in error via credit card will only be refunded upon motion and order of the court except when a filing fee is an unintended duplicate payment caused by an error in the court's CM/ECF system or Internet credit card program. Refunds will be processed through the electronic credit card system. Refund checks will not be issued.

[Comment: See Local Rule 7067–1 (registry funds).]

[Effective December 1, 1998. Amended effective December 1, 2002; June 2, 2008; December 1, 2009; December 1, 2015.]

RULE 5091–1. SIGNATURES. JUDGES

Any order entered electronically without the judge's original signature has the same force and effect as if the judge signed a paper copy of the order and it was entered on the docket conventionally.

[Effective June 2, 2008.]

RULE 6004–1. SALE OF PROPERTY

(A) Motion and Service. A motion seeking authority to sell property of the estate pursuant to 11 U.S.C. § 363, shall comply with Bankruptcy Rules 2002, 6003, and 6004, and this rule. Unless otherwise ordered by the court, notice of any use, sale, or lease of property shall be served on the debtor, the debtor's attorney, the trustee, the trustee's attorney, the U.S. Trustee, any party holding an interest in the property, all parties who have filed notices of appearance or requests for copies of notices, and all creditors. In a chapter 11 case, the notice need not be served on any creditors except those who are members of any creditors' committee formed under 11 U.S.C. § 1102, or when applicable, those creditors pursuant to Local Rule 2002–1(H); provided, however, that when the proposed use, sale, or lease is of substantially all the property of the estate notice must also be served on all creditors.

[Comment: See also Bankruptcy Rules 2002(h) and 2002(i) and Local Rule 2002–1(F).]

(B) Contents of Motion. The motion shall consist of, or (if the motion is more than five pages in length) begin with, a concise statement of the relief requested, not to exceed five pages, that lists or summarizes, and sets out the location within the relevant documents of all material provisions, including:

(1) the identity of the purchaser, if any, and whether the purchaser is an insider of the debtor;

(2) the terms of the sale including the price, any warranties, closing date and any closing conditions;

(3) whether the sale is subject to higher and better offers and, if so, the auction terms including:

(a) proposed auction date;

(b) minimum incremental bids;

(c) initial overbid amount; and

(d) the proposed last date for submitting competing bids.

(4) the requirements of any competing bidder including:

(a) minimum deposit;

(b) any documentation requirements; and

(c) any other qualifying conditions.

(5) any purchaser protections not otherwise described, including, but not limited to:

(a) any proposed break up fee;

(b) any matching rights.

(6) a statement regarding whether the debtor has a policy of prohibiting the transfer of personally identifiable information, whether the sale would be inconsistent with that policy, and whether the debtor believes a consumer privacy ombudsman is required under § 332 of the Bankruptcy Code;

(7) the identity of all known potential lienholders or interest holders including the nature and extent of their liens or interests and whether such liens or interests are disputed; and

(8) a statement setting forth the need for any critical path or accelerated hearings, requesting the dates for any necessary hearings or events to be scheduled by the court.

(C) Motions Seeking Relief Under 11 U.S.C. § 363(h). Any motion to seek relief under 11 U.S.C. § 363(h), shall also comply with the provisions of Bankruptcy Rule 7001.

(D) Use, Sale, or Lease on Negative Notice. Unless otherwise ordered by the court, notice of a proposed use, sale or lease of property—other than the proposed use of cash collateral, not in the ordinary course of business, pursuant to Bankruptcy Rule 6004(a) and 11 U.S.C. § 363(b), a motion seeking relief under 11 U.S.C. §§ 363(f), (g) or (h), or a motion seeking relief affecting a pro se debtor—may use the following negative notice procedures:

(1) Any motion using these procedures shall include above the preamble and below the title of the notice the following bulletin in bold print:

Pursuant to Bankruptcy Rule 6004 and Local Rule 6004–1(D), this proposed use, sale or lease will be deemed approved without necessity of a hearing or order if no objection to the use, sale or lease is filed and served within 21 days from the date of service of this [notice][motion].

An interested party's failure to timely file an objection shall be deemed a consent to the use, sale, or lease.

(2) If no objection is filed or served, the proponent shall file a report pursuant to Bankruptcy Rule 6004(f) certifying the lack of any response to the notice and the effectuation of the use, sale, or lease, or if the proposal is by motion the proponent shall submit a proposed order pursuant to Local Rule 5005–1(G), including the following language in the order's preamble:

"and the movant by submitting this form of order having represented that the motion was served on all parties required by Bankruptcy Rule 2002 or Local Rule 2002–1(H) or (J), that the 21–day response time provided by Local Rule 6004–1(D) has expired, that no one has filed, or served on the movant, a response to the motion, and that [either] the form of order was attached as an exhibit to the motion [or] the relief to be granted in this order is the identical relief requested in the motion,"

(3) If an objection to the proposed use, sale, or lease of property is received or filed, the proponent of the use, sale, or lease of property shall promptly submit the Local Form "Certificate of Contested Matter". If a certificate of contested matter is filed, the court will schedule a hearing in accordance with the procedures contained in Local Rule 9073–1(A). The "Notice of Hearing" shall be served by movant in accordance with the procedures contained in Local Rule 9073–1(B).

[Comment: This procedure may be used for notices of a use, sale or lease of property under Bankruptcy Rule 6004(a) and 11 U.S.C. § 363(b). Certain notices of sale do not require orders to effectuate the sale if no objection is filed. Nevertheless, this rule allows the proponent to submit an order where an order approving the sale is requested by the proponent for title or reporting purposes.]

[Effective December 1, 1998. Amended effective December 1, 2002; June 2, 2008; December 1, 2009; August 1, 2011; December 1, 2015.]

RULE 6005–1. AUCTIONEERS

(A) Local Form Application, Affidavit, Order Required. Applications for court approval of the employment of an auctioneer under 11 U.S.C. § 327(a), must substantially conform to the Local Form "Application for Approval of Employment of Auctioneer". Applications shall not include copies of the auctioneer's standard auction contract in lieu of this statement of costs and expenses and summary of terms of employment and proposed compensation. The application must be accompanied by an affidavit that substantially conforms with the Local Form "Affidavit of Auctioneer"; and (b) a proposed order granting the application that substantially conforms with the Local Form "Order Approving Employment of Auctioneer".

(B) Requirements for Auctioneer. Auctioneers whose employment is proposed must (1) be licensed pursuant to Florida Statutes § 468.381 *et seq.*, or § 468.387, for out-of-state auctioneers, (2) be covered by the Florida Auctioneer Recovery Fund as required by Florida Statute § 468.392, and (3) must either post a blanket (or case specific) fiduciary and faithful performance bond or surety bond, issued by a surety company approved by the Department of the Treasury, in an amount not less than the maximum expected proceeds of any proposed auction or combination of auctions, if a blanket bond. The bond must be in favor of the United States of America and the original bond shall be forwarded to the U.S. Trustee, who will maintain and safeguard the original. A copy of the bond should be provided to the trustee and should be included as an attachment to the application to employ auctioneer, as required by subdivision (A) of this rule.

(C) Compensation. Compensation may be approved by the court upon any reasonable terms and conditions negotiated with the auctioneer including a flat fee, guaranteed return, percentage of gross revenue, buyer's premium or any other reasonable method, provided that the basis for determining the fee is clearly described.

(D) Notice and Hearing. The application may be granted without notice or hearing, if the application reflects that the facts and circumstances so warrant including the size of the auction, the size of the estate, or a special need for haste. The applicant must request a hearing on the application if any aspect of the proposed employment or auction is irregular.

(E) Service of Order. Upon entry of an order approving the employment, the applicant shall serve copies of the order together with the sale notice in accordance with Bankruptcy Rules 2002(a)(2) and (c)(1) and 6004.

(F) Auctioneer's Report Summarizing Sale; Payment of Fees. Upon the completion of the auction, the auctioneer shall file with the court a report (a) summarizing the results of the auction and (b) stating the fees and expenses which will be paid in accordance with the order. Copies of the report shall be served only on the U.S. Trustee, the trustee, and any other party who specifically requests a copy, or if applicable, those parties required to be served pursuant to Local Rule 2002-1(H). The auctioneer's fees and expenses may be paid without the necessity of further notice or hearing unless a party in interest files an objection to the report within 14 days after the report is filed.

[Effective December 1, 1998. Amended effective December 1, 2002; June 2, 2008; December 1, 2009.]

RULE 6006-1. EXECUTORY CONTRACTS AND UNEXPIRED LEASES

(A) Required Bulletin in Orders. Unless otherwise ordered by the court, orders rejecting an executory contract or unexpired lease shall include the following bulletin at the conclusion of the body of the order, in print either highlighted or bold so as to make it more prominent than any other text:

Any proof of claim for damages arising from the rejection must be filed with the court on or before the latest of: i) the time for filing a proof of claim pursuant to Bankruptcy Rule 3002(c); ii) 30 days after the entry of the order compelling or approving the rejection of the contract or lease; or iii) 30 days after the effective date of the rejection of the contract or lease.

(B) Chapter 13 Cases. Any executory contract or unexpired lease of a chapter 13 debtor, which has not been assumed pursuant to court order prior to entry of an order confirming the debtor's chapter 13 plan, or which is not assumed in the chapter 13 plan confirmed by the court, is deemed rejected upon entry of the confirmation order. The confirmation order shall contain language to this effect.

[Comment: See also Local Rule 3003-1(C) (deadline for claims arising from rejection of executory contracts).]

[Effective December 1, 1998. Amended effective December 1, 2002; June 2, 2008; December 1, 2009; December 1, 2015.]

RULE 6007-1. ABANDONMENT OF PROPERTY

(A) Abandonment by Chapter 7 Trustee at § 341 Meeting. Notice shall be provided under Local Rule 2002-1(C)(1), that the chapter 7 trustee may abandon at the § 341 meeting or postconversion meeting, all property that the trustee has determined is of no value to the estate. The trustee shall, within two business days after the meeting, file a report of property abandoned at the meeting of creditors, and any objection to the abandonment must be filed within 14 days after the meeting. The trustee's filing of a report of no distribution shall constitute an abandonment of all scheduled assets, but the withdrawal of a report of no distribution shall revest ownership of scheduled assets in the estate. If the chapter 7 trustee wishes to abandon property other than at the § 341 or post-conversion meeting, the provisions of subdivision (B)(1) of this rule must be followed.

(B) Other Abandonment. Except for abandonment by a chapter 7 trustee at the § 341 meeting or post-conversion meeting, the following provisions apply to abandonment by a trustee or debtor in possession in all cases:

(1) *Abandonment by Chapter 7, 11 or 12 Trustee or Debtor in Possession by Negative Notice.* Notices of proposed abandonment either by a trustee (other than by a chapter 7 trustee at the § 341 meeting) or by a chapter 11 or 12 debtor in possession, shall include the following bulletin at the conclusion of the body of the notice, in print either highlighted or bold, so as to make it more prominent than any other text:

Pursuant to Bankruptcy Rule 6007, the proposed abandonment will be deemed approved without necessity of a hearing or order, if no objection is filed and served within 14 days after the date of service of this notice.

Upon receipt of a timely filed objection or other response, the proponent of the abandonment shall promptly file the Local Form "Certificate of Contested Matter". If a certificate of contested matter is filed, the court will schedule a hearing in accordance with the procedures contained in Local Rule 9073-1(A). The "Notice of Hearing" shall be served by movant in accordance with the procedures contained in Local Rule 9073-1(B).

When the bulletin in this subdivision is included in the notice, the failure of a party, properly served, to file an objection within 14 days after service of the notice, shall be deemed a consent to the proposed abandonment.

(2) *Abandonment by Chapter 13 Trustee.* Abandonment by the chapter 13 trustee shall be pursuant to Bankruptcy Rule 6007.

[Effective December 1, 1998. Amended effective December 1, 2002; June 2, 2008; December 1, 2009; December 1, 2015.]

RULE 7003-1. COMMENCEMENT OF ADVERSARY PROCEEDINGS

(A) Title of Complaint. The title of the complaint must indicate, briefly, the nature of the relief sought.

[Comment: See also Local Rule 9015-1 (demand for jury trial).]

(B) Cover Sheet, Corporate Ownership Statement.

(1) *Cover Sheet Required When Filing Conventionally.* Conventionally filed adversary complaints must be accompanied by the Administrative Office of the U.S. Courts Director's Form "Adversary Proceeding Cover Sheet".

(2) *Corporate Ownership Statement.* A corporate ownership statement shall be filed as required by Bankruptcy Rule 7007-1 and Local Rule 1002-1(A)(2).

(C) Judicial Assignment. Adversary proceedings arising in or related to an existing bankruptcy case shall be assigned to the judge assigned to the existing case. Adversary proceedings transferred from another district shall be assigned randomly.

(D) Permissible Joinder of Parties in Adversary Proceedings.

(1) *Complaint Requirements.* Adversary complaints listing multiple defendants joined pursuant to Bankruptcy Rule 7020, shall set forth in the complaint the justifications for permissive joinder consistent with the provisions of Bankruptcy Rule 7020.

(2) *Dismissal for Improper Joinder.* In an adversary complaint listing multiple defendants not properly joined in accordance with the Bankruptcy Rules, the court shall, pursuant to Bankruptcy Rule 7021, and without further advance notice or hearing, retain the first listed defendant in the complaint and dismiss, without prejudice, all other defendants in the adversary proceeding.

(3) *Consolidation by Court.* This rule shall not be construed to preclude court consideration of consolidation of adversary cases pursuant to Bankruptcy Rule 7042, which makes Rule 42, Fed. R. Civ. P., applicable in adversary proceedings.

[Comment: See Bankruptcy Rules 7020 and 7021—The plaintiff cannot obtain permissible joinder of multiple defendants based solely on the existence of similar or identical causes of action absent evidence that such right to relief was predicated on, or arising out of a single transaction or occurrence or series of occurrences. For example, an adversary complaint to avoid a preferential transfer or for turnover of property which lists multiple defendants in which a debtor (or trustee) is asserting joinder based on various payments that may be preferential or various claims for goods or services sold or provided to multiple defendants where each transaction was distinct and unrelated does not constitute a "series of transactions or occurrences" that would permit joinder within the meaning of the rule.]

[Effective December 1, 1998. Amended effective December 1, 2002; July 1, 2004; June 2, 2008; December 1, 2009; December 1, 2015.]

RULE 7004-1. RESERVED

[Note: 7004-1 is a reserved rule number.]

RULE 7004-2. SUMMONS IN ADVERSARY PROCEEDING. ALIAS SUMMONS

(A) General. The clerk will generate and docket the summons or, if applicable, an alias summons, and electronically transmit it to the plaintiff, who must serve it together with the complaint and pretrial order, on all defendants in accordance with the Bankruptcy Rules and these local rules. The electronic summons is a valid summons, signed, sealed and issued by the clerk. The clerk shall issue an alias summons upon receipt of a notice of non-service and request for issuance of alias summons, and a third party summons, when applicable. Requests for issuance of an alias summons that will require rescheduling of the pretrial conference date shall be considered in accordance with subdivision (B) of this Rule.

(B) Alias Summons. A request for issuance of an alias summons that would provide for an answer deadline of less than 30 days prior to the date of the originally scheduled pretrial conference must be accompanied by a motion to continue the pretrial conference to a date such that the answer shall be due not later than 30 days prior to the proposed, rescheduled pretrial conference. The court shall either set the motion for hearing or enter an order directing the clerk to issue an alias summons which shall include a rescheduled pretrial conference that provides for an answer deadline of no later than 30 days before the date of the pretrial conference.

2011 Amendment: Subdivisions (A) and (B) of this rule are set forth procedures for seeking issuance of an alias summons.

[Effective December 1, 1998. Amended effective December 1, 2002; July 1, 2004; June 2, 2008; August 1, 2011.]

RULE 7012-1. RESERVED

[Note: 7012-1 is a reserved rule number.]

RULE 7016-1. PRETRIAL PROCEDURE

(A) Scheduling Conference Requirements Inapplicable. The provisions of Rule 16(b) of the Federal Rules of Civil Procedure shall be inapplicable to cases or proceedings in this court.

[Comment: See Federal Rule 16(b) (opt-out provision) and Local Rule 87.1 of the United States District Court (bankruptcy court's authority to enact local rules).]

(B) Pretrial Orders. The clerk will electronically generate and docket the "Order Setting Filing and Disclosure Requirements" in an adversary proceeding and transmit it to the plaintiff who must serve the order together with the summons and complaint on all defendants in accordance with the federal and local rules.

[Comment: See also Local Rule 7026-1 (discovery).]

[Effective December 1, 1998. Amended effective December 1, 2002; June 2, 2008.]

RULE 7026-1. DISCOVERY—GENERAL

(A) Affirmative Disclosure Requirements. Except as otherwise ordered by the court, the provisions of Rules 26(a), (d) and (f) of the Federal Rules of Civil Procedure, shall apply to cases and proceedings in this court only to the extent set forth in the "Order Setting Filing and Disclosure Requirements for Pretrial and Trial".

(B) Subpoena Forms. Subpoenas served in adversary proceedings or main cases shall conform to, as applicable, the Administrative Office of the U.S. Courts Director's Procedural Form "Subpoena to Appear and Testify at a Hearing or Trial in a Bankruptcy Case (or Adversary Proceeding)", the Administrative Office of the U.S. Courts Director's Procedural Form "Subpoena to Testify at a Deposition in a Bankruptcy Case (or Adversary Proceeding)" or the Administrative Office of the U.S. Courts Director's Procedural Form "Subpoena to Produce Documents, Information, or Objects or To Permit Inspection of Premises in a Bankruptcy Case (or Adversary Proceeding)".

2013 Amendment: Local Rule 7026-1 includes Interim Local Rule 7026-1(B) adopted by Administrative Order 13-02, effective December 1, 2013.

(C) Service and Filing of Discovery Material. The following discovery requests and responses:

- notices of deposition upon oral examination;
- transcripts of deposition upon oral examination;
- depositions upon written questions;

- responses or objections to depositions upon written questions;

- written interrogatories;

- answers or objections to written interrogatories;

- requests for production of documents or to inspect any tangible thing;

- objections to requests for the production of documents or to inspect any tangible thing;

- written requests for admission; and

- answers or objections to written requests for admission;

shall be served upon other attorneys and parties, but shall not be filed with the court, nor shall proof of service be filed, unless upon order of the court or as provided in subdivision (D). The party responsible for service of the discovery material shall retain the original and become the custodian. The original of all depositions upon oral examination shall be retained by the party taking the depositions.

(D) Filing of Discovery Materials Permitted in Certain Circumstances. If depositions, interrogatories, requests for documents, requests for admission, answers or responses are to be used at an evidentiary hearing or trial or are necessary to a pretrial or post-trial motion, the portions to be used shall be filed with the clerk at the outset of the evidentiary hearing or trial or at the filing of the motion insofar as their use can be reasonably anticipated by the parties having custody of the materials. When documentation of discovery not previously in the record is needed for appeal purposes, upon order of the court or by written stipulation of attorneys, the necessary discovery papers may be filed with the clerk.

(E) Motions to Compel, Motions for Protective Order, Required Certification.

(1) *Motions to Compel.* Except for motions grounded upon complete failure to respond to the discovery sought to be compelled, or upon assertion of general or blanket objections to discovery, motions to compel discovery in accordance with Bankruptcy Rules 7033, 7034, 7036 and 7037, shall quote verbatim each interrogatory, request for admission or request for production and the response to which objection is taken followed by: (a) the specific objections, (b) the grounds assigned for the objection (if not apparent from the objection); and (c) the reasons assigned as supporting the motion, all of which shall be written in immediate succession to one another. Such objections and grounds shall be addressed to the specific interrogatory or request and may not be made generally.

(2) *Motions for Protective Order.* A party may file, prior to the date of a proposed deposition or other discovery deadline, a motion for a protective order stating the reasons for prohibiting, limiting or rescheduling the deposition or other discovery request, and the deposition or response deadline shall be stayed until the court rules on the motion.

(F) Certificate of Attorney as to Motion to Compel or Motion for Protective Order. Prior to filing a motion to compel discovery or a motion for protective order pursuant to Bankruptcy Rule 7026, the attorney for the moving party shall confer with the attorney for the opposing party and shall file with the clerk at the time of filing the motion a statement certifying that the movant's attorney has conferred with the attorney for the opposing party in a good faith effort to resolve by agreement the issues raised and that the attorneys have been unable to do so. If certain of the issues have been resolved by agreement, the statement shall specify the issues so resolved and the issues remaining unresolved.

[Comment: See also Local Rule 9073-1(D) (conference with opposing attorneys required generally).]

[Effective December 1, 1998. Amended effective December 1, 2002; June 2, 2008. Amended on an interim basis effective December 1, 2013.]

RULE 7030-2. DEPOSITIONS UPON ORAL EXAMINATION—REASONABLE NOTICE OF TAKING DEPOSITIONS

Unless otherwise stipulated by all interested parties or directed by the court or by these rules, the deposition of any person upon oral examination may be taken upon actual delivery of at least 14 days' notice in writing to the deponent and to every other party to the action.

[Comment: See also Bankruptcy Rule 9014 and Local Rule 9014-1 (contested matters are subject to discovery rules).]

[Effective June 2, 2008. Amended effective December 1, 2009.]

RULE 7041-1. DISMISSAL OF ADVERSARY PROCEEDING

(A) Failure to Pay Adversary Filing Fee. If the required adversary complaint filing fee is not paid, the case shall be dismissed.

[Comment: See Local Rules 7003-1 (commencement of adversary proceeding) and 7004-2 (summons).]

(B) When Main Case Has Been Dismissed. The court may, sua sponte, dismiss all adversary proceedings arising in any case which has been dismissed.

[Effective December 1, 1998. Amended effective December 1, 2002; June 2, 2008.]

RULE 7054-1. TAXATION OF COSTS BY CLERK; DEADLINE FOR MOTIONS FOR ATTORNEY FEES AND MOTIONS FOR COSTS REQUIRING COURT ORDER

(A) Costs Taxable by the Clerk. The clerk shall tax costs only where the judgment entered by the court specifically awards costs to the prevailing party. The clerk shall tax only those costs permitted by the court's "Guidelines for Taxation of Costs" and any costs not identified under 28 U.S.C. § 1920 but awarded as recoverable in a Bill of Costs by a separate court order. Request for attorney fees shall not be presented or taxed in a Bill of Costs.

(B) Local Form Bill of Costs. Parties requesting taxation of awarded costs shall submit to the clerk a proposed Local Form "Bill of Costs" and file a certificate of service in accordance with Local Rule 2002-1(F). The clerk may require the submission of supporting documentation prior to determination of the bill of costs.

(C) Deadline for Filing. The proposed bill of costs shall be submitted not later than 14 days after entry of final judgment or order allowing costs.

(D) Notice to Parties of Costs Taxed by Clerk. The clerk shall review the proposed bill of costs and tax costs on 14 days' notice. The issued bill of costs shall be served by the clerk on all parties.

(E) Court Review of Costs Taxed by Clerk. On motion timely filed and served within seven days as provided by Bankruptcy Rule 7054(b)(1), the action of the clerk under section (D) of this Rule, may be reviewed by the court.

(F) Deadline for Motions for Attorney Fees and Motions for Costs Requiring Separate Court Order. Motions for attorney fees required under Bankruptcy Rule 7054(b)(2)(a) and requests for costs which require a separate order under subdivision (A) of this Rule shall be considered only upon motion to the court filed within 14 days after entry of the judgment. A certificate of service must be filed in accordance with Local Rule 2002–1(F).

[Comment: See also "Guidelines for Preparing, Submitting, and Serving Orders", Bankruptcy Rule 8014 and Local Rule 8014–1 (taxation of costs on appeal) and 28 U.S.C. §§ 1920–1924.]

[Effective December 1, 1998. Amended effective December 1, 2002; June 2, 2008; December 1, 2009; December 1, 2015.]

RULE 7055–1. DEFAULT

Motions for entry of default shall be verified (sworn under penalty of perjury) and shall state that the defendant has been properly served with the complaint, that no response has been served on the plaintiff, and that the defendant-if an individual-is not a member of the military service. If defaults have been entered against all defendants, the plaintiff may submit a motion for judgment by default, a supporting affidavit calculating the amount of the damages sought, and a proposed judgment based on the allegations deemed admitted.

[Effective December 1, 1998. Amended effective December 1, 2002; July 1, 2004; June 2, 2008.]

RULE 7056–1. NOTICE TO INDIVIDUALS REGARDING OPPOSING MOTIONS FOR SUMMARY JUDGMENT

In any adversary proceeding or contested matter, a party serving a motion for summary judgment adverse to an individual must also serve upon each such individual the Local Form "Notice Regarding Opposing Motions For Summary Judgment." A motion for summary judgment adverse to an individual will not be acted upon or set for hearing absent filing of a certificate of service of the Local Form "Notice Regarding Opposing Motions For Summary Judgment" certifying that each individual who was served with a motion for summary judgment has also been served with the Local Form "Notice Regarding Opposing Motions For Summary Judgment."

[Effective December 1, 2009.]

RULE 7067–1. REGISTRY FUNDS. EXCEPTIONS TO REGISTRY FUND DEPOSIT REQUIREMENT.

(A) Court Registry Investment System. By administrative order, the Court has authorized that funds deposited in the court interest-bearing registry account be maintained in the Court Registry Investment System ("CRIS"), which is administered by the Administrative Office of the United States Courts.

(B) Fee. Registry account funds shall be assessed fees from interest earnings in the amount set forth in the Bankruptcy Court Miscellaneous Fee Schedule and in the manner described in this Court's administrative order authorizing "CRIS".

(C) Deposit and Withdrawal. In addition to the requirements of Local Rules 5080–1 and 5081–1, registry account funds shall be deposited and withdrawn only pursuant to order of the court or a statute.

(D) Exceptions.

(1) *Funds Deposited Under 11 U.S.C. § 362(1).* Notwithstanding provision (A) of this rule, any funds deposited with the clerk under § 362(1), shall be deposited into the non-interest bearing treasury account of the court. The court shall order the clerk to disburse these funds only upon the filing of a motion served on all affected parties. Reference in this rule to funds deposited under § 362(1), is not a finding by this court that the prerequisite for depositing money into the court registry under § 362(1)(1)(A), exists under Florida law.

(2) *Funds Deposited Directly Into U.S. Treasury Account.* Unclaimed funds deposited under Local Rule 3011–1 by a trustee or disbursement agent in a chapter 11 case, shall be deposited directly into the U.S. Treasury Registry Account. Neither registry fees nor interest shall accrue on these funds.

[Effective December 1, 1998. Amended effective December 1, 2002; June 2, 2008; December 1, 2015. Amended on an interim basis effective May 20, 2016.]

RULE 7069–1. EXECUTION

(A) Authority. Procedures in aid of execution of a judgment of this court may be conducted in the same proceeding in which the judgment was entered.

(B) Registration of Judgment from Another District. Judgments entered in another district may be registered in this district prior to or at the time a writ of execution or garnishment is sought by filing, with the clerk, a copy of the judgment (including any bill of costs entered), accompanied by the miscellaneous proceeding fee and the Administrative Office of the U.S. Courts Director's Form "Certification of Judgment for Registration in Another District", or a certified copy of an order allowing the judgment to be registered in this district.

(C) Writ of Execution. The party seeking the issuance of a writ of execution shall prepare the Local Form "Writ of Execution to the United States Marshal" for the clerk to issue. The writ shall be accompanied by a motion for writ and a certified copy of the judgment, including any bill of costs entered.

(D) Writs of Garnishment. Writs of garnishments shall be issued in accordance with Florida law.

(1) *Issuance of Writ. Required Notice to Garnishee.* The party seeking issuance of a writ of garnishment shall file a motion accompanied by a prepared writ, a certified copy of the judgment, and any bill of costs entered. If the writ is issued against an individual, the clerk shall attach to the writ a copy of the Local Form "Notice to Defendant of Right Against Garnishment of Wages, Money and Other Property" with attached "Claim of Exemption and Request for Hearing" (with the caption of the case filled in on the form "Claim of Exemption and Request for Hearing"). The following notice must accompany service of the writ: **"Under Florida Statutes § 77.28, upon issuance of any writ of garnishment, the party applying for it shall pay $100 to the garnishee on the garnishee's demand at any time after the service of the writ, for the payment or part payment of his or her attorney's fees which the garnishee expends or agrees to expend in obtaining representation in response to the writ."** In addition to service of other garnishment papers, a copy of this rule shall be served on the defendant. If the writ is being sought pursuant to Florida Statute § 77.0305 (continuing writ of garnishment against salary or wages) or Florida Statutes § 77.031 (issuance of writ before judgment), the filing of the writ must be accompanied by a motion and a proposed order.

(2) *Objection to Claim of Exemption.* An objection to a defendant's "Claim of Exemption and Request for Hearing" shall be set for hearing in accordance with Local Rule 9073–1.

(3) *Dissolution of Writ by Clerk.* The clerk shall automatically dissolve the writ and notify the parties of the dissolution by mail upon failure of the plaintiff to timely contest the defendant's claim of exemption.

(4) *Deadlines.* Absent further order of the court, the procedures and deadlines set forth in Florida Statute § 77.041, shall apply to writs of garnishments issued in this court.

(E) Satisfaction of Judgment. Satisfaction of judgment shall be filed with the court promptly upon collection of the judgment.

(F) Effect of Appeal. The filing of a notice of appeal shall not stay issuance of a writ absent entry of an order granting stay of execution prior to the expiration of the time for appeal of the judgment.

[Effective December 1, 1998. Amended effective December 1, 2002; July 1, 2004; June 2, 2008; December 1, 2009; September 15, 2014; December 1, 2015.]

RULE 7090–1. CONTINUANCE OF PRETRIAL AND TRIAL

Requests for continuance of a pretrial conference or trial must be requested by written motion filed no later than two business days before the pretrial conference. The motion must set forth (1) why the parties seek a continuance; (2) whether a continuance has previously been granted; (3) whether the client and opposing party consent to a continuance; and (3) the status of the litigation, including exchange of initial disclosures and status of discovery. The moving party shall submit a proposed order which provides blank spaces for the date and time of the rescheduled trial or pretrial conference in the event that the court grants the motion without hearing. Motions for continuance will be granted only under exceptional circumstances, and the stipulation of all parties is not sufficient grounds, standing alone, for a continuance.

[Comment: Compare Local Rule 5071–1 (continuances of hearings), and Local Rule 9013–1(C)(8) (no hearing necessary on motion for continuance).]

[Effective December 1, 1998. Amended effective December 1, 2002; June 2, 2008.]

RULE 8002–1. TIME FOR FILING NOTICE OF APPEAL

(A) Dismissal of Untimely Appeal. A notice of appeal filed after the time period specified in Bankruptcy Rule 8002 will be dismissed by this court as authorized by District Court Local Rule 87.4(c).

(B) Premature Appeal. If a notice of appeal is filed after the announcement of a ruling by the court but before entry on the docket of the written judgment, order, or decree, the notice will be docketed but not served in accordance with Bankruptcy Rule 8003. Once the judgment is entered on the docket, the notice of appeal will be served by the clerk, noting the date the judgment was entered on the docket as the filing date of the notice of appeal.

[Effective December 1, 1998. Amended effective December 1, 2002; June 2, 2008; April 15, 2010; August 1, 2011; December 1, 2015.]

RULE 8003–1. NOTICE OF APPEAL. REQUIRED CONTENT AND FEE

A notice of appeal must conform substantially to the Official Bankruptcy Form. A separate notice of appeal and filing fee is required for each order or judgment being appealed except that a single notice of appeal may commence an appeal of an order or judgment and subsequent orders addressing amendment to or requested relief from the same underlying order or judgment. If the prescribed fee does not accompany the notice of appeal, after service by the clerk of a fee due notice the appeal shall be dismissed by this court as authorized by District Court Local Rule 87.4(c).

[Effective December 1, 2015.]

RULE 8004–1. MOTIONS FOR LEAVE TO APPEAL

(A) Filing Fee Must Accompany Motion. A motion for leave to appeal shall be accompanied by the prescribed filing fee. A motion for leave to appeal not accompanied by the fee shall be dismissed by this court after service of notice by the clerk of the fee requirement, as authorized by District Court Local Rule 87.4(c).

(B) Appellate Docketing Fee Payment Deadline. Within seven days from the entry of the district court order granting a motion for leave to appeal, the appellant shall pay the prescribed appellate docketing fee to the clerk of the bankruptcy court.

[Comment: See "Clerk's Instructions for Appeals".]

[Former Rule 8003-1, effective December 1, 1998. Amended effective December 1, 2002; June 2, 2008; December 1, 2009; April 15, 2010; August 1, 2011. Amended and renumbered effective December 1, 2015.]

RULE 8007-1. MOTIONS FOR STAY PENDING APPEAL

Motions for stay pending appeal that request relief from the district court must be filed directly with the district court in accordance with District Court Local Rule 87.4(d). If a stay pending appeal has been granted by the district court the movant shall immediately file a copy of the district court ruling with the clerk of the bankruptcy court.

[Comment: See Local Rule 7069-1(F). (Writs shall issue absent entry of an order granting stay of execution).]

[Former Rule 8005-1, effective December 1, 1998. Amended effective December 1, 2002; June 2, 2008; December 1, 2009; April 15, 2010; August 1, 2011. Amended and renumbered effective December 1, 2015.]

RULE 8009-1. RECORD AND ISSUES ON APPEAL

(A) Dismissal for Failure to File Designation of Record or Statement of Issues. If the appellant fails to timely file a designation of record or statement of the issues as required by Bankruptcy Rule 8009, this court shall dismiss the appeal as authorized by District Court Local Rule 87.4(c).

(B) Ordering Transcripts. The Local Form "Transcript Request Form" provided by the clerk shall be used to order any untranscribed portion of the record. Charges for transcripts shall be in accordance with the rates adopted by administrative order of this court.

[Comment: See "Clerk's Instructions for Appeals".]

[Former Rule 8006-1, effective December 1, 1998. Amended effective December 1, 2002; June 2, 2008; April 15, 2010; August 1, 2011. Amended and renumbered effective December 1, 2015.]

RULE 8010-3. DETERMINATION OF MOTION—APPEAL

A motion to dismiss or other request for intermediate relief as contemplated under Bankruptcy Rule 8010(c) shall be filed directly with the district court in accordance with District Court Local Rule 87.4(d).

[Former Rule 8011-3, effective December 1, 1998. Amended effective December 1, 2002; June 2, 2008; April 15, 2010; August 1, 2011. Amended and renumbered effective December 1, 2015.]

RULE 8013-4. EMERGENCY MOTION—APPEAL; REQUEST TO EXPEDITE APPEAL

Emergency motions shall comply with the requirements under Bankruptcy Rule 8013(d). Requests to expedite an appeal under Bankruptcy Rule 8013(a)(2)(B) shall be brought to the attention of the clerk of the bankruptcy court by filing the Local Form "Request to Expedite Appeal" at any time prior to transmittal of the record. This request shall be brought to the attention of the clerk of the district court by the clerk of the bankruptcy court upon transmittal of the record on appeal.

[Former Rule 8011-4, effective December 1, 1998. Amended effective December 1, 2002; June 2, 2008. Amended and renumbered effective December 1, 2015.]

RULE 8021-1. TAXATION OF APPELLATE COSTS BY CLERK

(A) Authority to Tax Costs. The clerk shall only tax those costs as permitted by Bankruptcy Rule 8021(c) and in accordance with the court's "Guidelines for Taxation of Costs".

(B) Local Form Bill of Costs. Parties requesting taxation of allowed costs shall submit to the clerk a proposed Local Form "Bill of Costs" and file a certificate of service in accordance with Local Rule 2002-1(F). The clerk may require the submission of supporting documentation prior to determination of the bill of costs.

(C) Deadline for Filing. The proposed bill of costs shall be submitted not later than 14 days after entry of the judgment on appeal of the district court.

(D) Notice to Parties of Costs Taxed by Clerk. The clerk shall review the proposed bill of costs and tax costs on 14 days' notice. The issued bill of costs shall be served by the clerk on all required parties.

(E) Court Review of Costs Taxed by Clerk. On an objection filed and served within 14 days as provided under Bankruptcy Rule 8021(d), the action of the clerk under section (D) of this Rule, may be reviewed by the court.

[Comment: See also Bankruptcy Rule 7054 and Local Rule 7054-1 (taxation of costs in adversary proceeding) and 28 U.S.C. §§ 1920—1924.]

[Former Rule 8014-1, effective December 1, 1998. Amended effective December 1, 2002; June 2, 2008; December 1, 2009. Amended and renumbered effective December 1, 2015.]

RULE 9004-1. REQUIREMENTS FOR FORM AND STYLE OF PAPERS

Papers tendered for filing shall meet the following requirements of form and style:

(A) Official Forms and Local Forms. Papers in the form prescribed by a local form or other form specifically authorized by the Bankruptcy Rules or these rules shall be deemed in compliance with this rule. All forms must be completed in their entirety.

[Comment: In accordance with the federal judiciary privacy policy, local and internal forms either exclude the debtor's social security or other individual taxpayer identification number entirely or to redact the number to the last four digits.]

(B) Format. All papers shall be plainly and legibly typewritten, printed or reproduced on one side of standard weight white/opaque paper only, with not less than 1 1/2 spaces between lines except for quoted material. Margins shall be at least 3/4 inch at the bottom and both sides and 1 inch at the top of each page (except as otherwise required in the court's "Guidelines for Preparing, Submitting and Serving Orders"). All papers of more than one page, must be securely fastened, but not stapled, at the top left-hand corner and must be paginated at the bottom of each page.

(C) Title of Paper. The title of every paper filed, except exhibits, shall be in bold, identify the filing party and shall be descriptive of the paper, indicating the relief sought or the action proposed. Agreed matters must be designated as "agreed" in the title. The titles of orders must comply with the requirements in the court's "Guidelines for Preparing, Submitting and Serving Orders".

(D) Attachments. Documents filed with the court shall not have as an attachment any document already filed in the case or proceeding. Instead, when referencing previously filed documents in a document being filed, include, in parentheses next to the name of the referenced document, the referenced document's electronic docket entry or claim number.

[Comment: See also Local Rule 2002-1(H) (copies for service purposes may be 2-sided, but not "sandwiched").]

2011 Amendment: Subdivision (D) of this rule is amended to clarify how previously filed documents are to be referenced and not attached.

[Effective December 1, 1998. Amended effective December 1, 2002; July 1, 2004; June 2, 2008; August 1, 2011.]

RULE 9004-2. CAPTION—PAPERS

(A) Caption—General. The caption of all papers, except for orders, shall conform to applicable Official Form "Caption". The court style shall be centered at the top of the first page, and the case number shall include the judge's initials and chapter of the case shall appear to the right of the case style. Captions for miscellaneous proceedings filed in this court shall contain the court style for this district and the case name for the district where the case is pending and shall include the out-of-district case number and the court name below the space provided for the case number assigned by this court.

2013 Amendment: Local Rule 9004-2 includes Interim Local Rule 9004-2(A) adopted by Administrative Order 13-02, effective December 1, 2013.

(B) Caption—Jointly Administered Cases. All papers, other than in the lead case, shall be captioned under the lead case name and case number followed by the words "(Jointly Administered)" and, beneath that caption, the case names and numbers for the cases in which the paper is being filed. However, a proof of claim shall indicate only the case name and number of the case in which the claim is asserted. The style shall not use the word "Consolidated" to refer to joint administration, unless the estates have been substantively consolidated by court order.

(C) Caption—Substantively Consolidated Cases. All papers in substantively consolidated cases of two or more individual debtors shall contain in the case style the name of each debtor and the case number of the case into which the cases have been consolidated. In all other instances, all papers in substantively consolidated cases shall contain in the case style only the name and case number of the case into which the cases have been consolidated.

[Comment: See also Local Rules 7003-1(A), 9004-1(C), 9015-1(A), and 9075-1 (particular requirements in title) and this court's "Guidelines for Preparing, Submitting and Serving Orders".]

2011 Amendment: Subdivision (C) of this rule is amended to reflect change in manner of reflecting style of case in substantively consolidated cases of two or more individual debtors.

[Effective December 1, 1998. Amended effective December 1, 2002; June 2, 2008; August 1, 2011. Amended on an interim basis effective December 1, 2013.]

RULE 9005-1. HARMLESS ERRORS IN SETTING DEADLINES

The clerk is authorized to correct any deadline established in error and to provide notice of the corrected deadline. [Effective December 1, 1998. Amended effective December 1, 2002; June 2, 2008.]

RULE 9009-1. LOCAL FORMS

The court may promulgate local forms which supplement or modify the Official Forms promulgated by the Judicial Conference of the United States and the additional forms promulgated by the Director of the Administrative Office of the United States Courts, and which complement these rules and the Bankruptcy Rules. Unless otherwise directed by the court, the applicable local forms must be used in every case or proceeding. Local forms shall be used without any variation, to the extent possible, and any variation or fill-in-the-blank portion must be underlined or bold. The clerk shall maintain a current set and list of all local forms, each bearing the date of its most recent revision, copies of which shall be made available in each office and on the court web site.

[Comment: See also Local Rule 9004-1(A) (official forms and local forms comply with format requirements for papers).]

[Effective December 1, 1998. Amended effective December 1, 2002; June 2, 2008.]

RULE 9010-1. NOTICE OF APPEARANCE

(A) Requirement of Notice of Appearance. Every attorney representing a party or witness in any case or proceeding in this court must file a notice of appearance in the case or proceeding, except that the notice need not be filed when the appearance has previously been evidenced by the filing of a paper on behalf of the client. For the purpose of this rule, the filing of any paper (other than a ballot or proof of claim) shall, unless otherwise specified, constitute an appearance by the attorney who signs or electronically files it. An appearance filed in the main bankruptcy case is not an appearance in the adversary proceeding nor is an appearance in an adversary proceeding an appearance in the main case. To receive service in both a main case and a related adversary proceeding, a notice of appearance must be filed in the main case and another notice of appearance must be filed in the adversary proceeding.

(B) Appearing Without an Attorney.

(1) *Corporations and Other Artificial Entities.* A corporation, partnership, trust, or other artificial entity cannot appear or act on its own behalf without an attorney in a case or proceeding, except that it may take the following actions without an attorney: file requests for service of notices pursuant to Bankruptcy Rule 2002, file proofs of claim, file notices under Local Rule 3070–1(B), or file a ballot, and attend and participate at the meeting of creditors held under 11 U.S.C. § 341.

(2) *Parties Already Represented by Attorney.* A party who has appeared by attorney cannot thereafter appear or act in his or her own behalf in the case or proceeding—unless the attorney shall first have withdrawn as the attorney pursuant to Local Rule 2091–1—except to file a proof of claim, notices filed under Local Rule 3070–1(B), or a ballot, or to attend and inquire at the meeting of creditors; provided, that the court may in its discretion hear a party in open court, notwithstanding the fact that the party has appeared by or is represented by an attorney.

2011 Amendment: Subdivision (B)(1) of this rule is amended to remove provision that previously permitted non individual parties to file a response to an objection to a claim and to reflect stylistic changes.

[Effective December 1, 1998. Amended effective December 1, 2002; June 2, 2008; August 1, 2011.]

RULE 9011–4. SIGNATURES

(A) Identification of Attorney.

(1) *Required Signature Block.* In the signature block on all court papers signed electronically or conventionally, the attorney must be identified by name, state bar number, complete mailing address, e-mail address, telephone number and the name of the party who the attorney represents.

(2) *Login and Password for Attorneys Filing as "Registered Users" of CM/ECF.*

(a) The clerk will assign a unique login and an initial password to each registered user which is that registered user's signature on electronic documents for all purposes, including those under Bankruptcy Rule 9011, 28 U.S.C. § 1746, and this court's local rules. A registered user's electronic signature has the same force and effect as if the registered user signed a paper copy of the document being filed. If a registered user authorizes one or more employees to use the login and password or if the registered user's login and password is used without authorization, the registered user is responsible for such use and, in the event of unauthorized use, must notify the clerk and immediately take the necessary steps to deactivate access.

(b) Attorneys shall not share an assigned login and password with other attorneys for the purpose of having documents filed in CM/ECF. The typewritten name of the filing registered user must appear on the document and match the login name of that registered user's ECF account.

(B) Certification of Attorney. Papers filed by an attorney appearing:

(1) as a qualified attorney pursuant to Local Rule 2090–1(A), must contain this certification: "I hereby certify that I am admitted to the Bar of the United States District Court for the Southern District of Florida and I am in compliance with the additional qualifications to practice in this court set forth in Local Rule 2090–1(A)". The certification requirement of this provision shall not apply to registered users of CM/ECF appearing in this court under Local Rule 2090–1(A), if they have previously signed a "CM/ECF Full Filing Attorney Agreement" which contains the same certification requirements.

(2) pro hac vice pursuant to Local Rule 2090–1(B)(2), must contain this certification: "I hereby certify that the undersigned attorney is appearing pro hac vice in this matter pursuant to court order dated (date)". This certification shall be placed in papers in the locations described in subdivision (1) above.

(C) Verification of Debtor's Social Security Number. In individual debtor cases filed in CM/ECF, the registered user must obtain the debtor(s)' original signature(s) on a paper copy of the Official Bankruptcy Form "Statement About Your Social Security Numbers" (including any amendments), and must keep the original signed document for the time provided by Local Rule 5005–4(C) and file the form with the court. In accordance with the federal judiciary's privacy policy, the PDF image of the document which contains the debtor's complete social security or other individual taxpayer identification number will not be available for public viewing. The registered user must verify that the social security number (or other individual taxpayer identification number provided on the Official Bankruptcy Form "Statement About Your Social Security Numbers" is the same number entered in CM/ECF and appearing on the § 341 notice of commencement of case to ensure correct numbers are reflected in the court's records.

(D) Registered users must retain electronically filed documents signed by other than the registered user for as provided under Local Rule 5005–4(C).

[Comment: See Local Rules 1007–2(B) and 1009–1(D) (debtor must sign schedules, statements and lists), 2090–1 (attorneys) and Bankruptcy Rules 9010 (attorneys) and 9011 (effect of signature).]

[Effective December 1, 1998. Amended effective December 1, 2002; June 2, 2008; December 1, 2015.]

RULE 9013–1. MOTIONS

(A) Preamble. This rule applies to all motion practice. Local Rule 9075–1 describes the procedures to be followed in emergency motion practice.

(B) Form, Content, Service of Motions. The form of motions and other requests for court action or relief is governed by Local Rules 5005–3, 5005–4, 9004–1, 9004–2, 9011–4 and 9072–1. All motions must state with particularity the grounds for the motion and must request specific relief.

(C) Motions That May Be Considered Without a Hearing (Ex Parte Motions). In addition to those matters that may be considered without a hearing pursuant to the Bankruptcy Rules or other provisions in these rules, unless otherwise directed by the court no hearing is required for the following motions. For each motion indicated below, the moving party shall follow the procedure in Local Rule 5005–1(G)(1)(a) and not the procedure in Local Rule 9073–1.

Upon entry of an order, the motion and entered order shall be served as required by these rules. This subdivision is not intended to restrict a judge's authority to grant relief without a hearing on other motions.

(1) Motions in which the movant certifies that all affected parties have consented to the requested relief.

(2) Motions to extend the time for filing schedules, statements, or lists, where the requested extended deadline is not later than seven days before the § 341 meeting or post-conversion meeting. The motion must be served on the debtor, the trustee, the U.S. Trustee, and all parties who have requested notices. In a chapter 11 case, where applicable, the notice must also be served on the parties listed on the "Master Service List" filed pursuant to Local Rule 2002–1(H).

[Comment: See also Local Rules 1007–1(B) and 1019–1(A) (extension of time to file schedules, statements, and lists).]

(3) Subject to the requirements of Bankruptcy Rule 6003, motions to approve employment of professionals, where the motion does not seek approval of a postpetition retainer or a particular fee arrangement, and the motion does not reveal any actual or potential conflict of interest or any other facts that could preclude retention. The motion must be served on the debtor, the trustee, the U.S. Trustee, and the attorney for or members of any creditors' committee or, in the absence of a committee, the 20 largest unsecured creditors in a chapter 11 case, and all parties who have requested notices. In a chapter 11 case, when applicable, the notice must also be served on the parties listed on the "Master Service List" filed pursuant to Local Rule 2002–1(H).

[Comment: See also Local Rules 2014–1 (employment of professionals) and 6005–1 (employment of auctioneers).]

(4) Subject to the requirements of Bankruptcy Rule 6003, motions to approve employment of real estate brokers, and to fix compensation for brokers, where the motion seeks to fix the compensation at the standard rate charged for similar services. The motion must be served on the debtor, the trustee, the U.S. Trustee, and the attorney for or members of any creditors' committee or, in the absence of a committee, the 20 largest unsecured creditors in a chapter 11 case, and all parties who have requested notice. In a chapter 11 case, where applicable, the notice must also be served on the parties listed on the "Master Service List" filed pursuant to Local Rule 2002–1(H).

[Comment: See also Local Rules 2014–1 and 9013–1(C)(3) (employment of professionals).]

(5) Motions to extend time to file objections to claimed exemptions, where the motion reflects that:

(a) the debtor has consented to the requested relief;

(b) the debtor has failed to appear at a properly scheduled Bankruptcy Rule 2004 examination;

(c) the debtor has failed to produce properly requested documents; or

(d) despite reasonable diligence by the movant, discovery has been propounded which is not due until after the deadline, or Bankruptcy Rule 2004 examinations have been noticed for a date after the deadline and the discovery is necessary to evaluate whether to file an objection.

Unless the debtor agrees to a longer extension, the requested extension cannot be longer than 30 days after the original (or previously extended) deadline. The motion shall be served on the debtor, the trustee, and any creditor included in the moving party's request for extension.

(6) Motions to extend time to file complaints or motions objecting to discharge under § 727, motions objecting to discharge under § 1328(f), and complaints objecting to dischargeability under § 523, but only if the debtor consents to the requested extension. The motion must indicate in the body if it is an agreed motion and indicate the date the petition was filed.

[Comment: See Bankruptcy Rules 4004 and 4007.]

(7) Motions to shorten or extend time for responding to discovery requests. The motion must be served on all interested parties or if applicable, pursuant to Local Rule 2002–1(H).

[Comment: See also Local Rules 4001–1(G) (discovery in stay relief matters), 7016–1 (judges' pre-trial procedures), and 7030–2 (depositions).]

(8) Agreed motions for continuances of hearings, trials or pre-trial conferences. The motion must be served on all interested parties or if applicable, pursuant to Local Rule 2002–1(H).

[Comment: See Local Rules 5071–1 (continuance of hearings) and 7090–1 (continuances of trials or pre-trial conferences).]

(9) Motions for pro hac vice appearance. The motion must be served on the debtor, the trustee, the U.S. Trustee, and all interested parties or if applicable, pursuant to Local Rule 2002–1(H).

[Comment: See Local Rule 2090–1 (attorneys).]

(10) Motions by the chapter 7 trustee to approve sales of property for $2,500 or less. The motion must be served on the debtor and the U.S. Trustee.

[Comment: See also Bankruptcy Rule 6004 and Local Rule 6004–1 (sales).]

(11) Motions to reopen chapter 7 cases to administer additional assets. The motion must be served on the debtor and the U.S. Trustee.

[Comment: See Local Rules 5010–1(C) (reopening closed case).]

(12) Motions by debtors to convert under 11 U.S.C. § 1112(a). The motion must be served on the U.S. Trustee and the trustee, if applicable, or when applicable, pursuant to Local Rule 2002–1(H).

(13) Motions by debtors to dismiss under 11 U.S.C. § 1307(b) or under 11 U.S.C. § 1208(b).

(14) Motions for joint administration of **non individual** chapter 11 cases.

[Comment: See Local Rule 3017–2.]

(15) Motions for Orders Confirming Termination of Automatic Stay Under 11 U.S.C. § 362(c)(3)(A). Such motions shall be considered upon expiration of the 30–day period after the case was filed if accompanied by a certificate which (a) recites the facts which establish that the status of the debtor is that as described in § 362(c)(3), and (b) includes a statement that no order continuing the stay has been entered under

§ 362(c)(3)(B), and a proposed order confirming termination of the stay which sets forth the statement attested to by the creditor in the required certificate.

(16) Motions for Orders Confirming That Automatic Stay is Not in Effect Under 11 U.S.C. § 362(c)(4)(A)(i). Such motions shall be accompanied by a certificate which (a) recites the facts which establish that the status of the debtor is that as described in § 362(c)(4)(A)(i), and (b) includes a statement that no order imposing the stay has been entered under § 362(c)(4)(B), and a proposed order confirming that no stay is in effect which sets forth the statements attested to by the creditor in the required certificate.

(17) Motions for Order Confirming That Automatic Stay is Not in Effect Under 11 U.S.C. § 362(b)(23). Such motions shall be considered without hearing if the debtor has not filed an objection under 11 U.S.C. § 362(m)(2), within the 14–day period after the lessor files and serves the certification described in 11 U.S.C. § 362(b)(23), and upon the movant's submittal of a proposed order including in the order's preamble the following: "and the movant by submitting this form of order having represented that the motion was served on the debtor and counsel for the debtor, that the 14–day response time has expired, that the debtor has not filed, or served on the movant, a response to the motion, and that the relief to be granted in this order is the identical relief requested in the motion."

(18) Trustee's motions to pay debtors their allocable portion of any tax refund.

(19) Trustee's motions to waive the balance of debtor's settlement payments where the amount waived is the lesser of $100 or 1% of the total settlement amount.

(20) Debtor's motions to terminate wage deduction order so long as the motion represents that all payments have been completed under the debtor's chapter 13 plan and the chapter 13 trustee is served with a copy of the motion.

(21) Debtor's motion to reopen case to file Official Bankruptcy Form "Certification About a Financial Management Course".

[Comment: See Local Rule 5010–1(G).]

(22) Debtor's motion to amend petition to correct debtor's name.

[Comment: see Local Rule 1009–1(B)]

(23) Joint motions for substitution of counsel under Local Rule 2091–1.

(24) Motions to continue a pretrial conference in an adversary proceeding, following issuance of an alias summons under Local Rule 7004–2, to permit the timely filing of an answer not later than 30 days prior to the proposed, re-scheduled pretrial conference.

(25) Motions to redact personal information under Local Rule 5005–1(A)(3).

(D) Motions Considered on Negative Notice.

(1) *Introduction.* Certain motions may be considered by the court without a hearing if appropriate notice and an opportunity to object to the relief requested is provided to interested parties ("negative notice"). The option provided in this rule is not intended to limit the court's discretion to grant or deny relief sooner than 21 days after service of the motion.

(a) In addition to those motions listed under subdivision (D)(4), the negative notice procedure may not be used for any motion including a request for relief against a pro se debtor, or for those motions governed by the negative notice procedures described in Local Rules 3007–1(C) (objections to claims), 4001–1(C) (motions for stay relief), 6004–1(B) (certain notices of sale) and 6007–1(B)(1) (certain notices of abandonment).

(b) Motions may not combine requests for relief under more than one negative notice rule or combine any motion seeking relief on negative notice with a motion seeking relief for which negative notice is unavailable. In such instances, the court may deny the relief requested or require the filing of separate motions.

(2) *Use of Bulletin; Procedures.* Subject to the limitations of Local Rule 9013(D)(1), whenever the Bankruptcy Code or Bankruptcy Rules provide that an order may be entered "after notice and a hearing" or similar phrase, the motion may include above the preamble and below the title of the motion the following bulletin in bold print:

Any interested party who fails to file and serve a written response to this motion within 21 days after the date of service stated in this motion shall, pursuant to Local Rule 9013–1(D), be deemed to have consented to the entry of an order in the form attached to this motion. Any scheduled hearing may then be canceled.

Each motion filed under this subdivision must attach a proposed order as an exhibit. When this bulletin is included in the motion, a party properly served who fails to file a written response within 21 days after service of the motion shall be deemed to have consented to the entry of the order. Within seven days after the expiration of the 21 days notice period, the moving party shall submit to the court the following: (a) if no response is received or filed, a proposed order pursuant to Local Rule 5005–1(G), including the following language in the order's preamble:

"and the movant by submitting this form of order having represented that the motion was served on all parties required by Local Rule 9013–1(D), that the 21–day response time provided by that rule has expired, that no one has filed, or served on the movant, a response to the motion, and that the form of order was attached as an exhibit to the motion;"

or (b) if a response contesting the relief requested is received or filed, the Local Form "Certificate of Contested Matter". If a certificate of contested matter is filed, the court will schedule a hearing in accordance with the procedures contained in Local Rule 9073–1(A). The "Notice of Hearing" shall be served by movant in accordance with the procedures contained in Local Rule 9073–1(B).

(3) *Motions For Which Negative Notice May Be Used.* The following is a nonexclusive list of motions that may be considered without a hearing, provided such motions do not affect the rights of a pro se debtor.

(a) motions to compel abandonment of property (Bankruptcy Rule 6007(b));

(b) motions to approve compromise or settlement (Bankruptcy Rule 9019);

(c) motions to approve accounting by prior custodian (Bankruptcy Rule 6002);

(d) motions to extend time to object to exemptions (Bankruptcy Rule 4003(b));

(e) motions to temporarily allow claim for voting purposes (Bankruptcy Rule 3018(a));

(f) motions to avoid liens on exempt property (Bankruptcy Rule 4003(d));

(g) motions to obtain credit (11 U.S.C. § 364);

(h) motions to convert case pursuant to 11 U.S.C. § 706(a);

(i) motions to reopen chapter 7 cases to amend schedules to add omitted creditors; and

(j) motions seeking entry of an order under 11 U.S.C. § 362(j), confirming that the automatic stay has terminated under 11 U.S.C. § 362(c)(1). The motion shall recite the facts which establish that the stay has terminated, including, if applicable, a statement that the debtor has failed to comply with 11 U.S.C. § 521(a)(6), by either (i) failing to timely reaffirm a debt described in that section; or (ii) failing to timely redeem the collateral securing such debt. The statement shall also confirm that the trustee has not filed a motion under § 521(a)(6)(B), to determine that the property is of consequential value or benefit to the estate. The motion shall be served on the debtor, the trustee, and any other party of record claiming an interest in the collateral;

(k) multi-part motions to reopen case and to avoid judicial lien on exempt property (Bankruptcy Rule 4003(d)).

(4) *Motions Not Within Scope of Rule.* The following motions may not be considered by negative notice under Local Rule 9013-1(D):

(a) motions to assume or reject executory contracts or unexpired leases, or to compel assumption or rejection;

(b) motions to use, sell, or lease property except motions by a chapter 7 trustee to sell property for $2,500 or less as described in subdivision (C)(10) of this rule;

[Comment: See Bankruptcy Rule 6004; see also Local Rule 6004-1(B) (notice of sale).]

(c) motions to approve employment of professionals except those described in subdivision (C)(3) of this rule;

[Comment: See Bankruptcy Rule 2014.]

(d) motions to extend exclusivity period;

[Comment: See 11 U.S.C. § 1121(d).]

(e) motions for payment of administrative expenses, including professional fees;

[Comment: See 11 U.S.C. § 503(a), § 330 and § 331, but see special notice requirements in Bankruptcy Rule 2002(c)(2) and Local Rule 2002-1(C)(9).]

(f) motions to appoint trustee or examiner;

[Comment: See 11 U.S.C. § 303(g) or § 1104.]

(g) motions which seek alternative relief;

(h) motions to modify chapter 13 plans; and

(i) motions for joint administration in cases other than chapter 11 and motions requesting joint administration of a CHAPTER 11 case involving an individual debtor with one or more cases involving a non-individual debtor.

(j) motions for relief against a pro se debtor which affect a pro se debtor's rights.

(k) motions to dismiss a chapter 7 or chapter 11 case.

(*l*) motions to dismiss a chapter 12 or 13 case filed by a party other than the debtor.

(E) Motions to Rehear, Reconsider or Reinstate Dismissed Chapter 13 Cases. A motion to rehear, reconsider or vacate an order dismissing a chapter 13 case must be:

(1) If filed by an attorney, be accompanied by a certificate which states that the debtor has tendered to the attorney all funds required to be paid under the debtor's plan to bring the plan current as of the date of the motion and that said funds are in the attorney's trust account, unless the motion includes a request that the case be immediately converted to another chapter; or

(2) If the debtor is pro se, be accompanied by a photocopy of the cashier's check(s) or money order(s), made payable to the chapter 13 trustee, which will be tendered to the chapter 13 trustee by the debtor to bring the plan current if the case is reinstated, unless the motion includes a request that the case be immediately converted to another chapter.

Motions in chapter 13 cases complying with this provision shall be scheduled for hearing before the respective judge at the monthly chapter 13 calendar or, at the judge's discretion, set for hearing on an emergency basis. Motions not in compliance with these provisions will be denied without further notice or hearing.

In addition, a dismissed chapter 13 case shall not be reopened unless the debtor is current under the previously confirmed plan as of the hearing on the debtor's motion to rehear, reconsider or reinstate a dismissed case.

[Comment: See Bankruptcy Rule 1017 and Local Rules 1017-2 (dismissal), 5005-1 (filing and transmittal of papers), and Local Rule 5010-1(D) (reopening chapter 13 cases), and 11 U.S.C. § 350 (closing case).]

(F) Expedited Hearings for Certain Motions Filed in Chapter 11 Cases. Subject to Bankruptcy Rule 6003, the motions specified in subdivisions (G), (H), (I), (J), and (K) of this rule filed in a chapter 11 case, shall be filed in accordance with Local Rule 9075-1(A), scheduled for hearing within two business days if reasonably possible, and served, as applicable, pursuant to Local Rules 2002-1(H) or 9073-1(B). If the judge assigned to the case is unable to hear the motions within two business days, the motions shall be scheduled by the clerk, whenever possible, before the judge's designated alternative judge within the required time.

(G) Motion Seeking Authority to Use Cash Collateral. A motion seeking authority to use cash collateral pursuant to 11 U.S.C. § 363, shall comply with Bankruptcy Rule 4001(b) or (d), and the court's "Guidelines for Motions Seeking Authority to Use Cash Collateral and Motions Seeking Approval of Postpetition Financing".

(H) Motions for Approval of Postpetition Financing. A motion seeking approval of postpetition financing pursuant to 11 U.S.C. § 364, shall comply with Bankruptcy Rule 4001(c) or (d), and the court's "Guidelines for Motions Seeking Authority to Use Cash Collateral and Motions Seeking Approval of Postpetition Financing".

(I) Motions for Authority for the Payment of Prepetition Wages. A motion seeking authority to pay employees of the debtor prepetition wages outstanding as of the petition date shall comply with Bankruptcy Rule 6003 and

(1) include a schedule setting forth:

(a) the name of each employee to whom such wages are sought to be paid:

(b) the amount due such employee as of the petition date;

(c) the amounts to be withheld from such wages, including all applicable payroll taxes and related benefits;

(d) the period of time for which prepetition wages are due;

(e) whether the employee is presently employed by the debtor; and

(2) identify whether any of the employees constitute insiders as defined in 11 U.S.C. § 101(31).

The motion shall also include a representation by the debtor that all applicable payroll taxes and related benefits due to the debtor's employees will be paid concurrently with payment of the wages.

(J) Motions for Authority to Maintain Prepetition Bank Accounts. A motion seeking authority to maintain prepetition bank accounts shall include:

(1) a schedule listing each prepetition bank account which the debtor seeks to maintain postpetition;

(2) the amount on deposit in each such account as of the petition date; and

(3) whether the depository is an authorized depository pursuant to 11 U.S.C. § 345(b).

If the debtor is unable to provide the foregoing information, the motion shall set forth the reason why such information is not available, and provide an estimate as to when the debtor shall be able to supplement its motion with such information.

(K) Motions for Authority to Pay Prepetition Claims. A motion seeking authority to pay prepetition claims deemed critical by the debtor shall include:

(1) a schedule of the names of each claimant;

(2) the amount due each claimant;

(3) a description of the goods or services provided to the debtor by each claimant;

(4) facts and law supporting payment of the prepetition debt under the doctrine of necessity and Bankruptcy Rule 6003; and

(5) whether the claimant has made any concession or other agreement in consideration for the proposed payment, including the extension of postpetition trade credit.

(L) Utility Service—Adequate Assurance Motion.

(1) *When a Motion is Required.* No motion is required where the trustee or the debtor have reached an agreement with the utility company on the adequate assurance of future payment pursuant to 11 U.S.C. §§ 366(b) or (c). Where there is no agreement, the trustee or the debtor shall file a motion that complies with the requirements stated in subdivision (2) below seeking a determination by the court that the assurance of payment furnished by the trustee or the debtor constitutes adequate assurance of payment necessary under 11 U.S.C. §§ 366(b) or (c).

(2) *Content of Motion.* A motion to determine adequate assurance of payment for debtor's utility services shall be filed and served timely so that it may be heard prior to expiration of the applicable time period set forth in sections 366(b) or (c)(2) and include:

(a) a schedule of the names and addresses of the utilities;

(b) a certification that movant's attorney has contacted the utility service provider(s) and made a good faith effort to comply with the requirements under § 366, prior to the filing of the motion;

(c) the amount of the assurance payment required or paid and the form of adequate assurance the debtor has offered to furnish; and

(d) any request for an order scheduling a hearing to resolve disputes regarding assurance.

(3) *Objection.* The utility company shall serve a written objection no later than 4:30 p.m. on the second business day prior to the scheduled hearing, or the papers submitted may not be considered at the hearing (except when the hearing is set in less than five days notice). The objection shall set forth the location and account number for the utility service and specify the form and amount of assurance of payment that the utility demands.

(4) *Notice.* The trustee or debtor shall serve notice in compliance with the Bankruptcy Rules and Local Rule 2002–1, and specifically provide notice to any and all employee or representative of the utility company who negotiated the terms and conditions of the adequate assurance of payment.

(5) *Request for Evidentiary Hearing.* Unless otherwise requested, a motion filed in compliance with subdivision (2) above will be scheduled as an evidentiary hearing.

[Effective December 1, 1998. Amended effective December 1, 2002; July 1, 2004; April 9, 2007; June 2, 2008; December 1, 2009. Amended, on an interim basis, effective December 1, 2010. Amended effective August 1, 2011; November 19, 2014; December 1, 2015.]

RULE 9013–2. RESERVED

[Note: 9013–2 is a reserved rule number.]

RULE 9013–3. CERTIFICATE OF SERVICE

The service of motions is governed by this rule, Local Rules 2002–1(A) and 9076–1, and Bankruptcy Rules 7004, 9013 and 9014. Service of motions shall be reflected by the filing of the certificate of service filed in accordance with Local Rule 2002-1(F).

[Effective December 1, 1998. Amended effective December 1, 2002; June 2, 2008.]

RULE 9014-1. CONTESTED MATTERS

(A) Local Rule 7026-1, regarding discovery, is applicable to all contested matters.

(B) In a contested matter, the party to whom a request is directed under Bankruptcy Rules 9014(c) and 7034 must respond in writing within 14 days after being served.

[Comment (A): See also Local Rules 4001-1(G) (discovery in stay relief matters), 5071-1, 9013-1, 9019-1, 9073-1, 9074-1, and 9075-1 (motions and hearings). Comment (B): The 14-day deadline to respond to a document request applies only to contested matters. The deadline to respond to a document request in an adversary proceeding remains as set forth in Federal Rule of Civil Procedure 34(b)(2); see also Local Rule 2004-1(B) (creating a 14-day deadline to respond to document requests made pursuant to Federal Rule of Bankruptcy Procedure 2004).]

2011 Amendment: This rule is amended to shorten the time period for response to production of documents in contested matters to 14 days after service.

[Effective December 1, 1998. Amended effective December 1, 2002; June 2, 2008; August 1, 2011.]

RULE 9015-1. PLEADING AND RESPONDING TO JURY TRIAL DEMAND

(A) Title of Pleading. If the complaint, answer or other pleading includes a demand for a jury trial, the words "Demand for Jury Trial" shall be included in the title of the pleading.

(B) Deadline to File Statement of Consent. Parties may consent to have a jury trial conducted by a bankruptcy judge under 28 U.S.C. § 157(e), by jointly or separately filing a statement of consent within the latter of 14 days of service of a demand for jury trial or, if contained in the complaint, the deadline for filing an answer or other responsive pleading.

[Effective December 1, 1998. Amended effective December 1, 2002; June 2, 2008; December 1, 2009.]

RULE 9016-1. SUBPOENAS FROM CASES IN OTHER DISTRICTS

A motion seeking a compliance determination in this court as provided for by Fed. R. Civ. P. 45 regarding a subpoena issued in another district must be initiated by filing a miscellaneous proceeding, accompanied by the required filing fee.

[Effective December 1, 1998. Amended effective December 1, 2002; June 2, 2008. Amended on an interim basis effective December 1, 2013. Amended effective December 1, 2015.]

RULE 9019-1. SETTLEMENT OF MATTERS

(A) If a motion to compromise or settle pursuant to Bankruptcy Rule 9019 is filed on negative notice as otherwise permitted by Local Rule 9013-1(D)(3)(b), and no opposition to the motion is timely filed with the court, the movant shall submit a proposed order pursuant to Local Rule 5005-1(G), including the following language in the order's preamble:

> "and the movant by submitting this form of order having represented that the motion was served on all parties required by Bankruptcy Rule 2002 or Local Rule 2002-1(H), (I) or (J), that the 21-day response time provided by Local Rule 9013-1(D) has expired, that no one has filed, or served on the movant, a response to the motion, and that the form of order was attached as an exhibit to the motion".

If a motion to compromise or settle relates in whole or in part to an adversary proceeding, the motion to compromise or settle pursuant to Bankruptcy Rule 9019 shall be filed in the main bankruptcy case and a notice of the filing of the motion shall be filed in the affected adversary proceeding. If such a motion is granted in the main bankruptcy case, in addition to submitting a proposed order for entry in the main bankruptcy case granting the motion to compromise or settle, counsel for the movant shall submit a proposed order or judgment for entry in the adversary proceeding resolving the adversary proceeding consistent with the approved compromise or settlement, and such order or judgment shall include a direction to the clerk to close the adversary proceeding, if appropriate.

(B) Any stipulation to settle an adversary proceeding or contested matter with a pro se debtor must be set for hearing.

[Effective December 1, 1998. Amended effective December 1, 2002; June 2, 2008; August 1, 2011; December 1, 2015.]

RULE 9019-2. MEDIATION

(A) Registration of Mediators.

(1) *Mediation Register.* The clerk shall establish and maintain a register of qualified attorneys and retired federal and state judges who have registered to serve as mediators in adversary proceedings and contested matters in cases pending in the court. Attorneys and retired federal and state judges who meet the qualifications described in subdivision (2) shall be so registered. This subdivision shall not preclude an individual from serving as a mediator if the parties to the dispute agree upon the selection of that mediator. However, a mediator selected by the parties and not registered under this rule nonetheless shall comply with the other provisions of this rule where applicable.

(2) *Qualifications of Mediator.* To qualify for service as a mediator under this rule, a mediator must:

(a) (i) have completed a minimum of 40 hours in a circuit mediation training program certified by the Florida Supreme Court, (ii) have completed the American Bankruptcy Institute/St. John's University School of Law Bankruptcy Mediation Training, or (iii) be certified by the Florida Supreme Court as a circuit court mediator; and

(b) agree to accept at least 2 mediation assignments per year in cases where at least one party lacks the ability to compensate the mediator, in which case the mediator's fees shall be reduced accordingly or the mediator shall serve pro bono if no litigant is able to contribute compensation.

(3) *Procedures for Registration.* Each mediator who wishes to be included on the register must file the Local Form "Verification of Qualification to Act as Mediator".

(4) *Removal from Register.* The clerk shall remove a mediator from the register of mediators at the mediator's request or at the direction of a majority of the judges of the court in the exercise of their discretion. If removed at the mediator's request, the mediator may later request to be added to the register by submitting a new verification form. Upon receipt of such request, the clerk shall add the qualified mediator to the register.

(5) *Mediator's Oath.* Every mediator shall take the oath or affirmation prescribed by 28 U.S.C. § 453, before serving as a mediator. The oath may be administered by any person authorized to administer oaths, and proof of the oath or affirmation shall be included on the Local Form "Verification of Qualification to Act as Mediator".

(6) *Compensation of Mediators.* Mediators shall be compensated at the rate set by the U.S. District Court for the Southern District of Florida, and as adopted by this court by local rule or administrative order or at such rate as may be agreed to in writing by the parties and the mediator selected by the parties. Absent agreement of the parties to the contrary, the cost of the mediator's services shall be borne equally by the parties to the mediation conference, but a case trustee's or debtor in possession's share of the cost shall be an expense of the estate.

(B) Referral of Matters to Mediation.

(1) *Manner of Referral.* The court may order the assignment of a matter or proceeding to mediation at a pretrial conference or other hearing, upon the request of any party in interest or the U.S. Trustee, or upon the court's own motion. The court shall use the Local Form "Order of Referral to Mediation", which shall: (a) designate the trial or hearing date, (b) direct that mediation be conducted not later than 14 days before the scheduled trial or hearing, and (c) require the parties to agree upon a mediator within seven days after the date of the order. The parties shall timely file the Local Form "Notice of Selection of Mediator", failing which the clerk shall designate a mediator from the clerk's register on a random basis within court divisions using the Local Form "Notice of Clerk's Designation of Mediator" and serve this notice on the required parties. Notwithstanding the assignment of a matter or proceeding to mediation, the court shall set such matter or proceeding for trial final hearing, pretrial conference or other proceeding as is appropriate in accordance with the Bankruptcy Rules and these rules.

(2) *Disqualification of Mediator for Cause.* Any person selected as a mediator may be disqualified for bias or prejudice as provided in 28 U.S.C. § 144, and shall be disqualified in any action in which the mediator would be required to do so if the mediator were a judge governed by 28 U.S.C. § 455.

(3) *Replacement of Mediator.* If any party to the mediation conference, for any reason, objects to the designated mediator, then within three business days from the date of the notice of designation, the objecting party shall file with the clerk, and serve upon the mediator and all other parties to the mediation, a request for an alternate mediator including in the request the name of any alternate mediator already agreed upon by the parties. If the alternate mediator has been agreed upon, the clerk shall designate that mediator. Otherwise, the clerk shall designate a second mediator from the register of mediators on a random basis and shall serve a second notice of designation on all parties to the mediation conference and on the designated mediator. Each party shall be entitled to one challenge to any clerk-designated mediator. A mediator who is unable to serve shall, within seven days from the date of the notice of designation, serve on the clerk and all parties to the mediation a written notice of inability to serve, and the clerk shall designate an alternate mediator in the manner described above.

(4) *No Stay.* Notwithstanding a matter being referred to mediation, discovery and preparation for trial or final hearing shall not be stayed by mediation.

(5) *Types of Cases Subject to Mediation.* Any adversary proceeding or contested matter may be referred by the court to mediation.

(C) Mediation Conference.

(1) *Notice and Procedures.* Upon consultation with the parties and their attorneys, the mediator shall fix a reasonable time and place for the mediation conference, except as otherwise agreed by the parties or by order of the court, and shall give the parties at least 14 days' advance written notice of the conference. The conference shall be set as soon after the entry of the mediation order and as far in advance of the final evidentiary hearing as practicable. In keeping with the goal of prompt dispute resolution, the mediator shall have the duty and authority to establish the time for all mediation activities including a deadline for the parties to act upon a settlement or upon mediated recommendations.

(2) *Attendance of Parties Mandatory.* An attorney who is responsible for each party's case shall attend the mediation conference. Each individual party and the representatives of each non-individual party shall appear with the full authority to negotiate the amount and issues in dispute without further consultation. The mediator shall determine when the parties are to be present in the conference room. No party can be required to participate in a mediation conference for more than two hours.

(3) *Public Entity as Party.* If a party to mediation is a public entity, either a federal agency or an entity required to conduct its business pursuant to Chapter 286, Florida Statutes, that party shall be deemed to appear at a mediation conference by the physical presence of a representative with full authority to negotiate on behalf of the entity and to recommend settlement to the appropriate decision-making body of the entity.

(4) *Failure to Attend or to Participate in Good Faith.* The mediator shall report to the court the complete failure of any party to attend the mediation conference and shall report to the court the failure of any party to participate in the mediation process in good faith, either of which failures may result in the imposition of sanctions by the court.

(D) Recommendations of Mediator. The mediator shall have no obligation to make any written comments or recommendations other than the report required by subdivision (E). If a written recommendation is prepared, no copy shall be filed with the court.

(E) Post–Mediation Procedures. Within seven days after the mediation conference, the mediator shall file with the court a report showing compliance or non-compliance by the parties with the mediation order and the results of the mediation, using the Local Form "Report of Mediator". In the event there is an impasse, the mediator shall report that there is a lack of agreement, and shall make no further comment or recommendation. If the parties have reached an agreement regarding the disposition of the matter or proceeding, they shall prepare and submit to the court within 14 days after the filing of the mediator's report an appropriate stipulation of settlement and joint motion for its approval. Failure to file such a motion shall be a basis for the court to impose appropriate sanctions. If the mediator's report shows mediation has ended in an impasse, the matter will be tried as scheduled.

(F) Confidentiality. Conduct or statements made in the course of mediation proceedings constitute "conduct or statements made in compromise negotiations" within the meaning of Rule 408 of the Federal Rules of Evidence, and no evidence inadmissible under Rule 408, shall be admitted or otherwise disclosed to the court.

(G) Withdrawal from Mediation. Any action or claim referred to mediation pursuant to this rule may be exempt or withdrawn from mediation by the presiding judge at any time, before or after reference, upon motion of a party and/or a determination for any reason that the case is not suitable for mediation.

(H) Compliance with Bankruptcy Code and Rules. Nothing in this rule shall relieve any debtor, party in interest, or the U.S. Trustee from complying with any other orders of the court, the Bankruptcy Code, the Federal Rules of Bankruptcy Procedure, or these rules.

[Effective December 1, 1998. Amended effective December 1, 2002; June 2, 2008; December 1, 2009; December 1, 2015.]

RULE 9021–1. JUDGMENTS AND ORDERS—ENTRY OF

(A) Generally. The clerk will enter all the court's orders, decrees and judgments in CM/ECF which is the docket entry required of the clerk under Bankruptcy Rules 5003 and 9021. Orders may also be issued as "text-only" entries on the docket, without an attached document. Such orders are official and binding. Where the clerk is directed to serve notice, transmitting the NEF or, if applicable, service through the BNC or U.S. Mail constitutes the notice required under Bankruptcy Rule 9022. Parties directed to serve notice by the court must file a certificate of service filed in accordance with Local Rule 2002–1(F).

(B) Judgment. Judgments shall conform to the requirements of Local Rule 9072–1. Every judgment shall contain the name and mailing address of the judgment creditor and, to the extent practicable, shall state the last four digits of the social security number or other individual taxpayer identification number of the judgment debtor.

[Comment: Conforms to 1993 Florida statute requiring this information on all judgments to be recorded as liens and 28 U.S.C. § 1962 (state law governs judgment lien) except that only the last four digits of the social security or other individual taxpayer identification number shall be provided in accordance with the federal judiciary privacy policy.]

(C) Notification to Clerk of Matters Under Advisement. If any order on any contested matter or ruling after trial has been under advisement for more than 90 days, upon written notification and request sent to the Clerk of Court by any party in interest, the clerk or the clerk's designees shall send to the court and to all parties a "Notification of Matter Under Advisement for 90 Days". The clerk shall not file the request in the court file nor indicate the identity of the party making the request. When the court receives such notification, it shall set the matter for hearing within 30 days of receipt of the notification or shall issue an order resolving the matter during that same 30 day period.

[Effective December 1, 1998. Amended effective December 1, 2002; July 1, 2004; June 2, 2008; December 1, 2009.]

RULE 9027–1. REMOVAL; DEADLINE FOR MOTION TO REMAND

Motions for remand after removal of a case, proceeding, or civil action, must be filed not later than 21 days after removal.

[Effective December 1, 1998. Amended effective December 1, 2002; June 2, 2008; December 1, 2009.]

RULE 9036–1. NOTICE BY ELECTRONIC TRANSMISSION

(A) For Registered Users of CM/ECF.

(1) *Electronic Appearances.* Filing a document in CM/ECF for the first time (except for filing a proof of claim or ballot) is that registered user's electronic notice of appearance in that case or proceeding only. However, if a party has previously conventionally filed a notice of appearance or request for notice in a main case or proceeding prior to becoming a CM/ECF registered user, it is not necessary to enter an electronic appearance in such main case or proceeding.

(2) *Notice Provided Registered Users.* Every registered user who has made an electronic appearance in a specific case will automatically be sent an NEF (or Daily Summary Report—DSR) for each electronic entry in the case to the current e-mail address provided to the court. If a PDF document is attached to that NEF, the registered user will be able to view the document once at no charge for a period of 15 days from the date the document is entered on the docket. Subsequent access to that document or any other docketed items in CM/ECF cases will be available through PACER which provides electronic access to publicly filed electronic documents at the published fees or at the public computer terminals in each divisional clerk's office.

(3) *Withdrawal of Electronic Appearance.* A registered user seeking to withdraw an electronic appearance in a specific case or adversary proceeding must comply with Local Rule 2091–1.

(B) Electronic Notice in Lieu of Paper Notice from the BNC. Conventional filers and those registered users who have not yet made an electronic appearance in a specific case will receive notices generated by the clerk and served through the BNC in paper form unless they have elected to receive notices electronically in lieu of U.S. Mail service by either registering directly with the BNC EBN Program or, for debtors only, by registering directly with the clerk of court for DeBN noticing as provided under subdivision (C) of this Rule.

(C) Debtor Electronic Bankruptcy Noticing (DeBN). Debtors may elect to receive documents served by the clerk of the U.S. Bankruptcy Court electronically from the BNC under the DeBN program in lieu of by paper notice by filing the Local Form "Debtor's Request to Receive Notices Electronically Under DeBN Program". Debtor participation in DeBN does not constitute consent by the debtor to receive electronic notice from other parties, including attorneys and trustees. Documents not served by the clerk under DeBN must be served conventionally (non-electronic) on debtors as authorized under FRBP 7004 and 7005(b).

[Effective June 2, 2008. Amended effective December 1, 2009. Amended on an interim basis effective June 1, 2016.]

RULE 9070-1. EXHIBITS

(A) Submission and Service of Exhibits. Unless directed by the court, exhibits shall not be filed with the clerk of court. Exhibits shall be accompanied by the Local Form "Exhibit Register", and copies of the register and all exhibits should be submitted for each party and the judge. Unless ordered otherwise and except where the party receiving the exhibits is appearing pro se in a case or proceeding, parties may serve exhibits in electronic format. At the conclusion of the hearing or trial, the completed Exhibit Register will be filed by the courtroom deputy on the case or adversary docket.

(B) Format for Exhibits.

(1) Exhibits must be pre-marked prior to the commencement of any hearing or trial. Plaintiff/movant and defendant/respondent exhibits shall be identified by corresponding exhibit tags. Plaintiff(s)' exhibits shall be marked numerically and defendant(s)' exhibits shall be marked alphabetically.

(2) *Electronic Exhibits.* Unless otherwise directed by the court, ALL exhibits shall be submitted in electronic Portable Document Format (PDF) and stored on a USB flash drive or compact disc. Each individual PDF file shall be limited to a single exhibit of a file size no greater than 10MB and shall contain a unique identification name (e.g., Plaintiff's Exhibit 1 or Defendant's Exhibit A).

(3) *Oversized Exhibits.* Any physically large exhibit that cannot be submitted electronically may be submitted to the court in paper format. An exhibit that is unsuitable for storage at the court shall be returned to the party introducing it for retention until the matter is no longer subject to appellate review. Parties receiving such exhibits shall be responsible for producing them if required for an appellate record or for review by interested parties.

(C) Temporary Release of Exhibits. No exhibit received in evidence will be released from the court during the evidentiary proceedings without an order of court, except as provided in subdivision (B) of this Rule. Upon the entry of an order, the party to whom the exhibit is to be released shall prepare a receipt, precisely describing the exhibit and its corresponding number, for temporary release. The receipt must be signed by the attorney or other court-approved agent receiving the exhibit.

(D) Withdrawal or Disposal Upon Finality. After a matter is no longer subject to appellate review an exhibit may be returned to the party offering it without court order upon a written request stating that no appeal is pending and the case or proceeding is final. The requesting party shall furnish the clerk with an adequately sized, self-addressed, stamped envelope or shall make other appropriate arrangements for return of the exhibit. Any exhibit not returned within 30 days after a matter is no longer subject to appellate review may be destroyed or otherwise disposed of by the clerk without further notice.

[Effective December 1, 1998. Amended effective December 1, 2002; June 2, 2008; December 1, 2009; December 1, 2015.]

RULE 9071-1. RESERVED

[Note: 9071-1 is a Reserved Rule Number.]

2011 Amendment: This rule is abrogated to reflect relocation of settlement provisions to Local Rule 9019-1.

[Effective December 1, 1998. Amended effective December 1, 2002; June 2, 2008; August 1, 2011.]

RULE 9071-2. REFERRAL OF PRO SE PARTIES TO PRO BONO REPRESENTATION

In any adversary proceeding in which a party is proceeding pro se and the court finds either that, in the case of a pro se debtor defendant there is a reasonable doubt as to the validity of the creditor's claim, or in the case of any other pro se party, that the party would likely qualify for pro bono representation, the court will refer the party to the pro bono committee of the Bankruptcy Bar Association of the Southern District of Florida for the purpose of obtaining pro bono representation in a trial of the adversary proceeding.

[Effective June 2, 2008.]

RULE 9072-1. ORDERS—PROPOSED

Registered Users shall submit proposed orders and judgments to the judge in electronic format using the E-Orders program in CM/ECF, or in word processing format to an electronic mailbox designated by the court in accordance with the court's "Guidelines for Preparing, Submitting and Serving Orders". Conventional filers shall conform to the format requirements set forth in the "Guidelines" when submitting proposed orders and judgments in paper. Notwithstanding this provision, proposed orders submitted pursuant to Local Rule 5005-1(G)(1)(b), which requires parties in matters set for hearing on an emergency basis to bring proposed orders to court hearings, shall continue to be brought to the hearings and submitted conventionally. Conventionally signed orders will be converted to electronic format and docketed by the clerk.

[Comment: See Local Rules 5005-1(G) (submittal and service of proposed orders) and 9021-1 (judgments), and Bankruptcy Rules 7054 and 9021 (judgments).]

[Effective December 1, 1998. Amended effective December 1, 2002; June 2, 2008; December 1, 2009.]

RULE 9073-1. HEARINGS

(A) Notice of Hearing. Preparation by Clerk for Service by Required Party. Except for those matters self-calendared under section (C) of this rule, for any paper filed requiring a hearing, the clerk will prepare a notice of hearing and return it to the party required to serve the notice within the time required by any applicable rule or order of the court, either electronically via the NEF or by mail from the BNC, depending on whether the attorney for the movant is a registered user who has filed an electronic notice of appearance in the case or proceeding.

(B) Filing of Certificate of Service of Notice of Hearing. The movant shall file a certificate of service for that notice of hearing as required under Local Rule 2002-1(F). A request for relief as to which a notice of hearing is not timely served or a certificate of service timely filed may be denied sua sponte by the court without further notice or hearing.

(C) Self-Calendaring of Certain Matters. The court has issued guidelines for self-calendaring. Attorneys and trustees who self-calendar hearings must serve notice and file a certificate of service as required by subsections (A) and (B) of this rule. If the self-calendaring option is used to schedule a hearing on a motion for relief from stay, and the next available hearing date is scheduled beyond the 30 or 60 day provisions set forth in 11 U.S.C. § 362(e), the movant will be deemed to have consented to voluntarily extending the deadline to the date of the next available calendar.

(D) Conference With Opposing Attorneys Required. If a motion seeks relief involving a debtor that is represented by an attorney, the trustee, or another particular adverse party that is represented by an attorney, the certificate of service for the notice of hearing shall include a certification that movant's attorney has contacted counsel for all adverse parties to attempt to resolve the matter without hearing.

[Comment: See also Bankruptcy Rule 9011 (effect of signature) and Local Rules 7026-1(E) (motions to compel discovery) and 9076-1 (electronic service).]

[Effective December 1, 1998. Amended effective December 1, 2002; June 2, 2008; August 1, 2011; December 1, 2015.]

RULE 9074-1. APPEARANCE BY TELEPHONE

(A) General Eligibility Requirements. Unless the judge otherwise specifically directs, the appearance by telephone procedure in this rule is available only to parties who are not residents of the county in which the hearing is scheduled. For attorneys, residence shall mean the county in which the appearing attorney's law office is located.

(B) Restrictions. Telephone hearings will not be permitted for (1) evidentiary hearing; and (2) matters scheduled on a regular Chapter 13 calendar. When a land line is available, parties will not be permitted to appear by cellular telephone except with specific permission from the court.

(C) Procedure. Parties requesting to participate in hearings by telephone must contact the judge's calendar clerk at least two business days prior to the date of the hearing. Telephone hearings may be deferred by the judge to the end of the hearing calendar, so the party must remain available for the court's call from the scheduled hearing time until the end of the day's hearing calendar. The court generally will not postpone the hearing because of the party's unavailability or telephonic transmission problems.

[Effective December 1, 1998. Amended effective December 1, 2002; June 2, 2008; December 1, 2009.]

RULE 9075-1. EMERGENCY MOTIONS

If a motion or other paper requests an emergency hearing, the title of the motion or paper shall include the words "Emergency Hearing Requested". Any motion or paper requesting an emergency hearing shall set forth with particularity, under a separate heading in the text:

(A) the reason for the exigency and the date by which movant reasonably believes such hearing must be held; and

(B) a certification that the proponent has made a bona fide effort to resolve the matter without hearing.

Emergency hearings shall be held only where direct, immediate and substantial harm will occur to the interest of an entity in property, to the bankruptcy estate, or to the debtor's ability to reorganize if the parties are not able to obtain an immediate resolution of any dispute.

[Comment: See also Local Rules 5005-1(B) (papers to be filed with clerk, not court) and 5005-1(F)(2) (emergency submittal of papers).]

[Effective December 1, 1998. Amended effective December 1, 2002; June 2, 2008; December 1, 2009.]

RULE 9076-1. ELECTRONIC SERVICE

(A) Registered Users Consent to Waiver of Non-Electronic Service. Registered users (1) waive the right to receive notice by first class mail and consent to receive notice electronically via the CM/ECF generated NEF; and (2) waive the right to service by personal service or first class mail and consent to electronic service via the NEF, except with regard to service of a summons and complaint under Bankruptcy Rule 7004. Waiver of service and notice by first class mail applies to notice of the entry of an order or judgment under Bankruptcy Rule 9022.

(B) Electronic Appearance in that Case Constitutes Consent. Consent to electronic service becomes effective in a particular case when a registered user files a document that generates an NEF (except a proof of claim or ballot).

(C) Elimination of Duplicate Noticing. To reduce noticing costs and unnecessary duplication of service, registered users who are served with an NEF will not receive duplicate notice served via the BNC. This elimination of duplicate noticing will also apply to those registered users who have separately entered into an agreement for e-mail or fax service with the BNC. Registered users receiving notice under this rule shall have access to electronic dockets and case documents as provided under Local Rule 9036.

Note: Chapter 7 and 13 trustees are automatically added at case initiation and therefore always will receive service via the NEF; thus conventional filers need not serve a paper copy of a document on a trustee.

(D) Certificate of Service Required. As provided by subdivision (A) and (B) of this Rule, service may occur via the NEF (in lieu of service by U.S. Mail) for certain registered users in the case (absent a specific statutory or court requirement for conventional paper service), however, all certificates of service must comply with Local Rule 2002-1(F).

[Effective June 2, 2008. Amended effective December 1, 2009. Amended effective December 1, 2015.]

LOCAL FORMS, CLERK'S INSTRUCTIONS AND COURT GUIDELINES

LF-1. NOTICE OF DEADLINE TO OBJECT TO DEBTOR'S STATEMENT RE: 11 U.S.C. § 522(q)(1) APPLICABILITY, PAYMENT OF DOMESTIC SUPPORT OBLIGATIONS, AND [FOR CHAPTER 11 CASES ONLY] APPLICABILITY OF FINANCIAL MANAGEMENT COURSE AND STATEMENT REGARDING ELIGIBILITY TO RECEIVE A DISCHARGE

UNITED STATES BANKRUPTCY COURT
SOUTHERN DISTRICT OF FLORIDA
www.flsb.uscourts.gov

In re: Case No.
Chapter 11 (or 12)
Individual

______Debtor(s) /

Notice of Deadline to Object to Debtor's Statement Re: 11 U.S.C. §522(q)(1) Applicability, Payment of Domestic Support Obligations, and [For Chapter 11 Cases Only] Applicability of Financial Management Course and Statement Regarding Eligibility to Receive a Discharge

NOTICE: Any interested party who fails to file and serve a written objection to this statement within 30 days after the date of service of this statement shall, pursuant to Local Rule 2082-1(B), for chapter 12 cases or Local Rule 3022-1(B), for chapter 11 cases, be deemed to have consented to the entry of an order of discharge if the court determines that all other requirement for discharge of the debtor(s) have been met.

The Debtor(s), ____________________, in the above captioned matter certify(ies) as follows:

A. Compliance with 11 U.S.C. §1141(d)(5)(C) (chapter 11) or 11 U.S.C. §1228(f) (chapter 12): [select one]

___ 1. The Debtor has not claimed an exemption under 11 U.S.C. §522(b)(3) in an amount in excess of $155,675 in property of the kind described in 11 U.S.C. §522(q)(1) [generally the Debtor's homestead];

or

____ 2. The Debtor has claimed an exemption under 11 U.S.C. §522(b)(3) in an amount in excess of $155,675 in property of the kind described in 11 U.S.C. §522(q)(1) but there is no pending proceeding in which the Debtor may be found guilty of a felony of a kind described in 11 U.S.C. §522(q)(1)(A) or found liable for a debt of the kind described in 11 U.S.C. §522(q)(1)(B).

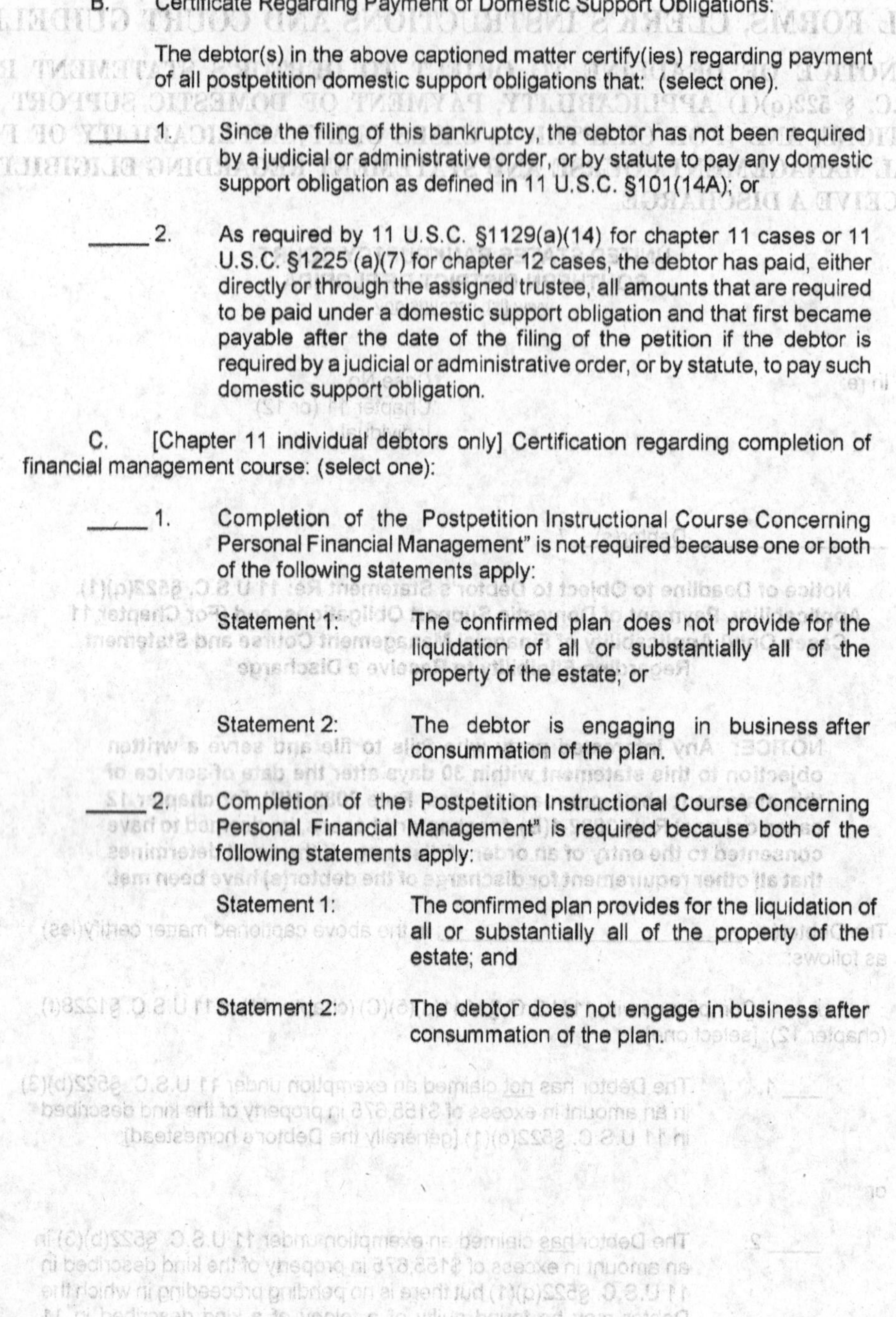

B. Certificate Regarding Payment of Domestic Support Obligations:

The debtor(s) in the above captioned matter certify(ies) regarding payment of all postpetition domestic support obligations that: (select one).

_____ 1. Since the filing of this bankruptcy, the debtor has not been required by a judicial or administrative order, or by statute to pay any domestic support obligation as defined in 11 U.S.C. §101(14A); or

_____ 2. As required by 11 U.S.C. §1129(a)(14) for chapter 11 cases or 11 U.S.C. §1225 (a)(7) for chapter 12 cases, the debtor has paid, either directly or through the assigned trustee, all amounts that are required to be paid under a domestic support obligation and that first became payable after the date of the filing of the petition if the debtor is required by a judicial or administrative order, or by statute, to pay such domestic support obligation.

C. [Chapter 11 individual debtors only] Certification regarding completion of financial management course: (select one):

_____ 1. Completion of the Postpetition Instructional Course Concerning Personal Financial Management" is not required because one or both of the following statements apply:

Statement 1: The confirmed plan does not provide for the liquidation of all or substantially all of the property of the estate; or

Statement 2: The debtor is engaging in business after consummation of the plan.

_____ 2. Completion of the Postpetition Instructional Course Concerning Personal Financial Management" is required because both of the following statements apply:

Statement 1: The confirmed plan provides for the liquidation of all or substantially all of the property of the estate; and

Statement 2: The debtor does not engage in business after consummation of the plan.

D. [Chapter 11 individual debtors only] Statement Regarding Eligibility To Receive A Discharge (select one):

_____ 1. I am eligible to receive a discharge because: (all must apply for the debtor to receive a discharge):

a) All payments under the plan have been completed;
b) If required by (C) above, I have filed Official Bankruptcy Form B23 "Debtor's Certification of Completion of Postpetition Instructional Course Concerning Personal Financial Management" (unless the course provider filed a certificate of completion of the financial management course on my behalf);
c) 11 U.S.C. §1141(d)(3) does not apply to me; and
d) There are no pending objections to discharge and no order denying discharge has been entered in this case.

_____ 2. By separate motion, I am seeking entry of a discharge under 11 U.S.C. §1141(d)(5).

_____ 3. I am not eligible for and am not seeking a discharge in my case.

I declare under penalty of perjury that the information provided in this Certificate is true and correct. A certificate of service shall be filed as provided by Local Rule 2002-1(F).

____
Debtor's Signature

Dated: _______________________
Joint Debtor's Signature (if applicable)

LF-1 (rev. 12/01/13)

[Effective December 1, 1998. Amended effective December 1, 2002; December 1, 2003; October 17, 2005; January 10, 2006; August 1, 2006; June 2, 2008; April 27, 2009; December 1, 2009; April 1, 2010; April 1, 2013; December 1, 2013.]

LF-2. ORDER REINSTATING CHAPTER 7 CASE

UNITED STATES BANKRUPTCY COURT
SOUTHERN DISTRICT OF FLORIDA
www.flsb.uscourts.gov

In re: Case No.
Chapter 7

_______________ Debtor /

ORDER REINSTATING CHAPTER 7 CASE

This matter came before the Court, ☐ after a hearing held on __________ ☐ without a hearing, upon the debtor's/debtors' motion for reinstatement [ECF No. ________] of the above captioned case, which case had been dismissed by prior order of the Court.

Upon consideration of the debtor's/debtors' motion and the presentation at the hearing, if applicable, the Court **ORDERS** as follows:

A. The above captioned case is reinstated effective upon entry of this order.

B. Pursuant to 11 U.S.C. §362(c)(2)(B), the automatic stay terminated on the date this case was dismissed and was not in effect from such date until the entry of this order. The automatic stay under 11 U.S.C. §362 shall become effective as of the date of entry of this order.

C. The Order Discharging Trustee, if entered, is vacated.

LF-2 (rev. 12/01/15) Page 1 of 2

D. If not previously filed, any and all documents required to be filed by the debtor(s) under 11 U.S.C. §521(a)(1), Bankruptcy Rule 1007, and Local Rule 1007-1 shall be filed no later than 14 days after entry of this order.

E. If the debtor(s) fail(s) to timely comply with any requirements of this order, the above captioned case will be dismissed without further notice or hearing.

F. Status of meeting of creditors under 11 U.S.C. §341 and related deadlines [select 1 or 2]:

☐ 1. Because this case was dismissed prior to the conclusion of the meeting of creditors under 11 U.S.C. §341, the previously scheduled meeting of creditors was canceled. In accordance with Local Rules 3002-1(B)(2)(a), 4004-2(B)(1) and 4007-1(B)(1), the Clerk will provide notice to all parties of record of the date of the rescheduled meeting of creditors and applicable deadlines for the filing of proof of claim, objections to discharge and objections to the dischargeability of particular debts.

☐ 2. This case was dismissed after the meeting of creditors under 11 U.S.C. §341. Any applicable deadlines in accordance with Local Rules 3002-1(B)(2)(a), 4004-2(A)(2)(a), 4004-2(B)(1) and 4007-1(B)(1) will be reset by separate order upon reinstatement of case.

###

Copies to:
All parties of record by Clerk

LF-2 (rev. 12/01/15) Page 2 of 2

[Effective January 28, 2013. Amended effective April 12, 2013; December 1, 2015.]

LF–3. APPLICATION TO PAY FILING FEE IN INSTALLMENTS

UNITED STATES BANKRUPTCY COURT
SOUTHERN DISTRICT OF FLORIDA
www.flsb.uscourts.gov

In re: Case No.
Chapter

_______________ Debtor/

APPLICATION FOR INDIVIDUALS TO PAY THE FILING FEE IN INSTALLMENTS

1. Which chapter of the Bankruptcy Code are you choosing to file under:

Petition Filing Fee	Initial Installment Payment	Final Installment Payment
☐ Chapter 7: **$335**	**$167.50**	**$167.50**
☐ Chapter 11: **$1,717**	**$858.50**	**$858.50**
☐ Chapter 12: **$275**	**$137.50**	**$137.50**
☐ Chapter 13: **$310**	**$155.00**	**$155.00**

2. I am unable to pay the full filing fee with the petition and apply to pay in installments in accordance with Bankruptcy Rule 1006, Local Rule 1006-1 and the current mandatory payment schedule established by this court.

3. I understand that, in order for this application to be approved absent further order of the court, I must have paid half of the filing fee due at the time of filing my petition and I must pay the remaining half which equals $ ____________ on or before 60 days from the filing date of my petition.

4. I understand that payment must be in cash or cashier's check unless submitted electronically by an attorney.

5. I understand that if I fail to pay the fee when due, my bankruptcy case may be dismissed and I may not receive a discharge of my debts. If I am a chapter 13 debtor, I understand that upon confirmation of my plan, the unpaid balance of the filing fee must be paid in full. If I am a chapter 7 debtor, I understand my discharge will not be entered until my filing fee is paid in full.

6. I understand that I must pay the entire filing fee before making any more payments or transfer any more property to an attorney, bankruptcy petition preparer, or anyone else for services in connection with this bankruptcy case.

_______________________________ _______________________________
Signature of Attorney Date Signature of Debtor Date
(In a joint case, both spouses must sign.)

_______________________________ _______________________________
Name of Attorney Signature of Joint Debtor (if any) Date

LF-3 (rev. 12/01/15)

[Effective December 1, 1998. Amended effective November 16, 1999; February 14, 2000; March 29, 2000; December 1, 2002; November 1, 2003; July 1, 2004; October 17, 2005; March 26, 2007; June 2, 2008; December 1, 2009; June 15, 2011; August 1, 2011; November 1, 2011; March 6, 2012; December 1, 2013; June 30, 2014; December 1, 2015.]

LF-4. DEBTOR'S NOTICE OF COMPLIANCE WITH REQUIREMENTS FOR AMENDING CREDITOR INFORMATION

UNITED STATES BANKRUPTCY COURT
SOUTHERN DISTRICT OF FLORIDA
www.flsb.uscourts.gov

In re: Case No.
Chapter

_______________ Debtor /

DEBTOR'S NOTICE OF COMPLIANCE WITH REQUIREMENTS FOR AMENDING CREDITOR INFORMATION

This notice is being filed in accordance with Local Rules 1007-2(B), 1009-1(D), or 1019-1(B) upon the filing of an amendment to the debtor's lists, schedules or statements, pursuant to Bankruptcy Rules 1007, 1009, 1019 or 5010-1(B). I certify that:

[ ] The paper filed **adds** creditor(s) as reflected on the attached list (include name and address of each creditor being added). I have:

1. remitted the required fee (unless the paper is a Bankruptcy Rule 1019(5) report);
2. provided the court with a supplemental matrix **of only the added creditors** on a CD or memory stick in electronic text format (ASCII or MS-DOS text), or electronically uploaded the added creditors in CM/ECF;
3. provided notice to affected parties, including service of a copy of this notice and a copy of the §341 or post conversion meeting notice [see Local Rule 1009-1(D)(2)] and filed a certificate of service in compliance with the court [see Local Rule 2002-1(F)];
4. filed an amended schedule(s) and summary of schedules; and
5. filed a motion to reopen accompanied by the required filing fee (if adding creditors pursuant to Local Rule 5010-1(B)).

[ ] The paper filed **deletes** a creditor(s) as reflected on the attached list (include name and address of each creditor being deleted). **I have:**

1. remitted the required fee;
2. provided notice to affected parties and filed a certificate of service in compliance with the court [see Local Rule 2002-1(F)]; and
3. filed an amended schedule(s) and summary of schedules.

[ ] The paper filed **corrects** the name and/or address of a creditor(s) as reflected on the attached list. **I have:**

1. provided notice to affected parties, including service of a copy of this notice and a copy of the §341 or post conversion meeting notice [see Local Rule 1009-1(D)(2)] and filed a certificate of service in compliance with the court [see Local Rule 2002-1(F)]; and
2. filed an amended schedule(s) or other paper.

[ ] The paper filed **corrects** schedule D or E/F amount(s) or classification(s). **I have:**

1. remitted the required fee;
2. provided notice to affected parties and filed a certificate of service in compliance with the court [see Local Rule 2002-1(F)]; and
3. filed an amended schedule(s) and summary of schedules.

[ ] None of the above apply. The paper filed does not require an additional fee, a supplemental matrix, or notice to affected parties. It □ does □ does not require the filing of an amended schedule and summary of schedules.

I also certify that, if filing amended schedules, Bankruptcy Form 106 "Declaration About an Individual Debtor's Schedules" (signed by both debtors) or Bankruptcy Form 202 , "Declaration Under Penalty of Perjury for Non-Individual Debtors" has been filed as required by Local Rules 1007-2(B), 1009-1(A)(2) and (D)(1), or 1019-1(B).

Dated: ___________

_______________	_______________
Attorney for Debtor (or Debtor, if pro se)	Joint Debtor (if applicable)
Print Name	Address
Florida Bar Number	Phone Number

LF-4 (rev. 12/01/15)

[Effective December 1, 1998. Amended effective September 26, 2000; September 18, 2003; November 1, 2003; October 17, 2005; June 2, 2008; December 1, 2009; January 17, 2014; December 1, 2015; January 15, 2016.]

LF-5. TRANSCRIPT REQUEST FORM

UNITED STATES BANKRUPTCY COURT
SOUTHERN DISTRICT OF FLORIDA
www.flsb.uscourts.gov

Transcript Request Form

Submit this form to the transcription company by email, fax or postal mail:

Transcriber:

Email: Telephone No.: Fax:

Case Number:______ Adversary Number:______ Judge:______

Date of Hearing or Trial: ______ Time of Hearing or Trial: ______

Debtor(s) Name:______

☐ The transcript being requested is included as a designated item for a pending appeal. **(If this box is checked, the requestor must also file this form with the clerk pursuant to Bankruptcy Rule 8009. The transcriber is responsible for notifying the clerk by electronic docket entry in the case the date the request was received and the date on which the transcriber expects to have the transcript completed (See Bankruptcy Rule 8010)).**

Select Delivery Method:

✔		Original	First Copy to Each Party	Each Additional Copy to the Same Party
	Ordinary Transcript A transcript to be delivered within thirty (30) calendar days after receipt of an order.	$3.65	.90	.60
	14-Day Transcript A transcript to be delivered within fourteen (14) calendar days after receipt of an order.	$4.25	.90	.60
	Expedited Transcript A transcript to be delivered within seven (7) calendar days after receipt of an order.	$4.85	.90	.60
	Daily Transcript A transcript to be delivered following adjournment and prior to the normal opening hour of the court on the following morning whether or not it actually is a court day.	$6.05	1.20	.90
	Hourly Transcript A transcript of proceedings ordered under unusual circumstances to be delivered within two (2) hours.	$7.25	1.20	.90

By submitting this request, it is understood that:

- A separate order must be placed for each transcript being requested.
- All transcript requests must be submitted directly to the transcriber. Do not contact the clerk's office regarding the status of a request.
- It is the responsibility of the requestor to verify that the transcript has not already been filed with the court.
- It is the responsibility of parties to request redaction. See Local Bankruptcy Rule 5005-1(A)(2)(b), Local Form "Notice of Intent to Request Redaction of Transcript" (LF-61), and "Guidelines on Electronic Availability of Transcripts and Procedures for Transcript Redaction".

Print Your Name:______

Mailing Address:______

Email Address:______ Telephone No.:______

LF-05 (rev. 12/01/15)

[Effective December 1, 1998. Amended effective May 8, 2001; December 1, 2002; December 1, 2003; February 15, 2005; October 17, 2005; April 9, 2006; January 8, 2007; June 2, 2008; December 1, 2009; October 1, 2013; December 1, 2015.]

LF–6. ORDER CONVERTING CASE UNDER CHAPTER 7 TO CASE UNDER CHAPTER 11

UNITED STATES BANKRUPTCY COURT
SOUTHERN DISTRICT OF FLORIDA
www.flsb.uscourts.gov

In re: Case No.
Chapter 7

_____ Debtor /

ORDER CONVERTING CASE UNDER CHAPTER 7 TO CASE UNDER CHAPTER 11

( ) The debtor has filed a motion to convert this case to a case under chapter 11 of the Bankruptcy Code pursuant to 11 U.S.C. §706(a) and served it on required parties in accordance with Local Rule 9013-1(D)(3)(h). Interested parties are deemed to have consented to entry of this order under Local Rule 9013-1(D)(2).

Since this case has not been previously converted under 11 U.S.C. §1112, §1208 or §1307, the court finds that the debtor is entitled to be a debtor under chapter 11.

( ) A party in interest has filed a motion to convert this case to a case under chapter 11 of the Bankruptcy Code pursuant to 11 U.S.C. §706(b). The court finds, after notice and hearing, that the motion should be granted.

It is **ORDERED** that:

1. This chapter 7 case is converted to a case under chapter 11.
2. The debtor shall:
   a. within 14 days of the date of this order, file a list of the debtor's equity security holders of each class, showing the number and kind of interests registered in the name of each holder and the last known

LF-6 (rev. 03/11/16) Page 1 of 4

name and address or place of business of each holder, as required by Bankruptcy Rule 1007(a)(3) and Local Rule 1019-1(C); and in accordance with Local Rules 1007-2 and 1009-1(D);

b. within 14 days from the date of this order and if such documents have not already been filed, the statements, schedules and, if the debtor is an individual, payment advices or the required statement regarding payment advices and Official Form 122B "Chapter 11 Statement of Your Current Monthly Income". [see Bankruptcy Rule 1007(b), Bankruptcy Rules 1007(b)(1) and 1007(c), Local Rules 1007-1(E), 1007-2, 1009-1(D), 1019-1(C) and 1019-1(L)]; and

c. As required under Local Rule 2081-1, file required payroll and sales tax reports utilizing the Local Form "Debtor's Notice of Filing Payroll and Sales Tax Reports" and file the Local Form "Chapter 11 Case Management Summary".

d. if the debtor is a small business in a case, file the most recent balance sheet, statement of operations, cash flow statement and Federal income tax return or a statement made under penalty of perjury that no balance sheet, statement of operations, or cash flow statement has been prepared and no Federal tax return has been filed. Access to filed tax returns filed by an individual debtor will be restricted as provided under Local Rule 5005-1(A)(2)(c).

3. Within 2 business days of the date of this order, the debtor shall file, as applicable either Bankruptcy Form B 104 "For Individual Chapter 11 Cases:

LF-6 (rev. 03/11/16) Page 2 of 4

The List of Creditors Who Have the 20 Largest Unsecured Claims Against You Who Are Not Insiders" or, for non individual debtors, Bankruptcy Form 204 "For Chapter 11 Cases: The List of Creditors Who Have the 20 Largest Unsecured Claims Against You Who Are Not Insiders" as required by Bankruptcy Rule 1007(d).

4. If the debtor was the moving party, the debtor shall immediately pay a conversion fee of $922.00, if not previously paid. Failure to pay the required fees will result in dismissal of this case.
5. The chapter 7 trustee shall:
   a. forthwith turn over to the debtor in possession, (or chapter 11 trustee, if one has been appointed), all records and property of the estate under the chapter 7 trustee's custody and control; and
   b. within 30 days of the date of this order, file an accounting of all receipts and distributions made, together with a report on administration of the case, as required by 11 U.S.C. §704(9).
6. The debtor shall provide notice to affected parties of the deadline set pursuant to Local Rule 1019-1(J)(1) for filing by a nongovernmental unit a request for payment of an administrative expense.
7. Failure of the debtor to comply with the provisions of this order may result in dismissal of this case without further hearing or notice.
8. If the debtor is an individual and 11 U.S.C. §1141(d)(3) applies, before a discharge can be issued, the debtor must complete a postpetition instructional course concerning personal financial management and file

LF-6 (rev. 03/11/16) Page 3 of 4

Official Form 423 "Certification About a Financial Management Course" (unless the course provider files a certificate of completion on the debtor's behalf).

#

Submitted by:

The party submitting this order shall serve a copy of the signed order on all parties listed below and file with the court a certificate of service conforming with Local Rule 2002-1(F).

Debtor
Attorney for Debtor
Attorney for Trustee (if applicable) Chapter 7
Trustee
U.S. Trustee

[Effective December 1, 1998. Amended effective December 1, 2002; October 17, 2005; April 9, 2006; January 8, 2007; April 5, 2007; June 2, 2008; December 1, 2008; December 1, 2009; November 21, 2012; December 1, 2013; January 28, 2015; December 1, 2015; March 11, 2016.]

LF–7. ORDER CONVERTING CASE UNDER CHAPTER 7 TO CASE UNDER CHAPTER 12

UNITED STATES BANKRUPTCY COURT
SOUTHERN DISTRICT OF FLORIDA
www.flsb.uscourts.gov

In re: Case No.
Chapter 7

_______________ Debtor /

ORDER CONVERTING CASE UNDER CHAPTER 7 TO CASE UNDER CHAPTER 12

The debtor has filed a motion to convert this case to a case under chapter 12 pursuant to 11 U.S.C. §706(a) and served it on required parties in accordance with Local Rule 9013-1(D)(3)(h). Interested parties are deemed to have consented to entry of this order under Local Rule 9013-1(D)(2). Since this case has not been previously converted under 11 U.S.C. §1112, §1208 or §1307, the court finds that the debtor is entitled to be a debtor under chapter 12.

It is **ORDERED** that:

1. This chapter 7 case is converted to a case under chapter 12.
2. The chapter 7 trustee, within 30 days of the date of this order, shall file:
   A. A final report accounting for all receipts and disbursements made in the chapter 7 case; and
   B. A report on the administration of the case pursuant to 11 U.S.C. §704(9).
3. The chapter 7 trustee forthwith shall turn over to the debtor in possession,

LF-7 (rev. 03/11/16) Page 1 of 2

all records and property of the estate remaining in the chapter 7 trustee's custody and control.

4. The debtor shall provide notice to affected parties of the deadline set pursuant to Local Rule 1019-1(J)(1) for filing by a nongovernmental unit a request for payment of an administrative expense.

5. The debtor shall file, within 14 days from the date of this order and if such documents have not already been filed, the statements, schedules and, if required, payment advices or the required statement regarding payment advices. [see Bankruptcy Rule 1007(b), Bankruptcy Rules 1007(b)(1) and 1007(c), Local Rules 1007-1(E), 1007-2, 1009-1(D) and 1019-1(C).

6. The debtor shall file, within 90 days from the date of this order, a chapter 12 plan pursuant to 11 U.S.C. §1221 and Local Rule 3015-1(A).

7. Failure of the debtor to comply with the provisions of this order may result in dismissal of this case without further hearing or notice.

###

Submitted by:

The party submitting this order shall serve a copy of the signed order on all parties listed below and file with the court a certificate of service conforming with Local Rule 2002-1(F).

Debtor
Attorney for Debtor
U.S. Trustee
Chapter 7 Trustee
Chapter 12
Trustee

LF-7 (rev. 03/11/16) Page 2 of 2

[Effective December 1, 1998. Amended effective December 1, 2002; October 17, 2005; April 5, 2007; June 2, 2008; December 1, 2008; December 1, 2009; December 1, 2015; March 11, 2016.]

LF–8A. ORDER CONVERTING CASE UNDER CHAPTER 7 TO CASE UNDER CHAPTER 13 (NEGATIVE NOTICE)

UNITED STATES BANKRUPTCY COURT
SOUTHERN DISTRICT OF FLORIDA
www.flsb.uscourts.gov

In re: **Case No.**
Chapter 7

_______________ **Debtor** /

ORDER CONVERTING CASE UNDER CHAPTER 7
TO CASE UNDER CHAPTER 13 (NEGATIVE NOTICE)

The debtor has filed a motion to convert this case to a case under chapter 13 pursuant to 11 U.S.C. §706(a) and served it on required parties in accordance with local rule 9013-1(D)(3)(h). Interested parties are deemed to have consented to entry of this order under Local Rule 9013-1(D)(2). Since the case has not been previously converted under 11 U.S.C. §1112, §1208 or §1307, the court finds that the debtor is eligible to be a debtor under chapter 13.

It is **ORDERED** that:

1. This chapter 7 case is converted to a case under chapter 13.

LF-8A (rev 03/11/16) Page 1 of 3

all records and property of the estate remaining in the chapter 7 trustee's custody and control.

4. The debtor shall provide notice to affected parties of the deadline set pursuant to Local Rule 1019-1(J)(1) for filing by a nongovernmental unit a request for payment of an administrative expense.

5. The debtor shall file, within 14 days from the date of this order and if such documents have not already been filed, the statements, schedules and, if required, payment advices or the required statement regarding payment advices. [see Bankruptcy Rule 1007(b), Bankruptcy Rules 1007(b)(1) and 1007(c), Local Rules 1007-1(E), 1007-2, 1009-1(D) and 1019-1(C).

6. The debtor shall file, within 90 days from the date of this order, a chapter 12 plan pursuant to 11 U.S.C. §1221 and Local Rule 3015-1(A).

7. Failure of the debtor to comply with the provisions of this order may result in dismissal of this case without further hearing or notice.

###

Submitted by:

The party submitting this order shall serve a copy of the signed order on all parties listed below and file with the court a certificate of service conforming with Local Rule 2002-1(F).

Debtor
Attorney for Debtor
U.S. Trustee
Chapter 7 Trustee
Chapter 12
Trustee

8. The debtor shall commence plan payments to the chapter 13 trustee within 30 days from the date of this order in the manner prescribed by that trustee as required by Local Rule 3070-1(A). If, at the first meeting of creditors, the debtor is not current in plan payments under the plan as originally filed, the chapter 13 trustee may submit a proposed order dismissing the debtor's chapter 13 case and the case may be dismissed without further notice of hearing. Dismissal shall be with prejudice to the debtor filing any bankruptcy case for a period of 180 days from entry of the order of dismissal (see Local Rule 3070-1(C)(1).

9. The debtor shall file, no later than the date of the past payment made as required by the plan or the filing of a motion for entry of a discharge under 11 U.S.C. § 1328(b), "Certification About a Financial Management Course" (Official Form 423) [See Bankruptcy Rules 1007(b)(7)(A) and (c)] (unless the course provider files a certificate of completion on the debtor's behalf).

10. Failure of the debtor to comply with the provisions of this order may result in dismissal of this case without further hearing or notice.

###

Submitted by:

Copies to:
The clerk shall serve a copy of this order on the Debtor, Attorney for Debtor, Chapter 7 Trustee and the Chapter 13 Trustee.

LF-8A (rev 03/11/16) Page 3 of 3

[Effective March 1, 2013. Amended effective December 1, 2013; January 28, 2015; December 1, 2015; March 11, 2016.]

LF–8B. ORDER CONVERTING CASE UNDER CHAPTER 7 TO CASE UNDER CHAPTER 13 (AFTER HEARING)

UNITED STATES BANKRUPTCY COURT
SOUTHERN DISTRICT OF FLORIDA
www.flsb.uscourts.gov

In re: Case No.
Chapter 7

____________________________/
Debtor

ORDER CONVERTING CASE UNDER CHAPTER 7
TO CASE UNDER CHAPTER 13 (AFTER HEARING)

The Court conducted a hearing on ____________ on the debtor's motion to convert this case to a case under chapter 13 pursuant to 11 U.S.C. §706(a). The motion was served on required parties in accordance with local rule 9013-1(D)(3)(h). The debtor is eligible to be a debtor under chapter 13 since the case has not previously been converted under 11 U.S.C. § 1112, § 1208 or § 1307 and the Court otherwise finds that conversion is justified.

It is **ORDERED** that:

1. This chapter 7 case is converted to a case under chapter 13.

LF-8B (rev. 03/30/16) Page 1 of 3

2. The chapter 7 trustee shall file, within 30 days of the date of this order:

   a. a final accounting for all receipts and disbursements made in the chapter 7 case; and

   b. a report on the administration of the case pursuant to 11 U.S.C. §704(9).

3. The chapter 7 trustee forthwith shall turn over to the debtor, all records and property of the estate remaining in the chapter 7 trustee's custody and control.

4. The debtor shall provide notice to affected parties of the deadline set pursuant to Local Rule 1019-1(J)(1) for filing by a nongovernmental unit a request for payment of an administrative expense.

5. The debtor shall file, within 14 days from the date of this order and if such documents have not already been filed, the statements, schedules, Official Form(s) 122C-1 "Chapter 13 Statement of Your Current Monthly Income and Calculation of Commitment Period", 122C-2 "Chapter 13 Calculation of Your Disposable Income", and, if required, payment advices or the required statement regarding payment advices. [see Bankruptcy Rule 1007(b), Bankruptcy Rules 1007(b)(1) and 1007(c), Local Rules 1007-1(E), 1007-2, 1009-1(D), 1019-1(C) and 1019-1(L)]; and

6. The debtor shall file, within 14 days from the date of this order, a chapter 13 plan using the Local Form required by Local Rule 3015-1(B)(1). Amendments to the plan shall be filed by the deadline set forth in Local Rule 3015-2.

7. If the chapter 7 filing fee was waived, the debtor shall pay the full chapter 13 filing fee of $____________ or file a local form application to pay the fee in installments within 14 days after entry of this order.

LF-8B (rev. 03/30/16) Page 2 of 3

8. The debtor shall commence plan payments to the chapter 13 trustee within 30 days from the date of this order in the manner prescribed by that trustee as required by Local Rule 3070-1(A). If, at the first meeting of creditors, the debtor is not current in plan payments under the plan as originally filed, the chapter 13 trustee may submit a proposed order dismissing the debtor's chapter 13 case and the case may be dismissed without further notice of hearing. Dismissal shall be with prejudice to the debtor filing any bankruptcy case for a period of 180 days from entry of the order of dismissal (see Local Rule 3070-1(C)(1).

9. The debtor shall file, no later than the date of the last payment made as required by the plan or the filing of a motion for entry of a discharge under 11 U.S.C. § 1328(b), "Certification About a Financial Management Course" (Official Form 423) [See Bankruptcy Rules 1007(b)(7)(A) and (c)] (unless the course provider files a certificate of completion on the debtor's behalf).

10. Failure of the debtor to comply with the provisions of this order may result in dismissal of this case without further hearing or notice.

###

Submitted by:

Copies to:
The clerk shall serve a copy of this order on the Debtor, Attorney for Debtor, Chapter 7 Trustee and the Chapter 13 Trustee.

LF-8B (rev. 03/30/16) Page 3 of 3

[Effective March 1, 2013. Amended effective December 1, 2013; January 28, 2015; December 1, 2015; March 30, 2016.]

LF–9. ORDER CONVERTING CASE UNDER CHAPTER 11 TO CASE UNDER CHAPTER 7

UNITED STATES BANKRUPTCY COURT
SOUTHERN DISTRICT OF FLORIDA
www.flsb.uscourts.gov

In re: Case No.
Chapter 11

_______________ Debtor /

ORDER CONVERTING CASE UNDER CHAPTER 11 TO CASE UNDER CHAPTER 7

The debtor in possession has filed a motion to convert this case to a case under chapter 7 pursuant to 11 U.S.C. §1112(a). Since the case was not commenced as an involuntary case under chapter 11, nor has the case been converted to a case under chapter 11 other than on the debtor's request, the court finds that the debtor is entitled to be a debtor under chapter 7.

It is **ORDERED** that:

1. This chapter 11 case is converted to a case under chapter 7.

2. If applicable, the debtor shall immediately remit to the clerk of court the $15.00 trustee surcharge fee prescribed by the Judicial Conference of the United States (if

Page 1 of 4

LF-9 (rev. 03/11/16)

not previously paid by the debtor). Failure to pay this fee will result in dismissal of this case.

3. The debtor or the chapter 11 trustee, shall:

   a. Forthwith turn over to the chapter 7 trustee all records and property of the estate under its custody and control as required by Bankruptcy Rule 1019(4);

   b. Within 30 days of the date of this order, file an accounting of all receipts and distributions made. A copy of this report must be served on the U.S. Trustee; and

   c. File, within 14 days of the date of this order, a schedule of unpaid debts incurred after the commencement of the chapter 11 case as required by Bankruptcy Rule 1019(5) and a supplemental matrix and certification in the format required by Local Rule 1019-1(B). The debtor or debtor's attorney is required to provide notice to those creditors pursuant to Local Rule 1019-1(B). Failure to comply may also result in sanctions being imposed by the court. Debts not listed or noticed timely will not be discharged. A copy of this schedule shall be served on the chapter 7 trustee.

4. The debtor shall:

   a. file, within 14 days of the date of this order, the statements and schedules required by Bankruptcy Rule 1019(1)(A) and Bankruptcy Rule 1007(c) and in accordance with Local Rule 1019-1(B).

   b. file, if the debtor is an individual, within 14 days of the date of this order, the Official Bankruptcy Form(s) 122A-1 "Chapter 7 Statement of Your Current Monthly Income and Means-Test Calculation", 122A-1Supp "Chapter 7 Means Test Exemption Attachment", 122A-2 "Chapter 7 Means Test Calculation" as required under Local Rule 1019-1(L), and, if not already filed under chapter 11, payment advices as required by Bankruptcy Rules 1007(b)(1) and 1007(c) and, the certificate and debt repayment plan, if any, required by §521(b), a certification under §109(h)(3) or a request for a determination by the court under 109(h)(4).

   c. file, if the debtor is an individual, within 30 days of the date of this order, a statement of intention with respect to retention or surrender of property securing consumer debts, as required by 11 U.S.C. §521(a)(2)(A) and Bankruptcy Rule 1019(1)(B), and conforming to Official Form 108.

d. file, if the debtor is an individual, within 60 days after the first date set for the meeting of creditors under § 341, "Certification About a Financial Management Course (Official Form 423), [See Bankruptcy Rules 1007(b)(7)(A) and (c)] (unless the course provider files a certificate of completion on the debtor's behalf).

5. Pursuant to Local Rule 2016-1(C)(2), the debtor's attorney, any examiner or trustee appointed by the court, or any other professional person employed under 11 U.S.C. §327 or 1103 shall, file within 90 days after the date of the post-conversion meeting, an application for compensation for outstanding fees and expenses incurred during the chapter 11 administration including an application justifying retention of any retainer received which has not been approved by a prior award. Any retainers received which are not approved will be subject to turnover to the chapter 7 trustee.

The attorney for the debtor in possession, or the chapter 11 trustee (if one was appointed) shall notify all such professionals of this deadline by serving them with a copy of this order.

6. The debtor shall provide notice to affected parties of the deadline set pursuant to Local Rule 1019-1(J)(1) for filing by a nongovernmental unit a request for payment of an administrative expense.

7. If this case is being converted after the confirmation of a plan, the debtor, within 30 days of the date of this order, shall file:

a. A schedule of all property not listed in the final report and account of the debtor in possession or chapter 11 trustee which was acquired after the commencement of the chapter 11 case but before the entry of this conversion order;

b. A schedule of unpaid debts (and a supplemental matrix as described in paragraph 3(c)) not listed in the final report and account of the debtor in possession or chapter 11 trustee, which were incurred after the commencement of the chapter 11 case but before the entry of this conversion order, as required by Bankruptcy Rule 1019(5) and provide notice of the claims deadline as required by Bankruptcy Rule 1019(6) and Local Rule 1019-1(B) and (J); and

c. A schedule of executory contracts and unexpired leases entered into or assumed after the commencement of the chapter 11 case, but before the entry of this conversion order.

8. Failure of the debtor to comply with the provisions of this order may result in dismissal of this case without further hearing or notice.

###

Submitted by:

The party submitting this order shall serve a copy of the signed order on all parties listed below and file with the court a certificate of service conforming with Local Rule 2002-1(F).

Debtor
Attorney for Debtor
U.S. Trustee
Chapter 11 Trustee (if applicable)
Attorney for Chapter 11 Trustee (if applicable)

Page 4 of 4

LF-9 (rev. 03/11/16)

[Effective December 1, 1998. Amended effective December 1, 2002; October 17, 2005; January 11, 2007; June 2, 2008; December 1, 2008; December 1, 2009; December 1, 2013; January 28, 2015; December 1, 2015; March 11, 2016.]

LF-10. DECLARATION REGARDING PAYMENT ADVICES

UNITED STATES BANKRUPTCY COURT
SOUTHERN DISTRICT OF FLORIDA
www.flsb.uscourts.gov

In re: Case No.
Chapter

_______________ Debtor _______ /

DECLARATION REGARDING PAYMENT ADVICES

Debtor:

_____ Copies of all payment advices, pay stubs or other evidence of payment received by the debtor from any employer within 60 days prior to the filing of the bankruptcy petition are attached. (Note: If you worked some, but not all of the 60 days prior, attach copies of any and all received and provide explanation that you didn't work the full 60 days. ____)

_____ Copies of all payment advices **are not** attached because the debtor had no income from any employer during the 60 days prior to filing the bankruptcy petition.

_____ Copies of all payment advices **are not** attached because the debtor:
__receives disability payments
__is unemployed and does not receive unemployment compensation
__receives Social Security payments
__receives a pension
__does not work outside the home
__is self employed and does not receive payment advices

_____ None of the statements above apply, however, the debtor is unable to timely provide some or all copies of payment advices or other evidence of payment received
Explain:____

Joint Debtor (if applicable):

_____ Copies of payment advices, pay stubs or other evidence of payment received by the joint debtor from any employer within 60 days prior to the filing of the bankruptcy petition are attached. (Note: If you worked some, but not all of the 60 days prior, attach copies of any and all received and provide explanation that you didn't work the full 60 days. ____)

_____ Copies of payment advices **are not** attached because the joint debtor had no income from any employer during the 60 days prior to filing the bankruptcy petition.

_____ Copies of payment advices **are not** attached because the joint debtor:
____receives disability payments
____is unemployed and does not receive unemployment compensation
____receives Social Security payments
____receives a pension
____does not work outside the home
____is self employed and does not receive payment advices

_____ None of the statements above apply, however, the joint debtor is unable to timely provide some or all copies of payment advices or other evidence of payment received
Explain: ____

NOTE: When submitting copies of evidence of payment such as pay stubs or payment advices, it is your responsibility to redact (blackout) any social security numbers, names of minor children, dates of birth or financial account numbers before attaching for filing with the court. See Local Rule 5005-1(A)(2).

______________________________ Date:______________
Signature of Attorney or Debtor

______________________________ Date:______________
Signature of Joint Debtor, if applicable

LF-10 (rev. 12/01/09)

[Effective December 1, 1998. Amended effective February 14, 2000; December 1, 2002; October 17, 2005; June 2, 2008; December 1, 2009.]

LF–12. ORDER CONVERTING CASE UNDER CHAPTER 13 TO CASE UNDER CHAPTER 7

UNITED STATES BANKRUPTCY COURT
SOUTHERN DISTRICT OF FLORIDA
www.flsb.uscourts.gov

In re: Case No.
Chapter

_______________ Debtor _______/

ORDER CONVERTING CASE UNDER CHAPTER 13 TO CASE UNDER CHAPTER 7

( ) At a hearing held in this case on ____________, the trustee recommended and the debtor consented to conversion of this case to a case under chapter 7.

( ) A party in interest other than the debtor has filed a motion to convert this case to a case under chapter 7 pursuant to 11 U.S.C. §1307(c). A hearing was held on ____________ at which time the court heard from all interested parties.

It is **ORDERED** that:

1. This case is converted to a case under chapter 7.

2. The chapter 13 trustee, within 30 days of the date of this order, shall file an

Page 1 of 4

LF-12 (rev. 03/11/16)

accounting of all receipts and distributions made, and list any pending obligations incurred under the plan. A copy of the report shall be served on the U.S. trustee.

3. The debtor, within 14 days of the date of this order, shall file a schedule of unpaid debts incurred after the commencement of the chapter 13 case as required by Bankruptcy Rule 1019(5) and Local Rule 1019-1(B). The schedule must be accompanied by a matrix of creditors as required by the "Clerk's Instructions for Preparing, Submitting and Obtaining Service Matrices". The debtor or debtor's attorney is required to provide notice to those creditors pursuant to Local Rule 1019-1(B). Failure to comply may also result in sanctions being imposed by the court. Debts not listed or noticed timely will not be discharged. A copy of this schedule shall be served on the chapter 7 trustee.

4. The chapter 13 trustee shall, within 14 days from the date of this order, turn over to the chapter 7 trustee all records of the estate remaining in the chapter 13 trustee's custody and control, as required by Bankruptcy Rule 1019(4).

5. The chapter 13 trustee shall dispose of funds in the trustee's possession in accordance with Local Rule 1019-1(E), unless otherwise ordered by the court.

6. The debtor shall file, within 14 days of the date of this order:

   a. the statements and schedules required by Bankruptcy Rules 1007(c) and 1019(1)(A) in accordance with Local Rules 1007-2 and 1009-1(E), if such documents have not already been filed.

   b. the Official Form(s) 122A-1 "Chapter 7 Statement of Your Current Monthly Income and Means-Test Calculation", 122A-1Supp "Chapter 7 Means Test Exemption Attachment, 122A-2 Chapter 7 Means Test Calculation, required under Local Rule 1019-1(L);

c. payment advices as required by Bankruptcy Rules 1007(b)(1) and 1007(c) and Local Rule 1007-1(F); and

d. if not already filed, the certificate and debt repayment plan, if any, required by §521(b), a certification under §109(h)(3) or a request for a determination by the court under §109(h)(4).

7. The debtor shall file, within 30 days of the date of this order, a statement of intention with respect to retention or surrender of property securing consumer debts, as required by 11 U.S.C. §521(a)(2)(A) and Bankruptcy Rule 1019(1)(B), and conforming to Official Form 108.

8. The debtor shall file, within 60 days after the first date set for the meeting of creditors under § 341, "Certification About a Financial Management Course" (Official Form 423) [See Bankruptcy Rules 1007(b)(7)(A) and (c)] (unless the course provider files a certificate of completion on the debtor's behalf).

9. If this case is being converted after the confirmation of a plan, the debtor shall file, within 30 days of the date of this order:

a. A schedule of all property not listed in the final report and account of the chapter 13 trustee which was acquired after the commencement of the chapter 13 case but before the entry of this conversion order;

b. A schedule of unpaid debts (and matrix as described in paragraph 3) not listed in the final report and account of the chapter 13 trustee which were incurred after the commencement of the chapter 13 case but before the entry of this conversion order, as required by Bankruptcy Rule 1019(5) and provide notice of claims deadline as required by Bankruptcy Rule 1019(6) and Local Rule 1019-1(B); and

c. A schedule of executory contracts and unexpired leases entered into or assumed after the commencement of the chapter 13 case but before the entry of this conversion order.

10. The debtor shall provide notice to affected parties of the deadline set pursuant to Local Rule 1019-1(J)(1) for filing by a nongovernmental unit a request for payment of an administrative expense.

11. If the debtor had been granted permission to pay the chapter 13 filing fee in installments and the debtor seeks waiver of the balance of the filing fee due, the debtor must file the waiver application prior to the next installment payment date to avoid dismissal of the case for nonpayment.

12. Failure of the debtor to comply with the provisions of this order may result in dismissal of this case without further hearing or notice.

###

Submitted by:

The party submitting this order shall serve a copy of the signed order on all parties listed below and file with the court a certificate of service conforming with Local Rule 2002-1(F).

Debtor
Attorney for Debtor
Chapter 13 Trustee
U.S. Trustee

Page 4 of 4

LF-12 (rev. 03/11/16)

[Effective December 1, 1998. Amended effective December 1, 2002; February 12, 2004; October 17, 2005; January 11, 2007; June 2, 2008; December 1, 2008; December 1, 2009; December 1, 2013; January 28, 2015; December 1, 2015; March 11, 2016.]

LF-13. REQUEST FOR COMPACT DISC (CD) OF AUDIO RECORDING OF COURT PROCEEDING

UNITED STATES BANKRUPTCY COURT
SOUTHERN DISTRICT OF FLORIDA
www.flsb.uscourts.gov

Request for Compact Disc (CD) of Audio Recording of Court Proceeding

Form may be submitted at any clerk's office location, U.S. mail, or email to: Audio_Recording_Request@flsb.uscourts.gov
[**NOTE:** All requests for 341 meeting recordings should be addressed to the Office of the U.S. Trustee.]

Case Number:__________ Adversary Number: __________ Judge: __________

Date of Hearing or Trial: __________ Time of Hearing or Trial: __________

Debtor(s) Name:__________

Quantity		Rate
	Audio CD This format will play on standard pc media players and on most CD-R and CD-RW compatible players. This option should be selected if the audio will be played in a vehicle or on a personal CD player. **Note:** This format is compatible with Apple or Mac computers.	$31.00* each Payable to: Clerk, U.S. Court

*See Bankruptcy Court Miscellaneous Fee Schedule

By submitting this request, it is understood that:

- A separate order must be placed for each hearing requested.
- All requests will be completed within two business days following receipt of the request.
- The requestor will be contacted when the CD is available for pick up at the clerk's intake office.
- CD of audio recording will remain available for a period of 14 days.
- Payment is due at time of pick up.
- If requesting the CD to be mailed, payment must be made in advance and a self-addressed, stamped padded envelope must be provided to the clerk.

Today's Date: __________ ☐ Pickup CD from Clerk's Office ☐ Mail CD

Print Your Name:

Mailing Address: __________

Email Address: __________ Telephone No.: __________

To be completed by clerk:

CD Completion Date: __________ *By:* __________

Date Requestor Contacted: __________ *Date CD Picked Up/Mailed:* __________

LF-13 (rev. 12/01/16)

[Effective October 1, 2013. Amended effective June 27, 2016; December 1, 2016.]

LF-14. NOTICE OF RULE 2004 EXAMINATION

UNITED STATES BANKRUPTCY COURT
SOUTHERN DISTRICT OF FLORIDA
www.flsb.uscourts.gov

In re: Case No.
Chapter

_______________ Debtor /

NOTICE OF RULE 2004 EXAMINATION

_______________, by the undersigned attorney, will examine _______________ under oath on _____ at _____ m. at _______________.
The examination may continue from day to day until completed. If the examinee receives this notice less than 14 days prior to the scheduled examination date, the examination will be rescheduled upon timely request to a mutually agreeable time.

The examination is pursuant to Bankruptcy Rule 2004 and Local Rule 2004-1, and will be recorded by this method: _______________. The scope of the examination shall be as described in Bankruptcy Rule 2004.

Pursuant to Local Rule 2004-1 no order shall be necessary. [If the examination is of a witness other than the debtor, the Local Form "Subpoena for Rule 2004 Examination" is included with this notice.]

☐ Production: [The examinee or your representatives, must also bring with you to the examination the documents, electronically stored information, or objects described on the attached schedule (or if the examination is of a witness other than the debtor, on the attached subpoena), and must permit inspection, copying, testing, or sampling of the materials.]

I CERTIFY that a true copy of this notice was filed with the court and served on the examinee, attorney for examinee, the debtor, the attorney for the debtor and the trustee [indicate name of party served, manner of service and date of service].

____
signature

____
print name

____
attorney for

____
address

____
phone

____
Attorney Bar No.

LF-14 (rev. 12/01/15)

[Effective December 1, 1998. Amended effective February 14, 2000; December 1, 2002; June 2, 2008; December 1, 2009; December 1, 2013; December 1, 2015.]

LF–15. DEBTOR IN POSSESSION'S APPLICATION FOR EMPLOYMENT OF ATTORNEY

UNITED STATES BANKRUPTCY COURT
SOUTHERN DISTRICT OF FLORIDA
www.flsb.uscourts.gov

In re: Case No.
Chapter 11

_______________ Debtor /

DEBTOR IN POSSESSION'S APPLICATION FOR EMPLOYMENT OF ATTORNEY

____________________, debtor in possession respectfully requests an order of the court authorizing the employment of ____________________ of the law firm of ________________________to represent the debtor in this case and states:

1. On ______________, the debtor filed a voluntary petition under chapter 11 of the United States Bankruptcy Code.

2. The debtor desires to employ ________________________________ as attorney(s) in this case.

3. The debtor believes that the attorney is qualified to practice in this court and is qualified to advise the debtor on its relations with, and responsibilities to, the creditors and other interested parties.

4. The professional services the attorney will render are summarized as follows:

(a) To give advice to the debtor with respect to its powers and duties as a debtor in possession and the continued management of its business operations;

(b) To advise the debtor with respect to its responsibilities in complying with the U.S. Trustee's Operating Guidelines and Reporting Requirements and with the rules of the court;

(c) To prepare motions, pleadings, orders, applications, adversary proceedings, and other legal documents necessary in the administration of the case;

(d) To protect the interest of the debtor in all matters pending before the court;

(e) To represent the debtor in negotiation with its creditors in the preparation of a plan.

5. To the best of the debtor's knowledge, neither said attorney nor said law firm have any connection with the creditors or other parties in interest or their respective attorneys. Neither said attorney nor said law firm represent any interest adverse to the debtor.

6. Attached to this motion is the proposed attorney's affidavit demonstrating [name of attorney and law firm] are disinterested as required by 11 U.S.C. §327(a) and a verified statement as required under Bankruptcy Rule 2014.

The debtor respectfully requests an order authorizing retention of [name of attorney and law firm] on a general retainer, pursuant to 11 U.S.C. §§327 and 330.

I CERTIFY that a true copy of this application was mailed on ___________ to the parties indicated below.

____
signature

____
print name and title

____
address

____
phone

Attach or file separately a Local Rule 2002-1(F) certificate of service reflecting manner and date of service on the following parties.

Debtor
U.S. trustee
Attorney for Creditor's Committee (or
if none 20 largest unsecured creditors)
All Appearances

LF-15 (rev. 12/01/09)

[Effective December 1, 1998. Amended effective February 14, 2000; December 1, 2002; June 2, 2008; December 1, 2009.]

LF–16. TRUSTEE'S APPLICATION FOR EMPLOYMENT OF ATTORNEY

UNITED STATES BANKRUPTCY COURT
SOUTHERN DISTRICT OF FLORIDA
www.flsb.uscourts.gov

In re: Case No.
Chapter

_______________ Debtor _____/

TRUSTEE'S APPLICATION FOR EMPLOYMENT OF ATTORNEY

Trustee, ______________________, respectfully requests an order of the court authorizing the employment of ______________________ of the law firm of ______________________ to represent the trustee in this case and states:

1. It is necessary that the trustee employ an attorney to represent the trustee in this case to perform ordinary and necessary legal services required in the administration of the estate.

2. The attorney does not hold or represent any interest adverse to the estate and the trustee believes that the employment of this attorney would be in the best interest of the estate.

3. Attached to this motion is the proposed attorney's affidavit demonstrating [name of attorney and law firm] are disinterested as required by 11 U.S.C. §327(a) and a verified statement as required under Bankruptcy Rule 2014.

4. The attorney has agreed to be compensated in accordance with 11 U.S.C. §330.

5. The trustee believes that the attorney is qualified to practice in the Bankruptcy Court and is qualified to advise the trustee on its relations with and responsibilities to the

debtor, creditors and other parties.

The trustee respectfully requests an Order authorizing the employment of [name of attorney and law firm] to represent the trustee on a general retainer, pursuant to 11 U.S.C. §§327 and 330.

(Trustee)

(Print Name)

(Address)

(Phone)

Attach or file separately a Local Rule 2002-1(F) certificate of service reflecting manner and date of service on all affected parties including the following:

Debtor
Trustee
Attorney for Debtor
U.S. Trustee
All appearances

LF-16 (rev. 12/01/09)

[Effective December 1, 1998. Amended effective December 1, 2002; June 2, 2008; December 1, 2009.]

LF-17. AFFIDAVIT OF PROPOSED ATTORNEY FOR DEBTOR IN POSSESSION

UNITED STATES BANKRUPTCY COURT
SOUTHERN DISTRICT OF FLORIDA
www.flsb.uscourts.gov

In re: Case No.
Chapter 11

__________ Debtor ______/

AFFIDAVIT OF PROPOSED ATTORNEY FOR DEBTOR IN POSSESSION

STATE OF)
) ss
COUNTY OF)

________________________________, being duly sworn, says:

1. I am [an attorney admitted to practice in the State of Florida, the United States District Court for the Southern District of Florida and qualified to practice in the U.S. Bankruptcy Court for the Southern District of Florida] [appearing pro hac vice pursuant to Local Rule 2090-1(C)(2)].

2. I am employed by the law firm of ______________________with offices located at____.

3. Neither I nor the firm represent any interest adverse to the debtor, or the estate, and we are disinterested persons as required by 11 U.S.C. §327(a).

4. (Disclose any connections with the debtor, creditors, any other party in interest, their respective attorneys and accountants, the U.S. Trustee, or any person employed in the Office of the U.S. Trustee as required by Bankruptcy Rule 2014.)

5. Except for the continuing representation of the debtor, neither I nor the firm has or will represent any other entity in connection with this case and neither I nor the firm will accept any fee from any other party or parties in this case, except the debtor in possession.

6. (State any additional exceptions including any prepetition fees owed and whether those fees are being waived.)

FURTHER AFFIANT SAYETH NAUGHT.

____
Signature
____
(Print Attorney's name here)

Sworn to and Subscribed before
on ____________________

____
Notary Public, State of

My Commission Expires:

Copies to:
All parties served with application for employment.

LF-17 (rev. 12/01/16)

[Effective December 1, 1998. Amended effective February 14, 2000; December 1, 2002; June 2, 2008; December 1, 2009; December 1, 2016.]

LF-18. AFFIDAVIT OF PROPOSED ATTORNEY FOR TRUSTEE

UNITED STATES BANKRUPTCY COURT
SOUTHERN DISTRICT OF FLORIDA
www.flsb.uscourts.gov

In re: Case No.
Chapter

_________ Debtor _______/

AFFIDAVIT OF PROPOSED ATTORNEY FOR TRUSTEE

STATE OF)
) SS:
COUNTY OF)

________________________________, being duly sworn, says:

1. I am [an attorney admitted to practice in the State of Florida, the United States District Court for the Southern District of Florida and am qualified to practice in the U.S. Bankruptcy Court for the Southern District of Florida] [appearing pro hac vice pursuant to Local Rule 2090-1(C)(2)].

2. I am employed by the law firm of ________________________, with offices located at________________________________.

3. Neither I nor the firm hold or represent any interest adverse to the estate, and we are disinterested persons as required by 11 U.S.C. §327(a).

4. (Disclose any connections with the debtor, creditors, any other party in interest, their respective attorneys and accountants, the U.S. Trustee, or any person employed in the office of the U.S. Trustee as required by Bankruptcy Rule 2014.)

5. (State any additional exceptions.)

FURTHER AFFIANT SAYETH NAUGHT.

____
Signature

____
(Print Attorney's name here)

Sworn and Subscribed before me
on _______________.

____
Notary Public, State of

My Commission Expires:

Copies to:
All parties served with application for employment

LF-18 (rev. 12/01/16)

[Effective December 1, 1998. Amended effective February 14, 2000; December 1, 2002; June 2, 2008; December 1, 2009; December 1, 2016.]

LF–19. ORDER APPROVING EMPLOYMENT OF DEBTOR IN POSSESSION'S ATTORNEY

UNITED STATES BANKRUPTCY COURT
SOUTHERN DISTRICT OF FLORIDA
www.flsb.uscourts.gov

In re: Case No.
Chapter 11

_______________ Debtor /

ORDER APPROVING EMPLOYMENT OF DEBTOR IN POSSESSION'S ATTORNEY

THIS CAUSE came on before the court upon the application of debtor in possession for authority to retain an attorney, and upon the affidavit of [name of attorney and law firm]. Upon the representations that [attorney] is [duly qualified under Local Rule 2090-1(A) to practice in this court] [admitted to appear pro hac vice pursuant to Local Rule 2090-1(C)(2)], that [name of attorney and law firm] hold no interest adverse to the estate in the matters upon which they are engaged, that [name of attorney and law firm] are disinterested persons as required by 11 U.S.C. §327(a), and have disclosed any

LF-19 (rev. 12/01/16) Page 1 of 2

connections with parties set forth in Bankruptcy Rule 2014, and that their employment is necessary and would be in the best interest of the estate, it is

ORDERED that the debtor in possession is authorized to retain ________________ of the law firm of ________________________________, on a general retainer, pursuant to 11 U.S.C. §§327 and 330.

###

Submitted by:

The party submitting this order shall serve a copy of the signed order on all parties listed below and file with the court a certificate of service conforming with Local Rule 2002-1(F).

Debtor
Attorney for Debtor
U.S. Trustee
Attorney for Creditor's Committee or
if none, 20 largest unsecured creditors
All appearances

LF-19 (rev. 12/01/16) Page 2 of 2

[Effective December 1, 1998. Amended effective December 1, 2002; October 17, 2005; June 2, 2008; December 1, 2009; December 1, 2016.]

LF–20. ORDER APPROVING EMPLOYMENT OF TRUSTEE'S ATTORNEY

UNITED STATES BANKRUPTCY COURT
SOUTHERN DISTRICT OF FLORIDA
www.flsb.uscourts.gov

In re: Case No.
Chapter

______________ Debtor __________/

ORDER APPROVING EMPLOYMENT OF TRUSTEE'S ATTORNEY

THIS CAUSE came on before the court upon the Trustee's Application for Employment of __________________ of the law firm of ______________________ in this case. Upon the representations that ___[Name of attorney]___ is [duly qualified to practice in this court pursuant to Local Rule 2090-1(A)] [appearing pro hac vice pursuant to Local Rule 2090-1(C)(2)], that ___[Name of attorney and law firm]___ hold no interest adverse to the estate in the matters upon which they are engaged, that ___[Name of attorney and law firm]___ are disinterested persons as required by 11 U.S.C §327(a), and have

LF-20 (rev. 12/01/16) Page 1 of 2

disclosed any connections with parties set forth in Bankruptcy Rule 2014, and that their employment is necessary and would be in the best interests of the estate, it is

ORDERED that the trustee is authorized to employ ______________________ of the law firm of __________________________________ as attorney for the trustee, on a general retainer, pursuant to 11 U.S.C. §§327 and 330.

###

Submitted by:

The party submitting this order shall serve a copy of the signed order on all parties listed below and file with the court a certificate of service conforming with Local Rule 2002-1(F).

LF-20 (rev. 12/01/16) Page 2 of 2

[Effective December 1, 1998. Amended effective December 1, 2002; October 17, 2005; June 2, 2008; December 1, 2009; December 1, 2016.]

LF-21. APPLICATION FOR APPROVAL OF EMPLOYMENT OF AUCTIONEER

UNITED STATES BANKRUPTCY COURT
SOUTHERN DISTRICT OF FLORIDA
www.flsb.uscourts.gov

In re: Case No.
Chapter

_______________ Debtor ____/

APPLICATION FOR APPROVAL OF EMPLOYMENT OF AUCTIONEER

Trustee [or Debtor in Possession] ("Trustee"), pursuant to 11 U.S.C. §327 and Local Rule 6005-1 applies for entry of an order approving the retention of [Name of Auctioneer] ("Auctioneer"), subject to the terms and conditions delineated herein, relative to a proposed auction of [general description of property] (the "Property"), and states:

1. Trustee believes that the highest and best value for the Property will be generated via auction and that an auction is in the best interest of the estate.

2. Auctioneer was selected after consideration of competitive bids obtained from at least one other qualified auctioneer. The terms of the rejected bids are available from the trustee upon request of the court or interested parties. [In the alternative, state reason why it was not necessary or appropriate to seek competitive bids.]

3. Trustee believes that retention of Auctioneer is in the best interest of the estate.

4. Trustee believes that Auctioneer is disinterested as defined in the Bankruptcy Code pursuant to the Affidavit of Auctioneer attached hereto as Exhibit **"A"**.

5. Auctioneer is licensed and bonded as an auctioneer and is authorized to conduct auctions in the State of Florida pursuant to Florida Statutes §468.381 <u>et seq</u> or §468.387 for out-of-state auctioneers and Local Rule 6005-1(B) and is covered by the

Florida Auctioneer Recovery Fund as required by Florida Statute 468.392. In addition, Auctioneer has posted a blanket bond in the amount of ______________ (or a case specific bond in the amount of ______________.) The blanket or case specific fiduciary and faithful performance bond or surety bond was issued by a surety company approved by the Department of the Treasury and the amount indicated is not less than the maximum expected proceeds of any proposed auction or combination of auctions, if a blanket bond. The bond is in favor of the United States of America and the original bond has been forwarded to the United States trustee. True copies of the appropriate licenses and bonds are attached to the Affidavit of Auctioneer attached hereto as Exhibit **"A"**.

6. The maximum amount of costs and expenses to be expended by and reimbursed to Auctioneer is ________ [for items including ______________], as indicated on the budget attached as Exhibit **"B"**.

7. Compensation of Auctioneer will be based on _______ percentage of gross revenue, (_______ % buyers premium), (flat fee of $__________), (guaranteed return of $__________), or [any other reasonable method described in sufficient detail].

8. Trustee requests approval of this Application after notice and hearing [or trustee submits that this Application should be approved without notice or hearing because (describe circumstances, e.g. amounts involved and/or time constraints, etc.)].

9. Trustee will serve copies of the Order granting this motion together with the sale notice required by Bankruptcy Rule 6004 and Bankruptcy Rule 2002(a)(2) and (c)(1) Bankruptcy Rule and Local Rule 6005-1(E).

10. Upon completion of the auction, the Auctioneer will file with the court a report summarizing the results of the auction and stating the fees and expenses which will be paid to Auctioneer in accordance with the Order approving the retention. The report shall be

served only on the U.S. Trustee, the trustee and any other interested party who specifically requests a copy. The fees and expenses will be paid without the necessity of further notice or hearing unless any party in interest files an objection within 14 days from the filing of the report with the court and service of the report on the above parties.

WHEREFORE, trustee moves for the entry of an order granting this Application, approving the retention and compensation of Auctioneer upon the terms and conditions stated herein.

I HEREBY CERTIFY that a true and correct copy of the foregoing APPLICATION FOR APPROVAL OF EMPLOYMENT OF AUCTIONEER was served upon the U.S. Trustee [all creditors] [twenty largest unsecured creditors] [all committees] [or otherwise per order of court], on ____________________

____
signature

____
print name

____
attorney for

____
address

____
phone

____
Florida Bar No.

LF-21 (rev. 12/01/09)

[Effective December 1, 1998. Amended effective February 15, 2000; December 1, 2002; June 2, 2008; December 1, 2009.]

LF–22. AFFIDAVIT OF AUCTIONEER

UNITED STATES BANKRUPTCY COURT
SOUTHERN DISTRICT OF FLORIDA
www.flsb.uscourts.gov

In re: Case No.
Chapter

______Debtor /

AFFIDAVIT OF AUCTIONEER

STATE OF FLORIDA)
) ss.
COUNTY OF__________)

BEFORE ME, the undersigned authority, this date personally appeared ______________________ who being first duly sworn under oath, deposes and states:

1. That I am an officer of [Auctioneer Co.], and am authorized to make this declaration on behalf of the corporation in accordance with Bankruptcy Rule 2014 and Local Rule 6005-1.

2. That neither I nor [Auctioneer Co.] nor any of its officers or directors have any connection to the debtor, the debtor's estate, the trustee [or debtor in possession] ("trustee") or the U.S. Trustee, and that same are disinterested persons within the meaning of 11 U.S.C. §327(a).

3. That [Auctioneer Co.] is duly licensed as an auctioneer and covered by the Florida Auctioneer Recovery Fund and is authorized to conduct auctions in the State of Florida pursuant to Florida Statutes §468.381 et seq or §468.387 for out-of-state auctioneers and Local Rule 6005-1(B). True copies of said license and bond are attached hereto.

EXHIBIT A

4. That in addition to the foregoing, I have attached hereto a copy of a Fiduciary and Faithful Performance (or Surety) Bond in the amount of ___________ [an amount greater than the revenues expected to be generated by the auction of the Property] a true copy of which is attached hereto. [Alternatively, I have attached an annual blanket bond in the amount of ___________, which is an amount greater than the revenues expected to be generated by the auction of the Property]. The bonds are issued by a surety company approved by the Department of the Treasury and in favor of the United States of America.

5. That I have read the application of the trustee regarding the retention and compensation of [Auctioneer Co.] and agree to be bound by the terms and conditions represented therein.

6. The property subject to this proposed auction will not be sold together with any non-bankruptcy property.

7. That I further understand that the court, in its discretion, may alter the terms and conditions of employment and compensation as it deems appropriate.

By: ______________________________
(Signature)

____
(Print Name)

SWORN TO AND SUBSCRIBED before me

on ____________________.

____
NOTARY PUBLIC, State of Florida at Large

My Commission Expires:

EXHIBIT A

LF-22 (rev. 12/01/09)

[Effective December 1, 1998. Amended effective February 14, 2000; December 1, 2002; June 2, 2008; December 1, 2009.]

LF-23. ORDER APPROVING EMPLOYMENT OF AUCTIONEER

UNITED STATES BANKRUPTCY COURT
SOUTHERN DISTRICT OF FLORIDA
www.flsb.uscourts.gov

In re: Case No.
Chapter

________________ Debtor ____________/

ORDER APPROVING EMPLOYMENT OF AUCTIONEER

THIS CAUSE having come before the court upon the application of the trustee [debtor in possession] ("trustee"), pursuant to 11 U.S.C. §327, Bankruptcy Rule 2014, and Local Rule 6005-1, seeking the entry of an order approving the retention of [name of auctioneer] _____, ("Auctioneer") subject to the terms and conditions delineated therein, relative to a potential auction of [general description of property] ("Property"). The application was considered ex parte and the court finds that no notice or hearing was necessary under the circumstances [or the application was heard by the court on

____________________]. The court having considered the record finds good cause to approve the retention and compensation of Auctioneer pursuant to the terms and conditions stated in the application. It is

ORDERED that the application is **GRANTED**, as follows:

1. The retention of Auctioneer is **APPROVED** with compensation to be based upon [describe method of compensation delineated in application]. The maximum amount of costs and expenses to be expended by and reimbursed to the Auctioneer is ________.

2. Auctioneer is disinterested as defined in the Bankruptcy Code pursuant to the Affidavit of Auctioneer attached to the Application. The Auctioneer and trustee have certified that (i) Auctioneer is licensed as an auctioneer and covered by the Florida Auctioneer Recovery Fund and is authorized to conduct auctions in the State of Florida pursuant to Florida Statutes §468.381 et seq or 468.387 for out-of-state auctioneer; (ii) Auctioneer has posted a Fiduciary and Faithful Performance (Surety) Bond in the amount of $ _____________ [an amount greater than the revenues expected to be generated by the auction of the Property]; [Alternatively, Auctioneer has posted an annual blanket bond in the amount of________________, which is greater than the revenues expected to be generated by the auction of the Property]; (iii) The bonds are issued by a surety company approved by the Department of the Treasury and in favor of the United States of America; and (iv) True copies of the license and bond were attached to the Application.

3. Trustee shall serve this order on the U.S. Trustee and all creditors together with service of the notice pursuant to Bankruptcy Rules 2002(a)(2), 2002(c)(1), and 6004.

4. Upon completion of the auction, Auctioneer shall file with the court a report summarizing the results of the auction and stating the fees and expenses which will be paid to the Auctioneer in accordance with this order. The report shall be served only on the U.S.

Trustee, the trustee and any other party who specifically requests a copy. The fees and expenses may be paid without the necessity of further notice or hearing unless a party in interest files an objection within 14 days from the filing of the report with the court and service of the report on the parties set forth above.

###

Submitted by:

The party submitting this order shall serve a copy of the signed order on all required parties and file with the court a certificate of service conforming with Local Rule 2002-1(F).

LF-23 (rev. 12/01/09)

[Effective December 1, 1998. Amended effective December 1, 2002; October 17, 2005; June 2, 2008; December 1, 2009.]

LF–24. OBJECTION TO CLAIM

UNITED STATES BANKRUPTCY COURT
SOUTHERN DISTRICT OF FLORIDA
www.flsb.uscourts.gov

In re: ______________________ Case No.
Chapter

______________________ Debtor /

OBJECTION TO CLAIM

**IMPORTANT NOTICE TO CREDITOR:
THIS IS AN OBJECTION TO YOUR CLAIM**

This objection seeks either to disallow or reduce the amount or change the priority status of the claim filed by you or on your behalf. Please read this objection carefully to identify which claim is objected to and what disposition of your claim is recommended.

If you disagree with the objection or the recommended treatment, you must file a written response WITHIN 30 DAYS from the date of service of this objection, explaining why your claim should be allowed as presently filed, and you must serve a copy to the undersigned [attorney][trustee] OR YOUR CLAIM MAY BE DISPOSED OF IN ACCORDANCE WITH THE RECOMMENDATION IN THIS OBJECTION.

If your entire claim is objected to and this is a chapter 11 case, you will not have the right to vote to accept or reject any proposed plan of reorganization until the objection is resolved, unless you request an order pursuant to Bankruptcy Rule 3018(a) temporarily allowing your claim for voting purposes.

The written response must contain the case name, case number, and must be filed with the Clerk of the United States Bankruptcy Court.

Pursuant to Bankruptcy Rule 3007 and Local Rule 3007-1, the [trustee][debtor(s)] object(s) to the following claim filed in this case *:

Claim No.	Name of Claimant	Amount of Claim	Basis for Objection and Recommended Disposition
____	____________	______	______________________
____	____________	______	______________________
____	____________	______	______________________
____	____________	______	______________________
____	____________	______	______________________

*Notwithstanding the requirements of Bankruptcy Rule 3007, up to five objections to claim may be included in one pleading. (See Local Rule 3007-1(C).)

____
Name of Attorney

____
Signature

____
[Attorney for]

____
Address

____
Telephone

____
Bar Number and State

The party filing this objection to claim must file a certificate of service in accordance with Local Rule 2002-1(F).

LF-24 (rev. 12/01/09)

[Effective December 1, 1998. Amended effective May 8, 2001; December 1, 2002; February 15, 2005; January 8, 2007; June 2, 2008; December 1, 2009.]

LF–25. ORDER SUSTAINING OBJECTION TO CLAIM

UNITED STATES BANKRUPTCY COURT
SOUTHERN DISTRICT OF FLORIDA
www.flsb.uscourts.gov

In re: Case No.
Chapter

________________ Debtor ______ /

ORDER SUSTAINING ________'s OBJECTION TO CLAIM

This matter having been considered without hearing upon the [Trustee's][Debtor's] Objection to Claim[s] [DE #____], and the objector by submitting this form order having represented that the objection was served on the parties listed below, that the 30-day response time provided by Local Rule 3007-1(D) has expired, that no one listed below has filed, or served on the objector, a response to the objection, and that the relief to be granted in this order is the identical relief requested in the objection, and this court having considered the basis for the objection to the claim, it is

ORDERED that [Trustee's][Debtor's] objection[s] to the following claim[s] is [are] sustained:

Claim holder Claim No. Disposition

LF-25 (rev. 12/01/15) Page 1 of 2

[Indicate claim holder name and claim number and insert disposition of the claim, using the statements below, as applicable].* and the claim is stricken [without prejudice to Claimant to pursue its interest in the collateral]; or as duplicative; Claim #_____ is stricken and Claim #_____ is allowed; or

as a late filed claim and subject to further consideration upon the determination that sufficient funds exist to pay the claim in its order of priority;

and the claim shall be classified as a ______ claim in the amount of $____.

###

Submitted by:

The party submitting the order shall serve a copy of the signed order on all required parties and file with the court a certificate of service conforming with Local Rule 2002-1(F).

LF-25 (rev. 12/01/15) Page 2 of 2

[Effective December 1, 1998. Amended effective December 1, 2002; October 17, 2005; June 2, 2008; December 1, 2009; August 28, 2013; December 1, 2015.]

LF–26. NOTICE OF DEPOSIT OF FUNDS WITH THE U.S. BANKRUPTCY COURT CLERK

UNITED STATES BANKRUPTCY COURT
SOUTHERN DISTRICT OF FLORIDA
www.flsb.uscourts.gov

In re: Case No.
Chapter

________________ Debtor /

NOTICE OF DEPOSIT OF FUNDS WITH THE U.S. BANKRUPTCY COURT CLERK

Notice is given that:

( ) The trustee has a balance of $________ remaining in the trustee's account which represents unpresented checks drawn and mailed to entities pursuant to the final distribution under U.S.C. §§726, 1226 or 1326 in a case under chapter 7, 12 or 13. The trustee has made a good faith effort to verify the correct mailing addresses for said entities and deliver the funds before presenting this notice. More than sufficient time has passed for these checks to be presented for payment; or

( ) The trustee has a balance of $________ remaining in the trustee's account which represents small dividends as defined by Bankruptcy Rule 3010; or

( ) the disbursing agent in a chapter 11 liquidating plan has $ ______ in funds unclaimed 120 calendar days after the final distribution under the plan. The disbursing agent has made a good faith effort to verify the correct mailing addresses for said entities and deliver the funds.

Attached and made a part of this notice is a list, pursuant to Bankruptcy Rule 3011, of the names, claim numbers and addresses of the claimants and the amount to which each is entitled.

Notice is given that the above stated sum has been deposited with the Clerk of the U.S. Bankruptcy Court, Southern District of Florida, to effect closing of this estate.

Dated: ________________
Trustee [or disbursing agent]

____
print name

Copies to:
Debtor (at last current address)
Attorney for Debtor
U.S. Trustee

____
address

____
phone

LF-26 (rev. 12/01/09)

[Effective December 1, 1998. Amended effective December 1, 2002; June 2, 2008; December 1, 2009.]

LF–27. APPLICATION TO WITHDRAW UNCLAIMED FUNDS

UNITED STATES BANKRUPTCY COURT
SOUTHERN DISTRICT OF FLORIDA
www.flsb.uscourts.gov

In re: Case No.
Chapter

________________ Debtor ____________/

APPLICATION TO WITHDRAW UNCLAIMED FUNDS

Applicant, ______________________________, applies to this court for entry of an order directing the clerk of the court to remit to the applicant the sum of $, said funds having been deposited into the Treasury of the United States pursuant to 28 U.S.C. §2041 as unclaimed funds held in the name of ____________________. Applicant further states that:

1. (Indicate one of the following items:)

___ Applicant is the individual listed in the "Notice of Deposit of Funds with the U.S. Bankruptcy Court Clerk" under whose name these funds were deposited and states that no other application for this claim has been submitted by or at the request of this applicant. If funds were deposited in the names of both husband and wife, both must sign this application, or if one spouse is requesting release of funds in the name of that spouse only, applicant must attach a notarized affidavit stating why the funds should be released to only one spouse and not in the name of both. Also attached is a copy of an official government photo id of applicant to prove applicant's identity.

___ Applicant is either a family member or other authorized personal representative of an incapacitated or deceased individual in whose name funds were deposited or a successor in interest to the individual or business under whose name the funds were deposited. **An original "power of attorney" conforming to the applicable Administrative Office of the US Court's Director's Form and/or other supporting documents, including probate documents which indicate applicant's entitlement to this claim are attached and made a part of this application.** Also attached is a copy of an official government photo id of applicant to prove applicant's identity.

___ Applicant is the duly authorized representative for the business or corporation listed in the "Notice of Deposit of Funds with the U.S. Bankruptcy Court Clerk" under whose name these funds were deposited. Applicant has reviewed all applicable records and states that no other application for this claim has been submitted by or at the request of this claimant. **A Local Form "Affidavit of Claimant" (LF-28) and an original "power of attorney" conforming to the applicable Administrative Office of the US Court's Director's Form are attached and made a part of this application.**

___ Applicant is an attorney or a "funds locator" who has been retained by an individual or business or corporation under whose name the funds were deposited. Applicant has obtained an original "power of attorney" **conforming to the applicable Administrative Office of the US Court's Director's Form** from the individual claimant or the duly authorized representative for the business or corporation named as the claimant in the notice of deposit of funds into the court. **An original "power of attorney", conforming to the Official Bankruptcy Form and a Local Form "Affidavit of Claimant" (LF-28) are attached and made a part of this application.**

___ Applicant is an attorney or a "funds locator" who has been retained by the debtor in this case to claim funds deposited in the name of another individual or business or corporation. Applicant has obtained and attached to this application an original "power of attorney" **conforming to the applicable Administrative Office of the US Court's Director's Form** from the debtor (if joint case, both debtors) who are seeking to claim these funds. Applicant has also attached to this application a notarized affidavit from the debtor detailing debtor's right to the funds deposited in the name of the creditor and has attached copies of any exhibits to substantiate this right. Also attached is a copy of an official government photo id of the debtor to prove debtor's identity. The applicant has also attached a certificate of service reflecting that a copy of this application and required attachments has been served on the creditor whose funds the debtor is seeking to claim and on the trustee who deposited the funds with the clerk of court. If this is a joint debtor case, both husband and wife must sign the power of attorney, or if one spouse is requesting release of funds in the name of that spouse only, applicant must attach a notarized affidavit stating why the funds should be released to only one spouse and not in the name of both.

___ Applicant is the debtor seeking to claim funds deposited in the name of another individual or business or corporation. Applicant has attached to this application a sworn affidavit detailing debtor's right to the funds deposited in the name of the creditor and has attached copies of any exhibits to substantiate this right. Also attached is a copy of an official government photo id of applicant to prove debtor's identity. The debtor has also attached a certificate of service reflecting that a copy of this application and required attachments has been served on the creditor whose funds the debtor is seeking to claim and on the trustee who deposited the funds with the clerk of court. If this is a joint case, both husband and wife must sign this application, or if one spouse is requesting release of funds in the name of that spouse only, applicant must attach a notarized affidavit stating why the funds should be released to only one spouse and not in the name of both.

2. Applicant has made sufficient inquiry and has no knowledge that this claim has been previously paid, that any other application for this claim is currently pending before this court, or that any party other than the applicant is entitled to submit an application for this claim.

3. Applicant has provided notice to the U.S. Attorney pursuant to 28 U.S.C. §2042.

Dated: ________

____
Name Under Which Funds Were Deposited

____
Claim Number

____
Name of Party on Whose Behalf Application Was Filed*

Address: ________________________
____
____

____
Signature of Applicant
(Note: In addition to signing, complete all information below)

Last Four Digits of SS# ________

Tax ID (EIN #) ________

____
Print Name and Title of Applicant

____
Print Company Name

____
Print Street Address

____
Print City and State

____
Telephone (including area code)

*Attach copy of official government photo id for all parties on whose behalf this application is being filed.

Sworn to and Subscribed before me

on ________

____
NOTARY PUBLIC, AT LARGE
STATE OF ________________

[Effective December 1, 1998. Amended effective February 14, 2000; December 1, 2002; December 1, 2003; March 26, 2007; July 17, 2007; June 2, 2008; December 1, 2009; December 1, 2015.]

LF–28. AFFIDAVIT OF CLAIMANT

UNITED STATES BANKRUPTCY COURT
SOUTHERN DISTRICT OF FLORIDA
www.flsb.uscourts.gov

In re: Case No.
Chapter

_______ Debtor ______/

AFFIDAVIT OF CLAIMANT

1. I, ______________________________, am (indicate status of claimant)

( ) the individual creditor (or authorized personal representative of the individual creditor) in whose name funds were deposited with the court who has granted a power of attorney to ______________________, a "funds locator" or attorney to submit an application to withdraw unclaimed funds on my behalf; or

( ) the duly authorized representative for the claimant "business" ____________ ______________________; or

( ) the debtor claiming funds deposited in the name of a creditor in this case who has granted a power of attorney to ______________________, a "funds locator" or attorney, to submit an application on my behalf; or

( ) the debtor claiming funds deposited in the name of the debtor in this case who has granted a power of attorney to ______________________, a "funds locator" or attorney, to submit an application on my behalf; or

( ) the duly authorized representative for claimant "business" as indicated in the attached corporate power of attorney who has granted a power of attorney to ______________________a "funds locator" or attorney, to submit an application to withdraw unclaimed funds on my behalf;

and I am seeking payment of unclaimed funds in the amount of $ __________deposited in this court in the name of ______________________ and representing claim number________________ (if no claim was filed write "scheduled" in blank space).

2. Claimant History: Substantiate claimant's right to funds, including but not limited to documents relating to sale of company, i.e. purchase agreements and/or stipulation by prior and new owner as to right of ownership of funds. Attach certified copies of all necessary documentation, including those which establish the chain of

Page 1 of 2

LF-28 (rev. 12/01/15)

ownership of the original corporate claimant. Also attach a copy of an official government photo id to prove your identity.

3. I (or the "business" I represent as claimant) have neither previously received remittance for these funds nor have contracted with any other party other than the person named as a "funds locator" or attorney in paragraph one above to recover these funds.

I hereby certify that the foregoing statements are true and correct to the best of my knowledge and belief.

Dated:__________

____
signature of claimant or representative of "business" claimant

____
print name

____
title

____
Last Four Digits of Social Security # or Tax ID# (EIN #)
(Note: attach a copy of an official government photo id such as a driver's license or passport")

____
address

____
Phone number

____
signature of joint debtor (if applicable)

____
print name

____
Last Four Digits of Social Security # or Tax ID# (EIN #)
(Note: attach a copy of an official government photo id such as a driver's license or passport")

Sworn to and Subscribed before me
on____________________.

____
NOTARY PUBLIC, AT LARGE

STATE OF____________________

Page 2 of 2

LF-28 (rev. 12/01/15)

[Effective December 1, 1998. Amended effective February 14, 2000; December 1, 2002; December 1, 2003; July 17, 2007; August 10, 2007; June 2, 2008; December 1, 2009; December 1, 2015.]

LF-29. ORDER FOR PAYMENT OF UNCLAIMED FUNDS

UNITED STATES BANKRUPTCY COURT
SOUTHERN DISTRICT OF FLORIDA
www.flsb.uscourts.gov

In re: Case No.
Chapter

__________ Debtor __________/

ORDER FOR PAYMENT OF UNCLAIMED FUNDS

Upon application by __________________________________ on behalf of ______________________________ and in accordance with the provisions of 28 U.S.C. §2042 and Local Rule 3011-1(D), it is

ORDERED that, following review by the clerk of the sufficiency of the Application to Withdraw Unclaimed Funds and all supporting documents submitted, the clerk is directed to remit to ____________________________ and, if applicable, the "funds locator" or attorney submitting the application, ____________________________, the sum of $__________ now held as unclaimed funds in the treasury for the original claimant ____________________________________.

If the applicant is a "funds locator" or attorney, the check for these funds shall issue in the name of the party on whose behalf the funds are being claimed and the "funds locator" or attorney.

###

Copies to:
Funds Recipient(s)
Funds Locator or Attorney (if applicable)
Creditor (if applicable)

LF-29 (rev. 12/01/09)

[Effective December 1, 1998. Amended effective December 1, 2002; October 17, 2005; July 17, 2007; June 2, 2008; December 1, 2009.]

LF–30. ORDER (I) SETTING HEARING ON CONFIRMATION OF PLAN; (II) SETTING DEADLINE FOR FILING OBJECTIONS TO CONFIRMATION; (III) SETTING HEARING ON FEE APPLICATIONS; AND (IV) DIRECTING DEBTOR TO SERVE NOTICE

UNITED STATES BANKRUPTCY COURT
SOUTHERN DISTRICT OF FLORIDA
www.flsb.uscourts.gov

In re: Case No.
Chapter 12

_______________ Debtor _______ /

ORDER (I) SETTING HEARING ON CONFIRMATION OF PLAN;
(II) SETTING DEADLINE FOR FILING OBJECTIONS TO CONFIRMATION;
(III) SETTING HEARING ON FEE APPLICATIONS; AND
(IV) DIRECTING DEBTOR TO SERVE NOTICE

A plan has been filed by the debtor as required by 11 U.S.C. §1221. The hearing on confirmation of the plan will be held on __________________ at ______________ at____.

Pursuant to Local Rule 3015-1(A)(2), any objections to the confirmation of the plan shall be filed with the court on or before __________________ (three business days prior to the confirmation hearing) and a copy must be served on the debtor, the trustee, and the U.S. Trustee.

NOTICE IS GIVEN that at any hearing scheduled by this order, this court will consider dismissal of this case or its conversion to a chapter 7 liquidation under 11 U.S.C. §1208(c) upon the request of any interested party made at or before the hearing.

LF-30 (rev. 12/01/15) Page 1 of 2

NOTICE IS GIVEN to all prospective applicants for compensation, including attorneys, accountants and other professionals that pursuant to Local Rule 2016-1(C)(3) the deadline to file fee applications in this case is _______________ (two business days prior to confirmation hearing). Fee applications shall be filed with the court and a copy shall be served on the debtor, the trustee, and the U.S. Trustee. Fee applications timely filed, shall be considered at the confirmation hearing.

_____________________, attorney for the debtor, **SHALL MAIL AT LEAST 21 DAYS BEFORE THE CONFIRMATION HEARING A COPY OF THIS ORDER AND THE PLAN** to every creditor, chapter 12 trustee, equity security holder, the U.S. Trustee and every other party in interest. The attorney shall file a certificate of these mailings.

###

Submitted by:

LF-30 (rev. 12/01/15) Page 2 of 2

[Effective December 1, 1998. Amended effective December 1, 2002; October 17, 2005; June 2, 2008; December 1, 2009; December 1, 2015.]

LF–31. CHAPTER 13 PLAN (INDIVIDUAL ADJUSTMENT OF DEBTS)

UNITED STATES BANKRUPTCY COURT, SOUTHERN DISTRICT OF FLORIDA
www.flsb.uscourts.gov
CHAPTER 13 PLAN (Individual Adjustment of Debts)

☐ ________ Amended Plan (Indicate 1st, 2nd, etc. amended, if applicable)
☐ ________ Modified Plan (Indicate 1st, 2nd, etc. amended, if applicable)

DEBTOR:__________ JOINT DEBTOR:__________ CASE NO.:__________
Last Four Digits of SS# ________ Last Four Digits of SS# ________

MONTHLY PLAN PAYMENT: Including trustee's fee of 10% and beginning 30 days from filing/conversion date, Debtor(s) to pay to the trustee for the period of ______ months. In the event the trustee does not collect the full 10%, any portion not collected will be paid to creditors pro-rata under the plan:

A. $________ for months _____ to _____;
B. $________ for months _____ to _____;
C. $________ for months _____ to _____; in order to pay the following creditors:

Administrative: Attorney's Fee - $__________ TOTAL PAID $__________
Balance Due $__________ payable $______/month (Months ____ to ____)

Secured Creditors: [Retain Liens pursuant to 11 U.S.C. §1325 (a)(5)] Mortgage(s)/Liens on Real or Personal Property:

1. __________________ Arrearage on Petition Date $__________
Address:______________ Arrears Payment $________/month (Months _____ to _____)
______________ Regular Payment $________/month (Months _____ to _____)
Account No:______________

2. __________________ Arrearage on Petition Date $__________
Address:______________ Arrears Payment $________/month (Months _____ to _____)
______________ Regular Payment $________/month (Months _____ to _____)
Account No:______________

3. __________________ Arrearage on Petition Date $__________
Address:______________ Arrears Payment $________/month (Months _____ to _____)
______________ Regular Payment $________/month (Months _____ to _____)
Account No:______________

IF YOU ARE A SECURED CREDITOR LISTED BELOW, THE PLAN SEEKS TO VALUE THE COLLATERAL SECURING YOUR CLAIM IN THE AMOUNT INDICATED. A SEPARATE MOTION WILL ALSO BE SERVED ON YOU PURSUANT TO BR 7004 and LR 3015-3.

Secured Creditor	Description of Collateral and Value of Collateral	Interest Rate	Plan Payments	Months of Payment	Total Plan Payments
	$	%	$	_____ To _____	
	$	%	$	_____ To _____	
	$	%	$	_____ To _____	

Priority Creditors: [as defined in 11 U.S.C. §507]

1. __________________ Total Due $________
Payable $________/month (Months____ to ___) Regular Payment $_______
2. __________________ Total Due $________
Payable $________/month (Months____ to ___) Regular Payment $_______

Unsecured Creditors: Pay $__________/month (Months______ to ______).
Pro rata dividend will be calculated by the Trustee upon review of filed claims after bar date.

Other Provisions Not Included Above:

I declare that the foregoing chapter 13 plan is true and correct under penalty of perjury.

______________________ ______________________
Debtor Joint Debtor
Date:____________ Date:____________

LF-31 (rev. 01/08/10)

[Effective October 17, 2005, for cases filed on or after October 17, 2005. Amended effective August 1, 2006; June 2, 2008; January 8, 2010.]

LF–32A. ORDER (I) SETTING HEARING TO CONSIDER APPROVAL OF DISCLOSURE STATEMENT; (II) SETTING DEADLINE FOR FILING OBJECTIONS TO DISCLOSURE STATEMENT; AND (III) DIRECTING PLAN PROPONENT TO SERVE NOTICE

UNITED STATES BANKRUPTCY COURT
SOUTHERN DISTRICT OF FLORIDA
www.flsb.uscourts.gov

In re: Case No.
Chapter 11

_______________ Debtor /

ORDER (I) SETTING HEARING TO CONSIDER APPROVAL OF DISCLOSURE STATEMENT; (II) SETTING DEADLINE FOR FILING OBJECTIONS TO DISCLOSURE STATEMENT; AND (III) DIRECTING PLAN PROPONENT TO SERVE NOTICE

DISCLOSURE HEARING:

_______________ at _______________ m.

LOCATION:
United States Bankruptcy Court
(address)

DEADLINE FOR SERVICE OF ORDER, DISCLOSURE STATEMENT AND PLAN:

_______________ (30 days before Disclosure Hearing)

DEADLINE FOR OBJECTIONS TO DISCLOSURE STATEMENT:

_______________ (seven days before Disclosure Hearing)

[Effective October 17, 2005, for cases filed on or after October 17, 2005. Amended effective August 1, 2006; June 2, 2008; January 5, 2010.]

PLAN PROPONENT:

______________________ (name of Plan Proponent)

______________________ (name and address of **Plan Proponent's Attorney)**

____

A Disclosure Statement and Plan were filed pursuant to 11 U.S.C. §§1121 and 1125 on ____________ by the plan proponent named above. This order sets a hearing to consider approval of the disclosure statement ("disclosure hearing"), and sets forth the deadlines and requirements relating to the disclosure statement provided in the Bankruptcy Code, Bankruptcy Rules and Local Rules of this court.

The disclosure statement is on file with the court, and may be accessed electronically or you may obtain a copy at your expense from the clerk or view a copy at the public terminals in the clerk's office. Copies also may be obtained from the plan proponent by written request, pursuant to paragraph 3(B) of this order.

1. HEARING TO CONSIDER APPROVAL OF DISCLOSURE STATEMENT

The court has set a hearing to consider approval of the disclosure statement for the date and time indicated above as "DISCLOSURE HEARING". The disclosure hearing may be continued to a future date by notice given in open court at the disclosure hearing. At the disclosure hearing, the court will consider the disclosure statement, and any modifications or objections to it.

2. DEADLINE FOR OBJECTIONS TO DISCLOSURE STATEMENT

The last day for filing and serving objections to the disclosure statement is indicated above as "DEADLINE FOR OBJECTIONS TO DISCLOSURE STATEMENT". Objections to the disclosure statement shall be filed with the court and served on (i) the debtor; (ii) the plan proponent (if other than the debtor); (iii) all committees that have been appointed; (iv) any chapter 11 trustee or examiner that has been appointed; and (v) the U.S. Trustee. Pursuant to Local Rule 3017-1(A), any objecting party shall confer with the plan proponent's counsel at least three business days before the disclosure hearing in an effort to resolve any objections to the disclosure statement.

3. PLAN PROPONENT TO SERVE NOTICE

(A) On or before the date indicated above as "DEADLINE FOR SERVICE OF ORDER, DISCLOSURE STATEMENT AND PLAN", the Plan Proponent shall serve a copy of this order on (i) all creditors; (ii) all equity security holders; (iii) all persons who have requested notice; and (iv) all other interested parties, pursuant to Bankruptcy Rules 2002, and 3017 (including those entities as described in Bankruptcy Rule 3017(f)), and Local Rule 3017-1(B) and including those on a Master Service List required to be filed pursuant to Local Rule 2002-1(H). The plan proponent shall file a certificate of service as required under Local Rule 2002-1(F).

(B) On or before the date indicated above as "DEADLINE FOR SERVICE OF ORDER, DISCLOSURE STATEMENT AND PLAN", the plan proponent shall serve a copy of the disclosure statement and plan, together with this order, on (i) the debtor; (ii) all committees that have been appointed; (iii) any chapter 11 trustee or examiner that has been appointed; (iv) the Securities and Exchange Commission; (v) the Internal Revenue Service; (vi) the U.S. Trustee; and (vii) any party in interest who requests in writing a copy of the disclosure statement and plan, pursuant to Bankruptcy Rule 3017(a), and Local Rule 3017-1(B).

The plan proponent shall file a certificate of service as required under Local Rule 2002-1(F).

If the plan proponent does not timely comply with any of the requirements of this order, the court may impose sanctions at the disclosure hearing without further notice, including dismissal, conversion of the case to chapter 7, or the striking of the plan. The court will also consider dismissal or conversion at the disclosure hearing at the request of any party that has requested such relief in a timely filed objection or on the court's own motion.

###

Submitted by:

LF-32A (rev. 12/01/09)

[Effective December 1, 1998. Amended effective December 1, 2002; October 17, 2005; June 2, 2008; December 1, 2009.]

LF–32B. ORDER (I) APPROVING DISCLOSURE STATEMENT; (II) SETTING HEARING ON CONFIRMATION OF PLAN; (III) SETTING HEARING ON FEE APPLICATIONS; (IV) SETTING VARIOUS DEADLINES; AND (V) DESCRIBING PLAN PROPONENT'S OBLIGATIONS

UNITED STATES BANKRUPTCY COURT
SOUTHERN DISTRICT OF FLORIDA
www.flsb.uscourts.gov

In re: Case No.
Chapter 11

____________________ Debtor __________ /

ORDER (I) APPROVING DISCLOSURE STATEMENT;
(II) SETTING HEARING ON CONFIRMATION OF PLAN;
(III) SETTING HEARING ON FEE APPLICATIONS;
(IV) SETTING VARIOUS DEADLINES; AND
(V) DESCRIBING PLAN PROPONENT'S OBLIGATIONS

CONFIRMATION HEARING AND HEARING ON FEE APPLICATIONS

______________________________ at _________________ m.

LOCATION:
United States Bankruptcy Court

(address)

PROPONENT'S DEADLINE FOR SERVING THIS ORDER,
DISCLOSURE STATEMENT, PLAN, AND BALLOT:

________________________ (40 days before Confirmation Hearing)

DEADLINE FOR OBJECTIONS TO CLAIMS:

________________________ (40 days before Confirmation Hearing)

DEADLINE FOR FEE APPLICATIONS:

________________ (21 days before Confirmation Hearing)

PROPONENT'S DEADLINE FOR SERVING NOTICE OF FEE APPLICATIONS:

________________ (14 days before Confirmation Hearing)

DEADLINE FOR OBJECTIONS TO CONFIRMATION:

________________ (14 days before Confirmation Hearing)

DEADLINE FOR FILING BALLOTS ACCEPTING OR REJECTING PLAN:

________________ (14 days before Confirmation Hearing)

PROPONENT'S DEADLINE FOR FILING
PROPONENT'S REPORT AND CONFIRMATION AFFIDAVIT:

________________ (three business days before Confirmation Hearing)

DEADLINE FOR INDIVIDUAL DEBTOR TO FILE "CERTIFICATE FOR CONFIRMATION REGARDING PAYMENT OF DOMESTIC SUPPORT OBLIGATIONS AND FILING OF REQUIRED TAX RETURNS":

________________ (three business days before Confirmation Hearing)

The court conducted a hearing on ________________ to consider approval of the disclosure statement filed by ________________________ (the "plan proponent"). The court finds that the disclosure statement (as amended, if amendments were announced by the plan proponent or required by the court at the hearing) contains "adequate information" regarding the plan in accordance with 11 U.S.C. §1125(a). Therefore, pursuant to 11 U.S.C. §1125(b) and Bankruptcy Rule 3017(b), the disclosure statement is approved.

This order sets a hearing to consider confirmation of the plan ("confirmation hearing"), a hearing on fee applications and sets forth the deadlines and requirements relating to confirmation provided in the Bankruptcy Code, Bankruptcy Rules and Local Rules of this court.

1. HEARING TO CONSIDER CONFIRMATION OF PLAN

The court has set a hearing to consider confirmation of the plan for the date and time indicated above as "CONFIRMATION HEARING". The confirmation hearing may be continued to a future date by notice given in open court at the confirmation hearing.

2. DEADLINE FOR FILING AND HEARING ON FEE APPLICATIONS

The last day for filing and serving fee applications is indicated above as "DEADLINE FOR FEE APPLICATIONS". All prospective applicants for compensation, including attorneys, accountants and other professionals, shall file applications which include actual time and costs, plus an estimate of additional time and costs to be incurred through confirmation. At or prior to confirmation, applicants must file a supplement with documentation supporting the estimated time and costs. Fee applications shall be timely filed with the court and served (with all exhibits, including documentation of estimated time) on (i) the debtor; (ii) the plan proponent (if other than the debtor); (iii) all committees that have been appointed; (iv) any chapter 11 trustee or Examiner that has been appointed; and (v) the U.S. Trustee.

Fee applications will be set for hearing together with the confirmation hearing. The plan proponent shall serve notice of all fee applications pursuant to paragraph 6 below. The plan proponent shall file a certificate of service as required under Local Rule 2002-1(F).

3. DEADLINE FOR OBJECTIONS TO CONFIRMATION

The last day for filing and serving objections to confirmation of the plan is indicated above as "DEADLINE FOR OBJECTIONS TO CONFIRMATION". Objections to confirmation shall be filed with the court and served on (i) the debtor; (ii) the plan proponent (if other than the debtor); (iii) all committees that have been appointed; (iv) any chapter 11 trustee or examiner that has been appointed; and (v) the U.S. Trustee.

4. DEADLINE FOR FILING BALLOTS ACCEPTING OR REJECTING PLAN

The last day for filing a ballot accepting or rejecting the plan is indicated above as "DEADLINE FOR FILING BALLOTS ACCEPTING OR REJECTING PLAN". All parties entitled to vote should receive a ballot from the plan proponent by U.S. Mail pursuant to paragraph 6(A) of this order. If you receive a ballot but your entire claim has been objected to, you will not have the right to vote until the objection is resolved, unless you request an order under Bankruptcy Rule 3018(a) temporarily allowing your claim for voting purposes.

5. DEADLINE FOR OBJECTIONS TO CLAIMS

The last day for filing and serving objections to claims is indicated above as "DEADLINE FOR OBJECTIONS TO CLAIMS". All objections to claims must be filed before this date unless the deadline is extended by further order.

6. PLAN PROPONENT'S OBLIGATIONS

(A) On or before the date indicated above as "PROPONENT'S DEADLINE FOR SERVING THIS ORDER, DISCLOSURE STATEMENT, PLAN, AND BALLOT" the plan proponent shall serve a copy of this order, the approved disclosure statement (with all amendments, if amendments were announced by the plan proponent or required by the court at the disclosure hearing), and the plan on all creditors, all equity security holders, and all other parties in interest, as required by the Bankruptcy Rules (including those entities as described in Bankruptcy Rule 3017(f)) and the Local Rules, including those listed on a "Master Service List" required to be filed pursuant to Local Rules 2002-1(H). At the time of serving this order, the Local Form "Ballot and Deadline for Filing Ballot Accepting or Rejecting Plan", customized as required by Local Rule 3018-1 shall be served via U.S. Mail on all creditors and equity security holders entitled to vote on the plan. The plan proponent shall file a certificate of service as required under Local Rule 2002-1(F).

(B) On or before the date indicated above as "PROPONENT'S DEADLINE FOR SERVING NOTICE OF FEE APPLICATIONS", the plan proponent shall serve a notice of hearing of all fee applications, identifying each applicant and the amounts requested. The notice shall be served on all creditors, all equity security holders, and all other parties in interest as required by the Bankruptcy and Local Rules, including those listed on a "Master Service List" required to be filed pursuant to Local Rules 2002-1(H). The plan proponent shall file a certificate of service as required under Local Rule 2002-1(F).

(C) On or before 5:00 p.m. on the date indicated above as "PROPONENT'S DEADLINE FOR FILING PROPONENT'S REPORT AND CONFIRMATION AFFIDAVIT", the plan proponent shall file with the court the Local Form "Certificate of Proponent of Plan on Acceptance of Plan, Report on Amount to be Deposited, Certificate of Amount Deposited and Payment of Fees," and the Local Form "Confirmation Affidavit". The "Confirmation Affidavit" shall set forth the facts upon which the plan proponent relies to establish that each of the requirements of 11 U.S.C. §1129 are satisfied. The "Confirmation Affidavit" should be prepared so that by reading it, the court can easily understand the significant terms of the plan and other material facts relating to confirmation of the plan. The individual executing the "Confirmation Affidavit" shall be present at the confirmation hearing.

If the plan proponent does not timely comply with any of the requirements of this order, the court may impose sanctions at the confirmation hearing without further notice including dismissal, conversion of the case to chapter 7, or the striking of the plan. The court will also consider dismissal or conversion at the confirmation hearing at the request of any party or on the court's own motion.

7. [If debtor is an individual] the debtor shall file, on or before the date indicated above, the Local Form "Certificate for Confirmation Regarding Payment of Domestic Support Obligations and Filing of Required Tax Returns".

###

Submitted by:

LF-32B (rev. 12/01/09)

[Effective December 1, 1998. Amended effective December 1, 2002; October 17, 2005; June 2, 2008; December 1, 2009.]

LF–33. BALLOT AND DEADLINE FOR FILING BALLOT ACCEPTING OR REJECTING PLAN

UNITED STATES BANKRUPTCY COURT FOR THE SOUTHERN DISTRICT OF FLORIDA
www.flsb.uscourts.gov

In re: Case No.
Chapter 11

____________ Debtor ____________/

BALLOT AND DEADLINE FOR FILING BALLOT ACCEPTING OR REJECTING PLAN

TO HAVE YOUR VOTE COUNT YOU MUST COMPLETE AND RETURN THIS BALLOT BY THE DEADLINE INDICATED BELOW [AS SET PURSUANT TO LOCAL RULE 3018-1(B)]

The plan filed by ______________________________ on ______________ can be confirmed by the court and thereby made binding on you if it is accepted by the holders of two-thirds in amount and more than one-half in number of claims in each class and the holders of two-thirds in amount of equity security interests in each class voting on the plan. In the event the requisite acceptances are not obtained, the court may nevertheless confirm the plan if the court finds that the plan accords fair and equitable treatment to the class rejecting it.

This ballot is for creditor (insert name)______________________________ for the following type of claim placed in the indicated class in the indicated amount:

TYPE OF CLAIM	CLASS IN PLAN	AMOUNT OF CLAIM
☐ General Secured		$____________
☐ General Unsecured		$____________
☐ Bond Holder		Amount of Bond/debenture $__________
☐ Equity Security Holder		Number of Shares of Stock __________

The undersigned [Check One Box] ☐ Accepts ☐ Rejects

the plan for reorganization of the above-named debtor.

Signed:

Print Name:

Address:

Phone:

Date:

★★★FILE THIS BALLOT ON OR BEFORE ____________________★★★

with: Clerk of Bankruptcy Court
☐ 301 N. Miami Ave., Room 150, Miami, FL 33128
☐ 299 E. Broward Blvd., Room 112, Ft. Lauderdale, FL 33301
☐ 1515 North Flagler Drive, Room 801, West Palm Beach, FL 33401

If you have more than one type of claim against this debtor, separate ballots must be filed and you should receive a ballot for each type of claim eligible to vote. Contact the plan proponent regarding incorrect or insufficient ballot(s).

LF-33 (rev. 10/10/14)

[Effective December 1, 1998. Amended effective May 8, 2001; December 1, 2002; February 15, 2005; October 17, 2005; January 8, 2007; June 2, 2008; December 1, 2009; October 10, 2014.]

LF–34. CERTIFICATE OF PROPONENT OF PLAN ON ACCEPTANCE OF PLAN, REPORT ON AMOUNT TO BE DEPOSITED, CERTIFICATE OF AMOUNT DEPOSITED AND PAYMENT OF FEES

UNITED STATES BANKRUPTCY COURT
SOUTHERN DISTRICT OF FLORIDA
www.flsb.uscourts.gov

In re: Case No.
Chapter 11

________Debtor___________/

CERTIFICATE OF PROPONENT OF PLAN ON ACCEPTANCE OF PLAN, REPORT ON AMOUNT TO BE DEPOSITED, CERTIFICATE OF AMOUNT DEPOSITED AND PAYMENT OF FEES

The undersigned attorney for the [debtor] [proponent of the plan] certifies the following:

1. I have examined the court files in this proceeding, particularly as to claims, schedules and ballots filed.

2. A total of _____ ballots were filed on or before the deadline date of ___________, set by court order dated ___________. Exhibit A is a summary of ballots submitted by class. Exhibit B is a list of all ballots filed. Class[es] _______________ are unimpaired and a ballot was not required.

3. Exhibit C lists each creditor to be paid pursuant to the plan. Exhibit D lists disputed, contingent or unliquidated claims included in Exhibit C. Below is a summary of the amount of money to be deposited for confirmation pursuant to plan:

<u>CLASS</u> <u>DOLLAR AMOUNT NEEDED FOR CONFIRMATION</u>

TOTAL: $______________

4. The amount of $ ____________ is available in my trust account for confirmation.

5. All fees required by 28 U.S.C. §1930 have been paid.

DATED____________ ____________________________________
[Attorney for Proponent of Plan]

EXHIBIT A SUMMARY OF BALLOTS

CLASS: ________

Total Acceptances in Dollar Amount	$________	% of total = $________	
Total Rejections in Dollar Amount	$________	% of total = $________	
Total # of Acceptances Filed	________	% of total =	________
Total # of Rejections Filed	________	% of total =	________

CLASS: ________

Total Acceptances in Dollar Amount	$________	% of total = $________	
Total Rejections in Dollar Amount	$________	% of total = $________	
Total # of Acceptances Filed	________	% of total =	________
Total # of Rejections Filed	________	% of total =	________

CLASS: ________

Total Acceptances in Dollar Amount	$________	% of total = $________	
Total Rejections in Dollar Amount	$________	% of total = $________	
Total # of Acceptances Filed	________	% of total =	________
Total # of Rejections Filed	________	% of total =	________

CLASS: ________

Total Acceptances in Dollar Amount	$________	% of total = $________	
Total Rejections in Dollar Amount	$________	% of total = $________	
Total # of Acceptances Filed	________	% of total =	________
Total # of Rejections Filed	________	% of total =	________

CLASS: ________

Total Acceptances in Dollar Amount	$________	% of total = $________	
Total Rejections in Dollar Amount	$________	% of total = $________	
Total # of Acceptances Filed	________	% of total =	________
Total # of Rejections Filed	________	% of total =	________

CLASS: ________

Total Acceptances in Dollar Amount	$________	% of total = $________	
Total Rejections in Dollar Amount	$________	% of total = $________	
Total # of Acceptances Filed	________	% of total =	________
Total # of Rejections Filed	________	% of total =	________

CLASS: ________

Total Acceptances in Dollar Amount	$________	% of total = $________	
Total Rejections in Dollar Amount	$________	% of total = $________	
Total # of Acceptances Filed	________	% of total =	________
Total # of Rejections Filed	________	% of total =	________

EXHIBIT B LIST OF ALL BALLOTS FILED

BALLOT #	CLASS	NAME OF CREDITOR	AMOUNT SCHEDULED OR CLAIMED	DATE BALLOT FILED WITH COURT	ACCEPTS	REJECTS	SHOULD BE ALLOWED TO VOTE IF NOT, WHY?

EXHIBIT C LIST OF CREDITORS TO BE PAID PURSUANT TO THE PLAN

The following is a list of creditors as provided for by the plan under consideration. These creditors are indicated by class and amount as scheduled or claimed. The dividend to be paid pursuant to the plan is indicated. (Indicate claim number as reflected in the claims register). Total each individual class.

CLASS	*NAME OF CREDITOR*	*CLAIM NUMBER*	*SCHEDULED AND/OR CLAIMED AMOUNT*	*FIRST DIVIDEND TO BE PAID PURSUANT TO PLAN*

(if more space needed use continuation sheet)

EXHIBIT C LIST OF CREDITORS TO BE PAID PURSUANT TO THE PLAN (CONTINUATION SHEET)

CLASS	NAME OF CREDITOR	CLAIM NUMBER	SCHEDULED AND/OR CLAIMED AMOUNT	FIRST DIVIDEND TO BE PAID PURSUANT TO PLAN

EXHIBIT D LIST OF DISPUTED, CONTINGENT OR UNLIQUIDATED CLAIMS

The following is a list of disputed, contingent or unliquidated claims which are also included in Exhibit C.

Note: If a claim was filed and is still in dispute, indicate claim number as is reflected in the claims register and give status of dispute (e.g. objection pending, etc.). Until there is an order on an objection, you must have enough money in the trust account to cover these creditors. If a person was listed in the schedules as disputed and they did not file a claim by the deadline date to file claims, you need not list them below or have money in your trust account to cover them. They are automatically taken off the case as creditors.

CLASS	NAME OF CREDITOR	CLAIM #	SCHEDULED AND/OR CLAIMED AMOUNT	STATUS OF CLAIM

LF-34 (rev. 12/01/09)

[Effective December 1, 1998. Amended effective December 1, 2002; June 2, 2008; December 1, 2009.]

LF–35. FINAL REPORT AND MOTION FOR ENTRY OF FINAL DECREE

UNITED STATES BANKRUPTCY COURT
SOUTHERN DISTRICT OF FLORIDA
www.flsb.uscourts.gov

In re: Case No.
Chapter 11

__________ Debtor __________/

FINAL REPORT AND MOTION FOR ENTRY OF FINAL DECREE

Pursuant to Local Rule 3022-1(A), the undersigned files this Final Report and Motion for Final Decree and represents:

1. The plan of reorganization in this case was confirmed on _______________. The plan provided for a _______% dividend to unsecured creditors.

2. The deposit required by the plan has been distributed [and if the debtor is an individual all payments under the plan have been completed or the debtor has filed a motion requesting discharge prior to completion of payments under the plan under 11 U.S.C. §1141(d)(5)] and all matters to be completed upon the effective date of the confirmed plan have been fulfilled or completed.

3. There are no longer any pending adversary proceedings or contested matters which would affect the substantial consummation of this case and the debtor, if an individual, has filed the Local Form "Notice of Deadline to Object to Debtor's Statement Re: 11 U.S.C. §522(q)(1) Applicability, Payment of Domestic Support Obligations, and [For Chapter 11 Cases Only] Applicability of Financial Management Course and Statement Regarding Eligibility to Receive a Discharge".

4. All administrative claims and expenses have been paid in full, or appropriate arrangements have been made for the full payment thereof. A summary of fees and expenses is as follows:

$_____________ Trustee Compensation (If trustee received compensation under more than one chapter)

$__________	$__________	$__________	$__________
Ch. 7	Ch. 9 or 11	Ch. 12	Ch. 13

$_______ Fee for Attorney for Trustee
$_______ Fee for Attorney for Debtor
$_______ U.S. Trustee (fees required by 28 U.S.C. §1930)
$_______ Clerk of Court (fees required by 28 U.S.C. §1930)
$_______ Other Professionals
$_______ <u>ALL</u> expenses, including Trustee's

5. Attached as Exhibit A is a distribution report detailing the payments made under the plan on the effective date.

The undersigned respectfully requests that this court enter a final decree and close this fully administered case.

I certify that a copy of this report and attachments was mailed to the U.S. Trustee's office on ______________________.

By:______________________________

Print Name and Title:______________________________

Address:______________________________

Phone: ______________________________

EXHIBIT A

CASE NAME: ______________________

CASE NUMBER: ______________________

The following payments have been made pursuant to the plan of reorganization:

LIST ALL PAYMENTS MADE ON OR BEFORE THE EFFECTIVE DATE OF THE PLAN, OR IF INDIVIDUAL CHAPTER 11, ALL PAYMENTS MADE UNDER THE PLAN. SEPARATE CLAIMANTS BY CLASSIFICATION UNDER THE PLAN AND PROVIDE A TOTAL FOR EACH CLASSIFICATION. LIST THE NAME OF EACH RECIPIENT, AMOUNT OF THE ALLOWED CLAIM AND THE AMOUNT THAT WAS PAID (USE CONTINUATION PAGE IF NECESSARY).

RECIPIENT	ALLOWED AMOUNT OF CLAIM	DIVIDEND PAID
	$	$
	$	$
	$	$
	$	$
	$	$
	$	$
	$	$
	$	$
	$	$
	$	$
	$	$
	$	$
	$	$
	$	$
	$	$
	$	$

LF-35 (rev. 12/01/09)

[Effective December 1, 1998. Amended effective December 1, 2002; June 2, 2008; April 27, 2009; December 1, 2009.]

LF-36. NOTICE OF LATE FILING OF PAPER PURSUANT TO LOCAL RULE 5005-1(F)(2)

UNITED STATES BANKRUPTCY COURT
SOUTHERN DISTRICT OF FLORIDA
www.flsb.uscourts.gov

In re: Case No.
Chapter

_______________ Debtor /

NOTICE OF LATE FILING OF PAPER
PURSUANT TO LOCAL RULE 5005-1(F)(2)

_______________ ("Movant") files this Notice of Late
[Name of Party]

Filing of Paper Pursuant to Local Rule 5005-1(F)(2) and states as follows:

1. The attached _______________ is filed for consideration at the hearing scheduled on _______ at _______ at _______________ to consider _______________.

2. Movant has been unable to comply with the requirement of Local Rule 5005-1(F)(1) for timely submission of papers in matters already set for hearing due to the following circumstances:

(Indicate emergency nature of filing or exceptional circumstances for the untimely filing.)

Movant respectfully requests that the court consider this paper at the above scheduled hearing.

I CERTIFY that a true copy of this notice was served on all parties noticed for the hearing for which the document was filed [indicate name of party served, manner of service and date of service].

____
[Signature]
By:_______________
[Movant's Name]
____
[Address]
____
[Phone number]

LF-36 (rev. 12/01/09)

[Effective December 1, 1998. Amended effective February 14, 2000; December 1, 2002; June 2, 2008; December 1, 2009.]

LF–37. ORDER REOPENING CASE TO AMEND SCHEDULES TO ADD OMITTED CREDITOR(S)

UNITED STATES BANKRUPTCY COURT
SOUTHERN DISTRICT OF FLORIDA
www.flsb.uscourts.gov

In re: Case No.
Chapter 7

______________________ Debtor /

ORDER REOPENING CASE TO AMEND SCHEDULES TO ADD OMITTED CREDITOR(S)

THIS MATTER came before the Court:

☐ upon the debtor's Motion to Reopen Case to Amend Schedules to Add Omitted Creditors (the "Motion") pursuant to 11 U.S.C. §350, Bankruptcy Rule 5010, and Local Rule 5010-1(B), filed pursuant to Local Rule 9013-1(D)(3)(i). Since the debtor has filed a certificate of no response, it is

☐ for hearing on ____________ upon the debtor's Motion to Reopen Case to Amend Schedules to Add Omitted Creditors (the "Motion") pursuant to 11 U.S.C. §350, Bankruptcy Rule 5010, and Local Rule 5010-1(B). For the reasons stated on the record, it is

ORDERED as follows:

1. This case is reopened. No trustee shall be appointed.

LF-37 (rev. 01/11/17)

Page 1 of 2

2. Within 14 days from the entry of this order, the debtor shall amend the schedules (and pay applicable amendment fee) to add the name(s) and address(es) of the creditor(s) and related information previously omitted from the original schedules. A supplemental matrix of creditors as required by the "Clerk's Instructions for Preparing, Submitting and Obtaining Service Matrices" and Local Form "Debtor's Notice of Compliance with Requirements for Amending Creditor Information" must accompany the amended schedules.

3. The debtor (or the debtor's attorney) is directed to furnish to all affected creditors a complete copy of (a) this order; (b) the clerk's original notice of meeting of creditors as required under Local Rule 1009-1(D); and (c) the order discharging the debtor. The debtor shall file a certificate of service as required under Local Rule 2002-1(F).

4. Each affected creditor shall have sixty (60) days from the date of service of_this order to file an adversary proceeding to determine whether the debt subject to amendment is dischargeable under 11 U.S.C. §523(a)(3)(B) because it is of a kind specified in paragraph (2), (4), or (6) of 11 U.S.C. §523(a). If a creditor fails to timely file such a complaint, then such creditor has waived the right to argue that the debt subject to such amendment is excepted from discharge under §523(a)(3)(b).

###

Submitted by:

Copies to:
Debtor (or Debtor's Attorney)

LF-37 (rev. 12/01/15)

Page 2 of 2

[Effective December 1, 1998. Amended effective December 1, 2002; September 16, 2003; October 17, 2005; June 2, 2008; December 1, 2009; June 21, 2012; December 1, 2015; January 11, 2017.]

LF-38. ORDER REOPENING CASE TO ADMINISTER ADDITIONAL ASSETS AND DIRECTING UNITED STATES TRUSTEE TO APPOINT A TRUSTEE

UNITED STATES BANKRUPTCY COURT
SOUTHERN DISTRICT OF FLORIDA
www.flsb.uscourts.gov

In re: Case No.
Chapter 7

________________Debtor________________/

ORDER REOPENING CASE TO ADMINISTER ADDITIONAL ASSETS AND DIRECTING UNITED STATES TRUSTEE TO APPOINT A TRUSTEE

THIS CAUSE having come before the court upon the Motion to Reopen Case pursuant to 11 U.S.C. §350, Bankruptcy Rule 5010, and Local Rule 5010-1(C), and the court having considered the motion, having determined that good cause has been shown, and being otherwise fully advised in the premises, it is

ORDERED that this case is reopened. The United States Trustee is directed to appoint a trustee in this case. The trustee appointed by the United States Trustee to oversee administration of the case shall advise the court if there are funds available for distribution to creditors by filing a "Notice of Assets". Eligibility for receipt of distributions

LF-38 (rev. 12/01/15) Page 1 of 2

from these funds shall be determined pursuant to Local Rule 3002-1(D). If, in lieu of full payment at the time of filing the motion to reopen, a motion to defer payment was filed, the fee shall be due upon recovery of assets by the trustee.

###

Submitted by:

The party submitting the order shall serve a copy of the signed order on all required parties and file with the court a certificate of service conforming with Local Rule 2002-1(F).

LF-38 (rev. 12/01/15) Page 2 of 2

[Effective December 1, 1998. Amended effective December 1, 2002; October 17, 2005; June 2, 2008; December 1, 2009; December 1, 2015.]

LF-41. BILL OF COSTS

UNITED STATES BANKRUPTCY COURT
SOUTHERN DISTRICT OF FLORIDA
www.flsb.uscourts.gov

In re | *Case No.*
Chapter

Debtor

Plaintiff

Adversary Proceeding No.

Defendant

Case No. of Appeal

BILL OF COSTS

Notice is given that the following Bill of Costs is presented to the bankruptcy clerk for consideration pursuant to Local Rule 7054-1 (or Local Rule 8014-1 for appellate costs) and in accordance with this court's Guidelines for Taxation of Costs by the Clerk.

Judgment was entered in the above entitled action on ________ (date) against ________________________.

The clerk of the bankruptcy court is requested to tax the following as costs:

Fees of the clerk .... $________
Fees for service of summons and complaint .... $________
Fees of the court reporter for any and all part of the transcript necessarily obtained for use in the case .... $________
Fees for witnesses (itemized on reverse) taxable as costs .... $________
Fees for exemplifications and copies of papers necessarily obtained for use in this case .... $________
Filing and Docketing fees for Notice of Appeal .... $________
Costs incident to taking of depositions taxable as costs .... $________
Other costs [Please itemize] .... $________
$________
$________
TOTAL $________

DECLARATION

I, attorney for ________________________ (name of party) declare under penalties of perjury that the foregoing costs are correct and were necessarily incurred in the action, that the services for which fees have been charged were actually and necessarily performed, that the fees requested are allowable pursuant to this court's Guidelines for Taxation of Costs by the Clerk.

Name and Address of Judgement Debtor:

Date ________ Signature of Attorney ________ Print Name ________ Phone ________

COSTS ARE TAXED IN THE FOLLOWING AMOUNT AND INCLUDED IN THE JUDGMENT: $________

CLERK OF COURT

________ Date

By: ________________ Deputy Clerk

WITNESS FEES (computation, cf. 28 U.S.C. §1821 for statutory fees)							
NAME AND RESIDENCE	ATTENDANCE		SUBSISTENCE		MILEAGE		TOTAL COST EACH WITNESS
	Days	Total Cost	Days	Total Cost	Miles	Total Cost	
						TOTAL:	

NOTICE

Section 1924, Title 28, U.S.C. provides:

"Before any bill of costs is taxed, the party claiming any item of cost or disbursement shall attach thereto an affidavit, made by himself or by his duly authorized attorney or agent having knowledge of the facts, that such item is correct and has been necessarily incurred in the case and that the services for which fees have been charged were actually and necessarily performed".

Section 1920 of Title 28 reads in part as follows:

"A bill of costs shall be filed in the case and, upon allowance, included in the judgment or decree".

The Federal Rules of Bankruptcy Procedure contain the following provisions:
Bankruptcy Rule 7054(b)

"COSTS. The court may allow costs to the prevailing party except when a statute of the United States or these rules otherwise provides. Costs against the United States, its officers and agencies shall be imposed only to the extent permitted by law. Costs may be taxed by the clerk on fourteen days' notice; on motion served within seven days thereafter, the action of the clerk may be reviewed by the court."

Bankruptcy Rule 9006(f)

"ADDITIONAL TIME AFTER SERVICE BY MAIL. When there is a right or requirement to do some act or undertake some proceedings within a prescribed period after service of a notice or other paper and the notice or paper other than process is served by mail, three days shall be added to the prescribed period".

Rule 9021, Incorporating Federal Rule of Civil Procedure 58

"Ordinarily, the entry of judgment may not be delayed . . . in order to tax costs or award fees."

LF-41 (rev. 12/01/12)

[Effective December 1, 1998. Amended effective December 1, 2002; November 1, 2006; June 2, 2008; December 1, 2009; December 1, 2012.]

LF–44. MOTION TO APPEAR PRO HAC VICE

UNITED STATES BANKRUPTCY COURT
SOUTHERN DISTRICT OF FLORIDA
www.flsb.uscourts.gov

In re: Case No:
Chapter

________________________ Debtor(s) /

MOTION TO APPEAR PRO HAC VICE

Motion and Affidavit of Local Counsel

I, ____________________ ("Movant"), a member in good standing of the bar of the United States District Court for the Southern District of Florida and qualified to practice in this court, request that this court admit *pro hac vice* ________________ ("Visiting Attorney"), an attorney admitted to practice and currently in good standing in the United States District Court(s) for [identify all districts], and qualified to practice in this court, who proposes to act as counsel for [list client or clients] ________________________ ("Client(s)") in the case listed above, and in any adversary proceedings therein in which the Visiting Attorney appears on behalf of such Client(s).

I am aware that the local rules of this court require a member in good standing of the bar of the United States District Court for the Southern District of Florida and qualified to practice in this court to act as local counsel for such Client(s), unless the court specifically authorizes an attorney not so admitted to act as local counsel. I understand that local counsel is required to participate in the preparation and presentation of, and accept service of all papers in, the case identified above and any adversary proceedings in which the Visiting Attorney appears on behalf of such Client(s).

I am a member in good standing of the bar of the United States District Court for the Southern District of Florida and qualified to practice in this court, and agree to act as local counsel for the above-referenced Client(s) in this case and in any adversary proceedings in this case in which the Visiting Attorney appears on behalf of the

LF-44 (rev. 12/01/16) Page 1 of 3

Client(s). I understand that I am required to participate in the preparation and the presentation of the case above and any such adversary proceedings and to accept service of all papers served in such case and proceedings.

The order granting this Motion will serve to admit the Visiting Attorney to practice in the case noted above on behalf of the Client(s) and in any adversary proceedings in that case in which the Visiting Attorney appears on behalf of such Client(s). I understand that if I decline to serve as local counsel in any such adversary proceeding, separate local counsel must file an additional *Motion to Appear Pro Hac Vice*, and that absent such separate motion and an order of this court approving the same I will continue to act as local counsel for the Client(s) in all such proceedings.

The affidavit of the Visiting Attorney required under Local Rule 2090-1(C)(2) is filed concurrently herewith.

WHEREFORE, upon the foregoing representations, Movant respectfully requests an order of this court authorizing the Visiting Attorney to appear *pro hac vice* in this case and in any adversary proceedings in this case on behalf of the Client(s) and indicating Movant as local counsel for the Client(s), and for such other and further relief as may be just.

Dated:

[Name of Movant
Name of Firm
Address
Main Tel. Number
Direct Dial Tel. Number
Facsimile Number
E-mail Address
Florida Bar No.]

BY: ____________________
[Signature of Movant]

Affidavit of Proposed Visiting Attorney

I, ____________________, am a member in good standing of the bar of the [State/Commonwealth/Territory/U.S. Possession] of ____________________. I am a member in good standing of the bar of the United States District Court for the [identify all relevant district(s)] ____________________, but am not admitted to the bar of the United States District Court for the Southern District of Florida. I certify that I have never been disbarred, that I am not currently suspended from the practice of law in the State of Florida or any other state, and that I am not currently suspended from the practice of law before any United States Court of Appeals, United States District Court, or United States Bankruptcy Court.

I hereby request authority to appear *pro hac vice* in this case and in any adversary proceedings in this case on behalf of [list client or clients]__________ ("Client(s)"). I designate ____________________ ("Local Counsel"), who is qualified to practice in this court, as local counsel for the Client(s). I understand that Local Counsel is required to participate in the preparation and the presentation of the case above and any adversary proceedings in which I appear on behalf of such Client(s), and accept service of all papers served in such case and proceedings, unless and until other local counsel is designated and accepts such designation by filing a separate *Motion to Appear Pro Hac Vice* on my behalf.

I certify that I am familiar with and shall and shall be governed by the local rules of this court, the rules of professional conduct and all other requirements governing the professional behavior of members of the Florida Bar.

Dated:

[Name of Visiting Attorney
Name of Firm
Address
Main Tel. Number
Direct Dial Tel. Number
Facsimile Number
E-mail Address
[State] Bar No. __________]

BY: ____________________
[Signature of Visiting Attorney]

LF-44 (rev. 12/01/16) Page 3 of 3

[Effective June 2, 2008. Amended effective December 1, 2009; April 29, 2011; August 1, 2011; December 1, 2016.]

LF-45. ORDER ADMITTING ATTORNEY PRO HAC VICE

UNITED STATES BANKRUPTCY COURT
SOUTHERN DISTRICT OF FLORIDA
www.flsb.uscourts.gov

In re Case No:
Chapter

______ Debtor /

ORDER ADMITTING ATTORNEY PRO HAC VICE

This matter came before the court without a hearing on the Motion to Appear Pro Hac Vice [ECF No.______]. The court having reviewed the motion and good cause appearing, it is

ORDERED that [name of visiting attorney] ("Visiting Attorney") may appear before this court *pro hac vice* as counsel for [list client or clients] ("Client(s)") in this case and in each adversary proceeding in this case where Visiting Attorney appears on behalf of Client(s), subject to the local rules of this court. Visiting Attorney shall include the certification required by Local Rule 9011-4(B)(2) in all papers filed with this court.

Visiting Attorney may apply to become a registered user of CM/ECF in this district with full filing privileges in this case and in any other case in which this court has entered an

LF45 (rev. 12/01/16) Page 1 of 2

order admitting Visiting Attorney *pro hac vice*.

The following attorney ("Local Attorney") is designated as the attorney qualified to practice in this court with whom the court and other counsel may readily communicate and upon whom papers may be served:

[Name of Local Attorney
Name of Firm
Address
Main Tel. Number
Direct Dial Tel. Number
Facsimile Number
E-mail Address
Florida Bar No. ________]

Local Attorney shall act as the local attorney as required by Local Rule 2090-1(C)(2) in this case and in each adversary proceeding in this case in which the Visiting Attorney appears on behalf of the Client(s). If Local Attorney declines to serve as the local attorney in any such adversary proceeding, a separate local attorney must file an additional *Motion to Appear Pro Hac Vice*, and absent such separate motion and an order of this court approving the same Local Attorney will continue to act as local attorney for the Client(s) in all such proceedings.

###

Submitted by:

COPIES TO:

[Visiting Attorney]

[Local Attorney], who shall serve a copy of this order on the United States Trustee, all parties who have filed appearances in this case, and all parties who have appeared in each applicable adversary proceeding, and shall file a certificate of service thereof.

LF-45 (rev. 12/01/16) Page 2 of 2

[Effective December 1, 1998. Amended effective December 1, 2002; October 17, 2005; June 2, 2008; December 1, 2009; April 29, 2011; August 1, 2011; December 1, 2016.]

LF–46. CERTIFICATE OF SERVICE AND [IF SERVICE OF NOTICE OF HEARING] CERTIFICATE OF COMPLIANCE WITH LOCAL RULE 9073–1(D)

UNITED STATES BANKRUPTCY COURT
SOUTHERN DISTRICT OF FLORIDA
www.flsb.uscourts.gov

In re: Case No.
Chapter

________________ Debtor /

CERTIFICATE OF SERVICE
and
[If service of notice of hearing] CERTIFICATE OF COMPLIANCE WITH LOCAL RULE 9073-1(D)

I certify that a true copy of *[this motion/this notice of hearing/identify any other type of paper being served]* and *[if notice of hearing: a true copy of the motion or other paper that is the subject of the notice of hearing (if not previously served)]* were served as follows:

[Note to party preparing this certificate of service: In this space (or as an attachment to this certificate) list the names and addresses and date and manner of service of all parties served. Note: The "Notice of Electronic Filing" (NEF) is not a substitute for the filing of a separate certificate of service but may be incorporated by reference into the certificate of service for the purpose of identifying those parties who were served electronically. The certificate of service must reflect that non-registered users or registered users who have yet to appear electronically in a specific case were served by conventional paper or other manner of service required under the federal rules and this court's local rules.]

[If filing the certificate for service of a Notice of Hearing: I further certify that I have conferred with opposing counsel in an attempt to resolve these issues without a hearing.]

____
Signature of Attorney for Serving Party

____
Print Name

____
Address

____
Telephone Phone

____
Fla. Bar No.

Dated:

LF-46 (rev. 12/01/09)

[Effective December 1, 1998. Amended effective December 1, 2002; February 11, 2005; October 17, 2005; June 2, 2008; December 1, 2009.]

LF–47. CERTIFICATE OF CONTESTED MATTER

UNITED STATES BANKRUPTCY COURT
SOUTHERN DISTRICT OF FLORIDA
www.flsb.uscourts.gov

In re: Case No.
Chapter

____________________ Debtor ______/

CERTIFICATE OF CONTESTED MATTER

__________________________, movant, has filed a ____________________ ______________________, dated ____________________, pursuant to Local Rule * ________. Movant represents:

1. Service was timely made on all interested parties pursuant to the referenced rule as is evidenced by a copy of the attached certificate of service previously filed.

2. If applicable, the motion contained the bulletin required by the referenced rule.

3. The deadline for a response was ____________________.

4. The only objections or requests for hearing filed in response, which have been received, are the following:

5. As of ____________________, a check of the electronic entries docketed in this case confirms that no other objections or requests for hearing on this matter have been filed.

DATED:

____
Signature

____
Print Name

Attorneys for____________________

____
Address

____
Phone

____
Fla. Bar No.

[*fill in Local Rule No.: 1013-1(A), 3007-1(D), 4001-1(C), 6004-1(D), 6007-1(B)(1) or 9013-1(D)(2)]

LF-47 (rev. 12/01/09)

[Effective December 1, 1998. Amended effective February 14, 2000; December 1, 2002; October 17, 2005; June 2, 2008; December 1, 2009.]

LF–49. EXHIBIT REGISTER

UNITED STATES BANKRUPTCY COURT
SOUTHERN DISTRICT OF FLORIDA
www.flsb.uscourts.gov

In re: Case No.
Chapter

______________________/

Plaintiff Adv. No.

vs.

Defendant
______________________/

EXHIBIT REGISTER

Exhibits Submitted on behalf of:

[ ] Plaintiff [ ] Defendant [ ] Debtor [ ] Other______________________

Date of Hearing/Trial: ______________________

Type of Hearing/Trial: ______________________

SUBMITTED BY: ______________________

____

(Tel.) ______________________

Exhibit Number/Letter	Description	Admitted	Refused	Not Introduced

Exhibit Register Continuation Page

Exhibit Number/Letter	**Description**	**Admitted**	**Refused**	**Not Introduced**

LF-49 (rev. 12/01/09)

[Effective June 2, 2008. Amended effective December 1, 2009.]

LF–50. VERIFICATION OF QUALIFICATION TO ACT AS MEDIATOR

UNITED STATES BANKRUPTCY COURT
SOUTHERN DISTRICT OF FLORIDA
www.flsb.uscourts.gov

VERIFICATION OF QUALIFICATION TO ACT AS MEDIATOR

In accordance with Local Rule 9019-2 and Administrative Order 13-01 of the U.S. Bankruptcy Court for the Southern District of Florida, I verify that I qualify for and agree to serve as a mediator under this rule as follows:

1. I have (check one or more)
   [ ] completed a minimum of 40 hours in a circuit court mediation training program certified by the Florida Supreme Court;
   [ ] completed the American Bankruptcy Institute/St. John's University School of Law Bankruptcy Mediation Training
   [ ] a certification by the Florida Supreme Court as a circuit court mediator.

2. I agree to accept at least 2 mediation assignments per year in cases where at least one party lacks the ability to compensate the mediator, in which case I understand that my mediator's fees will be reduced accordingly or I will serve as mediator pro bono if no litigant is able to contribute compensation.

3. I have taken the oath or affirmation prescribed by 28 U.S.C. §453 and have attached proof thereof to this Verification.

4. I agree to accept the current compensation rate established by the U.S. District Court for the Southern District of Florida and adopted by this court and, where applicable, as provided by Rules 9019-2(A)(2)(b) and (A)(6). I also agree to accept the compensation rate established by AO 13-01 of the U.S. Bankruptcy Court for the Southern District of Florida if I intend to accept assignments in the Mortgage Modification Mediation Program.

5. I am familiar with and will comply with all notice and report requirements contained in Rule 9019-2.

6. I will disclose to the court any bias or prejudice which may disqualify me as a mediator under Rule 9019-2(B)(2).

7. I will accept referrals for cases in the following divisions:
   [ ] Miami [ ] Ft. Lauderdale [ ] West Palm Beach

8. I [ ] will <u>or</u> [ ] will not accept assignments in the Mortgage Modification Program.

I certify under penalty of perjury that all the information on this form is true.

____
Signature

Date: Name:__________________________
(Printed or typed)

Florida Bar No.(if applicable)__________
Address:__________________________

Attach proof of item #3

Phone:__________________________
email:__________________________

THIS FORM MUST BE FILED WITH THE CLERK'S OFFICE.
YOU MAY ATTACH A ONE PAGE RESUME TO THIS VERIFICATION.

Page 1 of 2

LF-50 (rev. 12/01/15)

UNITED STATES BANKRUPTCY COURT
SOUTHERN DISTRICT OF FLORIDA

MEDIATOR'S OATH

Each mediator of the United States Bankruptcy Court shall take the following oath or affirmation before performing the duties of his office:

"I, ________ ________ do solemnly swear that I will administer justice without respect to persons, and do equal rights to the poor and to the rich, and that I will faithfully and impartially discharge and perform all the duties incumbent upon me as a mediator for the United States Bankruptcy Court, Southern District of Florida, under the Constitution and laws of the United States, so help me God".

By: ______________________________
(Signature)

____
(Print Name)

SWORN TO AND SUBSCRIBED

before me on ______________.

by ____________________________________.

NOTARY PUBLIC, State of Florida at Large

My Commission Expires:

Page 2 of 2

LF-50 (rev. 12/01/15)

[Effective June 2, 2008. Amended effective December 1, 2009; February 26, 2013; March 1, 2013; June 25, 2013; August 1, 2014; December 1, 2015.]

LF–51. ORDER OF REFERRAL TO MEDIATION

UNITED STATES BANKRUPTCY COURT
SOUTHERN DISTRICT OF FLORIDA
www.flsb.uscourts.gov

In re: Case No.
Chapter

______ Debtor ______/

Plaintiff

vs. Adversary Proceeding No.

______ Defendant ______/

ORDER OF REFERRAL TO MEDIATION

Pursuant to Local Rule 9019-2 of this court, [this adversary proceeding] [name of contested matter] between [names of contested matter and parties] is referred to mediation. Accordingly, it is

ORDERED as follows:

1. All parties are required to participate in mediation. The mediation shall be

conducted no later than 14 days before the scheduled trial/hearing date, which is set for ____________, at ____________.m.

2. Plaintiff's [or movant's] counsel, or another attorney agreed upon by all counsel of record and any unrepresented parties, shall be responsible for scheduling the mediation conference. The parties shall agree upon a mediator within seven days of the date of this order, and indicate their selection by the timely filing of the Local Form "Notice of Selection of Mediator". If there is no agreement, lead counsel shall promptly notify the clerk in writing, and the clerk shall randomly designate a mediator from the "List of Certified Mediators". The clerk's designation shall be set forth in the Local Form "Notice of Clerk's Designation of Mediator".

3. If any party to the mediation conference, for any reason, objects to the appointed mediator, then, within three business days from the date of the "Notice of Clerk's Designation of Mediator", the objecting party shall file with the clerk, and serve upon the mediator and all other parties to the mediation, a request for an alternate mediator -- including in the request the name of any alternate mediator already agreed upon by the parties. If the alternate mediator has been agreed upon, the clerk shall appoint that mediator. Otherwise, the clerk shall appoint a second mediator from the "List of Certified Mediators" on a random basis and shall serve a second "Notice of Clerk's Designation of Mediator". Each party shall be entitled to one challenge to any clerk-appointed mediator. If a mediator appointed by the clerk is unable to serve, he or she shall, within seven days from the date of the "Notice of Clerk's Designation of Mediator", serve on the clerk and all parties to the mediation a written notice of inability to serve, and the clerk shall appoint an alternate mediator in the manner described above.

4. Upon consultation with the parties and their attorneys, the mediator shall fix a reasonable time and place for the mediation conference, except as otherwise agreed by the parties or by order of the court, and shall give the parties at least 14 days advance written notice of the conference.

5. The appearance of counsel and each party or representatives of each party with full authority to enter into full and complete compromise and settlement is

mandatory.

6. The mediator may report to the court the complete failure of any party to attend the mediation conference, which failure may result in the imposition of sanctions by the court.

7. The mediator shall be compensated in accordance with the current rate established by the U.S. District Court for the Southern District of Florida and adopted by this court. The cost of mediation shall be shared equally by the parties [or indicate that the matter is being mediated pro bono in whole or in part pursuant to Local Rule 9019-2(A)(2)(b) and list parties]. All payments shall be remitted to the mediator within 30 days of the date of the bill. Notice to the mediator of cancellation or settlement prior to the scheduled mediation conference must be given at least two full business days in advance. Failure to do so will result in imposition of a fee for one hour.

8. Within seven days after the mediation conference, the mediator shall file the Local Form "Report of Mediator" required by Local Rule 9019-2(E). In the event there is an impasse, the mediator shall report that there is a lack of agreement, with no further comment or recommendation, and the matter will be tried as scheduled.

9. If the parties have reached an agreement regarding the disposition of the matter or proceeding, they shall prepare and submit to the court within 14 days after the filing of the "Report of Mediator" an appropriate stipulation of settlement and joint motion for its approval. Failure to file such a motion shall be a basis for the court to impose appropriate sanctions.

###

Submitted by:

The party submitting the order shall serve a copy of the signed order on all required parties and file a certificate of service as required under Local Rule 2002-1(F).

Page 3 of 3

LF-51 (rev. 12/01/15)

[Effective December 1, 1998. Amended effective December 1, 2002; October 17, 2005; June 2, 2008; December 1, 2009; October 15, 2013; December 1, 2015.]

LF–52. NOTICE OF SELECTION OF MEDIATOR

UNITED STATES BANKRUPTCY COURT
SOUTHERN DISTRICT OF FLORIDA
www.flsb.uscourts.gov

In re: Case No.
Chapter

_______________ Debtor _______________/

Plaintiff

vs. Adversary Proceeding No.

_______________ Defendant _______________/

NOTICE OF SELECTION OF MEDIATOR

Pursuant to Local Rule 9019-2(B)(1) of this court, the parties agree to and select the following mediator in this matter:

____
Name of Mediator

____
Address

____
City, State, Zip Code

____
Telephone

Signature of party or counsel for party	Signature of adverse party or counsel for adverse party
Print Name	Print Name
Address	Address
Telephone	Telephone
Counsel for ____________	Counsel for ____________
Dated: ____________	Submitted By: ____________

copies to:
(all parties to the mediation)

LF-52 (rev. 12/01/09)

[Effective June 2, 2008. Amended effective December 1, 2009.]

LF–53. NOTICE OF CLERK'S DESIGNATION OF MEDIATOR

UNITED STATES BANKRUPTCY COURT
SOUTHERN DISTRICT OF FLORIDA
www.flsb.uscourts.gov

In re: Case No.
Chapter

__________ Debtor __________/

Plaintiff
vs. Adversary Proceeding No.

__________ Defendant __________/

NOTICE OF CLERK'S DESIGNATION OF MEDIATOR

The parties have failed to agree on the selection of a mediator in this action. Pursuant to Local Rule 9019-2(B)(1) of this court, this matter is assigned the following mediator:

MEDIATOR

Name ____________________

Address ____________________

City, State, Zip Code ____________________

Telephone ____________________

CLERK OF COURT

By: ____________________
Deputy Clerk

Phone: ____________________

Dated: ____________________

Copies to:
[all parties to the mediation]

LF-53 (rev. 12/01/09)

[Effective June 2, 2008. Amended effective December 1, 2009.]

LF–54. REPORT OF MEDIATOR

UNITED STATES BANKRUPTCY COURT
SOUTHERN DISTRICT OF FLORIDA
www.flsb.uscourts.gov

In re: Case No.
Chapter

_______________ Debtor _______________/

Plaintiff

vs. Adversary Proceeding No.

_______________ Defendant _______________/

REPORT OF MEDIATOR

The undersigned court-appointed mediator, reports to the court as follows:

A. A mediation conference was conducted on ____________________
B. The conference resulted in the following:

Agreement signed (total resolution).

__________ The parties reached an impasse.

__________ The parties settled the following issues:

(a)

(b)

(c)

__________ C. The conference was continued and an additional mediation conference will be scheduled.

__________ D. The matter was settled prior to mediation conference.

Attendance:

Parties and Counsel present:

Parties and Counsel not present:

Dated: ______________

____
signature of mediator

____
print name

____
address

____
city, state, zip code

____
telephone

Copies to:
[all parties to mediation]

LF-54 (rev. 12/01/09)

[Effective June 2, 2008. Amended effective December 1, 2009.]

LF–57. WRIT OF EXECUTION TO THE UNITED STATES MARSHALL

UNITED STATES BANKRUPTCY COURT
Southern District of Florida
www.flsb.uscourts.gov

In re ______________________,) Case No. ______________
Debtor)
______________________,) Chapter ______________
Plaintiff)
vs.)
______________________,) Adv. Proc. No. ______________
Defendant)

WRIT OF EXECUTION TO THE UNITED STATES MARSHAL

Name and Address of Judgment Creditor	Amount of Judgment: $______________ Other Costs: $______________
vs.	
Name and Address of Judgment Debtor	Date of Entry of Judgment: ______________

TO THE UNITED STATES MARSHAL FOR THE SOUTHERN DISTRICT OF FLORIDA:

You are directed to levy upon the property of the above named judgment debtor to satisfy a money judgment in accordance with the attached instructions.

TO THE JUDGMENT DEBTOR:

You are notified that federal and state exemptions may be available to you and that you have a right to seek a court order releasing as exempt any property specified in the marshal's schedule from the levy.

CLERK OF COURT

______________ By: ______________________
Date Deputy Clerk

LF-57 (rev. 12/01/09)

[Effective December 1, 1998. Amended effective December 1, 2002; November 1, 2006; June 2, 2008; December 1, 2009.]

LF–58A. ORDER JOINTLY ADMINISTERING CHAPTER 7 CASES

UNITED STATES BANKRUPTCY COURT
SOUTHERN DISTRICT OF FLORIDA
www.flsb.uscourts.gov

In re: Case No.
Chapter 7

Jointly Administered
Case No(s), Names, and Chapter(s)

Debtor /

ORDER JOINTLY ADMINISTERING CHAPTER 7 CASES

This matter came before the court at a hearing on ____________________ on a motion filed pursuant to Bankruptcy Rule 1015 and Local Rule 1015-1(A)(2)(b).

The cases identified in the caption of this order are pending in this court by or against (1) a husband and wife, or (2) a partnership and one or more of its general partners, or (3) two or more general members of a partnership, or (4) a debtor and an affiliate. It appears that these cases should be jointly administered as authorized under Bankruptcy Rule 1015 and Local Rule 1015-1. Accordingly it is

ORDERED that:

1. These cases shall be jointly administered. Case No. ____________________ is designated the "lead case". If applicable, case number(s) ________________________ is

LF-58A (rev. 12/01/15) Page 1 of 2

(are) transferred to the undersigned judge.

2. A single case docket and court file will be maintained hereafter under the "lead case" number.

3. Pleadings filed in other than the lead case shall be captioned under the lead case name(s) and case number followed by the words "(Jointly Administered)" and beneath that caption, the case names and numbers for the cases in which the document is being filed. Claims filed shall indicate only the case name and number of the case in which the claim is asserted. Separate claims registers shall be maintained for each case.

4. The trustee will not commingle assets or liabilities unless and until it is determined, after notice and hearing, that these cases involve the same debtor or that another ground exists to order substantive consolidation of these cases.

###

Submitted by:

The party submitting the order shall serve a copy of the signed order on all parties listed below and file with the court a certificate of service conforming with Local Rule 2002-1(F).

Debtor
Attorney for Debtor
U.S. Trustee
Trustee
Attorney for Trustee (if applicable)

LF-58A (rev. 12/01/15) Page 2 of 2

[Effective December 1, 1998. Amended effective December 1, 2002; October 17, 2005; June 2, 2008; December 1, 2009; December 1, 2015.]

LF–58B. ORDER JOINTLY ADMINISTERING CHAPTER 11 CASES

UNITED STATES BANKRUPTCY COURT
SOUTHERN DISTRICT OF FLORIDA
www.flsb.uscourts.gov

In re: Case No.
Chapter 11

Jointly Administered
Case No(s), Names, and Chapter(s)

Debtor /

ORDER JOINTLY ADMINISTERING CHAPTER 11 CASES

This matter came before the court

☐ ex parte or ;

☐ at a hearing on ____________________

on a motion filed pursuant to Bankruptcy Rule 1015 and Local Rule 1015-1(A)(2).

The cases identified in the caption of this order are pending in this court by or against (1) a husband and wife, or (2) a partnership and one or more of its general partners, or (3) two or more general members of a partnership, or (4) a debtor and an affiliate. It appears that these cases

LF-58B (rev. 12/01/15) Page 1 of 2

should be jointly administered as authorized under Bankruptcy Rule 1015 and Local Rule 1015-1.

Accordingly it is

ORDERED that:

1. These cases shall be jointly administered. Case No. ____________________ is designated the "lead case". If applicable, case number(s) ________________________ is (are) transferred to the undersigned judge.

2. A single case docket and court file will be maintained hereafter under the "lead case" number.

3. Pleadings filed in other than the lead case shall be captioned under the lead case name(s) and case number followed by the words "(Jointly Administered)" and beneath that caption, the case names and numbers for the cases in which the document is being filed. Claims filed shall indicate only the case name and number of the case in which the claim is asserted. Separate claims registers shall be maintained for each case. Ballots shall be styled and filed only in the case name and number of the member case for which the plan being voted on was filed.

4. The debtor-in-possession, or if applicable, trustee, will not commingle assets or liabilities unless and until it is determined, after notice and hearing, that these cases involve the same debtor or that another ground exists to order substantive consolidation of these cases.

###

Submitted by:

The party submitting the order shall serve a copy of the signed order on all parties of record and file with the court a certificate of service conforming with Local Rule 2002-1(F).

LF-58B (rev. 12/01/15) Page 2 of 2

[Effective December 1, 1998. Amended effective December 1, 2002; October 17, 2005; June 2, 2008; December 1, 2009; December 1, 2015.]

LF–59. REQUEST FOR COPIES OF ARCHIVED CASE FILES FROM U.S. BANKRUPTCY COURT, SOUTHERN DISTRICT OF FLORIDA

REQUEST FOR COPIES OF ARCHIVED CASE FILES FROM U.S. BANKRUPTCY COURT,
SOUTHERN DISTRICT OF FLORIDA
NATIONAL ARCHIVES AND RECORDS ADMINISTRATION (NARA)
BANKRUPTCY CASES – ORDERING INSTRUCTIONS

Expedite your order; submit it online at: https://eservices.archives.gov/orderonline/

NARA receives orders more quickly when you submit them online. NARA will send you an email confirming that they have your request and you will be able to track the order online at no additional cost.

Copy Packages Available

- **Pre-Selected Documents (Individual only):** Includes the following documents, to the extent that they are contained in the case file: **Discharge of Debtor** (or Order of Dismissal or Final Decree), **Voluntary Petition**, **Summary of Debts and Property**, **Schedules D, E** and **F** (Note in some jurisdictions Schedules may be listed as A1, A2 and A3). No substitutions will be made for these documents.
- **Entire Case File:** Includes all documents in a Business and Individual case file.
- **Docket Sheet:** A list of documents filed in a Bankruptcy case; an outline of the case.
- **Certification:** A seal certifying copies to be a valid reproduction of the file. This is available for an additional charge of $15.00 for all packages delivered by mail or express shipping. A package may contain a maximum of 150 pages. Each additional 150 pages or part thereof requires an additional certification at an additional charge of $15.00. Certification for faxed and scanned copies is not available.

Instructions

How to Order

- Use a separate NATF Form 90 for each file that you request.
- Steps 1-6 must be completed on the order form to perform a search for the file. Steps 1-6 begin on page 2.
- Provide the case number, transfer number, and box number for the file that you request. You must obtain this information from the Court where the case was filed.
- Please discard this instruction sheet; only return the order form on page 2.

Payment

- When paying by check or money order for your request, a separate payment is required for each individual request. Make your check or money order payable to: National Archives Trust Fund (NATF).
- If paying by credit card, you may fax your request form to the fax number provided in Step 1. Please do not send credit card information via email.
- The Entire Case File option in Step 2 includes up to the first 150 pages. Copies of additional pages are subject to an additional labor charge of $22.00 per 15 minutes of work done. You will be notified of any additional labor charges before they are incurred.

Delivery

- Allow 1-3 work days from receipt of payment for processing your order.
- In addition to photocopies, orders can be faxed and/or scanned. Faxed and scanned orders cannot be certified.
- A valid email address is necessary for electronic transfer via secure FTP site. Download speeds will vary based upon file size and your internet connection.
- Orders can be sent by overnight delivery at an additional charge.
- Requests may be returned if the necessary information is not supplied or if the credit card is declined.
- Please note that contents of recent cases may be in both electronic and paper form. If NARA cannot provide the documents you requested, we will refer you to the Court that adjudicated the case.
- Additional information may be found online: http://www.archives.gov/research/court-records/

Privacy Act Statement

Collection of this information is authorized by 44 U.S.C. 2108. Disclosure of the information is voluntary; however, we will be unable to respond to your request if you do not furnish your name and address and the minimum required information about the records. The information is used by NARA employees to search for the record; to respond to you; to maintain control over information requests received and answered; and to facilitate preparation of internal statistical reports. If you provide credit card information, that information is used to bill you for copies.

LF-59 (rev. 06/01/16) NATF FORM 90 (10-15)

REQUEST FOR COPIES OF ARCHIVED CASE FILES FROM U.S. BANKRUPTCY COURT, SOUTHERN DISTRICT OF FLORIDA

NATIONAL ARCHIVES AND RECORDS ADMINISTRATION
BANKRUPTCY CASES – ORDER FORM

Save time by ordering online: https://eservices.archives.gov/orderonline/

STEP 1. SELECT THE STATE WHERE THE COURT CASE WAS FILED (select only one)

ADDRESS TO SEND COMPLETED FORM	AREAS SERVED
NARA, Atlanta Federal Records Center - U.S. Court Reference Program 4712 Southpark Boulevard Ellenwood, GA 30294 Telephone: 404-736-2900; Fax: 404-736-2927 Email: atlanta.reference@nara.gov	Alabama, Florida, Georgia, Kentucky, Mississippi, North Carolina, South Carolina, Tennessee

STEP 2. SELECT COPY PACKAGE (select only one)

Copy Package – <u>Not Certified</u>	Copy Package – <u>Certified</u>
	Certification for faxed, scanned, & electronic transfer copies is not available
☐ Pre-Selected Documents — **$35.00**	☐ Pre-Selected Documents Certified — **$50.00**
☐ Entire Case File — **$90.00** (150 page maximum)	☐ Entire Case File Certified — **$105.00** ***($15.00 per additional 150 pages or part thereof)***
☐ Docket Sheet — **$35.00**	☐ Docket Sheet — **$50.00**

STEP 3. CASE INFORMATION (obtain from the court in which the case was filed)

COURT LOCATION (city & state)	DEBTOR NAME(S)	CASE NUMBER
Miami, FL		
TRANSFER NUMBER	BOX NUMBER	

STEP 4. DELIVERY OPTIONS (if no selection is made, paper copies will be delivered via mail)

DELIVERY METHOD: (select one)	EXPEDITED DELIVERY: (optional, select one)
☐ Paper Copies by Mail	☐ Overnight express (additional $30.00)
☐ Fax	☐ Charge FedEx Account
☐ Scanned on CD/DVD by Mail	☐ Charge UPS Account
☐ Electronic Transfer via Secure FTP Site	

STEP 5. YOUR DELIVERY INFORMATION

NAME (or send to the attention of)		DAYTIME TELEPHONE NUMBER (required)
ADDRESS LINE 1		ALTERNATE TELEPHONE NUMBER (preferred)
ADDRESS LINE 2		FAX NUMBER
CITY	STATE ZIP CODE	EMAIL ADDRESS (for delivery by electronic transfer)

STEP 6. YOUR PAYMENT INFORMATION

Credit Card (please do not send credit card information via email)		**Check or Money Order**
CARD TYPE ☐ VISA ☐ MasterCard ☐ American Express ☐ Discover		Make your check or money order payable to: **National Archives Trust Fund (NATF)** Mail your request **with payment** to the address shown in **Step 1**.
ACCOUNT NUMBER	EXPIRATION DATE (MM/YYYY)	
NAME ON CARD	3 OR 4 DIGIT SECURITY CODE (CVV)	
SIGNATURE (Order <u>cannot</u> be processed without a signature unless the 3 or 4 digit security code is provided above)		

NARA USE *ONLY*

RESEARCHER	DATE (DD/MM/YYYY)	**PAYMENT PAID**
REMARKS	REVIEW – DATE TIME	☐ **CHECK #**

LF-59 (rev. 06/01/16) NATF FORM 90 (10-15)

[Effective December 1, 1998. Amended effective January 26, 2001; December 1, 2002; May 8, 2003; December 1, 2003; August 31, 2004; March 4, 2005; November 18, 2005; October 17, 2007; June 2, 2008; December 1, 2009; October 19, 2010; July 1, 2011; February 14, 2012; June 1, 2016.]

LF–60. REQUEST TO EXPEDITE APPEAL

UNITED STATES BANKRUPTCY COURT
SOUTHERN DISTRICT OF FLORIDA
www.flsb.uscourts.gov

In re: Case No.
Chapter

______________ Debtor ______________/

Plaintiff Adversary No.

vs.

______________ Defendant ______________/

Appellant

vs.

______________ Appellee ______________/

REQUEST TO EXPEDITE APPEAL

(Appellant) (Appellee) requests that the appeal of ______________________ filed on______________ in the above referenced case be expedited pursuant to Local Rule 8013-4 and that the clerk of the bankruptcy court expressly call this request to the attention of the clerk of the district court at the time the record is transmitted to the district court. This request is based upon the following:

1. [Include a one paragraph statement explaining the history, facts and issues of the case.]
2. [Indicate the urgency that would justify expediting this appeal.]

Page 1 of 2

LF-60 (rev. 12/01/15)

3. [Indicate any date certain deadline being delayed pending decision of this appeal and explain.]

4. [Indicate what damages will occur and to whom if this appeal is not decided by a date certain.]

____
Signature of Attorney for
[appellant/appellee]

____
Print Name

____
Address

____

____
Phone

____
Florida Bar Number

Attach or file separately a Local Rule 2002-1(F) certificate of service reflecting manner and date of service on all affected parties.

Page 2 of 2

LF-60 (rev. 12/01/15)

[Effective December 1, 1998. Amended effective December 1, 2002; June 2, 2008; December 1, 2009; December 1, 2015.]

LF–61. NOTICE OF INTENT TO REQUEST REDACTION OF TRANSCRIPT

UNITED STATES BANKRUPTCY COURT
SOUTHERN DISTRICT OF FLORIDA
www.flsb.uscourts.gov

In re: **Case No.**
Chapter

________________**Debtor**________/

[if adversary, include adversary caption]

NOTICE OF INTENT TO REQUEST REDACTION OF TRANSCRIPT

Notice is hereby given that a Statement of Personal Data Identifier Redaction Request and/or a Motion for Additional Redactions with respect to the official transcript of the proceeding held on ____________________, in the above referenced case or proceeding will be filed with the court within 21 days from the date the unredacted transcript was filed by the court reporter with the clerk of court.

____
Name

____
Address

____
City, State, Zip Code

____
Appearing on behalf of

Dated:________________________

Copy to:
Court Reporter

LF-61 (rev. 12/01/09)

[Effective December 1, 1998. Amended effective April 1, 2004; June 1, 2005; October 2005; June 2, 2008; December 1, 2009.]

LF–62. CONFIRMATION AFFIDAVIT OF [NAME OF AFFIANT]

UNITED STATES BANKRUPTCY COURT
SOUTHERN DISTRICT OF FLORIDA
www.flsb.uscourts.gov

In re	)	CASE NO.
	)	CHAPTER 11
Debtor	)	

CONFIRMATION AFFIDAVIT OF [NAME OF AFFIANT]

STATE OF FLORIDA)
) ss:
COUNTY OF DADE)

________________, being duly sworn, hereby deposes and says:
[Name of Affiant]

1. My name, is ______________________________[Name of Affiant]. I am over 21 years of age and fully competent to make this declaration. Unless otherwise stated, I have personal knowledge of the facts set forth in this affidavit.

2. I am the ____________________ [title of affiant] of ________________[name of debtor] (the "debtor"), which position I have held since __________[date]. [Briefly state educational background and professional certifications, if any, e.g., certified public accountant].

3. I make this declaration in support of the confirmation of the debtor's plan of reorganization, dated _______________ (the "plan").

4. [Describe debtor, e.g., debtor is a Florida corporation engaged in the manufacturing and sale of widgets].

5. As ______________________________[title with the debtor], I am familiar with the business, operations and assets of the company. My duties include [briefly describe, e.g., preparation of financial statements, supervision of daily financial and business affairs].

6. I am also familiar with and participated in, the negotiations leading to, and the terms and conditions of the plan, the debtor's disclosure statement, dated ________ [insert date] (the "disclosure statement"), and the documents related thereto. More specifically, I was directly responsible for supervising the preparation of financial projections and the liquidation analysis contained in these documents and I reviewed them for accuracy and completeness.

7. The plan includes the following principal features: [Describe the plan.]

8. [Describe benefits of the plan, e.g., as a result of the debt restructuring contemplated by this chapter 11 reorganization, the debtor will have reduced its debt service requirements by more than $[ ] annually and will be better placed to compete effectively in the marketplace].

Liquidation Analysis

9. As set forth in the analysis contained in the disclosure statement, a liquidation of the debtor would result in approximately $[ ] to $[ ] of value for distribution to the debtor's unsecured creditors.

10. The methodology I used in preparing or supervising the preparation of the liquidation analysis included: [describe]

Feasibility

11. [Describe why the plan is feasible and any changes since the approval of the disclosure statement. If appropriate, the most recent financial results can be attached as an exhibit.]

12. I believe the debtor will be able to meet all its obligations under the plan. In particular:

a. Assuming the effective date of the plan is [date], the debtor will have sufficient cash available to it to make all payments required to be made on such date. Such funds will be derived from [describe source of funds, e.g., cash infusion as part of plan or debtor's ongoing operations].

b. Based on the projections, the debtor will be in compliance with all the financial covenants under its loan and lease agreements.

c. Based on the projections, the debtor will be able to meet all payment obligations required by the plan.

14. [State any additional facts necessary to establish that each of the requirements of U.S.C. §1129 are met].

____
[Name of Affiant]

Sworn to and Subscribed
before me on __________.

____
NOTARY PUBLIC

LF-62 (rev. 12/01/09)

[Effective December 1, 1998. Amended effective February 14, 2000; December 1, 2002; June 2, 2008; December 1, 2009.]

LF–63A. PRETRIAL ORDER

UNITED STATES BANKRUPTCY COURT
SOUTHERN DISTRICT OF FLORIDA
www.flsb.uscourts.gov

In re: Case No.
Chapter

Debtor

ADV. NO.___-_____-BKC-___-A

Plaintiff
[or Counterplaintiff]

vs.

Defendant
[or Counterdefendant]

PRETRIAL ORDER

In accordance with the Order Setting Filing and Disclosure Requirements for Pretrial and Trial, plaintiff [or counterplaintiff] and defendant [or counterdefendant] have agreed to the terms of this Pretrial Order. Thereupon, it is-

ORDERED AND ADJUDGED that:

1. "The following facts are admitted and require no proof": [Set forth a concise statement of each.];

2. "The following issues of fact and no others remain to be litigated": [Set forth a concise statement of each.];

3. "The following issues of law, and no others, remain to be litigated": [Set forth a concise statement of each.];

4. "Attached is a list of exhibits intended to be offered at the trial by each party, other than exhibits to be used for impeachment or rebuttal only".

5. "Attached is a list of each party's witnesses including their names and addresses together with a designation of those witnesses whose testimony is expected to be presented by means of a deposition".

6. "All discovery has been completed" or "All discovery has been completed except..." [Describe any additional discovery required together with a statement of good cause and exceptional circumstances justifying discovery after the pretrial conference].

7. "The estimated length of trial is ____________________".

8. "[Name of attorney] will try the proceeding for the plaintiff [or counterplaintiff] and [name of attorney] will try the proceeding for the defendant [or counterdefendant], each of whom have certified that they are qualified to practice before this court or have been specially admitted for purposes of this proceeding".

9. "The foregoing admissions have been made by the parties, and the parties have specified the foregoing issues of fact and law remaining to be litigated. Therefore, this order shall supersede the pleadings and govern the course of this proceeding".

10. [If applicable] "The parties request a special setting..." [Specify the circumstances justifying a special setting].

###

We,_________________________, attorney for plaintiff [or counterplaintiff] and ________________________, attorney for defendant [or counterdefendant], certify that we have met to discuss settlement and that a good faith settlement attempt has been made.

ENTRY OF THIS ORDER IS STIPULATED AND AGREED TO BY:

________________________ Attorney for Plaintiff [or Counterplaintiff]	________________________ Attorney for Defendant [or Counterdefendant]
________________________ [Name and address of Plaintiff's or Counterplaintiff's counsel]	________________________ [Name and address of Defendant's or Counterdefendant's counsel]

Submitted by:

The party submitting this order shall serve a copy of the signed order on all interested parties and file with the court a certificate of service conforming with Local Rule 2002-1(F).

LF-63A (rev. 12/01/09)

[Effective October 17, 2005. Amended effective June 2, 2008; December 1, 2009.]

LF-63B. DIRECT TESTIMONY OF JOHN SMITH

UNITED STATES BANKRUPTCY COURT
SOUTHERN DISTRICT OF FLORIDA
www.flsb.uscourts.gov

In re: Bankruptcy Case No. ________

JOHN (NMI) SMITH (Chapter ____)

Debtor /

JOHN SMITH,
Plaintiff

Adversary Proceeding ________

v.

RICHARD ROE,
Defendant
________/

DIRECT TESTIMONY OF JOHN SMITH

1. My name is John Smith and I am the Plaintiff in this action.

2. On February 1, 1983, Richard Roe and I entered into a written agreement bearing the same date and marked as Plaintiff's Exhibit 1.

3. At the time of signing the agreement, I gave the Defendant, Richard Roe, my personal check for $50,000.00.

4. One week before we signed the contract, Mr. Roe showed me a special carburetor attachment which he claimed he had invented and had a patent therefor. At that time, Mr. Roe said to me that the attachment would reduce by 50% gasoline consumption of any engine to which it was attached.

5. At the same time, Mr. Roe said that he was negotiating with General Motors, who had offered $20,000.000.00 for an exclusive license to use and manufacture the patented device. However, Mr. Roe said he felt he was negotiating for a non-exclusive license to use and manufacture the patented device so that the product could subsequently be licensed to Ford, Chrysler, and other automobile manufacturers.

6. Three months after the contract was signed, I still had not received assignment of one-half interest in the patent rights to the device and in fact Mr. Roe has stopped returning my calls; his phone was disconnected and he had moved out of the apartment where he had been residing.

7. I next saw Mr. Roe on August 31, 1983, at the United States District Court in Miami, Florida, where he was being arraigned on charges of using the United States Mail to defraud. I spoke to him briefly at which time he admitted to me that the entire story about his inventing and patenting the carburetor device was false, including his purported negotiations with General Motors. He did, however, promise at the time that he would somehow or other pay back to me my $50,000.00, plus interest.

Executed at Miami, Florida, August 4, 1987. I declare under penalty of perjury that the foregoing is true and correct.

____
John Smith

APPROVED AS TO FORM:

____

____

____

____

ATTORNEY FOR ______________

LF-63B (rev. 12/01/09)

[Effective June 2, 2008. Amended effective December 1, 2009.]

LF-63C. JOINT PRETRIAL STIPULATION

UNITED STATES BANKRUPTCY COURT
SOUTHERN DISTRICT OF FLORIDA
www.flsb.uscourts.gov

In re: Case No.
Chapter

____
Debtor

ADV. NO.___-______-BKC-___-A

Plaintiff
[or Counterplaintiff]

vs.

Defendant
[or Counterdefendant]
____

JOINT PRETRIAL STIPULATION

In accordance with the Order Setting Filing and Disclosure Requirements for Pretrial and Trial, plaintiff [or counterplaintiff] and defendant [or counterdefendant] stipulate that the following facts are admitted and require no proof at trial:

1. [Set forth a concise statement of each stipulated fact]
2.
3. [etc.]

We, ______________________________, attorney for plaintiff [or counterplaintiff] and ______________________________, attorney for defendant [or counterdefendant], certify that we have met to discuss settlement and that a good faith settlement attempt has been made.

STIPULATED AND AGREED TO BY:

______________________________	______________________________
Attorney for Plaintiff [or Counterplaintiff]	Attorney for Defendant [or Counterdefendant]
______________________________	______________________________
[Name and address of Plaintiff's or Counterplaintiff's counsel]	[Name and address of Defendant's or Counterdefendant's counsel]

LF-63C (05/07/10)

[Effective May 7, 2010.]

LF–64A. ORDER CONDITIONALLY APPROVING DISCLOSURE STATEMENT, SETTING HEARING ON FINAL APPROVAL OF DISCLOSURE STATEMENT AND CONFIRMATION OF CHAPTER 11 PLAN, SETTING VARIOUS DEADLINES AND DESCRIBING PLAN PROPONENT'S OBLIGATIONS

UNITED STATES BANKRUPTCY COURT
SOUTHERN DISTRICT OF FLORIDA
www.flsb.uscourts.gov

In re: Case No.

Debtor Chapter 11
(small business)

Address:

ORDER CONDITIONALLY APPROVING DISCLOSURE STATEMENT, SETTING HEARING ON FINAL APPROVAL OF DISCLOSURE STATEMENT AND CONFIRMATION OF CHAPTER 11 PLAN, SETTING VARIOUS DEADLINES AND DESCRIBING PLAN PROPONENT'S OBLIGATIONS

HEARING ON FINAL APPROVAL OF DISCLOSURE STATEMENT, CONFIRMATION HEARING AND HEARING ON FEE APPLICATIONS

_______________________________ at _______________ m.

LOCATION:
United States Bankruptcy Court

(address)

PROPONENT'S DEADLINE FOR SERVING THIS ORDER,
DISCLOSURE STATEMENT, PLAN, AND BALLOT:

______________________ (30 days before Confirmation Hearing)

DEADLINE FOR OBJECTIONS TO CLAIMS:

______________________ (14 days before Confirmation Hearing)

DEADLINE FOR FEE APPLICATIONS:

______________________ (14 days before Confirmation Hearing)

DEADLINE FOR FILING BALLOTS ACCEPTING OR REJECTING PLAN:

______________________ (seven days before Confirmation Hearing)

DEADLINE FOR OBJECTIONS TO CONFIRMATION:

______________________ (three business days before Confirmation Hearing)

DEADLINE FOR OBJECTIONS TO FINAL APPROVAL OF THE DISCLOSURE STATEMENT:

______________________ (three business days before Confirmation Hearing)

PROPONENT'S DEADLINE FOR FILING
PROPONENT'S REPORT AND CONFIRMATION AFFIDAVIT:

______________________ (three business days before Confirmation Hearing)

DEADLINE FOR INDIVIDUAL DEBTOR TO FILE "CERTIFICATE FOR CONFIRMATION REGARDING PAYMENT OF DOMESTIC SUPPORT OBLIGATIONS AND FILING OF REQUIRED TAX RETURNS":

______________________ (three business days before Confirmation Hearing)

A disclosure statement [a combined plan and disclosure statement][a plan containing the disclosures required by 11 U.S.C. §1125(a)] (the "disclosure statement") under chapter 11 of the Bankruptcy Code having been filed under Local Rule 3017-2(A) by ______________, on __________ with respect to a plan under chapter 11 of the Bankruptcy Code filed by ______________, on __________, and the debtor being a small business:

IT IS ORDERED, and notice is hereby given, that:

A. The disclosure statement filed by ____________________ is conditionally approved.

B. DEADLINE FOR FILING BALLOTS ACCEPTING OR REJECTING PLAN

Pursuant to Local Rule 3018-1, ____________________ is fixed as the last day for filing written acceptances or rejections of the plan referred to above (seven days before hearing on confirmation of the plan ("confirmation hearing")).

C. PLAN PROPONENT'S OBLIGATIONS

(1) On or before the date indicated above as "PROPONENT'S DEADLINE FOR SERVING THIS ORDER, DISCLOSURE STATEMENT, PLAN, AND BALLOT" the plan proponent shall serve a copy of this order, the conditionally approved disclosure statement and the plan on all creditors, all equity security holders, the U.S. Trustee, and all other parties in interest, as required by the Bankruptcy Rules (including those entities as described in Bankruptcy Rule 3017(f)) and the Local Rules, including those listed on a "Master Service List" required to be filed pursuant to Local Rules 2002-1(H). At the time of serving this order, the Local Form "Ballot and Deadline for Filing Ballot Accepting or Rejecting Plan," customized as required by Local Rule 3018-1, shall be served via U.S. Mail on all creditors and equity security holders entitled to vote on the plan.

(2) On or before 5:00 p.m. on the date indicated above as "PROPONENT'S DEADLINE FOR FILING PROPONENT'S REPORT AND CONFIRMATION AFFIDAVIT," the plan proponent shall file with the court the Local Form "Certificate of Proponent of Plan on Acceptance of Plan, Report on Amount to be Deposited, Certificate of Amount Deposited and Payment of Fees," and the Local Form "Confirmation Affidavit." The "Confirmation Affidavit" shall set forth the facts upon which the plan proponent relies to establish that each of the requirements of 11 U.S.C. §1129 are satisfied. The "Confirmation Affidavit" should be prepared so that by reading it the court can easily understand the significant terms of the plan and other material facts relating to confirmation of the plan. The individual executing the "Confirmation Affidavit" shall be present at the confirmation hearing.

If the plan proponent does not timely comply with any of the requirements of this order, the court may impose sanctions at the confirmation hearing, without further notice, including dismissal, conversion of the case to chapter 7, or the striking of the plan. The court will also consider dismissal or conversion at the confirmation hearing at the request of any party or on the court's own motion.

D. HEARING TO CONSIDER CONFIRMATION OF PLAN

The hearing on final approval of the disclosure statement and confirmation of the plan (45 days after the plan is filed unless extended by the court prior to the expiration of this deadline) has been set for the date and time indicated above as "CONFIRMATION HEARING." The confirmation hearing may be continued to a future date by notice given in open court at the confirmation hearing.

E. Pursuant to Local Rules 3017-2(B) and 3020-1(A), ______________ is fixed as the last day for filing and serving written objections to the disclosure statement and confirmation of the plan (three business days before the confirmation hearing). Objections shall be served as required by Bankruptcy Rule 3017.1.

F. DEADLINE FOR OBJECTIONS TO CLAIMS

The last day for filing and serving objections to claims is indicated above as "DEADLINE FOR OBJECTIONS TO CLAIMS." All objections to claims must be filed before this date unless the deadline is extended by further order.

G. DEADLINE FOR FILING AND HEARING ON FEE APPLICATIONS

The last day for filing and serving fee applications is indicated above as "DEADLINE FOR FEE APPLICATIONS." All prospective applicants for compensation, including attorneys, accountants and other professionals, shall file applications which include actual time and costs, plus an estimate of additional time and costs to be incurred through confirmation. At or prior to confirmation, applicants must file a supplement with documentation supporting the estimated time and costs. Fee applications shall be timely filed with the court and served (with all exhibits including documentation of estimated time) on (i) the debtor; (ii) the plan proponent (if other than the debtor); (iii) all committees; (iv) any chapter 11 trustee or examiner; and (v) the U.S. Trustee.

Fee applications will be set for hearing together with the confirmation hearing.

H. DEADLINE FOR INDIVIDUAL DEBTOR TO FILE "CERTIFICATE FOR CONFIRMATION REGARDING PAYMENT OF DOMESTIC SUPPORT OBLIGATIONS AND FILING OF REQUIRED TAX RETURNS":

[If debtor is an individual] the debtor shall file, on or before the date indicated above, the Local Form "Certificate for Confirmation Regarding Payment of Domestic Support Obligations and Filing of Required Tax Returns."

###

Copy to: plan proponent by clerk of court

LF-64A (rev. 12/01/09)

[Effective September 19, 2008. Amended effective December 1, 2008; December 1, 2009.]

LF-64B. ORDER SETTING HEARING ON APPROVAL OF DISCLOSURE STATEMENT AND CONFIRMATION OF CHAPTER 11 PLAN, SETTING VARIOUS DEADLINES AND DESCRIBING PLAN PROPONENT'S OBLIGATIONS

UNITED STATES BANKRUPTCY COURT
SOUTHERN DISTRICT OF FLORIDA
www.flsb.uscourts.gov

In re: Case No.

Debtor Chapter 11
(small business)

Address:

ORDER SETTING HEARING ON APPROVAL OF DISCLOSURE STATEMENT AND CONFIRMATION OF CHAPTER 11 PLAN, SETTING VARIOUS DEADLINES AND DESCRIBING PLAN PROPONENT'S OBLIGATIONS

HEARING ON APPROVAL OF DISCLOSURE STATEMENT, CONFIRMATION HEARING AND HEARING ON FEE APPLICATIONS

____________ at ____________ m.

LOCATION:
United States Bankruptcy Court

(address)

PROPONENT'S DEADLINE FOR SERVING THIS ORDER, DISCLOSURE STATEMENT, PLAN, AND BALLOT:

________________________ (28 days before Confirmation Hearing)

DEADLINE FOR OBJECTIONS TO CLAIMS:

________________________ (14 days before Confirmation Hearing)

DEADLINE FOR FEE APPLICATIONS:

________________________ (21 days before Confirmation Hearing)

DEADLINE FOR FILING BALLOTS ACCEPTING OR REJECTING PLAN:

________________________ (seven business days before Confirmation Hearing)

DEADLINE FOR OBJECTIONS TO CONFIRMATION:

________________________ (three business days before Confirmation Hearing)

DEADLINE FOR OBJECTIONS TO APPROVAL OF THE DISCLOSURE STATEMENT:

________________________ (three business days before Confirmation Hearing)

PROPONENT'S DEADLINE FOR FILING PROPONENT'S REPORT AND CONFIRMATION AFFIDAVIT:

________________________ (three business days before Confirmation Hearing)

DEADLINE FOR INDIVIDUAL DEBTOR TO FILE "CERTIFICATE FOR CONFIRMATION REGARDING PAYMENT OF DOMESTIC SUPPORT OBLIGATIONS AND FILING OF REQUIRED TAX RETURNS":

________________________ (three business days before Confirmation Hearing)

A disclosure statement [a combined plan and disclosure statement][a plan containing the disclosures required by 11 U.S.C. §1125(a)] (the "disclosure statement") under chapter 11 of the Bankruptcy Code having been filed under Local Rule 3017-2(B) by ____________ ________, on ___________ with respect to a plan under chapter 11 of the Bankruptcy Code filed by ____________________, on ________, and the debtor being a small business:

IT IS ORDERED, and notice is hereby given, that:

A. DEADLINE FOR FILING BALLOTS ACCEPTING OR REJECTING PLAN

Pursuant to Local Rule 3018-1, ________________ is fixed as the last day for filing written acceptances or rejections of the plan referred to above (seven business days before hearing on confirmation of the plan ("confirmation hearing")).

B. PLAN PROPONENT'S OBLIGATIONS

(1) On or before the date indicated above as "PROPONENT'S DEADLINE FOR SERVING THIS ORDER, DISCLOSURE STATEMENT, PLAN, AND BALLOT" the plan proponent shall serve a copy of this order, the disclosure statement and the plan on all creditors, all equity security holders, the U.S. Trustee, and all other parties in interest, as required by the Bankruptcy Rules (including those entities as described in Bankruptcy Rule 3017(f)) and the Local Rules, including those listed on a "Master Service List" required to be filed pursuant to Local Rules 2002-1(H). At the time of serving this order, the Local Form "Ballot and Deadline for Filing Ballot Accepting or Rejecting Plan," customized as required by Local Rule 3018-1, shall be served via U.S. Mail on all creditors and equity security holders entitled to vote on the plan.

(2) On or before 5:00 p.m. on the date indicated above as "PROPONENT'S DEADLINE FOR FILING PROPONENT'S REPORT AND CONFIRMATION AFFIDAVIT," the plan proponent shall file with the court the Local Form "Certificate of Proponent of Plan on Acceptance of Plan, Report on Amount to be Deposited, Certificate of Amount Deposited and Payment of Fees," and the Local Form "Confirmation Affidavit." The "Confirmation Affidavit" shall set forth the facts upon which the plan proponent relies to establish that each of the requirements of 11 U.S.C. §1129 are satisfied. The "Confirmation Affidavit" should be prepared so that by reading it the court can easily understand the significant terms of the plan and other material facts relating to confirmation of the plan. The individual executing the "Confirmation Affidavit" shall be present at the confirmation hearing.

If the plan proponent does not timely comply with any of the requirements of this order, the court may impose sanctions at the confirmation hearing, without further notice, including dismissal, conversion of the case to chapter 7, or the striking of the plan. The court will also consider dismissal or conversion at the confirmation hearing at the request of any party or on the court's own motion.

C. HEARING TO CONSIDER CONFIRMATION OF PLAN

The hearing on approval of the disclosure statement and confirmation of the plan (45 days after the plan is filed unless extended by the court prior to the expiration of this deadline) has been set for the date and time indicated above as "CONFIRMATION HEARING." The confirmation hearing may be continued to a future date by notice given in open court at the confirmation hearing.

D. Pursuant to Local Rules 3017-2(B) and 3020-1(A), ________________ is fixed as the last day for filing and serving written objections to the disclosure statement and confirmation of the plan (three business days before the confirmation hearing). Objections shall be served as required by Bankruptcy Rule 3017.1.

E. DEADLINE FOR OBJECTIONS TO CLAIMS

The last day for filing and serving objections to claims is indicated above as "DEADLINE FOR OBJECTIONS TO CLAIMS." All objections to claims must be filed before this date unless the deadline is extended by further order.

F. DEADLINE FOR FILING AND HEARING ON FEE APPLICATIONS

The last day for filing and serving fee applications is indicated above as "DEADLINE FOR FEE APPLICATIONS." All prospective applicants for compensation, including attorneys, accountants and other professionals, shall file applications which include actual time and costs, plus an estimate of additional time and costs to be incurred through confirmation. At or prior to confirmation, applicants must file a supplement with documentation supporting the estimated time and costs. Fee applications shall be timely filed with the court and served (with all exhibits including documentation of estimated time) on (i) the debtor; (ii) the plan proponent (if other than the debtor); (iii) all committees; (iv) any chapter 11 trustee or examiner; and (v) the U.S. Trustee.

Fee applications will be set for hearing together with the confirmation hearing.

G. DEADLINE FOR INDIVIDUAL DEBTOR TO FILE "CERTIFICATE FOR CONFIRMATION REGARDING PAYMENT OF DOMESTIC SUPPORT OBLIGATIONS AND FILING OF REQUIRED TAX RETURNS":

[If debtor is an individual] the debtor shall file, on or before the date indicated above, the Local Form "Certificate for Confirmation Regarding Payment of Domestic Support Obligations and Filing of Required Tax Returns."

###

Copy to: plan proponent by clerk of court

LF-64B (rev. 12/01/09)

[Effective September 9, 2008. Amended effective December 1, 2008; December 1, 2009.]

LF–65. CHAPTER 7 TRUSTEE'S MOTION TO DISMISS CASE FOR FAILURE BY DEBTOR TO APPEAR AT THE FIRST MEETING OF CREDITORS

UNITED STATES BANKRUPTCY COURT
SOUTHERN DISTRICT OF FLORIDA
www.flsb.uscourts.gov

In re: Case No.
Chapter 7

________________Debtor______/

CHAPTER 7 TRUSTEE'S MOTION TO DISMISS CASE FOR FAILURE BY DEBTOR TO APPEAR AT THE FIRST MEETING OF CREDITORS

________________________, trustee, files this ex-parte Motion to Dismiss Case for Failure by Debtor to Appear at the First Meeting of Creditors, and in support, states as follows:

1. A first meeting of creditors was scheduled in this case on __________.

2. The debtor failed to appear at the first meeting of creditors as required by 11 U.S.C. §343.

The trustee respectfully requests that this court enter an order dismissing this case pursuant to Local Rule 1017-2(B)(1), and that the dismissal be "with prejudice" to the filing of any bankruptcy case in any federal bankruptcy court in the United States of America by the debtor earlier than 180 days from entry of this order.

____
Trustee

Attach or file separately a Local Rule 2002-1(F) certificate of service reflecting manner and date of service on the debtor and the attorney for the debtor.

LF-65 (rev. 12/01/15)

[Effective December 1, 1998. Amended effective February 14, 2000; December 1, 2002; June 2, 2008; December 1, 2009; December 1, 2015.]

LF–66. ORDER REINSTATING CHAPTER 13 CASE

UNITED STATES BANKRUPTCY COURT
SOUTHERN DISTRICT OF FLORIDA
www.flsb.uscourts.gov

In re: Case No.
Chapter 13

_______Debtor_______/

ORDER REINSTATING CHAPTER 13 CASE

This matter came to be heard on__________on the debtor's motion to reinstate case. The court, if applicable, has entered an order reopening the case and the debtor has paid all required reopening fees. Based on the record, it is

ORDERED as follows:

1) The motion is granted and this case is **REINSTATED**. Pursuant to 11 U.S.C. §362(c)(2)(B), the automatic stay terminated on the date this case was dismissed and was not in effect from that date until the entry of this order.

2) The Trustee's Final Report, if any filed, is deemed withdrawn and the Order Discharging Trustee, if entered, is deemed vacated.

3) If not previously filed, any and all documents required to be filed by the debtor(s) under 11 U.S.C. §521(a)(1), Bankruptcy Rule 1007, and Local Rule 1007-1 shall be filed no later than 14 days after entry of this order.

4) The following checked provision(s) also apply:

[ ] This case was dismissed prior to the conclusion of the meeting of creditors, under 11 U.S.C. §341. A new §341 meeting of creditors

Page 1 of 3

LF-66 (rev. 05/10/16)

and confirmation hearing shall be set and noticed to all parties of record by the Clerk of Court. The notice shall also establish a new deadline to file proofs of claims and deadline to file a motion objecting to discharge under §1328(f) or to file a complaint objecting to dischargeability of certain debts.

[ ] This case was dismissed after the §341 meeting of creditors was concluded but prior to or at the hearing on confirmation. (If applicable) A further §341 meeting will be conducted at______________. A new confirmation hearing is scheduled for____________________, at____.m. in courtroom________at_________________.The deadline to file a motion objecting to discharge under §1328(f) or to file a complaint objecting to dischargeability of certain debts, is______________. The deadline for filing claims (except for governmental units) is __________. Previously filed claims need not be refiled.

[ ] This case was dismissed after the §341 meeting of creditors was conducted and after the expiration of the deadline to file a motion objecting to discharge under §1328(f) or to file a complaint objecting to dischargeability of certain debts and the original deadline to file claims, but prior to or at the hearing on confirmation. No new deadlines shall be reset. (If applicable) A further §341 meeting will be conducted at____. A new confirmation hearing is scheduled for__________________________, at__________.m. in courtroom________at_________________

[ ] This case was dismissed after the §341 meeting of creditors and confirmation hearing and expiration of the deadline to file a motion objecting to discharge under §1328(f) or to file a complaint objecting to dischargeability of certain debts and the original claims bar date. No new §341 meeting, confirmation hearing, or deadlines shall be set, and the case shall proceed in the normal course under the confirmed plan.

[ ] If this box is checked, the following provision applies:

As a condition of reinstatement of this case and in order to provide protection of creditors' vested interests, in the event of conversion to another chapter or dismissal of this reinstated case prior to confirmation, all plan payments held by the Chapter 13 trustee shall be non-refundable and held in trust for the secured creditors as adequate protection, and in trust for priority and administrative creditors. If this case is dismissed or converted, the Trustee shall disburse all funds which were received prior to the order of conversion or dismissal and held in trust. The disbursement shall be on a pro rata basis, less Trustee fees, to the secured, priority or administrative creditors pursuant to the proposed Chapter 13 Plan which was filed at least one day prior to the last confirmation hearing date. (see Local Rule 1017-2(F) and Interim Local Rule 1019-1 (E), (F), (G), AND (H)).

###

Submitted by:

Copies to:
All parties of record by the Clerk of Court

Page 3 of 3

LF-66 (rev. 05/10/16)

[Effective December 1, 1998. Amended effective February 14, 2000; December 1, 2002; February 9, 2004; October 17, 2005; May 5, 2006; June 2, 2008; December 1, 2009; December 21, 2010; April 29, 2011; April 12, 2013; December 1, 2015; May 10, 2016.]

LF–67. DEBTOR CERTIFICATE OF COMPLIANCE AND REQUEST FOR CONFIRMATION OF CHAPTER 13 PLAN

UNITED STATES BANKRUPTCY COURT
SOUTHERN DISTRICT OF FLORIDA
www.flsb.uscourts.gov

In re: Case No.
Chapter 13

__________ Debtor __________/

DEBTOR CERTIFICATE OF COMPLIANCE AND REQUEST FOR CONFIRMATION OF CHAPTER 13 PLAN

As required under Local Rule 3015-3(B)(2), the debtor in the above captioned matter certifies as follows:

1. Payment of all postpetition domestic support obligations (check which paragraph applies).

_____ A. Since the filing of this bankruptcy, the debtor has not been required by a judicial or administrative order, or by statute to pay any domestic support obligation as defined in 11 U.S.C. §101(14A); or

_____ B. The debtor has paid, either directly or to the chapter 13 trustee under the last filed plan, all amounts that are required to be paid under a domestic support obligation and that first became payable after the date of the filing of the petition if the debtor is required by a judicial or administrative order, or by statute, to pay such domestic support obligation.

2. The debtor has filed all federal, state and local tax returns required by law to be filed under 11 U.S.C. §1308 for all taxable periods ending during the four year period ending on the date of the filing of the petition commencing this bankruptcy case.

I declare under penalty of perjury that the information provided in this Certificate is true and correct.

____
Debtor's Signature

Dated: __________

____
Joint Debtor's Signature (if applicable)

LF-67 (rev. 12/01/09)

[Effective November 21, 2005. Amended effective June 2, 2008; December 1, 2009.]

LF–69. APPLICATION FOR COMPENSATION FOR PROFESSIONAL SERVICES OR REIMBURSEMENT OF EXPENSES BY ATTORNEY FOR CHAPTER 13 DEBTOR

UNITED STATES BANKRUPTCY COURT
SOUTHERN DISTRICT OF FLORIDA
www.flsb.uscourts.gov

In re: Case No.
Chapter 13

_______________ Debtor _________ /

APPLICATION FOR COMPENSATION FOR PROFESSIONAL SERVICES OR REIMBURSEMENT OF EXPENSES BY ATTORNEY FOR CHAPTER 13 DEBTOR

Applicant, ________________________________, was retained by the debtor to serve in this bankruptcy case as attorney for debtor. A copy of the retainer agreement is attached as Exhibit "A". Pursuant to Local Rule 2016-1(B)(2) and the "Chapter 13 Fee Guidelines", applicant hereby requests the court to approve compensation and reimbursement of expenses as follows:

Total Fees Requested: $ __________

Total Expenses to be Reimbursed: $ __________

Amount Received To-Date: $ __________
(exclusive of filing fees)

Amount to be Paid through Plan: $ __________

1. The amount requested, if allowed, will be paid in full after ______ monthly payments under the plan.

2. A detailed itemization of the services rendered to date and corresponding time entries is attached as Exhibit "B".

3. Applicant estimates that an additional _____ hours will be required to be expended in providing legal services on behalf of the debtor(s) described below:

____

____

____.

4. The following is a short statement of any unusual, troublesome or unique aspects of this case which resulted in or will result in more than the usual amount of time being expended and more than the usual amount of costs being incurred:

____

____

____.

5. The source of compensation previously paid to applicant was __________

____.

6. Applicant has not shared or agreed to share any compensation received in connection with the bankruptcy case with any person or entity other than a member or regular associate of applicant's firm. (If such a sharing arrangement exists, it should be disclosed in this paragraph.)

DATED:______________

____
Applicant's Signature

____
Name

____
Address

____

____
Phone

c: Debtor
Chapter 13 Trustee

LF-69 (rev. 12/01/09)

[Effective June 2, 2008. Amended effective December 1, 2009.]

LF-70. OBJECTION TO CLAIM ON SHORTENED NOTICE

UNITED STATES BANKRUPTCY COURT
SOUTHERN DISTRICT OF FLORIDA
www.flsb.uscourts.gov

In re: Case No.
Chapter 13

_______________ Debtor ______/

OBJECTION TO CLAIM ON SHORTENED NOTICE

IMPORTANT NOTICE TO CREDITOR: THIS IS AN OBJECTION TO YOUR CLAIM

This objection seeks either to disallow or reduce the amount or change the priority status of the claim filed by you or on your behalf. Please read this objection carefully to identify which claim is objected to and what disposition of your claim is recommended. Upon the filing of this objection an expedited hearing on this objection will be scheduled on the date already scheduled for the confirmation hearing in accordance with Local Rule 3007-1(B)(2).

Pursuant to Bankruptcy Rule 3007 and Local Rule 3007-1(B)(2), the [trustee][debtor] objects to the following claim filed in this case:

[IDENTIFY CLAIM AND STATE BASIS FOR OBJECTION AND REQUESTED DISPOSITION]

The undersigned acknowledges that this objection and the notice of hearing for this objection will be served on the claimant and the debtor at least 14 days prior to the confirmation hearing date and that a certificate of service conforming to Local Rule 2002-1(F) must be filed with the court when the objection and notice of hearing are served.

DATED:___________

____
Name of Attorney

____
[Signature of Attorney or Debtor if the Debtor is pro se]

____
[Attorney for]

____
Address

____
Telephone

LF-70 (rev. 12/01/09)

[Effective July 8, 1999. Amended effective February 28, 2000; October 1, 2001; June 12, 2003; February 15, 2005; April 12, 2005; February 22, 2006; January 8, 2007; January 22, 2007; June 2, 2008; December 1, 2009.]

LF-71. INDIVIDUAL DEBTOR CERTIFICATE FOR CONFIRMATION REGARDING PAYMENT OF DOMESTIC SUPPORT OBLIGATIONS AND [FOR CHAPTER 11 CASES] FILING OF REQUIRED TAX RETURNS

UNITED STATES BANKRUPTCY COURT
SOUTHERN DISTRICT OF FLORIDA
www.flsb.uscourts.gov

In re:

Case No.
Chapter 11 [or 12]

________Debtor________/

INDIVIDUAL DEBTOR CERTIFICATE FOR CONFIRMATION REGARDING PAYMENT OF DOMESTIC SUPPORT OBLIGATIONS AND [FOR CHAPTER 11 CASES] FILING OF REQUIRED TAX RETURNS

As required under Local Rule 3020-1(B), the debtor in the above captioned matter certifies as follows:

1. Payment of all postpetition domestic support obligations (check which paragraph applies).

_____ A. Since the filing of this bankruptcy, the debtor has not been required by a judicial or administrative order, or by statute to pay any domestic support obligation as defined in 11 U.S.C. §101(14A); or

_____ B. As required by 11 U.S.C. §1129(a)(14) for chapter 11 cases or 11 U.S.C. §1225(a)(7) for chapter 12 cases, the debtor has paid, either directly or through the assigned trustee, all amounts that are required to be paid under a domestic support obligation and that first became payable after the date of the filing of the petition if the debtor is required by a judicial or administrative order, or by statute, to pay such domestic support obligation.

2. [If a chapter 11 case] As required by section 1228(b) of the Bankruptcy Abuse Prevention and Consumer Protection Act of 2005, all requested tax documents have been filed with the court.

I declare under penalty of perjury that the information provided in this certificate is true and correct.

____
Debtor's Signature

Dated: ___________

____
Joint Debtor's Signature (if applicable)

LF-71 (12/01/09)

[Effective August 12, 1999. Amended effective December 1, 2002; September 29, 2006; January, 2007; June 2, 2008; December 1, 2009.]

LF–72. COVER SHEET TO ACCOMPANY ITEMS SUBMITTED FOR SEALING OR IN CAMERA REVIEW

UNITED STATES BANKRUPTCY COURT
SOUTHERN DISTRICT OF FLORIDA
www.flsb.uscourts.gov

COVER SHEET TO ACCOMPANY ITEMS SUBMITTED FOR SEALING OR IN CAMERA REVIEW

Instructions: Items I through III must be completed by party submitting item for sealing or review. See Local Rule 5005-1(A)(4).

I. CASE INFORMATION:

Name of Case/Adversary Proceeding______________________________

Case/Adversary # ______________ Chapter ________

II. FILING INFORMATION:

Name of Filing Party:______________________________

Address of Filing Party: ______________________________

Phone # of Filing Party:______________________________

Filed on behalf of:______________________________

III. TYPE OF SUBMISSION: Submitted to: ☐ judge ☐ clerk's office intake

☐ sealed document and ____ sealed ____ unsealed motion to seal dated ____________.

[If request is filed sealed, a notice of filing request to seal or conduct in camera review should accompany the sealed item.]

or

☐ sealed item pursuant to court order entered on ____________

[Attach notice of filing sealed item and a copy of order directing sealing (unless order is sealed also).]

IV. DISPOSITION: (To be completed by court or clerk's office staff)

1. **ID number assigned upon receipt:** ____________

2. **Action by Judge:**

☐ **Request to file as "sealed" has been granted by order dated ____________. [attached]**

Additional Instructions for clerk's office (not contained in order):

☐ seal motion/request and order (entries will only read "SEALED")
☐ transcripts of proceedings relating to matters under seal including transcripts of hearing, if any, at which request to file pleadings or other papers under seal is made.
☐ final disposition instructions
☐ unseal only pursuant to court order
☐ unseal at closing absent other disposition
☐ other instructions: ______________________________

☐ **Request to file as "sealed" has been denied by order.**

☐ File request, order, item as unsealed
☐ return item to filer - docket request, order as ☐ sealed ☐ unsealed
☐ other: ______________________________

3. **Docket Entry Number Assigned:** motion _____ order_____ sealed item______

LF-72 (rev. 12/01/15)

[Amended effective October 3, 2001; December 1, 2002; June 2, 2008; December 1, 2009; December 1, 2015.]

LF–73. NOTICE TO DEFENDANT OF RIGHT AGAINST GARNISHMENT OF WAGES, MONEY AND OTHER PROPERTY

UNITED STATES BANKRUPTCY COURT SOUTHERN DISTRICT OF FLORIDA

www.flsb.uscourts.gov

NOTICE TO DEFENDANT OF RIGHT AGAINST GARNISHMENT OF WAGES, MONEY AND OTHER PROPERTY

This notice is provided pursuant to Florida Statute 77.041 in accordance with Local Rule 7069-1(D).

The Writ of Garnishment delivered to you with this Notice means that wages, money, and other property belonging to you have been garnished to pay a court judgment against you.

HOWEVER, YOU MAY BE ABLE TO KEEP OR RECOVER YOUR WAGES, MONEY, OR PROPERTY. READ THIS NOTICE CAREFULLY.

State and federal laws provide that certain wages, money, and property, even if deposited in a bank, savings and loan, or credit union, may not be taken to pay certain types of court judgments. Such wages, money, and property are exempt from garnishment. The major exemptions are listed below on the form for Claim of Exemption and Request for Hearing. This list does not include all possible exemptions. You should consult a lawyer for specific advice.

If an exemption from garnishment applies to you and you want to keep your wages, money, and other property from being garnished, or to recover anything already taken, you must complete a form for claim of exemption and request for hearing as set forth below and have the form notarized. If you have a valid exemption, you must file the form with the clerk's office within 20 days after the date you receive this notice or you may lose important rights. You must also mail or deliver a copy of this form to the plaintiff or the plaintiff's attorney and the garnishee or the garnishee's attorney at the addresses listed on the writ of garnishment. Note that the form requires you to complete a certification that you mailed or hand delivered copies to the plaintiff or the plaintiff's attorney and the garnishee or the garnishee's attorney.

If you request a hearing, it will be held as soon as possible after your request is received by the court. The plaintiff or the plaintiff's attorney must file any objection within 8 business days if you hand delivered to the plaintiff or the plaintiff's attorney a copy of the form for Claim of Exemption and Request for Hearing or, alternatively, 14 business days if you mailed a copy of the form for claim and request to the plaintiff or the plaintiff's attorney. If the plaintiff or the plaintiff's attorney files an objection to your Claim of Exemption and Request for Hearing, the clerk will notify you and the other parties of the time and date of the hearing. You may attend the hearing with or without an attorney. If the plaintiff or the plaintiff's attorney fails to file an objection, no hearing is required, the writ of garnishment will be dissolved and your wages, money, or property will be released.

If you have a valid exemption, you should file the form for claim of exemption immediately to keep your wages, money, or property from being applied to the court judgment. The clerk cannot give you legal advice. If you need legal assistance you should see a lawyer. If you cannot afford a private lawyer, legal services may be available. Contact your local bar association or ask the clerk's office about any legal services program in your area.

Clerk of Court (SEE REVERSE FOR SERVICE REQUIREMENT)

LF-73 (rev. 12/01/15) Page 1 of 4

PLAINTIFF'S SERVICE REQUIREMENTS: The plaintiff must mail, by first class, a copy of the writ of garnishment, a copy of the motion for writ of garnishment, a copy of this court's Local Form "Notice to Defendant of Right Against Garnishment of Wages, Money and Other Property" to the defendant's last known address within 5 business days after the writ is issued or 3 business days after the writ is served on the garnishee, whichever is later. However, if such documents are returned as undeliverable by the post office, or if the last known address is not discoverable after diligent search, the plaintiff must mail, by first class, the documents to the defendant at the defendant's place of employment. The plaintiff shall file in the proceeding a certificate of such service.

Upon the filing by a defendant of the "Claim of Exemption and Request for Hearing", a hearing will be held as soon as is practicable to determine the validity of the claimed exceptions. If the plaintiff or the plaintiff's attorney does not file a sworn written statement that answers the defendant's claim of exemption within 8 business days after hand delivery of the claim and request or, alternatively, 14 business days, if the claim and request were served by mail, no hearing is required and the clerk must automatically dissolve the writ and notify the parties of the dissolution by mail.

**Local Rule 7069-1(D) Writ of Garnishment. Writs of garnishments shall be issued in accordance with Florida law.*

(1) Issuance of Writ. Required Notice To Garnishee. The party seeking issuance of a writ of garnishment shall file a motion accompanied by a prepared writ, a certified copy of the judgment, and any bill of costs entered. If the writ is issued against an individual, the clerk shall attach to the writ a copy of the Local Form "Notice Pursuant to Florida Statute §77.041 to Defendant of Right Against Garnishment of Wages, Money and Other Property" with attached "Claim of Exemption and Request for Hearing" (with the caption of the case filled in on the form "Claim of Exemption and Request for Hearing"). The following notice must accompany service of the writ: ***"Under Florida Statute 77.28, upon issuance of any writ of garnishment, the party applying for it shall pay $100 to the garnishee on the garnishee's demand at any time after the service of the writ for the payment or part payment of his or her attorney fee which the garnishee expends or agrees to expend in obtaining representation in response to the writ."*** *In addition to service of other garnishment papers, a copy of this rule shall be served on the defendant. If the writ is being sought pursuant to Florida Statute §77.0305 (continuing writ of garnishment against salary or wages) or Florida Statute §77.031 (issuance of writ before judgment), the filing of the writ must be accompanied by a motion and a proposed order.*

(2) Objection to Claim of Exemption. An objection to a defendant's "Claim of Exemption and Request for Hearing" shall be set for hearing in accordance with Local Rule 9073-1.

(3) Dissolution of Writ by Clerk. The clerk shall automatically dissolve the writ and notify the parties of the dissolution by mail upon failure of the plaintiff to timely contest the defendant's claim of exemption.

(4) Deadlines. Absent further order of the court, the procedures and deadlines set forth in Florida Statute §77.041, shall apply to writs of garnishments issued in this court.

LF-73 (rev. 12/01/15) Page 2 of 4

UNITED STATES BANKRUPTCY COURT
Southern District of Florida

In re ____________________________)
Debtor) Case No. ____________________
____________________________,)
Plaintiff) Chapter ____________________
vs.)
____________________________,) Adv. Proc. No. ____________________
Defendant)
____________________________)
Garnishee

CLAIM OF EXEMPTION AND REQUEST FOR HEARING

I claim exemptions from garnishment under the following categories as checked:

☐ 1. Head of family wages. (Check either a. or b. below, if applicable.)

☐ a. I provide more than one-half of the support for a child or other dependent and have net earnings of $750 or less per week.

☐ b. I provide more than one-half of the support for a child or other dependent, have net earnings of more than $750 per week, but have not agreed in writing to have my wages garnished.

☐ 2. Social Security benefits.

☐ 3. Supplemental Security Income benefits.

☐ 4. Public assistance (welfare).

☐ 5. Workers' Compensation.

☐ 6. Reemployment assistance or unemployment compensation.

☐ 7. Veterans' benefits.

☐ 8. Retirement or profit-sharing benefits or pension money.

☐ 9. Life insurance benefits or cash surrender value of a life insurance policy or proceeds of annuity contract.

☐ 10. Disability income benefits.

☐ 11. Prepaid College Trust Fund or Medical Savings Account.

☐ 12. Other exemptions as provided by law. ____________________________(explain)

I request a hearing to decide the validity of my claim. Notice of the hearing should be given to me at:

Address: ______________________________

Telephone number: ______________________________

I CERTIFY UNDER OATH AND PENALTY OF PERJURY that a copy of this CLAIM OF EXEMPTION AND REQUEST FOR HEARING has been furnished by (circle one)United States mail or hand delivery on (insert date) , to: (insert names and addresses of Plaintiff or Plaintiff's attorney and of Garnishee or Garnishee's attorney to whom this document was furnished).

I FURTHER CERTIFY UNDER OATH AND PENALTY OF PERJURY that the statements made in this request are true to the best of my knowledge and belief.

______________________________ ______________________________
Defendant's signature Date

STATE OF FLORIDA

COUNTY OF ____________________

Sworn and subscribed to before me this ________ **day of** ____________________ (month and year),

By ______________________________ (name of person making statement).

Notary Public/Deputy Clerk

☐ Personally Known

OR

☐ Produced Identification

Type of Identification Produced: ______________________________

LF-73 (rev. 12/01/15) Page 4 of 4

[Effective April 25, 2001. Amended effective December 1, 2002; October 30, 2006; June 2, 2008; December 1, 2009; September 15, 2014; December 1, 2015.]

LF–74. THIRD–PARTY SUMMONS

UNITED STATES BANKRUPTCY COURT
Southern District of Florida
www.flsb.uscourts.gov

In re: Case No.
Chapter

__________________________/
Debtor

__________________________ **Adversary Proceeding No.**
Plaintiff

vs.

____
Defendant and Third-Party Plaintiff

__________________________/
Third-Party Defendant

THIRD-PARTY SUMMONS

YOU ARE SUMMONED and required to file a motion or answer to the third-party complaint which is attached to this summons with the clerk of the bankruptcy court within 30 days afer the date of issuance of this summons, except that the United States and its offices and agencies shall file a motion or answer to the third-party complaint within 35 days.

☐ Clerk, 301 N. Miami Ave., #150 Miami, FL 33128	☐ Clerk, 299 E. Broward Blvd., #112 Ft. Lauderdale, FL 33301	☐ Clerk, 1515 North Flagler Drive Room 801 West Palm Beach, FL 33401

At the same time, you must also serve a copy of the motion or answer upon the defendant's attorney.

Name and Address of Defendant's Attorney

At the same time, you must also serve a copy of the motion or answer upon the plaintiff's attorney.

Name and Address of Plaintiff's Attorney

If you make a motion, your time to answer is governed by Fed. R. Bankr. P. 7012. If you are also being served with a copy of the complaint of the plaintiff, you have the option of not answering the plaintiff's complaint **unless** this is an admiralty or maritime action subject to the provisions of Fed. R. Civ. P. 9(h) and 14(c), in which case you are required to file a motion or an answer to both the plaintiff's complaint and the third-party complaint, and to serve a copy of your motion or answer upon the appropriate parties.

Pretrial Conference Information	
Address:	Date:
	Time:
	Courtroom Number:

Trial Information: A Trial Will Be Held During the One-week Trial Period Indicated Below	
Address:	Trial Week: ☐ To be set at pretrial conference
	Time:
	Courtroom Number:

IF YOU FAIL TO RESPOND TO THIS SUMMONS, YOUR FAILURE WILL BE DEEMED TO BE YOUR CONSENT TO ENTRY OF A JUDGMENT BY THE BANKRUPTCY COURT AND JUDGMENT BY DEFAULT MAY BE TAKEN AGAINST YOU FOR THE RELIEF DEMANDED IN THE THIRD-PARTY COMPLAINT.

Clerk of the Bankruptcy Court

By: ________________
Date Deputy Clerk

LF-74 (rev. 10/10/14) Page 1 of 2

CERTIFICATE OF SERVICE

I, ______________(name)______________, certify that service of this summons and a copy of the third-party complaint was made____(date)_____by:

☐ Mail service: Regular, first class United States mail, postage fully pre-paid, addressed to:

☐ Personal Service: By leaving the process with the third-party defendant or with an officer or agent of third-party defendant at:

☐ Residence Service: By leaving the process with the following adult at:

☐ Certified Mail Service on an Insured Depository Institution: By sending the process by certified mail addressed to the following officer of the third-party defendant at:

☐ Publication: The third-party defendant was served as follows: [Describe briefly]

☐ State Law: The third-party defendant was served pursuant to the laws of the State of ___(name of state)_______, as follows: [Describe briefly]

If service was made by personal service, by residence service, or pursuant to state law, I further certify that I am, and at all times during the service of process was, not less than 18 years of age and not a party to the matter concerning which service of process was made.

Under penalty of perjury, I declare that the foregoing is true and correct.

Date	Signature

Print Name		
Business Address		
City	State	Zip

LF-74 (rev. 10/10/14) Page 2 of 2

[Amended effective December 1, 2003; February 15, 2005; November 1, 2006; January 8, 2007; June 2, 2008; December 1, 2009; October 10, 2014.]

LF–75. AGREED ORDER TO EMPLOYER TO DEDUCT AND REMIT AND FOR RELATED MATTERS

UNITED STATES BANKRUPTCY COURT
SOUTHERN DISTRICT OF FLORIDA
www.flsb.uscourts.gov

In re: Case No.
Chapter 13

_______________ Debtor ___________/

AGREED ORDER TO EMPLOYER TO DEDUCT AND REMIT AND FOR RELATED MATTERS

TO: ______________________________ (The Employer)

____

____

The above-named debtor has voluntarily filed a petition and plan under chapter 13 of the United States Bankruptcy Code, seeking to pay, in whole or in part, certain debts under the protection of this court. These debts are to be paid by the chapter 13 trustee from the debtor's future earnings. It is public policy that the employer shall assist in the rehabilitation of the debtor to avoid a chapter 7 liquidation pursuant to 11 U.S.C. § 1325(b). Accordingly, pursuant to Local Rule 3070-1(D), this court orders:

1. The employer immediately shall begin withholding from wages, salary, commission, or other earnings or income of said debtor $ _______________ per month and remit this amount by check (with the debtor's name and case number indicated on the check) payable to following assigned chapter 13 trustee: (indicate assigned trustee by checking the applicable box):

_____ Robin R. Weiner, P.O. Box 2258, Memphis, TN, 38101-2258

_____ Nancy K. Neidich, P.O. Box 2099, Memphis, TN 38101-2099

2. The employer is enjoined and restrained from discharging, terminating, suspending, or discriminating against the debtor for any reason whatsoever in connection with the filing of the chapter 13 petition or this wage-deduction order, the employer is ordered further to notify the trustee of the discharge, termination, suspension, or discriminatory action, and the specific reason(s).

3. If a summons of garnishment concerning the debtor has been served on the employer, this chapter 13 case automatically enjoins and stays the continuation of that garnishment proceeding pursuant to 11 U.S.C. § 362(a); and the employer is enjoined and stayed from making any further deductions from the debtor's earnings on account of the garnishment, and is ordered to remit immediately to the chapter 13 trustee any sums already deducted and not yet paid over to the garnishment court.

4. This order supersedes any previous order of garnishment or other order issued with respect to the debtor's wages, except for income deduction orders regarding child support, alimony and related support arrearages. Such support orders shall remain

in full force and effect. Failure to comply with the provisions of this order may result in an order to show cause why said employer should not be found in contempt of this court.

5. The debtor shall mail a copy of this order to any garnishment court with an action against the debtor and any garnishing creditor. The attorney for the debtor or the clerk of court, if the debtor is pro se, must serve copies on the employer. A certificate of service in accordance with Local Rule 2002-1(F) reflecting service on all required parties must be filed with the court.

6. This order shall be effective immediately upon service on the employer. This order shall remain in full force and effect until modified, suspended or terminated either in writing by the debtor's attorney or by further order of the Court. This order shall also terminate upon dismissal of this bankruptcy case, conversion of this case to chapter 7, or entry of a discharge of the debtor.

###

Agreed to by: (Both debtor and attorney for debtor, if any, must sign)

______________________________ (The Debtor)
Print name, address and telephone number

______________________________ (The Debtor's Attorney)
Print name, address and telephone number

Submitted by:

LF-75 (rev. 02/07/13)

[Amended effective September 18, 2003; October 17, 2005; October 17, 2006; June 2, 2008; December 1, 2009; April 29, 2011; February 7, 2013.]

LF–76. NOTICE OF COMPLIANCE BY ATTORNEY FOR DEBTOR WITH LOCAL RULE 2083–1(B) CLAIMS REVIEW REQUIREMENT

UNITED STATES BANKRUPTCY COURT
SOUTHERN DISTRICT OF FLORIDA
www.flsb.uscourts.gov

In re: Case No:
Chapter 13

______________ Debtor ______/

NOTICE OF COMPLIANCE BY ATTORNEY FOR DEBTOR WITH LOCAL RULE 2083-1(B) CLAIMS REVIEW REQUIREMENT

The undersigned attorney for debtor certifies that a review of the claims register and all claims filed in the above referenced case has been completed in accordance with Local Rule 2083-1(B) and that:

1) ☐ No further action is necessary.

2) The following actions have been taken:

☐ The debtor has filed an objection to the proof of claim filed by ______________.

☐ The debtor has filed a ______ amended plan or modified plan to provide for the proof of claim filed by ______________.

☐ Other: ____
____.

A copy of this certificate of compliance was served on the chapter 13 trustee via the NEF and the debtor via U.S. Mail on ______________.

Submitted by: ______________
[Signature]

[Print Name of Attorney
Florida Bar Number
Firm
Address
Telephone Number
Facsimile Number]

LF-76 (rev. 12/01/09)

[Effective December 1, 2002. Amended effective June 2, 2008; December 1, 2009.]

LF-77. MOTION TO VALUE AND DETERMINE SECURED STATUS OF LIEN ON REAL PROPERTY

UNITED STATES BANKRUPTCY COURT
SOUTHERN DISTRICT OF FLORIDA
____________ DIVISION
www.flsb.uscourts.gov

In re: Case No:
Chapter 13

__________ Debtor __________ /

MOTION TO VALUE AND DETERMINE SECURED STATUS OF LIEN ON REAL PROPERTY

IMPORTANT NOTICE TO CREDITORS:
THIS IS A MOTION TO VALUE YOUR COLLATERAL

This Motion seeks to value collateral described below securing the claim of the creditor listed below.

____

IF YOU DISPUTE THE VALUE ALLEGED OR TREATMENT OF YOUR CLAIM PROPOSED IN THIS MOTION, YOU MUST FILE A WRITTEN OBJECTION NO LATER THAN TWO BUSINESS DAYS PRIOR TO THE SCHEDULED HEARING [SEE LOCAL RULE 3015-3(A)(2)]

If you have not filed a proof of claim, you have until the later of the claims bar date or 21 days from the date this Motion was served upon you to file a proof of claim or you will be deemed to have waived the right to payment of any unsecured claim to which you might otherwise be entitled. [See Local Rule 3015-3(A)(4)]

1. Pursuant to 11 U.S.C. §506, Bankruptcy Rule 3012, and Local Rule 3015-3, the debtor seeks to value real property securing the claim of ___(lien holder's name)___ (the "Lender"). Lender holds a mortgage recorded at OR Book _____ Page _____ in the official records of ____________ County, Florida.

2. The real property is located at ___(address)___, and is more particularly described as follows:

(Legal description)

3. At the time of the filing of this case, the value of the real property is $_________ as determined by ______(insert method of valuation)______.

4. ____(names of parties holding liens senior to lender)____ hold liens on the real property, senior to priority to Lender, securing claims in the aggregate amount of $_________.

5. *(Select only one)*:

___ Lender's collateral consists solely of the debtor's principal residence. As there is no equity in the real property after payment in full of the claims secured by liens senior to that of Lender, the value of Lender's secured interest in the real property is $0.

___ Lender's collateral is not solely the debtor's principal residence. After payment in full of the claims secured by liens senior to that of Lender, there is equity of $ __________ remaining in the real property. Accordingly, the value of Lender's secured interest in the real property is $ _______ and the value of the Lender's unsecured, deficiency claim is $ __________.

6. The undersigned reviewed the docket and claims register and states (select only one):

___ Lender has not filed a proof of claim in this case. The trustee shall not disburse any payments to Lender unless a proof of claim is timely filed. In the event a proof of claim is timely filed, it shall be classified as a secured claim to the extent provided in paragraph 5, above, and as a general unsecured claim for any deficiency, regardless of the original classification in the proof of claim as filed.

or

___ Lender filed a proof of claim in this case. It shall be classified as a secured claim to the extent provided in paragraph 5, above, and as a general unsecured claim for any deficiency, regardless of the original classification in the proof of claim.

7. The subject real property may not be sold or refinanced without proper notice and further order of the court.

WHEREFORE, the debtor respectfully requests an order of the Court (a) determining the value of the real property in the amount asserted in this Motion, (b) determining the secured status of the Lender's lien as stated above, (c) determining that any timely filed proof of claim is classified as stated above, (d) if Lender's secured interest in the real property is determined to be $0, deeming Lender's mortgage on the real property void and extinguished automatically, without further order of the Court, upon entry of the debtor's discharge in this chapter 13 case, and (e) providing such other and further relief as is just.

NOTICE IS HEREBY GIVEN THAT:

1. In accordance with the rules of this Court, unless an objection is filed with the Court and served upon the debtor, the debtor's attorney, and the trustee at least two (2) business days prior to the hearing scheduled on this Motion, the value of the collateral may be established at the amount stated above without further notice, hearing or order of the Court. Pursuant to Local Rule 3015-3, timely raised objections will be heard at the hearing scheduled on the Motion.

2. The undersigned acknowledges that this Motion and the notice of hearing thereon must be served pursuant to Bankruptcy Rule 7004 and Local Rule 3015-3 at least 21 days prior to the hearing date and that a certificate of service must be filed when the Motion and notice of hearing thereon are served.

Submitted by:

[Attorney or Debtor if the Debtor is pro se]
Address
Phone:
Email:

LF-77 (rev. 08/01/11)

[Amended effective July 1, 2004; February 10, 2005; January 8, 2007; June 2, 2008; January 8, 2010; April 29, 2011; August 1, 2011.]

LF–78. DEBTOR'S NOTICE OF FILING PAYROLL AND SALES TAX REPORTS

UNITED STATES BANKRUPTCY COURT
SOUTHERN DISTRICT OF FLORIDA
www.flsb.uscourts.gov

In re: Case No.
Chapter 11

________________ Debtor /

DEBTOR'S NOTICE OF FILING PAYROLL AND SALES TAX REPORTS

________________, Debtor-in-Possession, ("Debtor") pursuant to Local Rule 2081-1(A), having filed its Chapter 11 Petition on ________, (the "Filing Date") files its Payroll and Sales Tax Reports as follows:

PAYROLL TAXES:

I. Payroll taxes accrued for 1st month prior to filing: ________
Date Paid: ________ Amount Paid________
Place of Payment:________

II. Payroll taxes accrued for 2nd month prior to filing: ________
Date Paid: ________ Amount Paid________
Place of Payment:________

III. Payroll taxes accrued for 3rd month prior to filing: ________
Date Paid: ________ Amount Paid________
Place of Payment:________

IV. Payroll taxes accrued for 4th month prior to filing: ________
Date Paid: ________ Amount Paid________
Place of Payment:________

V. Payroll taxes accrued for 5th month prior to filing ________
Date Paid: ________ Amount Paid________
Place of Payment:________

VI. Payroll taxes accrued for 6th month prior to filing: ________
Date Paid: ________ Amount Paid________
Place of Payment:________

VII. Amount still due and owing for six month period preceding filing:________

VIII. Amount still due and owing for earlier periods: ________

SALES TAXES:

I. Gross Sales subject to Sales Tax for 1st month prior to filing: ____________
Sales taxes accrued for 1st month prior to filing: ____________
Date Paid: ____________ Amount Paid____________
Place of Payment:____________________

II. Gross Sales subject to Sales Tax for 2nd month prior to filing: ____________
Sales taxes accrued for 2nd month prior to filing: ____________
Date Paid: ____________ Amount Paid____________
Place of Payment:____________________

III. Gross Sales subject to Sales Tax for 3rd month prior to filing: ____________
Sales taxes accrued for 3rd month prior to filing: ____________
Date Paid: ____________ Amount Paid____________
Place of Payment:____________________

IV. Gross Sales subject to Sales Tax for 4th month prior to filing: ____________
Sales taxes accrued for 4th month prior to filing: ____________
Date Paid: ____________ Amount Paid____________
Place of Payment:____________________

V. Gross Sales subject to Sales Tax for 5th month prior to filing: ____________
Sales taxes accrued for 5th month prior to filing ____________
Date Paid: ____________ Amount Paid____________
Place of Payment:____________________

VI. Gross Sales subject to Sales Tax for 6th month prior to filing: ____________
Sales taxes accrued for 6th month prior to filing: ____________
Date Paid: ____________ Amount Paid____________
Place of Payment:____________________

VII. Amount still due and owing for six month period preceding filing: ____________

VIII. Amount still due and owing for earlier periods: ____________

Attached are copies of proof of all payments made for payroll taxes and sales taxes for the 6 months preceding the filing date.

I, ____________________, president of ____________________ declare under penalty of perjury that the foregoing information is true and correct to the best of my knowledge, information and belief.

Date____________________ By____________________

____
print name of individual signing

A certificate of service complying with Local Rules 2002-1(F) and 2081-1(A)(3) reflecting service on the U.S. Trustee, the Internal Revenue Service, the Florida Department of Revenue and any other taxing authority named in the report must accompany the filing of this document.

LF-78 (rev. 12/01/09)

[Effective December 1, 2002. Amended effective June 2, 2008; December 1, 2009.]

LF–81. ORDER DETERMINING DEBTOR HAS CURED DEFAULT AND PAID ALL REQUIRED POSTPETITION AMOUNTS TO [INSERT NAME OF CREDITOR HERE]

UNITED STATES BANKRUPTCY COURT
SOUTHERN DISTRICT OF FLORIDA
www.flsb.uscourts.gov

In re: Case No.:
Chapter 13

_______________________________/

Order Determining Debtor Has Cured Default and Paid All Required Postpetition Amounts to [insert name of Creditor here]

( ) The [chapter 13 trustee] [debtor] filed a notice of final cure payment on ___________. The [chapter 13 trustee] [debtor] has filed a motion stating that no response has been filed by the holder to the notice of final cure payment as required under Bankruptcy Rule 3002.1(g) or, if applicable, Local Rule 3070-1(E), and requesting entry of an ex parte order determining that the debtor has cured the default and paid all required postpetition amounts.

( ) This matter came before the court on ________________, ________ at on [chapter 13 trustee's] [debtor's] motion (ECF #____) to determine that the debtor has cured the default and paid all required postpetition amounts. The motion states that the holder of the claim filed a response objecting to the notice of final cure payment on _________ and therefore, as provided under Bankruptcy Rule 3002.1(h), the [chapter 13 trustee] [debtor] seeks determination as to whether the debtor has cured the default and paid all required postpetition amounts. The court finds after hearing and notice that the motion shall be granted.

Page 1 of 2

LF-81 (rev. 12/01/15)

Accordingly, pursuant to Bankruptcy Rule 3002.1(h), the court determines that the debtor has cured the default and paid all required postpetition amounts.

###

Copies furnished to:
[Movant] is directed to serve a copy of this Order on all parties in interest and file a certificate of service. [If the debtor is pro se, the Clerk shall serve notice of entry of this Order on all parties in interest via the Bankruptcy Noticing Center, who shall file a "Certificate of Notice" with the court.]

Page 2 of 2

LF-81 (rev. 12/01/15)

[Amended effective June 10, 2003; September 29, 2006; January, 2007; June 2, 2008; December 1, 2009; December 1, 2011; December 1, 2015.]

LF–84. SUBPOENA FOR RULE 2004 EXAMINATION

UNITED STATES BANKRUPTCY COURT

Southern District of Florida

In re ______________________ Case No. ____________
Debtor

Chapter ________

SUBPOENA FOR RULE 2004 EXAMINATION

To: ____
(Name of person to whom the subpoena is directed)

☐ *Testimony:* **YOU ARE COMMANDED** to appear at the time, date, and place set forth below to testify at an examination under Rule 2004, Federal Rules of Bankruptcy Procedure and Local Rule 2004-1.

PLACE	DATE AND TIME

The examination will be recorded by this method: ______________________________________

☐ *Production:* You, or your representatives, must also bring with you to the examination the following documents, electronically stored information, or objects, and must permit inspection, copying, testing, or sampling of the material:

____

The following provisions of Fed. R. Civ. P. 45, made applicable in bankruptcy cases by Fed. R. Bankr. P. 9016, are attached – Rule 45(c), relating to the place of compliance; Rule 45(d), relating to your protection as a person subject to a subpoena; and Rule 45(e) and 45(g), relating to your duty to respond to this subpoena and the potential consequences of not doing so.

Date: ____________

CLERK OF COURT

OR

______________________ ______________________
Signature of Clerk or Deputy Clerk Attorney's signature

The name, address, email address, and telephone number of the attorney representing (name of party)________________ ______________________who issues or requests this subpoena, are:

____

Notice to the person who issues or requests this subpoena

If this subpoena commands the production of documents, electronically stored information, or tangible things, or the inspection of premises before trial, a notice and a copy of this subpoena must be served on each party before it is served on the person to whom it is directed. Fed. R. Civ. P. 45(a)(4).

Page 1 of 3

LF-84 (rev. 12/01/15)

PROOF OF SERVICE
(This section should not be filed with the court unless required by Fed. R. Civ. P. 45.)

I received this subpoena for (name of individual and title, if any): ______________________
on (date) __________.

☐ I served the subpoena by delivering a copy to the named person as follows: ______________________
____
______________________ on (date) ______________ ; or

☐ I returned the subpoena unexecuted because: ______________________
____

Unless the subpoena was issued on behalf of the United States, or one of its officers or agents, I have also tendered to the witness the fees for one day's attendance, and the mileage allowed by law, in the amount of $ ________.

My fees are $ ________for travel and $________for services, for a total of $________.

I declare under penalty of perjury that this information is true and correct.

Date: ____________

____
Server's signature

____
Printed name and title

____
Server's address

Additional information concerning attempted service, etc.:

Federal Rule of Civil Procedure 45(c), (d), (e), and (g) (Effective 12/1/13)
(made applicable in bankruptcy cases by Rule 9016, Federal Rules of Bankruptcy Procedure)

(c) Place of compliance.

(1) For a Trial, Hearing, or Deposition. A subpoena may command a person to attend a trial, hearing, or deposition only as follows:

(A) within 100 miles of where the person resides, is employed, or regularly transacts business in person; or

(B) within the state where the person resides, is employed, or regularly transacts business in person, if the person

(i) is a party or a party's officer; or

(ii) is commanded to attend a trial and would not incur substantial expense.

(2) For Other Discovery. A subpoena may command:

(A) production of documents, or electronically stored information, or things at a place within 100 miles of where the person resides, is employed, or regularly transacts business in person; and

(B) inspection of premises, at the premises to be inspected.

(d) Protecting a Person Subject to a Subpoena; Enforcement.

(1) Avoiding Undue Burden or Expense; Sanctions. A party or attorney responsible for issuing and serving a subpoena must take reasonable steps to avoid imposing undue burden or expense on a person subject to the subpoena. The court for the district where compliance is required must enforce this duty and impose an appropriate sanction — which may include lost earnings and reasonable attorney's fees on a party or attorney who fails to comply.

(2) Command to Produce Materials or Permit Inspection.

(A) Appearance Not Required. A person commanded to produce documents, electronically stored information, or tangible things, or to permit the inspection of premises, need not appear in person at the place of production or inspection unless also commanded to appear for a deposition, hearing, or trial.

(B) Objections. A person commanded to produce documents or tangible things or to permit inspection may serve on the party or attorney designated in the subpoena a written objection to inspecting, copying, testing or sampling any or all of the materials or to inspecting the premises — or to producing electronically stored information in the form or forms requested. The objection must be served before the earlier of the time specified for compliance or 14 days after the subpoena is served. If an objection is made, the following rules apply:

(i) At any time, on notice to the commanded person, the serving party may move the court for the district where compliance is required for an order compelling production or inspection.

(ii) These acts may be required only as directed in the order, and the order must protect a person who is neither a party nor a party's officer from significant expense resulting from compliance.

(3) Quashing or Modifying a Subpoena.

(A) When Required. On timely motion, the court for the district where compliance is required must quash or modify a subpoena that:

(i) fails to allow a reasonable time to comply;

(ii) requires a person to comply beyond the geographical limits specified in Rule 45(c);

(iii) requires disclosure of privileged or other protected matter, if no exception or waiver applies; or

(iv) subjects a person to undue burden.

(B) When Permitted. To protect a person subject to or affected by a subpoena, the court for the district where compliance is required may, on motion, quash or modify the subpoena if it requires:

(i) disclosing a trade secret or other confidential research, development, or commercial information; or

(ii) disclosing an unretained expert's opinion or information that does not describe specific occurrences in dispute and results from the expert's study that was not requested by a party.

(C) Specifying Conditions as an Alternative. In the circumstances described in Rule 45(d)(3)(B), the court may, instead of quashing or modifying a subpoena, order appearance or production under specified conditions if the serving party:

(i) shows a substantial need for the testimony or material that cannot be otherwise met without undue hardship; and

(ii) ensures that the subpoenaed person will be reasonably compensated.

(e) Duties in Responding to a Subpoena.

(1) Producing Documents or Electronically Stored Information. These procedures apply to producing documents or electronically stored information:

(A) Documents. A person responding to a subpoena to produce documents must produce them as they are kept in the ordinary course of business or must organize and label them to correspond to the categories in the demand.

(B) Form for Producing Electronically Stored Information Not Specified. If a subpoena does not specify a form for producing electronically stored information, the person responding must produce it in a form or forms in which it is ordinarily maintained or in a reasonably usable form or forms.

(C) Electronically Stored Information Produced in Only One Form. The person responding need not produce the same electronically stored information in more than one form.

(D) Inaccessible Electronically Stored Information. The person responding need not provide discovery of electronically stored information from sources that the person identifies as not reasonably accessible because of undue burden or cost. On motion to compel discovery or for a protective order, the person responding must show that the information is not reasonably accessible because of undue burden or cost. If that showing is made, the court may nonetheless order discovery from such sources if the requesting party shows good cause, considering the limitations of Rule 26(b)(2)(C). The court may specify conditions for the discovery.

(2) Claiming Privilege or Protection.

(A) Information Withheld. A person withholding subpoenaed information under a claim that it is privileged or subject to protection as trial-preparation material must:

(i) expressly make the claim; and

(ii) describe the nature of the withheld documents, communications, or tangible things in a manner that, without revealing information itself privileged or protected, will enable the parties to assess the claim.

(B) Information Produced. If information produced in response to a subpoena is subject to a claim of privilege or of protection as trial-preparation material, the person making the claim may notify any party that received the information of the claim and the basis for it. After being notified, a party must promptly return, sequester, or destroy the specified information and any copies it has; must not use or disclose the information until the claim is resolved; must take reasonable steps to retrieve the information if the party disclosed it before being notified; and may promptly present the information under seal to the court for the district where compliance is required for a determination of the claim. The person who produced the information must preserve the information until the claim is resolved.

(g) Contempt. The court for the district where compliance is required – and also, after a motion is transferred, the issuing court may hold in contempt a person who, having been served, fails without adequate excuse to obey the subpoena or an order related to it

For Access to Subpoena Materials
Fed. R. Civ. P. 45(a) Committee Note (2013)

- Parties desiring access to information produced in response to this subpoena will need to follow up with the party serving the subpoena to obtain such access.
- The party serving the subpoena should make reasonable provisions for prompt access.
- The court for the district where compliance with the subpoena is required has authority to order notice of receipt of produced materials or access to them.

Page 3 of 3

LF-84 (rev. 12/01/15)

[Effective February 13, 2003. Amended effective March 26, 2007; April 5, 2007; June 2, 2008; December 1, 2009; December 1, 2013; December 1, 2015.]

LF-85. APPLICATION FOR SEARCH OF BANKRUPTCY RECORDS

UNITED STATES BANKRUPTCY COURT
SOUTHERN DISTRICT OF FLORIDA
www.flsb.uscourts.gov

APPLICATION FOR SEARCH OF BANKRUPTCY RECORDS

Name of individual or business that is subject of the search:	Social Security No. or Individual Taxpayer-Identification No. (ITIN) of Subject: Employer Tax I.D. No. (EIN) of Subject: (if any):

Please search your records for the following information regarding the individual or business named above:
☐ pending or closed bankruptcy cases in this district;
☐ pending or closed adversary proceedings;
☐ judgments/evidence of satisfaction of judgments; and
☐ other [describe briefly]

A fee of $31.00 is charged for each name or item searched plus $11.00 per certification.
Payment by money order or check must be made payable to "Clerk, U.S. Court" and must accompany the request. DO NOT SEND CASH THROUGH THE MAIL.

Name, address, and phone number of the person requesting the search:

CERTIFICATE OF SEARCH

The undersigned clerk hereby certifies the following results of a diligent search of the records of the court: [Check only the items for which a search was requested and a fee paid.]

TYPE OF CASE: ☐ Bankruptcy ☐ Adversary ☐ Other ________

CASE FILED ON: ________ **CASE NO:** ________ ☐ None Found

CASE NAME: ________________________

The following information pertains to the main bankruptcy case only:

TYPE: ☐ Voluntary ☐ Involuntary Chapter ______

CLAIMS DEADLINE: Date:________

STATUS: ☐ Pending
☐ Closed on ________ (date) ☐ Discharge granted on ________ (date)

The following information pertains to the adversary case only:

STATUS: ☐ Pending ☐ Closed on ________ (date)

DISPOSITION: ☐ Dismissed on ________
[Seal of Court]
☐ Final Judgment entered on ________ (date)
Case Number(s) of Related Bankruptcy Case(s) ________

CLERK OF COURT

By: ________________________
Deputy Clerk

Record Searched on: Date

Telephone:________________

* **This form may contain complete social-security numbers. It should not be filed electronically.**

LF-85 (rev. 12/01/16)

[Effective June 2, 2008. Amended effective December 1, 2009; November 1, 2011; December 1, 2015; December 1, 2016.]

LF–88. ARCHIVES REQUEST FORM

UNITED STATES BANKRUPTCY COURT
SOUTHERN DISTRICT OF FLORIDA
www.flsb.uscourts.gov

PLEASE REPLY TO:

☐ 301 N. Miami Ave., Room 150, Miami, FL 33128, (305) 714-1800
☐ 299 E. Broward Blvd., Room 112, Ft. Lauderdale, FL 33301, (954) 769-5700
☐ 1515 North Flagler Drive, Room 801, West Palm Beach, FL 33401, (561) 514-4100

ARCHIVES REQUEST FORM

This form is used to request and retrieve archived personal, corporate and/or adversary proceeding cases from the Federal Records Center in Ellenwood, Georgia to the clerk's office.

The file you have requested has been archived at the Federal Records Center in Ellenwood, GA. There is a $64.00 retrieval fee payable in advance for one box. Retrievals involving multiple boxes is $39.00 for each additional box. Payment by money order or check must be made payable to Clerk, U.S. Court. DO NOT SEND CASH THROUGH THE MAIL. The files are usually received within two weeks after the request has been processed. You will be notified of the arrival of the file via telephone or email. Files are automatically returned to the Federal Records Center in Georgia two weeks after their arrival.

If the document is 100 pages or less, not sealed, restricted or requiring certification then it may be retrieved via SmartScan in Adobe Portable Document Format (PDF) via email. The service fee per document is $10.00 (Judiciary Administrative Fee) + $9.90 (FRC Fee) + $ 0.65 per PDF page. If your request is available through SmartScan, and would like to receive the document via email, we will contact you prior to processing the retrieval with the exact amount owed.

SECTION A: **FOR COMPLETION BY REQUESTOR (Please Print)**

Requested by: ______________________________ Date: ____________

Address: ______________________________ Email: ____________

______________________________ Phone: (   ) ____________

File Information

Case number: ____________ Name: ______________________________

Adv. No.: ____________

Applicable docket/claim entry number(s): ______________________________

Document/Claim Description: ______________________________

____

"MAKE SURE YOU HAVE ENCLOSED FEE"

SECTION B: **FOR CLERK'S OFFICE USE ONLY**

Accession # 021 - ____ - ____ Loc. # ________ Box # ________ SmartScan G Yes G No

Request verified by ______ Date __/__/__ Amount Paid $ ________ Receipt # ________ Clerk ________

Express Acct# ____________ Requested from FRC __/__/__ by ____________ RMS changed ☐

Date Rec'd __/__/__ Notified via ☐ Email ☐ telephone ☐ forward to ____________ division

Comments:

Request No. ____________

LF-88 (rev. 10/18/16)

[Amended effective December 1, 2003; November 18, 2005; January 8, 2007; June 2, 2008; December 1, 2009; November 1, 2011; December 1, 2013; October 10, 2014; September 26, 2016; October 18, 2016.]

LF–89. SUMMARY OF [FIRST] INTERIM [OR FINAL] FEE APPLICATION OF [ ] [COUNSEL] [ACCOUNTANT]

UNITED STATES BANKRUPTCY COURT
SOUTHERN DISTRICT OF FLORIDA
__________ DIVISION

IN RE: : CHAPTER __

: CASE NO. __________

Debtor

SUMMARY OF [FIRST] INTERIM (or FINAL) FEE APPLICATION OF __________

1. Name of Applicant: ____________________
2. Role of Applicant: ____________________
3. Name of Certifying Professional: ____________________
4. Date case filed: ____________________
5. Date of Retention Order: ____________________

IF INTERIM APPLICATION, COMPLETE 6, 7 AND 8 BELOW:

6. Period for this Application: ____________________
7. Amount of Compensation Sought: ____________________
8. Amount of Expense Reimbursement Sought: ____________________

IF FINAL APPLICATION, COMPLETE 9 AND 10 BELOW:

9. Total Amount of Compensation Sought during case: ____________________
10. Total Amount of Expense Reimbursement Sought during case: __________
11. Amount of Original Retainer (s) Please disclose both Fee Retainer and Cost Retainer if such a Retainer has been received: ____________________
12. Current Balance of Retainer(s) remaining: ____________________
13. Last monthly operating report filed (Month/Year and ECF No.): __________
14. If case is Chapter 11, current funds in the Chapter 11 estate: __________
15. If case is Chapter 7, current funds held by Chapter 7 trustee: __________

COMPLETE THE ATTACHED FEE APPLICATION SUMMARY CHART. PLEASE INCLUDE THE INFORMATION FOR EACH PRIOR APPLICATION FILED WITH THE COURT:

____

LF-89 (rev. 12/01/15)

Fee Application

, counsel [accountant] to the , applies for interim [final] compensation for fees for services rendered and costs incurred in this Chapter proceeding. This application is filed pursuant to 11 U.S.C. §330 and Bankruptcy Rule 2016, and meets all of the requirements set forth in the Guidelines incorporated in Local Rule 2016-1(B)(1). The exhibits attached to this application, pursuant to the Guidelines, are:

Exhibits "1-A" and "1-B"- Summary of Professional and Paraprofessional Time.

Exhibit "2" - Summary of Requested Reimbursements of Expenses.

Exhibit "3" - The applicant's complete time records, in chronological order, by activity code category, for the time period covered by this application. The requested fees are itemized to the tenth of an hour.

Exhibit "4" – Fee Application Summary Chart

The applicant believes that the requested fee, of $________ for________ hours worked, is reasonable considering the twelve factors enumerated in Johnson v. Georgia Highway Express, Inc., 488 F.2d 714 (5th Circuit 1974), made applicable to bankruptcy proceedings by In re First Colonial Corp. of America, 544 F.2d 1291 (5th Cir. 1977), as follows:

The Time and Labor Required:

The Novelty and Difficulty of the Services Rendered:

The Skill Requisite to Perform the Services Properly:

The Preclusion of Other Employment by the Professional Due to the Acceptance of the Case:

The Customary Fee:

Whether the Fee is Fixed or Contingent:

Time Limitations Imposed by the Client or Other Circumstances:

The Experience, Reputation, and Ability of the Professional:

The Undesirability of the Case:

The Nature and Length of the Professional Relationship of the Client:

Awards in Similar Cases:

The applicant seeks an interim award of fees in the amount of $__________ and costs in the amount of $_______.

LF-89 [rev. 12/01/15]

CERTIFICATION

1. I have been designated by ____________ (the "Applicant") as the professional with responsibility in this case for compliance with the "Guidelines for Fee Applications for Professionals in the Southern District of Florida in Bankruptcy Cases" (the "Guidelines").

2. I have read the Applicant's application for compensation and reimbursement of expenses (the "Application"). The application complies with the Guidelines, and the fees and expenses sought fall within the Guidelines, except as specifically noted in this certification and described in the application.

3. The fees and expenses sought are billed at rates and in accordance with practices customarily employed by the Applicant and generally accepted by the Applicant's clients.

4. In seeking reimbursement for the expenditures described on Exhibit 2, the Applicant is seeking reimbursement only for the actual expenditure and has not marked up the actual cost to provide a profit or to recover the amortized cost of investment in staff time or equipment or capital outlay (except to the extent that the Applicant has elected to charge for in-house photocopies and outgoing facsimile transmissions at the maximum rates permitted by the Guidelines).

5. In seeking reimbursement for any service provided by a third party, the Applicant is seeking reimbursement only for the amount actually paid by the Applicant to the third party.

6. The following are the variances with the provisions of the Guidelines, the date of each court order approving the variance, and the justification for the variance: ____________ ____________.

LF-89 (rev. 12/01/15)

CERTIFICATE OF SERVICE

[Include a certificate of service conforming to Local Rule 2002-1(F)]

[Applicant]
Attorneys/Accountant for
[address]
[phone]

By: ______________________________
[name of certifying professional]
Fla. Bar No.:______________________

LF-89 [rev. 12/01/15]

Summary of Professional and
Paraprofessional Time Total
per Individual
for this Period Only
(EXHIBIT "1-A")

[If this is a final application, and does not cumulate fee details from prior interim applications, then a separate Exhibit 1-A showing cumulative time summary from all applications is attached as well]

Name	Partner, Associate or Paraprofessional	Year Licensed	Total Hours	Average Hourly Rate*	Fee
					$

Blended Average Hourly Rate: $

Total fees: $

* Indicate any changes in hourly rate and the date of such change:

EXHIBIT "1"

LF-89 [rev. 12/01/15]

Summary of Professional and Paraprofessional Time by Activity Code Category for this Time Period Only
(EXHIBIT "1-B")

Activity Code: ______:

	Name	Rate	Hours	Fees
Partners:				
Associates:				
Paralegals:				
	Activity Subtotal:			$

Activity Code: ______:

	Name	Rate	Hours	Fees
Partners:				
Associates:				
Paralegals:				
	Activity Subtotal:			$

LF-89 [rev. 12/01/15]

Activity Code: ______:

	Name	Rate	Hours	Fees
Partners:				
Associates:				
Paralegals:				
	Activity Subtotal:			$

Activity Code: ______:

	Name	Rate	Hours	Fees
Partners:				
Associates:				
Paralegals:				
	Activity Subtotal:			$

Activity Code: ______:

	Name	Rate	Hours	Fees
Partners:				
Associates:				
Paralegals:				
	Activity Subtotal:			$

LF-89 [rev. 12/01/15]

Summary of Requested Reimbursement Of Expenses
for this Time Period Only

[If this is a final application which does not cumulate prior interim applications, a separate summary showing cumulative expenses for all applications is attached as well]

1. Filing Fees $________

2. Process Service Fees $________

3. Witness Fees $________

4. Court Reporter Fees and Transcripts $________

5. Lien and Title Searches $________

6. Photocopies

(a) In-house copies ($_____ at 15¢/page) $________

(b) Outside copies ($______) $________

7. Postage $________

8. Overnight Delivery Charges $________

9. Outside Courier/Messenger Services $________

10. Long Distance Telephone Charges $________

11. Long Distance Fax Transmissions

(copies at $1/page) $________

12. Computerized Research $________

13. Out-of-Southern-District-of-Florida Travel $________

(a) Transportation ($__________)

(b) Lodging ($__________)

(c) Meals ($__________)

LF-89 [rev. 12/01/15]

14. Other Permissible Expenses (must specify and justify) $________________

(a) ($____________)
(b) ($____________)

Total Expense Reimbursement Requested $________________

EXHIBIT "2"

LF-89 [rev. 12/01/15]

[The applicant's complete time records, in chronological order, by activity code category, for the time period covered by this application. The requested fees are itemized to the tenth of an hour.]

EXHIBIT "3"

LF-89 [rev. 12/01/15]

FEE APPLICATION SUMMARY CHART

REQUEST					APPROVAL				PAID		HOLDBACK	
Date Filed	ECF #	Period Covered	Fees Requested	Expenses Requested	Date Order Entered	ECF #	Fees Approved	Expenses Approved	Fees Paid	Expenses Paid	Fees Holdback	Expenses Holdback
TOTALS												

EXHIBIT "4"

LF-89 [rev. 12/01/15]

[Effective December 1, 1998. Amended effective December 1, 2002; July 1, 2004; June 2, 2008; December 1, 2009; December 1, 2015.]

LF-90. RIGHTS AND RESPONSIBILITIES AGREEMENT BETWEEN CHAPTER 13 DEBTOR(S) AND CHAPTER 13 DEBTOR(S)' ATTORNEY FOR CASES FILED IN THE UNITED STATES BANKRUPTCY COURT, SOUTHERN DISTRICT OF FLORIDA

UNITED STATES BANKRUPTCY COURT
SOUTHERN DISTRICT OF FLORIDA
www.flsb.uscourts.gov

RIGHTS AND RESPONSIBILITIES AGREEMENT BETWEEN CHAPTER 13 DEBTOR(S) AND CHAPTER 13 DEBTOR(S)' ATTORNEY FOR CASES FILED IN THE UNITED STATES BANKRUPTCY COURT, SOUTHERN DISTRICT OF FLORIDA

This agreement between the debtor(s) and the debtor(s)' attorney which is required under Local Rule 2016-1(B)(2)(a) and acknowledges that it is important for debtor(s) to understand the debtor(s)' rights and responsibilities to the court, the chapter 13 trustee and creditors and that the debtor(s)'attorney is expected to perform certain services that the debtor(s) is entitled to receive, including but not limited to the following:

BEFORE THE CASE IS FILED:

THE DEBTOR(S) AGREE TO:

1. Discuss debtor(s)'objectives for filing the case with the attorney.
2. Timely provide the attorney with full and accurate financial and other information, including properly documented proof of income and payment advices reflecting payment within 60 calendar days prior to the date of filing the bankruptcy petition and a copy of the debtor's Federal tax return for the most recent tax year ending immediately before the commencement of the case and for which a Federal income tax return was filed.
3. Inform attorney of any changes in address or telephone number.
4. Obtain consumer credit counseling from an authorized provider before filing a petition for bankruptcy.

THE ATTORNEY AGREES TO:

1. Personally counsel debtor(s) regarding the advisability of filing under Chapter 7 or Chapter 13, as well as non-bankruptcy options, and answer debtor(s)' questions.
2. Personally explain to debtor(s) that the attorney is being retained to represent debtor(s) on all matters arising in the bankruptcy case, and explain how and when the attorney's fees and the trustee's fees are determined and paid.
3. Personally review with debtor(s) and obtain debtor(s)' signatures on the completed petition, schedules, plan and statement of financial affairs, whether filed with the petition or later, and all amendments thereto. These documents may be prepared initially with the help of clerical or paralegal staff of the attorney's office, but personal attention of the attorney is required for the review and signing by debtor(s).

LF-90 (rev. 01/13/12) Page 1 of 4

4. Timely prepare, file and serve debtor(s)' petition, plan, schedules, statement of financial affairs and all other required pleadings.
5. Provide debtor(s) with a copy of the petition, plan, schedules, statement of financial affairs immediately upon execution.
6. Explain to debtor(s) how, when and where to make all plan payments as well as all direct payments made outside the plan, with particular attention to mortgage payments and the likely consequences for failure to make such payments.
7. Advise debtor(s) to maintain appropriate insurance on all assets.
8. Obtain from the debtors a signed Local Form "Declaration Under Penalty of Perjury to Accompany Petitions, Schedules and Statements Filed Electronically" and retain original signed papers as required under Local Rule 5005-4(C).

AFTER THE CASE IS FILED

THE DEBTOR(S) AGREES TO:

1. Timely provide the attorney with all information and documents requested by trustee including any tax returns required under the Bankruptcy Code or by court order to be filed with the court or provided to the trustee or other party in interest under the Bankruptcy Court.
2. Inform the attorney and trustee of any changes in address or telephone number.
3. Appear punctually at the 341 meeting of creditors with original proof of identification and proof of social security number. Acceptable forms of proof of identification are state issued driver's license, government-issued identification card, U.S. issued passport, military identification and resident alien card. Acceptable forms of proof of social security number are a social security card, a medical insurance card, a paystub, a W-2 form, an IRS Form 1099 and a Social Security Administration Report.
4. Make the first required plan payment to trustee no later than 30 days after the filing of the petition under or conversion to chapter 13 and timely make all subsequent payments.
5. Inform the attorney of any garnishments, liens or levies on assets that occur or continue after the filing of the case.
6. Inform the attorney immediately if debtor(s) loses employment, is 'laid off' or furloughed from work, or experiences any other significant change in financial situation, including serious illness, personal injury, lottery winnings, inheritance or any other material increase or decrease in income or assets.
7. Notify the attorney immediately if debtor(s) is sued or wishes to file a lawsuit, including divorce and matters regarding personal or property injury.
8. Notify the attorney if the debtor(s) finds it necessary to incur additional debt.
9. Advise the attorney before purchasing, selling or refinancing any real property or before entering into any loan agreements to determine required procedures for court approval.
10. Timely file the Local Form "Debtor Certificate of Compliance and Request for Confirmation of Chapter 13 Plan".

11. Timely complete the required financial management course and file the Official Bankruptcy Form "Certification of Completion of Course in Personal Financial Management".
12. Timely file and serve the Local Form "Debtor's Certificate of Compliance, Motion for Issuance of Discharge and Notice of Deadline to Object".
13. Submit a proposed Local Form "Agreed Order to Employer to Deduct and Remit and for Related Matters" signed by the debtors to the court prior to the meeting of creditors.

THE ATTORNEY AGREES TO:

1. Advise debtor(s) of the requirement to attend the meeting of creditors, and notify or remind debtor(s) of the date, time, and place of the meeting in such detail as is helpful or necessary to insure debtor(s)' appearance.
2. Advise debtor(s) of the necessity of being punctual to the meeting of creditors and, in the case of a joint filing, that both spouses must appear at the same meeting of creditors with the required identification.
3. Provide competent legal representation for debtor(s) at all times.
4. Appear timely at all meetings of creditors and court hearings.
5. Personally explain to debtor(s) if an attorney not employed by debtor(s)' attorney's law firm ("appearance attorney") will represent them at any meeting of creditors or court hearing. Personally explain to debtor(s), in advance, the role and identity of the appearance attorney, obtain debtor(s) written permission for the appearance attorney to represent debtor(s), and provide the appearance attorney with the file in sufficient time to review it and be prepared to answer all questions.
6. Timely submit to trustee all requested information and documentation, including, but not limited to properly documented proof of income for debtor(s) and business documentation for self-employed debtors after requesting and receipt of same from the debtor(s).
7. Timely prepare, file and serve all amendments on trustee, creditors and all interested parties.
8. Review and respond, if necessary, to all pleadings, correspondence, inquiries and trustee status reports and promptly take the appropriate action.
9. Promptly respond to debtor(s)' questions during the pendency of the case.
10. Timely prepare, file and serve all necessary modifications to the plan and amended schedules after confirmation.
11. Timely prepare, file and serve all necessary motions, including but not limited, to motions to value collateral; motions to purchase, sell or refinance property; motions to avoid liens; and motions to incur additional debt and, if applicable, "Motion to Determine Final Cure and Mortgage Payments".
12. Timely certify attorney has reviewed proofs of claim with debtor(s) and prepared, filed and served necessary objections.
13. Timely file proofs of claim for creditors when applicable.

14. Timely appear at and defend all motions against debtor(s) until discharge, conversion or dismissal of the case.
15. Provide any other bankruptcy legal services necessary for the administration of the case in accordance with applicable federal and local laws, rules and procedures.
16. Provide a copy of this agreement immediately upon execution to debtor(s) and to trustee upon filing of the case.

______________________	______________________
Debtor	Attorney
Address ______________	Address ______________
Address ______________	Address ______________
Phone ______________	Phone ______________
DATED: ______________	DATED: ______________

____
Debtor
Address ______________
Address ______________
Phone ______________

DATED: ______________

LF-90 (rev. 01/13/12) Page 4 of 4

[Effective July 1, 2004. Amended effective June 2, 2008; December 1, 2008; January 13, 2012; December 1, 2015.]

LF–91. ORDER ESTABLISHING PROCEDURES TO PERMIT MONTHLY PAYMENT OF INTERIM FEE APPLICATIONS OF CHAPTER 11 PROFESSIONALS

UNITED STATES BANKRUPTCY COURT
SOUTHERN DISTRICT OF FLORIDA
www.flsb.uscourts.gov

In re: Chapter 11
Case No.

Debtor. /

ORDER ESTABLISHING PROCEDURES TO PERMIT MONTHLY PAYMENT OF INTERIM FEE APPLICATIONS OF CHAPTER 11 PROFESSIONALS

THIS CAUSE came for hearing before the Court on _________ at _______a.m/p.m. in _________________, Florida upon the Debtor's Motion to Establish Procedures to Permit Monthly Payment of Interim Fee Applications of Chapter 11 Professionals pursuant to Local Rule 2016-1 (B)(3) (the "Motion to Establish Procedures"). The Court, having determined that the relief requested in the Motion to Establish Procedures is in the best interests of the Debtor, the estates, and creditors; and it appearing that proper and adequate notice has been given by service of the Motion to Establish Procedures on the Office of the United States trustee, counsel for each official committee [if no committee is appointed, the 20 unsecured creditors holding the largest claims], counsel for all postpetition lenders (or counsel for their agent(s)), and all parties who filed a notice of appearance, and that no other or further notice is necessary; having heard argument of counsel, and considered the record; upon the representation of the Debtor that the estate is administratively solvent; finding that good and sufficient cause exists to grant the Motion to Establish Procedures it is **ORDERED** as follows:

1. The Motion to Establish Procedures is Granted.

2. Interim compensation and reimbursement of the Chapter 11 professionals in this case shall be in accordance with this Order.

3. Except as may otherwise be provided in Court orders authorizing the retention of specific professionals, all professionals in these cases may seek monthly compensation in accordance with the following procedure:

(a) On or before the 20th day of each month following the month for which compensation is sought, each professional whose employment was approved by order of this Court authorized to seek compensation under this Order will serve a monthly statement, by hand or overnight delivery on (i)__________, the officer designated by the Debtor to be responsible for such matters; (ii) counsel for the Debtors; (iii) counsel for all official committees; (iv) counsel for the Office of the United States trustee,; (vi) counsel for all postpetition lenders or their agent(s); and ________________ (anyone else the Court may designate) (the "Service Parties").

(b) The monthly statement need not be filed with the Court and a courtesy copy need not be delivered to the presiding judge's chambers since this Order is not intended to alter the fee application requirements outlined in §§ 330 and 331 of the Code and since professionals are still required to serve and file interim and final applications for approval of fees and expenses in accordance with the relevant provisions of the Code, the Bankruptcy Rules and the Local Rules for the United States Bankruptcy Court, Southern District of Florida.

(c) Each monthly fee statement must contain a printout or schedule of the reimbursable expenses incurred and the professional and paraprofessional time spent (in sufficient detail to allow the review of this time by the Service Parties), which shall ordinarily be for services rendered through a particular calendar month.

(d) The following shall not be compensable time entries:

Preparing, reviewing, or revising monthly fee statements, invoices or other informal interim compensation requests to the extent duplicative of the preparation of the related interim or final application filed with the court under § 330 of the Code (or vice versa).

(e) Each Service Party receiving a statement may object to the payment of the fees or the reimbursement of costs set forth therein by serving a written objection (which shall not be filed with the Court) upon the other Service Parties on the last day of the month in which the statement is received. The objection shall state the nature of the objection and identify the amount of the fees or costs to which objection is made. The objecting party shall attempt in good faith to object only to the portion of the statement that is deemed to be objectionable.

(f) In the absence of any timely objection, the Debtor is authorized to pay 80% of the fees and 100% of the expenses identified in each monthly statement to which no objection has been served in accordance with paragraph (e).

(g) If the Debtors receive an objection to a particular fee statement, they shall withhold payment of that portion of the fee statement to which the objection is directed and promptly pay the remainder of the fees and disbursements in the percentages set forth in paragraph (f). All professionals subject to this Order shall establish a separate billing number for any time spent on the resolution of fee disputes. Any fees incurred in connection with such fees disputes shall not be paid pursuant to the monthly statement but may only be sought and paid upon the filing of an interim fee application as set forth in paragraph 3(k) below and after order of court.

(h) Similarly, if the parties to an objection are able to resolve their dispute following the service of an objection and if the party whose statement was objected to serves on all of the parties listed in paragraph (a) a statement indicating that the objection is withdrawn and describing in detail the terms of the resolution, then the Debtor is authorized to pay, in accordance with paragraph (f), that portion of the fee statement which is no longer subject to an objection.

(i) All objections that are not resolved by the parties shall be preserved and presented to the Court by the objecting party at the next interim or final fee application hearing to be heard by the Court. See paragraph (k), below.

(j) The service of an objection in accordance with paragraph (e) shall not prejudice the objecting party's right to object to any fee application on any ground, whether or not raised in the objection. Furthermore, the decision by any party not to object to a fee statement shall not be a waiver of, nor otherwise prejudice, that party's right to object to any subsequent fee application.

(k) Unless the Court orders otherwise, each of the professionals utilizing the procedures described in the Order shall file interim fee applications, for the amount of fees and costs sought in paragraph 3(f) above, in accordance with the 120-day guideline set forth in Section 331 of the Bankruptcy Code as follows:

i) First Interim Fee Applications may be filed on or before ________ (the "First Interim Fee Applications"). The First Interim Fee Applications shall represent fees and costs incurred by the professionals from ________ through ________.

ii) Second Interim Fee Applications may be filed on or before ________ (the "Second Interim Fee Applications"). The Second Interim Fee Applications shall represent fees and costs incurred by the professionals from ________ through ________.

iii) Thereafter, interim fee applications may be filed in accordance with the schedule set forth above covering the preceding four month time period. All interim fee applications shall comply with the Guidelines for Fee Applications for Professionals in the Southern District of Florida Bankruptcy Cases. The Court shall schedule and conduct a hearing, upon proper notice served by the party filing the interim fee application in accordance with Bankruptcy Rule 2002(a)(6), to determine all interim fee applications pending before it.

(l) A professional who fails to file an application seeking approval of compensation and expenses previously paid under this Order when such application is due shall preclude such professional from utilizing the automatic pay procedures as provided herein until an interim fee application has been filed and heard by the Court.

(m) A determination, by the Court, that payment of compensation or reimbursement of expenses was improper as to a particular monthly statement shall not disqualify a professional from the future payment of compensation or reimbursement of expenses as set forth above, unless otherwise ordered by the Court.

(n) Neither the payment of, nor the failure to pay, in whole or in part, monthly compensation and reimbursement as provided herein shall have any effect on this Court's interim or final allowance of compensation and reimbursement of expenses of any professionals.

4. The Debtor shall include all payments to professionals on its monthly operating reports, detailed so as to state the amount paid to each of the professionals.

5. The Debtor may not make any payments under this Order if the Debtor has not timely filed monthly operating reports or remained current with its administrative expenses and 28 U.S.C. §1930. Otherwise, this Order shall continue and shall remain in effect during the pendency of this case unless otherwise ordered by the Court.

6. All time periods set forth in this Order shall be calculated in accordance with Bankruptcy Rule 9006(a).

7. Upon motion or application, and after due notice to all parties set forth on the Master Service List, additional professionals employed by the Debtor or the Committee may be authorized to participate in modified interim compensation procedures as set forth in this Order.

8. All professionals subject to this Order shall be required to monitor their own compliance with the terms of this Order and shall include the following certification on each monthly invoice: I hereby certify that I am in compliance with the terms of the Order Establishing Procedures to Permit Monthly Payment of Interim Fee Applications of Chapter 11 Professionals.

###

Submitted by:

The party submitting the order shall serve a copy of the signed order on all required parties and file with the court a certificate of service conforming with Local Rule 2002-1(F).

Page 5 of 5

LF-91 (rev. 12/01/15)

[Effective July 1, 2004. Amended effective October 17, 2005; June 2, 2008; December 1, 2009; December 1, 2015.]

LF–92. ORDER GRANTING MOTION TO VALUE AND DETERMINE SECURED STATUS OF LIEN ON REAL PROPERTY

UNITED STATES BANKRUPTCY COURT
SOUTHERN DISTRICT OF FLORIDA
www.flsb.uscourts.gov

In re: Case No:
Chapter 13

_____________Debtor___________/

ORDER GRANTING MOTION TO VALUE AND DETERMINE SECURED STATUS OF LIEN ON REAL PROPERTY HELD BY _________

THIS CASE came to be heard on __________________ on the Debtor's *Motion to Value and Determine Secured Status of Lien on Real Property* (DE _____; the "Motion").

Based upon the debtor's assertions made in support of the Motion, without objection, having considered the record in this case, and being duly advised in the premises, the Court FINDS as follows:

A. The value of the debtor's real property (the "Real Property") located at ____________(address)____________, and more particularly described as

(Legal description)

is $ ________ at the time of the filing of this case.

B. The total of all claims secured by liens on the Real Property senior to the lien of ____(creditor's name)____ (the "Lender") is $ ___________.

C. The equity remaining in the Real Property after payment of all claims secured by liens senior to the lien of Lender is $ _______ and Lender has a secured interest in the Real Property in such amount.

Consequently, it is **ORDERED** as follows:

1. The Motion is **GRANTED**.

2. Lender has an allowed secured claim in the amount of $ ___________.

3. [*Include only if appropriate*: Because Lender's secured interest in the Real Property is $0, Lender's mortgage recorded on ____(date)____ at OR BOOK __________ Page ________ of the official records of __________ County, Florida shall be deemed void and shall be extinguished automatically, without further order of the Court, upon entry of the debtor's discharge in this chapter 13 case. If this case is converted to a case under any other chapter or if the chapter 13 case is dismissed, Lender's mortgage will no longer be considered void and shall be restored as a lien on the Real Property.]

4. (Select only one):

__ Lender has not filed a proof of claim in this case. The trustee shall not disburse any payments to Lender unless a proof of claim is timely filed. In the event a proof of claim is timely filed, it shall be classified as a secured claim in the amount stated in paragraph 2, above, and as a general unsecured claim for any amount in excess of such secured claim, regardless of the original classification in the proof of claim as filed.

or

___ Lender filed a proof of claim in this case. It shall be classified as a secured claim in the amount provided in paragraph 2, above, and as a general unsecured claim in the amount of $ _________, regardless of the original classification in the proof of claim as filed.

5. The Real Property may not be sold or refinanced without proper notice and further order of the Court.

6. Notwithstanding the foregoing, this Order is not recordable or enforceable until the debtor receives a discharge in this chapter 13 case.

###

Submitted By:
____

Address: ________________
____

Phone: _________________

Attorney _________________ is directed to serve a conformed copy of this Order on all interested parties immediately upon receipt hereof and to file a certificate of service.

LF-92 (rev. 01/08/10)

[Effective November 23, 2004. Amended effective June 2, 2008; January 8, 2010.]

LF–93. CHAPTER 11 CASE MANAGEMENT SUMMARY

UNITED STATES BANKRUPTCY COURT
SOUTHERN DISTRICT OF FLORIDA
www.flsb.uscourts.gov

_________________ Division

In re: Case No.
Chapter 11

_________ Debtor ___/

CHAPTER 11 CASE MANAGEMENT SUMMARY

In compliance with Local Rule 2081-1(B), the Debtor-in-Possession [Trustee], ________________________, files this Chapter 11 Case Management Summary and states:

The following data represents approximations for background information only and the information may represent the Debtor's [Trustee's] best estimate in response to some of the ensuing questions.

1. Date of Order for Relief under chapter 11 (filing date of petition if voluntary chapter 11 petition):
2. Names, case numbers and dates of filing of related debtors:
3. Description of debtor's business:
4. Locations of debtor's operations and whether the business premises are leased or owned:
5. Reasons for filing chapter 11:
6. List of officers and directors, if applicable, and their salaries and benefits at the time of filing and during the 1 year prior to filing:
7. Debtor's fiscal or calendar year to date gross income and the debtor's gross income for the calendar or fiscal year prior to the filing of this petition:
8. Amounts owed to various creditors:

   a. Obligations owed to priority creditors including priority tax obligations:

b. With respect to creditors holding secured claims, the name of and amounts owed to such creditors and a description and estimated value of all collateral of the debtor securing their claims, and

c. Amount of unsecured claims:

9. General description and approximate value of the debtor's assets:

10. List of all insurance policies, the property covered under the policy, the name of the insurer, the policy number, amount of coverage, whether the premium is current, the date the next premium is due and date the policy expires;

11. Number of employees and amounts of wages owed as of petition date:

12. Status of debtor's payroll and sales tax obligations, if applicable. This does not eliminate the obligation of chapter 11 debtors (other than individuals not engaged in business) to provide the more detailed payroll tax information required by Local Rule 2081-1(A):

13. Anticipated emergency relief to be requested within 14 days from the petition date:

Signature

(Name of Corporate Officer or Authorized Representative)

Signature

Name and Address of Debtor's Attorney

Florida Bar No.

Attach or file separately a Local Rule 2002-1(F) certificate of service reflecting manner and date of service on all affected parties.

LF-93 (rev. 12/01/09)

[Effective July 1, 2005. Amended effective June 2, 2008; December 1, 2009.]

LF–94. ACKNOWLEDGMENT OF RESPONSIBILITY AND REQUEST FOR LOGIN ID AND PASSWORD FOR LIVE ACCESS TO CM/ECF WITH TRUSTEE/US TRUSTEE FILING PRIVILEGES

United States Bankruptcy Court, Southern District of Florida
Acknowledgment of Responsibility and Request for Login ID and Password for Live Access to CM/ECF with Trustee/US Trustee Filing Privileges
www.flsb.uscourts.gov

Use this form to request a live account to access this court's CM/ECF system with trustee or US Trustee filing privileges. Trustees may use this access only for those cases in which they are acting as case trustee. If a trustee is also an attorney, a separate attorney account must be utilized for cases in which the attorney is not acting as the assigned trustee for that case. ***Submit only the signed first page of this form to:*** *CMECF_Support@flsb.uscourts.gov.*

I. Type of Applicant: ☐ **US Trustee** ☐ **Chapter 7 Trustee** ☐ **Chapter 13 Trustee:** (Please type)

First:__________ Middle:__________ Last Name:__________ Generation (Sr., Jr.):______

Bar ID #: (if applicable)__________ (and/or if other than Florida Bar, indicate state:______)

Mailing Address: ______________________________

Telephone #:__________ Fax #:__________

E-Mail address where Notices of Electronic Filing will be sent: ______________________

Number of Additional Logins Requested Under My Name:______

[NOTE: The email address provided will be used for all logins and passwords assigned to the applicant. Attach a list with all the names in your office for whom access is being requested. An attorney appearing as an attorney in a non trustee capacity will be required to register separately as attorneys with full filing privileges.]

I have a current Trading Partner Agreement with the BNC for EDI Noticing: ☐ No ☐ Yes

II. CM/ECF Training Requirements Certification:

I and my designated staff have attended USBC SDFL classroom training and received a certificate of completion on __________, and Completed the Proof of Proficiency exercises.

III. Acknowledgment of Responsibility:

My signature below reflects that I have read and agree to the statements contained in the "CM/ECF Trustee/US Trustee Agreement" and any future requirements of the court with respect to my electronic filing privileges.

______________________ **Send Live Login/Password via:**
(Signature of Attorney/Trustee (Date) ☐ email (if other than above)__________
☐ fax __________

CLERK'S OFFICE USE ONLY

Approved by:______________ **Date:**______________

Date of Notification: ______________ **By:**______________

Email Completed Form (first page only) to: CMECF_Support@flsb.uscourts.gov.

United States Bankruptcy Court, Southern District of Florida
CM/ECF Trustee/US Trustee Agreement

[Note: Detach and retain this agreement before submitting signed application (page one of this form) to the court.]

By signing and submitting to the court the "Acknowledgment of Responsibility" contained in Part III of Local Form **Acknowledgment of Responsibility and Request for Login ID and Password for Live Access to CM/ECF with Trustee/US Trustee Filing Privileges**, I understand that:

1. I agree to adhere to all of the rules, orders, guidelines, requirements, instructions and local forms (including subsequent amendments) or any other directives issued by this court or the clerk of this court in conjunction with use of this court's CM/ECF system.

2. I must maintain a valid primary e-mail address to receive Notices of Electronic Filing, individually or in summary. I must immediately notify the clerk's CM/ECF help desk via e-mail (CMECF_support@flsb.uscourts.gov) of any change in my mailing address. Registered users who have also registered with the BNC for noticing purposes must also notify the BNC of changes in service address information.

3. It is my responsibility to pay any and all fees for transactions made in CM/ECF in accordance with the U.S. Bankruptcy Court's Fee Schedule and any court guidelines or clerk's instructions.

4. Pursuant to Bankruptcy Rule 9011, use of my login and password constitutes my signature on an electronically filed document for all purposes, including those under Rule 9011 and 28 U.S.C. § 1746, and shall have the same force and effect as if I had affixed my signature on a paper copy of the document being filed. I must type or print my name on any document filed by me either above or below the signature line.

5. I may authorize one or more employees or office staff members to use any of my assigned logins and passwords for the electronic filing of a document. I will not knowingly permit use of my login(s) and password(s) by anyone not so authorized, I will take steps to prevent such unauthorized use, and I will be fully responsible for all use whether authorized or unauthorized. If authorization to use a login and password is withdrawn (e.g., when a staff member leaves employment) or if unauthorized use of a login and password is suspected, I will immediately select and activate a new password for that login. I shall also immediately notify the court's CM/ECF help desk via e-mail (CMECF_support@flsb.uscourts.gov) upon learning of any unauthorized use. I understand that failure to change the password and notify the court under the aforementioned circumstances may result in sanctions.

6. Registration for filing in CM/ECF constitutes: (1) consent to receive service and notice electronically via the CM/ECF generated Notice of Electronic Filing ("NEF") or Daily Summary Report ("DSR") and waiver of the right to receive notice by first class mail pursuant to Federal Rule of Civil Procedure 5(b)(2)(D) and Bankruptcy Rule 7005; (2) consent to electronic service via the CM/ECF generated NEF or DSR and waiver of the right to service by personal service or first class mail pursuant to Federal Rule of Civil Procedure 5(b)(2)(D) and Bankruptcy Rule 7005, except with regard to service of a summons and complaint. Waiver of service and notice by first class mail applies to notice of the entry of an order or

judgment. In cases wherein service of documents filed electronically is required to be made on the United States and its agencies, corporations or officers, full compliance with Bankruptcy Rules 2002(j) and 7004(b)(4), (5) and (6) is required.

7. Prior to electronically filing any document with the court that requires an original third-party signature, I must obtain the original signature of that party or parties on a paper copy of the document and must retain the original of that signed document for the length of time as required under Local Rule 5005-4(C). I attest that I will advise the signing party that the document will be submitted to the court electronically and the paper version of any electronic document filed by me will be an exact copy of the printed version with the sole exception that the paper version will contain original signatures. I must type or print the name of any signer on any document filed by me either above or below the signature line and inclusion of the typed names shall be deemed a representation by me that the document was signed in original by that party, regardless of whether /s/, /s, or s/ is reflected by the typed name.

8. The trustee/US Trustee login and password assigned to me is to be used only for those cases in which I am acting in the capacity of trustee or US Trustee in that specific case and that I must register separately as an attorney user for all other cases in which I intend to file documents in this court.

LF-94 (rev. 04/09/13)

[Effective October 17, 2005. Amended effective June 2, 2008; December 1, 2009; April 9, 2013.]

LF-95. ACKNOWLEDGMENT OF RESPONSIBILITY AND REQUEST FOR LOGIN ID AND PASSWORD FOR LIVE ACCESS TO CM/ECF WITH FULL ATTORNEY FILING PRIVILEGES

United States Bankruptcy Court, Southern District of Florida
Acknowledgment of Responsibility and Request for Login ID and Password for Live Access to CM/ECF with Full Attorney Filing Privileges
www.flsb.uscourts.gov

Use this form to request a live account to access this court's CM/ECF system with full attorney filing privileges and the ability to pay filing fees by credit card for all cases and adversary proceedings in this court. This form must be submitted ***only in the name of and by the filing attorney*** *regardless of number of logins and passwords requested. Attorneys who also serve as trustees in cases in this district must obtain a separate trustee login account and sign a trustee acknowledgment of responsibility. Parties not eligible for full filing attorney privilege accounts may request a limited filer account.* ***Submit only the signed first page of this form to:*** *CMECF_Support@flsb.uscourts.gov.*

I. Attorney Applicant Information: (Please type)
First: Middle: Last Name: Generation (Sr., Jr.):____

Bar ID #:____________________ (if other than Florida Bar, indicate state:________________)

Mailing Address: (if multiple addresses exist, one registration form per mailing address must be submitted)

____

Telephone #:________________ Fax #:________________

E-Mail address where Notices of Electronic Filing will be sent: ______________________

Number of Additional Logins Requested Under My Name: _____

I have a current Trading Partner Agreement with the BNC for EDI Noticing: ☐ No ☐ Yes

II. Basis for Request for Full Filing Privileges: I certify that I am qualified to register as:

☐ An attorney qualified to practice before this court pursuant to Local Rule 2090-1(A); or

☐ An attorney approved by this court to appear pro hac vice in Case(s) # ____________pursuant to Local Rule 2090-1(C)(2); or

☐ A government attorney appearing pursuant to Local Rule 2090-1(C)(3) [except for an attorney appearing on behalf of the US Trustee's office].

III. CM/ECF Training Requirements Certification: I hereby certify that I have:

☐ Attended USBC SDFL classroom training and received a certificate of completion on ____________, and Completed the Proof of Proficiency exercises; or,

☐ I am a registered user with full CM/ECF privileges in another United States Bankruptcy Court and have completed that court's Proof of Proficiency. (Indicate bankruptcy court(s): ______________________________.

IV. Acknowledgment of Responsibility:
My signature below reflects that I have read and agree to the statements contained in the "CM/ECF Full Filing Attorney Agreement" and any future requirements of the court with respect to my electronic filing privileges.

________________________ __________
(Signature of Attorney) **(Date)**

Send Live Login/Password via:
☐ email (if other than above) ____________
☐ fax ____________

CLERK'S OFFICE USE ONLY	
Approved by:____________________	**Date:**__________
Date of Notification:____________	**By:**__________

Email Completed Form (first page only) to: *CMECF_Support@flsb.uscourts.gov*

LF-95 (rev. 12/01/16) -1-

United States Bankruptcy Court, Southern District of Florida
CM/ECF Full Filing Attorney Agreement

[Note: Detach and retain this agreement before submitting signed application (page one of this form) to the court.]

By signing and submitting to the court the **"Acknowledgment of Responsibility"** contained in Part IV of Local Form **Acknowledgment of Responsibility and Request for Login ID and Password for Live Access to CM/ECF with Full Attorney Filing Privileges**, I understand that:

1. I agree to adhere to all of the rules, orders, guidelines, requirements, instructions and local forms (including subsequent amendments) or any other directives issued by this court or the clerk of this court in conjunction with use of this court's CM/ECF system.

2. I must obtain and maintain a PACER account login, in addition to the CM/ECF login issued by this court.

3. I must maintain a valid primary e-mail address and elect to receive Notices of Electronic Filing, individually or in summary, via e-mail in cases in which I am involved. I must file a notice of change of mailing address in each case in which I am involved. Registered users who have also registered with the BNC for noticing purposes must also notify the BNC of changes in service address information.

4. I must pay by credit card over the Internet for any fees incurred for transactions made in CM/ECF in accordance with the U.S. Bankruptcy Court's Fee Schedule. Failure to timely do so will result in temporary loss of access to CM/ECF under that login and may result in dismissal of a bankruptcy petition or adversary proceeding, striking of a document and/or sanctions.

5. Pursuant to Bankruptcy Rule 9011, every petition, pleading, motion and other paper (except a list, schedule, statement, or amendments thereto) shall be signed by at least one attorney of record. Use of my login and password constitutes my signature on an electronically filed document for all purposes, including those under Rule 9011 and 28 U.S.C. §1746, and shall have the same force and effect as if I had affixed my signature on a paper copy of the document being filed. [See Local Rule 9011-4.] I must type or print my name on any document filed by me either above or below the signature line. If I am appearing pro hac vice under Local Rule 2090-1(C)(2), I must include the certification required by Local Rule 9011-4(B)(2) on each paper filed.

6. I may authorize one or more employees or office staff members to use any of my assigned logins and passwords for the electronic filing of a document. However, such use constitutes my signature on the electronically filed document. I will not knowingly permit use of my login(s) and password(s) by anyone not so authorized, I shall take steps to prevent such unauthorized use, and I shall be fully responsible for all use whether authorized or unauthorized. If authorization to use a login and password is withdrawn (e.g., when a staff member leaves employment) or if unauthorized use of a login and password is suspected, I shall forthwith select and activate a new password for that login. I shall also immediately notify the court's CM/ECF help desk via e-mail (CMECF_support@flsb.uscourts.gov) upon learning of any unauthorized use. I understand that failure to change the password and notify the clerk under the aforementioned circumstances may result in sanctions.

7. Registration for filing in CM/ECF constitutes: (1) consent to receive service and notice electronically via the CM/ECF generated Notice of Electronic Filing ("NEF") or Daily Summary Report ("DSR") and waiver of the right to receive notice by first class mail pursuant to Federal Rule of Civil Procedure 5(b)(2)(D) and

LF-95 (rev. 12/01/16) -2-

Bankruptcy Rule 7005; and (2) consent to electronic service via the NEF or DSR and waiver of the right to service by personal service or first class mail pursuant to Federal Rule of Civil Procedure 5(b)(2)(D) and Bankruptcy Rule 7005, except with regard to service of a summons and complaint. Waiver of service and notice by first class mail applies to notice of the entry of an order or judgment. In cases wherein service of electronically filed documents is required to be made on the United States and its agencies, corporations or officers, full compliance with Bankruptcy Rules 2002(j) and 7004(b)(4), (5) and (6) is required.

8. Prior to electronically filing any document with the court, I must verify the identity and obtain the original signature of the party or parties I represent on a paper copy of the document and must retain the original of that signed document for the length of time as required under Local Rule 5005-4(C). I attest that I will advise the signing party that the document will be submitted to the court electronically and the paper version of any electronic document filed by me will be an exact copy of the printed version and that no changes, alterations or other modifications will be made with the sole exception that the paper version will contain original signatures. I must type or print the name of any signer on any document filed by me either above or below the signature line and inclusion of the typed names shall be deemed a representation by me that the document was signed in original by that party, regardless of whether /s/, /s, or s/ is reflected by the typed name.

9. For individual debtor cases filed electronically, I must obtain the original signature(s) of the debtor(s) I represent on a paper copy of Official Bankruptcy Form 121 "Your Statement About Your Social Security Number(s)", and that I must retain the original of that signed document for the length of time set forth by the court. I must compare the social security number(s) provided by the debtor(s) on Official Form to the numbers entered into CM/ECF to ensure they are the same.

10. The use of my login and password in filing a document containing the signature of another person is my representation to the court that, to the best of my knowledge, the document is a true and correct copy of the original document bearing such other person's signature. In the filing of a bankruptcy petition, the use of my login and password is my representation to the court that I have in my possession a copy of the voluntary petition with the original signature of the debtor.

LF-95 (rev. 12/01/16) -3-

[Effective January 1, 2006. Amended effective June 2, 2008; December 1, 2009; April 9, 2013; October 30, 2014; December 1, 2015; December 1, 2016.]

LF–96. ACKNOWLEDGMENT OF RESPONSIBILITY AND REQUEST FOR LOGIN ID AND PASSWORD FOR LIVE ACCESS TO CM/ECF WITH LIMITED FILING PRIVILEGES

United States Bankruptcy Court, Southern District of Florida Acknowledgment of Responsibility and Request for Login ID and Password for Live Access to CM/ECF with Limited Filing Privileges
www.flsb.uscourts.gov

Use this form to request a live account to access this court's CM/ECF system with limited filing privileges. This access does not permit the filing of any document for which a fee is due and is limited to filing those events listed under Local Rule 5005-4(B)(3). Auditors pursuant to 28 U.S.C. §586(f) will only have access to file audit reports. ***Submit only the signed first page of this form to:*** *CMECF_Support@flsb.uscourts.gov.*

I. Limited Filer Applicant Information: (Please type)

First: ________ Middle: ________ Last Name: ________ Generation (Sr., Jr.): ______

Bar ID #: ____________________ (if other than Florida Bar, indicate state: ____________)

Business Name and Mailing Address: (if multiple addresses exist, one registration form per mailing address must be submitted)

____

____

Telephone #: ________ Fax #: ________

E-Mail address where Notices of Electronic Filing will be sent: ____________________

I have a current Trading Partner Agreement with the BNC for EDI Noticing: ☐ No ☐ Yes

II. CM/ECF Training Requirements Certification: I hereby certify that I have:

☐ Attended USBC SDFL classroom training and received a certificate of completion on ________, and Completed the Proof of Proficiency exercises; or,

☐ I am a registered user with CM/ECF efiling privileges in another United States Bankruptcy Court and have completed that court's Proof of Proficiency. (Indicate bankruptcy court(s): ____________

III. Acknowledgment of Responsibility:
My signature below reflects that I have read and agree to the statements contained in the "CM/ECF Limited Filer Party Agreement" and any future requirements of the court with respect to my electronic filing privileges.

____
(Signature of Limited Filer Party) (Date)

Send Live Login/Password via:
☐ email (if other than above) ____________
☐ fax ____________

CLERK'S OFFICE USE ONLY

Approved by: ____________________ **Date:** ____________

Date of Notification: ____________ **By:** ____________

Email Completed Form (first page only) to: *CMECF_Support@flsb.uscourts.gov.*

LF-96 (rev. 12/01/16) -1

United States Bankruptcy Court, Southern District of Florida
CM/ECF Limited Filer Party Agreement

[Note: Detach and retain this agreement before submitting signed application (page one of this form) to the court.]

By signing and submitting to the court the "Acknowledgment of Responsibility" contained in Part III of Local Form **Acknowledgment of Responsibility and Request for Login ID and Password for Live Access to CM/ECF with Limited Filing Privileges**, I understand that:

1. I agree to adhere to all of the rules, orders, guidelines, requirements, instructions and local forms (including subsequent amendments) or any other directives issued by this court or the clerk of this court in conjunction with use of this court's CM/ECF system.

2. By requesting limited access, I understand that I will have limited access status to perform those events listed under Local Rule 5005-4(B)(3) or other directives of the court or clerk. Auditors pursuant to 28 U.S.C. §586(f) will only have access to file audit reports. I agree that any document that I am unable to file electronically must be filed in conventionally in paper format in a timely manner. I understand that I may notify the court to terminate my status as a registered user at any time.

3. I must maintain a valid primary e-mail address and elect to receive Notices of Electronic Filing, individually or in summary, via e-mail in cases in which I am involved. I must file a notice of change of mailing address in each case in which I am involved. Registered users who have also registered with the Bankruptcy Noticing Center (BNC) for noticing purposes must also notify the BNC of changes in service address information.

4. I must pay by credit card over the Internet for any fees incurred for transactions made in CM/ECF in accordance with the U.S. Bankruptcy Court's Fee Schedule. Failure to timely do so will result in temporary loss of access to CM/ECF under that login and may result in striking of a document and/or sanctions.

5. I understand that use of my login and password constitutes my signature on an electronically filed document for all purposes, including those under Rule 9011 and 28 U.S.C. § 1746, and shall have the same force and effect as if I had affixed my signature on a paper copy of the document being filed. I must type or print my name on any document filed by me either above or below the signature line.

6. I may authorize one or more employees or office staff members to use any of my assigned login and passwords for the electronic filing of a document. However, such use constitutes my signature on the electronically filed document. I will not knowingly permit use of my login(s) and password(s) by anyone not so authorized, I shall take steps to prevent such unauthorized use, and I shall be fully responsible for all use whether authorized or unauthorized. If authorization to use a login and password is withdrawn (e.g., when a staff member leaves employment) or if unauthorized use of a login and password is suspected, I shall forthwith select and activate a new password for that login. I shall also immediately notify the court's CM/ECF help desk via e-mail (CMECF_support@flsb.uscourts.gov) upon learning of any unauthorized use. I understand that failure to change the password and notify the court under the aforementioned circumstances may result in sanctions.

LF-96 (rev. 12/01/16) -2

7. Registration for filing in CM/ECF constitutes: (1) consent to receive service and notice electronically via the CM/ECF generated Notice of Electronic Filing ("NEF") or Daily Summary Report ("DSR") and waiver of the right to receive notice by first class mail pursuant to Federal Rule of Civil Procedure 5(b)(2)(D) and Bankruptcy Rule 7005; and (2) consent to electronic service via the NEF or DSR and waiver of the right to service by personal service or first class mail pursuant to Federal Rule of Civil Procedure 5(b)(2)(D) and Bankruptcy Rule 7005, except with regard to service of a summons and complaint. Waiver of service and notice by first class mail applies to notice of the entry of an order or judgment. In cases wherein service of electronically filed documents is required to be made on the United States and its agencies, corporations or officers, full compliance with Bankruptcy Rules 2002(j) and 7004(b)(4), (5) and (6) is required.

8. Prior to electronically filing any document with the court, I must verify the identity and obtain the original signature of the party or parties I represent on a paper copy of the document and must retain the original of that signed document for the length of time as required under Local Rule 5005-4(C). I attest that I will advise the signing party that the document will be submitted to the court electronically and the paper version of any electronic document filed by me will be an exact copy of the printed version and that no changes, alterations or other modifications will be made with the sole exception that the paper version will contain original signatures. I must type or print the name of any signer on any document filed by me either above or below the signature line and inclusion of the typed names shall be deemed a representation by me that the document was signed in original by that party, regardless of whether /s/, /s, or s/ is reflected by the typed name.

9. I understand that I may **NOT** file electronically any document that requires the filer to be qualified to appear as an attorney before this court pursuant to Local Rule 2090-1, other than appearances permitted by attorneys pursuant to Local Rule 2090-1(C)(1), or if non attorney filer, those permitted by pro se filers.

10. If a registered user ceases to be an employee or agent of a creditor on whose behalf documents are being electronically filed with the court, or for any other reason ceases to be authorized to file electronically on behalf of the creditor, the registered user will promptly notify the clerk.

11. If a creditor is appearing pro se as a registered user and subsequently obtains other representation, the creditor must notify the court to terminate the user's registration.

12. The court may, *sua sponte*, terminate a registered user's login and password for any reason and require future documents to be filed conventionally or in any other format specified by the court.

LF-96 (rev. 12/01/16) -3

[Effective January 6, 2006. Amended effective October 24, 2006; June 2, 2008; December 1, 2009; April 9, 2013; October 30, 2014; December 1, 2016.]

LF-97A. DEBTOR'S CERTIFICATE OF COMPLIANCE, MOTION FOR ISSUANCE OF DISCHARGE AND NOTICE OF DEADLINE TO OBJECT

UNITED STATES BANKRUPTCY COURT
SOUTHERN DISTRICT OF FLORIDA
www.flsb.uscourts.gov

In re: Case No.
Chapter 13

_______________ Debtor(s) /

DEBTOR'S CERTIFICATE OF COMPLIANCE,
MOTION FOR ISSUANCE OF DISCHARGE AND
NOTICE OF DEADLINE TO OBJECT

NOTICE OF TIME TO OBJECT

Any interested party who fails to file and serve a written response to this motion within 21 days after the date of service of this motion shall, pursuant to Local Rules 4004-3(A)(3) and 9013-1(D), be deemed to have consented to the entry of an order of discharge.

The debtor(s)*, ____________________________, in the above captioned matter certifies as follows:

1. The chapter 13 trustee has issued a Notice of Completion of Plan Payments on __________. The debtor is requesting the court issue a discharge in this case.
2. The debtor has completed an instructional course concerning personal financial management described in 11 U.S.C. §111 and proof of completion of the course was filed with the court on __________.
3. Compliance with 11 U.S.C. §101(14A):

_____ A. The debtor has not been required by a judicial or administrative order, or by statute to pay any domestic support obligation as defined in 11 U.S.C. §101(14A) either before this bankruptcy was filed or at any time after the filing of this bankruptcy,

or

*All further references to "debtor" shall include and refer to both of the debtors in a case filed jointly by two individuals, unless any information is noted as specifically applying to only one debtor.

LF-97A (rev. 4/01/16) Page 1 of 3

_____ B. The debtor certifies that as of the date of this certification, the debtor has paid all amounts due under any and all domestic support obligations as defined in 11 U.S.C. §101(14A), required by a judicial or administrative order or by statute, including amounts due before, during and after this case was filed. The name and address of each holder of a domestic support obligation is as follows:

(NAME)
(ADDRESS)

4. The debtor's mailing address for receipt of court notices is as follows: [Note: Providing an updated debtor address here constitutes a change of address pursuant to Local Rule 2002-1(G). No separate Notice of Change of Address is required to be filed.]

(ADDRESS)

5. The name and address of the debtor's most recent employer is as follows:

(NAME)
(ADDRESS)

6. The following creditors hold a claim that is not discharged under 11 U.S.C. §523(a)(2) or (a)(4) or a claim that was reaffirmed under 11 U.S.C. §524(c):

(NAME)
(NAME)

7. Compliance with 11 U.S.C. §1328(h):

_____ A. The debtor has <u>not</u> claimed an exemption under §522(b)(3) in an amount in excess of $160,375* in property of the kind described in §522(q)(1) [generally the debtor's homestead];

- or -

*Amounts are subject to adjustment on 4/01/19, and every 3 years thereafter with respect to cases commenced on or after the date of adjustment.

LF-97A (rev. 4/01/16) Page 2 of 3

____ B. The debtor has claimed an exemption under §522(b)(3) in an amount in excess of $160,375* in property of the kind described in §522(q)(1) but there is no pending proceeding in which the debtor may be found guilty of a felony of a kind described in §522(q)(1)(A) or found liable for a debt of the kind described in §522(q)(1)(B).

8. The debtor has not received a discharge in a case filed under chapter 7, 11, or 12 during the 4 year period preceding the filing of the instant case or in a case filed under chapter 13 during the 2 year period preceding the filing of the instant case.

I declare under penalty of perjury that the information provided in this Certificate is true and correct.

/s/ ______________________
Debtor

/s/ ______________________
Debtor

CERTIFICATE OF SERVICE

Attach or file separately a Local Rule 2002-1(F) certificate of service reflecting manner and date of service on parties in interest.

If the debtor is appearing pro-se, the clerk's office will serve this Certificate and Motion.

*Amounts are subject to adjustment on 4/01/19, and every 3 years thereafter with respect to cases commenced on or after the date of adjustment.

LF-97A (rev. 4/01/16) Page 3 of 3

[Effective October 17, 2006. Amended effective June 2, 2008; December 1, 2009; April 1, 2010; December 1, 2011; April 1, 2013; December 1, 2013; December 16, 2014; December 1, 2015; April 1, 2016.]

LF–97B. DEBTOR'S CERTIFICATE OF COMPLIANCE, MOTION FOR ISSUANCE OF DISCHARGE BEFORE COMPLETION OF PLAN PAYMENTS, AND NOTICE OF DEADLINE TO OBJECT

UNITED STATES BANKRUPTCY COURT
SOUTHERN DISTRICT OF FLORIDA
www.flsb.uscourts.gov

In re: Case No.
Chapter 13

Debtor(s) /

DEBTOR'S CERTIFICATE OF COMPLIANCE, MOTION FOR ISSUANCE OF DISCHARGE BEFORE COMPLETION OF PLAN PAYMENTS, AND NOTICE OF DEADLINE TO OBJECT

NOTICE OF TIME TO OBJECT

Any interested party who fails to file and serve a written response to this motion within 21 days after the date of service of this motion shall, pursuant to Local Rules 4004-3(A)(3) and 9013-1(D), be deemed to have consented to the entry of an order of discharge.

The debtor(s)*, ______________________, in the above captioned matter moves this court for entry of discharge prior to completion of all payments under the plan pursuant to 11 U.S.C. §1328(b) and certifies as follows:

1. A. The debtor is unable to complete payments under the confirmed plan due to the following circumstances for which the debtor should not justly be held accountable:

   B. The value, as of the effective date of the plan, of property actually distributed under the plan on account of each allowed unsecured claim is not less than the amount that would have been paid on such claim if the estate of the debtor had been liquidated under chapter 7 of the Bankruptcy Code, on such date. The debtor offers the following in support of this allegation:

   C. Modification of the plan under section 1329 of the Bankruptcy Code is not practicable because:

*Unless otherwise specified, each reference to the "debtor" shall include and refer to both debtors in a case filed jointly by two individuals.

Page 1 of 3

LF-97B (rev. 4/1/16)

2. The debtor has completed an instructional course concerning personal financial management described in 11 U.S.C. §111 and proof of completion of the course was filed with the court on ____________.

3. Compliance with 11 U.S.C. §101(14A):

_____A. The debtor has not been required by a judicial or administrative order, or by statute, to pay any domestic support obligation as defined in 11 U.S.C. §101(14A) either before this bankruptcy was filed or at any time after the filing of this bankruptcy.

or

_____B. The debtor certifies that as of the date of this certification, the debtor has paid all amounts due under any and all domestic support obligations as defined in 11 U.S.C. §101(14A), required by a judicial or administrative order or by statute, including amounts due before, during and after this case was filed. The name and address of each holder of a domestic support obligation is as follows:

(NAME)
(ADDRESS)

4. The debtor's mailing address for receipt of court notices is as follows: [Note: Providing an updated debtor address here constitutes a change of address pursuant to Local Rule 2002-1(G). No separate Notice of Change of Address is required to be filed.]

(ADDRESS)

5. The name and address of the debtor's most recent employer is as follows:

(NAME)
(ADDRESS)

6. The following creditors hold a claim that is not discharged under 11 U.S.C. §523(a)(2) or (a)(4) or a claim that was reaffirmed under 11 U.S.C. §524(c):

(NAME)
(NAME)

7. Compliance with 11 U.S.C. §1328(h):

____ A. The debtor has <u>not</u> claimed an exemption under §522(b)(3) in an amount in excess of $160,375* in property of the kind described in §522(q)(1) [generally the debtor's homestead];

or

____ B. The debtor <u>has</u> claimed an exemption under §522(b)(3) in an amount in excess of $160,375* in property of the kind described in §522(q)(1) but there is no pending proceeding in which the debtor may be found guilty of a felony of a kind described in §522(q)(1)(A) or found liable for a debt of the kind described in §522(q)(1)(B).

8. The debtor has not received a discharge in a case filed under chapter 7, 11, or 12 during the 4 year period preceding the filing of the instant case or in a case filed under chapter 13 during the 2 year period preceding the filing of the instant case.

I declare under penalty of perjury that the information provided in this Certificate is true and correct. I respectfully request that the Court grant a discharge under 11 U.S.C. §1328(b) and provide such other and further relief as is just.

/s/ ______________________
Debtor

/s/
Debtor

CERTIFICATE OF SERVICE

Attach or file separately a Local Rule 2002-1(F) certificate of service reflecting manner and date of service on parties in interest.

If the debtor is appearing pro-se, the clerk's office will serve this Certificate and Motion.

*Amounts are subject to adjustment on 4/01/19, and every 3 years thereafter with respect to cases commenced on or after the date of adjustment.

Page 3 of 3

LF-97B (rev. 4/1/16)

[Effective August 1, 2011. Amended effective December 1, 2011; April 1, 2013; December 1, 2013; December 16, 2014; April 1, 2016.]

LF–98. EX PARTE MOTION TO EXCUSE COMPLIANCE UNDER LOCAL RULE 5005–4(B)

UNITED STATES BANKRUPTCY COURT
SOUTHERN DISTRICT OF FLORIDA
www.flsb.uscourts.gov

IN RE: CASE NO.
Chapter

_____________ Debtor /

***EX PARTE* MOTION TO EXCUSE COMPLIANCE UNDER LOCAL RULE 5005-4(B)**

_____________, counsel to the Debtor in this bankruptcy case, moves this court to excuse compliance under Local Rule 5005-4(B).

Local Rule 5005-4(B) requires any attorney filing a bankruptcy petition to be a registered user on the CM/ECF system. _____________ has agreed to provide pro bono representation to the Debtor. _______ is not a registered user that would permit _______ to file pleadings electronically. _____________ does not regularly appear in bankruptcy court, and, but for this pro bono case, or subsequent cases that _________ might agree to accept on a pro bono basis, _________ does not intend to file bankruptcy petitions or any other documents that otherwise would require this attorney to become a registered user under Local Rule 5005-4(B).

[If applicable] Simultaneous herewith local counsel has filed Local Form "Motion to Appear Pro Hac Vice" and proposed Local Form "Order Admitting Attorney Pro Hac Vice" as required under Local Rule 2090-1(C)(2).

WHEREFORE, ____________________ respectfully requests this court excuse compliance under Local Rule 5005-4(B) in this case.

A proposed order granting this motion is attached.

Respectfully submitted,

____

____

____

CERTIFICATE OF SERVICE

LF-98 (rev. 12/01/16)

[Effective January 23, 2009. Amended effective December 1, 2009; December 1, 2015; December 1, 2016.]

LF-99. ORDER GRANTING EX PARTE MOTION TO EXCUSE COMPLIANCE UNDER LOCAL RULE 5005-4

UNITED STATES BANKRUPTCY COURT
SOUTHERN DISTRICT OF FLORIDA
www.flsb.uscourts.gov

IN RE: CASE NO.
Chapter

_______________ Debtor /

ORDER GRANTING EX PARTE MOTION TO EXCUSE COMPLIANCE UNDER LOCAL RULE 5005-4

This matter came before the court on Motion of ____ to Excuse Compliance under Local Rule 5005-4. The court having reviewed the motion, and having granted ______ Motion to Appear *Pro Hac Vice*, the Motion to Excuse Compliance is granted.

________ may, but is not required to, file all papers in this bankruptcy case through traditional, non-electronic filing. However, _______ must otherwise comply with all Local Rules, including with respect to service of all papers and filing certificates of service.

###

Copies furnished to:

Attorney_____ shall serve a conformed copy of this order upon all parties in interest and shall file a Certificate of Service of same with the Clerk of the Court.

LF-99 (rev. 12/01/09)

[Effective January 23, 2009. Amended effective December 1, 2009.]

LF–100. TRUSTEE'S SUMMARY OF REQUESTED FEES AND EXPENSES

UNITED STATES BANKRUPTCY COURT
SOUTHERN DISTRICT OF FLORIDA
www.flsb.uscourts.gov

In re: Case No.
Chapter 7

________ Debtor ____/

Trustee's Summary of Requested Fees and Expenses

☐ [If Checked] The chapter 7 trustee is **not required** to file and serve a Notice of Trustee's Final Report and Applications for Compensation on all parties of record because the amount of net proceeds realized does not exceed the amount set forth in Bankruptcy Rule 2002(f)(8) and the amount of any application for compensation does not exceed the amount set forth in Bankruptcy Rule 2002(a)(6). See Local Rule 3009-1.

Docket Entry #	Applicant Name and Role	Total Fees Total Expenses	Interim Fees Paid Interim Expenses Paid	Additional Fees Requested Additional Expenses Requested
		$ $	$ $	$ $
		$ $	$ $	$ $

Dated: ________

Submitted by:

____
Chapter 7 Trustee
[Address]

LF- 100 (rev. 12/01/09)

[Effective May 4, 2009. Amended effective December 1, 2009.]

LF–101. NOTICE REGARDING OPPOSING MOTIONS FOR SUMMARY JUDGMENT

UNITED STATES BANKRUPTCY COURT
SOUTHERN DISTRICT OF FLORIDA
www.flsb.uscourts.gov

In re: Case No.
Chapter

_______________ Debtor _______________/

Plaintiff

vs. Adversary Proceeding No.

_______________ Defendant _______________/

NOTICE REGARDING OPPOSING MOTIONS FOR SUMMARY JUDGMENT

[Name of Movant] (the "Movant") has moved for summary judgment pursuant to Rule 7056 of the Federal Rules of Bankruptcy Procedure, which adopts by reference Rule 56 of the Federal Rules of Civil Procedure. This means that the Movant has asked the Court to decide this matter in the Movant's favor without a trial, based on written materials, which may include affidavits and other evidence, submitted in support of the motion. The claims asserted by the Movant may be decided without a trial if the Court determines that there is no genuine dispute as to any material fact and the Movant is entitled to judgment as a matter of law.

You have a right to respond to the motion under Rule 56(c). Your response may include affidavits, declarations or other evidence in opposition to the motion. You may NOT oppose summary judgment simply by relying on the statements you made in your answer or original response. If you do not respond with affidavits or other evidence contradicting the facts asserted by the Movant, the Court may accept these factual assertions as true. Therefore, it is important that you provide support to show that there is an issue for trial based on a dispute of the material facts. On the last page of this notice, you will find a form of affidavit which you may wish to use in responding to the motion for summary judgment.

Rule 56, which governs motions for summary judgment, provides as follows:

Rule 56. Summary Judgment

(a) Motion for Summary Judgment or Partial Summary Judgment. *A party may move for summary judgment, identifying each claim or defense — or the part of each claim or defense — on which summary judgment is sought. The court shall grant summary judgment if the movant shows that there is no genuine dispute as to any material fact and the movant is entitled to judgment as a matter of law. The court should state on the record the reasons for granting or denying the motion.*

(b) Time to File a Motion. *Unless a different time is set by local rule or the court orders otherwise, a party may file a motion for summary judgment at any time until 30 days after the close of all discovery.*

(c) Procedures.

(1) Supporting Factual Positions. *A party asserting that a fact cannot be or is genuinely disputed must support the assertion by:*

(A) *citing to particular parts of materials in the record, including depositions, documents, electronically stored information, affidavits or declarations, stipulations (including those made for purposes of the motion only), admissions, interrogatory answers, or other materials; or*

(B) *showing that the materials cited do not establish the absence or presence of a genuine dispute, or that an adverse party cannot produce admissible evidence to support the fact.*

(2) Objection That a Fact Is Not Supported by Admissible Evidence. *A party may object that the material cited to support or dispute a fact cannot be presented in a form that would be admissible in evidence.*

(3) Materials Not Cited. *The court need consider only the cited materials, but it may consider other materials in the record.*

(4) Affidavits or Declarations. *An affidavit or declaration used to support or oppose a motion must be made on personal knowledge, set out facts that would be admissible in evidence, and show that the affiant or declarant is competent to testify on the matters stated.*

(d) When Facts Are Unavailable to the Nonmovant. *If a nonmovant shows by affidavit or declaration that, for specified reasons, it cannot present facts essential to justify its opposition, the court may:*

(1) defer considering the motion or deny it;

(2) allow time to obtain affidavits or declarations or to take discovery; or

(3) issue any other appropriate order.

(e) Failing to Properly Support or Address a Fact. *If a party fails to properly support an assertion of fact or fails to properly address another party's assertion of fact as required by Rule 56(c), the court may:*

(1) give an opportunity to properly support or address the fact;

(2) consider the fact undisputed for purposes of the motion;

(3) *grant summary judgment if the motion and supporting materials — including the facts considered undisputed — show that the movant is entitled to it; or*

(4) *issue any other appropriate order.*

(f) ***Judgment Independent of the Motion.*** *After giving notice and a reasonable time to respond, the court may:*

(1) *grant summary judgment for a nonmovant;*

(2) *grant the motion on grounds not raised by a party; or*

(3) *consider summary judgment on its own after identifying for the parties material facts that may not be genuinely in dispute.*

(g) ***Failing to Grant All the Requested Relief.*** *If the court does not grant all the relief requested by the motion, it may enter an order stating any material fact — including an item of damages or other relief — that is not genuinely in dispute and treating the fact as established in the case.*

(h) ***Affidavit or Declaration Submitted in Bad Faith.*** *If satisfied that an affidavit or declaration under this rule is submitted in bad faith or solely for delay, the court — after notice and a reasonable time to respond — may order the submitting party to pay the other party the reasonable expenses, including attorney's fees, it incurred as a result. An offending party or attorney may also be held in contempt or subjected to other appropriate sanctions.*

UNITED STATES BANKRUPTCY COURT
SOUTHERN DISTRICT OF FLORIDA
[division name] **DIVISION**

In re: **CASE NO.**:[number]

[debtor name(s)], **CHAPTER** [chapter number 7, 11 or 13]

Debtor(s).
__________________________/

[use this section only for adversary proceedings]

[name(s) of plaintiff(s)], **ADV. NO.:** [number]

Plaintiff(s),

v.

[name(s) of defendant(s)],

Defendant(s).
__________________________/

DECLARATION UNDER PENALTY OF PERJURY

I, [name of person making statements], **being at least 18 years of age, hereby declare based on my personal knowledge:**

[numbered paragraphs stating facts in support of your position]

I declare under penalty of perjury under the laws of the United States of America that the foregoing is true and correct. Executed on [date signed].

____
[name of person signing declaration - you need to print or type the name clearly below the line and then have the person making the declaration sign his or her name above the line]

LF-101 (rev. 02/02/11)

[Effective December 1, 2009. Amended effective February 2, 2011.]

LF–102. MOTION TO VALUE AND DETERMINE SECURED STATUS OF LIEN ON PERSONAL PROPERTY

UNITED STATES BANKRUPTCY COURT
SOUTHERN DISTRICT OF FLORIDA
www.flsb.uscourts.gov

In re: Case No:
Chapter 13

_______________ Debtor _______ /

MOTION TO VALUE AND DETERMINE SECURED STATUS OF LIEN ON PERSONAL PROPERTY

IMPORTANT NOTICE TO CREDITORS:
THIS IS A MOTION TO VALUE YOUR COLLATERAL

This Motion seeks to value collateral described below securing the claim of the creditor listed below.

IF YOU DISPUTE THE VALUE ALLEGED OR TREATMENT OF YOUR CLAIM PROPOSED IN THIS MOTION, YOU MUST FILE A WRITTEN OBJECTION NO LATER THAN TWO BUSINESS DAYS PRIOR TO THE SCHEDULED HEARING [SEE LOCAL RULE 3015-3(A)(2)]

If you have not filed a proof of claim, you have until the later of the claims bar date or 21 days from the date this Motion was served upon you to file a proof of claim or you will be deemed to have waived the right to payment of any unsecured claim to which you might otherwise be entitled. [See Local Rule 3015-3(A)(4)]

1. Pursuant to 11 U.S.C. §506, Bankruptcy Rule 3012, and Local Rule 3015-3, the debtor seeks to value personal property securing the claim of (lien holder's name) ("Lender").

2. *(Select only one)*:

___ Lender's collateral consists of a motor vehicle and is particularly described as follows:

Year and Model of motor vehicle:
Vehicle Identification Number (VIN #):
Odometer reading:

___ Lender's collateral consists of a lien on personal property other than a motor vehicle and is particularly described as follows:

3. At the time of the filing of this case, the value of the personal property is $______ as determined by (insert method of valuation) .

4. The undersigned reviewed the docket and claims register and states (select only one):

___ Lender has not filed a proof of claim in this case. The trustee shall not disburse any payments to Lender unless a proof of claim is timely filed. In the event a proof of claim is timely filed, it shall be classified as a secured claim to the extent provided in paragraph 3, above, and as a general unsecured claim for any deficiency, regardless of the original classification in the proof of claim as filed. Lender's secured claim shall be paid through the plan at ____% and for a total of $________.

or

___ Lender filed a proof of claim in this case. It shall be classified as a secured claim to the extent provided in paragraph 3, above, and as a general unsecured claim for any deficiency, regardless of the original classification in the proof of claim. Lender's secured claim shall be paid through the plan at ____% and for a total of $________.

5. The subject personal property may not be sold or refinanced without proper notice and further order of the court.

WHEREFORE, the debtor respectfully requests an order of the Court (a) determining the value of the personal property in the amount asserted in this Motion, (b) determining the secured status of the Lender's lien as stated above, (c) determining that any timely filed proof of claim is classified as stated above, and (d) providing such other and further relief as is just.

NOTICE IS HEREBY GIVEN THAT:

1. In accordance with the rules of this Court, unless an objection is filed with the Court and served upon the debtor, the debtor's attorney, and the trustee at least two (2) business days prior to the hearing scheduled on this Motion, the value of the collateral may be established at the amount stated above without

further notice, hearing, or order of the Court. Pursuant to Local Rule 3015-3, timely raised objections will be heard at the hearing scheduled on the Motion.

2. The undersigned acknowledges that this Motion and the notice of hearing thereon must be served pursuant to Bankruptcy Rule 7004 and Local Rule 3015-3 at least 21 days prior to the hearing date and that a certificate of service must be filed when the Motion and notice of hearing thereon are served.

Submitted by:

[Attorney or Debtor if the Debtor is pro se]
Address
Phone:
Email:

LF-102 (rev. 08/01/11)

[Effective January 8, 2010. Amended effective April 29, 2011; August 1, 2011.]

LF–103. ORDER GRANTING MOTION TO VALUE AND DETERMINE SECURED STATUS OF LIEN ON PERSONAL PROPERTY

UNITED STATES BANKRUPTCY COURT
SOUTHERN DISTRICT OF FLORIDA
www.flsb.uscourts.gov

In re: Case No:
Chapter 13

_____________ Debtor /

ORDER GRANTING MOTION TO VALUE AND DETERMINE SECURED STATUS OF LIEN ON PERSONAL PROPERTY HELD BY _______

THIS CASE came to be heard on _____________ on the *Debtor's Motion to Value and Determine Secured Status of Lien on Personal Property* (DE __; the "Motion"). Based upon the debtor's assertions made in support of the Motion, without objection, having considered the record in this case, and being duly advised in the premises, the Court FINDS as follows:

A. The value of the debtor's personal property (the "Personal Property") more particularly described as follows *(Select only one)*:

__ Motor vehicle described as follows:

Year and Model of motor vehicle:
Vehicle Identification Number (VIN #):
Odometer reading:

__ Personal property other than a motor vehicle described as follows:

is $ _________ at the time of the filing of this case.

Consequently, it is **ORDERED** as follows:

1. The Motion is **GRANTED**.

2. Lender has an allowed secured claim in the amount of $______________.

3. (Select only one):

__ Lender has not filed a proof of claim in this case. The trustee shall not disburse any payments to Lender unless a proof of claim is timely filed. In the event a proof of claim is timely filed, it shall be classified as a secured claim in the amount stated in paragraph 2, above, and as a general unsecured claim for any amount in excess of scheduled secured claim, regardless of the original classification in the proof of claim as filed. Lender's secured claim shall be paid through the plan at _____% for a total of $__________.

or

__ Lender filed a proof of claim in this case. It shall be classified as a secured claim in the amount provided in paragraph 2, above, and as a general unsecured claim in the amount of $ _______________, regardless of the original classification in the proof of claim as filed. Lender's secured claim shall be paid through the plan at _____% for a total of $__________.

4. The Personal Property may not be sold or refinanced without proper notice and further order of the Court.

5. Notwithstanding the foregoing, this Order is not recordable or enforceable until the debtor receives a discharge in this chapter 13 case.

6. Upon notification that the debtor has received a discharge, the creditor shall take all steps necessary to release the lien upon the personal property.

###

Submitted By:

____

Address: ________________

____

Phone: ________________

Attorney ________________ is directed to serve a conformed copy of this Order on all interested parties immediately upon receipt hereof and to file a certificate of service.

LF-103 (06/14/10)

[Effective January 8, 2010. Amended effective June 14, 2010.]

LF–104. ORDER AWARDING FINAL TRUSTEE'S FEES AND EXPENSES

UNITED STATES BANKRUPTCY COURT
SOUTHERN DISTRICT OF FLORIDA
www.flsb.uscourts.gov

In re: Case No.
Chapter 7

_____________ Debtor __________/

ORDER AWARDING FINAL TRUSTEE'S FEES AND EXPENSES

THIS MATTER came before the court upon the final application for compensation and expenses [ECF # ___] filed by trustee, ___________. The court having examined the fee application(s) presented and having considered all relevant material thereto, finds that the following allowances are reasonable under the applicable provisions of the Bankruptcy Code. Therefore, it is **ORDERED** as follows:

1. ___________, trustee is allowed total final fees of $__________ and total final expenses in the amount of $ ________, which includes the fees and expenses sought in the pending application and all previously awarded interim fees and expenses, if any.

2. The trustee is authorized to make the balance of payments set forth in this order or to pay the awards pro rata if there are insufficient funds.

In allowing the foregoing fees, the court has considered the criteria specified in 11 U.S.C. §§326 and 330, and the requirements of Bankruptcy Rule 2016.

###

Copy furnished to:
_______________, Chapter 7 trustee

The trustee shall serve a copy of this order on all required parties and file with the court a certificate of service conforming with Local Rule 2002-1(F).

LF-104 (rev. 01/28/13)

[Effective June 15, 2011. Amended effective January 28, 2013.]

LF–105. ORDER AWARDING FINAL TRUSTEE AND PROFESSIONAL FEES AND EXPENSES

UNITED STATES BANKRUPTCY COURT
SOUTHERN DISTRICT OF FLORIDA
www.flsb.uscourts.gov

In re: Case No.
Chapter 7

Debtor /

ORDER AWARDING FINAL TRUSTEE AND PROFESSIONAL FEES AND EXPENSES

THIS MATTER came before the court upon the final application for compensation and expenses [ECF # ___] filed by trustee, ___________, the final application for compensation and expenses [ECF #___] filed by _________________, attorneys for the trustee, and the final application for compensation and expenses [ECF #_____] filed by _________________, accountant for the trustee [*list any other applications*]. After notice to all creditors (if applicable), the court has considered the applications and finds that the following allowances are reasonable under the applicable provisions of the Bankruptcy Code. Therefore, it is **ORDERED** as follows:

1. The trustee, __________, is allowed total final fees of $ ______ and total final expenses of $ ________, which include the fees and expenses sought in the pending application and all previously awarded interim fees and expenses, if any.

2. ______________, attorney for the trustee, is allowed total final fees of $ __________ and total final expenses of $ __________, which include the fees and expenses sought in the pending application and all previously awarded interim fees and expenses, if any. [strike if not applicable]

3. ____________________, accountant for the trustee, is allowed total final fees of $ _________ and total final expenses of $ _________, which include the fees and expenses sought in the pending application and all previously awarded interim fees and expenses, if any. [strike if not applicable]

4. __________________, [any other professional] for the trustee, is allowed total final fees of $ _______ and total final expenses of $ _______, which include the fees and expenses sought in the pending application and all previously awarded interim fees and expenses, if any. [additional professionals as necessary] [strike if not applicable]

5. The trustee is authorized to make the balance of payments set forth in this order or to pay the awards pro rata if there are insufficient funds.

In allowing the foregoing fees, this court has considered the criteria specified in 11 U.S.C. §§ 326, 328 and 330, and the requirements of Bankruptcy Rule 2016, in light of the principles stated in *Pennsylvania v. Delaware Valley Citizens' Council for Clean Air*, 478 U.S. 546 (1986); *Hensley v. Eckerhart*, 461 U.S. 424, 433 (1983); and *Norman v. Housing Auth. of Montgomery*, 836 F.2d 1292, 1299 (11th Cir. 1988).

###

Copies furnished to:
Chapter 7 trustee

The trustee shall serve a copy of this order on all required parties and file with the court a certificate of service conforming with Local Rule 2002-1(F).

LF-105 (rev. 01/28/13)

[Effective June 15, 2011. Amended effective January 28, 2013.]

LF–106. ORDER JOINTLY ADMINISTERING CHAPTER 15 CASES

UNITED STATES BANKRUPTCY COURT
SOUTHERN DISTRICT OF FLORIDA
www.flsb.uscourts.gov

In re: Case No.
Chapter 15

Jointly Administered
Case No(s), Names, and Chapter(s)

_______Debtor_______/

ORDER JOINTLY ADMINISTERING CHAPTER 15 CASES

This matter came before the court for hearing on ______________upon the [motion] filed pursuant to Bankruptcy Rule 1015 and Local Rule 1015-1(B)(2)(b).

The petitions for recognition identified in the caption of this order relate to the same debtor. It appears that these cases should be jointly administered as authorized under Bankruptcy Rule 1015 and Local Rule 1015-1.

Accordingly it is

ORDERED that:

1. These cases shall be jointly administered. Case No. __________is designated the "lead case." If applicable, case number(s) ________________________is (are) transferred to the undersigned judge.

2. A single case docket and court file will be maintained hereafter under the "lead case" number.

3. Pleadings filed in other than the lead case shall be captioned under the lead case name and case number followed by the words "(Jointly Administered)" and beneath that caption the case name(s) and number(s) for the cases in which the document is being filed.

###

Submitted by:

The party submitting the order shall serve a copy of the signed order on all appropriate parties and file with the court a certificate of service conforming with Local Rule 2002-1(F).

LF-106 (08/01/11)

[Effective August 1, 2011.]

LF–107. ORDER CONVERTING CASE UNDER CHAPTER 13 TO CASE UNDER CHAPTER 11

UNITED STATES BANKRUPTCY COURT
SOUTHERN DISTRICT OF FLORIDA
__________ DIVISION
www.flsb.uscourts.gov

In re: Case No.
Chapter 13

Debtor /

ORDER CONVERTING CASE UNDER CHAPTER 13 TO CASE UNDER CHAPTER 11

The *[Debtor][Creditor][Third Party]* filed a motion to convert this case to a case under chapter 11 of the Bankruptcy Code pursuant to 11 U.S.C. § 1307(d). On *(month)(date), (year)*, the motion came before the Court for hearing. The Court notes that this matter was properly noticed, [that no party appeared at the hearing to object to the motion,] that no order has been entered confirming a plan under § 1325, and that the debtor may be a debtor under chapter 11. Accordingly, it is

ORDERED that:

1. This chapter 13 case is converted to a case under chapter 11.

Page 1 of 3

LF-107 (rev. 03/11/16)

2. The debtor shall:

a. within 14 days of the date of this order, file a list of the debtor's equity security holders of each class, showing the number and kind of interests registered in the name of each holder and the last known name and address or place of business of each holder, as required by Bankruptcy Rule 1007(a)(3) and Local Rule 1019-1(C); and in accordance with Local Rules 1007-2 and 1009-1(D);

b. within 14 days of the date of this order and if such documents have not already been filed, file the statements, schedules and, if the debtor is an individual, payment advices or the required statement regarding payment advices and Official Bankruptcy Form 122B "Chapter 11 Statement of Your Current Monthly Income"; and

c. as required under Local Rule 2081-1, file required payroll and sales tax reports utilizing the Local Form "Debtor's Notice of Filing Payroll and Sales Tax Reports" and file the Local Form "Chapter 11 Case Management Summary";

d. if the debtor is a small business debtor, file the most recent balance sheet, statement of operations, cash flow statement and federal income tax return or a statement made under penalty of perjury that no balance sheet, statement of operations, or cash flow statement has been prepared and no federal tax return has been filed. Access to filed tax returns will be restricted for individual debtors as provided under Local Rule 5005-1(A)(2)(c).

3. Within 2 business days of the date of this order, the debtor shall file, as applicable either Bankruptcy Form B 104 "For Individual Chapter 11 Cases: The List of Creditors Who Have the 20 Largest Unsecured Claims Against You Who Are Not Insiders" or, for non individual debtors, Bankruptcy Form B 204 "For Chapter 11 Cases: The List of Creditors Who Have the 20 Largest Unsecured Claims Against You Who Are Not Insiders" as required by Bankruptcy Rule 1007(d).

4. If the debtor was the moving party, the debtor shall immediately pay a conversion fee of $932.00, if not previously paid. Failure to pay the required fees will result in dismissal of this case.

5. The Chapter 13 Trustee shall dispose of funds in the Trustee's possession in accordance with Local Rulés 1019-1(E), unless otherwise ordered by the Court.

6. The debtor shall provide notice to affected parties of the deadline set pursuant to Local Rule 1019-1(J)(1) filing by a nongovernmental unit a request for payment of an

administrative expense.

7. Failure of the debtor to comply with the provisions of this order may result in dismissal of this case without further hearing or notice.

8. If 11 U.S.C. § 1141(d)(3) applies, before a discharge can be issued, the debtor must complete a postpetition instructional course concerning personal financial management and file Official Bankruptcy Form 423 "Certification About a Financial Management Course" (unless the course provider files a certificate of completion on the debtor's behalf).

###

Submitted by:

The party submitting this order shall serve a copy of the signed order on all parties listed below and file with the Court a certificate of service conforming with Local Rule 2002-1(F).

Debtor
Attorney for Debtor
U.S. Trustee
Chapter 13 Trustee (if applicable)
Attorney for Chapter 13 Trustee (if applicable)

Page 3 of 3

LF-107 (rev. 03/11/16)

[Effective August 1, 2011. Amended effective November 1, 2011; November 21, 2012; December 1, 2013; January 28, 2015; December 1, 2015; March 11, 2016.]

CI–1. CLERK'S FILING INSTRUCTIONS

UNITED STATES BANKRUPTCY COURT
SOUTHERN DISTRICT OF FLORIDA
www.flsb.uscourts.gov

CLERK'S FILING INSTRUCTIONS

Please visit the court's website address above for additional information, including the web pages for pro se (without attorney) parties.

A. GEOGRAPHIC BOUNDARIES

This court is the United States Bankruptcy Court for the Southern District of Florida.

The Southern District of Florida is comprised of the following counties:

- Dade, Monroe (Miami Division)
- Broward - (Ft. Lauderdale Division)
- Palm Beach, Indian River, Okeechobee, Highlands, Martin, St. Lucie - (West Palm Beach Division)

B. LOCATION OF CLERK'S OFFICES

The Clerk maintains three staffed offices.

Location	Open To the Public*
C. Clyde Atkins United States Courthouse 301 N. Miami Avenue #150 Miami, Florida 33128 (305) 714-1800	Monday - Friday 8:30 am - 4:00 pm
299 E. Broward Blvd. Room 112 Ft. Lauderdale, FL 33301 (954) 769-5700	Monday - Friday 8:30 am - 4:00 pm
The Flagler Waterview Building 1515 North Flagler Drive Room 801 West Palm Beach, FL 33401 (561) 514-4100	Monday - Friday 8:30 am - 4:00 pm

*Any party seeking to conventionally file an emergency or otherwise time sensitive paper during a time period when the clerk's office is not open to the public shall, in advance, contact the clerk or chief deputy clerk to request after hours, holiday, or weekend filing accommodations. [See Local Rule 5001-2(B)]

CI-1 (rev. 12/01/16)

Page 1 of 36

C. SEARCHING FOR CASE INFORMATION

See "Clerk's Instructions for Electronic Public Access Services". Limited case information will be provided by the clerk's office in response to telephone inquiries. This information includes: case type, case number, chapter, assigned judge, date filed, date discharged, date closed, primary party names, addresses, phone numbers, and NARA's (National Archives and Records Administration) case file location numbers.

D. LOCATION OF FILES

Paper case files are not maintained for cases filed on or after October 17, 2005. Documents filed in cases filed prior to October 17, 2005, and still pending before the court are located in the clerk's office in the division where the assigned judge is chambered. Documents filed in any case on or after October 17, 2005, must be accessed electronically, either by using the clerk's office public terminals or by obtaining an account with the PACER Service Center. See "Clerk's Instructions for Obtaining Copies of Court Records."

E. BANKRUPTCY RULES AND FORMS

The Bankruptcy Code and the Bankruptcy Rules and the local rules, administrative orders, court guidelines and clerk's instructions of this court set forth the requirements for filing bankruptcy petitions, complaints, and other proceedings and papers in this court.

The current versions of the Official Bankruptcy Forms and Administrative Office of the United States Courts Director's Procedural Forms and this court's local forms must be used.

Official Bankruptcy Forms (petition, schedules and other related forms), Administrative Office of the United States Courts Director's Procedural Forms, and this court's local rules, administrative orders, local forms, clerk's instructions and court guidelines are available on the court's web site, www.flsb.uscourts.gov.

F. FILING FEES, GENERALLY

The clerk may refuse to accept for filing any petition or other paper tendered without the required clerk's fees. Payment for filing fees by non attorney filers must be in the form of cash (exact change required), money order, or cashier's or "official" check made payable to "Clerk, U.S. Court". The clerk will accept a personal or business check ONLY for payment of copy, certification or research fees and fees for compact disc of court proceedings upon presentation of an official government photo identification of the person who is presenting the check. **DO NOT SEND CASH THROUGH THE MAIL**. Child support creditors seeking fee waivers must file the Administrative Office of the United States Courts Directors' Procedural Form 2810 "Appearance of Child Support Creditor or Representative". [See Local Rules 1006-1, 5080-1 and 5081-1 and the Clerk's Summary of Fees.]

Filing fees for petitions and other fee based documents filed electronically by registered users of CM/ECF must be paid utilizing the CM/ECF credit card payment module. Failure to pay fees for electronically filed documents by 3:00 a.m. the following day will result in the temporary suspension of electronic filing privileges until all fees are paid.

For information on installment payments and chapter 7 fee waiver applications for voluntary petitions, please refer to section K(1), "Filing Fee for Petitions".

G. REQUIRED SIGNATURES AND OTHER INFORMATION

The clerk may refuse to accept for filing any petition presented without required original signature(s) and address(es) or filed by a pro se individual debtor that is not accompanied by documentary proof of the debtor's identity. (See section K(2) below). Other nonconforming papers may be stricken from the court record or, if filed in a closed or dismissed case, returned without filing. [See Local Rules 1002-1(B) and 1003-1, and 5005-1(C).]

H. PHOTO ID REQUIREMENT FOR PRO SE PETITIONS

For information about this requirement see section L, "Additional Information for Filing Petitions".

I. PLACE OF FILING PAPERS

Conventionally filed (in paper) documents may be filed in any division. Unless directed by the court, do not deliver any papers to a judge's chambers. [See Local Rule 5005-1(B).] Any creditor with internet access may file a proof of claim electronically and print a copy of the claim at the time of filing by using the electronic claims filing program available on the court website: www.flsb.uscourts.gov.

J. COURTESY COPY NOT REQUIRED

Documents filed electronically or conventionally, including petitions, notices of appeal and other documents need no additional paper copies for the court's use, unless otherwise directed by the court or clerk. **Conventional paper filers may if desired, provide an extra copy when the original is filed in order to receive a conformed copy. Please include an adequate sized stamped self-addressed envelope if return by mail is desired.**

K. OPTION FOR DEBTOR(S) TO RECEIVE COURT NOTICES ELECTRONICALLY

Debtors may voluntarily elect to receive court-generated notices and orders served by the clerk by email instead of U.S. mail by filing Local Form "Debtor's Request to Receive Notices Electronically Under DeBN Program" [see Interim Local Rule 9036-1(B) and (C)]. Notice provided under this program is limited to receipt of notices and orders served **only** by the clerk of court and that notice by all other parties must continue to be served on the debtor via U.S. mail or in person.

L. ADDITIONAL INFORMATION FOR FILING PETITIONS

To: All Potential or Current Debtors

In addition to the other informational guidelines supplied by the clerk's office, please review the following items 1 through 15 below to ensure that your papers are prepared in the correct format using the correct forms and that other clerk's instructions are followed. The following pages list the papers required by chapter (and type) of petition, complaint or other proceeding. A "Notice Required by 11 U.S.C. §342(b) for Individuals Filing for Bankruptcy" "Notice to Pro Se Debtors" and a "Notice of New Photo Identification Requirement for Debtors Filing a Petition Without Attorney Representation Effective August 1, 2011" are attached to these instructions.

PLEASE NOTE: THE STAFFS OF THE JUDGES' AND CLERK'S OFFICES ARE NOT PERMITTED TO ASSIST YOU WITH PREPARING YOUR PETITION OR OTHER DOCUMENTS, OR PROVIDE YOU WITH LEGAL ADVICE.

1. Filing Fee for Petition

If spouses are filing a joint petition, only one filing fee is required (see also item "F" "Filing Fees, Generally"). Filing fees are due at the time of filing, unless an individual debtor is requesting payment in installments or a chapter 7 individual debtor is seeking a fee waiver. The following requirements must be met:

A. Installment payments

Only individual debtors (including joint petitions filed) may apply to pay the filing fee in installments. You must use the Local Form "Application for Individuals to Pay the Filing Fee in Installments" available from the clerk's office. Both debtors, if joint petition, must sign the application. A minimum installment payment of one half the filing fee at the time of filing of the petition is required. The clerk will not accept a voluntary petition presented for filing by a debtor seeking to pay filing fee in installments if filing fees remain due from any previous case filed by that debtor unless the application is accompanied by payment of all previously due fees. [See Local Rules 1002-1(B)(1)(b) and 1006-1(A)]

B. Chapter 7 Fee Waiver Applications.

Individual debtors in chapter 7 cases who meet certain financial requirements may apply for a waiver of the filing and certain other fees. Bankruptcy Form 103B "Application to Have the Chapter 7 Filing Fee Waived" must be submitted in accordance with the Judicial Conference of the United States' approved policy implementing Chapter 7 Fee Waiver Provision and Local Rule 1006-1(B). These documents are posted on the court website on the pro se web page under the information for chapter 7 fee waivers along with a link to the poverty guidelines that must be met in order to qualify for this waiver.

2. **Photo Identification Requirement for Pro Se Petitions**

Debtors who are not represented by an attorney must present current official government photo identification at the time the petition is presented for filing. [See the clerk's public notice "New Photo Identification Requirement for Debtors Filing a Petition Without Attorney Representation Effective August 1, 2011" attached to these instructions] and Local Rule 1002-1(B)(1)(d).

3. **Petition**

A. The petition must be completed fully and signed by debtors. For a joint petition, wherever signatures are required, both spouses must sign, even if the form you are using does not provide enough lines for both to sign. Original signatures must be on all documents for conventionally filed documents.

B. An individual and a corporation, trust or partnership cannot file in the same petition. Separate petitions must be filed. [See also Local Rule 1015-1(A) for joint administration.] A corporation, trust or partnership filing a petition must be represented by an attorney.

C. If you have not filed any prior bankruptcy case within the last eight years, you must indicate "NO" in the section of the petition requesting prior filing information.

D. All information requested in the petition must be completed. If complete schedules are not filed with the petition, please estimate statistical information.

E. All originals and copies must be legible (including handwritten papers).

4. **Statement of Social Security**

All individual debtors must submit a Bankruptcy Form 121 "Statement About Your Social Security Numbers" at the time the petition is filed. This document will not be placed in the public records.

5. **Requirement of Debtor to Complete Part 5 of the Voluntary Bankruptcy Petition Regarding Consumer Credit Counseling Requirement**

Individual debtors must comply with credit counseling requirements under 11 U.S.C. §§109(h) and 521(b), and Bankruptcy Rule 1007(b)(3), and indicate the debtor's status by completing Part 5 of the Official Bankruptcy Form 101 "Voluntary Petition for Individuals Filing for Bankruptcy" and submit any required attachments. If a joint case, both spouses must each complete this section and include attachments.

FAILURE TO COMPLY WITH THESE REQUIREMENTS MAY RESULT IN DISMISSAL OF YOUR CASE WITHOUT FURTHER NOTICE. Make sure you are using the most recent version of the official forms available on the court's website since major forms revisions took effect on December 1, 2015.

6. **List of Creditors (Creditor Service Matrix)**

Follow the instructions contained in "Clerk's Instructions for Preparing, Submitting and Obtaining Service Matrices". Do not follow the instructions that come with the kit you may have purchased from an office supply store. **DO NOT PUT ANY OTHER INFORMATION ON THIS MATRIX OTHER THAN WHICH THE INSTRUCTIONS REQUIRE. FAILURE TO COMPLY WITH MATRIX REQUIREMENTS MAY RESULT IN DISMISSAL OF YOUR CASE.**

7. **Schedules**

Use the latest version linked to on the court website. **IMPORTANT: MAJOR REVISIONS WERE MADE TO THE OFFICIAL BANKRUPTCY FORMS AND ADMINISTRATIVE OFFICE DIRECTOR'S PROCEDURAL FORMS EFFECTIVE 12/01/15.** When filing schedules, submit everything listed in these Instructions required for the chapter you are filing, even if you indicate **"NONE"**. Do not omit the schedules you think are unnecessary because you don't have any real property, secured creditors, etc. because your case may be dismissed without further notice for failure to file documents. Debtors must sign their own schedules and statements and any amendments. [See Clerk's Instructions for Preparing, Submitting and Obtaining Service Matrices". Local Rules 1007-1, 1007-2, and 1009-1; and see also Local Rule 1009-1(D)(4) Re: Deadline for Amendments in Unconfirmed Chapter 13 Cases.]

8. **Chapter 13 Plan**

If filing a chapter 13 case, the plan must be submitted on the local form required by Local Rule 3015-1(B)(1). [See Local Rule 3015-1(B)(2), and Local Rule 3015-2(A) "Deadline for Filing Amended Plan".] You must start making your plan payments to your chapter 13 trustee no later than 30 days after filing your petition. [See Local Rule 3070-1.]

9. **Use of Bankruptcy Kits**

The instructions contained in the "bankruptcy kit" you purchased will differ from this court's clerk's instructions, and this court requires you to use a local version of some forms instead of the national version (i.e., "Application to Pay Filing Fee in Installments"). Please make sure you follow the clerk's instructions and use the latest version of all required forms when filing a case in this district.

10. **Refiling after Dismissal**

If the petition is being filed after dismissal of the debtor's previous case by any bankruptcy court, a copy of the dismissal order and any other orders which set forth the conditions under which the subsequent case may be filed must accompany the petition. [See Local Rule 1002-1(A)(3).]

The clerk will not accept any voluntary petition presented for filing by a debtor who had a prior case dismissed by an order which prohibited the debtor from filing for a period of time that has not yet expired, or where a court order sets forth conditions for refiling and those conditions have not been met. [See Local Rule 1002-1(B)(1)(a).]

Individual debtors filing a chapter 7, 11, or 13 case who have filed a previous case or case(s) at any time should be aware that, protection of the automatic stay may be limited or may not be available at all. [See 11 U.S.C. §362(c)(3) and 11 U.S.C. §362(c)(4).]

11. Debtors Filing Without an Attorney or with Assistance from a Bankruptcy Petition Preparer

If the debtor is not represented by an attorney on the voluntary petition, the debtor should provide the court with a phone number where the debtor can be reached. An attorney is required for all petitions filed by corporations and other non-individual business entities. [Local Rule 9010-1(B)(1)].

Bankruptcy petition preparers who prepare documents for filing by debtors must sign the documents and include the preparer's name, address, social security number and telephone number [see 11 U.S.C. §110], and file Official Form 2800 "Disclosure of Compensation of Bankruptcy Petition Preparer". [See also Local Rule 2016-1(D).] Any document prepared by a bankruptcy petition preparer must include the required Bankruptcy Form 119 "Bankruptcy Petition Preparer's Notice, Declaration, and Signature" [See also section 2 above regarding pro se debtor photo identification requirement.]

12. Form of Petitions and Attachments and Other Papers Filed with the Court

Review the Local Rules for form requirements for conventional paper and registered CM/ECF filers. When filing schedules, file every schedule listed for that chapter and type (individual or non-individual) even if you will indicate "None" on the document. When filing copies of payment advices under 11 U.S.C. §521(a)(1)(B)(iv), or notifying the court that payment advices will not be filed, submit the Local Form "Declaration Regarding Payment Advices". [See Local Rule 1007-1(E).]

[See also Local Rules 5005-1, 5005-3, 5005-4, 9004-1, 9004-2, 9011-4, and 9072-1 for additional format requirements and "Guidelines for Preparing, Submitting and Serving Orders"].

13. Amendments to Petitions, Schedules, Lists, and Statements

For information on fee, format and service requirements for submitting amendments to petitions, lists, schedules and statements, see Local Rules 1007-2 and 1009-1, the "Clerk's Instructions for Preparing, Submitting and Obtaining Service Matrices" and Local Form "Debtor's Notice of Compliance with Requirements for Amending Creditor Information". Requests for amendments to a debtor's social security number must comply with Local Rule 1009-1(C). If attempting to amend schedules to add creditors after a case is closed, please refer to Local Rule 5010-1(B).

14. Debtor's Tax Returns

Debtors must provide the trustee with a copy of their federal income tax return if required under 11 U.S.C. §521(e) or the case may be dismissed. [See Local Rule 1007-1(F).] [Do not file the return with the court unless directed by the court.]

15. Documents Required by Chapter or Proceeding Type

Following are lists by chapter or type of proceeding of the documents (indicating format of submission) required in this court. Certain documents are required at the time of initiating the filing and are indicated by an "*". The other required documents may be either filed at the time of the initial filing or by the deadlines stated in the federal statutes, rules and local rules and orders. You must use the most current version of the Official Bankruptcy Forms, Administrative Office of the United States Courts Director's Forms and this court's local forms. **PLEASE NOTE THESE FORMS WERE SUBSTANTIALLY AMENDED EFFECTIVE 12/01/15.**

If seeking joint administration or substantive consolidation of cases, please refer to Local Rule 1015-1. Conventional paper filers: Assemble original papers in the order listed below for the chapter you are filing under.

*minimum initial filing requirements

CI-1 (rev. 12/01/16)

CHAPTER 7 (Attorney needed for Non-Individual Cases)

Debtors must provide the trustee with a copy of their federal income tax return if required under 11 U.S.C. §521(e) or the case may be dismissed. [Do not file the return with the court unless directed by the court.]

Original and, if desired, 1 copy for return to filer
Filing Fee: $335.00

OFFICIAL FORM	FORM TITLE – CHAPTER 7 INDIVIDUAL CASES ONLY
*101	**Voluntary Petition** • Individual debtors must obtain credit counseling before filing the petition, unless an exception applies. (See clerk's "Stop" notice attached to these instructions.) • Debtors filing without attorney representation (pro se) must provide a current government issued photo identification at the time of filing the petition. See the clerk's public notice "New Photo Identification Requirement for Debtors Filing a Petition without Attorney Representation Effective August 1, 2011" [attached to these instructions.]
*101A	Initial Statement About an Eviction Judgement Against You. • File IF you marked "Yes" to both questions in #11 of the Voluntary Petition.
106Sum	Summary of Your Assets and Liabilities and Certain Statistical Information
106A/B	Schedule A/B: Property
106C	Schedule C: The Property You Claim as Exempt
106D	Schedule D: Creditors Who Have Claims Secured by Property
106E/F	Schedule E/F: Creditors Who Have Unsecured Claims
106G	Schedule G: Executory Contracts and Unexpired Leases
106H	Schedule H: Your Codebtors
106I	Schedule I: Your Income
106J	Schedule J: Your Expenses
106J-2	Schedule J-2: Expenses for Separate Household of Debtor 2. • File IF you marked "Yes" to both questions in 106J, Part 1.
106Dec	Declaration About an Individual Debtor's Schedules
107	Statement of Financial Affairs for Individuals Filing for Bankruptcy
*119	Bankruptcy Petition Preparer's Notice, Declaration, and Signature (if applicable)
*121	Statement About Your Social Security Numbers – Note this document will not be placed in public records.

CI-1 (rev. 12/01/16)
*minimum initial filing requirements

OFFICIAL FORM	FORM TITLE – CHAPTER 7 INDIVIDUAL CASES ONLY
*	Creditor Matrix filed in accordance with the "Clerk's Instructions for Preparing, Submitting and Obtaining Service Matrices".

Additional Requirements

FORM NUMBER	FORM TITLE
108	Statement of Intention for Individuals Filing Under Chapter 7.
2030	Director's Form "Disclosure of Compensation of Attorney for Debtor" (if debtor is represented by an attorney).
2800	Disclosure of Compensation of Bankruptcy Petition Preparer (if applicable).
122A-1	Chapter 7 Statement of Your Current Monthly Income. File Official Form 122A-1Supp, Statement of Exemption from Presumption of Abuse Under §707(b)(2), and Official Form 122A-2, Chapter 7 Means Test Calculation, if applicable.
LF-10	Declaration Regarding Payment Advices. File this cover sheet with attached copies of all payment advices or other evidence of payment received within 60 days before the date of the filing of the petition as required by 11 U.S.C. §521(a)(1)(b)(iv). If copies are not attached, file the "Declaration" and indicate the reason(s).
*	Certificate of Credit Counseling: This certification is issued by a credit counseling agency to each debtor AFTER a debtor has completed a credit counseling course.
*LF-03	Application to Pay Filing Fee in Installments. If a debtor is unable to pay the filing fee in full, use this court's local form application to pay the filing fee in installments.(if applicable)
*103B	Application to Have the Chapter 7 Filing Fee Waived. (if applicable)
	Certificate of Personal Financial Management: Before a discharge can be entered, each individual debtor must take an approved course about personal financial management. In some instances, a vendor may file the debtor's certificate with the court. If the vendor does not, the debtor must obtain the certificate, and file the certificate or Official Form 423, Certification About a Financial Management Course.

*minimum initial filing requirements

CI-1 (rev. 12/01/16)

OFFICIAL FORM	FORM TITLE – CHAPTER 7 NON-INDIVIDUAL CASES ONLY
*201	Voluntary Petition
202	Declaration Under Penalty of Perjury for Non-Individual Debtors
206Sum	Summary of Assets and Liabilities for Non-Individuals
206A/B	Schedule A/B: Property
206D	Schedule D: Creditors Who Have Claims Secured by Property
206E/F	Schedule E/F: Creditors Who Have Unsecured Claims
206G	Schedule G: Executory Contracts and Unexpired Leases
206H	Schedule H: Your Codebtors
207	Statement of Financial Affairs for Non-Individuals Filing for Bankruptcy
*	Creditor Matrix filed in accordance with the "Clerk's Instructions for Preparing, Submitting and Obtaining Service Matrices".

Additional Requirements

FORM NUMBER	FORM TITLE
	Corporate Ownership Statement (as required by Bankruptcy Rule 1007(a)(1) and Local Rule 1002-1(A)(2)). [Please note Local Rule 1002-1(A)(2) definition of parties falling under the classification of "corporation" required to file this statement.]
2030	Director's Form "Disclosure of Compensation of Attorney for Debtor"

CI-1 (rev. 12/01/16)
*minimum initial filing requirements

CHAPTER 9 Original and, if desired, 1 copy for return to filer
Filing Fee: $ 1,717.00

OFFICIAL FORM	FORM TITLE – CHAPTER 9 NON-INDIVIDUAL CASES ONLY
*201	Voluntary Petition
202	Declaration Under Penalty of Perjury for Non-Individual Debtors
204	For Chapter 11 or Chapter 9 Cases: List of Creditors Who Have the 20 Largest Unsecured Claims and are Not Insiders.

Additional Requirements

FORM NUMBER	FORM TITLE
2030	Director's Form "Disclosure of Compensation of Attorney for Debtor"
	List of Creditors (deadline for filing set by court)
	Plan

*minimum initial filing requirements
CI-1 (rev. 12/01/16)

CHAPTER 11 (Attorney Needed for Non-Individual Cases)

Debtors must provide the trustee with a copy of their federal income tax return if required under 11 U.S.C. §521(e) or the case may be dismissed. [Do not file the return with the court unless directed by the court.] See Below under "Additional Requirement" for chapter 11 small business requirement to file tax return with the petition.

For additional chapter 11 requirements and forms, please refer to the "Clerk's Instructions for Chapter 11 Cases", court "Guidelines for Prepackaged Chapter 11 Cases" and to the U.S. Trustee Guideline letter you will receive from the U.S. Trustee after your case is filed and the forms listed on the Miami U.S. Trustee website: http://www.justice.gov/ust-regions-r21/region-21-chapter-11-2.

Original and 1 copy to be returned to filer
Filing Fee: $ 1,717.00

OFFICIAL FORM	FORM TITLE – CHAPTER 11 INDIVIDUAL CASES ONLY
*101	Voluntary Petition • Individual debtors must obtain credit counseling before filing the petition, unless an exception applies. (See clerk's "Stop" notice attached to these instructions.) • Debtors filing without attorney representation (pro se) must provide a current government issued photo identification at the time of filing the petition. See the clerk's public notice "New Photo Identification Requirement for Debtors Filing a Petition Without Attorney Representation Effective August 1, 2011" [attached to these instructions.]
*101A	Initial Statement About an Eviction Judgement Against You. • File IF you marked "Yes" to both questions in #11 of the Voluntary Petition.
*104	List of Creditors Who Have the 20 Largest Unsecured Claims Against You and Are Not Insiders
106Sum	Summary of Your Assets and Liabilities and Certain Statistical Information
106A/B	Schedule A/B: Property
106C	Schedule C: The Property You Claim as Exempt
106D	Schedule D: Creditors Who Have Claims Secured by Property
106E/F	Schedule E/F: Creditors Who Have Unsecured Claims
106G	Schedule G: Executory Contracts and Unexpired Leases

CI-1 (rev. 12/01/16)
*minimum initial filing requirements

OFFICIAL FORM	FORM TITLE – CHAPTER 11 INDIVIDUAL CASES ONLY
106H	Schedule H: Your Codebtors
106I	Schedule I: Your Income
106J	Schedule J: Your Expenses
106J-2	Schedule J-2: Expenses for Separate Household of Debtor 2. • File IF you marked "Yes" to both questions in 106J, Part 1.
106Dec	Declaration About an Individual Debtor's Schedules
107	Statement of Financial Affairs for Individuals Filing for Bankruptcy
*119	Bankruptcy Petition Preparer's Notice, Declaration, and Signature (If applicable)
*121	Statement About Your Social Security Numbers
*	Creditor Matrix filed in accordance with the "Clerk's Instructions for Preparing, Submitting and Obtaining Service Matrices".

Additional Requirements

FORM NUMBER	FORM TITLE
2030	Director's Form "Disclosure of Compensation of Attorney for Debtor" (if debtor is represented by an attorney).
2800	Disclosure of Compensation of Bankruptcy Petition Preparer (if applicable).
122B	Chapter 11 Statement of Your Monthly Income
LF-10	Declaration Regarding Payment Advices. File this cover sheet with attached copies of all payment advices or other evidence of payment received within 60 days before the date of the filing of the petition as required by 11 U.S.C. §521(a)(1)(b)(iv). If copies are not attached, file the "Declaration" and indicate the reason(s).
*	Certificate of Credit Counseling: This certification is issued by a credit counseling agency to each debtor AFTER a debtor has completed a credit counseling course.
*	Plan and Disclosure Statement. Note: See Clerk's Instructions for Chapter 11 cases for the forms available.
*LF-03	Application to Pay Filing Fee in Installments. If a debtor is unable to pay the filing fee in full, use this court's local form application to pay the filing fee in installments.
LF-93	Local Form "Chapter 11 Case Management Summary" as required under Local Rule 2081-1(B) must be filed within the earlier of three business days after relief is entered or one business day prior to the date of the first scheduled hearing. This summary must be served on all parties of record.

CI-1 (rev. 12/01/16)
*minimum initial filing requirements

FORM NUMBER	FORM TITLE
	If debtor is a small business, as required by 11 U.S.C. §1116(1), debtors' most recent balance sheet, statement of operations, cash-flow statement, and Federal income tax return; or a statement made under penalty of perjury that no balance sheet, statement of operations, or cash-flow statement has been prepared and no Federal tax return has been filed. For individual debtors only, the tax return will be docketed as a non-public "restricted" documents and requests for copies must comply with Local Rules 1007-1(F) and 5005-1(A)(2)(c).
	Certificate of Personal Financial Management: Before a discharge can be entered, each individual debtor must take an approved course about personal financial management. In some instances, a vendor may file the debtor's certificate with the court. If the vendor does not, the debtor must obtain the certificate, and file the certificate or Official Form 423, Certification About a Financial Management Course.
	If debtor is an individual, as required under Local Rules 3022-1(B) and 4004-3(A)(9), the Local Form "Notice of Deadline to Object to Debtor's Statements Re: 11 U.S.C. §522(q)(1) Applicability, Payment of Domestic Support Obligations and [For Chapter 11 Cases Only] Applicability of Financial Management Course and Statement Regarding Eligibility to Receive a Discharge" must be filed and served before the court may consider entry of the discharge.

OFFICIAL FORM	FORM TITLE – CHAPTER 11 NON-INDIVIDUAL CASES ONLY
*201	Voluntary Petition
201A	Attachment to Voluntary Petition for Non-Individuals Filing for Bankruptcy Under Chapter 11 (if applicable)
202	Declaration Under Penalty of Perjury for Non-Individual Debtors
*204	List of Creditors Who Have the 20 Largest Unsecured Claims and Are Not Insiders
206Sum	Summary of Assets and Liabilities for Non-Individuals
206A/B	Schedule A/B: Property
206D	Schedule D: Creditors Who Have Claims Secured by Property
206E/F	Schedule E/F: Creditors Who Have Unsecured Claims
206G	Schedule G: Executory Contracts and Unexpired Leases
206H	Schedule H: Your Codebtors
207	Statement of Financial Affairs for Non-Individuals Filing for Bankruptcy
*	Creditor Matrix filed in accordance with the "Clerk's Instructions for Preparing, Submitting and Obtaining Service Matrices".

CI-1 (rev. 12/01/16)
*minimum initial filing requirements

Additional Requirements

FORM NUMBER	FORM TITLE
	Names and addresses of equity security holders of the debtor.
2030	Disclosure of Compensation of Attorney for Debtor
	Plan and Disclosure Statement. Note: See Clerk's Instructions for Chapter 11 cases for the forms available.
	Pursuant to Local Rule 2081-1(A), chapter 11 debtors, except individual debtors not engaged in business, are required to file within 14 days after filing the petition, a certified report containing financial information regarding payroll and sales taxes using Local Form "Debtor's Notice of Filing Payroll and Sales Tax Reports". Only the original (with certificate of service included) need be filed with the court.
	Corporate Ownership Statement (as required by Bankruptcy Rule 1007(a)(1) and Local Rule 1002-1(A)(2)). Please note Local Rule 1002-1(A)(2) definition of parties falling under the classification of "corporation" required to file this statement.
	If debtor is a small business, as required by 11 U.S.C. §1116(1), debtors' most recent balance sheet, statement of operations, cash-flow statement, and Federal income tax return; or a statement made under penalty of perjury that no balance sheet, statement of operations, or cash-flow statement has been prepared and no Federal tax return has been filed. For individual debtors only, the tax return will be docketed as a non-public "restricted" documents and requests for copies must comply with Local Rules 1007-1(F) and 5005-1(A)(2)(c).
LF-93	Local Form "Chapter 11 Case Management Summary" as required under Local Rule 2081-1(B) must be filed within the earlier of three business days after relief is entered or one business day prior to the date of the first scheduled hearing. This summary must be served on all parties of record.

CI-1 (rev. 12/01/16)
*minimum initial filing requirements

CHAPTER 12 (Attorney Needed for Non-Individual Cases)

Debtors must provide the trustee with a copy of their federal income tax return if required under 11 U.S.C. §521(e) or the case may be dismissed. [Do not file the return with the court unless directed by the court.]

Original and, if desired, 1 copy for return to filer
Filing Fee: $ 275.00

OFFICIAL FORM	FORM TITLE – CHAPTER 12
*101 or 201	**Voluntary Petition** • Individual debtors must obtain credit counseling before filing the petition, unless an exception applies. (See clerk's "Stop" notice attached to these instructions.) • Debtors filing without attorney representation (pro se) must provide a current government issued photo identification at the time of filing the petition. See the clerk's public notice "New Photo Identification Requirement for Debtors Filing a Petition without Attorney Representation Effective August 1, 2011" [attached to these instructions.]
*101A	Initial Statement About an Eviction Judgement Against You. • File IF you marked "Yes" to both questions in #11 of the Voluntary Petition.
202	Declaration Under Penalty of Perjury for Non-Individual Debtor's (if applicable)
106/206Sum	Summary of Your Assets and Liabilities and Certain Statistical Information
106/206A/B	Schedule A/B: Property
106C	Schedule C: The Property You Claim as Exempt
106/206D	Schedule D: Creditors Who Have Claims Secured by Property
106/206E/F	Schedule E/F: Creditors Who Have Unsecured Claims
106/206G	Schedule G: Executory Contracts and Unexpired Leases
106/206H	Schedule H: Your Codebtors
106I	Schedule I: Your Income
106J	Schedule J: Your Expenses
106J-2	Schedule J-2: Expenses for Separate Household of Debtor 2 (if applicable)
106/Dec	Declaration About an Individual Debtor's Schedules
107/207	Statement of Financial Affairs for Individuals Filing for Bankruptcy
*119	Bankruptcy Petition Preparer's Notice, Declaration, and Signature (If applicable)
*121	Statement About Your Social Security Numbers (if applicable)
*	Creditor Matrix filed in accordance with the "Clerk's Instructions for Preparing, Submitting and Obtaining Service Matrices".

CI-1 (rev. 12/01/16)
*minimum initial filing requirements

Page 17 of 36

Additional Requirements (Filed separately)

FORM NUMBER	FORM TITLE
2030	Director's Form "Disclosure of Compensation of Attorney for Debtor" (if applicable).
2800	Disclosure of Compensation of Bankruptcy Petition Preparer (if applicable).
	Corporate Ownership Statement (as required by Bankruptcy Rule 1007(a)(1) and Local Rule 1002-1(A)(2)). [Please note Local Rule 1002-1(A)(2) definition of parties falling under the classification of "corporation" required to file this statement.] (if applicable)
LF-10	Local Form "Declaration Regarding Payment Advices" with attached copies of all payment advices or other evidence of payment received within 60 days before the date of the filing of the petition as required by 11 U.S.C. §521(a)(1)(b)(iv). If copies are not attached, file the "Declaration" and indicate the reason(s). (required for all individual debtors). (if applicable)
	If debtor is an individual, as required under Local Rules 2080-1(B) and 4004-3(A)(9), the Local Form "Notice of Deadline to Object to Debtor's Statements Re: 11 U.S.C. §522(q)(1) Applicability, Payment of Domestic Support Obligations and [For Chapter 11 Cases Only] Applicability of Financial Management Course and Statement Regarding Eligibility to Receive a Discharge" must be filed and served before the court may consider entry of the discharge. (if applicable)
	Certificate of Personal Financial Management: Before a discharge can be entered, each individual debtor must take an approved course about personal financial management. In some instances, a vendor may file the debtor's certificate with the court. If the vendor does not, the debtor must obtain the certificate, and file the certificate or Official Form 423, Certification About a Financial Management Course. (if applicable)

CI-1 (rev. 12/01/16)
*minimum initial filing requirements

CHAPTER 13

Note to Chapter 13 Debtors - You must start making plan payments to the chapter 13 trustee 30 days after you file your petition. [See Local Rule 3070-1(A)(1).]

The local form "Rights and Responsibilities Agreement" must be entered into by the attorney and debtor but is not filed with the court (see Chapter 13 Guidelines for Compensation for Chapter 13 Attorneys).

You must provide the trustee with a copy of your Federal income tax return as required under 11 U.S.C. §521(e) or your case may be dismissed. Do not file the return with the court unless directed by the court.

For additional information see "Chapter 13 Suggestions" posted on the court website and the chapter 13 trustees' web sites.

Original and, if desired 1 copy for return to filer
Filing Fee: $ 310.00

OFFICIAL FORM	FORM TITLE – CHAPTER 13
*101	Voluntary Petition • Individual debtors must obtain credit counseling before filing the petition, unless an exception applies. (See clerk's "Stop" notice attached to these instructions.) • Debtors filing without attorney representation (pro se) must provide a current government issued photo identification at the time of filing the petition. See the clerk's public notice "New Photo Identification Requirement for Debtors Filing a Petition Without Attorney Representation Effective August 1, 2011" [attached to these instructions.]
*101A	Initial Statement About an Eviction Judgement Against You. • File IF you marked "Yes" to both questions in #11 of the Voluntary Petition.
106Sum	Summary of Your Assets and Liabilities and Certain Statistical Information
106A/B	Schedule A/B: Property
106C	Schedule C: The Property You Claim as Exempt (Individual Cases Only)
106D	Schedule D: Creditors Who Have Claims Secured by Property
106E/F	Schedule E/F: Creditors Who Have Unsecured Claims
106G	Schedule G: Executory Contracts and Unexpired Leases
106H	Schedule H: Your Codebtors
106I	Schedule I: Your Income (Individual Cases Only)

CI-1 (rev. 12/01/16)
*minimum initial filing requirements

OFFICIAL FORM	FORM TITLE – CHAPTER 13
106J	Schedule J: Your Expenses (Individual Cases Only)
106Dec	Declaration About an Individual Debtor's Schedules (Individual Cases Only)
107	Statement of Financial Affairs for Individuals Filing for Bankruptcy
*119	Bankruptcy Petition Preparer's Notice, Declaration, and Signature (if applicable)
*121	Statement About Your Social Security Numbers
*	Creditor Matrix filed in accordance with the "Clerk's Instructions for Preparing, Submitting and Obtaining Service Matrices".

<u>Additional Requirements</u> (Filed separately)

FORM NUMBER	FORM TITLE
2030	Director's Form "Disclosure of Compensation of Attorney for Debtor" (if applicable).
2800	Disclosure of Compensation of Bankruptcy Petition Preparer (if applicable).
122C-1	Bankruptcy Form 122C-1 "Chapter 13 Statement of Your Current Monthly Income and Calculation of Commitment Period". If applicable, Official Form 122C-2 "Chapter 13 Calculation of Your Disposable Income".
LF-10	Declaration Regarding Payment Advices. File this cover sheet with attached copies of all payment advices or other evidence of payment received within 60 days before the date of the filing of the petition as required by 11 U.S.C. §521(a)(1)(b)(iv). If copies are not attached, file the "Declaration" and indicate the reason(s).
*	Certificate of Credit Counseling: This certification is issued by a credit counseling agency to each debtor AFTER a debtor has completed a credit counseling course.
LF-31	Chapter 13 Plan
*LF-03	Application to Pay Filing Fee in Installments. If a debtor is unable to pay the filing fee in full, use this court's local form application to pay the filing fee in installments.
	Certificate of Personal Financial Management: Before a discharge can be entered, each individual debtor must take an approved course about personal financial management. In some instances, a vendor may file the debtor's certificate with the court. If the vendor does not, the debtor must obtain the certificate, and file the certificate or Official Form 423, Certification About a Financial Management Course.

CI-1 (rev. 12/01/16)
*minimum initial filing requirements

INVOLUNTARY PETITIONS (joint involuntary petitions are not permitted)
[See Local Rule 1003-1(B)]

Original and, if desired, 1 copy for return to filer
Filing Fee: Same as chapter fee

OFFICIAL FORM	FORM TITLE – INVOLUNTARY PETITION - INIDIVIDUAL
*105	Involuntary Petition Against an Individual **NOTE:** If the petition is being filed electronically by a registered user, a scanned copy of the petitioning creditor signature page with original signatures of all petitioning creditors must be submitted with the petition.

OFFICIAL FORM	FORM TITLE – INVOLUNTARY PETITION – NON-INDIVIDUAL
*205	Involuntary Petition Against a Non-Individual **NOTE:** If the petition is being filed electronically by a registered user, a scanned copy of the petitioning creditor signature page with original signatures of all petitioning creditors must be submitted with the petition.
*	Corporate ownership statements as required by Bankruptcy Rule 1010(b).

NOTE: The clerk will generate the Bankruptcy Form 2500E "Summons to Debtor in Involuntary Case" and provide a copy to the petitioners for service on the debtor. See Local Rule 1010-1(A).

CI-1 (rev. 12/01/16)
*minimum initial filing requirements

CHAPTER 15 PETITION FOR RECOGNITION OF A FOREIGN PROCEEDING UNDER

Original and, if desired, 1 copy for return to filer
Filing Fee: $ 1,717.00

If the petition is being filed by a foreign representative where an order granting recognition of the foreign main proceeding has been entered, a certified copy of the order granting recognition of the foreign main proceeding must accompany the petition. [See also 11 U.S.C. §1511 and Bankruptcy Rules 1004.2, 1007, 1012 and 2002(q).]

OFFICIAL FORM	FORM TITLE
*401	Chapter 15 Petition for Recognition of a Foreign Proceeding and any applicable attachments listed as required in petition.
	List containing the name and address of those designated by Bankruptcy Rule 1007(a)(4).
	Corporate ownership statement as required by Bankruptcy Rule 1007(a)(4).

MOTIONS TO REOPEN CASES

Original and, if desired, 1 copy for return to filer

1. **Reopening to Amend Schedules to Add an Omitted Creditor (see Local Rule 5010-1(B): Chapter 7 Reopening Filing Fee $260; Chapter 13 Reopening Filing Fee $235; and Chapter 11 Reopening Filing Fee $1,167.** List fees required by Local Rule 5010-1(B) amended schedules must be accompanied by a $30 fee and filed in accordance with Local Rule 1009-1(D). Proposed order conforming to the Local Form "Order Reopening Case to Amend Schedules to Add Omitted Creditor" must accompany the motion.

2. **To avoid a judicial lien:** Chapter 7 filing fee $260; chapter 13 filing fee $235; and chapter 11 filing fee $1,167. **If case has been archived a $53 archive retrieval fee is required**. See also Local Rule 5010-1 (F).

3. **To correct an administrative clerk's error or for actions related to the debtor's discharge:** No fee required.

4. **To request issuance of a discharge in a chapter 7 or 13 case upon the filing of the Bankruptcy Form 423 "Certification About a Financial Management Course" accompanied by a motion to reopen case (See Local Rule 5010-1(G) and (H)):** Chapter 7 filing fee $260; chapter 12 filing fee $200; chapter 13 filing fee $235.
5. **To correct Social Security Number or Other Individual Taxpayer Identification Number:** Chapter 7 filing fee $260; chapter 12 filing fee $200; chapter 13 filing fee

CI-1 (rev. 12/01/16)
*minimum initial filing requirements

$235; and chapter 11 filing fee $1,167. **If case has been archived a $53 archive retrieval fee is required.** See also Local Rule 5010-1(E).

6. **To shorten the "with prejudice" period provision of a prior order of dismissal:** No fee required.

7. **To reopen a chapter 11 case involving an individual debtor whose case was previously closed after confirmation of a plan but prior to entry of discharge:** No fee required.

ADVERSARY PROCEEDING

Original and, if desired, 1 copy for return to filer (complaint only) - Filing Fee: $350.00 [Note: No fee required if filed by chapter 7 or chapter 13 debtors.]

FORM NUMBER	FORM TITLE
416D	Use this Official Form "Form 416D Caption for Use in Adversary Proceeding" as a template. Original Complaint [See Local Rule 7003-1(A)]
*1040	Adversary Proceeding Cover Sheet [See Local Rule 7003-1(A)] **NOTE:** Adversary complaints filed by registered users in CM/ECF do not need form cover sheet. The information required by the cover sheet is captured from data input directly into CM/ECF by the filer.
	Corporate Ownership Statement as required by Bankruptcy Rule 7007-1 and Local Rule 7003-1(B)(2). Please note Local Rule 1002-1(A)(2) definition of parties falling under the classification of "corporation" required to file this statement.

Upon the filing of an adversary proceeding, the clerk will generate and docket an electronic "Summons and Notice of Pretrial" and "Order Setting Filing and Disclosure Requirements" and transmit to the plaintiff electronically or via mail, who must serve them together with the complaint on all defendants in accordance with the federal and local rules. See also Local Rules 7004-2 and 7016-1(B).

*minimum initial filing requirements

REGISTRATION OF JUDGMENT FROM ANOTHER DISTRICT
[See also Local Rule 7069-1(B)]

Original and one copy – Filing Fee: $46.00

*1. Certified copy of Judgment (including Bill of Costs entered)

*2. Bankruptcy Form 2650 "Certification of Judgment for Registration in Another District" or certified copy of an order allowing the judgment to be registered in this district.

WRIT OF EXECUTION [See also Local Rule 7069-1]

Original and, if desired, 1 copy for return to filer

*1. Writ to U.S. Marshal
*2. Motion for Writ of Execution
*3. Certified copy of the judgment (including any Bill of Costs entered)

WRIT OF GARNISHMENT [See also Local Rule 7069-1(D)]

Original and, if desired, 1 copy for return to filer

*1. Writ of Garnishment
*2. Motion for Writ of Garnishment
*3. Proposed Order (when required by Florida law)
*4. Certified copy of the judgment (including any Bill of Costs entered)

OTHER MISCELLANEOUS PROCEEDINGS

Registration of a judgment in another district (see above); a motion for a protective order, or to quash a subpoena issued in a case pending in another district, a request to perpetuate testimony concerning a potential adversary proceeding under Rule 7027, a request to register a discharge order under Rule 4004(f), or any other request to register with the court a document not in a case or proceeding.

Original and, if desired, 1 copy for return to filer - Filing Fee: $46.00

CLAIMS [For filing transfers of claims - see Local Rule 3001-1(C).] (Transfer of Claims Fee $25)

Original and, if desired, 1 copy for return to filer (Note: In a chapter 13 case where the debtor is not represented by an attorney, a copy of the claim must be mailed to the debtor. See Local Rule 3002-1(E).

Unless the court directs otherwise, all **original** proofs of claim must be filed with the court using the Bankruptcy Form 410 "Proof of Claim" and if applicable Bankruptcy Form 410A "Proof of Claim, Attachment A", Bankruptcy Form 410S1 "Notice of Mortgage Payment Claim", and/or Bankruptcy Form 410S2 "Notice Postpetition Mortgage Fees, Expenses, and Charges" of If you wish to receive an acknowledgment from the clerk that your claim has been filed, you must include a copy of your claim with an adequate size self-addressed envelope containing sufficient postage so that the clerk may return a date-stamped copy of your claim to you.

Any creditor with internet access may file a proof of claim electronically and print a copy of the claim at the time of filing by using the electronic claims filing program available on the court website: www.flsb.uscourts.gov

*minimum initial filing requirements

UNITED STATES BANKRUPTCY COURT
SOUTHERN DISTRICT OF FLORIDA

NOTICE TO PRO SE DEBTORS

READ THIS IMPORTANT NOTICE TO AVOID THE DISMISSAL OF YOUR CASE.

As a debtor you must attend a meeting of creditors and timely pay filing fee installments (if applicable) or chapter 13 plan payments (if applicable) on time or your case may be dismissed without further notice to you. You are responsible for following up with your case after filing your petition to make sure you are aware of the date set for you to appear at your first meeting of creditors. The questions and answers which follow are provided to assist you in meeting your responsibility to attend your first meeting of creditors on the scheduled date and time.

Before you file you must complete pre bankruptcy credit counseling using one of the approved credit counseling providers listed on the United States Trustee website http://www.justice.gov/ust/ under the "Bankruptcy Reform Information" link http://www.justice.gov/ust/eo/bapcpa/index.htm. See clerk's "Stop" notice attached to these instructions for more information. Both debtor and joint debtor must complete the requirement.

Before a chapter 7 or 13 debtor can receive a discharge, the debtors must complete the required financial management course after filing the petition using one of the approved providers listed on the United States Trustee website http://www.justice.gov/ust/ under the "Bankruptcy Reform Information" link http://www.justice.gov/ust/eo/bapcpa/index.htm and file the required certificate.

Debtors who are not represented by an attorney must present current official government photo identification at the time the petition is presented for filing. [See the clerk's public notice "New Photo Identification Requirement for Debtors Filing a Petition Without Attorney Representation Effective August 1, 2011" attached to these instructions.]

Please view the video posted on this court's pro se webpage on line or at clerk's office which follows a debtor through the bankruptcy process. The link is: http://www.flsb.uscourts.gov/?page_id=4824

1. WHAT IS A MEETING OF CREDITORS?

Bankruptcy law requires each debtor (or both debtors if filing jointly) who files a bankruptcy petition to appear at a "first meeting of creditors". The meeting is not presided over by the judge. Instead the trustee assigned to your case (or a representative from the U.S. Trustee's office if you filed a chapter 11 case) will ask you questions under oath about your estate. Creditors who attend will also be permitted time to ask you questions. Your presence at the meeting of creditors is mandatory and continuances are granted only in exceptional

CI-1 (rev. 12/01/16)

circumstances. [See Local Rule 2003-1.]

[**Note:** Each individual debtor must present to the presiding officer at the meeting of creditors two pieces of identification as follows: 1) original government-issued photo identification; and 2) original social security card, or if applicable, Tax Identification Number (or other acceptable confirmation of each debtor's social security number, or if applicable, Tax Identification Number). [See also Local Rules 5072-2 and 5073-1 regarding security regulations and access to the court and prohibited electronic devices.]

2. HOW WILL MY CREDITORS AND I KNOW THE DATE SCHEDULED FOR MY MEETING OF CREDITORS?

The clerk of court will serve you and to all of the creditors listed on the initial service matrix filed with your petition, a notice which will provide the date, time and location of your first meeting of creditors. This notice will also contain other important information regarding your case, including the name of the trustee (if you filed a chapter 7, 12 or 13 case) assigned to your case. It is your responsibility as the debtor to verify that this notice contains your correct name, address, and social security number (or, if applicable, tax identification number) and to notify the clerk's office if you find an error. Notices mailed to your creditors will have your address or, if represented by an attorney, your attorney's address in the return address section of the envelope so that mail incorrectly addressed to your creditors will be returned to you. The clerk will mail your copy of the notice to you at the mailing address listed on your bankruptcy petition. The clerk will use the addresses provided in your creditor service matrix to mail copies to your creditors. **IT IS VERY IMPORTANT FOR YOU TO SUPPLY CORRECT ADDRESS INFORMATION FOR YOURSELF AND YOUR CREDITORS AND TO NOTIFY THE COURT IN WRITING IF THERE ARE ANY CHANGES. IF YOU ADD CREDITORS AFTER THE FILING OF YOUR INITIAL SERVICE MATRIX YOU MUST SERVE THE NEW CREDITORS WITH A COPY OF THE NOTICE. SEE LOCAL RULE 1007-2 AND 1009-1(D)(2).**

3. WHEN WILL MY CREDITORS AND I RECEIVE THIS NOTICE AND WHAT SHOULD I DO IF I DON'T RECEIVE IT?

Chapter 7, 11 and 12 Cases

If you filed a chapter 7, 11 or 12 case, you and your creditors should receive a copy of this notice no later than 7-10 days after you filed your bankruptcy petition and creditor service matrix. If you do not receive this notice within 10 days from the filing of your petition you must notify the clerk's office immediately by calling in Miami at (305) 714-1800, the divisional office in Ft. Lauderdale at (954) 769-5700, or the divisional office in West Palm Beach at (561) 514-4100. You may call our multi-court voice case information system (available 24 hours a day) at (866) 222-8029 to determine if the date has been set in the computer; however you still must notify the court if you do not receive a copy within the time indicated.

Chapter 13 Cases

If you file a chapter 13 case, your meeting of creditors and the confirmation hearing on your plan cannot be set until your plan and a creditor service matrix have been filed. If you did not file a plan with your petition, the clerk will serve, on you and all parties of record, an initial notice advising that the case was filed. After the plan is filed, a notice of meeting of creditors and other deadlines and information will be served on all parties of record. Your plan must be filed using the one page Local Form "Chapter 13 Plan". You must pay your first payment to the chapter 13 trustee within 30 days from the date of filing. [See Local Rule 3070-1.] Prior to the first scheduled meeting of creditors, the debtor shall provide to the trustee all documents listed in the Trustee's Notice of Required Documents and provide tax returns in accordance with 11 U.S.C. §521(e) and (f) and §1308. **DO NOT FILE THESE DOCUMENTS OR A CERTIFICATE OF SERVICE OF THESE DOCUMENTS WITH THE COURT, UNLESS ORDERED BY THE COURT TO DO SO.** See the document "Chapter 13 Trustees' Suggestions" for additional requirements.

If you do not receive notice of your meeting of creditors within 7 days after you file your plan and creditor service matrix, you must notify the clerk's office immediately by calling in Miami at (305) 714-1800, the office in Ft. Lauderdale at (954) 769-5700 or the office in West Palm Beach at (561) 514-4100. You may call our multi-court voice case information system (available 24 hours a day) at (866) 222-8029 to determine if the date has been set in the computer; however, you still must call the clerk's office if you do not receive a copy of the notice within the time indicated.

4. WHAT SHOULD I DO WITH THE MAIL THAT WAS ADDRESSED TO MY CREDITORS THAT IS BEING RETURNED TO ME?

These notices are being returned to you because the address you provided on your creditor service matrix is not correct or the creditor has moved. It is your responsibility to ensure that the clerk's office is provided with correct address information in order to provide any future noticing in your case. If you receive mail back from a creditor you must immediately mail the notice to the creditor at the new or corrected address. A certificate of service must be filed with the clerk's office which contains the new or corrected address information for the affected creditor and must state the date that you mailed the notice. You must also file a supplemental creditor matrix with the clerk which lists only those creditors with address changes. [See "Clerk's Instructions for Preparing, Submitting and Obtaining Service Matrices" (CI-3).] **DO NOT RETURN THESE NOTICES TO THE CLERK'S OFFICE. The exception to this requirement is if a debtor has received a bypass notice from the Bankruptcy Noticing Center (BNC) and is using it to change a previously submitted creditor address.**

UNITED STATES BANKRUPTCY COURT
SOUTHERN DISTRICT OF FLORIDA

NOTICE TO ALL DEBTORS:
READ THIS *BEFORE* YOU FILE YOUR CASE

DID YOU (AND JOINT DEBTOR, IF APPLICABLE) COMPLETE THE REQUIRED APPROVED PRE-FILING BANKRUPTCY CREDIT COUNSELING COURSE?

- If you completed the counseling and you have the certificate with you confirming you took the course, check box 1 in Part 5 and file the certificate with your petition.
- If you completed the counseling and you do NOT have the certificate with you, check box 2 in Part 5. **You will have 14 days after your case is filed to file the certificate or your case may be dismissed.**
- If you did NOT complete the counseling yet, you must check box 3 Part 5, if it applies, and attach an explanation as to WHY you did not receive the counseling. You must get the counseling as soon as possible, but no later than the date ordered by the court, and you must file the certificate. The court will enter an order that will require you to appear in court and explain why you did not get counseling before you filed bankruptcy. The court could dismiss your case if the court finds you did not have a good reason to file bankruptcy without taking the course.
- If you meet the requirements for an exemption from counseling (mentally ill or disabled or persons on military duty in an active combat zone) you must check box 4 of Part 5 and file a motion for determination by the court. See 11 U.S.C. §109(h)(4), and Local Rule 1007-1(D) and clerk's filing instructions for more information.

Under the bankruptcy laws, the court can only allow you to complete the course **after filing** if you meet **all** of the following conditions. [See 11 U.S.C. §109(h)(3).]

1) You must have tried to get counseling from an approved agency within at least a seven day period before filing and the agency could not provide it; AND

2) There are exigent (emergency) circumstances that prevented you from obtaining credit counseling before filing. (Important: The court will determine what qualifies as an emergency circumstance).

Please be advised that most debtors will not be able to meet these conditions because credit counseling is readily available in this district. The decision to file your petition is up to you but *if* you file without taking the course, you are risking dismissal of your case. ***The clerk cannot provide legal advice or predict in advance how a judge will decide your request for an extension to complete this requirement.***

To complete this requirement before filing, obtain from the clerk a list of United States Trustee approved pre-bankruptcy credit counseling agencies or go to this website:

http://www.justice.gov/ust/list-credit-counseling-agencies-approved-pursuant-11-usc-111

Page 29 of 36

(Form 2010)

Notice Required by 11 U.S.C. § 342(b) for Individuals Filing for Bankruptcy (Form 2010)

This notice is for you if:

- **You are an individual filing for bankruptcy,**

and

- **Your debts are primarily consumer debts.** *Consumer debts* are defined in 11 U.S.C. § 101(8) as "incurred by an individual primarily for a personal, family, or household purpose."

The types of bankruptcy that are available to individuals

Individuals who meet the qualifications may file under one of four different chapters of the Bankruptcy Code:

- Chapter 7 — Liquidation
- Chapter 11— Reorganization
- Chapter 12— Voluntary repayment plan for family farmers or fishermen
- Chapter 13— Voluntary repayment plan for individuals with regular income

You should have an attorney review your decision to file for bankruptcy and the choice of chapter.

Chapter 7: Liquidation

	$245	filing fee
	$75	administrative fee
+	$15	trustee surcharge
	$335	total fee

Chapter 7 is for individuals who have financial difficulty preventing them from paying their debts and who are willing to allow their non-exempt property to be used to pay their creditors. The primary purpose of filing under chapter 7 is to have your debts discharged. The bankruptcy discharge relieves you after bankruptcy from having to pay many of your pre-bankruptcy debts. Exceptions exist for particular debts, and liens on property may still be enforced after discharge. For example, a creditor may have the right to foreclose a home mortgage or repossess an automobile.

However, if the court finds that you have committed certain kinds of improper conduct described in the Bankruptcy Code, the court may deny your discharge.

You should know that even if you file chapter 7 and you receive a discharge, some debts are not discharged under the law. Therefore, you may still be responsible to pay:

- most taxes;
- most student loans;
- domestic support and property settlement obligations;

- most fines, penalties, forfeitures, and criminal restitution obligations; and
- certain debts that are not listed in your bankruptcy papers.

You may also be required to pay debts arising from:

- fraud or theft;
- fraud or defalcation while acting in breach of fiduciary capacity;
- intentional injuries that you inflicted; and
- death or personal injury caused by operating a motor vehicle, vessel, or aircraft while intoxicated from alcohol or drugs.

If your debts are primarily consumer debts, the court can dismiss your chapter 7 case if it finds that you have enough income to repay creditors a certain amount. You must file *Chapter 7 Statement of Your Current Monthly Income* (Official Form 122A–1) if you are an individual filing for bankruptcy under chapter 7. This form will determine your current monthly income and compare whether your income is more than the median income that applies in your state.

If your income is not above the median for your state, you will not have to complete the other chapter 7 form, the *Chapter 7 Means Test Calculation* (Official Form 122A–2).

If your income is above the median for your state, you must file a second form —the *Chapter 7 Means Test Calculation* (Official Form 122A–2). The calculations on the form— sometimes called the *Means Test*—deduct from your income living expenses and payments on certain debts to determine any amount available to pay unsecured creditors. If your income is more than the median income for your state of residence and family size, depending on the results of the *Means Test*, the U.S. trustee, bankruptcy administrator, or creditors can file a motion to dismiss your case under § 707(b) of the Bankruptcy Code. If a motion is filed, the court will decide if your case should be dismissed. To avoid dismissal, you may choose to proceed under another chapter of the Bankruptcy Code.

If you are an individual filing for chapter 7 bankruptcy, the trustee may sell your property to pay your debts, subject to your right to exempt the property or a portion of the proceeds from the sale of the property. The property, and the proceeds from property that your bankruptcy trustee sells or liquidates that you are entitled to, is called *exempt property*. Exemptions may enable you to keep your home, a car, clothing, and household items or to receive some of the proceeds if the property is sold.

Exemptions are not automatic. To exempt property, you must list it on *Schedule C: The Property You Claim as Exempt* (Official Form 106C). If you do not list the property, the trustee may sell it and pay all of the proceeds to your creditors.

Chapter 11: Reorganization

	$1,167	filing fee
+	$550	administrative fee
	$1,717	total fee

Chapter 11 is often used for reorganizing a business, but is also available to individuals. The provisions of chapter 11 are too complicated to summarize briefly.

Read These Important Warnings

Because bankruptcy can have serious long-term financial and legal consequences, including loss of your property, you should hire an attorney and carefully consider all of your options before you file. Only an attorney can give you legal advice about what can happen as a result of filing for bankruptcy and what your options are. If you do file for bankruptcy, an attorney can help you fill out the forms properly and protect you, your family, your home, and your possessions.

Although the law allows you to represent yourself in bankruptcy court, you should understand that many people find it difficult to represent themselves successfully. The rules are technical, and a mistake or inaction may harm you. If you file without an attorney, you are still responsible for knowing and following all of the legal requirements.

You should not file for bankruptcy if you are not eligible to file or if you do not intend to file the necessary documents.

Bankruptcy fraud is a serious crime; you could be fined and imprisoned if you commit fraud in your bankruptcy case. Making a false statement, concealing property, or obtaining money or property by fraud in connection with a bankruptcy case can result in fines up to $250,000, or imprisonment for up to 20 years, or both. 18 U.S.C. §§ 152, 1341, 1519, and 3571.

Chapter 12: Repayment plan for family farmers or fishermen

	$200	filing fee
+	$75	administrative fee
	$275	total fee

Similar to chapter 13, chapter 12 permits family farmers and fishermen to repay their debts over a period of time using future earnings and to discharge some debts that are not paid.

Chapter 13: Repayment plan for individuals with regular income

	$235	filing fee
+	$75	administrative fee
	$310	total fee

Chapter 13 is for individuals who have regular income and would like to pay all or part of their debts in installments over a period of time and to discharge some debts that are not paid. You are eligible for chapter 13 only if your debts are not more than certain dollar amounts set forth in 11 U.S.C. § 109.

Under chapter 13, you must file with the court a plan to repay your creditors all or part of the money that you owe them, usually using your future earnings. If the court approves your plan, the court will allow you to repay your debts, as adjusted by the plan, within 3 years or 5 years, depending on your income and other factors.

After you make all the payments under your plan, many of your debts are discharged. The debts that are not discharged and that you may still be responsible to pay include:

- domestic support obligations,
- most student loans,
- certain taxes,
- debts for fraud or theft,
- debts for fraud or defalcation while acting in a fiduciary capacity,
- most criminal fines and restitution obligations,
- certain debts that are not listed in your bankruptcy papers,
- certain debts for acts that caused death or personal injury, and
- certain long-term secured debts.

Warning: File Your Forms on Time

Section 521(a)(1) of the Bankruptcy Code requires that you promptly file detailed information about your creditors, assets, liabilities, income, expenses and general financial condition. The court may dismiss your bankruptcy case if you do not file this information within the deadlines set by the Bankruptcy Code, the Bankruptcy Rules, and the local rules of the court.

For more information about the documents and their deadlines, go to: http://www.uscourts.gov/bkforms/bankruptcy_forms.html #procedure.

Bankruptcy crimes have serious consequences

- If you knowingly and fraudulently conceal assets or make a false oath or statement under penalty of perjury—either orally or in writing—in connection with a bankruptcy case, you may be fined, imprisoned, or both.
- All information you supply in connection with a bankruptcy case is subject to examination by the Attorney General acting through the Office of the U.S. Trustee, the Office of the U.S. Attorney, and other offices and employees of the U.S. Department of Justice.

Make sure the court has your mailing address

The bankruptcy court sends notices to the mailing address you list on *Voluntary Petition for Individuals Filing for Bankruptcy* (Official Form 101). To ensure that you receive information about your case, Bankruptcy Rule 4002 requires that you notify the court of any changes in your address.

A married couple may file a bankruptcy case together—called a *joint case*. If you file a joint case and each spouse lists the same mailing address on the bankruptcy petition, the bankruptcy court generally will mail you and your spouse one copy of each notice, unless you file a statement with the court asking that each spouse receive separate copies.

Understand which services you could receive from credit counseling agencies

The law generally requires that you receive a credit counseling briefing from an approved credit counseling agency. 11 U.S.C. § 109(h). If you are filing a joint case, both spouses must receive the briefing. With limited exceptions, you must receive it within the 180 days ***before*** you file your bankruptcy petition. This briefing is usually conducted by telephone or on the Internet.

In addition, after filing a bankruptcy case, you generally must complete a financial management instructional course before you can receive a discharge. If you are filing a joint case, both spouses must complete the course.

You can obtain the list of agencies approved to provide both the briefing and the instructional course from: http://justice.gov/ust/eo/hapcpa/ccde/cc_approved.html.

In Alabama and North Carolina, go to: http://www.uscourts.gov/FederalCourts/Bankruptcy/BankruptcyResources/ApprovedCreditAndDebtCounselors.aspx.

If you do not have access to a computer, the clerk of the bankruptcy court may be able to help you obtain the list.

UNITED STATES BANKRUPTCY COURT
SOUTHERN DISTRICT OF FLORIDA

NEW PHOTO IDENTIFICATION REQUIREMENT FOR DEBTORS FILING A PETITION WITHOUT ATTORNEY REPRESENTATION

EFFECTIVE AUGUST 1, 2011

If you file a bankruptcy petition on or after August 1, 2011 with this court and you are not represented by an attorney, you must provide a current government issued photo identification when you bring in or mail your petition to the clerk of the U.S. Bankruptcy Court or your petition will not be accepted for filing.

Below are the new requirements and information as to what is considered proper identification. ***(See also Local Rule 1002-1(B)(1)(d) and the "Clerk's Instructions For Filing", amended effective December 1, 2015.)***

1) **Filing in person:** Only the individual debtor or a person presenting a notarized power of attorney authorizing that person to file the petition on the debtor's behalf may bring a petition to the clerk's office. The debtors (and any person holding power of attorney authorizing that person to file on behalf of the debtor) must present photo identification. If the petition is a joint case and only one spouse appears in person to file the petition, a legible copy of the absent spouse's identification card must be provided at the time the petition is filed.

2) **Filing by mail:** A photocopy of the debtor(s)' government issued identification must accompany the petition.

3) **Required identification:** When filing in person or by mail, identification presented must:

   - contain a photograph
   - be ***government*** issued such as a state driver's license, state or federal issued identification card, U.S. passport, federal, state or local U.S. government employee photo identification card
   - be current
   - be legible

4) **Retention of identification photocopies by the clerk:** The clerk will convert identification photocopies collected to pdf documents for retention under a restricted docket event which will be inaccessible to the public. Any paper copies submitted will be destroyed.

Page 35 of 36

UNITED STATES BANKRUPTCY COURT, SDFL
IMPORTANT INFORMATION FOR CHAPTER 13 DEBTORS

- Each debtor must obtain counseling prior to filing bankruptcy unless an exception applies. The law requires that you receive a briefing about credit counseling before you file for bankruptcy. You must truthfully check one of the petition choices. If you cannot do so, you are not eligible to file. If you file anyway, the court can dismiss your case, you will lose whatever filing fee you paid, and your creditors can begin collection activities again. FAILURE TO COMPLY WITH THESE REQUIREMENTS MAY RESULT IN DISMISSAL OF YOUR CASE WITHOUT FURTHER NOTICE. See Local Rule 1007-1(D).
- You must use this court's current local plan form to file your plan. See Local Rule 3015-1(B).
- Within 30 days of **filing** your chapter 13 petition, you must begin making your plan payments to the chapter 13 trustee assigned to your case. (See address below). If you are not current with your payments at the meeting of creditors, your case will be dismissed without further notice or hearing. See Local Rule 3070-1.
- You must provide the trustee with a copy of your Federal income tax return as required by 11 U.S.C. §521(e) and Bankruptcy Rule 4002(b)(3) or your case may be dismissed. See Local Rules 1017-2(C) and 4002-1.
- All required schedules, statements, copies of payment advices [see 11 U.S.C. §521(a)(1)(b)(iv), Local Rule 1007-1(E) and Local Form *"Declaration Regarding Payment Advices"*] lists and your plan are due within 14 days of filing your petition (if you didn't file them when you filed your petition). If you do not timely file these papers, your case will be dismissed without further notice or hearing.
- Each debtor must attend the meeting of creditors scheduled for your case or the case will be dismissed.
- Each debtor must present to the trustee at the meeting of creditors your original government issued photo ID and original (not a copy) proof of your Social Security or Taxpayer ID numbers.
- Each debtor must complete the required financial management course and file the Bankruptcy Form B423 *"Certification About a Financial Management Course"* and the Local Form *"Debtor's Certificate of Compliance, Motion for Issuance of Discharge and Notice of Deadline to Object"* as required by Local Rule 4004-3(A)(4), before a discharge will be issued.
- If you are paying your filing fee in installments and fail to timely make a payment, your case will be dismissed without further notice. See Local Rule 1006-1(A)(4).
- See Local Rule 3070-1 for information on the status pre-confirmation payments.
- See Local Rule 3015-3(B) for information on the chapter 13 confirmation process.

CHAPTER 13 DEBTORS AND ATTORNEYS ARE REQUIRED TO SIGN THIS COURT'S LOCAL FORM "RIGHTS AND RESPONSIBILITIES AGREEMENT".

(SEE COURT GUIDELINES FOR CHAPTER 13 COMPENSATION and Local Rule 2016-1(B)(2))

CHAPTER 13 TRUSTEES' CONTACT INFORMATION

DADE AND NORTH DADE DIVISION CODE 5 CASES: NANCY K. NEIDICH, P.O. Box 279806, Miramar, FL 33027; Phone: (954) 443-4402; Web page http://www.ch13herkert.com All chapter 13 plan payments must be mailed to a lock box at the following address: NANCY K. NEIDICH, CHAPTER 13 TRUSTEE, P.O. BOX 2099, MEMPHIS, TN 38101-2099.
BROWARD AND PALM BEACH DIVISION CASES: ROBIN WEINER, P.O. Box 559007, Ft. Lauderdale, FL 33355-9007; Phone: (954) 382-2001; Web page http://www.ch13weiner.com. All chapter 13 plan payments must be mailed to a lock box at the following address: ROBIN R. WEINER, CHAPTER 13 TRUSTEE, P.O. BOX 2258, MEMPHIS, TN 38101-2258.

Page 36 of 36

[Amended effective February 4, 2013; June 30, 2014 ; December 1, 2014; December 1, 2015; June 1, 2016; July 20, 2016; July 28, 2016; December 1, 2016.]

CI–2. CLERK'S SUMMARY OF FEES (SEE ALSO 28 USC § 1930)

UNITED STATES BANKRUPTCY COURT SOUTHERN DISTRICT OF FLORIDA
CLERK'S SUMMARY OF FEES (See also 28 USC §1930)

Debtors may only pay filing fees by cash, money order or cashier's or "official" checks. Do not send cash through the mail. Non cash payments must be made payable to "Clerk, U.S. Court". Overpayments of less than $25 are not refundable [see LR 5081-1(D)]. Child support creditors seeking fee waivers must file the U.S. Courts Director's Form "Appearance of Child Support Creditor or Representative".

Chapter 7 Petition Fee (Fee to reopen - $260.00*)	$ 335.00
Chapter 9 Petition Fee (Fee to reopen - $1,167.00*)	$ 1,717.00
Chapter 11 Petition Fee (Fee to reopen - $1,167.00*)	$ 1,717.00
Chapter 12 Petition Fee (Fee to reopen - $200.00*)	$ 275.00
Chapter 13 Petition Fee (Fee to reopen - $235.00*)	$ 310.00
Chapter 15 - Recognition of a Foreign Proceeding (fee to reopen $1,167.00*)	$ 1,717.00
Conversions; Motion to Convert or Notice of Conversion Chapter 7 to Chapter 13 Chapter 7 to Chapter 11 (by Debtor Only other than reconversion) Chapter 11 to Chapter 7 Chapter 12 to Chapter 7 Chapter 12 to Chapter 11 or Chapter 13 Chapter 13 to Chapter 7 Chapter 13 to Chapter 11 (by Debtor Only other than reconversion)	 No Fee Due $922.00 $15.00 $60.00 No Fee Due $25.00 $932.00
Dividing (splitting) a joint (husband and wife) case: Fee is equal to the current filing fee for the chapter under which the new case will commence and is due upon the filing of the motion requesting division of a joint case: Chapter 7 Chapter 13 Chapter 11 Chapter 12	 $ 335.00 $ 310.00 $ 1,717.00 $ 275.00
Adversary Proceeding (no fee if filed by Chapter 7 or 13 Debtors)	$ 350.00
Amendments to debtor's schedules D, E, or F; or to amend creditor matrix (See CI-3 for details)	$ 31.00
Appeal, (or Cross Appeal), Notice of (Filing Fee $5.00 + Docketing Fee of $293.00) Note: Request for Direct/Cross Appeal to the 11th Circuit Court of Appeals from the Bankruptcy Court will result in an additional charge of $207 if the Court of Appeals authorizes the direct appeal/cross appeal.	$ 298.00 $207.00
Motion for Leave to file Notice of Appeal (Appeal Docketing Fee of $293.00 will be due when court grants motion for Leave to file Notice of Appeal)	$ 5.00
Certification of a document (Note: Exemplification of a document - $22.00)	$11.00
Copies, reproduction of any document (per page) (Non electronic)	$ .50
Copies of any electronic record printed at a public terminal in the courthouse (per page)	$ .10
Transfer of Claims	$ 25.00
Miscellaneous Proceeding (filing or indexing a paper where no previous fee was paid, i.e. Registration of Foreign Judgment)	$ 47.00
Motion to Appear Pro Hac Vice (due at filing of motion)	$75.00
Motion to Redact Court Record(s)	$ 25.00
Motion to Compel Abandonment of Property of the Estate pursuant to Bankruptcy Rule 6007(b)	$ 181.00
Motion to Vacate or Modify the Automatic Stay pursuant to 11 U.S.C. § 362(d)	$ 181.00
Motion to Withdraw the Reference of a Case pursuant to 28 U.S.C. § 157(d)	$ 181.00
Motion to Sell Property of the Estate Free and Clear of Liens Under 11 U.S.C. § 363(f)	$ 181.00
Returned Check	$ 53.00
Registry, Handling Charge (See Administrative Order 02-3)	
Removal, Notice of (unless Notice is filed by the debtor or on behalf of the U.S.A.)	$ 350.00
Reproduction of an audio recording of a court proceeding	$31.00
Retrieval by clerk of records from Federal Archives Center (Note: see Local Form 88) Retrievals involving multiple boxes, $39.00 for each additional box ****For electronic retrievals, $10 plus any charges assessed by the Federal Records Center, National Archives, or other storage location removed from the place of business of the courts.**	$ 64.00 $ 39.00 **$ 10.00
Search of records conducted by the clerk (per each name or item researched)	$ 31.00
Per diem Witness Fees (not a filing fee)	$ 40.00

***NOTE:** Pursuant to Local Rule 5010-1(A) the filing fee for a motion to reopen a Bankruptcy Code case is due at the time of filing of the motion. The court may waive this fee under appropriate circumstances or may defer payment of the fee from trustees pending discovery of additional assets. Also see Local Rule 5010-1(A) for exceptions to the reopening fee requirement. Information for individual debtor on paying filing fees in installments or obtaining a chapter 7 waiver is contained in the "Clerk's Filing Instructions" and posted on the court's website.

CI-2 (rev. 12/01/16)

[Effective December 1, 1998. Amended effective November 16, 1999; November 1, 2003; October 29, 2004; July 1, 2005; October 17, 2005; April 9, 2006; January 1, 2007; June 2, 2008; October 1, 2008; December 1, 2009; August 1, 2011; January 23, 2012; November 21, 2012; June 18, 2013; December 1, 2013; June 1, 2014; December 1, 2014; July 1, 2015; December 1, 2015; March 11, 2016; June 1, 2016; December 1, 2016.]

CI-3. CLERK'S INSTRUCTIONS FOR PREPARING, SUBMITTING AND OBTAINING SERVICE MATRICES

I. Initial Creditor Service Matrix to Accompany Petition

Pursuant to Local Rule 1007-2, an initial creditor service matrix (list of all creditors) must be prepared in accordance with the attached instructions (***see Exhibit A: Preparing a Creditor Matrix***), and submitted at the time the petition is filed.

Debtors not represented by an attorney <u>**must**</u> submit the matrix on a 3½ inch High Density diskette, CD-ROM or memory stick in ASCII or MS-DOS text format. Debtors who do not have access to a computer may submit a service matrix on 8 ½ × 11″ unlined, white paper in accordance with the attached instructions. CM/ECF registered efiling attorneys <u>**must**</u> upload the creditor matrix directly into the CM/ECF application by selecting the <u>**Creditor Maintenance . . .**</u> option from the <u>Bankruptcy</u> events menu link.

II. Requirements for Submitting Subsequent Amendments

a. Local Form Required: Pursuant to Local Rules 1007-2(B) and 1009-1(D), Local Form **"Debtor's Notice of Compliance with Requirements for Amending Creditor Information" (LF-4)** must accompany any paper filed pursuant to Bankruptcy Rule l007 subsequent to the filing of the initial service matrix or any paper filed pursuant to Bankruptcy Rule 1007 that renders the initial service matrix inaccurate or incomplete due to the addition, deletion, or modification of data [including information listed on the report required by Bankruptcy Rule 1019(5) or list required by Local Rule 2002-1(H)]. This form requires the debtor to certify that, in conjunction with the filing of subsequent amended information, the debtor has complied with other court requirements, including payment of any schedule amendment fees, the filing of any required amended papers and service of notice and other documents on affected parties. The exception to this requirement is if a debtor or the attorney for a debtor has received a bypass notice from the Bankruptcy Noticing Center (BNC) and is using it to change a previously submitted creditor address. In those instances, the bypass notice may be filed in lieu of LF-4 to notify the court of a change of creditor address. [See Local Rule 1009-1(D)(1)]

Note: Amended schedules, summaries or other amended paper must be filed to reflect the change(s) noted on LF-4. Even if the attorney for the debtor is signing and submitting LF-4, the **debtors must still sign** schedules and other documents using the Official Form "Declaration Concerning Debtor's Schedules" as required by the Bankruptcy Rules and Local Rules 1007-2(B) and 1009-1(D). Also, Local Form "Declaration Under Penalty of Perjury to Accompany Petitions, Schedules and Statements Filed Electronically," is required unless documents contain an imaged signature of the debtor. [See Local Rule 9011-4(C)].

b. Correcting or Deleting Creditor Information: When submitting corrections or deletions to creditor information submitted on a previous service matrix you must attach a separate list to LF-4 entitled "Deletions to Creditor Information" and/or "Corrections to Creditor Information" which includes the correct name and address of the affected creditors. As noted in section (a) above, a debtor or debtor's attorney may file a signed BNC bypass notice in lieu of filing LF-4 when correcting a creditor's address previously submitted on a matrix or schedule.

c. Adding New Creditors: When adding new creditors, including creditors added pursuant to Bankruptcy Rule 1019(5), to a previously submitted service matrix, the debtor must submit the new creditors in the same format required for an initial service matrix (***see sec. I. Initial Creditor Service Matrix***). **ONLY** the newly added creditors should be listed on the diskette, unlined paper, or for efiling attorneys, uploaded into the CM/ECF application, along with a copy attached to the LF-4.

d. Fee Requirement for Certain Amendments: A $30.00 filing fee is required at the time of filing the amendment to add or delete a creditor from a schedule, list or creditor service matrix, or to change amounts or classifications of creditors listed on schedules D, E or F. This fee is for each paper filed, not each amendment listed on the paper. **NO** fee is required when the nature of the amendment is to change the address of a creditor or an attorney for a creditor listed on the schedules, to add the name and address of an attorney for a listed creditor or to add creditors pursuant to Bankruptcy Rule 1019(5).

e. Notice Requirement: A copy of LF-4, amended schedules, summaries or other papers and a copy of the § 341 Meeting of Creditors notice must be served on the affected party(ies). A copy of the amended schedules, summaries or other amended paper must also be provided to the U.S. Trustee or panel trustee.

III. Obtaining Service Matrices

The clerk maintains separate service matrices in CM/ECF (ECF PACER). Verification that a particular party or creditor appears complete and/or accurate on any service list or claims register is the responsibility of the party providing notice and of the listed party. Omissions of a party on any service list maintained in the CM/ECF application due to a failure by the debtor or other responsible party to provide the clerk with a supplemental matrix, or where applicable, a notice of change of address, shall be the responsibility of that party to correct. Determination as to the appropriate parties to serve shall be the responsibility of the party providing such service. When used by the clerk to designate service, "Parties of record", shall mean all parties listed on all service matrices maintained in CM/ECF. Available service matrices in CM/ECF (ECF PACER) are as follows:

1) List of Creditors. Displays a list of all parties who have filed an appearance in a case, or have automatically been added to the case by the clerk; all creditors who have been uploaded into the court's creditor database by filing of the initial or amended creditor matrix, and all creditors who have filed proofs of claim. This list is available in 3–column label format, or raw data format (delimited data fields).

2) Mailing Information for a Case. Displays a list of all registered efilers who have either made an electronic appearance in a case, or have automatically been added to the case by the clerk. List does not include registered efilers who have filed proofs of claim. This option also displays a list of non-efiling parties who have filed an appearance in a case.

3) Creditor List. Displays a list of creditors who have been uploaded into the court's creditor database by filing of the initial or amended creditor matrix, or have automatically been added to the case by the clerk. List also includes all creditors who have filed proofs of claim and/or assignments of claim. This list does not include those parties who have filed an appearance in a case.

4) Attorney List. Displays a list of attorneys and the party(ies) whom they represent who have filed an appearance in a case. This list does not include those parties who have been uploaded in the court's creditor database by filing of the initial or amended creditor matrix, or whom have filed a proof of claim.

5) Party List. Displays a list of parties, and (if applicable), their attorney(ies) who have filed an appearance in a case, or have automatically been added to the case by the clerk. This list does not include those parties who have been uploaded in the court's creditor database by filing of the initial or amended creditor matrix, or whom have filed a proof of claim.

IV. Creditor's Preferred Mailing Address

Section 11 U.S.C. § 342(f) of The Bankruptcy Code, along with Bankruptcy Rule 2002(g), permits a creditor in a chapter 7 or 13 case, to specify a preferred address or addresses for all notices transmitted by the bankruptcy courts, or by a particular bankruptcy court. If a creditor maintains a "preferred mailing address" on file with the Federal Judiciary's Bankruptcy Noticing Center's (BNC) National Creditor Registration Service (NCRS), the BNC will redirect the bankruptcy court's notice(s) to a preferred mailing address. The address listed in CM/ECF will be substituted automatically, unless a notice of override of preferred creditor address is filed in the case.

Exhibit A: Preparing a Creditor Matrix

In order for the clerk's office to process your service matrix, the following instructions <u>MUST</u> be followed. Failure to comply with matrix requirements may result in dismissal of your case.

I. Standards for Creating a Creditor List

(a) Lists MUST be typed in one of the following standard typefaces or print styles: Courier 10 Pitch, Prestige Elite or Letter Gothic [***see sec. II. Sample Creditor Matrix****]. Debtors who do not have access to a computer may submit a service matrix on 8½ × 11″ unlined white paper, in a neat and legible handwritten format;

(b) Lists must be typed in a single column on the page;

(c) No letters or numbers can be closer than 1 inch from any margin;

(d) Each line must not exceed 40 characters in length;

(e) Each name and address must consist of no more than 5 (five) total lines, with one blank line between creditors;

(f) List the creditors first name first, last name last, without titles (i.e., Dr., Mr., Mrs., Ms.);

(g) Attention or c/o references, if needed, should be listed on the second line followed by the party's name;

(h) Zip codes must be on the last line along with the city and state. Use a hyphen for nine digit zip codes. Use the standard abbreviations for states (***see sec. III U.S. Postal Service Abbreviations List***) which consists of two capital-letters with no periods;

(i) Do not include the following parties on your matrix: debtor, joint debtor, attorney for the debtor, U.S. trustee or case trustee. These parties will automatically be added by the clerk's office and retrieved from the system for noticing;

(j) Do not include duplicate creditor information (i.e. same name and address);

(k) Do not put any other information on the matrix, such as a heading, date, lines, or page numbers. Case number and debtor's name should be written on the diskette label or reverse side of a paper matrix;

(*l*) Do not include account numbers in the address;

(m) Do not use ALL CAPITAL LETTERS. Use both upper and lower case, where appropriate; and,

(n) Do not substitute:

- Letter "l" for the number "1"
- Use \ for /
- Use ~ for –
- Use % for **c/o**
- Use the + sign for ***and*** or ***&***
- Use [ ] for ( )

II. Sample List of Creditors

MBSA Americo Banco
PO Box 15168
Wilmington DE 19850

First Union National Bank
POB 13765
Roanoke VA 24037

Banco of America
PO Drawer 2601
Greensburg NC 27419

Video Expeditions
Attn: John Miller
345 N 98 St
Hoqiam WA 98550

Household Retail Services
c/o Mary Jones
4141 Fourth Ave #900
Seattle WA 98121

III. U.S. Postal Service Abbreviation List

AA	Armed Forces the Americas	MO	Missouri
AE	Armed Forces Europe	MP	Northern Mariana Islands
AK	Alaska	MS	Mississippi
AL	Alabama	MT	Montana
AP	Armed Forces Pacific	NC	North Carolina

AR	Arkansas	ND	North Dakota
AS	American Samoa	NE	Nebraska
AZ	Arizona	NH	New Hampshire
CA	California	NJ	New Jersey
CO	Colorado	NM	New Mexico
CT	Connecticut	NV	Nevada
DC	District of Columbia	NY	New York
DE	Delaware	OH	Ohio
FL	Florida	OK	Oklahoma
FM	Federated States of Micronesia	OR	Oregon
GA	Georgia	PA	Pennsylvania
GU	Guam	PR	Puerto Rico
HI	Hawaii	RI	Rhode Island
IA	Iowa	SC	South Carolina
ID	Idaho	SD	South Dakota
IL	Illinois	TN	Tennessee
IN	Indiana	TX	Texas
KS	Kansas	UT	Utah
KY	Kentucky	VA	Virginia
LA	Louisiana	VI	Virgin Islands, U.S.
MA	Massachusetts	VT	Vermont
MD	Maryland	WA	Washington
ME	Maine	WI	Wisconsin
MH	Marshall Islands	WV	West Virginia
MI	Michigan	WY	Wyoming
MN	Minnesota		

IV. Saving a creditor.scn file in WordPerfect (sample below is with version X3)

1. Insert a blank 3½″ floppy disk or a flash memory drive into your computer.
2. If necessary, launch WordPerfect.
3. Type or enter creditor text.
4. Click on File from the main menu bar.
5. Select Save As. The Save As dialog box will appear (see Figure 1A**).
6. From "Save in", use the drop-down list to click on a directory, usually "3½ Floppy [A:]" (see Figure 1B**) or the directory of an inserted flash drive.
7. From "File type", use the drop-down list to select **ASCII DOS Text** (see Figure 1C**).
8. At "File name", erase any text and enter **"creditor.scn"**. Use the quotation marks when naming your file to prevent the program from adding an additional extension (see Figure 1D**).
9. Click on Save.

V. Saving a creditor.txt file in MS Word (sample below is with version Word 2003)

1. Insert a blank 3½″ floppy disk or a flash memory drive into your computer.
2. If necessary, launch MS Word.
3. Type or enter creditor text.
4. Click on File from the main menu bar.
5. Select Save As. The Save As dialog box will appear (see Figure 1A**).
6. From "Save in", use the drop-down list to click on a directory, usually "3½ Floppy [A:]" (see Figure 1B**) or the directory of an inserted flash drive.
7. From "Save as type", use the drop-down list to select **Plain Text** (see Figure 1C**).

[NOTE—Some versions may have **MS–DOS Text.**]

8. At "File name", erase any text and enter **"creditor.txt"**. Use the quotation marks when naming your file to prevent the program from adding an additional extension (see Figure 1D**).

9. Click on Save.

10. *IF* a File Conversion dialog box appears, click Windows Default *or* MS–DOS, then OK (see Figure 1E**).

C1–3 (rev. 04/25/13)

[Effective December 1, 1998. Amended effective November 1, 2003; June 2, 2008; December 1, 2009; August 3, 2010; August 1, 2011; November 1, 2011; April 25, 2013.]

* **[Publisher's Note:** So in original. Probably should be "Sample List of Creditors".]

** **[Publisher's Note:** Screen shots accompanying the Court's original document are not displayed in this publication.]

CI-4. CLERK'S INSTRUCTIONS FOR ELECTRONIC PUBLIC ACCESS SERVICES

DIRECTORY OF PUBLIC ACCESS SERVICES

McVCIS (Multi-Court Voice Case Information System)

(866) 222-8029

McVCIS is a free interactive voice response system available 24 hours a day that allows anyone with a touchtone phone to determine whether a party has filed for bankruptcy, and gain a considerable amount of case information. One main advantage of McVCIS over the old VCIS system is that case information may be obtained from most bankruptcy courts in the United States by dialing one toll-free number: (866) 222-8029. Additionally, the speech recognition software employed by the system makes the caller's experience more enjoyable, and is available in both English and Spanish languages.

McVCIS is easy to use. After speaking the name of the desired state, then district, if applicable, the caller is connected to that district's CM/ECF database. Using the letters on the telephone keypad, enter the debtor's name (last name first) using up to ten characters, then press the # key. If the debtor is a corporation, enter the first ten characters of the name, then press the # key. Punctuation is irrelevant but it is recommended that all ten allotted characters be used, if necessary, to refine the search results. If more than one match is found, the caller is able to select the desired debtor from the choices given by the system. The information accessible includes debtor(s)' name(s), date of filing, chapter, attorney for the debtor(s), trustee (if applicable), date and time of any pending meeting of creditors, date of discharge, date of closing, and case status such as "Awaiting Discharge" or "Awaiting Closing."

Court Web Site: http://www.flsb.uscourts.gov

Anyone with access to the Internet can visit our web site to obtain a wide array of court information. Information available on our web site includes: general court information (such as court locations, office hours, and staff directory), local rules, administrative orders, local and official forms, filing and fee information, judges' hearing calendars, court opinions, latest court news, access to the court's electronic filing of proof of claim program, information for individuals filing without an attorney, links to related web sites and a copy of the most recent court newsletter.

If you have questions or comments regarding our web site, you may send us an e-mail by addressing it to: Webmaster_FLSB@flsb.uscourts.gov

ECF/PACER—https://ecf.flsb.uscourts.gov

ECF/PACER is a federal Judiciary fee-based electronic public access service that allows Internet users to obtain case and docket information from federal appellate, district and/or bankruptcy court case management systems (CM/ECF). Updated case information, including hyperlinks to all imaged case documents in PDF format, are immediately available and accessible through the ECF/PACER system.

ECF/PACER will provide the following information: listings of new bankruptcy case filings, including cases discharged, dismissed, converted and/or closed, case information accessible by case number, participant's name, and/or by social security or tax I.D. number, court docket reports and information for non-archived cases, claim registers, creditor mailing lists, and written opinions. Viewed information may be printed to a printer and/or saved to a computer.

To access the ECF/PACER system users will need to establish a subscriber account and register with the PACER Billing and Support Center (http://www.pacer.gov). An access fee of $.10 per viewable page is assessed for access to PACER service on the Internet, with certain exceptions (see Electronic Public Access Fee Schedule and information regarding Public Access to Copies of Court Records). This service is available 24/7, except for brief periods for necessary system maintenance.

For more information on ECF/PACER, inquire at the Intake counter, register by calling 1-800-676-6856, or visit the PACER Service Center web site at http://www.pacer.gov

Public Query Terminals

For viewing and/or printing case documents, docket sheets or claims registers, public query terminals are located at the clerk's office intake sections in the Miami, Fort Lauderdale and Palm Beach divisional offices. (See Clerk's Instructions for Obtaining Copies of Court Records.)

ELECTRONIC PUBLIC ACCESS FEE SCHEDULE

(Issued in accordance with 28 U.S.C. § 1913, 1914, 1926, 1930, 1932)

The fees included in the Electronic Public Access Fee Schedule are to be charged for providing electronic public access to court records.

Fees for Public Access to Court Electronic Records (PACER)

(1) Except as provided below, for electronic access to any case document, docket sheet, or case-specific report via PACER: $0.10 per page, not to exceed the fee for thirty pages.

(2) For electronic access to transcripts and non-case specific reports via PACER (such as reports obtained from the PACER Case Locator or docket activity reports): $0.10 per page.

(3) For electronic access to an audio file of a court hearing via PACER: $2.40 per audio file.

Fees for Courthouse Electronic Access

(4) For printing copies of any record or document accessed electronically at a public terminal in a courthouse: $0.10 per page.

PACER Service Center Fees

(5) For every search of court records conducted by the PACER Service Center, $30 per name or item searched.

(6) For the PACER Service Center to reproduce on paper any record pertaining to a PACER account, if this information is remotely available through electronic access: $0.50 per page.

(7) For any payment returned or denied for insufficient funds, $53.

Free Access and Exemptions

(8) Automatic Fee Exemptions

- No fee is owed for electronic access to court data or audio files via PACER until an account holder accrues charges of more than $15.00 in a quarterly billing cycle.
- Parties in a case (including pro se litigants) and attorneys of record receive one free electronic copy, via the notice of electronic filing or notice of docket activity, of all documents filed electronically, if receipt is required by law or directed by the filer.
- No fee is charged for access to judicial opinions.
- No fee is charged for viewing case information or documents at courthouse public access terminals.

(9) Discretionary Fee Exemptions:

- Courts may exempt certain persons or classes of persons from payment of the user access fee. Examples of individuals and groups that a court may consider exempting include: indigents, bankruptcy case trustees, pro bono attorneys, pro bono alternative dispute resolution neutrals, Section 501(c)(3) not-for-profit organizations, and individual researchers associated with educational institutions. Courts should not, however, exempt individuals or groups that have the ability to pay the statutorily established access fee. Examples of individuals and groups that a court should not exempt include: local, state or federal government agencies, members of the media, privately paid attorneys or others who have the ability to pay the fee.
- In considering granting an exemption, courts must find:
- that those seeking an exemption have demonstrated that an exemption is necessary in order to avoid unreasonable burdens and to promote public access to information;

- that individual researchers requesting an exemption have shown that the defined research project is intended for scholarly research, that it is limited in scope, and that it is not intended for redistribution on the internet or for commercial purposes.
- If the court grants an exemption:
- the user receiving the exemption must agree not to sell the data obtained as a result, and must not transfer any data obtained as the result of a fee exemption, unless expressly authorized by the court; and
- the exemption should be granted for a definite period of time, should be limited in scope, and may be revoked at the discretion of the court granting the exemption.
- Courts may provide local court information at no cost (e.g., local rules, court forms, news items, court calendars, and other information) to benefit the public.

Applicability to the United States and State and Local Governments

(10) Unless otherwise authorized by the Judicial Conference, these fees must be charged to the United States, except to federal agencies or programs that are funded from judiciary appropriations (including, but not limited to, agencies, organizations, and individuals providing services authorized by the Criminal Justice Act [18 U.S.C. § 3006A], and bankruptcy administrators).

(11) The fee for printing copies of any record or document accessed electronically at a public terminal ($0.10 per page) described in (4) above does not apply to services rendered on behalf of the United States if the record requested is not remotely available through electronic access.

(12) The fee for local, state, and federal government entities, shall be $0.08 per page until April 1, 2015, after which time, the fee shall be $0.10 per page.

JUDICIAL CONFERENCE POLICY NOTES

The Electronic Public Access (EPA) fee and its exemptions are directly related to the requirement that the judiciary charge user-based fees for the development and maintenance of electronic public access services. The fee schedule provides examples of users that may not be able to afford reasonable user fees (such as indigents, bankruptcy case trustees, individual researchers associated with educational institutions, 501(c)(3) not-for-profit organizations, and court-appointed pro bono attorneys), but requires those seeking an exemption to demonstrate that an exemption is limited in scope and is necessary in order to avoid an unreasonable burden. In addition, the fee schedule includes examples of other entities that courts should not exempt from the fee (such as local, state or federal government agencies, members of the media, and attorneys). The goal is to provide courts with guidance in evaluating a requestor's ability to pay the fee.

Judicial Conference policy also limits exemptions in other ways. First, it requires exempted users to agree not to sell the data they receive through an exemption (unless expressly authorized by the court). This prohibition is not intended to bar a quote or reference to information received as a result of a fee exemption in a scholarly or other similar work. Second, it permits courts to grant exemptions for a definite period of time, to limit the scope of the exemptions, and to revoke exemptions. Third, it cautions that exemptions should be granted as the exception, not the rule, and prohibits courts from exempting all users from EPA fees.

Application for Exemption from the
Judicial Conference's Electronic Public Access Fees
in the District of __________

In support of this application, I provide the following:

1) I am an individual researcher associated with __________.

2) The data received will be used in my research project: __________ (Attach additional sheets as necessary)

3) An exemption from the Judicial Conference's Electronic Public Access Fee is necessary in order to avoid unreasonable burdens and to promote public access to information.

4) I understand that this fee exemption will apply only to me, will be valid only for the purposes stated above, and will apply only to the electronic case files of this court that are available through the PACER service.

5) I agree that any data received through this exemption will not be sold for profit, will not be transferred, will not be used for commercial purposes, and will not be redistributed via the Internet.

Declaration: I declare that the above information is true and understand that a false statement may result in abolishment of my exempt access and an assessment of Electronic Public Access usage fees.

Date: ____________________

____
Applicant's signature

____
Printed name

[Effective December 1, 1998. Amended effective December 1, 2003; December 27, 2004; November 17, 2005; July 1, 2006; September 28, 2006; October 1, 2007; March 31, 2008; June 2, 2008; December 1, 2009; August 1, 2010; September 19, 2011; April 2, 2012; December 1, 2013.]

CI–5. CLERK'S INSTRUCTIONS FOR DEPOSITS INTO AND WITHDRAWALS FROM UNCLAIMED FUNDS

Local Rule 3011–1 sets forth the provisions for depositing and withdrawing unclaimed funds in this court.

I. Deposits Into Unclaimed Funds.

Trustees or others depositing funds into the court pursuant to Local Rule 3011–1(A) or (B) must submit the court's Local Form "Notice of Deposit of Funds With the U.S. Bankruptcy Court Clerk" (LF–26), which also requires the attachment of a list of all claimants containing required information, including name, amount of claim, amount allowed and last known address.

II. Withdrawals from Unclaimed Funds.

A. General Instructions. Modifications to forms **are not** permitted. Applications submitted on modified or nonconforming forms will be returned unprocessed.

If you are a "funds locator" or attorney (i.e. a person who **is not** the original claimant or successor in interest to the original claimant, or an officer of an original claimant corporation or an officer of a successor in interest to an original claimant corporation) and you are claiming funds in the name of a party in whose name funds were deposited with the clerk, you must complete all information on the Local Form "Affidavit of Claimant" ***before*** it is given to the claimant to sign **and have notarized.** This is necessary to ensure that the claimant has sufficient information to verify that the claimant is in fact entitled to the funds.

Applicants must provide notice to the U.S. Attorney pursuant to 28 U.S.C. § 2042. The address is: 99 NE Fourth Street, Miami, FL 33132.

B. Required Forms and Other Supporting Documents.

1. *Individuals Applying as Original Claimants (Including Those Claiming as Probate Successors).* Individuals applying on behalf of themselves must submit the court's Local Form "Application to Withdraw Unclaimed Funds" (LF–27), which must be notarized, a copy of an official government photo id to prove identity (for example driver's license, passport) and Local Form "Order For Payment of Unclaimed Funds" (LF–29).

If funds were deposited in the names of both husband and wife, both must sign this application and provide identification, or if one spouse is requesting release of funds in the name of that spouse only, applicant must attach a notarized affidavit stating why the funds should be released to only one spouse and not in the name of both.

2. *Funds Locators, Attorneys Or Employees of Corporations Representing.* In addition to the Local Form, "Application to Withdraw Unclaimed Funds" (LF–27), and Local Form, "Order For Payment of Unclaimed Funds" (LF–29), **you must also submit:**

- this court's Local Form "Affidavit of Claimant" (LF–28) (claimant must complete the form and have it notarized.);
- a "Power of Attorney" conforming to Director's Form 4011A "General Power of Attorney". If the claimant is a non individual, a corporate power of attorney, signed by the CEO (or other authorized signatory) of the company, sealed with the corporate seal and accompanied by a statement of the signing officer's authority, as well as documents which established the chain of ownership of the original corporate claimant must be provided.
- copy of an official government photo id to prove identity (for example driver's license, passport) of the person you are representing
- any documentation that will support the claimant or successor in interest to the original claimant's right to this claim (i.e. probate orders, purchase of business contracts, etc.).

3. *Debtors Claiming Funds Deposited in the Name of a Creditor.* Debtors seeking to claim funds deposited in the name of a creditor must:

Submit the Local Form, "Application to Withdraw Unclaimed Funds" (LF–27), "Order for Payment of Unclaimed Funds" (LF–29) **and** attach to the local form application a copy of an official government photo id to prove debtor's identity (for example driver's license, passport) and a sworn affidavit detailing debtor's right to the funds deposited in the name of the creditor and attach copies of any exhibits to substantiate this right. The debtor must also attach a certificate of service reflecting that a copy of the application and required attachments has been served on the creditor whose funds the debtor is seeking to claim and on the trustee who deposited the funds with the clerk of court. If funds were deposited in a joint debtor case, both husband and wife must sign this application, or if one spouse is requesting release of funds in the name of that spouse only, applicant must attach an affidavit stating why the funds should be released to only one spouse and not in the name of both.

4. *Funds Locators or Attorneys Representing Debtors who are Seeking to Claim Funds Deposited in the Name of a Creditor.* Funds locators or attorneys representing a debtor who is seeking to claim funds deposited in the name of a creditor must:

Submit the Local Form, "Application to Withdraw Unclaimed Funds" (LF–27), and Local Form, "Order For Payment of Unclaimed Funds" (LF–29) **and** attach to the local form application a copy of an official government photo id to prove debtor's identity (for example driver's license, passport) and a sworn affidavit detailing debtor's right to the funds deposited in the name of the creditor and attach copies of any exhibits to substantiate this right. Also attach a certificate of service reflecting that a copy of the application and required attachments has been served on the creditor whose funds the debtor is seeking to claim and on the trustee who deposited the funds with the clerk of court. If funds were deposited in a joint debtor case, both husband and wife must sign the affidavit, or if one spouse is requesting release of funds in the name of that spouse only, that spouse must provide an affidavit stating why the funds should be released to only one spouse and not in the name of both.

The funds locator or attorney must also submit a "Power of Attorney" conforming to the Director's Form 4011A "General Power of Attorney". If the debtor is a non individual, a corporate power of attorney, signed by the CEO (or other authorized signatory) of the company, sealed with the corporate seal and accompanied by a statement of the signing officer's authority, as well as documents which established the chain of ownership of the original corporate claimant must be provided.

C. Issuance of Checks. All checks issued as a result of an application submitted by an attorney or "funds locator" shall be made payable to the person on whose behalf application was submitted and to the "funds locator" or attorney who submitted the application so that the person on whose behalf the application was submitted is aware that a check has been issued. If the application is signed by an individual on behalf of a non individual, the check will be issued in the non individual (i.e. company) name. If the court approves an application for funds deposited in a joint debtor case, the check shall issue in the name of both debtors, unless the court determines that the funds shall be made payable to only one of the joint debtors.

Individuals applying for unclaimed funds must submit an AO213 Form along with all required documentation. An AO213 must filled out for **each payee** in which the check will be issued to. This includes attorneys and fund locators. Failure to do so will result in a returned application.

Note: Any indication of fraud related to unclaimed funds withdrawal requests will be reported to the U.S. Attorney.

D. Submittal of Application. Completed applications along with all required documentation and forms, must be mailed to the Financial Section, United States Bankruptcy Court, Southern District of Florida, C. Clyde Atkins United States Courthouse, Room 150, 301 N. Miami Avenue, Miami, FL 33128.

If you have any questions regarding depositing or claiming funds or these guidelines and related forms, please contact this court's financial section at (305) 714–1841 or 714–1848 or write to: Financial Section, United States Bankruptcy Court, Southern District of Florida, C. Clyde Atkins United States Courthouse, Room 150, 301 N. Miami Avenue, Miami, FL 33128.

[Effective June 2, 2008. Amended effective December 1, 2009; October 10, 2014; September 2, 2016.]

CI–6. CLERK'S INSTRUCTIONS FOR APPEALS

1. All notices of appeal filed in the Bankruptcy Court under Federal Rule of Bankruptcy Procedure 8003 and 8004 shall be transmitted promptly to the Clerk of the District Court for docketing and the opening of a new civil case [see U.S. District Court Local Rule 87.4]. Within 14 days after filing the notice of appeal or entry of an order disposing of the last timely motion of a type specified in Bankruptcy Rule 8002(b) (whichever is later), or entry of an order by the District Court granting leave to appeal, the appellant shall file with the clerk of the bankruptcy court a designation of the items to be included in the record on appeal and a statement of issues to be presented (Bankruptcy Rule 8009). **Failure to timely file this designation and statement of issues may result in dismissal of the appeal pursuant to this court's Local Rule** 8009–1(A) **and Local Rule 87.4(c), United States District Court, Southern District of Florida.** The designation shall include the title and docket number of each paper designated.

2. Within 14 days after the service of the designation and the statement of issues of the appellant the appellee may file and serve on the appellant a designation of additional items to be included in the record on appeal, and if the appellee has filed a cross appeal, the appellee as cross appellant shall file and serve a statement of issues to be presented on the cross appeal, and a designation of additional items to be included in the record. The appellee's designation shall include the title and docket number of each additional item designated.

3. If any transcripts of untranscribed proceedings are designated by a party, that party shall immediately, upon the filing of the designation, order the transcript(s) from the court reporter and make satisfactory arrangements for payment of its costs. All transcript orders must be made on the local form "Transcript Request Form" enclosed for this purpose, and a copy filed with the clerk at the time of filing the designation (Bankruptcy Rule 8009). On receipt of a request for a transcript, the reporter shall complete the Reporter's Acknowledgment and file a copy with the clerk (Bankruptcy Rule 8010). [See also "Guidelines on Electronic Availability of Transcripts and Procedures for Transcript Redaction."]

4. When the record is complete for purposes of the appeal, the bankruptcy clerk will electronically transmit the record to the clerk of the district court. Once the record has been transmitted to the district court, any subsequently filed document relating to the appeal must be filed in the district court.

5. Motions for Leave to Appeal (Bankruptcy Rule 8004). The clerk will electronically transmit the motion, notice of appeal and any answer to the clerk of the district court as soon as all parties have filed answers or the time for filing an answer has expired. The designation and statement of the issues should not be filed with the clerk of the bankruptcy court as required under Bankruptcy Rule 8009, until entry of an order by the district court granting leave to appeal (Local Rule 8004–1).

[Effective December 1, 1998. Amended effective December 1, 2002; October 17, 2005; November 2, 2007; June 2, 2008; December 1, 2009; October 1, 2013; April 11, 2016.]

CI–7. CLERK'S INSTRUCTIONS FOR CHAPTER 11 CASES

I. ADDITIONAL FILING REQUIREMENT FOR CHAPTER 11 DEBTORS

Pursuant to Local Rule 2081–1, chapter 11 debtors, except individual debtors not engaged in business, are required to file:

- within 14 days after filing the petition or after conversion to chapter 11, a certified report containing financial information regarding payroll and sales taxes using Local Form "Debtor's Notice of Filing Payroll and Sales Tax Reports". Only the original (with certificate of service included) need be filed with the court and
- within the earlier of three business days after relief is entered or one business day prior to the date of the first scheduled hearing, the Local Form "Chapter 11 Case Management Summary". This summary must be served on all parties of record.

Small Business Debtors must file the Official Bankruptcy Form 25c "Small Business Monthly Operating Report" [See 11 U.S.C. § 308(b)].

Official Bankruptcy Form **B 26** "Periodic Report Regarding Value, Operations and Profitability of Entities in Which the Debtor's Estate Holds a Substantial or Controlling Interest" must be filed as required under Bankruptcy Rule 2015.3.

II. PROCEDURES FOR DISCLOSURE AND CONFIRMATION HEARING

(1) In advance of filing the plan and disclosure statement, the attorney is responsible for obtaining current service matrices in accordance with Local Rule 2002–1(D) and if applicable, the "Master Service List" (as described in Local Rule 2002–1(H). If the claims bar date has not yet expired at the time the disclosure statement and plan are filed, the attorney must obtain an updated claims service list prior to the confirmation hearing.

(2) Disclosure and Confirmation Hearings.

A. *Standard Cases.* [See Local Rules 3016–2 and 3017–1]

(i) Order Setting Disclosure Hearing: Upon filing of the original plan and disclosure statement, an ORDER (I) SETTING HEARING TO CONSIDER APPROVAL OF DISCLOSURE STATEMENT; (II) SETTING DEADLINE FOR FILING OBJECTIONS TO DISCLOSURE STATEMENT; AND (III) DIRECTING PLAN PROPONENT TO SERVE NOTICE will be entered. The attorney for plan proponent shall serve the order pursuant to the instructions contained in the order and file a certificate of service as required under Local Rule 2002–1(F).

(ii) Order Setting Confirmation Hearing: Upon approval of the disclosure statement, the court shall enter the ORDER (I) APPROVING DISCLOSURE STATEMENT; (II) SETTING HEARING ON CONFIRMATION OF PLAN; (III) SETTING HEARING ON FEE APPLICATIONS; (IV) SETTING VARIOUS DEADLINES; AND (V) DESCRIBING PLAN PROPONENT'S OBLIGATIONS. The attorney for plan proponent shall serve the order pursuant to the instructions contained in the order and file a certificate of service as required under Local Rule 2002–1(F).

B. *Small Business Cases.* [See Local Rules 3016–1 and 3017–2]

C. *Prepackaged Chapter 11 Cases.* See the court's "Guidelines for Prepackaged Chapter 11 Cases." [See Local Rule 3017–3]

III. REPORTS ON CONFIRMATION. INDIVIDUAL DEBTOR CERTIFICATION

The Local Forms "Certificate of Proponent of Plan on Acceptance of Plan, Report on Amount to be Deposited, Certificate of Amount Deposited and Payment of Fees", and the Local Form "Confirmation Affidavit" must also be submitted at least three business days before the confirmation hearing. [See Local Rule 3020–1(B)]

If the debtor is an individual, the debtor shall also file the Local Form "Certificate for Confirmation Regarding Payment of Domestic Support Obligations and Filing of Required Tax Returns" at least three business days before the confirmation hearing.

IV. CONVERSIONS

Motions to convert by the debtor under LR 9013-1(C)(12), must be accompanied by the local form order of conversion as required under Local Rule 1017-1(A). **If converting to Chapter 7, the motion must be accompanied by a $15.00 filing fee.**

V. NOTICE OF REQUIREMENTS FOR FILING SCHEDULE OF POSTPETITION DEBTS AND BANCAP MATRIX UPON CONVERSION OF CASE TO CHAPTER 7

Pursuant to Bankruptcy Rule 1019(5), a Chapter 11 debtor in possession (or trustee if one was appointed) must file, within 15 days of entry of the order of conversion, a schedule of unpaid debts incurred after commencement of the superseded case, including the name and address of each creditor. Local Rule 1019-1(B) provides that this schedule must also be accompanied by a supplemental service matrix in the form required by the "Clerk's Instructions for Preparing, Submitting and Obtaining Service Matrices". The debtor is responsible for providing notice to those creditors. [See Local Rule 1019-1(B)]. If no unpaid debts have been incurred since the commencement of the case, a certification to this effect shall be filed.

VI. NOTICE OF PROCEDURE FOR CLOSING A CONFIRMED CHAPTER 11 CASE

Local Rule 3022-1(A) requires the debtor to file a Local Form "Final Report and Motion for Final Decree Closing Case", unless otherwise provided in the confirmation order, in a non-individual chapter 11 case, not later than 60 days after the order confirming the plan becomes final, and in an individual chapter 11 case, upon completion of all payments under the confirmed plan, or if applicable, upon the filing of a motion by an individual debtor seeking entry of a discharge prior to completion of payments under the plan under 11 U.S.C. § 1141(d)(5). A 30 day deadline will be set for the U.S. Trustee's Office to object to the report. Absent any objections or upon resolution of any objections, a Final Decree closing the case will be prepared by the clerk's office and a copy mailed to the attorney for the debtor.

Local Rule 3022-1(B) requires that, in an individual chapter 11 case, not later than 60 calendar days after completion of all payments under the confirmed plan, the debtor shall also file the Local Form "Notice of Deadline to Object to Debtor's Statements Re: 11 U.S.C. § 522(q)(1) Applicability, Payment of Domestic Support Obligations and [For Chapter 11 Cases Only] Applicability of Financial Management Course and Statement Regarding Eligibility to Receive a Discharge". This statement shall be served on negative notice on all parties of record. Any interested party who fails to file and serve a written objection to the statement within 30 days shall be deemed to have consented to entry of the final decree and discharge of debtor. A certificate of service shall be filed as provided by Local Rule 2002-1(F).

VII. FORMS LIST

A. Forms for Setting Disclosure and Confirmation Hearings. Please note: The four orders listed below with an "*" will be prepared by the court for service by the plan proponent. The form is published for information only.

Standard Chapter 11

*"Order (I) Setting Hearing to Consider Approval of Disclosure Statement; (II) Setting Deadline for Filing Objections to Disclosure Statement; and (III) Directing Plan Proponent to Serve Notice"

*"Order (I) Approving Disclosure Statement; (II) Setting Hearing On Confirmation of Plan; (III) Setting Hearing On Fee Applications; (IV) Setting Various Deadlines; And (V) Describing Plan Proponent's Obligations"

Small Business Chapter 11

*"Order (I) Conditionally Approving Proposed Disclosure Document; (II) Setting Hearing on Final Approval of Proposed Disclosure Document and Confirmation of Plan; (III) Setting

Hearing on Fee Applications; (IV) Setting Various Deadlines and (V) Describing Plan Proponent's Obligations". See Local Rule 3017–2(A).

*"Order (I) Setting Hearing on Approval of the Disclosure Statement and Confirmation of Plan; (II) Setting Hearing on Fee Applications; (III) Setting Various Deadlines; and (IV) Describing Plan Proponent's Obligations". See Local Rule 3017–2(B).

B. Other Forms Related to Confirmation Process. "Ballot and Deadline for Filing Ballot Accepting or Rejecting Plan" [Local Rule 3018–1(A)]

"Certificate of Proponent of Plan on Acceptance of Plan, Report on Amount to be Deposited, Certificate of Amount Deposited and Payment of Fees"

"Confirmation Affidavit"

"Certificate for Confirmation Regarding Payment of Domestic Support Obligations and Filing of Required Tax Returns"

C. Other Chapter 11 Forms and Instructions. "Clerk's Instructions for Preparing, Submitting and Obtaining Service Matrices"

Local Form "Order Converting Case Under Chapter 11 To Case Under Chapter 7"

Local Form "Final Report and Motion for Final Decree Closing Case"

Local Form "Debtor's Notice of Filing Payroll and Sales Tax Reports"

Local Form "Chapter 11 Case Management Summary"

Local Form "Notice of Deadline to Object to Debtor's Statements Re: 11 U.S.C. § 522(q)(1) Applicability, Payment of Domestic Support Obligations and [For Chapter 11 Cases Only] Applicability of Financial Management Course and Statement Regarding Eligibility to Receive a Discharge"

Official Bankruptcy Form 25c "Small Business Monthly Operating Report"

Official Bankruptcy Form **B 26** "Periodic Report Regarding Value, Operations and Profitability of Entities in Which the Debtor's Estate Holds a Substantial or Controlling Interest"

Official Bankruptcy Form "Plan of Reorganization in Small Business Case under Chapter 11"

Official Bankruptcy Form "Disclosure Statement in Small Business Case under Chapter 11"

VIII. CONTACT ADDRESSES

A list on reverse side of this notice is provided for your assistance in chapter 11 bankruptcy cases. It is the responsibility of the serving party to determine the correct address for and manner of service.

Clerk of Court
U.S. Bankruptcy Court

QUESTIONS CONCERNING THESE PROCEDURES SHOULD BE DIRECTED TO THE COURTROOM DEPUTY FOR THE ASSIGNED JUDGE.

The following addresses are provided for your assistance in noticing Chapter 11 Bankruptcy Cases:

1) **U.S. BANKRUPTCY COURT**

Clerk's Office—Miami Division
C. Clyde Atkins United States Courthouse (305) 714–1800
301 N. Miami Avenue, #150
Miami, FL 33128

Judge Robert A. Mark Courtroom #417
Judge A. Jay Cristol Courtroom #717
Judge Laurel Myerson Isicoff Courtroom #817

Clerk's Office—FTL Division
U.S. Courthouse (954) 769–5700
Room 112

299 East Broward Blvd.
Ft. Lauderdale, FL 33301

Judge Raymond B. Ray — Courtroom #308
Judge John K. Olson — Courtroom #301

Clerk's Office—WPB Division
The Flagler Waterview Building — (561) 514–4100
1515 North Flagler Drive
Room 801
West Palm Beach, FL 33401

Chief Judge Paul G. Hyman, Jr. — Courtroom #A
Judge Erik P. Kimball — Courtroom #B

2) **Office of U.S. Trustee**
51 S.W. First Ave. — (305) 536–7285
Room 1204
Miami, FL 33130

3) **Internal Revenue Service**
Internal Revenue Service
P.O. Box 21126
Philadelphia, PA 19114

Insolvency Unit
7850 S.W. 6th Court
Mail Stop 5730
Plantation, FL 33324

[NOTE: Payments for Chapter 11 cases MUST be sent to the local office.]

4) **State of Florida/Dept. of Revenue**
Bankruptcy Section
P.O. Box 6668
Tallahassee, FL 32314–6668

CI-7 (rev. 10/10/14)

[Effective December 1, 1998. Amended effective December 1, 2002; February 15, 2005; August 16, 2005; February 17, 2006; September 25, 2006; November 1, 2006; January 8, 2007; June 2, 2008; June 24, 2008; September 23, 2008; December 11, 2008; May 7, 2009; December 1, 2009; October 10, 2014.]

CI–8. CLERK'S INSTRUCTIONS FOR OBTAINING COPIES OF COURT RECORDS

Except for documents under SEAL, documents containing individual debtors' full Social security numbers, individual debtors' small business tax returns and any other document restricted pursuant to local rule or court order, documents are available as follows:

I. Clerk's Office. Copies of paper court documents in pending or recently closed cases filed **prior to** October 17, 2005, may be obtained from the clerk's office at a cost of $0.50 per page. These files are normally located in the clerk's divisional office where the assigned judge is chambered.

The following court documents can be viewed for free at all clerk's office locations or printed from public access terminals at a cost of $0.10 per page or may be obtained from the clerk's office at a cost of $0.50 per page.

- Court electronic documents filed in cases on or after October 17, 2005
- Court dockets/claim registers for cases filed on or after May 1, 1989
- Proofs of claim images for cases filed on or after September 1, 1993

Certified copies of court records for any document available at the clerk's office will cost $11.00 for each certified document plus a per page copy cost of $0.50. The fee for a search conducted by the clerk's office is $30.00 per name or item.

II. Internet Access Via Pacer. Images of court electronic documents filed in cases on or after October 17, 2005, court dockets for cases filed on or after May 1, 1989, and proofs of claim or claim registers for cases filed on or after September 1, 1993, may be viewed and printed using PACER (**P**ublic **A**ccess to **C**ourt **E**lectronic **R**ecords), a nationwide electronic access service of the federal judiciary. A PACER login account may be obtained by registering at: www.pacer.gov or by contacting the PACER service center at (800) 676–6856.

PACER charges $0.10 per page retrieved. The charge for any single document is capped at $3.00, the equivalent of 30 pages. The cap does not apply to name searches, reports that are not case-specific, and transcripts of federal court proceedings. *If a PACER account accrues a total of less than $10.00 of charges in any given quarter, fees are waived for that quarter.*

NOTE: The Judicial Conference of the United States has amended the policy on privacy and public access to electronic case files by restricting public access through PACER to documents in bankruptcy cases that were filed before December 1, 2003 that have been closed for more than one year, with the following conditions:

- *Docket sheet and docket information will remain available to the public via PACER.*
- *Any party that filed a Notice of Appearance in a case prior to October 10, 2011 will continue to have PACER access to ALL documents in that case provided that the party first logs into CM/ECF, then into ECF/PACER.*
- *ALL documents will remain accessible at the clerk's office public query terminals.*
- *If you are not a case participant and wish to obtain a copy of a restricted document, you must contact the clerk's office, who can provide you with a copy of the document at a cost of $.50 per page (a research fee may apply-see Clerk's Summary of Fees). The clerk's office will not provide copies of restricted documents electronically via email. Also, the clerk's office will not modify any printed document by redacting a social security number or other personal identifier.*

III. Federal Records Center. Copies of documents in closed cases which have been sent to the Federal Records Center (FRC) in Ellenwood, Georgia should be ordered directly from National Archives and Records Administration. You must first contact the court for the transfer and box information, then complete Local Form "Request for Copies of Archived Case Files from U.S. Bankruptcy Court, Southern District of Florida." Pre–Selected Documents for **Individual Debtor(s) Cases ONLY** (Voluntary Petition, Summary of Debts and Property, Schedules D, E/F, and Discharge of Debtor or Order of Dismissal may be obtained from the FRC at a cost of $35.00. Copies of all documents (150 page maximum) for **ALL CASE TYPES (Individual, Business and Adversary cases)** may be obtained from the FRC at a cost of $90.00. Additional fees will be incurred for a case exceeding the 150 page maximum. Copies of Documents from the FRC may be delivered via FAX or U.S. Mail. Either package can also be certified for an additional $15.00 at the time of ordering.

Files may also be retrieved from the FRC back to the court for a fee of $64.00 by submitting the Local Form "Archives Request Form" (LF–88). Retrievals involving multiple boxes is $39.00 for each additional box. Copies of any retrieved case document will cost $0.50 per page and are only available in paper format. Certified copies of those documents will cost $11.00 for each document plus a per page copy charge of $0.50. The fee for a search conducted by the clerk's office is $30.00 per name or item.

If the document is 100 pages or less, not sealed, restricted or requiring certification then it may be retrieved via SmartScan in Adobe Portable Document Format (PDF) via email. The service fee per document is $10.00 (Judiciary Administrative Fee) + $9.90 (FRC Fee) + $ 0.65 per PDF page. If your request is available through SmartScan, and would like to receive the document via email, we will contact you prior to processing the retrieval with the exact amount owed. This method requires submission of Local Form "Archives Request Form" (LF–88).

Local forms are available on the court website at www.flsb.uscourts.gov. Please contact the clerk's office at one of the following numbers if you have questions about obtaining copies of court documents:

Miami: (305) 714–1800

Ft. Lauderdale: (954) 769–5700

West Palm Beach: (561) 514–4100

[Amended effective April 2, 2012; December 1, 2013; September 26, 2016; October 18, 2016.]

CG–1. GUIDELINES FOR FEE APPLICATIONS FOR PROFESSIONALS IN THE SOUTHERN DISTRICT OF FLORIDA IN BANKRUPTCY CASES[1]

Pursuant to Local Rule 2016–1(B)(1), the following Guidelines For Fees And Disbursements For Professionals In The Southern District Of Florida In Bankruptcy Cases (the "Guidelines") apply in all bankruptcy cases in the Southern District of Florida except as provided in Local Rule 2016–1(B)(2) with respect to attorneys for chapter 13 debtors. They delineate information that each interim and final application for professional fees and expenses (the "Application") must contain, and guidelines for reimbursement of disbursements. The Guidelines are mandatory guidelines to which an applicant for compensation (the "Applicant") must certify the Application complies. Such certification shall be by way of the certification required to be attached to the Application by Section A herein (the "Certification"). The "Application" and the "Certification" must substantially conform to the local forms "Application" and "Certification" included in these Guidelines. No deviation from these Guidelines is permissible, regardless of circumstances, without prior order of the presiding judge in such case, entered after notice and hearing on a motion of the Applicant setting forth why the Applicant believes departure from the Guidelines is justified in the circumstances. If such an order is obtained, the Application must comply with the remainder of these Guidelines and the Certification shall specifically so state. Failure to comply with these Guidelines shall result in the denial, without prejudice, of the Application. Pursuant to Local Rule 2016–1(B)(1), applications for cumulative compensation that do not exceed $2,500 need not include a breakdown by categories of work performed.

A. Certification.

1. Each Application for fees and disbursements must contain the Certification by the professional designated by the Applicant with the responsibility in the particular case for compliance with these Guidelines (the "Certifying Professional"), certifying that: (a) the Certifying Professional has read the Application; (b) to the best of the Certifying Professionals knowledge, information and belief formed after reasonable inquiry, the Application complies with the mandatory Guidelines set forth herein; (c) to the best of the Certifying Professional's knowledge, information and belief formed after reasonable inquiry, the fees and disbursements sought fall within these Guidelines, except as specifically noted in the Certification and described in the Application; and (d) except to the extent that fees or disbursements are prohibited by the Guidelines, the fees and disbursements sought are billed at rates and in accordance with practices customarily employed by the Applicant and generally accepted by Applicant's clients.

2. Each Application for fees and disbursements must contain a certification by the Certifying Professional that the trustee (if any), the examiner (if any), the chair of each official committee (if any), the debtor, the U.S. trustee, and the respective counsel for the foregoing, have all been provided, simultaneously with the filing of the Application with the court, with a complete copy of the relevant Application (together with all exhibits).

3. Each Application requesting reimbursement for services and expenses must contain a certification by the Applicant that: (a) in providing a reimbursable service, the Applicant does not make a profit on that service; (b) in charging for a particular service, the Applicant does not include in the amount for which reimbursement is sought the amortization of the cost of any investment, equipment, or capital outlay (except to the extent that any such amortization is included within the permitted allowable amounts set forth herein for photocopies and facsimile transmission); and (c) in seeking reimbursement for a service which the Applicant justifiably purchased or contracted for from a third party (such as messenger service, over-night courier, computerized research, and title and lien searches), the Applicant requests reimbursement only for the amount billed to the Applicant by the third-party vendor and paid by the Applicant to such vendor.

4. The certifications set forth in these Guidelines shall be set forth in a separate exhibit to the Application and shall substantially conform to the local form "Certification" (and "Certificate of Service") included in these Guidelines.

B. Attendance at Hearing on Application.

1. The Certifying Professional shall notify its client that it should be present at the hearing to consider the Application.

C. Time Records Required to Support Fee Applications.

1. Each professional and paraprofessional must record time in increments of tenths of an hour, and must keep contemporaneous time records on a daily basis.

2. Time records must set forth in reasonable detail an appropriate narrative description of the services rendered. Without limiting the foregoing, the description should include indications of the participants in, as well as the scope, identification and purpose of the activity that is reasonable in the circumstances, especially in relation to the hours sought to be charged to the estate for that particular activity.

3. In recording time, each professional and paraprofessional may, subject to Section C(4), describe in one entry the nature of the services rendered during that day and the aggregate time expended for that day in an Activity Code Category (as herein defined) without delineating the actual time spent on each discrete activity in an Activity Code Category, provided, however, single time entries of more than one hour in an Activity Code Category that include two or more activities must include a notation of the approximate time spent on each activity within the Activity Code Category.

4. Time records shall be in chronological order by Activity Code Category. The following is a list of Activity Code Categories (the "Activity Code Category") that are applicable to most bankruptcy cases. Only one category should be used for any given activity and professionals and paraprofessionals should make their best effort to be consistent in their use of categories. This applies both within and across firms. Thus, it may be appropriate for all professionals to discuss the categories in advance and agree generally on how activities will be categorized. The Application may contain additional categories as the case requires. For example, each litigation matter should have its own category. But every effort should be made to use the listed categories in the first instance and to coordinate the use of additional categories with other professionals in the case.

(a) The following categories are generally more applicable to attorneys but may be used by all professionals as appropriate:

ASSET ANALYSIS AND RECOVERY: Identification and review of potential assets including causes of action and non-litigation recoveries.

ASSET DISPOSITION: Sales, leases (Section 365 matters), abandonment and related transaction work. Where extended series of sales or other disposition of assets is contemplated, a separate category should be established for each major transaction.

BUSINESS OPERATIONS: Issues related to debtor in possession operations in chapter 11 such as employee, vendor, tenant issues and other similar problems.

CASE ADMINISTRATION: Coordination and compliance activities, including preparation of statement of financial affairs; schedules; list of contracts; United States trustee Guideline compliance; United States trustee "Debtor in Possession Reports"; contacts with the U.S. trustee; general creditor inquiries.

CLAIMS ADMINISTRATION AND OBJECTIONS: Specific claim inquiries; bar date motions; analysis, objections and allowances of claims.

EMPLOYEE BENEFITS/PENSIONS: Review issues such as severance, retention, 401K coverage and continuance of pension plan.

FEE/EMPLOYMENT APPLICATIONS: Preparation of employment and fee applications for self and others; motions to establish interim procedures.

FEE/EMPLOYMENT OBJECTIONS: Review of and objections to the employment and fee applications of others.

FINANCING: Matters under Sections 361, 363 and 364 including cash collateral and secured claims; loan document analysis.

LITIGATION: There should be a separate category established for each matter (e.g. XYZ Stay Litigation).

MEETINGS OF CREDITORS: Preparing for and attending the first meeting of creditors and other creditors' committee meetings.

PLAN AND DISCLOSURE STATEMENT: Formulation, presentation and confirmation; compliance with the plan confirmation order, related orders and rules; disbursement and case closing activities, except those related to the allowance and objections to allowance of claims.

(b) The following categories are generally more applicable to accountants and financial advisors, but may be used by all professionals as appropriate:

ACCOUNTING/AUDITING: Activities related to maintaining and auditing books of account, preparation of financial statements and account analysis.

BUSINESS ANALYSIS: Preparation and review of company business plan; development and review of strategies; preparation and review of cash flow forecasts and feasibility studies.

CORPORATE FINANCE: Review financial aspects of potential mergers, acquisitions and disposition of company or subsidiaries.

DATA ANALYSIS: Management information systems review, installation and analysis, construction, maintenance and reporting of significant case financial data, lease rejection, claims, etc.

PREPARATION AND REVIEW OF REPORTS REQUIRED BY U.S. TRUSTEE: Preparation and review of the monthly debtor in possession reports, trustee or examiner reports, or other reports required by the U.S. trustee.

LITIGATION CONSULTING: Providing consulting and expert witness services relating to various bankruptcy matters such as insolvency, feasibility, avoidance actions; forensic accounting; etc.

RECONSTRUCTION ACCOUNTING: Reconstructing books and records from past transactions and bringing accounting current.

TAX ISSUES: Analysis of tax issues and preparation of state and federal tax returns.

VALUATION: Appraise or review appraisals of assets.

D. Reimbursement of Expenses and Services.

1. *Presentation of Disbursements and Expenses in Fee Application.*

(a) In requesting reimbursement for disbursements and expenses, Applicants are specifically reminded of other certifications required by these Guidelines, and in particular the certification under Section A(1)(c) hereof. Excessive charges shall not be reimbursed and all charges must be necessary and reasonable. To the extent that an Applicant seeks reimbursement for expenses and services, the Application shall categorize them and shall attach to the Application as an exhibit a summary of the total costs and Disbursements for the period covered by the Application which the Applicant is seeking, in substantially the format included in these Guidelines as local form labeled Exhibit 2.

(b) Support for each disbursement or expense item for which reimbursement is sought must be kept. Such support shall be provided on request to the court and the United States trustee, and in appropriate circumstances to any party in interest provided that, where applicable, privilege or confidentiality can be preserved.

2. *Allowable and Non–Allowable Reimbursable Disbursements and Expenses.*

(a) Filing Fees Process Service Fees, Witness Fees and Expert Witness Fees. Filing fees (including for necessary adversaries), process service fees, witness fees, and expert witness fees (subject to court approval of the employment of any professionals and the reasonableness of such fees) shall be allowable to the extent of the actual cost incurred by the Applicant.

(b) Court Reporter Fees and Transcripts. Court reporter fees and copies of transcripts shall be allowable to the extent of the actual cost incurred by the Applicant.

(c) Lien and Title Searches. The cost for lien and title searches (whether done in-house or by an outside vendor) is allowable to the extent of the actual cost incurred by, or invoiced to, the Applicant.

(d) Photocopying. Photocopying shall be allowable at a cost not to exceed $.15 per page. The Applicant shall set forth in its fee application the total number of copies. Outside vendor photocopying charges are allowable at the actual cost invoiced to the Applicant. Necessary copies obtained from the Clerk of the Bankruptcy Court (including certified copies) will be permitted at the actual cost incurred by the Applicant. The Applicant shall not seek reimbursement for any copies which the Applicant has provided to a third party if the third party has reimbursed Applicant for the copies.

(e) Postage, Over-night Delivered Courier/Messenger Services. The cost of postage, over-night delivery, and outside courier/messenger services are reimbursable for the actual cost incurred, if reasonably incurred. Charges should be minimized whenever possible. For example, couriers/messengers and over-night delivery service should be used only when first-class mail is impracticable.

(f) Telephone. Long distance telephone charges are allowable to the Applicant for the actual cost invoiced from the telephone carrier. Charges for local telephone exchange service and cellular telephone service shall not be reimbursable.

(g) Facsimile Transmission. A charge for out-going facsimile transmission to long distance telephone numbers are reimbursable at the lower of (a) toll charges or (b) if such amount is not readily determinable, $1.00 per page for domestic and $2.00 per page for international transmissions. Charges for in-coming facsimiles are not reimbursable. The Applicant's fee application shall state the total number of pages of the out-going transmissions.

(h) Computerized Research. Computerized legal research services such as Lexis and Westlaw are reimbursable to the extent of the invoiced cost from the vendor.

(i) Parking. Reimbursement for parking shall not be allowable, including parking by a professional to attend court proceedings, depositions or case conferences, parking at the airport, and client and third party parking (including validation).

(j) Travel Expenses and Meals. Travel expenses (mileage, taxis, etc.) and meals (including staff meals) incurred within a fifty (50) mile radius of the Applicant's office shall not be reimbursable. Mileage charges for out-of-town travel (outside a fifty (50) mile radius the Applicant's office) with one's own car are reimbursable at the lesser of the amount charged clients in the non-bankruptcy context or the amount allowed by the Internal Revenue Service for per mile deductions. The Applicant shall seek and use the lowest airfare available to the Applicant. Luxury accommodations and deluxe meals are not reimbursable, nor are personal, incidental charges such as telephone and laundry unless necessary as a result of a reasonably unforeseen extended stay not due to the fault of the traveler. Expenses for travel over a fifty (50) mile radius of the Applicant's office shall be substantiated with copies of all receipts for such travel, and the Application shall include the date of the travel, the purpose of the travel, the cost of each trip, and the name of the person traveling. For purposes of the foregoing, the Applicant's office shall be the office in which the person incurring the travel expense is located.

(k) Word Processing, Document Preparation, Data Processing, Proofreading. Secretarial and Other Staff Services. Secretarial, library, word processing, document preparation (other than by professionals or paraprofessionals), data processing, and other staff services (exclusive of paraprofessional services), including overtime for the foregoing, shall <u>not</u> be reimbursable. Charges for proofreading for typographical or similar errors are <u>not</u> reimbursable whether the services are performed by a paralegal, secretary, or temporary staff.

E. Content of Application.

1. The Application (including both interim and final Applications) shall address the twelve factors for consideration when awarding fees as enumerated in *Johnson v. Georgia Highway Express, Inc.*[2] (and made applicable to bankruptcy proceedings in *Matter of First Colonial Corp. of America*[3]). The Application shall provide a brief narrative of the significant events in the case during the time period covered by the Application, and a brief statement for each major Activity Code Category used during the period of the Application, noting the total hours and fees charged for that category during the period covered by the Application and the particular benefits generated to the estate.

2. *Exhibits to the Application.* Each Application must include:

(a) The Applicant shall complete and attach to <u>front (as the first page)</u> of the Application, the Summary Of Fee Application in substantially the format included in the local form "Summary of [First][Interim] [Final] Fee Application of __________ [Counsel][Accountant]" included in these Guidelines.

(b) The Certificate required by Section A, attached as exhibit to the Application, in substantially the format included in the local form "Application" included in these Guidelines.

(c) Exhibits, in substantially the format included in these Guidelines as local forms Exhibits 1–A and 1–B, showing the name of each professional, with his or her position in the firm, the name of each paraprofessional who worked on the case during the fee period, the year that the professional was licensed to practice or the number of years of work experience by the paraprofessional, the hours worked by each professional and paraprofessional, the hourly rate for each professional and paraprofessional, and the total dollar amount of the professional fees attributable to such professional or paraprofessional, in the case of Exhibit 1–A; and a summary of time during the period covered by the Application, by Activity Code Category, showing the name of the professional or paraprofessional, the hourly billing rate, the total number of hours spent during the period of the application on the particular Activity Code Category, and the total fee of that professional or paraprofessional during the period of the Application on the particular Activity Code Category, in the case of Exhibit 1–B. Any change in hourly rates or billing practices from those utilized in the prior Application period must be noted on the exhibit.

(d) The Summary of Requested Reimbursement of Expenses and Disbursements, in substantially the format attached to these Guidelines as Exhibit 2, as an exhibit to the Application.

(e) The Applicant shall attach, as an exhibit, the daily time entries of each professional, separated by Activity Code Category, reflecting the name of the billing professional or paraprofessional, the date of the entry, the detailed time entry, and the total number of hours billed. The Applicant shall conform with the provisions of Section C when completing such exhibit.

3. Interim Applications shall cover only the time period since the date covered by the previous interim Application, if any. Such interim Applications shall disclose all previous interim awards, if any.

4. Final Applications shall disclose all previous interim awards. The final Application shall include the time period since the date covered by the last interim Application. Unless fees or expenses were specifically disallowed in interim awards, the final Application may also seek payment of fees and expenses requested, but not previously awarded, in interim Applications.

5. Prior interim awards are subject to final review and allowance at the hearing on the final Application, and, at the request of a party in interest, or on the court's own motion, prior interim awards are subject to reconsideration.

[1] These Guidelines shall apply to all professional persons employed under 11 U.S.C. §§ 327 and 1103 seeking compensation pursuant to 11 U.S.C. §§ 328, 329, 330 and 331, including investment bankers and real estate advisors, unless the court, in the order of retention, after notice and hearing, specifically provides otherwise (upon an application demonstrating good cause for a variance from these Guidelines). In considering other requests for award of fees and costs (including, but not limited to, under 11 U.S.C. §§ 503(b) and 506(b)), the court will consider and apply, where appropriate, these Guidelines.

[2] 488 F.2d 714 (5th Cir. 1974).

[3] 544 F.2d 1291 (5th Cir. 1977).

UNITED STATES BANKRUPTCY COURT
SOUTHERN DISTRICT OF FLORIDA

www.flsb.uscourts.gov

In re: Case No.

Chapter

Debtor /

SUMMARY OF [FIRST] INTERIM [OR FINAL] FEE APPLICATION OF [ ] [COUNSEL] [ACCOUNTANT]

1. Name of applicant:
2. Role of applicant: **[Counsel] [Accountant] for [ ]**
3. Name of certifying professional:
4. Date case filed:
5. Date of application for employment:
6. Date of order approving employment:
7. If debtor's counsel, date of Disclosure of Compensation form:

8. Date of this application:
9. Dates of services covered:

10. If case is chapter 7, amount trustee has on hand: $

Fees . . .

11. Total fee requested for this period (from Exhibit 1) $
12. Balance remaining in fee retainer account, not yet awarded ($)
13. Fees paid or advanced for this period, by other sources ($)
14. **Net amount of fee requested for this period** $

Expenses

15. Total expense reimbursement requested for this period $
16. Balance remaining in expense retainer account, not yet received ($)
17. Expenses paid or advanced for this period, by other sources ($)
18. **Net amount of expense reimbursements requested for this period** $
19. Gross award requested for this period (#11 + #15) $
20. **Net award requested for this period** (#14 + #18) $
21. **If Final Fee Application, amounts of net awards requested in interim Applications but not previously awarded (total from History of Fees and Expenses, following pages):** $
22. **Final fee and expense award requested (#20 + #21)** $

History of Fees and Expenses

1. Dates, sources, and amounts of retainers received:

Dates	Sources	Amounts	For fees or costs?

2. Dates, sources, and amounts of third party payments received:

Dates	Sources	Amounts	For fees or costs?

3. Prior fee and expense awards . . .

	Prior Fee Awards	**Prior Expense Awards**
First interim application . . .		
Dates covered by first application:		
Amount of fees requested:	$	$
Amount of expenses requested:	$	$
Amount of fees awarded:	$	$
Amount of expenses awarded:	$	$
Amount of fee retainer authorized to be used:	$	
Amount of expense retainer authorized to be used:		$

	Prior Fee Awards	**Prior Expense Awards**
Fee award, net of retainer	$	$
Expense award, net of retainer		$
Date of first award:		

Amount of fees actually paid:	$	
Amount of expense reimbursement actually paid:		$
Amount of fees requested but not awarded, that applicant wishes to defer to final fee application:	$	
Amount of expenses requested but not awarded, that applicant wishes to defer to final fee application	$	

Second interim application . . .	**Prior Fee Awards**	**Prior Expense Awards**
Dates covered by first application:		
Amount of fees requested:	$	$
Amount of expenses requested:		$
Amount of fees awarded:	$	
Amount of expenses awarded:		$
Amount of fee retainer authorized to be used:	$	
Amount of expense retainer authorized to be used:		$
Fee award, net of retainer	$	
Expense award, net of retainer		$
Date of first award:		

	Prior Fee Awards	**Prior Expense Awards**
Amount of fees actually paid:	$	
Amount of expense reimbursement actually paid:		$
Amount of fees requested but not awarded, that applicant wishes to defer to final fee application:	$	
Amount of expenses requested but not awarded, that applicant wishes to defer to final fee application:	$	

Third interim application . . .		
Dates covered by first application:		
Amount of fees requested:	$	
Amount of expenses requested:	$	
Amount of fees awarded:	$	
Amount of expenses awarded:	$	
Amount of fee retainer authorized to be used:	$	
Amount of expense retainer authorized to be used:		$
Fee award, net of retainer	$	
Expense award, net of retainer		$
Date of first award:		
Amount of fees actually paid:	$	

Amount of expense reimbursement actually paid:	$	
Amount of fees requested but not awarded, that applicant wishes to defer to final fee application:	$	
Amount of expenses requested but not awarded, that applicant wishes to defer to final fee application:	$	

	Prior Fee Awards	**Prior Expense Awards**
Fourth interim application . . .		
Dates covered by first application:		
Amount of fees requested:	$	
Amount of expenses requested:		$
Amount of fees awarded:	$	
Amount of expenses awarded:		$
Amount of fee retainer authorized to be used:	$	
Amount of expense retainer authorized to be used:		$
Fee award, net of retainer	$	
Expense award, net of retainer		$
Date of first award:		
Amount of fees actually paid:	$	
Amount of expense reimbursement actually paid:	$	
Amount of fees requested but not awarded, that applicant wishes to defer to final fee application:	$	
Amount of expenses requested but not awarded, that applicant wishes to defer to final fee application:	$	

Summary of All Prior Applications and Awards

Total fees requested	$
Total fees awarded	$
Prior fees awarded but not yet paid, if any (Do not include holdbacks in this number)	$
Total prior fees requested but not awarded, deferred to final fee application	$
Total expenses requested	$
Total expenses awarded	$
Prior expenses awarded but not yet paid, if any (Do not include holdbacks in this number)	$

Total prior expenses requested but not awarded, deferred to final fee application $

Fee Application

______, counsel [accountant] to the ______, applies for interim [final] compensation for fees for services rendered and costs incurred in this Chapter ______ proceeding. This application is filed pursuant to 11 U.S.C. § 330 and Bankruptcy Rule 2016, and meets all of the requirements set forth in the Guidelines incorporated in Local Rule 2016–1(B)(1). The exhibits attached to this application, pursuant to the Guidelines, are:

Exhibits "1–A" and "1–B"—Summary of Professional and Paraprofessional Time.

Exhibit "2"—Summary of Requested Reimbursements of Expenses.

Exhibit "3"—The applicant's complete time records, in chronological order, by activity code category, for the time period covered by this application. The requested fees are itemized to the tenth of an hour.

The applicant believes that the requested fee, of $ for ______ hours worked, is reasonable considering the twelve factors enumerated in *Johnson v. Georgia Highway Express, Inc.*, 488 F.2d 714 (5th Circuit 1974), made applicable to bankruptcy proceedings by In re First Colonial Corp. of America, 544 F.2d 1291 (5th Cir. 1977), as follows:

The Time and Labor Required:

The Novelty and Difficulty of the Services Rendered:

The Skill Requisite to Perform the Services Properly:

The Preclusion of Other Employment by the Professional Due to the Acceptance of the Case:

The Customary Fee:

Whether the Fee is Fixed or Contingent:

Time Limitations Imposed by the Client or Other Circumstances:

The Experience, Reputation, and Ability of the Professional:

The Undesirability of the Case:

The Nature and Length of the Professional Relationship of the Client:

Awards in Similar Cases:

The applicant seeks an interim award of fees in the amount of $ ___ and costs in the amount of $ ___.

Certification

1. I have been designated by ______ (the "Applicant") as the professional with responsibility in this case for compliance with the "Guidelines for Fee Applications for Professionals in the Southern District of Florida in Bankruptcy Cases" (the "Guidelines").

2. I have read the Applicant's application for compensation and reimbursement of expenses (the "Application"). The application complies with the Guidelines, and the fees and expenses sought fall within the Guidelines, except as specifically noted in this certification and described in the application.

3. The fees and expenses sought are billed at rates and in accordance with practices customarily employed by the Applicant and generally accepted by the Applicant's clients.

4. In seeking reimbursement for the expenditures described on Exhibit 2, the Applicant is seeking reimbursement only for the actual expenditure and has not marked up the actual cost to provide a profit or to recover the amortized cost of investment in staff time or equipment or capital outlay (except to the extent that the Applicant has elected to charge for in-house photocopies and outgoing facsimile transmissions at the maximum rates permitted by the Guidelines).

5. In seeking reimbursement for any service provided by a third party, the Applicant is seeking reimbursement only for the amount actually paid by the Applicant to the third party.

6. The following are the variances with the provisions of the Guidelines, the date of each court order approving the variance, and the justification for the variance: ________ ________.

CERTIFICATE OF SERVICE

[Include a certificate of service conforming to Local Rule 2002–1(F) which reflects date and manner of service on the debtor, the U.S. Trustee, the trustee (if any), the examiner (if any), the chair of each official committee (if any), and their respective counsel]

[Applicant]

Attorneys/Accountant for

[address]

[phone]

By: ________________________

[name of certifying professional]

Fla. Bar No.: ________________

Summary of Professional and
Paraprofessional Time
Total per Individual
for this Period Only
(Exhibit "1–A")

[If this is a final application, and does not cumulate fee details from prior interim applications, then a separate Exhibit 1–A showing cumulative time summary from all applications is attached as well]

Name	Partner, Associate or Paraprofessional	Year Licensed	Total Hours	Average Hourly Rate *	Fee
					$
Blended Average Hourly Rate:				$	
Total fees:					$

* Indicate any changes in hourly rate and the date of such change.

EXHIBIT "1"

Summary of Professional and
Paraprofessional Time by
Activity Code Category
for this Time Period Only
(Exhibit "1–B")

Activity Code: ________;

	Name	Rate	Hours	Fees
Partners:				
Associates:				

Paralegals:

Activity Subtotal: $

Activity Code: __________:

	Name	Rate	Hours	Fees
Partners:				
Associates:				
Paralegals:				

Activity Subtotal: $

Activity Code: __________:

	Name	Rate	Hours	Fees
Partners:				
Associates:				
Paralegals:				

Activity Subtotal: $

Activity Code: __________:

	Name	Rate	Hours	Fees
Partners:				
Associates:				
Paralegals:				

Activity Subtotal: $

Activity Code: __________:

	Name	Rate	Hours	Fees
Partners:				
Associates:				
Paralegals:				

Activity Subtotal: $

Activity Code: __________:

	Name	Rate	Hours	Fees
Partners:				
Associates:				

Paralegals:

Activity Subtotal: $

Summary of Requested Reimbursement Of Expenses
for this Time Period Only

[If this is a final application which does not cumulate prior interim applications, a separate summary showing cumulative expenses for all applications is attached as well]

1. Filing Fees $ ______
2. Process Service Fees $ ______
3. Witness Fees $ ______
4. Court Reporter Fees and Transcripts $ ______
5. Lien and Title Searches $ ______
6. Photocopies
   (a) In–house copies ($ ____ at 15¢/page) $ ______
   (b) Outside copies ($ ____) $ ______
7. Postage $ ______
8. Overnight Delivery Charges $ ______
9. Outside Courier/Messenger Services $ ______
10. Long Distance Telephone Charges $ ______
11. Long Distance Fax Transmissions (copies at $1/page) $ ______
12. Computerized Research $ ______
13. Out-of-Southern–District-of-Florida Travel $ ______
   (a) Transportation ($ ______)
   (b) Lodging ($ ______)
   (c) Meals ($ ______)
14. Other Permissible Expenses (must specify and justify) $ ______
   (a) ($ ______)
   (b) ($ ______)

Total Expense Reimbursement Requested $______

EXHIBIT "2"

[Effective December 1, 1998. Amended effective December 1, 2002; July 1, 2004; June 2, 2008; December 1, 2009.]

CG–2. GUIDELINES FOR TAXATION OF COSTS BY THE CLERK

The following is a statement of the custom of the court concerning costs permitted to be taxed by the clerk in adversary proceedings, contested matters, miscellaneous proceedings and appeals pursuant to 28 U.S.C. § 1920, Local Rules 7054–1 and 8014–1 and Bankruptcy Rules 7054, 8014 and 9014.

I. FEES OF THE CLERK

The following items are taxable:

a. Filing fee for adversary complaint

b. Fee for filing or indexing any paper not in a case or proceeding for which a filing fee has been paid.

c. Filing fee for removal action.

d. Fee on interest earned on registry deposits.

The following item is not taxable:

Filing fee in an adversary proceeding instituted by the debtor (except for a chapter 11 debtor).

II. SERVICE FEES

The following items are taxable:

a. Service fees for summons, attachment and other process.

b. Service fees for trial subpoenas.

c. Service fees for deposition subpoenas for depositions taxed as costs.

d. Publication fees where service by publication is ordered by the court.

The following item is not taxable:

Service fees for discovery subpoenas

III. FEES OF COURT REPORTER FOR ALL OR ANY PART OF THE TRANSCRIPT NECESSARILY OBTAINED FOR USE IN THE CASE

a. The costs of the original of a trial transcript, daily transcript (see "c" below) and of a transcript of matters prior or subsequent to trial, is taxable—

(1) when requested by the court. Mere acceptance for filing does not constitute a request.

(2) at trial stage when, prior to incurring expense, the court determines that it is necessary.

(3) prepared pursuant to stipulation of parties with agreement to tax as costs.

(4) when used on appeal.

b. If forma pauperis party prevails, and the United States paid for the transcript, it is taxed in favor of the United States.

c. Daily transcript (when taxable) is taxed at ordinary rate unless there exists (a) advance determination by court that it is to be taxed or (b) agreement of parties to tax.

The following items are not taxable:

a. Costs of copies

b. Costs of daily copy solely for convenience of counsel

IV. FEES OF WITNESSES

Fees are provided by statute at the rate in effect when the witness appeared are strictly adhered to. No distinction is made between the fact and expert witness.

a. Attendance Fee. Allowed amount pursuant to 28 U.S.C. § 1821 for each day (1) in attendance and (2) days necessarily occupied in going to and returning from the place of attendance.

b. Travel. Allowed amount pursuant to 28 U.S.C. § 1821. When subsistence is allowed, only one round trip is allowed unless the court adjourns for a weekend or for some other reason.

c. Miscellaneous Allowances. Toll charges, bridges, tunnels, ferries, taxicab between places of lodging and carrier terminals, and parking fees within subpoena jurisdiction as allowed pursuant to 28 U.S.C. § 1821(c)(3).

d. Subsistence is Allowed for Witnesses Pursuant to 28 U.S.C. § 1821 (d).

e. Settlements. Trial witnesses' fees are taxed even though they did not appear.

f. Corporate Parties. Stockholders, directors, officers, and employees of a corporate party are taxed unless the witness is the real party in interest.

The following items are not taxable:

a. Discovery witness fees.

b. Expert witness fees in an amount exceeding that of any other witness.

c. Witnesses beyond subpoena jurisdiction.

V. FEES FOR EXEMPLIFICATION AND COPIES OF PAPERS NECESSARILY OBTAINED FOR USE IN CASE

The following items are taxable:

a. Cost of one copy of a document is taxed when introduced into evidence in lieu of original. Copy costs shall be allowed only in the amount set forth in the court's Guidelines for Fee Applications.

b. The fee of an official certification or proof re non-existence of a document is taxable when introduced into evidence.

c. The cost of securing translation if the document translated is taxable or the translation is necessary for exemplification of matters before the court.

d. Exhibits such as maps, graphs, charts, models, surveys and one copy of photographs introduced into evidence.

VI. COSTS INCIDENT TO TAKING DEPOSITIONS

The following items are taxable—

a. Depositions put into evidence.

b. Discovery depositions used on motion for summary judgement if the prevailing party in the case prevailed on summary judgement.

c. Discovery depositions used to defeat a motion for summary judgement.

d. The costs of videotaped deposition allowed only when authorizing order or stipulation provides for taxing of these costs.

e. Discovery depositions used for impeachment at a trial or hearing.

VII. INTERPRETERS

Interpreter charges are taxable where the court has determined compensation and directed it to be taxed as costs.

VIII. MEDIATION

Mediation costs are taxable where the court has determined compensation and directed it to be taxed as costs.

IX. APPELLATE COSTS (BANKRUPTCY RULE 8014)

a. Filing and docketing fees for notice of appeal.

b. Copy costs for production of appellate briefs and appendices.*

c. Cost of designated transcripts necessary to determine the appeal.

d. Bond premiums.

*Copy costs shall be allowed only in the amount set forth in the court's "Guidelines for Fee Applications for Professionals in the Southern District of Florida in Bankruptcy Cases".

CG–2 (rev. 12/01/09)

[Effective June 2, 2008. Amended effective December 1, 2009; November 25, 2014.]

CG–3. GUIDELINES FOR COURTROOM DECORUM [PURSUANT TO LOCAL RULE 2090–2(E)]

(A) The purpose of these guidelines is to state, for the guidance of those unfamiliar with the traditions of this court, certain basic principles concerning courtroom behavior and decorum. And to set forth additional requirements for courtrooms with DAR equipment. The requirements stated in this rule are minimal, not all-inclusive; and are intended to emphasize and supplement, not supplant or limit, the ethical obligations of counsel under the Rules of Professional Conduct or the time-honored customs of experienced trial counsel. Individual judges of the court may, in any case, or generally, announce and enforce additional prohibitions or requirements; or may excuse compliance with any one or more of the provisions of this rule.

(B) When appearing in this court, unless excused by the presiding judge, all counsel (including, where the context applies, all persons at counsel table) shall abide by the following:

1. Dress in business attire appropriate to the dignity of the court.
2. Stand as court is opened, recessed or adjourned.
3. Stand when addressing, or being addressed by, the court.
4. Stand at the lectern while examining any witness; except that counsel may approach the witness with court permission, for purposes of handling or tendering exhibits.
5. Stand at the lectern while making opening statements or closing arguments.
6. Address all remarks to the court, not to opposing counsel.
7. Counsel must begin all remarks by stating counsel's name and the parties they represent, spelling names as needed.
8. Do NOT speak over another person.
9. Avoid disparaging personal remarks or acrimony toward opposing counsel and remain wholly detached from any ill feeling between the litigants or witnesses.
10. Refer to all persons, including witnesses, other counsel and the parties by their surnames and not by their first or given names.
11. Only one attorney for each party shall examine, or cross examine each witness. The attorney stating objections, if any, during direct examination, shall be the attorney recognized for cross examination.
12. Counsel should request permission before approaching the bench; and any documents counsel wish to have the court examine should be handed to the clerk, or to the court reporter or other court designee if no clerk is present.
13. Any paper or exhibit not previously marked for identification should first be handed to the clerk, or to the court reporter or other court designee if no clerk is present, to be marked before it is tendered to a witness for examination; and any exhibit offered in evidence should, at the time of such offer, be handed to opposing counsel.
14. In making objections counsel should state only the legal grounds for the objection and should withhold all further comment or argument unless elaboration is requested by the court.
15. In examining a witness, counsel shall not repeat or echo the answer given by the witness.
16. Counsel shall admonish and discourage all persons at counsel table from making gestures, facial expressions, audible comments, or the like, as manifestations of approval or disapproval during the testimony of witnesses, or at any other time.
17. Smoking, eating, food and drink are prohibited in the courtroom at all times.
18. Do Not recite personal data and other sensitive information into the record.
    a. Limit SSN and financial account numbers to the last 4 digits.
    b. Limit names and birth dates to initials and birth year.
    c. Exhibits submitted to the court that contain personal identifiers must be redacted.
19. Conversations not necessary to the courtroom proceedings are not permitted while court is in session.

20. For courtrooms equipped with Digital Audio Recording (DAR) equipment:

a. Speak clearly and directly into the microphone.

b. Be aware that the microphone is recording at all times and conversations not intended to be recorded on the record must take place outside the courtroom.

c. If use of portable, clip-on microphones will be required when court is in session, request them from the Electronic Court Recorder Operator (ECRO) before the proceedings begin.

[Effective December 1, 1998. Amended effective December 1, 2002; June 2, 2008; December 1, 2009; October 1, 2013.]

CG–4. GUIDELINES FOR REIMBURSEMENT TO CHAPTER 7 TRUSTEES FOR COSTS WITHOUT PRIOR COURT ORDER PURSUANT TO LOCAL RULE 2016–1(A)

The following "Guidelines for Reimbursement to Chapter 7 Trustees for Costs Without Prior Court Order", issued with the approval of the U.S. Trustee, apply in all chapter 7 bankruptcy cases in the Southern District of Florida.

These Guidelines do not apply to any expenses relating to, or incurred by, a professional, such as an accountant, attorney, auctioneer, or real estate broker, which requires an order of the court regardless of the amount. All disbursement will continue to be subject to review by the Office of the United States trustee and ultimately the court at any time during the administration of the case. The chapter 7 trustee shall maintain proper documentation in the trustee's case file of all expenses paid pursuant to these Guidelines, and all such expenses shall be paid by a check from estate funds and all such expenses shall be clearly identified as to the nature of the expense on the trustee's semi-annual reports and on the trustee's final report of estate.

Chapter 7 trustees may pay the following specific expenses in a chapter 7 case without the necessity of seeking a court order prior to making the disbursement or incurring the expense:

(a) Changing of locks, up to an aggregate case total of $250.00;

(b) Retention of emergency security service (one week maximum), however a motion seeking Court approval of such retention should be filed within one week of employment of the security service;

(c) Towing when necessary, up to an aggregate case total of $200.00;

(d) Court reporter and transcript fees up to an aggregate case total of $500.00;

(e) U.C.C. searches and title searches up to an aggregate case total of $75.00;

(f) Process servers and subpoena fees up to an aggregate case total of $200.00;

(g) Witness fees, limited to the fee and mileage required by Federal Rule of Civil Procedure 45(b);

(h) Actual clerk's fees and filing fees;

(i) One copy of the claims register from court authorized copying service, including PACER use, up to an aggregate case total of $50.00;[1]

(j) Necessary insurance on property of the estate (non-operating business), limited to the lesser of one month's coverage or $250.00 maximum;

(k) Premiums on the trustee's bond;

(*l*) Post-petition expenses for non-operating cases (utilities and alarm expenses) limited to the lesser of one month's expenses or an aggregate case total of $250.00;

(m) Postage for mailing notices to creditors and parties in interest required by of Bankruptcy Rule 2002 when directed by the Clerk of the Bankruptcy Court (pursuant to Local Rule 2002–1(B)) and sent by the trustee; and

(n) Advertising expenses in connection with sale(s) of estate assets up to an aggregate case total of $100.00.

[Effective December 1, 1998. Amended effective December 1, 2002; July 1, 2004; June 2, 2008; December 1, 2009.]

1 The court has waived PACER fees for all Standing Chapter 7 and Chapter 13 Trustees.

CG–5. GUIDELINES FOR PREPARING, SUBMITTING AND SERVING ORDERS

Note: Please refer to the judge's court web page for any additional requirements specific to that judge. To access from the court web site, click on "Court Information" and then "Judges Information".

Preface: Pursuant to Local Rule 5005–1(G) these guidelines are intended to set forth: 1) how proposed orders should be delivered to the court; 2) the formatting requirements for all orders; 3) how entered orders will be served; and 4) the required general content for all orders.

PART ONE: HOW TO SUBMIT ORDERS

There are three methods for submitting proposed orders to the court as set forth below. Submission of a proposed order electronically or conventionally on a matter scheduled for hearing does not remove the matter from the judge's calendar. The parties must receive confirmation from the court that the hearing has been cancelled.

1. Electronic Submission of Orders Via CM/ECF: The court has adopted an electronic orders processing program referred to as "E–Orders." E–Orders replaces the conventional process by which proposed orders are delivered to the court, except as otherwise specified in the local rules and supplemented by these "Guidelines." E–Orders provides the ability to upload PDF-formatted proposed orders directly into CM/ECF without appearing prematurely on the public docket (except for proposed "sample" orders attached as exhibits to motions served on negative notice). Orders uploaded in CM/ECF can be electronically routed to and signed by the judge without the need to print any paper. Additionally, attorneys and trustees can check the status of uploaded proposed orders. Because E–Orders requires a proposed order to be uploaded in PDF format, the court can only make minor edits or modifications to the proposed order. "E–Orders" should be used to submit local form orders, routine ex-parte or uncontested orders and orders for matters heard at a nonemergency hearing. See Local Rule 5005–1(G)(1).

All local form orders have been converted to the E–Orders format and should be submitted via E–Orders as indicated on the attached "Summary List of Orders and Method of Submission" ("Summary") **[see Exhibit 1]. The "Summary" also lists several local form orders that will be generated internally by the court.**

The E–Orders Upload program is accessible as a separate menu item after logging into CM/ECF. *(See "User's Guide for Electronic Case Filing", Chapter III, Section 13.)*

2. Conventional (Paper) Submission of Orders: This method will ONLY be used by conventional paper filers AND for proposed orders brought to an emergency hearing pursuant to Local Rule 5005–1(G), or submission of a local form order for payment of unclaimed funds.

3. Submission to Judge's Dedicated E-mail Box: This method will ONLY be used when specifically directed by the court for (1) submission of competing orders following a contested hearing or trial or orders setting forth Findings of Fact and Conclusions of Law submitted before or after a contested hearing or trial; or (2) submission of an alternative version of a proposed order when the opposing party disputes the form or content of the initial proposed order submitted by the prevailing party. Proposed orders submitted in a word processing format to an electronic mailbox permit the judge to make additional modifications, as opposed to orders submitted in PDF format via E–Orders which cannot be easily edited. Each judge's electronic E–Mail address is listed in Section III of the "Summary" **[Exhibit 1].**

PART TWO: FORMATTING REQUIREMENTS

A. General Requirements for Both Paper and Electronically Submitted Orders. These requirements apply to all orders, whether submitted electronically or conventionally in paper **[sample order attached—Exhibit 2].**

1. The top margin on the FIRST PAGE must be four (4) inches. All other pages of the order will have a top margin of one (1) inch. Page size (and orientation) should be 8.5 × 11, portrait (note that this is not the same as 11 × 8.5 landscape).

2. To assist the court in verifying that the "entire" body of the submitted order has been properly transmitted, the last line in the order must consist of three (3) pound symbols (# # #), centered in the middle of the page, to indicate the order is complete. Any signatures or attachment notations should be placed below the line containing the ### symbols.

3. Do not include a line for the signature of the judge and date signed, as that will be included in the top margin on the first page of the order.

4. All proposed orders must include the name, law firm, mailing address, phone/fax number and, an active hyperlink to the e-mail address of the party who submitted the order. This information shall be included on the order, after the line containing the "###" symbols.

5. After the line containing # # #, list all parties who are to receive a conformed copy of the order and if the attorney submitting the proposed order is required to serve the order, include the following statement: "[submitting attorney's name] is directed to serve copies of this order on the parties listed and file a certificate of service."

6. Do not include any *colored* highlighting when submitting orders.

B. Technical Requirements for Uploading Proposed Orders in E–Orders.

1. Orders can ONLY be uploaded in PDF format and must contain a ".pdf" extension. No security should be applied to the PDF.

2. If you use Adobe Acrobat Writer version 5 or greater, your orders should be prepared using the Arial, Courier, or Times New Roman font (regular, bold, italic, and bold italic). Other fonts will not process correctly through the court's noticing center. **E–Orders cannot electronically sign orders which have been created using Adobe Distiller 6.0 default settings.**

C. Requirements for Submission of Proposed Orders to Judge's Dedicated E-mail Box.

1. Submit files created in a word processing format.

2. The subject line of the email should include the case number and a description of the order submitted (i.e., "Competing Order from Hearing Held <u>date</u>" or "Findings and Conclusions for Trial on <u>date</u>").

3. The submitting party must comply with Local Rule 5005–1(G)1(c) by serving a copy of the proposed order and any cover E-mail text to all adverse parties. [See Local Rule 9072–1]

PART THREE: SERVICE OF ORDERS

Local Rules 2002–1(F), 5005–1, 5005–4(G), 9021–1, 9036–1, 9072–1 set forth the provisions addressing electronic docketing of orders, service and certificate of service requirements. In general, the following guidelines apply:

1. If the attorney submitting the order is required to serve the order, include the following statement: "[attorney's name] is directed to serve copies of this order on the parties listed and file a certificate of service."] See Part Two A of these Guidelines and Exhibit 2.

2. Orders entered on the electronic docket will be served by the clerk via the Bankruptcy Noticing Center (BNC) on the designated serving party unless the order specifically directs the clerk to serve the order. Parties who have appeared electronically in the case at the time the order is entered on the docket will receive their copy of the order via the NEF only. It is the responsibility of the serving party to timely serve the order on all required parties and file a certificate of service with the court reflecting the date and manner of service as required under Local Rule 2002–1(F).

3. Unless requested by the court, no additional copies of orders and service envelopes should be submitted. If a party wishes to receive a conformed copy of a conventional paper order entered in open court, the party must bring an extra copy of the order to the hearing.

4. Conventional paper filers responsible for service will not have access to the Notice of Electronic Filing (NEF) generated by CM/ECF when the order is electronically entered on the docket, thus they will be required to serve all necessary parties by US Mail, absent other agreement among the parties.

PART FOUR: CONTENT REQUIREMENTS

I. General Requirements for All Proposed Orders.

A. Title. Include in the title a description of the order.

1. For example:

a. "Order Modifying Automatic Stay in Favor of Creditor, Rock Solid Bank"

b. "Order Allowing Claim No. 9"

Note #1: The title "Order" is insufficient. It provides no help when searching the docket for a particular order.

Note #2: Proposed orders submitted pursuant to the court's direction should be in a form that can be signed and entered by the court without modification. Do not include the word "proposed" in the title of the order.

2. Orders addressing agreed matters should include in the title that the matter is agreed.

3. See also Local Rule 9072–1 and these Guidelines.

B. Introduction. Always refer to the motion that brought the matter before the court. See Local Rule 9072–1(C). If a hearing was held, always include the date of the hearing. For example:

a. "On [date], [party] filed an "ex parte" motion for . . ."

b. "On [date], the court conducted a hearing on [party]'s motion for . . ."

c. "Without holding a hearing, the court considered the matter on the papers submitted . . ."

C. The Decision or Determination. Next recite what happened and the reasons why the Court is entering the order.

1. Avoid the use of the word "default". That is a Fed.R.Civ.P. 55 term of art. If the court has directed a response to a motion and the respondent has failed to respond, then the court will grant the motion because the respondent has not opposed the motion. Simply recite all of this as the reason for the order.

2. If the court's oral ruling at the hearing is to constitute the basis for its decision, simply recite that. For example:

a. If Rule 52 findings and conclusions are required: "The court made findings of fact and conclusions of law stated orally and recorded in open court".

b. If Rule 52 findings and conclusions are not required: "For the reasons stated orally and recorded in open court that shall constitute the decision of the court, ..."

3. If the matter is before the court as an agreed matter, the body of the order should state that the matter is an agreed matter.

D. The Disposition. Next state what the court ruled. For example:

a. "The motion is granted".

b. "The objection is sustained".

E. The Relief. Next state the relief that flows from the disposition.

1. For example:

a. "Accordingly, the complaint is dismissed without prejudice to the right of the plaintiff to file an amended complaint within ten days of the date of notice of the entry of this order, failing which the complaint will stand and be taken as dismissed with prejudice without further order".

b. "Accordingly, Claim No. 9 filed by Rock Solid Bank is disallowed in its entirety".

2. If there are different components to the relief ordered, these should be described in separately numbered paragraphs, for example:

"Accordingly, it is

ORDERED AS FOLLOWS:

a. Defendant's Motion to Dismiss Count I of the Complaint is granted.

b. Plaintiff shall have ten days to file an amended complaint.

c. Defendant's Motion for Sanctions is denied."

F. The Date. Do not include a date provision in the proposed order (e.g., "ORDERED in the Southern District of Florida on ________)." It will be inserted by the court at the top of the first page [see Ex. 2].

G. Signature Section. Do not include a signature section in the proposed order. It will be inserted by the court at the top of the first page [see Exhibit 2].

H. Service Section. A proposed order must not indicate in the service section that the clerk will serve the order unless the clerk is required to provide service under these rules or directed by the court for a specific case or order.

II. Orders Granting Relief From the Stay.

Stay relief orders typically require greater specificity:

A. The Relief. State precisely what relief is provided: state what it is that the creditor can do.

1. For example:

a. "Accordingly, the automatic stay is modified to permit [creditor movant] to commence and prosecute a mortgage foreclosure action in state court against real property, the legal description of which is . . ."

b. "Accordingly, the automatic stay is modified to permit [movant] to take possession of and sell its collateral more fully described as . . ."

2. Note especially:

a. What the creditor can do is specifically stated. Generalities, such as "to enforce its rights", are not sufficient.

b. The property must be described specifically.

B. The In Rem Limitation. If the scope of relief is limited to in rem only and not in personam against the debtor, so specify. For example:

"The relief granted here permits the creditor to [seek and obtain an in rem judgment] [take action] against the property only and does not permit the creditor to seek or obtain in personam relief against the debtor".

II.* Judgments and Orders, Especially (But Not Limited to) Those in Adversary Proceedings.

A. The federal rules make a significant distinction between a decision and a judgment. The rules further provide that the judgment be set forth in a separate document, not added to the end of a decision. Bankruptcy Rule 9021; Fed.R.Civ.P. 58. This is called the separate judgment rule.

B. Examples of decisions include:

1. Findings of fact and conclusions of law entered under Fed.R.Civ.P. 52.

2. An order granting a motion for summary judgment under Fed.R.Civ.P. 56.

3. An order granting a motion for judgment by default under Fed.R.Civ.P. 55.

C. A decision must include the reasons of fact and law that cause the court to grant the relief requested. In a money judgment situation, the decision should contain the amount to which the plaintiff is entitled and how it is calculated. On appeal, the reviewing authority will look to the decision to see why the trial court entered the judgment. If there are no reasons, or if the reasons are insufficiently stated, the judgment may be reversed summarily.

D. The decision should contain words like:

1. "In accordance with Bankruptcy Rule 9021, the court is contemporaneously entering a separate judgment".

2. "Counsel for the plaintiff is directed to submit a separate judgment for consideration and entry by the court".

E. The judgment should then generally be in the form contained in Fed.R.Civ.P. Form 32 appropriately modified. However, it should be prepared for entry by the court and not for entry by the clerk.

F. The federal rules also include a single judgment rule. If the complaint seeks relief against multiple parties or involves multiple claims, one judgment only is entered after all of the claims against all of the parties have been determined. Bankruptcy Rule 7054(a); Fed.R.Civ.P. 54(b). In this event, there may be several decisions entered by the court throughout the course of the proceeding upon which the single judgment, entered at the end, is based. In extraordinary circumstances, but only with express determinations and directions, the court may direct entry of judgment when fewer than all claims are determined. Id.

G. Post-judgment interest is controlled by 28 U.S.C. § 1961, not the Florida statutes. If you are entitled to post-judgment interest, recite in the judgment that the plaintiff is "owed $ ___ in principal plus interest at the rate of (determine federal interest rate and fill it in here)% from (date certain) to (date of judgment)". Leave a blank line in the judgment for entry of the amount. Determine the applicable federal interest rate and provide a memorandum indicating the amount owed if the judgment is entered on a particular date.

H. The memorandum shall conform to the following example:

a. Memorandum on interest

3 May 2004—$1,070.00

4 May 2004—$1,098.15

5 May 2004—$1,136.21

I. The court may grant costs to the prevailing party pursuant to Bankruptcy Rule 7054(b) and Local Rule 7054–1. The amount of costs is not included in the text of the judgment. After the entry of judgment, the party entitled to costs may file a Local Form "Bill of Costs". 28 U.S.C. § 1920; Bankruptcy Rule 7054(b); Bankruptcy Rule 9021; Fed.R.Civ.P. 58. If you object to the clerk's action in taxing costs, file a motion to review the clerk's taxation of costs. Bankruptcy Rule 7054(b); Local Rule 7054–1(E).

J. Motions for judgment by default after a default has been entered pursuant to Fed.R.Civ.P. 55 shall be submitted in accordance with Local Rule 7055–1. Remember especially that attorneys fees must be specifically alleged, Bankruptcy Rule 7008(b); and that the relief contained in the judgment cannot exceed the amount requested in the complaint, Fed.R.Civ.P. 54(c).

Exhibit 1

Summary List of Orders and Methods of Submission

I. E–ORDERS: THE FOLLOWING ORDERS MUST BE SUBMITTED BY REGISTERED USERS TO THE E–ORDERS PROGRAM

A. Local Form Orders (where motion is uncontested) except as listed in Section II.

B. Other orders to be uploaded in E–Orders:

1. Orders on motions which were served on negative notice if a certificate of no response or settlement has been filed. [Note: Proposed order must also be filed as an attachment to the motion.]

2. Ex parte orders submitted for requests for relief which may be considered immediately by the court without opportunity for objection or hearing.

3. Proposed orders on motions for continuances. The proposed order should contain blank spaces for the date and time of the rescheduled hearing in the event that the court grants the motion for continuance without hearing.

4. Proposed orders extending deadlines for filing documents. The proposed order should be uploaded immediately following the filing of the motion and include the new requested deadline that complies with any applicable rules.

5. Proposed Pretrial Orders in accordance with the Order Setting Filing and Disclosure Requirements for Pretrial and Trial unless otherwise directed by the assigned judge.

6. Agreed Orders.

II. THE FOLLOWING LOCAL FORM ORDERS WILL BE PREPARED BY THE COURT AND SHOULD NOT BE SUBMITTED WITH ELECTRONICALLY OR CONVENTIONALLY FILED MOTIONS:

A. Order Upon Conversion of Case Under Chapter 13 to Case Under Chapter 7 by the Debtor

B. Pretrial Order in an Adversary Proceeding and Sworn Declaration of Fact in an Adversary Proceeding

C. Order Dismissing Chapter 7 Case for Failure to Appear at the § 341 Meeting of Creditors

D. Order Conditionally Approving Disclosure Statement and Setting Hearing on Final Approval of Disclosure Statement and Confirmation of Chapter 11 Plan

E. Order (I) Setting Hearing to Consider Approval of Disclosure Statement; (II) Setting Deadline for Filing Objections to Disclosure Statement; and (III) Directing Plan Proponent to Serve Notice

F. Order (I) Approving Disclosure Statement; (II) Setting Hearing on Confirmation of Plan; (III) Setting Hearing on Fee Applications; (IV) Setting Various Deadlines; and (V) Describing Plan Proponent's Obligations

G. Order Conditionally Approving Disclosure Statement, Setting Hearing on Final Approval of Disclosure Statement and Confirmation of Chapter 11 Plan, Setting Various Deadlines and Describing Plan Proponent's Obligations

H. Order Setting Hearing on Approval of Disclosure Statement and Confirmation of Chapter 11 Plan, Setting Various Deadlines and Describing Plan Proponent's Obligations

I. Order Confirming Chapter 13 Plan

J. Order for Relief in Involuntary Case and Order Setting Deadline for Filing Schedules, Statements and Other Documents

K. Order Upon Conversion of Case Under Chapter 12 to Case Under Chapter 7 by the Debtor

L. Order Allowing Installment Payments

III. JUDGES' E-MAIL BOXES:

These e-mail boxes are solely for the purpose of submitting proposed orders as directed by the judge:

Chief Judge Paul G. Hyman	**PGH_Chambers@flsb.uscourts.gov**
Judge A. Jay Cristol	**AJC_Chambers@flsb.uscourts.gov**
Judge Robert A. Mark	**RAM_Chambers@flsb.uscourts.gov**
Judge Raymond B. Ray	**RBR_Chambers@flsb.uscourts.gov**
Judge John K. Olson	**JKO_Chambers@flsb.uscourts.gov**
Judge Laurel Myerson Isicoff	**LMI_Chambers@flsb.uscourts.gov**
Judge Erik P. Kimball	**EPK_Chambers@flsb.uscourts.gov**

Exhibit 2

UNITED STATES BANKRUPTCY COURT
SOUTHERN DISTRICT OF FLORIDA
www.flsb.uscourts.gov

In re: Case No.
Chapter

SAMPLE

Debtor /

ORDER APPROVING EMPLOYMENT OF TRUSTEE'S ATTORNEY

THIS CAUSE came on before the court upon the Trustee's Application for Employment of ________ of the law firm of ________ in this case. Upon the representations that[Name of attorney] is [duly qualified to practice in this court pursuant to Local Rule 2090–1(A)] [appearing pro hac vice pursuant to Local Rule 2090–1(B)(2)], that [Name of attorney and law firm] hold no interest adverse to the estate in the matters upon which they are engaged, that [Name of attorney and law firm] are disinterested persons as required by 11 U.S.C. § 327(a), and have disclosed any connections with parties set forth in Bankruptcy Rule 2014, and that their employment is necessary and would be in the best interests of the estate, it is

ORDERED that the trustee is authorized to employ ________ of the law firm of ________ as attorney for the trustee, on a general retainer, pursuant to 11 U.S.C. §§ 327 and 330.

###

Submitted by:

John Smith, Esq.

123 Flagler Street

Miami, FL 33130

(305) 714–1234

johnsmith@email.com

The party submitting this order shall serve a copy of the signed order on all parties listed below and file with the court a certificate of service conforming with Local Rule 2002–1(F).

[Effective December 1, 1998. Amended effective December 1, 2002; March 22, 2004; February 17, 2006; September 25, 2006; June 2, 2008; June 24, 2008; December 1, 2009; August 1, 2011.]

* [Publisher's Note: So in original. Probably should be "III".]

CG-6. GUIDELINES FOR COMPENSATION FOR PROFESSIONAL SERVICES OR REIMBURSEMENT OF EXPENSES BY ATTORNEYS FOR CHAPTER 13 DEBTORS PURSUANT TO LOCAL RULE 2016–1(B)(2)(a)

The following Guidelines apply in all chapter 13 cases in the Southern District of Florida.

These Guidelines also apply to payments by other parties on behalf of debtors. Notwithstanding these Guidelines, any fees paid by debtors shall continue to be subject to the bankruptcy and local rules which govern payment of filing fees in installments.

(A) Compensation and Expenses Allowed Without Application to the Court. Limits on Compensation and Expenses Allowed. Without application to the court, attorneys for debtors in chapter 13 cases shall be permitted to charge an attorney's fee not to exceed, unless all payments have been vested to creditors by earlier order, a base fee of $3500.00 per case, whether individual or joint, and to receive expenses, including the filing fee and up to $150.00 in other estimated expenses.

The base fee shall be presumed to compensate debtor(s)' attorney for a level of service to debtors that at a minimum shall include the following services:

1. Verification of debtors' identity, social security number and eligibility for Chapter 13;

2. Timely preparation and filing of petition, schedules, statement of financial affairs, chapter 13 plan, all amendments and all required documents pursuant to the Bankruptcy Code, and Bankruptcy and Local Rules;

3. Service of copies of all filed plans to all creditors and interested parties;

4. Explanation to debtors regarding all debtors' responsibilities, including, but not limited to payments and attendance at the first meeting of creditors;

5. Preparation for and attendance at all first meetings of creditors;

6. Preparation of and attendance at all necessary pre-confirmation motions brought on behalf of debtors;

7. Timely review of all proofs of claim in accordance with Local Rule 2083–1(B);

8. Timely objection to all improper or invalid proofs of claim in accordance with Local Rule 2083–1(B);

9. Preparation for and attendance at all confirmation hearings;

10. Attendance at and defense of all motions against debtors until discharge, conversion or dismissal of the case;

11. Preparation, filing and service of notices of conversions or voluntary dismissals;

12. Preparation, filing and service of motions to deem mortgage current.

Without application to the court, upon filing and serving of an amended disclosure of compensation, pursuant to BR 2016(b), attorneys for debtors in chapter 13 cases may be permitted to charge an additional fee plus $25.00 in costs for the following services, if the retainer agreement authorizes these fees, not to exceed the following amounts:

1.	Post-confirmation modification of plan	$500
2.	Motion for hardship discharge	$500
3.	Motion to purchase, sell or refinance real property	$500
4.	Motion to rehear, vacate dismissal, shorten prejudice period or reinstate case	$500
5.	Motion to avoid lien	$500
6.	Motion to value a motor vehicle, a motor home, or a manufactured home	$500
7.	Motion to value real property	$750
8.	Home Mortgage Loan Modification	$500

The following conditions also apply:

(1) If the case is dismissed or converted prior to confirmation and if the retainer agreement so provides, the attorney for the debtor may request and receive fees from monies paid to the chapter

13 trustee without separate application to the court, but the total fee, including any fees previously paid, may not exceed $2,500.00, unless, pursuant to court order, plan payments were not returned to the debtor and were paid pursuant to the terms of the last filed plan.

(2) Reimbursement for general expenses, other than the filing fee, that exceed $150.00 shall require a separate application for reimbursement of expenses filed pursuant to paragraph (C) of these Guidelines. Reimbursement for expenses in excess of $150.00 shall be permitted only as allowed pursuant to section D, "Reimbursement of Expenses and Services", of the court's "Guidelines for Fee Applications for Professionals in the Southern District of Florida in Bankruptcy Cases".

Reimbursement for the following expenses shall also be permitted without a separate application for reimbursement:

1. Court reporter expenses no greater than $125.00;
2. Interpreter fees no greater than $75.00;
3. Credit report retrieval fees no greater than $75.00.

(B) Compensation and Expenses Requiring Application and Court Approval. Attorneys seeking compensation or expenses which exceed the limits set forth in paragraph (A) of these Guidelines shall submit the court's Local Form "Application for Compensation for Professional Services or Reimbursement of Expenses by Attorney for Chapter 13 Debtor" on or before the deadlines established by Local Rule 2016–1(C)(4). This requirement applies to initial fee applications as well as to additional or supplemental applications. The application shall:

(1) describe in detail the actual or estimated services or expenses for which compensation or reimbursement is sought; and

(2) include as an attachment a copy of the retainer agreement, if any.

(C) Requirement of Rights and Responsibilities Agreement Between Chapter 13 Debtor(s) and Chapter 13 Debtor(s)' Attorneys. As required by Local Rule 2016–1(B)(2), Chapter 13 debtors and their attorneys must execute the local form "Rights and Responsibilities Agreement Between Chapter 13 Debtor(s) and Chapter 13 Debtor(s)' Attorney for Cases Filed in the United States Bankruptcy Court, Southern District of Florida" prior to filing a chapter 13 case in this court. The form shall be retained by the parties and not filed with the court. A copy of the agreement must be made available to the chapter 13 trustee at the meeting of creditors.

CG–6 (rev. 02/24/12)

[Effective December 1, 1998. Amended effective December 1, 2002; July 1, 2004; August 1, 2006; June 2, 2008; August 10, 2009; December 1, 2009; February 24, 2012.]

CG-7. GUIDELINES FOR MOTIONS SEEKING AUTHORITY TO USE CASH COLLATERAL AND MOTIONS SEEKING APPROVAL OF POST-PETITION FINANCING

The following guidelines apply to all motions filed pursuant to Bankruptcy Rule 4001 and Local Rules 4001-2, 4001-3 and 9013-1(G) and (H) seeking authority to use cash collateral and motions seeking approval of postpetition financing filed in this court.

I. Motions—General

Except as otherwise ordered by the court, all cash collateral and financing requests under 11 U.S.C. §§ 363 and 364 shall be heard by motion filed pursuant to Bankruptcy Rules 4001, 6003 and 9014 ("Cash Collateral or Financing Motion"). A motion seeking authority to use cash collateral pursuant to 11 U.S.C. § 363 shall comply with Bankruptcy Rule 4001(b) or (d) and Local Rules 9013-1(F) and (G). A motion seeking approval of postpetition financing pursuant to 11 U.S.C. § 364 shall comply with Bankruptcy Rule 4001(c) and (d) and Local Rules 9013-1(F) and (H).

II. Motions—Content

(A) All Cash Collateral or Financing Motions must (1) recite whether the proposed form of order and/or underlying cash collateral stipulation or loan agreement contains any provision of the type indicated in Bankruptcy Rule 4001 and these Guidelines, (2) highlight any such provision in the proposed form of order, cash collateral stipulation or loan agreement as required by Bankruptcy Rule 4001 and herein, and (3) provide the justification for the inclusion of such provision.

Note: *Provisions that grant cross-collateralization protection (other than replacement liens or other adequate protection) to the prepetition secured creditors (i.e., clauses that secure prepetition debt by post petition assets in which the secured creditor would not otherwise have a security interest by virtue of its prepetition security agreement or applicable law)* ***shall not be permitted.*** *(See In re Saybrook Manufacturing Co., Inc., 963 F.2d 1490 (11 Cir.1992).*

(B) A request for the following provisions shall be in print either highlighted or bold as to make them more prominent than the remainder of the text:

(1) **ALL THE PROVISIONS DESCRIBED IN BANKRUPTCY RULE 4001(B) AND (C).**

(2) Provisions or findings of fact that bind the estate or all parties in interest with respect to the validity, perfection or amount of the secured creditor's prepetition lien, claim or debt or the waiver of claims against the secured creditor without first giving parties-in-interest at least 75 days from the entry of the order and the creditors' committee, if formed, at least 60 days from the date of its formation to investigate such matters, and, if different than these time frames, the period of time after which any challenge is barred.

(3) Provisions or findings of fact that bind a subsequently appointed trustee.

(4) Provisions that grant liens on the debtor's property that is unencumbered by consensual liens.

(5) Provisions that deem prepetition secured debt to be postpetition debt or that use postpetition loans from a prepetition secured creditor to pay part or all of that secured creditor's prepetition debt, other than as provided in 11 U.S.C. § 552(b).

(6) Provisions that provide disparate treatment for the professionals retained by a creditors' committee from that provided for the professionals retained by the debtor with respect to a professional fee carveout.

(7) Provisions that subordinate any lien, without the consent of that lienor.

(8) Provisions that grant the secured creditor the right to exercise remedies upon a default by the debtor, without notice to the debtor and other parties-in-interest, a hearing, and further order of the court.

(C) All Cash Collateral or Financing Motions, even if less than five (5) pages, shall provide a bullet point summary of the essential terms of the proposed use of cash collateral or financing described in the Bankruptcy Rule 4001 and these Guidelines, and shall have as an attachment a budget setting forth the projected cash flow of the debtor for the period of time for which the credit is sought. If the debtor seeks authority for the use of cash collateral or authority to obtain credit sooner than 14 days after service of the motion, the motion must detail the amount of cash collateral the debtor seeks authority to use, or the amount of credit the debtor seeks authority to obtain, from the date of the preliminary hearing on the motion through and until the final hearing on the motion.

(D) The proposed form of order submitted with the motion shall expressly provide for a carveout for fees due the clerk of the court or the United States trustee pursuant to 28 U.S.C. § 1930.

III. Additional Requirements for Motions Seeking Authority to Use Cash Collateral

(A) In addition to the requirements of subsection II above, any motion seeking authority to use cash collateral shall identify:

(1) the basis upon which the secured creditor is entitled to assert a security interest in the cash collateral; and

(2) the amount owed to the secured creditor.

IV. Interim Relief.

When Cash Collateral or Financing Motions are filed with the court on or shortly after the date of the entry of the order for relief, the court may grant interim relief, after notice and a hearing, pending review by the interested parties of the proposed debtor-in-possession financing arrangements. Such interim relief is intended solely to avoid immediate and irreparable harm to the estate pending a final hearing. Even if interim relief is granted, in the absence of extraordinary circumstances, the court shall not approve interim financing orders that include any of the provisions listed in section II (B) (1) through (8) of these Guidelines.

V. Final Orders.

A final order shall be entered only after notice and a hearing pursuant to Bankruptcy Rule 4001 and Local Rule 2002–1(A). The final hearing shall not be held until at least 7 days following the organizational meeting of the creditors' committee contemplated by 11 U.S.C. § 1102, unless the court orders otherwise.

VI. Agreement in Settlement of Objection to Cash Collateral or Financing Motion.

All agreements in settlement of an objection to a Cash Collateral or Financing Motion must be in writing and must comply with the requirements of Bankruptcy Rule 4001(d).

[Effective July 1, 2004. Amended effective June 2, 2008; December 1, 2009.]

CG–8. GUIDELINES FOR SELF–CALENDARING CERTAIN CHAPTER 13 MATTERS

GUIDELINES FOR SELF–CALENDARING

The following guidelines apply when utilizing the court's self-calendaring process for scheduling non-emergency matters in chapter 7 and 13 cases in all divisions, and for chapter 11 cases and adversary proceedings in the West Palm Beach division. This automated process allows CM/ECF registered users ("the efiler") to select an available hearing date and time from the assigned judge's calendar at the time the motion is filed. The self-calendaring program will also display a hyperlink to the court-generated Notice of Hearing form that will contain the selected hearing date and time.

For chapter 13 cases, a list of each judge's motion/confirmation hearing dates and times are posted on the court's website at www.flsb.uscourts.gov and at the chapter 13 trustee's website: www.ch13herkert.com and www.ch13weiner.com.

SELF–CALENDARING PROCEDURE

A) Selecting a Hearing Date. The CM/ECF system has been programmed with the available calendar dates and times for each judge. Selectable dates that comply with applicable noticing requirements set forth in the federal and local bankruptcy rules will display when a motion is filed. In order to self-calendar a motion, it must be filed at least 14 days prior to the hearing and the selected hearing date must allow for at least 10 days' notice to all interested parties. The hearing date and time must be selected from the available list. If a matter is not properly calendared in accordance with these guidelines, the trustee or the clerk may docket an entry that will CANCEL the hearing and the matter will be removed from the calendar. It is the responsibility of the filing party to select the correct hearing date and time from the Self–Calendaring Utility (SCU) based on applicable noticing requirements.

B) Matters for Which Self–Calendaring May Not Be Used. The self-calendaring process may not be used to set a hearing for an emergency motion (including chapter 11 first-day motions filed pursuant to LR 9013–1(G), (H), (I), (J) & (K)), motion to rehear or reconsider, motion for summary judgment, evidentiary hearing or a hearing on a contested motion that was initially filed on negative notice, and any other designated relief as authorized by the court.

C) Motions for Relief From Stay. If a motion for relief from stay is self-calendared and the next available hearing date is more than 30 days after the date the motion is filed, the movant will be deemed to have consented to voluntarily waiving the 30–day limitation established by U.S.C. § 362(e) [see Local Rule 9073–1(C)].

D) Motions Requiring Service Pursuant to BR 7004. Any motion requiring service pursuant to BR 7004 must be served in accordance with that rule.

E) Notice of Hearing. The SCU will automatically generate a Notice of Hearing form with the designated date, time and location for the self-calendared matter. The Notice of Hearing form will be available via a hyperlink in CM/ECF at the conclusion of the filing process so that it may be printed locally and served on (non-electronic) interested parties via U.S. Mail.

F) Certificate of Service. A certificate of service substantially conforming to the local form certificate of service required under Local Rule 2002–1(F), must be filed in accordance with Local Rule 9073–1(B).

G) Continuances. Once a matter is set using the self-calendaring procedure and notice served on interested parties, continuances may **ONLY** be requested by motion and granted by court order. The parties must appear at the hearing unless an order has been entered (at least two business days prior to the hearing) continuing the hearing or the motion is withdrawn (at least two business days before the hearing). Notwithstanding this requirement, any matter continued at the hearing may be continued by notice or court order pursuant to the court's instructions.

Self–Calendaring FAQs

Is self-calendaring available for all chapters?

Currently, self-calendaring is only available for use in chapter 7 and 13 cases in all divisions, and for chapter 11 cases and adversary proceedings in the West Palm Beach division.

Are there any matters for which self-calendaring may not be used?

The self-calendaring process may not be used to set a hearing for an emergency motion (including chapter 11 first-day motions filed pursuant to LR 9013-1(G, H, I, J & K)), motion to rehear or reconsider, motion for summary judgment, evidentiary hearing or a hearing on a contested motion that was initially filed on negative notice, and any other designated relief as authorized by the court.

How do I serve non-electronic recipients?

The efiler will be able to view the automated Notice of Hearing form from a link provided on the Notice of Electronic Filing (NEF) screen immediately upon the electronic setting of the hearing. The Notice of Hearing form can be printed locally and served on all required parties. A certificate of service conforming to Local Rule 2002-1(F) must be filed by the movant.

Do I still have to file a Certificate of Service with the court?

Pursuant to Local Rule 9073-1(B), the movant is required to file, not later than two business days after service of the notice of hearing, a certificate of service for that notice of hearing as required under Local rule 2002-1(F).

What if I make a mistake?

If the efiler inadvertently selects an incorrect date or time block the efiler must file a notice to withdraw the motion and file a new motion and select the correct hearing date and time.

What do I do if the date I want to select for my hearing does not display?

The efiler should contact the courtroom deputy for the assigned judge.

What if I exit the SCU screens AFTER I have filed my motion but before I produce my Notice of Hearing form?

No further action by the efiler is necessary, as the courtroom deputy for the assigned judge will set the motion for hearing and generate a Notice of Hearing form.

I was ordered by the Judge during a hearing to reschedule my matter on the next calendar date which is outside the allowable date range. How do I do this and provide adequate Notice of Hearing?

The courtroom deputy will usually handle matters that require a hearing to be rescheduled, continued or renoticed. However, the judge may request the movant upload an order rescheduling the hearing.

I am a chapter 7 or 13 Trustee. Does the new process change trustee batch events to reschedule hearings for exemptions to objections?

No, the SCU will not be added to batch events. Continue using your current procedure.

I closed the Adobe Acrobat window that displayed the Notice of Hearing form before I was able to print it. How do I get back to it?

Each registered case participant will receive an NEF of all activity in a case, including one-free-look at the document(s) being filed. Alternatively, the Notice of Hearing hyperlink in the NEF may still be accessible by using the browser's "Back" button. If you have logged out of CM/ECF or attempted to file another document you will need to review the case docket to view the Notice of Hearing form (PACER fees will apply).

Who do I call if I am experiencing technical difficulties or do not understand how to proceed?

For questions regarding self-calendaring contact our CM/ECF Help Desks Miami (305) 714-1800; Ft. Lauderdale (954) 769-5700; and West Palm Beach (561) 514-4100. Case related questions should be directed to the division where the assigned judge is chambered.

CG-8 (rev. 01/02/14)

[Effective October 17, 2005. Amended effective February 27, 2006; June 2, 2008; December 1, 2009; February 1, 2013; August 1, 2013; January 2, 2014.]

CG–9. GUIDELINES FOR PREPACKAGED CHAPTER 11 CASES

1. GOALS.

The purpose of this guideline is to establish a uniform approach for commencing and administering "prepackaged chapter 11 cases" in the United States Bankruptcy Court for the Southern District of Florida under Local Rule 3017–3. This guideline defines what a "prepackaged chapter 11 case" is and attempts to assist practitioners with procedures that are not completely or specifically addressed by statute or rules. Although each case is different, many issues are common to all prepackaged cases. Judicial economy, as well as procedural predictability for debtors and creditors, will be enhanced by promulgation of the following guidelines to deal with these common issues. The guidelines are advisory only; the court retains the authority to depart from them at any time.

2. DEFINITION OF PREPACKAGED CHAPTER 11 CASE.

For purpose of these guidelines, a "prepackaged chapter 11 case" is one in which the debtor negotiates terms of a plan, and solicits acceptances thereof, prior to filing the chapter 11 petition. In these circumstances, the debtor shall file a motion requesting the court to schedule a preliminary status conference and subsequent confirmation hearing for the prepackaged plan (the "Prepackaged Scheduling Motion") as set forth below.

3. CRITERIA FOR PREPACKAGED CHAPTER 11 CASE; CONTENTS OF PREPACKAGED SCHEDULING MOTION.

A. Content of Prepackaged Scheduling Motion. The Prepackaged Scheduling Motion shall:

(1)(a) represent that the solicitation of votes to accept or reject the debtor's plan required for confirmation of that plan was completed prior to commencement of the case, and that no additional solicitation of votes on that plan is contemplated by the debtor, or (b) seek a determination that the solicitation of all votes to accept or reject the debtor's plan required for confirmation of that plan has been deemed adequate by the court pursuant to paragraph 3.C.(2) below such that no additional solicitation will be required;

(2) represent that the requisite acceptances of such plan have been obtained from each class of claims or interests as to which solicitation is required, except as provided in paragraph 3.A.(3) below;

(3) with respect to any class of interests that has not accepted the plan, whether or not it is deemed not to have accepted the plan under 11 U.S.C. § 1126(g), represent that the debtor is requesting confirmation under 11 U.S.C. § 1129(b);

(4) request entry of an Order scheduling an expedited preliminary hearing and status conference pursuant to 11 U.S.C. § 105(d). The Debtor may request a hearing within two business days of the commencement of the case if the motion sets forth cause for scheduling the hearing on short notice and the motion is served, as applicable, pursuant to Local Rules 2002–1(H) or 9073–1(B), for the court to hear any motions pursuant to which the debtor seeks entry of orders on or shortly after the filing of the petition ("First Day Motions") and set the hearing contemplated by paragraph 3.A.(5) below. If the motion requests a hearing within two business days and the judge assigned to the case is unable to conduct the preliminary hearing and status conference within two business days of the commencement of the case, the judge assigned to the case will schedule the hearing as soon as feasibly possible;

(5) request entry of an order scheduling the hearing (a) on confirmation of the plan and (b) to determine whether the debtor has satisfied the requirements of either 11 U.S.C. § 1126(b)(1) or 11 U.S.C. § 1126(b)(2), for a date that is not more than ninety (90) days following the petition date; and

(6) be supported by the Report and Affidavit required by Local Rule 3020–1(B) and have attached (a) a copy of the form of Ballot utilized for acceptance or rejection of the debtor's plan; and (b) copies of all solicitation materials used to solicit those votes.

B. Confirmation Pursuant to 11 U.S.C. § 1129(b)(2)(C). A chapter 11 case may constitute a "prepackaged chapter 11 case" for purposes of these guidelines notwithstanding the fact that the debtor proposes to confirm the plan pursuant to 11 U.S.C. § 1129(b)(2)(C) as to a class of interests.

C. Filing of Petition After Solicitation has Commenced but Before Expiration of Voting Deadline. Unless the court orders otherwise, if a chapter 11 case is commenced by or against the debtor, or if a chapter 7 case is commenced against the debtor and converted to a chapter 11 case by the debtor pursuant to 11 U.S.C. § 706(a), after the debtor has transmitted all solicitation materials to holders of claims and interests whose vote is sought, but before the deadline for casting acceptances or rejections of the debtor's plan (the "Voting Deadline"),

(1) the debtor and other parties in interest shall be permitted to accept but not solicit ballots until the Voting Deadline; and

(2) after further notice and a hearing the court shall determine the effect of any and all such votes.

D. Applicability of Guidelines to Cases Involving Cramdown of Classes of Claims and "Partial Prepackaged Chapter 11 Cases." The debtor or other party in interest, either as set forth in the scheduling motion or on separate notice and hearing, may request that the court, in an appropriate case, apply some or all of these guidelines to,

(1) cases in which the debtor has satisfied the requirements of paragraph 3.A.(1) above but intends to seek confirmation of the plan pursuant to 11 U.S.C. § 1129(b) as to a class of claims (a) which is deemed not to have accepted the plan under 11 U.S.C. § 1126(g); (b) which is receiving or retaining property under or pursuant to the plan but whose members' votes were not solicited prepetition and whose rejection of the plan has been assumed by the debtor for purposes of confirming the plan; or (c) which is receiving or retaining property under or pursuant to the plan and which voted prepetition to reject the plan, as long as no class junior to such rejecting class is receiving or retaining any property under or pursuant to the plan; and

(2) "Partial Prepackaged Chapter 11 Cases"—i.e.; cases in which acceptances of the debtor's plan were solicited prior to the commencement of the case from some, but not all, classes of claims or interests whose solicitation is required to confirm the debtor's plan.

4. FILING OR PREPACKAGED CHAPTER 11 CASE.

As soon as practicable following filing of a prepackaged chapter 11 case, the debtor shall furnish to the judge assigned to the case a copy of the plan, the disclosure statement (or other solicitation materials), the Reports and Affidavits of balloting as required by Local Bankruptcy Rule 3020(B), the First Day Motions, and any other filed motion.

[Effective June 2, 2008. Amended effective December 1, 2009.]

CG-10. GUIDELINES FOR MOTIONS FOR RELIEF FROM THE AUTOMATIC STAY

UNITED STATES BANKRUPTCY COURT
SOUTHERN DISTRICT OF FLORIDA

www.flsb.uscourts.gov

GUIDELINES FOR MOTIONS FOR RELIEF FROM THE AUTOMATIC STAY

As provided by Local Rule 4001-1(B), the following guidelines apply to the contents of all motions for relief from the automatic stay. Failure to comply may result in denial of relief even if no objection to the motion is filed.

A. Contents of Motion—General. All motions for relief from the automatic stay must contain:

(1) a short and plain statement of the facts upon which the request for relief is based, including a statement of any "cause" if based on 11 U.S.C. § 362(d)(1);

(2) a statement of the amount of the debt, the estimated value of the collateral and the source of the valuation if based on 11 U.S.C. § 362(d)(2); and

(3) if a chapter 7 individual case, a statement whether or not the property has been claimed exempt by the debtor or abandoned by the trustee.

B. Contents of Motion—Required exhibits for motions for relief to enforce a lien. If the motion seeks relief to enforce a lien, the following exhibits must be attached to the motion:

(1) a copy, showing recording information, of any security agreement, mortgage or other evidence of the lien that the moving party seeks to enforce;

(2) a copy of any note or evidence of the obligation secured by the lien; and

(3) an affidavit attesting that the amount of the indebtedness and the nature and extent of default set forth in the motion is information derived from records that were made at or near the time of the occurrence of the matters set forth by, or from information transmitted by, a person with knowledge of those matters, the records were kept in the course of the regularly conducted activity and were made by the regularly conducted activity as a regular practice. The affidavit must also certify that all of the documents attached to the motion as an exhibit are true and accurate copies of the original documents. The affidavit must be signed under penalty of perjury as being true and correct based on personal knowledge of the movant's books and business records.

C. Contents of Motion—Requirements for any motion for relief to enforce a lien secured by an interest in real property. If the motion seeks relief to enforce a lien secured by an interest in real property, the motion must include all of the following (or indicate in the motion whether any of the following information is not applicable):

(1) The name of the movant, and if the movant is not the holder of the note and mortgage or other security instrument (the "Lender"), a description of the movant's standing to bring the motion on behalf of the Lender;

(2) A description of the real property that is the subject of the motion including the address and legal description;

(3) A description of the mortgage and other lien documents including the date of the instrument, the original parties to the instrument (if not the debtor or the movant), and the applicable recording information;

(4) The post-petition payment address;

(5) The total pre-petition and post-petition indebtedness at the time of the filing of the motion allegedly owed by debtor to the movant (or to the Lender if the movant is not the Lender) expressed as a total number, which number must match the number on the Indebtedness Worksheet referenced below;

(6) The movant's estimated market value of the real property and the source of that estimated value.

(7) The motion must have the following attachments, identified clearly by exhibit number:

(a) The Indebtedness Worksheet that is included in these Guidelines;

(b) Copies of the documents that support the movant's interest in the real property. For purposes of example only, these documents should include a complete and legible copy of the promissory note or other debt instrument together with a complete and legible copy of the copy of the mortgages recorded in the public record as well as all assignments in the chain from the original mortgagee to the current moving party; and

(c) Copies of all documents establishing proof of movant's standing to bring the motion for stay relief.

(8) Notwithstanding subparagraphs (1) through (7), if a final judgment of foreclosure has been entered with respect to the real property in favor or Lender or movant, then the motion for relief from stay need only include a signed copy of the final judgment, the information required in subparagraph (6) and, if the movant is not the named judgment holder, the information required in subparagraph (7)(c).

D. Exceptions. The following motions shall not be subject to these Guidelines:

(1) Motions for relief from the automatic stay where the Debtor holds only a fractional interest in the subject property as a result of a transfer of such interest to the Debtor by a non-affiliate third party without the Debtor's acceptance.

(2) Motions seeking relief solely from the co-debtor stay imposed by 11 U.S.C. § 1301.

INDEBTEDNESS WORKSHEET

DEBT AS OF THE PETITION DATE

A. Total pre-petition indebtedness of debtor(s) to movant (if movant is not the lender, this refers to the indebtedness owed to the lender) as of petition filing date: $ ____________

1. Amount of principal: $ ____________
2. Amount of interest: $ ____________
3. Amount of escrow (taxes and insurance): $ ____________
4. Amount of forced placed insurance expended by movant: $ ____________
5. Amount of attorneys' fees billed to debtor(s) pre–petition: $ ____________
6. Amount of pre-petition late fees, if any, billed to debtor(s): $ ____________
7. Any additional pre-petition fees, charges or amounts charged to debtors/debtors account and not listed above: ________ (if additional space is needed, list the amounts on a separate sheet and attach the sheet as an exhibit to this form; please list the exhibit number here: ________.)

B. Contractual interest rate: ________ (if interest rate is (or was) adjustable, list the rate(s) and date(s) the rate(s) was/were in effect on a separate sheet and attach the sheet as an exhibit to this form; list the exhibit number here: ________.)

AMOUNT OF ALLEGED POST–PETITION DEFAULT

(As of <MM/DD/YYYY>)

C. Date last payment was received: ________ <mm/dd/yyyy>

D. Alleged total number of payments due postpetition from filing of petition through payment due on <mm/dd/yyyy>: ________.

E. All postpetition payments alleged to be in default:

Alleged Amount Due Date	Alleged Amount Due	Amount Received	Amount Applied To Principal	Amount Applied To Interest	Amount Applied To Escrow	Late fee Charged (If any)

Totals: $ $ $ $ $ $ $

F. Amount of movant's attorneys fees billed to debtor for the preparation, and filing and prosecution of this motion: $ ________

G. Amount of movant's filing fee for this motion: $ ________

H. Other attorneys' fees billed to debtor post–petition: $ ________

I. Amount of movant's post-petition inspection fees: $ ________

J. Amount of movant's post-petition appraisal broker's price opinion: $ ________

K. Amount of forced placed insurance or insurance provided by the movant post-petition: $ ________

L. Sum held in suspense by movant in connection with this contract, if applicable: $ ________

M. Amount of other post-petition advances or charges, for example taxes, insurance incurred by debtor etc. (itemize each charge): $ ________

CG–10 (rev. 08/01/11)

[Effective June 2, 2008. Amended effective December 1, 2009; August 1, 2011.]

CG–11. GUIDELINES ON ELECTRONIC AVAILABILITY OF TRANSCRIPTS AND PROCEDURES FOR TRANSCRIPT REDACTION

UNITED STATES BANKRUPTCY COURT
SOUTHERN DISTRICT OF FLORIDA
www.flsb.uscourts.gov

GUIDELINES ON ELECTRONIC AVAILABILITY OF TRANSCRIPTS AND PROCEDURES FOR TRANSCRIPT REDACTION

As provided under Local Rule 5005-1(A)(2)(b), filed transcripts shall be made available, and shall, where required to comply with privacy requirements, be redacted in accordance with the following guidelines, which are adopted from the Judicial Conference of the United States national policy addressing electronic availability of transcripts of court proceedings filed with the court. The Judicial Conference Policy on Electronic Availability of Transcripts applies to any transcript of a court proceeding that is subsequently filed with the court and made available to the public via electronic access. These Guidelines are effective for any transcript filed after February 16, 2009 (regardless of when the proceeding took place).

1. Transcripts of court proceedings may only be electronically filed by the court reporter. For a period of 90 days from the filing of the transcript electronic access via PACER will not be permitted except as provided under paragraph 2 below. However, the transcript will be available for viewing at the office of the clerk of court, free of charge, at any public terminal located in any of the three divisional clerk's offices, but it will not be available for copying during this period.

2. During this 90-day restriction period, a copy of the transcript may be obtained from the court reporter at the rate established by the Judicial Conference of the United States. An attorney in the case who purchases the transcript from the court reporter will also be given remote electronic access to the transcript through the court's CM/ECF system via PACER, for purposes of creating hyperlinks to the transcript in court filings and for other purposes. PACER fees apply at all times when accessing transcripts remotely and the 30-page cap does not apply to viewing or printing a transcript via PACER. After the 90-day restriction period expires, members of the public and media will be granted electronic access to the transcript.

3. Upon the filing of a transcript, the clerk shall issue, as applicable, an electronic or paper "Notice Regarding Filing of Transcript and Deadline for Filing Notice of Intent or Motions to Request Redactions of Transcript". The parties shall have seven days from the date of filing of the transcript to file Local Form "Notice of Intent to Request Redaction of Transcript".

4. Parties who timely file the Local Form "Notice of Intent to Request Redaction of Transcript," shall, within 21 days of the filing of the transcript, unless otherwise ordered by the court, file a "Statement of Personal Data Identifier Redaction Request" ("Statement") which shall indicate, by page and line number, the location of the personal

CG-11 (12/01/09)

Page 1 of 3

data identifiers for which redaction is being requested. For purposes of this procedure, personal data identifiers shall include: individual social security numbers, individual taxpayer identification numbers, financial account numbers, names of minor children, and dates of birth. Since the "Statement," once filed, will appear as a public document on the docket, the "Statement" should be worded so as not to contain unredacted personal identifiers. A copy of the "Statement" shall be served on the court reporter. Only these personal identifiers may be automatically redacted as provided by paragraph 6 below. Parties seeking to redact additional information shall file a motion in accordance with Local Rule 5003-1(D). A copy of the motion shall be served on the court reporter.

5. Redaction responsibilities are solely the responsibility of the attorneys and pro-se parties who attended the hearing. Each party is responsible for reviewing and indicating redactions in the testimony of the witnesses that were called by that party and for that party's own statements. In order to avoid redaction responsibilities, parties should refrain from eliciting testimony that includes personal identifiers listed in paragraph 6 below.

6. If a Local Form "Notice of Intent to Request Redaction of Transcript" has been filed and subsequently a "Statement" is filed within the 21 day deadline set forth in paragraph 4, the court reporter shall partially redact the personal data identifiers identified in the "Statement" as follows:

- for Social Security numbers and taxpayer-identification numbers use only the last four digits;
- for financial account numbers, use only the last four digits;
- for names of minor children, use only their initials; and
- for dates of birth, use only the year.

The court reporter shall then file, within 31 days from the filing of the transcript, a redacted transcript with an amended certification indicating that the transcript was amended by the redaction of certain personal identifiers at the request of the parties. Parties who have previously ordered the unredacted transcript shall be given remote access to the redacted transcript.

7. After the 90-day period has expired (unless there are pending related redaction motions), the filed transcript (or if a redacted transcript was filed the redacted transcript) will be available for inspection and copying at the clerk's office and for downloading from the court's CM/ECF system via PACER. If a redacted transcript has been filed in accordance with the provisions of this Order, the unredacted version will NOT be available via remote electronic access but will be available for inspection and copying at the clerk's office. Copy fees and PACER access fees apply.

8. The policy set forth in these Guidelines:

A. Does not affect in any way the obligation of the court reporter to file promptly with the clerk of court the court reporter's original records of a proceeding or the inclusion of a filed transcript with the records of the court pursuant to 28 U.S.C. §753.

B. Does not affect the obligation of the clerk to make the official transcript available for copying by the public without further compensation to the court reporter 90 days after the transcript is filed pursuant to Judicial Conference policy.

C. Is not intended to create a private right of action.

D. Is intended to apply the Judicial Conference policy on privacy and public access to electronic case files to transcripts that are electronically available to the public. It is not intended to change any rules or policies with respect to sealing or redaction of court records for any other purpose.

E. Does not prevent the production of a transcript on an expedited basis for a party, or any other person or entity, that may order such a transcript, subject to whatever court rules or orders are currently imposed to protect sealed materials. Any non-party that orders a transcript on an expedited basis should be alerted to the Judicial Conference policy on privacy and public access to electronic case files by the entity providing the transcript to the party.

CG-11 (12/01/09)

Page 3 of 3

[Effective December 1, 2009. Amended effective December 1, 2015.]

SELECTED ADMINISTRATIVE ORDERS

ADMINISTRATIVE ORDER 07-2. IN RE: ORDER ESTABLISHING PROCEDURES FOR REFERRALS OF CERTAIN SUSPECTED BANKRUPTCY CRIMES

In addition to meeting the obligations imposed under 18 U.S.C. § 3057 for reporting bankruptcy crimes, the court is required under 18 U.S.C. § 158(d), to establish procedures for referrals of cases where violations of 18 U.S.C. § 152 or § 157 may have occurred relating to (a) abusive reaffirmations of debt, or (b) materially fraudulent statements in bankruptcy schedules that are intentionally false or intentionally misleading. Accordingly, to meet these statutory requirements, it is **ORDERED** that:

1. Referrals of potential violations of the above referenced statutes shall be documented utilizing the attached "Notification Statement", and shall be accompanied by a referral letter from the presiding judge.

2. The judge may either:

A. Directly submit the referral to each of the individuals designated below:

United States Attorney's Office
Attn: Carolyn Bell, Esquire
Assistant U.S. Attorney/Criminal Bankruptcy Fraud Coordinator
Southern District of FL
500 Australian Avenue, North, Suite 400
West Palm Beach, FL 33401

Federal Bureau of Investigation
Attn: Alice D. McLaughlin, Special Agent
16320 N.W. 2nd Avenue
North Miami Beach, FL 33169

Office of the United States Trustee
Attn: Steven R. Turner, Assistant U.S. Trustee
Suite 1204, Claude Pepper Federal Building
51 S.W. First Avenue
Miami, FL 33130

or

B. Elect first to submit the referral to the United States Trustee for further investigation and review. The United States Trustee may elect to make a referral to the United States Attorney based upon the further investigation, in which case, the United States Trustee shall notify the referring Judge and the Clerk of Court that such a referral was made to the appropriate authority. If the United States Trustee has not made a referral within ninety (90) days from receipt of the court's ***referral***, the United States Trustee shall notify the referring Judge in writing every ninety (90) days thereafter, with a copy to the Clerk, that she is continuing her investigation or, that she has declined to refer the matter to the United States Attorney's Office.

3. Any court employee who discovers an apparent violation of 18 U.S.C. §§ 152 or 157 shall notify the Clerk of Court. The Clerk shall make reasonable inquiry and, if appropriate, shall report such information to the presiding Judge and furnish the Judge with copies of any documents the Clerk deems relevant to the suspected violation. If appropriate, the Judge shall refer the matter as provided under paragraph (2) of this order.

4. If the criminal referral is made by court order which directs that the records of the entire case file be sealed or expunged, the order shall direct that the Clerk of Court provide a copy of the record to the United States Trustee before the records are expunged or sealed, and that the order to seal also direct that the United States Trustee can reveal the records to the United States Attorney's Office, who are directed to publish the records for whatever purposes deemed necessary in the interests of justice.

[Effective February 12, 2007.]

UNITED STATES BANKRUPTCY COURT SOUTHERN DISTRICT OF FLORIDA

www.flsb.uscourts.gov

NOTIFICATION STATEMENT REGARDING REFERRAL OF SUSPECTED BANKRUPTCY CRIMES PURSUANT TO ADMINISTRATIVE ORDER 07–2

TO: ________ POSITION: ________

FROM: ________ POSITION: ________

DATE: ________

SIGNATURE OF PREPARER ________

PREPARER'S POSITION ________

1. **Background Information**

a. Name of Debtor ________

i. Case Number ________

ii. Debtor's Address ________

iii. Debtor's Telephone No. ________

b. Debtor's Attorney ________

i. Address ________

ii. Telephone No. ________

c. Name of Trustee (if any) ________

i. Address ________

ii. Telephone No. ________

d. *Case Chapter*

i. Chapter under which case was originally filed:

7 ( ); 11 ( ); 12 ( ); 13 ( )

ii. Chapter under which case now pending:

7 ( ); 11 ( ); 12 ( ); 13 ( )

e. Type of Case: Voluntary ( ); Involuntary ( )

f. *Additional Information*:

i. Petition and schedules attached for lists of claimholders, debts, assets, exempt property, and other information:

Yes ( ) No ( )

ii. If chapter 7 case, § 705 creditors' committee appointed:

Yes ( ) No ( )

If yes, date of appointment: ________

Name, address and telephone nos. of contact persons:

____

____

iii. If chapter 11 case, § 1102 creditors' committee appointed:

Yes ( ) No ( )

If yes, date of appointment: ________

Name, address and telephone nos. of contact persons:

____

____

iv. Other information regarding the debtor's case:

____

____

2. Basis for Notification and Possible Estate loss:

a. Suspected violation of 18 U.S.C. Section:

152( ); 153( ); 154( ); 155( ); 156( ); 157( ); 1341( ); 1342( ); 1343( ); 1344( )

b. Other suspected criminal violation ______________________________

c. Possible Estate Loss $ ______________________________

Other ______________________________

3. Circumstances Relating to Suspected Violation of Chapter 9 of Title 18, United State Code, or other Laws of the United States Relating to the Debtor's Case

a. *Subject of Notification*:

i. Role

( ) Debtor (principal/responsible person)

( ) Trustee

( ) Professional (Specify Title) ______________________________

( ) Claimholder/Equity Security Holder

( ) Public Official

( ) Other ______________________________

ii. Subject's address: ______________________________

Telephone numbers: ______________________________

iii. Other identification information:

____

____

b. **Report all facts and circumstances of the case, the names of witnesses, and the offense or offenses believed to have been committed (provide as complete a description as possible) by:**

(i) Providing full and complete account of the suspected violation, including identifying document(s) that contain information relating to the violation

(ii) Providing the names, addresses, and telephone numbers of persons with knowledge of and information relating to suspected offense.

(iii) Indicating, (based on available information) whether the suspected offense relates only to a single incident in a debtor's case or whether the suspected offense relates to multiple transactions/bankruptcies.

(iv) Indicating whether the subject of the notification has been the subject of a prior notification and, if so, relating the relevant circumstances surrounding the earlier notification.

(v) Disclosing other pertinent information.

ADMINISTRATIVE ORDER 07-8. IN RE: ADOPTION OF REVISED SCHEDULE OF TRANSCRIPT FEE RATES

In September 2007, the Judicial Conference approved an increase of ten percent to the maximum original and copy transcript fee rates that may be charged for court transcripts to be effective in fiscal year 2008, subject to the availability of funding. The Judicial Conference also approved a new rate for the delivery of transcripts within 14 days and agreed that the rate be set at the mid-point between the rates authorized for expedited (7-day) and ordinary (30-day) delivery, to be effective in fiscal year 2008. Pursuant to a Memorandum from the Director of the Administrative Office of the United States Courts dated October 18, 2007, implementation of these adjustments to transcript fee rates can take effect immediately upon adoption by the court of the new rates. Accordingly, it is ordered that:

1. Effective for all transcripts ordered on or after October 29, 2007, the court adopts a schedule of transcript fees subject to the maximum rates established by the Judicial Conference as set forth in the attached "Notice of Judicial Conference Maximum Transcript Rates Effective October 29, 2007".

2. Transcript orders placed prior to October 29, 2007 shall be billed at the rates established under this court's administrative orders setting transcript rates in effect on and applicable to the date the transcript was ordered.

3. This order replaces and abrogates Administrative Order 03-2, for purposes of establishing the current transcript rate in effect in this court.

[Effective October 22, 2007.]

NOTICE OF JUDICIAL CONFERENCE MAXIMUM TRANSCRIPT RATES EFFECTIVE OCTOBER 29, 2007

	Original	First Copy to Each Party	Each Add'l Copy to the Same Party
Ordinary Transcript A transcript to be delivered within thirty (30) calendar days after receipt of an order.	$3.65	.90	.60
14-Day Transcript A transcript to be delivered within fourteen (14) calendar days after receipt of an order.	$4.25	.90	.60
Expedited Transcript A transcript to be delivered within seven (7) calendar days after receipt of an order.	$4.85	.90	.60
Daily Transcript A transcript to be delivered following adjournment and prior to the normal opening hour of the court on the following morning whether or not it actually is a court day.	$6.05	1.20	.90
Hourly Transcript A transcript of proceedings ordered under unusual circumstances to be delivered within two (2) hours.	$7.25	1.20	.90
Realtime Transcript A draft unedited transcript produced by a certified realtime reporter as a byproduct of realtime to be delivered electronically during proceedings or immediately following adjournment.	$3.05	1.20	

For information regarding fee rates and transcript format requirements established by the Judicial Conference and procedures for addressing issues regarding fees, please contact the Clerk's Procurement Office at (305) 714-1824.

[Effective October 22, 2007.]

ADMINISTRATIVE ORDER 08-2. IN RE: ORDER ESTABLISHING NEW COMPENSATION RATE FOR MEDIATORS AND CLARIFYING EFFECTIVE DATE OF NEW RATE

In conformity with the rate established by the United States District Court for the Southern District of Florida, and in accordance with Local Rule 9019-2(A)(6), the Court hereby **ORDERS** as follows:

1. The compensation rate for qualified mediators selected or appointed pursuant to an "Order of Referral to Mediation" entered after the entry date of this Administrative Order shall be $250.00 per hour and the compensation rate for all previously selected or appointed mediators shall remain as $175.00 per hour unless (1) a different rate is or was agreed to in writing by the parties and the mediator selected by the parties; or (2) the matter is or was being mediated pro bono, in whole or in part, pursuant to Local Rule 9019-2(A)(2)(d).

2. This Order replaces Administrative Order 98-2 "ORDER ESTABLISHING NEW COMPENSATION RATE FOR MEDIATORS AND CLARIFYING EFFECTIVE DATE OF NEW RATE".

[Effective June 9, 2008.]

ADMINISTRATIVE ORDER 12-03. IN RE: ORDER CLARIFYING STATUS OF ADOPTION OF INTERIM BANKRUPTCY RULE 1007-I

Interim Bankruptcy Rule 1007-I implemented the The National Guard and Reservists Debt Relief Act of 2008, Pub. L. No. 110-438, as amended by Public Law No. 112-64, which provides a temporary exclusion from the bankruptcy means test for certain reservists and members of the National Guard.

Interim Bankruptcy Rule 1007-I incorporates provisions of Bankruptcy Rule 1007(c) and is currently in effect under Administrative Order 12-1 "Order Clarifying Status of Adoption of Interim Bankruptcy Rule 1007-I".

On December 1, 2012, unless Congress takes action to reject, modify, or defer the amendment, Bankruptcy Rule 1007(c) will be amended to eliminate from Rule 1007(c) the existing time limit for filing the list of creditors in an involuntary bankruptcy case. The existing time limit in Rule 1007(c) is inconsistent with the time limit in Rule 1007(a)(2), as amended effective December 1, 2010.

Accordingly, it is **ORDERED** that:

1. Interim Bankruptcy Rule 1007-I, currently in effect under Administrative Order 12-1, shall be amended, effective December 1, 2012, to eliminate inclusion of a time limit for filing the list of creditors in an involuntary bankruptcy case. (See attached Exhibit A.)

2. Interim Bankruptcy Rule 1007-I shall remain adopted by this court through the extended December 18, 2015 terminal date and, without further order, through any future extension of this Act.

3. This Order supersedes and replaces Administrative Order 12-01.

ORDERED in the Southern District of Florida on November 30, 2012.

Exhibit A

Interim Rule 1007-I.[1] Lists, Schedules, Statements, and Other Documents; Time Limits; Expiration of Temporary Means Testing Exclusion[2]

* * * * *

(b) Schedules, Statements, and Other Documents Required.

* * * * *

(4) *Unless Either*: (A) § 707(b)(2)(D)(1) applies, or (B) § 707(b)(2)(D)(ii) applies and the exclusion from means testing granted therein extends beyond the period specified by Rule 1017(e), an individual debtor in a chapter 7 case shall file a statement of current monthly income prepared as prescribed by the appropriate Official Form, and, if the current monthly income exceeds the median family income for the applicable state and household size, the information, including calculations, required by § 707(b), prepared as prescribed by the appropriate Official Form,

* * * * *

(c) Time Limits. In a voluntary' case, the schedules, statements, and other documents required by subdivision (b)(1), (4), (5), and (6) shall be filed with the petition or within 14 days thereafter, except as otherwise provided in subdivisions (d), (e), (f), (h), and (n) of this rule. In an involuntary case, the schedules, statements, and other documents required by subdivision (b)(1) shall be filed by the debtor within 14 days of the entry of the order for relief. In a voluntary case, the documents required by paragraphs (A), (C), and (D) of subdivision (b)(3) shall be filed with the petition. Unless the court orders otherwise, a debtor who has filed a statement under subdivision (b)(3)(B), shall file the documents required by subdivision (b)(3)(A) within 14 days of the order for relief. In a chapter 7 case, the debtor shall file the statement required by subdivision (b)(7) within 60 days after the first date set for the meeting of creditors under § 341 of the Code, and in a chapter 11 or 13 case no later than the date when the last payment was made by the debtor as required by the plan or the filing of a motion for a discharge under § 1141(d)(5)(B) or § 1328(b) of the Code. The court may, at any time and in its discretion, enlarge the time to file the statement required by subdivision (b)(7). The debtor shall file the statement required by subdivision (b)(8) no earlier than the date of the last payment made under the plan or the date of the filing of a motion for a discharge under §§ 1 141(d)(5)(B), 1228(b), or 1328(b) of the Code. Lists, schedules, statements, and other documents filed prior to the conversion of a case to another chapter shall be deemed filed in the converted case unless the court directs otherwise. Except as provided in § 1116(3), any extension of time to file schedules, statements, and other documents required under this rule may be granted only on motion for cause shown and on notice to the United States trustee, any committee elected under § 705 or appointed under § 1102 of the Code, trustee, examiner, or other party as the court may direct. Notice of an extension shall be given to the United States trustee and to any committee, trustee, or other party as the court may direct.

* * * * *

(n) Time Limits for, and Notice to, Debtors Temporarily Excluded from Means Testing.

(1) An individual debtor who is temporarily excluded from means testing pursuant to § 707(b)(2)(D)(ii) of the Code shall file any statement and calculations required by subdivision (b)(4) no later than 14 days after the expiration of the temporary exclusion if the expiration occurs within the time specified by Rule 1017(e) for filing a motion pursuant to § 707(b)(2).

(2) If the temporary exclusion from means testing under § 707(b)(2)(D)(ii) terminates due to the circumstances specified in subdivision (n)(1), and if the debtor has not previously filed a statement and calculations required by subdivision (b)(4), the clerk shall promptly notify the debtor that the required statement and calculations must be filed within the lime specified in subdivision (n)(1).

[Effective December 1, 2012.]

1 Interim Rule 1007–I has been adopted by the bankruptcy courts to implement the National Guard and Reservists Debt Relief Act of 2008, Public Law No: 110–438, as amended by Public Law No. 112–64. The amended Act, which provides a temporary exclusion from the application of the means test for certain members of the National Guard and reserve components of the Armed Forces, applies to bankruptcy cases commenced in the seven-year period beginning December 19, 2008.

2 Incorporates (1) time amendments to Rule 1007 which took effect on December 1, 2009, (2) an amendment, effective December 1, 2010, which extended the time to file the statement of completion of a course in personal financial management in a chapter 7 case filed by an individual debtor, and (3) a conforming amendment, effective December 1, 2012, which removed an inconsistency created by the 2010 amendment.

ADMINISTRATIVE ORDER 12–25. IN THE MATTER OF BANKRUPTCY PROCEEDINGS [DISTRICT COURT ORDER]

ORDER OF REFERENCE

Pursuant to 28 U.S.C. Section 157(a) any and all cases under title 11 and any proceedings arising under title 11 or arising in or related to a case under title 11 are referred to the bankruptcy judges of this district.

If a bankruptcy judge or district judge determines that entry of a final order or judgment by a bankruptcy judge would not be consistent with Article III of the United States Constitution in a particular proceeding referred under this order and determined to be a core matter, the bankruptcy judge shall, unless otherwise ordered by the district court, hear the proceeding and submit proposed findings of fact and conclusions of law to the district court made in compliance with Fed. R. Civ. P. 52(a)(1) in the form of findings of fact and conclusions stated on the record or in an opinion or memorandum of decision.

The district court may treat any order of the bankruptcy court as proposed findings of fact and conclusions of law in the event that the district court concludes that the bankruptcy judge could not have entered a final order or judgment consistent with Article III of the United States Constitution.

This Order of Reference amends and supersedes the Order of Reference entered by this Court on July 11, 1984, 84–12–Civ–Misc.

DONE AND ORDERED in Chambers in Miami, Florida this 21st day of March, 2012.

[Effective March 27, 2012.]

ADMINISTRATIVE ORDER 13-01. IN RE: IMPLEMENTATION OF LOSS MITIGATION MEDIATION PROGRAM

In determining whether a uniform, comprehensive, court-supervised loss mitigation mediation program would facilitate consensual resolutions between lenders and individual debtors whose real property is at risk of loss due to foreclosure or surrender, the Court sought input from a loss mitigation mediation working group and other local practitioners. Having considered the input received, the Court has determined that a loss mitigation mediation program may avoid the need for litigation, reduce costs to participants, and enable debtors to reorganize or otherwise address their most significant debts and assets under the United States Bankruptcy Code.

Accordingly, effective April 1, 2013, it is **ORDERED** as follows:

1. A Loss Mitigation Mediation program ("LMM") is adopted in accordance with 11 U.S.C. § 105(a), and shall be implemented by the LMM Program Procedures and Forms attached as Exhibit A to this Administrative Order.

2. LMM shall be effective for:

a. Individual debtor cases filed or reopened under or converted to an eligible chapter on or after April 1, 2013 as set forth in the program procedures;

b. Individual debtor cases pending under an eligible chapter before April 1, 2013, as set forth in the program procedures, provided that those debtors seek to commence LMM not later than September 30, 2013; and,

c. Individual debtor cases where the court has authorized, after motion and hearing, an application to participate in LMM outside the time periods established in (a) and (b) of this paragraph.

3. The compensation and cost amounts allowed for participants in the LMM program shall be set forth in the LMM Program Procedures and Local Forms and may be amended from time to time as provided under paragraph 4 of this order. This Court's Local Rule 9019-2(A)(6) and related administrative order setting compensation rate for mediators shall not apply to mediations under the LMM program, except for sessions extending beyond the initial two, one-hour sessions.

4. The Court may modify the LMM Procedures and Forms from time to time without prior notice, by publication of a clerk's notice of revised procedures and/or forms on the court website.

5. Copies of this Administrative Order and the LMM Program Procedures and Forms shall be posted on the court website and copies may be obtained from the Clerk's Office.

[Dated: February 26, 2013.]

EXHIBIT A. LOSS MITIGATION MEDIATION PROGRAM PROCEDURES

Effective April 1, 2013

I. PURPOSE

These procedures and forms implement the Loss Mitigation Mediation (LMM) program adopted under Administrative Order 13-1. This program is designed to function as a forum for eligible Debtors to explore loss mitigation options with their lenders ("Lender") for real property in which the Debtors have an interest and are obligated on the promissory note or mortgage. The goal of LMM is to facilitate communication and exchange of information in a confidential setting and encourage the parties to finalize a feasible and beneficial agreement with the assistance and supervision of the United States Bankruptcy Court for the Southern District of Florida. Loss mitigation options include modification of a mortgage or surrender of real property owned by an individual Debtor(s).

II. DEBTORS ELIGIBLE TO PARTICIPATE

Subject to the effective dates set forth in Administrative Order 13-1, individuals who have filed for bankruptcy protection under or converted to Chapters 7, 11, 12 and 13, are eligible to participate in LMM, with respect to not more than four units of real property, as follows:

A. Chapter 7: an individual Debtor may request LMM to surrender any real property in which the Debtor holds an interest;

B. Chapter 11: an individual Debtor may request LMM to modify a mortgage or surrender real property in which the Debtor holds an interest and is used as the Debtor's primary residence;

C. Chapter 12: an individual Debtor may request LMM to modify a mortgage or surrender real property in which the Debtor holds an interest and is used as the Debtor's primary residence; and

D. Chapter 13: an individual Debtor may request LMM to modify a mortgage or surrender any real property in which the Debtor holds an interest.

Individuals who seek to modify a mortgage must have paid their bankruptcy filing fee in full prior to filing a motion to participate in LMM.

III. LOSS MEDIATION MITIGATION PORTAL AND DOCUMENT PREPARATION SOFTWARE

In an effort to expedite the exchange of information between the Debtor and the Lender, the Court has mandated the use of a secure online portal (the "LMM Portal") **and** an on-line program that facilitates the preparation of the Debtor's loan modification package (Document Preparation Software). Submitting documents to the LMM Portal provides transparency in the loss mitigation process making information immediately available to the parties through a secure internet site. The use of the Document Preparation Software further ensures that the initial submission to the Lender is complete and accurate and should expedite the Lender's review. The use of an LMM Portal and Document Preparation Software eliminates the need for multiple submissions of documents that were not received and unnecessary delay based upon incomplete documentation.

All communication between the parties to the mediation shall be sent through the LMM Portal, unless otherwise ordered by the Court. Mediators will also be able to use the LMM Portal to send messages and file reports.

The current LMM Portal provider approved by the Court is managed and maintained by Default Mitigation Management LLC ("DMM"). Free training on the use of the LMM Portal shall be available to all attorneys and lenders. The Court's web page on LMM also includes LMM Portal training materials on loss mitigation, including contact information for the portal vendor and information on the Document Preparation Software. In the event other providers are approved by the Court, those providers will be listed on the Court's website.

IV. COMMENCEMENT OF LOSS MITIGATION MEDIATION

Referral to LMM may be initiated as follows:

A. By an Attorney–Represented Debtor on Negative Notice.

1. An eligible Debtor seeking to participate in LMM must file, within 45 days from the date of filing the Voluntary Petition, the LMM Local Form "Attorney–Represented Debtor's Verified Motion for Referral to Loss Mitigation Mediation" ("Verified Motion") and must attach as an exhibit the LMM Local Form "Order of Referral to Loss Mitigation Mediation" ("Order").

2. Prior to filing the Verified Motion:

(a) Debtor's information shall be submitted and processed through the Document Preparation Software;

(b) Debtor's initial loan modification forms shall be ready for signature and submission;

(c) Debtor's required supporting documentation as required by the Document Preparation Software has been collected in order to submit Debtor's initial package ("Debtor's Prepared Package") to the Lender for review through the LMM Portal; and

(d) The non-refundable Document Preparation Software fee of $40.00 has been paid directly to the approved vendor.

3. The Debtor's attorney shall serve the Verified Motion and proposed Order by U.S. Mail and, if possible, also by email, on the Lender and Lender's counsel, if known. The Debtor's attorney must also serve the proposed Mediator at the email address listed on the Verified Motion, and file a Certificate of Service pursuant to Local Rule 2002–1(F).

4. The Lender shall have 14 days from the date of service of Debtor's Verified Motion to file a response. Failure by the Lender or other party who has been properly served with the Verified Motion to file a timely response, shall be deemed a consent to the entry of the Order. Within seven days after the expiration of the 14 days' notice period, the Debtor's attorney shall file the LMM Local Form "Certificate of No Response and Request for Entry of Order". The Lender may also file the LMM Local Form "Lender's Consent to Participate in LMM" at any time after filing of the Verified Motion. Upon the filing of a "Certificate of No Response and Request for Entry of Order" or a "Lender's Consent to Participate in LMM" the Debtor's attorney shall upload the proposed Order in electronic format using the E-orders program in CM/ECF.

5. If the Lender or other party served with the Verified Motion files a timely response, the Debtor's attorney must file the LMM Local Form "Certificate of Contested Matter" and the Court will promptly schedule a hearing in accordance with the procedures set forth in Local Rule 9073-1.

6. If the objection is limited solely to the Debtor's designation of a Mediator, the objecting party must file the LMM Local Form "Certificate of Contested Matter Regarding Selection of Mediator and Request for the Clerk to Appoint Mediator". The Court shall then direct the clerk to randomly select a Mediator from the clerk's Mediation Register pursuant to Local Rule 9019-2(B)(3), without the necessity of a hearing. The clerk shall serve notice of the Mediator selection on the required parties using the LMM Local Form "Notice of Clerk's Designation of Mediator". Local Rule 9019-2(B)(3) shall apply to challenges to the clerk's designation of mediator.

B. By a Self-Represented Debtor.

1. An eligible Debtor seeking to participate in LMM who is not represented by an attorney, must file, within 45 days from the date of filing the Voluntary Petition, the LMM Local Form "Self-Represented Debtor's Verified Motion for Referral to Loss Mitigation Mediation" ("Verified Pro Se Motion"), which will promptly be set for hearing by the Court in accordance with the procedures contained in Local Rule 9073-1.

2. If the Debtor is seeking waiver of the mediation fee (see section X.3.a. below), the Debtor shall include this request in the Verified Pro Se Motion. If the use of the LMM Portal or the Document Preparation Software creates an undue hardship because the Debtor does not have access to a computer, the Debtor shall also include a request in the Verified Pro Se Motion to exchange documents with the Lender by fax or U.S. Mail.

3. The Debtor must serve the Pro Se Verified Motion and proposed LMM Local Form "Order of Referral of Pro Se Debtor to Loss Mitigation Mediation" ("Pro Se Order") by U.S. Mail and, if possible, also by email, on the Lender, the Lender's counsel, if known, the proposed Mediator and any other party required to participate in the mediation, and file a Certificate of Service pursuant to Local Rule 2002-1(F).

4. A response to the Debtor's Pro Se Verified Motion must be filed within 14 days from the date of service of the motion on the Lender.

C. By a Lender. A Lender may request referral to LMM by filing and serving upon the Debtor and Debtor's counsel, a motion requesting referral to LMM, together with a proposed order that substantially conform to the LMM Local Forms. The Lender must also file a Certificate or Service pursuant to Local Rule 2002-1(F). The Debtor shall have 14 days from the date of service of the motion to file a written response. If the Debtor fails to file a response objecting to the Lender's motion, the Court may enter the Order or, if the Debtor is not represented by counsel, the Court will set the matter for hearing in accordance with the procedures set forth in Local Rule 9073-1.

D. By the Bankruptcy Court. The Court may order the assignment of a loss mitigation matter to LMM upon the Court's own motion.

V. FILING A REQUEST OUT OF TIME

A Debtor seeking to engage in LMM under paragraph 2.c. of Administrative Order 13-01, must file a motion with the Court, on notice to the Lender and any co-obligor, co-borrower or third party whose participation is required, and the Court will promptly schedule a hearing in accordance with the procedures set forth in Local Rule 9073-1.

VI. ADDITIONAL PARTIES

CO–OBLIGORS/CO–BORROWERS OR OTHER THIRD PARTIES: Any co-obligor, co-borrower or other third party must participate in the LMM process. If the participation of a co-obligor, co-borrower or other third party is necessary, any party may request that such co-obligor, co-borrower or other third party participate in LMM. The co-obligor, co-borrower or other third party shall sign, and the Debtor or attorney for the Debtor shall file, simultaneously with the Debtor's Verified Motion, or Verified Pro Se Motion, the LMM Local Form "Consent to Attend and Participate in Loss Mitigation Mediation".

VII. ORDER OF REFERRAL TO LOSS MITIGATION MEDIATION

Upon entry of the Order, the moving party (or the clerk, if the Debtor is not represented by an attorney), shall serve the Order on the required parties and file a Certificate of Service pursuant to Local Rule 2002–1(F). The moving party shall also upload a copy of the Order on to the LMM Portal unless, by Court order, the Debtor has been excused from using the LMM Portal because the Debtor does not have access to a computer.

The parties are required to comply with all deadlines set forth in the Order. However, any deadlines imposed by the Order may be extended by Court order or by stipulation of the parties.

The parties are required to participate in LMM in good faith or be subject to possible sanctions by the Court.

A. Lender Requirements. Within seven days after entry of the Order, the Lender, if not already registered on the LMM Portal, shall ensure that it is registered and, if the Lender has counsel, that the Lender's counsel is registered as well. (Registration on the LMM Portal is a one-time event—i.e., once the Lender is registered on the LMM Portal, the Lender will not have to register again).

Within seven days after entry of the Order, the Lender will also confirm that all of the Lender's initial loss mitigation requirements ("Lender's Initial Package") are available on the LMM Portal. Lender's Initial Package shall specify the forms and documentation the Lender requires to initiate a review of Debtor's request for loss mitigation options.

Within seven days after Debtor's delivery of the information provided for in section VII.B. below, the Lender shall, on the LMM Portal, (i) acknowledge receipt of Debtor's information and advise Debtor of any additional or missing information required for Lender to proceed with its review; and (ii) designate its single point of contact and its outside legal counsel, if any. Such Lender's counsel or representative shall have the authority (within the investor's guidelines) to settle and will attend and continuously participate in all LMM conferences in this case.

B. Debtor Requirements. Within seven days after entry of the Order, or the Lender's registration on the LMM Portal, whichever occurs later, the Debtor shall upload and submit through the LMM Portal, Debtor's Prepared Package, together with any additional forms or documents which Lender may post on the LMM Portal, and pay a non-refundable LMM Portal submission fee in the amount of $25.00.

If the Debtor has been excused by Court order from using the LMM Portal because the Debtor does not have a computer, then within seven days after entry of the Order, the Debtor shall mail or fax to the Lender and the Mediator the Debtor's Prepared Package, with any additional forms or documents that the Lender has, in writing, advised the Debtor are required.

C. Mediator Requirements. The designated Mediator shall log in to the LMM Portal within seven days of the entry of the Order and use the LMM Portal to facilitate the exchange of information and documentation between Debtor and Lender in an effort to perfect the documentation needed for Lender to complete its analysis of Debtor's loss mitigation options.

If the Debtor does not have a computer and has been excused from using the LMM Portal, the Mediator shall contact the Debtor by phone or mail and contact the Lender in which ever manner the Lender and Mediator agree to communicate.

The Mediator shall schedule the initial LMM conference no later than seven days after the Mediator determines that the Lender has received and reviewed all the required information through the LMM Portal, or from the Debtor if use of the LMM Portal has been excused. In the event the Mediator cannot determine that the Lender has received and reviewed all the required information, the Mediator shall schedule the initial LLM conference within 60 days of entry of the Order. The initial LMM conference shall not exceed one hour. The Mediator shall report the scheduling of any LMM conference(s) on the LMM Portal.

VIII. LOSS MITIGATION MEDIATION CONFERENCE

All parties are required to attend the LMM conference and must be authorized to settle all matters requested in the Verified Motion.

A. Lender. The Lender and Lender's representative may participate in the LMM conference by telephone.

B. Debtor.

1. A Debtor represented by an attorney, and any co-obligor, co-borrower or other third party obligated on the note or mortgage, may also participate in the LMM conference by telephone provided they are physically present with Debtor's attorney and present identification to Debtor's attorney during all LMM conferences. The Debtor shall provide a foreign language interpreter, if necessary, at the Debtor's own expense.

2. A Debtor not represented by an attorney, and any co-obligor, co-borrower or other third party obligated on the note/mortgage, must be physically present with the Mediator at the Mediator's selected location and present identification to the Mediator for all LMM conferences. The Debtor shall provide a foreign language interpreter, if necessary, at the Debtor's own expense.

C. Settlement Agreement. All parties attending the LMM conference shall be ready, willing and able to sign a binding settlement agreement at the LMM conference and have the ability to scan, send and receive documents by facsimile, email or other electronic means at the time of the LMM conference.

D. Procedure. The initial LMM conference shall not exceed one hour. In the event the parties are unable to reach an agreement and require a second LMM conference, the Mediator shall schedule a final LMM conference not later than 30 days thereafter. The second LMM conference shall not exceed one hour.

Notwithstanding, the Mediator may continue the LMM conference, if necessary, beyond the two, one-hour conferences upon written agreement of the parties.

LMM shall be concluded not later than 150 days from the date of the Order, unless extended by order or by stipulation of the parties as provided in Section VII.

E. Confidential Communication. All communication and information exchanged during the LMM conference shall remain confidential and shall be inadmissible in any subsequent proceeding pursuant to Federal Rules of Evidence 408 and Chapter 44 of the Florida Statutes.

IX. EFFECT OF MEDIATION

A. Automatic Stay. The automatic stay will be modified to the extent necessary to facilitate LMM pursuant to the Order.

Once the Order has been entered:

(1) Any pending motion for stay relief with respect to property that is subject to LMM shall be continued until such time as the LMM has been concluded; the pendency of LMM constitutes good cause and compelling circumstances under 11 U.S.C. § 362(e) to delay entry of any final decision on a pending request for stay relief. Any Lender seeking relief prior to the conclusion of the LMM must file a motion requesting a hearing, setting forth the reasons why relief must be considered prior to conclusion of the LMM.

(2) No motion for stay relief with respect to the property subject of the LMM may be filed on negative notice.

B. No Delay. The referral of a matter to LMM does not relieve the parties from complying with any other court orders or applicable provisions of the Bankruptcy Code, the Federal Rules of Bankruptcy Procedure, Administrative Orders or Local Rules. Notwithstanding a loss mitigation matter being referred to LMM, the case shall not be stayed or delayed without further order of the Court.

C. If the Debtor's case is otherwise in a posture for administrative closing, the case shall remain open during the pendency of LMM, unless otherwise ordered by the Court.

X. POST LOSS MITIGATION MEDIATION

In the event the parties reach a final resolution or, if no agreement has been reached, the Mediator shall report the results of the LMM on the LMM Portal not later than seven days after the conclusion of the final LMM conference. The Mediator shall also complete and file the LMM Local Form "Final Report of Loss Mitigation Mediator" ("Final Report") with the Court, either electronically or by conventional filing, not later than two business days following entry of the "Final Report" data on the LMM Portal.

Within 14 days of the filing of the Final Report, if the Debtor and the Lender have reached a resolution through the LMM conference, the Debtor's attorney shall file the LMM Local Form "Motion to Approve Loss Mitigation Agreement with Lender" and must attach as an exhibit the proposed LMM Local Form "Order Granting Motion to Approve Loss Mitigation Agreement with Lender". If the Debtor is self-represented, the Debtor shall file the LMM Local Form "Self-Represented Debtor's Verified Motion for Referral to Loss Mitigation Mediation".

If any interested party files a timely response objecting to the Debtor's motion, the Debtor's attorney shall promptly file the LMM Local Form "Certificate of Contested Matter" and the Court will schedule a hearing in accordance with the procedures set forth in Local Rule 9073-1.

If no response is filed, the Debtor shall file the LMM Local Form "Certificate of No Response and Request for Entry of Order" and upload the LMM Local Form "Order Granting Motion to Approve Loss Mitigation Agreement with Lender".

If the Debtor is not represented by counsel, the Court will promptly schedule a hearing on the "Motion to Approve Loss Mitigation Agreement with Lender" in accordance with the procedures set forth in Local Rule 9073-1.

The parties shall formalize any required legal documents in a timely fashion thereafter.

XI. CHAPTER 13 PLAN LANGUAGE

When mortgage modification is sought as part of LMM in a chapter 13 case, the Debtor shall include the following language in "Other Provisions" of the chapter 13 plan:

> "The Debtor has filed a Verified Motion for Referral to LMM with ________ ("Lender"), loan number ___, for real property located at ________. The parties shall timely comply with all requirements of the Order of Referral to LMM and all Administrative Orders/Local Rules regarding LMM. While the LMM is pending and until the trial/interim payment plan or the permanent mortgage modification/permanent payment is established by the parties, the Debtor has included a post-petition plan payment, absent Court order to the contrary, of no less than 31% of the Debtor's gross monthly income as a good faith adequate protection payment to the Lender. All payments shall be considered timely upon receipt by the trustee and not upon receipt by the Lender.
>
> Until the LMM is completed and the Final Report of Loss Mitigation Mediator is filed, any objection to the Lender's Proof of Claim on the real property described above shall be held in abeyance as to the regular payment and mortgage arrearage stated in the Proof of Claim only. The Debtor shall assert any and all other objections to the Proof of Claim prior to confirmation of the plan or modified plan.
>
> If the Debtor, co-obligor/co-borrower or other third party (if applicable) and the Lender agree to a settlement as a result of the pending LMM, the Debtor will file a Motion to Approve Loss Mitigation Agreement with Lender no later than 14 calendar days following settlement. Once the settlement is approved by the Court, the Debtor shall immediately amend or modify the plan to reflect the settlement and the Lender shall amend its Proof of Claim to reflect the settlement, as applicable.
>
> If a settlement is reached after the plan is confirmed, the Debtor will file a motion to modify the plan no later than 30 calendar days following approval of the settlement by the Court and the Lender shall have leave to amend its Proof of Claim to reflect the settlement reached after

confirmation of the plan. The parties will then timely comply with any and all requirements necessary to complete the settlement.

In the event the Debtor receives any financial benefit from the Lender as part of any agreement, the Debtor shall immediately disclose the financial benefit to the Court and the trustee and amend or modify the plan accordingly.

If the Lender and the Debtor fail to reach a settlement, then no later than 14 calendar days after the Mediator's Final Report is filed, the Debtor will amend or modify the plan to (a) conform to the Lender's Proof of Claim (if the Lender has filed a Proof of Claim) or (b) provide that the real property will be surrendered. If the amended or modified plan provides that the real property is to be surrendered, then the obligations to the Lender will be considered "treated outside the plan" and the Lender shall have in rem relief from the automatic stay as to the real property being surrendered. Notwithstanding the foregoing, Lender may file a motion to confirm that the automatic stay is not in effect as to the real property.

Confirmation of the plan will be without prejudice to the assertion of any rights the Lender has to address payment of its Proof of Claim."

XII. LOSS MITIGATION MEDIATOR

Unless otherwise agreed to by the parties, the Mediator shall be selected from the Clerk's Register of Mediators maintained under Local Rule 9019–2(A)(1).

1. **Registration.** Each Mediator shall be registered on the LMM Portal.

2. **Standards of Professional Conduct.** The Mediator shall be governed by the standards of professional conduct set forth in the Florida Rules for Certified and Court-appointed Mediators and shall have judicial immunity in the same manner and to the same extent as a judge.

3. **Compensation.** Mediators shall be paid equally by the parties as follows:

   a. Unless the Debtor's case has been accepted as a pro bono case, the Debtor shall pay a non-refundable fee in the amount of $300.00 directly to the Mediator within seven days of the Order. A Debtor may request a Mediator to serve pro bono only if Debtor's income is less than 150% above the poverty level.

   b. The Lender shall pay a non-refundable fee in the amount of $300.00 directly to the Mediator within seven days of the Order.

   c. The fee includes the Mediator's assistance in determining all documentation is uploaded to the LMM Portal, or, for a Debtor with no computer, otherwise exchanged between the Debtor and Lender, scheduling of the mediation, and participation in a maximum of two, one-hour loss mitigation conferences.

   d. For sessions that extend beyond the initial two, one-hour sessions, the Mediator shall be compensated in accordance with Local Rule 9019–2(A)(6).

   e. Fees for LMM conferences that extend beyond the initial two, one-hour sessions shall be divided equally between the parties, except in the case of a pro bono matter in which case the Mediator will be paid one half of his or her fee by the Lender and the balance will be credited to the Mediator's pro bono commitment. Payment shall be made by the Debtor and the Lender prior to the beginning of each successive LMM conference. If the Debtor is not represented by an attorney, the Debtor shall bring a money order or cashier's check to the LMM conference in an amount equal to the Debtor's share of the one hour session. Any balance owed for a session that extends beyond the pre-paid session shall be paid as soon as possible, or within two business days following conclusion of the final session.

XIII. COMPENSATION OF DEBTOR'S COUNSEL

Without application to the Court, attorneys for Debtors shall be permitted to charge an attorney's fee not to exceed $1,800.00, and $65 in costs for LMM, subject to the compensation requirements for the chapter under which the case is filed. In chapter 13 cases, charges shall be made in accordance with the "Guidelines for Compensation For Professional Services or Reimbursement of Expense by Attorneys for Chapter 13 Debtors Pursuant to Local Rule 2016–1(B)(2)(a)".

1. The $1,800.00 fee shall include:

a. Filing of the Verified Motion and proposed Order;

b. Filing of other required pleadings and preparation of proposed orders, as applicable;

c. Communicating with the Lender and the Mediator; and

d. Attendance at all LMM conferences and Court hearings.

2. In a chapter 13 case the $1,800.00 fee shall be paid as follows:

a. The sum of $900.00 shall be presumed to compensate Debtor's attorney for initial services relating to LMM, including but not limited, collecting and uploading documents to the LMM Portal, drafting and filing the Verified Motion and communicating with the Lender and Mediator.

b. The remaining balance of $900.00 shall become payable once the Mediator has scheduled the initial LMM conference.

c. If modification of a chapter 13 plan after confirmation becomes necessary, the Debtor's attorney may charge an additional $500.00 in fees and $25 in costs in accordance with the "Guidelines for Compensation For Professional Services or Reimbursement of Expense by Attorneys for Chapter 13 Debtors Pursuant to Local Rule 2016–1(B)(2)(a)".

ADMINISTRATIVE ORDER 14–03. IN RE: ADOPTION OF MORTGAGE MODIFICATION MEDIATION PROGRAM AND STATUS OF LOSS MITIGATION MEDIATION PROGRAM ADOPTED UNDER AO 13–01

In accordance with 11 U.S.C. § 105(a), this court entered Administrative Order 13–01 "Adoption of Loss Mitigation Mediation Program" which implemented a mortgage modification program in this court effective April 1, 2013.

In February 2014, the United States Bankruptcy Court for the Middle District of Florida hosted a statewide Chapter 13 Mortgage Modification Mediation Summit (Summit) to provide an open forum for debtors' attorneys, mediators, lenders and chapter 13 trustees to discuss and compare the three mortgage modification mediation programs offered in the Southern, Middle and Northern Districts of Florida.

As a result of the Summit, the bankruptcy judges of the Southern, Middle and Northern Districts of Florida agreed to strive toward uniformity in all three districts and have identified and agreed upon certain provisions that should be included in each court's program,* with a focus on what is working well and on possible efficiencies that could be implemented to improve the respective programs.

The court, in accordance with the findings of the Summit, and in continued determination that a mortgage modification program may avoid the need for litigation, reduce costs to participants, and enable debtors to reorganize or otherwise address their most significant debts and assets under the United States Bankruptcy Code,

ORDERS as follows:

1. The Loss Mitigation Mediation (LMM) Program and implementing procedures and local forms adopted under Administrative Order 13–1 shall be replaced by the Mortgage Modification Mediation (MMM) Program and implementing procedures and forms. The MMM Program shall become effective August 1, 2014, for the following cases:

(a) Individual debtor cases filed or reopened under an eligible chapter on or after August 1, 2014, as set forth in the MMM Program Procedures;

(b) Individual debtor cases filed prior to August 1, 2014, in which no motion under LMM has ever been filed as of the effective date of the MMM Program, as set forth in the MMM Program Procedures, provided that those debtors seek to commence MMM on or after August 1, 2014, and not later than September 30, 2014; and,

(c) Individual debtor cases where the court has authorized, after motion and hearing, an application to participate in MMM outside the time periods established in paragraphs (a) and (b) above.

2. The compensation and cost amounts allowed for participants in the MMM Program shall be set forth in the MMM Program Procedures and local forms and may be amended from time to time as provided under paragraph 4 of this order. This court's Local Rule 9019–2(A)(6) and related

administrative order setting compensation rate for mediators shall not apply to mediations under the MMM Program, except for sessions extending beyond the initial two, one-hour sessions.

3. The Court may modify the MMM Program Procedures and local forms from time to time without prior notice, by publication of a clerk's notice of revised procedures and/or forms on the court website,

4. Copies of this Administrative Order, the MMM Program Procedures and local forms shall be posted on the court website and copies may be obtained from the Clerk's Office.

5. The Loss Mitigation Mediation Program procedures and local forms in effect under AO 13–1 shall remain in effect for those cases in which LMM was commenced prior to August 1, 2014. Upon determination by the clerk that no further LMM cases are pending, the forms and procedures shall be removed from the list of current procedures and forms for this court and Administrative Order 13–1 shall be deemed moot.

[Dated: July 24, 2014.]

*** Publisher's Note:** *See* Memorandum, dated April 13, 2014, re: Uniform State-Wide Procedures on mediation of mortgage modifications, set forth in this publication following the local forms of the United States Bankruptcy Court for the Northern District of Florida, *ante*.

MORTGAGE MODIFICATION MEDIATION PROGRAM PROCEDURES

Revised Effective August 1, 2014 as provided under Administrative Order 14–03 and Further Amended on April 1, 2015

I. PURPOSE

These procedures and forms implement the Mortgage Modification Mediation (MMM) program established under Administrative Order 14–03 and further amended on April 1, 2015. This program is designed to function as a forum for individual debtors to explore mortgage modification options with their lenders for real property in which the debtors have an interest or are obligated on the promissory note or mortgage. The goal of MMM is to facilitate communication and exchange of information in a confidential setting and encourage the parties to finalize a feasible and beneficial agreement with the assistance and supervision of the United States Bankruptcy Court for the Southern District of Florida. Mortgage Modification Mediation options include modification of a mortgage or surrender of real property owned by an individual debtor(s).

II. DEBTORS ELIGIBLE TO PARTICIPATE

Subject to implementation provisions set forth in Administrative Order 14–03 and further amended on April 1, 2015, individuals who have filed for bankruptcy protection and currently have a case pending under any chapter are eligible to participate in MMM with respect to real property. The party seeking MMM shall include the address of the relevant property and the last four digits of the mortgage loan number in the MMM motion.

Individuals who seek to modify a mortgage must have paid their bankruptcy filing fee in full prior to filing a motion to participate in MMM.

III. MORTGAGE MODIFICATION MEDIATION PORTAL AND DOCUMENT PREPARATION SOFTWARE

In an effort to expedite the exchange of information between the debtor and the lender, the Court has mandated the use of a secure online portal (the "MMM Portal") and an on-line program that facilitates the preparation of the debtor's loan modification package (Document Preparation Software). Submitting documents to the MMM Portal provides transparency in the mortgage modification process making information immediately available to the parties through a secure internet site. The use of the Document Preparation Software further ensures that the initial submission to the lender is complete and accurate and should expedite the lender's review. The use of an MMM Portal and Document Preparation Software eliminates the need for multiple submissions of documents that were not received and unnecessary delay based upon incomplete documentation.

All written communication between the parties regarding the mediation must be sent through the MMM Portal only, unless otherwise ordered by the Court. Any litigated matters incidental to the mediation shall be considered as separate matters and not subject to the portal communication requirement. (For example, a motion to compel mediation or motions related to discovery, must be filed in the main bankruptcy case, not through the portal.) The current MMM Portal provider approved by the Court is managed and maintained by Default Mitigation Management LLC ("DMM"). Free training on the use of the MMM Portal shall be available to all attorneys and lenders. The Court's web page on MMM also includes MMM Portal training materials on mortgage modification, including contact information for the portal vendor and information on the Document Preparation Software. In the event other providers are approved by the Court, those providers will be listed on the Court's website.

IV. REQUEST FOR ORDER OF REFERRAL TO MMM

Unless otherwise ordered by the Court, requests for an order of referral to MMM must be filed within 90 days from the date of filing the Voluntary Petition.

A. Ex Parte by Attorney Represented Debtor

1. *Requirements for filing ex parte motion.* A debtor seeking entry of an order of referral to MMM within 90 days of filing the Voluntary Petition may seek entry of an ex parte order of referral by filing the MMM Local Form "Attorney–Represented Debtor's Verified Ex Parte Motion for Referral to Mortgage Modification Mediation ("Ex Parte Motion") and attach as an exhibit the Local Form "Order Granting Debtor's Ex Parte Motion for Referral to Mortgage Modification Mediation" ("Ex Parte Order"). The debtor shall serve the Ex Parte Motion and proposed Ex Parte Order on the debtor, trustee, if applicable, lender, lender's counsel, if applicable, and any other required parties, and upload the Ex Parte Order to the Court's E–Orders program.

Prior to filing the Ex Parte Motion:

(a) The non-refundable Document Preparation Software fee of $40.00 shall have been paid directly to the approved vendor.

(b) Debtor's initial loan modification forms shall have been completed using the court-approved Document Preparation Software and ready for signature and submission. This includes collecting Debtor's required supporting documentation in order to submit Debtor's initial package ("Debtor's Prepared Package") to the Lender for review through the MMM Portal.

2. *Entry of Order of Referral–deadlines for Seeking Reconsideration.* Upon filing of the Ex Parte Motion, the Court shall enter the Ex Parte Order. The Ex Parte Order shall establish a 14 day deadline for the Lender to seek reconsideration of the Order ("Reconsideration Deadline"). If a timely motion for reconsideration is filed, the Court will promptly schedule a hearing in accordance with Local Rule 9073–1.

3. *Process for Selection of Mediator.* The parties shall, in consultation with one another, select a mediator by the later of (i) the Reconsideration Deadline, or (ii) 14 days after the entry of an order denying the motion for reconsideration, if a timely motion for reconsideration is filed (such period of time, the "Mediator Selection Period").

(a) If the parties agree on the selection of a mediator during the Mediator Selection Period, the Debtor shall file the MMM Local Form "Debtor's Notice of Selection of Mortgage Modification Mediator" (Check Box 1 and insert mediator name and contact information), serve a copy of the Notice on all required parties, and file a Certificate of Service pursuant to Local Rule 2002–1(F).

(b) If the lender fails to communicate with the debtor during the Mediator Selection Period, the debtor shall, within seven days, independently select a mediator and file the MMM Local Form "Debtor's Notice of Selection of Mortgage Modification Mediator" (Check Box 2 and insert mediator name and contact information), serve a copy of the Notice on all required parties, and file a Certificate of Service pursuant to Local Rule 2002–1(F). In this instance, it shall be deemed that the Lender has waived the right to challenge debtor's selection of a mediator.

(c) If the parties attempt to reach agreement on the selection of a mediator, but fail to do so during the Mediator Selection Period, the Debtor shall file the MMM Local Form "Debtor's Notice of Selection of Mortgage Modification Mediator" (Check Box 3 indicating the impasse), serve a copy of the Notice on all required parties, and file a Certificate of Service pursuant to Local Rule 2002–1(F). The clerk shall then randomly select a mediator from the clerk's Mediation Register pursuant to Local Rule 9019–2(B)(3), without the necessity of a hearing. The clerk shall serve notice of the mediator selection on the required parties using the MMM Local Form "Notice of Clerk's Designation of Mortgage Modification Mediator". Local Rule 9019–2(B) shall apply to any challenge to the clerk's designation of mediator.

B. Filing a Request Out of Time on Negative Notice.

1. An attorney-represented debtor seeking to initiate MMM later than 90 days from the date of filing the Voluntary Petition, must file the MMM Local Form Attorney–Represented Debtor's Verified Motion for Referral to Mortgage Modification Mediation ("Out of Time Motion"), on notice to the lender and any co-obligor, co-borrower or third party whose participation is required, and must attach as an exhibit the MMM Local Form "Order Granting Debtor's Verified "Out of Time Motion for Referral to Mortgage Modification Mediation ("Order"). A Certificate of Service must also be filed pursuant to Local Rule 2002–1(F).

2. Prior to filing the Out of Time Motion:

(a) The non-refundable Document Preparation Software fee of $40.00 shall have been paid directly to the approved vendor.

(b) Debtor's initial loan modification forms shall have been completed using the court-approved Document Preparation Software and ready for signature and submission. This includes collecting debtor's required supporting documentation in order to submit debtor's initial package ("Debtor's Prepared Package") to the lender for review through the LMM Portal.

3. The lender shall have 14 days from the date of service of debtor's Out of Time Motion to file a response. Failure by the lender or other party, who has been properly served with the Out of Time Motion to file a timely response, shall be deemed consent to the entry of the Order. Within seven days after the expiration of the 14 day response deadline, the debtor's attorney shall file the MMM Local Form "Certificate of No Response and Request for Entry of Order". The Lender may also file the MMM Local Form "Lender's Consent to Attend and Participate in Mortgage Modification Mediation" at any time after filing of the Negative Notice Motion.

4. If the lender or other party served with the Out of Time Motion files a timely response, the debtor's attorney shall file the MMM Local Form "Certificate of Contested Matter" and the Court will promptly schedule a hearing in accordance with the procedures set forth in Local Rule 9073–1.

5. If the Court grants the debtor's Out of Time Motion, the Order shall establish a 14 day deadline for selection of a mediator in accordance with the Section IV. A. 3. above.

C. By a Self–Represented Debtor.

1. An eligible debtor seeking to participate in MMM who is not represented by an attorney, must file the MMM Local Form "Self–Represented Debtor's Verified Motion for Referral to Mortgage Modification Mediation" ("Pro Se Motion"), which will promptly be set for hearing by the Court in accordance with the procedures contained in Local Rule 9073–1.

2. If the debtor is seeking waiver of the mediation fee (see section XIII.3.a. below), the debtor shall include this request in the Pro Se Motion. If the use of the MMM Portal or the Document Preparation Software creates an undue hardship because the debtor does not have access to a computer, the Debtor shall also include a request in the Pro Se Motion to exchange documents with the Lender by fax or U.S. Mail.

3. The debtor must serve the Pro Se Motion and proposed MMM Local Form Order Granting Self–Represented Debtor's Motion for Referral to Mortgage Modification Mediation ("Pro Se Order") by U.S. Mail and, if possible, also by email, on the lender, the lender's counsel, if known, and any other party required to participate in the mediation, and file a Certificate of Service pursuant to Local Rule 2002–1(F).

4. A response to the debtor's Pro Se Motion must be filed within 14 days from the date of service of the motion on the lender.

5. If the Debtor's Pro Se Motion is granted, the Pro Se Order shall establish a 14 day deadline for the parties to agree upon the selection of a mediator.

6. Process for Selection of Mediator:

(a) Within seven days after expiration of the 14 day deadline, if the parties agree on the selection of a mediator, the debtor shall file the MMM Local Form "Debtor's Notice of Selection of Mortgage Modification Mediator" (Check Box 1 and insert mediator name and contact information), serve a copy of the Notice on all required parties, and file a Certificate of Service pursuant to Local Rule 2002–1(F).

(b) If the parties fail to agree, within seven days after expiration of the 14 day deadline, the Debtor shall file the MMM Local Form "Debtor's Notice of Selection of MMM Mediator" (Check Box 3 indicating the impasse), serve a copy of the notice on all required parties, and file a Certificate of Service pursuant to Local Rule 2002–1(F). The clerk shall then randomly select a mediator from the clerk's Mediation Register pursuant to Local Rule 9019–2(B)(1), without the necessity of a hearing. The clerk shall serve notice of the mediator selection on the required parties using the MMM Local Form "Notice of Clerk's Designation of Mortgage Modification Mediator". Local Rule 9019–2(B)(3) shall apply to any challenge to the clerk's designation of mediator.

D. By A Lender. A Lender May Request Referral To MMM By Filing And Serving.

1. *Attorney–represented debtor.* upon the debtor and debtor's counsel, a motion requesting referral to MMM, together with a proposed order that substantially conforms to the MMM Local Form Ex Parte Order, except the provisions in paragraph one permitting reconsideration of the order shall not be included.

2. *Self–represented debtor.* upon the Debtor a motion requesting referral to MMM, together with a proposed order that substantially conforms to the MMM Local Form Pro Se Order.

The lender must file a Certificate or Service pursuant to Local Rule 2002–1(F). The debtor shall have 14 days from the date of service of the motion to file a written response. If the debtor fails to file a response objecting to the Lender's motion, the Court may enter the Order or, if the debtor is not represented by counsel, the Court will set the matter for hearing in accordance with the procedures set forth in Local Rule 9073–1.

If the lender's motion for referral to MMM is granted, the Order shall establish a 14 day deadline for the parties to agree upon the selection of a mediator. Within seven days after expiration of the 14 day deadline, if the parties agree on the selection of a mediator, the Debtor shall file the MMM Local Form "Debtor's Notice of Selection of MMM Mediator" (Check Box 1 and insert mediator name and contact information), serve a copy of the Notice on all required parties, and file a Certificate of Service pursuant to Local Rule 2002–1(F).

If the parties fail to agree, within seven days after expiration of the 14 day deadline, the Debtor shall file the MMM Local Form "Debtor's Notice of Selection of MMM Mediator" (Check Box 3 indicating the impasse), serve a copy of the Notice on all required parties, and file a Certificate of Service pursuant to Local Rule 2002–1(F). The clerk shall then randomly select a mediator from the clerk's Mediation Register pursuant to Local Rule 9019–2(B)(1), without the necessity of a hearing. The clerk shall serve notice of the mediator selection on the required parties using the MMM Local Form "Notice of Clerk's Designation of Mediator". Local Rule 9019–2(B)(3) shall apply to any challenge to the clerk's designation of mediator.

E. By the Bankruptcy Court. The Court may order the assignment of a mortgage modification matter to MMM upon the Court's own motion.

V. ADDITIONAL PARTIES

CO–OBLIGORS/CO–BORROWERS OR OTHER THIRD PARTIES: Any co-obligor, co-borrower or other third party must participate in the MMM process. If the participation of a co-obligor, co-borrower or other third party is necessary, any party may request that such co-obligor, co-borrower or other third party participates in MMM. The co-obligor, co-borrower or other third party shall sign, and the debtor or attorney for the debtor shall file, simultaneously with the debtor's Ex Parte Motion, or Pro–Se Motion, the MMM Local Form "Third Party's Consent to Attend and Participate in Mortgage Modification Mediation".

VI. ORDER OF REFERRAL TO MORTGAGE MODIFICATION MEDIATION

Upon entry of the Order the moving party shall serve the Order on the required parties, including the designated mediator, once determined, and file a Certificate of Service pursuant to Local Rule 2002–1(F). The moving party shall also upload a copy of the Order to the MMM Portal within seven days after filing of the Debtor's Notice of Selection of Mortgage Modification Mediator (or Notice of

Clerk's Designation of Mortgage Modification Mediator) or the lender's registration on the MMM Portal, whichever occurs later, unless by Court order, the debtor has been excused from using the MMM Portal. The parties are required to comply with all deadlines set forth in the Order. However, any deadlines imposed by the Order may be extended by Court order or by stipulation of the parties.

The parties are required to participate in MMM in good faith or be subject to possible sanctions by the Court, including vacating the Order.

A. Lender Requirements. Within seven days after entry of the Order (or after all motions for reconsideration have been heard and determined), the lender, if not already registered on the MMM Portal, shall ensure that it is registered, and if the lender has counsel, that the lender's counsel is registered as well. (Registration on the MMM Portal is a one-time event—i.e., once the lender is registered on the MMM Portal, the lender will not have to register again).

Within seven days after entry of the Order (or after all motions for reconsideration have been heard and determined), the lender will also confirm that all of the lender's initial mortgage modification requirements ("Lender's Initial Package") are available on the MMM Portal. Lender's Initial Package shall specify the forms and documentation the Lender requires to initiate a review of debtor's request for mortgage modification options. (Note: Lender's Initial Package should be provided to the MMM Portal vendor at the time of lender registration on the MMM Portal.)

If the lender transfers the loan, the lender must provide a copy of the Order to the new holder of the loan ("Successor Lender"), and the Successor Lender will be obligated to comply with all terms of the Order.

Within seven days after delivery of the information provided for in section VI.B. below, the lender shall, on the MMM Portal, (i) acknowledge receipt of debtor's information and advise debtor of any additional or missing information required for lender to proceed with its review; and (ii) designate its single point of contact and its outside legal counsel, if any. Such lender's counsel or representative shall have the authority (within the investor's guidelines) to settle and will attend and continuously participate in all MMM conferences in this case. The lender shall timely underwrite the loan modification request.

B. Debtor Requirements. Within seven days after filing the Debtor's Notice of Selection of Mortgage Modification Mediator (or Notice of Clerk's Designation of Mortgage Modification Mediator) or the lender's registration on the MMM Portal, whichever occurs later, the debtor shall upload and submit through the MMM Portal, Debtor's Prepared Package, together with any additional forms or documents which lender may post on the MMM Portal, and pay a nonrefundable MMM Portal submission fee in the amount of $40.00.

If the debtor has been excused by Court order from using the MMM Portal, then within seven days after entry of the Order, the debtor shall mail or fax to the lender and the mediator the Debtor's Prepared Package, with any additional forms or documents that the lender has, in writing, advised the debtor are required.

If the debtor fails to comply with these requirements, the Court will consider vacating the Order upon motion by the lender and after notice and hearing.

C. Mediator Requirements. The designated mediator shall, within seven days of designation, or within seven days after the debtor has complied with requirements in section VI.B above, log in to the MMM Portal to facilitate the exchange of information and documentation between debtor and lender in an effort to perfect the documentation needed for lender to complete its analysis of debtor's mortgage modification options.

If the debtor has been excused from using the MMM Portal, the mediator shall contact the debtor by phone or mail and contact the lender in which ever manner the lender and mediator agree to communicate.

The mediator shall schedule the initial MMM conference no later than seven days after the mediator determines that the lender has received and reviewed all the required information through the MMM Portal, or from the debtor if use of the MMM Portal has been excused. In the event the mediator cannot determine that the lender has received and reviewed all the required information, the mediator shall schedule the initial MMM conference within 90 days of entry of the Order. The initial MMM conference shall not exceed one hour. The mediator shall report the scheduling of any MMM conference(s) on the MMM Portal.

VII. MORTGAGE MODIFICATION MEDIATION CONFERENCE

All parties are required to attend the MMM conference and must be authorized to settle all matters requested in the motion.

A. Lender. The lender and lender's representative may participate in the MMM conference by telephone.

B. Debtor.

1. A debtor represented by an attorney, and any co-obligor, co-borrower or other third party obligated on the note or mortgage, may also participate in the MMM conference by telephone provided they are physically present with debtor's attorney and present identification to debtor's attorney during all MMM conferences. **The debtor shall provide a foreign language interpreter, if necessary, at the debtor's own expense.**

2. A self-represented debtor, and any co-obligor, co-borrower or other third party obligated on the note/mortgage, must be physically present with the mediator at the mediator's selected location and present identification to the Mediator for all MMM conferences. **The debtor shall provide a foreign language interpreter, if necessary, at the debtor's own expense.**

C. Settlement Agreement. All parties attending the MMM conference shall be ready, willing and able to sign a binding settlement agreement at the MMM conference and have the ability to scan, send and receive documents by facsimile, email or other electronic means at the time of the MMM conference.

D. Procedure. The initial MMM conference shall not exceed one hour. In the event the parties are unable to reach an agreement and require a second MMM conference, the mediator shall schedule a final MMM conference not later than 30 days thereafter. The second MMM conference shall not exceed one hour.

Notwithstanding, the mediator may continue the MMM conference, if necessary, beyond the two, one-hour conferences upon written agreement of the parties.

MMM shall be concluded not later than 150 days from the date of the Order, unless extended by written consent on the portal, or, as provided in Section VI, by court order or by stipulation of the parties.

E. Confidential Communication. All communication and information exchanged during the MMM conference shall remain confidential and shall be inadmissible in any subsequent proceeding pursuant to Federal Rules of Evidence 408 and Chapter 44 of the Florida Statutes.

VIII. EFFECT OF MEDIATION

A. Automatic Stay. The automatic stay will be modified to the extent necessary to facilitate MMM pursuant to the Order.

Once the Order has been entered:

1. Any pending motion for stay relief with respect to property that is subject to MMM shall be continued until such time as the MMM has been concluded; the pendency of MMM constitutes good cause and compelling circumstances under 11 U.S.C. § 362(e) to delay entry of any final decision on a pending request for stay relief. Any lender seeking relief prior to the conclusion of the MMM must file a motion requesting a hearing, setting forth the reasons why relief must be considered prior to conclusion of the MMM.

2. No motion for stay relief with respect to the property subject of the MMM may be filed on an ex parte basis.

B. No Delay. The referral of a matter to MMM does not relieve the parties from complying with any other court orders or applicable provisions of the Bankruptcy Code, the Federal Rules of Bankruptcy Procedure, Administrative Orders or Local Rules. Notwithstanding a mortgage modification matter being referred to MMM, the case shall not be stayed or delayed without further order of the Court.

C. If the debtor's case is otherwise in a posture for administrative closing, the case shall remain open during the pendency of MMM, unless otherwise ordered by the Court.

IX. POST MORTGAGE MODIFICATION MEDIATION

In the event the parties reach a final resolution or, if no agreement has been reached, the mediator shall report the results of the MMM on the MMM Portal not later than seven days after the conclusion of the final MMM conference. The Mediator shall also complete and file the MMM Local Form "Final Report of Mortgage Modification Mediator" ("Final Report") with the Court, either electronically or by conventional filing, not later than two business days following entry of the "Final Report" data on the MMM Portal.

Within 14 days of the filing of the Final Report, if the debtor and the lender have reached a resolution through the MMM conference, the debtor's attorney shall file the MMM Local Form "Ex–Parte Motion to Approve Mortgage Modification Mediation Agreement with Lender" and upload to the Court's E–Orders program the proposed MMM Local Form "Order Granting Motion to Approve Mortgage Modification Agreement with Lender". The debtor shall serve the ex-parte motion and proposed order on all required parties and file a certificate of service pursuant to Local Rule 2002–1(F).

If the debtor is not represented by an attorney, and the debtor and the lender have reached a resolution through the MMM conference, within 14 days of the filing of the Final Report, the debtor shall file the MMM Local Form "Self–Represented Debtor's Motion to Approve Mortgage Modification Mediation Agreement with Lender", and the Court will promptly schedule a hearing in accordance with the procedures set forth in Local Rule 9073–1. The Debtor shall serve the motion on all required parties and file a certificate of service pursuant to Local Rule 2002–1(F).

The parties shall formalize any required legal documents in a timely fashion thereafter.

X. TRIAL PAYMENTS DURING THE MMM PROCESS

A. Chapter 7 and Chapter 11 Payments. In a chapter 7 or chapter 11 case, if the lender requests trial payments as part of MMM, absent a court order to the contrary, the debtor must pay to the lender a monthly payment (a) with respect to the debtor's homestead, of no less than the lower of the prepetition monthly contractual mortgage payment or 31% of the debtor's gross monthly income (after deducting any amount paid toward HOA fees due for the property) and (b) with respect to income producing property, of no less than 75% of the gross income generated by such property. Payments will be made by the debtor directly to the lender as agreed by the parties and without requiring Court approval or any modification of the automatic stay.

Unless otherwise agreed to by the lender trial payments shall continue until the MMM is completed and either (a) the payments are superseded by whatever agreement is reached between the debtor and the lender during the MMM process or (b) the parties have reached impasse and no agreement is reached. If the parties reach impasse, the lender may seek relief including stay relief, dismissal or, in a chapter 11, 12 or 13 cases, an order compelling the debtor to amend the plan. If the court requires adequate protection payments in its order on the lender's post MMM motion, the amount of such adequate protection payments may be different than the amounts required during the MMM process.

B. Chapter 12 and Chapter 13 Plan Language. When mortgage modification is sought as part of MMM in a chapter 12 case or chapter 13 case, the debtor shall include the following language in "Other Provisions" of the plan, which plan must be filed at the time that the Ex–Parte Motion, the Out of Time Motion or the Pro Se Motion is filed:

"The debtor has filed a Verified Motion for Referral to MMM with ________ ("Lender"), loan number ___, for real property located at ___________. The parties shall timely comply with all requirements of the Order of Referral to MMM and all Administrative Orders/Local Rules regarding MMM. While the MMM is pending and until the trial/interim payment plan or the permanent mortgage modification/permanent payment is established by the parties, absent Court order to the contrary, the debtor has included a post-petition monthly plan payment (a) with respect to the debtor's homestead, of no less than the lower of the prepetition monthly contractual mortgage payment or 31% of the debtor's gross monthly income (after deducting any amount paid toward HOA fees due for the property) and (b) with respect to income producing property, of no less than 75% of the gross income generated by such property, as a good faith adequate protection payment to the lender. All payments shall be considered timely upon receipt by the trustee and not upon receipt by the lender.

Until the MMM is completed and the Final Report of Mortgage Modification Mediator is filed, any objection to the lender's proof of claim on the real property described above shall be held in abeyance as to the regular payment and mortgage arrearage stated in the proof of claim only. The debtor shall assert any and all other objections to the proof of claim prior to confirmation of the plan or modified plan.

If the debtor, co–obligor/co–borrower or other third party (if applicable) and the lender agree to a settlement as a result of the pending MMM, the debtor will file the MMM Local Form "Ex Parte Motion to Approve Mortgage Modification Agreement with Lender" (or Self–Represented Debtor's Motion to Approve Mortgage Modification Agreement with Lender) no later than 14 calendar days following settlement. Once the settlement is approved by the Court, the debtor shall immediately amend or modify the plan to reflect the settlement and the lender shall amend its Proof of Claim to reflect the settlement, as applicable.

If a settlement is reached after the plan is confirmed, the debtor will file a motion to modify the plan no later than 30 calendar days following approval of the settlement by the Court and the Lender shall have leave to amend its Proof of Claim to reflect the settlement reached after confirmation of the plan. The parties will then timely comply with any and all requirements necessary to complete the settlement.

In the event the debtor receives any financial benefit from the lender as part of any agreement, the debtor shall immediately disclose the financial benefit to the Court and the trustee and amend or modify the plan accordingly.

If the lender and the debtor fail to reach a settlement, then no later than 14 calendar days after the mediator's Final Report is filed, the debtor will amend or modify the plan to (a) conform to the lender's Proof of Claim (if the lender has filed a Proof of Claim) or (b) provide that the real property will be surrendered. If the amended or modified plan provides that the real property is to be surrendered, then the obligations to the lender will be considered "treated outside the plan" and the lender shall have in rem relief from the automatic stay as to the real property being surrendered. Notwithstanding the foregoing, lender may file a motion to confirm that the automatic stay is not in effect as to the real property.

Confirmation of the plan will be without prejudice to the assertion of any rights the lender has to address payment of its Proof of Claim."

C. Application of MMM Payments. Unless the parties have agreed to the contrary, MMM payments made during the MMM process will be applied in accordance with applicable loan documents and non-bankruptcy law.

When the MMM is concluded, if all payments provided by a chapter 12 or chapter 13 bankruptcy plan have not been distributed to the lender then the balance held by the trustee shall be distributed:

1. If MMM is successful, as specifically agreed to by the parties in the agreement reached by the parties (which may include the lender's decision to decline receipt of the additional funds);

2. If MMM is not successful, then the balance

(a) shall be distributed to the lender to be applied by the lender in accordance with the applicable loan documents and nonbankruptcy law, or

(b) or the lender may affirmatively reject the balance of the payments (failure to object is not sufficient).

XI. DELAY OF DISCHARGE FOR CHAPTER 7 DEBTOR

Until the MMM process is completed and either an agreement is reached or the parties reach impasse, the debtor's discharge shall be delayed. Note: This provision is effective for chapter 7 debtors filing motions for referral to MMM after April 1, 2015.

XII. MORTAGE MODIFICATION MEDIATOR

Unless otherwise agreed to by the parties, the mediator shall be selected from the Clerk's Register of Mediators maintained under Local Rule 9019–2(A)(1).

1. **Registration.** Each mediator shall be registered on the MMM Portal.

2. **Standards of Professional Conduct.** The mediator shall be governed by the standards of professional conduct set forth in the Florida Rules for Certified and Court-appointed Mediators and shall have judicial immunity in the same manner and to the same extent as a judge.

3. **Compensation.** Mediators shall be paid equally by the parties as follows:

(a) Unless the debtor's case has been accepted as a *pro bono* case, the debtor shall pay a non-refundable fee in the amount of $300.00 directly to the mediator within seven days of designation of the mediator. A debtor may request a mediator to serve pro bono only if debtor's income is less than 150% above the poverty level.

(b) The lender shall pay a non-refundable fee in the amount of $300.00 directly to the mediator within seven days of the designation of mediator.

(c) The fee includes the mediator's assistance in determining all documentation is uploaded to the MMM Portal, or, for a debtor with no computer, otherwise exchanged between the debtor and lender, scheduling of the mediation, and participation in a maximum of two, one–hour mortgage modification conferences.

(d) For sessions that extend beyond the initial two, one-hour sessions, the mediator shall be compensated in accordance with Local Rule 9019–2(A)(6).

(e) Fees for MMM conferences that extend beyond the initial two, one-hour sessions shall be divided equally between the parties, except in the case of a pro bono matter in which case the mediator will be paid one half of his or her fee by the lender and the balance will be credited to the mediator's pro bono commitment. Payment shall be made by the debtor and the lender prior to the beginning of each successive MMM conference. If the debtor is not represented by an attorney, the debtor shall bring a money order or cashier's check to the MMM conference in an amount equal to the debtor's share of the one hour session. Any balance owed for a session that extends beyond the pre-paid session shall be paid as soon as possible, or within two business days following conclusion of the final session.

XIII. COMPENSATION OF DEBTOR'S COUNSEL

Without application to the Court, attorneys for debtors shall be permitted to charge an attorney's fee not to exceed $2500.00, and $100.00 in costs for MMM, subject to the compensation requirements for the chapter under which the case is filed. In chapter 13 cases, charges shall be made in accordance with the "Guidelines for Compensation For Professional Services or Reimbursement of Expense by Attorneys for Chapter 13 Debtors Pursuant to Local Rule 2016–1(B)(2)(a)".

1. The $2500.00 fee shall include:

(a) Filing of the Motion and proposed Order;

(b) Preparation of all forms required for mediation;

(c) Filing of other required pleadings and preparation of proposed orders, and settlement papers, as applicable;

(d) Communicating with the lender and the mediator, including communications through the portal; and

(e) Attendance at all MMM conferences and Court hearings.

(f) Review of all modified loan documents.

2. In a chapter 13 case the $2500.00 fee shall be paid as follows:

(a) The sum of $1500.00 shall be presumed to compensate debtor's attorney for initial services relating to MMM, including but not limited, collecting and uploading documents to the MMM Portal, drafting and filing the motion and communicating with the lender and mediator.

(b) The remaining balance of $1000.00 shall become payable once the mediator has scheduled the initial MMM conference.

(c) If modification of a chapter 13 plan after confirmation becomes necessary, the debtor's attorney may charge an additional $500.00 in fees and $25 in costs in accordance with the "Guidelines for Compensation for Professional Services or Reimbursement of Expense by Attorneys for Chapter 13 Debtors Pursuant to Local Rule 2016–1(B)(2)(a)".

[Dated: April 1, 2015.]

RESOLUTION OF THE FLORIDA STATE—FEDERAL JUDICIAL COUNCIL REGARDING CALENDAR CONFLICTS BETWEEN STATE AND FEDERAL COURTS

Adopted January 13, 1995

WHEREAS, the great volume of cases filed in the state and federal courts of Florida creates calendar conflicts between the state and federal courts of Florida which should be resolved in a fair, efficient and orderly manner to allow for judicial efficiency and economy; and

WHEREAS, the Florida State—Federal Judicial Council which represents the Bench and Bar of the State of Florida believes that it would be beneficial to formally agree upon and publish recommended procedures and priorities for resolving calendar conflicts between the state and federal courts of Florida;

NOW, THEREFORE, BE IT RESOLVED

In resolving calendar conflicts between the state and federal courts of Florida, the following case priorities should be considered:

1. Criminal cases should prevail over civil cases.

2. Jury trials should prevail over non-jury trials.

3. Appellate arguments, hearings, and conferences should prevail over trials.

4. The case in which the trial date has been first set should take precedence.

5. Circumstances such as cost, numbers of witnesses and attorneys involved, travel, length of trial, age of case and other relevant matters may warrant deviation from this policy. Such matters are encouraged to be resolved through communication between the courts involved.

Where an attorney is scheduled to appear in two courts—trial or appellate, state or federal—at the same time and cannot arrange for other counsel in his or her firm or in the case to represent his or her client's interest, the attorney shall give prompt written notice to opposing counsel, the clerk of each court, and the presiding judge of each case, if known, of the conflict. If the presiding judge of a case cannot be identified, written notice of the conflict shall be given to the chief judge of the court having jurisdiction over the case, or to his or her designee. The judges or their designees shall confer and undertake to avoid the conflict by agreement among themselves. Absent agreement, conflicts should be promptly resolved by the judges or their designees in accordance with the above case priorities.

In jurisdictions where calendar conflicts arise with frequency, it is recommended that each court involved consider appointing a calendar conflict coordinator to assist the judges in resolving calendar conflicts by obtaining information regarding the conflicts and performing such other ministerial duties as directed by the judges.

RULES OF PROCEDURE OF THE JUDICIAL PANEL ON MULTIDISTRICT LITIGATION

Renumbered and Amended Effective November 2, 1998

Including Amendments Effective October 4, 2016

I. RULES FOR MULTIDISTRICT LITIGATION UNDER 28 U.S.C. § 1407

RULE 1.1 DEFINITIONS

(a) "Panel" means the members of the United States Judicial Panel on Multidistrict Litigation appointed by the Chief Justice of the United States pursuant to 28 U.S.C. § 1407.

(b) "Chair" means the Chair of the Panel appointed by the Chief Justice of the United States pursuant to Section 1407, or the member of the Panel properly designated to act as Chair.

(c) "Clerk of the Panel" means the official that the Panel appoints to that position. The Clerk of the Panel shall perform such duties that the Panel or the Panel Executive delegates.

(d) "Electronic Case Filing (ECF)" refers to the Panel's automated system that receives and stores documents filed in electronic form. All attorneys filing pleadings with the Panel must do so using ECF. All pro se individuals are non-ECF users, unless the Panel orders otherwise.

(e) "MDL" means a multidistrict litigation docket which the Panel is either considering or has created by transferring cases to a transferee district for coordinated or consolidated pretrial proceedings pursuant to Section 1407.

(f) "Panel Executive" means the official appointed to act as the Panel's Chief Executive and Legal Officer. The Panel Executive may appoint, with the approval of the Panel, necessary deputies, clerical assistants and other employees to perform or assist in the performance of the duties of the Panel Executive. The Panel Executive, with the approval of the Panel, may make such delegations of authority as are necessary for the Panel's efficient operation.

(g) "Pleadings" means all papers, motions, responses, or replies of any kind filed with the Panel, including exhibits attached thereto, as well as all orders and notices that the Panel issues.

(h) "Tag-along action" refers to a civil action pending in a district court which involves common questions of fact with either (1) actions on a pending motion to transfer to create an MDL or (2) actions previously transferred to an existing MDL, and which the Panel would consider transferring under Section 1407.

(i) "Transferee district" is the federal district court to which the Panel transfers an action pursuant to Section 1407, for inclusion in an MDL.

(j) "Transferor district" is the federal district court where an action was pending prior to its transfer pursuant to Section 1407, for inclusion in an MDL, and where the Panel may remand that action at or before the conclusion of pretrial proceedings.

[Former Rule 1 adopted May 3, 1993, effective July 1, 1993. Renumbered Rule 1.1 September 1, 1998, effective November 2, 1998. Amended September 8, 2010, effective October 4, 2010.]

RULE 2.1 RULES AND PRACTICE

(a) Customary Practice. The Panel's customary practice shall govern, unless otherwise fixed by statute or these Rules.

(b) Failure to Comply With Rules. When a pleading does not comply with these Rules, the Clerk of the Panel may advise counsel of the deficiencies and set a date for full compliance. If counsel does not fully comply within the established time, the Clerk of the Panel shall file the non-complying pleading, but the Chair may thereafter order it stricken.

(c) Admission to Practice Before the Panel. Every member in good standing of the Bar of any district court of the United States is entitled to practice before the Panel, provided, however, that he or she has established and maintains a CM/ECF account with any United States federal court. Any attorney of record in any action transferred under Section 1407 may continue to represent his or her client in any district court of the United States to which such action is transferred. Parties are not required to obtain local counsel.

(d) Pendency of Motion or Conditional Order. The pendency of a motion, order to show cause, conditional transfer order or conditional remand order before the Panel pursuant to 28 U.S.C. § 1407 does not affect or suspend orders and pretrial proceedings in any pending federal district court action and does not limit the pretrial jurisdiction of that court. An order to transfer or remand pursuant to 28 U.S.C. § 1407 shall be effective only upon its filing with the clerk of the transferee district court.

(e) Reassignment. If for any reason the transferee judge is unable to continue those responsibilities, the Panel shall make the reassignment of a new transferee judge.

[Former Rule 5 adopted May 3, 1993, effective July 1, 1993. Renumbered Rule 1.2 September 1, 1998, effective November 2, 1998. Former Rule 4 adopted May 3, 1993, effective July 1, 1993. Renumbered Rule 1.3 and amended September 1, 1998, effective November 2, 1998. Former Rule 6 adopted May 3, 1993, effective July 1, 1993. Renumbered Rule 1.4 September 1, 1998, effective November 2, 1998. Former Rule 18 adopted May 3, 1993, effective July 1, 1993. Renumbered Rule 1.5 September 1, 1998, effective November 2, 1998. Former Rules 1.2, 1.3, 1.4, and 1.5 redesignated and amended September 8, 2010, effective October 4, 2010.]

RULE 3.1 ELECTRONIC RECORDS AND FILES; COPY FEES

(a) Electronic Record. Effective October 4, 2010, the official Panel record shall be the electronic file maintained on the Panel's servers. This record includes, but is not limited to, Panel pleadings, documents filed in paper and then scanned and made part of the electronic record, and Panel orders and notices filed. The official record also includes any documents or exhibits that may be impractical to scan. These documents and exhibits shall be kept in the Panel offices.

(b) Maintaining Records. Records and files generated prior to October 4, 2010, may be (i) maintained at the Panel offices, (ii) temporarily or permanently removed to such places at such times as the Clerk of the Panel or the Chair shall direct, or (iii) transferred whenever appropriate to the Federal Records Center.

(c) Fees. The Clerk of the Panel may charge fees for duplicating records and files, as prescribed by the Judicial Conference of the United States.

[Former Rule 2 adopted May 3, 1993, effective July 1, 1993. Renumbered Rule 5.1 and amended September 1, 1998, effective November 2, 1998. Former Rule 5.1 redesignated and amended September 8, 2010, effective October 4, 2010.]

RULE 3.2 ECF USERS: FILING REQUIREMENTS

(a) Form of Pleadings. This Rule applies to pleadings that ECF users file with the Panel.

(i) Each pleading shall bear the heading "Before the United States Judicial Panel on Multidistrict Litigation," the identification "MDL No.___" and the descriptive title designated by the Panel. If the Panel has not yet designated a title, counsel shall use an appropriate description.

(ii) The final page of each pleading shall contain the name, address, telephone number, fax number and email address of the attorney or party designated to receive service of pleadings in the case, and the name of each party represented.

(iii) Each brief submitted with a motion and any response to it shall not exceed 20 pages, exclusive of exhibits. Each reply shall not exceed 10 pages and shall address arguments raised in the response(s). Absent exceptional circumstances and those set forth in Rule 6.1(d), the Panel will not grant motions to exceed page limits.

(iv) Each pleading shall be typed in size 12 point font (for both text and footnotes), double spaced (text only), in a letter size document (8½ × 11 inch) with sequentially numbered pages.

(v) Each exhibit shall be separately numbered and clearly identified.

(vi) Proposed Panel orders shall not be submitted.

(b) Place of Filing. Counsel shall sign and verify all pleadings electronically in accordance with these Rules and the Panel's Administrative Policies and Procedures for Electronic Case Filing found at www.jpml.uscourts.gov. A pleading filed electronically constitutes a written document for the purpose of these Rules and the Federal Rules of Civil Procedure and is deemed the electronically signed original thereof. All pleadings, except by pro se litigants, shall conform with this Rule beginning on October 4, 2010.

(i)* Pleadings shall not be transmitted directly to any Panel member.

(c) Attorney Registration. Only attorneys identified, or to be identified, pursuant to Rule 4.1, shall file pleadings. Each of these attorneys must register as a Panel CM/ECF user through www.jpml.uscourts.gov. Registration/possession of a CM/ECF account with any United States federal court shall be deemed consent to receive electronic service of all Panel orders and notices as well as electronic service of pleadings from other parties before the Panel.

(d) Courtesy Copy of Specified Pleadings. Counsel shall serve the Clerk of the Panel, for delivery within 1 business day of filing, with a courtesy paper copy of any of the following pleadings: (i) a motion to transfer and its supporting brief; (ii) a response to a show cause order; (iii) a motion to vacate a conditional transfer order or a conditional remand order; and (iv) any response, reply, supplemental information or interested party response related to the pleadings listed in (i), (ii) and (iii). No courtesy copies of any other pleadings are required. Courtesy copies of pleadings totaling 10 pages or less (including any attachments) may be faxed to the Panel. The courtesy copy shall include all exhibits, shall be clearly marked "Courtesy Copy–Do Not File," shall contain the CM/ECF pleading number (if known), and shall be mailed or delivered to:

Clerk of the Panel
United States Judicial Panel on Multidistrict Litigation
Thurgood Marshall Federal Judiciary Building
One Columbus Circle, NE, Room G–255, North Lobby
Washington, DC 20002–8041

(e) Privacy Protections. The privacy protections contained in Rule 5.2 of the Federal Rules of Civil Procedure shall apply to all Panel filings.

[Former Rule 3 adopted May 3, 1993, effective July 1, 1993. Renumbered Rule 5.11 and amended September 1, 1998, effective November 2, 1998; renumbered Rule 5.1.1 and amended March 25, 2010, effective April 1, 2010. Former Rule 7 adopted May 3, 1993, effective July 1, 1993. Renumbered Rule 5.12 and amended September 1, 1998, effective November 2, 1998. Amended April 2, 2001, effective April 2, 2001; paragraph (a) suspended in part by Order filed April 19, 2005; renumbered Rule 5.1.2 and amended March 25, 2010, effective April 1, 2010. Former Rule 9 adopted May 3, 1993, effective July 1, 1993. Renumbered Rule 7.1 and amended September 1, 1998, effective November 2, 1998. Amended April 2, 2001, effective April 2, 2001. Former Rules 5.1.1, 5.1.2, and 7.1 redesignated in part and amended September 8, 2010, effective October 4, 2010. Amended effective July 6, 2011; October 4, 2016.]

* So in original. No subdivision (ii) promulgated.

RULE 3.3 NON–ECF USERS: FILING REQUIREMENTS

(a) Definition of Non–ECF Users. Non–ECF users are all pro se individuals, unless the Panel orders otherwise. This Rule shall apply to all motions, responses and replies that non-ECF users file with the Panel.

(b) Form of Pleadings. Unless otherwise set forth in this Rule, the provisions of Rule 3.2 shall apply to non-ECF users.

(i) Each pleading shall be flat and unfolded; plainly written or typed in size 12 point font (for both text and footnotes), double spaced (text only), and printed single-sided on letter size (8 ½ × 11 inch) white paper with sequentially numbered pages; and fastened at the top-left corner without side binding or front or back covers.

(ii) Each exhibit shall be separately numbered and clearly identified. Any exhibits exceeding a cumulative total of 50 pages shall be bound separately.

(c) Place of Filing. File an original and one copy of all pleadings with the Clerk of the Panel by mailing or delivering to:

Clerk of the Panel
United States Judicial Panel on Multidistrict Litigation
Thurgood Marshall Federal Judiciary Building
One Columbus Circle, NE,
Room G–255, North Lobby
Washington, DC 20002–8041

(i) Pleadings not exceeding a total of 10 pages, including exhibits, may be faxed to the Panel office.

(ii) The Clerk of the Panel shall endorse the date for filing on all pleadings submitted for filing.

[Former Rule 3 adopted May 3, 1993, effective July 1, 1993. Renumbered Rule 5.11 and amended September 1, 1998, effective November 2, 1998; renumbered Rule 5.1.1 and amended March 25, 2010, effective April 1, 2010. Former Rule 7 adopted May 3, 1993, effective July 1, 1993. Renumbered Rule 5.12 and amended September 1, 1998, effective November 2, 1998. Amended April 2, 2001, effective April 2, 2001; paragraph (a) suspended in part by Order filed April 19, 2005; renumbered Rule 5.1.2 and amended March 25, 2010, effective April 1, 2010. Former Rule 9 adopted May 3, 1993, effective July 1, 1993. Renumbered Rule 7.1 and amended September 1, 1998, effective November 2, 1998. Amended April 2, 2001, effective April 2, 2001. Former Rules 5.1.1, 5.1.2, and 7.1 redesignated in part and amended September 8, 2010, effective October 4, 2010.]

RULE 4.1 SERVICE OF PLEADINGS

(a) Proof of Service. The Panel's notice of electronic filing shall constitute service of pleadings. Registration/possession by counsel of a CM/ECF account with any United States federal court shall be deemed consent to receive electronic service of all pleadings. All pleadings shall contain a proof of service on all other parties in all involved actions. The proof of service shall indicate the name and manner of service. If a party is not represented by counsel, the proof of service shall indicate the name of the party and the party's last known address. The proof of service shall indicate why any person named as a party in a constituent complaint was not served with the Section 1407 pleading.

(b) Service Upon Transferor Court. The proof of service pertaining to motions for a transfer or remand pursuant to 28 U.S.C. § 1407 shall certify that counsel has transmitted a copy of the motion for filing to the clerk of each district court where an affected action is pending.

(c) Notice of Appearance. Within 14 days after the issuance of a (i) notice of filing of a motion to initiate transfer under Rule 6.2, (ii) notice of filed opposition to a CTO under Rule 7.1, (iii) a show cause order under Rules* 8.1, (iv) notice of filed opposition to a CRO under Rule 10.2, or (v) notice of filing of a motion to remand under Rule 10.3, each party or designated attorney as required hereinafter shall file a Notice of Appearance notifying the Clerk of the Panel of the name, address and email address of the attorney designated to file and receive service of all pleadings. Each party shall designate only one attorney. Any party not represented by counsel shall be served by mailing such pleadings to the party's last known address. Except in extraordinary circumstances, the Panel will not grant requests for an extension of time to file the Notice of Appearance.

(d) Liaison Counsel. If the transferee district court appoints liaison counsel, this Rule shall be satisfied by serving each party in each affected action and all liaison counsel. Liaison counsel shall receive copies of all Panel orders concerning their particular litigation and shall be responsible for distribution to the parties for whom he or she serves as liaison counsel.

[Former Rule 8 adopted May 3, 1993, effective July 1, 1993. Renumbered Rule 5.2 and amended September 1, 1998, effective November 2, 1998; March 26, 2009, effective December 1, 2009. Former Rule 5.2 redesignated and amended September 8, 2010, effective October 4, 2010. Technical revisions effective July 6, 2011.]

* So in original.

RULE 5.1 CORPORATE DISCLOSURE STATEMENT

(a) Requirements. A nongovernmental corporate party must file a disclosure statement that: (1) identifies any parent corporation and any publicly held corporation owning 10% or more of its stock; or (2) states that there is no such corporation.

(b) Deadline. A party shall file the corporate disclosure statement within 14 days after issuance of a notice of the filing of a motion to transfer or remand, an order to show cause, or a motion to vacate a conditional transfer order or a conditional remand order.

(c) Updating. Each party must update its corporate disclosure statement to reflect any change in the information therein (i) until the matter before the Panel is decided, and (ii) within 14 days after issuance of a notice of the filing of any subsequent motion to transfer or remand, order to show cause, or motion to vacate a conditional transfer order or a conditional remand order in that docket.

[Former Rule 2 adopted May 3, 1993, effective July 1, 1993. Renumbered Rule 5.1 and amended September 1, 1998, effective November 2, 1998. Former Rule 5.3 redesignated and amended September 8, 2010, effective October 4, 2010. Amended effective July 6, 2011.]

RULE 5.1.3 FILING OF PAPERS: COMPUTER GENERATED DISK REQUIRED [DELETED SEPT. 8, 2010, EFF. OCT. 4, 2010]

[Added May 22, 2000, effective June 1, 2000. And amended July 30, 2007, effective July 30, 2007; renumbered Rule 5.1.3 and amended March 25, 2010, effective April 1, 2010. Deleted September 8, 2010, effective October 4, 2010.]

RULE 6.1 MOTION PRACTICE

(a) Application. This Rule governs all motions requesting Panel action generally. More specific provisions may apply to motions to transfer (Rule 6.2), miscellaneous motions (Rule 6.3), conditional transfer orders (Rule 7.1), show cause orders (Rule 8.1), conditional remand orders (Rule 10.2) and motions to remand (Rule 10.3).

(b) Form of Motions. All motions shall briefly describe the action or relief sought and shall include:

(i) a brief which concisely states the background of the litigation and movant's factual and legal contentions;

(ii) a numbered schedule providing

(A) the complete name of each action involved, listing the full name of each party included as such on the district court's docket sheet, not shortened by the use of references such as "et al." or "etc.";

(B) the district court and division where each action is pending;

(C) the civil action number of each action; and

(D) the name of the judge assigned each action, if known;

(iii) a proof of service providing

(A) a service list listing the full name of each party included on the district court's docket sheet and the complaint, including opt-in plaintiffs not listed on the docket sheet; and

(B) in actions where there are 25 or more plaintiffs listed on the docket sheet, list the first named plaintiff with the reference "et al." if all the plaintiffs are represented by the same attorney(s);

(iv) a copy of all complaints and docket sheets for all actions listed on the Schedule; and

(v) exhibits, if any, identified by number or letter and a descriptive title.

(c) Responses and Joinders. Any other party may file a response within 21 days after filing of a motion. Failure to respond to a motion shall be treated as that party's acquiescence to it. A joinder in a motion shall not add any action to that motion.

(d) Replies. The movant may file a reply within 7 days after the lapse of the time period for filing a response. Where a movant is replying to more than one response in opposition, the movant may file a consolidated reply with a limit of 20 pages.

(e) Alteration of Time Periods. The Clerk of the Panel has the discretion to shorten or enlarge the time periods set forth in this Rule as necessary.

(f) Notification of Developments. Counsel shall promptly notify the Clerk of the Panel of any development that would partially or completely moot any Panel matter.

[Former Rule 10 adopted May 3, 1993, effective July 1, 1993. Renumbered Rule 7.2 and amended September 1, 1998, effective November 2, 1998. Amended April 2, 2001, effective April 2, 2001; March 26, 2009, December 1, 2009. Former Rule 7.2 redesignated in part and amended September 8, 2010, effective October 4, 2010.]

RULE 6.2 MOTIONS TO TRANSFER FOR COORDINATED OR CONSOLIDATED PRETRIAL PROCEEDINGS

(a) Initiation of Transfer. A party to an action may initiate proceedings to transfer under Section 1407 by filing a motion in accordance with these Rules. A copy of the motion shall be filed in each district court where the motion affects a pending action.

(b) Notice of Filing of Motion to Transfer. Upon receipt of a motion, the Clerk of the Panel shall issue a "Notice of Filing of Motion to Transfer" to the service list recipients. The Notice shall contain the following: the filing date of the motion, caption, MDL docket number, briefing schedule and pertinent Panel policies. After a motion is filed, the Clerk of the Panel shall consider any other pleading to be a response unless the pleading adds an action. The Clerk of the Panel may designate such a pleading as a motion, and distribute a briefing schedule applicable to all or some of the parties, as appropriate.

(c) Notice of Appearance. Within 14 days of issuance of a "Notice of the Filing of a Motion to Transfer," each party or designated attorney shall file a Notice of Appearance in accordance with Rule 4.1(c).

(d) Notice of Potential Tag-along Actions. Any party or counsel in a new group of actions under consideration for transfer under Section 1407 shall promptly notify the Clerk of the Panel of any potential tag-along actions in which that party is also named or in which that counsel appears.

(e) Interested Party Responses. Any party or counsel in one or more potential tag-along actions as well as amicus curiae may file a response to a pending motion to transfer. Such a pleading shall be deemed an Interested Party Response.

(f) Amendment to a Motion. Before amending a motion to transfer, a party shall first contact the Clerk of the Panel to ascertain whether such amendment is feasible and permissible considering the Panel's hearing schedule. Any such amendment shall be entitled "Amendment to Motion for Transfer," and shall clearly and specifically identify and describe the nature of the amendment.

(i) Where the amended motion includes new civil actions, the amending party shall file a "Schedule of Additional Actions" and a revised Proof of Service.

(ii) The Proof of Service shall state (A) that all new counsel have been served with a copy of the amendment and all previously-filed motion papers, and (B) that all counsel previously served with the original motion have been served with a copy of the amendment.

(iii) The Clerk of the Panel may designate the amendment with a different denomination (*e.g.*, a notice of potential tag-along action(s)) and treatment.

(h) Oral Argument*. The Panel shall schedule oral arguments as needed and as set forth in Rule 11.1.

[Former Rule 10 adopted May 3, 1993, effective July 1, 1993. Renumbered Rule 7.2 and amended September 1, 1998, effective November 2, 1998. Amended April 2, 2001, effective April 2, 2001; March 26, 2009, December 1, 2009. Former Rule 15 adopted May 3, 1993, effective July 1, 1993. Renumbered Rule 6.2 and amended September 1, 1998, effective November 2, 1998. Former Rule 7.2 redesignated in part and amended September 8, 2010, effective October 4, 2010. Technical revisions effective July 6, 2011.]

* So in original.

RULE 6.3 MOTIONS FOR MISCELLANEOUS RELIEF

(a) Definition. Motions for miscellaneous relief include, but are not limited to, requests for extensions of time, exemption from ECF requirements, page limit extensions, or expedited consideration of any motion.

(b) Panel Action. The Panel, through the Clerk, may act upon any motion for miscellaneous relief, at any time, without waiting for a response. A motion for extension of time to file a pleading or perform an act under these Rules must state specifically the revised date sought and must be filed before the deadline for filing the pleading or performing the act. Any party aggrieved by the Clerk of the Panel's action may file objections for consideration. Absent exceptional circumstances, the Panel will not grant any extensions of time to file a notice of opposition to either a conditional transfer order or a conditional remand order.

[Former Rule 15 adopted May 3, 1993, effective July 1, 1993. Renumbered Rule 6.2 and amended September 1, 1998, effective November 2, 1998. Former Rule 6.2 redesignated and amended September 8, 2010, effective October 4, 2010.]

RULE 7.1 CONDITIONAL TRANSFER ORDERS (CTO) FOR TAG–ALONG ACTIONS

(a) Notice of Potential Tag-along Actions. Any party or counsel in actions previously transferred under Section 1407 shall promptly notify the Clerk of the Panel of any potential tag-along actions in which that party is also named or in which that counsel appears. The Panel has several options: (i) filing a CTO under Rule 7.1, (ii) filing a show cause order under Rule 8.1, or (iii) declining to act (Rule 7.1(b)(i)).

(b) Initiation of CTO. Upon learning of the pendency of a potential tag-along action, the Clerk of the Panel may enter a conditional order transferring that action to the previously designated transferee district court for the reasons expressed in the Panel's previous opinions and orders. The Clerk of the Panel shall serve this order on each party to the litigation but shall not send the order to the clerk of the transferee district court until 7 days after its entry.

(i)* If the Clerk of the Panel determines that a potential tag-along action is not appropriate for inclusion in an MDL proceeding and does not enter a CTO, an involved party may move for its transfer pursuant to Rule 6.1.

(c) Notice of Opposition to CTO. Any party opposing the transfer shall file a notice of opposition with the Clerk of the Panel within the 7-day period. In such event, the Clerk of the Panel shall not transmit the transfer order to the clerk of the transferee district court, but shall notify the parties of the briefing schedule.

(d) Failure to Respond. Failure to respond to a CTO shall be treated as that party's acquiescence to it.

(e) Notice of Appearance. Within 14 days after the issuance of a "Notice of Filed Opposition" to a CTO, each opposing party or designated attorney shall file a Notice of Appearance in accordance with Rule 4.1(c).

(f) Motion to Vacate CTO. Within 14 days of the filing of its notice of opposition, the party opposing transfer shall file a motion to vacate the CTO and brief in support thereof. The Clerk of the Panel shall set the motion for the next appropriate hearing session. Failure to file and serve a motion and brief shall be treated as withdrawal of the opposition and the Clerk of the Panel shall forthwith transmit the order to the clerk of the transferee district court.

(g) Notification of Developments. Parties to an action subject to a CTO shall notify the Clerk of the Panel if that action is no longer pending in its transferor district court.

(h) Effective Date of CTO. CTOs are effective when filed with the clerk of the transferee district court.

[Former Rule 12 adopted May 3, 1993, effective July 1, 1993. Renumbered Rule 7.4 and amended September 1, 1998, effective November 2, 1998. Amended April 2, 2001, effective April 2, 2001; March 26, 2009, December 1, 2009. Former Rule 7.4 redesignated and amended September 8, 2010, effective October 4, 2010. Technical revisions effective July 6, 2011.]

* So in original. No subdivision (ii) promulgated.

RULE 7.2 MISCELLANEOUS PROVISIONS CONCERNING TAG–ALONG ACTIONS

(a) Potential Tag-alongs in Transferee Court. Potential tag-along actions filed in the transferee district do not require Panel action. A party should request assignment of such actions to the Section 1407 transferee judge in accordance with applicable local rules.

(b) Failure to Serve. Failure to serve one or more of the defendants in a potential tag-along action with the complaint and summons as required by Rule 4 of the Federal Rules of Civil Procedure does not preclude transfer of such action under Section 1407. Such failure, however, may constitute grounds for denying the proposed transfer where prejudice can be shown. The failure of the Clerk of the Panel to serve a CTO on all plaintiffs or defendants or their counsel may constitute grounds for the Clerk to reinstate the CTO or for the aggrieved party to seek § 1407(c) remand.

[Former Rule 13 adopted May 3, 1993, effective July 1, 1993. Renumbered Rule 7.5 and amended September 1, 1998, effective November 2, 1998. Amended April 2, 2001, effective April 2, 2001. Former Rule 7.5 redesignated and amended September 8, 2010, effective October 4, 2010. Amended effective July 6, 2011.]

RULE 8.1 SHOW CAUSE ORDERS

(a) Entry of Show Cause Order. When transfer of multidistrict litigation is being considered on the initiative of the Panel pursuant to 28 U.S.C. § 1407(c)(i), the Clerk of the Panel may enter an order directing the parties to show cause why a certain civil action or actions should not be transferred for coordinated or consolidated pretrial proceedings. Any party shall also promptly notify the Clerk of the Panel whenever they learn of any other federal district court actions which are similar to those which the show cause order encompasses.

(b) Notice of Appearance. Within 14 days of the issuance of an order to show cause, each party or designated attorney shall file a Notice of Appearance in accordance with Rule 4.1(c).

(c) Responses. Unless otherwise provided by order, any party may file a response within 21 days of the filing of the show cause order. Failure to respond to a show cause order shall be treated as that party's acquiescence to the Panel action.

(d) Replies. Within 7 days after the lapse of the time period for filing a response, any party may file a reply.

(e) Notification of Developments. Counsel shall promptly notify the Clerk of the Panel of any development that would partially or completely moot any matter subject to a show cause order.

[Former Rule 7.3 adopted May 3, 1993, effective July 1, 1993. Renumbered Rule 7.3 and amended September 1, 1998, effective November 2, 1998; March 26, 2009, effective December 1, 2009. Former Rule 7.3 redesignated and amended September 8, 2010, effective October 4, 2010.]

RULE 9.1 TRANSFER OF FILES; NOTIFICATION REQUIREMENTS

(a) Notice to Transferee Court Clerk. The Clerk of the Panel, via a notice of electronic filing, will notify the clerk of the transferee district whenever a Panel transfer order should be filed in the transferee district court. Upon receipt of an electronically certified copy of a Panel transfer order from the clerk of the transferee district, the clerk of the transferor district shall transmit the record of each transferred action to the transferee district and then, unless Rule 9.1(b) applies, close the transferred action in the transferor district.

(b) Retention of Claims. If the transfer order provides for the separation and simultaneous remand of any claim, cross-claim, counterclaim, or third-party claim, the clerk of the transferor district shall retain jurisdiction over any such claim and shall not close the action.

(c) Notice to Clerk of Panel. The clerk of the transferee district shall promptly provide the Clerk of the Panel with the civil action numbers assigned to all transferred actions and the identity of liaison counsel, if or when designated. The clerk of the transferee district shall also promptly notify the Clerk of the Panel of any dispositive ruling that terminates a transferred action.

[Former Rule 19 adopted May 3, 1993, effective July 1, 1993. Renumbered Rule 1.6 and amended September 1, 1998, effective November 2, 1998. Former Rule 1.6 redesignated in part and amended September 8, 2010, effective October 4, 2010.]

RULE 10.1 TERMINATION AND REMAND

(a) Termination. Where the transferee district court terminates an action by valid order, including but not limited to summary judgment, judgment of dismissal and judgment upon stipulation, the transferee district court clerk shall transmit a copy of that order to the Clerk of the Panel. The terminated action shall not be remanded to the transferor court and the transferee court shall retain the original files and records unless the transferee judge or the Panel directs otherwise.

(b) Initiation of Remand. Typically, the transferee judge recommends remand of an action, or a part of it, to the transferor court at any time by filing a suggestion of remand with the Panel. However, the Panel may remand an action or any separable claim, cross-claim, counterclaim or third-party claim within it, upon

(i) the transferee court's suggestion of remand,

(ii) the Panel's own initiative by entry of an order to show cause, a conditional remand order or other appropriate order, or

(iii) motion of any party.

[Former Rule 14 adopted May 3, 1993, effective July 1, 1993. Renumbered Rule 7.6 and amended September 1, 1998, effective November 2, 1998. Amended April 2, 2001, effective April 2, 2001; March 26, 2009, effective December 1, 2009. Former Rule 7.6 redesignated in part and amended September 8, 2010, effective October 4, 2010.]

RULE 10.2 CONDITIONAL REMAND ORDERS (CRO)

(a) Entering a CRO. Upon the suggestion of the transferee judge or the Panel's own initiative, the Clerk of the Panel shall enter a conditional order remanding the action or actions to the transferor district court. The Clerk of the Panel shall serve this order on each party to the litigation but shall not send the order to the clerk of the transferee district court for 7 days from the entry thereof.

(i)* The Panel may, on its own initiative, also enter an order that the parties show cause why a matter should not be remanded. Rule 8.1 applies to responses and replies with respect to such a show cause order.

(b) Notice of Opposition. Any party opposing the CRO shall file a notice of opposition with the Clerk of the Panel within the 7–day period. In such event, the Clerk of the Panel shall not transmit the remand order to the clerk of the transferee district court and shall notify the parties of the briefing schedule.

(c) Failure to Respond. Failure to respond to a CRO shall be treated as that party's acquiescence to it.

(d) Notice of Appearance. Within 14 days after the issuance of a "Notice of Filed Opposition" to a CRO, each opposing party or designated attorney shall file a Notice of Appearance in accordance with Rule 4.1(c).

(e) Motion to Vacate CRO. Within 14 days of the filing of its notice of opposition, the party opposing remand shall file a motion to vacate the CRO and brief in support thereof. The Clerk of the Panel shall set the motion for the next appropriate Panel hearing session. Failure to file and serve a motion and brief shall be treated as a withdrawal of the opposition and the Clerk of the Panel shall forthwith transmit the order to the clerk of the transferee district court.

(f) Effective Date of CRO. CROs are not effective until filed with the clerk of the transferee district court.

[Former Rule 14 adopted May 3, 1993, effective July 1, 1993. Renumbered Rule 7.6 and amended September 1, 1998, effective November 2, 1998. Amended April 2, 2001, effective April 2, 2001; March 26, 2009, effective December 1, 2009. Former Rule 7.6 redesignated in part and amended September 8, 2010, effective October 4, 2010. Technical revisions effective July 6, 2011.]

* So in original. No subdivision (ii) promulgated.

RULE 10.3 MOTION TO REMAND

(a) Requirements of the Motion. If the Clerk of the Panel does not enter a CRO, a party may file a motion to remand to the transferor court pursuant to these Rules. Because the Panel is reluctant to order a remand absent the suggestion of the transferee judge, the motion must include:

(i) An affidavit reciting whether the movant has requested a suggestion of remand and the judge's response, whether the parties have completed common discovery and other pretrial proceedings, and whether the parties have complied with all transferee court orders.

(ii) A copy of the transferee district court's final pretrial order, if entered.

(b) Filing Copy of Motion. Counsel shall file a copy of the motion to remand in the affected transferee district court.

(c) Notice of Appearance. Within 14 days of the issuance of a "Notice of Filing" of a motion to remand, each party or designated attorney shall file a Notice of Appearance in accordance with Rule 4.1(c).

[Former Rule 14 adopted May 3, 1993, effective July 1, 1993. Renumbered Rule 7.6 and amended September 1, 1998, effective November 2, 1998. Amended April 2, 2001, effective April 2, 2001; March 26, 2009, effective December 1, 2009. Former Rule 7.6 redesignated in part and amended September 8, 2010, effective October 4, 2010. Technical revisions effective July 6, 2011.]

RULE 10.4 TRANSFER OF FILES ON REMAND

(a) Designating the Record. Upon receipt of an order to remand from the Clerk of the Panel, the parties shall furnish forthwith to the transferee district clerk a stipulation or designation of the contents of the record or part thereof to be remanded.

(b) Transfer of Files. Upon receipt of an order to remand from the Clerk of the Panel, the transferee district shall transmit to the clerk of the transferor district the following concerning each remanded action:

(i) a copy of the individual docket sheet for each action remanded;

(ii) a copy of the master docket sheet, if applicable;

(iii) the entire file for each action remanded, as originally received from the transferor district and augmented as set out in this Rule;

(iv) a copy of the final pretrial order, if applicable; and

(v) a "record on remand" as designated by the parties in accordance with 10.4(a).

[Former Rule 19 adopted May 3, 1993, effective July 1, 1993. Renumbered Rule 1.6 and amended September 1, 1998, effective November 2, 1998. Former Rule 1.6 redesignated in part and amended September 8, 2010, effective October 4, 2010.]

RULE 11.1 HEARING SESSIONS AND ORAL ARGUMENT

(a) Schedule. The Panel shall schedule sessions for oral argument and consideration of other matters as desirable or necessary. The Chair shall determine the time, place and agenda for each hearing session. The Clerk of the Panel shall give appropriate notice to counsel for all parties. The Panel may continue its consideration of any scheduled matters.

(b) Oral Argument Statement. Any party affected by a motion may file a separate statement setting forth reasons why oral argument should, or need not, be heard. Such statements shall be captioned "Reasons Why Oral Argument Should [Need Not] Be Heard" and shall be limited to 2 pages.

(i)* The parties affected by a motion to transfer may agree to waive oral argument. The Panel will take this into consideration in determining the need for oral argument.

(c) Hearing Session. The Panel shall not consider transfer or remand of any action pending in a federal district court when any party timely opposes such transfer or remand without first holding a hearing session for the presentation of oral argument. The Panel may dispense with oral argument if it determines that:

(i) the dispositive issue(s) have been authoritatively decided; or

(ii) the facts and legal arguments are adequately presented and oral argument would not significantly aid the decisional process.

Unless otherwise ordered, the Panel shall consider all other matters, such as a motion for reconsideration, upon the basis of the pleadings.

(d) Notification of Oral Argument. The Panel shall promptly notify counsel of those matters in which oral argument is scheduled, as well as those matters that the Panel will consider on the pleadings. The Clerk of the Panel shall require counsel to file and serve notice of their intent to either make or waive oral argument. Failure to do so shall be deemed a waiver of oral argument. If counsel does not attend oral argument, the matter shall not be rescheduled and that party's position shall be treated as submitted for decision on the basis of the pleadings filed.

(i) Absent Panel approval and for good cause shown, only those parties to actions who have filed a motion or written response to a motion or order shall be permitted to present oral argument.

(ii) The Panel will not receive oral testimony except upon notice, motion and an order expressly providing for it.

(e) Duty to Confer. Counsel in an action set for oral argument shall confer separately prior to that argument for the purpose of organizing their arguments and selecting representatives to present all views without duplication. Oral argument is a means for counsel to emphasize the key points of their arguments, and to update the Panel on any events since the conclusion of briefing.

(f) Time Limit for Oral Argument. Barring exceptional circumstances, the Panel shall allot a maximum of 20 minutes for oral argument in each matter. The time shall be divided among those with varying viewpoints. Counsel for the moving party or parties shall generally be heard first.

[Former Rule 16 adopted May 3, 1998, effective July 1, 1993. Renumbered Rule 16.1 and amended September 1, 1998, effective November 2, 1998. Amended April 2, 2001, effective April 2, 2001. Former Rule 16.1 redesignated and amended September 8, 2010, effective October 4, 2010.]

* So in original. No subdivision (ii) promulgated.

RULES 12 TO 15. [RESERVED]

II. RULES FOR MULTICIRCUIT PETITIONS FOR REVIEW UNDER 28 U.S.C. § 2112(a)(3)

RULE 25.1 DEFINITIONS

The Panel promulgates these Rules pursuant to its authority under 28 U.S.C. § 2112(a)(3) to provide a means for the random selection of one circuit court of appeals to hear consolidated petitions for review of agency decisions.

An "Agency" means an agency, board, commission or officer of the United States government, that has received two or more petitions for review in a circuit court of appeals to enjoin, set aside, suspend, modify or otherwise review or enforce an action.

[Former Rule 20 adopted May 3, 1993, effective July 1, 1993. Renumbered Rule 25.1 and amended September 1, 1998, effective November 2, 1998. Amended September 8, 2010, effective October 4, 2010.]

RULE 25.2 FILING OF NOTICES

(a) Submitting Notice. An affected agency shall submit a notice of multicircuit petitions for review pursuant to 28 U.S.C. § 2112(a)(3) to the Clerk of the Panel by electronic means in the manner these Rules require and in accordance with the Panel's Administrative Policies and Procedures for Electronic Case Filing, except that the portion of Rule 3.2(d) requiring a courtesy copy is suspended in its entirety.

(b) Accompaniments to Notices. All notices of multicircuit petitions for review shall include:

(i) a copy of each involved petition for review as the petition for review is defined in 28 U.S.C. § 2112(a)(2);

(ii) a schedule giving

(A) the date of the relevant agency order;

(B) the case name of each petition for review involved;

(C) the circuit court of appeals in which each petition for review is pending;

(D) the appellate docket number of each petition for review;

(E) the date of filing by the court of appeals of each petition for review; and

(F) the date of receipt by the agency of each petition for review; and

(iii) proof of service (*see* Rule 25.3).

(c) Scope of Notice. All notices of multicircuit petitions for review shall embrace exclusively petitions for review filed in the courts of appeals within 10 days after issuance of an agency order and received by the affected agency from the petitioners within that 10–day period.

(d) Filing at the Panel. The Clerk of the Panel shall file the notice of multicircuit petitions for review and endorse thereon the date of filing.

(e) Filing With Each Circuit Clerk. The affected agency shall file copies of notices of multicircuit petitions for review with the clerk of each circuit court of appeals in which a petition for review is pending.

[Former Rule 21 adopted May 3, 1993, effective July 1, 1993. Renumbered Rule 25.2 and amended September 1, 1998, effective November 2, 1998. Amended September 8, 2010, effective October 4, 2010. Technical revisions effective July 6, 2011.]

RULE 25.3 SERVICE OF NOTICES

(a) Proof of Service. Notices of multicircuit petitions for review shall include proof of service on all other parties in the petitions for review included in the notice. Rule 25 of the Federal Rules of Appellate Procedure governs service and proof of service. The proof of service shall state the name, address and email address of each person served and shall indicate the party represented by each and the manner in which service was accomplished on each party. If a party is not represented by counsel, the proof of service shall indicate the name of the party and his or her last known address. The affected party shall submit proof of service for filing with the Clerk of the Panel and shall send copies thereof to each person included within the proof of service.

(b) Service on Clerk of Circuit. The proof of service pertaining to notices of multicircuit petitions for review shall certify the affected party has mailed or delivered copies of the notices to the clerk of each circuit court of appeals in which a petition for review is pending that is included in the notice. The Clerk shall file the notice with the circuit court.

[Former Rule 22 adopted May 3, 1993, effective July 1, 1993. Renumbered Rule 25.3 September 1, 1998, effective November 2, 1998. Amended September 8, 2010, effective October 4, 2010.]

RULE 25.4 FORM OF NOTICES; PLACE OF FILING

(a) Unless otherwise provided here, Rule 3.2 governs the form of a notice of multicircuit petitions for review. Each notice shall bear the heading "Notice to the United States Judicial Panel on Multidistrict Litigation of Multicircuit Petitions for Review," followed by a brief caption identifying the involved agency, the relevant agency order, and the date of the order.

(b) Rule 3.2(b) and (c) govern the manner of filing a notice of multicircuit petitions for review.

[Former Rule 23 adopted May 3, 1993, effective July 1, 1993. Renumbered Rule 25.4 and amended September 1, 1998, effective November 2, 1998. Amended September 8, 2010, effective October 4, 2010.]

RULE 25.5 RANDOM SELECTION

(a) Selection Process. Upon filing a notice of multicircuit petitions for review, the Clerk of the Panel shall randomly select a circuit court of appeals from a drum containing an entry for each circuit wherein a constituent petition for review is pending. Multiple petitions for review pending in a single circuit shall be allotted only a single entry in the drum. A designated deputy other than the random selector shall witness the random selection. Thereafter, an order on behalf of the Panel shall be issued, signed by the random selector and the witness,

(i) consolidating the petitions for review in the court of appeals for the circuit that was randomly selected; and

(ii) designating that circuit as the one in which the record is to be filed pursuant to Rules 16 and 17 of the Federal Rules of Appellate Procedure.

(b) Effective Date. A consolidation of petitions for review shall be effective when the Clerk of the Panel enters the consolidation order.

[Former Rule 24 adopted May 3, 1993, effective July 1, 1993. Renumbered Rule 17.1 September 1, 1998, effective November 2, 1998. Former Rule 17.1 redesignated and amended September 8, 2010, effective October 4, 2010.]

RULE 25.6 SERVICE OF PANEL CONSOLIDATION ORDER

(a) The Clerk of the Panel shall serve the Panel's consolidation order on the affected agency through the individual or individuals, as identified in Rule 25.2(a), who submitted the notice of multicircuit petitions for review on behalf of the agency.

(b) That individual or individuals, or anyone else designated by the agency, shall promptly serve the Panel's consolidation order on all other parties in all petitions for review included in the Panel's consolidation order, and shall promptly submit a proof of that service to the Clerk of the Panel. Rule 25.3 governs service.

(c) The Clerk of the Panel shall serve the Panel's consolidation order on the clerks of all circuit courts of appeals that were among the candidates for the Panel's random selection.

[Former Rule 25 adopted May 3, 1993, effective July 1, 1993. Renumbered Rule 25.5 and amended September 1, 1998, effective November 2, 1998. Former Rule 25.5 redesignated and amended September 8, 2010, effective October 4, 2010.]

III. CONVERSION TABLE

New to Old:

New Rule	Previous Rule
1.1	1.1
2.1	1.2, 1.3, 1.4, 1.5
3.1	5.1
3.2	5.1.1, 5.1.2, 7.1
3.3	5.1.1, 5.1.2, 7.1
4.1	5.2
5.1	5.3
6.1	7.2
6.2	7.2
6.3	6.2
7.1	7.4
7.2	7.5
8.1	7.3
9.1	1.6
10.1	7.6
10.2	7.6
10.3	7.6
10.4	1.6
11.1	16.1
25.1	25.1
25.2	25.1, 25.2
25.3	25.3
25.4	25.1, 25.4
25.5	17.1
25.6	25.5

Old to New:

Previous Rule	New Rule
1.1	1.1
1.2	2.1
1.3	2.1
1.4	2.1
1.5	2.1
1.6	10.4
5.1	3.1
5.1.1	3.2, 3.3
5.1.2	3.2, 3.3
5.1.3	-
5.2	4.1
5.3	5.1
6.2	6.3
7.1	3.2, 3.3
7.2	6.1
7.3	8.1
7.4	7.1
7.5	7.2
7.6	10.1
16.1	11.1
17.1	25.5
25.1	25.1, 25.2, 25.4
25.2	25.2
25.3	25.3
25.4	25.4
25.5	25.6

[October 2010.]

ELECTRONIC CASE FILING ADMINISTRATIVE POLICIES AND PROCEDURES

1. DEFINITIONS.

1.1 "ELECTRONIC FILING SYSTEM" (ECF) refers to the United States Judicial Panel on Multidistrict Litigation's (the Panel's) automated system that receives and stores documents filed in electronic form. The program is part of the CM/ECF (Case Management/Electronic Case Files) software which was developed for the Federal Judiciary by the Administrative Office of the United States Courts.

1.2 "CLERK OF THE PANEL" means the official appointed by the Panel to act as Clerk of the Panel and shall include those deputized by the Clerk of the Panel to perform or assist in the performance of the duties of the Clerk of the Panel.

1.3 "FILING USER" is an individual who has a Panel-issued login and password to file documents electronically. In accordance with Rule 1.4 of the Rules of Procedure of the United States Judicial Panel on Multidistrict Litigation (the Panel Rules), every member in good standing of the Bar of any district court of the United States is entitled to practice before the Judicial Panel on Multidistrict Litigation.

1.4 "NOTICE OF ELECTRONIC FILING" (NEF) is a notice automatically generated by the Electronic Filing System at the time a document is filed with the system, setting forth the time of filing, the date the document is entered on the docket, the name of the party and attorney filing the document, the type of document, the text of the docket entry, the name of the party and/or attorney receiving the notice, and an electronic link (hyperlink) to the filed document, which allows recipients to retrieve the document automatically. A document shall not be considered filed for the purposes of the Panel's Rules until the filing party receives a system generated Notice of Electronic Filing with a hyperlink to the electronically filed document.

1.5 "PACER" (Public Access to Court Electronic Records) is an automated system that allows an individual to view, print and download Panel docket information over the Internet.

1.6 "PDF" (Portable Document Format). A document file created with a word processor, or a paper document which has been scanned, must be converted to portable document format to be filed electronically with the Panel. Converted files contain the extension ".pdf".

1.7 "TECHNICAL FAILURE" is defined as a failure of Panel owned/leased hardware, software, and/or telecommunications facility which results in the inability of a Filing User to submit a filing electronically. Technical failure does not include malfunctioning of a Filing User's equipment.

2. SCOPE OF ELECTRONIC FILING.

(a) All multidistrict litigation matters (MDLs) brought before the Panel under 28 U.S.C. § 1407 shall be assigned to the Electronic Filing System. Effective October 1, 2010, all MDLs, proceedings, motions, memoranda of law and other pleadings or documents filed with the Panel in new and existing dockets must be filed using CM/ECF unless otherwise specified herein.

(b) The filing of all MDL papers shall be accomplished electronically under procedures outlined in the Panel's CM/ECF User Manual.

(c) A party proceeding pro se shall not file electronically, unless otherwise permitted by the Panel. Pro se filers shall file paper originals of all documents. The clerk's office will scan these original documents into the JPML's electronic system, unless otherwise sealed.

3. ELIGIBILITY, REGISTRATION, PASSWORDS.

(a) Any attorney admitted to the Bar of any United States district court is eligible to practice before the Panel. Unless otherwise exempt as set forth herein, to become a Filing User, an attorney must register as a Filing User by completing the prescribed registration form and submitting it to the Clerk of the Panel.

(b) Registration as a Filing User constitutes consent to electronic service of all documents filed with or issued by the Panel in accordance with the Panel Rules.

(c) By submitting the online registration form, the Filing Users certify that they have read and are familiar with the Panel Rules and these administrative policies and procedures governing electronic filing and the method of training in the System used prior to becoming a Filing User. Filing users must also have a PACER account. An individual may register more than one Internet email address. The clerk's office will email the login and password to the attorney.

(d) Once the registration is processed by the clerk, the Filing User shall protect the security of the User password and immediately notify the clerk if the Filing User learns that the password has been compromised. Filing Users may be subject to sanctions for failure to comply with this provision. After registering, attorneys may change their passwords. If an attorney comes to believe that the security of an existing password has been compromised and that a threat to the System exists, the attorney must change his or her password immediately.

(e) Exemptions from mandatory electronic filing may be granted upon submission of a written request to the clerk. The written request shall include a supporting affidavit showing a substantial undue hardship. Final authority to grant such request is vested in the Clerk of the Panel or his/her designee.

(f)(1) Each attorney is responsible for keeping his/her contact information up to date. If an attorney is leaving a law firm and is the attorney of record on an existing case and representation in the case will remain with the law firm, withdrawal and substitution of counsel must be made prior to the attorney's termination in the law firm, for the following reason:

The attorney leaving the firm has an email address with the law firm he or she is leaving on record with the Panel. This email address may be disabled by the law firm as soon as the attorney terminates his/her employment. The electronic notices in CM/ECF will continue to go to the terminated attorney's email address at the former firm. If the email address is disabled at the law firm, the attorney will not receive the electronic notice. If a withdrawal/substitution of counsel has not been filed prior to the attorney leaving the firm, the law firm should not disable the email account of the attorney leaving the firm until another attorney in the firm enters his/her appearance. The law firm should designate someone in the firm to check this email account for CM/ECF notices until substitution of counsel has been filed with the Panel.

(2) If the attorney leaving the firm is taking active cases from the firm, the attorney needs to change his/her email address as soon as possible, otherwise the attorney will not receive electronic notices from CM/ECF. The email will continue to be sent to the former law firm's email address still on record. Procedures for changing an email address may be found in the Panel's CM/ECF User Manual.

4. ELECTRONIC FILING AND SERVICE OF DOCUMENTS.

(a) Electronic transmission of a document to the Electronic Filing System in accordance with these procedures, together with the transmission of a (System) Notice of Electronic Filing from the Panel with a hyperlink to the electronically filed document, constitutes filing of the document for all purposes of the Panel Rules of Procedure.

(b) Emailing a document to the clerk's office does not constitute filing the document. A document shall not be considered filed until the System generates a Notice of Electronic Filing (NEF) with a hyperlink to the electronically filed document.

(c) Before filing a scanned document with the court, a Filing User must verify its legibility.

(d) When a document has been filed electronically, the official record of that document is the electronic recording as stored by the Panel and the filing party is bound by the document as filed. A document filed electronically is deemed filed on the date and time stated on the Notice of Electronic Filing (NEF) from the Panel.

(e) Filing a document electronically does not alter the filing deadline for that document. Filing must be completed before midnight, **EASTERN TIME**, in order to be considered timely filed that day. However, if time of day is of the essence, the Clerk of the Panel may order a document filed by a certain time.

(f) Upon the filing of a document, a docket entry will be created using the information provided by the Filing User. The clerk will, where necessary and appropriate, modify the docket entry description to comply with quality control standards. In the event a Filing User electronically files a document in the wrong MDL or associated civil action, or the incorrect PDF document is attached, the Clerk of the Panel, or his/her designee, shall be authorized to strike the document from the record. A notice of the action striking a document from the record shall be served on all parties in the case.

(g) By participating in the electronic filing process, the parties consent to the electronic service of all documents, and shall make available electronic mail addresses for service. Upon the filing of a document by a Filing User, a Notice of Electronic Filing (NEF), with a hyperlink to the electronic document and an email message will be automatically generated by the electronic filing system, and sent via electronic mail to the email addresses of all parties who have registered in the MDL. In addition to receiving email notifications of filing activity, the Filing User is strongly encouraged to sign on to the electronic filing system at regular intervals to check the docket in his/her MDL and/or civil action.

(h) If the filing of an electronically submitted document requires leave of the Panel, such as a request to file out-of-time, the attorney shall attach the proposed document as an attachment to the motion requesting leave to file. If the Clerk of the Panel grants the motion, the document will be electronically filed without further action by the Filing User.

(i) A certificate of service must be included with all documents filed electronically. Such certificate shall indicate that service was accomplished pursuant to the Panel's electronic filing procedures. Service by electronic mail shall constitute service pursuant to Panel Rule 5.2.

A party who is not a registered CM/ECF participant with any United States federal court is entitled to a paper copy of any electronically filed pleading, document, or order pursuant to Panel Rule 5.1.1.(b). The filing party must therefore provide the non-registered attorney or party, including a terminated party or attorney, if appropriate, with the pleading, document, or order pursuant to Panel Rule 5.2. Under the Rule, they can be served with a paper copy of the electronically filed document, or they can consent in writing to service by any other method, including other forms of electronic service such as fax or direct email.

The following is a suggested certificate of service for electronic filing:

CERTIFICATE OF SERVICE

On [Date], I electronically filed this document through the CM/ECF system, which will send a notice of electronic filing to: [Attorney Name (attach list if necessary)]; and I [mailed] [hand delivered] [faxed] this document and the notice of electronic filing to: [Attorney/Party Name], [Address], [Parties Represented], [Civil Action(s)] (attach list if necessary).

/s/ [typed name of attorney]
Attorney's name
Law Firm Name (if applicable)
Address
Phone Number
Fax Number
Attorney's Email address
Attorney for:

5. ENTRY OF PANEL DOCUMENTS.

(a) A document entered or issued by the Panel will be filed in accordance with these procedures and such filing shall constitute entry on the docket kept by the Clerk.

(b) All signed orders will be electronically filed or entered. An order containing the electronic signature of a Panel Judge or the Clerk of the Panel shall have the same force and effect as if the Panel Judge or Clerk of the Panel had affixed a signature to a paper copy of the order and the order had been entered on the docket in a conventional manner.

(c) Orders may also be issued as "text-only" entries on the docket, without an attached document. Such orders are official and binding.

6. NOTICE OF PANEL ORDERS AND NOTICES.

Immediately upon the entry of an order or notice by the Panel, the clerk will transmit to Filing Users in affected cases in the MDL, in electronic form, a Notice of Electronic Filing (NEF), with a hyperlink to the electronic document. Electronic transmission of the NEF, along with a hyperlink to the electronic document, constitutes the notice required by Panel Rule 5.2. The clerk must give notice in paper form to a pro se party or an attorney who is not a Filing User to the extent notice is required.

7. ATTACHMENTS AND EXHIBITS.

Documents referenced as exhibits or attachments shall be filed in accordance with these administrative policies and procedures and the Panel's CM/ECF User Manual, unless otherwise ordered by the Panel. A Filing User shall submit as exhibits or attachments only those excerpts of the referenced documents that are directly germane to the matter under consideration by the Panel. Excerpted material must be clearly and prominently identified as such. Filing Users who file excerpts of documents as exhibits or attachments under these procedures do so without prejudice to their right to file timely additional excerpts or the complete document. Responding parties may timely file additional excerpts or the complete document that they believe are directly germane. The Panel may require parties to file additional excerpts or the complete document.

8. **SEALED DOCUMENTS.**

To ensure proper storage of a document, a document subject to a sealing order must be filed with the Panel on paper in a sealed envelope marked "sealed", citing thereon the MDL docket number and title and the associated case caption and case number; or by attaching thereto a paper copy of the Panel's order sealing the document or a copy of the NEF citing the entry of the court's order sealing the document. The clerk may require the document to be accompanied by a disk or CD–ROM containing the document in .pdf format. Only a motion to file a document under seal may be filed electronically, unless prohibited by law. The order of the Panel authorizing the filing of documents under seal may be filed electronically, unless prohibited by law or otherwise directed by the Panel. If a document is filed under seal pursuant to the E–Government Act of 2002, the filing party is nevertheless required to file a redacted copy for the public record along with the unredacted sealed document.

9. **SPECIAL FILING REQUIREMENTS AND EXCEPTIONS.**

9.1 Special Filing Requirements

The documents listed below shall be presented for filing on paper. The clerk may require the document be accompanied by a disk or CD–ROM containing the document in .pdf format:

Sealed

MDL dockets involving Qui Tam Cases (under seal)

9.2 Exceptions

All documents shall be filed electronically unless otherwise ordered by the Panel or specifically exempt herein.

10. **RETENTION REQUIREMENTS.**

(a) A document that is electronically filed and requires an original signature other than that of the Filing User must be maintained in paper form by counsel and/or the firm representing the party on whose behalf the document was filed until one year after all periods for appeals expire. On request of the Panel, said counsel must provide the original document for review.

(b) The clerk's office may choose to discard certain documents brought to the clerk's office for filing in paper form after those documents are scanned and uploaded to the System (to include pro se filings). Therefore, counsel and pro se filers shall provide the Panel with a copy of the original documents with intrinsic value for scanning and maintain the original signature in accordance with 10(a).

11. **SIGNATURES.**

(a) The user login and password required to submit documents to the Electronic Filing System serve as the Filing User signature on all electronic documents filed with the court. They serve as a signature for purposes of the Panel Rules and any other purpose for which a signature is required in connection with proceedings before the Panel.

(b) Each document filed electronically must indicate in the caption that it has been electronically filed. An electronically filed document must include a signature block in compliance with Panel Rule 7.1(e), and must set forth the name, address, telephone number, fax number, and email address. In addition, the name of the Filing User under whose login and password the document is submitted must be preceded by an "/s/" and typed in the space where the signature would otherwise appear. No Filing User or other person may knowingly permit or cause to permit a Filing User password to be used by anyone other than an authorized agent of the Filing User.

(c) A document requiring signatures of more than one party must be filed either by:

(1) electronically filing a scanned document containing all necessary signatures; or

(2) representing the consent of the other parties on the document; or

(3) identifying on the document the party whose signature is required and by the submission of a notice of endorsement by the other parties no later than three (3) business days after filing; or

(4) any other manner approved by the Panel.

(d) A non-filing signatory or party who disputes the authenticity of an electronically filed document with a non-attorney signature, or the authenticity of the signature on that document; or the authenticity of an electronically filed document containing multiple signatures or the authenticity of the signature themselves, must file an objection to the document within fourteen (14) days of service of the document.

(e) Any party challenging the authenticity of an electronically filed document or the attorney's signature on that document must file an objection to the document within fourteen (14) days of service of the document.

(f) If a party wishes to challenge the authenticity of an electronically filed document or signature after the fourteen (14) day period, the party shall file a motion to seek a ruling from the Panel.

12. SERVICE OF DOCUMENTS BY ELECTRONIC MEANS.

12.1 Service

12.1.1 Filing User

Upon the electronic filing of a pleading or other document, the Panel's Electronic Case Filing System will automatically generate and send a Notice of Electronic Filing (NEF) to all Filing Users associated with that MDL and/or associated cases, along with a hyperlink to the electronic document. Transmission of the Notice of Electronic Filing with a hyperlink to the electronic document constitutes service of the filed document.

The NEF must include the time of filing, the date the document was entered on the docket, the name of the party and attorney filing the document, the type of document, the text of the docket entry, and an electronic link (hyperlink) to the filed document, allowing anyone receiving the notice by email to retrieve the document automatically. If the Filing User becomes aware that the NEF was not transmitted successfully to a party, or that the notice is deficient, *i.e.,* the electronic link to the document is defective, the filer shall serve the electronically filed document by email, hand, facsimile, or by first-class mail postage prepaid immediately upon notification of the NEF deficiency.

12.1.2 Individual who is not a Filing User

A non-registered participant is entitled to receive a paper copy of any electronically filed document from the party making such filing. Service of such paper copy must be made according to the Panel Rules.

13. TECHNICAL FAILURES.

(a) If the site is unable to accept filings continuously or intermittently for more than one (1) hour occurring after 12:00 noon Eastern Time that day, the Clerk of the Panel shall deem the Panel's Electronic Case Filing web site to be subject to a technical failure.

(b) If a Filing User experiences a technical failure as defined herein, the Filing User may submit the document to the Clerk of the Panel, provided that the document is accompanied by a certification, signed by the Filing User, that the Filing User has attempted to file the document electronically at least twice, with those unsuccessful attempts occurring at least one (1) hour apart after 12:00 noon Eastern Time that day. The Clerk may require the document to be accompanied by a disk or CD–ROM which contains the document in .pdf format.

(c) The initial point of contact for a Filing User experiencing technical difficulty filing a document electronically will be the Panel's CM/ECF Help Desk at the numbers listed on the Panel's web site and in the CM/ECF User Manual.

(d) A Filing User who suffers prejudice as a result of a technical failure as defined herein or a Filing User who cannot file a time-sensitive document electronically due to unforeseen technical difficulties, such as the malfunctioning of a Filing User's equipment, may seek relief from the Clerk of the Panel.

14. PUBLIC ACCESS.

14.1 (a) A person may receive information from the Electronic Filing System at the Panel's Internet site by obtaining a PACER login and password. A person who has PACER access may retrieve docket sheets and documents (unless otherwise sealed or restricted) in MDL dockets and associated civil cases. Any case or document under seal shall not be available electronically or through any other means.

(b) If a case or document has been restricted, a PACER user may retrieve the docket sheet over the Internet, but only a Filing User who is counsel of record may retrieve restricted documents electronically. However, a restricted case or document will be available for viewing by the public at the clerk's office.

(c) Electronic access to electronic docket sheets and all documents filed in the System, unless sealed, is available to the public for viewing at no charge during regular business hours at the clerk's office. A copy fee for an electronic reproduction is required in accordance with 28 U.S.C. § 1932.

(d) Conventional copies and certified copies of electronically filed documents may be purchased at the clerk's office. The fee for copying and certifying will be in accordance with 28 U.S.C. § 1932.

14.2 Sensitive Information

Since the public may access certain case information over the Internet through the Panel's Electronic Filing System, sensitive information should not be included in any document filed with the court unless such inclusion is necessary and relevant. In accordance with these Administrative Policies and Procedures, if sensitive information must be included, certain personal and identifying information such as Social Security numbers, financial account numbers, dates of birth and names of minor children shall be redacted from the pleading, whether it is filed electronically or on paper.

The Panel recognizes that parties may need to include in the record a document containing information such as driver's license number; medical records, treatment and diagnosis; employment history; individual financial information; and proprietary or trade secret information. To avoid unnecessary disclosure of private, personal or financial information, a party may:

(a) **RESTRICTED MDL DOCKETS OR DOCUMENTS.**

File a "Motion to Seal" or "Motion to Seal Document". The motion must state the reason and show good cause for restricting remote access to the case. If the motion is granted, remote access to documents will be limited to Filing Users who are counsel of record. However, the MDL docket sheet and/or documents will be available for viewing by the public at the clerk's office.

(b) **EXHIBITS.**

File an exhibit containing private, personal or financial information as an attachment to a pleading entitled "Notice of Filing Restricted Exhibit". The notice and the attached exhibit shall be filed as a separate docket entry, rather than as an attachment to the pleading supported by the exhibit. Remote public access to the notice and exhibit will be limited to Filing Users who are counsel of record. The notice and exhibit will, however, be available for viewing by the public at the clerk's office.

(c) **DOCUMENTS UNDER SEAL.**

(1) File a redacted copy of a pleading or exhibit containing private, personal or financial information, whether electronically or on paper, while concurrently filing an unredacted copy under seal. This document shall be retained by the Panel as part of the record.

OR

(2) File a reference list under seal. The reference list shall contain the complete personal data identifier(s) and the redacted identifier(s) used in its (their) place in the filing. All references in the case to the redacted identifier(s) included in the reference list will be construed to refer to the corresponding complete identifier. The reference list must be filed under seal, and may be amended as of right. It shall be retained by the Panel as part of the record.

(d) **MOTION TO SEAL.**

File a motion to seal the document or MDL associated case. The motion must state the reason and show good cause for sealing the document or MDL associated case. If the motion to seal is granted, the document or case under seal will not be available electronically or through any other means.

It is the sole responsibility of counsel and the parties to ensure that all documents filed with the Panel comply with these Administrative Policies and Procedures, regarding public access to electronic case files. The Clerk will not review any document for redaction.

Counsel are strongly urged to share this information with all clients so that an informed decision about the inclusion, redaction, and/or exclusion of certain materials may be made.

[Effective May 2010.]

FEDERAL COURTS MISCELLANEOUS FEE SCHEDULES

COURT OF APPEALS FEE SCHEDULE

(Effective December 1, 2016)

The fees included in the Court of Appeals Miscellaneous Fee Schedule[1] are to be charged for services provided by the courts of appeals, including relevant services[2] provided by the bankruptcy appellate panels established under 28 U.S.C. § 158(b)(1).

- The United States should not be charged fees under this schedule, except as prescribed in Items 2, 4, and 5 when the information requested is available through remote electronic access.
- Federal agencies or programs that are funded from judiciary appropriations (agencies, organizations, and individuals providing services authorized by the Criminal Justice Act, 18 U.S.C. § 3006A, and bankruptcy administrators) should not be charged any fees under this schedule.

(1) For docketing a case on appeal or review, or docketing any other proceeding, $500.

- Each party filing a notice of appeal pays a separate fee to the district court, but parties filing a joint notice of appeal pay only one fee.
- There is no docketing fee for an application for an interlocutory appeal under 28 U.S.C. § 1292(b) or other petition for permission to appeal under Fed. R. App. P. 5, unless the appeal is allowed.
- There is no docketing fee for a direct bankruptcy appeal or a direct bankruptcy cross appeal, when the fee has been collected by the bankruptcy court in accordance with item 14 of the Bankruptcy Court Miscellaneous Fee Schedule.
- This fee is collected in addition to the statutory fee of $5 that is collected under 28 U.S.C. § 1917.

(2) For conducting a search of the court of appeals or bankruptcy appellate panel records, $31 per name or item searched. This fee applies to services rendered on behalf of the United States if the information requested is available through remote electronic access.

(3) For certification of any document, $11.

(4) For reproducing any document, $.50 per page. This fee applies to services rendered on behalf of the United States if the document requested is available through remote electronic access.

(5) For reproducing recordings of proceedings, regardless of the medium, $31, including the cost of materials. This fee applies to services rendered on behalf of the United States if the recording is available through remote electronic access.

(6) For reproducing the record in any appeal in which the court of appeals does not require an appendix pursuant to Fed. R. App. P.30(f), (or, in appeals before a bankruptcy appellate panel, pursuant to Fed. R. Bankr. P. 8018(e)), $86.

(7) For retrieval of one box of records from a Federal Records Center, National Archives, or other storage location removed from the place of business of the court, $64. For retrievals involving multiple boxes, $39 for each additional box. For electronic retrievals, $10 plus any charges assessed by the Federal Records Center, National Archives, or other storage location removed from the place of business of the courts.

(8) For any payment returned or denied for insufficient funds, $53.

(9) For copies of opinions, a fee commensurate with the cost of printing, as fixed by each court of appeals.

(10) For copies of the local rules of court, a fee commensurate with the cost of distributing the copies. The court may also distribute copies of the local rules without charge.

(11) For filing:

- Any separate or joint notice of appeal or application for appeal from the bankruptcy appellate panel, $5;
- A notice of the allowance of an appeal from the bankruptcy appellate panel, $5.

(12) For counsel's requested use of the court's videoconferencing equipment in connection with each oral argument, the court may charge and collect a fee of $200 per remote location.

(13) For original admission of attorney to practice, including a certificate of admission, $181. For a duplicate certificate of admission or certificate of good standing, $19.

1 Issued in accordance with 28 U.S.C. § 1913.

2 Item 13 does not apply to bankruptcy appellate panels.

DISTRICT COURT FEE SCHEDULE

(Effective December 1, 2016)

The fees included in the District Court Miscellaneous Fee Schedule[1] are to be charged for services provided by the district courts.

- The United States should not be charged fees under this schedule, with the exception of those specifically prescribed in Items 2, 4 and 5, when the information requested is available through remote electronic access.
- Federal agencies or programs that are funded from judiciary appropriations (agencies, organizations, and individuals providing services authorized by the Criminal Justice Act, 18 U.S.C. § 3006 and bankruptcy administrators) should not be charged any fees under this schedule.

1. For filing any document that is not related to a pending case or proceeding, $47.

2. For conducting a search of the district court records, $31 per name or item searched. This fee applies to services rendered on behalf of the United States if the information requested is available through electronic access.

3. For certification of any document, $11. For exemplification of any document, $22.

4. For reproducing any record or paper, $.50 per page. This fee shall apply to paper copies made from either: (1) original documents; or (2) microfiche or microfilm reproductions of the original records. This fee shall apply to services rendered on behalf of the United States if the record or paper requested is available through electronic access.

5. For reproduction of an audio recording of a court proceeding, $31. This fee applies to services rendered on behalf of the United States, if the recording is available electronically.

6. For each microfiche sheet of film or microfilm jacket copy of any court record, where available, $6.

7. For retrieval of one box of records from a Federal Records Center, National Archives, or other storage location removed from the place of business of the court, $64. For retrievals involving multiple boxes, $39 for each additional box. For electronic retrievals, $10 plus any charges assessed by the Federal Records Center, National Archives, or other storage location removed from the place of business of the courts.

8. For any payment returned or denied for insufficient funds, $53.

9. For an appeal to a district judge from a judgment of conviction by a magistrate judge in a misdemeanor case, $38.

10. For original admission of attorneys to practice, $181 each, including a certificate of admission. For a duplicate certificate of admission or certificate of good standing, $19.

11. The court may charge and collect fees commensurate with the cost of providing copies of the local rules of court. The court may also distribute copies of the local rules without charge.

12.

- For handling registry funds deposited with and held by the court, the clerk shall assess a charge from interest earnings, in accordance with the detailed fee schedule issued by the Director of the Administrative Office of the United States Courts.
- For management of registry funds invested through the Court Registry Investment System, a fee at an annual rate of 10 basis points of assets on deposit shall be assessed from interest earnings, excluding registry funds from disputed ownership interpleader cases deposited under 28 U.S.C. § 1335 and held in a Court Registry Investment System Disputed Ownership Fund.
- For management of funds deposited under 28 U.S.C. § 1335 and invested in a Disputed Ownership Fund through the Court Registry Investment System, a fee at an annual rate of 20 basis points of assets on deposit shall be assessed from interest earnings.
- The Director of the Administrative Office has the authority to waive these fees for cause.

13. For filing an action brought under Title III of the Cuban Liberty and Democratic Solidarity (LIBERTAD) Act of 1996, P.L. 104–114, 110 Stat. § 785 (1996), $6,548. (This fee is in addition to the

filing fee prescribed in 28 U.S.C. § 1914(a) for instituting any civil action other than a writ of habeas corpus.)

14. Administrative fee for filing a civil action, suit, or proceeding in a district court, $50. This fee does not apply to applications for a writ of habeas corpus or to persons granted in forma pauperis status under 28 U.S.C. § 1915.

15. Processing fee for a petty offense charged on a federal violation notice, $30.

1 Issued in accordance with 28 U.S.C. § 1914.

BANKRUPTCY COURT MISCELLANEOUS FEE SCHEDULE

(Effective December 1, 2016)

The fees included in the Bankruptcy Court Miscellaneous Fee Schedule[1] are to be charged for services provided by the bankruptcy courts.

- The United States should not be charged fees under this schedule, with the exception of those specifically prescribed in Items 1, 3 and 5 when the information requested is available through remote electronic access.
- Federal agencies or programs that are funded from judiciary appropriations (agencies, organizations, and individuals providing services authorized by the Criminal Justice Act, 18 U.S.C. § 3006A, and bankruptcy administrators) should not be charged any fees under this schedule.

1. For reproducing any document, $.50 per page. This fee applies to services rendered on behalf of the United States if the document requested is available through electronic access.

2. For certification of any document, $11.

For exemplification of any document, $22.

3. For reproduction of an audio recording of a court proceeding, $31. This fee applies to services rendered on behalf of the United States if the recording is available electronically.

4. For filing an amendment to the debtor's schedules of creditors, lists of creditors, or mailing list, $31, except:

- The bankruptcy judge may, for good cause, waive the charge in any case.
- This fee must not be charged if -
  - the amendment is to change the address of a creditor or an attorney for a creditor listed on the schedules; or
  - the amendment is to add the name and address of an attorney for a creditor listed on the schedules.

5. For conducting a search of the bankruptcy court records, $31 per name or item searched. This fee applies to services rendered on behalf of the United States if the information requested is available through electronic access.

6. For filing a complaint, $350, except:

- If the trustee or debtor-in-possession files the complaint, the fee must be paid only by the estate, to the extent there is an estate.
- This fee must not be charged if -
  - the debtor is the plaintiff; or
  - a child support creditor or representative files the complaint and submits the form required by § 304(g) of the Bankruptcy Reform Act of 1994.

7. For filing any document that is not related to a pending case or proceeding, $47.

8. Administrative fee:

- For filing a petition under Chapter 7, 12, or 13, $75.
- For filing a petition under Chapter 9, 11, or 15, $550.
- When a motion to divide a joint case under Chapter 7, 12, or 13 is filed, $75
- When a motion to divide a joint case under Chapter 11 is filed, $550.

9. For payment to trustees pursuant to 11 U.S.C. § 330(b)(2), a $15 fee applies in the following circumstances:

- For filing a petition under Chapter 7.
- For filing a notice of conversion to a Chapter 7 case.
- For filing a motion to convert a case to a Chapter 7 case.
- For filing a motion to divide a joint Chapter 7 case.

- For filing a motion to reopen a Chapter 7 case.

10. In addition to any fees imposed under Item 9, above, the following fees must be collected:

- For filing a motion to convert a Chapter 12 case to a Chapter 7 case or a notice of conversion pursuant to 11 U.S.C. § 1208(a), $45.
- For filing a motion to convert a Chapter 13 case to a Chapter 7 case or a notice of conversion pursuant to 11 U.S.C. § 1307(a), $10.

The fee amounts in this item are derived from the fees prescribed in 28 U.S.C. § 1930(a).

If the trustee files the motion to convert, the fee is payable only from the estate that exists prior to conversion.

If the filing fee for the chapter to which the case is requested to be converted is less than the fee paid at the commencement of the case, no refund may be provided.

11. For filing a motion to reopen, the following fees apply:

- For filing a motion to reopen a Chapter 7 case, $245.
- For filing a motion to reopen a Chapter 9 case, $1167.
- For filing a motion to reopen a Chapter 11 case, $1167.
- For filing a motion to reopen a Chapter 12 case, $200.
- For filing a motion to reopen a Chapter 13 case, $235.
- For filing a motion to reopen a Chapter 15 case, $1167.

The fee amounts in this item are derived from the fees prescribed in 28 U.S.C. § 1930(a).

The reopening fee must be charged when a case has been closed without a discharge being entered.

The court may waive this fee under appropriate circumstances or may defer payment of the fee from trustees pending discovery of additional assets. If payment is deferred, the fee should be waived if no additional assets are discovered.

The reopening fee must not be charged in the following situations:

- to permit a party to file a complaint to obtain a determination under Rule 4007(b); or
- when a debtor files a motion to reopen a case based upon an alleged violation of the terms of the discharge under 11 U.S.C. § 524; or
- when the reopening is to correct an administrative error.
- to redact a record already filed in a case, pursuant to Fed. R. Bankr. P. 9037, if redaction is the only reason for reopening.

12. For retrieval of one box of records from a Federal Records Center, National Archives, or other storage location removed from the place of business of the court, $64. For retrievals involving multiple boxes, $39 for each additional box. For electronic retrievals, $10 plus any charges assessed by the Federal Records Center, National Archives, or other storage location removed from the place of business of the courts.

13. For any payment returned or denied for insufficient funds, $53.

14. For filing an appeal or cross appeal from a judgment, order, or decree, $293.

This fee is collected in addition to the statutory fee of $5 that is collected under 28 U.S.C. § 1930(c) when a notice of appeal is filed.

Parties filing a joint notice of appeal should pay only one fee.

If a trustee or debtor-in-possession is the appellant, the fee must be paid only by the estate, to the extent there is an estate.

Upon notice from the court of appeals that a direct appeal or direct cross-appeal has been authorized, an additional fee of $207 must be collected.

15. For filing a case under Chapter 15 of the Bankruptcy Code, $1167.

This fee is derived from and equal to the fee prescribed in 28 U.S.C. § 1930(a)(3) for filing a case commenced under Chapter 11 of Title 11.

16. The court may charge and collect fees commensurate with the cost of providing copies of the local rules of court. The court may also distribute copies of the local rules without charge.

17.

- For handling registry funds deposited with and held by the court, the clerk shall assess a charge from interest earnings, in accordance with the detailed fee schedule issued by the Director of the Administrative Office of the United States Courts.
- For management of registry funds invested through the Court Registry Investment System, a fee at an annual rate of 10 basis points of assets on deposit shall be assessed from interest earnings, excluding registry funds from disputed ownership interpleader cases deposited under 28 U.S.C. § 1335 and held in a Court Registry Investment System Disputed Ownership Fund.
- For management of funds deposited under 28 U.S.C. § 1335 and invested in a Disputed Ownership Fund through the Court Registry Investment System, a fee at an annual rate of 20 basis points of assets on deposit shall be assessed from interest earnings.
- The Director of the Administrative Office has the authority to waive these fees for cause.

18. For a motion filed by the debtor to divide a joint case filed under 11 U.S.C. § 302, the following fees apply:

- For filing a motion to divide a joint Chapter 7 case, $245.
- For filing a motion to divide a joint Chapter 11 case, $1167.
- For filing a motion to divide a joint Chapter 12 case, $200.
- For filing a motion to divide a joint Chapter 13 case, $235.

These fees are derived from and equal to the filing fees prescribed in 28 U.S.C. § 1930(a).

19. For filing the following motions, $181:

- To terminate, annul, modify or condition the automatic stay;
- To compel abandonment of property of the estate pursuant to Rule 6007(b) of the Federal Rules of Bankruptcy Procedure;
- To withdraw the reference of a case or proceeding under 28 U.S.C. § 157(d); or
- To sell property of the estate free and clear of liens under 11 U.S.C. § 363(f).

This fee must not be collected in the following situations:

- For a motion for relief from the co-debtor stay;
- For a stipulation for court approval of an agreement for relief from a stay; or
- For a motion filed by a child support creditor or its representative, if the form required by § 304(g) of the Bankruptcy Reform Act of 1994 is filed.

20. For filing a transfer of claim, $25 per claim transferred.

21. For filing a motion to redact a record, $25 per affected case. The court may waive this fee under appropriate circumstances.

1 Issued in accordance with 28 U.S.C. § 1930.

JUDICIAL PANEL ON MULTIDISTRICT LITIGATION FEE SCHEDULE

(Effective December 1, 2016)

Following are fees to be charged for services to be performed by the clerk of the Judicial Panel on Multidistrict Litigation. No fees are to be charged for services rendered on behalf of the United States, with the exception of those specifically prescribed in items 1 and 3. No fees under this schedule shall be charged to federal agencies or programs which are funded from judiciary appropriations, including, but not limited to, agencies, organizations, and individuals providing services authorized by the Criminal Justice Act, 18 U.S.C. § 3006A.

(1) For every search of the records of the court conducted by the clerk of the court or a deputy clerk, $31 per name or item searched. This fee shall apply to services rendered on behalf of the United States if the information requested is available through electronic access.

(2) For certification of any document or paper, whether the certification is made directly on the document or by separate instrument, $11.

(3) For reproducing any record or paper, $.50 per page. This fee shall apply to paper copies made from either: (1) original documents; or (2) microfiche or microfilm reproductions of the original records. This fee shall apply to services rendered on behalf of the United States if the record or paper requested is available through electronic access.

(4) For retrieval of one box of records from a Federal Records Center, National Archives, or other storage location removed from the place of business of the court, $64. For retrievals involving multiple boxes, $39 for each additional box. For electronic retrievals, $10 plus any charges assessed by the Federal Records Center, National Archives, or other storage location removed from the place of business of the courts.

(5) For any payment returned or denied for insufficient funds, $53.

ELECTRONIC PUBLIC ACCESS FEE SCHEDULE

(Issued in accordance with 28 U.S.C. §§ 1913, 1914, 1926, 1930, 1932)
(Effective December 1, 2013)

The fees included in the Electronic Public Access Fee Schedule are to be charged for providing electronic public access to court records.

Fees for Public Access to Court Electronic Records (PACER)

(1) Except as provided below, for electronic access to any case document, docket sheet, or case-specific report via PACER: $0.10 per page, not to exceed the fee for thirty pages.

(2) For electronic access to transcripts and non-case specific reports via PACER (such as reports obtained from the PACER Case Locator or docket activity reports): $0.10 per page.

(3) For electronic access to an audio file of a court hearing via PACER: $2.40 per audio file.

Fees for Courthouse Electronic Access

(4) For printing copies of any record or document accessed electronically at a public terminal in a courthouse: $0.10 per page.

PACER Service Center Fees

(5) For every search of court records conducted by the PACER Service Center, $30 per name or item searched.

(6) For the PACER Service Center to reproduce on paper any record pertaining to a PACER account, if this information is remotely available through electronic access: $0.50 per page.

(7) For any payment returned or denied for insufficient funds, $53.

Free Access and Exemptions

(8) **Automatic Fee Exemptions.**

- No fee is owed for electronic access to court data or audio files via PACER until an account holder accrues charges of more than $15.00 in a quarterly billing cycle.
- Parties in a case (including pro se litigants) and attorneys of record receive one free electronic copy, via the notice of electronic filing or notice of docket activity, of all documents filed electronically, if receipt is required by law or directed by the filer.
- No fee is charged for access to judicial opinions.
- No fee is charged for viewing case information or documents at courthouse public access terminals.

(9) **Discretionary Fee Exemptions.**

- Courts may exempt certain persons or classes of persons from payment of the user access fee. Examples of individuals and groups that a court may consider exempting include: indigents, bankruptcy case trustees, pro bono attorneys, pro bono alternative dispute resolution neutrals, Section 501(c)(3) not-for-profit organizations, and individual researchers associated with educational institutions. Courts should not, however, exempt individuals or groups that have the ability to pay the statutorily established access fee. Examples of individuals and groups that a court should not exempt include: local, state or federal government agencies, members of the media, privately paid attorneys or others who have the ability to pay the fee.
- In considering granting an exemption, courts must find:
  - that those seeking an exemption have demonstrated that an exemption is necessary in order to avoid unreasonable burdens and to promote public access to information;
  - that individual researchers requesting an exemption have shown that the defined research project is intended for scholarly research, that it is limited in scope, and that it is not intended for redistribution on the internet or for commercial purposes.
- If the court grants an exemption:

- the user receiving the exemption must agree not to sell the data obtained as a result, and must not transfer any data obtained as the result of a fee exemption, unless expressly authorized by the court; and
- the exemption should be granted for a definite period of time, should be limited in scope, and may be revoked at the discretion of the court granting the exemption.

- Courts may provide local court information at no cost (e.g., local rules, court forms, news items, court calendars, and other information) to benefit the public.

Applicability to the United States and State and Local Governments

(10) Unless otherwise authorized by the Judicial Conference, these fees must be charged to the United States, except to federal agencies or programs that are funded from judiciary appropriations (including, but not limited to, agencies, organizations, and individuals providing services authorized by the Criminal Justice Act [18 U.S.C. § 3006A], and bankruptcy administrators).

(11) The fee for printing copies of any record or document accessed electronically at a public terminal ($0.10 per page) described in (4) above does not apply to services rendered on behalf of the United States if the record requested is not remotely available through electronic access.

(12) The fee for local, state, and federal government entities, shall be $0.08 per page until April 1, 2015, after which time, the fee shall be $0.10 per page.

JUDICIAL CONFERENCE POLICY NOTES

The Electronic Public Access (EPA) fee and its exemptions are directly related to the requirement that the judiciary charge user-based fees for the development and maintenance of electronic public access services. The fee schedule provides examples of users that may not be able to afford reasonable user fees (such as indigents, bankruptcy case trustees, individual researchers associated with educational institutions, 501(c)(3) not-for-profit organizations, and court-appointed pro bono attorneys), but requires those seeking an exemption to demonstrate that an exemption is limited in scope and is necessary in order to avoid an unreasonable burden. In addition, the fee schedule includes examples of other entities that courts should not exempt from the fee (such as local, state or federal government agencies, members of the media, and attorneys). The goal is to provide courts with guidance in evaluating a requestor's ability to pay the fee.

Judicial Conference policy also limits exemptions in other ways. First, it requires exempted users to agree not to sell the data they receive through an exemption (unless expressly authorized by the court). This prohibition is not intended to bar a quote or reference to information received as a result of a fee exemption in a scholarly or other similar work. Second, it permits courts to grant exemptions for a definite period of time, to limit the scope of the exemptions, and to revoke exemptions. Third, it cautions that exemptions should be granted as the exception, not the rule, and prohibits courts from exempting all users from EPA fees.